America's
Top-Rated Smaller Cities:
A Statistical Handbook

Volume 2: Nevada – Wyoming

2018/19

Twelfth Edition

America's Top-Rated Smaller Cities: A Statistical Handbook

Volume 2: Nevada – Wyoming

A UNIVERSAL REFERENCE BOOK

Grey House Publishing

PRESIDENT: Richard Gottlieb
PUBLISHER: Leslie Mackenzie
EDITORIAL DIRECTOR: Laura Mars
SENIOR EDITOR: David Garoogian

CONTRIBUTING WRITER: Alyssa Garoogian
PRODUCTION MANAGER: Kristen Thatcher
MARKETING DIRECTOR: Jessica Moody

A Universal Reference Book
Grey House Publishing, Inc.
4919 Route 22
Amenia, NY 12501
518.789.8700
Fax 845.373.6390
www.greyhouse.com
e-mail: books @greyhouse.com

Twelfth Edition
Printed in Canada

America's top-rated smaller cities : a statistical handbook. — 1st ed. (1994–1995)-

2 v.; 27.5 cm.
Biennial
Title varies.
ISSN: 1094-4893

1. Cities and towns—Ratings—United States—Statistics. 2. Cities and towns—United States—Statistics. 3. Social indicators—United States. 4. Quality of life—United States—Statistics.
HT123.A6692
307.76/0973/05

ISBN: 978-1-68217-773-0

Table of Contents

Marlboro, New Jersey

Princeton, New Jersey

Randolph, New Jersey

South Brunswick, New Jersey

Rio Rancho, New Mexico

Bethlehem, New York

Cicero, New York

East Fishkill, New York

Orchard Park, New York

Rye, New York

Vestal, New York

Webster, New York

Apex, North Carolina

Chapel Hill, North Carolina

Cornelius, North Carolina

Holly Springs, North Carolina

West Fargo, North Dakota

Beavercreek, Ohio

Dublin, Ohio

Hilliard, Ohio

Mason, Ohio

North Ridgeville, Ohio

Edmond, Oklahoma

Bend, Oregon

Lake Oswego, Oregon

Cranberry, Pennsylvania

Hampden, Pennsylvania

Lower Macungie, Pennsylvania

Moon, Pennsylvania

Radnor, Pennsylvania

State College, Pennsylvania

Tredyffrin, Pennsylvania

Upper Dublin, Pennsylvania

South Kingstown, Rhode Island

Mount Pleasant, South Carolina

Aberdeen, South Dakota

Brentwood, Tennessee

Collierville, Tennessee

Allen, Texas

Cedar Park, Texas

Cibolo, Texas

Coppell, Texas

Flower Mound, Texas

Friendswood, Texas

Lehi, Utah

Pleasant Grove, Utah

South Jordan, Utah

Syracuse, Utah

Burlington, Vermont

Blacksburg, Virginia

Leesburg, Virginia

Maple Valley, Washington

Sammamish, Washington

Morgantown, West Virginia

Menomonee Falls, Wisconsin

Sun Prairie, Wisconsin

Laramie, Wyoming

Places profiled in this edition of *America's Top-Rated Smaller Cities*

By City

Aberdeen (city), SD
Aliso Viejo (city), CA
Allen (city), TX
Ames (city), IA
Amherst (town), MA
Apex (town), NC
Beavercreek (city), OH
Bellevue (city), NE
Bend (city), OR
Benicia (city), CA
Bentonville (city), AR
Bethlehem (town), NY
Blacksburg (town), VA
Bowie (city), MD
Bozeman (city), MT
Brentwood (city), TN
Burlington (city), VT
Cabot (city), AR
Carmel (city), IN
Cedar Falls (city), IA
Cedar Park (city), TX
Central (city), LA
Chapel Hill (town), NC
Cheshire (town), CT
Chino Hills (city), CA
Cibolo (city), TX
Cicero (town), NY
Collierville (town), TN
Coppell (city), TX
Cornelius (town), NC
Cranberry (township), PA
Crown Point (city), IN
Dublin (city), OH
East Fishkill (town), NY
Eden Prairie (city), MN
Edmond (city), OK
Edwardsville (city), IL
Evesham (township), NJ
Flower Mound (town), TX
Folsom (city), CA
Friendswood (city), TX
Gaines (township), MI
Glastonbury (town), CT
Grand Blanc (township), MI
Hampden (township), PA
Hilliard (city), OH
Hillsborough (township), NJ
Holly Springs (town), NC
Independence (city), KY
Juneau (city and borough), AK
Kaysville (city), UT
Keller (city), TX
Lafayette (city), CA
Lafayette (city), CO
Lake Oswego (city), OR
Laramie (city), WY
Leander (city), TX
Leawood (city), KS
Lee's Summit (city), MO
Leesburg (town), VA
Lehi (city), UT
Lexington (town), MA
Los Altos (city), CA
Loveland (city), CO
Lower Macungie (township), PA
Madison (city), AL
Madison (city), MS
Maple Valley (city), WA
Marion (city), IA
Marlboro (township), NJ
Mason (city), OH
Menomonee Falls (village), WI
Meridian (city), ID
Meridian (township), MI
Merrimack (town), NH
Milton (city), GA
Moon (township), PA
Moorpark (city), CA
Morgantown (city), WV
Mount Pleasant (town), SC
Newark (city), DE
Newtown (town), CT
North Attleborough (town), MA
North Port (city), FL
North Ridgeville (city), OH
Northville (township), MI
O'Fallon (city), MO
Orchard Park (town), NY
Oro Valley (town), AZ
Oviedo (city), FL
Parker (town), CO
Parkland (city), FL
Peachtree City (city), GA
Pittsfield (township), MI
Plainfield (village), IL
Pleasant Grove (city), UT
Poway (city), CA
Princeton (municipality), NJ
Queen Creek (town), AZ
Radnor (township), PA
Randolph (township), NJ
Rexburg (city), ID
Rio Rancho (city), NM
Rye (town), NY
Sammamish (city), WA
San Ramon (city), CA
Saratoga (city), CA
Shrewsbury (town), MA
South Brunswick (township), NJ
South Jordan (city), UT
South Kingstown (town), RI
South Portland (city), ME
Sparks (city), NV
State College (borough), PA
Sugar Land (city), TX
Sun Prairie (city), WI
Syracuse (city), UT
Tredyffrin (township), PA
Upper Dublin (township), PA
Urbandale (city), IA
Vestal (town), NY
Vestavia Hills (city), AL
Webster (town), NY
Wellesley (town), MA
West Fargo (city), ND
West Lafayette (city), IN
Weston (city), FL
Wilmette (village), IL
Yorba Linda (city), CA
Zionsville (town), IN

By State

Madison (city), AL
Vestavia Hills (city), AL
Juneau (city and borough), AK
Oro Valley (town), AZ
Queen Creek (town), AZ
Bentonville (city), AR
Cabot (city), AR
Aliso Viejo (city), CA
Benicia (city), CA
Chino Hills (city), CA
Folsom (city), CA
Lafayette (city), CA
Los Altos (city), CA
Moorpark (city), CA
Poway (city), CA
San Ramon (city), CA
Saratoga (city), CA
Yorba Linda (city), CA
Lafayette (city), CO
Loveland (city), CO
Parker (town), CO
Cheshire (town), CT
Glastonbury (town), CT
Newtown (town), CT
Newark (city), DE
North Port (city), FL
Oviedo (city), FL
Parkland (city), FL
Weston (city), FL
Milton (city), GA
Peachtree City (city), GA
Meridian (city), ID
Rexburg (city), ID
Edwardsville (city), IL
Plainfield (village), IL
Wilmette (village), IL
Carmel (city), IN
Crown Point (city), IN
West Lafayette (city), IN
Zionsville (town), IN
Ames (city), IA
Cedar Falls (city), IA
Marion (city), IA
Urbandale (city), IA
Leawood (city), KS
Independence (city), KY
Central (city), LA
South Portland (city), ME
Bowie (city), MD
Amherst (town), MA
Lexington (town), MA
North Attleborough (town), MA
Shrewsbury (town), MA
Wellesley (town), MA
Gaines (township), MI
Grand Blanc (township), MI
Meridian (township), MI
Northville (township), MI
Pittsfield (township), MI
Eden Prairie (city), MN
Madison (city), MS
Lee's Summit (city), MO
O'Fallon (city), MO
Bozeman (city), MT
Bellevue (city), NE
Sparks (city), NV
Merrimack (town), NH
Evesham (township), NJ
Hillsborough (township), NJ
Marlboro (township), NJ
Princeton (municipality), NJ
Randolph (township), NJ
South Brunswick (township), NJ
Rio Rancho (city), NM
Bethlehem (town), NY
Cicero (town), NY
East Fishkill (town), NY
Orchard Park (town), NY
Rye (town), NY
Vestal (town), NY
Webster (town), NY
Apex (town), NC
Chapel Hill (town), NC
Cornelius (town), NC
Holly Springs (town), NC
West Fargo (city), ND
Beavercreek (city), OH
Dublin (city), OH
Hilliard (city), OH
Mason (city), OH
North Ridgeville (city), OH
Edmond (city), OK
Bend (city), OR
Lake Oswego (city), OR
Cranberry (township), PA
Hampden (township), PA
Lower Macungie (township), PA
Moon (township), PA
Radnor (township), PA
State College (borough), PA
Tredyffrin (township), PA
Upper Dublin (township), PA
South Kingstown (town), RI
Mount Pleasant (town), SC
Aberdeen (city), SD
Brentwood (city), TN
Collierville (town), TN
Allen (city), TX
Cedar Park (city), TX
Cibolo (city), TX
Coppell (city), TX
Flower Mound (town), TX
Friendswood (city), TX
Keller (city), TX
Leander (city), TX
Sugar Land (city), TX
Kaysville (city), UT
Lehi (city), UT
Pleasant Grove (city), UT
South Jordan (city), UT
Syracuse (city), UT
Burlington (city), VT
Blacksburg (town), VA
Leesburg (town), VA
Maple Valley (city), WA
Sammamish (city), WA
Morgantown (city), WV
Menomonee Falls (village), WI
Sun Prairie (city), WI
Laramie (city), WY

Introduction

This is the twelfth edition of *America's Top-Rated Smaller Cities*—current, concise statistical profiles of top U.S. cities with populations between 25,000 and 100,000. The 2018/19 edition features 130 cities, 55 which are new to this edition, including 29 never before profiled. There are many ways to research new places to live. The Internet can provide important details, like the cost of various lifestyles in various cities, and which schools are top rated, but only *America's Top-Rated Smaller Cities* gives you a complete picture. We've done the extensive research necessary to compile comprehensive profiles and comparative statistics that will educate and prepare you—and your business—for relocation.

Praise for previous editions:

> *"Patrons…will value this compilation of statistics on the 124 most desirable (statistically speaking)…cities…An exhaustive [resource] essential for libraries."*
>
> —Library Journal

> *"…These volumes provide excellent, comprehensive information on smaller urban communities…a valuable resource for graduating college students. Career professionals…will find these volumes useful…"*
>
> —Choice

> *"A quick and handy reference tool, this work will have a wide and grateful audience…recommended for public and academic libraries."*
>
> —ARBA

To expand our available city choices, selection is not limited to incorporated cities and villages, but includes towns and townships. This availed us many top-rated communities not designated as cities. Final selection was based on our unique rating system, using six key criteria: population growth, income, housing affordability, crime rate, educational attainment, and unemployment.

FEATURES

The city rankings for each of the 130 city chapters now comprise information from hundreds of books, magazines, newspapers and research reports. Interesting "top-city" rankings include...**Best Cities for Real Estate Investment**, **Best Cities for Sucessful Aging**, and **Best Cities for Asthma Sufferers**. You'll also learn which cities are the most...**Allergy Prone**, **Literate**, and **Safe**.

New topics include *Home Value Distribution* and *Segregation.* Expanded topic: *Recreational Marijuana Tax* added to Various State Sales and Excise Tax Rates.

ARRANGEMENT

America's Top-Rated Smaller Cities is arranged in two volumes—Volume 1 has 65 city chapters, Alabama to Nebraska, and Volume 2 also has 65 city chapters, Nevada to Wyoming. Each city chapter is divided into three sections: **Background & Rankings; Business Environment;** and **Living Environment**. Both volumes include **100 Honorable Mention Cities,** five **Maps** that indicate the location of each of the 130 cities, and five **Appendices**, with comparative rankings and resource information on all cities. Here is a detailed look:

City Background

Each of the 130 city chapters begins with an informative background. These combine history with current events, and touch on the city's environment, politics, employment, and cultural offerings, along with some interesting trivia.

Rankings

This section has 17 ranking categories, including *Business/Finance, Health, Women/Minorities, Retirement, Family, Safety, Sports/Recreation,* and *Dating/Romance.* It contains data from 257 books, articles, and research reports, and is presented in an easy-to-read, bulleted format. You'll find rankings—and several scores and figures—on a wide variety of topics, such as **Best Places for Business and Careers**, **Fastest-Growing Cities**, **Cleanest Metro Areas**, **Most Affordable Cities**, **Fittest Cities**, **Most Educated Cities**, and hundreds more.

Sources for these Rankings include both well-known magazines and other media, including *Forbes, Fortune, USA Today, Condé Nast Traveler, Gallup, Kiplinger's Personal Finance, Men's Journal,* and *Travel + Leisure,* as well as *Asthma & Allergy Foundation of America, Christopher & Dana Reeve Foundation, American Lung Association, League of American Bicyclists, The Advocate, National Civic League, National Alliance to End Homelessness, MovieMaker Magazine, Trulia.com, National Insurance Crime Bureau, Center for Digital Government, National Association of Home Builders,* and the *Milken Institute.*

Rankings cover a variety of geographic areas; see Appendix B for full geographic definitions.

Business Environment—Statistical Tables

Each city chapter in *America's Top-Rated Smaller Cities* includes 39 tables with business related data for seven topics. Over 95% of statistical data has been updated. Here is where you will find hard facts and figures on city finances, population demographics, income, bankruptcy rates, employment, and taxes. Again, our editors have used well-known sources, such as the *U.S. Census Bureau* and the *Bureau of Labor Statistics,* and more obscure ones, like *The Council for Community and Economic Research, Texas Transportation Institute,* and *Federation of Tax Administrators.*

Living Environment—Statistical Tables

The business tables are followed by 42 tables with data related to nine living environment topics. These include information on housing, healthcare, cost-of-living, education, air quality, and climate. Sources include the *Federal Trade Commission, U.S. Environmental Protection Agency, Federal Bureau of Investigation, Centers for Disease Control and Prevention,* and *National Center for Education Statistics.*

The availability of statistics is related to both a city's size and how data is gathered. Some statistics represent the Metropolitan Statistical Area the city is part of, and some are not available at all, indicated by n/a.

Five Appendices

- **A—Comparative Statistics:** A city-by-city comparison of hundreds of variables spread out over 77 tables that offers both an overview of the city, and a broader geographical profile.
- **B—Metropolitan Area Definitions:** In straight alpha-by-city order, this includes the counties/cities that combine to form each city's Metropolitan Statistical Area, Micropolitan Statistical Area, Metropolitan Division, New England City and Town Area, and New England City and Town Area Division.
- **C—Government Type & Primary County:** This appendix includes the government structure of each place included in this book. It also includes the county or county equivalent in which each place is located.
- **D—Chambers of Commerce:** Alpha-by-city, includes address, phone and fax numbers, and websites of additional city resources.
- **E—State Departments of Labor:** Another source for additional economic and employment data for each city, with address and phone number for easy access.

The material provided by public and private agencies and organizations was supplemented by library sources and Internet sites. This edition is designed for individuals considering relocating a residence or business; professionals considering expanding a business or changing careers; corporations considering relocation or additional offices; government agencies; general and market researchers; real estate consultants; human resource personnel; urban planners; investors; and urban government students. With more content and more coverage, this edition is our strongest and most informative to date.

Honorable Mentions

These places did not make our editor's final cut, however, they were on our preliminary list.

By City

Algonquin (village), IL
Alpharetta (city), GA
Andover (town), MA
Ankeny (city), IA
Arlington (town), MA
Ballwin (city), MO
Belmont (town), MA
Bernards (township), NJ
Bloomfield (township), MI
Bridgewater (township), NJ
Brookfield (city), WI
Broomfield (city), CO
Buffalo Grove (village), IL
Canton (township), MI
Castle Rock (town), CO
Chaska (city), MN
Chelmsford (town), MA
Chesterfield (city), MO
Commerce (township), MI
Cupertino (city), CA
Danville (town), CA
Downers Grove (village), IL
Draper (city), UT
Eagan (city), MN
Eastchester (town), NY
Edina (city), MN
Elmhurst (city), IL
Fairfield (town), CT
Fishers (city), IN
Foster City (city), CA
Franklin (city), TN
Franklin Town (city), MA
Germantown (city), TN
Glen Ellyn (village), IL
Glenview (village), IL
Guilderland (town), NY
Haverford (township), PA
Highland Park (city), IL
Hoover (city), AL
Huntersville (town), NC
Huntley (village), IL
Independence (township), MI
Johns Creek (city), GA
Kirkland (city), WA
Kirkwood (city), MO
Lakeville (city), MN
League City (city), TX
Lenexa (city), KS
Livingston (township), NJ
Lower Merion (township), PA
Mahwah (township), NJ
Manalapan (township), NJ
Manlius (town), NY
Mansfield (city), TX
Maple Grove (city), MN
McCandless (township), PA
Melrose (city), MA
Milton (town), MA
Minnetonka (city), MN
Mount Juliet (city), TN
Mount Lebanon (township), PA
Natick (town), MA
Needham (town), MA
New Berlin (city), WI
New Lenox (village), IL
Newton (city), MA
North Andover (town), MA
Northampton (township), PA
Northbrook (village), IL
Novi (city), MI
Orion (township), MI
Oswego (village), IL
Palo Alto (city), CA
Park Ridge (city), IL
Pleasanton (city), CA
Plymouth (township), MI
Plymouth (city), MN
Rancho Palos Verdes (city), CA
Reading (town), MA
Ridgefield (town), CT
Ridgewood (village), NJ
Rochester Hills (city), MI
Savage (city), MN
Shoreview (city), MN
South Windsor (town), CT
Southlake (city), TX
Spring Hill (city), TN
Troy (city), MI
Upper Arlington (city), OH
Vernon Hills (village), IL
Wake Forest (town), NC
West Bloomfield (township), MI
West Windsor (township), NJ
Westerville (city), OH
Westfield (city), IN
Westfield (town), NJ
Westlake (city), OH
Westport (town), CT
Wheaton (city), IL
Woodbury (city), MN

By State

Hoover (city), AL
Cupertino (city), CA
Danville (town), CA
Foster City (city), CA
Palo Alto (city), CA
Pleasanton (city), CA
Rancho Palos Verdes (city), CA
Broomfield (city), CO
Castle Rock (town), CO
Fairfield (town), CT
Ridgefield (town), CT
South Windsor (town), CT
Westport (town), CT
Alpharetta (city), GA
Johns Creek (city), GA
Algonquin (village), IL
Buffalo Grove (village), IL
Downers Grove (village), IL
Elmhurst (city), IL
Glen Ellyn (village), IL
Glenview (village), IL
Highland Park (city), IL
Huntley (village), IL
New Lenox (village), IL
Northbrook (village), IL
Oswego (village), IL
Park Ridge (city), IL
Vernon Hills (village), IL
Wheaton (city), IL
Fishers (city), IN
Westfield (city), IN
Ankeny (city), IA
Lenexa (city), KS
Andover (town), MA
Arlington (town), MA
Belmont (town), MA
Chelmsford (town), MA
Franklin Town (city), MA
Melrose (city), MA
Milton (town), MA
Natick (town), MA
Needham (town), MA
Newton (city), MA
North Andover (town), MA
Reading (town), MA
Bloomfield (township), MI
Canton (township), MI
Commerce (township), MI
Independence (township), MI
Novi (city), MI
Orion (township), MI
Plymouth (township), MI
Rochester Hills (city), MI
Troy (city), MI
West Bloomfield (township), MI
Chaska (city), MN
Eagan (city), MN
Edina (city), MN
Lakeville (city), MN
Maple Grove (city), MN
Minnetonka (city), MN
Plymouth (city), MN
Savage (city), MN
Shoreview (city), MN
Woodbury (city), MN
Ballwin (city), MO
Chesterfield (city), MO
Kirkwood (city), MO
Bernards (township), NJ
Bridgewater (township), NJ
Livingston (township), NJ
Mahwah (township), NJ
Manalapan (township), NJ
Ridgewood (village), NJ
West Windsor (township), NJ
Westfield (town), NJ
Eastchester (town), NY
Guilderland (town), NY
Manlius (town), NY
Huntersville (town), NC
Wake Forest (town), NC
Upper Arlington (city), OH
Westerville (city), OH
Westlake (city), OH
Haverford (township), PA
Lower Merion (township), PA
McCandless (township), PA
Mount Lebanon (township), PA
Northampton (township), PA
Franklin (city), TN
Germantown (city), TN
Mount Juliet (city), TN
Spring Hill (city), TN
League City (city), TX
Mansfield (city), TX
Southlake (city), TX
Draper (city), UT
Kirkland (city), WA
Brookfield (city), WI
New Berlin (city), WI

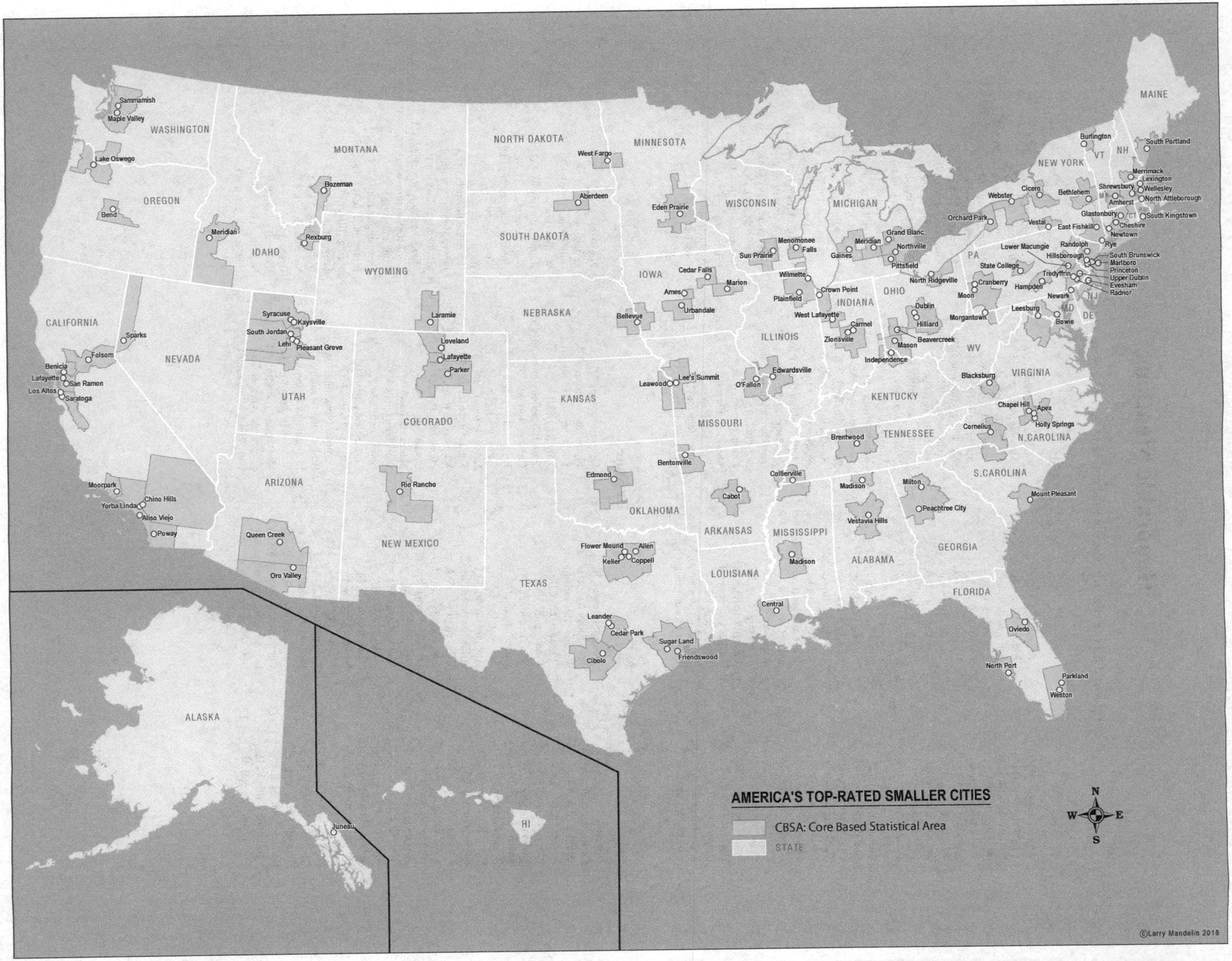
AMERICA'S TOP-RATED SMALLER CITIES
CBSA: Core Based Statistical Area
STATE
N
W
E
S
©Larry Mandelin 2018
WASHINGTON
OREGON
CALIFORNIA
NEVADA
IDAHO
MONTANA
WYOMING
UTAH
ARIZONA
COLORADO
NEW MEXICO
NORTH DAKOTA
SOUTH DAKOTA
NEBRASKA
KANSAS
OKLAHOMA
TEXAS
MINNESOTA
IOWA
MISSOURI
ARKANSAS
LOUISIANA
WISCONSIN
ILLINOIS
MICHIGAN
INDIANA
OHIO
KENTUCKY
TENNESSEE
MISSISSIPPI
ALABAMA
GEORGIA
FLORIDA
S.CAROLINA
N.CAROLINA
VIRGINIA
WV
PA
NEW YORK
VT
NH
MAINE
MA
CT
RI
NJ
MD
DE
ALASKA
HI
Sammamish
Maple Valley
Lake Oswego
Bend
Meridian
Bozeman
Rexburg
Syracuse
Kaysville
South Jordan
Lehi
Pleasant Grove
Sparks
Folsom
Benicia
Lafayette
San Ramon
Los Altos
Saratoga
Moorpark
Yorba Linda
Chino Hills
Aliso Viejo
Poway
Queen Creek
Oro Valley
Laramie
Loveland
Lafayette
Parker
Rio Rancho
West Fargo
Aberdeen
Eden Prairie
Bellevue
Ames
Urbandale
Cedar Falls
Marion
Leawood
Lee's Summit
Edmond
Bentonville
Flower Mound
Allen
Keller
Coppell
Leander
Cedar Park
Cibolo
Sugar Land
Friendswood
Cabot
Collierville
Central
Madison
Sun Prairie
Menomonee Falls
Wilmette
Plainfield
Crown Point
West Lafayette
Carmel
Zionsville
O'Fallon
Edwardsville
Meridian
Gaines
Grand Blanc
Northville
Pittsfield
North Ridgeville
Dublin
Hilliard
Beavercreek
Mason
Independence
Brentwood
Madison
Vestavia Hills
Milton
Peachtree City
Blacksburg
Chapel Hill
Apex
Holly Springs
Cornelius
Mount Pleasant
Oviedo
North Port
Parkland
Weston
Moon
Cranberry
Morgantown
State College
Orchard Park
Webster
Cicero
Vestal
Bethlehem
Burlington
East Fishkill
Lower Macungie
Hampden
Leesburg
Bowie
Newark
Randolph
Hillsborough
Tredyffrin
Rye
South Brunswick
Marlboro
Princeton
Upper Dublin
Evesham
Radnor
Newtown
Glastonbury
Cheshire
South Kingstown
Amherst
Shrewsbury
North Attleborough
Wellesley
Lexington
Merrimack
South Portland
Juneau

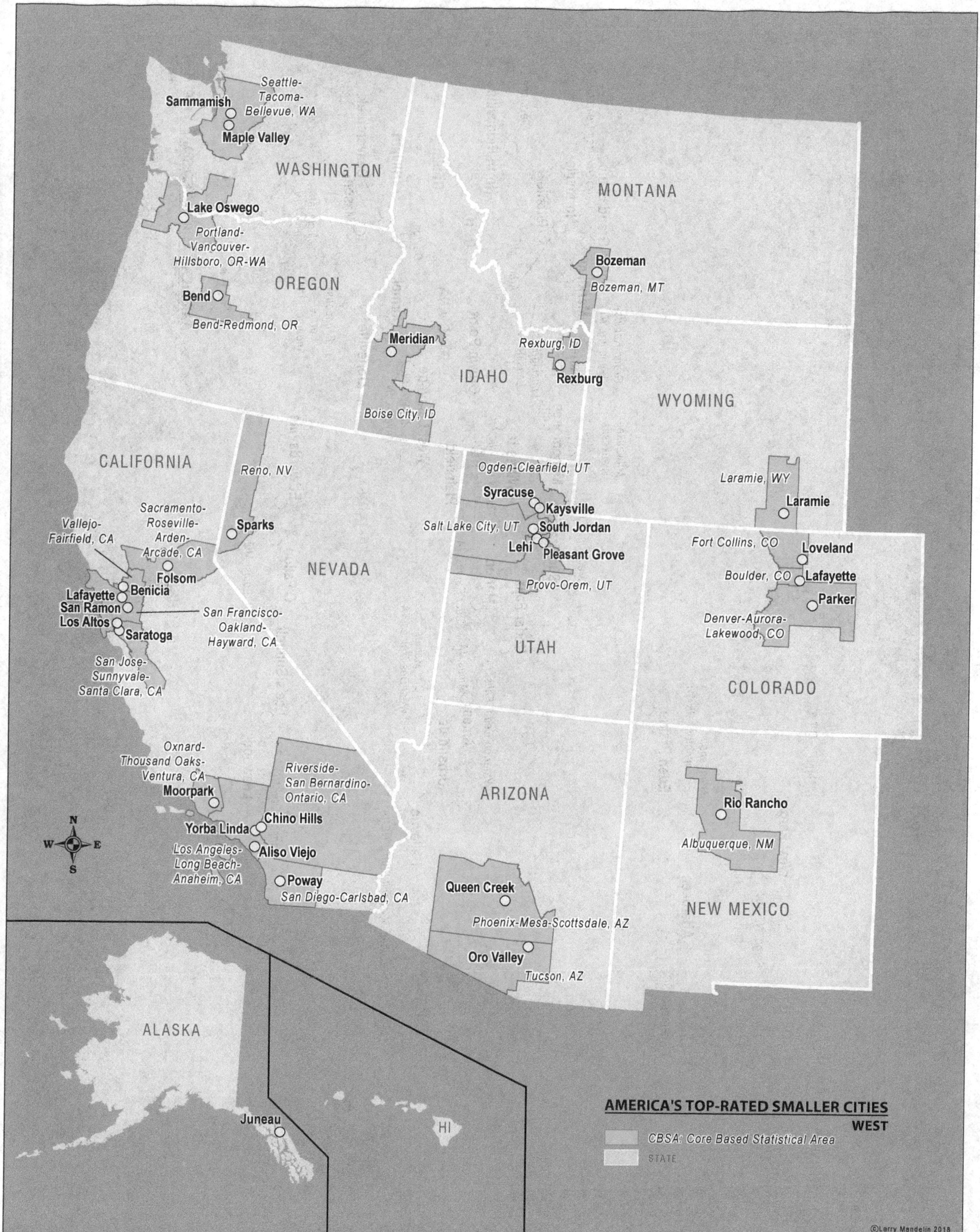

WASHINGTON
Sammamish
Maple Valley
Seattle-Tacoma-Bellevue, WA
Lake Oswego
Portland-Vancouver-Hillsboro, OR-WA
OREGON
Bend
Bend-Redmond, OR
MONTANA
Bozeman
Bozeman, MT
IDAHO
Meridian
Boise City, ID
Rexburg, ID
Rexburg
WYOMING
Laramie, WY
Laramie
CALIFORNIA
Reno, NV
Sparks
Sacramento-Roseville-Arden-Arcade, CA
Folsom
Vallejo-Fairfield, CA
Benicia
Lafayette
San Ramon
Los Altos
Saratoga
San Francisco-Oakland-Hayward, CA
San Jose-Sunnyvale-Santa Clara, CA
NEVADA
Ogden-Clearfield, UT
Syracuse
Kaysville
Salt Lake City, UT
South Jordan
Lehi
Pleasant Grove
Provo-Orem, UT
UTAH
Fort Collins, CO
Loveland
Boulder, CO
Lafayette
Parker
Denver-Aurora-Lakewood, CO
COLORADO
Oxnard-Thousand Oaks-Ventura, CA
Moorpark
Riverside-San Bernardino-Ontario, CA
Chino Hills
Yorba Linda
Aliso Viejo
Los Angeles-Long Beach-Anaheim, CA
Poway
San Diego-Carlsbad, CA
ARIZONA
Queen Creek
Phoenix-Mesa-Scottsdale, AZ
Oro Valley
Tucson, AZ
Rio Rancho
Albuquerque, NM
NEW MEXICO
N
W
E
S
ALASKA
Juneau
HI
AMERICA'S TOP-RATED SMALLER CITIES
WEST
CBSA: Core Based Statistical Area
STATE
©Larry Mandelin 2018

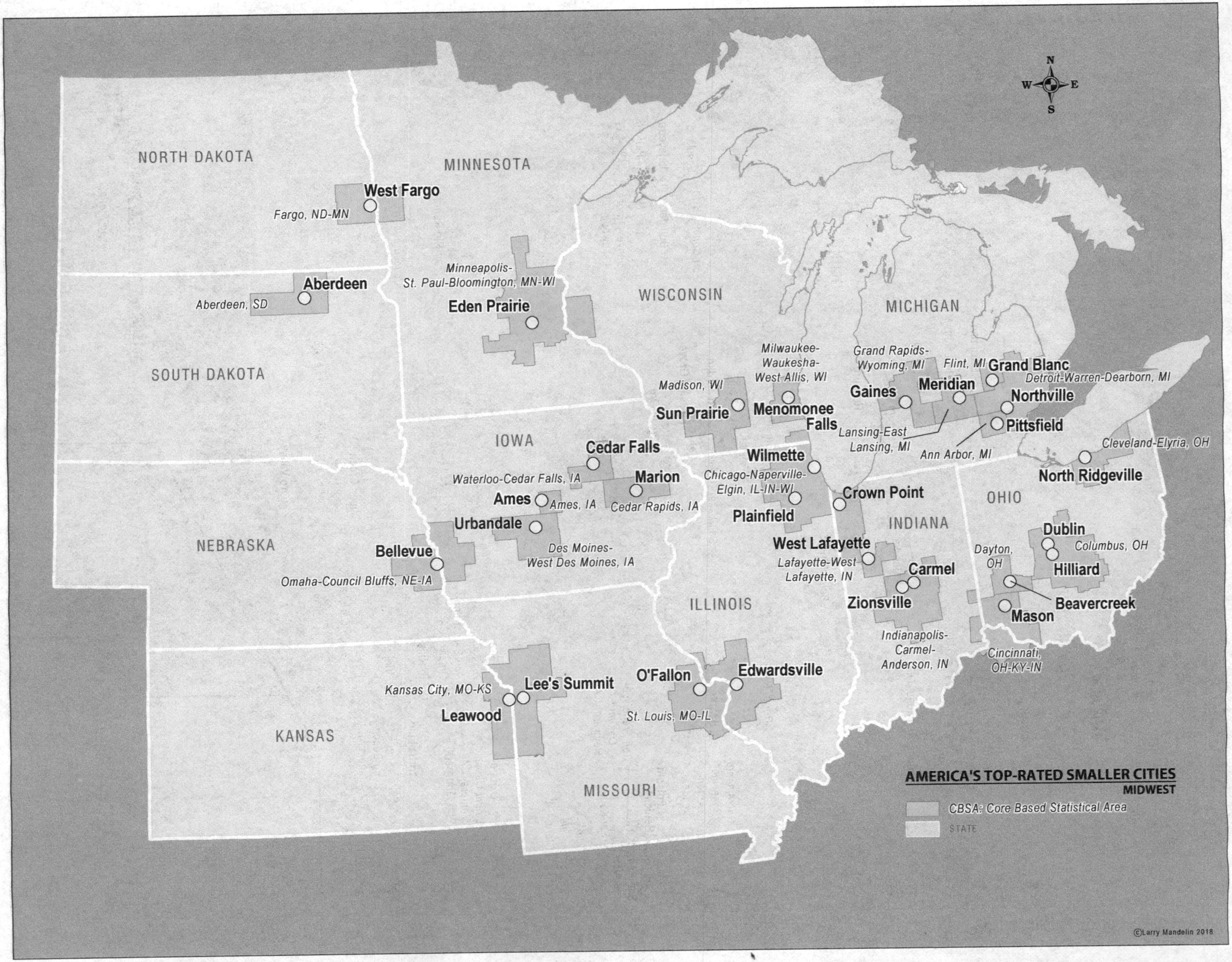

AMERICA'S TOP-RATED SMALLER CITIES
MIDWEST
CBSA: Core Based Statistical Area
STATE
NORTH DAKOTA
MINNESOTA
SOUTH DAKOTA
WISCONSIN
MICHIGAN
IOWA
NEBRASKA
ILLINOIS
INDIANA
OHIO
KANSAS
MISSOURI
West Fargo
Fargo, ND-MN
Aberdeen
Aberdeen, SD
Minneapolis-St. Paul-Bloomington, MN-WI
Eden Prairie
Madison, WI
Sun Prairie
Milwaukee-Waukesha-West Allis, WI
Menomonee Falls
Grand Rapids-Wyoming, MI
Gaines
Lansing-East Lansing, MI
Meridian
Flint, MI
Grand Blanc
Detroit-Warren-Dearborn, MI
Northville
Pittsfield
Ann Arbor, MI
Cleveland-Elyria, OH
North Ridgeville
Cedar Falls
Waterloo-Cedar Falls, IA
Marion
Cedar Rapids, IA
Ames
Ames, IA
Urbandale
Des Moines-West Des Moines, IA
Bellevue
Omaha-Council Bluffs, NE-IA
Wilmette
Chicago-Naperville-Elgin, IL-IN-WI
Plainfield
Crown Point
West Lafayette
Lafayette-West Lafayette, IN
Carmel
Zionsville
Indianapolis-Carmel-Anderson, IN
Dayton, OH
Dublin
Columbus, OH
Hilliard
Beavercreek
Mason
Cincinnati, OH-KY-IN
Kansas City, MO-KS
Lee's Summit
Leawood
O'Fallon
Edwardsville
St. Louis, MO-IL
©Larry Mandelin 2018

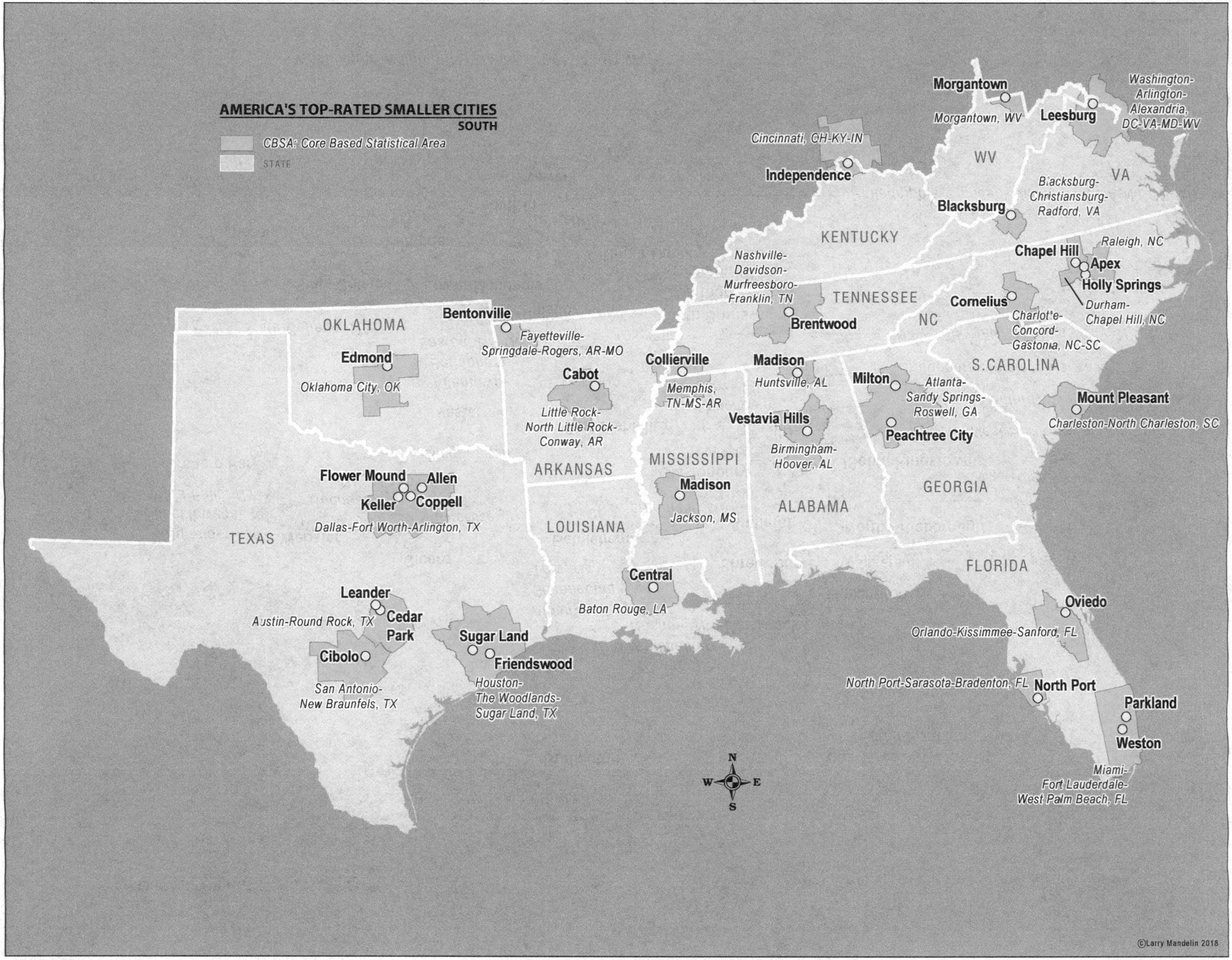
AMERICA'S TOP-RATED SMALLER CITIES
SOUTH
CBSA: Core Based Statistical Area
STATE
Morgantown
Morgantown, WV
Leesburg
Washington-Arlington-Alexandria, DC-VA-MD-WV
Cincinnati, CH-KY-IN
Independence
WV
VA
Blacksburg
Blacksburg-Christiansburg-Radford, VA
KENTUCKY
Raleigh, NC
Chapel Hill
Apex
Holly Springs
Durham-Chapel Hill, NC
Nashville-Davidson-Murfreesboro-Franklin, TN
TENNESSEE
Brentwood
Cornelius
Charlotte-Concord-Gastonia, NC-SC
NC
OKLAHOMA
Bentonville
Fayetteville-Springdale-Rogers, AR-MO
Edmond
Oklahoma City, OK
Cabot
Little Rock-North Little Rock-Conway, AR
Collierville
Memphis, TN-MS-AR
Madison
Huntsville, AL
Milton
Atlanta-Sandy Springs-Roswell, GA
Peachtree City
S.CAROLINA
Mount Pleasant
Charleston-North Charleston, SC
Vestavia Hills
Birmingham-Hoover, AL
MISSISSIPPI
Madison
Jackson, MS
ARKANSAS
ALABAMA
GEORGIA
Flower Mound
Allen
Keller
Coppell
Dallas-Fort Worth-Arlington, TX
TEXAS
LOUISIANA
FLORIDA
Central
Baton Rouge, LA
Leander
Austin-Round Rock, TX
Cedar Park
Sugar Land
Friendswood
Cibolo
San Antonio-New Braunfels, TX
Houston-The Woodlands-Sugar Land, TX
Oviedo
Orlando-Kissimmee-Sanford, FL
North Port-Sarasota-Bradenton, FL
North Port
Parkland
Weston
Miami-Fort Lauderdale-West Palm Beach, FL
N
W
E
S
©Larry Mandelin 2018

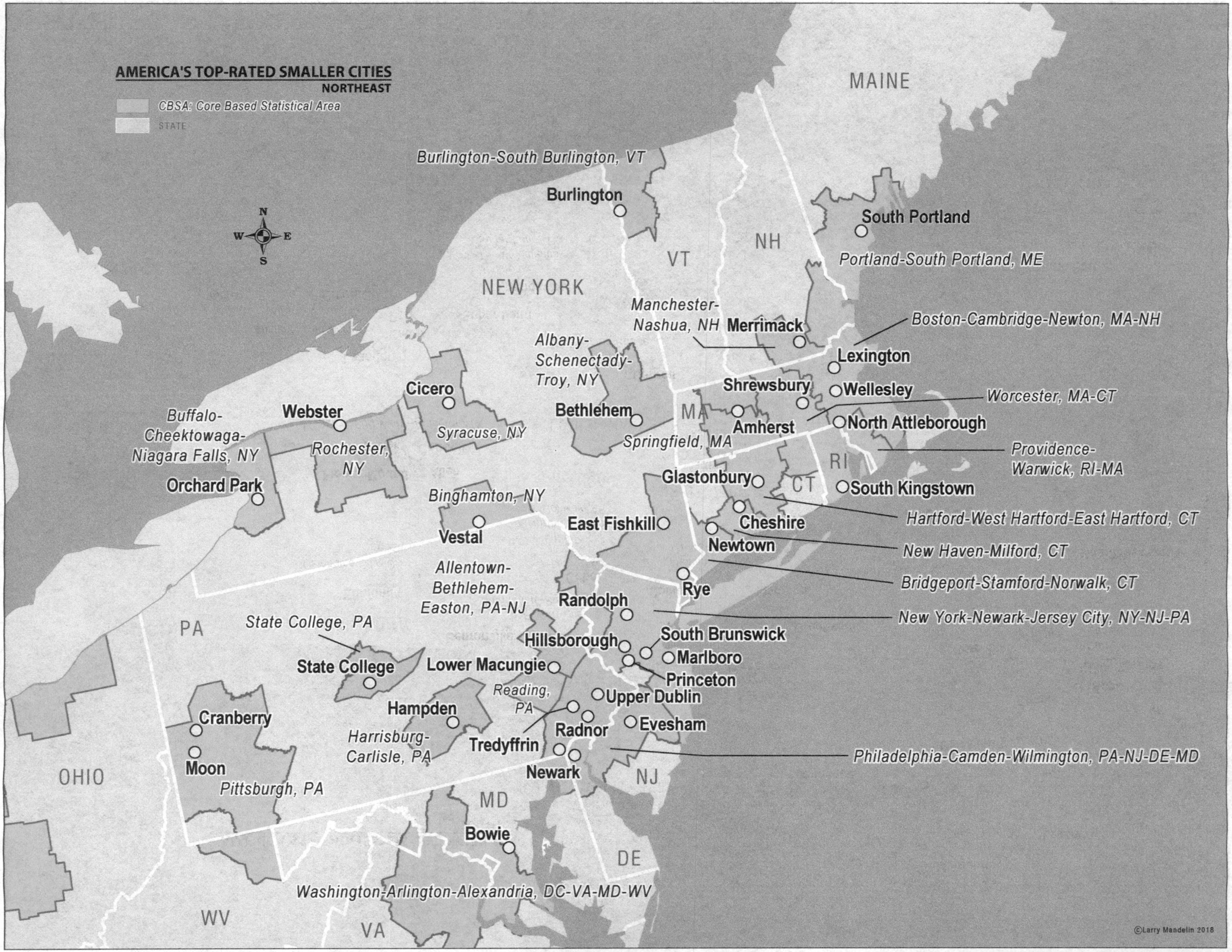
AMERICA'S TOP-RATED SMALLER CITIES
NORTHEAST
CBSA: Core Based Statistical Area
STATE
N
W
E
S
MAINE
NH
VT
NEW YORK
MA
RI
CT
PA
NJ
MD
DE
OHIO
WV
VA
Burlington-South Burlington, VT
Burlington
South Portland
Portland-South Portland, ME
Manchester-Nashua, NH
Merrimack
Boston-Cambridge-Newton, MA-NH
Lexington
Albany-Schenectady-Troy, NY
Shrewsbury
Wellesley
Worcester, MA-CT
Cicero
Bethlehem
Amherst
North Attleborough
Buffalo-Cheektowaga-Niagara Falls, NY
Webster
Syracuse, NY
Springfield, MA
Providence-Warwick, RI-MA
Rochester, NY
Glastonbury
South Kingstown
Orchard Park
Binghamton, NY
Hartford-West Hartford-East Hartford, CT
East Fishkill
Cheshire
Vestal
Newtown
New Haven-Milford, CT
Allentown-Bethlehem-Easton, PA-NJ
Bridgeport-Stamford-Norwalk, CT
Rye
Randolph
New York-Newark-Jersey City, NY-NJ-PA
State College, PA
South Brunswick
Hillsborough
Marlboro
State College
Lower Macungie
Princeton
Reading, PA
Upper Dublin
Hampden
Evesham
Cranberry
Radnor
Harrisburg-Carlisle, PA
Tredyffrin
Philadelphia-Camden-Wilmington, PA-NJ-DE-MD
Moon
Newark
Pittsburgh, PA
Bowie
Washington-Arlington-Alexandria, DC-VA-MD-WV
©Larry Mandelin 2018

Sparks, Nevada

Background

At an elevation of nearly 4,500 feet, Sparks lies just north of Reno, Nevada. Situated along Interstate 80 in Washoe County on the banks of the Truckee River, Sparks is Nevada's fifth-largest city, with a strong downtown business core and expanding residential neighborhoods. The city is a major center for distribution, warehousing, and light manufacturing, harboring the business facilities of more than 100 national companies, including Kmart Corporation, Ralston-Purina, Federal Express, and United Parcel Service.

Sparks was created in 1904 to replace Wadsworth as the large switching yard on that section of the Southern Pacific Railroad. The city was incorporated in 1905. Originally named Harriman after the railroad tycoon, Sparks was quickly renamed in honor of Governor John T. Sparks to cool the anti-railroad sentiment brewing in the state legislature over uncontrolled railroad tariffs.

For the first half of the twentieth century, Sparks was a very sleepy, unassuming place. In the 1950s, the city's northeast pasturelands became covered with subdivisions built to entice more families to the area. They served the purpose; Sparks became an even quieter, more residential community. By the 1970s, however, businesses became attracted to the city's potential, sparking truly dynamic growth.

In 1984, the tower for the Nugget Casino Resort was finished, giving Sparks its first, and currently only, high-rise casino. In 1996, the redevelopment effort of the B Street business district across from the Nugget that started in the early 1980s took a step forward with the opening of a multi-screen movie complex and the construction of a plaza area. This area, now known as Victorian Square, is a pedestrian-friendly district that hosts many open-air events.

Schools in Sparks are managed by the Washoe County School District, and comprise four high schools, four middle schools, and 22 elementary schools. Truckee Meadows Community College and the University of Nevada, Reno, are within an easy commute of the city.

The convenience of nearby Reno-Tahoe International Airport is an added boon to Sparks residents. It is among the fastest-growing airports in the nation. The region is served by many medical facilities, including Northern Nevada Adult Mental Health Services, and Northern Nevada Medical Center. Nursing homes and licensed child care centers are also available in the city.

Magnificent surroundings provide a myriad of outdoor activities. Sparks is less than an hour's drive from Lake Tahoe, with 18 world-class ski and snowboarding resorts. Sparks itself contains more than 50 park sites, including Sparks Marina Park, two sports complexes, two outdoor swimming venues, and three community centers.

The Sparks Heritage Foundation and Museum features early regional and railroad memorabilia, and Wild Island offers outdoor water rides, an arcade, new Laser Mazes, bowling and three miniature golf courses. The Reno metropolitan area has 40 casinos, nine of which are located in Sparks.

Located on a semi-arid plateau east of the Sierra Nevada, Sparks has a mild climate, with 80% sunshine throughout the year, accompanied by low humidity. Temperatures vary widely from day to night.

Rankings

Business/Finance Rankings

- The personal finance site NerdWallet analyzed 183 American metropolitan areas with populations over 250,000 and more than 15,000 businesses to rank where entrepreneurs find the most success. Criteria included area economy, annual income, housing cost, unemployment rate, and the success rate of area businesses. Reno* ranked #56. *www.nerdwallet.com, "Best Places to Start a Business," April 27, 2015*
- The Reno* metro area appeared on the Milken Institute "2017 Best Performing Cities" list. Rank: #37 out of 200 large metro areas. Criteria: job growth; wage and salary growth; high-tech output growth. *Milken Institute, "Best-Performing Cities 2017," January 2018*
- *Forbes* ranked the 200 most populous metro areas to determine the nation's "Best Places for Business and Careers." The Reno* metro area was ranked #40. Criteria: costs (business and living); job growth (past and projected); income growth; quality of life; educational attainment (college and high school); projected economic growth; cultural and recreational opportunities; net migration patterns; number of highly ranked colleges. *Forbes, "The Best Places for Business and Careers 2017," October 24, 2017*

Education Rankings

- Personal finance website *WalletHub* analyzed the 150 largest U.S. metropolitan statistical areas to determine where the most educated Americans are choosing to settle. Criteria: education quality and attainment gap; education levels; percentage of workers with degrees; public school rankings; quality and size of each metro area's universities. Reno* was ranked #63 (#1 = most educated city). *www.WalletHub.com, "2017's Most and Least Educated Cities in America," July 25, 2017*

Environmental Rankings

- Sperling's BestPlaces assessed 379 metropolitan areas of the United States for the likelihood of dangerously extreme weather events or earthquakes. In general the Southeast and South-Central regions have the highest risk of weather extremes and earthquakes, while the Pacific Northwest enjoys the lowest risk. Of the least risky metropolitan areas, the Reno* metro area was ranked #66. *www.bestplaces.net, "Safest Places from Natural Disasters," April 2011*
- Reno* was highlighted as one of the 25 metro areas most polluted by short-term particle pollution (24-hour PM 2.5) in the U.S. during 2013 through 2015. The area ranked #10. *American Lung Association, State of the Air 2017*

Health/Fitness Rankings

- The Reno* metro area ranked #124 out of 189 in The Gallup-Healthways Well-Being Index. Criteria: purpose; social well being; financial health; community and physical health. Results are based on telephone interviews with adults, aged 18 and older, living in metropolitan areas in the 50 U.S. states and the District of Columbia. *Gallup-Healthways, "State of American Well-Being, 2017 Community Well-Being Rankings" March 2018*

Real Estate Rankings

- Reno* was ranked #11 in the top 20 out of 265 metro areas in terms of house price appreciation in 2017 (#1 = highest rate). *Federal Housing Finance Agency, House Price Index, 4th Quarter 2017. February 27, 2018*
- The Reno* metro area was identified as one of the 20 best housing markets in the U.S. in 2017. The area ranked #2 out of 180 markets. Criteria: year-over-year change of median sales price of existing single-family homes between the 4th quarter of 2016 and the 4th quarter of 2017. *National Association of Realtors®, Median Sales Price of Existing Single-Family Homes for Metropolitan Areas, 4th Quarter 2017*

- The Reno* metro area was identified as one of the 20 least affordable housing markets in the U.S. in 2017. The area ranked #17 out of 180 markets. Criteria: qualification for a mortgage loan on a typical home. *National Association of Realtors®, Affordability Index of Existing Single-Family Homes for Metropolitan Areas, 2017*

- Reno* was ranked #220 out of 238 metro areas in terms of housing affordability in 2017 by the National Association of Home Builders (#1 = most affordable). Criteria: the share of homes sold in that area affordable to a family earning the local median income, based on standard mortgage underwriting criteria. *National Association of Home Builders®, NAHB-Wells Fargo Housing Opportunity Index, 4th Quarter 2017*

Safety Rankings

- The National Insurance Crime Bureau ranked 382 metro areas in the U.S. in terms of per capita rates of vehicle theft. The Reno* metro area ranked #49 (#1 = highest rate). Criteria: number of vehicle theft offenses per 100,000 inhabitants in 2016. *National Insurance Crime Bureau, "Hot Spots 2016," June 8, 2017*

Seniors/Retirement Rankings

- From its Best Cities for Successful Aging indexes, the Milken Institute generated rankings for metropolitan areas, weighing data in nine categories—health care, wellness, living arrangements, transportation and convenience, financial characteristics, education, employment, community engagement, and overall livability. The Reno* metro area was ranked #101 overall in the small metro area category. *Milken Institute, "Best Cities for Successful Aging, 2017" March 14, 2017*

*Sparks is located within the Reno, NV Metropolitan Statistical Area.

Business Environment

CITY FINANCES

City Government Finances

Component	2015 ($000)	2015 ($ per capita)
Total Revenues	129,517	1,348
Total Expenditures	98,448	1,024
Debt Outstanding	198,001	2,060
Cash and Securities[1]	113,320	1,179

Note: (1) Cash and security holdings of a government at the close of its fiscal year,, including those of its dependent agencies, utilities, and liquor stores.
Source: U.S Census Bureau, State & Local Government Finances 2015

City Government Revenue by Source

Source	2015 ($000)	2015 ($ per capita)	2015 (%)
General Revenue			
From Federal Government	710	7	0.5
From State Government	35,887	373	27.7
From Local Governments	5,908	61	4.6
Taxes			
Property	24,030	250	18.6
Sales and Gross Receipts	5,533	58	4.3
Personal Income	0	0	0.0
Corporate Income	0	0	0.0
Motor Vehicle License	0	0	0.0
Other Taxes	12,205	127	9.4
Current Charges	30,212	314	23.3
Liquor Store	0	0	0.0
Utility	0	0	0.0
Employee Retirement	0	0	0.0

Source: U.S Census Bureau, State & Local Government Finances 2015

City Government Expenditures by Function

Function	2015 ($000)	2015 ($ per capita)	2015 (%)
General Direct Expenditures			
Air Transportation	0	0	0.0
Corrections	0	0	0.0
Education	0	0	0.0
Employment Security Administration	0	0	0.0
Financial Administration	2,496	26	2.5
Fire Protection	14,622	152	14.9
General Public Buildings	98	1	0.1
Governmental Administration, Other	4,826	50	4.9
Health	0	0	0.0
Highways	4,211	43	4.3
Hospitals	0	0	0.0
Housing and Community Development	1,003	10	1.0
Interest on General Debt	12,441	129	12.6
Judicial and Legal	3,409	35	3.5
Libraries	0	0	0.0
Parking	0	0	0.0
Parks and Recreation	7,029	73	7.1
Police Protection	22,259	231	22.6
Public Welfare	0	0	0.0
Sewerage	21,497	223	21.8
Solid Waste Management	0	0	0.0
Veterans' Services	0	0	0.0
Liquor Store	0	0	0.0
Utility	0	0	0.0
Employee Retirement	0	0	0.0

Source: U.S Census Bureau, State & Local Government Finances 2015

DEMOGRAPHICS

Population Growth

Area	1990 Census	2000 Census	2010 Census	2016* Estimate	Population Growth (%) 1990-2016	Population Growth (%) 2010-2016
City	54,716	66,346	90,264	94,718	73.1	4.9
MSA[1]	257,193	342,885	425,417	443,855	72.6	4.3
U.S.	248,709,873	281,421,906	308,745,538	318,558,162	28.1	3.2

Note: (1) Figures cover the Reno, NV Metropolitan Statistical Area—see Appendix B for areas included; (*) 2012-2016 5-year estimated population
Source: U.S. Census Bureau, 1990 Census, Census 2000, Census 2010, 2012-2016 American Community Survey 5-Year Estimates

Household Size

Area	Persons in Household (%)							Average Household Size
	One	Two	Three	Four	Five	Six	Seven or More	
City	27.9	33.3	15.3	14.1	6.3	2.1	1.0	2.60
MSA[1]	29.3	35.0	15.0	11.8	5.1	2.4	1.4	2.60
U.S.	27.7	33.7	15.7	13.1	6.0	2.3	1.5	2.60

Note: (1) Figures cover the Reno, NV Metropolitan Statistical Area—see Appendix B for areas included
Source: U.S. Census Bureau, 2012-2016 American Community Survey 5-Year Estimates

Race

Area	White Alone[2] (%)	Black Alone[2] (%)	Asian Alone[2] (%)	AIAN[3] Alone[2] (%)	NHOPI[4] Alone[2] (%)	Other Race Alone[2] (%)	Two or More Races (%)
City	78.4	2.8	5.8	1.5	0.4	6.8	4.4
MSA[1]	80.6	2.3	5.4	1.6	0.6	5.6	4.0
U.S.	73.3	12.6	5.2	0.8	0.2	4.8	3.1

Note: (1) Figures cover the Reno, NV Metropolitan Statistical Area—see Appendix B for areas included; (2) Alone is defined as not being in combination with one or more other races; (3) American Indian and Alaska Native; (4) Native Hawaiian and Other Pacific Islander
Source: U.S. Census Bureau, 2012-2016 American Community Survey 5-Year Estimates

Hispanic or Latino Origin

Area	Total (%)	Mexican (%)	Puerto Rican (%)	Cuban (%)	Other (%)
City	27.6	22.8	0.4	0.1	4.3
MSA[1]	23.4	18.5	0.5	0.1	4.2
U.S.	17.3	11.0	1.7	0.7	4.0

Note: Persons of Hispanic or Latino origin can be of any race; (1) Figures cover the Reno, NV Metropolitan Statistical Area—see Appendix B for areas included
Source: U.S. Census Bureau, 2012-2016 American Community Survey 5-Year Estimates

Segregation

Type	Segregation Indices[1]				Percent Change		
	1990	2000	2010	2010 Rank[2]	1990-2000	1990-2010	2000-2010
Black/White	n/a	n/a	n/a	n/a	n/a	n/a	n/a
Asian/White	n/a	n/a	n/a	n/a	n/a	n/a	n/a
Hispanic/White	n/a	n/a	n/a	n/a	n/a	n/a	n/a

Note: All figures cover the Metropolitan Statistical Area—see Appendix B for areas included; Figures are based on an analysis of 1990, 2000, and 2010 Census Decennial Census tract data by William H. Frey, Brookings Institution and the University of Michigan Social Science Data Analysis Network. In this analysis all racial groups (whites, blacks, and asians) are non-Hispanic members of those races. Hispanics are shown as a separate category; (1) Segregation Indices are Dissimilarity Indices that measure the degree to which the minority group is distributed differently than whites across census tracts. They range from 0 (complete integration) to 100 (complete segregation) where the value indicates the percentage of the minority group that needs to move to be distributed exactly like whites; (2) Ranges from 1 (most segregated) to 102 (least segregated); n/a not available.
Source: www.CensusScope.org

Ancestry

Area	German	Irish	English	American	Italian	Polish	French[2]	Scottish	Dutch
City	13.4	11.0	8.9	5.5	6.8	2.1	2.7	2.4	1.3
MSA[1]	14.5	11.8	9.4	5.5	6.7	1.9	2.8	2.5	1.5
U.S.	14.4	10.4	7.7	6.9	5.4	2.9	2.6	1.7	1.3

Note: Figures are the percentage of the total population reporting a particular ancestry. The nine most commonly reported ancestries in the U.S. are shown. Figures include multiple ancestries (e.g. if a person reported being Irish and Italian, they were included in both columns); (1) Figures cover the Reno, NV Metropolitan Statistical Area—see Appendix B for areas included; (2) Excludes Basque
Source: U.S. Census Bureau, 2012-2016 American Community Survey 5-Year Estimates

Foreign-Born Population

Area	Percent of Population Born in								
	Any Foreign Country	Asia	Mexico	Europe	Carribean	Central America[2]	South America	Africa	Canada
City	16.3	3.8	8.6	0.8	0.1	1.7	0.5	0.4	0.2
MSA[1]	14.7	3.9	6.8	1.2	0.1	1.6	0.4	0.2	0.3
U.S.	13.2	4.0	3.6	1.5	1.3	1.0	0.9	0.6	0.3

Note: (1) Figures cover the Reno, NV Metropolitan Statistical Area—see Appendix B for areas included; (2) Excludes Mexico.
Source: U.S. Census Bureau, 2012-2016 American Community Survey 5-Year Estimates

Marital Status

Area	Never Married	Now Married[2]	Separated	Widowed	Divorced
City	29.1	49.2	1.9	5.4	14.4
MSA[1]	31.2	47.4	1.9	5.1	14.5
U.S.	33.0	48.1	2.1	5.9	11.0

Note: Figures are percentages and cover the population 15 years of age and older; (1) Figures cover the Reno, NV Metropolitan Statistical Area—see Appendix B for areas included; (2) Excludes separated
Source: U.S. Census Bureau, 2012-2016 American Community Survey 5-Year Estimates

Disability Status

Area	All Ages	Under 18 Years Old	18 to 64 Years Old	65 Years and Over
City	12.0	4.1	9.9	34.6
MSA[1]	12.3	4.4	10.4	32.3
U.S.	12.5	4.1	10.3	35.7

Note: Figures show percent of the civilian noninstitutionalized population that reported having a disability. Disability status is determined from six types of difficulty: vision, hearing, cognitive, ambulatory, self-care, and independent living. For children under 5 years old, hearing and vision difficulty are used to determine disability status. For children between the ages of 5 and 14, disability status is determined from hearing, vision, cognitive, ambulatory, and self-care difficulties. For people aged 15 years and older, they are considered to have a disability if they have difficulty with any one of the six difficulty types; Note: (1) Figures cover the Reno, NV Metropolitan Statistical Area—see Appendix B for areas included
Source: U.S. Census Bureau, 2012-2016 American Community Survey 5-Year Estimates

Age

Area	Percent of Population									Median Age
	Under Age 5	Age 5–19	Age 20–34	Age 35–44	Age 45–54	Age 55–64	Age 65–74	Age 75–84	Age 85+	
City	6.4	19.9	20.2	13.3	13.2	12.9	9.0	3.4	1.8	37.5
MSA[1]	6.1	18.7	21.3	12.3	13.6	13.3	9.3	3.9	1.5	38.1
U.S.	6.2	19.6	20.7	12.7	13.6	12.6	8.3	4.3	1.9	37.7

Note: (1) Figures cover the Reno, NV Metropolitan Statistical Area—see Appendix B for areas included
Source: U.S. Census Bureau, 2012-2016 American Community Survey 5-Year Estimates

Gender

Area	Males	Females	Males per 100 Females
City	46,253	48,465	95.4
MSA[1]	223,053	220,802	101.0
U.S.	156,765,322	161,792,840	96.9

Note: (1) Figures cover the Reno, NV Metropolitan Statistical Area—see Appendix B for areas included
Source: U.S. Census Bureau, 2012-2016 American Community Survey 5-Year Estimates

Religious Groups by Family

Area	Catholic	Baptist	Non-Den.	Methodist[2]	Lutheran	LDS[3]	Pente-costal	Presby-terian[4]	Muslim[5]	Judaism
MSA[1]	14.3	1.5	3.2	0.9	0.8	4.6	2.0	0.4	0.1	0.2
U.S.	19.1	9.3	4.0	4.0	2.3	2.0	1.9	1.6	0.8	0.7

Note: Figures are the number of adherents as a percentage of the total population; (1) Figures cover the Reno, NV Metropolitan Statistical Area see Appendix B for areas included; (2) Methodist/Pietist; (3) Latter Day Saints; (4) Reformed; (5) Figures are estimates
Source: Association of Statisticians of American Religious Bodies, 2010 U.S. Religion Census: Religious Congregations & Membership Study

Religious Groups by Tradition

Area	Catholic	Evangelical Protestant	Mainline Protestant	Other Tradition	Black Protestant	Orthodox
MSA[1]	14.3	7.7	1.9	5.1	0.2	0.1
U.S.	19.1	16.2	7.3	4.3	1.6	0.3

Note: Figures are the number of adherents as a percentage of the total population; (1) Figures cover the Reno, NV Metropolitan Statistical Area—see Appendix B for areas included
Source: Association of Statisticians of American Religious Bodies, 2010 U.S. Religion Census: Religious Congregations & Membership Study

ECONOMY

Gross Metropolitan Product

Area	2014	2015	2016	2017	Rank[2]
MSA[1]	21.0	21.8	22.6	24.1	112

Note: Figures are in billions of dollars; (1) Figures cover the Reno, NV Metropolitan Statistical Area—see Appendix B for areas included; (2) Rank is based on 2015 data and ranges from 1 to 381
Source: The U.S. Conference of Mayors, U.S. Metro Economies: GMP and Employment Report, 2015-2017

Economic Growth

Area	2012-14 (%)	2015 (%)	2016 (%)	2017 (%)	Rank[2]
MSA[1]	2.6	3.1	1.9	4.4	86
U.S.	2.0	2.4	1.9	2.6	–

Note: Figures are real gross metropolitan product (GMP) growth rates and represent average annual percent change; (1) Figures cover the Reno, NV Metropolitan Statistical Area—see Appendix B for areas included; (2) Rank is based on 2012-2014 average annual percent change and ranges from 1 to 381
Source: The U.S. Conference of Mayors, U.S. Metro Economies: GMP and Employment Report, 2015-2017

Metropolitan Area Exports

Area	2011	2012	2013	2014	2015	2016	Rank[2]
MSA[1]	1,687.4	2,019.0	2,117.4	2,138.9	1,943.3	2,382.1	86

Note: Figures are in millions of dollars; (1) Figures cover the Reno, NV Metropolitan Statistical Area—see Appendix B for areas included; (2) Rank is based on 2016 data and ranges from 1 to 385
Source: U.S. Department of Commerce, International Trade Administration, Office of Trade & Industry Information, Manufacturing & Services, data extracted March 15, 2018

Building Permits

Area	Single-Family			Multi-Family			Total		
	2016	2017p	Pct. Chg.	2016	2017p	Pct. Chg.	2016	2017p	Pct. Chg.
City	490	602	22.9	417	1,242	197.8	907	1,844	103.3
MSA[1]	1,867	2,091	12.0	1,732	2,473	42.8	3,599	4,564	26.8
U.S.	750,800	817,300	8.9	455,800	446,800	-2.0	1,206,600	1,264,100	4.8

Note: (1) Figures cover the Reno, NV Metropolitan Statistical Area—see Appendix B for areas included; Figures represent new, privately-owned housing units authorized (unadjusted data); All permit data are based on estimates with imputation; (p) preliminary data.
Source: U.S. Census Bureau, Manufacturing, Mining, and Construction Statistics, Building Permits, 2016, 2017

Bankruptcy Filings

Area	Business Filings			Nonbusiness Filings		
	2016	2017	% Chg.	2016	2017	% Chg.
Washoe County	32	43	34.4	1,037	920	-11.3
U.S.	24,114	23,157	-4.0	770,846	765,863	-0.6

Note: Business filings include Chapter 7, Chapter 11, Chapter 12, and Chapter 13; Nonbusiness filings include Chapter 7, Chapter 11, and Chapter 13
Source: Administrative Office of the U.S. Courts, Business and Nonbusiness Bankruptcy, County Cases Commenced by Chapter of the Bankruptcy Code, During the 12-Month Period Ending December 31, 2016 and Business and Nonbusiness Bankruptcy, County Cases Commenced by Chapter of the Bankruptcy Code, During the 12-Month Period Ending December 31, 2017

Housing Vacancy Rates

Area	Gross Vacancy Rate[2] (%)			Year-Round Vacancy Rate[3] (%)			Rental Vacancy Rate[4] (%)			Homeowner Vacancy Rate[5] (%)		
	2015	2016	2017	2015	2016	2017	2015	2016	2017	2015	2016	2017
MSA[1]	n/a	n/a	n/a	n/a	n/a	n/a	n/a	n/a	n/a	n/a	n/a	n/a
U.S.	12.9	12.8	12.7	10.0	9.9	9.9	7.1	6.9	7.2	1.8	1.7	1.6

Note: (1) Figures cover the Reno, NV Metropolitan Statistical Area—see Appendix B for areas included; (2) The percentage of the total housing inventory that is vacant; (3) The percentage of the housing inventory (excluding seasonal units) that is year-round vacant; (4) The percentage of rental inventory that is vacant for rent; (5) The percentage of homeowner inventory that is vacant for sale; n/a not available
Source: U.S. Census Bureau, Housing Vacancies and Homeownership Annual Statistics: 2015, 2016, 2017

INCOME

Income

Area	Per Capita ($)	Median Household ($)	Average Household ($)
City	27,039	54,196	68,455
MSA[1]	29,987	55,103	75,030
U.S.	29,829	55,322	77,866

Note: (1) Figures cover the Reno, NV Metropolitan Statistical Area—see Appendix B for areas included
Source: U.S. Census Bureau, 2012-2016 American Community Survey 5-Year Estimates

Household Income Distribution

Area	Percent of Households Earning							
	Under $15,000	$15,000 -$24,999	$25,000 -$34,999	$35,000 -$49,999	$50,000 -$74,999	$75,000 -$99,999	$100,000 -$149,999	$150,000 and up
City	9.3	10.9	10.1	15.1	21.1	12.7	13.7	7.1
MSA[1]	11.2	10.9	9.8	13.9	18.5	12.5	13.6	9.6
U.S.	12.1	10.2	9.9	13.2	17.8	12.2	13.5	11.1

Note: (1) Figures cover the Reno, NV Metropolitan Statistical Area—see Appendix B for areas included
Source: U.S. Census Bureau, 2012-2016 American Community Survey 5-Year Estimates

Poverty Rate

Area	All Ages	Under 18 Years Old	18 to 64 Years Old	65 Years and Over
City	12.3	18.1	11.1	7.5
MSA[1]	14.9	20.0	14.8	7.5
U.S.	15.1	21.2	14.2	9.3

Note: Figures are percentage of people whose income during the past 12 months was below the poverty level; (1) Figures cover the Reno, NV Metropolitan Statistical Area—see Appendix B for areas included
Source: U.S. Census Bureau, 2012-2016 American Community Survey 5-Year Estimates

EMPLOYMENT

Labor Force and Employment

Area	Civilian Labor Force			Workers Employed		
	Dec. 2016	Dec. 2017	% Chg.	Dec. 2016	Dec. 2017	% Chg.
City	50,706	52,900	4.3	48,480	50,951	5.1
MSA[1]	235,149	245,311	4.3	224,830	236,289	5.1
U.S.	158,968,000	159,880,000	0.6	151,798,000	153,602,000	1.2

Note: Data is not seasonally adjusted and covers workers 16 years of age and older; (1) Figures cover the Reno, NV Metropolitan Statistical Area—see Appendix B for areas included
Source: Bureau of Labor Statistics, Local Area Unemployment Statistics

Unemployment Rate

Area	2017											
	Jan.	Feb.	Mar.	Apr.	May	Jun.	Jul.	Aug.	Sep.	Oct.	Nov.	Dec.
City	5.3	4.8	4.6	4.3	4.1	4.3	4.0	3.8	3.8	3.7	3.6	3.7
MSA[1]	5.2	4.8	4.6	4.3	4.1	4.3	4.1	4.0	3.9	3.7	3.7	3.7
U.S.	5.1	4.9	4.6	4.1	4.1	4.5	4.6	4.5	4.1	3.9	3.9	3.9

Note: Data is not seasonally adjusted and covers workers 16 years of age and older; (1) Figures cover the Reno, NV Metropolitan Statistical Area—see Appendix B for areas included
Source: Bureau of Labor Statistics, Local Area Unemployment Statistics

Average Wages

Occupation	$/Hr.	Occupation	$/Hr.
Accountants and Auditors	33.90	Maids and Housekeeping Cleaners	10.20
Automotive Mechanics	22.20	Maintenance and Repair Workers	18.60
Bookkeepers	20.40	Marketing Managers	61.60
Carpenters	25.00	Nuclear Medicine Technologists	n/a
Cashiers	10.50	Nurses, Licensed Practical	25.20
Clerks, General Office	18.20	Nurses, Registered	37.70
Clerks, Receptionists/Information	14.30	Nursing Assistants	15.90
Clerks, Shipping/Receiving	17.70	Packers and Packagers, Hand	12.00
Computer Programmers	39.90	Physical Therapists	40.70
Computer Systems Analysts	34.40	Postal Service Mail Carriers	24.20
Computer User Support Specialists	22.10	Real Estate Brokers	31.00
Cooks, Restaurant	12.90	Retail Salespersons	12.90
Dentists	126.90	Sales Reps., Exc. Tech./Scientific	31.10
Electrical Engineers	44.00	Sales Reps., Tech./Scientific	39.30
Electricians	27.20	Secretaries, Exc. Legal/Med./Exec.	18.30
Financial Managers	59.40	Security Guards	11.60
First-Line Supervisors/Managers, Sales	19.10	Surgeons	n/a
Food Preparation Workers	9.70	Teacher Assistants*	13.40
General and Operations Managers	56.90	Teachers, Elementary School*	27.60
Hairdressers/Cosmetologists	10.40	Teachers, Secondary School*	27.90
Internists, General	n/a	Telemarketers	13.70
Janitors and Cleaners	11.50	Truck Drivers, Heavy/Tractor-Trailer	23.40
Landscaping/Groundskeeping Workers	14.60	Truck Drivers, Light/Delivery Svcs.	18.60
Lawyers	77.20	Waiters and Waitresses	9.70

Note: Wage data covers the Reno, NV Metropolitan Statistical Area—see Appendix B for areas included; (*) Hourly wages for elementary/secondary school teachers and teacher assistants were calculated by the editors from annual wage data based on a 40 hour work week; n/a not available.
Source: Bureau of Labor Statistics, Metro Area Occupational Employment & Wage Estimates, May 2017

Employment by Occupation

Occupation Classification	City (%)	MSA[1] (%)	U.S. (%)
Management, Business, Science, and Arts	29.8	33.7	37.0
Natural Resources, Construction, and Maintenance	8.7	7.9	8.9
Production, Transportation, and Material Moving	12.5	11.2	12.2
Sales and Office	28.3	26.1	23.8
Service	20.8	21.1	18.1

Note: Figures cover employed civilians 16 years of age and older; (1) Figures cover the Reno, NV Metropolitan Statistical Area—see Appendix B for areas included
Source: U.S. Census Bureau, 2012-2016 American Community Survey 5-Year Estimates

Employment by Industry

Sector	MSA[1] Number of Employees	MSA[1] Percent of Total	U.S. Percent of Total
Construction	16,500	6.9	4.7
Education and Health Services	26,500	11.1	15.9
Financial Activities	10,600	4.5	5.7
Government	32,000	13.5	15.3
Information	2,200	0.9	1.9
Leisure and Hospitality	37,500	15.8	10.7
Manufacturing	19,100	8.0	8.5
Mining and Logging	300	0.1	0.5
Other Services	6,400	2.7	3.9
Professional and Business Services	32,000	13.5	14.0
Retail Trade	23,900	10.1	11.0
Transportation, Warehousing, and Utilities	20,900	8.8	4.1
Wholesale Trade	9,900	4.2	4.0

Note: Figures are non-farm employment as of December 2017. Figures are not seasonally adjusted and include workers 16 years of age and older; (1) Figures cover the Reno, NV Metropolitan Statistical Area—see Appendix B for areas included
Source: Bureau of Labor Statistics, Current Employment Statistics, Employment, Hours, and Earnings

Occupations with Greatest Projected Employment Growth: 2017 – 2019

Occupation[1]	2017 Employment	2019 Projected Employment	Numeric Employment Change	Percent Employment Change
Combined Food Preparation and Serving Workers, Including Fast Food	32,640	35,070	2,430	7.5
Retail Salespersons	49,790	52,170	2,380	4.8
Laborers and Freight, Stock, and Material Movers, Hand	28,360	30,720	2,360	8.3
Registered Nurses	23,000	24,640	1,640	7.1
Waiters and Waitresses	40,820	42,330	1,510	3.7
Office Clerks, General	29,630	31,110	1,480	5.0
General and Operations Managers	18,800	20,220	1,420	7.6
Carpenters	14,710	16,020	1,310	8.9
Customer Service Representatives	25,080	26,380	1,300	5.2
Personal Care Aides	12,220	13,490	1,270	10.4

Note: Projections cover Nevada; (1) Sorted by numeric employment change
Source: www.projectionscentral.com, State Occupational Projections, 2017–2019 Short-Term Projections

Fastest Growing Occupations: 2017 – 2019

Occupation[1]	2017 Employment	2019 Projected Employment	Numeric Employment Change	Percent Employment Change
Electrical and Electronic Equipment Assemblers	1,070	2,120	1,050	96.9
Etchers and Engravers	140	240	100	73.0
Mechanical Drafters	250	390	140	54.7
Electrical and Electronics Repairers, Commercial and Industrial Equipment	390	570	180	47.3
Mechanical Engineers	750	1,090	340	45.4
Solar Photovoltaic Installers	290	410	120	39.9
Electrical Engineers	770	1,050	280	37.0
Industrial Engineers	450	590	140	31.0
Software Developers, Systems Software	980	1,250	270	27.6
Procurement Clerks	560	690	130	21.5

Note: Projections cover Nevada; (1) Sorted by percent employment change and excludes occupations with numeric employment change less than 50
Source: www.projectionscentral.com, State Occupational Projections, 2017–2019 Short-Term Projections

TAXES

State Corporate Income Tax Rates

State	Tax Rate (%)	Income Brackets ($)	Num. of Brackets	Financial Institution Tax Rate (%)[a]	Federal Income Tax Ded.
Nevada	None	–	–	–	–

Note: Tax rates as of January 1, 2018; (a) Rates listed are the corporate income tax rate applied to financial institutions or excise taxes based on income. Some states have other taxes based upon the value of deposits or shares.
Source: Federation of Tax Administrators, Range of State Corporate Income Tax Rates, January 1, 2018

State Individual Income Tax Rates

State	Tax Rate (%)	Income Brackets ($)	Num. of Brackets	Personal Exempt. ($)[1]		Fed. Inc. Tax Ded.
				Single	Dependents	
Nevada	None	–	–	–	–	–

Note: Tax rates as of January 1, 2018; Local- and county-level taxes are not included; n/a not applicable; (1) Married joint filers generally receive double the single exemption
Source: Federation of Tax Administrators, State Individual Income Tax Rates, January 1, 2018

Various State Sales and Excise Tax Rates

State	State Sales Tax (%)	Gasoline[1] (¢/gal.)	Cigarette[2] ($/pack)	Spirits[3] ($/gal.)	Wine[4] ($/gal.)	Beer[5] ($/gal.)	Recreational Marijuana (%)
Nevada	6.85	33.52	1.80	3.60 (f)	0.70 (l)	0.16	(z)

Note: All tax rates as of January 1, 2018; (1) The American Petroleum Institute has developed a methodology for determining the average tax rate on a gallon of fuel. Rates may include any of the following: excise taxes, environmental fees, storage tank fees, other fees or taxes, general sales tax, and local taxes. In states where gasoline is subject to the general sales tax, or where the fuel tax is based on the average sale price, the average rate determined by API is sensitive to changes in the price of gasoline. States that fully or partially apply general sales taxes to gasoline: CA, CO, GA, IL, IN, MI, NY; (2) The federal excise tax of $1.0066 per pack and local taxes are not included; (3) Rates are those applicable to off-premise sales of 40% alcohol by volume (a.b.v.) distilled spirits in 750ml containers. Local excise taxes are excluded; (4) Rates are those applicable to off-premise sales of 11% a.b.v. non-carbonated wine in 750ml containers; (5) Rates are those applicable to off-premise sales of 4.7% a.b.v. beer in 12 ounce containers; (f) Different rates also applicable according to alcohol content, place of production, size of container, or place purchased (on- or off-premise or onboard airlines); (l) Different rates also applicable to alcohol content, place of production, size of container, place purchased (on- or off-premise or on board airlines) or type of wine (carbonated, vermouth, etc.); (z) 15% excise tax (wholesale price) and 10% retail sales tax
Source: Tax Foundation, 2018 Facts & Figures: How Does Your State Compare?

State Business Tax Climate Index Rankings

State	Overall Rank	Corporate Tax Rank	Individual Income Tax Rank	Sales Tax Rank	Unemployment Insurance Tax Rank	Property Tax Rank
Nevada	5	33	1	42	45	8

Note: The index is a measure of how each state's tax laws affect economic performance. The lower the rank, the more favorable a state's tax system is for business. States without a given tax are given a ranking of 1. The scores/rankings for the District of Columbia do not affect other states. The 2018 index represents the tax climate as of July 1, 2017.
Source: Tax Foundation, State Business Tax Climate Index 2018

TRANSPORTATION

Means of Transportation to Work

Area	Car/Truck/Van		Public Transportation			Bicycle	Walked	Other Means	Worked at Home
	Drove Alone	Car-pooled	Bus	Subway	Railroad				
City	81.0	11.3	1.6	0.0	0.0	0.4	1.7	1.1	3.0
MSA[1]	77.7	11.1	2.0	0.0	0.0	0.5	2.9	1.5	4.2
U.S.	76.4	9.3	2.6	1.9	0.6	0.6	2.8	1.3	4.6

Note: Figures are percentages and cover workers 16 years of age and older; (1) Figures cover the Reno, NV Metropolitan Statistical Area—see Appendix B for areas included
Source: U.S. Census Bureau, 2012-2016 American Community Survey 5-Year Estimates

Travel Time to Work

Area	Less Than 10 Minutes	10 to 19 Minutes	20 to 29 Minutes	30 to 44 Minutes	45 to 59 Minutes	60 to 89 Minutes	90 Minutes or More
City	9.0	40.2	27.8	16.8	2.6	1.8	1.8
MSA[1]	12.3	40.0	25.4	14.4	3.7	2.5	1.7
U.S.	12.9	29.2	20.9	20.4	8.0	6.0	2.7

Note: Note: Figures are percentages and include workers 16 years old and over; (1) Figures cover the Reno, NV Metropolitan Statistical Area—see Appendix B for areas included
Source: U.S. Census Bureau, 2012-2016 American Community Survey 5-Year Estimates

Freeway Travel Time Index

Area	1985	1990	1995	2000	2005	2010	2014
Urban Area Rank[1,2]	n/a	n/a	n/a	n/a	n/a	n/a	n/a
Urban Area Index[1]	n/a	n/a	n/a	n/a	n/a	n/a	n/a
Average Index[3]	1.09	1.11	1.14	1.17	1.20	1.19	1.20

Note: Freeway Travel Time Index—the ratio of travel time in the peak period to the travel time at free-flow conditions. For example, a value of 1.30 indicates a 20-minute free-flow trip takes 26 minutes in the peak (20 minutes x 1.30 = 26 minutes); (1) Data for the Reno, NV urban area was not available; (2) Rank is based on 101 urban areas (#1 = highest travel time index); (3) Average of 101 urban areas
Source: Texas Transportation Institute, 2015 Urban Mobility Scorecard, August 2015

Freeway Commuter Stress Index

Area	1985	1990	1995	2000	2005	2010	2014
Urban Area Rank[1,2]	n/a	n/a	n/a	n/a	n/a	n/a	n/a
Urban Area Index[1]	n/a	n/a	n/a	n/a	n/a	n/a	n/a
Average Index[3]	1.13	1.16	1.19	1.22	1.25	1.24	1.25

Note: The Freeway Commuter Stress Index is the same as the Freeway Travel Time Index (see table above) except that it includes only the travel in the peak directions during the peak periods; the TTI includes travel in all directions during the peak period. Thus, the CSI is more indicative of the work trip experienced by each commuter on a daily basis; (1) Data for the Reno, NV urban area was not available; (2) Rank is based on 101 urban areas (#1 = highest travel time index); (3) Average of 101 urban areas
Source: Texas Transportation Institute, 2015 Urban Mobility Scorecard, August 2015

Living Environment

COST OF LIVING

Cost of Living Index

Composite Index	Groceries	Housing	Utilities	Trans-portation	Health Care	Misc. Goods/ Services
106.6	100.1	106.8	84.6	113.0	110.2	113.1

Note: The Cost of Living Index measures regional differences in the cost of consumer goods and services, excluding taxes and non-consumer expenditures, for professional and managerial households in the top income quintile. It is based on more than 50,000 prices covering almost 60 different items for which prices are collected three times a year by chambers of commerce, economic development organizations or university applied economic centers in each participating urban area. The numbers shown should be read as a percentage above or below the national average of 100. For example, a value of 115.4 in the groceries column indicates that grocery prices are 15.4% higher than the national average. Small differences in the index numbers should not be interpreted as significant; Figures cover the Reno-Sparks NV urban area.
Source: The Council for Community and Economic Research, ACCRA Cost of Living Index, 2017

Grocery Prices

Area[1]	T-Bone Steak ($/pound)	Frying Chicken ($/pound)	Whole Milk ($/half gal.)	Eggs ($/dozen)	Orange Juice ($/64 oz.)	Coffee ($/11.5 oz.)
City[2]	12.86	1.55	2.16	1.43	3.47	5.35
Avg.	11.29	1.40	2.02	1.47	3.55	4.37
Min.	7.71	0.93	1.04	0.70	2.86	3.24
Max.	15.83	2.39	4.03	3.92	6.29	8.16

*Note: (1) Values for the local area are compared with the average, minimum and maximum values for all 294 areas in the Cost of Living Index; (2) Figures cover the Reno-Sparks NV urban area; **T-Bone Steak** (price per pound); **Frying Chicken** (price per pound, whole fryer); **Whole Milk** (half gallon carton); **Eggs** (price per dozen, Grade A, large); **Orange Juice** (64 oz. Tropicana or Florida Natural); **Coffee** (11.5 oz. can, vacuum-packed, Maxwell House, Hills Bros, or Folgers).*
Source: The Council for Community and Economic Research, ACCRA Cost of Living Index, 2017

Housing and Utility Costs

Area[1]	New Home Price ($)	Apartment Rent ($/month)	All Electric ($/month)	Part Electric ($/month)	Other Energy ($/month)	Telephone ($/month)
City[2]	347,722	1,164	-	68.86	44.40	30.01
Avg.	335,956	1,047	175.01	97.34	67.93	28.71
Min.	187,788	491	109.48	49.33	35.44	12.39
Max.	1,739,087	4,559	432.62	227.09	353.33	44.61

*Note: (1) Values for the local area are compared with the average, minimum and maximum values for all 294 areas in the Cost of Living Index; (2) Figures cover the Reno-Sparks NV urban area; **New Home Price** (2,400 sf living area, 8,000 sf lot, in urban area with full utilities); **Apartment Rent** (950 sf 2 bedroom/1.5 or 2 bath, unfurnished, excluding all utilities except water); **All Electric** (average monthly cost for an all-electric home); **Part Electric** (average monthly cost for a part-electric home); **Other Energy** (average monthly cost for natural gas, fuel oil, coal, wood, and any other forms of energy except electricity); **Telephone** (price includes basic monthly rate for a private residential line plus additional local usage charges incurred by a family of four).*
Source: The Council for Community and Economic Research, ACCRA Cost of Living Index, 2017

Health Care, Transportation, and Other Costs

Area[1]	Doctor ($/visit)	Dentist ($/visit)	Optometrist ($/visit)	Gasoline ($/gallon)	Beauty Salon ($/visit)	Men's Shirt ($)
City[2]	138.14	99.33	108.47	2.73	46.47	34.11
Avg.	108.00	92.54	101.93	2.25	37.58	30.92
Min.	30.39	60.00	49.75	1.82	16.11	11.20
Max.	193.50	161.94	229.28	3.16	77.35	59.13

*Note: (1) Values for the local area are compared with the average, minimum and maximum values for all 294 areas in the Cost of Living Index; (2) Figures cover the Reno-Sparks NV urban area; **Doctor** (general practitioners routine exam of an established patient); **Dentist** (adult teeth cleaning and periodic oral examination); **Optometrist** (full vision eye exam for established adult patient); **Gasoline** (one gallon regular unleaded, national brand, including all taxes, cash price at self-service pump if available); **Beauty Salon** (woman's shampoo, trim, and blow-dry); **Men's Shirt** (cotton/polyester dress shirt, pinpoint weave, long sleeves).*
Source: The Council for Community and Economic Research, ACCRA Cost of Living Index, 2017

HOUSING

House Price Index (HPI)

Area	National Ranking[2]	Quarterly Change (%)	One-Year Change (%)	Five-Year Change (%)
MSA[1]	11	2.69	11.81	93.61
U.S.[3]	–	1.61	6.68	34.71

Note: The HPI is a weighted repeat sales index. It measures average price changes in repeat sales or refinancings on the same properties. This information is obtained by reviewing repeat mortgage transactions on single-family properties whose mortgages have been purchased or securitized by Fannie Mae or Freddie Mac in January 1975; (1) Figures cover the Reno, NV Metropolitan Statistical Area—see Appendix B for areas included; (2) Rankings are based on annual percentage change for all metro areas containing at least 15,000 transactions over the last 10 years and ranges from 1 to 253; (3) figures based on a weighted average of Census Division estimates using a seasonally adjusted, purchase-only index; all figures are for the period ending December 31, 2017

Source: Federal Housing Finance Agency, House Price Index, February 28, 2018

Median Single-Family Home Prices

Area	2015	2016	2017p	Percent Change 2016 to 2017
MSA[1]	283.6	306.0	345.1	12.8
U.S. Average	223.9	235.5	248.8	5.6

Note: Figures are median sales prices of existing single-family homes in thousands of dollars; (p) preliminary; (1) Figures cover the Reno, NV Metropolitan Statistical Area—see Appendix B for areas included

Source: National Association of Realtors, Median Sales Price of Existing Single-Family Homes for Metropolitan Areas, 4th Quarter 2017

Qualifying Income Based on Median Sales Price of Existing Single-Family Homes

Area	With 5% Down ($)	With 10% Down ($)	With 20% Down ($)
MSA[1]	80,057	75,844	67,417
U.S. Average	55,585	52,659	46,808

Note: Figures are preliminary; Qualifying income is based on a mortgage rate of 4.17%. Monthly principal and interest payment is limited to 25% of income; (1) Figures cover the Reno, NV Metropolitan Statistical Area—see Appendix B for areas included

Source: National Association of Realtors, Qualifying Income Based on Median Sales Price of Existing Single-Family Homes for Metropolitan Areas, 4th Quarter 2017

Median Apartment Condo-Coop Home Prices

Area	2015	2016	2017p	Percent Change 2016 to 2017
MSA[1]	143.7	169.8	187.1	10.2
U.S. Average	210.7	220.7	234.3	6.2

Note: Figures are median sales prices of existing apartment condo-coop homes in thousands of dollars; (p) preliminary; (1) Figures cover the Reno, NV Metropolitan Statistical Area—see Appendix B for areas included

Source: National Association of Realtors, Median Sales Price of Existing Apartment Condo-Coop Homes for Metropolitan Areas, 4th Quarter 2017

Home Value Distribution

Area	Under $50,000	$50,000 -$99,999	$100,000 -$149,999	$150,000 -$199,999	$200,000 -$299,999	$300,000 -$499,999	$500,000 -$999,999	$1,000,000 or more
City	5.4	7.4	14.0	20.2	30.8	19.6	2.2	0.5
MSA[1]	6.5	7.6	11.1	14.8	25.9	22.8	8.8	2.5
U.S.	8.8	14.8	15.3	14.9	18.4	16.4	9.0	2.5

Note: Figures are percentages and cover owner-occupied housing units; (1) Figures cover the Reno, NV Metropolitan Statistical Area—see Appendix B for areas included

Source: U.S. Census Bureau, 2012-2016 American Community Survey 5-Year Estimates

Homeownership Rate

Area	2009 (%)	2010 (%)	2011 (%)	2012 (%)	2013 (%)	2014 (%)	2015 (%)	2016 (%)	2017 (%)
MSA[1]	n/a	n/a	n/a	n/a	n/a	n/a	n/a	n/a	n/a
U.S.	67.4	66.9	66.1	65.4	65.1	64.5	63.7	63.4	63.9

Note: (1) Figures cover the Reno, NV Metropolitan Statistical Area—see Appendix B for areas included; n/a not available

Source: U.S. Census Bureau, Housing Vacancies and Homeownership Annual Statistics: 2009-2017

Year Housing Structure Built

Area	2010 or Later	2000 -2009	1990 -1999	1980 -1989	1970 -1979	1960 -1969	1950 -1959	1940 -1949	Before 1940	Median Year
City	2.2	28.4	17.9	15.9	17.6	9.0	6.0	1.5	1.6	1989
MSA[1]	1.9	23.2	20.3	16.1	18.9	9.2	5.5	2.2	2.7	1987
U.S.	2.3	14.7	14.0	13.7	15.6	10.9	10.6	5.2	13.0	1977

Note: Figures are percentages except for Median Year; Note: (1) Figures cover the Reno, NV Metropolitan Statistical Area—see Appendix B for areas included
Source: U.S. Census Bureau, 2012-2016 American Community Survey 5-Year Estimates

Gross Monthly Rent

Area	Under $500	$500 -$999	$1,000 -$1,499	$1,500 -$1,999	$2,000 -$2,499	$2,500 -$2,999	$3,000 and up	Median ($)
City	3.6	49.2	34.0	9.2	2.9	0.1	1.0	971
MSA[1]	7.5	50.7	29.2	9.7	2.0	0.4	0.5	917
U.S.	11.3	43.3	27.7	10.7	4.0	1.6	1.5	949

Note: Figures are percentages except for Median; Gross rent is the contract rent plus the estimated average monthly cost of utilities (electricity, gas, and water and sewer) and fuels (oil, coal, kerosene, wood, etc.) if these are paid by the renter (or paid for the renter by someone else); (1) Figures cover the Reno, NV Metropolitan Statistical Area—see Appendix B for areas included
Source: U.S. Census Bureau, 2012-2016 American Community Survey 5-Year Estimates

HEALTH

Health Risk Factors

Category	MSA[1] (%)	U.S. (%)
Adults aged 18–64 who have any kind of health care coverage	85.8	87.7
Adults who reported being in good or excellent health	81.4	83.6
Adults who are current smokers	15.6	17.1
Adults who currently use E-cigarettes	6.2	4.7
Adults who currently use chewing tobacco, snuff, or snus	4.2	4.0
Adults who are heavy drinkers[2]	8.1	6.5
Adults who are binge drinkers[3]	19.1	16.9
Adults who are overweight (BMI 25.0 - 29.9)	36.1	35.3
Adults who are obese (BMI 30.0 - 99.8)	26.4	29.9
Adults who participated in any physical activities in the past month	77.9	76.9
Adults who always or nearly always wears a seat belt	94.7	94.3

Note: (1) Figures cover the Reno, NV Metropolitan Statistical Area—see Appendix B for areas included; (2) Heavy drinkers are classified as adult men having more than 14 drinks per week and adult women having more than 7 drinks per week; (3) Binge drinkers are classified as males having five or more drinks on one occasion or females having four or more drinks on one occasion
Source: Centers for Disease Control and Prevention, Behaviorial Risk Factor Surveillance System, SMART: Selected Metropolitan Area Risk Trends, 2016

Health Screening Rates

Category	MSA[1] (%)	U.S. (%)
Adults 50-75 who have had a blood stool test within the past year	8.6	8.0
Adults 50-75 who have had a colonoscopy in the past 10 years	65.1	63.5
Adults aged 65+ who have had flu shot within the past year	52.3	58.6
Adults aged 65+ who have ever had a pneumonia vaccination	75.2	73.4
Adults who have ever been tested for HIV	39.4	35.6
Women aged 21-65 who have had a pap test in the past three years	77.3	79.8
Men aged 40+ who have had a PSA test within the past two years	41.8	39.5
Women aged 40+ who have had a mammogram within the past two years	66.4	72.5

Note: (1) Figures cover the Reno, NV Metropolitan Statistical Area—see Appendix B for areas included;
Source: Centers for Disease Control and Prevention, Behaviorial Risk Factor Surveillance System, SMART: Selected Metropolitan Area Risk Trends, 2016

Chronic Health Conditions

Category	MSA[1] (%)	U.S. (%)
Adults who have ever been told they had a heart attack	4.3	4.4
Adults who have ever been told they have angina or coronary heart disease	4.1	4.1
Adults who have ever been told they had a stroke	2.8	3.1
Adults who have been told they currently have asthma	8.5	9.3
Adults who have ever been told they have arthritis	25.9	25.8
Adults who have ever been told they have diabetes[2]	10.0	10.5
Adults who have ever been told they had skin cancer	6.7	5.9
Adults who have ever been told they had any other types of cancer	6.8	6.7
Adults who have ever been told they have COPD	5.5	6.3
Adults who have ever been told they have kidney disease	2.5	2.8
Adults who have ever been told they have a form of depression	15.4	17.4

Note: (1) Figures cover the Reno, NV Metropolitan Statistical Area—see Appendix B for areas included; (2) Figures do not include pregnancy-related, borderline, or pre-diabetes
Source: Centers for Disease Control and Prevention, Behaviorial Risk Factor Surveillance System, SMART: Selected Metropolitan Area Risk Trends, 2016

Mortality Rates for the Top 10 Causes of Death in the U.S.

ICD-10[a] Sub-Chapter	ICD-10[a] Code	Age-Adjusted Mortality Rate[1] per 100,000 population	
		County[2]	U.S.
Malignant neoplasms	C00-C97	158.4	158.5
Ischaemic heart diseases	I20-I25	126.2	96.8
Other forms of heart disease	I30-I51	30.5	52.4
Chronic lower respiratory diseases	J40-J47	49.0	40.9
Cerebrovascular diseases	I60-I69	33.5	37.2
Organic, including symptomatic, mental disorders	F01-F09	20.2	33.3
Other degenerative diseases of the nervous system	G30-G31	34.8	32.1
Other external causes of accidental injury	W00-X59	34.7	31.2
Diabetes mellitus	E10-E14	16.5	21.1
Hypertensive diseases	I10-I15	33.4	20.8

Note: (a) ICD-10 = International Classification of Diseases 10th Revision; (1) Mortality rates are a three year average covering 2014-2016; (2) Figures cover Washoe County.
Source: Centers for Disease Control and Prevention, National Center for Health Statistics. Underlying Cause of Death 1999-2016 on CDC WONDER Online Database, released December 2017

Mortality Rates for Selected Causes of Death

ICD-10[a] Sub-Chapter	ICD-10[a] Code	Age-Adjusted Mortality Rate[1] per 100,000 population	
		County[2]	U.S.
Assault	X85-Y09	4.9	5.6
Diseases of the liver	K70-K76	19.7	14.0
Human immunodeficiency virus (HIV) disease	B20-B24	1.6	1.9
Influenza and pneumonia	J09-J18	17.3	14.6
Intentional self-harm	X60-X84	22.8	13.2
Malnutrition	E40-E46	1.7	1.3
Obesity and other hyperalimentation	E65-E68	Unreliable	2.1
Renal failure	N17-N19	8.0	13.0
Transport accidents	V01-V99	12.9	12.0
Viral hepatitis	B15-B19	3.4	1.9

Note: (a) ICD-10 = International Classification of Diseases 10th Revision; (1) Mortality rates are a three year average covering 2014-2016; (2) Figures cover Washoe County; Data are Suppressed when the data meet the criteria for confidentiality constraints; Mortality rates are flagged as Unreliable when the rate would be calculated with a numerator of 20 or less.
Source: Centers for Disease Control and Prevention, National Center for Health Statistics. Underlying Cause of Death 1999-2016 on CDC WONDER Online Database, released December 2017

Health Insurance Coverage

Area	With Health Insurance	With Private Health Insurance	With Public Health Insurance	Without Health Insurance	Population Under Age 18 Without Health Insurance
City	86.6	67.4	29.8	13.4	8.7
MSA[1]	85.9	66.7	30.0	14.1	10.5
U.S.	88.3	66.7	33.0	11.7	5.9

Note: Figures are percentages that cover the civilian noninstitutionalized population; (1) Figures cover the Reno, NV Metropolitan Statistical Area—see Appendix B for areas included
Source: U.S. Census Bureau, 2012-2016 American Community Survey 5-Year Estimates

Number of Medical Professionals

Area	MDs[3]	DOs[3,4]	Dentists	Podiatrists	Chiropractors	Optometrists
County[1] (number)	1,291	90	315	19	116	93
County[1] (rate[2])	290.5	20.3	69.6	4.2	25.6	20.6
U.S. (rate[2])	276.5	22.3	67.3	6.0	26.7	15.9

Note: Data as of 2016 unless noted; (1) Data covers Washoe County; (2) Rate per 100,000 population; (3) Data as of 2015 and includes all active, non-federal physicians; (4) Doctor of Osteopathic Medicine
Source: U.S. Department of Health and Human Services, Health Resources and Services Administration, Bureau of Health Professions, Area Resource File (ARF) 2016-2017

EDUCATION

Public School District Statistics

District Name	Schls	Pupils	Pupil/ Teacher Ratio	Minority Pupils[1] (%)	Free Lunch Eligible[2] (%)	IEP[3] (%)
State-sponsored Charter Schools	25	25,748	27.3	48.5	n/a	8.1
Storey County School District	4	411	11.6	19.0	n/a	14.4
Washoe County School District	112	66,504	20.7	54.8	42.5	13.4

Note: Table includes school districts with 100 or more students; (1) Percentage of students that are not non-Hispanic white; (2) Percentage of students that are eligible for the free lunch program; (3) Percentage of students that have an Individualized Education Program.
Source: U.S. Department of Education, National Center for Education Statistics, Common Core of Data, Local Education Agency (School District) Universe Survey: School Year 2015-2016; U.S. Department of Education, National Center for Education Statistics, Common Core of Data, Public Elementary/Secondary School Universe Survey: School Year 2015-2016

Highest Level of Education

Area	Less than H.S.	H.S. Diploma	Some College, No Deg.	Associate Degree	Bachelor's Degree	Master's Degree	Prof. School Degree	Doctorate Degree
City	14.0	27.1	26.9	9.4	15.3	5.6	1.0	0.6
MSA[1]	12.9	23.9	26.3	7.9	18.2	7.1	2.0	1.6
U.S.	13.0	27.5	21.0	8.2	18.8	8.2	2.0	1.3

Note: Figures cover persons age 25 and over; (1) Figures cover the Reno, NV Metropolitan Statistical Area—see Appendix B for areas included
Source: U.S. Census Bureau, 2012-2016 American Community Survey 5-Year Estimates

Educational Attainment by Race

Area	High School Graduate or Higher (%)					Bachelor's Degree or Higher (%)				
	Total	White	Black	Asian	Hisp.[2]	Total	White	Black	Asian	Hisp.[2]
City	86.0	87.2	88.4	91.8	58.4	22.6	22.8	24.0	38.0	9.6
MSA[1]	87.1	88.6	88.6	87.0	58.3	28.9	30.2	19.9	38.7	10.1
U.S.	87.0	88.9	84.3	86.3	65.7	30.3	31.6	20.0	52.1	14.7

Note: Figures shown cover persons 25 years old and over; (1) Figures cover the Reno, NV Metropolitan Statistical Area—see Appendix B for areas included; (2) People of Hispanic origin can be of any race
Source: U.S. Census Bureau, 2012-2016 American Community Survey 5-Year Estimates

School Enrollment by Grade and Control

Area	Preschool (%)		Kindergarten (%)		Grades 1 - 4 (%)		Grades 5 - 8 (%)		Grades 9 - 12 (%)	
	Public	Private	Public	Private	Public	Private	Public	Private	Public	Private
City	59.6	40.4	89.4	10.6	93.8	6.2	93.0	7.0	96.9	3.1
MSA[1]	54.4	45.6	90.1	9.9	92.5	7.5	91.6	8.4	94.6	5.4
U.S.	58.4	41.6	87.7	12.3	89.8	10.2	89.7	10.3	90.4	9.6

Note: Figures shown cover persons 3 years old and over; (1) Figures cover the Reno, NV Metropolitan Statistical Area—see Appendix B for areas included
Source: U.S. Census Bureau, 2012-2016 American Community Survey 5-Year Estimates

Average Salaries of Public School Classroom Teachers

Area	2015		2016		Change from 2015 to 2016	
	Dollars	Rank[1]	Dollars	Rank[1]	Percent	Rank[2]
Nevada	56,703	18	56,943	18	0.4	38
U.S. Average	57,611	–	58,353	–	1.3	–

Note: (1) Rank ranges from 1 to 51 where 1 indicates highest salary; (2) Rank ranges from 1 to 51 where 1 indicates highest percent change.
Source: National Education Association, Rankings & Estimates: Rankings of the States 2016 and Estimates of School Statistics 2017

Higher Education

Four-Year Colleges			Two-Year Colleges			Medical Schools[1]	Law Schools[2]	Voc/ Tech[3]
Public	Private Non-profit	Private For-profit	Public	Private Non-profit	Private For-profit			
0	0	0	0	0	1	0	0	1

Note: Figures cover institutions located within the city limits and include main campuses only; (1) includes schools accredited by the Liaison Committee on Medical Education and the American Osteopathic Association's Commission on Osteopathic College Accreditation; (2) includes ABA-accredited schools, schools with provisional ABA accreditation, and state accredited schools; (3) includes all schools with programs that are less than 2 years.
Source: National Center for Education Statistics, Integrated Postsecondary Education System (IPEDS), 2016-17; Wikipedia, List of Medical Schools in the United States, accessed April 2, 2018; Wikipedia, List of Law Schools in the United States, accessed April 2, 2018

According to *U.S. News & World Report,* the Reno, NV metro area is home to one of the best national universities in the U.S.: **University of Nevada—Reno** (#202 tie). The indicators used to capture academic quality fall into a number of categories: assessment by administrators at peer institutions; retention of students; faculty resources; student selectivity; financial resources; alumni giving; high school counselor ratings of colleges; and graduation rate. *U.S. News & World Report, "America's Best Colleges 2018"*

PRESIDENTIAL ELECTION

2016 Presidential Election Results

Area	Clinton	Trump	Johnson	Stein	Other
Washoe County	46.4	45.1	4.4	0.0	4.0
U.S.	48.0	45.9	3.3	1.1	1.7

Note: Results are percentages and may not add to 100% due to rounding
Source: Dave Leip's Atlas of U.S. Presidential Elections

EMPLOYERS

Major Employers

Company Name	Industry
Atlantis Casino Resort	Casino hotels
Bellagio	Casino hotels
Circus Circus Casinos - Reno	Casino hotels
City of Reno	Executive & legislative offices combined
Desert Palace	Casino hotels
Eldorado Hotel & Casino	Casino hotels
Grand Sierra Resort & Casino	Casino hotels
Harrahs Reno	Casino hotels
IGT	All other miscellaneous manufacturing
Integrity Staffing Solutions	Temporary help services
Mandalay Corp	Casino hotels
Peppermill Hotel Casino - Reno	Casino hotels
Renown Regional Medical Center	General medical & surgical hospitals
Saint Marys	General medical & surgical hospitals
Sierra Nevada Healthcare System	General medical & surgical hospitals
Silver Legacy Resort Casino	Casino hotels
Sparks Nugget	Casino hotels
Truckee Meadows Community Coll	Junior colleges
United Parcel Service	Couriers
University of Nevada-Reno	Colleges & universities
Washoe County Comptroller	Executive & legislative offices combined
Washoe County School District	Elementary & secondary schools
West Business Solutions	Telemarketing bureaus

Note: Companies shown are located within the Reno, NV Metropolitan Statistical Area.
Source: Hoovers.com; Wikipedia

PUBLIC SAFETY

Crime Rate

Area	All Crimes	Violent Crimes: Murder	Violent Crimes: Rape[3]	Violent Crimes: Robbery	Violent Crimes: Aggrav. Assault	Property Crimes: Burglary	Property Crimes: Larceny -Theft	Property Crimes: Motor Vehicle Theft
City	2,966.0	3.1	26.7	91.5	325.9	460.6	1,708.7	349.5
Metro[1]	3,107.8	3.1	42.2	107.3	361.9	419.4	1,777.7	396.2
U.S.	2,847.8	5.3	40.4	102.8	248.5	468.9	1,745.0	236.9

Note: Figures are crimes per 100,000 population; (1) Figures cover the Reno, NV Metropolitan Statistical Area—see Appendix B for areas included; (3) The city and U.S. figures shown were reported using the revised Uniform Crime Reporting (UCR) definition of rape. The metro area figures shown are an aggregate total of the data submitted using both the revised and legacy UCR definitions.
Source: FBI Uniform Crime Reports, 2016

Hate Crimes

Area	Number of Quarters Reported	Race/Ethnicity/ Ancestry	Religion	Sexual Orientation	Disability	Gender	Gender Identity
		Number of Incidents per Bias Motivation					
City	4	0	0	0	0	0	0
U.S.	4	3,489	1,273	1,076	70	31	124

Source: Federal Bureau of Investigation, Hate Crime Statistics 2016

Identity Theft Consumer Reports

Area	Reports	Reports per 100,000 Population	Rank[2]
MSA[1]	461	101	97
U.S.	371,061	114	-

Note: (1) Figures cover the Reno, NV Metropolitan Statistical Area—see Appendix B for areas included; (2) Rank ranges from 1 to 389 where 1 indicates greatest number of identity theft reports per 100,000 population
Source: Federal Trade Commission, Consumer Sentinel Network Data Book for January–December 2017

Fraud and Other Consumer Reports

Area	Reports	Reports per 100,000 Population	Rank[2]
MSA[1]	2,475	541	78
U.S.	2,304,550	708	-

Note: (1) Figures cover the Reno, NV Metropolitan Statistical Area—see Appendix B for areas included; (2) Rank ranges from 1 to 389 where 1 indicates greatest number of fraud and other consumer reports per 100,000 population
Source: Federal Trade Commission, Consumer Sentinel Network Data Book for January–December 2017

SPORTS

Professional Sports Teams

Team Name	League	Year Established
No teams are located in the metro area		

Source: Wikipedia, Major Professional Sports Teams of the United States and Canada, April 5, 2018

CLIMATE

Average and Extreme Temperatures

Temperature	Jan	Feb	Mar	Apr	May	Jun	Jul	Aug	Sep	Oct	Nov	Dec	Yr.
Extreme High (°F)	70	75	83	89	96	103	104	105	101	91	77	70	105
Average High (°F)	45	51	56	64	73	82	91	89	81	70	55	46	67
Average Temp. (°F)	32	38	41	48	56	63	70	68	61	51	40	33	50
Average Low (°F)	19	23	26	31	38	44	49	47	40	32	25	20	33
Extreme Low (°F)	-16	-16	0	13	18	25	33	24	20	8	1	-16	-16

Note: Figures cover the years 1949-1992
Source: National Climatic Data Center, International Station Meteorological Climate Summary, 9/96

Average Precipitation/Snowfall/Humidity

Precip./Humidity	Jan	Feb	Mar	Apr	May	Jun	Jul	Aug	Sep	Oct	Nov	Dec	Yr.
Avg. Precip. (in.)	1.0	0.9	0.7	0.4	0.7	0.4	0.3	0.2	0.3	0.4	0.8	1.0	7.2
Avg. Snowfall (in.)	6	5	4	1	1	Tr	0	0	Tr	Tr	2	4	24
Avg. Rel. Hum. 7am (%)	79	77	71	61	55	51	49	55	64	72	78	80	66
Avg. Rel. Hum. 4pm (%)	51	41	34	27	26	22	19	19	22	27	41	51	32

Note: Figures cover the years 1949-1992; Tr = Trace amounts (<0.05 in. of rain; <0.5 in. of snow)
Source: National Climatic Data Center, International Station Meteorological Climate Summary, 9/96

Weather Conditions

Temperature			Daytime Sky			Precipitation		
10°F & below	32°F & below	90°F & above	Clear	Partly cloudy	Cloudy	0.01 inch or more precip.	0.1 inch or more snow/ice	Thunder-storms
14	178	50	143	139	83	50	17	14

Note: Figures are average number of days per year and cover the years 1949-1992
Source: National Climatic Data Center, International Station Meteorological Climate Summary, 9/96

HAZARDOUS WASTE

Superfund Sites

The Reno, NV metro area has no sites on the EPA's Superfund Final National Priorities List. There are a total of 1,396 Superfund sites with a status of proposed or final on the list in the U.S. *U.S. Environmental Protection Agency, National Priorities List, April 4, 2018*

AIR & WATER QUALITY

Air Quality Trends: Ozone

	1990	1995	2000	2005	2010	2012	2013	2014	2015	2016
MSA[1]	0.074	0.070	0.067	0.069	0.068	0.072	0.067	0.069	0.071	0.070
U.S.	0.087	0.089	0.081	0.079	0.073	0.075	0.069	0.067	0.068	0.069

Note: (1) Data covers the Reno, NV Metropolitan Statistical Area—see Appendix B for areas included. The values shown are the composite ozone concentration averages among trend sites based on the highest fourth daily maximum 8-hour concentration in parts per million. These trends are based on sites having an adequate record of monitoring data during the trend period. Data from exceptional events are included.
Source: U.S. Environmental Protection Agency, Air Quality Monitoring Information, "Air Quality Trends by City, 1990-2016"

Air Quality Index

Area	Percent of Days when Air Quality was...[2]					AQI Statistics[2]	
	Good	Moderate	Unhealthy for Sensitive Groups	Unhealthy	Very Unhealthy	Maximum	Median
MSA[1]	55.3	43.6	1.1	0.0	0.0	126	49

Note: (1) Data covers the Reno, NV Metropolitan Statistical Area—see Appendix B for areas included; (2) Based on 365 days with AQI data in 2017. Air Quality Index (AQI) is an index for reporting daily air quality. EPA calculates the AQI for five major air pollutants regulated by the Clean Air Act: ground-level ozone, particle pollution (aka particulate matter), carbon monoxide, sulfur dioxide, and nitrogen dioxide. The AQI runs from 0 to 500. The higher the AQI value, the greater the level of air pollution and the greater the health concern. There are six AQI categories: "Good" AQI is between 0 and 50. Air quality is considered satisfactory; "Moderate" AQI is between 51 and 100. Air quality is acceptable; "Unhealthy for Sensitive Groups" When AQI values are between 101 and 150, members of sensitive groups may experience health effects; "Unhealthy" When AQI values are between 151 and 200 everyone may begin to experience health effects; "Very Unhealthy" AQI values between 201 and 300 trigger a health alert; "Hazardous" AQI values over 300 trigger warnings of emergency conditions (not shown).
Source: U.S. Environmental Protection Agency, Air Quality Index Report, 2017

Air Quality Index Pollutants

Area	Percent of Days when AQI Pollutant was...[2]					
	Carbon Monoxide	Nitrogen Dioxide	Ozone	Sulfur Dioxide	Particulate Matter 2.5	Particulate Matter 10
MSA[1]	0.0	1.9	74.5	0.0	20.8	2.7

Note: (1) Data covers the Reno, NV Metropolitan Statistical Area—see Appendix B for areas included; (2) Based on 365 days with AQI data in 2017. The Air Quality Index (AQI) is an index for reporting daily air quality. EPA calculates the AQI for five major air pollutants regulated by the Clean Air Act: ground-level ozone, particle pollution (also known as particulate matter), carbon monoxide, sulfur dioxide, and nitrogen dioxide. The AQI runs from 0 to 500. The higher the AQI value, the greater the level of air pollution and the greater the health concern.
Source: U.S. Environmental Protection Agency, Air Quality Index Report, 2017

Maximum Air Pollutant Concentrations: Particulate Matter, Ozone, CO and Lead

	Particulate Matter 10 (ug/m^3)	Particulate Matter 2.5 Wtd AM (ug/m^3)	Particulate Matter 2.5 24-Hr (ug/m^3)	Ozone (ppm)	Carbon Monoxide (ppm)	Lead (ug/m^3)
MSA[1] Level	78	7	21	0.073	2	n/a
NAAQS[2]	150	15	35	0.075	9	0.15
Met NAAQS[2]	Yes	Yes	Yes	Yes	Yes	n/a

Note: (1) Data covers the Reno, NV Metropolitan Statistical Area—see Appendix B for areas included; Data from exceptional events are included; (2) National Ambient Air Quality Standards; ppm = parts per million; ug/m^3 = micrograms per cubic meter; n/a not available.
Concentrations: Particulate Matter 10 (coarse particulate)—highest second maximum 24-hour concentration; Particulate Matter 2.5 Wtd AM (fine particulate)—highest weighted annual mean concentration; Particulate Matter 2.5 24-Hour (fine particulate)—highest 98th percentile 24-hour concentration; Ozone—highest fourth daily maximum 8-hour concentration; Carbon Monoxide—highest second maximum non-overlapping 8-hour concentration; Lead—maximum running 3-month average
Source: U.S. Environmental Protection Agency, Air Quality Monitoring Information, "Air Quality Statistics by City, 2016"

Maximum Air Pollutant Concentrations: Nitrogen Dioxide and Sulfur Dioxide

	Nitrogen Dioxide AM (ppb)	Nitrogen Dioxide 1-Hr (ppb)	Sulfur Dioxide AM (ppb)	Sulfur Dioxide 1-Hr (ppb)	Sulfur Dioxide 24-Hr (ppb)
MSA[1] Level	13	46	n/a	5	n/a
NAAQS[2]	53	100	30	75	140
Met NAAQS[2]	Yes	Yes	n/a	Yes	n/a

Note: (1) Data covers the Reno, NV Metropolitan Statistical Area—see Appendix B for areas included; Data from exceptional events are included; (2) National Ambient Air Quality Standards; ppm = parts per million; ug/m³ = micrograms per cubic meter; n/a not available.
Concentrations: Nitrogen Dioxide AM—highest arithmetic mean concentration; Nitrogen Dioxide 1-Hr—highest 98th percentile 1-hour daily maximum concentration; Sulfur Dioxide AM—highest annual mean concentration; Sulfur Dioxide 1-Hr—highest 99th percentile 1-hour daily maximum concentration; Sulfur Dioxide 24-Hr—highest second maximum 24-hour concentration
Source: U.S. Environmental Protection Agency, Air Quality Monitoring Information, "Air Quality Statistics by City, 2016"

Drinking Water

Water System Name	Pop. Served	Primary Water Source Type	Violations[1] Health Based	Violations[1] Monitoring/ Reporting
Truckee Meadows Water Auth.	311,932	Surface	0	0

Note: (1) Based on violation data from January 1, 2017 to December 31, 2017
Source: U.S. Environmental Protection Agency, Office of Ground Water and Drinking Water, Safe Drinking Water Information System (based on data extracted April 5, 2018)

Merrimack, New Hampshire

Background

The town of Merrimack is located in southern New Hampshire, just north and adjacent to Nashua along the west bank of the Merrimack River. The township includes four villages: Reeds Ferry in the north; Merrimack Village (originally Souhegan Village) near the Souhegan River; and Thornton's Ferry and South Merrimack on the southern border. Thornton's Ferry was named after Matthew Thornton, a signer of the Declaration of Independence.

Originally the town was in Massachusetts: In 1734, the Commonwealth of Massachusetts granted the town organization under the name Naticook. In 1746, after the border between Massachusetts and New Hampshire was redrawn to its present line, Governor Wentworth of New Hampshire signed a charter awarding the lands between the Pennichuck and Souhegan Rivers to the town of "Merrymac." In 1750 the charter was ratified with the addition of lands north of the Souhegan River.

At first the four villages were fairly autonomous, each with its own schools, stores, and social life. Most of the people were farmers; what industry there was consisted of sawmills and grist mills. Later on, a central meetinghouse was built. In the nineteenth century, sawmills and grist mills gave way to brickyards: Bricks were floated down the Merrimack River on barges, to the city of Lowell.

In 1839, when Henry David Thoreau and his brother passed by Merrimack on the journey described in *A Week on the Concord and Merrimack Rivers*, the town was placid and rural, and it retained its character well into the twentieth century. After the 1950s, the pace of life picked up and the town grew quickly, as the Everett Turnpike was built and travel to and from Nashua, Lowell, and Boston became easier. During the 1960s, and later during the prosperous 1980s, the town became more and more of a bedroom community for Nashua and cities in Massachusetts, as hundreds of high-tech firms sprang up, especially along Route 128 and I-495 around Boston. Merrimack, along with southeastern New Hampshire in general, was among the fastest-growing areas in the nation. New roads and housing developments now occupied what had once been farm or woodland.

In addition, major businesses moved to town. The Anheuser-Busch Company built a bottling plant and moved its famous Clydesdale horses to Merrimack, where they remain a popular attraction for visitors. PC Connection, a leading provider of electronics and computer equipment, has its headquarters in Merrimack, as does Brookstone, the specialty retailer.

To serve this knowledgeable and sophisticated work force, the town has gourmet restaurants, specialty shops, and other features.

Merrimack, like the rest of New England, enjoys a four-season climate, with pleasant summers and falls, cold winters, and late springs. Located in the low-lying Merrimack River valley, the town enjoys warmer temperatures than the hills and mountains of western and northern New Hampshire; its climate more closely resembles that of northeastern Massachusetts and Boston. Snow can begin in late November and December, but consistent ground cover is not expected until January.

Rankings

Business/Finance Rankings

- The personal finance site NerdWallet analyzed 183 American metropolitan areas with populations over 250,000 and more than 15,000 businesses to rank where entrepreneurs find the most success. Criteria included area economy, annual income, housing cost, unemployment rate, and the success rate of area businesses. Manchester* ranked #46. *www.nerdwallet.com, "Best Places to Start a Business," April 27, 2015*
- The Manchester* metro area appeared on the Milken Institute "2017 Best Performing Cities" list. Rank: #100 out of 200 large metro areas. Criteria: job growth; wage and salary growth; high-tech output growth. *Milken Institute, "Best-Performing Cities 2017," January 2018*
- *Forbes* ranked the 200 most populous metro areas to determine the nation's "Best Places for Business and Careers." The Manchester* metro area was ranked #114. Criteria: costs (business and living); job growth (past and projected); income growth; quality of life; educational attainment (college and high school); projected economic growth; cultural and recreational opportunities; net migration patterns; number of highly ranked colleges. *Forbes, "The Best Places for Business and Careers 2017," October 24, 2017*

Education Rankings

- Personal finance website *WalletHub* analyzed the 150 largest U.S. metropolitan statistical areas to determine where the most educated Americans are choosing to settle. Criteria: education quality and attainment gap; education levels; percentage of workers with degrees; public school rankings; quality and size of each metro area's universities. Manchester* was ranked #50 (#1 = most educated city). *www.WalletHub.com, "2017's Most and Least Educated Cities in America," July 25, 2017*

Environmental Rankings

- Sperling's BestPlaces assessed 379 metropolitan areas of the United States for the likelihood of dangerously extreme weather events or earthquakes. In general the Southeast and South-Central regions have the highest risk of weather extremes and earthquakes, while the Pacific Northwest enjoys the lowest risk. Of the least risky metropolitan areas, the Manchester* metro area was ranked #273. *www.bestplaces.net, "Safest Places from Natural Disasters," April 2011*

Health/Fitness Rankings

- The Manchester* metro area ranked #59 out of 189 in The Gallup-Healthways Well-Being Index. Criteria: purpose; social well being; financial health; community and physical health. Results are based on telephone interviews with adults, aged 18 and older, living in metropolitan areas in the 50 U.S. states and the District of Columbia. *Gallup-Healthways, "State of American Well-Being, 2017 Community Well-Being Rankings" March 2018*

Real Estate Rankings

- Manchester* was ranked #126 out of 238 metro areas in terms of housing affordability in 2017 by the National Association of Home Builders (#1 = most affordable). Criteria: the share of homes sold in that area affordable to a family earning the local median income, based on standard mortgage underwriting criteria. *National Association of Home Builders®, NAHB-Wells Fargo Housing Opportunity Index, 4th Quarter 2017*

Safety Rankings

- The National Insurance Crime Bureau ranked 382 metro areas in the U.S. in terms of per capita rates of vehicle theft. The Manchester* metro area ranked #353 (#1 = highest rate). Criteria: number of vehicle theft offenses per 100,000 inhabitants in 2016. *National Insurance Crime Bureau, "Hot Spots 2016," June 8, 2017*

Seniors/Retirement Rankings

- From its Best Cities for Successful Aging indexes, the Milken Institute generated rankings for metropolitan areas, weighing data in nine categories—health care, wellness, living arrangements, transportation and convenience, financial characteristics, education, employment, community engagement, and overall livability. The Manchester* metro area was ranked #181 overall in the small metro area category. *Milken Institute, "Best Cities for Successful Aging, 2017" March 14, 2017*

*Merrimack is located within the Manchester-Nashua, NH Metropolitan Statistical Area.

Business Environment

CITY FINANCES

City Government Finances

Component	2015 ($000)	2015 ($ per capita)
Total Revenues	25,895	1,010
Total Expenditures	32,598	1,271
Debt Outstanding	4,912	192
Cash and Securities[1]	47,417	1,849

Note: (1) Cash and security holdings of a government at the close of its fiscal year,, including those of its dependent agencies, utilities, and liquor stores.
Source: U.S Census Bureau, State & Local Government Finances 2015

City Government Revenue by Source

Source	2015 ($000)	2015 ($ per capita)	2015 (%)
General Revenue			
From Federal Government	0	0	0.0
From State Government	2,343	91	9.0
From Local Governments	0	0	0.0
Taxes			
Property	20,221	788	78.1
Sales and Gross Receipts	0	0	0.0
Personal Income	0	0	0.0
Corporate Income	0	0	0.0
Motor Vehicle License	0	0	0.0
Other Taxes	661	26	2.6
Current Charges	1,702	66	6.6
Liquor Store	0	0	0.0
Utility	0	0	0.0
Employee Retirement	0	0	0.0

Source: U.S Census Bureau, State & Local Government Finances 2015

City Government Expenditures by Function

Function	2015 ($000)	2015 ($ per capita)	2015 (%)
General Direct Expenditures			
Air Transportation	0	0	0.0
Corrections	0	0	0.0
Education	0	0	0.0
Employment Security Administration	0	0	0.0
Financial Administration	768	29	2.4
Fire Protection	5,324	207	16.3
General Public Buildings	205	8	0.6
Governmental Administration, Other	1,772	69	5.4
Health	327	12	1.0
Highways	4,759	185	14.6
Hospitals	0	0	0.0
Housing and Community Development	11	< 1	< 0.1
Interest on General Debt	146	5	0.4
Judicial and Legal	0	0	0.0
Libraries	1,066	41	3.3
Parking	0	0	0.0
Parks and Recreation	580	22	1.8
Police Protection	5,953	232	18.3
Public Welfare	143	5	0.4
Sewerage	7,820	304	24.0
Solid Waste Management	1,396	54	4.3
Veterans' Services	0	0	0.0
Liquor Store	0	0	0.0
Utility	83	3	0.3
Employee Retirement	0	0	0.0

Source: U.S Census Bureau, State & Local Government Finances 2015

DEMOGRAPHICS

Population Growth

Area	1990 Census	2000 Census	2010 Census	2016* Estimate	Population Growth (%) 1990-2016	Population Growth (%) 2010-2016
City	22,156	25,119	25,494	25,580	15.5	0.3
MSA[1]	336,073	380,841	400,721	404,948	20.5	1.1
U.S.	248,709,873	281,421,906	308,745,538	318,558,162	28.1	3.2

Note: (1) Figures cover the Manchester-Nashua, NH Metropolitan Statistical Area—see Appendix B for areas included; (*) 2012-2016 5-year estimated population
Source: U.S. Census Bureau, 1990 Census, Census 2000, Census 2010, 2012-2016 American Community Survey 5-Year Estimates

Household Size

Area	Persons in Household (%)							Average Household Size
	One	Two	Three	Four	Five	Six	Seven or More	
City	20.8	39.0	17.4	13.9	6.1	2.1	0.8	2.60
MSA[1]	24.7	36.6	16.7	14.1	5.4	1.6	1.0	2.50
U.S.	27.7	33.7	15.7	13.1	6.0	2.3	1.5	2.60

Note: (1) Figures cover the Manchester-Nashua, NH Metropolitan Statistical Area—see Appendix B for areas included
Source: U.S. Census Bureau, 2012-2016 American Community Survey 5-Year Estimates

Race

Area	White Alone[2] (%)	Black Alone[2] (%)	Asian Alone[2] (%)	AIAN[3] Alone[2] (%)	NHOPI[4] Alone[2] (%)	Other Race Alone[2] (%)	Two or More Races (%)
City	95.2	0.4	2.1	0.1	0.1	0.6	1.5
MSA[1]	90.7	2.4	3.7	0.1	0.0	0.9	2.2
U.S.	73.3	12.6	5.2	0.8	0.2	4.8	3.1

Note: (1) Figures cover the Manchester-Nashua, NH Metropolitan Statistical Area—see Appendix B for areas included; (2) Alone is defined as not being in combination with one or more other races; (3) American Indian and Alaska Native; (4) Native Hawaiian and Other Pacific Islander
Source: U.S. Census Bureau, 2012-2016 American Community Survey 5-Year Estimates

Hispanic or Latino Origin

Area	Total (%)	Mexican (%)	Puerto Rican (%)	Cuban (%)	Other (%)
City	2.6	0.8	0.8	0.1	0.9
MSA[1]	6.0	1.5	1.9	0.2	2.5
U.S.	17.3	11.0	1.7	0.7	4.0

Note: Persons of Hispanic or Latino origin can be of any race; (1) Figures cover the Manchester-Nashua, NH Metropolitan Statistical Area—see Appendix B for areas included
Source: U.S. Census Bureau, 2012-2016 American Community Survey 5-Year Estimates

Segregation

Type	Segregation Indices[1]				Percent Change		
	1990	2000	2010	2010 Rank[2]	1990-2000	1990-2010	2000-2010
Black/White	n/a	n/a	n/a	n/a	n/a	n/a	n/a
Asian/White	n/a	n/a	n/a	n/a	n/a	n/a	n/a
Hispanic/White	n/a	n/a	n/a	n/a	n/a	n/a	n/a

Note: All figures cover the Metropolitan Statistical Area—see Appendix B for areas included; Figures are based on an analysis of 1990, 2000, and 2010 Census Decennial Census tract data by William H. Frey, Brookings Institution and the University of Michigan Social Science Data Analysis Network. In this analysis all racial groups (whites, blacks, and asians) are non-Hispanic members of those races. Hispanics are shown as a separate category; (1) Segregation Indices are Dissimilarity Indices that measure the degree to which the minority group is distributed differently than whites across census tracts. They range from 0 (complete integration) to 100 (complete segregation) where the value indicates the percentage of the minority group that needs to move to be distributed exactly like whites; (2) Ranges from 1 (most segregated) to 102 (least segregated); n/a not available.
Source: www.CensusScope.org

Ancestry

Area	German	Irish	English	American	Italian	Polish	French[2]	Scottish	Dutch
City	8.2	22.5	17.1	4.0	10.9	5.3	15.2	4.1	0.7
MSA[1]	8.2	20.7	13.1	4.3	10.3	4.7	14.4	3.2	0.8
U.S.	14.4	10.4	7.7	6.9	5.4	2.9	2.6	1.7	1.3

Note: Figures are the percentage of the total population reporting a particular ancestry. The nine most commonly reported ancestries in the U.S. are shown. Figures include multiple ancestries (e.g. if a person reported being Irish and Italian, they were included in both columns); (1) Figures cover the Manchester-Nashua, NH Metropolitan Statistical Area—see Appendix B for areas included; (2) Excludes Basque

Source: U.S. Census Bureau, 2012-2016 American Community Survey 5-Year Estimates

Foreign-Born Population

Area	Percent of Population Born in								
	Any Foreign Country	Asia	Mexico	Europe	Carribean	Central America[2]	South America	Africa	Canada
City	4.6	1.6	0.0	1.6	0.0	0.0	0.5	0.2	0.3
MSA[1]	9.1	3.1	0.6	1.8	0.7	0.4	0.8	0.7	1.0
U.S.	13.2	4.0	3.6	1.5	1.3	1.0	0.9	0.6	0.3

Note: (1) Figures cover the Manchester-Nashua, NH Metropolitan Statistical Area—see Appendix B for areas included; (2) Excludes Mexico.

Source: U.S. Census Bureau, 2012-2016 American Community Survey 5-Year Estimates

Marital Status

Area	Never Married	Now Married[2]	Separated	Widowed	Divorced
City	26.9	55.6	0.9	4.5	12.0
MSA[1]	30.2	51.5	1.4	5.3	11.7
U.S.	33.0	48.1	2.1	5.9	11.0

Note: Figures are percentages and cover the population 15 years of age and older; (1) Figures cover the Manchester-Nashua, NH Metropolitan Statistical Area—see Appendix B for areas included; (2) Excludes separated

Source: U.S. Census Bureau, 2012-2016 American Community Survey 5-Year Estimates

Disability Status

Area	All Ages	Under 18 Years Old	18 to 64 Years Old	65 Years and Over
City	8.8	3.8	7.5	24.2
MSA[1]	11.1	4.7	8.9	32.1
U.S.	12.5	4.1	10.3	35.7

Note: Figures show percent of the civilian noninstitutionalized population that reported having a disability. Disability status is determined from six types of difficulty: vision, hearing, cognitive, ambulatory, self-care, and independent living. For children under 5 years old, hearing and vision difficulty are used to determine disability status. For children between the ages of 5 and 14, disability status is determined from hearing, vision, cognitive, ambulatory, and self-care difficulties. For people aged 15 years and older, they are considered to have a disability if they have difficulty with any one of the six difficulty types; Note: (1) Figures cover the Manchester-Nashua, NH Metropolitan Statistical Area—see Appendix B for areas included

Source: U.S. Census Bureau, 2012-2016 American Community Survey 5-Year Estimates

Age

Area	Percent of Population									Median Age
	Under Age 5	Age 5–19	Age 20–34	Age 35–44	Age 45–54	Age 55–64	Age 65–74	Age 75–84	Age 85+	
City	4.5	19.1	15.5	14.3	18.5	15.6	8.5	3.0	1.0	43.0
MSA[1]	5.5	18.8	19.2	12.8	16.2	13.8	8.0	4.0	1.8	40.3
U.S.	6.2	19.6	20.7	12.7	13.6	12.6	8.3	4.3	1.9	37.7

Note: (1) Figures cover the Manchester-Nashua, NH Metropolitan Statistical Area—see Appendix B for areas included

Source: U.S. Census Bureau, 2012-2016 American Community Survey 5-Year Estimates

Gender

Area	Males	Females	Males per 100 Females
City	12,878	12,702	101.4
MSA[1]	200,979	203,969	98.5
U.S.	156,765,322	161,792,840	96.9

Note: (1) Figures cover the Manchester-Nashua, NH Metropolitan Statistical Area—see Appendix B for areas included
Source: U.S. Census Bureau, 2012-2016 American Community Survey 5-Year Estimates

Religious Groups by Family

Area	Catholic	Baptist	Non-Den.	Methodist[2]	Lutheran	LDS[3]	Pente-costal	Presby-terian[4]	Muslim[5]	Judaism
MSA[1]	31.2	1.4	2.4	1.2	0.5	0.6	0.5	2.0	0.3	0.5
U.S.	19.1	9.3	4.0	4.0	2.3	2.0	1.9	1.6	0.8	0.7

Note: Figures are the number of adherents as a percentage of the total population; (1) Figures cover the Manchester-Nashua, NH Metropolitan Statistical Area—see Appendix B for areas included; (2) Methodist/Pietist; (3) Latter Day Saints; (4) Reformed; (5) Figures are estimates
Source: Association of Statisticians of American Religious Bodies, 2010 U.S. Religion Census: Religious Congregations & Membership Study

Religious Groups by Tradition

Area	Catholic	Evangelical Protestant	Mainline Protestant	Other Tradition	Black Protestant	Orthodox
MSA[1]	31.2	5.1	4.4	1.8	<0.1	0.7
U.S.	19.1	16.2	7.3	4.3	1.6	0.3

Note: Figures are the number of adherents as a percentage of the total population; (1) Figures cover the Manchester-Nashua, NH Metropolitan Statistical Area—see Appendix B for areas included
Source: Association of Statisticians of American Religious Bodies, 2010 U.S. Religion Census: Religious Congregations & Membership Study

ECONOMY

Gross Metropolitan Product

Area	2014	2015	2016	2017	Rank[2]
MSA[1]	24.5	25.0	25.8	27.0	98

Note: Figures are in billions of dollars; (1) Figures cover the Manchester-Nashua, NH Metropolitan Statistical Area—see Appendix B for areas included; (2) Rank is based on 2015 data and ranges from 1 to 381
Source: The U.S. Conference of Mayors, U.S. Metro Economies: GMP and Employment Report, 2015-2017

Economic Growth

Area	2012-14 (%)	2015 (%)	2016 (%)	2017 (%)	Rank[2]
MSA[1]	1.1	0.0	2.0	2.8	200
U.S.	2.0	2.4	1.9	2.6	–

Note: Figures are real gross metropolitan product (GMP) growth rates and represent average annual percent change; (1) Figures cover the Manchester-Nashua, NH Metropolitan Statistical Area—see Appendix B for areas included; (2) Rank is based on 2012-2014 average annual percent change and ranges from 1 to 381
Source: The U.S. Conference of Mayors, U.S. Metro Economies: GMP and Employment Report, 2015-2017

Metropolitan Area Exports

Area	2011	2012	2013	2014	2015	2016	Rank[2]
MSA[1]	2,494.1	1,634.9	1,445.8	1,575.4	1,556.6	1,465.2	117

Note: Figures are in millions of dollars; (1) Figures cover the Manchester-Nashua, NH Metropolitan Statistical Area—see Appendix B for areas included; (2) Rank is based on 2016 data and ranges from 1 to 385
Source: U.S. Department of Commerce, International Trade Administration, Office of Trade & Industry Information, Manufacturing & Services, data extracted March 15, 2018

Building Permits

Area	Single-Family			Multi-Family			Total		
	2016	2017p	Pct. Chg.	2016	2017p	Pct. Chg.	2016	2017p	Pct. Chg.
City	n/a	n/a	n/a	n/a	n/a	n/a	n/a	n/a	n/a
MSA[1]	435	453	4.1	394	150	-61.9	829	603	-27.3
U.S.	750,800	817,300	8.9	455,800	446,800	-2.0	1,206,600	1,264,100	4.8

Note: (1) Figures cover the Manchester-Nashua, NH Metropolitan Statistical Area—see Appendix B for areas included; Figures represent new, privately-owned housing units authorized (unadjusted data); All permit data are based on estimates with imputation; (p) preliminary data.
Source: U.S. Census Bureau, Manufacturing, Mining, and Construction Statistics, Building Permits, 2016, 2017

Bankruptcy Filings

Area	Business Filings 2016	Business Filings 2017	Business Filings % Chg.	Nonbusiness Filings 2016	Nonbusiness Filings 2017	Nonbusiness Filings % Chg.
Hillsborough County	47	30	-36.2	545	591	8.4
U.S.	24,114	23,157	-4.0	770,846	765,863	-0.6

Note: Business filings include Chapter 7, Chapter 11, Chapter 12, and Chapter 13; Nonbusiness filings include Chapter 7, Chapter 11, and Chapter 13
Source: Administrative Office of the U.S. Courts, Business and Nonbusiness Bankruptcy, County Cases Commenced by Chapter of the Bankruptcy Code, During the 12-Month Period Ending December 31, 2016 and Business and Nonbusiness Bankruptcy, County Cases Commenced by Chapter of the Bankruptcy Code, During the 12-Month Period Ending December 31, 2017

Housing Vacancy Rates

Area	Gross Vacancy Rate[2] (%)			Year-Round Vacancy Rate[3] (%)			Rental Vacancy Rate[4] (%)			Homeowner Vacancy Rate[5] (%)		
	2015	2016	2017	2015	2016	2017	2015	2016	2017	2015	2016	2017
MSA[1]	n/a	n/a	n/a	n/a	n/a	n/a	n/a	n/a	n/a	n/a	n/a	n/a
U.S.	12.9	12.8	12.7	10.0	9.9	9.9	7.1	6.9	7.2	1.8	1.7	1.6

Note: (1) Figures cover the Manchester-Nashua, NH Metropolitan Statistical Area—see Appendix B for areas included; (2) The percentage of the total housing inventory that is vacant; (3) The percentage of the housing inventory (excluding seasonal units) that is year-round vacant; (4) The percentage of rental inventory that is vacant for rent; (5) The percentage of homeowner inventory that is vacant for sale; n/a not available
Source: U.S. Census Bureau, Housing Vacancies and Homeownership Annual Statistics: 2015, 2016, 2017

INCOME

Income

Area	Per Capita ($)	Median Household ($)	Average Household ($)
City	40,980	93,798	106,535
MSA[1]	36,012	73,189	91,648
U.S.	29,829	55,322	77,866

Note: (1) Figures cover the Manchester-Nashua, NH Metropolitan Statistical Area—see Appendix B for areas included
Source: U.S. Census Bureau, 2012-2016 American Community Survey 5-Year Estimates

Household Income Distribution

Area	Percent of Households Earning							
	Under $15,000	$15,000 -$24,999	$25,000 -$34,999	$35,000 -$49,999	$50,000 -$74,999	$75,000 -$99,999	$100,000 -$149,999	$150,000 and up
City	4.3	3.8	4.0	10.1	15.6	16.9	22.7	22.7
MSA[1]	7.1	7.4	7.8	11.4	17.3	14.6	18.7	15.6
U.S.	12.1	10.2	9.9	13.2	17.8	12.2	13.5	11.1

Note: (1) Figures cover the Manchester-Nashua, NH Metropolitan Statistical Area—see Appendix B for areas included
Source: U.S. Census Bureau, 2012-2016 American Community Survey 5-Year Estimates

Poverty Rate

Area	All Ages	Under 18 Years Old	18 to 64 Years Old	65 Years and Over
City	4.6	4.8	4.7	3.3
MSA[1]	8.6	11.3	8.3	6.1
U.S.	15.1	21.2	14.2	9.3

Note: Figures are percentage of people whose income during the past 12 months was below the poverty level; (1) Figures cover the Manchester-Nashua, NH Metropolitan Statistical Area—see Appendix B for areas included
Source: U.S. Census Bureau, 2012-2016 American Community Survey 5-Year Estimates

EMPLOYMENT

Labor Force and Employment

Area	Civilian Labor Force			Workers Employed		
	Dec. 2016	Dec. 2017	% Chg.	Dec. 2016	Dec. 2017	% Chg.
City	15,718	15,680	-0.2	15,292	15,311	0.1
NECTAD[1]	169,304	169,049	-0.2	164,446	164,679	0.1
U.S.	158,968,000	159,880,000	0.6	151,798,000	153,602,000	1.2

Note: Data is not seasonally adjusted and covers workers 16 years of age and older; (1) Figures cover the Nashua, NH-MA New England City and Town Area Division—see Appendix B for areas included
Source: Bureau of Labor Statistics, Local Area Unemployment Statistics

Unemployment Rate

Area	2017											
	Jan.	Feb.	Mar.	Apr.	May	Jun.	Jul.	Aug.	Sep.	Oct.	Nov.	Dec.
City	3.2	3.0	2.8	2.5	2.5	2.4	2.5	2.5	2.4	2.3	2.5	2.4
NECTAD[1]	3.6	3.6	3.4	3.0	2.8	3.0	3.0	3.0	2.8	2.7	2.7	2.6
U.S.	5.1	4.9	4.6	4.1	4.1	4.5	4.6	4.5	4.1	3.9	3.9	3.9

Note: Data is not seasonally adjusted and covers workers 16 years of age and older; (1) Figures cover the Nashua, NH-MA New England City and Town Area Division—see Appendix B for areas included
Source: Bureau of Labor Statistics, Local Area Unemployment Statistics

Average Wages

Occupation	$/Hr.	Occupation	$/Hr.
Accountants and Auditors	36.10	Maids and Housekeeping Cleaners	10.80
Automotive Mechanics	20.90	Maintenance and Repair Workers	20.60
Bookkeepers	20.50	Marketing Managers	69.90
Carpenters	23.70	Nuclear Medicine Technologists	n/a
Cashiers	10.70	Nurses, Licensed Practical	24.00
Clerks, General Office	19.60	Nurses, Registered	33.60
Clerks, Receptionists/Information	13.70	Nursing Assistants	15.20
Clerks, Shipping/Receiving	17.10	Packers and Packagers, Hand	11.10
Computer Programmers	31.90	Physical Therapists	38.00
Computer Systems Analysts	46.10	Postal Service Mail Carriers	24.10
Computer User Support Specialists	26.90	Real Estate Brokers	n/a
Cooks, Restaurant	13.10	Retail Salespersons	14.00
Dentists	106.70	Sales Reps., Exc. Tech./Scientific	38.90
Electrical Engineers	53.60	Sales Reps., Tech./Scientific	51.10
Electricians	26.60	Secretaries, Exc. Legal/Med./Exec.	17.80
Financial Managers	60.40	Security Guards	17.40
First-Line Supervisors/Managers, Sales	25.00	Surgeons	n/a
Food Preparation Workers	10.70	Teacher Assistants*	16.50
General and Operations Managers	67.40	Teachers, Elementary School*	29.00
Hairdressers/Cosmetologists	14.20	Teachers, Secondary School*	29.10
Internists, General	123.20	Telemarketers	16.80
Janitors and Cleaners	14.30	Truck Drivers, Heavy/Tractor-Trailer	22.30
Landscaping/Groundskeeping Workers	14.60	Truck Drivers, Light/Delivery Svcs.	17.00
Lawyers	53.00	Waiters and Waitresses	10.50

Note: Wage data covers the Nashua, NH-MA New England City and Town Area Division—see Appendix B for areas included; (*) Hourly wages for elementary/secondary school teachers and teacher assistants were calculated by the editors from annual wage data based on a 40 hour work week; n/a not available.
Source: Bureau of Labor Statistics, Metro Area Occupational Employment & Wage Estimates, May 2017

Employment by Occupation

Occupation Classification	City (%)	MSA[1] (%)	U.S. (%)
Management, Business, Science, and Arts	48.6	41.1	37.0
Natural Resources, Construction, and Maintenance	6.0	8.2	8.9
Production, Transportation, and Material Moving	7.8	10.9	12.2
Sales and Office	27.2	25.0	23.8
Service	10.3	14.9	18.1

Note: Figures cover employed civilians 16 years of age and older; (1) Figures cover the Manchester-Nashua, NH Metropolitan Statistical Area—see Appendix B for areas included
Source: U.S. Census Bureau, 2012-2016 American Community Survey 5-Year Estimates

Employment by Industry

Sector	NECTAD[1] Number of Employees	NECTAD[1] Percent of Total	U.S. Percent of Total
Construction, Mining, and Logging	5,400	4.1	5.2
Education and Health Services	19,400	14.9	15.9
Financial Activities	7,700	5.9	5.7
Government	13,800	10.6	15.3
Information	1,800	1.4	1.9
Leisure and Hospitality	11,400	8.7	10.7
Manufacturing	20,700	15.9	8.5
Other Services	5,300	4.1	3.9
Professional and Business Services	15,100	11.6	14.0
Retail Trade	20,800	15.9	11.0
Transportation, Warehousing, and Utilities	3,600	2.8	4.1
Wholesale Trade	5,500	4.2	4.0

Note: Figures are non-farm employment as of December 2017. Figures are not seasonally adjusted and include workers 16 years of age and older; (1) Figures cover the Nashua, NH-MA New England City and Town Area Division—see Appendix B for areas included
Source: Bureau of Labor Statistics, Current Employment Statistics, Employment, Hours, and Earnings

Occupations with Greatest Projected Employment Growth: 2017 – 2019

Occupation[1]	2017 Employment	2019 Projected Employment	Numeric Employment Change	Percent Employment Change
Combined Food Preparation and Serving Workers, Including Fast Food	13,270	13,800	530	3.9
Personal Care Aides	7,840	8,310	470	5.9
Registered Nurses	13,530	13,940	410	3.0
Waiters and Waitresses	12,820	13,190	370	2.8
Janitors and Cleaners, Except Maids and Housekeeping Cleaners	10,770	11,060	290	2.7
Software Developers, Applications	5,490	5,760	270	4.9
General and Operations Managers	11,540	11,800	260	2.2
Landscaping and Groundskeeping Workers	6,840	7,090	250	3.7
Cooks, Restaurant	5,840	6,060	220	3.9
Stock Clerks and Order Fillers	13,610	13,830	220	1.7

Note: Projections cover New Hampshire; (1) Sorted by numeric employment change
Source: www.projectionscentral.com, State Occupational Projections, 2017–2019 Short-Term Projections

Fastest Growing Occupations: 2017 – 2019

Occupation[1]	2017 Employment	2019 Projected Employment	Numeric Employment Change	Percent Employment Change
Nurse Practitioners	1,040	1,110	70	7.3
Home Health Aides	1,310	1,400	90	6.5
Personal Care Aides	7,840	8,310	470	5.9
Nonfarm Animal Caretakers	1,110	1,170	60	5.8
Veterinary Technologists and Technicians	910	970	60	5.7
Medical Assistants	2,650	2,790	140	5.4
Market Research Analysts and Marketing Specialists	2,060	2,170	110	5.3
Mental Health Counselors	1,060	1,110	50	5.0
Software Developers, Applications	5,490	5,760	270	4.9
Medical Secretaries	2,260	2,360	100	4.7

Note: Projections cover New Hampshire; (1) Sorted by percent employment change and excludes occupations with numeric employment change less than 50
Source: www.projectionscentral.com, State Occupational Projections, 2017–2019 Short-Term Projections

TAXES

State Corporate Income Tax Rates

State	Tax Rate (%)	Income Brackets ($)	Num. of Brackets	Financial Institution Tax Rate (%)[a]	Federal Income Tax Ded.
New Hampshire	8.2 (p)	Flat rate	1	8.2 (p)	No

Note: Tax rates as of January 1, 2018; (a) Rates listed are the corporate income tax rate applied to financial institutions or excise taxes based on income. Some states have other taxes based upon the value of deposits or shares; (p) New Hampshire's 8.2% Business Profits Tax is imposed on both corporations and unincorporated associations with gross income over $50,000. In addition, New Hampshire levies a Business Enterprise Tax of 0.75% on the enterprise base (total compensation, interest and dividends paid) for businesses with gross income over $150,000 or base over $75,000. The Business Profits Tax is scheduled to decrease to 7.9% for tax years beginning after 2018 if certain revenue conditions are met.
Source: Federation of Tax Administrators, Range of State Corporate Income Tax Rates, January 1, 2018

State Individual Income Tax Rates

State	Tax Rate (%)	Income Brackets ($)	Num. of Brackets	Personal Exempt. ($)[1]		Fed. Inc. Tax Ded.
				Single	Dependents	
New Hampshire	State income tax of 5% on dividends and interest income only					

Note: Tax rates as of January 1, 2018; Local- and county-level taxes are not included; n/a not applicable; (1) Married joint filers generally receive double the single exemption
Source: Federation of Tax Administrators, State Individual Income Tax Rates, January 1, 2018

Various State Sales and Excise Tax Rates

State	State Sales Tax (%)	Gasoline[1] (¢/gal.)	Cigarette[2] ($/pack)	Spirits[3] ($/gal.)	Wine[4] ($/gal.)	Beer[5] ($/gal.)	Recreational Marijuana (%)
New Hampshire	None	23.83	1.78	0 (g)	(l)(m)	0.30	Not legal

Note: All tax rates as of January 1, 2018; (1) The American Petroleum Institute has developed a methodology for determining the average tax rate on a gallon of fuel. Rates may include any of the following: excise taxes, environmental fees, storage tank fees, other fees or taxes, general sales tax, and local taxes. In states where gasoline is subject to the general sales tax, or where the fuel tax is based on the average sale price, the average rate determined by API is sensitive to changes in the price of gasoline. States that fully or partially apply general sales taxes to gasoline: CA, CO, GA, IL, IN, MI, NY; (2) The federal excise tax of $1.0066 per pack and local taxes are not included; (3) Rates are those applicable to off-premise sales of 40% alcohol by volume (a.b.v.) distilled spirits in 750ml containers. Local excise taxes are excluded; (4) Rates are those applicable to off-premise sales of 11% a.b.v. non-carbonated wine in 750ml containers; (5) Rates are those applicable to off-premise sales of 4.7% a.b.v. beer in 12 ounce containers; (g) Control states, where the government controls all sales. Products can be subject to ad valorem mark-up as well as excise taxes; (l) Different rates also applicable to alcohol content, place of production, size of container, place purchased (on- or off-premise or on board airlines) or type of wine (carbonated, vermouth, etc.); (m) Control states, where the government controls all sales. Products can be subject to ad valorem mark-up as well as excise taxes.
Source: Tax Foundation, 2018 Facts & Figures: How Does Your State Compare?

State Business Tax Climate Index Rankings

State	Overall Rank	Corporate Tax Rank	Individual Income Tax Rank	Sales Tax Rank	Unemployment Insurance Tax Rank	Property Tax Rank
New Hampshire	7	45	9	2	43	44

Note: The index is a measure of how each state's tax laws affect economic performance. The lower the rank, the more favorable a state's tax system is for business. States without a given tax are given a ranking of 1. The scores/rankings for the District of Columbia do not affect other states. The 2018 index represents the tax climate as of July 1, 2017.
Source: Tax Foundation, State Business Tax Climate Index 2018

TRANSPORTATION

Means of Transportation to Work

Area	Car/Truck/Van		Public Transportation			Bicycle	Walked	Other Means	Worked at Home
	Drove Alone	Car-pooled	Bus	Subway	Railroad				
City	85.6	4.9	0.3	0.0	0.0	0.1	0.8	0.9	7.4
MSA[1]	81.6	8.5	0.7	0.0	0.1	0.1	2.3	0.7	5.9
U.S.	76.4	9.3	2.6	1.9	0.6	0.6	2.8	1.3	4.6

Note: Figures are percentages and cover workers 16 years of age and older; (1) Figures cover the Manchester-Nashua, NH Metropolitan Statistical Area—see Appendix B for areas included
Source: U.S. Census Bureau, 2012-2016 American Community Survey 5-Year Estimates

Travel Time to Work

Area	Less Than 10 Minutes	10 to 19 Minutes	20 to 29 Minutes	30 to 44 Minutes	45 to 59 Minutes	60 to 89 Minutes	90 Minutes or More
City	9.7	30.2	27.8	13.2	7.3	8.6	3.1
MSA[1]	12.3	29.3	19.9	19.6	8.3	7.1	3.4
U.S.	12.9	29.2	20.9	20.4	8.0	6.0	2.7

Note: Note: Figures are percentages and include workers 16 years old and over; (1) Figures cover the Manchester-Nashua, NH Metropolitan Statistical Area—see Appendix B for areas included
Source: U.S. Census Bureau, 2012-2016 American Community Survey 5-Year Estimates

Freeway Travel Time Index

Area	1985	1990	1995	2000	2005	2010	2014
Urban Area Rank[1,2]	n/a	n/a	n/a	n/a	n/a	n/a	n/a
Urban Area Index[1]	n/a	n/a	n/a	n/a	n/a	n/a	n/a
Average Index[3]	1.09	1.11	1.14	1.17	1.20	1.19	1.20

Note: Freeway Travel Time Index—the ratio of travel time in the peak period to the travel time at free-flow conditions. For example, a value of 1.30 indicates a 20-minute free-flow trip takes 26 minutes in the peak (20 minutes x 1.30 = 26 minutes); (1) Data for the Manchester-Nashua, NH urban area was not available; (2) Rank is based on 101 urban areas (#1 = highest travel time index); (3) Average of 101 urban areas
Source: Texas Transportation Institute, 2015 Urban Mobility Scorecard, August 2015

Freeway Commuter Stress Index

Area	1985	1990	1995	2000	2005	2010	2014
Urban Area Rank[1,2]	n/a	n/a	n/a	n/a	n/a	n/a	n/a
Urban Area Index[1]	n/a	n/a	n/a	n/a	n/a	n/a	n/a
Average Index[3]	1.13	1.16	1.19	1.22	1.25	1.24	1.25

Note: The Freeway Commuter Stress Index is the same as the Freeway Travel Time Index (see table above) except that it includes only the travel in the peak directions during the peak periods; the TTI includes travel in all directions during the peak period. Thus, the CSI is more indicative of the work trip experienced by each commuter on a daily basis; (1) Data for the Manchester-Nashua, NH urban area was not available; (2) Rank is based on 101 urban areas (#1 = highest travel time index); (3) Average of 101 urban areas
Source: Texas Transportation Institute, 2015 Urban Mobility Scorecard, August 2015

Living Environment

COST OF LIVING

Cost of Living Index

Composite Index	Groceries	Housing	Utilities	Transportation	Health Care	Misc. Goods/ Services
114.7	113.6	110.1	131.2	105.1	115.0	116.7

Note: The Cost of Living Index measures regional differences in the cost of consumer goods and services, excluding taxes and non-consumer expenditures, for professional and managerial households in the top income quintile. It is based on more than 50,000 prices covering almost 60 different items for which prices are collected three times a year by chambers of commerce, economic development organizations or university applied economic centers in each participating urban area. The numbers shown should be read as a percentage above or below the national average of 100. For example, a value of 115.4 in the groceries column indicates that grocery prices are 15.4% higher than the national average. Small differences in the index numbers should not be interpreted as significant; Figures cover the Manchester NH urban area.
Source: The Council for Community and Economic Research, ACCRA Cost of Living Index, 2017

Grocery Prices

Area[1]	T-Bone Steak ($/pound)	Frying Chicken ($/pound)	Whole Milk ($/half gal.)	Eggs ($/dozen)	Orange Juice ($/64 oz.)	Coffee ($/11.5 oz.)
City[2]	12.82	1.82	3.56	1.66	3.52	4.62
Avg.	11.29	1.40	2.02	1.47	3.55	4.37
Min.	7.71	0.93	1.04	0.70	2.86	3.24
Max.	15.83	2.39	4.03	3.92	6.29	8.16

*Note: (1) Values for the local area are compared with the average, minimum and maximum values for all 294 areas in the Cost of Living Index; (2) Figures cover the Manchester NH urban area; **T-Bone Steak** (price per pound); **Frying Chicken** (price per pound, whole fryer); **Whole Milk** (half gallon carton); **Eggs** (price per dozen, Grade A, large); **Orange Juice** (64 oz. Tropicana or Florida Natural); **Coffee** (11.5 oz. can, vacuum-packed, Maxwell House, Hills Bros, or Folgers).*
Source: The Council for Community and Economic Research, ACCRA Cost of Living Index, 2017

Housing and Utility Costs

Area[1]	New Home Price ($)	Apartment Rent ($/month)	All Electric ($/month)	Part Electric ($/month)	Other Energy ($/month)	Telephone ($/month)
City[2]	342,782	1,358	-	121.03	105.09	36.25
Avg.	335,956	1,047	175.01	97.34	67.93	28.71
Min.	187,788	491	109.48	49.33	35.44	12.39
Max.	1,739,087	4,559	432.62	227.09	353.33	44.61

*Note: (1) Values for the local area are compared with the average, minimum and maximum values for all 294 areas in the Cost of Living Index; (2) Figures cover the Manchester NH urban area; **New Home Price** (2,400 sf living area, 8,000 sf lot, in urban area with full utilities); **Apartment Rent** (950 sf 2 bedroom/1.5 or 2 bath, unfurnished, excluding all utilities except water); **All Electric** (average monthly cost for an all-electric home); **Part Electric** (average monthly cost for a part-electric home); **Other Energy** (average monthly cost for natural gas, fuel oil, coal, wood, and any other forms of energy except electricity); **Telephone** (price includes basic monthly rate for a private residential line plus additional local usage charges incurred by a family of four).*
Source: The Council for Community and Economic Research, ACCRA Cost of Living Index, 2017

Health Care, Transportation, and Other Costs

Area[1]	Doctor ($/visit)	Dentist ($/visit)	Optometrist ($/visit)	Gasoline ($/gallon)	Beauty Salon ($/visit)	Men's Shirt ($)
City[2]	145.00	106.67	102.92	2.21	39.33	31.66
Avg.	108.00	92.54	101.93	2.25	37.58	30.92
Min.	30.39	60.00	49.75	1.82	16.11	11.20
Max.	193.50	161.94	229.28	3.16	77.35	59.13

*Note: (1) Values for the local area are compared with the average, minimum and maximum values for all 294 areas in the Cost of Living Index; (2) Figures cover the Manchester NH urban area; **Doctor** (general practitioners routine exam of an established patient); **Dentist** (adult teeth cleaning and periodic oral examination); **Optometrist** (full vision eye exam for established adult patient); **Gasoline** (one gallon regular unleaded, national brand, including all taxes, cash price at self-service pump if available); **Beauty Salon** (woman's shampoo, trim, and blow-dry); **Men's Shirt** (cotton/polyester dress shirt, pinpoint weave, long sleeves).*
Source: The Council for Community and Economic Research, ACCRA Cost of Living Index, 2017

HOUSING

House Price Index (HPI)

Area	National Ranking[2]	Quarterly Change (%)	One-Year Change (%)	Five-Year Change (%)
MSA[1]	96	1.00	7.05	22.90
U.S.[3]	–	1.61	6.68	34.71

Note: The HPI is a weighted repeat sales index. It measures average price changes in repeat sales or refinancings on the same properties. This information is obtained by reviewing repeat mortgage transactions on single-family properties whose mortgages have been purchased or securitized by Fannie Mae or Freddie Mac in January 1975; (1) Figures cover the Manchester-Nashua, NH Metropolitan Statistical Area—see Appendix B for areas included; (2) Rankings are based on annual percentage change for all metro areas containing at least 15,000 transactions over the last 10 years and ranges from 1 to 253; (3) figures based on a weighted average of Census Division estimates using a seasonally adjusted, purchase-only index; all figures are for the period ending December 31, 2017
Source: Federal Housing Finance Agency, House Price Index, February 28, 2018

Median Single-Family Home Prices

Area	2015	2016	2017[p]	Percent Change 2016 to 2017
MSA[1]	253.2	262.1	281.9	7.6
U.S. Average	223.9	235.5	248.8	5.6

Note: Figures are median sales prices of existing single-family homes in thousands of dollars; (p) preliminary; (1) Figures cover the Manchester-Nashua, NH Metropolitan Statistical Area—see Appendix B for areas included
Source: National Association of Realtors, Median Sales Price of Existing Single-Family Homes for Metropolitan Areas, 4th Quarter 2017

Qualifying Income Based on Median Sales Price of Existing Single-Family Homes

Area	With 5% Down ($)	With 10% Down ($)	With 20% Down ($)
MSA[1]	62,359	59,077	52,513
U.S. Average	55,585	52,659	46,808

Note: Figures are preliminary; Qualifying income is based on a mortgage rate of 4.17%. Monthly principal and interest payment is limited to 25% of income; (1) Figures cover the Manchester-Nashua, NH Metropolitan Statistical Area—see Appendix B for areas included
Source: National Association of Realtors, Qualifying Income Based on Median Sales Price of Existing Single-Family Homes for Metropolitan Areas, 4th Quarter 2017

Median Apartment Condo-Coop Home Prices

Area	2015	2016	2017[p]	Percent Change 2016 to 2017
MSA[1]	164.7	172.1	181.3	5.3
U.S. Average	210.7	220.7	234.3	6.2

Note: Figures are median sales prices of existing apartment condo-coop homes in thousands of dollars; (p) preliminary; (1) Figures cover the Manchester-Nashua, NH Metropolitan Statistical Area—see Appendix B for areas included
Source: National Association of Realtors, Median Sales Price of Existing Apartment Condo-Coop Homes for Metropolitan Areas, 4th Quarter 2017

Home Value Distribution

Area	Under $50,000	$50,000 -$99,999	$100,000 -$149,999	$150,000 -$199,999	$200,000 -$299,999	$300,000 -$499,999	$500,000 -$999,999	$1,000,000 or more
City	2.2	1.3	9.1	13.7	44.0	27.6	1.9	0.2
MSA[1]	2.8	2.9	7.2	16.5	39.4	25.6	4.8	0.8
U.S.	8.8	14.8	15.3	14.9	18.4	16.4	9.0	2.5

Note: Figures are percentages and cover owner-occupied housing units; (1) Figures cover the Manchester-Nashua, NH Metropolitan Statistical Area—see Appendix B for areas included
Source: U.S. Census Bureau, 2012-2016 American Community Survey 5-Year Estimates

Homeownership Rate

Area	2009 (%)	2010 (%)	2011 (%)	2012 (%)	2013 (%)	2014 (%)	2015 (%)	2016 (%)	2017 (%)
MSA[1]	n/a	n/a	n/a	n/a	n/a	n/a	n/a	n/a	n/a
U.S.	67.4	66.9	66.1	65.4	65.1	64.5	63.7	63.4	63.9

Note: (1) Figures cover the Manchester-Nashua, NH Metropolitan Statistical Area—see Appendix B for areas included; n/a not available
Source: U.S. Census Bureau, Housing Vacancies and Homeownership Annual Statistics: 2009-2017

Year Housing Structure Built

Area	2010 or Later	2000 -2009	1990 -1999	1980 -1989	1970 -1979	1960 -1969	1950 -1959	1940 -1949	Before 1940	Median Year
City	0.7	7.3	12.7	33.5	25.8	11.0	4.9	1.1	2.9	1981
MSA[1]	1.4	10.1	10.3	21.2	15.5	9.5	7.5	3.6	20.9	1976
U.S.	2.3	14.7	14.0	13.7	15.6	10.9	10.6	5.2	13.0	1977

Note: Figures are percentages except for Median Year; Note: (1) Figures cover the Manchester-Nashua, NH Metropolitan Statistical Area—see Appendix B for areas included
Source: U.S. Census Bureau, 2012-2016 American Community Survey 5-Year Estimates

Gross Monthly Rent

Area	Under $500	$500 -$999	$1,000 -$1,499	$1,500 -$1,999	$2,000 -$2,499	$2,500 -$2,999	$3,000 and up	Median ($)
City	3.6	8.5	56.7	27.1	4.1	0.0	0.0	1,375
MSA[1]	7.5	31.8	43.5	14.6	2.0	0.5	0.2	1,099
U.S.	11.3	43.3	27.7	10.7	4.0	1.6	1.5	949

Note: Figures are percentages except for Median; Gross rent is the contract rent plus the estimated average monthly cost of utilities (electricity, gas, and water and sewer) and fuels (oil, coal, kerosene, wood, etc.) if these are paid by the renter (or paid for the renter by someone else); (1) Figures cover the Manchester-Nashua, NH Metropolitan Statistical Area—see Appendix B for areas included
Source: U.S. Census Bureau, 2012-2016 American Community Survey 5-Year Estimates

HEALTH

Health Risk Factors

Category	MSA[1] (%)	U.S. (%)
Adults aged 18–64 who have any kind of health care coverage	n/a	87.7
Adults who reported being in good or excellent health	n/a	83.6
Adults who are current smokers	n/a	17.1
Adults who currently use E-cigarettes	n/a	4.7
Adults who currently use chewing tobacco, snuff, or snus	n/a	4.0
Adults who are heavy drinkers[2]	n/a	6.5
Adults who are binge drinkers[3]	n/a	16.9
Adults who are overweight (BMI 25.0 - 29.9)	n/a	35.3
Adults who are obese (BMI 30.0 - 99.8)	n/a	29.9
Adults who participated in any physical activities in the past month	n/a	76.9
Adults who always or nearly always wears a seat belt	n/a	94.3

Note: n/a not available; (1) Figures cover the Manchester-Nashua, NH Metropolitan Statistical Area—see Appendix B for areas included; (2) Heavy drinkers are classified as adult men having more than 14 drinks per week and adult women having more than 7 drinks per week; (3) Binge drinkers are classified as males having five or more drinks on one occasion or females having four or more drinks on one occasion
Source: Centers for Disease Control and Prevention, Behaviorial Risk Factor Surveillance System, SMART: Selected Metropolitan Area Risk Trends, 2016

Health Screening Rates

Category	MSA[1] (%)	U.S. (%)
Adults 50-75 who have had a blood stool test within the past year	n/a	8.0
Adults 50-75 who have had a colonoscopy in the past 10 years	n/a	63.5
Adults aged 65+ who have had flu shot within the past year	n/a	58.6
Adults aged 65+ who have ever had a pneumonia vaccination	n/a	73.4
Adults who have ever been tested for HIV	n/a	35.6
Women aged 21-65 who have had a pap test in the past three years	n/a	79.8
Men aged 40+ who have had a PSA test within the past two years	n/a	39.5
Women aged 40+ who have had a mammogram within the past two years	n/a	72.5

Note: n/a not available; (1) Figures cover the Manchester-Nashua, NH Metropolitan Statistical Area—see Appendix B for areas included; Source: Centers for Disease Control and Prevention, Behaviorial Risk Factor Surveillance System, SMART: Selected Metropolitan Area Risk Trends, 2016

Chronic Health Conditions

Category	MSA[1] (%)	U.S. (%)
Adults who have ever been told they had a heart attack	n/a	4.4
Adults who have ever been told they have angina or coronary heart disease	n/a	4.1
Adults who have ever been told they had a stroke	n/a	3.1
Adults who have been told they currently have asthma	n/a	9.3
Adults who have ever been told they have arthritis	n/a	25.8
Adults who have ever been told they have diabetes[2]	n/a	10.5
Adults who have ever been told they had skin cancer	n/a	5.9
Adults who have ever been told they had any other types of cancer	n/a	6.7
Adults who have ever been told they have COPD	n/a	6.3
Adults who have ever been told they have kidney disease	n/a	2.8
Adults who have ever been told they have a form of depression	n/a	17.4

Note: n/a not available; (1) Figures cover the Manchester-Nashua, NH Metropolitan Statistical Area—see Appendix B for areas included; (2) Figures do not include pregnancy-related, borderline, or pre-diabetes
Source: Centers for Disease Control and Prevention, Behaviorial Risk Factor Surveillance System, SMART: Selected Metropolitan Area Risk Trends, 2016

Mortality Rates for the Top 10 Causes of Death in the U.S.

ICD-10[a] Sub-Chapter	ICD-10[a] Code	Age-Adjusted Mortality Rate[1] per 100,000 population	
		County[2]	U.S.
Malignant neoplasms	C00-C97	156.2	158.5
Ischaemic heart diseases	I20-I25	80.3	96.8
Other forms of heart disease	I30-I51	56.8	52.4
Chronic lower respiratory diseases	J40-J47	38.5	40.9
Cerebrovascular diseases	I60-I69	25.8	37.2
Organic, including symptomatic, mental disorders	F01-F09	46.9	33.3
Other degenerative diseases of the nervous system	G30-G31	28.7	32.1
Other external causes of accidental injury	W00-X59	54.1	31.2
Diabetes mellitus	E10-E14	18.7	21.1
Hypertensive diseases	I10-I15	14.2	20.8

Note: (a) ICD-10 = International Classification of Diseases 10th Revision; (1) Mortality rates are a three year average covering 2014-2016; (2) Figures cover Hillsborough County.
Source: Centers for Disease Control and Prevention, National Center for Health Statistics. Underlying Cause of Death 1999-2016 on CDC WONDER Online Database, released December 2017

Mortality Rates for Selected Causes of Death

ICD-10[a] Sub-Chapter	ICD-10[a] Code	Age-Adjusted Mortality Rate[1] per 100,000 population	
		County[2]	U.S.
Assault	X85-Y09	2.0	5.6
Diseases of the liver	K70-K76	14.0	14.0
Human immunodeficiency virus (HIV) disease	B20-B24	Unreliable	1.9
Influenza and pneumonia	J09-J18	14.6	14.6
Intentional self-harm	X60-X84	18.3	13.2
Malnutrition	E40-E46	Unreliable	1.3
Obesity and other hyperalimentation	E65-E68	3.2	2.1
Renal failure	N17-N19	12.3	13.0
Transport accidents	V01-V99	7.3	12.0
Viral hepatitis	B15-B19	1.4	1.9

Note: (a) ICD-10 = International Classification of Diseases 10th Revision; (1) Mortality rates are a three year average covering 2014-2016; (2) Figures cover Hillsborough County; Data are Suppressed when the data meet the criteria for confidentiality constraints; Mortality rates are flagged as Unreliable when the rate would be calculated with a numerator of 20 or less.
Source: Centers for Disease Control and Prevention, National Center for Health Statistics. Underlying Cause of Death 1999-2016 on CDC WONDER Online Database, released December 2017

Health Insurance Coverage

Area	With Health Insurance	With Private Health Insurance	With Public Health Insurance	Without Health Insurance	Population Under Age 18 Without Health Insurance
City	94.5	87.2	20.3	5.5	2.1
MSA[1]	91.8	76.8	26.1	8.2	2.4
U.S.	88.3	66.7	33.0	11.7	5.9

Note: Figures are percentages that cover the civilian noninstitutionalized population; (1) Figures cover the Manchester-Nashua, NH Metropolitan Statistical Area—see Appendix B for areas included
Source: U.S. Census Bureau, 2012-2016 American Community Survey 5-Year Estimates

Number of Medical Professionals

Area	MDs[3]	DOs[3,4]	Dentists	Podiatrists	Chiropractors	Optometrists
County[1] (number)	936	88	313	20	106	76
County[1] (rate[2])	230.5	21.7	76.8	4.9	26.0	18.6
U.S. (rate[2])	276.5	22.3	67.3	6.0	26.7	15.9

Note: Data as of 2016 unless noted; (1) Data covers Hillsborough County; (2) Rate per 100,000 population; (3) Data as of 2015 and includes all active, non-federal physicians; (4) Doctor of Osteopathic Medicine
Source: U.S. Department of Health and Human Services, Health Resources and Services Administration, Bureau of Health Professions, Area Resource File (ARF) 2016-2017

EDUCATION

Public School District Statistics

District Name	Schls	Pupils	Pupil/ Teacher Ratio	Minority Pupils[1] (%)	Free Lunch Eligible[2] (%)	IEP[3] (%)
Merrimack School District	6	3,787	12.8	9.0	7.4	16.0

Note: Table includes school districts with 100 or more students; (1) Percentage of students that are not non-Hispanic white; (2) Percentage of students that are eligible for the free lunch program; (3) Percentage of students that have an Individualized Education Program.
Source: U.S. Department of Education, National Center for Education Statistics, Common Core of Data, Local Education Agency (School District) Universe Survey: School Year 2015-2016; U.S. Department of Education, National Center for Education Statistics, Common Core of Data, Public Elementary/Secondary School Universe Survey: School Year 2015-2016

Highest Level of Education

Area	Less than H.S.	H.S. Diploma	Some College, No Deg.	Associate Degree	Bachelor's Degree	Master's Degree	Prof. School Degree	Doctorate Degree
City	3.9	24.8	17.5	9.4	29.7	12.1	1.0	1.6
MSA[1]	8.4	27.1	18.6	9.6	23.3	10.3	1.5	1.2
U.S.	13.0	27.5	21.0	8.2	18.8	8.2	2.0	1.3

Note: Figures cover persons age 25 and over; (1) Figures cover the Manchester-Nashua, NH Metropolitan Statistical Area—see Appendix B for areas included
Source: U.S. Census Bureau, 2012-2016 American Community Survey 5-Year Estimates

Educational Attainment by Race

Area	High School Graduate or Higher (%)					Bachelor's Degree or Higher (%)				
	Total	White	Black	Asian	Hisp.[2]	Total	White	Black	Asian	Hisp.[2]
City	96.1	96.1	70.6	95.6	100.0	44.4	43.0	35.3	73.5	75.0
MSA[1]	91.6	92.0	85.9	87.3	71.9	36.3	35.8	23.8	61.6	17.7
U.S.	87.0	88.9	84.3	86.3	65.7	30.3	31.6	20.0	52.1	14.7

Note: Figures shown cover persons 25 years old and over; (1) Figures cover the Manchester-Nashua, NH Metropolitan Statistical Area—see Appendix B for areas included; (2) People of Hispanic origin can be of any race
Source: U.S. Census Bureau, 2012-2016 American Community Survey 5-Year Estimates

School Enrollment by Grade and Control

Area	Preschool (%)		Kindergarten (%)		Grades 1 - 4 (%)		Grades 5 - 8 (%)		Grades 9 - 12 (%)	
	Public	Private	Public	Private	Public	Private	Public	Private	Public	Private
City	38.1	61.9	79.5	20.5	95.0	5.0	90.1	9.9	85.3	14.7
MSA[1]	38.3	61.7	78.5	21.5	89.0	11.0	90.2	9.8	89.2	10.8
U.S.	58.4	41.6	87.7	12.3	89.8	10.2	89.7	10.3	90.4	9.6

Note: Figures shown cover persons 3 years old and over; (1) Figures cover the Manchester-Nashua, NH Metropolitan Statistical Area—see Appendix B for areas included
Source: U.S. Census Bureau, 2012-2016 American Community Survey 5-Year Estimates

Average Salaries of Public School Classroom Teachers

Area	2015 Dollars	2015 Rank[1]	2016 Dollars	2016 Rank[1]	Change from 2015 to 2016 Percent	Change from 2015 to 2016 Rank[2]
New Hampshire	55,986	20	56,616	20	1.1	23
U.S. Average	57,611	–	58,353	–	1.3	–

Note: (1) Rank ranges from 1 to 51 where 1 indicates highest salary; (2) Rank ranges from 1 to 51 where 1 indicates highest percent change.
Source: National Education Association, Rankings & Estimates: Rankings of the States 2016 and Estimates of School Statistics 2017

Higher Education

Four-Year Colleges			Two-Year Colleges			Medical Schools[1]	Law Schools[2]	Voc/ Tech[3]
Public	Private Non-profit	Private For-profit	Public	Private Non-profit	Private For-profit			
0	1	0	0	0	0	0	0	0

Note: Figures cover institutions located within the city limits and include main campuses only; (1) includes schools accredited by the Liaison Committee on Medical Education and the American Osteopathic Association's Commission on Osteopathic College Accreditation; (2) includes ABA-accredited schools, schools with provisional ABA accreditation, and state accredited schools; (3) includes all schools with programs that are less than 2 years.
Source: National Center for Education Statistics, Integrated Postsecondary Education System (IPEDS), 2016-17; Wikipedia, List of Medical Schools in the United States, accessed April 2, 2018; Wikipedia, List of Law Schools in the United States, accessed April 2, 2018

According to *U.S. News & World Report,* the Manchester-Nashua, NH metro area is home to one of the best liberal arts colleges in the U.S.: **Saint Anselm College** (#106 tie). The indicators used to capture academic quality fall into a number of categories: assessment by administrators at peer institutions; retention of students; faculty resources; student selectivity; financial resources; alumni giving; high school counselor ratings of colleges; and graduation rate. *U.S. News & World Report, "America's Best Colleges 2018"*

PRESIDENTIAL ELECTION

2016 Presidential Election Results

Area	Clinton	Trump	Johnson	Stein	Other
Hillsborough County	46.5	46.7	4.3	0.8	1.7
U.S.	48.0	45.9	3.3	1.1	1.7

Note: Results are percentages and may not add to 100% due to rounding
Source: Dave Leip's Atlas of U.S. Presidential Elections

EMPLOYERS

Major Employers

Company Name	Industry
C & S Wholesale Grocers Inc	Grocery
Concord Hospital	Healthcare
Dartmouth-Hitchcock Keene	Healthcare
Dartmouth-Hitchcock Med Ctr	Healthcare
Elliot Hospital	Healthcare
Fidelity Investments	Financial services
Freudenberg-Nok	Healthcare
Hypertherm	Technology
J Jill	Retailer
Liberty Life Assurance Co	Insurance companies/services
Southern New Hampshire Health	Healthcare
St Joseph's Hospital	Healthcare
Sturm Ruger & Co. Inc	Firearms
Trustees of Dartmouth College	Education
UA Local 788 Marine Pipefitter	Union
United Physical Therapy	Healthcare
University of New Hampshire	Education
University System of NH	Education

Note: Companies shown are located within the Manchester-Nashua, NH Metropolitan Statistical Area.
Source: Hoovers.com; Wikipedia

PUBLIC SAFETY

Crime Rate

Area	All Crimes	Violent Crimes: Murder	Violent Crimes: Rape[3]	Violent Crimes: Robbery	Violent Crimes: Aggrav. Assault	Property Crimes: Burglary	Property Crimes: Larceny-Theft	Property Crimes: Motor Vehicle Theft
City	743.9	0.0	0.0	0.0	0.0	85.7	646.5	11.7
Metro[1]	1,794.1	1.2	39.7	61.0	166.6	209.4	1,245.6	70.5
U.S.	2,847.8	5.3	40.4	102.8	248.5	468.9	1,745.0	236.9

Note: Figures are crimes per 100,000 population; (1) Figures cover the Manchester-Nashua, NH Metropolitan Statistical Area—see Appendix B for areas included; (3) The city and U.S. figures shown were reported using the revised Uniform Crime Reporting (UCR) definition of rape. The metro area figures shown are an aggregate total of the data submitted using both the revised and legacy UCR definitions.
Source: FBI Uniform Crime Reports, 2016

Hate Crimes

Area	Number of Quarters Reported	Number of Incidents per Bias Motivation: Race/Ethnicity/ Ancestry	Religion	Sexual Orientation	Disability	Gender	Gender Identity
City	4	0	0	0	0	0	0
U.S.	4	3,489	1,273	1,076	70	31	124

Source: Federal Bureau of Investigation, Hate Crime Statistics 2016

Identity Theft Consumer Reports

Area	Reports	Reports per 100,000 Population	Rank[2]
MSA[1]	367	90	139
U.S.	371,061	114	-

Note: (1) Figures cover the Manchester-Nashua, NH Metropolitan Statistical Area—see Appendix B for areas included; (2) Rank ranges from 1 to 389 where 1 indicates greatest number of identity theft reports per 100,000 population
Source: Federal Trade Commission, Consumer Sentinel Network Data Book for January–December 2017

Fraud and Other Consumer Reports

Area	Reports	Reports per 100,000 Population	Rank[2]
MSA[1]	1,971	483	133
U.S.	2,304,550	708	-

Note: (1) Figures cover the Manchester-Nashua, NH Metropolitan Statistical Area—see Appendix B for areas included; (2) Rank ranges from 1 to 389 where 1 indicates greatest number of fraud and other consumer reports per 100,000 population
Source: Federal Trade Commission, Consumer Sentinel Network Data Book for January–December 2017

SPORTS

Professional Sports Teams

Team Name	League	Year Established
No teams are located in the metro area		

Source: Wikipedia, Major Professional Sports Teams of the United States and Canada, April 5, 2018

CLIMATE

Average and Extreme Temperatures

Temperature	Jan	Feb	Mar	Apr	May	Jun	Jul	Aug	Sep	Oct	Nov	Dec	Yr.
Extreme High (°F)	68	66	85	95	97	98	102	101	98	90	80	68	102
Average High (°F)	31	34	43	57	69	77	83	80	72	61	48	35	57
Average Temp. (°F)	20	23	33	44	56	65	70	68	59	48	38	25	46
Average Low (°F)	9	11	22	32	42	51	57	55	46	35	28	15	34
Extreme Low (°F)	-33	-27	-16	8	21	30	35	29	22	10	-5	-22	-33

Note: Figures cover the years 1948-1990
Source: National Climatic Data Center, International Station Meteorological Climate Summary, 9/96

Average Precipitation/Snowfall/Humidity

Precip./Humidity	Jan	Feb	Mar	Apr	May	Jun	Jul	Aug	Sep	Oct	Nov	Dec	Yr.
Avg. Precip. (in.)	2.8	2.5	2.9	3.1	3.2	3.1	3.1	3.3	2.9	3.1	3.8	3.2	36.9
Avg. Snowfall (in.)	18	15	11	2	Tr	0	0	0	0	Tr	4	14	63
Avg. Rel. Hum. 7am (%)	76	76	76	75	75	80	82	87	89	86	83	79	80
Avg. Rel. Hum. 4pm (%)	59	55	52	46	47	52	51	53	55	53	61	63	54

Note: Figures cover the years 1948-1990; Tr = Trace amounts (<0.05 in. of rain; <0.5 in. of snow)
Source: National Climatic Data Center, International Station Meteorological Climate Summary, 9/96

Weather Conditions

Temperature			Daytime Sky			Precipitation		
5°F & below	32°F & below	90°F & above	Clear	Partly cloudy	Cloudy	0.01 inch or more precip.	0.1 inch or more snow/ice	Thunder-storms
32	171	12	87	131	147	125	32	19

Note: Figures are average number of days per year and cover the years 1948-1990
Source: National Climatic Data Center, International Station Meteorological Climate Summary, 9/96

HAZARDOUS WASTE

Superfund Sites

The Manchester-Nashua, NH metro area is home to six sites on the EPA's Superfund National Priorities List: **Fletcher's Paint Works & Storage** (final); **Mohawk Tannery** (proposed); **New Hampshire Plating Co.** (final); **Savage Municipal Water Supply** (final); **South Municipal Water Supply Well** (final); **Sylvester** (final). There are a total of 1,396 Superfund sites with a status of proposed or final on the list in the U.S. *U.S. Environmental Protection Agency, National Priorities List, April 4, 2018*

AIR & WATER QUALITY

Air Quality Trends: Ozone

	1990	1995	2000	2005	2010	2012	2013	2014	2015	2016
MSA[1]	n/a	n/a	n/a	n/a	n/a	n/a	n/a	n/a	n/a	n/a
U.S.	0.087	0.089	0.081	0.079	0.073	0.075	0.069	0.067	0.068	0.069

Note: (1) Data covers the Manchester-Nashua, NH Metropolitan Statistical Area—see Appendix B for areas included; n/a not available. The values shown are the composite ozone concentration averages among trend sites based on the highest fourth daily maximum 8-hour concentration in parts per million. These trends are based on sites having an adequate record of monitoring data during the trend period. Data from exceptional events are included.
Source: U.S. Environmental Protection Agency, Air Quality Monitoring Information, "Air Quality Trends by City, 1990-2016"

Air Quality Index

Area	Percent of Days when Air Quality was...[2]					AQI Statistics[2]	
	Good	Moderate	Unhealthy for Sensitive Groups	Unhealthy	Very Unhealthy	Maximum	Median
MSA[1]	93.7	6.0	0.3	0.0	0.0	101	37

Note: (1) Data covers the Manchester-Nashua, NH Metropolitan Statistical Area—see Appendix B for areas included; (2) Based on 365 days with AQI data in 2017. Air Quality Index (AQI) is an index for reporting daily air quality. EPA calculates the AQI for five major air pollutants regulated by the Clean Air Act: ground-level ozone, particle pollution (aka particulate matter), carbon monoxide, sulfur dioxide, and nitrogen dioxide. The AQI runs from 0 to 500. The higher the AQI value, the greater the level of air pollution and the greater the health concern. There are six AQI categories: "Good" AQI is between 0 and 50. Air quality is considered satisfactory; "Moderate" AQI is between 51 and 100. Air quality is acceptable; "Unhealthy for Sensitive Groups" When AQI values are between 101 and 150, members of sensitive groups may experience health effects; "Unhealthy" When AQI values are between 151 and 200 everyone may begin to experience health effects; "Very Unhealthy" AQI values between 201 and 300 trigger a health alert; "Hazardous" AQI values over 300 trigger warnings of emergency conditions (not shown).
Source: U.S. Environmental Protection Agency, Air Quality Index Report, 2017

Air Quality Index Pollutants

Area	Percent of Days when AQI Pollutant was...[2]					
	Carbon Monoxide	Nitrogen Dioxide	Ozone	Sulfur Dioxide	Particulate Matter 2.5	Particulate Matter 10
MSA[1]	0.0	0.0	96.4	0.3	3.3	0.0

Note: (1) Data covers the Manchester-Nashua, NH Metropolitan Statistical Area—see Appendix B for areas included; (2) Based on 365 days with AQI data in 2017. The Air Quality Index (AQI) is an index for reporting daily air quality. EPA calculates the AQI for five major air pollutants regulated by the Clean Air Act: ground-level ozone, particle pollution (also known as particulate matter), carbon monoxide, sulfur dioxide, and nitrogen dioxide. The AQI runs from 0 to 500. The higher the AQI value, the greater the level of air pollution and the greater the health concern.
Source: U.S. Environmental Protection Agency, Air Quality Index Report, 2017

Maximum Air Pollutant Concentrations: Particulate Matter, Ozone, CO and Lead

	Particulate Matter 10 (ug/m^3)	Particulate Matter 2.5 Wtd AM (ug/m^3)	Particulate Matter 2.5 24-Hr (ug/m^3)	Ozone (ppm)	Carbon Monoxide (ppm)	Lead (ug/m^3)
MSA[1] Level	n/a	4.2	10	0.069	0	n/a
NAAQS[2]	150	15	35	0.075	9	0.15
Met NAAQS[2]	n/a	Yes	Yes	Yes	Yes	n/a

Note: (1) Data covers the Manchester-Nashua, NH Metropolitan Statistical Area—see Appendix B for areas included; Data from exceptional events are included; (2) National Ambient Air Quality Standards; ppm = parts per million; ug/m^3 = micrograms per cubic meter; n/a not available.
Concentrations: Particulate Matter 10 (coarse particulate)—highest second maximum 24-hour concentration; Particulate Matter 2.5 Wtd AM (fine particulate)—highest weighted annual mean concentration; Particulate Matter 2.5 24-Hour (fine particulate)—highest 98th percentile 24-hour concentration; Ozone—highest fourth daily maximum 8-hour concentration; Carbon Monoxide—highest second maximum non-overlapping 8-hour concentration; Lead—maximum running 3-month average
Source: U.S. Environmental Protection Agency, Air Quality Monitoring Information, "Air Quality Statistics by City, 2016"

Maximum Air Pollutant Concentrations: Nitrogen Dioxide and Sulfur Dioxide

	Nitrogen Dioxide AM (ppb)	Nitrogen Dioxide 1-Hr (ppb)	Sulfur Dioxide AM (ppb)	Sulfur Dioxide 1-Hr (ppb)	Sulfur Dioxide 24-Hr (ppb)
MSA[1] Level	n/a	n/a	n/a	2	n/a
NAAQS[2]	53	100	30	75	140
Met NAAQS[2]	n/a	n/a	n/a	Yes	n/a

Note: (1) Data covers the Manchester-Nashua, NH Metropolitan Statistical Area—see Appendix B for areas included; Data from exceptional events are included; (2) National Ambient Air Quality Standards; ppm = parts per million; ug/m^3 = micrograms per cubic meter; n/a not available.
Concentrations: Nitrogen Dioxide AM—highest arithmetic mean concentration; Nitrogen Dioxide 1-Hr—highest 98th percentile 1-hour daily maximum concentration; Sulfur Dioxide AM—highest annual mean concentration; Sulfur Dioxide 1-Hr—highest 99th percentile 1-hour daily maximum concentration; Sulfur Dioxide 24-Hr—highest second maximum 24-hour concentration
Source: U.S. Environmental Protection Agency, Air Quality Monitoring Information, "Air Quality Statistics by City, 2016"

Drinking Water

Water System Name	Pop. Served	Primary Water Source Type	Violations[1]	
			Health Based	Monitoring/ Reporting
Merrimack Village District	25,000	Ground	0	0

Note: (1) Based on violation data from January 1, 2017 to December 31, 2017
Source: U.S. Environmental Protection Agency, Office of Ground Water and Drinking Water, Safe Drinking Water Information System (based on data extracted April 5, 2018)

Evesham, New Jersey

Background

Evesham is located in Burlington County, 13 miles southwest of Camden and 17 miles southwest of Philadelphia. The city borders Mount Laurel, Medford, and Camden County.

Present-day Evesham was settled by Quakers in 1672 and probably named for a town in England of the same name. The city was divided twice in its history, in 1847 and 1872, creating Medford and Mount Laurel, respectively. In 1955, the United States Army opened the PH-32 Nike Ajax facility in Evesham, one of 12 facilities intended to shield Philadelphia from an aerial assault during the Cold War. The facility was decommissioned in the mid-1960s and is currently used as a civil defense center. It is also the site of an upscale housing development.

The commercial center of Evesham is the historic Marlton Village, easily accessible from routes 70 and 73. This center offers businesses modern office space and upscale shopping, while still maintaining its old-time beauty.

Each fall, Evesham hosts the Olde Marlton Fall Festival, which features arts, crafts, food, and live entertainment in the city's historic downtown. Another major attraction in Evesham is the Indian Spring Country Club, with a 141-acre, 18-hole public golf course established in 1952.

A 14,000-square foot office building in the Evesham Corporate Center industrial park, is home to Lot Two, LLC, and the Elmwood Village Office Center along Route 70. More exciting to some than office space, however, is the state sponsored bikeway transportation system in the planning stages.

Evesham has a moderate climate with hot summers and cold winters. Median summer temperatures average 70 degrees, while winter averages are as low as 35 degrees during of December and January. The city averages 4.5 inches of rainfall per month from April to August and 6 inches of snowfall per month from December to March.

Rankings

Business/Finance Rankings

- The personal finance site NerdWallet analyzed 183 American metropolitan areas with populations over 250,000 and more than 15,000 businesses to rank where entrepreneurs find the most success. Criteria included area economy, annual income, housing cost, unemployment rate, and the success rate of area businesses. Camden* ranked #60. *www.nerdwallet.com, "Best Places to Start a Business," April 27, 2015*
- In a survey of economic confidence in the nation's 50 largest metropolitan areas conducted January–December 2014, the Philadelphia* metro area placed #33, according to Gallup's 2014 Economic Confidence Index. *Gallup, "San Jose and San Francisco Lead in Economic Confidence," March 19, 2015*
- The Brookings Institution ranked the 100 largest metro areas in the U.S. based on income inequality. Philadelphia* was ranked #12 (#1 = greatest ineqality). Criteria: the "95/20 ratio," a figure representing the income at which a household earns more than 95 percent of all other households, divided by the income at which a household earns more than only 20 percent of all other households. *Brookings Institution, "Household Income Inequality, 100 Largest U.S. Metro Areas, 2014-2016," February 5, 2018*
- Payscale.com ranked the largest metro areas in terms of wage growth. The Philadelphia* metro area ranked #29. Criteria: private-sector wage growth between the 4th quarter of 2016 and the 4th quarter of 2017. *PayScale, "Wage Trends by Metro Area-4th Quarter," January 17, 2018*
- The Philadelphia* metro area was identified as one of the most debt-ridden places in America by the finance site Credit.com. The metro area was ranked #11. Criteria: residents' average credit card debt as well as median income. *Credit.com, "25 Cities With the Most Credit Card Debt," February 28, 2018*
- Philadelphia* was identified as one of America's most frugal metro areas by *Coupons.com.* The city ranked #6 out of 25. Criteria: digital coupon usage. *Coupons.com, "America's Most Frugal Cities of 2017," March 22, 2018*
- The Camden* metro area appeared on the Milken Institute "2017 Best Performing Cities" list. Rank: #135 out of 200 large metro areas. Criteria: job growth; wage and salary growth; high-tech output growth. *Milken Institute, "Best-Performing Cities 2017," January 2018*
- *Forbes* ranked the 200 most populous metro areas to determine the nation's "Best Places for Business and Careers." The Camden* metro area was ranked #150. Criteria: costs (business and living); job growth (past and projected); income growth; quality of life; educational attainment (college and high school); projected economic growth; cultural and recreational opportunities; net migration patterns; number of highly ranked colleges. *Forbes, "The Best Places for Business and Careers 2017," October 24, 2017*

Education Rankings

- Personal finance website *WalletHub* analyzed the 150 largest U.S. metropolitan statistical areas to determine where the most educated Americans are choosing to settle. Criteria: education quality and attainment gap; education levels; percentage of workers with degrees; public school rankings; quality and size of each metro area's universities. Philadelphia* was ranked #44 (#1 = most educated city). *www.WalletHub.com, "2017's Most and Least Educated Cities in America, " July 25, 2017*

Environmental Rankings

- Sperling's BestPlaces assessed 379 metropolitan areas of the United States for the likelihood of dangerously extreme weather events or earthquakes. In general the Southeast and South-Central regions have the highest risk of weather extremes and earthquakes, while the Pacific Northwest enjoys the lowest risk. Of the least risky metropolitan areas, the Camden* metro area was ranked #331. *www.bestplaces.net, "Safest Places from Natural Disasters," April 2011*

- The U.S. Environmental Protection Agency (EPA) released a list of U.S. metropolitan areas with the most ENERGY STAR certified buildings in 2016. The Philadelphia* metro area was ranked #11 out of 25. *U.S. Environmental Protection Agency, "2017 Energy Star Top Cities," June 2017*

- Philadelphia* was highlighted as one of the 25 most ozone-polluted metro areas in the U.S. during 2013 through 2015. The area ranked #22. *American Lung Association, State of the Air 2017*

- Philadelphia* was highlighted as one of the 25 metro areas most polluted by year-round particle pollution (Annual PM 2.5) in the U.S. during 2013 through 2015. The area ranked #13. *American Lung Association, State of the Air 2017*

- Philadelphia* was highlighted as one of the 25 metro areas most polluted by short-term particle pollution (24-hour PM 2.5) in the U.S. during 2013 through 2015. The area ranked #20. *American Lung Association, State of the Air 2017*

Health/Fitness Rankings

- For each of the 50 most populous metro areas in the United States, the American College of Sports Medicine's American Fitness Index evaluated infrastructure, community assets, and policies that encourage healthy and fit lifestyles, including preventive health behaviors, levels of chronic disease conditions, health care access, and community resources and policies that support physical activity. The Philadelphia* metro area ranked #32 for "community fitness." *www.americanfitnessindex.org, "ACSM American Fitness Index Health and Community Fitness Status of the 50 Largest Metropolitan Areas," May 2017*

- The Philadelphia* metro area was identified as one of the worst cities for bed bugs in America by pest control company Orkin. The area ranked #12 out of 50 based on the number of bed bug treatments Orkin performed from December 2016 to November 2017. *Orkin, "Baltimore and Washington D.C. Continue to Hold Top Spots," January 8, 2018*

- Philadelphia* was identified as a "2016 Spring Allergy Capital." The area ranked #21 out of 100. Three groups of factors were used to identify the most severe cities for people with allergies during the spring season: annual pollen levels; medicine utilization; access to board-certified allergists. *Asthma and Allergy Foundation of America, "Spring Allergy Capitals 2016"*

- Philadelphia* was identified as a "2016 Fall Allergy Capital." The area ranked #32 out of 100. Three groups of factors were used to identify the most severe cities for people with allergies during the fall season: annual pollen levels; medicine utilization; access to board-certified allergists. *Asthma and Allergy Foundation of America, "Fall Allergy Capitals 2016"*

- Philadelphia* was identified as a "2015 Asthma Capital." The area ranked #3 out of the nation's 100 largest metropolitan areas. Criteria: estimated prevalence; self-reported prevalence; crude death rate for asthma; annual pollen score; annual air quality; public smoking laws; number of board-certified asthma specialists; school inhaler access laws; rescue medication use; controller medication use; ER visits for asthma; uninsured rate; poverty rate. *Asthma and Allergy Foundation of America, "Asthma Capitals 2015"*

- The Philadelphia* metro area ranked #132 out of 189 in The Gallup-Healthways Well-Being Index. Criteria: purpose; social well being; financial health; community and physical health. Results are based on telephone interviews with adults, aged 18 and older, living in metropolitan areas in the 50 U.S. states and the District of Columbia. *Gallup-Healthways, "State of American Well-Being, 2017 Community Well-Being Rankings" March 2018*

Real Estate Rankings

- FitSmallBusiness looked at 50 of the largest metropolitan areas in the U.S. to determine which metro was the best to start a real estate business. Data was compiled from such sources as: Zillow, Trulia, U.S. Census Bureau, and the Bureau of Labor Statistics. Criteria: location; inventory; annual wages; median sales price of homes; days on the market; median price cut percentage; and other factors that would influence real estate professional growth. The Philadelphia* metro area ranked #17. *fitsmallbusiness.com, "The Best Cities to Become a Real Estate Agent in 2018," January 30, 2018*

- Camden* was ranked #42 out of 238 metro areas in terms of housing affordability in 2017 by the National Association of Home Builders (#1 = most affordable). Criteria: the share of homes sold in that area affordable to a family earning the local median income, based on standard mortgage underwriting criteria. *National Association of Home Builders®, NAHB-Wells Fargo Housing Opportunity Index, 4th Quarter 2017*

- The nation's largest metro areas were analyzed in terms of the percentage of households entering some stage of foreclosure in 2017. The Philadelphia* metro area ranked #3 out of 10 (#1 = highest foreclosure rate). *RealtyTrac, "2017 Year-End U.S. Foreclosure Market Report™," January 16, 2018*

Safety Rankings

- The National Insurance Crime Bureau ranked 382 metro areas in the U.S. in terms of per capita rates of vehicle theft. The Philadelphia* metro area ranked #208 (#1 = highest rate). Criteria: number of vehicle theft offenses per 100,000 inhabitants in 2016. *National Insurance Crime Bureau, "Hot Spots 2016," June 8, 2017*

Seniors/Retirement Rankings

- From its Best Cities for Successful Aging indexes, the Milken Institute generated rankings for metropolitan areas, weighing data in nine categories—health care, wellness, living arrangements, transportation and convenience, financial characteristics, education, employment, community engagement, and overall livability. The Philadelphia* metro area was ranked #52 overall in the large metro area category. *Milken Institute, "Best Cities for Successful Aging, 2017" March 14, 2017*

Sports/Recreation Rankings

- According to the personal finance website NerdWallet, the Philadelphia* metro area, at #10, is one of the nation's top dozen metro areas for sports fans. Criteria included the presence of all four major sports—MLB, NFL, NHL, and NBA, fan enthusiasm (as measured by game attendance), ticket affordability, and "sports culture," that is, number of sports bars. *www.nerdwallet.com, "Best Cities for Sports Fans," May 5, 2013*

Transportation Rankings

- The Philadelphia* metro area appeared on *Forbes* list of places with the most extreme commutes. The metro area ranked #9 out of 10. Criteria: average travel time; percentage of mega commuters. Mega-commuters travel more than 90 minutes and 50 miles each way to work. *Forbes.com, "The Cities with the Most Extreme Commutes," March 5, 2013*

Miscellaneous Rankings

- The watchdog site Charity Navigator conducts an annual study of charities in the nation's major markets both to analyze statistical differences in their financial, accountability, and transparency practices and to track year-to-year variations in individual philanthropic communities. Charity Navigator's analysis demonstrated that the financial, accountability and transparency behaviors of America's largest charities can be influenced by the metropolitan market within which the charity operates. The Philadelphia* metro area was ranked #20 among the 30 metro markets in the rating category of Overall Score. *www.charitynavigator.org, "2017 Metro Market Study," May 1, 2017*

- The Harris Poll's Happiness Index survey revealed that of the top ten U.S. markets, the Philadelphia* metro area residents ranked #3 in happiness. Criteria included strong assent to positive statements and strong disagreement with negative ones, and degree of agreement with a series of statements about respondents' personal relationships and general outlook. *www.theharrispoll.com, "Dallas/Fort Worth Is "Happiest" City among America's Top Ten Markets," September 4, 2013*

- Energizer Personal Care, the makers of Edge® shave gel, in partnership with Sperling's BestPlaces, ranked 50 major metro areas in terms of everyday irritations. The Philadelphia* metro area ranked #4 the 50 metro area most irritating to guys. Criteria: high male-to-female ratio; poor sports team performance and high ticket prices; slow traffic; lack of job availability; unaffordable housing; extreme weather; lack of nightlife and fitness options. *Energizer Personal Care, "Most Irritating Cities for Guys," August 26, 2013*

- The National Alliance to End Homelessness listed the 25 most populous metro areas with the highest rate of homelessness. The Philadelphia* metro area had a high rate of homelessness. Criteria: number of homeless people per 10,000 population in 2016. *National Alliance to End Homelessness, "Homelessness in the 25 Most Populous U.S. Metro Areas," September 1, 2017*

*Evesham is located within the Philadelphia-Camden-Wilmington, PA-NJ-DE-MD Metropolitan Statistical Area and the Camden, NJ Metropolitan Division.

Business Environment

CITY FINANCES

City Government Finances

Component	2015 ($000)	2015 ($ per capita)
Total Revenues	55,354	1,215
Total Expenditures	50,425	1,106
Debt Outstanding	56,517	1,240
Cash and Securities[1]	35,079	770

Note: (1) Cash and security holdings of a government at the close of its fiscal year,, including those of its dependent agencies, utilities, and liquor stores.
Source: U.S Census Bureau, State & Local Government Finances 2015

City Government Revenue by Source

Source	2015 ($000)	2015 ($ per capita)	2015 (%)
General Revenue			
From Federal Government	0	0	0.0
From State Government	4,290	94	7.8
From Local Governments	24	1	0.0
Taxes			
Property	25,373	557	45.8
Sales and Gross Receipts	699	15	1.3
Personal Income	0	0	0.0
Corporate Income	0	0	0.0
Motor Vehicle License	0	0	0.0
Other Taxes	982	22	1.8
Current Charges	13,067	287	23.6
Liquor Store	0	0	0.0
Utility	6,240	137	11.3
Employee Retirement	0	0	0.0

Source: U.S Census Bureau, State & Local Government Finances 2015

City Government Expenditures by Function

Function	2015 ($000)	2015 ($ per capita)	2015 (%)
General Direct Expenditures			
Air Transportation	0	0	0.0
Corrections	0	0	0.0
Education	0	0	0.0
Employment Security Administration	0	0	0.0
Financial Administration	1,154	25	2.3
Fire Protection	14	< 1	< 0.1
General Public Buildings	342	7	0.7
Governmental Administration, Other	882	19	1.7
Health	29	< 1	< 0.1
Highways	2,143	47	4.2
Hospitals	0	0	0.0
Housing and Community Development	0	0	0.0
Interest on General Debt	1,960	43	3.9
Judicial and Legal	471	10	0.9
Libraries	0	0	0.0
Parking	0	0	0.0
Parks and Recreation	1,248	27	2.5
Police Protection	8,096	177	16.1
Public Welfare	0	0	0.0
Sewerage	6,358	139	12.6
Solid Waste Management	2,566	56	5.1
Veterans' Services	0	0	0.0
Liquor Store	0	0	0.0
Utility	3,834	84	7.6
Employee Retirement	0	0	0.0

Source: U.S Census Bureau, State & Local Government Finances 2015

DEMOGRAPHICS

Population Growth

Area	1990 Census	2000 Census	2010 Census	2016* Estimate	Population Growth (%) 1990-2016	Population Growth (%) 2010-2016
City	35,309	42,275	45,538	45,578	29.1	0.1
MSA[1]	5,435,470	5,687,147	5,965,343	6,047,721	11.3	1.4
U.S.	248,709,873	281,421,906	308,745,538	318,558,162	28.1	3.2

Note: (1) Figures cover the Philadelphia-Camden-Wilmington, PA-NJ-DE-MD Metropolitan Statistical Area—see Appendix B for areas included; (*) 2012-2016 5-year estimated population
Source: U.S. Census Bureau, 1990 Census, Census 2000, Census 2010, 2012-2016 American Community Survey 5-Year Estimates

Household Size

Area	Persons in Household (%) One	Two	Three	Four	Five	Six	Seven or More	Average Household Size
City	25.7	32.8	17.7	15.8	6.3	1.2	0.4	2.60
MSA[1]	29.3	31.8	16.4	13.5	5.9	2.1	1.1	2.60
U.S.	27.7	33.7	15.7	13.1	6.0	2.3	1.5	2.60

Note: (1) Figures cover the Philadelphia-Camden-Wilmington, PA-NJ-DE-MD Metropolitan Statistical Area—see Appendix B for areas included
Source: U.S. Census Bureau, 2012-2016 American Community Survey 5-Year Estimates

Race

Area	White Alone[2] (%)	Black Alone[2] (%)	Asian Alone[2] (%)	AIAN[3] Alone[2] (%)	NHOPI[4] Alone[2] (%)	Other Race Alone[2] (%)	Two or More Races (%)
City	86.1	4.7	5.9	0.0	0.0	1.6	1.6
MSA[1]	67.5	20.9	5.6	0.2	0.0	3.2	2.6
U.S.	73.3	12.6	5.2	0.8	0.2	4.8	3.1

Note: (1) Figures cover the Philadelphia-Camden-Wilmington, PA-NJ-DE-MD Metropolitan Statistical Area—see Appendix B for areas included; (2) Alone is defined as not being in combination with one or more other races; (3) American Indian and Alaska Native; (4) Native Hawaiian and Other Pacific Islander
Source: U.S. Census Bureau, 2012-2016 American Community Survey 5-Year Estimates

Hispanic or Latino Origin

Area	Total (%)	Mexican (%)	Puerto Rican (%)	Cuban (%)	Other (%)
City	4.9	1.0	2.0	0.3	1.6
MSA[1]	8.8	1.8	4.4	0.2	2.3
U.S.	17.3	11.0	1.7	0.7	4.0

Note: Persons of Hispanic or Latino origin can be of any race; (1) Figures cover the Philadelphia-Camden-Wilmington, PA-NJ-DE-MD Metropolitan Statistical Area—see Appendix B for areas included
Source: U.S. Census Bureau, 2012-2016 American Community Survey 5-Year Estimates

Segregation

Type	Segregation Indices[1] 1990	2000	2010	2010 Rank[2]	Percent Change 1990-2000	1990-2010	2000-2010
Black/White	75.2	71.0	68.4	9	-4.2	-6.8	-2.6
Asian/White	42.4	44.1	42.3	42	1.7	0.0	-1.8
Hispanic/White	60.9	58.5	55.1	12	-2.5	-5.9	-3.4

Note: All figures cover the Metropolitan Statistical Area—see Appendix B for areas included; Figures are based on an analysis of 1990, 2000, and 2010 Census Decennial Census tract data by William H. Frey, Brookings Institution and the University of Michigan Social Science Data Analysis Network. In this analysis all racial groups (whites, blacks, and asians) are non-Hispanic members of those races. Hispanics are shown as a separate category; (1) Segregation Indices are Dissimilarity Indices that measure the degree to which the minority group is distributed differently than whites across census tracts. They range from 0 (complete integration) to 100 (complete segregation) where the value indicates the percentage of the minority group that needs to move to be distributed exactly like whites; (2) Ranges from 1 (most segregated) to 102 (least segregated); n/a not available.
Source: www.CensusScope.org

Ancestry

Area	German	Irish	English	American	Italian	Polish	French[2]	Scottish	Dutch
City	18.5	25.7	9.0	3.2	23.8	8.5	2.0	2.0	1.3
MSA[1]	15.7	19.2	7.1	3.6	13.7	5.2	1.5	1.3	0.9
U.S.	14.4	10.4	7.7	6.9	5.4	2.9	2.6	1.7	1.3

Note: Figures are the percentage of the total population reporting a particular ancestry. The nine most commonly reported ancestries in the U.S. are shown. Figures include multiple ancestries (e.g. if a person reported being Irish and Italian, they were included in both columns); (1) Figures cover the Philadelphia-Camden-Wilmington, PA-NJ-DE-MD Metropolitan Statistical Area—see Appendix B for areas included; (2) Excludes Basque
Source: U.S. Census Bureau, 2012-2016 American Community Survey 5-Year Estimates

Foreign-Born Population

Area	Percent of Population Born in								
	Any Foreign Country	Asia	Mexico	Europe	Carribean	Central America[2]	South America	Africa	Canada
City	8.3	4.3	0.5	1.3	0.6	0.1	0.6	0.7	0.1
MSA[1]	10.3	4.2	0.9	1.9	1.2	0.4	0.6	0.9	0.1
U.S.	13.2	4.0	3.6	1.5	1.3	1.0	0.9	0.6	0.3

Note: (1) Figures cover the Philadelphia-Camden-Wilmington, PA-NJ-DE-MD Metropolitan Statistical Area—see Appendix B for areas included; (2) Excludes Mexico.
Source: U.S. Census Bureau, 2012-2016 American Community Survey 5-Year Estimates

Marital Status

Area	Never Married	Now Married[2]	Separated	Widowed	Divorced
City	28.8	54.3	1.6	6.0	9.3
MSA[1]	37.4	45.1	2.2	6.2	9.1
U.S.	33.0	48.1	2.1	5.9	11.0

Note: Figures are percentages and cover the population 15 years of age and older; (1) Figures cover the Philadelphia-Camden-Wilmington, PA-NJ-DE-MD Metropolitan Statistical Area—see Appendix B for areas included; (2) Excludes separated
Source: U.S. Census Bureau, 2012-2016 American Community Survey 5-Year Estimates

Disability Status

Area	All Ages	Under 18 Years Old	18 to 64 Years Old	65 Years and Over
City	9.0	2.6	5.5	32.1
MSA[1]	12.3	4.6	10.2	34.0
U.S.	12.5	4.1	10.3	35.7

Note: Figures show percent of the civilian noninstitutionalized population that reported having a disability. Disability status is determined from six types of difficulty: vision, hearing, cognitive, ambulatory, self-care, and independent living. For children under 5 years old, hearing and vision difficulty are used to determine disability status. For children between the ages of 5 and 14, disability status is determined from hearing, vision, cognitive, ambulatory, and self-care difficulties. For people aged 15 years and older, they are considered to have a disability if they have difficulty with any one of the six difficulty types; Note: (1) Figures cover the Philadelphia-Camden-Wilmington, PA-NJ-DE-MD Metropolitan Statistical Area—see Appendix B for areas included
Source: U.S. Census Bureau, 2012-2016 American Community Survey 5-Year Estimates

Age

Area	Percent of Population									Median Age
	Under Age 5	Age 5–19	Age 20–34	Age 35–44	Age 45–54	Age 55–64	Age 65–74	Age 75–84	Age 85+	
City	4.7	18.0	19.0	12.4	16.9	13.3	8.3	4.7	2.8	42.3
MSA[1]	6.0	19.1	20.8	12.4	14.3	13.0	8.0	4.4	2.2	38.4
U.S.	6.2	19.6	20.7	12.7	13.6	12.6	8.3	4.3	1.9	37.7

Note: (1) Figures cover the Philadelphia-Camden-Wilmington, PA-NJ-DE-MD Metropolitan Statistical Area—see Appendix B for areas included
Source: U.S. Census Bureau, 2012-2016 American Community Survey 5-Year Estimates

Gender

Area	Males	Females	Males per 100 Females
City	22,116	23,462	94.3
MSA[1]	2,923,439	3,124,282	93.6
U.S.	156,765,322	161,792,840	96.9

Note: (1) Figures cover the Philadelphia-Camden-Wilmington, PA-NJ-DE-MD Metropolitan Statistical Area—see Appendix B for areas included
Source: U.S. Census Bureau, 2012-2016 American Community Survey 5-Year Estimates

Religious Groups by Family

Area	Catholic	Baptist	Non-Den.	Methodist[2]	Lutheran	LDS[3]	Pente-costal	Presby-terian[4]	Muslim[5]	Judaism
MSA[1]	33.5	3.9	2.9	3.0	1.9	0.3	0.9	2.1	1.3	1.4
U.S.	19.1	9.3	4.0	4.0	2.3	2.0	1.9	1.6	0.8	0.7

Note: Figures are the number of adherents as a percentage of the total population; (1) Figures cover the Philadelphia-Camden-Wilmington, PA-NJ-DE-MD Metropolitan Statistical Area—see Appendix B for areas included; (2) Methodist/Pietist; (3) Latter Day Saints; (4) Reformed; (5) Figures are estimates
Source: Association of Statisticians of American Religious Bodies, 2010 U.S. Religion Census: Religious Congregations & Membership Study

Religious Groups by Tradition

Area	Catholic	Evangelical Protestant	Mainline Protestant	Other Tradition	Black Protestant	Orthodox
MSA[1]	33.5	6.3	8.9	3.7	1.8	0.4
U.S.	19.1	16.2	7.3	4.3	1.6	0.3

Note: Figures are the number of adherents as a percentage of the total population; (1) Figures cover the Philadelphia-Camden-Wilmington, PA-NJ-DE-MD Metropolitan Statistical Area—see Appendix B for areas included
Source: Association of Statisticians of American Religious Bodies, 2010 U.S. Religion Census: Religious Congregations & Membership Study

ECONOMY

Gross Metropolitan Product

Area	2014	2015	2016	2017	Rank[2]
MSA[1]	389.2	403.6	416.4	433.9	8

Note: Figures are in billions of dollars; (1) Figures cover the Philadelphia-Camden-Wilmington, PA-NJ-DE-MD Metropolitan Statistical Area—see Appendix B for areas included; (2) Rank is based on 2015 data and ranges from 1 to 381
Source: The U.S. Conference of Mayors, U.S. Metro Economies: GMP and Employment Report, 2015-2017

Economic Growth

Area	2012-14 (%)	2015 (%)	2016 (%)	2017 (%)	Rank[2]
MSA[1]	0.9	2.2	1.6	2.1	216
U.S.	2.0	2.4	1.9	2.6	–

Note: Figures are real gross metropolitan product (GMP) growth rates and represent average annual percent change; (1) Figures cover the Philadelphia-Camden-Wilmington, PA-NJ-DE-MD Metropolitan Statistical Area—see Appendix B for areas included; (2) Rank is based on 2012-2014 average annual percent change and ranges from 1 to 381
Source: The U.S. Conference of Mayors, U.S. Metro Economies: GMP and Employment Report, 2015-2017

Metropolitan Area Exports

Area	2011	2012	2013	2014	2015	2016	Rank[2]
MSA[1]	26,155.8	22,991.6	24,929.2	26,321.3	24,236.1	21,359.9	14

Note: Figures are in millions of dollars; (1) Figures cover the Philadelphia-Camden-Wilmington, PA-NJ-DE-MD Metropolitan Statistical Area—see Appendix B for areas included; (2) Rank is based on 2016 data and ranges from 1 to 385
Source: U.S. Department of Commerce, International Trade Administration, Office of Trade & Industry Information, Manufacturing & Services, data extracted March 15, 2018

Building Permits

Area	Single-Family			Multi-Family			Total		
	2016	2017p	Pct. Chg.	2016	2017p	Pct. Chg.	2016	2017p	Pct. Chg.
City	13	49	276.9	64	18	-71.9	77	67	-13.0
MSA[1]	6,820	7,278	6.7	5,295	6,021	13.7	12,115	13,299	9.8
U.S.	750,800	817,300	8.9	455,800	446,800	-2.0	1,206,600	1,264,100	4.8

Note: (1) Figures cover the Philadelphia-Camden-Wilmington, PA-NJ-DE-MD Metropolitan Statistical Area—see Appendix B for areas included; Figures represent new, privately-owned housing units authorized (unadjusted data); All permit data are based on estimates with imputation; (p) preliminary data.
Source: U.S. Census Bureau, Manufacturing, Mining, and Construction Statistics, Building Permits, 2016, 2017

Bankruptcy Filings

Area	Business Filings			Nonbusiness Filings		
	2016	2017	% Chg.	2016	2017	% Chg.
Burlington County	49	40	-18.4	1,598	1,764	10.4
U.S.	24,114	23,157	-4.0	770,846	765,863	-0.6

Note: Business filings include Chapter 7, Chapter 11, Chapter 12, and Chapter 13; Nonbusiness filings include Chapter 7, Chapter 11, and Chapter 13
Source: Administrative Office of the U.S. Courts, Business and Nonbusiness Bankruptcy, County Cases Commenced by Chapter of the Bankruptcy Code, During the 12-Month Period Ending December 31, 2016 and Business and Nonbusiness Bankruptcy, County Cases Commenced by Chapter of the Bankruptcy Code, During the 12-Month Period Ending December 31, 2017

Housing Vacancy Rates

Area	Gross Vacancy Rate[2] (%)			Year-Round Vacancy Rate[3] (%)			Rental Vacancy Rate[4] (%)			Homeowner Vacancy Rate[5] (%)		
	2015	2016	2017	2015	2016	2017	2015	2016	2017	2015	2016	2017
MSA[1]	10.7	9.3	8.6	10.2	8.6	8.3	7.6	6.8	7.3	2.4	1.4	1.6
U.S.	12.9	12.8	12.7	10.0	9.9	9.9	7.1	6.9	7.2	1.8	1.7	1.6

Note: (1) Figures cover the Philadelphia-Camden-Wilmington, PA-NJ-DE-MD Metropolitan Statistical Area—see Appendix B for areas included; (2) The percentage of the total housing inventory that is vacant; (3) The percentage of the housing inventory (excluding seasonal units) that is year-round vacant; (4) The percentage of rental inventory that is vacant for rent; (5) The percentage of homeowner inventory that is vacant for sale
Source: U.S. Census Bureau, Housing Vacancies and Homeownership Annual Statistics: 2015, 2016, 2017

INCOME

Income

Area	Per Capita ($)	Median Household ($)	Average Household ($)
City	43,130	90,315	110,180
MSA[1]	34,118	63,952	88,881
U.S.	29,829	55,322	77,866

Note: (1) Figures cover the Philadelphia-Camden-Wilmington, PA-NJ-DE-MD Metropolitan Statistical Area—see Appendix B for areas included
Source: U.S. Census Bureau, 2012-2016 American Community Survey 5-Year Estimates

Household Income Distribution

Area	Percent of Households Earning							
	Under $15,000	$15,000 -$24,999	$25,000 -$34,999	$35,000 -$49,999	$50,000 -$74,999	$75,000 -$99,999	$100,000 -$149,999	$150,000 and up
City	5.7	5.1	6.3	7.6	15.7	14.2	21.1	24.4
MSA[1]	11.3	8.8	8.4	11.6	16.4	12.3	16.0	15.2
U.S.	12.1	10.2	9.9	13.2	17.8	12.2	13.5	11.1

Note: (1) Figures cover the Philadelphia-Camden-Wilmington, PA-NJ-DE-MD Metropolitan Statistical Area—see Appendix B for areas included
Source: U.S. Census Bureau, 2012-2016 American Community Survey 5-Year Estimates

Poverty Rate

Area	All Ages	Under 18 Years Old	18 to 64 Years Old	65 Years and Over
City	4.8	6.1	4.0	6.3
MSA[1]	13.1	18.1	12.3	8.9
U.S.	15.1	21.2	14.2	9.3

Note: Figures are percentage of people whose income during the past 12 months was below the poverty level; (1) Figures cover the Philadelphia-Camden-Wilmington, PA-NJ-DE-MD Metropolitan Statistical Area—see Appendix B for areas included
Source: U.S. Census Bureau, 2012-2016 American Community Survey 5-Year Estimates

EMPLOYMENT

Labor Force and Employment

Area	Civilian Labor Force			Workers Employed		
	Dec. 2016	Dec. 2017	% Chg.	Dec. 2016	Dec. 2017	% Chg.
City	26,177	26,122	-0.2	25,374	25,372	0.0
MD[1]	641,023	640,625	-0.1	614,203	613,865	-0.1
U.S.	158,968,000	159,880,000	0.6	151,798,000	153,602,000	1.2

Note: Data is not seasonally adjusted and covers workers 16 years of age and older; (1) Figures cover the Camden, NJ Metropolitan Division—see Appendix B for areas included
Source: Bureau of Labor Statistics, Local Area Unemployment Statistics

Unemployment Rate

Area	2017											
	Jan.	Feb.	Mar.	Apr.	May	Jun.	Jul.	Aug.	Sep.	Oct.	Nov.	Dec.
City	3.5	3.4	3.0	2.9	3.2	3.2	3.7	3.6	3.5	3.2	3.2	2.9
MD[1]	4.9	4.9	4.5	4.1	4.4	4.7	5.3	5.1	4.7	4.5	4.4	4.2
U.S.	5.1	4.9	4.6	4.1	4.1	4.5	4.6	4.5	4.1	3.9	3.9	3.9

Note: Data is not seasonally adjusted and covers workers 16 years of age and older; (1) Figures cover the Camden, NJ Metropolitan Division—see Appendix B for areas included
Source: Bureau of Labor Statistics, Local Area Unemployment Statistics

Average Wages

Occupation	$/Hr.	Occupation	$/Hr.
Accountants and Auditors	40.50	Maids and Housekeeping Cleaners	12.20
Automotive Mechanics	23.80	Maintenance and Repair Workers	21.90
Bookkeepers	20.60	Marketing Managers	66.60
Carpenters	26.70	Nuclear Medicine Technologists	42.80
Cashiers	10.50	Nurses, Licensed Practical	25.10
Clerks, General Office	16.80	Nurses, Registered	37.20
Clerks, Receptionists/Information	14.70	Nursing Assistants	13.30
Clerks, Shipping/Receiving	18.00	Packers and Packagers, Hand	12.30
Computer Programmers	39.70	Physical Therapists	46.80
Computer Systems Analysts	46.00	Postal Service Mail Carriers	24.00
Computer User Support Specialists	24.10	Real Estate Brokers	28.20
Cooks, Restaurant	14.90	Retail Salespersons	14.10
Dentists	75.90	Sales Reps., Exc. Tech./Scientific	37.90
Electrical Engineers	60.30	Sales Reps., Tech./Scientific	50.40
Electricians	34.90	Secretaries, Exc. Legal/Med./Exec.	19.30
Financial Managers	80.50	Security Guards	15.00
First-Line Supervisors/Managers, Sales	24.40	Surgeons	n/a
Food Preparation Workers	11.40	Teacher Assistants*	12.50
General and Operations Managers	73.00	Teachers, Elementary School*	32.40
Hairdressers/Cosmetologists	15.60	Teachers, Secondary School*	35.50
Internists, General	94.80	Telemarketers	13.30
Janitors and Cleaners	14.40	Truck Drivers, Heavy/Tractor-Trailer	22.40
Landscaping/Groundskeeping Workers	13.50	Truck Drivers, Light/Delivery Svcs.	16.60
Lawyers	58.00	Waiters and Waitresses	12.00

Note: Wage data covers the Camden, NJ Metropolitan Division—see Appendix B for areas included; (*) Hourly wages for elementary/secondary school teachers and teacher assistants were calculated by the editors from annual wage data based on a 40 hour work week; n/a not available.
Source: Bureau of Labor Statistics, Metro Area Occupational Employment & Wage Estimates, May 2017

Employment by Occupation

Occupation Classification	City (%)	MSA[1] (%)	U.S. (%)
Management, Business, Science, and Arts	50.8	42.4	37.0
Natural Resources, Construction, and Maintenance	4.9	6.9	8.9
Production, Transportation, and Material Moving	7.0	9.6	12.2
Sales and Office	25.2	24.0	23.8
Service	12.1	17.2	18.1

Note: Figures cover employed civilians 16 years of age and older; (1) Figures cover the Philadelphia-Camden-Wilmington, PA-NJ-DE-MD Metropolitan Statistical Area—see Appendix B for areas included
Source: U.S. Census Bureau, 2012-2016 American Community Survey 5-Year Estimates

Employment by Industry

Sector	MD[1] Number of Employees	MD[1] Percent of Total	U.S. Percent of Total
Construction, Mining, and Logging	22,000	4.0	5.2
Education and Health Services	99,900	18.0	15.9
Financial Activities	29,300	5.3	5.7
Government	81,300	14.7	15.3
Information	6,600	1.2	1.9
Leisure and Hospitality	48,900	8.8	10.7
Manufacturing	39,000	7.0	8.5
Other Services	18,900	3.4	3.9
Professional and Business Services	81,200	14.7	14.0
Retail Trade	70,200	12.7	11.0
Transportation, Warehousing, and Utilities	26,500	4.8	4.1
Wholesale Trade	29,700	5.4	4.0

Note: Figures are non-farm employment as of December 2017. Figures are not seasonally adjusted and include workers 16 years of age and older; (1) Figures cover the Camden, NJ Metropolitan Division—see Appendix B for areas included
Source: Bureau of Labor Statistics, Current Employment Statistics, Employment, Hours, and Earnings

Occupations with Greatest Projected Employment Growth: 2016 – 2018

Occupation[1]	2016 Employment	2018 Projected Employment	Numeric Employment Change	Percent Employment Change
Laborers and Freight, Stock, and Material Movers, Hand	97,040	101,030	3,990	4.1
Registered Nurses	84,890	87,480	2,590	3.1
Home Health Aides	36,970	39,030	2,060	5.6
Combined Food Preparation and Serving Workers, Including Fast Food	55,230	57,260	2,030	3.7
Software Developers, Applications	42,830	44,770	1,940	4.5
Heavy and Tractor-Trailer Truck Drivers	45,100	46,980	1,880	4.2
Construction Laborers	32,430	34,110	1,680	5.2
Carpenters	25,870	27,440	1,570	6.1
Waiters and Waitresses	63,080	64,600	1,520	2.4
Receptionists and Information Clerks	52,840	54,340	1,500	2.8

Note: Projections cover New Jersey; (1) Sorted by numeric employment change
Source: www.projectionscentral.com, State Occupational Projections, 2016–2018 Short-Term Projections

Fastest Growing Occupations: 2016 – 2018

Occupation[1]	2016 Employment	2018 Projected Employment	Numeric Employment Change	Percent Employment Change
Brickmasons and Blockmasons	1,920	2,080	160	8.3
Helpers—Electricians	1,620	1,740	120	8.0
Cement Masons and Concrete Finishers	2,440	2,610	170	7.2
Roofers	2,450	2,620	170	7.2
Helpers—Pipelayers, Plumbers, Pipefitters, and Steamfitters	1,100	1,180	80	7.2
Helpers—Carpenters	1,070	1,150	80	7.1
Electricians	15,320	16,370	1,050	6.8
Operations Research Analysts	1,470	1,560	90	6.3
Carpenters	25,870	27,440	1,570	6.1
Drywall and Ceiling Tile Installers	1,510	1,600	90	6.0

Note: Projections cover New Jersey; (1) Sorted by percent employment change and excludes occupations with numeric employment change less than 50
Source: www.projectionscentral.com, State Occupational Projections, 2016–2018 Short-Term Projections

TAXES

State Corporate Income Tax Rates

State	Tax Rate (%)	Income Brackets ($)	Num. of Brackets	Financial Institution Tax Rate (%)[a]	Federal Income Tax Ded.
New Jersey	9.0 (q)	Flat rate	1	9.0 (q)	No

Note: Tax rates as of January 1, 2018; (a) Rates listed are the corporate income tax rate applied to financial institutions or excise taxes based on income. Some states have other taxes based upon the value of deposits or shares; (q) In New Jersey small businesses with annual entire net income under $100,000 pay a tax rate of 7.5%; businesses with income under $50,000 pay 6.5%. The minimum Corporation Business Tax is based on New Jersey gross receipts. It ranges from $500 for a corporation with gross receipts less than $100,000, to $2,000 for a corporation with gross receipts of $1 million or more.
Source: Federation of Tax Administrators, Range of State Corporate Income Tax Rates, January 1, 2018

State Individual Income Tax Rates

State	Tax Rate (%)	Income Brackets ($)	Num. of Brackets	Personal Exempt. ($)[1] Single	Personal Exempt. ($)[1] Dependents	Fed. Inc. Tax Ded.
New Jersey	1.4 - 8.97	20,000 - 500,000 (q)	6	1,000	1,500	No

Note: Tax rates as of January 1, 2018; Local- and county-level taxes are not included; n/a not applicable; (1) Married joint filers generally receive double the single exemption; (q) The New Jersey rates reported are for single individuals. For married couples filing jointly, the tax rates also range from 1.4% to 8.97%, with 7 brackets and the same high and low income ranges.
Source: Federation of Tax Administrators, State Individual Income Tax Rates, January 1, 2018

Various State Sales and Excise Tax Rates

State	State Sales Tax (%)	Gasoline[1] (¢/gal.)	Cigarette[2] ($/pack)	Spirits[3] ($/gal.)	Wine[4] ($/gal.)	Beer[5] ($/gal.)	Recreational Marijuana (%)
New Jersey	6.625 (e)	37.1	2.70	5.50	0.88	0.12	Not legal

Note: All tax rates as of January 1, 2018; (1) The American Petroleum Institute has developed a methodology for determining the average tax rate on a gallon of fuel. Rates may include any of the following: excise taxes, environmental fees, storage tank fees, other fees or taxes, general sales tax, and local taxes. In states where gasoline is subject to the general sales tax, or where the fuel tax is based on the average sale price, the average rate determined by API is sensitive to changes in the price of gasoline. States that fully or partially apply general sales taxes to gasoline: CA, CO, GA, IL, IN, MI, NY; (2) The federal excise tax of $1.0066 per pack and local taxes are not included; (3) Rates are those applicable to off-premise sales of 40% alcohol by volume (a.b.v.) distilled spirits in 750ml containers. Local excise taxes are excluded; (4) Rates are those applicable to off-premise sales of 11% a.b.v. non-carbonated wine in 750ml containers; (5) Rates are those applicable to off-premise sales of 4.7% a.b.v. beer in 12 ounce containers; (e) Salem County is not subject to the statewide sales tax rate and collects a local rate of 3.3125%. New Jersey's average local score is represented as a negative.
Source: Tax Foundation, 2018 Facts & Figures: How Does Your State Compare?

State Business Tax Climate Index Rankings

State	Overall Rank	Corporate Tax Rank	Individual Income Tax Rank	Sales Tax Rank	Unemployment Insurance Tax Rank	Property Tax Rank
New Jersey	50	42	48	46	36	50

Note: The index is a measure of how each state's tax laws affect economic performance. The lower the rank, the more favorable a state's tax system is for business. States without a given tax are given a ranking of 1. The scores/rankings for the District of Columbia do not affect other states. The 2018 index represents the tax climate as of July 1, 2017.
Source: Tax Foundation, State Business Tax Climate Index 2018

TRANSPORTATION

Means of Transportation to Work

Area	Car/Truck/Van		Public Transportation			Bicycle	Walked	Other Means	Worked at Home
	Drove Alone	Car-pooled	Bus	Subway	Railroad				
City	84.8	5.8	0.6	1.2	1.1	0.1	0.6	0.7	5.1
MSA[1]	73.1	7.7	5.4	1.7	2.3	0.6	3.7	1.0	4.3
U.S.	76.4	9.3	2.6	1.9	0.6	0.6	2.8	1.3	4.6

Note: Figures are percentages and cover workers 16 years of age and older; (1) Figures cover the Philadelphia-Camden-Wilmington, PA-NJ-DE-MD Metropolitan Statistical Area—see Appendix B for areas included
Source: U.S. Census Bureau, 2012-2016 American Community Survey 5-Year Estimates

Travel Time to Work

Area	Less Than 10 Minutes	10 to 19 Minutes	20 to 29 Minutes	30 to 44 Minutes	45 to 59 Minutes	60 to 89 Minutes	90 Minutes or More
City	9.2	28.5	21.7	18.8	9.9	8.0	3.9
MSA[1]	9.8	24.7	20.5	23.5	10.7	7.9	3.0
U.S.	12.9	29.2	20.9	20.4	8.0	6.0	2.7

Note: Note: Figures are percentages and include workers 16 years old and over; (1) Figures cover the Philadelphia-Camden-Wilmington, PA-NJ-DE-MD Metropolitan Statistical Area—see Appendix B for areas included
Source: U.S. Census Bureau, 2012-2016 American Community Survey 5-Year Estimates

Freeway Travel Time Index

Area	1985	1990	1995	2000	2005	2010	2014
Urban Area Rank[1,2]	20	21	26	26	24	22	25
Urban Area Index[1]	1.12	1.15	1.18	1.21	1.25	1.24	1.24
Average Index[3]	1.09	1.11	1.14	1.17	1.20	1.19	1.20

Note: Freeway Travel Time Index—the ratio of travel time in the peak period to the travel time at free-flow conditions. For example, a value of 1.30 indicates a 20-minute free-flow trip takes 26 minutes in the peak (20 minutes x 1.30 = 26 minutes); (1) Covers the Philadelphia PA-NJ-DE-MD urban area; (2) Rank is based on 101 urban areas (#1 = highest travel time index); (3) Average of 101 urban areas
Source: Texas Transportation Institute, 2015 Urban Mobility Scorecard, August 2015

Freeway Commuter Stress Index

Area	1985	1990	1995	2000	2005	2010	2014
Urban Area Rank[1,2]	31	28	33	34	30	31	31
Urban Area Index[1]	1.15	1.19	1.22	1.25	1.29	1.28	1.28
Average Index[3]	1.13	1.16	1.19	1.22	1.25	1.24	1.25

Note: The Freeway Commuter Stress Index is the same as the Freeway Travel Time Index (see table above) except that it includes only the travel in the peak directions during the peak periods; the TTI includes travel in all directions during the peak period. Thus, the CSI is more indicative of the work trip experienced by each commuter on a daily basis; (1) Covers the Philadelphia PA-NJ-DE-MD urban area; (2) Rank is based on 101 urban areas (#1 = highest travel time index); (3) Average of 101 urban areas
Source: Texas Transportation Institute, 2015 Urban Mobility Scorecard, August 2015

Living Environment

COST OF LIVING

Cost of Living Index

Composite Index	Groceries	Housing	Utilities	Trans- portation	Health Care	Misc. Goods/ Services
117.0	116.2	129.5	124.5	114.9	105.7	107.2

Note: The Cost of Living Index measures regional differences in the cost of consumer goods and services, excluding taxes and non-consumer expenditures, for professional and managerial households in the top income quintile. It is based on more than 50,000 prices covering almost 60 different items for which prices are collected three times a year by chambers of commerce, economic development organizations or university applied economic centers in each participating urban area. The numbers shown should be read as a percentage above or below the national average of 100. For example, a value of 115.4 in the groceries column indicates that grocery prices are 15.4% higher than the national average. Small differences in the index numbers should not be interpreted as significant; Figures cover the Philadelphia PA urban area.
Source: The Council for Community and Economic Research, ACCRA Cost of Living Index, 2017

Grocery Prices

Area[1]	T-Bone Steak ($/pound)	Frying Chicken ($/pound)	Whole Milk ($/half gal.)	Eggs ($/dozen)	Orange Juice ($/64 oz.)	Coffee ($/11.5 oz.)
City[2]	11.82	1.46	2.11	1.74	3.92	4.10
Avg.	11.29	1.40	2.02	1.47	3.55	4.37
Min.	7.71	0.93	1.04	0.70	2.86	3.24
Max.	15.83	2.39	4.03	3.92	6.29	8.16

*Note: (1) Values for the local area are compared with the average, minimum and maximum values for all 294 areas in the Cost of Living Index; (2) Figures cover the Philadelphia PA urban area; **T-Bone Steak** (price per pound); **Frying Chicken** (price per pound, whole fryer); **Whole Milk** (half gallon carton); **Eggs** (price per dozen, Grade A, large); **Orange Juice** (64 oz. Tropicana or Florida Natural); **Coffee** (11.5 oz. can, vacuum-packed, Maxwell House, Hills Bros, or Folgers).*
Source: The Council for Community and Economic Research, ACCRA Cost of Living Index, 2017

Housing and Utility Costs

Area[1]	New Home Price ($)	Apartment Rent ($/month)	All Electric ($/month)	Part Electric ($/month)	Other Energy ($/month)	Telephone ($/month)
City[2]	424,983	1,411	-	107.26	69.96	42.00
Avg.	335,956	1,047	175.01	97.34	67.93	28.71
Min.	187,788	491	109.48	49.33	35.44	12.39
Max.	1,739,087	4,559	432.62	227.09	353.33	44.61

*Note: (1) Values for the local area are compared with the average, minimum and maximum values for all 294 areas in the Cost of Living Index; (2) Figures cover the Philadelphia PA urban area; **New Home Price** (2,400 sf living area, 8,000 sf lot, in urban area with full utilities); **Apartment Rent** (950 sf 2 bedroom/1.5 or 2 bath, unfurnished, excluding all utilities except water); **All Electric** (average monthly cost for an all-electric home); **Part Electric** (average monthly cost for a part-electric home); **Other Energy** (average monthly cost for natural gas, fuel oil, coal, wood, and any other forms of energy except electricity); **Telephone** (price includes basic monthly rate for a private residential line plus additional local usage charges incurred by a family of four).*
Source: The Council for Community and Economic Research, ACCRA Cost of Living Index, 2017

Health Care, Transportation, and Other Costs

Area[1]	Doctor ($/visit)	Dentist ($/visit)	Optometrist ($/visit)	Gasoline ($/gallon)	Beauty Salon ($/visit)	Men's Shirt ($)
City[2]	130.24	96.14	100.71	2.48	56.27	31.77
Avg.	108.00	92.54	101.93	2.25	37.58	30.92
Min.	30.39	60.00	49.75	1.82	16.11	11.20
Max.	193.50	161.94	229.28	3.16	77.35	59.13

*Note: (1) Values for the local area are compared with the average, minimum and maximum values for all 294 areas in the Cost of Living Index; (2) Figures cover the Philadelphia PA urban area; **Doctor** (general practitioners routine exam of an established patient); **Dentist** (adult teeth cleaning and periodic oral examination); **Optometrist** (full vision eye exam for established adult patient); **Gasoline** (one gallon regular unleaded, national brand, including all taxes, cash price at self-service pump if available); **Beauty Salon** (woman's shampoo, trim, and blow-dry); **Men's Shirt** (cotton/polyester dress shirt, pinpoint weave, long sleeves).*
Source: The Council for Community and Economic Research, ACCRA Cost of Living Index, 2017

HOUSING

House Price Index (HPI)

Area	National Ranking[2]	Quarterly Change (%)	One-Year Change (%)	Five-Year Change (%)
MD[1]	231	0.47	2.08	9.04
U.S.[3]	–	1.61	6.68	34.71

Note: The HPI is a weighted repeat sales index. It measures average price changes in repeat sales or refinancings on the same properties. This information is obtained by reviewing repeat mortgage transactions on single-family properties whose mortgages have been purchased or securitized by Fannie Mae or Freddie Mac in January 1975; (1) Figures cover the Camden, NJ Metropolitan Division—see Appendix B for areas included; (2) Rankings are based on annual percentage change for all metro areas containing at least 15,000 transactions over the last 10 years and ranges from 1 to 253; (3) figures based on a weighted average of Census Division estimates using a seasonally adjusted, purchase-only index; all figures are for the period ending December 31, 2017
Source: Federal Housing Finance Agency, House Price Index, February 28, 2018

Median Single-Family Home Prices

Area	2015	2016	2017p	Percent Change 2016 to 2017
MSA[1]	223.7	225.4	230.0	2.0
U.S. Average	223.9	235.5	248.8	5.6

Note: Figures are median sales prices of existing single-family homes in thousands of dollars; (p) preliminary; (1) Figures cover the Philadelphia-Camden-Wilmington, PA-NJ-DE-MD Metropolitan Statistical Area—see Appendix B for areas included
Source: National Association of Realtors, Median Sales Price of Existing Single-Family Homes for Metropolitan Areas, 4th Quarter 2017

Qualifying Income Based on Median Sales Price of Existing Single-Family Homes

Area	With 5% Down ($)	With 10% Down ($)	With 20% Down ($)
MSA[1]	50,381	47,729	42,426
U.S. Average	55,585	52,659	46,808

Note: Figures are preliminary; Qualifying income is based on a mortgage rate of 4.17%. Monthly principal and interest payment is limited to 25% of income; (1) Figures cover the Philadelphia-Camden-Wilmington, PA-NJ-DE-MD Metropolitan Statistical Area—see Appendix B for areas included
Source: National Association of Realtors, Qualifying Income Based on Median Sales Price of Existing Single-Family Homes for Metropolitan Areas, 4th Quarter 2017

Median Apartment Condo-Coop Home Prices

Area	2015	2016	2017p	Percent Change 2016 to 2017
MSA[1]	176.5	182.7	185.1	1.3
U.S. Average	210.7	220.7	234.3	6.2

Note: Figures are median sales prices of existing apartment condo-coop homes in thousands of dollars; (p) preliminary; (1) Figures cover the Philadelphia-Camden-Wilmington, PA-NJ-DE-MD Metropolitan Statistical Area—see Appendix B for areas included
Source: National Association of Realtors, Median Sales Price of Existing Apartment Condo-Coop Homes for Metropolitan Areas, 4th Quarter 2017

Home Value Distribution

Area	Under $50,000	$50,000 -$99,999	$100,000 -$149,999	$150,000 -$199,999	$200,000 -$299,999	$300,000 -$499,999	$500,000 -$999,999	$1,000,000 or more
City	1.8	0.5	5.0	11.9	40.3	35.9	4.5	0.1
MSA[1]	4.7	7.9	10.8	15.6	27.1	23.9	8.5	1.4
U.S.	8.8	14.8	15.3	14.9	18.4	16.4	9.0	2.5

Note: Figures are percentages and cover owner-occupied housing units; (1) Figures cover the Philadelphia-Camden-Wilmington, PA-NJ-DE-MD Metropolitan Statistical Area—see Appendix B for areas included
Source: U.S. Census Bureau, 2012-2016 American Community Survey 5-Year Estimates

Homeownership Rate

Area	2009 (%)	2010 (%)	2011 (%)	2012 (%)	2013 (%)	2014 (%)	2015 (%)	2016 (%)	2017 (%)
MSA[1]	69.7	70.7	69.7	69.5	69.1	67.0	67.0	64.7	65.6
U.S.	67.4	66.9	66.1	65.4	65.1	64.5	63.7	63.4	63.9

Note: (1) Figures cover the Philadelphia-Camden-Wilmington, PA-NJ-DE-MD Metropolitan Statistical Area—see Appendix B for areas included
Source: U.S. Census Bureau, Housing Vacancies and Homeownership Annual Statistics: 2009-2017

Year Housing Structure Built

Area	2010 or Later	2000 -2009	1990 -1999	1980 -1989	1970 -1979	1960 -1969	1950 -1959	1940 -1949	Before 1940	Median Year
City	1.3	11.2	20.0	30.9	18.8	11.1	5.1	0.6	1.1	1984
MSA[1]	1.4	8.3	9.4	10.2	12.3	12.1	15.9	8.5	21.8	1963
U.S.	2.3	14.7	14.0	13.7	15.6	10.9	10.6	5.2	13.0	1977

Note: Figures are percentages except for Median Year; Note: (1) Figures cover the Philadelphia-Camden-Wilmington, PA-NJ-DE-MD Metropolitan Statistical Area—see Appendix B for areas included
Source: U.S. Census Bureau, 2012-2016 American Community Survey 5-Year Estimates

Gross Monthly Rent

Area	Under $500	$500 -$999	$1,000 -$1,499	$1,500 -$1,999	$2,000 -$2,499	$2,500 -$2,999	$3,000 and up	Median ($)
City	4.1	12.0	43.1	23.8	15.0	1.4	0.6	1,355
MSA[1]	9.0	37.4	35.4	11.9	3.9	1.3	1.1	1,040
U.S.	11.3	43.3	27.7	10.7	4.0	1.6	1.5	949

Note: Figures are percentages except for Median; Gross rent is the contract rent plus the estimated average monthly cost of utilities (electricity, gas, and water and sewer) and fuels (oil, coal, kerosene, wood, etc.) if these are paid by the renter (or paid for the renter by someone else); (1) Figures cover the Philadelphia-Camden-Wilmington, PA-NJ-DE-MD Metropolitan Statistical Area—see Appendix B for areas included
Source: U.S. Census Bureau, 2012-2016 American Community Survey 5-Year Estimates

HEALTH

Health Risk Factors

Category	MD[1] (%)	U.S. (%)
Adults aged 18–64 who have any kind of health care coverage	91.0	87.7
Adults who reported being in good or excellent health	82.5	83.6
Adults who are current smokers	16.0	17.1
Adults who currently use E-cigarettes	5.3	4.7
Adults who currently use chewing tobacco, snuff, or snus	2.5	4.0
Adults who are heavy drinkers[2]	4.3	6.5
Adults who are binge drinkers[3]	16.6	16.9
Adults who are overweight (BMI 25.0 - 29.9)	39.5	35.3
Adults who are obese (BMI 30.0 - 99.8)	30.7	29.9
Adults who participated in any physical activities in the past month	71.6	76.9
Adults who always or nearly always wears a seat belt	96.2	94.3

Note: (1) Figures cover the Camden, NJ Metropolitan Division—see Appendix B for areas included; (2) Heavy drinkers are classified as adult men having more than 14 drinks per week and adult women having more than 7 drinks per week; (3) Binge drinkers are classified as males having five or more drinks on one occasion or females having four or more drinks on one occasion
Source: Centers for Disease Control and Prevention, Behaviorial Risk Factor Surveillance System, SMART: Selected Metropolitan Area Risk Trends, 2016

Health Screening Rates

Category	MD[1] (%)	U.S. (%)
Adults 50-75 who have had a blood stool test within the past year	4.8	8.0
Adults 50-75 who have had a colonoscopy in the past 10 years	70.6	63.5
Adults aged 65+ who have had flu shot within the past year	65.7	58.6
Adults aged 65+ who have ever had a pneumonia vaccination	76.5	73.4
Adults who have ever been tested for HIV	45.3	35.6
Women aged 21-65 who have had a pap test in the past three years	82.2	79.8
Men aged 40+ who have had a PSA test within the past two years	55.7	39.5
Women aged 40+ who have had a mammogram within the past two years	75.7	72.5

Note: n/a not available; (1) Figures cover the Camden, NJ Metropolitan Division—see Appendix B for areas included; Source: Centers for Disease Control and Prevention, Behaviorial Risk Factor Surveillance System, SMART: Selected Metropolitan Area Risk Trends, 2016

Chronic Health Conditions

Category	MD[1] (%)	U.S. (%)
Adults who have ever been told they had a heart attack	6.3	4.4
Adults who have ever been told they have angina or coronary heart disease	6.6	4.1
Adults who have ever been told they had a stroke	3.8	3.1
Adults who have been told they currently have asthma	9.0	9.3
Adults who have ever been told they have arthritis	28.0	25.8
Adults who have ever been told they have diabetes[2]	10.2	10.5
Adults who have ever been told they had skin cancer	7.4	5.9
Adults who have ever been told they had any other types of cancer	6.9	6.7
Adults who have ever been told they have COPD	5.6	6.3
Adults who have ever been told they have kidney disease	2.9	2.8
Adults who have ever been told they have a form of depression	14.0	17.4

Note: (1) Figures cover the Camden, NJ Metropolitan Division—see Appendix B for areas included; (2) Figures do not include pregnancy-related, borderline, or pre-diabetes
Source: Centers for Disease Control and Prevention, Behaviorial Risk Factor Surveillance System, SMART: Selected Metropolitan Area Risk Trends, 2016

Mortality Rates for the Top 10 Causes of Death in the U.S.

ICD-10[a] Sub-Chapter	ICD-10[a] Code	Age-Adjusted Mortality Rate[1] per 100,000 population	
		County[2]	U.S.
Malignant neoplasms	C00-C97	166.2	158.5
Ischaemic heart diseases	I20-I25	88.2	96.8
Other forms of heart disease	I30-I51	68.5	52.4
Chronic lower respiratory diseases	J40-J47	31.0	40.9
Cerebrovascular diseases	I60-I69	34.6	37.2
Organic, including symptomatic, mental disorders	F01-F09	32.1	33.3
Other degenerative diseases of the nervous system	G30-G31	26.1	32.1
Other external causes of accidental injury	W00-X59	31.3	31.2
Diabetes mellitus	E10-E14	18.7	21.1
Hypertensive diseases	I10-I15	11.5	20.8

Note: (a) ICD-10 = International Classification of Diseases 10th Revision; (1) Mortality rates are a three year average covering 2014-2016; (2) Figures cover Burlington County.
Source: Centers for Disease Control and Prevention, National Center for Health Statistics. Underlying Cause of Death 1999-2016 on CDC WONDER Online Database, released December 2017

Mortality Rates for Selected Causes of Death

ICD-10[a] Sub-Chapter	ICD-10[a] Code	Age-Adjusted Mortality Rate[1] per 100,000 population	
		County[2]	U.S.
Assault	X85-Y09	3.5	5.6
Diseases of the liver	K70-K76	11.4	14.0
Human immunodeficiency virus (HIV) disease	B20-B24	Unreliable	1.9
Influenza and pneumonia	J09-J18	11.0	14.6
Intentional self-harm	X60-X84	10.5	13.2
Malnutrition	E40-E46	Unreliable	1.3
Obesity and other hyperalimentation	E65-E68	1.6	2.1
Renal failure	N17-N19	17.6	13.0
Transport accidents	V01-V99	9.1	12.0
Viral hepatitis	B15-B19	Unreliable	1.9

Note: (a) ICD-10 = International Classification of Diseases 10th Revision; (1) Mortality rates are a three year average covering 2014-2016; (2) Figures cover Burlington County; Data are Suppressed when the data meet the criteria for confidentiality constraints; Mortality rates are flagged as Unreliable when the rate would be calculated with a numerator of 20 or less.
Source: Centers for Disease Control and Prevention, National Center for Health Statistics. Underlying Cause of Death 1999-2016 on CDC WONDER Online Database, released December 2017

Health Insurance Coverage

Area	With Health Insurance	With Private Health Insurance	With Public Health Insurance	Without Health Insurance	Population Under Age 18 Without Health Insurance
City	96.2	86.9	23.4	3.8	2.8
MSA[1]	92.0	72.6	31.5	8.0	3.5
U.S.	88.3	66.7	33.0	11.7	5.9

Note: Figures are percentages that cover the civilian noninstitutionalized population; (1) Figures cover the Philadelphia-Camden-Wilmington, PA-NJ-DE-MD Metropolitan Statistical Area—see Appendix B for areas included
Source: U.S. Census Bureau, 2012-2016 American Community Survey 5-Year Estimates

Number of Medical Professionals

Area	MDs[3]	DOs[3,4]	Dentists	Podiatrists	Chiropractors	Optometrists
County[1] (number)	1,153	330	316	36	111	72
County[1] (rate[2])	256.9	73.5	70.5	8.0	24.8	16.1
U.S. (rate[2])	276.5	22.3	67.3	6.0	26.7	15.9

Note: Data as of 2016 unless noted; (1) Data covers Burlington County; (2) Rate per 100,000 population; (3) Data as of 2015 and includes all active, non-federal physicians; (4) Doctor of Osteopathic Medicine
Source: U.S. Department of Health and Human Services, Health Resources and Services Administration, Bureau of Health Professions, Area Resource File (ARF) 2016-2017

EDUCATION

Public School District Statistics

District Name	Schls	Pupils	Pupil/ Teacher Ratio	Minority Pupils[1] (%)	Free Lunch Eligible[2] (%)	IEP[3] (%)
Evesham Township School District	9	4,523	12.5	20.4	9.0	21.6
Lenape Regional High School District	4	6,887	11.8	18.5	8.3	16.1

Note: Table includes school districts with 100 or more students; (1) Percentage of students that are not non-Hispanic white; (2) Percentage of students that are eligible for the free lunch program; (3) Percentage of students that have an Individualized Education Program.
Source: U.S. Department of Education, National Center for Education Statistics, Common Core of Data, Local Education Agency (School District) Universe Survey: School Year 2015-2016; U.S. Department of Education, National Center for Education Statistics, Common Core of Data, Public Elementary/Secondary School Universe Survey: School Year 2015-2016

Highest Level of Education

Area	Less than H.S.	H.S. Diploma	Some College, No Deg.	Associate Degree	Bachelor's Degree	Master's Degree	Prof. School Degree	Doctorate Degree
City	4.4	22.7	18.9	8.1	30.6	11.1	2.8	1.4
MSA[1]	10.3	30.0	17.3	6.9	21.3	9.9	2.5	1.8
U.S.	13.0	27.5	21.0	8.2	18.8	8.2	2.0	1.3

Note: Figures cover persons age 25 and over; (1) Figures cover the Philadelphia-Camden-Wilmington, PA-NJ-DE-MD Metropolitan Statistical Area—see Appendix B for areas included
Source: U.S. Census Bureau, 2012-2016 American Community Survey 5-Year Estimates

Educational Attainment by Race

Area	High School Graduate or Higher (%)					Bachelor's Degree or Higher (%)				
	Total	White	Black	Asian	Hisp.[2]	Total	White	Black	Asian	Hisp.[2]
City	95.6	96.0	93.8	95.2	86.9	45.9	46.0	31.7	64.4	33.5
MSA[1]	89.7	92.3	85.7	83.4	68.1	35.5	39.5	19.2	55.0	16.3
U.S.	87.0	88.9	84.3	86.3	65.7	30.3	31.6	20.0	52.1	14.7

Note: Figures shown cover persons 25 years old and over; (1) Figures cover the Philadelphia-Camden-Wilmington, PA-NJ-DE-MD Metropolitan Statistical Area—see Appendix B for areas included; (2) People of Hispanic origin can be of any race
Source: U.S. Census Bureau, 2012-2016 American Community Survey 5-Year Estimates

School Enrollment by Grade and Control

Area	Preschool (%)		Kindergarten (%)		Grades 1 - 4 (%)		Grades 5 - 8 (%)		Grades 9 - 12 (%)	
	Public	Private	Public	Private	Public	Private	Public	Private	Public	Private
City	30.1	69.9	90.7	9.3	96.0	4.0	90.8	9.2	93.0	7.0
MSA[1]	43.6	56.4	81.7	18.3	85.0	15.0	83.6	16.4	83.6	16.4
U.S.	58.4	41.6	87.7	12.3	89.8	10.2	89.7	10.3	90.4	9.6

Note: Figures shown cover persons 3 years old and over; (1) Figures cover the Philadelphia-Camden-Wilmington, PA-NJ-DE-MD Metropolitan Statistical Area—see Appendix B for areas included
Source: U.S. Census Bureau, 2012-2016 American Community Survey 5-Year Estimates

Average Salaries of Public School Classroom Teachers

Area	2015		2016		Change from 2015 to 2016	
	Dollars	Rank[1]	Dollars	Rank[1]	Percent	Rank[2]
New Jersey	69,038	6	69,330	6	0.4	41
U.S. Average	57,611	–	58,353	–	1.3	–

Note: (1) Rank ranges from 1 to 51 where 1 indicates highest salary; (2) Rank ranges from 1 to 51 where 1 indicates highest percent change.
Source: National Education Association, Rankings & Estimates: Rankings of the States 2016 and Estimates of School Statistics 2017

Higher Education

Four-Year Colleges			Two-Year Colleges			Medical Schools[1]	Law Schools[2]	Voc/ Tech[3]
Public	Private Non-profit	Private For-profit	Public	Private Non-profit	Private For-profit			
0	0	0	0	0	0	0	0	0

Note: Figures cover institutions located within the city limits and include main campuses only; (1) includes schools accredited by the Liaison Committee on Medical Education and the American Osteopathic Association's Commission on Osteopathic College Accreditation; (2) includes ABA-accredited schools, schools with provisional ABA accreditation, and state accredited schools; (3) includes all schools with programs that are less than 2 years.
Source: National Center for Education Statistics, Integrated Postsecondary Education System (IPEDS), 2016-17; Wikipedia, List of Medical Schools in the United States, accessed April 2, 2018; Wikipedia, List of Law Schools in the United States, accessed April 2, 2018

According to *U.S. News & World Report,* the Camden, NJ metro division is home to one of the best national universities in the U.S.: **Rowan University** (#171 tie). The indicators used to capture academic quality fall into a number of categories: assessment by administrators at peer institutions; retention of students; faculty resources; student selectivity; financial resources; alumni giving; high school counselor ratings of colleges; and graduation rate. *U.S. News & World Report, "America's Best Colleges 2018"*

PRESIDENTIAL ELECTION

2016 Presidential Election Results

Area	Clinton	Trump	Johnson	Stein	Other
Burlington County	55.0	40.3	2.2	1.1	1.4
U.S.	48.0	45.9	3.3	1.1	1.7

Note: Results are percentages and may not add to 100% due to rounding
Source: Dave Leip's Atlas of U.S. Presidential Elections

EMPLOYERS

Major Employers

Company Name	Industry
Abington Memorial Hospital	General medical & surgical hospitals
AstraZeneca Pharmaceuticals	Pharmaceutical preparations
City of Philadelphia	Police protection
Comcast Holdings Corporation	Cable & other pay television services
Cooper Health Care	Hospital management
E.I. du Pont de Nemours and Company	Agricultural chemicals
Einstein Community Health Associates	Offices & clinics of medical doctors
Glaxosmithkline	Commerical physical research
Lockheed Martin Corporation	Defense systems & equipment
Mercy Health System of SE Pennsylvania	General medical & surgical hospitals
On Time Staffing	Employment agencies
Richlieu Associates	Apartment building operators
Temple University	General medical & surgical hospitals
The University of Pennsylvania	Colleges & universities
The US Navy	Navy
The Vanguard Group	Management, investment, open-end
Thomas Jefferson University Hospital	General medical & surgical hospitals
Trustees of the University of Penn	General medical & surgical hospitals
Unisys Corporation	Computer integrated systems design
University of Delaware	Colleges & universities

Note: Companies shown are located within the Philadelphia-Camden-Wilmington, PA-NJ-DE-MD Metropolitan Statistical Area.
Source: Hoovers.com; Wikipedia

PUBLIC SAFETY

Crime Rate

Area	All Crimes	Violent Crimes				Property Crimes		
		Murder	Rape[3]	Robbery	Aggrav. Assault	Burglary	Larceny -Theft	Motor Vehicle Theft
City	1,520.4	0.0	6.6	28.5	35.1	173.3	1,226.4	50.5
Metro[1]	2,221.1	6.7	22.6	89.2	153.9	411.9	1,422.1	114.6
U.S.	2,847.8	5.3	40.4	102.8	248.5	468.9	1,745.0	236.9

Note: Figures are crimes per 100,000 population; (1) Figures cover the Camden, NJ Metropolitan Division—see Appendix B for areas included; (3) The city and U.S. figures shown were reported using the revised Uniform Crime Reporting (UCR) definition of rape. The metro area figures shown are an aggregate total of the data submitted using both the revised and legacy UCR definitions.
Source: FBI Uniform Crime Reports, 2016

Hate Crimes

Area	Number of Quarters Reported	Number of Incidents per Bias Motivation					
		Race/Ethnicity/ Ancestry	Religion	Sexual Orientation	Disability	Gender	Gender Identity
Area[1]	4	4	1	1	0	0	0
U.S.	4	3,489	1,273	1,076	70	31	124

Note: (1) Figures cover the Evesham Township.
Source: Federal Bureau of Investigation, Hate Crime Statistics 2016

Identity Theft Consumer Reports

Area	Reports	Reports per 100,000 Population	Rank[2]
MSA[1]	8,444	139	23
U.S.	371,061	114	-

Note: (1) Figures cover the Philadelphia-Camden-Wilmington, PA-NJ-DE-MD Metropolitan Statistical Area—see Appendix B for areas included; (2) Rank ranges from 1 to 389 where 1 indicates greatest number of identity theft reports per 100,000 population
Source: Federal Trade Commission, Consumer Sentinel Network Data Book for January–December 2017

Fraud and Other Consumer Reports

Area	Reports	Reports per 100,000 Population	Rank[2]
MSA[1]	34,068	561	60
U.S.	2,304,550	708	-

Note: (1) Figures cover the Philadelphia-Camden-Wilmington, PA-NJ-DE-MD Metropolitan Statistical Area—see Appendix B for areas included; (2) Rank ranges from 1 to 389 where 1 indicates greatest number of fraud and other consumer reports per 100,000 population
Source: Federal Trade Commission, Consumer Sentinel Network Data Book for January–December 2017

SPORTS

Professional Sports Teams

Team Name	League	Year Established
Philadelphia 76ers	National Basketball Association (NBA)	1963
Philadelphia Eagles	National Football League (NFL)	1933
Philadelphia Flyers	National Hockey League (NHL)	1967
Philadelphia Phillies	Major League Baseball (MLB)	1883
Philadelphia Union	Major League Soccer (MLS)	2010

Note: Includes teams located in the Philadelphia-Camden-Wilmington, PA-NJ-DE-MD Metropolitan Statistical Area.
Source: Wikipedia, Major Professional Sports Teams of the United States and Canada, April 5, 2018

CLIMATE

Average and Extreme Temperatures

Temperature	Jan	Feb	Mar	Apr	May	Jun	Jul	Aug	Sep	Oct	Nov	Dec	Yr.
Extreme High (°F)	74	74	85	94	96	100	104	101	100	89	84	72	104
Average High (°F)	39	42	51	63	73	82	86	85	78	67	55	43	64
Average Temp. (°F)	32	34	42	53	63	72	77	76	68	57	47	36	55
Average Low (°F)	24	26	33	43	53	62	67	66	59	47	38	28	45
Extreme Low (°F)	-7	-4	7	19	28	44	51	44	35	25	15	1	-7

Note: Figures cover the years 1948-1990
Source: National Climatic Data Center, International Station Meteorological Climate Summary, 9/96

Average Precipitation/Snowfall/Humidity

Precip./Humidity	Jan	Feb	Mar	Apr	May	Jun	Jul	Aug	Sep	Oct	Nov	Dec	Yr.
Avg. Precip. (in.)	3.2	2.8	3.7	3.5	3.7	3.6	4.1	4.0	3.3	2.7	3.4	3.3	41.4
Avg. Snowfall (in.)	7	7	4	Tr	Tr	0	0	0	0	Tr	1	4	22
Avg. Rel. Hum. 7am (%)	74	73	73	72	75	77	80	82	84	83	79	75	77
Avg. Rel. Hum. 4pm (%)	60	55	51	48	51	52	54	55	55	54	57	60	54

Note: Figures cover the years 1948-1990; Tr = Trace amounts (<0.05 in. of rain; <0.5 in. of snow)
Source: National Climatic Data Center, International Station Meteorological Climate Summary, 9/96

Weather Conditions

Temperature			Daytime Sky			Precipitation		
10°F & below	32°F & below	90°F & above	Clear	Partly cloudy	Cloudy	0.01 inch or more precip.	0.1 inch or more snow/ice	Thunder-storms
5	94	23	81	146	138	117	14	27

Note: Figures are average number of days per year and cover the years 1948-1990
Source: National Climatic Data Center, International Station Meteorological Climate Summary, 9/96

HAZARDOUS WASTE

Superfund Sites

The Camden, NJ metro division is home to 30 sites on the EPA's Superfund National Priorities List: **Bridgeport Rental & Oil Services** (final); **Chemical Leaman Tank Lines, Inc.** (final); **Cinnaminson Township (Block 702) Ground Water Contamination** (final); **Cosden Chemical Coatings Corp.** (final); **Ellis Property** (final); **Ewan Property** (final); **Franklin Burn** (final); **Gems Landfill** (final); **Helen Kramer Landfill** (final); **Hercules, Inc. (Gibbstown Plant)** (final); **Kauffman & Minteer, Inc.** (final); **King of Prussia** (final); **Landfill & Development Co.** (final); **Lang Property** (final); **Lightman Drum Company** (final); **Lipari Landfill** (final); **Martin Aaron, Inc.** (final); **Matlack, Inc.** (final); **Matteo & Sons Inc.** (final); **Mcguire Air Force Base #1** (final); **Puchack Well Field** (final); **Roebling Steel Co.** (final); **Route 561 Dump** (proposed);

Sherwin-Williams/Hilliards Creek (final); **Shieldalloy Corp.** (final); **Swope Oil & Chemical Co.** (final); **United States Avenue Burn** (final); **Welsbach & General Gas Mantle (Camden Radiation)** (final); **Woodland Route 532 Dump** (final); **Woodland Route 72 Dump** (final).
There are a total of 1,396 Superfund sites with a status of proposed or final on the list in the U.S.
U.S. Environmental Protection Agency, National Priorities List, April 4, 2018

AIR & WATER QUALITY

Air Quality Trends: Ozone

	1990	1995	2000	2005	2010	2012	2013	2014	2015	2016
MSA[1]	0.102	0.109	0.099	0.091	0.083	0.084	0.069	0.071	0.074	0.075
U.S.	0.087	0.089	0.081	0.079	0.073	0.075	0.069	0.067	0.068	0.069

Note: (1) Data covers the Philadelphia-Camden-Wilmington, PA-NJ-DE-MD Metropolitan Statistical Area—see Appendix B for areas included. The values shown are the composite ozone concentration averages among trend sites based on the highest fourth daily maximum 8-hour concentration in parts per million. These trends are based on sites having an adequate record of monitoring data during the trend period. Data from exceptional events are included.
Source: U.S. Environmental Protection Agency, Air Quality Monitoring Information, "Air Quality Trends by City, 1990-2016"

Air Quality Index

Area	Percent of Days when Air Quality was...[2]					AQI Statistics[2]	
	Good	Moderate	Unhealthy for Sensitive Groups	Unhealthy	Very Unhealthy	Maximum	Median
MSA[1]	34.5	59.5	5.5	0.5	0.0	166	55

Note: (1) Data covers the Philadelphia-Camden-Wilmington, PA-NJ-DE-MD Metropolitan Statistical Area—see Appendix B for areas included; (2) Based on 365 days with AQI data in 2017. Air Quality Index (AQI) is an index for reporting daily air quality. EPA calculates the AQI for five major air pollutants regulated by the Clean Air Act: ground-level ozone, particle pollution (aka particulate matter), carbon monoxide, sulfur dioxide, and nitrogen dioxide. The AQI runs from 0 to 500. The higher the AQI value, the greater the level of air pollution and the greater the health concern. There are six AQI categories: "Good" AQI is between 0 and 50. Air quality is considered satisfactory; "Moderate" AQI is between 51 and 100. Air quality is acceptable; "Unhealthy for Sensitive Groups" When AQI values are between 101 and 150, members of sensitive groups may experience health effects; "Unhealthy" When AQI values are between 151 and 200 everyone may begin to experience health effects; "Very Unhealthy" AQI values between 201 and 300 trigger a health alert; "Hazardous" AQI values over 300 trigger warnings of emergency conditions (not shown).
Source: U.S. Environmental Protection Agency, Air Quality Index Report, 2017

Air Quality Index Pollutants

Area	Percent of Days when AQI Pollutant was...[2]					
	Carbon Monoxide	Nitrogen Dioxide	Ozone	Sulfur Dioxide	Particulate Matter 2.5	Particulate Matter 10
MSA[1]	0.0	0.3	31.2	0.5	67.7	0.3

Note: (1) Data covers the Philadelphia-Camden-Wilmington, PA-NJ-DE-MD Metropolitan Statistical Area—see Appendix B for areas included; (2) Based on 365 days with AQI data in 2017. The Air Quality Index (AQI) is an index for reporting daily air quality. EPA calculates the AQI for five major air pollutants regulated by the Clean Air Act: ground-level ozone, particle pollution (also known as particulate matter), carbon monoxide, sulfur dioxide, and nitrogen dioxide. The AQI runs from 0 to 500. The higher the AQI value, the greater the level of air pollution and the greater the health concern.
Source: U.S. Environmental Protection Agency, Air Quality Index Report, 2017

Maximum Air Pollutant Concentrations: Particulate Matter, Ozone, CO and Lead

	Particulate Matter 10 (ug/m^3)	Particulate Matter 2.5 Wtd AM (ug/m^3)	Particulate Matter 2.5 24-Hr (ug/m^3)	Ozone (ppm)	Carbon Monoxide (ppm)	Lead (ug/m^3)
MSA[1] Level	113	11	24	0.08	2	0.04
NAAQS[2]	150	15	35	0.075	9	0.15
Met NAAQS[2]	Yes	Yes	Yes	No	Yes	Yes

Note: (1) Data covers the Philadelphia-Camden-Wilmington, PA-NJ-DE-MD Metropolitan Statistical Area—see Appendix B for areas included; Data from exceptional events are included; (2) National Ambient Air Quality Standards; ppm = parts per million; ug/m^3 = micrograms per cubic meter; n/a not available.
Concentrations: Particulate Matter 10 (coarse particulate)—highest second maximum 24-hour concentration; Particulate Matter 2.5 Wtd AM (fine particulate)—highest weighted annual mean concentration; Particulate Matter 2.5 24-Hour (fine particulate)—highest 98th percentile 24-hour concentration; Ozone—highest fourth daily maximum 8-hour concentration; Carbon Monoxide—highest second maximum non-overlapping 8-hour concentration; Lead—maximum running 3-month average
Source: U.S. Environmental Protection Agency, Air Quality Monitoring Information, "Air Quality Statistics by City, 2016"

Maximum Air Pollutant Concentrations: Nitrogen Dioxide and Sulfur Dioxide

	Nitrogen Dioxide AM (ppb)	Nitrogen Dioxide 1-Hr (ppb)	Sulfur Dioxide AM (ppb)	Sulfur Dioxide 1-Hr (ppb)	Sulfur Dioxide 24-Hr (ppb)
MSA[1] Level	16	58	n/a	19	n/a
NAAQS[2]	53	100	30	75	140
Met NAAQS[2]	Yes	Yes	n/a	Yes	n/a

Note: (1) Data covers the Philadelphia-Camden-Wilmington, PA-NJ-DE-MD Metropolitan Statistical Area—see Appendix B for areas included; Data from exceptional events are included; (2) National Ambient Air Quality Standards; ppm = parts per million; ug/m^3 = micrograms per cubic meter; n/a not available.
Concentrations: Nitrogen Dioxide AM—highest arithmetic mean concentration; Nitrogen Dioxide 1-Hr—highest 98th percentile 1-hour daily maximum concentration; Sulfur Dioxide AM—highest annual mean concentration; Sulfur Dioxide 1-Hr—highest 99th percentile 1-hour daily maximum concentration; Sulfur Dioxide 24-Hr—highest second maximum 24-hour concentration
Source: U.S. Environmental Protection Agency, Air Quality Monitoring Information, "Air Quality Statistics by City, 2016"

Drinking Water

Water System Name	Pop. Served	Primary Water Source Type	Violations[1]	
			Health Based	Monitoring/ Reporting
Evesham MUA	45,538	Purchased Surface	0	2

Note: (1) Based on violation data from January 1, 2017 to December 31, 2017
Source: U.S. Environmental Protection Agency, Office of Ground Water and Drinking Water, Safe Drinking Water Information System (based on data extracted April 5, 2018)

Hillsborough, New Jersey

Background

Hillsborough is the largest township in Central New Jersey's Somerset County—#6 on *Forbes* list of the nation's ten wealthiest counties—located 30 miles east of Staten Island, NY and about 35 miles from Manhattan. The town is an hour's drive from Philadelphia, PA and 20 minutes from Princeton, NJ.

The township is comprised of five villages: Belle Mead, Blackwells Mills, Flagtown, Neshanic, and South Branch. The area is known to have been occupied by Native Americans going back thousands of years; the Dutch arrived in the middle of the 17th century. Farm and land records indicate settlement activity was well underway when William Penn purchased West Jersey in 1676. The township of Hillsborough was incorporated in 1771, and retains its early claim to fame as the place where George Washington and his troops passed through from the Battle of Princeton. In what may be an apocryphal story, Washington drilled his troops on Sourland Mountain using corn stalks for guns, and the sun glinting off the stalks convinced the British that Washington had reinforcements, allowing Washington to proceed to his winter headquarters at Morristown. Once-rural Hillsborough drew city dwellers to its pastoral setting as the 20th century progressed.

Reckitt Benckiser North America, a manufacturer of cleaning supplies, operates a 39,000-square foot facility in Hillsborough. However, all of the county's largest employers are located outside of town, such as AT&T and Verizon Wireless, and pharmaceutical manufacturers Alpharma, Catalent Pharma Solutions, Sanofi-Aventis US, and Ethicon. Ortho-McNeil Pharmaceutical and Ortho Biotech Products also operate within the county.

The Hillsborough Township Public Schools serve the community's 7700 students with six elementary schools, one intermediate school, one middle school, and one high school. The Hillsborough Education Foundation dedicates itself to promoting education within the township and awards grants for curriculum innovation. In addition, the township is within easy access of such institutions of higher learning such as the Ivy League's Princeton University, Rutgers University, Rider University, and The College of New Jersey—not to mention the numerous other major universities in New York City and the metro area.

The township offers numerous recreational opportunities, from music camps to sports leagues as well as 14 parks and recreational facilities including soccer fields and the Triangle Football/Lacrosse Complex. The nine-acre Ann Van Middlesworth Park, with its fishing pond, skate park, baseball/softball fields, basketball courts and playground, provides a centerpiece park for Hillsborough.

The Hillsborough Cultural Arts Commission sponsors an annual fine art and photography exhibition with prizes such as a one year, expenses-paid classical art apprenticeship.

One of Hillsborough's jewels is Duke Farms, a 2,740-acre former horse farm—and one of New Jersey's largest, privately-owned undeveloped land parcels—where residents enjoy 18 miles of walking trails, 12 miles of bicycle trails, and four miles of paved wheelchair-accessible lanes. Another recreational favorite is Sourland Mountain Preserve, owned by the county at 3,196.7 acres, with numerous opportunities for hiking, birding, biking or horseback riding.

The area has a moderate climate, with July highs averaging in the mid-80s, January lows dipping to an average of about 20 degrees, and snowfall averaging just above eight inches at its peak month of February.

Rankings

General Rankings

- New York* was identified as one of America's fastest-growing cities in terms of population growth by CNNMoney.com. The area ranked #1 out of 10. Criteria: population growth between July 2015 and July 2016; cities and towns with populations of 50,000. *CNNMoney, "10 Fastest-Growing Cities," June 2, 2017*

Business/Finance Rankings

- The personal finance site NerdWallet analyzed 183 American metropolitan areas with populations over 250,000 and more than 15,000 businesses to rank where entrepreneurs find the most success. Criteria included area economy, annual income, housing cost, unemployment rate, and the success rate of area businesses. New York* ranked #32. *www.nerdwallet.com, "Best Places to Start a Business," April 27, 2015*
- Metro areas with the largest gap in income between rich and poor residents were identified by 24/7 Wall Street using the U.S. Census Bureau's 2013 American Community Survey. The New York* metro area placed #7 among metro areas with the widest wealth gap between rich and poor. *247wallst.com, "20 Cities with the Widest Gap between the Rich and Poor," July 8, 2015*
- In a survey of economic confidence in the nation's 50 largest metropolitan areas conducted January–December 2014, the New York* metro area placed #23, according to Gallup's 2014 Economic Confidence Index. *Gallup, "San Jose and San Francisco Lead in Economic Confidence," March 19, 2015*
- The Brookings Institution ranked the 100 largest metro areas in the U.S. based on income inequality. New York* was ranked #2 (#1 = greatest ineqality). Criteria: the "95/20 ratio," a figure representing the income at which a household earns more than 95 percent of all other households, divided by the income at which a household earns more than only 20 percent of all other households. *Brookings Institution, "Household Income Inequality, 100 Largest U.S. Metro Areas, 2014-2016," February 5, 2018*
- Payscale.com ranked the largest metro areas in terms of wage growth. The New York* metro area ranked #1. Criteria: private-sector wage growth between the 4th quarter of 2016 and the 4th quarter of 2017. *PayScale, "Wage Trends by Metro Area-4th Quarter," January 17, 2018*
- The New York* metro area was identified as one of the most debt-ridden places in America by the finance site Credit.com. The metro area was ranked #3. Criteria: residents' average credit card debt as well as median income. *Credit.com, "25 Cities With the Most Credit Card Debt," February 28, 2018*
- New York* was identified as one of America's most frugal metro areas by *Coupons.com.* The city ranked #15 out of 25. Criteria: digital coupon usage. *Coupons.com, "America's Most Frugal Cities of 2017," March 22, 2018*
- New York* was cited as one of America's top metros for new and expanded facility projects in 2017. The area ranked #5 in the large metro area category (population over 1 million). *Site Selection, "Top Metropolitans of 2017," March 2018*
- The New York* metro area appeared on the Milken Institute "2017 Best Performing Cities" list. Rank: #82 out of 200 large metro areas. Criteria: job growth; wage and salary growth; high-tech output growth. *Milken Institute, "Best-Performing Cities 2017," January 2018*
- *Forbes* ranked the 200 most populous metro areas to determine the nation's "Best Places for Business and Careers." The Newark* metro area was ranked #152. Criteria: costs (business and living); job growth (past and projected); income growth; quality of life; educational attainment (college and high school); projected economic growth; cultural and recreational opportunities; net migration patterns; number of highly ranked colleges. *Forbes, "The Best Places for Business and Careers 2017," October 24, 2017*

Dating/Romance Rankings

- *Apartment List* conducted its annual survey of renters to compile a list of metros that have the best opportunities for dating. Nearly 11,000 respondents, from February 2017 through January 2018, rated their current city or neighborhood for opportunities to date and make friends. The New York* metro area ranked #10 out of 70 where single residents were very satisfied or somewhat satisfied, making it among the ten best metros for dating opportunities. Other criteria analyzed included gender and education levels of renters. *Apartment List, "Best Metros for Dating 2018," February 6, 2018*

Education Rankings

- Personal finance website *WalletHub* analyzed the 150 largest U.S. metropolitan statistical areas to determine where the most educated Americans are choosing to settle. Criteria: education quality and attainment gap; education levels; percentage of workers with degrees; public school rankings; quality and size of each metro area's universities. New York* was ranked #36 (#1 = most educated city). *www.WalletHub.com, "2017's Most and Least Educated Cities in America," July 25, 2017*

Environmental Rankings

- Sperling's BestPlaces assessed 379 metropolitan areas of the United States for the likelihood of dangerously extreme weather events or earthquakes. In general the Southeast and South-Central regions have the highest risk of weather extremes and earthquakes, while the Pacific Northwest enjoys the lowest risk. Of the least risky metropolitan areas, the Newark* metro area was ranked #208. *www.bestplaces.net, "Safest Places from Natural Disasters," April 2011*

- The U.S. Environmental Protection Agency (EPA) released a list of U.S. metropolitan areas with the most ENERGY STAR certified buildings in 2016. The New York* metro area was ranked #3 out of 25. *U.S. Environmental Protection Agency, "2017 Energy Star Top Cities," June 2017*

- New York* was highlighted as one of the 25 most ozone-polluted metro areas in the U.S. during 2013 through 2015. The area ranked #9. *American Lung Association, State of the Air 2017*

- New York* was highlighted as one of the 25 metro areas most polluted by year-round particle pollution (Annual PM 2.5) in the U.S. during 2013 through 2015. The area ranked #22. *American Lung Association, State of the Air 2017*

Health/Fitness Rankings

- For each of the 50 most populous metro areas in the United States, the American College of Sports Medicine's American Fitness Index evaluated infrastructure, community assets, and policies that encourage healthy and fit lifestyles, including preventive health behaviors, levels of chronic disease conditions, health care access, and community resources and policies that support physical activity. The New York* metro area ranked #18 for "community fitness." *www.americanfitnessindex.org, "ACSM American Fitness Index Health and Community Fitness Status of the 50 Largest Metropolitan Areas," May 2017*

- The New York* metro area was identified as one of the worst cities for bed bugs in America by pest control company Orkin. The area ranked #8 out of 50 based on the number of bed bug treatments Orkin performed from December 2016 to November 2017. *Orkin, "Baltimore and Washington D.C. Continue to Hold Top Spots," January 8, 2018*

- New York* was identified as a "2016 Spring Allergy Capital." The area ranked #31 out of 100. Three groups of factors were used to identify the most severe cities for people with allergies during the spring season: annual pollen levels; medicine utilization; access to board-certified allergists. *Asthma and Allergy Foundation of America, "Spring Allergy Capitals 2016"*

- New York* was identified as a "2016 Fall Allergy Capital." The area ranked #52 out of 100. Three groups of factors were used to identify the most severe cities for people with allergies during the fall season: annual pollen levels; medicine utilization; access to board-certified allergists. *Asthma and Allergy Foundation of America, "Fall Allergy Capitals 2016"*
- New York* was identified as a "2015 Asthma Capital." The area ranked #35 out of the nation's 100 largest metropolitan areas. Criteria: estimated prevalence; self-reported prevalence; crude death rate for asthma; annual pollen score; annual air quality; public smoking laws; number of board-certified asthma specialists; school inhaler access laws; rescue medication use; controller medication use; ER visits for asthma; uninsured rate; poverty rate. *Asthma and Allergy Foundation of America, "Asthma Capitals 2015"*
- The New York* metro area ranked #75 out of 189 in The Gallup-Healthways Well-Being Index. Criteria: purpose; social well being; financial health; community and physical health. Results are based on telephone interviews with adults, aged 18 and older, living in metropolitan areas in the 50 U.S. states and the District of Columbia. *Gallup-Healthways, "State of American Well-Being, 2017 Community Well-Being Rankings" March 2018*

Real Estate Rankings

- FitSmallBusiness looked at 50 of the largest metropolitan areas in the U.S. to determine which metro was the best to start a real estate business. Data was compiled from such sources as: Zillow, Trulia, U.S. Census Bureau, and the Bureau of Labor Statistics. Criteria: location; inventory; annual wages; median sales price of homes; days on the market; median price cut percentage; and other factors that would influence real estate professional growth. The New York* metro area ranked #6. *fitsmallbusiness.com, "The Best Cities to Become a Real Estate Agent in 2018," January 30, 2018*
- With data from RealtyTrac, Yahoo! Finance researchers listed the housing markets in which housing affordability is improving most, factoring in interest rates as well as median home prices. The New York* metro area was among the least affordable housing markets. *news.yahoo.com, "10 Cities Where Ordinary People Can No Longer Afford Homes," March 5, 2014*
- The New York* metro area was identified as one of the 20 least affordable housing markets in the U.S. in 2017. The area ranked #12 out of 180 markets. Criteria: qualification for a mortgage loan on a typical home. *National Association of Realtors®, Affordability Index of Existing Single-Family Homes for Metropolitan Areas, 2017*
- Newark* was ranked #143 out of 238 metro areas in terms of housing affordability in 2017 by the National Association of Home Builders (#1 = most affordable). Criteria: the share of homes sold in that area affordable to a family earning the local median income, based on standard mortgage underwriting criteria. *National Association of Home Builders®, NAHB-Wells Fargo Housing Opportunity Index, 4th Quarter 2017*

Safety Rankings

- The National Insurance Crime Bureau ranked 382 metro areas in the U.S. in terms of per capita rates of vehicle theft. The New York* metro area ranked #292 (#1 = highest rate). Criteria: number of vehicle theft offenses per 100,000 inhabitants in 2016. *National Insurance Crime Bureau, "Hot Spots 2016," June 8, 2017*

Seniors/Retirement Rankings

- From its Best Cities for Successful Aging indexes, the Milken Institute generated rankings for metropolitan areas, weighing data in nine categories—health care, wellness, living arrangements, transportation and convenience, financial characteristics, education, employment, community engagement, and overall livability. The New York* metro area was ranked #11 overall in the large metro area category. *Milken Institute, "Best Cities for Successful Aging, 2017" March 14, 2017*

Sports/Recreation Rankings

- According to the personal finance website NerdWallet, the New York* metro area, at #4, is one of the nation's top dozen metro areas for sports fans. Criteria included the presence of all four major sports—MLB, NFL, NHL, and NBA, fan enthusiasm (as measured by game attendance), ticket affordability, and "sports culture," that is, number of sports bars. *www.nerdwallet.com, "Best Cities for Sports Fans," May 5, 2013*

Transportation Rankings

- New York* was identified as one of the most congested metro areas in the U.S. The area ranked #4 out of 10. Criteria: yearly delay per auto commuter in hours. *Texas A&M Transportation Institute, "2015 Urban Mobility Scorecard," August 2015*
- The New York* metro area appeared on *Forbes* list of places with the most extreme commutes. The metro area ranked #2 out of 10. Criteria: average travel time; percentage of mega commuters. Mega-commuters travel more than 90 minutes and 50 miles each way to work. *Forbes.com, "The Cities with the Most Extreme Commutes," March 5, 2013*

Women/Minorities Rankings

- The *Houston Chronicle* listed the New York* metro area as #4 in top places for young Latinos to live in the U.S. Research was largely based on housing and occupational data from the largest metropolitan areas performed by *Forbes* and NBC Universo. Criteria: percentage of 18-34 year-olds; Latino college grad rates; and diversity. *blog.chron.com, "The 15 Best Big Cities for Latino Millenials," January 26, 2016*

Miscellaneous Rankings

- The watchdog site Charity Navigator conducts an annual study of charities in the nation's major markets both to analyze statistical differences in their financial, accountability, and transparency practices and to track year-to-year variations in individual philanthropic communities. Charity Navigator's analysis demonstrated that the financial, accountability and transparency behaviors of America's largest charities can be influenced by the metropolitan market within which the charity operates. The New York* metro area was ranked #19 among the 30 metro markets in the rating category of Overall Score. *www.charitynavigator.org, "2017 Metro Market Study," May 1, 2017*
- The Harris Poll's Happiness Index survey revealed that of the top ten U.S. markets, the New York* metro area residents ranked #6 in happiness. Criteria included strong assent to positive statements and strong disagreement with negative ones, and degree of agreement with a series of statements about respondents' personal relationships and general outlook. *www.theharrispoll.com, "Dallas/Fort Worth Is "Happiest" City among America's Top Ten Markets," September 4, 2013*
- Energizer Personal Care, the makers of Edge® shave gel, in partnership with Sperling's BestPlaces, ranked 50 major metro areas in terms of everyday irritations. The New York* metro area ranked #2 the 50 metro area most irritating to guys. Criteria: high male-to-female ratio; poor sports team performance and high ticket prices; slow traffic; lack of job availability; unaffordable housing; extreme weather; lack of nightlife and fitness options. *Energizer Personal Care, "Most Irritating Cities for Guys," August 26, 2013*
- The National Alliance to End Homelessness listed the 25 most populous metro areas with the highest rate of homelessness. The New York* metro area had a high rate of homelessness. Criteria: number of homeless people per 10,000 population in 2016. *National Alliance to End Homelessness, "Homelessness in the 25 Most Populous U.S. Metro Areas," September 1, 2017*

*Hillsborough is located within the New York-Newark-Jersey City, NY-NJ-PA Metropolitan Statistical Area and the Newark, NJ-PA Metropolitan Division.

Business Environment

CITY FINANCES

City Government Finances

Component	2015 ($000)	2015 ($ per capita)
Total Revenues	35,252	885
Total Expenditures	31,378	788
Debt Outstanding	9,665	243
Cash and Securities[1]	14,681	369

Note: (1) Cash and security holdings of a government at the close of its fiscal year,, including those of its dependent agencies, utilities, and liquor stores.
Source: U.S Census Bureau, State & Local Government Finances 2015

City Government Revenue by Source

Source	2015 ($000)	2015 ($ per capita)	2015 (%)
General Revenue			
From Federal Government	0	0	0.0
From State Government	3,428	86	9.7
From Local Governments	15	0	0.0
Taxes			
Property	21,273	534	60.3
Sales and Gross Receipts	48	1	0.1
Personal Income	0	0	0.0
Corporate Income	0	0	0.0
Motor Vehicle License	0	0	0.0
Other Taxes	1,723	43	4.9
Current Charges	6,057	152	17.2
Liquor Store	0	0	0.0
Utility	0	0	0.0
Employee Retirement	0	0	0.0

Source: U.S Census Bureau, State & Local Government Finances 2015

City Government Expenditures by Function

Function	2015 ($000)	2015 ($ per capita)	2015 (%)
General Direct Expenditures			
Air Transportation	0	0	0.0
Corrections	0	0	0.0
Education	0	0	0.0
Employment Security Administration	0	0	0.0
Financial Administration	836	21	2.7
Fire Protection	928	23	3.0
General Public Buildings	137	3	0.4
Governmental Administration, Other	714	17	2.3
Health	756	19	2.4
Highways	3,171	79	10.1
Hospitals	0	0	0.0
Housing and Community Development	0	0	0.0
Interest on General Debt	337	8	1.1
Judicial and Legal	563	14	1.8
Libraries	0	0	0.0
Parking	0	0	0.0
Parks and Recreation	492	12	1.6
Police Protection	7,215	181	23.0
Public Welfare	183	4	0.6
Sewerage	2,682	67	8.5
Solid Waste Management	407	10	1.3
Veterans' Services	0	0	0.0
Liquor Store	0	0	0.0
Utility	0	0	0.0
Employee Retirement	0	0	0.0

Source: U.S Census Bureau, State & Local Government Finances 2015

DEMOGRAPHICS

Population Growth

Area	1990 Census	2000 Census	2010 Census	2016* Estimate	Population Growth (%) 1990-2016	Population Growth (%) 2010-2016
City	28,842	36,634	38,303	39,517	37.0	3.2
MSA[1]	16,845,992	18,323,002	18,897,109	20,031,443	18.9	6.0
U.S.	248,709,873	281,421,906	308,745,538	318,558,162	28.1	3.2

Note: (1) Figures cover the New York-Newark-Jersey City, NY-NJ-PA Metropolitan Statistical Area—see Appendix B for areas included; (*) 2012-2016 5-year estimated population
Source: U.S. Census Bureau, 1990 Census, Census 2000, Census 2010, 2012-2016 American Community Survey 5-Year Estimates

Household Size

Area	Persons in Household (%) One	Two	Three	Four	Five	Six	Seven or More	Average Household Size
City	19.0	31.3	19.9	20.0	6.7	2.4	0.7	2.90
MSA[1]	28.0	29.1	17.0	14.7	6.7	2.6	1.9	2.80
U.S.	27.7	33.7	15.7	13.1	6.0	2.3	1.5	2.60

Note: (1) Figures cover the New York-Newark-Jersey City, NY-NJ-PA Metropolitan Statistical Area—see Appendix B for areas included
Source: U.S. Census Bureau, 2012-2016 American Community Survey 5-Year Estimates

Race

Area	White Alone[2] (%)	Black Alone[2] (%)	Asian Alone[2] (%)	AIAN[3] Alone[2] (%)	NHOPI[4] Alone[2] (%)	Other Race Alone[2] (%)	Two or More Races (%)
City	75.5	5.1	15.8	0.2	0.0	1.2	2.3
MSA[1]	58.7	17.1	10.6	0.3	0.0	10.3	2.9
U.S.	73.3	12.6	5.2	0.8	0.2	4.8	3.1

Note: (1) Figures cover the New York-Newark-Jersey City, NY-NJ-PA Metropolitan Statistical Area—see Appendix B for areas included; (2) Alone is defined as not being in combination with one or more other races; (3) American Indian and Alaska Native; (4) Native Hawaiian and Other Pacific Islander
Source: U.S. Census Bureau, 2012-2016 American Community Survey 5-Year Estimates

Hispanic or Latino Origin

Area	Total (%)	Mexican (%)	Puerto Rican (%)	Cuban (%)	Other (%)
City	7.5	0.9	2.8	0.2	3.6
MSA[1]	23.8	3.1	6.3	0.7	13.7
U.S.	17.3	11.0	1.7	0.7	4.0

Note: Persons of Hispanic or Latino origin can be of any race; (1) Figures cover the New York-Newark-Jersey City, NY-NJ-PA Metropolitan Statistical Area—see Appendix B for areas included
Source: U.S. Census Bureau, 2012-2016 American Community Survey 5-Year Estimates

Segregation

Type	Segregation Indices[1] 1990	2000	2010	2010 Rank[2]	Percent Change 1990-2000	1990-2010	2000-2010
Black/White	80.9	80.2	78.0	2	-0.7	-2.9	-2.2
Asian/White	47.4	50.8	51.9	3	3.5	4.5	1.0
Hispanic/White	66.2	65.6	62.0	3	-0.6	-4.2	-3.6

Note: All figures cover the Metropolitan Statistical Area—see Appendix B for areas included; Figures are based on an analysis of 1990, 2000, and 2010 Census Decennial Census tract data by William H. Frey, Brookings Institution and the University of Michigan Social Science Data Analysis Network. In this analysis all racial groups (whites, blacks, and asians) are non-Hispanic members of those races. Hispanics are shown as a separate category; (1) Segregation Indices are Dissimilarity Indices that measure the degree to which the minority group is distributed differently than whites across census tracts. They range from 0 (complete integration) to 100 (complete segregation) where the value indicates the percentage of the minority group that needs to move to be distributed exactly like whites; (2) Ranges from 1 (most segregated) to 102 (least segregated); n/a not available.
Source: www.CensusScope.org

Ancestry

Area	German	Irish	English	American	Italian	Polish	French[2]	Scottish	Dutch
City	12.6	14.3	5.3	5.1	18.0	9.6	1.6	1.7	1.3
MSA[1]	6.8	10.0	2.9	4.8	13.1	4.0	1.0	0.7	0.7
U.S.	14.4	10.4	7.7	6.9	5.4	2.9	2.6	1.7	1.3

Note: Figures are the percentage of the total population reporting a particular ancestry. The nine most commonly reported ancestries in the U.S. are shown. Figures include multiple ancestries (e.g. if a person reported being Irish and Italian, they were included in both columns); (1) Figures cover the New York-Newark-Jersey City, NY-NJ-PA Metropolitan Statistical Area—see Appendix B for areas included; (2) Excludes Basque
Source: U.S. Census Bureau, 2012-2016 American Community Survey 5-Year Estimates

Foreign-Born Population

Area	Percent of Population Born in								
	Any Foreign Country	Asia	Mexico	Europe	Carribean	Central America[2]	South America	Africa	Canada
City	17.9	9.9	0.2	3.8	1.0	0.5	1.2	1.2	0.2
MSA[1]	28.7	8.3	1.6	4.5	6.6	1.9	4.2	1.2	0.2
U.S.	13.2	4.0	3.6	1.5	1.3	1.0	0.9	0.6	0.3

Note: (1) Figures cover the New York-Newark-Jersey City, NY-NJ-PA Metropolitan Statistical Area—see Appendix B for areas included; (2) Excludes Mexico.
Source: U.S. Census Bureau, 2012-2016 American Community Survey 5-Year Estimates

Marital Status

Area	Never Married	Now Married[2]	Separated	Widowed	Divorced
City	26.7	61.3	0.4	4.7	7.0
MSA[1]	38.1	45.7	2.4	5.8	7.9
U.S.	33.0	48.1	2.1	5.9	11.0

Note: Figures are percentages and cover the population 15 years of age and older; (1) Figures cover the New York-Newark-Jersey City, NY-NJ-PA Metropolitan Statistical Area—see Appendix B for areas included; (2) Excludes separated
Source: U.S. Census Bureau, 2012-2016 American Community Survey 5-Year Estimates

Disability Status

Area	All Ages	Under 18 Years Old	18 to 64 Years Old	65 Years and Over
City	7.8	2.1	5.3	35.9
MSA[1]	10.0	3.2	7.4	33.3
U.S.	12.5	4.1	10.3	35.7

Note: Figures show percent of the civilian noninstitutionalized population that reported having a disability. Disability status is determined from six types of difficulty: vision, hearing, cognitive, ambulatory, self-care, and independent living. For children under 5 years old, hearing and vision difficulty are used to determine disability status. For children between the ages of 5 and 14, disability status is determined from hearing, vision, cognitive, ambulatory, and self-care difficulties. For people aged 15 years and older, they are considered to have a disability if they have difficulty with any one of the six difficulty types; Note: (1) Figures cover the New York-Newark-Jersey City, NY-NJ-PA Metropolitan Statistical Area—see Appendix B for areas included
Source: U.S. Census Bureau, 2012-2016 American Community Survey 5-Year Estimates

Age

Area	Percent of Population									Median Age
	Under Age 5	Age 5–19	Age 20–34	Age 35–44	Age 45–54	Age 55–64	Age 65–74	Age 75–84	Age 85+	
City	6.6	20.2	15.4	14.5	18.3	14.2	6.7	3.0	1.4	40.7
MSA[1]	6.1	18.4	21.3	13.3	14.3	12.3	7.8	4.2	2.1	38.0
U.S.	6.2	19.6	20.7	12.7	13.6	12.6	8.3	4.3	1.9	37.7

Note: (1) Figures cover the New York-Newark-Jersey City, NY-NJ-PA Metropolitan Statistical Area—see Appendix B for areas included
Source: U.S. Census Bureau, 2012-2016 American Community Survey 5-Year Estimates

Gender

Area	Males	Females	Males per 100 Females
City	19,167	20,350	94.2
MSA[1]	9,684,087	10,347,356	93.6
U.S.	156,765,322	161,792,840	96.9

Note: (1) Figures cover the New York-Newark-Jersey City, NY-NJ-PA Metropolitan Statistical Area—see Appendix B for areas included
Source: U.S. Census Bureau, 2012-2016 American Community Survey 5-Year Estimates

Religious Groups by Family

Area	Catholic	Baptist	Non-Den.	Methodist[2]	Lutheran	LDS[3]	Pentecostal	Presbyterian[4]	Muslim[5]	Judaism
MSA[1]	36.9	1.9	1.8	1.3	0.8	0.4	0.9	1.1	2.3	4.8
U.S.	19.1	9.3	4.0	4.0	2.3	2.0	1.9	1.6	0.8	0.7

Note: Figures are the number of adherents as a percentage of the total population; (1) Figures cover the New York-Newark-Jersey City, NY-NJ-PA Metropolitan Statistical Area—see Appendix B for areas included; (2) Methodist/Pietist; (3) Latter Day Saints; (4) Reformed; (5) Figures are estimates
Source: Association of Statisticians of American Religious Bodies, 2010 U.S. Religion Census: Religious Congregations & Membership Study

Religious Groups by Tradition

Area	Catholic	Evangelical Protestant	Mainline Protestant	Other Tradition	Black Protestant	Orthodox
MSA[1]	36.9	4.0	4.1	8.4	1.2	1.0
U.S.	19.1	16.2	7.3	4.3	1.6	0.3

Note: Figures are the number of adherents as a percentage of the total population; (1) Figures cover the New York-Newark-Jersey City, NY-NJ-PA Metropolitan Statistical Area—see Appendix B for areas included
Source: Association of Statisticians of American Religious Bodies, 2010 U.S. Religion Census: Religious Congregations & Membership Study

ECONOMY

Gross Metropolitan Product

Area	2014	2015	2016	2017	Rank[2]
MSA[1]	1,551.3	1,613.8	1,664.0	1,735.1	1

Note: Figures are in billions of dollars; (1) Figures cover the New York-Newark-Jersey City, NY-NJ-PA Metropolitan Statistical Area—see Appendix B for areas included; (2) Rank is based on 2015 data and ranges from 1 to 381
Source: The U.S. Conference of Mayors, U.S. Metro Economies: GMP and Employment Report, 2015-2017

Economic Growth

Area	2012-14 (%)	2015 (%)	2016 (%)	2017 (%)	Rank[2]
MSA[1]	1.6	1.9	1.6	2.2	151
U.S.	2.0	2.4	1.9	2.6	–

Note: Figures are real gross metropolitan product (GMP) growth rates and represent average annual percent change; (1) Figures cover the New York-Newark-Jersey City, NY-NJ-PA Metropolitan Statistical Area—see Appendix B for areas included; (2) Rank is based on 2012-2014 average annual percent change and ranges from 1 to 381
Source: The U.S. Conference of Mayors, U.S. Metro Economies: GMP and Employment Report, 2015-2017

Metropolitan Area Exports

Area	2011	2012	2013	2014	2015	2016	Rank[2]
MSA[1]	105,102.0	102,298.0	106,922.8	105,266.6	95,645.4	89,649.5	1

Note: Figures are in millions of dollars; (1) Figures cover the New York-Newark-Jersey City, NY-NJ-PA Metropolitan Statistical Area—see Appendix B for areas included; (2) Rank is based on 2016 data and ranges from 1 to 385
Source: U.S. Department of Commerce, International Trade Administration, Office of Trade & Industry Information, Manufacturing & Services, data extracted March 15, 2018

Building Permits

Area	Single-Family			Multi-Family			Total		
	2016	2017p	Pct. Chg.	2016	2017p	Pct. Chg.	2016	2017p	Pct. Chg.
City	63	73	15.9	48	116	141.7	111	189	70.3
MSA[1]	9,987	10,549	5.6	32,479	39,344	21.1	42,466	49,893	17.5
U.S.	750,800	817,300	8.9	455,800	446,800	-2.0	1,206,600	1,264,100	4.8

Note: (1) Figures cover the New York-Newark-Jersey City, NY-NJ-PA Metropolitan Statistical Area—see Appendix B for areas included; Figures represent new, privately-owned housing units authorized (unadjusted data); All permit data are based on estimates with imputation; (p) preliminary data.
Source: U.S. Census Bureau, Manufacturing, Mining, and Construction Statistics, Building Permits, 2016, 2017

Bankruptcy Filings

Area	Business Filings			Nonbusiness Filings		
	2016	2017	% Chg.	2016	2017	% Chg.
Somerset County	29	25	-13.8	568	596	4.9
U.S.	24,114	23,157	-4.0	770,846	765,863	-0.6

Note: Business filings include Chapter 7, Chapter 11, Chapter 12, and Chapter 13; Nonbusiness filings include Chapter 7, Chapter 11, and Chapter 13
Source: Administrative Office of the U.S. Courts, Business and Nonbusiness Bankruptcy, County Cases Commenced by Chapter of the Bankruptcy Code, During the 12-Month Period Ending December 31, 2016 and Business and Nonbusiness Bankruptcy, County Cases Commenced by Chapter of the Bankruptcy Code, During the 12-Month Period Ending December 31, 2017

Housing Vacancy Rates

Area	Gross Vacancy Rate[2] (%)			Year-Round Vacancy Rate[3] (%)			Rental Vacancy Rate[4] (%)			Homeowner Vacancy Rate[5] (%)		
	2015	2016	2017	2015	2016	2017	2015	2016	2017	2015	2016	2017
MSA[1]	9.8	10.3	10.7	8.6	9.1	9.6	4.2	4.7	4.6	2.1	2.2	1.9
U.S.	12.9	12.8	12.7	10.0	9.9	9.9	7.1	6.9	7.2	1.8	1.7	1.6

Note: (1) Figures cover the New York-Newark-Jersey City, NY-NJ-PA Metropolitan Statistical Area—see Appendix B for areas included; (2) The percentage of the total housing inventory that is vacant; (3) The percentage of the housing inventory (excluding seasonal units) that is year-round vacant; (4) The percentage of rental inventory that is vacant for rent; (5) The percentage of homeowner inventory that is vacant for sale
Source: U.S. Census Bureau, Housing Vacancies and Homeownership Annual Statistics: 2015, 2016, 2017

INCOME

Income

Area	Per Capita ($)	Median Household ($)	Average Household ($)
City	48,515	114,731	138,347
MSA[1]	37,510	69,211	101,617
U.S.	29,829	55,322	77,866

Note: (1) Figures cover the New York-Newark-Jersey City, NY-NJ-PA Metropolitan Statistical Area—see Appendix B for areas included
Source: U.S. Census Bureau, 2012-2016 American Community Survey 5-Year Estimates

Household Income Distribution

Area	Percent of Households Earning							
	Under $15,000	$15,000 -$24,999	$25,000 -$34,999	$35,000 -$49,999	$50,000 -$74,999	$75,000 -$99,999	$100,000 -$149,999	$150,000 and up
City	3.3	3.6	3.3	8.6	10.0	14.3	20.6	36.3
MSA[1]	11.7	8.5	7.7	10.2	15.0	11.7	15.9	19.3
U.S.	12.1	10.2	9.9	13.2	17.8	12.2	13.5	11.1

Note: (1) Figures cover the New York-Newark-Jersey City, NY-NJ-PA Metropolitan Statistical Area—see Appendix B for areas included
Source: U.S. Census Bureau, 2012-2016 American Community Survey 5-Year Estimates

Poverty Rate

Area	All Ages	Under 18 Years Old	18 to 64 Years Old	65 Years and Over
City	3.6	3.0	4.0	2.3
MSA[1]	14.2	20.0	12.7	11.7
U.S.	15.1	21.2	14.2	9.3

Note: Figures are percentage of people whose income during the past 12 months was below the poverty level; (1) Figures cover the New York-Newark-Jersey City, NY-NJ-PA Metropolitan Statistical Area—see Appendix B for areas included
Source: U.S. Census Bureau, 2012-2016 American Community Survey 5-Year Estimates

EMPLOYMENT

Labor Force and Employment

Area	Civilian Labor Force			Workers Employed		
	Dec. 2016	Dec. 2017	% Chg.	Dec. 2016	Dec. 2017	% Chg.
City	21,747	21,597	-0.7	21,108	20,912	-0.9
MD[1]	1,240,075	1,228,255	-1.0	1,188,742	1,178,033	-0.9
U.S.	158,968,000	159,880,000	0.6	151,798,000	153,602,000	1.2

Note: Data is not seasonally adjusted and covers workers 16 years of age and older; (1) Figures cover the Newark, NJ-PA Metropolitan Division—see Appendix B for areas included
Source: Bureau of Labor Statistics, Local Area Unemployment Statistics

Unemployment Rate

Area	2017											
	Jan.	Feb.	Mar.	Apr.	May	Jun.	Jul.	Aug.	Sep.	Oct.	Nov.	Dec.
City	3.6	3.6	3.2	3.1	3.3	3.5	3.9	4.0	3.7	3.4	3.2	3.2
MD[1]	4.9	4.9	4.5	4.2	4.4	4.6	5.1	5.0	4.7	4.4	4.3	4.1
U.S.	5.1	4.9	4.6	4.1	4.1	4.5	4.6	4.5	4.1	3.9	3.9	3.9

Note: Data is not seasonally adjusted and covers workers 16 years of age and older; (1) Figures cover the Newark, NJ-PA Metropolitan Division—see Appendix B for areas included
Source: Bureau of Labor Statistics, Local Area Unemployment Statistics

Average Wages

Occupation	$/Hr.	Occupation	$/Hr.
Accountants and Auditors	45.10	Maids and Housekeeping Cleaners	12.60
Automotive Mechanics	23.50	Maintenance and Repair Workers	21.90
Bookkeepers	22.70	Marketing Managers	91.50
Carpenters	33.00	Nuclear Medicine Technologists	46.40
Cashiers	10.80	Nurses, Licensed Practical	27.30
Clerks, General Office	17.60	Nurses, Registered	40.50
Clerks, Receptionists/Information	16.00	Nursing Assistants	14.40
Clerks, Shipping/Receiving	16.70	Packers and Packagers, Hand	11.20
Computer Programmers	42.90	Physical Therapists	48.40
Computer Systems Analysts	48.10	Postal Service Mail Carriers	24.50
Computer User Support Specialists	34.60	Real Estate Brokers	50.30
Cooks, Restaurant	15.40	Retail Salespersons	13.50
Dentists	n/a	Sales Reps., Exc. Tech./Scientific	37.60
Electrical Engineers	49.80	Sales Reps., Tech./Scientific	45.90
Electricians	33.80	Secretaries, Exc. Legal/Med./Exec.	20.20
Financial Managers	85.60	Security Guards	14.90
First-Line Supervisors/Managers, Sales	23.40	Surgeons	135.40
Food Preparation Workers	11.30	Teacher Assistants*	14.50
General and Operations Managers	82.50	Teachers, Elementary School*	33.10
Hairdressers/Cosmetologists	18.60	Teachers, Secondary School*	36.40
Internists, General	98.40	Telemarketers	13.80
Janitors and Cleaners	15.10	Truck Drivers, Heavy/Tractor-Trailer	23.60
Landscaping/Groundskeeping Workers	14.40	Truck Drivers, Light/Delivery Svcs.	17.80
Lawyers	69.70	Waiters and Waitresses	14.30

Note: Wage data covers the Newark, NJ-PA Metropolitan Division—see Appendix B for areas included; (*) Hourly wages for elementary/secondary school teachers and teacher assistants were calculated by the editors from annual wage data based on a 40 hour work week; n/a not available.
Source: Bureau of Labor Statistics, Metro Area Occupational Employment & Wage Estimates, May 2017

Employment by Occupation

Occupation Classification	City (%)	MSA[1] (%)	U.S. (%)
Management, Business, Science, and Arts	56.2	41.2	37.0
Natural Resources, Construction, and Maintenance	5.1	6.9	8.9
Production, Transportation, and Material Moving	4.9	9.0	12.2
Sales and Office	24.4	23.7	23.8
Service	9.4	19.3	18.1

Note: Figures cover employed civilians 16 years of age and older; (1) Figures cover the New York-Newark-Jersey City, NY-NJ-PA Metropolitan Statistical Area—see Appendix B for areas included
Source: U.S. Census Bureau, 2012-2016 American Community Survey 5-Year Estimates

Employment by Industry

Sector	MD[1] Number of Employees	MD[1] Percent of Total	U.S. Percent of Total
Construction, Mining, and Logging	45,000	3.7	5.2
Education and Health Services	191,300	15.7	15.9
Financial Activities	76,600	6.3	5.7
Government	177,900	14.6	15.3
Information	20,600	1.7	1.9
Leisure and Hospitality	95,900	7.9	10.7
Manufacturing	75,400	6.2	8.5
Other Services	54,800	4.5	3.9
Professional and Business Services	225,000	18.5	14.0
Retail Trade	123,100	10.1	11.0
Transportation, Warehousing, and Utilities	68,900	5.7	4.1
Wholesale Trade	63,700	5.2	4.0

Note: Figures are non-farm employment as of December 2017. Figures are not seasonally adjusted and include workers 16 years of age and older; (1) Figures cover the Newark, NJ-PA Metropolitan Division—see Appendix B for areas included
Source: Bureau of Labor Statistics, Current Employment Statistics, Employment, Hours, and Earnings

Occupations with Greatest Projected Employment Growth: 2016 – 2018

Occupation[1]	2016 Employment	2018 Projected Employment	Numeric Employment Change	Percent Employment Change
Laborers and Freight, Stock, and Material Movers, Hand	97,040	101,030	3,990	4.1
Registered Nurses	84,890	87,480	2,590	3.1
Home Health Aides	36,970	39,030	2,060	5.6
Combined Food Preparation and Serving Workers, Including Fast Food	55,230	57,260	2,030	3.7
Software Developers, Applications	42,830	44,770	1,940	4.5
Heavy and Tractor-Trailer Truck Drivers	45,100	46,980	1,880	4.2
Construction Laborers	32,430	34,110	1,680	5.2
Carpenters	25,870	27,440	1,570	6.1
Waiters and Waitresses	63,080	64,600	1,520	2.4
Receptionists and Information Clerks	52,840	54,340	1,500	2.8

Note: Projections cover New Jersey; (1) Sorted by numeric employment change
Source: www.projectionscentral.com, State Occupational Projections, 2016–2018 Short-Term Projections

Fastest Growing Occupations: 2016 – 2018

Occupation[1]	2016 Employment	2018 Projected Employment	Numeric Employment Change	Percent Employment Change
Brickmasons and Blockmasons	1,920	2,080	160	8.3
Helpers—Electricians	1,620	1,740	120	8.0
Cement Masons and Concrete Finishers	2,440	2,610	170	7.2
Roofers	2,450	2,620	170	7.2
Helpers—Pipelayers, Plumbers, Pipefitters, and Steamfitters	1,100	1,180	80	7.2
Helpers—Carpenters	1,070	1,150	80	7.1
Electricians	15,320	16,370	1,050	6.8
Operations Research Analysts	1,470	1,560	90	6.3
Carpenters	25,870	27,440	1,570	6.1
Drywall and Ceiling Tile Installers	1,510	1,600	90	6.0

Note: Projections cover New Jersey; (1) Sorted by percent employment change and excludes occupations with numeric employment change less than 50
Source: www.projectionscentral.com, State Occupational Projections, 2016–2018 Short-Term Projections

TAXES

State Corporate Income Tax Rates

State	Tax Rate (%)	Income Brackets ($)	Num. of Brackets	Financial Institution Tax Rate (%)[a]	Federal Income Tax Ded.
New Jersey	9.0 (q)	Flat rate	1	9.0 (q)	No

Note: Tax rates as of January 1, 2018; (a) Rates listed are the corporate income tax rate applied to financial institutions or excise taxes based on income. Some states have other taxes based upon the value of deposits or shares; (q) In New Jersey small businesses with annual entire net income under $100,000 pay a tax rate of 7.5%; businesses with income under $50,000 pay 6.5%. The minimum Corporation Business Tax is based on New Jersey gross receipts. It ranges from $500 for a corporation with gross receipts less than $100,000, to $2,000 for a corporation with gross receipts of $1 million or more.
Source: Federation of Tax Administrators, Range of State Corporate Income Tax Rates, January 1, 2018

State Individual Income Tax Rates

State	Tax Rate (%)	Income Brackets ($)	Num. of Brackets	Personal Exempt. ($)[1] Single	Personal Exempt. ($)[1] Dependents	Fed. Inc. Tax Ded.
New Jersey	1.4 - 8.97	20,000 - 500,000 (q)	6	1,000	1,500	No

Note: Tax rates as of January 1, 2018; Local- and county-level taxes are not included; n/a not applicable; (1) Married joint filers generally receive double the single exemption; (q) The New Jersey rates reported are for single individuals. For married couples filing jointly, the tax rates also range from 1.4% to 8.97%, with 7 brackets and the same high and low income ranges.
Source: Federation of Tax Administrators, State Individual Income Tax Rates, January 1, 2018

Various State Sales and Excise Tax Rates

State	State Sales Tax (%)	Gasoline[1] (¢/gal.)	Cigarette[2] ($/pack)	Spirits[3] ($/gal.)	Wine[4] ($/gal.)	Beer[5] ($/gal.)	Recreational Marijuana (%)
New Jersey	6.625 (e)	37.1	2.70	5.50	0.88	0.12	Not legal

Note: All tax rates as of January 1, 2018; (1) The American Petroleum Institute has developed a methodology for determining the average tax rate on a gallon of fuel. Rates may include any of the following: excise taxes, environmental fees, storage tank fees, other fees or taxes, general sales tax, and local taxes. In states where gasoline is subject to the general sales tax, or where the fuel tax is based on the average sale price, the average rate determined by API is sensitive to changes in the price of gasoline. States that fully or partially apply general sales taxes to gasoline: CA, CO, GA, IL, IN, MI, NY; (2) The federal excise tax of $1.0066 per pack and local taxes are not included; (3) Rates are those applicable to off-premise sales of 40% alcohol by volume (a.b.v.) distilled spirits in 750ml containers. Local excise taxes are excluded; (4) Rates are those applicable to off-premise sales of 11% a.b.v. non-carbonated wine in 750ml containers; (5) Rates are those applicable to off-premise sales of 4.7% a.b.v. beer in 12 ounce containers; (e) Salem County is not subject to the statewide sales tax rate and collects a local rate of 3.3125%. New Jersey's average local score is represented as a negative.
Source: Tax Foundation, 2018 Facts & Figures: How Does Your State Compare?

State Business Tax Climate Index Rankings

State	Overall Rank	Corporate Tax Rank	Individual Income Tax Rank	Sales Tax Rank	Unemployment Insurance Tax Rank	Property Tax Rank
New Jersey	50	42	48	46	36	50

Note: The index is a measure of how each state's tax laws affect economic performance. The lower the rank, the more favorable a state's tax system is for business. States without a given tax are given a ranking of 1. The scores/rankings for the District of Columbia do not affect other states. The 2018 index represents the tax climate as of July 1, 2017.
Source: Tax Foundation, State Business Tax Climate Index 2018

TRANSPORTATION

Means of Transportation to Work

Area	Car/Truck/Van		Public Transportation			Bicycle	Walked	Other Means	Worked at Home
	Drove Alone	Car-pooled	Bus	Subway	Railroad				
City	84.3	5.2	0.4	0.0	2.7	0.1	0.6	0.5	6.1
MSA[1]	50.1	6.6	7.7	19.1	3.8	0.6	6.0	1.8	4.2
U.S.	76.4	9.3	2.6	1.9	0.6	0.6	2.8	1.3	4.6

Note: Figures are percentages and cover workers 16 years of age and older; (1) Figures cover the New York-Newark-Jersey City, NY-NJ-PA Metropolitan Statistical Area—see Appendix B for areas included
Source: U.S. Census Bureau, 2012-2016 American Community Survey 5-Year Estimates

Travel Time to Work

Area	Less Than 10 Minutes	10 to 19 Minutes	20 to 29 Minutes	30 to 44 Minutes	45 to 59 Minutes	60 to 89 Minutes	90 Minutes or More
City	7.8	20.2	18.7	27.5	12.3	8.9	4.5
MSA[1]	7.4	19.3	16.4	23.7	12.4	14.4	6.5
U.S.	12.9	29.2	20.9	20.4	8.0	6.0	2.7

Note: Note: Figures are percentages and include workers 16 years old and over; (1) Figures cover the New York-Newark-Jersey City, NY-NJ-PA Metropolitan Statistical Area—see Appendix B for areas included
Source: U.S. Census Bureau, 2012-2016 American Community Survey 5-Year Estimates

Freeway Travel Time Index

Area	1985	1990	1995	2000	2005	2010	2014
Urban Area Rank[1,2]	11	9	8	7	7	8	8
Urban Area Index[1]	1.16	1.20	1.24	1.29	1.33	1.33	1.34
Average Index[3]	1.09	1.11	1.14	1.17	1.20	1.19	1.20

Note: Freeway Travel Time Index—the ratio of travel time in the peak period to the travel time at free-flow conditions. For example, a value of 1.30 indicates a 20-minute free-flow trip takes 26 minutes in the peak (20 minutes x 1.30 = 26 minutes); (1) Covers the New York-Newark NY-NJ-CT urban area; (2) Rank is based on 101 urban areas (#1 = highest travel time index); (3) Average of 101 urban areas
Source: Texas Transportation Institute, 2015 Urban Mobility Scorecard, August 2015

Freeway Commuter Stress Index

Area	1985	1990	1995	2000	2005	2010	2014
Urban Area Rank[1,2]	19	19	13	12	11	11	12
Urban Area Index[1]	1.21	1.24	1.29	1.34	1.38	1.38	1.39
Average Index[3]	1.13	1.16	1.19	1.22	1.25	1.24	1.25

Note: The Freeway Commuter Stress Index is the same as the Freeway Travel Time Index (see table above) except that it includes only the travel in the peak directions during the peak periods; the TTI includes travel in all directions during the peak period. Thus, the CSI is more indicative of the work trip experienced by each commuter on a daily basis; (1) Covers the New York-Newark NY-NJ-CT urban area; (2) Rank is based on 101 urban areas (#1 = highest travel time index); (3) Average of 101 urban areas
Source: Texas Transportation Institute, 2015 Urban Mobility Scorecard, August 2015

Living Environment

COST OF LIVING

Cost of Living Index

Composite Index	Groceries	Housing	Utilities	Transportation	Health Care	Misc. Goods/ Services
122.9	106.7	152.8	115.4	112.7	101.9	112.5

Note: The Cost of Living Index measures regional differences in the cost of consumer goods and services, excluding taxes and non-consumer expenditures, for professional and managerial households in the top income quintile. It is based on more than 50,000 prices covering almost 60 different items for which prices are collected three times a year by chambers of commerce, economic development organizations or university applied economic centers in each participating urban area. The numbers shown should be read as a percentage above or below the national average of 100. For example, a value of 115.4 in the groceries column indicates that grocery prices are 15.4% higher than the national average. Small differences in the index numbers should not be interpreted as significant; Figures cover the Newark-Elizabeth NJ urban area.
Source: The Council for Community and Economic Research, ACCRA Cost of Living Index, 2017

Grocery Prices

Area[1]	T-Bone Steak ($/pound)	Frying Chicken ($/pound)	Whole Milk ($/half gal.)	Eggs ($/dozen)	Orange Juice ($/64 oz.)	Coffee ($/11.5 oz.)
City[2]	11.80	1.69	2.27	1.72	3.04	3.82
Avg.	11.29	1.40	2.02	1.47	3.55	4.37
Min.	7.71	0.93	1.04	0.70	2.86	3.24
Max.	15.83	2.39	4.03	3.92	6.29	8.16

*Note: (1) Values for the local area are compared with the average, minimum and maximum values for all 294 areas in the Cost of Living Index; (2) Figures cover the Newark-Elizabeth NJ urban area; **T-Bone Steak** (price per pound); **Frying Chicken** (price per pound, whole fryer); **Whole Milk** (half gallon carton); **Eggs** (price per dozen, Grade A, large); **Orange Juice** (64 oz. Tropicana or Florida Natural); **Coffee** (11.5 oz. can, vacuum-packed, Maxwell House, Hills Bros, or Folgers).*
Source: The Council for Community and Economic Research, ACCRA Cost of Living Index, 2017

Housing and Utility Costs

Area[1]	New Home Price ($)	Apartment Rent ($/month)	All Electric ($/month)	Part Electric ($/month)	Other Energy ($/month)	Telephone ($/month)
City[2]	507,404	1,663	-	126.69	64.16	33.50
Avg.	335,956	1,047	175.01	97.34	67.93	28.71
Min.	187,788	491	109.48	49.33	35.44	12.39
Max.	1,739,087	4,559	432.62	227.09	353.33	44.61

*Note: (1) Values for the local area are compared with the average, minimum and maximum values for all 294 areas in the Cost of Living Index; (2) Figures cover the Newark-Elizabeth NJ urban area; **New Home Price** (2,400 sf living area, 8,000 sf lot, in urban area with full utilities); **Apartment Rent** (950 sf 2 bedroom/1.5 or 2 bath, unfurnished, excluding all utilities except water); **All Electric** (average monthly cost for an all-electric home); **Part Electric** (average monthly cost for a part-electric home); **Other Energy** (average monthly cost for natural gas, fuel oil, coal, wood, and any other forms of energy except electricity); **Telephone** (price includes basic monthly rate for a private residential line plus additional local usage charges incurred by a family of four).*
Source: The Council for Community and Economic Research, ACCRA Cost of Living Index, 2017

Health Care, Transportation, and Other Costs

Area[1]	Doctor ($/visit)	Dentist ($/visit)	Optometrist ($/visit)	Gasoline ($/gallon)	Beauty Salon ($/visit)	Men's Shirt ($)
City[2]	96.29	99.80	100.58	2.39	37.53	38.16
Avg.	108.00	92.54	101.93	2.25	37.58	30.92
Min.	30.39	60.00	49.75	1.82	16.11	11.20
Max.	193.50	161.94	229.28	3.16	77.35	59.13

*Note: (1) Values for the local area are compared with the average, minimum and maximum values for all 294 areas in the Cost of Living Index; (2) Figures cover the Newark-Elizabeth NJ urban area; **Doctor** (general practitioners routine exam of an established patient); **Dentist** (adult teeth cleaning and periodic oral examination); **Optometrist** (full vision eye exam for established adult patient); **Gasoline** (one gallon regular unleaded, national brand, including all taxes, cash price at self-service pump if available); **Beauty Salon** (woman's shampoo, trim, and blow-dry); **Men's Shirt** (cotton/polyester dress shirt, pinpoint weave, long sleeves).*
Source: The Council for Community and Economic Research, ACCRA Cost of Living Index, 2017

HOUSING

House Price Index (HPI)

Area	National Ranking[2]	Quarterly Change (%)	One-Year Change (%)	Five-Year Change (%)
MD[1]	213	0.97	3.29	14.23
U.S.[3]	–	1.61	6.68	34.71

Note: The HPI is a weighted repeat sales index. It measures average price changes in repeat sales or refinancings on the same properties. This information is obtained by reviewing repeat mortgage transactions on single-family properties whose mortgages have been purchased or securitized by Fannie Mae or Freddie Mac in January 1975; (1) Figures cover the Newark, NJ-PA Metropolitan Division—see Appendix B for areas included; (2) Rankings are based on annual percentage change for all metro areas containing at least 15,000 transactions over the last 10 years and ranges from 1 to 253; (3) figures based on a weighted average of Census Division estimates using a seasonally adjusted, purchase-only index; all figures are for the period ending December 31, 2017

Source: Federal Housing Finance Agency, House Price Index, February 28, 2018

Median Single-Family Home Prices

Area	2015	2016	2017p	Percent Change 2016 to 2017
MD[1]	383.9	374.8	379.3	1.2
U.S. Average	223.9	235.5	248.8	5.6

Note: Figures are median sales prices of existing single-family homes in thousands of dollars; (p) preliminary; (1) Figures cover the Newark, NJ-PA Metropolitan Division—see Appendix B for areas included

Source: National Association of Realtors, Median Sales Price of Existing Single-Family Homes for Metropolitan Areas, 4th Quarter 2017

Qualifying Income Based on Median Sales Price of Existing Single-Family Homes

Area	With 5% Down ($)	With 10% Down ($)	With 20% Down ($)
MD[1]	80,596	76,354	67,870
U.S. Average	55,585	52,659	46,808

Note: Figures are preliminary; Qualifying income is based on a mortgage rate of 4.17%. Monthly principal and interest payment is limited to 25% of income; (1) Figures cover the Newark, NJ-PA Metropolitan Division—see Appendix B for areas included

Source: National Association of Realtors, Qualifying Income Based on Median Sales Price of Existing Single-Family Homes for Metropolitan Areas, 4th Quarter 2017

Median Apartment Condo-Coop Home Prices

Area	2015	2016	2017p	Percent Change 2016 to 2017
MD[1]	261.7	259.3	263.4	1.6
U.S. Average	210.7	220.7	234.3	6.2

Note: Figures are median sales prices of existing apartment condo-coop homes in thousands of dollars; (p) preliminary; (1) Figures cover the Newark, NJ-PA Metropolitan Division—see Appendix B for areas included

Source: National Association of Realtors, Median Sales Price of Existing Apartment Condo-Coop Homes for Metropolitan Areas, 4th Quarter 2017

Home Value Distribution

Area	Under $50,000	$50,000 -$99,999	$100,000 -$149,999	$150,000 -$199,999	$200,000 -$299,999	$300,000 -$499,999	$500,000 -$999,999	$1,000,000 or more
City	1.4	0.4	1.6	3.1	25.6	37.3	30.0	0.7
MSA[1]	2.8	1.8	2.9	5.0	16.2	37.0	26.9	7.3
U.S.	8.8	14.8	15.3	14.9	18.4	16.4	9.0	2.5

Note: Figures are percentages and cover owner-occupied housing units; (1) Figures cover the New York-Newark-Jersey City, NY-NJ-PA Metropolitan Statistical Area—see Appendix B for areas included

Source: U.S. Census Bureau, 2012-2016 American Community Survey 5-Year Estimates

Homeownership Rate

Area	2009 (%)	2010 (%)	2011 (%)	2012 (%)	2013 (%)	2014 (%)	2015 (%)	2016 (%)	2017 (%)
MSA[1]	51.7	51.6	50.9	51.5	50.6	50.7	49.9	50.4	49.9
U.S.	67.4	66.9	66.1	65.4	65.1	64.5	63.7	63.4	63.9

Note: (1) Figures cover the New York-Newark-Jersey City, NY-NJ-PA Metropolitan Statistical Area—see Appendix B for areas included

Source: U.S. Census Bureau, Housing Vacancies and Homeownership Annual Statistics: 2009-2017

Year Housing Structure Built

Area	2010 or Later	2000 -2009	1990 -1999	1980 -1989	1970 -1979	1960 -1969	1950 -1959	1940 -1949	Before 1940	Median Year
City	3.3	6.8	17.1	30.6	21.4	8.6	6.8	1.6	3.8	1983
MSA[1]	1.3	7.2	6.1	7.9	10.0	13.8	16.2	9.1	28.3	1958
U.S.	2.3	14.7	14.0	13.7	15.6	10.9	10.6	5.2	13.0	1977

Note: Figures are percentages except for Median Year; Note: (1) Figures cover the New York-Newark-Jersey City, NY-NJ-PA Metropolitan Statistical Area—see Appendix B for areas included
Source: U.S. Census Bureau, 2012-2016 American Community Survey 5-Year Estimates

Gross Monthly Rent

Area	Under $500	$500 -$999	$1,000 -$1,499	$1,500 -$1,999	$2,000 -$2,499	$2,500 -$2,999	$3,000 and up	Median ($)
City	0.5	1.2	52.2	26.9	13.8	1.6	3.9	1,445
MSA[1]	9.7	18.7	35.2	19.8	8.3	3.8	4.5	1,297
U.S.	11.3	43.3	27.7	10.7	4.0	1.6	1.5	949

Note: Figures are percentages except for Median; Gross rent is the contract rent plus the estimated average monthly cost of utilities (electricity, gas, and water and sewer) and fuels (oil, coal, kerosene, wood, etc.) if these are paid by the renter (or paid for the renter by someone else); (1) Figures cover the New York-Newark-Jersey City, NY-NJ-PA Metropolitan Statistical Area—see Appendix B for areas included
Source: U.S. Census Bureau, 2012-2016 American Community Survey 5-Year Estimates

HEALTH

Health Risk Factors

Category	MD[1] (%)	U.S. (%)
Adults aged 18–64 who have any kind of health care coverage	86.9	87.7
Adults who reported being in good or excellent health	84.4	83.6
Adults who are current smokers	12.2	17.1
Adults who currently use E-cigarettes	2.7	4.7
Adults who currently use chewing tobacco, snuff, or snus	2.2	4.0
Adults who are heavy drinkers[2]	5.5	6.5
Adults who are binge drinkers[3]	16.2	16.9
Adults who are overweight (BMI 25.0 - 29.9)	39.7	35.3
Adults who are obese (BMI 30.0 - 99.8)	23.1	29.9
Adults who participated in any physical activities in the past month	72.8	76.9
Adults who always or nearly always wears a seat belt	95.8	94.3

Note: (1) Figures cover the Newark, NJ-PA Metropolitan Division—see Appendix B for areas included; (2) Heavy drinkers are classified as adult men having more than 14 drinks per week and adult women having more than 7 drinks per week; (3) Binge drinkers are classified as males having five or more drinks on one occasion or females having four or more drinks on one occasion
Source: Centers for Disease Control and Prevention, Behaviorial Risk Factor Surveillance System, SMART: Selected Metropolitan Area Risk Trends, 2016

Health Screening Rates

Category	MD[1] (%)	U.S. (%)
Adults 50-75 who have had a blood stool test within the past year	7.3	8.0
Adults 50-75 who have had a colonoscopy in the past 10 years	61.1	63.5
Adults aged 65+ who have had flu shot within the past year	58.5	58.6
Adults aged 65+ who have ever had a pneumonia vaccination	64.6	73.4
Adults who have ever been tested for HIV	44.0	35.6
Women aged 21-65 who have had a pap test in the past three years	84.9	79.8
Men aged 40+ who have had a PSA test within the past two years	48.5	39.5
Women aged 40+ who have had a mammogram within the past two years	79.8	72.5

Note: n/a not available; (1) Figures cover the Newark, NJ-PA Metropolitan Division—see Appendix B for areas included; Source: Centers for Disease Control and Prevention, Behaviorial Risk Factor Surveillance System, SMART: Selected Metropolitan Area Risk Trends, 2016

Chronic Health Conditions

Category	MD[1] (%)	U.S. (%)
Adults who have ever been told they had a heart attack	3.7	4.4
Adults who have ever been told they have angina or coronary heart disease	3.7	4.1
Adults who have ever been told they had a stroke	2.0	3.1
Adults who have been told they currently have asthma	7.2	9.3
Adults who have ever been told they have arthritis	22.1	25.8
Adults who have ever been told they have diabetes[2]	9.6	10.5
Adults who have ever been told they had skin cancer	4.1	5.9
Adults who have ever been told they had any other types of cancer	5.4	6.7
Adults who have ever been told they have COPD	5.3	6.3
Adults who have ever been told they have kidney disease	2.8	2.8
Adults who have ever been told they have a form of depression	11.6	17.4

Note: (1) Figures cover the Newark, NJ-PA Metropolitan Division—see Appendix B for areas included; (2) Figures do not include pregnancy-related, borderline, or pre-diabetes
Source: Centers for Disease Control and Prevention, Behaviorial Risk Factor Surveillance System, SMART: Selected Metropolitan Area Risk Trends, 2016

Mortality Rates for the Top 10 Causes of Death in the U.S.

ICD-10[a] Sub-Chapter	ICD-10[a] Code	Age-Adjusted Mortality Rate[1] per 100,000 population	
		County[2]	U.S.
Malignant neoplasms	C00-C97	136.7	158.5
Ischaemic heart diseases	I20-I25	75.0	96.8
Other forms of heart disease	I30-I51	48.1	52.4
Chronic lower respiratory diseases	J40-J47	24.6	40.9
Cerebrovascular diseases	I60-I69	29.1	37.2
Organic, including symptomatic, mental disorders	F01-F09	31.7	33.3
Other degenerative diseases of the nervous system	G30-G31	20.5	32.1
Other external causes of accidental injury	W00-X59	21.5	31.2
Diabetes mellitus	E10-E14	14.9	21.1
Hypertensive diseases	I10-I15	15.1	20.8

Note: (a) ICD-10 = International Classification of Diseases 10th Revision; (1) Mortality rates are a three year average covering 2014-2016; (2) Figures cover Somerset County.
Source: Centers for Disease Control and Prevention, National Center for Health Statistics. Underlying Cause of Death 1999-2016 on CDC WONDER Online Database, released December 2017

Mortality Rates for Selected Causes of Death

ICD-10[a] Sub-Chapter	ICD-10[a] Code	Age-Adjusted Mortality Rate[1] per 100,000 population	
		County[2]	U.S.
Assault	X85-Y09	Unreliable	5.6
Diseases of the liver	K70-K76	7.9	14.0
Human immunodeficiency virus (HIV) disease	B20-B24	Unreliable	1.9
Influenza and pneumonia	J09-J18	11.0	14.6
Intentional self-harm	X60-X84	6.6	13.2
Malnutrition	E40-E46	Unreliable	1.3
Obesity and other hyperalimentation	E65-E68	Unreliable	2.1
Renal failure	N17-N19	10.4	13.0
Transport accidents	V01-V99	5.7	12.0
Viral hepatitis	B15-B19	Suppressed	1.9

Note: (a) ICD-10 = International Classification of Diseases 10th Revision; (1) Mortality rates are a three year average covering 2014-2016; (2) Figures cover Somerset County; Data are Suppressed when the data meet the criteria for confidentiality constraints; Mortality rates are flagged as Unreliable when the rate would be calculated with a numerator of 20 or less.
Source: Centers for Disease Control and Prevention, National Center for Health Statistics. Underlying Cause of Death 1999-2016 on CDC WONDER Online Database, released December 2017

Health Insurance Coverage

Area	With Health Insurance	With Private Health Insurance	With Public Health Insurance	Without Health Insurance	Population Under Age 18 Without Health Insurance
City	95.4	88.9	14.6	4.6	3.2
MSA[1]	89.8	65.8	33.7	10.2	3.6
U.S.	88.3	66.7	33.0	11.7	5.9

Note: Figures are percentages that cover the civilian noninstitutionalized population; (1) Figures cover the New York-Newark-Jersey City, NY-NJ-PA Metropolitan Statistical Area—see Appendix B for areas included
Source: U.S. Census Bureau, 2012-2016 American Community Survey 5-Year Estimates

Number of Medical Professionals

Area	MDs[3]	DOs[3,4]	Dentists	Podiatrists	Chiropractors	Optometrists
County[1] (number)	1,474	99	318	24	99	54
County[1] (rate[2])	442.1	29.7	95.1	7.2	29.6	16.1
U.S. (rate[2])	276.5	22.3	67.3	6.0	26.7	15.9

Note: Data as of 2016 unless noted; (1) Data covers Somerset County; (2) Rate per 100,000 population; (3) Data as of 2015 and includes all active, non-federal physicians; (4) Doctor of Osteopathic Medicine
Source: U.S. Department of Health and Human Services, Health Resources and Services Administration, Bureau of Health Professions, Area Resource File (ARF) 2016-2017

Best Hospitals

According to *U.S. News,* the Newark, NJ-PA metro area is home to two of the best hospitals in the U.S.: **Kessler Institute for Rehabilitation** (1 adult specialty); **Morristown Medical Center** (2 adult specialties). The hospitals listed were nationally ranked in at least one of 16 specialties. Only 152 hospitals nationwide were nationally ranked in one or more specialties. Twenty hospitals in the U.S. made the Honor Roll. The Best Hospitals Honor Roll was revamped last year to take both the national rankings and the procedure and condition ratings into account. Hospitals received points if they were nationally ranked in one of the 16 specialties—the higher they ranked, the more points they got—and how many ratings of "high performing" they earned in the nine procedures and conditions. *U.S. News Online, "America's Best Hospitals 2017-18"*

EDUCATION

Public School District Statistics

District Name	Schls	Pupils	Pupil/ Teacher Ratio	Minority Pupils[1] (%)	Free Lunch Eligible[2] (%)	IEP[3] (%)
Hillsborough Township Public SD	9	7,318	11.0	36.3	6.5	18.3

Note: Table includes school districts with 100 or more students; (1) Percentage of students that are not non-Hispanic white; (2) Percentage of students that are eligible for the free lunch program; (3) Percentage of students that have an Individualized Education Program.
Source: U.S. Department of Education, National Center for Education Statistics, Common Core of Data, Local Education Agency (School District) Universe Survey: School Year 2015-2016; U.S. Department of Education, National Center for Education Statistics, Common Core of Data, Public Elementary/Secondary School Universe Survey: School Year 2015-2016

Highest Level of Education

Area	Less than H.S.	H.S. Diploma	Some College, No Deg.	Associate Degree	Bachelor's Degree	Master's Degree	Prof. School Degree	Doctorate Degree
City	2.5	20.8	14.0	6.8	34.5	16.5	2.5	2.4
MSA[1]	14.3	25.3	15.5	6.7	22.3	11.3	3.0	1.5
U.S.	13.0	27.5	21.0	8.2	18.8	8.2	2.0	1.3

Note: Figures cover persons age 25 and over; (1) Figures cover the New York-Newark-Jersey City, NY-NJ-PA Metropolitan Statistical Area—see Appendix B for areas included
Source: U.S. Census Bureau, 2012-2016 American Community Survey 5-Year Estimates

Educational Attainment by Race

Area	High School Graduate or Higher (%)					Bachelor's Degree or Higher (%)				
	Total	White	Black	Asian	Hisp.[2]	Total	White	Black	Asian	Hisp.[2]
City	97.5	97.7	96.9	97.3	93.5	55.9	50.9	55.3	81.8	30.2
MSA[1]	85.7	90.0	84.1	82.9	68.9	38.1	43.2	23.8	53.1	17.7
U.S.	87.0	88.9	84.3	86.3	65.7	30.3	31.6	20.0	52.1	14.7

Note: Figures shown cover persons 25 years old and over; (1) Figures cover the New York-Newark-Jersey City, NY-NJ-PA Metropolitan Statistical Area—see Appendix B for areas included; (2) People of Hispanic origin can be of any race
Source: U.S. Census Bureau, 2012-2016 American Community Survey 5-Year Estimates

School Enrollment by Grade and Control

Area	Preschool (%)		Kindergarten (%)		Grades 1 - 4 (%)		Grades 5 - 8 (%)		Grades 9 - 12 (%)	
	Public	Private	Public	Private	Public	Private	Public	Private	Public	Private
City	38.2	61.8	80.2	19.8	93.9	6.1	90.8	9.2	90.9	9.1
MSA[1]	51.9	48.1	81.6	18.4	86.1	13.9	86.3	13.7	85.9	14.1
U.S.	58.4	41.6	87.7	12.3	89.8	10.2	89.7	10.3	90.4	9.6

Note: Figures shown cover persons 3 years old and over; (1) Figures cover the New York-Newark-Jersey City, NY-NJ-PA Metropolitan Statistical Area—see Appendix B for areas included
Source: U.S. Census Bureau, 2012-2016 American Community Survey 5-Year Estimates

Average Salaries of Public School Classroom Teachers

Area	2015		2016		Change from 2015 to 2016	
	Dollars	Rank[1]	Dollars	Rank[1]	Percent	Rank[2]
New Jersey	69,038	6	69,330	6	0.4	41
U.S. Average	57,611	–	58,353	–	1.3	–

Note: (1) Rank ranges from 1 to 51 where 1 indicates highest salary; (2) Rank ranges from 1 to 51 where 1 indicates highest percent change.
Source: National Education Association, Rankings & Estimates: Rankings of the States 2016 and Estimates of School Statistics 2017

Higher Education

Four-Year Colleges			Two-Year Colleges			Medical Schools[1]	Law Schools[2]	Voc/ Tech[3]
Public	Private Non-profit	Private For-profit	Public	Private Non-profit	Private For-profit			
0	0	0	0	0	0	0	0	0

Note: Figures cover institutions located within the city limits and include main campuses only; (1) includes schools accredited by the Liaison Committee on Medical Education and the American Osteopathic Association's Commission on Osteopathic College Accreditation; (2) includes ABA-accredited schools, schools with provisional ABA accreditation, and state accredited schools; (3) includes all schools with programs that are less than 2 years.
Source: National Center for Education Statistics, Integrated Postsecondary Education System (IPEDS), 2016-17; Wikipedia, List of Medical Schools in the United States, accessed April 2, 2018; Wikipedia, List of Law Schools in the United States, accessed April 2, 2018

According to *U.S. News & World Report,* the Newark, NJ-PA metro division is home to four of the best national universities in the U.S.: **Seton Hall University** (#124 tie); **Rutgers University—Newark** (#133 tie); **New Jersey Institute of Technology** (#140 tie); **Montclair State University** (#187 tie). The indicators used to capture academic quality fall into a number of categories: assessment by administrators at peer institutions; retention of students; faculty resources; student selectivity; financial resources; alumni giving; high school counselor ratings of colleges; and graduation rate. *U.S. News & World Report, "America's Best Colleges 2018"*

According to *U.S. News & World Report,* the Newark, NJ-PA metro division is home to one of the best liberal arts colleges in the U.S.: **Drew University** (#112 tie). The indicators used to capture academic quality fall into a number of categories: assessment by administrators at peer institutions; retention of students; faculty resources; student selectivity; financial resources; alumni giving; high school counselor ratings of colleges; and graduation rate. *U.S. News & World Report, "America's Best Colleges 2018"*

According to *U.S. News & World Report,* the Newark, NJ-PA metro division is home to two of the top 100 law schools in the U.S.: **Seton Hall University** (#59 tie); **Rutgers—The State University of New Jersey** (#74 tie). The rankings are based on a weighted average of 12 measures of quality: peer assessment score; assessment score by lawyers/judges; median LSAT scores; median undergrad GPA; acceptance rate; employment rates for graduates; placement success; bar passage rate; faculty resources; expenditures per student; student/faculty ratio; and library resources. *U.S. News & World Report, "America's Best Graduate Schools, Law, 2019"*

According to *U.S. News & World Report,* the Newark, NJ-PA metro division is home to one of the top 75 business schools in the U.S.: **Rutgers—The State University of New Jersey-Newark and New Brunswick** (#44 tie). The rankings are based on a weighted average of the following nine measures: quality assessment; peer assessment; recruiter assessment; placement success; mean starting salary and bonus; student selectivity; mean GMAT and GRE scores; mean undergraduate GPA; and acceptance rate. *U.S. News & World Report, "America's Best Graduate Schools, Business, 2019"*

PRESIDENTIAL ELECTION

2016 Presidential Election Results

Area	Clinton	Trump	Johnson	Stein	Other
Somerset County	54.5	41.7	2.4	1.0	0.4
U.S.	48.0	45.9	3.3	1.1	1.7

Note: Results are percentages and may not add to 100% due to rounding
Source: Dave Leip's Atlas of U.S. Presidential Elections

EMPLOYERS

Major Employers

Company Name	Industry
American Express Company	Personal credit institutions
American International Group	Life insurance
Deloitte Consulting	Management consulting services
Hackensack University Medical Center	University
Merrill Lynch and Co	Security brokers & dealers
Mount Sinai Hospital	General medical & surgical hospitals
Mount Sinai School of Medicine	Medical training services
NewYork-Presbyterian Hospital	General medical & surgical hospitals
NYC Health and Hospitals Corp	Psychiatric hospitals
NYU School of Medicine	Offices & clinics of medical doctors
Paramount Comm Acq Corp	Investment holding companies, except banks
Patriarch Partners	Investment offices
Rutgers, The State Univ of NJ	Colleges & universities
Standard Americas	Agencies of foreign banks
The Long Island Rail Road Company	Local & suburban transit
U of Med and Dentistry of NJ	Colleges & universities
UMASS Memorial Health Care	Psychiatrist
United States Postal Service	U.S. postal service
Wellchoice	Health insurance carriers

Note: Companies shown are located within the New York-Newark-Jersey City, NY-NJ-PA Metropolitan Statistical Area.
Source: Hoovers.com; Wikipedia

PUBLIC SAFETY

Crime Rate

Area	All Crimes	Violent Crimes				Property Crimes		
		Murder	Rape[3]	Robbery	Aggrav. Assault	Burglary	Larceny -Theft	Motor Vehicle Theft
City	694.4	0.0	25.0	5.0	7.5	124.9	514.5	17.5
Metro[1]	1,683.1	6.0	16.9	134.2	126.5	248.6	943.7	207.1
U.S.	2,847.8	5.3	40.4	102.8	248.5	468.9	1,745.0	236.9

Note: Figures are crimes per 100,000 population; (1) Figures cover the Newark, NJ-PA Metropolitan Division—see Appendix B for areas included; (3) The city and U.S. figures shown were reported using the revised Uniform Crime Reporting (UCR) definition of rape. The metro area figures shown are an aggregate total of the data submitted using both the revised and legacy UCR definitions.
Source: FBI Uniform Crime Reports, 2016

Hate Crimes

Area	Number of Quarters Reported	Number of Incidents per Bias Motivation					
		Race/Ethnicity/ Ancestry	Religion	Sexual Orientation	Disability	Gender	Gender Identity
Area[1]	2	1	0	0	0	0	0
U.S.	4	3,489	1,273	1,076	70	31	124

Note: (1) Figures cover the Hillsborough Township.
Source: Federal Bureau of Investigation, Hate Crime Statistics 2016

Identity Theft Consumer Reports

Area	Reports	Reports per 100,000 Population	Rank[2]
MSA[1]	23,624	117	64
U.S.	371,061	114	-

Note: (1) Figures cover the New York-Newark-Jersey City, NY-NJ-PA Metropolitan Statistical Area—see Appendix B for areas included; (2) Rank ranges from 1 to 389 where 1 indicates greatest number of identity theft reports per 100,000 population
Source: Federal Trade Commission, Consumer Sentinel Network Data Book for January–December 2017

Fraud and Other Consumer Reports

Area	Reports	Reports per 100,000 Population	Rank[2]
MSA[1]	90,589	449	173
U.S.	2,304,550	708	-

Note: (1) Figures cover the New York-Newark-Jersey City, NY-NJ-PA Metropolitan Statistical Area—see Appendix B for areas included; (2) Rank ranges from 1 to 389 where 1 indicates greatest number of fraud and other consumer reports per 100,000 population
Source: Federal Trade Commission, Consumer Sentinel Network Data Book for January–December 2017

SPORTS

Professional Sports Teams

Team Name	League	Year Established
Brooklyn Nets	National Basketball Association (NBA)	1967
New Jersey Devils	National Hockey League (NHL)	1982
New York City FC	Major League Soccer (MLS)	2015
New York Giants	National Football League (NFL)	1925
New York Islanders	National Hockey League (NHL)	1972
New York Jets	National Football League (NFL)	1960
New York Knicks	National Basketball Association (NBA)	1946
New York Mets	Major League Baseball (MLB)	1962
New York Rangers	National Hockey League (NHL)	1926
New York Red Bulls	Major League Soccer (MLS)	1996
New York Yankees	Major League Baseball (MLB)	1903

Note: Includes teams located in the New York-Newark-Jersey City, NY-NJ-PA Metropolitan Statistical Area.
Source: Wikipedia, Major Professional Sports Teams of the United States and Canada, April 5, 2018

CLIMATE

Average and Extreme Temperatures

Temperature	Jan	Feb	Mar	Apr	May	Jun	Jul	Aug	Sep	Oct	Nov	Dec	Yr.
Extreme High (°F)	68	75	85	96	97	101	104	99	99	88	81	72	104
Average High (°F)	38	41	50	61	72	80	85	84	76	65	54	43	62
Average Temp. (°F)	32	34	43	53	63	72	77	76	68	58	48	37	55
Average Low (°F)	26	27	35	44	54	63	68	67	60	49	41	31	47
Extreme Low (°F)	-2	-2	8	21	36	46	53	50	40	29	17	-1	-2

Note: Figures cover the years 1962-1992
Source: National Climatic Data Center, International Station Meteorological Climate Summary, 9/96

Average Precipitation/Snowfall/Humidity

Precip./Humidity	Jan	Feb	Mar	Apr	May	Jun	Jul	Aug	Sep	Oct	Nov	Dec	Yr.
Avg. Precip. (in.)	3.5	3.1	4.0	3.9	4.5	3.8	4.5	4.1	4.1	3.3	4.5	3.8	47.0
Avg. Snowfall (in.)	7	8	4	Tr	Tr	0	0	0	0	Tr	Tr	3	23
Avg. Rel. Hum. 7am (%)	67	67	66	64	72	74	74	76	78	75	72	69	71
Avg. Rel. Hum. 4pm (%)	55	53	50	45	52	55	53	54	56	55	57	58	53

Note: Figures cover the years 1962-1992; Tr = Trace amounts (<0.05 in. of rain; <0.5 in. of snow)
Source: National Climatic Data Center, International Station Meteorological Climate Summary, 9/96

Weather Conditions

Temperature			Daytime Sky			Precipitation		
32°F & below	45°F & below	90°F & above	Clear	Partly cloudy	Cloudy	0.01 inch or more precip.	0.1 inch or more snow/ice	Thunder-storms
75	170	18	85	166	114	120	11	20

Note: Figures are average number of days per year and cover the years 1962-1992
Source: National Climatic Data Center, International Station Meteorological Climate Summary, 9/96

HAZARDOUS WASTE

Superfund Sites

The Newark, NJ-PA metro division is home to 31 sites on the EPA's Superfund National Priorities List: **A. O. Polymer** (final); **American Cyanamid Co** (final); **Brook Industrial Park** (final); **Caldwell Trucking Co.** (final); **Chemical Control** (final); **Combe Fill South Landfill** (final); **Curtis Specialty Papers, Inc** (final); **Dayco Corp./L.e Carpenter Co.** (final); **De Rewal Chemical Co.** (final); **Diamond Alkali Co.** (final); **Dover Municipal Well 4** (final); **Higgins Disposal** (final); **Higgins Farm** (final); **LCP Chemicals Inc.** (final); **Mansfield Trail Dump** (final); **Metaltec/Aerosystems** (final); **Montgomery Township Housing Development** (final); **Myers Property** (final); **Orange Valley Regional Ground Water Contamination** (final); **Picatinny Arsenal (USARMY)** (final); **Pierson's Creek** (final); **Radiation Technology, Inc.** (final); **Riverside Industrial Park** (final); **Rockaway Borough Well Field** (final); **Rockaway Township Wells** (final); **Rocky Hill Municipal Well** (final); **Rolling Knolls Lf** (final); **Sharkey Landfill** (final); **U.S. Radium Corp.** (final); **Unimatic Manufacturing Corporation** (final); **White Chemical Corp.** (final). There are a total of 1,396 Superfund sites with a status of proposed or final on the list in the U.S. *U.S. Environmental Protection Agency, National Priorities List, April 4, 2018*

AIR & WATER QUALITY

Air Quality Trends: Ozone

	1990	1995	2000	2005	2010	2012	2013	2014	2015	2016
MSA[1]	0.101	0.106	0.090	0.091	0.081	0.079	0.071	0.069	0.075	0.073
U.S.	0.087	0.089	0.081	0.079	0.073	0.075	0.069	0.067	0.068	0.069

Note: (1) Data covers the New York-Newark-Jersey City, NY-NJ-PA Metropolitan Statistical Area—see Appendix B for areas included. The values shown are the composite ozone concentration averages among trend sites based on the highest fourth daily maximum 8-hour concentration in parts per million. These trends are based on sites having an adequate record of monitoring data during the trend period. Data from exceptional events are included.
Source: U.S. Environmental Protection Agency, Air Quality Monitoring Information, "Air Quality Trends by City, 1990-2016"

Air Quality Index

Area	Percent of Days when Air Quality was...[2]					AQI Statistics[2]	
	Good	Moderate	Unhealthy for Sensitive Groups	Unhealthy	Very Unhealthy	Maximum	Median
MSA[1]	42.2	52.6	4.7	0.5	0.0	159	52

Note: (1) Data covers the New York-Newark-Jersey City, NY-NJ-PA Metropolitan Statistical Area—see Appendix B for areas included; (2) Based on 365 days with AQI data in 2017. Air Quality Index (AQI) is an index for reporting daily air quality. EPA calculates the AQI for five major air pollutants regulated by the Clean Air Act: ground-level ozone, particle pollution (aka particulate matter), carbon monoxide, sulfur dioxide, and nitrogen dioxide. The AQI runs from 0 to 500. The higher the AQI value, the greater the level of air pollution and the greater the health concern. There are six AQI categories: "Good" AQI is between 0 and 50. Air quality is considered satisfactory; "Moderate" AQI is between 51 and 100. Air quality is acceptable; "Unhealthy for Sensitive Groups" When AQI values are between 101 and 150, members of sensitive groups may experience health effects; "Unhealthy" When AQI values are between 151 and 200 everyone may begin to experience health effects; "Very Unhealthy" AQI values between 201 and 300 trigger a health alert; "Hazardous" AQI values over 300 trigger warnings of emergency conditions (not shown).
Source: U.S. Environmental Protection Agency, Air Quality Index Report, 2017

Air Quality Index Pollutants

Area	Percent of Days when AQI Pollutant was...[2]					
	Carbon Monoxide	Nitrogen Dioxide	Ozone	Sulfur Dioxide	Particulate Matter 2.5	Particulate Matter 10
MSA[1]	0.0	13.2	31.8	0.0	55.1	0.0

Note: (1) Data covers the New York-Newark-Jersey City, NY-NJ-PA Metropolitan Statistical Area—see Appendix B for areas included; (2) Based on 365 days with AQI data in 2017. The Air Quality Index (AQI) is an index for reporting daily air quality. EPA calculates the AQI for five major air pollutants regulated by the Clean Air Act: ground-level ozone, particle pollution (also known as particulate matter), carbon monoxide, sulfur dioxide, and nitrogen dioxide. The AQI runs from 0 to 500. The higher the AQI value, the greater the level of air pollution and the greater the health concern.
Source: U.S. Environmental Protection Agency, Air Quality Index Report, 2017

Maximum Air Pollutant Concentrations: Particulate Matter, Ozone, CO and Lead

	Particulate Matter 10 (ug/m^3)	Particulate Matter 2.5 Wtd AM (ug/m^3)	Particulate Matter 2.5 24-Hr (ug/m^3)	Ozone (ppm)	Carbon Monoxide (ppm)	Lead (ug/m^3)
MSA[1] Level	33	9.2	20	0.078	3	0.03
NAAQS[2]	150	15	35	0.075	9	0.15
Met NAAQS[2]	Yes	Yes	Yes	No	Yes	Yes

Note: (1) Data covers the New York-Newark-Jersey City, NY-NJ-PA Metropolitan Statistical Area—see Appendix B for areas included; Data from exceptional events are included; (2) National Ambient Air Quality Standards; ppm = parts per million; ug/m^3 = micrograms per cubic meter; n/a not available.
Concentrations: Particulate Matter 10 (coarse particulate)—highest second maximum 24-hour concentration; Particulate Matter 2.5 Wtd AM (fine particulate)—highest weighted annual mean concentration; Particulate Matter 2.5 24-Hour (fine particulate)—highest 98th percentile 24-hour concentration; Ozone—highest fourth daily maximum 8-hour concentration; Carbon Monoxide—highest second maximum non-overlapping 8-hour concentration; Lead—maximum running 3-month average
Source: U.S. Environmental Protection Agency, Air Quality Monitoring Information, "Air Quality Statistics by City, 2016"

Maximum Air Pollutant Concentrations: Nitrogen Dioxide and Sulfur Dioxide

	Nitrogen Dioxide AM (ppb)	Nitrogen Dioxide 1-Hr (ppb)	Sulfur Dioxide AM (ppb)	Sulfur Dioxide 1-Hr (ppb)	Sulfur Dioxide 24-Hr (ppb)
MSA[1] Level	20	60	n/a	7	n/a
NAAQS[2]	53	100	30	75	140
Met NAAQS[2]	Yes	Yes	n/a	Yes	n/a

Note: (1) Data covers the New York-Newark-Jersey City, NY-NJ-PA Metropolitan Statistical Area—see Appendix B for areas included; Data from exceptional events are included; (2) National Ambient Air Quality Standards; ppm = parts per million; ug/m^3 = micrograms per cubic meter; n/a not available.
Concentrations: Nitrogen Dioxide AM—highest arithmetic mean concentration; Nitrogen Dioxide 1-Hr—highest 98th percentile 1-hour daily maximum concentration; Sulfur Dioxide AM—highest annual mean concentration; Sulfur Dioxide 1-Hr—highest 99th percentile 1-hour daily maximum concentration; Sulfur Dioxide 24-Hr—highest second maximum 24-hour concentration
Source: U.S. Environmental Protection Agency, Air Quality Monitoring Information, "Air Quality Statistics by City, 2016"

Drinking Water

Water System Name	Pop. Served	Primary Water Source Type	Violations[1]	
			Health Based	Monitoring/ Reporting
NJ American Water Co.	n/a	n/a	n/a	n/a

Note: (1) Based on violation data from January 1, 2017 to December 31, 2017; n/a not available
Source: U.S. Environmental Protection Agency, Office of Ground Water and Drinking Water, Safe Drinking Water Information System (based on data extracted April 5, 2018)

Marlboro, New Jersey

Background

Marlboro rests 43 miles south of New York City in Monmouth County and less than 18 miles west of the Jersey shore, making it accessible to both a bustling urban center and peaceful seaside recreational opportunities.

The Township was established in 1848, largely as a farming community. From its earliest settlements until fairly recently, Marlboro was a rural community composed of a number of small hamlets. Although each had small inns or taverns, the hub of activity centered around what is still referred to today as Marlboro Village. Historical research reveals that the name came from the discovery of marl on a farm just east of the village in 1768. Marl, composed of the remains of prehistoric fish, clams, etc., dates back to the period when New Jersey was part of the ocean bed. Farmers used the heavily demanded marl to improve the soil in the days before commercial fertilizers, and the export of marl to all parts of the country became one of Marlboro's first industries.

During the Revolutionary War, Marlboro was the scene of many skirmishes between British and American forces. When retreating from the Battle of Monmouth in 1778, the British troops passed through Marlboro on their way to ships at nearby Sandy Hook. They were attacked by American militiamen who mobilized along their route.

Today, Marlboro is a largely residential suburban community which, although surrounded by urban sprawl, continues to encourage reclamation of its remaining open spaces. The now 415-acre Big Brook Park, once part of the Marlboro State Hospital facility, was acquired by the county to help protect the Navesink Watershed. This protected open space is adjacent to Camp Arrowhead Reserves, and includes a piece of the Henry Hudson Trail along its westerly edge.

In 2004, Marlboro Township launched an education and government television station. Informational and educational programming, produced by Marlboro Township, can be seen in households throughout the municipality. The video messaging system features public information from the Township, the Board of Education, and local not-for-profit entities.

The school systems in Marlboro offer several innovative opportunities. The Marlboro Early Learning Center serves all pre-school handicapped, as well as all kindergarten children in the district. Students in grades one through five attend one of five elementary schools in the district. A district wide approach to curriculum development results in a common and equal teaching guide in all the schools. Each school, however, is unique in its implementation of the curricula.

The district's newest school, finished in 2003, Marlboro Memorial Middle School houses all students in the sixth through eighth grades. Seventh and eighth grade students are offered an Enrichment Opportunity Period, which enables them to select several electives throughout the year.

The marl that gave the township its name have played a major role in preserving fossils in the area. Marlboro is regarded as one of the top three dinosaur fossil sites in the state. Multiple dinosaur finds have been found in this area. In 2009, a leg section from a duckbilled dinosaur called a hadrosaur was found. The first dinosaur discovery in North America was made in 1858 in this area. Several bones from a Mastodon were found in 2009 by an individual fossil hunting.

Marlboro Township has a humid sub-tropical climate placing it in Zone 7B on the USDA hardiness scale. This extends from Monmouth County, NJ to Northern Georgia. Because of its sheltered location and proximity to the Atlantic Ocean, some Palm trees can survive with minimal winter protection. Also, many Southern Magnolias, Crepe Myrtles, Musa Basjoo (Hardy Japanese Banana plants), native bamboo, native opuntia cactus, and bald cypress can be seen throughout commercial and private landscapes.

Rankings

General Rankings

- New York* was identified as one of America's fastest-growing cities in terms of population growth by CNNMoney.com. The area ranked #1 out of 10. Criteria: population growth between July 2015 and July 2016; cities and towns with populations of 50,000. *CNNMoney, "10 Fastest-Growing Cities," June 2, 2017*

Business/Finance Rankings

- The personal finance site NerdWallet analyzed 183 American metropolitan areas with populations over 250,000 and more than 15,000 businesses to rank where entrepreneurs find the most success. Criteria included area economy, annual income, housing cost, unemployment rate, and the success rate of area businesses. New York* ranked #32. *www.nerdwallet.com, "Best Places to Start a Business," April 27, 2015*

- Metro areas with the largest gap in income between rich and poor residents were identified by 24/7 Wall Street using the U.S. Census Bureau's 2013 American Community Survey. The New York* metro area placed #7 among metro areas with the widest wealth gap between rich and poor. *247wallst.com, "20 Cities with the Widest Gap between the Rich and Poor," July 8, 2015*

- In a survey of economic confidence in the nation's 50 largest metropolitan areas conducted January–December 2014, the New York* metro area placed #23, according to Gallup's 2014 Economic Confidence Index. *Gallup, "San Jose and San Francisco Lead in Economic Confidence," March 19, 2015*

- The Brookings Institution ranked the 100 largest metro areas in the U.S. based on income inequality. New York* was ranked #2 (#1 = greatest ineqality). Criteria: the "95/20 ratio," a figure representing the income at which a household earns more than 95 percent of all other households, divided by the income at which a household earns more than only 20 percent of all other households. *Brookings Institution, "Household Income Inequality, 100 Largest U.S. Metro Areas, 2014-2016," February 5, 2018*

- Payscale.com ranked the largest metro areas in terms of wage growth. The New York* metro area ranked #1. Criteria: private-sector wage growth between the 4th quarter of 2016 and the 4th quarter of 2017. *PayScale, "Wage Trends by Metro Area-4th Quarter," January 17, 2018*

- The New York* metro area was identified as one of the most debt-ridden places in America by the finance site Credit.com. The metro area was ranked #3. Criteria: residents' average credit card debt as well as median income. *Credit.com, "25 Cities With the Most Credit Card Debt," February 28, 2018*

- New York* was identified as one of America's most frugal metro areas by *Coupons.com.* The city ranked #15 out of 25. Criteria: digital coupon usage. *Coupons.com, "America's Most Frugal Cities of 2017," March 22, 2018*

- New York* was cited as one of America's top metros for new and expanded facility projects in 2017. The area ranked #5 in the large metro area category (population over 1 million). *Site Selection, "Top Metropolitans of 2017," March 2018*

- The New York* metro area appeared on the Milken Institute "2017 Best Performing Cities" list. Rank: #82 out of 200 large metro areas. Criteria: job growth; wage and salary growth; high-tech output growth. *Milken Institute, "Best-Performing Cities 2017," January 2018*

- *Forbes* ranked the 200 most populous metro areas to determine the nation's "Best Places for Business and Careers." The New York* metro area was ranked #113. Criteria: costs (business and living); job growth (past and projected); income growth; quality of life; educational attainment (college and high school); projected economic growth; cultural and recreational opportunities; net migration patterns; number of highly ranked colleges. *Forbes, "The Best Places for Business and Careers 2017," October 24, 2017*

Dating/Romance Rankings

- *Apartment List* conducted its annual survey of renters to compile a list of metros that have the best opportunities for dating. Nearly 11,000 respondents, from February 2017 through January 2018, rated their current city or neighborhood for opportunities to date and make friends. The New York* metro area ranked #10 out of 70 where single residents were very satisfied or somewhat satisfied, making it among the ten best metros for dating opportunities. Other criteria analyzed included gender and education levels of renters. *Apartment List, "Best Metros for Dating 2018," February 6, 2018*

Education Rankings

- Personal finance website *WalletHub* analyzed the 150 largest U.S. metropolitan statistical areas to determine where the most educated Americans are choosing to settle. Criteria: education quality and attainment gap; education levels; percentage of workers with degrees; public school rankings; quality and size of each metro area's universities. New York* was ranked #36 (#1 = most educated city). *www.WalletHub.com, "2017's Most and Least Educated Cities in America," July 25, 2017*

Environmental Rankings

- Sperling's BestPlaces assessed 379 metropolitan areas of the United States for the likelihood of dangerously extreme weather events or earthquakes. In general the Southeast and South-Central regions have the highest risk of weather extremes and earthquakes, while the Pacific Northwest enjoys the lowest risk. Of the least risky metropolitan areas, the New York* metro area was ranked #207. *www.bestplaces.net, "Safest Places from Natural Disasters," April 2011*

- The U.S. Environmental Protection Agency (EPA) released a list of U.S. metropolitan areas with the most ENERGY STAR certified buildings in 2016. The New York* metro area was ranked #3 out of 25. *U.S. Environmental Protection Agency, "2017 Energy Star Top Cities," June 2017*

- New York* was highlighted as one of the 25 most ozone-polluted metro areas in the U.S. during 2013 through 2015. The area ranked #9. *American Lung Association, State of the Air 2017*

- New York* was highlighted as one of the 25 metro areas most polluted by year-round particle pollution (Annual PM 2.5) in the U.S. during 2013 through 2015. The area ranked #22. *American Lung Association, State of the Air 2017*

Health/Fitness Rankings

- For each of the 50 most populous metro areas in the United States, the American College of Sports Medicine's American Fitness Index evaluated infrastructure, community assets, and policies that encourage healthy and fit lifestyles, including preventive health behaviors, levels of chronic disease conditions, health care access, and community resources and policies that support physical activity. The New York* metro area ranked #18 for "community fitness." *www.americanfitnessindex.org, "ACSM American Fitness Index Health and Community Fitness Status of the 50 Largest Metropolitan Areas," May 2017*

- The New York* metro area was identified as one of the worst cities for bed bugs in America by pest control company Orkin. The area ranked #8 out of 50 based on the number of bed bug treatments Orkin performed from December 2016 to November 2017. *Orkin, "Baltimore and Washington D.C. Continue to Hold Top Spots," January 8, 2018*

- New York* was identified as a "2016 Spring Allergy Capital." The area ranked #31 out of 100. Three groups of factors were used to identify the most severe cities for people with allergies during the spring season: annual pollen levels; medicine utilization; access to board-certified allergists. *Asthma and Allergy Foundation of America, "Spring Allergy Capitals 2016"*

Business Environment

CITY FINANCES

City Government Finances

Component	2015 ($000)	2015 ($ per capita)
Total Revenues	45,240	1,112
Total Expenditures	43,311	1,065
Debt Outstanding	55,952	1,376
Cash and Securities[1]	33,580	826

Note: (1) Cash and security holdings of a government at the close of its fiscal year,, including those of its dependent agencies, utilities, and liquor stores.
Source: U.S Census Bureau, State & Local Government Finances 2015

City Government Revenue by Source

Source	2015 ($000)	2015 ($ per capita)	2015 (%)
General Revenue			
From Federal Government	35	1	0.1
From State Government	2,754	68	6.1
From Local Governments	0	0	0.0
Taxes			
Property	28,505	701	63.0
Sales and Gross Receipts	192	5	0.4
Personal Income	0	0	0.0
Corporate Income	0	0	0.0
Motor Vehicle License	0	0	0.0
Other Taxes	629	15	1.4
Current Charges	2,362	58	5.2
Liquor Store	0	0	0.0
Utility	9,205	226	20.3
Employee Retirement	0	0	0.0

Source: U.S Census Bureau, State & Local Government Finances 2015

City Government Expenditures by Function

Function	2015 ($000)	2015 ($ per capita)	2015 (%)
General Direct Expenditures			
Air Transportation	0	0	0.0
Corrections	0	0	0.0
Education	0	0	0.0
Employment Security Administration	0	0	0.0
Financial Administration	767	18	1.8
Fire Protection	158	3	0.4
General Public Buildings	337	8	0.8
Governmental Administration, Other	921	22	2.1
Health	251	6	0.6
Highways	3,417	84	7.9
Hospitals	0	0	0.0
Housing and Community Development	0	0	0.0
Interest on General Debt	783	19	1.8
Judicial and Legal	576	14	1.3
Libraries	3	< 1	< 0.1
Parking	0	0	0.0
Parks and Recreation	3,782	93	8.7
Police Protection	9,638	237	22.3
Public Welfare	0	0	0.0
Sewerage	0	0	0.0
Solid Waste Management	925	22	2.1
Veterans' Services	0	0	0.0
Liquor Store	0	0	0.0
Utility	8,282	203	19.1
Employee Retirement	0	0	0.0

Source: U.S Census Bureau, State & Local Government Finances 2015

DEMOGRAPHICS

Population Growth

Area	1990 Census	2000 Census	2010 Census	2016* Estimate	Population Growth (%) 1990-2016	2010-2016
City	27,974	36,398	40,191	40,416	44.5	0.6
MSA[1]	16,845,992	18,323,002	18,897,109	20,031,443	18.9	6.0
U.S.	248,709,873	281,421,906	308,745,538	318,558,162	28.1	3.2

Note: (1) Figures cover the New York-Newark-Jersey City, NY-NJ-PA Metropolitan Statistical Area—see Appendix B for areas included; (*) 2012-2016 5-year estimated population
Source: U.S. Census Bureau, 1990 Census, Census 2000, Census 2010, 2012-2016 American Community Survey 5-Year Estimates

Household Size

Area	Persons in Household (%) One	Two	Three	Four	Five	Six	Seven or More	Average Household Size
City	12.6	30.1	17.7	26.4	9.0	2.4	1.7	3.20
MSA[1]	28.0	29.1	17.0	14.7	6.7	2.6	1.9	2.80
U.S.	27.7	33.7	15.7	13.1	6.0	2.3	1.5	2.60

Note: (1) Figures cover the New York-Newark-Jersey City, NY-NJ-PA Metropolitan Statistical Area—see Appendix B for areas included
Source: U.S. Census Bureau, 2012-2016 American Community Survey 5-Year Estimates

Race

Area	White Alone[2] (%)	Black Alone[2] (%)	Asian Alone[2] (%)	AIAN[3] Alone[2] (%)	NHOPI[4] Alone[2] (%)	Other Race Alone[2] (%)	Two or More Races (%)
City	76.9	2.3	18.5	0.1	0.0	0.7	1.6
MSA[1]	58.7	17.1	10.6	0.3	0.0	10.3	2.9
U.S.	73.3	12.6	5.2	0.8	0.2	4.8	3.1

Note: (1) Figures cover the New York-Newark-Jersey City, NY-NJ-PA Metropolitan Statistical Area—see Appendix B for areas included; (2) Alone is defined as not being in combination with one or more other races; (3) American Indian and Alaska Native; (4) Native Hawaiian and Other Pacific Islander
Source: U.S. Census Bureau, 2012-2016 American Community Survey 5-Year Estimates

Hispanic or Latino Origin

Area	Total (%)	Mexican (%)	Puerto Rican (%)	Cuban (%)	Other (%)
City	4.3	0.1	2.2	0.5	1.5
MSA[1]	23.8	3.1	6.3	0.7	13.7
U.S.	17.3	11.0	1.7	0.7	4.0

Note: Persons of Hispanic or Latino origin can be of any race; (1) Figures cover the New York-Newark-Jersey City, NY-NJ-PA Metropolitan Statistical Area—see Appendix B for areas included
Source: U.S. Census Bureau, 2012-2016 American Community Survey 5-Year Estimates

Segregation

Type	Segregation Indices[1] 1990	2000	2010	2010 Rank[2]	Percent Change 1990-2000	1990-2010	2000-2010
Black/White	80.9	80.2	78.0	2	-0.7	-2.9	-2.2
Asian/White	47.4	50.8	51.9	3	3.5	4.5	1.0
Hispanic/White	66.2	65.6	62.0	3	-0.6	-4.2	-3.6

Note: All figures cover the Metropolitan Statistical Area—see Appendix B for areas included; Figures are based on an analysis of 1990, 2000, and 2010 Census Decennial Census tract data by William H. Frey, Brookings Institution and the University of Michigan Social Science Data Analysis Network. In this analysis all racial groups (whites, blacks, and asians) are non-Hispanic members of those races. Hispanics are shown as a separate category; (1) Segregation Indices are Dissimilarity Indices that measure the degree to which the minority group is distributed differently than whites across census tracts. They range from 0 (complete integration) to 100 (complete segregation) where the value indicates the percentage of the minority group that needs to move to be distributed exactly like whites; (2) Ranges from 1 (most segregated) to 102 (least segregated); n/a not available.
Source: www.CensusScope.org

Ancestry

Area	German	Irish	English	American	Italian	Polish	French[2]	Scottish	Dutch
City	6.7	8.2	2.3	5.1	24.7	8.1	0.6	0.4	0.3
MSA[1]	6.8	10.0	2.9	4.8	13.1	4.0	1.0	0.7	0.7
U.S.	14.4	10.4	7.7	6.9	5.4	2.9	2.6	1.7	1.3

Note: Figures are the percentage of the total population reporting a particular ancestry. The nine most commonly reported ancestries in the U.S. are shown. Figures include multiple ancestries (e.g. if a person reported being Irish and Italian, they were included in both columns); (1) Figures cover the New York-Newark-Jersey City, NY-NJ-PA Metropolitan Statistical Area—see Appendix B for areas included; (2) Excludes Basque
Source: U.S. Census Bureau, 2012-2016 American Community Survey 5-Year Estimates

Foreign-Born Population

Area	Percent of Population Born in								
	Any Foreign Country	Asia	Mexico	Europe	Carribean	Central America[2]	South America	Africa	Canada
City	21.2	12.9	0.1	5.3	1.0	0.1	0.7	1.1	0.1
MSA[1]	28.7	8.3	1.6	4.5	6.6	1.9	4.2	1.2	0.2
U.S.	13.2	4.0	3.6	1.5	1.3	1.0	0.9	0.6	0.3

Note: (1) Figures cover the New York-Newark-Jersey City, NY-NJ-PA Metropolitan Statistical Area—see Appendix B for areas included; (2) Excludes Mexico.
Source: U.S. Census Bureau, 2012-2016 American Community Survey 5-Year Estimates

Marital Status

Area	Never Married	Now Married[2]	Separated	Widowed	Divorced
City	25.7	64.6	0.5	4.5	4.8
MSA[1]	38.1	45.7	2.4	5.8	7.9
U.S.	33.0	48.1	2.1	5.9	11.0

Note: Figures are percentages and cover the population 15 years of age and older; (1) Figures cover the New York-Newark-Jersey City, NY-NJ-PA Metropolitan Statistical Area—see Appendix B for areas included; (2) Excludes separated
Source: U.S. Census Bureau, 2012-2016 American Community Survey 5-Year Estimates

Disability Status

Area	All Ages	Under 18 Years Old	18 to 64 Years Old	65 Years and Over
City	7.0	1.4	4.5	29.9
MSA[1]	10.0	3.2	7.4	33.3
U.S.	12.5	4.1	10.3	35.7

Note: Figures show percent of the civilian noninstitutionalized population that reported having a disability. Disability status is determined from six types of difficulty: vision, hearing, cognitive, ambulatory, self-care, and independent living. For children under 5 years old, hearing and vision difficulty are used to determine disability status. For children between the ages of 5 and 14, disability status is determined from hearing, vision, cognitive, ambulatory, and self-care difficulties. For people aged 15 years and older, they are considered to have a disability if they have difficulty with any one of the six difficulty types; Note: (1) Figures cover the New York-Newark-Jersey City, NY-NJ-PA Metropolitan Statistical Area—see Appendix B for areas included
Source: U.S. Census Bureau, 2012-2016 American Community Survey 5-Year Estimates

Age

Area	Percent of Population									Median Age
	Under Age 5	Age 5–19	Age 20–34	Age 35–44	Age 45–54	Age 55–64	Age 65–74	Age 75–84	Age 85+	
City	4.3	24.0	13.0	12.2	19.0	14.3	8.5	3.6	1.2	43.0
MSA[1]	6.1	18.4	21.3	13.3	14.3	12.3	7.8	4.2	2.1	38.0
U.S.	6.2	19.6	20.7	12.7	13.6	12.6	8.3	4.3	1.9	37.7

Note: (1) Figures cover the New York-Newark-Jersey City, NY-NJ-PA Metropolitan Statistical Area—see Appendix B for areas included
Source: U.S. Census Bureau, 2012-2016 American Community Survey 5-Year Estimates

Gender

Area	Males	Females	Males per 100 Females
City	19,361	21,055	92.0
MSA[1]	9,684,087	10,347,356	93.6
U.S.	156,765,322	161,792,840	96.9

Note: (1) Figures cover the New York-Newark-Jersey City, NY-NJ-PA Metropolitan Statistical Area—see Appendix B for areas included
Source: U.S. Census Bureau, 2012-2016 American Community Survey 5-Year Estimates

Religious Groups by Family

Area	Catholic	Baptist	Non-Den.	Methodist[2]	Lutheran	LDS[3]	Pente-costal	Presby-terian[4]	Muslim[5]	Judaism
MSA[1]	36.9	1.9	1.8	1.3	0.8	0.4	0.9	1.1	2.3	4.8
U.S.	19.1	9.3	4.0	4.0	2.3	2.0	1.9	1.6	0.8	0.7

Note: Figures are the number of adherents as a percentage of the total population; (1) Figures cover the New York-Newark-Jersey City, NY-NJ-PA Metropolitan Statistical Area—see Appendix B for areas included; (2) Methodist/Pietist; (3) Latter Day Saints; (4) Reformed; (5) Figures are estimates
Source: Association of Statisticians of American Religious Bodies, 2010 U.S. Religion Census: Religious Congregations & Membership Study

Religious Groups by Tradition

Area	Catholic	Evangelical Protestant	Mainline Protestant	Other Tradition	Black Protestant	Orthodox
MSA[1]	36.9	4.0	4.1	8.4	1.2	1.0
U.S.	19.1	16.2	7.3	4.3	1.6	0.3

Note: Figures are the number of adherents as a percentage of the total population; (1) Figures cover the New York-Newark-Jersey City, NY-NJ-PA Metropolitan Statistical Area—see Appendix B for areas included
Source: Association of Statisticians of American Religious Bodies, 2010 U.S. Religion Census: Religious Congregations & Membership Study

ECONOMY

Gross Metropolitan Product

Area	2014	2015	2016	2017	Rank[2]
MSA[1]	1,551.3	1,613.8	1,664.0	1,735.1	1

Note: Figures are in billions of dollars; (1) Figures cover the New York-Newark-Jersey City, NY-NJ-PA Metropolitan Statistical Area—see Appendix B for areas included; (2) Rank is based on 2015 data and ranges from 1 to 381
Source: The U.S. Conference of Mayors, U.S. Metro Economies: GMP and Employment Report, 2015-2017

Economic Growth

Area	2012-14 (%)	2015 (%)	2016 (%)	2017 (%)	Rank[2]
MSA[1]	1.6	1.9	1.6	2.2	151
U.S.	2.0	2.4	1.9	2.6	-

Note: Figures are real gross metropolitan product (GMP) growth rates and represent average annual percent change; (1) Figures cover the New York-Newark-Jersey City, NY-NJ-PA Metropolitan Statistical Area—see Appendix B for areas included; (2) Rank is based on 2012-2014 average annual percent change and ranges from 1 to 381
Source: The U.S. Conference of Mayors, U.S. Metro Economies: GMP and Employment Report, 2015-2017

Metropolitan Area Exports

Area	2011	2012	2013	2014	2015	2016	Rank[2]
MSA[1]	105,102.0	102,298.0	106,922.8	105,266.6	95,645.4	89,649.5	1

Note: Figures are in millions of dollars; (1) Figures cover the New York-Newark-Jersey City, NY-NJ-PA Metropolitan Statistical Area—see Appendix B for areas included; (2) Rank is based on 2016 data and ranges from 1 to 385
Source: U.S. Department of Commerce, International Trade Administration, Office of Trade & Industry Information, Manufacturing & Services, data extracted March 15, 2018

Building Permits

Area	Single-Family			Multi-Family			Total		
	2016	2017p	Pct. Chg.	2016	2017p	Pct. Chg.	2016	2017p	Pct. Chg.
City	9	87	866.7	0	0	0.0	9	87	866.7
MSA[1]	9,987	10,549	5.6	32,479	39,344	21.1	42,466	49,893	17.5
U.S.	750,800	817,300	8.9	455,800	446,800	-2.0	1,206,600	1,264,100	4.8

Note: (1) Figures cover the New York-Newark-Jersey City, NY-NJ-PA Metropolitan Statistical Area—see Appendix B for areas included; Figures represent new, privately-owned housing units authorized (unadjusted data); All permit data are based on estimates with imputation; (p) preliminary data.
Source: U.S. Census Bureau, Manufacturing, Mining, and Construction Statistics, Building Permits, 2016, 2017

Bankruptcy Filings

Area	Business Filings			Nonbusiness Filings		
	2016	2017	% Chg.	2016	2017	% Chg.
Monmouth County	66	54	-18.2	1,587	1,697	6.9
U.S.	24,114	23,157	-4.0	770,846	765,863	-0.6

Note: Business filings include Chapter 7, Chapter 11, Chapter 12, and Chapter 13; Nonbusiness filings include Chapter 7, Chapter 11, and Chapter 13
Source: Administrative Office of the U.S. Courts, Business and Nonbusiness Bankruptcy, County Cases Commenced by Chapter of the Bankruptcy Code, During the 12-Month Period Ending December 31, 2016 and Business and Nonbusiness Bankruptcy, County Cases Commenced by Chapter of the Bankruptcy Code, During the 12-Month Period Ending December 31, 2017

Housing Vacancy Rates

Area	Gross Vacancy Rate[2] (%)			Year-Round Vacancy Rate[3] (%)			Rental Vacancy Rate[4] (%)			Homeowner Vacancy Rate[5] (%)		
	2015	2016	2017	2015	2016	2017	2015	2016	2017	2015	2016	2017
MSA[1]	9.8	10.3	10.7	8.6	9.1	9.6	4.2	4.7	4.6	2.1	2.2	1.9
U.S.	12.9	12.8	12.7	10.0	9.9	9.9	7.1	6.9	7.2	1.8	1.7	1.6

Note: (1) Figures cover the New York-Newark-Jersey City, NY-NJ-PA Metropolitan Statistical Area—see Appendix B for areas included; (2) The percentage of the total housing inventory that is vacant; (3) The percentage of the housing inventory (excluding seasonal units) that is year-round vacant; (4) The percentage of rental inventory that is vacant for rent; (5) The percentage of homeowner inventory that is vacant for sale
Source: U.S. Census Bureau, Housing Vacancies and Homeownership Annual Statistics: 2015, 2016, 2017

INCOME

Income

Area	Per Capita ($)	Median Household ($)	Average Household ($)
City	55,618	140,403	173,465
MSA[1]	37,510	69,211	101,617
U.S.	29,829	55,322	77,866

Note: (1) Figures cover the New York-Newark-Jersey City, NY-NJ-PA Metropolitan Statistical Area—see Appendix B for areas included
Source: U.S. Census Bureau, 2012-2016 American Community Survey 5-Year Estimates

Household Income Distribution

Area	Percent of Households Earning							
	Under $15,000	$15,000 -$24,999	$25,000 -$34,999	$35,000 -$49,999	$50,000 -$74,999	$75,000 -$99,999	$100,000 -$149,999	$150,000 and up
City	2.9	3.0	3.6	4.9	9.4	9.5	21.0	45.7
MSA[1]	11.7	8.5	7.7	10.2	15.0	11.7	15.9	19.3
U.S.	12.1	10.2	9.9	13.2	17.8	12.2	13.5	11.1

Note: (1) Figures cover the New York-Newark-Jersey City, NY-NJ-PA Metropolitan Statistical Area—see Appendix B for areas included
Source: U.S. Census Bureau, 2012-2016 American Community Survey 5-Year Estimates

Poverty Rate

Area	All Ages	Under 18 Years Old	18 to 64 Years Old	65 Years and Over
City	1.6	0.9	1.7	2.4
MSA[1]	14.2	20.0	12.7	11.7
U.S.	15.1	21.2	14.2	9.3

Note: Figures are percentage of people whose income during the past 12 months was below the poverty level; (1) Figures cover the New York-Newark-Jersey City, NY-NJ-PA Metropolitan Statistical Area—see Appendix B for areas included
Source: U.S. Census Bureau, 2012-2016 American Community Survey 5-Year Estimates

EMPLOYMENT

Labor Force and Employment

Area	Civilian Labor Force			Workers Employed		
	Dec. 2016	Dec. 2017	% Chg.	Dec. 2016	Dec. 2017	% Chg.
City	20,177	19,993	-0.9	19,545	19,459	-0.4
MD[1]	7,114,448	7,115,615	0.0	6,809,258	6,832,994	0.3
U.S.	158,968,000	159,880,000	0.6	151,798,000	153,602,000	1.2

Note: Data is not seasonally adjusted and covers workers 16 years of age and older; (1) Figures cover the New York-Jersey City-White Plains, NY-NJ Metropolitan Division—see Appendix B for areas included
Source: Bureau of Labor Statistics, Local Area Unemployment Statistics

Unemployment Rate

Area	2017											
	Jan.	Feb.	Mar.	Apr.	May	Jun.	Jul.	Aug.	Sep.	Oct.	Nov.	Dec.
City	3.5	3.5	3.1	3.1	3.5	3.6	4.1	3.9	3.7	3.4	3.1	2.7
MD[1]	4.9	4.9	4.4	4.1	4.3	4.5	4.9	4.9	4.5	4.3	4.1	4.0
U.S.	5.1	4.9	4.6	4.1	4.1	4.5	4.6	4.5	4.1	3.9	3.9	3.9

Note: Data is not seasonally adjusted and covers workers 16 years of age and older; (1) Figures cover the New York-Jersey City-White Plains, NY-NJ Metropolitan Division—see Appendix B for areas included
Source: Bureau of Labor Statistics, Local Area Unemployment Statistics

Average Wages

Occupation	$/Hr.	Occupation	$/Hr.
Accountants and Auditors	48.80	Maids and Housekeeping Cleaners	17.60
Automotive Mechanics	21.70	Maintenance and Repair Workers	22.70
Bookkeepers	22.50	Marketing Managers	93.90
Carpenters	33.00	Nuclear Medicine Technologists	43.30
Cashiers	11.50	Nurses, Licensed Practical	25.90
Clerks, General Office	16.60	Nurses, Registered	43.70
Clerks, Receptionists/Information	16.20	Nursing Assistants	17.10
Clerks, Shipping/Receiving	17.40	Packers and Packagers, Hand	12.10
Computer Programmers	46.80	Physical Therapists	44.60
Computer Systems Analysts	55.20	Postal Service Mail Carriers	24.30
Computer User Support Specialists	30.40	Real Estate Brokers	49.20
Cooks, Restaurant	14.30	Retail Salespersons	13.20
Dentists	78.00	Sales Reps., Exc. Tech./Scientific	35.80
Electrical Engineers	52.00	Sales Reps., Tech./Scientific	51.20
Electricians	40.30	Secretaries, Exc. Legal/Med./Exec.	20.10
Financial Managers	102.00	Security Guards	16.30
First-Line Supervisors/Managers, Sales	25.10	Surgeons	119.70
Food Preparation Workers	12.50	Teacher Assistants*	14.70
General and Operations Managers	82.40	Teachers, Elementary School*	38.30
Hairdressers/Cosmetologists	18.10	Teachers, Secondary School*	41.30
Internists, General	99.10	Telemarketers	13.70
Janitors and Cleaners	16.80	Truck Drivers, Heavy/Tractor-Trailer	24.50
Landscaping/Groundskeeping Workers	16.80	Truck Drivers, Light/Delivery Svcs.	18.60
Lawyers	86.30	Waiters and Waitresses	15.30

Note: Wage data covers the New York-Jersey City-White Plains, NY-NJ Metropolitan Division—see Appendix B for areas included; (*) Hourly wages for elementary/secondary school teachers and teacher assistants were calculated by the editors from annual wage data based on a 40 hour work week; n/a not available.
Source: Bureau of Labor Statistics, Metro Area Occupational Employment & Wage Estimates, May 2017

Employment by Occupation

Occupation Classification	City (%)	MSA[1] (%)	U.S. (%)
Management, Business, Science, and Arts	57.3	41.2	37.0
Natural Resources, Construction, and Maintenance	3.7	6.9	8.9
Production, Transportation, and Material Moving	4.3	9.0	12.2
Sales and Office	25.4	23.7	23.8
Service	9.2	19.3	18.1

Note: Figures cover employed civilians 16 years of age and older; (1) Figures cover the New York-Newark-Jersey City, NY-NJ-PA Metropolitan Statistical Area—see Appendix B for areas included
Source: U.S. Census Bureau, 2012-2016 American Community Survey 5-Year Estimates

Employment by Industry

Sector	MD[1] Number of Employees	MD[1] Percent of Total	U.S. Percent of Total
Construction, Mining, and Logging	265,600	3.7	5.2
Education and Health Services	1,478,800	20.8	15.9
Financial Activities	628,100	8.8	5.7
Government	913,000	12.8	15.3
Information	247,400	3.5	1.9
Leisure and Hospitality	670,100	9.4	10.7
Manufacturing	207,300	2.9	8.5
Other Services	304,700	4.3	3.9
Professional and Business Services	1,148,400	16.2	14.0
Retail Trade	685,200	9.6	11.0
Transportation, Warehousing, and Utilities	275,800	3.9	4.1
Wholesale Trade	284,100	4.0	4.0

Note: Figures are non-farm employment as of December 2017. Figures are not seasonally adjusted and include workers 16 years of age and older; (1) Figures cover the New York-Jersey City-White Plains, NY-NJ Metropolitan Division—see Appendix B for areas included
Source: Bureau of Labor Statistics, Current Employment Statistics, Employment, Hours, and Earnings

Occupations with Greatest Projected Employment Growth: 2016 – 2018

Occupation[1]	2016 Employment	2018 Projected Employment	Numeric Employment Change	Percent Employment Change
Laborers and Freight, Stock, and Material Movers, Hand	97,040	101,030	3,990	4.1
Registered Nurses	84,890	87,480	2,590	3.1
Home Health Aides	36,970	39,030	2,060	5.6
Combined Food Preparation and Serving Workers, Including Fast Food	55,230	57,260	2,030	3.7
Software Developers, Applications	42,830	44,770	1,940	4.5
Heavy and Tractor-Trailer Truck Drivers	45,100	46,980	1,880	4.2
Construction Laborers	32,430	34,110	1,680	5.2
Carpenters	25,870	27,440	1,570	6.1
Waiters and Waitresses	63,080	64,600	1,520	2.4
Receptionists and Information Clerks	52,840	54,340	1,500	2.8

Note: Projections cover New Jersey; (1) Sorted by numeric employment change
Source: www.projectionscentral.com, State Occupational Projections, 2016–2018 Short-Term Projections

Fastest Growing Occupations: 2016 – 2018

Occupation[1]	2016 Employment	2018 Projected Employment	Numeric Employment Change	Percent Employment Change
Brickmasons and Blockmasons	1,920	2,080	160	8.3
Helpers—Electricians	1,620	1,740	120	8.0
Cement Masons and Concrete Finishers	2,440	2,610	170	7.2
Roofers	2,450	2,620	170	7.2
Helpers—Pipelayers, Plumbers, Pipefitters, and Steamfitters	1,100	1,180	80	7.2
Helpers—Carpenters	1,070	1,150	80	7.1
Electricians	15,320	16,370	1,050	6.8
Operations Research Analysts	1,470	1,560	90	6.3
Carpenters	25,870	27,440	1,570	6.1
Drywall and Ceiling Tile Installers	1,510	1,600	90	6.0

Note: Projections cover New Jersey; (1) Sorted by percent employment change and excludes occupations with numeric employment change less than 50
Source: www.projectionscentral.com, State Occupational Projections, 2016–2018 Short-Term Projections

TAXES

State Corporate Income Tax Rates

State	Tax Rate (%)	Income Brackets ($)	Num. of Brackets	Financial Institution Tax Rate (%)[a]	Federal Income Tax Ded.
New Jersey	9.0 (q)	Flat rate	1	9.0 (q)	No

Note: Tax rates as of January 1, 2018; (a) Rates listed are the corporate income tax rate applied to financial institutions or excise taxes based on income. Some states have other taxes based upon the value of deposits or shares; (q) In New Jersey small businesses with annual entire net income under $100,000 pay a tax rate of 7.5%; businesses with income under $50,000 pay 6.5%. The minimum Corporation Business Tax is based on New Jersey gross receipts. It ranges from $500 for a corporation with gross receipts less than $100,000, to $2,000 for a corporation with gross receipts of $1 million or more.
Source: Federation of Tax Administrators, Range of State Corporate Income Tax Rates, January 1, 2018

State Individual Income Tax Rates

State	Tax Rate (%)	Income Brackets ($)	Num. of Brackets	Personal Exempt. ($)[1]		Fed. Inc. Tax Ded.
				Single	Dependents	
New Jersey	1.4 - 8.97	20,000 - 500,000 (q)	6	1,000	1,500	No

Note: Tax rates as of January 1, 2018; Local- and county-level taxes are not included; n/a not applicable; (1) Married joint filers generally receive double the single exemption; (q) The New Jersey rates reported are for single individuals. For married couples filing jointly, the tax rates also range from 1.4% to 8.97%, with 7 brackets and the same high and low income ranges.
Source: Federation of Tax Administrators, State Individual Income Tax Rates, January 1, 2018

Various State Sales and Excise Tax Rates

State	State Sales Tax (%)	Gasoline[1] (¢/gal.)	Cigarette[2] ($/pack)	Spirits[3] ($/gal.)	Wine[4] ($/gal.)	Beer[5] ($/gal.)	Recreational Marijuana (%)
New Jersey	6.625 (e)	37.1	2.70	5.50	0.88	0.12	Not legal

Note: All tax rates as of January 1, 2018; (1) The American Petroleum Institute has developed a methodology for determining the average tax rate on a gallon of fuel. Rates may include any of the following: excise taxes, environmental fees, storage tank fees, other fees or taxes, general sales tax, and local taxes. In states where gasoline is subject to the general sales tax, or where the fuel tax is based on the average sale price, the average rate determined by API is sensitive to changes in the price of gasoline. States that fully or partially apply general sales taxes to gasoline: CA, CO, GA, IL, IN, MI, NY; (2) The federal excise tax of $1.0066 per pack and local taxes are not included; (3) Rates are those applicable to off-premise sales of 40% alcohol by volume (a.b.v.) distilled spirits in 750ml containers. Local excise taxes are excluded; (4) Rates are those applicable to off-premise sales of 11% a.b.v. non-carbonated wine in 750ml containers; (5) Rates are those applicable to off-premise sales of 4.7% a.b.v. beer in 12 ounce containers; (e) Salem County is not subject to the statewide sales tax rate and collects a local rate of 3.3125%. New Jersey's average local score is represented as a negative.
Source: Tax Foundation, 2018 Facts & Figures: How Does Your State Compare?

State Business Tax Climate Index Rankings

State	Overall Rank	Corporate Tax Rank	Individual Income Tax Rank	Sales Tax Rank	Unemployment Insurance Tax Rank	Property Tax Rank
New Jersey	50	42	48	46	36	50

Note: The index is a measure of how each state's tax laws affect economic performance. The lower the rank, the more favorable a state's tax system is for business. States without a given tax are given a ranking of 1. The scores/rankings for the District of Columbia do not affect other states. The 2018 index represents the tax climate as of July 1, 2017.
Source: Tax Foundation, State Business Tax Climate Index 2018

TRANSPORTATION

Means of Transportation to Work

Area	Car/Truck/Van		Public Transportation			Bicycle	Walked	Other Means	Worked at Home
	Drove Alone	Car-pooled	Bus	Subway	Railroad				
City	72.0	6.3	11.3	0.4	3.5	0.0	0.6	1.0	4.8
MSA[1]	50.1	6.6	7.7	19.1	3.8	0.6	6.0	1.8	4.2
U.S.	76.4	9.3	2.6	1.9	0.6	0.6	2.8	1.3	4.6

Note: Figures are percentages and cover workers 16 years of age and older; (1) Figures cover the New York-Newark-Jersey City, NY-NJ-PA Metropolitan Statistical Area—see Appendix B for areas included
Source: U.S. Census Bureau, 2012-2016 American Community Survey 5-Year Estimates

Travel Time to Work

Area	Less Than 10 Minutes	10 to 19 Minutes	20 to 29 Minutes	30 to 44 Minutes	45 to 59 Minutes	60 to 89 Minutes	90 Minutes or More
City	6.5	16.2	13.9	16.7	11.8	17.7	17.2
MSA[1]	7.4	19.3	16.4	23.7	12.4	14.4	6.5
U.S.	12.9	29.2	20.9	20.4	8.0	6.0	2.7

Note: Note: Figures are percentages and include workers 16 years old and over; (1) Figures cover the New York-Newark-Jersey City, NY-NJ-PA Metropolitan Statistical Area—see Appendix B for areas included
Source: U.S. Census Bureau, 2012-2016 American Community Survey 5-Year Estimates

Freeway Travel Time Index

Area	1985	1990	1995	2000	2005	2010	2014
Urban Area Rank[1,2]	11	9	8	7	7	8	8
Urban Area Index[1]	1.16	1.20	1.24	1.29	1.33	1.33	1.34
Average Index[3]	1.09	1.11	1.14	1.17	1.20	1.19	1.20

Note: Freeway Travel Time Index—the ratio of travel time in the peak period to the travel time at free-flow conditions. For example, a value of 1.30 indicates a 20-minute free-flow trip takes 26 minutes in the peak (20 minutes x 1.30 = 26 minutes); (1) Covers the New York-Newark NY-NJ-CT urban area; (2) Rank is based on 101 urban areas (#1 = highest travel time index); (3) Average of 101 urban areas
Source: Texas Transportation Institute, 2015 Urban Mobility Scorecard, August 2015

Freeway Commuter Stress Index

Area	1985	1990	1995	2000	2005	2010	2014
Urban Area Rank[1,2]	19	19	13	12	11	11	12
Urban Area Index[1]	1.21	1.24	1.29	1.34	1.38	1.38	1.39
Average Index[3]	1.13	1.16	1.19	1.22	1.25	1.24	1.25

Note: The Freeway Commuter Stress Index is the same as the Freeway Travel Time Index (see table above) except that it includes only the travel in the peak directions during the peak periods; the TTI includes travel in all directions during the peak period. Thus, the CSI is more indicative of the work trip experienced by each commuter on a daily basis; (1) Covers the New York-Newark NY-NJ-CT urban area; (2) Rank is based on 101 urban areas (#1 = highest travel time index); (3) Average of 101 urban areas
Source: Texas Transportation Institute, 2015 Urban Mobility Scorecard, August 2015

Living Environment

COST OF LIVING

Cost of Living Index

Composite Index	Groceries	Housing	Utilities	Trans-portation	Health Care	Misc. Goods/ Services
116.7	104.2	134.1	114.5	111.1	106.7	110.9

Note: The Cost of Living Index measures regional differences in the cost of consumer goods and services, excluding taxes and non-consumer expenditures, for professional and managerial households in the top income quintile. It is based on more than 50,000 prices covering almost 60 different items for which prices are collected three times a year by chambers of commerce, economic development organizations or university applied economic centers in each participating urban area. The numbers shown should be read as a percentage above or below the national average of 100. For example, a value of 115.4 in the groceries column indicates that grocery prices are 15.4% higher than the national average. Small differences in the index numbers should not be interpreted as significant; Figures cover the Middlesex-Monmouth NJ urban area.
Source: The Council for Community and Economic Research, ACCRA Cost of Living Index, 2017

Grocery Prices

Area[1]	T-Bone Steak ($/pound)	Frying Chicken ($/pound)	Whole Milk ($/half gal.)	Eggs ($/dozen)	Orange Juice ($/64 oz.)	Coffee ($/11.5 oz.)
City[2]	11.10	1.47	2.24	1.66	3.35	3.57
Avg.	11.29	1.40	2.02	1.47	3.55	4.37
Min.	7.71	0.93	1.04	0.70	2.86	3.24
Max.	15.83	2.39	4.03	3.92	6.29	8.16

Note: (1) Values for the local area are compared with the average, minimum and maximum values for all 294 areas in the Cost of Living Index; (2) Figures cover the Middlesex-Monmouth NJ urban area; ***T-Bone Steak*** *(price per pound);* ***Frying Chicken*** *(price per pound, whole fryer);* ***Whole Milk*** *(half gallon carton);* ***Eggs*** *(price per dozen, Grade A, large);* ***Orange Juice*** *(64 oz. Tropicana or Florida Natural);* ***Coffee*** *(11.5 oz. can, vacuum-packed, Maxwell House, Hills Bros, or Folgers).*
Source: The Council for Community and Economic Research, ACCRA Cost of Living Index, 2017

Housing and Utility Costs

Area[1]	New Home Price ($)	Apartment Rent ($/month)	All Electric ($/month)	Part Electric ($/month)	Other Energy ($/month)	Telephone ($/month)
City[2]	456,663	1,380	-	124.44	63.78	33.50
Avg.	335,956	1,047	175.01	97.34	67.93	28.71
Min.	187,788	491	109.48	49.33	35.44	12.39
Max.	1,739,087	4,559	432.62	227.09	353.33	44.61

Note: (1) Values for the local area are compared with the average, minimum and maximum values for all 294 areas in the Cost of Living Index; (2) Figures cover the Middlesex-Monmouth NJ urban area; ***New Home Price*** *(2,400 sf living area, 8,000 sf lot, in urban area with full utilities);* ***Apartment Rent*** *(950 sf 2 bedroom/1.5 or 2 bath, unfurnished, excluding all utilities except water);* ***All Electric*** *(average monthly cost for an all-electric home);* ***Part Electric*** *(average monthly cost for a part-electric home);* ***Other Energy*** *(average monthly cost for natural gas, fuel oil, coal, wood, and any other forms of energy except electricity);* ***Telephone*** *(price includes basic monthly rate for a private residential line plus additional local usage charges incurred by a family of four).*
Source: The Council for Community and Economic Research, ACCRA Cost of Living Index, 2017

Health Care, Transportation, and Other Costs

Area[1]	Doctor ($/visit)	Dentist ($/visit)	Optometrist ($/visit)	Gasoline ($/gallon)	Beauty Salon ($/visit)	Men's Shirt ($)
City[2]	93.87	115.62	108.67	2.36	36.33	38.93
Avg.	108.00	92.54	101.93	2.25	37.58	30.92
Min.	30.39	60.00	49.75	1.82	16.11	11.20
Max.	193.50	161.94	229.28	3.16	77.35	59.13

Note: (1) Values for the local area are compared with the average, minimum and maximum values for all 294 areas in the Cost of Living Index; (2) Figures cover the Middlesex-Monmouth NJ urban area; ***Doctor*** *(general practitioners routine exam of an established patient);* ***Dentist*** *(adult teeth cleaning and periodic oral examination);* ***Optometrist*** *(full vision eye exam for established adult patient);* ***Gasoline*** *(one gallon regular unleaded, national brand, including all taxes, cash price at self-service pump if available);* ***Beauty Salon*** *(woman's shampoo, trim, and blow-dry);* ***Men's Shirt*** *(cotton/polyester dress shirt, pinpoint weave, long sleeves).*
Source: The Council for Community and Economic Research, ACCRA Cost of Living Index, 2017

HOUSING

House Price Index (HPI)

Area	National Ranking[2]	Quarterly Change (%)	One-Year Change (%)	Five-Year Change (%)
MD[1]	148	1.22	5.35	20.60
U.S.[3]	–	1.61	6.68	34.71

Note: The HPI is a weighted repeat sales index. It measures average price changes in repeat sales or refinancings on the same properties. This information is obtained by reviewing repeat mortgage transactions on single-family properties whose mortgages have been purchased or securitized by Fannie Mae or Freddie Mac in January 1975; (1) Figures cover the New York-Jersey City-White Plains, NY-NJ Metropolitan Division—see Appendix B for areas included; (2) Rankings are based on annual percentage change for all metro areas containing at least 15,000 transactions over the last 10 years and ranges from 1 to 253; (3) figures based on a weighted average of Census Division estimates using a seasonally adjusted, purchase-only index; all figures are for the period ending December 31, 2017
Source: Federal Housing Finance Agency, House Price Index, February 28, 2018

Median Single-Family Home Prices

Area	2015	2016	2017p	Percent Change 2016 to 2017
MD[1]	398.5	370.2	382.5	3.3
U.S. Average	223.9	235.5	248.8	5.6

Note: Figures are median sales prices of existing single-family homes in thousands of dollars; (p) preliminary; (1) Figures cover the New York-Jersey City-White Plains, NY-NJ Metropolitan Division—see Appendix B for areas included
Source: National Association of Realtors, Median Sales Price of Existing Single-Family Homes for Metropolitan Areas, 4th Quarter 2017

Qualifying Income Based on Median Sales Price of Existing Single-Family Homes

Area	With 5% Down ($)	With 10% Down ($)	With 20% Down ($)
MD[1]	83,646	79,244	70,439
U.S. Average	55,585	52,659	46,808

Note: Figures are preliminary; Qualifying income is based on a mortgage rate of 4.17%. Monthly principal and interest payment is limited to 25% of income; (1) Figures cover the New York-Jersey City-White Plains, NY-NJ Metropolitan Division—see Appendix B for areas included
Source: National Association of Realtors, Qualifying Income Based on Median Sales Price of Existing Single-Family Homes for Metropolitan Areas, 4th Quarter 2017

Median Apartment Condo-Coop Home Prices

Area	2015	2016	2017p	Percent Change 2016 to 2017
MD[1]	245.7	257.2	270.7	5.2
U.S. Average	210.7	220.7	234.3	6.2

Note: Figures are median sales prices of existing apartment condo-coop homes in thousands of dollars; (p) preliminary; (1) Figures cover the New York-Jersey City-White Plains, NY-NJ Metropolitan Division—see Appendix B for areas included
Source: National Association of Realtors, Median Sales Price of Existing Apartment Condo-Coop Homes for Metropolitan Areas, 4th Quarter 2017

Home Value Distribution

Area	Under $50,000	$50,000 -$99,999	$100,000 -$149,999	$150,000 -$199,999	$200,000 -$299,999	$300,000 -$499,999	$500,000 -$999,999	$1,000,000 or more
City	2.6	1.7	0.6	1.2	7.7	34.7	47.7	3.8
MSA[1]	2.8	1.8	2.9	5.0	16.2	37.0	26.9	7.3
U.S.	8.8	14.8	15.3	14.9	18.4	16.4	9.0	2.5

Note: Figures are percentages and cover owner-occupied housing units; (1) Figures cover the New York-Newark-Jersey City, NY-NJ-PA Metropolitan Statistical Area—see Appendix B for areas included
Source: U.S. Census Bureau, 2012-2016 American Community Survey 5-Year Estimates

Homeownership Rate

Area	2009 (%)	2010 (%)	2011 (%)	2012 (%)	2013 (%)	2014 (%)	2015 (%)	2016 (%)	2017 (%)
MSA[1]	51.7	51.6	50.9	51.5	50.6	50.7	49.9	50.4	49.9
U.S.	67.4	66.9	66.1	65.4	65.1	64.5	63.7	63.4	63.9

Note: (1) Figures cover the New York-Newark-Jersey City, NY-NJ-PA Metropolitan Statistical Area—see Appendix B for areas included
Source: U.S. Census Bureau, Housing Vacancies and Homeownership Annual Statistics: 2009-2017

Year Housing Structure Built

Area	2010 or Later	2000 -2009	1990 -1999	1980 -1989	1970 -1979	1960 -1969	1950 -1959	1940 -1949	Before 1940	Median Year
City	1.8	13.3	25.5	27.3	13.9	12.2	2.6	0.8	2.6	1987
MSA[1]	1.3	7.2	6.1	7.9	10.0	13.8	16.2	9.1	28.3	1958
U.S.	2.3	14.7	14.0	13.7	15.6	10.9	10.6	5.2	13.0	1977

Note: Figures are percentages except for Median Year; Note: (1) Figures cover the New York-Newark-Jersey City, NY-NJ-PA Metropolitan Statistical Area—see Appendix B for areas included
Source: U.S. Census Bureau, 2012-2016 American Community Survey 5-Year Estimates

Gross Monthly Rent

Area	Under $500	$500 -$999	$1,000 -$1,499	$1,500 -$1,999	$2,000 -$2,499	$2,500 -$2,999	$3,000 and up	Median ($)
City	1.0	8.0	11.9	21.5	51.9	2.5	3.2	2,074
MSA[1]	9.7	18.7	35.2	19.8	8.3	3.8	4.5	1,297
U.S.	11.3	43.3	27.7	10.7	4.0	1.6	1.5	949

Note: Figures are percentages except for Median; Gross rent is the contract rent plus the estimated average monthly cost of utilities (electricity, gas, and water and sewer) and fuels (oil, coal, kerosene, wood, etc.) if these are paid by the renter (or paid for the renter by someone else); (1) Figures cover the New York-Newark-Jersey City, NY-NJ-PA Metropolitan Statistical Area—see Appendix B for areas included
Source: U.S. Census Bureau, 2012-2016 American Community Survey 5-Year Estimates

HEALTH

Health Risk Factors

Category	MD[1] (%)	U.S. (%)
Adults aged 18–64 who have any kind of health care coverage	86.5	87.7
Adults who reported being in good or excellent health	82.3	83.6
Adults who are current smokers	11.9	17.1
Adults who currently use E-cigarettes	3.9	4.7
Adults who currently use chewing tobacco, snuff, or snus	2.0	4.0
Adults who are heavy drinkers[2]	5.0	6.5
Adults who are binge drinkers[3]	16.8	16.9
Adults who are overweight (BMI 25.0 - 29.9)	34.4	35.3
Adults who are obese (BMI 30.0 - 99.8)	24.0	29.9
Adults who participated in any physical activities in the past month	71.7	76.9
Adults who always or nearly always wears a seat belt	92.3	94.3

Note: (1) Figures cover the New York-Jersey City-White Plains, NY-NJ Metropolitan Division—see Appendix B for areas included; (2) Heavy drinkers are classified as adult men having more than 14 drinks per week and adult women having more than 7 drinks per week; (3) Binge drinkers are classified as males having five or more drinks on one occasion or females having four or more drinks on one occasion
Source: Centers for Disease Control and Prevention, Behaviorial Risk Factor Surveillance System, SMART: Selected Metropolitan Area Risk Trends, 2016

Health Screening Rates

Category	MD[1] (%)	U.S. (%)
Adults 50-75 who have had a blood stool test within the past year	7.2	8.0
Adults 50-75 who have had a colonoscopy in the past 10 years	63.9	63.5
Adults aged 65+ who have had flu shot within the past year	61.0	58.6
Adults aged 65+ who have ever had a pneumonia vaccination	64.0	73.4
Adults who have ever been tested for HIV	50.7	35.6
Women aged 21-65 who have had a pap test in the past three years	79.5	79.8
Men aged 40+ who have had a PSA test within the past two years	39.3	39.5
Women aged 40+ who have had a mammogram within the past two years	73.3	72.5

Note: (1) Figures cover the New York-Jersey City-White Plains, NY-NJ Metropolitan Division—see Appendix B for areas included; Source: Centers for Disease Control and Prevention, Behaviorial Risk Factor Surveillance System, SMART: Selected Metropolitan Area Risk Trends, 2016

Chronic Health Conditions

Category	MD[1] (%)	U.S. (%)
Adults who have ever been told they had a heart attack	3.3	4.4
Adults who have ever been told they have angina or coronary heart disease	3.5	4.1
Adults who have ever been told they had a stroke	2.5	3.1
Adults who have been told they currently have asthma	8.5	9.3
Adults who have ever been told they have arthritis	20.1	25.8
Adults who have ever been told they have diabetes[2]	10.1	10.5
Adults who have ever been told they had skin cancer	3.4	5.9
Adults who have ever been told they had any other types of cancer	4.9	6.7
Adults who have ever been told they have COPD	4.5	6.3
Adults who have ever been told they have kidney disease	2.3	2.8
Adults who have ever been told they have a form of depression	10.6	17.4

Note: (1) Figures cover the New York-Jersey City-White Plains, NY-NJ Metropolitan Division—see Appendix B for areas included; (2) Figures do not include pregnancy-related, borderline, or pre-diabetes
Source: Centers for Disease Control and Prevention, Behaviorial Risk Factor Surveillance System, SMART: Selected Metropolitan Area Risk Trends, 2016

Mortality Rates for the Top 10 Causes of Death in the U.S.

ICD-10[a] Sub-Chapter	ICD-10[a] Code	Age-Adjusted Mortality Rate[1] per 100,000 population	
		County[2]	U.S.
Malignant neoplasms	C00-C97	143.2	158.5
Ischaemic heart diseases	I20-I25	92.6	96.8
Other forms of heart disease	I30-I51	54.4	52.4
Chronic lower respiratory diseases	J40-J47	31.1	40.9
Cerebrovascular diseases	I60-I69	30.8	37.2
Organic, including symptomatic, mental disorders	F01-F09	34.8	33.3
Other degenerative diseases of the nervous system	G30-G31	22.3	32.1
Other external causes of accidental injury	W00-X59	29.7	31.2
Diabetes mellitus	E10-E14	17.6	21.1
Hypertensive diseases	I10-I15	12.9	20.8

Note: (a) ICD-10 = International Classification of Diseases 10th Revision; (1) Mortality rates are a three year average covering 2014-2016; (2) Figures cover Monmouth County.
Source: Centers for Disease Control and Prevention, National Center for Health Statistics. Underlying Cause of Death 1999-2016 on CDC WONDER Online Database, released December 2017

Mortality Rates for Selected Causes of Death

ICD-10[a] Sub-Chapter	ICD-10[a] Code	Age-Adjusted Mortality Rate[1] per 100,000 population	
		County[2]	U.S.
Assault	X85-Y09	1.6	5.6
Diseases of the liver	K70-K76	9.5	14.0
Human immunodeficiency virus (HIV) disease	B20-B24	1.5	1.9
Influenza and pneumonia	J09-J18	9.3	14.6
Intentional self-harm	X60-X84	8.6	13.2
Malnutrition	E40-E46	1.1	1.3
Obesity and other hyperalimentation	E65-E68	1.5	2.1
Renal failure	N17-N19	13.6	13.0
Transport accidents	V01-V99	7.3	12.0
Viral hepatitis	B15-B19	Unreliable	1.9

Note: (a) ICD-10 = International Classification of Diseases 10th Revision; (1) Mortality rates are a three year average covering 2014-2016; (2) Figures cover Monmouth County; Data are Suppressed when the data meet the criteria for confidentiality constraints; Mortality rates are flagged as Unreliable when the rate would be calculated with a numerator of 20 or less.
Source: Centers for Disease Control and Prevention, National Center for Health Statistics. Underlying Cause of Death 1999-2016 on CDC WONDER Online Database, released December 2017

Health Insurance Coverage

Area	With Health Insurance	With Private Health Insurance	With Public Health Insurance	Without Health Insurance	Population Under Age 18 Without Health Insurance
City	96.6	88.8	17.7	3.4	2.4
MSA[1]	89.8	65.8	33.7	10.2	3.6
U.S.	88.3	66.7	33.0	11.7	5.9

Note: Figures are percentages that cover the civilian noninstitutionalized population; (1) Figures cover the New York-Newark-Jersey City, NY-NJ-PA Metropolitan Statistical Area—see Appendix B for areas included
Source: U.S. Census Bureau, 2012-2016 American Community Survey 5-Year Estimates

Number of Medical Professionals

Area	MDs[3]	DOs[3,4]	Dentists	Podiatrists	Chiropractors	Optometrists
County[1] (number)	2,458	247	639	95	340	123
County[1] (rate[2])	391.8	39.4	101.9	15.2	54.2	19.6
U.S. (rate[2])	276.5	22.3	67.3	6.0	26.7	15.9

Note: Data as of 2016 unless noted; (1) Data covers Monmouth County; (2) Rate per 100,000 population; (3) Data as of 2015 and includes all active, non-federal physicians; (4) Doctor of Osteopathic Medicine
Source: U.S. Department of Health and Human Services, Health Resources and Services Administration, Bureau of Health Professions, Area Resource File (ARF) 2016-2017

Best Hospitals

According to *U.S. News,* the New York-Jersey City-White Plains, NY-NJ metro area is home to nine of the best hospitals in the U.S.: **Hackensack University Medical Center** (3 adult specialties and 1 pediatric specialty); **Hospital for Special Surgery** (2 adult specialties and 1 pediatric specialty); **Memorial Sloan Kettering Cancer Center** (4 adult specialties and 1 pediatric specialty); **Montefiore Medical Center** (1 adult specialty and 7 pediatric specialties); **Mount Sinai Hospital** (Honor Roll/10 adult specialties and 6 pediatric specialties); **NYU Langone Medical Center** (Honor Roll/12 adult specialties); **New York Eye and Ear Infirmary** (2 adult specialties); **New York-Presbyterian Hospital-Columbia and Cornell** (Honor Roll/14 adult specialties and 10 pediatric specialties); **Robert Wood Johnson University Hospital** (1 pediatric specialty). The hospitals listed were nationally ranked in at least one of 16 specialties. Only 152 hospitals nationwide were nationally ranked in one or more specialties. Twenty hospitals in the U.S. made the Honor Roll. The Best Hospitals Honor Roll was revamped last year to take both the national rankings and the procedure and condition ratings into account. Hospitals received points if they were nationally ranked in one of the 16 specialties—the higher they ranked, the more points they got—and how many ratings of "high performing" they earned in the nine procedures and conditions. *U.S. News Online, "America's Best Hospitals 2017-18"*

According to *U.S. News,* the New York-Jersey City-White Plains, NY-NJ metro area is home to seven of the best children's hospitals in the U.S.: **Bristol-Myers Squibb Children's Hospital at RWJ Univ. Hosp.** (1 pediatric specialty); **Children's Hospital at Montefiore** (7 pediatric specialties); **Memorial Sloan Kettering Cancer Center** (1 pediatric specialty); **Mount Sinai Kravis Children's Hospital** (6 pediatric specialties); **New York-Presbyterian Morgan Stanley-Komansky Children's Hospital** (10 pediatric specialties); **Hospital for Special Surgery, New York** (1 pediatric specialty); **Joseph M. Sanzari Children's Hospital at Hackensack University Medical Center** (1 pediatric specialty). The hospitals listed were highly ranked in at least one of 10 pediatric specialties. Eighty-two children's hospitals in the U.S. were nationally ranked in at least one specialty. Hospitals received points for being ranked in a specialty, and the 10 hospitals with the most points across the 10 specialties make up the Honor Roll. *U.S. News Online, "America's Best Children's Hospitals 2017-18"*

EDUCATION

Public School District Statistics

District Name	Schls	Pupils	Pupil/ Teacher Ratio	Minority Pupils[1] (%)	Free Lunch Eligible[2] (%)	IEP[3] (%)
Freehold Regional High School District	6	10,827	14.1	22.5	8.6	17.7
Marlboro Township School District	8	5,041	11.5	34.4	2.7	17.9

Note: Table includes school districts with 100 or more students; (1) Percentage of students that are not non-Hispanic white; (2) Percentage of students that are eligible for the free lunch program; (3) Percentage of students that have an Individualized Education Program.
Source: U.S. Department of Education, National Center for Education Statistics, Common Core of Data, Local Education Agency (School District) Universe Survey: School Year 2015-2016; U.S. Department of Education, National Center for Education Statistics, Common Core of Data, Public Elementary/Secondary School Universe Survey: School Year 2015-2016

Highest Level of Education

Area	Less than H.S.	H.S. Diploma	Some College, No Deg.	Associate Degree	Bachelor's Degree	Master's Degree	Prof. School Degree	Doctorate Degree
City	4.2	16.9	12.3	6.1	33.5	18.4	5.7	3.0
MSA[1]	14.3	25.3	15.5	6.7	22.3	11.3	3.0	1.5
U.S.	13.0	27.5	21.0	8.2	18.8	8.2	2.0	1.3

Note: Figures cover persons age 25 and over; (1) Figures cover the New York-Newark-Jersey City, NY-NJ-PA Metropolitan Statistical Area—see Appendix B for areas included
Source: U.S. Census Bureau, 2012-2016 American Community Survey 5-Year Estimates

Educational Attainment by Race

Area	High School Graduate or Higher (%)					Bachelor's Degree or Higher (%)				
	Total	White	Black	Asian	Hisp.[2]	Total	White	Black	Asian	Hisp.[2]
City	95.8	96.6	100.0	92.2	88.6	60.6	57.1	45.6	76.9	40.1
MSA[1]	85.7	90.0	84.1	82.9	68.9	38.1	43.2	23.8	53.1	17.7
U.S.	87.0	88.9	84.3	86.3	65.7	30.3	31.6	20.0	52.1	14.7

Note: Figures shown cover persons 25 years old and over; (1) Figures cover the New York-Newark-Jersey City, NY-NJ-PA Metropolitan Statistical Area—see Appendix B for areas included; (2) People of Hispanic origin can be of any race
Source: U.S. Census Bureau, 2012-2016 American Community Survey 5-Year Estimates

School Enrollment by Grade and Control

Area	Preschool (%)		Kindergarten (%)		Grades 1 - 4 (%)		Grades 5 - 8 (%)		Grades 9 - 12 (%)	
	Public	Private	Public	Private	Public	Private	Public	Private	Public	Private
City	19.6	80.4	87.5	12.5	98.4	1.6	98.2	1.8	91.3	8.7
MSA[1]	51.9	48.1	81.6	18.4	86.1	13.9	86.3	13.7	85.9	14.1
U.S.	58.4	41.6	87.7	12.3	89.8	10.2	89.7	10.3	90.4	9.6

Note: Figures shown cover persons 3 years old and over; (1) Figures cover the New York-Newark-Jersey City, NY-NJ-PA Metropolitan Statistical Area—see Appendix B for areas included
Source: U.S. Census Bureau, 2012-2016 American Community Survey 5-Year Estimates

Average Salaries of Public School Classroom Teachers

Area	2015		2016		Change from 2015 to 2016	
	Dollars	Rank[1]	Dollars	Rank[1]	Percent	Rank[2]
New Jersey	69,038	6	69,330	6	0.4	41
U.S. Average	57,611	–	58,353	–	1.3	–

Note: (1) Rank ranges from 1 to 51 where 1 indicates highest salary; (2) Rank ranges from 1 to 51 where 1 indicates highest percent change.
Source: National Education Association, Rankings & Estimates: Rankings of the States 2016 and Estimates of School Statistics 2017

Higher Education

Four-Year Colleges			Two-Year Colleges			Medical Schools[1]	Law Schools[2]	Voc/ Tech[3]
Public	Private Non-profit	Private For-profit	Public	Private Non-profit	Private For-profit			
0	0	0	0	0	0	0	0	0

Note: Figures cover institutions located within the city limits and include main campuses only; (1) includes schools accredited by the Liaison Committee on Medical Education and the American Osteopathic Association's Commission on Osteopathic College Accreditation; (2) includes ABA-accredited schools, schools with provisional ABA accreditation, and state accredited schools; (3) includes all schools with programs that are less than 2 years.
Source: National Center for Education Statistics, Integrated Postsecondary Education System (IPEDS), 2016-17; Wikipedia, List of Medical Schools in the United States, accessed April 2, 2018; Wikipedia, List of Law Schools in the United States, accessed April 2, 2018

According to *U.S. News & World Report,* the New York-Jersey City-White Plains, NY-NJ metro division is home to seven of the best national universities in the U.S.: **Columbia University** (#5 tie); **New York University** (#30 tie); **Fordham University** (#61 tie); **Yeshiva University** (#94 tie); **The New School** (#133 tie); **Saint John's University (Jamaica)** (#165 tie); **Pace University** (#187 tie). The indicators used to capture academic quality fall into a number of categories: assessment by administrators at peer institutions; retention of students; faculty resources; student selectivity; financial resources; alumni giving; high school counselor ratings of colleges; and graduation rate. *U.S. News & World Report, "America's Best Colleges 2018"*

According to *U.S. News & World Report,* the New York-Jersey City-White Plains, NY-NJ metro division is home to one of the best liberal arts colleges in the U.S.: **Barnard College** (#26 tie).

The indicators used to capture academic quality fall into a number of categories: assessment by administrators at peer institutions; retention of students; faculty resources; student selectivity; financial resources; alumni giving; high school counselor ratings of colleges; and graduation rate. *U.S. News & World Report, "America's Best Colleges 2018"*

According to *U.S. News & World Report,* the New York-Jersey City-White Plains, NY-NJ metro division is home to six of the top 100 law schools in the U.S.: **Columbia University** (#5); **New York University** (#6); **Fordham University** (#37 tie); **Yeshiva University (Cardozo)** (#56 tie); **Brooklyn Law School** (#83 tie); **Saint John's University (Jamaica)** (#83 tie). The rankings are based on a weighted average of 12 measures of quality: peer assessment score; assessment score by lawyers/judges; median LSAT scores; median undergrad GPA; acceptance rate; employment rates for graduates; placement success; bar passage rate; faculty resources; expenditures per student; student/faculty ratio; and library resources. *U.S. News & World Report, "America's Best Graduate Schools, Law, 2019"*

According to *U.S. News & World Report,* the New York-Jersey City-White Plains, NY-NJ metro division is home to five of the top 75 medical schools for research in the U.S.: **New York University (Langone)** (#3 tie); **Columbia University** (#11 tie); **Icahn School of Medicine at Mount Sinai** (#18 tie); **Cornell University (Weill)** (#21); **Yeshiva University (Einstein)** (#39 tie). The rankings are based on a weighted average of 11 measures of quality: quality assessment; peer assessment score; assessment score by residency directors; research activity; total research activity; average research activity per faculty member; student selectivity; median MCAT total score; median undergraduate GPA; acceptance rate; and faculty resources. *U.S. News & World Report, "America's Best Graduate Schools, Medical, 2019"*

According to *U.S. News & World Report,* the New York-Jersey City-White Plains, NY-NJ metro division is home to four of the top 75 business schools in the U.S.: **Columbia University** (#9); **New York University (Stern)** (#13 tie); **CUNY Bernard M. Baruch College (Zicklin)** (#55 tie); **Fordham University (Gabelli)** (#63 tie). The rankings are based on a weighted average of the following nine measures: quality assessment; peer assessment; recruiter assessment; placement success; mean starting salary and bonus; student selectivity; mean GMAT and GRE scores; mean undergraduate GPA; and acceptance rate. *U.S. News & World Report, "America's Best Graduate Schools, Business, 2019"*

PRESIDENTIAL ELECTION

2016 Presidential Election Results

Area	Clinton	Trump	Johnson	Stein	Other
Monmouth County	43.2	52.5	2.0	1.0	1.3
U.S.	48.0	45.9	3.3	1.1	1.7

Note: Results are percentages and may not add to 100% due to rounding
Source: Dave Leip's Atlas of U.S. Presidential Elections

EMPLOYERS

Major Employers

Company Name	Industry
American Express Company	Personal credit institutions
American International Group	Life insurance
Deloitte Consulting	Management consulting services
Hackensack University Medical Center	University
Merrill Lynch and Co	Security brokers & dealers
Mount Sinai Hospital	General medical & surgical hospitals
Mount Sinai School of Medicine	Medical training services
NewYork-Presbyterian Hospital	General medical & surgical hospitals
NYC Health and Hospitals Corp	Psychiatric hospitals
NYU School of Medicine	Offices & clinics of medical doctors
Paramount Comm Acq Corp	Investment holding companies, except banks
Patriarch Partners	Investment offices
Rutgers, The State Univ of NJ	Colleges & universities
Standard Americas	Agencies of foreign banks
The Long Island Rail Road Company	Local & suburban transit
U of Med and Dentistry of NJ	Colleges & universities
UMASS Memorial Health Care	Psychiatrist
United States Postal Service	U.S. postal service
Wellchoice	Health insurance carriers

Note: Companies shown are located within the New York-Newark-Jersey City, NY-NJ-PA Metropolitan Statistical Area.
Source: Hoovers.com; Wikipedia

PUBLIC SAFETY

Crime Rate

Area	All Crimes	Violent Crimes				Property Crimes		
		Murder	Rape[3]	Robbery	Aggrav. Assault	Burglary	Larceny -Theft	Motor Vehicle Theft
City	620.6	0.0	2.5	4.9	17.2	61.3	495.5	39.3
Metro[1]	1,805.2	3.1	22.2	136.2	255.9	160.0	1,152.5	75.3
U.S.	2,847.8	5.3	40.4	102.8	248.5	468.9	1,745.0	236.9

Note: Figures are crimes per 100,000 population; (1) Figures cover the New York-Jersey City-White Plains, NY-NJ Metropolitan Division—see Appendix B for areas included; (3) The city and U.S. figures shown were reported using the revised Uniform Crime Reporting (UCR) definition of rape. The metro area figures shown are an aggregate total of the data submitted using both the revised and legacy UCR definitions.
Source: FBI Uniform Crime Reports, 2016

Hate Crimes

Area	Number of Quarters Reported	Number of Incidents per Bias Motivation					
		Race/Ethnicity/ Ancestry	Religion	Sexual Orientation	Disability	Gender	Gender Identity
Area[1]	3	0	0	0	0	0	0
U.S.	4	3,489	1,273	1,076	70	31	124

Note: (1) Figures cover the Marlboro Township.
Source: Federal Bureau of Investigation, Hate Crime Statistics 2016

Identity Theft Consumer Reports

Area	Reports	Reports per 100,000 Population	Rank[2]
MSA[1]	23,624	117	64
U.S.	371,061	114	-

Note: (1) Figures cover the New York-Newark-Jersey City, NY-NJ-PA Metropolitan Statistical Area—see Appendix B for areas included; (2) Rank ranges from 1 to 389 where 1 indicates greatest number of identity theft reports per 100,000 population
Source: Federal Trade Commission, Consumer Sentinel Network Data Book for January–December 2017

Fraud and Other Consumer Reports

Area	Reports	Reports per 100,000 Population	Rank[2]
MSA[1]	90,589	449	173
U.S.	2,304,550	708	-

Note: (1) Figures cover the New York-Newark-Jersey City, NY-NJ-PA Metropolitan Statistical Area—see Appendix B for areas included; (2) Rank ranges from 1 to 389 where 1 indicates greatest number of fraud and other consumer reports per 100,000 population
Source: Federal Trade Commission, Consumer Sentinel Network Data Book for January–December 2017

SPORTS

Professional Sports Teams

Team Name	League	Year Established
Brooklyn Nets	National Basketball Association (NBA)	1967
New Jersey Devils	National Hockey League (NHL)	1982
New York City FC	Major League Soccer (MLS)	2015
New York Giants	National Football League (NFL)	1925
New York Islanders	National Hockey League (NHL)	1972
New York Jets	National Football League (NFL)	1960
New York Knicks	National Basketball Association (NBA)	1946
New York Mets	Major League Baseball (MLB)	1962
New York Rangers	National Hockey League (NHL)	1926
New York Red Bulls	Major League Soccer (MLS)	1996
New York Yankees	Major League Baseball (MLB)	1903

Note: Includes teams located in the New York-Newark-Jersey City, NY-NJ-PA Metropolitan Statistical Area.
Source: Wikipedia, Major Professional Sports Teams of the United States and Canada, April 5, 2018

CLIMATE

Average and Extreme Temperatures

Temperature	Jan	Feb	Mar	Apr	May	Jun	Jul	Aug	Sep	Oct	Nov	Dec	Yr.
Extreme High (°F)	68	75	85	96	97	101	104	99	99	88	81	72	104
Average High (°F)	38	41	50	61	72	80	85	84	76	65	54	43	62
Average Temp. (°F)	32	34	43	53	63	72	77	76	68	58	48	37	55
Average Low (°F)	26	27	35	44	54	63	68	67	60	49	41	31	47
Extreme Low (°F)	-2	-2	8	21	36	46	53	50	40	29	17	-1	-2

Note: Figures cover the years 1962-1992
Source: National Climatic Data Center, International Station Meteorological Climate Summary, 9/96

Average Precipitation/Snowfall/Humidity

Precip./Humidity	Jan	Feb	Mar	Apr	May	Jun	Jul	Aug	Sep	Oct	Nov	Dec	Yr.
Avg. Precip. (in.)	3.5	3.1	4.0	3.9	4.5	3.8	4.5	4.1	4.1	3.3	4.5	3.8	47.0
Avg. Snowfall (in.)	7	8	4	Tr	Tr	0	0	0	0	Tr	Tr	3	23
Avg. Rel. Hum. 7am (%)	67	67	66	64	72	74	74	76	78	75	72	69	71
Avg. Rel. Hum. 4pm (%)	55	53	50	45	52	55	53	54	56	55	57	58	53

Note: Figures cover the years 1962-1992; Tr = Trace amounts (<0.05 in. of rain; <0.5 in. of snow)
Source: National Climatic Data Center, International Station Meteorological Climate Summary, 9/96

Weather Conditions

Temperature			Daytime Sky			Precipitation		
32°F & below	45°F & below	90°F & above	Clear	Partly cloudy	Cloudy	0.01 inch or more precip.	0.1 inch or more snow/ice	Thunder-storms
75	170	18	85	166	114	120	11	20

Note: Figures are average number of days per year and cover the years 1962-1992
Source: National Climatic Data Center, International Station Meteorological Climate Summary, 9/96

HAZARDOUS WASTE

Superfund Sites

The New York-Jersey City-White Plains, NY-NJ metro division is home to 48 sites on the EPA's Superfund National Priorities List: **Atlantic Resources** (final); **Bog Creek Farm** (final); **Brick Township Landfill** (final); **Burnt Fly Bog** (final); **Carroll & Dubies Sewage Disposal** (final); **Chemical Insecticide Corp.** (final); **Chemsol, Inc.** (final); **Ciba-geigy Corp.** (final); **Cornell**

Dubilier Electronics Inc. (final); **CPS/Madison Industries** (final); **Curcio Scrap Metal, Inc.** (final); **Diamond Head Oil Refinery Div.** (final); **Evor Phillips Leasing** (final); **Fair Lawn Well Field** (final); **Fried Industries** (final); **Garfield Ground Water Contamination** (final); **Global Sanitary Landfill** (final); **Goose Farm** (final); **Gowanus Canal** (final); **Horseshoe Road** (final); **Hudson Technologies, Inc.** (proposed); **Imperial Oil Co., Inc./Champion Chemicals** (final); **JIS Landfill** (final); **Kin-Buc Landfill** (final); **Lone Pine Landfill** (final); **Maywood Chemical Co.** (final); **Middlesex Sampling Plant (USDOE)** (final); **Monitor Devices, Inc./Intercircuits, Inc.** (final); **Naval Air Engineering Center** (final); **Naval Weapons Station Earle (Site A)** (final); **Nepera Chemical Co., Inc.** (final); **Newtown Creek** (final); **Pjp Landfill** (final); **Quanta Resources** (final); **Ramapo Landfill** (final); **Raritan Bay Slag** (final); **Reich Farms** (final); **Ringwood Mines/Landfill** (final); **Scientific Chemical Processing** (final); **Standard Chlorine** (final); **Syncon Resins** (final); **Universal Oil Products (Chemical Division)** (final); **Ventron/Velsicol** (final); **Waldick Aerospace Devices, Inc.** (final); **White Swan Laundry and Cleaner Inc.** (final); **Wolff-Alport Chemical Company** (final); **Woodbrook Road Dump** (final); **Zschiegner Refining** (final). There are a total of 1,396 Superfund sites with a status of proposed or final on the list in the U.S. *U.S. Environmental Protection Agency, National Priorities List, April 4, 2018*

AIR & WATER QUALITY

Air Quality Trends: Ozone

	1990	1995	2000	2005	2010	2012	2013	2014	2015	2016
MSA[1]	0.101	0.106	0.090	0.091	0.081	0.079	0.071	0.069	0.075	0.073
U.S.	0.087	0.089	0.081	0.079	0.073	0.075	0.069	0.067	0.068	0.069

Note: (1) Data covers the New York-Newark-Jersey City, NY-NJ-PA Metropolitan Statistical Area—see Appendix B for areas included. The values shown are the composite ozone concentration averages among trend sites based on the highest fourth daily maximum 8-hour concentration in parts per million. These trends are based on sites having an adequate record of monitoring data during the trend period. Data from exceptional events are included.
Source: U.S. Environmental Protection Agency, Air Quality Monitoring Information, "Air Quality Trends by City, 1990-2016"

Air Quality Index

Area	Percent of Days when Air Quality was...[2]					AQI Statistics[2]	
	Good	Moderate	Unhealthy for Sensitive Groups	Unhealthy	Very Unhealthy	Maximum	Median
MSA[1]	42.2	52.6	4.7	0.5	0.0	159	52

Note: (1) Data covers the New York-Newark-Jersey City, NY-NJ-PA Metropolitan Statistical Area—see Appendix B for areas included; (2) Based on 365 days with AQI data in 2017. Air Quality Index (AQI) is an index for reporting daily air quality. EPA calculates the AQI for five major air pollutants regulated by the Clean Air Act: ground-level ozone, particle pollution (aka particulate matter), carbon monoxide, sulfur dioxide, and nitrogen dioxide. The AQI runs from 0 to 500. The higher the AQI value, the greater the level of air pollution and the greater the health concern. There are six AQI categories: "Good" AQI is between 0 and 50. Air quality is considered satisfactory; "Moderate" AQI is between 51 and 100. Air quality is acceptable; "Unhealthy for Sensitive Groups" When AQI values are between 101 and 150, members of sensitive groups may experience health effects; "Unhealthy" When AQI values are between 151 and 200 everyone may begin to experience health effects; "Very Unhealthy" AQI values between 201 and 300 trigger a health alert; "Hazardous" AQI values over 300 trigger warnings of emergency conditions (not shown).
Source: U.S. Environmental Protection Agency, Air Quality Index Report, 2017

Air Quality Index Pollutants

Area	Percent of Days when AQI Pollutant was...[2]					
	Carbon Monoxide	Nitrogen Dioxide	Ozone	Sulfur Dioxide	Particulate Matter 2.5	Particulate Matter 10
MSA[1]	0.0	13.2	31.8	0.0	55.1	0.0

Note: (1) Data covers the New York-Newark-Jersey City, NY-NJ-PA Metropolitan Statistical Area—see Appendix B for areas included; (2) Based on 365 days with AQI data in 2017. The Air Quality Index (AQI) is an index for reporting daily air quality. EPA calculates the AQI for five major air pollutants regulated by the Clean Air Act: ground-level ozone, particle pollution (also known as particulate matter), carbon monoxide, sulfur dioxide, and nitrogen dioxide. The AQI runs from 0 to 500. The higher the AQI value, the greater the level of air pollution and the greater the health concern.
Source: U.S. Environmental Protection Agency, Air Quality Index Report, 2017

Maximum Air Pollutant Concentrations: Particulate Matter, Ozone, CO and Lead

	Particulate Matter 10 (ug/m^3)	Particulate Matter 2.5 Wtd AM (ug/m^3)	Particulate Matter 2.5 24-Hr (ug/m^3)	Ozone (ppm)	Carbon Monoxide (ppm)	Lead (ug/m^3)
MSA[1] Level	33	9.2	20	0.078	3	0.03
NAAQS[2]	150	15	35	0.075	9	0.15
Met NAAQS[2]	Yes	Yes	Yes	No	Yes	Yes

Note: (1) Data covers the New York-Newark-Jersey City, NY-NJ-PA Metropolitan Statistical Area—see Appendix B for areas included; Data from exceptional events are included; (2) National Ambient Air Quality Standards; ppm = parts per million; ug/m^3 = micrograms per cubic meter; n/a not available.
Concentrations: Particulate Matter 10 (coarse particulate)—highest second maximum 24-hour concentration; Particulate Matter 2.5 Wtd AM (fine particulate)—highest weighted annual mean concentration; Particulate Matter 2.5 24-Hour (fine particulate)—highest 98th percentile 24-hour concentration; Ozone—highest fourth daily maximum 8-hour concentration; Carbon Monoxide—highest second maximum non-overlapping 8-hour concentration; Lead—maximum running 3-month average
Source: U.S. Environmental Protection Agency, Air Quality Monitoring Information, "Air Quality Statistics by City, 2016"

Maximum Air Pollutant Concentrations: Nitrogen Dioxide and Sulfur Dioxide

	Nitrogen Dioxide AM (ppb)	Nitrogen Dioxide 1-Hr (ppb)	Sulfur Dioxide AM (ppb)	Sulfur Dioxide 1-Hr (ppb)	Sulfur Dioxide 24-Hr (ppb)
MSA[1] Level	20	60	n/a	7	n/a
NAAQS[2]	53	100	30	75	140
Met NAAQS[2]	Yes	Yes	n/a	Yes	n/a

Note: (1) Data covers the New York-Newark-Jersey City, NY-NJ-PA Metropolitan Statistical Area—see Appendix B for areas included; Data from exceptional events are included; (2) National Ambient Air Quality Standards; ppm = parts per million; ug/m^3 = micrograms per cubic meter; n/a not available.
Concentrations: Nitrogen Dioxide AM—highest arithmetic mean concentration; Nitrogen Dioxide 1-Hr—highest 98th percentile 1-hour daily maximum concentration; Sulfur Dioxide AM—highest annual mean concentration; Sulfur Dioxide 1-Hr—highest 99th percentile 1-hour daily maximum concentration; Sulfur Dioxide 24-Hr—highest second maximum 24-hour concentration
Source: U.S. Environmental Protection Agency, Air Quality Monitoring Information, "Air Quality Statistics by City, 2016"

Drinking Water

Water System Name	Pop. Served	Primary Water Source Type	Violations[1]	
			Health Based	Monitoring/ Reporting
Marlboro Twp Water Utility Div	29,480	Purchased Surface	0	5

Note: (1) Based on violation data from January 1, 2017 to December 31, 2017
Source: U.S. Environmental Protection Agency, Office of Ground Water and Drinking Water, Safe Drinking Water Information System (based on data extracted April 5, 2018)

Princeton, New Jersey

Background

Princeton is located in Mercer County, in the heart of central New Jersey, covering about 18.1 square miles. The town's borough form of government was established in 2013 when the Borough of Princeton merged with Princeton Township. Princeton is situated equidistant from New York City and Philadelphia and is close to the many major roadways that serve both cities. US Highway Route 206 runs through the city and there is ready access to US Highway Route 1, the New Jersey Turnpike, the Garden State Parkway and Amtrak and New Jersey Transit which provide direct rail services to New York and Philadelphia.

Princeton is well known for being the home of Princeton University, the prestigious higher education institution that was founded in 1756. Princeton's long history with the university makes it primarily a college town. A substantial portion of the property of Princeton University lies within the borders of Princeton as does the property of the Institute for Advanced Study. Princeton is a hub for excellent public and private schools such as the Hun School, the Princeton Day School, and the Stuart Country Day School of the Sacred Heart. The area is also home to a variety of other well-known institutions such as the Dow Jones and Company, Siemens Corporate Research, and the Princeton Theological Seminary.

Despite a long history of being divided between two separate municipalities, Princeton's residents have strong community ties. The central borough, which was originally surrounded by the township, seceded in 1894 over a dispute regarding school taxes. The two municipalities would later form the Princeton Public Schools, with a few other combined public services before being officially reunited in 2013. Nassau Street is the main commercial street that runs through the town and most of the Princeton University campus. Before reunification, the borough and the township had similar populations.

While New Jersey's state capital is the city of Trenton, the governor's official residence has been in Princeton since 1945 when the Morven property was designated as the governor's mansion. An historic 18th century home at 55 Stockton Street, it served as the governor's mansion for nearly four decades from 1944 to 1981. Today, the governor's mansion is at Drumthwacket, at 354 Stockton Street, also in Princeton. It is one of three official governor's residences in the country that is not located in the state's capital city.

Princeton consistently ranks high on the list of most liveable cities, with a high quality of life and a vibrant community. The mixture of history, picturesque ivy covered walls and buildings, a bustling arts scene, and an array of fine and eclectic dining make it a desirable city to live and work in. It is also conveniently located to NYC and Philadelphia, and the endless offerings of these two major cities.

Historic Nassau Street is lined with bookshops, local stores, restaurants, and entertainment venues. Palmer Square is home to the historic Nassau Inn, and a variety of gift shops and outdoor dining options. Princeton University sits in the midst of the town, home to many of the country's leading scholars, scientists, and scribes. The gothic style Princeton University chapel is particularly exquisite in its architecture and mood. Princeton University also has its own art museum that houses renowned Chinese and classical art collections. There is also the famed McCarter Theater for theatrical performances and the Westminster Choir College for contemporary and classical vocal performances.

There are numerous recreation facilities in the area including a large pool complex, tennis and paddle tennis courts, athletic playing fields and various parks and playgrounds. Throughout the year, there are many different programs and activities on offer through the city's Recreation Department.

Princeton, like much of the northeastern United States, experiences a humid continental climate with cold winters and hot, humid summers. Highs in winter hover just above freezing and can drop well below zero, along with snowfall and precipitation. In summer, temperatures can reach into the 80s with a high percentage of humidity with balmy, warm evenings.

Rankings

Business/Finance Rankings

- The personal finance site NerdWallet analyzed 183 American metropolitan areas with populations over 250,000 and more than 15,000 businesses to rank where entrepreneurs find the most success. Criteria included area economy, annual income, housing cost, unemployment rate, and the success rate of area businesses. Trenton* ranked #27. *www.nerdwallet.com, "Best Places to Start a Business," April 27, 2015*
- The Trenton* metro area appeared on the Milken Institute "2017 Best Performing Cities" list. Rank: #101 out of 200 large metro areas. Criteria: job growth; wage and salary growth; high-tech output growth. *Milken Institute, "Best-Performing Cities 2017," January 2018*

Education Rankings

- Personal finance website *WalletHub* analyzed the 150 largest U.S. metropolitan statistical areas to determine where the most educated Americans are choosing to settle. Criteria: education quality and attainment gap; education levels; percentage of workers with degrees; public school rankings; quality and size of each metro area's universities. Trenton* was ranked #18 (#1 = most educated city). *www.WalletHub.com, "2017's Most and Least Educated Cities in America," July 25, 2017*

Environmental Rankings

- Sperling's BestPlaces assessed 379 metropolitan areas of the United States for the likelihood of dangerously extreme weather events or earthquakes. In general the Southeast and South-Central regions have the highest risk of weather extremes and earthquakes, while the Pacific Northwest enjoys the lowest risk. Of the least risky metropolitan areas, the Trenton* metro area was ranked #316. *www.bestplaces.net, "Safest Places from Natural Disasters," April 2011*

Health/Fitness Rankings

- The Trenton* metro area ranked #80 out of 189 in The Gallup-Healthways Well-Being Index. Criteria: purpose; social well being; financial health; community and physical health. Results are based on telephone interviews with adults, aged 18 and older, living in metropolitan areas in the 50 U.S. states and the District of Columbia. *Gallup-Healthways, "State of American Well-Being, 2017 Community Well-Being Rankings" March 2018*

Real Estate Rankings

- The Trenton* metro area was identified as one of the 10 worst condo markets in the U.S. in 2017. The area ranked #5 out of 66 markets. Criteria: year-over-year change of median sales price of existing apartment condo-coop homes between the 4th quarter of 2016 and the 4th quarter of 2017. *National Association of Realtors®, Median Sales Price of Existing Apartment Condo-Coop Homes for Metropolitan Areas, 4th Quarter 2017*
- Trenton* was ranked #95 out of 238 metro areas in terms of housing affordability in 2017 by the National Association of Home Builders (#1 = most affordable). Criteria: the share of homes sold in that area affordable to a family earning the local median income, based on standard mortgage underwriting criteria. *National Association of Home Builders®, NAHB-Wells Fargo Housing Opportunity Index, 4th Quarter 2017*
- The nation's largest metro areas were analyzed in terms of the percentage of households entering some stage of foreclosure in 2017. The Trenton* metro area ranked #2 out of 10 (#1 = highest foreclosure rate). *RealtyTrac, "2017 Year-End U.S. Foreclosure Market Report™," January 16, 2018*

Safety Rankings

- The National Insurance Crime Bureau ranked 382 metro areas in the U.S. in terms of per capita rates of vehicle theft. The Trenton* metro area ranked #183 (#1 = highest rate). Criteria: number of vehicle theft offenses per 100,000 inhabitants in 2016. *National Insurance Crime Bureau, "Hot Spots 2016," June 8, 2017*

Seniors/Retirement Rankings

- From its Best Cities for Successful Aging indexes, the Milken Institute generated rankings for metropolitan areas, weighing data in nine categories—health care, wellness, living arrangements, transportation and convenience, financial characteristics, education, employment, community engagement, and overall livability. The Trenton* metro area was ranked #93 overall in the small metro area category. *Milken Institute, "Best Cities for Successful Aging, 2017" March 14, 2017*

Transportation Rankings

- The Trenton* metro area appeared on *Forbes* list of places with the most extreme commutes. The metro area ranked #4 out of 10. Criteria: average travel time; percentage of mega commuters. Mega-commuters travel more than 90 minutes and 50 miles each way to work. *Forbes.com, "The Cities with the Most Extreme Commutes," March 5, 2013*

*Princeton is located within the Trenton, NJ Metropolitan Statistical Area.

Business Environment

CITY FINANCES

City Government Finances

Component	2015 ($000)	2015 ($ per capita)
Total Revenues	n/a	n/a
Total Expenditures	n/a	n/a
Debt Outstanding	n/a	n/a
Cash and Securities[1]	n/a	n/a

Note: (1) Cash and security holdings of a government at the close of its fiscal year,, including those of its dependent agencies, utilities, and liquor stores.
Source: U.S Census Bureau, State & Local Government Finances 2015

City Government Revenue by Source

Source	2015 ($000)	2015 ($ per capita)	2015 (%)
General Revenue			
From Federal Government	n/a	n/a	n/a
From State Government	n/a	n/a	n/a
From Local Governments	n/a	n/a	n/a
Taxes			
Property	n/a	n/a	n/a
Sales and Gross Receipts	n/a	n/a	n/a
Personal Income	n/a	n/a	n/a
Corporate Income	n/a	n/a	n/a
Motor Vehicle License	n/a	n/a	n/a
Other Taxes	n/a	n/a	n/a
Current Charges	n/a	n/a	n/a
Liquor Store	n/a	n/a	n/a
Utility	n/a	n/a	n/a
Employee Retirement	n/a	n/a	n/a

Source: U.S Census Bureau, State & Local Government Finances 2015

City Government Expenditures by Function

Function	2015 ($000)	2015 ($ per capita)	2015 (%)
General Direct Expenditures			
Air Transportation	n/a	n/a	n/a
Corrections	n/a	n/a	n/a
Education	n/a	n/a	n/a
Employment Security Administration	n/a	n/a	n/a
Financial Administration	n/a	n/a	n/a
Fire Protection	n/a	n/a	n/a
General Public Buildings	n/a	n/a	n/a
Governmental Administration, Other	n/a	n/a	n/a
Health	n/a	n/a	n/a
Highways	n/a	n/a	n/a
Hospitals	n/a	n/a	n/a
Housing and Community Development	n/a	n/a	n/a
Interest on General Debt	n/a	n/a	n/a
Judicial and Legal	n/a	n/a	n/a
Libraries	n/a	n/a	n/a
Parking	n/a	n/a	n/a
Parks and Recreation	n/a	n/a	n/a
Police Protection	n/a	n/a	n/a
Public Welfare	n/a	n/a	n/a
Sewerage	n/a	n/a	n/a
Solid Waste Management	n/a	n/a	n/a
Veterans' Services	n/a	n/a	n/a
Liquor Store	n/a	n/a	n/a
Utility	n/a	n/a	n/a
Employee Retirement	n/a	n/a	n/a

Source: U.S Census Bureau, State & Local Government Finances 2015

DEMOGRAPHICS

Population Growth

Area	1990 Census	2000 Census	2010 Census	2016* Estimate	Population Growth (%) 1990-2016	2010-2016
City	12,064	14,203	12,307	30,168	150.1	145.1
MSA[1]	325,804	350,761	366,513	371,101	13.9	1.3
U.S.	248,709,873	281,421,906	308,745,538	318,558,162	28.1	3.2

Note: (1) Figures cover the Trenton, NJ Metropolitan Statistical Area—see Appendix B for areas included; (*) 2012-2016 5-year estimated population
Source: U.S. Census Bureau, 1990 Census, Census 2000, Census 2010, 2012-2016 American Community Survey 5-Year Estimates

Household Size

Area	Persons in Household (%) One	Two	Three	Four	Five	Six	Seven or More	Average Household Size
City	26.6	37.7	15.5	12.6	6.2	0.9	0.5	2.50
MSA[1]	26.8	31.1	16.9	15.2	6.5	2.2	1.2	2.70
U.S.	27.7	33.7	15.7	13.1	6.0	2.3	1.5	2.60

Note: (1) Figures cover the Trenton, NJ Metropolitan Statistical Area—see Appendix B for areas included
Source: U.S. Census Bureau, 2012-2016 American Community Survey 5-Year Estimates

Race

Area	White Alone[2] (%)	Black Alone[2] (%)	Asian Alone[2] (%)	AIAN[3] Alone[2] (%)	NHOPI[4] Alone[2] (%)	Other Race Alone[2] (%)	Two or More Races (%)
City	74.6	6.1	15.4	0.1	0.0	1.3	2.5
MSA[1]	63.4	20.5	10.4	0.1	0.0	3.7	1.9
U.S.	73.3	12.6	5.2	0.8	0.2	4.8	3.1

Note: (1) Figures cover the Trenton, NJ Metropolitan Statistical Area—see Appendix B for areas included; (2) Alone is defined as not being in combination with one or more other races; (3) American Indian and Alaska Native; (4) Native Hawaiian and Other Pacific Islander
Source: U.S. Census Bureau, 2012-2016 American Community Survey 5-Year Estimates

Hispanic or Latino Origin

Area	Total (%)	Mexican (%)	Puerto Rican (%)	Cuban (%)	Other (%)
City	8.4	1.5	0.8	0.4	5.7
MSA[1]	16.4	1.8	4.5	0.3	9.8
U.S.	17.3	11.0	1.7	0.7	4.0

Note: Persons of Hispanic or Latino origin can be of any race; (1) Figures cover the Trenton, NJ Metropolitan Statistical Area—see Appendix B for areas included
Source: U.S. Census Bureau, 2012-2016 American Community Survey 5-Year Estimates

Segregation

Type	Segregation Indices[1] 1990	2000	2010	2010 Rank[2]	Percent Change 1990-2000	1990-2010	2000-2010
Black/White	n/a	n/a	n/a	n/a	n/a	n/a	n/a
Asian/White	n/a	n/a	n/a	n/a	n/a	n/a	n/a
Hispanic/White	n/a	n/a	n/a	n/a	n/a	n/a	n/a

Note: All figures cover the Metropolitan Statistical Area—see Appendix B for areas included; Figures are based on an analysis of 1990, 2000, and 2010 Census Decennial Census tract data by William H. Frey, Brookings Institution and the University of Michigan Social Science Data Analysis Network. In this analysis all racial groups (whites, blacks, and asians) are non-Hispanic members of those races. Hispanics are shown as a separate category; (1) Segregation Indices are Dissimilarity Indices that measure the degree to which the minority group is distributed differently than whites across census tracts. They range from 0 (complete integration) to 100 (complete segregation) where the value indicates the percentage of the minority group that needs to move to be distributed exactly like whites; (2) Ranges from 1 (most segregated) to 102 (least segregated); n/a not available.
Source: www.CensusScope.org

Ancestry

Area	German	Irish	English	American	Italian	Polish	French[2]	Scottish	Dutch
City	12.2	12.5	10.4	2.8	8.3	5.5	2.6	2.6	2.4
MSA[1]	10.5	11.5	5.7	2.6	13.2	6.2	1.5	1.4	0.9
U.S.	14.4	10.4	7.7	6.9	5.4	2.9	2.6	1.7	1.3

Note: Figures are the percentage of the total population reporting a particular ancestry. The nine most commonly reported ancestries in the U.S. are shown. Figures include multiple ancestries (e.g. if a person reported being Irish and Italian, they were included in both columns); (1) Figures cover the Trenton, NJ Metropolitan Statistical Area—see Appendix B for areas included; (2) Excludes Basque
Source: U.S. Census Bureau, 2012-2016 American Community Survey 5-Year Estimates

Foreign-Born Population

Area	Percent of Population Born in								
	Any Foreign Country	Asia	Mexico	Europe	Carribean	Central America[2]	South America	Africa	Canada
City	26.2	10.9	0.1	8.1	0.3	3.4	1.1	1.3	0.9
MSA[1]	21.8	7.3	0.9	3.7	2.7	3.9	1.6	1.5	0.3
U.S.	13.2	4.0	3.6	1.5	1.3	1.0	0.9	0.6	0.3

Note: (1) Figures cover the Trenton, NJ Metropolitan Statistical Area—see Appendix B for areas included; (2) Excludes Mexico.
Source: U.S. Census Bureau, 2012-2016 American Community Survey 5-Year Estimates

Marital Status

Area	Never Married	Now Married[2]	Separated	Widowed	Divorced
City	43.5	47.0	0.7	2.8	6.1
MSA[1]	37.4	47.0	1.8	5.7	8.1
U.S.	33.0	48.1	2.1	5.9	11.0

Note: Figures are percentages and cover the population 15 years of age and older; (1) Figures cover the Trenton, NJ Metropolitan Statistical Area—see Appendix B for areas included; (2) Excludes separated
Source: U.S. Census Bureau, 2012-2016 American Community Survey 5-Year Estimates

Disability Status

Area	All Ages	Under 18 Years Old	18 to 64 Years Old	65 Years and Over
City	6.0	2.9	4.3	17.9
MSA[1]	10.0	3.4	7.9	31.0
U.S.	12.5	4.1	10.3	35.7

Note: Figures show percent of the civilian noninstitutionalized population that reported having a disability. Disability status is determined from six types of difficulty: vision, hearing, cognitive, ambulatory, self-care, and independent living. For children under 5 years old, hearing and vision difficulty are used to determine disability status. For children between the ages of 5 and 14, disability status is determined from hearing, vision, cognitive, ambulatory, and self-care difficulties. For people aged 15 years and older, they are considered to have a disability if they have difficulty with any one of the six difficulty types; Note: (1) Figures cover the Trenton, NJ Metropolitan Statistical Area—see Appendix B for areas included
Source: U.S. Census Bureau, 2012-2016 American Community Survey 5-Year Estimates

Age

Area	Percent of Population									Median Age
	Under Age 5	Age 5–19	Age 20–34	Age 35–44	Age 45–54	Age 55–64	Age 65–74	Age 75–84	Age 85+	
City	3.7	23.3	25.0	9.2	12.6	11.2	8.0	4.9	1.9	32.8
MSA[1]	5.7	19.6	20.5	13.2	14.6	12.6	7.5	4.1	2.1	38.5
U.S.	6.2	19.6	20.7	12.7	13.6	12.6	8.3	4.3	1.9	37.7

Note: (1) Figures cover the Trenton, NJ Metropolitan Statistical Area—see Appendix B for areas included
Source: U.S. Census Bureau, 2012-2016 American Community Survey 5-Year Estimates

Gender

Area	Males	Females	Males per 100 Females
City	15,544	14,624	106.3
MSA[1]	181,642	189,459	95.9
U.S.	156,765,322	161,792,840	96.9

Note: (1) Figures cover the Trenton, NJ Metropolitan Statistical Area—see Appendix B for areas included
Source: U.S. Census Bureau, 2012-2016 American Community Survey 5-Year Estimates

Religious Groups by Family

Area	Catholic	Baptist	Non-Den.	Methodist[2]	Lutheran	LDS[3]	Pente-costal	Presby-terian[4]	Muslim[5]	Judaism
MSA[1]	33.2	2.8	2.2	2.1	1.1	0.4	1.2	2.3	1.4	2.2
U.S.	19.1	9.3	4.0	4.0	2.3	2.0	1.9	1.6	0.8	0.7

Note: Figures are the number of adherents as a percentage of the total population; (1) Figures cover the Trenton, NJ Metropolitan Statistical Area—see Appendix B for areas included; (2) Methodist/Pietist; (3) Latter Day Saints; (4) Reformed; (5) Figures are estimates
Source: Association of Statisticians of American Religious Bodies, 2010 U.S. Religion Census: Religious Congregations & Membership Study

Religious Groups by Tradition

Area	Catholic	Evangelical Protestant	Mainline Protestant	Other Tradition	Black Protestant	Orthodox
MSA[1]	33.2	4.7	8.1	4.7	1.4	0.5
U.S.	19.1	16.2	7.3	4.3	1.6	0.3

Note: Figures are the number of adherents as a percentage of the total population; (1) Figures cover the Trenton, NJ Metropolitan Statistical Area—see Appendix B for areas included
Source: Association of Statisticians of American Religious Bodies, 2010 U.S. Religion Census: Religious Congregations & Membership Study

ECONOMY

Gross Metropolitan Product

Area	2014	2015	2016	2017	Rank[2]
MSA[1]	29.8	31.4	32.5	33.9	81

Note: Figures are in billions of dollars; (1) Figures cover the Trenton, NJ Metropolitan Statistical Area—see Appendix B for areas included; (2) Rank is based on 2015 data and ranges from 1 to 381
Source: The U.S. Conference of Mayors, U.S. Metro Economies: GMP and Employment Report, 2015-2017

Economic Growth

Area	2012-14 (%)	2015 (%)	2016 (%)	2017 (%)	Rank[2]
MSA[1]	1.3	3.4	2.1	2.1	178
U.S.	2.0	2.4	1.9	2.6	–

Note: Figures are real gross metropolitan product (GMP) growth rates and represent average annual percent change; (1) Figures cover the Trenton, NJ Metropolitan Statistical Area—see Appendix B for areas included; (2) Rank is based on 2012-2014 average annual percent change and ranges from 1 to 381
Source: The U.S. Conference of Mayors, U.S. Metro Economies: GMP and Employment Report, 2015-2017

Metropolitan Area Exports

Area	2011	2012	2013	2014	2015	2016	Rank[2]
MSA[1]	754.1	713.0	879.2	947.1	812.9	969.6	156

Note: Figures are in millions of dollars; (1) Figures cover the Trenton, NJ Metropolitan Statistical Area—see Appendix B for areas included; (2) Rank is based on 2016 data and ranges from 1 to 385
Source: U.S. Department of Commerce, International Trade Administration, Office of Trade & Industry Information, Manufacturing & Services, data extracted March 15, 2018

Building Permits

Area	Single-Family			Multi-Family			Total		
	2016	2017p	Pct. Chg.	2016	2017p	Pct. Chg.	2016	2017p	Pct. Chg.
City	28	41	46.4	0	0	0.0	28	41	46.4
MSA[1]	180	144	-20.0	525	463	-11.8	705	607	-13.9
U.S.	750,800	817,300	8.9	455,800	446,800	-2.0	1,206,600	1,264,100	4.8

Note: (1) Figures cover the Trenton, NJ Metropolitan Statistical Area—see Appendix B for areas included; Figures represent new, privately-owned housing units authorized (unadjusted data); All permit data are based on estimates with imputation; (p) preliminary data.
Source: U.S. Census Bureau, Manufacturing, Mining, and Construction Statistics, Building Permits, 2016, 2017

Bankruptcy Filings

Area	Business Filings			Nonbusiness Filings		
	2016	2017	% Chg.	2016	2017	% Chg.
Mercer County	43	81	88.4	910	961	5.6
U.S.	24,114	23,157	-4.0	770,846	765,863	-0.6

Note: Business filings include Chapter 7, Chapter 11, Chapter 12, and Chapter 13; Nonbusiness filings include Chapter 7, Chapter 11, and Chapter 13
Source: Administrative Office of the U.S. Courts, Business and Nonbusiness Bankruptcy, County Cases Commenced by Chapter of the Bankruptcy Code, During the 12-Month Period Ending December 31, 2016 and Business and Nonbusiness Bankruptcy, County Cases Commenced by Chapter of the Bankruptcy Code, During the 12-Month Period Ending December 31, 2017

Housing Vacancy Rates

Area	Gross Vacancy Rate[2] (%)			Year-Round Vacancy Rate[3] (%)			Rental Vacancy Rate[4] (%)			Homeowner Vacancy Rate[5] (%)		
	2015	2016	2017	2015	2016	2017	2015	2016	2017	2015	2016	2017
MSA[1]	n/a	n/a	n/a	n/a	n/a	n/a	n/a	n/a	n/a	n/a	n/a	n/a
U.S.	12.9	12.8	12.7	10.0	9.9	9.9	7.1	6.9	7.2	1.8	1.7	1.6

Note: (1) Figures cover the Trenton, NJ Metropolitan Statistical Area—see Appendix B for areas included; (2) The percentage of the total housing inventory that is vacant; (3) The percentage of the housing inventory (excluding seasonal units) that is year-round vacant; (4) The percentage of rental inventory that is vacant for rent; (5) The percentage of homeowner inventory that is vacant for sale; n/a not available
Source: U.S. Census Bureau, Housing Vacancies and Homeownership Annual Statistics: 2015, 2016, 2017

INCOME

Income

Area	Per Capita ($)	Median Household ($)	Average Household ($)
City	67,660	118,467	200,430
MSA[1]	38,652	73,966	106,676
U.S.	29,829	55,322	77,866

Note: (1) Figures cover the Trenton, NJ Metropolitan Statistical Area—see Appendix B for areas included
Source: U.S. Census Bureau, 2012-2016 American Community Survey 5-Year Estimates

Household Income Distribution

Area	Percent of Households Earning							
	Under $15,000	$15,000 -$24,999	$25,000 -$34,999	$35,000 -$49,999	$50,000 -$74,999	$75,000 -$99,999	$100,000 -$149,999	$150,000 and up
City	5.7	4.7	7.0	7.1	11.0	8.4	13.2	42.9
MSA[1]	9.6	7.7	7.3	9.6	16.4	12.0	16.5	20.9
U.S.	12.1	10.2	9.9	13.2	17.8	12.2	13.5	11.1

Note: (1) Figures cover the Trenton, NJ Metropolitan Statistical Area—see Appendix B for areas included
Source: U.S. Census Bureau, 2012-2016 American Community Survey 5-Year Estimates

Poverty Rate

Area	All Ages	Under 18 Years Old	18 to 64 Years Old	65 Years and Over
City	6.6	4.5	8.0	4.4
MSA[1]	11.2	15.6	10.4	7.5
U.S.	15.1	21.2	14.2	9.3

Note: Figures are percentage of people whose income during the past 12 months was below the poverty level; (1) Figures cover the Trenton, NJ Metropolitan Statistical Area—see Appendix B for areas included
Source: U.S. Census Bureau, 2012-2016 American Community Survey 5-Year Estimates

EMPLOYMENT

Labor Force and Employment

Area	Civilian Labor Force			Workers Employed		
	Dec. 2016	Dec. 2017	% Chg.	Dec. 2016	Dec. 2017	% Chg.
City	16,595	16,474	-0.7	16,233	16,156	-0.5
MSA[1]	198,967	198,071	-0.5	191,840	190,927	-0.5
U.S.	158,968,000	159,880,000	0.6	151,798,000	153,602,000	1.2

Note: Data is not seasonally adjusted and covers workers 16 years of age and older; (1) Figures cover the Trenton, NJ Metropolitan Statistical Area—see Appendix B for areas included
Source: Bureau of Labor Statistics, Local Area Unemployment Statistics

Unemployment Rate

Area	2017 Jan.	Feb.	Mar.	Apr.	May	Jun.	Jul.	Aug.	Sep.	Oct.	Nov.	Dec.
City	2.9	2.8	2.3	2.1	2.7	2.6	3.2	3.1	2.8	2.7	2.4	1.9
MSA[1]	4.4	4.4	4.0	3.7	3.9	4.1	4.7	4.6	4.2	3.9	3.8	3.6
U.S.	5.1	4.9	4.6	4.1	4.1	4.5	4.6	4.5	4.1	3.9	3.9	3.9

Note: Data is not seasonally adjusted and covers workers 16 years of age and older; (1) Figures cover the Trenton, NJ Metropolitan Statistical Area—see Appendix B for areas included
Source: Bureau of Labor Statistics, Local Area Unemployment Statistics

Average Wages

Occupation	$/Hr.	Occupation	$/Hr.
Accountants and Auditors	40.80	Maids and Housekeeping Cleaners	12.30
Automotive Mechanics	24.00	Maintenance and Repair Workers	22.40
Bookkeepers	22.70	Marketing Managers	n/a
Carpenters	30.30	Nuclear Medicine Technologists	45.60
Cashiers	10.80	Nurses, Licensed Practical	26.60
Clerks, General Office	19.20	Nurses, Registered	36.60
Clerks, Receptionists/Information	16.10	Nursing Assistants	13.30
Clerks, Shipping/Receiving	18.90	Packers and Packagers, Hand	13.80
Computer Programmers	41.80	Physical Therapists	44.90
Computer Systems Analysts	48.30	Postal Service Mail Carriers	24.30
Computer User Support Specialists	30.80	Real Estate Brokers	n/a
Cooks, Restaurant	13.70	Retail Salespersons	11.90
Dentists	n/a	Sales Reps., Exc. Tech./Scientific	39.40
Electrical Engineers	53.70	Sales Reps., Tech./Scientific	41.10
Electricians	36.50	Secretaries, Exc. Legal/Med./Exec.	22.90
Financial Managers	83.30	Security Guards	17.40
First-Line Supervisors/Managers, Sales	22.70	Surgeons	n/a
Food Preparation Workers	11.40	Teacher Assistants*	14.90
General and Operations Managers	84.80	Teachers, Elementary School*	34.20
Hairdressers/Cosmetologists	16.80	Teachers, Secondary School*	36.10
Internists, General	112.50	Telemarketers	13.30
Janitors and Cleaners	15.10	Truck Drivers, Heavy/Tractor-Trailer	22.10
Landscaping/Groundskeeping Workers	17.60	Truck Drivers, Light/Delivery Svcs.	16.10
Lawyers	63.90	Waiters and Waitresses	11.30

Note: Wage data covers the Trenton, NJ Metropolitan Statistical Area—see Appendix B for areas included; (*) Hourly wages for elementary/secondary school teachers and teacher assistants were calculated by the editors from annual wage data based on a 40 hour work week; n/a not available.
Source: Bureau of Labor Statistics, Metro Area Occupational Employment & Wage Estimates, May 2017

Employment by Occupation

Occupation Classification	City (%)	MSA[1] (%)	U.S. (%)
Management, Business, Science, and Arts	69.6	44.0	37.0
Natural Resources, Construction, and Maintenance	1.1	5.8	8.9
Production, Transportation, and Material Moving	1.8	9.5	12.2
Sales and Office	13.6	22.8	23.8
Service	13.9	17.9	18.1

Note: Figures cover employed civilians 16 years of age and older; (1) Figures cover the Trenton, NJ Metropolitan Statistical Area—see Appendix B for areas included
Source: U.S. Census Bureau, 2012-2016 American Community Survey 5-Year Estimates

Employment by Industry

Sector	MSA[1] Number of Employees	MSA[1] Percent of Total	U.S. Percent of Total
Construction, Mining, and Logging	5,300	1.9	5.2
Education and Health Services	48,800	17.9	15.9
Financial Activities	18,800	6.9	5.7
Government	74,900	27.5	15.3
Information	5,100	1.9	1.9
Leisure and Hospitality	16,200	5.9	10.7
Manufacturing	8,600	3.2	8.5
Other Services	10,500	3.9	3.9
Professional and Business Services	43,000	15.8	14.0
Retail Trade	21,000	7.7	11.0
Transportation, Warehousing, and Utilities	12,700	4.7	4.1
Wholesale Trade	7,400	2.7	4.0

Note: Figures are non-farm employment as of December 2017. Figures are not seasonally adjusted and include workers 16 years of age and older; (1) Figures cover the Trenton, NJ Metropolitan Statistical Area—see Appendix B for areas included
Source: Bureau of Labor Statistics, Current Employment Statistics, Employment, Hours, and Earnings

Occupations with Greatest Projected Employment Growth: 2016 – 2018

Occupation[1]	2016 Employment	2018 Projected Employment	Numeric Employment Change	Percent Employment Change
Laborers and Freight, Stock, and Material Movers, Hand	97,040	101,030	3,990	4.1
Registered Nurses	84,890	87,480	2,590	3.1
Home Health Aides	36,970	39,030	2,060	5.6
Combined Food Preparation and Serving Workers, Including Fast Food	55,230	57,260	2,030	3.7
Software Developers, Applications	42,830	44,770	1,940	4.5
Heavy and Tractor-Trailer Truck Drivers	45,100	46,980	1,880	4.2
Construction Laborers	32,430	34,110	1,680	5.2
Carpenters	25,870	27,440	1,570	6.1
Waiters and Waitresses	63,080	64,600	1,520	2.4
Receptionists and Information Clerks	52,840	54,340	1,500	2.8

Note: Projections cover New Jersey; (1) Sorted by numeric employment change
Source: www.projectionscentral.com, State Occupational Projections, 2016–2018 Short-Term Projections

Fastest Growing Occupations: 2016 – 2018

Occupation[1]	2016 Employment	2018 Projected Employment	Numeric Employment Change	Percent Employment Change
Brickmasons and Blockmasons	1,920	2,080	160	8.3
Helpers—Electricians	1,620	1,740	120	8.0
Cement Masons and Concrete Finishers	2,440	2,610	170	7.2
Roofers	2,450	2,620	170	7.2
Helpers—Pipelayers, Plumbers, Pipefitters, and Steamfitters	1,100	1,180	80	7.2
Helpers—Carpenters	1,070	1,150	80	7.1
Electricians	15,320	16,370	1,050	6.8
Operations Research Analysts	1,470	1,560	90	6.3
Carpenters	25,870	27,440	1,570	6.1
Drywall and Ceiling Tile Installers	1,510	1,600	90	6.0

Note: Projections cover New Jersey; (1) Sorted by percent employment change and excludes occupations with numeric employment change less than 50
Source: www.projectionscentral.com, State Occupational Projections, 2016–2018 Short-Term Projections

TAXES

State Corporate Income Tax Rates

State	Tax Rate (%)	Income Brackets ($)	Num. of Brackets	Financial Institution Tax Rate (%)[a]	Federal Income Tax Ded.
New Jersey	9.0 (q)	Flat rate	1	9.0 (q)	No

Note: Tax rates as of January 1, 2018; (a) Rates listed are the corporate income tax rate applied to financial institutions or excise taxes based on income. Some states have other taxes based upon the value of deposits or shares; (q) In New Jersey small businesses with annual entire net income under $100,000 pay a tax rate of 7.5%; businesses with income under $50,000 pay 6.5%. The minimum Corporation Business Tax is based on New Jersey gross receipts. It ranges from $500 for a corporation with gross receipts less than $100,000, to $2,000 for a corporation with gross receipts of $1 million or more.
Source: Federation of Tax Administrators, Range of State Corporate Income Tax Rates, January 1, 2018

State Individual Income Tax Rates

State	Tax Rate (%)	Income Brackets ($)	Num. of Brackets	Personal Exempt. ($)[1]		Fed. Inc. Tax Ded.
				Single	Dependents	
New Jersey	1.4 - 8.97	20,000 - 500,000 (q)	6	1,000	1,500	No

Note: Tax rates as of January 1, 2018; Local- and county-level taxes are not included; n/a not applicable; (1) Married joint filers generally receive double the single exemption; (q) The New Jersey rates reported are for single individuals. For married couples filing jointly, the tax rates also range from 1.4% to 8.97%, with 7 brackets and the same high and low income ranges.
Source: Federation of Tax Administrators, State Individual Income Tax Rates, January 1, 2018

Various State Sales and Excise Tax Rates

State	State Sales Tax (%)	Gasoline[1] (¢/gal.)	Cigarette[2] ($/pack)	Spirits[3] ($/gal.)	Wine[4] ($/gal.)	Beer[5] ($/gal.)	Recreational Marijuana (%)
New Jersey	6.625 (e)	37.1	2.70	5.50	0.88	0.12	Not legal

Note: All tax rates as of January 1, 2018; (1) The American Petroleum Institute has developed a methodology for determining the average tax rate on a gallon of fuel. Rates may include any of the following: excise taxes, environmental fees, storage tank fees, other fees or taxes, general sales tax, and local taxes. In states where gasoline is subject to the general sales tax, or where the fuel tax is based on the average sale price, the average rate determined by API is sensitive to changes in the price of gasoline. States that fully or partially apply general sales taxes to gasoline: CA, CO, GA, IL, IN, MI, NY; (2) The federal excise tax of $1.0066 per pack and local taxes are not included; (3) Rates are those applicable to off-premise sales of 40% alcohol by volume (a.b.v.) distilled spirits in 750ml containers. Local excise taxes are excluded; (4) Rates are those applicable to off-premise sales of 11% a.b.v. non-carbonated wine in 750ml containers; (5) Rates are those applicable to off-premise sales of 4.7% a.b.v. beer in 12 ounce containers; (e) Salem County is not subject to the statewide sales tax rate and collects a local rate of 3.3125%. New Jersey's average local score is represented as a negative.
Source: Tax Foundation, 2018 Facts & Figures: How Does Your State Compare?

State Business Tax Climate Index Rankings

State	Overall Rank	Corporate Tax Rank	Individual Income Tax Rank	Sales Tax Rank	Unemployment Insurance Tax Rank	Property Tax Rank
New Jersey	50	42	48	46	36	50

Note: The index is a measure of how each state's tax laws affect economic performance. The lower the rank, the more favorable a state's tax system is for business. States without a given tax are given a ranking of 1. The scores/rankings for the District of Columbia do not affect other states. The 2018 index represents the tax climate as of July 1, 2017.
Source: Tax Foundation, State Business Tax Climate Index 2018

TRANSPORTATION

Means of Transportation to Work

Area	Car/Truck/Van		Public Transportation			Bicycle	Walked	Other Means	Worked at Home
	Drove Alone	Car-pooled	Bus	Subway	Railroad				
City	49.6	4.3	4.9	0.7	5.9	5.8	15.8	0.3	12.8
MSA[1]	71.8	10.3	3.1	0.3	4.4	0.8	3.1	1.3	4.9
U.S.	76.4	9.3	2.6	1.9	0.6	0.6	2.8	1.3	4.6

Note: Figures are percentages and cover workers 16 years of age and older; (1) Figures cover the Trenton, NJ Metropolitan Statistical Area—see Appendix B for areas included
Source: U.S. Census Bureau, 2012-2016 American Community Survey 5-Year Estimates

Travel Time to Work

Area	Less Than 10 Minutes	10 to 19 Minutes	20 to 29 Minutes	30 to 44 Minutes	45 to 59 Minutes	60 to 89 Minutes	90 Minutes or More
City	20.7	37.9	11.1	12.4	4.7	5.5	7.7
MSA[1]	11.5	32.9	21.4	15.4	6.3	6.9	5.7
U.S.	12.9	29.2	20.9	20.4	8.0	6.0	2.7

Note: Note: Figures are percentages and include workers 16 years old and over; (1) Figures cover the Trenton, NJ Metropolitan Statistical Area—see Appendix B for areas included
Source: U.S. Census Bureau, 2012-2016 American Community Survey 5-Year Estimates

Freeway Travel Time Index

Area	1985	1990	1995	2000	2005	2010	2014
Urban Area Rank[1,2]	n/a	n/a	n/a	n/a	n/a	n/a	n/a
Urban Area Index[1]	n/a	n/a	n/a	n/a	n/a	n/a	n/a
Average Index[3]	1.09	1.11	1.14	1.17	1.20	1.19	1.20

Note: Freeway Travel Time Index—the ratio of travel time in the peak period to the travel time at free-flow conditions. For example, a value of 1.30 indicates a 20-minute free-flow trip takes 26 minutes in the peak (20 minutes x 1.30 = 26 minutes); (1) Data for the Trenton, NJ urban area was not available; (2) Rank is based on 101 urban areas (#1 = highest travel time index); (3) Average of 101 urban areas
Source: Texas Transportation Institute, 2015 Urban Mobility Scorecard, August 2015

Freeway Commuter Stress Index

Area	1985	1990	1995	2000	2005	2010	2014
Urban Area Rank[1,2]	n/a	n/a	n/a	n/a	n/a	n/a	n/a
Urban Area Index[1]	n/a	n/a	n/a	n/a	n/a	n/a	n/a
Average Index[3]	1.13	1.16	1.19	1.22	1.25	1.24	1.25

Note: The Freeway Commuter Stress Index is the same as the Freeway Travel Time Index (see table above) except that it includes only the travel in the peak directions during the peak periods; the TTI includes travel in all directions during the peak period. Thus, the CSI is more indicative of the work trip experienced by each commuter on a daily basis; (1) Data for the Trenton, NJ urban area was not available; (2) Rank is based on 101 urban areas (#1 = highest travel time index); (3) Average of 101 urban areas
Source: Texas Transportation Institute, 2015 Urban Mobility Scorecard, August 2015

Living Environment

COST OF LIVING

Cost of Living Index

Composite Index	Groceries	Housing	Utilities	Transportation	Health Care	Misc. Goods/ Services
n/a	n/a	n/a	n/a	n/a	n/a	n/a

Note: The Cost of Living Index measures regional differences in the cost of consumer goods and services, excluding taxes and non-consumer expenditures, for professional and managerial households in the top income quintile. It is based on more than 50,000 prices covering almost 60 different items for which prices are collected three times a year by chambers of commerce, economic development organizations or university applied economic centers in each participating urban area. The numbers shown should be read as a percentage above or below the national average of 100. For example, a value of 115.4 in the groceries column indicates that grocery prices are 15.4% higher than the national average. Small differences in the index numbers should not be interpreted as significant; n/a not available.
Source: The Council for Community and Economic Research, ACCRA Cost of Living Index, 2017

Grocery Prices

Area[1]	T-Bone Steak ($/pound)	Frying Chicken ($/pound)	Whole Milk ($/half gal.)	Eggs ($/dozen)	Orange Juice ($/64 oz.)	Coffee ($/11.5 oz.)
City[2]	n/a	n/a	n/a	n/a	n/a	n/a
Avg.	11.29	1.40	2.02	1.47	3.55	4.37
Min.	7.71	0.93	1.04	0.70	2.86	3.24
Max.	15.83	2.39	4.03	3.92	6.29	8.16

*Note: (1) Values for the local area are compared with the average, minimum and maximum values for all 294 areas in the Cost of Living Index; (2) Figures cover the Princeton NJ urban area; n/a not available; **T-Bone Steak** (price per pound); **Frying Chicken** (price per pound, whole fryer); **Whole Milk** (half gallon carton); **Eggs** (price per dozen, Grade A, large); **Orange Juice** (64 oz. Tropicana or Florida Natural); **Coffee** (11.5 oz. can, vacuum-packed, Maxwell House, Hills Bros, or Folgers).*
Source: The Council for Community and Economic Research, ACCRA Cost of Living Index, 2017

Housing and Utility Costs

Area[1]	New Home Price ($)	Apartment Rent ($/month)	All Electric ($/month)	Part Electric ($/month)	Other Energy ($/month)	Telephone ($/month)
City[2]	n/a	n/a	n/a	n/a	n/a	n/a
Avg.	335,956	1,047	175.01	97.34	67.93	28.71
Min.	187,788	491	109.48	49.33	35.44	12.39
Max.	1,739,087	4,559	432.62	227.09	353.33	44.61

*Note: (1) Values for the local area are compared with the average, minimum and maximum values for all 294 areas in the Cost of Living Index; (2) Figures cover the Princeton NJ urban area; n/a not available; **New Home Price** (2,400 sf living area, 8,000 sf lot, in urban area with full utilities); **Apartment Rent** (950 sf 2 bedroom/1.5 or 2 bath, unfurnished, excluding all utilities except water); **All Electric** (average monthly cost for an all-electric home); **Part Electric** (average monthly cost for a part-electric home); **Other Energy** (average monthly cost for natural gas, fuel oil, coal, wood, and any other forms of energy except electricity); **Telephone** (price includes basic monthly rate for a private residential line plus additional local usage charges incurred by a family of four).*
Source: The Council for Community and Economic Research, ACCRA Cost of Living Index, 2017

Health Care, Transportation, and Other Costs

Area[1]	Doctor ($/visit)	Dentist ($/visit)	Optometrist ($/visit)	Gasoline ($/gallon)	Beauty Salon ($/visit)	Men's Shirt ($)
City[2]	n/a	n/a	n/a	n/a	n/a	n/a
Avg.	108.00	92.54	101.93	2.25	37.58	30.92
Min.	30.39	60.00	49.75	1.82	16.11	11.20
Max.	193.50	161.94	229.28	3.16	77.35	59.13

*Note: (1) Values for the local area are compared with the average, minimum and maximum values for all 294 areas in the Cost of Living Index; (2) Figures cover the Princeton NJ urban area; n/a not available; **Doctor** (general practitioners routine exam of an established patient); **Dentist** (adult teeth cleaning and periodic oral examination); **Optometrist** (full vision eye exam for established adult patient); **Gasoline** (one gallon regular unleaded, national brand, including all taxes, cash price at self-service pump if available); **Beauty Salon** (woman's shampoo, trim, and blow-dry); **Men's Shirt** (cotton/polyester dress shirt, pinpoint weave, long sleeves).*
Source: The Council for Community and Economic Research, ACCRA Cost of Living Index, 2017

HOUSING

House Price Index (HPI)

Area	National Ranking[2]	Quarterly Change (%)	One-Year Change (%)	Five-Year Change (%)
MSA[1]	234	1.68	1.83	8.55
U.S.[3]	–	1.61	6.68	34.71

Note: The HPI is a weighted repeat sales index. It measures average price changes in repeat sales or refinancings on the same properties. This information is obtained by reviewing repeat mortgage transactions on single-family properties whose mortgages have been purchased or securitized by Fannie Mae or Freddie Mac in January 1975; (1) Figures cover the Trenton, NJ Metropolitan Statistical Area—see Appendix B for areas included; (2) Rankings are based on annual percentage change for all metro areas containing at least 15,000 transactions over the last 10 years and ranges from 1 to 253; (3) figures based on a weighted average of Census Division estimates using a seasonally adjusted, purchase-only index; all figures are for the period ending December 31, 2017

Source: Federal Housing Finance Agency, House Price Index, February 28, 2018

Median Single-Family Home Prices

Area	2015	2016	2017p	Percent Change 2016 to 2017
MSA[1]	262.3	253.1	251.8	-0.5
U.S. Average	223.9	235.5	248.8	5.6

Note: Figures are median sales prices of existing single-family homes in thousands of dollars; (p) preliminary; (1) Figures cover the Trenton, NJ Metropolitan Statistical Area—see Appendix B for areas included

Source: National Association of Realtors, Median Sales Price of Existing Single-Family Homes for Metropolitan Areas, 4th Quarter 2017

Qualifying Income Based on Median Sales Price of Existing Single-Family Homes

Area	With 5% Down ($)	With 10% Down ($)	With 20% Down ($)
MSA[1]	53,342	50,534	44,919
U.S. Average	55,585	52,659	46,808

Note: Figures are preliminary; Qualifying income is based on a mortgage rate of 4.17%. Monthly principal and interest payment is limited to 25% of income; (1) Figures cover the Trenton, NJ Metropolitan Statistical Area—see Appendix B for areas included

Source: National Association of Realtors, Qualifying Income Based on Median Sales Price of Existing Single-Family Homes for Metropolitan Areas, 4th Quarter 2017

Median Apartment Condo-Coop Home Prices

Area	2015	2016	2017p	Percent Change 2016 to 2017
MSA[1]	198.3	197.6	185.6	-6.1
U.S. Average	210.7	220.7	234.3	6.2

Note: Figures are median sales prices of existing apartment condo-coop homes in thousands of dollars; (p) preliminary; (1) Figures cover the Trenton, NJ Metropolitan Statistical Area—see Appendix B for areas included

Source: National Association of Realtors, Median Sales Price of Existing Apartment Condo-Coop Homes for Metropolitan Areas, 4th Quarter 2017

Home Value Distribution

Area	Under $50,000	$50,000 -$99,999	$100,000 -$149,999	$150,000 -$199,999	$200,000 -$299,999	$300,000 -$499,999	$500,000 -$999,999	$1,000,000 or more
City	0.9	1.1	0.5	0.5	2.9	10.4	50.8	32.8
MSA[1]	2.9	7.6	7.2	11.6	26.3	24.7	16.2	3.5
U.S.	8.8	14.8	15.3	14.9	18.4	16.4	9.0	2.5

Note: Figures are percentages and cover owner-occupied housing units; (1) Figures cover the Trenton, NJ Metropolitan Statistical Area—see Appendix B for areas included

Source: U.S. Census Bureau, 2012-2016 American Community Survey 5-Year Estimates

Homeownership Rate

Area	2009 (%)	2010 (%)	2011 (%)	2012 (%)	2013 (%)	2014 (%)	2015 (%)	2016 (%)	2017 (%)
MSA[1]	n/a	n/a	n/a	n/a	n/a	n/a	n/a	n/a	n/a
U.S.	67.4	66.9	66.1	65.4	65.1	64.5	63.7	63.4	63.9

Note: (1) Figures cover the Trenton, NJ Metropolitan Statistical Area—see Appendix B for areas included; n/a not available

Source: U.S. Census Bureau, Housing Vacancies and Homeownership Annual Statistics: 2009-2017

Year Housing Structure Built

Area	2010 or Later	2000 -2009	1990 -1999	1980 -1989	1970 -1979	1960 -1969	1950 -1959	1940 -1949	Before 1940	Median Year
City	1.5	8.5	9.1	9.6	7.9	11.9	18.6	5.9	27.0	1959
MSA[1]	1.2	9.0	9.0	11.5	10.7	12.9	15.8	7.1	22.7	1963
U.S.	2.3	14.7	14.0	13.7	15.6	10.9	10.6	5.2	13.0	1977

Note: Figures are percentages except for Median Year; Note: (1) Figures cover the Trenton, NJ Metropolitan Statistical Area—see Appendix B for areas included
Source: U.S. Census Bureau, 2012-2016 American Community Survey 5-Year Estimates

Gross Monthly Rent

Area	Under $500	$500 -$999	$1,000 -$1,499	$1,500 -$1,999	$2,000 -$2,499	$2,500 -$2,999	$3,000 and up	Median ($)
City	6.1	19.6	28.2	14.7	9.3	8.9	13.2	1,396
MSA[1]	10.5	26.0	37.9	14.9	6.4	2.4	1.9	1,144
U.S.	11.3	43.3	27.7	10.7	4.0	1.6	1.5	949

Note: Figures are percentages except for Median; Gross rent is the contract rent plus the estimated average monthly cost of utilities (electricity, gas, and water and sewer) and fuels (oil, coal, kerosene, wood, etc.) if these are paid by the renter (or paid for the renter by someone else); (1) Figures cover the Trenton, NJ Metropolitan Statistical Area—see Appendix B for areas included
Source: U.S. Census Bureau, 2012-2016 American Community Survey 5-Year Estimates

HEALTH

Health Risk Factors

Category	MSA[1] (%)	U.S. (%)
Adults aged 18–64 who have any kind of health care coverage	n/a	87.7
Adults who reported being in good or excellent health	n/a	83.6
Adults who are current smokers	n/a	17.1
Adults who currently use E-cigarettes	n/a	4.7
Adults who currently use chewing tobacco, snuff, or snus	n/a	4.0
Adults who are heavy drinkers[2]	n/a	6.5
Adults who are binge drinkers[3]	n/a	16.9
Adults who are overweight (BMI 25.0 - 29.9)	n/a	35.3
Adults who are obese (BMI 30.0 - 99.8)	n/a	29.9
Adults who participated in any physical activities in the past month	n/a	76.9
Adults who always or nearly always wears a seat belt	n/a	94.3

Note: n/a not available; (1) Figures cover the Trenton, NJ Metropolitan Statistical Area—see Appendix B for areas included; (2) Heavy drinkers are classified as adult men having more than 14 drinks per week and adult women having more than 7 drinks per week; (3) Binge drinkers are classified as males having five or more drinks on one occasion or females having four or more drinks on one occasion
Source: Centers for Disease Control and Prevention, Behaviorial Risk Factor Surveillance System, SMART: Selected Metropolitan Area Risk Trends, 2016

Health Screening Rates

Category	MSA[1] (%)	U.S. (%)
Adults 50-75 who have had a blood stool test within the past year	n/a	8.0
Adults 50-75 who have had a colonoscopy in the past 10 years	n/a	63.5
Adults aged 65+ who have had flu shot within the past year	n/a	58.6
Adults aged 65+ who have ever had a pneumonia vaccination	n/a	73.4
Adults who have ever been tested for HIV	n/a	35.6
Women aged 21-65 who have had a pap test in the past three years	n/a	79.8
Men aged 40+ who have had a PSA test within the past two years	n/a	39.5
Women aged 40+ who have had a mammogram within the past two years	n/a	72.5

Note: n/a not available; (1) Figures cover the Trenton, NJ Metropolitan Statistical Area—see Appendix B for areas included; Source: Centers for Disease Control and Prevention, Behaviorial Risk Factor Surveillance System, SMART: Selected Metropolitan Area Risk Trends, 2016

Chronic Health Conditions

Category	MSA[1] (%)	U.S. (%)
Adults who have ever been told they had a heart attack	n/a	4.4
Adults who have ever been told they have angina or coronary heart disease	n/a	4.1
Adults who have ever been told they had a stroke	n/a	3.1
Adults who have been told they currently have asthma	n/a	9.3
Adults who have ever been told they have arthritis	n/a	25.8
Adults who have ever been told they have diabetes[2]	n/a	10.5
Adults who have ever been told they had skin cancer	n/a	5.9
Adults who have ever been told they had any other types of cancer	n/a	6.7
Adults who have ever been told they have COPD	n/a	6.3
Adults who have ever been told they have kidney disease	n/a	2.8
Adults who have ever been told they have a form of depression	n/a	17.4

Note: n/a not available; (1) Figures cover the Trenton, NJ Metropolitan Statistical Area—see Appendix B for areas included; (2) Figures do not include pregnancy-related, borderline, or pre-diabetes
Source: Centers for Disease Control and Prevention, Behaviorial Risk Factor Surveillance System, SMART: Selected Metropolitan Area Risk Trends, 2016

Mortality Rates for the Top 10 Causes of Death in the U.S.

ICD-10[a] Sub-Chapter	ICD-10[a] Code	Age-Adjusted Mortality Rate[1] per 100,000 population	
		County[2]	U.S.
Malignant neoplasms	C00-C97	155.4	158.5
Ischaemic heart diseases	I20-I25	81.1	96.8
Other forms of heart disease	I30-I51	62.5	52.4
Chronic lower respiratory diseases	J40-J47	29.1	40.9
Cerebrovascular diseases	I60-I69	32.0	37.2
Organic, including symptomatic, mental disorders	F01-F09	31.9	33.3
Other degenerative diseases of the nervous system	G30-G31	18.2	32.1
Other external causes of accidental injury	W00-X59	26.4	31.2
Diabetes mellitus	E10-E14	18.9	21.1
Hypertensive diseases	I10-I15	16.8	20.8

Note: (a) ICD-10 = International Classification of Diseases 10th Revision; (1) Mortality rates are a three year average covering 2014-2016; (2) Figures cover Mercer County.
Source: Centers for Disease Control and Prevention, National Center for Health Statistics. Underlying Cause of Death 1999-2016 on CDC WONDER Online Database, released December 2017

Mortality Rates for Selected Causes of Death

ICD-10[a] Sub-Chapter	ICD-10[a] Code	Age-Adjusted Mortality Rate[1] per 100,000 population	
		County[2]	U.S.
Assault	X85-Y09	7.1	5.6
Diseases of the liver	K70-K76	12.4	14.0
Human immunodeficiency virus (HIV) disease	B20-B24	2.5	1.9
Influenza and pneumonia	J09-J18	8.6	14.6
Intentional self-harm	X60-X84	6.2	13.2
Malnutrition	E40-E46	Unreliable	1.3
Obesity and other hyperalimentation	E65-E68	2.0	2.1
Renal failure	N17-N19	10.4	13.0
Transport accidents	V01-V99	6.9	12.0
Viral hepatitis	B15-B19	1.7	1.9

Note: (a) ICD-10 = International Classification of Diseases 10th Revision; (1) Mortality rates are a three year average covering 2014-2016; (2) Figures cover Mercer County; Data are Suppressed when the data meet the criteria for confidentiality constraints; Mortality rates are flagged as Unreliable when the rate would be calculated with a numerator of 20 or less.
Source: Centers for Disease Control and Prevention, National Center for Health Statistics. Underlying Cause of Death 1999-2016 on CDC WONDER Online Database, released December 2017

Health Insurance Coverage

Area	With Health Insurance	With Private Health Insurance	With Public Health Insurance	Without Health Insurance	Population Under Age 18 Without Health Insurance
City	96.8	90.8	17.4	3.2	0.2
MSA[1]	90.3	73.1	28.1	9.7	3.8
U.S.	88.3	66.7	33.0	11.7	5.9

Note: Figures are percentages that cover the civilian noninstitutionalized population; (1) Figures cover the Trenton, NJ Metropolitan Statistical Area—see Appendix B for areas included
Source: U.S. Census Bureau, 2012-2016 American Community Survey 5-Year Estimates

Number of Medical Professionals

Area	MDs[3]	DOs[3,4]	Dentists	Podiatrists	Chiropractors	Optometrists
County[1] (number)	1,453	96	292	31	98	71
County[1] (rate[2])	389.4	25.7	78.1	8.3	26.2	19.0
U.S. (rate[2])	276.5	22.3	67.3	6.0	26.7	15.9

Note: Data as of 2016 unless noted; (1) Data covers Mercer County; (2) Rate per 100,000 population; (3) Data as of 2015 and includes all active, non-federal physicians; (4) Doctor of Osteopathic Medicine
Source: U.S. Department of Health and Human Services, Health Resources and Services Administration, Bureau of Health Professions, Area Resource File (ARF) 2016-2017

EDUCATION

Public School District Statistics

District Name	Schls	Pupils	Pupil/ Teacher Ratio	Minority Pupils[1] (%)	Free Lunch Eligible[2] (%)	IEP[3] (%)
Princeton Charter School	1	347	10.7	45.8	1.7	7.5
Princeton Public Schools	6	3,313	10.2	43.1	10.3	20.6

Note: Table includes school districts with 100 or more students; (1) Percentage of students that are not non-Hispanic white; (2) Percentage of students that are eligible for the free lunch program; (3) Percentage of students that have an Individualized Education Program.
Source: U.S. Department of Education, National Center for Education Statistics, Common Core of Data, Local Education Agency (School District) Universe Survey: School Year 2015-2016; U.S. Department of Education, National Center for Education Statistics, Common Core of Data, Public Elementary/Secondary School Universe Survey: School Year 2015-2016

Best High Schools

According to *U.S. News,* Princeton is home to one of the best high schools in the U.S.: **Princeton High School** (#155). More than 22,000 public, magnet and charter schools were ranked based on their performance on state assessments and how well they prepare students for college. Schools with the highest unrounded College Readiness Index values were numerically ranked from 1 to 500 and were classified as gold medal winners. *U.S. News & World Report, "Best High Schools 2017"*

Highest Level of Education

Area	Less than H.S.	H.S. Diploma	Some College, No Deg.	Associate Degree	Bachelor's Degree	Master's Degree	Prof. School Degree	Doctorate Degree
City	4.3	7.6	6.9	2.5	24.4	29.9	7.9	16.5
MSA[1]	12.3	25.2	16.3	5.8	21.0	13.1	2.6	3.7
U.S.	13.0	27.5	21.0	8.2	18.8	8.2	2.0	1.3

Note: Figures cover persons age 25 and over; (1) Figures cover the Trenton, NJ Metropolitan Statistical Area—see Appendix B for areas included
Source: U.S. Census Bureau, 2012-2016 American Community Survey 5-Year Estimates

Educational Attainment by Race

Area	High School Graduate or Higher (%)					Bachelor's Degree or Higher (%)				
	Total	White	Black	Asian	Hisp.[2]	Total	White	Black	Asian	Hisp.[2]
City	95.7	96.1	87.6	97.3	85.2	78.7	81.0	41.9	86.7	32.9
MSA[1]	87.7	89.2	84.5	93.6	61.6	40.4	42.8	18.2	77.4	13.3
U.S.	87.0	88.9	84.3	86.3	65.7	30.3	31.6	20.0	52.1	14.7

Note: Figures shown cover persons 25 years old and over; (1) Figures cover the Trenton, NJ Metropolitan Statistical Area—see Appendix B for areas included; (2) People of Hispanic origin can be of any race
Source: U.S. Census Bureau, 2012-2016 American Community Survey 5-Year Estimates

School Enrollment by Grade and Control

Area	Preschool (%)		Kindergarten (%)		Grades 1 - 4 (%)		Grades 5 - 8 (%)		Grades 9 - 12 (%)	
	Public	Private	Public	Private	Public	Private	Public	Private	Public	Private
City	13.6	86.4	66.4	33.6	85.5	14.5	88.3	11.7	83.0	17.0
MSA[1]	46.4	53.6	88.9	11.1	90.4	9.6	91.2	8.8	88.0	12.0
U.S.	58.4	41.6	87.7	12.3	89.8	10.2	89.7	10.3	90.4	9.6

Note: Figures shown cover persons 3 years old and over; (1) Figures cover the Trenton, NJ Metropolitan Statistical Area—see Appendix B for areas included
Source: U.S. Census Bureau, 2012-2016 American Community Survey 5-Year Estimates

Average Salaries of Public School Classroom Teachers

Area	2015		2016		Change from 2015 to 2016	
	Dollars	Rank[1]	Dollars	Rank[1]	Percent	Rank[2]
New Jersey	69,038	6	69,330	6	0.4	41
U.S. Average	57,611	–	58,353	–	1.3	–

Note: (1) Rank ranges from 1 to 51 where 1 indicates highest salary; (2) Rank ranges from 1 to 51 where 1 indicates highest percent change.
Source: National Education Association, Rankings & Estimates: Rankings of the States 2016 and Estimates of School Statistics 2017

Higher Education

Four-Year Colleges			Two-Year Colleges			Medical Schools[1]	Law Schools[2]	Voc/ Tech[3]
Public	Private Non-profit	Private For-profit	Public	Private Non-profit	Private For-profit			
0	2	0	0	0	0	0	0	0

Note: Figures cover institutions located within the city limits and include main campuses only; (1) includes schools accredited by the Liaison Committee on Medical Education and the American Osteopathic Association's Commission on Osteopathic College Accreditation; (2) includes ABA-accredited schools, schools with provisional ABA accreditation, and state accredited schools; (3) includes all schools with programs that are less than 2 years.
Source: National Center for Education Statistics, Integrated Postsecondary Education System (IPEDS), 2016-17; Wikipedia, List of Medical Schools in the United States, accessed April 2, 2018; Wikipedia, List of Law Schools in the United States, accessed April 2, 2018

According to *U.S. News & World Report,* the Trenton, NJ metro area is home to one of the best national universities in the U.S.: **Princeton University** (#1). The indicators used to capture academic quality fall into a number of categories: assessment by administrators at peer institutions; retention of students; faculty resources; student selectivity; financial resources; alumni giving; high school counselor ratings of colleges; and graduation rate. *U.S. News & World Report, "America's Best Colleges 2018"*

PRESIDENTIAL ELECTION

2016 Presidential Election Results

Area	Clinton	Trump	Johnson	Stein	Other
Mercer County	66.3	29.2	2.1	1.1	1.4
U.S.	48.0	45.9	3.3	1.1	1.7

Note: Results are percentages and may not add to 100% due to rounding
Source: Dave Leip's Atlas of U.S. Presidential Elections

EMPLOYERS

Major Employers

Company Name	Industry
Bayada Nurses	Healthcare
Board of Education	Education
Capital Health Systems	Healthcare
Cenlar Capital Corp.	Mortgage loan servicing
College of NJ	Education
Congoleum Corp.	Manufacturing
Covance	Drug development
Horizon NJ Health	Healthcare
Hough Petroleum Corp.	Motor fuels and lubricants
New Jersey Ed. Assn.	Education
New Jersey Housing & Mortgage Finance Assn	Financial services
New Jersey Re-Insurance Co.	Auto insurance
Novo Nordisk	Pharmaceuticals
Sandoz, Inc.	Pharmaceuticals
St Francis Medical Center	Healthcare
The Crest Group	Real estate
The Hibbert Company	Global fulfillment and distribution
The Times of Trenton Publishing Corp.	Publisher

Note: Companies shown are located within the Trenton, NJ Metropolitan Statistical Area.
Source: Hoovers.com; Wikipedia

PUBLIC SAFETY

Crime Rate

Area	All Crimes	Violent Crimes				Property Crimes		
		Murder	Rape[3]	Robbery	Aggrav. Assault	Burglary	Larceny -Theft	Motor Vehicle Theft
City	836.1	0.0	6.7	0.0	43.8	114.6	654.1	16.9
Metro[1]	2,181.1	6.8	28.9	158.6	208.3	429.5	1,203.1	146.1
U.S.	2,847.8	5.3	40.4	102.8	248.5	468.9	1,745.0	236.9

Note: Figures are crimes per 100,000 population; (1) Figures cover the Trenton, NJ Metropolitan Statistical Area—see Appendix B for areas included; (3) The city and U.S. figures shown were reported using the revised Uniform Crime Reporting (UCR) definition of rape. The metro area figures shown are an aggregate total of the data submitted using both the revised and legacy UCR definitions.
Source: FBI Uniform Crime Reports, 2016

Hate Crimes

Area	Number of Quarters Reported	Number of Incidents per Bias Motivation					
		Race/Ethnicity/ Ancestry	Religion	Sexual Orientation	Disability	Gender	Gender Identity
City	3	1	2	1	0	0	0
U.S.	4	3,489	1,273	1,076	70	31	124

Source: Federal Bureau of Investigation, Hate Crime Statistics 2016

Identity Theft Consumer Reports

Area	Reports	Reports per 100,000 Population	Rank[2]
MSA[1]	416	112	73
U.S.	371,061	114	-

Note: (1) Figures cover the Trenton, NJ Metropolitan Statistical Area—see Appendix B for areas included; (2) Rank ranges from 1 to 389 where 1 indicates greatest number of identity theft reports per 100,000 population
Source: Federal Trade Commission, Consumer Sentinel Network Data Book for January–December 2017

Fraud and Other Consumer Reports

Area	Reports	Reports per 100,000 Population	Rank[2]
MSA[1]	1,754	473	154
U.S.	2,304,550	708	-

Note: (1) Figures cover the Trenton, NJ Metropolitan Statistical Area—see Appendix B for areas included; (2) Rank ranges from 1 to 389 where 1 indicates greatest number of fraud and other consumer reports per 100,000 population
Source: Federal Trade Commission, Consumer Sentinel Network Data Book for January–December 2017

SPORTS

Professional Sports Teams

Team Name	League	Year Established
No teams are located in the metro area		

Source: Wikipedia, Major Professional Sports Teams of the United States and Canada, April 5, 2018

CLIMATE

Average and Extreme Temperatures

Temperature	Jan	Feb	Mar	Apr	May	Jun	Jul	Aug	Sep	Oct	Nov	Dec	Yr.
Extreme High (°F)	74	74	85	94	96	100	104	101	100	89	84	72	104
Average High (°F)	39	42	51	63	73	82	86	85	78	67	55	43	64
Average Temp. (°F)	32	34	42	53	63	72	77	76	68	57	47	36	55
Average Low (°F)	24	26	33	43	53	62	67	66	59	47	38	28	45
Extreme Low (°F)	-7	-4	7	19	28	44	51	44	35	25	15	1	-7

Note: Figures cover the years 1948-1990
Source: National Climatic Data Center, International Station Meteorological Climate Summary, 9/96

Average Precipitation/Snowfall/Humidity

Precip./Humidity	Jan	Feb	Mar	Apr	May	Jun	Jul	Aug	Sep	Oct	Nov	Dec	Yr.
Avg. Precip. (in.)	3.2	2.8	3.7	3.5	3.7	3.6	4.1	4.0	3.3	2.7	3.4	3.3	41.4
Avg. Snowfall (in.)	7	7	4	Tr	Tr	0	0	0	0	Tr	1	4	22
Avg. Rel. Hum. 7am (%)	74	73	73	72	75	77	80	82	84	83	79	75	77
Avg. Rel. Hum. 4pm (%)	60	55	51	48	51	52	54	55	55	54	57	60	54

Note: Figures cover the years 1948-1990; Tr = Trace amounts (<0.05 in. of rain; <0.5 in. of snow)
Source: National Climatic Data Center, International Station Meteorological Climate Summary, 9/96

Weather Conditions

Temperature			Daytime Sky			Precipitation		
10°F & below	32°F & below	90°F & above	Clear	Partly cloudy	Cloudy	0.01 inch or more precip.	0.1 inch or more snow/ice	Thunder-storms
5	94	23	81	146	138	117	14	27

Note: Figures are average number of days per year and cover the years 1948-1990
Source: National Climatic Data Center, International Station Meteorological Climate Summary, 9/96

HAZARDOUS WASTE

Superfund Sites

The Trenton, NJ metro area has no sites on the EPA's Superfund Final National Priorities List. There are a total of 1,396 Superfund sites with a status of proposed or final on the list in the U.S.
U.S. Environmental Protection Agency, National Priorities List, April 4, 2018

AIR & WATER QUALITY

Air Quality Trends: Ozone

	1990	1995	2000	2005	2010	2012	2013	2014	2015	2016
MSA[1]	0.105	0.107	0.099	0.089	0.086	0.080	0.070	0.071	0.073	0.074
U.S.	0.087	0.089	0.081	0.079	0.073	0.075	0.069	0.067	0.068	0.069

Note: (1) Data covers the Trenton, NJ Metropolitan Statistical Area—see Appendix B for areas included. The values shown are the composite ozone concentration averages among trend sites based on the highest fourth daily maximum 8-hour concentration in parts per million. These trends are based on sites having an adequate record of monitoring data during the trend period. Data from exceptional events are included.
Source: U.S. Environmental Protection Agency, Air Quality Monitoring Information, "Air Quality Trends by City, 1990-2016"

Air Quality Index

Area	Percent of Days when Air Quality was...[2]					AQI Statistics[2]	
	Good	Moderate	Unhealthy for Sensitive Groups	Unhealthy	Very Unhealthy	Maximum	Median
MSA[1]	76.4	22.5	1.1	0.0	0.0	133	40

Note: (1) Data covers the Trenton, NJ Metropolitan Statistical Area—see Appendix B for areas included; (2) Based on 365 days with AQI data in 2017. Air Quality Index (AQI) is an index for reporting daily air quality. EPA calculates the AQI for five major air pollutants regulated by the Clean Air Act: ground-level ozone, particle pollution (aka particulate matter), carbon monoxide, sulfur dioxide, and nitrogen dioxide. The AQI runs from 0 to 500. The higher the AQI value, the greater the level of air pollution and the greater the health concern. There are six AQI categories: "Good" AQI is between 0 and 50. Air quality is considered satisfactory; "Moderate" AQI is between 51 and 100. Air quality is acceptable; "Unhealthy for Sensitive Groups" When AQI values are between 101 and 150, members of sensitive groups may experience health effects; "Unhealthy" When AQI values are between 151 and 200 everyone may begin to experience health effects; "Very Unhealthy" AQI values between 201 and 300 trigger a health alert; "Hazardous" AQI values over 300 trigger warnings of emergency conditions (not shown).
Source: U.S. Environmental Protection Agency, Air Quality Index Report, 2017

Air Quality Index Pollutants

Area	Percent of Days when AQI Pollutant was...[2]					
	Carbon Monoxide	Nitrogen Dioxide	Ozone	Sulfur Dioxide	Particulate Matter 2.5	Particulate Matter 10
MSA[1]	0.0	0.0	58.1	0.0	41.9	0.0

Note: (1) Data covers the Trenton, NJ Metropolitan Statistical Area—see Appendix B for areas included; (2) Based on 365 days with AQI data in 2017. The Air Quality Index (AQI) is an index for reporting daily air quality. EPA calculates the AQI for five major air pollutants regulated by the Clean Air Act: ground-level ozone, particle pollution (also known as particulate matter), carbon monoxide, sulfur dioxide, and nitrogen dioxide. The AQI runs from 0 to 500. The higher the AQI value, the greater the level of air pollution and the greater the health concern.
Source: U.S. Environmental Protection Agency, Air Quality Index Report, 2017

Maximum Air Pollutant Concentrations: Particulate Matter, Ozone, CO and Lead

	Particulate Matter 10 (ug/m³)	Particulate Matter 2.5 Wtd AM (ug/m³)	Particulate Matter 2.5 24-Hr (ug/m³)	Ozone (ppm)	Carbon Monoxide (ppm)	Lead (ug/m³)
MSA[1] Level	n/a	8.6	17	0.074	n/a	n/a
NAAQS[2]	150	15	35	0.075	9	0.15
Met NAAQS[2]	n/a	Yes	Yes	Yes	n/a	n/a

Note: (1) Data covers the Trenton, NJ Metropolitan Statistical Area—see Appendix B for areas included; Data from exceptional events are included; (2) National Ambient Air Quality Standards; ppm = parts per million; ug/m³ = micrograms per cubic meter; n/a not available.
Concentrations: Particulate Matter 10 (coarse particulate)—highest second maximum 24-hour concentration; Particulate Matter 2.5 Wtd AM (fine particulate)—highest weighted annual mean concentration; Particulate Matter 2.5 24-Hour (fine particulate)—highest 98th percentile 24-hour concentration; Ozone—highest fourth daily maximum 8-hour concentration; Carbon Monoxide—highest second maximum non-overlapping 8-hour concentration; Lead—maximum running 3-month average
Source: U.S. Environmental Protection Agency, Air Quality Monitoring Information, "Air Quality Statistics by City, 2016"

Maximum Air Pollutant Concentrations: Nitrogen Dioxide and Sulfur Dioxide

	Nitrogen Dioxide AM (ppb)	Nitrogen Dioxide 1-Hr (ppb)	Sulfur Dioxide AM (ppb)	Sulfur Dioxide 1-Hr (ppb)	Sulfur Dioxide 24-Hr (ppb)
MSA[1] Level	n/a	n/a	n/a	n/a	n/a
NAAQS[2]	53	100	30	75	140
Met NAAQS[2]	n/a	n/a	n/a	n/a	n/a

Note: (1) Data covers the Trenton, NJ Metropolitan Statistical Area—see Appendix B for areas included; Data from exceptional events are included; (2) National Ambient Air Quality Standards; ppm = parts per million; ug/m^3 = micrograms per cubic meter; n/a not available.
Concentrations: Nitrogen Dioxide AM—highest arithmetic mean concentration; Nitrogen Dioxide 1-Hr—highest 98th percentile 1-hour daily maximum concentration; Sulfur Dioxide AM—highest annual mean concentration; Sulfur Dioxide 1-Hr—highest 99th percentile 1-hour daily maximum concentration; Sulfur Dioxide 24-Hr—highest second maximum 24-hour concentration
Source: U.S. Environmental Protection Agency, Air Quality Monitoring Information, "Air Quality Statistics by City, 2016"

Drinking Water

Water System Name	Pop. Served	Primary Water Source Type	Violations[1]	
			Health Based	Monitoring/ Reporting
Trenton Water Works	205,000	Surface	1	2

Note: (1) Based on violation data from January 1, 2017 to December 31, 2017
Source: U.S. Environmental Protection Agency, Office of Ground Water and Drinking Water, Safe Drinking Water Information System (based on data extracted April 5, 2018)

Randolph, New Jersey

Background

Centrally located in Morris County, Randolph lies within the New Jersey Highlands, which is part of the Appalachian Mountain range, and yet New York City is less than an hour away.

The territory of Randolph was inhabited by the Lenni Lenape Indian tribe. The earliest European settlers were Quakers. Incorporated in 1805 and named for Quaker Hartshorne Fitz-Randolph, it was populated mostly by Quaker farm families until the mid-1700s, when a significant Presbyterian population settled there.

The iron industry played an important role in the development of Randolph for 200 years, beginning in 1714 when New Jersey's first iron mine was registered. During the Revolutionary War, the city's mines supplied the continental army with ore for tools and weapons. Situated upstream of the Black River, the iron hills of Randolph attracted settlers and its streams provided power for industry.

Following the Civil War, local industries declined, as less expensive products from larger urban manufacturers became readily available. There was a brief boom in iron mining in the 1870s, but Randolph reverted to an agricultural economy as inexpensive land attracted newcomers. At the turn of the century, a large number of Jewish families, disillusioned with urban life, came to Randolph from New York City. They purchased farmland, but, unable to make a living from the land, instead opened summer boarding houses for Jewish visitors from New York City. In 1919, a wealthy New York garment maker bought 100 acres and opened the township's first bungalow community; eventually, there were 45. Two of the largest resorts, Ackerman's and Saltz's, survived into the 1970s.

Randolph's population began to rise in the 1940s and continued for the next fifty years. This growth was aided by the construction of Route 10, which became a state highway in 1931. Despite this growth, substantial tracts of undeveloped land remained, including the hills and fields that became the campus of County College of Morris in 1968. Though Randolph's landscape continued to change, especially during the development of the 1990s, acres of open space still exist. Farmhouses, mills and other historic structures remain as reminders of Randolph's agricultural and rural heritage.

Although not as prevalent as it was 200 years ago, metal manufacturing is still a large sector of the economy in Randolph.

Historical landmarks include the Liberty Tree that began growing in 1720, the 1869 Bryant Distillery, and the 1924 Millbrook School, which is now used as office space. Additionally, Gristmill Road, one of the oldest streets in Randolph, is on the National Register of Historic Places. Randolph celebrated its bicentennial in 2005. During this time, the Historical Society of Old Randolph moved the Randolph Museum to the historic Brundage House in Freedom Park.

The median July temperature in Randolph is 71.5 degrees, while in January, typically the coldest month, the median temperature is 25.5. The city averages 4.67 inches of rainfall per month from April to September and 3.95 inches of snowfall per month from December to February.

Rankings

General Rankings

- New York* was identified as one of America's fastest-growing cities in terms of population growth by CNNMoney.com. The area ranked #1 out of 10. Criteria: population growth between July 2015 and July 2016; cities and towns with populations of 50,000. *CNNMoney, "10 Fastest-Growing Cities," June 2, 2017*

Business/Finance Rankings

- The personal finance site NerdWallet analyzed 183 American metropolitan areas with populations over 250,000 and more than 15,000 businesses to rank where entrepreneurs find the most success. Criteria included area economy, annual income, housing cost, unemployment rate, and the success rate of area businesses. New York* ranked #32. *www.nerdwallet.com, "Best Places to Start a Business," April 27, 2015*
- Metro areas with the largest gap in income between rich and poor residents were identified by 24/7 Wall Street using the U.S. Census Bureau's 2013 American Community Survey. The New York* metro area placed #7 among metro areas with the widest wealth gap between rich and poor. *247wallst.com, "20 Cities with the Widest Gap between the Rich and Poor," July 8, 2015*
- In a survey of economic confidence in the nation's 50 largest metropolitan areas conducted January–December 2014, the New York* metro area placed #23, according to Gallup's 2014 Economic Confidence Index. *Gallup, "San Jose and San Francisco Lead in Economic Confidence," March 19, 2015*
- The Brookings Institution ranked the 100 largest metro areas in the U.S. based on income inequality. New York* was ranked #2 (#1 = greatest ineqality). Criteria: the "95/20 ratio," a figure representing the income at which a household earns more than 95 percent of all other households, divided by the income at which a household earns more than only 20 percent of all other households. *Brookings Institution, "Household Income Inequality, 100 Largest U.S. Metro Areas, 2014-2016," February 5, 2018*
- Payscale.com ranked the largest metro areas in terms of wage growth. The New York* metro area ranked #1. Criteria: private-sector wage growth between the 4th quarter of 2016 and the 4th quarter of 2017. *PayScale, "Wage Trends by Metro Area-4th Quarter," January 17, 2018*
- The New York* metro area was identified as one of the most debt-ridden places in America by the finance site Credit.com. The metro area was ranked #3. Criteria: residents' average credit card debt as well as median income. *Credit.com, "25 Cities With the Most Credit Card Debt," February 28, 2018*
- New York* was identified as one of America's most frugal metro areas by *Coupons.com.* The city ranked #15 out of 25. Criteria: digital coupon usage. *Coupons.com, "America's Most Frugal Cities of 2017," March 22, 2018*
- New York* was cited as one of America's top metros for new and expanded facility projects in 2017. The area ranked #5 in the large metro area category (population over 1 million). *Site Selection, "Top Metropolitans of 2017," March 2018*
- The New York* metro area appeared on the Milken Institute "2017 Best Performing Cities" list. Rank: #82 out of 200 large metro areas. Criteria: job growth; wage and salary growth; high-tech output growth. *Milken Institute, "Best-Performing Cities 2017," January 2018*
- *Forbes* ranked the 200 most populous metro areas to determine the nation's "Best Places for Business and Careers." The Newark* metro area was ranked #152. Criteria: costs (business and living); job growth (past and projected); income growth; quality of life; educational attainment (college and high school); projected economic growth; cultural and recreational opportunities; net migration patterns; number of highly ranked colleges. *Forbes, "The Best Places for Business and Careers 2017," October 24, 2017*

Dating/Romance Rankings

- *Apartment List* conducted its annual survey of renters to compile a list of metros that have the best opportunities for dating. Nearly 11,000 respondents, from February 2017 through January 2018, rated their current city or neighborhood for opportunities to date and make friends. The New York* metro area ranked #10 out of 70 where single residents were very satisfied or somewhat satisfied, making it among the ten best metros for dating opportunities. Other criteria analyzed included gender and education levels of renters. *Apartment List, "Best Metros for Dating 2018," February 6, 2018*

Education Rankings

- Personal finance website *WalletHub* analyzed the 150 largest U.S. metropolitan statistical areas to determine where the most educated Americans are choosing to settle. Criteria: education quality and attainment gap; education levels; percentage of workers with degrees; public school rankings; quality and size of each metro area's universities. New York* was ranked #36 (#1 = most educated city). *www.WalletHub.com, "2017's Most and Least Educated Cities in America," July 25, 2017*

Environmental Rankings

- Sperling's BestPlaces assessed 379 metropolitan areas of the United States for the likelihood of dangerously extreme weather events or earthquakes. In general the Southeast and South-Central regions have the highest risk of weather extremes and earthquakes, while the Pacific Northwest enjoys the lowest risk. Of the least risky metropolitan areas, the Newark* metro area was ranked #208. *www.bestplaces.net, "Safest Places from Natural Disasters," April 2011*

- The U.S. Environmental Protection Agency (EPA) released a list of U.S. metropolitan areas with the most ENERGY STAR certified buildings in 2016. The New York* metro area was ranked #3 out of 25. *U.S. Environmental Protection Agency, "2017 Energy Star Top Cities," June 2017*

- New York* was highlighted as one of the 25 most ozone-polluted metro areas in the U.S. during 2013 through 2015. The area ranked #9. *American Lung Association, State of the Air 2017*

- New York* was highlighted as one of the 25 metro areas most polluted by year-round particle pollution (Annual PM 2.5) in the U.S. during 2013 through 2015. The area ranked #22. *American Lung Association, State of the Air 2017*

Health/Fitness Rankings

- For each of the 50 most populous metro areas in the United States, the American College of Sports Medicine's American Fitness Index evaluated infrastructure, community assets, and policies that encourage healthy and fit lifestyles, including preventive health behaviors, levels of chronic disease conditions, health care access, and community resources and policies that support physical activity. The New York* metro area ranked #18 for "community fitness." *www.americanfitnessindex.org, "ACSM American Fitness Index Health and Community Fitness Status of the 50 Largest Metropolitan Areas," May 2017*

- The New York* metro area was identified as one of the worst cities for bed bugs in America by pest control company Orkin. The area ranked #8 out of 50 based on the number of bed bug treatments Orkin performed from December 2016 to November 2017. *Orkin, "Baltimore and Washington D.C. Continue to Hold Top Spots," January 8, 2018*

- New York* was identified as a "2016 Spring Allergy Capital." The area ranked #31 out of 100. Three groups of factors were used to identify the most severe cities for people with allergies during the spring season: annual pollen levels; medicine utilization; access to board-certified allergists. *Asthma and Allergy Foundation of America, "Spring Allergy Capitals 2016"*

- New York* was identified as a "2016 Fall Allergy Capital." The area ranked #52 out of 100. Three groups of factors were used to identify the most severe cities for people with allergies during the fall season: annual pollen levels; medicine utilization; access to board-certified allergists. *Asthma and Allergy Foundation of America, "Fall Allergy Capitals 2016"*
- New York* was identified as a "2015 Asthma Capital." The area ranked #35 out of the nation's 100 largest metropolitan areas. Criteria: estimated prevalence; self-reported prevalence; crude death rate for asthma; annual pollen score; annual air quality; public smoking laws; number of board-certified asthma specialists; school inhaler access laws; rescue medication use; controller medication use; ER visits for asthma; uninsured rate; poverty rate. *Asthma and Allergy Foundation of America, "Asthma Capitals 2015"*
- The New York* metro area ranked #75 out of 189 in The Gallup-Healthways Well-Being Index. Criteria: purpose; social well being; financial health; community and physical health. Results are based on telephone interviews with adults, aged 18 and older, living in metropolitan areas in the 50 U.S. states and the District of Columbia. *Gallup-Healthways, "State of American Well-Being, 2017 Community Well-Being Rankings" March 2018*

Real Estate Rankings

- FitSmallBusiness looked at 50 of the largest metropolitan areas in the U.S. to determine which metro was the best to start a real estate business. Data was compiled from such sources as: Zillow, Trulia, U.S. Census Bureau, and the Bureau of Labor Statistics. Criteria: location; inventory; annual wages; median sales price of homes; days on the market; median price cut percentage; and other factors that would influence real estate professional growth. The New York* metro area ranked #6. *fitsmallbusiness.com, "The Best Cities to Become a Real Estate Agent in 2018," January 30, 2018*
- With data from RealtyTrac, Yahoo! Finance researchers listed the housing markets in which housing affordability is improving most, factoring in interest rates as well as median home prices. The New York* metro area was among the least affordable housing markets. *news.yahoo.com, "10 Cities Where Ordinary People Can No Longer Afford Homes," March 5, 2014*
- The New York* metro area was identified as one of the 20 least affordable housing markets in the U.S. in 2017. The area ranked #12 out of 180 markets. Criteria: qualification for a mortgage loan on a typical home. *National Association of Realtors®, Affordability Index of Existing Single-Family Homes for Metropolitan Areas, 2017*
- Newark* was ranked #143 out of 238 metro areas in terms of housing affordability in 2017 by the National Association of Home Builders (#1 = most affordable). Criteria: the share of homes sold in that area affordable to a family earning the local median income, based on standard mortgage underwriting criteria. *National Association of Home Builders®, NAHB-Wells Fargo Housing Opportunity Index, 4th Quarter 2017*

Safety Rankings

- The National Insurance Crime Bureau ranked 382 metro areas in the U.S. in terms of per capita rates of vehicle theft. The New York* metro area ranked #292 (#1 = highest rate). Criteria: number of vehicle theft offenses per 100,000 inhabitants in 2016. *National Insurance Crime Bureau, "Hot Spots 2016," June 8, 2017*

Seniors/Retirement Rankings

- From its Best Cities for Successful Aging indexes, the Milken Institute generated rankings for metropolitan areas, weighing data in nine categories—health care, wellness, living arrangements, transportation and convenience, financial characteristics, education, employment, community engagement, and overall livability. The New York* metro area was ranked #11 overall in the large metro area category. *Milken Institute, "Best Cities for Successful Aging, 2017" March 14, 2017*

Sports/Recreation Rankings

- According to the personal finance website NerdWallet, the New York* metro area, at #4, is one of the nation's top dozen metro areas for sports fans. Criteria included the presence of all four major sports—MLB, NFL, NHL, and NBA, fan enthusiasm (as measured by game attendance), ticket affordability, and "sports culture," that is, number of sports bars. *www.nerdwallet.com, "Best Cities for Sports Fans," May 5, 2013*

Transportation Rankings

- New York* was identified as one of the most congested metro areas in the U.S. The area ranked #4 out of 10. Criteria: yearly delay per auto commuter in hours. *Texas A&M Transportation Institute, "2015 Urban Mobility Scorecard," August 2015*

- The New York* metro area appeared on *Forbes* list of places with the most extreme commutes. The metro area ranked #2 out of 10. Criteria: average travel time; percentage of mega commuters. Mega-commuters travel more than 90 minutes and 50 miles each way to work. *Forbes.com, "The Cities with the Most Extreme Commutes," March 5, 2013*

Women/Minorities Rankings

- The *Houston Chronicle* listed the New York* metro area as #4 in top places for young Latinos to live in the U.S. Research was largely based on housing and occupational data from the largest metropolitan areas performed by *Forbes* and NBC Universo. Criteria: percentage of 18-34 year-olds; Latino college grad rates; and diversity. *blog.chron.com, "The 15 Best Big Cities for Latino Millenials," January 26, 2016*

Miscellaneous Rankings

- The watchdog site Charity Navigator conducts an annual study of charities in the nation's major markets both to analyze statistical differences in their financial, accountability, and transparency practices and to track year-to-year variations in individual philanthropic communities. Charity Navigator's analysis demonstrated that the financial, accountability and transparency behaviors of America's largest charities can be influenced by the metropolitan market within which the charity operates. The New York* metro area was ranked #19 among the 30 metro markets in the rating category of Overall Score. *www.charitynavigator.org, "2017 Metro Market Study," May 1, 2017*

- The Harris Poll's Happiness Index survey revealed that of the top ten U.S. markets, the New York* metro area residents ranked #6 in happiness. Criteria included strong assent to positive statements and strong disagreement with negative ones, and degree of agreement with a series of statements about respondents' personal relationships and general outlook. *www.theharrispoll.com, "Dallas/Fort Worth Is "Happiest" City among America's Top Ten Markets," September 4, 2013*

- Energizer Personal Care, the makers of Edge® shave gel, in partnership with Sperling's BestPlaces, ranked 50 major metro areas in terms of everyday irritations. The New York* metro area ranked #2 the 50 metro area most irritating to guys. Criteria: high male-to-female ratio; poor sports team performance and high ticket prices; slow traffic; lack of job availability; unaffordable housing; extreme weather; lack of nightlife and fitness options. *Energizer Personal Care, "Most Irritating Cities for Guys," August 26, 2013*

- The National Alliance to End Homelessness listed the 25 most populous metro areas with the highest rate of homelessness. The New York* metro area had a high rate of homelessness. Criteria: number of homeless people per 10,000 population in 2016. *National Alliance to End Homelessness, "Homelessness in the 25 Most Populous U.S. Metro Areas," September 1, 2017*

*Randolph is located within the New York-Newark-Jersey City, NY-NJ-PA Metropolitan Statistical Area and the Newark, NJ-PA Metropolitan Division.

Business Environment

CITY FINANCES

City Government Finances

Component	2015 ($000)	2015 ($ per capita)
Total Revenues	n/a	n/a
Total Expenditures	n/a	n/a
Debt Outstanding	n/a	n/a
Cash and Securities[1]	n/a	n/a

Note: (1) Cash and security holdings of a government at the close of its fiscal year,, including those of its dependent agencies, utilities, and liquor stores.
Source: U.S Census Bureau, State & Local Government Finances 2015

City Government Revenue by Source

Source	2015 ($000)	2015 ($ per capita)	2015 (%)
General Revenue			
From Federal Government	n/a	n/a	n/a
From State Government	n/a	n/a	n/a
From Local Governments	n/a	n/a	n/a
Taxes			
Property	n/a	n/a	n/a
Sales and Gross Receipts	n/a	n/a	n/a
Personal Income	n/a	n/a	n/a
Corporate Income	n/a	n/a	n/a
Motor Vehicle License	n/a	n/a	n/a
Other Taxes	n/a	n/a	n/a
Current Charges	n/a	n/a	n/a
Liquor Store	n/a	n/a	n/a
Utility	n/a	n/a	n/a
Employee Retirement	n/a	n/a	n/a

Source: U.S Census Bureau, State & Local Government Finances 2015

City Government Expenditures by Function

Function	2015 ($000)	2015 ($ per capita)	2015 (%)
General Direct Expenditures			
Air Transportation	n/a	n/a	n/a
Corrections	n/a	n/a	n/a
Education	n/a	n/a	n/a
Employment Security Administration	n/a	n/a	n/a
Financial Administration	n/a	n/a	n/a
Fire Protection	n/a	n/a	n/a
General Public Buildings	n/a	n/a	n/a
Governmental Administration, Other	n/a	n/a	n/a
Health	n/a	n/a	n/a
Highways	n/a	n/a	n/a
Hospitals	n/a	n/a	n/a
Housing and Community Development	n/a	n/a	n/a
Interest on General Debt	n/a	n/a	n/a
Judicial and Legal	n/a	n/a	n/a
Libraries	n/a	n/a	n/a
Parking	n/a	n/a	n/a
Parks and Recreation	n/a	n/a	n/a
Police Protection	n/a	n/a	n/a
Public Welfare	n/a	n/a	n/a
Sewerage	n/a	n/a	n/a
Solid Waste Management	n/a	n/a	n/a
Veterans' Services	n/a	n/a	n/a
Liquor Store	n/a	n/a	n/a
Utility	n/a	n/a	n/a
Employee Retirement	n/a	n/a	n/a

Source: U.S Census Bureau, State & Local Government Finances 2015

DEMOGRAPHICS

Population Growth

Area	1990 Census	2000 Census	2010 Census	2016* Estimate	Population Growth (%) 1990-2016	2010-2016
City	19,974	24,847	25,734	25,916	29.7	0.7
MSA[1]	16,845,992	18,323,002	18,897,109	20,031,443	18.9	6.0
U.S.	248,709,873	281,421,906	308,745,538	318,558,162	28.1	3.2

Note: (1) Figures cover the New York-Newark-Jersey City, NY-NJ-PA Metropolitan Statistical Area—see Appendix B for areas included; (*) 2012-2016 5-year estimated population
Source: U.S. Census Bureau, 1990 Census, Census 2000, Census 2010, 2012-2016 American Community Survey 5-Year Estimates

Household Size

Area	Persons in Household (%) One	Two	Three	Four	Five	Six	Seven or More	Average Household Size
City	20.7	27.4	20.2	21.2	8.2	1.6	0.6	2.90
MSA[1]	28.0	29.1	17.0	14.7	6.7	2.6	1.9	2.80
U.S.	27.7	33.7	15.7	13.1	6.0	2.3	1.5	2.60

Note: (1) Figures cover the New York-Newark-Jersey City, NY-NJ-PA Metropolitan Statistical Area—see Appendix B for areas included
Source: U.S. Census Bureau, 2012-2016 American Community Survey 5-Year Estimates

Race

Area	White Alone[2] (%)	Black Alone[2] (%)	Asian Alone[2] (%)	AIAN[3] Alone[2] (%)	NHOPI[4] Alone[2] (%)	Other Race Alone[2] (%)	Two or More Races (%)
City	81.6	3.5	10.3	0.0	0.1	1.7	2.8
MSA[1]	58.7	17.1	10.6	0.3	0.0	10.3	2.9
U.S.	73.3	12.6	5.2	0.8	0.2	4.8	3.1

Note: (1) Figures cover the New York-Newark-Jersey City, NY-NJ-PA Metropolitan Statistical Area—see Appendix B for areas included; (2) Alone is defined as not being in combination with one or more other races; (3) American Indian and Alaska Native; (4) Native Hawaiian and Other Pacific Islander
Source: U.S. Census Bureau, 2012-2016 American Community Survey 5-Year Estimates

Hispanic or Latino Origin

Area	Total (%)	Mexican (%)	Puerto Rican (%)	Cuban (%)	Other (%)
City	9.5	0.9	2.3	0.2	6.1
MSA[1]	23.8	3.1	6.3	0.7	13.7
U.S.	17.3	11.0	1.7	0.7	4.0

Note: Persons of Hispanic or Latino origin can be of any race; (1) Figures cover the New York-Newark-Jersey City, NY-NJ-PA Metropolitan Statistical Area—see Appendix B for areas included
Source: U.S. Census Bureau, 2012-2016 American Community Survey 5-Year Estimates

Segregation

Type	Segregation Indices[1] 1990	2000	2010	2010 Rank[2]	Percent Change 1990-2000	1990-2010	2000-2010
Black/White	80.9	80.2	78.0	2	-0.7	-2.9	-2.2
Asian/White	47.4	50.8	51.9	3	3.5	4.5	1.0
Hispanic/White	66.2	65.6	62.0	3	-0.6	-4.2	-3.6

Note: All figures cover the Metropolitan Statistical Area—see Appendix B for areas included; Figures are based on an analysis of 1990, 2000, and 2010 Census Decennial Census tract data by William H. Frey, Brookings Institution and the University of Michigan Social Science Data Analysis Network. In this analysis all racial groups (whites, blacks, and asians) are non-Hispanic members of those races. Hispanics are shown as a separate category; (1) Segregation Indices are Dissimilarity Indices that measure the degree to which the minority group is distributed differently than whites across census tracts. They range from 0 (complete integration) to 100 (complete segregation) where the value indicates the percentage of the minority group that needs to move to be distributed exactly like whites; (2) Ranges from 1 (most segregated) to 102 (least segregated); n/a not available.
Source: www.CensusScope.org

Ancestry

Area	German	Irish	English	American	Italian	Polish	French[2]	Scottish	Dutch
City	14.2	16.1	6.3	4.2	20.6	8.2	1.7	1.5	0.8
MSA[1]	6.8	10.0	2.9	4.8	13.1	4.0	1.0	0.7	0.7
U.S.	14.4	10.4	7.7	6.9	5.4	2.9	2.6	1.7	1.3

Note: Figures are the percentage of the total population reporting a particular ancestry. The nine most commonly reported ancestries in the U.S. are shown. Figures include multiple ancestries (e.g. if a person reported being Irish and Italian, they were included in both columns); (1) Figures cover the New York-Newark-Jersey City, NY-NJ-PA Metropolitan Statistical Area—see Appendix B for areas included; (2) Excludes Basque
Source: U.S. Census Bureau, 2012-2016 American Community Survey 5-Year Estimates

Foreign-Born Population

Area	Percent of Population Born in								
	Any Foreign Country	Asia	Mexico	Europe	Carribean	Central America[2]	South America	Africa	Canada
City	18.7	8.1	0.7	3.7	0.9	0.6	3.2	1.2	0.3
MSA[1]	28.7	8.3	1.6	4.5	6.6	1.9	4.2	1.2	0.2
U.S.	13.2	4.0	3.6	1.5	1.3	1.0	0.9	0.6	0.3

Note: (1) Figures cover the New York-Newark-Jersey City, NY-NJ-PA Metropolitan Statistical Area—see Appendix B for areas included; (2) Excludes Mexico.
Source: U.S. Census Bureau, 2012-2016 American Community Survey 5-Year Estimates

Marital Status

Area	Never Married	Now Married[2]	Separated	Widowed	Divorced
City	26.2	63.3	1.0	3.6	5.9
MSA[1]	38.1	45.7	2.4	5.8	7.9
U.S.	33.0	48.1	2.1	5.9	11.0

Note: Figures are percentages and cover the population 15 years of age and older; (1) Figures cover the New York-Newark-Jersey City, NY-NJ-PA Metropolitan Statistical Area—see Appendix B for areas included; (2) Excludes separated
Source: U.S. Census Bureau, 2012-2016 American Community Survey 5-Year Estimates

Disability Status

Area	All Ages	Under 18 Years Old	18 to 64 Years Old	65 Years and Over
City	5.9	2.1	3.9	24.6
MSA[1]	10.0	3.2	7.4	33.3
U.S.	12.5	4.1	10.3	35.7

Note: Figures show percent of the civilian noninstitutionalized population that reported having a disability. Disability status is determined from six types of difficulty: vision, hearing, cognitive, ambulatory, self-care, and independent living. For children under 5 years old, hearing and vision difficulty are used to determine disability status. For children between the ages of 5 and 14, disability status is determined from hearing, vision, cognitive, ambulatory, and self-care difficulties. For people aged 15 years and older, they are considered to have a disability if they have difficulty with any one of the six difficulty types; Note: (1) Figures cover the New York-Newark-Jersey City, NY-NJ-PA Metropolitan Statistical Area—see Appendix B for areas included
Source: U.S. Census Bureau, 2012-2016 American Community Survey 5-Year Estimates

Age

Area	Percent of Population									Median Age
	Under Age 5	Age 5–19	Age 20–34	Age 35–44	Age 45–54	Age 55–64	Age 65–74	Age 75–84	Age 85+	
City	6.1	21.4	16.0	12.4	18.0	14.3	6.8	3.7	1.4	40.9
MSA[1]	6.1	18.4	21.3	13.3	14.3	12.3	7.8	4.2	2.1	38.0
U.S.	6.2	19.6	20.7	12.7	13.6	12.6	8.3	4.3	1.9	37.7

Note: (1) Figures cover the New York-Newark-Jersey City, NY-NJ-PA Metropolitan Statistical Area—see Appendix B for areas included
Source: U.S. Census Bureau, 2012-2016 American Community Survey 5-Year Estimates

Gender

Area	Males	Females	Males per 100 Females
City	12,428	13,488	92.1
MSA[1]	9,684,087	10,347,356	93.6
U.S.	156,765,322	161,792,840	96.9

Note: (1) Figures cover the New York-Newark-Jersey City, NY-NJ-PA Metropolitan Statistical Area—see Appendix B for areas included
Source: U.S. Census Bureau, 2012-2016 American Community Survey 5-Year Estimates

Religious Groups by Family

Area	Catholic	Baptist	Non-Den.	Methodist[2]	Lutheran	LDS[3]	Pente-costal	Presby-terian[4]	Muslim[5]	Judaism
MSA[1]	36.9	1.9	1.8	1.3	0.8	0.4	0.9	1.1	2.3	4.8
U.S.	19.1	9.3	4.0	4.0	2.3	2.0	1.9	1.6	0.8	0.7

Note: Figures are the number of adherents as a percentage of the total population; (1) Figures cover the New York-Newark-Jersey City, NY-NJ-PA Metropolitan Statistical Area—see Appendix B for areas included; (2) Methodist/Pietist; (3) Latter Day Saints; (4) Reformed; (5) Figures are estimates
Source: Association of Statisticians of American Religious Bodies, 2010 U.S. Religion Census: Religious Congregations & Membership Study

Religious Groups by Tradition

Area	Catholic	Evangelical Protestant	Mainline Protestant	Other Tradition	Black Protestant	Orthodox
MSA[1]	36.9	4.0	4.1	8.4	1.2	1.0
U.S.	19.1	16.2	7.3	4.3	1.6	0.3

Note: Figures are the number of adherents as a percentage of the total population; (1) Figures cover the New York-Newark-Jersey City, NY-NJ-PA Metropolitan Statistical Area—see Appendix B for areas included
Source: Association of Statisticians of American Religious Bodies, 2010 U.S. Religion Census: Religious Congregations & Membership Study

ECONOMY

Gross Metropolitan Product

Area	2014	2015	2016	2017	Rank[2]
MSA[1]	1,551.3	1,613.8	1,664.0	1,735.1	1

Note: Figures are in billions of dollars; (1) Figures cover the New York-Newark-Jersey City, NY-NJ-PA Metropolitan Statistical Area—see Appendix B for areas included; (2) Rank is based on 2015 data and ranges from 1 to 381
Source: The U.S. Conference of Mayors, U.S. Metro Economies: GMP and Employment Report, 2015-2017

Economic Growth

Area	2012-14 (%)	2015 (%)	2016 (%)	2017 (%)	Rank[2]
MSA[1]	1.6	1.9	1.6	2.2	151
U.S.	2.0	2.4	1.9	2.6	–

Note: Figures are real gross metropolitan product (GMP) growth rates and represent average annual percent change; (1) Figures cover the New York-Newark-Jersey City, NY-NJ-PA Metropolitan Statistical Area—see Appendix B for areas included; (2) Rank is based on 2012-2014 average annual percent change and ranges from 1 to 381
Source: The U.S. Conference of Mayors, U.S. Metro Economies: GMP and Employment Report, 2015-2017

Metropolitan Area Exports

Area	2011	2012	2013	2014	2015	2016	Rank[2]
MSA[1]	105,102.0	102,298.0	106,922.8	105,266.6	95,645.4	89,649.5	1

Note: Figures are in millions of dollars; (1) Figures cover the New York-Newark-Jersey City, NY-NJ-PA Metropolitan Statistical Area—see Appendix B for areas included; (2) Rank is based on 2016 data and ranges from 1 to 385
Source: U.S. Department of Commerce, International Trade Administration, Office of Trade & Industry Information, Manufacturing & Services, data extracted March 15, 2018

Building Permits

Area	Single-Family 2016	Single-Family 2017p	Single-Family Pct. Chg.	Multi-Family 2016	Multi-Family 2017p	Multi-Family Pct. Chg.	Total 2016	Total 2017p	Total Pct. Chg.
City	37	93	151.4	5	0	-100.0	42	93	121.4
MSA[1]	9,987	10,549	5.6	32,479	39,344	21.1	42,466	49,893	17.5
U.S.	750,800	817,300	8.9	455,800	446,800	-2.0	1,206,600	1,264,100	4.8

Note: (1) Figures cover the New York-Newark-Jersey City, NY-NJ-PA Metropolitan Statistical Area—see Appendix B for areas included; Figures represent new, privately-owned housing units authorized (unadjusted data); All permit data are based on estimates with imputation; (p) preliminary data.
Source: U.S. Census Bureau, Manufacturing, Mining, and Construction Statistics, Building Permits, 2016, 2017

Bankruptcy Filings

Area	Business Filings 2016	Business Filings 2017	Business Filings % Chg.	Nonbusiness Filings 2016	Nonbusiness Filings 2017	Nonbusiness Filings % Chg.
Morris County	53	61	15.1	799	801	0.3
U.S.	24,114	23,157	-4.0	770,846	765,863	-0.6

Note: Business filings include Chapter 7, Chapter 11, Chapter 12, and Chapter 13; Nonbusiness filings include Chapter 7, Chapter 11, and Chapter 13
Source: Administrative Office of the U.S. Courts, Business and Nonbusiness Bankruptcy, County Cases Commenced by Chapter of the Bankruptcy Code, During the 12-Month Period Ending December 31, 2016 and Business and Nonbusiness Bankruptcy, County Cases Commenced by Chapter of the Bankruptcy Code, During the 12-Month Period Ending December 31, 2017

Housing Vacancy Rates

Area	Gross Vacancy Rate[2] (%) 2015	2016	2017	Year-Round Vacancy Rate[3] (%) 2015	2016	2017	Rental Vacancy Rate[4] (%) 2015	2016	2017	Homeowner Vacancy Rate[5] (%) 2015	2016	2017
MSA[1]	9.8	10.3	10.7	8.6	9.1	9.6	4.2	4.7	4.6	2.1	2.2	1.9
U.S.	12.9	12.8	12.7	10.0	9.9	9.9	7.1	6.9	7.2	1.8	1.7	1.6

Note: (1) Figures cover the New York-Newark-Jersey City, NY-NJ-PA Metropolitan Statistical Area—see Appendix B for areas included; (2) The percentage of the total housing inventory that is vacant; (3) The percentage of the housing inventory (excluding seasonal units) that is year-round vacant; (4) The percentage of rental inventory that is vacant for rent; (5) The percentage of homeowner inventory that is vacant for sale
Source: U.S. Census Bureau, Housing Vacancies and Homeownership Annual Statistics: 2015, 2016, 2017

INCOME

Income

Area	Per Capita ($)	Median Household ($)	Average Household ($)
City	57,054	121,334	162,062
MSA[1]	37,510	69,211	101,617
U.S.	29,829	55,322	77,866

Note: (1) Figures cover the New York-Newark-Jersey City, NY-NJ-PA Metropolitan Statistical Area—see Appendix B for areas included
Source: U.S. Census Bureau, 2012-2016 American Community Survey 5-Year Estimates

Household Income Distribution

Area	Under $15,000	$15,000 -$24,999	$25,000 -$34,999	$35,000 -$49,999	$50,000 -$74,999	$75,000 -$99,999	$100,000 -$149,999	$150,000 and up
City	3.9	2.8	3.4	5.3	11.4	12.0	21.2	39.9
MSA[1]	11.7	8.5	7.7	10.2	15.0	11.7	15.9	19.3
U.S.	12.1	10.2	9.9	13.2	17.8	12.2	13.5	11.1

(Percent of Households Earning)

Note: (1) Figures cover the New York-Newark-Jersey City, NY-NJ-PA Metropolitan Statistical Area—see Appendix B for areas included
Source: U.S. Census Bureau, 2012-2016 American Community Survey 5-Year Estimates

Poverty Rate

Area	All Ages	Under 18 Years Old	18 to 64 Years Old	65 Years and Over
City	3.0	2.5	2.9	5.0
MSA[1]	14.2	20.0	12.7	11.7
U.S.	15.1	21.2	14.2	9.3

Note: Figures are percentage of people whose income during the past 12 months was below the poverty level; (1) Figures cover the New York-Newark-Jersey City, NY-NJ-PA Metropolitan Statistical Area—see Appendix B for areas included
Source: U.S. Census Bureau, 2012-2016 American Community Survey 5-Year Estimates

EMPLOYMENT

Labor Force and Employment

Area	Civilian Labor Force			Workers Employed		
	Dec. 2016	Dec. 2017	% Chg.	Dec. 2016	Dec. 2017	% Chg.
City	13,705	13,538	-1.2	13,267	13,145	-0.9
MD[1]	1,240,075	1,228,255	-1.0	1,188,742	1,178,033	-0.9
U.S.	158,968,000	159,880,000	0.6	151,798,000	153,602,000	1.2

Note: Data is not seasonally adjusted and covers workers 16 years of age and older; (1) Figures cover the Newark, NJ-PA Metropolitan Division—see Appendix B for areas included
Source: Bureau of Labor Statistics, Local Area Unemployment Statistics

Unemployment Rate

Area	2017											
	Jan.	Feb.	Mar.	Apr.	May	Jun.	Jul.	Aug.	Sep.	Oct.	Nov.	Dec.
City	3.7	3.6	3.4	3.2	3.4	3.5	3.9	3.8	3.5	3.2	3.0	2.9
MD[1]	4.9	4.9	4.5	4.2	4.4	4.6	5.1	5.0	4.7	4.4	4.3	4.1
U.S.	5.1	4.9	4.6	4.1	4.1	4.5	4.6	4.5	4.1	3.9	3.9	3.9

Note: Data is not seasonally adjusted and covers workers 16 years of age and older; (1) Figures cover the Newark, NJ-PA Metropolitan Division—see Appendix B for areas included
Source: Bureau of Labor Statistics, Local Area Unemployment Statistics

Average Wages

Occupation	$/Hr.	Occupation	$/Hr.
Accountants and Auditors	45.10	Maids and Housekeeping Cleaners	12.60
Automotive Mechanics	23.50	Maintenance and Repair Workers	21.90
Bookkeepers	22.70	Marketing Managers	91.50
Carpenters	33.00	Nuclear Medicine Technologists	46.40
Cashiers	10.80	Nurses, Licensed Practical	27.30
Clerks, General Office	17.60	Nurses, Registered	40.50
Clerks, Receptionists/Information	16.00	Nursing Assistants	14.40
Clerks, Shipping/Receiving	16.70	Packers and Packagers, Hand	11.20
Computer Programmers	42.90	Physical Therapists	48.40
Computer Systems Analysts	48.10	Postal Service Mail Carriers	24.50
Computer User Support Specialists	34.60	Real Estate Brokers	50.30
Cooks, Restaurant	15.40	Retail Salespersons	13.50
Dentists	n/a	Sales Reps., Exc. Tech./Scientific	37.60
Electrical Engineers	49.80	Sales Reps., Tech./Scientific	45.90
Electricians	33.80	Secretaries, Exc. Legal/Med./Exec.	20.20
Financial Managers	85.60	Security Guards	14.90
First-Line Supervisors/Managers, Sales	23.40	Surgeons	135.40
Food Preparation Workers	11.30	Teacher Assistants*	14.50
General and Operations Managers	82.50	Teachers, Elementary School*	33.10
Hairdressers/Cosmetologists	18.60	Teachers, Secondary School*	36.40
Internists, General	98.40	Telemarketers	13.80
Janitors and Cleaners	15.10	Truck Drivers, Heavy/Tractor-Trailer	23.60
Landscaping/Groundskeeping Workers	14.40	Truck Drivers, Light/Delivery Svcs.	17.80
Lawyers	69.70	Waiters and Waitresses	14.30

Note: Wage data covers the Newark, NJ-PA Metropolitan Division—see Appendix B for areas included; (*) Hourly wages for elementary/secondary school teachers and teacher assistants were calculated by the editors from annual wage data based on a 40 hour work week; n/a not available.
Source: Bureau of Labor Statistics, Metro Area Occupational Employment & Wage Estimates, May 2017

Employment by Occupation

Occupation Classification	City (%)	MSA[1] (%)	U.S. (%)
Management, Business, Science, and Arts	59.4	41.2	37.0
Natural Resources, Construction, and Maintenance	3.5	6.9	8.9
Production, Transportation, and Material Moving	5.3	9.0	12.2
Sales and Office	22.4	23.7	23.8
Service	9.5	19.3	18.1

Note: Figures cover employed civilians 16 years of age and older; (1) Figures cover the New York-Newark-Jersey City, NY-NJ-PA Metropolitan Statistical Area—see Appendix B for areas included
Source: U.S. Census Bureau, 2012-2016 American Community Survey 5-Year Estimates

Employment by Industry

Sector	MD[1]		U.S.
	Number of Employees	Percent of Total	Percent of Total
Construction, Mining, and Logging	45,000	3.7	5.2
Education and Health Services	191,300	15.7	15.9
Financial Activities	76,600	6.3	5.7
Government	177,900	14.6	15.3
Information	20,600	1.7	1.9
Leisure and Hospitality	95,900	7.9	10.7
Manufacturing	75,400	6.2	8.5
Other Services	54,800	4.5	3.9
Professional and Business Services	225,000	18.5	14.0
Retail Trade	123,100	10.1	11.0
Transportation, Warehousing, and Utilities	68,900	5.7	4.1
Wholesale Trade	63,700	5.2	4.0

Note: Figures are non-farm employment as of December 2017. Figures are not seasonally adjusted and include workers 16 years of age and older; (1) Figures cover the Newark, NJ-PA Metropolitan Division—see Appendix B for areas included
Source: Bureau of Labor Statistics, Current Employment Statistics, Employment, Hours, and Earnings

Occupations with Greatest Projected Employment Growth: 2016 – 2018

Occupation[1]	2016 Employment	2018 Projected Employment	Numeric Employment Change	Percent Employment Change
Laborers and Freight, Stock, and Material Movers, Hand	97,040	101,030	3,990	4.1
Registered Nurses	84,890	87,480	2,590	3.1
Home Health Aides	36,970	39,030	2,060	5.6
Combined Food Preparation and Serving Workers, Including Fast Food	55,230	57,260	2,030	3.7
Software Developers, Applications	42,830	44,770	1,940	4.5
Heavy and Tractor-Trailer Truck Drivers	45,100	46,980	1,880	4.2
Construction Laborers	32,430	34,110	1,680	5.2
Carpenters	25,870	27,440	1,570	6.1
Waiters and Waitresses	63,080	64,600	1,520	2.4
Receptionists and Information Clerks	52,840	54,340	1,500	2.8

Note: Projections cover New Jersey; (1) Sorted by numeric employment change
Source: www.projectionscentral.com, State Occupational Projections, 2016–2018 Short-Term Projections

Fastest Growing Occupations: 2016 – 2018

Occupation[1]	2016 Employment	2018 Projected Employment	Numeric Employment Change	Percent Employment Change
Brickmasons and Blockmasons	1,920	2,080	160	8.3
Helpers—Electricians	1,620	1,740	120	8.0
Cement Masons and Concrete Finishers	2,440	2,610	170	7.2
Roofers	2,450	2,620	170	7.2
Helpers—Pipelayers, Plumbers, Pipefitters, and Steamfitters	1,100	1,180	80	7.2
Helpers—Carpenters	1,070	1,150	80	7.1
Electricians	15,320	16,370	1,050	6.8
Operations Research Analysts	1,470	1,560	90	6.3
Carpenters	25,870	27,440	1,570	6.1
Drywall and Ceiling Tile Installers	1,510	1,600	90	6.0

Note: Projections cover New Jersey; (1) Sorted by percent employment change and excludes occupations with numeric employment change less than 50
Source: www.projectionscentral.com, State Occupational Projections, 2016–2018 Short-Term Projections

TAXES

State Corporate Income Tax Rates

State	Tax Rate (%)	Income Brackets ($)	Num. of Brackets	Financial Institution Tax Rate (%)[a]	Federal Income Tax Ded.
New Jersey	9.0 (q)	Flat rate	1	9.0 (q)	No

Note: Tax rates as of January 1, 2018; (a) Rates listed are the corporate income tax rate applied to financial institutions or excise taxes based on income. Some states have other taxes based upon the value of deposits or shares; (q) In New Jersey small businesses with annual entire net income under $100,000 pay a tax rate of 7.5%; businesses with income under $50,000 pay 6.5%. The minimum Corporation Business Tax is based on New Jersey gross receipts. It ranges from $500 for a corporation with gross receipts less than $100,000, to $2,000 for a corporation with gross receipts of $1 million or more.
Source: Federation of Tax Administrators, Range of State Corporate Income Tax Rates, January 1, 2018

State Individual Income Tax Rates

State	Tax Rate (%)	Income Brackets ($)	Num. of Brackets	Personal Exempt. ($)[1] Single	Personal Exempt. ($)[1] Dependents	Fed. Inc. Tax Ded.
New Jersey	1.4 - 8.97	20,000 - 500,000 (q)	6	1,000	1,500	No

Note: Tax rates as of January 1, 2018; Local- and county-level taxes are not included; n/a not applicable; (1) Married joint filers generally receive double the single exemption; (q) The New Jersey rates reported are for single individuals. For married couples filing jointly, the tax rates also range from 1.4% to 8.97%, with 7 brackets and the same high and low income ranges.
Source: Federation of Tax Administrators, State Individual Income Tax Rates, January 1, 2018

Various State Sales and Excise Tax Rates

State	State Sales Tax (%)	Gasoline[1] (¢/gal.)	Cigarette[2] ($/pack)	Spirits[3] ($/gal.)	Wine[4] ($/gal.)	Beer[5] ($/gal.)	Recreational Marijuana (%)
New Jersey	6.625 (e)	37.1	2.70	5.50	0.88	0.12	Not legal

Note: All tax rates as of January 1, 2018; (1) The American Petroleum Institute has developed a methodology for determining the average tax rate on a gallon of fuel. Rates may include any of the following: excise taxes, environmental fees, storage tank fees, other fees or taxes, general sales tax, and local taxes. In states where gasoline is subject to the general sales tax, or where the fuel tax is based on the average sale price, the average rate determined by API is sensitive to changes in the price of gasoline. States that fully or partially apply general sales taxes to gasoline: CA, CO, GA, IL, IN, MI, NY; (2) The federal excise tax of $1.0066 per pack and local taxes are not included; (3) Rates are those applicable to off-premise sales of 40% alcohol by volume (a.b.v.) distilled spirits in 750ml containers. Local excise taxes are excluded; (4) Rates are those applicable to off-premise sales of 11% a.b.v. non-carbonated wine in 750ml containers; (5) Rates are those applicable to off-premise sales of 4.7% a.b.v. beer in 12 ounce containers; (e) Salem County is not subject to the statewide sales tax rate and collects a local rate of 3.3125%. New Jersey's average local score is represented as a negative.
Source: Tax Foundation, 2018 Facts & Figures: How Does Your State Compare?

State Business Tax Climate Index Rankings

State	Overall Rank	Corporate Tax Rank	Individual Income Tax Rank	Sales Tax Rank	Unemployment Insurance Tax Rank	Property Tax Rank
New Jersey	50	42	48	46	36	50

Note: The index is a measure of how each state's tax laws affect economic performance. The lower the rank, the more favorable a state's tax system is for business. States without a given tax are given a ranking of 1. The scores/rankings for the District of Columbia do not affect other states. The 2018 index represents the tax climate as of July 1, 2017.
Source: Tax Foundation, State Business Tax Climate Index 2018

TRANSPORTATION

Means of Transportation to Work

Area	Car/Truck/Van		Public Transportation			Bicycle	Walked	Other Means	Worked at Home
	Drove Alone	Car-pooled	Bus	Subway	Railroad				
City	78.7	7.3	0.8	0.1	3.8	0.1	1.9	0.3	6.9
MSA[1]	50.1	6.6	7.7	19.1	3.8	0.6	6.0	1.8	4.2
U.S.	76.4	9.3	2.6	1.9	0.6	0.6	2.8	1.3	4.6

Note: Figures are percentages and cover workers 16 years of age and older; (1) Figures cover the New York-Newark-Jersey City, NY-NJ-PA Metropolitan Statistical Area—see Appendix B for areas included
Source: U.S. Census Bureau, 2012-2016 American Community Survey 5-Year Estimates

Travel Time to Work

Area	Less Than 10 Minutes	10 to 19 Minutes	20 to 29 Minutes	30 to 44 Minutes	45 to 59 Minutes	60 to 89 Minutes	90 Minutes or More
City	8.0	20.5	20.1	23.0	12.4	8.5	7.5
MSA[1]	7.4	19.3	16.4	23.7	12.4	14.4	6.5
U.S.	12.9	29.2	20.9	20.4	8.0	6.0	2.7

Note: Note: Figures are percentages and include workers 16 years old and over; (1) Figures cover the New York-Newark-Jersey City, NY-NJ-PA Metropolitan Statistical Area—see Appendix B for areas included
Source: U.S. Census Bureau, 2012-2016 American Community Survey 5-Year Estimates

Freeway Travel Time Index

Area	1985	1990	1995	2000	2005	2010	2014
Urban Area Rank[1,2]	11	9	8	7	7	8	8
Urban Area Index[1]	1.16	1.20	1.24	1.29	1.33	1.33	1.34
Average Index[3]	1.09	1.11	1.14	1.17	1.20	1.19	1.20

Note: Freeway Travel Time Index—the ratio of travel time in the peak period to the travel time at free-flow conditions. For example, a value of 1.30 indicates a 20-minute free-flow trip takes 26 minutes in the peak (20 minutes x 1.30 = 26 minutes); (1) Covers the New York-Newark NY-NJ-CT urban area; (2) Rank is based on 101 urban areas (#1 = highest travel time index); (3) Average of 101 urban areas
Source: Texas Transportation Institute, 2015 Urban Mobility Scorecard, August 2015

Freeway Commuter Stress Index

Area	1985	1990	1995	2000	2005	2010	2014
Urban Area Rank[1,2]	19	19	13	12	11	11	12
Urban Area Index[1]	1.21	1.24	1.29	1.34	1.38	1.38	1.39
Average Index[3]	1.13	1.16	1.19	1.22	1.25	1.24	1.25

Note: The Freeway Commuter Stress Index is the same as the Freeway Travel Time Index (see table above) except that it includes only the travel in the peak directions during the peak periods; the TTI includes travel in all directions during the peak period. Thus, the CSI is more indicative of the work trip experienced by each commuter on a daily basis; (1) Covers the New York-Newark NY-NJ-CT urban area; (2) Rank is based on 101 urban areas (#1 = highest travel time index); (3) Average of 101 urban areas
Source: Texas Transportation Institute, 2015 Urban Mobility Scorecard, August 2015

Living Environment

COST OF LIVING

Cost of Living Index

Composite Index	Groceries	Housing	Utilities	Trans-portation	Health Care	Misc. Goods/ Services
122.9	106.7	152.8	115.4	112.7	101.9	112.5

Note: The Cost of Living Index measures regional differences in the cost of consumer goods and services, excluding taxes and non-consumer expenditures, for professional and managerial households in the top income quintile. It is based on more than 50,000 prices covering almost 60 different items for which prices are collected three times a year by chambers of commerce, economic development organizations or university applied economic centers in each participating urban area. The numbers shown should be read as a percentage above or below the national average of 100. For example, a value of 115.4 in the groceries column indicates that grocery prices are 15.4% higher than the national average. Small differences in the index numbers should not be interpreted as significant; Figures cover the Newark-Elizabeth NJ urban area.
Source: The Council for Community and Economic Research, ACCRA Cost of Living Index, 2017

Grocery Prices

Area[1]	T-Bone Steak ($/pound)	Frying Chicken ($/pound)	Whole Milk ($/half gal.)	Eggs ($/dozen)	Orange Juice ($/64 oz.)	Coffee ($/11.5 oz.)
City[2]	11.80	1.69	2.27	1.72	3.04	3.82
Avg.	11.29	1.40	2.02	1.47	3.55	4.37
Min.	7.71	0.93	1.04	0.70	2.86	3.24
Max.	15.83	2.39	4.03	3.92	6.29	8.16

*Note: (1) Values for the local area are compared with the average, minimum and maximum values for all 294 areas in the Cost of Living Index; (2) Figures cover the Newark-Elizabeth NJ urban area; **T-Bone Steak** (price per pound); **Frying Chicken** (price per pound, whole fryer); **Whole Milk** (half gallon carton); **Eggs** (price per dozen, Grade A, large); **Orange Juice** (64 oz. Tropicana or Florida Natural); **Coffee** (11.5 oz. can, vacuum-packed, Maxwell House, Hills Bros, or Folgers).*
Source: The Council for Community and Economic Research, ACCRA Cost of Living Index, 2017

Housing and Utility Costs

Area[1]	New Home Price ($)	Apartment Rent ($/month)	All Electric ($/month)	Part Electric ($/month)	Other Energy ($/month)	Telephone ($/month)
City[2]	507,404	1,663	-	126.69	64.16	33.50
Avg.	335,956	1,047	175.01	97.34	67.93	28.71
Min.	187,788	491	109.48	49.33	35.44	12.39
Max.	1,739,087	4,559	432.62	227.09	353.33	44.61

*Note: (1) Values for the local area are compared with the average, minimum and maximum values for all 294 areas in the Cost of Living Index; (2) Figures cover the Newark-Elizabeth NJ urban area; **New Home Price** (2,400 sf living area, 8,000 sf lot, in urban area with full utilities); **Apartment Rent** (950 sf 2 bedroom/1.5 or 2 bath, unfurnished, excluding all utilities except water); **All Electric** (average monthly cost for an all-electric home); **Part Electric** (average monthly cost for a part-electric home); **Other Energy** (average monthly cost for natural gas, fuel oil, coal, wood, and any other forms of energy except electricity); **Telephone** (price includes basic monthly rate for a private residential line plus additional local usage charges incurred by a family of four).*
Source: The Council for Community and Economic Research, ACCRA Cost of Living Index, 2017

Health Care, Transportation, and Other Costs

Area[1]	Doctor ($/visit)	Dentist ($/visit)	Optometrist ($/visit)	Gasoline ($/gallon)	Beauty Salon ($/visit)	Men's Shirt ($)
City[2]	96.29	99.80	100.58	2.39	37.53	38.16
Avg.	108.00	92.54	101.93	2.25	37.58	30.92
Min.	30.39	60.00	49.75	1.82	16.11	11.20
Max.	193.50	161.94	229.28	3.16	77.35	59.13

*Note: (1) Values for the local area are compared with the average, minimum and maximum values for all 294 areas in the Cost of Living Index; (2) Figures cover the Newark-Elizabeth NJ urban area; **Doctor** (general practitioners routine exam of an established patient); **Dentist** (adult teeth cleaning and periodic oral examination); **Optometrist** (full vision eye exam for established adult patient); **Gasoline** (one gallon regular unleaded, national brand, including all taxes, cash price at self-service pump if available); **Beauty Salon** (woman's shampoo, trim, and blow-dry); **Men's Shirt** (cotton/polyester dress shirt, pinpoint weave, long sleeves).*
Source: The Council for Community and Economic Research, ACCRA Cost of Living Index, 2017

HOUSING

House Price Index (HPI)

Area	National Ranking[2]	Quarterly Change (%)	One-Year Change (%)	Five-Year Change (%)
MD[1]	213	0.97	3.29	14.23
U.S.[3]	–	1.61	6.68	34.71

Note: The HPI is a weighted repeat sales index. It measures average price changes in repeat sales or refinancings on the same properties. This information is obtained by reviewing repeat mortgage transactions on single-family properties whose mortgages have been purchased or securitized by Fannie Mae or Freddie Mac in January 1975; (1) Figures cover the Newark, NJ-PA Metropolitan Division—see Appendix B for areas included; (2) Rankings are based on annual percentage change for all metro areas containing at least 15,000 transactions over the last 10 years and ranges from 1 to 253; (3) figures based on a weighted average of Census Division estimates using a seasonally adjusted, purchase-only index; all figures are for the period ending December 31, 2017

Source: Federal Housing Finance Agency, House Price Index, February 28, 2018

Median Single-Family Home Prices

Area	2015	2016	2017[p]	Percent Change 2016 to 2017
MD[1]	383.9	374.8	379.3	1.2
U.S. Average	223.9	235.5	248.8	5.6

Note: Figures are median sales prices of existing single-family homes in thousands of dollars; (p) preliminary; (1) Figures cover the Newark, NJ-PA Metropolitan Division—see Appendix B for areas included

Source: National Association of Realtors, Median Sales Price of Existing Single-Family Homes for Metropolitan Areas, 4th Quarter 2017

Qualifying Income Based on Median Sales Price of Existing Single-Family Homes

Area	With 5% Down ($)	With 10% Down ($)	With 20% Down ($)
MD[1]	80,596	76,354	67,870
U.S. Average	55,585	52,659	46,808

Note: Figures are preliminary; Qualifying income is based on a mortgage rate of 4.17%. Monthly principal and interest payment is limited to 25% of income; (1) Figures cover the Newark, NJ-PA Metropolitan Division—see Appendix B for areas included

Source: National Association of Realtors, Qualifying Income Based on Median Sales Price of Existing Single-Family Homes for Metropolitan Areas, 4th Quarter 2017

Median Apartment Condo-Coop Home Prices

Area	2015	2016	2017[p]	Percent Change 2016 to 2017
MD[1]	261.7	259.3	263.4	1.6
U.S. Average	210.7	220.7	234.3	6.2

Note: Figures are median sales prices of existing apartment condo-coop homes in thousands of dollars; (p) preliminary; (1) Figures cover the Newark, NJ-PA Metropolitan Division—see Appendix B for areas included

Source: National Association of Realtors, Median Sales Price of Existing Apartment Condo-Coop Homes for Metropolitan Areas, 4th Quarter 2017

Home Value Distribution

Area	Under $50,000	$50,000 -$99,999	$100,000 -$149,999	$150,000 -$199,999	$200,000 -$299,999	$300,000 -$499,999	$500,000 -$999,999	$1,000,000 or more
City	1.1	0.6	0.3	0.9	5.3	41.0	48.6	2.1
MSA[1]	2.8	1.8	2.9	5.0	16.2	37.0	26.9	7.3
U.S.	8.8	14.8	15.3	14.9	18.4	16.4	9.0	2.5

Note: Figures are percentages and cover owner-occupied housing units; (1) Figures cover the New York-Newark-Jersey City, NY-NJ-PA Metropolitan Statistical Area—see Appendix B for areas included

Source: U.S. Census Bureau, 2012-2016 American Community Survey 5-Year Estimates

Homeownership Rate

Area	2009 (%)	2010 (%)	2011 (%)	2012 (%)	2013 (%)	2014 (%)	2015 (%)	2016 (%)	2017 (%)
MSA[1]	51.7	51.6	50.9	51.5	50.6	50.7	49.9	50.4	49.9
U.S.	67.4	66.9	66.1	65.4	65.1	64.5	63.7	63.4	63.9

Note: (1) Figures cover the New York-Newark-Jersey City, NY-NJ-PA Metropolitan Statistical Area—see Appendix B for areas included

Source: U.S. Census Bureau, Housing Vacancies and Homeownership Annual Statistics: 2009-2017

Year Housing Structure Built

Area	2010 or Later	2000 -2009	1990 -1999	1980 -1989	1970 -1979	1960 -1969	1950 -1959	1940 -1949	Before 1940	Median Year
City	0.2	5.9	17.9	16.9	24.4	15.9	11.5	3.5	3.8	1976
MSA[1]	1.3	7.2	6.1	7.9	10.0	13.8	16.2	9.1	28.3	1958
U.S.	2.3	14.7	14.0	13.7	15.6	10.9	10.6	5.2	13.0	1977

Note: Figures are percentages except for Median Year; Note: (1) Figures cover the New York-Newark-Jersey City, NY-NJ-PA Metropolitan Statistical Area—see Appendix B for areas included
Source: U.S. Census Bureau, 2012-2016 American Community Survey 5-Year Estimates

Gross Monthly Rent

Area	Under $500	$500 -$999	$1,000 -$1,499	$1,500 -$1,999	$2,000 -$2,499	$2,500 -$2,999	$3,000 and up	Median ($)
City	4.2	3.3	66.8	18.7	3.7	1.3	2.1	1,341
MSA[1]	9.7	18.7	35.2	19.8	8.3	3.8	4.5	1,297
U.S.	11.3	43.3	27.7	10.7	4.0	1.6	1.5	949

Note: Figures are percentages except for Median; Gross rent is the contract rent plus the estimated average monthly cost of utilities (electricity, gas, and water and sewer) and fuels (oil, coal, kerosene, wood, etc.) if these are paid by the renter (or paid for the renter by someone else); (1) Figures cover the New York-Newark-Jersey City, NY-NJ-PA Metropolitan Statistical Area—see Appendix B for areas included
Source: U.S. Census Bureau, 2012-2016 American Community Survey 5-Year Estimates

HEALTH

Health Risk Factors

Category	MD[1] (%)	U.S. (%)
Adults aged 18–64 who have any kind of health care coverage	86.9	87.7
Adults who reported being in good or excellent health	84.4	83.6
Adults who are current smokers	12.2	17.1
Adults who currently use E-cigarettes	2.7	4.7
Adults who currently use chewing tobacco, snuff, or snus	2.2	4.0
Adults who are heavy drinkers[2]	5.5	6.5
Adults who are binge drinkers[3]	16.2	16.9
Adults who are overweight (BMI 25.0 - 29.9)	39.7	35.3
Adults who are obese (BMI 30.0 - 99.8)	23.1	29.9
Adults who participated in any physical activities in the past month	72.8	76.9
Adults who always or nearly always wears a seat belt	95.8	94.3

Note: (1) Figures cover the Newark, NJ-PA Metropolitan Division—see Appendix B for areas included; (2) Heavy drinkers are classified as adult men having more than 14 drinks per week and adult women having more than 7 drinks per week; (3) Binge drinkers are classified as males having five or more drinks on one occasion or females having four or more drinks on one occasion
Source: Centers for Disease Control and Prevention, Behaviorial Risk Factor Surveillance System, SMART: Selected Metropolitan Area Risk Trends, 2016

Health Screening Rates

Category	MD[1] (%)	U.S. (%)
Adults 50-75 who have had a blood stool test within the past year	7.3	8.0
Adults 50-75 who have had a colonoscopy in the past 10 years	61.1	63.5
Adults aged 65+ who have had flu shot within the past year	58.5	58.6
Adults aged 65+ who have ever had a pneumonia vaccination	64.6	73.4
Adults who have ever been tested for HIV	44.0	35.6
Women aged 21-65 who have had a pap test in the past three years	84.9	79.8
Men aged 40+ who have had a PSA test within the past two years	48.5	39.5
Women aged 40+ who have had a mammogram within the past two years	79.8	72.5

Note: n/a not available; (1) Figures cover the Newark, NJ-PA Metropolitan Division—see Appendix B for areas included; Source: Centers for Disease Control and Prevention, Behaviorial Risk Factor Surveillance System, SMART: Selected Metropolitan Area Risk Trends, 2016

Chronic Health Conditions

Category	MD[1] (%)	U.S. (%)
Adults who have ever been told they had a heart attack	3.7	4.4
Adults who have ever been told they have angina or coronary heart disease	3.7	4.1
Adults who have ever been told they had a stroke	2.0	3.1
Adults who have been told they currently have asthma	7.2	9.3
Adults who have ever been told they have arthritis	22.1	25.8
Adults who have ever been told they have diabetes[2]	9.6	10.5
Adults who have ever been told they had skin cancer	4.1	5.9
Adults who have ever been told they had any other types of cancer	5.4	6.7
Adults who have ever been told they have COPD	5.3	6.3
Adults who have ever been told they have kidney disease	2.8	2.8
Adults who have ever been told they have a form of depression	11.6	17.4

Note: (1) Figures cover the Newark, NJ-PA Metropolitan Division—see Appendix B for areas included; (2) Figures do not include pregnancy-related, borderline, or pre-diabetes
Source: Centers for Disease Control and Prevention, Behaviorial Risk Factor Surveillance System, SMART: Selected Metropolitan Area Risk Trends, 2016

Mortality Rates for the Top 10 Causes of Death in the U.S.

ICD-10[a] Sub-Chapter	ICD-10[a] Code	Age-Adjusted Mortality Rate[1] per 100,000 population	
		County[2]	U.S.
Malignant neoplasms	C00-C97	136.9	158.5
Ischaemic heart diseases	I20-I25	82.1	96.8
Other forms of heart disease	I30-I51	51.9	52.4
Chronic lower respiratory diseases	J40-J47	23.8	40.9
Cerebrovascular diseases	I60-I69	26.9	37.2
Organic, including symptomatic, mental disorders	F01-F09	37.1	33.3
Other degenerative diseases of the nervous system	G30-G31	19.2	32.1
Other external causes of accidental injury	W00-X59	22.7	31.2
Diabetes mellitus	E10-E14	12.0	21.1
Hypertensive diseases	I10-I15	11.0	20.8

Note: (a) ICD-10 = International Classification of Diseases 10th Revision; (1) Mortality rates are a three year average covering 2014-2016; (2) Figures cover Morris County.
Source: Centers for Disease Control and Prevention, National Center for Health Statistics. Underlying Cause of Death 1999-2016 on CDC WONDER Online Database, released December 2017

Mortality Rates for Selected Causes of Death

ICD-10[a] Sub-Chapter	ICD-10[a] Code	Age-Adjusted Mortality Rate[1] per 100,000 population	
		County[2]	U.S.
Assault	X85-Y09	Unreliable	5.6
Diseases of the liver	K70-K76	7.4	14.0
Human immunodeficiency virus (HIV) disease	B20-B24	Unreliable	1.9
Influenza and pneumonia	J09-J18	8.3	14.6
Intentional self-harm	X60-X84	8.2	13.2
Malnutrition	E40-E46	Unreliable	1.3
Obesity and other hyperalimentation	E65-E68	1.3	2.1
Renal failure	N17-N19	11.1	13.0
Transport accidents	V01-V99	4.5	12.0
Viral hepatitis	B15-B19	Unreliable	1.9

Note: (a) ICD-10 = International Classification of Diseases 10th Revision; (1) Mortality rates are a three year average covering 2014-2016; (2) Figures cover Morris County; Data are Suppressed when the data meet the criteria for confidentiality constraints; Mortality rates are flagged as Unreliable when the rate would be calculated with a numerator of 20 or less.
Source: Centers for Disease Control and Prevention, National Center for Health Statistics. Underlying Cause of Death 1999-2016 on CDC WONDER Online Database, released December 2017

Health Insurance Coverage

Area	With Health Insurance	With Private Health Insurance	With Public Health Insurance	Without Health Insurance	Population Under Age 18 Without Health Insurance
City	95.6	90.1	15.3	4.4	2.4
MSA[1]	89.8	65.8	33.7	10.2	3.6
U.S.	88.3	66.7	33.0	11.7	5.9

Note: Figures are percentages that cover the civilian noninstitutionalized population; (1) Figures cover the New York-Newark-Jersey City, NY-NJ-PA Metropolitan Statistical Area—see Appendix B for areas included
Source: U.S. Census Bureau, 2012-2016 American Community Survey 5-Year Estimates

Number of Medical Professionals

Area	MDs[3]	DOs[3,4]	Dentists	Podiatrists	Chiropractors	Optometrists
County[1] (number)	1,994	195	553	60	213	86
County[1] (rate[2])	400.0	39.1	110.9	12.0	42.7	17.2
U.S. (rate[2])	276.5	22.3	67.3	6.0	26.7	15.9

Note: Data as of 2016 unless noted; (1) Data covers Morris County; (2) Rate per 100,000 population; (3) Data as of 2015 and includes all active, non-federal physicians; (4) Doctor of Osteopathic Medicine
Source: U.S. Department of Health and Human Services, Health Resources and Services Administration, Bureau of Health Professions, Area Resource File (ARF) 2016-2017

Best Hospitals

According to *U.S. News,* the Newark, NJ-PA metro area is home to two of the best hospitals in the U.S.: **Kessler Institute for Rehabilitation** (1 adult specialty); **Morristown Medical Center** (2 adult specialties). The hospitals listed were nationally ranked in at least one of 16 specialties. Only 152 hospitals nationwide were nationally ranked in one or more specialties. Twenty hospitals in the U.S. made the Honor Roll. The Best Hospitals Honor Roll was revamped last year to take both the national rankings and the procedure and condition ratings into account. Hospitals received points if they were nationally ranked in one of the 16 specialties—the higher they ranked, the more points they got—and how many ratings of "high performing" they earned in the nine procedures and conditions. *U.S. News Online, "America's Best Hospitals 2017-18"*

EDUCATION

Public School District Statistics

District Name	Schls	Pupils	Pupil/ Teacher Ratio	Minority Pupils[1] (%)	Free Lunch Eligible[2] (%)	IEP[3] (%)
Randolph Township School District	6	4,849	11.9	27.6	6.1	18.6

Note: Table includes school districts with 100 or more students; (1) Percentage of students that are not non-Hispanic white; (2) Percentage of students that are eligible for the free lunch program; (3) Percentage of students that have an Individualized Education Program.
Source: U.S. Department of Education, National Center for Education Statistics, Common Core of Data, Local Education Agency (School District) Universe Survey: School Year 2015-2016; U.S. Department of Education, National Center for Education Statistics, Common Core of Data, Public Elementary/Secondary School Universe Survey: School Year 2015-2016

Highest Level of Education

Area	Less than H.S.	H.S. Diploma	Some College, No Deg.	Associate Degree	Bachelor's Degree	Master's Degree	Prof. School Degree	Doctorate Degree
City	3.5	14.4	13.4	5.8	34.7	20.5	5.0	2.8
MSA[1]	14.3	25.3	15.5	6.7	22.3	11.3	3.0	1.5
U.S.	13.0	27.5	21.0	8.2	18.8	8.2	2.0	1.3

Note: Figures cover persons age 25 and over; (1) Figures cover the New York-Newark-Jersey City, NY-NJ-PA Metropolitan Statistical Area—see Appendix B for areas included
Source: U.S. Census Bureau, 2012-2016 American Community Survey 5-Year Estimates

Educational Attainment by Race

Area	High School Graduate or Higher (%)					Bachelor's Degree or Higher (%)				
	Total	White	Black	Asian	Hisp.[2]	Total	White	Black	Asian	Hisp.[2]
City	96.5	97.3	93.1	95.3	91.7	63.0	63.1	37.1	78.3	35.5
MSA[1]	85.7	90.0	84.1	82.9	68.9	38.1	43.2	23.8	53.1	17.7
U.S.	87.0	88.9	84.3	86.3	65.7	30.3	31.6	20.0	52.1	14.7

Note: Figures shown cover persons 25 years old and over; (1) Figures cover the New York-Newark-Jersey City, NY-NJ-PA Metropolitan Statistical Area—see Appendix B for areas included; (2) People of Hispanic origin can be of any race
Source: U.S. Census Bureau, 2012-2016 American Community Survey 5-Year Estimates

School Enrollment by Grade and Control

Area	Preschool (%)		Kindergarten (%)		Grades 1 - 4 (%)		Grades 5 - 8 (%)		Grades 9 - 12 (%)	
	Public	Private	Public	Private	Public	Private	Public	Private	Public	Private
City	34.3	65.7	66.7	33.3	89.2	10.8	95.7	4.3	90.3	9.7
MSA[1]	51.9	48.1	81.6	18.4	86.1	13.9	86.3	13.7	85.9	14.1
U.S.	58.4	41.6	87.7	12.3	89.8	10.2	89.7	10.3	90.4	9.6

Note: Figures shown cover persons 3 years old and over; (1) Figures cover the New York-Newark-Jersey City, NY-NJ-PA Metropolitan Statistical Area—see Appendix B for areas included
Source: U.S. Census Bureau, 2012-2016 American Community Survey 5-Year Estimates

Average Salaries of Public School Classroom Teachers

Area	2015		2016		Change from 2015 to 2016	
	Dollars	Rank[1]	Dollars	Rank[1]	Percent	Rank[2]
New Jersey	69,038	6	69,330	6	0.4	41
U.S. Average	57,611	–	58,353	–	1.3	–

Note: (1) Rank ranges from 1 to 51 where 1 indicates highest salary; (2) Rank ranges from 1 to 51 where 1 indicates highest percent change.
Source: National Education Association, Rankings & Estimates: Rankings of the States 2016 and Estimates of School Statistics 2017

Higher Education

Four-Year Colleges			Two-Year Colleges			Medical Schools[1]	Law Schools[2]	Voc/ Tech[3]
Public	Private Non-profit	Private For-profit	Public	Private Non-profit	Private For-profit			
0	0	0	1	0	0	0	0	0

Note: Figures cover institutions located within the city limits and include main campuses only; (1) includes schools accredited by the Liaison Committee on Medical Education and the American Osteopathic Association's Commission on Osteopathic College Accreditation; (2) includes ABA-accredited schools, schools with provisional ABA accreditation, and state accredited schools; (3) includes all schools with programs that are less than 2 years.
Source: National Center for Education Statistics, Integrated Postsecondary Education System (IPEDS), 2016-17; Wikipedia, List of Medical Schools in the United States, accessed April 2, 2018; Wikipedia, List of Law Schools in the United States, accessed April 2, 2018

According to *U.S. News & World Report,* the Newark, NJ-PA metro division is home to four of the best national universities in the U.S.: **Seton Hall University** (#124 tie); **Rutgers University—Newark** (#133 tie); **New Jersey Institute of Technology** (#140 tie); **Montclair State University** (#187 tie). The indicators used to capture academic quality fall into a number of categories: assessment by administrators at peer institutions; retention of students; faculty resources; student selectivity; financial resources; alumni giving; high school counselor ratings of colleges; and graduation rate. *U.S. News & World Report, "America's Best Colleges 2018"*

According to *U.S. News & World Report,* the Newark, NJ-PA metro division is home to one of the best liberal arts colleges in the U.S.: **Drew University** (#112 tie). The indicators used to capture academic quality fall into a number of categories: assessment by administrators at peer institutions; retention of students; faculty resources; student selectivity; financial resources; alumni giving; high school counselor ratings of colleges; and graduation rate. *U.S. News & World Report, "America's Best Colleges 2018"*

According to *U.S. News & World Report,* the Newark, NJ-PA metro division is home to two of the top 100 law schools in the U.S.: **Seton Hall University** (#59 tie); **Rutgers—The State University of New Jersey** (#74 tie). The rankings are based on a weighted average of 12 measures of quality: peer assessment score; assessment score by lawyers/judges; median LSAT scores; median undergrad GPA; acceptance rate; employment rates for graduates; placement success; bar passage rate; faculty resources; expenditures per student; student/faculty ratio; and library resources. *U.S. News & World Report, "America's Best Graduate Schools, Law, 2019"*

According to *U.S. News & World Report*, the Newark, NJ-PA metro division is home to one of the top 75 business schools in the U.S.: **Rutgers—The State University of New Jersey-Newark and New Brunswick** (#44 tie). The rankings are based on a weighted average of the following nine measures: quality assessment; peer assessment; recruiter assessment; placement success; mean starting salary and bonus; student selectivity; mean GMAT and GRE scores; mean undergraduate GPA; and acceptance rate. *U.S. News & World Report, "America's Best Graduate Schools, Business, 2019"*

PRESIDENTIAL ELECTION

2016 Presidential Election Results

Area	Clinton	Trump	Johnson	Stein	Other
Morris County	45.5	49.7	2.3	1.0	1.5
U.S.	48.0	45.9	3.3	1.1	1.7

Note: Results are percentages and may not add to 100% due to rounding
Source: Dave Leip's Atlas of U.S. Presidential Elections

EMPLOYERS

Major Employers

Company Name	Industry
American Express Company	Personal credit institutions
American International Group	Life insurance
Deloitte Consulting	Management consulting services
Hackensack University Medical Center	University
Merrill Lynch and Co	Security brokers & dealers
Mount Sinai Hospital	General medical & surgical hospitals
Mount Sinai School of Medicine	Medical training services
NewYork-Presbyterian Hospital	General medical & surgical hospitals
NYC Health and Hospitals Corp	Psychiatric hospitals
NYU School of Medicine	Offices & clinics of medical doctors
Paramount Comm Acq Corp	Investment holding companies, except banks
Patriarch Partners	Investment offices
Rutgers, The State Univ of NJ	Colleges & universities
Standard Americas	Agencies of foreign banks
The Long Island Rail Road Company	Local & suburban transit
U of Med and Dentistry of NJ	Colleges & universities
UMASS Memorial Health Care	Psychiatrist
United States Postal Service	U.S. postal service
Wellchoice	Health insurance carriers

Note: Companies shown are located within the New York-Newark-Jersey City, NY-NJ-PA Metropolitan Statistical Area.
Source: Hoovers.com; Wikipedia

PUBLIC SAFETY

Crime Rate

Area	All Crimes	Violent Crimes				Property Crimes		
		Murder	Rape[3]	Robbery	Aggrav. Assault	Burglary	Larceny -Theft	Motor Vehicle Theft
City	510.1	0.0	0.0	7.7	11.6	81.2	386.4	23.2
Metro[1]	1,683.1	6.0	16.9	134.2	126.5	248.6	943.7	207.1
U.S.	2,847.8	5.3	40.4	102.8	248.5	468.9	1,745.0	236.9

Note: Figures are crimes per 100,000 population; (1) Figures cover the Newark, NJ-PA Metropolitan Division—see Appendix B for areas included; (3) The city and U.S. figures shown were reported using the revised Uniform Crime Reporting (UCR) definition of rape. The metro area figures shown are an aggregate total of the data submitted using both the revised and legacy UCR definitions.
Source: FBI Uniform Crime Reports, 2016

Hate Crimes

Area	Number of Quarters Reported	Number of Incidents per Bias Motivation					
		Race/Ethnicity/ Ancestry	Religion	Sexual Orientation	Disability	Gender	Gender Identity
Area[1]	2	0	2	0	0	0	0
U.S.	4	3,489	1,273	1,076	70	31	124

Note: (1) Figures cover the Randolph Township.
Source: Federal Bureau of Investigation, Hate Crime Statistics 2016

Identity Theft Consumer Reports

Area	Reports	Reports per 100,000 Population	Rank[2]
MSA[1]	23,624	117	64
U.S.	371,061	114	-

Note: (1) Figures cover the New York-Newark-Jersey City, NY-NJ-PA Metropolitan Statistical Area—see Appendix B for areas included; (2) Rank ranges from 1 to 389 where 1 indicates greatest number of identity theft reports per 100,000 population
Source: Federal Trade Commission, Consumer Sentinel Network Data Book for January–December 2017

Fraud and Other Consumer Reports

Area	Reports	Reports per 100,000 Population	Rank[2]
MSA[1]	90,589	449	173
U.S.	2,304,550	708	-

Note: (1) Figures cover the New York-Newark-Jersey City, NY-NJ-PA Metropolitan Statistical Area—see Appendix B for areas included; (2) Rank ranges from 1 to 389 where 1 indicates greatest number of fraud and other consumer reports per 100,000 population
Source: Federal Trade Commission, Consumer Sentinel Network Data Book for January–December 2017

SPORTS

Professional Sports Teams

Team Name	League	Year Established
Brooklyn Nets	National Basketball Association (NBA)	1967
New Jersey Devils	National Hockey League (NHL)	1982
New York City FC	Major League Soccer (MLS)	2015
New York Giants	National Football League (NFL)	1925
New York Islanders	National Hockey League (NHL)	1972
New York Jets	National Football League (NFL)	1960
New York Knicks	National Basketball Association (NBA)	1946
New York Mets	Major League Baseball (MLB)	1962
New York Rangers	National Hockey League (NHL)	1926
New York Red Bulls	Major League Soccer (MLS)	1996
New York Yankees	Major League Baseball (MLB)	1903

Note: Includes teams located in the New York-Newark-Jersey City, NY-NJ-PA Metropolitan Statistical Area.
Source: Wikipedia, Major Professional Sports Teams of the United States and Canada, April 5, 2018

CLIMATE

Average and Extreme Temperatures

Temperature	Jan	Feb	Mar	Apr	May	Jun	Jul	Aug	Sep	Oct	Nov	Dec	Yr.
Extreme High (°F)	68	75	85	96	97	101	104	99	99	88	81	72	104
Average High (°F)	38	41	50	61	72	80	85	84	76	65	54	43	62
Average Temp. (°F)	32	34	43	53	63	72	77	76	68	58	48	37	55
Average Low (°F)	26	27	35	44	54	63	68	67	60	49	41	31	47
Extreme Low (°F)	-2	-2	8	21	36	46	53	50	40	29	17	-1	-2

Note: Figures cover the years 1962-1992
Source: National Climatic Data Center, International Station Meteorological Climate Summary, 9/96

Average Precipitation/Snowfall/Humidity

Precip./Humidity	Jan	Feb	Mar	Apr	May	Jun	Jul	Aug	Sep	Oct	Nov	Dec	Yr.
Avg. Precip. (in.)	3.5	3.1	4.0	3.9	4.5	3.8	4.5	4.1	4.1	3.3	4.5	3.8	47.0
Avg. Snowfall (in.)	7	8	4	Tr	Tr	0	0	0	0	Tr	Tr	3	23
Avg. Rel. Hum. 7am (%)	67	67	66	64	72	74	74	76	78	75	72	69	71
Avg. Rel. Hum. 4pm (%)	55	53	50	45	52	55	53	54	56	55	57	58	53

Note: Figures cover the years 1962-1992; Tr = Trace amounts (<0.05 in. of rain; <0.5 in. of snow)
Source: National Climatic Data Center, International Station Meteorological Climate Summary, 9/96

Weather Conditions

Temperature			Daytime Sky			Precipitation		
32°F & below	45°F & below	90°F & above	Clear	Partly cloudy	Cloudy	0.01 inch or more precip.	0.1 inch or more snow/ice	Thunder-storms
75	170	18	85	166	114	120	11	20

Note: Figures are average number of days per year and cover the years 1962-1992
Source: National Climatic Data Center, International Station Meteorological Climate Summary, 9/96

HAZARDOUS WASTE

Superfund Sites

The Newark, NJ-PA metro division is home to 31 sites on the EPA's Superfund National Priorities List: **A. O. Polymer** (final); **American Cyanamid Co** (final); **Brook Industrial Park** (final); **Caldwell Trucking Co.** (final); **Chemical Control** (final); **Combe Fill South Landfill** (final); **Curtis Specialty Papers, Inc** (final); **Dayco Corp./L.e Carpenter Co.** (final); **De Rewal Chemical Co.** (final); **Diamond Alkali Co.** (final); **Dover Municipal Well 4** (final); **Higgins Disposal** (final); **Higgins Farm** (final); **LCP Chemicals Inc.** (final); **Mansfield Trail Dump** (final); **Metaltec/Aerosystems** (final); **Montgomery Township Housing Development** (final); **Myers Property** (final); **Orange Valley Regional Ground Water Contamination** (final); **Picatinny Arsenal (USARMY)** (final); **Pierson's Creek** (final); **Radiation Technology, Inc.** (final); **Riverside Industrial Park** (final); **Rockaway Borough Well Field** (final); **Rockaway Township Wells** (final); **Rocky Hill Municipal Well** (final); **Rolling Knolls Lf** (final); **Sharkey Landfill** (final); **U.S. Radium Corp.** (final); **Unimatic Manufacturing Corporation** (final); **White Chemical Corp.** (final). There are a total of 1,396 Superfund sites with a status of proposed or final on the list in the U.S. *U.S. Environmental Protection Agency, National Priorities List, April 4, 2018*

AIR & WATER QUALITY

Air Quality Trends: Ozone

	1990	1995	2000	2005	2010	2012	2013	2014	2015	2016
MSA[1]	0.101	0.106	0.090	0.091	0.081	0.079	0.071	0.069	0.075	0.073
U.S.	0.087	0.089	0.081	0.079	0.073	0.075	0.069	0.067	0.068	0.069

Note: (1) Data covers the New York-Newark-Jersey City, NY-NJ-PA Metropolitan Statistical Area—see Appendix B for areas included. The values shown are the composite ozone concentration averages among trend sites based on the highest fourth daily maximum 8-hour concentration in parts per million. These trends are based on sites having an adequate record of monitoring data during the trend period. Data from exceptional events are included.
Source: U.S. Environmental Protection Agency, Air Quality Monitoring Information, "Air Quality Trends by City, 1990-2016"

Air Quality Index

Area	Percent of Days when Air Quality was...[2]					AQI Statistics[2]	
	Good	Moderate	Unhealthy for Sensitive Groups	Unhealthy	Very Unhealthy	Maximum	Median
MSA[1]	42.2	52.6	4.7	0.5	0.0	159	52

Note: (1) Data covers the New York-Newark-Jersey City, NY-NJ-PA Metropolitan Statistical Area—see Appendix B for areas included; (2) Based on 365 days with AQI data in 2017. Air Quality Index (AQI) is an index for reporting daily air quality. EPA calculates the AQI for five major air pollutants regulated by the Clean Air Act: ground-level ozone, particle pollution (aka particulate matter), carbon monoxide, sulfur dioxide, and nitrogen dioxide. The AQI runs from 0 to 500. The higher the AQI value, the greater the level of air pollution and the greater the health concern. There are six AQI categories: "Good" AQI is between 0 and 50. Air quality is considered satisfactory; "Moderate" AQI is between 51 and 100. Air quality is acceptable; "Unhealthy for Sensitive Groups" When AQI values are between 101 and 150, members of sensitive groups may experience health effects; "Unhealthy" When AQI values are between 151 and 200 everyone may begin to experience health effects; "Very Unhealthy" AQI values between 201 and 300 trigger a health alert; "Hazardous" AQI values over 300 trigger warnings of emergency conditions (not shown).
Source: U.S. Environmental Protection Agency, Air Quality Index Report, 2017

Air Quality Index Pollutants

Area	Percent of Days when AQI Pollutant was...[2]					
	Carbon Monoxide	Nitrogen Dioxide	Ozone	Sulfur Dioxide	Particulate Matter 2.5	Particulate Matter 10
MSA[1]	0.0	13.2	31.8	0.0	55.1	0.0

Note: (1) Data covers the New York-Newark-Jersey City, NY-NJ-PA Metropolitan Statistical Area—see Appendix B for areas included; (2) Based on 365 days with AQI data in 2017. The Air Quality Index (AQI) is an index for reporting daily air quality. EPA calculates the AQI for five major air pollutants regulated by the Clean Air Act: ground-level ozone, particle pollution (also known as particulate matter), carbon monoxide, sulfur dioxide, and nitrogen dioxide. The AQI runs from 0 to 500. The higher the AQI value, the greater the level of air pollution and the greater the health concern.
Source: U.S. Environmental Protection Agency, Air Quality Index Report, 2017

Maximum Air Pollutant Concentrations: Particulate Matter, Ozone, CO and Lead

	Particulate Matter 10 (ug/m^3)	Particulate Matter 2.5 Wtd AM (ug/m^3)	Particulate Matter 2.5 24-Hr (ug/m^3)	Ozone (ppm)	Carbon Monoxide (ppm)	Lead (ug/m^3)
MSA[1] Level	33	9.2	20	0.078	3	0.03
NAAQS[2]	150	15	35	0.075	9	0.15
Met NAAQS[2]	Yes	Yes	Yes	No	Yes	Yes

Note: (1) Data covers the New York-Newark-Jersey City, NY-NJ-PA Metropolitan Statistical Area—see Appendix B for areas included; Data from exceptional events are included; (2) National Ambient Air Quality Standards; ppm = parts per million; ug/m^3 = micrograms per cubic meter; n/a not available.
Concentrations: Particulate Matter 10 (coarse particulate)—highest second maximum 24-hour concentration; Particulate Matter 2.5 Wtd AM (fine particulate)—highest weighted annual mean concentration; Particulate Matter 2.5 24-Hour (fine particulate)—highest 98th percentile 24-hour concentration; Ozone—highest fourth daily maximum 8-hour concentration; Carbon Monoxide—highest second maximum non-overlapping 8-hour concentration; Lead—maximum running 3-month average
Source: U.S. Environmental Protection Agency, Air Quality Monitoring Information, "Air Quality Statistics by City, 2016"

Maximum Air Pollutant Concentrations: Nitrogen Dioxide and Sulfur Dioxide

	Nitrogen Dioxide AM (ppb)	Nitrogen Dioxide 1-Hr (ppb)	Sulfur Dioxide AM (ppb)	Sulfur Dioxide 1-Hr (ppb)	Sulfur Dioxide 24-Hr (ppb)
MSA[1] Level	20	60	n/a	7	n/a
NAAQS[2]	53	100	30	75	140
Met NAAQS[2]	Yes	Yes	n/a	Yes	n/a

Note: (1) Data covers the New York-Newark-Jersey City, NY-NJ-PA Metropolitan Statistical Area—see Appendix B for areas included; Data from exceptional events are included; (2) National Ambient Air Quality Standards; ppm = parts per million; ug/m^3 = micrograms per cubic meter; n/a not available.
Concentrations: Nitrogen Dioxide AM—highest arithmetic mean concentration; Nitrogen Dioxide 1-Hr—highest 98th percentile 1-hour daily maximum concentration; Sulfur Dioxide AM—highest annual mean concentration; Sulfur Dioxide 1-Hr—highest 99th percentile 1-hour daily maximum concentration; Sulfur Dioxide 24-Hr—highest second maximum 24-hour concentration
Source: U.S. Environmental Protection Agency, Air Quality Monitoring Information, "Air Quality Statistics by City, 2016"

Drinking Water

Water System Name	Pop. Served	Primary Water Source Type	Violations[1]	
			Health Based	Monitoring/ Reporting
Randolph Twp Pub Works Dept	14,820	Purchased Surface	0	1

Note: (1) Based on violation data from January 1, 2017 to December 31, 2017
Source: U.S. Environmental Protection Agency, Office of Ground Water and Drinking Water, Safe Drinking Water Information System (based on data extracted April 5, 2018)

South Brunswick, New Jersey

Background

South Brunswick is located in Middlesex County, 33 miles southwest of Newark and 46 miles from New York City.

South Brunswick was incorporated in 1798. In the 18th century, it was a rural agricultural region with small clustered settlements located on major transportation routes. Early settlers took advantage of fertile soils and favorable growing conditions. The 19th century brought increased commercial and residential growth, which coincided with new transportation routes. The Straight Turnpike, now Route 1, was built in 1804. In 1872, the state Legislature reduced the size of South Brunswick with the creation of Cranbury from the southern portion of South Brunswick. In 1919, the size of South Brunswick was further reduced with the formation of Plainsboro.

By 1980, South Brunswick's population approached 18,000; by 1990, it was over 25,000. Now it is a diverse community of over 43,000. Despite its rapid growth, much of South Brunswick's 42 square miles remain undeveloped with significant amounts of wetlands, woodlands and open space.

Manufacturing and wholesale trade make up most of the economic activity in South Brunswick. The township also benefits from its location along the Route 1 corridor between Princeton and New Brunswick, which is popular with high tech companies.

The South Brunswick School District is currently made up of nine school communities and continues to grow while maintaining its reputation as one of the finest public school systems in the state.

There are over 2,000 acres of municipal, county and state park land within South Brunswick. Recreational facilities include a Community Center and Senior Center. The township is also close to many art and music centers in nearby Princeton and New Brunswick.

South Brunswick has a seasonal climate with hot summers and cold winters. Median summer temperatures average 70 degrees, while winter averages can be as low as 20 degrees during the months of December and January. The city averages 4.5 inches of rainfall per month from April to October and 7.5 inches of snowfall per month from December to March.

Rankings

General Rankings

- New York* was identified as one of America's fastest-growing cities in terms of population growth by CNNMoney.com. The area ranked #1 out of 10. Criteria: population growth between July 2015 and July 2016; cities and towns with populations of 50,000. *CNNMoney, "10 Fastest-Growing Cities," June 2, 2017*

Business/Finance Rankings

- The personal finance site NerdWallet analyzed 183 American metropolitan areas with populations over 250,000 and more than 15,000 businesses to rank where entrepreneurs find the most success. Criteria included area economy, annual income, housing cost, unemployment rate, and the success rate of area businesses. New York* ranked #32. *www.nerdwallet.com, "Best Places to Start a Business," April 27, 2015*
- Metro areas with the largest gap in income between rich and poor residents were identified by 24/7 Wall Street using the U.S. Census Bureau's 2013 American Community Survey. The New York* metro area placed #7 among metro areas with the widest wealth gap between rich and poor. *247wallst.com, "20 Cities with the Widest Gap between the Rich and Poor," July 8, 2015*
- In a survey of economic confidence in the nation's 50 largest metropolitan areas conducted January–December 2014, the New York* metro area placed #23, according to Gallup's 2014 Economic Confidence Index. *Gallup, "San Jose and San Francisco Lead in Economic Confidence," March 19, 2015*
- The Brookings Institution ranked the 100 largest metro areas in the U.S. based on income inequality. New York* was ranked #2 (#1 = greatest ineqality). Criteria: the "95/20 ratio," a figure representing the income at which a household earns more than 95 percent of all other households, divided by the income at which a household earns more than only 20 percent of all other households. *Brookings Institution, "Household Income Inequality, 100 Largest U.S. Metro Areas, 2014-2016," February 5, 2018*
- Payscale.com ranked the largest metro areas in terms of wage growth. The New York* metro area ranked #1. Criteria: private-sector wage growth between the 4th quarter of 2016 and the 4th quarter of 2017. *PayScale, "Wage Trends by Metro Area-4th Quarter," January 17, 2018*
- The New York* metro area was identified as one of the most debt-ridden places in America by the finance site Credit.com. The metro area was ranked #3. Criteria: residents' average credit card debt as well as median income. *Credit.com, "25 Cities With the Most Credit Card Debt," February 28, 2018*
- New York* was identified as one of America's most frugal metro areas by *Coupons.com.* The city ranked #15 out of 25. Criteria: digital coupon usage. *Coupons.com, "America's Most Frugal Cities of 2017," March 22, 2018*
- New York* was cited as one of America's top metros for new and expanded facility projects in 2017. The area ranked #5 in the large metro area category (population over 1 million). *Site Selection, "Top Metropolitans of 2017," March 2018*
- The New York* metro area appeared on the Milken Institute "2017 Best Performing Cities" list. Rank: #82 out of 200 large metro areas. Criteria: job growth; wage and salary growth; high-tech output growth. *Milken Institute, "Best-Performing Cities 2017," January 2018*
- *Forbes* ranked the 200 most populous metro areas to determine the nation's "Best Places for Business and Careers." The New York* metro area was ranked #113. Criteria: costs (business and living); job growth (past and projected); income growth; quality of life; educational attainment (college and high school); projected economic growth; cultural and recreational opportunities; net migration patterns; number of highly ranked colleges. *Forbes, "The Best Places for Business and Careers 2017," October 24, 2017*

Dating/Romance Rankings

- *Apartment List* conducted its annual survey of renters to compile a list of metros that have the best opportunities for dating. Nearly 11,000 respondents, from February 2017 through January 2018, rated their current city or neighborhood for opportunities to date and make friends. The New York* metro area ranked #10 out of 70 where single residents were very satisfied or somewhat satisfied, making it among the ten best metros for dating opportunities. Other criteria analyzed included gender and education levels of renters. *Apartment List, "Best Metros for Dating 2018," February 6, 2018*

Education Rankings

- Personal finance website *WalletHub* analyzed the 150 largest U.S. metropolitan statistical areas to determine where the most educated Americans are choosing to settle. Criteria: education quality and attainment gap; education levels; percentage of workers with degrees; public school rankings; quality and size of each metro area's universities. New York* was ranked #36 (#1 = most educated city). *www.WalletHub.com, "2017's Most and Least Educated Cities in America," July 25, 2017*

Environmental Rankings

- Sperling's BestPlaces assessed 379 metropolitan areas of the United States for the likelihood of dangerously extreme weather events or earthquakes. In general the Southeast and South-Central regions have the highest risk of weather extremes and earthquakes, while the Pacific Northwest enjoys the lowest risk. Of the least risky metropolitan areas, the New York* metro area was ranked #207. *www.bestplaces.net, "Safest Places from Natural Disasters," April 2011*

- The U.S. Environmental Protection Agency (EPA) released a list of U.S. metropolitan areas with the most ENERGY STAR certified buildings in 2016. The New York* metro area was ranked #3 out of 25. *U.S. Environmental Protection Agency, "2017 Energy Star Top Cities," June 2017*

- New York* was highlighted as one of the 25 most ozone-polluted metro areas in the U.S. during 2013 through 2015. The area ranked #9. *American Lung Association, State of the Air 2017*

- New York* was highlighted as one of the 25 metro areas most polluted by year-round particle pollution (Annual PM 2.5) in the U.S. during 2013 through 2015. The area ranked #22. *American Lung Association, State of the Air 2017*

Health/Fitness Rankings

- For each of the 50 most populous metro areas in the United States, the American College of Sports Medicine's American Fitness Index evaluated infrastructure, community assets, and policies that encourage healthy and fit lifestyles, including preventive health behaviors, levels of chronic disease conditions, health care access, and community resources and policies that support physical activity. The New York* metro area ranked #18 for "community fitness." *www.americanfitnessindex.org, "ACSM American Fitness Index Health and Community Fitness Status of the 50 Largest Metropolitan Areas," May 2017*

- The New York* metro area was identified as one of the worst cities for bed bugs in America by pest control company Orkin. The area ranked #8 out of 50 based on the number of bed bug treatments Orkin performed from December 2016 to November 2017. *Orkin, "Baltimore and Washington D.C. Continue to Hold Top Spots," January 8, 2018*

- New York* was identified as a "2016 Spring Allergy Capital." The area ranked #31 out of 100. Three groups of factors were used to identify the most severe cities for people with allergies during the spring season: annual pollen levels; medicine utilization; access to board-certified allergists. *Asthma and Allergy Foundation of America, "Spring Allergy Capitals 2016"*

- New York* was identified as a "2016 Fall Allergy Capital." The area ranked #52 out of 100. Three groups of factors were used to identify the most severe cities for people with allergies during the fall season: annual pollen levels; medicine utilization; access to board-certified allergists. *Asthma and Allergy Foundation of America, "Fall Allergy Capitals 2016"*
- New York* was identified as a "2015 Asthma Capital." The area ranked #35 out of the nation's 100 largest metropolitan areas. Criteria: estimated prevalence; self-reported prevalence; crude death rate for asthma; annual pollen score; annual air quality; public smoking laws; number of board-certified asthma specialists; school inhaler access laws; rescue medication use; controller medication use; ER visits for asthma; uninsured rate; poverty rate. *Asthma and Allergy Foundation of America, "Asthma Capitals 2015"*
- The New York* metro area ranked #75 out of 189 in The Gallup-Healthways Well-Being Index. Criteria: purpose; social well being; financial health; community and physical health. Results are based on telephone interviews with adults, aged 18 and older, living in metropolitan areas in the 50 U.S. states and the District of Columbia. *Gallup-Healthways, "State of American Well-Being, 2017 Community Well-Being Rankings" March 2018*

Real Estate Rankings

- FitSmallBusiness looked at 50 of the largest metropolitan areas in the U.S. to determine which metro was the best to start a real estate business. Data was compiled from such sources as: Zillow, Trulia, U.S. Census Bureau, and the Bureau of Labor Statistics. Criteria: location; inventory; annual wages; median sales price of homes; days on the market; median price cut percentage; and other factors that would influence real estate professional growth. The New York* metro area ranked #6. *fitsmallbusiness.com, "The Best Cities to Become a Real Estate Agent in 2018," January 30, 2018*
- With data from RealtyTrac, Yahoo! Finance researchers listed the housing markets in which housing affordability is improving most, factoring in interest rates as well as median home prices. The New York* metro area was among the least affordable housing markets. *news.yahoo.com, "10 Cities Where Ordinary People Can No Longer Afford Homes," March 5, 2014*
- The New York* metro area was identified as one of the 20 least affordable housing markets in the U.S. in 2017. The area ranked #12 out of 180 markets. Criteria: qualification for a mortgage loan on a typical home. *National Association of Realtors®, Affordability Index of Existing Single-Family Homes for Metropolitan Areas, 2017*
- New York* was ranked #219 out of 238 metro areas in terms of housing affordability in 2017 by the National Association of Home Builders (#1 = most affordable). Criteria: the share of homes sold in that area affordable to a family earning the local median income, based on standard mortgage underwriting criteria. *National Association of Home Builders®, NAHB-Wells Fargo Housing Opportunity Index, 4th Quarter 2017*

Safety Rankings

- The National Insurance Crime Bureau ranked 382 metro areas in the U.S. in terms of per capita rates of vehicle theft. The New York* metro area ranked #292 (#1 = highest rate). Criteria: number of vehicle theft offenses per 100,000 inhabitants in 2016. *National Insurance Crime Bureau, "Hot Spots 2016," June 8, 2017*

Seniors/Retirement Rankings

- From its Best Cities for Successful Aging indexes, the Milken Institute generated rankings for metropolitan areas, weighing data in nine categories—health care, wellness, living arrangements, transportation and convenience, financial characteristics, education, employment, community engagement, and overall livability. The New York* metro area was ranked #11 overall in the large metro area category. *Milken Institute, "Best Cities for Successful Aging, 2017" March 14, 2017*

Sports/Recreation Rankings

- According to the personal finance website NerdWallet, the New York* metro area, at #4, is one of the nation's top dozen metro areas for sports fans. Criteria included the presence of all four major sports—MLB, NFL, NHL, and NBA, fan enthusiasm (as measured by game attendance), ticket affordability, and "sports culture," that is, number of sports bars. *www.nerdwallet.com, "Best Cities for Sports Fans," May 5, 2013*

Transportation Rankings

- New York* was identified as one of the most congested metro areas in the U.S. The area ranked #4 out of 10. Criteria: yearly delay per auto commuter in hours. *Texas A&M Transportation Institute, "2015 Urban Mobility Scorecard," August 2015*

- The New York* metro area appeared on *Forbes* list of places with the most extreme commutes. The metro area ranked #2 out of 10. Criteria: average travel time; percentage of mega commuters. Mega-commuters travel more than 90 minutes and 50 miles each way to work. *Forbes.com, "The Cities with the Most Extreme Commutes," March 5, 2013*

Women/Minorities Rankings

- The *Houston Chronicle* listed the New York* metro area as #4 in top places for young Latinos to live in the U.S. Research was largely based on housing and occupational data from the largest metropolitan areas performed by *Forbes* and NBC Universo. Criteria: percentage of 18-34 year-olds; Latino college grad rates; and diversity. *blog.chron.com, "The 15 Best Big Cities for Latino Millenials," January 26, 2016*

Miscellaneous Rankings

- The watchdog site Charity Navigator conducts an annual study of charities in the nation's major markets both to analyze statistical differences in their financial, accountability, and transparency practices and to track year-to-year variations in individual philanthropic communities. Charity Navigator's analysis demonstrated that the financial, accountability and transparency behaviors of America's largest charities can be influenced by the metropolitan market within which the charity operates. The New York* metro area was ranked #19 among the 30 metro markets in the rating category of Overall Score. *www.charitynavigator.org, "2017 Metro Market Study," May 1, 2017*

- The Harris Poll's Happiness Index survey revealed that of the top ten U.S. markets, the New York* metro area residents ranked #6 in happiness. Criteria included strong assent to positive statements and strong disagreement with negative ones, and degree of agreement with a series of statements about respondents' personal relationships and general outlook. *www.theharrispoll.com, "Dallas/Fort Worth Is "Happiest" City among America's Top Ten Markets," September 4, 2013*

- Energizer Personal Care, the makers of Edge® shave gel, in partnership with Sperling's BestPlaces, ranked 50 major metro areas in terms of everyday irritations. The New York* metro area ranked #2 the 50 metro area most irritating to guys. Criteria: high male-to-female ratio; poor sports team performance and high ticket prices; slow traffic; lack of job availability; unaffordable housing; extreme weather; lack of nightlife and fitness options. *Energizer Personal Care, "Most Irritating Cities for Guys," August 26, 2013*

- The National Alliance to End Homelessness listed the 25 most populous metro areas with the highest rate of homelessness. The New York* metro area had a high rate of homelessness. Criteria: number of homeless people per 10,000 population in 2016. *National Alliance to End Homelessness, "Homelessness in the 25 Most Populous U.S. Metro Areas," September 1, 2017*

*South Brunswick is located within the New York-Newark-Jersey City, NY-NJ-PA Metropolitan Statistical Area and the New York-Jersey City-White Plains, NY-NJ Metropolitan Division.

Business Environment

CITY FINANCES

City Government Finances

Component	2015 ($000)	2015 ($ per capita)
Total Revenues	74,910	1,640
Total Expenditures	72,032	1,577
Debt Outstanding	88,750	1,944
Cash and Securities[1]	22,752	498

Note: (1) Cash and security holdings of a government at the close of its fiscal year,, including those of its dependent agencies, utilities, and liquor stores.
Source: U.S Census Bureau, State & Local Government Finances 2015

City Government Revenue by Source

Source	2015 ($000)	2015 ($ per capita)	2015 (%)
General Revenue			
From Federal Government	518	11	0.7
From State Government	5,563	122	7.4
From Local Governments	480	11	0.6
Taxes			
Property	35,425	776	47.3
Sales and Gross Receipts	1,428	31	1.9
Personal Income	0	0	0.0
Corporate Income	0	0	0.0
Motor Vehicle License	0	0	0.0
Other Taxes	3,889	85	5.2
Current Charges	17,189	376	22.9
Liquor Store	0	0	0.0
Utility	8,590	188	11.5
Employee Retirement	0	0	0.0

Source: U.S Census Bureau, State & Local Government Finances 2015

City Government Expenditures by Function

Function	2015 ($000)	2015 ($ per capita)	2015 (%)
General Direct Expenditures			
Air Transportation	0	0	0.0
Corrections	0	0	0.0
Education	0	0	0.0
Employment Security Administration	0	0	0.0
Financial Administration	1,754	38	2.4
Fire Protection	626	13	0.9
General Public Buildings	262	5	0.4
Governmental Administration, Other	724	15	1.0
Health	1,323	29	1.8
Highways	3,086	67	4.3
Hospitals	0	0	0.0
Housing and Community Development	0	0	0.0
Interest on General Debt	1,369	30	1.9
Judicial and Legal	640	14	0.9
Libraries	2,618	57	3.6
Parking	0	0	0.0
Parks and Recreation	1,640	35	2.3
Police Protection	9,030	197	12.5
Public Welfare	74	1	0.1
Sewerage	17,170	376	23.8
Solid Waste Management	2,773	60	3.8
Veterans' Services	0	0	0.0
Liquor Store	0	0	0.0
Utility	10,095	221	14.0
Employee Retirement	0	0	0.0

Source: U.S Census Bureau, State & Local Government Finances 2015

DEMOGRAPHICS

Population Growth

Area	1990 Census	2000 Census	2010 Census	2016* Estimate	Population Growth (%) 1990-2016	2010-2016
City	25,792	37,734	43,417	45,097	74.8	3.9
MSA[1]	16,845,992	18,323,002	18,897,109	20,031,443	18.9	6.0
U.S.	248,709,873	281,421,906	308,745,538	318,558,162	28.1	3.2

Note: (1) Figures cover the New York-Newark-Jersey City, NY-NJ-PA Metropolitan Statistical Area—see Appendix B for areas included; (*) 2012-2016 5-year estimated population
Source: U.S. Census Bureau, 1990 Census, Census 2000, Census 2010, 2012-2016 American Community Survey 5-Year Estimates

Household Size

Area	Persons in Household (%) One	Two	Three	Four	Five	Six	Seven or More	Average Household Size
City	18.9	26.4	21.2	22.7	7.1	2.8	0.9	2.90
MSA[1]	28.0	29.1	17.0	14.7	6.7	2.6	1.9	2.80
U.S.	27.7	33.7	15.7	13.1	6.0	2.3	1.5	2.60

Note: (1) Figures cover the New York-Newark-Jersey City, NY-NJ-PA Metropolitan Statistical Area—see Appendix B for areas included
Source: U.S. Census Bureau, 2012-2016 American Community Survey 5-Year Estimates

Race

Area	White Alone[2] (%)	Black Alone[2] (%)	Asian Alone[2] (%)	AIAN[3] Alone[2] (%)	NHOPI[4] Alone[2] (%)	Other Race Alone[2] (%)	Two or More Races (%)
City	46.8	8.6	41.0	0.1	0.0	1.8	1.7
MSA[1]	58.7	17.1	10.6	0.3	0.0	10.3	2.9
U.S.	73.3	12.6	5.2	0.8	0.2	4.8	3.1

Note: (1) Figures cover the New York-Newark-Jersey City, NY-NJ-PA Metropolitan Statistical Area—see Appendix B for areas included; (2) Alone is defined as not being in combination with one or more other races; (3) American Indian and Alaska Native; (4) Native Hawaiian and Other Pacific Islander
Source: U.S. Census Bureau, 2012-2016 American Community Survey 5-Year Estimates

Hispanic or Latino Origin

Area	Total (%)	Mexican (%)	Puerto Rican (%)	Cuban (%)	Other (%)
City	6.2	0.4	2.5	0.2	3.0
MSA[1]	23.8	3.1	6.3	0.7	13.7
U.S.	17.3	11.0	1.7	0.7	4.0

Note: Persons of Hispanic or Latino origin can be of any race; (1) Figures cover the New York-Newark-Jersey City, NY-NJ-PA Metropolitan Statistical Area—see Appendix B for areas included
Source: U.S. Census Bureau, 2012-2016 American Community Survey 5-Year Estimates

Segregation

Type	Segregation Indices[1] 1990	2000	2010	2010 Rank[2]	Percent Change 1990-2000	1990-2010	2000-2010
Black/White	80.9	80.2	78.0	2	-0.7	-2.9	-2.2
Asian/White	47.4	50.8	51.9	3	3.5	4.5	1.0
Hispanic/White	66.2	65.6	62.0	3	-0.6	-4.2	-3.6

Note: All figures cover the Metropolitan Statistical Area—see Appendix B for areas included; Figures are based on an analysis of 1990, 2000, and 2010 Census Decennial Census tract data by William H. Frey, Brookings Institution and the University of Michigan Social Science Data Analysis Network. In this analysis all racial groups (whites, blacks, and asians) are non-Hispanic members of those races. Hispanics are shown as a separate category; (1) Segregation Indices are Dissimilarity Indices that measure the degree to which the minority group is distributed differently than whites across census tracts. They range from 0 (complete integration) to 100 (complete segregation) where the value indicates the percentage of the minority group that needs to move to be distributed exactly like whites; (2) Ranges from 1 (most segregated) to 102 (least segregated); n/a not available.
Source: www.CensusScope.org

Ancestry

Area	German	Irish	English	American	Italian	Polish	French[2]	Scottish	Dutch
City	6.6	8.0	2.5	7.0	9.9	3.6	0.5	0.7	0.6
MSA[1]	6.8	10.0	2.9	4.8	13.1	4.0	1.0	0.7	0.7
U.S.	14.4	10.4	7.7	6.9	5.4	2.9	2.6	1.7	1.3

Note: Figures are the percentage of the total population reporting a particular ancestry. The nine most commonly reported ancestries in the U.S. are shown. Figures include multiple ancestries (e.g. if a person reported being Irish and Italian, they were included in both columns); (1) Figures cover the New York-Newark-Jersey City, NY-NJ-PA Metropolitan Statistical Area—see Appendix B for areas included; (2) Excludes Basque
Source: U.S. Census Bureau, 2012-2016 American Community Survey 5-Year Estimates

Foreign-Born Population

Area	Percent of Population Born in								
	Any Foreign Country	Asia	Mexico	Europe	Carribean	Central America[2]	South America	Africa	Canada
City	37.0	28.5	0.2	2.3	1.3	0.8	1.5	1.9	0.3
MSA[1]	28.7	8.3	1.6	4.5	6.6	1.9	4.2	1.2	0.2
U.S.	13.2	4.0	3.6	1.5	1.3	1.0	0.9	0.6	0.3

Note: (1) Figures cover the New York-Newark-Jersey City, NY-NJ-PA Metropolitan Statistical Area—see Appendix B for areas included; (2) Excludes Mexico.
Source: U.S. Census Bureau, 2012-2016 American Community Survey 5-Year Estimates

Marital Status

Area	Never Married	Now Married[2]	Separated	Widowed	Divorced
City	27.2	61.1	0.7	4.5	6.5
MSA[1]	38.1	45.7	2.4	5.8	7.9
U.S.	33.0	48.1	2.1	5.9	11.0

Note: Figures are percentages and cover the population 15 years of age and older; (1) Figures cover the New York-Newark-Jersey City, NY-NJ-PA Metropolitan Statistical Area—see Appendix B for areas included; (2) Excludes separated
Source: U.S. Census Bureau, 2012-2016 American Community Survey 5-Year Estimates

Disability Status

Area	All Ages	Under 18 Years Old	18 to 64 Years Old	65 Years and Over
City	7.4	3.0	5.3	28.0
MSA[1]	10.0	3.2	7.4	33.3
U.S.	12.5	4.1	10.3	35.7

Note: Figures show percent of the civilian noninstitutionalized population that reported having a disability. Disability status is determined from six types of difficulty: vision, hearing, cognitive, ambulatory, self-care, and independent living. For children under 5 years old, hearing and vision difficulty are used to determine disability status. For children between the ages of 5 and 14, disability status is determined from hearing, vision, cognitive, ambulatory, and self-care difficulties. For people aged 15 years and older, they are considered to have a disability if they have difficulty with any one of the six difficulty types; Note: (1) Figures cover the New York-Newark-Jersey City, NY-NJ-PA Metropolitan Statistical Area—see Appendix B for areas included
Source: U.S. Census Bureau, 2012-2016 American Community Survey 5-Year Estimates

Age

Area	Percent of Population									Median Age
	Under Age 5	Age 5–19	Age 20–34	Age 35–44	Age 45–54	Age 55–64	Age 65–74	Age 75–84	Age 85+	
City	4.6	23.3	14.7	15.5	17.6	12.4	6.8	3.1	1.8	39.8
MSA[1]	6.1	18.4	21.3	13.3	14.3	12.3	7.8	4.2	2.1	38.0
U.S.	6.2	19.6	20.7	12.7	13.6	12.6	8.3	4.3	1.9	37.7

Note: (1) Figures cover the New York-Newark-Jersey City, NY-NJ-PA Metropolitan Statistical Area—see Appendix B for areas included
Source: U.S. Census Bureau, 2012-2016 American Community Survey 5-Year Estimates

Gender

Area	Males	Females	Males per 100 Females
City	21,787	23,310	93.5
MSA[1]	9,684,087	10,347,356	93.6
U.S.	156,765,322	161,792,840	96.9

Note: (1) Figures cover the New York-Newark-Jersey City, NY-NJ-PA Metropolitan Statistical Area—see Appendix B for areas included
Source: U.S. Census Bureau, 2012-2016 American Community Survey 5-Year Estimates

Religious Groups by Family

Area	Catholic	Baptist	Non-Den.	Methodist[2]	Lutheran	LDS[3]	Pente-costal	Presby-terian[4]	Muslim[5]	Judaism
MSA[1]	36.9	1.9	1.8	1.3	0.8	0.4	0.9	1.1	2.3	4.8
U.S.	19.1	9.3	4.0	4.0	2.3	2.0	1.9	1.6	0.8	0.7

Note: Figures are the number of adherents as a percentage of the total population; (1) Figures cover the New York-Newark-Jersey City, NY-NJ-PA Metropolitan Statistical Area—see Appendix B for areas included; (2) Methodist/Pietist; (3) Latter Day Saints; (4) Reformed; (5) Figures are estimates
Source: Association of Statisticians of American Religious Bodies, 2010 U.S. Religion Census: Religious Congregations & Membership Study

Religious Groups by Tradition

Area	Catholic	Evangelical Protestant	Mainline Protestant	Other Tradition	Black Protestant	Orthodox
MSA[1]	36.9	4.0	4.1	8.4	1.2	1.0
U.S.	19.1	16.2	7.3	4.3	1.6	0.3

Note: Figures are the number of adherents as a percentage of the total population; (1) Figures cover the New York-Newark-Jersey City, NY-NJ-PA Metropolitan Statistical Area—see Appendix B for areas included
Source: Association of Statisticians of American Religious Bodies, 2010 U.S. Religion Census: Religious Congregations & Membership Study

ECONOMY

Gross Metropolitan Product

Area	2014	2015	2016	2017	Rank[2]
MSA[1]	1,551.3	1,613.8	1,664.0	1,735.1	1

Note: Figures are in billions of dollars; (1) Figures cover the New York-Newark-Jersey City, NY-NJ-PA Metropolitan Statistical Area—see Appendix B for areas included; (2) Rank is based on 2015 data and ranges from 1 to 381
Source: The U.S. Conference of Mayors, U.S. Metro Economies: GMP and Employment Report, 2015-2017

Economic Growth

Area	2012-14 (%)	2015 (%)	2016 (%)	2017 (%)	Rank[2]
MSA[1]	1.6	1.9	1.6	2.2	151
U.S.	2.0	2.4	1.9	2.6	–

Note: Figures are real gross metropolitan product (GMP) growth rates and represent average annual percent change; (1) Figures cover the New York-Newark-Jersey City, NY-NJ-PA Metropolitan Statistical Area—see Appendix B for areas included; (2) Rank is based on 2012-2014 average annual percent change and ranges from 1 to 381
Source: The U.S. Conference of Mayors, U.S. Metro Economies: GMP and Employment Report, 2015-2017

Metropolitan Area Exports

Area	2011	2012	2013	2014	2015	2016	Rank[2]
MSA[1]	105,102.0	102,298.0	106,922.8	105,266.6	95,645.4	89,649.5	1

Note: Figures are in millions of dollars; (1) Figures cover the New York-Newark-Jersey City, NY-NJ-PA Metropolitan Statistical Area—see Appendix B for areas included; (2) Rank is based on 2016 data and ranges from 1 to 385
Source: U.S. Department of Commerce, International Trade Administration, Office of Trade & Industry Information, Manufacturing & Services, data extracted March 15, 2018

Building Permits

Area	Single-Family			Multi-Family			Total		
	2016	2017p	Pct. Chg.	2016	2017p	Pct. Chg.	2016	2017p	Pct. Chg.
City	217	72	-66.8	0	0	0.0	217	72	-66.8
MSA1	9,987	10,549	5.6	32,479	39,344	21.1	42,466	49,893	17.5
U.S.	750,800	817,300	8.9	455,800	446,800	-2.0	1,206,600	1,264,100	4.8

Note: (1) Figures cover the New York-Newark-Jersey City, NY-NJ-PA Metropolitan Statistical Area—see Appendix B for areas included; Figures represent new, privately-owned housing units authorized (unadjusted data); All permit data are based on estimates with imputation; (p) preliminary data.
Source: U.S. Census Bureau, Manufacturing, Mining, and Construction Statistics, Building Permits, 2016, 2017

Bankruptcy Filings

Area	Business Filings			Nonbusiness Filings		
	2016	2017	% Chg.	2016	2017	% Chg.
Middlesex County	62	55	-11.3	1,895	1,945	2.6
U.S.	24,114	23,157	-4.0	770,846	765,863	-0.6

Note: Business filings include Chapter 7, Chapter 11, Chapter 12, and Chapter 13; Nonbusiness filings include Chapter 7, Chapter 11, and Chapter 13
Source: Administrative Office of the U.S. Courts, Business and Nonbusiness Bankruptcy, County Cases Commenced by Chapter of the Bankruptcy Code, During the 12-Month Period Ending December 31, 2016 and Business and Nonbusiness Bankruptcy, County Cases Commenced by Chapter of the Bankruptcy Code, During the 12-Month Period Ending December 31, 2017

Housing Vacancy Rates

Area	Gross Vacancy Rate2 (%)			Year-Round Vacancy Rate3 (%)			Rental Vacancy Rate4 (%)			Homeowner Vacancy Rate5 (%)		
	2015	2016	2017	2015	2016	2017	2015	2016	2017	2015	2016	2017
MSA1	9.8	10.3	10.7	8.6	9.1	9.6	4.2	4.7	4.6	2.1	2.2	1.9
U.S.	12.9	12.8	12.7	10.0	9.9	9.9	7.1	6.9	7.2	1.8	1.7	1.6

Note: (1) Figures cover the New York-Newark-Jersey City, NY-NJ-PA Metropolitan Statistical Area—see Appendix B for areas included; (2) The percentage of the total housing inventory that is vacant; (3) The percentage of the housing inventory (excluding seasonal units) that is year-round vacant; (4) The percentage of rental inventory that is vacant for rent; (5) The percentage of homeowner inventory that is vacant for sale
Source: U.S. Census Bureau, Housing Vacancies and Homeownership Annual Statistics: 2015, 2016, 2017

INCOME

Income

Area	Per Capita ($)	Median Household ($)	Average Household ($)
City	46,504	109,893	133,824
MSA1	37,510	69,211	101,617
U.S.	29,829	55,322	77,866

Note: (1) Figures cover the New York-Newark-Jersey City, NY-NJ-PA Metropolitan Statistical Area—see Appendix B for areas included
Source: U.S. Census Bureau, 2012-2016 American Community Survey 5-Year Estimates

Household Income Distribution

Area	Percent of Households Earning							
	Under $15,000	$15,000 -$24,999	$25,000 -$34,999	$35,000 -$49,999	$50,000 -$74,999	$75,000 -$99,999	$100,000 -$149,999	$150,000 and up
City	4.8	4.1	3.3	7.1	12.8	12.4	22.6	32.8
MSA1	11.7	8.5	7.7	10.2	15.0	11.7	15.9	19.3
U.S.	12.1	10.2	9.9	13.2	17.8	12.2	13.5	11.1

Note: (1) Figures cover the New York-Newark-Jersey City, NY-NJ-PA Metropolitan Statistical Area—see Appendix B for areas included
Source: U.S. Census Bureau, 2012-2016 American Community Survey 5-Year Estimates

Poverty Rate

Area	All Ages	Under 18 Years Old	18 to 64 Years Old	65 Years and Over
City	4.3	5.5	4.0	3.4
MSA[1]	14.2	20.0	12.7	11.7
U.S.	15.1	21.2	14.2	9.3

Note: Figures are percentage of people whose income during the past 12 months was below the poverty level; (1) Figures cover the New York-Newark-Jersey City, NY-NJ-PA Metropolitan Statistical Area—see Appendix B for areas included
Source: U.S. Census Bureau, 2012-2016 American Community Survey 5-Year Estimates

EMPLOYMENT

Labor Force and Employment

Area	Civilian Labor Force			Workers Employed		
	Dec. 2016	Dec. 2017	% Chg.	Dec. 2016	Dec. 2017	% Chg.
City	25,125	24,981	-0.6	24,354	24,216	-0.6
MD[1]	7,114,448	7,115,615	0.0	6,809,258	6,832,994	0.3
U.S.	158,968,000	159,880,000	0.6	151,798,000	153,602,000	1.2

Note: Data is not seasonally adjusted and covers workers 16 years of age and older; (1) Figures cover the New York-Jersey City-White Plains, NY-NJ Metropolitan Division—see Appendix B for areas included
Source: Bureau of Labor Statistics, Local Area Unemployment Statistics

Unemployment Rate

Area	2017											
	Jan.	Feb.	Mar.	Apr.	May	Jun.	Jul.	Aug.	Sep.	Oct.	Nov.	Dec.
City	3.4	3.5	3.3	3.1	3.2	3.4	4.0	3.8	3.7	3.5	3.4	3.1
MD[1]	4.9	4.9	4.4	4.1	4.3	4.5	4.9	4.9	4.5	4.3	4.1	4.0
U.S.	5.1	4.9	4.6	4.1	4.1	4.5	4.6	4.5	4.1	3.9	3.9	3.9

Note: Data is not seasonally adjusted and covers workers 16 years of age and older; (1) Figures cover the New York-Jersey City-White Plains, NY-NJ Metropolitan Division—see Appendix B for areas included
Source: Bureau of Labor Statistics, Local Area Unemployment Statistics

Average Wages

Occupation	$/Hr.	Occupation	$/Hr.
Accountants and Auditors	48.80	Maids and Housekeeping Cleaners	17.60
Automotive Mechanics	21.70	Maintenance and Repair Workers	22.70
Bookkeepers	22.50	Marketing Managers	93.90
Carpenters	33.00	Nuclear Medicine Technologists	43.30
Cashiers	11.50	Nurses, Licensed Practical	25.90
Clerks, General Office	16.60	Nurses, Registered	43.70
Clerks, Receptionists/Information	16.20	Nursing Assistants	17.10
Clerks, Shipping/Receiving	17.40	Packers and Packagers, Hand	12.10
Computer Programmers	46.80	Physical Therapists	44.60
Computer Systems Analysts	55.20	Postal Service Mail Carriers	24.30
Computer User Support Specialists	30.40	Real Estate Brokers	49.20
Cooks, Restaurant	14.30	Retail Salespersons	13.20
Dentists	78.00	Sales Reps., Exc. Tech./Scientific	35.80
Electrical Engineers	52.00	Sales Reps., Tech./Scientific	51.20
Electricians	40.30	Secretaries, Exc. Legal/Med./Exec.	20.10
Financial Managers	102.00	Security Guards	16.30
First-Line Supervisors/Managers, Sales	25.10	Surgeons	119.70
Food Preparation Workers	12.50	Teacher Assistants*	14.70
General and Operations Managers	82.40	Teachers, Elementary School*	38.30
Hairdressers/Cosmetologists	18.10	Teachers, Secondary School*	41.30
Internists, General	99.10	Telemarketers	13.70
Janitors and Cleaners	16.80	Truck Drivers, Heavy/Tractor-Trailer	24.50
Landscaping/Groundskeeping Workers	16.80	Truck Drivers, Light/Delivery Svcs.	18.60
Lawyers	86.30	Waiters and Waitresses	15.30

Note: Wage data covers the New York-Jersey City-White Plains, NY-NJ Metropolitan Division—see Appendix B for areas included; (*) Hourly wages for elementary/secondary school teachers and teacher assistants were calculated by the editors from annual wage data based on a 40 hour work week; n/a not available.
Source: Bureau of Labor Statistics, Metro Area Occupational Employment & Wage Estimates, May 2017

Employment by Occupation

Occupation Classification	City (%)	MSA[1] (%)	U.S. (%)
Management, Business, Science, and Arts	59.6	41.2	37.0
Natural Resources, Construction, and Maintenance	3.6	6.9	8.9
Production, Transportation, and Material Moving	6.4	9.0	12.2
Sales and Office	19.4	23.7	23.8
Service	11.0	19.3	18.1

Note: Figures cover employed civilians 16 years of age and older; (1) Figures cover the New York-Newark-Jersey City, NY-NJ-PA Metropolitan Statistical Area—see Appendix B for areas included
Source: U.S. Census Bureau, 2012-2016 American Community Survey 5-Year Estimates

Employment by Industry

Sector	MD[1]		U.S.
	Number of Employees	Percent of Total	Percent of Total
Construction, Mining, and Logging	265,600	3.7	5.2
Education and Health Services	1,478,800	20.8	15.9
Financial Activities	628,100	8.8	5.7
Government	913,000	12.8	15.3
Information	247,400	3.5	1.9
Leisure and Hospitality	670,100	9.4	10.7
Manufacturing	207,300	2.9	8.5
Other Services	304,700	4.3	3.9
Professional and Business Services	1,148,400	16.2	14.0
Retail Trade	685,200	9.6	11.0
Transportation, Warehousing, and Utilities	275,800	3.9	4.1
Wholesale Trade	284,100	4.0	4.0

Note: Figures are non-farm employment as of December 2017. Figures are not seasonally adjusted and include workers 16 years of age and older; (1) Figures cover the New York-Jersey City-White Plains, NY-NJ Metropolitan Division—see Appendix B for areas included
Source: Bureau of Labor Statistics, Current Employment Statistics, Employment, Hours, and Earnings

Occupations with Greatest Projected Employment Growth: 2016 – 2018

Occupation[1]	2016 Employment	2018 Projected Employment	Numeric Employment Change	Percent Employment Change
Laborers and Freight, Stock, and Material Movers, Hand	97,040	101,030	3,990	4.1
Registered Nurses	84,890	87,480	2,590	3.1
Home Health Aides	36,970	39,030	2,060	5.6
Combined Food Preparation and Serving Workers, Including Fast Food	55,230	57,260	2,030	3.7
Software Developers, Applications	42,830	44,770	1,940	4.5
Heavy and Tractor-Trailer Truck Drivers	45,100	46,980	1,880	4.2
Construction Laborers	32,430	34,110	1,680	5.2
Carpenters	25,870	27,440	1,570	6.1
Waiters and Waitresses	63,080	64,600	1,520	2.4
Receptionists and Information Clerks	52,840	54,340	1,500	2.8

Note: Projections cover New Jersey; (1) Sorted by numeric employment change
Source: www.projectionscentral.com, State Occupational Projections, 2016–2018 Short-Term Projections

Fastest Growing Occupations: 2016 – 2018

Occupation[1]	2016 Employment	2018 Projected Employment	Numeric Employment Change	Percent Employment Change
Brickmasons and Blockmasons	1,920	2,080	160	8.3
Helpers—Electricians	1,620	1,740	120	8.0
Cement Masons and Concrete Finishers	2,440	2,610	170	7.2
Roofers	2,450	2,620	170	7.2
Helpers—Pipelayers, Plumbers, Pipefitters, and Steamfitters	1,100	1,180	80	7.2
Helpers—Carpenters	1,070	1,150	80	7.1
Electricians	15,320	16,370	1,050	6.8
Operations Research Analysts	1,470	1,560	90	6.3
Carpenters	25,870	27,440	1,570	6.1
Drywall and Ceiling Tile Installers	1,510	1,600	90	6.0

Note: Projections cover New Jersey; (1) Sorted by percent employment change and excludes occupations with numeric employment change less than 50
Source: www.projectionscentral.com, State Occupational Projections, 2016–2018 Short-Term Projections

TAXES

State Corporate Income Tax Rates

State	Tax Rate (%)	Income Brackets ($)	Num. of Brackets	Financial Institution Tax Rate (%)[a]	Federal Income Tax Ded.
New Jersey	9.0 (q)	Flat rate	1	9.0 (q)	No

Note: Tax rates as of January 1, 2018; (a) Rates listed are the corporate income tax rate applied to financial institutions or excise taxes based on income. Some states have other taxes based upon the value of deposits or shares; (q) In New Jersey small businesses with annual entire net income under $100,000 pay a tax rate of 7.5%; businesses with income under $50,000 pay 6.5%. The minimum Corporation Business Tax is based on New Jersey gross receipts. It ranges from $500 for a corporation with gross receipts less than $100,000, to $2,000 for a corporation with gross receipts of $1 million or more.
Source: Federation of Tax Administrators, Range of State Corporate Income Tax Rates, January 1, 2018

State Individual Income Tax Rates

State	Tax Rate (%)	Income Brackets ($)	Num. of Brackets	Personal Exempt. ($)[1] Single	Personal Exempt. ($)[1] Dependents	Fed. Inc. Tax Ded.
New Jersey	1.4 - 8.97	20,000 - 500,000 (q)	6	1,000	1,500	No

Note: Tax rates as of January 1, 2018; Local- and county-level taxes are not included; n/a not applicable; (1) Married joint filers generally receive double the single exemption; (q) The New Jersey rates reported are for single individuals. For married couples filing jointly, the tax rates also range from 1.4% to 8.97%, with 7 brackets and the same high and low income ranges.
Source: Federation of Tax Administrators, State Individual Income Tax Rates, January 1, 2018

Various State Sales and Excise Tax Rates

State	State Sales Tax (%)	Gasoline[1] (¢/gal.)	Cigarette[2] ($/pack)	Spirits[3] ($/gal.)	Wine[4] ($/gal.)	Beer[5] ($/gal.)	Recreational Marijuana (%)
New Jersey	6.625 (e)	37.1	2.70	5.50	0.88	0.12	Not legal

Note: All tax rates as of January 1, 2018; (1) The American Petroleum Institute has developed a methodology for determining the average tax rate on a gallon of fuel. Rates may include any of the following: excise taxes, environmental fees, storage tank fees, other fees or taxes, general sales tax, and local taxes. In states where gasoline is subject to the general sales tax, or where the fuel tax is based on the average sale price, the average rate determined by API is sensitive to changes in the price of gasoline. States that fully or partially apply general sales taxes to gasoline: CA, CO, GA, IL, IN, MI, NY; (2) The federal excise tax of $1.0066 per pack and local taxes are not included; (3) Rates are those applicable to off-premise sales of 40% alcohol by volume (a.b.v.) distilled spirits in 750ml containers. Local excise taxes are excluded; (4) Rates are those applicable to off-premise sales of 11% a.b.v. non-carbonated wine in 750ml containers; (5) Rates are those applicable to off-premise sales of 4.7% a.b.v. beer in 12 ounce containers; (e) Salem County is not subject to the statewide sales tax rate and collects a local rate of 3.3125%. New Jersey's average local score is represented as a negative.
Source: Tax Foundation, 2018 Facts & Figures: How Does Your State Compare?

State Business Tax Climate Index Rankings

State	Overall Rank	Corporate Tax Rank	Individual Income Tax Rank	Sales Tax Rank	Unemployment Insurance Tax Rank	Property Tax Rank
New Jersey	50	42	48	46	36	50

Note: The index is a measure of how each state's tax laws affect economic performance. The lower the rank, the more favorable a state's tax system is for business. States without a given tax are given a ranking of 1. The scores/rankings for the District of Columbia do not affect other states. The 2018 index represents the tax climate as of July 1, 2017.
Source: Tax Foundation, State Business Tax Climate Index 2018

TRANSPORTATION

Means of Transportation to Work

Area	Car/Truck/Van		Public Transportation			Bicycle	Walked	Other Means	Worked at Home
	Drove Alone	Car-pooled	Bus	Subway	Railroad				
City	77.2	7.2	6.4	0.3	2.8	0.1	0.8	1.1	4.2
MSA[1]	50.1	6.6	7.7	19.1	3.8	0.6	6.0	1.8	4.2
U.S.	76.4	9.3	2.6	1.9	0.6	0.6	2.8	1.3	4.6

Note: Figures are percentages and cover workers 16 years of age and older; (1) Figures cover the New York-Newark-Jersey City, NY-NJ-PA Metropolitan Statistical Area—see Appendix B for areas included
Source: U.S. Census Bureau, 2012-2016 American Community Survey 5-Year Estimates

Travel Time to Work

Area	Less Than 10 Minutes	10 to 19 Minutes	20 to 29 Minutes	30 to 44 Minutes	45 to 59 Minutes	60 to 89 Minutes	90 Minutes or More
City	6.1	20.7	19.8	20.2	10.9	11.2	11.0
MSA[1]	7.4	19.3	16.4	23.7	12.4	14.4	6.5
U.S.	12.9	29.2	20.9	20.4	8.0	6.0	2.7

Note: Note: Figures are percentages and include workers 16 years old and over; (1) Figures cover the New York-Newark-Jersey City, NY-NJ-PA Metropolitan Statistical Area—see Appendix B for areas included
Source: U.S. Census Bureau, 2012-2016 American Community Survey 5-Year Estimates

Freeway Travel Time Index

Area	1985	1990	1995	2000	2005	2010	2014
Urban Area Rank[1,2]	11	9	8	7	7	8	8
Urban Area Index[1]	1.16	1.20	1.24	1.29	1.33	1.33	1.34
Average Index[3]	1.09	1.11	1.14	1.17	1.20	1.19	1.20

Note: Freeway Travel Time Index—the ratio of travel time in the peak period to the travel time at free-flow conditions. For example, a value of 1.30 indicates a 20-minute free-flow trip takes 26 minutes in the peak (20 minutes x 1.30 = 26 minutes); (1) Covers the New York-Newark NY-NJ-CT urban area; (2) Rank is based on 101 urban areas (#1 = highest travel time index); (3) Average of 101 urban areas
Source: Texas Transportation Institute, 2015 Urban Mobility Scorecard, August 2015

Freeway Commuter Stress Index

Area	1985	1990	1995	2000	2005	2010	2014
Urban Area Rank[1,2]	19	19	13	12	11	11	12
Urban Area Index[1]	1.21	1.24	1.29	1.34	1.38	1.38	1.39
Average Index[3]	1.13	1.16	1.19	1.22	1.25	1.24	1.25

Note: The Freeway Commuter Stress Index is the same as the Freeway Travel Time Index (see table above) except that it includes only the travel in the peak directions during the peak periods; the TTI includes travel in all directions during the peak period. Thus, the CSI is more indicative of the work trip experienced by each commuter on a daily basis; (1) Covers the New York-Newark NY-NJ-CT urban area; (2) Rank is based on 101 urban areas (#1 = highest travel time index); (3) Average of 101 urban areas
Source: Texas Transportation Institute, 2015 Urban Mobility Scorecard, August 2015

Living Environment

COST OF LIVING

Cost of Living Index

Composite Index	Groceries	Housing	Utilities	Trans-portation	Health Care	Misc. Goods/ Services
116.7	104.2	134.1	114.5	111.1	106.7	110.9

Note: The Cost of Living Index measures regional differences in the cost of consumer goods and services, excluding taxes and non-consumer expenditures, for professional and managerial households in the top income quintile. It is based on more than 50,000 prices covering almost 60 different items for which prices are collected three times a year by chambers of commerce, economic development organizations or university applied economic centers in each participating urban area. The numbers shown should be read as a percentage above or below the national average of 100. For example, a value of 115.4 in the groceries column indicates that grocery prices are 15.4% higher than the national average. Small differences in the index numbers should not be interpreted as significant; Figures cover the Middlesex-Monmouth NJ urban area.
Source: The Council for Community and Economic Research, ACCRA Cost of Living Index, 2017

Grocery Prices

Area[1]	T-Bone Steak ($/pound)	Frying Chicken ($/pound)	Whole Milk ($/half gal.)	Eggs ($/dozen)	Orange Juice ($/64 oz.)	Coffee ($/11.5 oz.)
City[2]	11.10	1.47	2.24	1.66	3.35	3.57
Avg.	11.29	1.40	2.02	1.47	3.55	4.37
Min.	7.71	0.93	1.04	0.70	2.86	3.24
Max.	15.83	2.39	4.03	3.92	6.29	8.16

Note: (1) Values for the local area are compared with the average, minimum and maximum values for all 294 areas in the Cost of Living Index; (2) Figures cover the Middlesex-Monmouth NJ urban area; ***T-Bone Steak*** *(price per pound);* ***Frying Chicken*** *(price per pound, whole fryer);* ***Whole Milk*** *(half gallon carton);* ***Eggs*** *(price per dozen, Grade A, large);* ***Orange Juice*** *(64 oz. Tropicana or Florida Natural);* ***Coffee*** *(11.5 oz. can, vacuum-packed, Maxwell House, Hills Bros, or Folgers).*
Source: The Council for Community and Economic Research, ACCRA Cost of Living Index, 2017

Housing and Utility Costs

Area[1]	New Home Price ($)	Apartment Rent ($/month)	All Electric ($/month)	Part Electric ($/month)	Other Energy ($/month)	Telephone ($/month)
City[2]	456,663	1,380	-	124.44	63.78	33.50
Avg.	335,956	1,047	175.01	97.34	67.93	28.71
Min.	187,788	491	109.48	49.33	35.44	12.39
Max.	1,739,087	4,559	432.62	227.09	353.33	44.61

Note: (1) Values for the local area are compared with the average, minimum and maximum values for all 294 areas in the Cost of Living Index; (2) Figures cover the Middlesex-Monmouth NJ urban area; ***New Home Price*** *(2,400 sf living area, 8,000 sf lot, in urban area with full utilities);* ***Apartment Rent*** *(950 sf 2 bedroom/1.5 or 2 bath, unfurnished, excluding all utilities except water);* ***All Electric*** *(average monthly cost for an all-electric home);* ***Part Electric*** *(average monthly cost for a part-electric home);* ***Other Energy*** *(average monthly cost for natural gas, fuel oil, coal, wood, and any other forms of energy except electricity);* ***Telephone*** *(price includes basic monthly rate for a private residential line plus additional local usage charges incurred by a family of four).*
Source: The Council for Community and Economic Research, ACCRA Cost of Living Index, 2017

Health Care, Transportation, and Other Costs

Area[1]	Doctor ($/visit)	Dentist ($/visit)	Optometrist ($/visit)	Gasoline ($/gallon)	Beauty Salon ($/visit)	Men's Shirt ($)
City[2]	93.87	115.62	108.67	2.36	36.33	38.93
Avg.	108.00	92.54	101.93	2.25	37.58	30.92
Min.	30.39	60.00	49.75	1.82	16.11	11.20
Max.	193.50	161.94	229.28	3.16	77.35	59.13

Note: (1) Values for the local area are compared with the average, minimum and maximum values for all 294 areas in the Cost of Living Index; (2) Figures cover the Middlesex-Monmouth NJ urban area; ***Doctor*** *(general practitioners routine exam of an established patient);* ***Dentist*** *(adult teeth cleaning and periodic oral examination);* ***Optometrist*** *(full vision eye exam for established adult patient);* ***Gasoline*** *(one gallon regular unleaded, national brand, including all taxes, cash price at self-service pump if available);* ***Beauty Salon*** *(woman's shampoo, trim, and blow-dry);* ***Men's Shirt*** *(cotton/polyester dress shirt, pinpoint weave, long sleeves).*
Source: The Council for Community and Economic Research, ACCRA Cost of Living Index, 2017

HOUSING

House Price Index (HPI)

Area	National Ranking[2]	Quarterly Change (%)	One-Year Change (%)	Five-Year Change (%)
MD[1]	148	1.22	5.35	20.60
U.S.[3]	–	1.61	6.68	34.71

Note: The HPI is a weighted repeat sales index. It measures average price changes in repeat sales or refinancings on the same properties. This information is obtained by reviewing repeat mortgage transactions on single-family properties whose mortgages have been purchased or securitized by Fannie Mae or Freddie Mac in January 1975; (1) Figures cover the New York-Jersey City-White Plains, NY-NJ Metropolitan Division—see Appendix B for areas included; (2) Rankings are based on annual percentage change for all metro areas containing at least 15,000 transactions over the last 10 years and ranges from 1 to 253; (3) figures based on a weighted average of Census Division estimates using a seasonally adjusted, purchase-only index; all figures are for the period ending December 31, 2017
Source: Federal Housing Finance Agency, House Price Index, February 28, 2018

Median Single-Family Home Prices

Area	2015	2016	2017p	Percent Change 2016 to 2017
MD[1]	398.5	370.2	382.5	3.3
U.S. Average	223.9	235.5	248.8	5.6

Note: Figures are median sales prices of existing single-family homes in thousands of dollars; (p) preliminary; (1) Figures cover the New York-Jersey City-White Plains, NY-NJ Metropolitan Division—see Appendix B for areas included
Source: National Association of Realtors, Median Sales Price of Existing Single-Family Homes for Metropolitan Areas, 4th Quarter 2017

Qualifying Income Based on Median Sales Price of Existing Single-Family Homes

Area	With 5% Down ($)	With 10% Down ($)	With 20% Down ($)
MD[1]	83,646	79,244	70,439
U.S. Average	55,585	52,659	46,808

Note: Figures are preliminary; Qualifying income is based on a mortgage rate of 4.17%. Monthly principal and interest payment is limited to 25% of income; (1) Figures cover the New York-Jersey City-White Plains, NY-NJ Metropolitan Division—see Appendix B for areas included
Source: National Association of Realtors, Qualifying Income Based on Median Sales Price of Existing Single-Family Homes for Metropolitan Areas, 4th Quarter 2017

Median Apartment Condo-Coop Home Prices

Area	2015	2016	2017p	Percent Change 2016 to 2017
MD[1]	245.7	257.2	270.7	5.2
U.S. Average	210.7	220.7	234.3	6.2

Note: Figures are median sales prices of existing apartment condo-coop homes in thousands of dollars; (p) preliminary; (1) Figures cover the New York-Jersey City-White Plains, NY-NJ Metropolitan Division—see Appendix B for areas included
Source: National Association of Realtors, Median Sales Price of Existing Apartment Condo-Coop Homes for Metropolitan Areas, 4th Quarter 2017

Home Value Distribution

Area	Under $50,000	$50,000 -$99,999	$100,000 -$149,999	$150,000 -$199,999	$200,000 -$299,999	$300,000 -$499,999	$500,000 -$999,999	$1,000,000 or more
City	2.5	1.7	1.8	3.0	13.0	48.6	28.4	1.0
MSA[1]	2.8	1.8	2.9	5.0	16.2	37.0	26.9	7.3
U.S.	8.8	14.8	15.3	14.9	18.4	16.4	9.0	2.5

Note: Figures are percentages and cover owner-occupied housing units; (1) Figures cover the New York-Newark-Jersey City, NY-NJ-PA Metropolitan Statistical Area—see Appendix B for areas included
Source: U.S. Census Bureau, 2012-2016 American Community Survey 5-Year Estimates

Homeownership Rate

Area	2009 (%)	2010 (%)	2011 (%)	2012 (%)	2013 (%)	2014 (%)	2015 (%)	2016 (%)	2017 (%)
MSA[1]	51.7	51.6	50.9	51.5	50.6	50.7	49.9	50.4	49.9
U.S.	67.4	66.9	66.1	65.4	65.1	64.5	63.7	63.4	63.9

Note: (1) Figures cover the New York-Newark-Jersey City, NY-NJ-PA Metropolitan Statistical Area—see Appendix B for areas included
Source: U.S. Census Bureau, Housing Vacancies and Homeownership Annual Statistics: 2009-2017

Year Housing Structure Built

Area	2010 or Later	2000 -2009	1990 -1999	1980 -1989	1970 -1979	1960 -1969	1950 -1959	1940 -1949	Before 1940	Median Year
City	1.4	11.2	25.8	26.7	14.7	9.4	6.9	1.5	2.2	1986
MSA[1]	1.3	7.2	6.1	7.9	10.0	13.8	16.2	9.1	28.3	1958
U.S.	2.3	14.7	14.0	13.7	15.6	10.9	10.6	5.2	13.0	1977

Note: Figures are percentages except for Median Year; Note: (1) Figures cover the New York-Newark-Jersey City, NY-NJ-PA Metropolitan Statistical Area—see Appendix B for areas included
Source: U.S. Census Bureau, 2012-2016 American Community Survey 5-Year Estimates

Gross Monthly Rent

Area	Under $500	$500 -$999	$1,000 -$1,499	$1,500 -$1,999	$2,000 -$2,499	$2,500 -$2,999	$3,000 and up	Median ($)
City	5.0	6.6	40.7	35.7	7.1	2.3	2.7	1,475
MSA[1]	9.7	18.7	35.2	19.8	8.3	3.8	4.5	1,297
U.S.	11.3	43.3	27.7	10.7	4.0	1.6	1.5	949

Note: Figures are percentages except for Median; Gross rent is the contract rent plus the estimated average monthly cost of utilities (electricity, gas, and water and sewer) and fuels (oil, coal, kerosene, wood, etc.) if these are paid by the renter (or paid for the renter by someone else); (1) Figures cover the New York-Newark-Jersey City, NY-NJ-PA Metropolitan Statistical Area—see Appendix B for areas included
Source: U.S. Census Bureau, 2012-2016 American Community Survey 5-Year Estimates

HEALTH

Health Risk Factors

Category	MD[1] (%)	U.S. (%)
Adults aged 18–64 who have any kind of health care coverage	86.5	87.7
Adults who reported being in good or excellent health	82.3	83.6
Adults who are current smokers	11.9	17.1
Adults who currently use E-cigarettes	3.9	4.7
Adults who currently use chewing tobacco, snuff, or snus	2.0	4.0
Adults who are heavy drinkers[2]	5.0	6.5
Adults who are binge drinkers[3]	16.8	16.9
Adults who are overweight (BMI 25.0 - 29.9)	34.4	35.3
Adults who are obese (BMI 30.0 - 99.8)	24.0	29.9
Adults who participated in any physical activities in the past month	71.7	76.9
Adults who always or nearly always wears a seat belt	92.3	94.3

Note: (1) Figures cover the New York-Jersey City-White Plains, NY-NJ Metropolitan Division—see Appendix B for areas included; (2) Heavy drinkers are classified as adult men having more than 14 drinks per week and adult women having more than 7 drinks per week; (3) Binge drinkers are classified as males having five or more drinks on one occasion or females having four or more drinks on one occasion
Source: Centers for Disease Control and Prevention, Behaviorial Risk Factor Surveillance System, SMART: Selected Metropolitan Area Risk Trends, 2016

Health Screening Rates

Category	MD[1] (%)	U.S. (%)
Adults 50-75 who have had a blood stool test within the past year	7.2	8.0
Adults 50-75 who have had a colonoscopy in the past 10 years	63.9	63.5
Adults aged 65+ who have had flu shot within the past year	61.0	58.6
Adults aged 65+ who have ever had a pneumonia vaccination	64.0	73.4
Adults who have ever been tested for HIV	50.7	35.6
Women aged 21-65 who have had a pap test in the past three years	79.5	79.8
Men aged 40+ who have had a PSA test within the past two years	39.3	39.5
Women aged 40+ who have had a mammogram within the past two years	73.3	72.5

Note: (1) Figures cover the New York-Jersey City-White Plains, NY-NJ Metropolitan Division—see Appendix B for areas included; Source: Centers for Disease Control and Prevention, Behaviorial Risk Factor Surveillance System, SMART: Selected Metropolitan Area Risk Trends, 2016

Chronic Health Conditions

Category	MD[1] (%)	U.S. (%)
Adults who have ever been told they had a heart attack	3.3	4.4
Adults who have ever been told they have angina or coronary heart disease	3.5	4.1
Adults who have ever been told they had a stroke	2.5	3.1
Adults who have been told they currently have asthma	8.5	9.3
Adults who have ever been told they have arthritis	20.1	25.8
Adults who have ever been told they have diabetes[2]	10.1	10.5
Adults who have ever been told they had skin cancer	3.4	5.9
Adults who have ever been told they had any other types of cancer	4.9	6.7
Adults who have ever been told they have COPD	4.5	6.3
Adults who have ever been told they have kidney disease	2.3	2.8
Adults who have ever been told they have a form of depression	10.6	17.4

Note: (1) Figures cover the New York-Jersey City-White Plains, NY-NJ Metropolitan Division—see Appendix B for areas included; (2) Figures do not include pregnancy-related, borderline, or pre-diabetes
Source: Centers for Disease Control and Prevention, Behaviorial Risk Factor Surveillance System, SMART: Selected Metropolitan Area Risk Trends, 2016

Mortality Rates for the Top 10 Causes of Death in the U.S.

ICD-10[a] Sub-Chapter	ICD-10[a] Code	Age-Adjusted Mortality Rate[1] per 100,000 population	
		County[2]	U.S.
Malignant neoplasms	C00-C97	141.0	158.5
Ischaemic heart diseases	I20-I25	90.5	96.8
Other forms of heart disease	I30-I51	50.2	52.4
Chronic lower respiratory diseases	J40-J47	23.9	40.9
Cerebrovascular diseases	I60-I69	28.6	37.2
Organic, including symptomatic, mental disorders	F01-F09	28.6	33.3
Other degenerative diseases of the nervous system	G30-G31	16.4	32.1
Other external causes of accidental injury	W00-X59	24.9	31.2
Diabetes mellitus	E10-E14	16.8	21.1
Hypertensive diseases	I10-I15	14.0	20.8

Note: (a) ICD-10 = International Classification of Diseases 10th Revision; (1) Mortality rates are a three year average covering 2014-2016; (2) Figures cover Middlesex County.
Source: Centers for Disease Control and Prevention, National Center for Health Statistics. Underlying Cause of Death 1999-2016 on CDC WONDER Online Database, released December 2017

Mortality Rates for Selected Causes of Death

ICD-10[a] Sub-Chapter	ICD-10[a] Code	Age-Adjusted Mortality Rate[1] per 100,000 population	
		County[2]	U.S.
Assault	X85-Y09	1.7	5.6
Diseases of the liver	K70-K76	8.9	14.0
Human immunodeficiency virus (HIV) disease	B20-B24	1.3	1.9
Influenza and pneumonia	J09-J18	11.3	14.6
Intentional self-harm	X60-X84	7.0	13.2
Malnutrition	E40-E46	Unreliable	1.3
Obesity and other hyperalimentation	E65-E68	1.9	2.1
Renal failure	N17-N19	14.2	13.0
Transport accidents	V01-V99	5.0	12.0
Viral hepatitis	B15-B19	1.2	1.9

Note: (a) ICD-10 = International Classification of Diseases 10th Revision; (1) Mortality rates are a three year average covering 2014-2016; (2) Figures cover Middlesex County; Data are Suppressed when the data meet the criteria for confidentiality constraints; Mortality rates are flagged as Unreliable when the rate would be calculated with a numerator of 20 or less.
Source: Centers for Disease Control and Prevention, National Center for Health Statistics. Underlying Cause of Death 1999-2016 on CDC WONDER Online Database, released December 2017

Health Insurance Coverage

Area	With Health Insurance	With Private Health Insurance	With Public Health Insurance	Without Health Insurance	Population Under Age 18 Without Health Insurance
City	94.6	85.6	16.6	5.4	3.7
MSA[1]	89.8	65.8	33.7	10.2	3.6
U.S.	88.3	66.7	33.0	11.7	5.9

Note: Figures are percentages that cover the civilian noninstitutionalized population; (1) Figures cover the New York-Newark-Jersey City, NY-NJ-PA Metropolitan Statistical Area—see Appendix B for areas included
Source: U.S. Census Bureau, 2012-2016 American Community Survey 5-Year Estimates

Number of Medical Professionals

Area	MDs[3]	DOs[3,4]	Dentists	Podiatrists	Chiropractors	Optometrists
County[1] (number)	3,049	162	717	82	203	148
County[1] (rate[2])	363.7	19.3	85.4	9.8	24.2	17.6
U.S. (rate[2])	276.5	22.3	67.3	6.0	26.7	15.9

Note: Data as of 2016 unless noted; (1) Data covers Middlesex County; (2) Rate per 100,000 population; (3) Data as of 2015 and includes all active, non-federal physicians; (4) Doctor of Osteopathic Medicine
Source: U.S. Department of Health and Human Services, Health Resources and Services Administration, Bureau of Health Professions, Area Resource File (ARF) 2016-2017

Best Hospitals

According to *U.S. News,* the New York-Jersey City-White Plains, NY-NJ metro area is home to nine of the best hospitals in the U.S.: **Hackensack University Medical Center** (3 adult specialties and 1 pediatric specialty); **Hospital for Special Surgery** (2 adult specialties and 1 pediatric specialty); **Memorial Sloan Kettering Cancer Center** (4 adult specialties and 1 pediatric specialty); **Montefiore Medical Center** (1 adult specialty and 7 pediatric specialties); **Mount Sinai Hospital** (Honor Roll/10 adult specialties and 6 pediatric specialties); **NYU Langone Medical Center** (Honor Roll/12 adult specialties); **New York Eye and Ear Infirmary** (2 adult specialties); **New York-Presbyterian Hospital-Columbia and Cornell** (Honor Roll/14 adult specialties and 10 pediatric specialties); **Robert Wood Johnson University Hospital** (1 pediatric specialty). The hospitals listed were nationally ranked in at least one of 16 specialties. Only 152 hospitals nationwide were nationally ranked in one or more specialties. Twenty hospitals in the U.S. made the Honor Roll. The Best Hospitals Honor Roll was revamped last year to take both the national rankings and the procedure and condition ratings into account. Hospitals received points if they were nationally ranked in one of the 16 specialties—the higher they ranked, the more points they got—and how many ratings of "high performing" they earned in the nine procedures and conditions. *U.S. News Online, "America's Best Hospitals 2017-18"*

According to *U.S. News,* the New York-Jersey City-White Plains, NY-NJ metro area is home to seven of the best children's hospitals in the U.S.: **Bristol-Myers Squibb Children's Hospital at RWJ Univ. Hosp.** (1 pediatric specialty); **Children's Hospital at Montefiore** (7 pediatric specialties); **Memorial Sloan Kettering Cancer Center** (1 pediatric specialty); **Mount Sinai Kravis Children's Hospital** (6 pediatric specialties); **New York-Presbyterian Morgan Stanley-Komansky Children's Hospital** (10 pediatric specialties); **Hospital for Special Surgery, New York** (1 pediatric specialty); **Joseph M. Sanzari Children's Hospital at Hackensack University Medical Center** (1 pediatric specialty). The hospitals listed were highly ranked in at least one of 10 pediatric specialties. Eighty-two children's hospitals in the U.S. were nationally ranked in at least one specialty. Hospitals received points for being ranked in a specialty, and the 10 hospitals with the most points across the 10 specialties make up the Honor Roll. *U.S. News Online, "America's Best Children's Hospitals 2017-18"*

EDUCATION

Public School District Statistics

District Name	Schls	Pupils	Pupil/ Teacher Ratio	Minority Pupils[1] (%)	Free Lunch Eligible[2] (%)	IEP[3] (%)
South Brunswick School District	10	8,790	13.9	72.3	9.5	12.0

Note: Table includes school districts with 100 or more students; (1) Percentage of students that are not non-Hispanic white; (2) Percentage of students that are eligible for the free lunch program; (3) Percentage of students that have an Individualized Education Program.
Source: U.S. Department of Education, National Center for Education Statistics, Common Core of Data, Local Education Agency (School District) Universe Survey: School Year 2015-2016; U.S. Department of Education, National Center for Education Statistics, Common Core of Data, Public Elementary/Secondary School Universe Survey: School Year 2015-2016

Highest Level of Education

Area	Less than H.S.	H.S. Diploma	Some College, No Deg.	Associate Degree	Bachelor's Degree	Master's Degree	Prof. School Degree	Doctorate Degree
City	4.9	15.2	12.3	6.6	35.7	19.5	3.5	2.2
MSA[1]	14.3	25.3	15.5	6.7	22.3	11.3	3.0	1.5
U.S.	13.0	27.5	21.0	8.2	18.8	8.2	2.0	1.3

Note: Figures cover persons age 25 and over; (1) Figures cover the New York-Newark-Jersey City, NY-NJ-PA Metropolitan Statistical Area—see Appendix B for areas included
Source: U.S. Census Bureau, 2012-2016 American Community Survey 5-Year Estimates

Educational Attainment by Race

Area	High School Graduate or Higher (%)					Bachelor's Degree or Higher (%)				
	Total	White	Black	Asian	Hisp.[2]	Total	White	Black	Asian	Hisp.[2]
City	95.1	96.5	93.1	94.3	94.6	60.9	47.8	60.3	79.7	30.4
MSA[1]	85.7	90.0	84.1	82.9	68.9	38.1	43.2	23.8	53.1	17.7
U.S.	87.0	88.9	84.3	86.3	65.7	30.3	31.6	20.0	52.1	14.7

Note: Figures shown cover persons 25 years old and over; (1) Figures cover the New York-Newark-Jersey City, NY-NJ-PA Metropolitan Statistical Area—see Appendix B for areas included; (2) People of Hispanic origin can be of any race
Source: U.S. Census Bureau, 2012-2016 American Community Survey 5-Year Estimates

School Enrollment by Grade and Control

Area	Preschool (%)		Kindergarten (%)		Grades 1 - 4 (%)		Grades 5 - 8 (%)		Grades 9 - 12 (%)	
	Public	Private	Public	Private	Public	Private	Public	Private	Public	Private
City	31.1	68.9	77.1	22.9	95.6	4.4	94.5	5.5	93.3	6.7
MSA[1]	51.9	48.1	81.6	18.4	86.1	13.9	86.3	13.7	85.9	14.1
U.S.	58.4	41.6	87.7	12.3	89.8	10.2	89.7	10.3	90.4	9.6

Note: Figures shown cover persons 3 years old and over; (1) Figures cover the New York-Newark-Jersey City, NY-NJ-PA Metropolitan Statistical Area—see Appendix B for areas included
Source: U.S. Census Bureau, 2012-2016 American Community Survey 5-Year Estimates

Average Salaries of Public School Classroom Teachers

Area	2015		2016		Change from 2015 to 2016	
	Dollars	Rank[1]	Dollars	Rank[1]	Percent	Rank[2]
New Jersey	69,038	6	69,330	6	0.4	41
U.S. Average	57,611	–	58,353	–	1.3	–

Note: (1) Rank ranges from 1 to 51 where 1 indicates highest salary; (2) Rank ranges from 1 to 51 where 1 indicates highest percent change.
Source: National Education Association, Rankings & Estimates: Rankings of the States 2016 and Estimates of School Statistics 2017

Higher Education

Four-Year Colleges			Two-Year Colleges			Medical Schools[1]	Law Schools[2]	Voc/ Tech[3]
Public	Private Non-profit	Private For-profit	Public	Private Non-profit	Private For-profit			
0	0	0	0	0	0	0	0	0

Note: Figures cover institutions located within the city limits and include main campuses only; (1) includes schools accredited by the Liaison Committee on Medical Education and the American Osteopathic Association's Commission on Osteopathic College Accreditation; (2) includes ABA-accredited schools, schools with provisional ABA accreditation, and state accredited schools; (3) includes all schools with programs that are less than 2 years.
Source: National Center for Education Statistics, Integrated Postsecondary Education System (IPEDS), 2016-17; Wikipedia, List of Medical Schools in the United States, accessed April 2, 2018; Wikipedia, List of Law Schools in the United States, accessed April 2, 2018

According to *U.S. News & World Report,* the New York-Jersey City-White Plains, NY-NJ metro division is home to seven of the best national universities in the U.S.: **Columbia University** (#5 tie); **New York University** (#30 tie); **Fordham University** (#61 tie); **Yeshiva University** (#94 tie); **The New School** (#133 tie); **Saint John's University (Jamaica)** (#165 tie); **Pace University** (#187 tie). The indicators used to capture academic quality fall into a number of categories: assessment by administrators at peer institutions; retention of students; faculty resources; student selectivity; financial resources; alumni giving; high school counselor ratings of colleges; and graduation rate. *U.S. News & World Report, "America's Best Colleges 2018"*

According to *U.S. News & World Report,* the New York-Jersey City-White Plains, NY-NJ metro division is home to one of the best liberal arts colleges in the U.S.: **Barnard College** (#26 tie).

The indicators used to capture academic quality fall into a number of categories: assessment by administrators at peer institutions; retention of students; faculty resources; student selectivity; financial resources; alumni giving; high school counselor ratings of colleges; and graduation rate. *U.S. News & World Report, "America's Best Colleges 2018"*

According to *U.S. News & World Report,* the New York-Jersey City-White Plains, NY-NJ metro division is home to six of the top 100 law schools in the U.S.: **Columbia University** (#5); **New York University** (#6); **Fordham University** (#37 tie); **Yeshiva University (Cardozo)** (#56 tie); **Brooklyn Law School** (#83 tie); **Saint John's University (Jamaica)** (#83 tie). The rankings are based on a weighted average of 12 measures of quality: peer assessment score; assessment score by lawyers/judges; median LSAT scores; median undergrad GPA; acceptance rate; employment rates for graduates; placement success; bar passage rate; faculty resources; expenditures per student; student/faculty ratio; and library resources. *U.S. News & World Report, "America's Best Graduate Schools, Law, 2019"*

According to *U.S. News & World Report,* the New York-Jersey City-White Plains, NY-NJ metro division is home to five of the top 75 medical schools for research in the U.S.: **New York University (Langone)** (#3 tie); **Columbia University** (#11 tie); **Icahn School of Medicine at Mount Sinai** (#18 tie); **Cornell University (Weill)** (#21); **Yeshiva University (Einstein)** (#39 tie). The rankings are based on a weighted average of 11 measures of quality: quality assessment; peer assessment score; assessment score by residency directors; research activity; total research activity; average research activity per faculty member; student selectivity; median MCAT total score; median undergraduate GPA; acceptance rate; and faculty resources. *U.S. News & World Report, "America's Best Graduate Schools, Medical, 2019"*

According to *U.S. News & World Report,* the New York-Jersey City-White Plains, NY-NJ metro division is home to four of the top 75 business schools in the U.S.: **Columbia University** (#9); **New York University (Stern)** (#13 tie); **CUNY Bernard M. Baruch College (Zicklin)** (#55 tie); **Fordham University (Gabelli)** (#63 tie). The rankings are based on a weighted average of the following nine measures: quality assessment; peer assessment; recruiter assessment; placement success; mean starting salary and bonus; student selectivity; mean GMAT and GRE scores; mean undergraduate GPA; and acceptance rate. *U.S. News & World Report, "America's Best Graduate Schools, Business, 2019"*

PRESIDENTIAL ELECTION

2016 Presidential Election Results

Area	Clinton	Trump	Johnson	Stein	Other
Middlesex County	58.8	37.4	1.7	1.1	1.1
U.S.	48.0	45.9	3.3	1.1	1.7

Note: Results are percentages and may not add to 100% due to rounding
Source: Dave Leip's Atlas of U.S. Presidential Elections

EMPLOYERS

Major Employers

Company Name	Industry
American Express Company	Personal credit institutions
American International Group	Life insurance
Deloitte Consulting	Management consulting services
Hackensack University Medical Center	University
Merrill Lynch and Co	Security brokers & dealers
Mount Sinai Hospital	General medical & surgical hospitals
Mount Sinai School of Medicine	Medical training services
NewYork-Presbyterian Hospital	General medical & surgical hospitals
NYC Health and Hospitals Corp	Psychiatric hospitals
NYU School of Medicine	Offices & clinics of medical doctors
Paramount Comm Acq Corp	Investment holding companies, except banks
Patriarch Partners	Investment offices
Rutgers, The State Univ of NJ	Colleges & universities
Standard Americas	Agencies of foreign banks
The Long Island Rail Road Company	Local & suburban transit
U of Med and Dentistry of NJ	Colleges & universities
UMASS Memorial Health Care	Psychiatrist
United States Postal Service	U.S. postal service
Wellchoice	Health insurance carriers

Note: Companies shown are located within the New York-Newark-Jersey City, NY-NJ-PA Metropolitan Statistical Area.
Source: Hoovers.com; Wikipedia

PUBLIC SAFETY

Crime Rate

Area	All Crimes	Violent Crimes				Property Crimes		
		Murder	Rape[3]	Robbery	Aggrav. Assault	Burglary	Larceny -Theft	Motor Vehicle Theft
City	872.2	0.0	6.5	17.4	15.3	172.3	597.4	63.2
Metro[1]	1,805.2	3.1	22.2	136.2	255.9	160.0	1,152.5	75.3
U.S.	2,847.8	5.3	40.4	102.8	248.5	468.9	1,745.0	236.9

Note: Figures are crimes per 100,000 population; (1) Figures cover the New York-Jersey City-White Plains, NY-NJ Metropolitan Division—see Appendix B for areas included; (3) The city and U.S. figures shown were reported using the revised Uniform Crime Reporting (UCR) definition of rape. The metro area figures shown are an aggregate total of the data submitted using both the revised and legacy UCR definitions.
Source: FBI Uniform Crime Reports, 2016

Hate Crimes

Area	Number of Quarters Reported	Number of Incidents per Bias Motivation					
		Race/Ethnicity/ Ancestry	Religion	Sexual Orientation	Disability	Gender	Gender Identity
Area[1]	4	3	11	1	0	0	0
U.S.	4	3,489	1,273	1,076	70	31	124

Note: (1) Figures cover the South Brunswick Township.
Source: Federal Bureau of Investigation, Hate Crime Statistics 2016

Identity Theft Consumer Reports

Area	Reports	Reports per 100,000 Population	Rank[2]
MSA[1]	23,624	117	64
U.S.	371,061	114	-

Note: (1) Figures cover the New York-Newark-Jersey City, NY-NJ-PA Metropolitan Statistical Area—see Appendix B for areas included; (2) Rank ranges from 1 to 389 where 1 indicates greatest number of identity theft reports per 100,000 population
Source: Federal Trade Commission, Consumer Sentinel Network Data Book for January–December 2017

Fraud and Other Consumer Reports

Area	Reports	Reports per 100,000 Population	Rank[2]
MSA[1]	90,589	449	173
U.S.	2,304,550	708	-

Note: (1) Figures cover the New York-Newark-Jersey City, NY-NJ-PA Metropolitan Statistical Area—see Appendix B for areas included; (2) Rank ranges from 1 to 389 where 1 indicates greatest number of fraud and other consumer reports per 100,000 population
Source: Federal Trade Commission, Consumer Sentinel Network Data Book for January–December 2017

SPORTS

Professional Sports Teams

Team Name	League	Year Established
Brooklyn Nets	National Basketball Association (NBA)	1967
New Jersey Devils	National Hockey League (NHL)	1982
New York City FC	Major League Soccer (MLS)	2015
New York Giants	National Football League (NFL)	1925
New York Islanders	National Hockey League (NHL)	1972
New York Jets	National Football League (NFL)	1960
New York Knicks	National Basketball Association (NBA)	1946
New York Mets	Major League Baseball (MLB)	1962
New York Rangers	National Hockey League (NHL)	1926
New York Red Bulls	Major League Soccer (MLS)	1996
New York Yankees	Major League Baseball (MLB)	1903

Note: Includes teams located in the New York-Newark-Jersey City, NY-NJ-PA Metropolitan Statistical Area.
Source: Wikipedia, Major Professional Sports Teams of the United States and Canada, April 5, 2018

CLIMATE

Average and Extreme Temperatures

Temperature	Jan	Feb	Mar	Apr	May	Jun	Jul	Aug	Sep	Oct	Nov	Dec	Yr.
Extreme High (°F)	68	75	85	96	97	101	104	99	99	88	81	72	104
Average High (°F)	38	41	50	61	72	80	85	84	76	65	54	43	62
Average Temp. (°F)	32	34	43	53	63	72	77	76	68	58	48	37	55
Average Low (°F)	26	27	35	44	54	63	68	67	60	49	41	31	47
Extreme Low (°F)	-2	-2	8	21	36	46	53	50	40	29	17	-1	-2

Note: Figures cover the years 1962-1992
Source: National Climatic Data Center, International Station Meteorological Climate Summary, 9/96

Average Precipitation/Snowfall/Humidity

Precip./Humidity	Jan	Feb	Mar	Apr	May	Jun	Jul	Aug	Sep	Oct	Nov	Dec	Yr.
Avg. Precip. (in.)	3.5	3.1	4.0	3.9	4.5	3.8	4.5	4.1	4.1	3.3	4.5	3.8	47.0
Avg. Snowfall (in.)	7	8	4	Tr	Tr	0	0	0	0	Tr	Tr	3	23
Avg. Rel. Hum. 7am (%)	67	67	66	64	72	74	74	76	78	75	72	69	71
Avg. Rel. Hum. 4pm (%)	55	53	50	45	52	55	53	54	56	55	57	58	53

Note: Figures cover the years 1962-1992; Tr = Trace amounts (<0.05 in. of rain; <0.5 in. of snow)
Source: National Climatic Data Center, International Station Meteorological Climate Summary, 9/96

Weather Conditions

Temperature			Daytime Sky			Precipitation		
32°F & below	45°F & below	90°F & above	Clear	Partly cloudy	Cloudy	0.01 inch or more precip.	0.1 inch or more snow/ice	Thunder-storms
75	170	18	85	166	114	120	11	20

Note: Figures are average number of days per year and cover the years 1962-1992
Source: National Climatic Data Center, International Station Meteorological Climate Summary, 9/96

HAZARDOUS WASTE

Superfund Sites

The New York-Jersey City-White Plains, NY-NJ metro division is home to 48 sites on the EPA's Superfund National Priorities List: **Atlantic Resources** (final); **Bog Creek Farm** (final); **Brick Township Landfill** (final); **Burnt Fly Bog** (final); **Carroll & Dubies Sewage Disposal** (final); **Chemical Insecticide Corp.** (final); **Chemsol, Inc.** (final); **Ciba-geigy Corp.** (final); **Cornell**

Dubilier Electronics Inc. (final); **CPS/Madison Industries** (final); **Curcio Scrap Metal, Inc.** (final); **Diamond Head Oil Refinery Div.** (final); **Evor Phillips Leasing** (final); **Fair Lawn Well Field** (final); **Fried Industries** (final); **Garfield Ground Water Contamination** (final); **Global Sanitary Landfill** (final); **Goose Farm** (final); **Gowanus Canal** (final); **Horseshoe Road** (final); **Hudson Technologies, Inc.** (proposed); **Imperial Oil Co., Inc./Champion Chemicals** (final); **JIS Landfill** (final); **Kin-Buc Landfill** (final); **Lone Pine Landfill** (final); **Maywood Chemical Co.** (final); **Middlesex Sampling Plant (USDOE)** (final); **Monitor Devices, Inc./Intercircuits, Inc.** (final); **Naval Air Engineering Center** (final); **Naval Weapons Station Earle (Site A)** (final); **Nepera Chemical Co., Inc.** (final); **Newtown Creek** (final); **Pjp Landfill** (final); **Quanta Resources** (final); **Ramapo Landfill** (final); **Raritan Bay Slag** (final); **Reich Farms** (final); **Ringwood Mines/Landfill** (final); **Scientific Chemical Processing** (final); **Standard Chlorine** (final); **Syncon Resins** (final); **Universal Oil Products (Chemical Division)** (final); **Ventron/Velsicol** (final); **Waldick Aerospace Devices, Inc.** (final); **White Swan Laundry and Cleaner Inc.** (final); **Wolff-Alport Chemical Company** (final); **Woodbrook Road Dump** (final); **Zschiegner Refining** (final). There are a total of 1,396 Superfund sites with a status of proposed or final on the list in the U.S. *U.S. Environmental Protection Agency, National Priorities List, April 4, 2018*

AIR & WATER QUALITY

Air Quality Trends: Ozone

	1990	1995	2000	2005	2010	2012	2013	2014	2015	2016
MSA[1]	0.101	0.106	0.090	0.091	0.081	0.079	0.071	0.069	0.075	0.073
U.S.	0.087	0.089	0.081	0.079	0.073	0.075	0.069	0.067	0.068	0.069

Note: (1) Data covers the New York-Newark-Jersey City, NY-NJ-PA Metropolitan Statistical Area—see Appendix B for areas included. The values shown are the composite ozone concentration averages among trend sites based on the highest fourth daily maximum 8-hour concentration in parts per million. These trends are based on sites having an adequate record of monitoring data during the trend period. Data from exceptional events are included.
Source: U.S. Environmental Protection Agency, Air Quality Monitoring Information, "Air Quality Trends by City, 1990-2016"

Air Quality Index

Area	Percent of Days when Air Quality was...[2]					AQI Statistics[2]	
	Good	Moderate	Unhealthy for Sensitive Groups	Unhealthy	Very Unhealthy	Maximum	Median
MSA[1]	42.2	52.6	4.7	0.5	0.0	159	52

Note: (1) Data covers the New York-Newark-Jersey City, NY-NJ-PA Metropolitan Statistical Area—see Appendix B for areas included; (2) Based on 365 days with AQI data in 2017. Air Quality Index (AQI) is an index for reporting daily air quality. EPA calculates the AQI for five major air pollutants regulated by the Clean Air Act: ground-level ozone, particle pollution (aka particulate matter), carbon monoxide, sulfur dioxide, and nitrogen dioxide. The AQI runs from 0 to 500. The higher the AQI value, the greater the level of air pollution and the greater the health concern. There are six AQI categories: "Good" AQI is between 0 and 50. Air quality is considered satisfactory; "Moderate" AQI is between 51 and 100. Air quality is acceptable; "Unhealthy for Sensitive Groups" When AQI values are between 101 and 150, members of sensitive groups may experience health effects; "Unhealthy" When AQI values are between 151 and 200 everyone may begin to experience health effects; "Very Unhealthy" AQI values between 201 and 300 trigger a health alert; "Hazardous" AQI values over 300 trigger warnings of emergency conditions (not shown).
Source: U.S. Environmental Protection Agency, Air Quality Index Report, 2017

Air Quality Index Pollutants

Area	Percent of Days when AQI Pollutant was...[2]					
	Carbon Monoxide	Nitrogen Dioxide	Ozone	Sulfur Dioxide	Particulate Matter 2.5	Particulate Matter 10
MSA[1]	0.0	13.2	31.8	0.0	55.1	0.0

Note: (1) Data covers the New York-Newark-Jersey City, NY-NJ-PA Metropolitan Statistical Area—see Appendix B for areas included; (2) Based on 365 days with AQI data in 2017. The Air Quality Index (AQI) is an index for reporting daily air quality. EPA calculates the AQI for five major air pollutants regulated by the Clean Air Act: ground-level ozone, particle pollution (also known as particulate matter), carbon monoxide, sulfur dioxide, and nitrogen dioxide. The AQI runs from 0 to 500. The higher the AQI value, the greater the level of air pollution and the greater the health concern.
Source: U.S. Environmental Protection Agency, Air Quality Index Report, 2017

Maximum Air Pollutant Concentrations: Particulate Matter, Ozone, CO and Lead

	Particulate Matter 10 (ug/m³)	Particulate Matter 2.5 Wtd AM (ug/m³)	Particulate Matter 2.5 24-Hr (ug/m³)	Ozone (ppm)	Carbon Monoxide (ppm)	Lead (ug/m³)
MSA[1] Level	33	9.2	20	0.078	3	0.03
NAAQS[2]	150	15	35	0.075	9	0.15
Met NAAQS[2]	Yes	Yes	Yes	No	Yes	Yes

Note: (1) Data covers the New York-Newark-Jersey City, NY-NJ-PA Metropolitan Statistical Area—see Appendix B for areas included; Data from exceptional events are included; (2) National Ambient Air Quality Standards; ppm = parts per million; ug/m³ = micrograms per cubic meter; n/a not available.
Concentrations: Particulate Matter 10 (coarse particulate)—highest second maximum 24-hour concentration; Particulate Matter 2.5 Wtd AM (fine particulate)—highest weighted annual mean concentration; Particulate Matter 2.5 24-Hour (fine particulate)—highest 98th percentile 24-hour concentration; Ozone—highest fourth daily maximum 8-hour concentration; Carbon Monoxide—highest second maximum non-overlapping 8-hour concentration; Lead—maximum running 3-month average
Source: U.S. Environmental Protection Agency, Air Quality Monitoring Information, "Air Quality Statistics by City, 2016"

Maximum Air Pollutant Concentrations: Nitrogen Dioxide and Sulfur Dioxide

	Nitrogen Dioxide AM (ppb)	Nitrogen Dioxide 1-Hr (ppb)	Sulfur Dioxide AM (ppb)	Sulfur Dioxide 1-Hr (ppb)	Sulfur Dioxide 24-Hr (ppb)
MSA[1] Level	20	60	n/a	7	n/a
NAAQS[2]	53	100	30	75	140
Met NAAQS[2]	Yes	Yes	n/a	Yes	n/a

Note: (1) Data covers the New York-Newark-Jersey City, NY-NJ-PA Metropolitan Statistical Area—see Appendix B for areas included; Data from exceptional events are included; (2) National Ambient Air Quality Standards; ppm = parts per million; ug/m³ = micrograms per cubic meter; n/a not available.
Concentrations: Nitrogen Dioxide AM—highest arithmetic mean concentration; Nitrogen Dioxide 1-Hr—highest 98th percentile 1-hour daily maximum concentration; Sulfur Dioxide AM—highest annual mean concentration; Sulfur Dioxide 1-Hr—highest 99th percentile 1-hour daily maximum concentration; Sulfur Dioxide 24-Hr—highest second maximum 24-hour concentration
Source: U.S. Environmental Protection Agency, Air Quality Monitoring Information, "Air Quality Statistics by City, 2016"

Drinking Water

Water System Name	Pop. Served	Primary Water Source Type	Violations[1]	
			Health Based	Monitoring/ Reporting
South Brunswick Twp WDI	45,450	Purchased Surface	0	0

Note: (1) Based on violation data from January 1, 2017 to December 31, 2017
Source: U.S. Environmental Protection Agency, Office of Ground Water and Drinking Water, Safe Drinking Water Information System (based on data extracted April 5, 2018)

Rio Rancho, New Mexico

Background

Rio Rancho is located at the top of West Mesa, close to Albuquerque and Santa Fe, and 19 miles north of Albuquerque International Airport. Surrounded by majestic views of Albuquerque, the Sandia Mountains, and the Rio Grande Valley, Rio Rancho is one of the nation's fastest-growing communities, offering both a magnificent setting and a mild climate, as well as low land costs, high-quality education, and affordable housing.

The area was originally inhabited by Pueblo Indians, who farmed the rich soil and hunted along the Rio Grande. In 1540, Don Francisco Vasquez de Coronado explored the region in search of the fabled Seven Cities of Gold. However, the beginning of Rio Rancho occurred over 300 years later, in the early 1960s, when AMREP Corporation purchased 55,000 acres of land on the outskirts of Albuquerque, originally called Rio Rancho Estates. AMREP marketed the area to residents in the East and Midwest. Many of the first residents were retirees; 1966 saw the hundredth family move in. Through another purchase of land in 1971, Rio Rancho Estates grew to 92,000 acres, becoming larger geographically than Albuquerque. By the early 1980s, Rio Rancho was incorporated. A new financing program, offering low-interest home loans, transformed Rio Rancho from a retirement community to a city attracting young families.

The Rio Rancho Public School System includes two high schools, six elementary and three middle schools. There are approximately 50 private and/or parochial schools in the greater Albuquerque area, covering levels from elementary through high school.

The abundance of higher-education choices is one of the many benefits of living in Rio Rancho. Albuquerque-based Technical-Vocational Institute offers 35 classes in technology, arts and sciences, and business. The University of New Mexico is one of the top institutions in the Southwest, offering 4,000 courses in 150 disciplines, along with highly regarded business and law schools, and a school of medicine that is ranked among the country's 10 best primary-care learning centers. The University of Phoenix offers degrees in business management, technology, and nursing, while the College of Santa Fe in Albuquerque awards bachelor's and master's degrees in business, psychology, and teacher education. Aztech College trains students in computer-aided design, architecture, and mechanical drafting.

Rio Rancho offers some of the most varied and interesting historical and recreational attractions in the country: Bandelier National Monument on Jemez Mountain Trail features twelfth-century Indian pueblos and breathtaking scenery; Petroglyph National Monument, created in 1990, protects 15,000 ancient petroglyphs and other archaeological sites just west of Albuquerque; The Sandia Peak Tramway provides a ride up to Sandia Peak—over 11,000 feet—on the world's longest aerial tramway. Indoor recreation includes several casinos, the Albuquerque Aquarium, and New Mexico's largest shopping center, the Cottonwood Mall, with movie theaters and hundreds of shops.

One of the biggest events in the area is the Rio Grande Valley Celtic Festival held in the spring. This includes competitions in Highland dancing, individual piping and drumming, Scottish/Irish dancing, and athletic contents, as well as Celtic foods and other cultural attractions. And not far away is the annual Albuquerque International Balloon Festival, held each August.

The Intel Corporation is by far the largest employer in Rio Rancho. The services, retail, and government sectors are also major components of the local economy.

Numerous medical facilities are located in the area, such as St. Joseph West Mesa Hospital, a 128-bed family-centered hospital offering everything from general medical and surgical services and pediatric care to obstetrics. Other facilities include Lovelace Primary Care Center and St. Joseph's Urgent Care. Senior communities comprise Talbert Medical Group Nursing Homes, Ancantilado Vista Independent Living, Rio Rancho Nursing and Rehabilitation Center, and Sandia Springs Assisted Living.

Rio Rancho enjoys a dry, arid climate with plenty of sunshine, low humidity, and scant rainfall. More than three-fourths of the daylight hours have sunshine, summer and winter. As in all desert climates, temperatures can fluctuate widely between day and night. Precipitation is meager during the winter, more abundant in summer with afternoon and evening thunderstorms.

Rankings

Business/Finance Rankings

- The personal finance site NerdWallet analyzed 183 American metropolitan areas with populations over 250,000 and more than 15,000 businesses to rank where entrepreneurs find the most success. Criteria included area economy, annual income, housing cost, unemployment rate, and the success rate of area businesses. Albuquerque* ranked #127. *www.nerdwallet.com, "Best Places to Start a Business," April 27, 2015*
- The Brookings Institution ranked the 100 largest metro areas in the U.S. based on income inequality. Albuquerque* was ranked #21 (#1 = greatest ineqality). Criteria: the "95/20 ratio," a figure representing the income at which a household earns more than 95 percent of all other households, divided by the income at which a household earns more than only 20 percent of all other households. *Brookings Institution, "Household Income Inequality, 100 Largest U.S. Metro Areas, 2014-2016," February 5, 2018*
- The Albuquerque* metro area appeared on the Milken Institute "2017 Best Performing Cities" list. Rank: #160 out of 200 large metro areas. Criteria: job growth; wage and salary growth; high-tech output growth. *Milken Institute, "Best-Performing Cities 2017," January 2018*
- *Forbes* ranked the 200 most populous metro areas to determine the nation's "Best Places for Business and Careers." The Albuquerque* metro area was ranked #137. Criteria: costs (business and living); job growth (past and projected); income growth; quality of life; educational attainment (college and high school); projected economic growth; cultural and recreational opportunities; net migration patterns; number of highly ranked colleges. *Forbes, "The Best Places for Business and Careers 2017," October 24, 2017*

Dating/Romance Rankings

- *Apartment List* conducted its annual survey of renters to compile a list of metros that have the best opportunities for dating. Nearly 11,000 respondents, from February 2017 through January 2018, rated their current city or neighborhood for opportunities to date and make friends. The Albuquerque* metro area ranked #67 out of 70 where single residents were very satisfied or somewhat satisfied, making it among the ten worst metros for dating opportunities. Other criteria analyzed included gender and education levels of renters. *Apartment List, "Best Metros for Dating 2018," February 6, 2018*

Education Rankings

- Personal finance website *WalletHub* analyzed the 150 largest U.S. metropolitan statistical areas to determine where the most educated Americans are choosing to settle. Criteria: education quality and attainment gap; education levels; percentage of workers with degrees; public school rankings; quality and size of each metro area's universities. Albuquerque* was ranked #45 (#1 = most educated city). *www.WalletHub.com, "2017's Most and Least Educated Cities in America," July 25, 2017*

Environmental Rankings

- Sperling's BestPlaces assessed 379 metropolitan areas of the United States for the likelihood of dangerously extreme weather events or earthquakes. In general the Southeast and South-Central regions have the highest risk of weather extremes and earthquakes, while the Pacific Northwest enjoys the lowest risk. Of the least risky metropolitan areas, the Albuquerque* metro area was ranked #115. *www.bestplaces.net, "Safest Places from Natural Disasters," April 2011*

Health/Fitness Rankings

- Albuquerque* was identified as a "2016 Spring Allergy Capital." The area ranked #38 out of 100. Three groups of factors were used to identify the most severe cities for people with allergies during the spring season: annual pollen levels; medicine utilization; access to board-certified allergists. *Asthma and Allergy Foundation of America, "Spring Allergy Capitals 2016"*

- Albuquerque* was identified as a "2016 Fall Allergy Capital." The area ranked #61 out of 100. Three groups of factors were used to identify the most severe cities for people with allergies during the fall season: annual pollen levels; medicine utilization; access to board-certified allergists. *Asthma and Allergy Foundation of America, "Fall Allergy Capitals 2016"*

- Albuquerque* was identified as a "2015 Asthma Capital." The area ranked #47 out of the nation's 100 largest metropolitan areas. Criteria: estimated prevalence; self-reported prevalence; crude death rate for asthma; annual pollen score; annual air quality; public smoking laws; number of board-certified asthma specialists; school inhaler access laws; rescue medication use; controller medication use; ER visits for asthma; uninsured rate; poverty rate. *Asthma and Allergy Foundation of America, "Asthma Capitals 2015"*

- The Albuquerque* metro area ranked #120 out of 189 in The Gallup-Healthways Well-Being Index. Criteria: purpose; social well being; financial health; community and physical health. Results are based on telephone interviews with adults, aged 18 and older, living in metropolitan areas in the 50 U.S. states and the District of Columbia. *Gallup-Healthways, "State of American Well-Being, 2017 Community Well-Being Rankings" March 2018*

Real Estate Rankings

- Albuquerque* was ranked #119 out of 238 metro areas in terms of housing affordability in 2017 by the National Association of Home Builders (#1 = most affordable). Criteria: the share of homes sold in that area affordable to a family earning the local median income, based on standard mortgage underwriting criteria. *National Association of Home Builders®, NAHB-Wells Fargo Housing Opportunity Index, 4th Quarter 2017*

- The nation's largest metro areas were analyzed in terms of the percentage of households entering some stage of foreclosure in 2017. The Albuquerque* metro area ranked #10 out of 10 (#1 = highest foreclosure rate). *RealtyTrac, "2017 Year-End U.S. Foreclosure Market Report™," January 16, 2018*

Safety Rankings

- Statistics drawn from the FBI's Uniform Crime Report were used to rank the 25 metropolitan statistical areas where violent crime rose most over the years 2011–2016. 24/7 Wall Street found that the Albuquerque* metro area placed #18 of those with the largest increases in violent crime. *247wallst.com, "25 U.S. Cities Where Crime Is Soaring," March 8, 2018*

- The National Insurance Crime Bureau ranked 382 metro areas in the U.S. in terms of per capita rates of vehicle theft. The Albuquerque* metro area ranked #1 (#1 = highest rate). Criteria: number of vehicle theft offenses per 100,000 inhabitants in 2016. *National Insurance Crime Bureau, "Hot Spots 2016," June 8, 2017*

Seniors/Retirement Rankings

- From its Best Cities for Successful Aging indexes, the Milken Institute generated rankings for metropolitan areas, weighing data in nine categories—health care, wellness, living arrangements, transportation and convenience, financial characteristics, education, employment, community engagement, and overall livability. The Albuquerque* metro area was ranked #87 overall in the large metro area category. *Milken Institute, "Best Cities for Successful Aging, 2017" March 14, 2017*

*Rio Rancho is located within the Albuquerque, NM Metropolitan Statistical Area.

Business Environment

CITY FINANCES

City Government Finances

Component	2015 ($000)	2015 ($ per capita)
Total Revenues	125,313	1,331
Total Expenditures	124,070	1,317
Debt Outstanding	94,114	999
Cash and Securities[1]	68,324	726

Note: (1) Cash and security holdings of a government at the close of its fiscal year,, including those of its dependent agencies, utilities, and liquor stores.
Source: U.S Census Bureau, State & Local Government Finances 2015

City Government Revenue by Source

Source	2015 ($000)	2015 ($ per capita)	2015 (%)
General Revenue			
From Federal Government	4,636	49	3.7
From State Government	5,262	56	4.2
From Local Governments	663	7	0.5
Taxes			
Property	17,834	189	14.2
Sales and Gross Receipts	39,672	421	31.7
Personal Income	0	0	0.0
Corporate Income	0	0	0.0
Motor Vehicle License	876	9	0.7
Other Taxes	376	4	0.3
Current Charges	22,046	234	17.6
Liquor Store	0	0	0.0
Utility	23,637	251	18.9
Employee Retirement	0	0	0.0

Source: U.S Census Bureau, State & Local Government Finances 2015

City Government Expenditures by Function

Function	2015 ($000)	2015 ($ per capita)	2015 (%)
General Direct Expenditures			
Air Transportation	0	0	0.0
Corrections	385	4	0.3
Education	0	0	0.0
Employment Security Administration	0	0	0.0
Financial Administration	2,574	27	2.1
Fire Protection	11,734	124	9.5
General Public Buildings	1,305	13	1.1
Governmental Administration, Other	7,126	75	5.7
Health	0	0	0.0
Highways	14,556	154	11.7
Hospitals	0	0	0.0
Housing and Community Development	398	4	0.3
Interest on General Debt	4,257	45	3.4
Judicial and Legal	1,785	19	1.4
Libraries	2,613	27	2.1
Parking	0	0	0.0
Parks and Recreation	6,509	69	5.2
Police Protection	17,454	185	14.1
Public Welfare	562	6	0.5
Sewerage	15,007	159	12.1
Solid Waste Management	278	3	0.2
Veterans' Services	0	0	0.0
Liquor Store	0	0	0.0
Utility	29,594	314	23.9
Employee Retirement	0	0	0.0

Source: U.S Census Bureau, State & Local Government Finances 2015

DEMOGRAPHICS

Population Growth

Area	1990 Census	2000 Census	2010 Census	2016* Estimate	Population Growth (%)	
					1990-2016	2010-2016
City	32,674	51,765	87,521	92,966	184.5	6.2
MSA[1]	599,416	729,649	887,077	904,486	50.9	2.0
U.S.	248,709,873	281,421,906	308,745,538	318,558,162	28.1	3.2

Note: (1) Figures cover the Albuquerque, NM Metropolitan Statistical Area—see Appendix B for areas included; (*) 2012-2016 5-year estimated population
Source: U.S. Census Bureau, 1990 Census, Census 2000, Census 2010, 2012-2016 American Community Survey 5-Year Estimates

Household Size

Area	Persons in Household (%)							Average Household Size
	One	Two	Three	Four	Five	Six	Seven or More	
City	23.1	34.5	15.1	14.9	7.3	3.9	1.2	2.80
MSA[1]	30.2	34.1	14.8	11.9	5.6	2.3	1.2	2.60
U.S.	27.7	33.7	15.7	13.1	6.0	2.3	1.5	2.60

Note: (1) Figures cover the Albuquerque, NM Metropolitan Statistical Area—see Appendix B for areas included
Source: U.S. Census Bureau, 2012-2016 American Community Survey 5-Year Estimates

Race

Area	White Alone[2] (%)	Black Alone[2] (%)	Asian Alone[2] (%)	AIAN[3] Alone[2] (%)	NHOPI[4] Alone[2] (%)	Other Race Alone[2] (%)	Two or More Races (%)
City	79.6	2.9	1.5	2.4	0.1	8.6	4.9
MSA[1]	72.7	2.6	2.1	5.7	0.1	12.8	4.1
U.S.	73.3	12.6	5.2	0.8	0.2	4.8	3.1

Note: (1) Figures cover the Albuquerque, NM Metropolitan Statistical Area—see Appendix B for areas included; (2) Alone is defined as not being in combination with one or more other races; (3) American Indian and Alaska Native; (4) Native Hawaiian and Other Pacific Islander
Source: U.S. Census Bureau, 2012-2016 American Community Survey 5-Year Estimates

Hispanic or Latino Origin

Area	Total (%)	Mexican (%)	Puerto Rican (%)	Cuban (%)	Other (%)
City	40.3	21.3	0.5	0.2	18.2
MSA[1]	48.1	27.9	0.5	0.3	19.4
U.S.	17.3	11.0	1.7	0.7	4.0

Note: Persons of Hispanic or Latino origin can be of any race; (1) Figures cover the Albuquerque, NM Metropolitan Statistical Area—see Appendix B for areas included
Source: U.S. Census Bureau, 2012-2016 American Community Survey 5-Year Estimates

Segregation

Type	Segregation Indices[1]				Percent Change		
	1990	2000	2010	2010 Rank[2]	1990-2000	1990-2010	2000-2010
Black/White	38.0	32.0	30.9	99	-6.0	-7.1	-1.1
Asian/White	25.7	28.1	28.5	93	2.4	2.9	0.4
Hispanic/White	40.5	39.8	36.4	79	-0.8	-4.1	-3.4

Note: All figures cover the Metropolitan Statistical Area—see Appendix B for areas included; Figures are based on an analysis of 1990, 2000, and 2010 Census Decennial Census tract data by William H. Frey, Brookings Institution and the University of Michigan Social Science Data Analysis Network. In this analysis all racial groups (whites, blacks, and asians) are non-Hispanic members of those races. Hispanics are shown as a separate category; (1) Segregation Indices are Dissimilarity Indices that measure the degree to which the minority group is distributed differently than whites across census tracts. They range from 0 (complete integration) to 100 (complete segregation) where the value indicates the percentage of the minority group that needs to move to be distributed exactly like whites; (2) Ranges from 1 (most segregated) to 102 (least segregated); n/a not available.
Source: www.CensusScope.org

Ancestry

Area	German	Irish	English	American	Italian	Polish	French[2]	Scottish	Dutch
City	12.6	9.1	8.1	4.7	4.0	2.5	2.1	2.5	1.4
MSA[1]	9.9	7.1	6.4	4.4	3.0	1.4	1.8	1.7	0.9
U.S.	14.4	10.4	7.7	6.9	5.4	2.9	2.6	1.7	1.3

Note: Figures are the percentage of the total population reporting a particular ancestry. The nine most commonly reported ancestries in the U.S. are shown. Figures include multiple ancestries (e.g. if a person reported being Irish and Italian, they were included in both columns); (1) Figures cover the Albuquerque, NM Metropolitan Statistical Area—see Appendix B for areas included; (2) Excludes Basque
Source: U.S. Census Bureau, 2012-2016 American Community Survey 5-Year Estimates

Foreign-Born Population

Area	Percent of Population Born in								
	Any Foreign Country	Asia	Mexico	Europe	Carribean	Central America[2]	South America	Africa	Canada
City	5.6	1.1	2.7	0.8	0.1	0.2	0.4	0.1	0.2
MSA[1]	9.5	1.7	5.9	0.8	0.2	0.2	0.3	0.2	0.2
U.S.	13.2	4.0	3.6	1.5	1.3	1.0	0.9	0.6	0.3

Note: (1) Figures cover the Albuquerque, NM Metropolitan Statistical Area—see Appendix B for areas included; (2) Excludes Mexico.
Source: U.S. Census Bureau, 2012-2016 American Community Survey 5-Year Estimates

Marital Status

Area	Never Married	Now Married[2]	Separated	Widowed	Divorced
City	29.6	51.0	1.2	5.3	12.9
MSA[1]	34.4	44.9	1.7	5.6	13.4
U.S.	33.0	48.1	2.1	5.9	11.0

Note: Figures are percentages and cover the population 15 years of age and older; (1) Figures cover the Albuquerque, NM Metropolitan Statistical Area—see Appendix B for areas included; (2) Excludes separated
Source: U.S. Census Bureau, 2012-2016 American Community Survey 5-Year Estimates

Disability Status

Area	All Ages	Under 18 Years Old	18 to 64 Years Old	65 Years and Over
City	12.8	3.8	11.2	38.7
MSA[1]	13.8	3.8	12.0	37.8
U.S.	12.5	4.1	10.3	35.7

Note: Figures show percent of the civilian noninstitutionalized population that reported having a disability. Disability status is determined from six types of difficulty: vision, hearing, cognitive, ambulatory, self-care, and independent living. For children under 5 years old, hearing and vision difficulty are used to determine disability status. For children between the ages of 5 and 14, disability status is determined from hearing, vision, cognitive, ambulatory, and self-care difficulties. For people aged 15 years and older, they are considered to have a disability if they have difficulty with any one of the six difficulty types; Note: (1) Figures cover the Albuquerque, NM Metropolitan Statistical Area—see Appendix B for areas included
Source: U.S. Census Bureau, 2012-2016 American Community Survey 5-Year Estimates

Age

Area	Percent of Population									Median Age
	Under Age 5	Age 5–19	Age 20–34	Age 35–44	Age 45–54	Age 55–64	Age 65–74	Age 75–84	Age 85+	
City	6.2	22.3	18.6	13.9	13.7	12.3	7.9	3.5	1.6	37.4
MSA[1]	6.1	19.8	21.0	12.5	13.2	13.1	8.6	4.3	1.6	37.4
U.S.	6.2	19.6	20.7	12.7	13.6	12.6	8.3	4.3	1.9	37.7

Note: (1) Figures cover the Albuquerque, NM Metropolitan Statistical Area—see Appendix B for areas included
Source: U.S. Census Bureau, 2012-2016 American Community Survey 5-Year Estimates

Gender

Area	Males	Females	Males per 100 Females
City	45,469	47,497	95.7
MSA[1]	444,849	459,637	96.8
U.S.	156,765,322	161,792,840	96.9

Note: (1) Figures cover the Albuquerque, NM Metropolitan Statistical Area—see Appendix B for areas included
Source: U.S. Census Bureau, 2012-2016 American Community Survey 5-Year Estimates

Religious Groups by Family

Area	Catholic	Baptist	Non-Den.	Methodist[2]	Lutheran	LDS[3]	Pente-costal	Presby-terian[4]	Muslim[5]	Judaism
MSA[1]	27.2	3.8	4.2	1.5	1.0	2.4	1.5	1.1	0.2	0.3
U.S.	19.1	9.3	4.0	4.0	2.3	2.0	1.9	1.6	0.8	0.7

Note: Figures are the number of adherents as a percentage of the total population; (1) Figures cover the Albuquerque, NM Metropolitan Statistical Area—see Appendix B for areas included; (2) Methodist/Pietist; (3) Latter Day Saints; (4) Reformed; (5) Figures are estimates
Source: Association of Statisticians of American Religious Bodies, 2010 U.S. Religion Census: Religious Congregations & Membership Study

Religious Groups by Tradition

Area	Catholic	Evangelical Protestant	Mainline Protestant	Other Tradition	Black Protestant	Orthodox
MSA[1]	27.2	11.3	3.3	3.9	0.2	0.2
U.S.	19.1	16.2	7.3	4.3	1.6	0.3

Note: Figures are the number of adherents as a percentage of the total population; (1) Figures cover the Albuquerque, NM Metropolitan Statistical Area—see Appendix B for areas included
Source: Association of Statisticians of American Religious Bodies, 2010 U.S. Religion Census: Religious Congregations & Membership Study

ECONOMY

Gross Metropolitan Product

Area	2014	2015	2016	2017	Rank[2]
MSA[1]	41.6	41.3	42.4	44.3	64

Note: Figures are in billions of dollars; (1) Figures cover the Albuquerque, NM Metropolitan Statistical Area—see Appendix B for areas included; (2) Rank is based on 2015 data and ranges from 1 to 381
Source: The U.S. Conference of Mayors, U.S. Metro Economies: GMP and Employment Report, 2015-2017

Economic Growth

Area	2012-14 (%)	2015 (%)	2016 (%)	2017 (%)	Rank[2]
MSA[1]	-0.7	0.5	1.0	2.1	321
U.S.	2.0	2.4	1.9	2.6	–

Note: Figures are real gross metropolitan product (GMP) growth rates and represent average annual percent change; (1) Figures cover the Albuquerque, NM Metropolitan Statistical Area—see Appendix B for areas included; (2) Rank is based on 2012-2014 average annual percent change and ranges from 1 to 381
Source: The U.S. Conference of Mayors, U.S. Metro Economies: GMP and Employment Report, 2015-2017

Metropolitan Area Exports

Area	2011	2012	2013	2014	2015	2016	Rank[2]
MSA[1]	951.9	1,790.6	1,389.6	1,564.0	1,761.2	999.7	153

Note: Figures are in millions of dollars; (1) Figures cover the Albuquerque, NM Metropolitan Statistical Area—see Appendix B for areas included; (2) Rank is based on 2016 data and ranges from 1 to 385
Source: U.S. Department of Commerce, International Trade Administration, Office of Trade & Industry Information, Manufacturing & Services, data extracted March 15, 2018

Building Permits

Area	Single-Family			Multi-Family			Total		
	2016	2017p	Pct. Chg.	2016	2017p	Pct. Chg.	2016	2017p	Pct. Chg.
City	698	530	-24.1	32	5	-84.4	730	535	-26.7
MSA[1]	1,927	1,996	3.6	534	260	-51.3	2,461	2,256	-8.3
U.S.	750,800	817,300	8.9	455,800	446,800	-2.0	1,206,600	1,264,100	4.8

Note: (1) Figures cover the Albuquerque, NM Metropolitan Statistical Area—see Appendix B for areas included; Figures represent new, privately-owned housing units authorized (unadjusted data); All permit data are based on estimates with imputation; (p) preliminary data.
Source: U.S. Census Bureau, Manufacturing, Mining, and Construction Statistics, Building Permits, 2016, 2017

Bankruptcy Filings

Area	Business Filings			Nonbusiness Filings		
	2016	2017	% Chg.	2016	2017	% Chg.
Sandoval County	16	13	-18.8	284	298	4.9
U.S.	24,114	23,157	-4.0	770,846	765,863	-0.6

Note: Business filings include Chapter 7, Chapter 11, Chapter 12, and Chapter 13; Nonbusiness filings include Chapter 7, Chapter 11, and Chapter 13
Source: Administrative Office of the U.S. Courts, Business and Nonbusiness Bankruptcy, County Cases Commenced by Chapter of the Bankruptcy Code, During the 12-Month Period Ending December 31, 2016 and Business and Nonbusiness Bankruptcy, County Cases Commenced by Chapter of the Bankruptcy Code, During the 12-Month Period Ending December 31, 2017

Housing Vacancy Rates

Area	Gross Vacancy Rate[2] (%)			Year-Round Vacancy Rate[3] (%)			Rental Vacancy Rate[4] (%)			Homeowner Vacancy Rate[5] (%)		
	2015	2016	2017	2015	2016	2017	2015	2016	2017	2015	2016	2017
MSA[1]	9.3	9.2	8.9	8.3	8.9	8.6	7.2	8.1	9.0	2.7	1.9	2.1
U.S.	12.9	12.8	12.7	10.0	9.9	9.9	7.1	6.9	7.2	1.8	1.7	1.6

Note: (1) Figures cover the Albuquerque, NM Metropolitan Statistical Area—see Appendix B for areas included; (2) The percentage of the total housing inventory that is vacant; (3) The percentage of the housing inventory (excluding seasonal units) that is year-round vacant; (4) The percentage of rental inventory that is vacant for rent; (5) The percentage of homeowner inventory that is vacant for sale
Source: U.S. Census Bureau, Housing Vacancies and Homeownership Annual Statistics: 2015, 2016, 2017

INCOME

Income

Area	Per Capita ($)	Median Household ($)	Average Household ($)
City	27,537	62,637	75,295
MSA[1]	26,569	49,711	66,762
U.S.	29,829	55,322	77,866

Note: (1) Figures cover the Albuquerque, NM Metropolitan Statistical Area—see Appendix B for areas included
Source: U.S. Census Bureau, 2012-2016 American Community Survey 5-Year Estimates

Household Income Distribution

Area	Percent of Households Earning							
	Under $15,000	$15,000 -$24,999	$25,000 -$34,999	$35,000 -$49,999	$50,000 -$74,999	$75,000 -$99,999	$100,000 -$149,999	$150,000 and up
City	8.4	8.7	7.4	14.0	21.6	14.6	16.2	9.1
MSA[1]	14.1	11.9	10.6	13.6	18.0	11.8	12.1	7.9
U.S.	12.1	10.2	9.9	13.2	17.8	12.2	13.5	11.1

Note: (1) Figures cover the Albuquerque, NM Metropolitan Statistical Area—see Appendix B for areas included
Source: U.S. Census Bureau, 2012-2016 American Community Survey 5-Year Estimates

Poverty Rate

Area	All Ages	Under 18 Years Old	18 to 64 Years Old	65 Years and Over
City	11.7	15.8	10.8	8.4
MSA[1]	18.6	26.3	17.6	10.6
U.S.	15.1	21.2	14.2	9.3

Note: Figures are percentage of people whose income during the past 12 months was below the poverty level; (1) Figures cover the Albuquerque, NM Metropolitan Statistical Area—see Appendix B for areas included
Source: U.S. Census Bureau, 2012-2016 American Community Survey 5-Year Estimates

EMPLOYMENT

Labor Force and Employment

Area	Civilian Labor Force			Workers Employed		
	Dec. 2016	Dec. 2017	% Chg.	Dec. 2016	Dec. 2017	% Chg.
City	44,746	45,369	1.4	42,172	42,932	1.8
MSA[1]	425,294	430,911	1.3	401,812	408,815	1.7
U.S.	158,968,000	159,880,000	0.6	151,798,000	153,602,000	1.2

Note: Data is not seasonally adjusted and covers workers 16 years of age and older; (1) Figures cover the Albuquerque, NM Metropolitan Statistical Area—see Appendix B for areas included
Source: Bureau of Labor Statistics, Local Area Unemployment Statistics

Unemployment Rate

Area	2017											
	Jan.	Feb.	Mar.	Apr.	May	Jun.	Jul.	Aug.	Sep.	Oct.	Nov.	Dec.
City	6.3	6.2	5.9	5.5	5.7	6.6	6.5	6.2	6.0	5.8	5.6	5.4
MSA[1]	6.0	5.9	5.7	5.3	5.4	6.3	6.3	6.0	5.7	5.5	5.3	5.1
U.S.	5.1	4.9	4.6	4.1	4.1	4.5	4.6	4.5	4.1	3.9	3.9	3.9

Note: Data is not seasonally adjusted and covers workers 16 years of age and older; (1) Figures cover the Albuquerque, NM Metropolitan Statistical Area—see Appendix B for areas included
Source: Bureau of Labor Statistics, Local Area Unemployment Statistics

Average Wages

Occupation	$/Hr.	Occupation	$/Hr.
Accountants and Auditors	33.80	Maids and Housekeeping Cleaners	9.90
Automotive Mechanics	19.30	Maintenance and Repair Workers	17.20
Bookkeepers	17.50	Marketing Managers	42.50
Carpenters	17.60	Nuclear Medicine Technologists	37.80
Cashiers	10.30	Nurses, Licensed Practical	23.30
Clerks, General Office	12.40	Nurses, Registered	35.30
Clerks, Receptionists/Information	13.60	Nursing Assistants	13.50
Clerks, Shipping/Receiving	14.60	Packers and Packagers, Hand	11.00
Computer Programmers	39.10	Physical Therapists	42.20
Computer Systems Analysts	40.60	Postal Service Mail Carriers	24.00
Computer User Support Specialists	20.70	Real Estate Brokers	n/a
Cooks, Restaurant	11.30	Retail Salespersons	13.40
Dentists	79.70	Sales Reps., Exc. Tech./Scientific	26.10
Electrical Engineers	48.90	Sales Reps., Tech./Scientific	32.30
Electricians	22.30	Secretaries, Exc. Legal/Med./Exec.	17.00
Financial Managers	50.80	Security Guards	12.90
First-Line Supervisors/Managers, Sales	20.80	Surgeons	132.80
Food Preparation Workers	10.70	Teacher Assistants*	10.90
General and Operations Managers	50.90	Teachers, Elementary School*	29.40
Hairdressers/Cosmetologists	11.50	Teachers, Secondary School*	23.40
Internists, General	126.40	Telemarketers	11.40
Janitors and Cleaners	11.50	Truck Drivers, Heavy/Tractor-Trailer	20.40
Landscaping/Groundskeeping Workers	12.60	Truck Drivers, Light/Delivery Svcs.	16.90
Lawyers	49.00	Waiters and Waitresses	10.50

Note: Wage data covers the Albuquerque, NM Metropolitan Statistical Area—see Appendix B for areas included; (*) Hourly wages for elementary/secondary school teachers and teacher assistants were calculated by the editors from annual wage data based on a 40 hour work week; n/a not available.
Source: Bureau of Labor Statistics, Metro Area Occupational Employment & Wage Estimates, May 2017

Employment by Occupation

Occupation Classification	City (%)	MSA[1] (%)	U.S. (%)
Management, Business, Science, and Arts	40.0	38.9	37.0
Natural Resources, Construction, and Maintenance	9.4	9.4	8.9
Production, Transportation, and Material Moving	7.3	8.1	12.2
Sales and Office	26.8	23.9	23.8
Service	16.6	19.7	18.1

Note: Figures cover employed civilians 16 years of age and older; (1) Figures cover the Albuquerque, NM Metropolitan Statistical Area—see Appendix B for areas included
Source: U.S. Census Bureau, 2012-2016 American Community Survey 5-Year Estimates

Employment by Industry

Sector	MSA[1] Number of Employees	MSA[1] Percent of Total	U.S. Percent of Total
Construction, Mining, and Logging	23,500	6.0	5.2
Education and Health Services	63,800	16.2	15.9
Financial Activities	19,300	4.9	5.7
Government	83,800	21.3	15.3
Information	7,300	1.9	1.9
Leisure and Hospitality	42,200	10.7	10.7
Manufacturing	15,900	4.0	8.5
Other Services	11,800	3.0	3.9
Professional and Business Services	60,800	15.5	14.0
Retail Trade	42,700	10.9	11.0
Transportation, Warehousing, and Utilities	10,500	2.7	4.1
Wholesale Trade	11,700	3.0	4.0

Note: Figures are non-farm employment as of December 2017. Figures are not seasonally adjusted and include workers 16 years of age and older; (1) Figures cover the Albuquerque, NM Metropolitan Statistical Area—see Appendix B for areas included
Source: Bureau of Labor Statistics, Current Employment Statistics, Employment, Hours, and Earnings

Occupations with Greatest Projected Employment Growth: 2017 – 2019

Occupation[1]	2017 Employment	2019 Projected Employment	Numeric Employment Change	Percent Employment Change
Personal Care Aides	25,500	27,400	1,900	7.4
Combined Food Preparation and Serving Workers, Including Fast Food	20,970	21,790	820	3.9
Home Health Aides	8,340	8,890	550	6.6
Registered Nurses	17,700	18,160	460	2.6
Construction Laborers	13,210	13,610	400	3.0
Waiters and Waitresses	16,610	16,970	360	2.2
Roustabouts, Oil and Gas	2,260	2,600	340	15.0
General and Operations Managers	15,760	16,080	320	2.0
Maids and Housekeeping Cleaners	8,970	9,230	260	2.9
Janitors and Cleaners, Except Maids and Housekeeping Cleaners	13,090	13,340	250	1.9

Note: Projections cover New Mexico; (1) Sorted by numeric employment change
Source: www.projectionscentral.com, State Occupational Projections, 2017–2019 Short-Term Projections

Fastest Growing Occupations: 2017 – 2019

Occupation[1]	2017 Employment	2019 Projected Employment	Numeric Employment Change	Percent Employment Change
Roustabouts, Oil and Gas	2,260	2,600	340	15.0
Derrick Operators, Oil and Gas	990	1,140	150	14.2
Rotary Drill Operators, Oil and Gas	570	640	70	13.8
Service Unit Operators, Oil, Gas, and Mining	1,540	1,700	160	10.7
Helpers—Extraction Workers	700	750	50	8.0
Personal Care Aides	25,500	27,400	1,900	7.4
Home Health Aides	8,340	8,890	550	6.6
Nurse Practitioners	900	950	50	5.6
Combined Food Preparation and Serving Workers, Including Fast Food	20,970	21,790	820	3.9
Market Research Analysts and Marketing Specialists	1,300	1,350	50	3.8

Note: Projections cover New Mexico; (1) Sorted by percent employment change and excludes occupations with numeric employment change less than 50
Source: www.projectionscentral.com, State Occupational Projections, 2017–2019 Short-Term Projections

TAXES

State Corporate Income Tax Rates

State	Tax Rate (%)	Income Brackets ($)	Num. of Brackets	Financial Institution Tax Rate (%)[a]	Federal Income Tax Ded.
New Mexico	4.8 - 5.9	500,000	2	4.8 - 5.9	No

Note: Tax rates as of January 1, 2018; (a) Rates listed are the corporate income tax rate applied to financial institutions or excise taxes based on income. Some states have other taxes based upon the value of deposits or shares.
Source: Federation of Tax Administrators, Range of State Corporate Income Tax Rates, January 1, 2018

State Individual Income Tax Rates

State	Tax Rate (%)	Income Brackets ($)	Num. of Brackets	Personal Exempt. ($)[1] Single	Personal Exempt. ($)[1] Dependents	Fed. Inc. Tax Ded.
New Mexico	1.7 - 4.9	5,500 - 16,001 (r)	4	4,150 (d)	4,150 (d)	No

Note: Tax rates as of January 1, 2018; Local- and county-level taxes are not included; n/a not applicable; (1) Married joint filers generally receive double the single exemption; (d) These states use the personal exemption amounts provided in the federal Internal Revenue Code. Note, the Tax Cut and Reform Act of 2017 has eliminated personal exemptions from the IRC. These states will need to enact legislation to reinstate a personal exemption for tax year 2018. We have reported here the exemption amounts before the federal tax change; (r) The income brackets reported for New Mexico are for single individuals. For married couples filing jointly, the same tax rates apply to income brackets ranging from $8,000 to $24,000.
Source: Federation of Tax Administrators, State Individual Income Tax Rates, January 1, 2018

Various State Sales and Excise Tax Rates

State	State Sales Tax (%)	Gasoline[1] (¢/gal.)	Cigarette[2] ($/pack)	Spirits[3] ($/gal.)	Wine[4] ($/gal.)	Beer[5] ($/gal.)	Recreational Marijuana (%)
New Mexico	5.125 (c)	18.88	1.66	6.06	1.70 (l)	0.41	Not legal

Note: All tax rates as of January 1, 2018; (1) The American Petroleum Institute has developed a methodology for determining the average tax rate on a gallon of fuel. Rates may include any of the following: excise taxes, environmental fees, storage tank fees, other fees or taxes, general sales tax, and local taxes. In states where gasoline is subject to the general sales tax, or where the fuel tax is based on the average sale price, the average rate determined by API is sensitive to changes in the price of gasoline. States that fully or partially apply general sales taxes to gasoline: CA, CO, GA, IL, IN, MI, NY; (2) The federal excise tax of $1.0066 per pack and local taxes are not included; (3) Rates are those applicable to off-premise sales of 40% alcohol by volume (a.b.v.) distilled spirits in 750ml containers. Local excise taxes are excluded; (4) Rates are those applicable to off-premise sales of 11% a.b.v. non-carbonated wine in 750ml containers; (5) Rates are those applicable to off-premise sales of 4.7% a.b.v. beer in 12 ounce containers; (c) The sales taxes in Hawaii, New Mexico, North Dakota, and South Dakota have broad bases that include many services; (l) Different rates also applicable to alcohol content, place of production, size of container, place purchased (on- or off-premise or on board airlines) or type of wine (carbonated, vermouth, etc.).
Source: Tax Foundation, 2018 Facts & Figures: How Does Your State Compare?

State Business Tax Climate Index Rankings

State	Overall Rank	Corporate Tax Rank	Individual Income Tax Rank	Sales Tax Rank	Unemployment Insurance Tax Rank	Property Tax Rank
New Mexico	34	24	35	40	16	1

Note: The index is a measure of how each state's tax laws affect economic performance. The lower the rank, the more favorable a state's tax system is for business. States without a given tax are given a ranking of 1. The scores/rankings for the District of Columbia do not affect other states. The 2018 index represents the tax climate as of July 1, 2017.
Source: Tax Foundation, State Business Tax Climate Index 2018

TRANSPORTATION

Means of Transportation to Work

Area	Car/Truck/Van: Drove Alone	Car/Truck/Van: Car-pooled	Public Transportation: Bus	Public Transportation: Subway	Public Transportation: Railroad	Bicycle	Walked	Other Means	Worked at Home
City	84.4	8.1	0.5	0.0	0.7	0.1	0.9	1.4	3.9
MSA[1]	80.4	9.2	1.4	0.0	0.3	1.0	1.8	1.4	4.5
U.S.	76.4	9.3	2.6	1.9	0.6	0.6	2.8	1.3	4.6

Note: Figures are percentages and cover workers 16 years of age and older; (1) Figures cover the Albuquerque, NM Metropolitan Statistical Area—see Appendix B for areas included
Source: U.S. Census Bureau, 2012-2016 American Community Survey 5-Year Estimates

Travel Time to Work

Area	Less Than 10 Minutes	10 to 19 Minutes	20 to 29 Minutes	30 to 44 Minutes	45 to 59 Minutes	60 to 89 Minutes	90 Minutes or More
City	9.4	24.5	17.0	25.9	14.6	6.2	2.4
MSA[1]	11.5	32.9	25.3	19.7	5.8	3.2	1.7
U.S.	12.9	29.2	20.9	20.4	8.0	6.0	2.7

Note: Note: Figures are percentages and include workers 16 years old and over; (1) Figures cover the Albuquerque, NM Metropolitan Statistical Area—see Appendix B for areas included
Source: U.S. Census Bureau, 2012-2016 American Community Survey 5-Year Estimates

Freeway Travel Time Index

Area	1985	1990	1995	2000	2005	2010	2014
Urban Area Rank[1,2]	39	56	47	38	51	57	65
Urban Area Index[1]	1.08	1.09	1.13	1.17	1.17	1.16	1.16
Average Index[3]	1.09	1.11	1.14	1.17	1.20	1.19	1.20

Note: Freeway Travel Time Index—the ratio of travel time in the peak period to the travel time at free-flow conditions. For example, a value of 1.30 indicates a 20-minute free-flow trip takes 26 minutes in the peak (20 minutes x 1.30 = 26 minutes); (1) Covers the Albuquerque NM urban area; (2) Rank is based on 101 urban areas (#1 = highest travel time index); (3) Average of 101 urban areas
Source: Texas Transportation Institute, 2015 Urban Mobility Scorecard, August 2015

Freeway Commuter Stress Index

Area	1985	1990	1995	2000	2005	2010	2014
Urban Area Rank[1,2]	48	51	55	46	58	65	71
Urban Area Index[1]	1.10	1.12	1.15	1.20	1.19	1.18	1.18
Average Index[3]	1.13	1.16	1.19	1.22	1.25	1.24	1.25

Note: The Freeway Commuter Stress Index is the same as the Freeway Travel Time Index (see table above) except that it includes only the travel in the peak directions during the peak periods; the TTI includes travel in all directions during the peak period. Thus, the CSI is more indicative of the work trip experienced by each commuter on a daily basis; (1) Covers the Albuquerque NM urban area; (2) Rank is based on 101 urban areas (#1 = highest travel time index); (3) Average of 101 urban areas
Source: Texas Transportation Institute, 2015 Urban Mobility Scorecard, August 2015

Living Environment

COST OF LIVING

Cost of Living Index

Composite Index	Groceries	Housing	Utilities	Trans-portation	Health Care	Misc. Goods/ Services
94.7	92.9	93.5	83.9	101.4	101.0	96.9

Note: The Cost of Living Index measures regional differences in the cost of consumer goods and services, excluding taxes and non-consumer expenditures, for professional and managerial households in the top income quintile. It is based on more than 50,000 prices covering almost 60 different items for which prices are collected three times a year by chambers of commerce, economic development organizations or university applied economic centers in each participating urban area. The numbers shown should be read as a percentage above or below the national average of 100. For example, a value of 115.4 in the groceries column indicates that grocery prices are 15.4% higher than the national average. Small differences in the index numbers should not be interpreted as significant; Figures cover the Albuquerque NM urban area.
Source: The Council for Community and Economic Research, ACCRA Cost of Living Index, 2017

Grocery Prices

Area[1]	T-Bone Steak ($/pound)	Frying Chicken ($/pound)	Whole Milk ($/half gal.)	Eggs ($/dozen)	Orange Juice ($/64 oz.)	Coffee ($/11.5 oz.)
City[2]	10.82	1.11	1.52	1.40	3.44	4.27
Avg.	11.29	1.40	2.02	1.47	3.55	4.37
Min.	7.71	0.93	1.04	0.70	2.86	3.24
Max.	15.83	2.39	4.03	3.92	6.29	8.16

*Note: (1) Values for the local area are compared with the average, minimum and maximum values for all 294 areas in the Cost of Living Index; (2) Figures cover the Albuquerque NM urban area; **T-Bone Steak** (price per pound); **Frying Chicken** (price per pound, whole fryer); **Whole Milk** (half gallon carton); **Eggs** (price per dozen, Grade A, large); **Orange Juice** (64 oz. Tropicana or Florida Natural); **Coffee** (11.5 oz. can, vacuum-packed, Maxwell House, Hills Bros, or Folgers).*
Source: The Council for Community and Economic Research, ACCRA Cost of Living Index, 2017

Housing and Utility Costs

Area[1]	New Home Price ($)	Apartment Rent ($/month)	All Electric ($/month)	Part Electric ($/month)	Other Energy ($/month)	Telephone ($/month)
City[2]	314,655	968	-	95.47	54.10	22.15
Avg.	335,956	1,047	175.01	97.34	67.93	28.71
Min.	187,788	491	109.48	49.33	35.44	12.39
Max.	1,739,087	4,559	432.62	227.09	353.33	44.61

*Note: (1) Values for the local area are compared with the average, minimum and maximum values for all 294 areas in the Cost of Living Index; (2) Figures cover the Albuquerque NM urban area; **New Home Price** (2,400 sf living area, 8,000 sf lot, in urban area with full utilities); **Apartment Rent** (950 sf 2 bedroom/1.5 or 2 bath, unfurnished, excluding all utilities except water); **All Electric** (average monthly cost for an all-electric home); **Part Electric** (average monthly cost for a part-electric home); **Other Energy** (average monthly cost for natural gas, fuel oil, coal, wood, and any other forms of energy except electricity); **Telephone** (price includes basic monthly rate for a private residential line plus additional local usage charges incurred by a family of four).*
Source: The Council for Community and Economic Research, ACCRA Cost of Living Index, 2017

Health Care, Transportation, and Other Costs

Area[1]	Doctor ($/visit)	Dentist ($/visit)	Optometrist ($/visit)	Gasoline ($/gallon)	Beauty Salon ($/visit)	Men's Shirt ($)
City[2]	103.83	100.33	101.52	2.21	45.00	30.00
Avg.	108.00	92.54	101.93	2.25	37.58	30.92
Min.	30.39	60.00	49.75	1.82	16.11	11.20
Max.	193.50	161.94	229.28	3.16	77.35	59.13

*Note: (1) Values for the local area are compared with the average, minimum and maximum values for all 294 areas in the Cost of Living Index; (2) Figures cover the Albuquerque NM urban area; **Doctor** (general practitioners routine exam of an established patient); **Dentist** (adult teeth cleaning and periodic oral examination); **Optometrist** (full vision eye exam for established adult patient); **Gasoline** (one gallon regular unleaded, national brand, including all taxes, cash price at self-service pump if available); **Beauty Salon** (woman's shampoo, trim, and blow-dry); **Men's Shirt** (cotton/polyester dress shirt, pinpoint weave, long sleeves).*
Source: The Council for Community and Economic Research, ACCRA Cost of Living Index, 2017

HOUSING

House Price Index (HPI)

Area	National Ranking[2]	Quarterly Change (%)	One-Year Change (%)	Five-Year Change (%)
MSA[1]	184	-0.26	4.18	14.18
U.S.[3]	–	1.61	6.68	34.71

Note: The HPI is a weighted repeat sales index. It measures average price changes in repeat sales or refinancings on the same properties. This information is obtained by reviewing repeat mortgage transactions on single-family properties whose mortgages have been purchased or securitized by Fannie Mae or Freddie Mac in January 1975; (1) Figures cover the Albuquerque, NM Metropolitan Statistical Area—see Appendix B for areas included; (2) Rankings are based on annual percentage change for all metro areas containing at least 15,000 transactions over the last 10 years and ranges from 1 to 253; (3) figures based on a weighted average of Census Division estimates using a seasonally adjusted, purchase-only index; all figures are for the period ending December 31, 2017

Source: Federal Housing Finance Agency, House Price Index, February 28, 2018

Median Single-Family Home Prices

Area	2015	2016	2017p	Percent Change 2016 to 2017
MSA[1]	180.8	190.0	196.6	3.5
U.S. Average	223.9	235.5	248.8	5.6

Note: Figures are median sales prices of existing single-family homes in thousands of dollars; (p) preliminary; (1) Figures cover the Albuquerque, NM Metropolitan Statistical Area—see Appendix B for areas included

Source: National Association of Realtors, Median Sales Price of Existing Single-Family Homes for Metropolitan Areas, 4th Quarter 2017

Qualifying Income Based on Median Sales Price of Existing Single-Family Homes

Area	With 5% Down ($)	With 10% Down ($)	With 20% Down ($)
MSA[1]	44,279	41,949	37,288
U.S. Average	55,585	52,659	46,808

Note: Figures are preliminary; Qualifying income is based on a mortgage rate of 4.17%. Monthly principal and interest payment is limited to 25% of income; (1) Figures cover the Albuquerque, NM Metropolitan Statistical Area—see Appendix B for areas included

Source: National Association of Realtors, Qualifying Income Based on Median Sales Price of Existing Single-Family Homes for Metropolitan Areas, 4th Quarter 2017

Median Apartment Condo-Coop Home Prices

Area	2015	2016	2017p	Percent Change 2016 to 2017
MSA[1]	n/a	n/a	n/a	n/a
U.S. Average	210.7	220.7	234.3	6.2

Note: Figures are median sales prices of existing apartment condo-coop homes in thousands of dollars; (p) preliminary; n/a not available; (1) Figures cover the Albuquerque, NM Metropolitan Statistical Area—see Appendix B for areas included

Source: National Association of Realtors, Median Sales Price of Existing Apartment Condo-Coop Homes for Metropolitan Areas, 4th Quarter 2017

Home Value Distribution

Area	Under $50,000	$50,000 -$99,999	$100,000 -$149,999	$150,000 -$199,999	$200,000 -$299,999	$300,000 -$499,999	$500,000 -$999,999	$1,000,000 or more
City	2.9	6.5	23.7	29.0	26.9	9.4	1.4	0.1
MSA[1]	7.1	8.8	19.7	22.6	23.9	13.3	4.0	0.6
U.S.	8.8	14.8	15.3	14.9	18.4	16.4	9.0	2.5

Note: Figures are percentages and cover owner-occupied housing units; (1) Figures cover the Albuquerque, NM Metropolitan Statistical Area—see Appendix B for areas included

Source: U.S. Census Bureau, 2012-2016 American Community Survey 5-Year Estimates

Homeownership Rate

Area	2009 (%)	2010 (%)	2011 (%)	2012 (%)	2013 (%)	2014 (%)	2015 (%)	2016 (%)	2017 (%)
MSA[1]	65.7	65.5	67.1	62.8	65.9	64.4	64.3	66.9	67.0
U.S.	67.4	66.9	66.1	65.4	65.1	64.5	63.7	63.4	63.9

Note: (1) Figures cover the Albuquerque, NM Metropolitan Statistical Area—see Appendix B for areas included

Source: U.S. Census Bureau, Housing Vacancies and Homeownership Annual Statistics: 2009-2017

Year Housing Structure Built

Area	2010 or Later	2000 -2009	1990 -1999	1980 -1989	1970 -1979	1960 -1969	1950 -1959	1940 -1949	Before 1940	Median Year
City	3.8	37.8	21.2	21.9	11.9	2.3	0.7	0.1	0.2	1996
MSA[1]	1.9	18.8	18.3	16.7	18.0	9.9	9.5	3.7	3.1	1983
U.S.	2.3	14.7	14.0	13.7	15.6	10.9	10.6	5.2	13.0	1977

Note: Figures are percentages except for Median Year; Note: (1) Figures cover the Albuquerque, NM Metropolitan Statistical Area—see Appendix B for areas included
Source: U.S. Census Bureau, 2012-2016 American Community Survey 5-Year Estimates

Gross Monthly Rent

Area	Under $500	$500 -$999	$1,000 -$1,499	$1,500 -$1,999	$2,000 -$2,499	$2,500 -$2,999	$3,000 and up	Median ($)
City	1.0	38.1	42.5	14.1	3.0	0.0	1.2	1,114
MSA[1]	10.5	56.4	26.4	5.0	0.9	0.3	0.5	830
U.S.	11.3	43.3	27.7	10.7	4.0	1.6	1.5	949

Note: Figures are percentages except for Median; Gross rent is the contract rent plus the estimated average monthly cost of utilities (electricity, gas, and water and sewer) and fuels (oil, coal, kerosene, wood, etc.) if these are paid by the renter (or paid for the renter by someone else); (1) Figures cover the Albuquerque, NM Metropolitan Statistical Area—see Appendix B for areas included
Source: U.S. Census Bureau, 2012-2016 American Community Survey 5-Year Estimates

HEALTH

Health Risk Factors

Category	MSA[1] (%)	U.S. (%)
Adults aged 18–64 who have any kind of health care coverage	89.8	87.7
Adults who reported being in good or excellent health	79.1	83.6
Adults who are current smokers	16.3	17.1
Adults who currently use E-cigarettes	5.9	4.7
Adults who currently use chewing tobacco, snuff, or snus	2.6	4.0
Adults who are heavy drinkers[2]	5.5	6.5
Adults who are binge drinkers[3]	14.4	16.9
Adults who are overweight (BMI 25.0 - 29.9)	37.2	35.3
Adults who are obese (BMI 30.0 - 99.8)	27.1	29.9
Adults who participated in any physical activities in the past month	82.6	76.9
Adults who always or nearly always wears a seat belt	97.0	94.3

Note: (1) Figures cover the Albuquerque, NM Metropolitan Statistical Area—see Appendix B for areas included; (2) Heavy drinkers are classified as adult men having more than 14 drinks per week and adult women having more than 7 drinks per week; (3) Binge drinkers are classified as males having five or more drinks on one occasion or females having four or more drinks on one occasion
Source: Centers for Disease Control and Prevention, Behaviorial Risk Factor Surveillance System, SMART: Selected Metropolitan Area Risk Trends, 2016

Health Screening Rates

Category	MSA[1] (%)	U.S. (%)
Adults 50-75 who have had a blood stool test within the past year	6.3	8.0
Adults 50-75 who have had a colonoscopy in the past 10 years	60.7	63.5
Adults aged 65+ who have had flu shot within the past year	62.8	58.6
Adults aged 65+ who have ever had a pneumonia vaccination	81.8	73.4
Adults who have ever been tested for HIV	38.9	35.6
Women aged 21-65 who have had a pap test in the past three years	81.4	79.8
Men aged 40+ who have had a PSA test within the past two years	29.3	39.5
Women aged 40+ who have had a mammogram within the past two years	65.3	72.5

Note: n/a not available; (1) Figures cover the Albuquerque, NM Metropolitan Statistical Area—see Appendix B for areas included; Source: Centers for Disease Control and Prevention, Behaviorial Risk Factor Surveillance System, SMART: Selected Metropolitan Area Risk Trends, 2016

Chronic Health Conditions

Category	MSA[1] (%)	U.S. (%)
Adults who have ever been told they had a heart attack	4.6	4.4
Adults who have ever been told they have angina or coronary heart disease	3.9	4.1
Adults who have ever been told they had a stroke	3.4	3.1
Adults who have been told they currently have asthma	13.3	9.3
Adults who have ever been told they have arthritis	27.3	25.8
Adults who have ever been told they have diabetes[2]	9.3	10.5
Adults who have ever been told they had skin cancer	5.7	5.9
Adults who have ever been told they had any other types of cancer	7.0	6.7
Adults who have ever been told they have COPD	5.3	6.3
Adults who have ever been told they have kidney disease	2.9	2.8
Adults who have ever been told they have a form of depression	20.5	17.4

Note: (1) Figures cover the Albuquerque, NM Metropolitan Statistical Area—see Appendix B for areas included; (2) Figures do not include pregnancy-related, borderline, or pre-diabetes
Source: Centers for Disease Control and Prevention, Behaviorial Risk Factor Surveillance System, SMART: Selected Metropolitan Area Risk Trends, 2016

Mortality Rates for the Top 10 Causes of Death in the U.S.

ICD-10[a] Sub-Chapter	ICD-10[a] Code	Age-Adjusted Mortality Rate[1] per 100,000 population	
		County[2]	U.S.
Malignant neoplasms	C00-C97	136.1	158.5
Ischaemic heart diseases	I20-I25	83.0	96.8
Other forms of heart disease	I30-I51	31.5	52.4
Chronic lower respiratory diseases	J40-J47	34.4	40.9
Cerebrovascular diseases	I60-I69	29.5	37.2
Organic, including symptomatic, mental disorders	F01-F09	29.6	33.3
Other degenerative diseases of the nervous system	G30-G31	28.3	32.1
Other external causes of accidental injury	W00-X59	43.4	31.2
Diabetes mellitus	E10-E14	26.7	21.1
Hypertensive diseases	I10-I15	16.1	20.8

Note: (a) ICD-10 = International Classification of Diseases 10th Revision; (1) Mortality rates are a three year average covering 2014-2016; (2) Figures cover Sandoval County.
Source: Centers for Disease Control and Prevention, National Center for Health Statistics. Underlying Cause of Death 1999-2016 on CDC WONDER Online Database, released December 2017

Mortality Rates for Selected Causes of Death

ICD-10[a] Sub-Chapter	ICD-10[a] Code	Age-Adjusted Mortality Rate[1] per 100,000 population	
		County[2]	U.S.
Assault	X85-Y09	Unreliable	5.6
Diseases of the liver	K70-K76	24.9	14.0
Human immunodeficiency virus (HIV) disease	B20-B24	Suppressed	1.9
Influenza and pneumonia	J09-J18	14.0	14.6
Intentional self-harm	X60-X84	20.1	13.2
Malnutrition	E40-E46	Unreliable	1.3
Obesity and other hyperalimentation	E65-E68	Unreliable	2.1
Renal failure	N17-N19	9.5	13.0
Transport accidents	V01-V99	12.1	12.0
Viral hepatitis	B15-B19	Unreliable	1.9

Note: (a) ICD-10 = International Classification of Diseases 10th Revision; (1) Mortality rates are a three year average covering 2014-2016; (2) Figures cover Sandoval County; Data are Suppressed when the data meet the criteria for confidentiality constraints; Mortality rates are flagged as Unreliable when the rate would be calculated with a numerator of 20 or less.
Source: Centers for Disease Control and Prevention, National Center for Health Statistics. Underlying Cause of Death 1999-2016 on CDC WONDER Online Database, released December 2017

Health Insurance Coverage

Area	With Health Insurance	With Private Health Insurance	With Public Health Insurance	Without Health Insurance	Population Under Age 18 Without Health Insurance
City	92.2	70.9	33.2	7.8	3.3
MSA[1]	87.7	59.0	40.1	12.3	5.2
U.S.	88.3	66.7	33.0	11.7	5.9

Note: Figures are percentages that cover the civilian noninstitutionalized population; (1) Figures cover the Albuquerque, NM Metropolitan Statistical Area—see Appendix B for areas included
Source: U.S. Census Bureau, 2012-2016 American Community Survey 5-Year Estimates

Number of Medical Professionals

Area	MDs[3]	DOs[3,4]	Dentists	Podiatrists	Chiropractors	Optometrists
County[1] (number)	195	14	61	2	14	15
County[1] (rate[2])	141.0	10.1	43.5	1.4	10.0	10.7
U.S. (rate[2])	276.5	22.3	67.3	6.0	26.7	15.9

Note: Data as of 2016 unless noted; (1) Data covers Sandoval County; (2) Rate per 100,000 population; (3) Data as of 2015 and includes all active, non-federal physicians; (4) Doctor of Osteopathic Medicine
Source: U.S. Department of Health and Human Services, Health Resources and Services Administration, Bureau of Health Professions, Area Resource File (ARF) 2016-2017

EDUCATION

Public School District Statistics

District Name	Schls	Pupils	Pupil/ Teacher Ratio	Minority Pupils[1] (%)	Free Lunch Eligible[2] (%)	IEP[3] (%)
Rio Rancho Public Schools	19	17,215	16.5	64.7	33.7	13.7
The Ask Academy	1	359	16.3	48.7	16.2	13.1

Note: Table includes school districts with 100 or more students; (1) Percentage of students that are not non-Hispanic white; (2) Percentage of students that are eligible for the free lunch program; (3) Percentage of students that have an Individualized Education Program.
Source: U.S. Department of Education, National Center for Education Statistics, Common Core of Data, Local Education Agency (School District) Universe Survey: School Year 2015-2016; U.S. Department of Education, National Center for Education Statistics, Common Core of Data, Public Elementary/Secondary School Universe Survey: School Year 2015-2016

Highest Level of Education

Area	Less than H.S.	H.S. Diploma	Some College, No Deg.	Associate Degree	Bachelor's Degree	Master's Degree	Prof. School Degree	Doctorate Degree
City	7.1	24.0	28.1	10.8	18.2	9.1	1.3	1.4
MSA[1]	12.2	24.7	24.1	8.2	17.2	9.5	1.9	2.1
U.S.	13.0	27.5	21.0	8.2	18.8	8.2	2.0	1.3

Note: Figures cover persons age 25 and over; (1) Figures cover the Albuquerque, NM Metropolitan Statistical Area—see Appendix B for areas included
Source: U.S. Census Bureau, 2012-2016 American Community Survey 5-Year Estimates

Educational Attainment by Race

Area	High School Graduate or Higher (%)					Bachelor's Degree or Higher (%)				
	Total	White	Black	Asian	Hisp.[2]	Total	White	Black	Asian	Hisp.[2]
City	92.9	94.2	97.4	91.4	88.0	30.0	31.2	31.9	49.3	22.0
MSA[1]	87.8	89.9	91.3	84.8	78.8	30.8	34.1	29.8	44.6	17.6
U.S.	87.0	88.9	84.3	86.3	65.7	30.3	31.6	20.0	52.1	14.7

Note: Figures shown cover persons 25 years old and over; (1) Figures cover the Albuquerque, NM Metropolitan Statistical Area—see Appendix B for areas included; (2) People of Hispanic origin can be of any race
Source: U.S. Census Bureau, 2012-2016 American Community Survey 5-Year Estimates

School Enrollment by Grade and Control

Area	Preschool (%)		Kindergarten (%)		Grades 1 - 4 (%)		Grades 5 - 8 (%)		Grades 9 - 12 (%)	
	Public	Private	Public	Private	Public	Private	Public	Private	Public	Private
City	65.0	35.0	86.6	13.4	87.3	12.7	89.8	10.2	92.1	7.9
MSA[1]	62.8	37.2	87.7	12.3	90.5	9.5	88.8	11.2	90.0	10.0
U.S.	58.4	41.6	87.7	12.3	89.8	10.2	89.7	10.3	90.4	9.6

Note: Figures shown cover persons 3 years old and over; (1) Figures cover the Albuquerque, NM Metropolitan Statistical Area—see Appendix B for areas included
Source: U.S. Census Bureau, 2012-2016 American Community Survey 5-Year Estimates

Average Salaries of Public School Classroom Teachers

Area	2015		2016		Change from 2015 to 2016	
	Dollars	Rank[1]	Dollars	Rank[1]	Percent	Rank[2]
New Mexico	46,625	45	47,163	44	1.2	20
U.S. Average	57,611	–	58,353	–	1.3	–

Note: (1) Rank ranges from 1 to 51 where 1 indicates highest salary; (2) Rank ranges from 1 to 51 where 1 indicates highest percent change.
Source: National Education Association, Rankings & Estimates: Rankings of the States 2016 and Estimates of School Statistics 2017

Higher Education

Four-Year Colleges			Two-Year Colleges			Medical Schools[1]	Law Schools[2]	Voc/ Tech[3]
Public	Private Non-profit	Private For-profit	Public	Private Non-profit	Private For-profit			
0	0	0	0	0	0	0	0	0

Note: Figures cover institutions located within the city limits and include main campuses only; (1) includes schools accredited by the Liaison Committee on Medical Education and the American Osteopathic Association's Commission on Osteopathic College Accreditation; (2) includes ABA-accredited schools, schools with provisional ABA accreditation, and state accredited schools; (3) includes all schools with programs that are less than 2 years.
Source: National Center for Education Statistics, Integrated Postsecondary Education System (IPEDS), 2016-17; Wikipedia, List of Medical Schools in the United States, accessed April 2, 2018; Wikipedia, List of Law Schools in the United States, accessed April 2, 2018

According to *U.S. News & World Report,* the Albuquerque, NM metro area is home to one of the best national universities in the U.S.: **University of New Mexico** (#192 tie). The indicators used to capture academic quality fall into a number of categories: assessment by administrators at peer institutions; retention of students; faculty resources; student selectivity; financial resources; alumni giving; high school counselor ratings of colleges; and graduation rate. *U.S. News & World Report, "America's Best Colleges 2018"*

According to *U.S. News & World Report,* the Albuquerque, NM metro area is home to one of the top 100 law schools in the U.S.: **University of New Mexico** (#88 tie). The rankings are based on a weighted average of 12 measures of quality: peer assessment score; assessment score by lawyers/judges; median LSAT scores; median undergrad GPA; acceptance rate; employment rates for graduates; placement success; bar passage rate; faculty resources; expenditures per student; student/faculty ratio; and library resources. *U.S. News & World Report, "America's Best Graduate Schools, Law, 2019"*

According to *U.S. News & World Report,* the Albuquerque, NM metro area is home to one of the top 75 medical schools for research in the U.S.: **University of New Mexico** (#72 tie). The rankings are based on a weighted average of 11 measures of quality: quality assessment; peer assessment score; assessment score by residency directors; research activity; total research activity; average research activity per faculty member; student selectivity; median MCAT total score; median undergraduate GPA; acceptance rate; and faculty resources. *U.S. News & World Report, "America's Best Graduate Schools, Medical, 2019"*

PRESIDENTIAL ELECTION

2016 Presidential Election Results

Area	Clinton	Trump	Johnson	Stein	Other
Sandoval County	44.9	42.0	10.8	1.0	1.3
U.S.	48.0	45.9	3.3	1.1	1.7

Note: Results are percentages and may not add to 100% due to rounding
Source: Dave Leip's Atlas of U.S. Presidential Elections

EMPLOYERS

Major Employers

Company Name	Industry
Central New Mexico Community College	Vocational schools
City of Albuquerque	City & town managers' office
City of Albuquerque Police Department	Municipal police
Fish and Wildlife Service, United States	Fish & wildlife conservation agency, government
Jack Henry & Associates	Computers
Laguna Development Corporation	Grocery stores, independent
Mediplex of Massachusetts	Nursing home, exc skilled & intermediate care facility
Sandia Corporation	Noncommercial research organizations
The Boeing Company	Aircraft
United States Department of Energy	Energy development & conservation agency, government
United States Department of the Air Force	Testing laboratories
University of New Mexico	University
University of New Mexico Hospital	General medical & surgical hospitals
USAF	Air force
Veterans Health Administration	Administration of veterans' affiars
Veterans Hospital	General medical & surgical hospitals

Note: Companies shown are located within the Albuquerque, NM Metropolitan Statistical Area.
Source: Hoovers.com; Wikipedia

PUBLIC SAFETY

Crime Rate

Area	All Crimes	Violent Crimes				Property Crimes		
		Murder	Rape[3]	Robbery	Aggrav. Assault	Burglary	Larceny -Theft	Motor Vehicle Theft
City	2,582.4	1.0	44.0	34.6	145.6	371.9	1,660.5	324.8
Metro[1]	6,189.7	8.3	57.3	238.7	596.7	951.1	3,319.6	1,018.0
U.S.	2,837.0	5.3	29.6	102.8	248.5	468.9	1,745.0	236.9

Note: Figures are crimes per 100,000 population; (1) Figures cover the Albuquerque, NM Metropolitan Statistical Area—see Appendix B for areas included; (3) The city and U.S. figures shown were reported using the legacy Uniform Crime Reporting (UCR) definition of rape. The metro area figures shown are an aggregate total of the data submitted using both the revised and legacy UCR definitions.
Source: FBI Uniform Crime Reports, 2016

Hate Crimes

Area	Number of Quarters Reported	Number of Incidents per Bias Motivation					
		Race/Ethnicity/ Ancestry	Religion	Sexual Orientation	Disability	Gender	Gender Identity
City	n/a	n/a	n/a	n/a	n/a	n/a	n/a
U.S.	4	3,489	1,273	1,076	70	31	124

Note: n/a not available.
Source: Federal Bureau of Investigation, Hate Crime Statistics 2016

Identity Theft Consumer Reports

Area	Reports	Reports per 100,000 Population	Rank[2]
MSA[1]	1,103	121	51
U.S.	371,061	114	-

Note: (1) Figures cover the Albuquerque, NM Metropolitan Statistical Area—see Appendix B for areas included; (2) Rank ranges from 1 to 389 where 1 indicates greatest number of identity theft reports per 100,000 population
Source: Federal Trade Commission, Consumer Sentinel Network Data Book for January–December 2017

Fraud and Other Consumer Reports

Area	Reports	Reports per 100,000 Population	Rank[2]
MSA[1]	4,754	522	92
U.S.	2,304,550	708	-

Note: (1) Figures cover the Albuquerque, NM Metropolitan Statistical Area—see Appendix B for areas included; (2) Rank ranges from 1 to 389 where 1 indicates greatest number of fraud and other consumer reports per 100,000 population
Source: Federal Trade Commission, Consumer Sentinel Network Data Book for January–December 2017

SPORTS

Professional Sports Teams

Team Name	League	Year Established
No teams are located in the metro area		

Source: Wikipedia, Major Professional Sports Teams of the United States and Canada, April 5, 2018

CLIMATE

Average and Extreme Temperatures

Temperature	Jan	Feb	Mar	Apr	May	Jun	Jul	Aug	Sep	Oct	Nov	Dec	Yr.
Extreme High (°F)	69	76	85	89	98	105	105	101	100	91	77	72	105
Average High (°F)	47	53	61	71	80	90	92	89	83	72	57	48	70
Average Temp. (°F)	35	40	47	56	65	75	79	76	70	58	45	36	57
Average Low (°F)	23	27	33	41	50	59	65	63	56	44	31	24	43
Extreme Low (°F)	-17	-5	8	19	28	40	52	50	37	21	-7	-7	-17

Note: Figures cover the years 1948-1992
Source: National Climatic Data Center, International Station Meteorological Climate Summary, 9/96

Average Precipitation/Snowfall/Humidity

Precip./Humidity	Jan	Feb	Mar	Apr	May	Jun	Jul	Aug	Sep	Oct	Nov	Dec	Yr.
Avg. Precip. (in.)	0.4	0.4	0.5	0.4	0.5	0.5	1.4	1.5	0.9	0.9	0.4	0.5	8.5
Avg. Snowfall (in.)	3	2	2	1	Tr	0	0	0	Tr	Tr	1	3	11
Avg. Rel. Hum. 5am (%)	68	64	55	48	48	45	60	65	61	60	63	68	59
Avg. Rel. Hum. 5pm (%)	41	33	25	20	19	18	27	30	29	29	35	43	29

Note: Figures cover the years 1948-1992; Tr = Trace amounts (<0.05 in. of rain; <0.5 in. of snow)
Source: National Climatic Data Center, International Station Meteorological Climate Summary, 9/96

Weather Conditions

Temperature			Daytime Sky			Precipitation		
10°F & below	32°F & below	90°F & above	Clear	Partly cloudy	Cloudy	0.01 inch or more precip.	0.1 inch or more snow/ice	Thunderstorms
4	114	65	140	160	65	60	9	38

Note: Figures are average number of days per year and cover the years 1948-1992
Source: National Climatic Data Center, International Station Meteorological Climate Summary, 9/96

HAZARDOUS WASTE

Superfund Sites

The Albuquerque, NM metro area is home to three sites on the EPA's Superfund National Priorities List: **AT&SF (Albuquerque)** (final); **Fruit Avenue Plume** (final); **South Valley** (final). There are a total of 1,396 Superfund sites with a status of proposed or final on the list in the U.S. *U.S. Environmental Protection Agency, National Priorities List, April 4, 2018*

AIR & WATER QUALITY

Air Quality Trends: Ozone

	1990	1995	2000	2005	2010	2012	2013	2014	2015	2016
MSA[1]	0.072	0.070	0.072	0.073	0.066	0.070	0.067	0.062	0.066	0.065
U.S.	0.087	0.089	0.081	0.079	0.073	0.075	0.069	0.067	0.068	0.069

Note: (1) Data covers the Albuquerque, NM Metropolitan Statistical Area—see Appendix B for areas included. The values shown are the composite ozone concentration averages among trend sites based on the highest fourth daily maximum 8-hour concentration in parts per million. These trends are based on sites having an adequate record of monitoring data during the trend period. Data from exceptional events are included.
Source: U.S. Environmental Protection Agency, Air Quality Monitoring Information, "Air Quality Trends by City, 1990-2016"

Air Quality Index

Area	Percent of Days when Air Quality was...[2]					AQI Statistics[2]	
	Good	Moderate	Unhealthy for Sensitive Groups	Unhealthy	Very Unhealthy	Maximum	Median
MSA[1]	45.2	53.7	1.1	0.0	0.0	119	52

Note: (1) Data covers the Albuquerque, NM Metropolitan Statistical Area—see Appendix B for areas included; (2) Based on 365 days with AQI data in 2017. Air Quality Index (AQI) is an index for reporting daily air quality. EPA calculates the AQI for five major air pollutants regulated by the Clean Air Act: ground-level ozone, particle pollution (aka particulate matter), carbon monoxide, sulfur dioxide, and nitrogen dioxide. The AQI runs from 0 to 500. The higher the AQI value, the greater the level of air pollution and the greater the health concern. There are six AQI categories: "Good" AQI is between 0 and 50. Air quality is considered satisfactory; "Moderate" AQI is between 51 and 100. Air quality is acceptable; "Unhealthy for Sensitive Groups" When AQI values are between 101 and 150, members of sensitive groups may experience health effects; "Unhealthy" When AQI values are between 151 and 200 everyone may begin to experience health effects; "Very Unhealthy" AQI values between 201 and 300 trigger a health alert; "Hazardous" AQI values over 300 trigger warnings of emergency conditions (not shown).
Source: U.S. Environmental Protection Agency, Air Quality Index Report, 2017

Air Quality Index Pollutants

Area	Percent of Days when AQI Pollutant was...[2]					
	Carbon Monoxide	Nitrogen Dioxide	Ozone	Sulfur Dioxide	Particulate Matter 2.5	Particulate Matter 10
MSA[1]	0.0	0.5	68.8	0.0	8.8	21.9

Note: (1) Data covers the Albuquerque, NM Metropolitan Statistical Area—see Appendix B for areas included; (2) Based on 365 days with AQI data in 2017. The Air Quality Index (AQI) is an index for reporting daily air quality. EPA calculates the AQI for five major air pollutants regulated by the Clean Air Act: ground-level ozone, particle pollution (also known as particulate matter), carbon monoxide, sulfur dioxide, and nitrogen dioxide. The AQI runs from 0 to 500. The higher the AQI value, the greater the level of air pollution and the greater the health concern.
Source: U.S. Environmental Protection Agency, Air Quality Index Report, 2017

Maximum Air Pollutant Concentrations: Particulate Matter, Ozone, CO and Lead

	Particulate Matter 10 (ug/m^3)	Particulate Matter 2.5 Wtd AM (ug/m^3)	Particulate Matter 2.5 24-Hr (ug/m^3)	Ozone (ppm)	Carbon Monoxide (ppm)	Lead (ug/m^3)
MSA[1] Level	205	7.6	19	0.067	2	0
NAAQS[2]	150	15	35	0.075	9	0.15
Met NAAQS[2]	No	Yes	Yes	Yes	Yes	Yes

Note: (1) Data covers the Albuquerque, NM Metropolitan Statistical Area—see Appendix B for areas included; Data from exceptional events are included; (2) National Ambient Air Quality Standards; ppm = parts per million; ug/m^3 = micrograms per cubic meter; n/a not available.
Concentrations: Particulate Matter 10 (coarse particulate)—highest second maximum 24-hour concentration; Particulate Matter 2.5 Wtd AM (fine particulate)—highest weighted annual mean concentration; Particulate Matter 2.5 24-Hour (fine particulate)—highest 98th percentile 24-hour concentration; Ozone—highest fourth daily maximum 8-hour concentration; Carbon Monoxide—highest second maximum non-overlapping 8-hour concentration; Lead—maximum running 3-month average
Source: U.S. Environmental Protection Agency, Air Quality Monitoring Information, "Air Quality Statistics by City, 2016"

Maximum Air Pollutant Concentrations: Nitrogen Dioxide and Sulfur Dioxide

	Nitrogen Dioxide AM (ppb)	Nitrogen Dioxide 1-Hr (ppb)	Sulfur Dioxide AM (ppb)	Sulfur Dioxide 1-Hr (ppb)	Sulfur Dioxide 24-Hr (ppb)
MSA[1] Level	10	44	n/a	6	n/a
NAAQS[2]	53	100	30	75	140
Met NAAQS[2]	Yes	Yes	n/a	Yes	n/a

Note: (1) Data covers the Albuquerque, NM Metropolitan Statistical Area—see Appendix B for areas included; Data from exceptional events are included; (2) National Ambient Air Quality Standards; ppm = parts per million; ug/m^3 = micrograms per cubic meter; n/a not available.
Concentrations: Nitrogen Dioxide AM—highest arithmetic mean concentration; Nitrogen Dioxide 1-Hr—highest 98th percentile 1-hour daily maximum concentration; Sulfur Dioxide AM—highest annual mean concentration; Sulfur Dioxide 1-Hr—highest 99th percentile 1-hour daily maximum concentration; Sulfur Dioxide 24-Hr—highest second maximum 24-hour concentration
Source: U.S. Environmental Protection Agency, Air Quality Monitoring Information, "Air Quality Statistics by City, 2016"

Drinking Water

Water System Name	Pop. Served	Primary Water Source Type	Violations[1]	
			Health Based	Monitoring/ Reporting
Rio Rancho Water & Wastewater	87,000	Ground	0	0

Note: (1) Based on violation data from January 1, 2017 to December 31, 2017
Source: U.S. Environmental Protection Agency, Office of Ground Water and Drinking Water, Safe Drinking Water Information System (based on data extracted April 5, 2018)

Bethlehem, New York

Background

The town of Bethlehem, on the Hudson River six miles from the capital of New York state at Albany, is comprised of seven historic hamlets: Delmar, Elsmere, Glenmont, Selkirk, Slingerlands, and North and South Bethlehem. The area was initially settled by the Dutch, and this early heritage is reflected in the town's annual spring "Feestelijk" arts and entertainment festival.

Incorporated in 1793, Bethlehem is a prosperous and modern community that maintains a comfortable sense of its small-town past. With excellent schools, convenient access to the greater Albany metropolitan area, excellent recreational resources, and consistently higher median incomes and employment rates than the state as a whole, Bethlehem is a model of careful planning and development.

Bethlehem Central School District is widely held to be one of the state's best. An unusually high percentage of graduating high school seniors are college-bound. Many institutions of higher education are in the area, including Siena College, The College of St. Rose, Maria College, Rensselaer Polytechnic Institute, Union College, The Sage Colleges, State University at Albany, Hudson Valley Community College, Skidmore College, Schenectady County Community College, Albany Law School, Albany Medical College and Albany College of Pharmacy.

Bethlehem operates a number of its own parks and recreational facilities, and many other recreational resources are available in the surrounding area. Elm Avenue Park is a year-round 160-acre recreational center that offers swimming, tennis, basketball and volleyball courts, baseball, softball and soccer fields, a fitness trail, ice skating rinks, sledding, playground, supervised programs and picnic facilities.

There is an Audubon Society sanctuary in the immediate area, plus John Boyd Thacher State Park, and Five Rivers Environmental Education Center, a 450-acre environmental and natural history state-run learning center. Skiers and hikers enjoy the nearby Adirondack, Catskill and Berkshire mountains, while water sports enthusiasts are close to Lake George and Lake Placid.

Major medical facilities in the area, all less than half an hour away, include Albany Medical Center, Albany Memorial Hospital, St. Peter's Hospital, a major Veteran's Administration Hospital, and the Capital District Psychiatric Center. In Bethlehem itself there are two large privately run medical centers.

Although it retains its small-town ambiance, Bethlehem is efficiently connected to the greater metropolitan region, with an average commute of just over twenty minutes. The town is also conveniently located for travel, via road or rail, to major northeast coast destinations, including New York City, Boston and Montreal, with Albany International Airport less than twenty minutes away, and four smaller regional airports nearby.

The Bethlehem Town Board is comprised of a Supervisor and four Board Members. The Supervisor is elected every two years and town board members serve four year terms, with two of the seats elected every two years.

Rankings

Business/Finance Rankings

- The personal finance site NerdWallet analyzed 183 American metropolitan areas with populations over 250,000 and more than 15,000 businesses to rank where entrepreneurs find the most success. Criteria included area economy, annual income, housing cost, unemployment rate, and the success rate of area businesses. Albany* ranked #62. *www.nerdwallet.com, "Best Places to Start a Business," April 27, 2015*
- The Brookings Institution ranked the 100 largest metro areas in the U.S. based on income inequality. Albany* was ranked #67 (#1 = greatest ineqality). Criteria: the "95/20 ratio," a figure representing the income at which a household earns more than 95 percent of all other households, divided by the income at which a household earns more than only 20 percent of all other households. *Brookings Institution, "Household Income Inequality, 100 Largest U.S. Metro Areas, 2014-2016," February 5, 2018*
- *Forbes* ranked the 100 largest metro areas in the U.S. in terms of the "Best Cities for Young Professionals." The Albany* metro area ranked #21 out of 25. (Large metro areas were divided into metro divisions.) Criteria: median rent of a two-bedroom apartment; job growth and unemployment rate; median salary of college graduates with 5 or less years of work experience; networking opportunities; social outlook; percentage of population 25 years of age and older with college degrees. *Forbes.com, "America's 25 Best Cities for Young Professionals in 2017," May 22, 2017*
- The Albany* metro area appeared on the Milken Institute "2017 Best Performing Cities" list. Rank: #111 out of 200 large metro areas. Criteria: job growth; wage and salary growth; high-tech output growth. *Milken Institute, "Best-Performing Cities 2017," January 2018*
- *Forbes* ranked the 200 most populous metro areas to determine the nation's "Best Places for Business and Careers." The Albany* metro area was ranked #80. Criteria: costs (business and living); job growth (past and projected); income growth; quality of life; educational attainment (college and high school); projected economic growth; cultural and recreational opportunities; net migration patterns; number of highly ranked colleges. *Forbes, "The Best Places for Business and Careers 2017," October 24, 2017*

Education Rankings

- Personal finance website *WalletHub* analyzed the 150 largest U.S. metropolitan statistical areas to determine where the most educated Americans are choosing to settle. Criteria: education quality and attainment gap; education levels; percentage of workers with degrees; public school rankings; quality and size of each metro area's universities. Albany* was ranked #20 (#1 = most educated city). *www.WalletHub.com, "2017's Most and Least Educated Cities in America," July 25, 2017*

Environmental Rankings

- Sperling's BestPlaces assessed 379 metropolitan areas of the United States for the likelihood of dangerously extreme weather events or earthquakes. In general the Southeast and South-Central regions have the highest risk of weather extremes and earthquakes, while the Pacific Northwest enjoys the lowest risk. Of the least risky metropolitan areas, the Albany* metro area was ranked #136. *www.bestplaces.net, "Safest Places from Natural Disasters," April 2011*
- Albany* was highlighted as one of the top 99 cleanest metro areas for short-term particle pollution (24-hour PM 2.5) in the U.S. during 2013 through 2015. Monitors in these cities reported no days with unhealthful PM 2.5 levels. *American Lung Association, State of the Air 2017*

Health/Fitness Rankings

- The Albany* metro area was identified as one of the worst cities for bed bugs in America by pest control company Orkin. The area ranked #50 out of 50 based on the number of bed bug treatments Orkin performed from December 2016 to November 2017. *Orkin, "Baltimore and Washington D.C. Continue to Hold Top Spots," January 8, 2018*
- Albany* was identified as a "2016 Spring Allergy Capital." The area ranked #49 out of 100. Three groups of factors were used to identify the most severe cities for people with allergies during the spring season: annual pollen levels; medicine utilization; access to board-certified allergists. *Asthma and Allergy Foundation of America, "Spring Allergy Capitals 2016"*
- Albany* was identified as a "2016 Fall Allergy Capital." The area ranked #31 out of 100. Three groups of factors were used to identify the most severe cities for people with allergies during the fall season: annual pollen levels; medicine utilization; access to board-certified allergists. *Asthma and Allergy Foundation of America, "Fall Allergy Capitals 2016"*
- Albany* was identified as a "2015 Asthma Capital." The area ranked #70 out of the nation's 100 largest metropolitan areas. Criteria: estimated prevalence; self-reported prevalence; crude death rate for asthma; annual pollen score; annual air quality; public smoking laws; number of board-certified asthma specialists; school inhaler access laws; rescue medication use; controller medication use; ER visits for asthma; uninsured rate; poverty rate. *Asthma and Allergy Foundation of America, "Asthma Capitals 2015"*
- The Albany* metro area ranked #78 out of 189 in The Gallup-Healthways Well-Being Index. Criteria: purpose; social well being; financial health; community and physical health. Results are based on telephone interviews with adults, aged 18 and older, living in metropolitan areas in the 50 U.S. states and the District of Columbia. *Gallup-Healthways, "State of American Well-Being, 2017 Community Well-Being Rankings" March 2018*

Real Estate Rankings

- The Albany* metro area was identified as one of the 20 worst housing markets in the U.S. in 2017. The area ranked #11 out of 180 markets. Criteria: year-over-year change of median sales price of existing single-family homes between the 4th quarter of 2016 and the 4th quarter of 2017. *National Association of Realtors®, Median Sales Price of Existing Single-Family Homes for Metropolitan Areas, 4th Quarter 2017*
- Albany* was ranked #52 out of 238 metro areas in terms of housing affordability in 2017 by the National Association of Home Builders (#1 = most affordable). Criteria: the share of homes sold in that area affordable to a family earning the local median income, based on standard mortgage underwriting criteria. *National Association of Home Builders®, NAHB-Wells Fargo Housing Opportunity Index, 4th Quarter 2017*

Safety Rankings

- The National Insurance Crime Bureau ranked 382 metro areas in the U.S. in terms of per capita rates of vehicle theft. The Albany* metro area ranked #326 (#1 = highest rate). Criteria: number of vehicle theft offenses per 100,000 inhabitants in 2016. *National Insurance Crime Bureau, "Hot Spots 2016," June 8, 2017*

Seniors/Retirement Rankings

- From its Best Cities for Successful Aging indexes, the Milken Institute generated rankings for metropolitan areas, weighing data in nine categories—health care, wellness, living arrangements, transportation and convenience, financial characteristics, education, employment, community engagement, and overall livability. The Albany* metro area was ranked #21 overall in the large metro area category. *Milken Institute, "Best Cities for Successful Aging, 2017" March 14, 2017*

*Bethlehem is located within the Albany-Schenectady-Troy, NY Metropolitan Statistical Area.

Business Environment

CITY FINANCES

City Government Finances

Component	2015 ($000)	2015 ($ per capita)
Total Revenues	41,628	1,193
Total Expenditures	42,174	1,208
Debt Outstanding	26,308	754
Cash and Securities[1]	22,834	654

Note: (1) Cash and security holdings of a government at the close of its fiscal year,, including those of its dependent agencies, utilities, and liquor stores.
Source: U.S Census Bureau, State & Local Government Finances 2015

City Government Revenue by Source

Source	2015 ($000)	2015 ($ per capita)	2015 (%)
General Revenue			
From Federal Government	1,077	31	2.6
From State Government	2,441	70	5.9
From Local Governments	11,198	321	26.9
Taxes			
Property	12,699	364	30.5
Sales and Gross Receipts	639	18	1.5
Personal Income	0	0	0.0
Corporate Income	0	0	0.0
Motor Vehicle License	0	0	0.0
Other Taxes	1,279	37	3.1
Current Charges	4,215	121	10.1
Liquor Store	0	0	0.0
Utility	6,776	194	16.3
Employee Retirement	0	0	0.0

Source: U.S Census Bureau, State & Local Government Finances 2015

City Government Expenditures by Function

Function	2015 ($000)	2015 ($ per capita)	2015 (%)
General Direct Expenditures			
Air Transportation	0	0	0.0
Corrections	0	0	0.0
Education	0	0	0.0
Employment Security Administration	0	0	0.0
Financial Administration	1,263	36	3.0
Fire Protection	9	< 1	< 0.1
General Public Buildings	745	21	1.8
Governmental Administration, Other	1,361	39	3.2
Health	1,301	37	3.1
Highways	7,002	200	16.6
Hospitals	0	0	0.0
Housing and Community Development	0	0	0.0
Interest on General Debt	1,493	42	3.5
Judicial and Legal	640	18	1.5
Libraries	0	0	0.0
Parking	0	0	0.0
Parks and Recreation	1,654	47	3.9
Police Protection	6,392	183	15.2
Public Welfare	300	8	0.7
Sewerage	5,381	154	12.8
Solid Waste Management	914	26	2.2
Veterans' Services	0	0	0.0
Liquor Store	0	0	0.0
Utility	8,371	239	19.8
Employee Retirement	0	0	0.0

Source: U.S Census Bureau, State & Local Government Finances 2015

DEMOGRAPHICS

Population Growth

Area	1990 Census	2000 Census	2010 Census	2016* Estimate	Population Growth (%) 1990-2016	2010-2016
City	27,552	31,304	33,656	34,709	26.0	3.1
MSA[1]	809,443	825,875	870,716	879,291	8.6	1.0
U.S.	248,709,873	281,421,906	308,745,538	318,558,162	28.1	3.2

Note: (1) Figures cover the Albany-Schenectady-Troy, NY Metropolitan Statistical Area—see Appendix B for areas included; (*) 2012-2016 5-year estimated population
Source: U.S. Census Bureau, 1990 Census, Census 2000, Census 2010, 2012-2016 American Community Survey 5-Year Estimates

Household Size

Area	Persons in Household (%) One	Two	Three	Four	Five	Six	Seven or More	Average Household Size
City	28.3	34.7	15.3	15.2	4.6	1.7	0.2	2.50
MSA[1]	31.9	35.0	15.3	11.6	4.2	1.4	0.6	2.50
U.S.	27.7	33.7	15.7	13.1	6.0	2.3	1.5	2.60

Note: (1) Figures cover the Albany-Schenectady-Troy, NY Metropolitan Statistical Area—see Appendix B for areas included
Source: U.S. Census Bureau, 2012-2016 American Community Survey 5-Year Estimates

Race

Area	White Alone[2] (%)	Black Alone[2] (%)	Asian Alone[2] (%)	AIAN[3] Alone[2] (%)	NHOPI[4] Alone[2] (%)	Other Race Alone[2] (%)	Two or More Races (%)
City	91.6	2.1	3.9	0.0	0.0	0.5	1.9
MSA[1]	83.7	7.7	4.1	0.2	0.0	1.4	2.9
U.S.	73.3	12.6	5.2	0.8	0.2	4.8	3.1

Note: (1) Figures cover the Albany-Schenectady-Troy, NY Metropolitan Statistical Area—see Appendix B for areas included; (2) Alone is defined as not being in combination with one or more other races; (3) American Indian and Alaska Native; (4) Native Hawaiian and Other Pacific Islander
Source: U.S. Census Bureau, 2012-2016 American Community Survey 5-Year Estimates

Hispanic or Latino Origin

Area	Total (%)	Mexican (%)	Puerto Rican (%)	Cuban (%)	Other (%)
City	1.9	0.4	0.8	0.1	0.5
MSA[1]	4.8	0.6	2.4	0.2	1.6
U.S.	17.3	11.0	1.7	0.7	4.0

Note: Persons of Hispanic or Latino origin can be of any race; (1) Figures cover the Albany-Schenectady-Troy, NY Metropolitan Statistical Area—see Appendix B for areas included
Source: U.S. Census Bureau, 2012-2016 American Community Survey 5-Year Estimates

Segregation

Type	Segregation Indices[1] 1990	2000	2010	2010 Rank[2]	Percent Change 1990-2000	1990-2010	2000-2010
Black/White	61.6	62.4	61.3	37	0.8	-0.2	-1.0
Asian/White	40.9	42.8	43.1	38	1.8	2.2	0.4
Hispanic/White	32.1	37.9	38.9	70	5.8	6.8	1.0

Note: All figures cover the Metropolitan Statistical Area—see Appendix B for areas included; Figures are based on an analysis of 1990, 2000, and 2010 Census Decennial Census tract data by William H. Frey, Brookings Institution and the University of Michigan Social Science Data Analysis Network. In this analysis all racial groups (whites, blacks, and asians) are non-Hispanic members of those races. Hispanics are shown as a separate category; (1) Segregation Indices are Dissimilarity Indices that measure the degree to which the minority group is distributed differently than whites across census tracts. They range from 0 (complete integration) to 100 (complete segregation) where the value indicates the percentage of the minority group that needs to move to be distributed exactly like whites; (2) Ranges from 1 (most segregated) to 102 (least segregated); n/a not available.
Source: www.CensusScope.org

Ancestry

Area	German	Irish	English	American	Italian	Polish	French[2]	Scottish	Dutch
City	18.8	27.3	13.0	6.4	16.9	6.4	4.7	2.1	3.4
MSA[1]	16.1	22.4	9.6	4.7	17.2	6.7	6.5	1.9	3.3
U.S.	14.4	10.4	7.7	6.9	5.4	2.9	2.6	1.7	1.3

Note: Figures are the percentage of the total population reporting a particular ancestry. The nine most commonly reported ancestries in the U.S. are shown. Figures include multiple ancestries (e.g. if a person reported being Irish and Italian, they were included in both columns); (1) Figures cover the Albany-Schenectady-Troy, NY Metropolitan Statistical Area—see Appendix B for areas included; (2) Excludes Basque
Source: U.S. Census Bureau, 2012-2016 American Community Survey 5-Year Estimates

Foreign-Born Population

Area	Percent of Population Born in								
	Any Foreign Country	Asia	Mexico	Europe	Carribean	Central America[2]	South America	Africa	Canada
City	6.2	3.3	0.0	2.0	0.1	0.0	0.4	0.2	0.2
MSA[1]	7.3	3.1	0.2	1.7	0.6	0.1	1.0	0.4	0.2
U.S.	13.2	4.0	3.6	1.5	1.3	1.0	0.9	0.6	0.3

Note: (1) Figures cover the Albany-Schenectady-Troy, NY Metropolitan Statistical Area—see Appendix B for areas included; (2) Excludes Mexico.
Source: U.S. Census Bureau, 2012-2016 American Community Survey 5-Year Estimates

Marital Status

Area	Never Married	Now Married[2]	Separated	Widowed	Divorced
City	28.1	56.2	0.8	6.7	8.1
MSA[1]	36.3	45.9	2.0	6.2	9.7
U.S.	33.0	48.1	2.1	5.9	11.0

Note: Figures are percentages and cover the population 15 years of age and older; (1) Figures cover the Albany-Schenectady-Troy, NY Metropolitan Statistical Area—see Appendix B for areas included; (2) Excludes separated
Source: U.S. Census Bureau, 2012-2016 American Community Survey 5-Year Estimates

Disability Status

Area	All Ages	Under 18 Years Old	18 to 64 Years Old	65 Years and Over
City	9.7	4.2	6.2	30.0
MSA[1]	12.0	4.4	9.8	32.0
U.S.	12.5	4.1	10.3	35.7

Note: Figures show percent of the civilian noninstitutionalized population that reported having a disability. Disability status is determined from six types of difficulty: vision, hearing, cognitive, ambulatory, self-care, and independent living. For children under 5 years old, hearing and vision difficulty are used to determine disability status. For children between the ages of 5 and 14, disability status is determined from hearing, vision, cognitive, ambulatory, and self-care difficulties. For people aged 15 years and older, they are considered to have a disability if they have difficulty with any one of the six difficulty types; Note: (1) Figures cover the Albany-Schenectady-Troy, NY Metropolitan Statistical Area—see Appendix B for areas included
Source: U.S. Census Bureau, 2012-2016 American Community Survey 5-Year Estimates

Age

Area	Percent of Population									Median Age
	Under Age 5	Age 5–19	Age 20–34	Age 35–44	Age 45–54	Age 55–64	Age 65–74	Age 75–84	Age 85+	
City	5.3	20.3	13.9	12.6	15.3	15.9	9.7	4.1	2.9	43.4
MSA[1]	5.3	18.4	20.5	12.0	14.5	13.7	8.7	4.4	2.4	39.9
U.S.	6.2	19.6	20.7	12.7	13.6	12.6	8.3	4.3	1.9	37.7

Note: (1) Figures cover the Albany-Schenectady-Troy, NY Metropolitan Statistical Area—see Appendix B for areas included
Source: U.S. Census Bureau, 2012-2016 American Community Survey 5-Year Estimates

Gender

Area	Males	Females	Males per 100 Females
City	16,704	18,005	92.8
MSA[1]	430,051	449,240	95.7
U.S.	156,765,322	161,792,840	96.9

Note: (1) Figures cover the Albany-Schenectady-Troy, NY Metropolitan Statistical Area—see Appendix B for areas included
Source: U.S. Census Bureau, 2012-2016 American Community Survey 5-Year Estimates

Religious Groups by Family

Area	Catholic	Baptist	Non-Den.	Methodist[2]	Lutheran	LDS[3]	Pente-costal	Presby-terian[4]	Muslim[5]	Judaism
MSA[1]	26.8	1.3	2.3	2.9	1.6	0.4	0.5	2.1	1.2	1.0
U.S.	19.1	9.3	4.0	4.0	2.3	2.0	1.9	1.6	0.8	0.7

Note: Figures are the number of adherents as a percentage of the total population; (1) Figures cover the Albany-Schenectady-Troy, NY Metropolitan Statistical Area—see Appendix B for areas included; (2) Methodist/Pietist; (3) Latter Day Saints; (4) Reformed; (5) Figures are estimates
Source: Association of Statisticians of American Religious Bodies, 2010 U.S. Religion Census: Religious Congregations & Membership Study

Religious Groups by Tradition

Area	Catholic	Evangelical Protestant	Mainline Protestant	Other Tradition	Black Protestant	Orthodox
MSA[1]	26.8	4.5	7.4	3.2	0.5	0.4
U.S.	19.1	16.2	7.3	4.3	1.6	0.3

Note: Figures are the number of adherents as a percentage of the total population; (1) Figures cover the Albany-Schenectady-Troy, NY Metropolitan Statistical Area—see Appendix B for areas included
Source: Association of Statisticians of American Religious Bodies, 2010 U.S. Religion Census: Religious Congregations & Membership Study

ECONOMY

Gross Metropolitan Product

Area	2014	2015	2016	2017	Rank[2]
MSA[1]	49.2	50.8	52.0	54.0	58

Note: Figures are in billions of dollars; (1) Figures cover the Albany-Schenectady-Troy, NY Metropolitan Statistical Area—see Appendix B for areas included; (2) Rank is based on 2015 data and ranges from 1 to 381
Source: The U.S. Conference of Mayors, U.S. Metro Economies: GMP and Employment Report, 2015-2017

Economic Growth

Area	2012-14 (%)	2015 (%)	2016 (%)	2017 (%)	Rank[2]
MSA[1]	1.8	1.1	0.8	1.7	139
U.S.	2.0	2.4	1.9	2.6	–

Note: Figures are real gross metropolitan product (GMP) growth rates and represent average annual percent change; (1) Figures cover the Albany-Schenectady-Troy, NY Metropolitan Statistical Area—see Appendix B for areas included; (2) Rank is based on 2012-2014 average annual percent change and ranges from 1 to 381
Source: The U.S. Conference of Mayors, U.S. Metro Economies: GMP and Employment Report, 2015-2017

Metropolitan Area Exports

Area	2011	2012	2013	2014	2015	2016	Rank[2]
MSA[1]	3,525.1	3,420.1	3,946.1	4,547.0	4,470.3	4,135.0	59

Note: Figures are in millions of dollars; (1) Figures cover the Albany-Schenectady-Troy, NY Metropolitan Statistical Area—see Appendix B for areas included; (2) Rank is based on 2016 data and ranges from 1 to 385
Source: U.S. Department of Commerce, International Trade Administration, Office of Trade & Industry Information, Manufacturing & Services, data extracted March 15, 2018

Building Permits

Area	Single-Family			Multi-Family			Total		
	2016	2017p	Pct. Chg.	2016	2017p	Pct. Chg.	2016	2017p	Pct. Chg.
City	94	67	-28.7	46	0	-100.0	140	67	-52.1
MSA[1]	1,353	1,200	-11.3	1,437	1,255	-12.7	2,790	2,455	-12.0
U.S.	750,800	817,300	8.9	455,800	446,800	-2.0	1,206,600	1,264,100	4.8

Note: (1) Figures cover the Albany-Schenectady-Troy, NY Metropolitan Statistical Area—see Appendix B for areas included; Figures represent new, privately-owned housing units authorized (unadjusted data); All permit data are based on estimates with imputation; (p) preliminary data.
Source: U.S. Census Bureau, Manufacturing, Mining, and Construction Statistics, Building Permits, 2016, 2017

Bankruptcy Filings

Area	Business Filings			Nonbusiness Filings		
	2016	2017	% Chg.	2016	2017	% Chg.
Albany County	14	12	-14.3	505	513	1.6
U.S.	24,114	23,157	-4.0	770,846	765,863	-0.6

Note: Business filings include Chapter 7, Chapter 11, Chapter 12, and Chapter 13; Nonbusiness filings include Chapter 7, Chapter 11, and Chapter 13
Source: Administrative Office of the U.S. Courts, Business and Nonbusiness Bankruptcy, County Cases Commenced by Chapter of the Bankruptcy Code, During the 12-Month Period Ending December 31, 2016 and Business and Nonbusiness Bankruptcy, County Cases Commenced by Chapter of the Bankruptcy Code, During the 12-Month Period Ending December 31, 2017

Housing Vacancy Rates

Area	Gross Vacancy Rate[2] (%)			Year-Round Vacancy Rate[3] (%)			Rental Vacancy Rate[4] (%)			Homeowner Vacancy Rate[5] (%)		
	2015	2016	2017	2015	2016	2017	2015	2016	2017	2015	2016	2017
MSA[1]	13.2	11.8	10.5	8.9	8.7	8.3	6.5	3.8	8.5	1.8	2.1	2.1
U.S.	12.9	12.8	12.7	10.0	9.9	9.9	7.1	6.9	7.2	1.8	1.7	1.6

Note: (1) Figures cover the Albany-Schenectady-Troy, NY Metropolitan Statistical Area—see Appendix B for areas included; (2) The percentage of the total housing inventory that is vacant; (3) The percentage of the housing inventory (excluding seasonal units) that is year-round vacant; (4) The percentage of rental inventory that is vacant for rent; (5) The percentage of homeowner inventory that is vacant for sale
Source: U.S. Census Bureau, Housing Vacancies and Homeownership Annual Statistics: 2015, 2016, 2017

INCOME

Income

Area	Per Capita ($)	Median Household ($)	Average Household ($)
City	47,364	92,708	120,094
MSA[1]	33,284	63,758	81,749
U.S.	29,829	55,322	77,866

Note: (1) Figures cover the Albany-Schenectady-Troy, NY Metropolitan Statistical Area—see Appendix B for areas included
Source: U.S. Census Bureau, 2012-2016 American Community Survey 5-Year Estimates

Household Income Distribution

Area	Percent of Households Earning							
	Under $15,000	$15,000 -$24,999	$25,000 -$34,999	$35,000 -$49,999	$50,000 -$74,999	$75,000 -$99,999	$100,000 -$149,999	$150,000 and up
City	4.5	5.3	5.5	8.2	16.1	14.9	20.8	24.8
MSA[1]	9.7	8.8	8.6	12.1	18.3	13.9	16.8	11.7
U.S.	12.1	10.2	9.9	13.2	17.8	12.2	13.5	11.1

Note: (1) Figures cover the Albany-Schenectady-Troy, NY Metropolitan Statistical Area—see Appendix B for areas included
Source: U.S. Census Bureau, 2012-2016 American Community Survey 5-Year Estimates

Poverty Rate

Area	All Ages	Under 18 Years Old	18 to 64 Years Old	65 Years and Over
City	4.5	4.0	4.6	4.9
MSA[1]	11.0	15.0	10.8	6.5
U.S.	15.1	21.2	14.2	9.3

Note: Figures are percentage of people whose income during the past 12 months was below the poverty level; (1) Figures cover the Albany-Schenectady-Troy, NY Metropolitan Statistical Area—see Appendix B for areas included
Source: U.S. Census Bureau, 2012-2016 American Community Survey 5-Year Estimates

EMPLOYMENT

Labor Force and Employment

Area	Civilian Labor Force			Workers Employed		
	Dec. 2016	Dec. 2017	% Chg.	Dec. 2016	Dec. 2017	% Chg.
City	18,059	18,061	0.0	17,527	17,524	0.0
MSA[1]	444,458	445,967	0.3	426,777	427,121	0.1
U.S.	158,968,000	159,880,000	0.6	151,798,000	153,602,000	1.2

Note: Data is not seasonally adjusted and covers workers 16 years of age and older; (1) Figures cover the Albany-Schenectady-Troy, NY Metropolitan Statistical Area—see Appendix B for areas included
Source: Bureau of Labor Statistics, Local Area Unemployment Statistics

Unemployment Rate

Area	2017											
	Jan.	Feb.	Mar.	Apr.	May	Jun.	Jul.	Aug.	Sep.	Oct.	Nov.	Dec.
City	3.6	3.8	3.3	3.1	3.3	3.3	3.5	3.4	3.4	3.1	3.1	3.0
MSA[1]	4.9	4.8	4.2	4.0	4.1	4.3	4.4	4.3	4.3	4.1	4.2	4.2
U.S.	5.1	4.9	4.6	4.1	4.1	4.5	4.6	4.5	4.1	3.9	3.9	3.9

Note: Data is not seasonally adjusted and covers workers 16 years of age and older; (1) Figures cover the Albany-Schenectady-Troy, NY Metropolitan Statistical Area—see Appendix B for areas included
Source: Bureau of Labor Statistics, Local Area Unemployment Statistics

Average Wages

Occupation	$/Hr.	Occupation	$/Hr.
Accountants and Auditors	36.40	Maids and Housekeeping Cleaners	11.50
Automotive Mechanics	19.20	Maintenance and Repair Workers	20.30
Bookkeepers	19.90	Marketing Managers	76.40
Carpenters	24.60	Nuclear Medicine Technologists	41.20
Cashiers	11.10	Nurses, Licensed Practical	20.10
Clerks, General Office	16.70	Nurses, Registered	32.20
Clerks, Receptionists/Information	15.30	Nursing Assistants	13.50
Clerks, Shipping/Receiving	16.80	Packers and Packagers, Hand	16.40
Computer Programmers	37.30	Physical Therapists	37.30
Computer Systems Analysts	38.30	Postal Service Mail Carriers	23.80
Computer User Support Specialists	25.00	Real Estate Brokers	n/a
Cooks, Restaurant	13.20	Retail Salespersons	13.20
Dentists	89.60	Sales Reps., Exc. Tech./Scientific	31.90
Electrical Engineers	50.20	Sales Reps., Tech./Scientific	47.30
Electricians	29.50	Secretaries, Exc. Legal/Med./Exec.	19.40
Financial Managers	67.50	Security Guards	16.60
First-Line Supervisors/Managers, Sales	20.40	Surgeons	129.90
Food Preparation Workers	12.60	Teacher Assistants*	14.40
General and Operations Managers	60.10	Teachers, Elementary School*	30.20
Hairdressers/Cosmetologists	14.40	Teachers, Secondary School*	34.40
Internists, General	122.60	Telemarketers	12.90
Janitors and Cleaners	13.50	Truck Drivers, Heavy/Tractor-Trailer	20.60
Landscaping/Groundskeeping Workers	15.20	Truck Drivers, Light/Delivery Svcs.	17.70
Lawyers	52.30	Waiters and Waitresses	13.10

Note: Wage data covers the Albany-Schenectady-Troy, NY Metropolitan Statistical Area—see Appendix B for areas included; (*) Hourly wages for elementary/secondary school teachers and teacher assistants were calculated by the editors from annual wage data based on a 40 hour work week; n/a not available.
Source: Bureau of Labor Statistics, Metro Area Occupational Employment & Wage Estimates, May 2017

Employment by Occupation

Occupation Classification	City (%)	MSA[1] (%)	U.S. (%)
Management, Business, Science, and Arts	58.2	41.9	37.0
Natural Resources, Construction, and Maintenance	4.2	7.1	8.9
Production, Transportation, and Material Moving	4.8	8.9	12.2
Sales and Office	21.7	25.2	23.8
Service	11.1	16.9	18.1

Note: Figures cover employed civilians 16 years of age and older; (1) Figures cover the Albany-Schenectady-Troy, NY Metropolitan Statistical Area—see Appendix B for areas included
Source: U.S. Census Bureau, 2012-2016 American Community Survey 5-Year Estimates

Employment by Industry

Sector	MSA[1] Number of Employees	MSA[1] Percent of Total	U.S. Percent of Total
Construction, Mining, and Logging	18,900	4.0	5.2
Education and Health Services	97,700	20.5	15.9
Financial Activities	26,000	5.5	5.7
Government	103,500	21.7	15.3
Information	8,400	1.8	1.9
Leisure and Hospitality	41,700	8.7	10.7
Manufacturing	26,700	5.6	8.5
Other Services	19,200	4.0	3.9
Professional and Business Services	56,800	11.9	14.0
Retail Trade	50,200	10.5	11.0
Transportation, Warehousing, and Utilities	14,200	3.0	4.1
Wholesale Trade	13,600	2.9	4.0

Note: Figures are non-farm employment as of December 2017. Figures are not seasonally adjusted and include workers 16 years of age and older; (1) Figures cover the Albany-Schenectady-Troy, NY Metropolitan Statistical Area—see Appendix B for areas included
Source: Bureau of Labor Statistics, Current Employment Statistics, Employment, Hours, and Earnings

Occupations with Greatest Projected Employment Growth: 2017 – 2019

Occupation[1]	2017 Employment	2019 Projected Employment	Numeric Employment Change	Percent Employment Change
Home Health Aides	190,490	216,300	25,810	13.5
Personal Care Aides	174,700	189,420	14,720	8.4
Combined Food Preparation and Serving Workers, Including Fast Food	154,570	162,110	7,540	4.9
Registered Nurses	189,840	197,230	7,390	3.9
Janitors and Cleaners, Except Maids and Housekeeping Cleaners	211,280	217,380	6,100	2.9
Waiters and Waitresses	151,380	156,430	5,050	3.3
General and Operations Managers	165,860	169,970	4,110	2.5
Accountants and Auditors	124,740	128,070	3,330	2.7
Software Developers, Applications	52,730	55,940	3,210	6.1
Security Guards	114,180	117,140	2,960	2.6

Note: Projections cover New York; (1) Sorted by numeric employment change
Source: www.projectionscentral.com, State Occupational Projections, 2017–2019 Short-Term Projections

Fastest Growing Occupations: 2017 – 2019

Occupation[1]	2017 Employment	2019 Projected Employment	Numeric Employment Change	Percent Employment Change
Gaming and Sports Book Writers and Runners	660	810	150	24.0
Gaming Change Persons and Booth Cashiers	840	1,030	190	22.7
Solar Photovoltaic Installers	800	980	180	22.7
Gaming Dealers	960	1,150	190	19.4
Home Health Aides	190,490	216,300	25,810	13.5
Gaming Supervisors	580	660	80	12.3
Entertainment Attendants and Related Workers, All Other	490	540	50	9.8
Personal Care Aides	174,700	189,420	14,720	8.4
Physical Therapist Aides	3,110	3,330	220	6.9
Physical Therapists	18,480	19,750	1,270	6.9

Note: Projections cover New York; (1) Sorted by percent employment change and excludes occupations with numeric employment change less than 50
Source: www.projectionscentral.com, State Occupational Projections, 2017–2019 Short-Term Projections

TAXES

State Corporate Income Tax Rates

State	Tax Rate (%)	Income Brackets ($)	Num. of Brackets	Financial Institution Tax Rate (%)[a]	Federal Income Tax Ded.
New York	6.5 (r)	Flat rate	1	6.5 (r)	No

Note: Tax rates as of January 1, 2018; (a) Rates listed are the corporate income tax rate applied to financial institutions or excise taxes based on income. Some states have other taxes based upon the value of deposits or shares; (r) New York's General business corporate rate shown. Corporations may also be subject to a capital stocks tax, which is being phased out through 2021. A minimum tax ranges from $25 to $200,000, depending on receipts ($250 minimum for banks). Certain qualified New York manufacturers pay 0%.
Source: Federation of Tax Administrators, Range of State Corporate Income Tax Rates, January 1, 2018

State Individual Income Tax Rates

State	Tax Rate (%)	Income Brackets ($)	Num. of Brackets	Personal Exempt. ($)[1]		Fed. Inc. Tax Ded.
				Single	Dependents	
New York (a)	4.0 - 8.82	8,500 - 1,077,550 (b)	8	0	1,000	No

Note: Tax rates as of January 1, 2018; Local- and county-level taxes are not included; n/a not applicable; (1) Married joint filers generally receive double the single exemption; (a) 19 states have statutory provision for automatically adjusting to the rate of inflation the dollar values of the income tax brackets, standard deductions, and/or personal exemptions. Massachusetts, Michigan, and Nebraska index the personal exemption only. Oregon does not index the income brackets for $125,000 and over; (b) For joint returns, taxes are twice the tax on half the couple's income.
Source: Federation of Tax Administrators, State Individual Income Tax Rates, January 1, 2018

Various State Sales and Excise Tax Rates

State	State Sales Tax (%)	Gasoline[1] (¢/gal.)	Cigarette[2] ($/pack)	Spirits[3] ($/gal.)	Wine[4] ($/gal.)	Beer[5] ($/gal.)	Recreational Marijuana (%)
New York	4.0	44.3	4.35	6.44 (f)	0.30	0.14	Not legal

Note: All tax rates as of January 1, 2018; (1) The American Petroleum Institute has developed a methodology for determining the average tax rate on a gallon of fuel. Rates may include any of the following: excise taxes, environmental fees, storage tank fees, other fees or taxes, general sales tax, and local taxes. In states where gasoline is subject to the general sales tax, or where the fuel tax is based on the average sale price, the average rate determined by API is sensitive to changes in the price of gasoline. States that fully or partially apply general sales taxes to gasoline: CA, CO, GA, IL, IN, MI, NY; (2) The federal excise tax of $1.0066 per pack and local taxes are not included; (3) Rates are those applicable to off-premise sales of 40% alcohol by volume (a.b.v.) distilled spirits in 750ml containers. Local excise taxes are excluded; (4) Rates are those applicable to off-premise sales of 11% a.b.v. non-carbonated wine in 750ml containers; (5) Rates are those applicable to off-premise sales of 4.7% a.b.v. beer in 12 ounce containers; (f) Different rates also applicable according to alcohol content, place of production, size of container, or place purchased (on- or off-premise or onboard airlines).
Source: Tax Foundation, 2018 Facts & Figures: How Does Your State Compare?

State Business Tax Climate Index Rankings

State	Overall Rank	Corporate Tax Rank	Individual Income Tax Rank	Sales Tax Rank	Unemployment Insurance Tax Rank	Property Tax Rank
New York	49	7	49	43	30	47

Note: The index is a measure of how each state's tax laws affect economic performance. The lower the rank, the more favorable a state's tax system is for business. States without a given tax are given a ranking of 1. The scores/rankings for the District of Columbia do not affect other states. The 2018 index represents the tax climate as of July 1, 2017.
Source: Tax Foundation, State Business Tax Climate Index 2018

TRANSPORTATION

Means of Transportation to Work

Area	Car/Truck/Van		Public Transportation			Bicycle	Walked	Other Means	Worked at Home
	Drove Alone	Car-pooled	Bus	Subway	Railroad				
City	84.3	6.0	1.2	0.0	0.2	0.1	1.0	0.9	6.3
MSA[1]	79.8	7.9	3.3	0.1	0.1	0.3	3.7	0.9	4.0
U.S.	76.4	9.3	2.6	1.9	0.6	0.6	2.8	1.3	4.6

Note: Figures are percentages and cover workers 16 years of age and older; (1) Figures cover the Albany-Schenectady-Troy, NY Metropolitan Statistical Area—see Appendix B for areas included
Source: U.S. Census Bureau, 2012-2016 American Community Survey 5-Year Estimates

Travel Time to Work

Area	Less Than 10 Minutes	10 to 19 Minutes	20 to 29 Minutes	30 to 44 Minutes	45 to 59 Minutes	60 to 89 Minutes	90 Minutes or More
City	10.9	36.4	32.1	14.6	2.9	1.9	1.2
MSA[1]	12.9	32.3	24.6	20.4	5.8	2.6	1.4
U.S.	12.9	29.2	20.9	20.4	8.0	6.0	2.7

Note: Note: Figures are percentages and include workers 16 years old and over; (1) Figures cover the Albany-Schenectady-Troy, NY Metropolitan Statistical Area—see Appendix B for areas included
Source: U.S. Census Bureau, 2012-2016 American Community Survey 5-Year Estimates

Freeway Travel Time Index

Area	1985	1990	1995	2000	2005	2010	2014
Urban Area Rank[1,2]	81	86	84	77	61	57	54
Urban Area Index[1]	1.04	1.06	1.08	1.12	1.16	1.16	1.17
Average Index[3]	1.09	1.11	1.14	1.17	1.20	1.19	1.20

Note: Freeway Travel Time Index—the ratio of travel time in the peak period to the travel time at free-flow conditions. For example, a value of 1.30 indicates a 20-minute free-flow trip takes 26 minutes in the peak (20 minutes x 1.30 = 26 minutes); (1) Covers the Albany-Schenectady NY urban area; (2) Rank is based on 101 urban areas (#1 = highest travel time index); (3) Average of 101 urban areas
Source: Texas Transportation Institute, 2015 Urban Mobility Scorecard, August 2015

Freeway Commuter Stress Index

Area	1985	1990	1995	2000	2005	2010	2014
Urban Area Rank[1,2]	91	84	88	85	68	74	71
Urban Area Index[1]	1.05	1.08	1.10	1.13	1.18	1.17	1.18
Average Index[3]	1.13	1.16	1.19	1.22	1.25	1.24	1.25

Note: The Freeway Commuter Stress Index is the same as the Freeway Travel Time Index (see table above) except that it includes only the travel in the peak directions during the peak periods; the TTI includes travel in all directions during the peak period. Thus, the CSI is more indicative of the work trip experienced by each commuter on a daily basis; (1) Covers the Albany-Schenectady NY urban area; (2) Rank is based on 101 urban areas (#1 = highest travel time index); (3) Average of 101 urban areas
Source: Texas Transportation Institute, 2015 Urban Mobility Scorecard, August 2015

Living Environment

COST OF LIVING

Cost of Living Index

Composite Index	Groceries	Housing	Utilities	Trans-portation	Health Care	Misc. Goods/ Services
107.3	107.7	115.8	98.4	104.8	99.1	104.6

Note: The Cost of Living Index measures regional differences in the cost of consumer goods and services, excluding taxes and non-consumer expenditures, for professional and managerial households in the top income quintile. It is based on more than 50,000 prices covering almost 60 different items for which prices are collected three times a year by chambers of commerce, economic development organizations or university applied economic centers in each participating urban area. The numbers shown should be read as a percentage above or below the national average of 100. For example, a value of 115.4 in the groceries column indicates that grocery prices are 15.4% higher than the national average. Small differences in the index numbers should not be interpreted as significant; Figures cover the Albany NY urban area.
Source: The Council for Community and Economic Research, ACCRA Cost of Living Index, 2017

Grocery Prices

Area[1]	T-Bone Steak ($/pound)	Frying Chicken ($/pound)	Whole Milk ($/half gal.)	Eggs ($/dozen)	Orange Juice ($/64 oz.)	Coffee ($/11.5 oz.)
City[2]	11.52	1.40	2.32	1.66	3.30	3.97
Avg.	11.29	1.40	2.02	1.47	3.55	4.37
Min.	7.71	0.93	1.04	0.70	2.86	3.24
Max.	15.83	2.39	4.03	3.92	6.29	8.16

*Note: (1) Values for the local area are compared with the average, minimum and maximum values for all 294 areas in the Cost of Living Index; (2) Figures cover the Albany NY urban area; **T-Bone Steak** (price per pound); **Frying Chicken** (price per pound, whole fryer); **Whole Milk** (half gallon carton); **Eggs** (price per dozen, Grade A, large); **Orange Juice** (64 oz. Tropicana or Florida Natural); **Coffee** (11.5 oz. can, vacuum-packed, Maxwell House, Hills Bros, or Folgers).*
Source: The Council for Community and Economic Research, ACCRA Cost of Living Index, 2017

Housing and Utility Costs

Area[1]	New Home Price ($)	Apartment Rent ($/month)	All Electric ($/month)	Part Electric ($/month)	Other Energy ($/month)	Telephone ($/month)
City[2]	389,074	1,207	-	82.48	66.79	31.34
Avg.	335,956	1,047	175.01	97.34	67.93	28.71
Min.	187,788	491	109.48	49.33	35.44	12.39
Max.	1,739,087	4,559	432.62	227.09	353.33	44.61

*Note: (1) Values for the local area are compared with the average, minimum and maximum values for all 294 areas in the Cost of Living Index; (2) Figures cover the Albany NY urban area; **New Home Price** (2,400 sf living area, 8,000 sf lot, in urban area with full utilities); **Apartment Rent** (950 sf 2 bedroom/1.5 or 2 bath, unfurnished, excluding all utilities except water); **All Electric** (average monthly cost for an all-electric home); **Part Electric** (average monthly cost for a part-electric home); **Other Energy** (average monthly cost for natural gas, fuel oil, coal, wood, and any other forms of energy except electricity); **Telephone** (price includes basic monthly rate for a private residential line plus additional local usage charges incurred by a family of four).*
Source: The Council for Community and Economic Research, ACCRA Cost of Living Index, 2017

Health Care, Transportation, and Other Costs

Area[1]	Doctor ($/visit)	Dentist ($/visit)	Optometrist ($/visit)	Gasoline ($/gallon)	Beauty Salon ($/visit)	Men's Shirt ($)
City[2]	102.72	93.90	99.72	2.35	30.79	28.31
Avg.	108.00	92.54	101.93	2.25	37.58	30.92
Min.	30.39	60.00	49.75	1.82	16.11	11.20
Max.	193.50	161.94	229.28	3.16	77.35	59.13

*Note: (1) Values for the local area are compared with the average, minimum and maximum values for all 294 areas in the Cost of Living Index; (2) Figures cover the Albany NY urban area; **Doctor** (general practitioners routine exam of an established patient); **Dentist** (adult teeth cleaning and periodic oral examination); **Optometrist** (full vision eye exam for established adult patient); **Gasoline** (one gallon regular unleaded, national brand, including all taxes, cash price at self-service pump if available); **Beauty Salon** (woman's shampoo, trim, and blow-dry); **Men's Shirt** (cotton/polyester dress shirt, pinpoint weave, long sleeves).*
Source: The Council for Community and Economic Research, ACCRA Cost of Living Index, 2017

HOUSING

House Price Index (HPI)

Area	National Ranking[2]	Quarterly Change (%)	One-Year Change (%)	Five-Year Change (%)
MSA[1]	192	0.96	3.96	9.14
U.S.[3]	–	1.61	6.68	34.71

Note: The HPI is a weighted repeat sales index. It measures average price changes in repeat sales or refinancings on the same properties. This information is obtained by reviewing repeat mortgage transactions on single-family properties whose mortgages have been purchased or securitized by Fannie Mae or Freddie Mac in January 1975; (1) Figures cover the Albany-Schenectady-Troy, NY Metropolitan Statistical Area—see Appendix B for areas included; (2) Rankings are based on annual percentage change for all metro areas containing at least 15,000 transactions over the last 10 years and ranges from 1 to 253; (3) figures based on a weighted average of Census Division estimates using a seasonally adjusted, purchase-only index; all figures are for the period ending December 31, 2017
Source: Federal Housing Finance Agency, House Price Index, February 28, 2018

Median Single-Family Home Prices

Area	2015	2016	2017p	Percent Change 2016 to 2017
MSA[1]	206.3	203.7	205.3	0.8
U.S. Average	223.9	235.5	248.8	5.6

Note: Figures are median sales prices of existing single-family homes in thousands of dollars; (p) preliminary; (1) Figures cover the Albany-Schenectady-Troy, NY Metropolitan Statistical Area—see Appendix B for areas included
Source: National Association of Realtors, Median Sales Price of Existing Single-Family Homes for Metropolitan Areas, 4th Quarter 2017

Qualifying Income Based on Median Sales Price of Existing Single-Family Homes

Area	With 5% Down ($)	With 10% Down ($)	With 20% Down ($)
MSA[1]	44,010	41,694	37,061
U.S. Average	55,585	52,659	46,808

Note: Figures are preliminary; Qualifying income is based on a mortgage rate of 4.17%. Monthly principal and interest payment is limited to 25% of income; (1) Figures cover the Albany-Schenectady-Troy, NY Metropolitan Statistical Area—see Appendix B for areas included
Source: National Association of Realtors, Qualifying Income Based on Median Sales Price of Existing Single-Family Homes for Metropolitan Areas, 4th Quarter 2017

Median Apartment Condo-Coop Home Prices

Area	2015	2016	2017p	Percent Change 2016 to 2017
MSA[1]	n/a	n/a	n/a	n/a
U.S. Average	210.7	220.7	234.3	6.2

Note: Figures are median sales prices of existing apartment condo-coop homes in thousands of dollars; (p) preliminary; n/a not available; (1) Figures cover the Albany-Schenectady-Troy, NY Metropolitan Statistical Area—see Appendix B for areas included
Source: National Association of Realtors, Median Sales Price of Existing Apartment Condo-Coop Homes for Metropolitan Areas, 4th Quarter 2017

Home Value Distribution

Area	Under $50,000	$50,000 -$99,999	$100,000 -$149,999	$150,000 -$199,999	$200,000 -$299,999	$300,000 -$499,999	$500,000 -$999,999	$1,000,000 or more
City	3.0	0.9	3.6	15.7	38.4	32.3	5.4	0.6
MSA[1]	5.2	8.1	14.3	22.3	29.1	17.1	3.4	0.5
U.S.	8.8	14.8	15.3	14.9	18.4	16.4	9.0	2.5

Note: Figures are percentages and cover owner-occupied housing units; (1) Figures cover the Albany-Schenectady-Troy, NY Metropolitan Statistical Area—see Appendix B for areas included
Source: U.S. Census Bureau, 2012-2016 American Community Survey 5-Year Estimates

Homeownership Rate

Area	2009 (%)	2010 (%)	2011 (%)	2012 (%)	2013 (%)	2014 (%)	2015 (%)	2016 (%)	2017 (%)
MSA[1]	71.1	72.8	72.4	70.6	67.9	67.5	65.9	61.3	64.1
U.S.	67.4	66.9	66.1	65.4	65.1	64.5	63.7	63.4	63.9

Note: (1) Figures cover the Albany-Schenectady-Troy, NY Metropolitan Statistical Area—see Appendix B for areas included
Source: U.S. Census Bureau, Housing Vacancies and Homeownership Annual Statistics: 2009-2017

Year Housing Structure Built

Area	2010 or Later	2000 -2009	1990 -1999	1980 -1989	1970 -1979	1960 -1969	1950 -1959	1940 -1949	Before 1940	Median Year
City	2.1	11.1	15.5	14.0	11.7	10.8	12.5	6.8	15.5	1974
MSA[1]	2.0	8.8	9.9	11.1	12.2	9.3	10.7	6.1	30.0	1963
U.S.	2.3	14.7	14.0	13.7	15.6	10.9	10.6	5.2	13.0	1977

Note: Figures are percentages except for Median Year; Note: (1) Figures cover the Albany-Schenectady-Troy, NY Metropolitan Statistical Area—see Appendix B for areas included
Source: U.S. Census Bureau, 2012-2016 American Community Survey 5-Year Estimates

Gross Monthly Rent

Area	Under $500	$500 -$999	$1,000 -$1,499	$1,500 -$1,999	$2,000 -$2,499	$2,500 -$2,999	$3,000 and up	Median ($)
City	1.9	40.3	42.0	9.6	3.8	1.0	1.4	1,098
MSA[1]	9.6	49.9	30.7	6.9	1.8	0.6	0.5	923
U.S.	11.3	43.3	27.7	10.7	4.0	1.6	1.5	949

Note: Figures are percentages except for Median; Gross rent is the contract rent plus the estimated average monthly cost of utilities (electricity, gas, and water and sewer) and fuels (oil, coal, kerosene, wood, etc.) if these are paid by the renter (or paid for the renter by someone else); (1) Figures cover the Albany-Schenectady-Troy, NY Metropolitan Statistical Area—see Appendix B for areas included
Source: U.S. Census Bureau, 2012-2016 American Community Survey 5-Year Estimates

HEALTH

Health Risk Factors

Category	MSA[1] (%)	U.S. (%)
Adults aged 18–64 who have any kind of health care coverage	94.0	87.7
Adults who reported being in good or excellent health	85.9	83.6
Adults who are current smokers	16.7	17.1
Adults who currently use E-cigarettes	4.1	4.7
Adults who currently use chewing tobacco, snuff, or snus	2.7	4.0
Adults who are heavy drinkers[2]	6.7	6.5
Adults who are binge drinkers[3]	17.4	16.9
Adults who are overweight (BMI 25.0 - 29.9)	36.0	35.3
Adults who are obese (BMI 30.0 - 99.8)	27.6	29.9
Adults who participated in any physical activities in the past month	77.9	76.9
Adults who always or nearly always wears a seat belt	96.8	94.3

Note: (1) Figures cover the Albany-Schenectady-Troy, NY Metropolitan Statistical Area—see Appendix B for areas included; (2) Heavy drinkers are classified as adult men having more than 14 drinks per week and adult women having more than 7 drinks per week; (3) Binge drinkers are classified as males having five or more drinks on one occasion or females having four or more drinks on one occasion
Source: Centers for Disease Control and Prevention, Behaviorial Risk Factor Surveillance System, SMART: Selected Metropolitan Area Risk Trends, 2016

Health Screening Rates

Category	MSA[1] (%)	U.S. (%)
Adults 50-75 who have had a blood stool test within the past year	9.1	8.0
Adults 50-75 who have had a colonoscopy in the past 10 years	74.6	63.5
Adults aged 65+ who have had flu shot within the past year	60.6	58.6
Adults aged 65+ who have ever had a pneumonia vaccination	75.0	73.4
Adults who have ever been tested for HIV	44.7	35.6
Women aged 21-65 who have had a pap test in the past three years	81.8	79.8
Men aged 40+ who have had a PSA test within the past two years	39.9	39.5
Women aged 40+ who have had a mammogram within the past two years	72.5	72.5

Note: (1) Figures cover the Albany-Schenectady-Troy, NY Metropolitan Statistical Area—see Appendix B for areas included; Source: Centers for Disease Control and Prevention, Behaviorial Risk Factor Surveillance System, SMART: Selected Metropolitan Area Risk Trends, 2016

Chronic Health Conditions

Category	MSA[1] (%)	U.S. (%)
Adults who have ever been told they had a heart attack	4.8	4.4
Adults who have ever been told they have angina or coronary heart disease	4.8	4.1
Adults who have ever been told they had a stroke	3.0	3.1
Adults who have been told they currently have asthma	12.7	9.3
Adults who have ever been told they have arthritis	26.9	25.8
Adults who have ever been told they have diabetes[2]	8.8	10.5
Adults who have ever been told they had skin cancer	4.3	5.9
Adults who have ever been told they had any other types of cancer	6.7	6.7
Adults who have ever been told they have COPD	6.4	6.3
Adults who have ever been told they have kidney disease	2.8	2.8
Adults who have ever been told they have a form of depression	15.1	17.4

Note: (1) Figures cover the Albany-Schenectady-Troy, NY Metropolitan Statistical Area—see Appendix B for areas included; (2) Figures do not include pregnancy-related, borderline, or pre-diabetes
Source: Centers for Disease Control and Prevention, Behaviorial Risk Factor Surveillance System, SMART: Selected Metropolitan Area Risk Trends, 2016

Mortality Rates for the Top 10 Causes of Death in the U.S.

ICD-10[a] Sub-Chapter	ICD-10[a] Code	Age-Adjusted Mortality Rate[1] per 100,000 population	
		County[2]	U.S.
Malignant neoplasms	C00-C97	158.0	158.5
Ischaemic heart diseases	I20-I25	100.4	96.8
Other forms of heart disease	I30-I51	59.7	52.4
Chronic lower respiratory diseases	J40-J47	35.0	40.9
Cerebrovascular diseases	I60-I69	27.2	37.2
Organic, including symptomatic, mental disorders	F01-F09	32.3	33.3
Other degenerative diseases of the nervous system	G30-G31	21.2	32.1
Other external causes of accidental injury	W00-X59	13.5	31.2
Diabetes mellitus	E10-E14	13.4	21.1
Hypertensive diseases	I10-I15	16.1	20.8

Note: (a) ICD-10 = International Classification of Diseases 10th Revision; (1) Mortality rates are a three year average covering 2014-2016; (2) Figures cover Albany County.
Source: Centers for Disease Control and Prevention, National Center for Health Statistics. Underlying Cause of Death 1999-2016 on CDC WONDER Online Database, released December 2017

Mortality Rates for Selected Causes of Death

ICD-10[a] Sub-Chapter	ICD-10[a] Code	Age-Adjusted Mortality Rate[1] per 100,000 population	
		County[2]	U.S.
Assault	X85-Y09	2.7	5.6
Diseases of the liver	K70-K76	10.7	14.0
Human immunodeficiency virus (HIV) disease	B20-B24	Unreliable	1.9
Influenza and pneumonia	J09-J18	13.6	14.6
Intentional self-harm	X60-X84	8.6	13.2
Malnutrition	E40-E46	Unreliable	1.3
Obesity and other hyperalimentation	E65-E68	Unreliable	2.1
Renal failure	N17-N19	12.9	13.0
Transport accidents	V01-V99	6.3	12.0
Viral hepatitis	B15-B19	1.6	1.9

Note: (a) ICD-10 = International Classification of Diseases 10th Revision; (1) Mortality rates are a three year average covering 2014-2016; (2) Figures cover Albany County; Data are Suppressed when the data meet the criteria for confidentiality constraints; Mortality rates are flagged as Unreliable when the rate would be calculated with a numerator of 20 or less.
Source: Centers for Disease Control and Prevention, National Center for Health Statistics. Underlying Cause of Death 1999-2016 on CDC WONDER Online Database, released December 2017

Health Insurance Coverage

Area	With Health Insurance	With Private Health Insurance	With Public Health Insurance	Without Health Insurance	Population Under Age 18 Without Health Insurance
City	97.3	90.2	22.8	2.7	1.8
MSA[1]	94.8	77.3	31.8	5.2	2.1
U.S.	88.3	66.7	33.0	11.7	5.9

Note: Figures are percentages that cover the civilian noninstitutionalized population; (1) Figures cover the Albany-Schenectady-Troy, NY Metropolitan Statistical Area—see Appendix B for areas included
Source: U.S. Census Bureau, 2012-2016 American Community Survey 5-Year Estimates

Number of Medical Professionals

Area	MDs[3]	DOs[3,4]	Dentists	Podiatrists	Chiropractors	Optometrists
County[1] (number)	1,748	120	276	26	59	50
County[1] (rate[2])	566.4	38.9	89.3	8.4	19.1	16.2
U.S. (rate[2])	276.5	22.3	67.3	6.0	26.7	15.9

Note: Data as of 2016 unless noted; (1) Data covers Albany County; (2) Rate per 100,000 population; (3) Data as of 2015 and includes all active, non-federal physicians; (4) Doctor of Osteopathic Medicine
Source: U.S. Department of Health and Human Services, Health Resources and Services Administration, Bureau of Health Professions, Area Resource File (ARF) 2016-2017

EDUCATION

Public School District Statistics

District Name	Schls	Pupils	Pupil/ Teacher Ratio	Minority Pupils[1] (%)	Free Lunch Eligible[2] (%)	IEP[3] (%)
Bethlehem Central School District	7	4,622	14.1	12.9	9.0	12.6
Ravena-Coeymans-Selkirk Central SD	4	1,878	9.5	16.3	35.8	16.0

Note: Table includes school districts with 100 or more students; (1) Percentage of students that are not non-Hispanic white; (2) Percentage of students that are eligible for the free lunch program; (3) Percentage of students that have an Individualized Education Program.
Source: U.S. Department of Education, National Center for Education Statistics, Common Core of Data, Local Education Agency (School District) Universe Survey: School Year 2015-2016; U.S. Department of Education, National Center for Education Statistics, Common Core of Data, Public Elementary/Secondary School Universe Survey: School Year 2015-2016

Highest Level of Education

Area	Less than H.S.	H.S. Diploma	Some College, No Deg.	Associate Degree	Bachelor's Degree	Master's Degree	Prof. School Degree	Doctorate Degree
City	3.0	16.2	12.0	10.1	25.1	22.4	7.8	3.5
MSA[1]	7.8	27.3	17.3	12.1	19.7	11.7	2.2	1.9
U.S.	13.0	27.5	21.0	8.2	18.8	8.2	2.0	1.3

Note: Figures cover persons age 25 and over; (1) Figures cover the Albany-Schenectady-Troy, NY Metropolitan Statistical Area—see Appendix B for areas included
Source: U.S. Census Bureau, 2012-2016 American Community Survey 5-Year Estimates

Educational Attainment by Race

Area	High School Graduate or Higher (%)					Bachelor's Degree or Higher (%)				
	Total	White	Black	Asian	Hisp.[2]	Total	White	Black	Asian	Hisp.[2]
City	97.0	97.7	82.0	93.3	85.1	58.7	58.7	35.0	79.5	43.2
MSA[1]	92.2	93.3	86.1	87.4	80.7	35.5	36.2	18.0	61.7	26.3
U.S.	87.0	88.9	84.3	86.3	65.7	30.3	31.6	20.0	52.1	14.7

Note: Figures shown cover persons 25 years old and over; (1) Figures cover the Albany-Schenectady-Troy, NY Metropolitan Statistical Area—see Appendix B for areas included; (2) People of Hispanic origin can be of any race
Source: U.S. Census Bureau, 2012-2016 American Community Survey 5-Year Estimates

School Enrollment by Grade and Control

Area	Preschool (%)		Kindergarten (%)		Grades 1 - 4 (%)		Grades 5 - 8 (%)		Grades 9 - 12 (%)	
	Public	Private	Public	Private	Public	Private	Public	Private	Public	Private
City	37.2	62.8	94.4	5.6	92.1	7.9	94.1	5.9	87.1	12.9
MSA[1]	47.9	52.1	88.0	12.0	91.0	9.0	91.3	8.7	91.1	8.9
U.S.	58.4	41.6	87.7	12.3	89.8	10.2	89.7	10.3	90.4	9.6

Note: Figures shown cover persons 3 years old and over; (1) Figures cover the Albany-Schenectady-Troy, NY Metropolitan Statistical Area—see Appendix B for areas included
Source: U.S. Census Bureau, 2012-2016 American Community Survey 5-Year Estimates

Average Salaries of Public School Classroom Teachers

Area	2015		2016		Change from 2015 to 2016	
	Dollars	Rank[1]	Dollars	Rank[1]	Percent	Rank[2]
New York	77,628	1	79,152	1	2.0	12
U.S. Average	57,611	–	58,353	–	1.3	–

Note: (1) Rank ranges from 1 to 51 where 1 indicates highest salary; (2) Rank ranges from 1 to 51 where 1 indicates highest percent change.
Source: National Education Association, Rankings & Estimates: Rankings of the States 2016 and Estimates of School Statistics 2017

Higher Education

Four-Year Colleges			Two-Year Colleges			Medical Schools[1]	Law Schools[2]	Voc/ Tech[3]
Public	Private Non-profit	Private For-profit	Public	Private Non-profit	Private For-profit			
0	0	0	0	0	0	0	0	0

Note: Figures cover institutions located within the city limits and include main campuses only; (1) includes schools accredited by the Liaison Committee on Medical Education and the American Osteopathic Association's Commission on Osteopathic College Accreditation; (2) includes ABA-accredited schools, schools with provisional ABA accreditation, and state accredited schools; (3) includes all schools with programs that are less than 2 years.
Source: National Center for Education Statistics, Integrated Postsecondary Education System (IPEDS), 2016-17; Wikipedia, List of Medical Schools in the United States, accessed April 2, 2018; Wikipedia, List of Law Schools in the United States, accessed April 2, 2018

According to *U.S. News & World Report,* the Albany-Schenectady-Troy, NY metro area is home to two of the best national universities in the U.S.: **Rensselaer Polytechnic Institute** (#42 tie); **University at Albany—SUNY** (#151 tie). The indicators used to capture academic quality fall into a number of categories: assessment by administrators at peer institutions; retention of students; faculty resources; student selectivity; financial resources; alumni giving; high school counselor ratings of colleges; and graduation rate. *U.S. News & World Report, "America's Best Colleges 2018"*

According to *U.S. News & World Report,* the Albany-Schenectady-Troy, NY metro area is home to two of the best liberal arts colleges in the U.S.: **Union College** (#36 tie); **Skidmore College** (#41 tie). The indicators used to capture academic quality fall into a number of categories: assessment by administrators at peer institutions; retention of students; faculty resources; student selectivity; financial resources; alumni giving; high school counselor ratings of colleges; and graduation rate. *U.S. News & World Report, "America's Best Colleges 2018"*

PRESIDENTIAL ELECTION

2016 Presidential Election Results

Area	Clinton	Trump	Johnson	Stein	Other
Albany County	59.4	34.2	3.4	1.8	1.2
U.S.	48.0	45.9	3.3	1.1	1.7

Note: Results are percentages and may not add to 100% due to rounding
Source: Dave Leip's Atlas of U.S. Presidential Elections

EMPLOYERS

Major Employers

Company Name	Industry
Albany Medical Center	Health care
Bechtel Marine Propulsion Corp.	Nuclear propulsion technology
Center For Disability Services	Disability services
County of Albany	County government
Ellis Hospital	Health care
General Electric Co.	Multinational conglomerate
GlobalFoundries	Semiconductor foundry
Hannaford Supermarkets	Grocery stores
Price Chopper	Retailing and restaurants
St. Peter's Hospital	Health care
State of New York	State government
United States Government	Federal government
Wal-Mart Stores	Retail stores

Note: Companies shown are located within the Albany-Schenectady-Troy, NY Metropolitan Statistical Area.
Source: Hoovers.com; Wikipedia

PUBLIC SAFETY

Crime Rate

Area	All Crimes	Violent Crimes				Property Crimes		
		Murder	Rape[3]	Robbery	Aggrav. Assault	Burglary	Larceny -Theft	Motor Vehicle Theft
City	1,394.1	0.0	31.3	5.7	25.6	150.8	1,163.7	17.1
Metro[1]	2,299.2	2.0	38.9	68.7	180.0	281.5	1,646.0	82.0
U.S.	2,847.8	5.3	40.4	102.8	248.5	468.9	1,745.0	236.9

Note: Figures are crimes per 100,000 population; (1) Figures cover the Albany-Schenectady-Troy, NY Metropolitan Statistical Area—see Appendix B for areas included; (3) The city and U.S. figures shown were reported using the revised Uniform Crime Reporting (UCR) definition of rape. The metro area figures shown are an aggregate total of the data submitted using both the revised and legacy UCR definitions.
Source: FBI Uniform Crime Reports, 2016

Hate Crimes

Area	Number of Quarters Reported	Number of Incidents per Bias Motivation					
		Race/Ethnicity/ Ancestry	Religion	Sexual Orientation	Disability	Gender	Gender Identity
Area[1]	4	0	0	0	0	0	0
U.S.	4	3,489	1,273	1,076	70	31	124

Note: (1) Figures cover the Bethlehem Town.
Source: Federal Bureau of Investigation, Hate Crime Statistics 2016

Identity Theft Consumer Reports

Area	Reports	Reports per 100,000 Population	Rank[2]
MSA[1]	595	67	271
U.S.	371,061	114	-

Note: (1) Figures cover the Albany-Schenectady-Troy, NY Metropolitan Statistical Area—see Appendix B for areas included; (2) Rank ranges from 1 to 389 where 1 indicates greatest number of identity theft reports per 100,000 population
Source: Federal Trade Commission, Consumer Sentinel Network Data Book for January–December 2017

Fraud and Other Consumer Reports

Area	Reports	Reports per 100,000 Population	Rank[2]
MSA[1]	3,908	443	187
U.S.	2,304,550	708	-

Note: (1) Figures cover the Albany-Schenectady-Troy, NY Metropolitan Statistical Area—see Appendix B for areas included; (2) Rank ranges from 1 to 389 where 1 indicates greatest number of fraud and other consumer reports per 100,000 population
Source: Federal Trade Commission, Consumer Sentinel Network Data Book for January–December 2017

SPORTS

Professional Sports Teams

Team Name	League	Year Established
No teams are located in the metro area		

Source: Wikipedia, Major Professional Sports Teams of the United States and Canada, April 5, 2018

CLIMATE

Average and Extreme Temperatures

Temperature	Jan	Feb	Mar	Apr	May	Jun	Jul	Aug	Sep	Oct	Nov	Dec	Yr.
Extreme High (°F)	64	67	86	92	94	99	100	99	100	89	82	71	100
Average High (°F)	31	33	43	58	69	78	83	81	73	62	48	35	58
Average Temp. (°F)	22	24	34	47	58	67	72	70	61	51	40	27	48
Average Low (°F)	13	14	25	36	46	55	60	58	50	39	31	19	37
Extreme Low (°F)	-28	-21	-21	10	26	36	40	34	24	16	5	-22	-28

Note: Figures cover the years 1945-1990
Source: National Climatic Data Center, International Station Meteorological Climate Summary, 9/96

Average Precipitation/Snowfall/Humidity

Precip./Humidity	Jan	Feb	Mar	Apr	May	Jun	Jul	Aug	Sep	Oct	Nov	Dec	Yr.
Avg. Precip. (in.)	2.4	2.3	2.8	2.9	3.6	3.4	3.1	3.3	3.1	2.9	3.1	2.9	35.8
Avg. Snowfall (in.)	16	14	11	3	Tr	0	0	0	0	Tr	4	14	63
Avg. Rel. Hum. 7am (%)	77	77	76	72	74	77	80	85	88	86	82	80	79
Avg. Rel. Hum. 4pm (%)	64	60	54	49	51	53	53	55	57	56	64	67	57

Note: Figures cover the years 1945-1990; Tr = Trace amounts (<0.05 in. of rain; <0.5 in. of snow)
Source: National Climatic Data Center, International Station Meteorological Climate Summary, 9/96

Weather Conditions

Temperature			Daytime Sky			Precipitation		
5°F & below	32°F & below	90°F & above	Clear	Partly cloudy	Cloudy	0.01 inch or more precip.	0.1 inch or more snow/ice	Thunder-storms
22	147	11	58	149	158	133	36	24

Note: Figures are average number of days per year and cover the years 1945-1990
Source: National Climatic Data Center, International Station Meteorological Climate Summary, 9/96

HAZARDOUS WASTE

Superfund Sites

The Albany-Schenectady-Troy, NY metro area is home to six sites on the EPA's Superfund National Priorities List: **Dewey Loeffel Landfill** (final); **Ge Moreau** (final); **Malta Rocket Fuel Area** (final); **Mercury Refining, Inc.** (final); **Niagara Mohawk Power Corp. (Saratoga Springs Plant)** (final); **Saint-Gobain Performance Plastics** (final). There are a total of 1,396 Superfund sites with a status of proposed or final on the list in the U.S. *U.S. Environmental Protection Agency, National Priorities List, April 4, 2018*

AIR & WATER QUALITY

Air Quality Trends: Ozone

	1990	1995	2000	2005	2010	2012	2013	2014	2015	2016
MSA[1]	0.086	0.079	0.070	0.082	0.072	0.071	0.063	0.061	0.062	0.068
U.S.	0.087	0.089	0.081	0.079	0.073	0.075	0.069	0.067	0.068	0.069

Note: (1) Data covers the Albany-Schenectady-Troy, NY Metropolitan Statistical Area—see Appendix B for areas included. The values shown are the composite ozone concentration averages among trend sites based on the highest fourth daily maximum 8-hour concentration in parts per million. These trends are based on sites having an adequate record of monitoring data during the trend period. Data from exceptional events are included.
Source: U.S. Environmental Protection Agency, Air Quality Monitoring Information, "Air Quality Trends by City, 1990-2016"

Air Quality Index

Area	Percent of Days when Air Quality was...[2]					AQI Statistics[2]	
	Good	Moderate	Unhealthy for Sensitive Groups	Unhealthy	Very Unhealthy	Maximum	Median
MSA[1]	83.8	16.2	0.0	0.0	0.0	90	39

Note: (1) Data covers the Albany-Schenectady-Troy, NY Metropolitan Statistical Area—see Appendix B for areas included; (2) Based on 365 days with AQI data in 2017. Air Quality Index (AQI) is an index for reporting daily air quality. EPA calculates the AQI for five major air pollutants regulated by the Clean Air Act: ground-level ozone, particle pollution (aka particulate matter), carbon monoxide, sulfur dioxide, and nitrogen dioxide. The AQI runs from 0 to 500. The higher the AQI value, the greater the level of air pollution and the greater the health concern. There are six AQI categories: "Good" AQI is between 0 and 50. Air quality is considered satisfactory; "Moderate" AQI is between 51 and 100. Air quality is acceptable; "Unhealthy for Sensitive Groups" When AQI values are between 101 and 150, members of sensitive groups may experience health effects; "Unhealthy" When AQI values are between 151 and 200 everyone may begin to experience health effects; "Very Unhealthy" AQI values between 201 and 300 trigger a health alert; "Hazardous" AQI values over 300 trigger warnings of emergency conditions (not shown).
Source: U.S. Environmental Protection Agency, Air Quality Index Report, 2017

Air Quality Index Pollutants

Area	Percent of Days when AQI Pollutant was...[2]					
	Carbon Monoxide	Nitrogen Dioxide	Ozone	Sulfur Dioxide	Particulate Matter 2.5	Particulate Matter 10
MSA[1]	0.0	0.0	67.7	0.0	32.3	0.0

Note: (1) Data covers the Albany-Schenectady-Troy, NY Metropolitan Statistical Area—see Appendix B for areas included; (2) Based on 365 days with AQI data in 2017. The Air Quality Index (AQI) is an index for reporting daily air quality. EPA calculates the AQI for five major air pollutants regulated by the Clean Air Act: ground-level ozone, particle pollution (also known as particulate matter), carbon monoxide, sulfur dioxide, and nitrogen dioxide. The AQI runs from 0 to 500. The higher the AQI value, the greater the level of air pollution and the greater the health concern.
Source: U.S. Environmental Protection Agency, Air Quality Index Report, 2017

Maximum Air Pollutant Concentrations: Particulate Matter, Ozone, CO and Lead

	Particulate Matter 10 (ug/m^3)	Particulate Matter 2.5 Wtd AM (ug/m^3)	Particulate Matter 2.5 24-Hr (ug/m^3)	Ozone (ppm)	Carbon Monoxide (ppm)	Lead (ug/m^3)
MSA[1] Level	n/a	6.3	18	0.068	1	n/a
NAAQS[2]	150	15	35	0.075	9	0.15
Met NAAQS[2]	n/a	Yes	Yes	Yes	Yes	n/a

Note: (1) Data covers the Albany-Schenectady-Troy, NY Metropolitan Statistical Area—see Appendix B for areas included; Data from exceptional events are included; (2) National Ambient Air Quality Standards; ppm = parts per million; ug/m^3 = micrograms per cubic meter; n/a not available.
Concentrations: Particulate Matter 10 (coarse particulate)—highest second maximum 24-hour concentration; Particulate Matter 2.5 Wtd AM (fine particulate)—highest weighted annual mean concentration; Particulate Matter 2.5 24-Hour (fine particulate)—highest 98th percentile 24-hour concentration; Ozone—highest fourth daily maximum 8-hour concentration; Carbon Monoxide—highest second maximum non-overlapping 8-hour concentration; Lead—maximum running 3-month average
Source: U.S. Environmental Protection Agency, Air Quality Monitoring Information, "Air Quality Statistics by City, 2016"

Maximum Air Pollutant Concentrations: Nitrogen Dioxide and Sulfur Dioxide

	Nitrogen Dioxide AM (ppb)	Nitrogen Dioxide 1-Hr (ppb)	Sulfur Dioxide AM (ppb)	Sulfur Dioxide 1-Hr (ppb)	Sulfur Dioxide 24-Hr (ppb)
MSA[1] Level	n/a	n/a	n/a	4	n/a
NAAQS[2]	53	100	30	75	140
Met NAAQS[2]	n/a	n/a	n/a	Yes	n/a

Note: (1) Data covers the Albany-Schenectady-Troy, NY Metropolitan Statistical Area—see Appendix B for areas included; Data from exceptional events are included; (2) National Ambient Air Quality Standards; ppm = parts per million; ug/m^3 = micrograms per cubic meter; n/a not available.
Concentrations: Nitrogen Dioxide AM—highest arithmetic mean concentration; Nitrogen Dioxide 1-Hr—highest 98th percentile 1-hour daily maximum concentration; Sulfur Dioxide AM—highest annual mean concentration; Sulfur Dioxide 1-Hr—highest 99th percentile 1-hour daily maximum concentration; Sulfur Dioxide 24-Hr—highest second maximum 24-hour concentration
Source: U.S. Environmental Protection Agency, Air Quality Monitoring Information, "Air Quality Statistics by City, 2016"

Drinking Water

Water System Name	Pop. Served	Primary Water Source Type	Violations[1]	
			Health Based	Monitoring/ Reporting
Bethlehem WD #1	31,000	Surface	1	0

Note: (1) Based on violation data from January 1, 2017 to December 31, 2017
Source: U.S. Environmental Protection Agency, Office of Ground Water and Drinking Water, Safe Drinking Water Information System (based on data extracted April 5, 2018)

Cicero, New York

Background

Cicero is a northern suburb of the city of Syracuse. It is situated in the northeast corner of Onondaga County, and includes the eastern half of the Village of North Syracuse. The original township of Cicero was comprised of both Cicero and Clay, formed in 1790. In 1827, the towns were separated, with Cicero becoming the eastern portion of the land.

The northern border of Cicero sits on the shores of Oneida Lake, one of the largest bodies of water in New York State. Cicero is home to the large Cicero Swamp, with the rest of the town consisting mainly of wetland, forests, farms, and an increasing number of housing developments which are slowly being built onto farmland.

Cicero is served by North Syracuse Central School District, which also serves the communities of North Syracuse, Clay, Bridgeport, and Mattydale/Hinsdale. Schools in Cicero include one high school, one middle school, and two elementary schools.

Areas of interest in Cicero include its local Museum & Learning Center, The Historical Log Frame House, and the Stone Arabia Schoolhouse, all of which are operated and maintained by the Cicero Historical Society. The community of Cicero also enjoys the Cicero Library branch of The Northern Onondaga Public Library, which also houses LibraryFarm, an organic community garden.

Cicero is home to a single runway general aviation airport, Michael Airfield.

Rankings

Business/Finance Rankings

- The personal finance site NerdWallet analyzed 183 American metropolitan areas with populations over 250,000 and more than 15,000 businesses to rank where entrepreneurs find the most success. Criteria included area economy, annual income, housing cost, unemployment rate, and the success rate of area businesses. Syracuse* ranked #43. *www.nerdwallet.com, "Best Places to Start a Business," April 27, 2015*
- The Brookings Institution ranked the 100 largest metro areas in the U.S. based on income inequality. Syracuse* was ranked #57 (#1 = greatest ineqality). Criteria: the "95/20 ratio," a figure representing the income at which a household earns more than 95 percent of all other households, divided by the income at which a household earns more than only 20 percent of all other households. *Brookings Institution, "Household Income Inequality, 100 Largest U.S. Metro Areas, 2014-2016," February 5, 2018*
- The Syracuse* metro area appeared on the Milken Institute "2017 Best Performing Cities" list. Rank: #153 out of 200 large metro areas. Criteria: job growth; wage and salary growth; high-tech output growth. *Milken Institute, "Best-Performing Cities 2017," January 2018*
- *Forbes* ranked the 200 most populous metro areas to determine the nation's "Best Places for Business and Careers." The Syracuse* metro area was ranked #105. Criteria: costs (business and living); job growth (past and projected); income growth; quality of life; educational attainment (college and high school); projected economic growth; cultural and recreational opportunities; net migration patterns; number of highly ranked colleges. *Forbes, "The Best Places for Business and Careers 2017," October 24, 2017*

Dating/Romance Rankings

- *Apartment List* conducted its annual survey of renters to compile a list of metros that have the best opportunities for dating. Nearly 11,000 respondents, from February 2017 through January 2018, rated their current city or neighborhood for opportunities to date and make friends. The Syracuse* metro area ranked #70 out of 70 where single residents were very satisfied or somewhat satisfied, making it among the ten worst metros for dating opportunities. Other criteria analyzed included gender and education levels of renters. *Apartment List, "Best Metros for Dating 2018," February 6, 2018*

Education Rankings

- Personal finance website *WalletHub* analyzed the 150 largest U.S. metropolitan statistical areas to determine where the most educated Americans are choosing to settle. Criteria: education quality and attainment gap; education levels; percentage of workers with degrees; public school rankings; quality and size of each metro area's universities. Syracuse* was ranked #53 (#1 = most educated city). *www.WalletHub.com, "2017's Most and Least Educated Cities in America, " July 25, 2017*

Environmental Rankings

- Sperling's BestPlaces assessed 379 metropolitan areas of the United States for the likelihood of dangerously extreme weather events or earthquakes. In general the Southeast and South-Central regions have the highest risk of weather extremes and earthquakes, while the Pacific Northwest enjoys the lowest risk. Of the least risky metropolitan areas, the Syracuse* metro area was ranked #111. *www.bestplaces.net, "Safest Places from Natural Disasters," April 2011*
- Syracuse* was highlighted as one of the top 25 cleanest metro areas for year-round particle pollution (Annual PM 2.5) in the U.S. during 2013 through 2015. The area ranked #21. *American Lung Association, State of the Air 2017*

- Syracuse* was highlighted as one of the top 99 cleanest metro areas for short-term particle pollution (24-hour PM 2.5) in the U.S. during 2013 through 2015. Monitors in these cities reported no days with unhealthful PM 2.5 levels. *American Lung Association, State of the Air 2017*

Health/Fitness Rankings

- The Syracuse* metro area was identified as one of the worst cities for bed bugs in America by pest control company Orkin. The area ranked #33 out of 50 based on the number of bed bug treatments Orkin performed from December 2016 to November 2017. *Orkin, "Baltimore and Washington D.C. Continue to Hold Top Spots," January 8, 2018*
- Syracuse* was identified as a "2016 Spring Allergy Capital." The area ranked #3 out of 100. Three groups of factors were used to identify the most severe cities for people with allergies during the spring season: annual pollen levels; medicine utilization; access to board-certified allergists. *Asthma and Allergy Foundation of America, "Spring Allergy Capitals 2016"*
- Syracuse* was identified as a "2016 Fall Allergy Capital." The area ranked #5 out of 100. Three groups of factors were used to identify the most severe cities for people with allergies during the fall season: annual pollen levels; medicine utilization; access to board-certified allergists. *Asthma and Allergy Foundation of America, "Fall Allergy Capitals 2016"*
- Syracuse* was identified as a "2015 Asthma Capital." The area ranked #62 out of the nation's 100 largest metropolitan areas. Criteria: estimated prevalence; self-reported prevalence; crude death rate for asthma; annual pollen score; annual air quality; public smoking laws; number of board-certified asthma specialists; school inhaler access laws; rescue medication use; controller medication use; ER visits for asthma; uninsured rate; poverty rate. *Asthma and Allergy Foundation of America, "Asthma Capitals 2015"*
- The Syracuse* metro area ranked #131 out of 189 in The Gallup-Healthways Well-Being Index. Criteria: purpose; social well being; financial health; community and physical health. Results are based on telephone interviews with adults, aged 18 and older, living in metropolitan areas in the 50 U.S. states and the District of Columbia. *Gallup-Healthways, "State of American Well-Being, 2017 Community Well-Being Rankings" March 2018*

Real Estate Rankings

- With data from RealtyTrac, Yahoo! Finance researchers listed the housing markets in which housing affordability is improving most, factoring in interest rates as well as median home prices. The Syracuse* metro area was among the most affordable housing markets. *news.yahoo.com, "10 Cities Where Ordinary People Can No Longer Afford Homes," March 5, 2014*
- The Syracuse* metro area was identified as one of the 20 most affordable housing markets in the U.S. in 2017. The area ranked #15 out of 180 markets. Criteria: qualification for a mortgage loan on a typical home. *National Association of Realtors®, Affordability Index of Existing Single-Family Homes for Metropolitan Areas, 2017*
- Syracuse* was ranked #20 out of 238 metro areas in terms of housing affordability in 2017 by the National Association of Home Builders (#1 = most affordable). Criteria: the share of homes sold in that area affordable to a family earning the local median income, based on standard mortgage underwriting criteria. *National Association of Home Builders®, NAHB-Wells Fargo Housing Opportunity Index, 4th Quarter 2017*

Safety Rankings

- The National Insurance Crime Bureau ranked 382 metro areas in the U.S. in terms of per capita rates of vehicle theft. The Syracuse* metro area ranked #327 (#1 = highest rate). Criteria: number of vehicle theft offenses per 100,000 inhabitants in 2016. *National Insurance Crime Bureau, "Hot Spots 2016," June 8, 2017*

Seniors/Retirement Rankings

- From its Best Cities for Successful Aging indexes, the Milken Institute generated rankings for metropolitan areas, weighing data in nine categories—health care, wellness, living arrangements, transportation and convenience, financial characteristics, education, employment, community engagement, and overall livability. The Syracuse* metro area was ranked #20 overall in the large metro area category. *Milken Institute, "Best Cities for Successful Aging, 2017" March 14, 2017*

*Cicero is located within the Syracuse, NY Metropolitan Statistical Area.

Business Environment

CITY FINANCES

City Government Finances

Component	2015 ($000)	2015 ($ per capita)
Total Revenues	14,302	454
Total Expenditures	15,191	482
Debt Outstanding	3,509	111
Cash and Securities[1]	5,078	161

Note: (1) Cash and security holdings of a government at the close of its fiscal year,, including those of its dependent agencies, utilities, and liquor stores.
Source: U.S Census Bureau, State & Local Government Finances 2015

City Government Revenue by Source

Source	2015 ($000)	2015 ($ per capita)	2015 (%)
General Revenue			
From Federal Government	0	0	0.0
From State Government	612	19	4.3
From Local Governments	391	12	2.7
Taxes			
Property	11,689	371	81.7
Sales and Gross Receipts	349	11	2.4
Personal Income	0	0	0.0
Corporate Income	0	0	0.0
Motor Vehicle License	0	0	0.0
Other Taxes	509	16	3.6
Current Charges	324	10	2.3
Liquor Store	0	0	0.0
Utility	0	0	0.0
Employee Retirement	0	0	0.0

Source: U.S Census Bureau, State & Local Government Finances 2015

City Government Expenditures by Function

Function	2015 ($000)	2015 ($ per capita)	2015 (%)
General Direct Expenditures			
Air Transportation	0	0	0.0
Corrections	0	0	0.0
Education	0	0	0.0
Employment Security Administration	0	0	0.0
Financial Administration	525	16	3.5
Fire Protection	1,590	50	10.5
General Public Buildings	153	4	1.0
Governmental Administration, Other	546	17	3.6
Health	67	2	0.4
Highways	3,616	114	23.8
Hospitals	0	0	0.0
Housing and Community Development	0	0	0.0
Interest on General Debt	211	6	1.4
Judicial and Legal	302	9	2.0
Libraries	0	0	0.0
Parking	0	0	0.0
Parks and Recreation	892	28	5.9
Police Protection	1,429	45	9.4
Public Welfare	0	0	0.0
Sewerage	213	6	1.4
Solid Waste Management	2,075	65	13.7
Veterans' Services	0	0	0.0
Liquor Store	0	0	0.0
Utility	53	1	0.3
Employee Retirement	0	0	0.0

Source: U.S Census Bureau, State & Local Government Finances 2015

DEMOGRAPHICS

Population Growth

Area	1990 Census	2000 Census	2010 Census	2016* Estimate	Population Growth (%)	
					1990-2016	2010-2016
City	25,560	27,982	31,632	31,495	23.2	-0.4
MSA[1]	659,864	650,154	662,577	660,652	0.1	-0.3
U.S.	248,709,873	281,421,906	308,745,538	318,558,162	28.1	3.2

Note: (1) Figures cover the Syracuse, NY Metropolitan Statistical Area—see Appendix B for areas included; (*) 2012-2016 5-year estimated population
Source: U.S. Census Bureau, 1990 Census, Census 2000, Census 2010, 2012-2016 American Community Survey 5-Year Estimates

Household Size

Area	Persons in Household (%)							Average Household Size
	One	Two	Three	Four	Five	Six	Seven or More	
City	24.4	33.3	18.4	16.4	5.3	1.5	0.7	2.60
MSA[1]	30.2	34.3	15.8	11.9	4.9	1.7	1.1	2.50
U.S.	27.7	33.7	15.7	13.1	6.0	2.3	1.5	2.60

Note: (1) Figures cover the Syracuse, NY Metropolitan Statistical Area—see Appendix B for areas included
Source: U.S. Census Bureau, 2012-2016 American Community Survey 5-Year Estimates

Race

Area	White Alone[2] (%)	Black Alone[2] (%)	Asian Alone[2] (%)	AIAN[3] Alone[2] (%)	NHOPI[4] Alone[2] (%)	Other Race Alone[2] (%)	Two or More Races (%)
City	94.8	1.6	1.2	0.5	0.0	0.2	1.7
MSA[1]	84.6	8.3	2.8	0.5	0.0	0.9	2.9
U.S.	73.3	12.6	5.2	0.8	0.2	4.8	3.1

Note: (1) Figures cover the Syracuse, NY Metropolitan Statistical Area—see Appendix B for areas included; (2) Alone is defined as not being in combination with one or more other races; (3) American Indian and Alaska Native; (4) Native Hawaiian and Other Pacific Islander
Source: U.S. Census Bureau, 2012-2016 American Community Survey 5-Year Estimates

Hispanic or Latino Origin

Area	Total (%)	Mexican (%)	Puerto Rican (%)	Cuban (%)	Other (%)
City	1.5	0.7	0.3	0.0	0.5
MSA[1]	3.9	0.5	1.9	0.3	1.2
U.S.	17.3	11.0	1.7	0.7	4.0

Note: Persons of Hispanic or Latino origin can be of any race; (1) Figures cover the Syracuse, NY Metropolitan Statistical Area—see Appendix B for areas included
Source: U.S. Census Bureau, 2012-2016 American Community Survey 5-Year Estimates

Segregation

Type	Segregation Indices[1]				Percent Change		
	1990	2000	2010	2010 Rank[2]	1990-2000	1990-2010	2000-2010
Black/White	73.0	71.4	67.8	11	-1.6	-5.2	-3.6
Asian/White	45.2	48.1	51.5	4	2.9	6.3	3.4
Hispanic/White	39.6	44.4	42.2	57	4.8	2.6	-2.3

Note: All figures cover the Metropolitan Statistical Area—see Appendix B for areas included; Figures are based on an analysis of 1990, 2000, and 2010 Census Decennial Census tract data by William H. Frey, Brookings Institution and the University of Michigan Social Science Data Analysis Network. In this analysis all racial groups (whites, blacks, and asians) are non-Hispanic members of those races. Hispanics are shown as a separate category; (1) Segregation Indices are Dissimilarity Indices that measure the degree to which the minority group is distributed differently than whites across census tracts. They range from 0 (complete integration) to 100 (complete segregation) where the value indicates the percentage of the minority group that needs to move to be distributed exactly like whites; (2) Ranges from 1 (most segregated) to 102 (least segregated); n/a not available.
Source: www.CensusScope.org

Ancestry

Area	German	Irish	English	American	Italian	Polish	French[2]	Scottish	Dutch
City	20.8	24.7	11.3	3.5	23.2	8.4	5.8	2.1	2.0
MSA[1]	17.3	21.1	11.3	7.1	15.6	6.2	4.9	1.9	2.1
U.S.	14.4	10.4	7.7	6.9	5.4	2.9	2.6	1.7	1.3

Note: Figures are the percentage of the total population reporting a particular ancestry. The nine most commonly reported ancestries in the U.S. are shown. Figures include multiple ancestries (e.g. if a person reported being Irish and Italian, they were included in both columns); (1) Figures cover the Syracuse, NY Metropolitan Statistical Area—see Appendix B for areas included; (2) Excludes Basque
Source: U.S. Census Bureau, 2012-2016 American Community Survey 5-Year Estimates

Foreign-Born Population

Area	Percent of Population Born in								
	Any Foreign Country	Asia	Mexico	Europe	Carribean	Central America[2]	South America	Africa	Canada
City	2.9	1.0	0.0	1.2	0.0	0.1	0.2	0.0	0.4
MSA[1]	5.8	2.4	0.1	1.5	0.6	0.1	0.3	0.6	0.3
U.S.	13.2	4.0	3.6	1.5	1.3	1.0	0.9	0.6	0.3

Note: (1) Figures cover the Syracuse, NY Metropolitan Statistical Area—see Appendix B for areas included; (2) Excludes Mexico.
Source: U.S. Census Bureau, 2012-2016 American Community Survey 5-Year Estimates

Marital Status

Area	Never Married	Now Married[2]	Separated	Widowed	Divorced
City	27.4	55.3	2.0	5.4	9.8
MSA[1]	36.0	45.1	2.3	6.0	10.6
U.S.	33.0	48.1	2.1	5.9	11.0

Note: Figures are percentages and cover the population 15 years of age and older; (1) Figures cover the Syracuse, NY Metropolitan Statistical Area—see Appendix B for areas included; (2) Excludes separated
Source: U.S. Census Bureau, 2012-2016 American Community Survey 5-Year Estimates

Disability Status

Area	All Ages	Under 18 Years Old	18 to 64 Years Old	65 Years and Over
City	10.3	3.8	9.3	26.8
MSA[1]	12.7	5.0	10.7	32.4
U.S.	12.5	4.1	10.3	35.7

Note: Figures show percent of the civilian noninstitutionalized population that reported having a disability. Disability status is determined from six types of difficulty: vision, hearing, cognitive, ambulatory, self-care, and independent living. For children under 5 years old, hearing and vision difficulty are used to determine disability status. For children between the ages of 5 and 14, disability status is determined from hearing, vision, cognitive, ambulatory, and self-care difficulties. For people aged 15 years and older, they are considered to have a disability if they have difficulty with any one of the six difficulty types; Note: (1) Figures cover the Syracuse, NY Metropolitan Statistical Area—see Appendix B for areas included
Source: U.S. Census Bureau, 2012-2016 American Community Survey 5-Year Estimates

Age

Area	Percent of Population									Median Age
	Under Age 5	Age 5–19	Age 20–34	Age 35–44	Age 45–54	Age 55–64	Age 65–74	Age 75–84	Age 85+	
City	6.3	19.6	17.3	13.3	16.6	13.7	8.2	3.6	1.5	40.5
MSA[1]	5.6	19.9	19.9	11.2	14.6	13.6	8.4	4.5	2.3	39.1
U.S.	6.2	19.6	20.7	12.7	13.6	12.6	8.3	4.3	1.9	37.7

Note: (1) Figures cover the Syracuse, NY Metropolitan Statistical Area—see Appendix B for areas included
Source: U.S. Census Bureau, 2012-2016 American Community Survey 5-Year Estimates

Gender

Area	Males	Females	Males per 100 Females
City	15,357	16,138	95.2
MSA[1]	321,835	338,817	95.0
U.S.	156,765,322	161,792,840	96.9

Note: (1) Figures cover the Syracuse, NY Metropolitan Statistical Area—see Appendix B for areas included
Source: U.S. Census Bureau, 2012-2016 American Community Survey 5-Year Estimates

Religious Groups by Family

Area	Catholic	Baptist	Non-Den.	Methodist[2]	Lutheran	LDS[3]	Pente-costal	Presby-terian[4]	Muslim[5]	Judaism
MSA[1]	30.1	2.1	1.9	4.9	1.3	0.4	1.1	1.4	1.0	0.6
U.S.	19.1	9.3	4.0	4.0	2.3	2.0	1.9	1.6	0.8	0.7

Note: Figures are the number of adherents as a percentage of the total population; (1) Figures cover the Syracuse, NY Metropolitan Statistical Area—see Appendix B for areas included; (2) Methodist/Pietist; (3) Latter Day Saints; (4) Reformed; (5) Figures are estimates
Source: Association of Statisticians of American Religious Bodies, 2010 U.S. Religion Census: Religious Congregations & Membership Study

Religious Groups by Tradition

Area	Catholic	Evangelical Protestant	Mainline Protestant	Other Tradition	Black Protestant	Orthodox
MSA[1]	30.1	5.1	9.2	3.0	0.9	0.6
U.S.	19.1	16.2	7.3	4.3	1.6	0.3

Note: Figures are the number of adherents as a percentage of the total population; (1) Figures cover the Syracuse, NY Metropolitan Statistical Area—see Appendix B for areas included
Source: Association of Statisticians of American Religious Bodies, 2010 U.S. Religion Census: Religious Congregations & Membership Study

ECONOMY

Gross Metropolitan Product

Area	2014	2015	2016	2017	Rank[2]
MSA[1]	31.1	31.7	32.4	33.5	80

Note: Figures are in billions of dollars; (1) Figures cover the Syracuse, NY Metropolitan Statistical Area—see Appendix B for areas included; (2) Rank is based on 2015 data and ranges from 1 to 381
Source: The U.S. Conference of Mayors, U.S. Metro Economies: GMP and Employment Report, 2015-2017

Economic Growth

Area	2012-14 (%)	2015 (%)	2016 (%)	2017 (%)	Rank[2]
MSA[1]	-0.5	-0.1	0.5	1.6	311
U.S.	2.0	2.4	1.9	2.6	–

Note: Figures are real gross metropolitan product (GMP) growth rates and represent average annual percent change; (1) Figures cover the Syracuse, NY Metropolitan Statistical Area—see Appendix B for areas included; (2) Rank is based on 2012-2014 average annual percent change and ranges from 1 to 381
Source: The U.S. Conference of Mayors, U.S. Metro Economies: GMP and Employment Report, 2015-2017

Metropolitan Area Exports

Area	2011	2012	2013	2014	2015	2016	Rank[2]
MSA[1]	2,054.1	1,915.5	1,753.3	1,922.5	1,930.3	1,853.1	103

Note: Figures are in millions of dollars; (1) Figures cover the Syracuse, NY Metropolitan Statistical Area—see Appendix B for areas included; (2) Rank is based on 2016 data and ranges from 1 to 385
Source: U.S. Department of Commerce, International Trade Administration, Office of Trade & Industry Information, Manufacturing & Services, data extracted March 15, 2018

Building Permits

Area	Single-Family			Multi-Family			Total		
	2016	2017p	Pct. Chg.	2016	2017p	Pct. Chg.	2016	2017p	Pct. Chg.
City	36	46	27.8	0	0	0.0	36	46	27.8
MSA[1]	375	307	-18.1	441	518	17.5	816	825	1.1
U.S.	750,800	817,300	8.9	455,800	446,800	-2.0	1,206,600	1,264,100	4.8

Note: (1) Figures cover the Syracuse, NY Metropolitan Statistical Area—see Appendix B for areas included; Figures represent new, privately-owned housing units authorized (unadjusted data); All permit data are based on estimates with imputation; (p) preliminary data.
Source: U.S. Census Bureau, Manufacturing, Mining, and Construction Statistics, Building Permits, 2016, 2017

Bankruptcy Filings

Area	Business Filings			Nonbusiness Filings		
	2016	2017	% Chg.	2016	2017	% Chg.
Onondaga County	30	13	-56.7	933	886	-5.0
U.S.	24,114	23,157	-4.0	770,846	765,863	-0.6

Note: Business filings include Chapter 7, Chapter 11, Chapter 12, and Chapter 13; Nonbusiness filings include Chapter 7, Chapter 11, and Chapter 13
Source: Administrative Office of the U.S. Courts, Business and Nonbusiness Bankruptcy, County Cases Commenced by Chapter of the Bankruptcy Code, During the 12-Month Period Ending December 31, 2016 and Business and Nonbusiness Bankruptcy, County Cases Commenced by Chapter of the Bankruptcy Code, During the 12-Month Period Ending December 31, 2017

Housing Vacancy Rates

Area	Gross Vacancy Rate[2] (%)			Year-Round Vacancy Rate[3] (%)			Rental Vacancy Rate[4] (%)			Homeowner Vacancy Rate[5] (%)		
	2015	2016	2017	2015	2016	2017	2015	2016	2017	2015	2016	2017
MSA[1]	11.1	12.0	13.0	10.4	10.2	11.1	9.2	6.5	6.5	2.3	2.3	1.8
U.S.	12.9	12.8	12.7	10.0	9.9	9.9	7.1	6.9	7.2	1.8	1.7	1.6

Note: (1) Figures cover the Syracuse, NY Metropolitan Statistical Area—see Appendix B for areas included; (2) The percentage of the total housing inventory that is vacant; (3) The percentage of the housing inventory (excluding seasonal units) that is year-round vacant; (4) The percentage of rental inventory that is vacant for rent; (5) The percentage of homeowner inventory that is vacant for sale
Source: U.S. Census Bureau, Housing Vacancies and Homeownership Annual Statistics: 2015, 2016, 2017

INCOME

Income

Area	Per Capita ($)	Median Household ($)	Average Household ($)
City	33,296	69,949	85,060
MSA[1]	28,770	54,581	71,507
U.S.	29,829	55,322	77,866

Note: (1) Figures cover the Syracuse, NY Metropolitan Statistical Area—see Appendix B for areas included
Source: U.S. Census Bureau, 2012-2016 American Community Survey 5-Year Estimates

Household Income Distribution

Area	Percent of Households Earning							
	Under $15,000	$15,000 -$24,999	$25,000 -$34,999	$35,000 -$49,999	$50,000 -$74,999	$75,000 -$99,999	$100,000 -$149,999	$150,000 and up
City	8.4	7.7	8.2	11.4	17.1	16.7	18.8	11.6
MSA[1]	12.7	9.9	9.7	13.7	18.6	12.8	14.0	8.6
U.S.	12.1	10.2	9.9	13.2	17.8	12.2	13.5	11.1

Note: (1) Figures cover the Syracuse, NY Metropolitan Statistical Area—see Appendix B for areas included
Source: U.S. Census Bureau, 2012-2016 American Community Survey 5-Year Estimates

Poverty Rate

Area	All Ages	Under 18 Years Old	18 to 64 Years Old	65 Years and Over
City	7.9	9.6	6.9	9.3
MSA[1]	15.4	22.4	14.6	8.4
U.S.	15.1	21.2	14.2	9.3

Note: Figures are percentage of people whose income during the past 12 months was below the poverty level; (1) Figures cover the Syracuse, NY Metropolitan Statistical Area—see Appendix B for areas included
Source: U.S. Census Bureau, 2012-2016 American Community Survey 5-Year Estimates

EMPLOYMENT

Labor Force and Employment

Area	Civilian Labor Force			Workers Employed		
	Dec. 2016	Dec. 2017	% Chg.	Dec. 2016	Dec. 2017	% Chg.
City	15,929	15,828	-0.6	15,278	15,143	-0.9
MSA[1]	304,859	303,285	-0.5	289,509	287,500	-0.7
U.S.	158,968,000	159,880,000	0.6	151,798,000	153,602,000	1.2

Note: Data is not seasonally adjusted and covers workers 16 years of age and older; (1) Figures cover the Syracuse, NY Metropolitan Statistical Area—see Appendix B for areas included
Source: Bureau of Labor Statistics, Local Area Unemployment Statistics

Unemployment Rate

Area	2017											
	Jan.	Feb.	Mar.	Apr.	May	Jun.	Jul.	Aug.	Sep.	Oct.	Nov.	Dec.
City	5.1	5.1	4.3	4.0	4.3	4.3	4.2	4.2	4.2	3.9	4.1	4.3
MSA[1]	5.8	5.9	5.2	4.8	4.8	5.0	5.1	5.0	5.0	4.7	5.0	5.2
U.S.	5.1	4.9	4.6	4.1	4.1	4.5	4.6	4.5	4.1	3.9	3.9	3.9

Note: Data is not seasonally adjusted and covers workers 16 years of age and older; (1) Figures cover the Syracuse, NY Metropolitan Statistical Area—see Appendix B for areas included
Source: Bureau of Labor Statistics, Local Area Unemployment Statistics

Average Wages

Occupation	$/Hr.	Occupation	$/Hr.
Accountants and Auditors	35.20	Maids and Housekeeping Cleaners	12.20
Automotive Mechanics	18.40	Maintenance and Repair Workers	19.10
Bookkeepers	19.20	Marketing Managers	71.00
Carpenters	21.10	Nuclear Medicine Technologists	38.60
Cashiers	10.90	Nurses, Licensed Practical	19.50
Clerks, General Office	15.60	Nurses, Registered	31.10
Clerks, Receptionists/Information	14.70	Nursing Assistants	13.90
Clerks, Shipping/Receiving	16.40	Packers and Packagers, Hand	13.70
Computer Programmers	37.20	Physical Therapists	37.90
Computer Systems Analysts	39.10	Postal Service Mail Carriers	23.70
Computer User Support Specialists	28.10	Real Estate Brokers	n/a
Cooks, Restaurant	12.50	Retail Salespersons	13.50
Dentists	88.50	Sales Reps., Exc. Tech./Scientific	35.90
Electrical Engineers	46.90	Sales Reps., Tech./Scientific	37.20
Electricians	27.10	Secretaries, Exc. Legal/Med./Exec.	17.70
Financial Managers	70.00	Security Guards	23.00
First-Line Supervisors/Managers, Sales	22.60	Surgeons	138.40
Food Preparation Workers	11.90	Teacher Assistants*	13.90
General and Operations Managers	55.80	Teachers, Elementary School*	30.90
Hairdressers/Cosmetologists	14.00	Teachers, Secondary School*	35.80
Internists, General	107.50	Telemarketers	12.10
Janitors and Cleaners	14.80	Truck Drivers, Heavy/Tractor-Trailer	21.80
Landscaping/Groundskeeping Workers	13.80	Truck Drivers, Light/Delivery Svcs.	16.80
Lawyers	45.40	Waiters and Waitresses	12.60

Note: Wage data covers the Syracuse, NY Metropolitan Statistical Area—see Appendix B for areas included; (*) Hourly wages for elementary/secondary school teachers and teacher assistants were calculated by the editors from annual wage data based on a 40 hour work week; n/a not available.
Source: Bureau of Labor Statistics, Metro Area Occupational Employment & Wage Estimates, May 2017

Employment by Occupation

Occupation Classification	City (%)	MSA[1] (%)	U.S. (%)
Management, Business, Science, and Arts	37.6	38.2	37.0
Natural Resources, Construction, and Maintenance	7.2	8.0	8.9
Production, Transportation, and Material Moving	11.8	11.0	12.2
Sales and Office	27.5	24.9	23.8
Service	15.9	17.9	18.1

Note: Figures cover employed civilians 16 years of age and older; (1) Figures cover the Syracuse, NY Metropolitan Statistical Area—see Appendix B for areas included
Source: U.S. Census Bureau, 2012-2016 American Community Survey 5-Year Estimates

Employment by Industry

Sector	MSA[1] Number of Employees	MSA[1] Percent of Total	U.S. Percent of Total
Construction, Mining, and Logging	11,900	3.7	5.2
Education and Health Services	64,800	20.2	15.9
Financial Activities	14,600	4.5	5.7
Government	59,100	18.4	15.3
Information	4,500	1.4	1.9
Leisure and Hospitality	29,500	9.2	10.7
Manufacturing	25,400	7.9	8.5
Other Services	12,300	3.8	3.9
Professional and Business Services	34,700	10.8	14.0
Retail Trade	36,400	11.3	11.0
Transportation, Warehousing, and Utilities	13,500	4.2	4.1
Wholesale Trade	14,700	4.6	4.0

Note: Figures are non-farm employment as of December 2017. Figures are not seasonally adjusted and include workers 16 years of age and older; (1) Figures cover the Syracuse, NY Metropolitan Statistical Area—see Appendix B for areas included
Source: Bureau of Labor Statistics, Current Employment Statistics, Employment, Hours, and Earnings

Occupations with Greatest Projected Employment Growth: 2017 – 2019

Occupation[1]	2017 Employment	2019 Projected Employment	Numeric Employment Change	Percent Employment Change
Home Health Aides	190,490	216,300	25,810	13.5
Personal Care Aides	174,700	189,420	14,720	8.4
Combined Food Preparation and Serving Workers, Including Fast Food	154,570	162,110	7,540	4.9
Registered Nurses	189,840	197,230	7,390	3.9
Janitors and Cleaners, Except Maids and Housekeeping Cleaners	211,280	217,380	6,100	2.9
Waiters and Waitresses	151,380	156,430	5,050	3.3
General and Operations Managers	165,860	169,970	4,110	2.5
Accountants and Auditors	124,740	128,070	3,330	2.7
Software Developers, Applications	52,730	55,940	3,210	6.1
Security Guards	114,180	117,140	2,960	2.6

Note: Projections cover New York; (1) Sorted by numeric employment change
Source: www.projectionscentral.com, State Occupational Projections, 2017–2019 Short-Term Projections

Fastest Growing Occupations: 2017 – 2019

Occupation[1]	2017 Employment	2019 Projected Employment	Numeric Employment Change	Percent Employment Change
Gaming and Sports Book Writers and Runners	660	810	150	24.0
Gaming Change Persons and Booth Cashiers	840	1,030	190	22.7
Solar Photovoltaic Installers	800	980	180	22.7
Gaming Dealers	960	1,150	190	19.4
Home Health Aides	190,490	216,300	25,810	13.5
Gaming Supervisors	580	660	80	12.3
Entertainment Attendants and Related Workers, All Other	490	540	50	9.8
Personal Care Aides	174,700	189,420	14,720	8.4
Physical Therapist Aides	3,110	3,330	220	6.9
Physical Therapists	18,480	19,750	1,270	6.9

Note: Projections cover New York; (1) Sorted by percent employment change and excludes occupations with numeric employment change less than 50
Source: www.projectionscentral.com, State Occupational Projections, 2017–2019 Short-Term Projections

TAXES

State Corporate Income Tax Rates

State	Tax Rate (%)	Income Brackets ($)	Num. of Brackets	Financial Institution Tax Rate (%)[a]	Federal Income Tax Ded.
New York	6.5 (r)	Flat rate	1	6.5 (r)	No

Note: Tax rates as of January 1, 2018; (a) Rates listed are the corporate income tax rate applied to financial institutions or excise taxes based on income. Some states have other taxes based upon the value of deposits or shares; (r) New York's General business corporate rate shown. Corporations may also be subject to a capital stocks tax, which is being phased out through 2021. A minimum tax ranges from $25 to $200,000, depending on receipts ($250 minimum for banks). Certain qualified New York manufacturers pay 0%.
Source: Federation of Tax Administrators, Range of State Corporate Income Tax Rates, January 1, 2018

State Individual Income Tax Rates

State	Tax Rate (%)	Income Brackets ($)	Num. of Brackets	Personal Exempt. ($)[1]		Fed. Inc. Tax Ded.
				Single	Dependents	
New York (a)	4.0 - 8.82	8,500 - 1,077,550 (b)	8	0	1,000	No

Note: Tax rates as of January 1, 2018; Local- and county-level taxes are not included; n/a not applicable; (1) Married joint filers generally receive double the single exemption; (a) 19 states have statutory provision for automatically adjusting to the rate of inflation the dollar values of the income tax brackets, standard deductions, and/or personal exemptions. Massachusetts, Michigan, and Nebraska index the personal exemption only. Oregon does not index the income brackets for $125,000 and over; (b) For joint returns, taxes are twice the tax on half the couple's income.
Source: Federation of Tax Administrators, State Individual Income Tax Rates, January 1, 2018

Various State Sales and Excise Tax Rates

State	State Sales Tax (%)	Gasoline[1] (¢/gal.)	Cigarette[2] ($/pack)	Spirits[3] ($/gal.)	Wine[4] ($/gal.)	Beer[5] ($/gal.)	Recreational Marijuana (%)
New York	4.0	44.3	4.35	6.44 (f)	0.30	0.14	Not legal

Note: All tax rates as of January 1, 2018; (1) The American Petroleum Institute has developed a methodology for determining the average tax rate on a gallon of fuel. Rates may include any of the following: excise taxes, environmental fees, storage tank fees, other fees or taxes, general sales tax, and local taxes. In states where gasoline is subject to the general sales tax, or where the fuel tax is based on the average sale price, the average rate determined by API is sensitive to changes in the price of gasoline. States that fully or partially apply general sales taxes to gasoline: CA, CO, GA, IL, IN, MI, NY; (2) The federal excise tax of $1.0066 per pack and local taxes are not included; (3) Rates are those applicable to off-premise sales of 40% alcohol by volume (a.b.v.) distilled spirits in 750ml containers. Local excise taxes are excluded; (4) Rates are those applicable to off-premise sales of 11% a.b.v. non-carbonated wine in 750ml containers; (5) Rates are those applicable to off-premise sales of 4.7% a.b.v. beer in 12 ounce containers; (f) Different rates also applicable according to alcohol content, place of production, size of container, or place purchased (on- or off-premise or onboard airlines).
Source: Tax Foundation, 2018 Facts & Figures: How Does Your State Compare?

State Business Tax Climate Index Rankings

State	Overall Rank	Corporate Tax Rank	Individual Income Tax Rank	Sales Tax Rank	Unemployment Insurance Tax Rank	Property Tax Rank
New York	49	7	49	43	30	47

Note: The index is a measure of how each state's tax laws affect economic performance. The lower the rank, the more favorable a state's tax system is for business. States without a given tax are given a ranking of 1. The scores/rankings for the District of Columbia do not affect other states. The 2018 index represents the tax climate as of July 1, 2017.
Source: Tax Foundation, State Business Tax Climate Index 2018

TRANSPORTATION

Means of Transportation to Work

Area	Car/Truck/Van		Public Transportation			Bicycle	Walked	Other Means	Worked at Home
	Drove Alone	Car-pooled	Bus	Subway	Railroad				
City	89.1	5.5	0.5	0.0	0.0	0.2	1.2	1.1	2.5
MSA[1]	80.0	8.2	2.4	0.0	0.0	0.4	4.6	0.8	3.6
U.S.	76.4	9.3	2.6	1.9	0.6	0.6	2.8	1.3	4.6

Note: Figures are percentages and cover workers 16 years of age and older; (1) Figures cover the Syracuse, NY Metropolitan Statistical Area—see Appendix B for areas included
Source: U.S. Census Bureau, 2012-2016 American Community Survey 5-Year Estimates

Travel Time to Work

Area	Less Than 10 Minutes	10 to 19 Minutes	20 to 29 Minutes	30 to 44 Minutes	45 to 59 Minutes	60 to 89 Minutes	90 Minutes or More
City	12.7	39.3	35.5	7.7	2.8	0.7	1.2
MSA[1]	15.8	36.1	25.5	14.6	4.1	2.3	1.5
U.S.	12.9	29.2	20.9	20.4	8.0	6.0	2.7

Note: Note: Figures are percentages and include workers 16 years old and over; (1) Figures cover the Syracuse, NY Metropolitan Statistical Area—see Appendix B for areas included
Source: U.S. Census Bureau, 2012-2016 American Community Survey 5-Year Estimates

Freeway Travel Time Index

Area	1985	1990	1995	2000	2005	2010	2014
Urban Area Rank[1,2]	n/a	n/a	n/a	n/a	n/a	n/a	n/a
Urban Area Index[1]	n/a	n/a	n/a	n/a	n/a	n/a	n/a
Average Index[3]	1.09	1.11	1.14	1.17	1.20	1.19	1.20

Note: Freeway Travel Time Index—the ratio of travel time in the peak period to the travel time at free-flow conditions. For example, a value of 1.30 indicates a 20-minute free-flow trip takes 26 minutes in the peak (20 minutes x 1.30 = 26 minutes); (1) Data for the Syracuse, NY urban area was not available; (2) Rank is based on 101 urban areas (#1 = highest travel time index); (3) Average of 101 urban areas
Source: Texas Transportation Institute, 2015 Urban Mobility Scorecard, August 2015

Freeway Commuter Stress Index

Area	1985	1990	1995	2000	2005	2010	2014
Urban Area Rank[1,2]	n/a	n/a	n/a	n/a	n/a	n/a	n/a
Urban Area Index[1]	n/a	n/a	n/a	n/a	n/a	n/a	n/a
Average Index[3]	1.13	1.16	1.19	1.22	1.25	1.24	1.25

Note: The Freeway Commuter Stress Index is the same as the Freeway Travel Time Index (see table above) except that it includes only the travel in the peak directions during the peak periods; the TTI includes travel in all directions during the peak period. Thus, the CSI is more indicative of the work trip experienced by each commuter on a daily basis; (1) Data for the Syracuse, NY urban area was not available; (2) Rank is based on 101 urban areas (#1 = highest travel time index); (3) Average of 101 urban areas
Source: Texas Transportation Institute, 2015 Urban Mobility Scorecard, August 2015

Living Environment

COST OF LIVING

Cost of Living Index

Composite Index	Groceries	Housing	Utilities	Trans-portation	Health Care	Misc. Goods/ Services
n/a	n/a	n/a	n/a	n/a	n/a	n/a

Note: The Cost of Living Index measures regional differences in the cost of consumer goods and services, excluding taxes and non-consumer expenditures, for professional and managerial households in the top income quintile. It is based on more than 50,000 prices covering almost 60 different items for which prices are collected three times a year by chambers of commerce, economic development organizations or university applied economic centers in each participating urban area. The numbers shown should be read as a percentage above or below the national average of 100. For example, a value of 115.4 in the groceries column indicates that grocery prices are 15.4% higher than the national average. Small differences in the index numbers should not be interpreted as significant; n/a not available.
Source: The Council for Community and Economic Research, ACCRA Cost of Living Index, 2017

Grocery Prices

Area[1]	T-Bone Steak ($/pound)	Frying Chicken ($/pound)	Whole Milk ($/half gal.)	Eggs ($/dozen)	Orange Juice ($/64 oz.)	Coffee ($/11.5 oz.)
City[2]	n/a	n/a	n/a	n/a	n/a	n/a
Avg.	11.29	1.40	2.02	1.47	3.55	4.37
Min.	7.71	0.93	1.04	0.70	2.86	3.24
Max.	15.83	2.39	4.03	3.92	6.29	8.16

*Note: (1) Values for the local area are compared with the average, minimum and maximum values for all 294 areas in the Cost of Living Index; (2) Figures cover the Cicero NY urban area; n/a not available; **T-Bone Steak** (price per pound); **Frying Chicken** (price per pound, whole fryer); **Whole Milk** (half gallon carton); **Eggs** (price per dozen, Grade A, large); **Orange Juice** (64 oz. Tropicana or Florida Natural); **Coffee** (11.5 oz. can, vacuum-packed, Maxwell House, Hills Bros, or Folgers).*
Source: The Council for Community and Economic Research, ACCRA Cost of Living Index, 2017

Housing and Utility Costs

Area[1]	New Home Price ($)	Apartment Rent ($/month)	All Electric ($/month)	Part Electric ($/month)	Other Energy ($/month)	Telephone ($/month)
City[2]	n/a	n/a	n/a	n/a	n/a	n/a
Avg.	335,956	1,047	175.01	97.34	67.93	28.71
Min.	187,788	491	109.48	49.33	35.44	12.39
Max.	1,739,087	4,559	432.62	227.09	353.33	44.61

*Note: (1) Values for the local area are compared with the average, minimum and maximum values for all 294 areas in the Cost of Living Index; (2) Figures cover the Cicero NY urban area; n/a not available; **New Home Price** (2,400 sf living area, 8,000 sf lot, in urban area with full utilities); **Apartment Rent** (950 sf 2 bedroom/1.5 or 2 bath, unfurnished, excluding all utilities except water); **All Electric** (average monthly cost for an all-electric home); **Part Electric** (average monthly cost for a part-electric home); **Other Energy** (average monthly cost for natural gas, fuel oil, coal, wood, and any other forms of energy except electricity); **Telephone** (price includes basic monthly rate for a private residential line plus additional local usage charges incurred by a family of four).*
Source: The Council for Community and Economic Research, ACCRA Cost of Living Index, 2017

Health Care, Transportation, and Other Costs

Area[1]	Doctor ($/visit)	Dentist ($/visit)	Optometrist ($/visit)	Gasoline ($/gallon)	Beauty Salon ($/visit)	Men's Shirt ($)
City[2]	n/a	n/a	n/a	n/a	n/a	n/a
Avg.	108.00	92.54	101.93	2.25	37.58	30.92
Min.	30.39	60.00	49.75	1.82	16.11	11.20
Max.	193.50	161.94	229.28	3.16	77.35	59.13

*Note: (1) Values for the local area are compared with the average, minimum and maximum values for all 294 areas in the Cost of Living Index; (2) Figures cover the Cicero NY urban area; n/a not available; **Doctor** (general practitioners routine exam of an established patient); **Dentist** (adult teeth cleaning and periodic oral examination); **Optometrist** (full vision eye exam for established adult patient); **Gasoline** (one gallon regular unleaded, national brand, including all taxes, cash price at self-service pump if available); **Beauty Salon** (woman's shampoo, trim, and blow-dry); **Men's Shirt** (cotton/polyester dress shirt, pinpoint weave, long sleeves).*
Source: The Council for Community and Economic Research, ACCRA Cost of Living Index, 2017

HOUSING

House Price Index (HPI)

Area	National Ranking[2]	Quarterly Change (%)	One-Year Change (%)	Five-Year Change (%)
MSA[1]	226	-2.00	2.51	9.09
U.S.[3]	–	1.61	6.68	34.71

Note: The HPI is a weighted repeat sales index. It measures average price changes in repeat sales or refinancings on the same properties. This information is obtained by reviewing repeat mortgage transactions on single-family properties whose mortgages have been purchased or securitized by Fannie Mae or Freddie Mac in January 1975; (1) Figures cover the Syracuse, NY Metropolitan Statistical Area—see Appendix B for areas included; (2) Rankings are based on annual percentage change for all metro areas containing at least 15,000 transactions over the last 10 years and ranges from 1 to 253; (3) figures based on a weighted average of Census Division estimates using a seasonally adjusted, purchase-only index; all figures are for the period ending December 31, 2017

Source: Federal Housing Finance Agency, House Price Index, February 28, 2018

Median Single-Family Home Prices

Area	2015	2016	2017p	Percent Change 2016 to 2017
MSA[1]	128.3	129.1	130.5	1.1
U.S. Average	223.9	235.5	248.8	5.6

Note: Figures are median sales prices of existing single-family homes in thousands of dollars; (p) preliminary; (1) Figures cover the Syracuse, NY Metropolitan Statistical Area—see Appendix B for areas included

Source: National Association of Realtors, Median Sales Price of Existing Single-Family Homes for Metropolitan Areas, 4th Quarter 2017

Qualifying Income Based on Median Sales Price of Existing Single-Family Homes

Area	With 5% Down ($)	With 10% Down ($)	With 20% Down ($)
MSA[1]	29,811	28,242	25,104
U.S. Average	55,585	52,659	46,808

Note: Figures are preliminary; Qualifying income is based on a mortgage rate of 4.17%. Monthly principal and interest payment is limited to 25% of income; (1) Figures cover the Syracuse, NY Metropolitan Statistical Area—see Appendix B for areas included

Source: National Association of Realtors, Qualifying Income Based on Median Sales Price of Existing Single-Family Homes for Metropolitan Areas, 4th Quarter 2017

Median Apartment Condo-Coop Home Prices

Area	2015	2016	2017p	Percent Change 2016 to 2017
MSA[1]	117.9	123.3	132.2	7.2
U.S. Average	210.7	220.7	234.3	6.2

Note: Figures are median sales prices of existing apartment condo-coop homes in thousands of dollars; (p) preliminary; (1) Figures cover the Syracuse, NY Metropolitan Statistical Area—see Appendix B for areas included

Source: National Association of Realtors, Median Sales Price of Existing Apartment Condo-Coop Homes for Metropolitan Areas, 4th Quarter 2017

Home Value Distribution

Area	Under $50,000	$50,000 -$99,999	$100,000 -$149,999	$150,000 -$199,999	$200,000 -$299,999	$300,000 -$499,999	$500,000 -$999,999	$1,000,000 or more
City	3.4	14.9	32.0	21.1	22.3	5.2	0.7	0.3
MSA[1]	7.6	26.1	26.9	17.4	13.8	5.9	1.8	0.5
U.S.	8.8	14.8	15.3	14.9	18.4	16.4	9.0	2.5

Note: Figures are percentages and cover owner-occupied housing units; (1) Figures cover the Syracuse, NY Metropolitan Statistical Area—see Appendix B for areas included

Source: U.S. Census Bureau, 2012-2016 American Community Survey 5-Year Estimates

Homeownership Rate

Area	2009 (%)	2010 (%)	2011 (%)	2012 (%)	2013 (%)	2014 (%)	2015 (%)	2016 (%)	2017 (%)
MSA[1]	61.3	61.1	61.5	57.0	58.9	60.4	62.8	61.0	63.1
U.S.	67.4	66.9	66.1	65.4	65.1	64.5	63.7	63.4	63.9

Note: (1) Figures cover the Syracuse, NY Metropolitan Statistical Area—see Appendix B for areas included

Source: U.S. Census Bureau, Housing Vacancies and Homeownership Annual Statistics: 2009-2017

Year Housing Structure Built

Area	2010 or Later	2000 -2009	1990 -1999	1980 -1989	1970 -1979	1960 -1969	1950 -1959	1940 -1949	Before 1940	Median Year
City	1.1	16.0	15.7	15.0	11.9	12.5	14.9	5.1	7.7	1978
MSA[1]	1.3	6.3	8.6	11.8	12.7	11.7	14.8	6.6	26.3	1962
U.S.	2.3	14.7	14.0	13.7	15.6	10.9	10.6	5.2	13.0	1977

Note: Figures are percentages except for Median Year; Note: (1) Figures cover the Syracuse, NY Metropolitan Statistical Area—see Appendix B for areas included
Source: U.S. Census Bureau, 2012-2016 American Community Survey 5-Year Estimates

Gross Monthly Rent

Area	Under $500	$500 -$999	$1,000 -$1,499	$1,500 -$1,999	$2,000 -$2,499	$2,500 -$2,999	$3,000 and up	Median ($)
City	20.2	44.7	27.2	7.5	0.1	0.3	0.0	835
MSA[1]	14.5	63.7	17.8	2.6	0.8	0.2	0.3	780
U.S.	11.3	43.3	27.7	10.7	4.0	1.6	1.5	949

Note: Figures are percentages except for Median; Gross rent is the contract rent plus the estimated average monthly cost of utilities (electricity, gas, and water and sewer) and fuels (oil, coal, kerosene, wood, etc.) if these are paid by the renter (or paid for the renter by someone else); (1) Figures cover the Syracuse, NY Metropolitan Statistical Area—see Appendix B for areas included
Source: U.S. Census Bureau, 2012-2016 American Community Survey 5-Year Estimates

HEALTH

Health Risk Factors

Category	MSA[1] (%)	U.S. (%)
Adults aged 18–64 who have any kind of health care coverage	90.6	87.7
Adults who reported being in good or excellent health	84.7	83.6
Adults who are current smokers	19.4	17.1
Adults who currently use E-cigarettes	5.7	4.7
Adults who currently use chewing tobacco, snuff, or snus	3.8	4.0
Adults who are heavy drinkers[2]	6.8	6.5
Adults who are binge drinkers[3]	19.9	16.9
Adults who are overweight (BMI 25.0 - 29.9)	34.4	35.3
Adults who are obese (BMI 30.0 - 99.8)	32.0	29.9
Adults who participated in any physical activities in the past month	75.4	76.9
Adults who always or nearly always wears a seat belt	97.1	94.3

Note: (1) Figures cover the Syracuse, NY Metropolitan Statistical Area—see Appendix B for areas included; (2) Heavy drinkers are classified as adult men having more than 14 drinks per week and adult women having more than 7 drinks per week; (3) Binge drinkers are classified as males having five or more drinks on one occasion or females having four or more drinks on one occasion
Source: Centers for Disease Control and Prevention, Behaviorial Risk Factor Surveillance System, SMART: Selected Metropolitan Area Risk Trends, 2016

Health Screening Rates

Category	MSA[1] (%)	U.S. (%)
Adults 50-75 who have had a blood stool test within the past year	9.9	8.0
Adults 50-75 who have had a colonoscopy in the past 10 years	70.9	63.5
Adults aged 65+ who have had flu shot within the past year	61.6	58.6
Adults aged 65+ who have ever had a pneumonia vaccination	77.5	73.4
Adults who have ever been tested for HIV	39.1	35.6
Women aged 21-65 who have had a pap test in the past three years	82.9	79.8
Men aged 40+ who have had a PSA test within the past two years	39.2	39.5
Women aged 40+ who have had a mammogram within the past two years	75.3	72.5

Note: n/a not available; (1) Figures cover the Syracuse, NY Metropolitan Statistical Area—see Appendix B for areas included; Source: Centers for Disease Control and Prevention, Behaviorial Risk Factor Surveillance System, SMART: Selected Metropolitan Area Risk Trends, 2016

Chronic Health Conditions

Category	MSA[1] (%)	U.S. (%)
Adults who have ever been told they had a heart attack	4.4	4.4
Adults who have ever been told they have angina or coronary heart disease	3.9	4.1
Adults who have ever been told they had a stroke	2.9	3.1
Adults who have been told they currently have asthma	10.5	9.3
Adults who have ever been told they have arthritis	30.4	25.8
Adults who have ever been told they have diabetes[2]	11.3	10.5
Adults who have ever been told they had skin cancer	5.6	5.9
Adults who have ever been told they had any other types of cancer	5.8	6.7
Adults who have ever been told they have COPD	7.3	6.3
Adults who have ever been told they have kidney disease	3.3	2.8
Adults who have ever been told they have a form of depression	13.2	17.4

Note: (1) Figures cover the Syracuse, NY Metropolitan Statistical Area—see Appendix B for areas included; (2) Figures do not include pregnancy-related, borderline, or pre-diabetes
Source: Centers for Disease Control and Prevention, Behaviorial Risk Factor Surveillance System, SMART: Selected Metropolitan Area Risk Trends, 2016

Mortality Rates for the Top 10 Causes of Death in the U.S.

ICD-10[a] Sub-Chapter	ICD-10[a] Code	Age-Adjusted Mortality Rate[1] per 100,000 population	
		County[2]	U.S.
Malignant neoplasms	C00-C97	166.0	158.5
Ischaemic heart diseases	I20-I25	100.2	96.8
Other forms of heart disease	I30-I51	46.8	52.4
Chronic lower respiratory diseases	J40-J47	36.0	40.9
Cerebrovascular diseases	I60-I69	32.5	37.2
Organic, including symptomatic, mental disorders	F01-F09	43.9	33.3
Other degenerative diseases of the nervous system	G30-G31	16.1	32.1
Other external causes of accidental injury	W00-X59	39.9	31.2
Diabetes mellitus	E10-E14	15.9	21.1
Hypertensive diseases	I10-I15	16.6	20.8

Note: (a) ICD-10 = International Classification of Diseases 10th Revision; (1) Mortality rates are a three year average covering 2014-2016; (2) Figures cover Onondaga County.
Source: Centers for Disease Control and Prevention, National Center for Health Statistics. Underlying Cause of Death 1999-2016 on CDC WONDER Online Database, released December 2017

Mortality Rates for Selected Causes of Death

ICD-10[a] Sub-Chapter	ICD-10[a] Code	Age-Adjusted Mortality Rate[1] per 100,000 population	
		County[2]	U.S.
Assault	X85-Y09	5.9	5.6
Diseases of the liver	K70-K76	11.7	14.0
Human immunodeficiency virus (HIV) disease	B20-B24	1.3	1.9
Influenza and pneumonia	J09-J18	19.5	14.6
Intentional self-harm	X60-X84	10.2	13.2
Malnutrition	E40-E46	1.4	1.3
Obesity and other hyperalimentation	E65-E68	2.3	2.1
Renal failure	N17-N19	12.4	13.0
Transport accidents	V01-V99	6.8	12.0
Viral hepatitis	B15-B19	1.2	1.9

Note: (a) ICD-10 = International Classification of Diseases 10th Revision; (1) Mortality rates are a three year average covering 2014-2016; (2) Figures cover Onondaga County; Data are Suppressed when the data meet the criteria for confidentiality constraints; Mortality rates are flagged as Unreliable when the rate would be calculated with a numerator of 20 or less.
Source: Centers for Disease Control and Prevention, National Center for Health Statistics. Underlying Cause of Death 1999-2016 on CDC WONDER Online Database, released December 2017

EDUCATION

Health Insurance Coverage

Area	With Health Insurance	With Private Health Insurance	With Public Health Insurance	Without Health Insurance	Population Under Age 18 Without Health Insurance
City	96.4	80.8	28.2	3.6	1.6
MSA[1]	94.0	71.8	36.6	6.0	3.1
U.S.	88.3	66.7	33.0	11.7	5.9

Note: Figures are percentages that cover the civilian noninstitutionalized population; (1) Figures cover the Syracuse, NY Metropolitan Statistical Area—see Appendix B for areas included
Source: U.S. Census Bureau, 2012-2016 American Community Survey 5-Year Estimates

Number of Medical Professionals

Area	MDs[3]	DOs[3,4]	Dentists	Podiatrists	Chiropractors	Optometrists
County[1] (number)	2,235	83	349	47	127	71
County[1] (rate[2])	477.3	17.7	74.8	10.1	27.2	15.2
U.S. (rate[2])	276.5	22.3	67.3	6.0	26.7	15.9

Note: Data as of 2016 unless noted; (1) Data covers Onondaga County; (2) Rate per 100,000 population; (3) Data as of 2015 and includes all active, non-federal physicians; (4) Doctor of Osteopathic Medicine
Source: U.S. Department of Health and Human Services, Health Resources and Services Administration, Bureau of Health Professions, Area Resource File (ARF) 2016-2017

Public School District Statistics

District Name	Schls	Pupils	Pupil/ Teacher Ratio	Minority Pupils[1] (%)	Free Lunch Eligible[2] (%)	IEP[3] (%)
North Syracuse Central School District	11	9,011	14.3	15.5	28.2	15.9

Note: Table includes school districts with 100 or more students; (1) Percentage of students that are not non-Hispanic white; (2) Percentage of students that are eligible for the free lunch program; (3) Percentage of students that have an Individualized Education Program.
Source: U.S. Department of Education, National Center for Education Statistics, Common Core of Data, Local Education Agency (School District) Universe Survey: School Year 2015-2016; U.S. Department of Education, National Center for Education Statistics, Common Core of Data, Public Elementary/Secondary School Universe Survey: School Year 2015-2016

Highest Level of Education

Area	Less than H.S.	H.S. Diploma	Some College, No Deg.	Associate Degree	Bachelor's Degree	Master's Degree	Prof. School Degree	Doctorate Degree
City	5.1	28.9	21.8	13.5	18.3	10.3	1.1	0.8
MSA[1]	10.2	29.1	18.3	11.9	17.2	9.8	2.0	1.5
U.S.	13.0	27.5	21.0	8.2	18.8	8.2	2.0	1.3

Note: Figures cover persons age 25 and over; (1) Figures cover the Syracuse, NY Metropolitan Statistical Area—see Appendix B for areas included
Source: U.S. Census Bureau, 2012-2016 American Community Survey 5-Year Estimates

Educational Attainment by Race

Area	High School Graduate or Higher (%)					Bachelor's Degree or Higher (%)				
	Total	White	Black	Asian	Hisp.[2]	Total	White	Black	Asian	Hisp.[2]
City	94.9	95.0	97.7	83.1	93.7	30.6	30.5	20.8	59.5	28.1
MSA[1]	89.8	91.4	77.5	71.0	78.2	30.6	31.5	14.6	47.0	26.8
U.S.	87.0	88.9	84.3	86.3	65.7	30.3	31.6	20.0	52.1	14.7

Note: Figures shown cover persons 25 years old and over; (1) Figures cover the Syracuse, NY Metropolitan Statistical Area—see Appendix B for areas included; (2) People of Hispanic origin can be of any race
Source: U.S. Census Bureau, 2012-2016 American Community Survey 5-Year Estimates

School Enrollment by Grade and Control

Area	Preschool (%)		Kindergarten (%)		Grades 1 - 4 (%)		Grades 5 - 8 (%)		Grades 9 - 12 (%)	
	Public	Private	Public	Private	Public	Private	Public	Private	Public	Private
City	57.9	42.1	92.1	7.9	90.4	9.6	96.1	3.9	93.6	6.4
MSA[1]	64.3	35.7	91.4	8.6	92.5	7.5	92.3	7.7	93.6	6.4
U.S.	58.4	41.6	87.7	12.3	89.8	10.2	89.7	10.3	90.4	9.6

Note: Figures shown cover persons 3 years old and over; (1) Figures cover the Syracuse, NY Metropolitan Statistical Area—see Appendix B for areas included
Source: U.S. Census Bureau, 2012-2016 American Community Survey 5-Year Estimates

Average Salaries of Public School Classroom Teachers

Area	2015 Dollars	2015 Rank[1]	2016 Dollars	2016 Rank[1]	Change from 2015 to 2016 Percent	Change from 2015 to 2016 Rank[2]
New York	77,628	1	79,152	1	2.0	12
U.S. Average	57,611	–	58,353	–	1.3	–

Note: (1) Rank ranges from 1 to 51 where 1 indicates highest salary; (2) Rank ranges from 1 to 51 where 1 indicates highest percent change.
Source: National Education Association, Rankings & Estimates: Rankings of the States 2016 and Estimates of School Statistics 2017

Higher Education

Four-Year Colleges			Two-Year Colleges			Medical Schools[1]	Law Schools[2]	Voc/ Tech[3]
Public	Private Non-profit	Private For-profit	Public	Private Non-profit	Private For-profit			
0	0	0	0	0	0	0	0	0

Note: Figures cover institutions located within the city limits and include main campuses only; (1) includes schools accredited by the Liaison Committee on Medical Education and the American Osteopathic Association's Commission on Osteopathic College Accreditation; (2) includes ABA-accredited schools, schools with provisional ABA accreditation, and state accredited schools; (3) includes all schools with programs that are less than 2 years.
Source: National Center for Education Statistics, Integrated Postsecondary Education System (IPEDS), 2016-17; Wikipedia, List of Medical Schools in the United States, accessed April 2, 2018; Wikipedia, List of Law Schools in the United States, accessed April 2, 2018

According to *U.S. News & World Report,* the Syracuse, NY metro area is home to two of the best national universities in the U.S.: **Syracuse University** (#61 tie); **SUNY College of Environmental Science and Forestry** (#97 tie). The indicators used to capture academic quality fall into a number of categories: assessment by administrators at peer institutions; retention of students; faculty resources; student selectivity; financial resources; alumni giving; high school counselor ratings of colleges; and graduation rate. *U.S. News & World Report, "America's Best Colleges 2018"*

According to *U.S. News & World Report,* the Syracuse, NY metro area is home to one of the best liberal arts colleges in the U.S.: **Colgate University** (#12 tie). The indicators used to capture academic quality fall into a number of categories: assessment by administrators at peer institutions; retention of students; faculty resources; student selectivity; financial resources; alumni giving; high school counselor ratings of colleges; and graduation rate. *U.S. News & World Report, "America's Best Colleges 2018"*

According to *U.S. News & World Report,* the Syracuse, NY metro area is home to one of the top 100 law schools in the U.S.: **Syracuse University** (#88 tie). The rankings are based on a weighted average of 12 measures of quality: peer assessment score; assessment score by lawyers/judges; median LSAT scores; median undergrad GPA; acceptance rate; employment rates for graduates; placement success; bar passage rate; faculty resources; expenditures per student; student/faculty ratio; and library resources. *U.S. News & World Report, "America's Best Graduate Schools, Law, 2019"*

According to *U.S. News & World Report,* the Syracuse, NY metro area is home to one of the top 75 business schools in the U.S.: **Syracuse University (Whitman)** (#70 tie). The rankings are based on a weighted average of the following nine measures: quality assessment; peer assessment; recruiter assessment; placement success; mean starting salary and bonus; student selectivity; mean GMAT and GRE scores; mean undergraduate GPA; and acceptance rate. *U.S. News & World Report, "America's Best Graduate Schools, Business, 2019"*

PRESIDENTIAL ELECTION

2016 Presidential Election Results

Area	Clinton	Trump	Johnson	Stein	Other
Onondaga County	53.9	40.1	4.1	1.5	0.4
U.S.	48.0	45.9	3.3	1.1	1.7

Note: Results are percentages and may not add to 100% due to rounding
Source: Dave Leip's Atlas of U.S. Presidential Elections

EMPLOYERS

Major Employers

Company Name	Industry
AXA Equitable Life Insurance	Finance & back office
Carrier Corporation	Environmental systems
Crouse Hospital	Life sciences
Excellus Blue Cross/Blue Shield	Finance & back office
L&JG Stickley, Inc.	Precision manufacturing
Lockheed Martin MS2	Radar & sensor devices
Loretto	Life sciences
National Grid	Finance & back office
Raymour & Flanigan	Misc. (service/retail)
Roman Catholic Diocese	Misc. (religious)
SRC, Inc.	Radar & sensor devices
St Joseph's Hospital Health Center	Life sciences
Syracuse University	Misc. (education)
Syracuse VA Medical Center	Life sciences
Time Warner Cable	Finance & back office
United Parcel Service	Misc. (service/retail)
Upstate University Health System	Life sciences
Verizon	Finance & back office
Wegmans	Misc. (service/retail)
Welch Allyn	Life sciences

Note: Companies shown are located within the Syracuse, NY Metropolitan Statistical Area.
Source: Hoovers.com; Wikipedia

PUBLIC SAFETY

Crime Rate

Area	All Crimes	Violent Crimes: Murder	Violent Crimes: Rape[3]	Violent Crimes: Robbery	Violent Crimes: Aggrav. Assault	Property Crimes: Burglary	Property Crimes: Larceny-Theft	Property Crimes: Motor Vehicle Theft
City	1,014.2	0.0	0.0	6.8	23.7	128.9	841.2	13.6
Metro[1]	2,234.6	5.3	51.3	65.6	154.2	347.9	1,516.3	94.0
U.S.	2,847.8	5.3	40.4	102.8	248.5	468.9	1,745.0	236.9

Note: Figures are crimes per 100,000 population; (1) Figures cover the Syracuse, NY Metropolitan Statistical Area—see Appendix B for areas included; (3) The city and U.S. figures shown were reported using the revised Uniform Crime Reporting (UCR) definition of rape. The metro area figures shown are an aggregate total of the data submitted using both the revised and legacy UCR definitions.
Source: FBI Uniform Crime Reports, 2016

Hate Crimes

Area	Number of Quarters Reported	Race/Ethnicity/ Ancestry	Religion	Sexual Orientation	Disability	Gender	Gender Identity
Area[1]	4	0	0	0	0	0	0
U.S.	4	3,489	1,273	1,076	70	31	124

Columns Race/Ethnicity/Ancestry through Gender Identity: Number of Incidents per Bias Motivation

Note: (1) Figures cover the Cicero Town.
Source: Federal Bureau of Investigation, Hate Crime Statistics 2016

Identity Theft Consumer Reports

Area	Reports	Reports per 100,000 Population	Rank[2]
MSA[1]	407	62	303
U.S.	371,061	114	-

Note: (1) Figures cover the Syracuse, NY Metropolitan Statistical Area—see Appendix B for areas included; (2) Rank ranges from 1 to 389 where 1 indicates greatest number of identity theft reports per 100,000 population
Source: Federal Trade Commission, Consumer Sentinel Network Data Book for January–December 2017

Fraud and Other Consumer Reports

Area	Reports	Reports per 100,000 Population	Rank[2]
MSA[1]	3,149	480	143
U.S.	2,304,550	708	-

Note: (1) Figures cover the Syracuse, NY Metropolitan Statistical Area—see Appendix B for areas included; (2) Rank ranges from 1 to 389 where 1 indicates greatest number of fraud and other consumer reports per 100,000 population

Source: Federal Trade Commission, Consumer Sentinel Network Data Book for January–December 2017

SPORTS

Professional Sports Teams

Team Name	League	Year Established
No teams are located in the metro area		

Source: Wikipedia, Major Professional Sports Teams of the United States and Canada, April 5, 2018

CLIMATE

Average and Extreme Temperatures

Temperature	Jan	Feb	Mar	Apr	May	Jun	Jul	Aug	Sep	Oct	Nov	Dec	Yr.
Extreme High (°F)	70	69	87	92	96	98	97	98	97	87	81	70	98
Average High (°F)	31	33	42	56	68	77	82	80	72	61	48	35	57
Average Temp. (°F)	23	25	34	46	57	66	71	70	62	52	41	29	48
Average Low (°F)	15	16	25	36	46	55	60	59	52	41	33	21	38
Extreme Low (°F)	-26	-26	-16	9	25	35	44	40	25	19	5	-22	-26

Note: Figures cover the years 1945-1990

Source: National Climatic Data Center, International Station Meteorological Climate Summary, 9/96

Average Precipitation/Snowfall/Humidity

Precip./Humidity	Jan	Feb	Mar	Apr	May	Jun	Jul	Aug	Sep	Oct	Nov	Dec	Yr.
Avg. Precip. (in.)	2.5	2.5	3.0	3.2	3.2	3.5	3.6	3.5	3.5	3.2	3.5	3.1	38.5
Avg. Snowfall (in.)	28	25	16	4	Tr	0	0	Tr	Tr	1	9	25	107
Avg. Rel. Hum. 7am (%)	77	78	78	76	76	77	79	85	86	84	80	79	80
Avg. Rel. Hum. 4pm (%)	69	67	60	53	53	54	53	56	60	60	68	72	60

Note: Figures cover the years 1945-1990; Tr = Trace amounts (<0.05 in. of rain; <0.5 in. of snow)

Source: National Climatic Data Center, International Station Meteorological Climate Summary, 9/96

Weather Conditions

Temperature			Daytime Sky			Precipitation		
5°F & below	32°F & below	90°F & above	Clear	Partly cloudy	Cloudy	0.01 inch or more precip.	0.1 inch or more snow/ice	Thunder-storms
17	136	9	56	135	174	170	67	27

Note: Figures are average number of days per year and cover the years 1945-1990

Source: National Climatic Data Center, International Station Meteorological Climate Summary, 9/96

HAZARDOUS WASTE

Superfund Sites

The Syracuse, NY metro area is home to four sites on the EPA's Superfund National Priorities List: **Fulton Terminals** (final); **Onondaga Lake** (final); **Pollution Abatement Services** (final); **Volney Municipal Landfill** (final). There are a total of 1,396 Superfund sites with a status of proposed or final on the list in the U.S. *U.S. Environmental Protection Agency, National Priorities List, April 4, 2018*

AIR & WATER QUALITY

Air Quality Trends: Ozone

	1990	1995	2000	2005	2010	2012	2013	2014	2015	2016
MSA[1]	0.089	0.090	0.074	0.077	0.073	0.074	0.065	0.063	0.063	0.067
U.S.	0.087	0.089	0.081	0.079	0.073	0.075	0.069	0.067	0.068	0.069

Note: (1) Data covers the Syracuse, NY Metropolitan Statistical Area—see Appendix B for areas included. The values shown are the composite ozone concentration averages among trend sites based on the highest fourth daily maximum 8-hour concentration in parts per million. These trends are based on sites having an adequate record of monitoring data during the trend period. Data from exceptional events are included.
Source: U.S. Environmental Protection Agency, Air Quality Monitoring Information, "Air Quality Trends by City, 1990-2016"

Air Quality Index

Area	Percent of Days when Air Quality was...[2]					AQI Statistics[2]	
	Good	Moderate	Unhealthy for Sensitive Groups	Unhealthy	Very Unhealthy	Maximum	Median
MSA[1]	92.6	7.4	0.0	0.0	0.0	93	36

Note: (1) Data covers the Syracuse, NY Metropolitan Statistical Area—see Appendix B for areas included; (2) Based on 365 days with AQI data in 2017. Air Quality Index (AQI) is an index for reporting daily air quality. EPA calculates the AQI for five major air pollutants regulated by the Clean Air Act: ground-level ozone, particle pollution (aka particulate matter), carbon monoxide, sulfur dioxide, and nitrogen dioxide. The AQI runs from 0 to 500. The higher the AQI value, the greater the level of air pollution and the greater the health concern. There are six AQI categories: "Good" AQI is between 0 and 50. Air quality is considered satisfactory; "Moderate" AQI is between 51 and 100. Air quality is acceptable; "Unhealthy for Sensitive Groups" When AQI values are between 101 and 150, members of sensitive groups may experience health effects; "Unhealthy" When AQI values are between 151 and 200 everyone may begin to experience health effects; "Very Unhealthy" AQI values between 201 and 300 trigger a health alert; "Hazardous" AQI values over 300 trigger warnings of emergency conditions (not shown).
Source: U.S. Environmental Protection Agency, Air Quality Index Report, 2017

Air Quality Index Pollutants

Area	Percent of Days when AQI Pollutant was...[2]					
	Carbon Monoxide	Nitrogen Dioxide	Ozone	Sulfur Dioxide	Particulate Matter 2.5	Particulate Matter 10
MSA[1]	0.0	0.0	86.0	0.0	14.0	0.0

Note: (1) Data covers the Syracuse, NY Metropolitan Statistical Area—see Appendix B for areas included; (2) Based on 365 days with AQI data in 2017. The Air Quality Index (AQI) is an index for reporting daily air quality. EPA calculates the AQI for five major air pollutants regulated by the Clean Air Act: ground-level ozone, particle pollution (also known as particulate matter), carbon monoxide, sulfur dioxide, and nitrogen dioxide. The AQI runs from 0 to 500. The higher the AQI value, the greater the level of air pollution and the greater the health concern.
Source: U.S. Environmental Protection Agency, Air Quality Index Report, 2017

Maximum Air Pollutant Concentrations: Particulate Matter, Ozone, CO and Lead

	Particulate Matter 10 (ug/m^3)	Particulate Matter 2.5 Wtd AM (ug/m^3)	Particulate Matter 2.5 24-Hr (ug/m^3)	Ozone (ppm)	Carbon Monoxide (ppm)	Lead (ug/m^3)
MSA[1] Level	n/a	5	12	0.067	n/a	n/a
NAAQS[2]	150	15	35	0.075	9	0.15
Met NAAQS[2]	n/a	Yes	Yes	Yes	n/a	n/a

Note: (1) Data covers the Syracuse, NY Metropolitan Statistical Area—see Appendix B for areas included; Data from exceptional events are included; (2) National Ambient Air Quality Standards; ppm = parts per million; ug/m^3 = micrograms per cubic meter; n/a not available.
Concentrations: Particulate Matter 10 (coarse particulate)—highest second maximum 24-hour concentration; Particulate Matter 2.5 Wtd AM (fine particulate)—highest weighted annual mean concentration; Particulate Matter 2.5 24-Hour (fine particulate)—highest 98th percentile 24-hour concentration; Ozone—highest fourth daily maximum 8-hour concentration; Carbon Monoxide—highest second maximum non-overlapping 8-hour concentration; Lead—maximum running 3-month average
Source: U.S. Environmental Protection Agency, Air Quality Monitoring Information, "Air Quality Statistics by City, 2016"

Maximum Air Pollutant Concentrations: Nitrogen Dioxide and Sulfur Dioxide

	Nitrogen Dioxide AM (ppb)	Nitrogen Dioxide 1-Hr (ppb)	Sulfur Dioxide AM (ppb)	Sulfur Dioxide 1-Hr (ppb)	Sulfur Dioxide 24-Hr (ppb)
MSA[1] Level	n/a	n/a	n/a	3	n/a
NAAQS[2]	53	100	30	75	140
Met NAAQS[2]	n/a	n/a	n/a	Yes	n/a

Note: (1) Data covers the Syracuse, NY Metropolitan Statistical Area—see Appendix B for areas included; Data from exceptional events are included; (2) National Ambient Air Quality Standards; ppm = parts per million; ug/m^3 = micrograms per cubic meter; n/a not available.
Concentrations: Nitrogen Dioxide AM—highest arithmetic mean concentration; Nitrogen Dioxide 1-Hr—highest 98th percentile 1-hour daily maximum concentration; Sulfur Dioxide AM—highest annual mean concentration; Sulfur Dioxide 1-Hr—highest 99th percentile 1-hour daily maximum concentration; Sulfur Dioxide 24-Hr—highest second maximum 24-hour concentration
Source: U.S. Environmental Protection Agency, Air Quality Monitoring Information, "Air Quality Statistics by City, 2016"

Drinking Water

Water System Name	Pop. Served	Primary Water Source Type	Violations[1] Health Based	Violations[1] Monitoring/ Reporting
OCWA	300,000	Surface	0	0

Note: (1) Based on violation data from January 1, 2017 to December 31, 2017
Source: U.S. Environmental Protection Agency, Office of Ground Water and Drinking Water, Safe Drinking Water Information System (based on data extracted April 5, 2018)

East Fishkill, New York

Background

East Fishkill, in Duchess County and sixty miles from New York City, is a prosperous town comprised of five hamlets: Hopewell Junction, Stormville, Wiccopee, Fishkill Plains, Hillside Lake, and Gayhead. The name is derived from Dutch ("Vis Kill") which means "Fish Creek," and it marks the old colonial character of the town and its surrounding region. East Fishkill is set amidst beautiful forested hills, offers excellent schools, and an unusually rich array of recreational resources.

Dutch settlers were in the area prior to 1700, and by the Revolutionary War there were a scattering of residences, several churches, a tavern, and a schoolhouse. Early in the war, colonials blocked nearby Wiccopee pass to prevent an overland advance by the British, and the town was crowded with refugees fleeing New York City. East Fishkill was incorporated as a town in 1849 and, until well into the 20th century, was a rural trading town serving the agricultural supply needs of the neighboring dairy farming region.

The town's rich historical heritage is reflected in many of the town's buildings, including the Brinckerhoff-Pudney-Palen House, an elegant exemplar of the Dutch colonial architecture of the 18th century. Originally owned by Roger Brett, in 1718, it was sold by his widow after Roger was drowned in the nearby Hudson River. The house was owned by various prosperous local citizens and finally came into the possession of Edward Palen, who utilized the estate's extensive lands for dairying. Acadia, as it came to be called, was entirely self-reliant, employed a horse-powered treadmill saw, and dog-powered treadmill butter churn.

Other local points of historical interest include the Storm-Adriance-Brinckerhoff House. the Van Wyck-Jay House, and a famous 1784 Reformed Dutch Church.

East Fishkill offers a wide variety of recreational facilities, including Red Wing Park, a 17-acre park with a spring fed lake and beach area, bath house, basketball, volleyball, and badminton courts, playing fields, and playground. East Fishkill Recreation Park is a larger area (60 acres), with six ball fields, lighted tennis, volleyball and basketball courts, a roller hockey rink, football and lacrosse fields, a skateboard park, a skating pond, fishing, and a walking/jogging trail. Four additional recreation areas offer ten soccer fields, fields for field hockey, football and lacrosse, and many children's playgrounds. The town is on the Appalachian Trail, at Stormville Mountain, and the surrounding area offers many opportunities for hiking, fishing, birding and other outdoor activities.

Nearby medical facilities include St. Francis Hospital, Vassar Brothers Hospital, and the Hudson River Psychiatric Center. East Fishkill is less than thirty miles away from Dutchess County, Stewart International, and Danbury Municipal Airports.

East Fishkill is served by four separate school districts. Institutions of higher learning in the area are many and varied, including Marist College, Duchess Community College, Vassar College, the Culinary Institute of America, the United States Military Academy, SUNY College at New Paltz, and Western Connecticut State University.

East Fishkill is governed by a town board which consists of four council members, elected to four-year terms, and the Town Supervisor, who is elected every two years.

Rankings

General Rankings

- New York* was identified as one of America's fastest-growing cities in terms of population growth by CNNMoney.com. The area ranked #1 out of 10. Criteria: population growth between July 2015 and July 2016; cities and towns with populations of 50,000. *CNNMoney, "10 Fastest-Growing Cities," June 2, 2017*

Business/Finance Rankings

- The personal finance site NerdWallet analyzed 183 American metropolitan areas with populations over 250,000 and more than 15,000 businesses to rank where entrepreneurs find the most success. Criteria included area economy, annual income, housing cost, unemployment rate, and the success rate of area businesses. New York* ranked #32. *www.nerdwallet.com, "Best Places to Start a Business," April 27, 2015*
- Metro areas with the largest gap in income between rich and poor residents were identified by 24/7 Wall Street using the U.S. Census Bureau's 2013 American Community Survey. The New York* metro area placed #7 among metro areas with the widest wealth gap between rich and poor. *247wallst.com, "20 Cities with the Widest Gap between the Rich and Poor," July 8, 2015*
- In a survey of economic confidence in the nation's 50 largest metropolitan areas conducted January–December 2014, the New York* metro area placed #23, according to Gallup's 2014 Economic Confidence Index. *Gallup, "San Jose and San Francisco Lead in Economic Confidence," March 19, 2015*
- The Brookings Institution ranked the 100 largest metro areas in the U.S. based on income inequality. New York* was ranked #2 (#1 = greatest ineqality). Criteria: the "95/20 ratio," a figure representing the income at which a household earns more than 95 percent of all other households, divided by the income at which a household earns more than only 20 percent of all other households. *Brookings Institution, "Household Income Inequality, 100 Largest U.S. Metro Areas, 2014-2016," February 5, 2018*
- Payscale.com ranked the largest metro areas in terms of wage growth. The New York* metro area ranked #1. Criteria: private-sector wage growth between the 4th quarter of 2016 and the 4th quarter of 2017. *PayScale, "Wage Trends by Metro Area-4th Quarter," January 17, 2018*
- The New York* metro area was identified as one of the most debt-ridden places in America by the finance site Credit.com. The metro area was ranked #3. Criteria: residents' average credit card debt as well as median income. *Credit.com, "25 Cities With the Most Credit Card Debt," February 28, 2018*
- New York* was identified as one of America's most frugal metro areas by *Coupons.com.* The city ranked #15 out of 25. Criteria: digital coupon usage. *Coupons.com, "America's Most Frugal Cities of 2017," March 22, 2018*
- New York* was cited as one of America's top metros for new and expanded facility projects in 2017. The area ranked #5 in the large metro area category (population over 1 million). *Site Selection, "Top Metropolitans of 2017," March 2018*
- The New York* metro area appeared on the Milken Institute "2017 Best Performing Cities" list. Rank: #82 out of 200 large metro areas. Criteria: job growth; wage and salary growth; high-tech output growth. *Milken Institute, "Best-Performing Cities 2017," January 2018*
- *Forbes* ranked the 200 most populous metro areas to determine the nation's "Best Places for Business and Careers." The New York* metro area was ranked #113. Criteria: costs (business and living); job growth (past and projected); income growth; quality of life; educational attainment (college and high school); projected economic growth; cultural and recreational opportunities; net migration patterns; number of highly ranked colleges. *Forbes, "The Best Places for Business and Careers 2017," October 24, 2017*

Dating/Romance Rankings

- *Apartment List* conducted its annual survey of renters to compile a list of metros that have the best opportunities for dating. Nearly 11,000 respondents, from February 2017 through January 2018, rated their current city or neighborhood for opportunities to date and make friends. The New York* metro area ranked #10 out of 70 where single residents were very satisfied or somewhat satisfied, making it among the ten best metros for dating opportunities. Other criteria analyzed included gender and education levels of renters. *Apartment List, "Best Metros for Dating 2018," February 6, 2018*

Education Rankings

- Personal finance website *WalletHub* analyzed the 150 largest U.S. metropolitan statistical areas to determine where the most educated Americans are choosing to settle. Criteria: education quality and attainment gap; education levels; percentage of workers with degrees; public school rankings; quality and size of each metro area's universities. New York* was ranked #36 (#1 = most educated city). *www.WalletHub.com, "2017's Most and Least Educated Cities in America," July 25, 2017*

Environmental Rankings

- Sperling's BestPlaces assessed 379 metropolitan areas of the United States for the likelihood of dangerously extreme weather events or earthquakes. In general the Southeast and South-Central regions have the highest risk of weather extremes and earthquakes, while the Pacific Northwest enjoys the lowest risk. Of the least risky metropolitan areas, the Dutchess County* metro area was ranked #191. *www.bestplaces.net, "Safest Places from Natural Disasters," April 2011*

- The U.S. Environmental Protection Agency (EPA) released a list of U.S. metropolitan areas with the most ENERGY STAR certified buildings in 2016. The New York* metro area was ranked #3 out of 25. *U.S. Environmental Protection Agency, "2017 Energy Star Top Cities," June 2017*

- New York* was highlighted as one of the 25 most ozone-polluted metro areas in the U.S. during 2013 through 2015. The area ranked #9. *American Lung Association, State of the Air 2017*
- New York* was highlighted as one of the 25 metro areas most polluted by year-round particle pollution (Annual PM 2.5) in the U.S. during 2013 through 2015. The area ranked #22. *American Lung Association, State of the Air 2017*

Health/Fitness Rankings

- For each of the 50 most populous metro areas in the United States, the American College of Sports Medicine's American Fitness Index evaluated infrastructure, community assets, and policies that encourage healthy and fit lifestyles, including preventive health behaviors, levels of chronic disease conditions, health care access, and community resources and policies that support physical activity. The New York* metro area ranked #18 for "community fitness." *www.americanfitnessindex.org, "ACSM American Fitness Index Health and Community Fitness Status of the 50 Largest Metropolitan Areas," May 2017*

- The New York* metro area was identified as one of the worst cities for bed bugs in America by pest control company Orkin. The area ranked #8 out of 50 based on the number of bed bug treatments Orkin performed from December 2016 to November 2017. *Orkin, "Baltimore and Washington D.C. Continue to Hold Top Spots," January 8, 2018*
- New York* was identified as a "2016 Spring Allergy Capital." The area ranked #31 out of 100. Three groups of factors were used to identify the most severe cities for people with allergies during the spring season: annual pollen levels; medicine utilization; access to board-certified allergists. *Asthma and Allergy Foundation of America, "Spring Allergy Capitals 2016"*

- New York* was identified as a "2016 Fall Allergy Capital." The area ranked #52 out of 100. Three groups of factors were used to identify the most severe cities for people with allergies during the fall season: annual pollen levels; medicine utilization; access to board-certified allergists. *Asthma and Allergy Foundation of America, "Fall Allergy Capitals 2016"*
- New York* was identified as a "2015 Asthma Capital." The area ranked #35 out of the nation's 100 largest metropolitan areas. Criteria: estimated prevalence; self-reported prevalence; crude death rate for asthma; annual pollen score; annual air quality; public smoking laws; number of board-certified asthma specialists; school inhaler access laws; rescue medication use; controller medication use; ER visits for asthma; uninsured rate; poverty rate. *Asthma and Allergy Foundation of America, "Asthma Capitals 2015"*
- The New York* metro area ranked #75 out of 189 in The Gallup-Healthways Well-Being Index. Criteria: purpose; social well being; financial health; community and physical health. Results are based on telephone interviews with adults, aged 18 and older, living in metropolitan areas in the 50 U.S. states and the District of Columbia. *Gallup-Healthways, "State of American Well-Being, 2017 Community Well-Being Rankings" March 2018*

Real Estate Rankings

- FitSmallBusiness looked at 50 of the largest metropolitan areas in the U.S. to determine which metro was the best to start a real estate business. Data was compiled from such sources as: Zillow, Trulia, U.S. Census Bureau, and the Bureau of Labor Statistics. Criteria: location; inventory; annual wages; median sales price of homes; days on the market; median price cut percentage; and other factors that would influence real estate professional growth. The New York* metro area ranked #6. *fitsmallbusiness.com, "The Best Cities to Become a Real Estate Agent in 2018," January 30, 2018*
- With data from RealtyTrac, Yahoo! Finance researchers listed the housing markets in which housing affordability is improving most, factoring in interest rates as well as median home prices. The New York* metro area was among the least affordable housing markets. *news.yahoo.com, "10 Cities Where Ordinary People Can No Longer Afford Homes," March 5, 2014*
- The Dutchess County* metro area was identified as one of the 20 best housing markets in the U.S. in 2017. The area ranked #3 out of 180 markets. Criteria: year-over-year change of median sales price of existing single-family homes between the 4th quarter of 2016 and the 4th quarter of 2017. *National Association of Realtors®, Median Sales Price of Existing Single-Family Homes for Metropolitan Areas, 4th Quarter 2017*
- The New York* metro area was identified as one of the 20 least affordable housing markets in the U.S. in 2017. The area ranked #12 out of 180 markets. Criteria: qualification for a mortgage loan on a typical home. *National Association of Realtors®, Affordability Index of Existing Single-Family Homes for Metropolitan Areas, 2017*
- New York* was ranked #219 out of 238 metro areas in terms of housing affordability in 2017 by the National Association of Home Builders (#1 = most affordable). Criteria: the share of homes sold in that area affordable to a family earning the local median income, based on standard mortgage underwriting criteria. *National Association of Home Builders®, NAHB-Wells Fargo Housing Opportunity Index, 4th Quarter 2017*

Safety Rankings

- The National Insurance Crime Bureau ranked 382 metro areas in the U.S. in terms of per capita rates of vehicle theft. The New York* metro area ranked #292 (#1 = highest rate). Criteria: number of vehicle theft offenses per 100,000 inhabitants in 2016. *National Insurance Crime Bureau, "Hot Spots 2016," June 8, 2017*

Seniors/Retirement Rankings

- From its Best Cities for Successful Aging indexes, the Milken Institute generated rankings for metropolitan areas, weighing data in nine categories—health care, wellness, living arrangements, transportation and convenience, financial characteristics, education, employment, community engagement, and overall livability. The New York* metro area was ranked #11 overall in the large metro area category. *Milken Institute, "Best Cities for Successful Aging, 2017" March 14, 2017*

Sports/Recreation Rankings

- According to the personal finance website NerdWallet, the New York* metro area, at #4, is one of the nation's top dozen metro areas for sports fans. Criteria included the presence of all four major sports—MLB, NFL, NHL, and NBA, fan enthusiasm (as measured by game attendance), ticket affordability, and "sports culture," that is, number of sports bars. *www.nerdwallet.com, "Best Cities for Sports Fans," May 5, 2013*

Transportation Rankings

- New York* was identified as one of the most congested metro areas in the U.S. The area ranked #4 out of 10. Criteria: yearly delay per auto commuter in hours. *Texas A&M Transportation Institute, "2015 Urban Mobility Scorecard," August 2015*

- The New York* metro area appeared on *Forbes* list of places with the most extreme commutes. The metro area ranked #2 out of 10. Criteria: average travel time; percentage of mega commuters. Mega-commuters travel more than 90 minutes and 50 miles each way to work. *Forbes.com, "The Cities with the Most Extreme Commutes," March 5, 2013*

Women/Minorities Rankings

- The *Houston Chronicle* listed the New York* metro area as #4 in top places for young Latinos to live in the U.S. Research was largely based on housing and occupational data from the largest metropolitan areas performed by *Forbes* and NBC Universo. Criteria: percentage of 18-34 year-olds; Latino college grad rates; and diversity. *blog.chron.com, "The 15 Best Big Cities for Latino Millenials," January 26, 2016*

Miscellaneous Rankings

- The watchdog site Charity Navigator conducts an annual study of charities in the nation's major markets both to analyze statistical differences in their financial, accountability, and transparency practices and to track year-to-year variations in individual philanthropic communities. Charity Navigator's analysis demonstrated that the financial, accountability and transparency behaviors of America's largest charities can be influenced by the metropolitan market within which the charity operates. The New York* metro area was ranked #19 among the 30 metro markets in the rating category of Overall Score. *www.charitynavigator.org, "2017 Metro Market Study," May 1, 2017*

- The Harris Poll's Happiness Index survey revealed that of the top ten U.S. markets, the New York* metro area residents ranked #6 in happiness. Criteria included strong assent to positive statements and strong disagreement with negative ones, and degree of agreement with a series of statements about respondents' personal relationships and general outlook. *www.theharrispoll.com, "Dallas/Fort Worth Is "Happiest" City among America's Top Ten Markets," September 4, 2013*

- Energizer Personal Care, the makers of Edge® shave gel, in partnership with Sperling's BestPlaces, ranked 50 major metro areas in terms of everyday irritations. The New York* metro area ranked #2 the 50 metro area most irritating to guys. Criteria: high male-to-female ratio; poor sports team performance and high ticket prices; slow traffic; lack of job availability; unaffordable housing; extreme weather; lack of nightlife and fitness options. *Energizer Personal Care, "Most Irritating Cities for Guys," August 26, 2013*

- The National Alliance to End Homelessness listed the 25 most populous metro areas with the highest rate of homelessness. The New York* metro area had a high rate of homelessness. Criteria: number of homeless people per 10,000 population in 2016. *National Alliance to End Homelessness, "Homelessness in the 25 Most Populous U.S. Metro Areas," September 1, 2017*

  *East Fishkill is located within the New York-Newark-Jersey City, NY-NJ-PA Metropolitan Statistical Area and the Dutchess County-Putnam County, NY Metropolitan Division.

Business Environment

CITY FINANCES

City Government Finances

Component	2015 ($000)	2015 ($ per capita)
Total Revenues	19,442	664
Total Expenditures	21,401	731
Debt Outstanding	24,357	832
Cash and Securities[1]	3,004	103

Note: (1) Cash and security holdings of a government at the close of its fiscal year,, including those of its dependent agencies, utilities, and liquor stores.
Source: U.S Census Bureau, State & Local Government Finances 2015

City Government Revenue by Source

Source	2015 ($000)	2015 ($ per capita)	2015 (%)
General Revenue			
From Federal Government	0	0	0.0
From State Government	467	16	2.4
From Local Governments	1,661	57	8.5
Taxes			
Property	12,164	415	62.6
Sales and Gross Receipts	427	15	2.2
Personal Income	0	0	0.0
Corporate Income	0	0	0.0
Motor Vehicle License	0	0	0.0
Other Taxes	1,152	39	5.9
Current Charges	958	33	4.9
Liquor Store	0	0	0.0
Utility	604	21	3.1
Employee Retirement	0	0	0.0

Source: U.S Census Bureau, State & Local Government Finances 2015

City Government Expenditures by Function

Function	2015 ($000)	2015 ($ per capita)	2015 (%)
General Direct Expenditures			
Air Transportation	0	0	0.0
Corrections	0	0	0.0
Education	0	0	0.0
Employment Security Administration	0	0	0.0
Financial Administration	610	20	2.9
Fire Protection	5	< 1	< 0.1
General Public Buildings	199	6	0.9
Governmental Administration, Other	407	13	1.9
Health	10	< 1	< 0.1
Highways	4,729	161	22.1
Hospitals	0	0	0.0
Housing and Community Development	0	0	0.0
Interest on General Debt	2,112	72	9.9
Judicial and Legal	427	14	2.0
Libraries	0	0	0.0
Parking	0	0	0.0
Parks and Recreation	1,259	43	5.9
Police Protection	4,048	138	18.9
Public Welfare	0	0	0.0
Sewerage	579	19	2.7
Solid Waste Management	42	1	0.2
Veterans' Services	0	0	0.0
Liquor Store	0	0	0.0
Utility	734	25	3.4
Employee Retirement	0	0	0.0

Source: U.S Census Bureau, State & Local Government Finances 2015

DEMOGRAPHICS

Population Growth

Area	1990 Census	2000 Census	2010 Census	2016* Estimate	Population Growth (%) 1990-2016	Population Growth (%) 2010-2016
City	22,101	25,589	29,029	29,282	32.5	0.9
MSA[1]	16,845,992	18,323,002	18,897,109	20,031,443	18.9	6.0
U.S.	248,709,873	281,421,906	308,745,538	318,558,162	28.1	3.2

Note: (1) Figures cover the New York-Newark-Jersey City, NY-NJ-PA Metropolitan Statistical Area—see Appendix B for areas included; (*) 2012-2016 5-year estimated population
Source: U.S. Census Bureau, 1990 Census, Census 2000, Census 2010, 2012-2016 American Community Survey 5-Year Estimates

Household Size

Area	Persons in Household (%) One	Two	Three	Four	Five	Six	Seven or More	Average Household Size
City	13.6	34.0	18.4	20.1	9.7	2.2	1.9	3.10
MSA[1]	28.0	29.1	17.0	14.7	6.7	2.6	1.9	2.80
U.S.	27.7	33.7	15.7	13.1	6.0	2.3	1.5	2.60

Note: (1) Figures cover the New York-Newark-Jersey City, NY-NJ-PA Metropolitan Statistical Area—see Appendix B for areas included
Source: U.S. Census Bureau, 2012-2016 American Community Survey 5-Year Estimates

Race

Area	White Alone[2] (%)	Black Alone[2] (%)	Asian Alone[2] (%)	AIAN[3] Alone[2] (%)	NHOPI[4] Alone[2] (%)	Other Race Alone[2] (%)	Two or More Races (%)
City	88.0	2.3	3.5	0.2	0.0	2.7	3.3
MSA[1]	58.7	17.1	10.6	0.3	0.0	10.3	2.9
U.S.	73.3	12.6	5.2	0.8	0.2	4.8	3.1

Note: (1) Figures cover the New York-Newark-Jersey City, NY-NJ-PA Metropolitan Statistical Area—see Appendix B for areas included; (2) Alone is defined as not being in combination with one or more other races; (3) American Indian and Alaska Native; (4) Native Hawaiian and Other Pacific Islander
Source: U.S. Census Bureau, 2012-2016 American Community Survey 5-Year Estimates

Hispanic or Latino Origin

Area	Total (%)	Mexican (%)	Puerto Rican (%)	Cuban (%)	Other (%)
City	7.4	1.0	3.1	0.4	2.9
MSA[1]	23.8	3.1	6.3	0.7	13.7
U.S.	17.3	11.0	1.7	0.7	4.0

Note: Persons of Hispanic or Latino origin can be of any race; (1) Figures cover the New York-Newark-Jersey City, NY-NJ-PA Metropolitan Statistical Area—see Appendix B for areas included
Source: U.S. Census Bureau, 2012-2016 American Community Survey 5-Year Estimates

Segregation

Type	Segregation Indices[1] 1990	2000	2010	2010 Rank[2]	Percent Change 1990-2000	1990-2010	2000-2010
Black/White	80.9	80.2	78.0	2	-0.7	-2.9	-2.2
Asian/White	47.4	50.8	51.9	3	3.5	4.5	1.0
Hispanic/White	66.2	65.6	62.0	3	-0.6	-4.2	-3.6

Note: All figures cover the Metropolitan Statistical Area—see Appendix B for areas included; Figures are based on an analysis of 1990, 2000, and 2010 Census Decennial Census tract data by William H. Frey, Brookings Institution and the University of Michigan Social Science Data Analysis Network. In this analysis all racial groups (whites, blacks, and asians) are non-Hispanic members of those races. Hispanics are shown as a separate category; (1) Segregation Indices are Dissimilarity Indices that measure the degree to which the minority group is distributed differently than whites across census tracts. They range from 0 (complete integration) to 100 (complete segregation) where the value indicates the percentage of the minority group that needs to move to be distributed exactly like whites; (2) Ranges from 1 (most segregated) to 102 (least segregated); n/a not available.
Source: www.CensusScope.org

Ancestry

Area	German	Irish	English	American	Italian	Polish	French[2]	Scottish	Dutch
City	13.6	23.3	6.8	4.3	30.5	5.5	2.1	1.3	1.7
MSA[1]	6.8	10.0	2.9	4.8	13.1	4.0	1.0	0.7	0.7
U.S.	14.4	10.4	7.7	6.9	5.4	2.9	2.6	1.7	1.3

Note: Figures are the percentage of the total population reporting a particular ancestry. The nine most commonly reported ancestries in the U.S. are shown. Figures include multiple ancestries (e.g. if a person reported being Irish and Italian, they were included in both columns); (1) Figures cover the New York-Newark-Jersey City, NY-NJ-PA Metropolitan Statistical Area—see Appendix B for areas included; (2) Excludes Basque
Source: U.S. Census Bureau, 2012-2016 American Community Survey 5-Year Estimates

Foreign-Born Population

Area	Percent of Population Born in								
	Any Foreign Country	Asia	Mexico	Europe	Carribean	Central America[2]	South America	Africa	Canada
City	9.9	3.6	0.6	2.9	0.7	0.1	1.5	0.4	0.1
MSA[1]	28.7	8.3	1.6	4.5	6.6	1.9	4.2	1.2	0.2
U.S.	13.2	4.0	3.6	1.5	1.3	1.0	0.9	0.6	0.3

Note: (1) Figures cover the New York-Newark-Jersey City, NY-NJ-PA Metropolitan Statistical Area—see Appendix B for areas included; (2) Excludes Mexico.
Source: U.S. Census Bureau, 2012-2016 American Community Survey 5-Year Estimates

Marital Status

Area	Never Married	Now Married[2]	Separated	Widowed	Divorced
City	26.0	60.7	1.3	4.5	7.5
MSA[1]	38.1	45.7	2.4	5.8	7.9
U.S.	33.0	48.1	2.1	5.9	11.0

Note: Figures are percentages and cover the population 15 years of age and older; (1) Figures cover the New York-Newark-Jersey City, NY-NJ-PA Metropolitan Statistical Area—see Appendix B for areas included; (2) Excludes separated
Source: U.S. Census Bureau, 2012-2016 American Community Survey 5-Year Estimates

Disability Status

Area	All Ages	Under 18 Years Old	18 to 64 Years Old	65 Years and Over
City	10.9	4.1	7.5	38.5
MSA[1]	10.0	3.2	7.4	33.3
U.S.	12.5	4.1	10.3	35.7

Note: Figures show percent of the civilian noninstitutionalized population that reported having a disability. Disability status is determined from six types of difficulty: vision, hearing, cognitive, ambulatory, self-care, and independent living. For children under 5 years old, hearing and vision difficulty are used to determine disability status. For children between the ages of 5 and 14, disability status is determined from hearing, vision, cognitive, ambulatory, and self-care difficulties. For people aged 15 years and older, they are considered to have a disability if they have difficulty with any one of the six difficulty types; Note: (1) Figures cover the New York-Newark-Jersey City, NY-NJ-PA Metropolitan Statistical Area—see Appendix B for areas included
Source: U.S. Census Bureau, 2012-2016 American Community Survey 5-Year Estimates

Age

Area	Percent of Population									Median Age
	Under Age 5	Age 5–19	Age 20–34	Age 35–44	Age 45–54	Age 55–64	Age 65–74	Age 75–84	Age 85+	
City	4.6	22.4	14.5	11.7	19.0	14.1	8.3	3.9	1.5	42.8
MSA[1]	6.1	18.4	21.3	13.3	14.3	12.3	7.8	4.2	2.1	38.0
U.S.	6.2	19.6	20.7	12.7	13.6	12.6	8.3	4.3	1.9	37.7

Note: (1) Figures cover the New York-Newark-Jersey City, NY-NJ-PA Metropolitan Statistical Area—see Appendix B for areas included
Source: U.S. Census Bureau, 2012-2016 American Community Survey 5-Year Estimates

ECONOMY

Gender

Area	Males	Females	Males per 100 Females
City	14,789	14,493	102.0
MSA[1]	9,684,087	10,347,356	93.6
U.S.	156,765,322	161,792,840	96.9

Note: (1) Figures cover the New York-Newark-Jersey City, NY-NJ-PA Metropolitan Statistical Area—see Appendix B for areas included
Source: U.S. Census Bureau, 2012-2016 American Community Survey 5-Year Estimates

Religious Groups by Family

Area	Catholic	Baptist	Non-Den.	Methodist[2]	Lutheran	LDS[3]	Pente-costal	Presby-terian[4]	Muslim[5]	Judaism
MSA[1]	36.9	1.9	1.8	1.3	0.8	0.4	0.9	1.1	2.3	4.8
U.S.	19.1	9.3	4.0	4.0	2.3	2.0	1.9	1.6	0.8	0.7

Note: Figures are the number of adherents as a percentage of the total population; (1) Figures cover the New York-Newark-Jersey City, NY-NJ-PA Metropolitan Statistical Area—see Appendix B for areas included; (2) Methodist/Pietist; (3) Latter Day Saints; (4) Reformed; (5) Figures are estimates
Source: Association of Statisticians of American Religious Bodies, 2010 U.S. Religion Census: Religious Congregations & Membership Study

Religious Groups by Tradition

Area	Catholic	Evangelical Protestant	Mainline Protestant	Other Tradition	Black Protestant	Orthodox
MSA[1]	36.9	4.0	4.1	8.4	1.2	1.0
U.S.	19.1	16.2	7.3	4.3	1.6	0.3

Note: Figures are the number of adherents as a percentage of the total population; (1) Figures cover the New York-Newark-Jersey City, NY-NJ-PA Metropolitan Statistical Area—see Appendix B for areas included
Source: Association of Statisticians of American Religious Bodies, 2010 U.S. Religion Census: Religious Congregations & Membership Study

Gross Metropolitan Product

Area	2014	2015	2016	2017	Rank[2]
MSA[1]	1,551.3	1,613.8	1,664.0	1,735.1	1

Note: Figures are in billions of dollars; (1) Figures cover the New York-Newark-Jersey City, NY-NJ-PA Metropolitan Statistical Area—see Appendix B for areas included; (2) Rank is based on 2015 data and ranges from 1 to 381
Source: The U.S. Conference of Mayors, U.S. Metro Economies: GMP and Employment Report, 2015-2017

Economic Growth

Area	2012-14 (%)	2015 (%)	2016 (%)	2017 (%)	Rank[2]
MSA[1]	1.6	1.9	1.6	2.2	151
U.S.	2.0	2.4	1.9	2.6	–

Note: Figures are real gross metropolitan product (GMP) growth rates and represent average annual percent change; (1) Figures cover the New York-Newark-Jersey City, NY-NJ-PA Metropolitan Statistical Area—see Appendix B for areas included; (2) Rank is based on 2012-2014 average annual percent change and ranges from 1 to 381
Source: The U.S. Conference of Mayors, U.S. Metro Economies: GMP and Employment Report, 2015-2017

Metropolitan Area Exports

Area	2011	2012	2013	2014	2015	2016	Rank[2]
MSA[1]	105,102.0	102,298.0	106,922.8	105,266.6	95,645.4	89,649.5	1

Note: Figures are in millions of dollars; (1) Figures cover the New York-Newark-Jersey City, NY-NJ-PA Metropolitan Statistical Area—see Appendix B for areas included; (2) Rank is based on 2016 data and ranges from 1 to 385
Source: U.S. Department of Commerce, International Trade Administration, Office of Trade & Industry Information, Manufacturing & Services, data extracted March 15, 2018

Building Permits

Area	Single-Family			Multi-Family			Total		
	2016	2017p	Pct. Chg.	2016	2017p	Pct. Chg.	2016	2017p	Pct. Chg.
City	62	69	11.3	0	0	0.0	62	69	11.3
MSA[1]	9,987	10,549	5.6	32,479	39,344	21.1	42,466	49,893	17.5
U.S.	750,800	817,300	8.9	455,800	446,800	-2.0	1,206,600	1,264,100	4.8

Note: (1) Figures cover the New York-Newark-Jersey City, NY-NJ-PA Metropolitan Statistical Area—see Appendix B for areas included; Figures represent new, privately-owned housing units authorized (unadjusted data); All permit data are based on estimates with imputation; (p) preliminary data.
Source: U.S. Census Bureau, Manufacturing, Mining, and Construction Statistics, Building Permits, 2016, 2017

Bankruptcy Filings

Area	Business Filings			Nonbusiness Filings		
	2016	2017	% Chg.	2016	2017	% Chg.
Dutchess County	29	22	-24.1	643	665	3.4
U.S.	24,114	23,157	-4.0	770,846	765,863	-0.6

Note: Business filings include Chapter 7, Chapter 11, Chapter 12, and Chapter 13; Nonbusiness filings include Chapter 7, Chapter 11, and Chapter 13
Source: Administrative Office of the U.S. Courts, Business and Nonbusiness Bankruptcy, County Cases Commenced by Chapter of the Bankruptcy Code, During the 12-Month Period Ending December 31, 2016 and Business and Nonbusiness Bankruptcy, County Cases Commenced by Chapter of the Bankruptcy Code, During the 12-Month Period Ending December 31, 2017

Housing Vacancy Rates

Area	Gross Vacancy Rate[2] (%)			Year-Round Vacancy Rate[3] (%)			Rental Vacancy Rate[4] (%)			Homeowner Vacancy Rate[5] (%)		
	2015	2016	2017	2015	2016	2017	2015	2016	2017	2015	2016	2017
MSA[1]	9.8	10.3	10.7	8.6	9.1	9.6	4.2	4.7	4.6	2.1	2.2	1.9
U.S.	12.9	12.8	12.7	10.0	9.9	9.9	7.1	6.9	7.2	1.8	1.7	1.6

Note: (1) Figures cover the New York-Newark-Jersey City, NY-NJ-PA Metropolitan Statistical Area—see Appendix B for areas included; (2) The percentage of the total housing inventory that is vacant; (3) The percentage of the housing inventory (excluding seasonal units) that is year-round vacant; (4) The percentage of rental inventory that is vacant for rent; (5) The percentage of homeowner inventory that is vacant for sale
Source: U.S. Census Bureau, Housing Vacancies and Homeownership Annual Statistics: 2015, 2016, 2017

INCOME

Income

Area	Per Capita ($)	Median Household ($)	Average Household ($)
City	41,074	104,980	123,722
MSA[1]	37,510	69,211	101,617
U.S.	29,829	55,322	77,866

Note: (1) Figures cover the New York-Newark-Jersey City, NY-NJ-PA Metropolitan Statistical Area—see Appendix B for areas included
Source: U.S. Census Bureau, 2012-2016 American Community Survey 5-Year Estimates

Household Income Distribution

Area	Percent of Households Earning							
	Under $15,000	$15,000 -$24,999	$25,000 -$34,999	$35,000 -$49,999	$50,000 -$74,999	$75,000 -$99,999	$100,000 -$149,999	$150,000 and up
City	3.2	4.8	5.7	7.3	14.1	12.1	23.3	29.5
MSA[1]	11.7	8.5	7.7	10.2	15.0	11.7	15.9	19.3
U.S.	12.1	10.2	9.9	13.2	17.8	12.2	13.5	11.1

Note: (1) Figures cover the New York-Newark-Jersey City, NY-NJ-PA Metropolitan Statistical Area—see Appendix B for areas included
Source: U.S. Census Bureau, 2012-2016 American Community Survey 5-Year Estimates

Poverty Rate

Area	All Ages	Under 18 Years Old	18 to 64 Years Old	65 Years and Over
City	3.4	4.8	3.0	2.9
MSA[1]	14.2	20.0	12.7	11.7
U.S.	15.1	21.2	14.2	9.3

Note: Figures are percentage of people whose income during the past 12 months was below the poverty level; (1) Figures cover the New York-Newark-Jersey City, NY-NJ-PA Metropolitan Statistical Area—see Appendix B for areas included

Source: U.S. Census Bureau, 2012-2016 American Community Survey 5-Year Estimates

EMPLOYMENT

Labor Force and Employment

Area	Civilian Labor Force			Workers Employed		
	Dec. 2016	Dec. 2017	% Chg.	Dec. 2016	Dec. 2017	% Chg.
City	14,146	14,264	0.8	13,564	13,656	0.7
MD[1]	192,703	194,103	0.7	185,083	186,184	0.6
U.S.	158,968,000	159,880,000	0.6	151,798,000	153,602,000	1.2

Note: Data is not seasonally adjusted and covers workers 16 years of age and older; (1) Figures cover the Dutchess County-Putnam County, NY Metropolitan Division—see Appendix B for areas included

Source: Bureau of Labor Statistics, Local Area Unemployment Statistics

Unemployment Rate

Area	2017											
	Jan.	Feb.	Mar.	Apr.	May	Jun.	Jul.	Aug.	Sep.	Oct.	Nov.	Dec.
City	4.6	4.5	4.0	3.9	4.0	4.4	4.3	4.3	4.5	4.5	4.4	4.3
MD[1]	4.7	4.8	4.1	4.0	4.1	4.4	4.4	4.4	4.4	4.2	4.2	4.1
U.S.	5.1	4.9	4.6	4.1	4.1	4.5	4.6	4.5	4.1	3.9	3.9	3.9

Note: Data is not seasonally adjusted and covers workers 16 years of age and older; (1) Figures cover the Dutchess County-Putnam County, NY Metropolitan Division—see Appendix B for areas included

Source: Bureau of Labor Statistics, Local Area Unemployment Statistics

Average Wages

Occupation	$/Hr.	Occupation	$/Hr.
Accountants and Auditors	41.40	Maids and Housekeeping Cleaners	11.90
Automotive Mechanics	24.70	Maintenance and Repair Workers	19.60
Bookkeepers	20.50	Marketing Managers	n/a
Carpenters	25.10	Nuclear Medicine Technologists	n/a
Cashiers	10.90	Nurses, Licensed Practical	22.20
Clerks, General Office	15.90	Nurses, Registered	38.00
Clerks, Receptionists/Information	15.80	Nursing Assistants	16.50
Clerks, Shipping/Receiving	17.20	Packers and Packagers, Hand	13.90
Computer Programmers	33.70	Physical Therapists	40.20
Computer Systems Analysts	48.20	Postal Service Mail Carriers	24.00
Computer User Support Specialists	27.40	Real Estate Brokers	n/a
Cooks, Restaurant	14.30	Retail Salespersons	13.30
Dentists	96.50	Sales Reps., Exc. Tech./Scientific	33.00
Electrical Engineers	45.20	Sales Reps., Tech./Scientific	49.00
Electricians	26.80	Secretaries, Exc. Legal/Med./Exec.	19.00
Financial Managers	66.80	Security Guards	18.40
First-Line Supervisors/Managers, Sales	22.40	Surgeons	n/a
Food Preparation Workers	12.70	Teacher Assistants*	13.60
General and Operations Managers	62.10	Teachers, Elementary School*	41.00
Hairdressers/Cosmetologists	13.90	Teachers, Secondary School*	39.00
Internists, General	n/a	Telemarketers	n/a
Janitors and Cleaners	15.10	Truck Drivers, Heavy/Tractor-Trailer	22.80
Landscaping/Groundskeeping Workers	15.80	Truck Drivers, Light/Delivery Svcs.	15.30
Lawyers	70.70	Waiters and Waitresses	14.30

Note: Wage data covers the Dutchess County-Putnam County, NY Metropolitan Division—see Appendix B for areas included; (*) Hourly wages for elementary/secondary school teachers and teacher assistants were calculated by the editors from annual wage data based on a 40 hour work week; n/a not available.

Source: Bureau of Labor Statistics, Metro Area Occupational Employment & Wage Estimates, May 2017

Employment by Occupation

Occupation Classification	City (%)	MSA[1] (%)	U.S. (%)
Management, Business, Science, and Arts	46.8	41.2	37.0
Natural Resources, Construction, and Maintenance	9.6	6.9	8.9
Production, Transportation, and Material Moving	5.7	9.0	12.2
Sales and Office	22.5	23.7	23.8
Service	15.5	19.3	18.1

Note: Figures cover employed civilians 16 years of age and older; (1) Figures cover the New York-Newark-Jersey City, NY-NJ-PA Metropolitan Statistical Area—see Appendix B for areas included
Source: U.S. Census Bureau, 2012-2016 American Community Survey 5-Year Estimates

Employment by Industry

Sector	MD[1] Number of Employees	MD[1] Percent of Total	U.S. Percent of Total
Construction, Mining, and Logging	8,000	5.3	5.2
Education and Health Services	41,100	27.1	15.9
Financial Activities	4,800	3.2	5.7
Government	26,600	17.5	15.3
Information	1,900	1.3	1.9
Leisure and Hospitality	14,900	9.8	10.7
Manufacturing	9,600	6.3	8.5
Other Services	7,200	4.7	3.9
Professional and Business Services	12,700	8.4	14.0
Retail Trade	17,500	11.5	11.0
Transportation, Warehousing, and Utilities	4,500	3.0	4.1
Wholesale Trade	3,000	2.0	4.0

Note: Figures are non-farm employment as of December 2017. Figures are not seasonally adjusted and include workers 16 years of age and older; (1) Figures cover the Dutchess County-Putnam County, NY Metropolitan Division—see Appendix B for areas included
Source: Bureau of Labor Statistics, Current Employment Statistics, Employment, Hours, and Earnings

Occupations with Greatest Projected Employment Growth: 2017 – 2019

Occupation[1]	2017 Employment	2019 Projected Employment	Numeric Employment Change	Percent Employment Change
Home Health Aides	190,490	216,300	25,810	13.5
Personal Care Aides	174,700	189,420	14,720	8.4
Combined Food Preparation and Serving Workers, Including Fast Food	154,570	162,110	7,540	4.9
Registered Nurses	189,840	197,230	7,390	3.9
Janitors and Cleaners, Except Maids and Housekeeping Cleaners	211,280	217,380	6,100	2.9
Waiters and Waitresses	151,380	156,430	5,050	3.3
General and Operations Managers	165,860	169,970	4,110	2.5
Accountants and Auditors	124,740	128,070	3,330	2.7
Software Developers, Applications	52,730	55,940	3,210	6.1
Security Guards	114,180	117,140	2,960	2.6

Note: Projections cover New York; (1) Sorted by numeric employment change
Source: www.projectionscentral.com, State Occupational Projections, 2017–2019 Short-Term Projections

Fastest Growing Occupations: 2017 – 2019

Occupation[1]	2017 Employment	2019 Projected Employment	Numeric Employment Change	Percent Employment Change
Gaming and Sports Book Writers and Runners	660	810	150	24.0
Gaming Change Persons and Booth Cashiers	840	1,030	190	22.7
Solar Photovoltaic Installers	800	980	180	22.7
Gaming Dealers	960	1,150	190	19.4
Home Health Aides	190,490	216,300	25,810	13.5
Gaming Supervisors	580	660	80	12.3
Entertainment Attendants and Related Workers, All Other	490	540	50	9.8
Personal Care Aides	174,700	189,420	14,720	8.4
Physical Therapist Aides	3,110	3,330	220	6.9
Physical Therapists	18,480	19,750	1,270	6.9

Note: Projections cover New York; (1) Sorted by percent employment change and excludes occupations with numeric employment change less than 50
Source: www.projectionscentral.com, State Occupational Projections, 2017–2019 Short-Term Projections

TAXES

State Corporate Income Tax Rates

State	Tax Rate (%)	Income Brackets ($)	Num. of Brackets	Financial Institution Tax Rate (%)[a]	Federal Income Tax Ded.
New York	6.5 (r)	Flat rate	1	6.5 (r)	No

Note: Tax rates as of January 1, 2018; (a) Rates listed are the corporate income tax rate applied to financial institutions or excise taxes based on income. Some states have other taxes based upon the value of deposits or shares; (r) New York's General business corporate rate shown. Corporations may also be subject to a capital stocks tax, which is being phased out through 2021. A minimum tax ranges from $25 to $200,000, depending on receipts ($250 minimum for banks). Certain qualified New York manufacturers pay 0%.
Source: Federation of Tax Administrators, Range of State Corporate Income Tax Rates, January 1, 2018

State Individual Income Tax Rates

State	Tax Rate (%)	Income Brackets ($)	Num. of Brackets	Personal Exempt. ($)[1]		Fed. Inc. Tax Ded.
				Single	Dependents	
New York (a)	4.0 - 8.82	8,500 - 1,077,550 (b)	8	0	1,000	No

Note: Tax rates as of January 1, 2018; Local- and county-level taxes are not included; n/a not applicable; (1) Married joint filers generally receive double the single exemption; (a) 19 states have statutory provision for automatically adjusting to the rate of inflation the dollar values of the income tax brackets, standard deductions, and/or personal exemptions. Massachusetts, Michigan, and Nebraska index the personal exemption only. Oregon does not index the income brackets for $125,000 and over; (b) For joint returns, taxes are twice the tax on half the couple's income.
Source: Federation of Tax Administrators, State Individual Income Tax Rates, January 1, 2018

Various State Sales and Excise Tax Rates

State	State Sales Tax (%)	Gasoline[1] (¢/gal.)	Cigarette[2] ($/pack)	Spirits[3] ($/gal.)	Wine[4] ($/gal.)	Beer[5] ($/gal.)	Recreational Marijuana (%)
New York	4.0	44.3	4.35	6.44 (f)	0.30	0.14	Not legal

Note: All tax rates as of January 1, 2018; (1) The American Petroleum Institute has developed a methodology for determining the average tax rate on a gallon of fuel. Rates may include any of the following: excise taxes, environmental fees, storage tank fees, other fees or taxes, general sales tax, and local taxes. In states where gasoline is subject to the general sales tax, or where the fuel tax is based on the average sale price, the average rate determined by API is sensitive to changes in the price of gasoline. States that fully or partially apply general sales taxes to gasoline: CA, CO, GA, IL, IN, MI, NY; (2) The federal excise tax of $1.0066 per pack and local taxes are not included; (3) Rates are those applicable to off-premise sales of 40% alcohol by volume (a.b.v.) distilled spirits in 750ml containers. Local excise taxes are excluded; (4) Rates are those applicable to off-premise sales of 11% a.b.v. non-carbonated wine in 750ml containers; (5) Rates are those applicable to off-premise sales of 4.7% a.b.v. beer in 12 ounce containers; (f) Different rates also applicable according to alcohol content, place of production, size of container, or place purchased (on- or off-premise or onboard airlines).
Source: Tax Foundation, 2018 Facts & Figures: How Does Your State Compare?

State Business Tax Climate Index Rankings

State	Overall Rank	Corporate Tax Rank	Individual Income Tax Rank	Sales Tax Rank	Unemployment Insurance Tax Rank	Property Tax Rank
New York	49	7	49	43	30	47

Note: The index is a measure of how each state's tax laws affect economic performance. The lower the rank, the more favorable a state's tax system is for business. States without a given tax are given a ranking of 1. The scores/rankings for the District of Columbia do not affect other states. The 2018 index represents the tax climate as of July 1, 2017.
Source: Tax Foundation, State Business Tax Climate Index 2018

TRANSPORTATION

Means of Transportation to Work

Area	Car/Truck/Van		Public Transportation			Bicycle	Walked	Other Means	Worked at Home
	Drove Alone	Car-pooled	Bus	Subway	Railroad				
City	85.2	4.8	0.3	0.0	3.3	0.1	0.4	0.5	5.3
MSA[1]	50.1	6.6	7.7	19.1	3.8	0.6	6.0	1.8	4.2
U.S.	76.4	9.3	2.6	1.9	0.6	0.6	2.8	1.3	4.6

Note: Figures are percentages and cover workers 16 years of age and older; (1) Figures cover the New York-Newark-Jersey City, NY-NJ-PA Metropolitan Statistical Area—see Appendix B for areas included
Source: U.S. Census Bureau, 2012-2016 American Community Survey 5-Year Estimates

Travel Time to Work

Area	Less Than 10 Minutes	10 to 19 Minutes	20 to 29 Minutes	30 to 44 Minutes	45 to 59 Minutes	60 to 89 Minutes	90 Minutes or More
City	7.4	17.0	19.2	23.5	13.0	11.4	8.4
MSA[1]	7.4	19.3	16.4	23.7	12.4	14.4	6.5
U.S.	12.9	29.2	20.9	20.4	8.0	6.0	2.7

Note: Note: Figures are percentages and include workers 16 years old and over; (1) Figures cover the New York-Newark-Jersey City, NY-NJ-PA Metropolitan Statistical Area—see Appendix B for areas included
Source: U.S. Census Bureau, 2012-2016 American Community Survey 5-Year Estimates

Freeway Travel Time Index

Area	1985	1990	1995	2000	2005	2010	2014
Urban Area Rank[1,2]	11	9	8	7	7	8	8
Urban Area Index[1]	1.16	1.20	1.24	1.29	1.33	1.33	1.34
Average Index[3]	1.09	1.11	1.14	1.17	1.20	1.19	1.20

Note: Freeway Travel Time Index—the ratio of travel time in the peak period to the travel time at free-flow conditions. For example, a value of 1.30 indicates a 20-minute free-flow trip takes 26 minutes in the peak (20 minutes x 1.30 = 26 minutes); (1) Covers the New York-Newark NY-NJ-CT urban area; (2) Rank is based on 101 urban areas (#1 = highest travel time index); (3) Average of 101 urban areas
Source: Texas Transportation Institute, 2015 Urban Mobility Scorecard, August 2015

Freeway Commuter Stress Index

Area	1985	1990	1995	2000	2005	2010	2014
Urban Area Rank[1,2]	19	19	13	12	11	11	12
Urban Area Index[1]	1.21	1.24	1.29	1.34	1.38	1.38	1.39
Average Index[3]	1.13	1.16	1.19	1.22	1.25	1.24	1.25

Note: The Freeway Commuter Stress Index is the same as the Freeway Travel Time Index (see table above) except that it includes only the travel in the peak directions during the peak periods; the TTI includes travel in all directions during the peak period. Thus, the CSI is more indicative of the work trip experienced by each commuter on a daily basis; (1) Covers the New York-Newark NY-NJ-CT urban area; (2) Rank is based on 101 urban areas (#1 = highest travel time index); (3) Average of 101 urban areas
Source: Texas Transportation Institute, 2015 Urban Mobility Scorecard, August 2015

Living Environment

COST OF LIVING

Cost of Living Index

Composite Index	Groceries	Housing	Utilities	Trans-portation	Health Care	Misc. Goods/ Services
n/a	n/a	n/a	n/a	n/a	n/a	n/a

Note: The Cost of Living Index measures regional differences in the cost of consumer goods and services, excluding taxes and non-consumer expenditures, for professional and managerial households in the top income quintile. It is based on more than 50,000 prices covering almost 60 different items for which prices are collected three times a year by chambers of commerce, economic development organizations or university applied economic centers in each participating urban area. The numbers shown should be read as a percentage above or below the national average of 100. For example, a value of 115.4 in the groceries column indicates that grocery prices are 15.4% higher than the national average. Small differences in the index numbers should not be interpreted as significant; n/a not available.
Source: The Council for Community and Economic Research, ACCRA Cost of Living Index, 2017

Grocery Prices

Area[1]	T-Bone Steak ($/pound)	Frying Chicken ($/pound)	Whole Milk ($/half gal.)	Eggs ($/dozen)	Orange Juice ($/64 oz.)	Coffee ($/11.5 oz.)
City[2]	n/a	n/a	n/a	n/a	n/a	n/a
Avg.	11.29	1.40	2.02	1.47	3.55	4.37
Min.	7.71	0.93	1.04	0.70	2.86	3.24
Max.	15.83	2.39	4.03	3.92	6.29	8.16

Note: (1) Values for the local area are compared with the average, minimum and maximum values for all 294 areas in the Cost of Living Index; (2) Figures cover the East Fishkill NY urban area; n/a not available; ***T-Bone Steak*** *(price per pound);* ***Frying Chicken*** *(price per pound, whole fryer);* ***Whole Milk*** *(half gallon carton);* ***Eggs*** *(price per dozen, Grade A, large);* ***Orange Juice*** *(64 oz. Tropicana or Florida Natural);* ***Coffee*** *(11.5 oz. can, vacuum-packed, Maxwell House, Hills Bros, or Folgers).*
Source: The Council for Community and Economic Research, ACCRA Cost of Living Index, 2017

Housing and Utility Costs

Area[1]	New Home Price ($)	Apartment Rent ($/month)	All Electric ($/month)	Part Electric ($/month)	Other Energy ($/month)	Telephone ($/month)
City[2]	n/a	n/a	n/a	n/a	n/a	n/a
Avg.	335,956	1,047	175.01	97.34	67.93	28.71
Min.	187,788	491	109.48	49.33	35.44	12.39
Max.	1,739,087	4,559	432.62	227.09	353.33	44.61

Note: (1) Values for the local area are compared with the average, minimum and maximum values for all 294 areas in the Cost of Living Index; (2) Figures cover the East Fishkill NY urban area; n/a not available; ***New Home Price*** *(2,400 sf living area, 8,000 sf lot, in urban area with full utilities);* ***Apartment Rent*** *(950 sf 2 bedroom/1.5 or 2 bath, unfurnished, excluding all utilities except water);* ***All Electric*** *(average monthly cost for an all-electric home);* ***Part Electric*** *(average monthly cost for a part-electric home);* ***Other Energy*** *(average monthly cost for natural gas, fuel oil, coal, wood, and any other forms of energy except electricity);* ***Telephone*** *(price includes basic monthly rate for a private residential line plus additional local usage charges incurred by a family of four).*
Source: The Council for Community and Economic Research, ACCRA Cost of Living Index, 2017

Health Care, Transportation, and Other Costs

Area[1]	Doctor ($/visit)	Dentist ($/visit)	Optometrist ($/visit)	Gasoline ($/gallon)	Beauty Salon ($/visit)	Men's Shirt ($)
City[2]	n/a	n/a	n/a	n/a	n/a	n/a
Avg.	108.00	92.54	101.93	2.25	37.58	30.92
Min.	30.39	60.00	49.75	1.82	16.11	11.20
Max.	193.50	161.94	229.28	3.16	77.35	59.13

Note: (1) Values for the local area are compared with the average, minimum and maximum values for all 294 areas in the Cost of Living Index; (2) Figures cover the East Fishkill NY urban area; n/a not available; ***Doctor*** *(general practitioners routine exam of an established patient);* ***Dentist*** *(adult teeth cleaning and periodic oral examination);* ***Optometrist*** *(full vision eye exam for established adult patient);* ***Gasoline*** *(one gallon regular unleaded, national brand, including all taxes, cash price at self-service pump if available);* ***Beauty Salon*** *(woman's shampoo, trim, and blow-dry);* ***Men's Shirt*** *(cotton/polyester dress shirt, pinpoint weave, long sleeves).*
Source: The Council for Community and Economic Research, ACCRA Cost of Living Index, 2017

HOUSING

House Price Index (HPI)

Area	National Ranking[2]	Quarterly Change (%)	One-Year Change (%)	Five-Year Change (%)
MD[1]	208	-0.39	3.44	10.16
U.S.[3]	–	1.61	6.68	34.71

Note: The HPI is a weighted repeat sales index. It measures average price changes in repeat sales or refinancings on the same properties. This information is obtained by reviewing repeat mortgage transactions on single-family properties whose mortgages have been purchased or securitized by Fannie Mae or Freddie Mac in January 1975; (1) Figures cover the Dutchess County-Putnam County, NY Metropolitan Division—see Appendix B for areas included; (2) Rankings are based on annual percentage change for all metro areas containing at least 15,000 transactions over the last 10 years and ranges from 1 to 253; (3) figures based on a weighted average of Census Division estimates using a seasonally adjusted, purchase-only index; all figures are for the period ending December 31, 2017

Source: Federal Housing Finance Agency, House Price Index, February 28, 2018

Median Single-Family Home Prices

Area	2015	2016	2017p	Percent Change 2016 to 2017
MSA[1]	386.8	388.5	404.3	4.1
U.S. Average	223.9	235.5	248.8	5.6

Note: Figures are median sales prices of existing single-family homes in thousands of dollars; (p) preliminary; (1) Figures cover the New York-Newark-Jersey City, NY-NJ-PA Metropolitan Statistical Area—see Appendix B for areas included

Source: National Association of Realtors, Median Sales Price of Existing Single-Family Homes for Metropolitan Areas, 4th Quarter 2017

Qualifying Income Based on Median Sales Price of Existing Single-Family Homes

Area	With 5% Down ($)	With 10% Down ($)	With 20% Down ($)
MSA[1]	88,805	84,131	74,784
U.S. Average	55,585	52,659	46,808

Note: Figures are preliminary; Qualifying income is based on a mortgage rate of 4.17%. Monthly principal and interest payment is limited to 25% of income; (1) Figures cover the New York-Newark-Jersey City, NY-NJ-PA Metropolitan Statistical Area—see Appendix B for areas included

Source: National Association of Realtors, Qualifying Income Based on Median Sales Price of Existing Single-Family Homes for Metropolitan Areas, 4th Quarter 2017

Median Apartment Condo-Coop Home Prices

Area	2015	2016	2017p	Percent Change 2016 to 2017
MSA[1]	n/a	n/a	n/a	n/a
U.S. Average	210.7	220.7	234.3	6.2

Note: Figures are median sales prices of existing apartment condo-coop homes in thousands of dollars; (p) preliminary; n/a not available; (1) Figures cover the New York-Newark-Jersey City, NY-NJ-PA Metropolitan Statistical Area—see Appendix B for areas included

Source: National Association of Realtors, Median Sales Price of Existing Apartment Condo-Coop Homes for Metropolitan Areas, 4th Quarter 2017

Home Value Distribution

Area	Under $50,000	$50,000 -$99,999	$100,000 -$149,999	$150,000 -$199,999	$200,000 -$299,999	$300,000 -$499,999	$500,000 -$999,999	$1,000,000 or more
City	2.1	0.8	1.4	4.2	25.8	49.2	16.2	0.5
MSA[1]	2.8	1.8	2.9	5.0	16.2	37.0	26.9	7.3
U.S.	8.8	14.8	15.3	14.9	18.4	16.4	9.0	2.5

Note: Figures are percentages and cover owner-occupied housing units; (1) Figures cover the New York-Newark-Jersey City, NY-NJ-PA Metropolitan Statistical Area—see Appendix B for areas included

Source: U.S. Census Bureau, 2012-2016 American Community Survey 5-Year Estimates

Homeownership Rate

Area	2009 (%)	2010 (%)	2011 (%)	2012 (%)	2013 (%)	2014 (%)	2015 (%)	2016 (%)	2017 (%)
MSA[1]	51.7	51.6	50.9	51.5	50.6	50.7	49.9	50.4	49.9
U.S.	67.4	66.9	66.1	65.4	65.1	64.5	63.7	63.4	63.9

Note: (1) Figures cover the New York-Newark-Jersey City, NY-NJ-PA Metropolitan Statistical Area—see Appendix B for areas included

Source: U.S. Census Bureau, Housing Vacancies and Homeownership Annual Statistics: 2009-2017

Year Housing Structure Built

Area	2010 or Later	2000 -2009	1990 -1999	1980 -1989	1970 -1979	1960 -1969	1950 -1959	1940 -1949	Before 1940	Median Year
City	1.7	15.2	13.2	16.9	21.3	13.7	9.0	2.8	6.2	1979
MSA[1]	1.3	7.2	6.1	7.9	10.0	13.8	16.2	9.1	28.3	1958
U.S.	2.3	14.7	14.0	13.7	15.6	10.9	10.6	5.2	13.0	1977

Note: Figures are percentages except for Median Year; Note: (1) Figures cover the New York-Newark-Jersey City, NY-NJ-PA Metropolitan Statistical Area—see Appendix B for areas included
Source: U.S. Census Bureau, 2012-2016 American Community Survey 5-Year Estimates

Gross Monthly Rent

Area	Under $500	$500 -$999	$1,000 -$1,499	$1,500 -$1,999	$2,000 -$2,499	$2,500 -$2,999	$3,000 and up	Median ($)
City	3.7	32.2	36.4	8.5	10.9	4.8	3.4	1,191
MSA[1]	9.7	18.7	35.2	19.8	8.3	3.8	4.5	1,297
U.S.	11.3	43.3	27.7	10.7	4.0	1.6	1.5	949

Note: Figures are percentages except for Median; Gross rent is the contract rent plus the estimated average monthly cost of utilities (electricity, gas, and water and sewer) and fuels (oil, coal, kerosene, wood, etc.) if these are paid by the renter (or paid for the renter by someone else); (1) Figures cover the New York-Newark-Jersey City, NY-NJ-PA Metropolitan Statistical Area—see Appendix B for areas included
Source: U.S. Census Bureau, 2012-2016 American Community Survey 5-Year Estimates

HEALTH

Health Risk Factors

Category	MD[1] (%)	U.S. (%)
Adults aged 18–64 who have any kind of health care coverage	91.4	87.7
Adults who reported being in good or excellent health	84.7	83.6
Adults who are current smokers	15.7	17.1
Adults who currently use E-cigarettes	3.5	4.7
Adults who currently use chewing tobacco, snuff, or snus	1.9	4.0
Adults who are heavy drinkers[2]	5.4	6.5
Adults who are binge drinkers[3]	16.8	16.9
Adults who are overweight (BMI 25.0 - 29.9)	34.8	35.3
Adults who are obese (BMI 30.0 - 99.8)	25.3	29.9
Adults who participated in any physical activities in the past month	75.1	76.9
Adults who always or nearly always wears a seat belt	97.6	94.3

Note: (1) Figures cover the Dutchess County-Putnam County, NY Metropolitan Division—see Appendix B for areas included; (2) Heavy drinkers are classified as adult men having more than 14 drinks per week and adult women having more than 7 drinks per week; (3) Binge drinkers are classified as males having five or more drinks on one occasion or females having four or more drinks on one occasion
Source: Centers for Disease Control and Prevention, Behaviorial Risk Factor Surveillance System, SMART: Selected Metropolitan Area Risk Trends, 2016

Health Screening Rates

Category	MD[1] (%)	U.S. (%)
Adults 50-75 who have had a blood stool test within the past year	11.3	8.0
Adults 50-75 who have had a colonoscopy in the past 10 years	67.9	63.5
Adults aged 65+ who have had flu shot within the past year	54.3	58.6
Adults aged 65+ who have ever had a pneumonia vaccination	66.5	73.4
Adults who have ever been tested for HIV	42.6	35.6
Women aged 21-65 who have had a pap test in the past three years	81.0	79.8
Men aged 40+ who have had a PSA test within the past two years	43.2	39.5
Women aged 40+ who have had a mammogram within the past two years	81.2	72.5

Note: n/a not available; (1) Figures cover the Dutchess County-Putnam County, NY Metropolitan Division—see Appendix B for areas included; Source: Centers for Disease Control and Prevention, Behaviorial Risk Factor Surveillance System, SMART: Selected Metropolitan Area Risk Trends, 2016

Chronic Health Conditions

Category	MD[1] (%)	U.S. (%)
Adults who have ever been told they had a heart attack	3.6	4.4
Adults who have ever been told they have angina or coronary heart disease	3.7	4.1
Adults who have ever been told they had a stroke	2.1	3.1
Adults who have been told they currently have asthma	10.5	9.3
Adults who have ever been told they have arthritis	25.5	25.8
Adults who have ever been told they have diabetes[2]	9.5	10.5
Adults who have ever been told they had skin cancer	5.4	5.9
Adults who have ever been told they had any other types of cancer	7.8	6.7
Adults who have ever been told they have COPD	4.7	6.3
Adults who have ever been told they have kidney disease	n/a	2.8
Adults who have ever been told they have a form of depression	12.1	17.4

Note: n/a not available; (1) Figures cover the Dutchess County-Putnam County, NY Metropolitan Division—see Appendix B for areas included; (2) Figures do not include pregnancy-related, borderline, or pre-diabetes
Source: Centers for Disease Control and Prevention, Behaviorial Risk Factor Surveillance System, SMART: Selected Metropolitan Area Risk Trends, 2016

Mortality Rates for the Top 10 Causes of Death in the U.S.

ICD-10[a] Sub-Chapter	ICD-10[a] Code	Age-Adjusted Mortality Rate[1] per 100,000 population	
		County[2]	U.S.
Malignant neoplasms	C00-C97	147.7	158.5
Ischaemic heart diseases	I20-I25	103.3	96.8
Other forms of heart disease	I30-I51	51.8	52.4
Chronic lower respiratory diseases	J40-J47	34.5	40.9
Cerebrovascular diseases	I60-I69	25.8	37.2
Organic, including symptomatic, mental disorders	F01-F09	23.7	33.3
Other degenerative diseases of the nervous system	G30-G31	11.4	32.1
Other external causes of accidental injury	W00-X59	29.9	31.2
Diabetes mellitus	E10-E14	12.7	21.1
Hypertensive diseases	I10-I15	27.1	20.8

Note: (a) ICD-10 = International Classification of Diseases 10th Revision; (1) Mortality rates are a three year average covering 2014-2016; (2) Figures cover Dutchess County.
Source: Centers for Disease Control and Prevention, National Center for Health Statistics. Underlying Cause of Death 1999-2016 on CDC WONDER Online Database, released December 2017

Mortality Rates for Selected Causes of Death

ICD-10[a] Sub-Chapter	ICD-10[a] Code	Age-Adjusted Mortality Rate[1] per 100,000 population	
		County[2]	U.S.
Assault	X85-Y09	Unreliable	5.6
Diseases of the liver	K70-K76	8.3	14.0
Human immunodeficiency virus (HIV) disease	B20-B24	Unreliable	1.9
Influenza and pneumonia	J09-J18	16.0	14.6
Intentional self-harm	X60-X84	10.8	13.2
Malnutrition	E40-E46	Suppressed	1.3
Obesity and other hyperalimentation	E65-E68	Unreliable	2.1
Renal failure	N17-N19	11.3	13.0
Transport accidents	V01-V99	7.1	12.0
Viral hepatitis	B15-B19	Unreliable	1.9

Note: (a) ICD-10 = International Classification of Diseases 10th Revision; (1) Mortality rates are a three year average covering 2014-2016; (2) Figures cover Dutchess County; Data are Suppressed when the data meet the criteria for confidentiality constraints; Mortality rates are flagged as Unreliable when the rate would be calculated with a numerator of 20 or less.
Source: Centers for Disease Control and Prevention, National Center for Health Statistics. Underlying Cause of Death 1999-2016 on CDC WONDER Online Database, released December 2017

Health Insurance Coverage

Area	With Health Insurance	With Private Health Insurance	With Public Health Insurance	Without Health Insurance	Population Under Age 18 Without Health Insurance
City	94.8	82.5	23.2	5.2	4.6
MSA[1]	89.8	65.8	33.7	10.2	3.6
U.S.	88.3	66.7	33.0	11.7	5.9

Note: Figures are percentages that cover the civilian noninstitutionalized population; (1) Figures cover the New York-Newark-Jersey City, NY-NJ-PA Metropolitan Statistical Area—see Appendix B for areas included
Source: U.S. Census Bureau, 2012-2016 American Community Survey 5-Year Estimates

Number of Medical Professionals

Area	MDs[3]	DOs[3,4]	Dentists	Podiatrists	Chiropractors	Optometrists
County[1] (number)	741	53	211	32	82	40
County[1] (rate[2])	250.9	17.9	71.6	10.9	27.8	13.6
U.S. (rate[2])	276.5	22.3	67.3	6.0	26.7	15.9

Note: Data as of 2016 unless noted; (1) Data covers Dutchess County; (2) Rate per 100,000 population; (3) Data as of 2015 and includes all active, non-federal physicians; (4) Doctor of Osteopathic Medicine
Source: U.S. Department of Health and Human Services, Health Resources and Services Administration, Bureau of Health Professions, Area Resource File (ARF) 2016-2017

EDUCATION

Public School District Statistics

District Name	Schls	Pupils	Pupil/ Teacher Ratio	Minority Pupils[1] (%)	Free Lunch Eligible[2] (%)	IEP[3] (%)
Wappingers Central School District	15	11,168	14.7	27.1	17.3	17.6

Note: Table includes school districts with 100 or more students; (1) Percentage of students that are not non-Hispanic white; (2) Percentage of students that are eligible for the free lunch program; (3) Percentage of students that have an Individualized Education Program.
Source: U.S. Department of Education, National Center for Education Statistics, Common Core of Data, Local Education Agency (School District) Universe Survey: School Year 2015-2016; U.S. Department of Education, National Center for Education Statistics, Common Core of Data, Public Elementary/Secondary School Universe Survey: School Year 2015-2016

Highest Level of Education

Area	Less than H.S.	H.S. Diploma	Some College, No Deg.	Associate Degree	Bachelor's Degree	Master's Degree	Prof. School Degree	Doctorate Degree
City	7.2	26.0	18.1	8.2	23.0	14.0	2.5	0.9
MSA[1]	14.3	25.3	15.5	6.7	22.3	11.3	3.0	1.5
U.S.	13.0	27.5	21.0	8.2	18.8	8.2	2.0	1.3

Note: Figures cover persons age 25 and over; (1) Figures cover the New York-Newark-Jersey City, NY-NJ-PA Metropolitan Statistical Area—see Appendix B for areas included
Source: U.S. Census Bureau, 2012-2016 American Community Survey 5-Year Estimates

Educational Attainment by Race

Area	High School Graduate or Higher (%)					Bachelor's Degree or Higher (%)				
	Total	White	Black	Asian	Hisp.[2]	Total	White	Black	Asian	Hisp.[2]
City	92.8	93.9	92.6	91.7	72.7	40.4	39.7	54.7	70.9	22.1
MSA[1]	85.7	90.0	84.1	82.9	68.9	38.1	43.2	23.8	53.1	17.7
U.S.	87.0	88.9	84.3	86.3	65.7	30.3	31.6	20.0	52.1	14.7

Note: Figures shown cover persons 25 years old and over; (1) Figures cover the New York-Newark-Jersey City, NY-NJ-PA Metropolitan Statistical Area—see Appendix B for areas included; (2) People of Hispanic origin can be of any race
Source: U.S. Census Bureau, 2012-2016 American Community Survey 5-Year Estimates

School Enrollment by Grade and Control

Area	Preschool (%)		Kindergarten (%)		Grades 1 - 4 (%)		Grades 5 - 8 (%)		Grades 9 - 12 (%)	
	Public	Private	Public	Private	Public	Private	Public	Private	Public	Private
City	5.1	94.9	87.0	13.0	84.5	15.5	89.6	10.4	91.7	8.3
MSA[1]	51.9	48.1	81.6	18.4	86.1	13.9	86.3	13.7	85.9	14.1
U.S.	58.4	41.6	87.7	12.3	89.8	10.2	89.7	10.3	90.4	9.6

Note: Figures shown cover persons 3 years old and over; (1) Figures cover the New York-Newark-Jersey City, NY-NJ-PA Metropolitan Statistical Area—see Appendix B for areas included
Source: U.S. Census Bureau, 2012-2016 American Community Survey 5-Year Estimates

Average Salaries of Public School Classroom Teachers

Area	2015 Dollars	2015 Rank[1]	2016 Dollars	2016 Rank[1]	Change from 2015 to 2016 Percent	Change from 2015 to 2016 Rank[2]
New York	77,628	1	79,152	1	2.0	12
U.S. Average	57,611	–	58,353	–	1.3	–

Note: (1) Rank ranges from 1 to 51 where 1 indicates highest salary; (2) Rank ranges from 1 to 51 where 1 indicates highest percent change.
Source: National Education Association, Rankings & Estimates: Rankings of the States 2016 and Estimates of School Statistics 2017

Higher Education

Four-Year Colleges			Two-Year Colleges			Medical Schools[1]	Law Schools[2]	Voc/ Tech[3]
Public	Private Non-profit	Private For-profit	Public	Private Non-profit	Private For-profit			
0	0	0	0	0	0	0	0	0

Note: Figures cover institutions located within the city limits and include main campuses only; (1) includes schools accredited by the Liaison Committee on Medical Education and the American Osteopathic Association's Commission on Osteopathic College Accreditation; (2) includes ABA-accredited schools, schools with provisional ABA accreditation, and state accredited schools; (3) includes all schools with programs that are less than 2 years.
Source: National Center for Education Statistics, Integrated Postsecondary Education System (IPEDS), 2016-17; Wikipedia, List of Medical Schools in the United States, accessed April 2, 2018; Wikipedia, List of Law Schools in the United States, accessed April 2, 2018

PRESIDENTIAL ELECTION

2016 Presidential Election Results

Area	Clinton	Trump	Johnson	Stein	Other
Dutchess County	47.5	47.2	2.7	1.5	1.0
U.S.	48.0	45.9	3.3	1.1	1.7

Note: Results are percentages and may not add to 100% due to rounding
Source: Dave Leip's Atlas of U.S. Presidential Elections

EMPLOYERS

Major Employers

Company Name	Industry
American Express Company	Personal credit institutions
American International Group	Life insurance
Deloitte Consulting	Management consulting services
Hackensack University Medical Center	University
Merrill Lynch and Co	Security brokers & dealers
Mount Sinai Hospital	General medical & surgical hospitals
Mount Sinai School of Medicine	Medical training services
NewYork-Presbyterian Hospital	General medical & surgical hospitals
NYC Health and Hospitals Corp	Psychiatric hospitals
NYU School of Medicine	Offices & clinics of medical doctors
Paramount Comm Acq Corp	Investment holding companies, except banks
Patriarch Partners	Investment offices
Rutgers, The State Univ of NJ	Colleges & universities
Standard Americas	Agencies of foreign banks
The Long Island Rail Road Company	Local & suburban transit
U of Med and Dentistry of NJ	Colleges & universities
UMASS Memorial Health Care	Psychiatrist
United States Postal Service	U.S. postal service
Wellchoice	Health insurance carriers

Note: Companies shown are located within the New York-Newark-Jersey City, NY-NJ-PA Metropolitan Statistical Area.
Source: Hoovers.com; Wikipedia

PUBLIC SAFETY

Crime Rate

Area	All Crimes	Violent Crimes				Property Crimes		
		Murder	Rape[3]	Robbery	Aggrav. Assault	Burglary	Larceny -Theft	Motor Vehicle Theft
City	624.2	0.0	10.2	0.0	34.1	37.5	508.3	34.1
Metro[1]	1,209.5	1.0	30.9	30.9	92.2	145.8	882.7	26.0
U.S.	2,847.8	5.3	40.4	102.8	248.5	468.9	1,745.0	236.9

Note: Figures are crimes per 100,000 population; (1) Figures cover the Dutchess County-Putnam County, NY Metropolitan Division—see Appendix B for areas included; (3) The city and U.S. figures shown were reported using the revised Uniform Crime Reporting (UCR) definition of rape. The metro area figures shown are an aggregate total of the data submitted using both the revised and legacy UCR definitions.
Source: FBI Uniform Crime Reports, 2016

Hate Crimes

Area	Number of Quarters Reported	Number of Incidents per Bias Motivation					
		Race/Ethnicity/ Ancestry	Religion	Sexual Orientation	Disability	Gender	Gender Identity
Area[1]	4	0	0	0	0	0	0
U.S.	4	3,489	1,273	1,076	70	31	124

Note: (1) Figures cover the East Fishkill Town.
Source: Federal Bureau of Investigation, Hate Crime Statistics 2016

Identity Theft Consumer Reports

Area	Reports	Reports per 100,000 Population	Rank[2]
MSA[1]	23,624	117	64
U.S.	371,061	114	-

Note: (1) Figures cover the New York-Newark-Jersey City, NY-NJ-PA Metropolitan Statistical Area—see Appendix B for areas included; (2) Rank ranges from 1 to 389 where 1 indicates greatest number of identity theft reports per 100,000 population
Source: Federal Trade Commission, Consumer Sentinel Network Data Book for January–December 2017

Fraud and Other Consumer Reports

Area	Reports	Reports per 100,000 Population	Rank[2]
MSA[1]	90,589	449	173
U.S.	2,304,550	708	-

Note: (1) Figures cover the New York-Newark-Jersey City, NY-NJ-PA Metropolitan Statistical Area—see Appendix B for areas included; (2) Rank ranges from 1 to 389 where 1 indicates greatest number of fraud and other consumer reports per 100,000 population
Source: Federal Trade Commission, Consumer Sentinel Network Data Book for January–December 2017

SPORTS

Professional Sports Teams

Team Name	League	Year Established
Brooklyn Nets	National Basketball Association (NBA)	1967
New Jersey Devils	National Hockey League (NHL)	1982
New York City FC	Major League Soccer (MLS)	2015
New York Giants	National Football League (NFL)	1925
New York Islanders	National Hockey League (NHL)	1972
New York Jets	National Football League (NFL)	1960
New York Knicks	National Basketball Association (NBA)	1946
New York Mets	Major League Baseball (MLB)	1962
New York Rangers	National Hockey League (NHL)	1926
New York Red Bulls	Major League Soccer (MLS)	1996
New York Yankees	Major League Baseball (MLB)	1903

Note: Includes teams located in the New York-Newark-Jersey City, NY-NJ-PA Metropolitan Statistical Area.
Source: Wikipedia, Major Professional Sports Teams of the United States and Canada, April 5, 2018

CLIMATE

Average and Extreme Temperatures

Temperature	Jan	Feb	Mar	Apr	May	Jun	Jul	Aug	Sep	Oct	Nov	Dec	Yr.
Extreme High (°F)	68	75	85	96	97	101	104	99	99	88	81	72	104
Average High (°F)	38	41	50	61	72	80	85	84	76	65	54	43	62
Average Temp. (°F)	32	34	43	53	63	72	77	76	68	58	48	37	55
Average Low (°F)	26	27	35	44	54	63	68	67	60	49	41	31	47
Extreme Low (°F)	-2	-2	8	21	36	46	53	50	40	29	17	-1	-2

Note: Figures cover the years 1962-1992
Source: National Climatic Data Center, International Station Meteorological Climate Summary, 9/96

Average Precipitation/Snowfall/Humidity

Precip./Humidity	Jan	Feb	Mar	Apr	May	Jun	Jul	Aug	Sep	Oct	Nov	Dec	Yr.
Avg. Precip. (in.)	3.5	3.1	4.0	3.9	4.5	3.8	4.5	4.1	4.1	3.3	4.5	3.8	47.0
Avg. Snowfall (in.)	7	8	4	Tr	Tr	0	0	0	0	Tr	Tr	3	23
Avg. Rel. Hum. 7am (%)	67	67	66	64	72	74	74	76	78	75	72	69	71
Avg. Rel. Hum. 4pm (%)	55	53	50	45	52	55	53	54	56	55	57	58	53

Note: Figures cover the years 1962-1992; Tr = Trace amounts (<0.05 in. of rain; <0.5 in. of snow)
Source: National Climatic Data Center, International Station Meteorological Climate Summary, 9/96

Weather Conditions

Temperature			Daytime Sky			Precipitation		
32°F & below	45°F & below	90°F & above	Clear	Partly cloudy	Cloudy	0.01 inch or more precip.	0.1 inch or more snow/ice	Thunder-storms
75	170	18	85	166	114	120	11	20

Note: Figures are average number of days per year and cover the years 1962-1992
Source: National Climatic Data Center, International Station Meteorological Climate Summary, 9/96

HAZARDOUS WASTE

Superfund Sites

The Dutchess County-Putnam County, NY metro division is home to six sites on the EPA's Superfund National Priorities List: **Brewster Well Field** (final); **Haviland Complex** (final); **Hopewell Precision** (final); **Sarney Farm** (final); **Shenandoah Road Groundwater Contamination** (final); **Wappinger Creek** (final). There are a total of 1,396 Superfund sites with a status of proposed or final on the list in the U.S. *U.S. Environmental Protection Agency, National Priorities List, April 4, 2018*

AIR & WATER QUALITY

Air Quality Trends: Ozone

	1990	1995	2000	2005	2010	2012	2013	2014	2015	2016
MSA[1]	0.101	0.106	0.090	0.091	0.081	0.079	0.071	0.069	0.075	0.073
U.S.	0.087	0.089	0.081	0.079	0.073	0.075	0.069	0.067	0.068	0.069

Note: (1) Data covers the New York-Newark-Jersey City, NY-NJ-PA Metropolitan Statistical Area—see Appendix B for areas included. The values shown are the composite ozone concentration averages among trend sites based on the highest fourth daily maximum 8-hour concentration in parts per million. These trends are based on sites having an adequate record of monitoring data during the trend period. Data from exceptional events are included.
Source: U.S. Environmental Protection Agency, Air Quality Monitoring Information, "Air Quality Trends by City, 1990-2016"

Air Quality Index

Area	Percent of Days when Air Quality was...[2]					AQI Statistics[2]	
	Good	Moderate	Unhealthy for Sensitive Groups	Unhealthy	Very Unhealthy	Maximum	Median
MSA[1]	42.2	52.6	4.7	0.5	0.0	159	52

Note: (1) Data covers the New York-Newark-Jersey City, NY-NJ-PA Metropolitan Statistical Area—see Appendix B for areas included; (2) Based on 365 days with AQI data in 2017. Air Quality Index (AQI) is an index for reporting daily air quality. EPA calculates the AQI for five major air pollutants regulated by the Clean Air Act: ground-level ozone, particle pollution (aka particulate matter), carbon monoxide, sulfur dioxide, and nitrogen dioxide. The AQI runs from 0 to 500. The higher the AQI value, the greater the level of air pollution and the greater the health concern. There are six AQI categories: "Good" AQI is between 0 and 50. Air quality is considered satisfactory; "Moderate" AQI is between 51 and 100. Air quality is acceptable; "Unhealthy for Sensitive Groups" When AQI values are between 101 and 150, members of sensitive groups may experience health effects; "Unhealthy" When AQI values are between 151 and 200 everyone may begin to experience health effects; "Very Unhealthy" AQI values between 201 and 300 trigger a health alert; "Hazardous" AQI values over 300 trigger warnings of emergency conditions (not shown).
Source: U.S. Environmental Protection Agency, Air Quality Index Report, 2017

Air Quality Index Pollutants

Area	Percent of Days when AQI Pollutant was...[2]					
	Carbon Monoxide	Nitrogen Dioxide	Ozone	Sulfur Dioxide	Particulate Matter 2.5	Particulate Matter 10
MSA[1]	0.0	13.2	31.8	0.0	55.1	0.0

Note: (1) Data covers the New York-Newark-Jersey City, NY-NJ-PA Metropolitan Statistical Area—see Appendix B for areas included; (2) Based on 365 days with AQI data in 2017. The Air Quality Index (AQI) is an index for reporting daily air quality. EPA calculates the AQI for five major air pollutants regulated by the Clean Air Act: ground-level ozone, particle pollution (also known as particulate matter), carbon monoxide, sulfur dioxide, and nitrogen dioxide. The AQI runs from 0 to 500. The higher the AQI value, the greater the level of air pollution and the greater the health concern.
Source: U.S. Environmental Protection Agency, Air Quality Index Report, 2017

Maximum Air Pollutant Concentrations: Particulate Matter, Ozone, CO and Lead

	Particulate Matter 10 (ug/m^3)	Particulate Matter 2.5 Wtd AM (ug/m^3)	Particulate Matter 2.5 24-Hr (ug/m^3)	Ozone (ppm)	Carbon Monoxide (ppm)	Lead (ug/m^3)
MSA[1] Level	33	9.2	20	0.078	3	0.03
NAAQS[2]	150	15	35	0.075	9	0.15
Met NAAQS[2]	Yes	Yes	Yes	No	Yes	Yes

Note: (1) Data covers the New York-Newark-Jersey City, NY-NJ-PA Metropolitan Statistical Area—see Appendix B for areas included; Data from exceptional events are included; (2) National Ambient Air Quality Standards; ppm = parts per million; ug/m^3 = micrograms per cubic meter; n/a not available.
Concentrations: Particulate Matter 10 (coarse particulate)—highest second maximum 24-hour concentration; Particulate Matter 2.5 Wtd AM (fine particulate)—highest weighted annual mean concentration; Particulate Matter 2.5 24-Hour (fine particulate)—highest 98th percentile 24-hour concentration; Ozone—highest fourth daily maximum 8-hour concentration; Carbon Monoxide—highest second maximum non-overlapping 8-hour concentration; Lead—maximum running 3-month average
Source: U.S. Environmental Protection Agency, Air Quality Monitoring Information, "Air Quality Statistics by City, 2016"

Maximum Air Pollutant Concentrations: Nitrogen Dioxide and Sulfur Dioxide

	Nitrogen Dioxide AM (ppb)	Nitrogen Dioxide 1-Hr (ppb)	Sulfur Dioxide AM (ppb)	Sulfur Dioxide 1-Hr (ppb)	Sulfur Dioxide 24-Hr (ppb)
MSA[1] Level	20	60	n/a	7	n/a
NAAQS[2]	53	100	30	75	140
Met NAAQS[2]	Yes	Yes	n/a	Yes	n/a

Note: (1) Data covers the New York-Newark-Jersey City, NY-NJ-PA Metropolitan Statistical Area—see Appendix B for areas included; Data from exceptional events are included; (2) National Ambient Air Quality Standards; ppm = parts per million; ug/m^3 = micrograms per cubic meter; n/a not available.
Concentrations: Nitrogen Dioxide AM—highest arithmetic mean concentration; Nitrogen Dioxide 1-Hr—highest 98th percentile 1-hour daily maximum concentration; Sulfur Dioxide AM—highest annual mean concentration; Sulfur Dioxide 1-Hr—highest 99th percentile 1-hour daily maximum concentration; Sulfur Dioxide 24-Hr—highest second maximum 24-hour concentration
Source: U.S. Environmental Protection Agency, Air Quality Monitoring Information, "Air Quality Statistics by City, 2016"

Drinking Water

Water System Name	Pop. Served	Primary Water Source Type	Violations[1]	
			Health Based	Monitoring/ Reporting
13 separate water districts	n/a	n/a	n/a	n/a

Note: (1) Based on violation data from January 1, 2017 to December 31, 2017; n/a not available
Source: U.S. Environmental Protection Agency, Office of Ground Water and Drinking Water, Safe Drinking Water Information System (based on data extracted April 5, 2018)

Orchard Park, New York

Background

Orchard Park lies about 11 miles southeast of Buffalo—a 20-minute drive—near Lake Erie with easy access to Niagara Falls and the Canadian border. The area that includes Orchard Park is known as Buffalo's Southtowns area.

The town grew from the Holland Land Company's decision to buy up much of Western New York. According to Orchard Park historian Suzanne S. Kulp, the company advertised "rich soil...finely watered with never failing springs and streams...reasonable terms." In 1803, settler Didymus C. Kinney and wife Phebe, built a cabin for their family and stayed until 1810.

Then came the 1804 completion of a road from Lake Erie into Orchard Park. Quakers moved in, and the Meeting House they built continues to serve the community. The city's association with Quakers went on for generations and today, the city hosts the annual Quaker Arts Festival, an outdoor arts and craft show. The Festival is held on the third week of September on the campus of Orchard Park Middle School.

Orchard Park was incorporated as a village in 1921. It became known as Orchard Park Township in 1934, and is about 40 square miles, including the village of Oyster Park, replete with shops, restaurants, and boutiques.

Today, the upscale community is full of farms and green space and is home to the NFL's Buffalo Bills—as well as a July 4 parade and fireworks. Institutions of higher education include Bryant and Stratton College, with its flexible courses, as well as the south campus of Erie Community College.

Major employers include the Krog Corporation, a construction company, and Al Hemer Music Corp., with strong ties to New York State's music education.

Local students attend the Orchard Park Central District Schools, which operates four K-5 elementary schools, one middle school, and one high school. The mascot for Orchard Park's athletic teams is a Quaker.

Health care providers include the Mercy Ambulatory Care Center, a diagnostic and treatment center of nearby Mercy Hospital, with senior living facilities close by. Local town-backed recreation includes numerous programs for all ages, including canoeing and sailing on Green Lake, youth camps, culinary camp, tennis and golf.

Orchard Park has four seasons with an average snowfall of 70 inches. Daily summer temperatures range from the high 70s to the low 80s.

Rankings

Business/Finance Rankings

- The personal finance site NerdWallet analyzed 183 American metropolitan areas with populations over 250,000 and more than 15,000 businesses to rank where entrepreneurs find the most success. Criteria included area economy, annual income, housing cost, unemployment rate, and the success rate of area businesses. Buffalo* ranked #39. *www.nerdwallet.com, "Best Places to Start a Business," April 27, 2015*
- In a survey of economic confidence in the nation's 50 largest metropolitan areas conducted January–December 2014, the Buffalo* metro area placed #41, according to Gallup's 2014 Economic Confidence Index. *Gallup, "San Jose and San Francisco Lead in Economic Confidence," March 19, 2015*
- The Brookings Institution ranked the 100 largest metro areas in the U.S. based on income inequality. Buffalo* was ranked #28 (#1 = greatest ineqality). Criteria: the "95/20 ratio," a figure representing the income at which a household earns more than 95 percent of all other households, divided by the income at which a household earns more than only 20 percent of all other households. *Brookings Institution, "Household Income Inequality, 100 Largest U.S. Metro Areas, 2014-2016," February 5, 2018*
- The Buffalo* metro area was identified as one of the most affordable metropolitan areas in America by *Forbes*. The area ranked #3 out of 20 based on the National Association of Home Builders/Wells Fargo Housing Affordability Index and Sperling's Best Places' cost-of-living index. *Forbes.com, "America's Most Affordable Cities in 2015," March 12, 2015*
- The Buffalo* metro area appeared on the Milken Institute "2017 Best Performing Cities" list. Rank: #170 out of 200 large metro areas. Criteria: job growth; wage and salary growth; high-tech output growth. *Milken Institute, "Best-Performing Cities 2017," January 2018*
- *Forbes* ranked the 200 most populous metro areas to determine the nation's "Best Places for Business and Careers." The Buffalo* metro area was ranked #108. Criteria: costs (business and living); job growth (past and projected); income growth; quality of life; educational attainment (college and high school); projected economic growth; cultural and recreational opportunities; net migration patterns; number of highly ranked colleges. *Forbes, "The Best Places for Business and Careers 2017," October 24, 2017*

Education Rankings

- Personal finance website *WalletHub* analyzed the 150 largest U.S. metropolitan statistical areas to determine where the most educated Americans are choosing to settle. Criteria: education quality and attainment gap; education levels; percentage of workers with degrees; public school rankings; quality and size of each metro area's universities. Buffalo* was ranked #49 (#1 = most educated city). *www.WalletHub.com, "2017's Most and Least Educated Cities in America, " July 25, 2017*

Environmental Rankings

- Sperling's BestPlaces assessed 379 metropolitan areas of the United States for the likelihood of dangerously extreme weather events or earthquakes. In general the Southeast and South-Central regions have the highest risk of weather extremes and earthquakes, while the Pacific Northwest enjoys the lowest risk. Of the least risky metropolitan areas, the Buffalo* metro area was ranked #118. *www.bestplaces.net, "Safest Places from Natural Disasters," April 2011*
- Buffalo* was highlighted as one of the top 99 cleanest metro areas for short-term particle pollution (24-hour PM 2.5) in the U.S. during 2013 through 2015. Monitors in these cities reported no days with unhealthful PM 2.5 levels. *American Lung Association, State of the Air 2017*

Health/Fitness Rankings

- For each of the 50 most populous metro areas in the United States, the American College of Sports Medicine's American Fitness Index evaluated infrastructure, community assets, and policies that encourage healthy and fit lifestyles, including preventive health behaviors, levels of chronic disease conditions, health care access, and community resources and policies that support physical activity. The Buffalo* metro area ranked #24 for "community fitness." *www.americanfitnessindex.org, "ACSM American Fitness Index Health and Community Fitness Status of the 50 Largest Metropolitan Areas," May 2017*
- The Buffalo* metro area was identified as one of the worst cities for bed bugs in America by pest control company Orkin. The area ranked #20 out of 50 based on the number of bed bug treatments Orkin performed from December 2016 to November 2017. *Orkin, "Baltimore and Washington D.C. Continue to Hold Top Spots," January 8, 2018*
- Buffalo* was identified as a "2016 Spring Allergy Capital." The area ranked #10 out of 100. Three groups of factors were used to identify the most severe cities for people with allergies during the spring season: annual pollen levels; medicine utilization; access to board-certified allergists. *Asthma and Allergy Foundation of America, "Spring Allergy Capitals 2016"*
- Buffalo* was identified as a "2016 Fall Allergy Capital." The area ranked #7 out of 100. Three groups of factors were used to identify the most severe cities for people with allergies during the fall season: annual pollen levels; medicine utilization; access to board-certified allergists. *Asthma and Allergy Foundation of America, "Fall Allergy Capitals 2016"*
- Buffalo* was identified as a "2015 Asthma Capital." The area ranked #59 out of the nation's 100 largest metropolitan areas. Criteria: estimated prevalence; self-reported prevalence; crude death rate for asthma; annual pollen score; annual air quality; public smoking laws; number of board-certified asthma specialists; school inhaler access laws; rescue medication use; controller medication use; ER visits for asthma; uninsured rate; poverty rate. *Asthma and Allergy Foundation of America, "Asthma Capitals 2015"*
- The Buffalo* metro area ranked #156 out of 189 in The Gallup-Healthways Well-Being Index. Criteria: purpose; social well being; financial health; community and physical health. Results are based on telephone interviews with adults, aged 18 and older, living in metropolitan areas in the 50 U.S. states and the District of Columbia. *Gallup-Healthways, "State of American Well-Being, 2017 Community Well-Being Rankings" March 2018*

Real Estate Rankings

- FitSmallBusiness looked at 50 of the largest metropolitan areas in the U.S. to determine which metro was the best to start a real estate business. Data was compiled from such sources as: Zillow, Trulia, U.S. Census Bureau, and the Bureau of Labor Statistics. Criteria: location; inventory; annual wages; median sales price of homes; days on the market; median price cut percentage; and other factors that would influence real estate professional growth. The Buffalo* metro area ranked #39. *fitsmallbusiness.com, "The Best Cities to Become a Real Estate Agent in 2018," January 30, 2018*
- The Buffalo* metro area was identified as one of the 20 most affordable housing markets in the U.S. in 2017. The area ranked #16 out of 180 markets. Criteria: qualification for a mortgage loan on a typical home. *National Association of Realtors®, Affordability Index of Existing Single-Family Homes for Metropolitan Areas, 2017*
- Buffalo* was ranked #70 out of 238 metro areas in terms of housing affordability in 2017 by the National Association of Home Builders (#1 = most affordable). Criteria: the share of homes sold in that area affordable to a family earning the local median income, based on standard mortgage underwriting criteria. *National Association of Home Builders®, NAHB-Wells Fargo Housing Opportunity Index, 4th Quarter 2017*

Safety Rankings

- The National Insurance Crime Bureau ranked 382 metro areas in the U.S. in terms of per capita rates of vehicle theft. The Buffalo* metro area ranked #258 (#1 = highest rate). Criteria: number of vehicle theft offenses per 100,000 inhabitants in 2016. *National Insurance Crime Bureau, "Hot Spots 2016," June 8, 2017*

Seniors/Retirement Rankings

- From its Best Cities for Successful Aging indexes, the Milken Institute generated rankings for metropolitan areas, weighing data in nine categories—health care, wellness, living arrangements, transportation and convenience, financial characteristics, education, employment, community engagement, and overall livability. The Buffalo* metro area was ranked #71 overall in the large metro area category. *Milken Institute, "Best Cities for Successful Aging, 2017" March 14, 2017*

*Orchard Park is located within the Buffalo-Cheektowaga-Niagara Falls, NY Metropolitan Statistical Area.

Business Environment

CITY FINANCES

City Government Finances

Component	2015 ($000)	2015 ($ per capita)
Total Revenues	n/a	n/a
Total Expenditures	n/a	n/a
Debt Outstanding	n/a	n/a
Cash and Securities[1]	n/a	n/a

Note: (1) Cash and security holdings of a government at the close of its fiscal year,, including those of its dependent agencies, utilities, and liquor stores.
Source: U.S Census Bureau, State & Local Government Finances 2015

City Government Revenue by Source

Source	2015 ($000)	2015 ($ per capita)	2015 (%)
General Revenue			
From Federal Government	n/a	n/a	n/a
From State Government	n/a	n/a	n/a
From Local Governments	n/a	n/a	n/a
Taxes			
Property	n/a	n/a	n/a
Sales and Gross Receipts	n/a	n/a	n/a
Personal Income	n/a	n/a	n/a
Corporate Income	n/a	n/a	n/a
Motor Vehicle License	n/a	n/a	n/a
Other Taxes	n/a	n/a	n/a
Current Charges	n/a	n/a	n/a
Liquor Store	n/a	n/a	n/a
Utility	n/a	n/a	n/a
Employee Retirement	n/a	n/a	n/a

Source: U.S Census Bureau, State & Local Government Finances 2015

City Government Expenditures by Function

Function	2015 ($000)	2015 ($ per capita)	2015 (%)
General Direct Expenditures			
Air Transportation	n/a	n/a	n/a
Corrections	n/a	n/a	n/a
Education	n/a	n/a	n/a
Employment Security Administration	n/a	n/a	n/a
Financial Administration	n/a	n/a	n/a
Fire Protection	n/a	n/a	n/a
General Public Buildings	n/a	n/a	n/a
Governmental Administration, Other	n/a	n/a	n/a
Health	n/a	n/a	n/a
Highways	n/a	n/a	n/a
Hospitals	n/a	n/a	n/a
Housing and Community Development	n/a	n/a	n/a
Interest on General Debt	n/a	n/a	n/a
Judicial and Legal	n/a	n/a	n/a
Libraries	n/a	n/a	n/a
Parking	n/a	n/a	n/a
Parks and Recreation	n/a	n/a	n/a
Police Protection	n/a	n/a	n/a
Public Welfare	n/a	n/a	n/a
Sewerage	n/a	n/a	n/a
Solid Waste Management	n/a	n/a	n/a
Veterans' Services	n/a	n/a	n/a
Liquor Store	n/a	n/a	n/a
Utility	n/a	n/a	n/a
Employee Retirement	n/a	n/a	n/a

Source: U.S Census Bureau, State & Local Government Finances 2015

DEMOGRAPHICS

Population Growth

Area	1990 Census	2000 Census	2010 Census	2016* Estimate	Population Growth (%) 1990-2016	2010-2016
City	24,632	27,637	29,054	29,521	19.8	1.6
MSA[1]	1,189,288	1,170,111	1,135,509	1,135,503	-4.5	0.0
U.S.	248,709,873	281,421,906	308,745,538	318,558,162	28.1	3.2

Note: (1) Figures cover the Buffalo-Cheektowaga-Niagara Falls, NY Metropolitan Statistical Area—see Appendix B for areas included; (*) 2012-2016 5-year estimated population
Source: U.S. Census Bureau, 1990 Census, Census 2000, Census 2010, 2012-2016 American Community Survey 5-Year Estimates

Household Size

Area	Persons in Household (%) One	Two	Three	Four	Five	Six	Seven or More	Average Household Size
City	25.9	34.7	16.0	15.2	5.9	1.6	0.7	2.50
MSA[1]	33.3	33.5	14.9	11.4	4.6	1.6	0.7	2.40
U.S.	27.7	33.7	15.7	13.1	6.0	2.3	1.5	2.60

Note: (1) Figures cover the Buffalo-Cheektowaga-Niagara Falls, NY Metropolitan Statistical Area—see Appendix B for areas included
Source: U.S. Census Bureau, 2012-2016 American Community Survey 5-Year Estimates

Race

Area	White Alone[2] (%)	Black Alone[2] (%)	Asian Alone[2] (%)	AIAN[3] Alone[2] (%)	NHOPI[4] Alone[2] (%)	Other Race Alone[2] (%)	Two or More Races (%)
City	96.2	1.0	1.7	0.1	0.0	0.4	0.7
MSA[1]	80.2	12.2	2.9	0.6	0.0	1.9	2.2
U.S.	73.3	12.6	5.2	0.8	0.2	4.8	3.1

Note: (1) Figures cover the Buffalo-Cheektowaga-Niagara Falls, NY Metropolitan Statistical Area—see Appendix B for areas included; (2) Alone is defined as not being in combination with one or more other races; (3) American Indian and Alaska Native; (4) Native Hawaiian and Other Pacific Islander
Source: U.S. Census Bureau, 2012-2016 American Community Survey 5-Year Estimates

Hispanic or Latino Origin

Area	Total (%)	Mexican (%)	Puerto Rican (%)	Cuban (%)	Other (%)
City	2.0	0.2	0.3	0.0	1.5
MSA[1]	4.6	0.4	3.1	0.1	1.0
U.S.	17.3	11.0	1.7	0.7	4.0

Note: Persons of Hispanic or Latino origin can be of any race; (1) Figures cover the Buffalo-Cheektowaga-Niagara Falls, NY Metropolitan Statistical Area—see Appendix B for areas included
Source: U.S. Census Bureau, 2012-2016 American Community Survey 5-Year Estimates

Segregation

Type	Segregation Indices[1] 1990	2000	2010	2010 Rank[2]	Percent Change 1990-2000	1990-2010	2000-2010
Black/White	80.1	78.0	73.2	6	-2.1	-6.9	-4.8
Asian/White	50.8	50.0	54.4	1	-0.8	3.6	4.4
Hispanic/White	54.9	56.2	50.7	21	1.3	-4.1	-5.4

Note: All figures cover the Metropolitan Statistical Area—see Appendix B for areas included; Figures are based on an analysis of 1990, 2000, and 2010 Census Decennial Census tract data by William H. Frey, Brookings Institution and the University of Michigan Social Science Data Analysis Network. In this analysis all racial groups (whites, blacks, and asians) are non-Hispanic members of those races. Hispanics are shown as a separate category; (1) Segregation Indices are Dissimilarity Indices that measure the degree to which the minority group is distributed differently than whites across census tracts. They range from 0 (complete integration) to 100 (complete segregation) where the value indicates the percentage of the minority group that needs to move to be distributed exactly like whites; (2) Ranges from 1 (most segregated) to 102 (least segregated); n/a not available.
Source: www.CensusScope.org

Ancestry

Area	German	Irish	English	American	Italian	Polish	French[2]	Scottish	Dutch
City	28.4	25.5	9.3	2.7	18.0	20.2	1.7	2.9	0.9
MSA[1]	24.7	16.7	7.5	4.3	16.6	16.5	2.4	1.7	0.9
U.S.	14.4	10.4	7.7	6.9	5.4	2.9	2.6	1.7	1.3

Note: Figures are the percentage of the total population reporting a particular ancestry. The nine most commonly reported ancestries in the U.S. are shown. Figures include multiple ancestries (e.g. if a person reported being Irish and Italian, they were included in both columns); (1) Figures cover the Buffalo-Cheektowaga-Niagara Falls, NY Metropolitan Statistical Area—see Appendix B for areas included; (2) Excludes Basque
Source: U.S. Census Bureau, 2012-2016 American Community Survey 5-Year Estimates

Foreign-Born Population

Area	Percent of Population Born in								
	Any Foreign Country	Asia	Mexico	Europe	Carribean	Central America[2]	South America	Africa	Canada
City	4.3	1.4	0.0	1.3	0.3	0.2	0.2	0.1	0.9
MSA[1]	6.1	2.6	0.1	1.5	0.4	0.1	0.3	0.5	0.6
U.S.	13.2	4.0	3.6	1.5	1.3	1.0	0.9	0.6	0.3

Note: (1) Figures cover the Buffalo-Cheektowaga-Niagara Falls, NY Metropolitan Statistical Area—see Appendix B for areas included; (2) Excludes Mexico.
Source: U.S. Census Bureau, 2012-2016 American Community Survey 5-Year Estimates

Marital Status

Area	Never Married	Now Married[2]	Separated	Widowed	Divorced
City	26.6	58.2	1.4	5.9	7.9
MSA[1]	35.8	44.7	1.9	7.0	10.6
U.S.	33.0	48.1	2.1	5.9	11.0

Note: Figures are percentages and cover the population 15 years of age and older; (1) Figures cover the Buffalo-Cheektowaga-Niagara Falls, NY Metropolitan Statistical Area—see Appendix B for areas included; (2) Excludes separated
Source: U.S. Census Bureau, 2012-2016 American Community Survey 5-Year Estimates

Disability Status

Area	All Ages	Under 18 Years Old	18 to 64 Years Old	65 Years and Over
City	8.7	2.9	4.9	27.7
MSA[1]	13.1	4.7	10.8	32.6
U.S.	12.5	4.1	10.3	35.7

Note: Figures show percent of the civilian noninstitutionalized population that reported having a disability. Disability status is determined from six types of difficulty: vision, hearing, cognitive, ambulatory, self-care, and independent living. For children under 5 years old, hearing and vision difficulty are used to determine disability status. For children between the ages of 5 and 14, disability status is determined from hearing, vision, cognitive, ambulatory, and self-care difficulties. For people aged 15 years and older, they are considered to have a disability if they have difficulty with any one of the six difficulty types; Note: (1) Figures cover the Buffalo-Cheektowaga-Niagara Falls, NY Metropolitan Statistical Area—see Appendix B for areas included
Source: U.S. Census Bureau, 2012-2016 American Community Survey 5-Year Estimates

Age

Area	Percent of Population									Median Age
	Under Age 5	Age 5–19	Age 20–34	Age 35–44	Age 45–54	Age 55–64	Age 65–74	Age 75–84	Age 85+	
City	4.1	20.2	12.6	11.0	17.6	15.0	10.9	5.6	3.0	45.7
MSA[1]	5.3	18.1	20.3	11.2	14.3	14.1	8.9	5.1	2.6	40.8
U.S.	6.2	19.6	20.7	12.7	13.6	12.6	8.3	4.3	1.9	37.7

Note: (1) Figures cover the Buffalo-Cheektowaga-Niagara Falls, NY Metropolitan Statistical Area—see Appendix B for areas included
Source: U.S. Census Bureau, 2012-2016 American Community Survey 5-Year Estimates

ECONOMY

Gender

Area	Males	Females	Males per 100 Females
City	14,192	15,329	92.6
MSA[1]	550,057	585,446	94.0
U.S.	156,765,322	161,792,840	96.9

Note: (1) Figures cover the Buffalo-Cheektowaga-Niagara Falls, NY Metropolitan Statistical Area—see Appendix B for areas included
Source: U.S. Census Bureau, 2012-2016 American Community Survey 5-Year Estimates

Religious Groups by Family

Area	Catholic	Baptist	Non-Den.	Methodist[2]	Lutheran	LDS[3]	Pente-costal	Presby-terian[4]	Muslim[5]	Judaism
MSA[1]	35.7	2.7	2.0	2.4	3.3	0.3	1.1	2.0	1.6	0.7
U.S.	19.1	9.3	4.0	4.0	2.3	2.0	1.9	1.6	0.8	0.7

Note: Figures are the number of adherents as a percentage of the total population; (1) Figures cover the Buffalo-Cheektowaga-Niagara Falls, NY Metropolitan Statistical Area—see Appendix B for areas included; (2) Methodist/Pietist; (3) Latter Day Saints; (4) Reformed; (5) Figures are estimates
Source: Association of Statisticians of American Religious Bodies, 2010 U.S. Religion Census: Religious Congregations & Membership Study

Religious Groups by Tradition

Area	Catholic	Evangelical Protestant	Mainline Protestant	Other Tradition	Black Protestant	Orthodox
MSA[1]	35.7	5.9	7.2	3.3	2.3	0.4
U.S.	19.1	16.2	7.3	4.3	1.6	0.3

Note: Figures are the number of adherents as a percentage of the total population; (1) Figures cover the Buffalo-Cheektowaga-Niagara Falls, NY Metropolitan Statistical Area—see Appendix B for areas included
Source: Association of Statisticians of American Religious Bodies, 2010 U.S. Religion Census: Religious Congregations & Membership Study

Gross Metropolitan Product

Area	2014	2015	2016	2017	Rank[2]
MSA[1]	54.6	56.2	57.5	59.7	53

Note: Figures are in billions of dollars; (1) Figures cover the Buffalo-Cheektowaga-Niagara Falls, NY Metropolitan Statistical Area—see Appendix B for areas included; (2) Rank is based on 2015 data and ranges from 1 to 381
Source: The U.S. Conference of Mayors, U.S. Metro Economies: GMP and Employment Report, 2015-2017

Economic Growth

Area	2012-14 (%)	2015 (%)	2016 (%)	2017 (%)	Rank[2]
MSA[1]	0.7	0.7	0.9	1.8	229
U.S.	2.0	2.4	1.9	2.6	–

Note: Figures are real gross metropolitan product (GMP) growth rates and represent average annual percent change; (1) Figures cover the Buffalo-Cheektowaga-Niagara Falls, NY Metropolitan Statistical Area—see Appendix B for areas included; (2) Rank is based on 2012-2014 average annual percent change and ranges from 1 to 381
Source: The U.S. Conference of Mayors, U.S. Metro Economies: GMP and Employment Report, 2015-2017

Metropolitan Area Exports

Area	2011	2012	2013	2014	2015	2016	Rank[2]
MSA[1]	4,179.7	4,305.1	4,376.6	4,798.7	4,684.6	4,783.4	55

Note: Figures are in millions of dollars; (1) Figures cover the Buffalo-Cheektowaga-Niagara Falls, NY Metropolitan Statistical Area—see Appendix B for areas included; (2) Rank is based on 2016 data and ranges from 1 to 385
Source: U.S. Department of Commerce, International Trade Administration, Office of Trade & Industry Information, Manufacturing & Services, data extracted March 15, 2018

Building Permits

Area	Single-Family			Multi-Family			Total		
	2016	2017p	Pct. Chg.	2016	2017p	Pct. Chg.	2016	2017p	Pct. Chg.
City	56	55	-1.8	0	0	0.0	56	55	-1.8
MSA[1]	935	958	2.5	1,057	678	-35.9	1,992	1,636	-17.9
U.S.	750,800	817,300	8.9	455,800	446,800	-2.0	1,206,600	1,264,100	4.8

Note: (1) Figures cover the Buffalo-Cheektowaga-Niagara Falls, NY Metropolitan Statistical Area—see Appendix B for areas included; Figures represent new, privately-owned housing units authorized (unadjusted data); All permit data are based on estimates with imputation; (p) preliminary data.
Source: U.S. Census Bureau, Manufacturing, Mining, and Construction Statistics, Building Permits, 2016, 2017

Bankruptcy Filings

Area	Business Filings			Nonbusiness Filings		
	2016	2017	% Chg.	2016	2017	% Chg.
Erie County	86	67	-22.1	1,639	1,858	13.4
U.S.	24,114	23,157	-4.0	770,846	765,863	-0.6

Note: Business filings include Chapter 7, Chapter 11, Chapter 12, and Chapter 13; Nonbusiness filings include Chapter 7, Chapter 11, and Chapter 13
Source: Administrative Office of the U.S. Courts, Business and Nonbusiness Bankruptcy, County Cases Commenced by Chapter of the Bankruptcy Code, During the 12-Month Period Ending December 31, 2016 and Business and Nonbusiness Bankruptcy, County Cases Commenced by Chapter of the Bankruptcy Code, During the 12-Month Period Ending December 31, 2017

Housing Vacancy Rates

Area	Gross Vacancy Rate[2] (%)			Year-Round Vacancy Rate[3] (%)			Rental Vacancy Rate[4] (%)			Homeowner Vacancy Rate[5] (%)		
	2015	2016	2017	2015	2016	2017	2015	2016	2017	2015	2016	2017
MSA[1]	12.3	11.6	12.4	11.8	10.1	11.2	11.9	9.3	6.4	2.5	1.2	3.3
U.S.	12.9	12.8	12.7	10.0	9.9	9.9	7.1	6.9	7.2	1.8	1.7	1.6

Note: (1) Figures cover the Buffalo-Cheektowaga-Niagara Falls, NY Metropolitan Statistical Area—see Appendix B for areas included; (2) The percentage of the total housing inventory that is vacant; (3) The percentage of the housing inventory (excluding seasonal units) that is year-round vacant; (4) The percentage of rental inventory that is vacant for rent; (5) The percentage of homeowner inventory that is vacant for sale
Source: U.S. Census Bureau, Housing Vacancies and Homeownership Annual Statistics: 2015, 2016, 2017

INCOME

Income

Area	Per Capita ($)	Median Household ($)	Average Household ($)
City	45,686	88,467	115,420
MSA[1]	29,479	52,303	69,343
U.S.	29,829	55,322	77,866

Note: (1) Figures cover the Buffalo-Cheektowaga-Niagara Falls, NY Metropolitan Statistical Area—see Appendix B for areas included
Source: U.S. Census Bureau, 2012-2016 American Community Survey 5-Year Estimates

Household Income Distribution

Area	Percent of Households Earning							
	Under $15,000	$15,000 -$24,999	$25,000 -$34,999	$35,000 -$49,999	$50,000 -$74,999	$75,000 -$99,999	$100,000 -$149,999	$150,000 and up
City	4.0	6.1	7.9	11.2	14.6	11.9	23.0	21.4
MSA[1]	13.7	10.9	10.2	13.2	17.7	12.8	13.7	7.9
U.S.	12.1	10.2	9.9	13.2	17.8	12.2	13.5	11.1

Note: (1) Figures cover the Buffalo-Cheektowaga-Niagara Falls, NY Metropolitan Statistical Area—see Appendix B for areas included
Source: U.S. Census Bureau, 2012-2016 American Community Survey 5-Year Estimates

Poverty Rate

Area	All Ages	Under 18 Years Old	18 to 64 Years Old	65 Years and Over
City	2.8	2.5	3.5	1.1
MSA[1]	14.5	21.7	13.7	8.4
U.S.	15.1	21.2	14.2	9.3

Note: Figures are percentage of people whose income during the past 12 months was below the poverty level; (1) Figures cover the Buffalo-Cheektowaga-Niagara Falls, NY Metropolitan Statistical Area—see Appendix B for areas included
Source: U.S. Census Bureau, 2012-2016 American Community Survey 5-Year Estimates

EMPLOYMENT

Labor Force and Employment

Area	Civilian Labor Force			Workers Employed		
	Dec. 2016	Dec. 2017	% Chg.	Dec. 2016	Dec. 2017	% Chg.
City	15,140	15,134	0.0	14,549	14,516	-0.2
MSA[1]	541,721	542,119	0.1	513,281	512,388	-0.2
U.S.	158,968,000	159,880,000	0.6	151,798,000	153,602,000	1.2

Note: Data is not seasonally adjusted and covers workers 16 years of age and older; (1) Figures cover the Buffalo-Cheektowaga-Niagara Falls, NY Metropolitan Statistical Area—see Appendix B for areas included
Source: Bureau of Labor Statistics, Local Area Unemployment Statistics

Unemployment Rate

Area	2017											
	Jan.	Feb.	Mar.	Apr.	May	Jun.	Jul.	Aug.	Sep.	Oct.	Nov.	Dec.
City	4.7	4.7	4.2	3.9	3.9	3.9	4.2	4.2	4.0	3.8	3.9	4.1
MSA[1]	6.2	6.2	5.5	5.1	5.0	5.2	5.4	5.4	5.0	4.9	5.2	5.5
U.S.	5.1	4.9	4.6	4.1	4.1	4.5	4.6	4.5	4.1	3.9	3.9	3.9

Note: Data is not seasonally adjusted and covers workers 16 years of age and older; (1) Figures cover the Buffalo-Cheektowaga-Niagara Falls, NY Metropolitan Statistical Area—see Appendix B for areas included
Source: Bureau of Labor Statistics, Local Area Unemployment Statistics

Average Wages

Occupation	$/Hr.	Occupation	$/Hr.
Accountants and Auditors	34.80	Maids and Housekeeping Cleaners	11.90
Automotive Mechanics	19.50	Maintenance and Repair Workers	18.60
Bookkeepers	18.70	Marketing Managers	66.80
Carpenters	22.00	Nuclear Medicine Technologists	34.70
Cashiers	10.90	Nurses, Licensed Practical	20.50
Clerks, General Office	15.20	Nurses, Registered	35.20
Clerks, Receptionists/Information	14.80	Nursing Assistants	14.20
Clerks, Shipping/Receiving	16.40	Packers and Packagers, Hand	11.80
Computer Programmers	35.10	Physical Therapists	35.20
Computer Systems Analysts	36.80	Postal Service Mail Carriers	23.80
Computer User Support Specialists	23.30	Real Estate Brokers	n/a
Cooks, Restaurant	13.00	Retail Salespersons	13.10
Dentists	96.40	Sales Reps., Exc. Tech./Scientific	31.40
Electrical Engineers	38.00	Sales Reps., Tech./Scientific	43.40
Electricians	27.50	Secretaries, Exc. Legal/Med./Exec.	17.20
Financial Managers	73.90	Security Guards	12.60
First-Line Supervisors/Managers, Sales	21.80	Surgeons	82.40
Food Preparation Workers	11.40	Teacher Assistants*	12.40
General and Operations Managers	55.70	Teachers, Elementary School*	32.10
Hairdressers/Cosmetologists	12.70	Teachers, Secondary School*	34.60
Internists, General	39.80	Telemarketers	14.70
Janitors and Cleaners	14.30	Truck Drivers, Heavy/Tractor-Trailer	20.80
Landscaping/Groundskeeping Workers	14.80	Truck Drivers, Light/Delivery Svcs.	15.90
Lawyers	54.30	Waiters and Waitresses	13.30

Note: Wage data covers the Buffalo-Cheektowaga-Niagara Falls, NY Metropolitan Statistical Area—see Appendix B for areas included; (*) Hourly wages for elementary/secondary school teachers and teacher assistants were calculated by the editors from annual wage data based on a 40 hour work week; n/a not available.
Source: Bureau of Labor Statistics, Metro Area Occupational Employment & Wage Estimates, May 2017

Employment by Occupation

Occupation Classification	City (%)	MSA[1] (%)	U.S. (%)
Management, Business, Science, and Arts	49.1	37.2	37.0
Natural Resources, Construction, and Maintenance	4.2	6.7	8.9
Production, Transportation, and Material Moving	7.8	11.9	12.2
Sales and Office	23.4	25.7	23.8
Service	15.4	18.5	18.1

Note: Figures cover employed civilians 16 years of age and older; (1) Figures cover the Buffalo-Cheektowaga-Niagara Falls, NY Metropolitan Statistical Area—see Appendix B for areas included
Source: U.S. Census Bureau, 2012-2016 American Community Survey 5-Year Estimates

Employment by Industry

Sector	MSA[1]		U.S.
	Number of Employees	Percent of Total	Percent of Total
Construction, Mining, and Logging	19,300	3.4	5.2
Education and Health Services	100,900	17.6	15.9
Financial Activities	37,300	6.5	5.7
Government	92,700	16.2	15.3
Information	7,000	1.2	1.9
Leisure and Hospitality	61,500	10.7	10.7
Manufacturing	52,100	9.1	8.5
Other Services	26,700	4.7	3.9
Professional and Business Services	70,800	12.4	14.0
Retail Trade	63,500	11.1	11.0
Transportation, Warehousing, and Utilities	18,600	3.3	4.1
Wholesale Trade	21,800	3.8	4.0

Note: Figures are non-farm employment as of December 2017. Figures are not seasonally adjusted and include workers 16 years of age and older; (1) Figures cover the Buffalo-Cheektowaga-Niagara Falls, NY Metropolitan Statistical Area—see Appendix B for areas included
Source: Bureau of Labor Statistics, Current Employment Statistics, Employment, Hours, and Earnings

Occupations with Greatest Projected Employment Growth: 2017 – 2019

Occupation[1]	2017 Employment	2019 Projected Employment	Numeric Employment Change	Percent Employment Change
Home Health Aides	190,490	216,300	25,810	13.5
Personal Care Aides	174,700	189,420	14,720	8.4
Combined Food Preparation and Serving Workers, Including Fast Food	154,570	162,110	7,540	4.9
Registered Nurses	189,840	197,230	7,390	3.9
Janitors and Cleaners, Except Maids and Housekeeping Cleaners	211,280	217,380	6,100	2.9
Waiters and Waitresses	151,380	156,430	5,050	3.3
General and Operations Managers	165,860	169,970	4,110	2.5
Accountants and Auditors	124,740	128,070	3,330	2.7
Software Developers, Applications	52,730	55,940	3,210	6.1
Security Guards	114,180	117,140	2,960	2.6

Note: Projections cover New York; (1) Sorted by numeric employment change
Source: www.projectionscentral.com, State Occupational Projections, 2017–2019 Short-Term Projections

Fastest Growing Occupations: 2017 – 2019

Occupation[1]	2017 Employment	2019 Projected Employment	Numeric Employment Change	Percent Employment Change
Gaming and Sports Book Writers and Runners	660	810	150	24.0
Gaming Change Persons and Booth Cashiers	840	1,030	190	22.7
Solar Photovoltaic Installers	800	980	180	22.7
Gaming Dealers	960	1,150	190	19.4
Home Health Aides	190,490	216,300	25,810	13.5
Gaming Supervisors	580	660	80	12.3
Entertainment Attendants and Related Workers, All Other	490	540	50	9.8
Personal Care Aides	174,700	189,420	14,720	8.4
Physical Therapist Aides	3,110	3,330	220	6.9
Physical Therapists	18,480	19,750	1,270	6.9

Note: Projections cover New York; (1) Sorted by percent employment change and excludes occupations with numeric employment change less than 50
Source: www.projectionscentral.com, State Occupational Projections, 2017–2019 Short-Term Projections

TAXES

State Corporate Income Tax Rates

State	Tax Rate (%)	Income Brackets ($)	Num. of Brackets	Financial Institution Tax Rate (%)[a]	Federal Income Tax Ded.
New York	6.5 (r)	Flat rate	1	6.5 (r)	No

Note: Tax rates as of January 1, 2018; (a) Rates listed are the corporate income tax rate applied to financial institutions or excise taxes based on income. Some states have other taxes based upon the value of deposits or shares; (r) New York's General business corporate rate shown. Corporations may also be subject to a capital stocks tax, which is being phased out through 2021. A minimum tax ranges from $25 to $200,000, depending on receipts ($250 minimum for banks). Certain qualified New York manufacturers pay 0%.
Source: Federation of Tax Administrators, Range of State Corporate Income Tax Rates, January 1, 2018

State Individual Income Tax Rates

State	Tax Rate (%)	Income Brackets ($)	Num. of Brackets	Personal Exempt. ($)[1]		Fed. Inc. Tax Ded.
				Single	Dependents	
New York (a)	4.0 - 8.82	8,500 - 1,077,550 (b)	8	0	1,000	No

Note: Tax rates as of January 1, 2018; Local- and county-level taxes are not included; n/a not applicable; (1) Married joint filers generally receive double the single exemption; (a) 19 states have statutory provision for automatically adjusting to the rate of inflation the dollar values of the income tax brackets, standard deductions, and/or personal exemptions. Massachusetts, Michigan, and Nebraska index the personal exemption only. Oregon does not index the income brackets for $125,000 and over; (b) For joint returns, taxes are twice the tax on half the couple's income.
Source: Federation of Tax Administrators, State Individual Income Tax Rates, January 1, 2018

Various State Sales and Excise Tax Rates

State	State Sales Tax (%)	Gasoline[1] (¢/gal.)	Cigarette[2] ($/pack)	Spirits[3] ($/gal.)	Wine[4] ($/gal.)	Beer[5] ($/gal.)	Recreational Marijuana (%)
New York	4.0	44.3	4.35	6.44 (f)	0.30	0.14	Not legal

Note: All tax rates as of January 1, 2018; (1) The American Petroleum Institute has developed a methodology for determining the average tax rate on a gallon of fuel. Rates may include any of the following: excise taxes, environmental fees, storage tank fees, other fees or taxes, general sales tax, and local taxes. In states where gasoline is subject to the general sales tax, or where the fuel tax is based on the average sale price, the average rate determined by API is sensitive to changes in the price of gasoline. States that fully or partially apply general sales taxes to gasoline: CA, CO, GA, IL, IN, MI, NY; (2) The federal excise tax of $1.0066 per pack and local taxes are not included; (3) Rates are those applicable to off-premise sales of 40% alcohol by volume (a.b.v.) distilled spirits in 750ml containers. Local excise taxes are excluded; (4) Rates are those applicable to off-premise sales of 11% a.b.v. non-carbonated wine in 750ml containers; (5) Rates are those applicable to off-premise sales of 4.7% a.b.v. beer in 12 ounce containers; (f) Different rates also applicable according to alcohol content, place of production, size of container, or place purchased (on- or off-premise or onboard airlines).
Source: Tax Foundation, 2018 Facts & Figures: How Does Your State Compare?

State Business Tax Climate Index Rankings

State	Overall Rank	Corporate Tax Rank	Individual Income Tax Rank	Sales Tax Rank	Unemployment Insurance Tax Rank	Property Tax Rank
New York	49	7	49	43	30	47

Note: The index is a measure of how each state's tax laws affect economic performance. The lower the rank, the more favorable a state's tax system is for business. States without a given tax are given a ranking of 1. The scores/rankings for the District of Columbia do not affect other states. The 2018 index represents the tax climate as of July 1, 2017.
Source: Tax Foundation, State Business Tax Climate Index 2018

TRANSPORTATION

Means of Transportation to Work

Area	Car/Truck/Van		Public Transportation			Bicycle	Walked	Other Means	Worked at Home
	Drove Alone	Car-pooled	Bus	Subway	Railroad				
City	89.1	5.1	0.6	0.0	0.0	0.1	1.2	0.7	3.2
MSA[1]	82.5	7.8	3.0	0.2	0.0	0.4	2.6	0.8	2.7
U.S.	76.4	9.3	2.6	1.9	0.6	0.6	2.8	1.3	4.6

Note: Figures are percentages and cover workers 16 years of age and older; (1) Figures cover the Buffalo-Cheektowaga-Niagara Falls, NY Metropolitan Statistical Area—see Appendix B for areas included
Source: U.S. Census Bureau, 2012-2016 American Community Survey 5-Year Estimates

Travel Time to Work

Area	Less Than 10 Minutes	10 to 19 Minutes	20 to 29 Minutes	30 to 44 Minutes	45 to 59 Minutes	60 to 89 Minutes	90 Minutes or More
City	14.2	30.1	25.8	23.0	3.7	1.9	1.4
MSA[1]	14.3	33.9	26.4	18.4	4.1	1.8	1.2
U.S.	12.9	29.2	20.9	20.4	8.0	6.0	2.7

Note: Note: Figures are percentages and include workers 16 years old and over; (1) Figures cover the Buffalo-Cheektowaga-Niagara Falls, NY Metropolitan Statistical Area—see Appendix B for areas included
Source: U.S. Census Bureau, 2012-2016 American Community Survey 5-Year Estimates

Freeway Travel Time Index

Area	1985	1990	1995	2000	2005	2010	2014
Urban Area Rank[1,2]	54	63	73	65	61	57	54
Urban Area Index[1]	1.06	1.08	1.10	1.14	1.16	1.16	1.17
Average Index[3]	1.09	1.11	1.14	1.17	1.20	1.19	1.20

Note: Freeway Travel Time Index—the ratio of travel time in the peak period to the travel time at free-flow conditions. For example, a value of 1.30 indicates a 20-minute free-flow trip takes 26 minutes in the peak (20 minutes x 1.30 = 26 minutes); (1) Covers the Buffalo NY urban area; (2) Rank is based on 101 urban areas (#1 = highest travel time index); (3) Average of 101 urban areas
Source: Texas Transportation Institute, 2015 Urban Mobility Scorecard, August 2015

Freeway Commuter Stress Index

Area	1985	1990	1995	2000	2005	2010	2014
Urban Area Rank[1,2]	66	75	88	76	76	74	71
Urban Area Index[1]	1.07	1.09	1.10	1.15	1.17	1.17	1.18
Average Index[3]	1.13	1.16	1.19	1.22	1.25	1.24	1.25

Note: The Freeway Commuter Stress Index is the same as the Freeway Travel Time Index (see table above) except that it includes only the travel in the peak directions during the peak periods; the TTI includes travel in all directions during the peak period. Thus, the CSI is more indicative of the work trip experienced by each commuter on a daily basis; (1) Covers the Buffalo NY urban area; (2) Rank is based on 101 urban areas (#1 = highest travel time index); (3) Average of 101 urban areas
Source: Texas Transportation Institute, 2015 Urban Mobility Scorecard, August 2015

Living Environment

COST OF LIVING

Cost of Living Index

Composite Index	Groceries	Housing	Utilities	Trans-portation	Health Care	Misc. Goods/ Services
100.1	97.2	102.5	108.7	102.5	85.5	98.0

Note: The Cost of Living Index measures regional differences in the cost of consumer goods and services, excluding taxes and non-consumer expenditures, for professional and managerial households in the top income quintile. It is based on more than 50,000 prices covering almost 60 different items for which prices are collected three times a year by chambers of commerce, economic development organizations or university applied economic centers in each participating urban area. The numbers shown should be read as a percentage above or below the national average of 100. For example, a value of 115.4 in the groceries column indicates that grocery prices are 15.4% higher than the national average. Small differences in the index numbers should not be interpreted as significant; Figures cover the Buffalo NY urban area.
Source: The Council for Community and Economic Research, ACCRA Cost of Living Index, 2017

Grocery Prices

Area[1]	T-Bone Steak ($/pound)	Frying Chicken ($/pound)	Whole Milk ($/half gal.)	Eggs ($/dozen)	Orange Juice ($/64 oz.)	Coffee ($/11.5 oz.)
City[2]	12.85	1.23	1.95	1.17	3.48	4.14
Avg.	11.29	1.40	2.02	1.47	3.55	4.37
Min.	7.71	0.93	1.04	0.70	2.86	3.24
Max.	15.83	2.39	4.03	3.92	6.29	8.16

Note: (1) Values for the local area are compared with the average, minimum and maximum values for all 294 areas in the Cost of Living Index; (2) Figures cover the Buffalo NY urban area; ***T-Bone Steak*** *(price per pound);* ***Frying Chicken*** *(price per pound, whole fryer);* ***Whole Milk*** *(half gallon carton);* ***Eggs*** *(price per dozen, Grade A, large);* ***Orange Juice*** *(64 oz. Tropicana or Florida Natural);* ***Coffee*** *(11.5 oz. can, vacuum-packed, Maxwell House, Hills Bros, or Folgers).*
Source: The Council for Community and Economic Research, ACCRA Cost of Living Index, 2017

Housing and Utility Costs

Area[1]	New Home Price ($)	Apartment Rent ($/month)	All Electric ($/month)	Part Electric ($/month)	Other Energy ($/month)	Telephone ($/month)
City[2]	369,768	866	-	81.57	69.97	37.33
Avg.	335,956	1,047	175.01	97.34	67.93	28.71
Min.	187,788	491	109.48	49.33	35.44	12.39
Max.	1,739,087	4,559	432.62	227.09	353.33	44.61

Note: (1) Values for the local area are compared with the average, minimum and maximum values for all 294 areas in the Cost of Living Index; (2) Figures cover the Buffalo NY urban area; ***New Home Price*** *(2,400 sf living area, 8,000 sf lot, in urban area with full utilities);* ***Apartment Rent*** *(950 sf 2 bedroom/1.5 or 2 bath, unfurnished, excluding all utilities except water);* ***All Electric*** *(average monthly cost for an all-electric home);* ***Part Electric*** *(average monthly cost for a part-electric home);* ***Other Energy*** *(average monthly cost for natural gas, fuel oil, coal, wood, and any other forms of energy except electricity);* ***Telephone*** *(price includes basic monthly rate for a private residential line plus additional local usage charges incurred by a family of four).*
Source: The Council for Community and Economic Research, ACCRA Cost of Living Index, 2017

Health Care, Transportation, and Other Costs

Area[1]	Doctor ($/visit)	Dentist ($/visit)	Optometrist ($/visit)	Gasoline ($/gallon)	Beauty Salon ($/visit)	Men's Shirt ($)
City[2]	86.67	78.97	60.23	2.36	37.27	17.38
Avg.	108.00	92.54	101.93	2.25	37.58	30.92
Min.	30.39	60.00	49.75	1.82	16.11	11.20
Max.	193.50	161.94	229.28	3.16	77.35	59.13

Note: (1) Values for the local area are compared with the average, minimum and maximum values for all 294 areas in the Cost of Living Index; (2) Figures cover the Buffalo NY urban area; ***Doctor*** *(general practitioners routine exam of an established patient);* ***Dentist*** *(adult teeth cleaning and periodic oral examination);* ***Optometrist*** *(full vision eye exam for established adult patient);* ***Gasoline*** *(one gallon regular unleaded, national brand, including all taxes, cash price at self-service pump if available);* ***Beauty Salon*** *(woman's shampoo, trim, and blow-dry);* ***Men's Shirt*** *(cotton/polyester dress shirt, pinpoint weave, long sleeves).*
Source: The Council for Community and Economic Research, ACCRA Cost of Living Index, 2017

HOUSING

House Price Index (HPI)

Area	National Ranking[2]	Quarterly Change (%)	One-Year Change (%)	Five-Year Change (%)
MSA[1]	111	0.42	6.57	23.19
U.S.[3]	–	1.61	6.68	34.71

Note: The HPI is a weighted repeat sales index. It measures average price changes in repeat sales or refinancings on the same properties. This information is obtained by reviewing repeat mortgage transactions on single-family properties whose mortgages have been purchased or securitized by Fannie Mae or Freddie Mac in January 1975; (1) Figures cover the Buffalo-Cheektowaga-Niagara Falls, NY Metropolitan Statistical Area—see Appendix B for areas included; (2) Rankings are based on annual percentage change for all metro areas containing at least 15,000 transactions over the last 10 years and ranges from 1 to 253; (3) figures based on a weighted average of Census Division estimates using a seasonally adjusted, purchase-only index; all figures are for the period ending December 31, 2017
Source: Federal Housing Finance Agency, House Price Index, February 28, 2018

Median Single-Family Home Prices

Area	2015	2016	2017p	Percent Change 2016 to 2017
MSA[1]	129.8	132.5	142.7	7.7
U.S. Average	223.9	235.5	248.8	5.6

Note: Figures are median sales prices of existing single-family homes in thousands of dollars; (p) preliminary; (1) Figures cover the Buffalo-Cheektowaga-Niagara Falls, NY Metropolitan Statistical Area—see Appendix B for areas included
Source: National Association of Realtors, Median Sales Price of Existing Single-Family Homes for Metropolitan Areas, 4th Quarter 2017

Qualifying Income Based on Median Sales Price of Existing Single-Family Homes

Area	With 5% Down ($)	With 10% Down ($)	With 20% Down ($)
MSA[1]	32,795	31,069	27,616
U.S. Average	55,585	52,659	46,808

Note: Figures are preliminary; Qualifying income is based on a mortgage rate of 4.17%. Monthly principal and interest payment is limited to 25% of income; (1) Figures cover the Buffalo-Cheektowaga-Niagara Falls, NY Metropolitan Statistical Area—see Appendix B for areas included
Source: National Association of Realtors, Qualifying Income Based on Median Sales Price of Existing Single-Family Homes for Metropolitan Areas, 4th Quarter 2017

Median Apartment Condo-Coop Home Prices

Area	2015	2016	2017p	Percent Change 2016 to 2017
MSA[1]	n/a	n/a	n/a	n/a
U.S. Average	210.7	220.7	234.3	6.2

Note: Figures are median sales prices of existing apartment condo-coop homes in thousands of dollars; (p) preliminary; n/a not available; (1) Figures cover the Buffalo-Cheektowaga-Niagara Falls, NY Metropolitan Statistical Area—see Appendix B for areas included
Source: National Association of Realtors, Median Sales Price of Existing Apartment Condo-Coop Homes for Metropolitan Areas, 4th Quarter 2017

Home Value Distribution

Area	Under $50,000	$50,000 -$99,999	$100,000 -$149,999	$150,000 -$199,999	$200,000 -$299,999	$300,000 -$499,999	$500,000 -$999,999	$1,000,000 or more
City	1.1	4.4	18.3	18.5	28.4	24.5	4.3	0.5
MSA[1]	9.5	24.0	25.7	17.1	14.8	6.8	1.7	0.4
U.S.	8.8	14.8	15.3	14.9	18.4	16.4	9.0	2.5

Note: Figures are percentages and cover owner-occupied housing units; (1) Figures cover the Buffalo-Cheektowaga-Niagara Falls, NY Metropolitan Statistical Area—see Appendix B for areas included
Source: U.S. Census Bureau, 2012-2016 American Community Survey 5-Year Estimates

Homeownership Rate

Area	2009 (%)	2010 (%)	2011 (%)	2012 (%)	2013 (%)	2014 (%)	2015 (%)	2016 (%)	2017 (%)
MSA[1]	60.3	64.5	67.6	63.5	65.5	64.1	63.9	62.6	62.4
U.S.	67.4	66.9	66.1	65.4	65.1	64.5	63.7	63.4	63.9

Note: (1) Figures cover the Buffalo-Cheektowaga-Niagara Falls, NY Metropolitan Statistical Area—see Appendix B for areas included
Source: U.S. Census Bureau, Housing Vacancies and Homeownership Annual Statistics: 2009-2017

Year Housing Structure Built

Area	2010 or Later	2000 -2009	1990 -1999	1980 -1989	1970 -1979	1960 -1969	1950 -1959	1940 -1949	Before 1940	Median Year
City	1.3	11.9	12.3	10.5	19.5	12.7	16.5	5.6	9.7	1973
MSA[1]	1.2	5.2	6.8	6.3	10.3	11.1	17.9	8.8	32.4	1955
U.S.	2.3	14.7	14.0	13.7	15.6	10.9	10.6	5.2	13.0	1977

Note: Figures are percentages except for Median Year; Note: (1) Figures cover the Buffalo-Cheektowaga-Niagara Falls, NY Metropolitan Statistical Area—see Appendix B for areas included
Source: U.S. Census Bureau, 2012-2016 American Community Survey 5-Year Estimates

Gross Monthly Rent

Area	Under $500	$500 -$999	$1,000 -$1,499	$1,500 -$1,999	$2,000 -$2,499	$2,500 -$2,999	$3,000 and up	Median ($)
City	4.5	64.4	24.1	6.0	0.5	0.0	0.6	915
MSA[1]	17.3	64.9	14.1	2.4	0.6	0.3	0.3	738
U.S.	11.3	43.3	27.7	10.7	4.0	1.6	1.5	949

Note: Figures are percentages except for Median; Gross rent is the contract rent plus the estimated average monthly cost of utilities (electricity, gas, and water and sewer) and fuels (oil, coal, kerosene, wood, etc.) if these are paid by the renter (or paid for the renter by someone else); (1) Figures cover the Buffalo-Cheektowaga-Niagara Falls, NY Metropolitan Statistical Area—see Appendix B for areas included
Source: U.S. Census Bureau, 2012-2016 American Community Survey 5-Year Estimates

HEALTH

Health Risk Factors

Category	MSA[1] (%)	U.S. (%)
Adults aged 18–64 who have any kind of health care coverage	89.2	87.7
Adults who reported being in good or excellent health	81.8	83.6
Adults who are current smokers	18.8	17.1
Adults who currently use E-cigarettes	4.8	4.7
Adults who currently use chewing tobacco, snuff, or snus	1.9	4.0
Adults who are heavy drinkers[2]	7.9	6.5
Adults who are binge drinkers[3]	20.0	16.9
Adults who are overweight (BMI 25.0 - 29.9)	38.7	35.3
Adults who are obese (BMI 30.0 - 99.8)	26.9	29.9
Adults who participated in any physical activities in the past month	73.6	76.9
Adults who always or nearly always wears a seat belt	95.0	94.3

Note: (1) Figures cover the Buffalo-Cheektowaga-Niagara Falls, NY Metropolitan Statistical Area—see Appendix B for areas included; (2) Heavy drinkers are classified as adult men having more than 14 drinks per week and adult women having more than 7 drinks per week; (3) Binge drinkers are classified as males having five or more drinks on one occasion or females having four or more drinks on one occasion
Source: Centers for Disease Control and Prevention, Behaviorial Risk Factor Surveillance System, SMART: Selected Metropolitan Area Risk Trends, 2016

Health Screening Rates

Category	MSA[1] (%)	U.S. (%)
Adults 50-75 who have had a blood stool test within the past year	6.3	8.0
Adults 50-75 who have had a colonoscopy in the past 10 years	66.2	63.5
Adults aged 65+ who have had flu shot within the past year	60.0	58.6
Adults aged 65+ who have ever had a pneumonia vaccination	77.1	73.4
Adults who have ever been tested for HIV	34.6	35.6
Women aged 21-65 who have had a pap test in the past three years	83.5	79.8
Men aged 40+ who have had a PSA test within the past two years	44.0	39.5
Women aged 40+ who have had a mammogram within the past two years	78.3	72.5

Note: n/a not available; (1) Figures cover the Buffalo-Cheektowaga-Niagara Falls, NY Metropolitan Statistical Area—see Appendix B for areas included; Source: Centers for Disease Control and Prevention, Behaviorial Risk Factor Surveillance System, SMART: Selected Metropolitan Area Risk Trends, 2016

Chronic Health Conditions

Category	MSA[1] (%)	U.S. (%)
Adults who have ever been told they had a heart attack	4.6	4.4
Adults who have ever been told they have angina or coronary heart disease	5.5	4.1
Adults who have ever been told they had a stroke	3.2	3.1
Adults who have been told they currently have asthma	11.0	9.3
Adults who have ever been told they have arthritis	29.9	25.8
Adults who have ever been told they have diabetes[2]	11.2	10.5
Adults who have ever been told they had skin cancer	3.9	5.9
Adults who have ever been told they had any other types of cancer	9.4	6.7
Adults who have ever been told they have COPD	7.3	6.3
Adults who have ever been told they have kidney disease	3.5	2.8
Adults who have ever been told they have a form of depression	14.9	17.4

Note: (1) Figures cover the Buffalo-Cheektowaga-Niagara Falls, NY Metropolitan Statistical Area—see Appendix B for areas included; (2) Figures do not include pregnancy-related, borderline, or pre-diabetes
Source: Centers for Disease Control and Prevention, Behaviorial Risk Factor Surveillance System, SMART: Selected Metropolitan Area Risk Trends, 2016

Mortality Rates for the Top 10 Causes of Death in the U.S.

ICD-10[a] Sub-Chapter	ICD-10[a] Code	Age-Adjusted Mortality Rate[1] per 100,000 population	
		County[2]	U.S.
Malignant neoplasms	C00-C97	173.6	158.5
Ischaemic heart diseases	I20-I25	105.2	96.8
Other forms of heart disease	I30-I51	61.9	52.4
Chronic lower respiratory diseases	J40-J47	39.5	40.9
Cerebrovascular diseases	I60-I69	37.0	37.2
Organic, including symptomatic, mental disorders	F01-F09	61.8	33.3
Other degenerative diseases of the nervous system	G30-G31	12.8	32.1
Other external causes of accidental injury	W00-X59	40.0	31.2
Diabetes mellitus	E10-E14	21.5	21.1
Hypertensive diseases	I10-I15	19.5	20.8

Note: (a) ICD-10 = International Classification of Diseases 10th Revision; (1) Mortality rates are a three year average covering 2014-2016; (2) Figures cover Erie County.
Source: Centers for Disease Control and Prevention, National Center for Health Statistics. Underlying Cause of Death 1999-2016 on CDC WONDER Online Database, released December 2017

Mortality Rates for Selected Causes of Death

ICD-10[a] Sub-Chapter	ICD-10[a] Code	Age-Adjusted Mortality Rate[1] per 100,000 population	
		County[2]	U.S.
Assault	X85-Y09	6.3	5.6
Diseases of the liver	K70-K76	12.7	14.0
Human immunodeficiency virus (HIV) disease	B20-B24	1.5	1.9
Influenza and pneumonia	J09-J18	15.5	14.6
Intentional self-harm	X60-X84	11.2	13.2
Malnutrition	E40-E46	1.1	1.3
Obesity and other hyperalimentation	E65-E68	2.9	2.1
Renal failure	N17-N19	12.9	13.0
Transport accidents	V01-V99	5.5	12.0
Viral hepatitis	B15-B19	1.3	1.9

Note: (a) ICD-10 = International Classification of Diseases 10th Revision; (1) Mortality rates are a three year average covering 2014-2016; (2) Figures cover Erie County; Data are Suppressed when the data meet the criteria for confidentiality constraints; Mortality rates are flagged as Unreliable when the rate would be calculated with a numerator of 20 or less.
Source: Centers for Disease Control and Prevention, National Center for Health Statistics. Underlying Cause of Death 1999-2016 on CDC WONDER Online Database, released December 2017

Health Insurance Coverage

Area	With Health Insurance	With Private Health Insurance	With Public Health Insurance	Without Health Insurance	Population Under Age 18 Without Health Insurance
City	98.2	89.4	25.4	1.8	0.5
MSA[1]	95.1	72.0	37.7	4.9	2.1
U.S.	88.3	66.7	33.0	11.7	5.9

Note: Figures are percentages that cover the civilian noninstitutionalized population; (1) Figures cover the Buffalo-Cheektowaga-Niagara Falls, NY Metropolitan Statistical Area—see Appendix B for areas included
Source: U.S. Census Bureau, 2012-2016 American Community Survey 5-Year Estimates

Number of Medical Professionals

Area	MDs[3]	DOs[3,4]	Dentists	Podiatrists	Chiropractors	Optometrists
County[1] (number)	3,525	218	742	77	360	141
County[1] (rate[2])	381.4	23.6	80.4	8.3	39.0	15.3
U.S. (rate[2])	276.5	22.3	67.3	6.0	26.7	15.9

Note: Data as of 2016 unless noted; (1) Data covers Erie County; (2) Rate per 100,000 population; (3) Data as of 2015 and includes all active, non-federal physicians; (4) Doctor of Osteopathic Medicine
Source: U.S. Department of Health and Human Services, Health Resources and Services Administration, Bureau of Health Professions, Area Resource File (ARF) 2016-2017

Best Hospitals

According to *U.S. News,* the Buffalo-Cheektowaga-Niagara Falls, NY metro area is home to one of the best hospitals in the U.S.: **Roswell Park Comprehensive Cancer Center** (1 adult specialty). The hospital listed was nationally ranked in at least one of 16 specialties. Only 152 hospitals nationwide were nationally ranked in one or more specialties. Twenty hospitals in the U.S. made the Honor Roll. The Best Hospitals Honor Roll was revamped last year to take both the national rankings and the procedure and condition ratings into account. Hospitals received points if they were nationally ranked in one of the 16 specialties—the higher they ranked, the more points they got—and how many ratings of "high performing" they earned in the nine procedures and conditions. *U.S. News Online, "America's Best Hospitals 2017-18"*

EDUCATION

Public School District Statistics

District Name	Schls	Pupils	Pupil/ Teacher Ratio	Minority Pupils[1] (%)	Free Lunch Eligible[2] (%)	IEP[3] (%)
Orchard Park Central School District	6	4,861	12.7	6.4	11.1	17.1

Note: Table includes school districts with 100 or more students; (1) Percentage of students that are not non-Hispanic white; (2) Percentage of students that are eligible for the free lunch program; (3) Percentage of students that have an Individualized Education Program.
Source: U.S. Department of Education, National Center for Education Statistics, Common Core of Data, Local Education Agency (School District) Universe Survey: School Year 2015-2016; U.S. Department of Education, National Center for Education Statistics, Common Core of Data, Public Elementary/Secondary School Universe Survey: School Year 2015-2016

Highest Level of Education

Area	Less than H.S.	H.S. Diploma	Some College, No Deg.	Associate Degree	Bachelor's Degree	Master's Degree	Prof. School Degree	Doctorate Degree
City	3.5	21.3	15.4	13.8	24.6	15.3	4.6	1.5
MSA[1]	9.2	29.5	18.9	11.9	17.0	10.2	2.0	1.3
U.S.	13.0	27.5	21.0	8.2	18.8	8.2	2.0	1.3

Note: Figures cover persons age 25 and over; (1) Figures cover the Buffalo-Cheektowaga-Niagara Falls, NY Metropolitan Statistical Area—see Appendix B for areas included
Source: U.S. Census Bureau, 2012-2016 American Community Survey 5-Year Estimates

Educational Attainment by Race

Area	High School Graduate or Higher (%)					Bachelor's Degree or Higher (%)				
	Total	White	Black	Asian	Hisp.[2]	Total	White	Black	Asian	Hisp.[2]
City	96.5	96.6	91.3	90.8	99.3	45.9	45.7	33.5	76.9	62.7
MSA[1]	90.8	92.8	82.8	78.6	74.2	30.5	32.2	15.5	55.3	20.1
U.S.	87.0	88.9	84.3	86.3	65.7	30.3	31.6	20.0	52.1	14.7

Note: Figures shown cover persons 25 years old and over; (1) Figures cover the Buffalo-Cheektowaga-Niagara Falls, NY Metropolitan Statistical Area—see Appendix B for areas included; (2) People of Hispanic origin can be of any race
Source: U.S. Census Bureau, 2012-2016 American Community Survey 5-Year Estimates

School Enrollment by Grade and Control

Area	Preschool (%)		Kindergarten (%)		Grades 1 - 4 (%)		Grades 5 - 8 (%)		Grades 9 - 12 (%)	
	Public	Private	Public	Private	Public	Private	Public	Private	Public	Private
City	61.3	38.7	72.9	27.1	83.7	16.3	82.0	18.0	85.9	14.1
MSA[1]	66.4	33.6	87.6	12.4	89.5	10.5	89.1	10.9	88.8	11.2
U.S.	58.4	41.6	87.7	12.3	89.8	10.2	89.7	10.3	90.4	9.6

Note: Figures shown cover persons 3 years old and over; (1) Figures cover the Buffalo-Cheektowaga-Niagara Falls, NY Metropolitan Statistical Area—see Appendix B for areas included
Source: U.S. Census Bureau, 2012-2016 American Community Survey 5-Year Estimates

Average Salaries of Public School Classroom Teachers

Area	2015		2016		Change from 2015 to 2016	
	Dollars	Rank[1]	Dollars	Rank[1]	Percent	Rank[2]
New York	77,628	1	79,152	1	2.0	12
U.S. Average	57,611	–	58,353	–	1.3	–

Note: (1) Rank ranges from 1 to 51 where 1 indicates highest salary; (2) Rank ranges from 1 to 51 where 1 indicates highest percent change.
Source: National Education Association, Rankings & Estimates: Rankings of the States 2016 and Estimates of School Statistics 2017

Higher Education

Four-Year Colleges			Two-Year Colleges			Medical Schools[1]	Law Schools[2]	Voc/ Tech[3]
Public	Private Non-profit	Private For-profit	Public	Private Non-profit	Private For-profit			
0	0	2	0	0	0	0	0	0

Note: Figures cover institutions located within the city limits and include main campuses only; (1) includes schools accredited by the Liaison Committee on Medical Education and the American Osteopathic Association's Commission on Osteopathic College Accreditation; (2) includes ABA-accredited schools, schools with provisional ABA accreditation, and state accredited schools; (3) includes all schools with programs that are less than 2 years.
Source: National Center for Education Statistics, Integrated Postsecondary Education System (IPEDS), 2016-17; Wikipedia, List of Medical Schools in the United States, accessed April 2, 2018; Wikipedia, List of Law Schools in the United States, accessed April 2, 2018

According to *U.S. News & World Report,* the Buffalo-Cheektowaga-Niagara Falls, NY metro area is home to one of the best national universities in the U.S.: **University at Buffalo—SUNY** (#97 tie). The indicators used to capture academic quality fall into a number of categories: assessment by administrators at peer institutions; retention of students; faculty resources; student selectivity; financial resources; alumni giving; high school counselor ratings of colleges; and graduation rate. *U.S. News & World Report, "America's Best Colleges 2018"*

According to *U.S. News & World Report,* the Buffalo-Cheektowaga-Niagara Falls, NY metro area is home to one of the top 75 medical schools for research in the U.S.: **University at Buffalo—SUNY (Jacobs)** (#61). The rankings are based on a weighted average of 11 measures of quality: quality assessment; peer assessment score; assessment score by residency directors; research activity; total research activity; average research activity per faculty member; student selectivity; median MCAT total score; median undergraduate GPA; acceptance rate; and faculty resources. *U.S. News & World Report, "America's Best Graduate Schools, Medical, 2019"*

According to *U.S. News & World Report,* the Buffalo-Cheektowaga-Niagara Falls, NY metro area is home to one of the top 75 business schools in the U.S.: **University at Buffalo—SUNY** (#70 tie). The rankings are based on a weighted average of the following nine measures: quality assessment; peer assessment; recruiter assessment; placement success; mean starting salary and bonus; student selectivity; mean GMAT and GRE scores; mean undergraduate GPA; and acceptance rate. *U.S. News & World Report, "America's Best Graduate Schools, Business, 2019"*

PRESIDENTIAL ELECTION

2016 Presidential Election Results

Area	Clinton	Trump	Johnson	Stein	Other
Erie County	50.9	44.5	3.0	1.5	0.2
U.S.	48.0	45.9	3.3	1.1	1.7

Note: Results are percentages and may not add to 100% due to rounding
Source: Dave Leip's Atlas of U.S. Presidential Elections

EMPLOYERS

Major Employers

Company Name	Industry
American Axle	Transportation
API Basco	Manufacturing
Bison Yard	Transportation
Bufalo Niagara Int'l Airport	Transportation
Calspan	Transportation
Cameron Industries	Manufacturing
Catholic Health System	Health care
Derrick Manufacturing	Manufacturing
DRS (Sierra Research)	Defense contractor
Elderwood Senior Care	Health care
FedEX Ground	Transportation
Frontier Yard	Transportation
Home Depot	Transportation
ICOR	Transportation
IRS	Government
Quebecor World Buffalo, Inc.	Printing
Sprint	Telecommunications
St Joseph Hospital	Health care
Target	Transportation
Tme Warner Cable	Telecommunications
Villa Maria College	Education
Wal-Mart/Sam's Club	Retail
Walden Galleria	Retail

Note: Companies shown are located within the Buffalo-Cheektowaga-Niagara Falls, NY Metropolitan Statistical Area.
Source: Hoovers.com; Wikipedia

PUBLIC SAFETY

Crime Rate

Area	All Crimes	Violent Crimes				Property Crimes		
		Murder	Rape[3]	Robbery	Aggrav. Assault	Burglary	Larceny -Theft	Motor Vehicle Theft
City	1,221.4	3.4	23.6	3.4	37.0	137.9	999.3	16.8
Metro[1]	2,828.4	4.9	33.1	138.9	234.2	461.7	1,822.8	132.9
U.S.	2,847.8	5.3	40.4	102.8	248.5	468.9	1,745.0	236.9

Note: Figures are crimes per 100,000 population; (1) Figures cover the Buffalo-Cheektowaga-Niagara Falls, NY Metropolitan Statistical Area—see Appendix B for areas included; (3) The city and U.S. figures shown were reported using the revised Uniform Crime Reporting (UCR) definition of rape. The metro area figures shown are an aggregate total of the data submitted using both the revised and legacy UCR definitions.
Source: FBI Uniform Crime Reports, 2016

Hate Crimes

Area	Number of Quarters Reported	Number of Incidents per Bias Motivation					
		Race/Ethnicity/ Ancestry	Religion	Sexual Orientation	Disability	Gender	Gender Identity
Area[1]	4	0	0	0	0	0	0
U.S.	4	3,489	1,273	1,076	70	31	124

Note: (1) Figures cover the Orchard Park Town.
Source: Federal Bureau of Investigation, Hate Crime Statistics 2016

Identity Theft Consumer Reports

Area	Reports	Reports per 100,000 Population	Rank[2]
MSA[1]	775	68	265
U.S.	371,061	114	-

Note: (1) Figures cover the Buffalo-Cheektowaga-Niagara Falls, NY Metropolitan Statistical Area—see Appendix B for areas included; (2) Rank ranges from 1 to 389 where 1 indicates greatest number of identity theft reports per 100,000 population
Source: Federal Trade Commission, Consumer Sentinel Network Data Book for January–December 2017

Fraud and Other Consumer Reports

Area	Reports	Reports per 100,000 Population	Rank[2]
MSA[1]	5,766	509	105
U.S.	2,304,550	708	-

Note: (1) Figures cover the Buffalo-Cheektowaga-Niagara Falls, NY Metropolitan Statistical Area—see Appendix B for areas included; (2) Rank ranges from 1 to 389 where 1 indicates greatest number of fraud and other consumer reports per 100,000 population
Source: Federal Trade Commission, Consumer Sentinel Network Data Book for January–December 2017

SPORTS

Professional Sports Teams

Team Name	League	Year Established
Buffalo Bills	National Football League (NFL)	1960
Buffalo Sabres	National Hockey League (NHL)	1970

Note: Includes teams located in the Buffalo-Cheektowaga-Niagara Falls, NY Metropolitan Statistical Area.
Source: Wikipedia, Major Professional Sports Teams of the United States and Canada, April 5, 2018

CLIMATE

Average and Extreme Temperatures

Temperature	Jan	Feb	Mar	Apr	May	Jun	Jul	Aug	Sep	Oct	Nov	Dec	Yr.
Extreme High (°F)	72	65	79	94	90	96	97	99	98	87	80	74	99
Average High (°F)	31	32	41	55	66	76	81	79	71	61	47	36	56
Average Temp. (°F)	25	26	34	46	57	66	71	70	62	52	41	30	48
Average Low (°F)	18	18	26	36	46	56	62	60	53	43	34	23	40
Extreme Low (°F)	-16	-20	-7	12	26	36	46	38	23	20	7	-10	-20

Note: Figures cover the years 1946-1990
Source: National Climatic Data Center, International Station Meteorological Climate Summary, 9/96

Average Precipitation/Snowfall/Humidity

Precip./Humidity	Jan	Feb	Mar	Apr	May	Jun	Jul	Aug	Sep	Oct	Nov	Dec	Yr.
Avg. Precip. (in.)	2.9	2.5	2.9	3.0	3.1	3.1	2.9	3.9	3.3	3.0	3.9	3.5	38.1
Avg. Snowfall (in.)	24	18	11	3	Tr	0	0	0	Tr	Tr	11	22	90
Avg. Rel. Hum. 7am (%)	79	80	80	77	76	77	78	83	83	82	80	80	80
Avg. Rel. Hum. 4pm (%)	73	70	65	57	55	55	53	56	59	60	70	74	62

Note: Figures cover the years 1946-1990; Tr = Trace amounts (<0.05 in. of rain; <0.5 in. of snow)
Source: National Climatic Data Center, International Station Meteorological Climate Summary, 9/96

Weather Conditions

Temperature			Daytime Sky			Precipitation		
5°F & below	32°F & below	90°F & above	Clear	Partly cloudy	Cloudy	0.01 inch or more precip.	0.1 inch or more snow/ice	Thunderstorms
11	131	4	47	144	174	169	65	30

Note: Figures are average number of days per year and cover the years 1946-1990
Source: National Climatic Data Center, International Station Meteorological Climate Summary, 9/96

HAZARDOUS WASTE

Superfund Sites

The Buffalo-Cheektowaga-Niagara Falls, NY metro area is home to three sites on the EPA's Superfund National Priorities List: **Eighteenmile Creek** (final); **Forest Glen Mobile Home Subdivision** (final); **Hooker (S Area)** (final). There are a total of 1,396 Superfund sites with a status of proposed or final on the list in the U.S. *U.S. Environmental Protection Agency, National Priorities List, April 4, 2018*

AIR & WATER QUALITY

Air Quality Trends: Ozone

	1990	1995	2000	2005	2010	2012	2013	2014	2015	2016
MSA[1]	0.089	0.088	0.083	0.090	0.072	0.081	0.068	0.062	0.069	0.072
U.S.	0.087	0.089	0.081	0.079	0.073	0.075	0.069	0.067	0.068	0.069

Note: (1) Data covers the Buffalo-Cheektowaga-Niagara Falls, NY Metropolitan Statistical Area—see Appendix B for areas included. The values shown are the composite ozone concentration averages among trend sites based on the highest fourth daily maximum 8-hour concentration in parts per million. These trends are based on sites having an adequate record of monitoring data during the trend period. Data from exceptional events are included.
Source: U.S. Environmental Protection Agency, Air Quality Monitoring Information, "Air Quality Trends by City, 1990-2016"

Air Quality Index

Area	Percent of Days when Air Quality was...[2]					AQI Statistics[2]	
	Good	Moderate	Unhealthy for Sensitive Groups	Unhealthy	Very Unhealthy	Maximum	Median
MSA[1]	78.9	20.8	0.3	0.0	0.0	119	39

Note: (1) Data covers the Buffalo-Cheektowaga-Niagara Falls, NY Metropolitan Statistical Area—see Appendix B for areas included; (2) Based on 365 days with AQI data in 2017. Air Quality Index (AQI) is an index for reporting daily air quality. EPA calculates the AQI for five major air pollutants regulated by the Clean Air Act: ground-level ozone, particle pollution (aka particulate matter), carbon monoxide, sulfur dioxide, and nitrogen dioxide. The AQI runs from 0 to 500. The higher the AQI value, the greater the level of air pollution and the greater the health concern. There are six AQI categories: "Good" AQI is between 0 and 50. Air quality is considered satisfactory; "Moderate" AQI is between 51 and 100. Air quality is acceptable; "Unhealthy for Sensitive Groups" When AQI values are between 101 and 150, members of sensitive groups may experience health effects; "Unhealthy" When AQI values are between 151 and 200 everyone may begin to experience health effects; "Very Unhealthy" AQI values between 201 and 300 trigger a health alert; "Hazardous" AQI values over 300 trigger warnings of emergency conditions (not shown).
Source: U.S. Environmental Protection Agency, Air Quality Index Report, 2017

Air Quality Index Pollutants

Area	Percent of Days when AQI Pollutant was...[2]					
	Carbon Monoxide	Nitrogen Dioxide	Ozone	Sulfur Dioxide	Particulate Matter 2.5	Particulate Matter 10
MSA[1]	0.0	3.8	53.2	0.0	43.0	0.0

Note: (1) Data covers the Buffalo-Cheektowaga-Niagara Falls, NY Metropolitan Statistical Area—see Appendix B for areas included; (2) Based on 365 days with AQI data in 2017. The Air Quality Index (AQI) is an index for reporting daily air quality. EPA calculates the AQI for five major air pollutants regulated by the Clean Air Act: ground-level ozone, particle pollution (also known as particulate matter), carbon monoxide, sulfur dioxide, and nitrogen dioxide. The AQI runs from 0 to 500. The higher the AQI value, the greater the level of air pollution and the greater the health concern.
Source: U.S. Environmental Protection Agency, Air Quality Index Report, 2017

Maximum Air Pollutant Concentrations: Particulate Matter, Ozone, CO and Lead

	Particulate Matter 10 (ug/m³)	Particulate Matter 2.5 Wtd AM (ug/m³)	Particulate Matter 2.5 24-Hr (ug/m³)	Ozone (ppm)	Carbon Monoxide (ppm)	Lead (ug/m³)
MSA[1] Level	n/a	6.8	15	0.074	1	n/a
NAAQS[2]	150	15	35	0.075	9	0.15
Met NAAQS[2]	n/a	Yes	Yes	Yes	Yes	n/a

Note: (1) Data covers the Buffalo-Cheektowaga-Niagara Falls, NY Metropolitan Statistical Area—see Appendix B for areas included; Data from exceptional events are included; (2) National Ambient Air Quality Standards; ppm = parts per million; ug/m³ = micrograms per cubic meter; n/a not available.
Concentrations: Particulate Matter 10 (coarse particulate)—highest second maximum 24-hour concentration; Particulate Matter 2.5 Wtd AM (fine particulate)—highest weighted annual mean concentration; Particulate Matter 2.5 24-Hour (fine particulate)—highest 98th percentile 24-hour concentration; Ozone—highest fourth daily maximum 8-hour concentration; Carbon Monoxide—highest second maximum non-overlapping 8-hour concentration; Lead—maximum running 3-month average
Source: U.S. Environmental Protection Agency, Air Quality Monitoring Information, "Air Quality Statistics by City, 2016"

Maximum Air Pollutant Concentrations: Nitrogen Dioxide and Sulfur Dioxide

	Nitrogen Dioxide AM (ppb)	Nitrogen Dioxide 1-Hr (ppb)	Sulfur Dioxide AM (ppb)	Sulfur Dioxide 1-Hr (ppb)	Sulfur Dioxide 24-Hr (ppb)
MSA[1] Level	11	48	n/a	18	n/a
NAAQS[2]	53	100	30	75	140
Met NAAQS[2]	Yes	Yes	n/a	Yes	n/a

Note: (1) Data covers the Buffalo-Cheektowaga-Niagara Falls, NY Metropolitan Statistical Area—see Appendix B for areas included; Data from exceptional events are included; (2) National Ambient Air Quality Standards; ppm = parts per million; ug/m^3 = micrograms per cubic meter; n/a not available.
Concentrations: Nitrogen Dioxide AM—highest arithmetic mean concentration; Nitrogen Dioxide 1-Hr—highest 98th percentile 1-hour daily maximum concentration; Sulfur Dioxide AM—highest annual mean concentration; Sulfur Dioxide 1-Hr—highest 99th percentile 1-hour daily maximum concentration; Sulfur Dioxide 24-Hr—highest second maximum 24-hour concentration
Source: U.S. Environmental Protection Agency, Air Quality Monitoring Information, "Air Quality Statistics by City, 2016"

Drinking Water

Water System Name	Pop. Served	Primary Water Source Type	Violations[1]	
			Health Based	Monitoring/ Reporting
ECWA Orchard Park	23,387	Purchased Surface	0	0

Note: (1) Based on violation data from January 1, 2017 to December 31, 2017
Source: U.S. Environmental Protection Agency, Office of Ground Water and Drinking Water, Safe Drinking Water Information System (based on data extracted April 5, 2018)

Rye, New York

Background

The Town of Rye, adjacent to the city of Rye, contains two villages: Port Chester and Rye Brook. It also contains a portion of the village of Mamaroneck (AKA Rye Neck), while the rest of that village is contained within the town of Mamaroneck. These villages encompass the entire area of Rye, which is nestled in Westchester County.

Begun as a small settlement on Manursing Island in 1660, Rye began as a land purchase by three settlers from the Mohegan Native Americans—Thomas Studwell, John Coe, and Peter Disbrow, regarded as the founders of Rye. In these early days, Connecticut and New York both claimed Rye, though the settlers considered themselves to be in Connecticut. Rye was officially ceded to New York in 1683, solidifying the Connecticut Panhandle. Over time, the town would grow and develop the area of Poningo Neck, which is the current business district of the City of Rye, and the Saw Pit area which is now known as Port Chester.

The Town of Rye, which totals 7.4 square miles, borders Long Island Sound and is a convenient commuting distance from the New York City metropolitan area.

Rye consists of four different school districts within its 3 villages: the Harrison School District, the Rye Neck School District, the Port Chester-Rye Union Free School District, and the Blind Brook-Rye Union Free School District.

Rye is home to two parks, Crawford Park and Rye Town Park and Beach. Crawford Park, donated to the Town of Rye in 1971, was originally established by the Crawford Family, whose estate was filled with gardens, lawns, and woods, surrounding a historic mansion, and the Friends of Crawford Park was formed in 1997 to restore the grounds to their former beauty. Rye Town Park and Beach, on the Long Island Sound, was placed on the National Register of Historic Places in 2003 after almost 100 years in operation. Today, the park offers 62 acres of grasslands, forests, open fields, duck pond, and beach. The Friends of Rye Town Park was established in 1991 to aid in restoring the park's landscape, and works to conserve the park's historic beauty. Within this park is the Mission Revival style Bathing Complex, which is comprised of six historic buildings: the Bathing Pavilion and two shelters, a restaurant, the Spring House, and the Women's Bath House.

The climate of Rye is primarily humid continental, which is fairly cooler than the humid subtropical climate of nearby New York City. Summers are hot inland but cooler towards the coast, while winters are cold.

Rankings

General Rankings

- New York* was identified as one of America's fastest-growing cities in terms of population growth by CNNMoney.com. The area ranked #1 out of 10. Criteria: population growth between July 2015 and July 2016; cities and towns with populations of 50,000. *CNNMoney, "10 Fastest-Growing Cities," June 2, 2017*

Business/Finance Rankings

- The personal finance site NerdWallet analyzed 183 American metropolitan areas with populations over 250,000 and more than 15,000 businesses to rank where entrepreneurs find the most success. Criteria included area economy, annual income, housing cost, unemployment rate, and the success rate of area businesses. New York* ranked #32. *www.nerdwallet.com, "Best Places to Start a Business," April 27, 2015*
- Metro areas with the largest gap in income between rich and poor residents were identified by 24/7 Wall Street using the U.S. Census Bureau's 2013 American Community Survey. The New York* metro area placed #7 among metro areas with the widest wealth gap between rich and poor. *247wallst.com, "20 Cities with the Widest Gap between the Rich and Poor," July 8, 2015*
- In a survey of economic confidence in the nation's 50 largest metropolitan areas conducted January–December 2014, the New York* metro area placed #23, according to Gallup's 2014 Economic Confidence Index. *Gallup, "San Jose and San Francisco Lead in Economic Confidence," March 19, 2015*
- The Brookings Institution ranked the 100 largest metro areas in the U.S. based on income inequality. New York* was ranked #2 (#1 = greatest ineqality). Criteria: the "95/20 ratio," a figure representing the income at which a household earns more than 95 percent of all other households, divided by the income at which a household earns more than only 20 percent of all other households. *Brookings Institution, "Household Income Inequality, 100 Largest U.S. Metro Areas, 2014-2016," February 5, 2018*
- Payscale.com ranked the largest metro areas in terms of wage growth. The New York* metro area ranked #1. Criteria: private-sector wage growth between the 4th quarter of 2016 and the 4th quarter of 2017. *PayScale, "Wage Trends by Metro Area-4th Quarter," January 17, 2018*
- The New York* metro area was identified as one of the most debt-ridden places in America by the finance site Credit.com. The metro area was ranked #3. Criteria: residents' average credit card debt as well as median income. *Credit.com, "25 Cities With the Most Credit Card Debt," February 28, 2018*
- New York* was identified as one of America's most frugal metro areas by *Coupons.com.* The city ranked #15 out of 25. Criteria: digital coupon usage. *Coupons.com, "America's Most Frugal Cities of 2017," March 22, 2018*
- New York* was cited as one of America's top metros for new and expanded facility projects in 2017. The area ranked #5 in the large metro area category (population over 1 million). *Site Selection, "Top Metropolitans of 2017," March 2018*
- The New York* metro area appeared on the Milken Institute "2017 Best Performing Cities" list. Rank: #82 out of 200 large metro areas. Criteria: job growth; wage and salary growth; high-tech output growth. *Milken Institute, "Best-Performing Cities 2017," January 2018*
- *Forbes* ranked the 200 most populous metro areas to determine the nation's "Best Places for Business and Careers." The New York* metro area was ranked #113. Criteria: costs (business and living); job growth (past and projected); income growth; quality of life; educational attainment (college and high school); projected economic growth; cultural and recreational opportunities; net migration patterns; number of highly ranked colleges. *Forbes, "The Best Places for Business and Careers 2017," October 24, 2017*

Dating/Romance Rankings

- *Apartment List* conducted its annual survey of renters to compile a list of metros that have the best opportunities for dating. Nearly 11,000 respondents, from February 2017 through January 2018, rated their current city or neighborhood for opportunities to date and make friends. The New York* metro area ranked #10 out of 70 where single residents were very satisfied or somewhat satisfied, making it among the ten best metros for dating opportunities. Other criteria analyzed included gender and education levels of renters. *Apartment List, "Best Metros for Dating 2018," February 6, 2018*

Education Rankings

- Personal finance website *WalletHub* analyzed the 150 largest U.S. metropolitan statistical areas to determine where the most educated Americans are choosing to settle. Criteria: education quality and attainment gap; education levels; percentage of workers with degrees; public school rankings; quality and size of each metro area's universities. New York* was ranked #36 (#1 = most educated city). *www.WalletHub.com, "2017's Most and Least Educated Cities in America," July 25, 2017*

Environmental Rankings

- Sperling's BestPlaces assessed 379 metropolitan areas of the United States for the likelihood of dangerously extreme weather events or earthquakes. In general the Southeast and South-Central regions have the highest risk of weather extremes and earthquakes, while the Pacific Northwest enjoys the lowest risk. Of the least risky metropolitan areas, the New York* metro area was ranked #207. *www.bestplaces.net, "Safest Places from Natural Disasters," April 2011*

- The U.S. Environmental Protection Agency (EPA) released a list of U.S. metropolitan areas with the most ENERGY STAR certified buildings in 2016. The New York* metro area was ranked #3 out of 25. *U.S. Environmental Protection Agency, "2017 Energy Star Top Cities," June 2017*

- New York* was highlighted as one of the 25 most ozone-polluted metro areas in the U.S. during 2013 through 2015. The area ranked #9. *American Lung Association, State of the Air 2017*

- New York* was highlighted as one of the 25 metro areas most polluted by year-round particle pollution (Annual PM 2.5) in the U.S. during 2013 through 2015. The area ranked #22. *American Lung Association, State of the Air 2017*

Health/Fitness Rankings

- For each of the 50 most populous metro areas in the United States, the American College of Sports Medicine's American Fitness Index evaluated infrastructure, community assets, and policies that encourage healthy and fit lifestyles, including preventive health behaviors, levels of chronic disease conditions, health care access, and community resources and policies that support physical activity. The New York* metro area ranked #18 for "community fitness." *www.americanfitnessindex.org, "ACSM American Fitness Index Health and Community Fitness Status of the 50 Largest Metropolitan Areas," May 2017*

- The New York* metro area was identified as one of the worst cities for bed bugs in America by pest control company Orkin. The area ranked #8 out of 50 based on the number of bed bug treatments Orkin performed from December 2016 to November 2017. *Orkin, "Baltimore and Washington D.C. Continue to Hold Top Spots," January 8, 2018*

- New York* was identified as a "2016 Spring Allergy Capital." The area ranked #31 out of 100. Three groups of factors were used to identify the most severe cities for people with allergies during the spring season: annual pollen levels; medicine utilization; access to board-certified allergists. *Asthma and Allergy Foundation of America, "Spring Allergy Capitals 2016"*

- New York* was identified as a "2016 Fall Allergy Capital." The area ranked #52 out of 100. Three groups of factors were used to identify the most severe cities for people with allergies during the fall season: annual pollen levels; medicine utilization; access to board-certified allergists. *Asthma and Allergy Foundation of America, "Fall Allergy Capitals 2016"*
- New York* was identified as a "2015 Asthma Capital." The area ranked #35 out of the nation's 100 largest metropolitan areas. Criteria: estimated prevalence; self-reported prevalence; crude death rate for asthma; annual pollen score; annual air quality; public smoking laws; number of board-certified asthma specialists; school inhaler access laws; rescue medication use; controller medication use; ER visits for asthma; uninsured rate; poverty rate. *Asthma and Allergy Foundation of America, "Asthma Capitals 2015"*
- The New York* metro area ranked #75 out of 189 in The Gallup-Healthways Well-Being Index. Criteria: purpose; social well being; financial health; community and physical health. Results are based on telephone interviews with adults, aged 18 and older, living in metropolitan areas in the 50 U.S. states and the District of Columbia. *Gallup-Healthways, "State of American Well-Being, 2017 Community Well-Being Rankings" March 2018*

Real Estate Rankings

- FitSmallBusiness looked at 50 of the largest metropolitan areas in the U.S. to determine which metro was the best to start a real estate business. Data was compiled from such sources as: Zillow, Trulia, U.S. Census Bureau, and the Bureau of Labor Statistics. Criteria: location; inventory; annual wages; median sales price of homes; days on the market; median price cut percentage; and other factors that would influence real estate professional growth. The New York* metro area ranked #6. *fitsmallbusiness.com, "The Best Cities to Become a Real Estate Agent in 2018," January 30, 2018*
- With data from RealtyTrac, Yahoo! Finance researchers listed the housing markets in which housing affordability is improving most, factoring in interest rates as well as median home prices. The New York* metro area was among the least affordable housing markets. *news.yahoo.com, "10 Cities Where Ordinary People Can No Longer Afford Homes," March 5, 2014*
- The New York* metro area was identified as one of the 20 least affordable housing markets in the U.S. in 2017. The area ranked #12 out of 180 markets. Criteria: qualification for a mortgage loan on a typical home. *National Association of Realtors®, Affordability Index of Existing Single-Family Homes for Metropolitan Areas, 2017*
- New York* was ranked #219 out of 238 metro areas in terms of housing affordability in 2017 by the National Association of Home Builders (#1 = most affordable). Criteria: the share of homes sold in that area affordable to a family earning the local median income, based on standard mortgage underwriting criteria. *National Association of Home Builders®, NAHB-Wells Fargo Housing Opportunity Index, 4th Quarter 2017*

Safety Rankings

- The National Insurance Crime Bureau ranked 382 metro areas in the U.S. in terms of per capita rates of vehicle theft. The New York* metro area ranked #292 (#1 = highest rate). Criteria: number of vehicle theft offenses per 100,000 inhabitants in 2016. *National Insurance Crime Bureau, "Hot Spots 2016," June 8, 2017*

Seniors/Retirement Rankings

- From its Best Cities for Successful Aging indexes, the Milken Institute generated rankings for metropolitan areas, weighing data in nine categories—health care, wellness, living arrangements, transportation and convenience, financial characteristics, education, employment, community engagement, and overall livability. The New York* metro area was ranked #11 overall in the large metro area category. *Milken Institute, "Best Cities for Successful Aging, 2017" March 14, 2017*

Sports/Recreation Rankings

- According to the personal finance website NerdWallet, the New York* metro area, at #4, is one of the nation's top dozen metro areas for sports fans. Criteria included the presence of all four major sports—MLB, NFL, NHL, and NBA, fan enthusiasm (as measured by game attendance), ticket affordability, and "sports culture," that is, number of sports bars. *www.nerdwallet.com, "Best Cities for Sports Fans," May 5, 2013*

Transportation Rankings

- New York* was identified as one of the most congested metro areas in the U.S. The area ranked #4 out of 10. Criteria: yearly delay per auto commuter in hours. *Texas A&M Transportation Institute, "2015 Urban Mobility Scorecard," August 2015*

- The New York* metro area appeared on *Forbes* list of places with the most extreme commutes. The metro area ranked #2 out of 10. Criteria: average travel time; percentage of mega commuters. Mega-commuters travel more than 90 minutes and 50 miles each way to work. *Forbes.com, "The Cities with the Most Extreme Commutes," March 5, 2013*

Women/Minorities Rankings

- The *Houston Chronicle* listed the New York* metro area as #4 in top places for young Latinos to live in the U.S. Research was largely based on housing and occupational data from the largest metropolitan areas performed by *Forbes* and NBC Universo. Criteria: percentage of 18-34 year-olds; Latino college grad rates; and diversity. *blog.chron.com, "The 15 Best Big Cities for Latino Millenials," January 26, 2016*

Miscellaneous Rankings

- The watchdog site Charity Navigator conducts an annual study of charities in the nation's major markets both to analyze statistical differences in their financial, accountability, and transparency practices and to track year-to-year variations in individual philanthropic communities. Charity Navigator's analysis demonstrated that the financial, accountability and transparency behaviors of America's largest charities can be influenced by the metropolitan market within which the charity operates. The New York* metro area was ranked #19 among the 30 metro markets in the rating category of Overall Score. *www.charitynavigator.org, "2017 Metro Market Study," May 1, 2017*

- The Harris Poll's Happiness Index survey revealed that of the top ten U.S. markets, the New York* metro area residents ranked #6 in happiness. Criteria included strong assent to positive statements and strong disagreement with negative ones, and degree of agreement with a series of statements about respondents' personal relationships and general outlook. *www.theharrispoll.com, "Dallas/Fort Worth Is "Happiest" City among America's Top Ten Markets," September 4, 2013*

- Energizer Personal Care, the makers of Edge® shave gel, in partnership with Sperling's BestPlaces, ranked 50 major metro areas in terms of everyday irritations. The New York* metro area ranked #2 the 50 metro area most irritating to guys. Criteria: high male-to-female ratio; poor sports team performance and high ticket prices; slow traffic; lack of job availability; unaffordable housing; extreme weather; lack of nightlife and fitness options. *Energizer Personal Care, "Most Irritating Cities for Guys," August 26, 2013*

- The National Alliance to End Homelessness listed the 25 most populous metro areas with the highest rate of homelessness. The New York* metro area had a high rate of homelessness. Criteria: number of homeless people per 10,000 population in 2016. *National Alliance to End Homelessness, "Homelessness in the 25 Most Populous U.S. Metro Areas," September 1, 2017*

*Rye is located within the New York-Newark-Jersey City, NY-NJ-PA Metropolitan Statistical Area and the New York-Jersey City-White Plains, NY-NJ Metropolitan Division.

Business Environment

CITY FINANCES

City Government Finances

Component	2015 ($000)	2015 ($ per capita)
Total Revenues	n/a	n/a
Total Expenditures	n/a	n/a
Debt Outstanding	n/a	n/a
Cash and Securities[1]	n/a	n/a

Note: (1) Cash and security holdings of a government at the close of its fiscal year,, including those of its dependent agencies, utilities, and liquor stores.
Source: U.S Census Bureau, State & Local Government Finances 2015

City Government Revenue by Source

Source	2015 ($000)	2015 ($ per capita)	2015 (%)
General Revenue			
From Federal Government	n/a	n/a	n/a
From State Government	n/a	n/a	n/a
From Local Governments	n/a	n/a	n/a
Taxes			
Property	n/a	n/a	n/a
Sales and Gross Receipts	n/a	n/a	n/a
Personal Income	n/a	n/a	n/a
Corporate Income	n/a	n/a	n/a
Motor Vehicle License	n/a	n/a	n/a
Other Taxes	n/a	n/a	n/a
Current Charges	n/a	n/a	n/a
Liquor Store	n/a	n/a	n/a
Utility	n/a	n/a	n/a
Employee Retirement	n/a	n/a	n/a

Source: U.S Census Bureau, State & Local Government Finances 2015

City Government Expenditures by Function

Function	2015 ($000)	2015 ($ per capita)	2015 (%)
General Direct Expenditures			
Air Transportation	n/a	n/a	n/a
Corrections	n/a	n/a	n/a
Education	n/a	n/a	n/a
Employment Security Administration	n/a	n/a	n/a
Financial Administration	n/a	n/a	n/a
Fire Protection	n/a	n/a	n/a
General Public Buildings	n/a	n/a	n/a
Governmental Administration, Other	n/a	n/a	n/a
Health	n/a	n/a	n/a
Highways	n/a	n/a	n/a
Hospitals	n/a	n/a	n/a
Housing and Community Development	n/a	n/a	n/a
Interest on General Debt	n/a	n/a	n/a
Judicial and Legal	n/a	n/a	n/a
Libraries	n/a	n/a	n/a
Parking	n/a	n/a	n/a
Parks and Recreation	n/a	n/a	n/a
Police Protection	n/a	n/a	n/a
Public Welfare	n/a	n/a	n/a
Sewerage	n/a	n/a	n/a
Solid Waste Management	n/a	n/a	n/a
Veterans' Services	n/a	n/a	n/a
Liquor Store	n/a	n/a	n/a
Utility	n/a	n/a	n/a
Employee Retirement	n/a	n/a	n/a

Source: U.S Census Bureau, State & Local Government Finances 2015

DEMOGRAPHICS

Population Growth

Area	1990 Census	2000 Census	2010 Census	2016* Estimate	Population Growth (%) 1990-2016	2010-2016
City	39,524	43,880	45,928	46,676	18.1	1.6
MSA[1]	16,845,992	18,323,002	18,897,109	20,031,443	18.9	6.0
U.S.	248,709,873	281,421,906	308,745,538	318,558,162	28.1	3.2

Note: (1) Figures cover the New York-Newark-Jersey City, NY-NJ-PA Metropolitan Statistical Area—see Appendix B for areas included; (*) 2012-2016 5-year estimated population
Source: U.S. Census Bureau, 1990 Census, Census 2000, Census 2010, 2012-2016 American Community Survey 5-Year Estimates

Household Size

Area	Persons in Household (%) One	Two	Three	Four	Five	Six	Seven or More	Average Household Size
City	22.6	26.8	18.8	18.5	6.4	3.4	3.4	3.00
MSA[1]	28.0	29.1	17.0	14.7	6.7	2.6	1.9	2.80
U.S.	27.7	33.7	15.7	13.1	6.0	2.3	1.5	2.60

Note: (1) Figures cover the New York-Newark-Jersey City, NY-NJ-PA Metropolitan Statistical Area—see Appendix B for areas included
Source: U.S. Census Bureau, 2012-2016 American Community Survey 5-Year Estimates

Race

Area	White Alone[2] (%)	Black Alone[2] (%)	Asian Alone[2] (%)	AIAN[3] Alone[2] (%)	NHOPI[4] Alone[2] (%)	Other Race Alone[2] (%)	Two or More Races (%)
City	63.7	5.5	2.8	0.7	0.0	25.0	2.2
MSA[1]	58.7	17.1	10.6	0.3	0.0	10.3	2.9
U.S.	73.3	12.6	5.2	0.8	0.2	4.8	3.1

Note: (1) Figures cover the New York-Newark-Jersey City, NY-NJ-PA Metropolitan Statistical Area—see Appendix B for areas included; (2) Alone is defined as not being in combination with one or more other races; (3) American Indian and Alaska Native; (4) Native Hawaiian and Other Pacific Islander
Source: U.S. Census Bureau, 2012-2016 American Community Survey 5-Year Estimates

Hispanic or Latino Origin

Area	Total (%)	Mexican (%)	Puerto Rican (%)	Cuban (%)	Other (%)
City	44.3	10.3	2.7	0.8	30.5
MSA[1]	23.8	3.1	6.3	0.7	13.7
U.S.	17.3	11.0	1.7	0.7	4.0

Note: Persons of Hispanic or Latino origin can be of any race; (1) Figures cover the New York-Newark-Jersey City, NY-NJ-PA Metropolitan Statistical Area—see Appendix B for areas included
Source: U.S. Census Bureau, 2012-2016 American Community Survey 5-Year Estimates

Segregation

Type	Segregation Indices[1] 1990	2000	2010	2010 Rank[2]	Percent Change 1990-2000	1990-2010	2000-2010
Black/White	80.9	80.2	78.0	2	-0.7	-2.9	-2.2
Asian/White	47.4	50.8	51.9	3	3.5	4.5	1.0
Hispanic/White	66.2	65.6	62.0	3	-0.6	-4.2	-3.6

Note: All figures cover the Metropolitan Statistical Area—see Appendix B for areas included; Figures are based on an analysis of 1990, 2000, and 2010 Census Decennial Census tract data by William H. Frey, Brookings Institution and the University of Michigan Social Science Data Analysis Network. In this analysis all racial groups (whites, blacks, and asians) are non-Hispanic members of those races. Hispanics are shown as a separate category; (1) Segregation Indices are Dissimilarity Indices that measure the degree to which the minority group is distributed differently than whites across census tracts. They range from 0 (complete integration) to 100 (complete segregation) where the value indicates the percentage of the minority group that needs to move to be distributed exactly like whites; (2) Ranges from 1 (most segregated) to 102 (least segregated); n/a not available.
Source: www.CensusScope.org

Ancestry

Area	German	Irish	English	American	Italian	Polish	French[2]	Scottish	Dutch
City	3.7	7.3	2.4	8.2	16.9	2.8	0.8	0.5	0.2
MSA[1]	6.8	10.0	2.9	4.8	13.1	4.0	1.0	0.7	0.7
U.S.	14.4	10.4	7.7	6.9	5.4	2.9	2.6	1.7	1.3

Note: Figures are the percentage of the total population reporting a particular ancestry. The nine most commonly reported ancestries in the U.S. are shown. Figures include multiple ancestries (e.g. if a person reported being Irish and Italian, they were included in both columns); (1) Figures cover the New York-Newark-Jersey City, NY-NJ-PA Metropolitan Statistical Area—see Appendix B for areas included; (2) Excludes Basque
Source: U.S. Census Bureau, 2012-2016 American Community Survey 5-Year Estimates

Foreign-Born Population

Area	Percent of Population Born in								
	Any Foreign Country	Asia	Mexico	Europe	Carribean	Central America[2]	South America	Africa	Canada
City	36.6	2.2	6.7	4.0	2.0	7.6	13.0	0.6	0.4
MSA[1]	28.7	8.3	1.6	4.5	6.6	1.9	4.2	1.2	0.2
U.S.	13.2	4.0	3.6	1.5	1.3	1.0	0.9	0.6	0.3

Note: (1) Figures cover the New York-Newark-Jersey City, NY-NJ-PA Metropolitan Statistical Area—see Appendix B for areas included; (2) Excludes Mexico.
Source: U.S. Census Bureau, 2012-2016 American Community Survey 5-Year Estimates

Marital Status

Area	Never Married	Now Married[2]	Separated	Widowed	Divorced
City	35.2	49.5	3.3	4.9	7.1
MSA[1]	38.1	45.7	2.4	5.8	7.9
U.S.	33.0	48.1	2.1	5.9	11.0

Note: Figures are percentages and cover the population 15 years of age and older; (1) Figures cover the New York-Newark-Jersey City, NY-NJ-PA Metropolitan Statistical Area—see Appendix B for areas included; (2) Excludes separated
Source: U.S. Census Bureau, 2012-2016 American Community Survey 5-Year Estimates

Disability Status

Area	All Ages	Under 18 Years Old	18 to 64 Years Old	65 Years and Over
City	9.0	2.1	6.8	32.1
MSA[1]	10.0	3.2	7.4	33.3
U.S.	12.5	4.1	10.3	35.7

Note: Figures show percent of the civilian noninstitutionalized population that reported having a disability. Disability status is determined from six types of difficulty: vision, hearing, cognitive, ambulatory, self-care, and independent living. For children under 5 years old, hearing and vision difficulty are used to determine disability status. For children between the ages of 5 and 14, disability status is determined from hearing, vision, cognitive, ambulatory, and self-care difficulties. For people aged 15 years and older, they are considered to have a disability if they have difficulty with any one of the six difficulty types; Note: (1) Figures cover the New York-Newark-Jersey City, NY-NJ-PA Metropolitan Statistical Area—see Appendix B for areas included
Source: U.S. Census Bureau, 2012-2016 American Community Survey 5-Year Estimates

Age

Area	Percent of Population									Median Age
	Under Age 5	Age 5–19	Age 20–34	Age 35–44	Age 45–54	Age 55–64	Age 65–74	Age 75–84	Age 85+	
City	6.0	19.9	18.5	15.7	13.9	12.7	6.9	4.0	2.4	38.5
MSA[1]	6.1	18.4	21.3	13.3	14.3	12.3	7.8	4.2	2.1	38.0
U.S.	6.2	19.6	20.7	12.7	13.6	12.6	8.3	4.3	1.9	37.7

Note: (1) Figures cover the New York-Newark-Jersey City, NY-NJ-PA Metropolitan Statistical Area—see Appendix B for areas included
Source: U.S. Census Bureau, 2012-2016 American Community Survey 5-Year Estimates

Gender

Area	Males	Females	Males per 100 Females
City	23,127	23,549	98.2
MSA[1]	9,684,087	10,347,356	93.6
U.S.	156,765,322	161,792,840	96.9

Note: (1) Figures cover the New York-Newark-Jersey City, NY-NJ-PA Metropolitan Statistical Area—see Appendix B for areas included
Source: U.S. Census Bureau, 2012-2016 American Community Survey 5-Year Estimates

Religious Groups by Family

Area	Catholic	Baptist	Non-Den.	Methodist[2]	Lutheran	LDS[3]	Pente-costal	Presby-terian[4]	Muslim[5]	Judaism
MSA[1]	36.9	1.9	1.8	1.3	0.8	0.4	0.9	1.1	2.3	4.8
U.S.	19.1	9.3	4.0	4.0	2.3	2.0	1.9	1.6	0.8	0.7

Note: Figures are the number of adherents as a percentage of the total population; (1) Figures cover the New York-Newark-Jersey City, NY-NJ-PA Metropolitan Statistical Area—see Appendix B for areas included; (2) Methodist/Pietist; (3) Latter Day Saints; (4) Reformed; (5) Figures are estimates
Source: Association of Statisticians of American Religious Bodies, 2010 U.S. Religion Census: Religious Congregations & Membership Study

Religious Groups by Tradition

Area	Catholic	Evangelical Protestant	Mainline Protestant	Other Tradition	Black Protestant	Orthodox
MSA[1]	36.9	4.0	4.1	8.4	1.2	1.0
U.S.	19.1	16.2	7.3	4.3	1.6	0.3

Note: Figures are the number of adherents as a percentage of the total population; (1) Figures cover the New York-Newark-Jersey City, NY-NJ-PA Metropolitan Statistical Area—see Appendix B for areas included
Source: Association of Statisticians of American Religious Bodies, 2010 U.S. Religion Census: Religious Congregations & Membership Study

ECONOMY

Gross Metropolitan Product

Area	2014	2015	2016	2017	Rank[2]
MSA[1]	1,551.3	1,613.8	1,664.0	1,735.1	1

Note: Figures are in billions of dollars; (1) Figures cover the New York-Newark-Jersey City, NY-NJ-PA Metropolitan Statistical Area—see Appendix B for areas included; (2) Rank is based on 2015 data and ranges from 1 to 381
Source: The U.S. Conference of Mayors, U.S. Metro Economies: GMP and Employment Report, 2015-2017

Economic Growth

Area	2012-14 (%)	2015 (%)	2016 (%)	2017 (%)	Rank[2]
MSA[1]	1.6	1.9	1.6	2.2	151
U.S.	2.0	2.4	1.9	2.6	–

Note: Figures are real gross metropolitan product (GMP) growth rates and represent average annual percent change; (1) Figures cover the New York-Newark-Jersey City, NY-NJ-PA Metropolitan Statistical Area—see Appendix B for areas included; (2) Rank is based on 2012-2014 average annual percent change and ranges from 1 to 381
Source: The U.S. Conference of Mayors, U.S. Metro Economies: GMP and Employment Report, 2015-2017

Metropolitan Area Exports

Area	2011	2012	2013	2014	2015	2016	Rank[2]
MSA[1]	105,102.0	102,298.0	106,922.8	105,266.6	95,645.4	89,649.5	1

Note: Figures are in millions of dollars; (1) Figures cover the New York-Newark-Jersey City, NY-NJ-PA Metropolitan Statistical Area—see Appendix B for areas included; (2) Rank is based on 2016 data and ranges from 1 to 385
Source: U.S. Department of Commerce, International Trade Administration, Office of Trade & Industry Information, Manufacturing & Services, data extracted March 15, 2018

Building Permits

Area	Single-Family			Multi-Family			Total		
	2016	2017p	Pct. Chg.	2016	2017p	Pct. Chg.	2016	2017p	Pct. Chg.
City	n/a	n/a	n/a	n/a	n/a	n/a	n/a	n/a	n/a
MSA[1]	9,987	10,549	5.6	32,479	39,344	21.1	42,466	49,893	17.5
U.S.	750,800	817,300	8.9	455,800	446,800	-2.0	1,206,600	1,264,100	4.8

Note: (1) Figures cover the New York-Newark-Jersey City, NY-NJ-PA Metropolitan Statistical Area—see Appendix B for areas included; Figures represent new, privately-owned housing units authorized (unadjusted data); All permit data are based on estimates with imputation; (p) preliminary data.
Source: U.S. Census Bureau, Manufacturing, Mining, and Construction Statistics, Building Permits, 2016, 2017

Bankruptcy Filings

Area	Business Filings			Nonbusiness Filings		
	2016	2017	% Chg.	2016	2017	% Chg.
Westchester County	101	102	1.0	1,191	1,243	4.4
U.S.	24,114	23,157	-4.0	770,846	765,863	-0.6

Note: Business filings include Chapter 7, Chapter 11, Chapter 12, and Chapter 13; Nonbusiness filings include Chapter 7, Chapter 11, and Chapter 13
Source: Administrative Office of the U.S. Courts, Business and Nonbusiness Bankruptcy, County Cases Commenced by Chapter of the Bankruptcy Code, During the 12-Month Period Ending December 31, 2016 and Business and Nonbusiness Bankruptcy, County Cases Commenced by Chapter of the Bankruptcy Code, During the 12-Month Period Ending December 31, 2017

Housing Vacancy Rates

Area	Gross Vacancy Rate[2] (%)			Year-Round Vacancy Rate[3] (%)			Rental Vacancy Rate[4] (%)			Homeowner Vacancy Rate[5] (%)		
	2015	2016	2017	2015	2016	2017	2015	2016	2017	2015	2016	2017
MSA[1]	9.8	10.3	10.7	8.6	9.1	9.6	4.2	4.7	4.6	2.1	2.2	1.9
U.S.	12.9	12.8	12.7	10.0	9.9	9.9	7.1	6.9	7.2	1.8	1.7	1.6

Note: (1) Figures cover the New York-Newark-Jersey City, NY-NJ-PA Metropolitan Statistical Area—see Appendix B for areas included; (2) The percentage of the total housing inventory that is vacant; (3) The percentage of the housing inventory (excluding seasonal units) that is year-round vacant; (4) The percentage of rental inventory that is vacant for rent; (5) The percentage of homeowner inventory that is vacant for sale
Source: U.S. Census Bureau, Housing Vacancies and Homeownership Annual Statistics: 2015, 2016, 2017

INCOME

Income

Area	Per Capita ($)	Median Household ($)	Average Household ($)
City	38,754	73,773	114,413
MSA[1]	37,510	69,211	101,617
U.S.	29,829	55,322	77,866

Note: (1) Figures cover the New York-Newark-Jersey City, NY-NJ-PA Metropolitan Statistical Area—see Appendix B for areas included
Source: U.S. Census Bureau, 2012-2016 American Community Survey 5-Year Estimates

Household Income Distribution

Area	Percent of Households Earning							
	Under $15,000	$15,000 -$24,999	$25,000 -$34,999	$35,000 -$49,999	$50,000 -$74,999	$75,000 -$99,999	$100,000 -$149,999	$150,000 and up
City	7.3	8.9	8.6	10.1	15.7	11.6	14.2	23.5
MSA[1]	11.7	8.5	7.7	10.2	15.0	11.7	15.9	19.3
U.S.	12.1	10.2	9.9	13.2	17.8	12.2	13.5	11.1

Note: (1) Figures cover the New York-Newark-Jersey City, NY-NJ-PA Metropolitan Statistical Area—see Appendix B for areas included
Source: U.S. Census Bureau, 2012-2016 American Community Survey 5-Year Estimates

Poverty Rate

Area	All Ages	Under 18 Years Old	18 to 64 Years Old	65 Years and Over
City	10.5	12.1	10.4	8.3
MSA[1]	14.2	20.0	12.7	11.7
U.S.	15.1	21.2	14.2	9.3

Note: Figures are percentage of people whose income during the past 12 months was below the poverty level; (1) Figures cover the New York-Newark-Jersey City, NY-NJ-PA Metropolitan Statistical Area—see Appendix B for areas included
Source: U.S. Census Bureau, 2012-2016 American Community Survey 5-Year Estimates

EMPLOYMENT

Labor Force and Employment

Area	Civilian Labor Force			Workers Employed		
	Dec. 2016	Dec. 2017	% Chg.	Dec. 2016	Dec. 2017	% Chg.
City	24,797	24,782	-0.1	23,952	23,838	-0.5
MD[1]	7,114,448	7,115,615	0.0	6,809,258	6,832,994	0.3
U.S.	158,968,000	159,880,000	0.6	151,798,000	153,602,000	1.2

Note: Data is not seasonally adjusted and covers workers 16 years of age and older; (1) Figures cover the New York-Jersey City-White Plains, NY-NJ Metropolitan Division—see Appendix B for areas included
Source: Bureau of Labor Statistics, Local Area Unemployment Statistics

Unemployment Rate

Area	2017											
	Jan.	Feb.	Mar.	Apr.	May	Jun.	Jul.	Aug.	Sep.	Oct.	Nov.	Dec.
City	4.5	4.5	3.9	3.2	3.1	3.4	3.8	3.8	3.5	3.4	3.5	3.8
MD[1]	4.9	4.9	4.4	4.1	4.3	4.5	4.9	4.9	4.5	4.3	4.1	4.0
U.S.	5.1	4.9	4.6	4.1	4.1	4.5	4.6	4.5	4.1	3.9	3.9	3.9

Note: Data is not seasonally adjusted and covers workers 16 years of age and older; (1) Figures cover the New York-Jersey City-White Plains, NY-NJ Metropolitan Division—see Appendix B for areas included
Source: Bureau of Labor Statistics, Local Area Unemployment Statistics

Average Wages

Occupation	$/Hr.	Occupation	$/Hr.
Accountants and Auditors	48.80	Maids and Housekeeping Cleaners	17.60
Automotive Mechanics	21.70	Maintenance and Repair Workers	22.70
Bookkeepers	22.50	Marketing Managers	93.90
Carpenters	33.00	Nuclear Medicine Technologists	43.30
Cashiers	11.50	Nurses, Licensed Practical	25.90
Clerks, General Office	16.60	Nurses, Registered	43.70
Clerks, Receptionists/Information	16.20	Nursing Assistants	17.10
Clerks, Shipping/Receiving	17.40	Packers and Packagers, Hand	12.10
Computer Programmers	46.80	Physical Therapists	44.60
Computer Systems Analysts	55.20	Postal Service Mail Carriers	24.30
Computer User Support Specialists	30.40	Real Estate Brokers	49.20
Cooks, Restaurant	14.30	Retail Salespersons	13.20
Dentists	78.00	Sales Reps., Exc. Tech./Scientific	35.80
Electrical Engineers	52.00	Sales Reps., Tech./Scientific	51.20
Electricians	40.30	Secretaries, Exc. Legal/Med./Exec.	20.10
Financial Managers	102.00	Security Guards	16.30
First-Line Supervisors/Managers, Sales	25.10	Surgeons	119.70
Food Preparation Workers	12.50	Teacher Assistants*	14.70
General and Operations Managers	82.40	Teachers, Elementary School*	38.30
Hairdressers/Cosmetologists	18.10	Teachers, Secondary School*	41.30
Internists, General	99.10	Telemarketers	13.70
Janitors and Cleaners	16.80	Truck Drivers, Heavy/Tractor-Trailer	24.50
Landscaping/Groundskeeping Workers	16.80	Truck Drivers, Light/Delivery Svcs.	18.60
Lawyers	86.30	Waiters and Waitresses	15.30

Note: Wage data covers the New York-Jersey City-White Plains, NY-NJ Metropolitan Division—see Appendix B for areas included; (*) Hourly wages for elementary/secondary school teachers and teacher assistants were calculated by the editors from annual wage data based on a 40 hour work week; n/a not available.
Source: Bureau of Labor Statistics, Metro Area Occupational Employment & Wage Estimates, May 2017

Employment by Occupation

Occupation Classification	City (%)	MSA[1] (%)	U.S. (%)
Management, Business, Science, and Arts	32.1	41.2	37.0
Natural Resources, Construction, and Maintenance	9.5	6.9	8.9
Production, Transportation, and Material Moving	8.5	9.0	12.2
Sales and Office	20.7	23.7	23.8
Service	29.2	19.3	18.1

Note: Figures cover employed civilians 16 years of age and older; (1) Figures cover the New York-Newark-Jersey City, NY-NJ-PA Metropolitan Statistical Area—see Appendix B for areas included
Source: U.S. Census Bureau, 2012-2016 American Community Survey 5-Year Estimates

Employment by Industry

Sector	MD[1]		U.S.
	Number of Employees	Percent of Total	Percent of Total
Construction, Mining, and Logging	265,600	3.7	5.2
Education and Health Services	1,478,800	20.8	15.9
Financial Activities	628,100	8.8	5.7
Government	913,000	12.8	15.3
Information	247,400	3.5	1.9
Leisure and Hospitality	670,100	9.4	10.7
Manufacturing	207,300	2.9	8.5
Other Services	304,700	4.3	3.9
Professional and Business Services	1,148,400	16.2	14.0
Retail Trade	685,200	9.6	11.0
Transportation, Warehousing, and Utilities	275,800	3.9	4.1
Wholesale Trade	284,100	4.0	4.0

Note: Figures are non-farm employment as of December 2017. Figures are not seasonally adjusted and include workers 16 years of age and older; (1) Figures cover the New York-Jersey City-White Plains, NY-NJ Metropolitan Division—see Appendix B for areas included
Source: Bureau of Labor Statistics, Current Employment Statistics, Employment, Hours, and Earnings

Occupations with Greatest Projected Employment Growth: 2017 – 2019

Occupation[1]	2017 Employment	2019 Projected Employment	Numeric Employment Change	Percent Employment Change
Home Health Aides	190,490	216,300	25,810	13.5
Personal Care Aides	174,700	189,420	14,720	8.4
Combined Food Preparation and Serving Workers, Including Fast Food	154,570	162,110	7,540	4.9
Registered Nurses	189,840	197,230	7,390	3.9
Janitors and Cleaners, Except Maids and Housekeeping Cleaners	211,280	217,380	6,100	2.9
Waiters and Waitresses	151,380	156,430	5,050	3.3
General and Operations Managers	165,860	169,970	4,110	2.5
Accountants and Auditors	124,740	128,070	3,330	2.7
Software Developers, Applications	52,730	55,940	3,210	6.1
Security Guards	114,180	117,140	2,960	2.6

Note: Projections cover New York; (1) Sorted by numeric employment change
Source: www.projectionscentral.com, State Occupational Projections, 2017–2019 Short-Term Projections

Fastest Growing Occupations: 2017 – 2019

Occupation[1]	2017 Employment	2019 Projected Employment	Numeric Employment Change	Percent Employment Change
Gaming and Sports Book Writers and Runners	660	810	150	24.0
Gaming Change Persons and Booth Cashiers	840	1,030	190	22.7
Solar Photovoltaic Installers	800	980	180	22.7
Gaming Dealers	960	1,150	190	19.4
Home Health Aides	190,490	216,300	25,810	13.5
Gaming Supervisors	580	660	80	12.3
Entertainment Attendants and Related Workers, All Other	490	540	50	9.8
Personal Care Aides	174,700	189,420	14,720	8.4
Physical Therapist Aides	3,110	3,330	220	6.9
Physical Therapists	18,480	19,750	1,270	6.9

Note: Projections cover New York; (1) Sorted by percent employment change and excludes occupations with numeric employment change less than 50
Source: www.projectionscentral.com, State Occupational Projections, 2017–2019 Short-Term Projections

TAXES

State Corporate Income Tax Rates

State	Tax Rate (%)	Income Brackets ($)	Num. of Brackets	Financial Institution Tax Rate (%)[a]	Federal Income Tax Ded.
New York	6.5 (r)	Flat rate	1	6.5 (r)	No

Note: Tax rates as of January 1, 2018; (a) Rates listed are the corporate income tax rate applied to financial institutions or excise taxes based on income. Some states have other taxes based upon the value of deposits or shares; (r) New York's General business corporate rate shown. Corporations may also be subject to a capital stocks tax, which is being phased out through 2021. A minimum tax ranges from $25 to $200,000, depending on receipts ($250 minimum for banks). Certain qualified New York manufacturers pay 0%.
Source: Federation of Tax Administrators, Range of State Corporate Income Tax Rates, January 1, 2018

State Individual Income Tax Rates

State	Tax Rate (%)	Income Brackets ($)	Num. of Brackets	Personal Exempt. ($)[1]		Fed. Inc. Tax Ded.
				Single	Dependents	
New York (a)	4.0 - 8.82	8,500 - 1,077,550 (b)	8	0	1,000	No

Note: Tax rates as of January 1, 2018; Local- and county-level taxes are not included; n/a not applicable; (1) Married joint filers generally receive double the single exemption; (a) 19 states have statutory provision for automatically adjusting to the rate of inflation the dollar values of the income tax brackets, standard deductions, and/or personal exemptions. Massachusetts, Michigan, and Nebraska index the personal exemption only. Oregon does not index the income brackets for $125,000 and over; (b) For joint returns, taxes are twice the tax on half the couple's income.
Source: Federation of Tax Administrators, State Individual Income Tax Rates, January 1, 2018

Various State Sales and Excise Tax Rates

State	State Sales Tax (%)	Gasoline[1] (¢/gal.)	Cigarette[2] ($/pack)	Spirits[3] ($/gal.)	Wine[4] ($/gal.)	Beer[5] ($/gal.)	Recreational Marijuana (%)
New York	4.0	44.3	4.35	6.44 (f)	0.30	0.14	Not legal

Note: All tax rates as of January 1, 2018; (1) The American Petroleum Institute has developed a methodology for determining the average tax rate on a gallon of fuel. Rates may include any of the following: excise taxes, environmental fees, storage tank fees, other fees or taxes, general sales tax, and local taxes. In states where gasoline is subject to the general sales tax, or where the fuel tax is based on the average sale price, the average rate determined by API is sensitive to changes in the price of gasoline. States that fully or partially apply general sales taxes to gasoline: CA, CO, GA, IL, IN, MI, NY; (2) The federal excise tax of $1.0066 per pack and local taxes are not included; (3) Rates are those applicable to off-premise sales of 40% alcohol by volume (a.b.v.) distilled spirits in 750ml containers. Local excise taxes are excluded; (4) Rates are those applicable to off-premise sales of 11% a.b.v. non-carbonated wine in 750ml containers; (5) Rates are those applicable to off-premise sales of 4.7% a.b.v. beer in 12 ounce containers; (f) Different rates also applicable according to alcohol content, place of production, size of container, or place purchased (on- or off-premise or onboard airlines).
Source: Tax Foundation, 2018 Facts & Figures: How Does Your State Compare?

State Business Tax Climate Index Rankings

State	Overall Rank	Corporate Tax Rank	Individual Income Tax Rank	Sales Tax Rank	Unemployment Insurance Tax Rank	Property Tax Rank
New York	49	7	49	43	30	47

Note: The index is a measure of how each state's tax laws affect economic performance. The lower the rank, the more favorable a state's tax system is for business. States without a given tax are given a ranking of 1. The scores/rankings for the District of Columbia do not affect other states. The 2018 index represents the tax climate as of July 1, 2017.
Source: Tax Foundation, State Business Tax Climate Index 2018

TRANSPORTATION

Means of Transportation to Work

Area	Car/Truck/Van		Public Transportation			Bicycle	Walked	Other Means	Worked at Home
	Drove Alone	Car-pooled	Bus	Subway	Railroad				
City	56.7	8.5	5.1	0.9	12.2	0.3	7.6	5.5	3.2
MSA[1]	50.1	6.6	7.7	19.1	3.8	0.6	6.0	1.8	4.2
U.S.	76.4	9.3	2.6	1.9	0.6	0.6	2.8	1.3	4.6

Note: Figures are percentages and cover workers 16 years of age and older; (1) Figures cover the New York-Newark-Jersey City, NY-NJ-PA Metropolitan Statistical Area—see Appendix B for areas included
Source: U.S. Census Bureau, 2012-2016 American Community Survey 5-Year Estimates

Travel Time to Work

Area	Less Than 10 Minutes	10 to 19 Minutes	20 to 29 Minutes	30 to 44 Minutes	45 to 59 Minutes	60 to 89 Minutes	90 Minutes or More
City	14.1	34.4	17.6	14.3	5.5	9.0	5.0
MSA[1]	7.4	19.3	16.4	23.7	12.4	14.4	6.5
U.S.	12.9	29.2	20.9	20.4	8.0	6.0	2.7

Note: Note: Figures are percentages and include workers 16 years old and over; (1) Figures cover the New York-Newark-Jersey City, NY-NJ-PA Metropolitan Statistical Area—see Appendix B for areas included
Source: U.S. Census Bureau, 2012-2016 American Community Survey 5-Year Estimates

Freeway Travel Time Index

Area	1985	1990	1995	2000	2005	2010	2014
Urban Area Rank[1,2]	11	9	8	7	7	8	8
Urban Area Index[1]	1.16	1.20	1.24	1.29	1.33	1.33	1.34
Average Index[3]	1.09	1.11	1.14	1.17	1.20	1.19	1.20

Note: Freeway Travel Time Index—the ratio of travel time in the peak period to the travel time at free-flow conditions. For example, a value of 1.30 indicates a 20-minute free-flow trip takes 26 minutes in the peak (20 minutes x 1.30 = 26 minutes); (1) Covers the New York-Newark NY-NJ-CT urban area; (2) Rank is based on 101 urban areas (#1 = highest travel time index); (3) Average of 101 urban areas
Source: Texas Transportation Institute, 2015 Urban Mobility Scorecard, August 2015

Freeway Commuter Stress Index

Area	1985	1990	1995	2000	2005	2010	2014
Urban Area Rank[1,2]	19	19	13	12	11	11	12
Urban Area Index[1]	1.21	1.24	1.29	1.34	1.38	1.38	1.39
Average Index[3]	1.13	1.16	1.19	1.22	1.25	1.24	1.25

Note: The Freeway Commuter Stress Index is the same as the Freeway Travel Time Index (see table above) except that it includes only the travel in the peak directions during the peak periods; the TTI includes travel in all directions during the peak period. Thus, the CSI is more indicative of the work trip experienced by each commuter on a daily basis; (1) Covers the New York-Newark NY-NJ-CT urban area; (2) Rank is based on 101 urban areas (#1 = highest travel time index); (3) Average of 101 urban areas
Source: Texas Transportation Institute, 2015 Urban Mobility Scorecard, August 2015

Living Environment

COST OF LIVING

Cost of Living Index

Composite Index	Groceries	Housing	Utilities	Trans-portation	Health Care	Misc. Goods/ Services
n/a	n/a	n/a	n/a	n/a	n/a	n/a

Note: The Cost of Living Index measures regional differences in the cost of consumer goods and services, excluding taxes and non-consumer expenditures, for professional and managerial households in the top income quintile. It is based on more than 50,000 prices covering almost 60 different items for which prices are collected three times a year by chambers of commerce, economic development organizations or university applied economic centers in each participating urban area. The numbers shown should be read as a percentage above or below the national average of 100. For example, a value of 115.4 in the groceries column indicates that grocery prices are 15.4% higher than the national average. Small differences in the index numbers should not be interpreted as significant; n/a not available.
Source: The Council for Community and Economic Research, ACCRA Cost of Living Index, 2017

Grocery Prices

Area[1]	T-Bone Steak ($/pound)	Frying Chicken ($/pound)	Whole Milk ($/half gal.)	Eggs ($/dozen)	Orange Juice ($/64 oz.)	Coffee ($/11.5 oz.)
City[2]	n/a	n/a	n/a	n/a	n/a	n/a
Avg.	11.29	1.40	2.02	1.47	3.55	4.37
Min.	7.71	0.93	1.04	0.70	2.86	3.24
Max.	15.83	2.39	4.03	3.92	6.29	8.16

*Note: (1) Values for the local area are compared with the average, minimum and maximum values for all 294 areas in the Cost of Living Index; (2) Figures cover the Rye NY urban area; n/a not available; **T-Bone Steak** (price per pound); **Frying Chicken** (price per pound, whole fryer); **Whole Milk** (half gallon carton); **Eggs** (price per dozen, Grade A, large); **Orange Juice** (64 oz. Tropicana or Florida Natural); **Coffee** (11.5 oz. can, vacuum-packed, Maxwell House, Hills Bros, or Folgers).*
Source: The Council for Community and Economic Research, ACCRA Cost of Living Index, 2017

Housing and Utility Costs

Area[1]	New Home Price ($)	Apartment Rent ($/month)	All Electric ($/month)	Part Electric ($/month)	Other Energy ($/month)	Telephone ($/month)
City[2]	n/a	n/a	n/a	n/a	n/a	n/a
Avg.	335,956	1,047	175.01	97.34	67.93	28.71
Min.	187,788	491	109.48	49.33	35.44	12.39
Max.	1,739,087	4,559	432.62	227.09	353.33	44.61

*Note: (1) Values for the local area are compared with the average, minimum and maximum values for all 294 areas in the Cost of Living Index; (2) Figures cover the Rye NY urban area; n/a not available; **New Home Price** (2,400 sf living area, 8,000 sf lot, in urban area with full utilities); **Apartment Rent** (950 sf 2 bedroom/1.5 or 2 bath, unfurnished, excluding all utilities except water); **All Electric** (average monthly cost for an all-electric home); **Part Electric** (average monthly cost for a part-electric home); **Other Energy** (average monthly cost for natural gas, fuel oil, coal, wood, and any other forms of energy except electricity); **Telephone** (price includes basic monthly rate for a private residential line plus additional local usage charges incurred by a family of four).*
Source: The Council for Community and Economic Research, ACCRA Cost of Living Index, 2017

Health Care, Transportation, and Other Costs

Area[1]	Doctor ($/visit)	Dentist ($/visit)	Optometrist ($/visit)	Gasoline ($/gallon)	Beauty Salon ($/visit)	Men's Shirt ($)
City[2]	n/a	n/a	n/a	n/a	n/a	n/a
Avg.	108.00	92.54	101.93	2.25	37.58	30.92
Min.	30.39	60.00	49.75	1.82	16.11	11.20
Max.	193.50	161.94	229.28	3.16	77.35	59.13

*Note: (1) Values for the local area are compared with the average, minimum and maximum values for all 294 areas in the Cost of Living Index; (2) Figures cover the Rye NY urban area; n/a not available; **Doctor** (general practitioners routine exam of an established patient); **Dentist** (adult teeth cleaning and periodic oral examination); **Optometrist** (full vision eye exam for established adult patient); **Gasoline** (one gallon regular unleaded, national brand, including all taxes, cash price at self-service pump if available); **Beauty Salon** (woman's shampoo, trim, and blow-dry); **Men's Shirt** (cotton/polyester dress shirt, pinpoint weave, long sleeves).*
Source: The Council for Community and Economic Research, ACCRA Cost of Living Index, 2017

HOUSING

House Price Index (HPI)

Area	National Ranking[2]	Quarterly Change (%)	One-Year Change (%)	Five-Year Change (%)
MD[1]	148	1.22	5.35	20.60
U.S.[3]	–	1.61	6.68	34.71

Note: The HPI is a weighted repeat sales index. It measures average price changes in repeat sales or refinancings on the same properties. This information is obtained by reviewing repeat mortgage transactions on single-family properties whose mortgages have been purchased or securitized by Fannie Mae or Freddie Mac in January 1975; (1) Figures cover the New York-Jersey City-White Plains, NY-NJ Metropolitan Division—see Appendix B for areas included; (2) Rankings are based on annual percentage change for all metro areas containing at least 15,000 transactions over the last 10 years and ranges from 1 to 253; (3) figures based on a weighted average of Census Division estimates using a seasonally adjusted, purchase-only index; all figures are for the period ending December 31, 2017
Source: Federal Housing Finance Agency, House Price Index, February 28, 2018

Median Single-Family Home Prices

Area	2015	2016	2017p	Percent Change 2016 to 2017
MD[1]	398.5	370.2	382.5	3.3
U.S. Average	223.9	235.5	248.8	5.6

Note: Figures are median sales prices of existing single-family homes in thousands of dollars; (p) preliminary; (1) Figures cover the New York-Jersey City-White Plains, NY-NJ Metropolitan Division—see Appendix B for areas included
Source: National Association of Realtors, Median Sales Price of Existing Single-Family Homes for Metropolitan Areas, 4th Quarter 2017

Qualifying Income Based on Median Sales Price of Existing Single-Family Homes

Area	With 5% Down ($)	With 10% Down ($)	With 20% Down ($)
MD[1]	83,646	79,244	70,439
U.S. Average	55,585	52,659	46,808

Note: Figures are preliminary; Qualifying income is based on a mortgage rate of 4.17%. Monthly principal and interest payment is limited to 25% of income; (1) Figures cover the New York-Jersey City-White Plains, NY-NJ Metropolitan Division—see Appendix B for areas included
Source: National Association of Realtors, Qualifying Income Based on Median Sales Price of Existing Single-Family Homes for Metropolitan Areas, 4th Quarter 2017

Median Apartment Condo-Coop Home Prices

Area	2015	2016	2017p	Percent Change 2016 to 2017
MD[1]	245.7	257.2	270.7	5.2
U.S. Average	210.7	220.7	234.3	6.2

Note: Figures are median sales prices of existing apartment condo-coop homes in thousands of dollars; (p) preliminary; (1) Figures cover the New York-Jersey City-White Plains, NY-NJ Metropolitan Division—see Appendix B for areas included
Source: National Association of Realtors, Median Sales Price of Existing Apartment Condo-Coop Homes for Metropolitan Areas, 4th Quarter 2017

Home Value Distribution

Area	Under $50,000	$50,000 -$99,999	$100,000 -$149,999	$150,000 -$199,999	$200,000 -$299,999	$300,000 -$499,999	$500,000 -$999,999	$1,000,000 or more
City	1.4	2.8	1.8	2.4	6.5	31.2	44.7	9.2
MSA[1]	2.8	1.8	2.9	5.0	16.2	37.0	26.9	7.3
U.S.	8.8	14.8	15.3	14.9	18.4	16.4	9.0	2.5

Note: Figures are percentages and cover owner-occupied housing units; (1) Figures cover the New York-Newark-Jersey City, NY-NJ-PA Metropolitan Statistical Area—see Appendix B for areas included
Source: U.S. Census Bureau, 2012-2016 American Community Survey 5-Year Estimates

Homeownership Rate

Area	2009 (%)	2010 (%)	2011 (%)	2012 (%)	2013 (%)	2014 (%)	2015 (%)	2016 (%)	2017 (%)
MSA[1]	51.7	51.6	50.9	51.5	50.6	50.7	49.9	50.4	49.9
U.S.	67.4	66.9	66.1	65.4	65.1	64.5	63.7	63.4	63.9

Note: (1) Figures cover the New York-Newark-Jersey City, NY-NJ-PA Metropolitan Statistical Area—see Appendix B for areas included
Source: U.S. Census Bureau, Housing Vacancies and Homeownership Annual Statistics: 2009-2017

Year Housing Structure Built

Area	2010 or Later	2000 -2009	1990 -1999	1980 -1989	1970 -1979	1960 -1969	1950 -1959	1940 -1949	Before 1940	Median Year
City	0.5	4.7	4.7	5.2	4.8	15.6	20.3	8.3	35.9	1953
MSA[1]	1.3	7.2	6.1	7.9	10.0	13.8	16.2	9.1	28.3	1958
U.S.	2.3	14.7	14.0	13.7	15.6	10.9	10.6	5.2	13.0	1977

Note: Figures are percentages except for Median Year; Note: (1) Figures cover the New York-Newark-Jersey City, NY-NJ-PA Metropolitan Statistical Area—see Appendix B for areas included
Source: U.S. Census Bureau, 2012-2016 American Community Survey 5-Year Estimates

Gross Monthly Rent

Area	Under $500	$500 -$999	$1,000 -$1,499	$1,500 -$1,999	$2,000 -$2,499	$2,500 -$2,999	$3,000 and up	Median ($)
City	8.4	10.5	29.0	32.3	11.1	5.9	2.9	1,532
MSA[1]	9.7	18.7	35.2	19.8	8.3	3.8	4.5	1,297
U.S.	11.3	43.3	27.7	10.7	4.0	1.6	1.5	949

Note: Figures are percentages except for Median; Gross rent is the contract rent plus the estimated average monthly cost of utilities (electricity, gas, and water and sewer) and fuels (oil, coal, kerosene, wood, etc.) if these are paid by the renter (or paid for the renter by someone else); (1) Figures cover the New York-Newark-Jersey City, NY-NJ-PA Metropolitan Statistical Area—see Appendix B for areas included
Source: U.S. Census Bureau, 2012-2016 American Community Survey 5-Year Estimates

HEALTH

Health Risk Factors

Category	MD[1] (%)	U.S. (%)
Adults aged 18–64 who have any kind of health care coverage	86.5	87.7
Adults who reported being in good or excellent health	82.3	83.6
Adults who are current smokers	11.9	17.1
Adults who currently use E-cigarettes	3.9	4.7
Adults who currently use chewing tobacco, snuff, or snus	2.0	4.0
Adults who are heavy drinkers[2]	5.0	6.5
Adults who are binge drinkers[3]	16.8	16.9
Adults who are overweight (BMI 25.0 - 29.9)	34.4	35.3
Adults who are obese (BMI 30.0 - 99.8)	24.0	29.9
Adults who participated in any physical activities in the past month	71.7	76.9
Adults who always or nearly always wears a seat belt	92.3	94.3

Note: (1) Figures cover the New York-Jersey City-White Plains, NY-NJ Metropolitan Division—see Appendix B for areas included; (2) Heavy drinkers are classified as adult men having more than 14 drinks per week and adult women having more than 7 drinks per week; (3) Binge drinkers are classified as males having five or more drinks on one occasion or females having four or more drinks on one occasion
Source: Centers for Disease Control and Prevention, Behaviorial Risk Factor Surveillance System, SMART: Selected Metropolitan Area Risk Trends, 2016

Health Screening Rates

Category	MD[1] (%)	U.S. (%)
Adults 50-75 who have had a blood stool test within the past year	7.2	8.0
Adults 50-75 who have had a colonoscopy in the past 10 years	63.9	63.5
Adults aged 65+ who have had flu shot within the past year	61.0	58.6
Adults aged 65+ who have ever had a pneumonia vaccination	64.0	73.4
Adults who have ever been tested for HIV	50.7	35.6
Women aged 21-65 who have had a pap test in the past three years	79.5	79.8
Men aged 40+ who have had a PSA test within the past two years	39.3	39.5
Women aged 40+ who have had a mammogram within the past two years	73.3	72.5

Note: (1) Figures cover the New York-Jersey City-White Plains, NY-NJ Metropolitan Division—see Appendix B for areas included; Source: Centers for Disease Control and Prevention, Behaviorial Risk Factor Surveillance System, SMART: Selected Metropolitan Area Risk Trends, 2016

Chronic Health Conditions

Category	MD[1] (%)	U.S. (%)
Adults who have ever been told they had a heart attack	3.3	4.4
Adults who have ever been told they have angina or coronary heart disease	3.5	4.1
Adults who have ever been told they had a stroke	2.5	3.1
Adults who have been told they currently have asthma	8.5	9.3
Adults who have ever been told they have arthritis	20.1	25.8
Adults who have ever been told they have diabetes[2]	10.1	10.5
Adults who have ever been told they had skin cancer	3.4	5.9
Adults who have ever been told they had any other types of cancer	4.9	6.7
Adults who have ever been told they have COPD	4.5	6.3
Adults who have ever been told they have kidney disease	2.3	2.8
Adults who have ever been told they have a form of depression	10.6	17.4

Note: (1) Figures cover the New York-Jersey City-White Plains, NY-NJ Metropolitan Division—see Appendix B for areas included; (2) Figures do not include pregnancy-related, borderline, or pre-diabetes
Source: Centers for Disease Control and Prevention, Behaviorial Risk Factor Surveillance System, SMART: Selected Metropolitan Area Risk Trends, 2016

Mortality Rates for the Top 10 Causes of Death in the U.S.

ICD-10[a] Sub-Chapter	ICD-10[a] Code	Age-Adjusted Mortality Rate[1] per 100,000 population	
		County[2]	U.S.
Malignant neoplasms	C00-C97	133.1	158.5
Ischaemic heart diseases	I20-I25	97.6	96.8
Other forms of heart disease	I30-I51	39.5	52.4
Chronic lower respiratory diseases	J40-J47	21.1	40.9
Cerebrovascular diseases	I60-I69	22.7	37.2
Organic, including symptomatic, mental disorders	F01-F09	23.5	33.3
Other degenerative diseases of the nervous system	G30-G31	10.8	32.1
Other external causes of accidental injury	W00-X59	22.3	31.2
Diabetes mellitus	E10-E14	10.8	21.1
Hypertensive diseases	I10-I15	14.9	20.8

Note: (a) ICD-10 = International Classification of Diseases 10th Revision; (1) Mortality rates are a three year average covering 2014-2016; (2) Figures cover Westchester County.
Source: Centers for Disease Control and Prevention, National Center for Health Statistics. Underlying Cause of Death 1999-2016 on CDC WONDER Online Database, released December 2017

Mortality Rates for Selected Causes of Death

ICD-10[a] Sub-Chapter	ICD-10[a] Code	Age-Adjusted Mortality Rate[1] per 100,000 population	
		County[2]	U.S.
Assault	X85-Y09	2.2	5.6
Diseases of the liver	K70-K76	6.0	14.0
Human immunodeficiency virus (HIV) disease	B20-B24	1.1	1.9
Influenza and pneumonia	J09-J18	16.0	14.6
Intentional self-harm	X60-X84	6.4	13.2
Malnutrition	E40-E46	Unreliable	1.3
Obesity and other hyperalimentation	E65-E68	0.8	2.1
Renal failure	N17-N19	9.0	13.0
Transport accidents	V01-V99	4.1	12.0
Viral hepatitis	B15-B19	1.0	1.9

Note: (a) ICD-10 = International Classification of Diseases 10th Revision; (1) Mortality rates are a three year average covering 2014-2016; (2) Figures cover Westchester County; Data are Suppressed when the data meet the criteria for confidentiality constraints; Mortality rates are flagged as Unreliable when the rate would be calculated with a numerator of 20 or less.
Source: Centers for Disease Control and Prevention, National Center for Health Statistics. Underlying Cause of Death 1999-2016 on CDC WONDER Online Database, released December 2017

Health Insurance Coverage

Area	With Health Insurance	With Private Health Insurance	With Public Health Insurance	Without Health Insurance	Population Under Age 18 Without Health Insurance
City	81.7	60.3	30.3	18.3	2.8
MSA[1]	89.8	65.8	33.7	10.2	3.6
U.S.	88.3	66.7	33.0	11.7	5.9

Note: Figures are percentages that cover the civilian noninstitutionalized population; (1) Figures cover the New York-Newark-Jersey City, NY-NJ-PA Metropolitan Statistical Area—see Appendix B for areas included
Source: U.S. Census Bureau, 2012-2016 American Community Survey 5-Year Estimates

Number of Medical Professionals

Area	MDs[3]	DOs[3,4]	Dentists	Podiatrists	Chiropractors	Optometrists
County[1] (number)	6,312	184	1,059	137	258	162
County[1] (rate[2])	646.7	18.9	108.2	14.0	26.4	16.6
U.S. (rate[2])	276.5	22.3	67.3	6.0	26.7	15.9

Note: Data as of 2016 unless noted; (1) Data covers Westchester County; (2) Rate per 100,000 population; (3) Data as of 2015 and includes all active, non-federal physicians; (4) Doctor of Osteopathic Medicine
Source: U.S. Department of Health and Human Services, Health Resources and Services Administration, Bureau of Health Professions, Area Resource File (ARF) 2016-2017

Best Hospitals

According to *U.S. News,* the New York-Jersey City-White Plains, NY-NJ metro area is home to nine of the best hospitals in the U.S.: **Hackensack University Medical Center** (3 adult specialties and 1 pediatric specialty); **Hospital for Special Surgery** (2 adult specialties and 1 pediatric specialty); **Memorial Sloan Kettering Cancer Center** (4 adult specialties and 1 pediatric specialty); **Montefiore Medical Center** (1 adult specialty and 7 pediatric specialties); **Mount Sinai Hospital** (Honor Roll/10 adult specialties and 6 pediatric specialties); **NYU Langone Medical Center** (Honor Roll/12 adult specialties); **New York Eye and Ear Infirmary** (2 adult specialties); **New York-Presbyterian Hospital-Columbia and Cornell** (Honor Roll/14 adult specialties and 10 pediatric specialties); **Robert Wood Johnson University Hospital** (1 pediatric specialty). The hospitals listed were nationally ranked in at least one of 16 specialties. Only 152 hospitals nationwide were nationally ranked in one or more specialties. Twenty hospitals in the U.S. made the Honor Roll. The Best Hospitals Honor Roll was revamped last year to take both the national rankings and the procedure and condition ratings into account. Hospitals received points if they were nationally ranked in one of the 16 specialties—the higher they ranked, the more points they got—and how many ratings of "high performing" they earned in the nine procedures and conditions. *U.S. News Online, "America's Best Hospitals 2017-18"*

According to *U.S. News,* the New York-Jersey City-White Plains, NY-NJ metro area is home to seven of the best children's hospitals in the U.S.: **Bristol-Myers Squibb Children's Hospital at RWJ Univ. Hosp.** (1 pediatric specialty); **Children's Hospital at Montefiore** (7 pediatric specialties); **Memorial Sloan Kettering Cancer Center** (1 pediatric specialty); **Mount Sinai Kravis Children's Hospital** (6 pediatric specialties); **New York-Presbyterian Morgan Stanley-Komansky Children's Hospital** (10 pediatric specialties); **Hospital for Special Surgery, New York** (1 pediatric specialty); **Joseph M. Sanzari Children's Hospital at Hackensack University Medical Center** (1 pediatric specialty). The hospitals listed were highly ranked in at least one of 10 pediatric specialties. Eighty-two children's hospitals in the U.S. were nationally ranked in at least one specialty. Hospitals received points for being ranked in a specialty, and the 10 hospitals with the most points across the 10 specialties make up the Honor Roll. *U.S. News Online, "America's Best Children's Hospitals 2017-18"*

EDUCATION

Public School District Statistics

District Name	Schls	Pupils	Pupil/ Teacher Ratio	Minority Pupils[1] (%)	Free Lunch Eligible[2] (%)	IEP[3] (%)
Rye City School District	5	3,332	13.1	15.8	1.9	9.9

Note: Table includes school districts with 100 or more students; (1) Percentage of students that are not non-Hispanic white; (2) Percentage of students that are eligible for the free lunch program; (3) Percentage of students that have an Individualized Education Program.
Source: U.S. Department of Education, National Center for Education Statistics, Common Core of Data, Local Education Agency (School District) Universe Survey: School Year 2015-2016; U.S. Department of Education, National Center for Education Statistics, Common Core of Data, Public Elementary/Secondary School Universe Survey: School Year 2015-2016

Best High Schools

According to *U.S. News,* Rye is home to one of the best high schools in the U.S.: **Rye High School** (#90). More than 22,000 public, magnet and charter schools were ranked based on their performance on state assessments and how well they prepare students for college. Schools with the highest unrounded College Readiness Index values were numerically ranked from 1 to 500 and were classified as gold medal winners. *U.S. News & World Report, "Best High Schools 2017"*

Highest Level of Education

Area	Less than H.S.	H.S. Diploma	Some College, No Deg.	Associate Degree	Bachelor's Degree	Master's Degree	Prof. School Degree	Doctorate Degree
City	22.5	23.4	14.5	4.4	19.7	11.7	3.1	0.8
MSA[1]	14.3	25.3	15.5	6.7	22.3	11.3	3.0	1.5
U.S.	13.0	27.5	21.0	8.2	18.8	8.2	2.0	1.3

Note: Figures cover persons age 25 and over; (1) Figures cover the New York-Newark-Jersey City, NY-NJ-PA Metropolitan Statistical Area—see Appendix B for areas included
Source: U.S. Census Bureau, 2012-2016 American Community Survey 5-Year Estimates

Educational Attainment by Race

Area	High School Graduate or Higher (%)					Bachelor's Degree or Higher (%)				
	Total	White	Black	Asian	Hisp.[2]	Total	White	Black	Asian	Hisp.[2]
City	77.5	84.5	83.4	93.6	55.3	35.3	43.7	29.1	70.0	11.1
MSA[1]	85.7	90.0	84.1	82.9	68.9	38.1	43.2	23.8	53.1	17.7
U.S.	87.0	88.9	84.3	86.3	65.7	30.3	31.6	20.0	52.1	14.7

Note: Figures shown cover persons 25 years old and over; (1) Figures cover the New York-Newark-Jersey City, NY-NJ-PA Metropolitan Statistical Area—see Appendix B for areas included; (2) People of Hispanic origin can be of any race
Source: U.S. Census Bureau, 2012-2016 American Community Survey 5-Year Estimates

School Enrollment by Grade and Control

Area	Preschool (%)		Kindergarten (%)		Grades 1 - 4 (%)		Grades 5 - 8 (%)		Grades 9 - 12 (%)	
	Public	Private	Public	Private	Public	Private	Public	Private	Public	Private
City	46.2	53.8	85.8	14.2	93.9	6.1	85.5	14.5	88.8	11.2
MSA[1]	51.9	48.1	81.6	18.4	86.1	13.9	86.3	13.7	85.9	14.1
U.S.	58.4	41.6	87.7	12.3	89.8	10.2	89.7	10.3	90.4	9.6

Note: Figures shown cover persons 3 years old and over; (1) Figures cover the New York-Newark-Jersey City, NY-NJ-PA Metropolitan Statistical Area—see Appendix B for areas included
Source: U.S. Census Bureau, 2012-2016 American Community Survey 5-Year Estimates

Average Salaries of Public School Classroom Teachers

Area	2015		2016		Change from 2015 to 2016	
	Dollars	Rank[1]	Dollars	Rank[1]	Percent	Rank[2]
New York	77,628	1	79,152	1	2.0	12
U.S. Average	57,611	–	58,353	–	1.3	–

Note: (1) Rank ranges from 1 to 51 where 1 indicates highest salary; (2) Rank ranges from 1 to 51 where 1 indicates highest percent change.
Source: National Education Association, Rankings & Estimates: Rankings of the States 2016 and Estimates of School Statistics 2017

Higher Education

Four-Year Colleges			Two-Year Colleges			Medical Schools[1]	Law Schools[2]	Voc/ Tech[3]
Public	Private Non-profit	Private For-profit	Public	Private Non-profit	Private For-profit			
0	0	0	0	0	0	0	0	0

Note: Figures cover institutions located within the city limits and include main campuses only; (1) includes schools accredited by the Liaison Committee on Medical Education and the American Osteopathic Association's Commission on Osteopathic College Accreditation; (2) includes ABA-accredited schools, schools with provisional ABA accreditation, and state accredited schools; (3) includes all schools with programs that are less than 2 years.
Source: National Center for Education Statistics, Integrated Postsecondary Education System (IPEDS), 2016-17; Wikipedia, List of Medical Schools in the United States, accessed April 2, 2018; Wikipedia, List of Law Schools in the United States, accessed April 2, 2018

According to *U.S. News & World Report,* the New York-Jersey City-White Plains, NY-NJ metro division is home to seven of the best national universities in the U.S.: **Columbia University** (#5 tie); **New York University** (#30 tie); **Fordham University** (#61 tie); **Yeshiva University** (#94 tie); **The New School** (#133 tie); **Saint John's University (Jamaica)** (#165 tie); **Pace University** (#187 tie). The indicators used to capture academic quality fall into a number of categories: assessment by administrators at peer institutions; retention of students; faculty resources; student selectivity; financial resources; alumni giving; high school counselor ratings of colleges; and graduation rate. *U.S. News & World Report, "America's Best Colleges 2018"*

According to *U.S. News & World Report,* the New York-Jersey City-White Plains, NY-NJ metro division is home to one of the best liberal arts colleges in the U.S.: **Barnard College** (#26 tie). The indicators used to capture academic quality fall into a number of categories: assessment by administrators at peer institutions; retention of students; faculty resources; student selectivity; financial resources; alumni giving; high school counselor ratings of colleges; and graduation rate. *U.S. News & World Report, "America's Best Colleges 2018"*

According to *U.S. News & World Report,* the New York-Jersey City-White Plains, NY-NJ metro division is home to six of the top 100 law schools in the U.S.: **Columbia University** (#5); **New York University** (#6); **Fordham University** (#37 tie); **Yeshiva University (Cardozo)** (#56 tie); **Brooklyn Law School** (#83 tie); **Saint John's University (Jamaica)** (#83 tie). The rankings are based on a weighted average of 12 measures of quality: peer assessment score; assessment score by lawyers/judges; median LSAT scores; median undergrad GPA; acceptance rate; employment rates for graduates; placement success; bar passage rate; faculty resources; expenditures per student; student/faculty ratio; and library resources. *U.S. News & World Report, "America's Best Graduate Schools, Law, 2019"*

According to *U.S. News & World Report,* the New York-Jersey City-White Plains, NY-NJ metro division is home to five of the top 75 medical schools for research in the U.S.: **New York University (Langone)** (#3 tie); **Columbia University** (#11 tie); **Icahn School of Medicine at Mount Sinai** (#18 tie); **Cornell University (Weill)** (#21); **Yeshiva University (Einstein)** (#39 tie). The rankings are based on a weighted average of 11 measures of quality: quality assessment; peer assessment score; assessment score by residency directors; research activity; total research activity; average research activity per faculty member; student selectivity; median MCAT total score; median undergraduate GPA; acceptance rate; and faculty resources. *U.S. News & World Report, "America's Best Graduate Schools, Medical, 2019"*

According to *U.S. News & World Report,* the New York-Jersey City-White Plains, NY-NJ metro division is home to four of the top 75 business schools in the U.S.: **Columbia University** (#9); **New York University (Stern)** (#13 tie); **CUNY Bernard M. Baruch College (Zicklin)** (#55 tie); **Fordham University (Gabelli)** (#63 tie). The rankings are based on a weighted average of the following nine measures: quality assessment; peer assessment; recruiter assessment; placement success; mean starting salary and bonus; student selectivity; mean GMAT and GRE scores; mean undergraduate GPA; and acceptance rate. *U.S. News & World Report, "America's Best Graduate Schools, Business, 2019"*

PRESIDENTIAL ELECTION

2016 Presidential Election Results

Area	Clinton	Trump	Johnson	Stein	Other
Westchester County	64.9	31.2	1.9	1.0	1.0
U.S.	48.0	45.9	3.3	1.1	1.7

Note: Results are percentages and may not add to 100% due to rounding
Source: Dave Leip's Atlas of U.S. Presidential Elections

EMPLOYERS

Major Employers

Company Name	Industry
American Express Company	Personal credit institutions
American International Group	Life insurance
Deloitte Consulting	Management consulting services
Hackensack University Medical Center	University
Merrill Lynch and Co	Security brokers & dealers
Mount Sinai Hospital	General medical & surgical hospitals
Mount Sinai School of Medicine	Medical training services
NewYork-Presbyterian Hospital	General medical & surgical hospitals
NYC Health and Hospitals Corp	Psychiatric hospitals
NYU School of Medicine	Offices & clinics of medical doctors
Paramount Comm Acq Corp	Investment holding companies, except banks
Patriarch Partners	Investment offices
Rutgers, The State Univ of NJ	Colleges & universities
Standard Americas	Agencies of foreign banks
The Long Island Rail Road Company	Local & suburban transit
U of Med and Dentistry of NJ	Colleges & universities
UMASS Memorial Health Care	Psychiatrist
United States Postal Service	U.S. postal service
Wellchoice	Health insurance carriers

Note: Companies shown are located within the New York-Newark-Jersey City, NY-NJ-PA Metropolitan Statistical Area.
Source: Hoovers.com; Wikipedia

PUBLIC SAFETY

Crime Rate

Area	All Crimes	Violent Crimes				Property Crimes		
		Murder	Rape[3]	Robbery	Aggrav. Assault	Burglary	Larceny -Theft	Motor Vehicle Theft
City	391.1	0.0	0.0	0.0	6.2	49.7	310.4	24.8
Metro[1]	1,805.2	3.1	22.2	136.2	255.9	160.0	1,152.5	75.3
U.S.	2,847.8	5.3	40.4	102.8	248.5	468.9	1,745.0	236.9

Note: Figures are crimes per 100,000 population; (1) Figures cover the New York-Jersey City-White Plains, NY-NJ Metropolitan Division—see Appendix B for areas included; (3) The city and U.S. figures shown were reported using the revised Uniform Crime Reporting (UCR) definition of rape. The metro area figures shown are an aggregate total of the data submitted using both the revised and legacy UCR definitions.
Source: FBI Uniform Crime Reports, 2016

Hate Crimes

Area	Number of Quarters Reported	Number of Incidents per Bias Motivation					
		Race/Ethnicity/ Ancestry	Religion	Sexual Orientation	Disability	Gender	Gender Identity
City	4	0	0	0	0	0	0
U.S.	4	3,489	1,273	1,076	70	31	124

Source: Federal Bureau of Investigation, Hate Crime Statistics 2016

Identity Theft Consumer Reports

Area	Reports	Reports per 100,000 Population	Rank[2]
MSA[1]	23,624	117	64
U.S.	371,061	114	-

Note: (1) Figures cover the New York-Newark-Jersey City, NY-NJ-PA Metropolitan Statistical Area—see Appendix B for areas included; (2) Rank ranges from 1 to 389 where 1 indicates greatest number of identity theft reports per 100,000 population
Source: Federal Trade Commission, Consumer Sentinel Network Data Book for January–December 2017

Fraud and Other Consumer Reports

Area	Reports	Reports per 100,000 Population	Rank[2]
MSA[1]	90,589	449	173
U.S.	2,304,550	708	-

Note: (1) Figures cover the New York-Newark-Jersey City, NY-NJ-PA Metropolitan Statistical Area—see Appendix B for areas included; (2) Rank ranges from 1 to 389 where 1 indicates greatest number of fraud and other consumer reports per 100,000 population
Source: Federal Trade Commission, Consumer Sentinel Network Data Book for January–December 2017

SPORTS

Professional Sports Teams

Team Name	League	Year Established
Brooklyn Nets	National Basketball Association (NBA)	1967
New Jersey Devils	National Hockey League (NHL)	1982
New York City FC	Major League Soccer (MLS)	2015
New York Giants	National Football League (NFL)	1925
New York Islanders	National Hockey League (NHL)	1972
New York Jets	National Football League (NFL)	1960
New York Knicks	National Basketball Association (NBA)	1946
New York Mets	Major League Baseball (MLB)	1962
New York Rangers	National Hockey League (NHL)	1926
New York Red Bulls	Major League Soccer (MLS)	1996
New York Yankees	Major League Baseball (MLB)	1903

Note: Includes teams located in the New York-Newark-Jersey City, NY-NJ-PA Metropolitan Statistical Area.
Source: Wikipedia, Major Professional Sports Teams of the United States and Canada, April 5, 2018

CLIMATE

Average and Extreme Temperatures

Temperature	Jan	Feb	Mar	Apr	May	Jun	Jul	Aug	Sep	Oct	Nov	Dec	Yr.
Extreme High (°F)	68	75	85	96	97	101	104	99	99	88	81	72	104
Average High (°F)	38	41	50	61	72	80	85	84	76	65	54	43	62
Average Temp. (°F)	32	34	43	53	63	72	77	76	68	58	48	37	55
Average Low (°F)	26	27	35	44	54	63	68	67	60	49	41	31	47
Extreme Low (°F)	-2	-2	8	21	36	46	53	50	40	29	17	-1	-2

Note: Figures cover the years 1962-1992
Source: National Climatic Data Center, International Station Meteorological Climate Summary, 9/96

Average Precipitation/Snowfall/Humidity

Precip./Humidity	Jan	Feb	Mar	Apr	May	Jun	Jul	Aug	Sep	Oct	Nov	Dec	Yr.
Avg. Precip. (in.)	3.5	3.1	4.0	3.9	4.5	3.8	4.5	4.1	4.1	3.3	4.5	3.8	47.0
Avg. Snowfall (in.)	7	8	4	Tr	Tr	0	0	0	0	Tr	Tr	3	23
Avg. Rel. Hum. 7am (%)	67	67	66	64	72	74	74	76	78	75	72	69	71
Avg. Rel. Hum. 4pm (%)	55	53	50	45	52	55	53	54	56	55	57	58	53

Note: Figures cover the years 1962-1992; Tr = Trace amounts (<0.05 in. of rain; <0.5 in. of snow)
Source: National Climatic Data Center, International Station Meteorological Climate Summary, 9/96

Weather Conditions

Temperature			Daytime Sky			Precipitation		
32°F & below	45°F & below	90°F & above	Clear	Partly cloudy	Cloudy	0.01 inch or more precip.	0.1 inch or more snow/ice	Thunder-storms
75	170	18	85	166	114	120	11	20

Note: Figures are average number of days per year and cover the years 1962-1992
Source: National Climatic Data Center, International Station Meteorological Climate Summary, 9/96

HAZARDOUS WASTE

Superfund Sites

The New York-Jersey City-White Plains, NY-NJ metro division is home to 48 sites on the EPA's Superfund National Priorities List: **Atlantic Resources** (final); **Bog Creek Farm** (final); **Brick Township Landfill** (final); **Burnt Fly Bog** (final); **Carroll & Dubies Sewage Disposal** (final); **Chemical Insecticide Corp.** (final); **Chemsol, Inc.** (final); **Ciba-geigy Corp.** (final); **Cornell**

Dubilier Electronics Inc. (final); **CPS/Madison Industries** (final); **Curcio Scrap Metal, Inc.** (final); **Diamond Head Oil Refinery Div.** (final); **Evor Phillips Leasing** (final); **Fair Lawn Well Field** (final); **Fried Industries** (final); **Garfield Ground Water Contamination** (final); **Global Sanitary Landfill** (final); **Goose Farm** (final); **Gowanus Canal** (final); **Horseshoe Road** (final); **Hudson Technologies, Inc.** (proposed); **Imperial Oil Co., Inc./Champion Chemicals** (final); **JIS Landfill** (final); **Kin-Buc Landfill** (final); **Lone Pine Landfill** (final); **Maywood Chemical Co.** (final); **Middlesex Sampling Plant (USDOE)** (final); **Monitor Devices, Inc./Intercircuits, Inc.** (final); **Naval Air Engineering Center** (final); **Naval Weapons Station Earle (Site A)** (final); **Nepera Chemical Co., Inc.** (final); **Newtown Creek** (final); **Pjp Landfill** (final); **Quanta Resources** (final); **Ramapo Landfill** (final); **Raritan Bay Slag** (final); **Reich Farms** (final); **Ringwood Mines/Landfill** (final); **Scientific Chemical Processing** (final); **Standard Chlorine** (final); **Syncon Resins** (final); **Universal Oil Products (Chemical Division)** (final); **Ventron/Velsicol** (final); **Waldick Aerospace Devices, Inc.** (final); **White Swan Laundry and Cleaner Inc.** (final); **Wolff-Alport Chemical Company** (final); **Woodbrook Road Dump** (final); **Zschiegner Refining** (final). There are a total of 1,396 Superfund sites with a status of proposed or final on the list in the U.S. *U.S. Environmental Protection Agency, National Priorities List, April 4, 2018*

AIR & WATER QUALITY

Air Quality Trends: Ozone

	1990	1995	2000	2005	2010	2012	2013	2014	2015	2016
MSA[1]	0.101	0.106	0.090	0.091	0.081	0.079	0.071	0.069	0.075	0.073
U.S.	0.087	0.089	0.081	0.079	0.073	0.075	0.069	0.067	0.068	0.069

Note: (1) Data covers the New York-Newark-Jersey City, NY-NJ-PA Metropolitan Statistical Area—see Appendix B for areas included. The values shown are the composite ozone concentration averages among trend sites based on the highest fourth daily maximum 8-hour concentration in parts per million. These trends are based on sites having an adequate record of monitoring data during the trend period. Data from exceptional events are included.

Source: U.S. Environmental Protection Agency, Air Quality Monitoring Information, "Air Quality Trends by City, 1990-2016"

Air Quality Index

Area	Percent of Days when Air Quality was...[2]					AQI Statistics[2]	
	Good	Moderate	Unhealthy for Sensitive Groups	Unhealthy	Very Unhealthy	Maximum	Median
MSA[1]	42.2	52.6	4.7	0.5	0.0	159	52

Note: (1) Data covers the New York-Newark-Jersey City, NY-NJ-PA Metropolitan Statistical Area—see Appendix B for areas included; (2) Based on 365 days with AQI data in 2017. Air Quality Index (AQI) is an index for reporting daily air quality. EPA calculates the AQI for five major air pollutants regulated by the Clean Air Act: ground-level ozone, particle pollution (aka particulate matter), carbon monoxide, sulfur dioxide, and nitrogen dioxide. The AQI runs from 0 to 500. The higher the AQI value, the greater the level of air pollution and the greater the health concern. There are six AQI categories: "Good" AQI is between 0 and 50. Air quality is considered satisfactory; "Moderate" AQI is between 51 and 100. Air quality is acceptable; "Unhealthy for Sensitive Groups" When AQI values are between 101 and 150, members of sensitive groups may experience health effects; "Unhealthy" When AQI values are between 151 and 200 everyone may begin to experience health effects; "Very Unhealthy" AQI values between 201 and 300 trigger a health alert; "Hazardous" AQI values over 300 trigger warnings of emergency conditions (not shown).

Source: U.S. Environmental Protection Agency, Air Quality Index Report, 2017

Air Quality Index Pollutants

Area	Percent of Days when AQI Pollutant was...[2]					
	Carbon Monoxide	Nitrogen Dioxide	Ozone	Sulfur Dioxide	Particulate Matter 2.5	Particulate Matter 10
MSA[1]	0.0	13.2	31.8	0.0	55.1	0.0

Note: (1) Data covers the New York-Newark-Jersey City, NY-NJ-PA Metropolitan Statistical Area—see Appendix B for areas included; (2) Based on 365 days with AQI data in 2017. The Air Quality Index (AQI) is an index for reporting daily air quality. EPA calculates the AQI for five major air pollutants regulated by the Clean Air Act: ground-level ozone, particle pollution (also known as particulate matter), carbon monoxide, sulfur dioxide, and nitrogen dioxide. The AQI runs from 0 to 500. The higher the AQI value, the greater the level of air pollution and the greater the health concern.

Source: U.S. Environmental Protection Agency, Air Quality Index Report, 2017

Maximum Air Pollutant Concentrations: Particulate Matter, Ozone, CO and Lead

	Particulate Matter 10 (ug/m^3)	Particulate Matter 2.5 Wtd AM (ug/m^3)	Particulate Matter 2.5 24-Hr (ug/m^3)	Ozone (ppm)	Carbon Monoxide (ppm)	Lead (ug/m^3)
MSA[1] Level	33	9.2	20	0.078	3	0.03
NAAQS[2]	150	15	35	0.075	9	0.15
Met NAAQS[2]	Yes	Yes	Yes	No	Yes	Yes

Note: (1) Data covers the New York-Newark-Jersey City, NY-NJ-PA Metropolitan Statistical Area—see Appendix B for areas included; Data from exceptional events are included; (2) National Ambient Air Quality Standards; ppm = parts per million; ug/m^3 = micrograms per cubic meter; n/a not available.
Concentrations: Particulate Matter 10 (coarse particulate)—highest second maximum 24-hour concentration; Particulate Matter 2.5 Wtd AM (fine particulate)—highest weighted annual mean concentration; Particulate Matter 2.5 24-Hour (fine particulate)—highest 98th percentile 24-hour concentration; Ozone—highest fourth daily maximum 8-hour concentration; Carbon Monoxide—highest second maximum non-overlapping 8-hour concentration; Lead—maximum running 3-month average
Source: U.S. Environmental Protection Agency, Air Quality Monitoring Information, "Air Quality Statistics by City, 2016"

Maximum Air Pollutant Concentrations: Nitrogen Dioxide and Sulfur Dioxide

	Nitrogen Dioxide AM (ppb)	Nitrogen Dioxide 1-Hr (ppb)	Sulfur Dioxide AM (ppb)	Sulfur Dioxide 1-Hr (ppb)	Sulfur Dioxide 24-Hr (ppb)
MSA[1] Level	20	60	n/a	7	n/a
NAAQS[2]	53	100	30	75	140
Met NAAQS[2]	Yes	Yes	n/a	Yes	n/a

Note: (1) Data covers the New York-Newark-Jersey City, NY-NJ-PA Metropolitan Statistical Area—see Appendix B for areas included; Data from exceptional events are included; (2) National Ambient Air Quality Standards; ppm = parts per million; ug/m^3 = micrograms per cubic meter; n/a not available.
Concentrations: Nitrogen Dioxide AM—highest arithmetic mean concentration; Nitrogen Dioxide 1-Hr—highest 98th percentile 1-hour daily maximum concentration; Sulfur Dioxide AM—highest annual mean concentration; Sulfur Dioxide 1-Hr—highest 99th percentile 1-hour daily maximum concentration; Sulfur Dioxide 24-Hr—highest second maximum 24-hour concentration
Source: U.S. Environmental Protection Agency, Air Quality Monitoring Information, "Air Quality Statistics by City, 2016"

Drinking Water

Water System Name	Pop. Served	Primary Water Source Type	Violations[1]	
			Health Based	Monitoring/ Reporting
Westchester Joint Water Works	59,629	Surface	0	0

Note: (1) Based on violation data from January 1, 2017 to December 31, 2017
Source: U.S. Environmental Protection Agency, Office of Ground Water and Drinking Water, Safe Drinking Water Information System (based on data extracted April 5, 2018)

Vestal, New York

Background

Vestal, a "Full Service Town" in the Southern Tier of New York, lies between the Susquehanna River and the Pennsylvania border. Situated in the southern border of Broome County, it lies west/south west of Binghamton, the county seat. Between Binghamton and Vestal is Binghamton University.

Arriving in Vestal around 1785, the first European settlers built upon land which was previously occupied by several Native American tribes. The conflict in this area between the natives and the settlers would be harsh during the American Revolution. After the war, European families would settle in the town of Union; the southern portion of Union would give rise to Vestal in 1823. Vestal is still closely linked to the towns around it, particularly Binghamton, Endicott, and Johnson City. During the 20th century, Vestal served as a residential suburb with its population commuting to and from companies such as Endicott Johnson Corporation, IBM, and Lockheed Martin. In 1961 Harpur College made its move to Vestal, eventually changed its name to Binghamton University, and is now the highest ranked public university in the Northeastern United States.

To the north of Vestal is Susquehanna River, which makes up its town line; to the west is Tioga County; and to the south is Susquehanna County, Pennsylvania. Vestal has a total area of 52.6 square miles. The town contains five official hamlets: Ross Corners, Tracy Creek, Twin Orchards, Vestal Center, and Willow Point.

Vestal is served by the Vestal Central School District, which is comprised of Vestal High School and Vestal Middle School, along with five elementary schools. The historic Vestal Central School, built in 1939, is on the National Register of Historic Places. Also within Vestal are the private Hillel Academy and Ross Corners Christian Academy.

Binghamton University dominates higher education in Vestal, with thousands of students and over 3,000 employees making up a grand portion of the town's population. Its entertainment, arts, and sporting events are highlights of the town, with the Binghamton University Events Center and the Bearcats Sports Complex hosting much of this excitement.

Recreation and retail are two major players in Vestal, with the area containing 21 town-operated parks to enjoy and the 1990s marking Vestal as the retail center of the Southern Tier region. A highlight of Vestal's natural recreational areas is the Vestal Rail Trail, a 2.1 mile trail for walking, skating, running, and cycling. The Town Square Mall, the Parkway Plaza, and the Shoppes at Vestal are only some of the retail opportunities in the city. The Kopernik Observatory & Science Center, the Drovers Inn and Round Family Residence, and the Vestal Museum are all points of interest. Vestal Museum programs are developed in concert with the Vestal Historical Society and community volunteers.

Vestal and surrounding municipalities are served by Broome County Transit for public bus transportation. The Greater Binghamton Airport, located in the nearby town of Maine, provides direct flights to Detroit, Philadelphia, and Newark.

Rankings

Business/Finance Rankings

- The personal finance site NerdWallet analyzed 183 American metropolitan areas with populations over 250,000 and more than 15,000 businesses to rank where entrepreneurs find the most success. Criteria included area economy, annual income, housing cost, unemployment rate, and the success rate of area businesses. Binghamton* ranked #126. *www.nerdwallet.com, "Best Places to Start a Business," April 27, 2015*
- The Binghamton* metro area appeared on the Milken Institute "2017 Best Performing Cities" list. Rank: #164 out of 201 small metro areas. Criteria: job growth; wage and salary growth; high-tech output growth. *Milken Institute, "Best-Performing Cities 2017," January 2018*
- *Forbes* ranked 200 smaller metro areas (population under 265,400) to determine the nation's "Best Small Places for Business and Careers." The Binghamton* metro area was ranked #110. Criteria: costs (business and living); job growth (past and projected); income growth; quality of life; educational attainment (college and high school); projected economic growth; cultural and recreational opportunities; net migration patterns; number of highly ranked colleges. *Forbes, "The Best Small Cities for Business and Careers 2017," November, 6 2017*

Environmental Rankings

- Sperling's BestPlaces assessed 379 metropolitan areas of the United States for the likelihood of dangerously extreme weather events or earthquakes. In general the Southeast and South-Central regions have the highest risk of weather extremes and earthquakes, while the Pacific Northwest enjoys the lowest risk. Of the least risky metropolitan areas, the Binghamton* metro area was ranked #102. *www.bestplaces.net, "Safest Places from Natural Disasters," April 2011*

Food/Drink Rankings

- For the Gallup-Healthways Well-Being Index, researchers interviewed at least 300 adults in each of 189 metropolitan areas on residents' access to affordable fresh produce. The Binghamton* metro area was found to be among the bottom ten communities for accessibility to affordable produce. *www.gallup.com, "In Anchorage, Access to Fruits and Vegetables Remains Lowest," April 8, 2014*

Health/Fitness Rankings

- The Gallup-Healthways Well-Being Index tracks Americans' optimism about their communities and satisfaction with the metro areas in which they live. At least 300 adult residents in each of 186 U.S. metropolitan areas were asked whether they liked what they did each day and were motivated to achieve their goals. The Binghamton* metro area was one of the five communities where residents' feeling of purpose was low. *www.gallup.com, "2017 Community Well-Being Rankings," March 2018*
- Gallup-Healthways Well-Being Index researchers asked at least 300 adult residents in each of 186 U.S. metropolitan areas how satisfied they were with the metro area in which they lived, if they felt safe and had community pride. The Binghamton* metro area was one of the five metros where residents had the lowest feeling of community. *www.gallup.com, "2017 Community Well-Being Rankings," March 2018*
- The Binghamton* metro area ranked #182 out of 189 in The Gallup-Healthways Well-Being Index. Criteria: purpose; social well being; financial health; community and physical health. Results are based on telephone interviews with adults, aged 18 and older, living in metropolitan areas in the 50 U.S. states and the District of Columbia. *Gallup-Healthways, "State of American Well-Being, 2017 Community Well-Being Rankings" March 2018*

Real Estate Rankings

- The Binghamton* metro area was identified as one of the 20 worst housing markets in the U.S. in 2017. The area ranked #14 out of 180 markets. Criteria: year-over-year change of median sales price of existing single-family homes between the 4th quarter of 2016 and the 4th quarter of 2017. *National Association of Realtors®, Median Sales Price of Existing Single-Family Homes for Metropolitan Areas, 4th Quarter 2017*
- The Binghamton* metro area was identified as one of the 20 most affordable housing markets in the U.S. in 2017. The area ranked #6 out of 180 markets. Criteria: qualification for a mortgage loan on a typical home. *National Association of Realtors®, Affordability Index of Existing Single-Family Homes for Metropolitan Areas, 2017*
- Binghamton* was ranked #8 out of 238 metro areas in terms of housing affordability in 2017 by the National Association of Home Builders (#1 = most affordable). Criteria: the share of homes sold in that area affordable to a family earning the local median income, based on standard mortgage underwriting criteria. *National Association of Home Builders®, NAHB-Wells Fargo Housing Opportunity Index, 4th Quarter 2017*

Safety Rankings

- Statistics drawn from the FBI's Uniform Crime Report were used to rank the 25 metropolitan statistical areas where violent crime rose most over the years 2011–2016. 24/7 Wall Street found that the Binghamton* metro area placed #23 of those with the largest increases in violent crime. *247wallst.com, "25 U.S. Cities Where Crime Is Soaring," March 8, 2018*
- The National Insurance Crime Bureau ranked 382 metro areas in the U.S. in terms of per capita rates of vehicle theft. The Binghamton* metro area ranked #339 (#1 = highest rate). Criteria: number of vehicle theft offenses per 100,000 inhabitants in 2016. *National Insurance Crime Bureau, "Hot Spots 2016," June 8, 2017*

Seniors/Retirement Rankings

- From its Best Cities for Successful Aging indexes, the Milken Institute generated rankings for metropolitan areas, weighing data in nine categories—health care, wellness, living arrangements, transportation and convenience, financial characteristics, education, employment, community engagement, and overall livability. The Binghamton* metro area was ranked #193 overall in the small metro area category. *Milken Institute, "Best Cities for Successful Aging, 2017" March 14, 2017*

*Vestal is located within the Binghamton, NY Metropolitan Statistical Area.

Business Environment

CITY FINANCES

City Government Finances

Component	2015 ($000)	2015 ($ per capita)
Total Revenues	28,362	1,005
Total Expenditures	27,290	967
Debt Outstanding	16,368	580
Cash and Securities[1]	9,866	350

Note: (1) Cash and security holdings of a government at the close of its fiscal year,, including those of its dependent agencies, utilities, and liquor stores.
Source: U.S Census Bureau, State & Local Government Finances 2015

City Government Revenue by Source

Source	2015 ($000)	2015 ($ per capita)	2015 (%)
General Revenue			
From Federal Government	1,825	65	6.4
From State Government	1,475	52	5.2
From Local Governments	5,950	211	21.0
Taxes			
Property	10,613	376	37.4
Sales and Gross Receipts	325	12	1.1
Personal Income	0	0	0.0
Corporate Income	0	0	0.0
Motor Vehicle License	0	0	0.0
Other Taxes	477	17	1.7
Current Charges	3,222	114	11.4
Liquor Store	0	0	0.0
Utility	2,579	91	9.1
Employee Retirement	0	0	0.0

Source: U.S Census Bureau, State & Local Government Finances 2015

City Government Expenditures by Function

Function	2015 ($000)	2015 ($ per capita)	2015 (%)
General Direct Expenditures			
Air Transportation	0	0	0.0
Corrections	0	0	0.0
Education	0	0	0.0
Employment Security Administration	0	0	0.0
Financial Administration	443	15	1.6
Fire Protection	1,270	45	4.7
General Public Buildings	153	5	0.6
Governmental Administration, Other	206	7	0.8
Health	55	1	0.2
Highways	6,733	238	24.7
Hospitals	0	0	0.0
Housing and Community Development	0	0	0.0
Interest on General Debt	302	10	1.1
Judicial and Legal	274	9	1.0
Libraries	624	22	2.3
Parking	0	0	0.0
Parks and Recreation	1,265	44	4.6
Police Protection	3,691	130	13.5
Public Welfare	0	0	0.0
Sewerage	3,228	114	11.8
Solid Waste Management	0	0	0.0
Veterans' Services	0	0	0.0
Liquor Store	0	0	0.0
Utility	1,897	67	7.0
Employee Retirement	0	0	0.0

Source: U.S Census Bureau, State & Local Government Finances 2015

DEMOGRAPHICS

Population Growth

Area	1990 Census	2000 Census	2010 Census	2016* Estimate	Population Growth (%) 1990-2016	2010-2016
City	26,733	26,535	28,043	28,267	5.7	0.8
MSA[1]	264,497	252,320	251,725	247,030	-6.6	-1.9
U.S.	248,709,873	281,421,906	308,745,538	318,558,162	28.1	3.2

Note: (1) Figures cover the Binghamton, NY Metropolitan Statistical Area—see Appendix B for areas included; (*) 2012-2016 5-year estimated population
Source: U.S. Census Bureau, 1990 Census, Census 2000, Census 2010, 2012-2016 American Community Survey 5-Year Estimates

Household Size

Area	Persons in Household (%) One	Two	Three	Four	Five	Six	Seven or More	Average Household Size
City	26.4	39.5	11.9	15.9	4.3	1.5	0.6	2.50
MSA[1]	30.6	35.8	14.4	11.8	4.7	1.7	0.9	2.40
U.S.	27.7	33.7	15.7	13.1	6.0	2.3	1.5	2.60

Note: (1) Figures cover the Binghamton, NY Metropolitan Statistical Area—see Appendix B for areas included
Source: U.S. Census Bureau, 2012-2016 American Community Survey 5-Year Estimates

Race

Area	White Alone[2] (%)	Black Alone[2] (%)	Asian Alone[2] (%)	AIAN[3] Alone[2] (%)	NHOPI[4] Alone[2] (%)	Other Race Alone[2] (%)	Two or More Races (%)
City	80.3	5.0	11.7	0.2	0.0	0.9	1.9
MSA[1]	88.5	4.6	3.4	0.2	0.0	0.9	2.4
U.S.	73.3	12.6	5.2	0.8	0.2	4.8	3.1

Note: (1) Figures cover the Binghamton, NY Metropolitan Statistical Area—see Appendix B for areas included; (2) Alone is defined as not being in combination with one or more other races; (3) American Indian and Alaska Native; (4) Native Hawaiian and Other Pacific Islander
Source: U.S. Census Bureau, 2012-2016 American Community Survey 5-Year Estimates

Hispanic or Latino Origin

Area	Total (%)	Mexican (%)	Puerto Rican (%)	Cuban (%)	Other (%)
City	4.8	0.6	1.4	0.2	2.5
MSA[1]	3.4	0.5	1.7	0.1	1.1
U.S.	17.3	11.0	1.7	0.7	4.0

Note: Persons of Hispanic or Latino origin can be of any race; (1) Figures cover the Binghamton, NY Metropolitan Statistical Area—see Appendix B for areas included
Source: U.S. Census Bureau, 2012-2016 American Community Survey 5-Year Estimates

Segregation

Type	Segregation Indices[1] 1990	2000	2010	2010 Rank[2]	Percent Change 1990-2000	1990-2010	2000-2010
Black/White	n/a	n/a	n/a	n/a	n/a	n/a	n/a
Asian/White	n/a	n/a	n/a	n/a	n/a	n/a	n/a
Hispanic/White	n/a	n/a	n/a	n/a	n/a	n/a	n/a

Note: All figures cover the Metropolitan Statistical Area—see Appendix B for areas included; Figures are based on an analysis of 1990, 2000, and 2010 Census Decennial Census tract data by William H. Frey, Brookings Institution and the University of Michigan Social Science Data Analysis Network. In this analysis all racial groups (whites, blacks, and asians) are non-Hispanic members of those races. Hispanics are shown as a separate category; (1) Segregation Indices are Dissimilarity Indices that measure the degree to which the minority group is distributed differently than whites across census tracts. They range from 0 (complete integration) to 100 (complete segregation) where the value indicates the percentage of the minority group that needs to move to be distributed exactly like whites; (2) Ranges from 1 (most segregated) to 102 (least segregated); n/a not available.
Source: www.CensusScope.org

Ancestry

Area	German	Irish	English	American	Italian	Polish	French[2]	Scottish	Dutch
City	14.7	15.4	10.4	4.5	11.8	4.9	3.0	1.0	2.0
MSA[1]	16.3	18.1	12.5	5.8	11.9	5.8	2.6	2.0	2.5
U.S.	14.4	10.4	7.7	6.9	5.4	2.9	2.6	1.7	1.3

Note: Figures are the percentage of the total population reporting a particular ancestry. The nine most commonly reported ancestries in the U.S. are shown. Figures include multiple ancestries (e.g. if a person reported being Irish and Italian, they were included in both columns); (1) Figures cover the Binghamton, NY Metropolitan Statistical Area—see Appendix B for areas included; (2) Excludes Basque
Source: U.S. Census Bureau, 2012-2016 American Community Survey 5-Year Estimates

Foreign-Born Population

Area	Percent of Population Born in								
	Any Foreign Country	Asia	Mexico	Europe	Carribean	Central America[2]	South America	Africa	Canada
City	11.1	7.6	0.1	1.4	1.2	0.1	0.3	0.1	0.3
MSA[1]	5.7	2.8	0.1	1.5	0.6	0.1	0.2	0.2	0.1
U.S.	13.2	4.0	3.6	1.5	1.3	1.0	0.9	0.6	0.3

Note: (1) Figures cover the Binghamton, NY Metropolitan Statistical Area—see Appendix B for areas included; (2) Excludes Mexico.
Source: U.S. Census Bureau, 2012-2016 American Community Survey 5-Year Estimates

Marital Status

Area	Never Married	Now Married[2]	Separated	Widowed	Divorced
City	46.5	41.2	0.6	5.0	6.7
MSA[1]	34.5	46.0	2.1	6.6	10.7
U.S.	33.0	48.1	2.1	5.9	11.0

Note: Figures are percentages and cover the population 15 years of age and older; (1) Figures cover the Binghamton, NY Metropolitan Statistical Area—see Appendix B for areas included; (2) Excludes separated
Source: U.S. Census Bureau, 2012-2016 American Community Survey 5-Year Estimates

Disability Status

Area	All Ages	Under 18 Years Old	18 to 64 Years Old	65 Years and Over
City	8.7	5.0	5.5	27.2
MSA[1]	14.9	6.5	12.1	35.1
U.S.	12.5	4.1	10.3	35.7

Note: Figures show percent of the civilian noninstitutionalized population that reported having a disability. Disability status is determined from six types of difficulty: vision, hearing, cognitive, ambulatory, self-care, and independent living. For children under 5 years old, hearing and vision difficulty are used to determine disability status. For children between the ages of 5 and 14, disability status is determined from hearing, vision, cognitive, ambulatory, and self-care difficulties. For people aged 15 years and older, they are considered to have a disability if they have difficulty with any one of the six difficulty types; Note: (1) Figures cover the Binghamton, NY Metropolitan Statistical Area—see Appendix B for areas included
Source: U.S. Census Bureau, 2012-2016 American Community Survey 5-Year Estimates

Age

Area	Percent of Population									Median Age
	Under Age 5	Age 5–19	Age 20–34	Age 35–44	Age 45–54	Age 55–64	Age 65–74	Age 75–84	Age 85+	
City	3.0	27.8	23.6	7.2	10.3	11.9	8.0	5.6	2.6	27.8
MSA[1]	5.2	18.8	20.0	10.4	13.9	14.0	9.2	5.7	2.8	40.7
U.S.	6.2	19.6	20.7	12.7	13.6	12.6	8.3	4.3	1.9	37.7

Note: (1) Figures cover the Binghamton, NY Metropolitan Statistical Area—see Appendix B for areas included
Source: U.S. Census Bureau, 2012-2016 American Community Survey 5-Year Estimates

Gender

Area	Males	Females	Males per 100 Females
City	13,814	14,453	95.6
MSA[1]	121,540	125,490	96.9
U.S.	156,765,322	161,792,840	96.9

Note: (1) Figures cover the Binghamton, NY Metropolitan Statistical Area—see Appendix B for areas included
Source: U.S. Census Bureau, 2012-2016 American Community Survey 5-Year Estimates

Religious Groups by Family

Area	Catholic	Baptist	Non-Den.	Methodist[2]	Lutheran	LDS[3]	Pente-costal	Presby-terian[4]	Muslim[5]	Judaism
MSA[1]	27.0	1.1	2.8	7.7	1.2	0.5	1.0	1.5	0.3	0.8
U.S.	19.1	9.3	4.0	4.0	2.3	2.0	1.9	1.6	0.8	0.7

Note: Figures are the number of adherents as a percentage of the total population; (1) Figures cover the Binghamton, NY Metropolitan Statistical Area—see Appendix B for areas included; (2) Methodist/Pietist; (3) Latter Day Saints; (4) Reformed; (5) Figures are estimates
Source: Association of Statisticians of American Religious Bodies, 2010 U.S. Religion Census: Religious Congregations & Membership Study

Religious Groups by Tradition

Area	Catholic	Evangelical Protestant	Mainline Protestant	Other Tradition	Black Protestant	Orthodox
MSA[1]	27.0	6.4	11.5	2.1	0.1	0.9
U.S.	19.1	16.2	7.3	4.3	1.6	0.3

Note: Figures are the number of adherents as a percentage of the total population; (1) Figures cover the Binghamton, NY Metropolitan Statistical Area—see Appendix B for areas included
Source: Association of Statisticians of American Religious Bodies, 2010 U.S. Religion Census: Religious Congregations & Membership Study

ECONOMY

Gross Metropolitan Product

Area	2014	2015	2016	2017	Rank[2]
MSA[1]	9.1	9.1	9.2	9.5	211

Note: Figures are in billions of dollars; (1) Figures cover the Binghamton, NY Metropolitan Statistical Area—see Appendix B for areas included; (2) Rank is based on 2015 data and ranges from 1 to 381
Source: The U.S. Conference of Mayors, U.S. Metro Economies: GMP and Employment Report, 2015-2017

Economic Growth

Area	2012-14 (%)	2015 (%)	2016 (%)	2017 (%)	Rank[2]
MSA[1]	-0.9	-1.2	-0.2	1.5	340
U.S.	2.0	2.4	1.9	2.6	–

Note: Figures are real gross metropolitan product (GMP) growth rates and represent average annual percent change; (1) Figures cover the Binghamton, NY Metropolitan Statistical Area—see Appendix B for areas included; (2) Rank is based on 2012-2014 average annual percent change and ranges from 1 to 381
Source: The U.S. Conference of Mayors, U.S. Metro Economies: GMP and Employment Report, 2015-2017

Metropolitan Area Exports

Area	2011	2012	2013	2014	2015	2016	Rank[2]
MSA[1]	605.6	508.3	388.5	471.0	431.4	404.8	226

Note: Figures are in millions of dollars; (1) Figures cover the Binghamton, NY Metropolitan Statistical Area—see Appendix B for areas included; (2) Rank is based on 2016 data and ranges from 1 to 385
Source: U.S. Department of Commerce, International Trade Administration, Office of Trade & Industry Information, Manufacturing & Services, data extracted March 15, 2018

Building Permits

Area	Single-Family			Multi-Family			Total		
	2016	2017p	Pct. Chg.	2016	2017p	Pct. Chg.	2016	2017p	Pct. Chg.
City	n/a	n/a	n/a	n/a	n/a	n/a	n/a	n/a	n/a
MSA[1]	1	5	400.0	0	0	0.0	1	5	400.0
U.S.	750,800	817,300	8.9	455,800	446,800	-2.0	1,206,600	1,264,100	4.8

Note: (1) Figures cover the Binghamton, NY Metropolitan Statistical Area—see Appendix B for areas included; Figures represent new, privately-owned housing units authorized (unadjusted data); All permit data are based on estimates with imputation; (p) preliminary data.
Source: U.S. Census Bureau, Manufacturing, Mining, and Construction Statistics, Building Permits, 2016, 2017

Bankruptcy Filings

Area	Business Filings			Nonbusiness Filings		
	2016	2017	% Chg.	2016	2017	% Chg.
Broome County	9	9	0.0	326	329	0.9
U.S.	24,114	23,157	-4.0	770,846	765,863	-0.6

Note: Business filings include Chapter 7, Chapter 11, Chapter 12, and Chapter 13; Nonbusiness filings include Chapter 7, Chapter 11, and Chapter 13
Source: Administrative Office of the U.S. Courts, Business and Nonbusiness Bankruptcy, County Cases Commenced by Chapter of the Bankruptcy Code, During the 12-Month Period Ending December 31, 2016 and Business and Nonbusiness Bankruptcy, County Cases Commenced by Chapter of the Bankruptcy Code, During the 12-Month Period Ending December 31, 2017

Housing Vacancy Rates

Area	Gross Vacancy Rate² (%)			Year-Round Vacancy Rate³ (%)			Rental Vacancy Rate⁴ (%)			Homeowner Vacancy Rate⁵ (%)		
	2015	2016	2017	2015	2016	2017	2015	2016	2017	2015	2016	2017
MSA[1]	n/a	n/a	n/a	n/a	n/a	n/a	n/a	n/a	n/a	n/a	n/a	n/a
U.S.	12.9	12.8	12.7	10.0	9.9	9.9	7.1	6.9	7.2	1.8	1.7	1.6

Note: (1) Figures cover the Binghamton, NY Metropolitan Statistical Area—see Appendix B for areas included; (2) The percentage of the total housing inventory that is vacant; (3) The percentage of the housing inventory (excluding seasonal units) that is year-round vacant; (4) The percentage of rental inventory that is vacant for rent; (5) The percentage of homeowner inventory that is vacant for sale; n/a not available
Source: U.S. Census Bureau, Housing Vacancies and Homeownership Annual Statistics: 2015, 2016, 2017

INCOME

Income

Area	Per Capita ($)	Median Household ($)	Average Household ($)
City	26,831	61,627	82,711
MSA[1]	26,638	49,707	65,240
U.S.	29,829	55,322	77,866

Note: (1) Figures cover the Binghamton, NY Metropolitan Statistical Area—see Appendix B for areas included
Source: U.S. Census Bureau, 2012-2016 American Community Survey 5-Year Estimates

Household Income Distribution

Area	Percent of Households Earning							
	Under $15,000	$15,000 -$24,999	$25,000 -$34,999	$35,000 -$49,999	$50,000 -$74,999	$75,000 -$99,999	$100,000 -$149,999	$150,000 and up
City	9.4	8.0	9.0	14.2	20.4	13.6	14.2	11.3
MSA[1]	13.3	12.5	10.8	13.6	18.6	12.1	12.2	6.8
U.S.	12.1	10.2	9.9	13.2	17.8	12.2	13.5	11.1

Note: (1) Figures cover the Binghamton, NY Metropolitan Statistical Area—see Appendix B for areas included
Source: U.S. Census Bureau, 2012-2016 American Community Survey 5-Year Estimates

Poverty Rate

Area	All Ages	Under 18 Years Old	18 to 64 Years Old	65 Years and Over
City	11.1	11.6	13.5	3.0
MSA[1]	16.1	22.1	16.6	7.1
U.S.	15.1	21.2	14.2	9.3

Note: Figures are percentage of people whose income during the past 12 months was below the poverty level; (1) Figures cover the Binghamton, NY Metropolitan Statistical Area—see Appendix B for areas included
Source: U.S. Census Bureau, 2012-2016 American Community Survey 5-Year Estimates

EMPLOYMENT

Labor Force and Employment

Area	Civilian Labor Force			Workers Employed		
	Dec. 2016	Dec. 2017	% Chg.	Dec. 2016	Dec. 2017	% Chg.
City	11,354	11,223	-1.2	10,795	10,649	-1.4
MSA[1]	108,011	106,915	-1.0	102,292	101,009	-1.3
U.S.	158,968,000	159,880,000	0.6	151,798,000	153,602,000	1.2

Note: Data is not seasonally adjusted and covers workers 16 years of age and older; (1) Figures cover the Binghamton, NY Metropolitan Statistical Area—see Appendix B for areas included
Source: Bureau of Labor Statistics, Local Area Unemployment Statistics

Unemployment Rate

Area	2017											
	Jan.	Feb.	Mar.	Apr.	May	Jun.	Jul.	Aug.	Sep.	Oct.	Nov.	Dec.
City	6.1	6.3	5.4	5.4	5.5	6.6	6.5	5.8	6.0	5.7	6.0	5.1
MSA[1]	6.6	6.5	5.8	5.3	5.1	5.5	5.5	5.3	5.1	4.9	5.3	5.5
U.S.	5.1	4.9	4.6	4.1	4.1	4.5	4.6	4.5	4.1	3.9	3.9	3.9

Note: Data is not seasonally adjusted and covers workers 16 years of age and older; (1) Figures cover the Binghamton, NY Metropolitan Statistical Area—see Appendix B for areas included
Source: Bureau of Labor Statistics, Local Area Unemployment Statistics

Average Wages

Occupation	$/Hr.	Occupation	$/Hr.
Accountants and Auditors	34.60	Maids and Housekeeping Cleaners	11.20
Automotive Mechanics	18.30	Maintenance and Repair Workers	18.00
Bookkeepers	17.60	Marketing Managers	82.70
Carpenters	22.00	Nuclear Medicine Technologists	n/a
Cashiers	10.60	Nurses, Licensed Practical	20.50
Clerks, General Office	14.00	Nurses, Registered	30.00
Clerks, Receptionists/Information	13.70	Nursing Assistants	13.40
Clerks, Shipping/Receiving	15.70	Packers and Packagers, Hand	14.80
Computer Programmers	43.40	Physical Therapists	40.30
Computer Systems Analysts	42.70	Postal Service Mail Carriers	23.90
Computer User Support Specialists	23.40	Real Estate Brokers	n/a
Cooks, Restaurant	12.50	Retail Salespersons	13.00
Dentists	97.90	Sales Reps., Exc. Tech./Scientific	25.10
Electrical Engineers	37.70	Sales Reps., Tech./Scientific	40.90
Electricians	26.70	Secretaries, Exc. Legal/Med./Exec.	17.60
Financial Managers	60.10	Security Guards	16.20
First-Line Supervisors/Managers, Sales	20.90	Surgeons	n/a
Food Preparation Workers	11.40	Teacher Assistants*	11.50
General and Operations Managers	51.50	Teachers, Elementary School*	28.90
Hairdressers/Cosmetologists	17.10	Teachers, Secondary School*	31.80
Internists, General	n/a	Telemarketers	n/a
Janitors and Cleaners	12.80	Truck Drivers, Heavy/Tractor-Trailer	19.20
Landscaping/Groundskeeping Workers	13.50	Truck Drivers, Light/Delivery Svcs.	15.80
Lawyers	40.60	Waiters and Waitresses	12.00

Note: Wage data covers the Binghamton, NY Metropolitan Statistical Area—see Appendix B for areas included; (*) Hourly wages for elementary/secondary school teachers and teacher assistants were calculated by the editors from annual wage data based on a 40 hour work week; n/a not available.
Source: Bureau of Labor Statistics, Metro Area Occupational Employment & Wage Estimates, May 2017

Employment by Occupation

Occupation Classification	City (%)	MSA[1] (%)	U.S. (%)
Management, Business, Science, and Arts	46.7	36.5	37.0
Natural Resources, Construction, and Maintenance	5.5	7.9	8.9
Production, Transportation, and Material Moving	6.2	12.1	12.2
Sales and Office	22.7	24.2	23.8
Service	18.9	19.4	18.1

Note: Figures cover employed civilians 16 years of age and older; (1) Figures cover the Binghamton, NY Metropolitan Statistical Area—see Appendix B for areas included
Source: U.S. Census Bureau, 2012-2016 American Community Survey 5-Year Estimates

Employment by Industry

Sector	MSA[1] Number of Employees	MSA[1] Percent of Total	U.S. Percent of Total
Construction, Mining, and Logging	4,200	4.0	5.2
Education and Health Services	17,100	16.2	15.9
Financial Activities	3,600	3.4	5.7
Government	23,200	22.0	15.3
Information	1,500	1.4	1.9
Leisure and Hospitality	10,700	10.2	10.7
Manufacturing	11,300	10.7	8.5
Other Services	5,600	5.3	3.9
Professional and Business Services	8,500	8.1	14.0
Retail Trade	12,300	11.7	11.0
Transportation, Warehousing, and Utilities	2,700	2.6	4.1
Wholesale Trade	4,600	4.4	4.0

Note: Figures are non-farm employment as of December 2017. Figures are not seasonally adjusted and include workers 16 years of age and older; (1) Figures cover the Binghamton, NY Metropolitan Statistical Area—see Appendix B for areas included
Source: Bureau of Labor Statistics, Current Employment Statistics, Employment, Hours, and Earnings

Occupations with Greatest Projected Employment Growth: 2017 – 2019

Occupation[1]	2017 Employment	2019 Projected Employment	Numeric Employment Change	Percent Employment Change
Home Health Aides	190,490	216,300	25,810	13.5
Personal Care Aides	174,700	189,420	14,720	8.4
Combined Food Preparation and Serving Workers, Including Fast Food	154,570	162,110	7,540	4.9
Registered Nurses	189,840	197,230	7,390	3.9
Janitors and Cleaners, Except Maids and Housekeeping Cleaners	211,280	217,380	6,100	2.9
Waiters and Waitresses	151,380	156,430	5,050	3.3
General and Operations Managers	165,860	169,970	4,110	2.5
Accountants and Auditors	124,740	128,070	3,330	2.7
Software Developers, Applications	52,730	55,940	3,210	6.1
Security Guards	114,180	117,140	2,960	2.6

Note: Projections cover New York; (1) Sorted by numeric employment change
Source: www.projectionscentral.com, State Occupational Projections, 2017–2019 Short-Term Projections

Fastest Growing Occupations: 2017 – 2019

Occupation[1]	2017 Employment	2019 Projected Employment	Numeric Employment Change	Percent Employment Change
Gaming and Sports Book Writers and Runners	660	810	150	24.0
Gaming Change Persons and Booth Cashiers	840	1,030	190	22.7
Solar Photovoltaic Installers	800	980	180	22.7
Gaming Dealers	960	1,150	190	19.4
Home Health Aides	190,490	216,300	25,810	13.5
Gaming Supervisors	580	660	80	12.3
Entertainment Attendants and Related Workers, All Other	490	540	50	9.8
Personal Care Aides	174,700	189,420	14,720	8.4
Physical Therapist Aides	3,110	3,330	220	6.9
Physical Therapists	18,480	19,750	1,270	6.9

Note: Projections cover New York; (1) Sorted by percent employment change and excludes occupations with numeric employment change less than 50
Source: www.projectionscentral.com, State Occupational Projections, 2017–2019 Short-Term Projections

TAXES

State Corporate Income Tax Rates

State	Tax Rate (%)	Income Brackets ($)	Num. of Brackets	Financial Institution Tax Rate (%)[a]	Federal Income Tax Ded.
New York	6.5 (r)	Flat rate	1	6.5 (r)	No

Note: Tax rates as of January 1, 2018; (a) Rates listed are the corporate income tax rate applied to financial institutions or excise taxes based on income. Some states have other taxes based upon the value of deposits or shares; (r) New York's General business corporate rate shown. Corporations may also be subject to a capital stocks tax, which is being phased out through 2021. A minimum tax ranges from $25 to $200,000, depending on receipts ($250 minimum for banks). Certain qualified New York manufacturers pay 0%.
Source: Federation of Tax Administrators, Range of State Corporate Income Tax Rates, January 1, 2018

State Individual Income Tax Rates

State	Tax Rate (%)	Income Brackets ($)	Num. of Brackets	Personal Exempt. ($)[1]		Fed. Inc. Tax Ded.
				Single	Dependents	
New York (a)	4.0 - 8.82	8,500 - 1,077,550 (b)	8	0	1,000	No

Note: Tax rates as of January 1, 2018; Local- and county-level taxes are not included; n/a not applicable; (1) Married joint filers generally receive double the single exemption; (a) 19 states have statutory provision for automatically adjusting to the rate of inflation the dollar values of the income tax brackets, standard deductions, and/or personal exemptions. Massachusetts, Michigan, and Nebraska index the personal exemption only. Oregon does not index the income brackets for $125,000 and over; (b) For joint returns, taxes are twice the tax on half the couple's income.
Source: Federation of Tax Administrators, State Individual Income Tax Rates, January 1, 2018

Various State Sales and Excise Tax Rates

State	State Sales Tax (%)	Gasoline[1] (¢/gal.)	Cigarette[2] ($/pack)	Spirits[3] ($/gal.)	Wine[4] ($/gal.)	Beer[5] ($/gal.)	Recreational Marijuana (%)
New York	4.0	44.3	4.35	6.44 (f)	0.30	0.14	Not legal

Note: All tax rates as of January 1, 2018; (1) The American Petroleum Institute has developed a methodology for determining the average tax rate on a gallon of fuel. Rates may include any of the following: excise taxes, environmental fees, storage tank fees, other fees or taxes, general sales tax, and local taxes. In states where gasoline is subject to the general sales tax, or where the fuel tax is based on the average sale price, the average rate determined by API is sensitive to changes in the price of gasoline. States that fully or partially apply general sales taxes to gasoline: CA, CO, GA, IL, IN, MI, NY; (2) The federal excise tax of $1.0066 per pack and local taxes are not included; (3) Rates are those applicable to off-premise sales of 40% alcohol by volume (a.b.v.) distilled spirits in 750ml containers. Local excise taxes are excluded; (4) Rates are those applicable to off-premise sales of 11% a.b.v. non-carbonated wine in 750ml containers; (5) Rates are those applicable to off-premise sales of 4.7% a.b.v. beer in 12 ounce containers; (f) Different rates also applicable according to alcohol content, place of production, size of container, or place purchased (on- or off-premise or onboard airlines).
Source: Tax Foundation, 2018 Facts & Figures: How Does Your State Compare?

State Business Tax Climate Index Rankings

State	Overall Rank	Corporate Tax Rank	Individual Income Tax Rank	Sales Tax Rank	Unemployment Insurance Tax Rank	Property Tax Rank
New York	49	7	49	43	30	47

Note: The index is a measure of how each state's tax laws affect economic performance. The lower the rank, the more favorable a state's tax system is for business. States without a given tax are given a ranking of 1. The scores/rankings for the District of Columbia do not affect other states. The 2018 index represents the tax climate as of July 1, 2017.
Source: Tax Foundation, State Business Tax Climate Index 2018

TRANSPORTATION

Means of Transportation to Work

Area	Car/Truck/Van		Public Transportation			Bicycle	Walked	Other Means	Worked at Home
	Drove Alone	Car-pooled	Bus	Subway	Railroad				
City	79.5	5.6	2.8	0.2	0.1	0.2	7.3	0.5	3.8
MSA[1]	80.7	8.4	2.6	0.2	0.0	0.4	3.8	0.8	3.2
U.S.	76.4	9.3	2.6	1.9	0.6	0.6	2.8	1.3	4.6

Note: Figures are percentages and cover workers 16 years of age and older; (1) Figures cover the Binghamton, NY Metropolitan Statistical Area—see Appendix B for areas included
Source: U.S. Census Bureau, 2012-2016 American Community Survey 5-Year Estimates

Travel Time to Work

Area	Less Than 10 Minutes	10 to 19 Minutes	20 to 29 Minutes	30 to 44 Minutes	45 to 59 Minutes	60 to 89 Minutes	90 Minutes or More
City	16.9	49.2	22.4	5.8	1.1	2.1	2.3
MSA[1]	17.3	40.0	22.9	12.1	3.2	2.7	1.8
U.S.	12.9	29.2	20.9	20.4	8.0	6.0	2.7

Note: Note: Figures are percentages and include workers 16 years old and over; (1) Figures cover the Binghamton, NY Metropolitan Statistical Area—see Appendix B for areas included
Source: U.S. Census Bureau, 2012-2016 American Community Survey 5-Year Estimates

Freeway Travel Time Index

Area	1985	1990	1995	2000	2005	2010	2014
Urban Area Rank[1,2]	n/a	n/a	n/a	n/a	n/a	n/a	n/a
Urban Area Index[1]	n/a	n/a	n/a	n/a	n/a	n/a	n/a
Average Index[3]	1.09	1.11	1.14	1.17	1.20	1.19	1.20

Note: Freeway Travel Time Index—the ratio of travel time in the peak period to the travel time at free-flow conditions. For example, a value of 1.30 indicates a 20-minute free-flow trip takes 26 minutes in the peak (20 minutes x 1.30 = 26 minutes); (1) Data for the Binghamton, NY urban area was not available; (2) Rank is based on 101 urban areas (#1 = highest travel time index); (3) Average of 101 urban areas
Source: Texas Transportation Institute, 2015 Urban Mobility Scorecard, August 2015

Freeway Commuter Stress Index

Area	1985	1990	1995	2000	2005	2010	2014
Urban Area Rank[1,2]	n/a	n/a	n/a	n/a	n/a	n/a	n/a
Urban Area Index[1]	n/a	n/a	n/a	n/a	n/a	n/a	n/a
Average Index[3]	1.13	1.16	1.19	1.22	1.25	1.24	1.25

Note: The Freeway Commuter Stress Index is the same as the Freeway Travel Time Index (see table above) except that it includes only the travel in the peak directions during the peak periods; the TTI includes travel in all directions during the peak period. Thus, the CSI is more indicative of the work trip experienced by each commuter on a daily basis; (1) Data for the Binghamton, NY urban area was not available; (2) Rank is based on 101 urban areas (#1 = highest travel time index); (3) Average of 101 urban areas
Source: Texas Transportation Institute, 2015 Urban Mobility Scorecard, August 2015

Living Environment

COST OF LIVING

Cost of Living Index

Composite Index	Groceries	Housing	Utilities	Transportation	Health Care	Misc. Goods/ Services
n/a	n/a	n/a	n/a	n/a	n/a	n/a

Note: The Cost of Living Index measures regional differences in the cost of consumer goods and services, excluding taxes and non-consumer expenditures, for professional and managerial households in the top income quintile. It is based on more than 50,000 prices covering almost 60 different items for which prices are collected three times a year by chambers of commerce, economic development organizations or university applied economic centers in each participating urban area. The numbers shown should be read as a percentage above or below the national average of 100. For example, a value of 115.4 in the groceries column indicates that grocery prices are 15.4% higher than the national average. Small differences in the index numbers should not be interpreted as significant; n/a not available.
Source: The Council for Community and Economic Research, ACCRA Cost of Living Index, 2017

Grocery Prices

Area[1]	T-Bone Steak ($/pound)	Frying Chicken ($/pound)	Whole Milk ($/half gal.)	Eggs ($/dozen)	Orange Juice ($/64 oz.)	Coffee ($/11.5 oz.)
City[2]	n/a	n/a	n/a	n/a	n/a	n/a
Avg.	11.29	1.40	2.02	1.47	3.55	4.37
Min.	7.71	0.93	1.04	0.70	2.86	3.24
Max.	15.83	2.39	4.03	3.92	6.29	8.16

Note: (1) Values for the local area are compared with the average, minimum and maximum values for all 294 areas in the Cost of Living Index; (2) Figures cover the Vestal NY urban area; n/a not available; ***T-Bone Steak*** *(price per pound);* ***Frying Chicken*** *(price per pound, whole fryer);* ***Whole Milk*** *(half gallon carton);* ***Eggs*** *(price per dozen, Grade A, large);* ***Orange Juice*** *(64 oz. Tropicana or Florida Natural);* ***Coffee*** *(11.5 oz. can, vacuum-packed, Maxwell House, Hills Bros, or Folgers).*
Source: The Council for Community and Economic Research, ACCRA Cost of Living Index, 2017

Housing and Utility Costs

Area[1]	New Home Price ($)	Apartment Rent ($/month)	All Electric ($/month)	Part Electric ($/month)	Other Energy ($/month)	Telephone ($/month)
City[2]	n/a	n/a	n/a	n/a	n/a	n/a
Avg.	335,956	1,047	175.01	97.34	67.93	28.71
Min.	187,788	491	109.48	49.33	35.44	12.39
Max.	1,739,087	4,559	432.62	227.09	353.33	44.61

Note: (1) Values for the local area are compared with the average, minimum and maximum values for all 294 areas in the Cost of Living Index; (2) Figures cover the Vestal NY urban area; n/a not available; ***New Home Price*** *(2,400 sf living area, 8,000 sf lot, in urban area with full utilities);* ***Apartment Rent*** *(950 sf 2 bedroom/1.5 or 2 bath, unfurnished, excluding all utilities except water);* ***All Electric*** *(average monthly cost for an all-electric home);* ***Part Electric*** *(average monthly cost for a part-electric home);* ***Other Energy*** *(average monthly cost for natural gas, fuel oil, coal, wood, and any other forms of energy except electricity);* ***Telephone*** *(price includes basic monthly rate for a private residential line plus additional local usage charges incurred by a family of four).*
Source: The Council for Community and Economic Research, ACCRA Cost of Living Index, 2017

Health Care, Transportation, and Other Costs

Area[1]	Doctor ($/visit)	Dentist ($/visit)	Optometrist ($/visit)	Gasoline ($/gallon)	Beauty Salon ($/visit)	Men's Shirt ($)
City[2]	n/a	n/a	n/a	n/a	n/a	n/a
Avg.	108.00	92.54	101.93	2.25	37.58	30.92
Min.	30.39	60.00	49.75	1.82	16.11	11.20
Max.	193.50	161.94	229.28	3.16	77.35	59.13

Note: (1) Values for the local area are compared with the average, minimum and maximum values for all 294 areas in the Cost of Living Index; (2) Figures cover the Vestal NY urban area; n/a not available; ***Doctor*** *(general practitioners routine exam of an established patient);* ***Dentist*** *(adult teeth cleaning and periodic oral examination);* ***Optometrist*** *(full vision eye exam for established adult patient);* ***Gasoline*** *(one gallon regular unleaded, national brand, including all taxes, cash price at self-service pump if available);* ***Beauty Salon*** *(woman's shampoo, trim, and blow-dry);* ***Men's Shirt*** *(cotton/polyester dress shirt, pinpoint weave, long sleeves).*
Source: The Council for Community and Economic Research, ACCRA Cost of Living Index, 2017

HOUSING

House Price Index (HPI)

Area	National Ranking[2]	Quarterly Change (%)	One-Year Change (%)	Five-Year Change (%)
MSA[1]	(a)	n/a	2.16	1.50
U.S.[3]	–	1.61	6.68	34.71

Note: The HPI is a weighted repeat sales index. It measures average price changes in repeat sales or refinancings on the same properties. This information is obtained by reviewing repeat mortgage transactions on single-family properties whose mortgages have been purchased or securitized by Fannie Mae or Freddie Mac in January 1975; (1) Figures cover the Binghamton, NY Metropolitan Statistical Area—see Appendix B for areas included; (2) Rankings are based on annual percentage change for all metro areas containing at least 15,000 transactions over the last 10 years and ranges from 1 to 253; (3) figures based on a weighted average of Census Division estimates using a seasonally adjusted, purchase-only index; all figures are for the period ending December 31, 2017; n/a not available; (a) Not ranked because of increased index variability due to smaller sample size

Source: Federal Housing Finance Agency, House Price Index, February 28, 2018

Median Single-Family Home Prices

Area	2015	2016	2017p	Percent Change 2016 to 2017
MSA[1]	113.0	108.4	109.6	1.1
U.S. Average	223.9	235.5	248.8	5.6

Note: Figures are median sales prices of existing single-family homes in thousands of dollars; (p) preliminary; (1) Figures cover the Binghamton, NY Metropolitan Statistical Area—see Appendix B for areas included

Source: National Association of Realtors, Median Sales Price of Existing Single-Family Homes for Metropolitan Areas, 4th Quarter 2017

Qualifying Income Based on Median Sales Price of Existing Single-Family Homes

Area	With 5% Down ($)	With 10% Down ($)	With 20% Down ($)
MSA[1]	24,428	23,142	20,571
U.S. Average	55,585	52,659	46,808

Note: Figures are preliminary; Qualifying income is based on a mortgage rate of 4.17%. Monthly principal and interest payment is limited to 25% of income; (1) Figures cover the Binghamton, NY Metropolitan Statistical Area—see Appendix B for areas included

Source: National Association of Realtors, Qualifying Income Based on Median Sales Price of Existing Single-Family Homes for Metropolitan Areas, 4th Quarter 2017

Median Apartment Condo-Coop Home Prices

Area	2015	2016	2017p	Percent Change 2016 to 2017
MSA[1]	n/a	n/a	n/a	n/a
U.S. Average	210.7	220.7	234.3	6.2

Note: Figures are median sales prices of existing apartment condo-coop homes in thousands of dollars; (p) preliminary; n/a not available; (1) Figures cover the Binghamton, NY Metropolitan Statistical Area—see Appendix B for areas included

Source: National Association of Realtors, Median Sales Price of Existing Apartment Condo-Coop Homes for Metropolitan Areas, 4th Quarter 2017

Home Value Distribution

Area	Under $50,000	$50,000 -$99,999	$100,000 -$149,999	$150,000 -$199,999	$200,000 -$299,999	$300,000 -$499,999	$500,000 -$999,999	$1,000,000 or more
City	4.8	19.1	27.2	21.4	16.3	8.1	2.4	0.6
MSA[1]	10.1	32.4	26.0	15.8	10.5	3.6	1.2	0.3
U.S.	8.8	14.8	15.3	14.9	18.4	16.4	9.0	2.5

Note: Figures are percentages and cover owner-occupied housing units; (1) Figures cover the Binghamton, NY Metropolitan Statistical Area—see Appendix B for areas included

Source: U.S. Census Bureau, 2012-2016 American Community Survey 5-Year Estimates

Homeownership Rate

Area	2009 (%)	2010 (%)	2011 (%)	2012 (%)	2013 (%)	2014 (%)	2015 (%)	2016 (%)	2017 (%)
MSA[1]	n/a	n/a	n/a	n/a	n/a	n/a	n/a	n/a	n/a
U.S.	67.4	66.9	66.1	65.4	65.1	64.5	63.7	63.4	63.9

Note: (1) Figures cover the Binghamton, NY Metropolitan Statistical Area—see Appendix B for areas included; n/a not available

Source: U.S. Census Bureau, Housing Vacancies and Homeownership Annual Statistics: 2009-2017

Year Housing Structure Built

Area	2010 or Later	2000 -2009	1990 -1999	1980 -1989	1970 -1979	1960 -1969	1950 -1959	1940 -1949	Before 1940	Median Year
City	1.6	5.3	8.1	9.5	16.3	18.7	20.8	7.5	12.1	1965
MSA[1]	1.1	4.3	6.6	10.3	11.0	13.0	14.1	9.1	30.5	1957
U.S.	2.3	14.7	14.0	13.7	15.6	10.9	10.6	5.2	13.0	1977

Note: Figures are percentages except for Median Year; Note: (1) Figures cover the Binghamton, NY Metropolitan Statistical Area—see Appendix B for areas included
Source: U.S. Census Bureau, 2012-2016 American Community Survey 5-Year Estimates

Gross Monthly Rent

Area	Under $500	$500 -$999	$1,000 -$1,499	$1,500 -$1,999	$2,000 -$2,499	$2,500 -$2,999	$3,000 and up	Median ($)
City	9.2	53.5	22.4	7.0	0.6	2.5	4.8	906
MSA[1]	16.4	67.2	12.5	2.4	0.5	0.3	0.7	709
U.S.	11.3	43.3	27.7	10.7	4.0	1.6	1.5	949

Note: Figures are percentages except for Median; Gross rent is the contract rent plus the estimated average monthly cost of utilities (electricity, gas, and water and sewer) and fuels (oil, coal, kerosene, wood, etc.) if these are paid by the renter (or paid for the renter by someone else); (1) Figures cover the Binghamton, NY Metropolitan Statistical Area—see Appendix B for areas included
Source: U.S. Census Bureau, 2012-2016 American Community Survey 5-Year Estimates

HEALTH

Health Risk Factors

Category	MSA[1] (%)	U.S. (%)
Adults aged 18–64 who have any kind of health care coverage	93.7	87.7
Adults who reported being in good or excellent health	80.8	83.6
Adults who are current smokers	23.3	17.1
Adults who currently use E-cigarettes	3.5	4.7
Adults who currently use chewing tobacco, snuff, or snus	4.1	4.0
Adults who are heavy drinkers[2]	10.1	6.5
Adults who are binge drinkers[3]	18.9	16.9
Adults who are overweight (BMI 25.0 - 29.9)	29.7	35.3
Adults who are obese (BMI 30.0 - 99.8)	30.0	29.9
Adults who participated in any physical activities in the past month	74.0	76.9
Adults who always or nearly always wears a seat belt	94.1	94.3

Note: (1) Figures cover the Binghamton, NY Metropolitan Statistical Area—see Appendix B for areas included; (2) Heavy drinkers are classified as adult men having more than 14 drinks per week and adult women having more than 7 drinks per week; (3) Binge drinkers are classified as males having five or more drinks on one occasion or females having four or more drinks on one occasion
Source: Centers for Disease Control and Prevention, Behaviorial Risk Factor Surveillance System, SMART: Selected Metropolitan Area Risk Trends, 2016

Health Screening Rates

Category	MSA[1] (%)	U.S. (%)
Adults 50-75 who have had a blood stool test within the past year	4.4	8.0
Adults 50-75 who have had a colonoscopy in the past 10 years	70.7	63.5
Adults aged 65+ who have had flu shot within the past year	58.5	58.6
Adults aged 65+ who have ever had a pneumonia vaccination	72.2	73.4
Adults who have ever been tested for HIV	37.3	35.6
Women aged 21-65 who have had a pap test in the past three years	80.8	79.8
Men aged 40+ who have had a PSA test within the past two years	35.9	39.5
Women aged 40+ who have had a mammogram within the past two years	72.7	72.5

Note: n/a not available; (1) Figures cover the Binghamton, NY Metropolitan Statistical Area—see Appendix B for areas included; Source: Centers for Disease Control and Prevention, Behaviorial Risk Factor Surveillance System, SMART: Selected Metropolitan Area Risk Trends, 2016

Chronic Health Conditions

Category	MSA[1] (%)	U.S. (%)
Adults who have ever been told they had a heart attack	5.5	4.4
Adults who have ever been told they have angina or coronary heart disease	6.0	4.1
Adults who have ever been told they had a stroke	3.3	3.1
Adults who have been told they currently have asthma	11.5	9.3
Adults who have ever been told they have arthritis	31.4	25.8
Adults who have ever been told they have diabetes[2]	10.5	10.5
Adults who have ever been told they had skin cancer	5.2	5.9
Adults who have ever been told they had any other types of cancer	9.2	6.7
Adults who have ever been told they have COPD	7.9	6.3
Adults who have ever been told they have kidney disease	2.8	2.8
Adults who have ever been told they have a form of depression	14.3	17.4

Note: (1) Figures cover the Binghamton, NY Metropolitan Statistical Area—see Appendix B for areas included; (2) Figures do not include pregnancy-related, borderline, or pre-diabetes
Source: Centers for Disease Control and Prevention, Behaviorial Risk Factor Surveillance System, SMART: Selected Metropolitan Area Risk Trends, 2016

Mortality Rates for the Top 10 Causes of Death in the U.S.

ICD-10[a] Sub-Chapter	ICD-10[a] Code	Age-Adjusted Mortality Rate[1] per 100,000 population	
		County[2]	U.S.
Malignant neoplasms	C00-C97	162.3	158.5
Ischaemic heart diseases	I20-I25	101.5	96.8
Other forms of heart disease	I30-I51	56.6	52.4
Chronic lower respiratory diseases	J40-J47	40.5	40.9
Cerebrovascular diseases	I60-I69	27.8	37.2
Organic, including symptomatic, mental disorders	F01-F09	36.5	33.3
Other degenerative diseases of the nervous system	G30-G31	23.9	32.1
Other external causes of accidental injury	W00-X59	42.6	31.2
Diabetes mellitus	E10-E14	20.6	21.1
Hypertensive diseases	I10-I15	20.3	20.8

Note: (a) ICD-10 = International Classification of Diseases 10th Revision; (1) Mortality rates are a three year average covering 2014-2016; (2) Figures cover Broome County.
Source: Centers for Disease Control and Prevention, National Center for Health Statistics. Underlying Cause of Death 1999-2016 on CDC WONDER Online Database, released December 2017

Mortality Rates for Selected Causes of Death

ICD-10[a] Sub-Chapter	ICD-10[a] Code	Age-Adjusted Mortality Rate[1] per 100,000 population	
		County[2]	U.S.
Assault	X85-Y09	Unreliable	5.6
Diseases of the liver	K70-K76	17.0	14.0
Human immunodeficiency virus (HIV) disease	B20-B24	Unreliable	1.9
Influenza and pneumonia	J09-J18	15.8	14.6
Intentional self-harm	X60-X84	12.2	13.2
Malnutrition	E40-E46	Unreliable	1.3
Obesity and other hyperalimentation	E65-E68	4.2	2.1
Renal failure	N17-N19	12.0	13.0
Transport accidents	V01-V99	7.9	12.0
Viral hepatitis	B15-B19	Unreliable	1.9

Note: (a) ICD-10 = International Classification of Diseases 10th Revision; (1) Mortality rates are a three year average covering 2014-2016; (2) Figures cover Broome County; Data are Suppressed when the data meet the criteria for confidentiality constraints; Mortality rates are flagged as Unreliable when the rate would be calculated with a numerator of 20 or less.
Source: Centers for Disease Control and Prevention, National Center for Health Statistics. Underlying Cause of Death 1999-2016 on CDC WONDER Online Database, released December 2017

Health Insurance Coverage

Area	With Health Insurance	With Private Health Insurance	With Public Health Insurance	Without Health Insurance	Population Under Age 18 Without Health Insurance
City	97.2	85.6	26.5	2.8	2.1
MSA[1]	94.1	69.6	39.8	5.9	3.3
U.S.	88.3	66.7	33.0	11.7	5.9

Note: Figures are percentages that cover the civilian noninstitutionalized population; (1) Figures cover the Binghamton, NY Metropolitan Statistical Area—see Appendix B for areas included
Source: U.S. Census Bureau, 2012-2016 American Community Survey 5-Year Estimates

Number of Medical Professionals

Area	MDs[3]	DOs[3,4]	Dentists	Podiatrists	Chiropractors	Optometrists
County[1] (number)	515	67	133	34	42	33
County[1] (rate[2])	262.4	34.1	68.3	17.5	21.6	16.9
U.S. (rate[2])	276.5	22.3	67.3	6.0	26.7	15.9

Note: Data as of 2016 unless noted; (1) Data covers Broome County; (2) Rate per 100,000 population; (3) Data as of 2015 and includes all active, non-federal physicians; (4) Doctor of Osteopathic Medicine
Source: U.S. Department of Health and Human Services, Health Resources and Services Administration, Bureau of Health Professions, Area Resource File (ARF) 2016-2017

EDUCATION

Public School District Statistics

District Name	Schls	Pupils	Pupil/ Teacher Ratio	Minority Pupils[1] (%)	Free Lunch Eligible[2] (%)	IEP[3] (%)
Vestal Central School District	7	3,353	12.3	17.6	20.7	14.0

Note: Table includes school districts with 100 or more students; (1) Percentage of students that are not non-Hispanic white; (2) Percentage of students that are eligible for the free lunch program; (3) Percentage of students that have an Individualized Education Program.
Source: U.S. Department of Education, National Center for Education Statistics, Common Core of Data, Local Education Agency (School District) Universe Survey: School Year 2015-2016; U.S. Department of Education, National Center for Education Statistics, Common Core of Data, Public Elementary/Secondary School Universe Survey: School Year 2015-2016

Highest Level of Education

Area	Less than H.S.	H.S. Diploma	Some College, No Deg.	Associate Degree	Bachelor's Degree	Master's Degree	Prof. School Degree	Doctorate Degree
City	4.2	22.5	16.7	12.4	21.2	16.0	3.6	3.3
MSA[1]	9.8	32.6	18.2	12.2	15.4	8.9	1.5	1.3
U.S.	13.0	27.5	21.0	8.2	18.8	8.2	2.0	1.3

Note: Figures cover persons age 25 and over; (1) Figures cover the Binghamton, NY Metropolitan Statistical Area—see Appendix B for areas included
Source: U.S. Census Bureau, 2012-2016 American Community Survey 5-Year Estimates

Educational Attainment by Race

Area	High School Graduate or Higher (%)					Bachelor's Degree or Higher (%)				
	Total	White	Black	Asian	Hisp.[2]	Total	White	Black	Asian	Hisp.[2]
City	95.8	96.2	89.6	93.5	97.3	44.1	42.0	37.4	72.9	52.8
MSA[1]	90.2	91.1	79.7	84.1	76.3	27.2	27.1	15.9	54.5	21.4
U.S.	87.0	88.9	84.3	86.3	65.7	30.3	31.6	20.0	52.1	14.7

Note: Figures shown cover persons 25 years old and over; (1) Figures cover the Binghamton, NY Metropolitan Statistical Area—see Appendix B for areas included; (2) People of Hispanic origin can be of any race
Source: U.S. Census Bureau, 2012-2016 American Community Survey 5-Year Estimates

School Enrollment by Grade and Control

Area	Preschool (%)		Kindergarten (%)		Grades 1 - 4 (%)		Grades 5 - 8 (%)		Grades 9 - 12 (%)	
	Public	Private	Public	Private	Public	Private	Public	Private	Public	Private
City	61.9	38.1	91.8	8.2	96.2	3.8	98.7	1.3	88.5	11.5
MSA[1]	74.1	25.9	90.9	9.1	91.9	8.1	94.0	6.0	93.8	6.2
U.S.	58.4	41.6	87.7	12.3	89.8	10.2	89.7	10.3	90.4	9.6

Note: Figures shown cover persons 3 years old and over; (1) Figures cover the Binghamton, NY Metropolitan Statistical Area—see Appendix B for areas included
Source: U.S. Census Bureau, 2012-2016 American Community Survey 5-Year Estimates

Average Salaries of Public School Classroom Teachers

Area	2015 Dollars	2015 Rank[1]	2016 Dollars	2016 Rank[1]	Change from 2015 to 2016 Percent	Change from 2015 to 2016 Rank[2]
New York	77,628	1	79,152	1	2.0	12
U.S. Average	57,611	–	58,353	–	1.3	–

Note: (1) Rank ranges from 1 to 51 where 1 indicates highest salary; (2) Rank ranges from 1 to 51 where 1 indicates highest percent change.
Source: National Education Association, Rankings & Estimates: Rankings of the States 2016 and Estimates of School Statistics 2017

Higher Education

Four-Year Colleges			Two-Year Colleges			Medical Schools[1]	Law Schools[2]	Voc/ Tech[3]
Public	Private Non-profit	Private For-profit	Public	Private Non-profit	Private For-profit			
1	0	0	0	0	0	0	0	0

Note: Figures cover institutions located within the city limits and include main campuses only; (1) includes schools accredited by the Liaison Committee on Medical Education and the American Osteopathic Association's Commission on Osteopathic College Accreditation; (2) includes ABA-accredited schools, schools with provisional ABA accreditation, and state accredited schools; (3) includes all schools with programs that are less than 2 years.
Source: National Center for Education Statistics, Integrated Postsecondary Education System (IPEDS), 2016-17; Wikipedia, List of Medical Schools in the United States, accessed April 2, 2018; Wikipedia, List of Law Schools in the United States, accessed April 2, 2018

According to *U.S. News & World Report,* the Binghamton, NY metro area is home to one of the best national universities in the U.S.: **Binghamton University—SUNY** (#87 tie). The indicators used to capture academic quality fall into a number of categories: assessment by administrators at peer institutions; retention of students; faculty resources; student selectivity; financial resources; alumni giving; high school counselor ratings of colleges; and graduation rate. *U.S. News & World Report, "America's Best Colleges 2018"*

PRESIDENTIAL ELECTION

2016 Presidential Election Results

Area	Clinton	Trump	Johnson	Stein	Other
Broome County	45.6	47.6	3.8	1.8	1.3
U.S.	48.0	45.9	3.3	1.1	1.7

Note: Results are percentages and may not add to 100% due to rounding
Source: Dave Leip's Atlas of U.S. Presidential Elections

EMPLOYERS

Major Employers

Company Name	Industry
BAE Systems	Manufacturing
Binghamton University	Public university
Broome County Government	Local government
Broome Developmental Center	Social assistance
Broome-Tioga BOCES	Local government
Endicott Interconnect Technologies	Manufacturing
Hitachi Metals Automotive Components	Automotive components
Lockheed Martin	Manufacturing
Lourdes Hospital	Health care
Maines Paper and Food Service	Wholesale trade
New York State Government	State government
Northern Tioga School District	School district
Southern Tioga School District	School district
Susquehanna Health System	Health care
United Health Services	Health care
Ward Manufacturing	Manufacturing

Note: Companies shown are located within the Binghamton, NY Metropolitan Statistical Area.
Source: Hoovers.com; Wikipedia

PUBLIC SAFETY

Crime Rate

Area	All Crimes	Violent Crimes				Property Crimes		
		Murder	Rape[3]	Robbery	Aggrav. Assault	Burglary	Larceny -Theft	Motor Vehicle Theft
City	1,773.3	0.0	14.2	21.2	21.2	120.3	1,571.5	24.8
Metro[1]	2,416.9	2.5	62.9	60.0	164.0	438.9	1,602.8	85.9
U.S.	2,847.8	5.3	40.4	102.8	248.5	468.9	1,745.0	236.9

Note: Figures are crimes per 100,000 population; (1) Figures cover the Binghamton, NY Metropolitan Statistical Area—see Appendix B for areas included; (3) The city and U.S. figures shown were reported using the revised Uniform Crime Reporting (UCR) definition of rape. The metro area figures shown are an aggregate total of the data submitted using both the revised and legacy UCR definitions.
Source: FBI Uniform Crime Reports, 2016

Hate Crimes

Area	Number of Quarters Reported	Number of Incidents per Bias Motivation					
		Race/Ethnicity/ Ancestry	Religion	Sexual Orientation	Disability	Gender	Gender Identity
Area[1]	4	0	0	0	0	0	0
U.S.	4	3,489	1,273	1,076	70	31	124

Note: (1) Figures cover the Vestal Town.
Source: Federal Bureau of Investigation, Hate Crime Statistics 2016

Identity Theft Consumer Reports

Area	Reports	Reports per 100,000 Population	Rank[2]
MSA[1]	119	49	362
U.S.	371,061	114	-

Note: (1) Figures cover the Binghamton, NY Metropolitan Statistical Area—see Appendix B for areas included; (2) Rank ranges from 1 to 389 where 1 indicates greatest number of identity theft reports per 100,000 population
Source: Federal Trade Commission, Consumer Sentinel Network Data Book for January–December 2017

Fraud and Other Consumer Reports

Area	Reports	Reports per 100,000 Population	Rank[2]
MSA[1]	1,068	438	196
U.S.	2,304,550	708	-

Note: (1) Figures cover the Binghamton, NY Metropolitan Statistical Area—see Appendix B for areas included; (2) Rank ranges from 1 to 389 where 1 indicates greatest number of fraud and other consumer reports per 100,000 population
Source: Federal Trade Commission, Consumer Sentinel Network Data Book for January–December 2017

SPORTS

Professional Sports Teams

Team Name	League	Year Established
No teams are located in the metro area		

Source: Wikipedia, Major Professional Sports Teams of the United States and Canada, April 5, 2018

CLIMATE

Average and Extreme Temperatures

Temperature	Jan	Feb	Mar	Apr	May	Jun	Jul	Aug	Sep	Oct	Nov	Dec	Yr.
Extreme High (°F)	69	66	82	88	89	94	98	98	96	87	80	65	98
Average High (°F)	29	31	40	54	66	74	79	77	69	58	45	33	55
Average Temp. (°F)	22	24	32	45	56	65	70	68	60	49	38	27	46
Average Low (°F)	15	16	24	35	46	55	60	58	50	40	31	20	38
Extreme Low (°F)	-26	-25	-14	9	25	33	39	37	25	17	3	-18	-26

Note: Figures cover the years 1948-1995
Source: National Climatic Data Center, International Station Meteorological Climate Summary, 9/96

Average Precipitation/Snowfall/Humidity

Precip./Humidity	Jan	Feb	Mar	Apr	May	Jun	Jul	Aug	Sep	Oct	Nov	Dec	Yr.
Avg. Precip. (in.)	2.4	2.3	2.9	3.3	3.3	3.6	3.6	3.5	3.2	2.9	3.2	2.9	37.1
Avg. Snowfall (in.)	19	17	14	5	Tr	0	0	0	Tr	1	8	18	81
Avg. Rel. Hum. 7am (%)	80	79	79	76	78	83	85	89	90	85	82	82	82
Avg. Rel. Hum. 4pm (%)	69	65	60	54	54	57	57	59	62	60	68	72	61

Note: Figures cover the years 1948-1995; Tr = Trace amounts (<0.05 in. of rain; <0.5 in. of snow)
Source: National Climatic Data Center, International Station Meteorological Climate Summary, 9/96

Weather Conditions

Temperature			Daytime Sky			Precipitation		
5°F & below	32°F & below	90°F & above	Clear	Partly cloudy	Cloudy	0.01 inch or more precip.	0.1 inch or more snow/ice	Thunder-storms
17	145	3	53	137	175	159	67	29

Note: Figures are average number of days per year and cover the years 1948-1995
Source: National Climatic Data Center, International Station Meteorological Climate Summary, 9/96

HAZARDOUS WASTE

Superfund Sites

The Binghamton, NY metro area is home to five sites on the EPA's Superfund National Priorities List: **Colesville Municipal Landfill** (final); **Endicott Village Well Field** (final); **Robintech, Inc./National Pipe Co.** (final); **Tri-cities Barrel Co., Inc.** (final); **Vestal Water Supply Well 1-1** (final). There are a total of 1,396 Superfund sites with a status of proposed or final on the list in the U.S. *U.S. Environmental Protection Agency, National Priorities List, April 4, 2018*

AIR & WATER QUALITY

Air Quality Trends: Ozone

	1990	1995	2000	2005	2010	2012	2013	2014	2015	2016
MSA[1]	n/a	n/a	n/a	n/a	n/a	n/a	n/a	n/a	n/a	n/a
U.S.	0.087	0.089	0.081	0.079	0.073	0.075	0.069	0.067	0.068	0.069

Note: (1) Data covers the Binghamton, NY Metropolitan Statistical Area—see Appendix B for areas included; n/a not available. The values shown are the composite ozone concentration averages among trend sites based on the highest fourth daily maximum 8-hour concentration in parts per million. These trends are based on sites having an adequate record of monitoring data during the trend period. Data from exceptional events are included.
Source: U.S. Environmental Protection Agency, Air Quality Monitoring Information, "Air Quality Trends by City, 1990-2016"

Air Quality Index

Area	Percent of Days when Air Quality was...[2]					AQI Statistics[2]	
	Good	Moderate	Unhealthy for Sensitive Groups	Unhealthy	Very Unhealthy	Maximum	Median
MSA[1]	n/a	n/a	n/a	n/a	n/a	n/a	n/a

Note: (1) Data covers the Binghamton, NY Metropolitan Statistical Area—see Appendix B for areas included; (2) Based on days with AQI data in 2017. Air Quality Index (AQI) is an index for reporting daily air quality. EPA calculates the AQI for five major air pollutants regulated by the Clean Air Act: ground-level ozone, particle pollution (aka particulate matter), carbon monoxide, sulfur dioxide, and nitrogen dioxide. The AQI runs from 0 to 500. The higher the AQI value, the greater the level of air pollution and the greater the health concern. There are six AQI categories: "Good" AQI is between 0 and 50. Air quality is considered satisfactory; "Moderate" AQI is between 51 and 100. Air quality is acceptable; "Unhealthy for Sensitive Groups" When AQI values are between 101 and 150, members of sensitive groups may experience health effects; "Unhealthy" When AQI values are between 151 and 200 everyone may begin to experience health effects; "Very Unhealthy" AQI values between 201 and 300 trigger a health alert; "Hazardous" AQI values over 300 trigger warnings of emergency conditions (not shown).
Source: U.S. Environmental Protection Agency, Air Quality Index Report, 2017

Air Quality Index Pollutants

Area	Percent of Days when AQI Pollutant was...[2]					
	Carbon Monoxide	Nitrogen Dioxide	Ozone	Sulfur Dioxide	Particulate Matter 2.5	Particulate Matter 10
MSA[1]	n/a	n/a	n/a	n/a	n/a	n/a

Note: (1) Data covers the Binghamton, NY Metropolitan Statistical Area—see Appendix B for areas included; (2) Based on days with AQI data in 2017. The Air Quality Index (AQI) is an index for reporting daily air quality. EPA calculates the AQI for five major air pollutants regulated by the Clean Air Act: ground-level ozone, particle pollution (also known as particulate matter), carbon monoxide, sulfur dioxide, and nitrogen dioxide. The AQI runs from 0 to 500. The higher the AQI value, the greater the level of air pollution and the greater the health concern.
Source: U.S. Environmental Protection Agency, Air Quality Index Report, 2017

Maximum Air Pollutant Concentrations: Particulate Matter, Ozone, CO and Lead

	Particulate Matter 10 (ug/m^3)	Particulate Matter 2.5 Wtd AM (ug/m^3)	Particulate Matter 2.5 24-Hr (ug/m^3)	Ozone (ppm)	Carbon Monoxide (ppm)	Lead (ug/m^3)
MSA[1] Level	n/a	n/a	n/a	n/a	n/a	n/a
NAAQS[2]	150	15	35	0.075	9	0.15
Met NAAQS[2]	n/a	n/a	n/a	n/a	n/a	n/a

Note: (1) Data covers the Binghamton, NY Metropolitan Statistical Area—see Appendix B for areas included; Data from exceptional events are included; (2) National Ambient Air Quality Standards; ppm = parts per million; ug/m^3 = micrograms per cubic meter; n/a not available.
Concentrations: Particulate Matter 10 (coarse particulate)—highest second maximum 24-hour concentration; Particulate Matter 2.5 Wtd AM (fine particulate)—highest weighted annual mean concentration; Particulate Matter 2.5 24-Hour (fine particulate)—highest 98th percentile 24-hour concentration; Ozone—highest fourth daily maximum 8-hour concentration; Carbon Monoxide—highest second maximum non-overlapping 8-hour concentration; Lead—maximum running 3-month average
Source: U.S. Environmental Protection Agency, Air Quality Monitoring Information, "Air Quality Statistics by City, 2016"

Maximum Air Pollutant Concentrations: Nitrogen Dioxide and Sulfur Dioxide

	Nitrogen Dioxide AM (ppb)	Nitrogen Dioxide 1-Hr (ppb)	Sulfur Dioxide AM (ppb)	Sulfur Dioxide 1-Hr (ppb)	Sulfur Dioxide 24-Hr (ppb)
MSA[1] Level	n/a	n/a	n/a	n/a	n/a
NAAQS[2]	53	100	30	75	140
Met NAAQS[2]	n/a	n/a	n/a	n/a	n/a

Note: (1) Data covers the Binghamton, NY Metropolitan Statistical Area—see Appendix B for areas included; Data from exceptional events are included; (2) National Ambient Air Quality Standards; ppm = parts per million; ug/m^3 = micrograms per cubic meter; n/a not available.
Concentrations: Nitrogen Dioxide AM—highest arithmetic mean concentration; Nitrogen Dioxide 1-Hr—highest 98th percentile 1-hour daily maximum concentration; Sulfur Dioxide AM—highest annual mean concentration; Sulfur Dioxide 1-Hr—highest 99th percentile 1-hour daily maximum concentration; Sulfur Dioxide 24-Hr—highest second maximum 24-hour concentration
Source: U.S. Environmental Protection Agency, Air Quality Monitoring Information, "Air Quality Statistics by City, 2016"

Drinking Water

Water System Name	Pop. Served	Primary Water Source Type	Violations[1]	
			Health Based	Monitoring/ Reporting
Vestal Consolidated WD No. 1	20,950	Purchased Surface	0	0

Note: (1) Based on violation data from January 1, 2017 to December 31, 2017
Source: U.S. Environmental Protection Agency, Office of Ground Water and Drinking Water, Safe Drinking Water Information System (based on data extracted April 5, 2018)

Webster, New York

Background

Webster is located in northeastern New York, in Monroe County, five miles from Rochester. The town is bordered on the north by Lake Ontario and on the west by Irondequoit Bay.

The town of Webster took its name from orator and statesman, Daniel Webster. Webster spoke to an assembly of Whigs farmers in nearby Rochester in 1837. The group was so impressed with Webster that, when the town was separated from North Penfield in 1840, town officials chose to name it in Webster's honor.

Webster began as an agricultural community. With fertile soil and optimum growing conditions, the area was a flourishing fruit growing center. Some of those fruit farms are still in operation today. Over the years, Webster has transformed from a rural village to a growing town attractive to business development and high-tech industries. Xerox, Eastman Kodak, Bausch & Lomb, JP Morgan Chase, Verizon, and PayChex have operations in Webster or in the surrounding area.

The town of Webster values its natural resources and seeks to make these areas available for its residents to enjoy. The community's nature preserves, hiking trails, parks and community centers, along with Webster Park and its views of Lake Ontario are all popular destinations. Webster's many miles of natural shoreline make it a popular spot for swimming, boating and fishing. Additionally, the Webster Arboretum, located in Kent Park, showcases a variety of trees, shrubs and plants.

Webster's public schools are managed by the Webster Central School District, with seven elementary schools, two middle schools and two high schools. High school athletics are very popular in Webster, with award-winning teams in football, hockey and lacrosse, along with many state of the art athletic facilities. Webster is also home to a number of private and parochial schools.

Nearby institutions of higher learning include the University of Rochester, Rochester Institute of Technology, Saint John Fisher College, Nazareth College of Rochester and Monroe Community College.

The area is served by the following Rochester hospitals: Genesee Hospital, Rochester General Hospital and Highland Hospital, all roughly 10 miles from Webster.

The Greater Rochester International Airport is located within convenient driving distance to Webster.

Lake Ontario keeps temperatures in Webster five degrees warmer in winter and five degrees cooler in summer. Summers are generally comfortable, with moderate humidity, while fall brings cooler temperatures and brilliant foliage. Webster avoids many of the area's severe winter storms, due to its close proximity to the Lake.

Rankings

Business/Finance Rankings

- The personal finance site NerdWallet analyzed 183 American metropolitan areas with populations over 250,000 and more than 15,000 businesses to rank where entrepreneurs find the most success. Criteria included area economy, annual income, housing cost, unemployment rate, and the success rate of area businesses. Rochester* ranked #90. *www.nerdwallet.com, "Best Places to Start a Business," April 27, 2015*
- The Brookings Institution ranked the 100 largest metro areas in the U.S. based on income inequality. Rochester* was ranked #72 (#1 = greatest ineqality). Criteria: the "95/20 ratio," a figure representing the income at which a household earns more than 95 percent of all other households, divided by the income at which a household earns more than only 20 percent of all other households. *Brookings Institution, "Household Income Inequality, 100 Largest U.S. Metro Areas, 2014-2016," February 5, 2018*
- The Rochester* metro area appeared on the Milken Institute "2017 Best Performing Cities" list. Rank: #136 out of 200 large metro areas. Criteria: job growth; wage and salary growth; high-tech output growth. *Milken Institute, "Best-Performing Cities 2017," January 2018*
- *Forbes* ranked the 200 most populous metro areas to determine the nation's "Best Places for Business and Careers." The Rochester* metro area was ranked #121. Criteria: costs (business and living); job growth (past and projected); income growth; quality of life; educational attainment (college and high school); projected economic growth; cultural and recreational opportunities; net migration patterns; number of highly ranked colleges. *Forbes, "The Best Places for Business and Careers 2017," October 24, 2017*

Education Rankings

- Personal finance website *WalletHub* analyzed the 150 largest U.S. metropolitan statistical areas to determine where the most educated Americans are choosing to settle. Criteria: education quality and attainment gap; education levels; percentage of workers with degrees; public school rankings; quality and size of each metro area's universities. Rochester* was ranked #38 (#1 = most educated city). *www.WalletHub.com, "2017's Most and Least Educated Cities in America," July 25, 2017*

Environmental Rankings

- Sperling's BestPlaces assessed 379 metropolitan areas of the United States for the likelihood of dangerously extreme weather events or earthquakes. In general the Southeast and South-Central regions have the highest risk of weather extremes and earthquakes, while the Pacific Northwest enjoys the lowest risk. Of the least risky metropolitan areas, the Rochester* metro area was ranked #83. *www.bestplaces.net, "Safest Places from Natural Disasters," April 2011*
- Rochester* was highlighted as one of the top 99 cleanest metro areas for short-term particle pollution (24-hour PM 2.5) in the U.S. during 2013 through 2015. Monitors in these cities reported no days with unhealthful PM 2.5 levels. *American Lung Association, State of the Air 2017*

Food/Drink Rankings

- For the Gallup-Healthways Well-Being Index, researchers interviewed at least 300 adults in each of 189 metropolitan areas on residents' access to affordable fresh produce. The Rochester* metro area was found to be among the top ten communities for accessibility to affordable produce. *www.gallup.com, "In Anchorage, Access to Fruits and Vegetables Remains Lowest," April 8, 2014*

Health/Fitness Rankings

- Analysts who tracked obesity rates in the nation's largest metro areas (populations above one million) found that the Rochester* metro area was one of the ten major metros where residents were most likely to be obese, defined as a BMI score of 30 or above. *www.gallup.com, "Boulder, Colo., Residents Still Least Likely to Be Obese," April 4, 2014*
- Rochester* was identified as a "2016 Spring Allergy Capital." The area ranked #61 out of 100. Three groups of factors were used to identify the most severe cities for people with allergies during the spring season: annual pollen levels; medicine utilization; access to board-certified allergists. *Asthma and Allergy Foundation of America, "Spring Allergy Capitals 2016"*
- Rochester* was identified as a "2016 Fall Allergy Capital." The area ranked #45 out of 100. Three groups of factors were used to identify the most severe cities for people with allergies during the fall season: annual pollen levels; medicine utilization; access to board-certified allergists. *Asthma and Allergy Foundation of America, "Fall Allergy Capitals 2016"*
- Rochester* was identified as a "2015 Asthma Capital." The area ranked #89 out of the nation's 100 largest metropolitan areas. Criteria: estimated prevalence; self-reported prevalence; crude death rate for asthma; annual pollen score; annual air quality; public smoking laws; number of board-certified asthma specialists; school inhaler access laws; rescue medication use; controller medication use; ER visits for asthma; uninsured rate; poverty rate. *Asthma and Allergy Foundation of America, "Asthma Capitals 2015"*
- The Rochester* metro area ranked #94 out of 189 in The Gallup-Healthways Well-Being Index. Criteria: purpose; social well being; financial health; community and physical health. Results are based on telephone interviews with adults, aged 18 and older, living in metropolitan areas in the 50 U.S. states and the District of Columbia. *Gallup-Healthways, "State of American Well-Being, 2017 Community Well-Being Rankings" March 2018*

Real Estate Rankings

- FitSmallBusiness looked at 50 of the largest metropolitan areas in the U.S. to determine which metro was the best to start a real estate business. Data was compiled from such sources as: Zillow, Trulia, U.S. Census Bureau, and the Bureau of Labor Statistics. Criteria: location; inventory; annual wages; median sales price of homes; days on the market; median price cut percentage; and other factors that would influence real estate professional growth. The Rochester* metro area ranked #45. *fitsmallbusiness.com, "The Best Cities to Become a Real Estate Agent in 2018," January 30, 2018*
- The Rochester* metro area was identified as one of the 20 most affordable housing markets in the U.S. in 2017. The area ranked #20 out of 180 markets. Criteria: qualification for a mortgage loan on a typical home. *National Association of Realtors®, Affordability Index of Existing Single-Family Homes for Metropolitan Areas, 2017*
- Rochester* was ranked #43 out of 238 metro areas in terms of housing affordability in 2017 by the National Association of Home Builders (#1 = most affordable). Criteria: the share of homes sold in that area affordable to a family earning the local median income, based on standard mortgage underwriting criteria. *National Association of Home Builders®, NAHB-Wells Fargo Housing Opportunity Index, 4th Quarter 2017*

Safety Rankings

- The National Insurance Crime Bureau ranked 382 metro areas in the U.S. in terms of per capita rates of vehicle theft. The Rochester* metro area ranked #320 (#1 = highest rate). Criteria: number of vehicle theft offenses per 100,000 inhabitants in 2016. *National Insurance Crime Bureau, "Hot Spots 2016," June 8, 2017*

Seniors/Retirement Rankings

- From its Best Cities for Successful Aging indexes, the Milken Institute generated rankings for metropolitan areas, weighing data in nine categories—health care, wellness, living arrangements, transportation and convenience, financial characteristics, education, employment, community engagement, and overall livability. The Rochester* metro area was ranked #17 overall in the large metro area category. *Milken Institute, "Best Cities for Successful Aging, 2017" March 14, 2017*

  *Webster is located within the Rochester, NY Metropolitan Statistical Area.

Business Environment

CITY FINANCES

City Government Finances

Component	2015 ($000)	2015 ($ per capita)
Total Revenues	n/a	n/a
Total Expenditures	n/a	n/a
Debt Outstanding	n/a	n/a
Cash and Securities[1]	n/a	n/a

Note: (1) Cash and security holdings of a government at the close of its fiscal year,, including those of its dependent agencies, utilities, and liquor stores.
Source: U.S Census Bureau, State & Local Government Finances 2015

City Government Revenue by Source

Source	2015 ($000)	2015 ($ per capita)	2015 (%)
General Revenue			
From Federal Government	n/a	n/a	n/a
From State Government	n/a	n/a	n/a
From Local Governments	n/a	n/a	n/a
Taxes			
Property	n/a	n/a	n/a
Sales and Gross Receipts	n/a	n/a	n/a
Personal Income	n/a	n/a	n/a
Corporate Income	n/a	n/a	n/a
Motor Vehicle License	n/a	n/a	n/a
Other Taxes	n/a	n/a	n/a
Current Charges	n/a	n/a	n/a
Liquor Store	n/a	n/a	n/a
Utility	n/a	n/a	n/a
Employee Retirement	n/a	n/a	n/a

Source: U.S Census Bureau, State & Local Government Finances 2015

City Government Expenditures by Function

Function	2015 ($000)	2015 ($ per capita)	2015 (%)
General Direct Expenditures			
Air Transportation	n/a	n/a	n/a
Corrections	n/a	n/a	n/a
Education	n/a	n/a	n/a
Employment Security Administration	n/a	n/a	n/a
Financial Administration	n/a	n/a	n/a
Fire Protection	n/a	n/a	n/a
General Public Buildings	n/a	n/a	n/a
Governmental Administration, Other	n/a	n/a	n/a
Health	n/a	n/a	n/a
Highways	n/a	n/a	n/a
Hospitals	n/a	n/a	n/a
Housing and Community Development	n/a	n/a	n/a
Interest on General Debt	n/a	n/a	n/a
Judicial and Legal	n/a	n/a	n/a
Libraries	n/a	n/a	n/a
Parking	n/a	n/a	n/a
Parks and Recreation	n/a	n/a	n/a
Police Protection	n/a	n/a	n/a
Public Welfare	n/a	n/a	n/a
Sewerage	n/a	n/a	n/a
Solid Waste Management	n/a	n/a	n/a
Veterans' Services	n/a	n/a	n/a
Liquor Store	n/a	n/a	n/a
Utility	n/a	n/a	n/a
Employee Retirement	n/a	n/a	n/a

Source: U.S Census Bureau, State & Local Government Finances 2015

DEMOGRAPHICS

Population Growth

Area	1990 Census	2000 Census	2010 Census	2016* Estimate	Population Growth (%) 1990-2016	Population Growth (%) 2010-2016
City	31,639	37,926	42,641	44,084	39.3	3.4
MSA[1]	1,002,410	1,037,831	1,054,323	1,082,226	8.0	2.6
U.S.	248,709,873	281,421,906	308,745,538	318,558,162	28.1	3.2

Note: (1) Figures cover the Rochester, NY Metropolitan Statistical Area—see Appendix B for areas included; (*) 2012-2016 5-year estimated population
Source: U.S. Census Bureau, 1990 Census, Census 2000, Census 2010, 2012-2016 American Community Survey 5-Year Estimates

Household Size

Area	Persons in Household (%) One	Two	Three	Four	Five	Six	Seven or More	Average Household Size
City	26.5	36.8	14.6	14.8	4.9	1.3	1.0	2.50
MSA[1]	30.7	35.2	15.1	11.8	4.7	1.6	0.9	2.40
U.S.	27.7	33.7	15.7	13.1	6.0	2.3	1.5	2.60

Note: (1) Figures cover the Rochester, NY Metropolitan Statistical Area—see Appendix B for areas included
Source: U.S. Census Bureau, 2012-2016 American Community Survey 5-Year Estimates

Race

Area	White Alone[2] (%)	Black Alone[2] (%)	Asian Alone[2] (%)	AIAN[3] Alone[2] (%)	NHOPI[4] Alone[2] (%)	Other Race Alone[2] (%)	Two or More Races (%)
City	92.4	1.7	3.7	0.0	0.0	0.4	1.8
MSA[1]	81.3	11.5	2.8	0.4	0.0	1.6	2.4
U.S.	73.3	12.6	5.2	0.8	0.2	4.8	3.1

Note: (1) Figures cover the Rochester, NY Metropolitan Statistical Area—see Appendix B for areas included; (2) Alone is defined as not being in combination with one or more other races; (3) American Indian and Alaska Native; (4) Native Hawaiian and Other Pacific Islander
Source: U.S. Census Bureau, 2012-2016 American Community Survey 5-Year Estimates

Hispanic or Latino Origin

Area	Total (%)	Mexican (%)	Puerto Rican (%)	Cuban (%)	Other (%)
City	2.7	0.3	1.9	0.0	0.5
MSA[1]	6.8	0.7	4.5	0.3	1.3
U.S.	17.3	11.0	1.7	0.7	4.0

Note: Persons of Hispanic or Latino origin can be of any race; (1) Figures cover the Rochester, NY Metropolitan Statistical Area—see Appendix B for areas included
Source: U.S. Census Bureau, 2012-2016 American Community Survey 5-Year Estimates

Segregation

Type	Segregation Indices[1] 1990	2000	2010	2010 Rank[2]	Percent Change 1990-2000	1990-2010	2000-2010
Black/White	67.4	67.9	65.3	21	0.5	-2.0	-2.5
Asian/White	40.7	43.4	45.1	24	2.7	4.4	1.6
Hispanic/White	55.4	54.1	48.9	29	-1.3	-6.5	-5.1

Note: All figures cover the Metropolitan Statistical Area—see Appendix B for areas included; Figures are based on an analysis of 1990, 2000, and 2010 Census Decennial Census tract data by William H. Frey, Brookings Institution and the University of Michigan Social Science Data Analysis Network. In this analysis all racial groups (whites, blacks, and asians) are non-Hispanic members of those races. Hispanics are shown as a separate category; (1) Segregation Indices are Dissimilarity Indices that measure the degree to which the minority group is distributed differently than whites across census tracts. They range from 0 (complete integration) to 100 (complete segregation) where the value indicates the percentage of the minority group that needs to move to be distributed exactly like whites; (2) Ranges from 1 (most segregated) to 102 (least segregated); n/a not available.
Source: www.CensusScope.org

Ancestry

Area	German	Irish	English	American	Italian	Polish	French[2]	Scottish	Dutch
City	22.9	18.6	12.1	3.9	27.2	6.3	2.7	2.3	3.3
MSA[1]	20.4	16.0	12.0	4.9	16.4	5.0	3.1	2.0	3.6
U.S.	14.4	10.4	7.7	6.9	5.4	2.9	2.6	1.7	1.3

Note: Figures are the percentage of the total population reporting a particular ancestry. The nine most commonly reported ancestries in the U.S. are shown. Figures include multiple ancestries (e.g. if a person reported being Irish and Italian, they were included in both columns); (1) Figures cover the Rochester, NY Metropolitan Statistical Area—see Appendix B for areas included; (2) Excludes Basque
Source: U.S. Census Bureau, 2012-2016 American Community Survey 5-Year Estimates

Foreign-Born Population

Area	Percent of Population Born in								
	Any Foreign Country	Asia	Mexico	Europe	Carribean	Central America[2]	South America	Africa	Canada
City	10.1	4.2	0.1	4.7	0.1	0.1	0.3	0.1	0.5
MSA[1]	6.9	2.5	0.2	2.0	0.9	0.2	0.3	0.5	0.4
U.S.	13.2	4.0	3.6	1.5	1.3	1.0	0.9	0.6	0.3

Note: (1) Figures cover the Rochester, NY Metropolitan Statistical Area—see Appendix B for areas included; (2) Excludes Mexico.
Source: U.S. Census Bureau, 2012-2016 American Community Survey 5-Year Estimates

Marital Status

Area	Never Married	Now Married[2]	Separated	Widowed	Divorced
City	24.6	58.1	1.5	6.5	9.3
MSA[1]	35.2	45.8	2.3	6.2	10.6
U.S.	33.0	48.1	2.1	5.9	11.0

Note: Figures are percentages and cover the population 15 years of age and older; (1) Figures cover the Rochester, NY Metropolitan Statistical Area—see Appendix B for areas included; (2) Excludes separated
Source: U.S. Census Bureau, 2012-2016 American Community Survey 5-Year Estimates

Disability Status

Area	All Ages	Under 18 Years Old	18 to 64 Years Old	65 Years and Over
City	10.2	2.3	7.0	30.9
MSA[1]	13.2	5.6	11.0	32.6
U.S.	12.5	4.1	10.3	35.7

Note: Figures show percent of the civilian noninstitutionalized population that reported having a disability. Disability status is determined from six types of difficulty: vision, hearing, cognitive, ambulatory, self-care, and independent living. For children under 5 years old, hearing and vision difficulty are used to determine disability status. For children between the ages of 5 and 14, disability status is determined from hearing, vision, cognitive, ambulatory, and self-care difficulties. For people aged 15 years and older, they are considered to have a disability if they have difficulty with any one of the six difficulty types; Note: (1) Figures cover the Rochester, NY Metropolitan Statistical Area—see Appendix B for areas included
Source: U.S. Census Bureau, 2012-2016 American Community Survey 5-Year Estimates

Age

Area	Percent of Population									Median Age
	Under Age 5	Age 5–19	Age 20–34	Age 35–44	Age 45–54	Age 55–64	Age 65–74	Age 75–84	Age 85+	
City	6.0	18.0	16.7	11.8	15.7	14.2	9.5	5.1	3.0	43.0
MSA[1]	5.5	19.0	20.2	11.3	14.4	13.6	8.9	4.6	2.4	39.9
U.S.	6.2	19.6	20.7	12.7	13.6	12.6	8.3	4.3	1.9	37.7

Note: (1) Figures cover the Rochester, NY Metropolitan Statistical Area—see Appendix B for areas included
Source: U.S. Census Bureau, 2012-2016 American Community Survey 5-Year Estimates

Gender

Area	Males	Females	Males per 100 Females
City	20,994	23,090	90.9
MSA[1]	526,580	555,646	94.8
U.S.	156,765,322	161,792,840	96.9

Note: (1) Figures cover the Rochester, NY Metropolitan Statistical Area—see Appendix B for areas included
Source: U.S. Census Bureau, 2012-2016 American Community Survey 5-Year Estimates

Religious Groups by Family

Area	Catholic	Baptist	Non-Den.	Methodist[2]	Lutheran	LDS[3]	Pente-costal	Presby-terian[4]	Muslim[5]	Judaism
MSA[1]	24.1	2.8	4.1	3.2	1.8	0.6	0.6	2.3	0.9	1.0
U.S.	19.1	9.3	4.0	4.0	2.3	2.0	1.9	1.6	0.8	0.7

Note: Figures are the number of adherents as a percentage of the total population; (1) Figures cover the Rochester, NY Metropolitan Statistical Area—see Appendix B for areas included; (2) Methodist/Pietist; (3) Latter Day Saints; (4) Reformed; (5) Figures are estimates
Source: Association of Statisticians of American Religious Bodies, 2010 U.S. Religion Census: Religious Congregations & Membership Study

Religious Groups by Tradition

Area	Catholic	Evangelical Protestant	Mainline Protestant	Other Tradition	Black Protestant	Orthodox
MSA[1]	24.1	7.3	8.5	3.0	0.9	0.3
U.S.	19.1	16.2	7.3	4.3	1.6	0.3

Note: Figures are the number of adherents as a percentage of the total population; (1) Figures cover the Rochester, NY Metropolitan Statistical Area—see Appendix B for areas included
Source: Association of Statisticians of American Religious Bodies, 2010 U.S. Religion Census: Religious Congregations & Membership Study

ECONOMY

Gross Metropolitan Product

Area	2014	2015	2016	2017	Rank[2]
MSA[1]	52.9	54.4	55.5	57.4	55

Note: Figures are in billions of dollars; (1) Figures cover the Rochester, NY Metropolitan Statistical Area—see Appendix B for areas included; (2) Rank is based on 2015 data and ranges from 1 to 381
Source: The U.S. Conference of Mayors, U.S. Metro Economies: GMP and Employment Report, 2015-2017

Economic Growth

Area	2012-14 (%)	2015 (%)	2016 (%)	2017 (%)	Rank[2]
MSA[1]	-0.5	0.8	0.4	1.5	314
U.S.	2.0	2.4	1.9	2.6	–

Note: Figures are real gross metropolitan product (GMP) growth rates and represent average annual percent change; (1) Figures cover the Rochester, NY Metropolitan Statistical Area—see Appendix B for areas included; (2) Rank is based on 2012-2014 average annual percent change and ranges from 1 to 381
Source: The U.S. Conference of Mayors, U.S. Metro Economies: GMP and Employment Report, 2015-2017

Metropolitan Area Exports

Area	2011	2012	2013	2014	2015	2016	Rank[2]
MSA[1]	5,492.9	5,329.8	5,092.0	5,150.2	5,038.4	4,627.5	56

Note: Figures are in millions of dollars; (1) Figures cover the Rochester, NY Metropolitan Statistical Area—see Appendix B for areas included; (2) Rank is based on 2016 data and ranges from 1 to 385
Source: U.S. Department of Commerce, International Trade Administration, Office of Trade & Industry Information, Manufacturing & Services, data extracted March 15, 2018

Building Permits

Area	Single-Family			Multi-Family			Total		
	2016	2017p	Pct. Chg.	2016	2017p	Pct. Chg.	2016	2017p	Pct. Chg.
City	102	90	-11.8	6	123	1,950.0	108	213	97.2
MSA[1]	1,282	1,089	-15.1	718	606	-15.6	2,000	1,695	-15.3
U.S.	750,800	817,300	8.9	455,800	446,800	-2.0	1,206,600	1,264,100	4.8

Note: (1) Figures cover the Rochester, NY Metropolitan Statistical Area—see Appendix B for areas included; Figures represent new, privately-owned housing units authorized (unadjusted data); All permit data are based on estimates with imputation; (p) preliminary data.
Source: U.S. Census Bureau, Manufacturing, Mining, and Construction Statistics, Building Permits, 2016, 2017

Bankruptcy Filings

Area	Business Filings			Nonbusiness Filings		
	2016	2017	% Chg.	2016	2017	% Chg.
Monroe County	39	44	12.8	902	854	-5.3
U.S.	24,114	23,157	-4.0	770,846	765,863	-0.6

Note: Business filings include Chapter 7, Chapter 11, Chapter 12, and Chapter 13; Nonbusiness filings include Chapter 7, Chapter 11, and Chapter 13
Source: Administrative Office of the U.S. Courts, Business and Nonbusiness Bankruptcy, County Cases Commenced by Chapter of the Bankruptcy Code, During the 12-Month Period Ending December 31, 2016 and Business and Nonbusiness Bankruptcy, County Cases Commenced by Chapter of the Bankruptcy Code, During the 12-Month Period Ending December 31, 2017

Housing Vacancy Rates

Area	Gross Vacancy Rate[2] (%)			Year-Round Vacancy Rate[3] (%)			Rental Vacancy Rate[4] (%)			Homeowner Vacancy Rate[5] (%)		
	2015	2016	2017	2015	2016	2017	2015	2016	2017	2015	2016	2017
MSA[1]	8.0	7.9	8.5	6.2	7.2	8.1	6.5	6.4	6.5	0.8	1.4	2.0
U.S.	12.9	12.8	12.7	10.0	9.9	9.9	7.1	6.9	7.2	1.8	1.7	1.6

Note: (1) Figures cover the Rochester, NY Metropolitan Statistical Area—see Appendix B for areas included; (2) The percentage of the total housing inventory that is vacant; (3) The percentage of the housing inventory (excluding seasonal units) that is year-round vacant; (4) The percentage of rental inventory that is vacant for rent; (5) The percentage of homeowner inventory that is vacant for sale
Source: U.S. Census Bureau, Housing Vacancies and Homeownership Annual Statistics: 2015, 2016, 2017

INCOME

Income

Area	Per Capita ($)	Median Household ($)	Average Household ($)
City	34,792	70,745	85,670
MSA[1]	29,293	53,480	71,174
U.S.	29,829	55,322	77,866

Note: (1) Figures cover the Rochester, NY Metropolitan Statistical Area—see Appendix B for areas included
Source: U.S. Census Bureau, 2012-2016 American Community Survey 5-Year Estimates

Household Income Distribution

Area	Percent of Households Earning							
	Under $15,000	$15,000 -$24,999	$25,000 -$34,999	$35,000 -$49,999	$50,000 -$74,999	$75,000 -$99,999	$100,000 -$149,999	$150,000 and up
City	7.3	7.0	8.4	12.0	17.4	16.9	18.0	13.1
MSA[1]	12.0	10.5	10.4	13.8	18.4	12.8	13.6	8.4
U.S.	12.1	10.2	9.9	13.2	17.8	12.2	13.5	11.1

Note: (1) Figures cover the Rochester, NY Metropolitan Statistical Area—see Appendix B for areas included
Source: U.S. Census Bureau, 2012-2016 American Community Survey 5-Year Estimates

Poverty Rate

Area	All Ages	Under 18 Years Old	18 to 64 Years Old	65 Years and Over
City	6.7	9.4	6.5	3.8
MSA[1]	14.1	20.9	13.7	6.8
U.S.	15.1	21.2	14.2	9.3

Note: Figures are percentage of people whose income during the past 12 months was below the poverty level; (1) Figures cover the Rochester, NY Metropolitan Statistical Area—see Appendix B for areas included
Source: U.S. Census Bureau, 2012-2016 American Community Survey 5-Year Estimates

EMPLOYMENT

Labor Force and Employment

Area	Civilian Labor Force			Workers Employed		
	Dec. 2016	Dec. 2017	% Chg.	Dec. 2016	Dec. 2017	% Chg.
City	22,250	22,146	-0.5	21,348	21,234	-0.5
MSA[1]	517,289	518,223	0.2	492,682	492,345	-0.1
U.S.	158,968,000	159,880,000	0.6	151,798,000	153,602,000	1.2

Note: Data is not seasonally adjusted and covers workers 16 years of age and older; (1) Figures cover the Rochester, NY Metropolitan Statistical Area—see Appendix B for areas included
Source: Bureau of Labor Statistics, Local Area Unemployment Statistics

Unemployment Rate

Area	2017											
	Jan.	Feb.	Mar.	Apr.	May	Jun.	Jul.	Aug.	Sep.	Oct.	Nov.	Dec.
City	4.6	4.6	3.9	3.6	3.8	3.9	3.9	3.8	4.0	3.9	4.0	4.1
MSA[1]	5.5	5.6	5.0	4.6	4.7	4.9	5.1	5.0	4.8	4.7	4.9	5.0
U.S.	5.1	4.9	4.6	4.1	4.1	4.5	4.6	4.5	4.1	3.9	3.9	3.9

Note: Data is not seasonally adjusted and covers workers 16 years of age and older; (1) Figures cover the Rochester, NY Metropolitan Statistical Area—see Appendix B for areas included
Source: Bureau of Labor Statistics, Local Area Unemployment Statistics

Average Wages

Occupation	$/Hr.	Occupation	$/Hr.
Accountants and Auditors	35.10	Maids and Housekeeping Cleaners	11.90
Automotive Mechanics	18.70	Maintenance and Repair Workers	19.80
Bookkeepers	19.10	Marketing Managers	66.10
Carpenters	21.20	Nuclear Medicine Technologists	38.60
Cashiers	10.60	Nurses, Licensed Practical	19.90
Clerks, General Office	15.60	Nurses, Registered	30.90
Clerks, Receptionists/Information	14.10	Nursing Assistants	13.60
Clerks, Shipping/Receiving	16.30	Packers and Packagers, Hand	12.70
Computer Programmers	38.90	Physical Therapists	36.60
Computer Systems Analysts	38.00	Postal Service Mail Carriers	23.70
Computer User Support Specialists	23.40	Real Estate Brokers	n/a
Cooks, Restaurant	12.70	Retail Salespersons	13.50
Dentists	86.80	Sales Reps., Exc. Tech./Scientific	32.00
Electrical Engineers	44.60	Sales Reps., Tech./Scientific	44.00
Electricians	28.00	Secretaries, Exc. Legal/Med./Exec.	17.70
Financial Managers	74.40	Security Guards	15.20
First-Line Supervisors/Managers, Sales	21.00	Surgeons	135.10
Food Preparation Workers	11.90	Teacher Assistants*	12.80
General and Operations Managers	61.80	Teachers, Elementary School*	30.60
Hairdressers/Cosmetologists	14.00	Teachers, Secondary School*	32.90
Internists, General	n/a	Telemarketers	14.70
Janitors and Cleaners	13.20	Truck Drivers, Heavy/Tractor-Trailer	21.90
Landscaping/Groundskeeping Workers	15.10	Truck Drivers, Light/Delivery Svcs.	16.20
Lawyers	45.30	Waiters and Waitresses	14.00

Note: Wage data covers the Rochester, NY Metropolitan Statistical Area—see Appendix B for areas included; (*) Hourly wages for elementary/secondary school teachers and teacher assistants were calculated by the editors from annual wage data based on a 40 hour work week; n/a not available.
Source: Bureau of Labor Statistics, Metro Area Occupational Employment & Wage Estimates, May 2017

Employment by Occupation

Occupation Classification	City (%)	MSA[1] (%)	U.S. (%)
Management, Business, Science, and Arts	47.0	40.3	37.0
Natural Resources, Construction, and Maintenance	7.6	7.2	8.9
Production, Transportation, and Material Moving	9.1	11.7	12.2
Sales and Office	23.3	23.4	23.8
Service	13.1	17.5	18.1

Note: Figures cover employed civilians 16 years of age and older; (1) Figures cover the Rochester, NY Metropolitan Statistical Area—see Appendix B for areas included
Source: U.S. Census Bureau, 2012-2016 American Community Survey 5-Year Estimates

Employment by Industry

Sector	MSA[1] Number of Employees	MSA[1] Percent of Total	U.S. Percent of Total
Construction	19,800	3.6	4.7
Education and Health Services	133,400	24.6	15.9
Financial Activities	21,600	4.0	5.7
Government	81,700	15.0	15.3
Information	8,000	1.5	1.9
Leisure and Hospitality	44,900	8.3	10.7
Manufacturing	57,800	10.6	8.5
Mining and Logging	600	0.1	0.5
Other Services	21,100	3.9	3.9
Professional and Business Services	68,300	12.6	14.0
Retail Trade	56,700	10.4	11.0
Transportation, Warehousing, and Utilities	11,500	2.1	4.1
Wholesale Trade	17,500	3.2	4.0

Note: Figures are non-farm employment as of December 2017. Figures are not seasonally adjusted and include workers 16 years of age and older; (1) Figures cover the Rochester, NY Metropolitan Statistical Area—see Appendix B for areas included
Source: Bureau of Labor Statistics, Current Employment Statistics, Employment, Hours, and Earnings

Occupations with Greatest Projected Employment Growth: 2017 – 2019

Occupation[1]	2017 Employment	2019 Projected Employment	Numeric Employment Change	Percent Employment Change
Home Health Aides	190,490	216,300	25,810	13.5
Personal Care Aides	174,700	189,420	14,720	8.4
Combined Food Preparation and Serving Workers, Including Fast Food	154,570	162,110	7,540	4.9
Registered Nurses	189,840	197,230	7,390	3.9
Janitors and Cleaners, Except Maids and Housekeeping Cleaners	211,280	217,380	6,100	2.9
Waiters and Waitresses	151,380	156,430	5,050	3.3
General and Operations Managers	165,860	169,970	4,110	2.5
Accountants and Auditors	124,740	128,070	3,330	2.7
Software Developers, Applications	52,730	55,940	3,210	6.1
Security Guards	114,180	117,140	2,960	2.6

Note: Projections cover New York; (1) Sorted by numeric employment change
Source: www.projectionscentral.com, State Occupational Projections, 2017–2019 Short-Term Projections

Fastest Growing Occupations: 2017 – 2019

Occupation[1]	2017 Employment	2019 Projected Employment	Numeric Employment Change	Percent Employment Change
Gaming and Sports Book Writers and Runners	660	810	150	24.0
Gaming Change Persons and Booth Cashiers	840	1,030	190	22.7
Solar Photovoltaic Installers	800	980	180	22.7
Gaming Dealers	960	1,150	190	19.4
Home Health Aides	190,490	216,300	25,810	13.5
Gaming Supervisors	580	660	80	12.3
Entertainment Attendants and Related Workers, All Other	490	540	50	9.8
Personal Care Aides	174,700	189,420	14,720	8.4
Physical Therapist Aides	3,110	3,330	220	6.9
Physical Therapists	18,480	19,750	1,270	6.9

Note: Projections cover New York; (1) Sorted by percent employment change and excludes occupations with numeric employment change less than 50
Source: www.projectionscentral.com, State Occupational Projections, 2017–2019 Short-Term Projections

TAXES

State Corporate Income Tax Rates

State	Tax Rate (%)	Income Brackets ($)	Num. of Brackets	Financial Institution Tax Rate (%)[a]	Federal Income Tax Ded.
New York	6.5 (r)	Flat rate	1	6.5 (r)	No

Note: Tax rates as of January 1, 2018; (a) Rates listed are the corporate income tax rate applied to financial institutions or excise taxes based on income. Some states have other taxes based upon the value of deposits or shares; (r) New York's General business corporate rate shown. Corporations may also be subject to a capital stocks tax, which is being phased out through 2021. A minimum tax ranges from $25 to $200,000, depending on receipts ($250 minimum for banks). Certain qualified New York manufacturers pay 0%.
Source: Federation of Tax Administrators, Range of State Corporate Income Tax Rates, January 1, 2018

State Individual Income Tax Rates

State	Tax Rate (%)	Income Brackets ($)	Num. of Brackets	Personal Exempt. ($)[1]		Fed. Inc. Tax Ded.
				Single	Dependents	
New York (a)	4.0 - 8.82	8,500 - 1,077,550 (b)	8	0	1,000	No

Note: Tax rates as of January 1, 2018; Local- and county-level taxes are not included; n/a not applicable; (1) Married joint filers generally receive double the single exemption; (a) 19 states have statutory provision for automatically adjusting to the rate of inflation the dollar values of the income tax brackets, standard deductions, and/or personal exemptions. Massachusetts, Michigan, and Nebraska index the personal exemption only. Oregon does not index the income brackets for $125,000 and over; (b) For joint returns, taxes are twice the tax on half the couple's income.
Source: Federation of Tax Administrators, State Individual Income Tax Rates, January 1, 2018

Various State Sales and Excise Tax Rates

State	State Sales Tax (%)	Gasoline[1] (¢/gal.)	Cigarette[2] ($/pack)	Spirits[3] ($/gal.)	Wine[4] ($/gal.)	Beer[5] ($/gal.)	Recreational Marijuana (%)
New York	4.0	44.3	4.35	6.44 (f)	0.30	0.14	Not legal

Note: All tax rates as of January 1, 2018; (1) The American Petroleum Institute has developed a methodology for determining the average tax rate on a gallon of fuel. Rates may include any of the following: excise taxes, environmental fees, storage tank fees, other fees or taxes, general sales tax, and local taxes. In states where gasoline is subject to the general sales tax, or where the fuel tax is based on the average sale price, the average rate determined by API is sensitive to changes in the price of gasoline. States that fully or partially apply general sales taxes to gasoline: CA, CO, GA, IL, IN, MI, NY; (2) The federal excise tax of $1.0066 per pack and local taxes are not included; (3) Rates are those applicable to off-premise sales of 40% alcohol by volume (a.b.v.) distilled spirits in 750ml containers. Local excise taxes are excluded; (4) Rates are those applicable to off-premise sales of 11% a.b.v. non-carbonated wine in 750ml containers; (5) Rates are those applicable to off-premise sales of 4.7% a.b.v. beer in 12 ounce containers; (f) Different rates also applicable according to alcohol content, place of production, size of container, or place purchased (on- or off-premise or onboard airlines).
Source: Tax Foundation, 2018 Facts & Figures: How Does Your State Compare?

State Business Tax Climate Index Rankings

State	Overall Rank	Corporate Tax Rank	Individual Income Tax Rank	Sales Tax Rank	Unemployment Insurance Tax Rank	Property Tax Rank
New York	49	7	49	43	30	47

Note: The index is a measure of how each state's tax laws affect economic performance. The lower the rank, the more favorable a state's tax system is for business. States without a given tax are given a ranking of 1. The scores/rankings for the District of Columbia do not affect other states. The 2018 index represents the tax climate as of July 1, 2017.
Source: Tax Foundation, State Business Tax Climate Index 2018

TRANSPORTATION

Means of Transportation to Work

Area	Car/Truck/Van		Public Transportation			Bicycle	Walked	Other Means	Worked at Home
	Drove Alone	Car-pooled	Bus	Subway	Railroad				
City	86.7	7.4	0.3	0.0	0.0	0.0	1.1	0.7	3.8
MSA[1]	81.3	7.9	2.3	0.1	0.0	0.5	3.5	0.8	3.7
U.S.	76.4	9.3	2.6	1.9	0.6	0.6	2.8	1.3	4.6

Note: Figures are percentages and cover workers 16 years of age and older; (1) Figures cover the Rochester, NY Metropolitan Statistical Area—see Appendix B for areas included
Source: U.S. Census Bureau, 2012-2016 American Community Survey 5-Year Estimates

Travel Time to Work

Area	Less Than 10 Minutes	10 to 19 Minutes	20 to 29 Minutes	30 to 44 Minutes	45 to 59 Minutes	60 to 89 Minutes	90 Minutes or More
City	14.6	30.0	33.0	17.6	2.8	1.4	0.6
MSA[1]	15.6	34.4	25.9	16.1	4.3	2.4	1.3
U.S.	12.9	29.2	20.9	20.4	8.0	6.0	2.7

Note: Note: Figures are percentages and include workers 16 years old and over; (1) Figures cover the Rochester, NY Metropolitan Statistical Area—see Appendix B for areas included
Source: U.S. Census Bureau, 2012-2016 American Community Survey 5-Year Estimates

Freeway Travel Time Index

Area	1985	1990	1995	2000	2005	2010	2014
Urban Area Rank[1,2]	48	46	59	72	51	57	65
Urban Area Index[1]	1.07	1.10	1.12	1.13	1.17	1.16	1.16
Average Index[3]	1.09	1.11	1.14	1.17	1.20	1.19	1.20

Note: Freeway Travel Time Index—the ratio of travel time in the peak period to the travel time at free-flow conditions. For example, a value of 1.30 indicates a 20-minute free-flow trip takes 26 minutes in the peak (20 minutes x 1.30 = 26 minutes); (1) Covers the Rochester NY urban area; (2) Rank is based on 101 urban areas (#1 = highest travel time index); (3) Average of 101 urban areas
Source: Texas Transportation Institute, 2015 Urban Mobility Scorecard, August 2015

Freeway Commuter Stress Index

Area	1985	1990	1995	2000	2005	2010	2014
Urban Area Rank[1,2]	53	51	61	70	58	65	61
Urban Area Index[1]	1.09	1.12	1.14	1.16	1.19	1.18	1.19
Average Index[3]	1.13	1.16	1.19	1.22	1.25	1.24	1.25

Note: The Freeway Commuter Stress Index is the same as the Freeway Travel Time Index (see table above) except that it includes only the travel in the peak directions during the peak periods; the TTI includes travel in all directions during the peak period. Thus, the CSI is more indicative of the work trip experienced by each commuter on a daily basis; (1) Covers the Rochester NY urban area; (2) Rank is based on 101 urban areas (#1 = highest travel time index); (3) Average of 101 urban areas
Source: Texas Transportation Institute, 2015 Urban Mobility Scorecard, August 2015

Living Environment

COST OF LIVING

Cost of Living Index

Composite Index	Groceries	Housing	Utilities	Trans-portation	Health Care	Misc. Goods/ Services
98.0	100.9	88.0	92.0	110.0	93.5	104.1

Note: The Cost of Living Index measures regional differences in the cost of consumer goods and services, excluding taxes and non-consumer expenditures, for professional and managerial households in the top income quintile. It is based on more than 50,000 prices covering almost 60 different items for which prices are collected three times a year by chambers of commerce, economic development organizations or university applied economic centers in each participating urban area. The numbers shown should be read as a percentage above or below the national average of 100. For example, a value of 115.4 in the groceries column indicates that grocery prices are 15.4% higher than the national average. Small differences in the index numbers should not be interpreted as significant; Figures cover the Rochester NY urban area.
Source: The Council for Community and Economic Research, ACCRA Cost of Living Index, 2017

Grocery Prices

Area[1]	T-Bone Steak ($/pound)	Frying Chicken ($/pound)	Whole Milk ($/half gal.)	Eggs ($/dozen)	Orange Juice ($/64 oz.)	Coffee ($/11.5 oz.)
City[2]	11.62	1.30	1.74	1.23	3.46	4.23
Avg.	11.29	1.40	2.02	1.47	3.55	4.37
Min.	7.71	0.93	1.04	0.70	2.86	3.24
Max.	15.83	2.39	4.03	3.92	6.29	8.16

*Note: (1) Values for the local area are compared with the average, minimum and maximum values for all 294 areas in the Cost of Living Index; (2) Figures cover the Rochester NY urban area; **T-Bone Steak** (price per pound); **Frying Chicken** (price per pound, whole fryer); **Whole Milk** (half gallon carton); **Eggs** (price per dozen, Grade A, large); **Orange Juice** (64 oz. Tropicana or Florida Natural); **Coffee** (11.5 oz. can, vacuum-packed, Maxwell House, Hills Bros, or Folgers).*
Source: The Council for Community and Economic Research, ACCRA Cost of Living Index, 2017

Housing and Utility Costs

Area[1]	New Home Price ($)	Apartment Rent ($/month)	All Electric ($/month)	Part Electric ($/month)	Other Energy ($/month)	Telephone ($/month)
City[2]	278,085	1,047	-	76.56	69.20	27.99
Avg.	335,956	1,047	175.01	97.34	67.93	28.71
Min.	187,788	491	109.48	49.33	35.44	12.39
Max.	1,739,087	4,559	432.62	227.09	353.33	44.61

*Note: (1) Values for the local area are compared with the average, minimum and maximum values for all 294 areas in the Cost of Living Index; (2) Figures cover the Rochester NY urban area; **New Home Price** (2,400 sf living area, 8,000 sf lot, in urban area with full utilities); **Apartment Rent** (950 sf 2 bedroom/1.5 or 2 bath, unfurnished, excluding all utilities except water); **All Electric** (average monthly cost for an all-electric home); **Part Electric** (average monthly cost for a part-electric home); **Other Energy** (average monthly cost for natural gas, fuel oil, coal, wood, and any other forms of energy except electricity); **Telephone** (price includes basic monthly rate for a private residential line plus additional local usage charges incurred by a family of four).*
Source: The Council for Community and Economic Research, ACCRA Cost of Living Index, 2017

Health Care, Transportation, and Other Costs

Area[1]	Doctor ($/visit)	Dentist ($/visit)	Optometrist ($/visit)	Gasoline ($/gallon)	Beauty Salon ($/visit)	Men's Shirt ($)
City[2]	91.47	94.93	111.54	2.42	38.00	29.43
Avg.	108.00	92.54	101.93	2.25	37.58	30.92
Min.	30.39	60.00	49.75	1.82	16.11	11.20
Max.	193.50	161.94	229.28	3.16	77.35	59.13

*Note: (1) Values for the local area are compared with the average, minimum and maximum values for all 294 areas in the Cost of Living Index; (2) Figures cover the Rochester NY urban area; **Doctor** (general practitioners routine exam of an established patient); **Dentist** (adult teeth cleaning and periodic oral examination); **Optometrist** (full vision eye exam for established adult patient); **Gasoline** (one gallon regular unleaded, national brand, including all taxes, cash price at self-service pump if available); **Beauty Salon** (woman's shampoo, trim, and blow-dry); **Men's Shirt** (cotton/polyester dress shirt, pinpoint weave, long sleeves).*
Source: The Council for Community and Economic Research, ACCRA Cost of Living Index, 2017

HOUSING

House Price Index (HPI)

Area	National Ranking[2]	Quarterly Change (%)	One-Year Change (%)	Five-Year Change (%)
MSA[1]	183	-0.11	4.20	12.33
U.S.[3]		1.61	6.68	34.71

Note: The HPI is a weighted repeat sales index. It measures average price changes in repeat sales or refinancings on the same properties. This information is obtained by reviewing repeat mortgage transactions on single-family properties whose mortgages have been purchased or securitized by Fannie Mae or Freddie Mac in January 1975; (1) Figures cover the Rochester, NY Metropolitan Statistical Area—see Appendix B for areas included; (2) Rankings are based on annual percentage change for all metro areas containing at least 15,000 transactions over the last 10 years and ranges from 1 to 253; (3) figures based on a weighted average of Census Division estimates using a seasonally adjusted, purchase-only index; all figures are for the period ending December 31, 2017

Source: Federal Housing Finance Agency, House Price Index, February 28, 2018

Median Single-Family Home Prices

Area	2015	2016	2017p	Percent Change 2016 to 2017
MSA[1]	134.0	133.4	137.7	3.2
U.S. Average	223.9	235.5	248.8	5.6

Note: Figures are median sales prices of existing single-family homes in thousands of dollars; (p) preliminary; (1) Figures cover the Rochester, NY Metropolitan Statistical Area—see Appendix B for areas included

Source: National Association of Realtors, Median Sales Price of Existing Single-Family Homes for Metropolitan Areas, 4th Quarter 2017

Qualifying Income Based on Median Sales Price of Existing Single-Family Homes

Area	With 5% Down ($)	With 10% Down ($)	With 20% Down ($)
MSA[1]	30,372	28,773	25,576
U.S. Average	55,585	52,659	46,808

Note: Figures are preliminary; Qualifying income is based on a mortgage rate of 4.17%. Monthly principal and interest payment is limited to 25% of income; (1) Figures cover the Rochester, NY Metropolitan Statistical Area—see Appendix B for areas included

Source: National Association of Realtors, Qualifying Income Based on Median Sales Price of Existing Single-Family Homes for Metropolitan Areas, 4th Quarter 2017

Median Apartment Condo-Coop Home Prices

Area	2015	2016	2017p	Percent Change 2016 to 2017
MSA[1]	124.8	118.5	131.3	10.8
U.S. Average	210.7	220.7	234.3	6.2

Note: Figures are median sales prices of existing apartment condo-coop homes in thousands of dollars; (p) preliminary; (1) Figures cover the Rochester, NY Metropolitan Statistical Area—see Appendix B for areas included

Source: National Association of Realtors, Median Sales Price of Existing Apartment Condo-Coop Homes for Metropolitan Areas, 4th Quarter 2017

Home Value Distribution

Area	Under $50,000	$50,000 -$99,999	$100,000 -$149,999	$150,000 -$199,999	$200,000 -$299,999	$300,000 -$499,999	$500,000 -$999,999	$1,000,000 or more
City	2.8	4.4	25.5	31.9	26.1	7.1	1.5	0.7
MSA[1]	6.9	22.0	29.1	19.3	14.3	6.4	1.7	0.4
U.S.	8.8	14.8	15.3	14.9	18.4	16.4	9.0	2.5

Note: Figures are percentages and cover owner-occupied housing units; (1) Figures cover the Rochester, NY Metropolitan Statistical Area—see Appendix B for areas included

Source: U.S. Census Bureau, 2012-2016 American Community Survey 5-Year Estimates

Homeownership Rate

Area	2009 (%)	2010 (%)	2011 (%)	2012 (%)	2013 (%)	2014 (%)	2015 (%)	2016 (%)	2017 (%)
MSA[1]	74.7	71.4	68.3	68.2	69.3	68.0	64.9	58.0	63.1
U.S.	67.4	66.9	66.1	65.4	65.1	64.5	63.7	63.4	63.9

Note: (1) Figures cover the Rochester, NY Metropolitan Statistical Area—see Appendix B for areas included

Source: U.S. Census Bureau, Housing Vacancies and Homeownership Annual Statistics: 2009-2017

Year Housing Structure Built

Area	2010 or Later	2000 -2009	1990 -1999	1980 -1989	1970 -1979	1960 -1969	1950 -1959	1940 -1949	Before 1940	Median Year
City	2.7	16.2	15.9	13.8	14.8	12.4	14.6	2.5	7.2	1979
MSA[1]	1.3	7.2	9.3	11.0	13.3	12.6	11.5	5.7	28.1	1964
U.S.	2.3	14.7	14.0	13.7	15.6	10.9	10.6	5.2	13.0	1977

Note: Figures are percentages except for Median Year; Note: (1) Figures cover the Rochester, NY Metropolitan Statistical Area—see Appendix B for areas included
Source: U.S. Census Bureau, 2012-2016 American Community Survey 5-Year Estimates

Gross Monthly Rent

Area	Under $500	$500 -$999	$1,000 -$1,499	$1,500 -$1,999	$2,000 -$2,499	$2,500 -$2,999	$3,000 and up	Median ($)
City	9.9	44.7	30.9	12.0	0.3	1.8	0.4	970
MSA[1]	12.1	60.7	21.4	3.4	1.1	0.6	0.7	821
U.S.	11.3	43.3	27.7	10.7	4.0	1.6	1.5	949

Note: Figures are percentages except for Median; Gross rent is the contract rent plus the estimated average monthly cost of utilities (electricity, gas, and water and sewer) and fuels (oil, coal, kerosene, wood, etc.) if these are paid by the renter (or paid for the renter by someone else); (1) Figures cover the Rochester, NY Metropolitan Statistical Area—see Appendix B for areas included
Source: U.S. Census Bureau, 2012-2016 American Community Survey 5-Year Estimates

HEALTH

Health Risk Factors

Category	MSA[1] (%)	U.S. (%)
Adults aged 18–64 who have any kind of health care coverage	91.4	87.7
Adults who reported being in good or excellent health	85.3	83.6
Adults who are current smokers	17.6	17.1
Adults who currently use E-cigarettes	3.7	4.7
Adults who currently use chewing tobacco, snuff, or snus	3.0	4.0
Adults who are heavy drinkers[2]	6.1	6.5
Adults who are binge drinkers[3]	18.4	16.9
Adults who are overweight (BMI 25.0 - 29.9)	33.1	35.3
Adults who are obese (BMI 30.0 - 99.8)	33.0	29.9
Adults who participated in any physical activities in the past month	77.5	76.9
Adults who always or nearly always wears a seat belt	95.4	94.3

Note: (1) Figures cover the Rochester, NY Metropolitan Statistical Area—see Appendix B for areas included; (2) Heavy drinkers are classified as adult men having more than 14 drinks per week and adult women having more than 7 drinks per week; (3) Binge drinkers are classified as males having five or more drinks on one occasion or females having four or more drinks on one occasion
Source: Centers for Disease Control and Prevention, Behaviorial Risk Factor Surveillance System, SMART: Selected Metropolitan Area Risk Trends, 2016

Health Screening Rates

Category	MSA[1] (%)	U.S. (%)
Adults 50-75 who have had a blood stool test within the past year	7.3	8.0
Adults 50-75 who have had a colonoscopy in the past 10 years	70.9	63.5
Adults aged 65+ who have had flu shot within the past year	67.9	58.6
Adults aged 65+ who have ever had a pneumonia vaccination	81.6	73.4
Adults who have ever been tested for HIV	40.4	35.6
Women aged 21-65 who have had a pap test in the past three years	79.4	79.8
Men aged 40+ who have had a PSA test within the past two years	37.1	39.5
Women aged 40+ who have had a mammogram within the past two years	78.2	72.5

Note: n/a not available; (1) Figures cover the Rochester, NY Metropolitan Statistical Area—see Appendix B for areas included; Source: Centers for Disease Control and Prevention, Behaviorial Risk Factor Surveillance System, SMART: Selected Metropolitan Area Risk Trends, 2016

Chronic Health Conditions

Category	MSA[1] (%)	U.S. (%)
Adults who have ever been told they had a heart attack	4.3	4.4
Adults who have ever been told they have angina or coronary heart disease	3.6	4.1
Adults who have ever been told they had a stroke	3.2	3.1
Adults who have been told they currently have asthma	10.6	9.3
Adults who have ever been told they have arthritis	29.0	25.8
Adults who have ever been told they have diabetes[2]	8.9	10.5
Adults who have ever been told they had skin cancer	5.0	5.9
Adults who have ever been told they had any other types of cancer	8.9	6.7
Adults who have ever been told they have COPD	5.9	6.3
Adults who have ever been told they have kidney disease	2.3	2.8
Adults who have ever been told they have a form of depression	18.6	17.4

Note: (1) Figures cover the Rochester, NY Metropolitan Statistical Area—see Appendix B for areas included; (2) Figures do not include pregnancy-related, borderline, or pre-diabetes
Source: Centers for Disease Control and Prevention, Behaviorial Risk Factor Surveillance System, SMART: Selected Metropolitan Area Risk Trends, 2016

Mortality Rates for the Top 10 Causes of Death in the U.S.

ICD-10[a] Sub-Chapter	ICD-10[a] Code	Age-Adjusted Mortality Rate[1] per 100,000 population	
		County[2]	U.S.
Malignant neoplasms	C00-C97	157.7	158.5
Ischaemic heart diseases	I20-I25	87.6	96.8
Other forms of heart disease	I30-I51	49.6	52.4
Chronic lower respiratory diseases	J40-J47	27.0	40.9
Cerebrovascular diseases	I60-I69	32.4	37.2
Organic, including symptomatic, mental disorders	F01-F09	62.6	33.3
Other degenerative diseases of the nervous system	G30-G31	19.0	32.1
Other external causes of accidental injury	W00-X59	32.1	31.2
Diabetes mellitus	E10-E14	13.1	21.1
Hypertensive diseases	I10-I15	12.0	20.8

Note: (a) ICD-10 = International Classification of Diseases 10th Revision; (1) Mortality rates are a three year average covering 2014-2016; (2) Figures cover Monroe County.
Source: Centers for Disease Control and Prevention, National Center for Health Statistics. Underlying Cause of Death 1999-2016 on CDC WONDER Online Database, released December 2017

Mortality Rates for Selected Causes of Death

ICD-10[a] Sub-Chapter	ICD-10[a] Code	Age-Adjusted Mortality Rate[1] per 100,000 population	
		County[2]	U.S.
Assault	X85-Y09	5.8	5.6
Diseases of the liver	K70-K76	10.8	14.0
Human immunodeficiency virus (HIV) disease	B20-B24	0.9	1.9
Influenza and pneumonia	J09-J18	19.2	14.6
Intentional self-harm	X60-X84	9.7	13.2
Malnutrition	E40-E46	1.1	1.3
Obesity and other hyperalimentation	E65-E68	1.5	2.1
Renal failure	N17-N19	12.5	13.0
Transport accidents	V01-V99	5.2	12.0
Viral hepatitis	B15-B19	1.0	1.9

Note: (a) ICD-10 = International Classification of Diseases 10th Revision; (1) Mortality rates are a three year average covering 2014-2016; (2) Figures cover Monroe County; Data are Suppressed when the data meet the criteria for confidentiality constraints; Mortality rates are flagged as Unreliable when the rate would be calculated with a numerator of 20 or less.
Source: Centers for Disease Control and Prevention, National Center for Health Statistics. Underlying Cause of Death 1999-2016 on CDC WONDER Online Database, released December 2017

Health Insurance Coverage

Area	With Health Insurance	With Private Health Insurance	With Public Health Insurance	Without Health Insurance	Population Under Age 18 Without Health Insurance
City	96.6	83.5	28.2	3.4	2.4
MSA[1]	94.1	73.0	35.6	5.9	3.9
U.S.	88.3	66.7	33.0	11.7	5.9

Note: Figures are percentages that cover the civilian noninstitutionalized population; (1) Figures cover the Rochester, NY Metropolitan Statistical Area—see Appendix B for areas included
Source: U.S. Census Bureau, 2012-2016 American Community Survey 5-Year Estimates

Number of Medical Professionals

Area	MDs[3]	DOs[3,4]	Dentists	Podiatrists	Chiropractors	Optometrists
County[1] (number)	3,587	124	600	47	205	133
County[1] (rate[2])	479.2	16.6	80.3	6.3	27.4	17.8
U.S. (rate[2])	276.5	22.3	67.3	6.0	26.7	15.9

Note: Data as of 2016 unless noted; (1) Data covers Monroe County; (2) Rate per 100,000 population; (3) Data as of 2015 and includes all active, non-federal physicians; (4) Doctor of Osteopathic Medicine
Source: U.S. Department of Health and Human Services, Health Resources and Services Administration, Bureau of Health Professions, Area Resource File (ARF) 2016-2017

Best Hospitals

According to *U.S. News,* the Rochester, NY metro area is home to two of the best hospitals in the U.S.: **Rochester General Hospital** (1 adult specialty); **UR Medicine Strong Memorial Hospital** (1 adult specialty and 3 pediatric specialties). The hospitals listed were nationally ranked in at least one of 16 specialties. Only 152 hospitals nationwide were nationally ranked in one or more specialties. Twenty hospitals in the U.S. made the Honor Roll. The Best Hospitals Honor Roll was revamped last year to take both the national rankings and the procedure and condition ratings into account. Hospitals received points if they were nationally ranked in one of the 16 specialties—the higher they ranked, the more points they got—and how many ratings of "high performing" they earned in the nine procedures and conditions. *U.S. News Online, "America's Best Hospitals 2017-18"*

According to *U.S. News,* the Rochester, NY metro area is home to one of the best children's hospitals in the U.S.: **University of Rochester-Golisano Children's Hospital** (3 pediatric specialties). The hospital listed was highly ranked in at least one of 10 pediatric specialties. Eighty-two children's hospitals in the U.S. were nationally ranked in at least one specialty. Hospitals received points for being ranked in a specialty, and the 10 hospitals with the most points across the 10 specialties make up the Honor Roll. *U.S. News Online, "America's Best Children's Hospitals 2017-18"*

EDUCATION

Public School District Statistics

District Name	Schls	Pupils	Pupil/ Teacher Ratio	Minority Pupils[1] (%)	Free Lunch Eligible[2] (%)	IEP[3] (%)
Webster Central School District	11	8,442	13.5	14.3	13.2	10.6

Note: Table includes school districts with 100 or more students; (1) Percentage of students that are not non-Hispanic white; (2) Percentage of students that are eligible for the free lunch program; (3) Percentage of students that have an Individualized Education Program.
Source: U.S. Department of Education, National Center for Education Statistics, Common Core of Data, Local Education Agency (School District) Universe Survey: School Year 2015-2016; U.S. Department of Education, National Center for Education Statistics, Common Core of Data, Public Elementary/Secondary School Universe Survey: School Year 2015-2016

Best High Schools

According to *U.S. News,* Webster is home to one of the best high schools in the U.S.: **Thomas High School** (#427). More than 22,000 public, magnet and charter schools were ranked based on their performance on state assessments and how well they prepare students for college. Schools with the highest unrounded College Readiness Index values were numerically ranked from 1 to 500 and were classified as gold medal winners. *U.S. News & World Report, "Best High Schools 2017"*

Highest Level of Education

Area	Less than H.S.	H.S. Diploma	Some College, No Deg.	Associate Degree	Bachelor's Degree	Master's Degree	Prof. School Degree	Doctorate Degree
City	4.7	20.9	16.9	13.8	24.3	15.4	1.6	2.4
MSA[1]	9.8	27.3	17.9	12.0	18.5	11.0	2.0	1.6
U.S.	13.0	27.5	21.0	8.2	18.8	8.2	2.0	1.3

Note: Figures cover persons age 25 and over; (1) Figures cover the Rochester, NY Metropolitan Statistical Area—see Appendix B for areas included
Source: U.S. Census Bureau, 2012-2016 American Community Survey 5-Year Estimates

Educational Attainment by Race

Area	High School Graduate or Higher (%)					Bachelor's Degree or Higher (%)				
	Total	White	Black	Asian	Hisp.[2]	Total	White	Black	Asian	Hisp.[2]
City	95.3	95.8	96.9	83.3	97.0	43.7	43.3	40.8	59.8	24.4
MSA[1]	90.2	92.3	78.8	81.0	70.4	33.0	35.0	13.8	53.0	16.0
U.S.	87.0	88.9	84.3	86.3	65.7	30.3	31.6	20.0	52.1	14.7

Note: Figures shown cover persons 25 years old and over; (1) Figures cover the Rochester, NY Metropolitan Statistical Area—see Appendix B for areas included; (2) People of Hispanic origin can be of any race
Source: U.S. Census Bureau, 2012-2016 American Community Survey 5-Year Estimates

School Enrollment by Grade and Control

Area	Preschool (%)		Kindergarten (%)		Grades 1 - 4 (%)		Grades 5 - 8 (%)		Grades 9 - 12 (%)	
	Public	Private	Public	Private	Public	Private	Public	Private	Public	Private
City	51.8	48.2	82.5	17.5	91.4	8.6	88.7	11.3	87.5	12.5
MSA[1]	60.3	39.7	89.9	10.1	90.6	9.4	90.0	10.0	90.1	9.9
U.S.	58.4	41.6	87.7	12.3	89.8	10.2	89.7	10.3	90.4	9.6

Note: Figures shown cover persons 3 years old and over; (1) Figures cover the Rochester, NY Metropolitan Statistical Area—see Appendix B for areas included
Source: U.S. Census Bureau, 2012-2016 American Community Survey 5-Year Estimates

Average Salaries of Public School Classroom Teachers

Area	2015		2016		Change from 2015 to 2016	
	Dollars	Rank[1]	Dollars	Rank[1]	Percent	Rank[2]
New York	77,628	1	79,152	1	2.0	12
U.S. Average	57,611	–	58,353	–	1.3	–

Note: (1) Rank ranges from 1 to 51 where 1 indicates highest salary; (2) Rank ranges from 1 to 51 where 1 indicates highest percent change.
Source: National Education Association, Rankings & Estimates: Rankings of the States 2016 and Estimates of School Statistics 2017

Higher Education

Four-Year Colleges			Two-Year Colleges			Medical Schools[1]	Law Schools[2]	Voc/ Tech[3]
Public	Private Non-profit	Private For-profit	Public	Private Non-profit	Private For-profit			
0	0	0	0	0	0	0	0	0

Note: Figures cover institutions located within the city limits and include main campuses only; (1) includes schools accredited by the Liaison Committee on Medical Education and the American Osteopathic Association's Commission on Osteopathic College Accreditation; (2) includes ABA-accredited schools, schools with provisional ABA accreditation, and state accredited schools; (3) includes all schools with programs that are less than 2 years.
Source: National Center for Education Statistics, Integrated Postsecondary Education System (IPEDS), 2016-17; Wikipedia, List of Medical Schools in the United States, accessed April 2, 2018; Wikipedia, List of Law Schools in the United States, accessed April 2, 2018

According to *U.S. News & World Report,* the Rochester, NY metro area is home to three of the best national universities in the U.S.: **University of Rochester** (#34 tie); **Rochester Institute of Technology** (#97 tie); **Saint John Fisher College** (#145 tie). The indicators used to capture academic quality fall into a number of categories: assessment by administrators at peer institutions; retention of students; faculty resources; student selectivity; financial resources; alumni giving; high school counselor ratings of colleges; and graduation rate. *U.S. News & World Report, "America's Best Colleges 2018"*

According to *U.S. News & World Report,* the Rochester, NY metro area is home to one of the best liberal arts colleges in the U.S.: **Hobart and William Smith Colleges** (#65 tie). The indicators used to capture academic quality fall into a number of categories: assessment by administrators at peer institutions; retention of students; faculty resources; student selectivity; financial resources; alumni giving; high school counselor ratings of colleges; and graduation rate. *U.S. News & World Report, "America's Best Colleges 2018"*

According to *U.S. News & World Report,* the Rochester, NY metro area is home to one of the top 75 medical schools for research in the U.S.: **University of Rochester** (#32 tie). The rankings are based on a weighted average of 11 measures of quality: quality assessment; peer assessment score; assessment score by residency directors; research activity; total research activity; average research activity per faculty member; student selectivity; median MCAT total score; median undergraduate GPA; acceptance rate; and faculty resources. *U.S. News & World Report, "America's Best Graduate Schools, Medical, 2019"*

According to *U.S. News & World Report,* the Rochester, NY metro area is home to two of the top 75 business schools in the U.S.: **University of Rochester (Simon)** (#44 tie); **Rochester Institute of Technology (Saunders)** (#73 tie). The rankings are based on a weighted average of the following nine measures: quality assessment; peer assessment; recruiter assessment; placement success; mean starting salary and bonus; student selectivity; mean GMAT and GRE scores; mean undergraduate GPA; and acceptance rate. *U.S. News & World Report, "America's Best Graduate Schools, Business, 2019"*

PRESIDENTIAL ELECTION

2016 Presidential Election Results

Area	Clinton	Trump	Johnson	Stein	Other
Monroe County	54.2	39.3	3.8	1.5	1.2
U.S.	48.0	45.9	3.3	1.1	1.7

Note: Results are percentages and may not add to 100% due to rounding
Source: Dave Leip's Atlas of U.S. Presidential Elections

EMPLOYERS

Major Employers

Company Name	Industry
American Packaging	Packaging
Auction Direct USA	Car dealership
Bergmann Associates	Civil engineering
Century Mold Company	Plastic injection molding
ConServe	Collection agency
Crosman	Air gun manufacturing
DDS Companies	Engineering
DeCarolis Truck Rental	Truck rental
Diamond packaging	Packaging
Erdman Anthony	Civil engineering
Fibertech Networls	Fiber-optic broadband
Flower City Printing	Commercial printing
Hammer Packaging	Packaging
Harris Beach	Law firm
Isaac Heating & Air Conditioning	HVAC contractor
Lapp Insulators	Electrical insulation
Lewis Tree Service	Arborist
Manning & Napier Advisors	Investments
Mindex Technologies	Software engineering
Pharma-Smart Int'l	Medical equipment
Pictometry Int'l	Aerial imagery
Sutherland Global Services	Business process outsourcing
Synergy Global Solutions	IT management
VP Supply	Plumbing product
Wegman's Food Markets	Supermarket chain

Note: Companies shown are located within the Rochester, NY Metropolitan Statistical Area.
Source: Hoovers.com; Wikipedia

PUBLIC SAFETY

Crime Rate

Area	All Crimes	Violent Crimes: Murder	Rape[3]	Robbery	Aggrav. Assault	Property Crimes: Burglary	Larceny -Theft	Motor Vehicle Theft
City	1,056.5	0.0	4.5	18.0	33.7	116.9	856.4	27.0
Metro[1]	2,276.5	4.7	42.7	85.1	148.3	329.9	1,562.2	103.6
U.S.	2,847.8	5.3	40.4	102.8	248.5	468.9	1,745.0	236.9

Note: Figures are crimes per 100,000 population; (1) Figures cover the Rochester, NY Metropolitan Statistical Area—see Appendix B for areas included; (3) The city and U.S. figures shown were reported using the revised Uniform Crime Reporting (UCR) definition of rape. The metro area figures shown are an aggregate total of the data submitted using both the revised and legacy UCR definitions.
Source: FBI Uniform Crime Reports, 2016

Hate Crimes

Area	Number of Quarters Reported	Number of Incidents per Bias Motivation: Race/Ethnicity/ Ancestry	Religion	Sexual Orientation	Disability	Gender	Gender Identity
Area[1]	4	0	0	0	0	0	0
U.S.	4	3,489	1,273	1,076	70	31	124

Note: (1) Figures cover the Webster Town and Village.
Source: Federal Bureau of Investigation, Hate Crime Statistics 2016

Identity Theft Consumer Reports

Area	Reports	Reports per 100,000 Population	Rank[2]
MSA[1]	847	79	206
U.S.	371,061	114	-

Note: (1) Figures cover the Rochester, NY Metropolitan Statistical Area—see Appendix B for areas included; (2) Rank ranges from 1 to 389 where 1 indicates greatest number of identity theft reports per 100,000 population
Source: Federal Trade Commission, Consumer Sentinel Network Data Book for January–December 2017

Fraud and Other Consumer Reports

Area	Reports	Reports per 100,000 Population	Rank[2]
MSA[1]	5,262	488	126
U.S.	2,304,550	708	-

Note: (1) Figures cover the Rochester, NY Metropolitan Statistical Area—see Appendix B for areas included; (2) Rank ranges from 1 to 389 where 1 indicates greatest number of fraud and other consumer reports per 100,000 population
Source: Federal Trade Commission, Consumer Sentinel Network Data Book for January–December 2017

SPORTS

Professional Sports Teams

Team Name	League	Year Established
No teams are located in the metro area		

Source: Wikipedia, Major Professional Sports Teams of the United States and Canada, April 5, 2018

CLIMATE

Average and Extreme Temperatures

Temperature	Jan	Feb	Mar	Apr	May	Jun	Jul	Aug	Sep	Oct	Nov	Dec	Yr.
Extreme High (°F)	74	67	83	93	94	100	98	99	99	91	81	72	100
Average High (°F)	31	33	42	56	68	78	82	80	72	61	48	36	57
Average Temp. (°F)	24	25	34	46	57	67	72	70	62	52	41	29	48
Average Low (°F)	17	17	25	36	46	56	60	59	52	42	33	23	39
Extreme Low (°F)	-16	-19	-6	13	26	35	42	36	30	20	5	-12	-19

Note: Figures cover the years 1945-1990
Source: National Climatic Data Center, International Station Meteorological Climate Summary, 9/96

Average Precipitation/Snowfall/Humidity

Precip./Humidity	Jan	Feb	Mar	Apr	May	Jun	Jul	Aug	Sep	Oct	Nov	Dec	Yr.
Avg. Precip. (in.)	2.2	2.3	2.5	2.6	2.7	2.8	2.6	3.3	2.8	2.5	2.8	2.6	31.8
Avg. Snowfall (in.)	24	23	14	4	Tr	0	0	0	Tr	Tr	7	20	92
Avg. Rel. Hum. 7am (%)	79	80	80	78	77	79	82	87	88	85	82	81	81
Avg. Rel. Hum. 4pm (%)	71	69	63	56	53	53	52	55	59	61	69	74	61

Note: Figures cover the years 1945-1990; Tr = Trace amounts (<0.05 in. of rain; <0.5 in. of snow)
Source: National Climatic Data Center, International Station Meteorological Climate Summary, 9/96

Weather Conditions

Temperature			Daytime Sky			Precipitation		
5°F & below	32°F & below	90°F & above	Clear	Partly cloudy	Cloudy	0.01 inch or more precip.	0.1 inch or more snow/ice	Thunder-storms
13	135	11	58	137	170	157	65	27

Note: Figures are average number of days per year and cover the years 1945-1990
Source: National Climatic Data Center, International Station Meteorological Climate Summary, 9/96

HAZARDOUS WASTE

Superfund Sites

The Rochester, NY metro area is home to three sites on the EPA's Superfund National Priorities List: **Diaz Chemical** (final); **FMC Corp. (Dublin Road Landfill)** (final); **Jones Chemicals, Inc.** (final). There are a total of 1,396 Superfund sites with a status of proposed or final on the list in the U.S. *U.S. Environmental Protection Agency, National Priorities List, April 4, 2018*

AIR & WATER QUALITY

Air Quality Trends: Ozone

	1990	1995	2000	2005	2010	2012	2013	2014	2015	2016
MSA[1]	0.087	0.096	0.070	0.065	0.071	0.072	0.066	0.064	0.061	0.067
U.S.	0.087	0.089	0.081	0.079	0.073	0.075	0.069	0.067	0.068	0.069

Note: (1) Data covers the Rochester, NY Metropolitan Statistical Area—see Appendix B for areas included. The values shown are the composite ozone concentration averages among trend sites based on the highest fourth daily maximum 8-hour concentration in parts per million. These trends are based on sites having an adequate record of monitoring data during the trend period. Data from exceptional events are included.
Source: U.S. Environmental Protection Agency, Air Quality Monitoring Information, "Air Quality Trends by City, 1990-2016"

Air Quality Index

Area	Percent of Days when Air Quality was...[2]					AQI Statistics[2]	
	Good	Moderate	Unhealthy for Sensitive Groups	Unhealthy	Very Unhealthy	Maximum	Median
MSA[1]	85.2	14.0	0.8	0.0	0.0	112	39

Note: (1) Data covers the Rochester, NY Metropolitan Statistical Area—see Appendix B for areas included; (2) Based on 365 days with AQI data in 2017. Air Quality Index (AQI) is an index for reporting daily air quality. EPA calculates the AQI for five major air pollutants regulated by the Clean Air Act: ground-level ozone, particle pollution (aka particulate matter), carbon monoxide, sulfur dioxide, and nitrogen dioxide. The AQI runs from 0 to 500. The higher the AQI value, the greater the level of air pollution and the greater the health concern. There are six AQI categories: "Good" AQI is between 0 and 50. Air quality is considered satisfactory; "Moderate" AQI is between 51 and 100. Air quality is acceptable; "Unhealthy for Sensitive Groups" When AQI values are between 101 and 150, members of sensitive groups may experience health effects; "Unhealthy" When AQI values are between 151 and 200 everyone may begin to experience health effects; "Very Unhealthy" AQI values between 201 and 300 trigger a health alert; "Hazardous" AQI values over 300 trigger warnings of emergency conditions (not shown).
Source: U.S. Environmental Protection Agency, Air Quality Index Report, 2017

Air Quality Index Pollutants

Area	Percent of Days when AQI Pollutant was...[2]					
	Carbon Monoxide	Nitrogen Dioxide	Ozone	Sulfur Dioxide	Particulate Matter 2.5	Particulate Matter 10
MSA[1]	0.0	0.3	66.3	0.3	33.2	0.0

Note: (1) Data covers the Rochester, NY Metropolitan Statistical Area—see Appendix B for areas included; (2) Based on 365 days with AQI data in 2017. The Air Quality Index (AQI) is an index for reporting daily air quality. EPA calculates the AQI for five major air pollutants regulated by the Clean Air Act: ground-level ozone, particle pollution (also known as particulate matter), carbon monoxide, sulfur dioxide, and nitrogen dioxide. The AQI runs from 0 to 500. The higher the AQI value, the greater the level of air pollution and the greater the health concern.

Source: U.S. Environmental Protection Agency, Air Quality Index Report, 2017

Maximum Air Pollutant Concentrations: Particulate Matter, Ozone, CO and Lead

	Particulate Matter 10 (ug/m^3)	Particulate Matter 2.5 Wtd AM (ug/m^3)	Particulate Matter 2.5 24-Hr (ug/m^3)	Ozone (ppm)	Carbon Monoxide (ppm)	Lead (ug/m^3)
MSA[1] Level	n/a	6.3	15	0.067	1	n/a
NAAQS[2]	150	15	35	0.075	9	0.15
Met NAAQS[2]	n/a	Yes	Yes	Yes	Yes	n/a

Note: (1) Data covers the Rochester, NY Metropolitan Statistical Area—see Appendix B for areas included; Data from exceptional events are included; (2) National Ambient Air Quality Standards; ppm = parts per million; ug/m^3 = micrograms per cubic meter; n/a not available.

Concentrations: Particulate Matter 10 (coarse particulate)—highest second maximum 24-hour concentration; Particulate Matter 2.5 Wtd AM (fine particulate)—highest weighted annual mean concentration; Particulate Matter 2.5 24-Hour (fine particulate)—highest 98th percentile 24-hour concentration; Ozone—highest fourth daily maximum 8-hour concentration; Carbon Monoxide—highest second maximum non-overlapping 8-hour concentration; Lead—maximum running 3-month average

Source: U.S. Environmental Protection Agency, Air Quality Monitoring Information, "Air Quality Statistics by City, 2016"

Maximum Air Pollutant Concentrations: Nitrogen Dioxide and Sulfur Dioxide

	Nitrogen Dioxide AM (ppb)	Nitrogen Dioxide 1-Hr (ppb)	Sulfur Dioxide AM (ppb)	Sulfur Dioxide 1-Hr (ppb)	Sulfur Dioxide 24-Hr (ppb)
MSA[1] Level	10	41	n/a	27	n/a
NAAQS[2]	53	100	30	75	140
Met NAAQS[2]	Yes	Yes	n/a	Yes	n/a

Note: (1) Data covers the Rochester, NY Metropolitan Statistical Area—see Appendix B for areas included; Data from exceptional events are included; (2) National Ambient Air Quality Standards; ppm = parts per million; ug/m^3 = micrograms per cubic meter; n/a not available.

Concentrations: Nitrogen Dioxide AM—highest arithmetic mean concentration; Nitrogen Dioxide 1-Hr—highest 98th percentile 1-hour daily maximum concentration; Sulfur Dioxide AM—highest annual mean concentration; Sulfur Dioxide 1-Hr—highest 99th percentile 1-hour daily maximum concentration; Sulfur Dioxide 24-Hr—highest second maximum 24-hour concentration

Source: U.S. Environmental Protection Agency, Air Quality Monitoring Information, "Air Quality Statistics by City, 2016"

Drinking Water

Water System Name	Pop. Served	Primary Water Source Type	Violations[1]	
			Health Based	Monitoring/ Reporting
MCWA	496,753	Surface	0	0

Note: (1) Based on violation data from January 1, 2017 to December 31, 2017

Source: U.S. Environmental Protection Agency, Office of Ground Water and Drinking Water, Safe Drinking Water Information System (based on data extracted April 5, 2018)

Apex, North Carolina

Background

Apex is located 15 miles southwest of Raleigh, in Wake County. Other neighboring cities include Cary to the northeast and Holly Springs to the south.

Incorporated in 1873, Apex's name is due to the fact that it is the highest point on the Chatham Railroad between Richmond, VA and Jacksonville, FL. The city grew slowly through its first few decades, partially due to several devastating fires, including a 1912 blaze that destroyed most of the downtown business district. The town center was rebuilt and still stands today. After a period of slowed growth during the Depression, the 1950s saw a population boom. The city's proximity to the highly regarded and innovative Research Triangle Park (RTF) fueled yet another growth spurt in the latter part of the 20th century, when the population of Apex more than quadrupled in the 1990s and 2000s. Apex prides itself in maintaining a small town character while experiencing rapid growth.

RTP, located between Duke University in Durham, North Carolina State University in Raleigh, and the University of North Carolina at Chapel Hill, is home to more than 170 global companies and is considered one of the world's premiere high-tech research and development centers, and has played an enormous part in Apex's growth.

IBM Corporation, GlaxoSmithKline, Cisco Systems, the National Institute of Environmental Health Sciences and the North Carolina Biotechnology Center are among the tenants. United Therapeutics Corp. recently purchased more buildings and property to increase its RTP workforce.

Students from Apex attend North Carolina's largest public school system, the Wake County Public School System. The town has 14 schools, including three high schools. The city is also home to a variety of healthcare options including Duke Medicine, UNC Healthcare and WakeMed Health and Hospitals.

Due to its history, Apex can boast of being one of the most intact railroad towns in the state. At the heart of the downtown stands the circa-1914 Apex Union Depot which was originally a passenger station for the Seaboard Air Line Railroad. Today it is the Apex Community Library.

The restored downtown area is listed on the National Register of Historic Places and offers shops and restaurants. Additionally, residents can enjoy their town's heyday aboard the New Hope Valley Railway, which offers rides on restored trains, and the North Carolina Railroad Museum. The annual Peakfest is held the first Saturday in May with hundreds of crafters, fine arts, food, and entertainment. The Beaver Creek Crossing shopping complex offers a range of restaurants and stores, as well as a multiplex movie theater.

Apex has a temperate southern climate with hot summers and cold winters. Median summer temperatures average 75 degrees, while winter averages can be as low as 30 degrees during of December and January. The city averages 4 inches of rainfall per month from April to October and 1.5 inches of snowfall per month from December to March.

Rankings

General Rankings

- *US News & World Report* conducted a survey of more than 2,000 people and analyzed the 125 largest metropolitan areas to determine what matters the most when selecting the next place to live. Raleigh* ranked #13 out of the top 25 as having the best combination of desirable factors. Criteria: cost of living; quality of education; job market, crime rates; and other factors. *realestate.usnews.com, "The 25 Best Places to Live in the U.S. in 2018," April 10, 2018*
- The Raleigh* metro area was identified as one of America's fastest-growing areas in terms of population and economy by *Forbes.* The area ranked #15 out of 25. The 100 most populous metro areas in the U.S. were evaluated on the following criteria: estimated population growth; employment; economic output; wages; home values. *Forbes, "America's Fastest-Growing Cities 2018," February 28, 2018*

Business/Finance Rankings

- The personal finance site NerdWallet analyzed 183 American metropolitan areas with populations over 250,000 and more than 15,000 businesses to rank where entrepreneurs find the most success. Criteria included area economy, annual income, housing cost, unemployment rate, and the success rate of area businesses. Raleigh* ranked #73. *www.nerdwallet.com, "Best Places to Start a Business," April 27, 2015*
- According to data by the Bureau of Economic Analysis (BEA) and the Bureau of Labor Statistics (BLS), the Raleigh* metro area has the fastest-growing GDP (gross domestic product) and positive employment trends, at #7. *247wallst.com, "Cities With the Fastest Growing (and Shrinking) Economies," September 26, 2016*
- 24/7 Wall Street used Brookings Institution research on 50 advanced industries to identify the proportion of workers in the nation's largest metropolitan areas that were employed in jobs requiring knowledge in the science, technology, engineering, or math (STEM) fields and where there was heavy investment in research and development (R&D). The Raleigh* metro area was #10. *247wallst.com, "15 Cities with the Most High-Tech Jobs," February 23, 2017*
- Based on metro area social media reviews, the employment opinion group Glassdoor surveyed 50 of the largest U.S. metro areas and equally weighed cost of living, hiring opportunity, and job satisfaction to compose a list of "25 Best Cities for Jobs." Median pay and home value, in-demand jobs and number of current job openings was also factored in. The Raleigh* metro area was ranked #4 in overall job satisfaction. *www.glassdoor.com, "Best Cities for Jobs," September 12, 2017*
- In a survey of economic confidence in the nation's 50 largest metropolitan areas conducted January–December 2014, the Raleigh* metro area placed #6, according to Gallup's 2014 Economic Confidence Index. *Gallup, "San Jose and San Francisco Lead in Economic Confidence," March 19, 2015*
- The Brookings Institution ranked the 100 largest metro areas in the U.S. based on income inequality. Raleigh* was ranked #80 (#1 = greatest ineqality). Criteria: the "95/20 ratio," a figure representing the income at which a household earns more than 95 percent of all other households, divided by the income at which a household earns more than only 20 percent of all other households. *Brookings Institution, "Household Income Inequality, 100 Largest U.S. Metro Areas, 2014-2016," February 5, 2018*
- *Forbes* ranked the 100 largest metro areas in the U.S. in terms of the "Best Cities for Young Professionals." The Raleigh* metro area ranked #10 out of 25. (Large metro areas were divided into metro divisions.) Criteria: median rent of a two-bedroom apartment; job growth and unemployment rate; median salary of college graduates with 5 or less years of work experience; networking opportunities; social outlook; percentage of population 25 years of age and older with college degrees. *Forbes.com, "America's 25 Best Cities for Young Professionals in 2017," May 22, 2017*

- Raleigh* was identified as one of America's most frugal metro areas by *Coupons.com.* The city ranked #3 out of 25. Criteria: digital coupon usage. *Coupons.com, "America's Most Frugal Cities of 2017," March 22, 2018*

- The Raleigh* metro area appeared on the Milken Institute "2017 Best Performing Cities" list. Rank: #2 out of 200 large metro areas. Criteria: job growth; wage and salary growth; high-tech output growth. *Milken Institute, "Best-Performing Cities 2017," January 2018*

- *Forbes* ranked the 200 most populous metro areas to determine the nation's "Best Places for Business and Careers." The Raleigh* metro area was ranked #2. Criteria: costs (business and living); job growth (past and projected); income growth; quality of life; educational attainment (college and high school); projected economic growth; cultural and recreational opportunities; net migration patterns; number of highly ranked colleges. *Forbes, "The Best Places for Business and Careers 2017," October 24, 2017*

Children/Family Rankings

- *Forbes* analyzed data on the 100 largest metropolitan areas in the United States to compile its 2016 ranking of the best cities for raising a family. The Raleigh* metro area was ranked #13. Criteria: median income; childcare costs; percent of population under 18; commuting delays; crime rate; percentage of families owning homes; education quality (mainly test scores). Overall cost of living and housing affordability was also unofficially considered. *Forbes, "America's Best Cities for Raising a Family 2016," August 30, 2016*

Dating/Romance Rankings

- *Apartment List* conducted its annual survey of renters to compile a list of metros that have the best opportunities for dating. Nearly 11,000 respondents, from February 2017 through January 2018, rated their current city or neighborhood for opportunities to date and make friends. The Raleigh* metro area ranked #1 out of 70 where single residents were very satisfied or somewhat satisfied, making it among the ten best metros for dating opportunities. Other criteria analyzed included gender and education levels of renters. *Apartment List, "Best Metros for Dating 2018," February 6, 2018*

Education Rankings

- Raleigh* was identified as one of America's "smartest" metropolitan areas by *The Business Journals.* The area ranked #8 out of 10. Criteria: percentage of adults (25 and older) with high school diplomas, bachelor's degrees and graduate degrees. *The Business Journals, "Where the Brainpower Is: Exclusive U.S. Rankings, Insights," February 27, 2014*

- Personal finance website *WalletHub* analyzed the 150 largest U.S. metropolitan statistical areas to determine where the most educated Americans are choosing to settle. Criteria: education quality and attainment gap; education levels; percentage of workers with degrees; public school rankings; quality and size of each metro area's universities. Raleigh* was ranked #15 (#1 = most educated city). *www.WalletHub.com, "2017's Most and Least Educated Cities in America," July 25, 2017*

Environmental Rankings

- Sperling's BestPlaces assessed 379 metropolitan areas of the United States for the likelihood of dangerously extreme weather events or earthquakes. In general the Southeast and South-Central regions have the highest risk of weather extremes and earthquakes, while the Pacific Northwest enjoys the lowest risk. Of the least risky metropolitan areas, the Raleigh* metro area was ranked #238. *www.bestplaces.net, "Safest Places from Natural Disasters," April 2011*

- The U.S. Environmental Protection Agency (EPA) released a list of mid-size U.S. metropolitan areas with the most ENERGY STAR certified buildings in 2016. The Raleigh* metro area was ranked #9 out of 10. *U.S. Environmental Protection Agency, "2017 Energy Star Top Cities," June 2017*

Health/Fitness Rankings

- For each of the 50 most populous metro areas in the United States, the American College of Sports Medicine's American Fitness Index evaluated infrastructure, community assets, and policies that encourage healthy and fit lifestyles, including preventive health behaviors, levels of chronic disease conditions, health care access, and community resources and policies that support physical activity. The Raleigh* metro area ranked #14 for "community fitness." *www.americanfitnessindex.org, "ACSM American Fitness Index Health and Community Fitness Status of the 50 Largest Metropolitan Areas," May 2017*
- The Raleigh* metro area was identified as one of the worst cities for bed bugs in America by pest control company Orkin. The area ranked #15 out of 50 based on the number of bed bug treatments Orkin performed from December 2016 to November 2017. *Orkin, "Baltimore and Washington D.C. Continue to Hold Top Spots," January 8, 2018*
- Raleigh* was identified as a "2016 Spring Allergy Capital." The area ranked #93 out of 100. Three groups of factors were used to identify the most severe cities for people with allergies during the spring season: annual pollen levels; medicine utilization; access to board-certified allergists. *Asthma and Allergy Foundation of America, "Spring Allergy Capitals 2016"*
- Raleigh* was identified as a "2016 Fall Allergy Capital." The area ranked #88 out of 100. Three groups of factors were used to identify the most severe cities for people with allergies during the fall season: annual pollen levels; medicine utilization; access to board-certified allergists. *Asthma and Allergy Foundation of America, "Fall Allergy Capitals 2016"*
- Raleigh* was identified as a "2015 Asthma Capital." The area ranked #92 out of the nation's 100 largest metropolitan areas. Criteria: estimated prevalence; self-reported prevalence; crude death rate for asthma; annual pollen score; annual air quality; public smoking laws; number of board-certified asthma specialists; school inhaler access laws; rescue medication use; controller medication use; ER visits for asthma; uninsured rate; poverty rate. *Asthma and Allergy Foundation of America, "Asthma Capitals 2015"*

Real Estate Rankings

- FitSmallBusiness looked at 50 of the largest metropolitan areas in the U.S. to determine which metro was the best to start a real estate business. Data was compiled from such sources as: Zillow, Trulia, U.S. Census Bureau, and the Bureau of Labor Statistics. Criteria: location; inventory; annual wages; median sales price of homes; days on the market; median price cut percentage; and other factors that would influence real estate professional growth. The Raleigh* metro area ranked #29. *fitsmallbusiness.com, "The Best Cities to Become a Real Estate Agent in 2018," January 30, 2018*
- The Raleigh* metro area was identified as one of the top 20 housing markets to invest in for 2018 by *Forbes*. The area ranked #4. Criteria: strong job and population growth; anticipated home price appreciation; and other factors. *Forbes.com, "Where to Invest in Housing in 2018," February 1, 2018*
- Raleigh* was ranked #144 out of 238 metro areas in terms of housing affordability in 2017 by the National Association of Home Builders (#1 = most affordable). Criteria: the share of homes sold in that area affordable to a family earning the local median income, based on standard mortgage underwriting criteria. *National Association of Home Builders®, NAHB-Wells Fargo Housing Opportunity Index, 4th Quarter 2017*

Safety Rankings

- The National Insurance Crime Bureau ranked 382 metro areas in the U.S. in terms of per capita rates of vehicle theft. The Raleigh* metro area ranked #239 (#1 = highest rate). Criteria: number of vehicle theft offenses per 100,000 inhabitants in 2016. *National Insurance Crime Bureau, "Hot Spots 2016," June 8, 2017*

Seniors/Retirement Rankings

- From its Best Cities for Successful Aging indexes, the Milken Institute generated rankings for metropolitan areas, weighing data in nine categories—health care, wellness, living arrangements, transportation and convenience, financial characteristics, education, employment, community engagement, and overall livability. The Raleigh* metro area was ranked #42 overall in the large metro area category. *Milken Institute, "Best Cities for Successful Aging, 2017" March 14, 2017*

  *Apex is located within the Raleigh, NC Metropolitan Statistical Area.

Business Environment

CITY FINANCES

City Government Finances

Component	2015 ($000)	2015 ($ per capita)
Total Revenues	94,767	2,079
Total Expenditures	99,895	2,191
Debt Outstanding	85,840	1,883
Cash and Securities[1]	588	13

Note: (1) Cash and security holdings of a government at the close of its fiscal year,, including those of its dependent agencies, utilities, and liquor stores.
Source: U.S Census Bureau, State & Local Government Finances 2015

City Government Revenue by Source

Source	2015 ($000)	2015 ($ per capita)	2015 (%)
General Revenue			
From Federal Government	0	0	0.0
From State Government	6,172	135	6.5
From Local Governments	2,287	50	2.4
Taxes			
Property	19,578	429	20.7
Sales and Gross Receipts	6,950	152	7.3
Personal Income	0	0	0.0
Corporate Income	0	0	0.0
Motor Vehicle License	227	5	0.2
Other Taxes	2,555	56	2.7
Current Charges	11,473	252	12.1
Liquor Store	0	0	0.0
Utility	39,671	870	41.9
Employee Retirement	73	2	0.1

Source: U.S Census Bureau, State & Local Government Finances 2015

City Government Expenditures by Function

Function	2015 ($000)	2015 ($ per capita)	2015 (%)
General Direct Expenditures			
Air Transportation	0	0	0.0
Corrections	0	0	0.0
Education	0	0	0.0
Employment Security Administration	0	0	0.0
Financial Administration	761	16	0.8
Fire Protection	5,678	124	5.7
General Public Buildings	1,278	28	1.3
Governmental Administration, Other	2,477	54	2.5
Health	1,439	31	1.4
Highways	4,838	106	4.8
Hospitals	0	0	0.0
Housing and Community Development	1,598	35	1.6
Interest on General Debt	2,133	46	2.1
Judicial and Legal	307	6	0.3
Libraries	0	0	0.0
Parking	0	0	0.0
Parks and Recreation	8,197	179	8.2
Police Protection	8,701	190	8.7
Public Welfare	0	0	0.0
Sewerage	7,236	158	7.2
Solid Waste Management	3,830	84	3.8
Veterans' Services	0	0	0.0
Liquor Store	0	0	0.0
Utility	48,212	1,057	48.3
Employee Retirement	48	1	0.0

Source: U.S Census Bureau, State & Local Government Finances 2015

DEMOGRAPHICS

Population Growth

Area	1990 Census	2000 Census	2010 Census	2016* Estimate	Population Growth (%) 1990-2016	2010-2016
City	7,092	20,212	37,476	43,893	518.9	17.1
MSA[1]	541,081	797,071	1,130,490	1,243,720	129.9	10.0
U.S.	248,709,873	281,421,906	308,745,538	318,558,162	28.1	3.2

Note: (1) Figures cover the Raleigh, NC Metropolitan Statistical Area—see Appendix B for areas included; (*) 2012-2016 5-year estimated population
Source: U.S. Census Bureau, 1990 Census, Census 2000, Census 2010, 2012-2016 American Community Survey 5-Year Estimates

Household Size

Area	Persons in Household (%)							Average Household Size
	One	Two	Three	Four	Five	Six	Seven or More	
City	19.1	26.5	21.3	21.1	9.4	2.0	0.6	2.90
MSA[1]	25.5	32.7	17.6	15.3	5.9	2.0	1.0	2.70
U.S.	27.7	33.7	15.7	13.1	6.0	2.3	1.5	2.60

Note: (1) Figures cover the Raleigh, NC Metropolitan Statistical Area—see Appendix B for areas included
Source: U.S. Census Bureau, 2012-2016 American Community Survey 5-Year Estimates

Race

Area	White Alone[2] (%)	Black Alone[2] (%)	Asian Alone[2] (%)	AIAN[3] Alone[2] (%)	NHOPI[4] Alone[2] (%)	Other Race Alone[2] (%)	Two or More Races (%)
City	79.7	8.5	7.0	0.3	0.0	1.6	2.9
MSA[1]	68.7	20.1	5.1	0.4	0.0	3.0	2.7
U.S.	73.3	12.6	5.2	0.8	0.2	4.8	3.1

Note: (1) Figures cover the Raleigh, NC Metropolitan Statistical Area—see Appendix B for areas included; (2) Alone is defined as not being in combination with one or more other races; (3) American Indian and Alaska Native; (4) Native Hawaiian and Other Pacific Islander
Source: U.S. Census Bureau, 2012-2016 American Community Survey 5-Year Estimates

Hispanic or Latino Origin

Area	Total (%)	Mexican (%)	Puerto Rican (%)	Cuban (%)	Other (%)
City	7.8	3.5	1.2	0.3	2.8
MSA[1]	10.3	5.8	1.1	0.3	3.1
U.S.	17.3	11.0	1.7	0.7	4.0

Note: Persons of Hispanic or Latino origin can be of any race; (1) Figures cover the Raleigh, NC Metropolitan Statistical Area—see Appendix B for areas included
Source: U.S. Census Bureau, 2012-2016 American Community Survey 5-Year Estimates

Segregation

Type	Segregation Indices[1]				Percent Change		
	1990	2000	2010	2010 Rank[2]	1990-2000	1990-2010	2000-2010
Black/White	41.9	40.8	42.1	87	-1.1	0.2	1.3
Asian/White	42.5	40.1	46.7	16	-2.4	4.2	6.6
Hispanic/White	19.9	34.9	37.1	76	15.1	17.3	2.2

Note: All figures cover the Metropolitan Statistical Area—see Appendix B for areas included; Figures are based on an analysis of 1990, 2000, and 2010 Census Decennial Census tract data by William H. Frey, Brookings Institution and the University of Michigan Social Science Data Analysis Network. In this analysis all racial groups (whites, blacks, and asians) are non-Hispanic members of those races. Hispanics are shown as a separate category; (1) Segregation Indices are Dissimilarity Indices that measure the degree to which the minority group is distributed differently than whites across census tracts. They range from 0 (complete integration) to 100 (complete segregation) where the value indicates the percentage of the minority group that needs to move to be distributed exactly like whites; (2) Ranges from 1 (most segregated) to 102 (least segregated); n/a not available.
Source: www.CensusScope.org

Ancestry

Area	German	Irish	English	American	Italian	Polish	French[2]	Scottish	Dutch
City	18.5	14.5	14.2	5.5	8.4	3.5	1.9	3.6	1.9
MSA[1]	11.2	9.9	10.6	11.3	4.8	2.1	1.9	2.7	1.0
U.S.	14.4	10.4	7.7	6.9	5.4	2.9	2.6	1.7	1.3

Note: Figures are the percentage of the total population reporting a particular ancestry. The nine most commonly reported ancestries in the U.S. are shown. Figures include multiple ancestries (e.g. if a person reported being Irish and Italian, they were included in both columns); (1) Figures cover the Raleigh, NC Metropolitan Statistical Area—see Appendix B for areas included; (2) Excludes Basque
Source: U.S. Census Bureau, 2012-2016 American Community Survey 5-Year Estimates

Foreign-Born Population

Area	Percent of Population Born in								
	Any Foreign Country	Asia	Mexico	Europe	Carribean	Central America[2]	South America	Africa	Canada
City	11.4	4.7	1.9	1.4	0.4	0.5	0.7	1.3	0.4
MSA[1]	11.8	4.1	3.0	1.2	0.6	1.0	0.6	1.0	0.4
U.S.	13.2	4.0	3.6	1.5	1.3	1.0	0.9	0.6	0.3

Note: (1) Figures cover the Raleigh, NC Metropolitan Statistical Area—see Appendix B for areas included; (2) Excludes Mexico.
Source: U.S. Census Bureau, 2012-2016 American Community Survey 5-Year Estimates

Marital Status

Area	Never Married	Now Married[2]	Separated	Widowed	Divorced
City	25.6	61.6	1.3	2.9	8.5
MSA[1]	31.7	51.7	2.5	4.4	9.7
U.S.	33.0	48.1	2.1	5.9	11.0

Note: Figures are percentages and cover the population 15 years of age and older; (1) Figures cover the Raleigh, NC Metropolitan Statistical Area—see Appendix B for areas included; (2) Excludes separated
Source: U.S. Census Bureau, 2012-2016 American Community Survey 5-Year Estimates

Disability Status

Area	All Ages	Under 18 Years Old	18 to 64 Years Old	65 Years and Over
City	5.9	3.0	5.3	25.6
MSA[1]	9.4	3.7	7.8	33.0
U.S.	12.5	4.1	10.3	35.7

Note: Figures show percent of the civilian noninstitutionalized population that reported having a disability. Disability status is determined from six types of difficulty: vision, hearing, cognitive, ambulatory, self-care, and independent living. For children under 5 years old, hearing and vision difficulty are used to determine disability status. For children between the ages of 5 and 14, disability status is determined from hearing, vision, cognitive, ambulatory, and self-care difficulties. For people aged 15 years and older, they are considered to have a disability if they have difficulty with any one of the six difficulty types; Note: (1) Figures cover the Raleigh, NC Metropolitan Statistical Area—see Appendix B for areas included
Source: U.S. Census Bureau, 2012-2016 American Community Survey 5-Year Estimates

Age

Area	Percent of Population									Median Age
	Under Age 5	Age 5–19	Age 20–34	Age 35–44	Age 45–54	Age 55–64	Age 65–74	Age 75–84	Age 85+	
City	7.4	25.6	15.5	19.3	16.5	8.7	4.5	1.5	0.8	35.9
MSA[1]	6.5	21.4	20.5	15.4	14.6	11.1	6.5	2.9	1.1	36.1
U.S.	6.2	19.6	20.7	12.7	13.6	12.6	8.3	4.3	1.9	37.7

Note: (1) Figures cover the Raleigh, NC Metropolitan Statistical Area—see Appendix B for areas included
Source: U.S. Census Bureau, 2012-2016 American Community Survey 5-Year Estimates

Gender

Area	Males	Females	Males per 100 Females
City	20,739	23,154	89.6
MSA[1]	605,735	637,985	94.9
U.S.	156,765,322	161,792,840	96.9

Note: (1) Figures cover the Raleigh, NC Metropolitan Statistical Area—see Appendix B for areas included
Source: U.S. Census Bureau, 2012-2016 American Community Survey 5-Year Estimates

Religious Groups by Family

Area	Catholic	Baptist	Non-Den.	Methodist[2]	Lutheran	LDS[3]	Pente-costal	Presby-terian[4]	Muslim[5]	Judaism
MSA[1]	9.2	12.1	6.0	6.7	0.9	0.9	2.3	2.3	0.9	0.3
U.S.	19.1	9.3	4.0	4.0	2.3	2.0	1.9	1.6	0.8	0.7

Note: Figures are the number of adherents as a percentage of the total population; (1) Figures cover the Raleigh, NC Metropolitan Statistical Area—see Appendix B for areas included; (2) Methodist/Pietist; (3) Latter Day Saints; (4) Reformed; (5) Figures are estimates
Source: Association of Statisticians of American Religious Bodies, 2010 U.S. Religion Census: Religious Congregations & Membership Study

Religious Groups by Tradition

Area	Catholic	Evangelical Protestant	Mainline Protestant	Other Tradition	Black Protestant	Orthodox
MSA[1]	9.2	19.9	10.1	3.3	1.7	0.2
U.S.	19.1	16.2	7.3	4.3	1.6	0.3

Note: Figures are the number of adherents as a percentage of the total population; (1) Figures cover the Raleigh, NC Metropolitan Statistical Area—see Appendix B for areas included
Source: Association of Statisticians of American Religious Bodies, 2010 U.S. Religion Census: Religious Congregations & Membership Study

ECONOMY

Gross Metropolitan Product

Area	2014	2015	2016	2017	Rank[2]
MSA[1]	71.4	75.9	79.7	84.8	44

Note: Figures are in billions of dollars; (1) Figures cover the Raleigh, NC Metropolitan Statistical Area—see Appendix B for areas included; (2) Rank is based on 2015 data and ranges from 1 to 381
Source: The U.S. Conference of Mayors, U.S. Metro Economies: GMP and Employment Report, 2015-2017

Economic Growth

Area	2012-14 (%)	2015 (%)	2016 (%)	2017 (%)	Rank[2]
MSA[1]	3.5	4.5	3.5	4.4	41
U.S.	2.0	2.4	1.9	2.6	–

Note: Figures are real gross metropolitan product (GMP) growth rates and represent average annual percent change; (1) Figures cover the Raleigh, NC Metropolitan Statistical Area—see Appendix B for areas included; (2) Rank is based on 2012-2014 average annual percent change and ranges from 1 to 381
Source: The U.S. Conference of Mayors, U.S. Metro Economies: GMP and Employment Report, 2015-2017

Metropolitan Area Exports

Area	2011	2012	2013	2014	2015	2016	Rank[2]
MSA[1]	2,254.4	2,308.1	2,280.6	2,713.1	2,553.4	2,620.4	81

Note: Figures are in millions of dollars; (1) Figures cover the Raleigh, NC Metropolitan Statistical Area—see Appendix B for areas included; (2) Rank is based on 2016 data and ranges from 1 to 385
Source: U.S. Department of Commerce, International Trade Administration, Office of Trade & Industry Information, Manufacturing & Services, data extracted March 15, 2018

Building Permits

Area	Single-Family			Multi-Family			Total		
	2016	2017p	Pct. Chg.	2016	2017p	Pct. Chg.	2016	2017p	Pct. Chg.
City	959	1,388	44.7	212	0	-100.0	1,171	1,388	18.5
MSA[1]	9,435	10,785	14.3	4,072	3,428	-15.8	13,507	14,213	5.2
U.S.	750,800	817,300	8.9	455,800	446,800	-2.0	1,206,600	1,264,100	4.8

Note: (1) Figures cover the Raleigh, NC Metropolitan Statistical Area—see Appendix B for areas included; Figures represent new, privately-owned housing units authorized (unadjusted data); All permit data are based on estimates with imputation; (p) preliminary data.
Source: U.S. Census Bureau, Manufacturing, Mining, and Construction Statistics, Building Permits, 2016, 2017

Bankruptcy Filings

Area	Business Filings 2016	Business Filings 2017	Business Filings % Chg.	Nonbusiness Filings 2016	Nonbusiness Filings 2017	Nonbusiness Filings % Chg.
Wake County	76	79	3.9	1,539	1,458	-5.3
U.S.	24,114	23,157	-4.0	770,846	765,863	-0.6

Note: Business filings include Chapter 7, Chapter 11, Chapter 12, and Chapter 13; Nonbusiness filings include Chapter 7, Chapter 11, and Chapter 13
Source: Administrative Office of the U.S. Courts, Business and Nonbusiness Bankruptcy, County Cases Commenced by Chapter of the Bankruptcy Code, During the 12-Month Period Ending December 31, 2016 and Business and Nonbusiness Bankruptcy, County Cases Commenced by Chapter of the Bankruptcy Code, During the 12-Month Period Ending December 31, 2017

Housing Vacancy Rates

Area	Gross Vacancy Rate[2] (%)			Year-Round Vacancy Rate[3] (%)			Rental Vacancy Rate[4] (%)			Homeowner Vacancy Rate[5] (%)		
	2015	2016	2017	2015	2016	2017	2015	2016	2017	2015	2016	2017
MSA[1]	6.8	6.8	8.0	6.7	6.7	7.8	6.6	4.3	5.8	1.7	1.9	1.7
U.S.	12.9	12.8	12.7	10.0	9.9	9.9	7.1	6.9	7.2	1.8	1.7	1.6

Note: (1) Figures cover the Raleigh, NC Metropolitan Statistical Area—see Appendix B for areas included; (2) The percentage of the total housing inventory that is vacant; (3) The percentage of the housing inventory (excluding seasonal units) that is year-round vacant; (4) The percentage of rental inventory that is vacant for rent; (5) The percentage of homeowner inventory that is vacant for sale
Source: U.S. Census Bureau, Housing Vacancies and Homeownership Annual Statistics: 2015, 2016, 2017

INCOME

Income

Area	Per Capita ($)	Median Household ($)	Average Household ($)
City	38,886	95,283	111,252
MSA[1]	33,233	65,834	87,616
U.S.	29,829	55,322	77,866

Note: (1) Figures cover the Raleigh, NC Metropolitan Statistical Area—see Appendix B for areas included
Source: U.S. Census Bureau, 2012-2016 American Community Survey 5-Year Estimates

Household Income Distribution

Area	Percent of Households Earning: Under $15,000	$15,000 -$24,999	$25,000 -$34,999	$35,000 -$49,999	$50,000 -$74,999	$75,000 -$99,999	$100,000 -$149,999	$150,000 and up
City	5.9	3.9	5.6	7.9	13.5	16.1	24.2	23.0
MSA[1]	8.4	7.7	9.0	13.0	17.7	13.6	16.4	14.2
U.S.	12.1	10.2	9.9	13.2	17.8	12.2	13.5	11.1

Note: (1) Figures cover the Raleigh, NC Metropolitan Statistical Area—see Appendix B for areas included
Source: U.S. Census Bureau, 2012-2016 American Community Survey 5-Year Estimates

Poverty Rate

Area	All Ages	Under 18 Years Old	18 to 64 Years Old	65 Years and Over
City	4.6	3.8	4.3	11.3
MSA[1]	11.6	15.7	10.8	6.9
U.S.	15.1	21.2	14.2	9.3

Note: Figures are percentage of people whose income during the past 12 months was below the poverty level; (1) Figures cover the Raleigh, NC Metropolitan Statistical Area—see Appendix B for areas included
Source: U.S. Census Bureau, 2012-2016 American Community Survey 5-Year Estimates

EMPLOYMENT

Labor Force and Employment

Area	Civilian Labor Force Dec. 2016	Civilian Labor Force Dec. 2017	Civilian Labor Force % Chg.	Workers Employed Dec. 2016	Workers Employed Dec. 2017	Workers Employed % Chg.
City	25,251	25,875	2.5	24,330	25,039	2.9
MSA[1]	679,166	696,216	2.5	650,915	669,860	2.9
U.S.	158,968,000	159,880,000	0.6	151,798,000	153,602,000	1.2

Note: Data is not seasonally adjusted and covers workers 16 years of age and older; (1) Figures cover the Raleigh, NC Metropolitan Statistical Area—see Appendix B for areas included
Source: Bureau of Labor Statistics, Local Area Unemployment Statistics

Unemployment Rate

Area	2017											
	Jan.	Feb.	Mar.	Apr.	May	Jun.	Jul.	Aug.	Sep.	Oct.	Nov.	Dec.
City	3.8	3.7	3.5	3.0	3.3	3.5	3.7	3.7	3.2	3.2	3.5	3.2
MSA[1]	4.5	4.3	4.0	3.6	3.8	4.0	4.2	4.3	3.8	3.7	3.9	3.8
U.S.	5.1	4.9	4.6	4.1	4.1	4.5	4.6	4.5	4.1	3.9	3.9	3.9

Note: Data is not seasonally adjusted and covers workers 16 years of age and older; (1) Figures cover the Raleigh, NC Metropolitan Statistical Area—see Appendix B for areas included
Source: Bureau of Labor Statistics, Local Area Unemployment Statistics

Average Wages

Occupation	$/Hr.	Occupation	$/Hr.
Accountants and Auditors	34.70	Maids and Housekeeping Cleaners	10.50
Automotive Mechanics	21.30	Maintenance and Repair Workers	20.20
Bookkeepers	19.90	Marketing Managers	73.10
Carpenters	19.00	Nuclear Medicine Technologists	33.40
Cashiers	9.80	Nurses, Licensed Practical	21.60
Clerks, General Office	15.50	Nurses, Registered	30.80
Clerks, Receptionists/Information	13.90	Nursing Assistants	12.00
Clerks, Shipping/Receiving	15.10	Packers and Packagers, Hand	12.10
Computer Programmers	47.20	Physical Therapists	41.10
Computer Systems Analysts	44.70	Postal Service Mail Carriers	24.10
Computer User Support Specialists	28.10	Real Estate Brokers	28.10
Cooks, Restaurant	12.00	Retail Salespersons	12.40
Dentists	114.20	Sales Reps., Exc. Tech./Scientific	34.20
Electrical Engineers	53.50	Sales Reps., Tech./Scientific	49.10
Electricians	19.80	Secretaries, Exc. Legal/Med./Exec.	17.60
Financial Managers	67.20	Security Guards	13.20
First-Line Supervisors/Managers, Sales	21.20	Surgeons	n/a
Food Preparation Workers	10.80	Teacher Assistants*	11.40
General and Operations Managers	67.90	Teachers, Elementary School*	23.40
Hairdressers/Cosmetologists	15.60	Teachers, Secondary School*	22.60
Internists, General	n/a	Telemarketers	12.80
Janitors and Cleaners	11.30	Truck Drivers, Heavy/Tractor-Trailer	22.00
Landscaping/Groundskeeping Workers	14.50	Truck Drivers, Light/Delivery Svcs.	16.20
Lawyers	70.10	Waiters and Waitresses	11.50

Note: Wage data covers the Raleigh, NC Metropolitan Statistical Area—see Appendix B for areas included; (*) Hourly wages for elementary/secondary school teachers and teacher assistants were calculated by the editors from annual wage data based on a 40 hour work week; n/a not available.
Source: Bureau of Labor Statistics, Metro Area Occupational Employment & Wage Estimates, May 2017

Employment by Occupation

Occupation Classification	City (%)	MSA[1] (%)	U.S. (%)
Management, Business, Science, and Arts	56.8	47.0	37.0
Natural Resources, Construction, and Maintenance	4.1	7.2	8.9
Production, Transportation, and Material Moving	4.1	7.6	12.2
Sales and Office	21.9	23.8	23.8
Service	13.1	14.5	18.1

Note: Figures cover employed civilians 16 years of age and older; (1) Figures cover the Raleigh, NC Metropolitan Statistical Area—see Appendix B for areas included
Source: U.S. Census Bureau, 2012-2016 American Community Survey 5-Year Estimates

Employment by Industry

Sector	MSA[1] Number of Employees	MSA[1] Percent of Total	U.S. Percent of Total
Construction, Mining, and Logging	38,100	6.1	5.2
Education and Health Services	75,400	12.0	15.9
Financial Activities	31,900	5.1	5.7
Government	98,600	15.8	15.3
Information	22,400	3.6	1.9
Leisure and Hospitality	69,500	11.1	10.7
Manufacturing	35,100	5.6	8.5
Other Services	23,700	3.8	3.9
Professional and Business Services	117,900	18.8	14.0
Retail Trade	71,900	11.5	11.0
Transportation, Warehousing, and Utilities	13,800	2.2	4.1
Wholesale Trade	27,600	4.4	4.0

Note: Figures are non-farm employment as of December 2017. Figures are not seasonally adjusted and include workers 16 years of age and older; (1) Figures cover the Raleigh, NC Metropolitan Statistical Area—see Appendix B for areas included
Source: Bureau of Labor Statistics, Current Employment Statistics, Employment, Hours, and Earnings

Occupations with Greatest Projected Employment Growth: 2017 – 2019

Occupation[1]	2017 Employment	2019 Projected Employment	Numeric Employment Change	Percent Employment Change
Combined Food Preparation and Serving Workers, Including Fast Food	150,940	161,640	10,700	7.1
Retail Salespersons	141,960	146,580	4,620	3.3
Waiters and Waitresses	78,300	82,440	4,140	5.3
Customer Service Representatives	98,260	102,060	3,800	3.9
Registered Nurses	99,040	102,730	3,690	3.7
Cashiers	112,380	115,690	3,310	3.0
Laborers and Freight, Stock, and Material Movers, Hand	86,000	89,280	3,280	3.8
Cooks, Restaurant	41,650	44,300	2,650	6.4
Home Health Aides	40,030	42,550	2,520	6.3
General and Operations Managers	55,710	58,180	2,470	4.4

Note: Projections cover North Carolina; (1) Sorted by numeric employment change
Source: www.projectionscentral.com, State Occupational Projections, 2017–2019 Short-Term Projections

Fastest Growing Occupations: 2017 – 2019

Occupation[1]	2017 Employment	2019 Projected Employment	Numeric Employment Change	Percent Employment Change
Solar Photovoltaic Installers	480	550	70	13.5
Helpers—Pipelayers, Plumbers, Pipefitters, and Steamfitters	3,340	3,670	330	9.9
Statisticians	1,220	1,340	120	9.8
Insurance Claims and Policy Processing Clerks	5,090	5,580	490	9.7
Insurance Sales Agents	12,990	14,230	1,240	9.5
Software Developers, Applications	26,360	28,620	2,260	8.6
Helpers—Brickmasons, Blockmasons, Stonemasons, and Tile and Marble Setters	1,060	1,150	90	8.5
Structural Iron and Steel Workers	1,560	1,690	130	8.5
Helpers—Carpenters	1,280	1,390	110	8.4
Plumbers, Pipefitters, and Steamfitters	11,560	12,520	960	8.3

Note: Projections cover North Carolina; (1) Sorted by percent employment change and excludes occupations with numeric employment change less than 50
Source: www.projectionscentral.com, State Occupational Projections, 2017–2019 Short-Term Projections

TAXES

State Corporate Income Tax Rates

State	Tax Rate (%)	Income Brackets ($)	Num. of Brackets	Financial Institution Tax Rate (%)[a]	Federal Income Tax Ded.
North Carolina	3.0	Flat rate	1	3.0	No

Note: Tax rates as of January 1, 2018; (a) Rates listed are the corporate income tax rate applied to financial institutions or excise taxes based on income. Some states have other taxes based upon the value of deposits or shares.
Source: Federation of Tax Administrators, Range of State Corporate Income Tax Rates, January 1, 2018

State Individual Income Tax Rates

State	Tax Rate (%)	Income Brackets ($)	Num. of Brackets	Personal Exempt. ($)[1]		Fed. Inc. Tax Ded.
				Single	Dependents	
North Carolina	5.499	Flat rate	1	None	None	No

Note: Tax rates as of January 1, 2018; Local- and county-level taxes are not included; n/a not applicable; (1) Married joint filers generally receive double the single exemption
Source: Federation of Tax Administrators, State Individual Income Tax Rates, January 1, 2018

Various State Sales and Excise Tax Rates

State	State Sales Tax (%)	Gasoline[1] (¢/gal.)	Cigarette[2] ($/pack)	Spirits[3] ($/gal.)	Wine[4] ($/gal.)	Beer[5] ($/gal.)	Recreational Marijuana (%)
North Carolina	4.75	35.35	0.45	14.63 (g)	1.00 (l)	0.62 (q)	Not legal

Note: All tax rates as of January 1, 2018; (1) The American Petroleum Institute has developed a methodology for determining the average tax rate on a gallon of fuel. Rates may include any of the following: excise taxes, environmental fees, storage tank fees, other fees or taxes, general sales tax, and local taxes. In states where gasoline is subject to the general sales tax, or where the fuel tax is based on the average sale price, the average rate determined by API is sensitive to changes in the price of gasoline. States that fully or partially apply general sales taxes to gasoline: CA, CO, GA, IL, IN, MI, NY; (2) The federal excise tax of $1.0066 per pack and local taxes are not included; (3) Rates are those applicable to off-premise sales of 40% alcohol by volume (a.b.v.) distilled spirits in 750ml containers. Local excise taxes are excluded; (4) Rates are those applicable to off-premise sales of 11% a.b.v. non-carbonated wine in 750ml containers; (5) Rates are those applicable to off-premise sales of 4.7% a.b.v. beer in 12 ounce containers; (g) Control states, where the government controls all sales. Products can be subject to ad valorem mark-up as well as excise taxes; (l) Different rates also applicable to alcohol content, place of production, size of container, place purchased (on- or off-premise or on board airlines) or type of wine (carbonated, vermouth, etc.); (q) Different rates also applicable according to alcohol content, place of production, size of container, or place purchased (on- or off-premise or onboard airlines).
Source: Tax Foundation, 2018 Facts & Figures: How Does Your State Compare?

State Business Tax Climate Index Rankings

State	Overall Rank	Corporate Tax Rank	Individual Income Tax Rank	Sales Tax Rank	Unemployment Insurance Tax Rank	Property Tax Rank
North Carolina	11	3	13	20	6	32

Note: The index is a measure of how each state's tax laws affect economic performance. The lower the rank, the more favorable a state's tax system is for business. States without a given tax are given a ranking of 1. The scores/rankings for the District of Columbia do not affect other states. The 2018 index represents the tax climate as of July 1, 2017.
Source: Tax Foundation, State Business Tax Climate Index 2018

TRANSPORTATION

Means of Transportation to Work

Area	Car/Truck/Van		Public Transportation			Bicycle	Walked	Other Means	Worked at Home
	Drove Alone	Car-pooled	Bus	Subway	Railroad				
City	81.4	7.8	0.4	0.0	0.0	0.2	0.6	0.9	8.7
MSA[1]	80.2	9.1	0.9	0.0	0.0	0.3	1.2	1.0	7.2
U.S.	76.4	9.3	2.6	1.9	0.6	0.6	2.8	1.3	4.6

Note: Figures are percentages and cover workers 16 years of age and older; (1) Figures cover the Raleigh, NC Metropolitan Statistical Area—see Appendix B for areas included
Source: U.S. Census Bureau, 2012-2016 American Community Survey 5-Year Estimates

Travel Time to Work

Area	Less Than 10 Minutes	10 to 19 Minutes	20 to 29 Minutes	30 to 44 Minutes	45 to 59 Minutes	60 to 89 Minutes	90 Minutes or More
City	10.2	25.5	31.6	24.8	4.6	1.9	1.3
MSA[1]	9.9	28.5	25.1	23.2	7.7	3.8	1.7
U.S.	12.9	29.2	20.9	20.4	8.0	6.0	2.7

Note: Note: Figures are percentages and include workers 16 years old and over; (1) Figures cover the Raleigh, NC Metropolitan Statistical Area—see Appendix B for areas included
Source: U.S. Census Bureau, 2012-2016 American Community Survey 5-Year Estimates

Freeway Travel Time Index

Area	1985	1990	1995	2000	2005	2010	2014
Urban Area Rank[1,2]	54	46	59	65	61	57	54
Urban Area Index[1]	1.06	1.10	1.12	1.14	1.16	1.16	1.17
Average Index[3]	1.09	1.11	1.14	1.17	1.20	1.19	1.20

Note: Freeway Travel Time Index—the ratio of travel time in the peak period to the travel time at free-flow conditions. For example, a value of 1.30 indicates a 20-minute free-flow trip takes 26 minutes in the peak (20 minutes x 1.30 = 26 minutes); (1) Covers the Raleigh NC urban area; (2) Rank is based on 101 urban areas (#1 = highest travel time index); (3) Average of 101 urban areas
Source: Texas Transportation Institute, 2015 Urban Mobility Scorecard, August 2015

Freeway Commuter Stress Index

Area	1985	1990	1995	2000	2005	2010	2014
Urban Area Rank[1,2]	58	51	61	63	58	58	61
Urban Area Index[1]	1.08	1.12	1.14	1.17	1.19	1.19	1.19
Average Index[3]	1.13	1.16	1.19	1.22	1.25	1.24	1.25

Note: The Freeway Commuter Stress Index is the same as the Freeway Travel Time Index (see table above) except that it includes only the travel in the peak directions during the peak periods; the TTI includes travel in all directions during the peak period. Thus, the CSI is more indicative of the work trip experienced by each commuter on a daily basis; (1) Covers the Raleigh NC urban area; (2) Rank is based on 101 urban areas (#1 = highest travel time index); (3) Average of 101 urban areas
Source: Texas Transportation Institute, 2015 Urban Mobility Scorecard, August 2015

Living Environment

COST OF LIVING

Cost of Living Index

Composite Index	Groceries	Housing	Utilities	Trans-portation	Health Care	Misc. Goods/ Services
96.2	105.7	83.4	97.5	99.7	100.5	101.1

Note: The Cost of Living Index measures regional differences in the cost of consumer goods and services, excluding taxes and non-consumer expenditures, for professional and managerial households in the top income quintile. It is based on more than 50,000 prices covering almost 60 different items for which prices are collected three times a year by chambers of commerce, economic development organizations or university applied economic centers in each participating urban area. The numbers shown should be read as a percentage above or below the national average of 100. For example, a value of 115.4 in the groceries column indicates that grocery prices are 15.4% higher than the national average. Small differences in the index numbers should not be interpreted as significant; Figures cover the Raleigh NC urban area.
Source: The Council for Community and Economic Research, ACCRA Cost of Living Index, 2017

Grocery Prices

Area[1]	T-Bone Steak ($/pound)	Frying Chicken ($/pound)	Whole Milk ($/half gal.)	Eggs ($/dozen)	Orange Juice ($/64 oz.)	Coffee ($/11.5 oz.)
City[2]	12.34	1.69	2.00	2.92	3.57	4.42
Avg.	11.29	1.40	2.02	1.47	3.55	4.37
Min.	7.71	0.93	1.04	0.70	2.86	3.24
Max.	15.83	2.39	4.03	3.92	6.29	8.16

Note: (1) Values for the local area are compared with the average, minimum and maximum values for all 294 areas in the Cost of Living Index; (2) Figures cover the Raleigh NC urban area; ***T-Bone Steak*** *(price per pound);* ***Frying Chicken*** *(price per pound, whole fryer);* ***Whole Milk*** *(half gallon carton);* ***Eggs*** *(price per dozen, Grade A, large);* ***Orange Juice*** *(64 oz. Tropicana or Florida Natural);* ***Coffee*** *(11.5 oz. can, vacuum-packed, Maxwell House, Hills Bros, or Folgers).*
Source: The Council for Community and Economic Research, ACCRA Cost of Living Index, 2017

Housing and Utility Costs

Area[1]	New Home Price ($)	Apartment Rent ($/month)	All Electric ($/month)	Part Electric ($/month)	Other Energy ($/month)	Telephone ($/month)
City[2]	261,414	1,013	-	81.95	61.55	31.92
Avg.	335,956	1,047	175.01	97.34	67.93	28.71
Min.	187,788	491	109.48	49.33	35.44	12.39
Max.	1,739,087	4,559	432.62	227.09	353.33	44.61

Note: (1) Values for the local area are compared with the average, minimum and maximum values for all 294 areas in the Cost of Living Index; (2) Figures cover the Raleigh NC urban area; ***New Home Price*** *(2,400 sf living area, 8,000 sf lot, in urban area with full utilities);* ***Apartment Rent*** *(950 sf 2 bedroom/1.5 or 2 bath, unfurnished, excluding all utilities except water);* ***All Electric*** *(average monthly cost for an all-electric home);* ***Part Electric*** *(average monthly cost for a part-electric home);* ***Other Energy*** *(average monthly cost for natural gas, fuel oil, coal, wood, and any other forms of energy except electricity);* ***Telephone*** *(price includes basic monthly rate for a private residential line plus additional local usage charges incurred by a family of four).*
Source: The Council for Community and Economic Research, ACCRA Cost of Living Index, 2017

Health Care, Transportation, and Other Costs

Area[1]	Doctor ($/visit)	Dentist ($/visit)	Optometrist ($/visit)	Gasoline ($/gallon)	Beauty Salon ($/visit)	Men's Shirt ($)
City[2]	99.19	98.93	103.10	2.26	51.86	23.44
Avg.	108.00	92.54	101.93	2.25	37.58	30.92
Min.	30.39	60.00	49.75	1.82	16.11	11.20
Max.	193.50	161.94	229.28	3.16	77.35	59.13

Note: (1) Values for the local area are compared with the average, minimum and maximum values for all 294 areas in the Cost of Living Index; (2) Figures cover the Raleigh NC urban area; ***Doctor*** *(general practitioners routine exam of an established patient);* ***Dentist*** *(adult teeth cleaning and periodic oral examination);* ***Optometrist*** *(full vision eye exam for established adult patient);* ***Gasoline*** *(one gallon regular unleaded, national brand, including all taxes, cash price at self-service pump if available);* ***Beauty Salon*** *(woman's shampoo, trim, and blow-dry);* ***Men's Shirt*** *(cotton/polyester dress shirt, pinpoint weave, long sleeves).*
Source: The Council for Community and Economic Research, ACCRA Cost of Living Index, 2017

HOUSING

House Price Index (HPI)

Area	National Ranking[2]	Quarterly Change (%)	One-Year Change (%)	Five-Year Change (%)
MSA[1]	95	0.62	7.09	29.98
U.S.[3]	–	1.61	6.68	34.71

Note: The HPI is a weighted repeat sales index. It measures average price changes in repeat sales or refinancings on the same properties. This information is obtained by reviewing repeat mortgage transactions on single-family properties whose mortgages have been purchased or securitized by Fannie Mae or Freddie Mac in January 1975; (1) Figures cover the Raleigh, NC Metropolitan Statistical Area—see Appendix B for areas included; (2) Rankings are based on annual percentage change for all metro areas containing at least 15,000 transactions over the last 10 years and ranges from 1 to 253; (3) figures based on a weighted average of Census Division estimates using a seasonally adjusted, purchase-only index; all figures are for the period ending December 31, 2017
Source: Federal Housing Finance Agency, House Price Index, February 28, 2018

Median Single-Family Home Prices

Area	2015	2016	2017p	Percent Change 2016 to 2017
MSA[1]	238.2	247.9	266.8	7.6
U.S. Average	223.9	235.5	248.8	5.6

Note: Figures are median sales prices of existing single-family homes in thousands of dollars; (p) preliminary; (1) Figures cover the Raleigh, NC Metropolitan Statistical Area—see Appendix B for areas included
Source: National Association of Realtors, Median Sales Price of Existing Single-Family Homes for Metropolitan Areas, 4th Quarter 2017

Qualifying Income Based on Median Sales Price of Existing Single-Family Homes

Area	With 5% Down ($)	With 10% Down ($)	With 20% Down ($)
MSA[1]	n/a	n/a	n/a
U.S. Average	55,585	52,659	46,808

Note: Figures are preliminary; Qualifying income is based on a mortgage rate of 4.17%. Monthly principal and interest payment is limited to 25% of income; n/a not available; (1) Figures cover the Raleigh, NC Metropolitan Statistical Area—see Appendix B for areas included
Source: National Association of Realtors, Qualifying Income Based on Median Sales Price of Existing Single-Family Homes for Metropolitan Areas, 4th Quarter 2017

Median Apartment Condo-Coop Home Prices

Area	2015	2016	2017p	Percent Change 2016 to 2017
MSA[1]	n/a	n/a	n/a	n/a
U.S. Average	210.7	220.7	234.3	6.2

Note: Figures are median sales prices of existing apartment condo-coop homes in thousands of dollars; (p) preliminary; n/a not available; (1) Figures cover the Raleigh, NC Metropolitan Statistical Area—see Appendix B for areas included
Source: National Association of Realtors, Median Sales Price of Existing Apartment Condo-Coop Homes for Metropolitan Areas, 4th Quarter 2017

Home Value Distribution

Area	Under $50,000	$50,000 -$99,999	$100,000 -$149,999	$150,000 -$199,999	$200,000 -$299,999	$300,000 -$499,999	$500,000 -$999,999	$1,000,000 or more
City	1.6	0.7	5.4	13.7	37.4	36.6	4.2	0.3
MSA[1]	4.5	6.5	16.2	18.2	24.8	21.9	6.9	1.1
U.S.	8.8	14.8	15.3	14.9	18.4	16.4	9.0	2.5

Note: Figures are percentages and cover owner-occupied housing units; (1) Figures cover the Raleigh, NC Metropolitan Statistical Area—see Appendix B for areas included
Source: U.S. Census Bureau, 2012-2016 American Community Survey 5-Year Estimates

Homeownership Rate

Area	2009 (%)	2010 (%)	2011 (%)	2012 (%)	2013 (%)	2014 (%)	2015 (%)	2016 (%)	2017 (%)
MSA[1]	65.7	65.9	66.7	67.7	65.5	65.5	67.4	65.9	68.2
U.S.	67.4	66.9	66.1	65.4	65.1	64.5	63.7	63.4	63.9

Note: (1) Figures cover the Raleigh, NC Metropolitan Statistical Area—see Appendix B for areas included
Source: U.S. Census Bureau, Housing Vacancies and Homeownership Annual Statistics: 2009-2017

Year Housing Structure Built

Area	2010 or Later	2000 -2009	1990 -1999	1980 -1989	1970 -1979	1960 -1969	1950 -1959	1940 -1949	Before 1940	Median Year
City	10.2	37.5	38.7	6.6	3.0	1.0	0.8	0.8	1.4	1999
MSA[1]	5.6	28.6	24.7	16.2	10.1	6.2	4.1	1.7	2.8	1994
U.S.	2.3	14.7	14.0	13.7	15.6	10.9	10.6	5.2	13.0	1977

Note: Figures are percentages except for Median Year; Note: (1) Figures cover the Raleigh, NC Metropolitan Statistical Area—see Appendix B for areas included
Source: U.S. Census Bureau, 2012-2016 American Community Survey 5-Year Estimates

Gross Monthly Rent

Area	Under $500	$500 -$999	$1,000 -$1,499	$1,500 -$1,999	$2,000 -$2,499	$2,500 -$2,999	$3,000 and up	Median ($)
City	0.1	32.2	47.8	16.8	2.7	0.5	0.0	1,162
MSA[1]	5.9	49.1	34.2	7.8	1.8	0.5	0.6	963
U.S.	11.3	43.3	27.7	10.7	4.0	1.6	1.5	949

Note: Figures are percentages except for Median; Gross rent is the contract rent plus the estimated average monthly cost of utilities (electricity, gas, and water and sewer) and fuels (oil, coal, kerosene, wood, etc.) if these are paid by the renter (or paid for the renter by someone else); (1) Figures cover the Raleigh, NC Metropolitan Statistical Area—see Appendix B for areas included
Source: U.S. Census Bureau, 2012-2016 American Community Survey 5-Year Estimates

HEALTH

Health Risk Factors

Category	MSA[1] (%)	U.S. (%)
Adults aged 18–64 who have any kind of health care coverage	84.0	87.7
Adults who reported being in good or excellent health	86.9	83.6
Adults who are current smokers	12.5	17.1
Adults who currently use E-cigarettes	3.2	4.7
Adults who currently use chewing tobacco, snuff, or snus	1.0	4.0
Adults who are heavy drinkers[2]	7.4	6.5
Adults who are binge drinkers[3]	15.8	16.9
Adults who are overweight (BMI 25.0 - 29.9)	33.9	35.3
Adults who are obese (BMI 30.0 - 99.8)	29.3	29.9
Adults who participated in any physical activities in the past month	84.2	76.9
Adults who always or nearly always wears a seat belt	98.4	94.3

Note: (1) Figures cover the Raleigh, NC Metropolitan Statistical Area—see Appendix B for areas included; (2) Heavy drinkers are classified as adult men having more than 14 drinks per week and adult women having more than 7 drinks per week; (3) Binge drinkers are classified as males having five or more drinks on one occasion or females having four or more drinks on one occasion
Source: Centers for Disease Control and Prevention, Behaviorial Risk Factor Surveillance System, SMART: Selected Metropolitan Area Risk Trends, 2016

Health Screening Rates

Category	MSA[1] (%)	U.S. (%)
Adults 50-75 who have had a blood stool test within the past year	7.3	8.0
Adults 50-75 who have had a colonoscopy in the past 10 years	72.6	63.5
Adults aged 65+ who have had flu shot within the past year	75.7	58.6
Adults aged 65+ who have ever had a pneumonia vaccination	76.1	73.4
Adults who have ever been tested for HIV	41.6	35.6
Women aged 21-65 who have had a pap test in the past three years	83.7	79.8
Men aged 40+ who have had a PSA test within the past two years	42.0	39.5
Women aged 40+ who have had a mammogram within the past two years	78.3	72.5

Note: n/a not available; (1) Figures cover the Raleigh, NC Metropolitan Statistical Area—see Appendix B for areas included; Source: Centers for Disease Control and Prevention, Behaviorial Risk Factor Surveillance System, SMART: Selected Metropolitan Area Risk Trends, 2016

Chronic Health Conditions

Category	MSA[1] (%)	U.S. (%)
Adults who have ever been told they had a heart attack	2.5	4.4
Adults who have ever been told they have angina or coronary heart disease	3.8	4.1
Adults who have ever been told they had a stroke	n/a	3.1
Adults who have been told they currently have asthma	9.4	9.3
Adults who have ever been told they have arthritis	20.9	25.8
Adults who have ever been told they have diabetes[2]	7.2	10.5
Adults who have ever been told they had skin cancer	8.2	5.9
Adults who have ever been told they had any other types of cancer	4.8	6.7
Adults who have ever been told they have COPD	4.2	6.3
Adults who have ever been told they have kidney disease	n/a	2.8
Adults who have ever been told they have a form of depression	17.4	17.4

Note: n/a not available; (1) Figures cover the Raleigh, NC Metropolitan Statistical Area—see Appendix B for areas included; (2) Figures do not include pregnancy-related, borderline, or pre-diabetes
Source: Centers for Disease Control and Prevention, Behaviorial Risk Factor Surveillance System, SMART: Selected Metropolitan Area Risk Trends, 2016

Mortality Rates for the Top 10 Causes of Death in the U.S.

ICD-10[a] Sub-Chapter	ICD-10[a] Code	Age-Adjusted Mortality Rate[1] per 100,000 population	
		County[2]	U.S.
Malignant neoplasms	C00-C97	142.5	158.5
Ischaemic heart diseases	I20-I25	63.0	96.8
Other forms of heart disease	I30-I51	43.3	52.4
Chronic lower respiratory diseases	J40-J47	27.8	40.9
Cerebrovascular diseases	I60-I69	37.7	37.2
Organic, including symptomatic, mental disorders	F01-F09	55.4	33.3
Other degenerative diseases of the nervous system	G30-G31	27.6	32.1
Other external causes of accidental injury	W00-X59	25.2	31.2
Diabetes mellitus	E10-E14	17.9	21.1
Hypertensive diseases	I10-I15	17.6	20.8

Note: (a) ICD-10 = International Classification of Diseases 10th Revision; (1) Mortality rates are a three year average covering 2014-2016; (2) Figures cover Wake County.
Source: Centers for Disease Control and Prevention, National Center for Health Statistics. Underlying Cause of Death 1999-2016 on CDC WONDER Online Database, released December 2017

Mortality Rates for Selected Causes of Death

ICD-10[a] Sub-Chapter	ICD-10[a] Code	Age-Adjusted Mortality Rate[1] per 100,000 population	
		County[2]	U.S.
Assault	X85-Y09	2.9	5.6
Diseases of the liver	K70-K76	8.7	14.0
Human immunodeficiency virus (HIV) disease	B20-B24	1.4	1.9
Influenza and pneumonia	J09-J18	10.1	14.6
Intentional self-harm	X60-X84	9.3	13.2
Malnutrition	E40-E46	1.4	1.3
Obesity and other hyperalimentation	E65-E68	1.3	2.1
Renal failure	N17-N19	12.1	13.0
Transport accidents	V01-V99	8.4	12.0
Viral hepatitis	B15-B19	1.3	1.9

Note: (a) ICD-10 = International Classification of Diseases 10th Revision; (1) Mortality rates are a three year average covering 2014-2016; (2) Figures cover Wake County; Data are Suppressed when the data meet the criteria for confidentiality constraints; Mortality rates are flagged as Unreliable when the rate would be calculated with a numerator of 20 or less.
Source: Centers for Disease Control and Prevention, National Center for Health Statistics. Underlying Cause of Death 1999-2016 on CDC WONDER Online Database, released December 2017

Health Insurance Coverage

Area	With Health Insurance	With Private Health Insurance	With Public Health Insurance	Without Health Insurance	Population Under Age 18 Without Health Insurance
City	94.2	88.7	11.1	5.8	2.8
MSA[1]	88.8	74.4	23.4	11.2	5.2
U.S.	88.3	66.7	33.0	11.7	5.9

Note: Figures are percentages that cover the civilian noninstitutionalized population; (1) Figures cover the Raleigh, NC Metropolitan Statistical Area—see Appendix B for areas included
Source: U.S. Census Bureau, 2012-2016 American Community Survey 5-Year Estimates

Number of Medical Professionals

Area	MDs[3]	DOs[3,4]	Dentists	Podiatrists	Chiropractors	Optometrists
County[1] (number)	2,798	100	715	34	256	158
County[1] (rate[2])	273.3	9.8	68.2	3.2	24.4	15.1
U.S. (rate[2])	276.5	22.3	67.3	6.0	26.7	15.9

Note: Data as of 2016 unless noted; (1) Data covers Wake County; (2) Rate per 100,000 population; (3) Data as of 2015 and includes all active, non-federal physicians; (4) Doctor of Osteopathic Medicine
Source: U.S. Department of Health and Human Services, Health Resources and Services Administration, Bureau of Health Professions, Area Resource File (ARF) 2016-2017

EDUCATION

Public School District Statistics

District Name	Schls	Pupils	Pupil/ Teacher Ratio	Minority Pupils[1] (%)	Free Lunch Eligible[2] (%)	IEP[3] (%)
Wake County Schools	181	157,839	15.8	52.5	30.3	13.2

Note: Table includes school districts with 100 or more students; (1) Percentage of students that are not non-Hispanic white; (2) Percentage of students that are eligible for the free lunch program; (3) Percentage of students that have an Individualized Education Program.
Source: U.S. Department of Education, National Center for Education Statistics, Common Core of Data, Local Education Agency (School District) Universe Survey: School Year 2015-2016; U.S. Department of Education, National Center for Education Statistics, Common Core of Data, Public Elementary/Secondary School Universe Survey: School Year 2015-2016

Highest Level of Education

Area	Less than H.S.	H.S. Diploma	Some College, No Deg.	Associate Degree	Bachelor's Degree	Master's Degree	Prof. School Degree	Doctorate Degree
City	4.9	10.2	15.3	8.9	39.1	16.5	2.6	2.4
MSA[1]	9.2	19.0	18.7	8.8	28.6	11.5	2.1	2.1
U.S.	13.0	27.5	21.0	8.2	18.8	8.2	2.0	1.3

Note: Figures cover persons age 25 and over; (1) Figures cover the Raleigh, NC Metropolitan Statistical Area—see Appendix B for areas included
Source: U.S. Census Bureau, 2012-2016 American Community Survey 5-Year Estimates

Educational Attainment by Race

Area	High School Graduate or Higher (%)					Bachelor's Degree or Higher (%)				
	Total	White	Black	Asian	Hisp.[2]	Total	White	Black	Asian	Hisp.[2]
City	95.1	95.5	89.6	94.6	67.0	60.7	61.1	40.5	80.5	28.1
MSA[1]	90.8	92.9	87.5	91.3	59.1	44.3	47.8	29.0	68.3	19.5
U.S.	87.0	88.9	84.3	86.3	65.7	30.3	31.6	20.0	52.1	14.7

Note: Figures shown cover persons 25 years old and over; (1) Figures cover the Raleigh, NC Metropolitan Statistical Area—see Appendix B for areas included; (2) People of Hispanic origin can be of any race
Source: U.S. Census Bureau, 2012-2016 American Community Survey 5-Year Estimates

School Enrollment by Grade and Control

Area	Preschool (%)		Kindergarten (%)		Grades 1 - 4 (%)		Grades 5 - 8 (%)		Grades 9 - 12 (%)	
	Public	Private	Public	Private	Public	Private	Public	Private	Public	Private
City	29.3	70.7	90.6	9.4	86.4	13.6	87.2	12.8	93.7	6.3
MSA[1]	40.5	59.5	87.6	12.4	89.6	10.4	89.5	10.5	89.8	10.2
U.S.	58.4	41.6	87.7	12.3	89.8	10.2	89.7	10.3	90.4	9.6

Note: Figures shown cover persons 3 years old and over; (1) Figures cover the Raleigh, NC Metropolitan Statistical Area—see Appendix B for areas included
Source: U.S. Census Bureau, 2012-2016 American Community Survey 5-Year Estimates

Average Salaries of Public School Classroom Teachers

Area	2015 Dollars	2015 Rank[1]	2016 Dollars	2016 Rank[1]	Change from 2015 to 2016 Percent	Change from 2015 to 2016 Rank[2]
North Carolina	47,792	40	47,941	41	0.3	44
U.S. Average	57,611	–	58,353	–	1.3	–

Note: (1) Rank ranges from 1 to 51 where 1 indicates highest salary; (2) Rank ranges from 1 to 51 where 1 indicates highest percent change.
Source: National Education Association, Rankings & Estimates: Rankings of the States 2016 and Estimates of School Statistics 2017

Higher Education

Four-Year Colleges			Two-Year Colleges			Medical Schools[1]	Law Schools[2]	Voc/ Tech[3]
Public	Private Non-profit	Private For-profit	Public	Private Non-profit	Private For-profit			
0	0	0	0	0	0	0	0	0

Note: Figures cover institutions located within the city limits and include main campuses only; (1) includes schools accredited by the Liaison Committee on Medical Education and the American Osteopathic Association's Commission on Osteopathic College Accreditation; (2) includes ABA-accredited schools, schools with provisional ABA accreditation, and state accredited schools; (3) includes all schools with programs that are less than 2 years.
Source: National Center for Education Statistics, Integrated Postsecondary Education System (IPEDS), 2016-17; Wikipedia, List of Medical Schools in the United States, accessed April 2, 2018; Wikipedia, List of Law Schools in the United States, accessed April 2, 2018

According to *U.S. News & World Report,* the Raleigh, NC metro area is home to one of the best national universities in the U.S.: **North Carolina State University—Raleigh** (#81 tie). The indicators used to capture academic quality fall into a number of categories: assessment by administrators at peer institutions; retention of students; faculty resources; student selectivity; financial resources; alumni giving; high school counselor ratings of colleges; and graduation rate. *U.S. News & World Report, "America's Best Colleges 2018"*

According to *U.S. News & World Report,* the Raleigh, NC metro area is home to one of the best liberal arts colleges in the U.S.: **Meredith College** (#163 tie). The indicators used to capture academic quality fall into a number of categories: assessment by administrators at peer institutions; retention of students; faculty resources; student selectivity; financial resources; alumni giving; high school counselor ratings of colleges; and graduation rate. *U.S. News & World Report, "America's Best Colleges 2018"*

PRESIDENTIAL ELECTION

2016 Presidential Election Results

Area	Clinton	Trump	Johnson	Stein	Other
Wake County	57.4	37.2	3.7	0.3	1.4
U.S.	48.0	45.9	3.3	1.1	1.7

Note: Results are percentages and may not add to 100% due to rounding
Source: Dave Leip's Atlas of U.S. Presidential Elections

EMPLOYERS

Major Employers

Company Name	Industry
Cisco Systems	Software
City of Raleigh	Government
Duke Energy	Electric services
Fidelity Investments	Financial services
GlaxoSmithKline	Healthcare
IBM Corporation	Technology
Lenovo	Technology
N.C. DHHS	Government
North Carolina State University	Education
Rex Healthcare	Healthcare
RTI International	Research & development
SAS Institute	Data management
State of North Carolina	Government
Wake County Government	Government
Wake County Public School System	Education
Wake Technical Community College	Education
WakeMed Health & Hospitals	Education
Wells Fargo	Financial services

Note: Companies shown are located within the Raleigh, NC Metropolitan Statistical Area.
Source: Hoovers.com; Wikipedia

PUBLIC SAFETY

Crime Rate

Area	All Crimes	Violent Crimes				Property Crimes		
		Murder	Rape[3]	Robbery	Aggrav. Assault	Burglary	Larceny -Theft	Motor Vehicle Theft
City	1,354.5	2.1	4.2	27.5	50.7	175.4	1,058.7	35.9
Metro[1]	n/a	n/a	n/a	n/a	n/a	n/a	n/a	n/a
U.S.	2,837.0	5.3	29.6	102.8	248.5	468.9	1,745.0	236.9

Note: Figures are crimes per 100,000 population; (1) Figures cover the Raleigh, NC Metropolitan Statistical Area—see Appendix B for areas included; n/a not available; (3) The city and U.S. figures shown were reported using the legacy Uniform Crime Reporting (UCR) definition of rape. The metro area figures shown are an aggregate total of the data submitted using both the revised and legacy UCR definitions.
Source: FBI Uniform Crime Reports, 2016

Hate Crimes

Area	Number of Quarters Reported	Number of Incidents per Bias Motivation					
		Race/Ethnicity/ Ancestry	Religion	Sexual Orientation	Disability	Gender	Gender Identity
City	3	3	0	0	0	0	0
U.S.	4	3,489	1,273	1,076	70	31	124

Source: Federal Bureau of Investigation, Hate Crime Statistics 2016

Identity Theft Consumer Reports

Area	Reports	Reports per 100,000 Population	Rank[2]
MSA[1]	1,516	116	65
U.S.	371,061	114	-

Note: (1) Figures cover the Raleigh, NC Metropolitan Statistical Area—see Appendix B for areas included; (2) Rank ranges from 1 to 389 where 1 indicates greatest number of identity theft reports per 100,000 population
Source: Federal Trade Commission, Consumer Sentinel Network Data Book for January–December 2017

Fraud and Other Consumer Reports

Area	Reports	Reports per 100,000 Population	Rank[2]
MSA[1]	6,887	529	86
U.S.	2,304,550	708	-

Note: (1) Figures cover the Raleigh, NC Metropolitan Statistical Area—see Appendix B for areas included; (2) Rank ranges from 1 to 389 where 1 indicates greatest number of fraud and other consumer reports per 100,000 population
Source: Federal Trade Commission, Consumer Sentinel Network Data Book for January–December 2017

SPORTS

Professional Sports Teams

Team Name	League	Year Established
Carolina Hurricanes	National Hockey League (NHL)	1997

Note: Includes teams located in the Raleigh, NC Metropolitan Statistical Area.
Source: Wikipedia, Major Professional Sports Teams of the United States and Canada, April 5, 2018

CLIMATE

Average and Extreme Temperatures

Temperature	Jan	Feb	Mar	Apr	May	Jun	Jul	Aug	Sep	Oct	Nov	Dec	Yr.
Extreme High (°F)	79	84	90	95	97	104	105	105	104	98	88	79	105
Average High (°F)	50	53	61	72	79	86	89	87	81	72	62	53	71
Average Temp. (°F)	40	43	50	59	67	75	78	77	71	60	51	42	60
Average Low (°F)	29	31	38	46	55	63	68	67	60	48	39	32	48
Extreme Low (°F)	-9	5	11	23	29	38	48	46	37	19	11	4	-9

Note: Figures cover the years 1948-1990
Source: National Climatic Data Center, International Station Meteorological Climate Summary, 9/96

Average Precipitation/Snowfall/Humidity

Precip./Humidity	Jan	Feb	Mar	Apr	May	Jun	Jul	Aug	Sep	Oct	Nov	Dec	Yr.
Avg. Precip. (in.)	3.4	3.6	3.6	2.9	3.9	3.6	4.4	4.4	3.2	2.9	3.0	3.1	42.0
Avg. Snowfall (in.)	2	3	1	Tr	0	0	0	0	0	0	Tr	1	8
Avg. Rel. Hum. 7am (%)	79	79	79	80	84	86	88	91	91	90	84	81	84
Avg. Rel. Hum. 4pm (%)	53	49	46	43	51	54	57	59	57	53	51	53	52

Note: Figures cover the years 1948-1990; Tr = Trace amounts (<0.05 in. of rain; <0.5 in. of snow)
Source: National Climatic Data Center, International Station Meteorological Climate Summary, 9/96

Weather Conditions

Temperature			Daytime Sky			Precipitation		
32°F & below	45°F & below	90°F & above	Clear	Partly cloudy	Cloudy	0.01 inch or more precip.	0.1 inch or more snow/ice	Thunder-storms
77	160	39	98	143	124	110	3	42

Note: Figures are average number of days per year and cover the years 1948-1990
Source: National Climatic Data Center, International Station Meteorological Climate Summary, 9/96

HAZARDOUS WASTE

Superfund Sites

The Raleigh, NC metro area is home to three sites on the EPA's Superfund National Priorities List: **Koppers Co., Inc. (Morrisville Plant)** (final); **North Carolina State University (Lot 86, Farm Unit #1)** (final); **Ward Transformer** (final). There are a total of 1,396 Superfund sites with a status of proposed or final on the list in the U.S. *U.S. Environmental Protection Agency, National Priorities List, April 4, 2018*

AIR & WATER QUALITY

Air Quality Trends: Ozone

	1990	1995	2000	2005	2010	2012	2013	2014	2015	2016
MSA[1]	0.093	0.081	0.087	0.082	0.071	0.071	0.061	0.063	0.065	0.069
U.S.	0.087	0.089	0.081	0.079	0.073	0.075	0.069	0.067	0.068	0.069

Note: (1) Data covers the Raleigh, NC Metropolitan Statistical Area—see Appendix B for areas included. The values shown are the composite ozone concentration averages among trend sites based on the highest fourth daily maximum 8-hour concentration in parts per million. These trends are based on sites having an adequate record of monitoring data during the trend period. Data from exceptional events are included.
Source: U.S. Environmental Protection Agency, Air Quality Monitoring Information, "Air Quality Trends by City, 1990-2016"

Air Quality Index

Area	Percent of Days when Air Quality was...[2]					AQI Statistics[2]	
	Good	Moderate	Unhealthy for Sensitive Groups	Unhealthy	Very Unhealthy	Maximum	Median
MSA[1]	66.3	33.7	0.0	0.0	0.0	100	45

Note: (1) Data covers the Raleigh, NC Metropolitan Statistical Area—see Appendix B for areas included; (2) Based on 365 days with AQI data in 2017. Air Quality Index (AQI) is an index for reporting daily air quality. EPA calculates the AQI for five major air pollutants regulated by the Clean Air Act: ground-level ozone, particle pollution (aka particulate matter), carbon monoxide, sulfur dioxide, and nitrogen dioxide. The AQI runs from 0 to 500. The higher the AQI value, the greater the level of air pollution and the greater the health concern. There are six AQI categories: "Good" AQI is between 0 and 50. Air quality is considered satisfactory; "Moderate" AQI is between 51 and 100. Air quality is acceptable; "Unhealthy for Sensitive Groups" When AQI values are between 101 and 150, members of sensitive groups may experience health effects; "Unhealthy" When AQI values are between 151 and 200 everyone may begin to experience health effects; "Very Unhealthy" AQI values between 201 and 300 trigger a health alert; "Hazardous" AQI values over 300 trigger warnings of emergency conditions (not shown).
Source: U.S. Environmental Protection Agency, Air Quality Index Report, 2017

Air Quality Index Pollutants

Area	Percent of Days when AQI Pollutant was...[2]					
	Carbon Monoxide	Nitrogen Dioxide	Ozone	Sulfur Dioxide	Particulate Matter 2.5	Particulate Matter 10
MSA[1]	0.0	0.5	42.7	0.0	56.7	0.0

Note: (1) Data covers the Raleigh, NC Metropolitan Statistical Area—see Appendix B for areas included; (2) Based on 365 days with AQI data in 2017. The Air Quality Index (AQI) is an index for reporting daily air quality. EPA calculates the AQI for five major air pollutants regulated by the Clean Air Act: ground-level ozone, particle pollution (also known as particulate matter), carbon monoxide, sulfur dioxide, and nitrogen dioxide. The AQI runs from 0 to 500. The higher the AQI value, the greater the level of air pollution and the greater the health concern.
Source: U.S. Environmental Protection Agency, Air Quality Index Report, 2017

Maximum Air Pollutant Concentrations: Particulate Matter, Ozone, CO and Lead

	Particulate Matter 10 (ug/m^3)	Particulate Matter 2.5 Wtd AM (ug/m^3)	Particulate Matter 2.5 24-Hr (ug/m^3)	Ozone (ppm)	Carbon Monoxide (ppm)	Lead (ug/m^3)
MSA[1] Level	26	7.6	16	0.069	2	n/a
NAAQS[2]	150	15	35	0.075	9	0.15
Met NAAQS[2]	Yes	Yes	Yes	Yes	Yes	n/a

Note: (1) Data covers the Raleigh, NC Metropolitan Statistical Area—see Appendix B for areas included; Data from exceptional events are included; (2) National Ambient Air Quality Standards; ppm = parts per million; ug/m^3 = micrograms per cubic meter; n/a not available.
Concentrations: Particulate Matter 10 (coarse particulate)—highest second maximum 24-hour concentration; Particulate Matter 2.5 Wtd AM (fine particulate)—highest weighted annual mean concentration; Particulate Matter 2.5 24-Hour (fine particulate)—highest 98th percentile 24-hour concentration; Ozone—highest fourth daily maximum 8-hour concentration; Carbon Monoxide—highest second maximum non-overlapping 8-hour concentration; Lead—maximum running 3-month average
Source: U.S. Environmental Protection Agency, Air Quality Monitoring Information, "Air Quality Statistics by City, 2016"

Maximum Air Pollutant Concentrations: Nitrogen Dioxide and Sulfur Dioxide

	Nitrogen Dioxide AM (ppb)	Nitrogen Dioxide 1-Hr (ppb)	Sulfur Dioxide AM (ppb)	Sulfur Dioxide 1-Hr (ppb)	Sulfur Dioxide 24-Hr (ppb)
MSA[1] Level	9	39	n/a	3	n/a
NAAQS[2]	53	100	30	75	140
Met NAAQS[2]	Yes	Yes	n/a	Yes	n/a

Note: (1) Data covers the Raleigh, NC Metropolitan Statistical Area—see Appendix B for areas included; Data from exceptional events are included; (2) National Ambient Air Quality Standards; ppm = parts per million; ug/m³ = micrograms per cubic meter; n/a not available.
Concentrations: Nitrogen Dioxide AM—highest arithmetic mean concentration; Nitrogen Dioxide 1-Hr—highest 98th percentile 1-hour daily maximum concentration; Sulfur Dioxide AM—highest annual mean concentration; Sulfur Dioxide 1-Hr—highest 99th percentile 1-hour daily maximum concentration; Sulfur Dioxide 24-Hr—highest second maximum 24-hour concentration
Source: U.S. Environmental Protection Agency, Air Quality Monitoring Information, "Air Quality Statistics by City, 2016"

Drinking Water

Water System Name	Pop. Served	Primary Water Source Type	Violations[1]	
			Health Based	Monitoring/ Reporting
Town of Apex	50,394	Purchased Surface	0	0

Note: (1) Based on violation data from January 1, 2017 to December 31, 2017
Source: U.S. Environmental Protection Agency, Office of Ground Water and Drinking Water, Safe Drinking Water Information System (based on data extracted April 5, 2018)

Chapel Hill, North Carolina

Background

Chapel Hill is located in central North Carolina, in the southeast corner of Orange County. The area is known for its natural beauty and Chapel Hill has been nicknamed, the "Southern Part of Heaven."

Chapel Hill took its name from its original inhabitants, New Hope Chapel, a small Anglican chapel built on the top of a hill. The Chapel Hill site was chosen as the location for the first State University in 1793, the University of North Carolina, Chapel Hill. As the University was constructed, the town of Chapel Hill grew up around it. Town plots were sold at auction to the highest bidder and Chapel Hill had its first permanent residents in 1795.

Culture and community in Chapel Hill are closely tied to the University. Chapel Hill's population consists of University faculty and staff, students, the research community, the business sector along with families with long histories in Chapel Hill. The town relies on the University as both a major employer and an epicenter for cultural and athletic programs.

In 1968, only a year after its schools became fully integrated, Chapel Hill became the first predominantly white municipality in the South to elect an African American mayor, Howard Lee. Lee served from 1969 until 1975 and, among other things, helped establish Chapel Hill Transit, the town's bus system. Some 30 years later, in 2002, legislation was passed to make the local buses free of fares to all riders, leading to a large increase in ridership; the buses are financed through Chapel Hill and Carrboro town taxes, federal grants, and UNC student fees. Several hybrid and articulated buses have been added recently. All buses carry GPS transmitters to report their location in real time to a tracking web site. Buses can transport bicycles and have wheelchair lifts.

Residents and visitors have ample opportunities for recreation. Chapel Hill has a lively city life, filled with music clubs, unique eateries, shopping venues and theaters. Street fairs and community events are plentiful.

Many large murals can be seen painted on the buildings in the Chapel Hill-Carrboro area. Most of these murals were painted by UNC alumnus Michael Brown. Also, for more than 30 years, Chapel Hill has sponsored the annual street fair, Festifall, in October. The fair offer booths to artists, craftsmakers, nonprofits, and food vendors. Performance space is also available for musicians, martial artists, and other groups. The fair is attended by tens of thousands each year.

Local cultural attractions include the Chapel Hill Museum, Chapel Hill Historical Society, The Arts Center, UNC's Ackland Art Museum and the Morehead Planetarium. The Chapel Hill Town Council allocates 1% of selected capital projects for the creation, installation or maintenance of works of public art.

The town is part of the Chapel Hill-Carrboro City School District, with nine elementary, four middle and two high schools. Both high schools in Chapel Hill have been acknowledged for educational excellence. Opportunities for higher education include the University of North Carolina, Chapel Hill and the University of North Carolina's Hospital School.

The University of North Carolina has been very successful at college basketball and women's soccer, and a passion for these sports has been a distinctive feature of the town's culture, fueled by the Tobacco Road rivalry among North Carolina's four ACC teams: the North Carolina Tar Heels, the Duke Blue Devils, the NC State Wolfpack, and the Wake Forest Demon Deacons.

Chapel Hill, together with Durham and Raleigh, make up the three points of the "Research Triangle." The research universities of University of North Carolina, Chapel Hill, North Carolina State University and Duke University have provided the region with a highly-educated workforce and make it attractive to several high technology companies. Research Triangle Park, built in 1959, is one of the country's premier research and development centers, with more than 100 research facilities and nearly 40,000 employees.

Rankings

General Rankings

- In their fifth annual survey, Livability.com looked at data for nearly 2,300 U.S. cities to determine the rankings for Livability's "Top 100 Best Places to Live" in 2018. Chapel Hill ranked #22. Criteria: vibrant economy; low cost of living; education, demographics, health care options; transportation & infrastructure; abundant lifestyle amenities. *Livability.com, "Top 100 Best Places to Live 2018" January 16, 2018*

Business/Finance Rankings

- The personal finance site NerdWallet analyzed 183 American metropolitan areas with populations over 250,000 and more than 15,000 businesses to rank where entrepreneurs find the most success. Criteria included area economy, annual income, housing cost, unemployment rate, and the success rate of area businesses. Durham* ranked #57. *www.nerdwallet.com, "Best Places to Start a Business," April 27, 2015*
- Metro areas with the largest gap in income between rich and poor residents were identified by 24/7 Wall Street using the U.S. Census Bureau's 2013 American Community Survey. The Durham* metro area placed #20 among metro areas with the widest wealth gap between rich and poor. *247wallst.com, "20 Cities with the Widest Gap between the Rich and Poor," July 8, 2015*
- Using data from the Council for Community and Economic Research's 2014 cost of living index, NerdWallet ranked the 100 most affordable cities in America. Median income was compared with cost of living to find truly affordable places. Chapel Hill ranked #11. *NerdWallet.com, "America's Most Affordable Places," May 18, 2015*
- The Durham* metro area appeared on the Milken Institute "2017 Best Performing Cities" list. Rank: #106 out of 200 large metro areas. Criteria: job growth; wage and salary growth; high-tech output growth. *Milken Institute, "Best-Performing Cities 2017," January 2018*
- *Forbes* ranked the 200 most populous metro areas to determine the nation's "Best Places for Business and Careers." The Durham* metro area was ranked #16. Criteria: costs (business and living); job growth (past and projected); income growth; quality of life; educational attainment (college and high school); projected economic growth; cultural and recreational opportunities; net migration patterns; number of highly ranked colleges. *Forbes, "The Best Places for Business and Careers 2017," October 24, 2017*

Education Rankings

- Durham* was identified as one of America's "smartest" metropolitan areas by *The Business Journals*. The area ranked #6 out of 10. Criteria: percentage of adults (25 and older) with high school diplomas, bachelor's degrees and graduate degrees. *The Business Journals, "Where the Brainpower Is: Exclusive U.S. Rankings, Insights," February 27, 2014*
- Personal finance website *WalletHub* analyzed the 150 largest U.S. metropolitan statistical areas to determine where the most educated Americans are choosing to settle. Criteria: education quality and attainment gap; education levels; percentage of workers with degrees; public school rankings; quality and size of each metro area's universities. Durham* was ranked #4 (#1 = most educated city). *www.WalletHub.com, "2017's Most and Least Educated Cities in America," July 25, 2017*

Environmental Rankings

- Sperling's BestPlaces assessed 379 metropolitan areas of the United States for the likelihood of dangerously extreme weather events or earthquakes. In general the Southeast and South-Central regions have the highest risk of weather extremes and earthquakes, while the Pacific Northwest enjoys the lowest risk. Of the least risky metropolitan areas, the Durham* metro area was ranked #240. *www.bestplaces.net, "Safest Places from Natural Disasters," April 2011*

Health/Fitness Rankings

- Durham* was identified as a "2016 Spring Allergy Capital." The area ranked #51 out of 100. Three groups of factors were used to identify the most severe cities for people with allergies during the spring season: annual pollen levels; medicine utilization; access to board-certified allergists. *Asthma and Allergy Foundation of America, "Spring Allergy Capitals 2016"*
- Durham* was identified as a "2016 Fall Allergy Capital." The area ranked #57 out of 100. Three groups of factors were used to identify the most severe cities for people with allergies during the fall season: annual pollen levels; medicine utilization; access to board-certified allergists. *Asthma and Allergy Foundation of America, "Fall Allergy Capitals 2016"*
- The Durham* metro area ranked #21 out of 189 in The Gallup-Healthways Well-Being Index. Criteria: purpose; social well being; financial health; community and physical health. Results are based on telephone interviews with adults, aged 18 and older, living in metropolitan areas in the 50 U.S. states and the District of Columbia. *Gallup-Healthways, "State of American Well-Being, 2017 Community Well-Being Rankings" March 2018*

Real Estate Rankings

- Durham* was ranked #137 out of 238 metro areas in terms of housing affordability in 2017 by the National Association of Home Builders (#1 = most affordable). Criteria: the share of homes sold in that area affordable to a family earning the local median income, based on standard mortgage underwriting criteria. *National Association of Home Builders®, NAHB-Wells Fargo Housing Opportunity Index, 4th Quarter 2017*

Safety Rankings

- The National Insurance Crime Bureau ranked 382 metro areas in the U.S. in terms of per capita rates of vehicle theft. The Durham* metro area ranked #137 (#1 = highest rate). Criteria: number of vehicle theft offenses per 100,000 inhabitants in 2016. *National Insurance Crime Bureau, "Hot Spots 2016," June 8, 2017*

Seniors/Retirement Rankings

- Chapel Hill made *Southern Living's* list of charming and unique southern places to retire or dream of retiring to. The favorite places focused on the following: presence of unique amenities; opportunities to volunteer; low cost of living; continued learning opportunities; stable housing market; access to medical care; availability of part-time work; and ease of travel. *Southern Living, "Best Places to Retire"*
- From its Best Cities for Successful Aging indexes, the Milken Institute generated rankings for metropolitan areas, weighing data in nine categories—health care, wellness, living arrangements, transportation and convenience, financial characteristics, education, employment, community engagement, and overall livability. The Durham* metro area was ranked #3 overall in the large metro area category. *Milken Institute, "Best Cities for Successful Aging, 2017" March 14, 2017*
- Chapel Hill was identified as one of the most popular places to retire by *Topretirements.com*. The list reflects the 100 cities that visitors to the website are most interested in for retirement, based on the number of times a city's review was viewed on the website. *Topretirements.com, "100 Most Popular Places to Retire for 2017," July 27, 2017*

Women/Minorities Rankings

- *24/7 Wall St.* compared median earnings over a 12-month period for men and women who worked full-time, year-round, and employment composition by sector to identify the best-paying cities for women. Of the largest 100 U.S. metropolitan areas, Durham* was ranked #1 in pay disparity. *24/7 Wall St., "The Best (and Worst) Paying Cities for Women," March 27, 2017*

*Chapel Hill is located within the Durham-Chapel Hill, NC Metropolitan Statistical Area.

Business Environment

CITY FINANCES

City Government Finances

Component	2015 ($000)	2015 ($ per capita)
Total Revenues	61,184	1,027
Total Expenditures	61,807	1,038
Debt Outstanding	50,407	846
Cash and Securities[1]	42,758	718

Note: (1) Cash and security holdings of a government at the close of its fiscal year,, including those of its dependent agencies, utilities, and liquor stores.
Source: U.S Census Bureau, State & Local Government Finances 2015

City Government Revenue by Source

Source	2015 ($000)	2015 ($ per capita)	2015 (%)
General Revenue			
From Federal Government	1,477	25	2.4
From State Government	5,318	89	8.7
From Local Governments	0	0	0.0
Taxes			
Property	28,918	485	47.3
Sales and Gross Receipts	12,544	211	20.5
Personal Income	0	0	0.0
Corporate Income	0	0	0.0
Motor Vehicle License	457	8	0.7
Other Taxes	1,794	30	2.9
Current Charges	7,664	129	12.5
Liquor Store	0	0	0.0
Utility	1,044	18	1.7
Employee Retirement	0	0	0.0

Source: U.S Census Bureau, State & Local Government Finances 2015

City Government Expenditures by Function

Function	2015 ($000)	2015 ($ per capita)	2015 (%)
General Direct Expenditures			
Air Transportation	0	0	0.0
Corrections	0	0	0.0
Education	0	0	0.0
Employment Security Administration	0	0	0.0
Financial Administration	1,697	28	2.7
Fire Protection	7,968	133	12.9
General Public Buildings	2,491	41	4.0
Governmental Administration, Other	6,081	102	9.8
Health	0	0	0.0
Highways	47	< 1	< 0.1
Hospitals	0	0	0.0
Housing and Community Development	2,154	36	3.5
Interest on General Debt	2,104	35	3.4
Judicial and Legal	303	5	0.5
Libraries	2,479	41	4.0
Parking	1,902	31	3.1
Parks and Recreation	6,519	109	10.5
Police Protection	12,369	207	20.0
Public Welfare	0	0	0.0
Sewerage	1,552	26	2.5
Solid Waste Management	0	0	0.0
Veterans' Services	0	0	0.0
Liquor Store	0	0	0.0
Utility	11,341	190	18.3
Employee Retirement	0	0	0.0

Source: U.S Census Bureau, State & Local Government Finances 2015

DEMOGRAPHICS

Population Growth

Area	1990 Census	2000 Census	2010 Census	2016* Estimate	Population Growth (%)	
					1990-2016	2010-2016
City	39,674	48,715	57,233	59,005	48.7	3.1
MSA[1]	344,646	426,493	504,357	542,399	57.4	7.5
U.S.	248,709,873	281,421,906	308,745,538	318,558,162	28.1	3.2

Note: (1) Figures cover the Durham-Chapel Hill, NC Metropolitan Statistical Area—see Appendix B for areas included; (*) 2012-2016 5-year estimated population
Source: U.S. Census Bureau, 1990 Census, Census 2000, Census 2010, 2012-2016 American Community Survey 5-Year Estimates

Household Size

Area	Persons in Household (%)							Average Household Size
	One	Two	Three	Four	Five	Six	Seven or More	
City	31.0	34.9	15.0	13.4	4.4	0.9	0.4	2.40
MSA[1]	30.8	36.0	15.1	11.6	4.3	1.5	0.7	2.40
U.S.	27.7	33.7	15.7	13.1	6.0	2.3	1.5	2.60

Note: (1) Figures cover the Durham-Chapel Hill, NC Metropolitan Statistical Area—see Appendix B for areas included
Source: U.S. Census Bureau, 2012-2016 American Community Survey 5-Year Estimates

Race

Area	White Alone[2] (%)	Black Alone[2] (%)	Asian Alone[2] (%)	AIAN[3] Alone[2] (%)	NHOPI[4] Alone[2] (%)	Other Race Alone[2] (%)	Two or More Races (%)
City	72.8	9.9	12.6	0.4	0.0	1.1	3.2
MSA[1]	62.2	26.8	4.6	0.4	0.0	3.0	2.8
U.S.	73.3	12.6	5.2	0.8	0.2	4.8	3.1

Note: (1) Figures cover the Durham-Chapel Hill, NC Metropolitan Statistical Area—see Appendix B for areas included; (2) Alone is defined as not being in combination with one or more other races; (3) American Indian and Alaska Native; (4) Native Hawaiian and Other Pacific Islander
Source: U.S. Census Bureau, 2012-2016 American Community Survey 5-Year Estimates

Hispanic or Latino Origin

Area	Total (%)	Mexican (%)	Puerto Rican (%)	Cuban (%)	Other (%)
City	5.9	2.2	0.4	0.3	3.0
MSA[1]	11.2	6.4	0.7	0.2	4.0
U.S.	17.3	11.0	1.7	0.7	4.0

Note: Persons of Hispanic or Latino origin can be of any race; (1) Figures cover the Durham-Chapel Hill, NC Metropolitan Statistical Area—see Appendix B for areas included
Source: U.S. Census Bureau, 2012-2016 American Community Survey 5-Year Estimates

Segregation

Type	Segregation Indices[1]				Percent Change		
	1990	2000	2010	2010 Rank[2]	1990-2000	1990-2010	2000-2010
Black/White	45.7	46.7	48.1	75	1.1	2.4	1.3
Asian/White	45.5	45.4	44.0	30	-0.2	-1.5	-1.3
Hispanic/White	23.4	53.8	48.0	33	30.4	24.6	-5.8

Note: All figures cover the Metropolitan Statistical Area—see Appendix B for areas included; Figures are based on an analysis of 1990, 2000, and 2010 Census Decennial Census tract data by William H. Frey, Brookings Institution and the University of Michigan Social Science Data Analysis Network. In this analysis all racial groups (whites, blacks, and asians) are non-Hispanic members of those races. Hispanics are shown as a separate category; (1) Segregation Indices are Dissimilarity Indices that measure the degree to which the minority group is distributed differently than whites across census tracts. They range from 0 (complete integration) to 100 (complete segregation) where the value indicates the percentage of the minority group that needs to move to be distributed exactly like whites; (2) Ranges from 1 (most segregated) to 102 (least segregated); n/a not available.
Source: www.CensusScope.org

Ancestry

Area	German	Irish	English	American	Italian	Polish	French[2]	Scottish	Dutch
City	13.8	9.9	12.3	3.6	5.2	3.5	2.7	3.4	1.3
MSA[1]	9.5	7.6	9.8	6.5	3.2	1.9	1.8	2.5	0.9
U.S.	14.4	10.4	7.7	6.9	5.4	2.9	2.6	1.7	1.3

Note: Figures are the percentage of the total population reporting a particular ancestry. The nine most commonly reported ancestries in the U.S. are shown. Figures include multiple ancestries (e.g. if a person reported being Irish and Italian, they were included in both columns); (1) Figures cover the Durham-Chapel Hill, NC Metropolitan Statistical Area—see Appendix B for areas included; (2) Excludes Basque
Source: U.S. Census Bureau, 2012-2016 American Community Survey 5-Year Estimates

Foreign-Born Population

Area	Percent of Population Born in								
	Any Foreign Country	Asia	Mexico	Europe	Carribean	Central America[2]	South America	Africa	Canada
City	16.4	8.8	0.8	3.5	0.2	0.4	1.1	0.9	0.5
MSA[1]	12.0	3.5	3.2	1.3	0.4	1.7	0.6	0.8	0.4
U.S.	13.2	4.0	3.6	1.5	1.3	1.0	0.9	0.6	0.3

Note: (1) Figures cover the Durham-Chapel Hill, NC Metropolitan Statistical Area—see Appendix B for areas included; (2) Excludes Mexico.
Source: U.S. Census Bureau, 2012-2016 American Community Survey 5-Year Estimates

Marital Status

Area	Never Married	Now Married[2]	Separated	Widowed	Divorced
City	52.6	37.1	0.8	2.6	7.0
MSA[1]	37.1	45.5	2.3	5.0	10.2
U.S.	33.0	48.1	2.1	5.9	11.0

Note: Figures are percentages and cover the population 15 years of age and older; (1) Figures cover the Durham-Chapel Hill, NC Metropolitan Statistical Area—see Appendix B for areas included; (2) Excludes separated
Source: U.S. Census Bureau, 2012-2016 American Community Survey 5-Year Estimates

Disability Status

Area	All Ages	Under 18 Years Old	18 to 64 Years Old	65 Years and Over
City	6.6	3.1	4.7	25.5
MSA[1]	10.9	3.5	9.0	32.9
U.S.	12.5	4.1	10.3	35.7

Note: Figures show percent of the civilian noninstitutionalized population that reported having a disability. Disability status is determined from six types of difficulty: vision, hearing, cognitive, ambulatory, self-care, and independent living. For children under 5 years old, hearing and vision difficulty are used to determine disability status. For children between the ages of 5 and 14, disability status is determined from hearing, vision, cognitive, ambulatory, and self-care difficulties. For people aged 15 years and older, they are considered to have a disability if they have difficulty with any one of the six difficulty types; Note: (1) Figures cover the Durham-Chapel Hill, NC Metropolitan Statistical Area—see Appendix B for areas included
Source: U.S. Census Bureau, 2012-2016 American Community Survey 5-Year Estimates

Age

Area	Percent of Population									Median Age
	Under Age 5	Age 5–19	Age 20–34	Age 35–44	Age 45–54	Age 55–64	Age 65–74	Age 75–84	Age 85+	
City	3.0	24.0	33.3	9.8	10.7	8.9	5.5	3.4	1.5	26.2
MSA[1]	6.0	19.0	23.1	13.4	13.0	12.3	7.8	3.7	1.7	36.4
U.S.	6.2	19.6	20.7	12.7	13.6	12.6	8.3	4.3	1.9	37.7

Note: (1) Figures cover the Durham-Chapel Hill, NC Metropolitan Statistical Area—see Appendix B for areas included
Source: U.S. Census Bureau, 2012-2016 American Community Survey 5-Year Estimates

Gender

Area	Males	Females	Males per 100 Females
City	27,334	31,671	86.3
MSA[1]	259,801	282,598	91.9
U.S.	156,765,322	161,792,840	96.9

Note: (1) Figures cover the Durham-Chapel Hill, NC Metropolitan Statistical Area—see Appendix B for areas included
Source: U.S. Census Bureau, 2012-2016 American Community Survey 5-Year Estimates

Religious Groups by Family

Area	Catholic	Baptist	Non-Den.	Methodist[2]	Lutheran	LDS[3]	Pente-costal	Presby-terian[4]	Muslim[5]	Judaism
MSA[1]	5.1	13.9	5.6	8.1	0.5	0.8	1.4	2.5	0.5	0.6
U.S.	19.1	9.3	4.0	4.0	2.3	2.0	1.9	1.6	0.8	0.7

Note: Figures are the number of adherents as a percentage of the total population; (1) Figures cover the Durham-Chapel Hill, NC Metropolitan Statistical Area—see Appendix B for areas included; (2) Methodist/Pietist; (3) Latter Day Saints; (4) Reformed; (5) Figures are estimates
Source: Association of Statisticians of American Religious Bodies, 2010 U.S. Religion Census: Religious Congregations & Membership Study

Religious Groups by Tradition

Area	Catholic	Evangelical Protestant	Mainline Protestant	Other Tradition	Black Protestant	Orthodox
MSA[1]	5.1	19.4	11.7	2.9	3.1	0.1
U.S.	19.1	16.2	7.3	4.3	1.6	0.3

Note: Figures are the number of adherents as a percentage of the total population; (1) Figures cover the Durham-Chapel Hill, NC Metropolitan Statistical Area—see Appendix B for areas included
Source: Association of Statisticians of American Religious Bodies, 2010 U.S. Religion Census: Religious Congregations & Membership Study

ECONOMY

Gross Metropolitan Product

Area	2014	2015	2016	2017	Rank[2]
MSA[1]	43.4	45.5	47.3	50.2	61

Note: Figures are in billions of dollars; (1) Figures cover the Durham-Chapel Hill, NC Metropolitan Statistical Area—see Appendix B for areas included; (2) Rank is based on 2015 data and ranges from 1 to 381
Source: The U.S. Conference of Mayors, U.S. Metro Economies: GMP and Employment Report, 2015-2017

Economic Growth

Area	2012-14 (%)	2015 (%)	2016 (%)	2017 (%)	Rank[2]
MSA[1]	4.3	3.1	2.5	4.0	25
U.S.	2.0	2.4	1.9	2.6	–

Note: Figures are real gross metropolitan product (GMP) growth rates and represent average annual percent change; (1) Figures cover the Durham-Chapel Hill, NC Metropolitan Statistical Area—see Appendix B for areas included; (2) Rank is based on 2012-2014 average annual percent change and ranges from 1 to 381
Source: The U.S. Conference of Mayors, U.S. Metro Economies: GMP and Employment Report, 2015-2017

Metropolitan Area Exports

Area	2011	2012	2013	2014	2015	2016	Rank[2]
MSA[1]	2,640.3	2,723.2	2,971.7	2,934.0	2,807.2	2,937.4	77

Note: Figures are in millions of dollars; (1) Figures cover the Durham-Chapel Hill, NC Metropolitan Statistical Area—see Appendix B for areas included; (2) Rank is based on 2016 data and ranges from 1 to 385
Source: U.S. Department of Commerce, International Trade Administration, Office of Trade & Industry Information, Manufacturing & Services, data extracted March 15, 2018

Building Permits

Area	Single-Family			Multi-Family			Total		
	2016	2017p	Pct. Chg.	2016	2017p	Pct. Chg.	2016	2017p	Pct. Chg.
City	38	71	86.8	88	477	442.0	126	548	334.9
MSA[1]	2,957	3,268	10.5	1,431	1,656	15.7	4,388	4,924	12.2
U.S.	750,800	817,300	8.9	455,800	446,800	-2.0	1,206,600	1,264,100	4.8

Note: (1) Figures cover the Durham-Chapel Hill, NC Metropolitan Statistical Area—see Appendix B for areas included; Figures represent new, privately-owned housing units authorized (unadjusted data); All permit data are based on estimates with imputation; (p) preliminary data.
Source: U.S. Census Bureau, Manufacturing, Mining, and Construction Statistics, Building Permits, 2016, 2017

Bankruptcy Filings

Area	Business Filings 2016	Business Filings 2017	Business Filings % Chg.	Nonbusiness Filings 2016	Nonbusiness Filings 2017	Nonbusiness Filings % Chg.
Orange County	7	4	-42.9	103	115	11.7
U.S.	24,114	23,157	-4.0	770,846	765,863	-0.6

Note: Business filings include Chapter 7, Chapter 11, Chapter 12, and Chapter 13; Nonbusiness filings include Chapter 7, Chapter 11, and Chapter 13
Source: Administrative Office of the U.S. Courts, Business and Nonbusiness Bankruptcy, County Cases Commenced by Chapter of the Bankruptcy Code, During the 12-Month Period Ending December 31, 2016 and Business and Nonbusiness Bankruptcy, County Cases Commenced by Chapter of the Bankruptcy Code, During the 12-Month Period Ending December 31, 2017

Housing Vacancy Rates

Area	Gross Vacancy Rate[2] (%)			Year-Round Vacancy Rate[3] (%)			Rental Vacancy Rate[4] (%)			Homeowner Vacancy Rate[5] (%)		
	2015	2016	2017	2015	2016	2017	2015	2016	2017	2015	2016	2017
MSA[1]	n/a	n/a	n/a	n/a	n/a	n/a	n/a	n/a	n/a	n/a	n/a	n/a
U.S.	12.9	12.8	12.7	10.0	9.9	9.9	7.1	6.9	7.2	1.8	1.7	1.6

Note: (1) Figures cover the Durham-Chapel Hill, NC Metropolitan Statistical Area—see Appendix B for areas included; (2) The percentage of the total housing inventory that is vacant; (3) The percentage of the housing inventory (excluding seasonal units) that is year-round vacant; (4) The percentage of rental inventory that is vacant for rent; (5) The percentage of homeowner inventory that is vacant for sale; n/a not available
Source: U.S. Census Bureau, Housing Vacancies and Homeownership Annual Statistics: 2015, 2016, 2017

INCOME

Income

Area	Per Capita ($)	Median Household ($)	Average Household ($)
City	38,854	65,373	110,561
MSA[1]	32,704	54,842	80,993
U.S.	29,829	55,322	77,866

Note: (1) Figures cover the Durham-Chapel Hill, NC Metropolitan Statistical Area—see Appendix B for areas included
Source: U.S. Census Bureau, 2012-2016 American Community Survey 5-Year Estimates

Household Income Distribution

Area	Percent of Households Earning							
	Under $15,000	$15,000 -$24,999	$25,000 -$34,999	$35,000 -$49,999	$50,000 -$74,999	$75,000 -$99,999	$100,000 -$149,999	$150,000 and up
City	15.0	7.0	7.3	12.6	12.1	8.5	13.4	24.2
MSA[1]	12.2	10.0	9.7	13.7	17.4	11.5	12.9	12.7
U.S.	12.1	10.2	9.9	13.2	17.8	12.2	13.5	11.1

Note: (1) Figures cover the Durham-Chapel Hill, NC Metropolitan Statistical Area—see Appendix B for areas included
Source: U.S. Census Bureau, 2012-2016 American Community Survey 5-Year Estimates

Poverty Rate

Area	All Ages	Under 18 Years Old	18 to 64 Years Old	65 Years and Over
City	20.1	5.2	26.9	3.8
MSA[1]	16.2	21.4	16.2	7.8
U.S.	15.1	21.2	14.2	9.3

Note: Figures are percentage of people whose income during the past 12 months was below the poverty level; (1) Figures cover the Durham-Chapel Hill, NC Metropolitan Statistical Area—see Appendix B for areas included
Source: U.S. Census Bureau, 2012-2016 American Community Survey 5-Year Estimates

EMPLOYMENT

Labor Force and Employment

Area	Civilian Labor Force			Workers Employed		
	Dec. 2016	Dec. 2017	% Chg.	Dec. 2016	Dec. 2017	% Chg.
City	29,418	29,861	1.5	28,033	28,608	2.1
MSA[1]	288,945	293,411	1.5	276,804	282,262	2.0
U.S.	158,968,000	159,880,000	0.6	151,798,000	153,602,000	1.2

Note: Data is not seasonally adjusted and covers workers 16 years of age and older; (1) Figures cover the Durham-Chapel Hill, NC Metropolitan Statistical Area—see Appendix B for areas included
Source: Bureau of Labor Statistics, Local Area Unemployment Statistics

Unemployment Rate

Area	2017											
	Jan.	Feb.	Mar.	Apr.	May	Jun.	Jul.	Aug.	Sep.	Oct.	Nov.	Dec.
City	5.0	4.8	4.8	4.0	4.4	4.9	5.2	5.3	4.0	4.0	4.2	4.2
MSA[1]	4.5	4.3	4.0	3.6	3.8	4.1	4.3	4.4	3.8	3.8	3.9	3.8
U.S.	5.1	4.9	4.6	4.1	4.1	4.5	4.6	4.5	4.1	3.9	3.9	3.9

Note: Data is not seasonally adjusted and covers workers 16 years of age and older; (1) Figures cover the Durham-Chapel Hill, NC Metropolitan Statistical Area—see Appendix B for areas included
Source: Bureau of Labor Statistics, Local Area Unemployment Statistics

Average Wages

Occupation	$/Hr.	Occupation	$/Hr.
Accountants and Auditors	38.70	Maids and Housekeeping Cleaners	10.50
Automotive Mechanics	21.40	Maintenance and Repair Workers	20.00
Bookkeepers	20.70	Marketing Managers	68.80
Carpenters	17.40	Nuclear Medicine Technologists	n/a
Cashiers	10.20	Nurses, Licensed Practical	22.40
Clerks, General Office	16.70	Nurses, Registered	32.40
Clerks, Receptionists/Information	13.60	Nursing Assistants	12.70
Clerks, Shipping/Receiving	15.10	Packers and Packagers, Hand	10.90
Computer Programmers	44.40	Physical Therapists	39.60
Computer Systems Analysts	41.20	Postal Service Mail Carriers	23.70
Computer User Support Specialists	26.10	Real Estate Brokers	26.50
Cooks, Restaurant	11.90	Retail Salespersons	13.00
Dentists	99.20	Sales Reps., Exc. Tech./Scientific	33.40
Electrical Engineers	50.80	Sales Reps., Tech./Scientific	51.60
Electricians	21.40	Secretaries, Exc. Legal/Med./Exec.	19.30
Financial Managers	72.40	Security Guards	16.10
First-Line Supervisors/Managers, Sales	21.20	Surgeons	n/a
Food Preparation Workers	11.50	Teacher Assistants*	11.90
General and Operations Managers	69.70	Teachers, Elementary School*	22.20
Hairdressers/Cosmetologists	21.40	Teachers, Secondary School*	23.50
Internists, General	n/a	Telemarketers	11.00
Janitors and Cleaners	11.70	Truck Drivers, Heavy/Tractor-Trailer	21.00
Landscaping/Groundskeeping Workers	13.70	Truck Drivers, Light/Delivery Svcs.	16.80
Lawyers	67.30	Waiters and Waitresses	11.40

Note: Wage data covers the Durham-Chapel Hill, NC Metropolitan Statistical Area—see Appendix B for areas included; (*) Hourly wages for elementary/secondary school teachers and teacher assistants were calculated by the editors from annual wage data based on a 40 hour work week; n/a not available.
Source: Bureau of Labor Statistics, Metro Area Occupational Employment & Wage Estimates, May 2017

Employment by Occupation

Occupation Classification	City (%)	MSA[1] (%)	U.S. (%)
Management, Business, Science, and Arts	59.8	48.4	37.0
Natural Resources, Construction, and Maintenance	2.1	7.2	8.9
Production, Transportation, and Material Moving	3.1	8.2	12.2
Sales and Office	17.9	18.9	23.8
Service	17.0	17.2	18.1

Note: Figures cover employed civilians 16 years of age and older; (1) Figures cover the Durham-Chapel Hill, NC Metropolitan Statistical Area—see Appendix B for areas included
Source: U.S. Census Bureau, 2012-2016 American Community Survey 5-Year Estimates

Employment by Industry

Sector	MSA[1] Number of Employees	MSA[1] Percent of Total	U.S. Percent of Total
Construction, Mining, and Logging	8,100	2.6	5.2
Education and Health Services	67,000	21.4	15.9
Financial Activities	15,100	4.8	5.7
Government	71,400	22.8	15.3
Information	4,600	1.5	1.9
Leisure and Hospitality	27,900	8.9	10.7
Manufacturing	27,900	8.9	8.5
Other Services	11,100	3.5	3.9
Professional and Business Services	42,300	13.5	14.0
Retail Trade	25,200	8.0	11.0
Transportation, Warehousing, and Utilities	4,500	1.4	4.1
Wholesale Trade	8,100	2.6	4.0

Note: Figures are non-farm employment as of December 2017. Figures are not seasonally adjusted and include workers 16 years of age and older; (1) Figures cover the Durham-Chapel Hill, NC Metropolitan Statistical Area—see Appendix B for areas included
Source: Bureau of Labor Statistics, Current Employment Statistics, Employment, Hours, and Earnings

Occupations with Greatest Projected Employment Growth: 2017 – 2019

Occupation[1]	2017 Employment	2019 Projected Employment	Numeric Employment Change	Percent Employment Change
Combined Food Preparation and Serving Workers, Including Fast Food	150,940	161,640	10,700	7.1
Retail Salespersons	141,960	146,580	4,620	3.3
Waiters and Waitresses	78,300	82,440	4,140	5.3
Customer Service Representatives	98,260	102,060	3,800	3.9
Registered Nurses	99,040	102,730	3,690	3.7
Cashiers	112,380	115,690	3,310	3.0
Laborers and Freight, Stock, and Material Movers, Hand	86,000	89,280	3,280	3.8
Cooks, Restaurant	41,650	44,300	2,650	6.4
Home Health Aides	40,030	42,550	2,520	6.3
General and Operations Managers	55,710	58,180	2,470	4.4

Note: Projections cover North Carolina; (1) Sorted by numeric employment change
Source: www.projectionscentral.com, State Occupational Projections, 2017–2019 Short-Term Projections

Fastest Growing Occupations: 2017 – 2019

Occupation[1]	2017 Employment	2019 Projected Employment	Numeric Employment Change	Percent Employment Change
Solar Photovoltaic Installers	480	550	70	13.5
Helpers—Pipelayers, Plumbers, Pipefitters, and Steamfitters	3,340	3,670	330	9.9
Statisticians	1,220	1,340	120	9.8
Insurance Claims and Policy Processing Clerks	5,090	5,580	490	9.7
Insurance Sales Agents	12,990	14,230	1,240	9.5
Software Developers, Applications	26,360	28,620	2,260	8.6
Helpers—Brickmasons, Blockmasons, Stonemasons, and Tile and Marble Setters	1,060	1,150	90	8.5
Structural Iron and Steel Workers	1,560	1,690	130	8.5
Helpers—Carpenters	1,280	1,390	110	8.4
Plumbers, Pipefitters, and Steamfitters	11,560	12,520	960	8.3

Note: Projections cover North Carolina; (1) Sorted by percent employment change and excludes occupations with numeric employment change less than 50
Source: www.projectionscentral.com, State Occupational Projections, 2017–2019 Short-Term Projections

TAXES

State Corporate Income Tax Rates

State	Tax Rate (%)	Income Brackets ($)	Num. of Brackets	Financial Institution Tax Rate (%)[a]	Federal Income Tax Ded.
North Carolina	3.0	Flat rate	1	3.0	No

Note: Tax rates as of January 1, 2018; (a) Rates listed are the corporate income tax rate applied to financial institutions or excise taxes based on income. Some states have other taxes based upon the value of deposits or shares.
Source: Federation of Tax Administrators, Range of State Corporate Income Tax Rates, January 1, 2018

State Individual Income Tax Rates

State	Tax Rate (%)	Income Brackets ($)	Num. of Brackets	Personal Exempt. ($)[1]		Fed. Inc. Tax Ded.
				Single	Dependents	
North Carolina	5.499	Flat rate	1	None	None	No

Note: Tax rates as of January 1, 2018; Local- and county-level taxes are not included; n/a not applicable; (1) Married joint filers generally receive double the single exemption
Source: Federation of Tax Administrators, State Individual Income Tax Rates, January 1, 2018

Various State Sales and Excise Tax Rates

State	State Sales Tax (%)	Gasoline[1] (¢/gal.)	Cigarette[2] ($/pack)	Spirits[3] ($/gal.)	Wine[4] ($/gal.)	Beer[5] ($/gal.)	Recreational Marijuana (%)
North Carolina	4.75	35.35	0.45	14.63 (g)	1.00 (l)	0.62 (q)	Not legal

Note: All tax rates as of January 1, 2018; (1) The American Petroleum Institute has developed a methodology for determining the average tax rate on a gallon of fuel. Rates may include any of the following: excise taxes, environmental fees, storage tank fees, other fees or taxes, general sales tax, and local taxes. In states where gasoline is subject to the general sales tax, or where the fuel tax is based on the average sale price, the average rate determined by API is sensitive to changes in the price of gasoline. States that fully or partially apply general sales taxes to gasoline: CA, CO, GA, IL, IN, MI, NY; (2) The federal excise tax of $1.0066 per pack and local taxes are not included; (3) Rates are those applicable to off-premise sales of 40% alcohol by volume (a.b.v.) distilled spirits in 750ml containers. Local excise taxes are excluded; (4) Rates are those applicable to off-premise sales of 11% a.b.v. non-carbonated wine in 750ml containers; (5) Rates are those applicable to off-premise sales of 4.7% a.b.v. beer in 12 ounce containers; (g) Control states, where the government controls all sales. Products can be subject to ad valorem mark-up as well as excise taxes; (l) Different rates also applicable to alcohol content, place of production, size of container, place purchased (on- or off-premise or on board airlines) or type of wine (carbonated, vermouth, etc.); (q) Different rates also applicable according to alcohol content, place of production, size of container, or place purchased (on- or off-premise or onboard airlines).
Source: Tax Foundation, 2018 Facts & Figures: How Does Your State Compare?

State Business Tax Climate Index Rankings

State	Overall Rank	Corporate Tax Rank	Individual Income Tax Rank	Sales Tax Rank	Unemployment Insurance Tax Rank	Property Tax Rank
North Carolina	11	3	13	20	6	32

Note: The index is a measure of how each state's tax laws affect economic performance. The lower the rank, the more favorable a state's tax system is for business. States without a given tax are given a ranking of 1. The scores/rankings for the District of Columbia do not affect other states. The 2018 index represents the tax climate as of July 1, 2017.
Source: Tax Foundation, State Business Tax Climate Index 2018

TRANSPORTATION

Means of Transportation to Work

Area	Car/Truck/Van		Public Transportation			Bicycle	Walked	Other Means	Worked at Home
	Drove Alone	Car-pooled	Bus	Subway	Railroad				
City	54.9	6.9	11.8	0.0	0.0	1.9	13.7	2.0	8.8
MSA[1]	74.2	10.1	4.4	0.0	0.0	0.9	3.4	1.1	5.9
U.S.	76.4	9.3	2.6	1.9	0.6	0.6	2.8	1.3	4.6

Note: Figures are percentages and cover workers 16 years of age and older; (1) Figures cover the Durham-Chapel Hill, NC Metropolitan Statistical Area—see Appendix B for areas included
Source: U.S. Census Bureau, 2012-2016 American Community Survey 5-Year Estimates

Travel Time to Work

Area	Less Than 10 Minutes	10 to 19 Minutes	20 to 29 Minutes	30 to 44 Minutes	45 to 59 Minutes	60 to 89 Minutes	90 Minutes or More
City	15.7	38.7	24.8	13.5	4.3	2.2	0.7
MSA[1]	10.6	34.4	24.3	19.4	5.9	3.6	1.7
U.S.	12.9	29.2	20.9	20.4	8.0	6.0	2.7

Note: Note: Figures are percentages and include workers 16 years old and over; (1) Figures cover the Durham-Chapel Hill, NC Metropolitan Statistical Area—see Appendix B for areas included
Source: U.S. Census Bureau, 2012-2016 American Community Survey 5-Year Estimates

Freeway Travel Time Index

Area	1985	1990	1995	2000	2005	2010	2014
Urban Area Rank[1,2]	n/a	n/a	n/a	n/a	n/a	n/a	n/a
Urban Area Index[1]	n/a	n/a	n/a	n/a	n/a	n/a	n/a
Average Index[3]	1.09	1.11	1.14	1.17	1.20	1.19	1.20

Note: Freeway Travel Time Index—the ratio of travel time in the peak period to the travel time at free-flow conditions. For example, a value of 1.30 indicates a 20-minute free-flow trip takes 26 minutes in the peak (20 minutes x 1.30 = 26 minutes); (1) Data for the Durham-Chapel Hill, NC urban area was not available; (2) Rank is based on 101 urban areas (#1 = highest travel time index); (3) Average of 101 urban areas
Source: Texas Transportation Institute, 2015 Urban Mobility Scorecard, August 2015

Freeway Commuter Stress Index

Area	1985	1990	1995	2000	2005	2010	2014
Urban Area Rank[1,2]	n/a	n/a	n/a	n/a	n/a	n/a	n/a
Urban Area Index[1]	n/a	n/a	n/a	n/a	n/a	n/a	n/a
Average Index[3]	1.13	1.16	1.19	1.22	1.25	1.24	1.25

Note: The Freeway Commuter Stress Index is the same as the Freeway Travel Time Index (see table above) except that it includes only the travel in the peak directions during the peak periods; the TTI includes travel in all directions during the peak period. Thus, the CSI is more indicative of the work trip experienced by each commuter on a daily basis; (1) Data for the Durham-Chapel Hill, NC urban area was not available; (2) Rank is based on 101 urban areas (#1 = highest travel time index); (3) Average of 101 urban areas
Source: Texas Transportation Institute, 2015 Urban Mobility Scorecard, August 2015

Living Environment

COST OF LIVING

Cost of Living Index

Composite Index	Groceries	Housing	Utilities	Transportation	Health Care	Misc. Goods/ Services
93.9	92.5	99.1	91.4	94.1	97.5	90.3

Note: The Cost of Living Index measures regional differences in the cost of consumer goods and services, excluding taxes and non-consumer expenditures, for professional and managerial households in the top income quintile. It is based on more than 50,000 prices covering almost 60 different items for which prices are collected three times a year by chambers of commerce, economic development organizations or university applied economic centers in each participating urban area. The numbers shown should be read as a percentage above or below the national average of 100. For example, a value of 115.4 in the groceries column indicates that grocery prices are 15.4% higher than the national average. Small differences in the index numbers should not be interpreted as significant; Figures cover the Chapel Hill NC urban area.
Source: The Council for Community and Economic Research, ACCRA Cost of Living Index, 2017

Grocery Prices

Area[1]	T-Bone Steak ($/pound)	Frying Chicken ($/pound)	Whole Milk ($/half gal.)	Eggs ($/dozen)	Orange Juice ($/64 oz.)	Coffee ($/11.5 oz.)
City[2]	9.70	1.22	2.42	1.49	3.16	3.33
Avg.	11.29	1.40	2.02	1.47	3.55	4.37
Min.	7.71	0.93	1.04	0.70	2.86	3.24
Max.	15.83	2.39	4.03	3.92	6.29	8.16

*Note: (1) Values for the local area are compared with the average, minimum and maximum values for all 294 areas in the Cost of Living Index; (2) Figures cover the Chapel Hill NC urban area; **T-Bone Steak** (price per pound); **Frying Chicken** (price per pound, whole fryer); **Whole Milk** (half gallon carton); **Eggs** (price per dozen, Grade A, large); **Orange Juice** (64 oz. Tropicana or Florida Natural); **Coffee** (11.5 oz. can, vacuum-packed, Maxwell House, Hills Bros, or Folgers).*
Source: The Council for Community and Economic Research, ACCRA Cost of Living Index, 2017

Housing and Utility Costs

Area[1]	New Home Price ($)	Apartment Rent ($/month)	All Electric ($/month)	Part Electric ($/month)	Other Energy ($/month)	Telephone ($/month)
City[2]	345,150	975	-	82.94	61.22	27.99
Avg.	335,956	1,047	175.01	97.34	67.93	28.71
Min.	187,788	491	109.48	49.33	35.44	12.39
Max.	1,739,087	4,559	432.62	227.09	353.33	44.61

*Note: (1) Values for the local area are compared with the average, minimum and maximum values for all 294 areas in the Cost of Living Index; (2) Figures cover the Chapel Hill NC urban area; **New Home Price** (2,400 sf living area, 8,000 sf lot, in urban area with full utilities); **Apartment Rent** (950 sf 2 bedroom/1.5 or 2 bath, unfurnished, excluding all utilities except water); **All Electric** (average monthly cost for an all-electric home); **Part Electric** (average monthly cost for a part-electric home); **Other Energy** (average monthly cost for natural gas, fuel oil, coal, wood, and any other forms of energy except electricity); **Telephone** (price includes basic monthly rate for a private residential line plus additional local usage charges incurred by a family of four).*
Source: The Council for Community and Economic Research, ACCRA Cost of Living Index, 2017

Health Care, Transportation, and Other Costs

Area[1]	Doctor ($/visit)	Dentist ($/visit)	Optometrist ($/visit)	Gasoline ($/gallon)	Beauty Salon ($/visit)	Men's Shirt ($)
City[2]	80.00	105.00	104.06	2.24	33.50	11.33
Avg.	108.00	92.54	101.93	2.25	37.58	30.92
Min.	30.39	60.00	49.75	1.82	16.11	11.20
Max.	193.50	161.94	229.28	3.16	77.35	59.13

*Note: (1) Values for the local area are compared with the average, minimum and maximum values for all 294 areas in the Cost of Living Index; (2) Figures cover the Chapel Hill NC urban area; **Doctor** (general practitioners routine exam of an established patient); **Dentist** (adult teeth cleaning and periodic oral examination); **Optometrist** (full vision eye exam for established adult patient); **Gasoline** (one gallon regular unleaded, national brand, including all taxes, cash price at self-service pump if available); **Beauty Salon** (woman's shampoo, trim, and blow-dry); **Men's Shirt** (cotton/polyester dress shirt, pinpoint weave, long sleeves).*
Source: The Council for Community and Economic Research, ACCRA Cost of Living Index, 2017

HOUSING

House Price Index (HPI)

Area	National Ranking[2]	Quarterly Change (%)	One-Year Change (%)	Five-Year Change (%)
MSA[1]	54	0.98	9.08	28.49
U.S.[3]	–	1.61	6.68	34.71

Note: The HPI is a weighted repeat sales index. It measures average price changes in repeat sales or refinancings on the same properties. This information is obtained by reviewing repeat mortgage transactions on single-family properties whose mortgages have been purchased or securitized by Fannie Mae or Freddie Mac in January 1975; (1) Figures cover the Durham-Chapel Hill, NC Metropolitan Statistical Area—see Appendix B for areas included; (2) Rankings are based on annual percentage change for all metro areas containing at least 15,000 transactions over the last 10 years and ranges from 1 to 253; (3) figures based on a weighted average of Census Division estimates using a seasonally adjusted, purchase-only index; all figures are for the period ending December 31, 2017
Source: Federal Housing Finance Agency, House Price Index, February 28, 2018

Median Single-Family Home Prices

Area	2015	2016	2017p	Percent Change 2016 to 2017
MSA[1]	222.9	239.4	254.7	6.4
U.S. Average	223.9	235.5	248.8	5.6

Note: Figures are median sales prices of existing single-family homes in thousands of dollars; (p) preliminary; (1) Figures cover the Durham-Chapel Hill, NC Metropolitan Statistical Area—see Appendix B for areas included
Source: National Association of Realtors, Median Sales Price of Existing Single-Family Homes for Metropolitan Areas, 4th Quarter 2017

Qualifying Income Based on Median Sales Price of Existing Single-Family Homes

Area	With 5% Down ($)	With 10% Down ($)	With 20% Down ($)
MSA[1]	56,415	53,445	47,507
U.S. Average	55,585	52,659	46,808

Note: Figures are preliminary; Qualifying income is based on a mortgage rate of 4.17%. Monthly principal and interest payment is limited to 25% of income; (1) Figures cover the Durham-Chapel Hill, NC Metropolitan Statistical Area—see Appendix B for areas included
Source: National Association of Realtors, Qualifying Income Based on Median Sales Price of Existing Single-Family Homes for Metropolitan Areas, 4th Quarter 2017

Median Apartment Condo-Coop Home Prices

Area	2015	2016	2017p	Percent Change 2016 to 2017
MSA[1]	n/a	n/a	n/a	n/a
U.S. Average	210.7	220.7	234.3	6.2

Note: Figures are median sales prices of existing apartment condo-coop homes in thousands of dollars; (p) preliminary; n/a not available; (1) Figures cover the Durham-Chapel Hill, NC Metropolitan Statistical Area—see Appendix B for areas included
Source: National Association of Realtors, Median Sales Price of Existing Apartment Condo-Coop Homes for Metropolitan Areas, 4th Quarter 2017

Home Value Distribution

Area	Under $50,000	$50,000 -$99,999	$100,000 -$149,999	$150,000 -$199,999	$200,000 -$299,999	$300,000 -$499,999	$500,000 -$999,999	$1,000,000 or more
City	1.1	2.0	6.2	6.4	16.2	36.0	27.9	4.1
MSA[1]	5.5	8.9	16.7	18.1	21.9	19.1	8.4	1.4
U.S.	8.8	14.8	15.3	14.9	18.4	16.4	9.0	2.5

Note: Figures are percentages and cover owner-occupied housing units; (1) Figures cover the Durham-Chapel Hill, NC Metropolitan Statistical Area—see Appendix B for areas included
Source: U.S. Census Bureau, 2012-2016 American Community Survey 5-Year Estimates

Homeownership Rate

Area	2009 (%)	2010 (%)	2011 (%)	2012 (%)	2013 (%)	2014 (%)	2015 (%)	2016 (%)	2017 (%)
MSA[1]	n/a	n/a	n/a	n/a	n/a	n/a	n/a	n/a	n/a
U.S.	67.4	66.9	66.1	65.4	65.1	64.5	63.7	63.4	63.9

Note: (1) Figures cover the Durham-Chapel Hill, NC Metropolitan Statistical Area—see Appendix B for areas included; n/a not available
Source: U.S. Census Bureau, Housing Vacancies and Homeownership Annual Statistics: 2009-2017

Year Housing Structure Built

Area	2010 or Later	2000 -2009	1990 -1999	1980 -1989	1970 -1979	1960 -1969	1950 -1959	1940 -1949	Before 1940	Median Year
City	2.5	18.3	18.7	19.0	14.2	13.1	8.3	2.7	3.3	1985
MSA[1]	4.3	20.7	19.1	16.8	13.0	9.8	6.9	3.5	5.8	1987
U.S.	2.3	14.7	14.0	13.7	15.6	10.9	10.6	5.2	13.0	1977

Note: Figures are percentages except for Median Year; Note: (1) Figures cover the Durham-Chapel Hill, NC Metropolitan Statistical Area—see Appendix B for areas included
Source: U.S. Census Bureau, 2012-2016 American Community Survey 5-Year Estimates

Gross Monthly Rent

Area	Under $500	$500 -$999	$1,000 -$1,499	$1,500 -$1,999	$2,000 -$2,499	$2,500 -$2,999	$3,000 and up	Median ($)
City	3.4	40.4	35.4	12.7	5.0	2.2	0.9	1,061
MSA[1]	8.5	52.9	28.4	6.8	1.9	0.8	0.7	910
U.S.	11.3	43.3	27.7	10.7	4.0	1.6	1.5	949

Note: Figures are percentages except for Median; Gross rent is the contract rent plus the estimated average monthly cost of utilities (electricity, gas, and water and sewer) and fuels (oil, coal, kerosene, wood, etc.) if these are paid by the renter (or paid for the renter by someone else); (1) Figures cover the Durham-Chapel Hill, NC Metropolitan Statistical Area—see Appendix B for areas included
Source: U.S. Census Bureau, 2012-2016 American Community Survey 5-Year Estimates

HEALTH

Health Risk Factors

Category	MSA[1] (%)	U.S. (%)
Adults aged 18–64 who have any kind of health care coverage	n/a	87.7
Adults who reported being in good or excellent health	n/a	83.6
Adults who are current smokers	n/a	17.1
Adults who currently use E-cigarettes	n/a	4.7
Adults who currently use chewing tobacco, snuff, or snus	n/a	4.0
Adults who are heavy drinkers[2]	n/a	6.5
Adults who are binge drinkers[3]	n/a	16.9
Adults who are overweight (BMI 25.0 - 29.9)	n/a	35.3
Adults who are obese (BMI 30.0 - 99.8)	n/a	29.9
Adults who participated in any physical activities in the past month	n/a	76.9
Adults who always or nearly always wears a seat belt	n/a	94.3

Note: n/a not available; (1) Figures cover the Durham-Chapel Hill, NC Metropolitan Statistical Area—see Appendix B for areas included; (2) Heavy drinkers are classified as adult men having more than 14 drinks per week and adult women having more than 7 drinks per week; (3) Binge drinkers are classified as males having five or more drinks on one occasion or females having four or more drinks on one occasion
Source: Centers for Disease Control and Prevention, Behaviorial Risk Factor Surveillance System, SMART: Selected Metropolitan Area Risk Trends, 2016

Health Screening Rates

Category	MSA[1] (%)	U.S. (%)
Adults 50-75 who have had a blood stool test within the past year	n/a	8.0
Adults 50-75 who have had a colonoscopy in the past 10 years	n/a	63.5
Adults aged 65+ who have had flu shot within the past year	n/a	58.6
Adults aged 65+ who have ever had a pneumonia vaccination	n/a	73.4
Adults who have ever been tested for HIV	n/a	35.6
Women aged 21-65 who have had a pap test in the past three years	n/a	79.8
Men aged 40+ who have had a PSA test within the past two years	n/a	39.5
Women aged 40+ who have had a mammogram within the past two years	n/a	72.5

Note: n/a not available; (1) Figures cover the Durham-Chapel Hill, NC Metropolitan Statistical Area—see Appendix B for areas included; Source: Centers for Disease Control and Prevention, Behaviorial Risk Factor Surveillance System, SMART: Selected Metropolitan Area Risk Trends, 2016

Chronic Health Conditions

Category	MSA[1] (%)	U.S. (%)
Adults who have ever been told they had a heart attack	n/a	4.4
Adults who have ever been told they have angina or coronary heart disease	n/a	4.1
Adults who have ever been told they had a stroke	n/a	3.1
Adults who have been told they currently have asthma	n/a	9.3
Adults who have ever been told they have arthritis	n/a	25.8
Adults who have ever been told they have diabetes[2]	n/a	10.5
Adults who have ever been told they had skin cancer	n/a	5.9
Adults who have ever been told they had any other types of cancer	n/a	6.7
Adults who have ever been told they have COPD	n/a	6.3
Adults who have ever been told they have kidney disease	n/a	2.8
Adults who have ever been told they have a form of depression	n/a	17.4

Note: n/a not available; (1) Figures cover the Durham-Chapel Hill, NC Metropolitan Statistical Area—see Appendix B for areas included; (2) Figures do not include pregnancy-related, borderline, or pre-diabetes
Source: Centers for Disease Control and Prevention, Behaviorial Risk Factor Surveillance System, SMART: Selected Metropolitan Area Risk Trends, 2016

Mortality Rates for the Top 10 Causes of Death in the U.S.

ICD-10[a] Sub-Chapter	ICD-10[a] Code	Age-Adjusted Mortality Rate[1] per 100,000 population	
		County[2]	U.S.
Malignant neoplasms	C00-C97	145.8	158.5
Ischaemic heart diseases	I20-I25	68.3	96.8
Other forms of heart disease	I30-I51	42.8	52.4
Chronic lower respiratory diseases	J40-J47	29.0	40.9
Cerebrovascular diseases	I60-I69	31.8	37.2
Organic, including symptomatic, mental disorders	F01-F09	47.4	33.3
Other degenerative diseases of the nervous system	G30-G31	30.7	32.1
Other external causes of accidental injury	W00-X59	24.7	31.2
Diabetes mellitus	E10-E14	16.4	21.1
Hypertensive diseases	I10-I15	13.3	20.8

Note: (a) ICD-10 = International Classification of Diseases 10th Revision; (1) Mortality rates are a three year average covering 2014-2016; (2) Figures cover Orange County.
Source: Centers for Disease Control and Prevention, National Center for Health Statistics. Underlying Cause of Death 1999-2016 on CDC WONDER Online Database, released December 2017

Mortality Rates for Selected Causes of Death

ICD-10[a] Sub-Chapter	ICD-10[a] Code	Age-Adjusted Mortality Rate[1] per 100,000 population	
		County[2]	U.S.
Assault	X85-Y09	Suppressed	5.6
Diseases of the liver	K70-K76	10.9	14.0
Human immunodeficiency virus (HIV) disease	B20-B24	Suppressed	1.9
Influenza and pneumonia	J09-J18	9.3	14.6
Intentional self-harm	X60-X84	8.0	13.2
Malnutrition	E40-E46	Suppressed	1.3
Obesity and other hyperalimentation	E65-E68	Unreliable	2.1
Renal failure	N17-N19	11.0	13.0
Transport accidents	V01-V99	8.0	12.0
Viral hepatitis	B15-B19	Suppressed	1.9

Note: (a) ICD-10 = International Classification of Diseases 10th Revision; (1) Mortality rates are a three year average covering 2014-2016; (2) Figures cover Orange County; Data are Suppressed when the data meet the criteria for confidentiality constraints; Mortality rates are flagged as Unreliable when the rate would be calculated with a numerator of 20 or less.
Source: Centers for Disease Control and Prevention, National Center for Health Statistics. Underlying Cause of Death 1999-2016 on CDC WONDER Online Database, released December 2017

Health Insurance Coverage

Area	With Health Insurance	With Private Health Insurance	With Public Health Insurance	Without Health Insurance	Population Under Age 18 Without Health Insurance
City	94.1	88.4	15.1	5.9	6.1
MSA[1]	87.8	71.0	28.0	12.2	6.4
U.S.	88.3	66.7	33.0	11.7	5.9

Note: Figures are percentages that cover the civilian noninstitutionalized population; (1) Figures cover the Durham-Chapel Hill, NC Metropolitan Statistical Area—see Appendix B for areas included
Source: U.S. Census Bureau, 2012-2016 American Community Survey 5-Year Estimates

Number of Medical Professionals

Area	MDs[3]	DOs[3,4]	Dentists	Podiatrists	Chiropractors	Optometrists
County[1] (number)	2,044	26	300	5	20	17
County[1] (rate[2])	1,443.9	18.4	210.2	3.5	14.0	11.9
U.S. (rate[2])	276.5	22.3	67.3	6.0	26.7	15.9

Note: Data as of 2016 unless noted; (1) Data covers Orange County; (2) Rate per 100,000 population; (3) Data as of 2015 and includes all active, non-federal physicians; (4) Doctor of Osteopathic Medicine
Source: U.S. Department of Health and Human Services, Health Resources and Services Administration, Bureau of Health Professions, Area Resource File (ARF) 2016-2017

Best Hospitals

According to *U.S. News,* the Durham-Chapel Hill, NC metro area is home to two of the best hospitals in the U.S.: **Duke University Hospital** (Honor Roll/13 adult specialties and 10 pediatric specialties); **University of North Carolina Hospitals** (6 adult specialties and 9 pediatric specialties). The hospitals listed were nationally ranked in at least one of 16 specialties. Only 152 hospitals nationwide were nationally ranked in one or more specialties. Twenty hospitals in the U.S. made the Honor Roll. The Best Hospitals Honor Roll was revamped last year to take both the national rankings and the procedure and condition ratings into account. Hospitals received points if they were nationally ranked in one of the 16 specialties—the higher they ranked, the more points they got—and how many ratings of "high performing" they earned in the nine procedures and conditions. *U.S. News Online, "America's Best Hospitals 2017-18"*

According to *U.S. News,* the Durham-Chapel Hill, NC metro area is home to two of the best children's hospitals in the U.S.: **Duke Children's Hospital and Health Center** (10 pediatric specialties); **North Carolina Children's Hospital at UNC** (9 pediatric specialties). The hospitals listed were highly ranked in at least one of 10 pediatric specialties. Eighty-two children's hospitals in the U.S. were nationally ranked in at least one specialty. Hospitals received points for being ranked in a specialty, and the 10 hospitals with the most points across the 10 specialties make up the Honor Roll. *U.S. News Online, "America's Best Children's Hospitals 2017-18"*

EDUCATION

Public School District Statistics

District Name	Schls	Pupils	Pupil/ Teacher Ratio	Minority Pupils[1] (%)	Free Lunch Eligible[2] (%)	IEP[3] (%)
Chapel Hill-Carrboro City Schools	20	11,982	12.9	48.3	23.7	10.1
Chatham County Schools	18	8,690	14.7	48.1	45.6	13.6
Orange County Schools	13	7,627	13.8	40.8	37.7	14.9
Willow Oak Montessori	1	149	9.5	18.8	6.7	11.4
Woods Charter School	1	503	11.0	17.5	1.6	16.9

Note: Table includes school districts with 100 or more students; (1) Percentage of students that are not non-Hispanic white; (2) Percentage of students that are eligible for the free lunch program; (3) Percentage of students that have an Individualized Education Program.
Source: U.S. Department of Education, National Center for Education Statistics, Common Core of Data, Local Education Agency (School District) Universe Survey: School Year 2015-2016; U.S. Department of Education, National Center for Education Statistics, Common Core of Data, Public Elementary/Secondary School Universe Survey: School Year 2015-2016

Best High Schools

According to *U.S. News,* Chapel Hill is home to three of the best high schools in the U.S.: **Woods Charter** (#104); **East Chapel Hill High** (#142); **Chapel Hill High** (#169). More than 22,000 public, magnet and charter schools were ranked based on their performance on state assessments and how well they prepare students for college. Schools with the highest unrounded College

Readiness Index values were numerically ranked from 1 to 500 and were classified as gold medal winners. *U.S. News & World Report, "Best High Schools 2017"*

Highest Level of Education

Area	Less than H.S.	H.S. Diploma	Some College, No Deg.	Associate Degree	Bachelor's Degree	Master's Degree	Prof. School Degree	Doctorate Degree
City	4.1	7.6	9.4	4.3	30.6	22.7	8.2	13.0
MSA[1]	11.7	18.8	16.9	6.7	23.7	13.1	3.9	5.2
U.S.	13.0	27.5	21.0	8.2	18.8	8.2	2.0	1.3

Note: Figures cover persons age 25 and over; (1) Figures cover the Durham-Chapel Hill, NC Metropolitan Statistical Area—see Appendix B for areas included
Source: U.S. Census Bureau, 2012-2016 American Community Survey 5-Year Estimates

Educational Attainment by Race

Area	High School Graduate or Higher (%)					Bachelor's Degree or Higher (%)				
	Total	White	Black	Asian	Hisp.[2]	Total	White	Black	Asian	Hisp.[2]
City	95.9	97.7	86.7	93.7	85.2	74.6	79.8	37.9	79.1	48.8
MSA[1]	88.3	90.8	86.0	91.6	48.6	45.9	52.4	29.2	72.9	15.0
U.S.	87.0	88.9	84.3	86.3	65.7	30.3	31.6	20.0	52.1	14.7

Note: Figures shown cover persons 25 years old and over; (1) Figures cover the Durham-Chapel Hill, NC Metropolitan Statistical Area—see Appendix B for areas included; (2) People of Hispanic origin can be of any race
Source: U.S. Census Bureau, 2012-2016 American Community Survey 5-Year Estimates

School Enrollment by Grade and Control

Area	Preschool (%)		Kindergarten (%)		Grades 1 - 4 (%)		Grades 5 - 8 (%)		Grades 9 - 12 (%)	
	Public	Private	Public	Private	Public	Private	Public	Private	Public	Private
City	28.7	71.3	85.6	14.4	93.4	6.6	93.5	6.5	89.2	10.8
MSA[1]	42.6	57.4	89.1	10.9	89.7	10.3	89.9	10.1	89.2	10.8
U.S.	58.4	41.6	87.7	12.3	89.8	10.2	89.7	10.3	90.4	9.6

Note: Figures shown cover persons 3 years old and over; (1) Figures cover the Durham-Chapel Hill, NC Metropolitan Statistical Area—see Appendix B for areas included
Source: U.S. Census Bureau, 2012-2016 American Community Survey 5-Year Estimates

Average Salaries of Public School Classroom Teachers

Area	2015		2016		Change from 2015 to 2016	
	Dollars	Rank[1]	Dollars	Rank[1]	Percent	Rank[2]
North Carolina	47,792	40	47,941	41	0.3	44
U.S. Average	57,611	–	58,353	–	1.3	–

Note: (1) Rank ranges from 1 to 51 where 1 indicates highest salary; (2) Rank ranges from 1 to 51 where 1 indicates highest percent change.
Source: National Education Association, Rankings & Estimates: Rankings of the States 2016 and Estimates of School Statistics 2017

Higher Education

Four-Year Colleges			Two-Year Colleges			Medical Schools[1]	Law Schools[2]	Voc/ Tech[3]
Public	Private Non-profit	Private For-profit	Public	Private Non-profit	Private For-profit			
1	0	0	0	0	0	1	1	1

Note: Figures cover institutions located within the city limits and include main campuses only; (1) includes schools accredited by the Liaison Committee on Medical Education and the American Osteopathic Association's Commission on Osteopathic College Accreditation; (2) includes ABA-accredited schools, schools with provisional ABA accreditation, and state accredited schools; (3) includes all schools with programs that are less than 2 years.
Source: National Center for Education Statistics, Integrated Postsecondary Education System (IPEDS), 2016-17; Wikipedia, List of Medical Schools in the United States, accessed April 2, 2018; Wikipedia, List of Law Schools in the United States, accessed April 2, 2018

According to *U.S. News & World Report,* the Durham-Chapel Hill, NC metro area is home to two of the best national universities in the U.S.: **Duke University** (#9); **University of North Carolina—Chapel Hill** (#30 tie). The indicators used to capture academic quality fall into a number of categories: assessment by administrators at peer institutions; retention of students; faculty resources; student selectivity; financial resources; alumni giving; high school counselor ratings of colleges; and graduation rate. *U.S. News & World Report, "America's Best Colleges 2018"*

According to *U.S. News & World Report,* the Durham-Chapel Hill, NC metro area is home to two of the top 100 law schools in the U.S.: **Duke University** (#11 tie); **University of North Carolina—Chapel Hill** (#45). The rankings are based on a weighted average of 12 measures of quality: peer assessment score; assessment score by lawyers/judges; median LSAT scores; median undergrad GPA; acceptance rate; employment rates for graduates; placement success; bar passage rate; faculty resources; expenditures per student; student/faculty ratio; and library resources. *U.S. News & World Report, "America's Best Graduate Schools, Law, 2019"*

According to *U.S. News & World Report,* the Durham-Chapel Hill, NC metro area is home to two of the top 75 medical schools for research in the U.S.: **Duke University** (#10); **University of North Carolina—Chapel Hill** (#23 tie). The rankings are based on a weighted average of 11 measures of quality: quality assessment; peer assessment score; assessment score by residency directors; research activity; total research activity; average research activity per faculty member; student selectivity; median MCAT total score; median undergraduate GPA; acceptance rate; and faculty resources. *U.S. News & World Report, "America's Best Graduate Schools, Medical, 2019"*

According to *U.S. News & World Report,* the Durham-Chapel Hill, NC metro area is home to two of the top 75 business schools in the U.S.: **Duke University (Fuqua)** (#11 tie); **University of North Carolina—Chapel Hill (Kenan-Flagler)** (#19). The rankings are based on a weighted average of the following nine measures: quality assessment; peer assessment; recruiter assessment; placement success; mean starting salary and bonus; student selectivity; mean GMAT and GRE scores; mean undergraduate GPA; and acceptance rate. *U.S. News & World Report, "America's Best Graduate Schools, Business, 2019"*

PRESIDENTIAL ELECTION

2016 Presidential Election Results

Area	Clinton	Trump	Johnson	Stein	Other
Orange County	72.8	22.5	2.9	0.6	1.2
U.S.	48.0	45.9	3.3	1.1	1.7

Note: Results are percentages and may not add to 100% due to rounding
Source: Dave Leip's Atlas of U.S. Presidential Elections

EMPLOYERS

Major Employers

Company Name	Industry
CISCO Systems	Data conversion equipment, media-to-media: computer
City of Durham	City & town managers' office
Duke University	Colleges & universities
Duke University Health System	General medical & surgical hospitals
Durham County Hospital Corporation	General medical & surgical hospitals
Environmental Protection Agency	Environmental protection agency, government
IBM	Computer peripheral equipment
National Institutes of Health	Environmental health program administration, govt
Netapp	Computer integrated systems design
North Carolina Central University	Colleges & universities
Patheon	Pharmaceutical preparations
Phyamerica Government Services	Hospital management
Research Triangle Institute	Commercial physical research
Sports Endeavors	Sporting goods & bicycle shops
University of NC at Chapel Hill	Hospital, med school affiliated with nursing & residency
University of NC at Chapel Hill	University
University of North Carolina Hospitals	General medical & surgical hospitals

Note: Companies shown are located within the Durham-Chapel Hill, NC Metropolitan Statistical Area.
Source: Hoovers.com; Wikipedia

PUBLIC SAFETY

Crime Rate

Area	All Crimes	Violent Crimes					Property Crimes		
		Murder	Rape[3]	Robbery	Aggrav. Assault		Burglary	Larceny -Theft	Motor Vehicle Theft
City	2,459.8	3.3	25.0	55.0	105.0		466.6	1,694.9	110.0
Metro[1]	n/a	n/a	n/a	n/a	n/a		n/a	n/a	n/a
U.S.	2,837.0	5.3	29.6	102.8	248.5		468.9	1,745.0	236.9

Note: Figures are crimes per 100,000 population; (1) Figures cover the Durham-Chapel Hill, NC Metropolitan Statistical Area—see Appendix B for areas included; n/a not available; (3) The city and U.S. figures shown were reported using the legacy Uniform Crime Reporting (UCR) definition of rape. The metro area figures shown are an aggregate total of the data submitted using both the revised and legacy UCR definitions.
Source: FBI Uniform Crime Reports, 2016

Hate Crimes

Area	Number of Quarters Reported	Number of Incidents per Bias Motivation					
		Race/Ethnicity/ Ancestry	Religion	Sexual Orientation	Disability	Gender	Gender Identity
City	4	0	0	0	0	0	0
U.S.	4	3,489	1,273	1,076	70	31	124

Source: Federal Bureau of Investigation, Hate Crime Statistics 2016

Identity Theft Consumer Reports

Area	Reports	Reports per 100,000 Population	Rank[2]
MSA[1]	730	130	40
U.S.	371,061	114	-

Note: (1) Figures cover the Durham-Chapel Hill, NC Metropolitan Statistical Area—see Appendix B for areas included; (2) Rank ranges from 1 to 389 where 1 indicates greatest number of identity theft reports per 100,000 population
Source: Federal Trade Commission, Consumer Sentinel Network Data Book for January–December 2017

Fraud and Other Consumer Reports

Area	Reports	Reports per 100,000 Population	Rank[2]
MSA[1]	2,610	466	159
U.S.	2,304,550	708	-

Note: (1) Figures cover the Durham-Chapel Hill, NC Metropolitan Statistical Area—see Appendix B for areas included; (2) Rank ranges from 1 to 389 where 1 indicates greatest number of fraud and other consumer reports per 100,000 population
Source: Federal Trade Commission, Consumer Sentinel Network Data Book for January–December 2017

SPORTS

Professional Sports Teams

Team Name	League	Year Established
Carolina Hurricanes	National Hockey League (NHL)	1997

Note: Includes teams located in the Durham-Chapel Hill, NC Metropolitan Statistical Area.
Source: Wikipedia, Major Professional Sports Teams of the United States and Canada, April 5, 2018

CLIMATE

Average and Extreme Temperatures

Temperature	Jan	Feb	Mar	Apr	May	Jun	Jul	Aug	Sep	Oct	Nov	Dec	Yr.
Extreme High (°F)	79	84	90	95	97	104	105	105	104	98	88	79	105
Average High (°F)	50	53	61	72	79	86	89	87	81	72	62	53	71
Average Temp. (°F)	40	43	50	59	67	75	78	77	71	60	51	42	60
Average Low (°F)	29	31	38	46	55	63	68	67	60	48	39	32	48
Extreme Low (°F)	-9	5	11	23	29	38	48	46	37	19	11	4	-9

Note: Figures cover the years 1948-1990
Source: National Climatic Data Center, International Station Meteorological Climate Summary, 9/96

Average Precipitation/Snowfall/Humidity

Precip./Humidity	Jan	Feb	Mar	Apr	May	Jun	Jul	Aug	Sep	Oct	Nov	Dec	Yr.
Avg. Precip. (in.)	3.4	3.6	3.6	2.9	3.9	3.6	4.4	4.4	3.2	2.9	3.0	3.1	42.0
Avg. Snowfall (in.)	2	3	1	Tr	0	0	0	0	0	0	Tr	1	8
Avg. Rel. Hum. 7am (%)	79	79	79	80	84	86	88	91	91	90	84	81	84
Avg. Rel. Hum. 4pm (%)	53	49	46	43	51	54	57	59	57	53	51	53	52

Note: Figures cover the years 1948-1990; Tr = Trace amounts (<0.05 in. of rain; <0.5 in. of snow)
Source: National Climatic Data Center, International Station Meteorological Climate Summary, 9/96

Weather Conditions

Temperature			Daytime Sky			Precipitation		
32°F & below	45°F & below	90°F & above	Clear	Partly cloudy	Cloudy	0.01 inch or more precip.	0.1 inch or more snow/ice	Thunder-storms
77	160	39	98	143	124	110	3	42

Note: Figures are average number of days per year and cover the years 1948-1990
Source: National Climatic Data Center, International Station Meteorological Climate Summary, 9/96

HAZARDOUS WASTE

Superfund Sites

The Durham-Chapel Hill, NC metro area is home to one site on the EPA's Superfund National Priorities List: **Gmh Electronics** (final). There are a total of 1,396 Superfund sites with a status of proposed or final on the list in the U.S. *U.S. Environmental Protection Agency, National Priorities List, April 4, 2018*

AIR & WATER QUALITY

Air Quality Trends: Ozone

	1990	1995	2000	2005	2010	2012	2013	2014	2015	2016
MSA[1]	n/a	n/a	n/a	n/a	n/a	n/a	n/a	n/a	n/a	n/a
U.S.	0.087	0.089	0.081	0.079	0.073	0.075	0.069	0.067	0.068	0.069

Note: (1) Data covers the Durham-Chapel Hill, NC Metropolitan Statistical Area—see Appendix B for areas included; n/a not available. The values shown are the composite ozone concentration averages among trend sites based on the highest fourth daily maximum 8-hour concentration in parts per million. These trends are based on sites having an adequate record of monitoring data during the trend period. Data from exceptional events are included.
Source: U.S. Environmental Protection Agency, Air Quality Monitoring Information, "Air Quality Trends by City, 1990-2016"

Air Quality Index

Area	Percent of Days when Air Quality was...[2]					AQI Statistics[2]	
	Good	Moderate	Unhealthy for Sensitive Groups	Unhealthy	Very Unhealthy	Maximum	Median
MSA[1]	72.3	27.4	0.3	0.0	0.0	110	44

Note: (1) Data covers the Durham-Chapel Hill, NC Metropolitan Statistical Area—see Appendix B for areas included; (2) Based on 365 days with AQI data in 2017. Air Quality Index (AQI) is an index for reporting daily air quality. EPA calculates the AQI for five major air pollutants regulated by the Clean Air Act: ground-level ozone, particle pollution (aka particulate matter), carbon monoxide, sulfur dioxide, and nitrogen dioxide. The AQI runs from 0 to 500. The higher the AQI value, the greater the level of air pollution and the greater the health concern. There are six AQI categories: "Good" AQI is between 0 and 50. Air quality is considered satisfactory; "Moderate" AQI is between 51 and 100. Air quality is acceptable; "Unhealthy for Sensitive Groups" When AQI values are between 101 and 150, members of sensitive groups may experience health effects; "Unhealthy" When AQI values are between 151 and 200 everyone may begin to experience health effects; "Very Unhealthy" AQI values between 201 and 300 trigger a health alert; "Hazardous" AQI values over 300 trigger warnings of emergency conditions (not shown).
Source: U.S. Environmental Protection Agency, Air Quality Index Report, 2017

Air Quality Index Pollutants

Area	Percent of Days when AQI Pollutant was...[2]					
	Carbon Monoxide	Nitrogen Dioxide	Ozone	Sulfur Dioxide	Particulate Matter 2.5	Particulate Matter 10
MSA[1]	0.0	0.0	47.4	0.5	52.1	0.0

Note: (1) Data covers the Durham-Chapel Hill, NC Metropolitan Statistical Area—see Appendix B for areas included; (2) Based on 365 days with AQI data in 2017. The Air Quality Index (AQI) is an index for reporting daily air quality. EPA calculates the AQI for five major air pollutants regulated by the Clean Air Act: ground-level ozone, particle pollution (also known as particulate matter), carbon monoxide, sulfur dioxide, and nitrogen dioxide. The AQI runs from 0 to 500. The higher the AQI value, the greater the level of air pollution and the greater the health concern.
Source: U.S. Environmental Protection Agency, Air Quality Index Report, 2017

Maximum Air Pollutant Concentrations: Particulate Matter, Ozone, CO and Lead

	Particulate Matter 10 (ug/m^3)	Particulate Matter 2.5 Wtd AM (ug/m^3)	Particulate Matter 2.5 24-Hr (ug/m^3)	Ozone (ppm)	Carbon Monoxide (ppm)	Lead (ug/m^3)
MSA[1] Level	29	8.9	20	0.063	n/a	n/a
NAAQS[2]	150	15	35	0.075	9	0.15
Met NAAQS[2]	Yes	Yes	Yes	Yes	n/a	n/a

Note: (1) Data covers the Durham-Chapel Hill, NC Metropolitan Statistical Area—see Appendix B for areas included; Data from exceptional events are included; (2) National Ambient Air Quality Standards; ppm = parts per million; ug/m^3 = micrograms per cubic meter; n/a not available.
Concentrations: Particulate Matter 10 (coarse particulate)—highest second maximum 24-hour concentration; Particulate Matter 2.5 Wtd AM (fine particulate)—highest weighted annual mean concentration; Particulate Matter 2.5 24-Hour (fine particulate)—highest 98th percentile 24-hour concentration; Ozone—highest fourth daily maximum 8-hour concentration; Carbon Monoxide—highest second maximum non-overlapping 8-hour concentration; Lead—maximum running 3-month average
Source: U.S. Environmental Protection Agency, Air Quality Monitoring Information, "Air Quality Statistics by City, 2016"

Maximum Air Pollutant Concentrations: Nitrogen Dioxide and Sulfur Dioxide

	Nitrogen Dioxide AM (ppb)	Nitrogen Dioxide 1-Hr (ppb)	Sulfur Dioxide AM (ppb)	Sulfur Dioxide 1-Hr (ppb)	Sulfur Dioxide 24-Hr (ppb)
MSA[1] Level	n/a	n/a	n/a	4	n/a
NAAQS[2]	53	100	30	75	140
Met NAAQS[2]	n/a	n/a	n/a	Yes	n/a

Note: (1) Data covers the Durham-Chapel Hill, NC Metropolitan Statistical Area—see Appendix B for areas included; Data from exceptional events are included; (2) National Ambient Air Quality Standards; ppm = parts per million; ug/m^3 = micrograms per cubic meter; n/a not available.
Concentrations: Nitrogen Dioxide AM—highest arithmetic mean concentration; Nitrogen Dioxide 1-Hr—highest 98th percentile 1-hour daily maximum concentration; Sulfur Dioxide AM—highest annual mean concentration; Sulfur Dioxide 1-Hr—highest 99th percentile 1-hour daily maximum concentration; Sulfur Dioxide 24-Hr—highest second maximum 24-hour concentration
Source: U.S. Environmental Protection Agency, Air Quality Monitoring Information, "Air Quality Statistics by City, 2016"

Drinking Water

Water System Name	Pop. Served	Primary Water Source Type	Violations[1]	
			Health Based	Monitoring/ Reporting
Orange Water & Sewer Authority	83,300	Surface	0	0

Note: (1) Based on violation data from January 1, 2017 to December 31, 2017
Source: U.S. Environmental Protection Agency, Office of Ground Water and Drinking Water, Safe Drinking Water Information System (based on data extracted April 5, 2018)

Cornelius, North Carolina

Background

Cornelius, in Mecklenburg County, is approximately 20 miles north of Charlotte located along the southeast coast of Lake Norman. Originally, the town's economy was based on cotton crops, but the creation of Lake Norman in 1963 reshaped Cornelius into a boating community.

The founding of Cornelius occurred due to the first gold rush in the United States in 1799, the emergence of the railroad, and the growth of the cotton industry in the 19th century, all of which led to the growth of Charlotte and its surrounding areas. Davidson College was founded in the area in 1837, followed by the town of Davidson, which prospered due to the trade of cotton. A dispute over the weight of the cotton crop led residents of Davidson to move their business elsewhere, and Cornelius sprung up. It was named after J.B. Cornelius, who never lived in the town, but recognized the potential of the cotton business and invested in a cotton mill. Cornelius was founded in 1893 and was officially incorporated in 1905.

The transformation of the town from a small suburb of Charlotte to an affluent community of North Carolina with a population of over 25,000 persons started with the creation of Lake Norman in 1963. This man-made body of water provides fresh water and hydroelectric power to Cornelius and several other communities along its 520-mile shoreline. The proximity of the town to Lake Norman along with the abundance of lakefront property has made Cornelius a desirable location for boating and fishing enthusiasts.

Cornelius has more than doubled in population during the last 15 years. This population boom coincides with a substantial increase in the town's median income, up from about $60,000 in 2001 to about $84,000 in 2010. As a suburb of Charlotte, the second largest banking center in the country, Cornelius, and Mecklenburg County as a whole, has benefited from the banking industry as many high-income individuals choose to commute from home in Cornelius to work in Charlotte.

Cornelius belongs to the Charlotte-Mecklenburg Schools, which services the entire county. William Amos Hough High was given an "A" grade from the State of North Carolina. The Thunderbird Preparatory School District offers children grades K-5 an alternative education option. Davidson College in Davidson is 3 miles from Cornelius, the closest institution of higher learning to the town.

The town is home to over a dozen parks. The James Hoyt Wilhelm Park is the newest, having opened in 2016. Westmoreland Athletic Complex offers premiere playing fields for recreational sports. Blythe Landing is a county operated park that offers beaches and a pier for boat launches. Cornelius is also home to the Peninsula Yacht Club with a marina, boating and sailing programs. The Peninsula Club features an 18-hole championship golf course along the coast of Lake Norman. Concord Regional Airport is the closest airport to Cornelius at 15 miles away. The closest international airport is Charlotte Douglas International Airport, 26 miles away.

Cornelius has a humid subtropical climate, with average temperatures above national averages—the July high is 90 degrees and the January low is 29 degrees. Cornelius also exceeds the national average for rainfall, with 44 inches yearly, but experiences less than an inch of snow annually.

Rankings

General Rankings

- *US News & World Report* conducted a survey of more than 2,000 people and analyzed the 125 largest metropolitan areas to determine what matters the most when selecting the next place to live. Charlotte* ranked #22 out of the top 25 as having the best combination of desirable factors. Criteria: cost of living; quality of education; job market, crime rates; and other factors. *realestate.usnews.com, "The 25 Best Places to Live in the U.S. in 2018," April 10, 2018*
- The Charlotte* metro area was identified as one of America's fastest-growing areas in terms of population and economy by *Forbes*. The area ranked #19 out of 25. The 100 most populous metro areas in the U.S. were evaluated on the following criteria: estimated population growth; employment; economic output; wages; home values. *Forbes, "America's Fastest-Growing Cities 2018," February 28, 2018*
- Charlotte* was identified as one of America's fastest-growing cities in terms of population growth by CNNMoney.com. The area ranked #10 out of 10. Criteria: population growth between July 2015 and July 2016; cities and towns with populations of 50,000. *CNNMoney, "10 Fastest-Growing Cities," June 2, 2017*

Business/Finance Rankings

- According to *Business Insider*, the Charlotte* metro area is where startup growth is on the rise. Based on the 2017 Kauffman Index of Growth Entrepreneurship, which measured in-depth national entrepreneurial trends in 40 metro areas, it ranked #16 in highest startup growth. *www.businessinsider.com, "The 21 U.S. Cities with the Highest Startup Growth," October 21, 2017*
- The personal finance site NerdWallet analyzed 183 American metropolitan areas with populations over 250,000 and more than 15,000 businesses to rank where entrepreneurs find the most success. Criteria included area economy, annual income, housing cost, unemployment rate, and the success rate of area businesses. Charlotte* ranked #146. *www.nerdwallet.com, "Best Places to Start a Business," April 27, 2015*
- Based on metro area social media reviews, the employment opinion group Glassdoor surveyed 50 of the largest U.S. metro areas and equally weighed cost of living, hiring opportunity, and job satisfaction to compose a list of "25 Best Cities for Jobs." Median pay and home value, in-demand jobs and number of current job openings was also factored in. The Charlotte* metro area was ranked #24 in overall job satisfaction. *www.glassdoor.com, "Best Cities for Jobs," September 12, 2017*
- In a survey of economic confidence in the nation's 50 largest metropolitan areas conducted January–December 2014, the Charlotte* metro area placed #30, according to Gallup's 2014 Economic Confidence Index. *Gallup, "San Jose and San Francisco Lead in Economic Confidence," March 19, 2015*
- The Brookings Institution ranked the 100 largest metro areas in the U.S. based on income inequality. Charlotte* was ranked #53 (#1 = greatest ineqality). Criteria: the "95/20 ratio," a figure representing the income at which a household earns more than 95 percent of all other households, divided by the income at which a household earns more than only 20 percent of all other households. *Brookings Institution, "Household Income Inequality, 100 Largest U.S. Metro Areas, 2014-2016," February 5, 2018*
- Payscale.com ranked the largest metro areas in terms of wage growth. The Charlotte* metro area ranked #22. Criteria: private-sector wage growth between the 4th quarter of 2016 and the 4th quarter of 2017. *PayScale, "Wage Trends by Metro Area-4th Quarter," January 17, 2018*
- The Charlotte* metro area was identified as one of the most debt-ridden places in America by the finance site Credit.com. The metro area was ranked #18. Criteria: residents' average credit card debt as well as median income. *Credit.com, "25 Cities With the Most Credit Card Debt," February 28, 2018*

- Charlotte* was identified as one of America's most frugal metro areas by *Coupons.com.* The city ranked #4 out of 25. Criteria: digital coupon usage. *Coupons.com, "America's Most Frugal Cities of 2017," March 22, 2018*
- The Charlotte* metro area appeared on the Milken Institute "2017 Best Performing Cities" list. Rank: #13 out of 200 large metro areas. Criteria: job growth; wage and salary growth; high-tech output growth. *Milken Institute, "Best-Performing Cities 2017," January 2018*
- *Forbes* ranked the 200 most populous metro areas to determine the nation's "Best Places for Business and Careers." The Charlotte* metro area was ranked #7. Criteria: costs (business and living); job growth (past and projected); income growth; quality of life; educational attainment (college and high school); projected economic growth; cultural and recreational opportunities; net migration patterns; number of highly ranked colleges. *Forbes, "The Best Places for Business and Careers 2017," October 24, 2017*

Dating/Romance Rankings

- *Apartment List* conducted its annual survey of renters to compile a list of metros that have the best opportunities for dating. Nearly 11,000 respondents, from February 2017 through January 2018, rated their current city or neighborhood for opportunities to date and make friends. The Charlotte* metro area ranked #4 out of 70 where single residents were very satisfied or somewhat satisfied, making it among the ten best metros for dating opportunities. Other criteria analyzed included gender and education levels of renters. *Apartment List, "Best Metros for Dating 2018," February 6, 2018*

Education Rankings

- Personal finance website *WalletHub* analyzed the 150 largest U.S. metropolitan statistical areas to determine where the most educated Americans are choosing to settle. Criteria: education quality and attainment gap; education levels; percentage of workers with degrees; public school rankings; quality and size of each metro area's universities. Charlotte* was ranked #71 (#1 = most educated city). *www.WalletHub.com, "2017's Most and Least Educated Cities in America," July 25, 2017*

Environmental Rankings

- Sperling's BestPlaces assessed 379 metropolitan areas of the United States for the likelihood of dangerously extreme weather events or earthquakes. In general the Southeast and South-Central regions have the highest risk of weather extremes and earthquakes, while the Pacific Northwest enjoys the lowest risk. Of the least risky metropolitan areas, the Charlotte* metro area was ranked #284. *www.bestplaces.net, "Safest Places from Natural Disasters," April 2011*
- Charlotte* was highlighted as one of the top 99 cleanest metro areas for short-term particle pollution (24-hour PM 2.5) in the U.S. during 2013 through 2015. Monitors in these cities reported no days with unhealthful PM 2.5 levels. *American Lung Association, State of the Air 2017*

Health/Fitness Rankings

- For each of the 50 most populous metro areas in the United States, the American College of Sports Medicine's American Fitness Index evaluated infrastructure, community assets, and policies that encourage healthy and fit lifestyles, including preventive health behaviors, levels of chronic disease conditions, health care access, and community resources and policies that support physical activity. The Charlotte* metro area ranked #47 for "community fitness." *www.americanfitnessindex.org, "ACSM American Fitness Index Health and Community Fitness Status of the 50 Largest Metropolitan Areas," May 2017*
- The Charlotte* metro area was identified as one of the worst cities for bed bugs in America by pest control company Orkin. The area ranked #19 out of 50 based on the number of bed bug treatments Orkin performed from December 2016 to November 2017. *Orkin, "Baltimore and Washington D.C. Continue to Hold Top Spots," January 8, 2018*

- Charlotte* was identified as a "2016 Spring Allergy Capital." The area ranked #37 out of 100. Three groups of factors were used to identify the most severe cities for people with allergies during the spring season: annual pollen levels; medicine utilization; access to board-certified allergists. *Asthma and Allergy Foundation of America, "Spring Allergy Capitals 2016"*
- Charlotte* was identified as a "2016 Fall Allergy Capital." The area ranked #55 out of 100. Three groups of factors were used to identify the most severe cities for people with allergies during the fall season: annual pollen levels; medicine utilization; access to board-certified allergists. *Asthma and Allergy Foundation of America, "Fall Allergy Capitals 2016"*
- Charlotte* was identified as a "2015 Asthma Capital." The area ranked #68 out of the nation's 100 largest metropolitan areas. Criteria: estimated prevalence; self-reported prevalence; crude death rate for asthma; annual pollen score; annual air quality; public smoking laws; number of board-certified asthma specialists; school inhaler access laws; rescue medication use; controller medication use; ER visits for asthma; uninsured rate; poverty rate. *Asthma and Allergy Foundation of America, "Asthma Capitals 2015"*
- The Charlotte* metro area ranked #64 out of 189 in The Gallup-Healthways Well-Being Index. Criteria: purpose; social well being; financial health; community and physical health. Results are based on telephone interviews with adults, aged 18 and older, living in metropolitan areas in the 50 U.S. states and the District of Columbia. *Gallup-Healthways, "State of American Well-Being, 2017 Community Well-Being Rankings" March 2018*

Real Estate Rankings

- FitSmallBusiness looked at 50 of the largest metropolitan areas in the U.S. to determine which metro was the best to start a real estate business. Data was compiled from such sources as: Zillow, Trulia, U.S. Census Bureau, and the Bureau of Labor Statistics. Criteria: location; inventory; annual wages; median sales price of homes; days on the market; median price cut percentage; and other factors that would influence real estate professional growth. The Charlotte* metro area ranked #20. *fitsmallbusiness.com, "The Best Cities to Become a Real Estate Agent in 2018," January 30, 2018*
- According to Penske Truck Rental, the Charlotte* metro area was named the #9 moving destination in 2017, based on one-way consumer truck rental reservations made through Penske's website, rental locations, and reservations call center. *blog.gopenske.com, "Penske Truck Rental's 2017 Top Moving Destinations List," January 22, 2018*
- The Charlotte* metro area was identified as one of the top 20 housing markets to invest in for 2018 by *Forbes*. The area ranked #16. Criteria: strong job and population growth; anticipated home price appreciation; and other factors. *Forbes.com, "Where to Invest in Housing in 2018," February 1, 2018*
- Charlotte* was ranked #132 out of 238 metro areas in terms of housing affordability in 2017 by the National Association of Home Builders (#1 = most affordable). Criteria: the share of homes sold in that area affordable to a family earning the local median income, based on standard mortgage underwriting criteria. *National Association of Home Builders®, NAHB-Wells Fargo Housing Opportunity Index, 4th Quarter 2017*

Safety Rankings

- The National Insurance Crime Bureau ranked 382 metro areas in the U.S. in terms of per capita rates of vehicle theft. The Charlotte* metro area ranked #72 (#1 = highest rate). Criteria: number of vehicle theft offenses per 100,000 inhabitants in 2016. *National Insurance Crime Bureau, "Hot Spots 2016," June 8, 2017*

Seniors/Retirement Rankings

- From its Best Cities for Successful Aging indexes, the Milken Institute generated rankings for metropolitan areas, weighing data in nine categories—health care, wellness, living arrangements, transportation and convenience, financial characteristics, education, employment, community engagement, and overall livability. The Charlotte* metro area was ranked #72 overall in the large metro area category. *Milken Institute, "Best Cities for Successful Aging, 2017" March 14, 2017*

Miscellaneous Rankings

- The finance and lifestyle site NerdWallet looked for the U.S. cities that topped the list in donating money and time to good causes. The Charlotte* metro area proved to be the #19-ranked metro area, judged by culture of volunteerism, depth of commitment in terms of volunteer hours per year, and monetary contributions. *www.nerdwallet.com, "Most Generous Cities," September 22, 2013*
- The National Alliance to End Homelessness listed the 25 most populous metro areas with the highest rate of homelessness. The Charlotte* metro area had a high rate of homelessness. Criteria: number of homeless people per 10,000 population in 2016. *National Alliance to End Homelessness, "Homelessness in the 25 Most Populous U.S. Metro Areas," September 1, 2017*

*Cornelius is located within the Charlotte-Concord-Gastonia, NC-SC Metropolitan Statistical Area.

Business Environment

CITY FINANCES

City Government Finances

Component	2015 ($000)	2015 ($ per capita)
Total Revenues	n/a	n/a
Total Expenditures	n/a	n/a
Debt Outstanding	n/a	n/a
Cash and Securities[1]	n/a	n/a

Note: (1) Cash and security holdings of a government at the close of its fiscal year,, including those of its dependent agencies, utilities, and liquor stores.
Source: U.S Census Bureau, State & Local Government Finances 2015

City Government Revenue by Source

Source	2015 ($000)	2015 ($ per capita)	2015 (%)
General Revenue			
From Federal Government	n/a	n/a	n/a
From State Government	n/a	n/a	n/a
From Local Governments	n/a	n/a	n/a
Taxes			
Property	n/a	n/a	n/a
Sales and Gross Receipts	n/a	n/a	n/a
Personal Income	n/a	n/a	n/a
Corporate Income	n/a	n/a	n/a
Motor Vehicle License	n/a	n/a	n/a
Other Taxes	n/a	n/a	n/a
Current Charges	n/a	n/a	n/a
Liquor Store	n/a	n/a	n/a
Utility	n/a	n/a	n/a
Employee Retirement	n/a	n/a	n/a

Source: U.S Census Bureau, State & Local Government Finances 2015

City Government Expenditures by Function

Function	2015 ($000)	2015 ($ per capita)	2015 (%)
General Direct Expenditures			
Air Transportation	n/a	n/a	n/a
Corrections	n/a	n/a	n/a
Education	n/a	n/a	n/a
Employment Security Administration	n/a	n/a	n/a
Financial Administration	n/a	n/a	n/a
Fire Protection	n/a	n/a	n/a
General Public Buildings	n/a	n/a	n/a
Governmental Administration, Other	n/a	n/a	n/a
Health	n/a	n/a	n/a
Highways	n/a	n/a	n/a
Hospitals	n/a	n/a	n/a
Housing and Community Development	n/a	n/a	n/a
Interest on General Debt	n/a	n/a	n/a
Judicial and Legal	n/a	n/a	n/a
Libraries	n/a	n/a	n/a
Parking	n/a	n/a	n/a
Parks and Recreation	n/a	n/a	n/a
Police Protection	n/a	n/a	n/a
Public Welfare	n/a	n/a	n/a
Sewerage	n/a	n/a	n/a
Solid Waste Management	n/a	n/a	n/a
Veterans' Services	n/a	n/a	n/a
Liquor Store	n/a	n/a	n/a
Utility	n/a	n/a	n/a
Employee Retirement	n/a	n/a	n/a

Source: U.S Census Bureau, State & Local Government Finances 2015

DEMOGRAPHICS

Population Growth

Area	1990 Census	2000 Census	2010 Census	2016* Estimate	Population Growth (%) 1990-2016	Population Growth (%) 2010-2016
City	5,815	11,969	24,866	27,426	371.6	10.3
MSA[1]	1,024,331	1,330,448	1,758,038	2,381,152	132.5	35.4
U.S.	248,709,873	281,421,906	308,745,538	318,558,162	28.1	3.2

Note: (1) Figures cover the Charlotte-Concord-Gastonia, NC-SC Metropolitan Statistical Area—see Appendix B for areas included; (*) 2012-2016 5-year estimated population
Source: U.S. Census Bureau, 1990 Census, Census 2000, Census 2010, 2012-2016 American Community Survey 5-Year Estimates

Household Size

Area	Persons in Household (%) One	Two	Three	Four	Five	Six	Seven or More	Average Household Size
City	28.8	39.9	16.2	8.5	5.5	1.1	0.1	2.30
MSA[1]	26.6	33.9	17.0	13.8	5.8	2.0	1.0	2.70
U.S.	27.7	33.7	15.7	13.1	6.0	2.3	1.5	2.60

Note: (1) Figures cover the Charlotte-Concord-Gastonia, NC-SC Metropolitan Statistical Area—see Appendix B for areas included
Source: U.S. Census Bureau, 2012-2016 American Community Survey 5-Year Estimates

Race

Area	White Alone[2] (%)	Black Alone[2] (%)	Asian Alone[2] (%)	AIAN[3] Alone[2] (%)	NHOPI[4] Alone[2] (%)	Other Race Alone[2] (%)	Two or More Races (%)
City	89.3	5.8	2.2	0.1	0.0	1.0	1.6
MSA[1]	68.4	22.2	3.3	0.4	0.0	3.4	2.3
U.S.	73.3	12.6	5.2	0.8	0.2	4.8	3.1

Note: (1) Figures cover the Charlotte-Concord-Gastonia, NC-SC Metropolitan Statistical Area—see Appendix B for areas included; (2) Alone is defined as not being in combination with one or more other races; (3) American Indian and Alaska Native; (4) Native Hawaiian and Other Pacific Islander
Source: U.S. Census Bureau, 2012-2016 American Community Survey 5-Year Estimates

Hispanic or Latino Origin

Area	Total (%)	Mexican (%)	Puerto Rican (%)	Cuban (%)	Other (%)
City	5.2	0.9	2.0	0.4	1.8
MSA[1]	9.6	4.7	0.9	0.4	3.7
U.S.	17.3	11.0	1.7	0.7	4.0

Note: Persons of Hispanic or Latino origin can be of any race; (1) Figures cover the Charlotte-Concord-Gastonia, NC-SC Metropolitan Statistical Area—see Appendix B for areas included
Source: U.S. Census Bureau, 2012-2016 American Community Survey 5-Year Estimates

Segregation

Type	Segregation Indices[1] 1990	2000	2010	2010 Rank[2]	Percent Change 1990-2000	1990-2010	2000-2010
Black/White	54.7	54.2	53.8	56	-0.5	-0.8	-0.4
Asian/White	41.8	42.6	43.6	34	0.8	1.8	1.0
Hispanic/White	32.8	50.8	47.6	35	18.0	14.8	-3.2

Note: All figures cover the Metropolitan Statistical Area—see Appendix B for areas included; Figures are based on an analysis of 1990, 2000, and 2010 Census Decennial Census tract data by William H. Frey, Brookings Institution and the University of Michigan Social Science Data Analysis Network. In this analysis all racial groups (whites, blacks, and asians) are non-Hispanic members of those races. Hispanics are shown as a separate category; (1) Segregation Indices are Dissimilarity Indices that measure the degree to which the minority group is distributed differently than whites across census tracts. They range from 0 (complete integration) to 100 (complete segregation) where the value indicates the percentage of the minority group that needs to move to be distributed exactly like whites; (2) Ranges from 1 (most segregated) to 102 (least segregated); n/a not available.
Source: www.CensusScope.org

Ancestry

Area	German	Irish	English	American	Italian	Polish	French[2]	Scottish	Dutch
City	19.1	12.0	11.3	8.8	8.8	3.6	3.8	4.0	1.7
MSA[1]	12.1	9.1	8.2	9.3	3.8	1.7	1.7	2.3	1.1
U.S.	14.4	10.4	7.7	6.9	5.4	2.9	2.6	1.7	1.3

Note: Figures are the percentage of the total population reporting a particular ancestry. The nine most commonly reported ancestries in the U.S. are shown. Figures include multiple ancestries (e.g. if a person reported being Irish and Italian, they were included in both columns); (1) Figures cover the Charlotte-Concord-Gastonia, NC-SC Metropolitan Statistical Area—see Appendix B for areas included; (2) Excludes Basque
Source: U.S. Census Bureau, 2012-2016 American Community Survey 5-Year Estimates

Foreign-Born Population

Area	Percent of Population Born in								
	Any Foreign Country	Asia	Mexico	Europe	Carribean	Central America[2]	South America	Africa	Canada
City	6.9	1.9	0.4	2.7	0.2	0.4	0.6	0.4	0.2
MSA[1]	9.6	2.6	2.3	1.0	0.6	1.3	0.9	0.8	0.2
U.S.	13.2	4.0	3.6	1.5	1.3	1.0	0.9	0.6	0.3

Note: (1) Figures cover the Charlotte-Concord-Gastonia, NC-SC Metropolitan Statistical Area—see Appendix B for areas included; (2) Excludes Mexico.
Source: U.S. Census Bureau, 2012-2016 American Community Survey 5-Year Estimates

Marital Status

Area	Never Married	Now Married[2]	Separated	Widowed	Divorced
City	24.7	55.2	1.1	4.4	14.6
MSA[1]	31.8	49.7	2.7	5.4	10.4
U.S.	33.0	48.1	2.1	5.9	11.0

Note: Figures are percentages and cover the population 15 years of age and older; (1) Figures cover the Charlotte-Concord-Gastonia, NC-SC Metropolitan Statistical Area—see Appendix B for areas included; (2) Excludes separated
Source: U.S. Census Bureau, 2012-2016 American Community Survey 5-Year Estimates

Disability Status

Area	All Ages	Under 18 Years Old	18 to 64 Years Old	65 Years and Over
City	7.6	2.3	5.7	26.4
MSA[1]	11.1	3.6	9.5	34.7
U.S.	12.5	4.1	10.3	35.7

Note: Figures show percent of the civilian noninstitutionalized population that reported having a disability. Disability status is determined from six types of difficulty: vision, hearing, cognitive, ambulatory, self-care, and independent living. For children under 5 years old, hearing and vision difficulty are used to determine disability status. For children between the ages of 5 and 14, disability status is determined from hearing, vision, cognitive, ambulatory, and self-care difficulties. For people aged 15 years and older, they are considered to have a disability if they have difficulty with any one of the six difficulty types; Note: (1) Figures cover the Charlotte-Concord-Gastonia, NC-SC Metropolitan Statistical Area—see Appendix B for areas included
Source: U.S. Census Bureau, 2012-2016 American Community Survey 5-Year Estimates

Age

Area	Percent of Population									Median Age
	Under Age 5	Age 5–19	Age 20–34	Age 35–44	Age 45–54	Age 55–64	Age 65–74	Age 75–84	Age 85+	
City	4.8	20.6	16.6	16.0	16.8	12.1	8.3	3.6	1.1	39.9
MSA[1]	6.4	20.7	20.0	14.5	14.4	11.6	7.5	3.5	1.3	37.1
U.S.	6.2	19.6	20.7	12.7	13.6	12.6	8.3	4.3	1.9	37.7

Note: (1) Figures cover the Charlotte-Concord-Gastonia, NC-SC Metropolitan Statistical Area—see Appendix B for areas included
Source: U.S. Census Bureau, 2012-2016 American Community Survey 5-Year Estimates

Gender

Area	Males	Females	Males per 100 Females
City	13,389	14,037	95.4
MSA[1]	1,154,769	1,226,383	94.2
U.S.	156,765,322	161,792,840	96.9

Note: (1) Figures cover the Charlotte-Concord-Gastonia, NC-SC Metropolitan Statistical Area—see Appendix B for areas included
Source: U.S. Census Bureau, 2012-2016 American Community Survey 5-Year Estimates

Religious Groups by Family

Area	Catholic	Baptist	Non-Den.	Methodist[2]	Lutheran	LDS[3]	Pente-costal	Presby-terian[4]	Muslim[5]	Judaism
MSA[1]	5.9	17.3	6.8	8.6	1.3	0.8	3.3	4.5	0.2	0.3
U.S.	19.1	9.3	4.0	4.0	2.3	2.0	1.9	1.6	0.8	0.7

Note: Figures are the number of adherents as a percentage of the total population; (1) Figures cover the Charlotte-Concord-Gastonia, NC-SC Metropolitan Statistical Area—see Appendix B for areas included; (2) Methodist/Pietist; (3) Latter Day Saints; (4) Reformed; (5) Figures are estimates
Source: Association of Statisticians of American Religious Bodies, 2010 U.S. Religion Census: Religious Congregations & Membership Study

Religious Groups by Tradition

Area	Catholic	Evangelical Protestant	Mainline Protestant	Other Tradition	Black Protestant	Orthodox
MSA[1]	5.9	27.6	13.3	1.7	2.8	0.5
U.S.	19.1	16.2	7.3	4.3	1.6	0.3

Note: Figures are the number of adherents as a percentage of the total population; (1) Figures cover the Charlotte-Concord-Gastonia, NC-SC Metropolitan Statistical Area—see Appendix B for areas included
Source: Association of Statisticians of American Religious Bodies, 2010 U.S. Religion Census: Religious Congregations & Membership Study

ECONOMY

Gross Metropolitan Product

Area	2014	2015	2016	2017	Rank[2]
MSA[1]	143.2	151.6	157.9	167.4	22

Note: Figures are in billions of dollars; (1) Figures cover the Charlotte-Concord-Gastonia, NC-SC Metropolitan Statistical Area—see Appendix B for areas included; (2) Rank is based on 2015 data and ranges from 1 to 381
Source: The U.S. Conference of Mayors, U.S. Metro Economies: GMP and Employment Report, 2015-2017

Economic Growth

Area	2012-14 (%)	2015 (%)	2016 (%)	2017 (%)	Rank[2]
MSA[1]	3.3	3.8	2.7	4.0	48
U.S.	2.0	2.4	1.9	2.6	–

Note: Figures are real gross metropolitan product (GMP) growth rates and represent average annual percent change; (1) Figures cover the Charlotte-Concord-Gastonia, NC-SC Metropolitan Statistical Area—see Appendix B for areas included; (2) Rank is based on 2012-2014 average annual percent change and ranges from 1 to 381
Source: The U.S. Conference of Mayors, U.S. Metro Economies: GMP and Employment Report, 2015-2017

Metropolitan Area Exports

Area	2011	2012	2013	2014	2015	2016	Rank[2]
MSA[1]	6,253.3	6,322.6	10,684.1	12,885.3	13,985.8	11,944.1	24

Note: Figures are in millions of dollars; (1) Figures cover the Charlotte-Concord-Gastonia, NC-SC Metropolitan Statistical Area—see Appendix B for areas included; (2) Rank is based on 2016 data and ranges from 1 to 385
Source: U.S. Department of Commerce, International Trade Administration, Office of Trade & Industry Information, Manufacturing & Services, data extracted March 15, 2018

Building Permits

Area	Single-Family			Multi-Family			Total		
	2016	2017p	Pct. Chg.	2016	2017p	Pct. Chg.	2016	2017p	Pct. Chg.
City	n/a	n/a	n/a	n/a	n/a	n/a	n/a	n/a	n/a
MSA[1]	12,989	13,974	7.6	6,364	7,451	17.1	19,353	21,425	10.7
U.S.	750,800	817,300	8.9	455,800	446,800	-2.0	1,206,600	1,264,100	4.8

Note: (1) Figures cover the Charlotte-Concord-Gastonia, NC-SC Metropolitan Statistical Area—see Appendix B for areas included; Figures represent new, privately-owned housing units authorized (unadjusted data); All permit data are based on estimates with imputation; (p) preliminary data.
Source: U.S. Census Bureau, Manufacturing, Mining, and Construction Statistics, Building Permits, 2016, 2017

Bankruptcy Filings

Area	Business Filings			Nonbusiness Filings		
	2016	2017	% Chg.	2016	2017	% Chg.
Mecklenburg County	49	81	65.3	1,312	1,262	-3.8
U.S.	24,114	23,157	-4.0	770,846	765,863	-0.6

Note: Business filings include Chapter 7, Chapter 11, Chapter 12, and Chapter 13; Nonbusiness filings include Chapter 7, Chapter 11, and Chapter 13
Source: Administrative Office of the U.S. Courts, Business and Nonbusiness Bankruptcy, County Cases Commenced by Chapter of the Bankruptcy Code, During the 12-Month Period Ending December 31, 2016 and Business and Nonbusiness Bankruptcy, County Cases Commenced by Chapter of the Bankruptcy Code, During the 12-Month Period Ending December 31, 2017

Housing Vacancy Rates

Area	Gross Vacancy Rate[2] (%)			Year-Round Vacancy Rate[3] (%)			Rental Vacancy Rate[4] (%)			Homeowner Vacancy Rate[5] (%)		
	2015	2016	2017	2015	2016	2017	2015	2016	2017	2015	2016	2017
MSA[1]	8.2	7.7	6.9	7.8	7.5	6.8	6.4	7.4	5.4	1.8	1.1	0.8
U.S.	12.9	12.8	12.7	10.0	9.9	9.9	7.1	6.9	7.2	1.8	1.7	1.6

Note: (1) Figures cover the Charlotte-Concord-Gastonia, NC-SC Metropolitan Statistical Area—see Appendix B for areas included; (2) The percentage of the total housing inventory that is vacant; (3) The percentage of the housing inventory (excluding seasonal units) that is year-round vacant; (4) The percentage of rental inventory that is vacant for rent; (5) The percentage of homeowner inventory that is vacant for sale
Source: U.S. Census Bureau, Housing Vacancies and Homeownership Annual Statistics: 2015, 2016, 2017

INCOME

Income

Area	Per Capita ($)	Median Household ($)	Average Household ($)
City	49,391	86,355	113,221
MSA[1]	29,969	55,191	77,959
U.S.	29,829	55,322	77,866

Note: (1) Figures cover the Charlotte-Concord-Gastonia, NC-SC Metropolitan Statistical Area—see Appendix B for areas included
Source: U.S. Census Bureau, 2012-2016 American Community Survey 5-Year Estimates

Household Income Distribution

Area	Percent of Households Earning							
	Under $15,000	$15,000 -$24,999	$25,000 -$34,999	$35,000 -$49,999	$50,000 -$74,999	$75,000 -$99,999	$100,000 -$149,999	$150,000 and up
City	5.4	8.2	5.5	11.4	12.9	14.2	20.1	22.4
MSA[1]	11.1	9.8	10.3	14.1	18.1	12.5	13.2	10.8
U.S.	12.1	10.2	9.9	13.2	17.8	12.2	13.5	11.1

Note: (1) Figures cover the Charlotte-Concord-Gastonia, NC-SC Metropolitan Statistical Area—see Appendix B for areas included
Source: U.S. Census Bureau, 2012-2016 American Community Survey 5-Year Estimates

Poverty Rate

Area	All Ages	Under 18 Years Old	18 to 64 Years Old	65 Years and Over
City	4.8	4.5	5.2	3.9
MSA[1]	14.1	19.4	13.0	8.8
U.S.	15.1	21.2	14.2	9.3

Note: Figures are percentage of people whose income during the past 12 months was below the poverty level; (1) Figures cover the Charlotte-Concord-Gastonia, NC-SC Metropolitan Statistical Area—see Appendix B for areas included
Source: U.S. Census Bureau, 2012-2016 American Community Survey 5-Year Estimates

EMPLOYMENT

Labor Force and Employment

Area	Civilian Labor Force			Workers Employed		
	Dec. 2016	Dec. 2017	% Chg.	Dec. 2016	Dec. 2017	% Chg.
City	16,784	17,459	4.0	16,187	16,818	3.9
MSA[1]	1,284,384	1,325,794	3.2	1,225,922	1,271,766	3.7
U.S.	158,968,000	159,880,000	0.6	151,798,000	153,602,000	1.2

Note: Data is not seasonally adjusted and covers workers 16 years of age and older; (1) Figures cover the Charlotte-Concord-Gastonia, NC-SC Metropolitan Statistical Area—see Appendix B for areas included
Source: Bureau of Labor Statistics, Local Area Unemployment Statistics

Unemployment Rate

Area	2017											
	Jan.	Feb.	Mar.	Apr.	May	Jun.	Jul.	Aug.	Sep.	Oct.	Nov.	Dec.
City	3.8	3.9	3.2	3.0	3.2	3.3	3.7	3.5	3.2	3.3	3.7	3.7
MSA[1]	4.9	4.7	4.2	3.9	4.1	4.3	4.5	4.6	4.1	4.1	4.2	4.1
U.S.	5.1	4.9	4.6	4.1	4.1	4.5	4.6	4.5	4.1	3.9	3.9	3.9

Note: Data is not seasonally adjusted and covers workers 16 years of age and older; (1) Figures cover the Charlotte-Concord-Gastonia, NC-SC Metropolitan Statistical Area—see Appendix B for areas included
Source: Bureau of Labor Statistics, Local Area Unemployment Statistics

Average Wages

Occupation	$/Hr.	Occupation	$/Hr.
Accountants and Auditors	38.30	Maids and Housekeeping Cleaners	10.00
Automotive Mechanics	21.00	Maintenance and Repair Workers	19.60
Bookkeepers	19.00	Marketing Managers	69.20
Carpenters	17.30	Nuclear Medicine Technologists	32.70
Cashiers	9.60	Nurses, Licensed Practical	20.90
Clerks, General Office	15.50	Nurses, Registered	30.00
Clerks, Receptionists/Information	13.70	Nursing Assistants	11.60
Clerks, Shipping/Receiving	16.50	Packers and Packagers, Hand	11.30
Computer Programmers	45.50	Physical Therapists	40.10
Computer Systems Analysts	45.30	Postal Service Mail Carriers	23.80
Computer User Support Specialists	27.50	Real Estate Brokers	37.50
Cooks, Restaurant	11.40	Retail Salespersons	12.40
Dentists	118.70	Sales Reps., Exc. Tech./Scientific	36.90
Electrical Engineers	49.90	Sales Reps., Tech./Scientific	44.70
Electricians	21.70	Secretaries, Exc. Legal/Med./Exec.	17.60
Financial Managers	74.60	Security Guards	13.60
First-Line Supervisors/Managers, Sales	22.30	Surgeons	127.10
Food Preparation Workers	11.00	Teacher Assistants*	11.50
General and Operations Managers	67.30	Teachers, Elementary School*	22.70
Hairdressers/Cosmetologists	16.10	Teachers, Secondary School*	23.50
Internists, General	125.10	Telemarketers	15.80
Janitors and Cleaners	11.70	Truck Drivers, Heavy/Tractor-Trailer	20.50
Landscaping/Groundskeeping Workers	13.20	Truck Drivers, Light/Delivery Svcs.	15.90
Lawyers	71.20	Waiters and Waitresses	10.00

Note: Wage data covers the Charlotte-Concord-Gastonia, NC-SC Metropolitan Statistical Area—see Appendix B for areas included; (*) Hourly wages for elementary/secondary school teachers and teacher assistants were calculated by the editors from annual wage data based on a 40 hour work week; n/a not available.
Source: Bureau of Labor Statistics, Metro Area Occupational Employment & Wage Estimates, May 2017

Employment by Occupation

Occupation Classification	City (%)	MSA[1] (%)	U.S. (%)
Management, Business, Science, and Arts	52.2	37.9	37.0
Natural Resources, Construction, and Maintenance	3.1	8.3	8.9
Production, Transportation, and Material Moving	5.5	12.8	12.2
Sales and Office	27.3	25.0	23.8
Service	11.8	16.1	18.1

Note: Figures cover employed civilians 16 years of age and older; (1) Figures cover the Charlotte-Concord-Gastonia, NC-SC Metropolitan Statistical Area—see Appendix B for areas included
Source: U.S. Census Bureau, 2012-2016 American Community Survey 5-Year Estimates

Employment by Industry

Sector	MSA[1]		U.S.
	Number of Employees	Percent of Total	Percent of Total
Construction, Mining, and Logging	62,900	5.2	5.2
Education and Health Services	124,600	10.3	15.9
Financial Activities	93,700	7.7	5.7
Government	163,300	13.5	15.3
Information	28,500	2.4	1.9
Leisure and Hospitality	137,900	11.4	10.7
Manufacturing	105,900	8.7	8.5
Other Services	41,300	3.4	3.9
Professional and Business Services	202,700	16.7	14.0
Retail Trade	130,800	10.8	11.0
Transportation, Warehousing, and Utilities	58,300	4.8	4.1
Wholesale Trade	61,400	5.1	4.0

Note: Figures are non-farm employment as of December 2017. Figures are not seasonally adjusted and include workers 16 years of age and older; (1) Figures cover the Charlotte-Concord-Gastonia, NC-SC Metropolitan Statistical Area—see Appendix B for areas included
Source: Bureau of Labor Statistics, Current Employment Statistics, Employment, Hours, and Earnings

Occupations with Greatest Projected Employment Growth: 2017 – 2019

Occupation[1]	2017 Employment	2019 Projected Employment	Numeric Employment Change	Percent Employment Change
Combined Food Preparation and Serving Workers, Including Fast Food	150,940	161,640	10,700	7.1
Retail Salespersons	141,960	146,580	4,620	3.3
Waiters and Waitresses	78,300	82,440	4,140	5.3
Customer Service Representatives	98,260	102,060	3,800	3.9
Registered Nurses	99,040	102,730	3,690	3.7
Cashiers	112,380	115,690	3,310	3.0
Laborers and Freight, Stock, and Material Movers, Hand	86,000	89,280	3,280	3.8
Cooks, Restaurant	41,650	44,300	2,650	6.4
Home Health Aides	40,030	42,550	2,520	6.3
General and Operations Managers	55,710	58,180	2,470	4.4

Note: Projections cover North Carolina; (1) Sorted by numeric employment change
Source: www.projectionscentral.com, State Occupational Projections, 2017–2019 Short-Term Projections

Fastest Growing Occupations: 2017 – 2019

Occupation[1]	2017 Employment	2019 Projected Employment	Numeric Employment Change	Percent Employment Change
Solar Photovoltaic Installers	480	550	70	13.5
Helpers—Pipelayers, Plumbers, Pipefitters, and Steamfitters	3,340	3,670	330	9.9
Statisticians	1,220	1,340	120	9.8
Insurance Claims and Policy Processing Clerks	5,090	5,580	490	9.7
Insurance Sales Agents	12,990	14,230	1,240	9.5
Software Developers, Applications	26,360	28,620	2,260	8.6
Helpers—Brickmasons, Blockmasons, Stonemasons, and Tile and Marble Setters	1,060	1,150	90	8.5
Structural Iron and Steel Workers	1,560	1,690	130	8.5
Helpers—Carpenters	1,280	1,390	110	8.4
Plumbers, Pipefitters, and Steamfitters	11,560	12,520	960	8.3

Note: Projections cover North Carolina; (1) Sorted by percent employment change and excludes occupations with numeric employment change less than 50
Source: www.projectionscentral.com, State Occupational Projections, 2017–2019 Short-Term Projections

TAXES

State Corporate Income Tax Rates

State	Tax Rate (%)	Income Brackets ($)	Num. of Brackets	Financial Institution Tax Rate (%)[a]	Federal Income Tax Ded.
North Carolina	3.0	Flat rate	1	3.0	No

Note: Tax rates as of January 1, 2018; (a) Rates listed are the corporate income tax rate applied to financial institutions or excise taxes based on income. Some states have other taxes based upon the value of deposits or shares.
Source: Federation of Tax Administrators, Range of State Corporate Income Tax Rates, January 1, 2018

State Individual Income Tax Rates

State	Tax Rate (%)	Income Brackets ($)	Num. of Brackets	Personal Exempt. ($)[1]		Fed. Inc. Tax Ded.
				Single	Dependents	
North Carolina	5.499	Flat rate	1	None	None	No

Note: Tax rates as of January 1, 2018; Local- and county-level taxes are not included; n/a not applicable; (1) Married joint filers generally receive double the single exemption
Source: Federation of Tax Administrators, State Individual Income Tax Rates, January 1, 2018

Various State Sales and Excise Tax Rates

State	State Sales Tax (%)	Gasoline[1] (¢/gal.)	Cigarette[2] ($/pack)	Spirits[3] ($/gal.)	Wine[4] ($/gal.)	Beer[5] ($/gal.)	Recreational Marijuana (%)
North Carolina	4.75	35.35	0.45	14.63 (g)	1.00 (l)	0.62 (q)	Not legal

Note: All tax rates as of January 1, 2018; (1) The American Petroleum Institute has developed a methodology for determining the average tax rate on a gallon of fuel. Rates may include any of the following: excise taxes, environmental fees, storage tank fees, other fees or taxes, general sales tax, and local taxes. In states where gasoline is subject to the general sales tax, or where the fuel tax is based on the average sale price, the average rate determined by API is sensitive to changes in the price of gasoline. States that fully or partially apply general sales taxes to gasoline: CA, CO, GA, IL, IN, MI, NY; (2) The federal excise tax of $1.0066 per pack and local taxes are not included; (3) Rates are those applicable to off-premise sales of 40% alcohol by volume (a.b.v.) distilled spirits in 750ml containers. Local excise taxes are excluded; (4) Rates are those applicable to off-premise sales of 11% a.b.v. non-carbonated wine in 750ml containers; (5) Rates are those applicable to off-premise sales of 4.7% a.b.v. beer in 12 ounce containers; (g) Control states, where the government controls all sales. Products can be subject to ad valorem mark-up as well as excise taxes; (l) Different rates also applicable to alcohol content, place of production, size of container, place purchased (on- or off-premise or on board airlines) or type of wine (carbonated, vermouth, etc.); (q) Different rates also applicable according to alcohol content, place of production, size of container, or place purchased (on- or off-premise or onboard airlines).
Source: Tax Foundation, 2018 Facts & Figures: How Does Your State Compare?

State Business Tax Climate Index Rankings

State	Overall Rank	Corporate Tax Rank	Individual Income Tax Rank	Sales Tax Rank	Unemployment Insurance Tax Rank	Property Tax Rank
North Carolina	11	3	13	20	6	32

Note: The index is a measure of how each state's tax laws affect economic performance. The lower the rank, the more favorable a state's tax system is for business. States without a given tax are given a ranking of 1. The scores/rankings for the District of Columbia do not affect other states. The 2018 index represents the tax climate as of July 1, 2017.
Source: Tax Foundation, State Business Tax Climate Index 2018

TRANSPORTATION

Means of Transportation to Work

Area	Car/Truck/Van		Public Transportation			Bicycle	Walked	Other Means	Worked at Home
	Drove Alone	Car-pooled	Bus	Subway	Railroad				
City	76.7	6.7	0.9	0.0	0.0	0.4	2.0	1.5	11.8
MSA[1]	80.7	9.6	1.4	0.1	0.1	0.1	1.4	1.1	5.4
U.S.	76.4	9.3	2.6	1.9	0.6	0.6	2.8	1.3	4.6

Note: Figures are percentages and cover workers 16 years of age and older; (1) Figures cover the Charlotte-Concord-Gastonia, NC-SC Metropolitan Statistical Area—see Appendix B for areas included
Source: U.S. Census Bureau, 2012-2016 American Community Survey 5-Year Estimates

Travel Time to Work

Area	Less Than 10 Minutes	10 to 19 Minutes	20 to 29 Minutes	30 to 44 Minutes	45 to 59 Minutes	60 to 89 Minutes	90 Minutes or More
City	12.8	23.5	17.8	26.0	11.7	6.1	2.1
MSA[1]	10.1	28.2	22.8	23.6	8.9	4.5	1.9
U.S.	12.9	29.2	20.9	20.4	8.0	6.0	2.7

Note: Note: Figures are percentages and include workers 16 years old and over; (1) Figures cover the Charlotte-Concord-Gastonia, NC-SC Metropolitan Statistical Area—see Appendix B for areas included
Source: U.S. Census Bureau, 2012-2016 American Community Survey 5-Year Estimates

Freeway Travel Time Index

Area	1985	1990	1995	2000	2005	2010	2014
Urban Area Rank[1,2]	26	25	29	28	27	25	29
Urban Area Index[1]	1.10	1.14	1.17	1.20	1.23	1.23	1.23
Average Index[3]	1.09	1.11	1.14	1.17	1.20	1.19	1.20

Note: Freeway Travel Time Index—the ratio of travel time in the peak period to the travel time at free-flow conditions. For example, a value of 1.30 indicates a 20-minute free-flow trip takes 26 minutes in the peak (20 minutes x 1.30 = 26 minutes); (1) Covers the Charlotte NC-SC urban area; (2) Rank is based on 101 urban areas (#1 = highest travel time index); (3) Average of 101 urban areas
Source: Texas Transportation Institute, 2015 Urban Mobility Scorecard, August 2015

Freeway Commuter Stress Index

Area	1985	1990	1995	2000	2005	2010	2014
Urban Area Rank[1,2]	31	28	31	32	30	31	30
Urban Area Index[1]	1.15	1.19	1.23	1.26	1.29	1.28	1.29
Average Index[3]	1.13	1.16	1.19	1.22	1.25	1.24	1.25

Note: The Freeway Commuter Stress Index is the same as the Freeway Travel Time Index (see table above) except that it includes only the travel in the peak directions during the peak periods; the TTI includes travel in all directions during the peak period. Thus, the CSI is more indicative of the work trip experienced by each commuter on a daily basis; (1) Covers the Charlotte NC-SC urban area; (2) Rank is based on 101 urban areas (#1 = highest travel time index); (3) Average of 101 urban areas
Source: Texas Transportation Institute, 2015 Urban Mobility Scorecard, August 2015

Living Environment

COST OF LIVING

Cost of Living Index

Composite Index	Groceries	Housing	Utilities	Transportation	Health Care	Misc. Goods/ Services
96.0	96.3	86.7	99.5	96.3	105.1	101.2

Note: The Cost of Living Index measures regional differences in the cost of consumer goods and services, excluding taxes and non-consumer expenditures, for professional and managerial households in the top income quintile. It is based on more than 50,000 prices covering almost 60 different items for which prices are collected three times a year by chambers of commerce, economic development organizations or university applied economic centers in each participating urban area. The numbers shown should be read as a percentage above or below the national average of 100. For example, a value of 115.4 in the groceries column indicates that grocery prices are 15.4% higher than the national average. Small differences in the index numbers should not be interpreted as significant; Figures cover the Charlotte NC urban area.
Source: The Council for Community and Economic Research, ACCRA Cost of Living Index, 2017

Grocery Prices

Area[1]	T-Bone Steak ($/pound)	Frying Chicken ($/pound)	Whole Milk ($/half gal.)	Eggs ($/dozen)	Orange Juice ($/64 oz.)	Coffee ($/11.5 oz.)
City[2]	10.92	1.17	1.87	1.53	3.44	3.82
Avg.	11.29	1.40	2.02	1.47	3.55	4.37
Min.	7.71	0.93	1.04	0.70	2.86	3.24
Max.	15.83	2.39	4.03	3.92	6.29	8.16

*Note: (1) Values for the local area are compared with the average, minimum and maximum values for all 294 areas in the Cost of Living Index; (2) Figures cover the Charlotte NC urban area; **T-Bone Steak** (price per pound); **Frying Chicken** (price per pound, whole fryer); **Whole Milk** (half gallon carton); **Eggs** (price per dozen, Grade A, large); **Orange Juice** (64 oz. Tropicana or Florida Natural); **Coffee** (11.5 oz. can, vacuum-packed, Maxwell House, Hills Bros, or Folgers).*
Source: The Council for Community and Economic Research, ACCRA Cost of Living Index, 2017

Housing and Utility Costs

Area[1]	New Home Price ($)	Apartment Rent ($/month)	All Electric ($/month)	Part Electric ($/month)	Other Energy ($/month)	Telephone ($/month)
City[2]	267,863	1,061	154.11	-	-	31.00
Avg.	335,956	1,047	175.01	97.34	67.93	28.71
Min.	187,788	491	109.48	49.33	35.44	12.39
Max.	1,739,087	4,559	432.62	227.09	353.33	44.61

*Note: (1) Values for the local area are compared with the average, minimum and maximum values for all 294 areas in the Cost of Living Index; (2) Figures cover the Charlotte NC urban area; **New Home Price** (2,400 sf living area, 8,000 sf lot, in urban area with full utilities); **Apartment Rent** (950 sf 2 bedroom/1.5 or 2 bath, unfurnished, excluding all utilities except water); **All Electric** (average monthly cost for an all-electric home); **Part Electric** (average monthly cost for a part-electric home); **Other Energy** (average monthly cost for natural gas, fuel oil, coal, wood, and any other forms of energy except electricity); **Telephone** (price includes basic monthly rate for a private residential line plus additional local usage charges incurred by a family of four).*
Source: The Council for Community and Economic Research, ACCRA Cost of Living Index, 2017

Health Care, Transportation, and Other Costs

Area[1]	Doctor ($/visit)	Dentist ($/visit)	Optometrist ($/visit)	Gasoline ($/gallon)	Beauty Salon ($/visit)	Men's Shirt ($)
City[2]	102.91	113.63	113.53	2.14	33.80	36.82
Avg.	108.00	92.54	101.93	2.25	37.58	30.92
Min.	30.39	60.00	49.75	1.82	16.11	11.20
Max.	193.50	161.94	229.28	3.16	77.35	59.13

*Note: (1) Values for the local area are compared with the average, minimum and maximum values for all 294 areas in the Cost of Living Index; (2) Figures cover the Charlotte NC urban area; **Doctor** (general practitioners routine exam of an established patient); **Dentist** (adult teeth cleaning and periodic oral examination); **Optometrist** (full vision eye exam for established adult patient); **Gasoline** (one gallon regular unleaded, national brand, including all taxes, cash price at self-service pump if available); **Beauty Salon** (woman's shampoo, trim, and blow-dry); **Men's Shirt** (cotton/polyester dress shirt, pinpoint weave, long sleeves).*
Source: The Council for Community and Economic Research, ACCRA Cost of Living Index, 2017

HOUSING

House Price Index (HPI)

Area	National Ranking[2]	Quarterly Change (%)	One-Year Change (%)	Five-Year Change (%)
MSA[1]	80	0.07	7.93	35.37
U.S.[3]	–	1.61	6.68	34.71

Note: The HPI is a weighted repeat sales index. It measures average price changes in repeat sales or refinancings on the same properties. This information is obtained by reviewing repeat mortgage transactions on single-family properties whose mortgages have been purchased or securitized by Fannie Mae or Freddie Mac in January 1975; (1) Figures cover the Charlotte-Concord-Gastonia, NC-SC Metropolitan Statistical Area—see Appendix B for areas included; (2) Rankings are based on annual percentage change for all metro areas containing at least 15,000 transactions over the last 10 years and ranges from 1 to 253; (3) figures based on a weighted average of Census Division estimates using a seasonally adjusted, purchase-only index; all figures are for the period ending December 31, 2017
Source: Federal Housing Finance Agency, House Price Index, February 28, 2018

Median Single-Family Home Prices

Area	2015	2016	2017[p]	Percent Change 2016 to 2017
MSA[1]	194.0	208.4	226.9	8.9
U.S. Average	223.9	235.5	248.8	5.6

Note: Figures are median sales prices of existing single-family homes in thousands of dollars; (p) preliminary; (1) Figures cover the Charlotte-Concord-Gastonia, NC-SC Metropolitan Statistical Area—see Appendix B for areas included
Source: National Association of Realtors, Median Sales Price of Existing Single-Family Homes for Metropolitan Areas, 4th Quarter 2017

Qualifying Income Based on Median Sales Price of Existing Single-Family Homes

Area	With 5% Down ($)	With 10% Down ($)	With 20% Down ($)
MSA[1]	50,134	47,495	42,218
U.S. Average	55,585	52,659	46,808

Note: Figures are preliminary; Qualifying income is based on a mortgage rate of 4.17%. Monthly principal and interest payment is limited to 25% of income; (1) Figures cover the Charlotte-Concord-Gastonia, NC-SC Metropolitan Statistical Area—see Appendix B for areas included
Source: National Association of Realtors, Qualifying Income Based on Median Sales Price of Existing Single-Family Homes for Metropolitan Areas, 4th Quarter 2017

Median Apartment Condo-Coop Home Prices

Area	2015	2016	2017[p]	Percent Change 2016 to 2017
MSA[1]	n/a	n/a	n/a	n/a
U.S. Average	210.7	220.7	234.3	6.2

Note: Figures are median sales prices of existing apartment condo-coop homes in thousands of dollars; (p) preliminary; n/a not available; (1) Figures cover the Charlotte-Concord-Gastonia, NC-SC Metropolitan Statistical Area—see Appendix B for areas included
Source: National Association of Realtors, Median Sales Price of Existing Apartment Condo-Coop Homes for Metropolitan Areas, 4th Quarter 2017

Home Value Distribution

Area	Under $50,000	$50,000 -$99,999	$100,000 -$149,999	$150,000 -$199,999	$200,000 -$299,999	$300,000 -$499,999	$500,000 -$999,999	$1,000,000 or more
City	2.2	2.0	14.9	14.2	26.6	18.9	12.6	8.6
MSA[1]	6.1	14.6	20.8	17.6	19.3	14.2	5.9	1.5
U.S.	8.8	14.8	15.3	14.9	18.4	16.4	9.0	2.5

Note: Figures are percentages and cover owner-occupied housing units; (1) Figures cover the Charlotte-Concord-Gastonia, NC-SC Metropolitan Statistical Area—see Appendix B for areas included
Source: U.S. Census Bureau, 2012-2016 American Community Survey 5-Year Estimates

Homeownership Rate

Area	2009 (%)	2010 (%)	2011 (%)	2012 (%)	2013 (%)	2014 (%)	2015 (%)	2016 (%)	2017 (%)
MSA[1]	66.1	66.1	63.6	58.3	58.9	58.1	62.3	66.2	64.6
U.S.	67.4	66.9	66.1	65.4	65.1	64.5	63.7	63.4	63.9

Note: (1) Figures cover the Charlotte-Concord-Gastonia, NC-SC Metropolitan Statistical Area—see Appendix B for areas included
Source: U.S. Census Bureau, Housing Vacancies and Homeownership Annual Statistics: 2009-2017

Year Housing Structure Built

Area	2010 or Later	2000 -2009	1990 -1999	1980 -1989	1970 -1979	1960 -1969	1950 -1959	1940 -1949	Before 1940	Median Year
City	5.4	39.6	30.3	14.8	5.6	1.7	0.5	0.5	1.6	1998
MSA[1]	3.8	25.7	20.4	14.5	12.2	8.8	6.8	3.3	4.5	1990
U.S.	2.3	14.7	14.0	13.7	15.6	10.9	10.6	5.2	13.0	1977

Note: Figures are percentages except for Median Year; Note: (1) Figures cover the Charlotte-Concord-Gastonia, NC-SC Metropolitan Statistical Area—see Appendix B for areas included
Source: U.S. Census Bureau, 2012-2016 American Community Survey 5-Year Estimates

Gross Monthly Rent

Area	Under $500	$500 -$999	$1,000 -$1,499	$1,500 -$1,999	$2,000 -$2,499	$2,500 -$2,999	$3,000 and up	Median ($)
City	1.3	32.7	43.5	18.0	3.6	0.3	0.6	1,149
MSA[1]	8.0	54.4	28.9	6.2	1.4	0.4	0.5	893
U.S.	11.3	43.3	27.7	10.7	4.0	1.6	1.5	949

Note: Figures are percentages except for Median; Gross rent is the contract rent plus the estimated average monthly cost of utilities (electricity, gas, and water and sewer) and fuels (oil, coal, kerosene, wood, etc.) if these are paid by the renter (or paid for the renter by someone else); (1) Figures cover the Charlotte-Concord-Gastonia, NC-SC Metropolitan Statistical Area—see Appendix B for areas included
Source: U.S. Census Bureau, 2012-2016 American Community Survey 5-Year Estimates

HEALTH

Health Risk Factors

Category	MSA[1] (%)	U.S. (%)
Adults aged 18–64 who have any kind of health care coverage	85.7	87.7
Adults who reported being in good or excellent health	86.0	83.6
Adults who are current smokers	17.1	17.1
Adults who currently use E-cigarettes	4.5	4.7
Adults who currently use chewing tobacco, snuff, or snus	3.9	4.0
Adults who are heavy drinkers[2]	6.1	6.5
Adults who are binge drinkers[3]	16.3	16.9
Adults who are overweight (BMI 25.0 - 29.9)	34.7	35.3
Adults who are obese (BMI 30.0 - 99.8)	30.5	29.9
Adults who participated in any physical activities in the past month	78.2	76.9
Adults who always or nearly always wears a seat belt	96.9	94.3

Note: (1) Figures cover the Charlotte-Concord-Gastonia, NC-SC Metropolitan Statistical Area—see Appendix B for areas included; (2) Heavy drinkers are classified as adult men having more than 14 drinks per week and adult women having more than 7 drinks per week; (3) Binge drinkers are classified as males having five or more drinks on one occasion or females having four or more drinks on one occasion
Source: Centers for Disease Control and Prevention, Behaviorial Risk Factor Surveillance System, SMART: Selected Metropolitan Area Risk Trends, 2016

Health Screening Rates

Category	MSA[1] (%)	U.S. (%)
Adults 50-75 who have had a blood stool test within the past year	7.7	8.0
Adults 50-75 who have had a colonoscopy in the past 10 years	69.7	63.5
Adults aged 65+ who have had flu shot within the past year	61.0	58.6
Adults aged 65+ who have ever had a pneumonia vaccination	69.2	73.4
Adults who have ever been tested for HIV	38.2	35.6
Women aged 21-65 who have had a pap test in the past three years	86.6	79.8
Men aged 40+ who have had a PSA test within the past two years	42.2	39.5
Women aged 40+ who have had a mammogram within the past two years	74.6	72.5

Note: n/a not available; (1) Figures cover the Charlotte-Concord-Gastonia, NC-SC Metropolitan Statistical Area—see Appendix B for areas included; Source: Centers for Disease Control and Prevention, Behaviorial Risk Factor Surveillance System, SMART: Selected Metropolitan Area Risk Trends, 2016

Chronic Health Conditions

Category	MSA[1] (%)	U.S. (%)
Adults who have ever been told they had a heart attack	3.7	4.4
Adults who have ever been told they have angina or coronary heart disease	3.6	4.1
Adults who have ever been told they had a stroke	3.4	3.1
Adults who have been told they currently have asthma	7.7	9.3
Adults who have ever been told they have arthritis	23.0	25.8
Adults who have ever been told they have diabetes[2]	9.8	10.5
Adults who have ever been told they had skin cancer	6.7	5.9
Adults who have ever been told they had any other types of cancer	6.9	6.7
Adults who have ever been told they have COPD	6.9	6.3
Adults who have ever been told they have kidney disease	2.2	2.8
Adults who have ever been told they have a form of depression	15.3	17.4

Note: (1) Figures cover the Charlotte-Concord-Gastonia, NC-SC Metropolitan Statistical Area—see Appendix B for areas included; (2) Figures do not include pregnancy-related, borderline, or pre-diabetes
Source: Centers for Disease Control and Prevention, Behaviorial Risk Factor Surveillance System, SMART: Selected Metropolitan Area Risk Trends, 2016

Mortality Rates for the Top 10 Causes of Death in the U.S.

ICD-10[a] Sub-Chapter	ICD-10[a] Code	Age-Adjusted Mortality Rate[1] per 100,000 population	
		County[2]	U.S.
Malignant neoplasms	C00-C97	146.0	158.5
Ischaemic heart diseases	I20-I25	56.7	96.8
Other forms of heart disease	I30-I51	59.7	52.4
Chronic lower respiratory diseases	J40-J47	30.5	40.9
Cerebrovascular diseases	I60-I69	38.2	37.2
Organic, including symptomatic, mental disorders	F01-F09	32.3	33.3
Other degenerative diseases of the nervous system	G30-G31	53.0	32.1
Other external causes of accidental injury	W00-X59	23.9	31.2
Diabetes mellitus	E10-E14	17.6	21.1
Hypertensive diseases	I10-I15	14.1	20.8

Note: (a) ICD-10 = International Classification of Diseases 10th Revision; (1) Mortality rates are a three year average covering 2014-2016; (2) Figures cover Mecklenburg County.
Source: Centers for Disease Control and Prevention, National Center for Health Statistics. Underlying Cause of Death 1999-2016 on CDC WONDER Online Database, released December 2017

Mortality Rates for Selected Causes of Death

ICD-10[a] Sub-Chapter	ICD-10[a] Code	Age-Adjusted Mortality Rate[1] per 100,000 population	
		County[2]	U.S.
Assault	X85-Y09	6.2	5.6
Diseases of the liver	K70-K76	11.4	14.0
Human immunodeficiency virus (HIV) disease	B20-B24	3.3	1.9
Influenza and pneumonia	J09-J18	14.9	14.6
Intentional self-harm	X60-X84	10.4	13.2
Malnutrition	E40-E46	3.8	1.3
Obesity and other hyperalimentation	E65-E68	1.6	2.1
Renal failure	N17-N19	17.7	13.0
Transport accidents	V01-V99	9.2	12.0
Viral hepatitis	B15-B19	1.5	1.9

Note: (a) ICD-10 = International Classification of Diseases 10th Revision; (1) Mortality rates are a three year average covering 2014-2016; (2) Figures cover Mecklenburg County; Data are Suppressed when the data meet the criteria for confidentiality constraints; Mortality rates are flagged as Unreliable when the rate would be calculated with a numerator of 20 or less.
Source: Centers for Disease Control and Prevention, National Center for Health Statistics. Underlying Cause of Death 1999-2016 on CDC WONDER Online Database, released December 2017

Health Insurance Coverage

Area	With Health Insurance	With Private Health Insurance	With Public Health Insurance	Without Health Insurance	Population Under Age 18 Without Health Insurance
City	93.9	86.4	16.6	6.1	2.9
MSA[1]	87.1	68.5	28.5	12.9	5.7
U.S.	88.3	66.7	33.0	11.7	5.9

Note: Figures are percentages that cover the civilian noninstitutionalized population; (1) Figures cover the Charlotte-Concord-Gastonia, NC-SC Metropolitan Statistical Area—see Appendix B for areas included
Source: U.S. Census Bureau, 2012-2016 American Community Survey 5-Year Estimates

Number of Medical Professionals

Area	MDs[3]	DOs[3,4]	Dentists	Podiatrists	Chiropractors	Optometrists
County[1] (number)	3,240	112	718	33	328	140
County[1] (rate[2])	313.2	10.8	67.9	3.1	31.0	13.2
U.S. (rate[2])	276.5	22.3	67.3	6.0	26.7	15.9

Note: Data as of 2016 unless noted; (1) Data covers Mecklenburg County; (2) Rate per 100,000 population; (3) Data as of 2015 and includes all active, non-federal physicians; (4) Doctor of Osteopathic Medicine
Source: U.S. Department of Health and Human Services, Health Resources and Services Administration, Bureau of Health Professions, Area Resource File (ARF) 2016-2017

Best Hospitals

According to *U.S. News,* the Charlotte-Concord-Gastonia, NC-SC metro area is home to one of the best hospitals in the U.S.: **Carolinas Medical Center** (2 adult specialties and 6 pediatric specialties). The hospital listed was nationally ranked in at least one of 16 specialties. Only 152 hospitals nationwide were nationally ranked in one or more specialties. Twenty hospitals in the U.S. made the Honor Roll. The Best Hospitals Honor Roll was revamped last year to take both the national rankings and the procedure and condition ratings into account. Hospitals received points if they were nationally ranked in one of the 16 specialties—the higher they ranked, the more points they got—and how many ratings of "high performing" they earned in the nine procedures and conditions. *U.S. News Online, "America's Best Hospitals 2017-18"*

According to *U.S. News,* the Charlotte-Concord-Gastonia, NC-SC metro area is home to one of the best children's hospitals in the U.S.: **Levine Children's Hospital** (6 pediatric specialties). The hospital listed was highly ranked in at least one of 10 pediatric specialties. Eighty-two children's hospitals in the U.S. were nationally ranked in at least one specialty. Hospitals received points for being ranked in a specialty, and the 10 hospitals with the most points across the 10 specialties make up the Honor Roll. *U.S. News Online, "America's Best Children's Hospitals 2017-18"*

EDUCATION

Public School District Statistics

District Name	Schls	Pupils	Pupil/ Teacher Ratio	Minority Pupils[1] (%)	Free Lunch Eligible[2] (%)	IEP[3] (%)
Charlotte-Mecklenburg Schools	170	146,211	16.7	70.6	58.0	9.6
Thunderbird Preparatory School	1	499	14.0	18.2	n/a	7.2

Note: Table includes school districts with 100 or more students; (1) Percentage of students that are not non-Hispanic white; (2) Percentage of students that are eligible for the free lunch program; (3) Percentage of students that have an Individualized Education Program.
Source: U.S. Department of Education, National Center for Education Statistics, Common Core of Data, Local Education Agency (School District) Universe Survey: School Year 2015-2016; U.S. Department of Education, National Center for Education Statistics, Common Core of Data, Public Elementary/Secondary School Universe Survey: School Year 2015-2016

Highest Level of Education

Area	Less than H.S.	H.S. Diploma	Some College, No Deg.	Associate Degree	Bachelor's Degree	Master's Degree	Prof. School Degree	Doctorate Degree
City	2.9	14.3	18.2	10.4	35.6	13.3	3.4	1.9
MSA[1]	12.2	24.5	21.7	8.7	22.3	8.0	1.6	0.9
U.S.	13.0	27.5	21.0	8.2	18.8	8.2	2.0	1.3

Note: Figures cover persons age 25 and over; (1) Figures cover the Charlotte-Concord-Gastonia, NC-SC Metropolitan Statistical Area—see Appendix B for areas included
Source: U.S. Census Bureau, 2012-2016 American Community Survey 5-Year Estimates

Educational Attainment by Race

Area	High School Graduate or Higher (%)					Bachelor's Degree or Higher (%)				
	Total	White	Black	Asian	Hisp.[2]	Total	White	Black	Asian	Hisp.[2]
City	97.1	97.8	89.2	94.0	92.1	54.2	55.6	37.9	54.5	40.1
MSA[1]	87.8	89.6	86.4	84.7	60.6	32.9	35.3	23.8	54.8	15.4
U.S.	87.0	88.9	84.3	86.3	65.7	30.3	31.6	20.0	52.1	14.7

Note: Figures shown cover persons 25 years old and over; (1) Figures cover the Charlotte-Concord-Gastonia, NC-SC Metropolitan Statistical Area—see Appendix B for areas included; (2) People of Hispanic origin can be of any race
Source: U.S. Census Bureau, 2012-2016 American Community Survey 5-Year Estimates

School Enrollment by Grade and Control

Area	Preschool (%)		Kindergarten (%)		Grades 1 - 4 (%)		Grades 5 - 8 (%)		Grades 9 - 12 (%)	
	Public	Private	Public	Private	Public	Private	Public	Private	Public	Private
City	17.8	82.2	77.0	23.0	87.1	12.9	85.1	14.9	90.8	9.2
MSA[1]	49.5	50.5	90.0	10.0	90.4	9.6	90.0	10.0	90.4	9.6
U.S.	58.4	41.6	87.7	12.3	89.8	10.2	89.7	10.3	90.4	9.6

Note: Figures shown cover persons 3 years old and over; (1) Figures cover the Charlotte-Concord-Gastonia, NC-SC Metropolitan Statistical Area—see Appendix B for areas included
Source: U.S. Census Bureau, 2012-2016 American Community Survey 5-Year Estimates

Average Salaries of Public School Classroom Teachers

Area	2015		2016		Change from 2015 to 2016	
	Dollars	Rank[1]	Dollars	Rank[1]	Percent	Rank[2]
North Carolina	47,792	40	47,941	41	0.3	44
U.S. Average	57,611	–	58,353	–	1.3	–

Note: (1) Rank ranges from 1 to 51 where 1 indicates highest salary; (2) Rank ranges from 1 to 51 where 1 indicates highest percent change.
Source: National Education Association, Rankings & Estimates: Rankings of the States 2016 and Estimates of School Statistics 2017

Higher Education

Four-Year Colleges			Two-Year Colleges			Medical Schools[1]	Law Schools[2]	Voc/ Tech[3]
Public	Private Non-profit	Private For-profit	Public	Private Non-profit	Private For-profit			
0	0	0	0	0	0	0	0	0

Note: Figures cover institutions located within the city limits and include main campuses only; (1) includes schools accredited by the Liaison Committee on Medical Education and the American Osteopathic Association's Commission on Osteopathic College Accreditation; (2) includes ABA-accredited schools, schools with provisional ABA accreditation, and state accredited schools; (3) includes all schools with programs that are less than 2 years.
Source: National Center for Education Statistics, Integrated Postsecondary Education System (IPEDS), 2016-17; Wikipedia, List of Medical Schools in the United States, accessed April 2, 2018; Wikipedia, List of Law Schools in the United States, accessed April 2, 2018

According to *U.S. News & World Report,* the Charlotte-Concord-Gastonia, NC-SC metro area is home to one of the best national universities in the U.S.: **University of North Carolina—Charlotte** (#198 tie). The indicators used to capture academic quality fall into a number of categories: assessment by administrators at peer institutions; retention of students; faculty resources; student selectivity; financial resources; alumni giving; high school counselor ratings of colleges; and graduation rate. *U.S. News & World Report, "America's Best Colleges 2018"*

According to *U.S. News & World Report,* the Charlotte-Concord-Gastonia, NC-SC metro area is home to one of the best liberal arts colleges in the U.S.: **Davidson College** (#10 tie). The indicators used to capture academic quality fall into a number of categories: assessment by administrators at peer institutions; retention of students; faculty resources; student selectivity; financial resources; alumni giving; high school counselor ratings of colleges; and graduation rate. *U.S. News & World Report, "America's Best Colleges 2018"*

PRESIDENTIAL ELECTION

2016 Presidential Election Results

Area	Clinton	Trump	Johnson	Stein	Other
Mecklenburg County	62.3	32.9	3.3	0.3	1.3
U.S.	48.0	45.9	3.3	1.1	1.7

Note: Results are percentages and may not add to 100% due to rounding
Source: Dave Leip's Atlas of U.S. Presidential Elections

EMPLOYERS

Major Employers

Company Name	Industry
Bank of America National Association	National commercial banks
Carlisle Companies Incorporated	Fabricated rubber products
Carolina Medical Center Northeast	General medical & surgical hospitals
Carolina Medical Center Union	General medical & surgical hospitals
Charlotte Mecklenburg Hosp Auth	General medical & surgical hospitals
Compass Group North America	Services
Duke Energy Corporation	Electric services
IBM	Office equipment
Insource Performance Solutions	Help supply services
Medcath Incorporated	Specialty hospitals, except psychiatric
Merchandising Corporation of America	Business consulting
Microsoft Corporation	Computer peripheral equipment
Polymer Group	Nonwoven fabrics
Presbyterian Hospital	General medical & surgical hospitals
RohrCredit Corporation	Aircraft engines & engine parts
University of NC at Chapel Hill	Colleges & universities
Wachovia Corporation	National commercial banks
Wells Fargo Bank	Banking & finance consultant

Note: Companies shown are located within the Charlotte-Concord-Gastonia, NC-SC Metropolitan Statistical Area.
Source: Hoovers.com; Wikipedia

PUBLIC SAFETY

Crime Rate

Area	All Crimes	Violent Crimes				Property Crimes		
		Murder	Rape[3]	Robbery	Aggrav. Assault	Burglary	Larceny -Theft	Motor Vehicle Theft
City	1,503.3	3.6	7.1	21.3	92.4	213.2	1,137.2	28.4
Metro[1]	n/a	n/a	n/a	n/a	n/a	n/a	n/a	n/a
U.S.	2,859.7	4.9	28.4	102.2	238.1	494.7	1,783.6	222.2

Note: Figures are crimes per 100,000 population; (1) Figures cover the Charlotte-Concord-Gastonia, NC-SC Metropolitan Statistical Area—see Appendix B for areas included; n/a not available; (3) The city and U.S. figures shown were reported using the legacy Uniform Crime Reporting (UCR) definition of rape. The metro area figures shown are an aggregate total of the data submitted using both the revised and legacy UCR definitions.
Source: FBI Uniform Crime Reports, 2015 (data for 2016 was not available)

Hate Crimes

Area	Number of Quarters Reported	Number of Incidents per Bias Motivation					
		Race/Ethnicity/ Ancestry	Religion	Sexual Orientation	Disability	Gender	Gender Identity
City	4	0	0	0	0	0	0
U.S.	4	3,489	1,273	1,076	70	31	124

Source: Federal Bureau of Investigation, Hate Crime Statistics 2016

Identity Theft Consumer Reports

Area	Reports	Reports per 100,000 Population	Rank[2]
MSA[1]	2,911	118	61
U.S.	371,061	114	-

Note: (1) Figures cover the Charlotte-Concord-Gastonia, NC-SC Metropolitan Statistical Area—see Appendix B for areas included; (2) Rank ranges from 1 to 389 where 1 indicates greatest number of identity theft reports per 100,000 population
Source: Federal Trade Commission, Consumer Sentinel Network Data Book for January–December 2017

Fraud and Other Consumer Reports

Area	Reports	Reports per 100,000 Population	Rank[2]
MSA[1]	16,666	674	16
U.S.	2,304,550	708	-

Note: (1) Figures cover the Charlotte-Concord-Gastonia, NC-SC Metropolitan Statistical Area—see Appendix B for areas included; (2) Rank ranges from 1 to 389 where 1 indicates greatest number of fraud and other consumer reports per 100,000 population
Source: Federal Trade Commission, Consumer Sentinel Network Data Book for January–December 2017

SPORTS

Professional Sports Teams

Team Name	League	Year Established
Carolina Panthers	National Football League (NFL)	1995
Charlotte Hornets	National Basketball Association (NBA)	2004

Note: Includes teams located in the Charlotte-Concord-Gastonia, NC-SC Metropolitan Statistical Area.
Source: Wikipedia, Major Professional Sports Teams of the United States and Canada, April 5, 2018

CLIMATE

Average and Extreme Temperatures

Temperature	Jan	Feb	Mar	Apr	May	Jun	Jul	Aug	Sep	Oct	Nov	Dec	Yr.
Extreme High (°F)	78	81	86	93	97	103	103	103	104	98	85	77	104
Average High (°F)	51	54	62	72	80	86	89	88	82	72	62	53	71
Average Temp. (°F)	41	44	51	61	69	76	79	78	72	61	51	43	61
Average Low (°F)	31	33	40	48	57	65	69	68	62	50	40	33	50
Extreme Low (°F)	-5	5	4	25	32	45	53	53	39	24	11	2	-5

Note: Figures cover the years 1948-1990
Source: National Climatic Data Center, International Station Meteorological Climate Summary, 9/96

Average Precipitation/Snowfall/Humidity

Precip./Humidity	Jan	Feb	Mar	Apr	May	Jun	Jul	Aug	Sep	Oct	Nov	Dec	Yr.
Avg. Precip. (in.)	3.6	3.8	4.5	3.0	3.7	3.4	3.9	3.9	3.4	3.2	3.1	3.4	42.8
Avg. Snowfall (in.)	2	2	1	Tr	0	0	0	0	0	0	Tr	1	6
Avg. Rel. Hum. 7am (%)	78	77	78	78	82	83	86	89	89	87	83	79	82
Avg. Rel. Hum. 4pm (%)	53	49	46	43	49	51	54	55	54	50	50	54	51

Note: Figures cover the years 1948-1990; Tr = Trace amounts (<0.05 in. of rain; <0.5 in. of snow)
Source: National Climatic Data Center, International Station Meteorological Climate Summary, 9/96

Weather Conditions

Temperature			Daytime Sky			Precipitation		
10°F & below	32°F & below	90°F & above	Clear	Partly cloudy	Cloudy	0.01 inch or more precip.	0.1 inch or more snow/ice	Thunder-storms
1	65	44	98	142	125	113	3	41

Note: Figures are average number of days per year and cover the years 1948-1990
Source: National Climatic Data Center, International Station Meteorological Climate Summary, 9/96

HAZARDOUS WASTE

Superfund Sites

The Charlotte-Concord-Gastonia, NC-SC metro area is home to 12 sites on the EPA's Superfund National Priorities List: **Bypass 601 Ground Water Contamination** (final); **Carolawn, Inc.** (final); **Davis Park Road Tce** (final); **Fcx, Inc. (Statesville Plant)** (final); **Hemphill Road Tce** (final); **Jadco-Hughes Facility** (final); **Leonard Chemical Co., Inc.** (final); **National Starch &**

Chemical Corp. (final); **North Belmont Pce** (final); **Ram Leather Care Site** (final); **Rock Hill Chemical Co.** (final); **Sigmon's Septic Tank Service** (final). There are a total of 1,396 Superfund sites with a status of proposed or final on the list in the U.S. *U.S. Environmental Protection Agency, National Priorities List, April 4, 2018*

AIR & WATER QUALITY

Air Quality Trends: Ozone

	1990	1995	2000	2005	2010	2012	2013	2014	2015	2016
MSA[1]	0.098	0.094	0.094	0.088	0.080	0.079	0.064	0.066	0.066	0.066
U.S.	0.087	0.089	0.081	0.079	0.073	0.075	0.069	0.067	0.068	0.069

Note: (1) Data covers the Charlotte-Concord-Gastonia, NC-SC Metropolitan Statistical Area—see Appendix B for areas included. The values shown are the composite ozone concentration averages among trend sites based on the highest fourth daily maximum 8-hour concentration in parts per million. These trends are based on sites having an adequate record of monitoring data during the trend period. Data from exceptional events are included.
Source: U.S. Environmental Protection Agency, Air Quality Monitoring Information, "Air Quality Trends by City, 1990-2016"

Air Quality Index

Area	Percent of Days when Air Quality was...[2]					AQI Statistics[2]	
	Good	Moderate	Unhealthy for Sensitive Groups	Unhealthy	Very Unhealthy	Maximum	Median
MSA[1]	58.6	40.0	1.4	0.0	0.0	115	48

Note: (1) Data covers the Charlotte-Concord-Gastonia, NC-SC Metropolitan Statistical Area—see Appendix B for areas included; (2) Based on 365 days with AQI data in 2017. Air Quality Index (AQI) is an index for reporting daily air quality. EPA calculates the AQI for five major air pollutants regulated by the Clean Air Act: ground-level ozone, particle pollution (aka particulate matter), carbon monoxide, sulfur dioxide, and nitrogen dioxide. The AQI runs from 0 to 500. The higher the AQI value, the greater the level of air pollution and the greater the health concern. There are six AQI categories: "Good" AQI is between 0 and 50. Air quality is considered satisfactory; "Moderate" AQI is between 51 and 100. Air quality is acceptable; "Unhealthy for Sensitive Groups" When AQI values are between 101 and 150, members of sensitive groups may experience health effects; "Unhealthy" When AQI values are between 151 and 200 everyone may begin to experience health effects; "Very Unhealthy" AQI values between 201 and 300 trigger a health alert; "Hazardous" AQI values over 300 trigger warnings of emergency conditions (not shown).
Source: U.S. Environmental Protection Agency, Air Quality Index Report, 2017

Air Quality Index Pollutants

Area	Percent of Days when AQI Pollutant was...[2]					
	Carbon Monoxide	Nitrogen Dioxide	Ozone	Sulfur Dioxide	Particulate Matter 2.5	Particulate Matter 10
MSA[1]	0.0	0.0	55.3	0.0	44.7	0.0

Note: (1) Data covers the Charlotte-Concord-Gastonia, NC-SC Metropolitan Statistical Area—see Appendix B for areas included; (2) Based on 365 days with AQI data in 2017. The Air Quality Index (AQI) is an index for reporting daily air quality. EPA calculates the AQI for five major air pollutants regulated by the Clean Air Act: ground-level ozone, particle pollution (also known as particulate matter), carbon monoxide, sulfur dioxide, and nitrogen dioxide. The AQI runs from 0 to 500. The higher the AQI value, the greater the level of air pollution and the greater the health concern.
Source: U.S. Environmental Protection Agency, Air Quality Index Report, 2017

Maximum Air Pollutant Concentrations: Particulate Matter, Ozone, CO and Lead

	Particulate Matter 10 (ug/m^3)	Particulate Matter 2.5 Wtd AM (ug/m^3)	Particulate Matter 2.5 24-Hr (ug/m^3)	Ozone (ppm)	Carbon Monoxide (ppm)	Lead (ug/m^3)
MSA[1] Level	44	9	21	0.074	1	n/a
NAAQS[2]	150	15	35	0.075	9	0.15
Met NAAQS[2]	Yes	Yes	Yes	Yes	Yes	n/a

Note: (1) Data covers the Charlotte-Concord-Gastonia, NC-SC Metropolitan Statistical Area—see Appendix B for areas included; Data from exceptional events are included; (2) National Ambient Air Quality Standards; ppm = parts per million; ug/m^3 = micrograms per cubic meter; n/a not available.
Concentrations: Particulate Matter 10 (coarse particulate)—highest second maximum 24-hour concentration; Particulate Matter 2.5 Wtd AM (fine particulate)—highest weighted annual mean concentration; Particulate Matter 2.5 24-Hour (fine particulate)—highest 98th percentile 24-hour concentration; Ozone—highest fourth daily maximum 8-hour concentration; Carbon Monoxide—highest second maximum non-overlapping 8-hour concentration; Lead—maximum running 3-month average
Source: U.S. Environmental Protection Agency, Air Quality Monitoring Information, "Air Quality Statistics by City, 2016"

Maximum Air Pollutant Concentrations: Nitrogen Dioxide and Sulfur Dioxide

	Nitrogen Dioxide AM (ppb)	Nitrogen Dioxide 1-Hr (ppb)	Sulfur Dioxide AM (ppb)	Sulfur Dioxide 1-Hr (ppb)	Sulfur Dioxide 24-Hr (ppb)
MSA[1] Level	11	40	n/a	4	n/a
NAAQS[2]	53	100	30	75	140
Met NAAQS[2]	Yes	Yes	n/a	Yes	n/a

Note: (1) Data covers the Charlotte-Concord-Gastonia, NC-SC Metropolitan Statistical Area—see Appendix B for areas included; Data from exceptional events are included; (2) National Ambient Air Quality Standards; ppm = parts per million; ug/m^3 = micrograms per cubic meter; n/a not available.
Concentrations: Nitrogen Dioxide AM—highest arithmetic mean concentration; Nitrogen Dioxide 1-Hr—highest 98th percentile 1-hour daily maximum concentration; Sulfur Dioxide AM—highest annual mean concentration; Sulfur Dioxide 1-Hr—highest 99th percentile 1-hour daily maximum concentration; Sulfur Dioxide 24-Hr—highest second maximum 24-hour concentration
Source: U.S. Environmental Protection Agency, Air Quality Monitoring Information, "Air Quality Statistics by City, 2016"

Drinking Water

Water System Name	Pop. Served	Primary Water Source Type	Violations[1] Health Based	Violations[1] Monitoring/ Reporting
Charlotte Water	954,644	Surface	0	0

Note: (1) Based on violation data from January 1, 2017 to December 31, 2017
Source: U.S. Environmental Protection Agency, Office of Ground Water and Drinking Water, Safe Drinking Water Information System (based on data extracted April 5, 2018)

Holly Springs, North Carolina

Background

Holly Springs is in Wake County, approximately 16 miles southeast of Raleigh. The township was incorporated in 1887, although settlers had lived in the area since the late 18th century. The town, and the county as a whole, has grown in the last 20 years from a quaint community to a bustling center for new business.

The Tuscarora Native American tribe, who was drawn there by its natural freshwater springs, originally inhabited the area of Holly Springs. A village sprung up around a crossroads that connected a few neighboring towns, most notably Raleigh. Until the 1980s, the town's land area was one square mile.

Holly Springs has gone through three difficult periods in its history, all nearly leading to the city's collapse. The first occurred at the start of the Civil War in 1861, when the town's men went to join the Confederate Army, leading to the closing of schools and the migration of the remaining residents. The town eventually recovered due in large part to George Alford, a businessman who invested in the industrial potential of Holly Springs. Just as the town was prospering, World War I caused the second difficult period, as the war stalled the town's growth. Finally, the town once again faltered from the Great Depression through World War II.

Today however, Holly Springs is one of the premier new business centers in North Carolina due to its proximity to Raleigh and Research Triangle Park. In 2006, pharmaceutical company Novartis built a flu vaccine manufacturing facility in the city, now the largest local employer in Holly Springs. In an effort to attract more new business, Holly Springs has attractive land packages available in the Holly Springs Business Park, and incentives to companies that will make a positive impact on the community.

The town takes great efforts towards preserving its natural beauty through well-maintained parks. Bass Lake Park features hiking trails, canoe rentals, fishing and a nature program for children. The disc golf course at Jones Park is one of the exciting new ways for people to get active in the community. The town also has two private golf courses located in the Sunset Ridge Community and the 12 Oaks Community.

State-of-the-art sports facilities and fields provide space for recreational play as well as youth and adult athletic programs. The North Main Athletic Complex is a massive outdoor facility with 12 tennis courts, two basketball courts, two regulation turf soccer fields, and an 1,800-seat stadium, home of the Holly Spring Salamanders, a collegiate summer baseball team. Parrish Womble Park also has a turf playing field, along with four baseball fields, horseshoe pits and a volleyball court. The town has youth and adult leagues for all major sports, including baseball, softball, soccer, basketball and tennis.

The Wake County Public School System serves Holly Springs with three public elementary schools, two public middle schools and one public high school. The New School Montessori Center is a private school for children grades K-8. North Carolina State University at Raleigh is the closest major college and is approximately 13 miles from Holly Springs.

Raleigh-Durham International Airport and Harnet Regional Jetport are the two closest airports to Holly Springs, each approximately 24 miles away. Fayetteville Regional Airport, the next closest, is just over 50 miles away.

The climate of Holly Springs is typical of Wake County, with the July average high at 88 degrees. The warm winters of Holly Springs is reflected through the January average low of 29 degrees and an average of 5 inches of annual snowfall. The town receives significantly more rain then the national average, at 49 inches per year.

Rankings

General Rankings

- *US News & World Report* conducted a survey of more than 2,000 people and analyzed the 125 largest metropolitan areas to determine what matters the most when selecting the next place to live. Raleigh* ranked #13 out of the top 25 as having the best combination of desirable factors. Criteria: cost of living; quality of education; job market, crime rates; and other factors. *realestate.usnews.com, "The 25 Best Places to Live in the U.S. in 2018," April 10, 2018*

- The Raleigh* metro area was identified as one of America's fastest-growing areas in terms of population and economy by *Forbes.* The area ranked #15 out of 25. The 100 most populous metro areas in the U.S. were evaluated on the following criteria: estimated population growth; employment; economic output; wages; home values. *Forbes, "America's Fastest-Growing Cities 2018," February 28, 2018*

Business/Finance Rankings

- The personal finance site NerdWallet analyzed 183 American metropolitan areas with populations over 250,000 and more than 15,000 businesses to rank where entrepreneurs find the most success. Criteria included area economy, annual income, housing cost, unemployment rate, and the success rate of area businesses. Raleigh* ranked #73. *www.nerdwallet.com, "Best Places to Start a Business," April 27, 2015*

- According to data by the Bureau of Economic Analysis (BEA) and the Bureau of Labor Statistics (BLS), the Raleigh* metro area has the fastest-growing GDP (gross domestic product) and positive employment trends, at #7. *247wallst.com, "Cities With the Fastest Growing (and Shrinking) Economies," September 26, 2016*

- 24/7 Wall Street used Brookings Institution research on 50 advanced industries to identify the proportion of workers in the nation's largest metropolitan areas that were employed in jobs requiring knowledge in the science, technology, engineering, or math (STEM) fields and where there was heavy investment in research and development (R&D). The Raleigh* metro area was #10. *247wallst.com, "15 Cities with the Most High-Tech Jobs," February 23, 2017*

- Based on metro area social media reviews, the employment opinion group Glassdoor surveyed 50 of the largest U.S. metro areas and equally weighed cost of living, hiring opportunity, and job satisfaction to compose a list of "25 Best Cities for Jobs." Median pay and home value, in-demand jobs and number of current job openings was also factored in. The Raleigh* metro area was ranked #4 in overall job satisfaction. *www.glassdoor.com, "Best Cities for Jobs," September 12, 2017*

- In a survey of economic confidence in the nation's 50 largest metropolitan areas conducted January–December 2014, the Raleigh* metro area placed #6, according to Gallup's 2014 Economic Confidence Index. *Gallup, "San Jose and San Francisco Lead in Economic Confidence," March 19, 2015*

- The Brookings Institution ranked the 100 largest metro areas in the U.S. based on income inequality. Raleigh* was ranked #80 (#1 = greatest ineqality). Criteria: the "95/20 ratio," a figure representing the income at which a household earns more than 95 percent of all other households, divided by the income at which a household earns more than only 20 percent of all other households. *Brookings Institution, "Household Income Inequality, 100 Largest U.S. Metro Areas, 2014-2016," February 5, 2018*

- *Forbes* ranked the 100 largest metro areas in the U.S. in terms of the "Best Cities for Young Professionals." The Raleigh* metro area ranked #10 out of 25. (Large metro areas were divided into metro divisions.) Criteria: median rent of a two-bedroom apartment; job growth and unemployment rate; median salary of college graduates with 5 or less years of work experience; networking opportunities; social outlook; percentage of population 25 years of age and older with college degrees. *Forbes.com, "America's 25 Best Cities for Young Professionals in 2017," May 22, 2017*

- Raleigh* was identified as one of America's most frugal metro areas by *Coupons.com*. The city ranked #3 out of 25. Criteria: digital coupon usage. *Coupons.com, "America's Most Frugal Cities of 2017," March 22, 2018*
- The Raleigh* metro area appeared on the Milken Institute "2017 Best Performing Cities" list. Rank: #2 out of 200 large metro areas. Criteria: job growth; wage and salary growth; high-tech output growth. *Milken Institute, "Best-Performing Cities 2017," January 2018*
- *Forbes* ranked the 200 most populous metro areas to determine the nation's "Best Places for Business and Careers." The Raleigh* metro area was ranked #2. Criteria: costs (business and living); job growth (past and projected); income growth; quality of life; educational attainment (college and high school); projected economic growth; cultural and recreational opportunities; net migration patterns; number of highly ranked colleges. *Forbes, "The Best Places for Business and Careers 2017," October 24, 2017*

Children/Family Rankings

- *Forbes* analyzed data on the 100 largest metropolitan areas in the United States to compile its 2016 ranking of the best cities for raising a family. The Raleigh* metro area was ranked #13. Criteria: median income; childcare costs; percent of population under 18; commuting delays; crime rate; percentage of families owning homes; education quality (mainly test scores). Overall cost of living and housing affordability was also unofficially considered. *Forbes, "America's Best Cities for Raising a Family 2016," August 30, 2016*

Dating/Romance Rankings

- *Apartment List* conducted its annual survey of renters to compile a list of metros that have the best opportunities for dating. Nearly 11,000 respondents, from February 2017 through January 2018, rated their current city or neighborhood for opportunities to date and make friends. The Raleigh* metro area ranked #1 out of 70 where single residents were very satisfied or somewhat satisfied, making it among the ten best metros for dating opportunities. Other criteria analyzed included gender and education levels of renters. *Apartment List, "Best Metros for Dating 2018," February 6, 2018*

Education Rankings

- Raleigh* was identified as one of America's "smartest" metropolitan areas by *The Business Journals*. The area ranked #8 out of 10. Criteria: percentage of adults (25 and older) with high school diplomas, bachelor's degrees and graduate degrees. *The Business Journals, "Where the Brainpower Is: Exclusive U.S. Rankings, Insights," February 27, 2014*
- Personal finance website *WalletHub* analyzed the 150 largest U.S. metropolitan statistical areas to determine where the most educated Americans are choosing to settle. Criteria: education quality and attainment gap; education levels; percentage of workers with degrees; public school rankings; quality and size of each metro area's universities. Raleigh* was ranked #15 (#1 = most educated city). *www.WalletHub.com, "2017's Most and Least Educated Cities in America," July 25, 2017*

Environmental Rankings

- Sperling's BestPlaces assessed 379 metropolitan areas of the United States for the likelihood of dangerously extreme weather events or earthquakes. In general the Southeast and South-Central regions have the highest risk of weather extremes and earthquakes, while the Pacific Northwest enjoys the lowest risk. Of the least risky metropolitan areas, the Raleigh* metro area was ranked #238. *www.bestplaces.net, "Safest Places from Natural Disasters," April 2011*
- The U.S. Environmental Protection Agency (EPA) released a list of mid-size U.S. metropolitan areas with the most ENERGY STAR certified buildings in 2016. The Raleigh* metro area was ranked #9 out of 10. *U.S. Environmental Protection Agency, "2017 Energy Star Top Cities," June 2017*

Health/Fitness Rankings

- For each of the 50 most populous metro areas in the United States, the American College of Sports Medicine's American Fitness Index evaluated infrastructure, community assets, and policies that encourage healthy and fit lifestyles, including preventive health behaviors, levels of chronic disease conditions, health care access, and community resources and policies that support physical activity. The Raleigh* metro area ranked #14 for "community fitness." *www.americanfitnessindex.org, "ACSM American Fitness Index Health and Community Fitness Status of the 50 Largest Metropolitan Areas," May 2017*
- The Raleigh* metro area was identified as one of the worst cities for bed bugs in America by pest control company Orkin. The area ranked #15 out of 50 based on the number of bed bug treatments Orkin performed from December 2016 to November 2017. *Orkin, "Baltimore and Washington D.C. Continue to Hold Top Spots," January 8, 2018*
- Raleigh* was identified as a "2016 Spring Allergy Capital." The area ranked #93 out of 100. Three groups of factors were used to identify the most severe cities for people with allergies during the spring season: annual pollen levels; medicine utilization; access to board-certified allergists. *Asthma and Allergy Foundation of America, "Spring Allergy Capitals 2016"*
- Raleigh* was identified as a "2016 Fall Allergy Capital." The area ranked #88 out of 100. Three groups of factors were used to identify the most severe cities for people with allergies during the fall season: annual pollen levels; medicine utilization; access to board-certified allergists. *Asthma and Allergy Foundation of America, "Fall Allergy Capitals 2016"*
- Raleigh* was identified as a "2015 Asthma Capital." The area ranked #92 out of the nation's 100 largest metropolitan areas. Criteria: estimated prevalence; self-reported prevalence; crude death rate for asthma; annual pollen score; annual air quality; public smoking laws; number of board-certified asthma specialists; school inhaler access laws; rescue medication use; controller medication use; ER visits for asthma; uninsured rate; poverty rate. *Asthma and Allergy Foundation of America, "Asthma Capitals 2015"*

Real Estate Rankings

- FitSmallBusiness looked at 50 of the largest metropolitan areas in the U.S. to determine which metro was the best to start a real estate business. Data was compiled from such sources as: Zillow, Trulia, U.S. Census Bureau, and the Bureau of Labor Statistics. Criteria: location; inventory; annual wages; median sales price of homes; days on the market; median price cut percentage; and other factors that would influence real estate professional growth. The Raleigh* metro area ranked #29. *fitsmallbusiness.com, "The Best Cities to Become a Real Estate Agent in 2018," January 30, 2018*
- The Raleigh* metro area was identified as one of the top 20 housing markets to invest in for 2018 by *Forbes*. The area ranked #4. Criteria: strong job and population growth; anticipated home price appreciation; and other factors. *Forbes.com, "Where to Invest in Housing in 2018," February 1, 2018*
- Raleigh* was ranked #144 out of 238 metro areas in terms of housing affordability in 2017 by the National Association of Home Builders (#1 = most affordable). Criteria: the share of homes sold in that area affordable to a family earning the local median income, based on standard mortgage underwriting criteria. *National Association of Home Builders®, NAHB-Wells Fargo Housing Opportunity Index, 4th Quarter 2017*

Safety Rankings

- Holly Springs was identified as one of the safest cities in America by NeighborhoodScout. The city ranked #63 out of 100 (100 = safest). Criteria: number of violent and property crimes per 1,000 residents. The editors only considered cities with 25,000 or more residents. *NeighborhoodScout, "Top 100 Safest Cities in the U.S. 2018" January 2, 2018*
- The National Insurance Crime Bureau ranked 382 metro areas in the U.S. in terms of per capita rates of vehicle theft. The Raleigh* metro area ranked #239 (#1 = highest rate). Criteria: number of vehicle theft offenses per 100,000 inhabitants in 2016. *National Insurance Crime Bureau, "Hot Spots 2016," June 8, 2017*

Seniors/Retirement Rankings

- From its Best Cities for Successful Aging indexes, the Milken Institute generated rankings for metropolitan areas, weighing data in nine categories—health care, wellness, living arrangements, transportation and convenience, financial characteristics, education, employment, community engagement, and overall livability. The Raleigh* metro area was ranked #42 overall in the large metro area category. *Milken Institute, "Best Cities for Successful Aging, 2017" March 14, 2017*

*Holly Springs is located within the Raleigh, NC Metropolitan Statistical Area.

Business Environment

CITY FINANCES

City Government Finances

Component	2015 ($000)	2015 ($ per capita)
Total Revenues	49,958	1,592
Total Expenditures	54,512	1,737
Debt Outstanding	93,013	2,964
Cash and Securities[1]	0	0

Note: (1) Cash and security holdings of a government at the close of its fiscal year,, including those of its dependent agencies, utilities, and liquor stores.
Source: U.S Census Bureau, State & Local Government Finances 2015

City Government Revenue by Source

Source	2015 ($000)	2015 ($ per capita)	2015 (%)
General Revenue			
From Federal Government	129	4	0.3
From State Government	4,691	150	9.4
From Local Governments	9	0	0.0
Taxes			
Property	16,286	519	32.6
Sales and Gross Receipts	4,644	148	9.3
Personal Income	0	0	0.0
Corporate Income	0	0	0.0
Motor Vehicle License	286	9	0.6
Other Taxes	1,069	34	2.1
Current Charges	12,698	405	25.4
Liquor Store	0	0	0.0
Utility	5,428	173	10.9
Employee Retirement	0	0	0.0

Source: U.S Census Bureau, State & Local Government Finances 2015

City Government Expenditures by Function

Function	2015 ($000)	2015 ($ per capita)	2015 (%)
General Direct Expenditures			
Air Transportation	0	0	0.0
Corrections	0	0	0.0
Education	0	0	0.0
Employment Security Administration	0	0	0.0
Financial Administration	738	23	1.4
Fire Protection	4,242	135	7.8
General Public Buildings	4,461	142	8.2
Governmental Administration, Other	1,456	46	2.7
Health	0	0	0.0
Highways	2,699	86	5.0
Hospitals	0	0	0.0
Housing and Community Development	2,818	89	5.2
Interest on General Debt	1,425	45	2.6
Judicial and Legal	0	0	0.0
Libraries	0	0	0.0
Parking	0	0	0.0
Parks and Recreation	17,749	565	32.6
Police Protection	5,049	160	9.3
Public Welfare	0	0	0.0
Sewerage	304	9	0.6
Solid Waste Management	2,409	76	4.4
Veterans' Services	0	0	0.0
Liquor Store	0	0	0.0
Utility	10,187	324	18.7
Employee Retirement	0	0	0.0

Source: U.S Census Bureau, State & Local Government Finances 2015

DEMOGRAPHICS

Population Growth

Area	1990 Census	2000 Census	2010 Census	2016* Estimate	Population Growth (%)	
					1990-2016	2010-2016
City	2,351	9,192	24,661	30,126	***.*	22.2
MSA[1]	541,081	797,071	1,130,490	1,243,720	129.9	10.0
U.S.	248,709,873	281,421,906	308,745,538	318,558,162	28.1	3.2

Note: (1) Figures cover the Raleigh, NC Metropolitan Statistical Area—see Appendix B for areas included; (*) 2012-2016 5-year estimated population
Source: U.S. Census Bureau, 1990 Census, Census 2000, Census 2010, 2012-2016 American Community Survey 5-Year Estimates

Household Size

Area	Persons in Household (%)							Average Household Size
	One	Two	Three	Four	Five	Six	Seven or More	
City	13.1	28.5	21.2	23.6	10.2	2.8	0.6	3.10
MSA[1]	25.5	32.7	17.6	15.3	5.9	2.0	1.0	2.70
U.S.	27.7	33.7	15.7	13.1	6.0	2.3	1.5	2.60

Note: (1) Figures cover the Raleigh, NC Metropolitan Statistical Area—see Appendix B for areas included
Source: U.S. Census Bureau, 2012-2016 American Community Survey 5-Year Estimates

Race

Area	White Alone[2] (%)	Black Alone[2] (%)	Asian Alone[2] (%)	AIAN[3] Alone[2] (%)	NHOPI[4] Alone[2] (%)	Other Race Alone[2] (%)	Two or More Races (%)
City	79.3	12.4	2.6	0.3	0.0	1.7	3.6
MSA[1]	68.7	20.1	5.1	0.4	0.0	3.0	2.7
U.S.	73.3	12.6	5.2	0.8	0.2	4.8	3.1

Note: (1) Figures cover the Raleigh, NC Metropolitan Statistical Area—see Appendix B for areas included; (2) Alone is defined as not being in combination with one or more other races; (3) American Indian and Alaska Native; (4) Native Hawaiian and Other Pacific Islander
Source: U.S. Census Bureau, 2012-2016 American Community Survey 5-Year Estimates

Hispanic or Latino Origin

Area	Total (%)	Mexican (%)	Puerto Rican (%)	Cuban (%)	Other (%)
City	5.1	1.9	1.1	0.8	1.3
MSA[1]	10.3	5.8	1.1	0.3	3.1
U.S.	17.3	11.0	1.7	0.7	4.0

Note: Persons of Hispanic or Latino origin can be of any race; (1) Figures cover the Raleigh, NC Metropolitan Statistical Area—see Appendix B for areas included
Source: U.S. Census Bureau, 2012-2016 American Community Survey 5-Year Estimates

Segregation

Type	Segregation Indices[1]				Percent Change		
	1990	2000	2010	2010 Rank[2]	1990-2000	1990-2010	2000-2010
Black/White	41.9	40.8	42.1	87	-1.1	0.2	1.3
Asian/White	42.5	40.1	46.7	16	-2.4	4.2	6.6
Hispanic/White	19.9	34.9	37.1	76	15.1	17.3	2.2

Note: All figures cover the Metropolitan Statistical Area—see Appendix B for areas included; Figures are based on an analysis of 1990, 2000, and 2010 Census Decennial Census tract data by William H. Frey, Brookings Institution and the University of Michigan Social Science Data Analysis Network. In this analysis all racial groups (whites, blacks, and asians) are non-Hispanic members of those races. Hispanics are shown as a separate category; (1) Segregation Indices are Dissimilarity Indices that measure the degree to which the minority group is distributed differently than whites across census tracts. They range from 0 (complete integration) to 100 (complete segregation) where the value indicates the percentage of the minority group that needs to move to be distributed exactly like whites; (2) Ranges from 1 (most segregated) to 102 (least segregated); n/a not available.
Source: www.CensusScope.org

Ancestry

Area	German	Irish	English	American	Italian	Polish	French²	Scottish	Dutch
City	16.6	13.3	10.9	7.7	9.9	3.8	2.4	4.5	0.9
MSA¹	11.2	9.9	10.6	11.3	4.8	2.1	1.9	2.7	1.0
U.S.	14.4	10.4	7.7	6.9	5.4	2.9	2.6	1.7	1.3

Note: Figures are the percentage of the total population reporting a particular ancestry. The nine most commonly reported ancestries in the U.S. are shown. Figures include multiple ancestries (e.g. if a person reported being Irish and Italian, they were included in both columns); (1) Figures cover the Raleigh, NC Metropolitan Statistical Area—see Appendix B for areas included; (2) Excludes Basque
Source: U.S. Census Bureau, 2012-2016 American Community Survey 5-Year Estimates

Foreign-Born Population

Area	Percent of Population Born in								
	Any Foreign Country	Asia	Mexico	Europe	Carribean	Central America²	South America	Africa	Canada
City	6.9	2.3	0.5	1.2	0.5	0.1	0.4	1.3	0.6
MSA¹	11.8	4.1	3.0	1.2	0.6	1.0	0.6	1.0	0.4
U.S.	13.2	4.0	3.6	1.5	1.3	1.0	0.9	0.6	0.3

Note: (1) Figures cover the Raleigh, NC Metropolitan Statistical Area—see Appendix B for areas included; (2) Excludes Mexico.
Source: U.S. Census Bureau, 2012-2016 American Community Survey 5-Year Estimates

Marital Status

Area	Never Married	Now Married²	Separated	Widowed	Divorced
City	22.5	64.3	2.0	3.4	7.8
MSA¹	31.7	51.7	2.5	4.4	9.7
U.S.	33.0	48.1	2.1	5.9	11.0

Note: Figures are percentages and cover the population 15 years of age and older; (1) Figures cover the Raleigh, NC Metropolitan Statistical Area—see Appendix B for areas included; (2) Excludes separated
Source: U.S. Census Bureau, 2012-2016 American Community Survey 5-Year Estimates

Disability Status

Area	All Ages	Under 18 Years Old	18 to 64 Years Old	65 Years and Over
City	6.4	3.7	5.3	28.2
MSA¹	9.4	3.7	7.8	33.0
U.S.	12.5	4.1	10.3	35.7

Note: Figures show percent of the civilian noninstitutionalized population that reported having a disability. Disability status is determined from six types of difficulty: vision, hearing, cognitive, ambulatory, self-care, and independent living. For children under 5 years old, hearing and vision difficulty are used to determine disability status. For children between the ages of 5 and 14, disability status is determined from hearing, vision, cognitive, ambulatory, and self-care difficulties. For people aged 15 years and older, they are considered to have a disability if they have difficulty with any one of the six difficulty types; Note: (1) Figures cover the Raleigh, NC Metropolitan Statistical Area—see Appendix B for areas included
Source: U.S. Census Bureau, 2012-2016 American Community Survey 5-Year Estimates

Age

Area	Percent of Population									Median Age
	Under Age 5	Age 5–19	Age 20–34	Age 35–44	Age 45–54	Age 55–64	Age 65–74	Age 75–84	Age 85+	
City	8.1	26.3	15.4	19.2	16.5	7.5	4.9	1.8	0.5	35.2
MSA¹	6.5	21.4	20.5	15.4	14.6	11.1	6.5	2.9	1.1	36.1
U.S.	6.2	19.6	20.7	12.7	13.6	12.6	8.3	4.3	1.9	37.7

Note: (1) Figures cover the Raleigh, NC Metropolitan Statistical Area—see Appendix B for areas included
Source: U.S. Census Bureau, 2012-2016 American Community Survey 5-Year Estimates

Gender

Area	Males	Females	Males per 100 Females
City	14,853	15,273	97.3
MSA¹	605,735	637,985	94.9
U.S.	156,765,322	161,792,840	96.9

Note: (1) Figures cover the Raleigh, NC Metropolitan Statistical Area—see Appendix B for areas included
Source: U.S. Census Bureau, 2012-2016 American Community Survey 5-Year Estimates

Religious Groups by Family

Area	Catholic	Baptist	Non-Den.	Methodist[2]	Lutheran	LDS[3]	Pentecostal	Presbyterian[4]	Muslim[5]	Judaism
MSA[1]	9.2	12.1	6.0	6.7	0.9	0.9	2.3	2.3	0.9	0.3
U.S.	19.1	9.3	4.0	4.0	2.3	2.0	1.9	1.6	0.8	0.7

Note: Figures are the number of adherents as a percentage of the total population; (1) Figures cover the Raleigh, NC Metropolitan Statistical Area—see Appendix B for areas included; (2) Methodist/Pietist; (3) Latter Day Saints; (4) Reformed; (5) Figures are estimates
Source: Association of Statisticians of American Religious Bodies, 2010 U.S. Religion Census: Religious Congregations & Membership Study

Religious Groups by Tradition

Area	Catholic	Evangelical Protestant	Mainline Protestant	Other Tradition	Black Protestant	Orthodox
MSA[1]	9.2	19.9	10.1	3.3	1.7	0.2
U.S.	19.1	16.2	7.3	4.3	1.6	0.3

Note: Figures are the number of adherents as a percentage of the total population; (1) Figures cover the Raleigh, NC Metropolitan Statistical Area—see Appendix B for areas included
Source: Association of Statisticians of American Religious Bodies, 2010 U.S. Religion Census: Religious Congregations & Membership Study

ECONOMY

Gross Metropolitan Product

Area	2014	2015	2016	2017	Rank[2]
MSA[1]	71.4	75.9	79.7	84.8	44

Note: Figures are in billions of dollars; (1) Figures cover the Raleigh, NC Metropolitan Statistical Area—see Appendix B for areas included; (2) Rank is based on 2015 data and ranges from 1 to 381
Source: The U.S. Conference of Mayors, U.S. Metro Economies: GMP and Employment Report, 2015-2017

Economic Growth

Area	2012-14 (%)	2015 (%)	2016 (%)	2017 (%)	Rank[2]
MSA[1]	3.5	4.5	3.5	4.4	41
U.S.	2.0	2.4	1.9	2.6	–

Note: Figures are real gross metropolitan product (GMP) growth rates and represent average annual percent change; (1) Figures cover the Raleigh, NC Metropolitan Statistical Area—see Appendix B for areas included; (2) Rank is based on 2012-2014 average annual percent change and ranges from 1 to 381
Source: The U.S. Conference of Mayors, U.S. Metro Economies: GMP and Employment Report, 2015-2017

Metropolitan Area Exports

Area	2011	2012	2013	2014	2015	2016	Rank[2]
MSA[1]	2,254.4	2,308.1	2,280.6	2,713.1	2,553.4	2,620.4	81

Note: Figures are in millions of dollars; (1) Figures cover the Raleigh, NC Metropolitan Statistical Area—see Appendix B for areas included; (2) Rank is based on 2016 data and ranges from 1 to 385
Source: U.S. Department of Commerce, International Trade Administration, Office of Trade & Industry Information, Manufacturing & Services, data extracted March 15, 2018

Building Permits

Area	Single-Family			Multi-Family			Total		
	2016	2017p	Pct. Chg.	2016	2017p	Pct. Chg.	2016	2017p	Pct. Chg.
City	683	633	-7.3	0	0	0.0	683	633	-7.3
MSA[1]	9,435	10,785	14.3	4,072	3,428	-15.8	13,507	14,213	5.2
U.S.	750,800	817,300	8.9	455,800	446,800	-2.0	1,206,600	1,264,100	4.8

Note: (1) Figures cover the Raleigh, NC Metropolitan Statistical Area—see Appendix B for areas included; Figures represent new, privately-owned housing units authorized (unadjusted data); All permit data are based on estimates with imputation; (p) preliminary data.
Source: U.S. Census Bureau, Manufacturing, Mining, and Construction Statistics, Building Permits, 2016, 2017

Bankruptcy Filings

Area	Business Filings			Nonbusiness Filings		
	2016	2017	% Chg.	2016	2017	% Chg.
Wake County	76	79	3.9	1,539	1,458	-5.3
U.S.	24,114	23,157	-4.0	770,846	765,863	-0.6

Note: Business filings include Chapter 7, Chapter 11, Chapter 12, and Chapter 13; Nonbusiness filings include Chapter 7, Chapter 11, and Chapter 13
Source: Administrative Office of the U.S. Courts, Business and Nonbusiness Bankruptcy, County Cases Commenced by Chapter of the Bankruptcy Code, During the 12-Month Period Ending December 31, 2016 and Business and Nonbusiness Bankruptcy, County Cases Commenced by Chapter of the Bankruptcy Code, During the 12-Month Period Ending December 31, 2017

Housing Vacancy Rates

Area	Gross Vacancy Rate[2] (%)			Year-Round Vacancy Rate[3] (%)			Rental Vacancy Rate[4] (%)			Homeowner Vacancy Rate[5] (%)		
	2015	2016	2017	2015	2016	2017	2015	2016	2017	2015	2016	2017
MSA[1]	6.8	6.8	8.0	6.7	6.7	7.8	6.6	4.3	5.8	1.7	1.9	1.7
U.S.	12.9	12.8	12.7	10.0	9.9	9.9	7.1	6.9	7.2	1.8	1.7	1.6

Note: (1) Figures cover the Raleigh, NC Metropolitan Statistical Area—see Appendix B for areas included; (2) The percentage of the total housing inventory that is vacant; (3) The percentage of the housing inventory (excluding seasonal units) that is year-round vacant; (4) The percentage of rental inventory that is vacant for rent; (5) The percentage of homeowner inventory that is vacant for sale
Source: U.S. Census Bureau, Housing Vacancies and Homeownership Annual Statistics: 2015, 2016, 2017

INCOME

Income

Area	Per Capita ($)	Median Household ($)	Average Household ($)
City	36,369	98,041	109,757
MSA[1]	33,233	65,834	87,616
U.S.	29,829	55,322	77,866

Note: (1) Figures cover the Raleigh, NC Metropolitan Statistical Area—see Appendix B for areas included
Source: U.S. Census Bureau, 2012-2016 American Community Survey 5-Year Estimates

Household Income Distribution

Area	Percent of Households Earning							
	Under $15,000	$15,000 -$24,999	$25,000 -$34,999	$35,000 -$49,999	$50,000 -$74,999	$75,000 -$99,999	$100,000 -$149,999	$150,000 and up
City	4.1	2.8	3.9	7.5	15.4	17.7	27.3	21.3
MSA[1]	8.4	7.7	9.0	13.0	17.7	13.6	16.4	14.2
U.S.	12.1	10.2	9.9	13.2	17.8	12.2	13.5	11.1

Note: (1) Figures cover the Raleigh, NC Metropolitan Statistical Area—see Appendix B for areas included
Source: U.S. Census Bureau, 2012-2016 American Community Survey 5-Year Estimates

Poverty Rate

Area	All Ages	Under 18 Years Old	18 to 64 Years Old	65 Years and Over
City	3.9	3.3	4.0	5.9
MSA[1]	11.6	15.7	10.8	6.9
U.S.	15.1	21.2	14.2	9.3

Note: Figures are percentage of people whose income during the past 12 months was below the poverty level; (1) Figures cover the Raleigh, NC Metropolitan Statistical Area—see Appendix B for areas included
Source: U.S. Census Bureau, 2012-2016 American Community Survey 5-Year Estimates

EMPLOYMENT

Labor Force and Employment

Area	Civilian Labor Force			Workers Employed		
	Dec. 2016	Dec. 2017	% Chg.	Dec. 2016	Dec. 2017	% Chg.
City	16,639	17,065	2.6	16,025	16,493	2.9
MSA[1]	679,166	696,216	2.5	650,915	669,860	2.9
U.S.	158,968,000	159,880,000	0.6	151,798,000	153,602,000	1.2

Note: Data is not seasonally adjusted and covers workers 16 years of age and older; (1) Figures cover the Raleigh, NC Metropolitan Statistical Area—see Appendix B for areas included
Source: Bureau of Labor Statistics, Local Area Unemployment Statistics

Unemployment Rate

Area	2017 Jan.	Feb.	Mar.	Apr.	May	Jun.	Jul.	Aug.	Sep.	Oct.	Nov.	Dec.
City	3.9	3.9	3.7	3.4	3.5	3.5	3.6	3.8	3.3	3.3	3.4	3.4
MSA[1]	4.5	4.3	4.0	3.6	3.8	4.0	4.2	4.3	3.8	3.7	3.9	3.8
U.S.	5.1	4.9	4.6	4.1	4.1	4.5	4.6	4.5	4.1	3.9	3.9	3.9

Note: Data is not seasonally adjusted and covers workers 16 years of age and older; (1) Figures cover the Raleigh, NC Metropolitan Statistical Area—see Appendix B for areas included
Source: Bureau of Labor Statistics, Local Area Unemployment Statistics

Average Wages

Occupation	$/Hr.	Occupation	$/Hr.
Accountants and Auditors	34.70	Maids and Housekeeping Cleaners	10.50
Automotive Mechanics	21.30	Maintenance and Repair Workers	20.20
Bookkeepers	19.90	Marketing Managers	73.10
Carpenters	19.00	Nuclear Medicine Technologists	33.40
Cashiers	9.80	Nurses, Licensed Practical	21.60
Clerks, General Office	15.50	Nurses, Registered	30.80
Clerks, Receptionists/Information	13.90	Nursing Assistants	12.00
Clerks, Shipping/Receiving	15.10	Packers and Packagers, Hand	12.10
Computer Programmers	47.20	Physical Therapists	41.10
Computer Systems Analysts	44.70	Postal Service Mail Carriers	24.10
Computer User Support Specialists	28.10	Real Estate Brokers	28.10
Cooks, Restaurant	12.00	Retail Salespersons	12.40
Dentists	114.20	Sales Reps., Exc. Tech./Scientific	34.20
Electrical Engineers	53.50	Sales Reps., Tech./Scientific	49.10
Electricians	19.80	Secretaries, Exc. Legal/Med./Exec.	17.60
Financial Managers	67.20	Security Guards	13.20
First-Line Supervisors/Managers, Sales	21.20	Surgeons	n/a
Food Preparation Workers	10.80	Teacher Assistants*	11.40
General and Operations Managers	67.90	Teachers, Elementary School*	23.40
Hairdressers/Cosmetologists	15.60	Teachers, Secondary School*	22.60
Internists, General	n/a	Telemarketers	12.80
Janitors and Cleaners	11.30	Truck Drivers, Heavy/Tractor-Trailer	22.00
Landscaping/Groundskeeping Workers	14.50	Truck Drivers, Light/Delivery Svcs.	16.20
Lawyers	70.10	Waiters and Waitresses	11.50

Note: Wage data covers the Raleigh, NC Metropolitan Statistical Area—see Appendix B for areas included; (*) Hourly wages for elementary/secondary school teachers and teacher assistants were calculated by the editors from annual wage data based on a 40 hour work week; n/a not available.
Source: Bureau of Labor Statistics, Metro Area Occupational Employment & Wage Estimates, May 2017

Employment by Occupation

Occupation Classification	City (%)	MSA[1] (%)	U.S. (%)
Management, Business, Science, and Arts	55.3	47.0	37.0
Natural Resources, Construction, and Maintenance	4.0	7.2	8.9
Production, Transportation, and Material Moving	7.2	7.6	12.2
Sales and Office	23.8	23.8	23.8
Service	9.7	14.5	18.1

Note: Figures cover employed civilians 16 years of age and older; (1) Figures cover the Raleigh, NC Metropolitan Statistical Area—see Appendix B for areas included
Source: U.S. Census Bureau, 2012-2016 American Community Survey 5-Year Estimates

Employment by Industry

Sector	MSA[1] Number of Employees	MSA[1] Percent of Total	U.S. Percent of Total
Construction, Mining, and Logging	38,100	6.1	5.2
Education and Health Services	75,400	12.0	15.9
Financial Activities	31,900	5.1	5.7
Government	98,600	15.8	15.3
Information	22,400	3.6	1.9
Leisure and Hospitality	69,500	11.1	10.7
Manufacturing	35,100	5.6	8.5
Other Services	23,700	3.8	3.9
Professional and Business Services	117,900	18.8	14.0
Retail Trade	71,900	11.5	11.0
Transportation, Warehousing, and Utilities	13,800	2.2	4.1
Wholesale Trade	27,600	4.4	4.0

Note: Figures are non-farm employment as of December 2017. Figures are not seasonally adjusted and include workers 16 years of age and older; (1) Figures cover the Raleigh, NC Metropolitan Statistical Area—see Appendix B for areas included

Source: Bureau of Labor Statistics, Current Employment Statistics, Employment, Hours, and Earnings

Occupations with Greatest Projected Employment Growth: 2017 – 2019

Occupation[1]	2017 Employment	2019 Projected Employment	Numeric Employment Change	Percent Employment Change
Combined Food Preparation and Serving Workers, Including Fast Food	150,940	161,640	10,700	7.1
Retail Salespersons	141,960	146,580	4,620	3.3
Waiters and Waitresses	78,300	82,440	4,140	5.3
Customer Service Representatives	98,260	102,060	3,800	3.9
Registered Nurses	99,040	102,730	3,690	3.7
Cashiers	112,380	115,690	3,310	3.0
Laborers and Freight, Stock, and Material Movers, Hand	86,000	89,280	3,280	3.8
Cooks, Restaurant	41,650	44,300	2,650	6.4
Home Health Aides	40,030	42,550	2,520	6.3
General and Operations Managers	55,710	58,180	2,470	4.4

Note: Projections cover North Carolina; (1) Sorted by numeric employment change

Source: www.projectionscentral.com, State Occupational Projections, 2017–2019 Short-Term Projections

Fastest Growing Occupations: 2017 – 2019

Occupation[1]	2017 Employment	2019 Projected Employment	Numeric Employment Change	Percent Employment Change
Solar Photovoltaic Installers	480	550	70	13.5
Helpers—Pipelayers, Plumbers, Pipefitters, and Steamfitters	3,340	3,670	330	9.9
Statisticians	1,220	1,340	120	9.8
Insurance Claims and Policy Processing Clerks	5,090	5,580	490	9.7
Insurance Sales Agents	12,990	14,230	1,240	9.5
Software Developers, Applications	26,360	28,620	2,260	8.6
Helpers—Brickmasons, Blockmasons, Stonemasons, and Tile and Marble Setters	1,060	1,150	90	8.5
Structural Iron and Steel Workers	1,560	1,690	130	8.5
Helpers—Carpenters	1,280	1,390	110	8.4
Plumbers, Pipefitters, and Steamfitters	11,560	12,520	960	8.3

Note: Projections cover North Carolina; (1) Sorted by percent employment change and excludes occupations with numeric employment change less than 50

Source: www.projectionscentral.com, State Occupational Projections, 2017–2019 Short-Term Projections

TAXES

State Corporate Income Tax Rates

State	Tax Rate (%)	Income Brackets ($)	Num. of Brackets	Financial Institution Tax Rate (%)[a]	Federal Income Tax Ded.
North Carolina	3.0	Flat rate	1	3.0	No

Note: Tax rates as of January 1, 2018; (a) Rates listed are the corporate income tax rate applied to financial institutions or excise taxes based on income. Some states have other taxes based upon the value of deposits or shares.
Source: Federation of Tax Administrators, Range of State Corporate Income Tax Rates, January 1, 2018

State Individual Income Tax Rates

State	Tax Rate (%)	Income Brackets ($)	Num. of Brackets	Personal Exempt. ($)[1]		Fed. Inc. Tax Ded.
				Single	Dependents	
North Carolina	5.499	Flat rate	1	None	None	No

Note: Tax rates as of January 1, 2018; Local- and county-level taxes are not included; n/a not applicable; (1) Married joint filers generally receive double the single exemption
Source: Federation of Tax Administrators, State Individual Income Tax Rates, January 1, 2018

Various State Sales and Excise Tax Rates

State	State Sales Tax (%)	Gasoline[1] (¢/gal.)	Cigarette[2] ($/pack)	Spirits[3] ($/gal.)	Wine[4] ($/gal.)	Beer[5] ($/gal.)	Recreational Marijuana (%)
North Carolina	4.75	35.35	0.45	14.63 (g)	1.00 (l)	0.62 (q)	Not legal

Note: All tax rates as of January 1, 2018; (1) The American Petroleum Institute has developed a methodology for determining the average tax rate on a gallon of fuel. Rates may include any of the following: excise taxes, environmental fees, storage tank fees, other fees or taxes, general sales tax, and local taxes. In states where gasoline is subject to the general sales tax, or where the fuel tax is based on the average sale price, the average rate determined by API is sensitive to changes in the price of gasoline. States that fully or partially apply general sales taxes to gasoline: CA, CO, GA, IL, IN, MI, NY; (2) The federal excise tax of $1.0066 per pack and local taxes are not included; (3) Rates are those applicable to off-premise sales of 40% alcohol by volume (a.b.v.) distilled spirits in 750ml containers. Local excise taxes are excluded; (4) Rates are those applicable to off-premise sales of 11% a.b.v. non-carbonated wine in 750ml containers; (5) Rates are those applicable to off-premise sales of 4.7% a.b.v. beer in 12 ounce containers; (g) Control states, where the government controls all sales. Products can be subject to ad valorem mark-up as well as excise taxes; (l) Different rates also applicable to alcohol content, place of production, size of container, place purchased (on- or off-premise or on board airlines) or type of wine (carbonated, vermouth, etc.); (q) Different rates also applicable according to alcohol content, place of production, size of container, or place purchased (on- or off-premise or onboard airlines).
Source: Tax Foundation, 2018 Facts & Figures: How Does Your State Compare?

State Business Tax Climate Index Rankings

State	Overall Rank	Corporate Tax Rank	Individual Income Tax Rank	Sales Tax Rank	Unemployment Insurance Tax Rank	Property Tax Rank
North Carolina	11	3	13	20	6	32

Note: The index is a measure of how each state's tax laws affect economic performance. The lower the rank, the more favorable a state's tax system is for business. States without a given tax are given a ranking of 1. The scores/rankings for the District of Columbia do not affect other states. The 2018 index represents the tax climate as of July 1, 2017.
Source: Tax Foundation, State Business Tax Climate Index 2018

TRANSPORTATION

Means of Transportation to Work

Area	Car/Truck/Van		Public Transportation			Bicycle	Walked	Other Means	Worked at Home
	Drove Alone	Car-pooled	Bus	Subway	Railroad				
City	80.4	7.1	0.5	0.0	0.0	0.0	0.5	1.6	9.9
MSA[1]	80.2	9.1	0.9	0.0	0.0	0.3	1.2	1.0	7.2
U.S.	76.4	9.3	2.6	1.9	0.6	0.6	2.8	1.3	4.6

Note: Figures are percentages and cover workers 16 years of age and older; (1) Figures cover the Raleigh, NC Metropolitan Statistical Area—see Appendix B for areas included
Source: U.S. Census Bureau, 2012-2016 American Community Survey 5-Year Estimates

Travel Time to Work

Area	Less Than 10 Minutes	10 to 19 Minutes	20 to 29 Minutes	30 to 44 Minutes	45 to 59 Minutes	60 to 89 Minutes	90 Minutes or More
City	6.7	18.0	27.1	33.9	9.5	3.4	1.4
MSA[1]	9.9	28.5	25.1	23.2	7.7	3.8	1.7
U.S.	12.9	29.2	20.9	20.4	8.0	6.0	2.7

Note: Note: Figures are percentages and include workers 16 years old and over; (1) Figures cover the Raleigh, NC Metropolitan Statistical Area—see Appendix B for areas included
Source: U.S. Census Bureau, 2012-2016 American Community Survey 5-Year Estimates

Freeway Travel Time Index

Area	1985	1990	1995	2000	2005	2010	2014
Urban Area Rank[1,2]	54	46	59	65	61	57	54
Urban Area Index[1]	1.06	1.10	1.12	1.14	1.16	1.16	1.17
Average Index[3]	1.09	1.11	1.14	1.17	1.20	1.19	1.20

Note: Freeway Travel Time Index—the ratio of travel time in the peak period to the travel time at free-flow conditions. For example, a value of 1.30 indicates a 20-minute free-flow trip takes 26 minutes in the peak (20 minutes x 1.30 = 26 minutes); (1) Covers the Raleigh NC urban area; (2) Rank is based on 101 urban areas (#1 = highest travel time index); (3) Average of 101 urban areas
Source: Texas Transportation Institute, 2015 Urban Mobility Scorecard, August 2015

Freeway Commuter Stress Index

Area	1985	1990	1995	2000	2005	2010	2014
Urban Area Rank[1,2]	58	51	61	63	58	58	61
Urban Area Index[1]	1.08	1.12	1.14	1.17	1.19	1.19	1.19
Average Index[3]	1.13	1.16	1.19	1.22	1.25	1.24	1.25

Note: The Freeway Commuter Stress Index is the same as the Freeway Travel Time Index (see table above) except that it includes only the travel in the peak directions during the peak periods; the TTI includes travel in all directions during the peak period. Thus, the CSI is more indicative of the work trip experienced by each commuter on a daily basis; (1) Covers the Raleigh NC urban area; (2) Rank is based on 101 urban areas (#1 = highest travel time index); (3) Average of 101 urban areas
Source: Texas Transportation Institute, 2015 Urban Mobility Scorecard, August 2015

Living Environment

COST OF LIVING

Cost of Living Index

Composite Index	Groceries	Housing	Utilities	Trans-portation	Health Care	Misc. Goods/ Services
96.2	105.7	83.4	97.5	99.7	100.5	101.1

Note: The Cost of Living Index measures regional differences in the cost of consumer goods and services, excluding taxes and non-consumer expenditures, for professional and managerial households in the top income quintile. It is based on more than 50,000 prices covering almost 60 different items for which prices are collected three times a year by chambers of commerce, economic development organizations or university applied economic centers in each participating urban area. The numbers shown should be read as a percentage above or below the national average of 100. For example, a value of 115.4 in the groceries column indicates that grocery prices are 15.4% higher than the national average. Small differences in the index numbers should not be interpreted as significant; Figures cover the Raleigh NC urban area.
Source: The Council for Community and Economic Research, ACCRA Cost of Living Index, 2017

Grocery Prices

Area[1]	T-Bone Steak ($/pound)	Frying Chicken ($/pound)	Whole Milk ($/half gal.)	Eggs ($/dozen)	Orange Juice ($/64 oz.)	Coffee ($/11.5 oz.)
City[2]	12.34	1.69	2.00	2.92	3.57	4.42
Avg.	11.29	1.40	2.02	1.47	3.55	4.37
Min.	7.71	0.93	1.04	0.70	2.86	3.24
Max.	15.83	2.39	4.03	3.92	6.29	8.16

*Note: (1) Values for the local area are compared with the average, minimum and maximum values for all 294 areas in the Cost of Living Index; (2) Figures cover the Raleigh NC urban area; **T-Bone Steak** (price per pound); **Frying Chicken** (price per pound, whole fryer); **Whole Milk** (half gallon carton); **Eggs** (price per dozen, Grade A, large); **Orange Juice** (64 oz. Tropicana or Florida Natural); **Coffee** (11.5 oz. can, vacuum-packed, Maxwell House, Hills Bros, or Folgers).*
Source: The Council for Community and Economic Research, ACCRA Cost of Living Index, 2017

Housing and Utility Costs

Area[1]	New Home Price ($)	Apartment Rent ($/month)	All Electric ($/month)	Part Electric ($/month)	Other Energy ($/month)	Telephone ($/month)
City[2]	261,414	1,013	-	81.95	61.55	31.92
Avg.	335,956	1,047	175.01	97.34	67.93	28.71
Min.	187,788	491	109.48	49.33	35.44	12.39
Max.	1,739,087	4,559	432.62	227.09	353.33	44.61

*Note: (1) Values for the local area are compared with the average, minimum and maximum values for all 294 areas in the Cost of Living Index; (2) Figures cover the Raleigh NC urban area; **New Home Price** (2,400 sf living area, 8,000 sf lot, in urban area with full utilities); **Apartment Rent** (950 sf 2 bedroom/1.5 or 2 bath, unfurnished, excluding all utilities except water); **All Electric** (average monthly cost for an all-electric home); **Part Electric** (average monthly cost for a part-electric home); **Other Energy** (average monthly cost for natural gas, fuel oil, coal, wood, and any other forms of energy except electricity); **Telephone** (price includes basic monthly rate for a private residential line plus additional local usage charges incurred by a family of four).*
Source: The Council for Community and Economic Research, ACCRA Cost of Living Index, 2017

Health Care, Transportation, and Other Costs

Area[1]	Doctor ($/visit)	Dentist ($/visit)	Optometrist ($/visit)	Gasoline ($/gallon)	Beauty Salon ($/visit)	Men's Shirt ($)
City[2]	99.19	98.93	103.10	2.26	51.86	23.44
Avg.	108.00	92.54	101.93	2.25	37.58	30.92
Min.	30.39	60.00	49.75	1.82	16.11	11.20
Max.	193.50	161.94	229.28	3.16	77.35	59.13

*Note: (1) Values for the local area are compared with the average, minimum and maximum values for all 294 areas in the Cost of Living Index; (2) Figures cover the Raleigh NC urban area; **Doctor** (general practitioners routine exam of an established patient); **Dentist** (adult teeth cleaning and periodic oral examination); **Optometrist** (full vision eye exam for established adult patient); **Gasoline** (one gallon regular unleaded, national brand, including all taxes, cash price at self-service pump if available); **Beauty Salon** (woman's shampoo, trim, and blow-dry); **Men's Shirt** (cotton/polyester dress shirt, pinpoint weave, long sleeves).*
Source: The Council for Community and Economic Research, ACCRA Cost of Living Index, 2017

HOUSING

House Price Index (HPI)

Area	National Ranking[2]	Quarterly Change (%)	One-Year Change (%)	Five-Year Change (%)
MSA[1]	95	0.62	7.09	29.98
U.S.[3]	–	1.61	6.68	34.71

Note: The HPI is a weighted repeat sales index. It measures average price changes in repeat sales or refinancings on the same properties. This information is obtained by reviewing repeat mortgage transactions on single-family properties whose mortgages have been purchased or securitized by Fannie Mae or Freddie Mac in January 1975; (1) Figures cover the Raleigh, NC Metropolitan Statistical Area—see Appendix B for areas included; (2) Rankings are based on annual percentage change for all metro areas containing at least 15,000 transactions over the last 10 years and ranges from 1 to 253; (3) figures based on a weighted average of Census Division estimates using a seasonally adjusted, purchase-only index; all figures are for the period ending December 31, 2017

Source: Federal Housing Finance Agency, House Price Index, February 28, 2018

Median Single-Family Home Prices

Area	2015	2016	2017p	Percent Change 2016 to 2017
MSA[1]	238.2	247.9	266.8	7.6
U.S. Average	223.9	235.5	248.8	5.6

Note: Figures are median sales prices of existing single-family homes in thousands of dollars; (p) preliminary; (1) Figures cover the Raleigh, NC Metropolitan Statistical Area—see Appendix B for areas included

Source: National Association of Realtors, Median Sales Price of Existing Single-Family Homes for Metropolitan Areas, 4th Quarter 2017

Qualifying Income Based on Median Sales Price of Existing Single-Family Homes

Area	With 5% Down ($)	With 10% Down ($)	With 20% Down ($)
MSA[1]	n/a	n/a	n/a
U.S. Average	55,585	52,659	46,808

Note: Figures are preliminary; Qualifying income is based on a mortgage rate of 4.17%. Monthly principal and interest payment is limited to 25% of income; n/a not available; (1) Figures cover the Raleigh, NC Metropolitan Statistical Area—see Appendix B for areas included

Source: National Association of Realtors, Qualifying Income Based on Median Sales Price of Existing Single-Family Homes for Metropolitan Areas, 4th Quarter 2017

Median Apartment Condo-Coop Home Prices

Area	2015	2016	2017p	Percent Change 2016 to 2017
MSA[1]	n/a	n/a	n/a	n/a
U.S. Average	210.7	220.7	234.3	6.2

Note: Figures are median sales prices of existing apartment condo-coop homes in thousands of dollars; (p) preliminary; n/a not available; (1) Figures cover the Raleigh, NC Metropolitan Statistical Area—see Appendix B for areas included

Source: National Association of Realtors, Median Sales Price of Existing Apartment Condo-Coop Homes for Metropolitan Areas, 4th Quarter 2017

Home Value Distribution

Area	Under $50,000	$50,000 -$99,999	$100,000 -$149,999	$150,000 -$199,999	$200,000 -$299,999	$300,000 -$499,999	$500,000 -$999,999	$1,000,000 or more
City	1.5	2.1	6.0	17.0	36.6	31.0	5.4	0.4
MSA[1]	4.5	6.5	16.2	18.2	24.8	21.9	6.9	1.1
U.S.	8.8	14.8	15.3	14.9	18.4	16.4	9.0	2.5

Note: Figures are percentages and cover owner-occupied housing units; (1) Figures cover the Raleigh, NC Metropolitan Statistical Area—see Appendix B for areas included

Source: U.S. Census Bureau, 2012-2016 American Community Survey 5-Year Estimates

Homeownership Rate

Area	2009 (%)	2010 (%)	2011 (%)	2012 (%)	2013 (%)	2014 (%)	2015 (%)	2016 (%)	2017 (%)
MSA[1]	65.7	65.9	66.7	67.7	65.5	65.5	67.4	65.9	68.2
U.S.	67.4	66.9	66.1	65.4	65.1	64.5	63.7	63.4	63.9

Note: (1) Figures cover the Raleigh, NC Metropolitan Statistical Area—see Appendix B for areas included

Source: U.S. Census Bureau, Housing Vacancies and Homeownership Annual Statistics: 2009-2017

Year Housing Structure Built

Area	2010 or Later	2000 -2009	1990 -1999	1980 -1989	1970 -1979	1960 -1969	1950 -1959	1940 -1949	Before 1940	Median Year
City	10.3	52.5	28.6	4.5	1.6	0.7	0.8	0.7	0.3	2002
MSA[1]	5.6	28.6	24.7	16.2	10.1	6.2	4.1	1.7	2.8	1994
U.S.	2.3	14.7	14.0	13.7	15.6	10.9	10.6	5.2	13.0	1977

Note: Figures are percentages except for Median Year; Note: (1) Figures cover the Raleigh, NC Metropolitan Statistical Area—see Appendix B for areas included
Source: U.S. Census Bureau, 2012-2016 American Community Survey 5-Year Estimates

Gross Monthly Rent

Area	Under $500	$500 -$999	$1,000 -$1,499	$1,500 -$1,999	$2,000 -$2,499	$2,500 -$2,999	$3,000 and up	Median ($)
City	13.5	20.4	36.1	20.0	6.9	3.1	0.0	1,231
MSA[1]	5.9	49.1	34.2	7.8	1.8	0.5	0.6	963
U.S.	11.3	43.3	27.7	10.7	4.0	1.6	1.5	949

Note: Figures are percentages except for Median; Gross rent is the contract rent plus the estimated average monthly cost of utilities (electricity, gas, and water and sewer) and fuels (oil, coal, kerosene, wood, etc.) if these are paid by the renter (or paid for the renter by someone else); (1) Figures cover the Raleigh, NC Metropolitan Statistical Area—see Appendix B for areas included
Source: U.S. Census Bureau, 2012-2016 American Community Survey 5-Year Estimates

HEALTH

Health Risk Factors

Category	MSA[1] (%)	U.S. (%)
Adults aged 18–64 who have any kind of health care coverage	84.0	87.7
Adults who reported being in good or excellent health	86.9	83.6
Adults who are current smokers	12.5	17.1
Adults who currently use E-cigarettes	3.2	4.7
Adults who currently use chewing tobacco, snuff, or snus	1.0	4.0
Adults who are heavy drinkers[2]	7.4	6.5
Adults who are binge drinkers[3]	15.8	16.9
Adults who are overweight (BMI 25.0 - 29.9)	33.9	35.3
Adults who are obese (BMI 30.0 - 99.8)	29.3	29.9
Adults who participated in any physical activities in the past month	84.2	76.9
Adults who always or nearly always wears a seat belt	98.4	94.3

Note: (1) Figures cover the Raleigh, NC Metropolitan Statistical Area—see Appendix B for areas included; (2) Heavy drinkers are classified as adult men having more than 14 drinks per week and adult women having more than 7 drinks per week; (3) Binge drinkers are classified as males having five or more drinks on one occasion or females having four or more drinks on one occasion
Source: Centers for Disease Control and Prevention, Behaviorial Risk Factor Surveillance System, SMART: Selected Metropolitan Area Risk Trends, 2016

Health Screening Rates

Category	MSA[1] (%)	U.S. (%)
Adults 50-75 who have had a blood stool test within the past year	7.3	8.0
Adults 50-75 who have had a colonoscopy in the past 10 years	72.6	63.5
Adults aged 65+ who have had flu shot within the past year	75.7	58.6
Adults aged 65+ who have ever had a pneumonia vaccination	76.1	73.4
Adults who have ever been tested for HIV	41.6	35.6
Women aged 21-65 who have had a pap test in the past three years	83.7	79.8
Men aged 40+ who have had a PSA test within the past two years	42.0	39.5
Women aged 40+ who have had a mammogram within the past two years	78.3	72.5

Note: n/a not available; (1) Figures cover the Raleigh, NC Metropolitan Statistical Area—see Appendix B for areas included; Source: Centers for Disease Control and Prevention, Behaviorial Risk Factor Surveillance System, SMART: Selected Metropolitan Area Risk Trends, 2016

Chronic Health Conditions

Category	MSA[1] (%)	U.S. (%)
Adults who have ever been told they had a heart attack	2.5	4.4
Adults who have ever been told they have angina or coronary heart disease	3.8	4.1
Adults who have ever been told they had a stroke	n/a	3.1
Adults who have been told they currently have asthma	9.4	9.3
Adults who have ever been told they have arthritis	20.9	25.8
Adults who have ever been told they have diabetes[2]	7.2	10.5
Adults who have ever been told they had skin cancer	8.2	5.9
Adults who have ever been told they had any other types of cancer	4.8	6.7
Adults who have ever been told they have COPD	4.2	6.3
Adults who have ever been told they have kidney disease	n/a	2.8
Adults who have ever been told they have a form of depression	17.4	17.4

Note: n/a not available; (1) Figures cover the Raleigh, NC Metropolitan Statistical Area—see Appendix B for areas included; (2) Figures do not include pregnancy-related, borderline, or pre-diabetes
Source: Centers for Disease Control and Prevention, Behaviorial Risk Factor Surveillance System, SMART: Selected Metropolitan Area Risk Trends, 2016

Mortality Rates for the Top 10 Causes of Death in the U.S.

ICD-10[a] Sub-Chapter	ICD-10[a] Code	Age-Adjusted Mortality Rate[1] per 100,000 population	
		County[2]	U.S.
Malignant neoplasms	C00-C97	142.5	158.5
Ischaemic heart diseases	I20-I25	63.0	96.8
Other forms of heart disease	I30-I51	43.3	52.4
Chronic lower respiratory diseases	J40-J47	27.8	40.9
Cerebrovascular diseases	I60-I69	37.7	37.2
Organic, including symptomatic, mental disorders	F01-F09	55.4	33.3
Other degenerative diseases of the nervous system	G30-G31	27.6	32.1
Other external causes of accidental injury	W00-X59	25.2	31.2
Diabetes mellitus	E10-E14	17.9	21.1
Hypertensive diseases	I10-I15	17.6	20.8

Note: (a) ICD-10 = International Classification of Diseases 10th Revision; (1) Mortality rates are a three year average covering 2014-2016; (2) Figures cover Wake County.
Source: Centers for Disease Control and Prevention, National Center for Health Statistics. Underlying Cause of Death 1999-2016 on CDC WONDER Online Database, released December 2017

Mortality Rates for Selected Causes of Death

ICD-10[a] Sub-Chapter	ICD-10[a] Code	Age-Adjusted Mortality Rate[1] per 100,000 population	
		County[2]	U.S.
Assault	X85-Y09	2.9	5.6
Diseases of the liver	K70-K76	8.7	14.0
Human immunodeficiency virus (HIV) disease	B20-B24	1.4	1.9
Influenza and pneumonia	J09-J18	10.1	14.6
Intentional self-harm	X60-X84	9.3	13.2
Malnutrition	E40-E46	1.4	1.3
Obesity and other hyperalimentation	E65-E68	1.3	2.1
Renal failure	N17-N19	12.1	13.0
Transport accidents	V01-V99	8.4	12.0
Viral hepatitis	B15-B19	1.3	1.9

Note: (a) ICD-10 = International Classification of Diseases 10th Revision; (1) Mortality rates are a three year average covering 2014-2016; (2) Figures cover Wake County; Data are Suppressed when the data meet the criteria for confidentiality constraints; Mortality rates are flagged as Unreliable when the rate would be calculated with a numerator of 20 or less.
Source: Centers for Disease Control and Prevention, National Center for Health Statistics. Underlying Cause of Death 1999-2016 on CDC WONDER Online Database, released December 2017

Health Insurance Coverage

Area	With Health Insurance	With Private Health Insurance	With Public Health Insurance	Without Health Insurance	Population Under Age 18 Without Health Insurance
City	95.5	89.1	12.9	4.5	2.4
MSA[1]	88.8	74.4	23.4	11.2	5.2
U.S.	88.3	66.7	33.0	11.7	5.9

Note: Figures are percentages that cover the civilian noninstitutionalized population; (1) Figures cover the Raleigh, NC Metropolitan Statistical Area—see Appendix B for areas included
Source: U.S. Census Bureau, 2012-2016 American Community Survey 5-Year Estimates

Number of Medical Professionals

Area	MDs[3]	DOs[3,4]	Dentists	Podiatrists	Chiropractors	Optometrists
County[1] (number)	2,798	100	715	34	256	158
County[1] (rate[2])	273.3	9.8	68.2	3.2	24.4	15.1
U.S. (rate[2])	276.5	22.3	67.3	6.0	26.7	15.9

Note: Data as of 2016 unless noted; (1) Data covers Wake County; (2) Rate per 100,000 population; (3) Data as of 2015 and includes all active, non-federal physicians; (4) Doctor of Osteopathic Medicine
Source: U.S. Department of Health and Human Services, Health Resources and Services Administration, Bureau of Health Professions, Area Resource File (ARF) 2016-2017

EDUCATION

Public School District Statistics

District Name	Schls	Pupils	Pupil/ Teacher Ratio	Minority Pupils[1] (%)	Free Lunch Eligible[2] (%)	IEP[3] (%)
Southern Wake Academy	1	370	11.0	12.7	3.8	26.2
Wake County Schools	181	157,839	15.8	52.5	30.3	13.2

Note: Table includes school districts with 100 or more students; (1) Percentage of students that are not non-Hispanic white; (2) Percentage of students that are eligible for the free lunch program; (3) Percentage of students that have an Individualized Education Program.
Source: U.S. Department of Education, National Center for Education Statistics, Common Core of Data, Local Education Agency (School District) Universe Survey: School Year 2015-2016; U.S. Department of Education, National Center for Education Statistics, Common Core of Data, Public Elementary/Secondary School Universe Survey: School Year 2015-2016

Highest Level of Education

Area	Less than H.S.	H.S. Diploma	Some College, No Deg.	Associate Degree	Bachelor's Degree	Master's Degree	Prof. School Degree	Doctorate Degree
City	4.3	12.8	17.2	9.0	38.6	14.7	1.2	2.1
MSA[1]	9.2	19.0	18.7	8.8	28.6	11.5	2.1	2.1
U.S.	13.0	27.5	21.0	8.2	18.8	8.2	2.0	1.3

Note: Figures cover persons age 25 and over; (1) Figures cover the Raleigh, NC Metropolitan Statistical Area—see Appendix B for areas included
Source: U.S. Census Bureau, 2012-2016 American Community Survey 5-Year Estimates

Educational Attainment by Race

Area	High School Graduate or Higher (%)					Bachelor's Degree or Higher (%)				
	Total	White	Black	Asian	Hisp.[2]	Total	White	Black	Asian	Hisp.[2]
City	95.7	98.4	84.8	95.6	77.0	56.7	60.6	35.3	66.9	44.5
MSA[1]	90.8	92.9	87.5	91.3	59.1	44.3	47.8	29.0	68.3	19.5
U.S.	87.0	88.9	84.3	86.3	65.7	30.3	31.6	20.0	52.1	14.7

Note: Figures shown cover persons 25 years old and over; (1) Figures cover the Raleigh, NC Metropolitan Statistical Area—see Appendix B for areas included; (2) People of Hispanic origin can be of any race
Source: U.S. Census Bureau, 2012-2016 American Community Survey 5-Year Estimates

School Enrollment by Grade and Control

Area	Preschool (%)		Kindergarten (%)		Grades 1 - 4 (%)		Grades 5 - 8 (%)		Grades 9 - 12 (%)	
	Public	Private	Public	Private	Public	Private	Public	Private	Public	Private
City	15.1	84.9	84.2	15.8	92.2	7.8	87.4	12.6	94.9	5.1
MSA[1]	40.5	59.5	87.6	12.4	89.6	10.4	89.5	10.5	89.8	10.2
U.S.	58.4	41.6	87.7	12.3	89.8	10.2	89.7	10.3	90.4	9.6

Note: Figures shown cover persons 3 years old and over; (1) Figures cover the Raleigh, NC Metropolitan Statistical Area—see Appendix B for areas included
Source: U.S. Census Bureau, 2012-2016 American Community Survey 5-Year Estimates

Average Salaries of Public School Classroom Teachers

Area	2015		2016		Change from 2015 to 2016	
	Dollars	Rank[1]	Dollars	Rank[1]	Percent	Rank[2]
North Carolina	47,792	40	47,941	41	0.3	44
U.S. Average	57,611	–	58,353	–	1.3	–

Note: (1) Rank ranges from 1 to 51 where 1 indicates highest salary; (2) Rank ranges from 1 to 51 where 1 indicates highest percent change.
Source: National Education Association, Rankings & Estimates: Rankings of the States 2016 and Estimates of School Statistics 2017

Higher Education

Four-Year Colleges			Two-Year Colleges			Medical Schools[1]	Law Schools[2]	Voc/ Tech[3]
Public	Private Non-profit	Private For-profit	Public	Private Non-profit	Private For-profit			
0	0	0	0	0	0	0	0	0

Note: Figures cover institutions located within the city limits and include main campuses only; (1) includes schools accredited by the Liaison Committee on Medical Education and the American Osteopathic Association's Commission on Osteopathic College Accreditation; (2) includes ABA-accredited schools, schools with provisional ABA accreditation, and state accredited schools; (3) includes all schools with programs that are less than 2 years.
Source: National Center for Education Statistics, Integrated Postsecondary Education System (IPEDS), 2016-17; Wikipedia, List of Medical Schools in the United States, accessed April 2, 2018; Wikipedia, List of Law Schools in the United States, accessed April 2, 2018

According to *U.S. News & World Report,* the Raleigh, NC metro area is home to one of the best national universities in the U.S.: **North Carolina State University—Raleigh** (#81 tie). The indicators used to capture academic quality fall into a number of categories: assessment by administrators at peer institutions; retention of students; faculty resources; student selectivity; financial resources; alumni giving; high school counselor ratings of colleges; and graduation rate. *U.S. News & World Report, "America's Best Colleges 2018"*

According to *U.S. News & World Report,* the Raleigh, NC metro area is home to one of the best liberal arts colleges in the U.S.: **Meredith College** (#163 tie). The indicators used to capture academic quality fall into a number of categories: assessment by administrators at peer institutions; retention of students; faculty resources; student selectivity; financial resources; alumni giving; high school counselor ratings of colleges; and graduation rate. *U.S. News & World Report, "America's Best Colleges 2018"*

PRESIDENTIAL ELECTION

2016 Presidential Election Results

Area	Clinton	Trump	Johnson	Stein	Other
Wake County	57.4	37.2	3.7	0.3	1.4
U.S.	48.0	45.9	3.3	1.1	1.7

Note: Results are percentages and may not add to 100% due to rounding
Source: Dave Leip's Atlas of U.S. Presidential Elections

EMPLOYERS

Major Employers

Company Name	Industry
Cisco Systems	Software
City of Raleigh	Government
Duke Energy	Electric services
Fidelity Investments	Financial services
GlaxoSmithKline	Healthcare
IBM Corporation	Technology
Lenovo	Technology
N.C. DHHS	Government
North Carolina State University	Education
Rex Healthcare	Healthcare
RTI International	Research & development
SAS Institute	Data management
State of North Carolina	Government
Wake County Government	Government
Wake County Public School System	Education
Wake Technical Community College	Education
WakeMed Health & Hospitals	Education
Wells Fargo	Financial services

Note: Companies shown are located within the Raleigh, NC Metropolitan Statistical Area.
Source: Hoovers.com; Wikipedia

PUBLIC SAFETY

Crime Rate

Area	All Crimes	Violent Crimes				Property Crimes		
		Murder	Rape[3]	Robbery	Aggrav. Assault	Burglary	Larceny -Theft	Motor Vehicle Theft
City	925.1	0.0	3.0	6.1	18.3	136.9	745.5	15.2
Metro[1]	n/a	n/a	n/a	n/a	n/a	n/a	n/a	n/a
U.S.	2,837.0	5.3	29.6	102.8	248.5	468.9	1,745.0	236.9

Note: Figures are crimes per 100,000 population; (1) Figures cover the Raleigh, NC Metropolitan Statistical Area—see Appendix B for areas included; n/a not available; (3) The city and U.S. figures shown were reported using the legacy Uniform Crime Reporting (UCR) definition of rape. The metro area figures shown are an aggregate total of the data submitted using both the revised and legacy UCR definitions.
Source: FBI Uniform Crime Reports, 2016

Hate Crimes

Area	Number of Quarters Reported	Number of Incidents per Bias Motivation					
		Race/Ethnicity/ Ancestry	Religion	Sexual Orientation	Disability	Gender	Gender Identity
City	4	0	0	0	0	0	0
U.S.	4	3,489	1,273	1,076	70	31	124

Source: Federal Bureau of Investigation, Hate Crime Statistics 2016

Identity Theft Consumer Reports

Area	Reports	Reports per 100,000 Population	Rank[2]
MSA[1]	1,516	116	65
U.S.	371,061	114	-

Note: (1) Figures cover the Raleigh, NC Metropolitan Statistical Area—see Appendix B for areas included; (2) Rank ranges from 1 to 389 where 1 indicates greatest number of identity theft reports per 100,000 population
Source: Federal Trade Commission, Consumer Sentinel Network Data Book for January–December 2017

Fraud and Other Consumer Reports

Area	Reports	Reports per 100,000 Population	Rank[2]
MSA[1]	6,887	529	86
U.S.	2,304,550	708	-

Note: (1) Figures cover the Raleigh, NC Metropolitan Statistical Area—see Appendix B for areas included; (2) Rank ranges from 1 to 389 where 1 indicates greatest number of fraud and other consumer reports per 100,000 population
Source: Federal Trade Commission, Consumer Sentinel Network Data Book for January–December 2017

SPORTS

Professional Sports Teams

Team Name	League	Year Established
Carolina Hurricanes	National Hockey League (NHL)	1997

Note: Includes teams located in the Raleigh, NC Metropolitan Statistical Area.
Source: Wikipedia, Major Professional Sports Teams of the United States and Canada, April 5, 2018

CLIMATE

Average and Extreme Temperatures

Temperature	Jan	Feb	Mar	Apr	May	Jun	Jul	Aug	Sep	Oct	Nov	Dec	Yr.
Extreme High (°F)	79	84	90	95	97	104	105	105	104	98	88	79	105
Average High (°F)	50	53	61	72	79	86	89	87	81	72	62	53	71
Average Temp. (°F)	40	43	50	59	67	75	78	77	71	60	51	42	60
Average Low (°F)	29	31	38	46	55	63	68	67	60	48	39	32	48
Extreme Low (°F)	-9	5	11	23	29	38	48	46	37	19	11	4	-9

Note: Figures cover the years 1948-1990
Source: National Climatic Data Center, International Station Meteorological Climate Summary, 9/96

Average Precipitation/Snowfall/Humidity

Precip./Humidity	Jan	Feb	Mar	Apr	May	Jun	Jul	Aug	Sep	Oct	Nov	Dec	Yr.
Avg. Precip. (in.)	3.4	3.6	3.6	2.9	3.9	3.6	4.4	4.4	3.2	2.9	3.0	3.1	42.0
Avg. Snowfall (in.)	2	3	1	Tr	0	0	0	0	0	0	Tr	1	8
Avg. Rel. Hum. 7am (%)	79	79	79	80	84	86	88	91	91	90	84	81	84
Avg. Rel. Hum. 4pm (%)	53	49	46	43	51	54	57	59	57	53	51	53	52

Note: Figures cover the years 1948-1990; Tr = Trace amounts (<0.05 in. of rain; <0.5 in. of snow)
Source: National Climatic Data Center, International Station Meteorological Climate Summary, 9/96

Weather Conditions

Temperature			Daytime Sky			Precipitation		
32°F & below	45°F & below	90°F & above	Clear	Partly cloudy	Cloudy	0.01 inch or more precip.	0.1 inch or more snow/ice	Thunder-storms
77	160	39	98	143	124	110	3	42

Note: Figures are average number of days per year and cover the years 1948-1990
Source: National Climatic Data Center, International Station Meteorological Climate Summary, 9/96

HAZARDOUS WASTE

Superfund Sites

The Raleigh, NC metro area is home to three sites on the EPA's Superfund National Priorities List: **Koppers Co., Inc. (Morrisville Plant)** (final); **North Carolina State University (Lot 86, Farm Unit #1)** (final); **Ward Transformer** (final). There are a total of 1,396 Superfund sites with a status of proposed or final on the list in the U.S. *U.S. Environmental Protection Agency, National Priorities List, April 4, 2018*

AIR & WATER QUALITY

Air Quality Trends: Ozone

	1990	1995	2000	2005	2010	2012	2013	2014	2015	2016
MSA[1]	0.093	0.081	0.087	0.082	0.071	0.071	0.061	0.063	0.065	0.069
U.S.	0.087	0.089	0.081	0.079	0.073	0.075	0.069	0.067	0.068	0.069

Note: (1) Data covers the Raleigh, NC Metropolitan Statistical Area—see Appendix B for areas included. The values shown are the composite ozone concentration averages among trend sites based on the highest fourth daily maximum 8-hour concentration in parts per million. These trends are based on sites having an adequate record of monitoring data during the trend period. Data from exceptional events are included.
Source: U.S. Environmental Protection Agency, Air Quality Monitoring Information, "Air Quality Trends by City, 1990-2016"

Air Quality Index

Area	Percent of Days when Air Quality was...[2]					AQI Statistics[2]	
	Good	Moderate	Unhealthy for Sensitive Groups	Unhealthy	Very Unhealthy	Maximum	Median
MSA[1]	66.3	33.7	0.0	0.0	0.0	100	45

Note: (1) Data covers the Raleigh, NC Metropolitan Statistical Area—see Appendix B for areas included; (2) Based on 365 days with AQI data in 2017. Air Quality Index (AQI) is an index for reporting daily air quality. EPA calculates the AQI for five major air pollutants regulated by the Clean Air Act: ground-level ozone, particle pollution (aka particulate matter), carbon monoxide, sulfur dioxide, and nitrogen dioxide. The AQI runs from 0 to 500. The higher the AQI value, the greater the level of air pollution and the greater the health concern. There are six AQI categories: "Good" AQI is between 0 and 50. Air quality is considered satisfactory; "Moderate" AQI is between 51 and 100. Air quality is acceptable; "Unhealthy for Sensitive Groups" When AQI values are between 101 and 150, members of sensitive groups may experience health effects; "Unhealthy" When AQI values are between 151 and 200 everyone may begin to experience health effects; "Very Unhealthy" AQI values between 201 and 300 trigger a health alert; "Hazardous" AQI values over 300 trigger warnings of emergency conditions (not shown).
Source: U.S. Environmental Protection Agency, Air Quality Index Report, 2017

Air Quality Index Pollutants

Area	Percent of Days when AQI Pollutant was...[2]					
	Carbon Monoxide	Nitrogen Dioxide	Ozone	Sulfur Dioxide	Particulate Matter 2.5	Particulate Matter 10
MSA[1]	0.0	0.5	42.7	0.0	56.7	0.0

Note: (1) Data covers the Raleigh, NC Metropolitan Statistical Area—see Appendix B for areas included; (2) Based on 365 days with AQI data in 2017. The Air Quality Index (AQI) is an index for reporting daily air quality. EPA calculates the AQI for five major air pollutants regulated by the Clean Air Act: ground-level ozone, particle pollution (also known as particulate matter), carbon monoxide, sulfur dioxide, and nitrogen dioxide. The AQI runs from 0 to 500. The higher the AQI value, the greater the level of air pollution and the greater the health concern.
Source: U.S. Environmental Protection Agency, Air Quality Index Report, 2017

Maximum Air Pollutant Concentrations: Particulate Matter, Ozone, CO and Lead

	Particulate Matter 10 (ug/m^3)	Particulate Matter 2.5 Wtd AM (ug/m^3)	Particulate Matter 2.5 24-Hr (ug/m^3)	Ozone (ppm)	Carbon Monoxide (ppm)	Lead (ug/m^3)
MSA[1] Level	26	7.6	16	0.069	2	n/a
NAAQS[2]	150	15	35	0.075	9	0.15
Met NAAQS[2]	Yes	Yes	Yes	Yes	Yes	n/a

Note: (1) Data covers the Raleigh, NC Metropolitan Statistical Area—see Appendix B for areas included; Data from exceptional events are included; (2) National Ambient Air Quality Standards; ppm = parts per million; ug/m^3 = micrograms per cubic meter; n/a not available.
Concentrations: Particulate Matter 10 (coarse particulate)—highest second maximum 24-hour concentration; Particulate Matter 2.5 Wtd AM (fine particulate)—highest weighted annual mean concentration; Particulate Matter 2.5 24-Hour (fine particulate)—highest 98th percentile 24-hour concentration; Ozone—highest fourth daily maximum 8-hour concentration; Carbon Monoxide—highest second maximum non-overlapping 8-hour concentration; Lead—maximum running 3-month average
Source: U.S. Environmental Protection Agency, Air Quality Monitoring Information, "Air Quality Statistics by City, 2016"

Maximum Air Pollutant Concentrations: Nitrogen Dioxide and Sulfur Dioxide

	Nitrogen Dioxide AM (ppb)	Nitrogen Dioxide 1-Hr (ppb)	Sulfur Dioxide AM (ppb)	Sulfur Dioxide 1-Hr (ppb)	Sulfur Dioxide 24-Hr (ppb)
MSA[1] Level	9	39	n/a	3	n/a
NAAQS[2]	53	100	30	75	140
Met NAAQS[2]	Yes	Yes	n/a	Yes	n/a

Note: (1) Data covers the Raleigh, NC Metropolitan Statistical Area—see Appendix B for areas included; Data from exceptional events are included; (2) National Ambient Air Quality Standards; ppm = parts per million; ug/m³ = micrograms per cubic meter; n/a not available.
Concentrations: Nitrogen Dioxide AM—highest arithmetic mean concentration; Nitrogen Dioxide 1-Hr—highest 98th percentile 1-hour daily maximum concentration; Sulfur Dioxide AM—highest annual mean concentration; Sulfur Dioxide 1-Hr—highest 99th percentile 1-hour daily maximum concentration; Sulfur Dioxide 24-Hr—highest second maximum 24-hour concentration
Source: U.S. Environmental Protection Agency, Air Quality Monitoring Information, "Air Quality Statistics by City, 2016"

Drinking Water

Water System Name	Pop. Served	Primary Water Source Type	Violations[1] Health Based	Violations[1] Monitoring/ Reporting
Town of Holly Springs	33,500	Purchased Surface	0	0

Note: (1) Based on violation data from January 1, 2017 to December 31, 2017
Source: U.S. Environmental Protection Agency, Office of Ground Water and Drinking Water, Safe Drinking Water Information System (based on data extracted April 5, 2018)

West Fargo, North Dakota

Background

West Fargo is one of the fastest growing communities in North Dakota. Its first European inhabitants were workers at a meat-packing plant run by the Equity Cooperative Packing Company in 1917, which built 24 houses for workers. After the plant went bankrupt in 1922, workers were broke and without options, until an event occurred that seemed nothing less than Biblical: "the summer of the frogs."

After heavy rainfall, thousands of frogs turned up along the Sheyenne River, and the former meat packers began to produce and package the delicacy, frogs' legs. This kept the area going until 1925, when Armour & Co. bought the plant and jobs returned to the area. Stockyards and meat-packing were a continuing presence in the city through the 1990s.

In 2000, the city created the West Fargo Renaissance Zone to revitalize and encourage private sector investment in a 20-block area making up the city's central business district, which officially ended in 2015. Approved projects in the zone were eligible for a five-year exemption from property taxes as well as state income tax exemptions.

The Sheyenne River, which runs through the city on its way to the Red River about 15 miles north of Fargo, twice flooded West Fargo, once in 1969 and again in 1975. The city now has flood protection in the form of a channel that diverts the river around the city. The $27.8 million project was completed in 1992, and has worked so far, withstanding record level floods in 1997 and 2009.

West Fargo's history is preserved at the West Fargo Historical Center in the public library, and at Bonanzaville, USA, a history museum complex run by the Cass County Historical Society. The 12-acre complex includes 47 buildings, including a historical general store, prairie church, and schoolhouse, and the newer aircraft museum.

West Fargo schools includes two kindergarten centers, eight elementary schools, two middle schools, the Sheyenne Ninth Grade Center (opened in 2007 in response to crowding at the high school), West Fargo High School, and West Fargo Community High School, an alternative high school.

Since it began in 2009, West Fargo School's Science, Technology, Engineering and Math (STEM) program has taken top honors in several competitions, including the Technology Student Association State Competition in 2012, the Bison BEST competition in 2009, and students won first place for Best Web Page Design at the 2009 Frontier Trails BEST Regional Robotics Competition. A group of Liberty Middle School students won 'Best of State' in the 2014-15, 2015-16 and 2016-17 Verizon Innovative App Challenge.

City-owned recreational spaces include Veterans Memorial Pool, an indoor skating rink and several outdoor rinks (some with warming houses), groomed cross-country ski trails, a BMX trail, playing fields, and courses for disc golf, a game played like golf but with a disc instead of a ball.

In 2016, the West Fargo school district began construction of an $18.5 million competitive pool facility at the L.E. Berger Elementary School. The facility includes the pool used for the USA Swimming trials for the 2016 Summer Olympics at the CenturyLink Center Omaha in which Michael Phelps and Ryan Lochte competed: the Omaha was dismantled after the competition and moved to West Fargo.

The Red River Valley Fairgrounds hosts the Big Iron Farm Show, the Red River Valley Fair, concerts, flea markets, auctions, rodeos, and trade shows.

West Fargo typically gets less rain than the rest of the country, but more snow. The average annual snowfall is 38 inches, as contrasted with 25 inches annual nationally. The average high temperature in July is 82 degrees, while the average low in January is 3 degrees below zero.

Rankings

Business/Finance Rankings

- The Fargo* metro area appeared on the Milken Institute "2017 Best Performing Cities" list. Rank: #21 out of 201 small metro areas. Criteria: job growth; wage and salary growth; high-tech output growth. *Milken Institute, "Best-Performing Cities 2017," January 2018*
- *Forbes* ranked 200 smaller metro areas (population under 265,400) to determine the nation's "Best Small Places for Business and Careers." The Fargo* metro area was ranked #14. Criteria: costs (business and living); job growth (past and projected); income growth; quality of life; educational attainment (college and high school); projected economic growth; cultural and recreational opportunities; net migration patterns; number of highly ranked colleges. *Forbes, "The Best Small Cities for Business and Careers 2017," November, 6 2017*

Environmental Rankings

- Sperling's BestPlaces assessed 379 metropolitan areas of the United States for the likelihood of dangerously extreme weather events or earthquakes. In general the Southeast and South-Central regions have the highest risk of weather extremes and earthquakes, while the Pacific Northwest enjoys the lowest risk. Of the least risky metropolitan areas, the Fargo* metro area was ranked #164. *www.bestplaces.net, "Safest Places from Natural Disasters," April 2011*
- Fargo* was highlighted as one of the cleanest metro areas for ozone air pollution in the U.S. during 2013 through 2015. The list represents cities with no monitored ozone air pollution in unhealthful ranges. *American Lung Association, State of the Air 2017*
- Fargo* was highlighted as one of the top 25 cleanest metro areas for year-round particle pollution (Annual PM 2.5) in the U.S. during 2013 through 2015. The area ranked #21. *American Lung Association, State of the Air 2017*

Safety Rankings

- The National Insurance Crime Bureau ranked 382 metro areas in the U.S. in terms of per capita rates of vehicle theft. The Fargo* metro area ranked #182 (#1 = highest rate). Criteria: number of vehicle theft offenses per 100,000 inhabitants in 2016. *National Insurance Crime Bureau, "Hot Spots 2016," June 8, 2017*

Seniors/Retirement Rankings

- From its Best Cities for Successful Aging indexes, the Milken Institute generated rankings for metropolitan areas, weighing data in nine categories—health care, wellness, living arrangements, transportation and convenience, financial characteristics, education, employment, community engagement, and overall livability. The Fargo* metro area was ranked #14 overall in the small metro area category. *Milken Institute, "Best Cities for Successful Aging, 2017" March 14, 2017*

*West Fargo is located within the Fargo, ND-MN Metropolitan Statistical Area.

Business Environment

CITY FINANCES

City Government Finances

Component	2015 ($000)	2015 ($ per capita)
Total Revenues	49,630	1,477
Total Expenditures	75,754	2,255
Debt Outstanding	214,962	6,398
Cash and Securities[1]	28,613	852

Note: (1) Cash and security holdings of a government at the close of its fiscal year,, including those of its dependent agencies, utilities, and liquor stores.
Source: U.S Census Bureau, State & Local Government Finances 2015

City Government Revenue by Source

Source	2015 ($000)	2015 ($ per capita)	2015 (%)
General Revenue			
From Federal Government	0	0	0.0
From State Government	4,842	144	9.8
From Local Governments	220	7	0.4
Taxes			
Property	8,701	259	17.5
Sales and Gross Receipts	4,517	134	9.1
Personal Income	0	0	0.0
Corporate Income	0	0	0.0
Motor Vehicle License	0	0	0.0
Other Taxes	1,030	31	2.1
Current Charges	5,504	164	11.1
Liquor Store	0	0	0.0
Utility	3,417	102	6.9
Employee Retirement	0	0	0.0

Source: U.S Census Bureau, State & Local Government Finances 2015

City Government Expenditures by Function

Function	2015 ($000)	2015 ($ per capita)	2015 (%)
General Direct Expenditures			
Air Transportation	191	5	0.3
Corrections	0	0	0.0
Education	0	0	0.0
Employment Security Administration	0	0	0.0
Financial Administration	993	29	1.3
Fire Protection	1,187	35	1.6
General Public Buildings	23	< 1	< 0.1
Governmental Administration, Other	1,163	34	1.5
Health	0	0	0.0
Highways	52,107	1,550	68.8
Hospitals	0	0	0.0
Housing and Community Development	0	0	0.0
Interest on General Debt	5,293	157	7.0
Judicial and Legal	380	11	0.5
Libraries	822	24	1.1
Parking	0	0	0.0
Parks and Recreation	0	0	0.0
Police Protection	5,152	153	6.8
Public Welfare	0	0	0.0
Sewerage	2,000	59	2.6
Solid Waste Management	2,650	78	3.5
Veterans' Services	0	0	0.0
Liquor Store	0	0	0.0
Utility	2,552	76	3.4
Employee Retirement	0	0	0.0

Source: U.S Census Bureau, State & Local Government Finances 2015

DEMOGRAPHICS

Population Growth

Area	1990 Census	2000 Census	2010 Census	2016* Estimate	Population Growth (%) 1990-2016	Population Growth (%) 2010-2016
City	12,276	14,940	25,830	31,557	157.1	22.2
MSA[1]	153,296	174,367	208,777	228,254	48.9	9.3
U.S.	248,709,873	281,421,906	308,745,538	318,558,162	28.1	3.2

Note: (1) Figures cover the Fargo, ND-MN Metropolitan Statistical Area—see Appendix B for areas included; (*) 2012-2016 5-year estimated population
Source: U.S. Census Bureau, 1990 Census, Census 2000, Census 2010, 2012-2016 American Community Survey 5-Year Estimates

Household Size

Area	Persons in Household (%)							Average Household Size
	One	Two	Three	Four	Five	Six	Seven or More	
City	23.7	36.3	17.7	13.1	7.2	1.0	1.0	2.60
MSA[1]	31.6	34.4	15.1	11.8	4.9	1.5	0.7	2.30
U.S.	27.7	33.7	15.7	13.1	6.0	2.3	1.5	2.60

Note: (1) Figures cover the Fargo, ND-MN Metropolitan Statistical Area—see Appendix B for areas included
Source: U.S. Census Bureau, 2012-2016 American Community Survey 5-Year Estimates

Race

Area	White Alone[2] (%)	Black Alone[2] (%)	Asian Alone[2] (%)	AIAN[3] Alone[2] (%)	NHOPI[4] Alone[2] (%)	Other Race Alone[2] (%)	Two or More Races (%)
City	92.5	2.6	2.0	1.2	0.0	0.0	1.8
MSA[1]	90.1	3.3	2.3	1.1	0.0	0.5	2.6
U.S.	73.3	12.6	5.2	0.8	0.2	4.8	3.1

Note: (1) Figures cover the Fargo, ND-MN Metropolitan Statistical Area—see Appendix B for areas included; (2) Alone is defined as not being in combination with one or more other races; (3) American Indian and Alaska Native; (4) Native Hawaiian and Other Pacific Islander
Source: U.S. Census Bureau, 2012-2016 American Community Survey 5-Year Estimates

Hispanic or Latino Origin

Area	Total (%)	Mexican (%)	Puerto Rican (%)	Cuban (%)	Other (%)
City	1.0	0.8	0.0	0.0	0.2
MSA[1]	2.9	2.0	0.2	0.0	0.7
U.S.	17.3	11.0	1.7	0.7	4.0

Note: Persons of Hispanic or Latino origin can be of any race; (1) Figures cover the Fargo, ND-MN Metropolitan Statistical Area—see Appendix B for areas included
Source: U.S. Census Bureau, 2012-2016 American Community Survey 5-Year Estimates

Segregation

Type	Segregation Indices[1]				Percent Change		
	1990	2000	2010	2010 Rank[2]	1990-2000	1990-2010	2000-2010
Black/White	n/a	n/a	n/a	n/a	n/a	n/a	n/a
Asian/White	n/a	n/a	n/a	n/a	n/a	n/a	n/a
Hispanic/White	n/a	n/a	n/a	n/a	n/a	n/a	n/a

Note: All figures cover the Metropolitan Statistical Area—see Appendix B for areas included; Figures are based on an analysis of 1990, 2000, and 2010 Census Decennial Census tract data by William H. Frey, Brookings Institution and the University of Michigan Social Science Data Analysis Network. In this analysis all racial groups (whites, blacks, and asians) are non-Hispanic members of those races. Hispanics are shown as a separate category; (1) Segregation Indices are Dissimilarity Indices that measure the degree to which the minority group is distributed differently than whites across census tracts. They range from 0 (complete integration) to 100 (complete segregation) where the value indicates the percentage of the minority group that needs to move to be distributed exactly like whites; (2) Ranges from 1 (most segregated) to 102 (least segregated); n/a not available.
Source: www.CensusScope.org

Ancestry

Area	German	Irish	English	American	Italian	Polish	French[2]	Scottish	Dutch
City	45.1	5.8	5.1	1.5	1.7	2.7	3.0	2.1	1.5
MSA[1]	39.9	8.0	4.2	2.1	1.2	2.9	3.4	1.4	1.2
U.S.	14.4	10.4	7.7	6.9	5.4	2.9	2.6	1.7	1.3

Note: Figures are the percentage of the total population reporting a particular ancestry. The nine most commonly reported ancestries in the U.S. are shown. Figures include multiple ancestries (e.g. if a person reported being Irish and Italian, they were included in both columns); (1) Figures cover the Fargo, ND-MN Metropolitan Statistical Area—see Appendix B for areas included; (2) Excludes Basque
Source: U.S. Census Bureau, 2012-2016 American Community Survey 5-Year Estimates

Foreign-Born Population

Area	Percent of Population Born in								
	Any Foreign Country	Asia	Mexico	Europe	Carribean	Central America[2]	South America	Africa	Canada
City	4.0	1.5	0.0	0.4	0.3	0.0	0.0	1.3	0.5
MSA[1]	5.7	2.5	0.1	0.9	0.1	0.1	0.1	1.6	0.3
U.S.	13.2	4.0	3.6	1.5	1.3	1.0	0.9	0.6	0.3

Note: (1) Figures cover the Fargo, ND-MN Metropolitan Statistical Area—see Appendix B for areas included; (2) Excludes Mexico.
Source: U.S. Census Bureau, 2012-2016 American Community Survey 5-Year Estimates

Marital Status

Area	Never Married	Now Married[2]	Separated	Widowed	Divorced
City	27.8	56.6	0.9	4.1	10.6
MSA[1]	37.8	47.8	0.9	4.5	9.0
U.S.	33.0	48.1	2.1	5.9	11.0

Note: Figures are percentages and cover the population 15 years of age and older; (1) Figures cover the Fargo, ND-MN Metropolitan Statistical Area—see Appendix B for areas included; (2) Excludes separated
Source: U.S. Census Bureau, 2012-2016 American Community Survey 5-Year Estimates

Disability Status

Area	All Ages	Under 18 Years Old	18 to 64 Years Old	65 Years and Over
City	9.8	3.5	8.5	38.6
MSA[1]	10.1	2.9	8.4	35.6
U.S.	12.5	4.1	10.3	35.7

Note: Figures show percent of the civilian noninstitutionalized population that reported having a disability. Disability status is determined from six types of difficulty: vision, hearing, cognitive, ambulatory, self-care, and independent living. For children under 5 years old, hearing and vision difficulty are used to determine disability status. For children between the ages of 5 and 14, disability status is determined from hearing, vision, cognitive, ambulatory, and self-care difficulties. For people aged 15 years and older, they are considered to have a disability if they have difficulty with any one of the six difficulty types; Note: (1) Figures cover the Fargo, ND-MN Metropolitan Statistical Area—see Appendix B for areas included
Source: U.S. Census Bureau, 2012-2016 American Community Survey 5-Year Estimates

Age

Area	Percent of Population									Median Age
	Under Age 5	Age 5–19	Age 20–34	Age 35–44	Age 45–54	Age 55–64	Age 65–74	Age 75–84	Age 85+	
City	8.4	20.1	24.5	14.3	13.4	10.6	5.6	2.3	0.9	33.4
MSA[1]	7.1	19.4	28.1	11.9	11.5	10.8	5.9	3.5	1.8	32.2
U.S.	6.2	19.6	20.7	12.7	13.6	12.6	8.3	4.3	1.9	37.7

Note: (1) Figures cover the Fargo, ND-MN Metropolitan Statistical Area—see Appendix B for areas included
Source: U.S. Census Bureau, 2012-2016 American Community Survey 5-Year Estimates

Gender

Area	Males	Females	Males per 100 Females
City	15,877	15,680	101.3
MSA[1]	114,611	113,643	100.9
U.S.	156,765,322	161,792,840	96.9

Note: (1) Figures cover the Fargo, ND-MN Metropolitan Statistical Area—see Appendix B for areas included
Source: U.S. Census Bureau, 2012-2016 American Community Survey 5-Year Estimates

Religious Groups by Family

Area	Catholic	Baptist	Non-Den.	Methodist[2]	Lutheran	LDS[3]	Pente-costal	Presby-terian[4]	Muslim[5]	Judaism
MSA[1]	17.4	0.4	0.5	3.3	32.5	0.6	1.5	1.9	0.1	<0.1
U.S.	19.1	9.3	4.0	4.0	2.3	2.0	1.9	1.6	0.8	0.7

Note: Figures are the number of adherents as a percentage of the total population; (1) Figures cover the Fargo, ND-MN Metropolitan Statistical Area—see Appendix B for areas included; (2) Methodist/Pietist; (3) Latter Day Saints; (4) Reformed; (5) Figures are estimates
Source: Association of Statisticians of American Religious Bodies, 2010 U.S. Religion Census: Religious Congregations & Membership Study

Religious Groups by Tradition

Area	Catholic	Evangelical Protestant	Mainline Protestant	Other Tradition	Black Protestant	Orthodox
MSA[1]	17.4	10.7	30.8	0.9	<0.1	<0.1
U.S.	19.1	16.2	7.3	4.3	1.6	0.3

Note: Figures are the number of adherents as a percentage of the total population; (1) Figures cover the Fargo, ND-MN Metropolitan Statistical Area—see Appendix B for areas included
Source: Association of Statisticians of American Religious Bodies, 2010 U.S. Religion Census: Religious Congregations & Membership Study

ECONOMY

Gross Metropolitan Product

Area	2014	2015	2016	2017	Rank[2]
MSA[1]	15.2	15.8	16.3	17.1	145

Note: Figures are in billions of dollars; (1) Figures cover the Fargo, ND-MN Metropolitan Statistical Area—see Appendix B for areas included; (2) Rank is based on 2015 data and ranges from 1 to 381
Source: The U.S. Conference of Mayors, U.S. Metro Economies: GMP and Employment Report, 2015-2017

Economic Growth

Area	2012-14 (%)	2015 (%)	2016 (%)	2017 (%)	Rank[2]
MSA[1]	2.6	4.1	1.5	3.1	79
U.S.	2.0	2.4	1.9	2.6	–

Note: Figures are real gross metropolitan product (GMP) growth rates and represent average annual percent change; (1) Figures cover the Fargo, ND-MN Metropolitan Statistical Area—see Appendix B for areas included; (2) Rank is based on 2012-2014 average annual percent change and ranges from 1 to 381
Source: The U.S. Conference of Mayors, U.S. Metro Economies: GMP and Employment Report, 2015-2017

Metropolitan Area Exports

Area	2011	2012	2013	2014	2015	2016	Rank[2]
MSA[1]	730.8	785.9	817.9	782.8	543.2	474.5	211

Note: Figures are in millions of dollars; (1) Figures cover the Fargo, ND-MN Metropolitan Statistical Area—see Appendix B for areas included; (2) Rank is based on 2016 data and ranges from 1 to 385
Source: U.S. Department of Commerce, International Trade Administration, Office of Trade & Industry Information, Manufacturing & Services, data extracted March 15, 2018

Building Permits

Area	Single-Family			Multi-Family			Total		
	2016	2017p	Pct. Chg.	2016	2017p	Pct. Chg.	2016	2017p	Pct. Chg.
City	409	341	-16.6	65	0	-100.0	474	341	-28.1
MSA[1]	1,197	1,062	-11.3	1,287	826	-35.8	2,484	1,888	-24.0
U.S.	750,800	817,300	8.9	455,800	446,800	-2.0	1,206,600	1,264,100	4.8

Note: (1) Figures cover the Fargo, ND-MN Metropolitan Statistical Area—see Appendix B for areas included; Figures represent new, privately-owned housing units authorized (unadjusted data); All permit data are based on estimates with imputation; (p) preliminary data.
Source: U.S. Census Bureau, Manufacturing, Mining, and Construction Statistics, Building Permits, 2016, 2017

Bankruptcy Filings

Area	Business Filings			Nonbusiness Filings		
	2016	2017	% Chg.	2016	2017	% Chg.
Cass County	7	14	100.0	188	177	-5.9
U.S.	24,114	23,157	-4.0	770,846	765,863	-0.6

Note: Business filings include Chapter 7, Chapter 11, Chapter 12, and Chapter 13; Nonbusiness filings include Chapter 7, Chapter 11, and Chapter 13
Source: Administrative Office of the U.S. Courts, Business and Nonbusiness Bankruptcy, County Cases Commenced by Chapter of the Bankruptcy Code, During the 12-Month Period Ending December 31, 2016 and Business and Nonbusiness Bankruptcy, County Cases Commenced by Chapter of the Bankruptcy Code, During the 12-Month Period Ending December 31, 2017

Housing Vacancy Rates

Area	Gross Vacancy Rate[2] (%)			Year-Round Vacancy Rate[3] (%)			Rental Vacancy Rate[4] (%)			Homeowner Vacancy Rate[5] (%)		
	2015	2016	2017	2015	2016	2017	2015	2016	2017	2015	2016	2017
MSA[1]	n/a	n/a	n/a	n/a	n/a	n/a	n/a	n/a	n/a	n/a	n/a	n/a
U.S.	12.9	12.8	12.7	10.0	9.9	9.9	7.1	6.9	7.2	1.8	1.7	1.6

Note: (1) Figures cover the Fargo, ND-MN Metropolitan Statistical Area—see Appendix B for areas included; (2) The percentage of the total housing inventory that is vacant; (3) The percentage of the housing inventory (excluding seasonal units) that is year-round vacant; (4) The percentage of rental inventory that is vacant for rent; (5) The percentage of homeowner inventory that is vacant for sale; n/a not available
Source: U.S. Census Bureau, Housing Vacancies and Homeownership Annual Statistics: 2015, 2016, 2017

INCOME

Income

Area	Per Capita ($)	Median Household ($)	Average Household ($)
City	33,489	71,516	84,689
MSA[1]	31,054	55,941	74,460
U.S.	29,829	55,322	77,866

Note: (1) Figures cover the Fargo, ND-MN Metropolitan Statistical Area—see Appendix B for areas included
Source: U.S. Census Bureau, 2012-2016 American Community Survey 5-Year Estimates

Household Income Distribution

Area	Percent of Households Earning							
	Under $15,000	$15,000 -$24,999	$25,000 -$34,999	$35,000 -$49,999	$50,000 -$74,999	$75,000 -$99,999	$100,000 -$149,999	$150,000 and up
City	5.0	8.0	7.9	11.8	20.8	17.6	17.2	11.7
MSA[1]	10.5	9.4	10.9	14.1	18.8	14.0	13.3	9.0
U.S.	12.1	10.2	9.9	13.2	17.8	12.2	13.5	11.1

Note: (1) Figures cover the Fargo, ND-MN Metropolitan Statistical Area—see Appendix B for areas included
Source: U.S. Census Bureau, 2012-2016 American Community Survey 5-Year Estimates

Poverty Rate

Area	All Ages	Under 18 Years Old	18 to 64 Years Old	65 Years and Over
City	6.8	8.4	6.4	5.2
MSA[1]	11.8	11.9	12.6	6.9
U.S.	15.1	21.2	14.2	9.3

Note: Figures are percentage of people whose income during the past 12 months was below the poverty level; (1) Figures cover the Fargo, ND-MN Metropolitan Statistical Area—see Appendix B for areas included
Source: U.S. Census Bureau, 2012-2016 American Community Survey 5-Year Estimates

EMPLOYMENT

Labor Force and Employment

Area	Civilian Labor Force			Workers Employed		
	Dec. 2016	Dec. 2017	% Chg.	Dec. 2016	Dec. 2017	% Chg.
City	20,940	20,950	0.0	20,480	20,492	0.1
MSA[1]	137,322	137,092	-0.2	133,698	133,678	0.0
U.S.	158,968,000	159,880,000	0.6	151,798,000	153,602,000	1.2

Note: Data is not seasonally adjusted and covers workers 16 years of age and older; (1) Figures cover the Fargo, ND-MN Metropolitan Statistical Area—see Appendix B for areas included
Source: Bureau of Labor Statistics, Local Area Unemployment Statistics

Unemployment Rate

Area	2017											
	Jan.	Feb.	Mar.	Apr.	May	Jun.	Jul.	Aug.	Sep.	Oct.	Nov.	Dec.
City	2.9	2.8	2.6	1.9	1.5	2.0	1.6	1.7	1.4	1.4	1.8	2.2
MSA[1]	3.3	3.2	3.0	2.3	2.0	2.4	2.1	2.1	1.9	1.6	2.1	2.5
U.S.	5.1	4.9	4.6	4.1	4.1	4.5	4.6	4.5	4.1	3.9	3.9	3.9

Note: Data is not seasonally adjusted and covers workers 16 years of age and older; (1) Figures cover the Fargo, ND-MN Metropolitan Statistical Area—see Appendix B for areas included
Source: Bureau of Labor Statistics, Local Area Unemployment Statistics

Average Wages

Occupation	$/Hr.	Occupation	$/Hr.
Accountants and Auditors	28.80	Maids and Housekeeping Cleaners	11.40
Automotive Mechanics	20.20	Maintenance and Repair Workers	19.40
Bookkeepers	18.70	Marketing Managers	50.90
Carpenters	19.10	Nuclear Medicine Technologists	n/a
Cashiers	10.70	Nurses, Licensed Practical	21.10
Clerks, General Office	16.30	Nurses, Registered	30.40
Clerks, Receptionists/Information	13.40	Nursing Assistants	15.20
Clerks, Shipping/Receiving	16.20	Packers and Packagers, Hand	12.40
Computer Programmers	32.40	Physical Therapists	37.00
Computer Systems Analysts	39.10	Postal Service Mail Carriers	23.50
Computer User Support Specialists	27.80	Real Estate Brokers	n/a
Cooks, Restaurant	14.20	Retail Salespersons	14.60
Dentists	107.00	Sales Reps., Exc. Tech./Scientific	31.00
Electrical Engineers	37.60	Sales Reps., Tech./Scientific	30.70
Electricians	25.30	Secretaries, Exc. Legal/Med./Exec.	18.20
Financial Managers	62.10	Security Guards	15.80
First-Line Supervisors/Managers, Sales	20.00	Surgeons	n/a
Food Preparation Workers	12.50	Teacher Assistants*	14.80
General and Operations Managers	50.60	Teachers, Elementary School*	24.80
Hairdressers/Cosmetologists	14.90	Teachers, Secondary School*	23.90
Internists, General	n/a	Telemarketers	14.20
Janitors and Cleaners	13.10	Truck Drivers, Heavy/Tractor-Trailer	22.90
Landscaping/Groundskeeping Workers	16.00	Truck Drivers, Light/Delivery Svcs.	17.50
Lawyers	54.40	Waiters and Waitresses	9.80

Note: Wage data covers the Fargo, ND-MN Metropolitan Statistical Area—see Appendix B for areas included; (*) Hourly wages for elementary/secondary school teachers and teacher assistants were calculated by the editors from annual wage data based on a 40 hour work week; n/a not available.
Source: Bureau of Labor Statistics, Metro Area Occupational Employment & Wage Estimates, May 2017

Employment by Occupation

Occupation Classification	City (%)	MSA[1] (%)	U.S. (%)
Management, Business, Science, and Arts	40.2	37.5	37.0
Natural Resources, Construction, and Maintenance	8.2	8.9	8.9
Production, Transportation, and Material Moving	14.4	12.5	12.2
Sales and Office	25.1	24.1	23.8
Service	12.1	17.0	18.1

Note: Figures cover employed civilians 16 years of age and older; (1) Figures cover the Fargo, ND-MN Metropolitan Statistical Area—see Appendix B for areas included
Source: U.S. Census Bureau, 2012-2016 American Community Survey 5-Year Estimates

Employment by Industry

Sector	MSA[1] Number of Employees	MSA[1] Percent of Total	U.S. Percent of Total
Construction, Mining, and Logging	8,100	5.7	5.2
Education and Health Services	24,500	17.3	15.9
Financial Activities	11,300	8.0	5.7
Government	20,000	14.1	15.3
Information	3,100	2.2	1.9
Leisure and Hospitality	13,300	9.4	10.7
Manufacturing	9,900	7.0	8.5
Other Services	5,500	3.9	3.9
Professional and Business Services	15,300	10.8	14.0
Retail Trade	15,800	11.2	11.0
Transportation, Warehousing, and Utilities	5,800	4.1	4.1
Wholesale Trade	8,900	6.3	4.0

Note: Figures are non-farm employment as of December 2017. Figures are not seasonally adjusted and include workers 16 years of age and older; (1) Figures cover the Fargo, ND-MN Metropolitan Statistical Area—see Appendix B for areas included
Source: Bureau of Labor Statistics, Current Employment Statistics, Employment, Hours, and Earnings

Occupations with Greatest Projected Employment Growth: 2017 – 2019

Occupation[1]	2017 Employment	2019 Projected Employment	Numeric Employment Change	Percent Employment Change
Heavy and Tractor-Trailer Truck Drivers	12,190	13,690	1,500	12.3
Roustabouts, Oil and Gas	2,810	3,690	880	31.5
Personal Care Aides	5,690	6,030	340	6.0
Registered Nurses	8,900	9,240	340	3.9
Laborers and Freight, Stock, and Material Movers, Hand	8,220	8,550	330	4.0
Rotary Drill Operators, Oil and Gas	890	1,180	290	32.0
Combined Food Preparation and Serving Workers, Including Fast Food	7,270	7,550	280	3.8
General and Operations Managers	6,860	7,140	280	4.1
Derrick Operators, Oil and Gas	650	880	230	35.2
Service Unit Operators, Oil, Gas, and Mining	760	980	220	28.2

Note: Projections cover North Dakota; (1) Sorted by numeric employment change
Source: www.projectionscentral.com, State Occupational Projections, 2017–2019 Short-Term Projections

Fastest Growing Occupations: 2017 – 2019

Occupation[1]	2017 Employment	2019 Projected Employment	Numeric Employment Change	Percent Employment Change
Derrick Operators, Oil and Gas	650	880	230	35.2
Extraction Workers, All Other	590	780	190	32.4
Rotary Drill Operators, Oil and Gas	890	1,180	290	32.0
Roustabouts, Oil and Gas	2,810	3,690	880	31.5
Service Unit Operators, Oil, Gas, and Mining	760	980	220	28.2
Wellhead Pumpers	660	790	130	19.0
Pump Operators, Except Wellhead Pumpers	480	570	90	17.9
Petroleum Pump System Operators, Refinery Operators, and Gaugers	660	780	120	17.5
Heavy and Tractor-Trailer Truck Drivers	12,190	13,690	1,500	12.3
Dispatchers, Except Police, Fire, and Ambulance	890	990	100	11.2

Note: Projections cover North Dakota; (1) Sorted by percent employment change and excludes occupations with numeric employment change less than 50
Source: www.projectionscentral.com, State Occupational Projections, 2017–2019 Short-Term Projections

TAXES

State Corporate Income Tax Rates

State	Tax Rate (%)	Income Brackets ($)	Num. of Brackets	Financial Institution Tax Rate (%)[a]	Federal Income Tax Ded.
North Dakota	1.41 - 4.31 (s)	25,000 - 50,001	3	1.41 - 4.31 (s)	No

Note: Tax rates as of January 1, 2018; (a) Rates listed are the corporate income tax rate applied to financial institutions or excise taxes based on income. Some states have other taxes based upon the value of deposits or shares; (s) North Dakota imposes a 3.5% surtax for filers electing to use the water's edge method to apportion income.
Source: Federation of Tax Administrators, Range of State Corporate Income Tax Rates, January 1, 2018

State Individual Income Tax Rates

State	Tax Rate (%)	Income Brackets ($)	Num. of Brackets	Personal Exempt. ($)[1]		Fed. Inc. Tax Ded.
				Single	Dependents	
North Dakota (a)	1.1 - 2.9	38,700 - 424,950 (s)	5	4,150 (d)	4,150 (d)	No

Note: Tax rates as of January 1, 2018; Local- and county-level taxes are not included; n/a not applicable; (1) Married joint filers generally receive double the single exemption; (a) 19 states have statutory provision for automatically adjusting to the rate of inflation the dollar values of the income tax brackets, standard deductions, and/or personal exemptions. Massachusetts, Michigan, and Nebraska index the personal exemption only. Oregon does not index the income brackets for $125,000 and over; (d) These states use the personal exemption amounts provided in the federal Internal Revenue Code. Note, the Tax Cut and Reform Act of 2017 has eliminated personal exemptions from the IRC. These states will need to enact legislation to reinstate a personal exemption for tax year 2018. We have reported here the exemption amounts before the federal tax change; (s) The income brackets reported for North Dakota are for single individuals. For married couples filing jointly, the same tax rates apply to income brackets ranging from $64,650 to $424,950.
Source: Federation of Tax Administrators, State Individual Income Tax Rates, January 1, 2018

Various State Sales and Excise Tax Rates

State	State Sales Tax (%)	Gasoline[1] (¢/gal.)	Cigarette[2] ($/pack)	Spirits[3] ($/gal.)	Wine[4] ($/gal.)	Beer[5] ($/gal.)	Recreational Marijuana (%)
North Dakota	5.0	23.0	0.44	4.66 (f)(j)	1.06 (l)	0.39 (q)	Not legal

Note: All tax rates as of January 1, 2018; (1) The American Petroleum Institute has developed a methodology for determining the average tax rate on a gallon of fuel. Rates may include any of the following: excise taxes, environmental fees, storage tank fees, other fees or taxes, general sales tax, and local taxes. In states where gasoline is subject to the general sales tax, or where the fuel tax is based on the average sale price, the average rate determined by API is sensitive to changes in the price of gasoline. States that fully or partially apply general sales taxes to gasoline: CA, CO, GA, IL, IN, MI, NY; (2) The federal excise tax of $1.0066 per pack and local taxes are not included; (3) Rates are those applicable to off-premise sales of 40% alcohol by volume (a.b.v.) distilled spirits in 750ml containers. Local excise taxes are excluded; (4) Rates are those applicable to off-premise sales of 11% a.b.v. non-carbonated wine in 750ml containers; (5) Rates are those applicable to off-premise sales of 4.7% a.b.v. beer in 12 ounce containers; (f) Different rates also applicable according to alcohol content, place of production, size of container, or place purchased (on- or off-premise or onboard airlines); (j) Includes sales taxes specific to alcoholic beverages; (l) Different rates also applicable to alcohol content, place of production, size of container, place purchased (on- or off-premise or on board airlines) or type of wine (carbonated, vermouth, etc.); (q) Different rates also applicable according to alcohol content, place of production, size of container, or place purchased (on- or off-premise or onboard airlines).
Source: Tax Foundation, 2018 Facts & Figures: How Does Your State Compare?

State Business Tax Climate Index Rankings

State	Overall Rank	Corporate Tax Rank	Individual Income Tax Rank	Sales Tax Rank	Unemployment Insurance Tax Rank	Property Tax Rank
North Dakota	30	16	36	34	14	2

Note: The index is a measure of how each state's tax laws affect economic performance. The lower the rank, the more favorable a state's tax system is for business. States without a given tax are given a ranking of 1. The scores/rankings for the District of Columbia do not affect other states. The 2018 index represents the tax climate as of July 1, 2017.
Source: Tax Foundation, State Business Tax Climate Index 2018

TRANSPORTATION

Means of Transportation to Work

Area	Car/Truck/Van		Public Transportation			Bicycle	Walked	Other Means	Worked at Home
	Drove Alone	Car-pooled	Bus	Subway	Railroad				
City	84.9	10.0	0.2	0.0	0.0	0.2	1.1	0.9	2.8
MSA[1]	82.1	8.6	0.8	0.0	0.0	0.5	3.4	0.8	3.7
U.S.	76.4	9.3	2.6	1.9	0.6	0.6	2.8	1.3	4.6

Note: Figures are percentages and cover workers 16 years of age and older; (1) Figures cover the Fargo, ND-MN Metropolitan Statistical Area—see Appendix B for areas included
Source: U.S. Census Bureau, 2012-2016 American Community Survey 5-Year Estimates

Travel Time to Work

Area	Less Than 10 Minutes	10 to 19 Minutes	20 to 29 Minutes	30 to 44 Minutes	45 to 59 Minutes	60 to 89 Minutes	90 Minutes or More
City	19.1	53.5	16.6	7.2	0.8	2.0	0.8
MSA[1]	20.2	49.6	18.2	7.6	1.9	1.6	0.9
U.S.	12.9	29.2	20.9	20.4	8.0	6.0	2.7

Note: Note: Figures are percentages and include workers 16 years old and over; (1) Figures cover the Fargo, ND-MN Metropolitan Statistical Area—see Appendix B for areas included
Source: U.S. Census Bureau, 2012-2016 American Community Survey 5-Year Estimates

Freeway Travel Time Index

Area	1985	1990	1995	2000	2005	2010	2014
Urban Area Rank[1,2]	n/a	n/a	n/a	n/a	n/a	n/a	n/a
Urban Area Index[1]	n/a	n/a	n/a	n/a	n/a	n/a	n/a
Average Index[3]	1.09	1.11	1.14	1.17	1.20	1.19	1.20

Note: Freeway Travel Time Index—the ratio of travel time in the peak period to the travel time at free-flow conditions. For example, a value of 1.30 indicates a 20-minute free-flow trip takes 26 minutes in the peak (20 minutes x 1.30 = 26 minutes); (1) Data for the Fargo, ND-MN urban area was not available; (2) Rank is based on 101 urban areas (#1 = highest travel time index); (3) Average of 101 urban areas
Source: Texas Transportation Institute, 2015 Urban Mobility Scorecard, August 2015

Freeway Commuter Stress Index

Area	1985	1990	1995	2000	2005	2010	2014
Urban Area Rank[1,2]	n/a	n/a	n/a	n/a	n/a	n/a	n/a
Urban Area Index[1]	n/a	n/a	n/a	n/a	n/a	n/a	n/a
Average Index[3]	1.13	1.16	1.19	1.22	1.25	1.24	1.25

Note: The Freeway Commuter Stress Index is the same as the Freeway Travel Time Index (see table above) except that it includes only the travel in the peak directions during the peak periods; the TTI includes travel in all directions during the peak period. Thus, the CSI is more indicative of the work trip experienced by each commuter on a daily basis; (1) Data for the Fargo, ND-MN urban area was not available; (2) Rank is based on 101 urban areas (#1 = highest travel time index); (3) Average of 101 urban areas
Source: Texas Transportation Institute, 2015 Urban Mobility Scorecard, August 2015

Living Environment

COST OF LIVING

Cost of Living Index

Composite Index	Groceries	Housing	Utilities	Trans-portation	Health Care	Misc. Goods/ Services
99.8	108.2	98.0	86.6	98.9	114.8	100.1

Note: The Cost of Living Index measures regional differences in the cost of consumer goods and services, excluding taxes and non-consumer expenditures, for professional and managerial households in the top income quintile. It is based on more than 50,000 prices covering almost 60 different items for which prices are collected three times a year by chambers of commerce, economic development organizations or university applied economic centers in each participating urban area. The numbers shown should be read as a percentage above or below the national average of 100. For example, a value of 115.4 in the groceries column indicates that grocery prices are 15.4% higher than the national average. Small differences in the index numbers should not be interpreted as significant; Figures cover the Fargo-Moorhead ND-MN urban area.
Source: The Council for Community and Economic Research, ACCRA Cost of Living Index, 2017

Grocery Prices

Area[1]	T-Bone Steak ($/pound)	Frying Chicken ($/pound)	Whole Milk ($/half gal.)	Eggs ($/dozen)	Orange Juice ($/64 oz.)	Coffee ($/11.5 oz.)
City[2]	12.56	1.84	2.96	1.24	4.12	4.32
Avg.	11.29	1.40	2.02	1.47	3.55	4.37
Min.	7.71	0.93	1.04	0.70	2.86	3.24
Max.	15.83	2.39	4.03	3.92	6.29	8.16

Note: (1) Values for the local area are compared with the average, minimum and maximum values for all 294 areas in the Cost of Living Index; (2) Figures cover the Fargo-Moorhead ND-MN urban area; ***T-Bone Steak*** *(price per pound);* ***Frying Chicken*** *(price per pound, whole fryer);* ***Whole Milk*** *(half gallon carton);* ***Eggs*** *(price per dozen, Grade A, large);* ***Orange Juice*** *(64 oz. Tropicana or Florida Natural);* ***Coffee*** *(11.5 oz. can, vacuum-packed, Maxwell House, Hills Bros, or Folgers).*
Source: The Council for Community and Economic Research, ACCRA Cost of Living Index, 2017

Housing and Utility Costs

Area[1]	New Home Price ($)	Apartment Rent ($/month)	All Electric ($/month)	Part Electric ($/month)	Other Energy ($/month)	Telephone ($/month)
City[2]	342,347	952	-	75.25	67.27	25.30
Avg.	335,956	1,047	175.01	97.34	67.93	28.71
Min.	187,788	491	109.48	49.33	35.44	12.39
Max.	1,739,087	4,559	432.62	227.09	353.33	44.61

Note: (1) Values for the local area are compared with the average, minimum and maximum values for all 294 areas in the Cost of Living Index; (2) Figures cover the Fargo-Moorhead ND-MN urban area; ***New Home Price*** *(2,400 sf living area, 8,000 sf lot, in urban area with full utilities);* ***Apartment Rent*** *(950 sf 2 bedroom/1.5 or 2 bath, unfurnished, excluding all utilities except water);* ***All Electric*** *(average monthly cost for an all-electric home);* ***Part Electric*** *(average monthly cost for a part-electric home);* ***Other Energy*** *(average monthly cost for natural gas, fuel oil, coal, wood, and any other forms of energy except electricity);* ***Telephone*** *(price includes basic monthly rate for a private residential line plus additional local usage charges incurred by a family of four).*
Source: The Council for Community and Economic Research, ACCRA Cost of Living Index, 2017

Health Care, Transportation, and Other Costs

Area[1]	Doctor ($/visit)	Dentist ($/visit)	Optometrist ($/visit)	Gasoline ($/gallon)	Beauty Salon ($/visit)	Men's Shirt ($)
City[2]	157.22	95.33	93.17	2.11	34.13	28.47
Avg.	108.00	92.54	101.93	2.25	37.58	30.92
Min.	30.39	60.00	49.75	1.82	16.11	11.20
Max.	193.50	161.94	229.28	3.16	77.35	59.13

Note: (1) Values for the local area are compared with the average, minimum and maximum values for all 294 areas in the Cost of Living Index; (2) Figures cover the Fargo-Moorhead ND-MN urban area; ***Doctor*** *(general practitioners routine exam of an established patient);* ***Dentist*** *(adult teeth cleaning and periodic oral examination);* ***Optometrist*** *(full vision eye exam for established adult patient);* ***Gasoline*** *(one gallon regular unleaded, national brand, including all taxes, cash price at self-service pump if available);* ***Beauty Salon*** *(woman's shampoo, trim, and blow-dry);* ***Men's Shirt*** *(cotton/polyester dress shirt, pinpoint weave, long sleeves).*
Source: The Council for Community and Economic Research, ACCRA Cost of Living Index, 2017

HOUSING

House Price Index (HPI)

Area	National Ranking[2]	Quarterly Change (%)	One-Year Change (%)	Five-Year Change (%)
MSA[1]	225	-0.33	2.56	33.44
U.S.[3]	–	1.61	6.68	34.71

Note: The HPI is a weighted repeat sales index. It measures average price changes in repeat sales or refinancings on the same properties. This information is obtained by reviewing repeat mortgage transactions on single-family properties whose mortgages have been purchased or securitized by Fannie Mae or Freddie Mac in January 1975; (1) Figures cover the Fargo, ND-MN Metropolitan Statistical Area—see Appendix B for areas included; (2) Rankings are based on annual percentage change for all metro areas containing at least 15,000 transactions over the last 10 years and ranges from 1 to 253; (3) figures based on a weighted average of Census Division estimates using a seasonally adjusted, purchase-only index; all figures are for the period ending December 31, 2017
Source: Federal Housing Finance Agency, House Price Index, February 28, 2018

Median Single-Family Home Prices

Area	2015	2016	2017p	Percent Change 2016 to 2017
MSA[1]	190.6	203.2	208.5	2.6
U.S. Average	223.9	235.5	248.8	5.6

Note: Figures are median sales prices of existing single-family homes in thousands of dollars; (p) preliminary; (1) Figures cover the Fargo, ND-MN Metropolitan Statistical Area—see Appendix B for areas included
Source: National Association of Realtors, Median Sales Price of Existing Single-Family Homes for Metropolitan Areas, 4th Quarter 2017

Qualifying Income Based on Median Sales Price of Existing Single-Family Homes

Area	With 5% Down ($)	With 10% Down ($)	With 20% Down ($)
MSA[1]	48,093	45,561	40,499
U.S. Average	55,585	52,659	46,808

Note: Figures are preliminary; Qualifying income is based on a mortgage rate of 4.17%. Monthly principal and interest payment is limited to 25% of income; (1) Figures cover the Fargo, ND-MN Metropolitan Statistical Area—see Appendix B for areas included
Source: National Association of Realtors, Qualifying Income Based on Median Sales Price of Existing Single-Family Homes for Metropolitan Areas, 4th Quarter 2017

Median Apartment Condo-Coop Home Prices

Area	2015	2016	2017p	Percent Change 2016 to 2017
MSA[1]	n/a	n/a	n/a	n/a
U.S. Average	210.7	220.7	234.3	6.2

Note: Figures are median sales prices of existing apartment condo-coop homes in thousands of dollars; (p) preliminary; n/a not available; (1) Figures cover the Fargo, ND-MN Metropolitan Statistical Area—see Appendix B for areas included
Source: National Association of Realtors, Median Sales Price of Existing Apartment Condo-Coop Homes for Metropolitan Areas, 4th Quarter 2017

Home Value Distribution

Area	Under $50,000	$50,000 -$99,999	$100,000 -$149,999	$150,000 -$199,999	$200,000 -$299,999	$300,000 -$499,999	$500,000 -$999,999	$1,000,000 or more
City	5.0	6.6	18.8	23.0	27.8	15.8	2.9	0.1
MSA[1]	5.0	8.7	22.1	23.4	25.6	12.5	2.5	0.3
U.S.	8.8	14.8	15.3	14.9	18.4	16.4	9.0	2.5

Note: Figures are percentages and cover owner-occupied housing units; (1) Figures cover the Fargo, ND-MN Metropolitan Statistical Area—see Appendix B for areas included
Source: U.S. Census Bureau, 2012-2016 American Community Survey 5-Year Estimates

Homeownership Rate

Area	2009 (%)	2010 (%)	2011 (%)	2012 (%)	2013 (%)	2014 (%)	2015 (%)	2016 (%)	2017 (%)
MSA[1]	n/a	n/a	n/a	n/a	n/a	n/a	n/a	n/a	n/a
U.S.	67.4	66.9	66.1	65.4	65.1	64.5	63.7	63.4	63.9

Note: (1) Figures cover the Fargo, ND-MN Metropolitan Statistical Area—see Appendix B for areas included; n/a not available
Source: U.S. Census Bureau, Housing Vacancies and Homeownership Annual Statistics: 2009-2017

Year Housing Structure Built

Area	2010 or Later	2000 -2009	1990 -1999	1980 -1989	1970 -1979	1960 -1969	1950 -1959	1940 -1949	Before 1940	Median Year
City	12.3	35.9	14.2	7.8	15.0	6.1	5.8	0.9	1.9	1999
MSA[1]	6.6	19.5	16.4	11.4	16.7	7.8	8.4	2.8	10.4	1983
U.S.	2.3	14.7	14.0	13.7	15.6	10.9	10.6	5.2	13.0	1977

Note: Figures are percentages except for Median Year; Note: (1) Figures cover the Fargo, ND-MN Metropolitan Statistical Area—see Appendix B for areas included
Source: U.S. Census Bureau, 2012-2016 American Community Survey 5-Year Estimates

Gross Monthly Rent

Area	Under $500	$500 -$999	$1,000 -$1,499	$1,500 -$1,999	$2,000 -$2,499	$2,500 -$2,999	$3,000 and up	Median ($)
City	9.3	63.8	21.8	3.4	0.6	0.7	0.4	770
MSA[1]	12.5	68.6	13.4	3.8	1.3	0.3	0.1	733
U.S.	11.3	43.3	27.7	10.7	4.0	1.6	1.5	949

Note: Figures are percentages except for Median; Gross rent is the contract rent plus the estimated average monthly cost of utilities (electricity, gas, and water and sewer) and fuels (oil, coal, kerosene, wood, etc.) if these are paid by the renter (or paid for the renter by someone else); (1) Figures cover the Fargo, ND-MN Metropolitan Statistical Area—see Appendix B for areas included
Source: U.S. Census Bureau, 2012-2016 American Community Survey 5-Year Estimates

HEALTH

Health Risk Factors

Category	MSA[1] (%)	U.S. (%)
Adults aged 18–64 who have any kind of health care coverage	92.6	87.7
Adults who reported being in good or excellent health	87.2	83.6
Adults who are current smokers	15.6	17.1
Adults who currently use E-cigarettes	2.7	4.7
Adults who currently use chewing tobacco, snuff, or snus	4.4	4.0
Adults who are heavy drinkers[2]	7.6	6.5
Adults who are binge drinkers[3]	24.8	16.9
Adults who are overweight (BMI 25.0 - 29.9)	35.5	35.3
Adults who are obese (BMI 30.0 - 99.8)	31.1	29.9
Adults who participated in any physical activities in the past month	83.7	76.9
Adults who always or nearly always wears a seat belt	93.6	94.3

Note: (1) Figures cover the Fargo, ND-MN Metropolitan Statistical Area—see Appendix B for areas included; (2) Heavy drinkers are classified as adult men having more than 14 drinks per week and adult women having more than 7 drinks per week; (3) Binge drinkers are classified as males having five or more drinks on one occasion or females having four or more drinks on one occasion
Source: Centers for Disease Control and Prevention, Behaviorial Risk Factor Surveillance System, SMART: Selected Metropolitan Area Risk Trends, 2016

Health Screening Rates

Category	MSA[1] (%)	U.S. (%)
Adults 50-75 who have had a blood stool test within the past year	5.6	8.0
Adults 50-75 who have had a colonoscopy in the past 10 years	72.9	63.5
Adults aged 65+ who have had flu shot within the past year	63.2	58.6
Adults aged 65+ who have ever had a pneumonia vaccination	80.5	73.4
Adults who have ever been tested for HIV	28.2	35.6
Women aged 21-65 who have had a pap test in the past three years	77.5	79.8
Men aged 40+ who have had a PSA test within the past two years	37.4	39.5
Women aged 40+ who have had a mammogram within the past two years	76.8	72.5

Note: n/a not available; (1) Figures cover the Fargo, ND-MN Metropolitan Statistical Area—see Appendix B for areas included; Source: Centers for Disease Control and Prevention, Behaviorial Risk Factor Surveillance System, SMART: Selected Metropolitan Area Risk Trends, 2016

Chronic Health Conditions

Category	MSA[1] (%)	U.S. (%)
Adults who have ever been told they had a heart attack	2.6	4.4
Adults who have ever been told they have angina or coronary heart disease	2.4	4.1
Adults who have ever been told they had a stroke	2.6	3.1
Adults who have been told they currently have asthma	8.2	9.3
Adults who have ever been told they have arthritis	20.0	25.8
Adults who have ever been told they have diabetes[2]	6.6	10.5
Adults who have ever been told they had skin cancer	2.8	5.9
Adults who have ever been told they had any other types of cancer	5.0	6.7
Adults who have ever been told they have COPD	4.2	6.3
Adults who have ever been told they have kidney disease	2.0	2.8
Adults who have ever been told they have a form of depression	17.4	17.4

Note: (1) Figures cover the Fargo, ND-MN Metropolitan Statistical Area—see Appendix B for areas included; (2) Figures do not include pregnancy-related, borderline, or pre-diabetes
Source: Centers for Disease Control and Prevention, Behaviorial Risk Factor Surveillance System, SMART: Selected Metropolitan Area Risk Trends, 2016

Mortality Rates for the Top 10 Causes of Death in the U.S.

ICD-10[a] Sub-Chapter	ICD-10[a] Code	Age-Adjusted Mortality Rate[1] per 100,000 population	
		County[2]	U.S.
Malignant neoplasms	C00-C97	145.6	158.5
Ischaemic heart diseases	I20-I25	69.4	96.8
Other forms of heart disease	I30-I51	43.0	52.4
Chronic lower respiratory diseases	J40-J47	37.7	40.9
Cerebrovascular diseases	I60-I69	29.1	37.2
Organic, including symptomatic, mental disorders	F01-F09	25.4	33.3
Other degenerative diseases of the nervous system	G30-G31	39.8	32.1
Other external causes of accidental injury	W00-X59	23.6	31.2
Diabetes mellitus	E10-E14	15.6	21.1
Hypertensive diseases	I10-I15	15.0	20.8

Note: (a) ICD-10 = International Classification of Diseases 10th Revision; (1) Mortality rates are a three year average covering 2014-2016; (2) Figures cover Cass County.
Source: Centers for Disease Control and Prevention, National Center for Health Statistics. Underlying Cause of Death 1999-2016 on CDC WONDER Online Database, released December 2017

Mortality Rates for Selected Causes of Death

ICD-10[a] Sub-Chapter	ICD-10[a] Code	Age-Adjusted Mortality Rate[1] per 100,000 population	
		County[2]	U.S.
Assault	X85-Y09	Unreliable	5.6
Diseases of the liver	K70-K76	14.4	14.0
Human immunodeficiency virus (HIV) disease	B20-B24	Suppressed	1.9
Influenza and pneumonia	J09-J18	16.6	14.6
Intentional self-harm	X60-X84	15.7	13.2
Malnutrition	E40-E46	Suppressed	1.3
Obesity and other hyperalimentation	E65-E68	Unreliable	2.1
Renal failure	N17-N19	9.4	13.0
Transport accidents	V01-V99	8.0	12.0
Viral hepatitis	B15-B19	Suppressed	1.9

Note: (a) ICD-10 = International Classification of Diseases 10th Revision; (1) Mortality rates are a three year average covering 2014-2016; (2) Figures cover Cass County; Data are Suppressed when the data meet the criteria for confidentiality constraints; Mortality rates are flagged as Unreliable when the rate would be calculated with a numerator of 20 or less.
Source: Centers for Disease Control and Prevention, National Center for Health Statistics. Underlying Cause of Death 1999-2016 on CDC WONDER Online Database, released December 2017

Health Insurance Coverage

Area	With Health Insurance	With Private Health Insurance	With Public Health Insurance	Without Health Insurance	Population Under Age 18 Without Health Insurance
City	94.2	86.7	18.0	5.8	4.7
MSA[1]	93.0	81.1	23.4	7.0	4.4
U.S.	88.3	66.7	33.0	11.7	5.9

Note: Figures are percentages that cover the civilian noninstitutionalized population; (1) Figures cover the Fargo, ND-MN Metropolitan Statistical Area—see Appendix B for areas included
Source: U.S. Census Bureau, 2012-2016 American Community Survey 5-Year Estimates

Number of Medical Professionals

Area	MDs[3]	DOs[3,4]	Dentists	Podiatrists	Chiropractors	Optometrists
County[1] (number)	673	29	137	5	108	51
County[1] (rate[2])	393.7	17.0	78.5	2.9	61.8	29.2
U.S. (rate[2])	276.5	22.3	67.3	6.0	26.7	15.9

Note: Data as of 2016 unless noted; (1) Data covers Cass County; (2) Rate per 100,000 population; (3) Data as of 2015 and includes all active, non-federal physicians; (4) Doctor of Osteopathic Medicine
Source: U.S. Department of Health and Human Services, Health Resources and Services Administration, Bureau of Health Professions, Area Resource File (ARF) 2016-2017

EDUCATION

Public School District Statistics

District Name	Schls	Pupils	Pupil/ Teacher Ratio	Minority Pupils[1] (%)	Free Lunch Eligible[2] (%)	IEP[3] (%)
West Fargo 6	17	9,549	12.7	22.7	24.1	12.9

Note: Table includes school districts with 100 or more students; (1) Percentage of students that are not non-Hispanic white; (2) Percentage of students that are eligible for the free lunch program; (3) Percentage of students that have an Individualized Education Program.
Source: U.S. Department of Education, National Center for Education Statistics, Common Core of Data, Local Education Agency (School District) Universe Survey: School Year 2015-2016; U.S. Department of Education, National Center for Education Statistics, Common Core of Data, Public Elementary/Secondary School Universe Survey: School Year 2015-2016

Highest Level of Education

Area	Less than H.S.	H.S. Diploma	Some College, No Deg.	Associate Degree	Bachelor's Degree	Master's Degree	Prof. School Degree	Doctorate Degree
City	4.3	19.2	22.9	17.1	25.6	8.1	1.2	1.6
MSA[1]	5.5	22.3	21.7	14.3	25.7	7.1	1.6	1.8
U.S.	13.0	27.5	21.0	8.2	18.8	8.2	2.0	1.3

Note: Figures cover persons age 25 and over; (1) Figures cover the Fargo, ND-MN Metropolitan Statistical Area—see Appendix B for areas included
Source: U.S. Census Bureau, 2012-2016 American Community Survey 5-Year Estimates

Educational Attainment by Race

Area	High School Graduate or Higher (%)					Bachelor's Degree or Higher (%)				
	Total	White	Black	Asian	Hisp.[2]	Total	White	Black	Asian	Hisp.[2]
City	95.7	96.8	65.6	68.3	96.2	36.6	37.1	24.6	32.1	46.9
MSA[1]	94.5	95.5	82.4	74.8	80.2	36.2	36.9	22.1	42.5	16.2
U.S.	87.0	88.9	84.3	86.3	65.7	30.3	31.6	20.0	52.1	14.7

Note: Figures shown cover persons 25 years old and over; (1) Figures cover the Fargo, ND-MN Metropolitan Statistical Area—see Appendix B for areas included; (2) People of Hispanic origin can be of any race
Source: U.S. Census Bureau, 2012-2016 American Community Survey 5-Year Estimates

School Enrollment by Grade and Control

Area	Preschool (%)		Kindergarten (%)		Grades 1 - 4 (%)		Grades 5 - 8 (%)		Grades 9 - 12 (%)	
	Public	Private	Public	Private	Public	Private	Public	Private	Public	Private
City	66.8	33.2	100.0	0.0	94.1	5.9	87.6	12.4	93.7	6.3
MSA[1]	63.9	36.1	90.7	9.3	88.5	11.5	88.4	11.6	91.8	8.2
U.S.	58.4	41.6	87.7	12.3	89.8	10.2	89.7	10.3	90.4	9.6

Note: Figures shown cover persons 3 years old and over; (1) Figures cover the Fargo, ND-MN Metropolitan Statistical Area—see Appendix B for areas included
Source: U.S. Census Bureau, 2012-2016 American Community Survey 5-Year Estimates

Average Salaries of Public School Classroom Teachers

Area	2015		2016		Change from 2015 to 2016	
	Dollars	Rank[1]	Dollars	Rank[1]	Percent	Rank[2]
North Dakota	48,944	35	50,472	33	3.1	5
U.S. Average	57,611	–	58,353	–	1.3	–

Note: (1) Rank ranges from 1 to 51 where 1 indicates highest salary; (2) Rank ranges from 1 to 51 where 1 indicates highest percent change.
Source: National Education Association, Rankings & Estimates: Rankings of the States 2016 and Estimates of School Statistics 2017

Higher Education

Four-Year Colleges			Two-Year Colleges			Medical Schools[1]	Law Schools[2]	Voc/ Tech[3]
Public	Private Non-profit	Private For-profit	Public	Private Non-profit	Private For-profit			
0	0	0	0	0	0	0	0	0

Note: Figures cover institutions located within the city limits and include main campuses only; (1) includes schools accredited by the Liaison Committee on Medical Education and the American Osteopathic Association's Commission on Osteopathic College Accreditation; (2) includes ABA-accredited schools, schools with provisional ABA accreditation, and state accredited schools; (3) includes all schools with programs that are less than 2 years.
Source: National Center for Education Statistics, Integrated Postsecondary Education System (IPEDS), 2016-17; Wikipedia, List of Medical Schools in the United States, accessed April 2, 2018; Wikipedia, List of Law Schools in the United States, accessed April 2, 2018

According to *U.S. News & World Report,* the Fargo, ND-MN metro area is home to one of the best national universities in the U.S.: **North Dakota State University** (#198 tie). The indicators used to capture academic quality fall into a number of categories: assessment by administrators at peer institutions; retention of students; faculty resources; student selectivity; financial resources; alumni giving; high school counselor ratings of colleges; and graduation rate. *U.S. News & World Report, "America's Best Colleges 2018"*

According to *U.S. News & World Report,* the Fargo, ND-MN metro area is home to one of the best liberal arts colleges in the U.S.: **Concordia College—Moorhead** (#117 tie). The indicators used to capture academic quality fall into a number of categories: assessment by administrators at peer institutions; retention of students; faculty resources; student selectivity; financial resources; alumni giving; high school counselor ratings of colleges; and graduation rate. *U.S. News & World Report, "America's Best Colleges 2018"*

PRESIDENTIAL ELECTION

2016 Presidential Election Results

Area	Clinton	Trump	Johnson	Stein	Other
Cass County	38.8	49.3	7.5	1.5	2.9
U.S.	48.0	45.9	3.3	1.1	1.7

Note: Results are percentages and may not add to 100% due to rounding
Source: Dave Leip's Atlas of U.S. Presidential Elections

EMPLOYERS

Major Employers

Company Name	Industry
Blue Cross Blue Shield of North Dakota	Insurance
City of Fargo	Government
CNH Industrial America	Agriculture equipment
Concordia College	Education
Essentia Health	Hospitals
Fargo Public School District	Education
John Deere Electronic Solutions	Manufacturers
Microsoft	Computer software
Minnesota State University Moorhead	Education
Moorhead Area Public Schools	Education
Noridian Heathcare Solutions	Insurance
North Dakota State University	Education
Sanford Fargo Medical Center	Healthcare services
U.S. Bank	Financial institutions
Veterans Affairs	Hospitals
West Fargo Public School	Education

Note: Companies shown are located within the Fargo, ND-MN Metropolitan Statistical Area.
Source: Hoovers.com; Wikipedia

PUBLIC SAFETY

Crime Rate

Area	All Crimes	Violent Crimes				Property Crimes		
		Murder	Rape[3]	Robbery	Aggrav. Assault	Burglary	Larceny -Theft	Motor Vehicle Theft
City	1,568.3	2.8	65.0	17.0	101.7	390.0	861.8	130.0
Metro[1]	2,742.3	2.1	57.5	38.7	172.0	414.6	1,846.2	211.1
U.S.	2,847.8	5.3	40.4	102.8	248.5	468.9	1,745.0	236.9

Note: Figures are crimes per 100,000 population; (1) Figures cover the Fargo, ND-MN Metropolitan Statistical Area—see Appendix B for areas included; (3) The city and U.S. figures shown were reported using the revised Uniform Crime Reporting (UCR) definition of rape. The metro area figures shown are an aggregate total of the data submitted using both the revised and legacy UCR definitions.
Source: FBI Uniform Crime Reports, 2016

Hate Crimes

Area	Number of Quarters Reported	Number of Incidents per Bias Motivation					
		Race/Ethnicity/ Ancestry	Religion	Sexual Orientation	Disability	Gender	Gender Identity
City	4	0	0	0	0	0	0
U.S.	4	3,489	1,273	1,076	70	31	124

Source: Federal Bureau of Investigation, Hate Crime Statistics 2016

Identity Theft Consumer Reports

Area	Reports	Reports per 100,000 Population	Rank[2]
MSA[1]	166	70	255
U.S.	371,061	114	-

Note: (1) Figures cover the Fargo, ND-MN Metropolitan Statistical Area—see Appendix B for areas included; (2) Rank ranges from 1 to 389 where 1 indicates greatest number of identity theft reports per 100,000 population
Source: Federal Trade Commission, Consumer Sentinel Network Data Book for January–December 2017

Fraud and Other Consumer Reports

Area	Reports	Reports per 100,000 Population	Rank[2]
MSA[1]	678	285	364
U.S.	2,304,550	708	-

Note: (1) Figures cover the Fargo, ND-MN Metropolitan Statistical Area—see Appendix B for areas included; (2) Rank ranges from 1 to 389 where 1 indicates greatest number of fraud and other consumer reports per 100,000 population
Source: Federal Trade Commission, Consumer Sentinel Network Data Book for January–December 2017

SPORTS

Professional Sports Teams

Team Name	League	Year Established
No teams are located in the metro area		

Source: Wikipedia, Major Professional Sports Teams of the United States and Canada, April 5, 2018

CLIMATE

Average and Extreme Temperatures

Temperature	Jan	Feb	Mar	Apr	May	Jun	Jul	Aug	Sep	Oct	Nov	Dec	Yr.
Extreme High (°F)	52	66	78	100	98	100	106	106	102	93	74	57	106
Average High (°F)	15	21	34	54	69	77	83	81	70	57	36	21	52
Average Temp. (°F)	6	12	26	43	56	66	71	69	58	46	28	13	41
Average Low (°F)	-3	3	17	32	44	54	59	57	46	35	19	4	31
Extreme Low (°F)	-36	-34	-34	-7	20	30	36	33	19	5	-24	-32	-36

Note: Figures cover the years 1948-1995
Source: National Climatic Data Center, International Station Meteorological Climate Summary, 9/96

Average Precipitation/Snowfall/Humidity

Precip./Humidity	Jan	Feb	Mar	Apr	May	Jun	Jul	Aug	Sep	Oct	Nov	Dec	Yr.
Avg. Precip. (in.)	0.6	0.5	1.0	1.7	2.3	3.1	3.2	2.4	1.8	1.5	0.8	0.6	19.6
Avg. Snowfall (in.)	9	6	7	3	Tr	0	0	0	Tr	1	6	7	40
Avg. Rel. Hum. 6am (%)	75	77	82	79	77	82	86	86	85	80	81	78	81
Avg. Rel. Hum. 3pm (%)	70	71	67	51	45	50	50	47	49	51	65	73	57

Note: Figures cover the years 1948-1995; Tr = Trace amounts (<0.05 in. of rain; <0.5 in. of snow)
Source: National Climatic Data Center, International Station Meteorological Climate Summary, 9/96

Weather Conditions

Temperature			Daytime Sky			Precipitation		
5°F & below	32°F & below	90°F & above	Clear	Partly cloudy	Cloudy	0.01 inch or more precip.	0.1 inch or more snow/ice	Thunder-storms
65	180	15	81	145	139	100	38	31

Note: Figures are average number of days per year and cover the years 1948-1995
Source: National Climatic Data Center, International Station Meteorological Climate Summary, 9/96

HAZARDOUS WASTE

Superfund Sites

The Fargo, ND-MN metro area has no sites on the EPA's Superfund Final National Priorities List. There are a total of 1,396 Superfund sites with a status of proposed or final on the list in the U.S.
U.S. Environmental Protection Agency, National Priorities List, April 4, 2018

AIR & WATER QUALITY

Air Quality Trends: Ozone

	1990	1995	2000	2005	2010	2012	2013	2014	2015	2016
MSA[1]	n/a	n/a	n/a	n/a	n/a	n/a	n/a	n/a	n/a	n/a
U.S.	0.087	0.089	0.081	0.079	0.073	0.075	0.069	0.067	0.068	0.069

Note: (1) Data covers the Fargo, ND-MN Metropolitan Statistical Area—see Appendix B for areas included; n/a not available. The values shown are the composite ozone concentration averages among trend sites based on the highest fourth daily maximum 8-hour concentration in parts per million. These trends are based on sites having an adequate record of monitoring data during the trend period. Data from exceptional events are included.
Source: U.S. Environmental Protection Agency, Air Quality Monitoring Information, "Air Quality Trends by City, 1990-2016"

Air Quality Index

Area	Percent of Days when Air Quality was...[2]					AQI Statistics[2]	
	Good	Moderate	Unhealthy for Sensitive Groups	Unhealthy	Very Unhealthy	Maximum	Median
MSA[1]	84.5	15.5	0.0	0.0	0.0	77	37.5

Note: (1) Data covers the Fargo, ND-MN Metropolitan Statistical Area—see Appendix B for areas included; (2) Based on 362 days with AQI data in 2017. Air Quality Index (AQI) is an index for reporting daily air quality. EPA calculates the AQI for five major air pollutants regulated by the Clean Air Act: ground-level ozone, particle pollution (aka particulate matter), carbon monoxide, sulfur dioxide, and nitrogen dioxide. The AQI runs from 0 to 500. The higher the AQI value, the greater the level of air pollution and the greater the health concern. There are six AQI categories: "Good" AQI is between 0 and 50. Air quality is considered satisfactory; "Moderate" AQI is between 51 and 100. Air quality is acceptable; "Unhealthy for Sensitive Groups" When AQI values are between 101 and 150, members of sensitive groups may experience health effects; "Unhealthy" When AQI values are between 151 and 200 everyone may begin to experience health effects; "Very Unhealthy" AQI values between 201 and 300 trigger a health alert; "Hazardous" AQI values over 300 trigger warnings of emergency conditions (not shown).
Source: U.S. Environmental Protection Agency, Air Quality Index Report, 2017

Air Quality Index Pollutants

Area	Percent of Days when AQI Pollutant was...[2]					
	Carbon Monoxide	Nitrogen Dioxide	Ozone	Sulfur Dioxide	Particulate Matter 2.5	Particulate Matter 10
MSA[1]	0.0	0.3	45.6	0.0	49.7	4.4

Note: (1) Data covers the Fargo, ND-MN Metropolitan Statistical Area—see Appendix B for areas included; (2) Based on 362 days with AQI data in 2017. The Air Quality Index (AQI) is an index for reporting daily air quality. EPA calculates the AQI for five major air pollutants regulated by the Clean Air Act: ground-level ozone, particle pollution (also known as particulate matter), carbon monoxide, sulfur dioxide, and nitrogen dioxide. The AQI runs from 0 to 500. The higher the AQI value, the greater the level of air pollution and the greater the health concern.
Source: U.S. Environmental Protection Agency, Air Quality Index Report, 2017

Maximum Air Pollutant Concentrations: Particulate Matter, Ozone, CO and Lead

	Particulate Matter 10 (ug/m^3)	Particulate Matter 2.5 Wtd AM (ug/m^3)	Particulate Matter 2.5 24-Hr (ug/m^3)	Ozone (ppm)	Carbon Monoxide (ppm)	Lead (ug/m^3)
MSA[1] Level	63	n/a	n/a	0.054	0	n/a
NAAQS[2]	150	15	35	0.075	9	0.15
Met NAAQS[2]	Yes	n/a	n/a	Yes	Yes	n/a

Note: (1) Data covers the Fargo, ND-MN Metropolitan Statistical Area—see Appendix B for areas included; Data from exceptional events are included; (2) National Ambient Air Quality Standards; ppm = parts per million; ug/m^3 = micrograms per cubic meter; n/a not available.
Concentrations: Particulate Matter 10 (coarse particulate)—highest second maximum 24-hour concentration; Particulate Matter 2.5 Wtd AM (fine particulate)—highest weighted annual mean concentration; Particulate Matter 2.5 24-Hour (fine particulate)—highest 98th percentile 24-hour concentration; Ozone—highest fourth daily maximum 8-hour concentration; Carbon Monoxide—highest second maximum non-overlapping 8-hour concentration; Lead—maximum running 3-month average
Source: U.S. Environmental Protection Agency, Air Quality Monitoring Information, "Air Quality Statistics by City, 2016"

Maximum Air Pollutant Concentrations: Nitrogen Dioxide and Sulfur Dioxide

	Nitrogen Dioxide AM (ppb)	Nitrogen Dioxide 1-Hr (ppb)	Sulfur Dioxide AM (ppb)	Sulfur Dioxide 1-Hr (ppb)	Sulfur Dioxide 24-Hr (ppb)
MSA[1] Level	4	27	n/a	2	n/a
NAAQS[2]	53	100	30	75	140
Met NAAQS[2]	Yes	Yes	n/a	Yes	n/a

Note: (1) Data covers the Fargo, ND-MN Metropolitan Statistical Area—see Appendix B for areas included; Data from exceptional events are included; (2) National Ambient Air Quality Standards; ppm = parts per million; ug/m^3 = micrograms per cubic meter; n/a not available.
Concentrations: Nitrogen Dioxide AM—highest arithmetic mean concentration; Nitrogen Dioxide 1-Hr—highest 98th percentile 1-hour daily maximum concentration; Sulfur Dioxide AM—highest annual mean concentration; Sulfur Dioxide 1-Hr—highest 99th percentile 1-hour daily maximum concentration; Sulfur Dioxide 24-Hr—highest second maximum 24-hour concentration
Source: U.S. Environmental Protection Agency, Air Quality Monitoring Information, "Air Quality Statistics by City, 2016"

Drinking Water

Water System Name	Pop. Served	Primary Water Source Type	Violations[1]	
			Health Based	Monitoring/ Reporting
City of West Fargo	34,858	Purchased Surface	0	0

Note: (1) Based on violation data from January 1, 2017 to December 31, 2017
Source: U.S. Environmental Protection Agency, Office of Ground Water and Drinking Water, Safe Drinking Water Information System (based on data extracted April 5, 2018)

Beavercreek, Ohio

Background

Beavercreek sits on over 27 square miles of wooded, rolling hills, 12 miles southeast of Dayton, which influences Beavercreek through its population, attractions and amenities, and politics.

A portion of Beavercreek lies in the Beavercreek Township, all of which is a part of Greene County. The area where Beavercreek currently sits was once a prominent hunting ground of the Shawnee and Miami Indians. In the late 1700s, European settlers arrived in the area, typically along the Little Beaver Creek or Big Beaver Creek. Greene County was formed in the early 1800s with Beavercreek as its county seat. Beavercreek traces its beginnings back to this time; however, the city itself was not incorporated until 1980, from a portion of the Beavercreek Township. Beavercreek includes the areas known as Apple Valley, Big Beaver Valley, Indian Ripple, Knollwood, New Germany, Spicer, Zimmermanville, and the village of Alpha.

Wright-Patterson Air Force Base has a large influence on Beavercreek, employing thousands of military personnel and civilians. The air force base has a positive impact on the Beavercreek economy, and the large number of technical and research jobs at the base pushed the city's median household income to over $75,000 per year. Furthermore, due to military base realignment, more jobs on Wright-Patterson AFB are available to local residents, encouraging people to move to the area to support the growth of the base.

Education within the city of Beavercreek is provided by the Beavercreek City School District. The city school district is growing rapidly and district officials are actively planning solutions to limit enrollment to ensure quality education for their students. The University of Dayton, a private Catholic institution, Wright State University, and several small colleges are available for those seeking higher education.

While Beavercreek's primary attractions include The Mall at Fairfield Common, the abundant bike trails, seasonal concerts, golfing and other outdoor activities, there are many other attractions available in the Dayton metropolitan area a short drive away. The area offers several museums, the Cox Arboretum and Gardens MetroPark, as well as many aviation-related attractions to commemorate the Wright Brothers who were from the area. In addition, there are ample opportunities to participate in the arts and sports.

Beavercreek has a humid continental climate with four distinct seasons. Average winter lows typically dip just below 20 degrees in January and average normal highs reach the mid-80s in July. Average precipitation ranges from two to four inches a month with the most precipitation in April, May, and June.

Beavercreek's transportation needs are served by the James M. Cox Dayton International Airport that offers non-stop flights to many hubs across the nation including Atlanta, Chicago, Denver, New York, and Orlando.

Rankings

Business/Finance Rankings

- The personal finance site NerdWallet analyzed 183 American metropolitan areas with populations over 250,000 and more than 15,000 businesses to rank where entrepreneurs find the most success. Criteria included area economy, annual income, housing cost, unemployment rate, and the success rate of area businesses. Dayton* ranked #121. *www.nerdwallet.com, "Best Places to Start a Business," April 27, 2015*
- The Brookings Institution ranked the 100 largest metro areas in the U.S. based on income inequality. Dayton* was ranked #43 (#1 = greatest ineqality). Criteria: the "95/20 ratio," a figure representing the income at which a household earns more than 95 percent of all other households, divided by the income at which a household earns more than only 20 percent of all other households. *Brookings Institution, "Household Income Inequality, 100 Largest U.S. Metro Areas, 2014-2016," February 5, 2018*
- The Dayton* metro area was identified as one of the most affordable metropolitan areas in America by *Forbes.* The area ranked #8 out of 20 based on the National Association of Home Builders/Wells Fargo Housing Affordability Index and Sperling's Best Places' cost-of-living index. *Forbes.com, "America's Most Affordable Cities in 2015," March 12, 2015*
- Dayton* was cited as one of America's top metros for new and expanded facility projects in 2017. The area ranked #8 in the mid-sized metro area category (population 200,000 to 1 million). *Site Selection, "Top Metropolitans of 2017," March 2018*
- The Dayton* metro area appeared on the Milken Institute "2017 Best Performing Cities" list. Rank: #149 out of 200 large metro areas. Criteria: job growth; wage and salary growth; high-tech output growth. *Milken Institute, "Best-Performing Cities 2017," January 2018*
- *Forbes* ranked the 200 most populous metro areas to determine the nation's "Best Places for Business and Careers." The Dayton* metro area was ranked #118. Criteria: costs (business and living); job growth (past and projected); income growth; quality of life; educational attainment (college and high school); projected economic growth; cultural and recreational opportunities; net migration patterns; number of highly ranked colleges. *Forbes, "The Best Places for Business and Careers 2017," October 24, 2017*

Dating/Romance Rankings

- *Apartment List* conducted its annual survey of renters to compile a list of metros that have the best opportunities for dating. Nearly 11,000 respondents, from February 2017 through January 2018, rated their current city or neighborhood for opportunities to date and make friends. The Dayton* metro area ranked #62 out of 70 where single residents were very satisfied or somewhat satisfied, making it among the ten worst metros for dating opportunities. Other criteria analyzed included gender and education levels of renters. *Apartment List, "Best Metros for Dating 2018," February 6, 2018*

Education Rankings

- Personal finance website *WalletHub* analyzed the 150 largest U.S. metropolitan statistical areas to determine where the most educated Americans are choosing to settle. Criteria: education quality and attainment gap; education levels; percentage of workers with degrees; public school rankings; quality and size of each metro area's universities. Dayton* was ranked #74 (#1 = most educated city). *www.WalletHub.com, "2017's Most and Least Educated Cities in America," July 25, 2017*

Environmental Rankings

- Sperling's BestPlaces assessed 379 metropolitan areas of the United States for the likelihood of dangerously extreme weather events or earthquakes. In general the Southeast and South-Central regions have the highest risk of weather extremes and earthquakes, while the Pacific Northwest enjoys the lowest risk. Of the least risky metropolitan areas, the Dayton* metro area was ranked #251. *www.bestplaces.net, "Safest Places from Natural Disasters," April 2011*

Health/Fitness Rankings

- Analysts who tracked obesity rates in 100 of the nation's most populous areas found that the Dayton* metro area was one of the ten communities where residents were most likely to be obese, defined as a BMI score of 30 or above. *www.gallup.com, "Colorado Springs Residents Least Likely to Be Obese," May 28, 2015*

- The Dayton* metro area was identified as one of the worst cities for bed bugs in America by pest control company Orkin. The area ranked #34 out of 50 based on the number of bed bug treatments Orkin performed from December 2016 to November 2017. *Orkin, "Baltimore and Washington D.C. Continue to Hold Top Spots," January 8, 2018*

- Dayton* was identified as a "2016 Spring Allergy Capital." The area ranked #11 out of 100. Three groups of factors were used to identify the most severe cities for people with allergies during the spring season: annual pollen levels; medicine utilization; access to board-certified allergists. *Asthma and Allergy Foundation of America, "Spring Allergy Capitals 2016"*

- Dayton* was identified as a "2016 Fall Allergy Capital." The area ranked #8 out of 100. Three groups of factors were used to identify the most severe cities for people with allergies during the fall season: annual pollen levels; medicine utilization; access to board-certified allergists. *Asthma and Allergy Foundation of America, "Fall Allergy Capitals 2016"*

- Dayton* was identified as a "2015 Asthma Capital." The area ranked #18 out of the nation's 100 largest metropolitan areas. Criteria: estimated prevalence; self-reported prevalence; crude death rate for asthma; annual pollen score; annual air quality; public smoking laws; number of board-certified asthma specialists; school inhaler access laws; rescue medication use; controller medication use; ER visits for asthma; uninsured rate; poverty rate. *Asthma and Allergy Foundation of America, "Asthma Capitals 2015"*

- The Dayton* metro area ranked #144 out of 189 in The Gallup-Healthways Well-Being Index. Criteria: purpose; social well being; financial health; community and physical health. Results are based on telephone interviews with adults, aged 18 and older, living in metropolitan areas in the 50 U.S. states and the District of Columbia. *Gallup-Healthways, "State of American Well-Being, 2017 Community Well-Being Rankings" March 2018*

Real Estate Rankings

- Dayton* was ranked #41 out of 238 metro areas in terms of housing affordability in 2017 by the National Association of Home Builders (#1 = most affordable). Criteria: the share of homes sold in that area affordable to a family earning the local median income, based on standard mortgage underwriting criteria. *National Association of Home Builders®, NAHB-Wells Fargo Housing Opportunity Index, 4th Quarter 2017*

Safety Rankings

- The National Insurance Crime Bureau ranked 382 metro areas in the U.S. in terms of per capita rates of vehicle theft. The Dayton* metro area ranked #117 (#1 = highest rate). Criteria: number of vehicle theft offenses per 100,000 inhabitants in 2016. *National Insurance Crime Bureau, "Hot Spots 2016," June 8, 2017*

Seniors/Retirement Rankings

- From its Best Cities for Successful Aging indexes, the Milken Institute generated rankings for metropolitan areas, weighing data in nine categories—health care, wellness, living arrangements, transportation and convenience, financial characteristics, education, employment, community engagement, and overall livability. The Dayton* metro area was ranked #29 overall in the large metro area category. *Milken Institute, "Best Cities for Successful Aging, 2017" March 14, 2017*

*Beavercreek is located within the Dayton, OH Metropolitan Statistical Area.

Business Environment

CITY FINANCES

City Government Finances

Component	2015 ($000)	2015 ($ per capita)
Total Revenues	25,841	558
Total Expenditures	29,533	638
Debt Outstanding	7,695	166
Cash and Securities[1]	6,866	148

Note: (1) Cash and security holdings of a government at the close of its fiscal year,, including those of its dependent agencies, utilities, and liquor stores.
Source: U.S Census Bureau, State & Local Government Finances 2015

City Government Revenue by Source

Source	2015 ($000)	2015 ($ per capita)	2015 (%)
General Revenue			
From Federal Government	0	0	0.0
From State Government	7,406	160	28.7
From Local Governments	0	0	0.0
Taxes			
Property	13,470	291	52.1
Sales and Gross Receipts	0	0	0.0
Personal Income	0	0	0.0
Corporate Income	0	0	0.0
Motor Vehicle License	0	0	0.0
Other Taxes	834	18	3.2
Current Charges	2,054	44	7.9
Liquor Store	0	0	0.0
Utility	0	0	0.0
Employee Retirement	0	0	0.0

Source: U.S Census Bureau, State & Local Government Finances 2015

City Government Expenditures by Function

Function	2015 ($000)	2015 ($ per capita)	2015 (%)
General Direct Expenditures			
Air Transportation	0	0	0.0
Corrections	0	0	0.0
Education	0	0	0.0
Employment Security Administration	0	0	0.0
Financial Administration	374	8	1.3
Fire Protection	0	0	0.0
General Public Buildings	111	2	0.4
Governmental Administration, Other	623	13	2.1
Health	0	0	0.0
Highways	14,381	310	48.7
Hospitals	0	0	0.0
Housing and Community Development	576	12	2.0
Interest on General Debt	679	14	2.3
Judicial and Legal	0	0	0.0
Libraries	0	0	0.0
Parking	0	0	0.0
Parks and Recreation	3,133	67	10.6
Police Protection	8,339	180	28.2
Public Welfare	0	0	0.0
Sewerage	0	0	0.0
Solid Waste Management	0	0	0.0
Veterans' Services	0	0	0.0
Liquor Store	0	0	0.0
Utility	0	0	0.0
Employee Retirement	0	0	0.0

Source: U.S Census Bureau, State & Local Government Finances 2015

DEMOGRAPHICS

Population Growth

Area	1990 Census	2000 Census	2010 Census	2016* Estimate	Population Growth (%) 1990-2016	2010-2016
City	33,946	37,984	45,193	46,086	35.8	2.0
MSA[1]	843,857	848,153	841,502	800,950	-5.1	-4.8
U.S.	248,709,873	281,421,906	308,745,538	318,558,162	28.1	3.2

Note: (1) Figures cover the Dayton, OH Metropolitan Statistical Area—see Appendix B for areas included; (*) 2012-2016 5-year estimated population
Source: U.S. Census Bureau, 1990 Census, Census 2000, Census 2010, 2012-2016 American Community Survey 5-Year Estimates

Household Size

Area	Persons in Household (%) One	Two	Three	Four	Five	Six	Seven or More	Average Household Size
City	25.0	37.5	17.4	12.3	5.2	2.0	0.6	2.50
MSA[1]	32.1	34.3	14.9	11.4	4.9	1.7	0.8	2.40
U.S.	27.7	33.7	15.7	13.1	6.0	2.3	1.5	2.60

Note: (1) Figures cover the Dayton, OH Metropolitan Statistical Area—see Appendix B for areas included
Source: U.S. Census Bureau, 2012-2016 American Community Survey 5-Year Estimates

Race

Area	White Alone[2] (%)	Black Alone[2] (%)	Asian Alone[2] (%)	AIAN[3] Alone[2] (%)	NHOPI[4] Alone[2] (%)	Other Race Alone[2] (%)	Two or More Races (%)
City	87.4	3.0	5.3	0.2	0.0	0.5	3.6
MSA[1]	78.8	15.5	2.1	0.2	0.0	0.6	2.9
U.S.	73.3	12.6	5.2	0.8	0.2	4.8	3.1

Note: (1) Figures cover the Dayton, OH Metropolitan Statistical Area—see Appendix B for areas included; (2) Alone is defined as not being in combination with one or more other races; (3) American Indian and Alaska Native; (4) Native Hawaiian and Other Pacific Islander
Source: U.S. Census Bureau, 2012-2016 American Community Survey 5-Year Estimates

Hispanic or Latino Origin

Area	Total (%)	Mexican (%)	Puerto Rican (%)	Cuban (%)	Other (%)
City	2.8	1.5	0.7	0.1	0.5
MSA[1]	2.5	1.5	0.4	0.1	0.5
U.S.	17.3	11.0	1.7	0.7	4.0

Note: Persons of Hispanic or Latino origin can be of any race; (1) Figures cover the Dayton, OH Metropolitan Statistical Area—see Appendix B for areas included
Source: U.S. Census Bureau, 2012-2016 American Community Survey 5-Year Estimates

Segregation

Type	Segregation Indices[1] 1990	2000	2010	2010 Rank[2]	Percent Change 1990-2000	1990-2010	2000-2010
Black/White	76.6	73.0	66.4	14	-3.6	-10.2	-6.6
Asian/White	36.4	36.7	39.8	58	0.3	3.4	3.1
Hispanic/White	28.9	25.9	27.3	99	-3.0	-1.7	1.3

Note: All figures cover the Metropolitan Statistical Area—see Appendix B for areas included; Figures are based on an analysis of 1990, 2000, and 2010 Census Decennial Census tract data by William H. Frey, Brookings Institution and the University of Michigan Social Science Data Analysis Network. In this analysis all racial groups (whites, blacks, and asians) are non-Hispanic members of those races. Hispanics are shown as a separate category; (1) Segregation Indices are Dissimilarity Indices that measure the degree to which the minority group is distributed differently than whites across census tracts. They range from 0 (complete integration) to 100 (complete segregation) where the value indicates the percentage of the minority group that needs to move to be distributed exactly like whites; (2) Ranges from 1 (most segregated) to 102 (least segregated); n/a not available.
Source: www.CensusScope.org

Ancestry

Area	German	Irish	English	American	Italian	Polish	French[2]	Scottish	Dutch
City	24.5	13.2	10.6	10.0	4.8	3.8	2.8	2.1	1.7
MSA[1]	24.3	12.7	8.6	7.9	3.5	2.0	2.3	2.0	1.5
U.S.	14.4	10.4	7.7	6.9	5.4	2.9	2.6	1.7	1.3

Note: Figures are the percentage of the total population reporting a particular ancestry. The nine most commonly reported ancestries in the U.S. are shown. Figures include multiple ancestries (e.g. if a person reported being Irish and Italian, they were included in both columns); (1) Figures cover the Dayton, OH Metropolitan Statistical Area—see Appendix B for areas included; (2) Excludes Basque
Source: U.S. Census Bureau, 2012-2016 American Community Survey 5-Year Estimates

Foreign-Born Population

Area	Percent of Population Born in								
	Any Foreign Country	Asia	Mexico	Europe	Carribean	Central America[2]	South America	Africa	Canada
City	7.9	5.7	0.1	0.9	0.1	0.0	0.4	0.5	0.2
MSA[1]	4.1	2.2	0.3	0.7	0.1	0.1	0.1	0.4	0.1
U.S.	13.2	4.0	3.6	1.5	1.3	1.0	0.9	0.6	0.3

Note: (1) Figures cover the Dayton, OH Metropolitan Statistical Area—see Appendix B for areas included; (2) Excludes Mexico.
Source: U.S. Census Bureau, 2012-2016 American Community Survey 5-Year Estimates

Marital Status

Area	Never Married	Now Married[2]	Separated	Widowed	Divorced
City	26.4	59.7	0.8	4.9	8.2
MSA[1]	31.9	46.6	1.7	6.8	13.0
U.S.	33.0	48.1	2.1	5.9	11.0

Note: Figures are percentages and cover the population 15 years of age and older; (1) Figures cover the Dayton, OH Metropolitan Statistical Area—see Appendix B for areas included; (2) Excludes separated
Source: U.S. Census Bureau, 2012-2016 American Community Survey 5-Year Estimates

Disability Status

Area	All Ages	Under 18 Years Old	18 to 64 Years Old	65 Years and Over
City	9.6	4.0	6.6	28.2
MSA[1]	14.4	4.8	12.4	35.5
U.S.	12.5	4.1	10.3	35.7

Note: Figures show percent of the civilian noninstitutionalized population that reported having a disability. Disability status is determined from six types of difficulty: vision, hearing, cognitive, ambulatory, self-care, and independent living. For children under 5 years old, hearing and vision difficulty are used to determine disability status. For children between the ages of 5 and 14, disability status is determined from hearing, vision, cognitive, ambulatory, and self-care difficulties. For people aged 15 years and older, they are considered to have a disability if they have difficulty with any one of the six difficulty types; Note: (1) Figures cover the Dayton, OH Metropolitan Statistical Area—see Appendix B for areas included
Source: U.S. Census Bureau, 2012-2016 American Community Survey 5-Year Estimates

Age

Area	Percent of Population									Median Age
	Under Age 5	Age 5–19	Age 20–34	Age 35–44	Age 45–54	Age 55–64	Age 65–74	Age 75–84	Age 85+	
City	5.0	17.1	21.6	11.2	14.5	14.1	9.8	4.8	1.8	41.1
MSA[1]	6.0	19.0	20.1	11.5	13.5	13.5	9.1	5.1	2.2	39.5
U.S.	6.2	19.6	20.7	12.7	13.6	12.6	8.3	4.3	1.9	37.7

Note: (1) Figures cover the Dayton, OH Metropolitan Statistical Area—see Appendix B for areas included
Source: U.S. Census Bureau, 2012-2016 American Community Survey 5-Year Estimates

Gender

Area	Males	Females	Males per 100 Females
City	23,536	22,550	104.4
MSA[1]	388,398	412,552	94.1
U.S.	156,765,322	161,792,840	96.9

Note: (1) Figures cover the Dayton, OH Metropolitan Statistical Area—see Appendix B for areas included
Source: U.S. Census Bureau, 2012-2016 American Community Survey 5-Year Estimates

Religious Groups by Family

Area	Catholic	Baptist	Non-Den.	Methodist[2]	Lutheran	LDS[3]	Pente-costal	Presby-terian[4]	Muslim[5]	Judaism
MSA[1]	12.4	9.6	4.3	4.5	2.1	0.8	1.5	2.1	0.2	0.3
U.S.	19.1	9.3	4.0	4.0	2.3	2.0	1.9	1.6	0.8	0.7

Note: Figures are the number of adherents as a percentage of the total population; (1) Figures cover the Dayton, OH Metropolitan Statistical Area—see Appendix B for areas included; (2) Methodist/Pietist; (3) Latter Day Saints; (4) Reformed; (5) Figures are estimates
Source: Association of Statisticians of American Religious Bodies, 2010 U.S. Religion Census: Religious Congregations & Membership Study

Religious Groups by Tradition

Area	Catholic	Evangelical Protestant	Mainline Protestant	Other Tradition	Black Protestant	Orthodox
MSA[1]	12.4	16.0	9.5	2.5	2.7	0.5
U.S.	19.1	16.2	7.3	4.3	1.6	0.3

Note: Figures are the number of adherents as a percentage of the total population; (1) Figures cover the Dayton, OH Metropolitan Statistical Area—see Appendix B for areas included
Source: Association of Statisticians of American Religious Bodies, 2010 U.S. Religion Census: Religious Congregations & Membership Study

ECONOMY

Gross Metropolitan Product

Area	2014	2015	2016	2017	Rank[2]
MSA[1]	37.7	38.9	40.1	41.7	69

Note: Figures are in billions of dollars; (1) Figures cover the Dayton, OH Metropolitan Statistical Area—see Appendix B for areas included; (2) Rank is based on 2015 data and ranges from 1 to 381
Source: The U.S. Conference of Mayors, U.S. Metro Economies: GMP and Employment Report, 2015-2017

Economic Growth

Area	2012-14 (%)	2015 (%)	2016 (%)	2017 (%)	Rank[2]
MSA[1]	-0.6	1.5	1.4	1.9	318
U.S.	2.0	2.4	1.9	2.6	–

Note: Figures are real gross metropolitan product (GMP) growth rates and represent average annual percent change; (1) Figures cover the Dayton, OH Metropolitan Statistical Area—see Appendix B for areas included; (2) Rank is based on 2012-2014 average annual percent change and ranges from 1 to 381
Source: The U.S. Conference of Mayors, U.S. Metro Economies: GMP and Employment Report, 2015-2017

Metropolitan Area Exports

Area	2011	2012	2013	2014	2015	2016	Rank[2]
MSA[1]	2,749.2	2,790.4	2,740.1	3,026.1	2,991.1	2,874.5	78

Note: Figures are in millions of dollars; (1) Figures cover the Dayton, OH Metropolitan Statistical Area—see Appendix B for areas included; (2) Rank is based on 2016 data and ranges from 1 to 385
Source: U.S. Department of Commerce, International Trade Administration, Office of Trade & Industry Information, Manufacturing & Services, data extracted March 15, 2018

Building Permits

Area	Single-Family			Multi-Family			Total		
	2016	2017p	Pct. Chg.	2016	2017p	Pct. Chg.	2016	2017p	Pct. Chg.
City	n/a	n/a	n/a	n/a	n/a	n/a	n/a	n/a	n/a
MSA[1]	901	994	10.3	323	176	-45.5	1,224	1,170	-4.4
U.S.	750,800	817,300	8.9	455,800	446,800	-2.0	1,206,600	1,264,100	4.8

Note: (1) Figures cover the Dayton, OH Metropolitan Statistical Area—see Appendix B for areas included; Figures represent new, privately-owned housing units authorized (unadjusted data); All permit data are based on estimates with imputation; (p) preliminary data.
Source: U.S. Census Bureau, Manufacturing, Mining, and Construction Statistics, Building Permits, 2016, 2017

Bankruptcy Filings

Area	Business Filings 2016	Business Filings 2017	Business Filings % Chg.	Nonbusiness Filings 2016	Nonbusiness Filings 2017	Nonbusiness Filings % Chg.
Greene County	7	2	-71.4	323	376	16.4
U.S.	24,114	23,157	-4.0	770,846	765,863	-0.6

Note: Business filings include Chapter 7, Chapter 11, Chapter 12, and Chapter 13; Nonbusiness filings include Chapter 7, Chapter 11, and Chapter 13
Source: Administrative Office of the U.S. Courts, Business and Nonbusiness Bankruptcy, County Cases Commenced by Chapter of the Bankruptcy Code, During the 12-Month Period Ending December 31, 2016 and Business and Nonbusiness Bankruptcy, County Cases Commenced by Chapter of the Bankruptcy Code, During the 12-Month Period Ending December 31, 2017

Housing Vacancy Rates

Area	Gross Vacancy Rate[2] (%)			Year-Round Vacancy Rate[3] (%)			Rental Vacancy Rate[4] (%)			Homeowner Vacancy Rate[5] (%)		
	2015	2016	2017	2015	2016	2017	2015	2016	2017	2015	2016	2017
MSA[1]	11.4	12.0	11.1	11.4	11.9	11.1	9.4	10.5	6.9	2.3	3.3	3.7
U.S.	12.9	12.8	12.7	10.0	9.9	9.9	7.1	6.9	7.2	1.8	1.7	1.6

Note: (1) Figures cover the Dayton, OH Metropolitan Statistical Area—see Appendix B for areas included; (2) The percentage of the total housing inventory that is vacant; (3) The percentage of the housing inventory (excluding seasonal units) that is year-round vacant; (4) The percentage of rental inventory that is vacant for rent; (5) The percentage of homeowner inventory that is vacant for sale
Source: U.S. Census Bureau, Housing Vacancies and Homeownership Annual Statistics: 2015, 2016, 2017

INCOME

Income

Area	Per Capita ($)	Median Household ($)	Average Household ($)
City	40,639	82,956	99,010
MSA[1]	27,628	49,223	65,799
U.S.	29,829	55,322	77,866

Note: (1) Figures cover the Dayton, OH Metropolitan Statistical Area—see Appendix B for areas included
Source: U.S. Census Bureau, 2012-2016 American Community Survey 5-Year Estimates

Household Income Distribution

Area	Under $15,000	$15,000 -$24,999	$25,000 -$34,999	$35,000 -$49,999	$50,000 -$74,999	$75,000 -$99,999	$100,000 -$149,999	$150,000 and up
City	4.8	5.6	5.4	10.6	18.6	15.4	21.9	17.8
MSA[1]	14.0	11.4	10.7	14.5	18.2	11.7	12.1	7.3
U.S.	12.1	10.2	9.9	13.2	17.8	12.2	13.5	11.1

Percent of Households Earning

Note: (1) Figures cover the Dayton, OH Metropolitan Statistical Area—see Appendix B for areas included
Source: U.S. Census Bureau, 2012-2016 American Community Survey 5-Year Estimates

Poverty Rate

Area	All Ages	Under 18 Years Old	18 to 64 Years Old	65 Years and Over
City	4.8	3.0	5.6	4.2
MSA[1]	16.4	24.8	15.5	8.1
U.S.	15.1	21.2	14.2	9.3

Note: Figures are percentage of people whose income during the past 12 months was below the poverty level; (1) Figures cover the Dayton, OH Metropolitan Statistical Area—see Appendix B for areas included
Source: U.S. Census Bureau, 2012-2016 American Community Survey 5-Year Estimates

EMPLOYMENT

Labor Force and Employment

Area	Civilian Labor Force Dec. 2016	Civilian Labor Force Dec. 2017	Civilian Labor Force % Chg.	Workers Employed Dec. 2016	Workers Employed Dec. 2017	Workers Employed % Chg.
City	23,178	23,733	2.4	22,326	22,906	2.6
MSA[1]	385,769	394,624	2.3	367,844	377,877	2.7
U.S.	158,968,000	159,880,000	0.6	151,798,000	153,602,000	1.2

Note: Data is not seasonally adjusted and covers workers 16 years of age and older; (1) Figures cover the Dayton, OH Metropolitan Statistical Area—see Appendix B for areas included
Source: Bureau of Labor Statistics, Local Area Unemployment Statistics

Unemployment Rate

Area	2017											
	Jan.	Feb.	Mar.	Apr.	May	Jun.	Jul.	Aug.	Sep.	Oct.	Nov.	Dec.
City	4.4	4.2	3.7	3.4	3.6	4.0	4.0	4.0	3.8	3.6	3.6	3.5
MSA[1]	5.7	5.3	4.7	4.2	4.3	4.9	4.9	4.9	4.4	4.2	4.2	4.2
U.S.	5.1	4.9	4.6	4.1	4.1	4.5	4.6	4.5	4.1	3.9	3.9	3.9

Note: Data is not seasonally adjusted and covers workers 16 years of age and older; (1) Figures cover the Dayton, OH Metropolitan Statistical Area—see Appendix B for areas included
Source: Bureau of Labor Statistics, Local Area Unemployment Statistics

Average Wages

Occupation	$/Hr.	Occupation	$/Hr.
Accountants and Auditors	36.70	Maids and Housekeeping Cleaners	10.50
Automotive Mechanics	17.80	Maintenance and Repair Workers	19.40
Bookkeepers	19.20	Marketing Managers	57.50
Carpenters	22.20	Nuclear Medicine Technologists	35.20
Cashiers	10.00	Nurses, Licensed Practical	21.10
Clerks, General Office	16.60	Nurses, Registered	32.30
Clerks, Receptionists/Information	12.90	Nursing Assistants	13.30
Clerks, Shipping/Receiving	15.70	Packers and Packagers, Hand	10.10
Computer Programmers	37.80	Physical Therapists	46.40
Computer Systems Analysts	43.30	Postal Service Mail Carriers	23.80
Computer User Support Specialists	22.40	Real Estate Brokers	n/a
Cooks, Restaurant	11.20	Retail Salespersons	12.10
Dentists	94.50	Sales Reps., Exc. Tech./Scientific	31.10
Electrical Engineers	41.70	Sales Reps., Tech./Scientific	37.40
Electricians	23.70	Secretaries, Exc. Legal/Med./Exec.	17.10
Financial Managers	62.90	Security Guards	12.90
First-Line Supervisors/Managers, Sales	20.90	Surgeons	117.20
Food Preparation Workers	11.00	Teacher Assistants*	13.00
General and Operations Managers	54.00	Teachers, Elementary School*	28.90
Hairdressers/Cosmetologists	11.60	Teachers, Secondary School*	30.50
Internists, General	115.00	Telemarketers	11.90
Janitors and Cleaners	13.20	Truck Drivers, Heavy/Tractor-Trailer	19.50
Landscaping/Groundskeeping Workers	13.50	Truck Drivers, Light/Delivery Svcs.	16.20
Lawyers	52.80	Waiters and Waitresses	11.20

Note: Wage data covers the Dayton, OH Metropolitan Statistical Area—see Appendix B for areas included; (*) Hourly wages for elementary/secondary school teachers and teacher assistants were calculated by the editors from annual wage data based on a 40 hour work week; n/a not available.
Source: Bureau of Labor Statistics, Metro Area Occupational Employment & Wage Estimates, May 2017

Employment by Occupation

Occupation Classification	City (%)	MSA[1] (%)	U.S. (%)
Management, Business, Science, and Arts	54.9	37.0	37.0
Natural Resources, Construction, and Maintenance	4.0	6.6	8.9
Production, Transportation, and Material Moving	7.1	14.6	12.2
Sales and Office	21.5	24.0	23.8
Service	12.5	17.7	18.1

Note: Figures cover employed civilians 16 years of age and older; (1) Figures cover the Dayton, OH Metropolitan Statistical Area—see Appendix B for areas included
Source: U.S. Census Bureau, 2012-2016 American Community Survey 5-Year Estimates

Employment by Industry

Sector	MSA[1] Number of Employees	MSA[1] Percent of Total	U.S. Percent of Total
Construction, Mining, and Logging	12,700	3.2	5.2
Education and Health Services	77,600	19.5	15.9
Financial Activities	18,300	4.6	5.7
Government	63,100	15.9	15.3
Information	8,200	2.1	1.9
Leisure and Hospitality	41,000	10.3	10.7
Manufacturing	43,000	10.8	8.5
Other Services	14,400	3.6	3.9
Professional and Business Services	51,500	12.9	14.0
Retail Trade	41,600	10.5	11.0
Transportation, Warehousing, and Utilities	13,200	3.3	4.1
Wholesale Trade	13,400	3.4	4.0

Note: Figures are non-farm employment as of December 2017. Figures are not seasonally adjusted and include workers 16 years of age and older; (1) Figures cover the Dayton, OH Metropolitan Statistical Area—see Appendix B for areas included
Source: Bureau of Labor Statistics, Current Employment Statistics, Employment, Hours, and Earnings

Occupations with Greatest Projected Employment Growth: 2017 – 2019

Occupation[1]	2017 Employment	2019 Projected Employment	Numeric Employment Change	Percent Employment Change
Combined Food Preparation and Serving Workers, Including Fast Food	160,970	170,100	9,130	5.7
Waiters and Waitresses	95,660	99,920	4,260	4.5
Home Health Aides	67,650	71,430	3,780	5.6
Registered Nurses	129,370	132,510	3,140	2.4
Heavy and Tractor-Trailer Truck Drivers	74,290	77,290	3,000	4.0
Laborers and Freight, Stock, and Material Movers, Hand	108,760	111,710	2,950	2.7
Personal Care Aides	30,510	32,800	2,290	7.5
Construction Laborers	40,630	42,780	2,150	5.3
Janitors and Cleaners, Except Maids and Housekeeping Cleaners	86,300	88,350	2,050	2.4
Software Developers, Applications	35,570	37,620	2,050	5.8

Note: Projections cover Ohio; (1) Sorted by numeric employment change
Source: www.projectionscentral.com, State Occupational Projections, 2017–2019 Short-Term Projections

Fastest Growing Occupations: 2017 – 2019

Occupation[1]	2017 Employment	2019 Projected Employment	Numeric Employment Change	Percent Employment Change
Rotary Drill Operators, Oil and Gas	230	280	50	21.7
Service Unit Operators, Oil, Gas, and Mining	710	850	140	19.7
Wellhead Pumpers	510	610	100	19.6
Roustabouts, Oil and Gas	720	860	140	19.4
Earth Drillers, Except Oil and Gas	460	510	50	10.9
Veterinary Technologists and Technicians	3,370	3,670	300	8.9
Veterinary Assistants and Laboratory Animal Caretakers	2,730	2,970	240	8.8
Veterinarians	3,330	3,610	280	8.4
Amusement and Recreation Attendants	8,950	9,650	700	7.8
Physician Assistants	3,210	3,460	250	7.8

Note: Projections cover Ohio; (1) Sorted by percent employment change and excludes occupations with numeric employment change less than 50
Source: www.projectionscentral.com, State Occupational Projections, 2017–2019 Short-Term Projections

TAXES

State Corporate Income Tax Rates

State	Tax Rate (%)	Income Brackets ($)	Num. of Brackets	Financial Institution Tax Rate (%)[a]	Federal Income Tax Ded.
Ohio	(t)	–	–	(t)	No

Note: Tax rates as of January 1, 2018; (a) Rates listed are the corporate income tax rate applied to financial institutions or excise taxes based on income. Some states have other taxes based upon the value of deposits or shares; (t) Ohio no longer levies a tax based on income (except for a particular subset of corporations), but instead imposes a Commercial Activity Tax (CAT) equal to $150 for gross receipts sitused to Ohio of between $150,000 and $1 million, plus 0.26% of gross receipts over $1 million. Banks continue to pay a franchise tax of 1.3% of net worth. For those few corporations for whom the franchise tax on net worth or net income still applies, a litter tax also applies.
Source: Federation of Tax Administrators, Range of State Corporate Income Tax Rates, January 1, 2018

State Individual Income Tax Rates

State	Tax Rate (%)	Income Brackets ($)	Num. of Brackets	Personal Exempt. ($)[1]		Fed. Inc. Tax Ded.
				Single	Dependents	
Ohio (a)	0.0 - 4.997	10,650 - 213,350	8	2,300 (t)	2,300 (t)	No

Note: Tax rates as of January 1, 2018; Local- and county-level taxes are not included; n/a not applicable; (1) Married joint filers generally receive double the single exemption; (a) 19 states have statutory provision for automatically adjusting to the rate of inflation the dollar values of the income tax brackets, standard deductions, and/or personal exemptions. Massachusetts, Michigan, and Nebraska index the personal exemption only. Oregon does not index the income brackets for $125,000 and over; (t) Ohio provides an additional tax credit of $20 per exemption. Exemption amounts reduced for higher income taxpayers.
Source: Federation of Tax Administrators, State Individual Income Tax Rates, January 1, 2018

Various State Sales and Excise Tax Rates

State	State Sales Tax (%)	Gasoline[1] (¢/gal.)	Cigarette[2] ($/pack)	Spirits[3] ($/gal.)	Wine[4] ($/gal.)	Beer[5] ($/gal.)	Recreational Marijuana (%)
Ohio	5.75	28.01	1.60	9.87 (g)	0.32 (l)	0.18 (q)	Not legal

Note: All tax rates as of January 1, 2018; (1) The American Petroleum Institute has developed a methodology for determining the average tax rate on a gallon of fuel. Rates may include any of the following: excise taxes, environmental fees, storage tank fees, other fees or taxes, general sales tax, and local taxes. In states where gasoline is subject to the general sales tax, or where the fuel tax is based on the average sale price, the average rate determined by API is sensitive to changes in the price of gasoline. States that fully or partially apply general sales taxes to gasoline: CA, CO, GA, IL, IN, MI, NY; (2) The federal excise tax of $1.0066 per pack and local taxes are not included; (3) Rates are those applicable to off-premise sales of 40% alcohol by volume (a.b.v.) distilled spirits in 750ml containers. Local excise taxes are excluded; (4) Rates are those applicable to off-premise sales of 11% a.b.v. non-carbonated wine in 750ml containers; (5) Rates are those applicable to off-premise sales of 4.7% a.b.v. beer in 12 ounce containers; (g) Control states, where the government controls all sales. Products can be subject to ad valorem mark-up as well as excise taxes; (l) Different rates also applicable to alcohol content, place of production, size of container, place purchased (on- or off-premise or on board airlines) or type of wine (carbonated, vermouth, etc.); (q) Different rates also applicable according to alcohol content, place of production, size of container, or place purchased (on- or off-premise or onboard airlines).
Source: Tax Foundation, 2018 Facts & Figures: How Does Your State Compare?

State Business Tax Climate Index Rankings

State	Overall Rank	Corporate Tax Rank	Individual Income Tax Rank	Sales Tax Rank	Unemployment Insurance Tax Rank	Property Tax Rank
Ohio	45	47	47	30	8	11

Note: The index is a measure of how each state's tax laws affect economic performance. The lower the rank, the more favorable a state's tax system is for business. States without a given tax are given a ranking of 1. The scores/rankings for the District of Columbia do not affect other states. The 2018 index represents the tax climate as of July 1, 2017.
Source: Tax Foundation, State Business Tax Climate Index 2018

TRANSPORTATION

Means of Transportation to Work

Area	Car/Truck/Van		Public Transportation			Bicycle	Walked	Other Means	Worked at Home
	Drove Alone	Car-pooled	Bus	Subway	Railroad				
City	88.7	5.2	0.1	0.0	0.0	0.1	1.3	0.6	4.0
MSA[1]	83.4	8.0	1.6	0.0	0.0	0.2	2.6	0.7	3.3
U.S.	76.4	9.3	2.6	1.9	0.6	0.6	2.8	1.3	4.6

Note: Figures are percentages and cover workers 16 years of age and older; (1) Figures cover the Dayton, OH Metropolitan Statistical Area—see Appendix B for areas included
Source: U.S. Census Bureau, 2012-2016 American Community Survey 5-Year Estimates

Travel Time to Work

Area	Less Than 10 Minutes	10 to 19 Minutes	20 to 29 Minutes	30 to 44 Minutes	45 to 59 Minutes	60 to 89 Minutes	90 Minutes or More
City	10.1	48.4	26.7	8.5	2.6	3.0	0.8
MSA[1]	15.1	35.5	25.7	15.8	3.8	2.7	1.4
U.S.	12.9	29.2	20.9	20.4	8.0	6.0	2.7

Note: Note: Figures are percentages and include workers 16 years old and over; (1) Figures cover the Dayton, OH Metropolitan Statistical Area—see Appendix B for areas included
Source: U.S. Census Bureau, 2012-2016 American Community Survey 5-Year Estimates

Freeway Travel Time Index

Area	1985	1990	1995	2000	2005	2010	2014
Urban Area Rank[1,2]	64	63	77	80	92	92	91
Urban Area Index[1]	1.05	1.08	1.09	1.11	1.11	1.11	1.12
Average Index[3]	1.09	1.11	1.14	1.17	1.20	1.19	1.20

Note: Freeway Travel Time Index—the ratio of travel time in the peak period to the travel time at free-flow conditions. For example, a value of 1.30 indicates a 20-minute free-flow trip takes 26 minutes in the peak (20 minutes x 1.30 = 26 minutes); (1) Covers the Dayton OH urban area; (2) Rank is based on 101 urban areas (#1 = highest travel time index); (3) Average of 101 urban areas
Source: Texas Transportation Institute, 2015 Urban Mobility Scorecard, August 2015

Freeway Commuter Stress Index

Area	1985	1990	1995	2000	2005	2010	2014
Urban Area Rank[1,2]	81	84	88	92	97	99	99
Urban Area Index[1]	1.06	1.08	1.10	1.12	1.12	1.11	1.12
Average Index[3]	1.13	1.16	1.19	1.22	1.25	1.24	1.25

Note: The Freeway Commuter Stress Index is the same as the Freeway Travel Time Index (see table above) except that it includes only the travel in the peak directions during the peak periods; the TTI includes travel in all directions during the peak period. Thus, the CSI is more indicative of the work trip experienced by each commuter on a daily basis; (1) Covers the Dayton OH urban area; (2) Rank is based on 101 urban areas (#1 = highest travel time index); (3) Average of 101 urban areas
Source: Texas Transportation Institute, 2015 Urban Mobility Scorecard, August 2015

Living Environment

COST OF LIVING

Cost of Living Index

Composite Index	Groceries	Housing	Utilities	Trans-portation	Health Care	Misc. Goods/ Services
90.8	96.0	68.1	83.5	104.0	87.0	106.4

Note: The Cost of Living Index measures regional differences in the cost of consumer goods and services, excluding taxes and non-consumer expenditures, for professional and managerial households in the top income quintile. It is based on more than 50,000 prices covering almost 60 different items for which prices are collected three times a year by chambers of commerce, economic development organizations or university applied economic centers in each participating urban area. The numbers shown should be read as a percentage above or below the national average of 100. For example, a value of 115.4 in the groceries column indicates that grocery prices are 15.4% higher than the national average. Small differences in the index numbers should not be interpreted as significant; Figures cover the Dayton OH urban area.
Source: The Council for Community and Economic Research, ACCRA Cost of Living Index, 2017

Grocery Prices

Area[1]	T-Bone Steak ($/pound)	Frying Chicken ($/pound)	Whole Milk ($/half gal.)	Eggs ($/dozen)	Orange Juice ($/64 oz.)	Coffee ($/11.5 oz.)
City[2]	13.13	1.77	1.57	1.10	3.67	4.27
Avg.	11.29	1.40	2.02	1.47	3.55	4.37
Min.	7.71	0.93	1.04	0.70	2.86	3.24
Max.	15.83	2.39	4.03	3.92	6.29	8.16

Note: (1) Values for the local area are compared with the average, minimum and maximum values for all 294 areas in the Cost of Living Index; (2) Figures cover the Dayton OH urban area; ***T-Bone Steak*** *(price per pound);* ***Frying Chicken*** *(price per pound, whole fryer);* ***Whole Milk*** *(half gallon carton);* ***Eggs*** *(price per dozen, Grade A, large);* ***Orange Juice*** *(64 oz. Tropicana or Florida Natural);* ***Coffee*** *(11.5 oz. can, vacuum-packed, Maxwell House, Hills Bros, or Folgers).*
Source: The Council for Community and Economic Research, ACCRA Cost of Living Index, 2017

Housing and Utility Costs

Area[1]	New Home Price ($)	Apartment Rent ($/month)	All Electric ($/month)	Part Electric ($/month)	Other Energy ($/month)	Telephone ($/month)
City[2]	222,925	747	-	76.40	66.28	23.32
Avg.	335,956	1,047	175.01	97.34	67.93	28.71
Min.	187,788	491	109.48	49.33	35.44	12.39
Max.	1,739,087	4,559	432.62	227.09	353.33	44.61

Note: (1) Values for the local area are compared with the average, minimum and maximum values for all 294 areas in the Cost of Living Index; (2) Figures cover the Dayton OH urban area; ***New Home Price*** *(2,400 sf living area, 8,000 sf lot, in urban area with full utilities);* ***Apartment Rent*** *(950 sf 2 bedroom/1.5 or 2 bath, unfurnished, excluding all utilities except water);* ***All Electric*** *(average monthly cost for an all-electric home);* ***Part Electric*** *(average monthly cost for a part-electric home);* ***Other Energy*** *(average monthly cost for natural gas, fuel oil, coal, wood, and any other forms of energy except electricity);* ***Telephone*** *(price includes basic monthly rate for a private residential line plus additional local usage charges incurred by a family of four).*
Source: The Council for Community and Economic Research, ACCRA Cost of Living Index, 2017

Health Care, Transportation, and Other Costs

Area[1]	Doctor ($/visit)	Dentist ($/visit)	Optometrist ($/visit)	Gasoline ($/gallon)	Beauty Salon ($/visit)	Men's Shirt ($)
City[2]	82.67	82.00	96.33	2.24	34.33	33.18
Avg.	108.00	92.54	101.93	2.25	37.58	30.92
Min.	30.39	60.00	49.75	1.82	16.11	11.20
Max.	193.50	161.94	229.28	3.16	77.35	59.13

Note: (1) Values for the local area are compared with the average, minimum and maximum values for all 294 areas in the Cost of Living Index; (2) Figures cover the Dayton OH urban area; ***Doctor*** *(general practitioners routine exam of an established patient);* ***Dentist*** *(adult teeth cleaning and periodic oral examination);* ***Optometrist*** *(full vision eye exam for established adult patient);* ***Gasoline*** *(one gallon regular unleaded, national brand, including all taxes, cash price at self-service pump if available);* ***Beauty Salon*** *(woman's shampoo, trim, and blow-dry);* ***Men's Shirt*** *(cotton/polyester dress shirt, pinpoint weave, long sleeves).*
Source: The Council for Community and Economic Research, ACCRA Cost of Living Index, 2017

HOUSING

House Price Index (HPI)

Area	National Ranking[2]	Quarterly Change (%)	One-Year Change (%)	Five-Year Change (%)
MSA[1]	136	0.69	5.68	15.17
U.S.[3]	–	1.61	6.68	34.71

Note: The HPI is a weighted repeat sales index. It measures average price changes in repeat sales or refinancings on the same properties. This information is obtained by reviewing repeat mortgage transactions on single-family properties whose mortgages have been purchased or securitized by Fannie Mae or Freddie Mac in January 1975; (1) Figures cover the Dayton, OH Metropolitan Statistical Area—see Appendix B for areas included; (2) Rankings are based on annual percentage change for all metro areas containing at least 15,000 transactions over the last 10 years and ranges from 1 to 253; (3) figures based on a weighted average of Census Division estimates using a seasonally adjusted, purchase-only index; all figures are for the period ending December 31, 2017

Source: Federal Housing Finance Agency, House Price Index, February 28, 2018

Median Single-Family Home Prices

Area	2015	2016	2017p	Percent Change 2016 to 2017
MSA[1]	121.7	131.6	138.7	5.4
U.S. Average	223.9	235.5	248.8	5.6

Note: Figures are median sales prices of existing single-family homes in thousands of dollars; (p) preliminary; (1) Figures cover the Dayton, OH Metropolitan Statistical Area—see Appendix B for areas included

Source: National Association of Realtors, Median Sales Price of Existing Single-Family Homes for Metropolitan Areas, 4th Quarter 2017

Qualifying Income Based on Median Sales Price of Existing Single-Family Homes

Area	With 5% Down ($)	With 10% Down ($)	With 20% Down ($)
MSA[1]	30,641	29,028	25,803
U.S. Average	55,585	52,659	46,808

Note: Figures are preliminary; Qualifying income is based on a mortgage rate of 4.17%. Monthly principal and interest payment is limited to 25% of income; (1) Figures cover the Dayton, OH Metropolitan Statistical Area—see Appendix B for areas included

Source: National Association of Realtors, Qualifying Income Based on Median Sales Price of Existing Single-Family Homes for Metropolitan Areas, 4th Quarter 2017

Median Apartment Condo-Coop Home Prices

Area	2015	2016	2017p	Percent Change 2016 to 2017
MSA[1]	n/a	n/a	n/a	n/a
U.S. Average	210.7	220.7	234.3	6.2

Note: Figures are median sales prices of existing apartment condo-coop homes in thousands of dollars; (p) preliminary; n/a not available; (1) Figures cover the Dayton, OH Metropolitan Statistical Area—see Appendix B for areas included

Source: National Association of Realtors, Median Sales Price of Existing Apartment Condo-Coop Homes for Metropolitan Areas, 4th Quarter 2017

Home Value Distribution

Area	Under $50,000	$50,000 -$99,999	$100,000 -$149,999	$150,000 -$199,999	$200,000 -$299,999	$300,000 -$499,999	$500,000 -$999,999	$1,000,000 or more
City	1.4	4.9	23.1	32.6	26.7	9.9	1.0	0.3
MSA[1]	9.2	29.4	23.2	17.2	13.5	5.9	1.3	0.3
U.S.	8.8	14.8	15.3	14.9	18.4	16.4	9.0	2.5

Note: Figures are percentages and cover owner-occupied housing units; (1) Figures cover the Dayton, OH Metropolitan Statistical Area—see Appendix B for areas included

Source: U.S. Census Bureau, 2012-2016 American Community Survey 5-Year Estimates

Homeownership Rate

Area	2009 (%)	2010 (%)	2011 (%)	2012 (%)	2013 (%)	2014 (%)	2015 (%)	2016 (%)	2017 (%)
MSA[1]	67.9	67.4	68.4	67.1	64.4	65.0	60.8	66.0	63.5
U.S.	67.4	66.9	66.1	65.4	65.1	64.5	63.7	63.4	63.9

Note: (1) Figures cover the Dayton, OH Metropolitan Statistical Area—see Appendix B for areas included

Source: U.S. Census Bureau, Housing Vacancies and Homeownership Annual Statistics: 2009-2017

Year Housing Structure Built

Area	2010 or Later	2000 -2009	1990 -1999	1980 -1989	1970 -1979	1960 -1969	1950 -1959	1940 -1949	Before 1940	Median Year
City	2.5	22.0	15.0	9.9	19.4	12.6	13.6	2.5	2.6	1980
MSA[1]	1.0	8.2	8.8	8.0	16.7	16.7	17.2	6.8	16.5	1966
U.S.	2.3	14.7	14.0	13.7	15.6	10.9	10.6	5.2	13.0	1977

Note: Figures are percentages except for Median Year; Note: (1) Figures cover the Dayton, OH Metropolitan Statistical Area—see Appendix B for areas included
Source: U.S. Census Bureau, 2012-2016 American Community Survey 5-Year Estimates

Gross Monthly Rent

Area	Under $500	$500 -$999	$1,000 -$1,499	$1,500 -$1,999	$2,000 -$2,499	$2,500 -$2,999	$3,000 and up	Median ($)
City	3.9	30.7	44.5	17.8	3.1	0.0	0.0	1,135
MSA[1]	16.8	61.5	17.5	2.9	0.8	0.2	0.3	756
U.S.	11.3	43.3	27.7	10.7	4.0	1.6	1.5	949

Note: Figures are percentages except for Median; Gross rent is the contract rent plus the estimated average monthly cost of utilities (electricity, gas, and water and sewer) and fuels (oil, coal, kerosene, wood, etc.) if these are paid by the renter (or paid for the renter by someone else); (1) Figures cover the Dayton, OH Metropolitan Statistical Area—see Appendix B for areas included
Source: U.S. Census Bureau, 2012-2016 American Community Survey 5-Year Estimates

HEALTH

Health Risk Factors

Category	MSA[1] (%)	U.S. (%)
Adults aged 18–64 who have any kind of health care coverage	93.6	87.7
Adults who reported being in good or excellent health	83.6	83.6
Adults who are current smokers	20.2	17.1
Adults who currently use E-cigarettes	6.5	4.7
Adults who currently use chewing tobacco, snuff, or snus	3.2	4.0
Adults who are heavy drinkers[2]	6.2	6.5
Adults who are binge drinkers[3]	16.6	16.9
Adults who are overweight (BMI 25.0 - 29.9)	35.5	35.3
Adults who are obese (BMI 30.0 - 99.8)	28.5	29.9
Adults who participated in any physical activities in the past month	76.0	76.9
Adults who always or nearly always wears a seat belt	93.2	94.3

Note: (1) Figures cover the Dayton, OH Metropolitan Statistical Area—see Appendix B for areas included; (2) Heavy drinkers are classified as adult men having more than 14 drinks per week and adult women having more than 7 drinks per week; (3) Binge drinkers are classified as males having five or more drinks on one occasion or females having four or more drinks on one occasion
Source: Centers for Disease Control and Prevention, Behaviorial Risk Factor Surveillance System, SMART: Selected Metropolitan Area Risk Trends, 2016

Health Screening Rates

Category	MSA[1] (%)	U.S. (%)
Adults 50-75 who have had a blood stool test within the past year	6.5	8.0
Adults 50-75 who have had a colonoscopy in the past 10 years	68.9	63.5
Adults aged 65+ who have had flu shot within the past year	59.9	58.6
Adults aged 65+ who have ever had a pneumonia vaccination	74.1	73.4
Adults who have ever been tested for HIV	32.1	35.6
Women aged 21-65 who have had a pap test in the past three years	74.8	79.8
Men aged 40+ who have had a PSA test within the past two years	40.8	39.5
Women aged 40+ who have had a mammogram within the past two years	72.5	72.5

Note: n/a not available; (1) Figures cover the Dayton, OH Metropolitan Statistical Area—see Appendix B for areas included; Source: Centers for Disease Control and Prevention, Behaviorial Risk Factor Surveillance System, SMART: Selected Metropolitan Area Risk Trends, 2016

Chronic Health Conditions

Category	MSA[1] (%)	U.S. (%)
Adults who have ever been told they had a heart attack	6.4	4.4
Adults who have ever been told they have angina or coronary heart disease	4.7	4.1
Adults who have ever been told they had a stroke	3.3	3.1
Adults who have been told they currently have asthma	10.5	9.3
Adults who have ever been told they have arthritis	33.2	25.8
Adults who have ever been told they have diabetes[2]	12.8	10.5
Adults who have ever been told they had skin cancer	6.9	5.9
Adults who have ever been told they had any other types of cancer	9.0	6.7
Adults who have ever been told they have COPD	10.8	6.3
Adults who have ever been told they have kidney disease	3.1	2.8
Adults who have ever been told they have a form of depression	17.8	17.4

Note: (1) Figures cover the Dayton, OH Metropolitan Statistical Area—see Appendix B for areas included; (2) Figures do not include pregnancy-related, borderline, or pre-diabetes
Source: Centers for Disease Control and Prevention, Behaviorial Risk Factor Surveillance System, SMART: Selected Metropolitan Area Risk Trends, 2016

Mortality Rates for the Top 10 Causes of Death in the U.S.

ICD-10[a] Sub-Chapter	ICD-10[a] Code	Age-Adjusted Mortality Rate[1] per 100,000 population	
		County[2]	U.S.
Malignant neoplasms	C00-C97	160.5	158.5
Ischaemic heart diseases	I20-I25	91.3	96.8
Other forms of heart disease	I30-I51	54.3	52.4
Chronic lower respiratory diseases	J40-J47	37.0	40.9
Cerebrovascular diseases	I60-I69	33.6	37.2
Organic, including symptomatic, mental disorders	F01-F09	38.6	33.3
Other degenerative diseases of the nervous system	G30-G31	42.7	32.1
Other external causes of accidental injury	W00-X59	42.1	31.2
Diabetes mellitus	E10-E14	21.5	21.1
Hypertensive diseases	I10-I15	18.7	20.8

Note: (a) ICD-10 = International Classification of Diseases 10th Revision; (1) Mortality rates are a three year average covering 2014-2016; (2) Figures cover Greene County.
Source: Centers for Disease Control and Prevention, National Center for Health Statistics. Underlying Cause of Death 1999-2016 on CDC WONDER Online Database, released December 2017

Mortality Rates for Selected Causes of Death

ICD-10[a] Sub-Chapter	ICD-10[a] Code	Age-Adjusted Mortality Rate[1] per 100,000 population	
		County[2]	U.S.
Assault	X85-Y09	Suppressed	5.6
Diseases of the liver	K70-K76	12.0	14.0
Human immunodeficiency virus (HIV) disease	B20-B24	Suppressed	1.9
Influenza and pneumonia	J09-J18	12.4	14.6
Intentional self-harm	X60-X84	13.6	13.2
Malnutrition	E40-E46	Unreliable	1.3
Obesity and other hyperalimentation	E65-E68	Suppressed	2.1
Renal failure	N17-N19	12.1	13.0
Transport accidents	V01-V99	8.2	12.0
Viral hepatitis	B15-B19	Suppressed	1.9

Note: (a) ICD-10 = International Classification of Diseases 10th Revision; (1) Mortality rates are a three year average covering 2014-2016; (2) Figures cover Greene County; Data are Suppressed when the data meet the criteria for confidentiality constraints; Mortality rates are flagged as Unreliable when the rate would be calculated with a numerator of 20 or less.
Source: Centers for Disease Control and Prevention, National Center for Health Statistics. Underlying Cause of Death 1999-2016 on CDC WONDER Online Database, released December 2017

Health Insurance Coverage

Area	With Health Insurance	With Private Health Insurance	With Public Health Insurance	Without Health Insurance	Population Under Age 18 Without Health Insurance
City	96.6	88.0	23.4	3.4	3.2
MSA[1]	91.6	68.4	36.6	8.4	4.0
U.S.	88.3	66.7	33.0	11.7	5.9

Note: Figures are percentages that cover the civilian noninstitutionalized population; (1) Figures cover the Dayton, OH Metropolitan Statistical Area—see Appendix B for areas included
Source: U.S. Census Bureau, 2012-2016 American Community Survey 5-Year Estimates

Number of Medical Professionals

Area	MDs[3]	DOs[3,4]	Dentists	Podiatrists	Chiropractors	Optometrists
County[1] (number)	513	115	136	9	37	42
County[1] (rate[2])	312.7	70.1	82.4	5.5	22.4	25.4
U.S. (rate[2])	276.5	22.3	67.3	6.0	26.7	15.9

Note: Data as of 2016 unless noted; (1) Data covers Greene County; (2) Rate per 100,000 population; (3) Data as of 2015 and includes all active, non-federal physicians; (4) Doctor of Osteopathic Medicine
Source: U.S. Department of Health and Human Services, Health Resources and Services Administration, Bureau of Health Professions, Area Resource File (ARF) 2016-2017

Best Hospitals

According to *U.S. News,* the Dayton, OH metro area is home to one of the best hospitals in the U.S.: **Miami Valley Hospital** (2 adult specialties). The hospital listed was nationally ranked in at least one of 16 specialties. Only 152 hospitals nationwide were nationally ranked in one or more specialties. Twenty hospitals in the U.S. made the Honor Roll. The Best Hospitals Honor Roll was revamped last year to take both the national rankings and the procedure and condition ratings into account. Hospitals received points if they were nationally ranked in one of the 16 specialties—the higher they ranked, the more points they got—and how many ratings of "high performing" they earned in the nine procedures and conditions. *U.S. News Online, "America's Best Hospitals 2017-18"*

EDUCATION

Public School District Statistics

District Name	Schls	Pupils	Pupil/ Teacher Ratio	Minority Pupils[1] (%)	Free Lunch Eligible[2] (%)	IEP[3] (%)
Beavercreek City	10	7,586	18.5	16.7	10.1	14.8

Note: Table includes school districts with 100 or more students; (1) Percentage of students that are not non-Hispanic white; (2) Percentage of students that are eligible for the free lunch program; (3) Percentage of students that have an Individualized Education Program.
Source: U.S. Department of Education, National Center for Education Statistics, Common Core of Data, Local Education Agency (School District) Universe Survey: School Year 2015-2016; U.S. Department of Education, National Center for Education Statistics, Common Core of Data, Public Elementary/Secondary School Universe Survey: School Year 2015-2016

Highest Level of Education

Area	Less than H.S.	H.S. Diploma	Some College, No Deg.	Associate Degree	Bachelor's Degree	Master's Degree	Prof. School Degree	Doctorate Degree
City	2.7	18.7	19.5	8.9	25.0	18.3	2.9	3.8
MSA[1]	9.8	28.7	24.1	9.5	16.3	8.8	1.5	1.2
U.S.	13.0	27.5	21.0	8.2	18.8	8.2	2.0	1.3

Note: Figures cover persons age 25 and over; (1) Figures cover the Dayton, OH Metropolitan Statistical Area—see Appendix B for areas included
Source: U.S. Census Bureau, 2012-2016 American Community Survey 5-Year Estimates

Educational Attainment by Race

Area	High School Graduate or Higher (%)					Bachelor's Degree or Higher (%)				
	Total	White	Black	Asian	Hisp.[2]	Total	White	Black	Asian	Hisp.[2]
City	97.3	97.4	98.2	93.0	96.7	50.0	48.2	62.3	76.7	55.4
MSA[1]	90.2	90.9	86.4	87.6	80.5	27.8	28.6	18.9	56.7	27.0
U.S.	87.0	88.9	84.3	86.3	65.7	30.3	31.6	20.0	52.1	14.7

Note: Figures shown cover persons 25 years old and over; (1) Figures cover the Dayton, OH Metropolitan Statistical Area—see Appendix B for areas included; (2) People of Hispanic origin can be of any race
Source: U.S. Census Bureau, 2012-2016 American Community Survey 5-Year Estimates

School Enrollment by Grade and Control

Area	Preschool (%)		Kindergarten (%)		Grades 1 - 4 (%)		Grades 5 - 8 (%)		Grades 9 - 12 (%)	
	Public	Private	Public	Private	Public	Private	Public	Private	Public	Private
City	32.7	67.3	74.0	26.0	87.6	12.4	85.9	14.1	84.4	15.6
MSA[1]	60.7	39.3	83.5	16.5	86.9	13.1	86.9	13.1	87.5	12.5
U.S.	58.4	41.6	87.7	12.3	89.8	10.2	89.7	10.3	90.4	9.6

Note: Figures shown cover persons 3 years old and over; (1) Figures cover the Dayton, OH Metropolitan Statistical Area—see Appendix B for areas included
Source: U.S. Census Bureau, 2012-2016 American Community Survey 5-Year Estimates

Average Salaries of Public School Classroom Teachers

Area	2015		2016		Change from 2015 to 2016	
	Dollars	Rank[1]	Dollars	Rank[1]	Percent	Rank[2]
Ohio	54,672	21	56,441	21	3.2	4
U.S. Average	57,611	–	58,353	–	1.3	–

Note: (1) Rank ranges from 1 to 51 where 1 indicates highest salary; (2) Rank ranges from 1 to 51 where 1 indicates highest percent change.
Source: National Education Association, Rankings & Estimates: Rankings of the States 2016 and Estimates of School Statistics 2017

Higher Education

Four-Year Colleges			Two-Year Colleges			Medical Schools[1]	Law Schools[2]	Voc/ Tech[3]
Public	Private Non-profit	Private For-profit	Public	Private Non-profit	Private For-profit			
0	0	0	0	0	0	0	0	0

Note: Figures cover institutions located within the city limits and include main campuses only; (1) includes schools accredited by the Liaison Committee on Medical Education and the American Osteopathic Association's Commission on Osteopathic College Accreditation; (2) includes ABA-accredited schools, schools with provisional ABA accreditation, and state accredited schools; (3) includes all schools with programs that are less than 2 years.
Source: National Center for Education Statistics, Integrated Postsecondary Education System (IPEDS), 2016-17; Wikipedia, List of Medical Schools in the United States, accessed April 2, 2018; Wikipedia, List of Law Schools in the United States, accessed April 2, 2018

According to *U.S. News & World Report,* the Dayton, OH metro area is home to one of the best national universities in the U.S.: **University of Dayton** (#124 tie). The indicators used to capture academic quality fall into a number of categories: assessment by administrators at peer institutions; retention of students; faculty resources; student selectivity; financial resources; alumni giving; high school counselor ratings of colleges; and graduation rate. *U.S. News & World Report, "America's Best Colleges 2018"*

PRESIDENTIAL ELECTION

2016 Presidential Election Results

Area	Clinton	Trump	Johnson	Stein	Other
Greene County	34.9	58.5	4.0	0.8	1.8
U.S.	48.0	45.9	3.3	1.1	1.7

Note: Results are percentages and may not add to 100% due to rounding
Source: Dave Leip's Atlas of U.S. Presidential Elections

EMPLOYERS

Major Employers

Company Name	Industry
AK Steel Holding Corp.	Steel manufacturer
Assurant Specialty Property	Mortgage lending
Behr Dayton Thermal Products	Auto parts facility
CareSource	Healthcare
City of Dayton	Government
Community Mercy Health Partners	Healthcare
Dayton Children's Hospital	Healthcare
Dayton Public Schools	Education
Emerson Climate Technologies	Heating, air conditioning
GE Capital	Financial services
Honda of America Manufacturing	Auto manufacturing
Kettering Health Network	Healthcare
Kroger Co.	Food chain
LexisNexis	Research
Meijer, Inc.	Supermarket chain
Miami University	Education
Montgomery County	Government
Premier Health	Healthcare
Reynolds and Reynolds	Auto dealer
Sinclair Community College	Education
Speedway LLC	Gas station and convenience store
University of Dayton	Education
VA Medical Center	Healthcare
Wright Patterson Air Force Base	Government
Wright State University	Education

Note: Companies shown are located within the Dayton, OH Metropolitan Statistical Area.
Source: Hoovers.com; Wikipedia

PUBLIC SAFETY

Crime Rate

Area	All Crimes	Violent Crimes				Property Crimes		
		Murder	Rape[3]	Robbery	Aggrav. Assault	Burglary	Larceny -Theft	Motor Vehicle Theft
City	2,359.6	0.0	30.1	28.0	10.8	137.7	2,084.3	68.8
Metro[1]	3,240.6	7.9	56.4	107.5	139.6	672.4	2,045.8	211.0
U.S.	2,847.8	5.3	40.4	102.8	248.5	468.9	1,745.0	236.9

Note: Figures are crimes per 100,000 population; (1) Figures cover the Dayton, OH Metropolitan Statistical Area—see Appendix B for areas included; (3) The city and U.S. figures shown were reported using the revised Uniform Crime Reporting (UCR) definition of rape. The metro area figures shown are an aggregate total of the data submitted using both the revised and legacy UCR definitions.
Source: FBI Uniform Crime Reports, 2016

Hate Crimes

Area	Number of Quarters Reported	Number of Incidents per Bias Motivation					
		Race/Ethnicity/ Ancestry	Religion	Sexual Orientation	Disability	Gender	Gender Identity
City	4	0	0	0	0	0	0
U.S.	4	3,489	1,273	1,076	70	31	124

Source: Federal Bureau of Investigation, Hate Crime Statistics 2016

Identity Theft Consumer Reports

Area	Reports	Reports per 100,000 Population	Rank[2]
MSA[1]	632	79	201
U.S.	371,061	114	-

Note: (1) Figures cover the Dayton, OH Metropolitan Statistical Area—see Appendix B for areas included; (2) Rank ranges from 1 to 389 where 1 indicates greatest number of identity theft reports per 100,000 population
Source: Federal Trade Commission, Consumer Sentinel Network Data Book for January–December 2017

Fraud and Other Consumer Reports

Area	Reports	Reports per 100,000 Population	Rank[2]
MSA[1]	4,156	519	93
U.S.	2,304,550	708	-

Note: (1) Figures cover the Dayton, OH Metropolitan Statistical Area—see Appendix B for areas included; (2) Rank ranges from 1 to 389 where 1 indicates greatest number of fraud and other consumer reports per 100,000 population
Source: Federal Trade Commission, Consumer Sentinel Network Data Book for January–December 2017

SPORTS

Professional Sports Teams

Team Name	League	Year Established

No teams are located in the metro area
Source: Wikipedia, Major Professional Sports Teams of the United States and Canada, April 5, 2018

CLIMATE

Average and Extreme Temperatures

Temperature	Jan	Feb	Mar	Apr	May	Jun	Jul	Aug	Sep	Oct	Nov	Dec	Yr.
Extreme High (°F)	71	69	82	89	93	102	102	102	101	89	79	72	102
Average High (°F)	35	39	49	62	72	81	85	83	76	65	51	39	62
Average Temp. (°F)	27	31	40	52	62	71	75	73	66	55	43	32	52
Average Low (°F)	19	22	31	41	51	60	65	62	55	44	34	24	42
Extreme Low (°F)	-25	-16	-7	15	26	40	44	40	32	21	-2	-20	-25

Note: Figures cover the years 1948-1995
Source: National Climatic Data Center, International Station Meteorological Climate Summary, 9/96

Average Precipitation/Snowfall/Humidity

Precip./Humidity	Jan	Feb	Mar	Apr	May	Jun	Jul	Aug	Sep	Oct	Nov	Dec	Yr.
Avg. Precip. (in.)	2.8	2.3	3.2	3.7	3.9	3.9	3.7	3.1	2.5	2.4	3.1	2.8	37.4
Avg. Snowfall (in.)	8	6	5	1	Tr	0	0	0	0	Tr	2	5	29
Avg. Rel. Hum. 7am (%)	80	79	79	77	78	80	83	86	87	83	81	81	81
Avg. Rel. Hum. 4pm (%)	68	64	59	53	52	52	53	53	52	52	63	69	57

Note: Figures cover the years 1948-1995; Tr = Trace amounts (<0.05 in. of rain; <0.5 in. of snow)
Source: National Climatic Data Center, International Station Meteorological Climate Summary, 9/96

Weather Conditions

Temperature			Daytime Sky			Precipitation		
10°F & below	32°F & below	90°F & above	Clear	Partly cloudy	Cloudy	0.01 inch or more precip.	0.1 inch or more snow/ice	Thunder-storms
18	117	17	80	121	164	133	28	40

Note: Figures are average number of days per year and cover the years 1948-1995
Source: National Climatic Data Center, International Station Meteorological Climate Summary, 9/96

HAZARDOUS WASTE

Superfund Sites

The Dayton, OH metro area is home to 13 sites on the EPA's Superfund National Priorities List: **Behr Dayton Thermal System Voc Plume** (final); **East Troy Contaminated Aquifer** (final); **Lammers Barrel Factory** (final); **Miami County Incinerator** (final); **Mound Plant (USDOE)** (final); **North Sanitary Landfill** (final); **Powell Road Landfill** (final); **Sanitary Landfill Co. (Industrial Waste Disposal Co., Inc.)** (final); **South Dayton Dump & Landfill** (proposed); **United Scrap Lead Co., Inc.** (final); **Valley Pike Vocs** (final); **West Troy Contaminated Aquifer** (final); **Wright-Patterson Air Force Base** (final). There are a total of 1,396 Superfund sites with a status of proposed or final on the list in the U.S. *U.S. Environmental Protection Agency, National Priorities List, April 4, 2018*

AIR & WATER QUALITY

Air Quality Trends: Ozone

	1990	1995	2000	2005	2010	2012	2013	2014	2015	2016
MSA[1]	0.074	0.087	0.074	0.080	0.071	0.077	0.067	0.065	0.067	0.069
U.S.	0.087	0.089	0.081	0.079	0.073	0.075	0.069	0.067	0.068	0.069

Note: (1) Data covers the Dayton, OH Metropolitan Statistical Area—see Appendix B for areas included. The values shown are the composite ozone concentration averages among trend sites based on the highest fourth daily maximum 8-hour concentration in parts per million. These trends are based on sites having an adequate record of monitoring data during the trend period. Data from exceptional events are included.
Source: U.S. Environmental Protection Agency, Air Quality Monitoring Information, "Air Quality Trends by City, 1990-2016"

Air Quality Index

Area	Percent of Days when Air Quality was...[2]					AQI Statistics[2]	
	Good	Moderate	Unhealthy for Sensitive Groups	Unhealthy	Very Unhealthy	Maximum	Median
MSA[1]	70.4	28.8	0.8	0.0	0.0	108	43

Note: (1) Data covers the Dayton, OH Metropolitan Statistical Area—see Appendix B for areas included; (2) Based on 365 days with AQI data in 2017. Air Quality Index (AQI) is an index for reporting daily air quality. EPA calculates the AQI for five major air pollutants regulated by the Clean Air Act: ground-level ozone, particle pollution (aka particulate matter), carbon monoxide, sulfur dioxide, and nitrogen dioxide. The AQI runs from 0 to 500. The higher the AQI value, the greater the level of air pollution and the greater the health concern. There are six AQI categories: "Good" AQI is between 0 and 50. Air quality is considered satisfactory; "Moderate" AQI is between 51 and 100. Air quality is acceptable; "Unhealthy for Sensitive Groups" When AQI values are between 101 and 150, members of sensitive groups may experience health effects; "Unhealthy" When AQI values are between 151 and 200 everyone may begin to experience health effects; "Very Unhealthy" AQI values between 201 and 300 trigger a health alert; "Hazardous" AQI values over 300 trigger warnings of emergency conditions (not shown).
Source: U.S. Environmental Protection Agency, Air Quality Index Report, 2017

Air Quality Index Pollutants

Area	Percent of Days when AQI Pollutant was...[2]					
	Carbon Monoxide	Nitrogen Dioxide	Ozone	Sulfur Dioxide	Particulate Matter 2.5	Particulate Matter 10
MSA[1]	0.0	0.0	56.7	0.0	43.3	0.0

Note: (1) Data covers the Dayton, OH Metropolitan Statistical Area—see Appendix B for areas included; (2) Based on 365 days with AQI data in 2017. The Air Quality Index (AQI) is an index for reporting daily air quality. EPA calculates the AQI for five major air pollutants regulated by the Clean Air Act: ground-level ozone, particle pollution (also known as particulate matter), carbon monoxide, sulfur dioxide, and nitrogen dioxide. The AQI runs from 0 to 500. The higher the AQI value, the greater the level of air pollution and the greater the health concern.
Source: U.S. Environmental Protection Agency, Air Quality Index Report, 2017

Maximum Air Pollutant Concentrations: Particulate Matter, Ozone, CO and Lead

	Particulate Matter 10 (ug/m^3)	Particulate Matter 2.5 Wtd AM (ug/m^3)	Particulate Matter 2.5 24-Hr (ug/m^3)	Ozone (ppm)	Carbon Monoxide (ppm)	Lead (ug/m^3)
MSA[1] Level	39	8.9	21	0.072	1	0
NAAQS[2]	150	15	35	0.075	9	0.15
Met NAAQS[2]	Yes	Yes	Yes	Yes	Yes	Yes

Note: (1) Data covers the Dayton, OH Metropolitan Statistical Area—see Appendix B for areas included; Data from exceptional events are included; (2) National Ambient Air Quality Standards; ppm = parts per million; ug/m^3 = micrograms per cubic meter; n/a not available.
Concentrations: Particulate Matter 10 (coarse particulate)—highest second maximum 24-hour concentration; Particulate Matter 2.5 Wtd AM (fine particulate)—highest weighted annual mean concentration; Particulate Matter 2.5 24-Hour (fine particulate)—highest 98th percentile 24-hour concentration; Ozone—highest fourth daily maximum 8-hour concentration; Carbon Monoxide—highest second maximum non-overlapping 8-hour concentration; Lead—maximum running 3-month average
Source: U.S. Environmental Protection Agency, Air Quality Monitoring Information, "Air Quality Statistics by City, 2016"

Maximum Air Pollutant Concentrations: Nitrogen Dioxide and Sulfur Dioxide

	Nitrogen Dioxide AM (ppb)	Nitrogen Dioxide 1-Hr (ppb)	Sulfur Dioxide AM (ppb)	Sulfur Dioxide 1-Hr (ppb)	Sulfur Dioxide 24-Hr (ppb)
MSA[1] Level	n/a	n/a	n/a	16	n/a
NAAQS[2]	53	100	30	75	140
Met NAAQS[2]	n/a	n/a	n/a	Yes	n/a

Note: (1) Data covers the Dayton, OH Metropolitan Statistical Area—see Appendix B for areas included; Data from exceptional events are included; (2) National Ambient Air Quality Standards; ppm = parts per million; ug/m^3 = micrograms per cubic meter; n/a not available.
Concentrations: Nitrogen Dioxide AM—highest arithmetic mean concentration; Nitrogen Dioxide 1-Hr—highest 98th percentile 1-hour daily maximum concentration; Sulfur Dioxide AM—highest annual mean concentration; Sulfur Dioxide 1-Hr—highest 99th percentile 1-hour daily maximum concentration; Sulfur Dioxide 24-Hr—highest second maximum 24-hour concentration
Source: U.S. Environmental Protection Agency, Air Quality Monitoring Information, "Air Quality Statistics by City, 2016"

Drinking Water

Water System Name	Pop. Served	Primary Water Source Type	Violations[1]	
			Health Based	Monitoring/ Reporting
Green Co. NW Regional Water	36,855	Ground	0	0

Note: (1) Based on violation data from January 1, 2017 to December 31, 2017
Source: U.S. Environmental Protection Agency, Office of Ground Water and Drinking Water, Safe Drinking Water Information System (based on data extracted April 5, 2018)

Dublin, Ohio

Background

Dublin, located in the central part of the state, lies on the banks of the Scioto River in Franklin County. The city is a 20-minute drive from Ohio's capital of Columbus. Dublin's phenomenal growth can be attributed to a number of factors, not the least being its energetic corporate climate, attracting family-owned businesses as well as several major corporations.

In short, Dublin has it all. Its stable and diverse economic base, direct regional highway access, top-rated school system, and high-quality city services make it a refreshingly pleasant place to live. In 2001, Dublin City Schools became the country's first school district to reach the highest possible level of accreditation given by the North Central Association, the nation's premier accrediting institution. In addition, Dublin offers indoor and outdoor recreation facilities, entertaining events, and eclectic shopping and dining, as well as varied residential property surrounded by open spaces, parks, bike paths, and a protected natural environment.

The settlement of Franklin County began in 1802 when Peter and Benjamin Sells of Huntington, Pennsylvania, purchased 400 acres of land in the area for their brother, John, who came with his family in 1808 to claim the land. When John Sells and John Shields began surveying lots for the town in 1810, Shields decided to name the new town after his birthplace of Dublin, Ireland. In 1881, Dublin was incorporated as a village. Nearly 90 years later, growth began and continued enough to warrant incorporation as a city in 1987.

More than 90% of Dublin students continue their education after graduating from high school and over 19% of the student population is culturally diverse, representing 65 countries. In 2003, 14 students were named as National Merit semifinalists.

Eleven colleges or universities, including Ohio State University, are within a 35-minute commuting distance from Dublin. Columbus State Community College-Dublin Center is the Dublin branch campus of Columbus State Community College. Franklin University offers both MBA and undergraduate courses at its Northwest Campus in Dublin.

As of 2011 Columbus has the highest concentration of Asians of any Ohio city. Many Japanese expatriates working at the Honda offices in the area live in Dublin. The community includes Japanese restaurants. A Coldwell Banker real estate agent named Akiko Miyamoto stated in Car Talk that the services provided for Japanese speakers by the Dublin City School District attract Japanese expatriates to Dublin.

In 2011, as part of a community-wide partnership, the city kicked off the Healthy Dublin program to help each citizen set personal health goals and achieve a greater state of well-being.

The original village of Dublin was located in what is now called Historic Dublin, a lovely district where the streets and sidewalks are brick, the teahouses are Irish, and the shops sell unique Irish imported goods. Brazenhead, a genuine Irish pub named for the oldest watering hole in Dublin, Ireland, offers Guinness, Irish whiskey, and authentic fish and chips. The Dublin Irish Festival, an annual arts and music festival showcasing all aspects of Irish culture, draws tens of thousands of people each year. It is produced and supported by the city.

Other attractions include the Columbus Zoo & Aquarium, featuring over 700 species of wildlife and over 400 acres of habitats and recreation areas, including Manatee Coast—one of only two facilities outside Florida to exhibit these endangered animals. Along those lines, the first gorilla born in captivity was born at the Columbus Zoo in 1956.

Listed on the national Register of Historic Places, the Fletcher-Coffman Homestead was built in the early 1860s. The Dublin Historical Society has restored the house to its original period and renovated the barn, which houses the early farm machinery used in the area.

Each year in late May or early June, the city hosts the Memorial Tournament, a stop on golf's PGA Tour. Consequently, numerous golf aficionados choose to make Dublin their home. There are also several other golf courses in Dublin. The Riviera Golf Club, which closed in 2014, was home to the American-Italian Golf Association. Tartan Fields Golf Club hosted the LPGA's Wendy's Championship for Children from 2002 through 2006. Dublin also has a public golf course financed by the Muirfield association, as well as the Jack Nicklaus-designed The Country Club of Muirfield Village.

Dublin has the usual four seasons associated with a continental climate. Extremes of high and low temperatures are possible. Summers are pleasant and mild. Though variable from year to year, rainfall is slightly in excess of the national average.

Rankings

Business/Finance Rankings

- According to *Business Insider*, the Columbus* metro area is where startup growth is on the rise. Based on the 2017 Kauffman Index of Growth Entrepreneurship, which measured in-depth national entrepreneurial trends in 40 metro areas, it ranked #3 in highest startup growth. *www.businessinsider.com, "The 21 U.S. Cities with the Highest Startup Growth," October 21, 2017*

- The personal finance site NerdWallet analyzed 183 American metropolitan areas with populations over 250,000 and more than 15,000 businesses to rank where entrepreneurs find the most success. Criteria included area economy, annual income, housing cost, unemployment rate, and the success rate of area businesses. Columbus* ranked #92. *www.nerdwallet.com, "Best Places to Start a Business," April 27, 2015*

- The editors of *Kiplinger's Personal Finance Magazine* named Columbus* to their list of ten of the best metro areas for start-ups. The area ranked #10.Criteria: well-educated workforce; low living costs for self-employed people, as measured by the Council for Community and Economic Research; a strong existing community of small business; low unemployment; low business costs. *www.kiplinger.com, "10 Great Cities for Starting a Business," October 2014*

- Based on metro area social media reviews, the employment opinion group Glassdoor surveyed 50 of the largest U.S. metro areas and equally weighed cost of living, hiring opportunity, and job satisfaction to compose a list of "25 Best Cities for Jobs." Median pay and home value, in-demand jobs and number of current job openings was also factored in. The Columbus* metro area was ranked #7 in overall job satisfaction. *www.glassdoor.com, "Best Cities for Jobs," September 12, 2017*

- In a survey of economic confidence in the nation's 50 largest metropolitan areas conducted January–December 2014, the Columbus* metro area placed #25, according to Gallup's 2014 Economic Confidence Index. *Gallup, "San Jose and San Francisco Lead in Economic Confidence," March 19, 2015*

- The Brookings Institution ranked the 100 largest metro areas in the U.S. based on income inequality. Columbus* was ranked #62 (#1 = greatest ineqality). Criteria: the "95/20 ratio," a figure representing the income at which a household earns more than 95 percent of all other households, divided by the income at which a household earns more than only 20 percent of all other households. *Brookings Institution, "Household Income Inequality, 100 Largest U.S. Metro Areas, 2014-2016," February 5, 2018*

- *Forbes* ranked the 100 largest metro areas in the U.S. in terms of the "Best Cities for Young Professionals." The Columbus* metro area ranked #9 out of 25. (Large metro areas were divided into metro divisions.) Criteria: median rent of a two-bedroom apartment; job growth and unemployment rate; median salary of college graduates with 5 or less years of work experience; networking opportunities; social outlook; percentage of population 25 years of age and older with college degrees. *Forbes.com, "America's 25 Best Cities for Young Professionals in 2017," May 22, 2017*

- The Columbus* metro area was identified as one of the most affordable metropolitan areas in America by *Forbes*. The area ranked #10 out of 20 based on the National Association of Home Builders/Wells Fargo Housing Affordability Index and Sperling's Best Places' cost-of-living index. *Forbes.com, "America's Most Affordable Cities in 2015," March 12, 2015*

- Columbus* was identified as one of America's most frugal metro areas by *Coupons.com*. The city ranked #20 out of 25. Criteria: digital coupon usage. *Coupons.com, "America's Most Frugal Cities of 2017," March 22, 2018*

- Columbus* was cited as one of America's top metros for new and expanded facility projects in 2017. The area ranked #7 in the large metro area category (population over 1 million). *Site Selection, "Top Metropolitans of 2017," March 2018*

- The Columbus* metro area appeared on the Milken Institute "2017 Best Performing Cities" list. Rank: #62 out of 200 large metro areas. Criteria: job growth; wage and salary growth; high-tech output growth. *Milken Institute, "Best-Performing Cities 2017," January 2018*
- *Forbes* ranked the 200 most populous metro areas to determine the nation's "Best Places for Business and Careers." The Columbus* metro area was ranked #11. Criteria: costs (business and living); job growth (past and projected); income growth; quality of life; educational attainment (college and high school); projected economic growth; cultural and recreational opportunities; net migration patterns; number of highly ranked colleges. *Forbes, "The Best Places for Business and Careers 2017," October 24, 2017*

Education Rankings

- Personal finance website *WalletHub* analyzed the 150 largest U.S. metropolitan statistical areas to determine where the most educated Americans are choosing to settle. Criteria: education quality and attainment gap; education levels; percentage of workers with degrees; public school rankings; quality and size of each metro area's universities. Columbus* was ranked #34 (#1 = most educated city). *www.WalletHub.com, "2017's Most and Least Educated Cities in America," July 25, 2017*

Environmental Rankings

- Sperling's BestPlaces assessed 379 metropolitan areas of the United States for the likelihood of dangerously extreme weather events or earthquakes. In general the Southeast and South-Central regions have the highest risk of weather extremes and earthquakes, while the Pacific Northwest enjoys the lowest risk. Of the least risky metropolitan areas, the Columbus* metro area was ranked #144. *www.bestplaces.net, "Safest Places from Natural Disasters," April 2011*
- Columbus* was highlighted as one of the top 99 cleanest metro areas for short-term particle pollution (24-hour PM 2.5) in the U.S. during 2013 through 2015. Monitors in these cities reported no days with unhealthful PM 2.5 levels. *American Lung Association, State of the Air 2017*

Health/Fitness Rankings

- Analysts who tracked obesity rates in the nation's largest metro areas (populations above one million) found that the Columbus* metro area was one of the ten major metros where residents were most likely to be obese, defined as a BMI score of 30 or above. *www.gallup.com, "Boulder, Colo., Residents Still Least Likely to Be Obese," April 4, 2014*
- For each of the 50 most populous metro areas in the United States, the American College of Sports Medicine's American Fitness Index evaluated infrastructure, community assets, and policies that encourage healthy and fit lifestyles, including preventive health behaviors, levels of chronic disease conditions, health care access, and community resources and policies that support physical activity. The Columbus* metro area ranked #41 for "community fitness." *www.americanfitnessindex.org, "ACSM American Fitness Index Health and Community Fitness Status of the 50 Largest Metropolitan Areas," May 2017*
- The Columbus* metro area was identified as one of the worst cities for bed bugs in America by pest control company Orkin. The area ranked #5 out of 50 based on the number of bed bug treatments Orkin performed from December 2016 to November 2017. *Orkin, "Baltimore and Washington D.C. Continue to Hold Top Spots," January 8, 2018*
- Columbus* was identified as a "2016 Spring Allergy Capital." The area ranked #55 out of 100. Three groups of factors were used to identify the most severe cities for people with allergies during the spring season: annual pollen levels; medicine utilization; access to board-certified allergists. *Asthma and Allergy Foundation of America, "Spring Allergy Capitals 2016"*
- Columbus* was identified as a "2016 Fall Allergy Capital." The area ranked #43 out of 100. Three groups of factors were used to identify the most severe cities for people with allergies during the fall season: annual pollen levels; medicine utilization; access to board-certified allergists. *Asthma and Allergy Foundation of America, "Fall Allergy Capitals 2016"*

- Columbus* was identified as a "2015 Asthma Capital." The area ranked #49 out of the nation's 100 largest metropolitan areas. Criteria: estimated prevalence; self-reported prevalence; crude death rate for asthma; annual pollen score; annual air quality; public smoking laws; number of board-certified asthma specialists; school inhaler access laws; rescue medication use; controller medication use; ER visits for asthma; uninsured rate; poverty rate. *Asthma and Allergy Foundation of America, "Asthma Capitals 2015"*
- The Columbus* metro area ranked #125 out of 189 in The Gallup-Healthways Well-Being Index. Criteria: purpose; social well being; financial health; community and physical health. Results are based on telephone interviews with adults, aged 18 and older, living in metropolitan areas in the 50 U.S. states and the District of Columbia. *Gallup-Healthways, "State of American Well-Being, 2017 Community Well-Being Rankings" March 2018*

Real Estate Rankings

- FitSmallBusiness looked at 50 of the largest metropolitan areas in the U.S. to determine which metro was the best to start a real estate business. Data was compiled from such sources as: Zillow, Trulia, U.S. Census Bureau, and the Bureau of Labor Statistics. Criteria: location; inventory; annual wages; median sales price of homes; days on the market; median price cut percentage; and other factors that would influence real estate professional growth. The Columbus* metro area ranked #44. *fitsmallbusiness.com, "The Best Cities to Become a Real Estate Agent in 2018," January 30, 2018*
- The Columbus* metro area was identified as one of the nations's 20 hottest housing markets in 2018. Criteria: listing views as an indicator of demand and median days on the market as an indicator of supply. The area ranked #16. *Realtor.com, "The 20 Hottest Real Estate Markets for February 2018," March 1, 2018*
- The Columbus* metro area was identified as one of the top 20 housing markets to invest in for 2018 by *Forbes*. The area ranked #20. Criteria: strong job and population growth; anticipated home price appreciation; and other factors. *Forbes.com, "Where to Invest in Housing in 2018," February 1, 2018*
- The Columbus* metro area was identified as one of the 20 best housing markets in the U.S. in 2017. The area ranked #16 out of 180 markets. Criteria: year-over-year change of median sales price of existing single-family homes between the 4th quarter of 2016 and the 4th quarter of 2017. *National Association of Realtors®, Median Sales Price of Existing Single-Family Homes for Metropolitan Areas, 4th Quarter 2017*
- Columbus* was ranked #97 out of 238 metro areas in terms of housing affordability in 2017 by the National Association of Home Builders (#1 = most affordable). Criteria: the share of homes sold in that area affordable to a family earning the local median income, based on standard mortgage underwriting criteria. *National Association of Home Builders®, NAHB-Wells Fargo Housing Opportunity Index, 4th Quarter 2017*

Safety Rankings

- The National Insurance Crime Bureau ranked 382 metro areas in the U.S. in terms of per capita rates of vehicle theft. The Columbus* metro area ranked #134 (#1 = highest rate). Criteria: number of vehicle theft offenses per 100,000 inhabitants in 2016. *National Insurance Crime Bureau, "Hot Spots 2016," June 8, 2017*

Seniors/Retirement Rankings

- From its Best Cities for Successful Aging indexes, the Milken Institute generated rankings for metropolitan areas, weighing data in nine categories—health care, wellness, living arrangements, transportation and convenience, financial characteristics, education, employment, community engagement, and overall livability. The Columbus* metro area was ranked #49 overall in the large metro area category. *Milken Institute, "Best Cities for Successful Aging, 2017" March 14, 2017*

*Dublin is located within the Columbus, OH Metropolitan Statistical Area.

Business Environment

CITY FINANCES

City Government Finances

Component	2015 ($000)	2015 ($ per capita)
Total Revenues	115,358	2,558
Total Expenditures	66,062	1,465
Debt Outstanding	65,050	1,442
Cash and Securities[1]	156,066	3,461

Note: (1) Cash and security holdings of a government at the close of its fiscal year,, including those of its dependent agencies, utilities, and liquor stores.
Source: U.S Census Bureau, State & Local Government Finances 2015

City Government Revenue by Source

Source	2015 ($000)	2015 ($ per capita)	2015 (%)
General Revenue			
From Federal Government	10	0	0.0
From State Government	2,286	51	2.0
From Local Governments	4,021	89	3.5
Taxes			
Property	3,372	75	2.9
Sales and Gross Receipts	2,006	44	1.7
Personal Income	77,076	1,709	66.8
Corporate Income	10,709	237	9.3
Motor Vehicle License	0	0	0.0
Other Taxes	3,007	67	2.6
Current Charges	6,336	140	5.5
Liquor Store	0	0	0.0
Utility	0	0	0.0
Employee Retirement	0	0	0.0

Source: U.S Census Bureau, State & Local Government Finances 2015

City Government Expenditures by Function

Function	2015 ($000)	2015 ($ per capita)	2015 (%)
General Direct Expenditures			
Air Transportation	0	0	0.0
Corrections	0	0	0.0
Education	0	0	0.0
Employment Security Administration	0	0	0.0
Financial Administration	1,872	41	2.8
Fire Protection	0	0	0.0
General Public Buildings	2,189	48	3.3
Governmental Administration, Other	13,608	301	20.6
Health	0	0	0.0
Highways	3,876	85	5.9
Hospitals	0	0	0.0
Housing and Community Development	0	0	0.0
Interest on General Debt	1,766	39	2.7
Judicial and Legal	343	7	0.5
Libraries	0	0	0.0
Parking	0	0	0.0
Parks and Recreation	14,233	315	21.5
Police Protection	11,049	245	16.7
Public Welfare	0	0	0.0
Sewerage	1,341	29	2.0
Solid Waste Management	3,348	74	5.1
Veterans' Services	0	0	0.0
Liquor Store	0	0	0.0
Utility	1,303	28	2.0
Employee Retirement	0	0	0.0

Source: U.S Census Bureau, State & Local Government Finances 2015

DEMOGRAPHICS

Population Growth

Area	1990 Census	2000 Census	2010 Census	2016* Estimate	Population Growth (%) 1990-2016	2010-2016
City	17,231	31,392	41,751	43,874	154.6	5.1
MSA[1]	1,405,176	1,612,694	1,836,536	1,995,004	42.0	8.6
U.S.	248,709,873	281,421,906	308,745,538	318,558,162	28.1	3.2

Note: (1) Figures cover the Columbus, OH Metropolitan Statistical Area—see Appendix B for areas included; (*) 2012-2016 5-year estimated population
Source: U.S. Census Bureau, 1990 Census, Census 2000, Census 2010, 2012-2016 American Community Survey 5-Year Estimates

Household Size

Area	Persons in Household (%) One	Two	Three	Four	Five	Six	Seven or More	Average Household Size
City	18.7	31.2	18.1	21.7	8.4	1.8	0.3	2.80
MSA[1]	28.6	33.5	16.0	13.1	5.7	2.0	1.0	2.50
U.S.	27.7	33.7	15.7	13.1	6.0	2.3	1.5	2.60

Note: (1) Figures cover the Columbus, OH Metropolitan Statistical Area—see Appendix B for areas included
Source: U.S. Census Bureau, 2012-2016 American Community Survey 5-Year Estimates

Race

Area	White Alone[2] (%)	Black Alone[2] (%)	Asian Alone[2] (%)	AIAN[3] Alone[2] (%)	NHOPI[4] Alone[2] (%)	Other Race Alone[2] (%)	Two or More Races (%)
City	76.4	2.3	16.9	0.3	0.0	0.8	3.3
MSA[1]	77.2	14.8	3.6	0.2	0.0	1.0	3.1
U.S.	73.3	12.6	5.2	0.8	0.2	4.8	3.1

Note: (1) Figures cover the Columbus, OH Metropolitan Statistical Area—see Appendix B for areas included; (2) Alone is defined as not being in combination with one or more other races; (3) American Indian and Alaska Native; (4) Native Hawaiian and Other Pacific Islander
Source: U.S. Census Bureau, 2012-2016 American Community Survey 5-Year Estimates

Hispanic or Latino Origin

Area	Total (%)	Mexican (%)	Puerto Rican (%)	Cuban (%)	Other (%)
City	5.5	1.8	0.7	0.2	2.8
MSA[1]	3.8	2.1	0.5	0.1	1.1
U.S.	17.3	11.0	1.7	0.7	4.0

Note: Persons of Hispanic or Latino origin can be of any race; (1) Figures cover the Columbus, OH Metropolitan Statistical Area—see Appendix B for areas included
Source: U.S. Census Bureau, 2012-2016 American Community Survey 5-Year Estimates

Segregation

Type	Segregation Indices[1] 1990	2000	2010	2010 Rank[2]	Percent Change 1990-2000	1990-2010	2000-2010
Black/White	67.6	63.4	62.2	33	-4.2	-5.5	-1.2
Asian/White	44.7	43.3	43.3	35	-1.4	-1.4	0.0
Hispanic/White	27.9	36.9	41.5	59	9.0	13.6	4.6

Note: All figures cover the Metropolitan Statistical Area—see Appendix B for areas included; Figures are based on an analysis of 1990, 2000, and 2010 Census Decennial Census tract data by William H. Frey, Brookings Institution and the University of Michigan Social Science Data Analysis Network. In this analysis all racial groups (whites, blacks, and asians) are non-Hispanic members of those races. Hispanics are shown as a separate category; (1) Segregation Indices are Dissimilarity Indices that measure the degree to which the minority group is distributed differently than whites across census tracts. They range from 0 (complete integration) to 100 (complete segregation) where the value indicates the percentage of the minority group that needs to move to be distributed exactly like whites; (2) Ranges from 1 (most segregated) to 102 (least segregated); n/a not available.
Source: www.CensusScope.org

Ancestry

Area	German	Irish	English	American	Italian	Polish	French[2]	Scottish	Dutch
City	27.3	14.1	10.7	6.3	7.2	4.5	3.2	2.0	1.2
MSA[1]	24.4	13.5	9.0	6.9	5.5	2.3	2.2	2.2	1.5
U.S.	14.4	10.4	7.7	6.9	5.4	2.9	2.6	1.7	1.3

Note: Figures are the percentage of the total population reporting a particular ancestry. The nine most commonly reported ancestries in the U.S. are shown. Figures include multiple ancestries (e.g. if a person reported being Irish and Italian, they were included in both columns); (1) Figures cover the Columbus, OH Metropolitan Statistical Area—see Appendix B for areas included; (2) Excludes Basque
Source: U.S. Census Bureau, 2012-2016 American Community Survey 5-Year Estimates

Foreign-Born Population

Area	Percent of Population Born in								
	Any Foreign Country	Asia	Mexico	Europe	Carribean	Central America[2]	South America	Africa	Canada
City	16.5	12.7	0.3	1.9	0.3	0.1	0.4	0.3	0.5
MSA[1]	7.3	3.0	0.8	0.8	0.2	0.2	0.2	1.8	0.1
U.S.	13.2	4.0	3.6	1.5	1.3	1.0	0.9	0.6	0.3

Note: (1) Figures cover the Columbus, OH Metropolitan Statistical Area—see Appendix B for areas included; (2) Excludes Mexico.
Source: U.S. Census Bureau, 2012-2016 American Community Survey 5-Year Estimates

Marital Status

Area	Never Married	Now Married[2]	Separated	Widowed	Divorced
City	21.6	67.7	0.4	3.0	7.2
MSA[1]	34.0	47.5	1.9	4.9	11.7
U.S.	33.0	48.1	2.1	5.9	11.0

Note: Figures are percentages and cover the population 15 years of age and older; (1) Figures cover the Columbus, OH Metropolitan Statistical Area—see Appendix B for areas included; (2) Excludes separated
Source: U.S. Census Bureau, 2012-2016 American Community Survey 5-Year Estimates

Disability Status

Area	All Ages	Under 18 Years Old	18 to 64 Years Old	65 Years and Over
City	5.7	3.1	4.0	25.1
MSA[1]	11.8	4.6	10.3	35.1
U.S.	12.5	4.1	10.3	35.7

Note: Figures show percent of the civilian noninstitutionalized population that reported having a disability. Disability status is determined from six types of difficulty: vision, hearing, cognitive, ambulatory, self-care, and independent living. For children under 5 years old, hearing and vision difficulty are used to determine disability status. For children between the ages of 5 and 14, disability status is determined from hearing, vision, cognitive, ambulatory, and self-care difficulties. For people aged 15 years and older, they are considered to have a disability if they have difficulty with any one of the six difficulty types; Note: (1) Figures cover the Columbus, OH Metropolitan Statistical Area—see Appendix B for areas included
Source: U.S. Census Bureau, 2012-2016 American Community Survey 5-Year Estimates

Age

Area	Percent of Population									Median Age
	Under Age 5	Age 5–19	Age 20–34	Age 35–44	Age 45–54	Age 55–64	Age 65–74	Age 75–84	Age 85+	
City	6.2	25.4	11.5	17.2	16.6	13.7	5.3	2.7	1.4	39.6
MSA[1]	6.8	20.0	22.2	13.6	13.6	11.8	7.1	3.4	1.5	35.7
U.S.	6.2	19.6	20.7	12.7	13.6	12.6	8.3	4.3	1.9	37.7

Note: (1) Figures cover the Columbus, OH Metropolitan Statistical Area—see Appendix B for areas included
Source: U.S. Census Bureau, 2012-2016 American Community Survey 5-Year Estimates

Gender

Area	Males	Females	Males per 100 Females
City	21,682	22,192	97.7
MSA[1]	981,638	1,013,366	96.9
U.S.	156,765,322	161,792,840	96.9

Note: (1) Figures cover the Columbus, OH Metropolitan Statistical Area—see Appendix B for areas included
Source: U.S. Census Bureau, 2012-2016 American Community Survey 5-Year Estimates

Religious Groups by Family

Area	Catholic	Baptist	Non-Den.	Methodist[2]	Lutheran	LDS[3]	Pente-costal	Presby-terian[4]	Muslim[5]	Judaism
MSA[1]	11.8	5.3	3.6	4.7	2.4	0.7	2.0	2.0	0.8	0.5
U.S.	19.1	9.3	4.0	4.0	2.3	2.0	1.9	1.6	0.8	0.7

Note: Figures are the number of adherents as a percentage of the total population; (1) Figures cover the Columbus, OH Metropolitan Statistical Area—see Appendix B for areas included; (2) Methodist/Pietist; (3) Latter Day Saints; (4) Reformed; (5) Figures are estimates
Source: Association of Statisticians of American Religious Bodies, 2010 U.S. Religion Census: Religious Congregations & Membership Study

Religious Groups by Tradition

Area	Catholic	Evangelical Protestant	Mainline Protestant	Other Tradition	Black Protestant	Orthodox
MSA[1]	11.8	11.9	9.5	3.1	1.1	0.3
U.S.	19.1	16.2	7.3	4.3	1.6	0.3

Note: Figures are the number of adherents as a percentage of the total population; (1) Figures cover the Columbus, OH Metropolitan Statistical Area—see Appendix B for areas included
Source: Association of Statisticians of American Religious Bodies, 2010 U.S. Religion Census: Religious Congregations & Membership Study

ECONOMY

Gross Metropolitan Product

Area	2014	2015	2016	2017	Rank[2]
MSA[1]	116.4	121.8	126.5	132.9	31

Note: Figures are in billions of dollars; (1) Figures cover the Columbus, OH Metropolitan Statistical Area—see Appendix B for areas included; (2) Rank is based on 2015 data and ranges from 1 to 381
Source: The U.S. Conference of Mayors, U.S. Metro Economies: GMP and Employment Report, 2015-2017

Economic Growth

Area	2012-14 (%)	2015 (%)	2016 (%)	2017 (%)	Rank[2]
MSA[1]	1.6	2.6	2.3	3.0	155
U.S.	2.0	2.4	1.9	2.6	–

Note: Figures are real gross metropolitan product (GMP) growth rates and represent average annual percent change; (1) Figures cover the Columbus, OH Metropolitan Statistical Area—see Appendix B for areas included; (2) Rank is based on 2012-2014 average annual percent change and ranges from 1 to 381
Source: The U.S. Conference of Mayors, U.S. Metro Economies: GMP and Employment Report, 2015-2017

Metropolitan Area Exports

Area	2011	2012	2013	2014	2015	2016	Rank[2]
MSA[1]	4,327.5	5,488.6	5,731.4	6,245.6	6,201.6	5,675.4	48

Note: Figures are in millions of dollars; (1) Figures cover the Columbus, OH Metropolitan Statistical Area—see Appendix B for areas included; (2) Rank is based on 2016 data and ranges from 1 to 385
Source: U.S. Department of Commerce, International Trade Administration, Office of Trade & Industry Information, Manufacturing & Services, data extracted March 15, 2018

Building Permits

Area	Single-Family			Multi-Family			Total		
	2016	2017p	Pct. Chg.	2016	2017p	Pct. Chg.	2016	2017p	Pct. Chg.
City	148	258	74.3	482	30	-93.8	630	288	-54.3
MSA[1]	4,040	4,166	3.1	4,209	4,593	9.1	8,249	8,759	6.2
U.S.	750,800	817,300	8.9	455,800	446,800	-2.0	1,206,600	1,264,100	4.8

Note: (1) Figures cover the Columbus, OH Metropolitan Statistical Area—see Appendix B for areas included; Figures represent new, privately-owned housing units authorized (unadjusted data); All permit data are based on estimates with imputation; (p) preliminary data.
Source: U.S. Census Bureau, Manufacturing, Mining, and Construction Statistics, Building Permits, 2016, 2017

Bankruptcy Filings

Area	Business Filings			Nonbusiness Filings		
	2016	2017	% Chg.	2016	2017	% Chg.
Franklin County	58	70	20.7	4,463	4,479	0.4
U.S.	24,114	23,157	-4.0	770,846	765,863	-0.6

Note: Business filings include Chapter 7, Chapter 11, Chapter 12, and Chapter 13; Nonbusiness filings include Chapter 7, Chapter 11, and Chapter 13
Source: Administrative Office of the U.S. Courts, Business and Nonbusiness Bankruptcy, County Cases Commenced by Chapter of the Bankruptcy Code, During the 12-Month Period Ending December 31, 2016 and Business and Nonbusiness Bankruptcy, County Cases Commenced by Chapter of the Bankruptcy Code, During the 12-Month Period Ending December 31, 2017

Housing Vacancy Rates

Area	Gross Vacancy Rate[2] (%)			Year-Round Vacancy Rate[3] (%)			Rental Vacancy Rate[4] (%)			Homeowner Vacancy Rate[5] (%)		
	2015	2016	2017	2015	2016	2017	2015	2016	2017	2015	2016	2017
MSA[1]	9.6	8.0	6.6	9.2	7.8	6.0	6.5	6.1	6.3	1.5	1.0	1.1
U.S.	12.9	12.8	12.7	10.0	9.9	9.9	7.1	6.9	7.2	1.8	1.7	1.6

Note: (1) Figures cover the Columbus, OH Metropolitan Statistical Area—see Appendix B for areas included; (2) The percentage of the total housing inventory that is vacant; (3) The percentage of the housing inventory (excluding seasonal units) that is year-round vacant; (4) The percentage of rental inventory that is vacant for rent; (5) The percentage of homeowner inventory that is vacant for sale
Source: U.S. Census Bureau, Housing Vacancies and Homeownership Annual Statistics: 2015, 2016, 2017

INCOME

Income

Area	Per Capita ($)	Median Household ($)	Average Household ($)
City	58,698	125,540	163,872
MSA[1]	30,399	57,440	77,221
U.S.	29,829	55,322	77,866

Note: (1) Figures cover the Columbus, OH Metropolitan Statistical Area—see Appendix B for areas included
Source: U.S. Census Bureau, 2012-2016 American Community Survey 5-Year Estimates

Household Income Distribution

Area	Percent of Households Earning							
	Under $15,000	$15,000 -$24,999	$25,000 -$34,999	$35,000 -$49,999	$50,000 -$74,999	$75,000 -$99,999	$100,000 -$149,999	$150,000 and up
City	3.2	2.3	2.0	5.3	12.3	13.0	22.2	39.7
MSA[1]	11.3	9.4	9.6	13.4	18.7	12.9	14.3	10.5
U.S.	12.1	10.2	9.9	13.2	17.8	12.2	13.5	11.1

Note: (1) Figures cover the Columbus, OH Metropolitan Statistical Area—see Appendix B for areas included
Source: U.S. Census Bureau, 2012-2016 American Community Survey 5-Year Estimates

Poverty Rate

Area	All Ages	Under 18 Years Old	18 to 64 Years Old	65 Years and Over
City	2.7	2.9	2.2	5.8
MSA[1]	14.4	20.3	13.5	7.7
U.S.	15.1	21.2	14.2	9.3

Note: Figures are percentage of people whose income during the past 12 months was below the poverty level; (1) Figures cover the Columbus, OH Metropolitan Statistical Area—see Appendix B for areas included
Source: U.S. Census Bureau, 2012-2016 American Community Survey 5-Year Estimates

EMPLOYMENT

Labor Force and Employment

Area	Civilian Labor Force			Workers Employed		
	Dec. 2016	Dec. 2017	% Chg.	Dec. 2016	Dec. 2017	% Chg.
City	24,862	25,161	1.2	24,005	24,405	1.7
MSA[1]	1,066,787	1,080,007	1.2	1,023,273	1,039,735	1.6
U.S.	158,968,000	159,880,000	0.6	151,798,000	153,602,000	1.2

Note: Data is not seasonally adjusted and covers workers 16 years of age and older; (1) Figures cover the Columbus, OH Metropolitan Statistical Area—see Appendix B for areas included
Source: Bureau of Labor Statistics, Local Area Unemployment Statistics

Unemployment Rate

Area	2017											
	Jan.	Feb.	Mar.	Apr.	May	Jun.	Jul.	Aug.	Sep.	Oct.	Nov.	Dec.
City	4.0	3.7	3.3	3.1	3.3	3.7	3.6	3.7	3.4	3.3	3.2	3.0
MSA[1]	4.9	4.6	4.1	3.7	3.7	4.3	4.3	4.2	3.9	3.7	3.7	3.7
U.S.	5.1	4.9	4.6	4.1	4.1	4.5	4.6	4.5	4.1	3.9	3.9	3.9

Note: Data is not seasonally adjusted and covers workers 16 years of age and older; (1) Figures cover the Columbus, OH Metropolitan Statistical Area—see Appendix B for areas included
Source: Bureau of Labor Statistics, Local Area Unemployment Statistics

Average Wages

Occupation	$/Hr.	Occupation	$/Hr.
Accountants and Auditors	35.90	Maids and Housekeeping Cleaners	10.60
Automotive Mechanics	20.00	Maintenance and Repair Workers	19.20
Bookkeepers	19.70	Marketing Managers	70.00
Carpenters	22.30	Nuclear Medicine Technologists	34.00
Cashiers	10.20	Nurses, Licensed Practical	20.20
Clerks, General Office	16.80	Nurses, Registered	32.30
Clerks, Receptionists/Information	13.30	Nursing Assistants	12.70
Clerks, Shipping/Receiving	15.10	Packers and Packagers, Hand	11.50
Computer Programmers	36.40	Physical Therapists	38.90
Computer Systems Analysts	47.10	Postal Service Mail Carriers	23.80
Computer User Support Specialists	25.00	Real Estate Brokers	65.00
Cooks, Restaurant	13.00	Retail Salespersons	13.00
Dentists	100.70	Sales Reps., Exc. Tech./Scientific	31.20
Electrical Engineers	38.50	Sales Reps., Tech./Scientific	37.40
Electricians	22.10	Secretaries, Exc. Legal/Med./Exec.	18.10
Financial Managers	66.60	Security Guards	15.30
First-Line Supervisors/Managers, Sales	21.00	Surgeons	123.60
Food Preparation Workers	10.70	Teacher Assistants*	13.90
General and Operations Managers	59.10	Teachers, Elementary School*	29.60
Hairdressers/Cosmetologists	13.20	Teachers, Secondary School*	30.30
Internists, General	122.30	Telemarketers	13.40
Janitors and Cleaners	13.30	Truck Drivers, Heavy/Tractor-Trailer	22.20
Landscaping/Groundskeeping Workers	13.80	Truck Drivers, Light/Delivery Svcs.	16.80
Lawyers	55.60	Waiters and Waitresses	11.00

Note: Wage data covers the Columbus, OH Metropolitan Statistical Area—see Appendix B for areas included; (*) Hourly wages for elementary/secondary school teachers and teacher assistants were calculated by the editors from annual wage data based on a 40 hour work week; n/a not available.
Source: Bureau of Labor Statistics, Metro Area Occupational Employment & Wage Estimates, May 2017

Employment by Occupation

Occupation Classification	City (%)	MSA[1] (%)	U.S. (%)
Management, Business, Science, and Arts	65.7	40.9	37.0
Natural Resources, Construction, and Maintenance	1.5	6.3	8.9
Production, Transportation, and Material Moving	3.8	11.9	12.2
Sales and Office	21.1	24.5	23.8
Service	7.9	16.3	18.1

Note: Figures cover employed civilians 16 years of age and older; (1) Figures cover the Columbus, OH Metropolitan Statistical Area—see Appendix B for areas included
Source: U.S. Census Bureau, 2012-2016 American Community Survey 5-Year Estimates

Employment by Industry

Sector	MSA[1] Number of Employees	MSA[1] Percent of Total	U.S. Percent of Total
Construction, Mining, and Logging	38,600	3.5	5.2
Education and Health Services	162,000	14.8	15.9
Financial Activities	86,000	7.8	5.7
Government	177,900	16.2	15.3
Information	17,200	1.6	1.9
Leisure and Hospitality	104,200	9.5	10.7
Manufacturing	74,000	6.7	8.5
Other Services	40,500	3.7	3.9
Professional and Business Services	180,800	16.5	14.0
Retail Trade	114,500	10.4	11.0
Transportation, Warehousing, and Utilities	58,700	5.4	4.1
Wholesale Trade	42,500	3.9	4.0

Note: Figures are non-farm employment as of December 2017. Figures are not seasonally adjusted and include workers 16 years of age and older; (1) Figures cover the Columbus, OH Metropolitan Statistical Area—see Appendix B for areas included
Source: Bureau of Labor Statistics, Current Employment Statistics, Employment, Hours, and Earnings

Occupations with Greatest Projected Employment Growth: 2017 – 2019

Occupation[1]	2017 Employment	2019 Projected Employment	Numeric Employment Change	Percent Employment Change
Combined Food Preparation and Serving Workers, Including Fast Food	160,970	170,100	9,130	5.7
Waiters and Waitresses	95,660	99,920	4,260	4.5
Home Health Aides	67,650	71,430	3,780	5.6
Registered Nurses	129,370	132,510	3,140	2.4
Heavy and Tractor-Trailer Truck Drivers	74,290	77,290	3,000	4.0
Laborers and Freight, Stock, and Material Movers, Hand	108,760	111,710	2,950	2.7
Personal Care Aides	30,510	32,800	2,290	7.5
Construction Laborers	40,630	42,780	2,150	5.3
Janitors and Cleaners, Except Maids and Housekeeping Cleaners	86,300	88,350	2,050	2.4
Software Developers, Applications	35,570	37,620	2,050	5.8

Note: Projections cover Ohio; (1) Sorted by numeric employment change
Source: www.projectionscentral.com, State Occupational Projections, 2017–2019 Short-Term Projections

Fastest Growing Occupations: 2017 – 2019

Occupation[1]	2017 Employment	2019 Projected Employment	Numeric Employment Change	Percent Employment Change
Rotary Drill Operators, Oil and Gas	230	280	50	21.7
Service Unit Operators, Oil, Gas, and Mining	710	850	140	19.7
Wellhead Pumpers	510	610	100	19.6
Roustabouts, Oil and Gas	720	860	140	19.4
Earth Drillers, Except Oil and Gas	460	510	50	10.9
Veterinary Technologists and Technicians	3,370	3,670	300	8.9
Veterinary Assistants and Laboratory Animal Caretakers	2,730	2,970	240	8.8
Veterinarians	3,330	3,610	280	8.4
Amusement and Recreation Attendants	8,950	9,650	700	7.8
Physician Assistants	3,210	3,460	250	7.8

Note: Projections cover Ohio; (1) Sorted by percent employment change and excludes occupations with numeric employment change less than 50
Source: www.projectionscentral.com, State Occupational Projections, 2017–2019 Short-Term Projections

TAXES

State Corporate Income Tax Rates

State	Tax Rate (%)	Income Brackets ($)	Num. of Brackets	Financial Institution Tax Rate (%)[a]	Federal Income Tax Ded.
Ohio	(t)	–	–	(t)	No

Note: Tax rates as of January 1, 2018; (a) Rates listed are the corporate income tax rate applied to financial institutions or excise taxes based on income. Some states have other taxes based upon the value of deposits or shares; (t) Ohio no longer levies a tax based on income (except for a particular subset of corporations), but instead imposes a Commercial Activity Tax (CAT) equal to $150 for gross receipts sitused to Ohio of between $150,000 and $1 million, plus 0.26% of gross receipts over $1 million. Banks continue to pay a franchise tax of 1.3% of net worth. For those few corporations for whom the franchise tax on net worth or net income still applies, a litter tax also applies.
Source: Federation of Tax Administrators, Range of State Corporate Income Tax Rates, January 1, 2018

State Individual Income Tax Rates

State	Tax Rate (%)	Income Brackets ($)	Num. of Brackets	Personal Exempt. ($)[1] Single	Personal Exempt. ($)[1] Dependents	Fed. Inc. Tax Ded.
Ohio (a)	0.0 - 4.997	10,650 - 213,350	8	2,300 (t)	2,300 (t)	No

Note: Tax rates as of January 1, 2018; Local- and county-level taxes are not included; n/a not applicable; (1) Married joint filers generally receive double the single exemption; (a) 19 states have statutory provision for automatically adjusting to the rate of inflation the dollar values of the income tax brackets, standard deductions, and/or personal exemptions. Massachusetts, Michigan, and Nebraska index the personal exemption only. Oregon does not index the income brackets for $125,000 and over; (t) Ohio provides an additional tax credit of $20 per exemption. Exemption amounts reduced for higher income taxpayers.
Source: Federation of Tax Administrators, State Individual Income Tax Rates, January 1, 2018

Various State Sales and Excise Tax Rates

State	State Sales Tax (%)	Gasoline[1] (¢/gal.)	Cigarette[2] ($/pack)	Spirits[3] ($/gal.)	Wine[4] ($/gal.)	Beer[5] ($/gal.)	Recreational Marijuana (%)
Ohio	5.75	28.01	1.60	9.87 (g)	0.32 (l)	0.18 (q)	Not legal

Note: All tax rates as of January 1, 2018; (1) The American Petroleum Institute has developed a methodology for determining the average tax rate on a gallon of fuel. Rates may include any of the following: excise taxes, environmental fees, storage tank fees, other fees or taxes, general sales tax, and local taxes. In states where gasoline is subject to the general sales tax, or where the fuel tax is based on the average sale price, the average rate determined by API is sensitive to changes in the price of gasoline. States that fully or partially apply general sales taxes to gasoline: CA, CO, GA, IL, IN, MI, NY; (2) The federal excise tax of $1.0066 per pack and local taxes are not included; (3) Rates are those applicable to off-premise sales of 40% alcohol by volume (a.b.v.) distilled spirits in 750ml containers. Local excise taxes are excluded; (4) Rates are those applicable to off-premise sales of 11% a.b.v. non-carbonated wine in 750ml containers; (5) Rates are those applicable to off-premise sales of 4.7% a.b.v. beer in 12 ounce containers; (g) Control states, where the government controls all sales. Products can be subject to ad valorem mark-up as well as excise taxes; (l) Different rates also applicable to alcohol content, place of production, size of container, place purchased (on- or off-premise or on board airlines) or type of wine (carbonated, vermouth, etc.); (q) Different rates also applicable according to alcohol content, place of production, size of container, or place purchased (on- or off-premise or onboard airlines).
Source: Tax Foundation, 2018 Facts & Figures: How Does Your State Compare?

State Business Tax Climate Index Rankings

State	Overall Rank	Corporate Tax Rank	Individual Income Tax Rank	Sales Tax Rank	Unemployment Insurance Tax Rank	Property Tax Rank
Ohio	45	47	47	30	8	11

Note: The index is a measure of how each state's tax laws affect economic performance. The lower the rank, the more favorable a state's tax system is for business. States without a given tax are given a ranking of 1. The scores/rankings for the District of Columbia do not affect other states. The 2018 index represents the tax climate as of July 1, 2017.
Source: Tax Foundation, State Business Tax Climate Index 2018

TRANSPORTATION

Means of Transportation to Work

Area	Car/Truck/Van		Public Transportation			Bicycle	Walked	Other Means	Worked at Home
	Drove Alone	Car-pooled	Bus	Subway	Railroad				
City	85.8	4.5	0.4	0.0	0.0	0.2	0.5	1.4	7.2
MSA[1]	82.5	7.9	1.7	0.0	0.0	0.4	2.2	0.9	4.4
U.S.	76.4	9.3	2.6	1.9	0.6	0.6	2.8	1.3	4.6

Note: Figures are percentages and cover workers 16 years of age and older; (1) Figures cover the Columbus, OH Metropolitan Statistical Area—see Appendix B for areas included
Source: U.S. Census Bureau, 2012-2016 American Community Survey 5-Year Estimates

Travel Time to Work

Area	Less Than 10 Minutes	10 to 19 Minutes	20 to 29 Minutes	30 to 44 Minutes	45 to 59 Minutes	60 to 89 Minutes	90 Minutes or More
City	15.2	22.3	26.0	27.8	5.1	2.0	1.7
MSA[1]	11.4	30.6	26.7	21.0	6.0	3.0	1.4
U.S.	12.9	29.2	20.9	20.4	8.0	6.0	2.7

Note: Note: Figures are percentages and include workers 16 years old and over; (1) Figures cover the Columbus, OH Metropolitan Statistical Area—see Appendix B for areas included
Source: U.S. Census Bureau, 2012-2016 American Community Survey 5-Year Estimates

Freeway Travel Time Index

Area	1985	1990	1995	2000	2005	2010	2014
Urban Area Rank[1,2]	35	34	36	38	42	48	46
Urban Area Index[1]	1.09	1.12	1.15	1.17	1.18	1.17	1.18
Average Index[3]	1.09	1.11	1.14	1.17	1.20	1.19	1.20

Note: Freeway Travel Time Index—the ratio of travel time in the peak period to the travel time at free-flow conditions. For example, a value of 1.30 indicates a 20-minute free-flow trip takes 26 minutes in the peak (20 minutes x 1.30 = 26 minutes); (1) Covers the Columbus OH urban area; (2) Rank is based on 101 urban areas (#1 = highest travel time index); (3) Average of 101 urban areas
Source: Texas Transportation Institute, 2015 Urban Mobility Scorecard, August 2015

Freeway Commuter Stress Index

Area	1985	1990	1995	2000	2005	2010	2014
Urban Area Rank[1,2]	36	41	40	40	44	49	49
Urban Area Index[1]	1.13	1.16	1.19	1.21	1.22	1.21	1.22
Average Index[3]	1.13	1.16	1.19	1.22	1.25	1.24	1.25

Note: The Freeway Commuter Stress Index is the same as the Freeway Travel Time Index (see table above) except that it includes only the travel in the peak directions during the peak periods; the TTI includes travel in all directions during the peak period. Thus, the CSI is more indicative of the work trip experienced by each commuter on a daily basis; (1) Covers the Columbus OH urban area; (2) Rank is based on 101 urban areas (#1 = highest travel time index); (3) Average of 101 urban areas
Source: Texas Transportation Institute, 2015 Urban Mobility Scorecard, August 2015

Living Environment

COST OF LIVING

Cost of Living Index

Composite Index	Groceries	Housing	Utilities	Trans-portation	Health Care	Misc. Goods/ Services
89.6	98.9	76.8	77.7	96.9	92.1	97.4

Note: The Cost of Living Index measures regional differences in the cost of consumer goods and services, excluding taxes and non-consumer expenditures, for professional and managerial households in the top income quintile. It is based on more than 50,000 prices covering almost 60 different items for which prices are collected three times a year by chambers of commerce, economic development organizations or university applied economic centers in each participating urban area. The numbers shown should be read as a percentage above or below the national average of 100. For example, a value of 115.4 in the groceries column indicates that grocery prices are 15.4% higher than the national average. Small differences in the index numbers should not be interpreted as significant; Figures cover the Columbus OH urban area.
Source: The Council for Community and Economic Research, ACCRA Cost of Living Index, 2017

Grocery Prices

Area[1]	T-Bone Steak ($/pound)	Frying Chicken ($/pound)	Whole Milk ($/half gal.)	Eggs ($/dozen)	Orange Juice ($/64 oz.)	Coffee ($/11.5 oz.)
City[2]	12.96	1.30	1.43	1.39	3.01	7.48
Avg.	11.29	1.40	2.02	1.47	3.55	4.37
Min.	7.71	0.93	1.04	0.70	2.86	3.24
Max.	15.83	2.39	4.03	3.92	6.29	8.16

*Note: (1) Values for the local area are compared with the average, minimum and maximum values for all 294 areas in the Cost of Living Index; (2) Figures cover the Columbus OH urban area; **T-Bone Steak** (price per pound); **Frying Chicken** (price per pound, whole fryer); **Whole Milk** (half gallon carton); **Eggs** (price per dozen, Grade A, large); **Orange Juice** (64 oz. Tropicana or Florida Natural); **Coffee** (11.5 oz. can, vacuum-packed, Maxwell House, Hills Bros, or Folgers).*
Source: The Council for Community and Economic Research, ACCRA Cost of Living Index, 2017

Housing and Utility Costs

Area[1]	New Home Price ($)	Apartment Rent ($/month)	All Electric ($/month)	Part Electric ($/month)	Other Energy ($/month)	Telephone ($/month)
City[2]	238,079	952	-	52.90	65.42	24.67
Avg.	335,956	1,047	175.01	97.34	67.93	28.71
Min.	187,788	491	109.48	49.33	35.44	12.39
Max.	1,739,087	4,559	432.62	227.09	353.33	44.61

*Note: (1) Values for the local area are compared with the average, minimum and maximum values for all 294 areas in the Cost of Living Index; (2) Figures cover the Columbus OH urban area; **New Home Price** (2,400 sf living area, 8,000 sf lot, in urban area with full utilities); **Apartment Rent** (950 sf 2 bedroom/1.5 or 2 bath, unfurnished, excluding all utilities except water); **All Electric** (average monthly cost for an all-electric home); **Part Electric** (average monthly cost for a part-electric home); **Other Energy** (average monthly cost for natural gas, fuel oil, coal, wood, and any other forms of energy except electricity); **Telephone** (price includes basic monthly rate for a private residential line plus additional local usage charges incurred by a family of four).*
Source: The Council for Community and Economic Research, ACCRA Cost of Living Index, 2017

Health Care, Transportation, and Other Costs

Area[1]	Doctor ($/visit)	Dentist ($/visit)	Optometrist ($/visit)	Gasoline ($/gallon)	Beauty Salon ($/visit)	Men's Shirt ($)
City[2]	99.16	86.52	59.51	2.29	33.40	29.68
Avg.	108.00	92.54	101.93	2.25	37.58	30.92
Min.	30.39	60.00	49.75	1.82	16.11	11.20
Max.	193.50	161.94	229.28	3.16	77.35	59.13

*Note: (1) Values for the local area are compared with the average, minimum and maximum values for all 294 areas in the Cost of Living Index; (2) Figures cover the Columbus OH urban area; **Doctor** (general practitioners routine exam of an established patient); **Dentist** (adult teeth cleaning and periodic oral examination); **Optometrist** (full vision eye exam for established adult patient); **Gasoline** (one gallon regular unleaded, national brand, including all taxes, cash price at self-service pump if available); **Beauty Salon** (woman's shampoo, trim, and blow-dry); **Men's Shirt** (cotton/polyester dress shirt, pinpoint weave, long sleeves).*
Source: The Council for Community and Economic Research, ACCRA Cost of Living Index, 2017

HOUSING

House Price Index (HPI)

Area	National Ranking[2]	Quarterly Change (%)	One-Year Change (%)	Five-Year Change (%)
MSA[1]	72	-0.08	8.20	30.85
U.S.[3]	–	1.61	6.68	34.71

Note: The HPI is a weighted repeat sales index. It measures average price changes in repeat sales or refinancings on the same properties. This information is obtained by reviewing repeat mortgage transactions on single-family properties whose mortgages have been purchased or securitized by Fannie Mae or Freddie Mac in January 1975; (1) Figures cover the Columbus, OH Metropolitan Statistical Area—see Appendix B for areas included; (2) Rankings are based on annual percentage change for all metro areas containing at least 15,000 transactions over the last 10 years and ranges from 1 to 253; (3) figures based on a weighted average of Census Division estimates using a seasonally adjusted, purchase-only index; all figures are for the period ending December 31, 2017
Source: Federal Housing Finance Agency, House Price Index, February 28, 2018

Median Single-Family Home Prices

Area	2015	2016	2017p	Percent Change 2016 to 2017
MSA[1]	164.7	175.5	189.9	8.2
U.S. Average	223.9	235.5	248.8	5.6

Note: Figures are median sales prices of existing single-family homes in thousands of dollars; (p) preliminary; (1) Figures cover the Columbus, OH Metropolitan Statistical Area—see Appendix B for areas included
Source: National Association of Realtors, Median Sales Price of Existing Single-Family Homes for Metropolitan Areas, 4th Quarter 2017

Qualifying Income Based on Median Sales Price of Existing Single-Family Homes

Area	With 5% Down ($)	With 10% Down ($)	With 20% Down ($)
MSA[1]	42,687	40,440	35,947
U.S. Average	55,585	52,659	46,808

Note: Figures are preliminary; Qualifying income is based on a mortgage rate of 4.17%. Monthly principal and interest payment is limited to 25% of income; (1) Figures cover the Columbus, OH Metropolitan Statistical Area—see Appendix B for areas included
Source: National Association of Realtors, Qualifying Income Based on Median Sales Price of Existing Single-Family Homes for Metropolitan Areas, 4th Quarter 2017

Median Apartment Condo-Coop Home Prices

Area	2015	2016	2017p	Percent Change 2016 to 2017
MSA[1]	132.0	138.2	149.8	8.4
U.S. Average	210.7	220.7	234.3	6.2

Note: Figures are median sales prices of existing apartment condo-coop homes in thousands of dollars; (p) preliminary; (1) Figures cover the Columbus, OH Metropolitan Statistical Area—see Appendix B for areas included
Source: National Association of Realtors, Median Sales Price of Existing Apartment Condo-Coop Homes for Metropolitan Areas, 4th Quarter 2017

Home Value Distribution

Area	Under $50,000	$50,000 -$99,999	$100,000 -$149,999	$150,000 -$199,999	$200,000 -$299,999	$300,000 -$499,999	$500,000 -$999,999	$1,000,000 or more
City	1.4	2.3	4.0	4.6	21.1	50.8	15.2	0.6
MSA[1]	5.9	16.9	21.7	19.7	19.7	12.0	3.6	0.5
U.S.	8.8	14.8	15.3	14.9	18.4	16.4	9.0	2.5

Note: Figures are percentages and cover owner-occupied housing units; (1) Figures cover the Columbus, OH Metropolitan Statistical Area—see Appendix B for areas included
Source: U.S. Census Bureau, 2012-2016 American Community Survey 5-Year Estimates

Homeownership Rate

Area	2009 (%)	2010 (%)	2011 (%)	2012 (%)	2013 (%)	2014 (%)	2015 (%)	2016 (%)	2017 (%)
MSA[1]	61.5	62.2	59.7	60.7	60.5	60.0	59.0	57.5	57.9
U.S.	67.4	66.9	66.1	65.4	65.1	64.5	63.7	63.4	63.9

Note: (1) Figures cover the Columbus, OH Metropolitan Statistical Area—see Appendix B for areas included
Source: U.S. Census Bureau, Housing Vacancies and Homeownership Annual Statistics: 2009-2017

Year Housing Structure Built

Area	2010 or Later	2000 -2009	1990 -1999	1980 -1989	1970 -1979	1960 -1969	1950 -1959	1940 -1949	Before 1940	Median Year
City	4.2	24.1	29.6	29.0	8.2	1.7	1.8	0.2	1.0	1993
MSA[1]	2.6	14.9	16.8	12.0	14.8	11.6	10.5	4.3	12.5	1977
U.S.	2.3	14.7	14.0	13.7	15.6	10.9	10.6	5.2	13.0	1977

Note: Figures are percentages except for Median Year; Note: (1) Figures cover the Columbus, OH Metropolitan Statistical Area—see Appendix B for areas included
Source: U.S. Census Bureau, 2012-2016 American Community Survey 5-Year Estimates

Gross Monthly Rent

Area	Under $500	$500 -$999	$1,000 -$1,499	$1,500 -$1,999	$2,000 -$2,499	$2,500 -$2,999	$3,000 and up	Median ($)
City	0.5	23.8	46.5	16.4	7.9	3.9	1.0	1,266
MSA[1]	9.9	58.4	25.2	4.6	1.3	0.3	0.3	855
U.S.	11.3	43.3	27.7	10.7	4.0	1.6	1.5	949

Note: Figures are percentages except for Median; Gross rent is the contract rent plus the estimated average monthly cost of utilities (electricity, gas, and water and sewer) and fuels (oil, coal, kerosene, wood, etc.) if these are paid by the renter (or paid for the renter by someone else); (1) Figures cover the Columbus, OH Metropolitan Statistical Area—see Appendix B for areas included
Source: U.S. Census Bureau, 2012-2016 American Community Survey 5-Year Estimates

HEALTH

Health Risk Factors

Category	MSA[1] (%)	U.S. (%)
Adults aged 18–64 who have any kind of health care coverage	92.0	87.7
Adults who reported being in good or excellent health	83.9	83.6
Adults who are current smokers	21.8	17.1
Adults who currently use E-cigarettes	5.5	4.7
Adults who currently use chewing tobacco, snuff, or snus	3.2	4.0
Adults who are heavy drinkers[2]	6.2	6.5
Adults who are binge drinkers[3]	18.7	16.9
Adults who are overweight (BMI 25.0 - 29.9)	34.2	35.3
Adults who are obese (BMI 30.0 - 99.8)	30.2	29.9
Adults who participated in any physical activities in the past month	77.3	76.9
Adults who always or nearly always wears a seat belt	91.2	94.3

Note: (1) Figures cover the Columbus, OH Metropolitan Statistical Area—see Appendix B for areas included; (2) Heavy drinkers are classified as adult men having more than 14 drinks per week and adult women having more than 7 drinks per week; (3) Binge drinkers are classified as males having five or more drinks on one occasion or females having four or more drinks on one occasion
Source: Centers for Disease Control and Prevention, Behaviorial Risk Factor Surveillance System, SMART: Selected Metropolitan Area Risk Trends, 2016

Health Screening Rates

Category	MSA[1] (%)	U.S. (%)
Adults 50-75 who have had a blood stool test within the past year	7.3	8.0
Adults 50-75 who have had a colonoscopy in the past 10 years	66.5	63.5
Adults aged 65+ who have had flu shot within the past year	60.2	58.6
Adults aged 65+ who have ever had a pneumonia vaccination	78.3	73.4
Adults who have ever been tested for HIV	38.1	35.6
Women aged 21-65 who have had a pap test in the past three years	86.0	79.8
Men aged 40+ who have had a PSA test within the past two years	40.8	39.5
Women aged 40+ who have had a mammogram within the past two years	76.4	72.5

Note: n/a not available; (1) Figures cover the Columbus, OH Metropolitan Statistical Area—see Appendix B for areas included; Source: Centers for Disease Control and Prevention, Behaviorial Risk Factor Surveillance System, SMART: Selected Metropolitan Area Risk Trends, 2016

Chronic Health Conditions

Category	MSA[1] (%)	U.S. (%)
Adults who have ever been told they had a heart attack	3.9	4.4
Adults who have ever been told they have angina or coronary heart disease	3.2	4.1
Adults who have ever been told they had a stroke	3.6	3.1
Adults who have been told they currently have asthma	9.2	9.3
Adults who have ever been told they have arthritis	25.8	25.8
Adults who have ever been told they have diabetes[2]	10.0	10.5
Adults who have ever been told they had skin cancer	5.1	5.9
Adults who have ever been told they had any other types of cancer	6.5	6.7
Adults who have ever been told they have COPD	7.3	6.3
Adults who have ever been told they have kidney disease	1.7	2.8
Adults who have ever been told they have a form of depression	20.1	17.4

Note: (1) Figures cover the Columbus, OH Metropolitan Statistical Area—see Appendix B for areas included; (2) Figures do not include pregnancy-related, borderline, or pre-diabetes
Source: Centers for Disease Control and Prevention, Behaviorial Risk Factor Surveillance System, SMART: Selected Metropolitan Area Risk Trends, 2016

Mortality Rates for the Top 10 Causes of Death in the U.S.

ICD-10[a] Sub-Chapter	ICD-10[a] Code	Age-Adjusted Mortality Rate[1] per 100,000 population	
		County[2]	U.S.
Malignant neoplasms	C00-C97	171.8	158.5
Ischaemic heart diseases	I20-I25	82.5	96.8
Other forms of heart disease	I30-I51	70.5	52.4
Chronic lower respiratory diseases	J40-J47	47.1	40.9
Cerebrovascular diseases	I60-I69	45.0	37.2
Organic, including symptomatic, mental disorders	F01-F09	48.4	33.3
Other degenerative diseases of the nervous system	G30-G31	33.4	32.1
Other external causes of accidental injury	W00-X59	40.4	31.2
Diabetes mellitus	E10-E14	24.8	21.1
Hypertensive diseases	I10-I15	25.9	20.8

Note: (a) ICD-10 = International Classification of Diseases 10th Revision; (1) Mortality rates are a three year average covering 2014-2016; (2) Figures cover Franklin County.
Source: Centers for Disease Control and Prevention, National Center for Health Statistics. Underlying Cause of Death 1999-2016 on CDC WONDER Online Database, released December 2017

Mortality Rates for Selected Causes of Death

ICD-10[a] Sub-Chapter	ICD-10[a] Code	Age-Adjusted Mortality Rate[1] per 100,000 population	
		County[2]	U.S.
Assault	X85-Y09	8.3	5.6
Diseases of the liver	K70-K76	14.0	14.0
Human immunodeficiency virus (HIV) disease	B20-B24	1.7	1.9
Influenza and pneumonia	J09-J18	18.6	14.6
Intentional self-harm	X60-X84	11.7	13.2
Malnutrition	E40-E46	2.1	1.3
Obesity and other hyperalimentation	E65-E68	2.2	2.1
Renal failure	N17-N19	16.4	13.0
Transport accidents	V01-V99	9.7	12.0
Viral hepatitis	B15-B19	1.4	1.9

Note: (a) ICD-10 = International Classification of Diseases 10th Revision; (1) Mortality rates are a three year average covering 2014-2016; (2) Figures cover Franklin County; Data are Suppressed when the data meet the criteria for confidentiality constraints; Mortality rates are flagged as Unreliable when the rate would be calculated with a numerator of 20 or less.
Source: Centers for Disease Control and Prevention, National Center for Health Statistics. Underlying Cause of Death 1999-2016 on CDC WONDER Online Database, released December 2017

Health Insurance Coverage

Area	With Health Insurance	With Private Health Insurance	With Public Health Insurance	Without Health Insurance	Population Under Age 18 Without Health Insurance
City	97.9	93.5	11.4	2.1	1.2
MSA[1]	91.0	71.2	29.7	9.0	4.3
U.S.	88.3	66.7	33.0	11.7	5.9

Note: Figures are percentages that cover the civilian noninstitutionalized population; (1) Figures cover the Columbus, OH Metropolitan Statistical Area—see Appendix B for areas included
Source: U.S. Census Bureau, 2012-2016 American Community Survey 5-Year Estimates

Number of Medical Professionals

Area	MDs[3]	DOs[3,4]	Dentists	Podiatrists	Chiropractors	Optometrists
County[1] (number)	5,205	811	1,076	86	306	334
County[1] (rate[2])	415.2	64.7	84.7	6.8	24.1	26.3
U.S. (rate[2])	276.5	22.3	67.3	6.0	26.7	15.9

Note: Data as of 2016 unless noted; (1) Data covers Franklin County; (2) Rate per 100,000 population; (3) Data as of 2015 and includes all active, non-federal physicians; (4) Doctor of Osteopathic Medicine
Source: U.S. Department of Health and Human Services, Health Resources and Services Administration, Bureau of Health Professions, Area Resource File (ARF) 2016-2017

Best Hospitals

According to *U.S. News,* the Columbus, OH metro area is home to three of the best hospitals in the U.S.: **Ohio State University James Cancer Hospital** (1 adult specialty); **Ohio State University Wexner Medical Center** (7 adult specialties); **OhioHealth Riverside Hospital** (1 adult specialty). The hospitals listed were nationally ranked in at least one of 16 specialties. Only 152 hospitals nationwide were nationally ranked in one or more specialties. Twenty hospitals in the U.S. made the Honor Roll. The Best Hospitals Honor Roll was revamped last year to take both the national rankings and the procedure and condition ratings into account. Hospitals received points if they were nationally ranked in one of the 16 specialties—the higher they ranked, the more points they got—and how many ratings of "high performing" they earned in the nine procedures and conditions. *U.S. News Online, "America's Best Hospitals 2017-18"*

According to *U.S. News,* the Columbus, OH metro area is home to one of the best children's hospitals in the U.S.: **Nationwide Children's Hospital** (Honor Roll/10 pediatric specialties). The hospital listed was highly ranked in at least one of 10 pediatric specialties. Eighty-two children's hospitals in the U.S. were nationally ranked in at least one specialty. Hospitals received points for being ranked in a specialty, and the 10 hospitals with the most points across the 10 specialties make up the Honor Roll. *U.S. News Online, "America's Best Children's Hospitals 2017-18"*

EDUCATION

Public School District Statistics

District Name	Schls	Pupils	Pupil/ Teacher Ratio	Minority Pupils[1] (%)	Free Lunch Eligible[2] (%)	IEP[3] (%)
Dublin City	19	15,432	19.1	36.0	11.3	10.3
Hilliard City	23	15,910	18.6	25.1	19.8	12.2

Note: Table includes school districts with 100 or more students; (1) Percentage of students that are not non-Hispanic white; (2) Percentage of students that are eligible for the free lunch program; (3) Percentage of students that have an Individualized Education Program.
Source: U.S. Department of Education, National Center for Education Statistics, Common Core of Data, Local Education Agency (School District) Universe Survey: School Year 2015-2016; U.S. Department of Education, National Center for Education Statistics, Common Core of Data, Public Elementary/Secondary School Universe Survey: School Year 2015-2016

Best High Schools

According to *U.S. News,* Dublin is home to two of the best high schools in the U.S.: **Dublin Jerome High School** (#291); **Dublin Coffman High School** (#439). More than 22,000 public, magnet and charter schools were ranked based on their performance on state assessments and how well they prepare students for college. Schools with the highest unrounded College Readiness Index values were numerically ranked from 1 to 500 and were classified as gold medal winners. *U.S. News & World Report, "Best High Schools 2017"*

Highest Level of Education

Area	Less than H.S.	H.S. Diploma	Some College, No Deg.	Associate Degree	Bachelor's Degree	Master's Degree	Prof. School Degree	Doctorate Degree
City	1.5	7.3	10.9	5.0	44.6	20.9	5.8	4.1
MSA[1]	9.3	28.5	20.1	7.4	22.3	8.8	2.1	1.5
U.S.	13.0	27.5	21.0	8.2	18.8	8.2	2.0	1.3

Note: Figures cover persons age 25 and over; (1) Figures cover the Columbus, OH Metropolitan Statistical Area—see Appendix B for areas included
Source: U.S. Census Bureau, 2012-2016 American Community Survey 5-Year Estimates

Educational Attainment by Race

Area	High School Graduate or Higher (%)					Bachelor's Degree or Higher (%)				
	Total	White	Black	Asian	Hisp.[2]	Total	White	Black	Asian	Hisp.[2]
City	98.5	98.6	99.6	98.2	95.4	75.3	74.1	58.9	84.6	76.3
MSA[1]	90.7	91.8	86.0	88.4	72.0	34.8	36.2	20.6	63.9	22.6
U.S.	87.0	88.9	84.3	86.3	65.7	30.3	31.6	20.0	52.1	14.7

Note: Figures shown cover persons 25 years old and over; (1) Figures cover the Columbus, OH Metropolitan Statistical Area—see Appendix B for areas included; (2) People of Hispanic origin can be of any race
Source: U.S. Census Bureau, 2012-2016 American Community Survey 5-Year Estimates

School Enrollment by Grade and Control

Area	Preschool (%)		Kindergarten (%)		Grades 1 - 4 (%)		Grades 5 - 8 (%)		Grades 9 - 12 (%)	
	Public	Private	Public	Private	Public	Private	Public	Private	Public	Private
City	27.6	72.4	73.1	26.9	89.6	10.4	87.4	12.6	92.0	8.0
MSA[1]	50.6	49.4	87.5	12.5	89.9	10.1	88.5	11.5	89.2	10.8
U.S.	58.4	41.6	87.7	12.3	89.8	10.2	89.7	10.3	90.4	9.6

Note: Figures shown cover persons 3 years old and over; (1) Figures cover the Columbus, OH Metropolitan Statistical Area—see Appendix B for areas included
Source: U.S. Census Bureau, 2012-2016 American Community Survey 5-Year Estimates

Average Salaries of Public School Classroom Teachers

Area	2015		2016		Change from 2015 to 2016	
	Dollars	Rank[1]	Dollars	Rank[1]	Percent	Rank[2]
Ohio	54,672	21	56,441	21	3.2	4
U.S. Average	57,611	–	58,353	–	1.3	–

Note: (1) Rank ranges from 1 to 51 where 1 indicates highest salary; (2) Rank ranges from 1 to 51 where 1 indicates highest percent change.
Source: National Education Association, Rankings & Estimates: Rankings of the States 2016 and Estimates of School Statistics 2017

Higher Education

Four-Year Colleges			Two-Year Colleges			Medical Schools[1]	Law Schools[2]	Voc/ Tech[3]
Public	Private Non-profit	Private For-profit	Public	Private Non-profit	Private For-profit			
0	0	0	0	0	0	0	0	0

Note: Figures cover institutions located within the city limits and include main campuses only; (1) includes schools accredited by the Liaison Committee on Medical Education and the American Osteopathic Association's Commission on Osteopathic College Accreditation; (2) includes ABA-accredited schools, schools with provisional ABA accreditation, and state accredited schools; (3) includes all schools with programs that are less than 2 years.
Source: National Center for Education Statistics, Integrated Postsecondary Education System (IPEDS), 2016-17; Wikipedia, List of Medical Schools in the United States, accessed April 2, 2018; Wikipedia, List of Law Schools in the United States, accessed April 2, 2018

According to *U.S. News & World Report,* the Columbus, OH metro area is home to one of the best national universities in the U.S.: **Ohio State University—Columbus** (#54 tie). The indicators used to capture academic quality fall into a number of categories: assessment by administrators at peer institutions; retention of students; faculty resources; student selectivity; financial resources; alumni giving; high school counselor ratings of colleges; and graduation rate. *U.S. News & World Report, "America's Best Colleges 2018"*

According to *U.S. News & World Report,* the Columbus, OH metro area is home to two of the best liberal arts colleges in the U.S.: **Denison University** (#46 tie); **Ohio Wesleyan University** (#101 tie). The indicators used to capture academic quality fall into a number of categories: assessment by administrators at peer institutions; retention of students; faculty resources; student selectivity;

financial resources; alumni giving; high school counselor ratings of colleges; and graduation rate. *U.S. News & World Report, "America's Best Colleges 2018"*

According to *U.S. News & World Report,* the Columbus, OH metro area is home to one of the top 100 law schools in the U.S.: **Ohio State University (Moritz)** (#32 tie). The rankings are based on a weighted average of 12 measures of quality: peer assessment score; assessment score by lawyers/judges; median LSAT scores; median undergrad GPA; acceptance rate; employment rates for graduates; placement success; bar passage rate; faculty resources; expenditures per student; student/faculty ratio; and library resources. *U.S. News & World Report, "America's Best Graduate Schools, Law, 2019"*

According to *U.S. News & World Report,* the Columbus, OH metro area is home to one of the top 75 medical schools for research in the U.S.: **Ohio State University** (#32 tie). The rankings are based on a weighted average of 11 measures of quality: quality assessment; peer assessment score; assessment score by residency directors; research activity; total research activity; average research activity per faculty member; student selectivity; median MCAT total score; median undergraduate GPA; acceptance rate; and faculty resources. *U.S. News & World Report, "America's Best Graduate Schools, Medical, 2019"*

According to *U.S. News & World Report,* the Columbus, OH metro area is home to one of the top 75 business schools in the U.S.: **Ohio State University (Fisher)** (#31 tie). The rankings are based on a weighted average of the following nine measures: quality assessment; peer assessment; recruiter assessment; placement success; mean starting salary and bonus; student selectivity; mean GMAT and GRE scores; mean undergraduate GPA; and acceptance rate. *U.S. News & World Report, "America's Best Graduate Schools, Business, 2019"*

PRESIDENTIAL ELECTION

2016 Presidential Election Results

Area	Clinton	Trump	Johnson	Stein	Other
Franklin County	59.8	33.9	3.4	1.0	1.9
U.S.	48.0	45.9	3.3	1.1	1.7

Note: Results are percentages and may not add to 100% due to rounding
Source: Dave Leip's Atlas of U.S. Presidential Elections

EMPLOYERS

Major Employers

Company Name	Industry
American Electric Power	Utilities
AT&T Ohio (formerly SBC Ohio)	Information
Battelle Memorial Institute	Professional services
Big Lots	Corp. mgt./retail trade
City of Columbus	Government
Columbus City Schools	Public education
Franklin County	Government
Honda of America Manufacturing	Manufacturing
Huntington Bancshares	Financial activities
JPMorgan Chase	Financial activities
Kroger Company	Retail trade
Limited Brands	Corp. mgt./retail trade
Medco Health Solutions	Health care/wholesale trade
Mount Carmel Health System	Health care
Nationwide	Financial activities
Nationwide Children's Hospital	Health care
OhioHealth	Health care
Retail Ventures	Corp. mgt./retail trade
Ross Products Division	Abbott Labs
South-Western City School District	Public education
The Ohio State University	Public education
The State of Ohio	Government
United States Government	Government
Wal-Mart Stores	Retail trade
Wendy's International	Corp. mgt./retail trade

Note: Companies shown are located within the Columbus, OH Metropolitan Statistical Area.
Source: Hoovers.com; Wikipedia

PUBLIC SAFETY

Crime Rate

Area	All Crimes	Violent Crimes: Murder	Violent Crimes: Rape[3]	Violent Crimes: Robbery	Violent Crimes: Aggrav. Assault	Property Crimes: Burglary	Property Crimes: Larceny -Theft	Property Crimes: Motor Vehicle Theft
City	1,175.3	0.0	19.6	10.9	17.4	211.5	885.3	30.5
Metro[1]	3,196.0	5.2	59.7	125.1	94.9	594.4	2,100.6	216.1
U.S.	2,847.8	5.3	40.4	102.8	248.5	468.9	1,745.0	236.9

Note: Figures are crimes per 100,000 population; (1) Figures cover the Columbus, OH Metropolitan Statistical Area—see Appendix B for areas included; (3) The city and U.S. figures shown were reported using the revised Uniform Crime Reporting (UCR) definition of rape. The metro area figures shown are an aggregate total of the data submitted using both the revised and legacy UCR definitions.
Source: FBI Uniform Crime Reports, 2016

Hate Crimes

Area	Number of Quarters Reported	Race/Ethnicity/ Ancestry	Religion	Sexual Orientation	Disability	Gender	Gender Identity
City	4	0	0	0	0	0	0
U.S.	4	3,489	1,273	1,076	70	31	124

(Columns 3–8: Number of Incidents per Bias Motivation)

Source: Federal Bureau of Investigation, Hate Crime Statistics 2016

Identity Theft Consumer Reports

Area	Reports	Reports per 100,000 Population	Rank[2]
MSA[1]	1,699	83	175
U.S.	371,061	114	-

Note: (1) Figures cover the Columbus, OH Metropolitan Statistical Area—see Appendix B for areas included; (2) Rank ranges from 1 to 389 where 1 indicates greatest number of identity theft reports per 100,000 population
Source: Federal Trade Commission, Consumer Sentinel Network Data Book for January–December 2017

Fraud and Other Consumer Reports

Area	Reports	Reports per 100,000 Population	Rank[2]
MSA[1]	10,447	512	101
U.S.	2,304,550	708	-

Note: (1) Figures cover the Columbus, OH Metropolitan Statistical Area—see Appendix B for areas included; (2) Rank ranges from 1 to 389 where 1 indicates greatest number of fraud and other consumer reports per 100,000 population
Source: Federal Trade Commission, Consumer Sentinel Network Data Book for January–December 2017

SPORTS

Professional Sports Teams

Team Name	League	Year Established
Columbus Blue Jackets	National Hockey League (NHL)	2000
Columbus Crew	Major League Soccer (MLS)	1996

Note: Includes teams located in the Columbus, OH Metropolitan Statistical Area.
Source: Wikipedia, Major Professional Sports Teams of the United States and Canada, April 5, 2018

CLIMATE

Average and Extreme Temperatures

Temperature	Jan	Feb	Mar	Apr	May	Jun	Jul	Aug	Sep	Oct	Nov	Dec	Yr.
Extreme High (°F)	74	73	82	89	93	101	104	101	100	90	80	76	104
Average High (°F)	36	39	50	62	73	82	85	83	77	65	51	40	62
Average Temp. (°F)	28	31	41	52	62	70	74	73	66	54	43	32	52
Average Low (°F)	20	22	31	40	50	59	63	62	55	43	34	24	42
Extreme Low (°F)	-19	-13	-6	14	25	35	43	39	31	17	-4	-17	-19

Note: Figures cover the years 1948-1990
Source: National Climatic Data Center, International Station Meteorological Climate Summary, 9/96

Average Precipitation/Snowfall/Humidity

Precip./Humidity	Jan	Feb	Mar	Apr	May	Jun	Jul	Aug	Sep	Oct	Nov	Dec	Yr.
Avg. Precip. (in.)	2.8	2.4	3.1	3.3	3.9	4.0	4.3	3.3	2.7	2.1	3.0	2.8	37.9
Avg. Snowfall (in.)	8	6	5	1	Tr	0	0	0	Tr	Tr	2	6	28
Avg. Rel. Hum. 7am (%)	78	78	76	76	79	81	84	87	87	83	80	79	81
Avg. Rel. Hum. 4pm (%)	66	62	55	51	52	53	53	54	53	53	61	68	57

Note: Figures cover the years 1948-1990; Tr = Trace amounts (<0.05 in. of rain; <0.5 in. of snow)
Source: National Climatic Data Center, International Station Meteorological Climate Summary, 9/96

Weather Conditions

Temperature			Daytime Sky			Precipitation		
5°F & below	32°F & below	90°F & above	Clear	Partly cloudy	Cloudy	0.01 inch or more precip.	0.1 inch or more snow/ice	Thunder-storms
10	118	19	72	137	156	136	29	40

Note: Figures are average number of days per year and cover the years 1948-1990
Source: National Climatic Data Center, International Station Meteorological Climate Summary, 9/96

HAZARDOUS WASTE

Superfund Sites

The Columbus, OH metro area is home to one site on the EPA's Superfund National Priorities List: **Air Force Plant 85** (proposed). There are a total of 1,396 Superfund sites with a status of proposed or final on the list in the U.S. *U.S. Environmental Protection Agency, National Priorities List, April 4, 2018*

AIR & WATER QUALITY

Air Quality Trends: Ozone

	1990	1995	2000	2005	2010	2012	2013	2014	2015	2016
MSA[1]	0.090	0.091	0.085	0.084	0.073	0.077	0.065	0.067	0.066	0.069
U.S.	0.087	0.089	0.081	0.079	0.073	0.075	0.069	0.067	0.068	0.069

Note: (1) Data covers the Columbus, OH Metropolitan Statistical Area—see Appendix B for areas included. The values shown are the composite ozone concentration averages among trend sites based on the highest fourth daily maximum 8-hour concentration in parts per million. These trends are based on sites having an adequate record of monitoring data during the trend period. Data from exceptional events are included.
Source: U.S. Environmental Protection Agency, Air Quality Monitoring Information, "Air Quality Trends by City, 1990-2016"

Air Quality Index

Area	Percent of Days when Air Quality was...[2]					AQI Statistics[2]	
	Good	Moderate	Unhealthy for Sensitive Groups	Unhealthy	Very Unhealthy	Maximum	Median
MSA[1]	77.3	21.9	0.8	0.0	0.0	112	42

Note: (1) Data covers the Columbus, OH Metropolitan Statistical Area—see Appendix B for areas included; (2) Based on 365 days with AQI data in 2017. Air Quality Index (AQI) is an index for reporting daily air quality. EPA calculates the AQI for five major air pollutants regulated by the Clean Air Act: ground-level ozone, particle pollution (aka particulate matter), carbon monoxide, sulfur dioxide, and nitrogen dioxide. The AQI runs from 0 to 500. The higher the AQI value, the greater the level of air pollution and the greater the health concern. There are six AQI categories: "Good" AQI is between 0 and 50. Air quality is considered satisfactory; "Moderate" AQI is between 51 and 100. Air quality is acceptable; "Unhealthy for Sensitive Groups" When AQI values are between 101 and 150, members of sensitive groups may experience health effects; "Unhealthy" When AQI values are between 151 and 200 everyone may begin to experience health effects; "Very Unhealthy" AQI values between 201 and 300 trigger a health alert; "Hazardous" AQI values over 300 trigger warnings of emergency conditions (not shown).
Source: U.S. Environmental Protection Agency, Air Quality Index Report, 2017

Air Quality Index Pollutants

Area	Percent of Days when AQI Pollutant was...[2]					
	Carbon Monoxide	Nitrogen Dioxide	Ozone	Sulfur Dioxide	Particulate Matter 2.5	Particulate Matter 10
MSA[1]	0.0	7.4	53.7	0.0	38.1	0.8

Note: (1) Data covers the Columbus, OH Metropolitan Statistical Area—see Appendix B for areas included; (2) Based on 365 days with AQI data in 2017. The Air Quality Index (AQI) is an index for reporting daily air quality. EPA calculates the AQI for five major air pollutants regulated by the Clean Air Act: ground-level ozone, particle pollution (also known as particulate matter), carbon monoxide, sulfur dioxide, and nitrogen dioxide. The AQI runs from 0 to 500. The higher the AQI value, the greater the level of air pollution and the greater the health concern.
Source: U.S. Environmental Protection Agency, Air Quality Index Report, 2017

Maximum Air Pollutant Concentrations: Particulate Matter, Ozone, CO and Lead

	Particulate Matter 10 (ug/m^3)	Particulate Matter 2.5 Wtd AM (ug/m^3)	Particulate Matter 2.5 24-Hr (ug/m^3)	Ozone (ppm)	Carbon Monoxide (ppm)	Lead (ug/m^3)
MSA[1] Level	52	8.7	18	0.072	2	0.01
NAAQS[2]	150	15	35	0.075	9	0.15
Met NAAQS[2]	Yes	Yes	Yes	Yes	Yes	Yes

Note: (1) Data covers the Columbus, OH Metropolitan Statistical Area—see Appendix B for areas included; Data from exceptional events are included; (2) National Ambient Air Quality Standards; ppm = parts per million; ug/m^3 = micrograms per cubic meter; n/a not available.
Concentrations: Particulate Matter 10 (coarse particulate)—highest second maximum 24-hour concentration; Particulate Matter 2.5 Wtd AM (fine particulate)—highest weighted annual mean concentration; Particulate Matter 2.5 24-Hour (fine particulate)—highest 98th percentile 24-hour concentration; Ozone—highest fourth daily maximum 8-hour concentration; Carbon Monoxide—highest second maximum non-overlapping 8-hour concentration; Lead—maximum running 3-month average
Source: U.S. Environmental Protection Agency, Air Quality Monitoring Information, "Air Quality Statistics by City, 2016"

Maximum Air Pollutant Concentrations: Nitrogen Dioxide and Sulfur Dioxide

	Nitrogen Dioxide AM (ppb)	Nitrogen Dioxide 1-Hr (ppb)	Sulfur Dioxide AM (ppb)	Sulfur Dioxide 1-Hr (ppb)	Sulfur Dioxide 24-Hr (ppb)
MSA[1] Level	12	42	n/a	4	n/a
NAAQS[2]	53	100	30	75	140
Met NAAQS[2]	Yes	Yes	n/a	Yes	n/a

Note: (1) Data covers the Columbus, OH Metropolitan Statistical Area—see Appendix B for areas included; Data from exceptional events are included; (2) National Ambient Air Quality Standards; ppm = parts per million; ug/m^3 = micrograms per cubic meter; n/a not available.
Concentrations: Nitrogen Dioxide AM—highest arithmetic mean concentration; Nitrogen Dioxide 1-Hr—highest 98th percentile 1-hour daily maximum concentration; Sulfur Dioxide AM—highest annual mean concentration; Sulfur Dioxide 1-Hr—highest 99th percentile 1-hour daily maximum concentration; Sulfur Dioxide 24-Hr—highest second maximum 24-hour concentration
Source: U.S. Environmental Protection Agency, Air Quality Monitoring Information, "Air Quality Statistics by City, 2016"

Drinking Water

Water System Name	Pop. Served	Primary Water Source Type	Violations[1]	
			Health Based	Monitoring/ Reporting
Columbus Public Water System	1,196,848	Surface	0	0

Note: (1) Based on violation data from January 1, 2017 to December 31, 2017
Source: U.S. Environmental Protection Agency, Office of Ground Water and Drinking Water, Safe Drinking Water Information System (based on data extracted April 5, 2018)

Hilliard, Ohio

Background

Hilliard is a family-oriented suburb of Columbus, located 11 miles northwest of the city in Franklin County with easy access to I-70 and I-71. Hilliard is adjacent to I-270.

The city, originally called Hilliard Station, began as ten acres of farmland purchased in 1852 by John Reed Hilliard. Due to its proximity to the Indiana Railroad, the town was an ideal shipping point for sending out agricultural products and receiving farming supplies. In 1854, the town got a post office and lost the word "station," but it wasn't incorporated until 1869. The first railroad station was built in town in 1886, which stood until 1962 when rail service ceased.

The construction of three large residential subdivisions in the 1950s brought major growth to Hilliard, which was further fueled when the city was connected to the Columbus regional sewer and water systems in the 1960s. The Village of Hilliard became a city in 1960, with a population of nearly 5,700. The completion of the Interstate 270 in the 1980s brought a second wave of rapid growth.

Today Hilliard is a mix of residential and commercial development, although its interest in its past extends to the multi-million dollar streetscape designed to spruce up Old Hilliard, the historic district in the center of town.

Significant local employers include the Hilliard City School District, as well as employers in the manufacturing, retail and wholesale trade sectors.

Local students attend the Hilliard City School District schools, which recently opened an Innovative Learning Center.

Hilliard's quality of life includes 23 diverse parks, from the Roger A. Reynolds Municipal Park with its fishing, skate park, bike path, and lighted ball fields to the small First Responders Park with its reflection pool and sculpture. The city backs three community gardens, a disc golf course, and is at work on a dog park. The Franklin County Fairgrounds are located in Hilliard.

The Old Hilliardfest Art & Street Fair is held in downtown Hilliard each year the second Saturday of each September and is sponsored by the Hilliard Civic Association. The festival includes several stages of music, ranging from professional acts to various talented community performers; a car show, featuring dozens of classic and modern cars; food vendors, including several food trucks; a large variety of community organizations, artists, and other various vendors; lots for kids to do, including inflatables, carnival games and rides, face painting, arts and crafts activities; and more.

Hilliard is also home to the only Early Television Museum in the country. It holds over 150 TV sets, ranging from the earliest models from the 1920s and 1930s to the early color sets of the 1950s and 1960s. Many of the sets are still in working condition.

Hilliard has a seasonal climate with hot summers and cold winters. Median summer temperatures average 70 degrees, while winter averages can be as low as 25 degrees during December and January. The city averages four inches of rainfall per month from April to October and seven inches of snowfall per month from December to March.

Rankings

Business/Finance Rankings

- According to *Business Insider*, the Columbus* metro area is where startup growth is on the rise. Based on the 2017 Kauffman Index of Growth Entrepreneurship, which measured in-depth national entrepreneurial trends in 40 metro areas, it ranked #3 in highest startup growth. *www.businessinsider.com, "The 21 U.S. Cities with the Highest Startup Growth," October 21, 2017*

- The personal finance site NerdWallet analyzed 183 American metropolitan areas with populations over 250,000 and more than 15,000 businesses to rank where entrepreneurs find the most success. Criteria included area economy, annual income, housing cost, unemployment rate, and the success rate of area businesses. Columbus* ranked #92. *www.nerdwallet.com, "Best Places to Start a Business," April 27, 2015*

- The editors of *Kiplinger's Personal Finance Magazine* named Columbus* to their list of ten of the best metro areas for start-ups. The area ranked #10.Criteria: well-educated workforce; low living costs for self-employed people, as measured by the Council for Community and Economic Research; a strong existing community of small business; low unemployment; low business costs. *www.kiplinger.com, "10 Great Cities for Starting a Business," October 2014*

- Based on metro area social media reviews, the employment opinion group Glassdoor surveyed 50 of the largest U.S. metro areas and equally weighed cost of living, hiring opportunity, and job satisfaction to compose a list of "25 Best Cities for Jobs." Median pay and home value, in-demand jobs and number of current job openings was also factored in. The Columbus* metro area was ranked #7 in overall job satisfaction. *www.glassdoor.com, "Best Cities for Jobs," September 12, 2017*

- In a survey of economic confidence in the nation's 50 largest metropolitan areas conducted January–December 2014, the Columbus* metro area placed #25, according to Gallup's 2014 Economic Confidence Index. *Gallup, "San Jose and San Francisco Lead in Economic Confidence," March 19, 2015*

- The Brookings Institution ranked the 100 largest metro areas in the U.S. based on income inequality. Columbus* was ranked #62 (#1 = greatest ineqality). Criteria: the "95/20 ratio," a figure representing the income at which a household earns more than 95 percent of all other households, divided by the income at which a household earns more than only 20 percent of all other households. *Brookings Institution, "Household Income Inequality, 100 Largest U.S. Metro Areas, 2014-2016," February 5, 2018*

- *Forbes* ranked the 100 largest metro areas in the U.S. in terms of the "Best Cities for Young Professionals." The Columbus* metro area ranked #9 out of 25. (Large metro areas were divided into metro divisions.) Criteria: median rent of a two-bedroom apartment; job growth and unemployment rate; median salary of college graduates with 5 or less years of work experience; networking opportunities; social outlook; percentage of population 25 years of age and older with college degrees. *Forbes.com, "America's 25 Best Cities for Young Professionals in 2017," May 22, 2017*

- The Columbus* metro area was identified as one of the most affordable metropolitan areas in America by *Forbes.* The area ranked #10 out of 20 based on the National Association of Home Builders/Wells Fargo Housing Affordability Index and Sperling's Best Places' cost-of-living index. *Forbes.com, "America's Most Affordable Cities in 2015," March 12, 2015*

- Columbus* was identified as one of America's most frugal metro areas by *Coupons.com.* The city ranked #20 out of 25. Criteria: digital coupon usage. *Coupons.com, "America's Most Frugal Cities of 2017," March 22, 2018*

- Columbus* was cited as one of America's top metros for new and expanded facility projects in 2017. The area ranked #7 in the large metro area category (population over 1 million). *Site Selection, "Top Metropolitans of 2017," March 2018*

- The Columbus* metro area appeared on the Milken Institute "2017 Best Performing Cities" list. Rank: #62 out of 200 large metro areas. Criteria: job growth; wage and salary growth; high-tech output growth. *Milken Institute, "Best-Performing Cities 2017," January 2018*

- *Forbes* ranked the 200 most populous metro areas to determine the nation's "Best Places for Business and Careers." The Columbus* metro area was ranked #11. Criteria: costs (business and living); job growth (past and projected); income growth; quality of life; educational attainment (college and high school); projected economic growth; cultural and recreational opportunities; net migration patterns; number of highly ranked colleges. *Forbes, "The Best Places for Business and Careers 2017," October 24, 2017*

Education Rankings

- Personal finance website *WalletHub* analyzed the 150 largest U.S. metropolitan statistical areas to determine where the most educated Americans are choosing to settle. Criteria: education quality and attainment gap; education levels; percentage of workers with degrees; public school rankings; quality and size of each metro area's universities. Columbus* was ranked #34 (#1 = most educated city). *www.WalletHub.com, "2017's Most and Least Educated Cities in America, " July 25, 2017*

Environmental Rankings

- Sperling's BestPlaces assessed 379 metropolitan areas of the United States for the likelihood of dangerously extreme weather events or earthquakes. In general the Southeast and South-Central regions have the highest risk of weather extremes and earthquakes, while the Pacific Northwest enjoys the lowest risk. Of the least risky metropolitan areas, the Columbus* metro area was ranked #144. *www.bestplaces.net, "Safest Places from Natural Disasters," April 2011*

- Columbus* was highlighted as one of the top 99 cleanest metro areas for short-term particle pollution (24-hour PM 2.5) in the U.S. during 2013 through 2015. Monitors in these cities reported no days with unhealthful PM 2.5 levels. *American Lung Association, State of the Air 2017*

Health/Fitness Rankings

- Analysts who tracked obesity rates in the nation's largest metro areas (populations above one million) found that the Columbus* metro area was one of the ten major metros where residents were most likely to be obese, defined as a BMI score of 30 or above. *www.gallup.com, "Boulder, Colo., Residents Still Least Likely to Be Obese," April 4, 2014*

- For each of the 50 most populous metro areas in the United States, the American College of Sports Medicine's American Fitness Index evaluated infrastructure, community assets, and policies that encourage healthy and fit lifestyles, including preventive health behaviors, levels of chronic disease conditions, health care access, and community resources and policies that support physical activity. The Columbus* metro area ranked #41 for "community fitness." *www.americanfitnessindex.org, "ACSM American Fitness Index Health and Community Fitness Status of the 50 Largest Metropolitan Areas," May 2017*

- The Columbus* metro area was identified as one of the worst cities for bed bugs in America by pest control company Orkin. The area ranked #5 out of 50 based on the number of bed bug treatments Orkin performed from December 2016 to November 2017. *Orkin, "Baltimore and Washington D.C. Continue to Hold Top Spots," January 8, 2018*

- Columbus* was identified as a "2016 Spring Allergy Capital." The area ranked #55 out of 100. Three groups of factors were used to identify the most severe cities for people with allergies during the spring season: annual pollen levels; medicine utilization; access to board-certified allergists. *Asthma and Allergy Foundation of America, "Spring Allergy Capitals 2016"*

- Columbus* was identified as a "2016 Fall Allergy Capital." The area ranked #43 out of 100. Three groups of factors were used to identify the most severe cities for people with allergies during the fall season: annual pollen levels; medicine utilization; access to board-certified allergists. *Asthma and Allergy Foundation of America, "Fall Allergy Capitals 2016"*

- Columbus* was identified as a "2015 Asthma Capital." The area ranked #49 out of the nation's 100 largest metropolitan areas. Criteria: estimated prevalence; self-reported prevalence; crude death rate for asthma; annual pollen score; annual air quality; public smoking laws; number of board-certified asthma specialists; school inhaler access laws; rescue medication use; controller medication use; ER visits for asthma; uninsured rate; poverty rate. *Asthma and Allergy Foundation of America, "Asthma Capitals 2015"*

- The Columbus* metro area ranked #125 out of 189 in The Gallup-Healthways Well-Being Index. Criteria: purpose; social well being; financial health; community and physical health. Results are based on telephone interviews with adults, aged 18 and older, living in metropolitan areas in the 50 U.S. states and the District of Columbia. *Gallup-Healthways, "State of American Well-Being, 2017 Community Well-Being Rankings" March 2018*

Real Estate Rankings

- FitSmallBusiness looked at 50 of the largest metropolitan areas in the U.S. to determine which metro was the best to start a real estate business. Data was compiled from such sources as: Zillow, Trulia, U.S. Census Bureau, and the Bureau of Labor Statistics. Criteria: location; inventory; annual wages; median sales price of homes; days on the market; median price cut percentage; and other factors that would influence real estate professional growth. The Columbus* metro area ranked #44. *fitsmallbusiness.com, "The Best Cities to Become a Real Estate Agent in 2018," January 30, 2018*

- The Columbus* metro area was identified as one of the nations's 20 hottest housing markets in 2018. Criteria: listing views as an indicator of demand and median days on the market as an indicator of supply. The area ranked #16. *Realtor.com, "The 20 Hottest Real Estate Markets for February 2018," March 1, 2018*

- The Columbus* metro area was identified as one of the top 20 housing markets to invest in for 2018 by *Forbes*. The area ranked #20. Criteria: strong job and population growth; anticipated home price appreciation; and other factors. *Forbes.com, "Where to Invest in Housing in 2018," February 1, 2018*

- The Columbus* metro area was identified as one of the 20 best housing markets in the U.S. in 2017. The area ranked #16 out of 180 markets. Criteria: year-over-year change of median sales price of existing single-family homes between the 4th quarter of 2016 and the 4th quarter of 2017. *National Association of Realtors®, Median Sales Price of Existing Single-Family Homes for Metropolitan Areas, 4th Quarter 2017*

- Columbus* was ranked #97 out of 238 metro areas in terms of housing affordability in 2017 by the National Association of Home Builders (#1 = most affordable). Criteria: the share of homes sold in that area affordable to a family earning the local median income, based on standard mortgage underwriting criteria. *National Association of Home Builders®, NAHB-Wells Fargo Housing Opportunity Index, 4th Quarter 2017*

Safety Rankings

- Hilliard was identified as one of the safest cities in America by NeighborhoodScout. The city ranked #92 out of 100 (100 = safest). Criteria: number of violent and property crimes per 1,000 residents. The editors only considered cities with 25,000 or more residents. *NeighborhoodScout, "Top 100 Safest Cities in the U.S. 2018" January 2, 2018*

- The National Insurance Crime Bureau ranked 382 metro areas in the U.S. in terms of per capita rates of vehicle theft. The Columbus* metro area ranked #134 (#1 = highest rate). Criteria: number of vehicle theft offenses per 100,000 inhabitants in 2016. *National Insurance Crime Bureau, "Hot Spots 2016," June 8, 2017*

Seniors/Retirement Rankings

- From its Best Cities for Successful Aging indexes, the Milken Institute generated rankings for metropolitan areas, weighing data in nine categories—health care, wellness, living arrangements, transportation and convenience, financial characteristics, education, employment, community engagement, and overall livability. The Columbus* metro area was ranked #49 overall in the large metro area category. *Milken Institute, "Best Cities for Successful Aging, 2017" March 14, 2017*

*Hilliard is located within the Columbus, OH Metropolitan Statistical Area.

Business Environment

CITY FINANCES

City Government Finances

Component	2015 ($000)	2015 ($ per capita)
Total Revenues	43,555	1,294
Total Expenditures	33,817	1,005
Debt Outstanding	71,408	2,122
Cash and Securities[1]	44,341	1,318

Note: (1) Cash and security holdings of a government at the close of its fiscal year,, including those of its dependent agencies, utilities, and liquor stores.
Source: U.S Census Bureau, State & Local Government Finances 2015

City Government Revenue by Source

Source	2015 ($000)	2015 ($ per capita)	2015 (%)
General Revenue			
From Federal Government	0	0	0.0
From State Government	2,136	63	4.9
From Local Governments	1,329	39	3.1
Taxes			
Property	1,226	36	2.8
Sales and Gross Receipts	180	5	0.4
Personal Income	19,631	583	45.1
Corporate Income	2,147	64	4.9
Motor Vehicle License	0	0	0.0
Other Taxes	1,324	39	3.0
Current Charges	6,103	181	14.0
Liquor Store	0	0	0.0
Utility	0	0	0.0
Employee Retirement	0	0	0.0

Source: U.S Census Bureau, State & Local Government Finances 2015

City Government Expenditures by Function

Function	2015 ($000)	2015 ($ per capita)	2015 (%)
General Direct Expenditures			
Air Transportation	0	0	0.0
Corrections	0	0	0.0
Education	0	0	0.0
Employment Security Administration	0	0	0.0
Financial Administration	602	17	1.8
Fire Protection	0	0	0.0
General Public Buildings	859	25	2.5
Governmental Administration, Other	805	23	2.4
Health	0	0	0.0
Highways	3,007	89	8.9
Hospitals	0	0	0.0
Housing and Community Development	0	0	0.0
Interest on General Debt	2,259	67	6.7
Judicial and Legal	434	12	1.3
Libraries	0	0	0.0
Parking	0	0	0.0
Parks and Recreation	2,465	73	7.3
Police Protection	9,349	277	27.6
Public Welfare	0	0	0.0
Sewerage	0	0	0.0
Solid Waste Management	0	0	0.0
Veterans' Services	0	0	0.0
Liquor Store	0	0	0.0
Utility	0	0	0.0
Employee Retirement	0	0	0.0

Source: U.S Census Bureau, State & Local Government Finances 2015

DEMOGRAPHICS

Population Growth

Area	1990 Census	2000 Census	2010 Census	2016* Estimate	Population Growth (%) 1990-2016	Population Growth (%) 2010-2016
City	12,516	24,230	28,435	33,108	164.5	16.4
MSA[1]	1,405,176	1,612,694	1,836,536	1,995,004	42.0	8.6
U.S.	248,709,873	281,421,906	308,745,538	318,558,162	28.1	3.2

Note: (1) Figures cover the Columbus, OH Metropolitan Statistical Area—see Appendix B for areas included; (*) 2012-2016 5-year estimated population
Source: U.S. Census Bureau, 1990 Census, Census 2000, Census 2010, 2012-2016 American Community Survey 5-Year Estimates

Household Size

Area	Persons in Household (%)							Average Household Size
	One	Two	Three	Four	Five	Six	Seven or More	
City	22.9	29.5	17.9	19.2	8.0	0.8	1.8	2.80
MSA[1]	28.6	33.5	16.0	13.1	5.7	2.0	1.0	2.50
U.S.	27.7	33.7	15.7	13.1	6.0	2.3	1.5	2.60

Note: (1) Figures cover the Columbus, OH Metropolitan Statistical Area—see Appendix B for areas included
Source: U.S. Census Bureau, 2012-2016 American Community Survey 5-Year Estimates

Race

Area	White Alone[2] (%)	Black Alone[2] (%)	Asian Alone[2] (%)	AIAN[3] Alone[2] (%)	NHOPI[4] Alone[2] (%)	Other Race Alone[2] (%)	Two or More Races (%)
City	88.2	3.4	6.5	0.1	0.1	0.2	1.4
MSA[1]	77.2	14.8	3.6	0.2	0.0	1.0	3.1
U.S.	73.3	12.6	5.2	0.8	0.2	4.8	3.1

Note: (1) Figures cover the Columbus, OH Metropolitan Statistical Area—see Appendix B for areas included; (2) Alone is defined as not being in combination with one or more other races; (3) American Indian and Alaska Native; (4) Native Hawaiian and Other Pacific Islander
Source: U.S. Census Bureau, 2012-2016 American Community Survey 5-Year Estimates

Hispanic or Latino Origin

Area	Total (%)	Mexican (%)	Puerto Rican (%)	Cuban (%)	Other (%)
City	2.6	1.8	0.2	0.1	0.7
MSA[1]	3.8	2.1	0.5	0.1	1.1
U.S.	17.3	11.0	1.7	0.7	4.0

Note: Persons of Hispanic or Latino origin can be of any race; (1) Figures cover the Columbus, OH Metropolitan Statistical Area—see Appendix B for areas included
Source: U.S. Census Bureau, 2012-2016 American Community Survey 5-Year Estimates

Segregation

Type	Segregation Indices[1]				Percent Change		
	1990	2000	2010	2010 Rank[2]	1990-2000	1990-2010	2000-2010
Black/White	67.6	63.4	62.2	33	-4.2	-5.5	-1.2
Asian/White	44.7	43.3	43.3	35	-1.4	-1.4	0.0
Hispanic/White	27.9	36.9	41.5	59	9.0	13.6	4.6

Note: All figures cover the Metropolitan Statistical Area—see Appendix B for areas included; Figures are based on an analysis of 1990, 2000, and 2010 Census Decennial Census tract data by William H. Frey, Brookings Institution and the University of Michigan Social Science Data Analysis Network. In this analysis all racial groups (whites, blacks, and asians) are non-Hispanic members of those races. Hispanics are shown as a separate category; (1) Segregation Indices are Dissimilarity Indices that measure the degree to which the minority group is distributed differently than whites across census tracts. They range from 0 (complete integration) to 100 (complete segregation) where the value indicates the percentage of the minority group that needs to move to be distributed exactly like whites; (2) Ranges from 1 (most segregated) to 102 (least segregated); n/a not available.
Source: www.CensusScope.org

Ancestry

Area	German	Irish	English	American	Italian	Polish	French[2]	Scottish	Dutch
City	28.6	14.5	11.2	5.8	8.4	3.6	3.0	2.7	1.6
MSA[1]	24.4	13.5	9.0	6.9	5.5	2.3	2.2	2.2	1.5
U.S.	14.4	10.4	7.7	6.9	5.4	2.9	2.6	1.7	1.3

Note: Figures are the percentage of the total population reporting a particular ancestry. The nine most commonly reported ancestries in the U.S. are shown. Figures include multiple ancestries (e.g. if a person reported being Irish and Italian, they were included in both columns); (1) Figures cover the Columbus, OH Metropolitan Statistical Area—see Appendix B for areas included; (2) Excludes Basque
Source: U.S. Census Bureau, 2012-2016 American Community Survey 5-Year Estimates

Foreign-Born Population

Area	Percent of Population Born in								
	Any Foreign Country	Asia	Mexico	Europe	Carribean	Central America[2]	South America	Africa	Canada
City	6.2	4.7	0.3	0.6	0.0	0.0	0.1	0.4	0.0
MSA[1]	7.3	3.0	0.8	0.8	0.2	0.2	0.2	1.8	0.1
U.S.	13.2	4.0	3.6	1.5	1.3	1.0	0.9	0.6	0.3

Note: (1) Figures cover the Columbus, OH Metropolitan Statistical Area—see Appendix B for areas included; (2) Excludes Mexico.
Source: U.S. Census Bureau, 2012-2016 American Community Survey 5-Year Estimates

Marital Status

Area	Never Married	Now Married[2]	Separated	Widowed	Divorced
City	26.7	59.1	1.3	5.0	8.0
MSA[1]	34.0	47.5	1.9	4.9	11.7
U.S.	33.0	48.1	2.1	5.9	11.0

Note: Figures are percentages and cover the population 15 years of age and older; (1) Figures cover the Columbus, OH Metropolitan Statistical Area—see Appendix B for areas included; (2) Excludes separated
Source: U.S. Census Bureau, 2012-2016 American Community Survey 5-Year Estimates

Disability Status

Area	All Ages	Under 18 Years Old	18 to 64 Years Old	65 Years and Over
City	7.7	4.4	5.2	33.1
MSA[1]	11.8	4.6	10.3	35.1
U.S.	12.5	4.1	10.3	35.7

Note: Figures show percent of the civilian noninstitutionalized population that reported having a disability. Disability status is determined from six types of difficulty: vision, hearing, cognitive, ambulatory, self-care, and independent living. For children under 5 years old, hearing and vision difficulty are used to determine disability status. For children between the ages of 5 and 14, disability status is determined from hearing, vision, cognitive, ambulatory, and self-care difficulties. For people aged 15 years and older, they are considered to have a disability if they have difficulty with any one of the six difficulty types; Note: (1) Figures cover the Columbus, OH Metropolitan Statistical Area—see Appendix B for areas included
Source: U.S. Census Bureau, 2012-2016 American Community Survey 5-Year Estimates

Age

Area	Percent of Population									Median Age
	Under Age 5	Age 5–19	Age 20–34	Age 35–44	Age 45–54	Age 55–64	Age 65–74	Age 75–84	Age 85+	
City	6.8	23.6	18.2	14.5	15.9	10.8	5.8	3.0	1.4	35.9
MSA[1]	6.8	20.0	22.2	13.6	13.6	11.8	7.1	3.4	1.5	35.7
U.S.	6.2	19.6	20.7	12.7	13.6	12.6	8.3	4.3	1.9	37.7

Note: (1) Figures cover the Columbus, OH Metropolitan Statistical Area—see Appendix B for areas included
Source: U.S. Census Bureau, 2012-2016 American Community Survey 5-Year Estimates

Gender

Area	Males	Females	Males per 100 Females
City	16,438	16,670	98.6
MSA[1]	981,638	1,013,366	96.9
U.S.	156,765,322	161,792,840	96.9

Note: (1) Figures cover the Columbus, OH Metropolitan Statistical Area—see Appendix B for areas included
Source: U.S. Census Bureau, 2012-2016 American Community Survey 5-Year Estimates

Religious Groups by Family

Area	Catholic	Baptist	Non-Den.	Methodist[2]	Lutheran	LDS[3]	Pente-costal	Presby-terian[4]	Muslim[5]	Judaism
MSA[1]	11.8	5.3	3.6	4.7	2.4	0.7	2.0	2.0	0.8	0.5
U.S.	19.1	9.3	4.0	4.0	2.3	2.0	1.9	1.6	0.8	0.7

Note: Figures are the number of adherents as a percentage of the total population; (1) Figures cover the Columbus, OH Metropolitan Statistical Area—see Appendix B for areas included; (2) Methodist/Pietist; (3) Latter Day Saints; (4) Reformed; (5) Figures are estimates
Source: Association of Statisticians of American Religious Bodies, 2010 U.S. Religion Census: Religious Congregations & Membership Study

Religious Groups by Tradition

Area	Catholic	Evangelical Protestant	Mainline Protestant	Other Tradition	Black Protestant	Orthodox
MSA[1]	11.8	11.9	9.5	3.1	1.1	0.3
U.S.	19.1	16.2	7.3	4.3	1.6	0.3

Note: Figures are the number of adherents as a percentage of the total population; (1) Figures cover the Columbus, OH Metropolitan Statistical Area—see Appendix B for areas included
Source: Association of Statisticians of American Religious Bodies, 2010 U.S. Religion Census: Religious Congregations & Membership Study

ECONOMY

Gross Metropolitan Product

Area	2014	2015	2016	2017	Rank[2]
MSA[1]	116.4	121.8	126.5	132.9	31

Note: Figures are in billions of dollars; (1) Figures cover the Columbus, OH Metropolitan Statistical Area—see Appendix B for areas included; (2) Rank is based on 2015 data and ranges from 1 to 381
Source: The U.S. Conference of Mayors, U.S. Metro Economies: GMP and Employment Report, 2015-2017

Economic Growth

Area	2012-14 (%)	2015 (%)	2016 (%)	2017 (%)	Rank[2]
MSA[1]	1.6	2.6	2.3	3.0	155
U.S.	2.0	2.4	1.9	2.6	–

Note: Figures are real gross metropolitan product (GMP) growth rates and represent average annual percent change; (1) Figures cover the Columbus, OH Metropolitan Statistical Area—see Appendix B for areas included; (2) Rank is based on 2012-2014 average annual percent change and ranges from 1 to 381
Source: The U.S. Conference of Mayors, U.S. Metro Economies: GMP and Employment Report, 2015-2017

Metropolitan Area Exports

Area	2011	2012	2013	2014	2015	2016	Rank[2]
MSA[1]	4,327.5	5,488.6	5,731.4	6,245.6	6,201.6	5,675.4	48

Note: Figures are in millions of dollars; (1) Figures cover the Columbus, OH Metropolitan Statistical Area—see Appendix B for areas included; (2) Rank is based on 2016 data and ranges from 1 to 385
Source: U.S. Department of Commerce, International Trade Administration, Office of Trade & Industry Information, Manufacturing & Services, data extracted March 15, 2018

Building Permits

Area	Single-Family			Multi-Family			Total		
	2016	2017p	Pct. Chg.	2016	2017p	Pct. Chg.	2016	2017p	Pct. Chg.
City	74	98	32.4	122	2	-98.4	196	100	-49.0
MSA[1]	4,040	4,166	3.1	4,209	4,593	9.1	8,249	8,759	6.2
U.S.	750,800	817,300	8.9	455,800	446,800	-2.0	1,206,600	1,264,100	4.8

Note: (1) Figures cover the Columbus, OH Metropolitan Statistical Area—see Appendix B for areas included; Figures represent new, privately-owned housing units authorized (unadjusted data); All permit data are based on estimates with imputation; (p) preliminary data.
Source: U.S. Census Bureau, Manufacturing, Mining, and Construction Statistics, Building Permits, 2016, 2017

Bankruptcy Filings

Area	Business Filings 2016	Business Filings 2017	Business Filings % Chg.	Nonbusiness Filings 2016	Nonbusiness Filings 2017	Nonbusiness Filings % Chg.
Franklin County	58	70	20.7	4,463	4,479	0.4
U.S.	24,114	23,157	-4.0	770,846	765,863	-0.6

Note: Business filings include Chapter 7, Chapter 11, Chapter 12, and Chapter 13; Nonbusiness filings include Chapter 7, Chapter 11, and Chapter 13
Source: Administrative Office of the U.S. Courts, Business and Nonbusiness Bankruptcy, County Cases Commenced by Chapter of the Bankruptcy Code, During the 12-Month Period Ending December 31, 2016 and Business and Nonbusiness Bankruptcy, County Cases Commenced by Chapter of the Bankruptcy Code, During the 12-Month Period Ending December 31, 2017

Housing Vacancy Rates

Area	Gross Vacancy Rate[2] (%)			Year-Round Vacancy Rate[3] (%)			Rental Vacancy Rate[4] (%)			Homeowner Vacancy Rate[5] (%)		
	2015	2016	2017	2015	2016	2017	2015	2016	2017	2015	2016	2017
MSA[1]	9.6	8.0	6.6	9.2	7.8	6.0	6.5	6.1	6.3	1.5	1.0	1.1
U.S.	12.9	12.8	12.7	10.0	9.9	9.9	7.1	6.9	7.2	1.8	1.7	1.6

Note: (1) Figures cover the Columbus, OH Metropolitan Statistical Area—see Appendix B for areas included; (2) The percentage of the total housing inventory that is vacant; (3) The percentage of the housing inventory (excluding seasonal units) that is year-round vacant; (4) The percentage of rental inventory that is vacant for rent; (5) The percentage of homeowner inventory that is vacant for sale
Source: U.S. Census Bureau, Housing Vacancies and Homeownership Annual Statistics: 2015, 2016, 2017

INCOME

Income

Area	Per Capita ($)	Median Household ($)	Average Household ($)
City	40,964	92,727	111,490
MSA[1]	30,399	57,440	77,221
U.S.	29,829	55,322	77,866

Note: (1) Figures cover the Columbus, OH Metropolitan Statistical Area—see Appendix B for areas included
Source: U.S. Census Bureau, 2012-2016 American Community Survey 5-Year Estimates

Household Income Distribution

Area	Percent of Households Earning							
	Under $15,000	$15,000 -$24,999	$25,000 -$34,999	$35,000 -$49,999	$50,000 -$74,999	$75,000 -$99,999	$100,000 -$149,999	$150,000 and up
City	4.9	4.9	7.5	7.7	15.6	13.3	21.3	24.8
MSA[1]	11.3	9.4	9.6	13.4	18.7	12.9	14.3	10.5
U.S.	12.1	10.2	9.9	13.2	17.8	12.2	13.5	11.1

Note: (1) Figures cover the Columbus, OH Metropolitan Statistical Area—see Appendix B for areas included
Source: U.S. Census Bureau, 2012-2016 American Community Survey 5-Year Estimates

Poverty Rate

Area	All Ages	Under 18 Years Old	18 to 64 Years Old	65 Years and Over
City	4.0	6.3	2.8	4.4
MSA[1]	14.4	20.3	13.5	7.7
U.S.	15.1	21.2	14.2	9.3

Note: Figures are percentage of people whose income during the past 12 months was below the poverty level; (1) Figures cover the Columbus, OH Metropolitan Statistical Area—see Appendix B for areas included
Source: U.S. Census Bureau, 2012-2016 American Community Survey 5-Year Estimates

EMPLOYMENT

Labor Force and Employment

Area	Civilian Labor Force Dec. 2016	Civilian Labor Force Dec. 2017	Civilian Labor Force % Chg.	Workers Employed Dec. 2016	Workers Employed Dec. 2017	Workers Employed % Chg.
City	19,044	19,326	1.5	18,435	18,752	1.7
MSA[1]	1,066,787	1,080,007	1.2	1,023,273	1,039,735	1.6
U.S.	158,968,000	159,880,000	0.6	151,798,000	153,602,000	1.2

Note: Data is not seasonally adjusted and covers workers 16 years of age and older; (1) Figures cover the Columbus, OH Metropolitan Statistical Area—see Appendix B for areas included
Source: Bureau of Labor Statistics, Local Area Unemployment Statistics

Unemployment Rate

Area	2017											
	Jan.	Feb.	Mar.	Apr.	May	Jun.	Jul.	Aug.	Sep.	Oct.	Nov.	Dec.
City	3.9	3.6	3.3	2.9	3.1	3.8	3.7	3.7	3.3	3.1	3.1	3.0
MSA[1]	4.9	4.6	4.1	3.7	3.7	4.3	4.3	4.2	3.9	3.7	3.7	3.7
U.S.	5.1	4.9	4.6	4.1	4.1	4.5	4.6	4.5	4.1	3.9	3.9	3.9

Note: Data is not seasonally adjusted and covers workers 16 years of age and older; (1) Figures cover the Columbus, OH Metropolitan Statistical Area—see Appendix B for areas included
Source: Bureau of Labor Statistics, Local Area Unemployment Statistics

Average Wages

Occupation	$/Hr.	Occupation	$/Hr.
Accountants and Auditors	35.90	Maids and Housekeeping Cleaners	10.60
Automotive Mechanics	20.00	Maintenance and Repair Workers	19.20
Bookkeepers	19.70	Marketing Managers	70.00
Carpenters	22.30	Nuclear Medicine Technologists	34.00
Cashiers	10.20	Nurses, Licensed Practical	20.20
Clerks, General Office	16.80	Nurses, Registered	32.30
Clerks, Receptionists/Information	13.30	Nursing Assistants	12.70
Clerks, Shipping/Receiving	15.10	Packers and Packagers, Hand	11.50
Computer Programmers	36.40	Physical Therapists	38.90
Computer Systems Analysts	47.10	Postal Service Mail Carriers	23.80
Computer User Support Specialists	25.00	Real Estate Brokers	65.00
Cooks, Restaurant	13.00	Retail Salespersons	13.00
Dentists	100.70	Sales Reps., Exc. Tech./Scientific	31.20
Electrical Engineers	38.50	Sales Reps., Tech./Scientific	37.40
Electricians	22.10	Secretaries, Exc. Legal/Med./Exec.	18.10
Financial Managers	66.60	Security Guards	15.30
First-Line Supervisors/Managers, Sales	21.00	Surgeons	123.60
Food Preparation Workers	10.70	Teacher Assistants*	13.90
General and Operations Managers	59.10	Teachers, Elementary School*	29.60
Hairdressers/Cosmetologists	13.20	Teachers, Secondary School*	30.30
Internists, General	122.30	Telemarketers	13.40
Janitors and Cleaners	13.30	Truck Drivers, Heavy/Tractor-Trailer	22.20
Landscaping/Groundskeeping Workers	13.80	Truck Drivers, Light/Delivery Svcs.	16.80
Lawyers	55.60	Waiters and Waitresses	11.00

Note: Wage data covers the Columbus, OH Metropolitan Statistical Area—see Appendix B for areas included; (*) Hourly wages for elementary/secondary school teachers and teacher assistants were calculated by the editors from annual wage data based on a 40 hour work week; n/a not available.
Source: Bureau of Labor Statistics, Metro Area Occupational Employment & Wage Estimates, May 2017

Employment by Occupation

Occupation Classification	City (%)	MSA[1] (%)	U.S. (%)
Management, Business, Science, and Arts	53.9	40.9	37.0
Natural Resources, Construction, and Maintenance	2.4	6.3	8.9
Production, Transportation, and Material Moving	6.8	11.9	12.2
Sales and Office	24.4	24.5	23.8
Service	12.4	16.3	18.1

Note: Figures cover employed civilians 16 years of age and older; (1) Figures cover the Columbus, OH Metropolitan Statistical Area—see Appendix B for areas included
Source: U.S. Census Bureau, 2012-2016 American Community Survey 5-Year Estimates

Employment by Industry

Sector	MSA[1] Number of Employees	MSA[1] Percent of Total	U.S. Percent of Total
Construction, Mining, and Logging	38,600	3.5	5.2
Education and Health Services	162,000	14.8	15.9
Financial Activities	86,000	7.8	5.7
Government	177,900	16.2	15.3
Information	17,200	1.6	1.9
Leisure and Hospitality	104,200	9.5	10.7
Manufacturing	74,000	6.7	8.5
Other Services	40,500	3.7	3.9
Professional and Business Services	180,800	16.5	14.0
Retail Trade	114,500	10.4	11.0
Transportation, Warehousing, and Utilities	58,700	5.4	4.1
Wholesale Trade	42,500	3.9	4.0

Note: Figures are non-farm employment as of December 2017. Figures are not seasonally adjusted and include workers 16 years of age and older; (1) Figures cover the Columbus, OH Metropolitan Statistical Area—see Appendix B for areas included
Source: Bureau of Labor Statistics, Current Employment Statistics, Employment, Hours, and Earnings

Occupations with Greatest Projected Employment Growth: 2017 – 2019

Occupation[1]	2017 Employment	2019 Projected Employment	Numeric Employment Change	Percent Employment Change
Combined Food Preparation and Serving Workers, Including Fast Food	160,970	170,100	9,130	5.7
Waiters and Waitresses	95,660	99,920	4,260	4.5
Home Health Aides	67,650	71,430	3,780	5.6
Registered Nurses	129,370	132,510	3,140	2.4
Heavy and Tractor-Trailer Truck Drivers	74,290	77,290	3,000	4.0
Laborers and Freight, Stock, and Material Movers, Hand	108,760	111,710	2,950	2.7
Personal Care Aides	30,510	32,800	2,290	7.5
Construction Laborers	40,630	42,780	2,150	5.3
Janitors and Cleaners, Except Maids and Housekeeping Cleaners	86,300	88,350	2,050	2.4
Software Developers, Applications	35,570	37,620	2,050	5.8

Note: Projections cover Ohio; (1) Sorted by numeric employment change
Source: www.projectionscentral.com, State Occupational Projections, 2017–2019 Short-Term Projections

Fastest Growing Occupations: 2017 – 2019

Occupation[1]	2017 Employment	2019 Projected Employment	Numeric Employment Change	Percent Employment Change
Rotary Drill Operators, Oil and Gas	230	280	50	21.7
Service Unit Operators, Oil, Gas, and Mining	710	850	140	19.7
Wellhead Pumpers	510	610	100	19.6
Roustabouts, Oil and Gas	720	860	140	19.4
Earth Drillers, Except Oil and Gas	460	510	50	10.9
Veterinary Technologists and Technicians	3,370	3,670	300	8.9
Veterinary Assistants and Laboratory Animal Caretakers	2,730	2,970	240	8.8
Veterinarians	3,330	3,610	280	8.4
Amusement and Recreation Attendants	8,950	9,650	700	7.8
Physician Assistants	3,210	3,460	250	7.8

Note: Projections cover Ohio; (1) Sorted by percent employment change and excludes occupations with numeric employment change less than 50
Source: www.projectionscentral.com, State Occupational Projections, 2017–2019 Short-Term Projections

TAXES

State Corporate Income Tax Rates

State	Tax Rate (%)	Income Brackets ($)	Num. of Brackets	Financial Institution Tax Rate (%)[a]	Federal Income Tax Ded.
Ohio	(t)	–	–	(t)	No

Note: Tax rates as of January 1, 2018; (a) Rates listed are the corporate income tax rate applied to financial institutions or excise taxes based on income. Some states have other taxes based upon the value of deposits or shares; (t) Ohio no longer levies a tax based on income (except for a particular subset of corporations), but instead imposes a Commercial Activity Tax (CAT) equal to $150 for gross receipts sitused to Ohio of between $150,000 and $1 million, plus 0.26% of gross receipts over $1 million. Banks continue to pay a franchise tax of 1.3% of net worth. For those few corporations for whom the franchise tax on net worth or net income still applies, a litter tax also applies.
Source: Federation of Tax Administrators, Range of State Corporate Income Tax Rates, January 1, 2018

State Individual Income Tax Rates

State	Tax Rate (%)	Income Brackets ($)	Num. of Brackets	Personal Exempt. ($)[1]		Fed. Inc. Tax Ded.
				Single	Dependents	
Ohio (a)	0.0 - 4.997	10,650 - 213,350	8	2,300 (t)	2,300 (t)	No

Note: Tax rates as of January 1, 2018; Local- and county-level taxes are not included; n/a not applicable; (1) Married joint filers generally receive double the single exemption; (a) 19 states have statutory provision for automatically adjusting to the rate of inflation the dollar values of the income tax brackets, standard deductions, and/or personal exemptions. Massachusetts, Michigan, and Nebraska index the personal exemption only. Oregon does not index the income brackets for $125,000 and over; (t) Ohio provides an additional tax credit of $20 per exemption. Exemption amounts reduced for higher income taxpayers.
Source: Federation of Tax Administrators, State Individual Income Tax Rates, January 1, 2018

Various State Sales and Excise Tax Rates

State	State Sales Tax (%)	Gasoline[1] (¢/gal.)	Cigarette[2] ($/pack)	Spirits[3] ($/gal.)	Wine[4] ($/gal.)	Beer[5] ($/gal.)	Recreational Marijuana (%)
Ohio	5.75	28.01	1.60	9.87 (g)	0.32 (l)	0.18 (q)	Not legal

Note: All tax rates as of January 1, 2018; (1) The American Petroleum Institute has developed a methodology for determining the average tax rate on a gallon of fuel. Rates may include any of the following: excise taxes, environmental fees, storage tank fees, other fees or taxes, general sales tax, and local taxes. In states where gasoline is subject to the general sales tax, or where the fuel tax is based on the average sale price, the average rate determined by API is sensitive to changes in the price of gasoline. States that fully or partially apply general sales taxes to gasoline: CA, CO, GA, IL, IN, MI, NY; (2) The federal excise tax of $1.0066 per pack and local taxes are not included; (3) Rates are those applicable to off-premise sales of 40% alcohol by volume (a.b.v.) distilled spirits in 750ml containers. Local excise taxes are excluded; (4) Rates are those applicable to off-premise sales of 11% a.b.v. non-carbonated wine in 750ml containers; (5) Rates are those applicable to off-premise sales of 4.7% a.b.v. beer in 12 ounce containers; (g) Control states, where the government controls all sales. Products can be subject to ad valorem mark-up as well as excise taxes; (l) Different rates also applicable to alcohol content, place of production, size of container, place purchased (on- or off-premise or on board airlines) or type of wine (carbonated, vermouth, etc.); (q) Different rates also applicable according to alcohol content, place of production, size of container, or place purchased (on- or off-premise or onboard airlines).
Source: Tax Foundation, 2018 Facts & Figures: How Does Your State Compare?

State Business Tax Climate Index Rankings

State	Overall Rank	Corporate Tax Rank	Individual Income Tax Rank	Sales Tax Rank	Unemployment Insurance Tax Rank	Property Tax Rank
Ohio	45	47	47	30	8	11

Note: The index is a measure of how each state's tax laws affect economic performance. The lower the rank, the more favorable a state's tax system is for business. States without a given tax are given a ranking of 1. The scores/rankings for the District of Columbia do not affect other states. The 2018 index represents the tax climate as of July 1, 2017.
Source: Tax Foundation, State Business Tax Climate Index 2018

TRANSPORTATION

Means of Transportation to Work

Area	Car/Truck/Van		Public Transportation			Bicycle	Walked	Other Means	Worked at Home
	Drove Alone	Car-pooled	Bus	Subway	Railroad				
City	84.2	8.3	0.4	0.0	0.0	0.1	1.0	0.8	5.2
MSA[1]	82.5	7.9	1.7	0.0	0.0	0.4	2.2	0.9	4.4
U.S.	76.4	9.3	2.6	1.9	0.6	0.6	2.8	1.3	4.6

Note: Figures are percentages and cover workers 16 years of age and older; (1) Figures cover the Columbus, OH Metropolitan Statistical Area—see Appendix B for areas included
Source: U.S. Census Bureau, 2012-2016 American Community Survey 5-Year Estimates

Travel Time to Work

Area	Less Than 10 Minutes	10 to 19 Minutes	20 to 29 Minutes	30 to 44 Minutes	45 to 59 Minutes	60 to 89 Minutes	90 Minutes or More
City	10.9	27.7	31.6	23.2	4.4	1.9	0.4
MSA[1]	11.4	30.6	26.7	21.0	6.0	3.0	1.4
U.S.	12.9	29.2	20.9	20.4	8.0	6.0	2.7

Note: Note: Figures are percentages and include workers 16 years old and over; (1) Figures cover the Columbus, OH Metropolitan Statistical Area—see Appendix B for areas included
Source: U.S. Census Bureau, 2012-2016 American Community Survey 5-Year Estimates

Freeway Travel Time Index

Area	1985	1990	1995	2000	2005	2010	2014
Urban Area Rank[1,2]	35	34	36	38	42	48	46
Urban Area Index[1]	1.09	1.12	1.15	1.17	1.18	1.17	1.18
Average Index[3]	1.09	1.11	1.14	1.17	1.20	1.19	1.20

Note: Freeway Travel Time Index—the ratio of travel time in the peak period to the travel time at free-flow conditions. For example, a value of 1.30 indicates a 20-minute free-flow trip takes 26 minutes in the peak (20 minutes x 1.30 = 26 minutes); (1) Covers the Columbus OH urban area; (2) Rank is based on 101 urban areas (#1 = highest travel time index); (3) Average of 101 urban areas
Source: Texas Transportation Institute, 2015 Urban Mobility Scorecard, August 2015

Freeway Commuter Stress Index

Area	1985	1990	1995	2000	2005	2010	2014
Urban Area Rank[1,2]	36	41	40	40	44	49	49
Urban Area Index[1]	1.13	1.16	1.19	1.21	1.22	1.21	1.22
Average Index[3]	1.13	1.16	1.19	1.22	1.25	1.24	1.25

Note: The Freeway Commuter Stress Index is the same as the Freeway Travel Time Index (see table above) except that it includes only the travel in the peak directions during the peak periods; the TTI includes travel in all directions during the peak period. Thus, the CSI is more indicative of the work trip experienced by each commuter on a daily basis; (1) Covers the Columbus OH urban area; (2) Rank is based on 101 urban areas (#1 = highest travel time index); (3) Average of 101 urban areas
Source: Texas Transportation Institute, 2015 Urban Mobility Scorecard, August 2015

Living Environment

COST OF LIVING

Cost of Living Index

Composite Index	Groceries	Housing	Utilities	Transportation	Health Care	Misc. Goods/ Services
89.6	98.9	76.8	77.7	96.9	92.1	97.4

Note: The Cost of Living Index measures regional differences in the cost of consumer goods and services, excluding taxes and non-consumer expenditures, for professional and managerial households in the top income quintile. It is based on more than 50,000 prices covering almost 60 different items for which prices are collected three times a year by chambers of commerce, economic development organizations or university applied economic centers in each participating urban area. The numbers shown should be read as a percentage above or below the national average of 100. For example, a value of 115.4 in the groceries column indicates that grocery prices are 15.4% higher than the national average. Small differences in the index numbers should not be interpreted as significant; Figures cover the Columbus OH urban area.
Source: The Council for Community and Economic Research, ACCRA Cost of Living Index, 2017

Grocery Prices

Area[1]	T-Bone Steak ($/pound)	Frying Chicken ($/pound)	Whole Milk ($/half gal.)	Eggs ($/dozen)	Orange Juice ($/64 oz.)	Coffee ($/11.5 oz.)
City[2]	12.96	1.30	1.43	1.39	3.01	7.48
Avg.	11.29	1.40	2.02	1.47	3.55	4.37
Min.	7.71	0.93	1.04	0.70	2.86	3.24
Max.	15.83	2.39	4.03	3.92	6.29	8.16

Note: (1) Values for the local area are compared with the average, minimum and maximum values for all 294 areas in the Cost of Living Index; (2) Figures cover the Columbus OH urban area; ***T-Bone Steak*** *(price per pound);* ***Frying Chicken*** *(price per pound, whole fryer);* ***Whole Milk*** *(half gallon carton);* ***Eggs*** *(price per dozen, Grade A, large);* ***Orange Juice*** *(64 oz. Tropicana or Florida Natural);* ***Coffee*** *(11.5 oz. can, vacuum-packed, Maxwell House, Hills Bros, or Folgers).*
Source: The Council for Community and Economic Research, ACCRA Cost of Living Index, 2017

Housing and Utility Costs

Area[1]	New Home Price ($)	Apartment Rent ($/month)	All Electric ($/month)	Part Electric ($/month)	Other Energy ($/month)	Telephone ($/month)
City[2]	238,079	952	-	52.90	65.42	24.67
Avg.	335,956	1,047	175.01	97.34	67.93	28.71
Min.	187,788	491	109.48	49.33	35.44	12.39
Max.	1,739,087	4,559	432.62	227.09	353.33	44.61

Note: (1) Values for the local area are compared with the average, minimum and maximum values for all 294 areas in the Cost of Living Index; (2) Figures cover the Columbus OH urban area; ***New Home Price*** *(2,400 sf living area, 8,000 sf lot, in urban area with full utilities);* ***Apartment Rent*** *(950 sf 2 bedroom/1.5 or 2 bath, unfurnished, excluding all utilities except water);* ***All Electric*** *(average monthly cost for an all-electric home);* ***Part Electric*** *(average monthly cost for a part-electric home);* ***Other Energy*** *(average monthly cost for natural gas, fuel oil, coal, wood, and any other forms of energy except electricity);* ***Telephone*** *(price includes basic monthly rate for a private residential line plus additional local usage charges incurred by a family of four).*
Source: The Council for Community and Economic Research, ACCRA Cost of Living Index, 2017

Health Care, Transportation, and Other Costs

Area[1]	Doctor ($/visit)	Dentist ($/visit)	Optometrist ($/visit)	Gasoline ($/gallon)	Beauty Salon ($/visit)	Men's Shirt ($)
City[2]	99.16	86.52	59.51	2.29	33.40	29.68
Avg.	108.00	92.54	101.93	2.25	37.58	30.92
Min.	30.39	60.00	49.75	1.82	16.11	11.20
Max.	193.50	161.94	229.28	3.16	77.35	59.13

Note: (1) Values for the local area are compared with the average, minimum and maximum values for all 294 areas in the Cost of Living Index; (2) Figures cover the Columbus OH urban area; ***Doctor*** *(general practitioners routine exam of an established patient);* ***Dentist*** *(adult teeth cleaning and periodic oral examination);* ***Optometrist*** *(full vision eye exam for established adult patient);* ***Gasoline*** *(one gallon regular unleaded, national brand, including all taxes, cash price at self-service pump if available);* ***Beauty Salon*** *(woman's shampoo, trim, and blow-dry);* ***Men's Shirt*** *(cotton/polyester dress shirt, pinpoint weave, long sleeves).*
Source: The Council for Community and Economic Research, ACCRA Cost of Living Index, 2017

HOUSING

House Price Index (HPI)

Area	National Ranking[2]	Quarterly Change (%)	One-Year Change (%)	Five-Year Change (%)
MSA[1]	72	-0.08	8.20	30.85
U.S.[3]	–	1.61	6.68	34.71

Note: The HPI is a weighted repeat sales index. It measures average price changes in repeat sales or refinancings on the same properties. This information is obtained by reviewing repeat mortgage transactions on single-family properties whose mortgages have been purchased or securitized by Fannie Mae or Freddie Mac in January 1975; (1) Figures cover the Columbus, OH Metropolitan Statistical Area—see Appendix B for areas included; (2) Rankings are based on annual percentage change for all metro areas containing at least 15,000 transactions over the last 10 years and ranges from 1 to 253; (3) figures based on a weighted average of Census Division estimates using a seasonally adjusted, purchase-only index; all figures are for the period ending December 31, 2017
Source: Federal Housing Finance Agency, House Price Index, February 28, 2018

Median Single-Family Home Prices

Area	2015	2016	2017p	Percent Change 2016 to 2017
MSA[1]	164.7	175.5	189.9	8.2
U.S. Average	223.9	235.5	248.8	5.6

Note: Figures are median sales prices of existing single-family homes in thousands of dollars; (p) preliminary; (1) Figures cover the Columbus, OH Metropolitan Statistical Area—see Appendix B for areas included
Source: National Association of Realtors, Median Sales Price of Existing Single-Family Homes for Metropolitan Areas, 4th Quarter 2017

Qualifying Income Based on Median Sales Price of Existing Single-Family Homes

Area	With 5% Down ($)	With 10% Down ($)	With 20% Down ($)
MSA[1]	42,687	40,440	35,947
U.S. Average	55,585	52,659	46,808

Note: Figures are preliminary; Qualifying income is based on a mortgage rate of 4.17%. Monthly principal and interest payment is limited to 25% of income; (1) Figures cover the Columbus, OH Metropolitan Statistical Area—see Appendix B for areas included
Source: National Association of Realtors, Qualifying Income Based on Median Sales Price of Existing Single-Family Homes for Metropolitan Areas, 4th Quarter 2017

Median Apartment Condo-Coop Home Prices

Area	2015	2016	2017p	Percent Change 2016 to 2017
MSA[1]	132.0	138.2	149.8	8.4
U.S. Average	210.7	220.7	234.3	6.2

Note: Figures are median sales prices of existing apartment condo-coop homes in thousands of dollars; (p) preliminary; (1) Figures cover the Columbus, OH Metropolitan Statistical Area—see Appendix B for areas included
Source: National Association of Realtors, Median Sales Price of Existing Apartment Condo-Coop Homes for Metropolitan Areas, 4th Quarter 2017

Home Value Distribution

Area	Under $50,000	$50,000 -$99,999	$100,000 -$149,999	$150,000 -$199,999	$200,000 -$299,999	$300,000 -$499,999	$500,000 -$999,999	$1,000,000 or more
City	1.2	4.7	20.2	18.7	36.0	18.3	0.9	0.0
MSA[1]	5.9	16.9	21.7	19.7	19.7	12.0	3.6	0.5
U.S.	8.8	14.8	15.3	14.9	18.4	16.4	9.0	2.5

Note: Figures are percentages and cover owner-occupied housing units; (1) Figures cover the Columbus, OH Metropolitan Statistical Area—see Appendix B for areas included
Source: U.S. Census Bureau, 2012-2016 American Community Survey 5-Year Estimates

Homeownership Rate

Area	2009 (%)	2010 (%)	2011 (%)	2012 (%)	2013 (%)	2014 (%)	2015 (%)	2016 (%)	2017 (%)
MSA[1]	61.5	62.2	59.7	60.7	60.5	60.0	59.0	57.5	57.9
U.S.	67.4	66.9	66.1	65.4	65.1	64.5	63.7	63.4	63.9

Note: (1) Figures cover the Columbus, OH Metropolitan Statistical Area—see Appendix B for areas included
Source: U.S. Census Bureau, Housing Vacancies and Homeownership Annual Statistics: 2009-2017

Year Housing Structure Built

Area	2010 or Later	2000 -2009	1990 -1999	1980 -1989	1970 -1979	1960 -1969	1950 -1959	1940 -1949	Before 1940	Median Year
City	6.4	15.3	39.0	14.0	5.7	4.3	13.1	0.8	1.5	1993
MSA[1]	2.6	14.9	16.8	12.0	14.8	11.6	10.5	4.3	12.5	1977
U.S.	2.3	14.7	14.0	13.7	15.6	10.9	10.6	5.2	13.0	1977

Note: Figures are percentages except for Median Year; Note: (1) Figures cover the Columbus, OH Metropolitan Statistical Area—see Appendix B for areas included
Source: U.S. Census Bureau, 2012-2016 American Community Survey 5-Year Estimates

Gross Monthly Rent

Area	Under $500	$500 -$999	$1,000 -$1,499	$1,500 -$1,999	$2,000 -$2,499	$2,500 -$2,999	$3,000 and up	Median ($)
City	8.6	41.0	39.6	9.2	1.2	0.0	0.4	1,004
MSA[1]	9.9	58.4	25.2	4.6	1.3	0.3	0.3	855
U.S.	11.3	43.3	27.7	10.7	4.0	1.6	1.5	949

Note: Figures are percentages except for Median; Gross rent is the contract rent plus the estimated average monthly cost of utilities (electricity, gas, and water and sewer) and fuels (oil, coal, kerosene, wood, etc.) if these are paid by the renter (or paid for the renter by someone else); (1) Figures cover the Columbus, OH Metropolitan Statistical Area—see Appendix B for areas included
Source: U.S. Census Bureau, 2012-2016 American Community Survey 5-Year Estimates

HEALTH

Health Risk Factors

Category	MSA[1] (%)	U.S. (%)
Adults aged 18–64 who have any kind of health care coverage	92.0	87.7
Adults who reported being in good or excellent health	83.9	83.6
Adults who are current smokers	21.8	17.1
Adults who currently use E-cigarettes	5.5	4.7
Adults who currently use chewing tobacco, snuff, or snus	3.2	4.0
Adults who are heavy drinkers[2]	6.2	6.5
Adults who are binge drinkers[3]	18.7	16.9
Adults who are overweight (BMI 25.0 - 29.9)	34.2	35.3
Adults who are obese (BMI 30.0 - 99.8)	30.2	29.9
Adults who participated in any physical activities in the past month	77.3	76.9
Adults who always or nearly always wears a seat belt	91.2	94.3

Note: (1) Figures cover the Columbus, OH Metropolitan Statistical Area—see Appendix B for areas included; (2) Heavy drinkers are classified as adult men having more than 14 drinks per week and adult women having more than 7 drinks per week; (3) Binge drinkers are classified as males having five or more drinks on one occasion or females having four or more drinks on one occasion
Source: Centers for Disease Control and Prevention, Behaviorial Risk Factor Surveillance System, SMART: Selected Metropolitan Area Risk Trends, 2016

Health Screening Rates

Category	MSA[1] (%)	U.S. (%)
Adults 50-75 who have had a blood stool test within the past year	7.3	8.0
Adults 50-75 who have had a colonoscopy in the past 10 years	66.5	63.5
Adults aged 65+ who have had flu shot within the past year	60.2	58.6
Adults aged 65+ who have ever had a pneumonia vaccination	78.3	73.4
Adults who have ever been tested for HIV	38.1	35.6
Women aged 21-65 who have had a pap test in the past three years	86.0	79.8
Men aged 40+ who have had a PSA test within the past two years	40.8	39.5
Women aged 40+ who have had a mammogram within the past two years	76.4	72.5

Note: n/a not available; (1) Figures cover the Columbus, OH Metropolitan Statistical Area—see Appendix B for areas included; Source: Centers for Disease Control and Prevention, Behaviorial Risk Factor Surveillance System, SMART: Selected Metropolitan Area Risk Trends, 2016

Chronic Health Conditions

Category	MSA[1] (%)	U.S. (%)
Adults who have ever been told they had a heart attack	3.9	4.4
Adults who have ever been told they have angina or coronary heart disease	3.2	4.1
Adults who have ever been told they had a stroke	3.6	3.1
Adults who have been told they currently have asthma	9.2	9.3
Adults who have ever been told they have arthritis	25.8	25.8
Adults who have ever been told they have diabetes[2]	10.0	10.5
Adults who have ever been told they had skin cancer	5.1	5.9
Adults who have ever been told they had any other types of cancer	6.5	6.7
Adults who have ever been told they have COPD	7.3	6.3
Adults who have ever been told they have kidney disease	1.7	2.8
Adults who have ever been told they have a form of depression	20.1	17.4

Note: (1) Figures cover the Columbus, OH Metropolitan Statistical Area—see Appendix B for areas included; (2) Figures do not include pregnancy-related, borderline, or pre-diabetes
Source: Centers for Disease Control and Prevention, Behaviorial Risk Factor Surveillance System, SMART: Selected Metropolitan Area Risk Trends, 2016

Mortality Rates for the Top 10 Causes of Death in the U.S.

ICD-10[a] Sub-Chapter	ICD-10[a] Code	Age-Adjusted Mortality Rate[1] per 100,000 population	
		County[2]	U.S.
Malignant neoplasms	C00-C97	171.8	158.5
Ischaemic heart diseases	I20-I25	82.5	96.8
Other forms of heart disease	I30-I51	70.5	52.4
Chronic lower respiratory diseases	J40-J47	47.1	40.9
Cerebrovascular diseases	I60-I69	45.0	37.2
Organic, including symptomatic, mental disorders	F01-F09	48.4	33.3
Other degenerative diseases of the nervous system	G30-G31	33.4	32.1
Other external causes of accidental injury	W00-X59	40.4	31.2
Diabetes mellitus	E10-E14	24.8	21.1
Hypertensive diseases	I10-I15	25.9	20.8

Note: (a) ICD-10 = International Classification of Diseases 10th Revision; (1) Mortality rates are a three year average covering 2014-2016; (2) Figures cover Franklin County.
Source: Centers for Disease Control and Prevention, National Center for Health Statistics. Underlying Cause of Death 1999-2016 on CDC WONDER Online Database, released December 2017

Mortality Rates for Selected Causes of Death

ICD-10[a] Sub-Chapter	ICD-10[a] Code	Age-Adjusted Mortality Rate[1] per 100,000 population	
		County[2]	U.S.
Assault	X85-Y09	8.3	5.6
Diseases of the liver	K70-K76	14.0	14.0
Human immunodeficiency virus (HIV) disease	B20-B24	1.7	1.9
Influenza and pneumonia	J09-J18	18.6	14.6
Intentional self-harm	X60-X84	11.7	13.2
Malnutrition	E40-E46	2.1	1.3
Obesity and other hyperalimentation	E65-E68	2.2	2.1
Renal failure	N17-N19	16.4	13.0
Transport accidents	V01-V99	9.7	12.0
Viral hepatitis	B15-B19	1.4	1.9

Note: (a) ICD-10 = International Classification of Diseases 10th Revision; (1) Mortality rates are a three year average covering 2014-2016; (2) Figures cover Franklin County; Data are Suppressed when the data meet the criteria for confidentiality constraints; Mortality rates are flagged as Unreliable when the rate would be calculated with a numerator of 20 or less.
Source: Centers for Disease Control and Prevention, National Center for Health Statistics. Underlying Cause of Death 1999-2016 on CDC WONDER Online Database, released December 2017

Health Insurance Coverage

Area	With Health Insurance	With Private Health Insurance	With Public Health Insurance	Without Health Insurance	Population Under Age 18 Without Health Insurance
City	94.6	84.7	18.3	5.4	2.2
MSA[1]	91.0	71.2	29.7	9.0	4.3
U.S.	88.3	66.7	33.0	11.7	5.9

Note: Figures are percentages that cover the civilian noninstitutionalized population; (1) Figures cover the Columbus, OH Metropolitan Statistical Area—see Appendix B for areas included
Source: U.S. Census Bureau, 2012-2016 American Community Survey 5-Year Estimates

Number of Medical Professionals

Area	MDs[3]	DOs[3,4]	Dentists	Podiatrists	Chiropractors	Optometrists
County[1] (number)	5,205	811	1,076	86	306	334
County[1] (rate[2])	415.2	64.7	84.7	6.8	24.1	26.3
U.S. (rate[2])	276.5	22.3	67.3	6.0	26.7	15.9

Note: Data as of 2016 unless noted; (1) Data covers Franklin County; (2) Rate per 100,000 population; (3) Data as of 2015 and includes all active, non-federal physicians; (4) Doctor of Osteopathic Medicine
Source: U.S. Department of Health and Human Services, Health Resources and Services Administration, Bureau of Health Professions, Area Resource File (ARF) 2016-2017

Best Hospitals

According to *U.S. News,* the Columbus, OH metro area is home to three of the best hospitals in the U.S.: **Ohio State University James Cancer Hospital** (1 adult specialty); **Ohio State University Wexner Medical Center** (7 adult specialties); **OhioHealth Riverside Hospital** (1 adult specialty). The hospitals listed were nationally ranked in at least one of 16 specialties. Only 152 hospitals nationwide were nationally ranked in one or more specialties. Twenty hospitals in the U.S. made the Honor Roll. The Best Hospitals Honor Roll was revamped last year to take both the national rankings and the procedure and condition ratings into account. Hospitals received points if they were nationally ranked in one of the 16 specialties—the higher they ranked, the more points they got—and how many ratings of "high performing" they earned in the nine procedures and conditions. *U.S. News Online, "America's Best Hospitals 2017-18"*

According to *U.S. News,* the Columbus, OH metro area is home to one of the best children's hospitals in the U.S.: **Nationwide Children's Hospital** (Honor Roll/10 pediatric specialties). The hospital listed was highly ranked in at least one of 10 pediatric specialties. Eighty-two children's hospitals in the U.S. were nationally ranked in at least one specialty. Hospitals received points for being ranked in a specialty, and the 10 hospitals with the most points across the 10 specialties make up the Honor Roll. *U.S. News Online, "America's Best Children's Hospitals 2017-18"*

EDUCATION

Public School District Statistics

District Name	Schls	Pupils	Pupil/ Teacher Ratio	Minority Pupils[1] (%)	Free Lunch Eligible[2] (%)	IEP[3] (%)
Hilliard City	23	15,910	18.6	25.1	19.8	12.2

Note: Table includes school districts with 100 or more students; (1) Percentage of students that are not non-Hispanic white; (2) Percentage of students that are eligible for the free lunch program; (3) Percentage of students that have an Individualized Education Program.
Source: U.S. Department of Education, National Center for Education Statistics, Common Core of Data, Local Education Agency (School District) Universe Survey: School Year 2015-2016; U.S. Department of Education, National Center for Education Statistics, Common Core of Data, Public Elementary/Secondary School Universe Survey: School Year 2015-2016

Highest Level of Education

Area	Less than H.S.	H.S. Diploma	Some College, No Deg.	Associate Degree	Bachelor's Degree	Master's Degree	Prof. School Degree	Doctorate Degree
City	3.7	18.3	17.9	8.0	31.6	13.4	4.6	2.4
MSA[1]	9.3	28.5	20.1	7.4	22.3	8.8	2.1	1.5
U.S.	13.0	27.5	21.0	8.2	18.8	8.2	2.0	1.3

Note: Figures cover persons age 25 and over; (1) Figures cover the Columbus, OH Metropolitan Statistical Area—see Appendix B for areas included
Source: U.S. Census Bureau, 2012-2016 American Community Survey 5-Year Estimates

Educational Attainment by Race

Area	High School Graduate or Higher (%)					Bachelor's Degree or Higher (%)				
	Total	White	Black	Asian	Hisp.[2]	Total	White	Black	Asian	Hisp.[2]
City	96.3	96.3	93.3	98.1	66.6	52.1	51.5	30.1	74.8	29.4
MSA[1]	90.7	91.8	86.0	88.4	72.0	34.8	36.2	20.6	63.9	22.6
U.S.	87.0	88.9	84.3	86.3	65.7	30.3	31.6	20.0	52.1	14.7

Note: Figures shown cover persons 25 years old and over; (1) Figures cover the Columbus, OH Metropolitan Statistical Area—see Appendix B for areas included; (2) People of Hispanic origin can be of any race
Source: U.S. Census Bureau, 2012-2016 American Community Survey 5-Year Estimates

School Enrollment by Grade and Control

Area	Preschool (%)		Kindergarten (%)		Grades 1 - 4 (%)		Grades 5 - 8 (%)		Grades 9 - 12 (%)	
	Public	Private	Public	Private	Public	Private	Public	Private	Public	Private
City	31.3	68.8	94.1	5.9	92.3	7.7	87.9	12.1	87.5	12.5
MSA[1]	50.6	49.4	87.5	12.5	89.9	10.1	88.5	11.5	89.2	10.8
U.S.	58.4	41.6	87.7	12.3	89.8	10.2	89.7	10.3	90.4	9.6

Note: Figures shown cover persons 3 years old and over; (1) Figures cover the Columbus, OH Metropolitan Statistical Area—see Appendix B for areas included
Source: U.S. Census Bureau, 2012-2016 American Community Survey 5-Year Estimates

Average Salaries of Public School Classroom Teachers

Area	2015		2016		Change from 2015 to 2016	
	Dollars	Rank[1]	Dollars	Rank[1]	Percent	Rank[2]
Ohio	54,672	21	56,441	21	3.2	4
U.S. Average	57,611	–	58,353	–	1.3	–

Note: (1) Rank ranges from 1 to 51 where 1 indicates highest salary; (2) Rank ranges from 1 to 51 where 1 indicates highest percent change.
Source: National Education Association, Rankings & Estimates: Rankings of the States 2016 and Estimates of School Statistics 2017

Higher Education

Four-Year Colleges			Two-Year Colleges			Medical Schools[1]	Law Schools[2]	Voc/ Tech[3]
Public	Private Non-profit	Private For-profit	Public	Private Non-profit	Private For-profit			
0	0	1	0	0	1	0	0	0

Note: Figures cover institutions located within the city limits and include main campuses only; (1) includes schools accredited by the Liaison Committee on Medical Education and the American Osteopathic Association's Commission on Osteopathic College Accreditation; (2) includes ABA-accredited schools, schools with provisional ABA accreditation, and state accredited schools; (3) includes all schools with programs that are less than 2 years.
Source: National Center for Education Statistics, Integrated Postsecondary Education System (IPEDS), 2016-17; Wikipedia, List of Medical Schools in the United States, accessed April 2, 2018; Wikipedia, List of Law Schools in the United States, accessed April 2, 2018

According to *U.S. News & World Report,* the Columbus, OH metro area is home to one of the best national universities in the U.S.: **Ohio State University—Columbus** (#54 tie). The indicators used to capture academic quality fall into a number of categories: assessment by administrators at peer institutions; retention of students; faculty resources; student selectivity; financial resources; alumni giving; high school counselor ratings of colleges; and graduation rate. *U.S. News & World Report, "America's Best Colleges 2018"*

According to *U.S. News & World Report,* the Columbus, OH metro area is home to two of the best liberal arts colleges in the U.S.: **Denison University** (#46 tie); **Ohio Wesleyan University** (#101 tie). The indicators used to capture academic quality fall into a number of categories: assessment by administrators at peer institutions; retention of students; faculty resources; student selectivity; financial resources; alumni giving; high school counselor ratings of colleges; and graduation rate. *U.S. News & World Report, "America's Best Colleges 2018"*

According to *U.S. News & World Report,* the Columbus, OH metro area is home to one of the top 100 law schools in the U.S.: **Ohio State University (Moritz)** (#32 tie). The rankings are based on a weighted average of 12 measures of quality: peer assessment score; assessment score by lawyers/judges; median LSAT scores; median undergrad GPA; acceptance rate; employment rates for graduates; placement success; bar passage rate; faculty resources; expenditures per student; student/faculty ratio; and library resources. *U.S. News & World Report, "America's Best Graduate Schools, Law, 2019"*

According to *U.S. News & World Report,* the Columbus, OH metro area is home to one of the top 75 medical schools for research in the U.S.: **Ohio State University** (#32 tie). The rankings are based on a weighted average of 11 measures of quality: quality assessment; peer assessment score; assessment score by residency directors; research activity; total research activity; average research activity per faculty member; student selectivity; median MCAT total score; median undergraduate GPA; acceptance rate; and faculty resources. *U.S. News & World Report, "America's Best Graduate Schools, Medical, 2019"*

According to *U.S. News & World Report,* the Columbus, OH metro area is home to one of the top 75 business schools in the U.S.: **Ohio State University (Fisher)** (#31 tie). The rankings are based on a weighted average of the following nine measures: quality assessment; peer assessment; recruiter assessment; placement success; mean starting salary and bonus; student selectivity; mean GMAT and GRE scores; mean undergraduate GPA; and acceptance rate. *U.S. News & World Report, "America's Best Graduate Schools, Business, 2019"*

PRESIDENTIAL ELECTION

2016 Presidential Election Results

Area	Clinton	Trump	Johnson	Stein	Other
Franklin County	59.8	33.9	3.4	1.0	1.9
U.S.	48.0	45.9	3.3	1.1	1.7

Note: Results are percentages and may not add to 100% due to rounding
Source: Dave Leip's Atlas of U.S. Presidential Elections

EMPLOYERS

Major Employers

Company Name	Industry
American Electric Power	Utilities
AT&T Ohio (formerly SBC Ohio)	Information
Battelle Memorial Institute	Professional services
Big Lots	Corp. mgt./retail trade
City of Columbus	Government
Columbus City Schools	Public education
Franklin County	Government
Honda of America Manufacturing	Manufacturing
Huntington Bancshares	Financial activities
JPMorgan Chase	Financial activities
Kroger Company	Retail trade
Limited Brands	Corp. mgt./retail trade
Medco Health Solutions	Health care/wholesale trade
Mount Carmel Health System	Health care
Nationwide	Financial activities
Nationwide Children's Hospital	Health care
OhioHealth	Health care
Retail Ventures	Corp. mgt./retail trade
Ross Products Division	Abbott Labs
South-Western City School District	Public education
The Ohio State University	Public education
The State of Ohio	Government
United States Government	Government
Wal-Mart Stores	Retail trade
Wendy's International	Corp. mgt./retail trade

Note: Companies shown are located within the Columbus, OH Metropolitan Statistical Area.
Source: Hoovers.com; Wikipedia

PUBLIC SAFETY

Crime Rate

Area	All Crimes	Violent Crimes: Murder	Violent Crimes: Rape[3]	Violent Crimes: Robbery	Violent Crimes: Aggrav. Assault	Property Crimes: Burglary	Property Crimes: Larceny -Theft	Property Crimes: Motor Vehicle Theft
City	1,082.3	0.0	31.6	25.8	37.3	192.4	726.3	68.9
Metro[1]	3,196.0	5.2	59.7	125.1	94.9	594.4	2,100.6	216.1
U.S.	2,847.8	5.3	40.4	102.8	248.5	468.9	1,745.0	236.9

Note: Figures are crimes per 100,000 population; (1) Figures cover the Columbus, OH Metropolitan Statistical Area—see Appendix B for areas included; (3) The city and U.S. figures shown were reported using the revised Uniform Crime Reporting (UCR) definition of rape. The metro area figures shown are an aggregate total of the data submitted using both the revised and legacy UCR definitions.
Source: FBI Uniform Crime Reports, 2016

Hate Crimes

Area	Number of Quarters Reported	Race/Ethnicity/ Ancestry	Religion	Sexual Orientation	Disability	Gender	Gender Identity
		Number of Incidents per Bias Motivation					
City	2	2	0	1	0	0	0
U.S.	4	3,489	1,273	1,076	70	31	124

Source: Federal Bureau of Investigation, Hate Crime Statistics 2016

Identity Theft Consumer Reports

Area	Reports	Reports per 100,000 Population	Rank[2]
MSA[1]	1,699	83	175
U.S.	371,061	114	-

Note: (1) Figures cover the Columbus, OH Metropolitan Statistical Area—see Appendix B for areas included; (2) Rank ranges from 1 to 389 where 1 indicates greatest number of identity theft reports per 100,000 population
Source: Federal Trade Commission, Consumer Sentinel Network Data Book for January–December 2017

Fraud and Other Consumer Reports

Area	Reports	Reports per 100,000 Population	Rank[2]
MSA[1]	10,447	512	101
U.S.	2,304,550	708	-

Note: (1) Figures cover the Columbus, OH Metropolitan Statistical Area—see Appendix B for areas included; (2) Rank ranges from 1 to 389 where 1 indicates greatest number of fraud and other consumer reports per 100,000 population
Source: Federal Trade Commission, Consumer Sentinel Network Data Book for January–December 2017

SPORTS

Professional Sports Teams

Team Name	League	Year Established
Columbus Blue Jackets	National Hockey League (NHL)	2000
Columbus Crew	Major League Soccer (MLS)	1996

Note: Includes teams located in the Columbus, OH Metropolitan Statistical Area.
Source: Wikipedia, Major Professional Sports Teams of the United States and Canada, April 5, 2018

CLIMATE

Average and Extreme Temperatures

Temperature	Jan	Feb	Mar	Apr	May	Jun	Jul	Aug	Sep	Oct	Nov	Dec	Yr.
Extreme High (°F)	74	73	82	89	93	101	104	101	100	90	80	76	104
Average High (°F)	36	39	50	62	73	82	85	83	77	65	51	40	62
Average Temp. (°F)	28	31	41	52	62	70	74	73	66	54	43	32	52
Average Low (°F)	20	22	31	40	50	59	63	62	55	43	34	24	42
Extreme Low (°F)	-19	-13	-6	14	25	35	43	39	31	17	-4	-17	-19

Note: Figures cover the years 1948-1990
Source: National Climatic Data Center, International Station Meteorological Climate Summary, 9/96

Average Precipitation/Snowfall/Humidity

Precip./Humidity	Jan	Feb	Mar	Apr	May	Jun	Jul	Aug	Sep	Oct	Nov	Dec	Yr.
Avg. Precip. (in.)	2.8	2.4	3.1	3.3	3.9	4.0	4.3	3.3	2.7	2.1	3.0	2.8	37.9
Avg. Snowfall (in.)	8	6	5	1	Tr	0	0	0	Tr	Tr	2	6	28
Avg. Rel. Hum. 7am (%)	78	78	76	76	79	81	84	87	87	83	80	79	81
Avg. Rel. Hum. 4pm (%)	66	62	55	51	52	53	53	54	53	53	61	68	57

Note: Figures cover the years 1948-1990; Tr = Trace amounts (<0.05 in. of rain; <0.5 in. of snow)
Source: National Climatic Data Center, International Station Meteorological Climate Summary, 9/96

Weather Conditions

Temperature			Daytime Sky			Precipitation		
5°F & below	32°F & below	90°F & above	Clear	Partly cloudy	Cloudy	0.01 inch or more precip.	0.1 inch or more snow/ice	Thunder-storms
10	118	19	72	137	156	136	29	40

Note: Figures are average number of days per year and cover the years 1948-1990
Source: National Climatic Data Center, International Station Meteorological Climate Summary, 9/96

HAZARDOUS WASTE

Superfund Sites

The Columbus, OH metro area is home to one site on the EPA's Superfund National Priorities List: **Air Force Plant 85** (proposed). There are a total of 1,396 Superfund sites with a status of proposed or final on the list in the U.S. *U.S. Environmental Protection Agency, National Priorities List, April 4, 2018*

AIR & WATER QUALITY

Air Quality Trends: Ozone

	1990	1995	2000	2005	2010	2012	2013	2014	2015	2016
MSA[1]	0.090	0.091	0.085	0.084	0.073	0.077	0.065	0.067	0.066	0.069
U.S.	0.087	0.089	0.081	0.079	0.073	0.075	0.069	0.067	0.068	0.069

Note: (1) Data covers the Columbus, OH Metropolitan Statistical Area—see Appendix B for areas included. The values shown are the composite ozone concentration averages among trend sites based on the highest fourth daily maximum 8-hour concentration in parts per million. These trends are based on sites having an adequate record of monitoring data during the trend period. Data from exceptional events are included.
Source: U.S. Environmental Protection Agency, Air Quality Monitoring Information, "Air Quality Trends by City, 1990-2016"

Air Quality Index

Area	Percent of Days when Air Quality was...[2]					AQI Statistics[2]	
	Good	Moderate	Unhealthy for Sensitive Groups	Unhealthy	Very Unhealthy	Maximum	Median
MSA[1]	77.3	21.9	0.8	0.0	0.0	112	42

Note: (1) Data covers the Columbus, OH Metropolitan Statistical Area—see Appendix B for areas included; (2) Based on 365 days with AQI data in 2017. Air Quality Index (AQI) is an index for reporting daily air quality. EPA calculates the AQI for five major air pollutants regulated by the Clean Air Act: ground-level ozone, particle pollution (aka particulate matter), carbon monoxide, sulfur dioxide, and nitrogen dioxide. The AQI runs from 0 to 500. The higher the AQI value, the greater the level of air pollution and the greater the health concern. There are six AQI categories: "Good" AQI is between 0 and 50. Air quality is considered satisfactory; "Moderate" AQI is between 51 and 100. Air quality is acceptable; "Unhealthy for Sensitive Groups" When AQI values are between 101 and 150, members of sensitive groups may experience health effects; "Unhealthy" When AQI values are between 151 and 200 everyone may begin to experience health effects; "Very Unhealthy" AQI values between 201 and 300 trigger a health alert; "Hazardous" AQI values over 300 trigger warnings of emergency conditions (not shown).
Source: U.S. Environmental Protection Agency, Air Quality Index Report, 2017

Air Quality Index Pollutants

Area	Carbon Monoxide	Nitrogen Dioxide	Ozone	Sulfur Dioxide	Particulate Matter 2.5	Particulate Matter 10
	Percent of Days when AQI Pollutant was...[2]					
MSA[1]	0.0	7.4	53.7	0.0	38.1	0.8

Note: (1) Data covers the Columbus, OH Metropolitan Statistical Area—see Appendix B for areas included; (2) Based on 365 days with AQI data in 2017. The Air Quality Index (AQI) is an index for reporting daily air quality. EPA calculates the AQI for five major air pollutants regulated by the Clean Air Act: ground-level ozone, particle pollution (also known as particulate matter), carbon monoxide, sulfur dioxide, and nitrogen dioxide. The AQI runs from 0 to 500. The higher the AQI value, the greater the level of air pollution and the greater the health concern.
Source: U.S. Environmental Protection Agency, Air Quality Index Report, 2017

Maximum Air Pollutant Concentrations: Particulate Matter, Ozone, CO and Lead

	Particulate Matter 10 (ug/m³)	Particulate Matter 2.5 Wtd AM (ug/m³)	Particulate Matter 2.5 24-Hr (ug/m³)	Ozone (ppm)	Carbon Monoxide (ppm)	Lead (ug/m³)
MSA[1] Level	52	8.7	18	0.072	2	0.01
NAAQS[2]	150	15	35	0.075	9	0.15
Met NAAQS[2]	Yes	Yes	Yes	Yes	Yes	Yes

Note: (1) Data covers the Columbus, OH Metropolitan Statistical Area—see Appendix B for areas included; Data from exceptional events are included; (2) National Ambient Air Quality Standards; ppm = parts per million; ug/m³ = micrograms per cubic meter; n/a not available.
Concentrations: Particulate Matter 10 (coarse particulate)—highest second maximum 24-hour concentration; Particulate Matter 2.5 Wtd AM (fine particulate)—highest weighted annual mean concentration; Particulate Matter 2.5 24-Hour (fine particulate)—highest 98th percentile 24-hour concentration; Ozone—highest fourth daily maximum 8-hour concentration; Carbon Monoxide—highest second maximum non-overlapping 8-hour concentration; Lead—maximum running 3-month average
Source: U.S. Environmental Protection Agency, Air Quality Monitoring Information, "Air Quality Statistics by City, 2016"

Maximum Air Pollutant Concentrations: Nitrogen Dioxide and Sulfur Dioxide

	Nitrogen Dioxide AM (ppb)	Nitrogen Dioxide 1-Hr (ppb)	Sulfur Dioxide AM (ppb)	Sulfur Dioxide 1-Hr (ppb)	Sulfur Dioxide 24-Hr (ppb)
MSA[1] Level	12	42	n/a	4	n/a
NAAQS[2]	53	100	30	75	140
Met NAAQS[2]	Yes	Yes	n/a	Yes	n/a

Note: (1) Data covers the Columbus, OH Metropolitan Statistical Area—see Appendix B for areas included; Data from exceptional events are included; (2) National Ambient Air Quality Standards; ppm = parts per million; ug/m³ = micrograms per cubic meter; n/a not available.
Concentrations: Nitrogen Dioxide AM—highest arithmetic mean concentration; Nitrogen Dioxide 1-Hr—highest 98th percentile 1-hour daily maximum concentration; Sulfur Dioxide AM—highest annual mean concentration; Sulfur Dioxide 1-Hr—highest 99th percentile 1-hour daily maximum concentration; Sulfur Dioxide 24-Hr—highest second maximum 24-hour concentration
Source: U.S. Environmental Protection Agency, Air Quality Monitoring Information, "Air Quality Statistics by City, 2016"

Drinking Water

Water System Name	Pop. Served	Primary Water Source Type	Violations[1]	
			Health Based	Monitoring/ Reporting
Columbus Public Water System	1,196,848	Surface	0	0

Note: (1) Based on violation data from January 1, 2017 to December 31, 2017
Source: U.S. Environmental Protection Agency, Office of Ground Water and Drinking Water, Safe Drinking Water Information System (based on data extracted April 5, 2018)

Mason, Ohio

Background

Mason is located in southwestern Ohio, in Warren County. Cincinnati is 22 miles to the southwest and Dayton is 30 miles to the north.

The 640 acres surrounding Mason were purchased at auction by Revolutionary War veteran, William Mason, in 1803. The village of Palmira was founded on Mason's lands. The town was officially renamed Mason when local officials learned that there was already a city named Palmyra in Ohio.

Mason is known as the resort area of southwest Ohio. Area attractions include Kings Island Amusement & Waterpark, The Beach Waterpark, Great Wolf Lodge & Conference Center and The Golf Center at Kings Island.

Mason has experienced significant growth in recent years. Mason's economy is supported by its resort attractions along with its growing business sector. The city's business-friendly atmosphere has attracted several major employers, including Procter & Gamble, Luxottica Retail, Cintas Corporation and the Lindner Family Tennis Center, home to the Cincinnati Masters tennis tournament and Intelligrated, which offers automated material handling solutions.

Mason is also known as a family-oriented community with one of Ohio's top-ranked school systems, attracting many new residents looking for a better place to raise a family. Mason's public schools are managed by the Mason City Schools and Kings Local Schools districts. Combined, the districts manage six elementary schools, three middle schools and two high schools. Three private schools are also located in Mason.

Mason is home to Sinclair Community College's Courseview Campus. Additional nearby institutions of higher education include the University of Cincinnati, Miami University, Northern Kentucky University, Xavier University, University of Dayton and Ohio State University.

The Cincinnati/Northern Kentucky International Airport is located 35 miles outside of Mason. Additional airports within convenient driving distance include Dayton Airport and Port Columbus Airport.

Mason, like much of Ohio, typically has hot and humid summers, with cold and snowy winters.

Rankings

Business/Finance Rankings

- The personal finance site NerdWallet analyzed 183 American metropolitan areas with populations over 250,000 and more than 15,000 businesses to rank where entrepreneurs find the most success. Criteria included area economy, annual income, housing cost, unemployment rate, and the success rate of area businesses. Cincinnati* ranked #67. *www.nerdwallet.com, "Best Places to Start a Business," April 27, 2015*
- Based on metro area social media reviews, the employment opinion group Glassdoor surveyed 50 of the largest U.S. metro areas and equally weighed cost of living, hiring opportunity, and job satisfaction to compose a list of "25 Best Cities for Jobs." Median pay and home value, in-demand jobs and number of current job openings was also factored in. The Cincinnati* metro area was ranked #8 in overall job satisfaction. *www.glassdoor.com, "Best Cities for Jobs," September 12, 2017*
- In a survey of economic confidence in the nation's 50 largest metropolitan areas conducted January–December 2014, the Cincinnati* metro area placed #43, according to Gallup's 2014 Economic Confidence Index. *Gallup, "San Jose and San Francisco Lead in Economic Confidence," March 19, 2015*
- The Brookings Institution ranked the 100 largest metro areas in the U.S. based on income inequality. Cincinnati* was ranked #40 (#1 = greatest ineqality). Criteria: the "95/20 ratio," a figure representing the income at which a household earns more than 95 percent of all other households, divided by the income at which a household earns more than only 20 percent of all other households. *Brookings Institution, "Household Income Inequality, 100 Largest U.S. Metro Areas, 2014-2016," February 5, 2018*
- Payscale.com ranked the largest metro areas in terms of wage growth. The Cincinnati* metro area ranked #14. Criteria: private-sector wage growth between the 4th quarter of 2016 and the 4th quarter of 2017. *PayScale, "Wage Trends by Metro Area-4th Quarter," January 17, 2018*
- The Cincinnati* metro area was identified as one of the most affordable metropolitan areas in America by *Forbes.* The area ranked #5 out of 20 based on the National Association of Home Builders/Wells Fargo Housing Affordability Index and Sperling's Best Places' cost-of-living index. *Forbes.com, "America's Most Affordable Cities in 2015," March 12, 2015*
- Cincinnati* was identified as one of America's most frugal metro areas by *Coupons.com.* The city ranked #24 out of 25. Criteria: digital coupon usage. *Coupons.com, "America's Most Frugal Cities of 2017," March 22, 2018*
- Cincinnati* was cited as one of America's top metros for new and expanded facility projects in 2017. The area ranked #6 in the large metro area category (population over 1 million). *Site Selection, "Top Metropolitans of 2017," March 2018*
- The Cincinnati* metro area appeared on the Milken Institute "2017 Best Performing Cities" list. Rank: #104 out of 200 large metro areas. Criteria: job growth; wage and salary growth; high-tech output growth. *Milken Institute, "Best-Performing Cities 2017," January 2018*
- *Forbes* ranked the 200 most populous metro areas to determine the nation's "Best Places for Business and Careers." The Cincinnati* metro area was ranked #50. Criteria: costs (business and living); job growth (past and projected); income growth; quality of life; educational attainment (college and high school); projected economic growth; cultural and recreational opportunities; net migration patterns; number of highly ranked colleges. *Forbes, "The Best Places for Business and Careers 2017," October 24, 2017*

Children/Family Rankings

- *Forbes* analyzed data on the 100 largest metropolitan areas in the United States to compile its 2016 ranking of the best cities for raising a family. The Cincinnati* metro area was ranked #16. Criteria: median income; childcare costs; percent of population under 18; commuting delays; crime rate; percentage of families owning homes; education quality (mainly test scores). Overall cost of living and housing affordability was also unofficially considered. *Forbes, "America's Best Cities for Raising a Family 2016," August 30, 2016*

Education Rankings

- Personal finance website *WalletHub* analyzed the 150 largest U.S. metropolitan statistical areas to determine where the most educated Americans are choosing to settle. Criteria: education quality and attainment gap; education levels; percentage of workers with degrees; public school rankings; quality and size of each metro area's universities. Cincinnati* was ranked #57 (#1 = most educated city). *www.WalletHub.com, "2017's Most and Least Educated Cities in America," July 25, 2017*

Environmental Rankings

- Sperling's BestPlaces assessed 379 metropolitan areas of the United States for the likelihood of dangerously extreme weather events or earthquakes. In general the Southeast and South-Central regions have the highest risk of weather extremes and earthquakes, while the Pacific Northwest enjoys the lowest risk. Of the least risky metropolitan areas, the Cincinnati* metro area was ranked #249. *www.bestplaces.net, "Safest Places from Natural Disasters," April 2011*
- The U.S. Environmental Protection Agency (EPA) released a list of U.S. metropolitan areas with the most ENERGY STAR certified buildings in 2016. The Cincinnati* metro area was ranked #23 out of 25. *U.S. Environmental Protection Agency, "2017 Energy Star Top Cities," June 2017*
- Cincinnati* was highlighted as one of the 25 metro areas most polluted by year-round particle pollution (Annual PM 2.5) in the U.S. during 2013 through 2015. The area ranked #20. *American Lung Association, State of the Air 2017*

Health/Fitness Rankings

- For each of the 50 most populous metro areas in the United States, the American College of Sports Medicine's American Fitness Index evaluated infrastructure, community assets, and policies that encourage healthy and fit lifestyles, including preventive health behaviors, levels of chronic disease conditions, health care access, and community resources and policies that support physical activity. The Cincinnati* metro area ranked #22 for "community fitness." *www.americanfitnessindex.org, "ACSM American Fitness Index Health and Community Fitness Status of the 50 Largest Metropolitan Areas," May 2017*
- The Cincinnati* metro area was identified as one of the worst cities for bed bugs in America by pest control company Orkin. The area ranked #6 out of 50 based on the number of bed bug treatments Orkin performed from December 2016 to November 2017. *Orkin, "Baltimore and Washington D.C. Continue to Hold Top Spots," January 8, 2018*
- Cincinnati* was identified as a "2016 Spring Allergy Capital." The area ranked #74 out of 100. Three groups of factors were used to identify the most severe cities for people with allergies during the spring season: annual pollen levels; medicine utilization; access to board-certified allergists. *Asthma and Allergy Foundation of America, "Spring Allergy Capitals 2016"*
- Cincinnati* was identified as a "2016 Fall Allergy Capital." The area ranked #66 out of 100. Three groups of factors were used to identify the most severe cities for people with allergies during the fall season: annual pollen levels; medicine utilization; access to board-certified allergists. *Asthma and Allergy Foundation of America, "Fall Allergy Capitals 2016"*
- Cincinnati* was identified as a "2015 Asthma Capital." The area ranked #34 out of the nation's 100 largest metropolitan areas. Criteria: estimated prevalence; self-reported prevalence; crude death rate for asthma; annual pollen score; annual air quality; public smoking laws; number of board-certified asthma specialists; school inhaler access laws; rescue medication use; controller medication use; ER visits for asthma; uninsured rate; poverty rate. *Asthma and Allergy Foundation of America, "Asthma Capitals 2015"*

- The Cincinnati* metro area ranked #121 out of 189 in The Gallup-Healthways Well-Being Index. Criteria: purpose; social well being; financial health; community and physical health. Results are based on telephone interviews with adults, aged 18 and older, living in metropolitan areas in the 50 U.S. states and the District of Columbia. *Gallup-Healthways, "State of American Well-Being, 2017 Community Well-Being Rankings" March 2018*

Real Estate Rankings

- FitSmallBusiness looked at 50 of the largest metropolitan areas in the U.S. to determine which metro was the best to start a real estate business. Data was compiled from such sources as: Zillow, Trulia, U.S. Census Bureau, and the Bureau of Labor Statistics. Criteria: location; inventory; annual wages; median sales price of homes; days on the market; median price cut percentage; and other factors that would influence real estate professional growth. The Cincinnati* metro area ranked #50. *fitsmallbusiness.com, "The Best Cities to Become a Real Estate Agent in 2018," January 30, 2018*
- The Cincinnati* metro area was identified as one of nine best housing markets to invest in. Criteria: single-family rental home investing in the first quarter of 2017 based on first-year returns. The area ranked #2. *The Business Insider, "Here are the 9 Best U.S. Housing Markets for Investment," May 11, 2017*
- Cincinnati* was ranked #39 out of 238 metro areas in terms of housing affordability in 2017 by the National Association of Home Builders (#1 = most affordable). Criteria: the share of homes sold in that area affordable to a family earning the local median income, based on standard mortgage underwriting criteria. *National Association of Home Builders®, NAHB-Wells Fargo Housing Opportunity Index, 4th Quarter 2017*

Safety Rankings

- Mason was identified as one of the safest cities in America by NeighborhoodScout. The city ranked #78 out of 100 (100 = safest). Criteria: number of violent and property crimes per 1,000 residents. The editors only considered cities with 25,000 or more residents. *NeighborhoodScout, "Top 100 Safest Cities in the U.S. 2018" January 2, 2018*
- The National Insurance Crime Bureau ranked 382 metro areas in the U.S. in terms of per capita rates of vehicle theft. The Cincinnati* metro area ranked #220 (#1 = highest rate). Criteria: number of vehicle theft offenses per 100,000 inhabitants in 2016. *National Insurance Crime Bureau, "Hot Spots 2016," June 8, 2017*

Seniors/Retirement Rankings

- From its Best Cities for Successful Aging indexes, the Milken Institute generated rankings for metropolitan areas, weighing data in nine categories—health care, wellness, living arrangements, transportation and convenience, financial characteristics, education, employment, community engagement, and overall livability. The Cincinnati* metro area was ranked #50 overall in the large metro area category. *Milken Institute, "Best Cities for Successful Aging, 2017" March 14, 2017*

Miscellaneous Rankings

- The watchdog site Charity Navigator conducts an annual study of charities in the nation's major markets both to analyze statistical differences in their financial, accountability, and transparency practices and to track year-to-year variations in individual philanthropic communities. Charity Navigator's analysis demonstrated that the financial, accountability and transparency behaviors of America's largest charities can be influenced by the metropolitan market within which the charity operates. The Cincinnati* metro area was ranked #30 among the 30 metro markets in the rating category of Overall Score. *www.charitynavigator.org, "2017 Metro Market Study," May 1, 2017*

*Mason is located within the Cincinnati, OH-KY-IN Metropolitan Statistical Area.

Business Environment

CITY FINANCES

City Government Finances

Component	2015 ($000)	2015 ($ per capita)
Total Revenues	65,437	2,003
Total Expenditures	72,948	2,233
Debt Outstanding	87,032	2,665
Cash and Securities[1]	90,183	2,761

Note: (1) Cash and security holdings of a government at the close of its fiscal year,, including those of its dependent agencies, utilities, and liquor stores.
Source: U.S Census Bureau, State & Local Government Finances 2015

City Government Revenue by Source

Source	2015 ($000)	2015 ($ per capita)	2015 (%)
General Revenue			
From Federal Government	0	0	0.0
From State Government	5,296	162	8.1
From Local Governments	0	0	0.0
Taxes			
Property	7,189	220	11.0
Sales and Gross Receipts	0	0	0.0
Personal Income	25,868	792	39.5
Corporate Income	0	0	0.0
Motor Vehicle License	0	0	0.0
Other Taxes	3,194	98	4.9
Current Charges	20,361	623	31.1
Liquor Store	0	0	0.0
Utility	0	0	0.0
Employee Retirement	0	0	0.0

Source: U.S Census Bureau, State & Local Government Finances 2015

City Government Expenditures by Function

Function	2015 ($000)	2015 ($ per capita)	2015 (%)
General Direct Expenditures			
Air Transportation	0	0	0.0
Corrections	0	0	0.0
Education	0	0	0.0
Employment Security Administration	0	0	0.0
Financial Administration	2,248	68	3.1
Fire Protection	7,203	220	9.9
General Public Buildings	682	20	0.9
Governmental Administration, Other	1,577	48	2.2
Health	0	0	0.0
Highways	10,638	325	14.6
Hospitals	0	0	0.0
Housing and Community Development	3,495	107	4.8
Interest on General Debt	4,768	146	6.5
Judicial and Legal	2,210	67	3.0
Libraries	0	0	0.0
Parking	0	0	0.0
Parks and Recreation	10,085	308	13.8
Police Protection	6,031	184	8.3
Public Welfare	0	0	0.0
Sewerage	5,371	164	7.4
Solid Waste Management	1,413	43	1.9
Veterans' Services	0	0	0.0
Liquor Store	0	0	0.0
Utility	0	0	0.0
Employee Retirement	0	0	0.0

Source: U.S Census Bureau, State & Local Government Finances 2015

DEMOGRAPHICS

Population Growth

Area	1990 Census	2000 Census	2010 Census	2016* Estimate	Population Growth (%) 1990-2016	Population Growth (%) 2010-2016
City	12,046	22,016	30,712	32,025	165.9	4.3
MSA[1]	1,844,917	2,009,632	2,130,151	2,146,410	16.3	0.8
U.S.	248,709,873	281,421,906	308,745,538	318,558,162	28.1	3.2

Note: (1) Figures cover the Cincinnati, OH-KY-IN Metropolitan Statistical Area—see Appendix B for areas included; (*) 2012-2016 5-year estimated population
Source: U.S. Census Bureau, 1990 Census, Census 2000, Census 2010, 2012-2016 American Community Survey 5-Year Estimates

Household Size

Area	Persons in Household (%) One	Two	Three	Four	Five	Six	Seven or More	Average Household Size
City	26.2	29.7	16.5	18.5	7.4	1.4	0.4	2.70
MSA[1]	28.5	34.3	15.3	13.0	5.9	2.0	1.1	2.50
U.S.	27.7	33.7	15.7	13.1	6.0	2.3	1.5	2.60

Note: (1) Figures cover the Cincinnati, OH-KY-IN Metropolitan Statistical Area—see Appendix B for areas included
Source: U.S. Census Bureau, 2012-2016 American Community Survey 5-Year Estimates

Race

Area	White Alone[2] (%)	Black Alone[2] (%)	Asian Alone[2] (%)	AIAN[3] Alone[2] (%)	NHOPI[4] Alone[2] (%)	Other Race Alone[2] (%)	Two or More Races (%)
City	84.6	3.9	8.8	0.0	0.0	1.0	1.8
MSA[1]	82.3	12.2	2.2	0.1	0.0	0.9	2.1
U.S.	73.3	12.6	5.2	0.8	0.2	4.8	3.1

Note: (1) Figures cover the Cincinnati, OH-KY-IN Metropolitan Statistical Area—see Appendix B for areas included; (2) Alone is defined as not being in combination with one or more other races; (3) American Indian and Alaska Native; (4) Native Hawaiian and Other Pacific Islander
Source: U.S. Census Bureau, 2012-2016 American Community Survey 5-Year Estimates

Hispanic or Latino Origin

Area	Total (%)	Mexican (%)	Puerto Rican (%)	Cuban (%)	Other (%)
City	3.4	0.2	0.2	0.9	2.1
MSA[1]	2.9	1.4	0.4	0.1	1.1
U.S.	17.3	11.0	1.7	0.7	4.0

Note: Persons of Hispanic or Latino origin can be of any race; (1) Figures cover the Cincinnati, OH-KY-IN Metropolitan Statistical Area—see Appendix B for areas included
Source: U.S. Census Bureau, 2012-2016 American Community Survey 5-Year Estimates

Segregation

Type	Segregation Indices[1] 1990	2000	2010	2010 Rank[2]	Percent Change 1990-2000	1990-2010	2000-2010
Black/White	75.9	73.7	69.4	8	-2.2	-6.5	-4.3
Asian/White	42.7	44.6	46.0	21	1.9	3.4	1.5
Hispanic/White	25.8	29.0	36.9	77	3.2	11.1	7.9

Note: All figures cover the Metropolitan Statistical Area—see Appendix B for areas included; Figures are based on an analysis of 1990, 2000, and 2010 Census Decennial Census tract data by William H. Frey, Brookings Institution and the University of Michigan Social Science Data Analysis Network. In this analysis all racial groups (whites, blacks, and asians) are non-Hispanic members of those races. Hispanics are shown as a separate category; (1) Segregation Indices are Dissimilarity Indices that measure the degree to which the minority group is distributed differently than whites across census tracts. They range from 0 (complete integration) to 100 (complete segregation) where the value indicates the percentage of the minority group that needs to move to be distributed exactly like whites; (2) Ranges from 1 (most segregated) to 102 (least segregated); n/a not available.
Source: www.CensusScope.org

Ancestry

Area	German	Irish	English	American	Italian	Polish	French[2]	Scottish	Dutch
City	29.0	11.8	9.4	5.7	6.1	2.2	2.1	1.9	2.2
MSA[1]	29.1	14.0	8.6	9.0	4.1	1.6	1.9	1.7	1.2
U.S.	14.4	10.4	7.7	6.9	5.4	2.9	2.6	1.7	1.3

Note: Figures are the percentage of the total population reporting a particular ancestry. The nine most commonly reported ancestries in the U.S. are shown. Figures include multiple ancestries (e.g. if a person reported being Irish and Italian, they were included in both columns); (1) Figures cover the Cincinnati, OH-KY-IN Metropolitan Statistical Area—see Appendix B for areas included; (2) Excludes Basque
Source: U.S. Census Bureau, 2012-2016 American Community Survey 5-Year Estimates

Foreign-Born Population

Area	Percent of Population Born in								
	Any Foreign Country	Asia	Mexico	Europe	Carribean	Central America[2]	South America	Africa	Canada
City	11.3	6.8	0.0	1.5	0.2	0.1	1.7	0.6	0.1
MSA[1]	4.3	1.9	0.4	0.7	0.1	0.3	0.2	0.5	0.1
U.S.	13.2	4.0	3.6	1.5	1.3	1.0	0.9	0.6	0.3

Note: (1) Figures cover the Cincinnati, OH-KY-IN Metropolitan Statistical Area—see Appendix B for areas included; (2) Excludes Mexico.
Source: U.S. Census Bureau, 2012-2016 American Community Survey 5-Year Estimates

Marital Status

Area	Never Married	Now Married[2]	Separated	Widowed	Divorced
City	24.4	59.8	1.4	5.5	8.9
MSA[1]	31.8	49.2	1.8	5.7	11.5
U.S.	33.0	48.1	2.1	5.9	11.0

Note: Figures are percentages and cover the population 15 years of age and older; (1) Figures cover the Cincinnati, OH-KY-IN Metropolitan Statistical Area—see Appendix B for areas included; (2) Excludes separated
Source: U.S. Census Bureau, 2012-2016 American Community Survey 5-Year Estimates

Disability Status

Area	All Ages	Under 18 Years Old	18 to 64 Years Old	65 Years and Over
City	8.3	3.2	4.2	34.9
MSA[1]	12.2	4.5	10.7	33.9
U.S.	12.5	4.1	10.3	35.7

Note: Figures show percent of the civilian noninstitutionalized population that reported having a disability. Disability status is determined from six types of difficulty: vision, hearing, cognitive, ambulatory, self-care, and independent living. For children under 5 years old, hearing and vision difficulty are used to determine disability status. For children between the ages of 5 and 14, disability status is determined from hearing, vision, cognitive, ambulatory, and self-care difficulties. For people aged 15 years and older, they are considered to have a disability if they have difficulty with any one of the six difficulty types; Note: (1) Figures cover the Cincinnati, OH-KY-IN Metropolitan Statistical Area—see Appendix B for areas included
Source: U.S. Census Bureau, 2012-2016 American Community Survey 5-Year Estimates

Age

Area	Percent of Population									Median Age
	Under Age 5	Age 5–19	Age 20–34	Age 35–44	Age 45–54	Age 55–64	Age 65–74	Age 75–84	Age 85+	
City	4.3	25.8	11.5	14.1	17.7	12.1	7.9	4.5	2.0	41.9
MSA[1]	6.4	20.4	19.9	12.5	14.1	13.0	7.8	4.0	1.8	37.6
U.S.	6.2	19.6	20.7	12.7	13.6	12.6	8.3	4.3	1.9	37.7

Note: (1) Figures cover the Cincinnati, OH-KY-IN Metropolitan Statistical Area—see Appendix B for areas included
Source: U.S. Census Bureau, 2012-2016 American Community Survey 5-Year Estimates

Gender

Area	Males	Females	Males per 100 Females
City	15,348	16,677	92.0
MSA[1]	1,050,706	1,095,704	95.9
U.S.	156,765,322	161,792,840	96.9

Note: (1) Figures cover the Cincinnati, OH-KY-IN Metropolitan Statistical Area—see Appendix B for areas included
Source: U.S. Census Bureau, 2012-2016 American Community Survey 5-Year Estimates

Religious Groups by Family

Area	Catholic	Baptist	Non-Den.	Methodist[2]	Lutheran	LDS[3]	Pente-costal	Presby-terian[4]	Muslim[5]	Judaism
MSA[1]	19.1	9.6	3.7	3.9	1.2	0.6	2.2	1.6	0.2	0.5
U.S.	19.1	9.3	4.0	4.0	2.3	2.0	1.9	1.6	0.8	0.7

Note: Figures are the number of adherents as a percentage of the total population; (1) Figures cover the Cincinnati, OH-KY-IN Metropolitan Statistical Area—see Appendix B for areas included; (2) Methodist/Pietist; (3) Latter Day Saints; (4) Reformed; (5) Figures are estimates
Source: Association of Statisticians of American Religious Bodies, 2010 U.S. Religion Census: Religious Congregations & Membership Study

Religious Groups by Tradition

Area	Catholic	Evangelical Protestant	Mainline Protestant	Other Tradition	Black Protestant	Orthodox
MSA[1]	19.1	15.5	7.2	1.6	1.2	0.2
U.S.	19.1	16.2	7.3	4.3	1.6	0.3

Note: Figures are the number of adherents as a percentage of the total population; (1) Figures cover the Cincinnati, OH-KY-IN Metropolitan Statistical Area—see Appendix B for areas included
Source: Association of Statisticians of American Religious Bodies, 2010 U.S. Religion Census: Religious Congregations & Membership Study

ECONOMY

Gross Metropolitan Product

Area	2014	2015	2016	2017	Rank[2]
MSA[1]	120.1	124.7	128.8	134.7	28

Note: Figures are in billions of dollars; (1) Figures cover the Cincinnati, OH-KY-IN Metropolitan Statistical Area—see Appendix B for areas included; (2) Rank is based on 2015 data and ranges from 1 to 381
Source: The U.S. Conference of Mayors, U.S. Metro Economies: GMP and Employment Report, 2015-2017

Economic Growth

Area	2012-14 (%)	2015 (%)	2016 (%)	2017 (%)	Rank[2]
MSA[1]	1.3	2.0	1.8	2.6	174
U.S.	2.0	2.4	1.9	2.6	-

Note: Figures are real gross metropolitan product (GMP) growth rates and represent average annual percent change; (1) Figures cover the Cincinnati, OH-KY-IN Metropolitan Statistical Area—see Appendix B for areas included; (2) Rank is based on 2012-2014 average annual percent change and ranges from 1 to 381
Source: The U.S. Conference of Mayors, U.S. Metro Economies: GMP and Employment Report, 2015-2017

Metropolitan Area Exports

Area	2011	2012	2013	2014	2015	2016	Rank[2]
MSA[1]	18,744.2	19,966.8	20,976.4	22,280.7	24,127.0	26,326.2	11

Note: Figures are in millions of dollars; (1) Figures cover the Cincinnati, OH-KY-IN Metropolitan Statistical Area—see Appendix B for areas included; (2) Rank is based on 2016 data and ranges from 1 to 385
Source: U.S. Department of Commerce, International Trade Administration, Office of Trade & Industry Information, Manufacturing & Services, data extracted March 15, 2018

Building Permits

Area	Single-Family			Multi-Family			Total		
	2016	2017p	Pct. Chg.	2016	2017p	Pct. Chg.	2016	2017p	Pct. Chg.
City	144	170	18.1	0	0	0.0	144	170	18.1
MSA[1]	3,932	4,425	12.5	1,927	1,886	-2.1	5,859	6,311	7.7
U.S.	750,800	817,300	8.9	455,800	446,800	-2.0	1,206,600	1,264,100	4.8

Note: (1) Figures cover the Cincinnati, OH-KY-IN Metropolitan Statistical Area—see Appendix B for areas included; Figures represent new, privately-owned housing units authorized (unadjusted data); All permit data are based on estimates with imputation; (p) preliminary data.
Source: U.S. Census Bureau, Manufacturing, Mining, and Construction Statistics, Building Permits, 2016, 2017

Bankruptcy Filings

Area	Business Filings 2016	Business Filings 2017	Business Filings % Chg.	Nonbusiness Filings 2016	Nonbusiness Filings 2017	Nonbusiness Filings % Chg.
Warren County	12	22	83.3	479	459	-4.2
U.S.	24,114	23,157	-4.0	770,846	765,863	-0.6

Note: Business filings include Chapter 7, Chapter 11, Chapter 12, and Chapter 13; Nonbusiness filings include Chapter 7, Chapter 11, and Chapter 13
Source: Administrative Office of the U.S. Courts, Business and Nonbusiness Bankruptcy, County Cases Commenced by Chapter of the Bankruptcy Code, During the 12-Month Period Ending December 31, 2016 and Business and Nonbusiness Bankruptcy, County Cases Commenced by Chapter of the Bankruptcy Code, During the 12-Month Period Ending December 31, 2017

Housing Vacancy Rates

Area	Gross Vacancy Rate[2] (%)			Year-Round Vacancy Rate[3] (%)			Rental Vacancy Rate[4] (%)			Homeowner Vacancy Rate[5] (%)		
	2015	2016	2017	2015	2016	2017	2015	2016	2017	2015	2016	2017
MSA[1]	10.5	9.2	8.4	10.0	8.3	7.5	10.1	5.8	7.5	2.2	1.4	1.9
U.S.	12.9	12.8	12.7	10.0	9.9	9.9	7.1	6.9	7.2	1.8	1.7	1.6

Note: (1) Figures cover the Cincinnati, OH-KY-IN Metropolitan Statistical Area—see Appendix B for areas included; (2) The percentage of the total housing inventory that is vacant; (3) The percentage of the housing inventory (excluding seasonal units) that is year-round vacant; (4) The percentage of rental inventory that is vacant for rent; (5) The percentage of homeowner inventory that is vacant for sale
Source: U.S. Census Bureau, Housing Vacancies and Homeownership Annual Statistics: 2015, 2016, 2017

INCOME

Income

Area	Per Capita ($)	Median Household ($)	Average Household ($)
City	46,005	92,819	121,969
MSA[1]	30,431	56,861	76,908
U.S.	29,829	55,322	77,866

Note: (1) Figures cover the Cincinnati, OH-KY-IN Metropolitan Statistical Area—see Appendix B for areas included
Source: U.S. Census Bureau, 2012-2016 American Community Survey 5-Year Estimates

Household Income Distribution

Area	Percent of Households Earning: Under $15,000	$15,000 -$24,999	$25,000 -$34,999	$35,000 -$49,999	$50,000 -$74,999	$75,000 -$99,999	$100,000 -$149,999	$150,000 and up
City	3.7	5.2	6.9	9.8	15.0	12.9	19.0	27.5
MSA[1]	12.2	9.8	9.4	12.9	18.3	12.6	14.0	10.8
U.S.	12.1	10.2	9.9	13.2	17.8	12.2	13.5	11.1

Note: (1) Figures cover the Cincinnati, OH-KY-IN Metropolitan Statistical Area—see Appendix B for areas included
Source: U.S. Census Bureau, 2012-2016 American Community Survey 5-Year Estimates

Poverty Rate

Area	All Ages	Under 18 Years Old	18 to 64 Years Old	65 Years and Over
City	2.6	1.8	2.4	4.6
MSA[1]	13.8	19.4	12.9	7.7
U.S.	15.1	21.2	14.2	9.3

Note: Figures are percentage of people whose income during the past 12 months was below the poverty level; (1) Figures cover the Cincinnati, OH-KY-IN Metropolitan Statistical Area—see Appendix B for areas included
Source: U.S. Census Bureau, 2012-2016 American Community Survey 5-Year Estimates

EMPLOYMENT

Labor Force and Employment

Area	Civilian Labor Force Dec. 2016	Civilian Labor Force Dec. 2017	Civilian Labor Force % Chg.	Workers Employed Dec. 2016	Workers Employed Dec. 2017	Workers Employed % Chg.
City	16,880	17,007	0.8	16,244	16,389	0.9
MSA[1]	1,094,195	1,099,941	0.5	1,048,073	1,057,790	0.9
U.S.	158,968,000	159,880,000	0.6	151,798,000	153,602,000	1.2

Note: Data is not seasonally adjusted and covers workers 16 years of age and older; (1) Figures cover the Cincinnati, OH-KY-IN Metropolitan Statistical Area—see Appendix B for areas included
Source: Bureau of Labor Statistics, Local Area Unemployment Statistics

Unemployment Rate

Area	2017											
	Jan.	Feb.	Mar.	Apr.	May	Jun.	Jul.	Aug.	Sep.	Oct.	Nov.	Dec.
City	4.5	4.2	3.8	3.6	3.7	4.4	4.5	4.4	4.0	3.8	3.6	3.6
MSA[1]	5.2	4.8	4.3	3.9	4.0	4.6	4.6	4.5	4.0	3.9	3.8	3.8
U.S.	5.1	4.9	4.6	4.1	4.1	4.5	4.6	4.5	4.1	3.9	3.9	3.9

Note: Data is not seasonally adjusted and covers workers 16 years of age and older; (1) Figures cover the Cincinnati, OH-KY-IN Metropolitan Statistical Area—see Appendix B for areas included
Source: Bureau of Labor Statistics, Local Area Unemployment Statistics

Average Wages

Occupation	$/Hr.	Occupation	$/Hr.
Accountants and Auditors	34.00	Maids and Housekeeping Cleaners	11.00
Automotive Mechanics	19.80	Maintenance and Repair Workers	20.20
Bookkeepers	19.30	Marketing Managers	61.00
Carpenters	21.50	Nuclear Medicine Technologists	33.30
Cashiers	10.20	Nurses, Licensed Practical	21.60
Clerks, General Office	16.20	Nurses, Registered	32.10
Clerks, Receptionists/Information	13.30	Nursing Assistants	13.50
Clerks, Shipping/Receiving	16.30	Packers and Packagers, Hand	12.10
Computer Programmers	31.90	Physical Therapists	41.60
Computer Systems Analysts	42.80	Postal Service Mail Carriers	24.40
Computer User Support Specialists	23.90	Real Estate Brokers	51.20
Cooks, Restaurant	11.20	Retail Salespersons	13.10
Dentists	96.40	Sales Reps., Exc. Tech./Scientific	35.60
Electrical Engineers	40.30	Sales Reps., Tech./Scientific	40.40
Electricians	22.90	Secretaries, Exc. Legal/Med./Exec.	17.70
Financial Managers	64.80	Security Guards	12.80
First-Line Supervisors/Managers, Sales	20.20	Surgeons	109.40
Food Preparation Workers	10.90	Teacher Assistants*	12.60
General and Operations Managers	58.90	Teachers, Elementary School*	30.50
Hairdressers/Cosmetologists	13.40	Teachers, Secondary School*	28.70
Internists, General	80.40	Telemarketers	13.00
Janitors and Cleaners	12.60	Truck Drivers, Heavy/Tractor-Trailer	21.40
Landscaping/Groundskeeping Workers	13.90	Truck Drivers, Light/Delivery Svcs.	17.00
Lawyers	57.80	Waiters and Waitresses	10.10

Note: Wage data covers the Cincinnati, OH-KY-IN Metropolitan Statistical Area—see Appendix B for areas included; (*) Hourly wages for elementary/secondary school teachers and teacher assistants were calculated by the editors from annual wage data based on a 40 hour work week; n/a not available.
Source: Bureau of Labor Statistics, Metro Area Occupational Employment & Wage Estimates, May 2017

Employment by Occupation

Occupation Classification	City (%)	MSA[1] (%)	U.S. (%)
Management, Business, Science, and Arts	55.7	38.8	37.0
Natural Resources, Construction, and Maintenance	4.0	7.1	8.9
Production, Transportation, and Material Moving	6.4	13.2	12.2
Sales and Office	22.9	24.5	23.8
Service	11.0	16.4	18.1

Note: Figures cover employed civilians 16 years of age and older; (1) Figures cover the Cincinnati, OH-KY-IN Metropolitan Statistical Area—see Appendix B for areas included
Source: U.S. Census Bureau, 2012-2016 American Community Survey 5-Year Estimates

Employment by Industry

Sector	MSA[1] Number of Employees	MSA[1] Percent of Total	U.S. Percent of Total
Construction, Mining, and Logging	46,700	4.3	5.2
Education and Health Services	164,000	15.0	15.9
Financial Activities	74,400	6.8	5.7
Government	131,900	12.0	15.3
Information	13,500	1.2	1.9
Leisure and Hospitality	116,400	10.6	10.7
Manufacturing	116,600	10.6	8.5
Other Services	43,300	3.9	3.9
Professional and Business Services	165,500	15.1	14.0
Retail Trade	111,800	10.2	11.0
Transportation, Warehousing, and Utilities	49,700	4.5	4.1
Wholesale Trade	62,500	5.7	4.0

Note: Figures are non-farm employment as of December 2017. Figures are not seasonally adjusted and include workers 16 years of age and older; (1) Figures cover the Cincinnati, OH-KY-IN Metropolitan Statistical Area—see Appendix B for areas included
Source: Bureau of Labor Statistics, Current Employment Statistics, Employment, Hours, and Earnings

Occupations with Greatest Projected Employment Growth: 2017 – 2019

Occupation[1]	2017 Employment	2019 Projected Employment	Numeric Employment Change	Percent Employment Change
Combined Food Preparation and Serving Workers, Including Fast Food	160,970	170,100	9,130	5.7
Waiters and Waitresses	95,660	99,920	4,260	4.5
Home Health Aides	67,650	71,430	3,780	5.6
Registered Nurses	129,370	132,510	3,140	2.4
Heavy and Tractor-Trailer Truck Drivers	74,290	77,290	3,000	4.0
Laborers and Freight, Stock, and Material Movers, Hand	108,760	111,710	2,950	2.7
Personal Care Aides	30,510	32,800	2,290	7.5
Construction Laborers	40,630	42,780	2,150	5.3
Janitors and Cleaners, Except Maids and Housekeeping Cleaners	86,300	88,350	2,050	2.4
Software Developers, Applications	35,570	37,620	2,050	5.8

Note: Projections cover Ohio; (1) Sorted by numeric employment change
Source: www.projectionscentral.com, State Occupational Projections, 2017–2019 Short-Term Projections

Fastest Growing Occupations: 2017 – 2019

Occupation[1]	2017 Employment	2019 Projected Employment	Numeric Employment Change	Percent Employment Change
Rotary Drill Operators, Oil and Gas	230	280	50	21.7
Service Unit Operators, Oil, Gas, and Mining	710	850	140	19.7
Wellhead Pumpers	510	610	100	19.6
Roustabouts, Oil and Gas	720	860	140	19.4
Earth Drillers, Except Oil and Gas	460	510	50	10.9
Veterinary Technologists and Technicians	3,370	3,670	300	8.9
Veterinary Assistants and Laboratory Animal Caretakers	2,730	2,970	240	8.8
Veterinarians	3,330	3,610	280	8.4
Amusement and Recreation Attendants	8,950	9,650	700	7.8
Physician Assistants	3,210	3,460	250	7.8

Note: Projections cover Ohio; (1) Sorted by percent employment change and excludes occupations with numeric employment change less than 50
Source: www.projectionscentral.com, State Occupational Projections, 2017–2019 Short-Term Projections

TAXES

State Corporate Income Tax Rates

State	Tax Rate (%)	Income Brackets ($)	Num. of Brackets	Financial Institution Tax Rate (%)[a]	Federal Income Tax Ded.
Ohio	(t)	–	–	(t)	No

Note: Tax rates as of January 1, 2018; (a) Rates listed are the corporate income tax rate applied to financial institutions or excise taxes based on income. Some states have other taxes based upon the value of deposits or shares; (t) Ohio no longer levies a tax based on income (except for a particular subset of corporations), but instead imposes a Commercial Activity Tax (CAT) equal to $150 for gross receipts sitused to Ohio of between $150,000 and $1 million, plus 0.26% of gross receipts over $1 million. Banks continue to pay a franchise tax of 1.3% of net worth. For those few corporations for whom the franchise tax on net worth or net income still applies, a litter tax also applies.
Source: Federation of Tax Administrators, Range of State Corporate Income Tax Rates, January 1, 2018

State Individual Income Tax Rates

State	Tax Rate (%)	Income Brackets ($)	Num. of Brackets	Personal Exempt. ($)[1]		Fed. Inc. Tax Ded.
				Single	Dependents	
Ohio (a)	0.0 - 4.997	10,650 - 213,350	8	2,300 (t)	2,300 (t)	No

Note: Tax rates as of January 1, 2018; Local- and county-level taxes are not included; n/a not applicable; (1) Married joint filers generally receive double the single exemption; (a) 19 states have statutory provision for automatically adjusting to the rate of inflation the dollar values of the income tax brackets, standard deductions, and/or personal exemptions. Massachusetts, Michigan, and Nebraska index the personal exemption only. Oregon does not index the income brackets for $125,000 and over; (t) Ohio provides an additional tax credit of $20 per exemption. Exemption amounts reduced for higher income taxpayers.
Source: Federation of Tax Administrators, State Individual Income Tax Rates, January 1, 2018

Various State Sales and Excise Tax Rates

State	State Sales Tax (%)	Gasoline[1] (¢/gal.)	Cigarette[2] ($/pack)	Spirits[3] ($/gal.)	Wine[4] ($/gal.)	Beer[5] ($/gal.)	Recreational Marijuana (%)
Ohio	5.75	28.01	1.60	9.87 (g)	0.32 (l)	0.18 (q)	Not legal

Note: All tax rates as of January 1, 2018; (1) The American Petroleum Institute has developed a methodology for determining the average tax rate on a gallon of fuel. Rates may include any of the following: excise taxes, environmental fees, storage tank fees, other fees or taxes, general sales tax, and local taxes. In states where gasoline is subject to the general sales tax, or where the fuel tax is based on the average sale price, the average rate determined by API is sensitive to changes in the price of gasoline. States that fully or partially apply general sales taxes to gasoline: CA, CO, GA, IL, IN, MI, NY; (2) The federal excise tax of $1.0066 per pack and local taxes are not included; (3) Rates are those applicable to off-premise sales of 40% alcohol by volume (a.b.v.) distilled spirits in 750ml containers. Local excise taxes are excluded; (4) Rates are those applicable to off-premise sales of 11% a.b.v. non-carbonated wine in 750ml containers; (5) Rates are those applicable to off-premise sales of 4.7% a.b.v. beer in 12 ounce containers; (g) Control states, where the government controls all sales. Products can be subject to ad valorem mark-up as well as excise taxes; (l) Different rates also applicable to alcohol content, place of production, size of container, place purchased (on- or off-premise or on board airlines) or type of wine (carbonated, vermouth, etc.); (q) Different rates also applicable according to alcohol content, place of production, size of container, or place purchased (on- or off-premise or onboard airlines).
Source: Tax Foundation, 2018 Facts & Figures: How Does Your State Compare?

State Business Tax Climate Index Rankings

State	Overall Rank	Corporate Tax Rank	Individual Income Tax Rank	Sales Tax Rank	Unemployment Insurance Tax Rank	Property Tax Rank
Ohio	45	47	47	30	8	11

Note: The index is a measure of how each state's tax laws affect economic performance. The lower the rank, the more favorable a state's tax system is for business. States without a given tax are given a ranking of 1. The scores/rankings for the District of Columbia do not affect other states. The 2018 index represents the tax climate as of July 1, 2017.
Source: Tax Foundation, State Business Tax Climate Index 2018

TRANSPORTATION

Means of Transportation to Work

Area	Car/Truck/Van		Public Transportation			Bicycle	Walked	Other Means	Worked at Home
	Drove Alone	Car-pooled	Bus	Subway	Railroad				
City	87.4	4.8	0.6	0.0	0.0	0.0	0.7	0.3	6.2
MSA[1]	82.8	8.0	1.9	0.0	0.0	0.2	2.1	0.7	4.2
U.S.	76.4	9.3	2.6	1.9	0.6	0.6	2.8	1.3	4.6

Note: Figures are percentages and cover workers 16 years of age and older; (1) Figures cover the Cincinnati, OH-KY-IN Metropolitan Statistical Area—see Appendix B for areas included
Source: U.S. Census Bureau, 2012-2016 American Community Survey 5-Year Estimates

Travel Time to Work

Area	Less Than 10 Minutes	10 to 19 Minutes	20 to 29 Minutes	30 to 44 Minutes	45 to 59 Minutes	60 to 89 Minutes	90 Minutes or More
City	10.8	25.0	28.7	24.0	7.5	2.6	1.4
MSA[1]	11.1	28.5	25.4	23.0	7.2	3.3	1.5
U.S.	12.9	29.2	20.9	20.4	8.0	6.0	2.7

Note: Note: Figures are percentages and include workers 16 years old and over; (1) Figures cover the Cincinnati, OH-KY-IN Metropolitan Statistical Area—see Appendix B for areas included
Source: U.S. Census Bureau, 2012-2016 American Community Survey 5-Year Estimates

Freeway Travel Time Index

Area	1985	1990	1995	2000	2005	2010	2014
Urban Area Rank[1,2]	54	41	36	38	51	57	46
Urban Area Index[1]	1.06	1.11	1.15	1.17	1.17	1.16	1.18
Average Index[3]	1.09	1.11	1.14	1.17	1.20	1.19	1.20

Note: Freeway Travel Time Index—the ratio of travel time in the peak period to the travel time at free-flow conditions. For example, a value of 1.30 indicates a 20-minute free-flow trip takes 26 minutes in the peak (20 minutes x 1.30 = 26 minutes); (1) Covers the Cincinnati OH-KY-IN urban area; (2) Rank is based on 101 urban areas (#1 = highest travel time index); (3) Average of 101 urban areas
Source: Texas Transportation Institute, 2015 Urban Mobility Scorecard, August 2015

Freeway Commuter Stress Index

Area	1985	1990	1995	2000	2005	2010	2014
Urban Area Rank[1,2]	58	45	43	46	53	58	52
Urban Area Index[1]	1.08	1.14	1.18	1.20	1.20	1.19	1.21
Average Index[3]	1.13	1.16	1.19	1.22	1.25	1.24	1.25

Note: The Freeway Commuter Stress Index is the same as the Freeway Travel Time Index (see table above) except that it includes only the travel in the peak directions during the peak periods; the TTI includes travel in all directions during the peak period. Thus, the CSI is more indicative of the work trip experienced by each commuter on a daily basis; (1) Covers the Cincinnati OH-KY-IN urban area; (2) Rank is based on 101 urban areas (#1 = highest travel time index); (3) Average of 101 urban areas
Source: Texas Transportation Institute, 2015 Urban Mobility Scorecard, August 2015

Living Environment

COST OF LIVING

Cost of Living Index

Composite Index	Groceries	Housing	Utilities	Trans-portation	Health Care	Misc. Goods/ Services
92.3	91.3	76.2	95.4	100.7	98.4	101.9

Note: The Cost of Living Index measures regional differences in the cost of consumer goods and services, excluding taxes and non-consumer expenditures, for professional and managerial households in the top income quintile. It is based on more than 50,000 prices covering almost 60 different items for which prices are collected three times a year by chambers of commerce, economic development organizations or university applied economic centers in each participating urban area. The numbers shown should be read as a percentage above or below the national average of 100. For example, a value of 115.4 in the groceries column indicates that grocery prices are 15.4% higher than the national average. Small differences in the index numbers should not be interpreted as significant; Figures cover the Cincinnati OH urban area.
Source: The Council for Community and Economic Research, ACCRA Cost of Living Index, 2017

Grocery Prices

Area[1]	T-Bone Steak ($/pound)	Frying Chicken ($/pound)	Whole Milk ($/half gal.)	Eggs ($/dozen)	Orange Juice ($/64 oz.)	Coffee ($/11.5 oz.)
City[2]	12.29	1.07	1.31	1.19	3.30	4.16
Avg.	11.29	1.40	2.02	1.47	3.55	4.37
Min.	7.71	0.93	1.04	0.70	2.86	3.24
Max.	15.83	2.39	4.03	3.92	6.29	8.16

Note: (1) Values for the local area are compared with the average, minimum and maximum values for all 294 areas in the Cost of Living Index; (2) Figures cover the Cincinnati OH urban area; ***T-Bone Steak*** *(price per pound);* ***Frying Chicken*** *(price per pound, whole fryer);* ***Whole Milk*** *(half gallon carton);* ***Eggs*** *(price per dozen, Grade A, large);* ***Orange Juice*** *(64 oz. Tropicana or Florida Natural);* ***Coffee*** *(11.5 oz. can, vacuum-packed, Maxwell House, Hills Bros, or Folgers).*
Source: The Council for Community and Economic Research, ACCRA Cost of Living Index, 2017

Housing and Utility Costs

Area[1]	New Home Price ($)	Apartment Rent ($/month)	All Electric ($/month)	Part Electric ($/month)	Other Energy ($/month)	Telephone ($/month)
City[2]	242,171	887	-	84.08	78.14	26.78
Avg.	335,956	1,047	175.01	97.34	67.93	28.71
Min.	187,788	491	109.48	49.33	35.44	12.39
Max.	1,739,087	4,559	432.62	227.09	353.33	44.61

Note: (1) Values for the local area are compared with the average, minimum and maximum values for all 294 areas in the Cost of Living Index; (2) Figures cover the Cincinnati OH urban area; ***New Home Price*** *(2,400 sf living area, 8,000 sf lot, in urban area with full utilities);* ***Apartment Rent*** *(950 sf 2 bedroom/1.5 or 2 bath, unfurnished, excluding all utilities except water);* ***All Electric*** *(average monthly cost for an all-electric home);* ***Part Electric*** *(average monthly cost for a part-electric home);* ***Other Energy*** *(average monthly cost for natural gas, fuel oil, coal, wood, and any other forms of energy except electricity);* ***Telephone*** *(price includes basic monthly rate for a private residential line plus additional local usage charges incurred by a family of four).*
Source: The Council for Community and Economic Research, ACCRA Cost of Living Index, 2017

Health Care, Transportation, and Other Costs

Area[1]	Doctor ($/visit)	Dentist ($/visit)	Optometrist ($/visit)	Gasoline ($/gallon)	Beauty Salon ($/visit)	Men's Shirt ($)
City[2]	100.96	95.10	95.13	2.30	38.07	39.56
Avg.	108.00	92.54	101.93	2.25	37.58	30.92
Min.	30.39	60.00	49.75	1.82	16.11	11.20
Max.	193.50	161.94	229.28	3.16	77.35	59.13

Note: (1) Values for the local area are compared with the average, minimum and maximum values for all 294 areas in the Cost of Living Index; (2) Figures cover the Cincinnati OH urban area; ***Doctor*** *(general practitioners routine exam of an established patient);* ***Dentist*** *(adult teeth cleaning and periodic oral examination);* ***Optometrist*** *(full vision eye exam for established adult patient);* ***Gasoline*** *(one gallon regular unleaded, national brand, including all taxes, cash price at self-service pump if available);* ***Beauty Salon*** *(woman's shampoo, trim, and blow-dry);* ***Men's Shirt*** *(cotton/polyester dress shirt, pinpoint weave, long sleeves).*
Source: The Council for Community and Economic Research, ACCRA Cost of Living Index, 2017

HOUSING

House Price Index (HPI)

Area	National Ranking[2]	Quarterly Change (%)	One-Year Change (%)	Five-Year Change (%)
MSA[1]	120	0.30	6.32	19.53
U.S.[3]	–	1.61	6.68	34.71

Note: The HPI is a weighted repeat sales index. It measures average price changes in repeat sales or refinancings on the same properties. This information is obtained by reviewing repeat mortgage transactions on single-family properties whose mortgages have been purchased or securitized by Fannie Mae or Freddie Mac in January 1975; (1) Figures cover the Cincinnati, OH-KY-IN Metropolitan Statistical Area—see Appendix B for areas included; (2) Rankings are based on annual percentage change for all metro areas containing at least 15,000 transactions over the last 10 years and ranges from 1 to 253; (3) figures based on a weighted average of Census Division estimates using a seasonally adjusted, purchase-only index; all figures are for the period ending December 31, 2017
Source: Federal Housing Finance Agency, House Price Index, February 28, 2018

Median Single-Family Home Prices

Area	2015	2016	2017[p]	Percent Change 2016 to 2017
MSA[1]	145.4	152.3	162.0	6.4
U.S. Average	223.9	235.5	248.8	5.6

Note: Figures are median sales prices of existing single-family homes in thousands of dollars; (p) preliminary; (1) Figures cover the Cincinnati, OH-KY-IN Metropolitan Statistical Area—see Appendix B for areas included
Source: National Association of Realtors, Median Sales Price of Existing Single-Family Homes for Metropolitan Areas, 4th Quarter 2017

Qualifying Income Based on Median Sales Price of Existing Single-Family Homes

Area	With 5% Down ($)	With 10% Down ($)	With 20% Down ($)
MSA[1]	35,643	33,767	30,015
U.S. Average	55,585	52,659	46,808

Note: Figures are preliminary; Qualifying income is based on a mortgage rate of 4.17%. Monthly principal and interest payment is limited to 25% of income; (1) Figures cover the Cincinnati, OH-KY-IN Metropolitan Statistical Area—see Appendix B for areas included
Source: National Association of Realtors, Qualifying Income Based on Median Sales Price of Existing Single-Family Homes for Metropolitan Areas, 4th Quarter 2017

Median Apartment Condo-Coop Home Prices

Area	2015	2016	2017[p]	Percent Change 2016 to 2017
MSA[1]	109.3	114.9	121.2	5.5
U.S. Average	210.7	220.7	234.3	6.2

Note: Figures are median sales prices of existing apartment condo-coop homes in thousands of dollars; (p) preliminary; (1) Figures cover the Cincinnati, OH-KY-IN Metropolitan Statistical Area—see Appendix B for areas included
Source: National Association of Realtors, Median Sales Price of Existing Apartment Condo-Coop Homes for Metropolitan Areas, 4th Quarter 2017

Home Value Distribution

Area	Under $50,000	$50,000 -$99,999	$100,000 -$149,999	$150,000 -$199,999	$200,000 -$299,999	$300,000 -$499,999	$500,000 -$999,999	$1,000,000 or more
City	2.5	5.8	16.8	18.5	22.3	25.9	7.1	1.1
MSA[1]	6.2	17.9	23.2	19.1	18.7	10.9	3.3	0.7
U.S.	8.8	14.8	15.3	14.9	18.4	16.4	9.0	2.5

Note: Figures are percentages and cover owner-occupied housing units; (1) Figures cover the Cincinnati, OH-KY-IN Metropolitan Statistical Area—see Appendix B for areas included
Source: U.S. Census Bureau, 2012-2016 American Community Survey 5-Year Estimates

Homeownership Rate

Area	2009 (%)	2010 (%)	2011 (%)	2012 (%)	2013 (%)	2014 (%)	2015 (%)	2016 (%)	2017 (%)
MSA[1]	62.4	62.8	65.2	63.4	63.3	65.5	65.9	64.9	65.7
U.S.	67.4	66.9	66.1	65.4	65.1	64.5	63.7	63.4	63.9

Note: (1) Figures cover the Cincinnati, OH-KY-IN Metropolitan Statistical Area—see Appendix B for areas included
Source: U.S. Census Bureau, Housing Vacancies and Homeownership Annual Statistics: 2009-2017

Year Housing Structure Built

Area	2010 or Later	2000 -2009	1990 -1999	1980 -1989	1970 -1979	1960 -1969	1950 -1959	1940 -1949	Before 1940	Median Year
City	1.5	27.2	35.9	10.3	11.8	1.8	8.5	0.5	2.6	1994
MSA[1]	1.8	12.6	14.7	10.8	13.4	11.0	12.3	5.3	18.1	1972
U.S.	2.3	14.7	14.0	13.7	15.6	10.9	10.6	5.2	13.0	1977

Note: Figures are percentages except for Median Year; Note: (1) Figures cover the Cincinnati, OH-KY-IN Metropolitan Statistical Area—see Appendix B for areas included
Source: U.S. Census Bureau, 2012-2016 American Community Survey 5-Year Estimates

Gross Monthly Rent

Area	Under $500	$500 -$999	$1,000 -$1,499	$1,500 -$1,999	$2,000 -$2,499	$2,500 -$2,999	$3,000 and up	Median ($)
City	4.4	41.1	40.7	10.2	1.5	0.3	1.8	1,056
MSA[1]	15.7	58.5	20.2	3.6	1.0	0.4	0.5	767
U.S.	11.3	43.3	27.7	10.7	4.0	1.6	1.5	949

Note: Figures are percentages except for Median; Gross rent is the contract rent plus the estimated average monthly cost of utilities (electricity, gas, and water and sewer) and fuels (oil, coal, kerosene, wood, etc.) if these are paid by the renter (or paid for the renter by someone else); (1) Figures cover the Cincinnati, OH-KY-IN Metropolitan Statistical Area—see Appendix B for areas included
Source: U.S. Census Bureau, 2012-2016 American Community Survey 5-Year Estimates

HEALTH

Health Risk Factors

Category	MSA[1] (%)	U.S. (%)
Adults aged 18–64 who have any kind of health care coverage	94.3	87.7
Adults who reported being in good or excellent health	82.6	83.6
Adults who are current smokers	21.7	17.1
Adults who currently use E-cigarettes	5.4	4.7
Adults who currently use chewing tobacco, snuff, or snus	5.0	4.0
Adults who are heavy drinkers[2]	7.8	6.5
Adults who are binge drinkers[3]	20.4	16.9
Adults who are overweight (BMI 25.0 - 29.9)	37.8	35.3
Adults who are obese (BMI 30.0 - 99.8)	31.3	29.9
Adults who participated in any physical activities in the past month	76.4	76.9
Adults who always or nearly always wears a seat belt	93.6	94.3

Note: (1) Figures cover the Cincinnati, OH-KY-IN Metropolitan Statistical Area—see Appendix B for areas included; (2) Heavy drinkers are classified as adult men having more than 14 drinks per week and adult women having more than 7 drinks per week; (3) Binge drinkers are classified as males having five or more drinks on one occasion or females having four or more drinks on one occasion
Source: Centers for Disease Control and Prevention, Behaviorial Risk Factor Surveillance System, SMART: Selected Metropolitan Area Risk Trends, 2016

Health Screening Rates

Category	MSA[1] (%)	U.S. (%)
Adults 50-75 who have had a blood stool test within the past year	11.0	8.0
Adults 50-75 who have had a colonoscopy in the past 10 years	63.1	63.5
Adults aged 65+ who have had flu shot within the past year	57.7	58.6
Adults aged 65+ who have ever had a pneumonia vaccination	76.5	73.4
Adults who have ever been tested for HIV	37.3	35.6
Women aged 21-65 who have had a pap test in the past three years	83.4	79.8
Men aged 40+ who have had a PSA test within the past two years	35.6	39.5
Women aged 40+ who have had a mammogram within the past two years	70.4	72.5

Note: n/a not available; (1) Figures cover the Cincinnati, OH-KY-IN Metropolitan Statistical Area—see Appendix B for areas included; Source: Centers for Disease Control and Prevention, Behaviorial Risk Factor Surveillance System, SMART: Selected Metropolitan Area Risk Trends, 2016

Chronic Health Conditions

Category	MSA[1] (%)	U.S. (%)
Adults who have ever been told they had a heart attack	4.7	4.4
Adults who have ever been told they have angina or coronary heart disease	5.6	4.1
Adults who have ever been told they had a stroke	3.9	3.1
Adults who have been told they currently have asthma	8.8	9.3
Adults who have ever been told they have arthritis	29.6	25.8
Adults who have ever been told they have diabetes[2]	11.4	10.5
Adults who have ever been told they had skin cancer	5.9	5.9
Adults who have ever been told they had any other types of cancer	6.8	6.7
Adults who have ever been told they have COPD	8.5	6.3
Adults who have ever been told they have kidney disease	3.0	2.8
Adults who have ever been told they have a form of depression	19.9	17.4

Note: (1) Figures cover the Cincinnati, OH-KY-IN Metropolitan Statistical Area—see Appendix B for areas included; (2) Figures do not include pregnancy-related, borderline, or pre-diabetes
Source: Centers for Disease Control and Prevention, Behaviorial Risk Factor Surveillance System, SMART: Selected Metropolitan Area Risk Trends, 2016

Mortality Rates for the Top 10 Causes of Death in the U.S.

ICD-10[a] Sub-Chapter	ICD-10[a] Code	Age-Adjusted Mortality Rate[1] per 100,000 population	
		County[2]	U.S.
Malignant neoplasms	C00-C97	158.1	158.5
Ischaemic heart diseases	I20-I25	87.9	96.8
Other forms of heart disease	I30-I51	53.7	52.4
Chronic lower respiratory diseases	J40-J47	39.7	40.9
Cerebrovascular diseases	I60-I69	35.0	37.2
Organic, including symptomatic, mental disorders	F01-F09	52.5	33.3
Other degenerative diseases of the nervous system	G30-G31	50.2	32.1
Other external causes of accidental injury	W00-X59	37.9	31.2
Diabetes mellitus	E10-E14	12.1	21.1
Hypertensive diseases	I10-I15	9.5	20.8

Note: (a) ICD-10 = International Classification of Diseases 10th Revision; (1) Mortality rates are a three year average covering 2014-2016; (2) Figures cover Warren County.
Source: Centers for Disease Control and Prevention, National Center for Health Statistics. Underlying Cause of Death 1999-2016 on CDC WONDER Online Database, released December 2017

Mortality Rates for Selected Causes of Death

ICD-10[a] Sub-Chapter	ICD-10[a] Code	Age-Adjusted Mortality Rate[1] per 100,000 population	
		County[2]	U.S.
Assault	X85-Y09	Unreliable	5.6
Diseases of the liver	K70-K76	8.6	14.0
Human immunodeficiency virus (HIV) disease	B20-B24	Suppressed	1.9
Influenza and pneumonia	J09-J18	13.3	14.6
Intentional self-harm	X60-X84	12.1	13.2
Malnutrition	E40-E46	3.4	1.3
Obesity and other hyperalimentation	E65-E68	Suppressed	2.1
Renal failure	N17-N19	9.5	13.0
Transport accidents	V01-V99	7.3	12.0
Viral hepatitis	B15-B19	Suppressed	1.9

Note: (a) ICD-10 = International Classification of Diseases 10th Revision; (1) Mortality rates are a three year average covering 2014-2016; (2) Figures cover Warren County; Data are Suppressed when the data meet the criteria for confidentiality constraints; Mortality rates are flagged as Unreliable when the rate would be calculated with a numerator of 20 or less.
Source: Centers for Disease Control and Prevention, National Center for Health Statistics. Underlying Cause of Death 1999-2016 on CDC WONDER Online Database, released December 2017

Health Insurance Coverage

Area	With Health Insurance	With Private Health Insurance	With Public Health Insurance	Without Health Insurance	Population Under Age 18 Without Health Insurance
City	96.7	89.4	17.1	3.3	2.0
MSA[1]	92.2	72.4	30.4	7.8	3.8
U.S.	88.3	66.7	33.0	11.7	5.9

Note: Figures are percentages that cover the civilian noninstitutionalized population; (1) Figures cover the Cincinnati, OH-KY-IN Metropolitan Statistical Area—see Appendix B for areas included
Source: U.S. Census Bureau, 2012-2016 American Community Survey 5-Year Estimates

Number of Medical Professionals

Area	MDs[3]	DOs[3,4]	Dentists	Podiatrists	Chiropractors	Optometrists
County[1] (number)	561	75	82	9	52	28
County[1] (rate[2])	250.7	33.5	36.2	4.0	23.0	12.4
U.S. (rate[2])	276.5	22.3	67.3	6.0	26.7	15.9

Note: Data as of 2016 unless noted; (1) Data covers Warren County; (2) Rate per 100,000 population; (3) Data as of 2015 and includes all active, non-federal physicians; (4) Doctor of Osteopathic Medicine
Source: U.S. Department of Health and Human Services, Health Resources and Services Administration, Bureau of Health Professions, Area Resource File (ARF) 2016-2017

Best Hospitals

According to *U.S. News,* the Cincinnati, OH-KY-IN metro area is home to two of the best hospitals in the U.S.: **Christ Hospital** (2 adult specialties); **University of Cincinnati Medical Center** (2 adult specialties). The hospitals listed were nationally ranked in at least one of 16 specialties. Only 152 hospitals nationwide were nationally ranked in one or more specialties. Twenty hospitals in the U.S. made the Honor Roll. The Best Hospitals Honor Roll was revamped last year to take both the national rankings and the procedure and condition ratings into account. Hospitals received points if they were nationally ranked in one of the 16 specialties—the higher they ranked, the more points they got—and how many ratings of "high performing" they earned in the nine procedures and conditions. *U.S. News Online, "America's Best Hospitals 2017-18"*

According to *U.S. News,* the Cincinnati, OH-KY-IN metro area is home to one of the best children's hospitals in the U.S.: **Cincinnati Children's Hospital Medical Center** (Honor Roll/10 pediatric specialties). The hospital listed was highly ranked in at least one of 10 pediatric specialties. Eighty-two children's hospitals in the U.S. were nationally ranked in at least one specialty. Hospitals received points for being ranked in a specialty, and the 10 hospitals with the most points across the 10 specialties make up the Honor Roll. *U.S. News Online, "America's Best Children's Hospitals 2017-18"*

EDUCATION

Public School District Statistics

District Name	Schls	Pupils	Pupil/ Teacher Ratio	Minority Pupils[1] (%)	Free Lunch Eligible[2] (%)	IEP[3] (%)
Mason City	5	10,605	22.4	33.5	6.1	9.1

Note: Table includes school districts with 100 or more students; (1) Percentage of students that are not non-Hispanic white; (2) Percentage of students that are eligible for the free lunch program; (3) Percentage of students that have an Individualized Education Program.
Source: U.S. Department of Education, National Center for Education Statistics, Common Core of Data, Local Education Agency (School District) Universe Survey: School Year 2015-2016; U.S. Department of Education, National Center for Education Statistics, Common Core of Data, Public Elementary/Secondary School Universe Survey: School Year 2015-2016

Highest Level of Education

Area	Less than H.S.	H.S. Diploma	Some College, No Deg.	Associate Degree	Bachelor's Degree	Master's Degree	Prof. School Degree	Doctorate Degree
City	2.5	18.6	13.3	6.2	33.4	18.9	4.4	2.7
MSA[1]	9.9	30.3	19.8	8.2	20.0	8.6	1.9	1.3
U.S.	13.0	27.5	21.0	8.2	18.8	8.2	2.0	1.3

Note: Figures cover persons age 25 and over; (1) Figures cover the Cincinnati, OH-KY-IN Metropolitan Statistical Area—see Appendix B for areas included
Source: U.S. Census Bureau, 2012-2016 American Community Survey 5-Year Estimates

Educational Attainment by Race

Area	High School Graduate or Higher (%)					Bachelor's Degree or Higher (%)				
	Total	White	Black	Asian	Hisp.[2]	Total	White	Black	Asian	Hisp.[2]
City	97.5	97.7	95.4	98.2	88.9	59.3	57.3	65.4	81.1	68.9
MSA[1]	90.1	91.0	84.9	87.4	72.2	31.7	33.0	17.2	63.4	24.7
U.S.	87.0	88.9	84.3	86.3	65.7	30.3	31.6	20.0	52.1	14.7

Note: Figures shown cover persons 25 years old and over; (1) Figures cover the Cincinnati, OH-KY-IN Metropolitan Statistical Area—see Appendix B for areas included; (2) People of Hispanic origin can be of any race
Source: U.S. Census Bureau, 2012-2016 American Community Survey 5-Year Estimates

School Enrollment by Grade and Control

Area	Preschool (%)		Kindergarten (%)		Grades 1 - 4 (%)		Grades 5 - 8 (%)		Grades 9 - 12 (%)	
	Public	Private	Public	Private	Public	Private	Public	Private	Public	Private
City	54.7	45.3	70.3	29.7	83.7	16.3	92.6	7.4	83.5	16.5
MSA[1]	54.2	45.8	80.9	19.1	82.7	17.3	83.1	16.9	82.8	17.2
U.S.	58.4	41.6	87.7	12.3	89.8	10.2	89.7	10.3	90.4	9.6

Note: Figures shown cover persons 3 years old and over; (1) Figures cover the Cincinnati, OH-KY-IN Metropolitan Statistical Area—see Appendix B for areas included
Source: U.S. Census Bureau, 2012-2016 American Community Survey 5-Year Estimates

Average Salaries of Public School Classroom Teachers

Area	2015		2016		Change from 2015 to 2016	
	Dollars	Rank[1]	Dollars	Rank[1]	Percent	Rank[2]
Ohio	54,672	21	56,441	21	3.2	4
U.S. Average	57,611	–	58,353	–	1.3	–

Note: (1) Rank ranges from 1 to 51 where 1 indicates highest salary; (2) Rank ranges from 1 to 51 where 1 indicates highest percent change.
Source: National Education Association, Rankings & Estimates: Rankings of the States 2016 and Estimates of School Statistics 2017

Higher Education

Four-Year Colleges			Two-Year Colleges			Medical Schools[1]	Law Schools[2]	Voc/ Tech[3]
Public	Private Non-profit	Private For-profit	Public	Private Non-profit	Private For-profit			
0	0	0	0	0	0	0	0	0

Note: Figures cover institutions located within the city limits and include main campuses only; (1) includes schools accredited by the Liaison Committee on Medical Education and the American Osteopathic Association's Commission on Osteopathic College Accreditation; (2) includes ABA-accredited schools, schools with provisional ABA accreditation, and state accredited schools; (3) includes all schools with programs that are less than 2 years.
Source: National Center for Education Statistics, Integrated Postsecondary Education System (IPEDS), 2016-17; Wikipedia, List of Medical Schools in the United States, accessed April 2, 2018; Wikipedia, List of Law Schools in the United States, accessed April 2, 2018

According to *U.S. News & World Report,* the Cincinnati, OH-KY-IN metro area is home to two of the best national universities in the U.S.: **Miami University—Oxford** (#78 tie); **University of Cincinnati** (#133 tie). The indicators used to capture academic quality fall into a number of categories: assessment by administrators at peer institutions; retention of students; faculty resources; student selectivity; financial resources; alumni giving; high school counselor ratings of colleges; and graduation rate. *U.S. News & World Report, "America's Best Colleges 2018"*

According to *U.S. News & World Report,* the Cincinnati, OH-KY-IN metro area is home to one of the top 100 law schools in the U.S.: **University of Cincinnati** (#65 tie). The rankings are based on a weighted average of 12 measures of quality: peer assessment score; assessment score by lawyers/judges; median LSAT scores; median undergrad GPA; acceptance rate; employment rates for graduates; placement success; bar passage rate; faculty resources; expenditures per student; student/faculty ratio; and library resources. *U.S. News & World Report, "America's Best Graduate Schools, Law, 2019"*

According to *U.S. News & World Report,* the Cincinnati, OH-KY-IN metro area is home to one of the top 75 medical schools for research in the U.S.: **University of Cincinnati** (#44 tie). The rankings are based on a weighted average of 11 measures of quality: quality assessment; peer assessment score; assessment score by residency directors; research activity; total research activity; average research activity per faculty member; student selectivity; median MCAT total score; median undergraduate GPA; acceptance rate; and faculty resources. *U.S. News & World Report, "America's Best Graduate Schools, Medical, 2019"*

PRESIDENTIAL ELECTION

2016 Presidential Election Results

Area	Clinton	Trump	Johnson	Stein	Other
Warren County	28.5	65.6	3.7	0.6	1.6
U.S.	48.0	45.9	3.3	1.1	1.7

Note: Results are percentages and may not add to 100% due to rounding
Source: Dave Leip's Atlas of U.S. Presidential Elections

EMPLOYERS

Major Employers

Company Name	Industry
Archdiocese of Cincinnati	Religious
Christ Hospital	Medical
Cincinnati Children's Hospital Med Ctr	Medical
Cincinnati Public Schools	Education
City of Cincinnati	Government
Fifth Third Bancorp	Banking
Frisch's Restaurants	Restaurant
GE Aviation	Aviation
Hamilton County	Government
Internal Revenue Service	Government
Kroger Company	Supermarket
Macy's	Retail
Mercy Health Partners	Medical
Miami University	Education
Procter & Gamble Company	Consumer products
St. Elizabeth Healthcare	Medical
TriHealth	Medical
University of Cincinnati	Education
US Postal Service	Government
Wal-Mart Stores	Retail

Note: Companies shown are located within the Cincinnati, OH-KY-IN Metropolitan Statistical Area.
Source: Hoovers.com; Wikipedia

PUBLIC SAFETY

Crime Rate

Area	All Crimes	Violent Crimes				Property Crimes		
		Murder	Rape[3]	Robbery	Aggrav. Assault	Burglary	Larceny -Theft	Motor Vehicle Theft
City	1,017.4	0.0	9.1	6.1	3.0	51.5	923.5	24.2
Metro[1]	2,873.9	4.7	41.1	102.3	109.2	525.9	1,954.4	136.2
U.S.	2,847.8	5.3	40.4	102.8	248.5	468.9	1,745.0	236.9

Note: Figures are crimes per 100,000 population; (1) Figures cover the Cincinnati, OH-KY-IN Metropolitan Statistical Area—see Appendix B for areas included; (3) The city and U.S. figures shown were reported using the revised Uniform Crime Reporting (UCR) definition of rape. The metro area figures shown are an aggregate total of the data submitted using both the revised and legacy UCR definitions.
Source: FBI Uniform Crime Reports, 2016

Hate Crimes

Area	Number of Quarters Reported	Number of Incidents per Bias Motivation					
		Race/Ethnicity/ Ancestry	Religion	Sexual Orientation	Disability	Gender	Gender Identity
City	4	0	0	0	0	0	0
U.S.	4	3,489	1,273	1,076	70	31	124

Source: Federal Bureau of Investigation, Hate Crime Statistics 2016

Identity Theft Consumer Reports

Area	Reports	Reports per 100,000 Population	Rank[2]
MSA[1]	1,969	91	135
U.S.	371,061	114	-

Note: (1) Figures cover the Cincinnati, OH-KY-IN Metropolitan Statistical Area—see Appendix B for areas included; (2) Rank ranges from 1 to 389 where 1 indicates greatest number of identity theft reports per 100,000 population
Source: Federal Trade Commission, Consumer Sentinel Network Data Book for January–December 2017

Fraud and Other Consumer Reports

Area	Reports	Reports per 100,000 Population	Rank[2]
MSA[1]	10,808	499	113
U.S.	2,304,550	708	-

Note: (1) Figures cover the Cincinnati, OH-KY-IN Metropolitan Statistical Area—see Appendix B for areas included; (2) Rank ranges from 1 to 389 where 1 indicates greatest number of fraud and other consumer reports per 100,000 population
Source: Federal Trade Commission, Consumer Sentinel Network Data Book for January–December 2017

SPORTS

Professional Sports Teams

Team Name	League	Year Established
Cincinnati Bengals	National Football League (NFL)	1968
Cincinnati Reds	Major League Baseball (MLB)	1882

Note: Includes teams located in the Cincinnati, OH-KY-IN Metropolitan Statistical Area.
Source: Wikipedia, Major Professional Sports Teams of the United States and Canada, April 5, 2018

CLIMATE

Average and Extreme Temperatures

Temperature	Jan	Feb	Mar	Apr	May	Jun	Jul	Aug	Sep	Oct	Nov	Dec	Yr.
Extreme High (°F)	74	72	84	89	93	102	103	102	102	89	81	75	103
Average High (°F)	38	42	52	64	74	82	86	85	78	67	53	42	64
Average Temp. (°F)	30	33	43	54	63	72	76	74	68	56	44	34	54
Average Low (°F)	21	24	33	43	52	61	65	63	56	45	35	26	44
Extreme Low (°F)	-25	-15	-11	17	27	39	47	43	33	16	0	-20	-25

Note: Figures cover the years 1948-1990
Source: National Climatic Data Center, International Station Meteorological Climate Summary, 9/96

Average Precipitation/Snowfall/Humidity

Precip./Humidity	Jan	Feb	Mar	Apr	May	Jun	Jul	Aug	Sep	Oct	Nov	Dec	Yr.
Avg. Precip. (in.)	3.2	2.9	3.9	3.5	4.0	3.9	4.2	3.1	2.8	2.8	3.4	3.1	40.9
Avg. Snowfall (in.)	7	5	4	1	Tr	0	0	0	0	Tr	2	4	23
Avg. Rel. Hum. 7am (%)	79	78	77	76	79	82	85	87	87	83	79	79	81
Avg. Rel. Hum. 4pm (%)	65	60	55	50	51	53	54	52	52	51	58	65	55

Note: Figures cover the years 1948-1990; Tr = Trace amounts (<0.05 in. of rain; <0.5 in. of snow)
Source: National Climatic Data Center, International Station Meteorological Climate Summary, 9/96

Weather Conditions

Temperature			Daytime Sky			Precipitation		
10°F & below	32°F & below	90°F & above	Clear	Partly cloudy	Cloudy	0.01 inch or more precip.	0.1 inch or more snow/ice	Thunder-storms
14	107	23	80	126	159	127	25	39

Note: Figures are average number of days per year and cover the years 1948-1990
Source: National Climatic Data Center, International Station Meteorological Climate Summary, 9/96

HAZARDOUS WASTE

Superfund Sites

The Cincinnati, OH-KY-IN metro area is home to seven sites on the EPA's Superfund National Priorities List: **Armco Incorporation-Hamilton Plant** (proposed); **Chem-dyne** (final); **Feed Materials Production Center (USDOE)** (final); **Milford Contaminated Aquifer** (final); **Peters Cartridge Factory** (final); **Pristine, Inc.** (final); **Skinner Landfill** (final). There are a total of

1,396 Superfund sites with a status of proposed or final on the list in the U.S. *U.S. Environmental Protection Agency, National Priorities List, April 4, 2018*

AIR & WATER QUALITY

Air Quality Trends: Ozone

	1990	1995	2000	2005	2010	2012	2013	2014	2015	2016
MSA[1]	0.092	0.090	0.082	0.086	0.076	0.082	0.065	0.069	0.069	0.072
U.S.	0.087	0.089	0.081	0.079	0.073	0.075	0.069	0.067	0.068	0.069

Note: (1) Data covers the Cincinnati, OH-KY-IN Metropolitan Statistical Area—see Appendix B for areas included. The values shown are the composite ozone concentration averages among trend sites based on the highest fourth daily maximum 8-hour concentration in parts per million. These trends are based on sites having an adequate record of monitoring data during the trend period. Data from exceptional events are included.
Source: U.S. Environmental Protection Agency, Air Quality Monitoring Information, "Air Quality Trends by City, 1990-2016"

Air Quality Index

Area	Percent of Days when Air Quality was...[2]					AQI Statistics[2]	
	Good	Moderate	Unhealthy for Sensitive Groups	Unhealthy	Very Unhealthy	Maximum	Median
MSA[1]	47.1	50.1	2.7	0.0	0.0	129	51

Note: (1) Data covers the Cincinnati, OH-KY-IN Metropolitan Statistical Area—see Appendix B for areas included; (2) Based on 365 days with AQI data in 2017. Air Quality Index (AQI) is an index for reporting daily air quality. EPA calculates the AQI for five major air pollutants regulated by the Clean Air Act: ground-level ozone, particle pollution (aka particulate matter), carbon monoxide, sulfur dioxide, and nitrogen dioxide. The AQI runs from 0 to 500. The higher the AQI value, the greater the level of air pollution and the greater the health concern. There are six AQI categories: "Good" AQI is between 0 and 50. Air quality is considered satisfactory; "Moderate" AQI is between 51 and 100. Air quality is acceptable; "Unhealthy for Sensitive Groups" When AQI values are between 101 and 150, members of sensitive groups may experience health effects; "Unhealthy" When AQI values are between 151 and 200 everyone may begin to experience health effects; "Very Unhealthy" AQI values between 201 and 300 trigger a health alert; "Hazardous" AQI values over 300 trigger warnings of emergency conditions (not shown).
Source: U.S. Environmental Protection Agency, Air Quality Index Report, 2017

Air Quality Index Pollutants

Area	Percent of Days when AQI Pollutant was...[2]					
	Carbon Monoxide	Nitrogen Dioxide	Ozone	Sulfur Dioxide	Particulate Matter 2.5	Particulate Matter 10
MSA[1]	0.0	3.3	35.6	1.4	59.7	0.0

Note: (1) Data covers the Cincinnati, OH-KY-IN Metropolitan Statistical Area—see Appendix B for areas included; (2) Based on 365 days with AQI data in 2017. The Air Quality Index (AQI) is an index for reporting daily air quality. EPA calculates the AQI for five major air pollutants regulated by the Clean Air Act: ground-level ozone, particle pollution (also known as particulate matter), carbon monoxide, sulfur dioxide, and nitrogen dioxide. The AQI runs from 0 to 500. The higher the AQI value, the greater the level of air pollution and the greater the health concern.
Source: U.S. Environmental Protection Agency, Air Quality Index Report, 2017

Maximum Air Pollutant Concentrations: Particulate Matter, Ozone, CO and Lead

	Particulate Matter 10 (ug/m³)	Particulate Matter 2.5 Wtd AM (ug/m³)	Particulate Matter 2.5 24-Hr (ug/m³)	Ozone (ppm)	Carbon Monoxide (ppm)	Lead (ug/m³)
MSA[1] Level	85	10.9	25	0.076	1	n/a
NAAQS[2]	150	15	35	0.075	9	0.15
Met NAAQS[2]	Yes	Yes	Yes	No	Yes	n/a

Note: (1) Data covers the Cincinnati, OH-KY-IN Metropolitan Statistical Area—see Appendix B for areas included; Data from exceptional events are included; (2) National Ambient Air Quality Standards; ppm = parts per million; ug/m³ = micrograms per cubic meter; n/a not available.
Concentrations: Particulate Matter 10 (coarse particulate)—highest second maximum 24-hour concentration; Particulate Matter 2.5 Wtd AM (fine particulate)—highest weighted annual mean concentration; Particulate Matter 2.5 24-Hour (fine particulate)—highest 98th percentile 24-hour concentration; Ozone—highest fourth daily maximum 8-hour concentration; Carbon Monoxide—highest second maximum non-overlapping 8-hour concentration; Lead—maximum running 3-month average
Source: U.S. Environmental Protection Agency, Air Quality Monitoring Information, "Air Quality Statistics by City, 2016"

Maximum Air Pollutant Concentrations: Nitrogen Dioxide and Sulfur Dioxide

	Nitrogen Dioxide AM (ppb)	Nitrogen Dioxide 1-Hr (ppb)	Sulfur Dioxide AM (ppb)	Sulfur Dioxide 1-Hr (ppb)	Sulfur Dioxide 24-Hr (ppb)
MSA[1] Level	21	56	n/a	43	n/a
NAAQS[2]	53	100	30	75	140
Met NAAQS[2]	Yes	Yes	n/a	Yes	n/a

Note: (1) Data covers the Cincinnati, OH-KY-IN Metropolitan Statistical Area—see Appendix B for areas included; Data from exceptional events are included; (2) National Ambient Air Quality Standards; ppm = parts per million; ug/m³ = micrograms per cubic meter; n/a not available.
Concentrations: Nitrogen Dioxide AM—highest arithmetic mean concentration; Nitrogen Dioxide 1-Hr—highest 98th percentile 1-hour daily maximum concentration; Sulfur Dioxide AM—highest annual mean concentration; Sulfur Dioxide 1-Hr—highest 99th percentile 1-hour daily maximum concentration; Sulfur Dioxide 24-Hr—highest second maximum 24-hour concentration
Source: U.S. Environmental Protection Agency, Air Quality Monitoring Information, "Air Quality Statistics by City, 2016"

Drinking Water

Water System Name	Pop. Served	Primary Water Source Type	Violations[1]	
			Health Based	Monitoring/ Reporting
Cincinnati Public Water System	749,000	Surface	0	0

Note: (1) Based on violation data from January 1, 2017 to December 31, 2017
Source: U.S. Environmental Protection Agency, Office of Ground Water and Drinking Water, Safe Drinking Water Information System (based on data extracted April 5, 2018)

North Ridgeville, Ohio

Background

This Cleveland suburb is located twenty minutes southwest of the city—and just south of Lake Erie—along I-80.

The city, in eastern Lorain County, was founded in 1810 by 14 men from Waterbury, Connecticut. Three of them were Revolutionary War veterans and one had fought in the French & Indian War. Originally known as Ridgeville Township, the area was divided by five geologic ridges that indicated the shorelines of the receding Lake Erie, which was created by a slow, northward migration of Ice Age glaciers. The early settlement's voting adult males approved the creation of Ridgeville Township in 1813, and served at Columbia Blockhouse during the War of 1812—including during the Battle of Lake Erie.

In 1828, the Postmaster General requested a change of name owing to another Ridgeville near Dayton, Ohio, which produced the name North Ridgefield. The town saw growth with stagecoach lines and steam railroads. After World War II, the township remained more or less a farming community until the 1960s and '70s. It incorporated as a city in 1960 and today, North Ridgeville is known as a family-friendly city.

Students attend the North Ridgeville City Schools, where the local North Ridgeville High School includes a Ranger Academy program to offer an alternative educational environment. The city's recreational offerings include the 37-acre Shady Drive Complex with 13 baseball/softball diamonds, batting cages and more. There's also a 12-acre soccer complex.

North Ridgeville is home to the North Ridgeville Corn Festival. The history started when the Bicentennial Committee for the City of North Ridgeville was formed in 1975 to celebrate the upcoming United States bicentennial in 1976. The first festival ran 6 hours and featured 13 booths around the North Ridgeville Middle School track. The proceeds were donated to the library to assist with the cost of relocating it from the old Lawson's store area to the Olde Town Hall building across the street. The next year, in 1976, in addition to celebrating the bicentennial, the festival was held in honor of Harold Sweet, a sweet corn grower in North Ridgeville, for all that he did for the youth and citizens of the city. The proceeds from this festival were donated to purchase trees for the then new Bainbridge Extension along with 2 bicentennial flags for City Hall. The Bicentennial Committee was renamed the North Ridgeville Corn Festival Committee in 1977.

Major employers in the city include Norlake Manufacturing, which designs and manufactures custom-made magnetics. The company recently built a 20,000 square foot facility dedicated to manufacturing large MV magnetics.

North Ridgeville's climate means average temperatures near 25 degrees in January and maximum July temperatures in the low 80s. Snowfall may top 50 inches annually.

Rankings

Business/Finance Rankings

- According to *Business Insider*, the Cleveland* metro area is where startup growth is on the rise. Based on the 2017 Kauffman Index of Growth Entrepreneurship, which measured in-depth national entrepreneurial trends in 40 metro areas, it ranked #18 in highest startup growth. *www.businessinsider.com, "The 21 U.S. Cities with the Highest Startup Growth," October 21, 2017*
- The personal finance site NerdWallet analyzed 183 American metropolitan areas with populations over 250,000 and more than 15,000 businesses to rank where entrepreneurs find the most success. Criteria included area economy, annual income, housing cost, unemployment rate, and the success rate of area businesses. Cleveland* ranked #50. *www.nerdwallet.com, "Best Places to Start a Business," April 27, 2015*
- USAA and Hiring Our Heroes worked with Sperlings's BestPlaces and the Institute for Veterans and Military Families at Syracuse University to rank major metropolitan areas where military-skills-related employment is strongest. Criteria for *mid-career* veterans included veteran wage growth; recent job growth; stability; and accessible health resources. Metro areas with a higher than national average crime or unemployment rate were excluded. At #8, the Cleveland* metro area made the top ten. *www.usaa.com, "2015 Best Places for Veterans"*
- Based on metro area social media reviews, the employment opinion group Glassdoor surveyed 50 of the largest U.S. metro areas and equally weighed cost of living, hiring opportunity, and job satisfaction to compose a list of "25 Best Cities for Jobs." Median pay and home value, in-demand jobs and number of current job openings was also factored in. The Cleveland* metro area was ranked #9 in overall job satisfaction. *www.glassdoor.com, "Best Cities for Jobs," September 12, 2017*
- In a survey of economic confidence in the nation's 50 largest metropolitan areas conducted January–December 2014, the Cleveland* metro area placed #36, according to Gallup's 2014 Economic Confidence Index. *Gallup, "San Jose and San Francisco Lead in Economic Confidence," March 19, 2015*
- The Brookings Institution ranked the 100 largest metro areas in the U.S. based on income inequality. Cleveland* was ranked #18 (#1 = greatest ineqality). Criteria: the "95/20 ratio," a figure representing the income at which a household earns more than 95 percent of all other households, divided by the income at which a household earns more than only 20 percent of all other households. *Brookings Institution, "Household Income Inequality, 100 Largest U.S. Metro Areas, 2014-2016," February 5, 2018*
- Payscale.com ranked the largest metro areas in terms of wage growth. The Cleveland* metro area ranked #16. Criteria: private-sector wage growth between the 4th quarter of 2016 and the 4th quarter of 2017. *PayScale, "Wage Trends by Metro Area-4th Quarter," January 17, 2018*
- Cleveland* was identified as one of America's most frugal metro areas by *Coupons.com.* The city ranked #10 out of 25. Criteria: digital coupon usage. *Coupons.com, "America's Most Frugal Cities of 2017," March 22, 2018*
- The Cleveland* metro area appeared on the Milken Institute "2017 Best Performing Cities" list. Rank: #169 out of 200 large metro areas. Criteria: job growth; wage and salary growth; high-tech output growth. *Milken Institute, "Best-Performing Cities 2017," January 2018*
- *Forbes* ranked the 200 most populous metro areas to determine the nation's "Best Places for Business and Careers." The Cleveland* metro area was ranked #101. Criteria: costs (business and living); job growth (past and projected); income growth; quality of life; educational attainment (college and high school); projected economic growth; cultural and recreational opportunities; net migration patterns; number of highly ranked colleges. *Forbes, "The Best Places for Business and Careers 2017," October 24, 2017*

Education Rankings

- Personal finance website *WalletHub* analyzed the 150 largest U.S. metropolitan statistical areas to determine where the most educated Americans are choosing to settle. Criteria: education quality and attainment gap; education levels; percentage of workers with degrees; public school rankings; quality and size of each metro area's universities. Cleveland* was ranked #64 (#1 = most educated city). *www.WalletHub.com, "2017's Most and Least Educated Cities in America," July 25, 2017*

Environmental Rankings

- Sperling's BestPlaces assessed 379 metropolitan areas of the United States for the likelihood of dangerously extreme weather events or earthquakes. In general the Southeast and South-Central regions have the highest risk of weather extremes and earthquakes, while the Pacific Northwest enjoys the lowest risk. Of the least risky metropolitan areas, the Cleveland* metro area was ranked #158. *www.bestplaces.net, "Safest Places from Natural Disasters," April 2011*

- Cleveland* was highlighted as one of the 25 metro areas most polluted by year-round particle pollution (Annual PM 2.5) in the U.S. during 2013 through 2015. The area ranked #9. *American Lung Association, State of the Air 2017*

Health/Fitness Rankings

- Analysts who tracked obesity rates in the nation's largest metro areas (populations above one million) found that the Cleveland* metro area was one of the ten major metros where residents were most likely to be obese, defined as a BMI score of 30 or above. *www.gallup.com, "Boulder, Colo., Residents Still Least Likely to Be Obese," April 4, 2014*

- For each of the 50 most populous metro areas in the United States, the American College of Sports Medicine's American Fitness Index evaluated infrastructure, community assets, and policies that encourage healthy and fit lifestyles, including preventive health behaviors, levels of chronic disease conditions, health care access, and community resources and policies that support physical activity. The Cleveland* metro area ranked #28 for "community fitness." *www.americanfitnessindex.org, "ACSM American Fitness Index Health and Community Fitness Status of the 50 Largest Metropolitan Areas," May 2017*

- The Cleveland* metro area was identified as one of the worst cities for bed bugs in America by pest control company Orkin. The area ranked #14 out of 50 based on the number of bed bug treatments Orkin performed from December 2016 to November 2017. *Orkin, "Baltimore and Washington D.C. Continue to Hold Top Spots," January 8, 2018*

- Cleveland* was identified as a "2016 Spring Allergy Capital." The area ranked #42 out of 100. Three groups of factors were used to identify the most severe cities for people with allergies during the spring season: annual pollen levels; medicine utilization; access to board-certified allergists. *Asthma and Allergy Foundation of America, "Spring Allergy Capitals 2016"*

- Cleveland* was identified as a "2016 Fall Allergy Capital." The area ranked #21 out of 100. Three groups of factors were used to identify the most severe cities for people with allergies during the fall season: annual pollen levels; medicine utilization; access to board-certified allergists. *Asthma and Allergy Foundation of America, "Fall Allergy Capitals 2016"*

- Cleveland* was identified as a "2015 Asthma Capital." The area ranked #20 out of the nation's 100 largest metropolitan areas. Criteria: estimated prevalence; self-reported prevalence; crude death rate for asthma; annual pollen score; annual air quality; public smoking laws; number of board-certified asthma specialists; school inhaler access laws; rescue medication use; controller medication use; ER visits for asthma; uninsured rate; poverty rate. *Asthma and Allergy Foundation of America, "Asthma Capitals 2015"*

- The Cleveland* metro area ranked #127 out of 189 in The Gallup-Healthways Well-Being Index. Criteria: purpose; social well being; financial health; community and physical health. Results are based on telephone interviews with adults, aged 18 and older, living in metropolitan areas in the 50 U.S. states and the District of Columbia. *Gallup-Healthways, "State of American Well-Being, 2017 Community Well-Being Rankings" March 2018*

Real Estate Rankings

- FitSmallBusiness looked at 50 of the largest metropolitan areas in the U.S. to determine which metro was the best to start a real estate business. Data was compiled from such sources as: Zillow, Trulia, U.S. Census Bureau, and the Bureau of Labor Statistics. Criteria: location; inventory; annual wages; median sales price of homes; days on the market; median price cut percentage; and other factors that would influence real estate professional growth. The Cleveland* metro area ranked #48. *fitsmallbusiness.com, "The Best Cities to Become a Real Estate Agent in 2018," January 30, 2018*
- The Cleveland* metro area was identified as #8 among the ten housing markets with the highest percentage of distressed property sales, based on the findings of the housing data website RealtyTrac. Criteria: short sales; income and poverty figures; and unemployment data. *247wallst.com, "Cities Selling the Most Distressed Homes," January 23, 2014*
- The Cleveland* metro area was identified as one of nine best housing markets to invest in. Criteria: single-family rental home investing in the first quarter of 2017 based on first-year returns. The area ranked #1. *The Business Insider, "Here are the 9 Best U.S. Housing Markets for Investment," May 11, 2017*
- Cleveland* was ranked #44 out of 238 metro areas in terms of housing affordability in 2017 by the National Association of Home Builders (#1 = most affordable). Criteria: the share of homes sold in that area affordable to a family earning the local median income, based on standard mortgage underwriting criteria. *National Association of Home Builders®, NAHB-Wells Fargo Housing Opportunity Index, 4th Quarter 2017*
- The nation's largest metro areas were analyzed in terms of the percentage of households entering some stage of foreclosure in 2017. The Cleveland* metro area ranked #6 out of 10 (#1 = highest foreclosure rate). *RealtyTrac, "2017 Year-End U.S. Foreclosure Market Report™," January 16, 2018*

Safety Rankings

- The National Insurance Crime Bureau ranked 382 metro areas in the U.S. in terms of per capita rates of vehicle theft. The Cleveland* metro area ranked #81 (#1 = highest rate). Criteria: number of vehicle theft offenses per 100,000 inhabitants in 2016. *National Insurance Crime Bureau, "Hot Spots 2016," June 8, 2017*

Seniors/Retirement Rankings

- From its Best Cities for Successful Aging indexes, the Milken Institute generated rankings for metropolitan areas, weighing data in nine categories—health care, wellness, living arrangements, transportation and convenience, financial characteristics, education, employment, community engagement, and overall livability. The Cleveland* metro area was ranked #36 overall in the large metro area category. *Milken Institute, "Best Cities for Successful Aging, 2017" March 14, 2017*

Miscellaneous Rankings

- The watchdog site Charity Navigator conducts an annual study of charities in the nation's major markets both to analyze statistical differences in their financial, accountability, and transparency practices and to track year-to-year variations in individual philanthropic communities. Charity Navigator's analysis demonstrated that the financial, accountability and transparency behaviors of America's largest charities can be influenced by the metropolitan market within which the charity operates. The Cleveland* metro area was ranked #6 among the 30 metro markets in the rating category of Overall Score. *www.charitynavigator.org, "2017 Metro Market Study," May 1, 2017*

*North Ridgeville is located within the Cleveland-Elyria, OH Metropolitan Statistical Area.

Business Environment

CITY FINANCES

City Government Finances

Component	2015 ($000)	2015 ($ per capita)
Total Revenues	38,320	1,180
Total Expenditures	40,431	1,245
Debt Outstanding	28,091	865
Cash and Securities[1]	30,015	924

Note: (1) Cash and security holdings of a government at the close of its fiscal year,, including those of its dependent agencies, utilities, and liquor stores.
Source: U.S Census Bureau, State & Local Government Finances 2015

City Government Revenue by Source

Source	2015 ($000)	2015 ($ per capita)	2015 (%)
General Revenue			
From Federal Government	474	15	1.2
From State Government	2,864	88	7.5
From Local Governments	0	0	0.0
Taxes			
Property	5,500	169	14.4
Sales and Gross Receipts	0	0	0.0
Personal Income	9,498	292	24.8
Corporate Income	0	0	0.0
Motor Vehicle License	476	15	1.2
Other Taxes	1,226	38	3.2
Current Charges	11,790	363	30.8
Liquor Store	0	0	0.0
Utility	4,180	129	10.9
Employee Retirement	0	0	0.0

Source: U.S Census Bureau, State & Local Government Finances 2015

City Government Expenditures by Function

Function	2015 ($000)	2015 ($ per capita)	2015 (%)
General Direct Expenditures			
Air Transportation	0	0	0.0
Corrections	0	0	0.0
Education	0	0	0.0
Employment Security Administration	0	0	0.0
Financial Administration	1,202	37	3.0
Fire Protection	4,106	126	10.2
General Public Buildings	802	24	2.0
Governmental Administration, Other	917	28	2.3
Health	994	30	2.5
Highways	4,105	126	10.2
Hospitals	0	0	0.0
Housing and Community Development	0	0	0.0
Interest on General Debt	997	30	2.5
Judicial and Legal	506	15	1.3
Libraries	0	0	0.0
Parking	0	0	0.0
Parks and Recreation	434	13	1.1
Police Protection	5,266	162	13.0
Public Welfare	0	0	0.0
Sewerage	7,909	243	19.6
Solid Waste Management	2,908	89	7.2
Veterans' Services	0	0	0.0
Liquor Store	0	0	0.0
Utility	4,980	153	12.3
Employee Retirement	0	0	0.0

Source: U.S Census Bureau, State & Local Government Finances 2015

DEMOGRAPHICS

Population Growth

Area	1990 Census	2000 Census	2010 Census	2016* Estimate	Population Growth (%) 1990-2016	Population Growth (%) 2010-2016
City	21,564	22,338	29,465	31,832	47.6	8.0
MSA[1]	2,102,219	2,148,143	2,077,240	2,061,630	-1.9	-0.8
U.S.	248,709,873	281,421,906	308,745,538	318,558,162	28.1	3.2

Note: (1) Figures cover the Cleveland-Elyria, OH Metropolitan Statistical Area—see Appendix B for areas included; (*) 2012-2016 5-year estimated population

Source: U.S. Census Bureau, 1990 Census, Census 2000, Census 2010, 2012-2016 American Community Survey 5-Year Estimates

Household Size

Area	Persons in Household (%)							Average Household Size
	One	Two	Three	Four	Five	Six	Seven or More	
City	24.7	36.8	15.3	13.9	6.6	2.1	0.6	2.60
MSA[1]	33.3	33.3	14.8	11.2	4.8	1.7	0.9	2.40
U.S.	27.7	33.7	15.7	13.1	6.0	2.3	1.5	2.60

Note: (1) Figures cover the Cleveland-Elyria, OH Metropolitan Statistical Area—see Appendix B for areas included

Source: U.S. Census Bureau, 2012-2016 American Community Survey 5-Year Estimates

Race

Area	White Alone[2] (%)	Black Alone[2] (%)	Asian Alone[2] (%)	AIAN[3] Alone[2] (%)	NHOPI[4] Alone[2] (%)	Other Race Alone[2] (%)	Two or More Races (%)
City	92.9	1.6	1.7	0.1	0.0	0.7	3.0
MSA[1]	74.0	20.0	2.1	0.2	0.0	1.1	2.5
U.S.	73.3	12.6	5.2	0.8	0.2	4.8	3.1

Note: (1) Figures cover the Cleveland-Elyria, OH Metropolitan Statistical Area—see Appendix B for areas included; (2) Alone is defined as not being in combination with one or more other races; (3) American Indian and Alaska Native; (4) Native Hawaiian and Other Pacific Islander

Source: U.S. Census Bureau, 2012-2016 American Community Survey 5-Year Estimates

Hispanic or Latino Origin

Area	Total (%)	Mexican (%)	Puerto Rican (%)	Cuban (%)	Other (%)
City	3.8	0.9	2.1	0.1	0.7
MSA[1]	5.3	1.1	3.2	0.1	0.9
U.S.	17.3	11.0	1.7	0.7	4.0

Note: Persons of Hispanic or Latino origin can be of any race; (1) Figures cover the Cleveland-Elyria, OH Metropolitan Statistical Area—see Appendix B for areas included

Source: U.S. Census Bureau, 2012-2016 American Community Survey 5-Year Estimates

Segregation

Type	Segregation Indices[1]				Percent Change		
	1990	2000	2010	2010 Rank[2]	1990-2000	1990-2010	2000-2010
Black/White	82.8	78.2	74.1	5	-4.7	-8.7	-4.0
Asian/White	38.1	39.9	41.3	48	1.8	3.2	1.4
Hispanic/White	58.3	58.5	52.3	20	0.2	-6.0	-6.3

Note: All figures cover the Metropolitan Statistical Area—see Appendix B for areas included; Figures are based on an analysis of 1990, 2000, and 2010 Census Decennial Census tract data by William H. Frey, Brookings Institution and the University of Michigan Social Science Data Analysis Network. In this analysis all racial groups (whites, blacks, and asians) are non-Hispanic members of those races. Hispanics are shown as a separate category; (1) Segregation Indices are Dissimilarity Indices that measure the degree to which the minority group is distributed differently than whites across census tracts. They range from 0 (complete integration) to 100 (complete segregation) where the value indicates the percentage of the minority group that needs to move to be distributed exactly like whites; (2) Ranges from 1 (most segregated) to 102 (least segregated); n/a not available.

Source: www.CensusScope.org

Ancestry

Area	German	Irish	English	American	Italian	Polish	French[2]	Scottish	Dutch
City	28.4	20.6	9.3	5.5	11.4	9.8	2.0	2.4	1.3
MSA[1]	19.9	14.1	7.4	3.8	9.9	7.8	1.6	1.6	1.0
U.S.	14.4	10.4	7.7	6.9	5.4	2.9	2.6	1.7	1.3

Note: Figures are the percentage of the total population reporting a particular ancestry. The nine most commonly reported ancestries in the U.S. are shown. Figures include multiple ancestries (e.g. if a person reported being Irish and Italian, they were included in both columns); (1) Figures cover the Cleveland-Elyria, OH Metropolitan Statistical Area—see Appendix B for areas included; (2) Excludes Basque
Source: U.S. Census Bureau, 2012-2016 American Community Survey 5-Year Estimates

Foreign-Born Population

Area	Percent of Population Born in								
	Any Foreign Country	Asia	Mexico	Europe	Carribean	Central America[2]	South America	Africa	Canada
City	4.7	2.0	0.3	2.1	0.0	0.0	0.1	0.1	0.1
MSA[1]	5.6	2.1	0.3	2.2	0.2	0.2	0.2	0.3	0.2
U.S.	13.2	4.0	3.6	1.5	1.3	1.0	0.9	0.6	0.3

Note: (1) Figures cover the Cleveland-Elyria, OH Metropolitan Statistical Area—see Appendix B for areas included; (2) Excludes Mexico.
Source: U.S. Census Bureau, 2012-2016 American Community Survey 5-Year Estimates

Marital Status

Area	Never Married	Now Married[2]	Separated	Widowed	Divorced
City	21.7	60.7	1.3	6.7	9.6
MSA[1]	34.3	45.3	1.8	6.8	11.9
U.S.	33.0	48.1	2.1	5.9	11.0

Note: Figures are percentages and cover the population 15 years of age and older; (1) Figures cover the Cleveland-Elyria, OH Metropolitan Statistical Area—see Appendix B for areas included; (2) Excludes separated
Source: U.S. Census Bureau, 2012-2016 American Community Survey 5-Year Estimates

Disability Status

Area	All Ages	Under 18 Years Old	18 to 64 Years Old	65 Years and Over
City	10.7	4.0	7.8	27.7
MSA[1]	14.0	5.3	11.7	34.9
U.S.	12.5	4.1	10.3	35.7

Note: Figures show percent of the civilian noninstitutionalized population that reported having a disability. Disability status is determined from six types of difficulty: vision, hearing, cognitive, ambulatory, self-care, and independent living. For children under 5 years old, hearing and vision difficulty are used to determine disability status. For children between the ages of 5 and 14, disability status is determined from hearing, vision, cognitive, ambulatory, and self-care difficulties. For people aged 15 years and older, they are considered to have a disability if they have difficulty with any one of the six difficulty types; Note: (1) Figures cover the Cleveland-Elyria, OH Metropolitan Statistical Area—see Appendix B for areas included
Source: U.S. Census Bureau, 2012-2016 American Community Survey 5-Year Estimates

Age

Area	Percent of Population									Median Age
	Under Age 5	Age 5–19	Age 20–34	Age 35–44	Age 45–54	Age 55–64	Age 65–74	Age 75–84	Age 85+	
City	7.3	17.2	16.2	13.1	14.0	12.7	12.3	5.2	2.0	41.7
MSA[1]	5.6	18.8	18.5	11.9	14.3	14.2	9.0	5.0	2.5	41.2
U.S.	6.2	19.6	20.7	12.7	13.6	12.6	8.3	4.3	1.9	37.7

Note: (1) Figures cover the Cleveland-Elyria, OH Metropolitan Statistical Area—see Appendix B for areas included
Source: U.S. Census Bureau, 2012-2016 American Community Survey 5-Year Estimates

Gender

Area	Males	Females	Males per 100 Females
City	16,071	15,761	102.0
MSA[1]	994,214	1,067,416	93.1
U.S.	156,765,322	161,792,840	96.9

Note: (1) Figures cover the Cleveland-Elyria, OH Metropolitan Statistical Area—see Appendix B for areas included
Source: U.S. Census Bureau, 2012-2016 American Community Survey 5-Year Estimates

Religious Groups by Family

Area	Catholic	Baptist	Non-Den.	Methodist[2]	Lutheran	LDS[3]	Pente-costal	Presby-terian[4]	Muslim[5]	Judaism
MSA[1]	28.9	4.4	3.3	2.9	2.5	0.4	1.1	2.1	0.2	1.5
U.S.	19.1	9.3	4.0	4.0	2.3	2.0	1.9	1.6	0.8	0.7

Note: Figures are the number of adherents as a percentage of the total population; (1) Figures cover the Cleveland-Elyria, OH Metropolitan Statistical Area—see Appendix B for areas included; (2) Methodist/Pietist; (3) Latter Day Saints; (4) Reformed; (5) Figures are estimates
Source: Association of Statisticians of American Religious Bodies, 2010 U.S. Religion Census: Religious Congregations & Membership Study

Religious Groups by Tradition

Area	Catholic	Evangelical Protestant	Mainline Protestant	Other Tradition	Black Protestant	Orthodox
MSA[1]	28.9	9.1	7.6	2.7	2.1	0.8
U.S.	19.1	16.2	7.3	4.3	1.6	0.3

Note: Figures are the number of adherents as a percentage of the total population; (1) Figures cover the Cleveland-Elyria, OH Metropolitan Statistical Area—see Appendix B for areas included
Source: Association of Statisticians of American Religious Bodies, 2010 U.S. Religion Census: Religious Congregations & Membership Study

ECONOMY

Gross Metropolitan Product

Area	2014	2015	2016	2017	Rank[2]
MSA[1]	123.1	126.3	129.3	134.6	27

Note: Figures are in billions of dollars; (1) Figures cover the Cleveland-Elyria, OH Metropolitan Statistical Area—see Appendix B for areas included; (2) Rank is based on 2015 data and ranges from 1 to 381
Source: The U.S. Conference of Mayors, U.S. Metro Economies: GMP and Employment Report, 2015-2017

Economic Growth

Area	2012-14 (%)	2015 (%)	2016 (%)	2017 (%)	Rank[2]
MSA[1]	0.3	0.7	0.9	2.1	273
U.S.	2.0	2.4	1.9	2.6	–

Note: Figures are real gross metropolitan product (GMP) growth rates and represent average annual percent change; (1) Figures cover the Cleveland-Elyria, OH Metropolitan Statistical Area—see Appendix B for areas included; (2) Rank is based on 2012-2014 average annual percent change and ranges from 1 to 381
Source: The U.S. Conference of Mayors, U.S. Metro Economies: GMP and Employment Report, 2015-2017

Metropolitan Area Exports

Area	2011	2012	2013	2014	2015	2016	Rank[2]
MSA[1]	11,276.1	11,063.7	11,137.9	10,706.5	9,629.7	8,752.9	34

Note: Figures are in millions of dollars; (1) Figures cover the Cleveland-Elyria, OH Metropolitan Statistical Area—see Appendix B for areas included; (2) Rank is based on 2016 data and ranges from 1 to 385
Source: U.S. Department of Commerce, International Trade Administration, Office of Trade & Industry Information, Manufacturing & Services, data extracted March 15, 2018

Building Permits

Area	Single-Family			Multi-Family			Total		
	2016	2017p	Pct. Chg.	2016	2017p	Pct. Chg.	2016	2017p	Pct. Chg.
City	193	207	7.3	8	8	0.0	201	215	7.0
MSA[1]	2,653	2,706	2.0	302	506	67.5	2,955	3,212	8.7
U.S.	750,800	817,300	8.9	455,800	446,800	-2.0	1,206,600	1,264,100	4.8

Note: (1) Figures cover the Cleveland-Elyria, OH Metropolitan Statistical Area—see Appendix B for areas included; Figures represent new, privately-owned housing units authorized (unadjusted data); All permit data are based on estimates with imputation; (p) preliminary data.
Source: U.S. Census Bureau, Manufacturing, Mining, and Construction Statistics, Building Permits, 2016, 2017

Bankruptcy Filings

Area	Business Filings			Nonbusiness Filings		
	2016	2017	% Chg.	2016	2017	% Chg.
Lorain County	14	11	-21.4	934	1,001	7.2
U.S.	24,114	23,157	-4.0	770,846	765,863	-0.6

Note: Business filings include Chapter 7, Chapter 11, Chapter 12, and Chapter 13; Nonbusiness filings include Chapter 7, Chapter 11, and Chapter 13
Source: Administrative Office of the U.S. Courts, Business and Nonbusiness Bankruptcy, County Cases Commenced by Chapter of the Bankruptcy Code, During the 12-Month Period Ending December 31, 2016 and Business and Nonbusiness Bankruptcy, County Cases Commenced by Chapter of the Bankruptcy Code, During the 12-Month Period Ending December 31, 2017

Housing Vacancy Rates

Area	Gross Vacancy Rate[2] (%)			Year-Round Vacancy Rate[3] (%)			Rental Vacancy Rate[4] (%)			Homeowner Vacancy Rate[5] (%)		
	2015	2016	2017	2015	2016	2017	2015	2016	2017	2015	2016	2017
MSA[1]	11.0	11.1	9.2	10.9	10.9	9.2	7.4	7.1	8.0	1.4	1.7	1.2
U.S.	12.9	12.8	12.7	10.0	9.9	9.9	7.1	6.9	7.2	1.8	1.7	1.6

Note: (1) Figures cover the Cleveland-Elyria, OH Metropolitan Statistical Area—see Appendix B for areas included; (2) The percentage of the total housing inventory that is vacant; (3) The percentage of the housing inventory (excluding seasonal units) that is year-round vacant; (4) The percentage of rental inventory that is vacant for rent; (5) The percentage of homeowner inventory that is vacant for sale
Source: U.S. Census Bureau, Housing Vacancies and Homeownership Annual Statistics: 2015, 2016, 2017

INCOME

Income

Area	Per Capita ($)	Median Household ($)	Average Household ($)
City	31,399	68,778	80,662
MSA[1]	29,822	51,001	70,884
U.S.	29,829	55,322	77,866

Note: (1) Figures cover the Cleveland-Elyria, OH Metropolitan Statistical Area—see Appendix B for areas included
Source: U.S. Census Bureau, 2012-2016 American Community Survey 5-Year Estimates

Household Income Distribution

Area	Percent of Households Earning							
	Under $15,000	$15,000 -$24,999	$25,000 -$34,999	$35,000 -$49,999	$50,000 -$74,999	$75,000 -$99,999	$100,000 -$149,999	$150,000 and up
City	4.3	5.3	9.5	13.6	22.1	16.9	18.5	9.9
MSA[1]	14.2	11.0	10.4	13.5	17.6	11.9	12.7	8.7
U.S.	12.1	10.2	9.9	13.2	17.8	12.2	13.5	11.1

Note: (1) Figures cover the Cleveland-Elyria, OH Metropolitan Statistical Area—see Appendix B for areas included
Source: U.S. Census Bureau, 2012-2016 American Community Survey 5-Year Estimates

Poverty Rate

Area	All Ages	Under 18 Years Old	18 to 64 Years Old	65 Years and Over
City	4.9	5.8	5.0	3.4
MSA[1]	15.2	22.0	14.3	9.1
U.S.	15.1	21.2	14.2	9.3

Note: Figures are percentage of people whose income during the past 12 months was below the poverty level; (1) Figures cover the Cleveland-Elyria, OH Metropolitan Statistical Area—see Appendix B for areas included
Source: U.S. Census Bureau, 2012-2016 American Community Survey 5-Year Estimates

EMPLOYMENT

Labor Force and Employment

Area	Civilian Labor Force			Workers Employed		
	Dec. 2016	Dec. 2017	% Chg.	Dec. 2016	Dec. 2017	% Chg.
City	17,341	17,173	-1.0	16,450	16,444	0.0
MSA[1]	1,013,960	1,005,220	-0.9	956,780	957,181	0.0
U.S.	158,968,000	159,880,000	0.6	151,798,000	153,602,000	1.2

Note: Data is not seasonally adjusted and covers workers 16 years of age and older; (1) Figures cover the Cleveland-Elyria, OH Metropolitan Statistical Area—see Appendix B for areas included
Source: Bureau of Labor Statistics, Local Area Unemployment Statistics

Unemployment Rate

Area	2017											
	Jan.	Feb.	Mar.	Apr.	May	Jun.	Jul.	Aug.	Sep.	Oct.	Nov.	Dec.
City	6.0	6.6	5.7	4.9	4.8	5.4	5.3	5.3	4.7	4.2	4.0	4.2
MSA[1]	6.6	7.1	6.1	5.4	5.5	6.1	6.0	5.9	5.1	4.7	4.5	4.8
U.S.	5.1	4.9	4.6	4.1	4.1	4.5	4.6	4.5	4.1	3.9	3.9	3.9

Note: Data is not seasonally adjusted and covers workers 16 years of age and older; (1) Figures cover the Cleveland-Elyria, OH Metropolitan Statistical Area—see Appendix B for areas included
Source: Bureau of Labor Statistics, Local Area Unemployment Statistics

Average Wages

Occupation	$/Hr.	Occupation	$/Hr.
Accountants and Auditors	36.50	Maids and Housekeeping Cleaners	10.90
Automotive Mechanics	21.20	Maintenance and Repair Workers	19.80
Bookkeepers	19.40	Marketing Managers	66.20
Carpenters	25.90	Nuclear Medicine Technologists	34.30
Cashiers	10.60	Nurses, Licensed Practical	21.90
Clerks, General Office	16.40	Nurses, Registered	32.90
Clerks, Receptionists/Information	13.30	Nursing Assistants	13.00
Clerks, Shipping/Receiving	16.40	Packers and Packagers, Hand	11.20
Computer Programmers	31.20	Physical Therapists	42.10
Computer Systems Analysts	39.40	Postal Service Mail Carriers	24.20
Computer User Support Specialists	22.80	Real Estate Brokers	n/a
Cooks, Restaurant	12.70	Retail Salespersons	15.20
Dentists	79.10	Sales Reps., Exc. Tech./Scientific	32.30
Electrical Engineers	41.50	Sales Reps., Tech./Scientific	40.00
Electricians	24.90	Secretaries, Exc. Legal/Med./Exec.	17.70
Financial Managers	66.80	Security Guards	15.00
First-Line Supervisors/Managers, Sales	18.80	Surgeons	130.60
Food Preparation Workers	11.30	Teacher Assistants*	13.30
General and Operations Managers	58.10	Teachers, Elementary School*	28.10
Hairdressers/Cosmetologists	13.90	Teachers, Secondary School*	31.00
Internists, General	100.20	Telemarketers	11.30
Janitors and Cleaners	12.80	Truck Drivers, Heavy/Tractor-Trailer	20.90
Landscaping/Groundskeeping Workers	13.70	Truck Drivers, Light/Delivery Svcs.	17.00
Lawyers	52.80	Waiters and Waitresses	11.40

Note: Wage data covers the Cleveland-Elyria, OH Metropolitan Statistical Area—see Appendix B for areas included; (*) Hourly wages for elementary/secondary school teachers and teacher assistants were calculated by the editors from annual wage data based on a 40 hour work week; n/a not available.
Source: Bureau of Labor Statistics, Metro Area Occupational Employment & Wage Estimates, May 2017

Employment by Occupation

Occupation Classification	City (%)	MSA[1] (%)	U.S. (%)
Management, Business, Science, and Arts	41.6	37.9	37.0
Natural Resources, Construction, and Maintenance	6.5	6.5	8.9
Production, Transportation, and Material Moving	11.5	13.4	12.2
Sales and Office	26.3	24.5	23.8
Service	14.1	17.6	18.1

Note: Figures cover employed civilians 16 years of age and older; (1) Figures cover the Cleveland-Elyria, OH Metropolitan Statistical Area—see Appendix B for areas included
Source: U.S. Census Bureau, 2012-2016 American Community Survey 5-Year Estimates

Employment by Industry

Sector	MSA[1] Number of Employees	MSA[1] Percent of Total	U.S. Percent of Total
Construction, Mining, and Logging	34,200	3.2	5.2
Education and Health Services	202,200	19.1	15.9
Financial Activities	67,300	6.3	5.7
Government	137,200	12.9	15.3
Information	14,000	1.3	1.9
Leisure and Hospitality	103,000	9.7	10.7
Manufacturing	123,800	11.7	8.5
Other Services	39,300	3.7	3.9
Professional and Business Services	151,100	14.3	14.0
Retail Trade	102,200	9.6	11.0
Transportation, Warehousing, and Utilities	32,800	3.1	4.1
Wholesale Trade	53,000	5.0	4.0

Note: Figures are non-farm employment as of December 2017. Figures are not seasonally adjusted and include workers 16 years of age and older; (1) Figures cover the Cleveland-Elyria, OH Metropolitan Statistical Area—see Appendix B for areas included
Source: Bureau of Labor Statistics, Current Employment Statistics, Employment, Hours, and Earnings

Occupations with Greatest Projected Employment Growth: 2017 – 2019

Occupation[1]	2017 Employment	2019 Projected Employment	Numeric Employment Change	Percent Employment Change
Combined Food Preparation and Serving Workers, Including Fast Food	160,970	170,100	9,130	5.7
Waiters and Waitresses	95,660	99,920	4,260	4.5
Home Health Aides	67,650	71,430	3,780	5.6
Registered Nurses	129,370	132,510	3,140	2.4
Heavy and Tractor-Trailer Truck Drivers	74,290	77,290	3,000	4.0
Laborers and Freight, Stock, and Material Movers, Hand	108,760	111,710	2,950	2.7
Personal Care Aides	30,510	32,800	2,290	7.5
Construction Laborers	40,630	42,780	2,150	5.3
Janitors and Cleaners, Except Maids and Housekeeping Cleaners	86,300	88,350	2,050	2.4
Software Developers, Applications	35,570	37,620	2,050	5.8

Note: Projections cover Ohio; (1) Sorted by numeric employment change
Source: www.projectionscentral.com, State Occupational Projections, 2017–2019 Short-Term Projections

Fastest Growing Occupations: 2017 – 2019

Occupation[1]	2017 Employment	2019 Projected Employment	Numeric Employment Change	Percent Employment Change
Rotary Drill Operators, Oil and Gas	230	280	50	21.7
Service Unit Operators, Oil, Gas, and Mining	710	850	140	19.7
Wellhead Pumpers	510	610	100	19.6
Roustabouts, Oil and Gas	720	860	140	19.4
Earth Drillers, Except Oil and Gas	460	510	50	10.9
Veterinary Technologists and Technicians	3,370	3,670	300	8.9
Veterinary Assistants and Laboratory Animal Caretakers	2,730	2,970	240	8.8
Veterinarians	3,330	3,610	280	8.4
Amusement and Recreation Attendants	8,950	9,650	700	7.8
Physician Assistants	3,210	3,460	250	7.8

Note: Projections cover Ohio; (1) Sorted by percent employment change and excludes occupations with numeric employment change less than 50
Source: www.projectionscentral.com, State Occupational Projections, 2017–2019 Short-Term Projections

TAXES

State Corporate Income Tax Rates

State	Tax Rate (%)	Income Brackets ($)	Num. of Brackets	Financial Institution Tax Rate (%)[a]	Federal Income Tax Ded.
Ohio	(t)	–	–	(t)	No

Note: Tax rates as of January 1, 2018; (a) Rates listed are the corporate income tax rate applied to financial institutions or excise taxes based on income. Some states have other taxes based upon the value of deposits or shares; (t) Ohio no longer levies a tax based on income (except for a particular subset of corporations), but instead imposes a Commercial Activity Tax (CAT) equal to $150 for gross receipts sitused to Ohio of between $150,000 and $1 million, plus 0.26% of gross receipts over $1 million. Banks continue to pay a franchise tax of 1.3% of net worth. For those few corporations for whom the franchise tax on net worth or net income still applies, a litter tax also applies.
Source: Federation of Tax Administrators, Range of State Corporate Income Tax Rates, January 1, 2018

State Individual Income Tax Rates

State	Tax Rate (%)	Income Brackets ($)	Num. of Brackets	Personal Exempt. ($)[1]		Fed. Inc. Tax Ded.
				Single	Dependents	
Ohio (a)	0.0 - 4.997	10,650 - 213,350	8	2,300 (t)	2,300 (t)	No

Note: Tax rates as of January 1, 2018; Local- and county-level taxes are not included; n/a not applicable; (1) Married joint filers generally receive double the single exemption; (a) 19 states have statutory provision for automatically adjusting to the rate of inflation the dollar values of the income tax brackets, standard deductions, and/or personal exemptions. Massachusetts, Michigan, and Nebraska index the personal exemption only. Oregon does not index the income brackets for $125,000 and over; (t) Ohio provides an additional tax credit of $20 per exemption. Exemption amounts reduced for higher income taxpayers.
Source: Federation of Tax Administrators, State Individual Income Tax Rates, January 1, 2018

Various State Sales and Excise Tax Rates

State	State Sales Tax (%)	Gasoline[1] (¢/gal.)	Cigarette[2] ($/pack)	Spirits[3] ($/gal.)	Wine[4] ($/gal.)	Beer[5] ($/gal.)	Recreational Marijuana (%)
Ohio	5.75	28.01	1.60	9.87 (g)	0.32 (l)	0.18 (q)	Not legal

Note: All tax rates as of January 1, 2018; (1) The American Petroleum Institute has developed a methodology for determining the average tax rate on a gallon of fuel. Rates may include any of the following: excise taxes, environmental fees, storage tank fees, other fees or taxes, general sales tax, and local taxes. In states where gasoline is subject to the general sales tax, or where the fuel tax is based on the average sale price, the average rate determined by API is sensitive to changes in the price of gasoline. States that fully or partially apply general sales taxes to gasoline: CA, CO, GA, IL, IN, MI, NY; (2) The federal excise tax of $1.0066 per pack and local taxes are not included; (3) Rates are those applicable to off-premise sales of 40% alcohol by volume (a.b.v.) distilled spirits in 750ml containers. Local excise taxes are excluded; (4) Rates are those applicable to off-premise sales of 11% a.b.v. non-carbonated wine in 750ml containers; (5) Rates are those applicable to off-premise sales of 4.7% a.b.v. beer in 12 ounce containers; (g) Control states, where the government controls all sales. Products can be subject to ad valorem mark-up as well as excise taxes; (l) Different rates also applicable to alcohol content, place of production, size of container, place purchased (on- or off-premise or on board airlines) or type of wine (carbonated, vermouth, etc.); (q) Different rates also applicable according to alcohol content, place of production, size of container, or place purchased (on- or off-premise or onboard airlines).
Source: Tax Foundation, 2018 Facts & Figures: How Does Your State Compare?

State Business Tax Climate Index Rankings

State	Overall Rank	Corporate Tax Rank	Individual Income Tax Rank	Sales Tax Rank	Unemployment Insurance Tax Rank	Property Tax Rank
Ohio	45	47	47	30	8	11

Note: The index is a measure of how each state's tax laws affect economic performance. The lower the rank, the more favorable a state's tax system is for business. States without a given tax are given a ranking of 1. The scores/rankings for the District of Columbia do not affect other states. The 2018 index represents the tax climate as of July 1, 2017.
Source: Tax Foundation, State Business Tax Climate Index 2018

TRANSPORTATION

Means of Transportation to Work

Area	Car/Truck/Van		Public Transportation			Bicycle	Walked	Other Means	Worked at Home
	Drove Alone	Car-pooled	Bus	Subway	Railroad				
City	87.1	6.8	0.8	0.1	0.0	0.2	0.5	0.9	3.6
MSA[1]	82.1	7.2	2.9	0.2	0.1	0.3	2.3	1.0	3.9
U.S.	76.4	9.3	2.6	1.9	0.6	0.6	2.8	1.3	4.6

Note: Figures are percentages and cover workers 16 years of age and older; (1) Figures cover the Cleveland-Elyria, OH Metropolitan Statistical Area—see Appendix B for areas included
Source: U.S. Census Bureau, 2012-2016 American Community Survey 5-Year Estimates

Travel Time to Work

Area	Less Than 10 Minutes	10 to 19 Minutes	20 to 29 Minutes	30 to 44 Minutes	45 to 59 Minutes	60 to 89 Minutes	90 Minutes or More
City	7.5	22.7	26.5	28.0	9.3	4.6	1.4
MSA[1]	11.2	28.1	25.0	23.6	7.4	3.4	1.4
U.S.	12.9	29.2	20.9	20.4	8.0	6.0	2.7

Note: Note: Figures are percentages and include workers 16 years old and over; (1) Figures cover the Cleveland-Elyria, OH Metropolitan Statistical Area—see Appendix B for areas included
Source: U.S. Census Bureau, 2012-2016 American Community Survey 5-Year Estimates

Freeway Travel Time Index

Area	1985	1990	1995	2000	2005	2010	2014
Urban Area Rank[1,2]	81	63	41	65	77	76	76
Urban Area Index[1]	1.04	1.08	1.14	1.14	1.14	1.14	1.15
Average Index[3]	1.09	1.11	1.14	1.17	1.20	1.19	1.20

Note: Freeway Travel Time Index—the ratio of travel time in the peak period to the travel time at free-flow conditions. For example, a value of 1.30 indicates a 20-minute free-flow trip takes 26 minutes in the peak (20 minutes x 1.30 = 26 minutes); (1) Covers the Cleveland OH urban area; (2) Rank is based on 101 urban areas (#1 = highest travel time index); (3) Average of 101 urban areas
Source: Texas Transportation Institute, 2015 Urban Mobility Scorecard, August 2015

Freeway Commuter Stress Index

Area	1985	1990	1995	2000	2005	2010	2014
Urban Area Rank[1,2]	81	59	46	63	76	74	71
Urban Area Index[1]	1.06	1.11	1.17	1.17	1.17	1.17	1.18
Average Index[3]	1.13	1.16	1.19	1.22	1.25	1.24	1.25

Note: The Freeway Commuter Stress Index is the same as the Freeway Travel Time Index (see table above) except that it includes only the travel in the peak directions during the peak periods; the TTI includes travel in all directions during the peak period. Thus, the CSI is more indicative of the work trip experienced by each commuter on a daily basis; (1) Covers the Cleveland OH urban area; (2) Rank is based on 101 urban areas (#1 = highest travel time index); (3) Average of 101 urban areas
Source: Texas Transportation Institute, 2015 Urban Mobility Scorecard, August 2015

Living Environment

COST OF LIVING

Cost of Living Index

Composite Index	Groceries	Housing	Utilities	Trans-portation	Health Care	Misc. Goods/ Services
101.1	111.2	88.3	104.7	102.5	101.2	106.0

Note: The Cost of Living Index measures regional differences in the cost of consumer goods and services, excluding taxes and non-consumer expenditures, for professional and managerial households in the top income quintile. It is based on more than 50,000 prices covering almost 60 different items for which prices are collected three times a year by chambers of commerce, economic development organizations or university applied economic centers in each participating urban area. The numbers shown should be read as a percentage above or below the national average of 100. For example, a value of 115.4 in the groceries column indicates that grocery prices are 15.4% higher than the national average. Small differences in the index numbers should not be interpreted as significant; Figures cover the Cleveland OH urban area.
Source: The Council for Community and Economic Research, ACCRA Cost of Living Index, 2017

Grocery Prices

Area[1]	T-Bone Steak ($/pound)	Frying Chicken ($/pound)	Whole Milk ($/half gal.)	Eggs ($/dozen)	Orange Juice ($/64 oz.)	Coffee ($/11.5 oz.)
City[2]	15.83	2.05	1.88	1.18	3.81	4.95
Avg.	11.29	1.40	2.02	1.47	3.55	4.37
Min.	7.71	0.93	1.04	0.70	2.86	3.24
Max.	15.83	2.39	4.03	3.92	6.29	8.16

*Note: (1) Values for the local area are compared with the average, minimum and maximum values for all 294 areas in the Cost of Living Index; (2) Figures cover the Cleveland OH urban area; **T-Bone Steak** (price per pound); **Frying Chicken** (price per pound, whole fryer); **Whole Milk** (half gallon carton); **Eggs** (price per dozen, Grade A, large); **Orange Juice** (64 oz. Tropicana or Florida Natural); **Coffee** (11.5 oz. can, vacuum-packed, Maxwell House, Hills Bros, or Folgers).*
Source: The Council for Community and Economic Research, ACCRA Cost of Living Index, 2017

Housing and Utility Costs

Area[1]	New Home Price ($)	Apartment Rent ($/month)	All Electric ($/month)	Part Electric ($/month)	Other Energy ($/month)	Telephone ($/month)
City[2]	281,845	1,041	-	87.85	69.95	33.53
Avg.	335,956	1,047	175.01	97.34	67.93	28.71
Min.	187,788	491	109.48	49.33	35.44	12.39
Max.	1,739,087	4,559	432.62	227.09	353.33	44.61

*Note: (1) Values for the local area are compared with the average, minimum and maximum values for all 294 areas in the Cost of Living Index; (2) Figures cover the Cleveland OH urban area; **New Home Price** (2,400 sf living area, 8,000 sf lot, in urban area with full utilities); **Apartment Rent** (950 sf 2 bedroom/1.5 or 2 bath, unfurnished, excluding all utilities except water); **All Electric** (average monthly cost for an all-electric home); **Part Electric** (average monthly cost for a part-electric home); **Other Energy** (average monthly cost for natural gas, fuel oil, coal, wood, and any other forms of energy except electricity); **Telephone** (price includes basic monthly rate for a private residential line plus additional local usage charges incurred by a family of four).*
Source: The Council for Community and Economic Research, ACCRA Cost of Living Index, 2017

Health Care, Transportation, and Other Costs

Area[1]	Doctor ($/visit)	Dentist ($/visit)	Optometrist ($/visit)	Gasoline ($/gallon)	Beauty Salon ($/visit)	Men's Shirt ($)
City[2]	110.20	90.67	80.26	2.24	36.88	33.63
Avg.	108.00	92.54	101.93	2.25	37.58	30.92
Min.	30.39	60.00	49.75	1.82	16.11	11.20
Max.	193.50	161.94	229.28	3.16	77.35	59.13

*Note: (1) Values for the local area are compared with the average, minimum and maximum values for all 294 areas in the Cost of Living Index; (2) Figures cover the Cleveland OH urban area; **Doctor** (general practitioners routine exam of an established patient); **Dentist** (adult teeth cleaning and periodic oral examination); **Optometrist** (full vision eye exam for established adult patient); **Gasoline** (one gallon regular unleaded, national brand, including all taxes, cash price at self-service pump if available); **Beauty Salon** (woman's shampoo, trim, and blow-dry); **Men's Shirt** (cotton/polyester dress shirt, pinpoint weave, long sleeves).*
Source: The Council for Community and Economic Research, ACCRA Cost of Living Index, 2017

HOUSING

House Price Index (HPI)

Area	National Ranking[2]	Quarterly Change (%)	One-Year Change (%)	Five-Year Change (%)
MSA[1]	177	-0.82	4.38	18.06
U.S.[3]	—	1.61	6.68	34.71

Note: The HPI is a weighted repeat sales index. It measures average price changes in repeat sales or refinancings on the same properties. This information is obtained by reviewing repeat mortgage transactions on single-family properties whose mortgages have been purchased or securitized by Fannie Mae or Freddie Mac in January 1975; (1) Figures cover the Cleveland-Elyria, OH Metropolitan Statistical Area—see Appendix B for areas included; (2) Rankings are based on annual percentage change for all metro areas containing at least 15,000 transactions over the last 10 years and ranges from 1 to 253; (3) figures based on a weighted average of Census Division estimates using a seasonally adjusted, purchase-only index; all figures are for the period ending December 31, 2017
Source: Federal Housing Finance Agency, House Price Index, February 28, 2018

Median Single-Family Home Prices

Area	2015	2016	2017p	Percent Change 2016 to 2017
MSA[1]	125.1	132.2	140.4	6.2
U.S. Average	223.9	235.5	248.8	5.6

Note: Figures are median sales prices of existing single-family homes in thousands of dollars; (p) preliminary; (1) Figures cover the Cleveland-Elyria, OH Metropolitan Statistical Area—see Appendix B for areas included
Source: National Association of Realtors, Median Sales Price of Existing Single-Family Homes for Metropolitan Areas, 4th Quarter 2017

Qualifying Income Based on Median Sales Price of Existing Single-Family Homes

Area	With 5% Down ($)	With 10% Down ($)	With 20% Down ($)
MSA[1]	31,494	29,836	26,521
U.S. Average	55,585	52,659	46,808

Note: Figures are preliminary; Qualifying income is based on a mortgage rate of 4.17%. Monthly principal and interest payment is limited to 25% of income; (1) Figures cover the Cleveland-Elyria, OH Metropolitan Statistical Area—see Appendix B for areas included
Source: National Association of Realtors, Qualifying Income Based on Median Sales Price of Existing Single-Family Homes for Metropolitan Areas, 4th Quarter 2017

Median Apartment Condo-Coop Home Prices

Area	2015	2016	2017p	Percent Change 2016 to 2017
MSA[1]	n/a	n/a	n/a	n/a
U.S. Average	210.7	220.7	234.3	6.2

Note: Figures are median sales prices of existing apartment condo-coop homes in thousands of dollars; (p) preliminary; n/a not available; (1) Figures cover the Cleveland-Elyria, OH Metropolitan Statistical Area—see Appendix B for areas included
Source: National Association of Realtors, Median Sales Price of Existing Apartment Condo-Coop Homes for Metropolitan Areas, 4th Quarter 2017

Home Value Distribution

Area	Under $50,000	$50,000 -$99,999	$100,000 -$149,999	$150,000 -$199,999	$200,000 -$299,999	$300,000 -$499,999	$500,000 -$999,999	$1,000,000 or more
City	5.0	10.0	28.7	26.4	26.9	2.6	0.1	0.3
MSA[1]	8.6	22.5	23.1	17.8	16.7	8.5	2.3	0.6
U.S.	8.8	14.8	15.3	14.9	18.4	16.4	9.0	2.5

Note: Figures are percentages and cover owner-occupied housing units; (1) Figures cover the Cleveland-Elyria, OH Metropolitan Statistical Area—see Appendix B for areas included
Source: U.S. Census Bureau, 2012-2016 American Community Survey 5-Year Estimates

Homeownership Rate

Area	2009 (%)	2010 (%)	2011 (%)	2012 (%)	2013 (%)	2014 (%)	2015 (%)	2016 (%)	2017 (%)
MSA[1]	70.9	70.7	69.8	64.2	65.8	69.2	68.4	64.8	66.6
U.S.	67.4	66.9	66.1	65.4	65.1	64.5	63.7	63.4	63.9

Note: (1) Figures cover the Cleveland-Elyria, OH Metropolitan Statistical Area—see Appendix B for areas included
Source: U.S. Census Bureau, Housing Vacancies and Homeownership Annual Statistics: 2009-2017

Year Housing Structure Built

Area	2010 or Later	2000 -2009	1990 -1999	1980 -1989	1970 -1979	1960 -1969	1950 -1959	1940 -1949	Before 1940	Median Year
City	6.5	30.1	10.9	5.7	20.6	10.8	8.4	2.4	4.6	1986
MSA[1]	1.0	7.4	8.6	6.6	12.5	13.3	18.6	8.0	24.1	1960
U.S.	2.3	14.7	14.0	13.7	15.6	10.9	10.6	5.2	13.0	1977

Note: Figures are percentages except for Median Year; Note: (1) Figures cover the Cleveland-Elyria, OH Metropolitan Statistical Area—see Appendix B for areas included
Source: U.S. Census Bureau, 2012-2016 American Community Survey 5-Year Estimates

Gross Monthly Rent

Area	Under $500	$500 -$999	$1,000 -$1,499	$1,500 -$1,999	$2,000 -$2,499	$2,500 -$2,999	$3,000 and up	Median ($)
City	4.0	40.7	40.2	9.8	1.0	0.0	4.4	1,071
MSA[1]	15.7	61.3	18.7	2.8	0.8	0.3	0.4	758
U.S.	11.3	43.3	27.7	10.7	4.0	1.6	1.5	949

Note: Figures are percentages except for Median; Gross rent is the contract rent plus the estimated average monthly cost of utilities (electricity, gas, and water and sewer) and fuels (oil, coal, kerosene, wood, etc.) if these are paid by the renter (or paid for the renter by someone else); (1) Figures cover the Cleveland-Elyria, OH Metropolitan Statistical Area—see Appendix B for areas included
Source: U.S. Census Bureau, 2012-2016 American Community Survey 5-Year Estimates

HEALTH

Health Risk Factors

Category	MSA[1] (%)	U.S. (%)
Adults aged 18–64 who have any kind of health care coverage	90.9	87.7
Adults who reported being in good or excellent health	84.3	83.6
Adults who are current smokers	21.9	17.1
Adults who currently use E-cigarettes	5.4	4.7
Adults who currently use chewing tobacco, snuff, or snus	3.0	4.0
Adults who are heavy drinkers[2]	4.3	6.5
Adults who are binge drinkers[3]	17.7	16.9
Adults who are overweight (BMI 25.0 - 29.9)	34.3	35.3
Adults who are obese (BMI 30.0 - 99.8)	29.8	29.9
Adults who participated in any physical activities in the past month	78.2	76.9
Adults who always or nearly always wears a seat belt	91.7	94.3

Note: (1) Figures cover the Cleveland-Elyria, OH Metropolitan Statistical Area—see Appendix B for areas included; (2) Heavy drinkers are classified as adult men having more than 14 drinks per week and adult women having more than 7 drinks per week; (3) Binge drinkers are classified as males having five or more drinks on one occasion or females having four or more drinks on one occasion
Source: Centers for Disease Control and Prevention, Behaviorial Risk Factor Surveillance System, SMART: Selected Metropolitan Area Risk Trends, 2016

Health Screening Rates

Category	MSA[1] (%)	U.S. (%)
Adults 50-75 who have had a blood stool test within the past year	9.6	8.0
Adults 50-75 who have had a colonoscopy in the past 10 years	64.1	63.5
Adults aged 65+ who have had flu shot within the past year	57.9	58.6
Adults aged 65+ who have ever had a pneumonia vaccination	76.1	73.4
Adults who have ever been tested for HIV	37.0	35.6
Women aged 21-65 who have had a pap test in the past three years	81.3	79.8
Men aged 40+ who have had a PSA test within the past two years	35.6	39.5
Women aged 40+ who have had a mammogram within the past two years	75.9	72.5

Note: n/a not available; (1) Figures cover the Cleveland-Elyria, OH Metropolitan Statistical Area—see Appendix B for areas included; Source: Centers for Disease Control and Prevention, Behaviorial Risk Factor Surveillance System, SMART: Selected Metropolitan Area Risk Trends, 2016

Chronic Health Conditions

Category	MSA[1] (%)	U.S. (%)
Adults who have ever been told they had a heart attack	4.1	4.4
Adults who have ever been told they have angina or coronary heart disease	4.9	4.1
Adults who have ever been told they had a stroke	2.9	3.1
Adults who have been told they currently have asthma	7.8	9.3
Adults who have ever been told they have arthritis	29.4	25.8
Adults who have ever been told they have diabetes[2]	9.1	10.5
Adults who have ever been told they had skin cancer	5.4	5.9
Adults who have ever been told they had any other types of cancer	6.7	6.7
Adults who have ever been told they have COPD	7.3	6.3
Adults who have ever been told they have kidney disease	4.2	2.8
Adults who have ever been told they have a form of depression	14.4	17.4

Note: (1) Figures cover the Cleveland-Elyria, OH Metropolitan Statistical Area—see Appendix B for areas included; (2) Figures do not include pregnancy-related, borderline, or pre-diabetes
Source: Centers for Disease Control and Prevention, Behaviorial Risk Factor Surveillance System, SMART: Selected Metropolitan Area Risk Trends, 2016

Mortality Rates for the Top 10 Causes of Death in the U.S.

ICD-10[a] Sub-Chapter	ICD-10[a] Code	Age-Adjusted Mortality Rate[1] per 100,000 population	
		County[2]	U.S.
Malignant neoplasms	C00-C97	171.3	158.5
Ischaemic heart diseases	I20-I25	106.1	96.8
Other forms of heart disease	I30-I51	47.4	52.4
Chronic lower respiratory diseases	J40-J47	56.2	40.9
Cerebrovascular diseases	I60-I69	33.3	37.2
Organic, including symptomatic, mental disorders	F01-F09	36.4	33.3
Other degenerative diseases of the nervous system	G30-G31	38.1	32.1
Other external causes of accidental injury	W00-X59	51.7	31.2
Diabetes mellitus	E10-E14	20.7	21.1
Hypertensive diseases	I10-I15	17.4	20.8

Note: (a) ICD-10 = International Classification of Diseases 10th Revision; (1) Mortality rates are a three year average covering 2014-2016; (2) Figures cover Lorain County.
Source: Centers for Disease Control and Prevention, National Center for Health Statistics. Underlying Cause of Death 1999-2016 on CDC WONDER Online Database, released December 2017

Mortality Rates for Selected Causes of Death

ICD-10[a] Sub-Chapter	ICD-10[a] Code	Age-Adjusted Mortality Rate[1] per 100,000 population	
		County[2]	U.S.
Assault	X85-Y09	4.5	5.6
Diseases of the liver	K70-K76	14.9	14.0
Human immunodeficiency virus (HIV) disease	B20-B24	Suppressed	1.9
Influenza and pneumonia	J09-J18	15.1	14.6
Intentional self-harm	X60-X84	13.1	13.2
Malnutrition	E40-E46	Unreliable	1.3
Obesity and other hyperalimentation	E65-E68	2.0	2.1
Renal failure	N17-N19	12.3	13.0
Transport accidents	V01-V99	11.1	12.0
Viral hepatitis	B15-B19	Unreliable	1.9

Note: (a) ICD-10 = International Classification of Diseases 10th Revision; (1) Mortality rates are a three year average covering 2014-2016; (2) Figures cover Lorain County; Data are Suppressed when the data meet the criteria for confidentiality constraints; Mortality rates are flagged as Unreliable when the rate would be calculated with a numerator of 20 or less.
Source: Centers for Disease Control and Prevention, National Center for Health Statistics. Underlying Cause of Death 1999-2016 on CDC WONDER Online Database, released December 2017

Health Insurance Coverage

Area	With Health Insurance	With Private Health Insurance	With Public Health Insurance	Without Health Insurance	Population Under Age 18 Without Health Insurance
City	95.5	83.1	27.6	4.5	1.6
MSA[1]	92.2	69.5	35.6	7.8	3.8
U.S.	88.3	66.7	33.0	11.7	5.9

Note: Figures are percentages that cover the civilian noninstitutionalized population; (1) Figures cover the Cleveland-Elyria, OH Metropolitan Statistical Area—see Appendix B for areas included
Source: U.S. Census Bureau, 2012-2016 American Community Survey 5-Year Estimates

Number of Medical Professionals

Area	MDs[3]	DOs[3,4]	Dentists	Podiatrists	Chiropractors	Optometrists
County[1] (number)	427	79	143	24	50	52
County[1] (rate[2])	139.9	25.9	46.6	7.8	16.3	17.0
U.S. (rate[2])	276.5	22.3	67.3	6.0	26.7	15.9

Note: Data as of 2016 unless noted; (1) Data covers Lorain County; (2) Rate per 100,000 population; (3) Data as of 2015 and includes all active, non-federal physicians; (4) Doctor of Osteopathic Medicine
Source: U.S. Department of Health and Human Services, Health Resources and Services Administration, Bureau of Health Professions, Area Resource File (ARF) 2016-2017

Best Hospitals

According to *U.S. News,* the Cleveland-Elyria, OH metro area is home to four of the best hospitals in the U.S.: **Cleveland Clinic** (Honor Roll/14 adult specialties and 9 pediatric specialties); **Cleveland Clinic Hillcrest Hospital** (1 adult specialty); **Fairview Hospital** (3 adult specialties); **University Hospitals Cleveland Medical Center** (8 adult specialties and 9 pediatric specialties). The hospitals listed were nationally ranked in at least one of 16 specialties. Only 152 hospitals nationwide were nationally ranked in one or more specialties. Twenty hospitals in the U.S. made the Honor Roll. The Best Hospitals Honor Roll was revamped last year to take both the national rankings and the procedure and condition ratings into account. Hospitals received points if they were nationally ranked in one of the 16 specialties—the higher they ranked, the more points they got—and how many ratings of "high performing" they earned in the nine procedures and conditions. *U.S. News Online, "America's Best Hospitals 2017-18"*

According to *U.S. News,* the Cleveland-Elyria, OH metro area is home to two of the best children's hospitals in the U.S.: **Cleveland Clinic Children's Hospital** (9 pediatric specialties); **Rainbow Babies and Children's Hospital** (9 pediatric specialties). The hospitals listed were highly ranked in at least one of 10 pediatric specialties. Eighty-two children's hospitals in the U.S. were nationally ranked in at least one specialty. Hospitals received points for being ranked in a specialty, and the 10 hospitals with the most points across the 10 specialties make up the Honor Roll. *U.S. News Online, "America's Best Children's Hospitals 2017-18"*

EDUCATION

Public School District Statistics

District Name	Schls	Pupils	Pupil/ Teacher Ratio	Minority Pupils[1] (%)	Free Lunch Eligible[2] (%)	IEP[3] (%)
North Ridgeville City	7	4,190	20.4	9.8	18.1	12.2

Note: Table includes school districts with 100 or more students; (1) Percentage of students that are not non-Hispanic white; (2) Percentage of students that are eligible for the free lunch program; (3) Percentage of students that have an Individualized Education Program.
Source: U.S. Department of Education, National Center for Education Statistics, Common Core of Data, Local Education Agency (School District) Universe Survey: School Year 2015-2016; U.S. Department of Education, National Center for Education Statistics, Common Core of Data, Public Elementary/Secondary School Universe Survey: School Year 2015-2016

Highest Level of Education

Area	Less than H.S.	H.S. Diploma	Some College, No Deg.	Associate Degree	Bachelor's Degree	Master's Degree	Prof. School Degree	Doctorate Degree
City	7.7	28.9	21.5	9.4	21.1	8.9	1.6	1.0
MSA[1]	10.4	29.7	22.0	8.1	18.1	8.2	2.3	1.2
U.S.	13.0	27.5	21.0	8.2	18.8	8.2	2.0	1.3

Note: Figures cover persons age 25 and over; (1) Figures cover the Cleveland-Elyria, OH Metropolitan Statistical Area—see Appendix B for areas included
Source: U.S. Census Bureau, 2012-2016 American Community Survey 5-Year Estimates

Educational Attainment by Race

Area	High School Graduate or Higher (%)					Bachelor's Degree or Higher (%)				
	Total	White	Black	Asian	Hisp.[2]	Total	White	Black	Asian	Hisp.[2]
City	92.3	93.4	89.1	72.2	84.6	32.6	32.2	30.4	45.7	26.6
MSA[1]	89.6	91.5	82.8	88.5	73.3	29.7	32.6	14.6	63.4	15.0
U.S.	87.0	88.9	84.3	86.3	65.7	30.3	31.6	20.0	52.1	14.7

Note: Figures shown cover persons 25 years old and over; (1) Figures cover the Cleveland-Elyria, OH Metropolitan Statistical Area—see Appendix B for areas included; (2) People of Hispanic origin can be of any race
Source: U.S. Census Bureau, 2012-2016 American Community Survey 5-Year Estimates

School Enrollment by Grade and Control

Area	Preschool (%)		Kindergarten (%)		Grades 1 - 4 (%)		Grades 5 - 8 (%)		Grades 9 - 12 (%)	
	Public	Private	Public	Private	Public	Private	Public	Private	Public	Private
City	36.3	63.7	70.4	29.6	83.0	17.0	82.5	17.5	84.5	15.5
MSA[1]	51.4	48.6	80.5	19.5	81.2	18.8	81.5	18.5	84.0	16.0
U.S.	58.4	41.6	87.7	12.3	89.8	10.2	89.7	10.3	90.4	9.6

Note: Figures shown cover persons 3 years old and over; (1) Figures cover the Cleveland-Elyria, OH Metropolitan Statistical Area—see Appendix B for areas included
Source: U.S. Census Bureau, 2012-2016 American Community Survey 5-Year Estimates

Average Salaries of Public School Classroom Teachers

Area	2015		2016		Change from 2015 to 2016	
	Dollars	Rank[1]	Dollars	Rank[1]	Percent	Rank[2]
Ohio	54,672	21	56,441	21	3.2	4
U.S. Average	57,611	–	58,353	–	1.3	–

Note: (1) Rank ranges from 1 to 51 where 1 indicates highest salary; (2) Rank ranges from 1 to 51 where 1 indicates highest percent change.
Source: National Education Association, Rankings & Estimates: Rankings of the States 2016 and Estimates of School Statistics 2017

Higher Education

Four-Year Colleges			Two-Year Colleges			Medical Schools[1]	Law Schools[2]	Voc/ Tech[3]
Public	Private Non-profit	Private For-profit	Public	Private Non-profit	Private For-profit			
0	0	0	0	0	0	0	0	0

Note: Figures cover institutions located within the city limits and include main campuses only; (1) includes schools accredited by the Liaison Committee on Medical Education and the American Osteopathic Association's Commission on Osteopathic College Accreditation; (2) includes ABA-accredited schools, schools with provisional ABA accreditation, and state accredited schools; (3) includes all schools with programs that are less than 2 years.
Source: National Center for Education Statistics, Integrated Postsecondary Education System (IPEDS), 2016-17; Wikipedia, List of Medical Schools in the United States, accessed April 2, 2018; Wikipedia, List of Law Schools in the United States, accessed April 2, 2018

According to *U.S. News & World Report,* the Cleveland-Elyria, OH metro area is home to one of the best national universities in the U.S.: **Case Western Reserve University** (#37 tie). The indicators used to capture academic quality fall into a number of categories: assessment by administrators at peer institutions; retention of students; faculty resources; student selectivity; financial resources; alumni giving; high school counselor ratings of colleges; and graduation rate. *U.S. News & World Report, "America's Best Colleges 2018"*

According to *U.S. News & World Report,* the Cleveland-Elyria, OH metro area is home to one of the best liberal arts colleges in the U.S.: **Oberlin College** (#26 tie). The indicators used to capture academic quality fall into a number of categories: assessment by administrators at peer institutions; retention of students; faculty resources; student selectivity; financial resources; alumni giving; high school counselor ratings of colleges; and graduation rate. *U.S. News & World Report, "America's Best Colleges 2018"*

According to *U.S. News & World Report,* the Cleveland-Elyria, OH metro area is home to one of the top 100 law schools in the U.S.: **Case Western Reserve University** (#65 tie). The rankings are based on a weighted average of 12 measures of quality: peer assessment score; assessment score by lawyers/judges; median LSAT scores; median undergrad GPA; acceptance rate; employment rates for graduates; placement success; bar passage rate; faculty resources; expenditures per student; student/faculty ratio; and library resources. *U.S. News & World Report, "America's Best Graduate Schools, Law, 2019"*

According to *U.S. News & World Report,* the Cleveland-Elyria, OH metro area is home to one of the top 75 medical schools for research in the U.S.: **Case Western Reserve University** (#25). The rankings are based on a weighted average of 11 measures of quality: quality assessment; peer assessment score; assessment score by residency directors; research activity; total research activity; average research activity per faculty member; student selectivity; median MCAT total score; median undergraduate GPA; acceptance rate; and faculty resources. *U.S. News & World Report, "America's Best Graduate Schools, Medical, 2019"*

According to *U.S. News & World Report,* the Cleveland-Elyria, OH metro area is home to one of the top 75 business schools in the U.S.: **Case Western Reserve University (Weatherhead)** (#55 tie). The rankings are based on a weighted average of the following nine measures: quality assessment; peer assessment; recruiter assessment; placement success; mean starting salary and bonus; student selectivity; mean GMAT and GRE scores; mean undergraduate GPA; and acceptance rate. *U.S. News & World Report, "America's Best Graduate Schools, Business, 2019"*

PRESIDENTIAL ELECTION

2016 Presidential Election Results

Area	Clinton	Trump	Johnson	Stein	Other
Lorain County	47.6	47.5	3.2	0.9	0.7
U.S.	48.0	45.9	3.3	1.1	1.7

Note: Results are percentages and may not add to 100% due to rounding
Source: Dave Leip's Atlas of U.S. Presidential Elections

EMPLOYERS

Major Employers

Company Name	Industry
Agilysys	Cloud-based property management
Aleris International	Aluminum producer
American Greetings	Greeting card company
Applied Ind. Technologies	Industrial distributor
Cliffs Natural Resources	Mining
Eaton Corporation	Power management company
Forest City Enterprises	Real estate management
Invacare	Medical equipment manufacturer
Jones Day	Law firm
KeyCorp	Investment banking
Lincoln Electric Holdings	Welding manufacturer
Lubrizol	Specialty chemicals producer
Medical Mutual of Ohio	Health insurance
Nacco Industries	Mining
NASA Glenn Research Center	Government
Parker Hannifin	Motion and control technologies
PNC Bank	Banking
PolyOne	Plastics material
Port of Cleveland	Shipping port
Progressive	Insurance
RPM International	Specialty coatings
Sherwin-Williams Company	Stains, supplies and coatings

Note: Companies shown are located within the Cleveland-Elyria, OH Metropolitan Statistical Area.
Source: Hoovers.com; Wikipedia

PUBLIC SAFETY

Crime Rate

Area	All Crimes	Violent Crimes: Murder	Violent Crimes: Rape[3]	Violent Crimes: Robbery	Violent Crimes: Aggrav. Assault	Property Crimes: Burglary	Property Crimes: Larceny -Theft	Property Crimes: Motor Vehicle Theft
City	619.4	3.0	12.1	9.1	12.1	111.8	465.3	6.0
Metro[1]	2,829.3	9.2	43.8	195.1	197.4	565.2	1,535.3	283.3
U.S.	2,847.8	5.3	40.4	102.8	248.5	468.9	1,745.0	236.9

Note: Figures are crimes per 100,000 population; (1) Figures cover the Cleveland-Elyria, OH Metropolitan Statistical Area—see Appendix B for areas included; (3) The city and U.S. figures shown were reported using the revised Uniform Crime Reporting (UCR) definition of rape. The metro area figures shown are an aggregate total of the data submitted using both the revised and legacy UCR definitions.
Source: FBI Uniform Crime Reports, 2016

Hate Crimes

Area	Number of Quarters Reported	Race/Ethnicity/ Ancestry	Religion	Sexual Orientation	Disability	Gender	Gender Identity
		Number of Incidents per Bias Motivation					
City	n/a	n/a	n/a	n/a	n/a	n/a	n/a
U.S.	4	3,489	1,273	1,076	70	31	124

Note: n/a not available.
Source: Federal Bureau of Investigation, Hate Crime Statistics 2016

Identity Theft Consumer Reports

Area	Reports	Reports per 100,000 Population	Rank[2]
MSA[1]	2,158	105	84
U.S.	371,061	114	-

Note: (1) Figures cover the Cleveland-Elyria, OH Metropolitan Statistical Area—see Appendix B for areas included; (2) Rank ranges from 1 to 389 where 1 indicates greatest number of identity theft reports per 100,000 population
Source: Federal Trade Commission, Consumer Sentinel Network Data Book for January–December 2017

Fraud and Other Consumer Reports

Area	Reports	Reports per 100,000 Population	Rank[2]
MSA[1]	11,933	581	48
U.S.	2,304,550	708	-

Note: (1) Figures cover the Cleveland-Elyria, OH Metropolitan Statistical Area—see Appendix B for areas included; (2) Rank ranges from 1 to 389 where 1 indicates greatest number of fraud and other consumer reports per 100,000 population
Source: Federal Trade Commission, Consumer Sentinel Network Data Book for January–December 2017

SPORTS

Professional Sports Teams

Team Name	League	Year Established
Cleveland Browns	National Football League (NFL)	1946
Cleveland Cavaliers	National Basketball Association (NBA)	1970
Cleveland Indians	Major League Baseball (MLB)	1900

Note: Includes teams located in the Cleveland-Elyria, OH Metropolitan Statistical Area.
Source: Wikipedia, Major Professional Sports Teams of the United States and Canada, April 5, 2018

CLIMATE

Average and Extreme Temperatures

Temperature	Jan	Feb	Mar	Apr	May	Jun	Jul	Aug	Sep	Oct	Nov	Dec	Yr.
Extreme High (°F)	73	69	82	88	92	104	100	102	101	89	82	77	104
Average High (°F)	33	36	46	58	69	79	83	81	74	63	50	38	59
Average Temp. (°F)	26	28	37	49	59	68	73	71	64	54	43	31	50
Average Low (°F)	19	20	28	38	48	58	62	61	54	44	35	24	41
Extreme Low (°F)	-19	-15	-5	10	25	31	41	38	34	19	3	-15	-19

Note: Figures cover the years 1948-1990
Source: National Climatic Data Center, International Station Meteorological Climate Summary, 9/96

Average Precipitation/Snowfall/Humidity

Precip./Humidity	Jan	Feb	Mar	Apr	May	Jun	Jul	Aug	Sep	Oct	Nov	Dec	Yr.
Avg. Precip. (in.)	2.4	2.3	3.1	3.4	3.5	3.5	3.5	3.4	3.2	2.6	3.2	2.9	37.1
Avg. Snowfall (in.)	13	12	10	2	Tr	0	0	0	0	1	5	12	55
Avg. Rel. Hum. 7am (%)	79	79	78	76	77	78	81	85	84	81	78	78	79
Avg. Rel. Hum. 4pm (%)	70	67	62	56	54	55	55	58	58	58	65	70	61

Note: Figures cover the years 1948-1990; Tr = Trace amounts (<0.05 in. of rain; <0.5 in. of snow)
Source: National Climatic Data Center, International Station Meteorological Climate Summary, 9/96

Weather Conditions

Temperature			Daytime Sky			Precipitation		
5°F & below	32°F & below	90°F & above	Clear	Partly cloudy	Cloudy	0.01 inch or more precip.	0.1 inch or more snow/ice	Thunder-storms
11	123	12	63	127	175	157	48	34

Note: Figures are average number of days per year and cover the years 1948-1990
Source: National Climatic Data Center, International Station Meteorological Climate Summary, 9/96

HAZARDOUS WASTE

Superfund Sites

The Cleveland-Elyria, OH metro area is home to one site on the EPA's Superfund National Priorities List: **Diamond Shamrock Corp. (Painesville Works)** (proposed). There are a total of 1,396 Superfund sites with a status of proposed or final on the list in the U.S. *U.S. Environmental Protection Agency, National Priorities List, April 4, 2018*

AIR & WATER QUALITY

Air Quality Trends: Ozone

	1990	1995	2000	2005	2010	2012	2013	2014	2015	2016
MSA[1]	0.085	0.092	0.076	0.083	0.077	0.087	0.068	0.069	0.071	0.072
U.S.	0.087	0.089	0.081	0.079	0.073	0.075	0.069	0.067	0.068	0.069

Note: (1) Data covers the Cleveland-Elyria, OH Metropolitan Statistical Area—see Appendix B for areas included. The values shown are the composite ozone concentration averages among trend sites based on the highest fourth daily maximum 8-hour concentration in parts per million. These trends are based on sites having an adequate record of monitoring data during the trend period. Data from exceptional events are included.
Source: U.S. Environmental Protection Agency, Air Quality Monitoring Information, "Air Quality Trends by City, 1990-2016"

Air Quality Index

Area	Percent of Days when Air Quality was...[2]					AQI Statistics[2]	
	Good	Moderate	Unhealthy for Sensitive Groups	Unhealthy	Very Unhealthy	Maximum	Median
MSA[1]	56.4	40.3	3.3	0.0	0.0	147	46

Note: (1) Data covers the Cleveland-Elyria, OH Metropolitan Statistical Area—see Appendix B for areas included; (2) Based on 365 days with AQI data in 2017. Air Quality Index (AQI) is an index for reporting daily air quality. EPA calculates the AQI for five major air pollutants regulated by the Clean Air Act: ground-level ozone, particle pollution (aka particulate matter), carbon monoxide, sulfur dioxide, and nitrogen dioxide. The AQI runs from 0 to 500. The higher the AQI value, the greater the level of air pollution and the greater the health concern. There are six AQI categories: "Good" AQI is between 0 and 50. Air quality is considered satisfactory; "Moderate" AQI is between 51 and 100. Air quality is acceptable; "Unhealthy for Sensitive Groups" When AQI values are between 101 and 150, members of sensitive groups may experience health effects; "Unhealthy" When AQI values are between 151 and 200 everyone may begin to experience health effects; "Very Unhealthy" AQI values between 201 and 300 trigger a health alert; "Hazardous" AQI values over 300 trigger warnings of emergency conditions (not shown).
Source: U.S. Environmental Protection Agency, Air Quality Index Report, 2017

Air Quality Index Pollutants

Area	Percent of Days when AQI Pollutant was...[2]					
	Carbon Monoxide	Nitrogen Dioxide	Ozone	Sulfur Dioxide	Particulate Matter 2.5	Particulate Matter 10
MSA[1]	0.3	1.9	46.8	2.5	47.4	1.1

Note: (1) Data covers the Cleveland-Elyria, OH Metropolitan Statistical Area—see Appendix B for areas included; (2) Based on 365 days with AQI data in 2017. The Air Quality Index (AQI) is an index for reporting daily air quality. EPA calculates the AQI for five major air pollutants regulated by the Clean Air Act: ground-level ozone, particle pollution (also known as particulate matter), carbon monoxide, sulfur dioxide, and nitrogen dioxide. The AQI runs from 0 to 500. The higher the AQI value, the greater the level of air pollution and the greater the health concern.
Source: U.S. Environmental Protection Agency, Air Quality Index Report, 2017

Maximum Air Pollutant Concentrations: Particulate Matter, Ozone, CO and Lead

	Particulate Matter 10 (ug/m^3)	Particulate Matter 2.5 Wtd AM (ug/m^3)	Particulate Matter 2.5 24-Hr (ug/m^3)	Ozone (ppm)	Carbon Monoxide (ppm)	Lead (ug/m^3)
MSA[1] Level	86	10.7	22	0.077	4	0.03
NAAQS[2]	150	15	35	0.075	9	0.15
Met NAAQS[2]	Yes	Yes	Yes	No	Yes	Yes

Note: (1) Data covers the Cleveland-Elyria, OH Metropolitan Statistical Area—see Appendix B for areas included; Data from exceptional events are included; (2) National Ambient Air Quality Standards; ppm = parts per million; ug/m^3 = micrograms per cubic meter; n/a not available.
Concentrations: Particulate Matter 10 (coarse particulate)—highest second maximum 24-hour concentration; Particulate Matter 2.5 Wtd AM (fine particulate)—highest weighted annual mean concentration; Particulate Matter 2.5 24-Hour (fine particulate)—highest 98th percentile 24-hour concentration; Ozone—highest fourth daily maximum 8-hour concentration; Carbon Monoxide—highest second maximum non-overlapping 8-hour concentration; Lead—maximum running 3-month average
Source: U.S. Environmental Protection Agency, Air Quality Monitoring Information, "Air Quality Statistics by City, 2016"

Maximum Air Pollutant Concentrations: Nitrogen Dioxide and Sulfur Dioxide

	Nitrogen Dioxide AM (ppb)	Nitrogen Dioxide 1-Hr (ppb)	Sulfur Dioxide AM (ppb)	Sulfur Dioxide 1-Hr (ppb)	Sulfur Dioxide 24-Hr (ppb)
MSA[1] Level	11	50	n/a	370	n/a
NAAQS[2]	53	100	30	75	140
Met NAAQS[2]	Yes	Yes	n/a	No	n/a

Note: (1) Data covers the Cleveland-Elyria, OH Metropolitan Statistical Area—see Appendix B for areas included; Data from exceptional events are included; (2) National Ambient Air Quality Standards; ppm = parts per million; ug/m^3 = micrograms per cubic meter; n/a not available.
Concentrations: Nitrogen Dioxide AM—highest arithmetic mean concentration; Nitrogen Dioxide 1-Hr—highest 98th percentile 1-hour daily maximum concentration; Sulfur Dioxide AM—highest annual mean concentration; Sulfur Dioxide 1-Hr—highest 99th percentile 1-hour daily maximum concentration; Sulfur Dioxide 24-Hr—highest second maximum 24-hour concentration
Source: U.S. Environmental Protection Agency, Air Quality Monitoring Information, "Air Quality Statistics by City, 2016"

Drinking Water

Water System Name	Pop. Served	Primary Water Source Type	Violations[1]	
			Health Based	Monitoring/ Reporting
North Ridgeville City PWS	29,465	Purchased Surface	0	0

Note: (1) Based on violation data from January 1, 2017 to December 31, 2017
Source: U.S. Environmental Protection Agency, Office of Ground Water and Drinking Water, Safe Drinking Water Information System (based on data extracted April 5, 2018)

Edmond, Oklahoma

Background

The city of Edmond lies in the central part of the state, 15 miles north of Oklahoma City. It has a city-council-manager form of government. There are four councilmen elected by the people, with the mayor acting as councilman-at-large; a city manager is appointed by the council.

Edmond is a rapidly growing, affluent city. Although Oklahoma's fastest-growing high-tech job base exists in Edmond, an agricultural spirit still permeates the city. Major employers include the University of Central Oklahoma, Edmond Public Schools, and OU Medical Center Edmond.

The Edmond site was originally explored by Washington Irving in 1832 and described in his publication, *A Tour on the Prairies*. In 1870, the U.S. Government issued a directive to survey the western portion of the Indian Territories. After establishing treaties with the Creek and Seminole Indian nations, and the assignment of other reservations within Indian Territory, it was discovered that a large area in the center of this region—of which Edmond was included—had been left unassigned. The region later became known as Oklahoma. In 1886, a route going through the state was surveyed for the Santa Fe Railroad. Several railroad workers were among the first to stake out claims during the Great Oklahoma Land Run of April 22, 1889, at 12:00 noon. At 12:05 p.m., a crew of surveyors began laying out the town of Edmond.

Two major universities, as well as the most honored public school system in Oklahoma, are located in Edmond. The state's first public college, the University of Central Oklahoma, is now the premier educational institution in the region, with many of the campus buildings dating back to the 1890s. The university offers undergraduate studies in business administration, education, liberal arts, mathematics and science, as well as eight master's degree programs.

Edmond's schools are innovative and comprehensive, with gifted programs and special education services. In each of the city's elementary schools, a media center is provided, along with instructional specialists in music, art, physical education, and gifted education. The high schools provide a wide array of subjects beyond the required curriculum, including fine arts, business and vocational education, foreign languages, computer technology, and professional internships.

OU Medical Center Edmond has been renovated and expanded to meet the needs of the area's growing population. Over 300 highly skilled physicians in more than 50 specialty areas, as well as comprehensive specialized services and facilities, ensure quality medical care for Edmond's residents within their own community.

The city is home to the famous Oak Tree National golf club, the host site of the 2014 U.S. Senior open. There are 10 golf courses in the area, but golf is only part of Edmond's recreational opportunities. Arcadia Lake offers fishing, skiing, camping, and 17 miles of hiking trails. Historic downtown Edmond features diverse shopping and the Fine Arts Institute sponsors and hosts art shows. Nearby Oklahoma City Zoo is one of the country's largest and best zoos, while Remington Park offers exciting thoroughbred horseracing.

The award-winning Cross Timbers Municipal Complex, the largest municipal project in Edmond's history, houses the town's Public Service Center, a fire station, fire department administrative and training offices, and an animal welfare facility.

The city of Edmond is making efforts to promote public art with murals, stained glass and steel sculptures. On a portion of Main Street, statuary lines nearly every corner. In 2015 the Dave McGary sculpture of Chief Touch the Clouds was relocated to Edmond from Houston's Astrodome. The 18 foot tall, 15 foot wide sculpture is located on Second Street at the entrance of the University of Central Oklahoma.

The climate of Edmond is affected mainly by winds from the continental Great Plains, though occasionally moist air comes up from the Gulf Coast. Pronounced changes in temperature, both daily and seasonally, are the rule. Winters are short and mild. Summers are hot, but the heat is mitigated by low humidity.

Rankings

General Rankings

- For its "Best Places to Live" rankings (formerly known as Best for Vets: Places to Live), *Military Times* evaluated 577 cities (79 large, 244 medium, 254 small) and compared the locations across three broad categories: veteran and military culture/services; economic indicators; and livability factors such as health, crime, traffic, and school quality. Edmond ranked #50 out of the top 50, in the small city category (populations of less than 75,000). Data points more specific to veterans and the military weighed more heavily than the rest. *rebootcamp.militarytimes.com, "Military Times Best Places to Live 2017," September 11, 2017*

Business/Finance Rankings

- The personal finance site NerdWallet analyzed 183 American metropolitan areas with populations over 250,000 and more than 15,000 businesses to rank where entrepreneurs find the most success. Criteria included area economy, annual income, housing cost, unemployment rate, and the success rate of area businesses. Oklahoma City* ranked #33. *www.nerdwallet.com, "Best Places to Start a Business," April 27, 2015*

- The editors of *Kiplinger's Personal Finance Magazine* named Oklahoma City* to their list of ten of the best metro areas for start-ups. The area ranked #1.Criteria: well-educated workforce; low living costs for self-employed people, as measured by the Council for Community and Economic Research; a strong existing community of small business; low unemployment; low business costs. *www.kiplinger.com, "10 Great Cities for Starting a Business," October 2014*

- USAA and Hiring Our Heroes worked with Sperlings's BestPlaces and the Institute for Veterans and Military Families at Syracuse University to rank major metropolitan areas where military-skills-related employment is strongest. Criteria for veterans *pursuing entrepreneurship* included veteran-owned businesses per capita; percentage of small businesses; colleges; certification/license transfers; airports nearby; and accessible health resources. Metro areas with a higher than national average crime or unemployment rate were excluded. At #9, the Oklahoma City* metro area made the top ten. *www.usaa.com, "2015 Best Places for Veterans"*

- USAA and Hiring Our Heroes worked with Sperlings's BestPlaces and the Institute for Veterans and Military Families at Syracuse University to rank major metropolitan areas where military-skills-related employment is strongest. Criteria for *mid-career* veterans included veteran wage growth; recent job growth; stability; and accessible health resources. Metro areas with a higher than national average crime or unemployment rate were excluded. At #1, the Oklahoma City* metro area made the top ten. *www.usaa.com, "2015 Best Places for Veterans"*

- Based on metro area social media reviews, the employment opinion group Glassdoor surveyed 50 of the largest U.S. metro areas and equally weighed cost of living, hiring opportunity, and job satisfaction to compose a list of "25 Best Cities for Jobs." Median pay and home value, in-demand jobs and number of current job openings was also factored in. The Oklahoma City* metro area was ranked #15 in overall job satisfaction. *www.glassdoor.com, "Best Cities for Jobs," September 12, 2017*

- In a survey of economic confidence in the nation's 50 largest metropolitan areas conducted January–December 2014, the Oklahoma City* metro area placed #48, according to Gallup's 2014 Economic Confidence Index. *Gallup, "San Jose and San Francisco Lead in Economic Confidence," March 19, 2015*

- Using data from the Council for Community and Economic Research's 2014 cost of living index, NerdWallet ranked the 100 most affordable cities in America. Median income was compared with cost of living to find truly affordable places. Edmond ranked #2. *NerdWallet.com, "America's Most Affordable Places," May 18, 2015*

- The Brookings Institution ranked the 100 largest metro areas in the U.S. based on income inequality. Oklahoma City* was ranked #47 (#1 = greatest ineqality). Criteria: the "95/20 ratio," a figure representing the income at which a household earns more than 95 percent of all other households, divided by the income at which a household earns more than only 20 percent of all other households. *Brookings Institution, "Household Income Inequality, 100 Largest U.S. Metro Areas, 2014-2016," February 5, 2018*

- The Oklahoma City* metro area was identified as one of the most affordable metropolitan areas in America by *Forbes*. The area ranked #4 out of 20 based on the National Association of Home Builders/Wells Fargo Housing Affordability Index and Sperling's Best Places' cost-of-living index. *Forbes.com, "America's Most Affordable Cities in 2015," March 12, 2015*

- The Oklahoma City* metro area appeared on the Milken Institute "2017 Best Performing Cities" list. Rank: #131 out of 200 large metro areas. Criteria: job growth; wage and salary growth; high-tech output growth. *Milken Institute, "Best-Performing Cities 2017," January 2018*

- *Forbes* ranked the 200 most populous metro areas to determine the nation's "Best Places for Business and Careers." The Oklahoma City* metro area was ranked #60. Criteria: costs (business and living); job growth (past and projected); income growth; quality of life; educational attainment (college and high school); projected economic growth; cultural and recreational opportunities; net migration patterns; number of highly ranked colleges. *Forbes, "The Best Places for Business and Careers 2017," October 24, 2017*

Education Rankings

- Personal finance website *WalletHub* analyzed the 150 largest U.S. metropolitan statistical areas to determine where the most educated Americans are choosing to settle. Criteria: education quality and attainment gap; education levels; percentage of workers with degrees; public school rankings; quality and size of each metro area's universities. Oklahoma City* was ranked #72 (#1 = most educated city). *www.WalletHub.com, "2017's Most and Least Educated Cities in America, " July 25, 2017*

Environmental Rankings

- Sperling's BestPlaces assessed 379 metropolitan areas of the United States for the likelihood of dangerously extreme weather events or earthquakes. In general the Southeast and South-Central regions have the highest risk of weather extremes and earthquakes, while the Pacific Northwest enjoys the lowest risk. Of the least risky metropolitan areas, the Oklahoma City* metro area was ranked #364. *www.bestplaces.net, "Safest Places from Natural Disasters," April 2011*

- Oklahoma City* was highlighted as one of the top 99 cleanest metro areas for short-term particle pollution (24-hour PM 2.5) in the U.S. during 2013 through 2015. Monitors in these cities reported no days with unhealthful PM 2.5 levels. *American Lung Association, State of the Air 2017*

Health/Fitness Rankings

- Analysts who tracked obesity rates in the nation's largest metro areas (populations above one million) found that the Oklahoma City* metro area was one of the ten major metros where residents were most likely to be obese, defined as a BMI score of 30 or above. *www.gallup.com, "Boulder, Colo., Residents Still Least Likely to Be Obese," April 4, 2014*

- For each of the 50 most populous metro areas in the United States, the American College of Sports Medicine's American Fitness Index evaluated infrastructure, community assets, and policies that encourage healthy and fit lifestyles, including preventive health behaviors, levels of chronic disease conditions, health care access, and community resources and policies that support physical activity. The Oklahoma City* metro area ranked #49 for "community fitness." *www.americanfitnessindex.org, "ACSM American Fitness Index Health and Community Fitness Status of the 50 Largest Metropolitan Areas," May 2017*

- Oklahoma City* was identified as a "2016 Spring Allergy Capital." The area ranked #7 out of 100. Three groups of factors were used to identify the most severe cities for people with allergies during the spring season: annual pollen levels; medicine utilization; access to board-certified allergists. *Asthma and Allergy Foundation of America, "Spring Allergy Capitals 2016"*

- Oklahoma City* was identified as a "2016 Fall Allergy Capital." The area ranked #6 out of 100. Three groups of factors were used to identify the most severe cities for people with allergies during the fall season: annual pollen levels; medicine utilization; access to board-certified allergists. *Asthma and Allergy Foundation of America, "Fall Allergy Capitals 2016"*

- Oklahoma City* was identified as a "2015 Asthma Capital." The area ranked #5 out of the nation's 100 largest metropolitan areas. Criteria: estimated prevalence; self-reported prevalence; crude death rate for asthma; annual pollen score; annual air quality; public smoking laws; number of board-certified asthma specialists; school inhaler access laws; rescue medication use; controller medication use; ER visits for asthma; uninsured rate; poverty rate. *Asthma and Allergy Foundation of America, "Asthma Capitals 2015"*

- The Oklahoma City* metro area ranked #173 out of 189 in The Gallup-Healthways Well-Being Index. Criteria: purpose; social well being; financial health; community and physical health. Results are based on telephone interviews with adults, aged 18 and older, living in metropolitan areas in the 50 U.S. states and the District of Columbia. *Gallup-Healthways, "State of American Well-Being, 2017 Community Well-Being Rankings" March 2018*

Real Estate Rankings

- FitSmallBusiness looked at 50 of the largest metropolitan areas in the U.S. to determine which metro was the best to start a real estate business. Data was compiled from such sources as: Zillow, Trulia, U.S. Census Bureau, and the Bureau of Labor Statistics. Criteria: location; inventory; annual wages; median sales price of homes; days on the market; median price cut percentage; and other factors that would influence real estate professional growth. The Oklahoma City* metro area ranked #35. *fitsmallbusiness.com, "The Best Cities to Become a Real Estate Agent in 2018," January 30, 2018*

- The Oklahoma City* metro area was identified as one of nine best housing markets to invest in. Criteria: single-family rental home investing in the first quarter of 2017 based on first-year returns. The area ranked #6. *The Business Insider, "Here are the 9 Best U.S. Housing Markets for Investment," May 11, 2017*

- The Oklahoma City* metro area was identified as one of the 20 worst housing markets in the U.S. in 2017. The area ranked #16 out of 180 markets. Criteria: year-over-year change of median sales price of existing single-family homes between the 4th quarter of 2016 and the 4th quarter of 2017. *National Association of Realtors®, Median Sales Price of Existing Single-Family Homes for Metropolitan Areas, 4th Quarter 2017*

- Oklahoma City* was ranked #74 out of 238 metro areas in terms of housing affordability in 2017 by the National Association of Home Builders (#1 = most affordable). Criteria: the share of homes sold in that area affordable to a family earning the local median income, based on standard mortgage underwriting criteria. *National Association of Home Builders®, NAHB-Wells Fargo Housing Opportunity Index, 4th Quarter 2017*

Safety Rankings

- The National Insurance Crime Bureau ranked 382 metro areas in the U.S. in terms of per capita rates of vehicle theft. The Oklahoma City* metro area ranked #59 (#1 = highest rate). Criteria: number of vehicle theft offenses per 100,000 inhabitants in 2016. *National Insurance Crime Bureau, "Hot Spots 2016," June 8, 2017*

Seniors/Retirement Rankings

- From its Best Cities for Successful Aging indexes, the Milken Institute generated rankings for metropolitan areas, weighing data in nine categories—health care, wellness, living arrangements, transportation and convenience, financial characteristics, education, employment, community engagement, and overall livability. The Oklahoma City* metro area was ranked #28 overall in the large metro area category. *Milken Institute, "Best Cities for Successful Aging, 2017" March 14, 2017*

*Edmond is located within the Oklahoma City, OK Metropolitan Statistical Area.

Business Environment

CITY FINANCES

City Government Finances

Component	2015 ($000)	2015 ($ per capita)
Total Revenues	223,804	2,484
Total Expenditures	219,968	2,442
Debt Outstanding	108,871	1,208
Cash and Securities[1]	254,465	2,825

Note: (1) Cash and security holdings of a government at the close of its fiscal year,, including those of its dependent agencies, utilities, and liquor stores.
Source: U.S Census Bureau, State & Local Government Finances 2015

City Government Revenue by Source

Source	2015 ($000)	2015 ($ per capita)	2015 (%)
General Revenue			
From Federal Government	464	5	0.2
From State Government	5,715	63	2.6
From Local Governments	517	6	0.2
Taxes			
Property	0	0	0.0
Sales and Gross Receipts	70,046	777	31.3
Personal Income	0	0	0.0
Corporate Income	0	0	0.0
Motor Vehicle License	0	0	0.0
Other Taxes	1,806	20	0.8
Current Charges	22,890	254	10.2
Liquor Store	0	0	0.0
Utility	112,973	1,254	50.5
Employee Retirement	-1,213	-13	-0.5

Source: U.S Census Bureau, State & Local Government Finances 2015

City Government Expenditures by Function

Function	2015 ($000)	2015 ($ per capita)	2015 (%)
General Direct Expenditures			
Air Transportation	93	1	0.0
Corrections	0	0	0.0
Education	0	0	0.0
Employment Security Administration	0	0	0.0
Financial Administration	4,371	48	2.0
Fire Protection	16,592	184	7.5
General Public Buildings	0	0	0.0
Governmental Administration, Other	6,215	69	2.8
Health	1,715	19	0.8
Highways	14,204	157	6.5
Hospitals	0	0	0.0
Housing and Community Development	269	3	0.1
Interest on General Debt	211	2	0.1
Judicial and Legal	1,331	14	0.6
Libraries	0	0	0.0
Parking	0	0	0.0
Parks and Recreation	8,990	99	4.1
Police Protection	36,887	409	16.8
Public Welfare	688	7	0.3
Sewerage	5,302	58	2.4
Solid Waste Management	5,340	59	2.4
Veterans' Services	0	0	0.0
Liquor Store	0	0	0.0
Utility	87,189	967	39.6
Employee Retirement	3,109	34	1.4

Source: U.S Census Bureau, State & Local Government Finances 2015

DEMOGRAPHICS

Population Growth

Area	1990 Census	2000 Census	2010 Census	2016* Estimate	Population Growth (%) 1990-2016	Population Growth (%) 2010-2016
City	52,239	68,315	81,405	88,342	69.1	8.5
MSA[1]	971,042	1,095,421	1,252,987	1,337,075	37.7	6.7
U.S.	248,709,873	281,421,906	308,745,538	318,558,162	28.1	3.2

Note: (1) Figures cover the Oklahoma City, OK Metropolitan Statistical Area—see Appendix B for areas included; (*) 2012-2016 5-year estimated population
Source: U.S. Census Bureau, 1990 Census, Census 2000, Census 2010, 2012-2016 American Community Survey 5-Year Estimates

Household Size

Area	Persons in Household (%) One	Two	Three	Four	Five	Six	Seven or More	Average Household Size
City	23.3	35.6	17.9	14.4	6.2	1.9	0.8	2.70
MSA[1]	28.4	34.1	15.6	12.7	5.8	2.2	1.2	2.60
U.S.	27.7	33.7	15.7	13.1	6.0	2.3	1.5	2.60

Note: (1) Figures cover the Oklahoma City, OK Metropolitan Statistical Area—see Appendix B for areas included
Source: U.S. Census Bureau, 2012-2016 American Community Survey 5-Year Estimates

Race

Area	White Alone[2] (%)	Black Alone[2] (%)	Asian Alone[2] (%)	AIAN[3] Alone[2] (%)	NHOPI[4] Alone[2] (%)	Other Race Alone[2] (%)	Two or More Races (%)
City	80.6	5.7	3.3	2.4	0.3	0.9	6.9
MSA[1]	74.1	10.2	3.1	3.5	0.1	2.6	6.4
U.S.	73.3	12.6	5.2	0.8	0.2	4.8	3.1

Note: (1) Figures cover the Oklahoma City, OK Metropolitan Statistical Area—see Appendix B for areas included; (2) Alone is defined as not being in combination with one or more other races; (3) American Indian and Alaska Native; (4) Native Hawaiian and Other Pacific Islander
Source: U.S. Census Bureau, 2012-2016 American Community Survey 5-Year Estimates

Hispanic or Latino Origin

Area	Total (%)	Mexican (%)	Puerto Rican (%)	Cuban (%)	Other (%)
City	5.6	4.2	0.2	0.2	1.0
MSA[1]	12.4	10.3	0.3	0.1	1.8
U.S.	17.3	11.0	1.7	0.7	4.0

Note: Persons of Hispanic or Latino origin can be of any race; (1) Figures cover the Oklahoma City, OK Metropolitan Statistical Area—see Appendix B for areas included
Source: U.S. Census Bureau, 2012-2016 American Community Survey 5-Year Estimates

Segregation

Type	Segregation Indices[1] 1990	2000	2010	2010 Rank[2]	Percent Change 1990-2000	1990-2010	2000-2010
Black/White	60.2	55.3	51.4	67	-4.8	-8.8	-4.0
Asian/White	39.8	40.8	39.2	60	1.0	-0.6	-1.7
Hispanic/White	33.4	44.2	47.0	38	10.7	13.6	2.9

Note: All figures cover the Metropolitan Statistical Area—see Appendix B for areas included; Figures are based on an analysis of 1990, 2000, and 2010 Census Decennial Census tract data by William H. Frey, Brookings Institution and the University of Michigan Social Science Data Analysis Network. In this analysis all racial groups (whites, blacks, and asians) are non-Hispanic members of those races. Hispanics are shown as a separate category; (1) Segregation Indices are Dissimilarity Indices that measure the degree to which the minority group is distributed differently than whites across census tracts. They range from 0 (complete integration) to 100 (complete segregation) where the value indicates the percentage of the minority group that needs to move to be distributed exactly like whites; (2) Ranges from 1 (most segregated) to 102 (least segregated); n/a not available.
Source: www.CensusScope.org

Ancestry

Area	German	Irish	English	American	Italian	Polish	French[2]	Scottish	Dutch
City	17.7	11.5	10.5	7.9	3.0	1.6	2.8	2.4	1.5
MSA[1]	13.6	10.3	7.8	8.0	1.9	1.0	2.0	1.8	1.4
U.S.	14.4	10.4	7.7	6.9	5.4	2.9	2.6	1.7	1.3

Note: Figures are the percentage of the total population reporting a particular ancestry. The nine most commonly reported ancestries in the U.S. are shown. Figures include multiple ancestries (e.g. if a person reported being Irish and Italian, they were included in both columns); (1) Figures cover the Oklahoma City, OK Metropolitan Statistical Area—see Appendix B for areas included; (2) Excludes Basque
Source: U.S. Census Bureau, 2012-2016 American Community Survey 5-Year Estimates

Foreign-Born Population

Area	Percent of Population Born in								
	Any Foreign Country	Asia	Mexico	Europe	Carribean	Central America[2]	South America	Africa	Canada
City	6.4	3.0	1.5	0.5	0.1	0.1	0.3	0.6	0.2
MSA[1]	8.1	2.5	3.7	0.4	0.1	0.6	0.2	0.4	0.1
U.S.	13.2	4.0	3.6	1.5	1.3	1.0	0.9	0.6	0.3

Note: (1) Figures cover the Oklahoma City, OK Metropolitan Statistical Area—see Appendix B for areas included; (2) Excludes Mexico.
Source: U.S. Census Bureau, 2012-2016 American Community Survey 5-Year Estimates

Marital Status

Area	Never Married	Now Married[2]	Separated	Widowed	Divorced
City	28.0	56.5	1.2	5.1	9.1
MSA[1]	30.6	48.8	2.2	5.7	12.7
U.S.	33.0	48.1	2.1	5.9	11.0

Note: Figures are percentages and cover the population 15 years of age and older; (1) Figures cover the Oklahoma City, OK Metropolitan Statistical Area—see Appendix B for areas included; (2) Excludes separated
Source: U.S. Census Bureau, 2012-2016 American Community Survey 5-Year Estimates

Disability Status

Area	All Ages	Under 18 Years Old	18 to 64 Years Old	65 Years and Over
City	9.5	3.7	7.0	33.4
MSA[1]	13.6	4.4	12.0	40.0
U.S.	12.5	4.1	10.3	35.7

Note: Figures show percent of the civilian noninstitutionalized population that reported having a disability. Disability status is determined from six types of difficulty: vision, hearing, cognitive, ambulatory, self-care, and independent living. For children under 5 years old, hearing and vision difficulty are used to determine disability status. For children between the ages of 5 and 14, disability status is determined from hearing, vision, cognitive, ambulatory, and self-care difficulties. For people aged 15 years and older, they are considered to have a disability if they have difficulty with any one of the six difficulty types; Note: (1) Figures cover the Oklahoma City, OK Metropolitan Statistical Area—see Appendix B for areas included
Source: U.S. Census Bureau, 2012-2016 American Community Survey 5-Year Estimates

Age

Area	Percent of Population									Median Age
	Under Age 5	Age 5–19	Age 20–34	Age 35–44	Age 45–54	Age 55–64	Age 65–74	Age 75–84	Age 85+	
City	7.2	22.1	21.2	12.0	12.5	12.1	7.4	3.7	1.7	34.6
MSA[1]	7.1	20.5	22.7	12.7	12.5	11.8	7.4	3.8	1.5	34.8
U.S.	6.2	19.6	20.7	12.7	13.6	12.6	8.3	4.3	1.9	37.7

Note: (1) Figures cover the Oklahoma City, OK Metropolitan Statistical Area—see Appendix B for areas included
Source: U.S. Census Bureau, 2012-2016 American Community Survey 5-Year Estimates

Gender

Area	Males	Females	Males per 100 Females
City	43,050	45,292	95.0
MSA[1]	659,180	677,895	97.2
U.S.	156,765,322	161,792,840	96.9

Note: (1) Figures cover the Oklahoma City, OK Metropolitan Statistical Area—see Appendix B for areas included
Source: U.S. Census Bureau, 2012-2016 American Community Survey 5-Year Estimates

Religious Groups by Family

Area	Catholic	Baptist	Non-Den.	Methodist[2]	Lutheran	LDS[3]	Pente-costal	Presby-terian[4]	Muslim[5]	Judaism
MSA[1]	6.4	25.4	7.1	10.6	0.7	1.3	3.2	1.0	0.2	0.1
U.S.	19.1	9.3	4.0	4.0	2.3	2.0	1.9	1.6	0.8	0.7

Note: Figures are the number of adherents as a percentage of the total population; (1) Figures cover the Oklahoma City, OK Metropolitan Statistical Area—see Appendix B for areas included; (2) Methodist/Pietist; (3) Latter Day Saints; (4) Reformed; (5) Figures are estimates
Source: Association of Statisticians of American Religious Bodies, 2010 U.S. Religion Census: Religious Congregations & Membership Study

Religious Groups by Tradition

Area	Catholic	Evangelical Protestant	Mainline Protestant	Other Tradition	Black Protestant	Orthodox
MSA[1]	6.4	39.1	9.9	2.8	1.9	0.2
U.S.	19.1	16.2	7.3	4.3	1.6	0.3

Note: Figures are the number of adherents as a percentage of the total population; (1) Figures cover the Oklahoma City, OK Metropolitan Statistical Area—see Appendix B for areas included
Source: Association of Statisticians of American Religious Bodies, 2010 U.S. Religion Census: Religious Congregations & Membership Study

ECONOMY

Gross Metropolitan Product

Area	2014	2015	2016	2017	Rank[2]
MSA[1]	72.5	72.7	73.8	77.6	46

Note: Figures are in billions of dollars; (1) Figures cover the Oklahoma City, OK Metropolitan Statistical Area—see Appendix B for areas included; (2) Rank is based on 2015 data and ranges from 1 to 381
Source: The U.S. Conference of Mayors, U.S. Metro Economies: GMP and Employment Report, 2015-2017

Economic Growth

Area	2012-14 (%)	2015 (%)	2016 (%)	2017 (%)	Rank[2]
MSA[1]	2.6	3.4	-0.4	2.3	81
U.S.	2.0	2.4	1.9	2.6	–

Note: Figures are real gross metropolitan product (GMP) growth rates and represent average annual percent change; (1) Figures cover the Oklahoma City, OK Metropolitan Statistical Area—see Appendix B for areas included; (2) Rank is based on 2012-2014 average annual percent change and ranges from 1 to 381
Source: The U.S. Conference of Mayors, U.S. Metro Economies: GMP and Employment Report, 2015-2017

Metropolitan Area Exports

Area	2011	2012	2013	2014	2015	2016	Rank[2]
MSA[1]	1,592.8	1,574.6	1,581.7	1,622.0	1,353.1	1,260.0	130

Note: Figures are in millions of dollars; (1) Figures cover the Oklahoma City, OK Metropolitan Statistical Area—see Appendix B for areas included; (2) Rank is based on 2016 data and ranges from 1 to 385
Source: U.S. Department of Commerce, International Trade Administration, Office of Trade & Industry Information, Manufacturing & Services, data extracted March 15, 2018

Building Permits

Area	Single-Family			Multi-Family			Total		
	2016	2017p	Pct. Chg.	2016	2017p	Pct. Chg.	2016	2017p	Pct. Chg.
City	394	526	33.5	6	74	1,133.3	400	600	50.0
MSA[1]	5,039	5,167	2.5	1,731	292	-83.1	6,770	5,459	-19.4
U.S.	750,800	817,300	8.9	455,800	446,800	-2.0	1,206,600	1,264,100	4.8

Note: (1) Figures cover the Oklahoma City, OK Metropolitan Statistical Area—see Appendix B for areas included; Figures represent new, privately-owned housing units authorized (unadjusted data); All permit data are based on estimates with imputation; (p) preliminary data.
Source: U.S. Census Bureau, Manufacturing, Mining, and Construction Statistics, Building Permits, 2016, 2017

Bankruptcy Filings

Area	Business Filings			Nonbusiness Filings		
	2016	2017	% Chg.	2016	2017	% Chg.
Oklahoma County	110	59	-46.4	2,113	2,098	-0.7
U.S.	24,114	23,157	-4.0	770,846	765,863	-0.6

Note: Business filings include Chapter 7, Chapter 11, Chapter 12, and Chapter 13; Nonbusiness filings include Chapter 7, Chapter 11, and Chapter 13
Source: Administrative Office of the U.S. Courts, Business and Nonbusiness Bankruptcy, County Cases Commenced by Chapter of the Bankruptcy Code, During the 12-Month Period Ending December 31, 2016 and Business and Nonbusiness Bankruptcy, County Cases Commenced by Chapter of the Bankruptcy Code, During the 12-Month Period Ending December 31, 2017

Housing Vacancy Rates

Area	Gross Vacancy Rate[2] (%)			Year-Round Vacancy Rate[3] (%)			Rental Vacancy Rate[4] (%)			Homeowner Vacancy Rate[5] (%)		
	2015	2016	2017	2015	2016	2017	2015	2016	2017	2015	2016	2017
MSA[1]	11.9	11.9	11.1	11.1	11.6	10.8	7.6	10.9	9.9	2.0	1.6	1.9
U.S.	12.9	12.8	12.7	10.0	9.9	9.9	7.1	6.9	7.2	1.8	1.7	1.6

Note: (1) Figures cover the Oklahoma City, OK Metropolitan Statistical Area—see Appendix B for areas included; (2) The percentage of the total housing inventory that is vacant; (3) The percentage of the housing inventory (excluding seasonal units) that is year-round vacant; (4) The percentage of rental inventory that is vacant for rent; (5) The percentage of homeowner inventory that is vacant for sale
Source: U.S. Census Bureau, Housing Vacancies and Homeownership Annual Statistics: 2015, 2016, 2017

INCOME

Income

Area	Per Capita ($)	Median Household ($)	Average Household ($)
City	39,643	74,632	105,799
MSA[1]	27,964	52,825	72,006
U.S.	29,829	55,322	77,866

Note: (1) Figures cover the Oklahoma City, OK Metropolitan Statistical Area—see Appendix B for areas included
Source: U.S. Census Bureau, 2012-2016 American Community Survey 5-Year Estimates

Household Income Distribution

Area	Percent of Households Earning							
	Under $15,000	$15,000 -$24,999	$25,000 -$34,999	$35,000 -$49,999	$50,000 -$74,999	$75,000 -$99,999	$100,000 -$149,999	$150,000 and up
City	8.5	7.0	6.3	12.3	16.1	12.2	18.3	19.4
MSA[1]	11.7	10.2	10.8	14.4	19.1	12.5	12.5	8.7
U.S.	12.1	10.2	9.9	13.2	17.8	12.2	13.5	11.1

Note: (1) Figures cover the Oklahoma City, OK Metropolitan Statistical Area—see Appendix B for areas included
Source: U.S. Census Bureau, 2012-2016 American Community Survey 5-Year Estimates

Poverty Rate

Area	All Ages	Under 18 Years Old	18 to 64 Years Old	65 Years and Over
City	10.0	11.1	10.7	4.4
MSA[1]	15.0	21.2	14.1	7.3
U.S.	15.1	21.2	14.2	9.3

Note: Figures are percentage of people whose income during the past 12 months was below the poverty level; (1) Figures cover the Oklahoma City, OK Metropolitan Statistical Area—see Appendix B for areas included
Source: U.S. Census Bureau, 2012-2016 American Community Survey 5-Year Estimates

EMPLOYMENT

Labor Force and Employment

Area	Civilian Labor Force			Workers Employed		
	Dec. 2016	Dec. 2017	% Chg.	Dec. 2016	Dec. 2017	% Chg.
City	46,484	47,372	1.9	45,132	46,033	2.0
MSA[1]	663,581	674,115	1.6	637,645	650,461	2.0
U.S.	158,968,000	159,880,000	0.6	151,798,000	153,602,000	1.2

Note: Data is not seasonally adjusted and covers workers 16 years of age and older; (1) Figures cover the Oklahoma City, OK Metropolitan Statistical Area—see Appendix B for areas included
Source: Bureau of Labor Statistics, Local Area Unemployment Statistics

Unemployment Rate

Area	2017											
	Jan.	Feb.	Mar.	Apr.	May	Jun.	Jul.	Aug.	Sep.	Oct.	Nov.	Dec.
City	3.5	3.7	3.3	2.9	3.5	3.6	3.3	3.3	3.1	2.9	2.9	2.8
MSA[1]	4.2	4.3	3.9	3.6	4.0	4.3	3.9	3.9	3.7	3.6	3.5	3.5
U.S.	5.1	4.9	4.6	4.1	4.1	4.5	4.6	4.5	4.1	3.9	3.9	3.9

Note: Data is not seasonally adjusted and covers workers 16 years of age and older; (1) Figures cover the Oklahoma City, OK Metropolitan Statistical Area—see Appendix B for areas included
Source: Bureau of Labor Statistics, Local Area Unemployment Statistics

Average Wages

Occupation	$/Hr.	Occupation	$/Hr.
Accountants and Auditors	33.50	Maids and Housekeeping Cleaners	9.70
Automotive Mechanics	20.00	Maintenance and Repair Workers	16.20
Bookkeepers	18.70	Marketing Managers	49.20
Carpenters	19.80	Nuclear Medicine Technologists	34.70
Cashiers	10.10	Nurses, Licensed Practical	19.80
Clerks, General Office	13.90	Nurses, Registered	30.70
Clerks, Receptionists/Information	13.20	Nursing Assistants	12.40
Clerks, Shipping/Receiving	16.20	Packers and Packagers, Hand	11.20
Computer Programmers	38.20	Physical Therapists	39.70
Computer Systems Analysts	34.00	Postal Service Mail Carriers	23.80
Computer User Support Specialists	21.90	Real Estate Brokers	n/a
Cooks, Restaurant	12.40	Retail Salespersons	14.30
Dentists	68.40	Sales Reps., Exc. Tech./Scientific	27.60
Electrical Engineers	45.40	Sales Reps., Tech./Scientific	35.20
Electricians	21.60	Secretaries, Exc. Legal/Med./Exec.	15.60
Financial Managers	52.30	Security Guards	14.50
First-Line Supervisors/Managers, Sales	20.80	Surgeons	113.40
Food Preparation Workers	9.60	Teacher Assistants*	9.80
General and Operations Managers	51.70	Teachers, Elementary School*	20.30
Hairdressers/Cosmetologists	12.60	Teachers, Secondary School*	20.70
Internists, General	89.70	Telemarketers	12.00
Janitors and Cleaners	11.50	Truck Drivers, Heavy/Tractor-Trailer	20.30
Landscaping/Groundskeeping Workers	12.90	Truck Drivers, Light/Delivery Svcs.	18.70
Lawyers	50.70	Waiters and Waitresses	10.60

Note: Wage data covers the Oklahoma City, OK Metropolitan Statistical Area—see Appendix B for areas included; (*) Hourly wages for elementary/secondary school teachers and teacher assistants were calculated by the editors from annual wage data based on a 40 hour work week; n/a not available.
Source: Bureau of Labor Statistics, Metro Area Occupational Employment & Wage Estimates, May 2017

Employment by Occupation

Occupation Classification	City (%)	MSA[1] (%)	U.S. (%)
Management, Business, Science, and Arts	48.0	36.4	37.0
Natural Resources, Construction, and Maintenance	5.6	10.8	8.9
Production, Transportation, and Material Moving	6.4	10.6	12.2
Sales and Office	24.6	25.0	23.8
Service	15.4	17.2	18.1

Note: Figures cover employed civilians 16 years of age and older; (1) Figures cover the Oklahoma City, OK Metropolitan Statistical Area—see Appendix B for areas included
Source: U.S. Census Bureau, 2012-2016 American Community Survey 5-Year Estimates

Employment by Industry

Sector	MSA[1] Number of Employees	MSA[1] Percent of Total	U.S. Percent of Total
Construction	29,700	4.6	4.7
Education and Health Services	93,100	14.4	15.9
Financial Activities	33,200	5.1	5.7
Government	132,100	20.4	15.3
Information	7,600	1.2	1.9
Leisure and Hospitality	72,300	11.2	10.7
Manufacturing	33,600	5.2	8.5
Mining and Logging	20,100	3.1	0.5
Other Services	28,200	4.4	3.9
Professional and Business Services	82,700	12.8	14.0
Retail Trade	67,800	10.5	11.0
Transportation, Warehousing, and Utilities	22,100	3.4	4.1
Wholesale Trade	24,000	3.7	4.0

Note: Figures are non-farm employment as of December 2017. Figures are not seasonally adjusted and include workers 16 years of age and older; (1) Figures cover the Oklahoma City, OK Metropolitan Statistical Area—see Appendix B for areas included
Source: Bureau of Labor Statistics, Current Employment Statistics, Employment, Hours, and Earnings

Occupations with Greatest Projected Employment Growth: 2017 – 2019

Occupation[1]	2017 Employment	2019 Projected Employment	Numeric Employment Change	Percent Employment Change
Laborers and Freight, Stock, and Material Movers, Hand	27,390	28,700	1,310	4.8
Combined Food Preparation and Serving Workers, Including Fast Food	34,310	35,490	1,180	3.4
Retail Salespersons	48,840	49,860	1,020	2.1
General and Operations Managers	29,350	30,330	980	3.3
Heavy and Tractor-Trailer Truck Drivers	25,300	26,230	930	3.7
Roustabouts, Oil and Gas	4,950	5,860	910	18.5
Customer Service Representatives	29,670	30,440	770	2.6
Janitors and Cleaners, Except Maids and Housekeeping Cleaners	22,420	23,150	730	3.3
Registered Nurses	32,680	33,360	680	2.1
Service Unit Operators, Oil, Gas, and Mining	3,370	3,980	610	18.2

Note: Projections cover Oklahoma; (1) Sorted by numeric employment change
Source: www.projectionscentral.com, State Occupational Projections, 2017–2019 Short-Term Projections

Fastest Growing Occupations: 2017 – 2019

Occupation[1]	2017 Employment	2019 Projected Employment	Numeric Employment Change	Percent Employment Change
Derrick Operators, Oil and Gas	1,140	1,380	240	20.8
Rotary Drill Operators, Oil and Gas	2,030	2,460	430	20.8
Helpers—Extraction Workers	740	890	150	19.9
Roustabouts, Oil and Gas	4,950	5,860	910	18.5
Service Unit Operators, Oil, Gas, and Mining	3,370	3,980	610	18.2
Pump Operators, Except Wellhead Pumpers	450	510	60	13.1
Geological and Petroleum Technicians	1,290	1,410	120	9.4
Production Workers, All Other	1,770	1,920	150	8.8
Mechanical Drafters	1,080	1,150	70	7.3
Helpers—Production Workers	4,830	5,170	340	6.9

Note: Projections cover Oklahoma; (1) Sorted by percent employment change and excludes occupations with numeric employment change less than 50
Source: www.projectionscentral.com, State Occupational Projections, 2017–2019 Short-Term Projections

TAXES

State Corporate Income Tax Rates

State	Tax Rate (%)	Income Brackets ($)	Num. of Brackets	Financial Institution Tax Rate (%)[a]	Federal Income Tax Ded.
Oklahoma	6.0	Flat rate	1	6.0	No

Note: Tax rates as of January 1, 2018; (a) Rates listed are the corporate income tax rate applied to financial institutions or excise taxes based on income. Some states have other taxes based upon the value of deposits or shares.
Source: Federation of Tax Administrators, Range of State Corporate Income Tax Rates, January 1, 2018

State Individual Income Tax Rates

State	Tax Rate (%)	Income Brackets ($)	Num. of Brackets	Personal Exempt. ($)[1]		Fed. Inc. Tax Ded.
				Single	Dependents	
Oklahoma	0.5 - 5.0	1,000 - 7,200 (u)	6	1,000	1,000	No

Note: Tax rates as of January 1, 2018; Local- and county-level taxes are not included; n/a not applicable; (1) Married joint filers generally receive double the single exemption; (u) The income brackets reported for Oklahoma are for single persons. For married persons filing jointly, the same tax rates apply to income brackets ranging from $2,000, to $12,200.
Source: Federation of Tax Administrators, State Individual Income Tax Rates, January 1, 2018

Various State Sales and Excise Tax Rates

State	State Sales Tax (%)	Gasoline[1] (¢/gal.)	Cigarette[2] ($/pack)	Spirits[3] ($/gal.)	Wine[4] ($/gal.)	Beer[5] ($/gal.)	Recreational Marijuana (%)
Oklahoma	4.5	17.0	1.03	5.56	0.72 (l)	0.40 (q)	Not legal

Note: All tax rates as of January 1, 2018; (1) The American Petroleum Institute has developed a methodology for determining the average tax rate on a gallon of fuel. Rates may include any of the following: excise taxes, environmental fees, storage tank fees, other fees or taxes, general sales tax, and local taxes. In states where gasoline is subject to the general sales tax, or where the fuel tax is based on the average sale price, the average rate determined by API is sensitive to changes in the price of gasoline. States that fully or partially apply general sales taxes to gasoline: CA, CO, GA, IL, IN, MI, NY; (2) The federal excise tax of $1.0066 per pack and local taxes are not included; (3) Rates are those applicable to off-premise sales of 40% alcohol by volume (a.b.v.) distilled spirits in 750ml containers. Local excise taxes are excluded; (4) Rates are those applicable to off-premise sales of 11% a.b.v. non-carbonated wine in 750ml containers; (5) Rates are those applicable to off-premise sales of 4.7% a.b.v. beer in 12 ounce containers; (l) Different rates also applicable to alcohol content, place of production, size of container, place purchased (on- or off-premise or on board airlines) or type of wine (carbonated, vermouth, etc.); (q) Different rates also applicable according to alcohol content, place of production, size of container, or place purchased (on- or off-premise or onboard airlines).
Source: Tax Foundation, 2018 Facts & Figures: How Does Your State Compare?

State Business Tax Climate Index Rankings

State	Overall Rank	Corporate Tax Rank	Individual Income Tax Rank	Sales Tax Rank	Unemployment Insurance Tax Rank	Property Tax Rank
Oklahoma	32	9	38	36	1	15

Note: The index is a measure of how each state's tax laws affect economic performance. The lower the rank, the more favorable a state's tax system is for business. States without a given tax are given a ranking of 1. The scores/rankings for the District of Columbia do not affect other states. The 2018 index represents the tax climate as of July 1, 2017.
Source: Tax Foundation, State Business Tax Climate Index 2018

TRANSPORTATION

Means of Transportation to Work

Area	Car/Truck/Van		Public Transportation			Bicycle	Walked	Other Means	Worked at Home
	Drove Alone	Car-pooled	Bus	Subway	Railroad				
City	84.7	6.3	0.3	0.0	0.0	0.2	2.0	1.0	5.4
MSA[1]	83.3	9.9	0.4	0.0	0.0	0.3	1.6	1.0	3.5
U.S.	76.4	9.3	2.6	1.9	0.6	0.6	2.8	1.3	4.6

Note: Figures are percentages and cover workers 16 years of age and older; (1) Figures cover the Oklahoma City, OK Metropolitan Statistical Area—see Appendix B for areas included
Source: U.S. Census Bureau, 2012-2016 American Community Survey 5-Year Estimates

Travel Time to Work

Area	Less Than 10 Minutes	10 to 19 Minutes	20 to 29 Minutes	30 to 44 Minutes	45 to 59 Minutes	60 to 89 Minutes	90 Minutes or More
City	13.5	31.2	28.3	20.5	3.9	1.1	1.5
MSA[1]	13.3	32.5	25.8	19.6	5.0	2.2	1.5
U.S.	12.9	29.2	20.9	20.4	8.0	6.0	2.7

Note: Note: Figures are percentages and include workers 16 years old and over; (1) Figures cover the Oklahoma City, OK Metropolitan Statistical Area—see Appendix B for areas included
Source: U.S. Census Bureau, 2012-2016 American Community Survey 5-Year Estimates

Freeway Travel Time Index

Area	1985	1990	1995	2000	2005	2010	2014
Urban Area Rank[1,2]	54	63	68	46	42	42	42
Urban Area Index[1]	1.06	1.08	1.11	1.16	1.18	1.18	1.19
Average Index[3]	1.09	1.11	1.14	1.17	1.20	1.19	1.20

Note: Freeway Travel Time Index—the ratio of travel time in the peak period to the travel time at free-flow conditions. For example, a value of 1.30 indicates a 20-minute free-flow trip takes 26 minutes in the peak (20 minutes x 1.30 = 26 minutes); (1) Covers the Oklahoma City OK urban area; (2) Rank is based on 101 urban areas (#1 = highest travel time index); (3) Average of 101 urban areas
Source: Texas Transportation Institute, 2015 Urban Mobility Scorecard, August 2015

Freeway Commuter Stress Index

Area	1985	1990	1995	2000	2005	2010	2014
Urban Area Rank[1,2]	66	75	71	54	53	58	52
Urban Area Index[1]	1.07	1.09	1.13	1.18	1.20	1.19	1.21
Average Index[3]	1.13	1.16	1.19	1.22	1.25	1.24	1.25

Note: The Freeway Commuter Stress Index is the same as the Freeway Travel Time Index (see table above) except that it includes only the travel in the peak directions during the peak periods; the TTI includes travel in all directions during the peak period. Thus, the CSI is more indicative of the work trip experienced by each commuter on a daily basis; (1) Covers the Oklahoma City OK urban area; (2) Rank is based on 101 urban areas (#1 = highest travel time index); (3) Average of 101 urban areas
Source: Texas Transportation Institute, 2015 Urban Mobility Scorecard, August 2015

Living Environment

COST OF LIVING

Cost of Living Index

Composite Index	Groceries	Housing	Utilities	Trans-portation	Health Care	Misc. Goods/ Services
89.5	87.9	86.4	84.5	95.4	91.7	92.2

Note: The Cost of Living Index measures regional differences in the cost of consumer goods and services, excluding taxes and non-consumer expenditures, for professional and managerial households in the top income quintile. It is based on more than 50,000 prices covering almost 60 different items for which prices are collected three times a year by chambers of commerce, economic development organizations or university applied economic centers in each participating urban area. The numbers shown should be read as a percentage above or below the national average of 100. For example, a value of 115.4 in the groceries column indicates that grocery prices are 15.4% higher than the national average. Small differences in the index numbers should not be interpreted as significant; Figures cover the Edmond OK urban area.
Source: The Council for Community and Economic Research, ACCRA Cost of Living Index, 2017

Grocery Prices

Area[1]	T-Bone Steak ($/pound)	Frying Chicken ($/pound)	Whole Milk ($/half gal.)	Eggs ($/dozen)	Orange Juice ($/64 oz.)	Coffee ($/11.5 oz.)
City[2]	12.13	1.17	1.83	0.98	3.14	3.54
Avg.	11.29	1.40	2.02	1.47	3.55	4.37
Min.	7.71	0.93	1.04	0.70	2.86	3.24
Max.	15.83	2.39	4.03	3.92	6.29	8.16

*Note: (1) Values for the local area are compared with the average, minimum and maximum values for all 294 areas in the Cost of Living Index; (2) Figures cover the Edmond OK urban area; **T-Bone Steak** (price per pound); **Frying Chicken** (price per pound, whole fryer); **Whole Milk** (half gallon carton); **Eggs** (price per dozen, Grade A, large); **Orange Juice** (64 oz. Tropicana or Florida Natural); **Coffee** (11.5 oz. can, vacuum-packed, Maxwell House, Hills Bros, or Folgers).*
Source: The Council for Community and Economic Research, ACCRA Cost of Living Index, 2017

Housing and Utility Costs

Area[1]	New Home Price ($)	Apartment Rent ($/month)	All Electric ($/month)	Part Electric ($/month)	Other Energy ($/month)	Telephone ($/month)
City[2]	301,277	837	-	91.58	62.81	21.55
Avg.	335,956	1,047	175.01	97.34	67.93	28.71
Min.	187,788	491	109.48	49.33	35.44	12.39
Max.	1,739,087	4,559	432.62	227.09	353.33	44.61

*Note: (1) Values for the local area are compared with the average, minimum and maximum values for all 294 areas in the Cost of Living Index; (2) Figures cover the Edmond OK urban area; **New Home Price** (2,400 sf living area, 8,000 sf lot, in urban area with full utilities); **Apartment Rent** (950 sf 2 bedroom/1.5 or 2 bath, unfurnished, excluding all utilities except water); **All Electric** (average monthly cost for an all-electric home); **Part Electric** (average monthly cost for a part-electric home); **Other Energy** (average monthly cost for natural gas, fuel oil, coal, wood, and any other forms of energy except electricity); **Telephone** (price includes basic monthly rate for a private residential line plus additional local usage charges incurred by a family of four).*
Source: The Council for Community and Economic Research, ACCRA Cost of Living Index, 2017

Health Care, Transportation, and Other Costs

Area[1]	Doctor ($/visit)	Dentist ($/visit)	Optometrist ($/visit)	Gasoline ($/gallon)	Beauty Salon ($/visit)	Men's Shirt ($)
City[2]	92.73	82.67	113.11	1.93	31.85	24.00
Avg.	108.00	92.54	101.93	2.25	37.58	30.92
Min.	30.39	60.00	49.75	1.82	16.11	11.20
Max.	193.50	161.94	229.28	3.16	77.35	59.13

*Note: (1) Values for the local area are compared with the average, minimum and maximum values for all 294 areas in the Cost of Living Index; (2) Figures cover the Edmond OK urban area; **Doctor** (general practitioners routine exam of an established patient); **Dentist** (adult teeth cleaning and periodic oral examination); **Optometrist** (full vision eye exam for established adult patient); **Gasoline** (one gallon regular unleaded, national brand, including all taxes, cash price at self-service pump if available); **Beauty Salon** (woman's shampoo, trim, and blow-dry); **Men's Shirt** (cotton/polyester dress shirt, pinpoint weave, long sleeves).*
Source: The Council for Community and Economic Research, ACCRA Cost of Living Index, 2017

HOUSING

House Price Index (HPI)

Area	National Ranking[2]	Quarterly Change (%)	One-Year Change (%)	Five-Year Change (%)
MSA[1]	206	-1.23	3.46	19.45
U.S.[3]	–	1.61	6.68	34.71

Note: The HPI is a weighted repeat sales index. It measures average price changes in repeat sales or refinancings on the same properties. This information is obtained by reviewing repeat mortgage transactions on single-family properties whose mortgages have been purchased or securitized by Fannie Mae or Freddie Mac in January 1975; (1) Figures cover the Oklahoma City, OK Metropolitan Statistical Area—see Appendix B for areas included; (2) Rankings are based on annual percentage change for all metro areas containing at least 15,000 transactions over the last 10 years and ranges from 1 to 253; (3) figures based on a weighted average of Census Division estimates using a seasonally adjusted, purchase-only index; all figures are for the period ending December 31, 2017

Source: Federal Housing Finance Agency, House Price Index, February 28, 2018

Median Single-Family Home Prices

Area	2015	2016	2017[p]	Percent Change 2016 to 2017
MSA[1]	149.6	150.8	154.3	2.3
U.S. Average	223.9	235.5	248.8	5.6

Note: Figures are median sales prices of existing single-family homes in thousands of dollars; (p) preliminary; (1) Figures cover the Oklahoma City, OK Metropolitan Statistical Area—see Appendix B for areas included

Source: National Association of Realtors, Median Sales Price of Existing Single-Family Homes for Metropolitan Areas, 4th Quarter 2017

Qualifying Income Based on Median Sales Price of Existing Single-Family Homes

Area	With 5% Down ($)	With 10% Down ($)	With 20% Down ($)
MSA[1]	34,297	32,492	28,882
U.S. Average	55,585	52,659	46,808

Note: Figures are preliminary; Qualifying income is based on a mortgage rate of 4.17%. Monthly principal and interest payment is limited to 25% of income; (1) Figures cover the Oklahoma City, OK Metropolitan Statistical Area—see Appendix B for areas included

Source: National Association of Realtors, Qualifying Income Based on Median Sales Price of Existing Single-Family Homes for Metropolitan Areas, 4th Quarter 2017

Median Apartment Condo-Coop Home Prices

Area	2015	2016	2017[p]	Percent Change 2016 to 2017
MSA[1]	n/a	n/a	n/a	n/a
U.S. Average	210.7	220.7	234.3	6.2

Note: Figures are median sales prices of existing apartment condo-coop homes in thousands of dollars; (p) preliminary; n/a not available; (1) Figures cover the Oklahoma City, OK Metropolitan Statistical Area—see Appendix B for areas included

Source: National Association of Realtors, Median Sales Price of Existing Apartment Condo-Coop Homes for Metropolitan Areas, 4th Quarter 2017

Home Value Distribution

Area	Under $50,000	$50,000 -$99,999	$100,000 -$149,999	$150,000 -$199,999	$200,000 -$299,999	$300,000 -$499,999	$500,000 -$999,999	$1,000,000 or more
City	2.7	4.1	18.9	22.5	23.3	19.2	8.2	1.1
MSA[1]	9.1	21.0	23.8	19.0	15.7	8.0	2.7	0.6
U.S.	8.8	14.8	15.3	14.9	18.4	16.4	9.0	2.5

Note: Figures are percentages and cover owner-occupied housing units; (1) Figures cover the Oklahoma City, OK Metropolitan Statistical Area—see Appendix B for areas included

Source: U.S. Census Bureau, 2012-2016 American Community Survey 5-Year Estimates

Homeownership Rate

Area	2009 (%)	2010 (%)	2011 (%)	2012 (%)	2013 (%)	2014 (%)	2015 (%)	2016 (%)	2017 (%)
MSA[1]	69.0	70.0	69.6	67.3	67.6	65.7	61.4	63.1	64.7
U.S.	67.4	66.9	66.1	65.4	65.1	64.5	63.7	63.4	63.9

Note: (1) Figures cover the Oklahoma City, OK Metropolitan Statistical Area—see Appendix B for areas included

Source: U.S. Census Bureau, Housing Vacancies and Homeownership Annual Statistics: 2009-2017

Year Housing Structure Built

Area	2010 or Later	2000 -2009	1990 -1999	1980 -1989	1970 -1979	1960 -1969	1950 -1959	1940 -1949	Before 1940	Median Year
City	6.8	20.4	19.6	20.8	19.0	7.1	3.3	1.2	1.8	1988
MSA[1]	4.7	15.9	11.5	15.3	17.8	12.6	10.1	5.4	6.8	1979
U.S.	2.3	14.7	14.0	13.7	15.6	10.9	10.6	5.2	13.0	1977

Note: Figures are percentages except for Median Year; Note: (1) Figures cover the Oklahoma City, OK Metropolitan Statistical Area—see Appendix B for areas included
Source: U.S. Census Bureau, 2012-2016 American Community Survey 5-Year Estimates

Gross Monthly Rent

Area	Under $500	$500 -$999	$1,000 -$1,499	$1,500 -$1,999	$2,000 -$2,499	$2,500 -$2,999	$3,000 and up	Median ($)
City	6.0	49.1	30.3	10.8	1.9	0.8	1.1	962
MSA[1]	10.6	62.4	20.6	4.7	1.1	0.3	0.3	800
U.S.	11.3	43.3	27.7	10.7	4.0	1.6	1.5	949

Note: Figures are percentages except for Median; Gross rent is the contract rent plus the estimated average monthly cost of utilities (electricity, gas, and water and sewer) and fuels (oil, coal, kerosene, wood, etc.) if these are paid by the renter (or paid for the renter by someone else); (1) Figures cover the Oklahoma City, OK Metropolitan Statistical Area—see Appendix B for areas included
Source: U.S. Census Bureau, 2012-2016 American Community Survey 5-Year Estimates

HEALTH

Health Risk Factors

Category	MSA[1] (%)	U.S. (%)
Adults aged 18–64 who have any kind of health care coverage	80.3	87.7
Adults who reported being in good or excellent health	82.2	83.6
Adults who are current smokers	17.5	17.1
Adults who currently use E-cigarettes	6.3	4.7
Adults who currently use chewing tobacco, snuff, or snus	3.9	4.0
Adults who are heavy drinkers[2]	3.7	6.5
Adults who are binge drinkers[3]	11.1	16.9
Adults who are overweight (BMI 25.0 - 29.9)	36.1	35.3
Adults who are obese (BMI 30.0 - 99.8)	31.4	29.9
Adults who participated in any physical activities in the past month	73.6	76.9
Adults who always or nearly always wears a seat belt	95.4	94.3

Note: (1) Figures cover the Oklahoma City, OK Metropolitan Statistical Area—see Appendix B for areas included; (2) Heavy drinkers are classified as adult men having more than 14 drinks per week and adult women having more than 7 drinks per week; (3) Binge drinkers are classified as males having five or more drinks on one occasion or females having four or more drinks on one occasion
Source: Centers for Disease Control and Prevention, Behaviorial Risk Factor Surveillance System, SMART: Selected Metropolitan Area Risk Trends, 2016

Health Screening Rates

Category	MSA[1] (%)	U.S. (%)
Adults 50-75 who have had a blood stool test within the past year	8.4	8.0
Adults 50-75 who have had a colonoscopy in the past 10 years	60.3	63.5
Adults aged 65+ who have had flu shot within the past year	61.8	58.6
Adults aged 65+ who have ever had a pneumonia vaccination	78.2	73.4
Adults who have ever been tested for HIV	30.1	35.6
Women aged 21-65 who have had a pap test in the past three years	80.7	79.8
Men aged 40+ who have had a PSA test within the past two years	46.5	39.5
Women aged 40+ who have had a mammogram within the past two years	73.7	72.5

Note: n/a not available; (1) Figures cover the Oklahoma City, OK Metropolitan Statistical Area—see Appendix B for areas included; Source: Centers for Disease Control and Prevention, Behaviorial Risk Factor Surveillance System, SMART: Selected Metropolitan Area Risk Trends, 2016

Chronic Health Conditions

Category	MSA[1] (%)	U.S. (%)
Adults who have ever been told they had a heart attack	4.0	4.4
Adults who have ever been told they have angina or coronary heart disease	4.5	4.1
Adults who have ever been told they had a stroke	3.8	3.1
Adults who have been told they currently have asthma	10.0	9.3
Adults who have ever been told they have arthritis	26.1	25.8
Adults who have ever been told they have diabetes[2]	10.8	10.5
Adults who have ever been told they had skin cancer	5.4	5.9
Adults who have ever been told they had any other types of cancer	5.2	6.7
Adults who have ever been told they have COPD	7.1	6.3
Adults who have ever been told they have kidney disease	2.7	2.8
Adults who have ever been told they have a form of depression	20.2	17.4

Note: (1) Figures cover the Oklahoma City, OK Metropolitan Statistical Area—see Appendix B for areas included; (2) Figures do not include pregnancy-related, borderline, or pre-diabetes
Source: Centers for Disease Control and Prevention, Behaviorial Risk Factor Surveillance System, SMART: Selected Metropolitan Area Risk Trends, 2016

Mortality Rates for the Top 10 Causes of Death in the U.S.

ICD-10[a] Sub-Chapter	ICD-10[a] Code	Age-Adjusted Mortality Rate[1] per 100,000 population	
		County[2]	U.S.
Malignant neoplasms	C00-C97	179.0	158.5
Ischaemic heart diseases	I20-I25	122.2	96.8
Other forms of heart disease	I30-I51	54.3	52.4
Chronic lower respiratory diseases	J40-J47	63.2	40.9
Cerebrovascular diseases	I60-I69	45.0	37.2
Organic, including symptomatic, mental disorders	F01-F09	38.7	33.3
Other degenerative diseases of the nervous system	G30-G31	44.2	32.1
Other external causes of accidental injury	W00-X59	46.6	31.2
Diabetes mellitus	E10-E14	33.2	21.1
Hypertensive diseases	I10-I15	42.0	20.8

Note: (a) ICD-10 = International Classification of Diseases 10th Revision; (1) Mortality rates are a three year average covering 2014-2016; (2) Figures cover Oklahoma County.
Source: Centers for Disease Control and Prevention, National Center for Health Statistics. Underlying Cause of Death 1999-2016 on CDC WONDER Online Database, released December 2017

Mortality Rates for Selected Causes of Death

ICD-10[a] Sub-Chapter	ICD-10[a] Code	Age-Adjusted Mortality Rate[1] per 100,000 population	
		County[2]	U.S.
Assault	X85-Y09	10.9	5.6
Diseases of the liver	K70-K76	19.6	14.0
Human immunodeficiency virus (HIV) disease	B20-B24	2.7	1.9
Influenza and pneumonia	J09-J18	12.1	14.6
Intentional self-harm	X60-X84	18.7	13.2
Malnutrition	E40-E46	2.4	1.3
Obesity and other hyperalimentation	E65-E68	1.6	2.1
Renal failure	N17-N19	13.4	13.0
Transport accidents	V01-V99	13.5	12.0
Viral hepatitis	B15-B19	3.5	1.9

Note: (a) ICD-10 = International Classification of Diseases 10th Revision; (1) Mortality rates are a three year average covering 2014-2016; (2) Figures cover Oklahoma County; Data are Suppressed when the data meet the criteria for confidentiality constraints; Mortality rates are flagged as Unreliable when the rate would be calculated with a numerator of 20 or less.
Source: Centers for Disease Control and Prevention, National Center for Health Statistics. Underlying Cause of Death 1999-2016 on CDC WONDER Online Database, released December 2017

Health Insurance Coverage

Area	With Health Insurance	With Private Health Insurance	With Public Health Insurance	Without Health Insurance	Population Under Age 18 Without Health Insurance
City	92.1	81.5	22.3	7.9	3.9
MSA[1]	85.7	66.9	29.8	14.3	7.0
U.S.	88.3	66.7	33.0	11.7	5.9

Note: Figures are percentages that cover the civilian noninstitutionalized population; (1) Figures cover the Oklahoma City, OK Metropolitan Statistical Area—see Appendix B for areas included
Source: U.S. Census Bureau, 2012-2016 American Community Survey 5-Year Estimates

Number of Medical Professionals

Area	MDs[3]	DOs[3,4]	Dentists	Podiatrists	Chiropractors	Optometrists
County[1] (number)	3,087	358	780	39	203	141
County[1] (rate[2])	397.5	46.1	99.5	5.0	25.9	18.0
U.S. (rate[2])	276.5	22.3	67.3	6.0	26.7	15.9

Note: Data as of 2016 unless noted; (1) Data covers Oklahoma County; (2) Rate per 100,000 population; (3) Data as of 2015 and includes all active, non-federal physicians; (4) Doctor of Osteopathic Medicine
Source: U.S. Department of Health and Human Services, Health Resources and Services Administration, Bureau of Health Professions, Area Resource File (ARF) 2016-2017

EDUCATION

Public School District Statistics

District Name	Schls	Pupils	Pupil/ Teacher Ratio	Minority Pupils[1] (%)	Free Lunch Eligible[2] (%)	IEP[3] (%)
Deer Creek	8	5,628	18.6	28.0	7.1	12.2
Edmond	25	23,994	18.8	36.1	21.6	10.7
Oakdale	1	618	15.0	21.0	13.1	6.5

Note: Table includes school districts with 100 or more students; (1) Percentage of students that are not non-Hispanic white; (2) Percentage of students that are eligible for the free lunch program; (3) Percentage of students that have an Individualized Education Program.
Source: U.S. Department of Education, National Center for Education Statistics, Common Core of Data, Local Education Agency (School District) Universe Survey: School Year 2015-2016; U.S. Department of Education, National Center for Education Statistics, Common Core of Data, Public Elementary/Secondary School Universe Survey: School Year 2015-2016

Highest Level of Education

Area	Less than H.S.	H.S. Diploma	Some College, No Deg.	Associate Degree	Bachelor's Degree	Master's Degree	Prof. School Degree	Doctorate Degree
City	3.9	15.6	21.5	5.9	31.6	14.4	4.3	2.7
MSA[1]	11.9	27.2	24.5	7.2	19.1	7.0	1.8	1.2
U.S.	13.0	27.5	21.0	8.2	18.8	8.2	2.0	1.3

Note: Figures cover persons age 25 and over; (1) Figures cover the Oklahoma City, OK Metropolitan Statistical Area—see Appendix B for areas included
Source: U.S. Census Bureau, 2012-2016 American Community Survey 5-Year Estimates

Educational Attainment by Race

Area	High School Graduate or Higher (%)					Bachelor's Degree or Higher (%)				
	Total	White	Black	Asian	Hisp.[2]	Total	White	Black	Asian	Hisp.[2]
City	96.1	96.7	96.3	94.0	75.8	53.0	53.9	40.0	73.2	33.0
MSA[1]	88.1	89.2	89.7	82.5	57.1	29.1	30.5	20.2	44.2	11.0
U.S.	87.0	88.9	84.3	86.3	65.7	30.3	31.6	20.0	52.1	14.7

Note: Figures shown cover persons 25 years old and over; (1) Figures cover the Oklahoma City, OK Metropolitan Statistical Area—see Appendix B for areas included; (2) People of Hispanic origin can be of any race
Source: U.S. Census Bureau, 2012-2016 American Community Survey 5-Year Estimates

School Enrollment by Grade and Control

Area	Preschool (%)		Kindergarten (%)		Grades 1 - 4 (%)		Grades 5 - 8 (%)		Grades 9 - 12 (%)	
	Public	Private	Public	Private	Public	Private	Public	Private	Public	Private
City	53.7	46.3	79.3	20.7	82.8	17.2	84.3	15.7	90.9	9.1
MSA[1]	72.0	28.0	89.9	10.1	91.3	8.7	90.7	9.3	91.7	8.3
U.S.	58.4	41.6	87.7	12.3	89.8	10.2	89.7	10.3	90.4	9.6

Note: Figures shown cover persons 3 years old and over; (1) Figures cover the Oklahoma City, OK Metropolitan Statistical Area—see Appendix B for areas included
Source: U.S. Census Bureau, 2012-2016 American Community Survey 5-Year Estimates

Average Salaries of Public School Classroom Teachers

Area	2015		2016		Change from 2015 to 2016	
	Dollars	Rank[1]	Dollars	Rank[1]	Percent	Rank[2]
Oklahoma	45,317	47	45,276	49	-0.1	47
U.S. Average	57,611	–	58,353	–	1.3	–

Note: (1) Rank ranges from 1 to 51 where 1 indicates highest salary; (2) Rank ranges from 1 to 51 where 1 indicates highest percent change.
Source: National Education Association, Rankings & Estimates: Rankings of the States 2016 and Estimates of School Statistics 2017

Higher Education

Four-Year Colleges			Two-Year Colleges			Medical Schools[1]	Law Schools[2]	Voc/ Tech[3]
Public	Private Non-profit	Private For-profit	Public	Private Non-profit	Private For-profit			
1	1	0	0	0	0	0	0	0

Note: Figures cover institutions located within the city limits and include main campuses only; (1) includes schools accredited by the Liaison Committee on Medical Education and the American Osteopathic Association's Commission on Osteopathic College Accreditation; (2) includes ABA-accredited schools, schools with provisional ABA accreditation, and state accredited schools; (3) includes all schools with programs that are less than 2 years.
Source: National Center for Education Statistics, Integrated Postsecondary Education System (IPEDS), 2016-17; Wikipedia, List of Medical Schools in the United States, accessed April 2, 2018; Wikipedia, List of Law Schools in the United States, accessed April 2, 2018

According to *U.S. News & World Report,* the Oklahoma City, OK metro area is home to one of the best national universities in the U.S.: **University of Oklahoma** (#97 tie). The indicators used to capture academic quality fall into a number of categories: assessment by administrators at peer institutions; retention of students; faculty resources; student selectivity; financial resources; alumni giving; high school counselor ratings of colleges; and graduation rate. *U.S. News & World Report, "America's Best Colleges 2018"*

According to *U.S. News & World Report,* the Oklahoma City, OK metro area is home to one of the top 100 law schools in the U.S.: **University of Oklahoma** (#63 tie). The rankings are based on a weighted average of 12 measures of quality: peer assessment score; assessment score by lawyers/judges; median LSAT scores; median undergrad GPA; acceptance rate; employment rates for graduates; placement success; bar passage rate; faculty resources; expenditures per student; student/faculty ratio; and library resources. *U.S. News & World Report, "America's Best Graduate Schools, Law, 2019"*

PRESIDENTIAL ELECTION

2016 Presidential Election Results

Area	Clinton	Trump	Johnson	Stein	Other
Oklahoma County	41.2	51.7	7.1	0.0	0.0
U.S.	48.0	45.9	3.3	1.1	1.7

Note: Results are percentages and may not add to 100% due to rounding
Source: Dave Leip's Atlas of U.S. Presidential Elections

EMPLOYERS

Major Employers

Company Name	Industry
AT&T	Telecommunications
Chesapeake Energy Corp	Oil & gas
City of Oklahoma City	Government
Devon Energy Corp	Oil & gas
FAA Mike Monroney Aeronautical Center	Aerospace
Hobby Lobby Stores Inc	Wholesale & retail
INTEGRIS Health	Health care
Mercy Health Center	Health care
Norman Regional Hospital	Health care
OGE Energy Corp	Utility
Oklahoma City Community College	Education
OU Medical Center	Health care
Sonic Corp	Wholesale & retail
SSM Health Care of Oklahoma	Health care
State of Oklahoma	Government
The Boeing Company	Aerospace
Tinker Air Force Base	Military
University of Central Oklahoma	Higher education
University of Oklahoma - Norman	Higher education
University of Oklahoma Health Sci Ctr	Higher education

Note: Companies shown are located within the Oklahoma City, OK Metropolitan Statistical Area.
Source: Hoovers.com; Wikipedia

PUBLIC SAFETY

Crime Rate

Area	All Crimes	Violent Crimes				Property Crimes		
		Murder	Rape[3]	Robbery	Aggrav. Assault	Burglary	Larceny -Theft	Motor Vehicle Theft
City	1,664.3	1.1	25.0	22.9	95.8	280.8	1,168.0	70.8
Metro[1]	3,600.1	6.7	54.8	104.4	324.9	686.7	2,093.3	329.3
U.S.	2,847.8	5.3	40.4	102.8	248.5	468.9	1,745.0	236.9

Note: Figures are crimes per 100,000 population; (1) Figures cover the Oklahoma City, OK Metropolitan Statistical Area—see Appendix B for areas included; (3) The city and U.S. figures shown were reported using the revised Uniform Crime Reporting (UCR) definition of rape. The metro area figures shown are an aggregate total of the data submitted using both the revised and legacy UCR definitions.
Source: FBI Uniform Crime Reports, 2016

Hate Crimes

Area	Number of Quarters Reported	Number of Incidents per Bias Motivation					
		Race/Ethnicity/ Ancestry	Religion	Sexual Orientation	Disability	Gender	Gender Identity
City	3	0	0	0	0	0	0
U.S.	4	3,489	1,273	1,076	70	31	124

Source: Federal Bureau of Investigation, Hate Crime Statistics 2016

Identity Theft Consumer Reports

Area	Reports	Reports per 100,000 Population	Rank[2]
MSA[1]	1,201	87	148
U.S.	371,061	114	-

Note: (1) Figures cover the Oklahoma City, OK Metropolitan Statistical Area—see Appendix B for areas included; (2) Rank ranges from 1 to 389 where 1 indicates greatest number of identity theft reports per 100,000 population
Source: Federal Trade Commission, Consumer Sentinel Network Data Book for January–December 2017

Fraud and Other Consumer Reports

Area	Reports	Reports per 100,000 Population	Rank[2]
MSA[1]	5,818	424	223
U.S.	2,304,550	708	-

Note: (1) Figures cover the Oklahoma City, OK Metropolitan Statistical Area—see Appendix B for areas included; (2) Rank ranges from 1 to 389 where 1 indicates greatest number of fraud and other consumer reports per 100,000 population
Source: Federal Trade Commission, Consumer Sentinel Network Data Book for January–December 2017

SPORTS

Professional Sports Teams

Team Name	League	Year Established
Oklahoma City Thunder	National Basketball Association (NBA)	2008

Note: Includes teams located in the Oklahoma City, OK Metropolitan Statistical Area.
Source: Wikipedia, Major Professional Sports Teams of the United States and Canada, April 5, 2018

CLIMATE

Average and Extreme Temperatures

Temperature	Jan	Feb	Mar	Apr	May	Jun	Jul	Aug	Sep	Oct	Nov	Dec	Yr.
Extreme High (°F)	80	84	93	100	104	105	109	110	104	96	87	86	110
Average High (°F)	47	52	61	72	79	87	93	92	84	74	60	50	71
Average Temp. (°F)	36	41	50	60	69	77	82	81	73	62	49	40	60
Average Low (°F)	26	30	38	49	58	66	71	70	62	51	38	29	49
Extreme Low (°F)	-4	-3	1	20	32	47	53	51	36	22	11	-8	-8

Note: Figures cover the years 1948-1990
Source: National Climatic Data Center, International Station Meteorological Climate Summary, 9/96

Average Precipitation/Snowfall/Humidity

Precip./Humidity	Jan	Feb	Mar	Apr	May	Jun	Jul	Aug	Sep	Oct	Nov	Dec	Yr.
Avg. Precip. (in.)	1.2	1.5	2.5	2.8	5.6	4.4	2.8	2.5	3.5	3.1	1.6	1.3	32.8
Avg. Snowfall (in.)	3	3	2	Tr	0	0	0	0	0	Tr	1	2	10
Avg. Rel. Hum. 6am (%)	78	78	76	77	84	84	81	81	82	79	78	77	80
Avg. Rel. Hum. 3pm (%)	53	52	47	46	52	51	46	44	47	46	48	52	49

Note: Figures cover the years 1948-1990; Tr = Trace amounts (<0.05 in. of rain; <0.5 in. of snow)
Source: National Climatic Data Center, International Station Meteorological Climate Summary, 9/96

Weather Conditions

Temperature			Daytime Sky			Precipitation		
10°F & below	32°F & below	90°F & above	Clear	Partly cloudy	Cloudy	0.01 inch or more precip.	0.1 inch or more snow/ice	Thunder-storms
5	79	70	124	131	110	80	8	50

Note: Figures are average number of days per year and cover the years 1948-1990
Source: National Climatic Data Center, International Station Meteorological Climate Summary, 9/96

HAZARDOUS WASTE

Superfund Sites

The Oklahoma City, OK metro area is home to three sites on the EPA's Superfund National Priorities List: **Eagle Industries** (final); **Hardage/Criner** (final); **Tinker Air Force Base (Soldier Creek/Building 3001)** (final). There are a total of 1,396 Superfund sites with a status of proposed or final on the list in the U.S. *U.S. Environmental Protection Agency, National Priorities List, April 4, 2018*

AIR & WATER QUALITY

Air Quality Trends: Ozone

	1990	1995	2000	2005	2010	2012	2013	2014	2015	2016
MSA[1]	0.078	0.086	0.082	0.077	0.071	0.080	0.071	0.068	0.067	0.066
U.S.	0.087	0.089	0.081	0.079	0.073	0.075	0.069	0.067	0.068	0.069

Note: (1) Data covers the Oklahoma City, OK Metropolitan Statistical Area—see Appendix B for areas included. The values shown are the composite ozone concentration averages among trend sites based on the highest fourth daily maximum 8-hour concentration in parts per million. These trends are based on sites having an adequate record of monitoring data during the trend period. Data from exceptional events are included.
Source: U.S. Environmental Protection Agency, Air Quality Monitoring Information, "Air Quality Trends by City, 1990-2016"

Air Quality Index

Area	Percent of Days when Air Quality was...[2]					AQI Statistics[2]	
	Good	Moderate	Unhealthy for Sensitive Groups	Unhealthy	Very Unhealthy	Maximum	Median
MSA[1]	62.2	35.9	1.9	0.0	0.0	119	47

Note: (1) Data covers the Oklahoma City, OK Metropolitan Statistical Area—see Appendix B for areas included; (2) Based on 365 days with AQI data in 2017. Air Quality Index (AQI) is an index for reporting daily air quality. EPA calculates the AQI for five major air pollutants regulated by the Clean Air Act: ground-level ozone, particle pollution (aka particulate matter), carbon monoxide, sulfur dioxide, and nitrogen dioxide. The AQI runs from 0 to 500. The higher the AQI value, the greater the level of air pollution and the greater the health concern. There are six AQI categories: "Good" AQI is between 0 and 50. Air quality is considered satisfactory; "Moderate" AQI is between 51 and 100. Air quality is acceptable; "Unhealthy for Sensitive Groups" When AQI values are between 101 and 150, members of sensitive groups may experience health effects; "Unhealthy" When AQI values are between 151 and 200 everyone may begin to experience health effects; "Very Unhealthy" AQI values between 201 and 300 trigger a health alert; "Hazardous" AQI values over 300 trigger warnings of emergency conditions (not shown).
Source: U.S. Environmental Protection Agency, Air Quality Index Report, 2017

Air Quality Index Pollutants

Area	Percent of Days when AQI Pollutant was...[2]					
	Carbon Monoxide	Nitrogen Dioxide	Ozone	Sulfur Dioxide	Particulate Matter 2.5	Particulate Matter 10
MSA[1]	0.0	4.1	58.1	0.0	37.8	0.0

Note: (1) Data covers the Oklahoma City, OK Metropolitan Statistical Area—see Appendix B for areas included; (2) Based on 365 days with AQI data in 2017. The Air Quality Index (AQI) is an index for reporting daily air quality. EPA calculates the AQI for five major air pollutants regulated by the Clean Air Act: ground-level ozone, particle pollution (also known as particulate matter), carbon monoxide, sulfur dioxide, and nitrogen dioxide. The AQI runs from 0 to 500. The higher the AQI value, the greater the level of air pollution and the greater the health concern.
Source: U.S. Environmental Protection Agency, Air Quality Index Report, 2017

Maximum Air Pollutant Concentrations: Particulate Matter, Ozone, CO and Lead

	Particulate Matter 10 (ug/m^3)	Particulate Matter 2.5 Wtd AM (ug/m^3)	Particulate Matter 2.5 24-Hr (ug/m^3)	Ozone (ppm)	Carbon Monoxide (ppm)	Lead (ug/m^3)
MSA[1] Level	68	7.8	17	0.068	1	n/a
NAAQS[2]	150	15	35	0.075	9	0.15
Met NAAQS[2]	Yes	Yes	Yes	Yes	Yes	n/a

Note: (1) Data covers the Oklahoma City, OK Metropolitan Statistical Area—see Appendix B for areas included; Data from exceptional events are included; (2) National Ambient Air Quality Standards; ppm = parts per million; ug/m^3 = micrograms per cubic meter; n/a not available.
Concentrations: Particulate Matter 10 (coarse particulate)—highest second maximum 24-hour concentration; Particulate Matter 2.5 Wtd AM (fine particulate)—highest weighted annual mean concentration; Particulate Matter 2.5 24-Hour (fine particulate)—highest 98th percentile 24-hour concentration; Ozone—highest fourth daily maximum 8-hour concentration; Carbon Monoxide—highest second maximum non-overlapping 8-hour concentration; Lead—maximum running 3-month average
Source: U.S. Environmental Protection Agency, Air Quality Monitoring Information, "Air Quality Statistics by City, 2016"

Maximum Air Pollutant Concentrations: Nitrogen Dioxide and Sulfur Dioxide

	Nitrogen Dioxide AM (ppb)	Nitrogen Dioxide 1-Hr (ppb)	Sulfur Dioxide AM (ppb)	Sulfur Dioxide 1-Hr (ppb)	Sulfur Dioxide 24-Hr (ppb)
MSA[1] Level	17	47	n/a	3	n/a
NAAQS[2]	53	100	30	75	140
Met NAAQS[2]	Yes	Yes	n/a	Yes	n/a

Note: (1) Data covers the Oklahoma City, OK Metropolitan Statistical Area—see Appendix B for areas included; Data from exceptional events are included; (2) National Ambient Air Quality Standards; ppm = parts per million; ug/m^3 = micrograms per cubic meter; n/a not available.
Concentrations: Nitrogen Dioxide AM—highest arithmetic mean concentration; Nitrogen Dioxide 1-Hr—highest 98th percentile 1-hour daily maximum concentration; Sulfur Dioxide AM—highest annual mean concentration; Sulfur Dioxide 1-Hr—highest 99th percentile 1-hour daily maximum concentration; Sulfur Dioxide 24-Hr—highest second maximum 24-hour concentration
Source: U.S. Environmental Protection Agency, Air Quality Monitoring Information, "Air Quality Statistics by City, 2016"

Drinking Water

Water System Name	Pop. Served	Primary Water Source Type	Violations[1]	
			Health Based	Monitoring/ Reporting
Edmond PWA - Arcadia	77,616	Surface	0	0

Note: (1) Based on violation data from January 1, 2017 to December 31, 2017
Source: U.S. Environmental Protection Agency, Office of Ground Water and Drinking Water, Safe Drinking Water Information System (based on data extracted April 5, 2018)

Bend, Oregon

Background

Located in the foothills of the Cascade Mountains, Bend is noted for its vibrant downtown area, scenic setting, mild climate, year-round recreation and growing economy. The city covers 32 square miles along the western border of Central Oregon's high desert plateau. Bend is the geological result of dynamic lava flows and volcanic ash that shaped the Deschutes River. Canyon walls still punctuate the area and many wildlife species inhabit Deschutes' corridor.

The first permanent settlement was established in 1870. By 1877 a land claim was filed for the "Farewell Bend" ranch, located at the dramatic 90 degree bend in the Deschutes River just south of the current downtown. A post office was granted in 1886, and the name changed to Bend.

Shortly after the turn of the century, East Coast developers formed the first irrigation companies in the area, and construction was begun on several large canals and dams needed to take water out of the Deschutes River to irrigate the desert. The main canals are still in operation today.

Bend was incorporated in 1905. In 1911 the Oregon Trunk Line Railroad, coming south from the Columbia River, was completed to Bend. Four years later, plans were announced to build large sawmills there. The railroad and lumber mills created an explosion in population, which led to a tremendous growth in commerce and housing that is still evident today. Bend's historic architecture is the direct product of the boom period of the first part of the 20th century.

In the 1970s the economy began to diversify, and the number of jobs in the county increased dramatically during the last quarter of the century. Most of this growth has been in non-manufacturing sectors, as small, innovative niche-product companies began relocating or expanding here to escape skyrocketing costs, electricity shortages and tight labor markets.

The abundance of scenic and recreational amenities is complemented by a diverse cultural climate, which includes performing arts at the Community Theatre of the Cascades and The Central Oregon Community College presentations of the Magic Circle Theatre, Central Oregon Symphony, jazz band, and choir performances. In Drake Park, along the banks of Deschutes River, the Cascade Festival of Music presents classical, pop, and jazz concerts. The Munch & Music evening concerts offer free music, fine food, and spectacular mountain sunsets.

Bend is also home to the Deschutes Brewery, the 8th largest craft brewery in the nation and the largest of over a dozen microbreweries in the city. Each year the city hosts many events celebrating its brewing culture including: The Bend Oktoberfest, The Little Woody Barrel Aged Brew and Whiskey Fest, Bend Brewfest, and Central Oregon Beer Week. Beer aficionados can also visit many of the breweries along the Bend Ale Trail. Since 2004, Bend has also hosted the one of the top indie film festivals in the nation The Bend Film Festival.

Many families choose Central Oregon because of its quality public schools. In 1991, Oregon passed legislation that offer students in grades 11 and 12 the Certificate of Advanced Mastery (CAM), which signifies that they are workforce ready. The college board is working on expanding Central Oregon Community College into a fully accredited, four-year college.

The Parks and School systems coordinate to complement one another, especially with regard to outdoor programs offered to school-aged children. The Bend Metro Park and Recreation District has dozens of parks, and over 900 acres of park land. The 600 acres of wildlife refuge along Tumolo Creek are used for hiking and picnicking. Pilot Butte State Scenic Viewpoint—a volcanic cinder cone in the center of town with a commanding view of the urban area—is a favorite spot for residents and visitors. Public parks and trails follow the Deschutes River which runs for eight miles through the city's center.

Bend's climate is typical of the high desert plateau, dry with low humidity, cool nights and sunny days. A typical Central Oregon summer is marked with daily temperatures in the 80s and 90s during the day, and the mid 40s and 50s during the night. Hard frosts are not unheard of during summer months. Autumn brings warm days and cooler nights, and "Indian Summer." The winter season provides typical daytime temperatures in the 40s to 50s. Nighttime temperatures range from 22 to 51 degrees.

Rankings

General Rankings

- *Insider* listed 33 places in the U.S. that were a must see vacation destination. Whether it is the great beaches, exploring a new city or experiencing the great outdoors, according to the website thisisinsider.com Bend is a place to visit in 2018. *Insider, "33 Trips Everyone Should Take in the U.S. in 2018," November 27, 2017*
- Bend was selected as one of the best places to live in America by *Outside Magazine.* Criteria included great access to trails and public lands, great for children, delicious food and drink, and welcoming to people of all backgrounds. Three decades of coverage was combined with the expertise of an advisory council to pick the finalists. *Outside Magazine, "The 25 Best Towns of 2017," July 2017*
- Bend was selected as one of the best places to live in the United States by *Money* magazine. The city ranked #44 out of 100. This year's list focused on cities with populations of 10,000 to 100,000. Beginning with a pool of over 2,400 candidates, editors looked at 70 data points, from local economy and housing market to schools, crime and healthcare—and then sent reporters to interview residents, search neighborhoods and look for other intangibles. *Money, "Best Places to Live, 2017" September 18, 2017*

Business/Finance Rankings

- According to data by the Bureau of Economic Analysis (BEA) and the Bureau of Labor Statistics (BLS), the Bend metro area has the fastest-growing GDP (gross domestic product) and positive employment trends, at #8. *247wallst.com, "Cities With the Fastest Growing (and Shrinking) Economies," September 26, 2016*
- The Bend metro area appeared on the Milken Institute "2017 Best Performing Cities" list. Rank: #1 out of 201 small metro areas. Criteria: job growth; wage and salary growth; high-tech output growth. *Milken Institute, "Best-Performing Cities 2017," January 2018*
- *Forbes* ranked 200 smaller metro areas (population under 265,400) to determine the nation's "Best Small Places for Business and Careers." The Bend metro area was ranked #7. Criteria: costs (business and living); job growth (past and projected); income growth; quality of life; educational attainment (college and high school); projected economic growth; cultural and recreational opportunities; net migration patterns; number of highly ranked colleges. *Forbes, "The Best Small Cities for Business and Careers 2017," November, 6 2017*

Dating/Romance Rankings

- Bend was selected as one of the most romantic cities in the U.S. by video-rental kiosk company Redbox. The city ranked #20 out of 20. Criteria: number of romance-related rentals in 2016. *Redbox, "20 Most Romantic Cities," February 6, 2017*

Environmental Rankings

- Sperling's BestPlaces assessed 379 metropolitan areas of the United States for the likelihood of dangerously extreme weather events or earthquakes. In general the Southeast and South-Central regions have the highest risk of weather extremes and earthquakes, while the Pacific Northwest enjoys the lowest risk. Of the least risky metropolitan areas, the Bend metro area was ranked #18. *www.bestplaces.net, "Safest Places from Natural Disasters," April 2011*
- Bend was highlighted as one of the 25 metro areas most polluted by short-term particle pollution (24-hour PM 2.5) in the U.S. during 2013 through 2015. The area ranked #25. *American Lung Association, State of the Air 2017*

Real Estate Rankings

- Bend was ranked #222 out of 238 metro areas in terms of housing affordability in 2017 by the National Association of Home Builders (#1 = most affordable). Criteria: the share of homes sold in that area affordable to a family earning the local median income, based on standard mortgage underwriting criteria. *National Association of Home Builders®, NAHB-Wells Fargo Housing Opportunity Index, 4th Quarter 2017*

Safety Rankings

- The National Insurance Crime Bureau ranked 382 metro areas in the U.S. in terms of per capita rates of vehicle theft. The Bend metro area ranked #250 (#1 = highest rate). Criteria: number of vehicle theft offenses per 100,000 inhabitants in 2016. *National Insurance Crime Bureau, "Hot Spots 2016," June 8, 2017*

Seniors/Retirement Rankings

- From its Best Cities for Successful Aging indexes, the Milken Institute generated rankings for metropolitan areas, weighing data in nine categories—health care, wellness, living arrangements, transportation and convenience, financial characteristics, education, employment, community engagement, and overall livability. The Bend metro area was ranked #196 overall in the small metro area category. *Milken Institute, "Best Cities for Successful Aging, 2017" March 14, 2017*
- Bend was identified as one of the most popular places to retire by *Topretirements.com*. The list reflects the 100 cities that visitors to the website are most interested in for retirement, based on the number of times a city's review was viewed on the website. *Topretirements.com, "100 Most Popular Places to Retire for 2017," July 27, 2017*

Business Environment

CITY FINANCES

City Government Finances

Component	2015 ($000)	2015 ($ per capita)
Total Revenues	127,716	1,468
Total Expenditures	156,806	1,802
Debt Outstanding	165,742	1,905
Cash and Securities[1]	134,867	1,550

Note: (1) Cash and security holdings of a government at the close of its fiscal year,, including those of its dependent agencies, utilities, and liquor stores.
Source: U.S Census Bureau, State & Local Government Finances 2015

City Government Revenue by Source

Source	2015 ($000)	2015 ($ per capita)	2015 (%)
General Revenue			
From Federal Government	973	11	0.8
From State Government	7,375	85	5.8
From Local Governments	3,772	43	3.0
Taxes			
Property	30,289	348	23.7
Sales and Gross Receipts	14,370	165	11.3
Personal Income	0	0	0.0
Corporate Income	0	0	0.0
Motor Vehicle License	0	0	0.0
Other Taxes	17,326	199	13.6
Current Charges	30,166	347	23.6
Liquor Store	0	0	0.0
Utility	17,430	200	13.6
Employee Retirement	0	0	0.0

Source: U.S Census Bureau, State & Local Government Finances 2015

City Government Expenditures by Function

Function	2015 ($000)	2015 ($ per capita)	2015 (%)
General Direct Expenditures			
Air Transportation	569	6	0.4
Corrections	0	0	0.0
Education	0	0	0.0
Employment Security Administration	0	0	0.0
Financial Administration	5,494	63	3.5
Fire Protection	15,563	178	9.9
General Public Buildings	1,726	19	1.1
Governmental Administration, Other	3,742	43	2.4
Health	0	0	0.0
Highways	17,660	203	11.3
Hospitals	0	0	0.0
Housing and Community Development	2,746	31	1.8
Interest on General Debt	4,276	49	2.7
Judicial and Legal	1,000	11	0.6
Libraries	0	0	0.0
Parking	452	5	0.3
Parks and Recreation	0	0	0.0
Police Protection	17,044	195	10.9
Public Welfare	0	0	0.0
Sewerage	27,688	318	17.7
Solid Waste Management	0	0	0.0
Veterans' Services	0	0	0.0
Liquor Store	0	0	0.0
Utility	43,600	501	27.8
Employee Retirement	0	0	0.0

Source: U.S Census Bureau, State & Local Government Finances 2015

DEMOGRAPHICS

Population Growth

Area	1990 Census	2000 Census	2010 Census	2016* Estimate	Population Growth (%) 1990-2016	Population Growth (%) 2010-2016
City	34,266	52,029	76,639	84,416	146.4	10.1
MSA[1]	74,958	115,367	157,733	170,813	127.9	8.3
U.S.	248,709,873	281,421,906	308,745,538	318,558,162	28.1	3.2

Note: (1) Figures cover the Bend-Redmond, OR Metropolitan Statistical Area—see Appendix B for areas included; (*) 2012-2016 5-year estimated population
Source: U.S. Census Bureau, 1990 Census, Census 2000, Census 2010, 2012-2016 American Community Survey 5-Year Estimates

Household Size

Area	Persons in Household (%) One	Two	Three	Four	Five	Six	Seven or More	Average Household Size
City	28.4	39.2	14.6	11.9	4.0	1.1	0.8	2.50
MSA[1]	25.3	42.5	14.5	11.6	3.9	1.4	0.9	2.50
U.S.	27.7	33.7	15.7	13.1	6.0	2.3	1.5	2.60

Note: (1) Figures cover the Bend-Redmond, OR Metropolitan Statistical Area—see Appendix B for areas included
Source: U.S. Census Bureau, 2012-2016 American Community Survey 5-Year Estimates

Race

Area	White Alone[2] (%)	Black Alone[2] (%)	Asian Alone[2] (%)	AIAN[3] Alone[2] (%)	NHOPI[4] Alone[2] (%)	Other Race Alone[2] (%)	Two or More Races (%)
City	93.1	0.5	1.6	0.2	0.1	1.7	2.9
MSA[1]	93.4	0.5	1.0	0.5	0.1	1.5	2.9
U.S.	73.3	12.6	5.2	0.8	0.2	4.8	3.1

Note: (1) Figures cover the Bend-Redmond, OR Metropolitan Statistical Area—see Appendix B for areas included; (2) Alone is defined as not being in combination with one or more other races; (3) American Indian and Alaska Native; (4) Native Hawaiian and Other Pacific Islander
Source: U.S. Census Bureau, 2012-2016 American Community Survey 5-Year Estimates

Hispanic or Latino Origin

Area	Total (%)	Mexican (%)	Puerto Rican (%)	Cuban (%)	Other (%)
City	8.7	6.6	0.5	0.4	1.2
MSA[1]	7.6	6.0	0.4	0.2	1.1
U.S.	17.3	11.0	1.7	0.7	4.0

Note: Persons of Hispanic or Latino origin can be of any race; (1) Figures cover the Bend-Redmond, OR Metropolitan Statistical Area—see Appendix B for areas included
Source: U.S. Census Bureau, 2012-2016 American Community Survey 5-Year Estimates

Segregation

Type	Segregation Indices[1] 1990	2000	2010	2010 Rank[2]	Percent Change 1990-2000	1990-2010	2000-2010
Black/White	n/a	n/a	n/a	n/a	n/a	n/a	n/a
Asian/White	n/a	n/a	n/a	n/a	n/a	n/a	n/a
Hispanic/White	n/a	n/a	n/a	n/a	n/a	n/a	n/a

Note: All figures cover the Metropolitan Statistical Area—see Appendix B for areas included; Figures are based on an analysis of 1990, 2000, and 2010 Census Decennial Census tract data by William H. Frey, Brookings Institution and the University of Michigan Social Science Data Analysis Network. In this analysis all racial groups (whites, blacks, and asians) are non-Hispanic members of those races. Hispanics are shown as a separate category; (1) Segregation Indices are Dissimilarity Indices that measure the degree to which the minority group is distributed differently than whites across census tracts. They range from 0 (complete integration) to 100 (complete segregation) where the value indicates the percentage of the minority group that needs to move to be distributed exactly like whites; (2) Ranges from 1 (most segregated) to 102 (least segregated); n/a not available.
Source: www.CensusScope.org

Ancestry

Area	German	Irish	English	American	Italian	Polish	French[2]	Scottish	Dutch
City	21.4	13.5	11.9	6.3	4.5	2.8	2.8	3.4	2.1
MSA[1]	21.4	13.2	12.5	6.6	3.8	2.1	2.9	3.4	2.3
U.S.	14.4	10.4	7.7	6.9	5.4	2.9	2.6	1.7	1.3

Note: Figures are the percentage of the total population reporting a particular ancestry. The nine most commonly reported ancestries in the U.S. are shown. Figures include multiple ancestries (e.g. if a person reported being Irish and Italian, they were included in both columns); (1) Figures cover the Bend-Redmond, OR Metropolitan Statistical Area—see Appendix B for areas included; (2) Excludes Basque
Source: U.S. Census Bureau, 2012-2016 American Community Survey 5-Year Estimates

Foreign-Born Population

Area	Percent of Population Born in								
	Any Foreign Country	Asia	Mexico	Europe	Carribean	Central America[2]	South America	Africa	Canada
City	4.8	1.0	1.5	1.1	0.0	0.3	0.1	0.1	0.5
MSA[1]	4.1	0.8	1.5	1.0	0.0	0.2	0.2	0.0	0.4
U.S.	13.2	4.0	3.6	1.5	1.3	1.0	0.9	0.6	0.3

Note: (1) Figures cover the Bend-Redmond, OR Metropolitan Statistical Area—see Appendix B for areas included; (2) Excludes Mexico.
Source: U.S. Census Bureau, 2012-2016 American Community Survey 5-Year Estimates

Marital Status

Area	Never Married	Now Married[2]	Separated	Widowed	Divorced
City	27.6	51.2	1.6	5.1	14.4
MSA[1]	25.1	53.7	1.5	5.3	14.4
U.S.	33.0	48.1	2.1	5.9	11.0

Note: Figures are percentages and cover the population 15 years of age and older; (1) Figures cover the Bend-Redmond, OR Metropolitan Statistical Area—see Appendix B for areas included; (2) Excludes separated
Source: U.S. Census Bureau, 2012-2016 American Community Survey 5-Year Estimates

Disability Status

Area	All Ages	Under 18 Years Old	18 to 64 Years Old	65 Years and Over
City	10.5	3.4	7.8	31.8
MSA[1]	12.8	3.9	10.2	32.1
U.S.	12.5	4.1	10.3	35.7

Note: Figures show percent of the civilian noninstitutionalized population that reported having a disability. Disability status is determined from six types of difficulty: vision, hearing, cognitive, ambulatory, self-care, and independent living. For children under 5 years old, hearing and vision difficulty are used to determine disability status. For children between the ages of 5 and 14, disability status is determined from hearing, vision, cognitive, ambulatory, and self-care difficulties. For people aged 15 years and older, they are considered to have a disability if they have difficulty with any one of the six difficulty types; Note: (1) Figures cover the Bend-Redmond, OR Metropolitan Statistical Area—see Appendix B for areas included
Source: U.S. Census Bureau, 2012-2016 American Community Survey 5-Year Estimates

Age

Area	Percent of Population									Median Age
	Under Age 5	Age 5–19	Age 20–34	Age 35–44	Age 45–54	Age 55–64	Age 65–74	Age 75–84	Age 85+	
City	6.1	18.8	20.1	14.4	12.7	12.4	8.7	4.2	2.6	38.3
MSA[1]	5.4	18.0	17.5	13.0	13.1	14.7	11.5	4.6	2.1	42.0
U.S.	6.2	19.6	20.7	12.7	13.6	12.6	8.3	4.3	1.9	37.7

Note: (1) Figures cover the Bend-Redmond, OR Metropolitan Statistical Area—see Appendix B for areas included
Source: U.S. Census Bureau, 2012-2016 American Community Survey 5-Year Estimates

Gender

Area	Males	Females	Males per 100 Females
City	40,755	43,661	93.3
MSA[1]	84,267	86,546	97.4
U.S.	156,765,322	161,792,840	96.9

Note: (1) Figures cover the Bend-Redmond, OR Metropolitan Statistical Area—see Appendix B for areas included
Source: U.S. Census Bureau, 2012-2016 American Community Survey 5-Year Estimates

Religious Groups by Family

Area	Catholic	Baptist	Non-Den.	Methodist[2]	Lutheran	LDS[3]	Pente-costal	Presby-terian[4]	Muslim[5]	Judaism
MSA[1]	7.4	1.8	3.5	0.6	1.8	3.5	3.2	0.9	<0.1	0.1
U.S.	19.1	9.3	4.0	4.0	2.3	2.0	1.9	1.6	0.8	0.7

Note: Figures are the number of adherents as a percentage of the total population; (1) Figures cover the Bend-Redmond, OR Metropolitan Statistical Area—see Appendix B for areas included; (2) Methodist/Pietist; (3) Latter Day Saints; (4) Reformed; (5) Figures are estimates
Source: Association of Statisticians of American Religious Bodies, 2010 U.S. Religion Census: Religious Congregations & Membership Study

Religious Groups by Tradition

Area	Catholic	Evangelical Protestant	Mainline Protestant	Other Tradition	Black Protestant	Orthodox
MSA[1]	7.4	11.0	3.1	4.1	<0.1	<0.1
U.S.	19.1	16.2	7.3	4.3	1.6	0.3

Note: Figures are the number of adherents as a percentage of the total population; (1) Figures cover the Bend-Redmond, OR Metropolitan Statistical Area—see Appendix B for areas included
Source: Association of Statisticians of American Religious Bodies, 2010 U.S. Religion Census: Religious Congregations & Membership Study

ECONOMY

Gross Metropolitan Product

Area	2014	2015	2016	2017	Rank[2]
MSA[1]	7.0	7.6	7.9	8.3	230

Note: Figures are in billions of dollars; (1) Figures cover the Bend-Redmond, OR Metropolitan Statistical Area—see Appendix B for areas included; (2) Rank is based on 2015 data and ranges from 1 to 381
Source: The U.S. Conference of Mayors, U.S. Metro Economies: GMP and Employment Report, 2015-2017

Economic Growth

Area	2012-14 (%)	2015 (%)	2016 (%)	2017 (%)	Rank[2]
MSA[1]	4.8	6.8	3.2	4.0	19
U.S.	2.0	2.4	1.9	2.6	–

Note: Figures are real gross metropolitan product (GMP) growth rates and represent average annual percent change; (1) Figures cover the Bend-Redmond, OR Metropolitan Statistical Area—see Appendix B for areas included; (2) Rank is based on 2012-2014 average annual percent change and ranges from 1 to 381
Source: The U.S. Conference of Mayors, U.S. Metro Economies: GMP and Employment Report, 2015-2017

Metropolitan Area Exports

Area	2011	2012	2013	2014	2015	2016	Rank[2]
MSA[1]	87.3	93.5	119.0	114.9	149.3	214.8	292

Note: Figures are in millions of dollars; (1) Figures cover the Bend-Redmond, OR Metropolitan Statistical Area—see Appendix B for areas included; (2) Rank is based on 2016 data and ranges from 1 to 385
Source: U.S. Department of Commerce, International Trade Administration, Office of Trade & Industry Information, Manufacturing & Services, data extracted March 15, 2018

Building Permits

Area	Single-Family			Multi-Family			Total		
	2016	2017p	Pct. Chg.	2016	2017p	Pct. Chg.	2016	2017p	Pct. Chg.
City	1,014	946	-6.7	457	266	-41.8	1,471	1,212	-17.6
MSA[1]	1,761	1,741	-1.1	457	320	-30.0	2,218	2,061	-7.1
U.S.	750,800	817,300	8.9	455,800	446,800	-2.0	1,206,600	1,264,100	4.8

Note: (1) Figures cover the Bend-Redmond, OR Metropolitan Statistical Area—see Appendix B for areas included; Figures represent new, privately-owned housing units authorized (unadjusted data); All permit data are based on estimates with imputation; (p) preliminary data.
Source: U.S. Census Bureau, Manufacturing, Mining, and Construction Statistics, Building Permits, 2016, 2017

Bankruptcy Filings

Area	Business Filings 2016	Business Filings 2017	% Chg.	Nonbusiness Filings 2016	Nonbusiness Filings 2017	% Chg.
Deschutes County	17	15	-11.8	514	459	-10.7
U.S.	24,114	23,157	-4.0	770,846	765,863	-0.6

Note: Business filings include Chapter 7, Chapter 11, Chapter 12, and Chapter 13; Nonbusiness filings include Chapter 7, Chapter 11, and Chapter 13
Source: Administrative Office of the U.S. Courts, Business and Nonbusiness Bankruptcy, County Cases Commenced by Chapter of the Bankruptcy Code, During the 12-Month Period Ending December 31, 2016 and Business and Nonbusiness Bankruptcy, County Cases Commenced by Chapter of the Bankruptcy Code, During the 12-Month Period Ending December 31, 2017

Housing Vacancy Rates

Area	Gross Vacancy Rate² (%)			Year-Round Vacancy Rate³ (%)			Rental Vacancy Rate⁴ (%)			Homeowner Vacancy Rate⁵ (%)		
	2015	2016	2017	2015	2016	2017	2015	2016	2017	2015	2016	2017
MSA[1]	n/a	n/a	n/a	n/a	n/a	n/a	n/a	n/a	n/a	n/a	n/a	n/a
U.S.	12.9	12.8	12.7	10.0	9.9	9.9	7.1	6.9	7.2	1.8	1.7	1.6

Note: (1) Figures cover the Bend-Redmond, OR Metropolitan Statistical Area—see Appendix B for areas included; (2) The percentage of the total housing inventory that is vacant; (3) The percentage of the housing inventory (excluding seasonal units) that is year-round vacant; (4) The percentage of rental inventory that is vacant for rent; (5) The percentage of homeowner inventory that is vacant for sale; n/a not available
Source: U.S. Census Bureau, Housing Vacancies and Homeownership Annual Statistics: 2015, 2016, 2017

INCOME

Income

Area	Per Capita ($)	Median Household ($)	Average Household ($)
City	32,162	55,625	77,559
MSA[1]	30,177	54,211	73,597
U.S.	29,829	55,322	77,866

Note: (1) Figures cover the Bend-Redmond, OR Metropolitan Statistical Area—see Appendix B for areas included
Source: U.S. Census Bureau, 2012-2016 American Community Survey 5-Year Estimates

Household Income Distribution

Area	Percent of Households Earning: Under $15,000	$15,000 -$24,999	$25,000 -$34,999	$35,000 -$49,999	$50,000 -$74,999	$75,000 -$99,999	$100,000 -$149,999	$150,000 and up
City	9.9	10.5	10.6	14.6	18.9	12.8	13.3	9.4
MSA[1]	10.8	10.7	10.4	14.8	18.7	13.2	13.4	8.1
U.S.	12.1	10.2	9.9	13.2	17.8	12.2	13.5	11.1

Note: (1) Figures cover the Bend-Redmond, OR Metropolitan Statistical Area—see Appendix B for areas included
Source: U.S. Census Bureau, 2012-2016 American Community Survey 5-Year Estimates

Poverty Rate

Area	All Ages	Under 18 Years Old	18 to 64 Years Old	65 Years and Over
City	12.4	15.0	12.3	9.2
MSA[1]	13.9	18.3	14.0	8.3
U.S.	15.1	21.2	14.2	9.3

Note: Figures are percentage of people whose income during the past 12 months was below the poverty level; (1) Figures cover the Bend-Redmond, OR Metropolitan Statistical Area—see Appendix B for areas included
Source: U.S. Census Bureau, 2012-2016 American Community Survey 5-Year Estimates

EMPLOYMENT

Labor Force and Employment

Area	Civilian Labor Force Dec. 2016	Civilian Labor Force Dec. 2017	% Chg.	Workers Employed Dec. 2016	Workers Employed Dec. 2017	% Chg.
City	49,242	51,296	4.2	47,749	49,402	3.5
MSA[1]	90,518	93,692	3.5	86,682	89,684	3.5
U.S.	158,968,000	159,880,000	0.6	151,798,000	153,602,000	1.2

Note: Data is not seasonally adjusted and covers workers 16 years of age and older; (1) Figures cover the Bend-Redmond, OR Metropolitan Statistical Area—see Appendix B for areas included
Source: Bureau of Labor Statistics, Local Area Unemployment Statistics

Unemployment Rate

Area	2017											
	Jan.	Feb.	Mar.	Apr.	May	Jun.	Jul.	Aug.	Sep.	Oct.	Nov.	Dec.
City	4.1	4.0	3.8	3.2	3.1	3.7	3.7	3.6	3.5	3.6	3.6	3.7
MSA[1]	5.1	4.8	4.5	3.8	3.6	4.1	4.2	4.1	3.8	4.0	4.1	4.3
U.S.	5.1	4.9	4.6	4.1	4.1	4.5	4.6	4.5	4.1	3.9	3.9	3.9

Note: Data is not seasonally adjusted and covers workers 16 years of age and older; (1) Figures cover the Bend-Redmond, OR Metropolitan Statistical Area—see Appendix B for areas included
Source: Bureau of Labor Statistics, Local Area Unemployment Statistics

Average Wages

Occupation	$/Hr.	Occupation	$/Hr.
Accountants and Auditors	30.70	Maids and Housekeeping Cleaners	12.10
Automotive Mechanics	22.10	Maintenance and Repair Workers	17.50
Bookkeepers	19.20	Marketing Managers	47.20
Carpenters	19.50	Nuclear Medicine Technologists	n/a
Cashiers	12.50	Nurses, Licensed Practical	24.30
Clerks, General Office	16.00	Nurses, Registered	43.60
Clerks, Receptionists/Information	15.10	Nursing Assistants	15.30
Clerks, Shipping/Receiving	17.40	Packers and Packagers, Hand	13.10
Computer Programmers	31.90	Physical Therapists	36.40
Computer Systems Analysts	40.20	Postal Service Mail Carriers	24.10
Computer User Support Specialists	23.40	Real Estate Brokers	25.70
Cooks, Restaurant	13.60	Retail Salespersons	14.90
Dentists	108.00	Sales Reps., Exc. Tech./Scientific	31.70
Electrical Engineers	41.10	Sales Reps., Tech./Scientific	n/a
Electricians	28.30	Secretaries, Exc. Legal/Med./Exec.	17.00
Financial Managers	47.30	Security Guards	13.30
First-Line Supervisors/Managers, Sales	19.40	Surgeons	n/a
Food Preparation Workers	12.20	Teacher Assistants*	16.50
General and Operations Managers	43.50	Teachers, Elementary School*	37.40
Hairdressers/Cosmetologists	12.70	Teachers, Secondary School*	32.10
Internists, General	n/a	Telemarketers	n/a
Janitors and Cleaners	15.40	Truck Drivers, Heavy/Tractor-Trailer	23.40
Landscaping/Groundskeeping Workers	14.80	Truck Drivers, Light/Delivery Svcs.	19.80
Lawyers	57.40	Waiters and Waitresses	14.00

Note: Wage data covers the Bend-Redmond, OR Metropolitan Statistical Area—see Appendix B for areas included; (*) Hourly wages for elementary/secondary school teachers and teacher assistants were calculated by the editors from annual wage data based on a 40 hour work week; n/a not available.
Source: Bureau of Labor Statistics, Metro Area Occupational Employment & Wage Estimates, May 2017

Employment by Occupation

Occupation Classification	City (%)	MSA[1] (%)	U.S. (%)
Management, Business, Science, and Arts	40.8	36.4	37.0
Natural Resources, Construction, and Maintenance	7.8	8.9	8.9
Production, Transportation, and Material Moving	7.9	10.1	12.2
Sales and Office	24.2	25.0	23.8
Service	19.2	19.6	18.1

Note: Figures cover employed civilians 16 years of age and older; (1) Figures cover the Bend-Redmond, OR Metropolitan Statistical Area—see Appendix B for areas included
Source: U.S. Census Bureau, 2012-2016 American Community Survey 5-Year Estimates

Employment by Industry

Sector	MSA[1] Number of Employees	MSA[1] Percent of Total	U.S. Percent of Total
Construction, Mining, and Logging	6,700	8.2	5.2
Education and Health Services	13,100	16.0	15.9
Financial Activities	4,800	5.8	5.7
Government	10,000	12.2	15.3
Information	1,700	2.1	1.9
Leisure and Hospitality	12,000	14.6	10.7
Manufacturing	5,600	6.8	8.5
Other Services	2,800	3.4	3.9
Professional and Business Services	9,700	11.8	14.0
Retail Trade	11,600	14.1	11.0
Transportation, Warehousing, and Utilities	2,100	2.6	4.1
Wholesale Trade	2,000	2.4	4.0

Note: Figures are non-farm employment as of December 2017. Figures are not seasonally adjusted and include workers 16 years of age and older; (1) Figures cover the Bend-Redmond, OR Metropolitan Statistical Area—see Appendix B for areas included
Source: Bureau of Labor Statistics, Current Employment Statistics, Employment, Hours, and Earnings

Occupations with Greatest Projected Employment Growth: 2017 – 2019

Occupation[1]	2017 Employment	2019 Projected Employment	Numeric Employment Change	Percent Employment Change
Carpenters	22,060	24,830	2,770	12.6
Retail Salespersons	69,050	71,620	2,570	3.7
Combined Food Preparation and Serving Workers, Including Fast Food	37,540	39,870	2,330	6.2
Construction Laborers	17,510	19,030	1,520	8.7
Waiters and Waitresses	32,960	34,470	1,510	4.6
Cooks, Restaurant	25,640	27,050	1,410	5.5
General and Operations Managers	31,040	32,340	1,300	4.2
Personal Care Aides	21,600	22,900	1,300	6.0
Registered Nurses	35,230	36,350	1,120	3.2
Office Clerks, General	36,770	37,740	970	2.6

Note: Projections cover Oregon; (1) Sorted by numeric employment change
Source: www.projectionscentral.com, State Occupational Projections, 2017–2019 Short-Term Projections

Fastest Growing Occupations: 2017 – 2019

Occupation[1]	2017 Employment	2019 Projected Employment	Numeric Employment Change	Percent Employment Change
Animal Trainers	230	300	70	32.3
Chemical Equipment Operators and Tenders	560	630	70	14.2
Carpenters	22,060	24,830	2,770	12.6
Nonfarm Animal Caretakers	3,430	3,860	430	12.4
Brickmasons and Blockmasons	990	1,100	110	11.1
Roofers	3,700	4,100	400	10.9
Structural Iron and Steel Workers	740	820	80	10.5
Physical Therapist Aides	780	860	80	10.4
Glaziers	900	990	90	10.3
Massage Therapists	3,650	4,030	380	10.3

Note: Projections cover Oregon; (1) Sorted by percent employment change and excludes occupations with numeric employment change less than 50
Source: www.projectionscentral.com, State Occupational Projections, 2017–2019 Short-Term Projections

TAXES

State Corporate Income Tax Rates

State	Tax Rate (%)	Income Brackets ($)	Num. of Brackets	Financial Institution Tax Rate (%)[a]	Federal Income Tax Ded.
Oregon	6.6 - 7.6 (u)	1 million	2	6.6 - 7.6 (u)	No

Note: Tax rates as of January 1, 2018; (a) Rates listed are the corporate income tax rate applied to financial institutions or excise taxes based on income. Some states have other taxes based upon the value of deposits or shares; (u) Oregon's minimum tax for C corporations depends on the Oregon sales of the filing group. The minimum tax ranges from $150 for corporations with sales under $500,000, up to $100,000 for companies with sales of $100 million or above.
Source: Federation of Tax Administrators, Range of State Corporate Income Tax Rates, January 1, 2018

State Individual Income Tax Rates

State	Tax Rate (%)	Income Brackets ($)	Num. of Brackets	Personal Exempt. ($)[1] Single	Personal Exempt. ($)[1] Dependents	Fed. Inc. Tax Ded.
Oregon (a)	5.0 - 9.9	3,450 -125,000 (b)	4	201 (c)	201 (c)	Yes (p)

Note: Tax rates as of January 1, 2018; Local- and county-level taxes are not included; n/a not applicable; (1) Married joint filers generally receive double the single exemption; (a) 19 states have statutory provision for automatically adjusting to the rate of inflation the dollar values of the income tax brackets, standard deductions, and/or personal exemptions. Massachusetts, Michigan, and Nebraska index the personal exemption only. Oregon does not index the income brackets for $125,000 and over; (b) For joint returns, taxes are twice the tax on half the couple's income; (c) The personal exemption takes the form of a tax credit instead of a deduction; (p) The deduction for federal income tax is limited to $5,000 for individuals and $10,000 for joint returns in Missouri and Montana, and to $6,350 for all filers in Oregon.
Source: Federation of Tax Administrators, State Individual Income Tax Rates, January 1, 2018

Various State Sales and Excise Tax Rates

State	State Sales Tax (%)	Gasoline[1] (¢/gal.)	Cigarette[2] ($/pack)	Spirits[3] ($/gal.)	Wine[4] ($/gal.)	Beer[5] ($/gal.)	Recreational Marijuana (%)
Oregon	None	36.77	1.33	22.75 (g)	0.67 (l)	0.08	17.0

Note: All tax rates as of January 1, 2018; (1) The American Petroleum Institute has developed a methodology for determining the average tax rate on a gallon of fuel. Rates may include any of the following: excise taxes, environmental fees, storage tank fees, other fees or taxes, general sales tax, and local taxes. In states where gasoline is subject to the general sales tax, or where the fuel tax is based on the average sale price, the average rate determined by API is sensitive to changes in the price of gasoline. States that fully or partially apply general sales taxes to gasoline: CA, CO, GA, IL, IN, MI, NY; (2) The federal excise tax of $1.0066 per pack and local taxes are not included; (3) Rates are those applicable to off-premise sales of 40% alcohol by volume (a.b.v.) distilled spirits in 750ml containers. Local excise taxes are excluded; (4) Rates are those applicable to off-premise sales of 11% a.b.v. non-carbonated wine in 750ml containers; (5) Rates are those applicable to off-premise sales of 4.7% a.b.v. beer in 12 ounce containers; (g) Control states, where the government controls all sales. Products can be subject to ad valorem mark-up as well as excise taxes; (l) Different rates also applicable to alcohol content, place of production, size of container, place purchased (on- or off-premise or on board airlines) or type of wine (carbonated, vermouth, etc.).
Source: Tax Foundation, 2018 Facts & Figures: How Does Your State Compare?

State Business Tax Climate Index Rankings

State	Overall Rank	Corporate Tax Rank	Individual Income Tax Rank	Sales Tax Rank	Unemployment Insurance Tax Rank	Property Tax Rank
Oregon	10	34	32	4	31	18

Note: The index is a measure of how each state's tax laws affect economic performance. The lower the rank, the more favorable a state's tax system is for business. States without a given tax are given a ranking of 1. The scores/rankings for the District of Columbia do not affect other states. The 2018 index represents the tax climate as of July 1, 2017.
Source: Tax Foundation, State Business Tax Climate Index 2018

TRANSPORTATION

Means of Transportation to Work

Area	Car/Truck/Van		Public Transportation			Bicycle	Walked	Other Means	Worked at Home
	Drove Alone	Car-pooled	Bus	Subway	Railroad				
City	75.1	7.5	0.6	0.0	0.0	3.1	3.3	1.0	9.4
MSA[1]	74.9	9.0	0.4	0.0	0.0	2.2	2.7	1.2	9.5
U.S.	76.4	9.3	2.6	1.9	0.6	0.6	2.8	1.3	4.6

Note: Figures are percentages and cover workers 16 years of age and older; (1) Figures cover the Bend-Redmond, OR Metropolitan Statistical Area—see Appendix B for areas included
Source: U.S. Census Bureau, 2012-2016 American Community Survey 5-Year Estimates

Travel Time to Work

Area	Less Than 10 Minutes	10 to 19 Minutes	20 to 29 Minutes	30 to 44 Minutes	45 to 59 Minutes	60 to 89 Minutes	90 Minutes or More
City	24.2	54.7	11.0	6.1	1.6	0.9	1.5
MSA[1]	21.7	43.8	15.9	12.7	2.9	1.4	1.6
U.S.	12.9	29.2	20.9	20.4	8.0	6.0	2.7

Note: Note: Figures are percentages and include workers 16 years old and over; (1) Figures cover the Bend-Redmond, OR Metropolitan Statistical Area—see Appendix B for areas included
Source: U.S. Census Bureau, 2012-2016 American Community Survey 5-Year Estimates

Freeway Travel Time Index

Area	1985	1990	1995	2000	2005	2010	2014
Urban Area Rank[1,2]	n/a	n/a	n/a	n/a	n/a	n/a	n/a
Urban Area Index[1]	n/a	n/a	n/a	n/a	n/a	n/a	n/a
Average Index[3]	1.09	1.11	1.14	1.17	1.20	1.19	1.20

Note: Freeway Travel Time Index—the ratio of travel time in the peak period to the travel time at free-flow conditions. For example, a value of 1.30 indicates a 20-minute free-flow trip takes 26 minutes in the peak (20 minutes x 1.30 = 26 minutes); (1) Data for the Bend-Redmond, OR urban area was not available; (2) Rank is based on 101 urban areas (#1 = highest travel time index); (3) Average of 101 urban areas
Source: Texas Transportation Institute, 2015 Urban Mobility Scorecard, August 2015

Freeway Commuter Stress Index

Area	1985	1990	1995	2000	2005	2010	2014
Urban Area Rank[1,2]	n/a	n/a	n/a	n/a	n/a	n/a	n/a
Urban Area Index[1]	n/a	n/a	n/a	n/a	n/a	n/a	n/a
Average Index[3]	1.13	1.16	1.19	1.22	1.25	1.24	1.25

Note: The Freeway Commuter Stress Index is the same as the Freeway Travel Time Index (see table above) except that it includes only the travel in the peak directions during the peak periods; the TTI includes travel in all directions during the peak period. Thus, the CSI is more indicative of the work trip experienced by each commuter on a daily basis; (1) Data for the Bend-Redmond, OR urban area was not available; (2) Rank is based on 101 urban areas (#1 = highest travel time index); (3) Average of 101 urban areas
Source: Texas Transportation Institute, 2015 Urban Mobility Scorecard, August 2015

Living Environment

COST OF LIVING

Cost of Living Index

Composite Index	Groceries	Housing	Utilities	Trans-portation	Health Care	Misc. Goods/ Services
n/a	n/a	n/a	n/a	n/a	n/a	n/a

Note: The Cost of Living Index measures regional differences in the cost of consumer goods and services, excluding taxes and non-consumer expenditures, for professional and managerial households in the top income quintile. It is based on more than 50,000 prices covering almost 60 different items for which prices are collected three times a year by chambers of commerce, economic development organizations or university applied economic centers in each participating urban area. The numbers shown should be read as a percentage above or below the national average of 100. For example, a value of 115.4 in the groceries column indicates that grocery prices are 15.4% higher than the national average. Small differences in the index numbers should not be interpreted as significant; n/a not available.
Source: The Council for Community and Economic Research, ACCRA Cost of Living Index, 2017

Grocery Prices

Area[1]	T-Bone Steak ($/pound)	Frying Chicken ($/pound)	Whole Milk ($/half gal.)	Eggs ($/dozen)	Orange Juice ($/64 oz.)	Coffee ($/11.5 oz.)
City[2]	n/a	n/a	n/a	n/a	n/a	n/a
Avg.	11.29	1.40	2.02	1.47	3.55	4.37
Min.	7.71	0.93	1.04	0.70	2.86	3.24
Max.	15.83	2.39	4.03	3.92	6.29	8.16

*Note: (1) Values for the local area are compared with the average, minimum and maximum values for all 294 areas in the Cost of Living Index; (2) Figures cover the Bend OR urban area; n/a not available; **T-Bone Steak** (price per pound); **Frying Chicken** (price per pound, whole fryer); **Whole Milk** (half gallon carton); **Eggs** (price per dozen, Grade A, large); **Orange Juice** (64 oz. Tropicana or Florida Natural); **Coffee** (11.5 oz. can, vacuum-packed, Maxwell House, Hills Bros, or Folgers).*
Source: The Council for Community and Economic Research, ACCRA Cost of Living Index, 2017

Housing and Utility Costs

Area[1]	New Home Price ($)	Apartment Rent ($/month)	All Electric ($/month)	Part Electric ($/month)	Other Energy ($/month)	Telephone ($/month)
City[2]	n/a	n/a	n/a	n/a	n/a	n/a
Avg.	335,956	1,047	175.01	97.34	67.93	28.71
Min.	187,788	491	109.48	49.33	35.44	12.39
Max.	1,739,087	4,559	432.62	227.09	353.33	44.61

*Note: (1) Values for the local area are compared with the average, minimum and maximum values for all 294 areas in the Cost of Living Index; (2) Figures cover the Bend OR urban area; n/a not available; **New Home Price** (2,400 sf living area, 8,000 sf lot, in urban area with full utilities); **Apartment Rent** (950 sf 2 bedroom/1.5 or 2 bath, unfurnished, excluding all utilities except water); **All Electric** (average monthly cost for an all-electric home); **Part Electric** (average monthly cost for a part-electric home); **Other Energy** (average monthly cost for natural gas, fuel oil, coal, wood, and any other forms of energy except electricity); **Telephone** (price includes basic monthly rate for a private residential line plus additional local usage charges incurred by a family of four).*
Source: The Council for Community and Economic Research, ACCRA Cost of Living Index, 2017

Health Care, Transportation, and Other Costs

Area[1]	Doctor ($/visit)	Dentist ($/visit)	Optometrist ($/visit)	Gasoline ($/gallon)	Beauty Salon ($/visit)	Men's Shirt ($)
City[2]	n/a	n/a	n/a	n/a	n/a	n/a
Avg.	108.00	92.54	101.93	2.25	37.58	30.92
Min.	30.39	60.00	49.75	1.82	16.11	11.20
Max.	193.50	161.94	229.28	3.16	77.35	59.13

*Note: (1) Values for the local area are compared with the average, minimum and maximum values for all 294 areas in the Cost of Living Index; (2) Figures cover the Bend OR urban area; n/a not available; **Doctor** (general practitioners routine exam of an established patient); **Dentist** (adult teeth cleaning and periodic oral examination); **Optometrist** (full vision eye exam for established adult patient); **Gasoline** (one gallon regular unleaded, national brand, including all taxes, cash price at self-service pump if available); **Beauty Salon** (woman's shampoo, trim, and blow-dry); **Men's Shirt** (cotton/polyester dress shirt, pinpoint weave, long sleeves).*
Source: The Council for Community and Economic Research, ACCRA Cost of Living Index, 2017

HOUSING

House Price Index (HPI)

Area	National Ranking[2]	Quarterly Change (%)	One-Year Change (%)	Five-Year Change (%)
MSA[1]	49	0.93	9.28	84.38
U.S.[3]	–	1.61	6.68	34.71

Note: The HPI is a weighted repeat sales index. It measures average price changes in repeat sales or refinancings on the same properties. This information is obtained by reviewing repeat mortgage transactions on single-family properties whose mortgages have been purchased or securitized by Fannie Mae or Freddie Mac in January 1975; (1) Figures cover the Bend-Redmond, OR Metropolitan Statistical Area—see Appendix B for areas included; (2) Rankings are based on annual percentage change for all metro areas containing at least 15,000 transactions over the last 10 years and ranges from 1 to 253; (3) figures based on a weighted average of Census Division estimates using a seasonally adjusted, purchase-only index; all figures are for the period ending December 31, 2017
Source: Federal Housing Finance Agency, House Price Index, February 28, 2018

Median Single-Family Home Prices

Area	2015	2016	2017p	Percent Change 2016 to 2017
MSA[1]	n/a	n/a	n/a	n/a
U.S. Average	223.9	235.5	248.8	5.6

Note: Figures are median sales prices of existing single-family homes in thousands of dollars; (p) preliminary; n/a not available; (1) Figures cover the Bend-Redmond, OR Metropolitan Statistical Area—see Appendix B for areas included
Source: National Association of Realtors, Median Sales Price of Existing Single-Family Homes for Metropolitan Areas, 4th Quarter 2017

Qualifying Income Based on Median Sales Price of Existing Single-Family Homes

Area	With 5% Down ($)	With 10% Down ($)	With 20% Down ($)
MSA[1]	n/a	n/a	n/a
U.S. Average	55,585	52,659	46,808

Note: Figures are preliminary; Qualifying income is based on a mortgage rate of 4.17%. Monthly principal and interest payment is limited to 25% of income; n/a not available; (1) Figures cover the Bend-Redmond, OR Metropolitan Statistical Area—see Appendix B for areas included
Source: National Association of Realtors, Qualifying Income Based on Median Sales Price of Existing Single-Family Homes for Metropolitan Areas, 4th Quarter 2017

Median Apartment Condo-Coop Home Prices

Area	2015	2016	2017p	Percent Change 2016 to 2017
MSA[1]	n/a	n/a	n/a	n/a
U.S. Average	210.7	220.7	234.3	6.2

Note: Figures are median sales prices of existing apartment condo-coop homes in thousands of dollars; (p) preliminary; n/a not available; (1) Figures cover the Bend-Redmond, OR Metropolitan Statistical Area—see Appendix B for areas included
Source: National Association of Realtors, Median Sales Price of Existing Apartment Condo-Coop Homes for Metropolitan Areas, 4th Quarter 2017

Home Value Distribution

Area	Under $50,000	$50,000 -$99,999	$100,000 -$149,999	$150,000 -$199,999	$200,000 -$299,999	$300,000 -$499,999	$500,000 -$999,999	$1,000,000 or more
City	6.3	2.3	7.1	10.4	25.2	31.6	14.8	2.4
MSA[1]	5.0	4.9	8.6	12.4	25.0	26.5	15.6	2.0
U.S.	8.8	14.8	15.3	14.9	18.4	16.4	9.0	2.5

Note: Figures are percentages and cover owner-occupied housing units; (1) Figures cover the Bend-Redmond, OR Metropolitan Statistical Area—see Appendix B for areas included
Source: U.S. Census Bureau, 2012-2016 American Community Survey 5-Year Estimates

Homeownership Rate

Area	2009 (%)	2010 (%)	2011 (%)	2012 (%)	2013 (%)	2014 (%)	2015 (%)	2016 (%)	2017 (%)
MSA[1]	n/a	n/a	n/a	n/a	n/a	n/a	n/a	n/a	n/a
U.S.	67.4	66.9	66.1	65.4	65.1	64.5	63.7	63.4	63.9

Note: (1) Figures cover the Bend-Redmond, OR Metropolitan Statistical Area—see Appendix B for areas included; n/a not available
Source: U.S. Census Bureau, Housing Vacancies and Homeownership Annual Statistics: 2009-2017

Year Housing Structure Built

Area	2010 or Later	2000 -2009	1990 -1999	1980 -1989	1970 -1979	1960 -1969	1950 -1959	1940 -1949	Before 1940	Median Year
City	3.4	33.1	24.1	12.0	15.4	3.3	2.3	1.2	5.0	1994
MSA[1]	2.6	29.7	24.9	13.7	18.0	3.7	2.4	1.3	3.7	1993
U.S.	2.3	14.7	14.0	13.7	15.6	10.9	10.6	5.2	13.0	1977

Note: Figures are percentages except for Median Year; Note: (1) Figures cover the Bend-Redmond, OR Metropolitan Statistical Area—see Appendix B for areas included
Source: U.S. Census Bureau, 2012-2016 American Community Survey 5-Year Estimates

Gross Monthly Rent

Area	Under $500	$500 -$999	$1,000 -$1,499	$1,500 -$1,999	$2,000 -$2,499	$2,500 -$2,999	$3,000 and up	Median ($)
City	5.1	42.9	34.9	12.1	3.1	0.5	1.4	1,024
MSA[1]	5.4	46.8	34.7	9.3	2.4	0.5	0.8	981
U.S.	11.3	43.3	27.7	10.7	4.0	1.6	1.5	949

Note: Figures are percentages except for Median; Gross rent is the contract rent plus the estimated average monthly cost of utilities (electricity, gas, and water and sewer) and fuels (oil, coal, kerosene, wood, etc.) if these are paid by the renter (or paid for the renter by someone else); (1) Figures cover the Bend-Redmond, OR Metropolitan Statistical Area—see Appendix B for areas included
Source: U.S. Census Bureau, 2012-2016 American Community Survey 5-Year Estimates

HEALTH

Health Risk Factors

Category	MSA[1] (%)	U.S. (%)
Adults aged 18–64 who have any kind of health care coverage	n/a	87.7
Adults who reported being in good or excellent health	n/a	83.6
Adults who are current smokers	n/a	17.1
Adults who currently use E-cigarettes	n/a	4.7
Adults who currently use chewing tobacco, snuff, or snus	n/a	4.0
Adults who are heavy drinkers[2]	n/a	6.5
Adults who are binge drinkers[3]	n/a	16.9
Adults who are overweight (BMI 25.0 - 29.9)	n/a	35.3
Adults who are obese (BMI 30.0 - 99.8)	n/a	29.9
Adults who participated in any physical activities in the past month	n/a	76.9
Adults who always or nearly always wears a seat belt	n/a	94.3

Note: n/a not available; (1) Figures cover the Bend-Redmond, OR Metropolitan Statistical Area—see Appendix B for areas included; (2) Heavy drinkers are classified as adult men having more than 14 drinks per week and adult women having more than 7 drinks per week; (3) Binge drinkers are classified as males having five or more drinks on one occasion or females having four or more drinks on one occasion
Source: Centers for Disease Control and Prevention, Behaviorial Risk Factor Surveillance System, SMART: Selected Metropolitan Area Risk Trends, 2016

Health Screening Rates

Category	MSA[1] (%)	U.S. (%)
Adults 50-75 who have had a blood stool test within the past year	n/a	8.0
Adults 50-75 who have had a colonoscopy in the past 10 years	n/a	63.5
Adults aged 65+ who have had flu shot within the past year	n/a	58.6
Adults aged 65+ who have ever had a pneumonia vaccination	n/a	73.4
Adults who have ever been tested for HIV	n/a	35.6
Women aged 21-65 who have had a pap test in the past three years	n/a	79.8
Men aged 40+ who have had a PSA test within the past two years	n/a	39.5
Women aged 40+ who have had a mammogram within the past two years	n/a	72.5

Note: n/a not available; (1) Figures cover the Bend-Redmond, OR Metropolitan Statistical Area—see Appendix B for areas included; Source: Centers for Disease Control and Prevention, Behaviorial Risk Factor Surveillance System, SMART: Selected Metropolitan Area Risk Trends, 2016

Chronic Health Conditions

Category	MSA[1] (%)	U.S. (%)
Adults who have ever been told they had a heart attack	n/a	4.4
Adults who have ever been told they have angina or coronary heart disease	n/a	4.1
Adults who have ever been told they had a stroke	n/a	3.1
Adults who have been told they currently have asthma	n/a	9.3
Adults who have ever been told they have arthritis	n/a	25.8
Adults who have ever been told they have diabetes[2]	n/a	10.5
Adults who have ever been told they had skin cancer	n/a	5.9
Adults who have ever been told they had any other types of cancer	n/a	6.7
Adults who have ever been told they have COPD	n/a	6.3
Adults who have ever been told they have kidney disease	n/a	2.8
Adults who have ever been told they have a form of depression	n/a	17.4

Note: n/a not available; (1) Figures cover the Bend-Redmond, OR Metropolitan Statistical Area—see Appendix B for areas included; (2) Figures do not include pregnancy-related, borderline, or pre-diabetes
Source: Centers for Disease Control and Prevention, Behaviorial Risk Factor Surveillance System, SMART: Selected Metropolitan Area Risk Trends, 2016

Mortality Rates for the Top 10 Causes of Death in the U.S.

ICD-10[a] Sub-Chapter	ICD-10[a] Code	Age-Adjusted Mortality Rate[1] per 100,000 population	
		County[2]	U.S.
Malignant neoplasms	C00-C97	134.4	158.5
Ischaemic heart diseases	I20-I25	69.6	96.8
Other forms of heart disease	I30-I51	47.8	52.4
Chronic lower respiratory diseases	J40-J47	36.4	40.9
Cerebrovascular diseases	I60-I69	33.9	37.2
Organic, including symptomatic, mental disorders	F01-F09	41.1	33.3
Other degenerative diseases of the nervous system	G30-G31	36.7	32.1
Other external causes of accidental injury	W00-X59	26.8	31.2
Diabetes mellitus	E10-E14	15.7	21.1
Hypertensive diseases	I10-I15	13.1	20.8

Note: (a) ICD-10 = International Classification of Diseases 10th Revision; (1) Mortality rates are a three year average covering 2014-2016; (2) Figures cover Deschutes County.
Source: Centers for Disease Control and Prevention, National Center for Health Statistics. Underlying Cause of Death 1999-2016 on CDC WONDER Online Database, released December 2017

Mortality Rates for Selected Causes of Death

ICD-10[a] Sub-Chapter	ICD-10[a] Code	Age-Adjusted Mortality Rate[1] per 100,000 population	
		County[2]	U.S.
Assault	X85-Y09	Suppressed	5.6
Diseases of the liver	K70-K76	12.4	14.0
Human immunodeficiency virus (HIV) disease	B20-B24	Suppressed	1.9
Influenza and pneumonia	J09-J18	7.3	14.6
Intentional self-harm	X60-X84	20.0	13.2
Malnutrition	E40-E46	Unreliable	1.3
Obesity and other hyperalimentation	E65-E68	Unreliable	2.1
Renal failure	N17-N19	6.1	13.0
Transport accidents	V01-V99	11.3	12.0
Viral hepatitis	B15-B19	Unreliable	1.9

Note: (a) ICD-10 = International Classification of Diseases 10th Revision; (1) Mortality rates are a three year average covering 2014-2016; (2) Figures cover Deschutes County; Data are Suppressed when the data meet the criteria for confidentiality constraints; Mortality rates are flagged as Unreliable when the rate would be calculated with a numerator of 20 or less.
Source: Centers for Disease Control and Prevention, National Center for Health Statistics. Underlying Cause of Death 1999-2016 on CDC WONDER Online Database, released December 2017

Health Insurance Coverage

Area	With Health Insurance	With Private Health Insurance	With Public Health Insurance	Without Health Insurance	Population Under Age 18 Without Health Insurance
City	86.3	66.7	33.1	13.7	9.9
MSA[1]	86.9	64.9	36.9	13.1	8.3
U.S.	88.3	66.7	33.0	11.7	5.9

Note: Figures are percentages that cover the civilian noninstitutionalized population; (1) Figures cover the Bend-Redmond, OR Metropolitan Statistical Area—see Appendix B for areas included
Source: U.S. Census Bureau, 2012-2016 American Community Survey 5-Year Estimates

Number of Medical Professionals

Area	MDs[3]	DOs[3,4]	Dentists	Podiatrists	Chiropractors	Optometrists
County[1] (number)	518	52	149	11	100	39
County[1] (rate[2])	297.2	29.8	82.5	6.1	55.3	21.6
U.S. (rate[2])	276.5	22.3	67.3	6.0	26.7	15.9

Note: Data as of 2016 unless noted; (1) Data covers Deschutes County; (2) Rate per 100,000 population; (3) Data as of 2015 and includes all active, non-federal physicians; (4) Doctor of Osteopathic Medicine
Source: U.S. Department of Health and Human Services, Health Resources and Services Administration, Bureau of Health Professions, Area Resource File (ARF) 2016-2017

EDUCATION

Public School District Statistics

District Name	Schls	Pupils	Pupil/ Teacher Ratio	Minority Pupils[1] (%)	Free Lunch Eligible[2] (%)	IEP[3] (%)
Bend-Lapine Administrative SD 1	31	17,517	21.6	17.0	35.8	11.4
Redmond SD 2J	12	7,364	21.4	22.2	51.1	14.5

Note: Table includes school districts with 100 or more students; (1) Percentage of students that are not non-Hispanic white; (2) Percentage of students that are eligible for the free lunch program; (3) Percentage of students that have an Individualized Education Program.
Source: U.S. Department of Education, National Center for Education Statistics, Common Core of Data, Local Education Agency (School District) Universe Survey: School Year 2015-2016; U.S. Department of Education, National Center for Education Statistics, Common Core of Data, Public Elementary/Secondary School Universe Survey: School Year 2015-2016

Highest Level of Education

Area	Less than H.S.	H.S. Diploma	Some College, No Deg.	Associate Degree	Bachelor's Degree	Master's Degree	Prof. School Degree	Doctorate Degree
City	5.3	17.3	26.2	9.6	26.9	10.2	3.1	1.4
MSA[1]	7.0	23.6	26.9	9.1	20.9	8.9	2.3	1.2
U.S.	13.0	27.5	21.0	8.2	18.8	8.2	2.0	1.3

Note: Figures cover persons age 25 and over; (1) Figures cover the Bend-Redmond, OR Metropolitan Statistical Area—see Appendix B for areas included
Source: U.S. Census Bureau, 2012-2016 American Community Survey 5-Year Estimates

Educational Attainment by Race

Area	High School Graduate or Higher (%)					Bachelor's Degree or Higher (%)				
	Total	White	Black	Asian	Hisp.[2]	Total	White	Black	Asian	Hisp.[2]
City	94.7	95.4	92.3	82.1	74.8	41.6	42.5	48.2	27.8	22.0
MSA[1]	93.0	93.7	92.5	86.4	72.7	33.3	33.9	32.2	24.5	18.8
U.S.	87.0	88.9	84.3	86.3	65.7	30.3	31.6	20.0	52.1	14.7

Note: Figures shown cover persons 25 years old and over; (1) Figures cover the Bend-Redmond, OR Metropolitan Statistical Area—see Appendix B for areas included; (2) People of Hispanic origin can be of any race
Source: U.S. Census Bureau, 2012-2016 American Community Survey 5-Year Estimates

School Enrollment by Grade and Control

Area	Preschool (%)		Kindergarten (%)		Grades 1 - 4 (%)		Grades 5 - 8 (%)		Grades 9 - 12 (%)	
	Public	Private	Public	Private	Public	Private	Public	Private	Public	Private
City	22.2	77.8	85.5	14.5	89.7	10.3	90.6	9.4	94.4	5.6
MSA[1]	30.0	70.0	92.5	7.5	90.1	9.9	89.6	10.4	95.0	5.0
U.S.	58.4	41.6	87.7	12.3	89.8	10.2	89.7	10.3	90.4	9.6

Note: Figures shown cover persons 3 years old and over; (1) Figures cover the Bend-Redmond, OR Metropolitan Statistical Area—see Appendix B for areas included
Source: U.S. Census Bureau, 2012-2016 American Community Survey 5-Year Estimates

Average Salaries of Public School Classroom Teachers

Area	2015		2016		Change from 2015 to 2016	
	Dollars	Rank[1]	Dollars	Rank[1]	Percent	Rank[2]
Oregon	59,464	14	60,359	13	1.5	17
U.S. Average	57,611	–	58,353	–	1.3	–

Note: (1) Rank ranges from 1 to 51 where 1 indicates highest salary; (2) Rank ranges from 1 to 51 where 1 indicates highest percent change.
Source: National Education Association, Rankings & Estimates: Rankings of the States 2016 and Estimates of School Statistics 2017

Higher Education

Four-Year Colleges			Two-Year Colleges			Medical Schools[1]	Law Schools[2]	Voc/ Tech[3]
Public	Private Non-profit	Private For-profit	Public	Private Non-profit	Private For-profit			
1	0	0	1	0	1	0	0	1

Note: Figures cover institutions located within the city limits and include main campuses only; (1) includes schools accredited by the Liaison Committee on Medical Education and the American Osteopathic Association's Commission on Osteopathic College Accreditation; (2) includes ABA-accredited schools, schools with provisional ABA accreditation, and state accredited schools; (3) includes all schools with programs that are less than 2 years.
Source: National Center for Education Statistics, Integrated Postsecondary Education System (IPEDS), 2016-17; Wikipedia, List of Medical Schools in the United States, accessed April 2, 2018; Wikipedia, List of Law Schools in the United States, accessed April 2, 2018

PRESIDENTIAL ELECTION

2016 Presidential Election Results

Area	Clinton	Trump	Johnson	Stein	Other
Deschutes County	43.1	46.4	5.2	2.0	3.3
U.S.	48.0	45.9	3.3	1.1	1.7

Note: Results are percentages and may not add to 100% due to rounding
Source: Dave Leip's Atlas of U.S. Presidential Elections

EMPLOYERS

Major Employers

Company Name	Industry
Bright Wood Corporation	Manufacturer of wood components and millwork
IBEX Global	Customer acquisition solutions
Les Schwab Tire Centers	Tire retail stores
McDonald's	Quick-service food
Mt. Bachelor	Ski resort
Safeway	Supermarket chain
St. Charles Medical Center	General medical and surgical hospital
Summit Med Group OR-Bend Mem Clinic	Multispecialty physician clinic
Sunriver Resort	Luxury resort and residential community
Wal-Mart	Discount retailer

Note: Companies shown are located within the Bend-Redmond, OR Metropolitan Statistical Area.
Source: Hoovers.com; Wikipedia

PUBLIC SAFETY

Crime Rate

Area	All Crimes	Violent Crimes				Property Crimes		
		Murder	Rape[3]	Robbery	Aggrav. Assault	Burglary	Larceny -Theft	Motor Vehicle Theft
City	2,359.8	0.0	19.0	22.4	66.1	199.5	1,949.7	103.1
Metro[1]	2,322.4	1.1	26.1	16.7	107.7	243.2	1,793.2	134.4
U.S.	2,847.8	5.3	40.4	102.8	248.5	468.9	1,745.0	236.9

Note: Figures are crimes per 100,000 population; (1) Figures cover the Bend-Redmond, OR Metropolitan Statistical Area—see Appendix B for areas included; (3) The city and U.S. figures shown were reported using the revised Uniform Crime Reporting (UCR) definition of rape. The metro area figures shown are an aggregate total of the data submitted using both the revised and legacy UCR definitions.
Source: FBI Uniform Crime Reports, 2016

Hate Crimes

Area	Number of Quarters Reported	Number of Incidents per Bias Motivation					
		Race/Ethnicity/ Ancestry	Religion	Sexual Orientation	Disability	Gender	Gender Identity
City	4	0	0	0	0	0	0
U.S.	4	3,489	1,273	1,076	70	31	124

Source: Federal Bureau of Investigation, Hate Crime Statistics 2016

Identity Theft Consumer Reports

Area	Reports	Reports per 100,000 Population	Rank[2]
MSA[1]	111	61	308
U.S.	371,061	114	-

Note: (1) Figures cover the Bend-Redmond, OR Metropolitan Statistical Area—see Appendix B for areas included; (2) Rank ranges from 1 to 389 where 1 indicates greatest number of identity theft reports per 100,000 population
Source: Federal Trade Commission, Consumer Sentinel Network Data Book for January–December 2017

Fraud and Other Consumer Reports

Area	Reports	Reports per 100,000 Population	Rank[2]
MSA[1]	702	387	276
U.S.	2,304,550	708	-

Note: (1) Figures cover the Bend-Redmond, OR Metropolitan Statistical Area—see Appendix B for areas included; (2) Rank ranges from 1 to 389 where 1 indicates greatest number of fraud and other consumer reports per 100,000 population
Source: Federal Trade Commission, Consumer Sentinel Network Data Book for January–December 2017

SPORTS

Professional Sports Teams

Team Name	League	Year Established
No teams are located in the metro area		

Source: Wikipedia, Major Professional Sports Teams of the United States and Canada, April 5, 2018

CLIMATE

Average and Extreme Temperatures

Temperature	Jan	Feb	Mar	Apr	May	Jun	Jul	Aug	Sep	Oct	Nov	Dec	Yr.
Extreme High (°F)	67	69	77	86	93	102	105	108	103	94	76	68	108
Average High (°F)	46	51	55	61	67	74	82	82	76	64	53	47	63
Average Temp. (°F)	40	44	46	50	55	61	67	67	62	53	46	41	53
Average Low (°F)	33	35	37	39	43	48	51	51	48	42	38	35	42
Extreme Low (°F)	-4	-3	20	27	28	32	39	38	32	19	12	-12	-12

Note: Figures cover the years 1948-1992
Source: National Climatic Data Center, International Station Meteorological Climate Summary, 9/96

Average Precipitation/Snowfall/Humidity

Precip./Humidity	Jan	Feb	Mar	Apr	May	Jun	Jul	Aug	Sep	Oct	Nov	Dec	Yr.
Avg. Precip. (in.)	7.8	5.6	5.3	3.0	2.2	1.4	0.4	0.8	1.4	3.6	7.6	8.2	47.3
Avg. Snowfall (in.)	4	1	1	Tr	Tr	0	0	0	0	Tr	Tr	1	7
Avg. Rel. Hum. 7am (%)	91	92	91	88	84	81	78	82	88	93	93	92	88
Avg. Rel. Hum. 4pm (%)	79	73	64	57	54	49	38	39	44	61	79	84	60

Note: Figures cover the years 1948-1992; Tr = Trace amounts (<0.05 in. of rain; <0.5 in. of snow)
Source: National Climatic Data Center, International Station Meteorological Climate Summary, 9/96

Weather Conditions

Temperature			Daytime Sky			Precipitation		
32°F & below	45°F & below	90°F & above	Clear	Partly cloudy	Cloudy	0.01 inch or more precip.	0.1 inch or more snow/ice	Thunder-storms
54	233	15	75	115	175	136	4	3

Note: Figures are average number of days per year and cover the years 1948-1992
Source: National Climatic Data Center, International Station Meteorological Climate Summary, 9/96

HAZARDOUS WASTE

Superfund Sites

The Bend-Redmond, OR metro area has no sites on the EPA's Superfund Final National Priorities List. There are a total of 1,396 Superfund sites with a status of proposed or final on the list in the U.S. *U.S. Environmental Protection Agency, National Priorities List, April 4, 2018*

AIR & WATER QUALITY

Air Quality Trends: Ozone

	1990	1995	2000	2005	2010	2012	2013	2014	2015	2016
MSA[1]	n/a	n/a	n/a	n/a	n/a	n/a	n/a	n/a	n/a	n/a
U.S.	0.087	0.089	0.081	0.079	0.073	0.075	0.069	0.067	0.068	0.069

Note: (1) Data covers the Bend-Redmond, OR Metropolitan Statistical Area—see Appendix B for areas included; n/a not available. The values shown are the composite ozone concentration averages among trend sites based on the highest fourth daily maximum 8-hour concentration in parts per million. These trends are based on sites having an adequate record of monitoring data during the trend period. Data from exceptional events are included.
Source: U.S. Environmental Protection Agency, Air Quality Monitoring Information, "Air Quality Trends by City, 1990-2016"

Air Quality Index

Area	Percent of Days when Air Quality was...[2]					AQI Statistics[2]	
	Good	Moderate	Unhealthy for Sensitive Groups	Unhealthy	Very Unhealthy	Maximum	Median
MSA[1]	79.9	9.9	0.7	5.5	4.0	365	18

Note: (1) Data covers the Bend-Redmond, OR Metropolitan Statistical Area—see Appendix B for areas included; (2) Based on 273 days with AQI data in 2017. Air Quality Index (AQI) is an index for reporting daily air quality. EPA calculates the AQI for five major air pollutants regulated by the Clean Air Act: ground-level ozone, particle pollution (aka particulate matter), carbon monoxide, sulfur dioxide, and nitrogen dioxide. The AQI runs from 0 to 500. The higher the AQI value, the greater the level of air pollution and the greater the health concern. There are six AQI categories: "Good" AQI is between 0 and 50. Air quality is considered satisfactory; "Moderate" AQI is between 51 and 100. Air quality is acceptable; "Unhealthy for Sensitive Groups" When AQI values are between 101 and 150, members of sensitive groups may experience health effects; "Unhealthy" When AQI values are between 151 and 200 everyone may begin to experience health effects; "Very Unhealthy" AQI values between 201 and 300 trigger a health alert; "Hazardous" AQI values over 300 trigger warnings of emergency conditions (not shown).
Source: U.S. Environmental Protection Agency, Air Quality Index Report, 2017

Air Quality Index Pollutants

Area	Percent of Days when AQI Pollutant was...[2]					
	Carbon Monoxide	Nitrogen Dioxide	Ozone	Sulfur Dioxide	Particulate Matter 2.5	Particulate Matter 10
MSA[1]	0.0	0.0	0.0	0.0	100.0	0.0

Note: (1) Data covers the Bend-Redmond, OR Metropolitan Statistical Area—see Appendix B for areas included; (2) Based on 273 days with AQI data in 2017. The Air Quality Index (AQI) is an index for reporting daily air quality. EPA calculates the AQI for five major air pollutants regulated by the Clean Air Act: ground-level ozone, particle pollution (also known as particulate matter), carbon monoxide, sulfur dioxide, and nitrogen dioxide. The AQI runs from 0 to 500. The higher the AQI value, the greater the level of air pollution and the greater the health concern.
Source: U.S. Environmental Protection Agency, Air Quality Index Report, 2017

Maximum Air Pollutant Concentrations: Particulate Matter, Ozone, CO and Lead

	Particulate Matter 10 (ug/m^3)	Particulate Matter 2.5 Wtd AM (ug/m^3)	Particulate Matter 2.5 24-Hr (ug/m^3)	Ozone (ppm)	Carbon Monoxide (ppm)	Lead (ug/m^3)
MSA[1] Level	n/a	n/a	n/a	n/a	n/a	n/a
NAAQS[2]	150	15	35	0.075	9	0.15
Met NAAQS[2]	n/a	n/a	n/a	n/a	n/a	n/a

Note: (1) Data covers the Bend-Redmond, OR Metropolitan Statistical Area—see Appendix B for areas included; Data from exceptional events are included; (2) National Ambient Air Quality Standards; ppm = parts per million; ug/m^3 = micrograms per cubic meter; n/a not available.
Concentrations: Particulate Matter 10 (coarse particulate)—highest second maximum 24-hour concentration; Particulate Matter 2.5 Wtd AM (fine particulate)—highest weighted annual mean concentration; Particulate Matter 2.5 24-Hour (fine particulate)—highest 98th percentile 24-hour concentration; Ozone—highest fourth daily maximum 8-hour concentration; Carbon Monoxide—highest second maximum non-overlapping 8-hour concentration; Lead—maximum running 3-month average
Source: U.S. Environmental Protection Agency, Air Quality Monitoring Information, "Air Quality Statistics by City, 2016"

Maximum Air Pollutant Concentrations: Nitrogen Dioxide and Sulfur Dioxide

	Nitrogen Dioxide AM (ppb)	Nitrogen Dioxide 1-Hr (ppb)	Sulfur Dioxide AM (ppb)	Sulfur Dioxide 1-Hr (ppb)	Sulfur Dioxide 24-Hr (ppb)
MSA[1] Level	n/a	n/a	n/a	n/a	n/a
NAAQS[2]	53	100	30	75	140
Met NAAQS[2]	n/a	n/a	n/a	n/a	n/a

Note: (1) Data covers the Bend-Redmond, OR Metropolitan Statistical Area—see Appendix B for areas included; Data from exceptional events are included; (2) National Ambient Air Quality Standards; ppm = parts per million; ug/m^3 = micrograms per cubic meter; n/a not available.
Concentrations: Nitrogen Dioxide AM—highest arithmetic mean concentration; Nitrogen Dioxide 1-Hr—highest 98th percentile 1-hour daily maximum concentration; Sulfur Dioxide AM—highest annual mean concentration; Sulfur Dioxide 1-Hr—highest 99th percentile 1-hour daily maximum concentration; Sulfur Dioxide 24-Hr—highest second maximum 24-hour concentration
Source: U.S. Environmental Protection Agency, Air Quality Monitoring Information, "Air Quality Statistics by City, 2016"

Drinking Water

Water System Name	Pop. Served	Primary Water Source Type	Violations[1]	
			Health Based	Monitoring/ Reporting
Bend Water Dept	62,091	Surface	0	3

Note: (1) Based on violation data from January 1, 2017 to December 31, 2017
Source: U.S. Environmental Protection Agency, Office of Ground Water and Drinking Water, Safe Drinking Water Information System (based on data extracted April 5, 2018)

Lake Oswego, Oregon

Background

Lake Oswego, in Clackamas County, is only six miles south of downtown Portland, and less than an hour north of the state capital at Salem. With its eastern boundary on the scenic Willamette River, Lake Oswego is primarily a residential community. Lake Oswego features a fascinating mix of housing, with many English Cottage and Tudor Revival homes, dating from 1920-1940, as well as more contemporary developments. Lake Oswego is considered one of the most elegant towns in Oregon.

Until the mid-1800s, the Lake Oswego area was rural and agricultural. The original inhabitants, the Clackamas Indians, who lent their name to the county, were badly affected by diseases brought by early European explorers, and were ultimately displaced by white settlers. The town was founded as Oswego in 1847 by Albert Durham, who named it after his hometown of Oswego, New York. Durham also established the town's first business, a lumbermill on Sucker, now Oswego, Creek. Until a rail link was provided in 1886, the town was difficult to reach, and was served only by river boats and poorly maintained dirt roads.

Deposits of iron ore were known to be in the area from an early time, but were not commercially exploited until 1865, when the Oregon Iron Company was founded. This was the first of several iron companies that would eventually be established, and the iron industry eventually became active enough so that Oswego was known for a while as the "Pittsburgh of the West." At peak production, in the late nineteenth century, iron provided employment for many in the town and the surrounding area, and Oswego was able to build many local businesses and churches, even an opera house, which did a profitable business for many years.

Oregon Iron & Steel, responding to a downturn in its original business, built a power plant on Oswego Creek in 1909, and by 1914 the whole town was electrified. Reliable train lines linked Oswego into the Portland economic and social communities, and the town grew quickly. In 1910, Oswego was incorporated as a city.

In 1926, the first City Hall was built. Shortly thereafter, the Oswego Lake Country Club was established to encourage a place where residents could "work and play." For several decades prior to World War II, city planners encouraged noted architects to design elegant homes which to this day are admired by residents as key features of the town's charm. In 1960, the city annexed part of the Lake Grove community to its west, and it became Lake Oswego.

Lake Oswego boasts its own police and fire departments, an excellent library, and an award-winning senior center. The city also maintains a comprehensive water sports center on the Willamette River, two public swimming facilities at Oswego Lake, a public golf course, and an indoor tennis center.

The public schools in Lake Oswego are highly rated, by both state and national standards, and there are also religiously affiliated primary, middle and high schools. Colleges in or near the city include Lewis & Clark College, Marylhurst University, Portland State University, University of Portland, Portland Community College and the unique Northwest Nannies Institute.

Lake Oswego is within a thirty minute drive of Portland International Airport and is also served by five smaller regional airports.

Local government takes the council-manager form, and local residents are very serious about participative democracy, serving on some 17 neighborhood associations and 12 citizen advisory boards. The Lake Oswego City Council consists of a mayor and six councilors who serve four-year terms.

Rankings

General Rankings

- *US News & World Report* conducted a survey of more than 2,000 people and analyzed the 125 largest metropolitan areas to determine what matters the most when selecting the next place to live. Portland* ranked #6 out of the top 25 as having the best combination of desirable factors. Criteria: cost of living; quality of education; job market, crime rates; and other factors. *realestate.usnews.com, "The 25 Best Places to Live in the U.S. in 2018," April 10, 2018*
- The Portland* metro area was identified as one of America's fastest-growing areas in terms of population and economy by *Forbes.* The area ranked #17 out of 25. The 100 most populous metro areas in the U.S. were evaluated on the following criteria: estimated population growth; employment; economic output; wages; home values. *Forbes, "America's Fastest-Growing Cities 2018," February 28, 2018*

Business/Finance Rankings

- According to *Business Insider,* the Portland* metro area is where startup growth is on the rise. Based on the 2017 Kauffman Index of Growth Entrepreneurship, which measured in-depth national entrepreneurial trends in 40 metro areas, it ranked #21 in highest startup growth. *www.businessinsider.com, "The 21 U.S. Cities with the Highest Startup Growth," October 21, 2017*
- The personal finance site NerdWallet analyzed 183 American metropolitan areas with populations over 250,000 and more than 15,000 businesses to rank where entrepreneurs find the most success. Criteria included area economy, annual income, housing cost, unemployment rate, and the success rate of area businesses. Portland* ranked #61. *www.nerdwallet.com, "Best Places to Start a Business," April 27, 2015*
- 24/7 Wall Street used Brookings Institution research on 50 advanced industries to identify the proportion of workers in the nation's largest metropolitan areas that were employed in jobs requiring knowledge in the science, technology, engineering, or math (STEM) fields and where there was heavy investment in research and development (R&D). The Portland* metro area was #15. *247wallst.com, "15 Cities with the Most High-Tech Jobs," February 23, 2017*
- In a survey of economic confidence in the nation's 50 largest metropolitan areas conducted January–December 2014, the Portland* metro area placed #15, according to Gallup's 2014 Economic Confidence Index. *Gallup, "San Jose and San Francisco Lead in Economic Confidence," March 19, 2015*
- The Brookings Institution ranked the 100 largest metro areas in the U.S. based on income inequality. Portland* was ranked #83 (#1 = greatest ineqality). Criteria: the "95/20 ratio," a figure representing the income at which a household earns more than 95 percent of all other households, divided by the income at which a household earns more than only 20 percent of all other households. *Brookings Institution, "Household Income Inequality, 100 Largest U.S. Metro Areas, 2014-2016," February 5, 2018*
- *Forbes* ranked the 100 largest metro areas in the U.S. in terms of the "Best Cities for Young Professionals." The Portland* metro area ranked #23 out of 25. (Large metro areas were divided into metro divisions.) Criteria: median rent of a two-bedroom apartment; job growth and unemployment rate; median salary of college graduates with 5 or less years of work experience; networking opportunities; social outlook; percentage of population 25 years of age and older with college degrees. *Forbes.com, "America's 25 Best Cities for Young Professionals in 2017," May 22, 2017*
- Payscale.com ranked the largest metro areas in terms of wage growth. The Portland* metro area ranked #14. Criteria: private-sector wage growth between the 4th quarter of 2016 and the 4th quarter of 2017. *PayScale, "Wage Trends by Metro Area-4th Quarter," January 17, 2018*
- The Portland* metro area was identified as one of the most debt-ridden places in America by the finance site Credit.com. The metro area was ranked #21. Criteria: residents' average credit card debt as well as median income. *Credit.com, "25 Cities With the Most Credit Card Debt," February 28, 2018*

- The Portland* metro area appeared on the Milken Institute "2017 Best Performing Cities" list. Rank: #24 out of 200 large metro areas. Criteria: job growth; wage and salary growth; high-tech output growth. *Milken Institute, "Best-Performing Cities 2017," January 2018*

- *Forbes* ranked the 200 most populous metro areas to determine the nation's "Best Places for Business and Careers." The Portland* metro area was ranked #1. Criteria: costs (business and living); job growth (past and projected); income growth; quality of life; educational attainment (college and high school); projected economic growth; cultural and recreational opportunities; net migration patterns; number of highly ranked colleges. *Forbes, "The Best Places for Business and Careers 2017," October 24, 2017*

Education Rankings

- Personal finance website *WalletHub* analyzed the 150 largest U.S. metropolitan statistical areas to determine where the most educated Americans are choosing to settle. Criteria: education quality and attainment gap; education levels; percentage of workers with degrees; public school rankings; quality and size of each metro area's universities. Portland* was ranked #28 (#1 = most educated city). *www.WalletHub.com, "2017's Most and Least Educated Cities in America," July 25, 2017*

Environmental Rankings

- Sperling's BestPlaces assessed 379 metropolitan areas of the United States for the likelihood of dangerously extreme weather events or earthquakes. In general the Southeast and South-Central regions have the highest risk of weather extremes and earthquakes, while the Pacific Northwest enjoys the lowest risk. Of the least risky metropolitan areas, the Portland* metro area was ranked #19. *www.bestplaces.net, "Safest Places from Natural Disasters," April 2011*

- The U.S. Environmental Protection Agency (EPA) released a list of U.S. metropolitan areas with the most ENERGY STAR certified buildings in 2016. The Portland* metro area was ranked #24 out of 25. *U.S. Environmental Protection Agency, "2017 Energy Star Top Cities," June 2017*

Health/Fitness Rankings

- For each of the 50 most populous metro areas in the United States, the American College of Sports Medicine's American Fitness Index evaluated infrastructure, community assets, and policies that encourage healthy and fit lifestyles, including preventive health behaviors, levels of chronic disease conditions, health care access, and community resources and policies that support physical activity. The Portland* metro area ranked #8 for "community fitness." *www.americanfitnessindex.org, "ACSM American Fitness Index Health and Community Fitness Status of the 50 Largest Metropolitan Areas," May 2017*

- Portland* was identified as a "2016 Spring Allergy Capital." The area ranked #92 out of 100. Three groups of factors were used to identify the most severe cities for people with allergies during the spring season: annual pollen levels; medicine utilization; access to board-certified allergists. *Asthma and Allergy Foundation of America, "Spring Allergy Capitals 2016"*

- Portland* was identified as a "2016 Fall Allergy Capital." The area ranked #98 out of 100. Three groups of factors were used to identify the most severe cities for people with allergies during the fall season: annual pollen levels; medicine utilization; access to board-certified allergists. *Asthma and Allergy Foundation of America, "Fall Allergy Capitals 2016"*

- Portland* was identified as a "2015 Asthma Capital." The area ranked #90 out of the nation's 100 largest metropolitan areas. Criteria: estimated prevalence; self-reported prevalence; crude death rate for asthma; annual pollen score; annual air quality; public smoking laws; number of board-certified asthma specialists; school inhaler access laws; rescue medication use; controller medication use; ER visits for asthma; uninsured rate; poverty rate. *Asthma and Allergy Foundation of America, "Asthma Capitals 2015"*

- The Portland* metro area ranked #92 out of 189 in The Gallup-Healthways Well-Being Index. Criteria: purpose; social well being; financial health; community and physical health. Results are based on telephone interviews with adults, aged 18 and older, living in metropolitan areas in the 50 U.S. states and the District of Columbia. *Gallup-Healthways, "State of American Well-Being, 2017 Community Well-Being Rankings" March 2018*

Real Estate Rankings

- FitSmallBusiness looked at 50 of the largest metropolitan areas in the U.S. to determine which metro was the best to start a real estate business. Data was compiled from such sources as: Zillow, Trulia, U.S. Census Bureau, and the Bureau of Labor Statistics. Criteria: location; inventory; annual wages; median sales price of homes; days on the market; median price cut percentage; and other factors that would influence real estate professional growth. The Portland* metro area ranked #24. *fitsmallbusiness.com, "The Best Cities to Become a Real Estate Agent in 2018," January 30, 2018*
- According to Penske Truck Rental, the Portland* metro area was named the #10 moving destination in 2017, based on one-way consumer truck rental reservations made through Penske's website, rental locations, and reservations call center. *blog.gopenske.com, "Penske Truck Rental's 2017 Top Moving Destinations List," January 22, 2018*
- With data from RealtyTrac, Yahoo! Finance researchers listed the housing markets in which housing affordability is improving most, factoring in interest rates as well as median home prices. The Portland* metro area was among the least affordable housing markets. *news.yahoo.com, "10 Cities Where Ordinary People Can No Longer Afford Homes," March 5, 2014*
- The Portland* metro area was identified as one of the 10 worst housing markets to invest in. Criteria: single-family rental home investing in the first quarter of 2017 based on first-year returns. The area ranked #10. *The Business Insider, "Here Are the 10 Worst U.S. Housing Markets for Investment," May 12, 2017*
- The Portland* metro area was identified as one of the 20 least affordable housing markets in the U.S. in 2017. The area ranked #13 out of 180 markets. Criteria: qualification for a mortgage loan on a typical home. *National Association of Realtors®, Affordability Index of Existing Single-Family Homes for Metropolitan Areas, 2017*
- Portland* was ranked #212 out of 238 metro areas in terms of housing affordability in 2017 by the National Association of Home Builders (#1 = most affordable). Criteria: the share of homes sold in that area affordable to a family earning the local median income, based on standard mortgage underwriting criteria. *National Association of Home Builders®, NAHB-Wells Fargo Housing Opportunity Index, 4th Quarter 2017*

Safety Rankings

- The National Insurance Crime Bureau ranked 382 metro areas in the U.S. in terms of per capita rates of vehicle theft. The Portland* metro area ranked #41 (#1 = highest rate). Criteria: number of vehicle theft offenses per 100,000 inhabitants in 2016. *National Insurance Crime Bureau, "Hot Spots 2016," June 8, 2017*

Seniors/Retirement Rankings

- From its Best Cities for Successful Aging indexes, the Milken Institute generated rankings for metropolitan areas, weighing data in nine categories—health care, wellness, living arrangements, transportation and convenience, financial characteristics, education, employment, community engagement, and overall livability. The Portland* metro area was ranked #40 overall in the large metro area category. *Milken Institute, "Best Cities for Successful Aging, 2017" March 14, 2017*

Miscellaneous Rankings

- Of the American metro areas that allow medical or recreational use of marijuana, the Portland* metro area was identified by CNBC editors as one of the most livable for marijuana lovers. Criteria included the Sperling's BestPlaces assessment of marijuana-friendly cities in terms of sound economy, cultural diversity, and a healthy population, plus cost-of-living index and high-quality schools. *www.cnbc.com, "The Best Cities to Live for Marijuana Lovers," February 5, 2014*
- The watchdog site Charity Navigator conducts an annual study of charities in the nation's major markets both to analyze statistical differences in their financial, accountability, and transparency practices and to track year-to-year variations in individual philanthropic communities. Charity Navigator's analysis demonstrated that the financial, accountability and transparency behaviors of America's largest charities can be influenced by the metropolitan market within which the charity operates. The Portland* metro area was ranked #10 among the 30 metro markets in the rating category of Overall Score. *www.charitynavigator.org, "2017 Metro Market Study," May 1, 2017*
- The National Alliance to End Homelessness listed the 25 most populous metro areas with the highest rate of homelessness. The Portland* metro area had a high rate of homelessness. Criteria: number of homeless people per 10,000 population in 2016. *National Alliance to End Homelessness, "Homelessness in the 25 Most Populous U.S. Metro Areas," September 1, 2017*

*Lake Oswego is located within the Portland-Vancouver-Hillsboro, OR-WA Metropolitan Statistical Area.

Business Environment

CITY FINANCES

City Government Finances

Component	2015 ($000)	2015 ($ per capita)
Total Revenues	149,500	3,884
Total Expenditures	187,099	4,860
Debt Outstanding	212,972	5,532
Cash and Securities[1]	98,904	2,569

Note: (1) Cash and security holdings of a government at the close of its fiscal year,, including those of its dependent agencies, utilities, and liquor stores.
Source: U.S Census Bureau, State & Local Government Finances 2015

City Government Revenue by Source

Source	2015 ($000)	2015 ($ per capita)	2015 (%)
General Revenue			
From Federal Government	68	2	0.0
From State Government	3,359	87	2.2
From Local Governments	62,701	1,629	41.9
Taxes			
Property	36,822	957	24.6
Sales and Gross Receipts	3,739	97	2.5
Personal Income	0	0	0.0
Corporate Income	0	0	0.0
Motor Vehicle License	0	0	0.0
Other Taxes	273	7	0.2
Current Charges	25,728	668	17.2
Liquor Store	0	0	0.0
Utility	11,807	307	7.9
Employee Retirement	0	0	0.0

Source: U.S Census Bureau, State & Local Government Finances 2015

City Government Expenditures by Function

Function	2015 ($000)	2015 ($ per capita)	2015 (%)
General Direct Expenditures			
Air Transportation	0	0	0.0
Corrections	0	0	0.0
Education	0	0	0.0
Employment Security Administration	0	0	0.0
Financial Administration	1,480	38	0.8
Fire Protection	11,161	289	6.0
General Public Buildings	996	25	0.5
Governmental Administration, Other	7,969	207	4.3
Health	0	0	0.0
Highways	7,152	185	3.8
Hospitals	0	0	0.0
Housing and Community Development	888	23	0.5
Interest on General Debt	5,847	151	3.1
Judicial and Legal	1,650	42	0.9
Libraries	3,951	102	2.1
Parking	0	0	0.0
Parks and Recreation	9,120	236	4.9
Police Protection	11,540	299	6.2
Public Welfare	0	0	0.0
Sewerage	7,792	202	4.2
Solid Waste Management	0	0	0.0
Veterans' Services	0	0	0.0
Liquor Store	0	0	0.0
Utility	107,590	2,794	57.5
Employee Retirement	0	0	0.0

Source: U.S Census Bureau, State & Local Government Finances 2015

DEMOGRAPHICS

Population Growth

Area	1990 Census	2000 Census	2010 Census	2016* Estimate	Population Growth (%) 1990-2016	Population Growth (%) 2010-2016
City	32,216	35,278	36,619	38,065	18.2	3.9
MSA[1]	1,523,741	1,927,881	2,226,009	2,351,319	54.3	5.6
U.S.	248,709,873	281,421,906	308,745,538	318,558,162	28.1	3.2

Note: (1) Figures cover the Portland-Vancouver-Hillsboro, OR-WA Metropolitan Statistical Area—see Appendix B for areas included; (*) 2012-2016 5-year estimated population

Source: U.S. Census Bureau, 1990 Census, Census 2000, Census 2010, 2012-2016 American Community Survey 5-Year Estimates

Household Size

Area	Persons in Household (%) One	Two	Three	Four	Five	Six	Seven or More	Average Household Size
City	29.8	36.3	14.9	13.0	4.6	1.2	0.1	2.30
MSA[1]	27.1	34.7	15.7	13.3	5.6	2.1	1.4	2.60
U.S.	27.7	33.7	15.7	13.1	6.0	2.3	1.5	2.60

Note: (1) Figures cover the Portland-Vancouver-Hillsboro, OR-WA Metropolitan Statistical Area—see Appendix B for areas included

Source: U.S. Census Bureau, 2012-2016 American Community Survey 5-Year Estimates

Race

Area	White Alone[2] (%)	Black Alone[2] (%)	Asian Alone[2] (%)	AIAN[3] Alone[2] (%)	NHOPI[4] Alone[2] (%)	Other Race Alone[2] (%)	Two or More Races (%)
City	88.9	0.4	6.2	0.1	0.1	0.9	3.4
MSA[1]	81.9	2.8	6.2	0.7	0.5	3.3	4.6
U.S.	73.3	12.6	5.2	0.8	0.2	4.8	3.1

Note: (1) Figures cover the Portland-Vancouver-Hillsboro, OR-WA Metropolitan Statistical Area—see Appendix B for areas included; (2) Alone is defined as not being in combination with one or more other races; (3) American Indian and Alaska Native; (4) Native Hawaiian and Other Pacific Islander

Source: U.S. Census Bureau, 2012-2016 American Community Survey 5-Year Estimates

Hispanic or Latino Origin

Area	Total (%)	Mexican (%)	Puerto Rican (%)	Cuban (%)	Other (%)
City	4.2	1.7	0.3	0.5	1.7
MSA[1]	11.4	9.2	0.3	0.2	1.7
U.S.	17.3	11.0	1.7	0.7	4.0

Note: Persons of Hispanic or Latino origin can be of any race; (1) Figures cover the Portland-Vancouver-Hillsboro, OR-WA Metropolitan Statistical Area—see Appendix B for areas included

Source: U.S. Census Bureau, 2012-2016 American Community Survey 5-Year Estimates

Segregation

Type	Segregation Indices[1] 1990	2000	2010	2010 Rank[2]	Percent Change 1990-2000	1990-2010	2000-2010
Black/White	63.2	51.8	46.0	81	-11.4	-17.2	-5.9
Asian/White	31.2	35.1	35.8	75	3.9	4.7	0.8
Hispanic/White	25.6	34.2	34.3	83	8.6	8.6	0.0

Note: All figures cover the Metropolitan Statistical Area—see Appendix B for areas included; Figures are based on an analysis of 1990, 2000, and 2010 Census Decennial Census tract data by William H. Frey, Brookings Institution and the University of Michigan Social Science Data Analysis Network. In this analysis all racial groups (whites, blacks, and asians) are non-Hispanic members of those races. Hispanics are shown as a separate category; (1) Segregation Indices are Dissimilarity Indices that measure the degree to which the minority group is distributed differently than whites across census tracts. They range from 0 (complete integration) to 100 (complete segregation) where the value indicates the percentage of the minority group that needs to move to be distributed exactly like whites; (2) Ranges from 1 (most segregated) to 102 (least segregated); n/a not available.

Source: www.CensusScope.org

Ancestry

Area	German	Irish	English	American	Italian	Polish	French[2]	Scottish	Dutch
City	21.2	14.0	14.7	5.1	5.4	3.0	3.3	6.4	2.1
MSA[1]	19.3	11.2	11.0	5.0	4.0	1.9	3.1	3.2	2.0
U.S.	14.4	10.4	7.7	6.9	5.4	2.9	2.6	1.7	1.3

Note: Figures are the percentage of the total population reporting a particular ancestry. The nine most commonly reported ancestries in the U.S. are shown. Figures include multiple ancestries (e.g. if a person reported being Irish and Italian, they were included in both columns); (1) Figures cover the Portland-Vancouver-Hillsboro, OR-WA Metropolitan Statistical Area—see Appendix B for areas included; (2) Excludes Basque
Source: U.S. Census Bureau, 2012-2016 American Community Survey 5-Year Estimates

Foreign-Born Population

Area	Percent of Population Born in								
	Any Foreign Country	Asia	Mexico	Europe	Carribean	Central America[2]	South America	Africa	Canada
City	10.5	5.6	0.4	2.6	0.2	0.1	0.2	0.2	1.0
MSA[1]	12.5	4.6	3.5	2.4	0.1	0.4	0.3	0.5	0.5
U.S.	13.2	4.0	3.6	1.5	1.3	1.0	0.9	0.6	0.3

Note: (1) Figures cover the Portland-Vancouver-Hillsboro, OR-WA Metropolitan Statistical Area—see Appendix B for areas included; (2) Excludes Mexico.
Source: U.S. Census Bureau, 2012-2016 American Community Survey 5-Year Estimates

Marital Status

Area	Never Married	Now Married[2]	Separated	Widowed	Divorced
City	21.8	59.0	1.4	5.9	11.9
MSA[1]	31.5	49.7	1.8	4.7	12.4
U.S.	33.0	48.1	2.1	5.9	11.0

Note: Figures are percentages and cover the population 15 years of age and older; (1) Figures cover the Portland-Vancouver-Hillsboro, OR-WA Metropolitan Statistical Area—see Appendix B for areas included; (2) Excludes separated
Source: U.S. Census Bureau, 2012-2016 American Community Survey 5-Year Estimates

Disability Status

Area	All Ages	Under 18 Years Old	18 to 64 Years Old	65 Years and Over
City	8.1	2.6	4.4	26.7
MSA[1]	12.3	4.0	10.4	36.0
U.S.	12.5	4.1	10.3	35.7

Note: Figures show percent of the civilian noninstitutionalized population that reported having a disability. Disability status is determined from six types of difficulty: vision, hearing, cognitive, ambulatory, self-care, and independent living. For children under 5 years old, hearing and vision difficulty are used to determine disability status. For children between the ages of 5 and 14, disability status is determined from hearing, vision, cognitive, ambulatory, and self-care difficulties. For people aged 15 years and older, they are considered to have a disability if they have difficulty with any one of the six difficulty types; Note: (1) Figures cover the Portland-Vancouver-Hillsboro, OR-WA Metropolitan Statistical Area—see Appendix B for areas included
Source: U.S. Census Bureau, 2012-2016 American Community Survey 5-Year Estimates

Age

Area	Percent of Population									Median Age
	Under Age 5	Age 5–19	Age 20–34	Age 35–44	Age 45–54	Age 55–64	Age 65–74	Age 75–84	Age 85+	
City	4.5	19.4	12.4	13.4	14.6	17.1	10.9	4.4	3.2	45.2
MSA[1]	6.1	18.6	21.2	14.5	13.6	12.7	8.0	3.5	1.7	37.6
U.S.	6.2	19.6	20.7	12.7	13.6	12.6	8.3	4.3	1.9	37.7

Note: (1) Figures cover the Portland-Vancouver-Hillsboro, OR-WA Metropolitan Statistical Area—see Appendix B for areas included
Source: U.S. Census Bureau, 2012-2016 American Community Survey 5-Year Estimates

Gender

Area	Males	Females	Males per 100 Females
City	17,591	20,474	85.9
MSA[1]	1,161,988	1,189,331	97.7
U.S.	156,765,322	161,792,840	96.9

Note: (1) Figures cover the Portland-Vancouver-Hillsboro, OR-WA Metropolitan Statistical Area—see Appendix B for areas included
Source: U.S. Census Bureau, 2012-2016 American Community Survey 5-Year Estimates

Religious Groups by Family

Area	Catholic	Baptist	Non-Den.	Methodist[2]	Lutheran	LDS[3]	Pente-costal	Presby-terian[4]	Muslim[5]	Judaism
MSA[1]	10.6	2.3	4.5	1.0	1.6	3.8	2.0	1.0	0.1	0.3
U.S.	19.1	9.3	4.0	4.0	2.3	2.0	1.9	1.6	0.8	0.7

Note: Figures are the number of adherents as a percentage of the total population; (1) Figures cover the Portland-Vancouver-Hillsboro, OR-WA Metropolitan Statistical Area—see Appendix B for areas included; (2) Methodist/Pietist; (3) Latter Day Saints; (4) Reformed; (5) Figures are estimates
Source: Association of Statisticians of American Religious Bodies, 2010 U.S. Religion Census: Religious Congregations & Membership Study

Religious Groups by Tradition

Area	Catholic	Evangelical Protestant	Mainline Protestant	Other Tradition	Black Protestant	Orthodox
MSA[1]	10.6	11.7	3.7	5.2	0.2	0.3
U.S.	19.1	16.2	7.3	4.3	1.6	0.3

Note: Figures are the number of adherents as a percentage of the total population; (1) Figures cover the Portland-Vancouver-Hillsboro, OR-WA Metropolitan Statistical Area—see Appendix B for areas included
Source: Association of Statisticians of American Religious Bodies, 2010 U.S. Religion Census: Religious Congregations & Membership Study

ECONOMY

Gross Metropolitan Product

Area	2014	2015	2016	2017	Rank[2]
MSA[1]	157.3	167.7	173.9	183.9	20

Note: Figures are in billions of dollars; (1) Figures cover the Portland-Vancouver-Hillsboro, OR-WA Metropolitan Statistical Area—see Appendix B for areas included; (2) Rank is based on 2015 data and ranges from 1 to 381
Source: The U.S. Conference of Mayors, U.S. Metro Economies: GMP and Employment Report, 2015-2017

Economic Growth

Area	2012-14 (%)	2015 (%)	2016 (%)	2017 (%)	Rank[2]
MSA[1]	0.5	4.0	2.0	3.5	247
U.S.	2.0	2.4	1.9	2.6	–

Note: Figures are real gross metropolitan product (GMP) growth rates and represent average annual percent change; (1) Figures cover the Portland-Vancouver-Hillsboro, OR-WA Metropolitan Statistical Area—see Appendix B for areas included; (2) Rank is based on 2012-2014 average annual percent change and ranges from 1 to 381
Source: The U.S. Conference of Mayors, U.S. Metro Economies: GMP and Employment Report, 2015-2017

Metropolitan Area Exports

Area	2011	2012	2013	2014	2015	2016	Rank[2]
MSA[1]	20,875.7	20,337.7	17,606.8	18,667.2	18,847.8	20,256.8	17

Note: Figures are in millions of dollars; (1) Figures cover the Portland-Vancouver-Hillsboro, OR-WA Metropolitan Statistical Area—see Appendix B for areas included; (2) Rank is based on 2016 data and ranges from 1 to 385
Source: U.S. Department of Commerce, International Trade Administration, Office of Trade & Industry Information, Manufacturing & Services, data extracted March 15, 2018

Building Permits

Area	Single-Family 2016	Single-Family 2017p	Single-Family Pct. Chg.	Multi-Family 2016	Multi-Family 2017p	Multi-Family Pct. Chg.	Total 2016	Total 2017p	Total Pct. Chg.
City	94	101	7.4	200	93	-53.5	294	194	-34.0
MSA[1]	7,344	6,684	-9.0	7,379	10,350	40.3	14,723	17,034	15.7
U.S.	750,800	817,300	8.9	455,800	446,800	-2.0	1,206,600	1,264,100	4.8

Note: (1) Figures cover the Portland-Vancouver-Hillsboro, OR-WA Metropolitan Statistical Area—see Appendix B for areas included; Figures represent new, privately-owned housing units authorized (unadjusted data); All permit data are based on estimates with imputation; (p) preliminary data.
Source: U.S. Census Bureau, Manufacturing, Mining, and Construction Statistics, Building Permits, 2016, 2017

Bankruptcy Filings

Area	Business Filings 2016	Business Filings 2017	Business Filings % Chg.	Nonbusiness Filings 2016	Nonbusiness Filings 2017	Nonbusiness Filings % Chg.
Clackamas County	22	35	59.1	834	898	7.7
U.S.	24,114	23,157	-4.0	770,846	765,863	-0.6

Note: Business filings include Chapter 7, Chapter 11, Chapter 12, and Chapter 13; Nonbusiness filings include Chapter 7, Chapter 11, and Chapter 13
Source: Administrative Office of the U.S. Courts, Business and Nonbusiness Bankruptcy, County Cases Commenced by Chapter of the Bankruptcy Code, During the 12-Month Period Ending December 31, 2016 and Business and Nonbusiness Bankruptcy, County Cases Commenced by Chapter of the Bankruptcy Code, During the 12-Month Period Ending December 31, 2017

Housing Vacancy Rates

Area	Gross Vacancy Rate[2] (%) 2015	2016	2017	Year-Round Vacancy Rate[3] (%) 2015	2016	2017	Rental Vacancy Rate[4] (%) 2015	2016	2017	Homeowner Vacancy Rate[5] (%) 2015	2016	2017
MSA[1]	6.0	6.7	6.4	5.5	6.2	6.1	3.4	5.0	4.8	1.0	1.0	1.1
U.S.	12.9	12.8	12.7	10.0	9.9	9.9	7.1	6.9	7.2	1.8	1.7	1.6

Note: (1) Figures cover the Portland-Vancouver-Hillsboro, OR-WA Metropolitan Statistical Area—see Appendix B for areas included; (2) The percentage of the total housing inventory that is vacant; (3) The percentage of the housing inventory (excluding seasonal units) that is year-round vacant; (4) The percentage of rental inventory that is vacant for rent; (5) The percentage of homeowner inventory that is vacant for sale
Source: U.S. Census Bureau, Housing Vacancies and Homeownership Annual Statistics: 2015, 2016, 2017

INCOME

Income

Area	Per Capita ($)	Median Household ($)	Average Household ($)
City	59,953	89,979	138,952
MSA[1]	32,654	62,772	83,175
U.S.	29,829	55,322	77,866

Note: (1) Figures cover the Portland-Vancouver-Hillsboro, OR-WA Metropolitan Statistical Area—see Appendix B for areas included
Source: U.S. Census Bureau, 2012-2016 American Community Survey 5-Year Estimates

Household Income Distribution

Area	Percent of Households Earning: Under $15,000	$15,000 -$24,999	$25,000 -$34,999	$35,000 -$49,999	$50,000 -$74,999	$75,000 -$99,999	$100,000 -$149,999	$150,000 and up
City	6.2	7.5	6.7	7.2	13.9	12.6	14.0	31.8
MSA[1]	9.5	8.6	8.9	12.8	18.3	13.9	15.9	12.1
U.S.	12.1	10.2	9.9	13.2	17.8	12.2	13.5	11.1

Note: (1) Figures cover the Portland-Vancouver-Hillsboro, OR-WA Metropolitan Statistical Area—see Appendix B for areas included
Source: U.S. Census Bureau, 2012-2016 American Community Survey 5-Year Estimates

Poverty Rate

Area	All Ages	Under 18 Years Old	18 to 64 Years Old	65 Years and Over
City	7.2	9.9	6.8	5.1
MSA[1]	12.8	16.3	12.7	7.6
U.S.	15.1	21.2	14.2	9.3

Note: Figures are percentage of people whose income during the past 12 months was below the poverty level; (1) Figures cover the Portland-Vancouver-Hillsboro, OR-WA Metropolitan Statistical Area—see Appendix B for areas included
Source: U.S. Census Bureau, 2012-2016 American Community Survey 5-Year Estimates

EMPLOYMENT

Labor Force and Employment

Area	Civilian Labor Force			Workers Employed		
	Dec. 2016	Dec. 2017	% Chg.	Dec. 2016	Dec. 2017	% Chg.
City	20,705	21,403	3.4	20,064	20,734	3.3
MSA[1]	1,283,618	1,324,396	3.2	1,234,956	1,276,346	3.4
U.S.	158,968,000	159,880,000	0.6	151,798,000	153,602,000	1.2

Note: Data is not seasonally adjusted and covers workers 16 years of age and older; (1) Figures cover the Portland-Vancouver-Hillsboro, OR-WA Metropolitan Statistical Area—see Appendix B for areas included
Source: Bureau of Labor Statistics, Local Area Unemployment Statistics

Unemployment Rate

Area	2017											
	Jan.	Feb.	Mar.	Apr.	May	Jun.	Jul.	Aug.	Sep.	Oct.	Nov.	Dec.
City	3.3	3.2	3.3	3.1	3.1	3.7	3.7	3.6	3.3	3.3	3.3	3.1
MSA[1]	4.2	4.1	4.0	3.6	3.6	4.1	4.2	4.3	3.9	3.8	3.7	3.6
U.S.	5.1	4.9	4.6	4.1	4.1	4.5	4.6	4.5	4.1	3.9	3.9	3.9

Note: Data is not seasonally adjusted and covers workers 16 years of age and older; (1) Figures cover the Portland-Vancouver-Hillsboro, OR-WA Metropolitan Statistical Area—see Appendix B for areas included
Source: Bureau of Labor Statistics, Local Area Unemployment Statistics

Average Wages

Occupation	$/Hr.	Occupation	$/Hr.
Accountants and Auditors	33.80	Maids and Housekeeping Cleaners	12.80
Automotive Mechanics	24.70	Maintenance and Repair Workers	20.40
Bookkeepers	20.40	Marketing Managers	60.80
Carpenters	25.30	Nuclear Medicine Technologists	41.90
Cashiers	12.50	Nurses, Licensed Practical	24.30
Clerks, General Office	17.80	Nurses, Registered	43.80
Clerks, Receptionists/Information	15.40	Nursing Assistants	15.60
Clerks, Shipping/Receiving	18.00	Packers and Packagers, Hand	13.80
Computer Programmers	40.80	Physical Therapists	41.50
Computer Systems Analysts	44.80	Postal Service Mail Carriers	23.70
Computer User Support Specialists	26.50	Real Estate Brokers	35.50
Cooks, Restaurant	13.60	Retail Salespersons	13.80
Dentists	87.80	Sales Reps., Exc. Tech./Scientific	34.00
Electrical Engineers	46.40	Sales Reps., Tech./Scientific	43.90
Electricians	33.90	Secretaries, Exc. Legal/Med./Exec.	19.40
Financial Managers	60.30	Security Guards	14.10
First-Line Supervisors/Managers, Sales	21.00	Surgeons	n/a
Food Preparation Workers	12.60	Teacher Assistants*	15.90
General and Operations Managers	57.10	Teachers, Elementary School*	32.70
Hairdressers/Cosmetologists	15.80	Teachers, Secondary School*	35.10
Internists, General	100.70	Telemarketers	14.70
Janitors and Cleaners	14.40	Truck Drivers, Heavy/Tractor-Trailer	22.80
Landscaping/Groundskeeping Workers	16.80	Truck Drivers, Light/Delivery Svcs.	18.10
Lawyers	60.20	Waiters and Waitresses	13.40

Note: Wage data covers the Portland-Vancouver-Hillsboro, OR-WA Metropolitan Statistical Area—see Appendix B for areas included; (*) Hourly wages for elementary/secondary school teachers and teacher assistants were calculated by the editors from annual wage data based on a 40 hour work week; n/a not available.
Source: Bureau of Labor Statistics, Metro Area Occupational Employment & Wage Estimates, May 2017

Employment by Occupation

Occupation Classification	City (%)	MSA[1] (%)	U.S. (%)
Management, Business, Science, and Arts	59.2	41.0	37.0
Natural Resources, Construction, and Maintenance	2.5	7.4	8.9
Production, Transportation, and Material Moving	4.2	11.4	12.2
Sales and Office	24.7	23.2	23.8
Service	9.4	17.0	18.1

Note: Figures cover employed civilians 16 years of age and older; (1) Figures cover the Portland-Vancouver-Hillsboro, OR-WA Metropolitan Statistical Area—see Appendix B for areas included
Source: U.S. Census Bureau, 2012-2016 American Community Survey 5-Year Estimates

Employment by Industry

Sector	MSA[1]		U.S.
	Number of Employees	Percent of Total	Percent of Total
Construction	67,000	5.6	4.7
Education and Health Services	174,300	14.6	15.9
Financial Activities	71,200	6.0	5.7
Government	159,100	13.3	15.3
Information	25,600	2.1	1.9
Leisure and Hospitality	122,300	10.3	10.7
Manufacturing	124,800	10.5	8.5
Mining and Logging	1,200	0.1	0.5
Other Services	42,200	3.5	3.9
Professional and Business Services	181,400	15.2	14.0
Retail Trade	123,200	10.3	11.0
Transportation, Warehousing, and Utilities	41,900	3.5	4.1
Wholesale Trade	58,200	4.9	4.0

Note: Figures are non-farm employment as of December 2017. Figures are not seasonally adjusted and include workers 16 years of age and older; (1) Figures cover the Portland-Vancouver-Hillsboro, OR-WA Metropolitan Statistical Area—see Appendix B for areas included
Source: Bureau of Labor Statistics, Current Employment Statistics, Employment, Hours, and Earnings

Occupations with Greatest Projected Employment Growth: 2017 – 2019

Occupation[1]	2017 Employment	2019 Projected Employment	Numeric Employment Change	Percent Employment Change
Carpenters	22,060	24,830	2,770	12.6
Retail Salespersons	69,050	71,620	2,570	3.7
Combined Food Preparation and Serving Workers, Including Fast Food	37,540	39,870	2,330	6.2
Construction Laborers	17,510	19,030	1,520	8.7
Waiters and Waitresses	32,960	34,470	1,510	4.6
Cooks, Restaurant	25,640	27,050	1,410	5.5
General and Operations Managers	31,040	32,340	1,300	4.2
Personal Care Aides	21,600	22,900	1,300	6.0
Registered Nurses	35,230	36,350	1,120	3.2
Office Clerks, General	36,770	37,740	970	2.6

Note: Projections cover Oregon; (1) Sorted by numeric employment change
Source: www.projectionscentral.com, State Occupational Projections, 2017–2019 Short-Term Projections

Fastest Growing Occupations: 2017 – 2019

Occupation[1]	2017 Employment	2019 Projected Employment	Numeric Employment Change	Percent Employment Change
Animal Trainers	230	300	70	32.3
Chemical Equipment Operators and Tenders	560	630	70	14.2
Carpenters	22,060	24,830	2,770	12.6
Nonfarm Animal Caretakers	3,430	3,860	430	12.4
Brickmasons and Blockmasons	990	1,100	110	11.1
Roofers	3,700	4,100	400	10.9
Structural Iron and Steel Workers	740	820	80	10.5
Physical Therapist Aides	780	860	80	10.4
Glaziers	900	990	90	10.3
Massage Therapists	3,650	4,030	380	10.3

Note: Projections cover Oregon; (1) Sorted by percent employment change and excludes occupations with numeric employment change less than 50
Source: www.projectionscentral.com, State Occupational Projections, 2017–2019 Short-Term Projections

TAXES

State Corporate Income Tax Rates

State	Tax Rate (%)	Income Brackets ($)	Num. of Brackets	Financial Institution Tax Rate (%)[a]	Federal Income Tax Ded.
Oregon	6.6 - 7.6 (u)	1 million	2	6.6 - 7.6 (u)	No

Note: Tax rates as of January 1, 2018; (a) Rates listed are the corporate income tax rate applied to financial institutions or excise taxes based on income. Some states have other taxes based upon the value of deposits or shares; (u) Oregon's minimum tax for C corporations depends on the Oregon sales of the filing group. The minimum tax ranges from $150 for corporations with sales under $500,000, up to $100,000 for companies with sales of $100 million or above.
Source: Federation of Tax Administrators, Range of State Corporate Income Tax Rates, January 1, 2018

State Individual Income Tax Rates

State	Tax Rate (%)	Income Brackets ($)	Num. of Brackets	Personal Exempt. ($)[1] Single	Personal Exempt. ($)[1] Dependents	Fed. Inc. Tax Ded.
Oregon (a)	5.0 - 9.9	3,450 -125,000 (b)	4	201 (c)	201 (c)	Yes (p)

Note: Tax rates as of January 1, 2018; Local- and county-level taxes are not included; n/a not applicable; (1) Married joint filers generally receive double the single exemption; (a) 19 states have statutory provision for automatically adjusting to the rate of inflation the dollar values of the income tax brackets, standard deductions, and/or personal exemptions. Massachusetts, Michigan, and Nebraska index the personal exemption only. Oregon does not index the income brackets for $125,000 and over; (b) For joint returns, taxes are twice the tax on half the couple's income; (c) The personal exemption takes the form of a tax credit instead of a deduction; (p) The deduction for federal income tax is limited to $5,000 for individuals and $10,000 for joint returns in Missouri and Montana, and to $6,350 for all filers in Oregon.
Source: Federation of Tax Administrators, State Individual Income Tax Rates, January 1, 2018

Various State Sales and Excise Tax Rates

State	State Sales Tax (%)	Gasoline[1] (¢/gal.)	Cigarette[2] ($/pack)	Spirits[3] ($/gal.)	Wine[4] ($/gal.)	Beer[5] ($/gal.)	Recreational Marijuana (%)
Oregon	None	36.77	1.33	22.75 (g)	0.67 (l)	0.08	17.0

Note: All tax rates as of January 1, 2018; (1) The American Petroleum Institute has developed a methodology for determining the average tax rate on a gallon of fuel. Rates may include any of the following: excise taxes, environmental fees, storage tank fees, other fees or taxes, general sales tax, and local taxes. In states where gasoline is subject to the general sales tax, or where the fuel tax is based on the average sale price, the average rate determined by API is sensitive to changes in the price of gasoline. States that fully or partially apply general sales taxes to gasoline: CA, CO, GA, IL, IN, MI, NY; (2) The federal excise tax of $1.0066 per pack and local taxes are not included; (3) Rates are those applicable to off-premise sales of 40% alcohol by volume (a.b.v.) distilled spirits in 750ml containers. Local excise taxes are excluded; (4) Rates are those applicable to off-premise sales of 11% a.b.v. non-carbonated wine in 750ml containers; (5) Rates are those applicable to off-premise sales of 4.7% a.b.v. beer in 12 ounce containers; (g) Control states, where the government controls all sales. Products can be subject to ad valorem mark-up as well as excise taxes; (l) Different rates also applicable to alcohol content, place of production, size of container, place purchased (on- or off-premise or on board airlines) or type of wine (carbonated, vermouth, etc.).
Source: Tax Foundation, 2018 Facts & Figures: How Does Your State Compare?

State Business Tax Climate Index Rankings

State	Overall Rank	Corporate Tax Rank	Individual Income Tax Rank	Sales Tax Rank	Unemployment Insurance Tax Rank	Property Tax Rank
Oregon	10	34	32	4	31	18

Note: The index is a measure of how each state's tax laws affect economic performance. The lower the rank, the more favorable a state's tax system is for business. States without a given tax are given a ranking of 1. The scores/rankings for the District of Columbia do not affect other states. The 2018 index represents the tax climate as of July 1, 2017.
Source: Tax Foundation, State Business Tax Climate Index 2018

TRANSPORTATION

Means of Transportation to Work

Area	Car/Truck/Van		Public Transportation			Bicycle	Walked	Other Means	Worked at Home
	Drove Alone	Car-pooled	Bus	Subway	Railroad				
City	72.3	7.9	3.9	0.1	0.0	0.8	1.5	0.5	13.1
MSA[1]	70.4	9.8	4.8	0.7	0.3	2.4	3.4	1.7	6.6
U.S.	76.4	9.3	2.6	1.9	0.6	0.6	2.8	1.3	4.6

Note: Figures are percentages and cover workers 16 years of age and older; (1) Figures cover the Portland-Vancouver-Hillsboro, OR-WA Metropolitan Statistical Area—see Appendix B for areas included
Source: U.S. Census Bureau, 2012-2016 American Community Survey 5-Year Estimates

Travel Time to Work

Area	Less Than 10 Minutes	10 to 19 Minutes	20 to 29 Minutes	30 to 44 Minutes	45 to 59 Minutes	60 to 89 Minutes	90 Minutes or More
City	12.1	27.3	26.1	24.2	6.6	2.2	1.5
MSA[1]	10.9	28.2	23.0	22.4	8.4	5.2	2.0
U.S.	12.9	29.2	20.9	20.4	8.0	6.0	2.7

Note: Note: Figures are percentages and include workers 16 years old and over; (1) Figures cover the Portland-Vancouver-Hillsboro, OR-WA Metropolitan Statistical Area—see Appendix B for areas included
Source: U.S. Census Bureau, 2012-2016 American Community Survey 5-Year Estimates

Freeway Travel Time Index

Area	1985	1990	1995	2000	2005	2010	2014
Urban Area Rank[1,2]	11	15	6	6	8	9	7
Urban Area Index[1]	1.16	1.19	1.25	1.30	1.32	1.32	1.35
Average Index[3]	1.09	1.11	1.14	1.17	1.20	1.19	1.20

Note: Freeway Travel Time Index—the ratio of travel time in the peak period to the travel time at free-flow conditions. For example, a value of 1.30 indicates a 20-minute free-flow trip takes 26 minutes in the peak (20 minutes x 1.30 = 26 minutes); (1) Covers the Portland OR-WA urban area; (2) Rank is based on 101 urban areas (#1 = highest travel time index); (3) Average of 101 urban areas
Source: Texas Transportation Institute, 2015 Urban Mobility Scorecard, August 2015

Freeway Commuter Stress Index

Area	1985	1990	1995	2000	2005	2010	2014
Urban Area Rank[1,2]	21	21	13	12	15	14	10
Urban Area Index[1]	1.20	1.23	1.29	1.34	1.36	1.36	1.40
Average Index[3]	1.13	1.16	1.19	1.22	1.25	1.24	1.25

Note: The Freeway Commuter Stress Index is the same as the Freeway Travel Time Index (see table above) except that it includes only the travel in the peak directions during the peak periods; the TTI includes travel in all directions during the peak period. Thus, the CSI is more indicative of the work trip experienced by each commuter on a daily basis; (1) Covers the Portland OR-WA urban area; (2) Rank is based on 101 urban areas (#1 = highest travel time index); (3) Average of 101 urban areas
Source: Texas Transportation Institute, 2015 Urban Mobility Scorecard, August 2015

Living Environment

COST OF LIVING

Cost of Living Index

Composite Index	Groceries	Housing	Utilities	Trans-portation	Health Care	Misc. Goods/ Services
129.1	115.2	178.9	78.0	106.4	107.1	117.6

Note: The Cost of Living Index measures regional differences in the cost of consumer goods and services, excluding taxes and non-consumer expenditures, for professional and managerial households in the top income quintile. It is based on more than 50,000 prices covering almost 60 different items for which prices are collected three times a year by chambers of commerce, economic development organizations or university applied economic centers in each participating urban area. The numbers shown should be read as a percentage above or below the national average of 100. For example, a value of 115.4 in the groceries column indicates that grocery prices are 15.4% higher than the national average. Small differences in the index numbers should not be interpreted as significant; Figures cover the Portland OR urban area.
Source: The Council for Community and Economic Research, ACCRA Cost of Living Index, 2017

Grocery Prices

Area[1]	T-Bone Steak ($/pound)	Frying Chicken ($/pound)	Whole Milk ($/half gal.)	Eggs ($/dozen)	Orange Juice ($/64 oz.)	Coffee ($/11.5 oz.)
City[2]	12.94	1.58	2.06	1.78	3.92	5.88
Avg.	11.29	1.40	2.02	1.47	3.55	4.37
Min.	7.71	0.93	1.04	0.70	2.86	3.24
Max.	15.83	2.39	4.03	3.92	6.29	8.16

Note: (1) Values for the local area are compared with the average, minimum and maximum values for all 294 areas in the Cost of Living Index; (2) Figures cover the Portland OR urban area; ***T-Bone Steak*** *(price per pound);* ***Frying Chicken*** *(price per pound, whole fryer);* ***Whole Milk*** *(half gallon carton);* ***Eggs*** *(price per dozen, Grade A, large);* ***Orange Juice*** *(64 oz. Tropicana or Florida Natural);* ***Coffee*** *(11.5 oz. can, vacuum-packed, Maxwell House, Hills Bros, or Folgers).*
Source: The Council for Community and Economic Research, ACCRA Cost of Living Index, 2017

Housing and Utility Costs

Area[1]	New Home Price ($)	Apartment Rent ($/month)	All Electric ($/month)	Part Electric ($/month)	Other Energy ($/month)	Telephone ($/month)
City[2]	507,368	2,482	-	76.08	69.16	19.33
Avg.	335,956	1,047	175.01	97.34	67.93	28.71
Min.	187,788	491	109.48	49.33	35.44	12.39
Max.	1,739,087	4,559	432.62	227.09	353.33	44.61

Note: (1) Values for the local area are compared with the average, minimum and maximum values for all 294 areas in the Cost of Living Index; (2) Figures cover the Portland OR urban area; ***New Home Price*** *(2,400 sf living area, 8,000 sf lot, in urban area with full utilities);* ***Apartment Rent*** *(950 sf 2 bedroom/1.5 or 2 bath, unfurnished, excluding all utilities except water);* ***All Electric*** *(average monthly cost for an all-electric home);* ***Part Electric*** *(average monthly cost for a part-electric home);* ***Other Energy*** *(average monthly cost for natural gas, fuel oil, coal, wood, and any other forms of energy except electricity);* ***Telephone*** *(price includes basic monthly rate for a private residential line plus additional local usage charges incurred by a family of four).*
Source: The Council for Community and Economic Research, ACCRA Cost of Living Index, 2017

Health Care, Transportation, and Other Costs

Area[1]	Doctor ($/visit)	Dentist ($/visit)	Optometrist ($/visit)	Gasoline ($/gallon)	Beauty Salon ($/visit)	Men's Shirt ($)
City[2]	107.61	102.69	131.19	2.88	48.67	33.62
Avg.	108.00	92.54	101.93	2.25	37.58	30.92
Min.	30.39	60.00	49.75	1.82	16.11	11.20
Max.	193.50	161.94	229.28	3.16	77.35	59.13

Note: (1) Values for the local area are compared with the average, minimum and maximum values for all 294 areas in the Cost of Living Index; (2) Figures cover the Portland OR urban area; ***Doctor*** *(general practitioners routine exam of an established patient);* ***Dentist*** *(adult teeth cleaning and periodic oral examination);* ***Optometrist*** *(full vision eye exam for established adult patient);* ***Gasoline*** *(one gallon regular unleaded, national brand, including all taxes, cash price at self-service pump if available);* ***Beauty Salon*** *(woman's shampoo, trim, and blow-dry);* ***Men's Shirt*** *(cotton/polyester dress shirt, pinpoint weave, long sleeves).*
Source: The Council for Community and Economic Research, ACCRA Cost of Living Index, 2017

HOUSING

House Price Index (HPI)

Area	National Ranking[2]	Quarterly Change (%)	One-Year Change (%)	Five-Year Change (%)
MSA[1]	78	0.16	8.04	61.46
U.S.[3]	–	1.61	6.68	34.71

Note: The HPI is a weighted repeat sales index. It measures average price changes in repeat sales or refinancings on the same properties. This information is obtained by reviewing repeat mortgage transactions on single-family properties whose mortgages have been purchased or securitized by Fannie Mae or Freddie Mac in January 1975; (1) Figures cover the Portland-Vancouver-Hillsboro, OR-WA Metropolitan Statistical Area—see Appendix B for areas included; (2) Rankings are based on annual percentage change for all metro areas containing at least 15,000 transactions over the last 10 years and ranges from 1 to 253; (3) figures based on a weighted average of Census Division estimates using a seasonally adjusted, purchase-only index; all figures are for the period ending December 31, 2017
Source: Federal Housing Finance Agency, House Price Index, February 28, 2018

Median Single-Family Home Prices

Area	2015	2016	2017[p]	Percent Change 2016 to 2017
MSA[1]	312.1	351.2	381.8	8.7
U.S. Average	223.9	235.5	248.8	5.6

Note: Figures are median sales prices of existing single-family homes in thousands of dollars; (p) preliminary; (1) Figures cover the Portland-Vancouver-Hillsboro, OR-WA Metropolitan Statistical Area—see Appendix B for areas included
Source: National Association of Realtors, Median Sales Price of Existing Single-Family Homes for Metropolitan Areas, 4th Quarter 2017

Qualifying Income Based on Median Sales Price of Existing Single-Family Homes

Area	With 5% Down ($)	With 10% Down ($)	With 20% Down ($)
MSA[1]	85,329	80,838	71,856
U.S. Average	55,585	52,659	46,808

Note: Figures are preliminary; Qualifying income is based on a mortgage rate of 4.17%. Monthly principal and interest payment is limited to 25% of income; (1) Figures cover the Portland-Vancouver-Hillsboro, OR-WA Metropolitan Statistical Area—see Appendix B for areas included
Source: National Association of Realtors, Qualifying Income Based on Median Sales Price of Existing Single-Family Homes for Metropolitan Areas, 4th Quarter 2017

Median Apartment Condo-Coop Home Prices

Area	2015	2016	2017[p]	Percent Change 2016 to 2017
MSA[1]	198.0	228.6	254.1	11.2
U.S. Average	210.7	220.7	234.3	6.2

Note: Figures are median sales prices of existing apartment condo-coop homes in thousands of dollars; (p) preliminary; (1) Figures cover the Portland-Vancouver-Hillsboro, OR-WA Metropolitan Statistical Area—see Appendix B for areas included
Source: National Association of Realtors, Median Sales Price of Existing Apartment Condo-Coop Homes for Metropolitan Areas, 4th Quarter 2017

Home Value Distribution

Area	Under $50,000	$50,000 -$99,999	$100,000 -$149,999	$150,000 -$199,999	$200,000 -$299,999	$300,000 -$499,999	$500,000 -$999,999	$1,000,000 or more
City	0.5	1.2	3.3	3.2	8.1	32.8	40.1	10.9
MSA[1]	4.8	1.8	5.2	12.0	30.0	31.9	12.6	1.6
U.S.	8.8	14.8	15.3	14.9	18.4	16.4	9.0	2.5

Note: Figures are percentages and cover owner-occupied housing units; (1) Figures cover the Portland-Vancouver-Hillsboro, OR-WA Metropolitan Statistical Area—see Appendix B for areas included
Source: U.S. Census Bureau, 2012-2016 American Community Survey 5-Year Estimates

Homeownership Rate

Area	2009 (%)	2010 (%)	2011 (%)	2012 (%)	2013 (%)	2014 (%)	2015 (%)	2016 (%)	2017 (%)
MSA[1]	64.0	63.7	63.7	63.9	60.9	59.8	58.9	61.8	61.1
U.S.	67.4	66.9	66.1	65.4	65.1	64.5	63.7	63.4	63.9

Note: (1) Figures cover the Portland-Vancouver-Hillsboro, OR-WA Metropolitan Statistical Area—see Appendix B for areas included
Source: U.S. Census Bureau, Housing Vacancies and Homeownership Annual Statistics: 2009-2017

Year Housing Structure Built

Area	2010 or Later	2000 -2009	1990 -1999	1980 -1989	1970 -1979	1960 -1969	1950 -1959	1940 -1949	Before 1940	Median Year
City	2.1	8.9	17.3	22.6	23.7	9.7	7.4	3.7	4.6	1980
MSA[1]	2.5	15.7	18.9	11.4	17.8	8.9	7.3	4.7	12.6	1979
U.S.	2.3	14.7	14.0	13.7	15.6	10.9	10.6	5.2	13.0	1977

Note: Figures are percentages except for Median Year; Note: (1) Figures cover the Portland-Vancouver-Hillsboro, OR-WA Metropolitan Statistical Area—see Appendix B for areas included
Source: U.S. Census Bureau, 2012-2016 American Community Survey 5-Year Estimates

Gross Monthly Rent

Area	Under $500	$500 -$999	$1,000 -$1,499	$1,500 -$1,999	$2,000 -$2,499	$2,500 -$2,999	$3,000 and up	Median ($)
City	2.7	11.6	46.7	25.1	4.9	3.0	6.0	1,371
MSA[1]	5.8	40.2	35.7	13.0	3.3	1.1	0.9	1,047
U.S.	11.3	43.3	27.7	10.7	4.0	1.6	1.5	949

Note: Figures are percentages except for Median; Gross rent is the contract rent plus the estimated average monthly cost of utilities (electricity, gas, and water and sewer) and fuels (oil, coal, kerosene, wood, etc.) if these are paid by the renter (or paid for the renter by someone else); (1) Figures cover the Portland-Vancouver-Hillsboro, OR-WA Metropolitan Statistical Area—see Appendix B for areas included
Source: U.S. Census Bureau, 2012-2016 American Community Survey 5-Year Estimates

HEALTH

Health Risk Factors

Category	MSA[1] (%)	U.S. (%)
Adults aged 18–64 who have any kind of health care coverage	90.7	87.7
Adults who reported being in good or excellent health	86.3	83.6
Adults who are current smokers	14.4	17.1
Adults who currently use E-cigarettes	4.7	4.7
Adults who currently use chewing tobacco, snuff, or snus	2.8	4.0
Adults who are heavy drinkers[2]	7.7	6.5
Adults who are binge drinkers[3]	17.5	16.9
Adults who are overweight (BMI 25.0 - 29.9)	34.7	35.3
Adults who are obese (BMI 30.0 - 99.8)	26.3	29.9
Adults who participated in any physical activities in the past month	85.0	76.9
Adults who always or nearly always wears a seat belt	98.8	94.3

Note: (1) Figures cover the Portland-Vancouver-Hillsboro, OR-WA Metropolitan Statistical Area—see Appendix B for areas included; (2) Heavy drinkers are classified as adult men having more than 14 drinks per week and adult women having more than 7 drinks per week; (3) Binge drinkers are classified as males having five or more drinks on one occasion or females having four or more drinks on one occasion
Source: Centers for Disease Control and Prevention, Behaviorial Risk Factor Surveillance System, SMART: Selected Metropolitan Area Risk Trends, 2016

Health Screening Rates

Category	MSA[1] (%)	U.S. (%)
Adults 50-75 who have had a blood stool test within the past year	18.1	8.0
Adults 50-75 who have had a colonoscopy in the past 10 years	62.2	63.5
Adults aged 65+ who have had flu shot within the past year	54.0	58.6
Adults aged 65+ who have ever had a pneumonia vaccination	78.7	73.4
Adults who have ever been tested for HIV	39.6	35.6
Women aged 21-65 who have had a pap test in the past three years	77.7	79.8
Men aged 40+ who have had a PSA test within the past two years	31.4	39.5
Women aged 40+ who have had a mammogram within the past two years	66.9	72.5

Note: (1) Figures cover the Portland-Vancouver-Hillsboro, OR-WA Metropolitan Statistical Area—see Appendix B for areas included; Source: Centers for Disease Control and Prevention, Behaviorial Risk Factor Surveillance System, SMART: Selected Metropolitan Area Risk Trends, 2016

Chronic Health Conditions

Category	MSA[1] (%)	U.S. (%)
Adults who have ever been told they had a heart attack	3.6	4.4
Adults who have ever been told they have angina or coronary heart disease	3.4	4.1
Adults who have ever been told they had a stroke	2.4	3.1
Adults who have been told they currently have asthma	9.1	9.3
Adults who have ever been told they have arthritis	23.7	25.8
Adults who have ever been told they have diabetes[2]	9.0	10.5
Adults who have ever been told they had skin cancer	6.3	5.9
Adults who have ever been told they had any other types of cancer	6.4	6.7
Adults who have ever been told they have COPD	4.7	6.3
Adults who have ever been told they have kidney disease	3.1	2.8
Adults who have ever been told they have a form of depression	23.2	17.4

Note: (1) Figures cover the Portland-Vancouver-Hillsboro, OR-WA Metropolitan Statistical Area—see Appendix B for areas included; (2) Figures do not include pregnancy-related, borderline, or pre-diabetes
Source: Centers for Disease Control and Prevention, Behaviorial Risk Factor Surveillance System, SMART: Selected Metropolitan Area Risk Trends, 2016

Mortality Rates for the Top 10 Causes of Death in the U.S.

ICD-10[a] Sub-Chapter	ICD-10[a] Code	Age-Adjusted Mortality Rate[1] per 100,000 population	
		County[2]	U.S.
Malignant neoplasms	C00-C97	151.4	158.5
Ischaemic heart diseases	I20-I25	53.8	96.8
Other forms of heart disease	I30-I51	55.5	52.4
Chronic lower respiratory diseases	J40-J47	34.4	40.9
Cerebrovascular diseases	I60-I69	37.6	37.2
Organic, including symptomatic, mental disorders	F01-F09	49.8	33.3
Other degenerative diseases of the nervous system	G30-G31	38.7	32.1
Other external causes of accidental injury	W00-X59	28.0	31.2
Diabetes mellitus	E10-E14	18.4	21.1
Hypertensive diseases	I10-I15	14.8	20.8

Note: (a) ICD-10 = International Classification of Diseases 10th Revision; (1) Mortality rates are a three year average covering 2014-2016; (2) Figures cover Clackamas County.
Source: Centers for Disease Control and Prevention, National Center for Health Statistics. Underlying Cause of Death 1999-2016 on CDC WONDER Online Database, released December 2017

Mortality Rates for Selected Causes of Death

ICD-10[a] Sub-Chapter	ICD-10[a] Code	Age-Adjusted Mortality Rate[1] per 100,000 population	
		County[2]	U.S.
Assault	X85-Y09	1.7	5.6
Diseases of the liver	K70-K76	12.4	14.0
Human immunodeficiency virus (HIV) disease	B20-B24	Suppressed	1.9
Influenza and pneumonia	J09-J18	8.2	14.6
Intentional self-harm	X60-X84	16.3	13.2
Malnutrition	E40-E46	2.2	1.3
Obesity and other hyperalimentation	E65-E68	2.3	2.1
Renal failure	N17-N19	7.1	13.0
Transport accidents	V01-V99	9.3	12.0
Viral hepatitis	B15-B19	2.1	1.9

Note: (a) ICD-10 = International Classification of Diseases 10th Revision; (1) Mortality rates are a three year average covering 2014-2016; (2) Figures cover Clackamas County; Data are Suppressed when the data meet the criteria for confidentiality constraints; Mortality rates are flagged as Unreliable when the rate would be calculated with a numerator of 20 or less.
Source: Centers for Disease Control and Prevention, National Center for Health Statistics. Underlying Cause of Death 1999-2016 on CDC WONDER Online Database, released December 2017

Health Insurance Coverage

Area	With Health Insurance	With Private Health Insurance	With Public Health Insurance	Without Health Insurance	Population Under Age 18 Without Health Insurance
City	95.5	85.8	22.8	4.5	2.9
MSA[1]	90.5	71.4	30.7	9.5	3.6
U.S.	88.3	66.7	33.0	11.7	5.9

Note: Figures are percentages that cover the civilian noninstitutionalized population; (1) Figures cover the Portland-Vancouver-Hillsboro, OR-WA Metropolitan Statistical Area—see Appendix B for areas included
Source: U.S. Census Bureau, 2012-2016 American Community Survey 5-Year Estimates

Number of Medical Professionals

Area	MDs[3]	DOs[3,4]	Dentists	Podiatrists	Chiropractors	Optometrists
County[1] (number)	995	101	317	15	152	58
County[1] (rate[2])	248.9	25.3	77.9	3.7	37.4	14.3
U.S. (rate[2])	276.5	22.3	67.3	6.0	26.7	15.9

Note: Data as of 2016 unless noted; (1) Data covers Clackamas County; (2) Rate per 100,000 population; (3) Data as of 2015 and includes all active, non-federal physicians; (4) Doctor of Osteopathic Medicine
Source: U.S. Department of Health and Human Services, Health Resources and Services Administration, Bureau of Health Professions, Area Resource File (ARF) 2016-2017

Best Hospitals

According to *U.S. News,* the Portland-Vancouver-Hillsboro, OR-WA metro area is home to two of the best hospitals in the U.S.: **OHSU Hospital** (7 adult specialties and 6 pediatric specialties); **Providence Portland Medical Center** (2 adult specialties). The hospitals listed were nationally ranked in at least one of 16 specialties. Only 152 hospitals nationwide were nationally ranked in one or more specialties. Twenty hospitals in the U.S. made the Honor Roll. The Best Hospitals Honor Roll was revamped last year to take both the national rankings and the procedure and condition ratings into account. Hospitals received points if they were nationally ranked in one of the 16 specialties—the higher they ranked, the more points they got—and how many ratings of "high performing" they earned in the nine procedures and conditions. *U.S. News Online, "America's Best Hospitals 2017-18"*

According to *U.S. News,* the Portland-Vancouver-Hillsboro, OR-WA metro area is home to one of the best children's hospitals in the U.S.: **Doernbecher Children's Hospital at Oregon Health and Science University** (6 pediatric specialties). The hospital listed was highly ranked in at least one of 10 pediatric specialties. Eighty-two children's hospitals in the U.S. were nationally ranked in at least one specialty. Hospitals received points for being ranked in a specialty, and the 10 hospitals with the most points across the 10 specialties make up the Honor Roll. *U.S. News Online, "America's Best Children's Hospitals 2017-18"*

EDUCATION

Public School District Statistics

District Name	Schls	Pupils	Pupil/ Teacher Ratio	Minority Pupils[1] (%)	Free Lunch Eligible[2] (%)	IEP[3] (%)
Lake Oswego SD 7J	10	7,078	21.2	24.0	8.1	9.0

Note: Table includes school districts with 100 or more students; (1) Percentage of students that are not non-Hispanic white; (2) Percentage of students that are eligible for the free lunch program; (3) Percentage of students that have an Individualized Education Program.
Source: U.S. Department of Education, National Center for Education Statistics, Common Core of Data, Local Education Agency (School District) Universe Survey: School Year 2015-2016; U.S. Department of Education, National Center for Education Statistics, Common Core of Data, Public Elementary/Secondary School Universe Survey: School Year 2015-2016

Highest Level of Education

Area	Less than H.S.	H.S. Diploma	Some College, No Deg.	Associate Degree	Bachelor's Degree	Master's Degree	Prof. School Degree	Doctorate Degree
City	1.5	9.0	17.8	4.7	39.3	16.7	8.2	2.8
MSA[1]	8.8	20.9	24.8	8.8	23.1	9.6	2.4	1.6
U.S.	13.0	27.5	21.0	8.2	18.8	8.2	2.0	1.3

Note: Figures cover persons age 25 and over; (1) Figures cover the Portland-Vancouver-Hillsboro, OR-WA Metropolitan Statistical Area—see Appendix B for areas included
Source: U.S. Census Bureau, 2012-2016 American Community Survey 5-Year Estimates

Educational Attainment by Race

Area	High School Graduate or Higher (%)					Bachelor's Degree or Higher (%)				
	Total	White	Black	Asian	Hisp.[2]	Total	White	Black	Asian	Hisp.[2]
City	98.5	98.7	100.0	99.9	90.6	67.0	67.6	46.7	69.0	55.1
MSA[1]	91.2	92.9	87.9	85.0	65.0	36.8	37.6	24.6	47.0	17.4
U.S.	87.0	88.9	84.3	86.3	65.7	30.3	31.6	20.0	52.1	14.7

Note: Figures shown cover persons 25 years old and over; (1) Figures cover the Portland-Vancouver-Hillsboro, OR-WA Metropolitan Statistical Area—see Appendix B for areas included; (2) People of Hispanic origin can be of any race
Source: U.S. Census Bureau, 2012-2016 American Community Survey 5-Year Estimates

School Enrollment by Grade and Control

Area	Preschool (%)		Kindergarten (%)		Grades 1 - 4 (%)		Grades 5 - 8 (%)		Grades 9 - 12 (%)	
	Public	Private	Public	Private	Public	Private	Public	Private	Public	Private
City	27.5	72.5	84.9	15.1	86.1	13.9	89.0	11.0	90.5	9.5
MSA[1]	40.3	59.7	84.9	15.1	88.9	11.1	89.9	10.1	91.2	8.8
U.S.	58.4	41.6	87.7	12.3	89.8	10.2	89.7	10.3	90.4	9.6

Note: Figures shown cover persons 3 years old and over; (1) Figures cover the Portland-Vancouver-Hillsboro, OR-WA Metropolitan Statistical Area—see Appendix B for areas included
Source: U.S. Census Bureau, 2012-2016 American Community Survey 5-Year Estimates

Average Salaries of Public School Classroom Teachers

Area	2015		2016		Change from 2015 to 2016	
	Dollars	Rank[1]	Dollars	Rank[1]	Percent	Rank[2]
Oregon	59,464	14	60,359	13	1.5	17
U.S. Average	57,611	–	58,353	–	1.3	–

Note: (1) Rank ranges from 1 to 51 where 1 indicates highest salary; (2) Rank ranges from 1 to 51 where 1 indicates highest percent change.
Source: National Education Association, Rankings & Estimates: Rankings of the States 2016 and Estimates of School Statistics 2017

Higher Education

Four-Year Colleges			Two-Year Colleges			Medical Schools[1]	Law Schools[2]	Voc/ Tech[3]
Public	Private Non-profit	Private For-profit	Public	Private Non-profit	Private For-profit			
0	0	0	0	0	0	0	0	0

Note: Figures cover institutions located within the city limits and include main campuses only; (1) includes schools accredited by the Liaison Committee on Medical Education and the American Osteopathic Association's Commission on Osteopathic College Accreditation; (2) includes ABA-accredited schools, schools with provisional ABA accreditation, and state accredited schools; (3) includes all schools with programs that are less than 2 years.
Source: National Center for Education Statistics, Integrated Postsecondary Education System (IPEDS), 2016-17; Wikipedia, List of Medical Schools in the United States, accessed April 2, 2018; Wikipedia, List of Law Schools in the United States, accessed April 2, 2018

According to *U.S. News & World Report,* the Portland-Vancouver-Hillsboro, OR-WA metro area is home to three of the best liberal arts colleges in the U.S.: **Lewis & Clark College** (#76 tie); **Reed College** (#82 tie); **Linfield College** (#117 tie). The indicators used to capture academic quality fall into a number of categories: assessment by administrators at peer institutions; retention of students; faculty resources; student selectivity; financial resources; alumni giving; high school counselor ratings of colleges; and graduation rate. *U.S. News & World Report, "America's Best Colleges 2018"*

According to *U.S. News & World Report,* the Portland-Vancouver-Hillsboro, OR-WA metro area is home to one of the top 100 law schools in the U.S.: **Lewis & Clark College (Northwestern)** (#95 tie). The rankings are based on a weighted average of 12 measures of quality: peer assessment score; assessment score by lawyers/judges; median LSAT scores; median undergrad GPA; acceptance rate; employment rates for graduates; placement success; bar passage rate; faculty resources; expenditures per student; student/faculty ratio; and library resources. *U.S. News & World Report, "America's Best Graduate Schools, Law, 2019"*

According to *U.S. News & World Report,* the Portland-Vancouver-Hillsboro, OR-WA metro area is home to one of the top 75 medical schools for research in the U.S.: **Oregon Health and Science University** (#29 tie). The rankings are based on a weighted average of 11 measures of quality: quality assessment; peer assessment score; assessment score by residency directors; research activity; total research activity; average research activity per faculty member; student selectivity;

median MCAT total score; median undergraduate GPA; acceptance rate; and faculty resources.
U.S. News & World Report, "America's Best Graduate Schools, Medical, 2019"

PRESIDENTIAL ELECTION

2016 Presidential Election Results

Area	Clinton	Trump	Johnson	Stein	Other
Clackamas County	47.7	41.3	5.2	1.9	4.0
U.S.	48.0	45.9	3.3	1.1	1.7

Note: Results are percentages and may not add to 100% due to rounding
Source: Dave Leip's Atlas of U.S. Presidential Elections

EMPLOYERS

Major Employers

Company Name	Industry
Children's Creative Learning Center	Child day care services
Clackamas Community College	Community college
Coho Distributing	Liquor
Con-Way Enterprise Services	Accounting, auditing, & bookkeeping
Legacy Emanuel Hospital and Health Center	General medical & surgical hospitals
Nike	Rubber & plastics footwear
Oregon Health & Science University	Colleges & universities
PCC Structurals	Aircraft parts & equipment, nec
Portland Adventist Medical Center	General medical & surgical hospitals
Portland Community College	Community college
Portland State University	Colleges & universities
Providence Health & Services - Oregon	Skilled nursing care facilities
School Dist 1 Multnomah County	Public elementary & secondary schools
Shilo Management Corp.	Motels
Southwest Washington Medical Center	General medical & surgical hospitals
Stancorp Mortgage Investors	Life insurance
SW Washington Hospital	General medical & surgical hospitals
Tektronix	Instruments to measure elasticity
The Evergreen Aviation and Space Museum	Museums & art galleries
Veterans Health Administration	Administration of veterans' affairs

Note: Companies shown are located within the Portland-Vancouver-Hillsboro, OR-WA Metropolitan Statistical Area.
Source: Hoovers.com; Wikipedia

PUBLIC SAFETY

Crime Rate

Area	All Crimes	Violent Crimes				Property Crimes		
		Murder	Rape[3]	Robbery	Aggrav. Assault	Burglary	Larceny -Theft	Motor Vehicle Theft
City	1,227.5	0.0	23.2	12.9	43.7	159.5	952.1	36.0
Metro[1]	3,070.3	1.7	49.2	68.4	156.8	370.7	2,033.5	390.0
U.S.	2,847.8	5.3	40.4	102.8	248.5	468.9	1,745.0	236.9

Note: Figures are crimes per 100,000 population; (1) Figures cover the Portland-Vancouver-Hillsboro, OR-WA Metropolitan Statistical Area—see Appendix B for areas included; (3) The city and U.S. figures shown were reported using the revised Uniform Crime Reporting (UCR) definition of rape. The metro area figures shown are an aggregate total of the data submitted using both the revised and legacy UCR definitions.
Source: FBI Uniform Crime Reports, 2016

Hate Crimes

Area	Number of Quarters Reported	Number of Incidents per Bias Motivation					
		Race/Ethnicity/ Ancestry	Religion	Sexual Orientation	Disability	Gender	Gender Identity
City	4	0	0	0	0	0	0
U.S.	4	3,489	1,273	1,076	70	31	124

Source: Federal Bureau of Investigation, Hate Crime Statistics 2016

Identity Theft Consumer Reports

Area	Reports	Reports per 100,000 Population	Rank[2]
MSA[1]	2,560	106	81
U.S.	371,061	114	-

Note: (1) Figures cover the Portland-Vancouver-Hillsboro, OR-WA Metropolitan Statistical Area—see Appendix B for areas included; (2) Rank ranges from 1 to 389 where 1 indicates greatest number of identity theft reports per 100,000 population
Source: Federal Trade Commission, Consumer Sentinel Network Data Book for January–December 2017

Fraud and Other Consumer Reports

Area	Reports	Reports per 100,000 Population	Rank[2]
MSA[1]	11,584	478	147
U.S.	2,304,550	708	-

Note: (1) Figures cover the Portland-Vancouver-Hillsboro, OR-WA Metropolitan Statistical Area—see Appendix B for areas included; (2) Rank ranges from 1 to 389 where 1 indicates greatest number of fraud and other consumer reports per 100,000 population
Source: Federal Trade Commission, Consumer Sentinel Network Data Book for January–December 2017

SPORTS

Professional Sports Teams

Team Name	League	Year Established
Portland Timbers	Major League Soccer (MLS)	2011
Portland Trail Blazers	National Basketball Association (NBA)	1970

Note: Includes teams located in the Portland-Vancouver-Hillsboro, OR-WA Metropolitan Statistical Area.
Source: Wikipedia, Major Professional Sports Teams of the United States and Canada, April 5, 2018

CLIMATE

Average and Extreme Temperatures

Temperature	Jan	Feb	Mar	Apr	May	Jun	Jul	Aug	Sep	Oct	Nov	Dec	Yr.
Extreme High (°F)	65	71	83	93	100	102	107	107	105	92	73	64	107
Average High (°F)	45	50	56	61	68	73	80	79	74	64	53	46	62
Average Temp. (°F)	39	43	48	52	58	63	68	68	63	55	46	41	54
Average Low (°F)	34	36	39	42	48	53	57	57	52	46	40	36	45
Extreme Low (°F)	-2	-3	19	29	29	39	43	44	34	26	13	6	-3

Note: Figures cover the years 1926-1992
Source: National Climatic Data Center, International Station Meteorological Climate Summary, 9/96

Average Precipitation/Snowfall/Humidity

Precip./Humidity	Jan	Feb	Mar	Apr	May	Jun	Jul	Aug	Sep	Oct	Nov	Dec	Yr.
Avg. Precip. (in.)	5.5	4.2	3.8	2.4	2.0	1.5	0.5	0.9	1.7	3.0	5.5	6.6	37.5
Avg. Snowfall (in.)	3	1	1	Tr	Tr	0	0	0	0	0	1	2	7
Avg. Rel. Hum. 7am (%)	85	86	86	84	80	78	77	81	87	90	88	87	84
Avg. Rel. Hum. 4pm (%)	75	67	60	55	53	50	45	45	49	61	74	79	59

Note: Figures cover the years 1926-1992; Tr = Trace amounts (<0.05 in. of rain; <0.5 in. of snow)
Source: National Climatic Data Center, International Station Meteorological Climate Summary, 9/96

Weather Conditions

Temperature			Daytime Sky			Precipitation		
5°F & below	32°F & below	90°F & above	Clear	Partly cloudy	Cloudy	0.01 inch or more precip.	0.1 inch or more snow/ice	Thunder-storms
< 1	37	11	67	116	182	152	4	7

Note: Figures are average number of days per year and cover the years 1926-1992
Source: National Climatic Data Center, International Station Meteorological Climate Summary, 9/96

HAZARDOUS WASTE

Superfund Sites

The Portland-Vancouver-Hillsboro, OR-WA metro area is home to seven sites on the EPA's Superfund National Priorities List: **Boomsnub/Airco** (final); **Frontier Hard Chrome, Inc.** (final); **Mccormick & Baxter Creosoting Co. (Portland Plant)** (final); **Northwest Pipe & Casing/Hall Process Company** (final); **Portland Harbor** (final); **Reynolds Metals Company** (final); **Taylor**

Lumber and Treating (final). There are a total of 1,396 Superfund sites with a status of proposed or final on the list in the U.S. *U.S. Environmental Protection Agency, National Priorities List, April 4, 2018*

AIR & WATER QUALITY

Air Quality Trends: Ozone

	1990	1995	2000	2005	2010	2012	2013	2014	2015	2016
MSA[1]	0.081	0.065	0.059	0.059	0.056	0.059	0.053	0.057	0.064	0.057
U.S.	0.087	0.089	0.081	0.079	0.073	0.075	0.069	0.067	0.068	0.069

Note: (1) Data covers the Portland-Vancouver-Hillsboro, OR-WA Metropolitan Statistical Area—see Appendix B for areas included. The values shown are the composite ozone concentration averages among trend sites based on the highest fourth daily maximum 8-hour concentration in parts per million. These trends are based on sites having an adequate record of monitoring data during the trend period. Data from exceptional events are included.
Source: U.S. Environmental Protection Agency, Air Quality Monitoring Information, "Air Quality Trends by City, 1990-2016"

Air Quality Index

Area	Percent of Days when Air Quality was...[2]					AQI Statistics[2]	
	Good	Moderate	Unhealthy for Sensitive Groups	Unhealthy	Very Unhealthy	Maximum	Median
MSA[1]	76.4	19.2	2.7	1.4	0.3	212	38

Note: (1) Data covers the Portland-Vancouver-Hillsboro, OR-WA Metropolitan Statistical Area—see Appendix B for areas included; (2) Based on 365 days with AQI data in 2017. Air Quality Index (AQI) is an index for reporting daily air quality. EPA calculates the AQI for five major air pollutants regulated by the Clean Air Act: ground-level ozone, particle pollution (aka particulate matter), carbon monoxide, sulfur dioxide, and nitrogen dioxide. The AQI runs from 0 to 500. The higher the AQI value, the greater the level of air pollution and the greater the health concern. There are six AQI categories: "Good" AQI is between 0 and 50. Air quality is considered satisfactory; "Moderate" AQI is between 51 and 100. Air quality is acceptable; "Unhealthy for Sensitive Groups" When AQI values are between 101 and 150, members of sensitive groups may experience health effects; "Unhealthy" When AQI values are between 151 and 200 everyone may begin to experience health effects; "Very Unhealthy" AQI values between 201 and 300 trigger a health alert; "Hazardous" AQI values over 300 trigger warnings of emergency conditions (not shown).
Source: U.S. Environmental Protection Agency, Air Quality Index Report, 2017

Air Quality Index Pollutants

Area	Percent of Days when AQI Pollutant was...[2]					
	Carbon Monoxide	Nitrogen Dioxide	Ozone	Sulfur Dioxide	Particulate Matter 2.5	Particulate Matter 10
MSA[1]	0.0	4.1	48.8	0.0	47.1	0.0

Note: (1) Data covers the Portland-Vancouver-Hillsboro, OR-WA Metropolitan Statistical Area—see Appendix B for areas included; (2) Based on 365 days with AQI data in 2017. The Air Quality Index (AQI) is an index for reporting daily air quality. EPA calculates the AQI for five major air pollutants regulated by the Clean Air Act: ground-level ozone, particle pollution (also known as particulate matter), carbon monoxide, sulfur dioxide, and nitrogen dioxide. The AQI runs from 0 to 500. The higher the AQI value, the greater the level of air pollution and the greater the health concern.
Source: U.S. Environmental Protection Agency, Air Quality Index Report, 2017

Maximum Air Pollutant Concentrations: Particulate Matter, Ozone, CO and Lead

	Particulate Matter 10 (ug/m^3)	Particulate Matter 2.5 Wtd AM (ug/m^3)	Particulate Matter 2.5 24-Hr (ug/m^3)	Ozone (ppm)	Carbon Monoxide (ppm)	Lead (ug/m^3)
MSA[1] Level	32	5.9	18	0.064	1	n/a
NAAQS[2]	150	15	35	0.075	9	0.15
Met NAAQS[2]	Yes	Yes	Yes	Yes	Yes	n/a

Note: (1) Data covers the Portland-Vancouver-Hillsboro, OR-WA Metropolitan Statistical Area—see Appendix B for areas included; Data from exceptional events are included; (2) National Ambient Air Quality Standards; ppm = parts per million; ug/m^3 = micrograms per cubic meter; n/a not available.
Concentrations: Particulate Matter 10 (coarse particulate)—highest second maximum 24-hour concentration; Particulate Matter 2.5 Wtd AM (fine particulate)—highest weighted annual mean concentration; Particulate Matter 2.5 24-Hour (fine particulate)—highest 98th percentile 24-hour concentration; Ozone—highest fourth daily maximum 8-hour concentration; Carbon Monoxide—highest second maximum non-overlapping 8-hour concentration; Lead—maximum running 3-month average
Source: U.S. Environmental Protection Agency, Air Quality Monitoring Information, "Air Quality Statistics by City, 2016"

Maximum Air Pollutant Concentrations: Nitrogen Dioxide and Sulfur Dioxide

	Nitrogen Dioxide AM (ppb)	Nitrogen Dioxide 1-Hr (ppb)	Sulfur Dioxide AM (ppb)	Sulfur Dioxide 1-Hr (ppb)	Sulfur Dioxide 24-Hr (ppb)
MSA[1] Level	13	35	n/a	3	n/a
NAAQS[2]	53	100	30	75	140
Met NAAQS[2]	Yes	Yes	n/a	Yes	n/a

Note: (1) Data covers the Portland-Vancouver-Hillsboro, OR-WA Metropolitan Statistical Area—see Appendix B for areas included; Data from exceptional events are included; (2) National Ambient Air Quality Standards; ppm = parts per million; ug/m^3 = micrograms per cubic meter; n/a not available.
Concentrations: Nitrogen Dioxide AM—highest arithmetic mean concentration; Nitrogen Dioxide 1-Hr—highest 98th percentile 1-hour daily maximum concentration; Sulfur Dioxide AM—highest annual mean concentration; Sulfur Dioxide 1-Hr—highest 99th percentile 1-hour daily maximum concentration; Sulfur Dioxide 24-Hr—highest second maximum 24-hour concentration
Source: U.S. Environmental Protection Agency, Air Quality Monitoring Information, "Air Quality Statistics by City, 2016"

Drinking Water

Water System Name	Pop. Served	Primary Water Source Type	Violations[1]	
			Health Based	Monitoring/ Reporting
Lake Oswego Municipal Water	36,093	Surface	0	0

Note: (1) Based on violation data from January 1, 2017 to December 31, 2017
Source: U.S. Environmental Protection Agency, Office of Ground Water and Drinking Water, Safe Drinking Water Information System (based on data extracted April 5, 2018)

Cranberry, Pennsylvania

Background

Cranberry Township is located about 20 miles north of Pittsburgh in the southwest corner of Butler County. Incorporated in 1803, it was originally named for the wild cranberries that grew rampant in the area. Cranberry is now a rapidly growing municipality, with a population that has nearly doubled since 1990. Interstate highways facilitate travel to and from the city and nearby Pittsburgh.

Surrounded by rolling wooded hills, Cranberry's landscape includes 250-year-old oak trees, and Brush Creek meanders through a corner of the township and in places its brush-covered banks are reminiscent of when the first settlers arrived in the late 1700s. The original bogs and marshes that were home to cranberries that gave the township its name were drained long ago, but efforts are ongoing to recreate them in city parks.

Oil was discovered in Pennsylvania in 1859 and the oil boom included the township of Cranberry. Historic remnants of the oil drilling can still be seen and, in 1940, there were about 150 registered active wells listed in the city. After World War II, the desire for "black gold" was replaced by the value and desire for surface real estate.

In the early part of the 1900s, Cranberry was often cut off from surrounding areas due to heavily rutted roads and trails leading in and out of town that became impassible in wet weather. The Harmony Line railroad helped make the local area accessible to the residents of Cranberry. In 1908, the railway began hourly travels through the township. Used first as a passenger train, the Harmony Line later added freight cars that allowed the farmers in Cranberry to sell their goods in Pittsburgh. Harmony Line eventually lost out to the ever-expanding world of Henry Ford's automobile but signs of the railway can still be seen today.

Activities and attractions in Cranberry include a water park, summer camps, sport leagues, golf courses and concerts. Free summer concerts can be enjoyed at the Rotary Amphitheater in Community Park and the Cranberry Municipal Center. Community Days is also celebrated in the summer, including games, food, informational booths, and fireworks.

In August 2015, the Pittsburgh Penguins and UPMC opened a new hockey practice and sports medicine facility in Cranberry near the PA 228/I-79 interchange. The UPMC Lemieux Sports Complex is named for former Penguin and current team co-owner Mario Lemieux.

Business in Cranberry is booming. There are over 3,000 national and international firms ranging from small businesses to major corporations, including the headquarters of Westinghouse Electric's nuclear energy complex, employing over 3,000 people. The Cranberry Board of Supervisors adopted a plan to ensure that present development does not hurt future generations. Local leaders are working hard to ensure the present level of development is sustainable.

Institutions of higher learning close to Cranberry are University of Pittsburgh, Penn State University, and Slippery Rock University.

The climate of Cranberry is varied, averaging around 165 days of sunshine throughout the year. Precipitation levels include 40 inches of rain in the summer and 41 inches of snow in the winter, both slightly above the national average. Summer highs are around 87 degrees and lows in the winter are close to 20 degrees.

Rankings

Business/Finance Rankings

- The personal finance site NerdWallet analyzed 183 American metropolitan areas with populations over 250,000 and more than 15,000 businesses to rank where entrepreneurs find the most success. Criteria included area economy, annual income, housing cost, unemployment rate, and the success rate of area businesses. Pittsburgh* ranked #17. *www.nerdwallet.com, "Best Places to Start a Business," April 27, 2015*
- USAA and Hiring Our Heroes worked with Sperlings's BestPlaces and the Institute for Veterans and Military Families at Syracuse University to rank major metropolitan areas where military-skills-related employment is strongest. Criteria for *mid-career* veterans included veteran wage growth; recent job growth; stability; and accessible health resources. Metro areas with a higher than national average crime or unemployment rate were excluded. At #2, the Pittsburgh* metro area made the top ten. *www.usaa.com, "2015 Best Places for Veterans"*
- Based on metro area social media reviews, the employment opinion group Glassdoor surveyed 50 of the largest U.S. metro areas and equally weighed cost of living, hiring opportunity, and job satisfaction to compose a list of "25 Best Cities for Jobs." Median pay and home value, in-demand jobs and number of current job openings was also factored in. The Pittsburgh* metro area was ranked #1 in overall job satisfaction. *www.glassdoor.com, "Best Cities for Jobs," September 12, 2017*
- In a survey of economic confidence in the nation's 50 largest metropolitan areas conducted January–December 2014, the Pittsburgh* metro area placed #45, according to Gallup's 2014 Economic Confidence Index. *Gallup, "San Jose and San Francisco Lead in Economic Confidence," March 19, 2015*
- The Brookings Institution ranked the 100 largest metro areas in the U.S. based on income inequality. Pittsburgh* was ranked #34 (#1 = greatest ineqality). Criteria: the "95/20 ratio," a figure representing the income at which a household earns more than 95 percent of all other households, divided by the income at which a household earns more than only 20 percent of all other households. *Brookings Institution, "Household Income Inequality, 100 Largest U.S. Metro Areas, 2014-2016," February 5, 2018*
- Payscale.com ranked the largest metro areas in terms of wage growth. The Pittsburgh* metro area ranked #1. Criteria: private-sector wage growth between the 4th quarter of 2016 and the 4th quarter of 2017. *PayScale, "Wage Trends by Metro Area-4th Quarter," January 17, 2018*
- Pittsburgh* was identified as one of America's most frugal metro areas by *Coupons.com.* The city ranked #25 out of 25. Criteria: digital coupon usage. *Coupons.com, "America's Most Frugal Cities of 2017," March 22, 2018*
- The Pittsburgh* metro area appeared on the Milken Institute "2017 Best Performing Cities" list. Rank: #143 out of 200 large metro areas. Criteria: job growth; wage and salary growth; high-tech output growth. *Milken Institute, "Best-Performing Cities 2017," January 2018*
- *Forbes* ranked the 200 most populous metro areas to determine the nation's "Best Places for Business and Careers." The Pittsburgh* metro area was ranked #85. Criteria: costs (business and living); job growth (past and projected); income growth; quality of life; educational attainment (college and high school); projected economic growth; cultural and recreational opportunities; net migration patterns; number of highly ranked colleges. *Forbes, "The Best Places for Business and Careers 2017," October 24, 2017*

Education Rankings

- Personal finance website *WalletHub* analyzed the 150 largest U.S. metropolitan statistical areas to determine where the most educated Americans are choosing to settle. Criteria: education quality and attainment gap; education levels; percentage of workers with degrees; public school rankings; quality and size of each metro area's universities. Pittsburgh* was ranked #47 (#1 = most educated city). *www.WalletHub.com, "2017's Most and Least Educated Cities in America," July 25, 2017*

Environmental Rankings

- Sperling's BestPlaces assessed 379 metropolitan areas of the United States for the likelihood of dangerously extreme weather events or earthquakes. In general the Southeast and South-Central regions have the highest risk of weather extremes and earthquakes, while the Pacific Northwest enjoys the lowest risk. Of the least risky metropolitan areas, the Pittsburgh* metro area was ranked #110. *www.bestplaces.net, "Safest Places from Natural Disasters," April 2011*

- Pittsburgh* was highlighted as one of the 25 metro areas most polluted by year-round particle pollution (Annual PM 2.5) in the U.S. during 2013 through 2015. The area ranked #8. *American Lung Association, State of the Air 2017*

- Pittsburgh* was highlighted as one of the 25 metro areas most polluted by short-term particle pollution (24-hour PM 2.5) in the U.S. during 2013 through 2015. The area ranked #17. *American Lung Association, State of the Air 2017*

Health/Fitness Rankings

- For each of the 50 most populous metro areas in the United States, the American College of Sports Medicine's American Fitness Index evaluated infrastructure, community assets, and policies that encourage healthy and fit lifestyles, including preventive health behaviors, levels of chronic disease conditions, health care access, and community resources and policies that support physical activity. The Pittsburgh* metro area ranked #29 for "community fitness." *www.americanfitnessindex.org, "ACSM American Fitness Index Health and Community Fitness Status of the 50 Largest Metropolitan Areas," May 2017*

- The Pittsburgh* metro area was identified as one of the worst cities for bed bugs in America by pest control company Orkin. The area ranked #24 out of 50 based on the number of bed bug treatments Orkin performed from December 2016 to November 2017. *Orkin, "Baltimore and Washington D.C. Continue to Hold Top Spots," January 8, 2018*

- Pittsburgh* was identified as a "2016 Spring Allergy Capital." The area ranked #54 out of 100. Three groups of factors were used to identify the most severe cities for people with allergies during the spring season: annual pollen levels; medicine utilization; access to board-certified allergists. *Asthma and Allergy Foundation of America, "Spring Allergy Capitals 2016"*

- Pittsburgh* was identified as a "2016 Fall Allergy Capital." The area ranked #30 out of 100. Three groups of factors were used to identify the most severe cities for people with allergies during the fall season: annual pollen levels; medicine utilization; access to board-certified allergists. *Asthma and Allergy Foundation of America, "Fall Allergy Capitals 2016"*

- Pittsburgh* was identified as a "2015 Asthma Capital." The area ranked #27 out of the nation's 100 largest metropolitan areas. Criteria: estimated prevalence; self-reported prevalence; crude death rate for asthma; annual pollen score; annual air quality; public smoking laws; number of board-certified asthma specialists; school inhaler access laws; rescue medication use; controller medication use; ER visits for asthma; uninsured rate; poverty rate. *Asthma and Allergy Foundation of America, "Asthma Capitals 2015"*

- The Pittsburgh* metro area ranked #65 out of 189 in The Gallup-Healthways Well-Being Index. Criteria: purpose; social well being; financial health; community and physical health. Results are based on telephone interviews with adults, aged 18 and older, living in metropolitan areas in the 50 U.S. states and the District of Columbia. *Gallup-Healthways, "State of American Well-Being, 2017 Community Well-Being Rankings" March 2018*

Real Estate Rankings

- FitSmallBusiness looked at 50 of the largest metropolitan areas in the U.S. to determine which metro was the best to start a real estate business. Data was compiled from such sources as: Zillow, Trulia, U.S. Census Bureau, and the Bureau of Labor Statistics. Criteria: location; inventory; annual wages; median sales price of homes; days on the market; median price cut percentage; and other factors that would influence real estate professional growth. The Pittsburgh* metro area ranked #49. *fitsmallbusiness.com, "The Best Cities to Become a Real Estate Agent in 2018," January 30, 2018*
- The Pittsburgh* metro area was identified as one of nine best housing markets to invest in. Criteria: single-family rental home investing in the first quarter of 2017 based on first-year returns. The area ranked #9. *The Business Insider, "Here are the 9 Best U.S. Housing Markets for Investment," May 11, 2017*
- Pittsburgh* was ranked #48 out of 238 metro areas in terms of housing affordability in 2017 by the National Association of Home Builders (#1 = most affordable). Criteria: the share of homes sold in that area affordable to a family earning the local median income, based on standard mortgage underwriting criteria. *National Association of Home Builders®, NAHB-Wells Fargo Housing Opportunity Index, 4th Quarter 2017*

Safety Rankings

- The National Insurance Crime Bureau ranked 382 metro areas in the U.S. in terms of per capita rates of vehicle theft. The Pittsburgh* metro area ranked #305 (#1 = highest rate). Criteria: number of vehicle theft offenses per 100,000 inhabitants in 2016. *National Insurance Crime Bureau, "Hot Spots 2016," June 8, 2017*

Seniors/Retirement Rankings

- From its Best Cities for Successful Aging indexes, the Milken Institute generated rankings for metropolitan areas, weighing data in nine categories—health care, wellness, living arrangements, transportation and convenience, financial characteristics, education, employment, community engagement, and overall livability. The Pittsburgh* metro area was ranked #44 overall in the large metro area category. *Milken Institute, "Best Cities for Successful Aging, 2017" March 14, 2017*

Miscellaneous Rankings

- The watchdog site Charity Navigator conducts an annual study of charities in the nation's major markets both to analyze statistical differences in their financial, accountability, and transparency practices and to track year-to-year variations in individual philanthropic communities. Charity Navigator's analysis demonstrated that the financial, accountability and transparency behaviors of America's largest charities can be influenced by the metropolitan market within which the charity operates. The Pittsburgh* metro area was ranked #27 among the 30 metro markets in the rating category of Overall Score. *www.charitynavigator.org, "2017 Metro Market Study," May 1, 2017*

*Cranberry is located within the Pittsburgh, PA Metropolitan Statistical Area.

Business Environment

CITY FINANCES

City Government Finances

Component	2015 ($000)	2015 ($ per capita)
Total Revenues	41,472	1,362
Total Expenditures	43,742	1,436
Debt Outstanding	48,794	1,602
Cash and Securities[1]	34,582	1,135

Note: (1) Cash and security holdings of a government at the close of its fiscal year,, including those of its dependent agencies, utilities, and liquor stores.
Source: U.S Census Bureau, State & Local Government Finances 2015

City Government Revenue by Source

Source	2015 ($000)	2015 ($ per capita)	2015 (%)
General Revenue			
From Federal Government	3	0	0.0
From State Government	2,034	67	4.9
From Local Governments	683	22	1.6
Taxes			
Property	4,862	160	11.7
Sales and Gross Receipts	0	0	0.0
Personal Income	7,085	233	17.1
Corporate Income	0	0	0.0
Motor Vehicle License	0	0	0.0
Other Taxes	5,168	170	12.5
Current Charges	13,839	454	33.4
Liquor Store	0	0	0.0
Utility	5,451	179	13.1
Employee Retirement	0	0	0.0

Source: U.S Census Bureau, State & Local Government Finances 2015

City Government Expenditures by Function

Function	2015 ($000)	2015 ($ per capita)	2015 (%)
General Direct Expenditures			
Air Transportation	0	0	0.0
Corrections	0	0	0.0
Education	0	0	0.0
Employment Security Administration	0	0	0.0
Financial Administration	691	22	1.6
Fire Protection	743	24	1.7
General Public Buildings	3,211	105	7.3
Governmental Administration, Other	1,413	46	3.2
Health	22	< 1	< 0.1
Highways	5,827	191	13.3
Hospitals	0	0	0.0
Housing and Community Development	1,071	35	2.4
Interest on General Debt	1,960	64	4.5
Judicial and Legal	0	0	0.0
Libraries	332	10	0.8
Parking	0	0	0.0
Parks and Recreation	6,262	205	14.3
Police Protection	8,157	267	18.6
Public Welfare	0	0	0.0
Sewerage	6,023	197	13.8
Solid Waste Management	2,032	66	4.6
Veterans' Services	0	0	0.0
Liquor Store	0	0	0.0
Utility	5,154	169	11.8
Employee Retirement	0	0	0.0

Source: U.S Census Bureau, State & Local Government Finances 2015

DEMOGRAPHICS

Population Growth

Area	1990 Census	2000 Census	2010 Census	2016* Estimate	Population Growth (%) 1990-2016	Population Growth (%) 2010-2016
City	14,764	23,625	28,098	29,914	102.6	6.5
MSA[1]	2,468,289	2,431,087	2,356,285	2,354,926	-4.6	-0.1
U.S.	248,709,873	281,421,906	308,745,538	318,558,162	28.1	3.2

Note: (1) Figures cover the Pittsburgh, PA Metropolitan Statistical Area—see Appendix B for areas included; (*) 2012-2016 5-year estimated population
Source: U.S. Census Bureau, 1990 Census, Census 2000, Census 2010, 2012-2016 American Community Survey 5-Year Estimates

Household Size

Area	Persons in Household (%)							Average Household Size
	One	Two	Three	Four	Five	Six	Seven or More	
City	19.8	32.9	16.8	19.8	8.0	2.0	0.6	2.70
MSA[1]	32.5	35.5	14.9	11.2	4.1	1.3	0.6	2.30
U.S.	27.7	33.7	15.7	13.1	6.0	2.3	1.5	2.60

Note: (1) Figures cover the Pittsburgh, PA Metropolitan Statistical Area—see Appendix B for areas included
Source: U.S. Census Bureau, 2012-2016 American Community Survey 5-Year Estimates

Race

Area	White Alone[2] (%)	Black Alone[2] (%)	Asian Alone[2] (%)	AIAN[3] Alone[2] (%)	NHOPI[4] Alone[2] (%)	Other Race Alone[2] (%)	Two or More Races (%)
City	93.4	1.3	3.1	0.0	0.1	0.7	1.4
MSA[1]	87.1	8.2	2.1	0.1	0.0	0.3	2.1
U.S.	73.3	12.6	5.2	0.8	0.2	4.8	3.1

Note: (1) Figures cover the Pittsburgh, PA Metropolitan Statistical Area—see Appendix B for areas included; (2) Alone is defined as not being in combination with one or more other races; (3) American Indian and Alaska Native; (4) Native Hawaiian and Other Pacific Islander
Source: U.S. Census Bureau, 2012-2016 American Community Survey 5-Year Estimates

Hispanic or Latino Origin

Area	Total (%)	Mexican (%)	Puerto Rican (%)	Cuban (%)	Other (%)
City	2.2	1.3	0.3	0.0	0.6
MSA[1]	1.6	0.5	0.4	0.1	0.6
U.S.	17.3	11.0	1.7	0.7	4.0

Note: Persons of Hispanic or Latino origin can be of any race; (1) Figures cover the Pittsburgh, PA Metropolitan Statistical Area—see Appendix B for areas included
Source: U.S. Census Bureau, 2012-2016 American Community Survey 5-Year Estimates

Segregation

Type	Segregation Indices[1]				Percent Change		
	1990	2000	2010	2010 Rank[2]	1990-2000	1990-2010	2000-2010
Black/White	70.8	68.9	65.8	17	-1.9	-5.1	-3.2
Asian/White	51.3	52.1	52.4	2	0.8	1.0	0.3
Hispanic/White	29.5	29.0	28.6	97	-0.5	-0.9	-0.4

Note: All figures cover the Metropolitan Statistical Area—see Appendix B for areas included; Figures are based on an analysis of 1990, 2000, and 2010 Census Decennial Census tract data by William H. Frey, Brookings Institution and the University of Michigan Social Science Data Analysis Network. In this analysis all racial groups (whites, blacks, and asians) are non-Hispanic members of those races. Hispanics are shown as a separate category; (1) Segregation Indices are Dissimilarity Indices that measure the degree to which the minority group is distributed differently than whites across census tracts. They range from 0 (complete integration) to 100 (complete segregation) where the value indicates the percentage of the minority group that needs to move to be distributed exactly like whites; (2) Ranges from 1 (most segregated) to 102 (least segregated); n/a not available.
Source: www.CensusScope.org

Ancestry

Area	German	Irish	English	American	Italian	Polish	French[2]	Scottish	Dutch
City	36.1	22.0	9.5	3.7	17.5	8.9	2.5	1.6	1.0
MSA[1]	27.8	18.4	8.1	4.2	16.3	8.7	1.8	1.9	1.2
U.S.	14.4	10.4	7.7	6.9	5.4	2.9	2.6	1.7	1.3

Note: Figures are the percentage of the total population reporting a particular ancestry. The nine most commonly reported ancestries in the U.S. are shown. Figures include multiple ancestries (e.g. if a person reported being Irish and Italian, they were included in both columns); (1) Figures cover the Pittsburgh, PA Metropolitan Statistical Area—see Appendix B for areas included; (2) Excludes Basque
Source: U.S. Census Bureau, 2012-2016 American Community Survey 5-Year Estimates

Foreign-Born Population

Area	Percent of Population Born in								
	Any Foreign Country	Asia	Mexico	Europe	Carribean	Central America[2]	South America	Africa	Canada
City	4.9	2.4	0.4	0.7	0.1	0.1	0.7	0.1	0.3
MSA[1]	3.7	1.8	0.1	1.0	0.1	0.1	0.2	0.2	0.1
U.S.	13.2	4.0	3.6	1.5	1.3	1.0	0.9	0.6	0.3

Note: (1) Figures cover the Pittsburgh, PA Metropolitan Statistical Area—see Appendix B for areas included; (2) Excludes Mexico.
Source: U.S. Census Bureau, 2012-2016 American Community Survey 5-Year Estimates

Marital Status

Area	Never Married	Now Married[2]	Separated	Widowed	Divorced
City	23.0	65.8	1.2	4.3	5.6
MSA[1]	31.8	48.9	1.8	7.7	9.8
U.S.	33.0	48.1	2.1	5.9	11.0

Note: Figures are percentages and cover the population 15 years of age and older; (1) Figures cover the Pittsburgh, PA Metropolitan Statistical Area—see Appendix B for areas included; (2) Excludes separated
Source: U.S. Census Bureau, 2012-2016 American Community Survey 5-Year Estimates

Disability Status

Area	All Ages	Under 18 Years Old	18 to 64 Years Old	65 Years and Over
City	6.9	4.1	4.6	30.1
MSA[1]	14.0	5.0	11.0	34.2
U.S.	12.5	4.1	10.3	35.7

Note: Figures show percent of the civilian noninstitutionalized population that reported having a disability. Disability status is determined from six types of difficulty: vision, hearing, cognitive, ambulatory, self-care, and independent living. For children under 5 years old, hearing and vision difficulty are used to determine disability status. For children between the ages of 5 and 14, disability status is determined from hearing, vision, cognitive, ambulatory, and self-care difficulties. For people aged 15 years and older, they are considered to have a disability if they have difficulty with any one of the six difficulty types; Note: (1) Figures cover the Pittsburgh, PA Metropolitan Statistical Area—see Appendix B for areas included
Source: U.S. Census Bureau, 2012-2016 American Community Survey 5-Year Estimates

Age

Area	Percent of Population									Median Age
	Under Age 5	Age 5–19	Age 20–34	Age 35–44	Age 45–54	Age 55–64	Age 65–74	Age 75–84	Age 85+	
City	6.6	22.6	14.3	15.9	17.6	12.7	6.1	2.9	1.3	39.4
MSA[1]	5.1	16.9	19.1	11.5	14.2	14.9	9.7	5.7	3.0	42.9
U.S.	6.2	19.6	20.7	12.7	13.6	12.6	8.3	4.3	1.9	37.7

Note: (1) Figures cover the Pittsburgh, PA Metropolitan Statistical Area—see Appendix B for areas included
Source: U.S. Census Bureau, 2012-2016 American Community Survey 5-Year Estimates

Gender

Area	Males	Females	Males per 100 Females
City	15,057	14,857	101.3
MSA[1]	1,144,208	1,210,718	94.5
U.S.	156,765,322	161,792,840	96.9

Note: (1) Figures cover the Pittsburgh, PA Metropolitan Statistical Area—see Appendix B for areas included
Source: U.S. Census Bureau, 2012-2016 American Community Survey 5-Year Estimates

Religious Groups by Family

Area	Catholic	Baptist	Non-Den.	Methodist[2]	Lutheran	LDS[3]	Pente-costal	Presby-terian[4]	Muslim[5]	Judaism
MSA[1]	32.8	2.3	2.8	5.7	3.4	0.4	1.1	4.7	0.3	0.7
U.S.	19.1	9.3	4.0	4.0	2.3	2.0	1.9	1.6	0.8	0.7

Note: Figures are the number of adherents as a percentage of the total population; (1) Figures cover the Pittsburgh, PA Metropolitan Statistical Area—see Appendix B for areas included; (2) Methodist/Pietist; (3) Latter Day Saints; (4) Reformed; (5) Figures are estimates
Source: Association of Statisticians of American Religious Bodies, 2010 U.S. Religion Census: Religious Congregations & Membership Study

Religious Groups by Tradition

Area	Catholic	Evangelical Protestant	Mainline Protestant	Other Tradition	Black Protestant	Orthodox
MSA[1]	32.8	7.4	13.8	2.1	0.9	0.7
U.S.	19.1	16.2	7.3	4.3	1.6	0.3

Note: Figures are the number of adherents as a percentage of the total population; (1) Figures cover the Pittsburgh, PA Metropolitan Statistical Area—see Appendix B for areas included
Source: Association of Statisticians of American Religious Bodies, 2010 U.S. Religion Census: Religious Congregations & Membership Study

ECONOMY

Gross Metropolitan Product

Area	2014	2015	2016	2017	Rank[2]
MSA[1]	134.7	138.6	142.1	147.9	24

Note: Figures are in billions of dollars; (1) Figures cover the Pittsburgh, PA Metropolitan Statistical Area—see Appendix B for areas included; (2) Rank is based on 2015 data and ranges from 1 to 381
Source: The U.S. Conference of Mayors, U.S. Metro Economies: GMP and Employment Report, 2015-2017

Economic Growth

Area	2012-14 (%)	2015 (%)	2016 (%)	2017 (%)	Rank[2]
MSA[1]	2.0	1.7	0.9	2.0	125
U.S.	2.0	2.4	1.9	2.6	–

Note: Figures are real gross metropolitan product (GMP) growth rates and represent average annual percent change; (1) Figures cover the Pittsburgh, PA Metropolitan Statistical Area—see Appendix B for areas included; (2) Rank is based on 2012-2014 average annual percent change and ranges from 1 to 381
Source: The U.S. Conference of Mayors, U.S. Metro Economies: GMP and Employment Report, 2015-2017

Metropolitan Area Exports

Area	2011	2012	2013	2014	2015	2016	Rank[2]
MSA[1]	15,165.5	14,134.7	10,444.4	10,015.8	9,137.1	7,971.0	39

Note: Figures are in millions of dollars; (1) Figures cover the Pittsburgh, PA Metropolitan Statistical Area—see Appendix B for areas included; (2) Rank is based on 2016 data and ranges from 1 to 385
Source: U.S. Department of Commerce, International Trade Administration, Office of Trade & Industry Information, Manufacturing & Services, data extracted March 15, 2018

Building Permits

Area	Single-Family			Multi-Family			Total		
	2016	2017p	Pct. Chg.	2016	2017p	Pct. Chg.	2016	2017p	Pct. Chg.
City	132	157	18.9	48	310	545.8	180	467	159.4
MSA[1]	999	1,053	5.4	510	815	59.8	1,509	1,868	23.8
U.S.	750,800	817,300	8.9	455,800	446,800	-2.0	1,206,600	1,264,100	4.8

Note: (1) Figures cover the Pittsburgh, PA Metropolitan Statistical Area—see Appendix B for areas included; Figures represent new, privately-owned housing units authorized (unadjusted data); All permit data are based on estimates with imputation; (p) preliminary data.
Source: U.S. Census Bureau, Manufacturing, Mining, and Construction Statistics, Building Permits, 2016, 2017

Bankruptcy Filings

Area	Business Filings 2016	Business Filings 2017	Business Filings % Chg.	Nonbusiness Filings 2016	Nonbusiness Filings 2017	Nonbusiness Filings % Chg.
Butler County	16	34	112.5	265	308	16.2
U.S.	24,114	23,157	-4.0	770,846	765,863	-0.6

Note: Business filings include Chapter 7, Chapter 11, Chapter 12, and Chapter 13; Nonbusiness filings include Chapter 7, Chapter 11, and Chapter 13
Source: Administrative Office of the U.S. Courts, Business and Nonbusiness Bankruptcy, County Cases Commenced by Chapter of the Bankruptcy Code, During the 12-Month Period Ending December 31, 2016 and Business and Nonbusiness Bankruptcy, County Cases Commenced by Chapter of the Bankruptcy Code, During the 12-Month Period Ending December 31, 2017

Housing Vacancy Rates

Area	Gross Vacancy Rate[2] (%)			Year-Round Vacancy Rate[3] (%)			Rental Vacancy Rate[4] (%)			Homeowner Vacancy Rate[5] (%)		
	2015	2016	2017	2015	2016	2017	2015	2016	2017	2015	2016	2017
MSA[1]	13.5	17.7	13.6	13.2	17.4	13.4	7.1	7.4	9.7	1.5	1.8	2.2
U.S.	12.9	12.8	12.7	10.0	9.9	9.9	7.1	6.9	7.2	1.8	1.7	1.6

Note: (1) Figures cover the Pittsburgh, PA Metropolitan Statistical Area—see Appendix B for areas included; (2) The percentage of the total housing inventory that is vacant; (3) The percentage of the housing inventory (excluding seasonal units) that is year-round vacant; (4) The percentage of rental inventory that is vacant for rent; (5) The percentage of homeowner inventory that is vacant for sale
Source: U.S. Census Bureau, Housing Vacancies and Homeownership Annual Statistics: 2015, 2016, 2017

INCOME

Income

Area	Per Capita ($)	Median Household ($)	Average Household ($)
City	46,315	103,276	125,734
MSA[1]	31,728	54,020	73,756
U.S.	29,829	55,322	77,866

Note: (1) Figures cover the Pittsburgh, PA Metropolitan Statistical Area—see Appendix B for areas included
Source: U.S. Census Bureau, 2012-2016 American Community Survey 5-Year Estimates

Household Income Distribution

Area	Percent of Households Earning							
	Under $15,000	$15,000 -$24,999	$25,000 -$34,999	$35,000 -$49,999	$50,000 -$74,999	$75,000 -$99,999	$100,000 -$149,999	$150,000 and up
City	3.4	4.2	4.2	6.7	16.2	13.9	21.8	29.6
MSA[1]	12.2	11.0	10.1	13.1	18.2	12.5	13.6	9.4
U.S.	12.1	10.2	9.9	13.2	17.8	12.2	13.5	11.1

Note: (1) Figures cover the Pittsburgh, PA Metropolitan Statistical Area—see Appendix B for areas included
Source: U.S. Census Bureau, 2012-2016 American Community Survey 5-Year Estimates

Poverty Rate

Area	All Ages	Under 18 Years Old	18 to 64 Years Old	65 Years and Over
City	3.1	3.4	2.6	5.0
MSA[1]	12.0	16.9	11.7	7.9
U.S.	15.1	21.2	14.2	9.3

Note: Figures are percentage of people whose income during the past 12 months was below the poverty level; (1) Figures cover the Pittsburgh, PA Metropolitan Statistical Area—see Appendix B for areas included
Source: U.S. Census Bureau, 2012-2016 American Community Survey 5-Year Estimates

EMPLOYMENT

Labor Force and Employment

Area	Civilian Labor Force Dec. 2016	Civilian Labor Force Dec. 2017	Civilian Labor Force % Chg.	Workers Employed Dec. 2016	Workers Employed Dec. 2017	Workers Employed % Chg.
City	17,082	17,184	0.6	16,486	16,661	1.1
MSA[1]	1,197,241	1,200,452	0.3	1,135,886	1,146,911	1.0
U.S.	158,968,000	159,880,000	0.6	151,798,000	153,602,000	1.2

Note: Data is not seasonally adjusted and covers workers 16 years of age and older; (1) Figures cover the Pittsburgh, PA Metropolitan Statistical Area—see Appendix B for areas included
Source: Bureau of Labor Statistics, Local Area Unemployment Statistics

Unemployment Rate

Area	2017											
	Jan.	Feb.	Mar.	Apr.	May	Jun.	Jul.	Aug.	Sep.	Oct.	Nov.	Dec.
City	3.8	3.9	3.4	3.2	3.6	3.6	3.7	3.8	3.4	3.3	3.2	3.0
MSA[1]	6.1	6.0	5.5	4.6	4.9	5.2	5.3	5.4	4.4	4.3	4.4	4.5
U.S.	5.1	4.9	4.6	4.1	4.1	4.5	4.6	4.5	4.1	3.9	3.9	3.9

Note: Data is not seasonally adjusted and covers workers 16 years of age and older; (1) Figures cover the Pittsburgh, PA Metropolitan Statistical Area—see Appendix B for areas included
Source: Bureau of Labor Statistics, Local Area Unemployment Statistics

Average Wages

Occupation	$/Hr.	Occupation	$/Hr.
Accountants and Auditors	34.60	Maids and Housekeeping Cleaners	11.10
Automotive Mechanics	18.80	Maintenance and Repair Workers	18.80
Bookkeepers	18.50	Marketing Managers	69.80
Carpenters	26.00	Nuclear Medicine Technologists	28.70
Cashiers	9.40	Nurses, Licensed Practical	21.30
Clerks, General Office	15.90	Nurses, Registered	31.40
Clerks, Receptionists/Information	12.80	Nursing Assistants	14.30
Clerks, Shipping/Receiving	16.90	Packers and Packagers, Hand	11.70
Computer Programmers	35.10	Physical Therapists	38.10
Computer Systems Analysts	44.80	Postal Service Mail Carriers	23.70
Computer User Support Specialists	23.60	Real Estate Brokers	37.50
Cooks, Restaurant	11.70	Retail Salespersons	12.80
Dentists	41.20	Sales Reps., Exc. Tech./Scientific	35.30
Electrical Engineers	46.80	Sales Reps., Tech./Scientific	41.60
Electricians	31.70	Secretaries, Exc. Legal/Med./Exec.	17.00
Financial Managers	74.70	Security Guards	11.70
First-Line Supervisors/Managers, Sales	21.10	Surgeons	135.90
Food Preparation Workers	11.20	Teacher Assistants*	13.10
General and Operations Managers	61.80	Teachers, Elementary School*	30.40
Hairdressers/Cosmetologists	12.10	Teachers, Secondary School*	32.70
Internists, General	n/a	Telemarketers	11.80
Janitors and Cleaners	13.10	Truck Drivers, Heavy/Tractor-Trailer	22.40
Landscaping/Groundskeeping Workers	13.80	Truck Drivers, Light/Delivery Svcs.	16.40
Lawyers	66.30	Waiters and Waitresses	10.80

Note: Wage data covers the Pittsburgh, PA Metropolitan Statistical Area—see Appendix B for areas included; (*) Hourly wages for elementary/secondary school teachers and teacher assistants were calculated by the editors from annual wage data based on a 40 hour work week; n/a not available.
Source: Bureau of Labor Statistics, Metro Area Occupational Employment & Wage Estimates, May 2017

Employment by Occupation

Occupation Classification	City (%)	MSA[1] (%)	U.S. (%)
Management, Business, Science, and Arts	53.5	39.6	37.0
Natural Resources, Construction, and Maintenance	4.5	7.9	8.9
Production, Transportation, and Material Moving	5.9	11.1	12.2
Sales and Office	25.0	24.2	23.8
Service	11.1	17.2	18.1

Note: Figures cover employed civilians 16 years of age and older; (1) Figures cover the Pittsburgh, PA Metropolitan Statistical Area—see Appendix B for areas included
Source: U.S. Census Bureau, 2012-2016 American Community Survey 5-Year Estimates

Employment by Industry

Sector	MSA[1] Number of Employees	MSA[1] Percent of Total	U.S. Percent of Total
Construction	59,800	5.0	4.7
Education and Health Services	254,600	21.3	15.9
Financial Activities	72,700	6.1	5.7
Government	117,300	9.8	15.3
Information	18,600	1.6	1.9
Leisure and Hospitality	120,400	10.1	10.7
Manufacturing	86,200	7.2	8.5
Mining and Logging	10,400	0.9	0.5
Other Services	51,600	4.3	3.9
Professional and Business Services	182,800	15.3	14.0
Retail Trade	127,300	10.7	11.0
Transportation, Warehousing, and Utilities	48,700	4.1	4.1
Wholesale Trade	43,500	3.6	4.0

Note: Figures are non-farm employment as of December 2017. Figures are not seasonally adjusted and include workers 16 years of age and older; (1) Figures cover the Pittsburgh, PA Metropolitan Statistical Area—see Appendix B for areas included
Source: Bureau of Labor Statistics, Current Employment Statistics, Employment, Hours, and Earnings

Occupations with Greatest Projected Employment Growth: 2017 – 2019

Occupation[1]	2017 Employment	2019 Projected Employment	Numeric Employment Change	Percent Employment Change
Personal Care Aides	95,040	101,150	6,110	6.4
Combined Food Preparation and Serving Workers, Including Fast Food	149,690	154,700	5,010	3.3
Registered Nurses	143,300	147,290	3,990	2.8
Laborers and Freight, Stock, and Material Movers, Hand	138,050	141,860	3,810	2.8
Home Health Aides	46,950	50,700	3,750	8.0
Waiters and Waitresses	100,790	102,540	1,750	1.7
Janitors and Cleaners, Except Maids and Housekeeping Cleaners	98,590	100,250	1,660	1.7
Cooks, Restaurant	49,820	51,120	1,300	2.6
Software Developers, Applications	25,890	27,190	1,300	5.0
Nursing Assistants	80,510	81,790	1,280	1.6

Note: Projections cover Pennsylvania; (1) Sorted by numeric employment change
Source: www.projectionscentral.com, State Occupational Projections, 2017–2019 Short-Term Projections

Fastest Growing Occupations: 2017 – 2019

Occupation[1]	2017 Employment	2019 Projected Employment	Numeric Employment Change	Percent Employment Change
Home Health Aides	46,950	50,700	3,750	8.0
Statisticians	2,710	2,880	170	6.5
Personal Care Aides	95,040	101,150	6,110	6.4
Physician Assistants	5,620	5,960	340	6.1
Nurse Practitioners	5,240	5,550	310	6.0
Operations Research Analysts	2,660	2,800	140	5.1
Information Security Analysts	3,020	3,170	150	5.0
Software Developers, Applications	25,890	27,190	1,300	5.0
Nonfarm Animal Caretakers	7,820	8,210	390	4.9
Physical Therapist Assistants	4,660	4,880	220	4.8

Note: Projections cover Pennsylvania; (1) Sorted by percent employment change and excludes occupations with numeric employment change less than 50
Source: www.projectionscentral.com, State Occupational Projections, 2017–2019 Short-Term Projections

TAXES

State Corporate Income Tax Rates

State	Tax Rate (%)	Income Brackets ($)	Num. of Brackets	Financial Institution Tax Rate (%)[a]	Federal Income Tax Ded.
Pennsylvania	9.99	Flat rate	1	(a)	No

Note: Tax rates as of January 1, 2018; (a) Rates listed are the corporate income tax rate applied to financial institutions or excise taxes based on income. Some states have other taxes based upon the value of deposits or shares.
Source: Federation of Tax Administrators, Range of State Corporate Income Tax Rates, January 1, 2018

State Individual Income Tax Rates

State	Tax Rate (%)	Income Brackets ($)	Num. of Brackets	Personal Exempt. ($)[1]		Fed. Inc. Tax Ded.
				Single	Dependents	
Pennsylvania	3.07	Flat rate	1	None	None	No

Note: Tax rates as of January 1, 2018; Local- and county-level taxes are not included; n/a not applicable; (1) Married joint filers generally receive double the single exemption
Source: Federation of Tax Administrators, State Individual Income Tax Rates, January 1, 2018

Various State Sales and Excise Tax Rates

State	State Sales Tax (%)	Gasoline[1] (¢/gal.)	Cigarette[2] ($/pack)	Spirits[3] ($/gal.)	Wine[4] ($/gal.)	Beer[5] ($/gal.)	Recreational Marijuana (%)
Pennsylvania	6.0	58.7	2.60	7.24 (g)	(m)	0.08	Not legal

Note: All tax rates as of January 1, 2018; (1) The American Petroleum Institute has developed a methodology for determining the average tax rate on a gallon of fuel. Rates may include any of the following: excise taxes, environmental fees, storage tank fees, other fees or taxes, general sales tax, and local taxes. In states where gasoline is subject to the general sales tax, or where the fuel tax is based on the average sale price, the average rate determined by API is sensitive to changes in the price of gasoline. States that fully or partially apply general sales taxes to gasoline: CA, CO, GA, IL, IN, MI, NY; (2) The federal excise tax of $1.0066 per pack and local taxes are not included; (3) Rates are those applicable to off-premise sales of 40% alcohol by volume (a.b.v.) distilled spirits in 750ml containers. Local excise taxes are excluded; (4) Rates are those applicable to off-premise sales of 11% a.b.v. non-carbonated wine in 750ml containers; (5) Rates are those applicable to off-premise sales of 4.7% a.b.v. beer in 12 ounce containers; (g) Control states, where the government controls all sales. Products can be subject to ad valorem mark-up as well as excise taxes; (m) Control states, where the government controls all sales. Products can be subject to ad valorem mark-up as well as excise taxes.
Source: Tax Foundation, 2018 Facts & Figures: How Does Your State Compare?

State Business Tax Climate Index Rankings

State	Overall Rank	Corporate Tax Rank	Individual Income Tax Rank	Sales Tax Rank	Unemployment Insurance Tax Rank	Property Tax Rank
Pennsylvania	26	44	17	21	50	33

Note: The index is a measure of how each state's tax laws affect economic performance. The lower the rank, the more favorable a state's tax system is for business. States without a given tax are given a ranking of 1. The scores/rankings for the District of Columbia do not affect other states. The 2018 index represents the tax climate as of July 1, 2017.
Source: Tax Foundation, State Business Tax Climate Index 2018

TRANSPORTATION

Means of Transportation to Work

Area	Car/Truck/Van		Public Transportation			Bicycle	Walked	Other Means	Worked at Home
	Drove Alone	Car-pooled	Bus	Subway	Railroad				
City	83.3	8.4	1.0	0.0	0.0	0.0	0.6	0.6	6.0
MSA[1]	77.5	8.4	4.9	0.2	0.0	0.4	3.4	1.1	4.1
U.S.	76.4	9.3	2.6	1.9	0.6	0.6	2.8	1.3	4.6

Note: Figures are percentages and cover workers 16 years of age and older; (1) Figures cover the Pittsburgh, PA Metropolitan Statistical Area—see Appendix B for areas included
Source: U.S. Census Bureau, 2012-2016 American Community Survey 5-Year Estimates

Travel Time to Work

Area	Less Than 10 Minutes	10 to 19 Minutes	20 to 29 Minutes	30 to 44 Minutes	45 to 59 Minutes	60 to 89 Minutes	90 Minutes or More
City	9.8	27.3	12.9	29.2	14.4	3.9	2.5
MSA[1]	12.1	27.3	21.4	22.1	9.3	5.9	2.0
U.S.	12.9	29.2	20.9	20.4	8.0	6.0	2.7

Note: Note: Figures are percentages and include workers 16 years old and over; (1) Figures cover the Pittsburgh, PA Metropolitan Statistical Area—see Appendix B for areas included
Source: U.S. Census Bureau, 2012-2016 American Community Survey 5-Year Estimates

Freeway Travel Time Index

Area	1985	1990	1995	2000	2005	2010	2014
Urban Area Rank[1,2]	39	33	36	46	42	42	42
Urban Area Index[1]	1.08	1.13	1.15	1.16	1.18	1.18	1.19
Average Index[3]	1.09	1.11	1.14	1.17	1.20	1.19	1.20

Note: Freeway Travel Time Index—the ratio of travel time in the peak period to the travel time at free-flow conditions. For example, a value of 1.30 indicates a 20-minute free-flow trip takes 26 minutes in the peak (20 minutes x 1.30 = 26 minutes); (1) Covers the Pittsburgh PA urban area; (2) Rank is based on 101 urban areas (#1 = highest travel time index); (3) Average of 101 urban areas
Source: Texas Transportation Institute, 2015 Urban Mobility Scorecard, August 2015

Freeway Commuter Stress Index

Area	1985	1990	1995	2000	2005	2010	2014
Urban Area Rank[1,2]	42	36	40	40	44	45	43
Urban Area Index[1]	1.11	1.17	1.19	1.21	1.22	1.22	1.23
Average Index[3]	1.13	1.16	1.19	1.22	1.25	1.24	1.25

Note: The Freeway Commuter Stress Index is the same as the Freeway Travel Time Index (see table above) except that it includes only the travel in the peak directions during the peak periods; the TTI includes travel in all directions during the peak period. Thus, the CSI is more indicative of the work trip experienced by each commuter on a daily basis; (1) Covers the Pittsburgh PA urban area; (2) Rank is based on 101 urban areas (#1 = highest travel time index); (3) Average of 101 urban areas
Source: Texas Transportation Institute, 2015 Urban Mobility Scorecard, August 2015

Living Environment

COST OF LIVING

Cost of Living Index

Composite Index	Groceries	Housing	Utilities	Trans-portation	Health Care	Misc. Goods/ Services
99.4	110.4	91.5	110.0	106.7	93.8	97.4

Note: The Cost of Living Index measures regional differences in the cost of consumer goods and services, excluding taxes and non-consumer expenditures, for professional and managerial households in the top income quintile. It is based on more than 50,000 prices covering almost 60 different items for which prices are collected three times a year by chambers of commerce, economic development organizations or university applied economic centers in each participating urban area. The numbers shown should be read as a percentage above or below the national average of 100. For example, a value of 115.4 in the groceries column indicates that grocery prices are 15.4% higher than the national average. Small differences in the index numbers should not be interpreted as significant; Figures cover the Pittsburgh PA urban area.
Source: The Council for Community and Economic Research, ACCRA Cost of Living Index, 2017

Grocery Prices

Area[1]	T-Bone Steak ($/pound)	Frying Chicken ($/pound)	Whole Milk ($/half gal.)	Eggs ($/dozen)	Orange Juice ($/64 oz.)	Coffee ($/11.5 oz.)
City[2]	13.40	1.57	1.90	1.05	3.91	4.74
Avg.	11.29	1.40	2.02	1.47	3.55	4.37
Min.	7.71	0.93	1.04	0.70	2.86	3.24
Max.	15.83	2.39	4.03	3.92	6.29	8.16

Note: (1) Values for the local area are compared with the average, minimum and maximum values for all 294 areas in the Cost of Living Index; (2) Figures cover the Pittsburgh PA urban area; ***T-Bone Steak*** *(price per pound);* ***Frying Chicken*** *(price per pound, whole fryer);* ***Whole Milk*** *(half gallon carton);* ***Eggs*** *(price per dozen, Grade A, large);* ***Orange Juice*** *(64 oz. Tropicana or Florida Natural);* ***Coffee*** *(11.5 oz. can, vacuum-packed, Maxwell House, Hills Bros, or Folgers).*
Source: The Council for Community and Economic Research, ACCRA Cost of Living Index, 2017

Housing and Utility Costs

Area[1]	New Home Price ($)	Apartment Rent ($/month)	All Electric ($/month)	Part Electric ($/month)	Other Energy ($/month)	Telephone ($/month)
City[2]	281,247	1,110	-	96.22	90.24	30.99
Avg.	335,956	1,047	175.01	97.34	67.93	28.71
Min.	187,788	491	109.48	49.33	35.44	12.39
Max.	1,739,087	4,559	432.62	227.09	353.33	44.61

Note: (1) Values for the local area are compared with the average, minimum and maximum values for all 294 areas in the Cost of Living Index; (2) Figures cover the Pittsburgh PA urban area; ***New Home Price*** *(2,400 sf living area, 8,000 sf lot, in urban area with full utilities);* ***Apartment Rent*** *(950 sf 2 bedroom/1.5 or 2 bath, unfurnished, excluding all utilities except water);* ***All Electric*** *(average monthly cost for an all-electric home);* ***Part Electric*** *(average monthly cost for a part-electric home);* ***Other Energy*** *(average monthly cost for natural gas, fuel oil, coal, wood, and any other forms of energy except electricity);* ***Telephone*** *(price includes basic monthly rate for a private residential line plus additional local usage charges incurred by a family of four).*
Source: The Council for Community and Economic Research, ACCRA Cost of Living Index, 2017

Health Care, Transportation, and Other Costs

Area[1]	Doctor ($/visit)	Dentist ($/visit)	Optometrist ($/visit)	Gasoline ($/gallon)	Beauty Salon ($/visit)	Men's Shirt ($)
City[2]	98.75	86.30	86.58	2.61	32.20	26.61
Avg.	108.00	92.54	101.93	2.25	37.58	30.92
Min.	30.39	60.00	49.75	1.82	16.11	11.20
Max.	193.50	161.94	229.28	3.16	77.35	59.13

Note: (1) Values for the local area are compared with the average, minimum and maximum values for all 294 areas in the Cost of Living Index; (2) Figures cover the Pittsburgh PA urban area; ***Doctor*** *(general practitioners routine exam of an established patient);* ***Dentist*** *(adult teeth cleaning and periodic oral examination);* ***Optometrist*** *(full vision eye exam for established adult patient);* ***Gasoline*** *(one gallon regular unleaded, national brand, including all taxes, cash price at self-service pump if available);* ***Beauty Salon*** *(woman's shampoo, trim, and blow-dry);* ***Men's Shirt*** *(cotton/polyester dress shirt, pinpoint weave, long sleeves).*
Source: The Council for Community and Economic Research, ACCRA Cost of Living Index, 2017

HOUSING

House Price Index (HPI)

Area	National Ranking[2]	Quarterly Change (%)	One-Year Change (%)	Five-Year Change (%)
MSA[1]	186	0.79	4.10	19.67
U.S.[3]	—	1.61	6.68	34.71

Note: The HPI is a weighted repeat sales index. It measures average price changes in repeat sales or refinancings on the same properties. This information is obtained by reviewing repeat mortgage transactions on single-family properties whose mortgages have been purchased or securitized by Fannie Mae or Freddie Mac in January 1975; (1) Figures cover the Pittsburgh, PA Metropolitan Statistical Area—see Appendix B for areas included; (2) Rankings are based on annual percentage change for all metro areas containing at least 15,000 transactions over the last 10 years and ranges from 1 to 253; (3) figures based on a weighted average of Census Division estimates using a seasonally adjusted, purchase-only index; all figures are for the period ending December 31, 2017
Source: Federal Housing Finance Agency, House Price Index, February 28, 2018

Median Single-Family Home Prices

Area	2015	2016	2017p	Percent Change 2016 to 2017
MSA[1]	n/a	n/a	n/a	n/a
U.S. Average	223.9	235.5	248.8	5.6

Note: Figures are median sales prices of existing single-family homes in thousands of dollars; (p) preliminary; n/a not available; (1) Figures cover the Pittsburgh, PA Metropolitan Statistical Area—see Appendix B for areas included
Source: National Association of Realtors, Median Sales Price of Existing Single-Family Homes for Metropolitan Areas, 4th Quarter 2017

Qualifying Income Based on Median Sales Price of Existing Single-Family Homes

Area	With 5% Down ($)	With 10% Down ($)	With 20% Down ($)
MSA[1]	n/a	n/a	n/a
U.S. Average	55,585	52,659	46,808

Note: Figures are preliminary; Qualifying income is based on a mortgage rate of 4.17%. Monthly principal and interest payment is limited to 25% of income; n/a not available; (1) Figures cover the Pittsburgh, PA Metropolitan Statistical Area—see Appendix B for areas included
Source: National Association of Realtors, Qualifying Income Based on Median Sales Price of Existing Single-Family Homes for Metropolitan Areas, 4th Quarter 2017

Median Apartment Condo-Coop Home Prices

Area	2015	2016	2017p	Percent Change 2016 to 2017
MSA[1]	n/a	n/a	n/a	n/a
U.S. Average	210.7	220.7	234.3	6.2

Note: Figures are median sales prices of existing apartment condo-coop homes in thousands of dollars; (p) preliminary; n/a not available; (1) Figures cover the Pittsburgh, PA Metropolitan Statistical Area—see Appendix B for areas included
Source: National Association of Realtors, Median Sales Price of Existing Apartment Condo-Coop Homes for Metropolitan Areas, 4th Quarter 2017

Home Value Distribution

Area	Under $50,000	$50,000 -$99,999	$100,000 -$149,999	$150,000 -$199,999	$200,000 -$299,999	$300,000 -$499,999	$500,000 -$999,999	$1,000,000 or more
City	3.9	3.1	9.1	13.6	26.5	33.3	9.4	1.0
MSA[1]	11.1	23.5	20.5	17.3	15.2	9.3	2.7	0.5
U.S.	8.8	14.8	15.3	14.9	18.4	16.4	9.0	2.5

Note: Figures are percentages and cover owner-occupied housing units; (1) Figures cover the Pittsburgh, PA Metropolitan Statistical Area—see Appendix B for areas included
Source: U.S. Census Bureau, 2012-2016 American Community Survey 5-Year Estimates

Homeownership Rate

Area	2009 (%)	2010 (%)	2011 (%)	2012 (%)	2013 (%)	2014 (%)	2015 (%)	2016 (%)	2017 (%)
MSA[1]	71.7	70.4	70.3	67.9	68.3	69.1	71.0	72.2	72.7
U.S.	67.4	66.9	66.1	65.4	65.1	64.5	63.7	63.4	63.9

Note: (1) Figures cover the Pittsburgh, PA Metropolitan Statistical Area—see Appendix B for areas included
Source: U.S. Census Bureau, Housing Vacancies and Homeownership Annual Statistics: 2009-2017

Year Housing Structure Built

Area	2010 or Later	2000 -2009	1990 -1999	1980 -1989	1970 -1979	1960 -1969	1950 -1959	1940 -1949	Before 1940	Median Year
City	6.8	21.6	28.4	18.6	13.9	4.6	4.4	0.5	1.1	1992
MSA[1]	1.3	6.7	7.6	7.4	12.1	11.4	17.0	9.2	27.4	1958
U.S.	2.3	14.7	14.0	13.7	15.6	10.9	10.6	5.2	13.0	1977

Note: Figures are percentages except for Median Year; Note: (1) Figures cover the Pittsburgh, PA Metropolitan Statistical Area—see Appendix B for areas included
Source: U.S. Census Bureau, 2012-2016 American Community Survey 5-Year Estimates

Gross Monthly Rent

Area	Under $500	$500 -$999	$1,000 -$1,499	$1,500 -$1,999	$2,000 -$2,499	$2,500 -$2,999	$3,000 and up	Median ($)
City	2.8	21.4	53.0	8.9	7.3	3.2	3.4	1,201
MSA[1]	19.5	56.6	17.3	4.0	1.5	0.5	0.5	749
U.S.	11.3	43.3	27.7	10.7	4.0	1.6	1.5	949

Note: Figures are percentages except for Median; Gross rent is the contract rent plus the estimated average monthly cost of utilities (electricity, gas, and water and sewer) and fuels (oil, coal, kerosene, wood, etc.) if these are paid by the renter (or paid for the renter by someone else); (1) Figures cover the Pittsburgh, PA Metropolitan Statistical Area—see Appendix B for areas included
Source: U.S. Census Bureau, 2012-2016 American Community Survey 5-Year Estimates

HEALTH

Health Risk Factors

Category	MSA[1] (%)	U.S. (%)
Adults aged 18–64 who have any kind of health care coverage	94.1	87.7
Adults who reported being in good or excellent health	85.0	83.6
Adults who are current smokers	17.4	17.1
Adults who currently use E-cigarettes	4.9	4.7
Adults who currently use chewing tobacco, snuff, or snus	4.9	4.0
Adults who are heavy drinkers[2]	6.6	6.5
Adults who are binge drinkers[3]	21.6	16.9
Adults who are overweight (BMI 25.0 - 29.9)	35.1	35.3
Adults who are obese (BMI 30.0 - 99.8)	31.8	29.9
Adults who participated in any physical activities in the past month	78.0	76.9
Adults who always or nearly always wears a seat belt	89.5	94.3

Note: (1) Figures cover the Pittsburgh, PA Metropolitan Statistical Area—see Appendix B for areas included; (2) Heavy drinkers are classified as adult men having more than 14 drinks per week and adult women having more than 7 drinks per week; (3) Binge drinkers are classified as males having five or more drinks on one occasion or females having four or more drinks on one occasion
Source: Centers for Disease Control and Prevention, Behaviorial Risk Factor Surveillance System, SMART: Selected Metropolitan Area Risk Trends, 2016

Health Screening Rates

Category	MSA[1] (%)	U.S. (%)
Adults 50-75 who have had a blood stool test within the past year	8.5	8.0
Adults 50-75 who have had a colonoscopy in the past 10 years	64.8	63.5
Adults aged 65+ who have had flu shot within the past year	69.5	58.6
Adults aged 65+ who have ever had a pneumonia vaccination	80.7	73.4
Adults who have ever been tested for HIV	26.8	35.6
Women aged 21-65 who have had a pap test in the past three years	80.8	79.8
Men aged 40+ who have had a PSA test within the past two years	40.0	39.5
Women aged 40+ who have had a mammogram within the past two years	74.2	72.5

Note: n/a not available; (1) Figures cover the Pittsburgh, PA Metropolitan Statistical Area—see Appendix B for areas included; Source: Centers for Disease Control and Prevention, Behaviorial Risk Factor Surveillance System, SMART: Selected Metropolitan Area Risk Trends, 2016

Chronic Health Conditions

Category	MSA[1] (%)	U.S. (%)
Adults who have ever been told they had a heart attack	5.3	4.4
Adults who have ever been told they have angina or coronary heart disease	5.0	4.1
Adults who have ever been told they had a stroke	3.9	3.1
Adults who have been told they currently have asthma	10.1	9.3
Adults who have ever been told they have arthritis	33.5	25.8
Adults who have ever been told they have diabetes[2]	11.1	10.5
Adults who have ever been told they had skin cancer	6.8	5.9
Adults who have ever been told they had any other types of cancer	6.5	6.7
Adults who have ever been told they have COPD	8.0	6.3
Adults who have ever been told they have kidney disease	2.6	2.8
Adults who have ever been told they have a form of depression	18.4	17.4

Note: (1) Figures cover the Pittsburgh, PA Metropolitan Statistical Area—see Appendix B for areas included; (2) Figures do not include pregnancy-related, borderline, or pre-diabetes
Source: Centers for Disease Control and Prevention, Behaviorial Risk Factor Surveillance System, SMART: Selected Metropolitan Area Risk Trends, 2016

Mortality Rates for the Top 10 Causes of Death in the U.S.

ICD-10[a] Sub-Chapter	ICD-10[a] Code	Age-Adjusted Mortality Rate[1] per 100,000 population	
		County[2]	U.S.
Malignant neoplasms	C00-C97	151.8	158.5
Ischaemic heart diseases	I20-I25	88.8	96.8
Other forms of heart disease	I30-I51	73.9	52.4
Chronic lower respiratory diseases	J40-J47	43.3	40.9
Cerebrovascular diseases	I60-I69	37.4	37.2
Organic, including symptomatic, mental disorders	F01-F09	42.1	33.3
Other degenerative diseases of the nervous system	G30-G31	33.4	32.1
Other external causes of accidental injury	W00-X59	45.6	31.2
Diabetes mellitus	E10-E14	23.3	21.1
Hypertensive diseases	I10-I15	11.9	20.8

Note: (a) ICD-10 = International Classification of Diseases 10th Revision; (1) Mortality rates are a three year average covering 2014-2016; (2) Figures cover Butler County.
Source: Centers for Disease Control and Prevention, National Center for Health Statistics. Underlying Cause of Death 1999-2016 on CDC WONDER Online Database, released December 2017

Mortality Rates for Selected Causes of Death

ICD-10[a] Sub-Chapter	ICD-10[a] Code	Age-Adjusted Mortality Rate[1] per 100,000 population	
		County[2]	U.S.
Assault	X85-Y09	Suppressed	5.6
Diseases of the liver	K70-K76	13.3	14.0
Human immunodeficiency virus (HIV) disease	B20-B24	Suppressed	1.9
Influenza and pneumonia	J09-J18	14.0	14.6
Intentional self-harm	X60-X84	13.0	13.2
Malnutrition	E40-E46	Unreliable	1.3
Obesity and other hyperalimentation	E65-E68	Suppressed	2.1
Renal failure	N17-N19	15.4	13.0
Transport accidents	V01-V99	12.2	12.0
Viral hepatitis	B15-B19	Suppressed	1.9

Note: (a) ICD-10 = International Classification of Diseases 10th Revision; (1) Mortality rates are a three year average covering 2014-2016; (2) Figures cover Butler County; Data are Suppressed when the data meet the criteria for confidentiality constraints; Mortality rates are flagged as Unreliable when the rate would be calculated with a numerator of 20 or less.
Source: Centers for Disease Control and Prevention, National Center for Health Statistics. Underlying Cause of Death 1999-2016 on CDC WONDER Online Database, released December 2017

Health Insurance Coverage

Area	With Health Insurance	With Private Health Insurance	With Public Health Insurance	Without Health Insurance	Population Under Age 18 Without Health Insurance
City	96.4	90.0	16.2	3.6	2.9
MSA[1]	94.1	76.7	33.5	5.9	2.4
U.S.	88.3	66.7	33.0	11.7	5.9

Note: Figures are percentages that cover the civilian noninstitutionalized population; (1) Figures cover the Pittsburgh, PA Metropolitan Statistical Area—see Appendix B for areas included
Source: U.S. Census Bureau, 2012-2016 American Community Survey 5-Year Estimates

Number of Medical Professionals

Area	MDs[3]	DOs[3,4]	Dentists	Podiatrists	Chiropractors	Optometrists
County[1] (number)	261	69	130	12	109	47
County[1] (rate[2])	140.4	37.1	69.8	6.4	58.5	25.2
U.S. (rate[2])	276.5	22.3	67.3	6.0	26.7	15.9

Note: Data as of 2016 unless noted; (1) Data covers Butler County; (2) Rate per 100,000 population; (3) Data as of 2015 and includes all active, non-federal physicians; (4) Doctor of Osteopathic Medicine
Source: U.S. Department of Health and Human Services, Health Resources and Services Administration, Bureau of Health Professions, Area Resource File (ARF) 2016-2017

Best Hospitals

According to *U.S. News,* the Pittsburgh, PA metro area is home to two of the best hospitals in the U.S.: **Magee-Womens Hospital of UPMC** (1 adult specialty); **UPMC Presbyterian Shadyside** (Honor Roll/14 adult specialties). The hospitals listed were nationally ranked in at least one of 16 specialties. Only 152 hospitals nationwide were nationally ranked in one or more specialties. Twenty hospitals in the U.S. made the Honor Roll. The Best Hospitals Honor Roll was revamped last year to take both the national rankings and the procedure and condition ratings into account. Hospitals received points if they were nationally ranked in one of the 16 specialties—the higher they ranked, the more points they got—and how many ratings of "high performing" they earned in the nine procedures and conditions. *U.S. News Online, "America's Best Hospitals 2017-18"*

According to *U.S. News,* the Pittsburgh, PA metro area is home to one of the best children's hospitals in the U.S.: **Children's Hospital of Pittsburgh of UPMC** (Honor Roll/10 pediatric specialties). The hospital listed was highly ranked in at least one of 10 pediatric specialties. Eighty-two children's hospitals in the U.S. were nationally ranked in at least one specialty. Hospitals received points for being ranked in a specialty, and the 10 hospitals with the most points across the 10 specialties make up the Honor Roll. *U.S. News Online, "America's Best Children's Hospitals 2017-18"*

EDUCATION

Public School District Statistics

District Name	Schls	Pupils	Pupil/ Teacher Ratio	Minority Pupils[1] (%)	Free Lunch Eligible[2] (%)	IEP[3] (%)
Seneca Valley SD	8	7,152	14.4	7.6	13.4	17.5

Note: Table includes school districts with 100 or more students; (1) Percentage of students that are not non-Hispanic white; (2) Percentage of students that are eligible for the free lunch program; (3) Percentage of students that have an Individualized Education Program.
Source: U.S. Department of Education, National Center for Education Statistics, Common Core of Data, Local Education Agency (School District) Universe Survey: School Year 2015-2016; U.S. Department of Education, National Center for Education Statistics, Common Core of Data, Public Elementary/Secondary School Universe Survey: School Year 2015-2016

Highest Level of Education

Area	Less than H.S.	H.S. Diploma	Some College, No Deg.	Associate Degree	Bachelor's Degree	Master's Degree	Prof. School Degree	Doctorate Degree
City	3.2	18.1	14.0	7.7	36.3	16.0	2.7	2.0
MSA[1]	7.1	34.3	16.3	9.8	19.9	9.0	2.1	1.5
U.S.	13.0	27.5	21.0	8.2	18.8	8.2	2.0	1.3

Note: Figures cover persons age 25 and over; (1) Figures cover the Pittsburgh, PA Metropolitan Statistical Area—see Appendix B for areas included
Source: U.S. Census Bureau, 2012-2016 American Community Survey 5-Year Estimates

Educational Attainment by Race

Area	High School Graduate or Higher (%)					Bachelor's Degree or Higher (%)				
	Total	White	Black	Asian	Hisp.[2]	Total	White	Black	Asian	Hisp.[2]
City	96.8	97.2	95.9	89.8	86.1	57.0	56.8	65.6	62.3	52.9
MSA[1]	92.9	93.3	88.9	88.4	86.2	32.5	32.9	18.6	71.7	35.8
U.S.	87.0	88.9	84.3	86.3	65.7	30.3	31.6	20.0	52.1	14.7

Note: Figures shown cover persons 25 years old and over; (1) Figures cover the Pittsburgh, PA Metropolitan Statistical Area—see Appendix B for areas included; (2) People of Hispanic origin can be of any race
Source: U.S. Census Bureau, 2012-2016 American Community Survey 5-Year Estimates

School Enrollment by Grade and Control

Area	Preschool (%)		Kindergarten (%)		Grades 1 - 4 (%)		Grades 5 - 8 (%)		Grades 9 - 12 (%)	
	Public	Private	Public	Private	Public	Private	Public	Private	Public	Private
City	32.7	67.3	80.8	19.2	82.1	17.9	85.7	14.3	85.4	14.6
MSA[1]	48.3	51.7	84.3	15.7	87.5	12.5	88.2	11.8	89.7	10.3
U.S.	58.4	41.6	87.7	12.3	89.8	10.2	89.7	10.3	90.4	9.6

Note: Figures shown cover persons 3 years old and over; (1) Figures cover the Pittsburgh, PA Metropolitan Statistical Area—see Appendix B for areas included
Source: U.S. Census Bureau, 2012-2016 American Community Survey 5-Year Estimates

Average Salaries of Public School Classroom Teachers

Area	2015		2016		Change from 2015 to 2016	
	Dollars	Rank[1]	Dollars	Rank[1]	Percent	Rank[2]
Pennsylvania	64,447	10	65,151	10	1.1	24
U.S. Average	57,611	–	58,353	–	1.3	–

Note: (1) Rank ranges from 1 to 51 where 1 indicates highest salary; (2) Rank ranges from 1 to 51 where 1 indicates highest percent change.
Source: National Education Association, Rankings & Estimates: Rankings of the States 2016 and Estimates of School Statistics 2017

Higher Education

Four-Year Colleges			Two-Year Colleges			Medical Schools[1]	Law Schools[2]	Voc/Tech[3]
Public	Private Non-profit	Private For-profit	Public	Private Non-profit	Private For-profit			
0	0	0	0	0	0	0	0	0

Note: Figures cover institutions located within the city limits and include main campuses only; (1) includes schools accredited by the Liaison Committee on Medical Education and the American Osteopathic Association's Commission on Osteopathic College Accreditation; (2) includes ABA-accredited schools, schools with provisional ABA accreditation, and state accredited schools; (3) includes all schools with programs that are less than 2 years.
Source: National Center for Education Statistics, Integrated Postsecondary Education System (IPEDS), 2016-17; Wikipedia, List of Medical Schools in the United States, accessed April 2, 2018; Wikipedia, List of Law Schools in the United States, accessed April 2, 2018

According to *U.S. News & World Report,* the Pittsburgh, PA metro area is home to four of the best national universities in the U.S.: **Carnegie Mellon University** (#25 tie); **University of Pittsburgh** (#68); **Duquesne University** (#120 tie); **Robert Morris University** (#176 tie). The indicators used to capture academic quality fall into a number of categories: assessment by administrators at peer institutions; retention of students; faculty resources; student selectivity; financial resources; alumni giving; high school counselor ratings of colleges; and graduation rate. *U.S. News & World Report, "America's Best Colleges 2018"*

According to *U.S. News & World Report,* the Pittsburgh, PA metro area is home to two of the best liberal arts colleges in the U.S.: **Washington and Jefferson College** (#106 tie); **Saint Vincent College** (#147 tie). The indicators used to capture academic quality fall into a number of categories: assessment by administrators at peer institutions; retention of students; faculty resources; student selectivity; financial resources; alumni giving; high school counselor ratings of colleges; and graduation rate. *U.S. News & World Report, "America's Best Colleges 2018"*

According to *U.S. News & World Report,* the Pittsburgh, PA metro area is home to one of the top 100 law schools in the U.S.: **University of Pittsburgh** (#74 tie). The rankings are based on a weighted average of 12 measures of quality: peer assessment score; assessment score by lawyers/judges; median LSAT scores; median undergrad GPA; acceptance rate; employment rates for graduates; placement success; bar passage rate; faculty resources; expenditures per student; student/faculty ratio; and library resources. *U.S. News & World Report, "America's Best Graduate Schools, Law, 2019"*

According to *U.S. News & World Report,* the Pittsburgh, PA metro area is home to one of the top 75 medical schools for research in the U.S.: **University of Pittsburgh** (#14). The rankings are based on a weighted average of 11 measures of quality: quality assessment; peer assessment score; assessment score by residency directors; research activity; total research activity; average research activity per faculty member; student selectivity; median MCAT total score; median undergraduate GPA; acceptance rate; and faculty resources. *U.S. News & World Report, "America's Best Graduate Schools, Medical, 2019"*

According to *U.S. News & World Report,* the Pittsburgh, PA metro area is home to two of the top 75 business schools in the U.S.: **Carnegie Mellon University (Tepper)** (#17 tie); **University of Pittsburgh (Katz)** (#52). The rankings are based on a weighted average of the following nine measures: quality assessment; peer assessment; recruiter assessment; placement success; mean starting salary and bonus; student selectivity; mean GMAT and GRE scores; mean undergraduate GPA; and acceptance rate. *U.S. News & World Report, "America's Best Graduate Schools, Business, 2019"*

PRESIDENTIAL ELECTION

2016 Presidential Election Results

Area	Clinton	Trump	Johnson	Stein	Other
Butler County	29.2	65.7	3.1	0.6	1.4
U.S.	48.0	45.9	3.3	1.1	1.7

Note: Results are percentages and may not add to 100% due to rounding
Source: Dave Leip's Atlas of U.S. Presidential Elections

EMPLOYERS

Major Employers

Company Name	Industry
Allegheny General Hospital	Extended care facility
Associated Cleaning Consultants	Janitorial service, contract basis
Bayer Corporation	Pharmaceutical preparations
Children's Hospital of Pittsburgh	Specialty hospitals, except psychiatric
Duquesne University of the Holy Spirit	Colleges & universities
Highmark	Hospital & medical service plans
Jefferson Regional Medical Center	General medical & surgical hospitals
Magee-Womens Hospital of UPMC	Hospital, affiliated with ama residency
Mercy Life Center Corporation	Charitable organizations
Mercy Life Center Corporation	Mental health clinic, outpatient
PNC Bank, National Association	National trust companies with deposits, commercial
United States Steel Corporation	Blast furnaces & steel mills
United States Steel International	Steel
University of Pittsburgh	Colleges & universities
UPMC Mercy	General medical & surgical hospitals
UPMC Shadyside	General medical & surgical hospitals
US Dept of Energy	Noncommercial research organizations
Veterans Health Administration	Administration of veterans' affairs
West Penn Allegheny Health System	Management services

Note: Companies shown are located within the Pittsburgh, PA Metropolitan Statistical Area.
Source: Hoovers.com; Wikipedia

PUBLIC SAFETY

Crime Rate

Area	All Crimes	Violent Crimes				Property Crimes		
		Murder	Rape[3]	Robbery	Aggrav. Assault	Burglary	Larceny -Theft	Motor Vehicle Theft
City	1,312.2	0.0	6.5	12.9	29.1	74.3	1,173.2	16.2
Metro[1]	2,035.5	5.1	22.9	82.9	178.1	309.5	1,349.8	87.2
U.S.	2,847.8	5.3	40.4	102.8	248.5	468.9	1,745.0	236.9

Note: Figures are crimes per 100,000 population; (1) Figures cover the Pittsburgh, PA Metropolitan Statistical Area—see Appendix B for areas included; (3) The city and U.S. figures shown were reported using the revised Uniform Crime Reporting (UCR) definition of rape. The metro area figures shown are an aggregate total of the data submitted using both the revised and legacy UCR definitions.
Source: FBI Uniform Crime Reports, 2016

Hate Crimes

Area	Number of Quarters Reported	Number of Incidents per Bias Motivation					
		Race/Ethnicity/ Ancestry	Religion	Sexual Orientation	Disability	Gender	Gender Identity
Area[1]	4	0	0	0	0	0	0
U.S.	4	3,489	1,273	1,076	70	31	124

Note: (1) Figures cover the Cranberry Township.
Source: Federal Bureau of Investigation, Hate Crime Statistics 2016

Identity Theft Consumer Reports

Area	Reports	Reports per 100,000 Population	Rank[2]
MSA[1]	1,992	85	163
U.S.	371,061	114	-

Note: (1) Figures cover the Pittsburgh, PA Metropolitan Statistical Area—see Appendix B for areas included; (2) Rank ranges from 1 to 389 where 1 indicates greatest number of identity theft reports per 100,000 population
Source: Federal Trade Commission, Consumer Sentinel Network Data Book for January–December 2017

Fraud and Other Consumer Reports

Area	Reports	Reports per 100,000 Population	Rank[2]
MSA[1]	12,250	523	91
U.S.	2,304,550	708	-

Note: (1) Figures cover the Pittsburgh, PA Metropolitan Statistical Area—see Appendix B for areas included; (2) Rank ranges from 1 to 389 where 1 indicates greatest number of fraud and other consumer reports per 100,000 population
Source: Federal Trade Commission, Consumer Sentinel Network Data Book for January–December 2017

SPORTS

Professional Sports Teams

Team Name	League	Year Established
Pittsburgh Penguins	National Hockey League (NHL)	1967
Pittsburgh Pirates	Major League Baseball (MLB)	1882
Pittsburgh Steelers	National Football League (NFL)	1933

Note: Includes teams located in the Pittsburgh, PA Metropolitan Statistical Area.
Source: Wikipedia, Major Professional Sports Teams of the United States and Canada, April 5, 2018

CLIMATE

Average and Extreme Temperatures

Temperature	Jan	Feb	Mar	Apr	May	Jun	Jul	Aug	Sep	Oct	Nov	Dec	Yr.
Extreme High (°F)	75	69	83	89	91	98	103	100	97	89	82	74	103
Average High (°F)	35	38	48	61	71	79	83	81	75	63	50	39	60
Average Temp. (°F)	28	30	39	50	60	68	73	71	64	53	42	32	51
Average Low (°F)	20	22	29	39	49	57	62	61	54	43	34	25	41
Extreme Low (°F)	-18	-12	-1	14	26	34	42	39	31	16	-1	-12	-18

Note: Figures cover the years 1948-1990
Source: National Climatic Data Center, International Station Meteorological Climate Summary, 9/96

Average Precipitation/Snowfall/Humidity

Precip./Humidity	Jan	Feb	Mar	Apr	May	Jun	Jul	Aug	Sep	Oct	Nov	Dec	Yr.
Avg. Precip. (in.)	2.8	2.4	3.4	3.3	3.6	3.9	3.8	3.2	2.8	2.4	2.7	2.8	37.1
Avg. Snowfall (in.)	11	9	8	2	Tr	0	0	0	0	Tr	4	8	43
Avg. Rel. Hum. 7am (%)	76	75	75	73	76	79	82	86	85	81	78	77	79
Avg. Rel. Hum. 4pm (%)	64	60	54	49	50	51	53	54	55	53	60	66	56

Note: Figures cover the years 1948-1990; Tr = Trace amounts (<0.05 in. of rain; <0.5 in. of snow)
Source: National Climatic Data Center, International Station Meteorological Climate Summary, 9/96

Weather Conditions

Temperature			Daytime Sky			Precipitation		
5°F & below	32°F & below	90°F & above	Clear	Partly cloudy	Cloudy	0.01 inch or more precip.	0.1 inch or more snow/ice	Thunder-storms
9	121	8	62	137	166	154	42	35

Note: Figures are average number of days per year and cover the years 1948-1990
Source: National Climatic Data Center, International Station Meteorological Climate Summary, 9/96

HAZARDOUS WASTE

Superfund Sites

The Pittsburgh, PA metro area is home to three sites on the EPA's Superfund National Priorities List: **Breslube-Penn, Inc.** (final); **Lindane Dump** (final); **Ohio River Park** (final). There are a total of 1,396 Superfund sites with a status of proposed or final on the list in the U.S. *U.S. Environmental Protection Agency, National Priorities List, April 4, 2018*

AIR & WATER QUALITY

Air Quality Trends: Ozone

	1990	1995	2000	2005	2010	2012	2013	2014	2015	2016
MSA[1]	0.080	0.095	0.082	0.082	0.075	0.079	0.067	0.065	0.069	0.068
U.S.	0.087	0.089	0.081	0.079	0.073	0.075	0.069	0.067	0.068	0.069

Note: (1) Data covers the Pittsburgh, PA Metropolitan Statistical Area—see Appendix B for areas included. The values shown are the composite ozone concentration averages among trend sites based on the highest fourth daily maximum 8-hour concentration in parts per million. These trends are based on sites having an adequate record of monitoring data during the trend period. Data from exceptional events are included.
Source: U.S. Environmental Protection Agency, Air Quality Monitoring Information, "Air Quality Trends by City, 1990-2016"

Air Quality Index

Area	Percent of Days when Air Quality was...[2]					AQI Statistics[2]	
	Good	Moderate	Unhealthy for Sensitive Groups	Unhealthy	Very Unhealthy	Maximum	Median
MSA[1]	25.2	66.0	8.5	0.3	0.0	164	59

Note: (1) Data covers the Pittsburgh, PA Metropolitan Statistical Area—see Appendix B for areas included; (2) Based on 365 days with AQI data in 2017. Air Quality Index (AQI) is an index for reporting daily air quality. EPA calculates the AQI for five major air pollutants regulated by the Clean Air Act: ground-level ozone, particle pollution (aka particulate matter), carbon monoxide, sulfur dioxide, and nitrogen dioxide. The AQI runs from 0 to 500. The higher the AQI value, the greater the level of air pollution and the greater the health concern. There are six AQI categories: "Good" AQI is between 0 and 50. Air quality is considered satisfactory; "Moderate" AQI is between 51 and 100. Air quality is acceptable; "Unhealthy for Sensitive Groups" When AQI values are between 101 and 150, members of sensitive groups may experience health effects; "Unhealthy" When AQI values are between 151 and 200 everyone may begin to experience health effects; "Very Unhealthy" AQI values between 201 and 300 trigger a health alert; "Hazardous" AQI values over 300 trigger warnings of emergency conditions (not shown).
Source: U.S. Environmental Protection Agency, Air Quality Index Report, 2017

Air Quality Index Pollutants

Area	Percent of Days when AQI Pollutant was...[2]					
	Carbon Monoxide	Nitrogen Dioxide	Ozone	Sulfur Dioxide	Particulate Matter 2.5	Particulate Matter 10
MSA[1]	0.0	0.0	22.7	7.4	69.6	0.3

Note: (1) Data covers the Pittsburgh, PA Metropolitan Statistical Area—see Appendix B for areas included; (2) Based on 365 days with AQI data in 2017. The Air Quality Index (AQI) is an index for reporting daily air quality. EPA calculates the AQI for five major air pollutants regulated by the Clean Air Act: ground-level ozone, particle pollution (also known as particulate matter), carbon monoxide, sulfur dioxide, and nitrogen dioxide. The AQI runs from 0 to 500. The higher the AQI value, the greater the level of air pollution and the greater the health concern.
Source: U.S. Environmental Protection Agency, Air Quality Index Report, 2017

Maximum Air Pollutant Concentrations: Particulate Matter, Ozone, CO and Lead

	Particulate Matter 10 (ug/m³)	Particulate Matter 2.5 Wtd AM (ug/m³)	Particulate Matter 2.5 24-Hr (ug/m³)	Ozone (ppm)	Carbon Monoxide (ppm)	Lead (ug/m³)
MSA[1] Level	84	12.8	40	0.073	3	0.02
NAAQS[2]	150	15	35	0.075	9	0.15
Met NAAQS[2]	Yes	Yes	No	Yes	Yes	Yes

Note: (1) Data covers the Pittsburgh, PA Metropolitan Statistical Area—see Appendix B for areas included; Data from exceptional events are included; (2) National Ambient Air Quality Standards; ppm = parts per million; ug/m³ = micrograms per cubic meter; n/a not available.
Concentrations: Particulate Matter 10 (coarse particulate)—highest second maximum 24-hour concentration; Particulate Matter 2.5 Wtd AM (fine particulate)—highest weighted annual mean concentration; Particulate Matter 2.5 24-Hour (fine particulate)—highest 98th percentile 24-hour concentration; Ozone—highest fourth daily maximum 8-hour concentration; Carbon Monoxide—highest second maximum non-overlapping 8-hour concentration; Lead—maximum running 3-month average
Source: U.S. Environmental Protection Agency, Air Quality Monitoring Information, "Air Quality Statistics by City, 2016"

Maximum Air Pollutant Concentrations: Nitrogen Dioxide and Sulfur Dioxide

	Nitrogen Dioxide AM (ppb)	Nitrogen Dioxide 1-Hr (ppb)	Sulfur Dioxide AM (ppb)	Sulfur Dioxide 1-Hr (ppb)	Sulfur Dioxide 24-Hr (ppb)
MSA[1] Level	11	40	n/a	64	n/a
NAAQS[2]	53	100	30	75	140
Met NAAQS[2]	Yes	Yes	n/a	Yes	n/a

Note: (1) Data covers the Pittsburgh, PA Metropolitan Statistical Area—see Appendix B for areas included; Data from exceptional events are included; (2) National Ambient Air Quality Standards; ppm = parts per million; ug/m³ = micrograms per cubic meter; n/a not available.
Concentrations: Nitrogen Dioxide AM—highest arithmetic mean concentration; Nitrogen Dioxide 1-Hr—highest 98th percentile 1-hour daily maximum concentration; Sulfur Dioxide AM—highest annual mean concentration; Sulfur Dioxide 1-Hr—highest 99th percentile 1-hour daily maximum concentration; Sulfur Dioxide 24-Hr—highest second maximum 24-hour concentration
Source: U.S. Environmental Protection Agency, Air Quality Monitoring Information, "Air Quality Statistics by City, 2016"

Drinking Water

Water System Name	Pop. Served	Primary Water Source Type	Violations[1]	
			Health Based	Monitoring/ Reporting
Cranberry Township WTP	36,930	Purchased Surface	0	0

Note: (1) Based on violation data from January 1, 2017 to December 31, 2017
Source: U.S. Environmental Protection Agency, Office of Ground Water and Drinking Water, Safe Drinking Water Information System (based on data extracted April 5, 2018)

Hampden, Pennsylvania

Background

Hampden is located across the Susquehanna River from Harrisburg, the state capital of Pennsylvania. With multiple bridges spanning the river, Hampden is one of fifteen municipalities in what is now called West Susquehanna, part of the greater Harrisburg-Carlisle metro area, situated in the south central part of the state in the Cumberland Valley.

The name Hampden is of English origin, and the area was originally settled in the 1800s by Scotch-Irish immigrants. In 1845 Hampden became a township. Until the 1970s the area was primarily farm land with small villages and residential pockets. Recent development includes housing in the suburbs of Hampden. Route 11, now Carlisle Turnpike, was originally a roadway to the West for the earliest settlers. Now it is the most commercially developed shopping area of southern Hampden, and distinct from the industrial north, which houses a Medical Technology Park and Cumberland Technology Development.

Hampden's government includes five elected commissioners and 100 employees. Hampden belongs to the West Shore Chamber of Commerce and is part of the Cumberland Valley School District. Nearby educational institutions include Dickens College, Elizabethtown College, Gettysburg College, Harrisburg Community College, and Penn State University campuses in York and Harrisburg.

Hampden employs its own police force and ambulance service, the latter transporting to Milton Hershey Medical Center and Harrisburg hospitals. A highly organized recreation department offers more than 80 acres of parks, and 2 large pools encircled with tennis and ball courts, and outdoor amenities. Hampden's golf course was willed to the township in the 1980s.

The nearby city of Harrisburg offers the Hershey Symphony Orchestra, the Hershey Museum, the National Apple Museum, National Watch and Clock Museum, and the State Museum of Pennsylvania. Eisenhower National Historic Site, Gettysburg National Military Park, and Milton S. Hershey Mansion are also worth the trip. Hampden offers expedient bus transportation to Philadelphia and New York City.

Midway between the eastern seaboard and northeast areas, Hampden's weather spans four seasons. Blizzards are a part of the winter and summer can be very humid. The trees provided by the many wooded areas throughout the region have a positive impact on the weather and air quality.

Rankings

Business/Finance Rankings

- The personal finance site NerdWallet analyzed 183 American metropolitan areas with populations over 250,000 and more than 15,000 businesses to rank where entrepreneurs find the most success. Criteria included area economy, annual income, housing cost, unemployment rate, and the success rate of area businesses. Harrisburg* ranked #44. *www.nerdwallet.com, "Best Places to Start a Business," April 27, 2015*
- The Brookings Institution ranked the 100 largest metro areas in the U.S. based on income inequality. Harrisburg* was ranked #96 (#1 = greatest ineqality). Criteria: the "95/20 ratio," a figure representing the income at which a household earns more than 95 percent of all other households, divided by the income at which a household earns more than only 20 percent of all other households. *Brookings Institution, "Household Income Inequality, 100 Largest U.S. Metro Areas, 2014-2016," February 5, 2018*
- The Harrisburg* metro area appeared on the Milken Institute "2017 Best Performing Cities" list. Rank: #124 out of 200 large metro areas. Criteria: job growth; wage and salary growth; high-tech output growth. *Milken Institute, "Best-Performing Cities 2017," January 2018*
- *Forbes* ranked the 200 most populous metro areas to determine the nation's "Best Places for Business and Careers." The Harrisburg* metro area was ranked #116. Criteria: costs (business and living); job growth (past and projected); income growth; quality of life; educational attainment (college and high school); projected economic growth; cultural and recreational opportunities; net migration patterns; number of highly ranked colleges. *Forbes, "The Best Places for Business and Careers 2017," October 24, 2017*

Children/Family Rankings

- *Forbes* analyzed data on the 100 largest metropolitan areas in the United States to compile its 2016 ranking of the best cities for raising a family. The Harrisburg* metro area was ranked #7. Criteria: median income; childcare costs; percent of population under 18; commuting delays; crime rate; percentage of families owning homes; education quality (mainly test scores). Overall cost of living and housing affordability was also unofficially considered. *Forbes, "America's Best Cities for Raising a Family 2016," August 30, 2016*

Education Rankings

- Personal finance website *WalletHub* analyzed the 150 largest U.S. metropolitan statistical areas to determine where the most educated Americans are choosing to settle. Criteria: education quality and attainment gap; education levels; percentage of workers with degrees; public school rankings; quality and size of each metro area's universities. Harrisburg* was ranked #99 (#1 = most educated city). *www.WalletHub.com, "2017's Most and Least Educated Cities in America, " July 25, 2017*

Environmental Rankings

- Sperling's BestPlaces assessed 379 metropolitan areas of the United States for the likelihood of dangerously extreme weather events or earthquakes. In general the Southeast and South-Central regions have the highest risk of weather extremes and earthquakes, while the Pacific Northwest enjoys the lowest risk. Of the least risky metropolitan areas, the Harrisburg* metro area was ranked #131. *www.bestplaces.net, "Safest Places from Natural Disasters," April 2011*
- Harrisburg* was highlighted as one of the 25 metro areas most polluted by year-round particle pollution (Annual PM 2.5) in the U.S. during 2013 through 2015. The area ranked #22. *American Lung Association, State of the Air 2017*
- Harrisburg* was highlighted as one of the 25 metro areas most polluted by short-term particle pollution (24-hour PM 2.5) in the U.S. during 2013 through 2015. The area ranked #21. *American Lung Association, State of the Air 2017*

Food/Drink Rankings

- For the Gallup-Healthways Well-Being Index, researchers interviewed at least 300 adults in each of 189 metropolitan areas on residents' access to affordable fresh produce. The Harrisburg* metro area was found to be among the top ten communities for accessibility to affordable produce. *www.gallup.com, "In Anchorage, Access to Fruits and Vegetables Remains Lowest," April 8, 2014*

Health/Fitness Rankings

- Analysts who tracked obesity rates in 100 of the nation's most populous areas found that the Harrisburg* metro area was one of the ten communities where residents were most likely to be obese, defined as a BMI score of 30 or above. *www.gallup.com, "Colorado Springs Residents Least Likely to Be Obese," May 28, 2015*
- Harrisburg* was identified as a "2016 Spring Allergy Capital." The area ranked #68 out of 100. Three groups of factors were used to identify the most severe cities for people with allergies during the spring season: annual pollen levels; medicine utilization; access to board-certified allergists. *Asthma and Allergy Foundation of America, "Spring Allergy Capitals 2016"*
- Harrisburg* was identified as a "2016 Fall Allergy Capital." The area ranked #69 out of 100. Three groups of factors were used to identify the most severe cities for people with allergies during the fall season: annual pollen levels; medicine utilization; access to board-certified allergists. *Asthma and Allergy Foundation of America, "Fall Allergy Capitals 2016"*
- Harrisburg* was identified as a "2015 Asthma Capital." The area ranked #43 out of the nation's 100 largest metropolitan areas. Criteria: estimated prevalence; self-reported prevalence; crude death rate for asthma; annual pollen score; annual air quality; public smoking laws; number of board-certified asthma specialists; school inhaler access laws; rescue medication use; controller medication use; ER visits for asthma; uninsured rate; poverty rate. *Asthma and Allergy Foundation of America, "Asthma Capitals 2015"*
- The Harrisburg* metro area ranked #114 out of 189 in The Gallup-Healthways Well-Being Index. Criteria: purpose; social well being; financial health; community and physical health. Results are based on telephone interviews with adults, aged 18 and older, living in metropolitan areas in the 50 U.S. states and the District of Columbia. *Gallup-Healthways, "State of American Well-Being, 2017 Community Well-Being Rankings" March 2018*

Real Estate Rankings

- Harrisburg* was ranked #29 out of 238 metro areas in terms of housing affordability in 2017 by the National Association of Home Builders (#1 = most affordable). Criteria: the share of homes sold in that area affordable to a family earning the local median income, based on standard mortgage underwriting criteria. *National Association of Home Builders®, NAHB-Wells Fargo Housing Opportunity Index, 4th Quarter 2017*

Safety Rankings

- The National Insurance Crime Bureau ranked 382 metro areas in the U.S. in terms of per capita rates of vehicle theft. The Harrisburg* metro area ranked #332 (#1 = highest rate). Criteria: number of vehicle theft offenses per 100,000 inhabitants in 2016. *National Insurance Crime Bureau, "Hot Spots 2016," June 8, 2017*

Seniors/Retirement Rankings

- From its Best Cities for Successful Aging indexes, the Milken Institute generated rankings for metropolitan areas, weighing data in nine categories—health care, wellness, living arrangements, transportation and convenience, financial characteristics, education, employment, community engagement, and overall livability. The Harrisburg* metro area was ranked #31 overall in the large metro area category. *Milken Institute, "Best Cities for Successful Aging, 2017" March 14, 2017*

*Hampden is located within the Harrisburg-Carlisle, PA Metropolitan Statistical Area.

Business Environment

CITY FINANCES

City Government Finances

Component	2015 ($000)	2015 ($ per capita)
Total Revenues	31,284	1,066
Total Expenditures	27,731	945
Debt Outstanding	45,267	1,542
Cash and Securities[1]	48,894	1,666

Note: (1) Cash and security holdings of a government at the close of its fiscal year,, including those of its dependent agencies, utilities, and liquor stores.
Source: U.S Census Bureau, State & Local Government Finances 2015

City Government Revenue by Source

Source	2015 ($000)	2015 ($ per capita)	2015 (%)
General Revenue			
From Federal Government	54	2	0.2
From State Government	1,482	50	4.7
From Local Governments	323	11	1.0
Taxes			
Property	719	24	2.3
Sales and Gross Receipts	0	0	0.0
Personal Income	5,647	192	18.1
Corporate Income	0	0	0.0
Motor Vehicle License	0	0	0.0
Other Taxes	3,581	122	11.4
Current Charges	14,988	511	47.9
Liquor Store	0	0	0.0
Utility	0	0	0.0
Employee Retirement	3,026	103	9.7

Source: U.S Census Bureau, State & Local Government Finances 2015

City Government Expenditures by Function

Function	2015 ($000)	2015 ($ per capita)	2015 (%)
General Direct Expenditures			
Air Transportation	0	0	0.0
Corrections	0	0	0.0
Education	0	0	0.0
Employment Security Administration	0	0	0.0
Financial Administration	1,021	34	3.7
Fire Protection	1,747	59	6.3
General Public Buildings	726	24	2.6
Governmental Administration, Other	775	26	2.8
Health	1,140	38	4.1
Highways	4,752	161	17.1
Hospitals	0	0	0.0
Housing and Community Development	0	0	0.0
Interest on General Debt	1,761	60	6.4
Judicial and Legal	0	0	0.0
Libraries	0	0	0.0
Parking	0	0	0.0
Parks and Recreation	2,506	85	9.0
Police Protection	2,850	97	10.3
Public Welfare	0	0	0.0
Sewerage	6,930	236	25.0
Solid Waste Management	1,781	60	6.4
Veterans' Services	0	0	0.0
Liquor Store	0	0	0.0
Utility	0	0	0.0
Employee Retirement	1,328	45	4.8

Source: U.S Census Bureau, State & Local Government Finances 2015

DEMOGRAPHICS

Population Growth

Area	1990 Census	2000 Census	2010 Census	2016* Estimate	Population Growth (%) 1990-2016	Population Growth (%) 2010-2016
City	20,384	24,135	28,044	28,962	42.1	3.3
MSA[1]	474,242	509,074	549,475	561,447	18.4	2.2
U.S.	248,709,873	281,421,906	308,745,538	318,558,162	28.1	3.2

Note: (1) Figures cover the Harrisburg-Carlisle, PA Metropolitan Statistical Area—see Appendix B for areas included; (*) 2012-2016 5-year estimated population
Source: U.S. Census Bureau, 1990 Census, Census 2000, Census 2010, 2012-2016 American Community Survey 5-Year Estimates

Household Size

Area	Persons in Household (%)							Average Household Size
	One	Two	Three	Four	Five	Six	Seven or More	
City	27.9	37.7	12.8	13.5	6.2	1.4	0.5	2.40
MSA[1]	29.8	35.7	15.4	12.0	4.3	1.7	1.1	2.40
U.S.	27.7	33.7	15.7	13.1	6.0	2.3	1.5	2.60

Note: (1) Figures cover the Harrisburg-Carlisle, PA Metropolitan Statistical Area—see Appendix B for areas included
Source: U.S. Census Bureau, 2012-2016 American Community Survey 5-Year Estimates

Race

Area	White Alone[2] (%)	Black Alone[2] (%)	Asian Alone[2] (%)	AIAN[3] Alone[2] (%)	NHOPI[4] Alone[2] (%)	Other Race Alone[2] (%)	Two or More Races (%)
City	84.0	1.9	11.1	0.2	0.0	0.6	2.2
MSA[1]	81.4	10.5	3.5	0.2	0.0	1.8	2.7
U.S.	73.3	12.6	5.2	0.8	0.2	4.8	3.1

Note: (1) Figures cover the Harrisburg-Carlisle, PA Metropolitan Statistical Area—see Appendix B for areas included; (2) Alone is defined as not being in combination with one or more other races; (3) American Indian and Alaska Native; (4) Native Hawaiian and Other Pacific Islander
Source: U.S. Census Bureau, 2012-2016 American Community Survey 5-Year Estimates

Hispanic or Latino Origin

Area	Total (%)	Mexican (%)	Puerto Rican (%)	Cuban (%)	Other (%)
City	2.6	1.3	0.9	0.0	0.5
MSA[1]	5.6	1.0	3.0	0.2	1.4
U.S.	17.3	11.0	1.7	0.7	4.0

Note: Persons of Hispanic or Latino origin can be of any race; (1) Figures cover the Harrisburg-Carlisle, PA Metropolitan Statistical Area—see Appendix B for areas included
Source: U.S. Census Bureau, 2012-2016 American Community Survey 5-Year Estimates

Segregation

Type	Segregation Indices[1]				Percent Change		
	1990	2000	2010	2010 Rank[2]	1990-2000	1990-2010	2000-2010
Black/White	74.3	71.1	65.7	18	-3.2	-8.6	-5.4
Asian/White	34.0	37.4	41.1	50	3.4	7.1	3.7
Hispanic/White	53.6	52.3	47.0	39	-1.4	-6.7	-5.3

Note: All figures cover the Metropolitan Statistical Area—see Appendix B for areas included; Figures are based on an analysis of 1990, 2000, and 2010 Census Decennial Census tract data by William H. Frey, Brookings Institution and the University of Michigan Social Science Data Analysis Network. In this analysis all racial groups (whites, blacks, and asians) are non-Hispanic members of those races. Hispanics are shown as a separate category; (1) Segregation Indices are Dissimilarity Indices that measure the degree to which the minority group is distributed differently than whites across census tracts. They range from 0 (complete integration) to 100 (complete segregation) where the value indicates the percentage of the minority group that needs to move to be distributed exactly like whites; (2) Ranges from 1 (most segregated) to 102 (least segregated); n/a not available.
Source: www.CensusScope.org

Ancestry

Area	German	Irish	English	American	Italian	Polish	French²	Scottish	Dutch
City	28.9	13.7	8.7	4.8	9.5	4.7	2.6	2.1	1.7
MSA¹	30.6	12.5	6.8	5.7	7.2	3.8	1.7	1.7	1.7
U.S.	14.4	10.4	7.7	6.9	5.4	2.9	2.6	1.7	1.3

Note: Figures are the percentage of the total population reporting a particular ancestry. The nine most commonly reported ancestries in the U.S. are shown. Figures include multiple ancestries (e.g. if a person reported being Irish and Italian, they were included in both columns); (1) Figures cover the Harrisburg-Carlisle, PA Metropolitan Statistical Area—see Appendix B for areas included; (2) Excludes Basque
Source: U.S. Census Bureau, 2012-2016 American Community Survey 5-Year Estimates

Foreign-Born Population

Area	Percent of Population Born in								
	Any Foreign Country	Asia	Mexico	Europe	Carribean	Central America²	South America	Africa	Canada
City	12.3	8.0	0.2	2.3	0.0	0.0	0.2	1.2	0.2
MSA¹	6.1	3.0	0.3	1.1	0.4	0.1	0.4	0.6	0.2
U.S.	13.2	4.0	3.6	1.5	1.3	1.0	0.9	0.6	0.3

Note: (1) Figures cover the Harrisburg-Carlisle, PA Metropolitan Statistical Area—see Appendix B for areas included; (2) Excludes Mexico.
Source: U.S. Census Bureau, 2012-2016 American Community Survey 5-Year Estimates

Marital Status

Area	Never Married	Now Married²	Separated	Widowed	Divorced
City	21.5	62.5	1.2	6.9	8.0
MSA¹	31.1	50.3	2.1	6.4	10.1
U.S.	33.0	48.1	2.1	5.9	11.0

Note: Figures are percentages and cover the population 15 years of age and older; (1) Figures cover the Harrisburg-Carlisle, PA Metropolitan Statistical Area—see Appendix B for areas included; (2) Excludes separated
Source: U.S. Census Bureau, 2012-2016 American Community Survey 5-Year Estimates

Disability Status

Area	All Ages	Under 18 Years Old	18 to 64 Years Old	65 Years and Over
City	9.0	2.5	4.8	31.0
MSA¹	12.4	4.4	10.1	32.5
U.S.	12.5	4.1	10.3	35.7

Note: Figures show percent of the civilian noninstitutionalized population that reported having a disability. Disability status is determined from six types of difficulty: vision, hearing, cognitive, ambulatory, self-care, and independent living. For children under 5 years old, hearing and vision difficulty are used to determine disability status. For children between the ages of 5 and 14, disability status is determined from hearing, vision, cognitive, ambulatory, and self-care difficulties. For people aged 15 years and older, they are considered to have a disability if they have difficulty with any one of the six difficulty types; Note: (1) Figures cover the Harrisburg-Carlisle, PA Metropolitan Statistical Area—see Appendix B for areas included
Source: U.S. Census Bureau, 2012-2016 American Community Survey 5-Year Estimates

Age

Area	Percent of Population									Median Age
	Under Age 5	Age 5–19	Age 20–34	Age 35–44	Age 45–54	Age 55–64	Age 65–74	Age 75–84	Age 85+	
City	4.9	19.8	13.3	14.1	14.5	15.5	10.2	5.4	2.4	43.9
MSA¹	5.8	18.4	19.5	12.2	14.2	13.8	9.0	4.9	2.3	40.3
U.S.	6.2	19.6	20.7	12.7	13.6	12.6	8.3	4.3	1.9	37.7

Note: (1) Figures cover the Harrisburg-Carlisle, PA Metropolitan Statistical Area—see Appendix B for areas included
Source: U.S. Census Bureau, 2012-2016 American Community Survey 5-Year Estimates

Gender

Area	Males	Females	Males per 100 Females
City	13,588	15,374	88.4
MSA[1]	275,187	286,260	96.1
U.S.	156,765,322	161,792,840	96.9

Note: (1) Figures cover the Harrisburg-Carlisle, PA Metropolitan Statistical Area—see Appendix B for areas included
Source: U.S. Census Bureau, 2012-2016 American Community Survey 5-Year Estimates

Religious Groups by Family

Area	Catholic	Baptist	Non-Den.	Methodist[2]	Lutheran	LDS[3]	Pente-costal	Presby-terian[4]	Muslim[5]	Judaism
MSA[1]	14.2	1.6	3.2	9.8	5.5	0.6	2.0	5.1	0.9	0.8
U.S.	19.1	9.3	4.0	4.0	2.3	2.0	1.9	1.6	0.8	0.7

Note: Figures are the number of adherents as a percentage of the total population; (1) Figures cover the Harrisburg-Carlisle, PA Metropolitan Statistical Area—see Appendix B for areas included; (2) Methodist/Pietist; (3) Latter Day Saints; (4) Reformed; (5) Figures are estimates
Source: Association of Statisticians of American Religious Bodies, 2010 U.S. Religion Census: Religious Congregations & Membership Study

Religious Groups by Tradition

Area	Catholic	Evangelical Protestant	Mainline Protestant	Other Tradition	Black Protestant	Orthodox
MSA[1]	14.2	11.4	17.7	4.0	1.3	0.4
U.S.	19.1	16.2	7.3	4.3	1.6	0.3

Note: Figures are the number of adherents as a percentage of the total population; (1) Figures cover the Harrisburg-Carlisle, PA Metropolitan Statistical Area—see Appendix B for areas included
Source: Association of Statisticians of American Religious Bodies, 2010 U.S. Religion Census: Religious Congregations & Membership Study

ECONOMY

Gross Metropolitan Product

Area	2014	2015	2016	2017	Rank[2]
MSA[1]	32.0	33.3	34.2	35.5	78

Note: Figures are in billions of dollars; (1) Figures cover the Harrisburg-Carlisle, PA Metropolitan Statistical Area—see Appendix B for areas included; (2) Rank is based on 2015 data and ranges from 1 to 381
Source: The U.S. Conference of Mayors, U.S. Metro Economies: GMP and Employment Report, 2015-2017

Economic Growth

Area	2012-14 (%)	2015 (%)	2016 (%)	2017 (%)	Rank[2]
MSA[1]	0.3	2.5	1.3	1.8	269
U.S.	2.0	2.4	1.9	2.6	–

Note: Figures are real gross metropolitan product (GMP) growth rates and represent average annual percent change; (1) Figures cover the Harrisburg-Carlisle, PA Metropolitan Statistical Area—see Appendix B for areas included; (2) Rank is based on 2012-2014 average annual percent change and ranges from 1 to 381
Source: The U.S. Conference of Mayors, U.S. Metro Economies: GMP and Employment Report, 2015-2017

Metropolitan Area Exports

Area	2011	2012	2013	2014	2015	2016	Rank[2]
MSA[1]	2,595.7	2,894.4	3,030.4	3,052.8	2,926.2	2,252.5	89

Note: Figures are in millions of dollars; (1) Figures cover the Harrisburg-Carlisle, PA Metropolitan Statistical Area—see Appendix B for areas included; (2) Rank is based on 2016 data and ranges from 1 to 385
Source: U.S. Department of Commerce, International Trade Administration, Office of Trade & Industry Information, Manufacturing & Services, data extracted March 15, 2018

Building Permits

Area	Single-Family			Multi-Family			Total		
	2016	2017p	Pct. Chg.	2016	2017p	Pct. Chg.	2016	2017p	Pct. Chg.
City	129	127	-1.6	120	52	-56.7	249	179	-28.1
MSA[1]	1,162	1,253	7.8	393	305	-22.4	1,555	1,558	0.2
U.S.	750,800	817,300	8.9	455,800	446,800	-2.0	1,206,600	1,264,100	4.8

Note: (1) Figures cover the Harrisburg-Carlisle, PA Metropolitan Statistical Area—see Appendix B for areas included; Figures represent new, privately-owned housing units authorized (unadjusted data); All permit data are based on estimates with imputation; (p) preliminary data.
Source: U.S. Census Bureau, Manufacturing, Mining, and Construction Statistics, Building Permits, 2016, 2017

Bankruptcy Filings

Area	Business Filings 2016	Business Filings 2017	Business Filings % Chg.	Nonbusiness Filings 2016	Nonbusiness Filings 2017	Nonbusiness Filings % Chg.
Cumberland County	19	22	15.8	361	374	3.6
U.S.	24,114	23,157	-4.0	770,846	765,863	-0.6

Note: Business filings include Chapter 7, Chapter 11, Chapter 12, and Chapter 13; Nonbusiness filings include Chapter 7, Chapter 11, and Chapter 13
Source: Administrative Office of the U.S. Courts, Business and Nonbusiness Bankruptcy, County Cases Commenced by Chapter of the Bankruptcy Code, During the 12-Month Period Ending December 31, 2016 and Business and Nonbusiness Bankruptcy, County Cases Commenced by Chapter of the Bankruptcy Code, During the 12-Month Period Ending December 31, 2017

Housing Vacancy Rates

Area	Gross Vacancy Rate[2] (%)			Year-Round Vacancy Rate[3] (%)			Rental Vacancy Rate[4] (%)			Homeowner Vacancy Rate[5] (%)		
	2015	2016	2017	2015	2016	2017	2015	2016	2017	2015	2016	2017
MSA[1]	n/a	n/a	n/a	n/a	n/a	n/a	n/a	n/a	n/a	n/a	n/a	n/a
U.S.	12.9	12.8	12.7	10.0	9.9	9.9	7.1	6.9	7.2	1.8	1.7	1.6

Note: (1) Figures cover the Harrisburg-Carlisle, PA Metropolitan Statistical Area—see Appendix B for areas included; (2) The percentage of the total housing inventory that is vacant; (3) The percentage of the housing inventory (excluding seasonal units) that is year-round vacant; (4) The percentage of rental inventory that is vacant for rent; (5) The percentage of homeowner inventory that is vacant for sale; n/a not available
Source: U.S. Census Bureau, Housing Vacancies and Homeownership Annual Statistics: 2015, 2016, 2017

INCOME

Income

Area	Per Capita ($)	Median Household ($)	Average Household ($)
City	44,012	82,967	106,351
MSA[1]	31,179	58,774	75,966
U.S.	29,829	55,322	77,866

Note: (1) Figures cover the Harrisburg-Carlisle, PA Metropolitan Statistical Area—see Appendix B for areas included
Source: U.S. Census Bureau, 2012-2016 American Community Survey 5-Year Estimates

Household Income Distribution

Area	Percent of Households Earning							
	Under $15,000	$15,000 -$24,999	$25,000 -$34,999	$35,000 -$49,999	$50,000 -$74,999	$75,000 -$99,999	$100,000 -$149,999	$150,000 and up
City	4.0	6.2	9.5	8.7	16.2	14.1	21.1	20.2
MSA[1]	9.0	9.1	10.0	14.0	20.2	13.8	14.5	9.3
U.S.	12.1	10.2	9.9	13.2	17.8	12.2	13.5	11.1

Note: (1) Figures cover the Harrisburg-Carlisle, PA Metropolitan Statistical Area—see Appendix B for areas included
Source: U.S. Census Bureau, 2012-2016 American Community Survey 5-Year Estimates

Poverty Rate

Area	All Ages	Under 18 Years Old	18 to 64 Years Old	65 Years and Over
City	3.0	2.7	2.7	4.4
MSA[1]	11.0	16.3	10.5	5.8
U.S.	15.1	21.2	14.2	9.3

Note: Figures are percentage of people whose income during the past 12 months was below the poverty level; (1) Figures cover the Harrisburg-Carlisle, PA Metropolitan Statistical Area—see Appendix B for areas included
Source: U.S. Census Bureau, 2012-2016 American Community Survey 5-Year Estimates

EMPLOYMENT

Labor Force and Employment

Area	Civilian Labor Force Dec. 2016	Civilian Labor Force Dec. 2017	Civilian Labor Force % Chg.	Workers Employed Dec. 2016	Workers Employed Dec. 2017	Workers Employed % Chg.
City	16,481	16,347	-0.8	16,037	15,912	-0.8
MSA[1]	293,946	291,194	-0.9	282,533	280,229	-0.8
U.S.	158,968,000	159,880,000	0.6	151,798,000	153,602,000	1.2

Note: Data is not seasonally adjusted and covers workers 16 years of age and older; (1) Figures cover the Harrisburg-Carlisle, PA Metropolitan Statistical Area—see Appendix B for areas included
Source: Bureau of Labor Statistics, Local Area Unemployment Statistics

Unemployment Rate

Area	2017											
	Jan.	Feb.	Mar.	Apr.	May	Jun.	Jul.	Aug.	Sep.	Oct.	Nov.	Dec.
City	3.2	3.2	2.8	2.7	3.1	3.1	3.3	3.3	2.9	2.6	2.7	2.7
MSA[1]	4.6	4.6	4.3	3.8	4.2	4.4	4.6	4.6	3.9	3.7	3.8	3.8
U.S.	5.1	4.9	4.6	4.1	4.1	4.5	4.6	4.5	4.1	3.9	3.9	3.9

Note: Data is not seasonally adjusted and covers workers 16 years of age and older; (1) Figures cover the Harrisburg-Carlisle, PA Metropolitan Statistical Area—see Appendix B for areas included
Source: Bureau of Labor Statistics, Local Area Unemployment Statistics

Average Wages

Occupation	$/Hr.	Occupation	$/Hr.
Accountants and Auditors	33.60	Maids and Housekeeping Cleaners	9.90
Automotive Mechanics	18.80	Maintenance and Repair Workers	19.00
Bookkeepers	19.20	Marketing Managers	60.50
Carpenters	22.80	Nuclear Medicine Technologists	n/a
Cashiers	9.70	Nurses, Licensed Practical	23.70
Clerks, General Office	16.80	Nurses, Registered	34.00
Clerks, Receptionists/Information	13.50	Nursing Assistants	15.10
Clerks, Shipping/Receiving	16.00	Packers and Packagers, Hand	13.90
Computer Programmers	36.90	Physical Therapists	42.70
Computer Systems Analysts	42.10	Postal Service Mail Carriers	24.30
Computer User Support Specialists	24.40	Real Estate Brokers	41.00
Cooks, Restaurant	12.10	Retail Salespersons	12.50
Dentists	68.00	Sales Reps., Exc. Tech./Scientific	32.90
Electrical Engineers	43.80	Sales Reps., Tech./Scientific	40.60
Electricians	25.10	Secretaries, Exc. Legal/Med./Exec.	18.00
Financial Managers	60.80	Security Guards	15.40
First-Line Supervisors/Managers, Sales	22.90	Surgeons	n/a
Food Preparation Workers	10.70	Teacher Assistants*	11.50
General and Operations Managers	58.90	Teachers, Elementary School*	29.30
Hairdressers/Cosmetologists	12.10	Teachers, Secondary School*	24.20
Internists, General	n/a	Telemarketers	10.00
Janitors and Cleaners	12.20	Truck Drivers, Heavy/Tractor-Trailer	22.00
Landscaping/Groundskeeping Workers	14.00	Truck Drivers, Light/Delivery Svcs.	15.70
Lawyers	64.30	Waiters and Waitresses	10.30

Note: Wage data covers the Harrisburg-Carlisle, PA Metropolitan Statistical Area—see Appendix B for areas included; (*) Hourly wages for elementary/secondary school teachers and teacher assistants were calculated by the editors from annual wage data based on a 40 hour work week; n/a not available.
Source: Bureau of Labor Statistics, Metro Area Occupational Employment & Wage Estimates, May 2017

Employment by Occupation

Occupation Classification	City (%)	MSA[1] (%)	U.S. (%)
Management, Business, Science, and Arts	51.5	38.1	37.0
Natural Resources, Construction, and Maintenance	3.1	6.8	8.9
Production, Transportation, and Material Moving	7.7	12.9	12.2
Sales and Office	25.1	25.5	23.8
Service	12.5	16.8	18.1

Note: Figures cover employed civilians 16 years of age and older; (1) Figures cover the Harrisburg-Carlisle, PA Metropolitan Statistical Area—see Appendix B for areas included
Source: U.S. Census Bureau, 2012-2016 American Community Survey 5-Year Estimates

Employment by Industry

Sector	MSA[1] Number of Employees	MSA[1] Percent of Total	U.S. Percent of Total
Construction, Mining, and Logging	11,700	3.4	5.2
Education and Health Services	57,900	16.9	15.9
Financial Activities	21,600	6.3	5.7
Government	58,500	17.0	15.3
Information	3,700	1.1	1.9
Leisure and Hospitality	30,800	9.0	10.7
Manufacturing	21,800	6.3	8.5
Other Services	14,800	4.3	3.9
Professional and Business Services	48,100	14.0	14.0
Retail Trade	33,000	9.6	11.0
Transportation, Warehousing, and Utilities	29,800	8.7	4.1
Wholesale Trade	11,800	3.4	4.0

Note: Figures are non-farm employment as of December 2017. Figures are not seasonally adjusted and include workers 16 years of age and older; (1) Figures cover the Harrisburg-Carlisle, PA Metropolitan Statistical Area—see Appendix B for areas included
Source: Bureau of Labor Statistics, Current Employment Statistics, Employment, Hours, and Earnings

Occupations with Greatest Projected Employment Growth: 2017 – 2019

Occupation[1]	2017 Employment	2019 Projected Employment	Numeric Employment Change	Percent Employment Change
Personal Care Aides	95,040	101,150	6,110	6.4
Combined Food Preparation and Serving Workers, Including Fast Food	149,690	154,700	5,010	3.3
Registered Nurses	143,300	147,290	3,990	2.8
Laborers and Freight, Stock, and Material Movers, Hand	138,050	141,860	3,810	2.8
Home Health Aides	46,950	50,700	3,750	8.0
Waiters and Waitresses	100,790	102,540	1,750	1.7
Janitors and Cleaners, Except Maids and Housekeeping Cleaners	98,590	100,250	1,660	1.7
Cooks, Restaurant	49,820	51,120	1,300	2.6
Software Developers, Applications	25,890	27,190	1,300	5.0
Nursing Assistants	80,510	81,790	1,280	1.6

Note: Projections cover Pennsylvania; (1) Sorted by numeric employment change
Source: www.projectionscentral.com, State Occupational Projections, 2017–2019 Short-Term Projections

Fastest Growing Occupations: 2017 – 2019

Occupation[1]	2017 Employment	2019 Projected Employment	Numeric Employment Change	Percent Employment Change
Home Health Aides	46,950	50,700	3,750	8.0
Statisticians	2,710	2,880	170	6.5
Personal Care Aides	95,040	101,150	6,110	6.4
Physician Assistants	5,620	5,960	340	6.1
Nurse Practitioners	5,240	5,550	310	6.0
Operations Research Analysts	2,660	2,800	140	5.1
Information Security Analysts	3,020	3,170	150	5.0
Software Developers, Applications	25,890	27,190	1,300	5.0
Nonfarm Animal Caretakers	7,820	8,210	390	4.9
Physical Therapist Assistants	4,660	4,880	220	4.8

Note: Projections cover Pennsylvania; (1) Sorted by percent employment change and excludes occupations with numeric employment change less than 50
Source: www.projectionscentral.com, State Occupational Projections, 2017–2019 Short-Term Projections

TAXES

State Corporate Income Tax Rates

State	Tax Rate (%)	Income Brackets ($)	Num. of Brackets	Financial Institution Tax Rate (%)[a]	Federal Income Tax Ded.
Pennsylvania	9.99	Flat rate	1	(a)	No

Note: Tax rates as of January 1, 2018; (a) Rates listed are the corporate income tax rate applied to financial institutions or excise taxes based on income. Some states have other taxes based upon the value of deposits or shares.
Source: Federation of Tax Administrators, Range of State Corporate Income Tax Rates, January 1, 2018

State Individual Income Tax Rates

State	Tax Rate (%)	Income Brackets ($)	Num. of Brackets	Personal Exempt. ($)[1]		Fed. Inc. Tax Ded.
				Single	Dependents	
Pennsylvania	3.07	Flat rate	1	None	None	No

Note: Tax rates as of January 1, 2018; Local- and county-level taxes are not included; n/a not applicable; (1) Married joint filers generally receive double the single exemption
Source: Federation of Tax Administrators, State Individual Income Tax Rates, January 1, 2018

Various State Sales and Excise Tax Rates

State	State Sales Tax (%)	Gasoline[1] (¢/gal.)	Cigarette[2] ($/pack)	Spirits[3] ($/gal.)	Wine[4] ($/gal.)	Beer[5] ($/gal.)	Recreational Marijuana (%)
Pennsylvania	6.0	58.7	2.60	7.24 (g)	(m)	0.08	Not legal

Note: All tax rates as of January 1, 2018; (1) The American Petroleum Institute has developed a methodology for determining the average tax rate on a gallon of fuel. Rates may include any of the following: excise taxes, environmental fees, storage tank fees, other fees or taxes, general sales tax, and local taxes. In states where gasoline is subject to the general sales tax, or where the fuel tax is based on the average sale price, the average rate determined by API is sensitive to changes in the price of gasoline. States that fully or partially apply general sales taxes to gasoline: CA, CO, GA, IL, IN, MI, NY; (2) The federal excise tax of $1.0066 per pack and local taxes are not included; (3) Rates are those applicable to off-premise sales of 40% alcohol by volume (a.b.v.) distilled spirits in 750ml containers. Local excise taxes are excluded; (4) Rates are those applicable to off-premise sales of 11% a.b.v. non-carbonated wine in 750ml containers; (5) Rates are those applicable to off-premise sales of 4.7% a.b.v. beer in 12 ounce containers; (g) Control states, where the government controls all sales. Products can be subject to ad valorem mark-up as well as excise taxes; (m) Control states, where the government controls all sales. Products can be subject to ad valorem mark-up as well as excise taxes.
Source: Tax Foundation, 2018 Facts & Figures: How Does Your State Compare?

State Business Tax Climate Index Rankings

State	Overall Rank	Corporate Tax Rank	Individual Income Tax Rank	Sales Tax Rank	Unemployment Insurance Tax Rank	Property Tax Rank
Pennsylvania	26	44	17	21	50	33

Note: The index is a measure of how each state's tax laws affect economic performance. The lower the rank, the more favorable a state's tax system is for business. States without a given tax are given a ranking of 1. The scores/rankings for the District of Columbia do not affect other states. The 2018 index represents the tax climate as of July 1, 2017.
Source: Tax Foundation, State Business Tax Climate Index 2018

TRANSPORTATION

Means of Transportation to Work

Area	Car/Truck/Van		Public Transportation			Bicycle	Walked	Other Means	Worked at Home
	Drove Alone	Car-pooled	Bus	Subway	Railroad				
City	87.5	6.8	0.4	0.0	0.0	0.3	0.4	0.4	4.0
MSA[1]	80.8	9.1	1.4	0.0	0.0	0.4	3.4	0.8	3.9
U.S.	76.4	9.3	2.6	1.9	0.6	0.6	2.8	1.3	4.6

Note: Figures are percentages and cover workers 16 years of age and older; (1) Figures cover the Harrisburg-Carlisle, PA Metropolitan Statistical Area—see Appendix B for areas included
Source: U.S. Census Bureau, 2012-2016 American Community Survey 5-Year Estimates

Travel Time to Work

Area	Less Than 10 Minutes	10 to 19 Minutes	20 to 29 Minutes	30 to 44 Minutes	45 to 59 Minutes	60 to 89 Minutes	90 Minutes or More
City	10.4	43.5	27.3	13.1	2.2	1.6	1.9
MSA[1]	14.2	34.3	24.3	16.7	5.8	3.0	1.8
U.S.	12.9	29.2	20.9	20.4	8.0	6.0	2.7

Note: Note: Figures are percentages and include workers 16 years old and over; (1) Figures cover the Harrisburg-Carlisle, PA Metropolitan Statistical Area—see Appendix B for areas included
Source: U.S. Census Bureau, 2012-2016 American Community Survey 5-Year Estimates

Freeway Travel Time Index

Area	1985	1990	1995	2000	2005	2010	2014
Urban Area Rank[1,2]	n/a	n/a	n/a	n/a	n/a	n/a	n/a
Urban Area Index[1]	n/a	n/a	n/a	n/a	n/a	n/a	n/a
Average Index[3]	1.09	1.11	1.14	1.17	1.20	1.19	1.20

Note: Freeway Travel Time Index—the ratio of travel time in the peak period to the travel time at free-flow conditions. For example, a value of 1.30 indicates a 20-minute free-flow trip takes 26 minutes in the peak (20 minutes x 1.30 = 26 minutes); (1) Data for the Harrisburg-Carlisle, PA urban area was not available; (2) Rank is based on 101 urban areas (#1 = highest travel time index); (3) Average of 101 urban areas
Source: Texas Transportation Institute, 2015 Urban Mobility Scorecard, August 2015

Freeway Commuter Stress Index

Area	1985	1990	1995	2000	2005	2010	2014
Urban Area Rank[1,2]	n/a	n/a	n/a	n/a	n/a	n/a	n/a
Urban Area Index[1]	n/a	n/a	n/a	n/a	n/a	n/a	n/a
Average Index[3]	1.13	1.16	1.19	1.22	1.25	1.24	1.25

Note: The Freeway Commuter Stress Index is the same as the Freeway Travel Time Index (see table above) except that it includes only the travel in the peak directions during the peak periods; the TTI includes travel in all directions during the peak period. Thus, the CSI is more indicative of the work trip experienced by each commuter on a daily basis; (1) Data for the Harrisburg-Carlisle, PA urban area was not available; (2) Rank is based on 101 urban areas (#1 = highest travel time index); (3) Average of 101 urban areas
Source: Texas Transportation Institute, 2015 Urban Mobility Scorecard, August 2015

Living Environment

COST OF LIVING

Cost of Living Index

Composite Index	Groceries	Housing	Utilities	Trans-portation	Health Care	Misc. Goods/ Services
99.3	98.8	92.6	119.1	105.9	88.3	98.9

Note: The Cost of Living Index measures regional differences in the cost of consumer goods and services, excluding taxes and non-consumer expenditures, for professional and managerial households in the top income quintile. It is based on more than 50,000 prices covering almost 60 different items for which prices are collected three times a year by chambers of commerce, economic development organizations or university applied economic centers in each participating urban area. The numbers shown should be read as a percentage above or below the national average of 100. For example, a value of 115.4 in the groceries column indicates that grocery prices are 15.4% higher than the national average. Small differences in the index numbers should not be interpreted as significant; Figures cover the Harrisburg PA urban area.
Source: The Council for Community and Economic Research, ACCRA Cost of Living Index, 2017

Grocery Prices

Area[1]	T-Bone Steak ($/pound)	Frying Chicken ($/pound)	Whole Milk ($/half gal.)	Eggs ($/dozen)	Orange Juice ($/64 oz.)	Coffee ($/11.5 oz.)
City[2]	12.35	1.42	2.10	1.55	3.09	3.55
Avg.	11.29	1.40	2.02	1.47	3.55	4.37
Min.	7.71	0.93	1.04	0.70	2.86	3.24
Max.	15.83	2.39	4.03	3.92	6.29	8.16

Note: (1) Values for the local area are compared with the average, minimum and maximum values for all 294 areas in the Cost of Living Index; (2) Figures cover the Harrisburg PA urban area; ***T-Bone Steak*** *(price per pound);* ***Frying Chicken*** *(price per pound, whole fryer);* ***Whole Milk*** *(half gallon carton);* ***Eggs*** *(price per dozen, Grade A, large);* ***Orange Juice*** *(64 oz. Tropicana or Florida Natural);* ***Coffee*** *(11.5 oz. can, vacuum-packed, Maxwell House, Hills Bros, or Folgers).*
Source: The Council for Community and Economic Research, ACCRA Cost of Living Index, 2017

Housing and Utility Costs

Area[1]	New Home Price ($)	Apartment Rent ($/month)	All Electric ($/month)	Part Electric ($/month)	Other Energy ($/month)	Telephone ($/month)
City[2]	322,594	888	210.14	-	-	31.90
Avg.	335,956	1,047	175.01	97.34	67.93	28.71
Min.	187,788	491	109.48	49.33	35.44	12.39
Max.	1,739,087	4,559	432.62	227.09	353.33	44.61

Note: (1) Values for the local area are compared with the average, minimum and maximum values for all 294 areas in the Cost of Living Index; (2) Figures cover the Harrisburg PA urban area; ***New Home Price*** *(2,400 sf living area, 8,000 sf lot, in urban area with full utilities);* ***Apartment Rent*** *(950 sf 2 bedroom/1.5 or 2 bath, unfurnished, excluding all utilities except water);* ***All Electric*** *(average monthly cost for an all-electric home);* ***Part Electric*** *(average monthly cost for a part-electric home);* ***Other Energy*** *(average monthly cost for natural gas, fuel oil, coal, wood, and any other forms of energy except electricity);* ***Telephone*** *(price includes basic monthly rate for a private residential line plus additional local usage charges incurred by a family of four).*
Source: The Council for Community and Economic Research, ACCRA Cost of Living Index, 2017

Health Care, Transportation, and Other Costs

Area[1]	Doctor ($/visit)	Dentist ($/visit)	Optometrist ($/visit)	Gasoline ($/gallon)	Beauty Salon ($/visit)	Men's Shirt ($)
City[2]	89.29	82.49	51.78	2.45	23.12	21.84
Avg.	108.00	92.54	101.93	2.25	37.58	30.92
Min.	30.39	60.00	49.75	1.82	16.11	11.20
Max.	193.50	161.94	229.28	3.16	77.35	59.13

Note: (1) Values for the local area are compared with the average, minimum and maximum values for all 294 areas in the Cost of Living Index; (2) Figures cover the Harrisburg PA urban area; ***Doctor*** *(general practitioners routine exam of an established patient);* ***Dentist*** *(adult teeth cleaning and periodic oral examination);* ***Optometrist*** *(full vision eye exam for established adult patient);* ***Gasoline*** *(one gallon regular unleaded, national brand, including all taxes, cash price at self-service pump if available);* ***Beauty Salon*** *(woman's shampoo, trim, and blow-dry);* ***Men's Shirt*** *(cotton/polyester dress shirt, pinpoint weave, long sleeves).*
Source: The Council for Community and Economic Research, ACCRA Cost of Living Index, 2017

HOUSING

House Price Index (HPI)

Area	National Ranking[2]	Quarterly Change (%)	One-Year Change (%)	Five-Year Change (%)
MSA[1]	224	1.40	2.62	9.23
U.S.[3]	–	1.61	6.68	34.71

Note: The HPI is a weighted repeat sales index. It measures average price changes in repeat sales or refinancings on the same properties. This information is obtained by reviewing repeat mortgage transactions on single-family properties whose mortgages have been purchased or securitized by Fannie Mae or Freddie Mac in January 1975; (1) Figures cover the Harrisburg-Carlisle, PA Metropolitan Statistical Area—see Appendix B for areas included; (2) Rankings are based on annual percentage change for all metro areas containing at least 15,000 transactions over the last 10 years and ranges from 1 to 253; (3) figures based on a weighted average of Census Division estimates using a seasonally adjusted, purchase-only index; all figures are for the period ending December 31, 2017
Source: Federal Housing Finance Agency, House Price Index, February 28, 2018

Median Single-Family Home Prices

Area	2015	2016	2017p	Percent Change 2016 to 2017
MSA[1]	159.0	160.4	165.9	3.4
U.S. Average	223.9	235.5	248.8	5.6

Note: Figures are median sales prices of existing single-family homes in thousands of dollars; (p) preliminary; (1) Figures cover the Harrisburg-Carlisle, PA Metropolitan Statistical Area—see Appendix B for areas included
Source: National Association of Realtors, Median Sales Price of Existing Single-Family Homes for Metropolitan Areas, 4th Quarter 2017

Qualifying Income Based on Median Sales Price of Existing Single-Family Homes

Area	With 5% Down ($)	With 10% Down ($)	With 20% Down ($)
MSA[1]	37,842	35,850	31,867
U.S. Average	55,585	52,659	46,808

Note: Figures are preliminary; Qualifying income is based on a mortgage rate of 4.17%. Monthly principal and interest payment is limited to 25% of income; (1) Figures cover the Harrisburg-Carlisle, PA Metropolitan Statistical Area—see Appendix B for areas included
Source: National Association of Realtors, Qualifying Income Based on Median Sales Price of Existing Single-Family Homes for Metropolitan Areas, 4th Quarter 2017

Median Apartment Condo-Coop Home Prices

Area	2015	2016	2017p	Percent Change 2016 to 2017
MSA[1]	n/a	n/a	n/a	n/a
U.S. Average	210.7	220.7	234.3	6.2

Note: Figures are median sales prices of existing apartment condo-coop homes in thousands of dollars; (p) preliminary; n/a not available; (1) Figures cover the Harrisburg-Carlisle, PA Metropolitan Statistical Area—see Appendix B for areas included
Source: National Association of Realtors, Median Sales Price of Existing Apartment Condo-Coop Homes for Metropolitan Areas, 4th Quarter 2017

Home Value Distribution

Area	Under $50,000	$50,000 -$99,999	$100,000 -$149,999	$150,000 -$199,999	$200,000 -$299,999	$300,000 -$499,999	$500,000 -$999,999	$1,000,000 or more
City	5.2	2.4	8.1	16.3	35.1	26.7	5.1	1.0
MSA[1]	6.2	10.8	19.7	24.6	23.8	11.4	2.8	0.5
U.S.	8.8	14.8	15.3	14.9	18.4	16.4	9.0	2.5

Note: Figures are percentages and cover owner-occupied housing units; (1) Figures cover the Harrisburg-Carlisle, PA Metropolitan Statistical Area—see Appendix B for areas included
Source: U.S. Census Bureau, 2012-2016 American Community Survey 5-Year Estimates

Homeownership Rate

Area	2009 (%)	2010 (%)	2011 (%)	2012 (%)	2013 (%)	2014 (%)	2015 (%)	2016 (%)	2017 (%)
MSA[1]	n/a	n/a	n/a	n/a	n/a	n/a	n/a	n/a	n/a
U.S.	67.4	66.9	66.1	65.4	65.1	64.5	63.7	63.4	63.9

Note: (1) Figures cover the Harrisburg-Carlisle, PA Metropolitan Statistical Area—see Appendix B for areas included; n/a not available
Source: U.S. Census Bureau, Housing Vacancies and Homeownership Annual Statistics: 2009-2017

Year Housing Structure Built

Area	2010 or Later	2000 -2009	1990 -1999	1980 -1989	1970 -1979	1960 -1969	1950 -1959	1940 -1949	Before 1940	Median Year
City	3.9	19.4	19.1	13.1	19.3	12.6	9.8	1.3	1.5	1984
MSA[1]	2.3	10.5	12.1	11.8	14.4	10.7	12.8	5.4	20.2	1971
U.S.	2.3	14.7	14.0	13.7	15.6	10.9	10.6	5.2	13.0	1977

Note: Figures are percentages except for Median Year; Note: (1) Figures cover the Harrisburg-Carlisle, PA Metropolitan Statistical Area—see Appendix B for areas included
Source: U.S. Census Bureau, 2012-2016 American Community Survey 5-Year Estimates

Gross Monthly Rent

Area	Under $500	$500 -$999	$1,000 -$1,499	$1,500 -$1,999	$2,000 -$2,499	$2,500 -$2,999	$3,000 and up	Median ($)
City	1.2	46.1	29.7	11.4	3.8	2.3	5.5	1,031
MSA[1]	10.7	55.6	26.5	4.9	1.0	0.5	0.7	873
U.S.	11.3	43.3	27.7	10.7	4.0	1.6	1.5	949

Note: Figures are percentages except for Median; Gross rent is the contract rent plus the estimated average monthly cost of utilities (electricity, gas, and water and sewer) and fuels (oil, coal, kerosene, wood, etc.) if these are paid by the renter (or paid for the renter by someone else); (1) Figures cover the Harrisburg-Carlisle, PA Metropolitan Statistical Area—see Appendix B for areas included
Source: U.S. Census Bureau, 2012-2016 American Community Survey 5-Year Estimates

HEALTH

Health Risk Factors

Category	MSA[1] (%)	U.S. (%)
Adults aged 18–64 who have any kind of health care coverage	n/a	87.7
Adults who reported being in good or excellent health	n/a	83.6
Adults who are current smokers	n/a	17.1
Adults who currently use E-cigarettes	n/a	4.7
Adults who currently use chewing tobacco, snuff, or snus	n/a	4.0
Adults who are heavy drinkers[2]	n/a	6.5
Adults who are binge drinkers[3]	n/a	16.9
Adults who are overweight (BMI 25.0 - 29.9)	n/a	35.3
Adults who are obese (BMI 30.0 - 99.8)	n/a	29.9
Adults who participated in any physical activities in the past month	n/a	76.9
Adults who always or nearly always wears a seat belt	n/a	94.3

Note: n/a not available; (1) Figures cover the Harrisburg-Carlisle, PA Metropolitan Statistical Area—see Appendix B for areas included; (2) Heavy drinkers are classified as adult men having more than 14 drinks per week and adult women having more than 7 drinks per week; (3) Binge drinkers are classified as males having five or more drinks on one occasion or females having four or more drinks on one occasion
Source: Centers for Disease Control and Prevention, Behaviorial Risk Factor Surveillance System, SMART: Selected Metropolitan Area Risk Trends, 2016

Health Screening Rates

Category	MSA[1] (%)	U.S. (%)
Adults 50-75 who have had a blood stool test within the past year	n/a	8.0
Adults 50-75 who have had a colonoscopy in the past 10 years	n/a	63.5
Adults aged 65+ who have had flu shot within the past year	n/a	58.6
Adults aged 65+ who have ever had a pneumonia vaccination	n/a	73.4
Adults who have ever been tested for HIV	n/a	35.6
Women aged 21-65 who have had a pap test in the past three years	n/a	79.8
Men aged 40+ who have had a PSA test within the past two years	n/a	39.5
Women aged 40+ who have had a mammogram within the past two years	n/a	72.5

Note: n/a not available; (1) Figures cover the Harrisburg-Carlisle, PA Metropolitan Statistical Area—see Appendix B for areas included; Source: Centers for Disease Control and Prevention, Behaviorial Risk Factor Surveillance System, SMART: Selected Metropolitan Area Risk Trends, 2016

Chronic Health Conditions

Category	MSA[1] (%)	U.S. (%)
Adults who have ever been told they had a heart attack	n/a	4.4
Adults who have ever been told they have angina or coronary heart disease	n/a	4.1
Adults who have ever been told they had a stroke	n/a	3.1
Adults who have been told they currently have asthma	n/a	9.3
Adults who have ever been told they have arthritis	n/a	25.8
Adults who have ever been told they have diabetes[2]	n/a	10.5
Adults who have ever been told they had skin cancer	n/a	5.9
Adults who have ever been told they had any other types of cancer	n/a	6.7
Adults who have ever been told they have COPD	n/a	6.3
Adults who have ever been told they have kidney disease	n/a	2.8
Adults who have ever been told they have a form of depression	n/a	17.4

Note: n/a not available; (1) Figures cover the Harrisburg-Carlisle, PA Metropolitan Statistical Area—see Appendix B for areas included; (2) Figures do not include pregnancy-related, borderline, or pre-diabetes
Source: Centers for Disease Control and Prevention, Behaviorial Risk Factor Surveillance System, SMART: Selected Metropolitan Area Risk Trends, 2016

Mortality Rates for the Top 10 Causes of Death in the U.S.

ICD-10[a] Sub-Chapter	ICD-10[a] Code	Age-Adjusted Mortality Rate[1] per 100,000 population	
		County[2]	U.S.
Malignant neoplasms	C00-C97	148.2	158.5
Ischaemic heart diseases	I20-I25	93.7	96.8
Other forms of heart disease	I30-I51	68.6	52.4
Chronic lower respiratory diseases	J40-J47	33.9	40.9
Cerebrovascular diseases	I60-I69	34.1	37.2
Organic, including symptomatic, mental disorders	F01-F09	32.3	33.3
Other degenerative diseases of the nervous system	G30-G31	19.2	32.1
Other external causes of accidental injury	W00-X59	31.2	31.2
Diabetes mellitus	E10-E14	16.0	21.1
Hypertensive diseases	I10-I15	13.6	20.8

Note: (a) ICD-10 = International Classification of Diseases 10th Revision; (1) Mortality rates are a three year average covering 2014-2016; (2) Figures cover Cumberland County.
Source: Centers for Disease Control and Prevention, National Center for Health Statistics. Underlying Cause of Death 1999-2016 on CDC WONDER Online Database, released December 2017

Mortality Rates for Selected Causes of Death

ICD-10[a] Sub-Chapter	ICD-10[a] Code	Age-Adjusted Mortality Rate[1] per 100,000 population	
		County[2]	U.S.
Assault	X85-Y09	Unreliable	5.6
Diseases of the liver	K70-K76	10.6	14.0
Human immunodeficiency virus (HIV) disease	B20-B24	Suppressed	1.9
Influenza and pneumonia	J09-J18	16.5	14.6
Intentional self-harm	X60-X84	13.3	13.2
Malnutrition	E40-E46	Suppressed	1.3
Obesity and other hyperalimentation	E65-E68	Unreliable	2.1
Renal failure	N17-N19	15.0	13.0
Transport accidents	V01-V99	8.9	12.0
Viral hepatitis	B15-B19	Unreliable	1.9

Note: (a) ICD-10 = International Classification of Diseases 10th Revision; (1) Mortality rates are a three year average covering 2014-2016; (2) Figures cover Cumberland County; Data are Suppressed when the data meet the criteria for confidentiality constraints; Mortality rates are flagged as Unreliable when the rate would be calculated with a numerator of 20 or less.
Source: Centers for Disease Control and Prevention, National Center for Health Statistics. Underlying Cause of Death 1999-2016 on CDC WONDER Online Database, released December 2017

Health Insurance Coverage

Area	With Health Insurance	With Private Health Insurance	With Public Health Insurance	Without Health Insurance	Population Under Age 18 Without Health Insurance
City	97.3	87.6	25.9	2.7	1.1
MSA[1]	92.5	76.5	30.7	7.5	5.3
U.S.	88.3	66.7	33.0	11.7	5.9

Note: Figures are percentages that cover the civilian noninstitutionalized population; (1) Figures cover the Harrisburg-Carlisle, PA Metropolitan Statistical Area—see Appendix B for areas included
Source: U.S. Census Bureau, 2012-2016 American Community Survey 5-Year Estimates

Number of Medical Professionals

Area	MDs[3]	DOs[3,4]	Dentists	Podiatrists	Chiropractors	Optometrists
County[1] (number)	597	109	177	18	58	54
County[1] (rate[2])	242.4	44.3	71.4	7.3	23.4	21.8
U.S. (rate[2])	276.5	22.3	67.3	6.0	26.7	15.9

Note: Data as of 2016 unless noted; (1) Data covers Cumberland County; (2) Rate per 100,000 population; (3) Data as of 2015 and includes all active, non-federal physicians; (4) Doctor of Osteopathic Medicine
Source: U.S. Department of Health and Human Services, Health Resources and Services Administration, Bureau of Health Professions, Area Resource File (ARF) 2016-2017

Best Hospitals

According to *U.S. News,* the Harrisburg-Carlisle, PA metro area is home to one of the best hospitals in the U.S.: **Penn State Milton S. Hershey Medical Center** (2 adult specialties and 4 pediatric specialties). The hospital listed was nationally ranked in at least one of 16 specialties. Only 152 hospitals nationwide were nationally ranked in one or more specialties. Twenty hospitals in the U.S. made the Honor Roll. The Best Hospitals Honor Roll was revamped last year to take both the national rankings and the procedure and condition ratings into account. Hospitals received points if they were nationally ranked in one of the 16 specialties—the higher they ranked, the more points they got—and how many ratings of "high performing" they earned in the nine procedures and conditions. *U.S. News Online, "America's Best Hospitals 2017-18"*

According to *U.S. News,* the Harrisburg-Carlisle, PA metro area is home to one of the best children's hospitals in the U.S.: **Penn State Children's Hospital** (4 pediatric specialties). The hospital listed was highly ranked in at least one of 10 pediatric specialties. Eighty-two children's hospitals in the U.S. were nationally ranked in at least one specialty. Hospitals received points for being ranked in a specialty, and the 10 hospitals with the most points across the 10 specialties make up the Honor Roll. *U.S. News Online, "America's Best Children's Hospitals 2017-18"*

EDUCATION

Public School District Statistics

District Name	Schls	Pupils	Pupil/ Teacher Ratio	Minority Pupils[1] (%)	Free Lunch Eligible[2] (%)	IEP[3] (%)
Cumberland Valley SD	10	8,512	16.4	22.5	16.7	13.2
Mechanicsburg Area SD	8	3,852	14.1	21.3	30.0	13.6
West Shore SD	14	7,800	15.6	17.3	26.5	17.6

Note: Table includes school districts with 100 or more students; (1) Percentage of students that are not non-Hispanic white; (2) Percentage of students that are eligible for the free lunch program; (3) Percentage of students that have an Individualized Education Program.
Source: U.S. Department of Education, National Center for Education Statistics, Common Core of Data, Local Education Agency (School District) Universe Survey: School Year 2015-2016; U.S. Department of Education, National Center for Education Statistics, Common Core of Data, Public Elementary/Secondary School Universe Survey: School Year 2015-2016

Highest Level of Education

Area	Less than H.S.	H.S. Diploma	Some College, No Deg.	Associate Degree	Bachelor's Degree	Master's Degree	Prof. School Degree	Doctorate Degree
City	6.0	21.4	15.1	7.4	30.4	14.1	3.5	2.1
MSA[1]	10.0	35.0	16.6	8.3	18.7	8.1	2.2	1.2
U.S.	13.0	27.5	21.0	8.2	18.8	8.2	2.0	1.3

Note: Figures cover persons age 25 and over; (1) Figures cover the Harrisburg-Carlisle, PA Metropolitan Statistical Area—see Appendix B for areas included
Source: U.S. Census Bureau, 2012-2016 American Community Survey 5-Year Estimates

Educational Attainment by Race

Area	High School Graduate or Higher (%)					Bachelor's Degree or Higher (%)				
	Total	White	Black	Asian	Hisp.[2]	Total	White	Black	Asian	Hisp.[2]
City	94.0	94.9	94.3	88.2	91.1	50.1	48.5	36.8	66.6	32.0
MSA[1]	90.0	91.3	85.6	81.5	71.1	30.1	31.2	16.4	50.5	16.3
U.S.	87.0	88.9	84.3	86.3	65.7	30.3	31.6	20.0	52.1	14.7

Note: Figures shown cover persons 25 years old and over; (1) Figures cover the Harrisburg-Carlisle, PA Metropolitan Statistical Area—see Appendix B for areas included; (2) People of Hispanic origin can be of any race
Source: U.S. Census Bureau, 2012-2016 American Community Survey 5-Year Estimates

School Enrollment by Grade and Control

Area	Preschool (%)		Kindergarten (%)		Grades 1 - 4 (%)		Grades 5 - 8 (%)		Grades 9 - 12 (%)	
	Public	Private	Public	Private	Public	Private	Public	Private	Public	Private
City	43.7	56.3	90.7	9.3	96.1	3.9	94.8	5.2	91.8	8.2
MSA[1]	49.4	50.6	80.3	19.7	85.7	14.3	88.0	12.0	88.6	11.4
U.S.	58.4	41.6	87.7	12.3	89.8	10.2	89.7	10.3	90.4	9.6

Note: Figures shown cover persons 3 years old and over; (1) Figures cover the Harrisburg-Carlisle, PA Metropolitan Statistical Area—see Appendix B for areas included
Source: U.S. Census Bureau, 2012-2016 American Community Survey 5-Year Estimates

Average Salaries of Public School Classroom Teachers

Area	2015		2016		Change from 2015 to 2016	
	Dollars	Rank[1]	Dollars	Rank[1]	Percent	Rank[2]
Pennsylvania	64,447	10	65,151	10	1.1	24
U.S. Average	57,611	–	58,353	–	1.3	–

Note: (1) Rank ranges from 1 to 51 where 1 indicates highest salary; (2) Rank ranges from 1 to 51 where 1 indicates highest percent change.
Source: National Education Association, Rankings & Estimates: Rankings of the States 2016 and Estimates of School Statistics 2017

Higher Education

Four-Year Colleges			Two-Year Colleges			Medical Schools[1]	Law Schools[2]	Voc/ Tech[3]
Public	Private Non-profit	Private For-profit	Public	Private Non-profit	Private For-profit			
0	0	0	0	0	0	0	0	0

Note: Figures cover institutions located within the city limits and include main campuses only; (1) includes schools accredited by the Liaison Committee on Medical Education and the American Osteopathic Association's Commission on Osteopathic College Accreditation; (2) includes ABA-accredited schools, schools with provisional ABA accreditation, and state accredited schools; (3) includes all schools with programs that are less than 2 years.
Source: National Center for Education Statistics, Integrated Postsecondary Education System (IPEDS), 2016-17; Wikipedia, List of Medical Schools in the United States, accessed April 2, 2018; Wikipedia, List of Law Schools in the United States, accessed April 2, 2018

According to *U.S. News & World Report,* the Harrisburg-Carlisle, PA metro area is home to one of the best liberal arts colleges in the U.S.: **Dickinson College** (#51 tie). The indicators used to capture academic quality fall into a number of categories: assessment by administrators at peer institutions; retention of students; faculty resources; student selectivity; financial resources; alumni giving; high school counselor ratings of colleges; and graduation rate. *U.S. News & World Report, "America's Best Colleges 2018"*

According to *U.S. News & World Report,* the Harrisburg-Carlisle, PA metro area is home to one of the top 100 law schools in the U.S.: **Pennsylvania State University—Carlisle (Dickinson)** (#59 tie). The rankings are based on a weighted average of 12 measures of quality: peer assessment score; assessment score by lawyers/judges; median LSAT scores; median undergrad GPA; acceptance rate; employment rates for graduates; placement success; bar passage rate; faculty resources; expenditures per student; student/faculty ratio; and library resources. *U.S. News & World Report, "America's Best Graduate Schools, Law, 2019"*

PRESIDENTIAL ELECTION

2016 Presidential Election Results

Area	Clinton	Trump	Johnson	Stein	Other
Cumberland County	38.1	55.9	3.2	0.8	2.0
U.S.	48.0	45.9	3.3	1.1	1.7

Note: Results are percentages and may not add to 100% due to rounding
Source: Dave Leip's Atlas of U.S. Presidential Elections

EMPLOYERS

Major Employers

Company Name	Industry
Capital Blue Cross	Health insurer
Central Dauphin SD	Education
Commonwealth of Pennsylvania	State government
Dauphin County	County government
Giant Food Stores	Retail grocery
Harley Davidson	Motorcycle manufacturer
Harrisburg Area Community College	Education
Highmark Blue Shield	Insurance
Holy Spirit Health System	Health care
JFC Personnel	Staffing
Kinsley Construction Inc.	General contractor
Lancaster County	County government
Lancaster General Health	Health care
Lancaster-Lebanon Intermediate Unit 13	Educational service agency
Penn State Milton S. Hershey Medical Center	Health care
Pinnaclehealth System	Health care
Rite Aid	Retail drug store
Rutter's Holdings, Inc.	Fluid dair, convenience store operations
Susquehanna Bancshares, Inc.	Financial services
The High Cos.	Manufacturing
Tyco Electronics Corp	Manufacturer
US Government	Federal government
Wal-Mart	Retailer
Wellspan Health	Health care
York County	Government

Note: Companies shown are located within the Harrisburg-Carlisle, PA Metropolitan Statistical Area.
Source: Hoovers.com; Wikipedia

PUBLIC SAFETY

Crime Rate

Area	All Crimes	Violent Crimes				Property Crimes		
		Murder	Rape[3]	Robbery	Aggrav. Assault	Burglary	Larceny -Theft	Motor Vehicle Theft
City	828.7	0.0	6.7	20.2	10.1	101.1	680.5	10.1
Metro[1]	1,734.5	3.4	38.0	54.7	159.1	272.4	1,144.8	62.1
U.S.	2,847.8	5.3	40.4	102.8	248.5	468.9	1,745.0	236.9

Note: Figures are crimes per 100,000 population; (1) Figures cover the Harrisburg-Carlisle, PA Metropolitan Statistical Area—see Appendix B for areas included; (3) The city and U.S. figures shown were reported using the revised Uniform Crime Reporting (UCR) definition of rape. The metro area figures shown are an aggregate total of the data submitted using both the revised and legacy UCR definitions.
Source: FBI Uniform Crime Reports, 2016

Hate Crimes

Area	Number of Quarters Reported	Number of Incidents per Bias Motivation					
		Race/Ethnicity/ Ancestry	Religion	Sexual Orientation	Disability	Gender	Gender Identity
Area[1]	4	0	0	0	0	0	0
U.S.	4	3,489	1,273	1,076	70	31	124

Note: (1) Figures cover the Hampden Township.
Source: Federal Bureau of Investigation, Hate Crime Statistics 2016

Identity Theft Consumer Reports

Area	Reports	Reports per 100,000 Population	Rank[2]
MSA[1]	460	81	190
U.S.	371,061	114	-

Note: (1) Figures cover the Harrisburg-Carlisle, PA Metropolitan Statistical Area—see Appendix B for areas included; (2) Rank ranges from 1 to 389 where 1 indicates greatest number of identity theft reports per 100,000 population
Source: Federal Trade Commission, Consumer Sentinel Network Data Book for January–December 2017

Fraud and Other Consumer Reports

Area	Reports	Reports per 100,000 Population	Rank[2]
MSA[1]	2,986	526	88
U.S.	2,304,550	708	-

Note: (1) Figures cover the Harrisburg-Carlisle, PA Metropolitan Statistical Area—see Appendix B for areas included; (2) Rank ranges from 1 to 389 where 1 indicates greatest number of fraud and other consumer reports per 100,000 population
Source: Federal Trade Commission, Consumer Sentinel Network Data Book for January–December 2017

SPORTS

Professional Sports Teams

Team Name	League	Year Established
No teams are located in the metro area		

Source: Wikipedia, Major Professional Sports Teams of the United States and Canada, April 5, 2018

CLIMATE

Average and Extreme Temperatures

Temperature	Jan	Feb	Mar	Apr	May	Jun	Jul	Aug	Sep	Oct	Nov	Dec	Yr.
Extreme High (°F)	73	75	84	93	95	100	107	100	102	90	84	75	107
Average High (°F)	37	40	50	62	73	81	86	84	76	65	53	41	62
Average Temp. (°F)	30	32	41	52	62	71	76	74	67	55	44	34	53
Average Low (°F)	23	24	32	42	51	61	66	64	56	45	36	26	44
Extreme Low (°F)	-9	-5	5	19	31	40	50	45	30	23	13	-8	-9

Note: Figures cover the years 1948-1991
Source: National Climatic Data Center, International Station Meteorological Climate Summary, 9/96

Average Precipitation/Snowfall/Humidity

Precip./Humidity	Jan	Feb	Mar	Apr	May	Jun	Jul	Aug	Sep	Oct	Nov	Dec	Yr.
Avg. Precip. (in.)	2.8	2.8	3.3	3.2	4.1	3.5	3.5	3.3	3.2	2.8	3.3	3.2	39.0
Avg. Snowfall (in.)	9	10	6	1	Tr	0	0	0	0	Tr	2	7	35
Avg. Rel. Hum. 7am (%)	71	71	70	71	75	77	79	83	85	82	77	72	76
Avg. Rel. Hum. 4pm (%)	56	53	49	47	51	51	52	54	55	53	56	58	53

Note: Figures cover the years 1948-1991; Tr = Trace amounts (<0.05 in. of rain; <0.5 in. of snow)
Source: National Climatic Data Center, International Station Meteorological Climate Summary, 9/96

Weather Conditions

Temperature			Daytime Sky			Precipitation		
5°F & below	32°F & below	90°F & above	Clear	Partly cloudy	Cloudy	0.01 inch or more precip.	0.1 inch or more snow/ice	Thunder-storms
3	106	22	83	134	148	124	20	31

Note: Figures are average number of days per year and cover the years 1948-1991
Source: National Climatic Data Center, International Station Meteorological Climate Summary, 9/96

HAZARDOUS WASTE

Superfund Sites

The Harrisburg-Carlisle, PA metro area is home to one site on the EPA's Superfund National Priorities List: **Navy Ships Parts Control Center** (final). There are a total of 1,396 Superfund sites with a status of proposed or final on the list in the U.S. *U.S. Environmental Protection Agency, National Priorities List, April 4, 2018*

AIR & WATER QUALITY

Air Quality Trends: Ozone

	1990	1995	2000	2005	2010	2012	2013	2014	2015	2016
MSA[1]	0.091	0.086	0.080	0.084	0.075	0.072	0.066	0.063	0.066	0.067
U.S.	0.087	0.089	0.081	0.079	0.073	0.075	0.069	0.067	0.068	0.069

Note: (1) Data covers the Harrisburg-Carlisle, PA Metropolitan Statistical Area—see Appendix B for areas included. The values shown are the composite ozone concentration averages among trend sites based on the highest fourth daily maximum 8-hour concentration in parts per million. These trends are based on sites having an adequate record of monitoring data during the trend period. Data from exceptional events are included.
Source: U.S. Environmental Protection Agency, Air Quality Monitoring Information, "Air Quality Trends by City, 1990-2016"

Air Quality Index

Area	Percent of Days when Air Quality was...[2]					AQI Statistics[2]	
	Good	Moderate	Unhealthy for Sensitive Groups	Unhealthy	Very Unhealthy	Maximum	Median
MSA[1]	72.9	26.8	0.3	0.0	0.0	110	43

Note: (1) Data covers the Harrisburg-Carlisle, PA Metropolitan Statistical Area—see Appendix B for areas included; (2) Based on 365 days with AQI data in 2017. Air Quality Index (AQI) is an index for reporting daily air quality. EPA calculates the AQI for five major air pollutants regulated by the Clean Air Act: ground-level ozone, particle pollution (aka particulate matter), carbon monoxide, sulfur dioxide, and nitrogen dioxide. The AQI runs from 0 to 500. The higher the AQI value, the greater the level of air pollution and the greater the health concern. There are six AQI categories: "Good" AQI is between 0 and 50. Air quality is considered satisfactory; "Moderate" AQI is between 51 and 100. Air quality is acceptable; "Unhealthy for Sensitive Groups" When AQI values are between 101 and 150, members of sensitive groups may experience health effects; "Unhealthy" When AQI values are between 151 and 200 everyone may begin to experience health effects; "Very Unhealthy" AQI values between 201 and 300 trigger a health alert; "Hazardous" AQI values over 300 trigger warnings of emergency conditions (not shown).
Source: U.S. Environmental Protection Agency, Air Quality Index Report, 2017

Air Quality Index Pollutants

Area	Percent of Days when AQI Pollutant was...[2]					
	Carbon Monoxide	Nitrogen Dioxide	Ozone	Sulfur Dioxide	Particulate Matter 2.5	Particulate Matter 10
MSA[1]	0.0	0.0	46.6	0.0	53.4	0.0

Note: (1) Data covers the Harrisburg-Carlisle, PA Metropolitan Statistical Area—see Appendix B for areas included; (2) Based on 365 days with AQI data in 2017. The Air Quality Index (AQI) is an index for reporting daily air quality. EPA calculates the AQI for five major air pollutants regulated by the Clean Air Act: ground-level ozone, particle pollution (also known as particulate matter), carbon monoxide, sulfur dioxide, and nitrogen dioxide. The AQI runs from 0 to 500. The higher the AQI value, the greater the level of air pollution and the greater the health concern.
Source: U.S. Environmental Protection Agency, Air Quality Index Report, 2017

Maximum Air Pollutant Concentrations: Particulate Matter, Ozone, CO and Lead

	Particulate Matter 10 (ug/m^3)	Particulate Matter 2.5 Wtd AM (ug/m^3)	Particulate Matter 2.5 24-Hr (ug/m^3)	Ozone (ppm)	Carbon Monoxide (ppm)	Lead (ug/m^3)
MSA[1] Level	41	8.9	25	0.07	n/a	n/a
NAAQS[2]	150	15	35	0.075	9	0.15
Met NAAQS[2]	Yes	Yes	Yes	Yes	n/a	n/a

Note: (1) Data covers the Harrisburg-Carlisle, PA Metropolitan Statistical Area—see Appendix B for areas included; Data from exceptional events are included; (2) National Ambient Air Quality Standards; ppm = parts per million; ug/m^3 = micrograms per cubic meter; n/a not available.
Concentrations: Particulate Matter 10 (coarse particulate)—highest second maximum 24-hour concentration; Particulate Matter 2.5 Wtd AM (fine particulate)—highest weighted annual mean concentration; Particulate Matter 2.5 24-Hour (fine particulate)—highest 98th percentile 24-hour concentration; Ozone—highest fourth daily maximum 8-hour concentration; Carbon Monoxide—highest second maximum non-overlapping 8-hour concentration; Lead—maximum running 3-month average
Source: U.S. Environmental Protection Agency, Air Quality Monitoring Information, "Air Quality Statistics by City, 2016"

Maximum Air Pollutant Concentrations: Nitrogen Dioxide and Sulfur Dioxide

	Nitrogen Dioxide AM (ppb)	Nitrogen Dioxide 1-Hr (ppb)	Sulfur Dioxide AM (ppb)	Sulfur Dioxide 1-Hr (ppb)	Sulfur Dioxide 24-Hr (ppb)
MSA[1] Level	n/a	n/a	n/a	n/a	n/a
NAAQS[2]	53	100	30	75	140
Met NAAQS[2]	n/a	n/a	n/a	n/a	n/a

Note: (1) Data covers the Harrisburg-Carlisle, PA Metropolitan Statistical Area—see Appendix B for areas included; Data from exceptional events are included; (2) National Ambient Air Quality Standards; ppm = parts per million; ug/m^3 = micrograms per cubic meter; n/a not available.

Concentrations: Nitrogen Dioxide AM—highest arithmetic mean concentration; Nitrogen Dioxide 1-Hr—highest 98th percentile 1-hour daily maximum concentration; Sulfur Dioxide AM—highest annual mean concentration; Sulfur Dioxide 1-Hr—highest 99th percentile 1-hour daily maximum concentration; Sulfur Dioxide 24-Hr—highest second maximum 24-hour concentration

Source: U.S. Environmental Protection Agency, Air Quality Monitoring Information, "Air Quality Statistics by City, 2016"

Drinking Water

Water System Name	Pop. Served	Primary Water Source Type	Violations[1] Health Based	Violations[1] Monitoring/ Reporting
Suez Mechanicsburg	32,336	Surface	1	0

Note: (1) Based on violation data from January 1, 2017 to December 31, 2017

Source: U.S. Environmental Protection Agency, Office of Ground Water and Drinking Water, Safe Drinking Water Information System (based on data extracted April 5, 2018)

Lower Macungie, Pennsylvania

Background

Lower Macungie Township is a suburb of Allentown, Pennsylvania, in the Lehigh Valley region. It is the fastest growing area in the state population-wise. Villages within the township include East Texas, Minesite, New Hensingersville (which also sits in Berks County), Weilersville, and Wescosville.

The area that includes Lower Macungie Township was previously occupied by the Lenni Lenape people, who mined and traded jasper from quarries outside present-day Macungie and Vera Cruz to people all over North America. The early 18th century brought German settlers to the area, who adopted the name "Lenape" for their new land after its prior occupants. The name "Macungie" eventually took over, which is Native American for bear swamp, or place where bears feed. Macungie Township was officially formed in 1743, and in 1832 was approved by Lehigh Country to be separated into Upper and Lower halves. For many generations, Lower Macungie was a rural community until the 1960s, when housing subdivisions began to sprout new homes, changing the area forever. Many farms have been sold in the latter half of the 20th century, with house construction replacing farmland. Presently, industrial and commercial growth reigns strongly beside residential growth.

The township, with a total of 22.6 square miles, has both Little Lehigh Creek and Swabia Creek running through it and draining into the Lehigh River in nearby Allentown. South Mountain crosses the southern tier of the township, slightly south of the Alburtis and Macungie Boroughs.

East Penn School District serves Lower Macungie Township along with the Boroughs of Alburtis, Emmaus, Macungie, and Upper Milford Township. One high school, two middle schools, and seven elementary schools reside within this district.

Lower Macungie Township offers 28 parks to explore, with walking trails/paths, ball fields, and multiple pavilions for the community to enjoy. Another area to experience is the Lower Macungie Community Center, built atop a plot of land which rises above the Lower Macungie Township Municipal Campus, housing a state-of-the-art gymnasium, two community rooms with numerous amenities, and a 10,000- square foot, hi-tech library. Programs include adult and children classes, and adult fitness sessions. The Township also provides free summer concerts for its community, boasting a wide range of music for people to enjoy.

Lower Macungie Township houses the main manufacturing facilities of Mack Trucks and special effects manufacturer Smooth-On.

The Township has a humid-continental climate with hot summers.

Rankings

Business/Finance Rankings

- The personal finance site NerdWallet analyzed 183 American metropolitan areas with populations over 250,000 and more than 15,000 businesses to rank where entrepreneurs find the most success. Criteria included area economy, annual income, housing cost, unemployment rate, and the success rate of area businesses. Allentown* ranked #114. *www.nerdwallet.com, "Best Places to Start a Business," April 27, 2015*
- The Brookings Institution ranked the 100 largest metro areas in the U.S. based on income inequality. Allentown* was ranked #87 (#1 = greatest ineqality). Criteria: the "95/20 ratio," a figure representing the income at which a household earns more than 95 percent of all other households, divided by the income at which a household earns more than only 20 percent of all other households. *Brookings Institution, "Household Income Inequality, 100 Largest U.S. Metro Areas, 2014-2016," February 5, 2018*
- The Allentown* metro area appeared on the Milken Institute "2017 Best Performing Cities" list. Rank: #119 out of 200 large metro areas. Criteria: job growth; wage and salary growth; high-tech output growth. *Milken Institute, "Best-Performing Cities 2017," January 2018*
- *Forbes* ranked the 200 most populous metro areas to determine the nation's "Best Places for Business and Careers." The Allentown* metro area was ranked #151. Criteria: costs (business and living); job growth (past and projected); income growth; quality of life; educational attainment (college and high school); projected economic growth; cultural and recreational opportunities; net migration patterns; number of highly ranked colleges. *Forbes, "The Best Places for Business and Careers 2017," October 24, 2017*

Children/Family Rankings

- *Forbes* analyzed data on the 100 largest metropolitan areas in the United States to compile its 2016 ranking of the best cities for raising a family. The Allentown* metro area was ranked #4. Criteria: median income; childcare costs; percent of population under 18; commuting delays; crime rate; percentage of families owning homes; education quality (mainly test scores). Overall cost of living and housing affordability was also unofficially considered. *Forbes, "America's Best Cities for Raising a Family 2016," August 30, 2016*

Education Rankings

- Personal finance website *WalletHub* analyzed the 150 largest U.S. metropolitan statistical areas to determine where the most educated Americans are choosing to settle. Criteria: education quality and attainment gap; education levels; percentage of workers with degrees; public school rankings; quality and size of each metro area's universities. Allentown* was ranked #90 (#1 = most educated city). *www.WalletHub.com, "2017's Most and Least Educated Cities in America," July 25, 2017*

Environmental Rankings

- Sperling's BestPlaces assessed 379 metropolitan areas of the United States for the likelihood of dangerously extreme weather events or earthquakes. In general the Southeast and South-Central regions have the highest risk of weather extremes and earthquakes, while the Pacific Northwest enjoys the lowest risk. Of the least risky metropolitan areas, the Allentown* metro area was ranked #152. *www.bestplaces.net, "Safest Places from Natural Disasters," April 2011*

Health/Fitness Rankings

- Allentown* was identified as a "2016 Spring Allergy Capital." The area ranked #46 out of 100. Three groups of factors were used to identify the most severe cities for people with allergies during the spring season: annual pollen levels; medicine utilization; access to board-certified allergists. *Asthma and Allergy Foundation of America, "Spring Allergy Capitals 2016"*

- Allentown* was identified as a "2016 Fall Allergy Capital." The area ranked #58 out of 100. Three groups of factors were used to identify the most severe cities for people with allergies during the fall season: annual pollen levels; medicine utilization; access to board-certified allergists. *Asthma and Allergy Foundation of America, "Fall Allergy Capitals 2016"*
- Allentown* was identified as a "2015 Asthma Capital." The area ranked #19 out of the nation's 100 largest metropolitan areas. Criteria: estimated prevalence; self-reported prevalence; crude death rate for asthma; annual pollen score; annual air quality; public smoking laws; number of board-certified asthma specialists; school inhaler access laws; rescue medication use; controller medication use; ER visits for asthma; uninsured rate; poverty rate. *Asthma and Allergy Foundation of America, "Asthma Capitals 2015"*
- The Allentown* metro area ranked #89 out of 189 in The Gallup-Healthways Well-Being Index. Criteria: purpose; social well being; financial health; community and physical health. Results are based on telephone interviews with adults, aged 18 and older, living in metropolitan areas in the 50 U.S. states and the District of Columbia. *Gallup-Healthways, "State of American Well-Being, 2017 Community Well-Being Rankings" March 2018*

Real Estate Rankings

- The Allentown* metro area was identified as one of the 20 worst housing markets in the U.S. in 2017. The area ranked #20 out of 180 markets. Criteria: year-over-year change of median sales price of existing single-family homes between the 4th quarter of 2016 and the 4th quarter of 2017. *National Association of Realtors®, Median Sales Price of Existing Single-Family Homes for Metropolitan Areas, 4th Quarter 2017*
- Allentown* was ranked #81 out of 238 metro areas in terms of housing affordability in 2017 by the National Association of Home Builders (#1 = most affordable). Criteria: the share of homes sold in that area affordable to a family earning the local median income, based on standard mortgage underwriting criteria. *National Association of Home Builders®, NAHB-Wells Fargo Housing Opportunity Index, 4th Quarter 2017*

Safety Rankings

- The National Insurance Crime Bureau ranked 382 metro areas in the U.S. in terms of per capita rates of vehicle theft. The Allentown* metro area ranked #300 (#1 = highest rate). Criteria: number of vehicle theft offenses per 100,000 inhabitants in 2016. *National Insurance Crime Bureau, "Hot Spots 2016," June 8, 2017*

Seniors/Retirement Rankings

- From its Best Cities for Successful Aging indexes, the Milken Institute generated rankings for metropolitan areas, weighing data in nine categories—health care, wellness, living arrangements, transportation and convenience, financial characteristics, education, employment, community engagement, and overall livability. The Allentown* metro area was ranked #73 overall in the large metro area category. *Milken Institute, "Best Cities for Successful Aging, 2017" March 14, 2017*

*Lower Macungie is located within the Allentown-Bethlehem-Easton, PA-NJ Metropolitan Statistical Area.

Business Environment

CITY FINANCES

City Government Finances

Component	2015 ($000)	2015 ($ per capita)
Total Revenues	17,704	557
Total Expenditures	14,890	468
Debt Outstanding	2,455	77
Cash and Securities[1]	9,929	312

Note: (1) Cash and security holdings of a government at the close of its fiscal year,, including those of its dependent agencies, utilities, and liquor stores.
Source: U.S Census Bureau, State & Local Government Finances 2015

City Government Revenue by Source

Source	2015 ($000)	2015 ($ per capita)	2015 (%)
General Revenue			
From Federal Government	0	0	0.0
From State Government	2,077	65	11.7
From Local Governments	0	0	0.0
Taxes			
Property	1,041	33	5.9
Sales and Gross Receipts	0	0	0.0
Personal Income	5,389	169	30.4
Corporate Income	0	0	0.0
Motor Vehicle License	0	0	0.0
Other Taxes	2,088	66	11.8
Current Charges	6,317	199	35.7
Liquor Store	0	0	0.0
Utility	0	0	0.0
Employee Retirement	0	0	0.0

Source: U.S Census Bureau, State & Local Government Finances 2015

City Government Expenditures by Function

Function	2015 ($000)	2015 ($ per capita)	2015 (%)
General Direct Expenditures			
Air Transportation	0	0	0.0
Corrections	0	0	0.0
Education	0	0	0.0
Employment Security Administration	0	0	0.0
Financial Administration	287	9	1.9
Fire Protection	571	18	3.8
General Public Buildings	730	23	4.9
Governmental Administration, Other	643	20	4.3
Health	0	0	0.0
Highways	2,352	73	15.8
Hospitals	0	0	0.0
Housing and Community Development	0	0	0.0
Interest on General Debt	79	2	0.5
Judicial and Legal	172	5	1.2
Libraries	0	0	0.0
Parking	0	0	0.0
Parks and Recreation	2,203	69	14.8
Police Protection	61	1	0.4
Public Welfare	0	0	0.0
Sewerage	2,723	85	18.3
Solid Waste Management	2,440	76	16.4
Veterans' Services	0	0	0.0
Liquor Store	0	0	0.0
Utility	0	0	0.0
Employee Retirement	0	0	0.0

Source: U.S Census Bureau, State & Local Government Finances 2015

DEMOGRAPHICS

Population Growth

Area	1990 Census	2000 Census	2010 Census	2016* Estimate	Population Growth (%) 1990-2016	Population Growth (%) 2010-2016
City	16,832	19,220	30,633	31,662	88.1	3.4
MSA[1]	686,666	740,395	821,173	830,737	21.0	1.2
U.S.	248,709,873	281,421,906	308,745,538	318,558,162	28.1	3.2

Note: (1) Figures cover the Allentown-Bethlehem-Easton, PA-NJ Metropolitan Statistical Area—see Appendix B for areas included; (*) 2012-2016 5-year estimated population
Source: U.S. Census Bureau, 1990 Census, Census 2000, Census 2010, 2012-2016 American Community Survey 5-Year Estimates

Household Size

Area	Persons in Household (%) One	Two	Three	Four	Five	Six	Seven or More	Average Household Size
City	23.8	36.0	15.4	17.2	5.1	1.7	0.7	2.60
MSA[1]	26.0	34.9	16.4	13.6	6.1	2.0	1.1	2.60
U.S.	27.7	33.7	15.7	13.1	6.0	2.3	1.5	2.60

Note: (1) Figures cover the Allentown-Bethlehem-Easton, PA-NJ Metropolitan Statistical Area—see Appendix B for areas included
Source: U.S. Census Bureau, 2012-2016 American Community Survey 5-Year Estimates

Race

Area	White Alone[2] (%)	Black Alone[2] (%)	Asian Alone[2] (%)	AIAN[3] Alone[2] (%)	NHOPI[4] Alone[2] (%)	Other Race Alone[2] (%)	Two or More Races (%)
City	85.9	3.6	5.2	0.0	0.0	1.9	3.4
MSA[1]	84.2	5.4	2.8	0.3	0.0	4.6	2.7
U.S.	73.3	12.6	5.2	0.8	0.2	4.8	3.1

Note: (1) Figures cover the Allentown-Bethlehem-Easton, PA-NJ Metropolitan Statistical Area—see Appendix B for areas included; (2) Alone is defined as not being in combination with one or more other races; (3) American Indian and Alaska Native; (4) Native Hawaiian and Other Pacific Islander
Source: U.S. Census Bureau, 2012-2016 American Community Survey 5-Year Estimates

Hispanic or Latino Origin

Area	Total (%)	Mexican (%)	Puerto Rican (%)	Cuban (%)	Other (%)
City	7.1	1.6	3.0	0.1	2.4
MSA[1]	15.2	1.2	8.4	0.3	5.3
U.S.	17.3	11.0	1.7	0.7	4.0

Note: Persons of Hispanic or Latino origin can be of any race; (1) Figures cover the Allentown-Bethlehem-Easton, PA-NJ Metropolitan Statistical Area—see Appendix B for areas included
Source: U.S. Census Bureau, 2012-2016 American Community Survey 5-Year Estimates

Segregation

Type	Segregation Indices[1] 1990	2000	2010	2010 Rank[2]	Percent Change 1990-2000	1990-2010	2000-2010
Black/White	53.6	51.7	47.2	78	-1.9	-6.4	-4.5
Asian/White	37.6	38.0	38.0	67	0.4	0.4	0.0
Hispanic/White	58.2	60.0	55.4	11	1.8	-2.8	-4.6

Note: All figures cover the Metropolitan Statistical Area—see Appendix B for areas included; Figures are based on an analysis of 1990, 2000, and 2010 Census Decennial Census tract data by William H. Frey, Brookings Institution and the University of Michigan Social Science Data Analysis Network. In this analysis all racial groups (whites, blacks, and asians) are non-Hispanic members of those races. Hispanics are shown as a separate category; (1) Segregation Indices are Dissimilarity Indices that measure the degree to which the minority group is distributed differently than whites across census tracts. They range from 0 (complete integration) to 100 (complete segregation) where the value indicates the percentage of the minority group that needs to move to be distributed exactly like whites; (2) Ranges from 1 (most segregated) to 102 (least segregated); n/a not available.
Source: www.CensusScope.org

Ancestry

Area	German	Irish	English	American	Italian	Polish	French[2]	Scottish	Dutch
City	30.2	16.3	7.6	5.7	11.8	5.2	2.3	1.3	2.3
MSA[1]	25.8	13.6	6.1	5.2	12.7	5.6	1.6	1.1	2.6
U.S.	14.4	10.4	7.7	6.9	5.4	2.9	2.6	1.7	1.3

Note: Figures are the percentage of the total population reporting a particular ancestry. The nine most commonly reported ancestries in the U.S. are shown. Figures include multiple ancestries (e.g. if a person reported being Irish and Italian, they were included in both columns); (1) Figures cover the Allentown-Bethlehem-Easton, PA-NJ Metropolitan Statistical Area—see Appendix B for areas included; (2) Excludes Basque
Source: U.S. Census Bureau, 2012-2016 American Community Survey 5-Year Estimates

Foreign-Born Population

Area	Percent of Population Born in								
	Any Foreign Country	Asia	Mexico	Europe	Carribean	Central America[2]	South America	Africa	Canada
City	9.2	4.3	0.2	2.3	0.7	0.0	1.1	0.4	0.1
MSA[1]	8.7	2.6	0.4	1.7	1.7	0.5	1.2	0.4	0.1
U.S.	13.2	4.0	3.6	1.5	1.3	1.0	0.9	0.6	0.3

Note: (1) Figures cover the Allentown-Bethlehem-Easton, PA-NJ Metropolitan Statistical Area—see Appendix B for areas included; (2) Excludes Mexico.
Source: U.S. Census Bureau, 2012-2016 American Community Survey 5-Year Estimates

Marital Status

Area	Never Married	Now Married[2]	Separated	Widowed	Divorced
City	21.1	63.5	1.4	6.5	7.5
MSA[1]	30.9	50.2	2.3	6.7	9.9
U.S.	33.0	48.1	2.1	5.9	11.0

Note: Figures are percentages and cover the population 15 years of age and older; (1) Figures cover the Allentown-Bethlehem-Easton, PA-NJ Metropolitan Statistical Area—see Appendix B for areas included; (2) Excludes separated
Source: U.S. Census Bureau, 2012-2016 American Community Survey 5-Year Estimates

Disability Status

Area	All Ages	Under 18 Years Old	18 to 64 Years Old	65 Years and Over
City	10.7	6.4	6.8	27.9
MSA[1]	13.4	5.8	10.9	33.5
U.S.	12.5	4.1	10.3	35.7

Note: Figures show percent of the civilian noninstitutionalized population that reported having a disability. Disability status is determined from six types of difficulty: vision, hearing, cognitive, ambulatory, self-care, and independent living. For children under 5 years old, hearing and vision difficulty are used to determine disability status. For children between the ages of 5 and 14, disability status is determined from hearing, vision, cognitive, ambulatory, and self-care difficulties. For people aged 15 years and older, they are considered to have a disability if they have difficulty with any one of the six difficulty types; Note: (1) Figures cover the Allentown-Bethlehem-Easton, PA-NJ Metropolitan Statistical Area—see Appendix B for areas included
Source: U.S. Census Bureau, 2012-2016 American Community Survey 5-Year Estimates

Age

Area	Percent of Population									Median Age
	Under Age 5	Age 5–19	Age 20–34	Age 35–44	Age 45–54	Age 55–64	Age 65–74	Age 75–84	Age 85+	
City	5.5	20.1	13.9	13.6	15.2	12.3	10.7	6.4	2.3	43.1
MSA[1]	5.4	19.0	18.3	12.2	14.8	13.7	9.0	5.0	2.7	41.3
U.S.	6.2	19.6	20.7	12.7	13.6	12.6	8.3	4.3	1.9	37.7

Note: (1) Figures cover the Allentown-Bethlehem-Easton, PA-NJ Metropolitan Statistical Area—see Appendix B for areas included
Source: U.S. Census Bureau, 2012-2016 American Community Survey 5-Year Estimates

Gender

Area	Males	Females	Males per 100 Females
City	15,474	16,188	95.6
MSA[1]	406,498	424,239	95.8
U.S.	156,765,322	161,792,840	96.9

Note: (1) Figures cover the Allentown-Bethlehem-Easton, PA-NJ Metropolitan Statistical Area—see Appendix B for areas included
Source: U.S. Census Bureau, 2012-2016 American Community Survey 5-Year Estimates

Religious Groups by Family

Area	Catholic	Baptist	Non-Den.	Methodist[2]	Lutheran	LDS[3]	Pente-costal	Presby-terian[4]	Muslim[5]	Judaism
MSA[1]	23.2	0.5	1.9	3.9	8.0	0.3	0.5	6.2	0.6	0.6
U.S.	19.1	9.3	4.0	4.0	2.3	2.0	1.9	1.6	0.8	0.7

Note: Figures are the number of adherents as a percentage of the total population; (1) Figures cover the Allentown-Bethlehem-Easton, PA-NJ Metropolitan Statistical Area—see Appendix B for areas included; (2) Methodist/Pietist; (3) Latter Day Saints; (4) Reformed; (5) Figures are estimates
Source: Association of Statisticians of American Religious Bodies, 2010 U.S. Religion Census: Religious Congregations & Membership Study

Religious Groups by Tradition

Area	Catholic	Evangelical Protestant	Mainline Protestant	Other Tradition	Black Protestant	Orthodox
MSA[1]	23.2	5.4	17.8	3.0	0.1	0.6
U.S.	19.1	16.2	7.3	4.3	1.6	0.3

Note: Figures are the number of adherents as a percentage of the total population; (1) Figures cover the Allentown-Bethlehem-Easton, PA-NJ Metropolitan Statistical Area—see Appendix B for areas included
Source: Association of Statisticians of American Religious Bodies, 2010 U.S. Religion Census: Religious Congregations & Membership Study

ECONOMY

Gross Metropolitan Product

Area	2014	2015	2016	2017	Rank[2]
MSA[1]	35.2	36.5	37.5	39.0	75

Note: Figures are in billions of dollars; (1) Figures cover the Allentown-Bethlehem-Easton, PA-NJ Metropolitan Statistical Area—see Appendix B for areas included; (2) Rank is based on 2015 data and ranges from 1 to 381
Source: The U.S. Conference of Mayors, U.S. Metro Economies: GMP and Employment Report, 2015-2017

Economic Growth

Area	2012-14 (%)	2015 (%)	2016 (%)	2017 (%)	Rank[2]
MSA[1]	1.7	2.1	1.3	2.0	148
U.S.	2.0	2.4	1.9	2.6	–

Note: Figures are real gross metropolitan product (GMP) growth rates and represent average annual percent change; (1) Figures cover the Allentown-Bethlehem-Easton, PA-NJ Metropolitan Statistical Area—see Appendix B for areas included; (2) Rank is based on 2012-2014 average annual percent change and ranges from 1 to 381
Source: The U.S. Conference of Mayors, U.S. Metro Economies: GMP and Employment Report, 2015-2017

Metropolitan Area Exports

Area	2011	2012	2013	2014	2015	2016	Rank[2]
MSA[1]	2,955.2	2,939.0	2,949.9	3,152.5	3,439.9	3,657.2	65

Note: Figures are in millions of dollars; (1) Figures cover the Allentown-Bethlehem-Easton, PA-NJ Metropolitan Statistical Area—see Appendix B for areas included; (2) Rank is based on 2016 data and ranges from 1 to 385
Source: U.S. Department of Commerce, International Trade Administration, Office of Trade & Industry Information, Manufacturing & Services, data extracted March 15, 2018

Building Permits

Area	Single-Family 2016	Single-Family 2017p	Single-Family Pct. Chg.	Multi-Family 2016	Multi-Family 2017p	Multi-Family Pct. Chg.	Total 2016	Total 2017p	Total Pct. Chg.
City	n/a	n/a	n/a	n/a	n/a	n/a	n/a	n/a	n/a
MSA[1]	329	298	-9.4	153	110	-28.1	482	408	-15.4
U.S.	750,800	817,300	8.9	455,800	446,800	-2.0	1,206,600	1,264,100	4.8

Note: (1) Figures cover the Allentown-Bethlehem-Easton, PA-NJ Metropolitan Statistical Area—see Appendix B for areas included; Figures represent new, privately-owned housing units authorized (unadjusted data); All permit data are based on estimates with imputation; (p) preliminary data.
Source: U.S. Census Bureau, Manufacturing, Mining, and Construction Statistics, Building Permits, 2016, 2017

Bankruptcy Filings

Area	Business Filings 2016	Business Filings 2017	Business Filings % Chg.	Nonbusiness Filings 2016	Nonbusiness Filings 2017	Nonbusiness Filings % Chg.
Lehigh County	25	27	8.0	603	585	-3.0
U.S.	24,114	23,157	-4.0	770,846	765,863	-0.6

Note: Business filings include Chapter 7, Chapter 11, Chapter 12, and Chapter 13; Nonbusiness filings include Chapter 7, Chapter 11, and Chapter 13
Source: Administrative Office of the U.S. Courts, Business and Nonbusiness Bankruptcy, County Cases Commenced by Chapter of the Bankruptcy Code, During the 12-Month Period Ending December 31, 2016 and Business and Nonbusiness Bankruptcy, County Cases Commenced by Chapter of the Bankruptcy Code, During the 12-Month Period Ending December 31, 2017

Housing Vacancy Rates

Area	Gross Vacancy Rate[2] (%) 2015	2016	2017	Year-Round Vacancy Rate[3] (%) 2015	2016	2017	Rental Vacancy Rate[4] (%) 2015	2016	2017	Homeowner Vacancy Rate[5] (%) 2015	2016	2017
MSA[1]	9.1	7.4	9.5	6.5	5.2	8.5	3.7	4.2	5.3	1.7	1.1	1.7
U.S.	12.9	12.8	12.7	10.0	9.9	9.9	7.1	6.9	7.2	1.8	1.7	1.6

Note: (1) Figures cover the Allentown-Bethlehem-Easton, PA-NJ Metropolitan Statistical Area—see Appendix B for areas included; (2) The percentage of the total housing inventory that is vacant; (3) The percentage of the housing inventory (excluding seasonal units) that is year-round vacant; (4) The percentage of rental inventory that is vacant for rent; (5) The percentage of homeowner inventory that is vacant for sale
Source: U.S. Census Bureau, Housing Vacancies and Homeownership Annual Statistics: 2015, 2016, 2017

INCOME

Income

Area	Per Capita ($)	Median Household ($)	Average Household ($)
City	41,369	81,929	105,584
MSA[1]	30,579	60,441	78,662
U.S.	29,829	55,322	77,866

Note: (1) Figures cover the Allentown-Bethlehem-Easton, PA-NJ Metropolitan Statistical Area—see Appendix B for areas included
Source: U.S. Census Bureau, 2012-2016 American Community Survey 5-Year Estimates

Household Income Distribution

Area	Percent of Households Earning: Under $15,000	$15,000 -$24,999	$25,000 -$34,999	$35,000 -$49,999	$50,000 -$74,999	$75,000 -$99,999	$100,000 -$149,999	$150,000 and up
City	4.0	6.1	8.4	11.4	16.6	13.7	20.9	18.9
MSA[1]	9.1	9.4	9.3	13.3	19.1	13.7	15.3	10.7
U.S.	12.1	10.2	9.9	13.2	17.8	12.2	13.5	11.1

Note: (1) Figures cover the Allentown-Bethlehem-Easton, PA-NJ Metropolitan Statistical Area—see Appendix B for areas included
Source: U.S. Census Bureau, 2012-2016 American Community Survey 5-Year Estimates

Poverty Rate

Area	All Ages	Under 18 Years Old	18 to 64 Years Old	65 Years and Over
City	2.8	2.5	3.2	2.1
MSA[1]	10.9	16.9	10.0	5.9
U.S.	15.1	21.2	14.2	9.3

Note: Figures are percentage of people whose income during the past 12 months was below the poverty level; (1) Figures cover the Allentown-Bethlehem-Easton, PA-NJ Metropolitan Statistical Area—see Appendix B for areas included
Source: U.S. Census Bureau, 2012-2016 American Community Survey 5-Year Estimates

EMPLOYMENT

Labor Force and Employment

Area	Civilian Labor Force			Workers Employed		
	Dec. 2016	Dec. 2017	% Chg.	Dec. 2016	Dec. 2017	% Chg.
City	16,533	16,308	-1.4	15,908	15,766	-0.9
MSA[1]	434,946	429,942	-1.2	415,241	411,484	-0.9
U.S.	158,968,000	159,880,000	0.6	151,798,000	153,602,000	1.2

Note: Data is not seasonally adjusted and covers workers 16 years of age and older; (1) Figures cover the Allentown-Bethlehem-Easton, PA-NJ Metropolitan Statistical Area—see Appendix B for areas included
Source: Bureau of Labor Statistics, Local Area Unemployment Statistics

Unemployment Rate

Area	2017											
	Jan.	Feb.	Mar.	Apr.	May	Jun.	Jul.	Aug.	Sep.	Oct.	Nov.	Dec.
City	4.1	4.3	3.9	3.6	3.8	3.9	4.2	4.5	3.5	3.3	3.4	3.3
MSA[1]	5.5	5.6	5.2	4.5	4.9	4.9	5.3	5.4	4.5	4.4	4.4	4.3
U.S.	5.1	4.9	4.6	4.1	4.1	4.5	4.6	4.5	4.1	3.9	3.9	3.9

Note: Data is not seasonally adjusted and covers workers 16 years of age and older; (1) Figures cover the Allentown-Bethlehem-Easton, PA-NJ Metropolitan Statistical Area—see Appendix B for areas included
Source: Bureau of Labor Statistics, Local Area Unemployment Statistics

Average Wages

Occupation	$/Hr.	Occupation	$/Hr.
Accountants and Auditors	37.00	Maids and Housekeeping Cleaners	11.00
Automotive Mechanics	20.90	Maintenance and Repair Workers	19.20
Bookkeepers	18.30	Marketing Managers	69.30
Carpenters	23.80	Nuclear Medicine Technologists	35.50
Cashiers	9.80	Nurses, Licensed Practical	23.20
Clerks, General Office	16.50	Nurses, Registered	32.70
Clerks, Receptionists/Information	13.90	Nursing Assistants	14.90
Clerks, Shipping/Receiving	17.30	Packers and Packagers, Hand	13.40
Computer Programmers	33.00	Physical Therapists	41.50
Computer Systems Analysts	42.60	Postal Service Mail Carriers	24.10
Computer User Support Specialists	25.20	Real Estate Brokers	n/a
Cooks, Restaurant	13.00	Retail Salespersons	12.70
Dentists	94.70	Sales Reps., Exc. Tech./Scientific	35.00
Electrical Engineers	39.40	Sales Reps., Tech./Scientific	43.50
Electricians	28.70	Secretaries, Exc. Legal/Med./Exec.	17.30
Financial Managers	72.60	Security Guards	12.70
First-Line Supervisors/Managers, Sales	22.40	Surgeons	82.60
Food Preparation Workers	11.50	Teacher Assistants*	12.60
General and Operations Managers	61.10	Teachers, Elementary School*	33.30
Hairdressers/Cosmetologists	14.00	Teachers, Secondary School*	32.00
Internists, General	n/a	Telemarketers	16.00
Janitors and Cleaners	14.60	Truck Drivers, Heavy/Tractor-Trailer	23.20
Landscaping/Groundskeeping Workers	13.10	Truck Drivers, Light/Delivery Svcs.	17.70
Lawyers	58.20	Waiters and Waitresses	11.60

Note: Wage data covers the Allentown-Bethlehem-Easton, PA-NJ Metropolitan Statistical Area—see Appendix B for areas included; (*) Hourly wages for elementary/secondary school teachers and teacher assistants were calculated by the editors from annual wage data based on a 40 hour work week; n/a not available.
Source: Bureau of Labor Statistics, Metro Area Occupational Employment & Wage Estimates, May 2017

Employment by Occupation

Occupation Classification	City (%)	MSA[1] (%)	U.S. (%)
Management, Business, Science, and Arts	52.5	34.4	37.0
Natural Resources, Construction, and Maintenance	4.4	8.2	8.9
Production, Transportation, and Material Moving	8.6	15.3	12.2
Sales and Office	23.0	24.8	23.8
Service	11.5	17.4	18.1

Note: Figures cover employed civilians 16 years of age and older; (1) Figures cover the Allentown-Bethlehem-Easton, PA-NJ Metropolitan Statistical Area—see Appendix B for areas included
Source: U.S. Census Bureau, 2012-2016 American Community Survey 5-Year Estimates

Employment by Industry

Sector	MSA[1] Number of Employees	MSA[1] Percent of Total	U.S. Percent of Total
Construction, Mining, and Logging	13,400	3.6	5.2
Education and Health Services	77,200	20.7	15.9
Financial Activities	14,400	3.9	5.7
Government	40,800	10.9	15.3
Information	5,400	1.4	1.9
Leisure and Hospitality	35,400	9.5	10.7
Manufacturing	36,700	9.8	8.5
Other Services	14,500	3.9	3.9
Professional and Business Services	48,600	13.0	14.0
Retail Trade	40,400	10.8	11.0
Transportation, Warehousing, and Utilities	31,400	8.4	4.1
Wholesale Trade	14,800	4.0	4.0

Note: Figures are non-farm employment as of December 2017. Figures are not seasonally adjusted and include workers 16 years of age and older; (1) Figures cover the Allentown-Bethlehem-Easton, PA-NJ Metropolitan Statistical Area—see Appendix B for areas included
Source: Bureau of Labor Statistics, Current Employment Statistics, Employment, Hours, and Earnings

Occupations with Greatest Projected Employment Growth: 2017 – 2019

Occupation[1]	2017 Employment	2019 Projected Employment	Numeric Employment Change	Percent Employment Change
Personal Care Aides	95,040	101,150	6,110	6.4
Combined Food Preparation and Serving Workers, Including Fast Food	149,690	154,700	5,010	3.3
Registered Nurses	143,300	147,290	3,990	2.8
Laborers and Freight, Stock, and Material Movers, Hand	138,050	141,860	3,810	2.8
Home Health Aides	46,950	50,700	3,750	8.0
Waiters and Waitresses	100,790	102,540	1,750	1.7
Janitors and Cleaners, Except Maids and Housekeeping Cleaners	98,590	100,250	1,660	1.7
Cooks, Restaurant	49,820	51,120	1,300	2.6
Software Developers, Applications	25,890	27,190	1,300	5.0
Nursing Assistants	80,510	81,790	1,280	1.6

Note: Projections cover Pennsylvania; (1) Sorted by numeric employment change
Source: www.projectionscentral.com, State Occupational Projections, 2017–2019 Short-Term Projections

Fastest Growing Occupations: 2017 – 2019

Occupation[1]	2017 Employment	2019 Projected Employment	Numeric Employment Change	Percent Employment Change
Home Health Aides	46,950	50,700	3,750	8.0
Statisticians	2,710	2,880	170	6.5
Personal Care Aides	95,040	101,150	6,110	6.4
Physician Assistants	5,620	5,960	340	6.1
Nurse Practitioners	5,240	5,550	310	6.0
Operations Research Analysts	2,660	2,800	140	5.1
Information Security Analysts	3,020	3,170	150	5.0
Software Developers, Applications	25,890	27,190	1,300	5.0
Nonfarm Animal Caretakers	7,820	8,210	390	4.9
Physical Therapist Assistants	4,660	4,880	220	4.8

Note: Projections cover Pennsylvania; (1) Sorted by percent employment change and excludes occupations with numeric employment change less than 50
Source: www.projectionscentral.com, State Occupational Projections, 2017–2019 Short-Term Projections

TAXES

State Corporate Income Tax Rates

State	Tax Rate (%)	Income Brackets ($)	Num. of Brackets	Financial Institution Tax Rate (%)[a]	Federal Income Tax Ded.
Pennsylvania	9.99	Flat rate	1	(a)	No

Note: Tax rates as of January 1, 2018; (a) Rates listed are the corporate income tax rate applied to financial institutions or excise taxes based on income. Some states have other taxes based upon the value of deposits or shares.
Source: Federation of Tax Administrators, Range of State Corporate Income Tax Rates, January 1, 2018

State Individual Income Tax Rates

State	Tax Rate (%)	Income Brackets ($)	Num. of Brackets	Personal Exempt. ($)[1]		Fed. Inc. Tax Ded.
				Single	Dependents	
Pennsylvania	3.07	Flat rate	1	None	None	No

Note: Tax rates as of January 1, 2018; Local- and county-level taxes are not included; n/a not applicable; (1) Married joint filers generally receive double the single exemption
Source: Federation of Tax Administrators, State Individual Income Tax Rates, January 1, 2018

Various State Sales and Excise Tax Rates

State	State Sales Tax (%)	Gasoline[1] (¢/gal.)	Cigarette[2] ($/pack)	Spirits[3] ($/gal.)	Wine[4] ($/gal.)	Beer[5] ($/gal.)	Recreational Marijuana (%)
Pennsylvania	6.0	58.7	2.60	7.24 (g)	(m)	0.08	Not legal

Note: All tax rates as of January 1, 2018; (1) The American Petroleum Institute has developed a methodology for determining the average tax rate on a gallon of fuel. Rates may include any of the following: excise taxes, environmental fees, storage tank fees, other fees or taxes, general sales tax, and local taxes. In states where gasoline is subject to the general sales tax, or where the fuel tax is based on the average sale price, the average rate determined by API is sensitive to changes in the price of gasoline. States that fully or partially apply general sales taxes to gasoline: CA, CO, GA, IL, IN, MI, NY; (2) The federal excise tax of $1.0066 per pack and local taxes are not included; (3) Rates are those applicable to off-premise sales of 40% alcohol by volume (a.b.v.) distilled spirits in 750ml containers. Local excise taxes are excluded; (4) Rates are those applicable to off-premise sales of 11% a.b.v. non-carbonated wine in 750ml containers; (5) Rates are those applicable to off-premise sales of 4.7% a.b.v. beer in 12 ounce containers; (g) Control states, where the government controls all sales. Products can be subject to ad valorem mark-up as well as excise taxes; (m) Control states, where the government controls all sales. Products can be subject to ad valorem mark-up as well as excise taxes.
Source: Tax Foundation, 2018 Facts & Figures: How Does Your State Compare?

State Business Tax Climate Index Rankings

State	Overall Rank	Corporate Tax Rank	Individual Income Tax Rank	Sales Tax Rank	Unemployment Insurance Tax Rank	Property Tax Rank
Pennsylvania	26	44	17	21	50	33

Note: The index is a measure of how each state's tax laws affect economic performance. The lower the rank, the more favorable a state's tax system is for business. States without a given tax are given a ranking of 1. The scores/rankings for the District of Columbia do not affect other states. The 2018 index represents the tax climate as of July 1, 2017.
Source: Tax Foundation, State Business Tax Climate Index 2018

TRANSPORTATION

Means of Transportation to Work

Area	Car/Truck/Van		Public Transportation			Bicycle	Walked	Other Means	Worked at Home
	Drove Alone	Car-pooled	Bus	Subway	Railroad				
City	87.1	3.9	1.0	0.1	0.0	0.2	0.6	0.3	6.9
MSA[1]	81.7	8.5	1.8	0.0	0.0	0.3	2.6	1.1	4.0
U.S.	76.4	9.3	2.6	1.9	0.6	0.6	2.8	1.3	4.6

Note: Figures are percentages and cover workers 16 years of age and older; (1) Figures cover the Allentown-Bethlehem-Easton, PA-NJ Metropolitan Statistical Area—see Appendix B for areas included
Source: U.S. Census Bureau, 2012-2016 American Community Survey 5-Year Estimates

Travel Time to Work

Area	Less Than 10 Minutes	10 to 19 Minutes	20 to 29 Minutes	30 to 44 Minutes	45 to 59 Minutes	60 to 89 Minutes	90 Minutes or More
City	15.5	33.2	21.0	13.8	5.8	7.6	3.0
MSA[1]	12.7	28.3	21.8	18.3	7.4	7.5	4.1
U.S.	12.9	29.2	20.9	20.4	8.0	6.0	2.7

Note: Note: Figures are percentages and include workers 16 years old and over; (1) Figures cover the Allentown-Bethlehem-Easton, PA-NJ Metropolitan Statistical Area—see Appendix B for areas included
Source: U.S. Census Bureau, 2012-2016 American Community Survey 5-Year Estimates

Freeway Travel Time Index

Area	1985	1990	1995	2000	2005	2010	2014
Urban Area Rank[1,2]	48	76	36	37	51	48	54
Urban Area Index[1]	1.07	1.07	1.15	1.18	1.17	1.17	1.17
Average Index[3]	1.09	1.11	1.14	1.17	1.20	1.19	1.20

Note: Freeway Travel Time Index—the ratio of travel time in the peak period to the travel time at free-flow conditions. For example, a value of 1.30 indicates a 20-minute free-flow trip takes 26 minutes in the peak (20 minutes x 1.30 = 26 minutes); (1) Covers the Allentown PA-NJ urban area; (2) Rank is based on 101 urban areas (#1 = highest travel time index); (3) Average of 101 urban areas
Source: Texas Transportation Institute, 2015 Urban Mobility Scorecard, August 2015

Freeway Commuter Stress Index

Area	1985	1990	1995	2000	2005	2010	2014
Urban Area Rank[1,2]	53	75	46	46	58	58	61
Urban Area Index[1]	1.09	1.09	1.17	1.20	1.19	1.19	1.19
Average Index[3]	1.13	1.16	1.19	1.22	1.25	1.24	1.25

Note: The Freeway Commuter Stress Index is the same as the Freeway Travel Time Index (see table above) except that it includes only the travel in the peak directions during the peak periods; the TTI includes travel in all directions during the peak period. Thus, the CSI is more indicative of the work trip experienced by each commuter on a daily basis; (1) Covers the Allentown PA-NJ urban area; (2) Rank is based on 101 urban areas (#1 = highest travel time index); (3) Average of 101 urban areas
Source: Texas Transportation Institute, 2015 Urban Mobility Scorecard, August 2015

Living Environment

COST OF LIVING

Cost of Living Index

Composite Index	Groceries	Housing	Utilities	Trans-portation	Health Care	Misc. Goods/ Services
105.7	100.1	115.9	97.7	109.5	101.4	101.6

Note: The Cost of Living Index measures regional differences in the cost of consumer goods and services, excluding taxes and non-consumer expenditures, for professional and managerial households in the top income quintile. It is based on more than 50,000 prices covering almost 60 different items for which prices are collected three times a year by chambers of commerce, economic development organizations or university applied economic centers in each participating urban area. The numbers shown should be read as a percentage above or below the national average of 100. For example, a value of 115.4 in the groceries column indicates that grocery prices are 15.4% higher than the national average. Small differences in the index numbers should not be interpreted as significant; Figures cover the Allentown PA urban area.
Source: The Council for Community and Economic Research, ACCRA Cost of Living Index, 2017

Grocery Prices

Area[1]	T-Bone Steak ($/pound)	Frying Chicken ($/pound)	Whole Milk ($/half gal.)	Eggs ($/dozen)	Orange Juice ($/64 oz.)	Coffee ($/11.5 oz.)
City[2]	11.88	1.41	1.86	1.24	3.21	3.68
Avg.	11.29	1.40	2.02	1.47	3.55	4.37
Min.	7.71	0.93	1.04	0.70	2.86	3.24
Max.	15.83	2.39	4.03	3.92	6.29	8.16

*Note: (1) Values for the local area are compared with the average, minimum and maximum values for all 294 areas in the Cost of Living Index; (2) Figures cover the Allentown PA urban area; **T-Bone Steak** (price per pound); **Frying Chicken** (price per pound, whole fryer); **Whole Milk** (half gallon carton); **Eggs** (price per dozen, Grade A, large); **Orange Juice** (64 oz. Tropicana or Florida Natural); **Coffee** (11.5 oz. can, vacuum-packed, Maxwell House, Hills Bros, or Folgers).*
Source: The Council for Community and Economic Research, ACCRA Cost of Living Index, 2017

Housing and Utility Costs

Area[1]	New Home Price ($)	Apartment Rent ($/month)	All Electric ($/month)	Part Electric ($/month)	Other Energy ($/month)	Telephone ($/month)
City[2]	354,972	1,436	-	101.48	75.53	25.24
Avg.	335,956	1,047	175.01	97.34	67.93	28.71
Min.	187,788	491	109.48	49.33	35.44	12.39
Max.	1,739,087	4,559	432.62	227.09	353.33	44.61

*Note: (1) Values for the local area are compared with the average, minimum and maximum values for all 294 areas in the Cost of Living Index; (2) Figures cover the Allentown PA urban area; **New Home Price** (2,400 sf living area, 8,000 sf lot, in urban area with full utilities); **Apartment Rent** (950 sf 2 bedroom/1.5 or 2 bath, unfurnished, excluding all utilities except water); **All Electric** (average monthly cost for an all-electric home); **Part Electric** (average monthly cost for a part-electric home); **Other Energy** (average monthly cost for natural gas, fuel oil, coal, wood, and any other forms of energy except electricity); **Telephone** (price includes basic monthly rate for a private residential line plus additional local usage charges incurred by a family of four).*
Source: The Council for Community and Economic Research, ACCRA Cost of Living Index, 2017

Health Care, Transportation, and Other Costs

Area[1]	Doctor ($/visit)	Dentist ($/visit)	Optometrist ($/visit)	Gasoline ($/gallon)	Beauty Salon ($/visit)	Men's Shirt ($)
City[2]	92.57	105.22	122.49	2.53	38.21	29.58
Avg.	108.00	92.54	101.93	2.25	37.58	30.92
Min.	30.39	60.00	49.75	1.82	16.11	11.20
Max.	193.50	161.94	229.28	3.16	77.35	59.13

*Note: (1) Values for the local area are compared with the average, minimum and maximum values for all 294 areas in the Cost of Living Index; (2) Figures cover the Allentown PA urban area; **Doctor** (general practitioners routine exam of an established patient); **Dentist** (adult teeth cleaning and periodic oral examination); **Optometrist** (full vision eye exam for established adult patient); **Gasoline** (one gallon regular unleaded, national brand, including all taxes, cash price at self-service pump if available); **Beauty Salon** (woman's shampoo, trim, and blow-dry); **Men's Shirt** (cotton/polyester dress shirt, pinpoint weave, long sleeves).*
Source: The Council for Community and Economic Research, ACCRA Cost of Living Index, 2017

HOUSING

House Price Index (HPI)

Area	National Ranking[2]	Quarterly Change (%)	One-Year Change (%)	Five-Year Change (%)
MSA[1]	168	0.38	4.57	11.64
U.S.[3]	–	1.61	6.68	34.71

Note: The HPI is a weighted repeat sales index. It measures average price changes in repeat sales or refinancings on the same properties. This information is obtained by reviewing repeat mortgage transactions on single-family properties whose mortgages have been purchased or securitized by Fannie Mae or Freddie Mac in January 1975; (1) Figures cover the Allentown-Bethlehem-Easton, PA-NJ Metropolitan Statistical Area—see Appendix B for areas included; (2) Rankings are based on annual percentage change for all metro areas containing at least 15,000 transactions over the last 10 years and ranges from 1 to 253; (3) figures based on a weighted average of Census Division estimates using a seasonally adjusted, purchase-only index; all figures are for the period ending December 31, 2017
Source: Federal Housing Finance Agency, House Price Index, February 28, 2018

Median Single-Family Home Prices

Area	2015	2016	2017p	Percent Change 2016 to 2017
MSA[1]	182.6	186.8	190.3	1.9
U.S. Average	223.9	235.5	248.8	5.6

Note: Figures are median sales prices of existing single-family homes in thousands of dollars; (p) preliminary; (1) Figures cover the Allentown-Bethlehem-Easton, PA-NJ Metropolitan Statistical Area—see Appendix B for areas included
Source: National Association of Realtors, Median Sales Price of Existing Single-Family Homes for Metropolitan Areas, 4th Quarter 2017

Qualifying Income Based on Median Sales Price of Existing Single-Family Homes

Area	With 5% Down ($)	With 10% Down ($)	With 20% Down ($)
MSA[1]	42,507	40,270	35,796
U.S. Average	55,585	52,659	46,808

Note: Figures are preliminary; Qualifying income is based on a mortgage rate of 4.17%. Monthly principal and interest payment is limited to 25% of income; (1) Figures cover the Allentown-Bethlehem-Easton, PA-NJ Metropolitan Statistical Area—see Appendix B for areas included
Source: National Association of Realtors, Qualifying Income Based on Median Sales Price of Existing Single-Family Homes for Metropolitan Areas, 4th Quarter 2017

Median Apartment Condo-Coop Home Prices

Area	2015	2016	2017p	Percent Change 2016 to 2017
MSA[1]	n/a	n/a	n/a	n/a
U.S. Average	210.7	220.7	234.3	6.2

Note: Figures are median sales prices of existing apartment condo-coop homes in thousands of dollars; (p) preliminary; n/a not available; (1) Figures cover the Allentown-Bethlehem-Easton, PA-NJ Metropolitan Statistical Area—see Appendix B for areas included
Source: National Association of Realtors, Median Sales Price of Existing Apartment Condo-Coop Homes for Metropolitan Areas, 4th Quarter 2017

Home Value Distribution

Area	Under $50,000	$50,000 -$99,999	$100,000 -$149,999	$150,000 -$199,999	$200,000 -$299,999	$300,000 -$499,999	$500,000 -$999,999	$1,000,000 or more
City	6.2	4.3	7.2	12.7	34.9	31.2	3.2	0.3
MSA[1]	4.9	8.7	15.5	20.9	27.8	18.3	3.4	0.5
U.S.	8.8	14.8	15.3	14.9	18.4	16.4	9.0	2.5

Note: Figures are percentages and cover owner-occupied housing units; (1) Figures cover the Allentown-Bethlehem-Easton, PA-NJ Metropolitan Statistical Area—see Appendix B for areas included
Source: U.S. Census Bureau, 2012-2016 American Community Survey 5-Year Estimates

Homeownership Rate

Area	2009 (%)	2010 (%)	2011 (%)	2012 (%)	2013 (%)	2014 (%)	2015 (%)	2016 (%)	2017 (%)
MSA[1]	72.4	71.5	75.7	75.5	71.5	68.2	69.2	68.9	73.1
U.S.	67.4	66.9	66.1	65.4	65.1	64.5	63.7	63.4	63.9

Note: (1) Figures cover the Allentown-Bethlehem-Easton, PA-NJ Metropolitan Statistical Area—see Appendix B for areas included
Source: U.S. Census Bureau, Housing Vacancies and Homeownership Annual Statistics: 2009-2017

Year Housing Structure Built

Area	2010 or Later	2000 -2009	1990 -1999	1980 -1989	1970 -1979	1960 -1969	1950 -1959	1940 -1949	Before 1940	Median Year
City	1.5	36.5	12.8	14.6	13.3	10.4	3.3	2.3	5.4	1991
MSA[1]	1.4	11.5	10.6	10.8	12.8	9.6	11.8	5.4	26.1	1967
U.S.	2.3	14.7	14.0	13.7	15.6	10.9	10.6	5.2	13.0	1977

Note: Figures are percentages except for Median Year; Note: (1) Figures cover the Allentown-Bethlehem-Easton, PA-NJ Metropolitan Statistical Area—see Appendix B for areas included
Source: U.S. Census Bureau, 2012-2016 American Community Survey 5-Year Estimates

Gross Monthly Rent

Area	Under $500	$500 -$999	$1,000 -$1,499	$1,500 -$1,999	$2,000 -$2,499	$2,500 -$2,999	$3,000 and up	Median ($)
City	0.0	18.6	53.4	26.5	1.6	0.0	0.0	1,247
MSA[1]	10.4	44.3	34.3	8.2	1.8	0.4	0.7	961
U.S.	11.3	43.3	27.7	10.7	4.0	1.6	1.5	949

Note: Figures are percentages except for Median; Gross rent is the contract rent plus the estimated average monthly cost of utilities (electricity, gas, and water and sewer) and fuels (oil, coal, kerosene, wood, etc.) if these are paid by the renter (or paid for the renter by someone else); (1) Figures cover the Allentown-Bethlehem-Easton, PA-NJ Metropolitan Statistical Area—see Appendix B for areas included
Source: U.S. Census Bureau, 2012-2016 American Community Survey 5-Year Estimates

HEALTH

Health Risk Factors

Category	MSA[1] (%)	U.S. (%)
Adults aged 18–64 who have any kind of health care coverage	90.8	87.7
Adults who reported being in good or excellent health	84.0	83.6
Adults who are current smokers	16.1	17.1
Adults who currently use E-cigarettes	4.8	4.7
Adults who currently use chewing tobacco, snuff, or snus	1.5	4.0
Adults who are heavy drinkers[2]	7.4	6.5
Adults who are binge drinkers[3]	19.9	16.9
Adults who are overweight (BMI 25.0 - 29.9)	32.6	35.3
Adults who are obese (BMI 30.0 - 99.8)	31.2	29.9
Adults who participated in any physical activities in the past month	73.0	76.9
Adults who always or nearly always wears a seat belt	90.9	94.3

Note: (1) Figures cover the Allentown-Bethlehem-Easton, PA-NJ Metropolitan Statistical Area—see Appendix B for areas included; (2) Heavy drinkers are classified as adult men having more than 14 drinks per week and adult women having more than 7 drinks per week; (3) Binge drinkers are classified as males having five or more drinks on one occasion or females having four or more drinks on one occasion
Source: Centers for Disease Control and Prevention, Behaviorial Risk Factor Surveillance System, SMART: Selected Metropolitan Area Risk Trends, 2016

Health Screening Rates

Category	MSA[1] (%)	U.S. (%)
Adults 50-75 who have had a blood stool test within the past year	n/a	8.0
Adults 50-75 who have had a colonoscopy in the past 10 years	65.4	63.5
Adults aged 65+ who have had flu shot within the past year	62.2	58.6
Adults aged 65+ who have ever had a pneumonia vaccination	71.4	73.4
Adults who have ever been tested for HIV	37.2	35.6
Women aged 21-65 who have had a pap test in the past three years	77.0	79.8
Men aged 40+ who have had a PSA test within the past two years	33.8	39.5
Women aged 40+ who have had a mammogram within the past two years	69.4	72.5

Note: n/a not available; (1) Figures cover the Allentown-Bethlehem-Easton, PA-NJ Metropolitan Statistical Area—see Appendix B for areas included; Source: Centers for Disease Control and Prevention, Behaviorial Risk Factor Surveillance System, SMART: Selected Metropolitan Area Risk Trends, 2016

Chronic Health Conditions

Category	MSA[1] (%)	U.S. (%)
Adults who have ever been told they had a heart attack	4.4	4.4
Adults who have ever been told they have angina or coronary heart disease	3.5	4.1
Adults who have ever been told they had a stroke	n/a	3.1
Adults who have been told they currently have asthma	8.8	9.3
Adults who have ever been told they have arthritis	28.1	25.8
Adults who have ever been told they have diabetes[2]	11.1	10.5
Adults who have ever been told they had skin cancer	6.0	5.9
Adults who have ever been told they had any other types of cancer	8.8	6.7
Adults who have ever been told they have COPD	6.1	6.3
Adults who have ever been told they have kidney disease	n/a	2.8
Adults who have ever been told they have a form of depression	19.4	17.4

Note: n/a not available; (1) Figures cover the Allentown-Bethlehem-Easton, PA-NJ Metropolitan Statistical Area—see Appendix B for areas included; (2) Figures do not include pregnancy-related, borderline, or pre-diabetes
Source: Centers for Disease Control and Prevention, Behaviorial Risk Factor Surveillance System, SMART: Selected Metropolitan Area Risk Trends, 2016

Mortality Rates for the Top 10 Causes of Death in the U.S.

ICD-10[a] Sub-Chapter	ICD-10[a] Code	Age-Adjusted Mortality Rate[1] per 100,000 population	
		County[2]	U.S.
Malignant neoplasms	C00-C97	157.2	158.5
Ischaemic heart diseases	I20-I25	78.9	96.8
Other forms of heart disease	I30-I51	59.8	52.4
Chronic lower respiratory diseases	J40-J47	31.3	40.9
Cerebrovascular diseases	I60-I69	30.2	37.2
Organic, including symptomatic, mental disorders	F01-F09	52.3	33.3
Other degenerative diseases of the nervous system	G30-G31	28.4	32.1
Other external causes of accidental injury	W00-X59	39.5	31.2
Diabetes mellitus	E10-E14	21.2	21.1
Hypertensive diseases	I10-I15	12.5	20.8

Note: (a) ICD-10 = International Classification of Diseases 10th Revision; (1) Mortality rates are a three year average covering 2014-2016; (2) Figures cover Lehigh County.
Source: Centers for Disease Control and Prevention, National Center for Health Statistics. Underlying Cause of Death 1999-2016 on CDC WONDER Online Database, released December 2017

Mortality Rates for Selected Causes of Death

ICD-10[a] Sub-Chapter	ICD-10[a] Code	Age-Adjusted Mortality Rate[1] per 100,000 population	
		County[2]	U.S.
Assault	X85-Y09	3.9	5.6
Diseases of the liver	K70-K76	11.5	14.0
Human immunodeficiency virus (HIV) disease	B20-B24	Unreliable	1.9
Influenza and pneumonia	J09-J18	10.4	14.6
Intentional self-harm	X60-X84	16.2	13.2
Malnutrition	E40-E46	Unreliable	1.3
Obesity and other hyperalimentation	E65-E68	1.7	2.1
Renal failure	N17-N19	12.2	13.0
Transport accidents	V01-V99	8.2	12.0
Viral hepatitis	B15-B19	1.7	1.9

Note: (a) ICD-10 = International Classification of Diseases 10th Revision; (1) Mortality rates are a three year average covering 2014-2016; (2) Figures cover Lehigh County; Data are Suppressed when the data meet the criteria for confidentiality constraints; Mortality rates are flagged as Unreliable when the rate would be calculated with a numerator of 20 or less.
Source: Centers for Disease Control and Prevention, National Center for Health Statistics. Underlying Cause of Death 1999-2016 on CDC WONDER Online Database, released December 2017

Health Insurance Coverage

Area	With Health Insurance	With Private Health Insurance	With Public Health Insurance	Without Health Insurance	Population Under Age 18 Without Health Insurance
City	94.9	85.0	25.2	5.1	2.5
MSA[1]	91.9	73.4	32.5	8.1	3.6
U.S.	88.3	66.7	33.0	11.7	5.9

Note: Figures are percentages that cover the civilian noninstitutionalized population; (1) Figures cover the Allentown-Bethlehem-Easton, PA-NJ Metropolitan Statistical Area—see Appendix B for areas included
Source: U.S. Census Bureau, 2012-2016 American Community Survey 5-Year Estimates

Number of Medical Professionals

Area	MDs[3]	DOs[3,4]	Dentists	Podiatrists	Chiropractors	Optometrists
County[1] (number)	1,222	306	307	52	106	68
County[1] (rate[2])	339.0	84.9	84.5	14.3	29.2	18.7
U.S. (rate[2])	276.5	22.3	67.3	6.0	26.7	15.9

Note: Data as of 2016 unless noted; (1) Data covers Lehigh County; (2) Rate per 100,000 population; (3) Data as of 2015 and includes all active, non-federal physicians; (4) Doctor of Osteopathic Medicine
Source: U.S. Department of Health and Human Services, Health Resources and Services Administration, Bureau of Health Professions, Area Resource File (ARF) 2016-2017

Best Hospitals

According to *U.S. News,* the Allentown-Bethlehem-Easton, PA-NJ metro area is home to one of the best hospitals in the U.S.: **Lehigh Valley Hospital** (1 adult specialty). The hospital listed was nationally ranked in at least one of 16 specialties. Only 152 hospitals nationwide were nationally ranked in one or more specialties. Twenty hospitals in the U.S. made the Honor Roll. The Best Hospitals Honor Roll was revamped last year to take both the national rankings and the procedure and condition ratings into account. Hospitals received points if they were nationally ranked in one of the 16 specialties—the higher they ranked, the more points they got—and how many ratings of "high performing" they earned in the nine procedures and conditions. *U.S. News Online, "America's Best Hospitals 2017-18"*

EDUCATION

Public School District Statistics

District Name	Schls	Pupils	Pupil/ Teacher Ratio	Minority Pupils[1] (%)	Free Lunch Eligible[2] (%)	IEP[3] (%)
East Penn Sd	11	8,011	16.5	22.2	20.6	16.8
Seven Generations Charter School	1	390	12.2	39.5	n/a	20.8

Note: Table includes school districts with 100 or more students; (1) Percentage of students that are not non-Hispanic white; (2) Percentage of students that are eligible for the free lunch program; (3) Percentage of students that have an Individualized Education Program.
Source: U.S. Department of Education, National Center for Education Statistics, Common Core of Data, Local Education Agency (School District) Universe Survey: School Year 2015-2016; U.S. Department of Education, National Center for Education Statistics, Common Core of Data, Public Elementary/Secondary School Universe Survey: School Year 2015-2016

Highest Level of Education

Area	Less than H.S.	H.S. Diploma	Some College, No Deg.	Associate Degree	Bachelor's Degree	Master's Degree	Prof. School Degree	Doctorate Degree
City	6.0	22.1	14.3	8.4	26.9	16.1	3.1	3.1
MSA[1]	10.7	35.0	17.7	8.9	17.5	7.6	1.5	1.2
U.S.	13.0	27.5	21.0	8.2	18.8	8.2	2.0	1.3

Note: Figures cover persons age 25 and over; (1) Figures cover the Allentown-Bethlehem-Easton, PA-NJ Metropolitan Statistical Area—see Appendix B for areas included
Source: U.S. Census Bureau, 2012-2016 American Community Survey 5-Year Estimates

Educational Attainment by Race

Area	High School Graduate or Higher (%)					Bachelor's Degree or Higher (%)				
	Total	White	Black	Asian	Hisp.[2]	Total	White	Black	Asian	Hisp.[2]
City	94.0	93.9	96.1	92.0	97.6	49.2	48.0	51.4	72.9	32.6
MSA[1]	89.3	90.5	87.2	87.6	73.2	27.7	28.1	19.7	57.5	12.6
U.S.	87.0	88.9	84.3	86.3	65.7	30.3	31.6	20.0	52.1	14.7

Note: Figures shown cover persons 25 years old and over; (1) Figures cover the Allentown-Bethlehem-Easton, PA-NJ Metropolitan Statistical Area—see Appendix B for areas included; (2) People of Hispanic origin can be of any race
Source: U.S. Census Bureau, 2012-2016 American Community Survey 5-Year Estimates

School Enrollment by Grade and Control

Area	Preschool (%)		Kindergarten (%)		Grades 1 - 4 (%)		Grades 5 - 8 (%)		Grades 9 - 12 (%)	
	Public	Private	Public	Private	Public	Private	Public	Private	Public	Private
City	16.5	83.5	62.9	37.1	91.2	8.8	89.2	10.8	93.6	6.4
MSA[1]	45.3	54.7	80.4	19.6	90.6	9.4	89.9	10.1	90.4	9.6
U.S.	58.4	41.6	87.7	12.3	89.8	10.2	89.7	10.3	90.4	9.6

Note: Figures shown cover persons 3 years old and over; (1) Figures cover the Allentown-Bethlehem-Easton, PA-NJ Metropolitan Statistical Area—see Appendix B for areas included
Source: U.S. Census Bureau, 2012-2016 American Community Survey 5-Year Estimates

Average Salaries of Public School Classroom Teachers

Area	2015		2016		Change from 2015 to 2016	
	Dollars	Rank[1]	Dollars	Rank[1]	Percent	Rank[2]
Pennsylvania	64,447	10	65,151	10	1.1	24
U.S. Average	57,611	–	58,353	–	1.3	–

Note: (1) Rank ranges from 1 to 51 where 1 indicates highest salary; (2) Rank ranges from 1 to 51 where 1 indicates highest percent change.
Source: National Education Association, Rankings & Estimates: Rankings of the States 2016 and Estimates of School Statistics 2017

Higher Education

Four-Year Colleges			Two-Year Colleges			Medical Schools[1]	Law Schools[2]	Voc/ Tech[3]
Public	Private Non-profit	Private For-profit	Public	Private Non-profit	Private For-profit			
0	0	0	0	0	0	0	0	0

Note: Figures cover institutions located within the city limits and include main campuses only; (1) includes schools accredited by the Liaison Committee on Medical Education and the American Osteopathic Association's Commission on Osteopathic College Accreditation; (2) includes ABA-accredited schools, schools with provisional ABA accreditation, and state accredited schools; (3) includes all schools with programs that are less than 2 years.
Source: National Center for Education Statistics, Integrated Postsecondary Education System (IPEDS), 2016-17; Wikipedia, List of Medical Schools in the United States, accessed April 2, 2018; Wikipedia, List of Law Schools in the United States, accessed April 2, 2018

According to *U.S. News & World Report,* the Allentown-Bethlehem-Easton, PA-NJ metro area is home to one of the best national universities in the U.S.: **Lehigh University** (#46 tie). The indicators used to capture academic quality fall into a number of categories: assessment by administrators at peer institutions; retention of students; faculty resources; student selectivity; financial resources; alumni giving; high school counselor ratings of colleges; and graduation rate. *U.S. News & World Report, "America's Best Colleges 2018"*

According to *U.S. News & World Report,* the Allentown-Bethlehem-Easton, PA-NJ metro area is home to three of the best liberal arts colleges in the U.S.: **Lafayette College** (#36 tie); **Muhlenberg College** (#71 tie); **Moravian College** (#165 tie). The indicators used to capture academic quality fall into a number of categories: assessment by administrators at peer institutions; retention of students; faculty resources; student selectivity; financial resources; alumni giving; high school counselor ratings of colleges; and graduation rate. *U.S. News & World Report, "America's Best Colleges 2018"*

PRESIDENTIAL ELECTION

2016 Presidential Election Results

Area	Clinton	Trump	Johnson	Stein	Other
Lehigh County	50.0	45.3	2.5	0.9	1.4
U.S.	48.0	45.9	3.3	1.1	1.7

Note: Results are percentages and may not add to 100% due to rounding
Source: Dave Leip's Atlas of U.S. Presidential Elections

EMPLOYERS

Major Employers

Company Name	Industry
Air Products	Manufacturer
Amazon.com	Retailer
B. Braun Medical	Healthcare
Crayola	Electronics
Easton Hospital	Healthcare
Giant Food Stores	Grocery stores
Good Shepard Rehabilitation Network	Healthcare
Guardian Life Insurance Co.	Life insurance
HCR Manorcare	Healthcare
KidsPeace	Healthcare
Lehigh Carbon Community College	Education
Lehigh University	Education
Lehigh Valley Hospital and Health Network	Healthcare
Lutron Electronics Co.	Electronics
Mack Trucks	Trucking
Northampton Community College	Education
PPL	Utilities
Sacred Heart Healthcare System	Healthcare
Sands Casino Resort Bethlehem	Gambling
Sodexo	Conglomerate
St. Luke's Hospital and Health Network	Healthcare
Wal-Mart Stores	Retailer
Wegman's	Grocery stores
Weis Markets	Grocery stores
Wells Fargo	Banking/loans

Note: Companies shown are located within the Allentown-Bethlehem-Easton, PA-NJ Metropolitan Statistical Area.
Source: Hoovers.com; Wikipedia

PUBLIC SAFETY

Crime Rate

Area	All Crimes	Violent Crimes				Property Crimes		
		Murder	Rape[3]	Robbery	Aggrav. Assault	Burglary	Larceny -Theft	Motor Vehicle Theft
City	n/a	n/a	n/a	n/a	n/a	n/a	n/a	n/a
Metro[1]	n/a	2.6	19.4	58.3	n/a	264.7	n/a	89.1
U.S.	2,847.8	5.3	40.4	102.8	248.5	468.9	1,745.0	236.9

Note: Figures are crimes per 100,000 population; (1) Figures cover the Allentown-Bethlehem-Easton, PA-NJ Metropolitan Statistical Area—see Appendix B for areas included; n/a not available; (3) The city and U.S. figures shown were reported using the revised Uniform Crime Reporting (UCR) definition of rape. The metro area figures shown are an aggregate total of the data submitted using both the revised and legacy UCR definitions.
Source: FBI Uniform Crime Reports, 2016

Hate Crimes

Area	Number of Quarters Reported	Number of Incidents per Bias Motivation: Race/Ethnicity/ Ancestry	Religion	Sexual Orientation	Disability	Gender	Gender Identity
City	n/a	n/a	n/a	n/a	n/a	n/a	n/a
U.S.	4	3,489	1,273	1,076	70	31	124

Note: n/a not available.
Source: Federal Bureau of Investigation, Hate Crime Statistics 2016

Identity Theft Consumer Reports

Area	Reports	Reports per 100,000 Population	Rank[2]
MSA[1]	779	93	129
U.S.	371,061	114	-

Note: (1) Figures cover the Allentown-Bethlehem-Easton, PA-NJ Metropolitan Statistical Area—see Appendix B for areas included; (2) Rank ranges from 1 to 389 where 1 indicates greatest number of identity theft reports per 100,000 population
Source: Federal Trade Commission, Consumer Sentinel Network Data Book for January–December 2017

Fraud and Other Consumer Reports

Area	Reports	Reports per 100,000 Population	Rank[2]
MSA[1]	4,050	485	131
U.S.	2,304,550	708	-

Note: (1) Figures cover the Allentown-Bethlehem-Easton, PA-NJ Metropolitan Statistical Area—see Appendix B for areas included; (2) Rank ranges from 1 to 389 where 1 indicates greatest number of fraud and other consumer reports per 100,000 population
Source: Federal Trade Commission, Consumer Sentinel Network Data Book for January–December 2017

SPORTS

Professional Sports Teams

Team Name	League	Year Established
No teams are located in the metro area		

Source: Wikipedia, Major Professional Sports Teams of the United States and Canada, April 5, 2018

CLIMATE

Average and Extreme Temperatures

Temperature	Jan	Feb	Mar	Apr	May	Jun	Jul	Aug	Sep	Oct	Nov	Dec	Yr.
Extreme High (°F)	72	76	84	93	97	100	105	100	99	90	81	72	105
Average High (°F)	35	38	48	61	71	80	85	82	75	64	52	39	61
Average Temp. (°F)	28	30	39	50	60	70	74	72	65	54	43	32	52
Average Low (°F)	20	22	29	39	49	58	63	62	54	43	34	24	42
Extreme Low (°F)	-12	-7	-1	16	30	39	48	41	31	21	11	-8	-12

Note: Figures cover the years 1948-1990
Source: National Climatic Data Center, International Station Meteorological Climate Summary, 9/96

Average Precipitation/Snowfall/Humidity

Precip./Humidity	Jan	Feb	Mar	Apr	May	Jun	Jul	Aug	Sep	Oct	Nov	Dec	Yr.
Avg. Precip. (in.)	3.2	3.0	3.5	3.8	4.2	3.6	4.3	4.4	3.9	2.9	3.8	3.6	44.2
Avg. Snowfall (in.)	9	9	6	1	Tr	0	0	0	0	Tr	1	6	32
Avg. Rel. Hum. 7am (%)	77	76	75	75	78	79	82	86	88	86	82	79	80
Avg. Rel. Hum. 4pm (%)	62	57	51	48	52	52	52	55	57	56	60	64	55

Note: Figures cover the years 1948-1990; Tr = Trace amounts (<0.05 in. of rain; <0.5 in. of snow)
Source: National Climatic Data Center, International Station Meteorological Climate Summary, 9/96

Weather Conditions

Temperature			Daytime Sky			Precipitation		
5°F & below	32°F & below	90°F & above	Clear	Partly cloudy	Cloudy	0.01 inch or more precip.	0.1 inch or more snow/ice	Thunder-storms
6	123	15	77	148	140	123	20	31

Note: Figures are average number of days per year and cover the years 1948-1990
Source: National Climatic Data Center, International Station Meteorological Climate Summary, 9/96

HAZARDOUS WASTE

Superfund Sites

The Allentown-Bethlehem-Easton, PA-NJ metro area is home to nine sites on the EPA's Superfund National Priorities List: **Dorney Road Landfill** (final); **Heleva Landfill** (final); **Hellertown Manufacturing Co.** (final); **Industrial Lane** (final); **Novak Sanitary Landfill** (final); **Palmerton Zinc Pile** (final); **Pohatcong Valley Ground Water Contamination** (final); **Rodale Manufacturing Co., Inc.** (final); **Tonolli Corp.** (final). There are a total of 1,396 Superfund sites with a status of proposed or final on the list in the U.S. *U.S. Environmental Protection Agency, National Priorities List, April 4, 2018*

AIR & WATER QUALITY

Air Quality Trends: Ozone

	1990	1995	2000	2005	2010	2012	2013	2014	2015	2016
MSA[1]	0.093	0.091	0.091	0.086	0.080	0.075	0.068	0.068	0.070	0.071
U.S.	0.087	0.089	0.081	0.079	0.073	0.075	0.069	0.067	0.068	0.069

Note: (1) Data covers the Allentown-Bethlehem-Easton, PA-NJ Metropolitan Statistical Area—see Appendix B for areas included. The values shown are the composite ozone concentration averages among trend sites based on the highest fourth daily maximum 8-hour concentration in parts per million. These trends are based on sites having an adequate record of monitoring data during the trend period. Data from exceptional events are included.
Source: U.S. Environmental Protection Agency, Air Quality Monitoring Information, "Air Quality Trends by City, 1990-2016"

Air Quality Index

Area	Percent of Days when Air Quality was...[2]					AQI Statistics[2]	
	Good	Moderate	Unhealthy for Sensitive Groups	Unhealthy	Very Unhealthy	Maximum	Median
MSA[1]	49.0	50.7	0.3	0.0	0.0	119	51

Note: (1) Data covers the Allentown-Bethlehem-Easton, PA-NJ Metropolitan Statistical Area—see Appendix B for areas included; (2) Based on 365 days with AQI data in 2017. Air Quality Index (AQI) is an index for reporting daily air quality. EPA calculates the AQI for five major air pollutants regulated by the Clean Air Act: ground-level ozone, particle pollution (aka particulate matter), carbon monoxide, sulfur dioxide, and nitrogen dioxide. The AQI runs from 0 to 500. The higher the AQI value, the greater the level of air pollution and the greater the health concern. There are six AQI categories: "Good" AQI is between 0 and 50. Air quality is considered satisfactory; "Moderate" AQI is between 51 and 100. Air quality is acceptable; "Unhealthy for Sensitive Groups" When AQI values are between 101 and 150, members of sensitive groups may experience health effects; "Unhealthy" When AQI values are between 151 and 200 everyone may begin to experience health effects; "Very Unhealthy" AQI values between 201 and 300 trigger a health alert; "Hazardous" AQI values over 300 trigger warnings of emergency conditions (not shown).
Source: U.S. Environmental Protection Agency, Air Quality Index Report, 2017

Air Quality Index Pollutants

Area	Percent of Days when AQI Pollutant was...[2]					
	Carbon Monoxide	Nitrogen Dioxide	Ozone	Sulfur Dioxide	Particulate Matter 2.5	Particulate Matter 10
MSA[1]	0.0	0.3	33.2	0.0	66.6	0.0

Note: (1) Data covers the Allentown-Bethlehem-Easton, PA-NJ Metropolitan Statistical Area—see Appendix B for areas included; (2) Based on 365 days with AQI data in 2017. The Air Quality Index (AQI) is an index for reporting daily air quality. EPA calculates the AQI for five major air pollutants regulated by the Clean Air Act: ground-level ozone, particle pollution (also known as particulate matter), carbon monoxide, sulfur dioxide, and nitrogen dioxide. The AQI runs from 0 to 500. The higher the AQI value, the greater the level of air pollution and the greater the health concern.
Source: U.S. Environmental Protection Agency, Air Quality Index Report, 2017

Maximum Air Pollutant Concentrations: Particulate Matter, Ozone, CO and Lead

	Particulate Matter 10 (ug/m³)	Particulate Matter 2.5 Wtd AM (ug/m³)	Particulate Matter 2.5 24-Hr (ug/m³)	Ozone (ppm)	Carbon Monoxide (ppm)	Lead (ug/m³)
MSA[1] Level	31	10.5	25	0.075	n/a	0.11
NAAQS[2]	150	15	35	0.075	9	0.15
Met NAAQS[2]	Yes	Yes	Yes	Yes	n/a	Yes

Note: (1) Data covers the Allentown-Bethlehem-Easton, PA-NJ Metropolitan Statistical Area—see Appendix B for areas included; Data from exceptional events are included; (2) National Ambient Air Quality Standards; ppm = parts per million; ug/m³ = micrograms per cubic meter; n/a not available.
Concentrations: Particulate Matter 10 (coarse particulate)—highest second maximum 24-hour concentration; Particulate Matter 2.5 Wtd AM (fine particulate)—highest weighted annual mean concentration; Particulate Matter 2.5 24-Hour (fine particulate)—highest 98th percentile 24-hour concentration; Ozone—highest fourth daily maximum 8-hour concentration; Carbon Monoxide—highest second maximum non-overlapping 8-hour concentration; Lead—maximum running 3-month average
Source: U.S. Environmental Protection Agency, Air Quality Monitoring Information, "Air Quality Statistics by City, 2016"

Maximum Air Pollutant Concentrations: Nitrogen Dioxide and Sulfur Dioxide

	Nitrogen Dioxide AM (ppb)	Nitrogen Dioxide 1-Hr (ppb)	Sulfur Dioxide AM (ppb)	Sulfur Dioxide 1-Hr (ppb)	Sulfur Dioxide 24-Hr (ppb)
MSA[1] Level	11	48	n/a	19	n/a
NAAQS[2]	53	100	30	75	140
Met NAAQS[2]	Yes	Yes	n/a	Yes	n/a

Note: (1) Data covers the Allentown-Bethlehem-Easton, PA-NJ Metropolitan Statistical Area—see Appendix B for areas included; Data from exceptional events are included; (2) National Ambient Air Quality Standards; ppm = parts per million; ug/m³ = micrograms per cubic meter; n/a not available.
Concentrations: Nitrogen Dioxide AM—highest arithmetic mean concentration; Nitrogen Dioxide 1-Hr—highest 98th percentile 1-hour daily maximum concentration; Sulfur Dioxide AM—highest annual mean concentration; Sulfur Dioxide 1-Hr—highest 99th percentile 1-hour daily maximum concentration; Sulfur Dioxide 24-Hr—highest second maximum 24-hour concentration
Source: U.S. Environmental Protection Agency, Air Quality Monitoring Information, "Air Quality Statistics by City, 2016"

Drinking Water

Water System Name	Pop. Served	Primary Water Source Type	Violations[1] Health Based	Violations[1] Monitoring/ Reporting
LCA WLSA Central Division	47,508	Purchased Surface	1	0

Note: (1) Based on violation data from January 1, 2017 to December 31, 2017
Source: U.S. Environmental Protection Agency, Office of Ground Water and Drinking Water, Safe Drinking Water Information System (based on data extracted April 5, 2018)

Moon, Pennsylvania

Background

Moon Township sits along the Ohio River, part of the Pittsburgh Metro Area, and 12 miles from Pittsburgh. Its name is said to derive from a crescent-shaped bend in the Ohio River.

Founded in 1788, Moon is the oldest township in Allegheny County. With its beginnings as a farm-based and hunting community, Moon has become economically diverse. As the Industrial Revolution brought railroads and roadways to Moon, both its economy and population exploded, significantly in 1952, with the establishment of the Greater Pittsburgh International Airport, now the Pittsburgh International Airport. Penn Lincoln Parkway was also completed one year later, which shortened the commute to downtown Pittsburgh. Moon would enjoy the fruits of this growth until the 1990s, when the airport was moved to Findlay Township nearby. The town persevered and refocused, and in shifting from airport commerce to corporate development it managed to maintain its economic prosperity. Today, Moon is home to multiple high-profile national corporations, including FedEx Ground, GlaxoSmithKline, Eaton Electrical Group, Nova Chemicals, Inc., and Michael Baker Corporation.

Moon Township's 24.1 square miles border five other townships and one borough: Crescent Township to the north-northwest, Hopewell Township (Beaver County) to the northwest, Findlay Township to the west and southwest, North Fayette Township to the south, Robinson Township to the southeast, east and northeast, and the borough of Coraopolis to the north-northeast. In the northwest, across the Ohio River are Edgeworth, Sewickley, and Glen Osborne. The Sewickley Bridge serves as the link between Moon Township and Sewickley.

The Moon Area School District serves Moon Township and is made up of students from both Moon and Crescent Townships. The district is comprised of five elementary schools, one middle school, and one high school. For higher education, the main campus of private, doctoral Robert Morris University also resides within Moon.

Moon's proximity to Pittsburgh allows residents to enjoy many urban amenities. Nearby attractions include Idlewild Park and Storybook Forest, the Pittsburgh Zoo & PPG Aquarium, and the Seven Spring Ski Resorts. Also popular are area parks, including the nine different parks within Allegheny County Parks. Museums are abundant in nearby Pittsburgh, as well, with the city boasting 11 museums and art galleries. The city is also home to 12 live theatres and six sports facilities.

Moon continues to be served by the Pittsburgh International Airport, which is a civil-military international airport. It is the busiest airport in western Pennsylvania and the second-busiest in the state, placing only behind Philadelphia International Airport.

Rankings

Business/Finance Rankings

- The personal finance site NerdWallet analyzed 183 American metropolitan areas with populations over 250,000 and more than 15,000 businesses to rank where entrepreneurs find the most success. Criteria included area economy, annual income, housing cost, unemployment rate, and the success rate of area businesses. Pittsburgh* ranked #17. *www.nerdwallet.com, "Best Places to Start a Business," April 27, 2015*

- USAA and Hiring Our Heroes worked with Sperlings's BestPlaces and the Institute for Veterans and Military Families at Syracuse University to rank major metropolitan areas where military-skills-related employment is strongest. Criteria for *mid-career* veterans included veteran wage growth; recent job growth; stability; and accessible health resources. Metro areas with a higher than national average crime or unemployment rate were excluded. At #2, the Pittsburgh* metro area made the top ten. *www.usaa.com, "2015 Best Places for Veterans"*

- Based on metro area social media reviews, the employment opinion group Glassdoor surveyed 50 of the largest U.S. metro areas and equally weighed cost of living, hiring opportunity, and job satisfaction to compose a list of "25 Best Cities for Jobs." Median pay and home value, in-demand jobs and number of current job openings was also factored in. The Pittsburgh* metro area was ranked #1 in overall job satisfaction. *www.glassdoor.com, "Best Cities for Jobs," September 12, 2017*

- In a survey of economic confidence in the nation's 50 largest metropolitan areas conducted January–December 2014, the Pittsburgh* metro area placed #45, according to Gallup's 2014 Economic Confidence Index. *Gallup, "San Jose and San Francisco Lead in Economic Confidence," March 19, 2015*

- The Brookings Institution ranked the 100 largest metro areas in the U.S. based on income inequality. Pittsburgh* was ranked #34 (#1 = greatest ineqality). Criteria: the "95/20 ratio," a figure representing the income at which a household earns more than 95 percent of all other households, divided by the income at which a household earns more than only 20 percent of all other households. *Brookings Institution, "Household Income Inequality, 100 Largest U.S. Metro Areas, 2014-2016," February 5, 2018*

- Payscale.com ranked the largest metro areas in terms of wage growth. The Pittsburgh* metro area ranked #1. Criteria: private-sector wage growth between the 4th quarter of 2016 and the 4th quarter of 2017. *PayScale, "Wage Trends by Metro Area-4th Quarter," January 17, 2018*

- Pittsburgh* was identified as one of America's most frugal metro areas by *Coupons.com.* The city ranked #25 out of 25. Criteria: digital coupon usage. *Coupons.com, "America's Most Frugal Cities of 2017," March 22, 2018*

- The Pittsburgh* metro area appeared on the Milken Institute "2017 Best Performing Cities" list. Rank: #143 out of 200 large metro areas. Criteria: job growth; wage and salary growth; high-tech output growth. *Milken Institute, "Best-Performing Cities 2017," January 2018*

- *Forbes* ranked the 200 most populous metro areas to determine the nation's "Best Places for Business and Careers." The Pittsburgh* metro area was ranked #85. Criteria: costs (business and living); job growth (past and projected); income growth; quality of life; educational attainment (college and high school); projected economic growth; cultural and recreational opportunities; net migration patterns; number of highly ranked colleges. *Forbes, "The Best Places for Business and Careers 2017," October 24, 2017*

Education Rankings

- Personal finance website *WalletHub* analyzed the 150 largest U.S. metropolitan statistical areas to determine where the most educated Americans are choosing to settle. Criteria: education quality and attainment gap; education levels; percentage of workers with degrees; public school rankings; quality and size of each metro area's universities. Pittsburgh* was ranked #47 (#1 = most educated city). *www.WalletHub.com, "2017's Most and Least Educated Cities in America," July 25, 2017*

Environmental Rankings

- Sperling's BestPlaces assessed 379 metropolitan areas of the United States for the likelihood of dangerously extreme weather events or earthquakes. In general the Southeast and South-Central regions have the highest risk of weather extremes and earthquakes, while the Pacific Northwest enjoys the lowest risk. Of the least risky metropolitan areas, the Pittsburgh* metro area was ranked #110. *www.bestplaces.net, "Safest Places from Natural Disasters," April 2011*

- Pittsburgh* was highlighted as one of the 25 metro areas most polluted by year-round particle pollution (Annual PM 2.5) in the U.S. during 2013 through 2015. The area ranked #8. *American Lung Association, State of the Air 2017*

- Pittsburgh* was highlighted as one of the 25 metro areas most polluted by short-term particle pollution (24-hour PM 2.5) in the U.S. during 2013 through 2015. The area ranked #17. *American Lung Association, State of the Air 2017*

Health/Fitness Rankings

- For each of the 50 most populous metro areas in the United States, the American College of Sports Medicine's American Fitness Index evaluated infrastructure, community assets, and policies that encourage healthy and fit lifestyles, including preventive health behaviors, levels of chronic disease conditions, health care access, and community resources and policies that support physical activity. The Pittsburgh* metro area ranked #29 for "community fitness." *www.americanfitnessindex.org, "ACSM American Fitness Index Health and Community Fitness Status of the 50 Largest Metropolitan Areas," May 2017*

- The Pittsburgh* metro area was identified as one of the worst cities for bed bugs in America by pest control company Orkin. The area ranked #24 out of 50 based on the number of bed bug treatments Orkin performed from December 2016 to November 2017. *Orkin, "Baltimore and Washington D.C. Continue to Hold Top Spots," January 8, 2018*

- Pittsburgh* was identified as a "2016 Spring Allergy Capital." The area ranked #54 out of 100. Three groups of factors were used to identify the most severe cities for people with allergies during the spring season: annual pollen levels; medicine utilization; access to board-certified allergists. *Asthma and Allergy Foundation of America, "Spring Allergy Capitals 2016"*

- Pittsburgh* was identified as a "2016 Fall Allergy Capital." The area ranked #30 out of 100. Three groups of factors were used to identify the most severe cities for people with allergies during the fall season: annual pollen levels; medicine utilization; access to board-certified allergists. *Asthma and Allergy Foundation of America, "Fall Allergy Capitals 2016"*

- Pittsburgh* was identified as a "2015 Asthma Capital." The area ranked #27 out of the nation's 100 largest metropolitan areas. Criteria: estimated prevalence; self-reported prevalence; crude death rate for asthma; annual pollen score; annual air quality; public smoking laws; number of board-certified asthma specialists; school inhaler access laws; rescue medication use; controller medication use; ER visits for asthma; uninsured rate; poverty rate. *Asthma and Allergy Foundation of America, "Asthma Capitals 2015"*

- The Pittsburgh* metro area ranked #65 out of 189 in The Gallup-Healthways Well-Being Index. Criteria: purpose; social well being; financial health; community and physical health. Results are based on telephone interviews with adults, aged 18 and older, living in metropolitan areas in the 50 U.S. states and the District of Columbia. *Gallup-Healthways, "State of American Well-Being, 2017 Community Well-Being Rankings" March 2018*

Real Estate Rankings

- FitSmallBusiness looked at 50 of the largest metropolitan areas in the U.S. to determine which metro was the best to start a real estate business. Data was compiled from such sources as: Zillow, Trulia, U.S. Census Bureau, and the Bureau of Labor Statistics. Criteria: location; inventory; annual wages; median sales price of homes; days on the market; median price cut percentage; and other factors that would influence real estate professional growth. The Pittsburgh* metro area ranked #49. *fitsmallbusiness.com, "The Best Cities to Become a Real Estate Agent in 2018," January 30, 2018*
- The Pittsburgh* metro area was identified as one of nine best housing markets to invest in. Criteria: single-family rental home investing in the first quarter of 2017 based on first-year returns. The area ranked #9. *The Business Insider, "Here are the 9 Best U.S. Housing Markets for Investment," May 11, 2017*
- Pittsburgh* was ranked #48 out of 238 metro areas in terms of housing affordability in 2017 by the National Association of Home Builders (#1 = most affordable). Criteria: the share of homes sold in that area affordable to a family earning the local median income, based on standard mortgage underwriting criteria. *National Association of Home Builders®, NAHB-Wells Fargo Housing Opportunity Index, 4th Quarter 2017*

Safety Rankings

- The National Insurance Crime Bureau ranked 382 metro areas in the U.S. in terms of per capita rates of vehicle theft. The Pittsburgh* metro area ranked #305 (#1 = highest rate). Criteria: number of vehicle theft offenses per 100,000 inhabitants in 2016. *National Insurance Crime Bureau, "Hot Spots 2016," June 8, 2017*

Seniors/Retirement Rankings

- From its Best Cities for Successful Aging indexes, the Milken Institute generated rankings for metropolitan areas, weighing data in nine categories—health care, wellness, living arrangements, transportation and convenience, financial characteristics, education, employment, community engagement, and overall livability. The Pittsburgh* metro area was ranked #44 overall in the large metro area category. *Milken Institute, "Best Cities for Successful Aging, 2017" March 14, 2017*

Miscellaneous Rankings

- The watchdog site Charity Navigator conducts an annual study of charities in the nation's major markets both to analyze statistical differences in their financial, accountability, and transparency practices and to track year-to-year variations in individual philanthropic communities. Charity Navigator's analysis demonstrated that the financial, accountability and transparency behaviors of America's largest charities can be influenced by the metropolitan market within which the charity operates. The Pittsburgh* metro area was ranked #27 among the 30 metro markets in the rating category of Overall Score. *www.charitynavigator.org, "2017 Metro Market Study," May 1, 2017*

*Moon is located within the Pittsburgh, PA Metropolitan Statistical Area.

Business Environment

CITY FINANCES

City Government Finances

Component	2015 ($000)	2015 ($ per capita)
Total Revenues	n/a	n/a
Total Expenditures	n/a	n/a
Debt Outstanding	n/a	n/a
Cash and Securities[1]	n/a	n/a

Note: (1) Cash and security holdings of a government at the close of its fiscal year,, including those of its dependent agencies, utilities, and liquor stores.
Source: U.S Census Bureau, State & Local Government Finances 2015

City Government Revenue by Source

Source	2015 ($000)	2015 ($ per capita)	2015 (%)
General Revenue			
From Federal Government	n/a	n/a	n/a
From State Government	n/a	n/a	n/a
From Local Governments	n/a	n/a	n/a
Taxes			
Property	n/a	n/a	n/a
Sales and Gross Receipts	n/a	n/a	n/a
Personal Income	n/a	n/a	n/a
Corporate Income	n/a	n/a	n/a
Motor Vehicle License	n/a	n/a	n/a
Other Taxes	n/a	n/a	n/a
Current Charges	n/a	n/a	n/a
Liquor Store	n/a	n/a	n/a
Utility	n/a	n/a	n/a
Employee Retirement	n/a	n/a	n/a

Source: U.S Census Bureau, State & Local Government Finances 2015

City Government Expenditures by Function

Function	2015 ($000)	2015 ($ per capita)	2015 (%)
General Direct Expenditures			
Air Transportation	n/a	n/a	n/a
Corrections	n/a	n/a	n/a
Education	n/a	n/a	n/a
Employment Security Administration	n/a	n/a	n/a
Financial Administration	n/a	n/a	n/a
Fire Protection	n/a	n/a	n/a
General Public Buildings	n/a	n/a	n/a
Governmental Administration, Other	n/a	n/a	n/a
Health	n/a	n/a	n/a
Highways	n/a	n/a	n/a
Hospitals	n/a	n/a	n/a
Housing and Community Development	n/a	n/a	n/a
Interest on General Debt	n/a	n/a	n/a
Judicial and Legal	n/a	n/a	n/a
Libraries	n/a	n/a	n/a
Parking	n/a	n/a	n/a
Parks and Recreation	n/a	n/a	n/a
Police Protection	n/a	n/a	n/a
Public Welfare	n/a	n/a	n/a
Sewerage	n/a	n/a	n/a
Solid Waste Management	n/a	n/a	n/a
Veterans' Services	n/a	n/a	n/a
Liquor Store	n/a	n/a	n/a
Utility	n/a	n/a	n/a
Employee Retirement	n/a	n/a	n/a

Source: U.S Census Bureau, State & Local Government Finances 2015

DEMOGRAPHICS

Population Growth

Area	1990 Census	2000 Census	2010 Census	2016* Estimate	Population Growth (%) 1990-2016	2010-2016
City	19,638	22,290	24,185	25,435	29.5	5.2
MSA[1]	2,468,289	2,431,087	2,356,285	2,354,926	-4.6	-0.1
U.S.	248,709,873	281,421,906	308,745,538	318,558,162	28.1	3.2

Note: (1) Figures cover the Pittsburgh, PA Metropolitan Statistical Area—see Appendix B for areas included; (*) 2012-2016 5-year estimated population
Source: U.S. Census Bureau, 1990 Census, Census 2000, Census 2010, 2012-2016 American Community Survey 5-Year Estimates

Household Size

Area	Persons in Household (%) One	Two	Three	Four	Five	Six	Seven or More	Average Household Size
City	29.4	32.5	18.5	11.7	5.5	1.2	1.3	2.50
MSA[1]	32.5	35.5	14.9	11.2	4.1	1.3	0.6	2.30
U.S.	27.7	33.7	15.7	13.1	6.0	2.3	1.5	2.60

Note: (1) Figures cover the Pittsburgh, PA Metropolitan Statistical Area—see Appendix B for areas included
Source: U.S. Census Bureau, 2012-2016 American Community Survey 5-Year Estimates

Race

Area	White Alone[2] (%)	Black Alone[2] (%)	Asian Alone[2] (%)	AIAN[3] Alone[2] (%)	NHOPI[4] Alone[2] (%)	Other Race Alone[2] (%)	Two or More Races (%)
City	88.6	4.4	4.3	0.2	0.0	0.5	1.9
MSA[1]	87.1	8.2	2.1	0.1	0.0	0.3	2.1
U.S.	73.3	12.6	5.2	0.8	0.2	4.8	3.1

Note: (1) Figures cover the Pittsburgh, PA Metropolitan Statistical Area—see Appendix B for areas included; (2) Alone is defined as not being in combination with one or more other races; (3) American Indian and Alaska Native; (4) Native Hawaiian and Other Pacific Islander
Source: U.S. Census Bureau, 2012-2016 American Community Survey 5-Year Estimates

Hispanic or Latino Origin

Area	Total (%)	Mexican (%)	Puerto Rican (%)	Cuban (%)	Other (%)
City	2.6	0.4	0.3	0.1	1.9
MSA[1]	1.6	0.5	0.4	0.1	0.6
U.S.	17.3	11.0	1.7	0.7	4.0

Note: Persons of Hispanic or Latino origin can be of any race; (1) Figures cover the Pittsburgh, PA Metropolitan Statistical Area—see Appendix B for areas included
Source: U.S. Census Bureau, 2012-2016 American Community Survey 5-Year Estimates

Segregation

Type	Segregation Indices[1] 1990	2000	2010	2010 Rank[2]	Percent Change 1990-2000	1990-2010	2000-2010
Black/White	70.8	68.9	65.8	17	-1.9	-5.1	-3.2
Asian/White	51.3	52.1	52.4	2	0.8	1.0	0.3
Hispanic/White	29.5	29.0	28.6	97	-0.5	-0.9	-0.4

Note: All figures cover the Metropolitan Statistical Area—see Appendix B for areas included; Figures are based on an analysis of 1990, 2000, and 2010 Census Decennial Census tract data by William H. Frey, Brookings Institution and the University of Michigan Social Science Data Analysis Network. In this analysis all racial groups (whites, blacks, and asians) are non-Hispanic members of those races. Hispanics are shown as a separate category; (1) Segregation Indices are Dissimilarity Indices that measure the degree to which the minority group is distributed differently than whites across census tracts. They range from 0 (complete integration) to 100 (complete segregation) where the value indicates the percentage of the minority group that needs to move to be distributed exactly like whites; (2) Ranges from 1 (most segregated) to 102 (least segregated); n/a not available.
Source: www.CensusScope.org

Ancestry

Area	German	Irish	English	American	Italian	Polish	French[2]	Scottish	Dutch
City	28.5	19.0	7.7	2.8	19.7	8.8	2.0	1.7	0.8
MSA[1]	27.8	18.4	8.1	4.2	16.3	8.7	1.8	1.9	1.2
U.S.	14.4	10.4	7.7	6.9	5.4	2.9	2.6	1.7	1.3

Note: Figures are the percentage of the total population reporting a particular ancestry. The nine most commonly reported ancestries in the U.S. are shown. Figures include multiple ancestries (e.g. if a person reported being Irish and Italian, they were included in both columns); (1) Figures cover the Pittsburgh, PA Metropolitan Statistical Area—see Appendix B for areas included; (2) Excludes Basque
Source: U.S. Census Bureau, 2012-2016 American Community Survey 5-Year Estimates

Foreign-Born Population

Area	Percent of Population Born in								
	Any Foreign Country	Asia	Mexico	Europe	Carribean	Central America[2]	South America	Africa	Canada
City	8.3	3.9	0.4	1.4	0.8	0.8	0.4	0.4	0.1
MSA[1]	3.7	1.8	0.1	1.0	0.1	0.1	0.2	0.2	0.1
U.S.	13.2	4.0	3.6	1.5	1.3	1.0	0.9	0.6	0.3

Note: (1) Figures cover the Pittsburgh, PA Metropolitan Statistical Area—see Appendix B for areas included; (2) Excludes Mexico.
Source: U.S. Census Bureau, 2012-2016 American Community Survey 5-Year Estimates

Marital Status

Area	Never Married	Now Married[2]	Separated	Widowed	Divorced
City	34.2	50.2	1.3	5.8	8.6
MSA[1]	31.8	48.9	1.8	7.7	9.8
U.S.	33.0	48.1	2.1	5.9	11.0

Note: Figures are percentages and cover the population 15 years of age and older; (1) Figures cover the Pittsburgh, PA Metropolitan Statistical Area—see Appendix B for areas included; (2) Excludes separated
Source: U.S. Census Bureau, 2012-2016 American Community Survey 5-Year Estimates

Disability Status

Area	All Ages	Under 18 Years Old	18 to 64 Years Old	65 Years and Over
City	9.3	2.7	7.7	27.3
MSA[1]	14.0	5.0	11.0	34.2
U.S.	12.5	4.1	10.3	35.7

Note: Figures show percent of the civilian noninstitutionalized population that reported having a disability. Disability status is determined from six types of difficulty: vision, hearing, cognitive, ambulatory, self-care, and independent living. For children under 5 years old, hearing and vision difficulty are used to determine disability status. For children between the ages of 5 and 14, disability status is determined from hearing, vision, cognitive, ambulatory, and self-care difficulties. For people aged 15 years and older, they are considered to have a disability if they have difficulty with any one of the six difficulty types; Note: (1) Figures cover the Pittsburgh, PA Metropolitan Statistical Area—see Appendix B for areas included
Source: U.S. Census Bureau, 2012-2016 American Community Survey 5-Year Estimates

Age

Area	Percent of Population									Median Age
	Under Age 5	Age 5–19	Age 20–34	Age 35–44	Age 45–54	Age 55–64	Age 65–74	Age 75–84	Age 85+	
City	5.6	20.6	18.8	12.8	15.5	13.5	7.6	3.8	1.8	39.4
MSA[1]	5.1	16.9	19.1	11.5	14.2	14.9	9.7	5.7	3.0	42.9
U.S.	6.2	19.6	20.7	12.7	13.6	12.6	8.3	4.3	1.9	37.7

Note: (1) Figures cover the Pittsburgh, PA Metropolitan Statistical Area—see Appendix B for areas included
Source: U.S. Census Bureau, 2012-2016 American Community Survey 5-Year Estimates

Gender

Area	Males	Females	Males per 100 Females
City	12,821	12,614	101.6
MSA[1]	1,144,208	1,210,718	94.5
U.S.	156,765,322	161,792,840	96.9

Note: (1) Figures cover the Pittsburgh, PA Metropolitan Statistical Area—see Appendix B for areas included
Source: U.S. Census Bureau, 2012-2016 American Community Survey 5-Year Estimates

Religious Groups by Family

Area	Catholic	Baptist	Non-Den.	Methodist[2]	Lutheran	LDS[3]	Pente-costal	Presby-terian[4]	Muslim[5]	Judaism
MSA[1]	32.8	2.3	2.8	5.7	3.4	0.4	1.1	4.7	0.3	0.7
U.S.	19.1	9.3	4.0	4.0	2.3	2.0	1.9	1.6	0.8	0.7

Note: Figures are the number of adherents as a percentage of the total population; (1) Figures cover the Pittsburgh, PA Metropolitan Statistical Area—see Appendix B for areas included; (2) Methodist/Pietist; (3) Latter Day Saints; (4) Reformed; (5) Figures are estimates
Source: Association of Statisticians of American Religious Bodies, 2010 U.S. Religion Census: Religious Congregations & Membership Study

Religious Groups by Tradition

Area	Catholic	Evangelical Protestant	Mainline Protestant	Other Tradition	Black Protestant	Orthodox
MSA[1]	32.8	7.4	13.8	2.1	0.9	0.7
U.S.	19.1	16.2	7.3	4.3	1.6	0.3

Note: Figures are the number of adherents as a percentage of the total population; (1) Figures cover the Pittsburgh, PA Metropolitan Statistical Area—see Appendix B for areas included
Source: Association of Statisticians of American Religious Bodies, 2010 U.S. Religion Census: Religious Congregations & Membership Study

ECONOMY

Gross Metropolitan Product

Area	2014	2015	2016	2017	Rank[2]
MSA[1]	134.7	138.6	142.1	147.9	24

Note: Figures are in billions of dollars; (1) Figures cover the Pittsburgh, PA Metropolitan Statistical Area—see Appendix B for areas included; (2) Rank is based on 2015 data and ranges from 1 to 381
Source: The U.S. Conference of Mayors, U.S. Metro Economies: GMP and Employment Report, 2015-2017

Economic Growth

Area	2012-14 (%)	2015 (%)	2016 (%)	2017 (%)	Rank[2]
MSA[1]	2.0	1.7	0.9	2.0	125
U.S.	2.0	2.4	1.9	2.6	–

Note: Figures are real gross metropolitan product (GMP) growth rates and represent average annual percent change; (1) Figures cover the Pittsburgh, PA Metropolitan Statistical Area—see Appendix B for areas included; (2) Rank is based on 2012-2014 average annual percent change and ranges from 1 to 381
Source: The U.S. Conference of Mayors, U.S. Metro Economies: GMP and Employment Report, 2015-2017

Metropolitan Area Exports

Area	2011	2012	2013	2014	2015	2016	Rank[2]
MSA[1]	15,165.5	14,134.7	10,444.4	10,015.8	9,137.1	7,971.0	39

Note: Figures are in millions of dollars; (1) Figures cover the Pittsburgh, PA Metropolitan Statistical Area—see Appendix B for areas included; (2) Rank is based on 2016 data and ranges from 1 to 385
Source: U.S. Department of Commerce, International Trade Administration, Office of Trade & Industry Information, Manufacturing & Services, data extracted March 15, 2018

Building Permits

Area	Single-Family			Multi-Family			Total		
	2016	2017p	Pct. Chg.	2016	2017p	Pct. Chg.	2016	2017p	Pct. Chg.
City	n/a	n/a	n/a	n/a	n/a	n/a	n/a	n/a	n/a
MSA[1]	999	1,053	5.4	510	815	59.8	1,509	1,868	23.8
U.S.	750,800	817,300	8.9	455,800	446,800	-2.0	1,206,600	1,264,100	4.8

Note: (1) Figures cover the Pittsburgh, PA Metropolitan Statistical Area—see Appendix B for areas included; Figures represent new, privately-owned housing units authorized (unadjusted data); All permit data are based on estimates with imputation; (p) preliminary data.
Source: U.S. Census Bureau, Manufacturing, Mining, and Construction Statistics, Building Permits, 2016, 2017

Bankruptcy Filings

Area	Business Filings 2016	Business Filings 2017	Business Filings % Chg.	Nonbusiness Filings 2016	Nonbusiness Filings 2017	Nonbusiness Filings % Chg.
Allegheny County	131	120	-8.4	2,299	2,583	12.4
U.S.	24,114	23,157	-4.0	770,846	765,863	-0.6

Note: Business filings include Chapter 7, Chapter 11, Chapter 12, and Chapter 13; Nonbusiness filings include Chapter 7, Chapter 11, and Chapter 13
Source: Administrative Office of the U.S. Courts, Business and Nonbusiness Bankruptcy, County Cases Commenced by Chapter of the Bankruptcy Code, During the 12-Month Period Ending December 31, 2016 and Business and Nonbusiness Bankruptcy, County Cases Commenced by Chapter of the Bankruptcy Code, During the 12-Month Period Ending December 31, 2017

Housing Vacancy Rates

Area	Gross Vacancy Rate[2] (%)			Year-Round Vacancy Rate[3] (%)			Rental Vacancy Rate[4] (%)			Homeowner Vacancy Rate[5] (%)		
	2015	2016	2017	2015	2016	2017	2015	2016	2017	2015	2016	2017
MSA[1]	13.5	17.7	13.6	13.2	17.4	13.4	7.1	7.4	9.7	1.5	1.8	2.2
U.S.	12.9	12.8	12.7	10.0	9.9	9.9	7.1	6.9	7.2	1.8	1.7	1.6

Note: (1) Figures cover the Pittsburgh, PA Metropolitan Statistical Area—see Appendix B for areas included; (2) The percentage of the total housing inventory that is vacant; (3) The percentage of the housing inventory (excluding seasonal units) that is year-round vacant; (4) The percentage of rental inventory that is vacant for rent; (5) The percentage of homeowner inventory that is vacant for sale
Source: U.S. Census Bureau, Housing Vacancies and Homeownership Annual Statistics: 2015, 2016, 2017

INCOME

Income

Area	Per Capita ($)	Median Household ($)	Average Household ($)
City	39,428	75,553	100,794
MSA[1]	31,728	54,020	73,756
U.S.	29,829	55,322	77,866

Note: (1) Figures cover the Pittsburgh, PA Metropolitan Statistical Area—see Appendix B for areas included
Source: U.S. Census Bureau, 2012-2016 American Community Survey 5-Year Estimates

Household Income Distribution

Area	Percent of Households Earning							
	Under $15,000	$15,000 -$24,999	$25,000 -$34,999	$35,000 -$49,999	$50,000 -$74,999	$75,000 -$99,999	$100,000 -$149,999	$150,000 and up
City	5.8	7.8	7.5	11.0	17.7	10.2	20.8	19.3
MSA[1]	12.2	11.0	10.1	13.1	18.2	12.5	13.6	9.4
U.S.	12.1	10.2	9.9	13.2	17.8	12.2	13.5	11.1

Note: (1) Figures cover the Pittsburgh, PA Metropolitan Statistical Area—see Appendix B for areas included
Source: U.S. Census Bureau, 2012-2016 American Community Survey 5-Year Estimates

Poverty Rate

Area	All Ages	Under 18 Years Old	18 to 64 Years Old	65 Years and Over
City	6.5	5.5	7.5	3.7
MSA[1]	12.0	16.9	11.7	7.9
U.S.	15.1	21.2	14.2	9.3

Note: Figures are percentage of people whose income during the past 12 months was below the poverty level; (1) Figures cover the Pittsburgh, PA Metropolitan Statistical Area—see Appendix B for areas included
Source: U.S. Census Bureau, 2012-2016 American Community Survey 5-Year Estimates

EMPLOYMENT

Labor Force and Employment

Area	Civilian Labor Force Dec. 2016	Civilian Labor Force Dec. 2017	Civilian Labor Force % Chg.	Workers Employed Dec. 2016	Workers Employed Dec. 2017	Workers Employed % Chg.
City	14,166	14,249	0.6	13,641	13,767	0.9
MSA[1]	1,197,241	1,200,452	0.3	1,135,886	1,146,911	1.0
U.S.	158,968,000	159,880,000	0.6	151,798,000	153,602,000	1.2

Note: Data is not seasonally adjusted and covers workers 16 years of age and older; (1) Figures cover the Pittsburgh, PA Metropolitan Statistical Area—see Appendix B for areas included
Source: Bureau of Labor Statistics, Local Area Unemployment Statistics

Unemployment Rate

Area	2017											
	Jan.	Feb.	Mar.	Apr.	May	Jun.	Jul.	Aug.	Sep.	Oct.	Nov.	Dec.
City	4.3	4.3	3.9	3.5	3.9	4.2	4.3	4.1	3.6	3.7	3.4	3.4
MSA[1]	6.1	6.0	5.5	4.6	4.9	5.2	5.3	5.4	4.4	4.3	4.4	4.5
U.S.	5.1	4.9	4.6	4.1	4.1	4.5	4.6	4.5	4.1	3.9	3.9	3.9

Note: Data is not seasonally adjusted and covers workers 16 years of age and older; (1) Figures cover the Pittsburgh, PA Metropolitan Statistical Area—see Appendix B for areas included
Source: Bureau of Labor Statistics, Local Area Unemployment Statistics

Average Wages

Occupation	$/Hr.	Occupation	$/Hr.
Accountants and Auditors	34.60	Maids and Housekeeping Cleaners	11.10
Automotive Mechanics	18.80	Maintenance and Repair Workers	18.80
Bookkeepers	18.50	Marketing Managers	69.80
Carpenters	26.00	Nuclear Medicine Technologists	28.70
Cashiers	9.40	Nurses, Licensed Practical	21.30
Clerks, General Office	15.90	Nurses, Registered	31.40
Clerks, Receptionists/Information	12.80	Nursing Assistants	14.30
Clerks, Shipping/Receiving	16.90	Packers and Packagers, Hand	11.70
Computer Programmers	35.10	Physical Therapists	38.10
Computer Systems Analysts	44.80	Postal Service Mail Carriers	23.70
Computer User Support Specialists	23.60	Real Estate Brokers	37.50
Cooks, Restaurant	11.70	Retail Salespersons	12.80
Dentists	41.20	Sales Reps., Exc. Tech./Scientific	35.30
Electrical Engineers	46.80	Sales Reps., Tech./Scientific	41.60
Electricians	31.70	Secretaries, Exc. Legal/Med./Exec.	17.00
Financial Managers	74.70	Security Guards	11.70
First-Line Supervisors/Managers, Sales	21.10	Surgeons	135.90
Food Preparation Workers	11.20	Teacher Assistants*	13.10
General and Operations Managers	61.80	Teachers, Elementary School*	30.40
Hairdressers/Cosmetologists	12.10	Teachers, Secondary School*	32.70
Internists, General	n/a	Telemarketers	11.80
Janitors and Cleaners	13.10	Truck Drivers, Heavy/Tractor-Trailer	22.40
Landscaping/Groundskeeping Workers	13.80	Truck Drivers, Light/Delivery Svcs.	16.40
Lawyers	66.30	Waiters and Waitresses	10.80

Note: Wage data covers the Pittsburgh, PA Metropolitan Statistical Area—see Appendix B for areas included; (*) Hourly wages for elementary/secondary school teachers and teacher assistants were calculated by the editors from annual wage data based on a 40 hour work week; n/a not available.
Source: Bureau of Labor Statistics, Metro Area Occupational Employment & Wage Estimates, May 2017

Employment by Occupation

Occupation Classification	City (%)	MSA[1] (%)	U.S. (%)
Management, Business, Science, and Arts	47.5	39.6	37.0
Natural Resources, Construction, and Maintenance	7.3	7.9	8.9
Production, Transportation, and Material Moving	7.3	11.1	12.2
Sales and Office	25.4	24.2	23.8
Service	12.5	17.2	18.1

Note: Figures cover employed civilians 16 years of age and older; (1) Figures cover the Pittsburgh, PA Metropolitan Statistical Area—see Appendix B for areas included
Source: U.S. Census Bureau, 2012-2016 American Community Survey 5-Year Estimates

Employment by Industry

Sector	MSA[1] Number of Employees	MSA[1] Percent of Total	U.S. Percent of Total
Construction	59,800	5.0	4.7
Education and Health Services	254,600	21.3	15.9
Financial Activities	72,700	6.1	5.7
Government	117,300	9.8	15.3
Information	18,600	1.6	1.9
Leisure and Hospitality	120,400	10.1	10.7
Manufacturing	86,200	7.2	8.5
Mining and Logging	10,400	0.9	0.5
Other Services	51,600	4.3	3.9
Professional and Business Services	182,800	15.3	14.0
Retail Trade	127,300	10.7	11.0
Transportation, Warehousing, and Utilities	48,700	4.1	4.1
Wholesale Trade	43,500	3.6	4.0

Note: Figures are non-farm employment as of December 2017. Figures are not seasonally adjusted and include workers 16 years of age and older; (1) Figures cover the Pittsburgh, PA Metropolitan Statistical Area—see Appendix B for areas included
Source: Bureau of Labor Statistics, Current Employment Statistics, Employment, Hours, and Earnings

Occupations with Greatest Projected Employment Growth: 2017 – 2019

Occupation[1]	2017 Employment	2019 Projected Employment	Numeric Employment Change	Percent Employment Change
Personal Care Aides	95,040	101,150	6,110	6.4
Combined Food Preparation and Serving Workers, Including Fast Food	149,690	154,700	5,010	3.3
Registered Nurses	143,300	147,290	3,990	2.8
Laborers and Freight, Stock, and Material Movers, Hand	138,050	141,860	3,810	2.8
Home Health Aides	46,950	50,700	3,750	8.0
Waiters and Waitresses	100,790	102,540	1,750	1.7
Janitors and Cleaners, Except Maids and Housekeeping Cleaners	98,590	100,250	1,660	1.7
Cooks, Restaurant	49,820	51,120	1,300	2.6
Software Developers, Applications	25,890	27,190	1,300	5.0
Nursing Assistants	80,510	81,790	1,280	1.6

Note: Projections cover Pennsylvania; (1) Sorted by numeric employment change
Source: www.projectionscentral.com, State Occupational Projections, 2017–2019 Short-Term Projections

Fastest Growing Occupations: 2017 – 2019

Occupation[1]	2017 Employment	2019 Projected Employment	Numeric Employment Change	Percent Employment Change
Home Health Aides	46,950	50,700	3,750	8.0
Statisticians	2,710	2,880	170	6.5
Personal Care Aides	95,040	101,150	6,110	6.4
Physician Assistants	5,620	5,960	340	6.1
Nurse Practitioners	5,240	5,550	310	6.0
Operations Research Analysts	2,660	2,800	140	5.1
Information Security Analysts	3,020	3,170	150	5.0
Software Developers, Applications	25,890	27,190	1,300	5.0
Nonfarm Animal Caretakers	7,820	8,210	390	4.9
Physical Therapist Assistants	4,660	4,880	220	4.8

Note: Projections cover Pennsylvania; (1) Sorted by percent employment change and excludes occupations with numeric employment change less than 50
Source: www.projectionscentral.com, State Occupational Projections, 2017–2019 Short-Term Projections

TAXES

State Corporate Income Tax Rates

State	Tax Rate (%)	Income Brackets ($)	Num. of Brackets	Financial Institution Tax Rate (%)[a]	Federal Income Tax Ded.
Pennsylvania	9.99	Flat rate	1	(a)	No

Note: Tax rates as of January 1, 2018; (a) Rates listed are the corporate income tax rate applied to financial institutions or excise taxes based on income. Some states have other taxes based upon the value of deposits or shares.
Source: Federation of Tax Administrators, Range of State Corporate Income Tax Rates, January 1, 2018

State Individual Income Tax Rates

State	Tax Rate (%)	Income Brackets ($)	Num. of Brackets	Personal Exempt. ($)[1]		Fed. Inc. Tax Ded.
				Single	Dependents	
Pennsylvania	3.07	Flat rate	1	None	None	No

Note: Tax rates as of January 1, 2018; Local- and county-level taxes are not included; n/a not applicable; (1) Married joint filers generally receive double the single exemption
Source: Federation of Tax Administrators, State Individual Income Tax Rates, January 1, 2018

Various State Sales and Excise Tax Rates

State	State Sales Tax (%)	Gasoline[1] (¢/gal.)	Cigarette[2] ($/pack)	Spirits[3] ($/gal.)	Wine[4] ($/gal.)	Beer[5] ($/gal.)	Recreational Marijuana (%)
Pennsylvania	6.0	58.7	2.60	7.24 (g)	(m)	0.08	Not legal

Note: All tax rates as of January 1, 2018; (1) The American Petroleum Institute has developed a methodology for determining the average tax rate on a gallon of fuel. Rates may include any of the following: excise taxes, environmental fees, storage tank fees, other fees or taxes, general sales tax, and local taxes. In states where gasoline is subject to the general sales tax, or where the fuel tax is based on the average sale price, the average rate determined by API is sensitive to changes in the price of gasoline. States that fully or partially apply general sales taxes to gasoline: CA, CO, GA, IL, IN, MI, NY; (2) The federal excise tax of $1.0066 per pack and local taxes are not included; (3) Rates are those applicable to off-premise sales of 40% alcohol by volume (a.b.v.) distilled spirits in 750ml containers. Local excise taxes are excluded; (4) Rates are those applicable to off-premise sales of 11% a.b.v. non-carbonated wine in 750ml containers; (5) Rates are those applicable to off-premise sales of 4.7% a.b.v. beer in 12 ounce containers; (g) Control states, where the government controls all sales. Products can be subject to ad valorem mark-up as well as excise taxes; (m) Control states, where the government controls all sales. Products can be subject to ad valorem mark-up as well as excise taxes.
Source: Tax Foundation, 2018 Facts & Figures: How Does Your State Compare?

State Business Tax Climate Index Rankings

State	Overall Rank	Corporate Tax Rank	Individual Income Tax Rank	Sales Tax Rank	Unemployment Insurance Tax Rank	Property Tax Rank
Pennsylvania	26	44	17	21	50	33

Note: The index is a measure of how each state's tax laws affect economic performance. The lower the rank, the more favorable a state's tax system is for business. States without a given tax are given a ranking of 1. The scores/rankings for the District of Columbia do not affect other states. The 2018 index represents the tax climate as of July 1, 2017.
Source: Tax Foundation, State Business Tax Climate Index 2018

TRANSPORTATION

Means of Transportation to Work

Area	Car/Truck/Van		Public Transportation			Bicycle	Walked	Other Means	Worked at Home
	Drove Alone	Car-pooled	Bus	Subway	Railroad				
City	79.5	10.0	3.3	0.0	0.0	0.0	2.5	1.1	3.6
MSA[1]	77.5	8.4	4.9	0.2	0.0	0.4	3.4	1.1	4.1
U.S.	76.4	9.3	2.6	1.9	0.6	0.6	2.8	1.3	4.6

Note: Figures are percentages and cover workers 16 years of age and older; (1) Figures cover the Pittsburgh, PA Metropolitan Statistical Area—see Appendix B for areas included
Source: U.S. Census Bureau, 2012-2016 American Community Survey 5-Year Estimates

Travel Time to Work

Area	Less Than 10 Minutes	10 to 19 Minutes	20 to 29 Minutes	30 to 44 Minutes	45 to 59 Minutes	60 to 89 Minutes	90 Minutes or More
City	13.8	35.4	16.0	18.9	8.7	5.3	1.8
MSA[1]	12.1	27.3	21.4	22.1	9.3	5.9	2.0
U.S.	12.9	29.2	20.9	20.4	8.0	6.0	2.7

Note: Note: Figures are percentages and include workers 16 years old and over; (1) Figures cover the Pittsburgh, PA Metropolitan Statistical Area—see Appendix B for areas included
Source: U.S. Census Bureau, 2012-2016 American Community Survey 5-Year Estimates

Freeway Travel Time Index

Area	1985	1990	1995	2000	2005	2010	2014
Urban Area Rank[1,2]	39	33	36	46	42	42	42
Urban Area Index[1]	1.08	1.13	1.15	1.16	1.18	1.18	1.19
Average Index[3]	1.09	1.11	1.14	1.17	1.20	1.19	1.20

Note: Freeway Travel Time Index—the ratio of travel time in the peak period to the travel time at free-flow conditions. For example, a value of 1.30 indicates a 20-minute free-flow trip takes 26 minutes in the peak (20 minutes x 1.30 = 26 minutes); (1) Covers the Pittsburgh PA urban area; (2) Rank is based on 101 urban areas (#1 = highest travel time index); (3) Average of 101 urban areas
Source: Texas Transportation Institute, 2015 Urban Mobility Scorecard, August 2015

Freeway Commuter Stress Index

Area	1985	1990	1995	2000	2005	2010	2014
Urban Area Rank[1,2]	42	36	40	40	44	45	43
Urban Area Index[1]	1.11	1.17	1.19	1.21	1.22	1.22	1.23
Average Index[3]	1.13	1.16	1.19	1.22	1.25	1.24	1.25

Note: The Freeway Commuter Stress Index is the same as the Freeway Travel Time Index (see table above) except that it includes only the travel in the peak directions during the peak periods; the TTI includes travel in all directions during the peak period. Thus, the CSI is more indicative of the work trip experienced by each commuter on a daily basis; (1) Covers the Pittsburgh PA urban area; (2) Rank is based on 101 urban areas (#1 = highest travel time index); (3) Average of 101 urban areas
Source: Texas Transportation Institute, 2015 Urban Mobility Scorecard, August 2015

Living Environment

COST OF LIVING

Cost of Living Index

Composite Index	Groceries	Housing	Utilities	Trans-portation	Health Care	Misc. Goods/ Services
99.4	110.4	91.5	110.0	106.7	93.8	97.4

Note: The Cost of Living Index measures regional differences in the cost of consumer goods and services, excluding taxes and non-consumer expenditures, for professional and managerial households in the top income quintile. It is based on more than 50,000 prices covering almost 60 different items for which prices are collected three times a year by chambers of commerce, economic development organizations or university applied economic centers in each participating urban area. The numbers shown should be read as a percentage above or below the national average of 100. For example, a value of 115.4 in the groceries column indicates that grocery prices are 15.4% higher than the national average. Small differences in the index numbers should not be interpreted as significant; Figures cover the Pittsburgh PA urban area.
Source: The Council for Community and Economic Research, ACCRA Cost of Living Index, 2017

Grocery Prices

Area[1]	T-Bone Steak ($/pound)	Frying Chicken ($/pound)	Whole Milk ($/half gal.)	Eggs ($/dozen)	Orange Juice ($/64 oz.)	Coffee ($/11.5 oz.)
City[2]	13.40	1.57	1.90	1.05	3.91	4.74
Avg.	11.29	1.40	2.02	1.47	3.55	4.37
Min.	7.71	0.93	1.04	0.70	2.86	3.24
Max.	15.83	2.39	4.03	3.92	6.29	8.16

Note: (1) Values for the local area are compared with the average, minimum and maximum values for all 294 areas in the Cost of Living Index; (2) Figures cover the Pittsburgh PA urban area; ***T-Bone Steak*** *(price per pound);* ***Frying Chicken*** *(price per pound, whole fryer);* ***Whole Milk*** *(half gallon carton);* ***Eggs*** *(price per dozen, Grade A, large);* ***Orange Juice*** *(64 oz. Tropicana or Florida Natural);* ***Coffee*** *(11.5 oz. can, vacuum-packed, Maxwell House, Hills Bros, or Folgers).*
Source: The Council for Community and Economic Research, ACCRA Cost of Living Index, 2017

Housing and Utility Costs

Area[1]	New Home Price ($)	Apartment Rent ($/month)	All Electric ($/month)	Part Electric ($/month)	Other Energy ($/month)	Telephone ($/month)
City[2]	281,247	1,110	-	96.22	90.24	30.99
Avg.	335,956	1,047	175.01	97.34	67.93	28.71
Min.	187,788	491	109.48	49.33	35.44	12.39
Max.	1,739,087	4,559	432.62	227.09	353.33	44.61

Note: (1) Values for the local area are compared with the average, minimum and maximum values for all 294 areas in the Cost of Living Index; (2) Figures cover the Pittsburgh PA urban area; ***New Home Price*** *(2,400 sf living area, 8,000 sf lot, in urban area with full utilities);* ***Apartment Rent*** *(950 sf 2 bedroom/1.5 or 2 bath, unfurnished, excluding all utilities except water);* ***All Electric*** *(average monthly cost for an all-electric home);* ***Part Electric*** *(average monthly cost for a part-electric home);* ***Other Energy*** *(average monthly cost for natural gas, fuel oil, coal, wood, and any other forms of energy except electricity);* ***Telephone*** *(price includes basic monthly rate for a private residential line plus additional local usage charges incurred by a family of four).*
Source: The Council for Community and Economic Research, ACCRA Cost of Living Index, 2017

Health Care, Transportation, and Other Costs

Area[1]	Doctor ($/visit)	Dentist ($/visit)	Optometrist ($/visit)	Gasoline ($/gallon)	Beauty Salon ($/visit)	Men's Shirt ($)
City[2]	98.75	86.30	86.58	2.61	32.20	26.61
Avg.	108.00	92.54	101.93	2.25	37.58	30.92
Min.	30.39	60.00	49.75	1.82	16.11	11.20
Max.	193.50	161.94	229.28	3.16	77.35	59.13

Note: (1) Values for the local area are compared with the average, minimum and maximum values for all 294 areas in the Cost of Living Index; (2) Figures cover the Pittsburgh PA urban area; ***Doctor*** *(general practitioners routine exam of an established patient);* ***Dentist*** *(adult teeth cleaning and periodic oral examination);* ***Optometrist*** *(full vision eye exam for established adult patient);* ***Gasoline*** *(one gallon regular unleaded, national brand, including all taxes, cash price at self-service pump if available);* ***Beauty Salon*** *(woman's shampoo, trim, and blow-dry);* ***Men's Shirt*** *(cotton/polyester dress shirt, pinpoint weave, long sleeves).*
Source: The Council for Community and Economic Research, ACCRA Cost of Living Index, 2017

HOUSING

House Price Index (HPI)

Area	National Ranking[2]	Quarterly Change (%)	One-Year Change (%)	Five-Year Change (%)
MSA[1]	186	0.79	4.10	19.67
U.S.[3]	–	1.61	6.68	34.71

Note: The HPI is a weighted repeat sales index. It measures average price changes in repeat sales or refinancings on the same properties. This information is obtained by reviewing repeat mortgage transactions on single-family properties whose mortgages have been purchased or securitized by Fannie Mae or Freddie Mac in January 1975; (1) Figures cover the Pittsburgh, PA Metropolitan Statistical Area—see Appendix B for areas included; (2) Rankings are based on annual percentage change for all metro areas containing at least 15,000 transactions over the last 10 years and ranges from 1 to 253; (3) figures based on a weighted average of Census Division estimates using a seasonally adjusted, purchase-only index; all figures are for the period ending December 31, 2017

Source: Federal Housing Finance Agency, House Price Index, February 28, 2018

Median Single-Family Home Prices

Area	2015	2016	2017[p]	Percent Change 2016 to 2017
MSA[1]	n/a	n/a	n/a	n/a
U.S. Average	223.9	235.5	248.8	5.6

Note: Figures are median sales prices of existing single-family homes in thousands of dollars; (p) preliminary; n/a not available; (1) Figures cover the Pittsburgh, PA Metropolitan Statistical Area—see Appendix B for areas included

Source: National Association of Realtors, Median Sales Price of Existing Single-Family Homes for Metropolitan Areas, 4th Quarter 2017

Qualifying Income Based on Median Sales Price of Existing Single-Family Homes

Area	With 5% Down ($)	With 10% Down ($)	With 20% Down ($)
MSA[1]	n/a	n/a	n/a
U.S. Average	55,585	52,659	46,808

Note: Figures are preliminary; Qualifying income is based on a mortgage rate of 4.17%. Monthly principal and interest payment is limited to 25% of income; n/a not available; (1) Figures cover the Pittsburgh, PA Metropolitan Statistical Area—see Appendix B for areas included

Source: National Association of Realtors, Qualifying Income Based on Median Sales Price of Existing Single-Family Homes for Metropolitan Areas, 4th Quarter 2017

Median Apartment Condo-Coop Home Prices

Area	2015	2016	2017[p]	Percent Change 2016 to 2017
MSA[1]	n/a	n/a	n/a	n/a
U.S. Average	210.7	220.7	234.3	6.2

Note: Figures are median sales prices of existing apartment condo-coop homes in thousands of dollars; (p) preliminary; n/a not available; (1) Figures cover the Pittsburgh, PA Metropolitan Statistical Area—see Appendix B for areas included

Source: National Association of Realtors, Median Sales Price of Existing Apartment Condo-Coop Homes for Metropolitan Areas, 4th Quarter 2017

Home Value Distribution

Area	Under $50,000	$50,000 -$99,999	$100,000 -$149,999	$150,000 -$199,999	$200,000 -$299,999	$300,000 -$499,999	$500,000 -$999,999	$1,000,000 or more
City	2.8	9.4	17.2	23.7	26.0	17.4	3.3	0.2
MSA[1]	11.1	23.5	20.5	17.3	15.2	9.3	2.7	0.5
U.S.	8.8	14.8	15.3	14.9	18.4	16.4	9.0	2.5

Note: Figures are percentages and cover owner-occupied housing units; (1) Figures cover the Pittsburgh, PA Metropolitan Statistical Area—see Appendix B for areas included

Source: U.S. Census Bureau, 2012-2016 American Community Survey 5-Year Estimates

Homeownership Rate

Area	2009 (%)	2010 (%)	2011 (%)	2012 (%)	2013 (%)	2014 (%)	2015 (%)	2016 (%)	2017 (%)
MSA[1]	71.7	70.4	70.3	67.9	68.3	69.1	71.0	72.2	72.7
U.S.	67.4	66.9	66.1	65.4	65.1	64.5	63.7	63.4	63.9

Note: (1) Figures cover the Pittsburgh, PA Metropolitan Statistical Area—see Appendix B for areas included

Source: U.S. Census Bureau, Housing Vacancies and Homeownership Annual Statistics: 2009-2017

Year Housing Structure Built

Area	2010 or Later	2000 -2009	1990 -1999	1980 -1989	1970 -1979	1960 -1969	1950 -1959	1940 -1949	Before 1940	Median Year
City	4.1	9.6	14.4	10.8	20.4	19.3	12.7	4.8	3.9	1975
MSA[1]	1.3	6.7	7.6	7.4	12.1	11.4	17.0	9.2	27.4	1958
U.S.	2.3	14.7	14.0	13.7	15.6	10.9	10.6	5.2	13.0	1977

Note: Figures are percentages except for Median Year; Note: (1) Figures cover the Pittsburgh, PA Metropolitan Statistical Area—see Appendix B for areas included
Source: U.S. Census Bureau, 2012-2016 American Community Survey 5-Year Estimates

Gross Monthly Rent

Area	Under $500	$500 -$999	$1,000 -$1,499	$1,500 -$1,999	$2,000 -$2,499	$2,500 -$2,999	$3,000 and up	Median ($)
City	1.4	61.2	30.9	3.7	2.7	0.0	0.0	919
MSA[1]	19.5	56.6	17.3	4.0	1.5	0.5	0.5	749
U.S.	11.3	43.3	27.7	10.7	4.0	1.6	1.5	949

Note: Figures are percentages except for Median; Gross rent is the contract rent plus the estimated average monthly cost of utilities (electricity, gas, and water and sewer) and fuels (oil, coal, kerosene, wood, etc.) if these are paid by the renter (or paid for the renter by someone else); (1) Figures cover the Pittsburgh, PA Metropolitan Statistical Area—see Appendix B for areas included
Source: U.S. Census Bureau, 2012-2016 American Community Survey 5-Year Estimates

HEALTH

Health Risk Factors

Category	MSA[1] (%)	U.S. (%)
Adults aged 18–64 who have any kind of health care coverage	94.1	87.7
Adults who reported being in good or excellent health	85.0	83.6
Adults who are current smokers	17.4	17.1
Adults who currently use E-cigarettes	4.9	4.7
Adults who currently use chewing tobacco, snuff, or snus	4.9	4.0
Adults who are heavy drinkers[2]	6.6	6.5
Adults who are binge drinkers[3]	21.6	16.9
Adults who are overweight (BMI 25.0 - 29.9)	35.1	35.3
Adults who are obese (BMI 30.0 - 99.8)	31.8	29.9
Adults who participated in any physical activities in the past month	78.0	76.9
Adults who always or nearly always wears a seat belt	89.5	94.3

Note: (1) Figures cover the Pittsburgh, PA Metropolitan Statistical Area—see Appendix B for areas included; (2) Heavy drinkers are classified as adult men having more than 14 drinks per week and adult women having more than 7 drinks per week; (3) Binge drinkers are classified as males having five or more drinks on one occasion or females having four or more drinks on one occasion
Source: Centers for Disease Control and Prevention, Behaviorial Risk Factor Surveillance System, SMART: Selected Metropolitan Area Risk Trends, 2016

Health Screening Rates

Category	MSA[1] (%)	U.S. (%)
Adults 50-75 who have had a blood stool test within the past year	8.5	8.0
Adults 50-75 who have had a colonoscopy in the past 10 years	64.8	63.5
Adults aged 65+ who have had flu shot within the past year	69.5	58.6
Adults aged 65+ who have ever had a pneumonia vaccination	80.7	73.4
Adults who have ever been tested for HIV	26.8	35.6
Women aged 21-65 who have had a pap test in the past three years	80.8	79.8
Men aged 40+ who have had a PSA test within the past two years	40.0	39.5
Women aged 40+ who have had a mammogram within the past two years	74.2	72.5

Note: n/a not available; (1) Figures cover the Pittsburgh, PA Metropolitan Statistical Area—see Appendix B for areas included; Source: Centers for Disease Control and Prevention, Behaviorial Risk Factor Surveillance System, SMART: Selected Metropolitan Area Risk Trends, 2016

Chronic Health Conditions

Category	MSA[1] (%)	U.S. (%)
Adults who have ever been told they had a heart attack	5.3	4.4
Adults who have ever been told they have angina or coronary heart disease	5.0	4.1
Adults who have ever been told they had a stroke	3.9	3.1
Adults who have been told they currently have asthma	10.1	9.3
Adults who have ever been told they have arthritis	33.5	25.8
Adults who have ever been told they have diabetes[2]	11.1	10.5
Adults who have ever been told they had skin cancer	6.8	5.9
Adults who have ever been told they had any other types of cancer	6.5	6.7
Adults who have ever been told they have COPD	8.0	6.3
Adults who have ever been told they have kidney disease	2.6	2.8
Adults who have ever been told they have a form of depression	18.4	17.4

Note: (1) Figures cover the Pittsburgh, PA Metropolitan Statistical Area—see Appendix B for areas included; (2) Figures do not include pregnancy-related, borderline, or pre-diabetes
Source: Centers for Disease Control and Prevention, Behaviorial Risk Factor Surveillance System, SMART: Selected Metropolitan Area Risk Trends, 2016

Mortality Rates for the Top 10 Causes of Death in the U.S.

ICD-10[a] Sub-Chapter	ICD-10[a] Code	Age-Adjusted Mortality Rate[1] per 100,000 population	
		County[2]	U.S.
Malignant neoplasms	C00-C97	170.5	158.5
Ischaemic heart diseases	I20-I25	117.4	96.8
Other forms of heart disease	I30-I51	55.0	52.4
Chronic lower respiratory diseases	J40-J47	37.5	40.9
Cerebrovascular diseases	I60-I69	35.0	37.2
Organic, including symptomatic, mental disorders	F01-F09	40.6	33.3
Other degenerative diseases of the nervous system	G30-G31	25.1	32.1
Other external causes of accidental injury	W00-X59	53.1	31.2
Diabetes mellitus	E10-E14	19.0	21.1
Hypertensive diseases	I10-I15	12.7	20.8

Note: (a) ICD-10 = International Classification of Diseases 10th Revision; (1) Mortality rates are a three year average covering 2014-2016; (2) Figures cover Allegheny County.
Source: Centers for Disease Control and Prevention, National Center for Health Statistics. Underlying Cause of Death 1999-2016 on CDC WONDER Online Database, released December 2017

Mortality Rates for Selected Causes of Death

ICD-10[a] Sub-Chapter	ICD-10[a] Code	Age-Adjusted Mortality Rate[1] per 100,000 population	
		County[2]	U.S.
Assault	X85-Y09	9.3	5.6
Diseases of the liver	K70-K76	16.2	14.0
Human immunodeficiency virus (HIV) disease	B20-B24	0.9	1.9
Influenza and pneumonia	J09-J18	15.8	14.6
Intentional self-harm	X60-X84	12.8	13.2
Malnutrition	E40-E46	1.2	1.3
Obesity and other hyperalimentation	E65-E68	1.5	2.1
Renal failure	N17-N19	15.1	13.0
Transport accidents	V01-V99	6.6	12.0
Viral hepatitis	B15-B19	1.2	1.9

Note: (a) ICD-10 = International Classification of Diseases 10th Revision; (1) Mortality rates are a three year average covering 2014-2016; (2) Figures cover Allegheny County; Data are Suppressed when the data meet the criteria for confidentiality constraints; Mortality rates are flagged as Unreliable when the rate would be calculated with a numerator of 20 or less.
Source: Centers for Disease Control and Prevention, National Center for Health Statistics. Underlying Cause of Death 1999-2016 on CDC WONDER Online Database, released December 2017

Health Insurance Coverage

Area	With Health Insurance	With Private Health Insurance	With Public Health Insurance	Without Health Insurance	Population Under Age 18 Without Health Insurance
City	96.4	88.0	20.9	3.6	0.3
MSA[1]	94.1	76.7	33.5	5.9	2.4
U.S.	88.3	66.7	33.0	11.7	5.9

Note: Figures are percentages that cover the civilian noninstitutionalized population; (1) Figures cover the Pittsburgh, PA Metropolitan Statistical Area—see Appendix B for areas included
Source: U.S. Census Bureau, 2012-2016 American Community Survey 5-Year Estimates

Number of Medical Professionals

Area	MDs[3]	DOs[3,4]	Dentists	Podiatrists	Chiropractors	Optometrists
County[1] (number)	7,639	462	1,159	129	522	235
County[1] (rate[2])	621.0	37.6	94.4	10.5	42.5	19.1
U.S. (rate[2])	276.5	22.3	67.3	6.0	26.7	15.9

Note: Data as of 2016 unless noted; (1) Data covers Allegheny County; (2) Rate per 100,000 population; (3) Data as of 2015 and includes all active, non-federal physicians; (4) Doctor of Osteopathic Medicine
Source: U.S. Department of Health and Human Services, Health Resources and Services Administration, Bureau of Health Professions, Area Resource File (ARF) 2016-2017

Best Hospitals

According to *U.S. News*, the Pittsburgh, PA metro area is home to two of the best hospitals in the U.S.: **Magee-Womens Hospital of UPMC** (1 adult specialty); **UPMC Presbyterian Shadyside** (Honor Roll/14 adult specialties). The hospitals listed were nationally ranked in at least one of 16 specialties. Only 152 hospitals nationwide were nationally ranked in one or more specialties. Twenty hospitals in the U.S. made the Honor Roll. The Best Hospitals Honor Roll was revamped last year to take both the national rankings and the procedure and condition ratings into account. Hospitals received points if they were nationally ranked in one of the 16 specialties—the higher they ranked, the more points they got—and how many ratings of "high performing" they earned in the nine procedures and conditions. *U.S. News Online, "America's Best Hospitals 2017-18"*

According to *U.S. News*, the Pittsburgh, PA metro area is home to one of the best children's hospitals in the U.S.: **Children's Hospital of Pittsburgh of UPMC** (Honor Roll/10 pediatric specialties). The hospital listed was highly ranked in at least one of 10 pediatric specialties. Eighty-two children's hospitals in the U.S. were nationally ranked in at least one specialty. Hospitals received points for being ranked in a specialty, and the 10 hospitals with the most points across the 10 specialties make up the Honor Roll. *U.S. News Online, "America's Best Children's Hospitals 2017-18"*

EDUCATION

Public School District Statistics

District Name	Schls	Pupils	Pupil/ Teacher Ratio	Minority Pupils[1] (%)	Free Lunch Eligible[2] (%)	IEP[3] (%)
Moon Area SD	9	3,715	12.4	15.8	19.5	15.5

Note: Table includes school districts with 100 or more students; (1) Percentage of students that are not non-Hispanic white; (2) Percentage of students that are eligible for the free lunch program; (3) Percentage of students that have an Individualized Education Program.
Source: U.S. Department of Education, National Center for Education Statistics, Common Core of Data, Local Education Agency (School District) Universe Survey: School Year 2015-2016; U.S. Department of Education, National Center for Education Statistics, Common Core of Data, Public Elementary/Secondary School Universe Survey: School Year 2015-2016

Highest Level of Education

Area	Less than H.S.	H.S. Diploma	Some College, No Deg.	Associate Degree	Bachelor's Degree	Master's Degree	Prof. School Degree	Doctorate Degree
City	5.2	20.9	15.2	8.9	31.3	13.6	2.6	2.2
MSA[1]	7.1	34.3	16.3	9.8	19.9	9.0	2.1	1.5
U.S.	13.0	27.5	21.0	8.2	18.8	8.2	2.0	1.3

Note: Figures cover persons age 25 and over; (1) Figures cover the Pittsburgh, PA Metropolitan Statistical Area—see Appendix B for areas included
Source: U.S. Census Bureau, 2012-2016 American Community Survey 5-Year Estimates

Educational Attainment by Race

Area	High School Graduate or Higher (%)					Bachelor's Degree or Higher (%)				
	Total	White	Black	Asian	Hisp.[2]	Total	White	Black	Asian	Hisp.[2]
City	94.8	96.0	87.8	82.0	76.6	49.8	49.6	35.9	73.6	35.6
MSA[1]	92.9	93.3	88.9	88.4	86.2	32.5	32.9	18.6	71.7	35.8
U.S.	87.0	88.9	84.3	86.3	65.7	30.3	31.6	20.0	52.1	14.7

Note: Figures shown cover persons 25 years old and over; (1) Figures cover the Pittsburgh, PA Metropolitan Statistical Area—see Appendix B for areas included; (2) People of Hispanic origin can be of any race
Source: U.S. Census Bureau, 2012-2016 American Community Survey 5-Year Estimates

School Enrollment by Grade and Control

Area	Preschool (%)		Kindergarten (%)		Grades 1 - 4 (%)		Grades 5 - 8 (%)		Grades 9 - 12 (%)	
	Public	Private	Public	Private	Public	Private	Public	Private	Public	Private
City	42.0	58.0	84.1	15.9	87.2	12.8	90.3	9.7	92.5	7.5
MSA[1]	48.3	51.7	84.3	15.7	87.5	12.5	88.2	11.8	89.7	10.3
U.S.	58.4	41.6	87.7	12.3	89.8	10.2	89.7	10.3	90.4	9.6

Note: Figures shown cover persons 3 years old and over; (1) Figures cover the Pittsburgh, PA Metropolitan Statistical Area—see Appendix B for areas included
Source: U.S. Census Bureau, 2012-2016 American Community Survey 5-Year Estimates

Average Salaries of Public School Classroom Teachers

Area	2015		2016		Change from 2015 to 2016	
	Dollars	Rank[1]	Dollars	Rank[1]	Percent	Rank[2]
Pennsylvania	64,447	10	65,151	10	1.1	24
U.S. Average	57,611	–	58,353	–	1.3	–

Note: (1) Rank ranges from 1 to 51 where 1 indicates highest salary; (2) Rank ranges from 1 to 51 where 1 indicates highest percent change.
Source: National Education Association, Rankings & Estimates: Rankings of the States 2016 and Estimates of School Statistics 2017

Higher Education

Four-Year Colleges			Two-Year Colleges			Medical Schools[1]	Law Schools[2]	Voc/ Tech[3]
Public	Private Non-profit	Private For-profit	Public	Private Non-profit	Private For-profit			
0	1	0	0	0	0	0	0	0

Note: Figures cover institutions located within the city limits and include main campuses only; (1) includes schools accredited by the Liaison Committee on Medical Education and the American Osteopathic Association's Commission on Osteopathic College Accreditation; (2) includes ABA-accredited schools, schools with provisional ABA accreditation, and state accredited schools; (3) includes all schools with programs that are less than 2 years.
Source: National Center for Education Statistics, Integrated Postsecondary Education System (IPEDS), 2016-17; Wikipedia, List of Medical Schools in the United States, accessed April 2, 2018; Wikipedia, List of Law Schools in the United States, accessed April 2, 2018

According to *U.S. News & World Report,* the Pittsburgh, PA metro area is home to four of the best national universities in the U.S.: **Carnegie Mellon University** (#25 tie); **University of Pittsburgh** (#68); **Duquesne University** (#120 tie); **Robert Morris University** (#176 tie). The indicators used to capture academic quality fall into a number of categories: assessment by administrators at peer institutions; retention of students; faculty resources; student selectivity; financial resources; alumni giving; high school counselor ratings of colleges; and graduation rate. *U.S. News & World Report, "America's Best Colleges 2018"*

According to *U.S. News & World Report,* the Pittsburgh, PA metro area is home to two of the best liberal arts colleges in the U.S.: **Washington and Jefferson College** (#106 tie); **Saint Vincent College** (#147 tie). The indicators used to capture academic quality fall into a number of categories: assessment by administrators at peer institutions; retention of students; faculty resources; student selectivity; financial resources; alumni giving; high school counselor ratings of colleges; and graduation rate. *U.S. News & World Report, "America's Best Colleges 2018"*

According to *U.S. News & World Report,* the Pittsburgh, PA metro area is home to one of the top 100 law schools in the U.S.: **University of Pittsburgh** (#74 tie). The rankings are based on a weighted average of 12 measures of quality: peer assessment score; assessment score by lawyers/judges; median LSAT scores; median undergrad GPA; acceptance rate; employment rates for graduates; placement success; bar passage rate; faculty resources; expenditures per student; student/faculty ratio; and library resources. *U.S. News & World Report, "America's Best Graduate Schools, Law, 2019"*

According to *U.S. News & World Report,* the Pittsburgh, PA metro area is home to one of the top 75 medical schools for research in the U.S.: **University of Pittsburgh** (#14). The rankings are based on a weighted average of 11 measures of quality: quality assessment; peer assessment score; assessment score by residency directors; research activity; total research activity; average research activity per faculty member; student selectivity; median MCAT total score; median undergraduate GPA; acceptance rate; and faculty resources. *U.S. News & World Report, "America's Best Graduate Schools, Medical, 2019"*

According to *U.S. News & World Report,* the Pittsburgh, PA metro area is home to two of the top 75 business schools in the U.S.: **Carnegie Mellon University (Tepper)** (#17 tie); **University of Pittsburgh (Katz)** (#52). The rankings are based on a weighted average of the following nine measures: quality assessment; peer assessment; recruiter assessment; placement success; mean starting salary and bonus; student selectivity; mean GMAT and GRE scores; mean undergraduate GPA; and acceptance rate. *U.S. News & World Report, "America's Best Graduate Schools, Business, 2019"*

PRESIDENTIAL ELECTION

2016 Presidential Election Results

Area	Clinton	Trump	Johnson	Stein	Other
Allegheny County	55.9	39.5	2.5	0.8	1.4
U.S.	48.0	45.9	3.3	1.1	1.7

Note: Results are percentages and may not add to 100% due to rounding
Source: Dave Leip's Atlas of U.S. Presidential Elections

EMPLOYERS

Major Employers

Company Name	Industry
Allegheny General Hospital	Extended care facility
Associated Cleaning Consultants	Janitorial service, contract basis
Bayer Corporation	Pharmaceutical preparations
Children's Hospital of Pittsburgh	Specialty hospitals, except psychiatric
Duquesne University of the Holy Spirit	Colleges & universities
Highmark	Hospital & medical service plans
Jefferson Regional Medical Center	General medical & surgical hospitals
Magee-Womens Hospital of UPMC	Hospital, affiliated with ama residency
Mercy Life Center Corporation	Charitable organizations
Mercy Life Center Corporation	Mental health clinic, outpatient
PNC Bank, National Association	National trust companies with deposits, commercial
United States Steel Corporation	Blast furnaces & steel mills
United States Steel International	Steel
University of Pittsburgh	Colleges & universities
UPMC Mercy	General medical & surgical hospitals
UPMC Shadyside	General medical & surgical hospitals
US Dept of Energy	Noncommercial research organizations
Veterans Health Administration	Administration of veterans' affairs
West Penn Allegheny Health System	Management services

Note: Companies shown are located within the Pittsburgh, PA Metropolitan Statistical Area.
Source: Hoovers.com; Wikipedia

PUBLIC SAFETY

Crime Rate

Area	All Crimes	Violent Crimes				Property Crimes		
		Murder	Rape[3]	Robbery	Aggrav. Assault	Burglary	Larceny -Theft	Motor Vehicle Theft
City	1,052.4	0.0	15.5	7.7	50.3	174.1	789.3	15.5
Metro[1]	2,035.5	5.1	22.9	82.9	178.1	309.5	1,349.8	87.2
U.S.	2,847.8	5.3	40.4	102.8	248.5	468.9	1,745.0	236.9

Note: Figures are crimes per 100,000 population; (1) Figures cover the Pittsburgh, PA Metropolitan Statistical Area—see Appendix B for areas included; (3) The city and U.S. figures shown were reported using the revised Uniform Crime Reporting (UCR) definition of rape. The metro area figures shown are an aggregate total of the data submitted using both the revised and legacy UCR definitions.
Source: FBI Uniform Crime Reports, 2016

Hate Crimes

Area	Number of Quarters Reported	Number of Incidents per Bias Motivation					
		Race/Ethnicity/ Ancestry	Religion	Sexual Orientation	Disability	Gender	Gender Identity
Area[1]	4	0	0	0	0	0	0
U.S.	4	3,489	1,273	1,076	70	31	124

Note: (1) Figures cover the Moon Township.
Source: Federal Bureau of Investigation, Hate Crime Statistics 2016

Identity Theft Consumer Reports

Area	Reports	Reports per 100,000 Population	Rank[2]
MSA[1]	1,992	85	163
U.S.	371,061	114	-

Note: (1) Figures cover the Pittsburgh, PA Metropolitan Statistical Area—see Appendix B for areas included; (2) Rank ranges from 1 to 389 where 1 indicates greatest number of identity theft reports per 100,000 population
Source: Federal Trade Commission, Consumer Sentinel Network Data Book for January–December 2017

Fraud and Other Consumer Reports

Area	Reports	Reports per 100,000 Population	Rank[2]
MSA[1]	12,250	523	91
U.S.	2,304,550	708	-

Note: (1) Figures cover the Pittsburgh, PA Metropolitan Statistical Area—see Appendix B for areas included; (2) Rank ranges from 1 to 389 where 1 indicates greatest number of fraud and other consumer reports per 100,000 population
Source: Federal Trade Commission, Consumer Sentinel Network Data Book for January–December 2017

SPORTS

Professional Sports Teams

Team Name	League	Year Established
Pittsburgh Penguins	National Hockey League (NHL)	1967
Pittsburgh Pirates	Major League Baseball (MLB)	1882
Pittsburgh Steelers	National Football League (NFL)	1933

Note: Includes teams located in the Pittsburgh, PA Metropolitan Statistical Area.
Source: Wikipedia, Major Professional Sports Teams of the United States and Canada, April 5, 2018

CLIMATE

Average and Extreme Temperatures

Temperature	Jan	Feb	Mar	Apr	May	Jun	Jul	Aug	Sep	Oct	Nov	Dec	Yr.
Extreme High (°F)	75	69	83	89	91	98	103	100	97	89	82	74	103
Average High (°F)	35	38	48	61	71	79	83	81	75	63	50	39	60
Average Temp. (°F)	28	30	39	50	60	68	73	71	64	53	42	32	51
Average Low (°F)	20	22	29	39	49	57	62	61	54	43	34	25	41
Extreme Low (°F)	-18	-12	-1	14	26	34	42	39	31	16	-1	-12	-18

Note: Figures cover the years 1948-1990
Source: National Climatic Data Center, International Station Meteorological Climate Summary, 9/96

Average Precipitation/Snowfall/Humidity

Precip./Humidity	Jan	Feb	Mar	Apr	May	Jun	Jul	Aug	Sep	Oct	Nov	Dec	Yr.
Avg. Precip. (in.)	2.8	2.4	3.4	3.3	3.6	3.9	3.8	3.2	2.8	2.4	2.7	2.8	37.1
Avg. Snowfall (in.)	11	9	8	2	Tr	0	0	0	0	Tr	4	8	43
Avg. Rel. Hum. 7am (%)	76	75	75	73	76	79	82	86	85	81	78	77	79
Avg. Rel. Hum. 4pm (%)	64	60	54	49	50	51	53	54	55	53	60	66	56

Note: Figures cover the years 1948-1990; Tr = Trace amounts (<0.05 in. of rain; <0.5 in. of snow)
Source: National Climatic Data Center, International Station Meteorological Climate Summary, 9/96

Weather Conditions

Temperature			Daytime Sky			Precipitation		
5°F & below	32°F & below	90°F & above	Clear	Partly cloudy	Cloudy	0.01 inch or more precip.	0.1 inch or more snow/ice	Thunder-storms
9	121	8	62	137	166	154	42	35

Note: Figures are average number of days per year and cover the years 1948-1990
Source: National Climatic Data Center, International Station Meteorological Climate Summary, 9/96

HAZARDOUS WASTE

Superfund Sites

The Pittsburgh, PA metro area is home to three sites on the EPA's Superfund National Priorities List: **Breslube-Penn, Inc.** (final); **Lindane Dump** (final); **Ohio River Park** (final). There are a total of 1,396 Superfund sites with a status of proposed or final on the list in the U.S. *U.S. Environmental Protection Agency, National Priorities List, April 4, 2018*

AIR & WATER QUALITY

Air Quality Trends: Ozone

	1990	1995	2000	2005	2010	2012	2013	2014	2015	2016
MSA[1]	0.080	0.095	0.082	0.082	0.075	0.079	0.067	0.065	0.069	0.068
U.S.	0.087	0.089	0.081	0.079	0.073	0.075	0.069	0.067	0.068	0.069

Note: (1) Data covers the Pittsburgh, PA Metropolitan Statistical Area—see Appendix B for areas included. The values shown are the composite ozone concentration averages among trend sites based on the highest fourth daily maximum 8-hour concentration in parts per million. These trends are based on sites having an adequate record of monitoring data during the trend period. Data from exceptional events are included.
Source: U.S. Environmental Protection Agency, Air Quality Monitoring Information, "Air Quality Trends by City, 1990-2016"

Air Quality Index

Area	Percent of Days when Air Quality was...[2]					AQI Statistics[2]	
	Good	Moderate	Unhealthy for Sensitive Groups	Unhealthy	Very Unhealthy	Maximum	Median
MSA[1]	25.2	66.0	8.5	0.3	0.0	164	59

Note: (1) Data covers the Pittsburgh, PA Metropolitan Statistical Area—see Appendix B for areas included; (2) Based on 365 days with AQI data in 2017. Air Quality Index (AQI) is an index for reporting daily air quality. EPA calculates the AQI for five major air pollutants regulated by the Clean Air Act: ground-level ozone, particle pollution (aka particulate matter), carbon monoxide, sulfur dioxide, and nitrogen dioxide. The AQI runs from 0 to 500. The higher the AQI value, the greater the level of air pollution and the greater the health concern. There are six AQI categories: "Good" AQI is between 0 and 50. Air quality is considered satisfactory; "Moderate" AQI is between 51 and 100. Air quality is acceptable; "Unhealthy for Sensitive Groups" When AQI values are between 101 and 150, members of sensitive groups may experience health effects; "Unhealthy" When AQI values are between 151 and 200 everyone may begin to experience health effects; "Very Unhealthy" AQI values between 201 and 300 trigger a health alert; "Hazardous" AQI values over 300 trigger warnings of emergency conditions (not shown).
Source: U.S. Environmental Protection Agency, Air Quality Index Report, 2017

Air Quality Index Pollutants

Area	Percent of Days when AQI Pollutant was...[2]					
	Carbon Monoxide	Nitrogen Dioxide	Ozone	Sulfur Dioxide	Particulate Matter 2.5	Particulate Matter 10
MSA[1]	0.0	0.0	22.7	7.4	69.6	0.3

Note: (1) Data covers the Pittsburgh, PA Metropolitan Statistical Area—see Appendix B for areas included; (2) Based on 365 days with AQI data in 2017. The Air Quality Index (AQI) is an index for reporting daily air quality. EPA calculates the AQI for five major air pollutants regulated by the Clean Air Act: ground-level ozone, particle pollution (also known as particulate matter), carbon monoxide, sulfur dioxide, and nitrogen dioxide. The AQI runs from 0 to 500. The higher the AQI value, the greater the level of air pollution and the greater the health concern.
Source: U.S. Environmental Protection Agency, Air Quality Index Report, 2017

Maximum Air Pollutant Concentrations: Particulate Matter, Ozone, CO and Lead

	Particulate Matter 10 (ug/m^3)	Particulate Matter 2.5 Wtd AM (ug/m^3)	Particulate Matter 2.5 24-Hr (ug/m^3)	Ozone (ppm)	Carbon Monoxide (ppm)	Lead (ug/m^3)
MSA[1] Level	84	12.8	40	0.073	3	0.02
NAAQS[2]	150	15	35	0.075	9	0.15
Met NAAQS[2]	Yes	Yes	No	Yes	Yes	Yes

Note: (1) Data covers the Pittsburgh, PA Metropolitan Statistical Area—see Appendix B for areas included; Data from exceptional events are included; (2) National Ambient Air Quality Standards; ppm = parts per million; ug/m^3 = micrograms per cubic meter; n/a not available.
Concentrations: Particulate Matter 10 (coarse particulate)—highest second maximum 24-hour concentration; Particulate Matter 2.5 Wtd AM (fine particulate)—highest weighted annual mean concentration; Particulate Matter 2.5 24-Hour (fine particulate)—highest 98th percentile 24-hour concentration; Ozone—highest fourth daily maximum 8-hour concentration; Carbon Monoxide—highest second maximum non-overlapping 8-hour concentration; Lead—maximum running 3-month average
Source: U.S. Environmental Protection Agency, Air Quality Monitoring Information, "Air Quality Statistics by City, 2016"

Maximum Air Pollutant Concentrations: Nitrogen Dioxide and Sulfur Dioxide

	Nitrogen Dioxide AM (ppb)	Nitrogen Dioxide 1-Hr (ppb)	Sulfur Dioxide AM (ppb)	Sulfur Dioxide 1-Hr (ppb)	Sulfur Dioxide 24-Hr (ppb)
MSA[1] Level	11	40	n/a	64	n/a
NAAQS[2]	53	100	30	75	140
Met NAAQS[2]	Yes	Yes	n/a	Yes	n/a

Note: (1) Data covers the Pittsburgh, PA Metropolitan Statistical Area—see Appendix B for areas included; Data from exceptional events are included; (2) National Ambient Air Quality Standards; ppm = parts per million; ug/m^3 = micrograms per cubic meter; n/a not available.
Concentrations: Nitrogen Dioxide AM—highest arithmetic mean concentration; Nitrogen Dioxide 1-Hr—highest 98th percentile 1-hour daily maximum concentration; Sulfur Dioxide AM—highest annual mean concentration; Sulfur Dioxide 1-Hr—highest 99th percentile 1-hour daily maximum concentration; Sulfur Dioxide 24-Hr—highest second maximum 24-hour concentration
Source: U.S. Environmental Protection Agency, Air Quality Monitoring Information, "Air Quality Statistics by City, 2016"

Drinking Water

Water System Name	Pop. Served	Primary Water Source Type	Violations[1]	
			Health Based	Monitoring/ Reporting
Moon Township Municipal Authority	38,000	Surface	0	0

Note: (1) Based on violation data from January 1, 2017 to December 31, 2017
Source: U.S. Environmental Protection Agency, Office of Ground Water and Drinking Water, Safe Drinking Water Information System (based on data extracted April 5, 2018)

Radnor, Pennsylvania

Background

Radnor Township is located in southeastern Pennsylvania, in northern Delaware County. Radnor Township is part of the upper Main Line, a group of affluent suburbs of western Philadelphia.

The first European settlers to reach the Radnor Township area were a group of 40 Quakers from Radnorshire, Wales, seeking religious freedom from their homeland. Radnor Township was officially founded in 1682. It later took on the more elaborate governmental structure of a first class township in 1901.

The Welsh Friends constructed their Quaker meetinghouse at the junction of the Conestoga Road and the Schuylkill and Susquehanna Rivers, and the township grew up around it. Early industry in Radnor Township included gristmills, saw mills and tanneries. The Conestoga Road, which connected Philadelphia and Lancaster, brought many travelers through Radnor Township. Radnor Township's Sorrel Horse Inn is rumored to have sheltered George Washington and General Lafayette during their encampment at Valley Forge.

The Lancaster Turnpike, the first toll road in America, came through Radnor Township in 1794, and later the Columbia Railroad crossed the Township in 1832. Both the Turnpike and the railroad brought traffic, continued development and population growth. Several wealthy industrialists from Philadelphia turned area farms into country estates along the outside of the township.

In 1865, one of the country's first planned suburban developments, with electricity, sewers, and a public water supply, was built on a former country estate in Radnor Township. At the time, the development doubled the community's population. Development and population growth saw significant increases following World War II, growing from 13,000 in 1950 to 30,000 in 2000. Many of the area's country estates have now been subdivided into housing developments.

Today, Radnor Township seeks to maintain a high quality of life for its residents. The Township has a dynamic downtown area, beautiful parks and community conservation efforts, award-winning schools and excellent municipal services, all of which contribute to its vibrant, thriving atmosphere.

The highly-regarded Radnor Township School District manages three elementary schools, one middle school and one high school. Radnor Township also has several private and parochial schools. Institutions of higher education in Radnor Township include Villanova University, Eastern University and Cabrini College along with Valley Forge Military Academy's two-year junior college.

Radnor Township has access to several nearby hospitals and healthcare facilities, including Penn Medicine at Radnor, a regional office of the Hospital of the University of Pennsylvania, the Graduate Hospital Human Performance & Sports Medical Center in Wayne, the Bryn Mawr Hospital in Bryn Mawr, Lankenau Hospital in Overbrook and Paoli Memorial Hospital in Paoli.

Radnor Township is served by the Philadelphia International Airport, a 20 minute drive from the Township.

The climate in Radnor Township can be characterized by hot and muggy summers, mild falls and springs, with cold, sometimes snowy, winters.

Rankings

Business/Finance Rankings

- The personal finance site NerdWallet analyzed 183 American metropolitan areas with populations over 250,000 and more than 15,000 businesses to rank where entrepreneurs find the most success. Criteria included area economy, annual income, housing cost, unemployment rate, and the success rate of area businesses. Philadelphia* ranked #60. *www.nerdwallet.com, "Best Places to Start a Business," April 27, 2015*
- In a survey of economic confidence in the nation's 50 largest metropolitan areas conducted January–December 2014, the Philadelphia* metro area placed #33, according to Gallup's 2014 Economic Confidence Index. *Gallup, "San Jose and San Francisco Lead in Economic Confidence," March 19, 2015*
- The Brookings Institution ranked the 100 largest metro areas in the U.S. based on income inequality. Philadelphia* was ranked #12 (#1 = greatest ineqality). Criteria: the "95/20 ratio," a figure representing the income at which a household earns more than 95 percent of all other households, divided by the income at which a household earns more than only 20 percent of all other households. *Brookings Institution, "Household Income Inequality, 100 Largest U.S. Metro Areas, 2014-2016," February 5, 2018*
- Payscale.com ranked the largest metro areas in terms of wage growth. The Philadelphia* metro area ranked #29. Criteria: private-sector wage growth between the 4th quarter of 2016 and the 4th quarter of 2017. *PayScale, "Wage Trends by Metro Area-4th Quarter," January 17, 2018*
- The Philadelphia* metro area was identified as one of the most debt-ridden places in America by the finance site Credit.com. The metro area was ranked #11. Criteria: residents' average credit card debt as well as median income. *Credit.com, "25 Cities With the Most Credit Card Debt," February 28, 2018*
- Philadelphia* was identified as one of America's most frugal metro areas by *Coupons.com.* The city ranked #6 out of 25. Criteria: digital coupon usage. *Coupons.com, "America's Most Frugal Cities of 2017," March 22, 2018*
- The Philadelphia* metro area appeared on the Milken Institute "2017 Best Performing Cities" list. Rank: #98 out of 200 large metro areas. Criteria: job growth; wage and salary growth; high-tech output growth. *Milken Institute, "Best-Performing Cities 2017," January 2018*
- *Forbes* ranked the 200 most populous metro areas to determine the nation's "Best Places for Business and Careers." The Philadelphia* metro area was ranked #83. Criteria: costs (business and living); job growth (past and projected); income growth; quality of life; educational attainment (college and high school); projected economic growth; cultural and recreational opportunities; net migration patterns; number of highly ranked colleges. *Forbes, "The Best Places for Business and Careers 2017," October 24, 2017*

Education Rankings

- Personal finance website *WalletHub* analyzed the 150 largest U.S. metropolitan statistical areas to determine where the most educated Americans are choosing to settle. Criteria: education quality and attainment gap; education levels; percentage of workers with degrees; public school rankings; quality and size of each metro area's universities. Philadelphia* was ranked #44 (#1 = most educated city). *www.WalletHub.com, "2017's Most and Least Educated Cities in America," July 25, 2017*

Environmental Rankings

- Sperling's BestPlaces assessed 379 metropolitan areas of the United States for the likelihood of dangerously extreme weather events or earthquakes. In general the Southeast and South-Central regions have the highest risk of weather extremes and earthquakes, while the Pacific Northwest enjoys the lowest risk. Of the least risky metropolitan areas, the Philadelphia* metro area was ranked #232. *www.bestplaces.net, "Safest Places from Natural Disasters," April 2011*

- The U.S. Environmental Protection Agency (EPA) released a list of U.S. metropolitan areas with the most ENERGY STAR certified buildings in 2016. The Philadelphia* metro area was ranked #11 out of 25. *U.S. Environmental Protection Agency, "2017 Energy Star Top Cities," June 2017*

- Philadelphia* was highlighted as one of the 25 most ozone-polluted metro areas in the U.S. during 2013 through 2015. The area ranked #22. *American Lung Association, State of the Air 2017*

- Philadelphia* was highlighted as one of the 25 metro areas most polluted by year-round particle pollution (Annual PM 2.5) in the U.S. during 2013 through 2015. The area ranked #13. *American Lung Association, State of the Air 2017*

- Philadelphia* was highlighted as one of the 25 metro areas most polluted by short-term particle pollution (24-hour PM 2.5) in the U.S. during 2013 through 2015. The area ranked #20. *American Lung Association, State of the Air 2017*

Health/Fitness Rankings

- For each of the 50 most populous metro areas in the United States, the American College of Sports Medicine's American Fitness Index evaluated infrastructure, community assets, and policies that encourage healthy and fit lifestyles, including preventive health behaviors, levels of chronic disease conditions, health care access, and community resources and policies that support physical activity. The Philadelphia* metro area ranked #32 for "community fitness." *www.americanfitnessindex.org, "ACSM American Fitness Index Health and Community Fitness Status of the 50 Largest Metropolitan Areas," May 2017*

- The Philadelphia* metro area was identified as one of the worst cities for bed bugs in America by pest control company Orkin. The area ranked #12 out of 50 based on the number of bed bug treatments Orkin performed from December 2016 to November 2017. *Orkin, "Baltimore and Washington D.C. Continue to Hold Top Spots," January 8, 2018*

- Philadelphia* was identified as a "2016 Spring Allergy Capital." The area ranked #21 out of 100. Three groups of factors were used to identify the most severe cities for people with allergies during the spring season: annual pollen levels; medicine utilization; access to board-certified allergists. *Asthma and Allergy Foundation of America, "Spring Allergy Capitals 2016"*

- Philadelphia* was identified as a "2016 Fall Allergy Capital." The area ranked #32 out of 100. Three groups of factors were used to identify the most severe cities for people with allergies during the fall season: annual pollen levels; medicine utilization; access to board-certified allergists. *Asthma and Allergy Foundation of America, "Fall Allergy Capitals 2016"*

- Philadelphia* was identified as a "2015 Asthma Capital." The area ranked #3 out of the nation's 100 largest metropolitan areas. Criteria: estimated prevalence; self-reported prevalence; crude death rate for asthma; annual pollen score; annual air quality; public smoking laws; number of board-certified asthma specialists; school inhaler access laws; rescue medication use; controller medication use; ER visits for asthma; uninsured rate; poverty rate. *Asthma and Allergy Foundation of America, "Asthma Capitals 2015"*

- The Philadelphia* metro area ranked #132 out of 189 in The Gallup-Healthways Well-Being Index. Criteria: purpose; social well being; financial health; community and physical health. Results are based on telephone interviews with adults, aged 18 and older, living in metropolitan areas in the 50 U.S. states and the District of Columbia. *Gallup-Healthways, "State of American Well-Being, 2017 Community Well-Being Rankings" March 2018*

Real Estate Rankings

- FitSmallBusiness looked at 50 of the largest metropolitan areas in the U.S. to determine which metro was the best to start a real estate business. Data was compiled from such sources as: Zillow, Trulia, U.S. Census Bureau, and the Bureau of Labor Statistics. Criteria: location; inventory; annual wages; median sales price of homes; days on the market; median price cut percentage; and other factors that would influence real estate professional growth. The Philadelphia* metro area ranked #17. *fitsmallbusiness.com, "The Best Cities to Become a Real Estate Agent in 2018," January 30, 2018*
- Philadelphia* was ranked #138 out of 238 metro areas in terms of housing affordability in 2017 by the National Association of Home Builders (#1 = most affordable). Criteria: the share of homes sold in that area affordable to a family earning the local median income, based on standard mortgage underwriting criteria. *National Association of Home Builders®, NAHB-Wells Fargo Housing Opportunity Index, 4th Quarter 2017*
- The nation's largest metro areas were analyzed in terms of the percentage of households entering some stage of foreclosure in 2017. The Philadelphia* metro area ranked #3 out of 10 (#1 = highest foreclosure rate). *RealtyTrac, "2017 Year-End U.S. Foreclosure Market Report™," January 16, 2018*

Safety Rankings

- The National Insurance Crime Bureau ranked 382 metro areas in the U.S. in terms of per capita rates of vehicle theft. The Philadelphia* metro area ranked #208 (#1 = highest rate). Criteria: number of vehicle theft offenses per 100,000 inhabitants in 2016. *National Insurance Crime Bureau, "Hot Spots 2016," June 8, 2017*

Seniors/Retirement Rankings

- From its Best Cities for Successful Aging indexes, the Milken Institute generated rankings for metropolitan areas, weighing data in nine categories—health care, wellness, living arrangements, transportation and convenience, financial characteristics, education, employment, community engagement, and overall livability. The Philadelphia* metro area was ranked #52 overall in the large metro area category. *Milken Institute, "Best Cities for Successful Aging, 2017" March 14, 2017*

Sports/Recreation Rankings

- According to the personal finance website NerdWallet, the Philadelphia* metro area, at #10, is one of the nation's top dozen metro areas for sports fans. Criteria included the presence of all four major sports—MLB, NFL, NHL, and NBA, fan enthusiasm (as measured by game attendance), ticket affordability, and "sports culture," that is, number of sports bars. *www.nerdwallet.com, "Best Cities for Sports Fans," May 5, 2013*

Transportation Rankings

- The Philadelphia* metro area appeared on *Forbes* list of places with the most extreme commutes. The metro area ranked #9 out of 10. Criteria: average travel time; percentage of mega commuters. Mega-commuters travel more than 90 minutes and 50 miles each way to work. *Forbes.com, "The Cities with the Most Extreme Commutes," March 5, 2013*

Miscellaneous Rankings

- The watchdog site Charity Navigator conducts an annual study of charities in the nation's major markets both to analyze statistical differences in their financial, accountability, and transparency practices and to track year-to-year variations in individual philanthropic communities. Charity Navigator's analysis demonstrated that the financial, accountability and transparency behaviors of America's largest charities can be influenced by the metropolitan market within which the charity operates. The Philadelphia* metro area was ranked #20 among the 30 metro markets in the rating category of Overall Score. *www.charitynavigator.org, "2017 Metro Market Study," May 1, 2017*

- The Harris Poll's Happiness Index survey revealed that of the top ten U.S. markets, the Philadelphia* metro area residents ranked #3 in happiness. Criteria included strong assent to positive statements and strong disagreement with negative ones, and degree of agreement with a series of statements about respondents' personal relationships and general outlook. *www.theharrispoll.com, "Dallas/Fort Worth Is "Happiest" City among America's Top Ten Markets," September 4, 2013*
- Energizer Personal Care, the makers of Edge® shave gel, in partnership with Sperling's BestPlaces, ranked 50 major metro areas in terms of everyday irritations. The Philadelphia* metro area ranked #4 the 50 metro area most irritating to guys. Criteria: high male-to-female ratio; poor sports team performance and high ticket prices; slow traffic; lack of job availability; unaffordable housing; extreme weather; lack of nightlife and fitness options. *Energizer Personal Care, "Most Irritating Cities for Guys," August 26, 2013*
- The National Alliance to End Homelessness listed the 25 most populous metro areas with the highest rate of homelessness. The Philadelphia* metro area had a high rate of homelessness. Criteria: number of homeless people per 10,000 population in 2016. *National Alliance to End Homelessness, "Homelessness in the 25 Most Populous U.S. Metro Areas," September 1, 2017*

*Radnor is located within the Philadelphia-Camden-Wilmington, PA-NJ-DE-MD Metropolitan Statistical Area and the Philadelphia, PA Metropolitan Division.

Business Environment

CITY FINANCES

City Government Finances

Component	2015 ($000)	2015 ($ per capita)
Total Revenues	46,704	1,477
Total Expenditures	56,777	1,796
Debt Outstanding	73,478	2,324
Cash and Securities[1]	61,249	1,938

Note: (1) Cash and security holdings of a government at the close of its fiscal year,, including those of its dependent agencies, utilities, and liquor stores.
Source: U.S Census Bureau, State & Local Government Finances 2015

City Government Revenue by Source

Source	2015 ($000)	2015 ($ per capita)	2015 (%)
General Revenue			
From Federal Government	0	0	0.0
From State Government	3,411	108	7.3
From Local Governments	0	0	0.0
Taxes			
Property	11,805	373	25.3
Sales and Gross Receipts	38	1	0.1
Personal Income	0	0	0.0
Corporate Income	0	0	0.0
Motor Vehicle License	0	0	0.0
Other Taxes	17,959	568	38.5
Current Charges	6,355	201	13.6
Liquor Store	0	0	0.0
Utility	1,073	34	2.3
Employee Retirement	4,477	142	9.6

Source: U.S Census Bureau, State & Local Government Finances 2015

City Government Expenditures by Function

Function	2015 ($000)	2015 ($ per capita)	2015 (%)
General Direct Expenditures			
Air Transportation	0	0	0.0
Corrections	0	0	0.0
Education	0	0	0.0
Employment Security Administration	0	0	0.0
Financial Administration	1,125	35	2.0
Fire Protection	1,004	31	1.8
General Public Buildings	544	17	1.0
Governmental Administration, Other	1,050	33	1.8
Health	752	23	1.3
Highways	6,464	204	11.4
Hospitals	0	0	0.0
Housing and Community Development	197	6	0.3
Interest on General Debt	1,825	57	3.2
Judicial and Legal	0	0	0.0
Libraries	899	28	1.6
Parking	0	0	0.0
Parks and Recreation	14,966	473	26.4
Police Protection	8,825	279	15.5
Public Welfare	0	0	0.0
Sewerage	4,900	155	8.6
Solid Waste Management	2,791	88	4.9
Veterans' Services	0	0	0.0
Liquor Store	0	0	0.0
Utility	0	0	0.0
Employee Retirement	6,624	209	11.7

Source: U.S Census Bureau, State & Local Government Finances 2015

DEMOGRAPHICS

Population Growth

Area	1990 Census	2000 Census	2010 Census	2016* Estimate	Population Growth (%) 1990-2016	Population Growth (%) 2010-2016
City	28,710	30,878	31,531	31,616	10.1	0.3
MSA[1]	5,435,470	5,687,147	5,965,343	6,047,721	11.3	1.4
U.S.	248,709,873	281,421,906	308,745,538	318,558,162	28.1	3.2

Note: (1) Figures cover the Philadelphia-Camden-Wilmington, PA-NJ-DE-MD Metropolitan Statistical Area—see Appendix B for areas included; (*) 2012-2016 5-year estimated population
Source: U.S. Census Bureau, 1990 Census, Census 2000, Census 2010, 2012-2016 American Community Survey 5-Year Estimates

Household Size

Area	Persons in Household (%) One	Two	Three	Four	Five	Six	Seven or More	Average Household Size
City	30.8	30.9	14.7	13.5	7.4	1.8	0.8	2.60
MSA[1]	29.3	31.8	16.4	13.5	5.9	2.1	1.1	2.60
U.S.	27.7	33.7	15.7	13.1	6.0	2.3	1.5	2.60

Note: (1) Figures cover the Philadelphia-Camden-Wilmington, PA-NJ-DE-MD Metropolitan Statistical Area—see Appendix B for areas included
Source: U.S. Census Bureau, 2012-2016 American Community Survey 5-Year Estimates

Race

Area	White Alone[2] (%)	Black Alone[2] (%)	Asian Alone[2] (%)	AIAN[3] Alone[2] (%)	NHOPI[4] Alone[2] (%)	Other Race Alone[2] (%)	Two or More Races (%)
City	82.9	6.5	7.4	0.0	0.0	1.2	2.0
MSA[1]	67.5	20.9	5.6	0.2	0.0	3.2	2.6
U.S.	73.3	12.6	5.2	0.8	0.2	4.8	3.1

Note: (1) Figures cover the Philadelphia-Camden-Wilmington, PA-NJ-DE-MD Metropolitan Statistical Area—see Appendix B for areas included; (2) Alone is defined as not being in combination with one or more other races; (3) American Indian and Alaska Native; (4) Native Hawaiian and Other Pacific Islander
Source: U.S. Census Bureau, 2012-2016 American Community Survey 5-Year Estimates

Hispanic or Latino Origin

Area	Total (%)	Mexican (%)	Puerto Rican (%)	Cuban (%)	Other (%)
City	4.0	0.8	1.1	0.2	1.9
MSA[1]	8.8	1.8	4.4	0.2	2.3
U.S.	17.3	11.0	1.7	0.7	4.0

Note: Persons of Hispanic or Latino origin can be of any race; (1) Figures cover the Philadelphia-Camden-Wilmington, PA-NJ-DE-MD Metropolitan Statistical Area—see Appendix B for areas included
Source: U.S. Census Bureau, 2012-2016 American Community Survey 5-Year Estimates

Segregation

Type	Segregation Indices[1] 1990	2000	2010	2010 Rank[2]	Percent Change 1990-2000	1990-2010	2000-2010
Black/White	75.2	71.0	68.4	9	-4.2	-6.8	-2.6
Asian/White	42.4	44.1	42.3	42	1.7	0.0	-1.8
Hispanic/White	60.9	58.5	55.1	12	-2.5	-5.9	-3.4

Note: All figures cover the Metropolitan Statistical Area—see Appendix B for areas included; Figures are based on an analysis of 1990, 2000, and 2010 Census Decennial Census tract data by William H. Frey, Brookings Institution and the University of Michigan Social Science Data Analysis Network. In this analysis all racial groups (whites, blacks, and asians) are non-Hispanic members of those races. Hispanics are shown as a separate category; (1) Segregation Indices are Dissimilarity Indices that measure the degree to which the minority group is distributed differently than whites across census tracts. They range from 0 (complete integration) to 100 (complete segregation) where the value indicates the percentage of the minority group that needs to move to be distributed exactly like whites; (2) Ranges from 1 (most segregated) to 102 (least segregated); n/a not available.
Source: www.CensusScope.org

Ancestry

Area	German	Irish	English	American	Italian	Polish	French[2]	Scottish	Dutch
City	15.0	25.5	9.4	4.1	16.5	4.4	2.3	1.7	0.8
MSA[1]	15.7	19.2	7.1	3.6	13.7	5.2	1.5	1.3	0.9
U.S.	14.4	10.4	7.7	6.9	5.4	2.9	2.6	1.7	1.3

Note: Figures are the percentage of the total population reporting a particular ancestry. The nine most commonly reported ancestries in the U.S. are shown. Figures include multiple ancestries (e.g. if a person reported being Irish and Italian, they were included in both columns); (1) Figures cover the Philadelphia-Camden-Wilmington, PA-NJ-DE-MD Metropolitan Statistical Area—see Appendix B for areas included; (2) Excludes Basque
Source: U.S. Census Bureau, 2012-2016 American Community Survey 5-Year Estimates

Foreign-Born Population

Area	Percent of Population Born in								
	Any Foreign Country	Asia	Mexico	Europe	Carribean	Central America[2]	South America	Africa	Canada
City	10.7	5.3	0.2	2.6	0.5	0.2	0.6	0.9	0.1
MSA[1]	10.3	4.2	0.9	1.9	1.2	0.4	0.6	0.9	0.1
U.S.	13.2	4.0	3.6	1.5	1.3	1.0	0.9	0.6	0.3

Note: (1) Figures cover the Philadelphia-Camden-Wilmington, PA-NJ-DE-MD Metropolitan Statistical Area—see Appendix B for areas included; (2) Excludes Mexico.
Source: U.S. Census Bureau, 2012-2016 American Community Survey 5-Year Estimates

Marital Status

Area	Never Married	Now Married[2]	Separated	Widowed	Divorced
City	48.8	40.1	1.0	3.9	6.2
MSA[1]	37.4	45.1	2.2	6.2	9.1
U.S.	33.0	48.1	2.1	5.9	11.0

Note: Figures are percentages and cover the population 15 years of age and older; (1) Figures cover the Philadelphia-Camden-Wilmington, PA-NJ-DE-MD Metropolitan Statistical Area—see Appendix B for areas included; (2) Excludes separated
Source: U.S. Census Bureau, 2012-2016 American Community Survey 5-Year Estimates

Disability Status

Area	All Ages	Under 18 Years Old	18 to 64 Years Old	65 Years and Over
City	5.9	2.2	3.6	25.7
MSA[1]	12.3	4.6	10.2	34.0
U.S.	12.5	4.1	10.3	35.7

Note: Figures show percent of the civilian noninstitutionalized population that reported having a disability. Disability status is determined from six types of difficulty: vision, hearing, cognitive, ambulatory, self-care, and independent living. For children under 5 years old, hearing and vision difficulty are used to determine disability status. For children between the ages of 5 and 14, disability status is determined from hearing, vision, cognitive, ambulatory, and self-care difficulties. For people aged 15 years and older, they are considered to have a disability if they have difficulty with any one of the six difficulty types; Note: (1) Figures cover the Philadelphia-Camden-Wilmington, PA-NJ-DE-MD Metropolitan Statistical Area—see Appendix B for areas included
Source: U.S. Census Bureau, 2012-2016 American Community Survey 5-Year Estimates

Age

Area	Percent of Population									Median Age
	Under Age 5	Age 5–19	Age 20–34	Age 35–44	Age 45–54	Age 55–64	Age 65–74	Age 75–84	Age 85+	
City	4.7	29.1	22.2	9.1	12.1	10.5	6.7	3.7	1.7	26.8
MSA[1]	6.0	19.1	20.8	12.4	14.3	13.0	8.0	4.4	2.2	38.4
U.S.	6.2	19.6	20.7	12.7	13.6	12.6	8.3	4.3	1.9	37.7

Note: (1) Figures cover the Philadelphia-Camden-Wilmington, PA-NJ-DE-MD Metropolitan Statistical Area—see Appendix B for areas included
Source: U.S. Census Bureau, 2012-2016 American Community Survey 5-Year Estimates

Gender

Area	Males	Females	Males per 100 Females
City	14,888	16,728	89.0
MSA[1]	2,923,439	3,124,282	93.6
U.S.	156,765,322	161,792,840	96.9

Note: (1) Figures cover the Philadelphia-Camden-Wilmington, PA-NJ-DE-MD Metropolitan Statistical Area—see Appendix B for areas included
Source: U.S. Census Bureau, 2012-2016 American Community Survey 5-Year Estimates

Religious Groups by Family

Area	Catholic	Baptist	Non-Den.	Methodist[2]	Lutheran	LDS[3]	Pente-costal	Presby-terian[4]	Muslim[5]	Judaism
MSA[1]	33.5	3.9	2.9	3.0	1.9	0.3	0.9	2.1	1.3	1.4
U.S.	19.1	9.3	4.0	4.0	2.3	2.0	1.9	1.6	0.8	0.7

Note: Figures are the number of adherents as a percentage of the total population; (1) Figures cover the Philadelphia-Camden-Wilmington, PA-NJ-DE-MD Metropolitan Statistical Area—see Appendix B for areas included; (2) Methodist/Pietist; (3) Latter Day Saints; (4) Reformed; (5) Figures are estimates
Source: Association of Statisticians of American Religious Bodies, 2010 U.S. Religion Census: Religious Congregations & Membership Study

Religious Groups by Tradition

Area	Catholic	Evangelical Protestant	Mainline Protestant	Other Tradition	Black Protestant	Orthodox
MSA[1]	33.5	6.3	8.9	3.7	1.8	0.4
U.S.	19.1	16.2	7.3	4.3	1.6	0.3

Note: Figures are the number of adherents as a percentage of the total population; (1) Figures cover the Philadelphia-Camden-Wilmington, PA-NJ-DE-MD Metropolitan Statistical Area—see Appendix B for areas included
Source: Association of Statisticians of American Religious Bodies, 2010 U.S. Religion Census: Religious Congregations & Membership Study

ECONOMY

Gross Metropolitan Product

Area	2014	2015	2016	2017	Rank[2]
MSA[1]	389.2	403.6	416.4	433.9	8

Note: Figures are in billions of dollars; (1) Figures cover the Philadelphia-Camden-Wilmington, PA-NJ-DE-MD Metropolitan Statistical Area—see Appendix B for areas included; (2) Rank is based on 2015 data and ranges from 1 to 381
Source: The U.S. Conference of Mayors, U.S. Metro Economies: GMP and Employment Report, 2015-2017

Economic Growth

Area	2012-14 (%)	2015 (%)	2016 (%)	2017 (%)	Rank[2]
MSA[1]	0.9	2.2	1.6	2.1	216
U.S.	2.0	2.4	1.9	2.6	–

Note: Figures are real gross metropolitan product (GMP) growth rates and represent average annual percent change; (1) Figures cover the Philadelphia-Camden-Wilmington, PA-NJ-DE-MD Metropolitan Statistical Area—see Appendix B for areas included; (2) Rank is based on 2012-2014 average annual percent change and ranges from 1 to 381
Source: The U.S. Conference of Mayors, U.S. Metro Economies: GMP and Employment Report, 2015-2017

Metropolitan Area Exports

Area	2011	2012	2013	2014	2015	2016	Rank[2]
MSA[1]	26,155.8	22,991.6	24,929.2	26,321.3	24,236.1	21,359.9	14

Note: Figures are in millions of dollars; (1) Figures cover the Philadelphia-Camden-Wilmington, PA-NJ-DE-MD Metropolitan Statistical Area—see Appendix B for areas included; (2) Rank is based on 2016 data and ranges from 1 to 385
Source: U.S. Department of Commerce, International Trade Administration, Office of Trade & Industry Information, Manufacturing & Services, data extracted March 15, 2018

Building Permits

Area	Single-Family			Multi-Family			Total		
	2016	2017p	Pct. Chg.	2016	2017p	Pct. Chg.	2016	2017p	Pct. Chg.
City	18	17	-5.6	3	0	-100.0	21	17	-19.0
MSA[1]	6,820	7,278	6.7	5,295	6,021	13.7	12,115	13,299	9.8
U.S.	750,800	817,300	8.9	455,800	446,800	-2.0	1,206,600	1,264,100	4.8

Note: (1) Figures cover the Philadelphia-Camden-Wilmington, PA-NJ-DE-MD Metropolitan Statistical Area—see Appendix B for areas included; Figures represent new, privately-owned housing units authorized (unadjusted data); All permit data are based on estimates with imputation; (p) preliminary data.
Source: U.S. Census Bureau, Manufacturing, Mining, and Construction Statistics, Building Permits, 2016, 2017

Bankruptcy Filings

Area	Business Filings			Nonbusiness Filings		
	2016	2017	% Chg.	2016	2017	% Chg.
Delaware County	44	25	-43.2	908	888	-2.2
U.S.	24,114	23,157	-4.0	770,846	765,863	-0.6

Note: Business filings include Chapter 7, Chapter 11, Chapter 12, and Chapter 13; Nonbusiness filings include Chapter 7, Chapter 11, and Chapter 13
Source: Administrative Office of the U.S. Courts, Business and Nonbusiness Bankruptcy, County Cases Commenced by Chapter of the Bankruptcy Code, During the 12-Month Period Ending December 31, 2016 and Business and Nonbusiness Bankruptcy, County Cases Commenced by Chapter of the Bankruptcy Code, During the 12-Month Period Ending December 31, 2017

Housing Vacancy Rates

Area	Gross Vacancy Rate[2] (%)			Year-Round Vacancy Rate[3] (%)			Rental Vacancy Rate[4] (%)			Homeowner Vacancy Rate[5] (%)		
	2015	2016	2017	2015	2016	2017	2015	2016	2017	2015	2016	2017
MSA[1]	10.7	9.3	8.6	10.2	8.6	8.3	7.6	6.8	7.3	2.4	1.4	1.6
U.S.	12.9	12.8	12.7	10.0	9.9	9.9	7.1	6.9	7.2	1.8	1.7	1.6

Note: (1) Figures cover the Philadelphia-Camden-Wilmington, PA-NJ-DE-MD Metropolitan Statistical Area—see Appendix B for areas included; (2) The percentage of the total housing inventory that is vacant; (3) The percentage of the housing inventory (excluding seasonal units) that is year-round vacant; (4) The percentage of rental inventory that is vacant for rent; (5) The percentage of homeowner inventory that is vacant for sale
Source: U.S. Census Bureau, Housing Vacancies and Homeownership Annual Statistics: 2015, 2016, 2017

INCOME

Income

Area	Per Capita ($)	Median Household ($)	Average Household ($)
City	53,456	106,209	170,904
MSA[1]	34,118	63,952	88,881
U.S.	29,829	55,322	77,866

Note: (1) Figures cover the Philadelphia-Camden-Wilmington, PA-NJ-DE-MD Metropolitan Statistical Area—see Appendix B for areas included
Source: U.S. Census Bureau, 2012-2016 American Community Survey 5-Year Estimates

Household Income Distribution

Area	Percent of Households Earning							
	Under $15,000	$15,000 -$24,999	$25,000 -$34,999	$35,000 -$49,999	$50,000 -$74,999	$75,000 -$99,999	$100,000 -$149,999	$150,000 and up
City	9.4	6.1	4.6	7.7	11.7	7.8	17.5	35.1
MSA[1]	11.3	8.8	8.4	11.6	16.4	12.3	16.0	15.2
U.S.	12.1	10.2	9.9	13.2	17.8	12.2	13.5	11.1

Note: (1) Figures cover the Philadelphia-Camden-Wilmington, PA-NJ-DE-MD Metropolitan Statistical Area—see Appendix B for areas included
Source: U.S. Census Bureau, 2012-2016 American Community Survey 5-Year Estimates

Poverty Rate

Area	All Ages	Under 18 Years Old	18 to 64 Years Old	65 Years and Over
City	8.9	7.3	10.0	7.6
MSA[1]	13.1	18.1	12.3	8.9
U.S.	15.1	21.2	14.2	9.3

Note: Figures are percentage of people whose income during the past 12 months was below the poverty level; (1) Figures cover the Philadelphia-Camden-Wilmington, PA-NJ-DE-MD Metropolitan Statistical Area—see Appendix B for areas included
Source: U.S. Census Bureau, 2012-2016 American Community Survey 5-Year Estimates

EMPLOYMENT

Labor Force and Employment

Area	Civilian Labor Force			Workers Employed		
	Dec. 2016	Dec. 2017	% Chg.	Dec. 2016	Dec. 2017	% Chg.
City	15,629	15,570	-0.4	15,109	15,102	0.0
MD[1]	995,008	992,557	-0.2	941,604	941,721	0.0
U.S.	158,968,000	159,880,000	0.6	151,798,000	153,602,000	1.2

Note: Data is not seasonally adjusted and covers workers 16 years of age and older; (1) Figures cover the Philadelphia, PA Metropolitan Division—see Appendix B for areas included
Source: Bureau of Labor Statistics, Local Area Unemployment Statistics

Unemployment Rate

Area	2017											
	Jan.	Feb.	Mar.	Apr.	May	Jun.	Jul.	Aug.	Sep.	Oct.	Nov.	Dec.
City	3.7	3.8	3.6	3.6	4.3	4.0	4.4	4.3	3.9	3.5	3.6	3.0
MD[1]	6.1	6.1	5.7	5.3	5.8	5.8	6.3	6.4	5.5	5.4	5.3	5.1
U.S.	5.1	4.9	4.6	4.1	4.1	4.5	4.6	4.5	4.1	3.9	3.9	3.9

Note: Data is not seasonally adjusted and covers workers 16 years of age and older; (1) Figures cover the Philadelphia, PA Metropolitan Division—see Appendix B for areas included
Source: Bureau of Labor Statistics, Local Area Unemployment Statistics

Average Wages

Occupation	$/Hr.	Occupation	$/Hr.
Accountants and Auditors	40.80	Maids and Housekeeping Cleaners	12.90
Automotive Mechanics	19.00	Maintenance and Repair Workers	20.40
Bookkeepers	21.30	Marketing Managers	77.60
Carpenters	31.20	Nuclear Medicine Technologists	41.10
Cashiers	10.60	Nurses, Licensed Practical	26.10
Clerks, General Office	18.00	Nurses, Registered	39.60
Clerks, Receptionists/Information	14.10	Nursing Assistants	15.00
Clerks, Shipping/Receiving	17.80	Packers and Packagers, Hand	11.70
Computer Programmers	42.10	Physical Therapists	42.80
Computer Systems Analysts	47.70	Postal Service Mail Carriers	24.70
Computer User Support Specialists	27.70	Real Estate Brokers	45.30
Cooks, Restaurant	12.90	Retail Salespersons	13.30
Dentists	67.90	Sales Reps., Exc. Tech./Scientific	36.20
Electrical Engineers	48.30	Sales Reps., Tech./Scientific	41.90
Electricians	35.80	Secretaries, Exc. Legal/Med./Exec.	18.90
Financial Managers	84.00	Security Guards	13.30
First-Line Supervisors/Managers, Sales	23.10	Surgeons	63.20
Food Preparation Workers	11.30	Teacher Assistants*	12.30
General and Operations Managers	72.50	Teachers, Elementary School*	33.10
Hairdressers/Cosmetologists	13.50	Teachers, Secondary School*	31.50
Internists, General	53.40	Telemarketers	11.20
Janitors and Cleaners	14.80	Truck Drivers, Heavy/Tractor-Trailer	22.70
Landscaping/Groundskeeping Workers	15.70	Truck Drivers, Light/Delivery Svcs.	18.90
Lawyers	75.60	Waiters and Waitresses	12.00

Note: Wage data covers the Philadelphia, PA Metropolitan Division—see Appendix B for areas included; (*) Hourly wages for elementary/secondary school teachers and teacher assistants were calculated by the editors from annual wage data based on a 40 hour work week; n/a not available.
Source: Bureau of Labor Statistics, Metro Area Occupational Employment & Wage Estimates, May 2017

Employment by Occupation

Occupation Classification	City (%)	MSA[1] (%)	U.S. (%)
Management, Business, Science, and Arts	57.9	42.4	37.0
Natural Resources, Construction, and Maintenance	2.9	6.9	8.9
Production, Transportation, and Material Moving	2.7	9.6	12.2
Sales and Office	22.7	24.0	23.8
Service	13.8	17.2	18.1

Note: Figures cover employed civilians 16 years of age and older; (1) Figures cover the Philadelphia-Camden-Wilmington, PA-NJ-DE-MD Metropolitan Statistical Area—see Appendix B for areas included
Source: U.S. Census Bureau, 2012-2016 American Community Survey 5-Year Estimates

Employment by Industry

Sector	MD[1]		U.S.
	Number of Employees	Percent of Total	Percent of Total
Construction, Mining, and Logging	23,600	2.5	5.2
Education and Health Services	297,200	30.9	15.9
Financial Activities	59,100	6.2	5.7
Government	128,500	13.4	15.3
Information	14,000	1.5	1.9
Leisure and Hospitality	96,200	10.0	10.7
Manufacturing	34,300	3.6	8.5
Other Services	39,500	4.1	3.9
Professional and Business Services	128,200	13.3	14.0
Retail Trade	77,400	8.1	11.0
Transportation, Warehousing, and Utilities	38,800	4.0	4.1
Wholesale Trade	23,600	2.5	4.0

Note: Figures are non-farm employment as of December 2017. Figures are not seasonally adjusted and include workers 16 years of age and older; (1) Figures cover the Philadelphia, PA Metropolitan Division—see Appendix B for areas included
Source: Bureau of Labor Statistics, Current Employment Statistics, Employment, Hours, and Earnings

Occupations with Greatest Projected Employment Growth: 2017 – 2019

Occupation[1]	2017 Employment	2019 Projected Employment	Numeric Employment Change	Percent Employment Change
Personal Care Aides	95,040	101,150	6,110	6.4
Combined Food Preparation and Serving Workers, Including Fast Food	149,690	154,700	5,010	3.3
Registered Nurses	143,300	147,290	3,990	2.8
Laborers and Freight, Stock, and Material Movers, Hand	138,050	141,860	3,810	2.8
Home Health Aides	46,950	50,700	3,750	8.0
Waiters and Waitresses	100,790	102,540	1,750	1.7
Janitors and Cleaners, Except Maids and Housekeeping Cleaners	98,590	100,250	1,660	1.7
Cooks, Restaurant	49,820	51,120	1,300	2.6
Software Developers, Applications	25,890	27,190	1,300	5.0
Nursing Assistants	80,510	81,790	1,280	1.6

Note: Projections cover Pennsylvania; (1) Sorted by numeric employment change
Source: www.projectionscentral.com, State Occupational Projections, 2017–2019 Short-Term Projections

Fastest Growing Occupations: 2017 – 2019

Occupation[1]	2017 Employment	2019 Projected Employment	Numeric Employment Change	Percent Employment Change
Home Health Aides	46,950	50,700	3,750	8.0
Statisticians	2,710	2,880	170	6.5
Personal Care Aides	95,040	101,150	6,110	6.4
Physician Assistants	5,620	5,960	340	6.1
Nurse Practitioners	5,240	5,550	310	6.0
Operations Research Analysts	2,660	2,800	140	5.1
Information Security Analysts	3,020	3,170	150	5.0
Software Developers, Applications	25,890	27,190	1,300	5.0
Nonfarm Animal Caretakers	7,820	8,210	390	4.9
Physical Therapist Assistants	4,660	4,880	220	4.8

Note: Projections cover Pennsylvania; (1) Sorted by percent employment change and excludes occupations with numeric employment change less than 50
Source: www.projectionscentral.com, State Occupational Projections, 2017–2019 Short-Term Projections

TAXES

State Corporate Income Tax Rates

State	Tax Rate (%)	Income Brackets ($)	Num. of Brackets	Financial Institution Tax Rate (%)[a]	Federal Income Tax Ded.
Pennsylvania	9.99	Flat rate	1	(a)	No

Note: Tax rates as of January 1, 2018; (a) Rates listed are the corporate income tax rate applied to financial institutions or excise taxes based on income. Some states have other taxes based upon the value of deposits or shares.
Source: Federation of Tax Administrators, Range of State Corporate Income Tax Rates, January 1, 2018

State Individual Income Tax Rates

State	Tax Rate (%)	Income Brackets ($)	Num. of Brackets	Personal Exempt. ($)[1] Single	Personal Exempt. ($)[1] Dependents	Fed. Inc. Tax Ded.
Pennsylvania	3.07	Flat rate	1	None	None	No

Note: Tax rates as of January 1, 2018; Local- and county-level taxes are not included; n/a not applicable; (1) Married joint filers generally receive double the single exemption
Source: Federation of Tax Administrators, State Individual Income Tax Rates, January 1, 2018

Various State Sales and Excise Tax Rates

State	State Sales Tax (%)	Gasoline[1] (¢/gal.)	Cigarette[2] ($/pack)	Spirits[3] ($/gal.)	Wine[4] ($/gal.)	Beer[5] ($/gal.)	Recreational Marijuana (%)
Pennsylvania	6.0	58.7	2.60	7.24 (g)	(m)	0.08	Not legal

Note: All tax rates as of January 1, 2018; (1) The American Petroleum Institute has developed a methodology for determining the average tax rate on a gallon of fuel. Rates may include any of the following: excise taxes, environmental fees, storage tank fees, other fees or taxes, general sales tax, and local taxes. In states where gasoline is subject to the general sales tax, or where the fuel tax is based on the average sale price, the average rate determined by API is sensitive to changes in the price of gasoline. States that fully or partially apply general sales taxes to gasoline: CA, CO, GA, IL, IN, MI, NY; (2) The federal excise tax of $1.0066 per pack and local taxes are not included; (3) Rates are those applicable to off-premise sales of 40% alcohol by volume (a.b.v.) distilled spirits in 750ml containers. Local excise taxes are excluded; (4) Rates are those applicable to off-premise sales of 11% a.b.v. non-carbonated wine in 750ml containers; (5) Rates are those applicable to off-premise sales of 4.7% a.b.v. beer in 12 ounce containers; (g) Control states, where the government controls all sales. Products can be subject to ad valorem mark-up as well as excise taxes; (m) Control states, where the government controls all sales. Products can be subject to ad valorem mark-up as well as excise taxes.
Source: Tax Foundation, 2018 Facts & Figures: How Does Your State Compare?

State Business Tax Climate Index Rankings

State	Overall Rank	Corporate Tax Rank	Individual Income Tax Rank	Sales Tax Rank	Unemployment Insurance Tax Rank	Property Tax Rank
Pennsylvania	26	44	17	21	50	33

Note: The index is a measure of how each state's tax laws affect economic performance. The lower the rank, the more favorable a state's tax system is for business. States without a given tax are given a ranking of 1. The scores/rankings for the District of Columbia do not affect other states. The 2018 index represents the tax climate as of July 1, 2017.
Source: Tax Foundation, State Business Tax Climate Index 2018

TRANSPORTATION

Means of Transportation to Work

Area	Car/Truck/Van		Public Transportation			Bicycle	Walked	Other Means	Worked at Home
	Drove Alone	Car-pooled	Bus	Subway	Railroad				
City	59.4	5.1	0.9	2.1	8.5	0.7	14.1	0.6	8.7
MSA[1]	73.1	7.7	5.4	1.7	2.3	0.6	3.7	1.0	4.3
U.S.	76.4	9.3	2.6	1.9	0.6	0.6	2.8	1.3	4.6

Note: Figures are percentages and cover workers 16 years of age and older; (1) Figures cover the Philadelphia-Camden-Wilmington, PA-NJ-DE-MD Metropolitan Statistical Area—see Appendix B for areas included
Source: U.S. Census Bureau, 2012-2016 American Community Survey 5-Year Estimates

Travel Time to Work

Area	Less Than 10 Minutes	10 to 19 Minutes	20 to 29 Minutes	30 to 44 Minutes	45 to 59 Minutes	60 to 89 Minutes	90 Minutes or More
City	19.9	26.6	17.9	17.9	10.6	4.9	2.2
MSA[1]	9.8	24.7	20.5	23.5	10.7	7.9	3.0
U.S.	12.9	29.2	20.9	20.4	8.0	6.0	2.7

Note: Note: Figures are percentages and include workers 16 years old and over; (1) Figures cover the Philadelphia-Camden-Wilmington, PA-NJ-DE-MD Metropolitan Statistical Area—see Appendix B for areas included
Source: U.S. Census Bureau, 2012-2016 American Community Survey 5-Year Estimates

Freeway Travel Time Index

Area	1985	1990	1995	2000	2005	2010	2014
Urban Area Rank[1,2]	20	21	26	26	24	22	25
Urban Area Index[1]	1.12	1.15	1.18	1.21	1.25	1.24	1.24
Average Index[3]	1.09	1.11	1.14	1.17	1.20	1.19	1.20

Note: Freeway Travel Time Index—the ratio of travel time in the peak period to the travel time at free-flow conditions. For example, a value of 1.30 indicates a 20-minute free-flow trip takes 26 minutes in the peak (20 minutes x 1.30 = 26 minutes); (1) Covers the Philadelphia PA-NJ-DE-MD urban area; (2) Rank is based on 101 urban areas (#1 = highest travel time index); (3) Average of 101 urban areas
Source: Texas Transportation Institute, 2015 Urban Mobility Scorecard, August 2015

Freeway Commuter Stress Index

Area	1985	1990	1995	2000	2005	2010	2014
Urban Area Rank[1,2]	31	28	33	34	30	31	31
Urban Area Index[1]	1.15	1.19	1.22	1.25	1.29	1.28	1.28
Average Index[3]	1.13	1.16	1.19	1.22	1.25	1.24	1.25

Note: The Freeway Commuter Stress Index is the same as the Freeway Travel Time Index (see table above) except that it includes only the travel in the peak directions during the peak periods; the TTI includes travel in all directions during the peak period. Thus, the CSI is more indicative of the work trip experienced by each commuter on a daily basis; (1) Covers the Philadelphia PA-NJ-DE-MD urban area; (2) Rank is based on 101 urban areas (#1 = highest travel time index); (3) Average of 101 urban areas
Source: Texas Transportation Institute, 2015 Urban Mobility Scorecard, August 2015

Living Environment

COST OF LIVING

Cost of Living Index

Composite Index	Groceries	Housing	Utilities	Trans-portation	Health Care	Misc. Goods/ Services
117.0	116.2	129.5	124.5	114.9	105.7	107.2

Note: The Cost of Living Index measures regional differences in the cost of consumer goods and services, excluding taxes and non-consumer expenditures, for professional and managerial households in the top income quintile. It is based on more than 50,000 prices covering almost 60 different items for which prices are collected three times a year by chambers of commerce, economic development organizations or university applied economic centers in each participating urban area. The numbers shown should be read as a percentage above or below the national average of 100. For example, a value of 115.4 in the groceries column indicates that grocery prices are 15.4% higher than the national average. Small differences in the index numbers should not be interpreted as significant; Figures cover the Philadelphia PA urban area.
Source: The Council for Community and Economic Research, ACCRA Cost of Living Index, 2017

Grocery Prices

Area[1]	T-Bone Steak ($/pound)	Frying Chicken ($/pound)	Whole Milk ($/half gal.)	Eggs ($/dozen)	Orange Juice ($/64 oz.)	Coffee ($/11.5 oz.)
City[2]	11.82	1.46	2.11	1.74	3.92	4.10
Avg.	11.29	1.40	2.02	1.47	3.55	4.37
Min.	7.71	0.93	1.04	0.70	2.86	3.24
Max.	15.83	2.39	4.03	3.92	6.29	8.16

Note: (1) Values for the local area are compared with the average, minimum and maximum values for all 294 areas in the Cost of Living Index; (2) Figures cover the Philadelphia PA urban area; ***T-Bone Steak*** *(price per pound);* ***Frying Chicken*** *(price per pound, whole fryer);* ***Whole Milk*** *(half gallon carton);* ***Eggs*** *(price per dozen, Grade A, large);* ***Orange Juice*** *(64 oz. Tropicana or Florida Natural);* ***Coffee*** *(11.5 oz. can, vacuum-packed, Maxwell House, Hills Bros, or Folgers).*
Source: The Council for Community and Economic Research, ACCRA Cost of Living Index, 2017

Housing and Utility Costs

Area[1]	New Home Price ($)	Apartment Rent ($/month)	All Electric ($/month)	Part Electric ($/month)	Other Energy ($/month)	Telephone ($/month)
City[2]	424,983	1,411	-	107.26	69.96	42.00
Avg.	335,956	1,047	175.01	97.34	67.93	28.71
Min.	187,788	491	109.48	49.33	35.44	12.39
Max.	1,739,087	4,559	432.62	227.09	353.33	44.61

Note: (1) Values for the local area are compared with the average, minimum and maximum values for all 294 areas in the Cost of Living Index; (2) Figures cover the Philadelphia PA urban area; ***New Home Price*** *(2,400 sf living area, 8,000 sf lot, in urban area with full utilities);* ***Apartment Rent*** *(950 sf 2 bedroom/1.5 or 2 bath, unfurnished, excluding all utilities except water);* ***All Electric*** *(average monthly cost for an all-electric home);* ***Part Electric*** *(average monthly cost for a part-electric home);* ***Other Energy*** *(average monthly cost for natural gas, fuel oil, coal, wood, and any other forms of energy except electricity);* ***Telephone*** *(price includes basic monthly rate for a private residential line plus additional local usage charges incurred by a family of four).*
Source: The Council for Community and Economic Research, ACCRA Cost of Living Index, 2017

Health Care, Transportation, and Other Costs

Area[1]	Doctor ($/visit)	Dentist ($/visit)	Optometrist ($/visit)	Gasoline ($/gallon)	Beauty Salon ($/visit)	Men's Shirt ($)
City[2]	130.24	96.14	100.71	2.48	56.27	31.77
Avg.	108.00	92.54	101.93	2.25	37.58	30.92
Min.	30.39	60.00	49.75	1.82	16.11	11.20
Max.	193.50	161.94	229.28	3.16	77.35	59.13

Note: (1) Values for the local area are compared with the average, minimum and maximum values for all 294 areas in the Cost of Living Index; (2) Figures cover the Philadelphia PA urban area; ***Doctor*** *(general practitioners routine exam of an established patient);* ***Dentist*** *(adult teeth cleaning and periodic oral examination);* ***Optometrist*** *(full vision eye exam for established adult patient);* ***Gasoline*** *(one gallon regular unleaded, national brand, including all taxes, cash price at self-service pump if available);* ***Beauty Salon*** *(woman's shampoo, trim, and blow-dry);* ***Men's Shirt*** *(cotton/polyester dress shirt, pinpoint weave, long sleeves).*
Source: The Council for Community and Economic Research, ACCRA Cost of Living Index, 2017

HOUSING

House Price Index (HPI)

Area	National Ranking[2]	Quarterly Change (%)	One-Year Change (%)	Five-Year Change (%)
MD[1]	99	0.25	6.92	20.17
U.S.[3]	–	1.61	6.68	34.71

Note: The HPI is a weighted repeat sales index. It measures average price changes in repeat sales or refinancings on the same properties. This information is obtained by reviewing repeat mortgage transactions on single-family properties whose mortgages have been purchased or securitized by Fannie Mae or Freddie Mac in January 1975; (1) Figures cover the Philadelphia, PA Metropolitan Division—see Appendix B for areas included; (2) Rankings are based on annual percentage change for all metro areas containing at least 15,000 transactions over the last 10 years and ranges from 1 to 253; (3) figures based on a weighted average of Census Division estimates using a seasonally adjusted, purchase-only index; all figures are for the period ending December 31, 2017

Source: Federal Housing Finance Agency, House Price Index, February 28, 2018

Median Single-Family Home Prices

Area	2015	2016	2017p	Percent Change 2016 to 2017
MSA[1]	223.7	225.4	230.0	2.0
U.S. Average	223.9	235.5	248.8	5.6

Note: Figures are median sales prices of existing single-family homes in thousands of dollars; (p) preliminary; (1) Figures cover the Philadelphia-Camden-Wilmington, PA-NJ-DE-MD Metropolitan Statistical Area—see Appendix B for areas included

Source: National Association of Realtors, Median Sales Price of Existing Single-Family Homes for Metropolitan Areas, 4th Quarter 2017

Qualifying Income Based on Median Sales Price of Existing Single-Family Homes

Area	With 5% Down ($)	With 10% Down ($)	With 20% Down ($)
MSA[1]	50,381	47,729	42,426
U.S. Average	55,585	52,659	46,808

Note: Figures are preliminary; Qualifying income is based on a mortgage rate of 4.17%. Monthly principal and interest payment is limited to 25% of income; (1) Figures cover the Philadelphia-Camden-Wilmington, PA-NJ-DE-MD Metropolitan Statistical Area—see Appendix B for areas included

Source: National Association of Realtors, Qualifying Income Based on Median Sales Price of Existing Single-Family Homes for Metropolitan Areas, 4th Quarter 2017

Median Apartment Condo-Coop Home Prices

Area	2015	2016	2017p	Percent Change 2016 to 2017
MSA[1]	176.5	182.7	185.1	1.3
U.S. Average	210.7	220.7	234.3	6.2

Note: Figures are median sales prices of existing apartment condo-coop homes in thousands of dollars; (p) preliminary; (1) Figures cover the Philadelphia-Camden-Wilmington, PA-NJ-DE-MD Metropolitan Statistical Area—see Appendix B for areas included

Source: National Association of Realtors, Median Sales Price of Existing Apartment Condo-Coop Homes for Metropolitan Areas, 4th Quarter 2017

Home Value Distribution

Area	Under $50,000	$50,000 -$99,999	$100,000 -$149,999	$150,000 -$199,999	$200,000 -$299,999	$300,000 -$499,999	$500,000 -$999,999	$1,000,000 or more
City	1.0	0.2	3.0	3.1	6.5	22.7	45.7	17.8
MSA[1]	4.7	7.9	10.8	15.6	27.1	23.9	8.5	1.4
U.S.	8.8	14.8	15.3	14.9	18.4	16.4	9.0	2.5

Note: Figures are percentages and cover owner-occupied housing units; (1) Figures cover the Philadelphia-Camden-Wilmington, PA-NJ-DE-MD Metropolitan Statistical Area—see Appendix B for areas included

Source: U.S. Census Bureau, 2012-2016 American Community Survey 5-Year Estimates

Homeownership Rate

Area	2009 (%)	2010 (%)	2011 (%)	2012 (%)	2013 (%)	2014 (%)	2015 (%)	2016 (%)	2017 (%)
MSA[1]	69.7	70.7	69.7	69.5	69.1	67.0	67.0	64.7	65.6
U.S.	67.4	66.9	66.1	65.4	65.1	64.5	63.7	63.4	63.9

Note: (1) Figures cover the Philadelphia-Camden-Wilmington, PA-NJ-DE-MD Metropolitan Statistical Area—see Appendix B for areas included

Source: U.S. Census Bureau, Housing Vacancies and Homeownership Annual Statistics: 2009-2017

Year Housing Structure Built

Area	2010 or Later	2000 -2009	1990 -1999	1980 -1989	1970 -1979	1960 -1969	1950 -1959	1940 -1949	Before 1940	Median Year
City	1.1	4.1	6.0	10.1	13.7	14.3	22.9	5.9	22.0	1960
MSA[1]	1.4	8.3	9.4	10.2	12.3	12.1	15.9	8.5	21.8	1963
U.S.	2.3	14.7	14.0	13.7	15.6	10.9	10.6	5.2	13.0	1977

Note: Figures are percentages except for Median Year; Note: (1) Figures cover the Philadelphia-Camden-Wilmington, PA-NJ-DE-MD Metropolitan Statistical Area—see Appendix B for areas included
Source: U.S. Census Bureau, 2012-2016 American Community Survey 5-Year Estimates

Gross Monthly Rent

Area	Under $500	$500 -$999	$1,000 -$1,499	$1,500 -$1,999	$2,000 -$2,499	$2,500 -$2,999	$3,000 and up	Median ($)
City	1.3	7.6	48.7	26.6	8.4	3.7	3.7	1,432
MSA[1]	9.0	37.4	35.4	11.9	3.9	1.3	1.1	1,040
U.S.	11.3	43.3	27.7	10.7	4.0	1.6	1.5	949

Note: Figures are percentages except for Median; Gross rent is the contract rent plus the estimated average monthly cost of utilities (electricity, gas, and water and sewer) and fuels (oil, coal, kerosene, wood, etc.) if these are paid by the renter (or paid for the renter by someone else); (1) Figures cover the Philadelphia-Camden-Wilmington, PA-NJ-DE-MD Metropolitan Statistical Area—see Appendix B for areas included
Source: U.S. Census Bureau, 2012-2016 American Community Survey 5-Year Estimates

HEALTH

Health Risk Factors

Category	MD[1] (%)	U.S. (%)
Adults aged 18–64 who have any kind of health care coverage	88.1	87.7
Adults who reported being in good or excellent health	79.8	83.6
Adults who are current smokers	20.6	17.1
Adults who currently use E-cigarettes	4.0	4.7
Adults who currently use chewing tobacco, snuff, or snus	1.5	4.0
Adults who are heavy drinkers[2]	6.2	6.5
Adults who are binge drinkers[3]	21.9	16.9
Adults who are overweight (BMI 25.0 - 29.9)	33.3	35.3
Adults who are obese (BMI 30.0 - 99.8)	28.7	29.9
Adults who participated in any physical activities in the past month	77.0	76.9
Adults who always or nearly always wears a seat belt	86.6	94.3

Note: (1) Figures cover the Philadelphia, PA Metropolitan Division—see Appendix B for areas included; (2) Heavy drinkers are classified as adult men having more than 14 drinks per week and adult women having more than 7 drinks per week; (3) Binge drinkers are classified as males having five or more drinks on one occasion or females having four or more drinks on one occasion
Source: Centers for Disease Control and Prevention, Behaviorial Risk Factor Surveillance System, SMART: Selected Metropolitan Area Risk Trends, 2016

Health Screening Rates

Category	MD[1] (%)	U.S. (%)
Adults 50-75 who have had a blood stool test within the past year	8.7	8.0
Adults 50-75 who have had a colonoscopy in the past 10 years	68.9	63.5
Adults aged 65+ who have had flu shot within the past year	72.2	58.6
Adults aged 65+ who have ever had a pneumonia vaccination	74.1	73.4
Adults who have ever been tested for HIV	54.8	35.6
Women aged 21-65 who have had a pap test in the past three years	78.1	79.8
Men aged 40+ who have had a PSA test within the past two years	41.8	39.5
Women aged 40+ who have had a mammogram within the past two years	72.4	72.5

Note: n/a not available; (1) Figures cover the Philadelphia, PA Metropolitan Division—see Appendix B for areas included; Source: Centers for Disease Control and Prevention, Behaviorial Risk Factor Surveillance System, SMART: Selected Metropolitan Area Risk Trends, 2016

Chronic Health Conditions

Category	MD[1] (%)	U.S. (%)
Adults who have ever been told they had a heart attack	4.3	4.4
Adults who have ever been told they have angina or coronary heart disease	5.0	4.1
Adults who have ever been told they had a stroke	3.7	3.1
Adults who have been told they currently have asthma	12.7	9.3
Adults who have ever been told they have arthritis	26.2	25.8
Adults who have ever been told they have diabetes[2]	9.8	10.5
Adults who have ever been told they had skin cancer	5.5	5.9
Adults who have ever been told they had any other types of cancer	5.3	6.7
Adults who have ever been told they have COPD	6.2	6.3
Adults who have ever been told they have kidney disease	3.2	2.8
Adults who have ever been told they have a form of depression	20.5	17.4

Note: (1) Figures cover the Philadelphia, PA Metropolitan Division—see Appendix B for areas included; (2) Figures do not include pregnancy-related, borderline, or pre-diabetes
Source: Centers for Disease Control and Prevention, Behaviorial Risk Factor Surveillance System, SMART: Selected Metropolitan Area Risk Trends, 2016

Mortality Rates for the Top 10 Causes of Death in the U.S.

ICD-10[a] Sub-Chapter	ICD-10[a] Code	Age-Adjusted Mortality Rate[1] per 100,000 population	
		County[2]	U.S.
Malignant neoplasms	C00-C97	170.1	158.5
Ischaemic heart diseases	I20-I25	99.8	96.8
Other forms of heart disease	I30-I51	57.8	52.4
Chronic lower respiratory diseases	J40-J47	39.6	40.9
Cerebrovascular diseases	I60-I69	42.3	37.2
Organic, including symptomatic, mental disorders	F01-F09	40.2	33.3
Other degenerative diseases of the nervous system	G30-G31	17.1	32.1
Other external causes of accidental injury	W00-X59	44.7	31.2
Diabetes mellitus	E10-E14	16.2	21.1
Hypertensive diseases	I10-I15	14.7	20.8

Note: (a) ICD-10 = International Classification of Diseases 10th Revision; (1) Mortality rates are a three year average covering 2014-2016; (2) Figures cover Delaware County.
Source: Centers for Disease Control and Prevention, National Center for Health Statistics. Underlying Cause of Death 1999-2016 on CDC WONDER Online Database, released December 2017

Mortality Rates for Selected Causes of Death

ICD-10[a] Sub-Chapter	ICD-10[a] Code	Age-Adjusted Mortality Rate[1] per 100,000 population	
		County[2]	U.S.
Assault	X85-Y09	8.2	5.6
Diseases of the liver	K70-K76	13.7	14.0
Human immunodeficiency virus (HIV) disease	B20-B24	2.0	1.9
Influenza and pneumonia	J09-J18	16.2	14.6
Intentional self-harm	X60-X84	13.0	13.2
Malnutrition	E40-E46	Unreliable	1.3
Obesity and other hyperalimentation	E65-E68	1.5	2.1
Renal failure	N17-N19	14.5	13.0
Transport accidents	V01-V99	6.6	12.0
Viral hepatitis	B15-B19	1.5	1.9

Note: (a) ICD-10 = International Classification of Diseases 10th Revision; (1) Mortality rates are a three year average covering 2014-2016; (2) Figures cover Delaware County; Data are Suppressed when the data meet the criteria for confidentiality constraints; Mortality rates are flagged as Unreliable when the rate would be calculated with a numerator of 20 or less.
Source: Centers for Disease Control and Prevention, National Center for Health Statistics. Underlying Cause of Death 1999-2016 on CDC WONDER Online Database, released December 2017

Health Insurance Coverage

Area	With Health Insurance	With Private Health Insurance	With Public Health Insurance	Without Health Insurance	Population Under Age 18 Without Health Insurance
City	97.0	89.5	16.6	3.0	0.2
MSA[1]	92.0	72.6	31.5	8.0	3.5
U.S.	88.3	66.7	33.0	11.7	5.9

Note: Figures are percentages that cover the civilian noninstitutionalized population; (1) Figures cover the Philadelphia-Camden-Wilmington, PA-NJ-DE-MD Metropolitan Statistical Area—see Appendix B for areas included
Source: U.S. Census Bureau, 2012-2016 American Community Survey 5-Year Estimates

Number of Medical Professionals

Area	MDs[3]	DOs[3,4]	Dentists	Podiatrists	Chiropractors	Optometrists
County[1] (number)	2,103	347	457	73	143	102
County[1] (rate[2])	373.1	61.6	81.0	12.9	25.4	18.1
U.S. (rate[2])	276.5	22.3	67.3	6.0	26.7	15.9

Note: Data as of 2016 unless noted; (1) Data covers Delaware County; (2) Rate per 100,000 population; (3) Data as of 2015 and includes all active, non-federal physicians; (4) Doctor of Osteopathic Medicine
Source: U.S. Department of Health and Human Services, Health Resources and Services Administration, Bureau of Health Professions, Area Resource File (ARF) 2016-2017

Best Hospitals

According to *U.S. News,* the Philadelphia, PA metro area is home to seven of the best hospitals in the U.S.: **Fox Chase Cancer Center** (2 adult specialties); **Hahnemann University Hospital** (1 adult specialty); **Hospitals of the University of Pennsylvania-Penn Presbyterian** (Honor Roll/11 adult specialties); **Magee Rehabilitation Hospital** (1 adult specialty); **Pennsylvania Hospital** (1 adult specialty); **Thomas Jefferson University Hospital** (Honor Roll/11 adult specialties); **Wills Eye Hospital** (1 adult specialty). The hospitals listed were nationally ranked in at least one of 16 specialties. Only 152 hospitals nationwide were nationally ranked in one or more specialties. Twenty hospitals in the U.S. made the Honor Roll. The Best Hospitals Honor Roll was revamped last year to take both the national rankings and the procedure and condition ratings into account. Hospitals received points if they were nationally ranked in one of the 16 specialties—the higher they ranked, the more points they got—and how many ratings of "high performing" they earned in the nine procedures and conditions. *U.S. News Online, "America's Best Hospitals 2017-18"*

According to *U.S. News,* the Philadelphia, PA metro area is home to one of the best children's hospitals in the U.S.: **Children's Hospital of Philadelphia** (Honor Roll/10 pediatric specialties). The hospital listed was highly ranked in at least one of 10 pediatric specialties. Eighty-two children's hospitals in the U.S. were nationally ranked in at least one specialty. Hospitals received points for being ranked in a specialty, and the 10 hospitals with the most points across the 10 specialties make up the Honor Roll. *U.S. News Online, "America's Best Children's Hospitals 2017-18"*

EDUCATION

Public School District Statistics

District Name	Schls	Pupils	Pupil/ Teacher Ratio	Minority Pupils[1] (%)	Free Lunch Eligible[2] (%)	IEP[3] (%)
Radnor Township SD	5	3,730	13.0	26.7	9.0	14.4

Note: Table includes school districts with 100 or more students; (1) Percentage of students that are not non-Hispanic white; (2) Percentage of students that are eligible for the free lunch program; (3) Percentage of students that have an Individualized Education Program.
Source: U.S. Department of Education, National Center for Education Statistics, Common Core of Data, Local Education Agency (School District) Universe Survey: School Year 2015-2016; U.S. Department of Education, National Center for Education Statistics, Common Core of Data, Public Elementary/Secondary School Universe Survey: School Year 2015-2016

Best High Schools

According to *U.S. News,* Radnor is home to one of the best high schools in the U.S.: **Radnor High School** (#432). More than 22,000 public, magnet and charter schools were ranked based on their performance on state assessments and how well they prepare students for college. Schools with the highest unrounded College Readiness Index values were numerically ranked from 1 to 500 and were classified as gold medal winners. *U.S. News & World Report, "Best High Schools 2017"*

Highest Level of Education

Area	Less than H.S.	H.S. Diploma	Some College, No Deg.	Associate Degree	Bachelor's Degree	Master's Degree	Prof. School Degree	Doctorate Degree
City	2.5	11.7	9.2	3.9	33.2	22.9	11.0	5.7
MSA[1]	10.3	30.0	17.3	6.9	21.3	9.9	2.5	1.8
U.S.	13.0	27.5	21.0	8.2	18.8	8.2	2.0	1.3

Note: Figures cover persons age 25 and over; (1) Figures cover the Philadelphia-Camden-Wilmington, PA-NJ-DE-MD Metropolitan Statistical Area—see Appendix B for areas included
Source: U.S. Census Bureau, 2012-2016 American Community Survey 5-Year Estimates

Educational Attainment by Race

Area	High School Graduate or Higher (%)					Bachelor's Degree or Higher (%)				
	Total	White	Black	Asian	Hisp.[2]	Total	White	Black	Asian	Hisp.[2]
City	97.5	97.5	94.6	98.6	98.2	72.7	73.6	40.2	83.6	69.7
MSA[1]	89.7	92.3	85.7	83.4	68.1	35.5	39.5	19.2	55.0	16.3
U.S.	87.0	88.9	84.3	86.3	65.7	30.3	31.6	20.0	52.1	14.7

Note: Figures shown cover persons 25 years old and over; (1) Figures cover the Philadelphia-Camden-Wilmington, PA-NJ-DE-MD Metropolitan Statistical Area—see Appendix B for areas included; (2) People of Hispanic origin can be of any race
Source: U.S. Census Bureau, 2012-2016 American Community Survey 5-Year Estimates

School Enrollment by Grade and Control

Area	Preschool (%)		Kindergarten (%)		Grades 1 - 4 (%)		Grades 5 - 8 (%)		Grades 9 - 12 (%)	
	Public	Private	Public	Private	Public	Private	Public	Private	Public	Private
City	10.4	89.6	77.4	22.6	74.0	26.0	78.1	21.9	78.2	21.8
MSA[1]	43.6	56.4	81.7	18.3	85.0	15.0	83.6	16.4	83.6	16.4
U.S.	58.4	41.6	87.7	12.3	89.8	10.2	89.7	10.3	90.4	9.6

Note: Figures shown cover persons 3 years old and over; (1) Figures cover the Philadelphia-Camden-Wilmington, PA-NJ-DE-MD Metropolitan Statistical Area—see Appendix B for areas included
Source: U.S. Census Bureau, 2012-2016 American Community Survey 5-Year Estimates

Average Salaries of Public School Classroom Teachers

Area	2015		2016		Change from 2015 to 2016	
	Dollars	Rank[1]	Dollars	Rank[1]	Percent	Rank[2]
Pennsylvania	64,447	10	65,151	10	1.1	24
U.S. Average	57,611	–	58,353	–	1.3	–

Note: (1) Rank ranges from 1 to 51 where 1 indicates highest salary; (2) Rank ranges from 1 to 51 where 1 indicates highest percent change.
Source: National Education Association, Rankings & Estimates: Rankings of the States 2016 and Estimates of School Statistics 2017

Higher Education

Four-Year Colleges			Two-Year Colleges			Medical Schools[1]	Law Schools[2]	Voc/ Tech[3]
Public	Private Non-profit	Private For-profit	Public	Private Non-profit	Private For-profit			
0	1	0	0	0	0	0	1	0

Note: Figures cover institutions located within the city limits and include main campuses only; (1) includes schools accredited by the Liaison Committee on Medical Education and the American Osteopathic Association's Commission on Osteopathic College Accreditation; (2) includes ABA-accredited schools, schools with provisional ABA accreditation, and state accredited schools; (3) includes all schools with programs that are less than 2 years.
Source: National Center for Education Statistics, Integrated Postsecondary Education System (IPEDS), 2016-17; Wikipedia, List of Medical Schools in the United States, accessed April 2, 2018; Wikipedia, List of Law Schools in the United States, accessed April 2, 2018

According to *U.S. News & World Report,* the Philadelphia, PA metro division is home to four of the best national universities in the U.S.: **University of Pennsylvania** (#8); **Drexel University** (#94 tie); **Temple University** (#115 tie); **Widener University** (#192 tie). The indicators used to capture academic quality fall into a number of categories: assessment by administrators at peer institutions; retention of students; faculty resources; student selectivity; financial resources; alumni giving; high school counselor ratings of colleges; and graduation rate. *U.S. News & World Report, "America's Best Colleges 2018"*

According to *U.S. News & World Report,* the Philadelphia, PA metro division is home to four of the best liberal arts colleges in the U.S.: **Swarthmore College** (#3 tie); **Haverford College** (#18 tie); **Bryn Mawr College** (#32); **Ursinus College** (#93 tie). The indicators used to capture academic quality fall into a number of categories: assessment by administrators at peer institutions; retention of students; faculty resources; student selectivity; financial resources; alumni giving; high school counselor ratings of colleges; and graduation rate. *U.S. News & World Report, "America's Best Colleges 2018"*

According to *U.S. News & World Report,* the Philadelphia, PA metro division is home to three of the top 100 law schools in the U.S.: **University of Pennsylvania** (#7); **Temple University (Beasley)** (#47 tie); **Villanova University** (#65 tie). The rankings are based on a weighted average of 12 measures of quality: peer assessment score; assessment score by lawyers/judges; median LSAT scores; median undergrad GPA; acceptance rate; employment rates for graduates; placement success; bar passage rate; faculty resources; expenditures per student; student/faculty ratio; and library resources. *U.S. News & World Report, "America's Best Graduate Schools, Law, 2019"*

According to *U.S. News & World Report,* the Philadelphia, PA metro division is home to three of the top 75 medical schools for research in the U.S.: **University of Pennsylvania (Perelman)** (#6 tie); **Thomas Jefferson University (Kimmel)** (#56); **Temple University (Katz)** (#57 tie). The rankings are based on a weighted average of 11 measures of quality: quality assessment; peer assessment score; assessment score by residency directors; research activity; total research activity; average research activity per faculty member; student selectivity; median MCAT total score; median undergraduate GPA; acceptance rate; and faculty resources. *U.S. News & World Report, "America's Best Graduate Schools, Medical, 2019"*

According to *U.S. News & World Report,* the Philadelphia, PA metro division is home to one of the top 75 business schools in the U.S.: **University of Pennsylvania (Wharton)** (#3). The rankings are based on a weighted average of the following nine measures: quality assessment; peer assessment; recruiter assessment; placement success; mean starting salary and bonus; student selectivity; mean GMAT and GRE scores; mean undergraduate GPA; and acceptance rate. *U.S. News & World Report, "America's Best Graduate Schools, Business, 2019"*

PRESIDENTIAL ELECTION

2016 Presidential Election Results

Area	Clinton	Trump	Johnson	Stein	Other
Delaware County	59.3	37.0	2.0	0.9	0.9
U.S.	48.0	45.9	3.3	1.1	1.7

Note: Results are percentages and may not add to 100% due to rounding
Source: Dave Leip's Atlas of U.S. Presidential Elections

EMPLOYERS

Major Employers

Company Name	Industry
Abington Memorial Hospital	General medical & surgical hospitals
AstraZeneca Pharmaceuticals	Pharmaceutical preparations
City of Philadelphia	Police protection
Comcast Holdings Corporation	Cable & other pay television services
Cooper Health Care	Hospital management
E.I. du Pont de Nemours and Company	Agricultural chemicals
Einstein Community Health Associates	Offices & clinics of medical doctors
Glaxosmithkline	Commerical physical research
Lockheed Martin Corporation	Defense systems & equipment
Mercy Health System of SE Pennsylvania	General medical & surgical hospitals
On Time Staffing	Employment agencies
Richlieu Associates	Apartment building operators
Temple University	General medical & surgical hospitals
The University of Pennsylvania	Colleges & universities
The US Navy	Navy
The Vanguard Group	Management, investment, open-end
Thomas Jefferson University Hospital	General medical & surgical hospitals
Trustees of the University of Penn	General medical & surgical hospitals
Unisys Corporation	Computer integrated systems design
University of Delaware	Colleges & universities

Note: Companies shown are located within the Philadelphia-Camden-Wilmington, PA-NJ-DE-MD Metropolitan Statistical Area.
Source: Hoovers.com; Wikipedia

PUBLIC SAFETY

Crime Rate

Area	All Crimes	Violent Crimes				Property Crimes		
		Murder	Rape[3]	Robbery	Aggrav. Assault	Burglary	Larceny -Theft	Motor Vehicle Theft
City	989.7	0.0	3.2	0.0	66.4	94.9	793.7	31.6
Metro[1]	3,618.8	14.6	62.8	324.5	424.8	389.4	2,117.7	285.0
U.S.	2,847.8	5.3	40.4	102.8	248.5	468.9	1,745.0	236.9

Note: Figures are crimes per 100,000 population; (1) Figures cover the Philadelphia, PA Metropolitan Division—see Appendix B for areas included; (3) The city and U.S. figures shown were reported using the revised Uniform Crime Reporting (UCR) definition of rape. The metro area figures shown are an aggregate total of the data submitted using both the revised and legacy UCR definitions.
Source: FBI Uniform Crime Reports, 2016

Hate Crimes

Area	Number of Quarters Reported	Number of Incidents per Bias Motivation					
		Race/Ethnicity/ Ancestry	Religion	Sexual Orientation	Disability	Gender	Gender Identity
Area[1]	4	0	0	0	0	0	0
U.S.	4	3,489	1,273	1,076	70	31	124

Note: (1) Figures cover the Radnor Township.
Source: Federal Bureau of Investigation, Hate Crime Statistics 2016

Identity Theft Consumer Reports

Area	Reports	Reports per 100,000 Population	Rank[2]
MSA[1]	8,444	139	23
U.S.	371,061	114	-

Note: (1) Figures cover the Philadelphia-Camden-Wilmington, PA-NJ-DE-MD Metropolitan Statistical Area—see Appendix B for areas included; (2) Rank ranges from 1 to 389 where 1 indicates greatest number of identity theft reports per 100,000 population
Source: Federal Trade Commission, Consumer Sentinel Network Data Book for January–December 2017

Fraud and Other Consumer Reports

Area	Reports	Reports per 100,000 Population	Rank[2]
MSA[1]	34,068	561	60
U.S.	2,304,550	708	-

Note: (1) Figures cover the Philadelphia-Camden-Wilmington, PA-NJ-DE-MD Metropolitan Statistical Area—see Appendix B for areas included; (2) Rank ranges from 1 to 389 where 1 indicates greatest number of fraud and other consumer reports per 100,000 population
Source: Federal Trade Commission, Consumer Sentinel Network Data Book for January–December 2017

SPORTS

Professional Sports Teams

Team Name	League	Year Established
Philadelphia 76ers	National Basketball Association (NBA)	1963
Philadelphia Eagles	National Football League (NFL)	1933
Philadelphia Flyers	National Hockey League (NHL)	1967
Philadelphia Phillies	Major League Baseball (MLB)	1883
Philadelphia Union	Major League Soccer (MLS)	2010

Note: Includes teams located in the Philadelphia-Camden-Wilmington, PA-NJ-DE-MD Metropolitan Statistical Area.
Source: Wikipedia, Major Professional Sports Teams of the United States and Canada, April 5, 2018

CLIMATE

Average and Extreme Temperatures

Temperature	Jan	Feb	Mar	Apr	May	Jun	Jul	Aug	Sep	Oct	Nov	Dec	Yr.
Extreme High (°F)	74	74	85	94	96	100	104	101	100	89	84	72	104
Average High (°F)	39	42	51	63	73	82	86	85	78	67	55	43	64
Average Temp. (°F)	32	34	42	53	63	72	77	76	68	57	47	36	55
Average Low (°F)	24	26	33	43	53	62	67	66	59	47	38	28	45
Extreme Low (°F)	-7	-4	7	19	28	44	51	44	35	25	15	1	-7

Note: Figures cover the years 1948-1990
Source: National Climatic Data Center, International Station Meteorological Climate Summary, 9/96

Average Precipitation/Snowfall/Humidity

Precip./Humidity	Jan	Feb	Mar	Apr	May	Jun	Jul	Aug	Sep	Oct	Nov	Dec	Yr.
Avg. Precip. (in.)	3.2	2.8	3.7	3.5	3.7	3.6	4.1	4.0	3.3	2.7	3.4	3.3	41.4
Avg. Snowfall (in.)	7	7	4	Tr	Tr	0	0	0	0	Tr	1	4	22
Avg. Rel. Hum. 7am (%)	74	73	73	72	75	77	80	82	84	83	79	75	77
Avg. Rel. Hum. 4pm (%)	60	55	51	48	51	52	54	55	55	54	57	60	54

Note: Figures cover the years 1948-1990; Tr = Trace amounts (<0.05 in. of rain; <0.5 in. of snow)
Source: National Climatic Data Center, International Station Meteorological Climate Summary, 9/96

Weather Conditions

Temperature			Daytime Sky			Precipitation		
10°F & below	32°F & below	90°F & above	Clear	Partly cloudy	Cloudy	0.01 inch or more precip.	0.1 inch or more snow/ice	Thunder-storms
5	94	23	81	146	138	117	14	27

Note: Figures are average number of days per year and cover the years 1948-1990
Source: National Climatic Data Center, International Station Meteorological Climate Summary, 9/96

HAZARDOUS WASTE

Superfund Sites

The Philadelphia, PA metro division is home to six sites on the EPA's Superfund National Priorities List: **East Tenth Street** (proposed); **Franklin Slag Pile (MDC)** (final); **Havertown Pcp** (final); **Lower Darby Creek Area** (final); **Metal Bank** (final); **Metro Container Corporation** (final). There are a total of 1,396 Superfund sites with a status of proposed or final on the list in the U.S.
U.S. Environmental Protection Agency, National Priorities List, April 4, 2018

AIR & WATER QUALITY

Air Quality Trends: Ozone

	1990	1995	2000	2005	2010	2012	2013	2014	2015	2016
MSA[1]	0.102	0.109	0.099	0.091	0.083	0.084	0.069	0.071	0.074	0.075
U.S.	0.087	0.089	0.081	0.079	0.073	0.075	0.069	0.067	0.068	0.069

Note: (1) Data covers the Philadelphia-Camden-Wilmington, PA-NJ-DE-MD Metropolitan Statistical Area—see Appendix B for areas included. The values shown are the composite ozone concentration averages among trend sites based on the highest fourth daily maximum 8-hour concentration in parts per million. These trends are based on sites having an adequate record of monitoring data during the trend period. Data from exceptional events are included.
Source: U.S. Environmental Protection Agency, Air Quality Monitoring Information, "Air Quality Trends by City, 1990-2016"

Air Quality Index

Area	Percent of Days when Air Quality was...[2]					AQI Statistics[2]	
	Good	Moderate	Unhealthy for Sensitive Groups	Unhealthy	Very Unhealthy	Maximum	Median
MSA[1]	34.5	59.5	5.5	0.5	0.0	166	55

Note: (1) Data covers the Philadelphia-Camden-Wilmington, PA-NJ-DE-MD Metropolitan Statistical Area—see Appendix B for areas included; (2) Based on 365 days with AQI data in 2017. Air Quality Index (AQI) is an index for reporting daily air quality. EPA calculates the AQI for five major air pollutants regulated by the Clean Air Act: ground-level ozone, particle pollution (aka particulate matter), carbon monoxide, sulfur dioxide, and nitrogen dioxide. The AQI runs from 0 to 500. The higher the AQI value, the greater the level of air pollution and the greater the health concern. There are six AQI categories: "Good" AQI is between 0 and 50. Air quality is considered satisfactory; "Moderate" AQI is between 51 and 100. Air quality is acceptable; "Unhealthy for Sensitive Groups" When AQI values are between 101 and 150, members of sensitive groups may experience health effects; "Unhealthy" When AQI values are between 151 and 200 everyone may begin to experience health effects; "Very Unhealthy" AQI values between 201 and 300 trigger a health alert; "Hazardous" AQI values over 300 trigger warnings of emergency conditions (not shown).
Source: U.S. Environmental Protection Agency, Air Quality Index Report, 2017

Air Quality Index Pollutants

Area	Percent of Days when AQI Pollutant was...[2]					
	Carbon Monoxide	Nitrogen Dioxide	Ozone	Sulfur Dioxide	Particulate Matter 2.5	Particulate Matter 10
MSA[1]	0.0	0.3	31.2	0.5	67.7	0.3

Note: (1) Data covers the Philadelphia-Camden-Wilmington, PA-NJ-DE-MD Metropolitan Statistical Area—see Appendix B for areas included; (2) Based on 365 days with AQI data in 2017. The Air Quality Index (AQI) is an index for reporting daily air quality. EPA calculates the AQI for five major air pollutants regulated by the Clean Air Act: ground-level ozone, particle pollution (also known as particulate matter), carbon monoxide, sulfur dioxide, and nitrogen dioxide. The AQI runs from 0 to 500. The higher the AQI value, the greater the level of air pollution and the greater the health concern.
Source: U.S. Environmental Protection Agency, Air Quality Index Report, 2017

Maximum Air Pollutant Concentrations: Particulate Matter, Ozone, CO and Lead

	Particulate Matter 10 (ug/m^3)	Particulate Matter 2.5 Wtd AM (ug/m^3)	Particulate Matter 2.5 24-Hr (ug/m^3)	Ozone (ppm)	Carbon Monoxide (ppm)	Lead (ug/m^3)
MSA[1] Level	113	11	24	0.08	2	0.04
NAAQS[2]	150	15	35	0.075	9	0.15
Met NAAQS[2]	Yes	Yes	Yes	No	Yes	Yes

Note: (1) Data covers the Philadelphia-Camden-Wilmington, PA-NJ-DE-MD Metropolitan Statistical Area—see Appendix B for areas included; Data from exceptional events are included; (2) National Ambient Air Quality Standards; ppm = parts per million; ug/m^3 = micrograms per cubic meter; n/a not available.
Concentrations: Particulate Matter 10 (coarse particulate)—highest second maximum 24-hour concentration; Particulate Matter 2.5 Wtd AM (fine particulate)—highest weighted annual mean concentration; Particulate Matter 2.5 24-Hour (fine particulate)—highest 98th percentile 24-hour concentration; Ozone—highest fourth daily maximum 8-hour concentration; Carbon Monoxide—highest second maximum non-overlapping 8-hour concentration; Lead—maximum running 3-month average
Source: U.S. Environmental Protection Agency, Air Quality Monitoring Information, "Air Quality Statistics by City, 2016"

Maximum Air Pollutant Concentrations: Nitrogen Dioxide and Sulfur Dioxide

	Nitrogen Dioxide AM (ppb)	Nitrogen Dioxide 1-Hr (ppb)	Sulfur Dioxide AM (ppb)	Sulfur Dioxide 1-Hr (ppb)	Sulfur Dioxide 24-Hr (ppb)
MSA[1] Level	16	58	n/a	19	n/a
NAAQS[2]	53	100	30	75	140
Met NAAQS[2]	Yes	Yes	n/a	Yes	n/a

Note: (1) Data covers the Philadelphia-Camden-Wilmington, PA-NJ-DE-MD Metropolitan Statistical Area—see Appendix B for areas included; Data from exceptional events are included; (2) National Ambient Air Quality Standards; ppm = parts per million; ug/m^3 = micrograms per cubic meter; n/a not available.
Concentrations: Nitrogen Dioxide AM—highest arithmetic mean concentration; Nitrogen Dioxide 1-Hr—highest 98th percentile 1-hour daily maximum concentration; Sulfur Dioxide AM—highest annual mean concentration; Sulfur Dioxide 1-Hr—highest 99th percentile 1-hour daily maximum concentration; Sulfur Dioxide 24-Hr—highest second maximum 24-hour concentration
Source: U.S. Environmental Protection Agency, Air Quality Monitoring Information, "Air Quality Statistics by City, 2016"

Drinking Water

Water System Name	Pop. Served	Primary Water Source Type	Violations[1]	
			Health Based	Monitoring/ Reporting
Chester Water Authority	138,453	Surface	0	0

Note: (1) Based on violation data from January 1, 2017 to December 31, 2017
Source: U.S. Environmental Protection Agency, Office of Ground Water and Drinking Water, Safe Drinking Water Information System (based on data extracted April 5, 2018)

State College, Pennsylvania

Background

State College, the largest designated borough in Pennsylvania, is a college town known primarily for the University Park campus of Pennsylvania State University. The area is often referred to as "Happy Valley," including College, Harris, Patton, and Ferguson. Together, these communities make up the Centre Region Council of Governments.

State College has grown from a village to a town in tandem with Pennsylvania State College, which was founded as the Farmers' High School of Pennsylvania in 1855. State College was incorporated as a borough in 1896, and Pennsylvania State College was officially renamed to what it is known as today, Pennsylvania State University, in 1953. When Pennsylvania State University's name was changed from College to University in 1953, its then-president, Milton S. Eisenhower, petitioned for the borough to change its name as well. A majority was not reached, and the borough's name was not changed.

With a total area of 4.5 square miles, State College is primarily surrounded by large tracts of farmland, mountains, and forests.

Although Pennsylvania State University is the primarily employer of the area, State College also offers employment in health care, retail, hospitality services, construction, and government. Other major employers of the area include Mount Nittany Medical Center, the Government of Pennsylvania, and Weis Markets.

The activities and events that occur in State College are endless, as it goes for a college town. One such event is the Central Pennsylvania Festival of the Arts, or "Arts Fest," which attracts national acts and visitors from around the country. The Penn State IFC/Panhellenic Dance Marathon, or THON, is another University event—a 46-hour dance marathon that raises money each year for the Four Diamonds Foundation. Other events include Blue-White Football Weekend and First Night State College. State College also offers a variety of museums, restaurants, and live shows throughout the year.

State College is under the State College Area School district, which serves the area with nine elementary schools, two middle schools, and one high school. Eleven private schools also populate State College. While Pennsylvania State University comprises much of State College's higher education, the South Hills School of Business and Technology also resides in the borough.

Penn State Nittany Lions Football attracts hundreds of thousands of fans to their home games at Beaver Stadium every year. The minor league baseball team, the State College Spikes, represent the borough itself. Other sports such as basketball, ice hockey, and soccer are also popular.

College Town is served by the Centre Area Transportation Authority for bus transit needs. The University Park Airport, located in Benner Township is the commercial airport.

State College has a humid continental climate, with the lowest temperature recorded in the area being -20 °F (-29 °C) in 1899, and the highest being 102 °F (39 °C) in both 1988 and 1936.

Rankings

General Rankings

- In their fifth annual survey, Livability.com looked at data for nearly 2,300 U.S. cities to determine the rankings for Livability's "Top 100 Best Places to Live" in 2018. State College ranked #52. Criteria: vibrant economy; low cost of living; education, demographics, health care options; transportation & infrastructure; abundant lifestyle amenities. *Livability.com, "Top 100 Best Places to Live 2018" January 16, 2018*

Business/Finance Rankings

- The State College metro area appeared on the Milken Institute "2017 Best Performing Cities" list. Rank: #84 out of 201 small metro areas. Criteria: job growth; wage and salary growth; high-tech output growth. *Milken Institute, "Best-Performing Cities 2017," January 2018*
- *Forbes* ranked 200 smaller metro areas (population under 265,400) to determine the nation's "Best Small Places for Business and Careers." The State College metro area was ranked #38. Criteria: costs (business and living); job growth (past and projected); income growth; quality of life; educational attainment (college and high school); projected economic growth; cultural and recreational opportunities; net migration patterns; number of highly ranked colleges. *Forbes, "The Best Small Cities for Business and Careers 2017," November, 6 2017*

Environmental Rankings

- Sperling's BestPlaces assessed 379 metropolitan areas of the United States for the likelihood of dangerously extreme weather events or earthquakes. In general the Southeast and South-Central regions have the highest risk of weather extremes and earthquakes, while the Pacific Northwest enjoys the lowest risk. Of the least risky metropolitan areas, the State College metro area was ranked #81. *www.bestplaces.net, "Safest Places from Natural Disasters," April 2011*

Safety Rankings

- The National Insurance Crime Bureau ranked 382 metro areas in the U.S. in terms of per capita rates of vehicle theft. The State College metro area ranked #380 (#1 = highest rate). Criteria: number of vehicle theft offenses per 100,000 inhabitants in 2016. *National Insurance Crime Bureau, "Hot Spots 2016," June 8, 2017*

Seniors/Retirement Rankings

- From its Best Cities for Successful Aging indexes, the Milken Institute generated rankings for metropolitan areas, weighing data in nine categories—health care, wellness, living arrangements, transportation and convenience, financial characteristics, education, employment, community engagement, and overall livability. The State College metro area was ranked #16 overall in the small metro area category. *Milken Institute, "Best Cities for Successful Aging, 2017" March 14, 2017*

Business Environment

CITY FINANCES

City Government Finances

Component	2015 ($000)	2015 ($ per capita)
Total Revenues	40,948	971
Total Expenditures	61,326	1,455
Debt Outstanding	8,457	201
Cash and Securities[1]	60,041	1,424

Note: (1) Cash and security holdings of a government at the close of its fiscal year,, including those of its dependent agencies, utilities, and liquor stores.
Source: U.S Census Bureau, State & Local Government Finances 2015

City Government Revenue by Source

Source	2015 ($000)	2015 ($ per capita)	2015 (%)
General Revenue			
From Federal Government	1,642	39	4.0
From State Government	2,080	49	5.1
From Local Governments	584	14	1.4
Taxes			
Property	4,955	118	12.1
Sales and Gross Receipts	0	0	0.0
Personal Income	4,495	107	11.0
Corporate Income	0	0	0.0
Motor Vehicle License	0	0	0.0
Other Taxes	2,872	68	7.0
Current Charges	18,732	444	45.7
Liquor Store	0	0	0.0
Utility	0	0	0.0
Employee Retirement	3,827	91	9.3

Source: U.S Census Bureau, State & Local Government Finances 2015

City Government Expenditures by Function

Function	2015 ($000)	2015 ($ per capita)	2015 (%)
General Direct Expenditures			
Air Transportation	0	0	0.0
Corrections	0	0	0.0
Education	0	0	0.0
Employment Security Administration	0	0	0.0
Financial Administration	1,356	32	2.2
Fire Protection	507	12	0.8
General Public Buildings	16,024	380	26.1
Governmental Administration, Other	2,355	55	3.8
Health	425	10	0.7
Highways	4,991	118	8.1
Hospitals	0	0	0.0
Housing and Community Development	1,632	38	2.7
Interest on General Debt	104	2	0.2
Judicial and Legal	78	1	0.1
Libraries	383	9	0.6
Parking	1,878	44	3.1
Parks and Recreation	1,496	35	2.4
Police Protection	9,779	231	15.9
Public Welfare	0	0	0.0
Sewerage	5,913	140	9.6
Solid Waste Management	3,725	88	6.1
Veterans' Services	0	0	0.0
Liquor Store	0	0	0.0
Utility	153	3	0.2
Employee Retirement	8,346	198	13.6

Source: U.S Census Bureau, State & Local Government Finances 2015

DEMOGRAPHICS

Population Growth

Area	1990 Census	2000 Census	2010 Census	2016* Estimate	Population Growth (%) 1990-2016	Population Growth (%) 2010-2016
City	38,933	38,420	42,034	42,074	8.1	0.1
MSA[1]	123,786	135,758	153,990	159,178	28.6	3.4
U.S.	248,709,873	281,421,906	308,745,538	318,558,162	28.1	3.2

Note: (1) Figures cover the State College, PA Metropolitan Statistical Area—see Appendix B for areas included; (*) 2012-2016 5-year estimated population
Source: U.S. Census Bureau, 1990 Census, Census 2000, Census 2010, 2012-2016 American Community Survey 5-Year Estimates

Household Size

Area	Persons in Household (%) One	Two	Three	Four	Five	Six	Seven or More	Average Household Size
City	38.3	30.7	15.4	10.4	4.2	0.6	0.4	2.50
MSA[1]	28.1	36.7	16.7	12.2	4.3	1.1	0.9	2.50
U.S.	27.7	33.7	15.7	13.1	6.0	2.3	1.5	2.60

Note: (1) Figures cover the State College, PA Metropolitan Statistical Area—see Appendix B for areas included
Source: U.S. Census Bureau, 2012-2016 American Community Survey 5-Year Estimates

Race

Area	White Alone[2] (%)	Black Alone[2] (%)	Asian Alone[2] (%)	AIAN[3] Alone[2] (%)	NHOPI[4] Alone[2] (%)	Other Race Alone[2] (%)	Two or More Races (%)
City	82.0	4.2	10.8	0.1	0.1	0.7	2.1
MSA[1]	88.0	3.8	5.8	0.2	0.0	0.5	1.7
U.S.	73.3	12.6	5.2	0.8	0.2	4.8	3.1

Note: (1) Figures cover the State College, PA Metropolitan Statistical Area—see Appendix B for areas included; (2) Alone is defined as not being in combination with one or more other races; (3) American Indian and Alaska Native; (4) Native Hawaiian and Other Pacific Islander
Source: U.S. Census Bureau, 2012-2016 American Community Survey 5-Year Estimates

Hispanic or Latino Origin

Area	Total (%)	Mexican (%)	Puerto Rican (%)	Cuban (%)	Other (%)
City	4.2	1.2	0.9	0.2	1.9
MSA[1]	2.8	0.8	0.8	0.1	1.1
U.S.	17.3	11.0	1.7	0.7	4.0

Note: Persons of Hispanic or Latino origin can be of any race; (1) Figures cover the State College, PA Metropolitan Statistical Area—see Appendix B for areas included
Source: U.S. Census Bureau, 2012-2016 American Community Survey 5-Year Estimates

Segregation

Type	Segregation Indices[1] 1990	2000	2010	2010 Rank[2]	Percent Change 1990-2000	1990-2010	2000-2010
Black/White	n/a	n/a	n/a	n/a	n/a	n/a	n/a
Asian/White	n/a	n/a	n/a	n/a	n/a	n/a	n/a
Hispanic/White	n/a	n/a	n/a	n/a	n/a	n/a	n/a

Note: All figures cover the Metropolitan Statistical Area—see Appendix B for areas included; Figures are based on an analysis of 1990, 2000, and 2010 Census Decennial Census tract data by William H. Frey, Brookings Institution and the University of Michigan Social Science Data Analysis Network. In this analysis all racial groups (whites, blacks, and asians) are non-Hispanic members of those races. Hispanics are shown as a separate category; (1) Segregation Indices are Dissimilarity Indices that measure the degree to which the minority group is distributed differently than whites across census tracts. They range from 0 (complete integration) to 100 (complete segregation) where the value indicates the percentage of the minority group that needs to move to be distributed exactly like whites; (2) Ranges from 1 (most segregated) to 102 (least segregated); n/a not available.
Source: www.CensusScope.org

Ancestry

Area	German	Irish	English	American	Italian	Polish	French²	Scottish	Dutch
City	18.5	11.6	5.6	1.8	10.0	5.7	2.1	1.5	1.1
MSA¹	25.1	11.9	7.5	5.1	7.4	5.2	1.9	1.8	1.6
U.S.	14.4	10.4	7.7	6.9	5.4	2.9	2.6	1.7	1.3

Note: Figures are the percentage of the total population reporting a particular ancestry. The nine most commonly reported ancestries in the U.S. are shown. Figures include multiple ancestries (e.g. if a person reported being Irish and Italian, they were included in both columns); (1) Figures cover the State College, PA Metropolitan Statistical Area—see Appendix B for areas included; (2) Excludes Basque
Source: U.S. Census Bureau, 2012-2016 American Community Survey 5-Year Estimates

Foreign-Born Population

Area	Percent of Population Born in								
	Any Foreign Country	Asia	Mexico	Europe	Carribean	Central America²	South America	Africa	Canada
City	13.5	9.1	0.2	1.9	0.4	0.2	0.5	0.3	0.7
MSA¹	8.1	5.6	0.1	1.1	0.2	0.1	0.2	0.4	0.3
U.S.	13.2	4.0	3.6	1.5	1.3	1.0	0.9	0.6	0.3

Note: (1) Figures cover the State College, PA Metropolitan Statistical Area—see Appendix B for areas included; (2) Excludes Mexico.
Source: U.S. Census Bureau, 2012-2016 American Community Survey 5-Year Estimates

Marital Status

Area	Never Married	Now Married²	Separated	Widowed	Divorced
City	79.7	15.5	0.5	1.5	2.8
MSA¹	47.0	40.7	1.0	4.2	7.1
U.S.	33.0	48.1	2.1	5.9	11.0

Note: Figures are percentages and cover the population 15 years of age and older; (1) Figures cover the State College, PA Metropolitan Statistical Area—see Appendix B for areas included; (2) Excludes separated
Source: U.S. Census Bureau, 2012-2016 American Community Survey 5-Year Estimates

Disability Status

Area	All Ages	Under 18 Years Old	18 to 64 Years Old	65 Years and Over
City	5.6	2.3	4.6	28.4
MSA¹	9.9	4.0	7.4	32.3
U.S.	12.5	4.1	10.3	35.7

Note: Figures show percent of the civilian noninstitutionalized population that reported having a disability. Disability status is determined from six types of difficulty: vision, hearing, cognitive, ambulatory, self-care, and independent living. For children under 5 years old, hearing and vision difficulty are used to determine disability status. For children between the ages of 5 and 14, disability status is determined from hearing, vision, cognitive, ambulatory, and self-care difficulties. For people aged 15 years and older, they are considered to have a disability if they have difficulty with any one of the six difficulty types; Note: (1) Figures cover the State College, PA Metropolitan Statistical Area—see Appendix B for areas included
Source: U.S. Census Bureau, 2012-2016 American Community Survey 5-Year Estimates

Age

Area	Percent of Population									Median Age
	Under Age 5	Age 5–19	Age 20–34	Age 35–44	Age 45–54	Age 55–64	Age 65–74	Age 75–84	Age 85+	
City	1.8	26.6	53.9	4.3	4.3	3.9	2.7	1.6	1.0	21.6
MSA¹	4.1	18.8	32.0	10.4	11.5	10.8	6.9	4.0	1.6	30.8
U.S.	6.2	19.6	20.7	12.7	13.6	12.6	8.3	4.3	1.9	37.7

Note: (1) Figures cover the State College, PA Metropolitan Statistical Area—see Appendix B for areas included
Source: U.S. Census Bureau, 2012-2016 American Community Survey 5-Year Estimates

Gender

Area	Males	Females	Males per 100 Females
City	22,705	19,369	117.2
MSA¹	83,558	75,620	110.5
U.S.	156,765,322	161,792,840	96.9

Note: (1) Figures cover the State College, PA Metropolitan Statistical Area—see Appendix B for areas included
Source: U.S. Census Bureau, 2012-2016 American Community Survey 5-Year Estimates

Religious Groups by Family

Area	Catholic	Baptist	Non-Den.	Methodist[2]	Lutheran	LDS[3]	Pente-costal	Presby-terian[4]	Muslim[5]	Judaism
MSA[1]	12.5	2.3	0.9	7.4	4.4	0.8	1.1	2.8	0.3	0.3
U.S.	19.1	9.3	4.0	4.0	2.3	2.0	1.9	1.6	0.8	0.7

Note: Figures are the number of adherents as a percentage of the total population; (1) Figures cover the State College, PA Metropolitan Statistical Area—see Appendix B for areas included; (2) Methodist/Pietist; (3) Latter Day Saints; (4) Reformed; (5) Figures are estimates
Source: Association of Statisticians of American Religious Bodies, 2010 U.S. Religion Census: Religious Congregations & Membership Study

Religious Groups by Tradition

Area	Catholic	Evangelical Protestant	Mainline Protestant	Other Tradition	Black Protestant	Orthodox
MSA[1]	12.5	7.6	15.6	1.6	0.1	0.1
U.S.	19.1	16.2	7.3	4.3	1.6	0.3

Note: Figures are the number of adherents as a percentage of the total population; (1) Figures cover the State College, PA Metropolitan Statistical Area—see Appendix B for areas included
Source: Association of Statisticians of American Religious Bodies, 2010 U.S. Religion Census: Religious Congregations & Membership Study

ECONOMY

Gross Metropolitan Product

Area	2014	2015	2016	2017	Rank[2]
MSA[1]	7.7	8.0	8.2	8.5	225

Note: Figures are in billions of dollars; (1) Figures cover the State College, PA Metropolitan Statistical Area—see Appendix B for areas included; (2) Rank is based on 2015 data and ranges from 1 to 381
Source: The U.S. Conference of Mayors, U.S. Metro Economies: GMP and Employment Report, 2015-2017

Economic Growth

Area	2012-14 (%)	2015 (%)	2016 (%)	2017 (%)	Rank[2]
MSA[1]	3.1	3.2	1.2	2.3	57
U.S.	2.0	2.4	1.9	2.6	–

Note: Figures are real gross metropolitan product (GMP) growth rates and represent average annual percent change; (1) Figures cover the State College, PA Metropolitan Statistical Area—see Appendix B for areas included; (2) Rank is based on 2012-2014 average annual percent change and ranges from 1 to 381
Source: The U.S. Conference of Mayors, U.S. Metro Economies: GMP and Employment Report, 2015-2017

Metropolitan Area Exports

Area	2011	2012	2013	2014	2015	2016	Rank[2]
MSA[1]	225.1	234.8	218.0	232.0	225.4	221.6	291

Note: Figures are in millions of dollars; (1) Figures cover the State College, PA Metropolitan Statistical Area—see Appendix B for areas included; (2) Rank is based on 2016 data and ranges from 1 to 385
Source: U.S. Department of Commerce, International Trade Administration, Office of Trade & Industry Information, Manufacturing & Services, data extracted March 15, 2018

Building Permits

Area	Single-Family			Multi-Family			Total		
	2016	2017p	Pct. Chg.	2016	2017p	Pct. Chg.	2016	2017p	Pct. Chg.
City	n/a	n/a	n/a	n/a	n/a	n/a	n/a	n/a	n/a
MSA[1]	72	73	1.4	0	74	n/a	72	147	104.2
U.S.	750,800	817,300	8.9	455,800	446,800	-2.0	1,206,600	1,264,100	4.8

Note: (1) Figures cover the State College, PA Metropolitan Statistical Area—see Appendix B for areas included; Figures represent new, privately-owned housing units authorized (unadjusted data); All permit data are based on estimates with imputation; (p) preliminary data.
Source: U.S. Census Bureau, Manufacturing, Mining, and Construction Statistics, Building Permits, 2016, 2017

Bankruptcy Filings

Area	Business Filings			Nonbusiness Filings		
	2016	2017	% Chg.	2016	2017	% Chg.
Centre County	6	6	0.0	83	69	-16.9
U.S.	24,114	23,157	-4.0	770,846	765,863	-0.6

Note: Business filings include Chapter 7, Chapter 11, Chapter 12, and Chapter 13; Nonbusiness filings include Chapter 7, Chapter 11, and Chapter 13
Source: Administrative Office of the U.S. Courts, Business and Nonbusiness Bankruptcy, County Cases Commenced by Chapter of the Bankruptcy Code, During the 12-Month Period Ending December 31, 2016 and Business and Nonbusiness Bankruptcy, County Cases Commenced by Chapter of the Bankruptcy Code, During the 12-Month Period Ending December 31, 2017

Housing Vacancy Rates

Area	Gross Vacancy Rate[2] (%)			Year-Round Vacancy Rate[3] (%)			Rental Vacancy Rate[4] (%)			Homeowner Vacancy Rate[5] (%)		
	2015	2016	2017	2015	2016	2017	2015	2016	2017	2015	2016	2017
MSA[1]	n/a	n/a	n/a	n/a	n/a	n/a	n/a	n/a	n/a	n/a	n/a	n/a
U.S.	12.9	12.8	12.7	10.0	9.9	9.9	7.1	6.9	7.2	1.8	1.7	1.6

Note: (1) Figures cover the State College, PA Metropolitan Statistical Area—see Appendix B for areas included; (2) The percentage of the total housing inventory that is vacant; (3) The percentage of the housing inventory (excluding seasonal units) that is year-round vacant; (4) The percentage of rental inventory that is vacant for rent; (5) The percentage of homeowner inventory that is vacant for sale; n/a not available
Source: U.S. Census Bureau, Housing Vacancies and Homeownership Annual Statistics: 2015, 2016, 2017

INCOME

Income

Area	Per Capita ($)	Median Household ($)	Average Household ($)
City	17,472	31,618	54,784
MSA[1]	27,584	54,407	73,047
U.S.	29,829	55,322	77,866

Note: (1) Figures cover the State College, PA Metropolitan Statistical Area—see Appendix B for areas included
Source: U.S. Census Bureau, 2012-2016 American Community Survey 5-Year Estimates

Household Income Distribution

Area	Percent of Households Earning							
	Under $15,000	$15,000 -$24,999	$25,000 -$34,999	$35,000 -$49,999	$50,000 -$74,999	$75,000 -$99,999	$100,000 -$149,999	$150,000 and up
City	29.5	12.9	10.3	12.0	12.8	6.6	9.2	6.6
MSA[1]	13.7	9.9	10.3	12.5	17.7	11.7	14.0	10.1
U.S.	12.1	10.2	9.9	13.2	17.8	12.2	13.5	11.1

Note: (1) Figures cover the State College, PA Metropolitan Statistical Area—see Appendix B for areas included
Source: U.S. Census Bureau, 2012-2016 American Community Survey 5-Year Estimates

Poverty Rate

Area	All Ages	Under 18 Years Old	18 to 64 Years Old	65 Years and Over
City	44.8	14.1	50.7	3.8
MSA[1]	19.1	13.6	23.1	5.7
U.S.	15.1	21.2	14.2	9.3

Note: Figures are percentage of people whose income during the past 12 months was below the poverty level; (1) Figures cover the State College, PA Metropolitan Statistical Area—see Appendix B for areas included
Source: U.S. Census Bureau, 2012-2016 American Community Survey 5-Year Estimates

EMPLOYMENT

Labor Force and Employment

Area	Civilian Labor Force			Workers Employed		
	Dec. 2016	Dec. 2017	% Chg.	Dec. 2016	Dec. 2017	% Chg.
City	16,383	16,351	-0.2	15,746	15,798	0.3
MSA[1]	79,179	79,021	-0.2	76,212	76,466	0.3
U.S.	158,968,000	159,880,000	0.6	151,798,000	153,602,000	1.2

Note: Data is not seasonally adjusted and covers workers 16 years of age and older; (1) Figures cover the State College, PA Metropolitan Statistical Area—see Appendix B for areas included
Source: Bureau of Labor Statistics, Local Area Unemployment Statistics

Unemployment Rate

Area	2017											
	Jan.	Feb.	Mar.	Apr.	May	Jun.	Jul.	Aug.	Sep.	Oct.	Nov.	Dec.
City	4.5	4.3	3.9	4.2	5.5	5.3	6.0	5.2	4.6	4.2	4.1	3.4
MSA[1]	4.4	4.2	3.7	3.2	4.0	3.9	4.2	3.9	3.3	3.1	3.2	3.2
U.S.	5.1	4.9	4.6	4.1	4.1	4.5	4.6	4.5	4.1	3.9	3.9	3.9

Note: Data is not seasonally adjusted and covers workers 16 years of age and older; (1) Figures cover the State College, PA Metropolitan Statistical Area—see Appendix B for areas included
Source: Bureau of Labor Statistics, Local Area Unemployment Statistics

Average Wages

Occupation	$/Hr.	Occupation	$/Hr.
Accountants and Auditors	31.40	Maids and Housekeeping Cleaners	11.50
Automotive Mechanics	18.30	Maintenance and Repair Workers	18.50
Bookkeepers	17.60	Marketing Managers	73.40
Carpenters	21.70	Nuclear Medicine Technologists	n/a
Cashiers	9.40	Nurses, Licensed Practical	18.20
Clerks, General Office	15.90	Nurses, Registered	28.10
Clerks, Receptionists/Information	11.60	Nursing Assistants	14.30
Clerks, Shipping/Receiving	16.00	Packers and Packagers, Hand	17.50
Computer Programmers	37.00	Physical Therapists	39.30
Computer Systems Analysts	41.50	Postal Service Mail Carriers	23.20
Computer User Support Specialists	25.80	Real Estate Brokers	n/a
Cooks, Restaurant	11.70	Retail Salespersons	12.10
Dentists	94.30	Sales Reps., Exc. Tech./Scientific	30.70
Electrical Engineers	48.70	Sales Reps., Tech./Scientific	n/a
Electricians	21.80	Secretaries, Exc. Legal/Med./Exec.	16.90
Financial Managers	65.70	Security Guards	13.60
First-Line Supervisors/Managers, Sales	18.60	Surgeons	n/a
Food Preparation Workers	11.40	Teacher Assistants*	12.90
General and Operations Managers	58.00	Teachers, Elementary School*	31.50
Hairdressers/Cosmetologists	14.30	Teachers, Secondary School*	30.40
Internists, General	n/a	Telemarketers	n/a
Janitors and Cleaners	14.00	Truck Drivers, Heavy/Tractor-Trailer	22.70
Landscaping/Groundskeeping Workers	14.90	Truck Drivers, Light/Delivery Svcs.	19.20
Lawyers	48.80	Waiters and Waitresses	11.60

Note: Wage data covers the State College, PA Metropolitan Statistical Area—see Appendix B for areas included; (*) Hourly wages for elementary/secondary school teachers and teacher assistants were calculated by the editors from annual wage data based on a 40 hour work week; n/a not available.
Source: Bureau of Labor Statistics, Metro Area Occupational Employment & Wage Estimates, May 2017

Employment by Occupation

Occupation Classification	City (%)	MSA[1] (%)	U.S. (%)
Management, Business, Science, and Arts	48.8	46.0	37.0
Natural Resources, Construction, and Maintenance	3.1	6.5	8.9
Production, Transportation, and Material Moving	5.6	8.9	12.2
Sales and Office	17.5	20.1	23.8
Service	25.0	18.5	18.1

Note: Figures cover employed civilians 16 years of age and older; (1) Figures cover the State College, PA Metropolitan Statistical Area—see Appendix B for areas included
Source: U.S. Census Bureau, 2012-2016 American Community Survey 5-Year Estimates

Employment by Industry

Sector	MSA[1] Number of Employees	MSA[1] Percent of Total	U.S. Percent of Total
Construction, Mining, and Logging	n/a	n/a	5.2
Education and Health Services	10,000	12.4	15.9
Financial Activities	n/a	n/a	5.7
Government	33,100	41.2	15.3
Information	n/a	n/a	1.9
Leisure and Hospitality	7,300	9.1	10.7
Manufacturing	4,000	5.0	8.5
Other Services	n/a	n/a	3.9
Professional and Business Services	6,800	8.5	14.0
Retail Trade	7,800	9.7	11.0
Transportation, Warehousing, and Utilities	n/a	n/a	4.1
Wholesale Trade	n/a	n/a	4.0

Note: Figures are non-farm employment as of December 2017. Figures are not seasonally adjusted and include workers 16 years of age and older; (1) Figures cover the State College, PA Metropolitan Statistical Area—see Appendix B for areas included; n/a not available
Source: Bureau of Labor Statistics, Current Employment Statistics, Employment, Hours, and Earnings

Occupations with Greatest Projected Employment Growth: 2017 – 2019

Occupation[1]	2017 Employment	2019 Projected Employment	Numeric Employment Change	Percent Employment Change
Personal Care Aides	95,040	101,150	6,110	6.4
Combined Food Preparation and Serving Workers, Including Fast Food	149,690	154,700	5,010	3.3
Registered Nurses	143,300	147,290	3,990	2.8
Laborers and Freight, Stock, and Material Movers, Hand	138,050	141,860	3,810	2.8
Home Health Aides	46,950	50,700	3,750	8.0
Waiters and Waitresses	100,790	102,540	1,750	1.7
Janitors and Cleaners, Except Maids and Housekeeping Cleaners	98,590	100,250	1,660	1.7
Cooks, Restaurant	49,820	51,120	1,300	2.6
Software Developers, Applications	25,890	27,190	1,300	5.0
Nursing Assistants	80,510	81,790	1,280	1.6

Note: Projections cover Pennsylvania; (1) Sorted by numeric employment change
Source: www.projectionscentral.com, State Occupational Projections, 2017–2019 Short-Term Projections

Fastest Growing Occupations: 2017 – 2019

Occupation[1]	2017 Employment	2019 Projected Employment	Numeric Employment Change	Percent Employment Change
Home Health Aides	46,950	50,700	3,750	8.0
Statisticians	2,710	2,880	170	6.5
Personal Care Aides	95,040	101,150	6,110	6.4
Physician Assistants	5,620	5,960	340	6.1
Nurse Practitioners	5,240	5,550	310	6.0
Operations Research Analysts	2,660	2,800	140	5.1
Information Security Analysts	3,020	3,170	150	5.0
Software Developers, Applications	25,890	27,190	1,300	5.0
Nonfarm Animal Caretakers	7,820	8,210	390	4.9
Physical Therapist Assistants	4,660	4,880	220	4.8

Note: Projections cover Pennsylvania; (1) Sorted by percent employment change and excludes occupations with numeric employment change less than 50
Source: www.projectionscentral.com, State Occupational Projections, 2017–2019 Short-Term Projections

TAXES

State Corporate Income Tax Rates

State	Tax Rate (%)	Income Brackets ($)	Num. of Brackets	Financial Institution Tax Rate (%)[a]	Federal Income Tax Ded.
Pennsylvania	9.99	Flat rate	1	(a)	No

Note: Tax rates as of January 1, 2018; (a) Rates listed are the corporate income tax rate applied to financial institutions or excise taxes based on income. Some states have other taxes based upon the value of deposits or shares.
Source: Federation of Tax Administrators, Range of State Corporate Income Tax Rates, January 1, 2018

State Individual Income Tax Rates

State	Tax Rate (%)	Income Brackets ($)	Num. of Brackets	Personal Exempt. ($)[1]		Fed. Inc. Tax Ded.
				Single	Dependents	
Pennsylvania	3.07	Flat rate	1	None	None	No

Note: Tax rates as of January 1, 2018; Local- and county-level taxes are not included; n/a not applicable; (1) Married joint filers generally receive double the single exemption
Source: Federation of Tax Administrators, State Individual Income Tax Rates, January 1, 2018

Various State Sales and Excise Tax Rates

State	State Sales Tax (%)	Gasoline[1] (¢/gal.)	Cigarette[2] ($/pack)	Spirits[3] ($/gal.)	Wine[4] ($/gal.)	Beer[5] ($/gal.)	Recreational Marijuana (%)
Pennsylvania	6.0	58.7	2.60	7.24 (g)	(m)	0.08	Not legal

Note: All tax rates as of January 1, 2018; (1) The American Petroleum Institute has developed a methodology for determining the average tax rate on a gallon of fuel. Rates may include any of the following: excise taxes, environmental fees, storage tank fees, other fees or taxes, general sales tax, and local taxes. In states where gasoline is subject to the general sales tax, or where the fuel tax is based on the average sale price, the average rate determined by API is sensitive to changes in the price of gasoline. States that fully or partially apply general sales taxes to gasoline: CA, CO, GA, IL, IN, MI, NY; (2) The federal excise tax of $1.0066 per pack and local taxes are not included; (3) Rates are those applicable to off-premise sales of 40% alcohol by volume (a.b.v.) distilled spirits in 750ml containers. Local excise taxes are excluded; (4) Rates are those applicable to off-premise sales of 11% a.b.v. non-carbonated wine in 750ml containers; (5) Rates are those applicable to off-premise sales of 4.7% a.b.v. beer in 12 ounce containers; (g) Control states, where the government controls all sales. Products can be subject to ad valorem mark-up as well as excise taxes; (m) Control states, where the government controls all sales. Products can be subject to ad valorem mark-up as well as excise taxes.
Source: Tax Foundation, 2018 Facts & Figures: How Does Your State Compare?

State Business Tax Climate Index Rankings

State	Overall Rank	Corporate Tax Rank	Individual Income Tax Rank	Sales Tax Rank	Unemployment Insurance Tax Rank	Property Tax Rank
Pennsylvania	26	44	17	21	50	33

Note: The index is a measure of how each state's tax laws affect economic performance. The lower the rank, the more favorable a state's tax system is for business. States without a given tax are given a ranking of 1. The scores/rankings for the District of Columbia do not affect other states. The 2018 index represents the tax climate as of July 1, 2017.
Source: Tax Foundation, State Business Tax Climate Index 2018

TRANSPORTATION

Means of Transportation to Work

Area	Car/Truck/Van		Public Transportation			Bicycle	Walked	Other Means	Worked at Home
	Drove Alone	Car-pooled	Bus	Subway	Railroad				
City	36.5	5.7	10.3	0.1	0.0	7.5	35.7	0.8	3.4
MSA[1]	68.2	9.4	4.3	0.1	0.0	2.0	9.8	1.2	4.9
U.S.	76.4	9.3	2.6	1.9	0.6	0.6	2.8	1.3	4.6

Note: Figures are percentages and cover workers 16 years of age and older; (1) Figures cover the State College, PA Metropolitan Statistical Area—see Appendix B for areas included
Source: U.S. Census Bureau, 2012-2016 American Community Survey 5-Year Estimates

Travel Time to Work

Area	Less Than 10 Minutes	10 to 19 Minutes	20 to 29 Minutes	30 to 44 Minutes	45 to 59 Minutes	60 to 89 Minutes	90 Minutes or More
City	22.2	48.9	17.0	7.1	2.1	1.1	1.4
MSA[1]	17.2	39.8	21.3	13.8	4.0	2.0	1.8
U.S.	12.9	29.2	20.9	20.4	8.0	6.0	2.7

Note: Note: Figures are percentages and include workers 16 years old and over; (1) Figures cover the State College, PA Metropolitan Statistical Area—see Appendix B for areas included
Source: U.S. Census Bureau, 2012-2016 American Community Survey 5-Year Estimates

Freeway Travel Time Index

Area	1985	1990	1995	2000	2005	2010	2014
Urban Area Rank[1,2]	n/a	n/a	n/a	n/a	n/a	n/a	n/a
Urban Area Index[1]	n/a	n/a	n/a	n/a	n/a	n/a	n/a
Average Index[3]	1.09	1.11	1.14	1.17	1.20	1.19	1.20

Note: Freeway Travel Time Index—the ratio of travel time in the peak period to the travel time at free-flow conditions. For example, a value of 1.30 indicates a 20-minute free-flow trip takes 26 minutes in the peak (20 minutes x 1.30 = 26 minutes); (1) Data for the State College, PA urban area was not available; (2) Rank is based on 101 urban areas (#1 = highest travel time index); (3) Average of 101 urban areas
Source: Texas Transportation Institute, 2015 Urban Mobility Scorecard, August 2015

Freeway Commuter Stress Index

Area	1985	1990	1995	2000	2005	2010	2014
Urban Area Rank[1,2]	n/a	n/a	n/a	n/a	n/a	n/a	n/a
Urban Area Index[1]	n/a	n/a	n/a	n/a	n/a	n/a	n/a
Average Index[3]	1.13	1.16	1.19	1.22	1.25	1.24	1.25

Note: The Freeway Commuter Stress Index is the same as the Freeway Travel Time Index (see table above) except that it includes only the travel in the peak directions during the peak periods; the TTI includes travel in all directions during the peak period. Thus, the CSI is more indicative of the work trip experienced by each commuter on a daily basis; (1) Data for the State College, PA urban area was not available; (2) Rank is based on 101 urban areas (#1 = highest travel time index); (3) Average of 101 urban areas
Source: Texas Transportation Institute, 2015 Urban Mobility Scorecard, August 2015

Living Environment

COST OF LIVING

Cost of Living Index

Composite Index	Groceries	Housing	Utilities	Trans-portation	Health Care	Misc. Goods/ Services
n/a	n/a	n/a	n/a	n/a	n/a	n/a

Note: The Cost of Living Index measures regional differences in the cost of consumer goods and services, excluding taxes and non-consumer expenditures, for professional and managerial households in the top income quintile. It is based on more than 50,000 prices covering almost 60 different items for which prices are collected three times a year by chambers of commerce, economic development organizations or university applied economic centers in each participating urban area. The numbers shown should be read as a percentage above or below the national average of 100. For example, a value of 115.4 in the groceries column indicates that grocery prices are 15.4% higher than the national average. Small differences in the index numbers should not be interpreted as significant; n/a not available.
Source: The Council for Community and Economic Research, ACCRA Cost of Living Index, 2017

Grocery Prices

Area[1]	T-Bone Steak ($/pound)	Frying Chicken ($/pound)	Whole Milk ($/half gal.)	Eggs ($/dozen)	Orange Juice ($/64 oz.)	Coffee ($/11.5 oz.)
City[2]	n/a	n/a	n/a	n/a	n/a	n/a
Avg.	11.29	1.40	2.02	1.47	3.55	4.37
Min.	7.71	0.93	1.04	0.70	2.86	3.24
Max.	15.83	2.39	4.03	3.92	6.29	8.16

*Note: (1) Values for the local area are compared with the average, minimum and maximum values for all 294 areas in the Cost of Living Index; (2) Figures cover the State College PA urban area; n/a not available; **T-Bone Steak** (price per pound); **Frying Chicken** (price per pound, whole fryer); **Whole Milk** (half gallon carton); **Eggs** (price per dozen, Grade A, large); **Orange Juice** (64 oz. Tropicana or Florida Natural); **Coffee** (11.5 oz. can, vacuum-packed, Maxwell House, Hills Bros, or Folgers).*
Source: The Council for Community and Economic Research, ACCRA Cost of Living Index, 2017

Housing and Utility Costs

Area[1]	New Home Price ($)	Apartment Rent ($/month)	All Electric ($/month)	Part Electric ($/month)	Other Energy ($/month)	Telephone ($/month)
City[2]	n/a	n/a	n/a	n/a	n/a	n/a
Avg.	335,956	1,047	175.01	97.34	67.93	28.71
Min.	187,788	491	109.48	49.33	35.44	12.39
Max.	1,739,087	4,559	432.62	227.09	353.33	44.61

*Note: (1) Values for the local area are compared with the average, minimum and maximum values for all 294 areas in the Cost of Living Index; (2) Figures cover the State College PA urban area; n/a not available; **New Home Price** (2,400 sf living area, 8,000 sf lot, in urban area with full utilities); **Apartment Rent** (950 sf 2 bedroom/1.5 or 2 bath, unfurnished, excluding all utilities except water); **All Electric** (average monthly cost for an all-electric home); **Part Electric** (average monthly cost for a part-electric home); **Other Energy** (average monthly cost for natural gas, fuel oil, coal, wood, and any other forms of energy except electricity); **Telephone** (price includes basic monthly rate for a private residential line plus additional local usage charges incurred by a family of four).*
Source: The Council for Community and Economic Research, ACCRA Cost of Living Index, 2017

Health Care, Transportation, and Other Costs

Area[1]	Doctor ($/visit)	Dentist ($/visit)	Optometrist ($/visit)	Gasoline ($/gallon)	Beauty Salon ($/visit)	Men's Shirt ($)
City[2]	n/a	n/a	n/a	n/a	n/a	n/a
Avg.	108.00	92.54	101.93	2.25	37.58	30.92
Min.	30.39	60.00	49.75	1.82	16.11	11.20
Max.	193.50	161.94	229.28	3.16	77.35	59.13

*Note: (1) Values for the local area are compared with the average, minimum and maximum values for all 294 areas in the Cost of Living Index; (2) Figures cover the State College PA urban area; n/a not available; **Doctor** (general practitioners routine exam of an established patient); **Dentist** (adult teeth cleaning and periodic oral examination); **Optometrist** (full vision eye exam for established adult patient); **Gasoline** (one gallon regular unleaded, national brand, including all taxes, cash price at self-service pump if available); **Beauty Salon** (woman's shampoo, trim, and blow-dry); **Men's Shirt** (cotton/polyester dress shirt, pinpoint weave, long sleeves).*
Source: The Council for Community and Economic Research, ACCRA Cost of Living Index, 2017

HOUSING

House Price Index (HPI)

Area	National Ranking[2]	Quarterly Change (%)	One-Year Change (%)	Five-Year Change (%)
MSA[1]	(a)	n/a	2.07	17.01
U.S.[3]	–	1.61	6.68	34.71

Note: The HPI is a weighted repeat sales index. It measures average price changes in repeat sales or refinancings on the same properties. This information is obtained by reviewing repeat mortgage transactions on single-family properties whose mortgages have been purchased or securitized by Fannie Mae or Freddie Mac in January 1975; (1) Figures cover the State College, PA Metropolitan Statistical Area—see Appendix B for areas included; (2) Rankings are based on annual percentage change for all metro areas containing at least 15,000 transactions over the last 10 years and ranges from 1 to 253; (3) figures based on a weighted average of Census Division estimates using a seasonally adjusted, purchase-only index; all figures are for the period ending December 31, 2017; n/a not available; (a) Not ranked because of increased index variability due to smaller sample size
Source: Federal Housing Finance Agency, House Price Index, February 28, 2018

Median Single-Family Home Prices

Area	2015	2016	2017p	Percent Change 2016 to 2017
MSA[1]	n/a	n/a	n/a	n/a
U.S. Average	223.9	235.5	248.8	5.6

Note: Figures are median sales prices of existing single-family homes in thousands of dollars; (p) preliminary; n/a not available; (1) Figures cover the State College, PA Metropolitan Statistical Area—see Appendix B for areas included
Source: National Association of Realtors, Median Sales Price of Existing Single-Family Homes for Metropolitan Areas, 4th Quarter 2017

Qualifying Income Based on Median Sales Price of Existing Single-Family Homes

Area	With 5% Down ($)	With 10% Down ($)	With 20% Down ($)
MSA[1]	n/a	n/a	n/a
U.S. Average	55,585	52,659	46,808

Note: Figures are preliminary; Qualifying income is based on a mortgage rate of 4.17%. Monthly principal and interest payment is limited to 25% of income; n/a not available; (1) Figures cover the State College, PA Metropolitan Statistical Area—see Appendix B for areas included
Source: National Association of Realtors, Qualifying Income Based on Median Sales Price of Existing Single-Family Homes for Metropolitan Areas, 4th Quarter 2017

Median Apartment Condo-Coop Home Prices

Area	2015	2016	2017p	Percent Change 2016 to 2017
MSA[1]	n/a	n/a	n/a	n/a
U.S. Average	210.7	220.7	234.3	6.2

Note: Figures are median sales prices of existing apartment condo-coop homes in thousands of dollars; (p) preliminary; n/a not available; (1) Figures cover the State College, PA Metropolitan Statistical Area—see Appendix B for areas included
Source: National Association of Realtors, Median Sales Price of Existing Apartment Condo-Coop Homes for Metropolitan Areas, 4th Quarter 2017

Home Value Distribution

Area	Under $50,000	$50,000 -$99,999	$100,000 -$149,999	$150,000 -$199,999	$200,000 -$299,999	$300,000 -$499,999	$500,000 -$999,999	$1,000,000 or more
City	2.4	2.1	5.0	11.4	37.3	32.8	8.6	0.4
MSA[1]	7.2	7.7	12.5	20.7	27.4	17.0	6.3	1.2
U.S.	8.8	14.8	15.3	14.9	18.4	16.4	9.0	2.5

Note: Figures are percentages and cover owner-occupied housing units; (1) Figures cover the State College, PA Metropolitan Statistical Area—see Appendix B for areas included
Source: U.S. Census Bureau, 2012-2016 American Community Survey 5-Year Estimates

Homeownership Rate

Area	2009 (%)	2010 (%)	2011 (%)	2012 (%)	2013 (%)	2014 (%)	2015 (%)	2016 (%)	2017 (%)
MSA[1]	n/a	n/a	n/a	n/a	n/a	n/a	n/a	n/a	n/a
U.S.	67.4	66.9	66.1	65.4	65.1	64.5	63.7	63.4	63.9

Note: (1) Figures cover the State College, PA Metropolitan Statistical Area—see Appendix B for areas included; n/a not available
Source: U.S. Census Bureau, Housing Vacancies and Homeownership Annual Statistics: 2009-2017

Year Housing Structure Built

Area	2010 or Later	2000 -2009	1990 -1999	1980 -1989	1970 -1979	1960 -1969	1950 -1959	1940 -1949	Before 1940	Median Year
City	0.7	3.8	9.9	17.0	17.1	20.2	13.9	7.1	10.2	1969
MSA[1]	2.3	12.8	14.4	14.5	14.9	12.0	9.5	4.7	15.0	1976
U.S.	2.3	14.7	14.0	13.7	15.6	10.9	10.6	5.2	13.0	1977

Note: Figures are percentages except for Median Year; Note: (1) Figures cover the State College, PA Metropolitan Statistical Area—see Appendix B for areas included
Source: U.S. Census Bureau, 2012-2016 American Community Survey 5-Year Estimates

Gross Monthly Rent

Area	Under $500	$500 -$999	$1,000 -$1,499	$1,500 -$1,999	$2,000 -$2,499	$2,500 -$2,999	$3,000 and up	Median ($)
City	4.3	50.1	25.3	11.2	6.1	2.5	0.6	968
MSA[1]	6.1	51.0	26.8	9.3	5.1	1.2	0.5	930
U.S.	11.3	43.3	27.7	10.7	4.0	1.6	1.5	949

Note: Figures are percentages except for Median; Gross rent is the contract rent plus the estimated average monthly cost of utilities (electricity, gas, and water and sewer) and fuels (oil, coal, kerosene, wood, etc.) if these are paid by the renter (or paid for the renter by someone else); (1) Figures cover the State College, PA Metropolitan Statistical Area—see Appendix B for areas included
Source: U.S. Census Bureau, 2012-2016 American Community Survey 5-Year Estimates

HEALTH

Health Risk Factors

Category	MSA[1] (%)	U.S. (%)
Adults aged 18–64 who have any kind of health care coverage	n/a	87.7
Adults who reported being in good or excellent health	n/a	83.6
Adults who are current smokers	n/a	17.1
Adults who currently use E-cigarettes	n/a	4.7
Adults who currently use chewing tobacco, snuff, or snus	n/a	4.0
Adults who are heavy drinkers[2]	n/a	6.5
Adults who are binge drinkers[3]	n/a	16.9
Adults who are overweight (BMI 25.0 - 29.9)	n/a	35.3
Adults who are obese (BMI 30.0 - 99.8)	n/a	29.9
Adults who participated in any physical activities in the past month	n/a	76.9
Adults who always or nearly always wears a seat belt	n/a	94.3

Note: n/a not available; (1) Figures cover the State College, PA Metropolitan Statistical Area—see Appendix B for areas included; (2) Heavy drinkers are classified as adult men having more than 14 drinks per week and adult women having more than 7 drinks per week; (3) Binge drinkers are classified as males having five or more drinks on one occasion or females having four or more drinks on one occasion
Source: Centers for Disease Control and Prevention, Behaviorial Risk Factor Surveillance System, SMART: Selected Metropolitan Area Risk Trends, 2016

Health Screening Rates

Category	MSA[1] (%)	U.S. (%)
Adults 50-75 who have had a blood stool test within the past year	n/a	8.0
Adults 50-75 who have had a colonoscopy in the past 10 years	n/a	63.5
Adults aged 65+ who have had flu shot within the past year	n/a	58.6
Adults aged 65+ who have ever had a pneumonia vaccination	n/a	73.4
Adults who have ever been tested for HIV	n/a	35.6
Women aged 21-65 who have had a pap test in the past three years	n/a	79.8
Men aged 40+ who have had a PSA test within the past two years	n/a	39.5
Women aged 40+ who have had a mammogram within the past two years	n/a	72.5

Note: n/a not available; (1) Figures cover the State College, PA Metropolitan Statistical Area—see Appendix B for areas included; Source: Centers for Disease Control and Prevention, Behaviorial Risk Factor Surveillance System, SMART: Selected Metropolitan Area Risk Trends, 2016

Chronic Health Conditions

Category	MSA[1] (%)	U.S. (%)
Adults who have ever been told they had a heart attack	n/a	4.4
Adults who have ever been told they have angina or coronary heart disease	n/a	4.1
Adults who have ever been told they had a stroke	n/a	3.1
Adults who have been told they currently have asthma	n/a	9.3
Adults who have ever been told they have arthritis	n/a	25.8
Adults who have ever been told they have diabetes[2]	n/a	10.5
Adults who have ever been told they had skin cancer	n/a	5.9
Adults who have ever been told they had any other types of cancer	n/a	6.7
Adults who have ever been told they have COPD	n/a	6.3
Adults who have ever been told they have kidney disease	n/a	2.8
Adults who have ever been told they have a form of depression	n/a	17.4

Note: n/a not available; (1) Figures cover the State College, PA Metropolitan Statistical Area—see Appendix B for areas included; (2) Figures do not include pregnancy-related, borderline, or pre-diabetes
Source: Centers for Disease Control and Prevention, Behaviorial Risk Factor Surveillance System, SMART: Selected Metropolitan Area Risk Trends, 2016

Mortality Rates for the Top 10 Causes of Death in the U.S.

ICD-10[a] Sub-Chapter	ICD-10[a] Code	Age-Adjusted Mortality Rate[1] per 100,000 population	
		County[2]	U.S.
Malignant neoplasms	C00-C97	132.0	158.5
Ischaemic heart diseases	I20-I25	59.6	96.8
Other forms of heart disease	I30-I51	85.4	52.4
Chronic lower respiratory diseases	J40-J47	24.7	40.9
Cerebrovascular diseases	I60-I69	33.2	37.2
Organic, including symptomatic, mental disorders	F01-F09	26.8	33.3
Other degenerative diseases of the nervous system	G30-G31	19.6	32.1
Other external causes of accidental injury	W00-X59	23.0	31.2
Diabetes mellitus	E10-E14	9.7	21.1
Hypertensive diseases	I10-I15	4.9	20.8

Note: (a) ICD-10 = International Classification of Diseases 10th Revision; (1) Mortality rates are a three year average covering 2014-2016; (2) Figures cover Centre County.
Source: Centers for Disease Control and Prevention, National Center for Health Statistics. Underlying Cause of Death 1999-2016 on CDC WONDER Online Database, released December 2017

Mortality Rates for Selected Causes of Death

ICD-10[a] Sub-Chapter	ICD-10[a] Code	Age-Adjusted Mortality Rate[1] per 100,000 population	
		County[2]	U.S.
Assault	X85-Y09	Suppressed	5.6
Diseases of the liver	K70-K76	8.0	14.0
Human immunodeficiency virus (HIV) disease	B20-B24	Suppressed	1.9
Influenza and pneumonia	J09-J18	18.1	14.6
Intentional self-harm	X60-X84	10.5	13.2
Malnutrition	E40-E46	Suppressed	1.3
Obesity and other hyperalimentation	E65-E68	Suppressed	2.1
Renal failure	N17-N19	12.3	13.0
Transport accidents	V01-V99	10.4	12.0
Viral hepatitis	B15-B19	Suppressed	1.9

Note: (a) ICD-10 = International Classification of Diseases 10th Revision; (1) Mortality rates are a three year average covering 2014-2016; (2) Figures cover Centre County; Data are Suppressed when the data meet the criteria for confidentiality constraints; Mortality rates are flagged as Unreliable when the rate would be calculated with a numerator of 20 or less.
Source: Centers for Disease Control and Prevention, National Center for Health Statistics. Underlying Cause of Death 1999-2016 on CDC WONDER Online Database, released December 2017

EDUCATION

Health Insurance Coverage

Area	With Health Insurance	With Private Health Insurance	With Public Health Insurance	Without Health Insurance	Population Under Age 18 Without Health Insurance
City	95.0	90.0	10.0	5.0	1.7
MSA[1]	93.4	83.5	21.8	6.6	6.1
U.S.	88.3	66.7	33.0	11.7	5.9

Note: Figures are percentages that cover the civilian noninstitutionalized population; (1) Figures cover the State College, PA Metropolitan Statistical Area—see Appendix B for areas included
Source: U.S. Census Bureau, 2012-2016 American Community Survey 5-Year Estimates

Number of Medical Professionals

Area	MDs[3]	DOs[3,4]	Dentists	Podiatrists	Chiropractors	Optometrists
County[1] (number)	334	61	92	7	51	29
County[1] (rate[2])	208.0	38.0	56.8	4.3	31.5	17.9
U.S. (rate[2])	276.5	22.3	67.3	6.0	26.7	15.9

Note: Data as of 2016 unless noted; (1) Data covers Centre County; (2) Rate per 100,000 population; (3) Data as of 2015 and includes all active, non-federal physicians; (4) Doctor of Osteopathic Medicine
Source: U.S. Department of Health and Human Services, Health Resources and Services Administration, Bureau of Health Professions, Area Resource File (ARF) 2016-2017

Public School District Statistics

District Name	Schls	Pupils	Pupil/ Teacher Ratio	Minority Pupils[1] (%)	Free Lunch Eligible[2] (%)	IEP[3] (%)
State College Area SD	11	6,763	12.9	19.3	14.2	11.8
Young Scholars of Central Pa CS	1	343	10.7	28.9	25.1	9.3

Note: Table includes school districts with 100 or more students; (1) Percentage of students that are not non-Hispanic white; (2) Percentage of students that are eligible for the free lunch program; (3) Percentage of students that have an Individualized Education Program.
Source: U.S. Department of Education, National Center for Education Statistics, Common Core of Data, Local Education Agency (School District) Universe Survey: School Year 2015-2016; U.S. Department of Education, National Center for Education Statistics, Common Core of Data, Public Elementary/Secondary School Universe Survey: School Year 2015-2016

Highest Level of Education

Area	Less than H.S.	H.S. Diploma	Some College, No Deg.	Associate Degree	Bachelor's Degree	Master's Degree	Prof. School Degree	Doctorate Degree
City	3.0	12.1	10.2	4.9	28.8	24.9	2.1	14.1
MSA[1]	6.7	31.1	12.1	7.6	22.3	12.7	1.7	5.7
U.S.	13.0	27.5	21.0	8.2	18.8	8.2	2.0	1.3

Note: Figures cover persons age 25 and over; (1) Figures cover the State College, PA Metropolitan Statistical Area—see Appendix B for areas included
Source: U.S. Census Bureau, 2012-2016 American Community Survey 5-Year Estimates

Educational Attainment by Race

Area	High School Graduate or Higher (%)					Bachelor's Degree or Higher (%)				
	Total	White	Black	Asian	Hisp.[2]	Total	White	Black	Asian	Hisp.[2]
City	97.0	97.3	100.0	98.7	89.4	69.8	68.8	46.9	88.2	51.8
MSA[1]	93.3	93.6	88.3	93.3	81.9	42.4	41.4	33.0	72.5	38.4
U.S.	87.0	88.9	84.3	86.3	65.7	30.3	31.6	20.0	52.1	14.7

Note: Figures shown cover persons 25 years old and over; (1) Figures cover the State College, PA Metropolitan Statistical Area—see Appendix B for areas included; (2) People of Hispanic origin can be of any race
Source: U.S. Census Bureau, 2012-2016 American Community Survey 5-Year Estimates

School Enrollment by Grade and Control

Area	Preschool (%)		Kindergarten (%)		Grades 1 - 4 (%)		Grades 5 - 8 (%)		Grades 9 - 12 (%)	
	Public	Private	Public	Private	Public	Private	Public	Private	Public	Private
City	29.3	70.7	96.7	3.3	89.1	10.9	72.1	27.9	91.2	8.8
MSA[1]	37.8	62.2	85.1	14.9	87.0	13.0	83.7	16.3	91.8	8.2
U.S.	58.4	41.6	87.7	12.3	89.8	10.2	89.7	10.3	90.4	9.6

Note: Figures shown cover persons 3 years old and over; (1) Figures cover the State College, PA Metropolitan Statistical Area—see Appendix B for areas included
Source: U.S. Census Bureau, 2012-2016 American Community Survey 5-Year Estimates

Average Salaries of Public School Classroom Teachers

Area	2015 Dollars	2015 Rank[1]	2016 Dollars	2016 Rank[1]	Change from 2015 to 2016 Percent	Change from 2015 to 2016 Rank[2]
Pennsylvania	64,447	10	65,151	10	1.1	24
U.S. Average	57,611	–	58,353	–	1.3	–

Note: (1) Rank ranges from 1 to 51 where 1 indicates highest salary; (2) Rank ranges from 1 to 51 where 1 indicates highest percent change.
Source: National Education Association, Rankings & Estimates: Rankings of the States 2016 and Estimates of School Statistics 2017

Higher Education

Four-Year Colleges			Two-Year Colleges			Medical Schools[1]	Law Schools[2]	Voc/ Tech[3]
Public	Private Non-profit	Private For-profit	Public	Private Non-profit	Private For-profit			
0	0	0	0	0	1	0	0	0

Note: Figures cover institutions located within the city limits and include main campuses only; (1) includes schools accredited by the Liaison Committee on Medical Education and the American Osteopathic Association's Commission on Osteopathic College Accreditation; (2) includes ABA-accredited schools, schools with provisional ABA accreditation, and state accredited schools; (3) includes all schools with programs that are less than 2 years.
Source: National Center for Education Statistics, Integrated Postsecondary Education System (IPEDS), 2016-17; Wikipedia, List of Medical Schools in the United States, accessed April 2, 2018; Wikipedia, List of Law Schools in the United States, accessed April 2, 2018

PRESIDENTIAL ELECTION

2016 Presidential Election Results

Area	Clinton	Trump	Johnson	Stein	Other
Centre County	48.0	45.6	3.4	1.0	1.9
U.S.	48.0	45.9	3.3	1.1	1.7

Note: Results are percentages and may not add to 100% due to rounding
Source: Dave Leip's Atlas of U.S. Presidential Elections

EMPLOYERS

Major Employers

Company Name	Industry
AccuWeather	Weather forecasting
Bellefonte Area School District	School district
Centre County	County government
Federal government	Federal government
Geisinger Clinic	Healthcare
Glenn O. Hawbaker Inc.	Excavation
Mount Nittany Medical Center	Regional health system
Penn State	State-related, land-grant, doctoral university
State College Area School District	School district
State of Pennsylvania	State government
Wal-Mart Associates	Discount retailer
Weis Markets	Supermarket chain

Note: Companies shown are located within the State College, PA Metropolitan Statistical Area.
Source: Hoovers.com; Wikipedia

PUBLIC SAFETY

Crime Rate

Area	All Crimes	Violent Crimes: Murder	Violent Crimes: Rape[3]	Violent Crimes: Robbery	Violent Crimes: Aggrav. Assault	Property Crimes: Burglary	Property Crimes: Larceny -Theft	Property Crimes: Motor Vehicle Theft
City	911.9	0.0	13.8	17.2	36.1	60.2	769.1	15.5
Metro[1]	1,159.2	1.2	40.3	11.8	40.9	147.5	899.6	18.0
U.S.	2,847.8	5.3	40.4	102.8	248.5	468.9	1,745.0	236.9

Note: Figures are crimes per 100,000 population; (1) Figures cover the State College, PA Metropolitan Statistical Area—see Appendix B for areas included; (3) The city and U.S. figures shown were reported using the revised Uniform Crime Reporting (UCR) definition of rape. The metro area figures shown are an aggregate total of the data submitted using both the revised and legacy UCR definitions.
Source: FBI Uniform Crime Reports, 2016

Hate Crimes

Area	Number of Quarters Reported	Number of Incidents per Bias Motivation: Race/Ethnicity/ Ancestry	Religion	Sexual Orientation	Disability	Gender	Gender Identity
City	3	2	0	0	1	0	0
U.S.	4	3,489	1,273	1,076	70	31	124

Source: Federal Bureau of Investigation, Hate Crime Statistics 2016

Identity Theft Consumer Reports

Area	Reports	Reports per 100,000 Population	Rank[2]
MSA[1]	101	63	299
U.S.	371,061	114	-

Note: (1) Figures cover the State College, PA Metropolitan Statistical Area—see Appendix B for areas included; (2) Rank ranges from 1 to 389 where 1 indicates greatest number of identity theft reports per 100,000 population
Source: Federal Trade Commission, Consumer Sentinel Network Data Book for January–December 2017

Fraud and Other Consumer Reports

Area	Reports	Reports per 100,000 Population	Rank[2]
MSA[1]	494	306	354
U.S.	2,304,550	708	-

Note: (1) Figures cover the State College, PA Metropolitan Statistical Area—see Appendix B for areas included; (2) Rank ranges from 1 to 389 where 1 indicates greatest number of fraud and other consumer reports per 100,000 population
Source: Federal Trade Commission, Consumer Sentinel Network Data Book for January–December 2017

SPORTS

Professional Sports Teams

Team Name	League	Year Established
No teams are located in the metro area		

Source: Wikipedia, Major Professional Sports Teams of the United States and Canada, April 5, 2018

CLIMATE

Average and Extreme Temperatures

Temperature	Jan	Feb	Mar	Apr	May	Jun	Jul	Aug	Sep	Oct	Nov	Dec	Yr.
Extreme High (°F)	73	75	84	93	95	100	107	100	102	90	84	75	107
Average High (°F)	37	40	50	62	73	81	86	84	76	65	53	41	62
Average Temp. (°F)	30	32	41	52	62	71	76	74	67	55	44	34	53
Average Low (°F)	23	24	32	42	51	61	66	64	56	45	36	26	44
Extreme Low (°F)	-9	-5	5	19	31	40	50	45	30	23	13	-8	-9

Note: Figures cover the years 1948-1991
Source: National Climatic Data Center, International Station Meteorological Climate Summary, 9/96

Average Precipitation/Snowfall/Humidity

Precip./Humidity	Jan	Feb	Mar	Apr	May	Jun	Jul	Aug	Sep	Oct	Nov	Dec	Yr.
Avg. Precip. (in.)	2.8	2.8	3.3	3.2	4.1	3.5	3.5	3.3	3.2	2.8	3.3	3.2	39.0
Avg. Snowfall (in.)	9	10	6	1	Tr	0	0	0	0	Tr	2	7	35
Avg. Rel. Hum. 7am (%)	71	71	70	71	75	77	79	83	85	82	77	72	76
Avg. Rel. Hum. 4pm (%)	56	53	49	47	51	51	52	54	55	53	56	58	53

Note: Figures cover the years 1948-1991; Tr = Trace amounts (<0.05 in. of rain; <0.5 in. of snow)
Source: National Climatic Data Center, International Station Meteorological Climate Summary, 9/96

Weather Conditions

Temperature: 5°F & below	32°F & below	90°F & above	Daytime Sky: Clear	Partly cloudy	Cloudy	Precipitation: 0.01 inch or more precip.	0.1 inch or more snow/ice	Thunder-storms
3	106	22	83	134	148	124	20	31

Note: Figures are average number of days per year and cover the years 1948-1991
Source: National Climatic Data Center, International Station Meteorological Climate Summary, 9/96

HAZARDOUS WASTE

Superfund Sites

The State College, PA metro area is home to one site on the EPA's Superfund National Priorities List: **Centre County Kepone** (final). There are a total of 1,396 Superfund sites with a status of proposed or final on the list in the U.S. *U.S. Environmental Protection Agency, National Priorities List, April 4, 2018*

AIR & WATER QUALITY

Air Quality Trends: Ozone

	1990	1995	2000	2005	2010	2012	2013	2014	2015	2016
MSA[1]	n/a	n/a	n/a	n/a	n/a	n/a	n/a	n/a	n/a	n/a
U.S.	0.087	0.089	0.081	0.079	0.073	0.075	0.069	0.067	0.068	0.069

Note: (1) Data covers the State College, PA Metropolitan Statistical Area—see Appendix B for areas included; n/a not available. The values shown are the composite ozone concentration averages among trend sites based on the highest fourth daily maximum 8-hour concentration in parts per million. These trends are based on sites having an adequate record of monitoring data during the trend period. Data from exceptional events are included.
Source: U.S. Environmental Protection Agency, Air Quality Monitoring Information, "Air Quality Trends by City, 1990-2016"

Air Quality Index

Area	Percent of Days when Air Quality was...[2]					AQI Statistics[2]	
	Good	Moderate	Unhealthy for Sensitive Groups	Unhealthy	Very Unhealthy	Maximum	Median
MSA[1]	69.3	30.7	0.0	0.0	0.0	100	45

Note: (1) Data covers the State College, PA Metropolitan Statistical Area—see Appendix B for areas included; (2) Based on 365 days with AQI data in 2017. Air Quality Index (AQI) is an index for reporting daily air quality. EPA calculates the AQI for five major air pollutants regulated by the Clean Air Act: ground-level ozone, particle pollution (aka particulate matter), carbon monoxide, sulfur dioxide, and nitrogen dioxide. The AQI runs from 0 to 500. The higher the AQI value, the greater the level of air pollution and the greater the health concern. There are six AQI categories: "Good" AQI is between 0 and 50. Air quality is considered satisfactory; "Moderate" AQI is between 51 and 100. Air quality is acceptable; "Unhealthy for Sensitive Groups" When AQI values are between 101 and 150, members of sensitive groups may experience health effects; "Unhealthy" When AQI values are between 151 and 200 everyone may begin to experience health effects; "Very Unhealthy" AQI values between 201 and 300 trigger a health alert; "Hazardous" AQI values over 300 trigger warnings of emergency conditions (not shown).
Source: U.S. Environmental Protection Agency, Air Quality Index Report, 2017

Air Quality Index Pollutants

Area	Percent of Days when AQI Pollutant was...[2]					
	Carbon Monoxide	Nitrogen Dioxide	Ozone	Sulfur Dioxide	Particulate Matter 2.5	Particulate Matter 10
MSA[1]	0.0	0.0	54.8	0.0	45.2	0.0

Note: (1) Data covers the State College, PA Metropolitan Statistical Area—see Appendix B for areas included; (2) Based on 365 days with AQI data in 2017. The Air Quality Index (AQI) is an index for reporting daily air quality. EPA calculates the AQI for five major air pollutants regulated by the Clean Air Act: ground-level ozone, particle pollution (also known as particulate matter), carbon monoxide, sulfur dioxide, and nitrogen dioxide. The AQI runs from 0 to 500. The higher the AQI value, the greater the level of air pollution and the greater the health concern.
Source: U.S. Environmental Protection Agency, Air Quality Index Report, 2017

Maximum Air Pollutant Concentrations: Particulate Matter, Ozone, CO and Lead

	Particulate Matter 10 (ug/m^3)	Particulate Matter 2.5 Wtd AM (ug/m^3)	Particulate Matter 2.5 24-Hr (ug/m^3)	Ozone (ppm)	Carbon Monoxide (ppm)	Lead (ug/m^3)
MSA[1] Level	n/a	n/a	n/a	0.065	n/a	n/a
NAAQS[2]	150	15	35	0.075	9	0.15
Met NAAQS[2]	n/a	n/a	n/a	Yes	n/a	n/a

Note: (1) Data covers the State College, PA Metropolitan Statistical Area—see Appendix B for areas included; Data from exceptional events are included; (2) National Ambient Air Quality Standards; ppm = parts per million; ug/m^3 = micrograms per cubic meter; n/a not available.
Concentrations: Particulate Matter 10 (coarse particulate)—highest second maximum 24-hour concentration; Particulate Matter 2.5 Wtd AM (fine particulate)—highest weighted annual mean concentration; Particulate Matter 2.5 24-Hour (fine particulate)—highest 98th percentile 24-hour concentration; Ozone—highest fourth daily maximum 8-hour concentration; Carbon Monoxide—highest second maximum non-overlapping 8-hour concentration; Lead—maximum running 3-month average
Source: U.S. Environmental Protection Agency, Air Quality Monitoring Information, "Air Quality Statistics by City, 2016"

Maximum Air Pollutant Concentrations: Nitrogen Dioxide and Sulfur Dioxide

	Nitrogen Dioxide AM (ppb)	Nitrogen Dioxide 1-Hr (ppb)	Sulfur Dioxide AM (ppb)	Sulfur Dioxide 1-Hr (ppb)	Sulfur Dioxide 24-Hr (ppb)
MSA[1] Level	5	31	n/a	7	n/a
NAAQS[2]	53	100	30	75	140
Met NAAQS[2]	Yes	Yes	n/a	Yes	n/a

Note: (1) Data covers the State College, PA Metropolitan Statistical Area—see Appendix B for areas included; Data from exceptional events are included; (2) National Ambient Air Quality Standards; ppm = parts per million; ug/m^3 = micrograms per cubic meter; n/a not available.
Concentrations: Nitrogen Dioxide AM—highest arithmetic mean concentration; Nitrogen Dioxide 1-Hr—highest 98th percentile 1-hour daily maximum concentration; Sulfur Dioxide AM—highest annual mean concentration; Sulfur Dioxide 1-Hr—highest 99th percentile 1-hour daily maximum concentration; Sulfur Dioxide 24-Hr—highest second maximum 24-hour concentration
Source: U.S. Environmental Protection Agency, Air Quality Monitoring Information, "Air Quality Statistics by City, 2016"

Drinking Water

Water System Name	Pop. Served	Primary Water Source Type	Violations[1]	
			Health Based	Monitoring/ Reporting
State College Boro Water Authority	72,000	Surface	0	0

Note: (1) Based on violation data from January 1, 2017 to December 31, 2017
Source: U.S. Environmental Protection Agency, Office of Ground Water and Drinking Water, Safe Drinking Water Information System (based on data extracted April 5, 2018)

Tredyffrin, Pennsylvania

Background

Tredyffrin Township is located on the eastern edge of Chester County, in Pennsylvania. A suburb of Philadelphia, the communities that make up Tredyffrin Township include Chesterbrook and Strafford, along with portions of Paoli and Wayne.

Tredyffrin Township was originally settled in 1682, as part of the Welsh Tract. Settlers purchased sections of land from William Penn in England, seeking religious freedom from their homeland. Tredyffrin takes its name from its Welsh heritage, Tre is Welsh for town and Dryffrin means a wide cultivated valley.

Tredyffrin was incorporated as a village in 1707. At that time, much of the area was made up of family farms, with a mill, a meetinghouse and a market. During the American Army's winter encampment at Valley Forge in 1777, many of Washington's generals spent the winter in Tredyffrin farmers' homes. Many of these houses still stand and are listed as historic sites. Part of Valley Forge National Historical Park lies in Tredyffrin.

Tredyffrin Township, a prosperous agricultural community through the 1950s, saw significant growth following World War II. The population went from 7,800 in 1950 to 16,000 in 1960 to well over 29,000 today. The Township has a unique combination of beautiful, quiet neighborhoods alongside some of the best shopping and artistic venues in the area.

There are over 300 acres of parkland in Tredyffrin Township, with 14 active parks and five open space areas. The Township runs a wide variety of recreational programs, from youth activities to community events.

The Township's public schools are managed by the Tredyffrin/Easttown School District, with five elementary schools, two middle schools and one high school. The district is ranked as one of the best in the Philadelphia area. Several private and parochial schools also operate in Tredyffrin.

Tredyffrin is served by the Philadelphia International Airport, less than 15 miles from the township.

Tredyffrin residents can expect hot and humid summers, mild weather in spring and fall, and cold, sometimes snowy, winters.

Rankings

Business/Finance Rankings

- The personal finance site NerdWallet analyzed 183 American metropolitan areas with populations over 250,000 and more than 15,000 businesses to rank where entrepreneurs find the most success. Criteria included area economy, annual income, housing cost, unemployment rate, and the success rate of area businesses. Philadelphia* ranked #60. *www.nerdwallet.com, "Best Places to Start a Business," April 27, 2015*
- In a survey of economic confidence in the nation's 50 largest metropolitan areas conducted January–December 2014, the Philadelphia* metro area placed #33, according to Gallup's 2014 Economic Confidence Index. *Gallup, "San Jose and San Francisco Lead in Economic Confidence," March 19, 2015*
- The Brookings Institution ranked the 100 largest metro areas in the U.S. based on income inequality. Philadelphia* was ranked #12 (#1 = greatest ineqality). Criteria: the "95/20 ratio," a figure representing the income at which a household earns more than 95 percent of all other households, divided by the income at which a household earns more than only 20 percent of all other households. *Brookings Institution, "Household Income Inequality, 100 Largest U.S. Metro Areas, 2014-2016," February 5, 2018*
- Payscale.com ranked the largest metro areas in terms of wage growth. The Philadelphia* metro area ranked #29. Criteria: private-sector wage growth between the 4th quarter of 2016 and the 4th quarter of 2017. *PayScale, "Wage Trends by Metro Area-4th Quarter," January 17, 2018*
- The Philadelphia* metro area was identified as one of the most debt-ridden places in America by the finance site Credit.com. The metro area was ranked #11. Criteria: residents' average credit card debt as well as median income. *Credit.com, "25 Cities With the Most Credit Card Debt," February 28, 2018*
- Philadelphia* was identified as one of America's most frugal metro areas by *Coupons.com.* The city ranked #6 out of 25. Criteria: digital coupon usage. *Coupons.com, "America's Most Frugal Cities of 2017," March 22, 2018*
- The Philadelphia* metro area appeared on the Milken Institute "2017 Best Performing Cities" list. Rank: #98 out of 200 large metro areas. Criteria: job growth; wage and salary growth; high-tech output growth. *Milken Institute, "Best-Performing Cities 2017," January 2018*
- *Forbes* ranked the 200 most populous metro areas to determine the nation's "Best Places for Business and Careers." The Philadelphia* metro area was ranked #83. Criteria: costs (business and living); job growth (past and projected); income growth; quality of life; educational attainment (college and high school); projected economic growth; cultural and recreational opportunities; net migration patterns; number of highly ranked colleges. *Forbes, "The Best Places for Business and Careers 2017," October 24, 2017*

Education Rankings

- Personal finance website *WalletHub* analyzed the 150 largest U.S. metropolitan statistical areas to determine where the most educated Americans are choosing to settle. Criteria: education quality and attainment gap; education levels; percentage of workers with degrees; public school rankings; quality and size of each metro area's universities. Philadelphia* was ranked #44 (#1 = most educated city). *www.WalletHub.com, "2017's Most and Least Educated Cities in America," July 25, 2017*

Environmental Rankings

- Sperling's BestPlaces assessed 379 metropolitan areas of the United States for the likelihood of dangerously extreme weather events or earthquakes. In general the Southeast and South-Central regions have the highest risk of weather extremes and earthquakes, while the Pacific Northwest enjoys the lowest risk. Of the least risky metropolitan areas, the Philadelphia* metro area was ranked #232. *www.bestplaces.net, "Safest Places from Natural Disasters," April 2011*

- The U.S. Environmental Protection Agency (EPA) released a list of U.S. metropolitan areas with the most ENERGY STAR certified buildings in 2016. The Philadelphia* metro area was ranked #11 out of 25. *U.S. Environmental Protection Agency, "2017 Energy Star Top Cities," June 2017*
- Philadelphia* was highlighted as one of the 25 most ozone-polluted metro areas in the U.S. during 2013 through 2015. The area ranked #22. *American Lung Association, State of the Air 2017*
- Philadelphia* was highlighted as one of the 25 metro areas most polluted by year-round particle pollution (Annual PM 2.5) in the U.S. during 2013 through 2015. The area ranked #13. *American Lung Association, State of the Air 2017*
- Philadelphia* was highlighted as one of the 25 metro areas most polluted by short-term particle pollution (24-hour PM 2.5) in the U.S. during 2013 through 2015. The area ranked #20. *American Lung Association, State of the Air 2017*

Health/Fitness Rankings

- For each of the 50 most populous metro areas in the United States, the American College of Sports Medicine's American Fitness Index evaluated infrastructure, community assets, and policies that encourage healthy and fit lifestyles, including preventive health behaviors, levels of chronic disease conditions, health care access, and community resources and policies that support physical activity. The Philadelphia* metro area ranked #32 for "community fitness." *www.americanfitnessindex.org, "ACSM American Fitness Index Health and Community Fitness Status of the 50 Largest Metropolitan Areas," May 2017*
- The Philadelphia* metro area was identified as one of the worst cities for bed bugs in America by pest control company Orkin. The area ranked #12 out of 50 based on the number of bed bug treatments Orkin performed from December 2016 to November 2017. *Orkin, "Baltimore and Washington D.C. Continue to Hold Top Spots," January 8, 2018*
- Philadelphia* was identified as a "2016 Spring Allergy Capital." The area ranked #21 out of 100. Three groups of factors were used to identify the most severe cities for people with allergies during the spring season: annual pollen levels; medicine utilization; access to board-certified allergists. *Asthma and Allergy Foundation of America, "Spring Allergy Capitals 2016"*
- Philadelphia* was identified as a "2016 Fall Allergy Capital." The area ranked #32 out of 100. Three groups of factors were used to identify the most severe cities for people with allergies during the fall season: annual pollen levels; medicine utilization; access to board-certified allergists. *Asthma and Allergy Foundation of America, "Fall Allergy Capitals 2016"*
- Philadelphia* was identified as a "2015 Asthma Capital." The area ranked #3 out of the nation's 100 largest metropolitan areas. Criteria: estimated prevalence; self-reported prevalence; crude death rate for asthma; annual pollen score; annual air quality; public smoking laws; number of board-certified asthma specialists; school inhaler access laws; rescue medication use; controller medication use; ER visits for asthma; uninsured rate; poverty rate. *Asthma and Allergy Foundation of America, "Asthma Capitals 2015"*
- The Philadelphia* metro area ranked #132 out of 189 in The Gallup-Healthways Well-Being Index. Criteria: purpose; social well being; financial health; community and physical health. Results are based on telephone interviews with adults, aged 18 and older, living in metropolitan areas in the 50 U.S. states and the District of Columbia. *Gallup-Healthways, "State of American Well-Being, 2017 Community Well-Being Rankings" March 2018*

Real Estate Rankings

- FitSmallBusiness looked at 50 of the largest metropolitan areas in the U.S. to determine which metro was the best to start a real estate business. Data was compiled from such sources as: Zillow, Trulia, U.S. Census Bureau, and the Bureau of Labor Statistics. Criteria: location; inventory; annual wages; median sales price of homes; days on the market; median price cut percentage; and other factors that would influence real estate professional growth. The Philadelphia* metro area ranked #17. *fitsmallbusiness.com, "The Best Cities to Become a Real Estate Agent in 2018," January 30, 2018*

- Philadelphia* was ranked #138 out of 238 metro areas in terms of housing affordability in 2017 by the National Association of Home Builders (#1 = most affordable). Criteria: the share of homes sold in that area affordable to a family earning the local median income, based on standard mortgage underwriting criteria. *National Association of Home Builders®, NAHB-Wells Fargo Housing Opportunity Index, 4th Quarter 2017*

- The nation's largest metro areas were analyzed in terms of the percentage of households entering some stage of foreclosure in 2017. The Philadelphia* metro area ranked #3 out of 10 (#1 = highest foreclosure rate). *RealtyTrac, "2017 Year-End U.S. Foreclosure Market Report™," January 16, 2018*

Safety Rankings

- The National Insurance Crime Bureau ranked 382 metro areas in the U.S. in terms of per capita rates of vehicle theft. The Philadelphia* metro area ranked #208 (#1 = highest rate). Criteria: number of vehicle theft offenses per 100,000 inhabitants in 2016. *National Insurance Crime Bureau, "Hot Spots 2016," June 8, 2017*

Seniors/Retirement Rankings

- From its Best Cities for Successful Aging indexes, the Milken Institute generated rankings for metropolitan areas, weighing data in nine categories—health care, wellness, living arrangements, transportation and convenience, financial characteristics, education, employment, community engagement, and overall livability. The Philadelphia* metro area was ranked #52 overall in the large metro area category. *Milken Institute, "Best Cities for Successful Aging, 2017" March 14, 2017*

Sports/Recreation Rankings

- According to the personal finance website NerdWallet, the Philadelphia* metro area, at #10, is one of the nation's top dozen metro areas for sports fans. Criteria included the presence of all four major sports—MLB, NFL, NHL, and NBA, fan enthusiasm (as measured by game attendance), ticket affordability, and "sports culture," that is, number of sports bars. *www.nerdwallet.com, "Best Cities for Sports Fans," May 5, 2013*

Transportation Rankings

- The Philadelphia* metro area appeared on *Forbes* list of places with the most extreme commutes. The metro area ranked #9 out of 10. Criteria: average travel time; percentage of mega commuters. Mega-commuters travel more than 90 minutes and 50 miles each way to work. *Forbes.com, "The Cities with the Most Extreme Commutes," March 5, 2013*

Miscellaneous Rankings

- The watchdog site Charity Navigator conducts an annual study of charities in the nation's major markets both to analyze statistical differences in their financial, accountability, and transparency practices and to track year-to-year variations in individual philanthropic communities. Charity Navigator's analysis demonstrated that the financial, accountability and transparency behaviors of America's largest charities can be influenced by the metropolitan market within which the charity operates. The Philadelphia* metro area was ranked #20 among the 30 metro markets in the rating category of Overall Score. *www.charitynavigator.org, "2017 Metro Market Study," May 1, 2017*

- The Harris Poll's Happiness Index survey revealed that of the top ten U.S. markets, the Philadelphia* metro area residents ranked #3 in happiness. Criteria included strong assent to positive statements and strong disagreement with negative ones, and degree of agreement with a series of statements about respondents' personal relationships and general outlook. *www.theharrispoll.com, "Dallas/Fort Worth Is "Happiest" City among America's Top Ten Markets," September 4, 2013*
- Energizer Personal Care, the makers of Edge® shave gel, in partnership with Sperling's BestPlaces, ranked 50 major metro areas in terms of everyday irritations. The Philadelphia* metro area ranked #4 the 50 metro area most irritating to guys. Criteria: high male-to-female ratio; poor sports team performance and high ticket prices; slow traffic; lack of job availability; unaffordable housing; extreme weather; lack of nightlife and fitness options. *Energizer Personal Care, "Most Irritating Cities for Guys," August 26, 2013*
- The National Alliance to End Homelessness listed the 25 most populous metro areas with the highest rate of homelessness. The Philadelphia* metro area had a high rate of homelessness. Criteria: number of homeless people per 10,000 population in 2016. *National Alliance to End Homelessness, "Homelessness in the 25 Most Populous U.S. Metro Areas," September 1, 2017*

*Tredyffrin is located within the Philadelphia-Camden-Wilmington, PA-NJ-DE-MD Metropolitan Statistical Area.

Business Environment

CITY FINANCES

City Government Finances

Component	2015 ($000)	2015 ($ per capita)
Total Revenues	30,122	1,019
Total Expenditures	27,989	947
Debt Outstanding	16,139	546
Cash and Securities[1]	76,211	2,578

Note: (1) Cash and security holdings of a government at the close of its fiscal year,, including those of its dependent agencies, utilities, and liquor stores.
Source: U.S Census Bureau, State & Local Government Finances 2015

City Government Revenue by Source

Source	2015 ($000)	2015 ($ per capita)	2015 (%)
General Revenue			
From Federal Government	0	0	0.0
From State Government	1,959	66	6.5
From Local Governments	176	6	0.6
Taxes			
Property	8,322	282	27.6
Sales and Gross Receipts	0	0	0.0
Personal Income	0	0	0.0
Corporate Income	0	0	0.0
Motor Vehicle License	0	0	0.0
Other Taxes	5,766	195	19.1
Current Charges	10,370	351	34.4
Liquor Store	0	0	0.0
Utility	0	0	0.0
Employee Retirement	2,665	90	8.8

Source: U.S Census Bureau, State & Local Government Finances 2015

City Government Expenditures by Function

Function	2015 ($000)	2015 ($ per capita)	2015 (%)
General Direct Expenditures			
Air Transportation	0	0	0.0
Corrections	0	0	0.0
Education	0	0	0.0
Employment Security Administration	0	0	0.0
Financial Administration	431	14	1.5
Fire Protection	1,012	34	3.6
General Public Buildings	0	0	0.0
Governmental Administration, Other	838	28	3.0
Health	0	0	0.0
Highways	6,089	206	21.8
Hospitals	0	0	0.0
Housing and Community Development	0	0	0.0
Interest on General Debt	426	14	1.5
Judicial and Legal	0	0	0.0
Libraries	1,017	34	3.6
Parking	0	0	0.0
Parks and Recreation	811	27	2.9
Police Protection	8,569	289	30.6
Public Welfare	0	0	0.0
Sewerage	5,675	192	20.3
Solid Waste Management	38	1	0.1
Veterans' Services	0	0	0.0
Liquor Store	0	0	0.0
Utility	0	0	0.0
Employee Retirement	1,324	44	4.7

Source: U.S Census Bureau, State & Local Government Finances 2015

DEMOGRAPHICS

Population Growth

Area	1990 Census	2000 Census	2010 Census	2016* Estimate	Population Growth (%) 1990-2016	2010-2016
City	28,021	29,062	29,332	29,491	5.2	0.5
MSA[1]	5,435,470	5,687,147	5,965,343	6,047,721	11.3	1.4
U.S.	248,709,873	281,421,906	308,745,538	318,558,162	28.1	3.2

Note: (1) Figures cover the Philadelphia-Camden-Wilmington, PA-NJ-DE-MD Metropolitan Statistical Area—see Appendix B for areas included; (*) 2012-2016 5-year estimated population
Source: U.S. Census Bureau, 1990 Census, Census 2000, Census 2010, 2012-2016 American Community Survey 5-Year Estimates

Household Size

Area	Persons in Household (%) One	Two	Three	Four	Five	Six	Seven or More	Average Household Size
City	29.0	32.2	15.4	15.9	5.8	1.3	0.4	2.50
MSA[1]	29.3	31.8	16.4	13.5	5.9	2.1	1.1	2.60
U.S.	27.7	33.7	15.7	13.1	6.0	2.3	1.5	2.60

Note: (1) Figures cover the Philadelphia-Camden-Wilmington, PA-NJ-DE-MD Metropolitan Statistical Area—see Appendix B for areas included
Source: U.S. Census Bureau, 2012-2016 American Community Survey 5-Year Estimates

Race

Area	White Alone[2] (%)	Black Alone[2] (%)	Asian Alone[2] (%)	AIAN[3] Alone[2] (%)	NHOPI[4] Alone[2] (%)	Other Race Alone[2] (%)	Two or More Races (%)
City	80.7	3.7	12.7	0.0	0.0	0.7	2.2
MSA[1]	67.5	20.9	5.6	0.2	0.0	3.2	2.6
U.S.	73.3	12.6	5.2	0.8	0.2	4.8	3.1

Note: (1) Figures cover the Philadelphia-Camden-Wilmington, PA-NJ-DE-MD Metropolitan Statistical Area—see Appendix B for areas included; (2) Alone is defined as not being in combination with one or more other races; (3) American Indian and Alaska Native; (4) Native Hawaiian and Other Pacific Islander
Source: U.S. Census Bureau, 2012-2016 American Community Survey 5-Year Estimates

Hispanic or Latino Origin

Area	Total (%)	Mexican (%)	Puerto Rican (%)	Cuban (%)	Other (%)
City	2.5	0.8	0.4	0.2	1.1
MSA[1]	8.8	1.8	4.4	0.2	2.3
U.S.	17.3	11.0	1.7	0.7	4.0

Note: Persons of Hispanic or Latino origin can be of any race; (1) Figures cover the Philadelphia-Camden-Wilmington, PA-NJ-DE-MD Metropolitan Statistical Area—see Appendix B for areas included
Source: U.S. Census Bureau, 2012-2016 American Community Survey 5-Year Estimates

Segregation

Type	Segregation Indices[1] 1990	2000	2010	2010 Rank[2]	Percent Change 1990-2000	1990-2010	2000-2010
Black/White	75.2	71.0	68.4	9	-4.2	-6.8	-2.6
Asian/White	42.4	44.1	42.3	42	1.7	0.0	-1.8
Hispanic/White	60.9	58.5	55.1	12	-2.5	-5.9	-3.4

Note: All figures cover the Metropolitan Statistical Area—see Appendix B for areas included; Figures are based on an analysis of 1990, 2000, and 2010 Census Decennial Census tract data by William H. Frey, Brookings Institution and the University of Michigan Social Science Data Analysis Network. In this analysis all racial groups (whites, blacks, and asians) are non-Hispanic members of those races. Hispanics are shown as a separate category; (1) Segregation Indices are Dissimilarity Indices that measure the degree to which the minority group is distributed differently than whites across census tracts. They range from 0 (complete integration) to 100 (complete segregation) where the value indicates the percentage of the minority group that needs to move to be distributed exactly like whites; (2) Ranges from 1 (most segregated) to 102 (least segregated); n/a not available.
Source: www.CensusScope.org

Ancestry

Area	German	Irish	English	American	Italian	Polish	French[2]	Scottish	Dutch
City	21.3	21.7	11.9	3.7	12.8	5.2	2.4	3.0	1.1
MSA[1]	15.7	19.2	7.1	3.6	13.7	5.2	1.5	1.3	0.9
U.S.	14.4	10.4	7.7	6.9	5.4	2.9	2.6	1.7	1.3

Note: Figures are the percentage of the total population reporting a particular ancestry. The nine most commonly reported ancestries in the U.S. are shown. Figures include multiple ancestries (e.g. if a person reported being Irish and Italian, they were included in both columns); (1) Figures cover the Philadelphia-Camden-Wilmington, PA-NJ-DE-MD Metropolitan Statistical Area—see Appendix B for areas included; (2) Excludes Basque
Source: U.S. Census Bureau, 2012-2016 American Community Survey 5-Year Estimates

Foreign-Born Population

Area	Percent of Population Born in								
	Any Foreign Country	Asia	Mexico	Europe	Carribean	Central America[2]	South America	Africa	Canada
City	15.0	9.4	0.2	3.7	0.2	0.0	0.5	0.6	0.4
MSA[1]	10.3	4.2	0.9	1.9	1.2	0.4	0.6	0.9	0.1
U.S.	13.2	4.0	3.6	1.5	1.3	1.0	0.9	0.6	0.3

Note: (1) Figures cover the Philadelphia-Camden-Wilmington, PA-NJ-DE-MD Metropolitan Statistical Area—see Appendix B for areas included; (2) Excludes Mexico.
Source: U.S. Census Bureau, 2012-2016 American Community Survey 5-Year Estimates

Marital Status

Area	Never Married	Now Married[2]	Separated	Widowed	Divorced
City	23.9	59.7	1.7	5.4	9.3
MSA[1]	37.4	45.1	2.2	6.2	9.1
U.S.	33.0	48.1	2.1	5.9	11.0

Note: Figures are percentages and cover the population 15 years of age and older; (1) Figures cover the Philadelphia-Camden-Wilmington, PA-NJ-DE-MD Metropolitan Statistical Area—see Appendix B for areas included; (2) Excludes separated
Source: U.S. Census Bureau, 2012-2016 American Community Survey 5-Year Estimates

Disability Status

Area	All Ages	Under 18 Years Old	18 to 64 Years Old	65 Years and Over
City	6.8	0.4	3.9	25.0
MSA[1]	12.3	4.6	10.2	34.0
U.S.	12.5	4.1	10.3	35.7

Note: Figures show percent of the civilian noninstitutionalized population that reported having a disability. Disability status is determined from six types of difficulty: vision, hearing, cognitive, ambulatory, self-care, and independent living. For children under 5 years old, hearing and vision difficulty are used to determine disability status. For children between the ages of 5 and 14, disability status is determined from hearing, vision, cognitive, ambulatory, and self-care difficulties. For people aged 15 years and older, they are considered to have a disability if they have difficulty with any one of the six difficulty types; Note: (1) Figures cover the Philadelphia-Camden-Wilmington, PA-NJ-DE-MD Metropolitan Statistical Area—see Appendix B for areas included
Source: U.S. Census Bureau, 2012-2016 American Community Survey 5-Year Estimates

Age

Area	Percent of Population									Median Age
	Under Age 5	Age 5–19	Age 20–34	Age 35–44	Age 45–54	Age 55–64	Age 65–74	Age 75–84	Age 85+	
City	4.8	20.2	14.6	11.8	16.2	15.0	9.7	5.6	2.0	43.8
MSA[1]	6.0	19.1	20.8	12.4	14.3	13.0	8.0	4.4	2.2	38.4
U.S.	6.2	19.6	20.7	12.7	13.6	12.6	8.3	4.3	1.9	37.7

Note: (1) Figures cover the Philadelphia-Camden-Wilmington, PA-NJ-DE-MD Metropolitan Statistical Area—see Appendix B for areas included
Source: U.S. Census Bureau, 2012-2016 American Community Survey 5-Year Estimates

Gender

Area	Males	Females	Males per 100 Females
City	14,052	15,439	91.0
MSA[1]	2,923,439	3,124,282	93.6
U.S.	156,765,322	161,792,840	96.9

Note: (1) Figures cover the Philadelphia-Camden-Wilmington, PA-NJ-DE-MD Metropolitan Statistical Area—see Appendix B for areas included
Source: U.S. Census Bureau, 2012-2016 American Community Survey 5-Year Estimates

Religious Groups by Family

Area	Catholic	Baptist	Non-Den.	Methodist[2]	Lutheran	LDS[3]	Pente-costal	Presby-terian[4]	Muslim[5]	Judaism
MSA[1]	33.5	3.9	2.9	3.0	1.9	0.3	0.9	2.1	1.3	1.4
U.S.	19.1	9.3	4.0	4.0	2.3	2.0	1.9	1.6	0.8	0.7

Note: Figures are the number of adherents as a percentage of the total population; (1) Figures cover the Philadelphia-Camden-Wilmington, PA-NJ-DE-MD Metropolitan Statistical Area—see Appendix B for areas included; (2) Methodist/Pietist; (3) Latter Day Saints; (4) Reformed; (5) Figures are estimates
Source: Association of Statisticians of American Religious Bodies, 2010 U.S. Religion Census: Religious Congregations & Membership Study

Religious Groups by Tradition

Area	Catholic	Evangelical Protestant	Mainline Protestant	Other Tradition	Black Protestant	Orthodox
MSA[1]	33.5	6.3	8.9	3.7	1.8	0.4
U.S.	19.1	16.2	7.3	4.3	1.6	0.3

Note: Figures are the number of adherents as a percentage of the total population; (1) Figures cover the Philadelphia-Camden-Wilmington, PA-NJ-DE-MD Metropolitan Statistical Area—see Appendix B for areas included
Source: Association of Statisticians of American Religious Bodies, 2010 U.S. Religion Census: Religious Congregations & Membership Study

ECONOMY

Gross Metropolitan Product

Area	2014	2015	2016	2017	Rank[2]
MSA[1]	389.2	403.6	416.4	433.9	8

Note: Figures are in billions of dollars; (1) Figures cover the Philadelphia-Camden-Wilmington, PA-NJ-DE-MD Metropolitan Statistical Area—see Appendix B for areas included; (2) Rank is based on 2015 data and ranges from 1 to 381
Source: The U.S. Conference of Mayors, U.S. Metro Economies: GMP and Employment Report, 2015-2017

Economic Growth

Area	2012-14 (%)	2015 (%)	2016 (%)	2017 (%)	Rank[2]
MSA[1]	0.9	2.2	1.6	2.1	216
U.S.	2.0	2.4	1.9	2.6	–

Note: Figures are real gross metropolitan product (GMP) growth rates and represent average annual percent change; (1) Figures cover the Philadelphia-Camden-Wilmington, PA-NJ-DE-MD Metropolitan Statistical Area—see Appendix B for areas included; (2) Rank is based on 2012-2014 average annual percent change and ranges from 1 to 381
Source: The U.S. Conference of Mayors, U.S. Metro Economies: GMP and Employment Report, 2015-2017

Metropolitan Area Exports

Area	2011	2012	2013	2014	2015	2016	Rank[2]
MSA[1]	26,155.8	22,991.6	24,929.2	26,321.3	24,236.1	21,359.9	14

Note: Figures are in millions of dollars; (1) Figures cover the Philadelphia-Camden-Wilmington, PA-NJ-DE-MD Metropolitan Statistical Area—see Appendix B for areas included; (2) Rank is based on 2016 data and ranges from 1 to 385
Source: U.S. Department of Commerce, International Trade Administration, Office of Trade & Industry Information, Manufacturing & Services, data extracted March 15, 2018

Building Permits

Area	Single-Family			Multi-Family			Total		
	2016	2017p	Pct. Chg.	2016	2017p	Pct. Chg.	2016	2017p	Pct. Chg.
City	63	0	n/a	0	0	0.0	63	0	n/a
MSA[1]	6,820	7,278	6.7	5,295	6,021	13.7	12,115	13,299	9.8
U.S.	750,800	817,300	8.9	455,800	446,800	-2.0	1,206,600	1,264,100	4.8

Note: (1) Figures cover the Philadelphia-Camden-Wilmington, PA-NJ-DE-MD Metropolitan Statistical Area—see Appendix B for areas included; Figures represent new, privately-owned housing units authorized (unadjusted data); All permit data are based on estimates with imputation; (p) preliminary data.
Source: U.S. Census Bureau, Manufacturing, Mining, and Construction Statistics, Building Permits, 2016, 2017

Bankruptcy Filings

Area	Business Filings			Nonbusiness Filings		
	2016	2017	% Chg.	2016	2017	% Chg.
Chester County	51	25	-51.0	562	556	-1.1
U.S.	24,114	23,157	-4.0	770,846	765,863	-0.6

Note: Business filings include Chapter 7, Chapter 11, Chapter 12, and Chapter 13; Nonbusiness filings include Chapter 7, Chapter 11, and Chapter 13
Source: Administrative Office of the U.S. Courts, Business and Nonbusiness Bankruptcy, County Cases Commenced by Chapter of the Bankruptcy Code, During the 12-Month Period Ending December 31, 2016 and Business and Nonbusiness Bankruptcy, County Cases Commenced by Chapter of the Bankruptcy Code, During the 12-Month Period Ending December 31, 2017

Housing Vacancy Rates

Area	Gross Vacancy Rate[2] (%)			Year-Round Vacancy Rate[3] (%)			Rental Vacancy Rate[4] (%)			Homeowner Vacancy Rate[5] (%)		
	2015	2016	2017	2015	2016	2017	2015	2016	2017	2015	2016	2017
MSA[1]	10.7	9.3	8.6	10.2	8.6	8.3	7.6	6.8	7.3	2.4	1.4	1.6
U.S.	12.9	12.8	12.7	10.0	9.9	9.9	7.1	6.9	7.2	1.8	1.7	1.6

Note: (1) Figures cover the Philadelphia-Camden-Wilmington, PA-NJ-DE-MD Metropolitan Statistical Area—see Appendix B for areas included; (2) The percentage of the total housing inventory that is vacant; (3) The percentage of the housing inventory (excluding seasonal units) that is year-round vacant; (4) The percentage of rental inventory that is vacant for rent; (5) The percentage of homeowner inventory that is vacant for sale
Source: U.S. Census Bureau, Housing Vacancies and Homeownership Annual Statistics: 2015, 2016, 2017

INCOME

Income

Area	Per Capita ($)	Median Household ($)	Average Household ($)
City	63,030	118,462	154,327
MSA[1]	34,118	63,952	88,881
U.S.	29,829	55,322	77,866

Note: (1) Figures cover the Philadelphia-Camden-Wilmington, PA-NJ-DE-MD Metropolitan Statistical Area—see Appendix B for areas included
Source: U.S. Census Bureau, 2012-2016 American Community Survey 5-Year Estimates

Household Income Distribution

Area	Percent of Households Earning							
	Under $15,000	$15,000 -$24,999	$25,000 -$34,999	$35,000 -$49,999	$50,000 -$74,999	$75,000 -$99,999	$100,000 -$149,999	$150,000 and up
City	3.8	5.6	3.7	6.3	11.5	10.1	20.9	38.1
MSA[1]	11.3	8.8	8.4	11.6	16.4	12.3	16.0	15.2
U.S.	12.1	10.2	9.9	13.2	17.8	12.2	13.5	11.1

Note: (1) Figures cover the Philadelphia-Camden-Wilmington, PA-NJ-DE-MD Metropolitan Statistical Area—see Appendix B for areas included
Source: U.S. Census Bureau, 2012-2016 American Community Survey 5-Year Estimates

Poverty Rate

Area	All Ages	Under 18 Years Old	18 to 64 Years Old	65 Years and Over
City	4.5	7.4	4.1	2.1
MSA[1]	13.1	18.1	12.3	8.9
U.S.	15.1	21.2	14.2	9.3

Note: Figures are percentage of people whose income during the past 12 months was below the poverty level; (1) Figures cover the Philadelphia-Camden-Wilmington, PA-NJ-DE-MD Metropolitan Statistical Area—see Appendix B for areas included
Source: U.S. Census Bureau, 2012-2016 American Community Survey 5-Year Estimates

EMPLOYMENT

Labor Force and Employment

Area	Civilian Labor Force			Workers Employed		
	Dec. 2016	Dec. 2017	% Chg.	Dec. 2016	Dec. 2017	% Chg.
City	15,841	15,877	0.2	15,373	15,452	0.5
MD[1]	1,060,053	1,058,151	-0.2	1,021,300	1,022,167	0.1
U.S.	158,968,000	159,880,000	0.6	151,798,000	153,602,000	1.2

Note: Data is not seasonally adjusted and covers workers 16 years of age and older; (1) Figures cover the Montgomery County-Bucks County-Chester County, PA Metropolitan Division—see Appendix B for areas included
Source: Bureau of Labor Statistics, Local Area Unemployment Statistics

Unemployment Rate

Area	2017											
	Jan.	Feb.	Mar.	Apr.	May	Jun.	Jul.	Aug.	Sep.	Oct.	Nov.	Dec.
City	3.4	3.5	3.0	3.0	3.4	3.3	3.4	3.3	3.0	3.0	2.8	2.7
MD[1]	4.3	4.4	4.0	3.6	3.9	4.0	4.3	4.3	3.7	3.5	3.6	3.4
U.S.	5.1	4.9	4.6	4.1	4.1	4.5	4.6	4.5	4.1	3.9	3.9	3.9

Note: Data is not seasonally adjusted and covers workers 16 years of age and older; (1) Figures cover the Montgomery County-Bucks County-Chester County, PA Metropolitan Division—see Appendix B for areas included
Source: Bureau of Labor Statistics, Local Area Unemployment Statistics

Average Wages

Occupation	$/Hr.	Occupation	$/Hr.
Accountants and Auditors	38.60	Maids and Housekeeping Cleaners	12.20
Automotive Mechanics	21.90	Maintenance and Repair Workers	20.50
Bookkeepers	21.00	Marketing Managers	78.40
Carpenters	28.20	Nuclear Medicine Technologists	38.30
Cashiers	10.20	Nurses, Licensed Practical	26.10
Clerks, General Office	17.30	Nurses, Registered	34.90
Clerks, Receptionists/Information	14.40	Nursing Assistants	14.70
Clerks, Shipping/Receiving	17.00	Packers and Packagers, Hand	14.20
Computer Programmers	41.80	Physical Therapists	41.20
Computer Systems Analysts	47.40	Postal Service Mail Carriers	24.30
Computer User Support Specialists	25.40	Real Estate Brokers	37.70
Cooks, Restaurant	14.50	Retail Salespersons	14.10
Dentists	68.00	Sales Reps., Exc. Tech./Scientific	38.60
Electrical Engineers	47.80	Sales Reps., Tech./Scientific	53.30
Electricians	33.00	Secretaries, Exc. Legal/Med./Exec.	18.30
Financial Managers	77.10	Security Guards	13.20
First-Line Supervisors/Managers, Sales	23.30	Surgeons	115.70
Food Preparation Workers	11.90	Teacher Assistants*	14.10
General and Operations Managers	71.40	Teachers, Elementary School*	36.60
Hairdressers/Cosmetologists	14.50	Teachers, Secondary School*	35.20
Internists, General	72.30	Telemarketers	15.40
Janitors and Cleaners	15.20	Truck Drivers, Heavy/Tractor-Trailer	23.30
Landscaping/Groundskeeping Workers	15.40	Truck Drivers, Light/Delivery Svcs.	17.30
Lawyers	65.40	Waiters and Waitresses	11.20

Note: Wage data covers the Montgomery County-Bucks County-Chester County, PA Metropolitan Division—see Appendix B for areas included; (*) Hourly wages for elementary/secondary school teachers and teacher assistants were calculated by the editors from annual wage data based on a 40 hour work week; n/a not available.
Source: Bureau of Labor Statistics, Metro Area Occupational Employment & Wage Estimates, May 2017

Employment by Occupation

Occupation Classification	City (%)	MSA[1] (%)	U.S. (%)
Management, Business, Science, and Arts	68.4	42.4	37.0
Natural Resources, Construction, and Maintenance	1.8	6.9	8.9
Production, Transportation, and Material Moving	2.1	9.6	12.2
Sales and Office	19.7	24.0	23.8
Service	7.9	17.2	18.1

Note: Figures cover employed civilians 16 years of age and older; (1) Figures cover the Philadelphia-Camden-Wilmington, PA-NJ-DE-MD Metropolitan Statistical Area—see Appendix B for areas included
Source: U.S. Census Bureau, 2012-2016 American Community Survey 5-Year Estimates

Employment by Industry

Sector	MD[1] Number of Employees	MD[1] Percent of Total	U.S. Percent of Total
Construction, Mining, and Logging	50,200	4.7	5.2
Education and Health Services	196,700	18.3	15.9
Financial Activities	82,800	7.7	5.7
Government	85,000	7.9	15.3
Information	20,800	1.9	1.9
Leisure and Hospitality	84,100	7.8	10.7
Manufacturing	91,300	8.5	8.5
Other Services	47,300	4.4	3.9
Professional and Business Services	207,000	19.3	14.0
Retail Trade	122,400	11.4	11.0
Transportation, Warehousing, and Utilities	29,700	2.8	4.1
Wholesale Trade	57,400	5.3	4.0

Note: Figures are non-farm employment as of December 2017. Figures are not seasonally adjusted and include workers 16 years of age and older; (1) Figures cover the Montgomery County-Bucks County-Chester County, PA Metropolitan Division—see Appendix B for areas included
Source: Bureau of Labor Statistics, Current Employment Statistics, Employment, Hours, and Earnings

Occupations with Greatest Projected Employment Growth: 2017 – 2019

Occupation[1]	2017 Employment	2019 Projected Employment	Numeric Employment Change	Percent Employment Change
Personal Care Aides	95,040	101,150	6,110	6.4
Combined Food Preparation and Serving Workers, Including Fast Food	149,690	154,700	5,010	3.3
Registered Nurses	143,300	147,290	3,990	2.8
Laborers and Freight, Stock, and Material Movers, Hand	138,050	141,860	3,810	2.8
Home Health Aides	46,950	50,700	3,750	8.0
Waiters and Waitresses	100,790	102,540	1,750	1.7
Janitors and Cleaners, Except Maids and Housekeeping Cleaners	98,590	100,250	1,660	1.7
Cooks, Restaurant	49,820	51,120	1,300	2.6
Software Developers, Applications	25,890	27,190	1,300	5.0
Nursing Assistants	80,510	81,790	1,280	1.6

Note: Projections cover Pennsylvania; (1) Sorted by numeric employment change
Source: www.projectionscentral.com, State Occupational Projections, 2017–2019 Short-Term Projections

Fastest Growing Occupations: 2017 – 2019

Occupation[1]	2017 Employment	2019 Projected Employment	Numeric Employment Change	Percent Employment Change
Home Health Aides	46,950	50,700	3,750	8.0
Statisticians	2,710	2,880	170	6.5
Personal Care Aides	95,040	101,150	6,110	6.4
Physician Assistants	5,620	5,960	340	6.1
Nurse Practitioners	5,240	5,550	310	6.0
Operations Research Analysts	2,660	2,800	140	5.1
Information Security Analysts	3,020	3,170	150	5.0
Software Developers, Applications	25,890	27,190	1,300	5.0
Nonfarm Animal Caretakers	7,820	8,210	390	4.9
Physical Therapist Assistants	4,660	4,880	220	4.8

Note: Projections cover Pennsylvania; (1) Sorted by percent employment change and excludes occupations with numeric employment change less than 50
Source: www.projectionscentral.com, State Occupational Projections, 2017–2019 Short-Term Projections

TAXES

State Corporate Income Tax Rates

State	Tax Rate (%)	Income Brackets ($)	Num. of Brackets	Financial Institution Tax Rate (%)[a]	Federal Income Tax Ded.
Pennsylvania	9.99	Flat rate	1	(a)	No

Note: Tax rates as of January 1, 2018; (a) Rates listed are the corporate income tax rate applied to financial institutions or excise taxes based on income. Some states have other taxes based upon the value of deposits or shares.
Source: Federation of Tax Administrators, Range of State Corporate Income Tax Rates, January 1, 2018

State Individual Income Tax Rates

State	Tax Rate (%)	Income Brackets ($)	Num. of Brackets	Personal Exempt. ($)[1]		Fed. Inc. Tax Ded.
				Single	Dependents	
Pennsylvania	3.07	Flat rate	1	None	None	No

Note: Tax rates as of January 1, 2018; Local- and county-level taxes are not included; n/a not applicable; (1) Married joint filers generally receive double the single exemption
Source: Federation of Tax Administrators, State Individual Income Tax Rates, January 1, 2018

Various State Sales and Excise Tax Rates

State	State Sales Tax (%)	Gasoline[1] (¢/gal.)	Cigarette[2] ($/pack)	Spirits[3] ($/gal.)	Wine[4] ($/gal.)	Beer[5] ($/gal.)	Recreational Marijuana (%)
Pennsylvania	6.0	58.7	2.60	7.24 (g)	(m)	0.08	Not legal

Note: All tax rates as of January 1, 2018; (1) The American Petroleum Institute has developed a methodology for determining the average tax rate on a gallon of fuel. Rates may include any of the following: excise taxes, environmental fees, storage tank fees, other fees or taxes, general sales tax, and local taxes. In states where gasoline is subject to the general sales tax, or where the fuel tax is based on the average sale price, the average rate determined by API is sensitive to changes in the price of gasoline. States that fully or partially apply general sales taxes to gasoline: CA, CO, GA, IL, IN, MI, NY; (2) The federal excise tax of $1.0066 per pack and local taxes are not included; (3) Rates are those applicable to off-premise sales of 40% alcohol by volume (a.b.v.) distilled spirits in 750ml containers. Local excise taxes are excluded; (4) Rates are those applicable to off-premise sales of 11% a.b.v. non-carbonated wine in 750ml containers; (5) Rates are those applicable to off-premise sales of 4.7% a.b.v. beer in 12 ounce containers; (g) Control states, where the government controls all sales. Products can be subject to ad valorem mark-up as well as excise taxes; (m) Control states, where the government controls all sales. Products can be subject to ad valorem mark-up as well as excise taxes.
Source: Tax Foundation, 2018 Facts & Figures: How Does Your State Compare?

State Business Tax Climate Index Rankings

State	Overall Rank	Corporate Tax Rank	Individual Income Tax Rank	Sales Tax Rank	Unemployment Insurance Tax Rank	Property Tax Rank
Pennsylvania	26	44	17	21	50	33

Note: The index is a measure of how each state's tax laws affect economic performance. The lower the rank, the more favorable a state's tax system is for business. States without a given tax are given a ranking of 1. The scores/rankings for the District of Columbia do not affect other states. The 2018 index represents the tax climate as of July 1, 2017.
Source: Tax Foundation, State Business Tax Climate Index 2018

TRANSPORTATION

Means of Transportation to Work

Area	Car/Truck/Van: Drove Alone	Car/Truck/Van: Car-pooled	Public Transportation: Bus	Public Transportation: Subway	Public Transportation: Railroad	Bicycle	Walked	Other Means	Worked at Home
City	74.5	4.9	0.4	0.9	7.4	0.4	2.5	0.7	8.3
MSA[1]	73.1	7.7	5.4	1.7	2.3	0.6	3.7	1.0	4.3
U.S.	76.4	9.3	2.6	1.9	0.6	0.6	2.8	1.3	4.6

Note: Figures are percentages and cover workers 16 years of age and older; (1) Figures cover the Philadelphia-Camden-Wilmington, PA-NJ-DE-MD Metropolitan Statistical Area—see Appendix B for areas included
Source: U.S. Census Bureau, 2012-2016 American Community Survey 5-Year Estimates

Travel Time to Work

Area	Less Than 10 Minutes	10 to 19 Minutes	20 to 29 Minutes	30 to 44 Minutes	45 to 59 Minutes	60 to 89 Minutes	90 Minutes or More
City	14.5	29.7	18.6	15.9	9.4	9.7	2.2
MSA[1]	9.8	24.7	20.5	23.5	10.7	7.9	3.0
U.S.	12.9	29.2	20.9	20.4	8.0	6.0	2.7

Note: Note: Figures are percentages and include workers 16 years old and over; (1) Figures cover the Philadelphia-Camden-Wilmington, PA-NJ-DE-MD Metropolitan Statistical Area—see Appendix B for areas included
Source: U.S. Census Bureau, 2012-2016 American Community Survey 5-Year Estimates

Freeway Travel Time Index

Area	1985	1990	1995	2000	2005	2010	2014
Urban Area Rank[1,2]	20	21	26	26	24	22	25
Urban Area Index[1]	1.12	1.15	1.18	1.21	1.25	1.24	1.24
Average Index[3]	1.09	1.11	1.14	1.17	1.20	1.19	1.20

Note: Freeway Travel Time Index—the ratio of travel time in the peak period to the travel time at free-flow conditions. For example, a value of 1.30 indicates a 20-minute free-flow trip takes 26 minutes in the peak (20 minutes x 1.30 = 26 minutes); (1) Covers the Philadelphia PA-NJ-DE-MD urban area; (2) Rank is based on 101 urban areas (#1 = highest travel time index); (3) Average of 101 urban areas
Source: Texas Transportation Institute, 2015 Urban Mobility Scorecard, August 2015

Freeway Commuter Stress Index

Area	1985	1990	1995	2000	2005	2010	2014
Urban Area Rank[1,2]	31	28	33	34	30	31	31
Urban Area Index[1]	1.15	1.19	1.22	1.25	1.29	1.28	1.28
Average Index[3]	1.13	1.16	1.19	1.22	1.25	1.24	1.25

Note: The Freeway Commuter Stress Index is the same as the Freeway Travel Time Index (see table above) except that it includes only the travel in the peak directions during the peak periods; the TTI includes travel in all directions during the peak period. Thus, the CSI is more indicative of the work trip experienced by each commuter on a daily basis; (1) Covers the Philadelphia PA-NJ-DE-MD urban area; (2) Rank is based on 101 urban areas (#1 = highest travel time index); (3) Average of 101 urban areas
Source: Texas Transportation Institute, 2015 Urban Mobility Scorecard, August 2015

Living Environment

COST OF LIVING

Cost of Living Index

Composite Index	Groceries	Housing	Utilities	Trans-portation	Health Care	Misc. Goods/ Services
117.0	116.2	129.5	124.5	114.9	105.7	107.2

Note: The Cost of Living Index measures regional differences in the cost of consumer goods and services, excluding taxes and non-consumer expenditures, for professional and managerial households in the top income quintile. It is based on more than 50,000 prices covering almost 60 different items for which prices are collected three times a year by chambers of commerce, economic development organizations or university applied economic centers in each participating urban area. The numbers shown should be read as a percentage above or below the national average of 100. For example, a value of 115.4 in the groceries column indicates that grocery prices are 15.4% higher than the national average. Small differences in the index numbers should not be interpreted as significant; Figures cover the Philadelphia PA urban area.
Source: The Council for Community and Economic Research, ACCRA Cost of Living Index, 2017

Grocery Prices

Area[1]	T-Bone Steak ($/pound)	Frying Chicken ($/pound)	Whole Milk ($/half gal.)	Eggs ($/dozen)	Orange Juice ($/64 oz.)	Coffee ($/11.5 oz.)
City[2]	11.82	1.46	2.11	1.74	3.92	4.10
Avg.	11.29	1.40	2.02	1.47	3.55	4.37
Min.	7.71	0.93	1.04	0.70	2.86	3.24
Max.	15.83	2.39	4.03	3.92	6.29	8.16

Note: (1) Values for the local area are compared with the average, minimum and maximum values for all 294 areas in the Cost of Living Index; (2) Figures cover the Philadelphia PA urban area; ***T-Bone Steak*** *(price per pound);* ***Frying Chicken*** *(price per pound, whole fryer);* ***Whole Milk*** *(half gallon carton);* ***Eggs*** *(price per dozen, Grade A, large);* ***Orange Juice*** *(64 oz. Tropicana or Florida Natural);* ***Coffee*** *(11.5 oz. can, vacuum-packed, Maxwell House, Hills Bros, or Folgers).*
Source: The Council for Community and Economic Research, ACCRA Cost of Living Index, 2017

Housing and Utility Costs

Area[1]	New Home Price ($)	Apartment Rent ($/month)	All Electric ($/month)	Part Electric ($/month)	Other Energy ($/month)	Telephone ($/month)
City[2]	424,983	1,411	-	107.26	69.96	42.00
Avg.	335,956	1,047	175.01	97.34	67.93	28.71
Min.	187,788	491	109.48	49.33	35.44	12.39
Max.	1,739,087	4,559	432.62	227.09	353.33	44.61

Note: (1) Values for the local area are compared with the average, minimum and maximum values for all 294 areas in the Cost of Living Index; (2) Figures cover the Philadelphia PA urban area; ***New Home Price*** *(2,400 sf living area, 8,000 sf lot, in urban area with full utilities);* ***Apartment Rent*** *(950 sf 2 bedroom/1.5 or 2 bath, unfurnished, excluding all utilities except water);* ***All Electric*** *(average monthly cost for an all-electric home);* ***Part Electric*** *(average monthly cost for a part-electric home);* ***Other Energy*** *(average monthly cost for natural gas, fuel oil, coal, wood, and any other forms of energy except electricity);* ***Telephone*** *(price includes basic monthly rate for a private residential line plus additional local usage charges incurred by a family of four).*
Source: The Council for Community and Economic Research, ACCRA Cost of Living Index, 2017

Health Care, Transportation, and Other Costs

Area[1]	Doctor ($/visit)	Dentist ($/visit)	Optometrist ($/visit)	Gasoline ($/gallon)	Beauty Salon ($/visit)	Men's Shirt ($)
City[2]	130.24	96.14	100.71	2.48	56.27	31.77
Avg.	108.00	92.54	101.93	2.25	37.58	30.92
Min.	30.39	60.00	49.75	1.82	16.11	11.20
Max.	193.50	161.94	229.28	3.16	77.35	59.13

Note: (1) Values for the local area are compared with the average, minimum and maximum values for all 294 areas in the Cost of Living Index; (2) Figures cover the Philadelphia PA urban area; ***Doctor*** *(general practitioners routine exam of an established patient);* ***Dentist*** *(adult teeth cleaning and periodic oral examination);* ***Optometrist*** *(full vision eye exam for established adult patient);* ***Gasoline*** *(one gallon regular unleaded, national brand, including all taxes, cash price at self-service pump if available);* ***Beauty Salon*** *(woman's shampoo, trim, and blow-dry);* ***Men's Shirt*** *(cotton/polyester dress shirt, pinpoint weave, long sleeves).*
Source: The Council for Community and Economic Research, ACCRA Cost of Living Index, 2017

HOUSING

House Price Index (HPI)

Area	National Ranking[2]	Quarterly Change (%)	One-Year Change (%)	Five-Year Change (%)
MD[1]	181	0.74	4.24	14.38
U.S.[3]	–	1.61	6.68	34.71

Note: The HPI is a weighted repeat sales index. It measures average price changes in repeat sales or refinancings on the same properties. This information is obtained by reviewing repeat mortgage transactions on single-family properties whose mortgages have been purchased or securitized by Fannie Mae or Freddie Mac in January 1975; (1) Figures cover the Montgomery County-Bucks County-Chester County, PA Metropolitan Division—see Appendix B for areas included; (2) Rankings are based on annual percentage change for all metro areas containing at least 15,000 transactions over the last 10 years and ranges from 1 to 253; (3) figures based on a weighted average of Census Division estimates using a seasonally adjusted, purchase-only index; all figures are for the period ending December 31, 2017
Source: Federal Housing Finance Agency, House Price Index, February 28, 2018

Median Single-Family Home Prices

Area	2015	2016	2017p	Percent Change 2016 to 2017
MSA[1]	223.7	225.4	230.0	2.0
U.S. Average	223.9	235.5	248.8	5.6

Note: Figures are median sales prices of existing single-family homes in thousands of dollars; (p) preliminary; (1) Figures cover the Philadelphia-Camden-Wilmington, PA-NJ-DE-MD Metropolitan Statistical Area—see Appendix B for areas included
Source: National Association of Realtors, Median Sales Price of Existing Single-Family Homes for Metropolitan Areas, 4th Quarter 2017

Qualifying Income Based on Median Sales Price of Existing Single-Family Homes

Area	With 5% Down ($)	With 10% Down ($)	With 20% Down ($)
MSA[1]	50,381	47,729	42,426
U.S. Average	55,585	52,659	46,808

Note: Figures are preliminary; Qualifying income is based on a mortgage rate of 4.17%. Monthly principal and interest payment is limited to 25% of income; (1) Figures cover the Philadelphia-Camden-Wilmington, PA-NJ-DE-MD Metropolitan Statistical Area—see Appendix B for areas included
Source: National Association of Realtors, Qualifying Income Based on Median Sales Price of Existing Single-Family Homes for Metropolitan Areas, 4th Quarter 2017

Median Apartment Condo-Coop Home Prices

Area	2015	2016	2017p	Percent Change 2016 to 2017
MSA[1]	176.5	182.7	185.1	1.3
U.S. Average	210.7	220.7	234.3	6.2

Note: Figures are median sales prices of existing apartment condo-coop homes in thousands of dollars; (p) preliminary; (1) Figures cover the Philadelphia-Camden-Wilmington, PA-NJ-DE-MD Metropolitan Statistical Area—see Appendix B for areas included
Source: National Association of Realtors, Median Sales Price of Existing Apartment Condo-Coop Homes for Metropolitan Areas, 4th Quarter 2017

Home Value Distribution

Area	Under $50,000	$50,000 -$99,999	$100,000 -$149,999	$150,000 -$199,999	$200,000 -$299,999	$300,000 -$499,999	$500,000 -$999,999	$1,000,000 or more
City	2.0	0.6	1.1	7.4	12.0	29.6	39.2	8.2
MSA[1]	4.7	7.9	10.8	15.6	27.1	23.9	8.5	1.4
U.S.	8.8	14.8	15.3	14.9	18.4	16.4	9.0	2.5

Note: Figures are percentages and cover owner-occupied housing units; (1) Figures cover the Philadelphia-Camden-Wilmington, PA-NJ-DE-MD Metropolitan Statistical Area—see Appendix B for areas included
Source: U.S. Census Bureau, 2012-2016 American Community Survey 5-Year Estimates

Homeownership Rate

Area	2009 (%)	2010 (%)	2011 (%)	2012 (%)	2013 (%)	2014 (%)	2015 (%)	2016 (%)	2017 (%)
MSA[1]	69.7	70.7	69.7	69.5	69.1	67.0	67.0	64.7	65.6
U.S.	67.4	66.9	66.1	65.4	65.1	64.5	63.7	63.4	63.9

Note: (1) Figures cover the Philadelphia-Camden-Wilmington, PA-NJ-DE-MD Metropolitan Statistical Area—see Appendix B for areas included
Source: U.S. Census Bureau, Housing Vacancies and Homeownership Annual Statistics: 2009-2017

Year Housing Structure Built

Area	2010 or Later	2000 -2009	1990 -1999	1980 -1989	1970 -1979	1960 -1969	1950 -1959	1940 -1949	Before 1940	Median Year
City	0.3	2.0	8.0	23.9	14.9	18.3	18.1	4.1	10.3	1970
MSA[1]	1.4	8.3	9.4	10.2	12.3	12.1	15.9	8.5	21.8	1963
U.S.	2.3	14.7	14.0	13.7	15.6	10.9	10.6	5.2	13.0	1977

Note: Figures are percentages except for Median Year; Note: (1) Figures cover the Philadelphia-Camden-Wilmington, PA-NJ-DE-MD Metropolitan Statistical Area—see Appendix B for areas included
Source: U.S. Census Bureau, 2012-2016 American Community Survey 5-Year Estimates

Gross Monthly Rent

Area	Under $500	$500 -$999	$1,000 -$1,499	$1,500 -$1,999	$2,000 -$2,499	$2,500 -$2,999	$3,000 and up	Median ($)
City	0.4	12.3	49.6	19.1	8.7	5.8	4.1	1,392
MSA[1]	9.0	37.4	35.4	11.9	3.9	1.3	1.1	1,040
U.S.	11.3	43.3	27.7	10.7	4.0	1.6	1.5	949

Note: Figures are percentages except for Median; Gross rent is the contract rent plus the estimated average monthly cost of utilities (electricity, gas, and water and sewer) and fuels (oil, coal, kerosene, wood, etc.) if these are paid by the renter (or paid for the renter by someone else); (1) Figures cover the Philadelphia-Camden-Wilmington, PA-NJ-DE-MD Metropolitan Statistical Area—see Appendix B for areas included
Source: U.S. Census Bureau, 2012-2016 American Community Survey 5-Year Estimates

HEALTH

Health Risk Factors

Category	MD[1] (%)	U.S. (%)
Adults aged 18–64 who have any kind of health care coverage	93.7	87.7
Adults who reported being in good or excellent health	86.3	83.6
Adults who are current smokers	13.3	17.1
Adults who currently use E-cigarettes	n/a	4.7
Adults who currently use chewing tobacco, snuff, or snus	2.0	4.0
Adults who are heavy drinkers[2]	7.3	6.5
Adults who are binge drinkers[3]	19.6	16.9
Adults who are overweight (BMI 25.0 - 29.9)	34.8	35.3
Adults who are obese (BMI 30.0 - 99.8)	23.1	29.9
Adults who participated in any physical activities in the past month	83.1	76.9
Adults who always or nearly always wears a seat belt	95.3	94.3

Note: n/a not available; (1) Figures cover the Montgomery County-Bucks County-Chester County, PA Metropolitan Division—see Appendix B for areas included; (2) Heavy drinkers are classified as adult men having more than 14 drinks per week and adult women having more than 7 drinks per week; (3) Binge drinkers are classified as males having five or more drinks on one occasion or females having four or more drinks on one occasion
Source: Centers for Disease Control and Prevention, Behaviorial Risk Factor Surveillance System, SMART: Selected Metropolitan Area Risk Trends, 2016

Health Screening Rates

Category	MD[1] (%)	U.S. (%)
Adults 50-75 who have had a blood stool test within the past year	5.6	8.0
Adults 50-75 who have had a colonoscopy in the past 10 years	65.8	63.5
Adults aged 65+ who have had flu shot within the past year	67.0	58.6
Adults aged 65+ who have ever had a pneumonia vaccination	75.4	73.4
Adults who have ever been tested for HIV	32.4	35.6
Women aged 21-65 who have had a pap test in the past three years	79.2	79.8
Men aged 40+ who have had a PSA test within the past two years	45.0	39.5
Women aged 40+ who have had a mammogram within the past two years	74.2	72.5

Note: n/a not available; (1) Figures cover the Montgomery County-Bucks County-Chester County, PA Metropolitan Division—see Appendix B for areas included; Source: Centers for Disease Control and Prevention, Behaviorial Risk Factor Surveillance System, SMART: Selected Metropolitan Area Risk Trends, 2016

Chronic Health Conditions

Category	MD[1] (%)	U.S. (%)
Adults who have ever been told they had a heart attack	3.1	4.4
Adults who have ever been told they have angina or coronary heart disease	3.8	4.1
Adults who have ever been told they had a stroke	n/a	3.1
Adults who have been told they currently have asthma	9.2	9.3
Adults who have ever been told they have arthritis	27.3	25.8
Adults who have ever been told they have diabetes[2]	10.6	10.5
Adults who have ever been told they had skin cancer	9.0	5.9
Adults who have ever been told they had any other types of cancer	9.0	6.7
Adults who have ever been told they have COPD	8.1	6.3
Adults who have ever been told they have kidney disease	n/a	2.8
Adults who have ever been told they have a form of depression	15.0	17.4

Note: n/a not available; (1) Figures cover the Montgomery County-Bucks County-Chester County, PA Metropolitan Division—see Appendix B for areas included; (2) Figures do not include pregnancy-related, borderline, or pre-diabetes
Source: Centers for Disease Control and Prevention, Behaviorial Risk Factor Surveillance System, SMART: Selected Metropolitan Area Risk Trends, 2016

Mortality Rates for the Top 10 Causes of Death in the U.S.

ICD-10[a] Sub-Chapter	ICD-10[a] Code	Age-Adjusted Mortality Rate[1] per 100,000 population	
		County[2]	U.S.
Malignant neoplasms	C00-C97	148.8	158.5
Ischaemic heart diseases	I20-I25	78.1	96.8
Other forms of heart disease	I30-I51	53.4	52.4
Chronic lower respiratory diseases	J40-J47	29.0	40.9
Cerebrovascular diseases	I60-I69	35.5	37.2
Organic, including symptomatic, mental disorders	F01-F09	40.9	33.3
Other degenerative diseases of the nervous system	G30-G31	18.5	32.1
Other external causes of accidental injury	W00-X59	32.2	31.2
Diabetes mellitus	E10-E14	12.2	21.1
Hypertensive diseases	I10-I15	14.0	20.8

Note: (a) ICD-10 = International Classification of Diseases 10th Revision; (1) Mortality rates are a three year average covering 2014-2016; (2) Figures cover Chester County.
Source: Centers for Disease Control and Prevention, National Center for Health Statistics. Underlying Cause of Death 1999-2016 on CDC WONDER Online Database, released December 2017

Mortality Rates for Selected Causes of Death

ICD-10[a] Sub-Chapter	ICD-10[a] Code	Age-Adjusted Mortality Rate[1] per 100,000 population	
		County[2]	U.S.
Assault	X85-Y09	1.7	5.6
Diseases of the liver	K70-K76	9.0	14.0
Human immunodeficiency virus (HIV) disease	B20-B24	Suppressed	1.9
Influenza and pneumonia	J09-J18	12.2	14.6
Intentional self-harm	X60-X84	11.5	13.2
Malnutrition	E40-E46	Suppressed	1.3
Obesity and other hyperalimentation	E65-E68	Unreliable	2.1
Renal failure	N17-N19	10.6	13.0
Transport accidents	V01-V99	7.7	12.0
Viral hepatitis	B15-B19	1.4	1.9

Note: (a) ICD-10 = International Classification of Diseases 10th Revision; (1) Mortality rates are a three year average covering 2014-2016; (2) Figures cover Chester County; Data are Suppressed when the data meet the criteria for confidentiality constraints; Mortality rates are flagged as Unreliable when the rate would be calculated with a numerator of 20 or less.
Source: Centers for Disease Control and Prevention, National Center for Health Statistics. Underlying Cause of Death 1999-2016 on CDC WONDER Online Database, released December 2017

Health Insurance Coverage

Area	With Health Insurance	With Private Health Insurance	With Public Health Insurance	Without Health Insurance	Population Under Age 18 Without Health Insurance
City	97.6	91.0	21.0	2.4	0.9
MSA[1]	92.0	72.6	31.5	8.0	3.5
U.S.	88.3	66.7	33.0	11.7	5.9

Note: Figures are percentages that cover the civilian noninstitutionalized population; (1) Figures cover the Philadelphia-Camden-Wilmington, PA-NJ-DE-MD Metropolitan Statistical Area—see Appendix B for areas included
Source: U.S. Census Bureau, 2012-2016 American Community Survey 5-Year Estimates

Number of Medical Professionals

Area	MDs[3]	DOs[3,4]	Dentists	Podiatrists	Chiropractors	Optometrists
County[1] (number)	1,246	230	342	48	141	99
County[1] (rate[2])	241.8	44.6	66.2	9.3	27.3	19.2
U.S. (rate[2])	276.5	22.3	67.3	6.0	26.7	15.9

Note: Data as of 2016 unless noted; (1) Data covers Chester County; (2) Rate per 100,000 population; (3) Data as of 2015 and includes all active, non-federal physicians; (4) Doctor of Osteopathic Medicine
Source: U.S. Department of Health and Human Services, Health Resources and Services Administration, Bureau of Health Professions, Area Resource File (ARF) 2016-2017

Best Hospitals

According to *U.S. News*, the Montgomery County-Bucks County-Chester County, PA metro area is home to one of the best hospitals in the U.S.: **MossRehab** (1 adult specialty). The hospital listed was nationally ranked in at least one of 16 specialties. Only 152 hospitals nationwide were nationally ranked in one or more specialties. Twenty hospitals in the U.S. made the Honor Roll. The Best Hospitals Honor Roll was revamped last year to take both the national rankings and the procedure and condition ratings into account. Hospitals received points if they were nationally ranked in one of the 16 specialties—the higher they ranked, the more points they got—and how many ratings of "high performing" they earned in the nine procedures and conditions. *U.S. News Online, "America's Best Hospitals 2017-18"*

EDUCATION

Public School District Statistics

District Name	Schls	Pupils	Pupil/ Teacher Ratio	Minority Pupils[1] (%)	Free Lunch Eligible[2] (%)	IEP[3] (%)
Education Plus Academy Cyber CS	1	412	9.9	47.3	n/a	n/a
Radnor Township SD	5	3,730	13.0	26.7	9.0	14.4
Tredyffrin-Easttown SD	8	6,569	15.2	27.4	5.7	16.4
Upper Merion Area SD	6	3,991	13.9	42.8	31.8	13.7

Note: Table includes school districts with 100 or more students; (1) Percentage of students that are not non-Hispanic white; (2) Percentage of students that are eligible for the free lunch program; (3) Percentage of students that have an Individualized Education Program.
Source: U.S. Department of Education, National Center for Education Statistics, Common Core of Data, Local Education Agency (School District) Universe Survey: School Year 2015-2016; U.S. Department of Education, National Center for Education Statistics, Common Core of Data, Public Elementary/Secondary School Universe Survey: School Year 2015-2016

Highest Level of Education

Area	Less than H.S.	H.S. Diploma	Some College, No Deg.	Associate Degree	Bachelor's Degree	Master's Degree	Prof. School Degree	Doctorate Degree
City	1.8	9.2	9.3	3.4	39.8	24.2	7.3	4.9
MSA[1]	10.3	30.0	17.3	6.9	21.3	9.9	2.5	1.8
U.S.	13.0	27.5	21.0	8.2	18.8	8.2	2.0	1.3

Note: Figures cover persons age 25 and over; (1) Figures cover the Philadelphia-Camden-Wilmington, PA-NJ-DE-MD Metropolitan Statistical Area—see Appendix B for areas included
Source: U.S. Census Bureau, 2012-2016 American Community Survey 5-Year Estimates

Educational Attainment by Race

Area	High School Graduate or Higher (%)					Bachelor's Degree or Higher (%)				
	Total	White	Black	Asian	Hisp.[2]	Total	White	Black	Asian	Hisp.[2]
City	98.2	98.9	96.1	94.5	87.0	76.2	75.5	51.9	88.5	61.0
MSA[1]	89.7	92.3	85.7	83.4	68.1	35.5	39.5	19.2	55.0	16.3
U.S.	87.0	88.9	84.3	86.3	65.7	30.3	31.6	20.0	52.1	14.7

Note: Figures shown cover persons 25 years old and over; (1) Figures cover the Philadelphia-Camden-Wilmington, PA-NJ-DE-MD Metropolitan Statistical Area—see Appendix B for areas included; (2) People of Hispanic origin can be of any race
Source: U.S. Census Bureau, 2012-2016 American Community Survey 5-Year Estimates

School Enrollment by Grade and Control

Area	Preschool (%)		Kindergarten (%)		Grades 1 - 4 (%)		Grades 5 - 8 (%)		Grades 9 - 12 (%)	
	Public	Private	Public	Private	Public	Private	Public	Private	Public	Private
City	18.5	81.5	86.6	13.4	92.1	7.9	90.5	9.5	85.9	14.1
MSA[1]	43.6	56.4	81.7	18.3	85.0	15.0	83.6	16.4	83.6	16.4
U.S.	58.4	41.6	87.7	12.3	89.8	10.2	89.7	10.3	90.4	9.6

Note: Figures shown cover persons 3 years old and over; (1) Figures cover the Philadelphia-Camden-Wilmington, PA-NJ-DE-MD Metropolitan Statistical Area—see Appendix B for areas included
Source: U.S. Census Bureau, 2012-2016 American Community Survey 5-Year Estimates

Average Salaries of Public School Classroom Teachers

Area	2015		2016		Change from 2015 to 2016	
	Dollars	Rank[1]	Dollars	Rank[1]	Percent	Rank[2]
Pennsylvania	64,447	10	65,151	10	1.1	24
U.S. Average	57,611	–	58,353	–	1.3	–

Note: (1) Rank ranges from 1 to 51 where 1 indicates highest salary; (2) Rank ranges from 1 to 51 where 1 indicates highest percent change.
Source: National Education Association, Rankings & Estimates: Rankings of the States 2016 and Estimates of School Statistics 2017

Higher Education

Four-Year Colleges			Two-Year Colleges			Medical Schools[1]	Law Schools[2]	Voc/ Tech[3]
Public	Private Non-profit	Private For-profit	Public	Private Non-profit	Private For-profit			
0	0	0	0	0	0	0	0	0

Note: Figures cover institutions located within the city limits and include main campuses only; (1) includes schools accredited by the Liaison Committee on Medical Education and the American Osteopathic Association's Commission on Osteopathic College Accreditation; (2) includes ABA-accredited schools, schools with provisional ABA accreditation, and state accredited schools; (3) includes all schools with programs that are less than 2 years.
Source: National Center for Education Statistics, Integrated Postsecondary Education System (IPEDS), 2016-17; Wikipedia, List of Medical Schools in the United States, accessed April 2, 2018; Wikipedia, List of Law Schools in the United States, accessed April 2, 2018

PRESIDENTIAL ELECTION

2016 Presidential Election Results

Area	Clinton	Trump	Johnson	Stein	Other
Chester County	51.9	42.5	2.9	0.8	1.8
U.S.	48.0	45.9	3.3	1.1	1.7

Note: Results are percentages and may not add to 100% due to rounding
Source: Dave Leip's Atlas of U.S. Presidential Elections

EMPLOYERS

Major Employers

Company Name	Industry
Abington Memorial Hospital	General medical & surgical hospitals
AstraZeneca Pharmaceuticals	Pharmaceutical preparations
City of Philadelphia	Police protection
Comcast Holdings Corporation	Cable & other pay television services
Cooper Health Care	Hospital management
E.I. du Pont de Nemours and Company	Agricultural chemicals
Einstein Community Health Associates	Offices & clinics of medical doctors
Glaxosmithkline	Commerical physical research
Lockheed Martin Corporation	Defense systems & equipment
Mercy Health System of SE Pennsylvania	General medical & surgical hospitals
On Time Staffing	Employment agencies
Richlieu Associates	Apartment building operators
Temple University	General medical & surgical hospitals
The University of Pennsylvania	Colleges & universities
The US Navy	Navy
The Vanguard Group	Management, investment, open-end
Thomas Jefferson University Hospital	General medical & surgical hospitals
Trustees of the University of Penn	General medical & surgical hospitals
Unisys Corporation	Computer integrated systems design
University of Delaware	Colleges & universities

Note: Companies shown are located within the Philadelphia-Camden-Wilmington, PA-NJ-DE-MD Metropolitan Statistical Area.
Source: Hoovers.com; Wikipedia

PUBLIC SAFETY

Crime Rate

Area	All Crimes	Violent Crimes				Property Crimes		
		Murder	Rape[3]	Robbery	Aggrav. Assault	Burglary	Larceny -Theft	Motor Vehicle Theft
City	817.5	3.4	6.8	20.3	43.9	84.5	625.0	33.8
Metro[1]	1,533.9	1.7	11.8	33.4	72.5	161.9	1,194.9	57.6
U.S.	2,847.8	5.3	40.4	102.8	248.5	468.9	1,745.0	236.9

Note: Figures are crimes per 100,000 population; (1) Figures cover the Montgomery County-Bucks County-Chester County, PA Metropolitan Division—see Appendix B for areas included; (3) The city and U.S. figures shown were reported using the revised Uniform Crime Reporting (UCR) definition of rape. The metro area figures shown are an aggregate total of the data submitted using both the revised and legacy UCR definitions.
Source: FBI Uniform Crime Reports, 2016

Hate Crimes

Area	Number of Quarters Reported	Number of Incidents per Bias Motivation					
		Race/Ethnicity/ Ancestry	Religion	Sexual Orientation	Disability	Gender	Gender Identity
Area[1]	4	0	0	0	0	0	0
U.S.	4	3,489	1,273	1,076	70	31	124

Note: (1) Figures cover the Tredyffrin Township.
Source: Federal Bureau of Investigation, Hate Crime Statistics 2016

Identity Theft Consumer Reports

Area	Reports	Reports per 100,000 Population	Rank[2]
MSA[1]	8,444	139	23
U.S.	371,061	114	-

Note: (1) Figures cover the Philadelphia-Camden-Wilmington, PA-NJ-DE-MD Metropolitan Statistical Area—see Appendix B for areas included; (2) Rank ranges from 1 to 389 where 1 indicates greatest number of identity theft reports per 100,000 population
Source: Federal Trade Commission, Consumer Sentinel Network Data Book for January–December 2017

Fraud and Other Consumer Reports

Area	Reports	Reports per 100,000 Population	Rank[2]
MSA[1]	34,068	561	60
U.S.	2,304,550	708	-

Note: (1) Figures cover the Philadelphia-Camden-Wilmington, PA-NJ-DE-MD Metropolitan Statistical Area—see Appendix B for areas included; (2) Rank ranges from 1 to 389 where 1 indicates greatest number of fraud and other consumer reports per 100,000 population
Source: Federal Trade Commission, Consumer Sentinel Network Data Book for January–December 2017

SPORTS

Professional Sports Teams

Team Name	League	Year Established
Philadelphia 76ers	National Basketball Association (NBA)	1963
Philadelphia Eagles	National Football League (NFL)	1933
Philadelphia Flyers	National Hockey League (NHL)	1967
Philadelphia Phillies	Major League Baseball (MLB)	1883
Philadelphia Union	Major League Soccer (MLS)	2010

Note: Includes teams located in the Philadelphia-Camden-Wilmington, PA-NJ-DE-MD Metropolitan Statistical Area.
Source: Wikipedia, Major Professional Sports Teams of the United States and Canada, April 5, 2018

CLIMATE

Average and Extreme Temperatures

Temperature	Jan	Feb	Mar	Apr	May	Jun	Jul	Aug	Sep	Oct	Nov	Dec	Yr.
Extreme High (°F)	74	74	85	94	96	100	104	101	100	89	84	72	104
Average High (°F)	39	42	51	63	73	82	86	85	78	67	55	43	64
Average Temp. (°F)	32	34	42	53	63	72	77	76	68	57	47	36	55
Average Low (°F)	24	26	33	43	53	62	67	66	59	47	38	28	45
Extreme Low (°F)	-7	-4	7	19	28	44	51	44	35	25	15	1	-7

Note: Figures cover the years 1948-1990
Source: National Climatic Data Center, International Station Meteorological Climate Summary, 9/96

Average Precipitation/Snowfall/Humidity

Precip./Humidity	Jan	Feb	Mar	Apr	May	Jun	Jul	Aug	Sep	Oct	Nov	Dec	Yr.
Avg. Precip. (in.)	3.2	2.8	3.7	3.5	3.7	3.6	4.1	4.0	3.3	2.7	3.4	3.3	41.4
Avg. Snowfall (in.)	7	7	4	Tr	Tr	0	0	0	0	Tr	1	4	22
Avg. Rel. Hum. 7am (%)	74	73	73	72	75	77	80	82	84	83	79	75	77
Avg. Rel. Hum. 4pm (%)	60	55	51	48	51	52	54	55	55	54	57	60	54

Note: Figures cover the years 1948-1990; Tr = Trace amounts (<0.05 in. of rain; <0.5 in. of snow)
Source: National Climatic Data Center, International Station Meteorological Climate Summary, 9/96

Weather Conditions

Temperature			Daytime Sky			Precipitation		
10°F & below	32°F & below	90°F & above	Clear	Partly cloudy	Cloudy	0.01 inch or more precip.	0.1 inch or more snow/ice	Thunder-storms
5	94	23	81	146	138	117	14	27

Note: Figures are average number of days per year and cover the years 1948-1990
Source: National Climatic Data Center, International Station Meteorological Climate Summary, 9/96

HAZARDOUS WASTE

Superfund Sites

The Montgomery County-Bucks County-Chester County, PA metro division is home to 36 sites on the EPA's Superfund National Priorities List: **A.I.W. Frank/Mid-county Mustang** (final); **Baghurst Drive** (final); **Blosenski Landfill** (final); **Boarhead Farms** (final); **Borit Asbestos** (final); **Chem-fab** (final); **Commodore Semiconductor Group** (final); **Crater Resources, Inc./Keystone Coke Co./Alan Wood Steel Co.** (final); **Croydon Tce** (final); **Dublin Tce Site** (final); **Fischer & Porter Co.** (final); **Foote Mineral Co.** (final); **Henderson Road** (final); **Kimberton** (final); **Malvern Tce** (final); **Naval Air Development Center (8 Waste Areas)** (final); **North Penn - Area 1** (final); **North Penn - Area 12** (final); **North Penn - Area 2** (final); **North Penn - Area 5** (final); **North Penn - Area 6** (final); **North Penn - Area 7** (final);

Occidental Chemical Corp./Firestone Tire & Rubber Co. (final); **Old Wilmington Road Gw Contamination** (final); **Paoli Rail Yard** (final); **Raymark** (final); **Recticon/Allied Steel Corp.** (final); **Revere Chemical Co.** (final); **Salford Quarry** (final); **Stanley Kessler** (final); **Strasburg Landfill** (final); **Tysons Dump** (final); **Walsh Landfill** (final); **Watson Johnson Landfill** (final); **William Dick Lagoons** (final); **Willow Grove Naval Air and Air Reserve Station** (final). There are a total of 1,396 Superfund sites with a status of proposed or final on the list in the U.S. *U.S. Environmental Protection Agency, National Priorities List, April 4, 2018*

AIR & WATER QUALITY

Air Quality Trends: Ozone

	1990	1995	2000	2005	2010	2012	2013	2014	2015	2016
MSA[1]	0.102	0.109	0.099	0.091	0.083	0.084	0.069	0.071	0.074	0.075
U.S.	0.087	0.089	0.081	0.079	0.073	0.075	0.069	0.067	0.068	0.069

Note: (1) Data covers the Philadelphia-Camden-Wilmington, PA-NJ-DE-MD Metropolitan Statistical Area—see Appendix B for areas included. The values shown are the composite ozone concentration averages among trend sites based on the highest fourth daily maximum 8-hour concentration in parts per million. These trends are based on sites having an adequate record of monitoring data during the trend period. Data from exceptional events are included.
Source: U.S. Environmental Protection Agency, Air Quality Monitoring Information, "Air Quality Trends by City, 1990-2016"

Air Quality Index

Area	Percent of Days when Air Quality was...[2]					AQI Statistics[2]	
	Good	Moderate	Unhealthy for Sensitive Groups	Unhealthy	Very Unhealthy	Maximum	Median
MSA[1]	34.5	59.5	5.5	0.5	0.0	166	55

Note: (1) Data covers the Philadelphia-Camden-Wilmington, PA-NJ-DE-MD Metropolitan Statistical Area—see Appendix B for areas included; (2) Based on 365 days with AQI data in 2017. Air Quality Index (AQI) is an index for reporting daily air quality. EPA calculates the AQI for five major air pollutants regulated by the Clean Air Act: ground-level ozone, particle pollution (aka particulate matter), carbon monoxide, sulfur dioxide, and nitrogen dioxide. The AQI runs from 0 to 500. The higher the AQI value, the greater the level of air pollution and the greater the health concern. There are six AQI categories: "Good" AQI is between 0 and 50. Air quality is considered satisfactory; "Moderate" AQI is between 51 and 100. Air quality is acceptable; "Unhealthy for Sensitive Groups" When AQI values are between 101 and 150, members of sensitive groups may experience health effects; "Unhealthy" When AQI values are between 151 and 200 everyone may begin to experience health effects; "Very Unhealthy" AQI values between 201 and 300 trigger a health alert; "Hazardous" AQI values over 300 trigger warnings of emergency conditions (not shown).
Source: U.S. Environmental Protection Agency, Air Quality Index Report, 2017

Air Quality Index Pollutants

Area	Percent of Days when AQI Pollutant was...[2]					
	Carbon Monoxide	Nitrogen Dioxide	Ozone	Sulfur Dioxide	Particulate Matter 2.5	Particulate Matter 10
MSA[1]	0.0	0.3	31.2	0.5	67.7	0.3

Note: (1) Data covers the Philadelphia-Camden-Wilmington, PA-NJ-DE-MD Metropolitan Statistical Area—see Appendix B for areas included; (2) Based on 365 days with AQI data in 2017. The Air Quality Index (AQI) is an index for reporting daily air quality. EPA calculates the AQI for five major air pollutants regulated by the Clean Air Act: ground-level ozone, particle pollution (also known as particulate matter), carbon monoxide, sulfur dioxide, and nitrogen dioxide. The AQI runs from 0 to 500. The higher the AQI value, the greater the level of air pollution and the greater the health concern.
Source: U.S. Environmental Protection Agency, Air Quality Index Report, 2017

Maximum Air Pollutant Concentrations: Particulate Matter, Ozone, CO and Lead

	Particulate Matter 10 (ug/m^3)	Particulate Matter 2.5 Wtd AM (ug/m^3)	Particulate Matter 2.5 24-Hr (ug/m^3)	Ozone (ppm)	Carbon Monoxide (ppm)	Lead (ug/m^3)
MSA[1] Level	113	11	24	0.08	2	0.04
NAAQS[2]	150	15	35	0.075	9	0.15
Met NAAQS[2]	Yes	Yes	Yes	No	Yes	Yes

Note: (1) Data covers the Philadelphia-Camden-Wilmington, PA-NJ-DE-MD Metropolitan Statistical Area—see Appendix B for areas included; Data from exceptional events are included; (2) National Ambient Air Quality Standards; ppm = parts per million; ug/m^3 = micrograms per cubic meter; n/a not available.
Concentrations: Particulate Matter 10 (coarse particulate)—highest second maximum 24-hour concentration; Particulate Matter 2.5 Wtd AM (fine particulate)—highest weighted annual mean concentration; Particulate Matter 2.5 24-Hour (fine particulate)—highest 98th percentile 24-hour concentration; Ozone—highest fourth daily maximum 8-hour concentration; Carbon Monoxide—highest second maximum non-overlapping 8-hour concentration; Lead—maximum running 3-month average
Source: U.S. Environmental Protection Agency, Air Quality Monitoring Information, "Air Quality Statistics by City, 2016"

Maximum Air Pollutant Concentrations: Nitrogen Dioxide and Sulfur Dioxide

	Nitrogen Dioxide AM (ppb)	Nitrogen Dioxide 1-Hr (ppb)	Sulfur Dioxide AM (ppb)	Sulfur Dioxide 1-Hr (ppb)	Sulfur Dioxide 24-Hr (ppb)
MSA[1] Level	16	58	n/a	19	n/a
NAAQS[2]	53	100	30	75	140
Met NAAQS[2]	Yes	Yes	n/a	Yes	n/a

Note: (1) Data covers the Philadelphia-Camden-Wilmington, PA-NJ-DE-MD Metropolitan Statistical Area—see Appendix B for areas included; Data from exceptional events are included; (2) National Ambient Air Quality Standards; ppm = parts per million; ug/m^3 = micrograms per cubic meter; n/a not available.
Concentrations: Nitrogen Dioxide AM—highest arithmetic mean concentration; Nitrogen Dioxide 1-Hr—highest 98th percentile 1-hour daily maximum concentration; Sulfur Dioxide AM—highest annual mean concentration; Sulfur Dioxide 1-Hr—highest 99th percentile 1-hour daily maximum concentration; Sulfur Dioxide 24-Hr—highest second maximum 24-hour concentration
Source: U.S. Environmental Protection Agency, Air Quality Monitoring Information, "Air Quality Statistics by City, 2016"

Drinking Water

Water System Name	Pop. Served	Primary Water Source Type	Violations[1]	
			Health Based	Monitoring/ Reporting
Aqua PA Main System	747,460	Surface	0	0

Note: (1) Based on violation data from January 1, 2017 to December 31, 2017
Source: U.S. Environmental Protection Agency, Office of Ground Water and Drinking Water, Safe Drinking Water Information System (based on data extracted April 5, 2018)

Upper Dublin, Pennsylvania

Background

Upper Dublin in Montgomery County is approximately 19 miles north of Philadelphia. Incorporated in 1719, it became a township in 1954, and is comprised of 10 small communities.

The area that is now Upper Dublin was founded in 1698 from land granted to Edward Tanner in 1684. He named the area Upper and Lower Dublin, the latter eventually becoming part of Philadelphia. Upper Dublin grew significantly during the 1950s as the suburbs expanded, and is home to Emlen House, where George Washington stayed before embarking on his journey to Valley Forge.

The Fort Washington Office Park is the city's premier business center. The office park is conveniently located next to PA Turnpike and PA Route 309 and is served by the Washington SEPTA regional rail station, providing easy access to Philadelphia and the rest of Pennsylvania. It currently contains over 65 buildings, with GE Financial, Nutrisystem and Honeywell among the companies located in the complex.

Upper Dublin has a wealth of recreational parks and facilities for residents to enjoy. The Upper Dublin Sports Park features two turf fields and is used by the city's high school. The park also has a half-mile track. Robbins Park captures the beauty of the Upper Dublin area and works with the school district to provide educational environmental classes held at Cheston Center, a historically replicated log cabin, and at an outdoor amphitheater. The park also has trails that are used to explore the natural wildlife. Mondauk Manor Park allows leashed dogs to enjoy the property, and is home to the popular enclosed dog park, MonDaug Bark Park.

The Upper Dublin Golf and Fitness Club offers a variety of amenities, including an 18-hole golf course, fitness center, driving range and golf academy.

Upper Dublin is served by the Upper Dublin School District. Upper Dublin High School has received the National Blue Ribbon School of Excellence. There are also several private school options in Upper Dublin, including the Montessori School for children grades K-6 and Open Door Christian Academy for children grades PK-8. Temple University and DeVry University both have campuses in nearby Fort Washington.

Philadelphia International Airport is the nearest major airport to Upper Dublin, 19 miles away.

Upper Dublin enjoys four seasons. The July average high is 88 degrees and the January average low is 26 degrees, both within a few degrees of the national average. The Township receives 49 inches of rain per year, 11 inches more then the national average. Due to hotter winters, Upper Dublin receives an average of 23 inches of snowfall per year, less then the national average.

Rankings

Business/Finance Rankings

- The personal finance site NerdWallet analyzed 183 American metropolitan areas with populations over 250,000 and more than 15,000 businesses to rank where entrepreneurs find the most success. Criteria included area economy, annual income, housing cost, unemployment rate, and the success rate of area businesses. Philadelphia* ranked #60. *www.nerdwallet.com, "Best Places to Start a Business," April 27, 2015*
- In a survey of economic confidence in the nation's 50 largest metropolitan areas conducted January–December 2014, the Philadelphia* metro area placed #33, according to Gallup's 2014 Economic Confidence Index. *Gallup, "San Jose and San Francisco Lead in Economic Confidence," March 19, 2015*
- The Brookings Institution ranked the 100 largest metro areas in the U.S. based on income inequality. Philadelphia* was ranked #12 (#1 = greatest ineqality). Criteria: the "95/20 ratio," a figure representing the income at which a household earns more than 95 percent of all other households, divided by the income at which a household earns more than only 20 percent of all other households. *Brookings Institution, "Household Income Inequality, 100 Largest U.S. Metro Areas, 2014-2016," February 5, 2018*
- Payscale.com ranked the largest metro areas in terms of wage growth. The Philadelphia* metro area ranked #29. Criteria: private-sector wage growth between the 4th quarter of 2016 and the 4th quarter of 2017. *PayScale, "Wage Trends by Metro Area-4th Quarter," January 17, 2018*
- The Philadelphia* metro area was identified as one of the most debt-ridden places in America by the finance site Credit.com. The metro area was ranked #11. Criteria: residents' average credit card debt as well as median income. *Credit.com, "25 Cities With the Most Credit Card Debt," February 28, 2018*
- Philadelphia* was identified as one of America's most frugal metro areas by *Coupons.com.* The city ranked #6 out of 25. Criteria: digital coupon usage. *Coupons.com, "America's Most Frugal Cities of 2017," March 22, 2018*
- The Philadelphia* metro area appeared on the Milken Institute "2017 Best Performing Cities" list. Rank: #98 out of 200 large metro areas. Criteria: job growth; wage and salary growth; high-tech output growth. *Milken Institute, "Best-Performing Cities 2017," January 2018*
- *Forbes* ranked the 200 most populous metro areas to determine the nation's "Best Places for Business and Careers." The Philadelphia* metro area was ranked #83. Criteria: costs (business and living); job growth (past and projected); income growth; quality of life; educational attainment (college and high school); projected economic growth; cultural and recreational opportunities; net migration patterns; number of highly ranked colleges. *Forbes, "The Best Places for Business and Careers 2017," October 24, 2017*

Education Rankings

- Personal finance website *WalletHub* analyzed the 150 largest U.S. metropolitan statistical areas to determine where the most educated Americans are choosing to settle. Criteria: education quality and attainment gap; education levels; percentage of workers with degrees; public school rankings; quality and size of each metro area's universities. Philadelphia* was ranked #44 (#1 = most educated city). *www.WalletHub.com, "2017's Most and Least Educated Cities in America," July 25, 2017*

Environmental Rankings

- Sperling's BestPlaces assessed 379 metropolitan areas of the United States for the likelihood of dangerously extreme weather events or earthquakes. In general the Southeast and South-Central regions have the highest risk of weather extremes and earthquakes, while the Pacific Northwest enjoys the lowest risk. Of the least risky metropolitan areas, the Philadelphia* metro area was ranked #232. *www.bestplaces.net, "Safest Places from Natural Disasters," April 2011*

- The U.S. Environmental Protection Agency (EPA) released a list of U.S. metropolitan areas with the most ENERGY STAR certified buildings in 2016. The Philadelphia* metro area was ranked #11 out of 25. *U.S. Environmental Protection Agency, "2017 Energy Star Top Cities," June 2017*
- Philadelphia* was highlighted as one of the 25 most ozone-polluted metro areas in the U.S. during 2013 through 2015. The area ranked #22. *American Lung Association, State of the Air 2017*
- Philadelphia* was highlighted as one of the 25 metro areas most polluted by year-round particle pollution (Annual PM 2.5) in the U.S. during 2013 through 2015. The area ranked #13. *American Lung Association, State of the Air 2017*
- Philadelphia* was highlighted as one of the 25 metro areas most polluted by short-term particle pollution (24-hour PM 2.5) in the U.S. during 2013 through 2015. The area ranked #20. *American Lung Association, State of the Air 2017*

Health/Fitness Rankings

- For each of the 50 most populous metro areas in the United States, the American College of Sports Medicine's American Fitness Index evaluated infrastructure, community assets, and policies that encourage healthy and fit lifestyles, including preventive health behaviors, levels of chronic disease conditions, health care access, and community resources and policies that support physical activity. The Philadelphia* metro area ranked #32 for "community fitness." *www.americanfitnessindex.org, "ACSM American Fitness Index Health and Community Fitness Status of the 50 Largest Metropolitan Areas," May 2017*
- The Philadelphia* metro area was identified as one of the worst cities for bed bugs in America by pest control company Orkin. The area ranked #12 out of 50 based on the number of bed bug treatments Orkin performed from December 2016 to November 2017. *Orkin, "Baltimore and Washington D.C. Continue to Hold Top Spots," January 8, 2018*
- Philadelphia* was identified as a "2016 Spring Allergy Capital." The area ranked #21 out of 100. Three groups of factors were used to identify the most severe cities for people with allergies during the spring season: annual pollen levels; medicine utilization; access to board-certified allergists. *Asthma and Allergy Foundation of America, "Spring Allergy Capitals 2016"*
- Philadelphia* was identified as a "2016 Fall Allergy Capital." The area ranked #32 out of 100. Three groups of factors were used to identify the most severe cities for people with allergies during the fall season: annual pollen levels; medicine utilization; access to board-certified allergists. *Asthma and Allergy Foundation of America, "Fall Allergy Capitals 2016"*
- Philadelphia* was identified as a "2015 Asthma Capital." The area ranked #3 out of the nation's 100 largest metropolitan areas. Criteria: estimated prevalence; self-reported prevalence; crude death rate for asthma; annual pollen score; annual air quality; public smoking laws; number of board-certified asthma specialists; school inhaler access laws; rescue medication use; controller medication use; ER visits for asthma; uninsured rate; poverty rate. *Asthma and Allergy Foundation of America, "Asthma Capitals 2015"*
- The Philadelphia* metro area ranked #132 out of 189 in The Gallup-Healthways Well-Being Index. Criteria: purpose; social well being; financial health; community and physical health. Results are based on telephone interviews with adults, aged 18 and older, living in metropolitan areas in the 50 U.S. states and the District of Columbia. *Gallup-Healthways, "State of American Well-Being, 2017 Community Well-Being Rankings" March 2018*

Real Estate Rankings

- FitSmallBusiness looked at 50 of the largest metropolitan areas in the U.S. to determine which metro was the best to start a real estate business. Data was compiled from such sources as: Zillow, Trulia, U.S. Census Bureau, and the Bureau of Labor Statistics. Criteria: location; inventory; annual wages; median sales price of homes; days on the market; median price cut percentage; and other factors that would influence real estate professional growth. The Philadelphia* metro area ranked #17. *fitsmallbusiness.com, "The Best Cities to Become a Real Estate Agent in 2018," January 30, 2018*
- Philadelphia* was ranked #138 out of 238 metro areas in terms of housing affordability in 2017 by the National Association of Home Builders (#1 = most affordable). Criteria: the share of homes sold in that area affordable to a family earning the local median income, based on standard mortgage underwriting criteria. *National Association of Home Builders®, NAHB-Wells Fargo Housing Opportunity Index, 4th Quarter 2017*
- The nation's largest metro areas were analyzed in terms of the percentage of households entering some stage of foreclosure in 2017. The Philadelphia* metro area ranked #3 out of 10 (#1 = highest foreclosure rate). *RealtyTrac, "2017 Year-End U.S. Foreclosure Market Report™," January 16, 2018*

Safety Rankings

- The National Insurance Crime Bureau ranked 382 metro areas in the U.S. in terms of per capita rates of vehicle theft. The Philadelphia* metro area ranked #208 (#1 = highest rate). Criteria: number of vehicle theft offenses per 100,000 inhabitants in 2016. *National Insurance Crime Bureau, "Hot Spots 2016," June 8, 2017*

Seniors/Retirement Rankings

- From its Best Cities for Successful Aging indexes, the Milken Institute generated rankings for metropolitan areas, weighing data in nine categories—health care, wellness, living arrangements, transportation and convenience, financial characteristics, education, employment, community engagement, and overall livability. The Philadelphia* metro area was ranked #52 overall in the large metro area category. *Milken Institute, "Best Cities for Successful Aging, 2017" March 14, 2017*

Sports/Recreation Rankings

- According to the personal finance website NerdWallet, the Philadelphia* metro area, at #10, is one of the nation's top dozen metro areas for sports fans. Criteria included the presence of all four major sports—MLB, NFL, NHL, and NBA, fan enthusiasm (as measured by game attendance), ticket affordability, and "sports culture," that is, number of sports bars. *www.nerdwallet.com, "Best Cities for Sports Fans," May 5, 2013*

Transportation Rankings

- The Philadelphia* metro area appeared on *Forbes* list of places with the most extreme commutes. The metro area ranked #9 out of 10. Criteria: average travel time; percentage of mega commuters. Mega-commuters travel more than 90 minutes and 50 miles each way to work. *Forbes.com, "The Cities with the Most Extreme Commutes," March 5, 2013*

Miscellaneous Rankings

- The watchdog site Charity Navigator conducts an annual study of charities in the nation's major markets both to analyze statistical differences in their financial, accountability, and transparency practices and to track year-to-year variations in individual philanthropic communities. Charity Navigator's analysis demonstrated that the financial, accountability and transparency behaviors of America's largest charities can be influenced by the metropolitan market within which the charity operates. The Philadelphia* metro area was ranked #20 among the 30 metro markets in the rating category of Overall Score. *www.charitynavigator.org, "2017 Metro Market Study," May 1, 2017*

- The Harris Poll's Happiness Index survey revealed that of the top ten U.S. markets, the Philadelphia* metro area residents ranked #3 in happiness. Criteria included strong assent to positive statements and strong disagreement with negative ones, and degree of agreement with a series of statements about respondents' personal relationships and general outlook. *www.theharrispoll.com, "Dallas/Fort Worth Is "Happiest" City among America's Top Ten Markets," September 4, 2013*

- Energizer Personal Care, the makers of Edge® shave gel, in partnership with Sperling's BestPlaces, ranked 50 major metro areas in terms of everyday irritations. The Philadelphia* metro area ranked #4 the 50 metro area most irritating to guys. Criteria: high male-to-female ratio; poor sports team performance and high ticket prices; slow traffic; lack of job availability; unaffordable housing; extreme weather; lack of nightlife and fitness options. *Energizer Personal Care, "Most Irritating Cities for Guys," August 26, 2013*

- The National Alliance to End Homelessness listed the 25 most populous metro areas with the highest rate of homelessness. The Philadelphia* metro area had a high rate of homelessness. Criteria: number of homeless people per 10,000 population in 2016. *National Alliance to End Homelessness, "Homelessness in the 25 Most Populous U.S. Metro Areas," September 1, 2017*

*Upper Dublin is located within the Philadelphia-Camden-Wilmington, PA-NJ-DE-MD Metropolitan Statistical Area.

Business Environment

CITY FINANCES

City Government Finances

Component	2015 ($000)	2015 ($ per capita)
Total Revenues	29,991	1,144
Total Expenditures	32,826	1,252
Debt Outstanding	31,036	1,184
Cash and Securities[1]	42,484	1,621

Note: (1) Cash and security holdings of a government at the close of its fiscal year,, including those of its dependent agencies, utilities, and liquor stores.
Source: U.S Census Bureau, State & Local Government Finances 2015

City Government Revenue by Source

Source	2015 ($000)	2015 ($ per capita)	2015 (%)
General Revenue			
From Federal Government	50	2	0.2
From State Government	2,067	79	6.9
From Local Governments	13	0	0.0
Taxes			
Property	12,036	459	40.1
Sales and Gross Receipts	0	0	0.0
Personal Income	7,340	280	24.5
Corporate Income	0	0	0.0
Motor Vehicle License	0	0	0.0
Other Taxes	2,911	111	9.7
Current Charges	2,841	108	9.5
Liquor Store	0	0	0.0
Utility	0	0	0.0
Employee Retirement	1,516	58	5.1

Source: U.S Census Bureau, State & Local Government Finances 2015

City Government Expenditures by Function

Function	2015 ($000)	2015 ($ per capita)	2015 (%)
General Direct Expenditures			
Air Transportation	0	0	0.0
Corrections	0	0	0.0
Education	0	0	0.0
Employment Security Administration	0	0	0.0
Financial Administration	566	21	1.7
Fire Protection	1,235	47	3.8
General Public Buildings	1,101	42	3.4
Governmental Administration, Other	1,927	73	5.9
Health	0	0	0.0
Highways	8,018	305	24.4
Hospitals	0	0	0.0
Housing and Community Development	524	20	1.6
Interest on General Debt	1,437	54	4.4
Judicial and Legal	0	0	0.0
Libraries	1,073	40	3.3
Parking	0	0	0.0
Parks and Recreation	2,071	79	6.3
Police Protection	6,882	262	21.0
Public Welfare	0	0	0.0
Sewerage	965	36	2.9
Solid Waste Management	4,543	173	13.8
Veterans' Services	0	0	0.0
Liquor Store	0	0	0.0
Utility	107	4	0.3
Employee Retirement	1,138	43	3.5

Source: U.S Census Bureau, State & Local Government Finances 2015

DEMOGRAPHICS

Population Growth

Area	1990 Census	2000 Census	2010 Census	2016* Estimate	Population Growth (%) 1990-2016	2010-2016
City	24,028	25,878	25,569	26,181	9.0	2.4
MSA[1]	5,435,470	5,687,147	5,965,343	6,047,721	11.3	1.4
U.S.	248,709,873	281,421,906	308,745,538	318,558,162	28.1	3.2

Note: (1) Figures cover the Philadelphia-Camden-Wilmington, PA-NJ-DE-MD Metropolitan Statistical Area—see Appendix B for areas included; (*) 2012-2016 5-year estimated population
Source: U.S. Census Bureau, 1990 Census, Census 2000, Census 2010, 2012-2016 American Community Survey 5-Year Estimates

Household Size

Area	Persons in Household (%) One	Two	Three	Four	Five	Six	Seven or More	Average Household Size
City	19.0	33.9	19.3	18.1	7.7	1.7	0.4	2.70
MSA[1]	29.3	31.8	16.4	13.5	5.9	2.1	1.1	2.60
U.S.	27.7	33.7	15.7	13.1	6.0	2.3	1.5	2.60

Note: (1) Figures cover the Philadelphia-Camden-Wilmington, PA-NJ-DE-MD Metropolitan Statistical Area—see Appendix B for areas included
Source: U.S. Census Bureau, 2012-2016 American Community Survey 5-Year Estimates

Race

Area	White Alone[2] (%)	Black Alone[2] (%)	Asian Alone[2] (%)	AIAN[3] Alone[2] (%)	NHOPI[4] Alone[2] (%)	Other Race Alone[2] (%)	Two or More Races (%)
City	85.3	5.4	7.9	0.0	0.0	0.0	1.4
MSA[1]	67.5	20.9	5.6	0.2	0.0	3.2	2.6
U.S.	73.3	12.6	5.2	0.8	0.2	4.8	3.1

Note: (1) Figures cover the Philadelphia-Camden-Wilmington, PA-NJ-DE-MD Metropolitan Statistical Area—see Appendix B for areas included; (2) Alone is defined as not being in combination with one or more other races; (3) American Indian and Alaska Native; (4) Native Hawaiian and Other Pacific Islander
Source: U.S. Census Bureau, 2012-2016 American Community Survey 5-Year Estimates

Hispanic or Latino Origin

Area	Total (%)	Mexican (%)	Puerto Rican (%)	Cuban (%)	Other (%)
City	2.0	0.6	0.3	0.0	1.1
MSA[1]	8.8	1.8	4.4	0.2	2.3
U.S.	17.3	11.0	1.7	0.7	4.0

Note: Persons of Hispanic or Latino origin can be of any race; (1) Figures cover the Philadelphia-Camden-Wilmington, PA-NJ-DE-MD Metropolitan Statistical Area—see Appendix B for areas included
Source: U.S. Census Bureau, 2012-2016 American Community Survey 5-Year Estimates

Segregation

Type	Segregation Indices[1] 1990	2000	2010	2010 Rank[2]	Percent Change 1990-2000	1990-2010	2000-2010
Black/White	75.2	71.0	68.4	9	-4.2	-6.8	-2.6
Asian/White	42.4	44.1	42.3	42	1.7	0.0	-1.8
Hispanic/White	60.9	58.5	55.1	12	-2.5	-5.9	-3.4

Note: All figures cover the Metropolitan Statistical Area—see Appendix B for areas included; Figures are based on an analysis of 1990, 2000, and 2010 Census Decennial Census tract data by William H. Frey, Brookings Institution and the University of Michigan Social Science Data Analysis Network. In this analysis all racial groups (whites, blacks, and asians) are non-Hispanic members of those races. Hispanics are shown as a separate category; (1) Segregation Indices are Dissimilarity Indices that measure the degree to which the minority group is distributed differently than whites across census tracts. They range from 0 (complete integration) to 100 (complete segregation) where the value indicates the percentage of the minority group that needs to move to be distributed exactly like whites; (2) Ranges from 1 (most segregated) to 102 (least segregated); n/a not available.
Source: www.CensusScope.org

Ancestry

Area	German	Irish	English	American	Italian	Polish	French[2]	Scottish	Dutch
City	20.4	23.6	8.2	4.9	16.1	8.1	1.4	1.8	0.8
MSA[1]	15.7	19.2	7.1	3.6	13.7	5.2	1.5	1.3	0.9
U.S.	14.4	10.4	7.7	6.9	5.4	2.9	2.6	1.7	1.3

Note: Figures are the percentage of the total population reporting a particular ancestry. The nine most commonly reported ancestries in the U.S. are shown. Figures include multiple ancestries (e.g. if a person reported being Irish and Italian, they were included in both columns); (1) Figures cover the Philadelphia-Camden-Wilmington, PA-NJ-DE-MD Metropolitan Statistical Area—see Appendix B for areas included; (2) Excludes Basque
Source: U.S. Census Bureau, 2012-2016 American Community Survey 5-Year Estimates

Foreign-Born Population

Area	Percent of Population Born in								
	Any Foreign Country	Asia	Mexico	Europe	Carribean	Central America[2]	South America	Africa	Canada
City	9.8	6.4	0.3	1.9	0.1	0.1	0.6	0.3	0.0
MSA[1]	10.3	4.2	0.9	1.9	1.2	0.4	0.6	0.9	0.1
U.S.	13.2	4.0	3.6	1.5	1.3	1.0	0.9	0.6	0.3

Note: (1) Figures cover the Philadelphia-Camden-Wilmington, PA-NJ-DE-MD Metropolitan Statistical Area—see Appendix B for areas included; (2) Excludes Mexico.
Source: U.S. Census Bureau, 2012-2016 American Community Survey 5-Year Estimates

Marital Status

Area	Never Married	Now Married[2]	Separated	Widowed	Divorced
City	25.3	62.6	1.3	5.1	5.8
MSA[1]	37.4	45.1	2.2	6.2	9.1
U.S.	33.0	48.1	2.1	5.9	11.0

Note: Figures are percentages and cover the population 15 years of age and older; (1) Figures cover the Philadelphia-Camden-Wilmington, PA-NJ-DE-MD Metropolitan Statistical Area—see Appendix B for areas included; (2) Excludes separated
Source: U.S. Census Bureau, 2012-2016 American Community Survey 5-Year Estimates

Disability Status

Area	All Ages	Under 18 Years Old	18 to 64 Years Old	65 Years and Over
City	7.7	2.3	5.4	22.6
MSA[1]	12.3	4.6	10.2	34.0
U.S.	12.5	4.1	10.3	35.7

Note: Figures show percent of the civilian noninstitutionalized population that reported having a disability. Disability status is determined from six types of difficulty: vision, hearing, cognitive, ambulatory, self-care, and independent living. For children under 5 years old, hearing and vision difficulty are used to determine disability status. For children between the ages of 5 and 14, disability status is determined from hearing, vision, cognitive, ambulatory, and self-care difficulties. For people aged 15 years and older, they are considered to have a disability if they have difficulty with any one of the six difficulty types; Note: (1) Figures cover the Philadelphia-Camden-Wilmington, PA-NJ-DE-MD Metropolitan Statistical Area—see Appendix B for areas included
Source: U.S. Census Bureau, 2012-2016 American Community Survey 5-Year Estimates

Age

Area	Percent of Population									Median Age
	Under Age 5	Age 5–19	Age 20–34	Age 35–44	Age 45–54	Age 55–64	Age 65–74	Age 75–84	Age 85+	
City	4.9	20.5	12.6	12.4	16.7	15.2	10.3	4.8	2.6	44.7
MSA[1]	6.0	19.1	20.8	12.4	14.3	13.0	8.0	4.4	2.2	38.4
U.S.	6.2	19.6	20.7	12.7	13.6	12.6	8.3	4.3	1.9	37.7

Note: (1) Figures cover the Philadelphia-Camden-Wilmington, PA-NJ-DE-MD Metropolitan Statistical Area—see Appendix B for areas included
Source: U.S. Census Bureau, 2012-2016 American Community Survey 5-Year Estimates

Gender

Area	Males	Females	Males per 100 Females
City	12,469	13,712	90.9
MSA[1]	2,923,439	3,124,282	93.6
U.S.	156,765,322	161,792,840	96.9

Note: (1) Figures cover the Philadelphia-Camden-Wilmington, PA-NJ-DE-MD Metropolitan Statistical Area—see Appendix B for areas included
Source: U.S. Census Bureau, 2012-2016 American Community Survey 5-Year Estimates

Religious Groups by Family

Area	Catholic	Baptist	Non-Den.	Methodist[2]	Lutheran	LDS[3]	Pente-costal	Presby-terian[4]	Muslim[5]	Judaism
MSA[1]	33.5	3.9	2.9	3.0	1.9	0.3	0.9	2.1	1.3	1.4
U.S.	19.1	9.3	4.0	4.0	2.3	2.0	1.9	1.6	0.8	0.7

Note: Figures are the number of adherents as a percentage of the total population; (1) Figures cover the Philadelphia-Camden-Wilmington, PA-NJ-DE-MD Metropolitan Statistical Area—see Appendix B for areas included; (2) Methodist/Pietist; (3) Latter Day Saints; (4) Reformed; (5) Figures are estimates
Source: Association of Statisticians of American Religious Bodies, 2010 U.S. Religion Census: Religious Congregations & Membership Study

Religious Groups by Tradition

Area	Catholic	Evangelical Protestant	Mainline Protestant	Other Tradition	Black Protestant	Orthodox
MSA[1]	33.5	6.3	8.9	3.7	1.8	0.4
U.S.	19.1	16.2	7.3	4.3	1.6	0.3

Note: Figures are the number of adherents as a percentage of the total population; (1) Figures cover the Philadelphia-Camden-Wilmington, PA-NJ-DE-MD Metropolitan Statistical Area—see Appendix B for areas included
Source: Association of Statisticians of American Religious Bodies, 2010 U.S. Religion Census: Religious Congregations & Membership Study

ECONOMY

Gross Metropolitan Product

Area	2014	2015	2016	2017	Rank[2]
MSA[1]	389.2	403.6	416.4	433.9	8

Note: Figures are in billions of dollars; (1) Figures cover the Philadelphia-Camden-Wilmington, PA-NJ-DE-MD Metropolitan Statistical Area—see Appendix B for areas included; (2) Rank is based on 2015 data and ranges from 1 to 381
Source: The U.S. Conference of Mayors, U.S. Metro Economies: GMP and Employment Report, 2015-2017

Economic Growth

Area	2012-14 (%)	2015 (%)	2016 (%)	2017 (%)	Rank[2]
MSA[1]	0.9	2.2	1.6	2.1	216
U.S.	2.0	2.4	1.9	2.6	–

Note: Figures are real gross metropolitan product (GMP) growth rates and represent average annual percent change; (1) Figures cover the Philadelphia-Camden-Wilmington, PA-NJ-DE-MD Metropolitan Statistical Area—see Appendix B for areas included; (2) Rank is based on 2012-2014 average annual percent change and ranges from 1 to 381
Source: The U.S. Conference of Mayors, U.S. Metro Economies: GMP and Employment Report, 2015-2017

Metropolitan Area Exports

Area	2011	2012	2013	2014	2015	2016	Rank[2]
MSA[1]	26,155.8	22,991.6	24,929.2	26,321.3	24,236.1	21,359.9	14

Note: Figures are in millions of dollars; (1) Figures cover the Philadelphia-Camden-Wilmington, PA-NJ-DE-MD Metropolitan Statistical Area—see Appendix B for areas included; (2) Rank is based on 2016 data and ranges from 1 to 385
Source: U.S. Department of Commerce, International Trade Administration, Office of Trade & Industry Information, Manufacturing & Services, data extracted March 15, 2018

Building Permits

Area	Single-Family 2016	Single-Family 2017p	Single-Family Pct. Chg.	Multi-Family 2016	Multi-Family 2017p	Multi-Family Pct. Chg.	Total 2016	Total 2017p	Total Pct. Chg.
City	72	69	-4.2	0	20	n/a	72	89	23.6
MSA[1]	6,820	7,278	6.7	5,295	6,021	13.7	12,115	13,299	9.8
U.S.	750,800	817,300	8.9	455,800	446,800	-2.0	1,206,600	1,264,100	4.8

Note: (1) Figures cover the Philadelphia-Camden-Wilmington, PA-NJ-DE-MD Metropolitan Statistical Area—see Appendix B for areas included; Figures represent new, privately-owned housing units authorized (unadjusted data); All permit data are based on estimates with imputation; (p) preliminary data.
Source: U.S. Census Bureau, Manufacturing, Mining, and Construction Statistics, Building Permits, 2016, 2017

Bankruptcy Filings

Area	Business Filings 2016	Business Filings 2017	Business Filings % Chg.	Nonbusiness Filings 2016	Nonbusiness Filings 2017	Nonbusiness Filings % Chg.
Montgomery County	65	59	-9.2	1,057	1,038	-1.8
U.S.	24,114	23,157	-4.0	770,846	765,863	-0.6

Note: Business filings include Chapter 7, Chapter 11, Chapter 12, and Chapter 13; Nonbusiness filings include Chapter 7, Chapter 11, and Chapter 13
Source: Administrative Office of the U.S. Courts, Business and Nonbusiness Bankruptcy, County Cases Commenced by Chapter of the Bankruptcy Code, During the 12-Month Period Ending December 31, 2016 and Business and Nonbusiness Bankruptcy, County Cases Commenced by Chapter of the Bankruptcy Code, During the 12-Month Period Ending December 31, 2017

Housing Vacancy Rates

Area	Gross Vacancy Rate[2] (%) 2015	2016	2017	Year-Round Vacancy Rate[3] (%) 2015	2016	2017	Rental Vacancy Rate[4] (%) 2015	2016	2017	Homeowner Vacancy Rate[5] (%) 2015	2016	2017
MSA[1]	10.7	9.3	8.6	10.2	8.6	8.3	7.6	6.8	7.3	2.4	1.4	1.6
U.S.	12.9	12.8	12.7	10.0	9.9	9.9	7.1	6.9	7.2	1.8	1.7	1.6

Note: (1) Figures cover the Philadelphia-Camden-Wilmington, PA-NJ-DE-MD Metropolitan Statistical Area—see Appendix B for areas included; (2) The percentage of the total housing inventory that is vacant; (3) The percentage of the housing inventory (excluding seasonal units) that is year-round vacant; (4) The percentage of rental inventory that is vacant for rent; (5) The percentage of homeowner inventory that is vacant for sale
Source: U.S. Census Bureau, Housing Vacancies and Homeownership Annual Statistics: 2015, 2016, 2017

INCOME

Income

Area	Per Capita ($)	Median Household ($)	Average Household ($)
City	55,003	111,516	150,599
MSA[1]	34,118	63,952	88,881
U.S.	29,829	55,322	77,866

Note: (1) Figures cover the Philadelphia-Camden-Wilmington, PA-NJ-DE-MD Metropolitan Statistical Area—see Appendix B for areas included
Source: U.S. Census Bureau, 2012-2016 American Community Survey 5-Year Estimates

Household Income Distribution

Area	Percent of Households Earning: Under $15,000	$15,000 -$24,999	$25,000 -$34,999	$35,000 -$49,999	$50,000 -$74,999	$75,000 -$99,999	$100,000 -$149,999	$150,000 and up
City	3.5	4.9	4.2	6.3	12.3	13.3	21.9	33.7
MSA[1]	11.3	8.8	8.4	11.6	16.4	12.3	16.0	15.2
U.S.	12.1	10.2	9.9	13.2	17.8	12.2	13.5	11.1

Note: (1) Figures cover the Philadelphia-Camden-Wilmington, PA-NJ-DE-MD Metropolitan Statistical Area—see Appendix B for areas included
Source: U.S. Census Bureau, 2012-2016 American Community Survey 5-Year Estimates

Poverty Rate

Area	All Ages	Under 18 Years Old	18 to 64 Years Old	65 Years and Over
City	3.0	3.9	2.5	3.7
MSA[1]	13.1	18.1	12.3	8.9
U.S.	15.1	21.2	14.2	9.3

Note: Figures are percentage of people whose income during the past 12 months was below the poverty level; (1) Figures cover the Philadelphia-Camden-Wilmington, PA-NJ-DE-MD Metropolitan Statistical Area—see Appendix B for areas included

Source: U.S. Census Bureau, 2012-2016 American Community Survey 5-Year Estimates

EMPLOYMENT

Labor Force and Employment

Area	Civilian Labor Force			Workers Employed		
	Dec. 2016	Dec. 2017	% Chg.	Dec. 2016	Dec. 2017	% Chg.
City	14,108	14,076	-0.2	13,657	13,646	-0.1
MD[1]	1,060,053	1,058,151	-0.2	1,021,300	1,022,167	0.1
U.S.	158,968,000	159,880,000	0.6	151,798,000	153,602,000	1.2

Note: Data is not seasonally adjusted and covers workers 16 years of age and older; (1) Figures cover the Montgomery County-Bucks County-Chester County, PA Metropolitan Division—see Appendix B for areas included

Source: Bureau of Labor Statistics, Local Area Unemployment Statistics

Unemployment Rate

Area	2017											
	Jan.	Feb.	Mar.	Apr.	May	Jun.	Jul.	Aug.	Sep.	Oct.	Nov.	Dec.
City	3.3	3.5	3.2	2.9	3.5	3.5	4.0	4.0	3.5	3.2	3.2	3.1
MD[1]	4.3	4.4	4.0	3.6	3.9	4.0	4.3	4.3	3.7	3.5	3.6	3.4
U.S.	5.1	4.9	4.6	4.1	4.1	4.5	4.6	4.5	4.1	3.9	3.9	3.9

Note: Data is not seasonally adjusted and covers workers 16 years of age and older; (1) Figures cover the Montgomery County-Bucks County-Chester County, PA Metropolitan Division—see Appendix B for areas included

Source: Bureau of Labor Statistics, Local Area Unemployment Statistics

Average Wages

Occupation	$/Hr.	Occupation	$/Hr.
Accountants and Auditors	38.60	Maids and Housekeeping Cleaners	12.20
Automotive Mechanics	21.90	Maintenance and Repair Workers	20.50
Bookkeepers	21.00	Marketing Managers	78.40
Carpenters	28.20	Nuclear Medicine Technologists	38.30
Cashiers	10.20	Nurses, Licensed Practical	26.10
Clerks, General Office	17.30	Nurses, Registered	34.90
Clerks, Receptionists/Information	14.40	Nursing Assistants	14.70
Clerks, Shipping/Receiving	17.00	Packers and Packagers, Hand	14.20
Computer Programmers	41.80	Physical Therapists	41.20
Computer Systems Analysts	47.40	Postal Service Mail Carriers	24.30
Computer User Support Specialists	25.40	Real Estate Brokers	37.70
Cooks, Restaurant	14.50	Retail Salespersons	14.10
Dentists	68.00	Sales Reps., Exc. Tech./Scientific	38.60
Electrical Engineers	47.80	Sales Reps., Tech./Scientific	53.30
Electricians	33.00	Secretaries, Exc. Legal/Med./Exec.	18.30
Financial Managers	77.10	Security Guards	13.20
First-Line Supervisors/Managers, Sales	23.30	Surgeons	115.70
Food Preparation Workers	11.90	Teacher Assistants*	14.10
General and Operations Managers	71.40	Teachers, Elementary School*	36.60
Hairdressers/Cosmetologists	14.50	Teachers, Secondary School*	35.20
Internists, General	72.30	Telemarketers	15.40
Janitors and Cleaners	15.20	Truck Drivers, Heavy/Tractor-Trailer	23.30
Landscaping/Groundskeeping Workers	15.40	Truck Drivers, Light/Delivery Svcs.	17.30
Lawyers	65.40	Waiters and Waitresses	11.20

Note: Wage data covers the Montgomery County-Bucks County-Chester County, PA Metropolitan Division—see Appendix B for areas included; (*) Hourly wages for elementary/secondary school teachers and teacher assistants were calculated by the editors from annual wage data based on a 40 hour work week; n/a not available.

Source: Bureau of Labor Statistics, Metro Area Occupational Employment & Wage Estimates, May 2017

Employment by Occupation

Occupation Classification	City (%)	MSA[1] (%)	U.S. (%)
Management, Business, Science, and Arts	60.4	42.4	37.0
Natural Resources, Construction, and Maintenance	3.3	6.9	8.9
Production, Transportation, and Material Moving	4.0	9.6	12.2
Sales and Office	20.6	24.0	23.8
Service	11.7	17.2	18.1

Note: Figures cover employed civilians 16 years of age and older; (1) Figures cover the Philadelphia-Camden-Wilmington, PA-NJ-DE-MD Metropolitan Statistical Area—see Appendix B for areas included
Source: U.S. Census Bureau, 2012-2016 American Community Survey 5-Year Estimates

Employment by Industry

Sector	MD[1] Number of Employees	MD[1] Percent of Total	U.S. Percent of Total
Construction, Mining, and Logging	50,200	4.7	5.2
Education and Health Services	196,700	18.3	15.9
Financial Activities	82,800	7.7	5.7
Government	85,000	7.9	15.3
Information	20,800	1.9	1.9
Leisure and Hospitality	84,100	7.8	10.7
Manufacturing	91,300	8.5	8.5
Other Services	47,300	4.4	3.9
Professional and Business Services	207,000	19.3	14.0
Retail Trade	122,400	11.4	11.0
Transportation, Warehousing, and Utilities	29,700	2.8	4.1
Wholesale Trade	57,400	5.3	4.0

Note: Figures are non-farm employment as of December 2017. Figures are not seasonally adjusted and include workers 16 years of age and older; (1) Figures cover the Montgomery County-Bucks County-Chester County, PA Metropolitan Division—see Appendix B for areas included
Source: Bureau of Labor Statistics, Current Employment Statistics, Employment, Hours, and Earnings

Occupations with Greatest Projected Employment Growth: 2017 – 2019

Occupation[1]	2017 Employment	2019 Projected Employment	Numeric Employment Change	Percent Employment Change
Personal Care Aides	95,040	101,150	6,110	6.4
Combined Food Preparation and Serving Workers, Including Fast Food	149,690	154,700	5,010	3.3
Registered Nurses	143,300	147,290	3,990	2.8
Laborers and Freight, Stock, and Material Movers, Hand	138,050	141,860	3,810	2.8
Home Health Aides	46,950	50,700	3,750	8.0
Waiters and Waitresses	100,790	102,540	1,750	1.7
Janitors and Cleaners, Except Maids and Housekeeping Cleaners	98,590	100,250	1,660	1.7
Cooks, Restaurant	49,820	51,120	1,300	2.6
Software Developers, Applications	25,890	27,190	1,300	5.0
Nursing Assistants	80,510	81,790	1,280	1.6

Note: Projections cover Pennsylvania; (1) Sorted by numeric employment change
Source: www.projectionscentral.com, State Occupational Projections, 2017–2019 Short-Term Projections

Fastest Growing Occupations: 2017 – 2019

Occupation[1]	2017 Employment	2019 Projected Employment	Numeric Employment Change	Percent Employment Change
Home Health Aides	46,950	50,700	3,750	8.0
Statisticians	2,710	2,880	170	6.5
Personal Care Aides	95,040	101,150	6,110	6.4
Physician Assistants	5,620	5,960	340	6.1
Nurse Practitioners	5,240	5,550	310	6.0
Operations Research Analysts	2,660	2,800	140	5.1
Information Security Analysts	3,020	3,170	150	5.0
Software Developers, Applications	25,890	27,190	1,300	5.0
Nonfarm Animal Caretakers	7,820	8,210	390	4.9
Physical Therapist Assistants	4,660	4,880	220	4.8

Note: Projections cover Pennsylvania; (1) Sorted by percent employment change and excludes occupations with numeric employment change less than 50
Source: www.projectionscentral.com, State Occupational Projections, 2017–2019 Short-Term Projections

TAXES

State Corporate Income Tax Rates

State	Tax Rate (%)	Income Brackets ($)	Num. of Brackets	Financial Institution Tax Rate (%)[a]	Federal Income Tax Ded.
Pennsylvania	9.99	Flat rate	1	(a)	No

Note: Tax rates as of January 1, 2018; (a) Rates listed are the corporate income tax rate applied to financial institutions or excise taxes based on income. Some states have other taxes based upon the value of deposits or shares.
Source: Federation of Tax Administrators, Range of State Corporate Income Tax Rates, January 1, 2018

State Individual Income Tax Rates

State	Tax Rate (%)	Income Brackets ($)	Num. of Brackets	Personal Exempt. ($)[1]		Fed. Inc. Tax Ded.
				Single	Dependents	
Pennsylvania	3.07	Flat rate	1	None	None	No

Note: Tax rates as of January 1, 2018; Local- and county-level taxes are not included; n/a not applicable; (1) Married joint filers generally receive double the single exemption
Source: Federation of Tax Administrators, State Individual Income Tax Rates, January 1, 2018

Various State Sales and Excise Tax Rates

State	State Sales Tax (%)	Gasoline[1] (¢/gal.)	Cigarette[2] ($/pack)	Spirits[3] ($/gal.)	Wine[4] ($/gal.)	Beer[5] ($/gal.)	Recreational Marijuana (%)
Pennsylvania	6.0	58.7	2.60	7.24 (g)	(m)	0.08	Not legal

Note: All tax rates as of January 1, 2018; (1) The American Petroleum Institute has developed a methodology for determining the average tax rate on a gallon of fuel. Rates may include any of the following: excise taxes, environmental fees, storage tank fees, other fees or taxes, general sales tax, and local taxes. In states where gasoline is subject to the general sales tax, or where the fuel tax is based on the average sale price, the average rate determined by API is sensitive to changes in the price of gasoline. States that fully or partially apply general sales taxes to gasoline: CA, CO, GA, IL, IN, MI, NY; (2) The federal excise tax of $1.0066 per pack and local taxes are not included; (3) Rates are those applicable to off-premise sales of 40% alcohol by volume (a.b.v.) distilled spirits in 750ml containers. Local excise taxes are excluded; (4) Rates are those applicable to off-premise sales of 11% a.b.v. non-carbonated wine in 750ml containers; (5) Rates are those applicable to off-premise sales of 4.7% a.b.v. beer in 12 ounce containers; (g) Control states, where the government controls all sales. Products can be subject to ad valorem mark-up as well as excise taxes; (m) Control states, where the government controls all sales. Products can be subject to ad valorem mark-up as well as excise taxes.
Source: Tax Foundation, 2018 Facts & Figures: How Does Your State Compare?

State Business Tax Climate Index Rankings

State	Overall Rank	Corporate Tax Rank	Individual Income Tax Rank	Sales Tax Rank	Unemployment Insurance Tax Rank	Property Tax Rank
Pennsylvania	26	44	17	21	50	33

Note: The index is a measure of how each state's tax laws affect economic performance. The lower the rank, the more favorable a state's tax system is for business. States without a given tax are given a ranking of 1. The scores/rankings for the District of Columbia do not affect other states. The 2018 index represents the tax climate as of July 1, 2017.
Source: Tax Foundation, State Business Tax Climate Index 2018

TRANSPORTATION

Means of Transportation to Work

Area	Car/Truck/Van		Public Transportation			Bicycle	Walked	Other Means	Worked at Home
	Drove Alone	Car-pooled	Bus	Subway	Railroad				
City	78.8	5.7	0.7	0.3	4.9	0.5	1.3	0.6	7.1
MSA[1]	73.1	7.7	5.4	1.7	2.3	0.6	3.7	1.0	4.3
U.S.	76.4	9.3	2.6	1.9	0.6	0.6	2.8	1.3	4.6

Note: Figures are percentages and cover workers 16 years of age and older; (1) Figures cover the Philadelphia-Camden-Wilmington, PA-NJ-DE-MD Metropolitan Statistical Area—see Appendix B for areas included
Source: U.S. Census Bureau, 2012-2016 American Community Survey 5-Year Estimates

Travel Time to Work

Area	Less Than 10 Minutes	10 to 19 Minutes	20 to 29 Minutes	30 to 44 Minutes	45 to 59 Minutes	60 to 89 Minutes	90 Minutes or More
City	12.1	24.6	18.3	24.1	11.3	7.0	2.8
MSA[1]	9.8	24.7	20.5	23.5	10.7	7.9	3.0
U.S.	12.9	29.2	20.9	20.4	8.0	6.0	2.7

Note: Note: Figures are percentages and include workers 16 years old and over; (1) Figures cover the Philadelphia-Camden-Wilmington, PA-NJ-DE-MD Metropolitan Statistical Area—see Appendix B for areas included
Source: U.S. Census Bureau, 2012-2016 American Community Survey 5-Year Estimates

Freeway Travel Time Index

Area	1985	1990	1995	2000	2005	2010	2014
Urban Area Rank[1,2]	20	21	26	26	24	22	25
Urban Area Index[1]	1.12	1.15	1.18	1.21	1.25	1.24	1.24
Average Index[3]	1.09	1.11	1.14	1.17	1.20	1.19	1.20

Note: Freeway Travel Time Index—the ratio of travel time in the peak period to the travel time at free-flow conditions. For example, a value of 1.30 indicates a 20-minute free-flow trip takes 26 minutes in the peak (20 minutes x 1.30 = 26 minutes); (1) Covers the Philadelphia PA-NJ-DE-MD urban area; (2) Rank is based on 101 urban areas (#1 = highest travel time index); (3) Average of 101 urban areas
Source: Texas Transportation Institute, 2015 Urban Mobility Scorecard, August 2015

Freeway Commuter Stress Index

Area	1985	1990	1995	2000	2005	2010	2014
Urban Area Rank[1,2]	31	28	33	34	30	31	31
Urban Area Index[1]	1.15	1.19	1.22	1.25	1.29	1.28	1.28
Average Index[3]	1.13	1.16	1.19	1.22	1.25	1.24	1.25

Note: The Freeway Commuter Stress Index is the same as the Freeway Travel Time Index (see table above) except that it includes only the travel in the peak directions during the peak periods; the TTI includes travel in all directions during the peak period. Thus, the CSI is more indicative of the work trip experienced by each commuter on a daily basis; (1) Covers the Philadelphia PA-NJ-DE-MD urban area; (2) Rank is based on 101 urban areas (#1 = highest travel time index); (3) Average of 101 urban areas
Source: Texas Transportation Institute, 2015 Urban Mobility Scorecard, August 2015

Living Environment

COST OF LIVING

Cost of Living Index

Composite Index	Groceries	Housing	Utilities	Trans-portation	Health Care	Misc. Goods/ Services
117.0	116.2	129.5	124.5	114.9	105.7	107.2

Note: The Cost of Living Index measures regional differences in the cost of consumer goods and services, excluding taxes and non-consumer expenditures, for professional and managerial households in the top income quintile. It is based on more than 50,000 prices covering almost 60 different items for which prices are collected three times a year by chambers of commerce, economic development organizations or university applied economic centers in each participating urban area. The numbers shown should be read as a percentage above or below the national average of 100. For example, a value of 115.4 in the groceries column indicates that grocery prices are 15.4% higher than the national average. Small differences in the index numbers should not be interpreted as significant; Figures cover the Philadelphia PA urban area.
Source: The Council for Community and Economic Research, ACCRA Cost of Living Index, 2017

Grocery Prices

Area[1]	T-Bone Steak ($/pound)	Frying Chicken ($/pound)	Whole Milk ($/half gal.)	Eggs ($/dozen)	Orange Juice ($/64 oz.)	Coffee ($/11.5 oz.)
City[2]	11.82	1.46	2.11	1.74	3.92	4.10
Avg.	11.29	1.40	2.02	1.47	3.55	4.37
Min.	7.71	0.93	1.04	0.70	2.86	3.24
Max.	15.83	2.39	4.03	3.92	6.29	8.16

Note: (1) Values for the local area are compared with the average, minimum and maximum values for all 294 areas in the Cost of Living Index; (2) Figures cover the Philadelphia PA urban area; ***T-Bone Steak*** *(price per pound);* ***Frying Chicken*** *(price per pound, whole fryer);* ***Whole Milk*** *(half gallon carton);* ***Eggs*** *(price per dozen, Grade A, large);* ***Orange Juice*** *(64 oz. Tropicana or Florida Natural);* ***Coffee*** *(11.5 oz. can, vacuum-packed, Maxwell House, Hills Bros, or Folgers).*
Source: The Council for Community and Economic Research, ACCRA Cost of Living Index, 2017

Housing and Utility Costs

Area[1]	New Home Price ($)	Apartment Rent ($/month)	All Electric ($/month)	Part Electric ($/month)	Other Energy ($/month)	Telephone ($/month)
City[2]	424,983	1,411	-	107.26	69.96	42.00
Avg.	335,956	1,047	175.01	97.34	67.93	28.71
Min.	187,788	491	109.48	49.33	35.44	12.39
Max.	1,739,087	4,559	432.62	227.09	353.33	44.61

Note: (1) Values for the local area are compared with the average, minimum and maximum values for all 294 areas in the Cost of Living Index; (2) Figures cover the Philadelphia PA urban area; ***New Home Price*** *(2,400 sf living area, 8,000 sf lot, in urban area with full utilities);* ***Apartment Rent*** *(950 sf 2 bedroom/1.5 or 2 bath, unfurnished, excluding all utilities except water);* ***All Electric*** *(average monthly cost for an all-electric home);* ***Part Electric*** *(average monthly cost for a part-electric home);* ***Other Energy*** *(average monthly cost for natural gas, fuel oil, coal, wood, and any other forms of energy except electricity);* ***Telephone*** *(price includes basic monthly rate for a private residential line plus additional local usage charges incurred by a family of four).*
Source: The Council for Community and Economic Research, ACCRA Cost of Living Index, 2017

Health Care, Transportation, and Other Costs

Area[1]	Doctor ($/visit)	Dentist ($/visit)	Optometrist ($/visit)	Gasoline ($/gallon)	Beauty Salon ($/visit)	Men's Shirt ($)
City[2]	130.24	96.14	100.71	2.48	56.27	31.77
Avg.	108.00	92.54	101.93	2.25	37.58	30.92
Min.	30.39	60.00	49.75	1.82	16.11	11.20
Max.	193.50	161.94	229.28	3.16	77.35	59.13

Note: (1) Values for the local area are compared with the average, minimum and maximum values for all 294 areas in the Cost of Living Index; (2) Figures cover the Philadelphia PA urban area; ***Doctor*** *(general practitioners routine exam of an established patient);* ***Dentist*** *(adult teeth cleaning and periodic oral examination);* ***Optometrist*** *(full vision eye exam for established adult patient);* ***Gasoline*** *(one gallon regular unleaded, national brand, including all taxes, cash price at self-service pump if available);* ***Beauty Salon*** *(woman's shampoo, trim, and blow-dry);* ***Men's Shirt*** *(cotton/polyester dress shirt, pinpoint weave, long sleeves).*
Source: The Council for Community and Economic Research, ACCRA Cost of Living Index, 2017

HOUSING

House Price Index (HPI)

Area	National Ranking[2]	Quarterly Change (%)	One-Year Change (%)	Five-Year Change (%)
MD[1]	181	0.74	4.24	14.38
U.S.[3]	–	1.61	6.68	34.71

Note: The HPI is a weighted repeat sales index. It measures average price changes in repeat sales or refinancings on the same properties. This information is obtained by reviewing repeat mortgage transactions on single-family properties whose mortgages have been purchased or securitized by Fannie Mae or Freddie Mac in January 1975; (1) Figures cover the Montgomery County-Bucks County-Chester County, PA Metropolitan Division—see Appendix B for areas included; (2) Rankings are based on annual percentage change for all metro areas containing at least 15,000 transactions over the last 10 years and ranges from 1 to 253; (3) figures based on a weighted average of Census Division estimates using a seasonally adjusted, purchase-only index; all figures are for the period ending December 31, 2017
Source: Federal Housing Finance Agency, House Price Index, February 28, 2018

Median Single-Family Home Prices

Area	2015	2016	2017p	Percent Change 2016 to 2017
MSA[1]	223.7	225.4	230.0	2.0
U.S. Average	223.9	235.5	248.8	5.6

Note: Figures are median sales prices of existing single-family homes in thousands of dollars; (p) preliminary; (1) Figures cover the Philadelphia-Camden-Wilmington, PA-NJ-DE-MD Metropolitan Statistical Area—see Appendix B for areas included
Source: National Association of Realtors, Median Sales Price of Existing Single-Family Homes for Metropolitan Areas, 4th Quarter 2017

Qualifying Income Based on Median Sales Price of Existing Single-Family Homes

Area	With 5% Down ($)	With 10% Down ($)	With 20% Down ($)
MSA[1]	50,381	47,729	42,426
U.S. Average	55,585	52,659	46,808

Note: Figures are preliminary; Qualifying income is based on a mortgage rate of 4.17%. Monthly principal and interest payment is limited to 25% of income; (1) Figures cover the Philadelphia-Camden-Wilmington, PA-NJ-DE-MD Metropolitan Statistical Area—see Appendix B for areas included
Source: National Association of Realtors, Qualifying Income Based on Median Sales Price of Existing Single-Family Homes for Metropolitan Areas, 4th Quarter 2017

Median Apartment Condo-Coop Home Prices

Area	2015	2016	2017p	Percent Change 2016 to 2017
MSA[1]	176.5	182.7	185.1	1.3
U.S. Average	210.7	220.7	234.3	6.2

Note: Figures are median sales prices of existing apartment condo-coop homes in thousands of dollars; (p) preliminary; (1) Figures cover the Philadelphia-Camden-Wilmington, PA-NJ-DE-MD Metropolitan Statistical Area—see Appendix B for areas included
Source: National Association of Realtors, Median Sales Price of Existing Apartment Condo-Coop Homes for Metropolitan Areas, 4th Quarter 2017

Home Value Distribution

Area	Under $50,000	$50,000 -$99,999	$100,000 -$149,999	$150,000 -$199,999	$200,000 -$299,999	$300,000 -$499,999	$500,000 -$999,999	$1,000,000 or more
City	2.0	0.5	1.5	2.6	18.4	49.5	24.9	0.6
MSA[1]	4.7	7.9	10.8	15.6	27.1	23.9	8.5	1.4
U.S.	8.8	14.8	15.3	14.9	18.4	16.4	9.0	2.5

Note: Figures are percentages and cover owner-occupied housing units; (1) Figures cover the Philadelphia-Camden-Wilmington, PA-NJ-DE-MD Metropolitan Statistical Area—see Appendix B for areas included
Source: U.S. Census Bureau, 2012-2016 American Community Survey 5-Year Estimates

Homeownership Rate

Area	2009 (%)	2010 (%)	2011 (%)	2012 (%)	2013 (%)	2014 (%)	2015 (%)	2016 (%)	2017 (%)
MSA[1]	69.7	70.7	69.7	69.5	69.1	67.0	67.0	64.7	65.6
U.S.	67.4	66.9	66.1	65.4	65.1	64.5	63.7	63.4	63.9

Note: (1) Figures cover the Philadelphia-Camden-Wilmington, PA-NJ-DE-MD Metropolitan Statistical Area—see Appendix B for areas included
Source: U.S. Census Bureau, Housing Vacancies and Homeownership Annual Statistics: 2009-2017

Year Housing Structure Built

Area	2010 or Later	2000 -2009	1990 -1999	1980 -1989	1970 -1979	1960 -1969	1950 -1959	1940 -1949	Before 1940	Median Year
City	1.4	4.9	12.9	14.0	19.5	20.0	14.9	4.0	8.3	1971
MSA[1]	1.4	8.3	9.4	10.2	12.3	12.1	15.9	8.5	21.8	1963
U.S.	2.3	14.7	14.0	13.7	15.6	10.9	10.6	5.2	13.0	1977

Note: Figures are percentages except for Median Year; Note: (1) Figures cover the Philadelphia-Camden-Wilmington, PA-NJ-DE-MD Metropolitan Statistical Area—see Appendix B for areas included
Source: U.S. Census Bureau, 2012-2016 American Community Survey 5-Year Estimates

Gross Monthly Rent

Area	Under $500	$500 -$999	$1,000 -$1,499	$1,500 -$1,999	$2,000 -$2,499	$2,500 -$2,999	$3,000 and up	Median ($)
City	2.3	7.7	42.2	21.0	11.1	11.7	4.0	1,463
MSA[1]	9.0	37.4	35.4	11.9	3.9	1.3	1.1	1,040
U.S.	11.3	43.3	27.7	10.7	4.0	1.6	1.5	949

Note: Figures are percentages except for Median; Gross rent is the contract rent plus the estimated average monthly cost of utilities (electricity, gas, and water and sewer) and fuels (oil, coal, kerosene, wood, etc.) if these are paid by the renter (or paid for the renter by someone else); (1) Figures cover the Philadelphia-Camden-Wilmington, PA-NJ-DE-MD Metropolitan Statistical Area—see Appendix B for areas included
Source: U.S. Census Bureau, 2012-2016 American Community Survey 5-Year Estimates

HEALTH

Health Risk Factors

Category	MD[1] (%)	U.S. (%)
Adults aged 18–64 who have any kind of health care coverage	93.7	87.7
Adults who reported being in good or excellent health	86.3	83.6
Adults who are current smokers	13.3	17.1
Adults who currently use E-cigarettes	n/a	4.7
Adults who currently use chewing tobacco, snuff, or snus	2.0	4.0
Adults who are heavy drinkers[2]	7.3	6.5
Adults who are binge drinkers[3]	19.6	16.9
Adults who are overweight (BMI 25.0 - 29.9)	34.8	35.3
Adults who are obese (BMI 30.0 - 99.8)	23.1	29.9
Adults who participated in any physical activities in the past month	83.1	76.9
Adults who always or nearly always wears a seat belt	95.3	94.3

Note: n/a not available; (1) Figures cover the Montgomery County-Bucks County-Chester County, PA Metropolitan Division—see Appendix B for areas included; (2) Heavy drinkers are classified as adult men having more than 14 drinks per week and adult women having more than 7 drinks per week; (3) Binge drinkers are classified as males having five or more drinks on one occasion or females having four or more drinks on one occasion
Source: Centers for Disease Control and Prevention, Behaviorial Risk Factor Surveillance System, SMART: Selected Metropolitan Area Risk Trends, 2016

Health Screening Rates

Category	MD[1] (%)	U.S. (%)
Adults 50-75 who have had a blood stool test within the past year	5.6	8.0
Adults 50-75 who have had a colonoscopy in the past 10 years	65.8	63.5
Adults aged 65+ who have had flu shot within the past year	67.0	58.6
Adults aged 65+ who have ever had a pneumonia vaccination	75.4	73.4
Adults who have ever been tested for HIV	32.4	35.6
Women aged 21-65 who have had a pap test in the past three years	79.2	79.8
Men aged 40+ who have had a PSA test within the past two years	45.0	39.5
Women aged 40+ who have had a mammogram within the past two years	74.2	72.5

Note: n/a not available; (1) Figures cover the Montgomery County-Bucks County-Chester County, PA Metropolitan Division—see Appendix B for areas included; Source: Centers for Disease Control and Prevention, Behaviorial Risk Factor Surveillance System, SMART: Selected Metropolitan Area Risk Trends, 2016

Chronic Health Conditions

Category	MD[1] (%)	U.S. (%)
Adults who have ever been told they had a heart attack	3.1	4.4
Adults who have ever been told they have angina or coronary heart disease	3.8	4.1
Adults who have ever been told they had a stroke	n/a	3.1
Adults who have been told they currently have asthma	9.2	9.3
Adults who have ever been told they have arthritis	27.3	25.8
Adults who have ever been told they have diabetes[2]	10.6	10.5
Adults who have ever been told they had skin cancer	9.0	5.9
Adults who have ever been told they had any other types of cancer	9.0	6.7
Adults who have ever been told they have COPD	8.1	6.3
Adults who have ever been told they have kidney disease	n/a	2.8
Adults who have ever been told they have a form of depression	15.0	17.4

Note: n/a not available; (1) Figures cover the Montgomery County-Bucks County-Chester County, PA Metropolitan Division—see Appendix B for areas included; (2) Figures do not include pregnancy-related, borderline, or pre-diabetes
Source: Centers for Disease Control and Prevention, Behaviorial Risk Factor Surveillance System, SMART: Selected Metropolitan Area Risk Trends, 2016

Mortality Rates for the Top 10 Causes of Death in the U.S.

ICD-10[a] Sub-Chapter	ICD-10[a] Code	Age-Adjusted Mortality Rate[1] per 100,000 population	
		County[2]	U.S.
Malignant neoplasms	C00-C97	150.5	158.5
Ischaemic heart diseases	I20-I25	82.3	96.8
Other forms of heart disease	I30-I51	49.4	52.4
Chronic lower respiratory diseases	J40-J47	30.1	40.9
Cerebrovascular diseases	I60-I69	43.0	37.2
Organic, including symptomatic, mental disorders	F01-F09	40.7	33.3
Other degenerative diseases of the nervous system	G30-G31	17.9	32.1
Other external causes of accidental injury	W00-X59	35.8	31.2
Diabetes mellitus	E10-E14	14.8	21.1
Hypertensive diseases	I10-I15	11.1	20.8

Note: (a) ICD-10 = International Classification of Diseases 10th Revision; (1) Mortality rates are a three year average covering 2014-2016; (2) Figures cover Montgomery County.
Source: Centers for Disease Control and Prevention, National Center for Health Statistics. Underlying Cause of Death 1999-2016 on CDC WONDER Online Database, released December 2017

Mortality Rates for Selected Causes of Death

ICD-10[a] Sub-Chapter	ICD-10[a] Code	Age-Adjusted Mortality Rate[1] per 100,000 population	
		County[2]	U.S.
Assault	X85-Y09	1.8	5.6
Diseases of the liver	K70-K76	10.5	14.0
Human immunodeficiency virus (HIV) disease	B20-B24	Unreliable	1.9
Influenza and pneumonia	J09-J18	13.7	14.6
Intentional self-harm	X60-X84	12.6	13.2
Malnutrition	E40-E46	0.6	1.3
Obesity and other hyperalimentation	E65-E68	1.3	2.1
Renal failure	N17-N19	12.4	13.0
Transport accidents	V01-V99	5.2	12.0
Viral hepatitis	B15-B19	1.1	1.9

Note: (a) ICD-10 = International Classification of Diseases 10th Revision; (1) Mortality rates are a three year average covering 2014-2016; (2) Figures cover Montgomery County; Data are Suppressed when the data meet the criteria for confidentiality constraints; Mortality rates are flagged as Unreliable when the rate would be calculated with a numerator of 20 or less.
Source: Centers for Disease Control and Prevention, National Center for Health Statistics. Underlying Cause of Death 1999-2016 on CDC WONDER Online Database, released December 2017

Health Insurance Coverage

Area	With Health Insurance	With Private Health Insurance	With Public Health Insurance	Without Health Insurance	Population Under Age 18 Without Health Insurance
City	96.7	88.4	22.5	3.3	0.9
MSA[1]	92.0	72.6	31.5	8.0	3.5
U.S.	88.3	66.7	33.0	11.7	5.9

Note: Figures are percentages that cover the civilian noninstitutionalized population; (1) Figures cover the Philadelphia-Camden-Wilmington, PA-NJ-DE-MD Metropolitan Statistical Area—see Appendix B for areas included
Source: U.S. Census Bureau, 2012-2016 American Community Survey 5-Year Estimates

Number of Medical Professionals

Area	MDs[3]	DOs[3,4]	Dentists	Podiatrists	Chiropractors	Optometrists
County[1] (number)	4,769	681	861	108	326	189
County[1] (rate[2])	583.1	83.3	104.9	13.2	39.7	23.0
U.S. (rate[2])	276.5	22.3	67.3	6.0	26.7	15.9

Note: Data as of 2016 unless noted; (1) Data covers Montgomery County; (2) Rate per 100,000 population; (3) Data as of 2015 and includes all active, non-federal physicians; (4) Doctor of Osteopathic Medicine
Source: U.S. Department of Health and Human Services, Health Resources and Services Administration, Bureau of Health Professions, Area Resource File (ARF) 2016-2017

Best Hospitals

According to *U.S. News,* the Montgomery County-Bucks County-Chester County, PA metro area is home to one of the best hospitals in the U.S.: **MossRehab** (1 adult specialty). The hospital listed was nationally ranked in at least one of 16 specialties. Only 152 hospitals nationwide were nationally ranked in one or more specialties. Twenty hospitals in the U.S. made the Honor Roll. The Best Hospitals Honor Roll was revamped last year to take both the national rankings and the procedure and condition ratings into account. Hospitals received points if they were nationally ranked in one of the 16 specialties—the higher they ranked, the more points they got—and how many ratings of "high performing" they earned in the nine procedures and conditions. *U.S. News Online, "America's Best Hospitals 2017-18"*

EDUCATION

Public School District Statistics

District Name	Schls	Pupils	Pupil/ Teacher Ratio	Minority Pupils[1] (%)	Free Lunch Eligible[2] (%)	IEP[3] (%)
Upper Dublin SD	6	4,183	13.9	24.8	13.1	12.1

Note: Table includes school districts with 100 or more students; (1) Percentage of students that are not non-Hispanic white; (2) Percentage of students that are eligible for the free lunch program; (3) Percentage of students that have an Individualized Education Program.
Source: U.S. Department of Education, National Center for Education Statistics, Common Core of Data, Local Education Agency (School District) Universe Survey: School Year 2015-2016; U.S. Department of Education, National Center for Education Statistics, Common Core of Data, Public Elementary/Secondary School Universe Survey: School Year 2015-2016

Highest Level of Education

Area	Less than H.S.	H.S. Diploma	Some College, No Deg.	Associate Degree	Bachelor's Degree	Master's Degree	Prof. School Degree	Doctorate Degree
City	3.2	15.9	11.5	6.1	32.7	19.7	7.3	3.6
MSA[1]	10.3	30.0	17.3	6.9	21.3	9.9	2.5	1.8
U.S.	13.0	27.5	21.0	8.2	18.8	8.2	2.0	1.3

Note: Figures cover persons age 25 and over; (1) Figures cover the Philadelphia-Camden-Wilmington, PA-NJ-DE-MD Metropolitan Statistical Area—see Appendix B for areas included
Source: U.S. Census Bureau, 2012-2016 American Community Survey 5-Year Estimates

Educational Attainment by Race

Area	High School Graduate or Higher (%)					Bachelor's Degree or Higher (%)				
	Total	White	Black	Asian	Hisp.[2]	Total	White	Black	Asian	Hisp.[2]
City	96.8	97.6	93.8	91.1	87.8	63.3	65.2	32.1	66.1	35.3
MSA[1]	89.7	92.3	85.7	83.4	68.1	35.5	39.5	19.2	55.0	16.3
U.S.	87.0	88.9	84.3	86.3	65.7	30.3	31.6	20.0	52.1	14.7

Note: Figures shown cover persons 25 years old and over; (1) Figures cover the Philadelphia-Camden-Wilmington, PA-NJ-DE-MD Metropolitan Statistical Area—see Appendix B for areas included; (2) People of Hispanic origin can be of any race
Source: U.S. Census Bureau, 2012-2016 American Community Survey 5-Year Estimates

School Enrollment by Grade and Control

Area	Preschool (%)		Kindergarten (%)		Grades 1 - 4 (%)		Grades 5 - 8 (%)		Grades 9 - 12 (%)	
	Public	Private	Public	Private	Public	Private	Public	Private	Public	Private
City	10.7	89.3	89.5	10.5	84.0	16.0	85.3	14.7	80.4	19.6
MSA[1]	43.6	56.4	81.7	18.3	85.0	15.0	83.6	16.4	83.6	16.4
U.S.	58.4	41.6	87.7	12.3	89.8	10.2	89.7	10.3	90.4	9.6

Note: Figures shown cover persons 3 years old and over; (1) Figures cover the Philadelphia-Camden-Wilmington, PA-NJ-DE-MD Metropolitan Statistical Area—see Appendix B for areas included
Source: U.S. Census Bureau, 2012-2016 American Community Survey 5-Year Estimates

Average Salaries of Public School Classroom Teachers

Area	2015		2016		Change from 2015 to 2016	
	Dollars	Rank[1]	Dollars	Rank[1]	Percent	Rank[2]
Pennsylvania	64,447	10	65,151	10	1.1	24
U.S. Average	57,611	–	58,353	–	1.3	–

Note: (1) Rank ranges from 1 to 51 where 1 indicates highest salary; (2) Rank ranges from 1 to 51 where 1 indicates highest percent change.
Source: National Education Association, Rankings & Estimates: Rankings of the States 2016 and Estimates of School Statistics 2017

Higher Education

Four-Year Colleges			Two-Year Colleges			Medical Schools[1]	Law Schools[2]	Voc/ Tech[3]
Public	Private Non-profit	Private For-profit	Public	Private Non-profit	Private For-profit			
0	0	0	0	0	0	0	0	0

Note: Figures cover institutions located within the city limits and include main campuses only; (1) includes schools accredited by the Liaison Committee on Medical Education and the American Osteopathic Association's Commission on Osteopathic College Accreditation; (2) includes ABA-accredited schools, schools with provisional ABA accreditation, and state accredited schools; (3) includes all schools with programs that are less than 2 years.
Source: National Center for Education Statistics, Integrated Postsecondary Education System (IPEDS), 2016-17; Wikipedia, List of Medical Schools in the United States, accessed April 2, 2018; Wikipedia, List of Law Schools in the United States, accessed April 2, 2018

PRESIDENTIAL ELECTION

2016 Presidential Election Results

Area	Clinton	Trump	Johnson	Stein	Other
Montgomery County	58.4	37.1	2.5	0.8	1.2
U.S.	48.0	45.9	3.3	1.1	1.7

Note: Results are percentages and may not add to 100% due to rounding
Source: Dave Leip's Atlas of U.S. Presidential Elections

EMPLOYERS

Major Employers

Company Name	Industry
Abington Memorial Hospital	General medical & surgical hospitals
AstraZeneca Pharmaceuticals	Pharmaceutical preparations
City of Philadelphia	Police protection
Comcast Holdings Corporation	Cable & other pay television services
Cooper Health Care	Hospital management
E.I. du Pont de Nemours and Company	Agricultural chemicals
Einstein Community Health Associates	Offices & clinics of medical doctors
Glaxosmithkline	Commerical physical research
Lockheed Martin Corporation	Defense systems & equipment
Mercy Health System of SE Pennsylvania	General medical & surgical hospitals
On Time Staffing	Employment agencies
Richlieu Associates	Apartment building operators
Temple University	General medical & surgical hospitals
The University of Pennsylvania	Colleges & universities
The US Navy	Navy
The Vanguard Group	Management, investment, open-end
Thomas Jefferson University Hospital	General medical & surgical hospitals
Trustees of the University of Penn	General medical & surgical hospitals
Unisys Corporation	Computer integrated systems design
University of Delaware	Colleges & universities

Note: Companies shown are located within the Philadelphia-Camden-Wilmington, PA-NJ-DE-MD Metropolitan Statistical Area.
Source: Hoovers.com; Wikipedia

PUBLIC SAFETY

Crime Rate

Area	All Crimes	Violent Crimes				Property Crimes		
		Murder	Rape[3]	Robbery	Aggrav. Assault	Burglary	Larceny -Theft	Motor Vehicle Theft
City	884.8	0.0	11.4	19.0	11.4	68.4	725.3	49.4
Metro[1]	1,533.9	1.7	11.8	33.4	72.5	161.9	1,194.9	57.6
U.S.	2,847.8	5.3	40.4	102.8	248.5	468.9	1,745.0	236.9

Note: Figures are crimes per 100,000 population; (1) Figures cover the Montgomery County-Bucks County-Chester County, PA Metropolitan Division—see Appendix B for areas included; (3) The city and U.S. figures shown were reported using the revised Uniform Crime Reporting (UCR) definition of rape. The metro area figures shown are an aggregate total of the data submitted using both the revised and legacy UCR definitions.
Source: FBI Uniform Crime Reports, 2016

Hate Crimes

Area	Number of Quarters Reported	Number of Incidents per Bias Motivation					
		Race/Ethnicity/ Ancestry	Religion	Sexual Orientation	Disability	Gender	Gender Identity
Area[1]	4	0	0	0	0	0	0
U.S.	4	3,489	1,273	1,076	70	31	124

Note: (1) Figures cover the Upper Dublin Township.
Source: Federal Bureau of Investigation, Hate Crime Statistics 2016

Identity Theft Consumer Reports

Area	Reports	Reports per 100,000 Population	Rank[2]
MSA[1]	8,444	139	23
U.S.	371,061	114	-

Note: (1) Figures cover the Philadelphia-Camden-Wilmington, PA-NJ-DE-MD Metropolitan Statistical Area—see Appendix B for areas included; (2) Rank ranges from 1 to 389 where 1 indicates greatest number of identity theft reports per 100,000 population
Source: Federal Trade Commission, Consumer Sentinel Network Data Book for January–December 2017

Fraud and Other Consumer Reports

Area	Reports	Reports per 100,000 Population	Rank[2]
MSA[1]	34,068	561	60
U.S.	2,304,550	708	-

Note: (1) Figures cover the Philadelphia-Camden-Wilmington, PA-NJ-DE-MD Metropolitan Statistical Area—see Appendix B for areas included; (2) Rank ranges from 1 to 389 where 1 indicates greatest number of fraud and other consumer reports per 100,000 population
Source: Federal Trade Commission, Consumer Sentinel Network Data Book for January–December 2017

SPORTS

Professional Sports Teams

Team Name	League	Year Established
Philadelphia 76ers	National Basketball Association (NBA)	1963
Philadelphia Eagles	National Football League (NFL)	1933
Philadelphia Flyers	National Hockey League (NHL)	1967
Philadelphia Phillies	Major League Baseball (MLB)	1883
Philadelphia Union	Major League Soccer (MLS)	2010

Note: Includes teams located in the Philadelphia-Camden-Wilmington, PA-NJ-DE-MD Metropolitan Statistical Area.
Source: Wikipedia, Major Professional Sports Teams of the United States and Canada, April 5, 2018

CLIMATE

Average and Extreme Temperatures

Temperature	Jan	Feb	Mar	Apr	May	Jun	Jul	Aug	Sep	Oct	Nov	Dec	Yr.
Extreme High (°F)	74	74	85	94	96	100	104	101	100	89	84	72	104
Average High (°F)	39	42	51	63	73	82	86	85	78	67	55	43	64
Average Temp. (°F)	32	34	42	53	63	72	77	76	68	57	47	36	55
Average Low (°F)	24	26	33	43	53	62	67	66	59	47	38	28	45
Extreme Low (°F)	-7	-4	7	19	28	44	51	44	35	25	15	1	-7

Note: Figures cover the years 1948-1990
Source: National Climatic Data Center, International Station Meteorological Climate Summary, 9/96

Average Precipitation/Snowfall/Humidity

Precip./Humidity	Jan	Feb	Mar	Apr	May	Jun	Jul	Aug	Sep	Oct	Nov	Dec	Yr.
Avg. Precip. (in.)	3.2	2.8	3.7	3.5	3.7	3.6	4.1	4.0	3.3	2.7	3.4	3.3	41.4
Avg. Snowfall (in.)	7	7	4	Tr	Tr	0	0	0	0	Tr	1	4	22
Avg. Rel. Hum. 7am (%)	74	73	73	72	75	77	80	82	84	83	79	75	77
Avg. Rel. Hum. 4pm (%)	60	55	51	48	51	52	54	55	55	54	57	60	54

Note: Figures cover the years 1948-1990; Tr = Trace amounts (<0.05 in. of rain; <0.5 in. of snow)
Source: National Climatic Data Center, International Station Meteorological Climate Summary, 9/96

Weather Conditions

Temperature			Daytime Sky			Precipitation		
10°F & below	32°F & below	90°F & above	Clear	Partly cloudy	Cloudy	0.01 inch or more precip.	0.1 inch or more snow/ice	Thunder-storms
5	94	23	81	146	138	117	14	27

Note: Figures are average number of days per year and cover the years 1948-1990
Source: National Climatic Data Center, International Station Meteorological Climate Summary, 9/96

HAZARDOUS WASTE

Superfund Sites

The Montgomery County-Bucks County-Chester County, PA metro division is home to 36 sites on the EPA's Superfund National Priorities List: **A.I.W. Frank/Mid-county Mustang** (final); **Baghurst Drive** (final); **Blosenski Landfill** (final); **Boarhead Farms** (final); **Borit Asbestos** (final); **Chem-fab** (final); **Commodore Semiconductor Group** (final); **Crater Resources, Inc./Keystone Coke Co./Alan Wood Steel Co.** (final); **Croydon Tce** (final); **Dublin Tce Site** (final); **Fischer & Porter Co.** (final); **Foote Mineral Co.** (final); **Henderson Road** (final); **Kimberton** (final); **Malvern Tce** (final); **Naval Air Development Center (8 Waste Areas)** (final); **North Penn - Area 1** (final); **North Penn - Area 12** (final); **North Penn - Area 2** (final); **North Penn - Area 5** (final); **North Penn - Area 6** (final); **North Penn - Area 7** (final);

Occidental Chemical Corp./Firestone Tire & Rubber Co. (final); **Old Wilmington Road Gw Contamination** (final); **Paoli Rail Yard** (final); **Raymark** (final); **Recticon/Allied Steel Corp.** (final); **Revere Chemical Co.** (final); **Salford Quarry** (final); **Stanley Kessler** (final); **Strasburg Landfill** (final); **Tysons Dump** (final); **Walsh Landfill** (final); **Watson Johnson Landfill** (final); **William Dick Lagoons** (final); **Willow Grove Naval Air and Air Reserve Station** (final). There are a total of 1,396 Superfund sites with a status of proposed or final on the list in the U.S. *U.S. Environmental Protection Agency, National Priorities List, April 4, 2018*

AIR & WATER QUALITY

Air Quality Trends: Ozone

	1990	1995	2000	2005	2010	2012	2013	2014	2015	2016
MSA[1]	0.102	0.109	0.099	0.091	0.083	0.084	0.069	0.071	0.074	0.075
U.S.	0.087	0.089	0.081	0.079	0.073	0.075	0.069	0.067	0.068	0.069

Note: (1) Data covers the Philadelphia-Camden-Wilmington, PA-NJ-DE-MD Metropolitan Statistical Area—see Appendix B for areas included. The values shown are the composite ozone concentration averages among trend sites based on the highest fourth daily maximum 8-hour concentration in parts per million. These trends are based on sites having an adequate record of monitoring data during the trend period. Data from exceptional events are included.
Source: U.S. Environmental Protection Agency, Air Quality Monitoring Information, "Air Quality Trends by City, 1990-2016"

Air Quality Index

Area	Percent of Days when Air Quality was...[2]					AQI Statistics[2]	
	Good	Moderate	Unhealthy for Sensitive Groups	Unhealthy	Very Unhealthy	Maximum	Median
MSA[1]	34.5	59.5	5.5	0.5	0.0	166	55

Note: (1) Data covers the Philadelphia-Camden-Wilmington, PA-NJ-DE-MD Metropolitan Statistical Area—see Appendix B for areas included; (2) Based on 365 days with AQI data in 2017. Air Quality Index (AQI) is an index for reporting daily air quality. EPA calculates the AQI for five major air pollutants regulated by the Clean Air Act: ground-level ozone, particle pollution (aka particulate matter), carbon monoxide, sulfur dioxide, and nitrogen dioxide. The AQI runs from 0 to 500. The higher the AQI value, the greater the level of air pollution and the greater the health concern. There are six AQI categories: "Good" AQI is between 0 and 50. Air quality is considered satisfactory; "Moderate" AQI is between 51 and 100. Air quality is acceptable; "Unhealthy for Sensitive Groups" When AQI values are between 101 and 150, members of sensitive groups may experience health effects; "Unhealthy" When AQI values are between 151 and 200 everyone may begin to experience health effects; "Very Unhealthy" AQI values between 201 and 300 trigger a health alert; "Hazardous" AQI values over 300 trigger warnings of emergency conditions (not shown).
Source: U.S. Environmental Protection Agency, Air Quality Index Report, 2017

Air Quality Index Pollutants

Area	Percent of Days when AQI Pollutant was...[2]					
	Carbon Monoxide	Nitrogen Dioxide	Ozone	Sulfur Dioxide	Particulate Matter 2.5	Particulate Matter 10
MSA[1]	0.0	0.3	31.2	0.5	67.7	0.3

Note: (1) Data covers the Philadelphia-Camden-Wilmington, PA-NJ-DE-MD Metropolitan Statistical Area—see Appendix B for areas included; (2) Based on 365 days with AQI data in 2017. The Air Quality Index (AQI) is an index for reporting daily air quality. EPA calculates the AQI for five major air pollutants regulated by the Clean Air Act: ground-level ozone, particle pollution (also known as particulate matter), carbon monoxide, sulfur dioxide, and nitrogen dioxide. The AQI runs from 0 to 500. The higher the AQI value, the greater the level of air pollution and the greater the health concern.
Source: U.S. Environmental Protection Agency, Air Quality Index Report, 2017

Maximum Air Pollutant Concentrations: Particulate Matter, Ozone, CO and Lead

	Particulate Matter 10 (ug/m^3)	Particulate Matter 2.5 Wtd AM (ug/m^3)	Particulate Matter 2.5 24-Hr (ug/m^3)	Ozone (ppm)	Carbon Monoxide (ppm)	Lead (ug/m^3)
MSA[1] Level	113	11	24	0.08	2	0.04
NAAQS[2]	150	15	35	0.075	9	0.15
Met NAAQS[2]	Yes	Yes	Yes	No	Yes	Yes

Note: (1) Data covers the Philadelphia-Camden-Wilmington, PA-NJ-DE-MD Metropolitan Statistical Area—see Appendix B for areas included; Data from exceptional events are included; (2) National Ambient Air Quality Standards; ppm = parts per million; ug/m^3 = micrograms per cubic meter; n/a not available.
Concentrations: Particulate Matter 10 (coarse particulate)—highest second maximum 24-hour concentration; Particulate Matter 2.5 Wtd AM (fine particulate)—highest weighted annual mean concentration; Particulate Matter 2.5 24-Hour (fine particulate)—highest 98th percentile 24-hour concentration; Ozone—highest fourth daily maximum 8-hour concentration; Carbon Monoxide—highest second maximum non-overlapping 8-hour concentration; Lead—maximum running 3-month average
Source: U.S. Environmental Protection Agency, Air Quality Monitoring Information, "Air Quality Statistics by City, 2016"

Maximum Air Pollutant Concentrations: Nitrogen Dioxide and Sulfur Dioxide

	Nitrogen Dioxide AM (ppb)	Nitrogen Dioxide 1-Hr (ppb)	Sulfur Dioxide AM (ppb)	Sulfur Dioxide 1-Hr (ppb)	Sulfur Dioxide 24-Hr (ppb)
MSA[1] Level	16	58	n/a	19	n/a
NAAQS[2]	53	100	30	75	140
Met NAAQS[2]	Yes	Yes	n/a	Yes	n/a

Note: (1) Data covers the Philadelphia-Camden-Wilmington, PA-NJ-DE-MD Metropolitan Statistical Area—see Appendix B for areas included; Data from exceptional events are included; (2) National Ambient Air Quality Standards; ppm = parts per million; ug/m^3 = micrograms per cubic meter; n/a not available.
Concentrations: Nitrogen Dioxide AM—highest arithmetic mean concentration; Nitrogen Dioxide 1-Hr—highest 98th percentile 1-hour daily maximum concentration; Sulfur Dioxide AM—highest annual mean concentration; Sulfur Dioxide 1-Hr—highest 99th percentile 1-hour daily maximum concentration; Sulfur Dioxide 24-Hr—highest second maximum 24-hour concentration
Source: U.S. Environmental Protection Agency, Air Quality Monitoring Information, "Air Quality Statistics by City, 2016"

Drinking Water

Water System Name	Pop. Served	Primary Water Source Type	Violations[1] Health Based	Violations[1] Monitoring/Reporting
Ambler Boro Water Dept	20,000	Surface	0	2
Aqua PA Main System	747,460	Surface	0	0
North Wales Water Authority	72,496	Surface	0	1

Note: (1) Based on violation data from January 1, 2017 to December 31, 2017
Source: U.S. Environmental Protection Agency, Office of Ground Water and Drinking Water, Safe Drinking Water Information System (based on data extracted April 5, 2018)

South Kingstown, Rhode Island

Background

South Kingstown lies in southern Rhode Island, adjacent to the town of Narragansett, on the west side of Narragansett Bay. Its history properly begins in 1674 with the formation of "Kings Towne," which then encompassed both North Kingstown and South Kingstown. The two were separated and incorporated as separate towns in 1723. Today South Kingstown is a combination of beautiful rural spaces and picturesque villages.

South Kingstown is the county seat for Washington County. Like other New England townships, it includes a number of villages. Wakefield, the primary commercial center, is also blessed with a number of fine buildings of eighteenth- and nineteenth-century architecture. Kingston, two miles northwest, is home of the University of Rhode Island. Other villages include West Kingston, Peace Dale, Green Hill, Matunuck, Usquepaugh, Middlebridge, Rocky Brook, Indian Lake Shores, Perryville, Tuckertown, Curtis Corner, and Snug Harbor. South Kingstown as a whole is governed by a town council and town manager, occupying a historic town hall in Wakefield.

Wakefield was the birthplace of Oliver Hazard Perry (1785-1819), the naval hero of the War of 1812 whose famous words "We have met the enemy and he is ours" signaled his victory over the British in the Battle of Lake Erie (1813). His birthplace is now a museum. In 1804, Rowland Hazard arrived here from Charleston, South Carolina, and gave Peace Dale its name. In 1847, the Hazard family founded the textile-manufacturing firm that was to be the dominant industry in town for four generations. Later Hazards built the Peace Dale Public Library, designed in the Richardsonian Romanesque style, and commissioned a bronze relief, The Weaver, sculpted by Daniel Chester French, who is best known for the massive seated figure of Lincoln in the Lincoln Memorial in Washington.

South Kingstown likewise has a distinguished library building. First built as a court house in 1775 and used as one of five rotating state houses for the Rhode Island General Assembly from 1776-1791, the library was remodeled in the Victorian style in 1876 and is now on the National Register of Historic Places. The city's University of Rhode Island is home to over 13,000 students and innumerable cultural and recreational opportunities, including a full schedule of concerts and theatrical performances.

Art galleries include the Hera Gallery (Wakefield), South County Art Association (Kingston), and sometimes the Courthouse Center for the Arts (or CCA, West Kingston). Theaters include The Contemporary Theatre (Wakefield), the Theatre-by-the-Sea (Matunuck), and the CCA. The sole cinema is South County Cinema 8 (Wakefield), which replaced the independently run Campus Cinema (Wakefield) in the early 2000s. There are numerous venues for music and other entertainment, including the University of Rhode Island's Ryan Center and smaller venues such as Lily Pads (Peace Dale), and the CCA.

The next township east, Narragansett, also offers opportunities for culture and recreation. The South County Museum celebrates Rhode Island's heritage. And from Narragansett, one can go fishing, swimming, sailing, whale-watching, or hop a ferry to Block Island. Also from Narragansett, it is but a short trip across the bridge to Newport, with its bustling streets, glittering mansions, and historic houses.

With its shoreline on Block Island Sound and its proximity to Narragansett Bay, South Kingstown enjoys a four-season climate that is moderated by the sea. Precipitation occurs evenly throughout the year. In winter, snow is generally light and mixed with rain, though occasionally storms do sweep up the Atlantic coast, to collide with cold air from interior New England and drop large amounts of snow along the shore. Spring is pleasant and early, though the warmest days of spring can be cooler here than farther inland. Summer is high season, with comfortable temperatures for all outdoor activities.

Rankings

Business/Finance Rankings

- The personal finance site NerdWallet analyzed 183 American metropolitan areas with populations over 250,000 and more than 15,000 businesses to rank where entrepreneurs find the most success. Criteria included area economy, annual income, housing cost, unemployment rate, and the success rate of area businesses. Providence* ranked #68. *www.nerdwallet.com, "Best Places to Start a Business," April 27, 2015*
- In a survey of economic confidence in the nation's 50 largest metropolitan areas conducted January–December 2014, the Providence* metro area placed #47, according to Gallup's 2014 Economic Confidence Index. *Gallup, "San Jose and San Francisco Lead in Economic Confidence," March 19, 2015*
- The Brookings Institution ranked the 100 largest metro areas in the U.S. based on income inequality. Providence* was ranked #20 (#1 = greatest ineqality). Criteria: the "95/20 ratio," a figure representing the income at which a household earns more than 95 percent of all other households, divided by the income at which a household earns more than only 20 percent of all other households. *Brookings Institution, "Household Income Inequality, 100 Largest U.S. Metro Areas, 2014-2016," February 5, 2018*
- Providence* was identified as one of America's most frugal metro areas by *Coupons.com.* The city ranked #22 out of 25. Criteria: digital coupon usage. *Coupons.com, "America's Most Frugal Cities of 2017," March 22, 2018*
- The Providence* metro area appeared on the Milken Institute "2017 Best Performing Cities" list. Rank: #133 out of 200 large metro areas. Criteria: job growth; wage and salary growth; high-tech output growth. *Milken Institute, "Best-Performing Cities 2017," January 2018*
- *Forbes* ranked the 200 most populous metro areas to determine the nation's "Best Places for Business and Careers." The Providence* metro area was ranked #133. Criteria: costs (business and living); job growth (past and projected); income growth; quality of life; educational attainment (college and high school); projected economic growth; cultural and recreational opportunities; net migration patterns; number of highly ranked colleges. *Forbes, "The Best Places for Business and Careers 2017," October 24, 2017*

Education Rankings

- Personal finance website *WalletHub* analyzed the 150 largest U.S. metropolitan statistical areas to determine where the most educated Americans are choosing to settle. Criteria: education quality and attainment gap; education levels; percentage of workers with degrees; public school rankings; quality and size of each metro area's universities. Providence* was ranked #84 (#1 = most educated city). *www.WalletHub.com, "2017's Most and Least Educated Cities in America, " July 25, 2017*

Environmental Rankings

- Sperling's BestPlaces assessed 379 metropolitan areas of the United States for the likelihood of dangerously extreme weather events or earthquakes. In general the Southeast and South-Central regions have the highest risk of weather extremes and earthquakes, while the Pacific Northwest enjoys the lowest risk. Of the least risky metropolitan areas, the Providence* metro area was ranked #195. *www.bestplaces.net, "Safest Places from Natural Disasters," April 2011*

Health/Fitness Rankings

- For each of the 50 most populous metro areas in the United States, the American College of Sports Medicine's American Fitness Index evaluated infrastructure, community assets, and policies that encourage healthy and fit lifestyles, including preventive health behaviors, levels of chronic disease conditions, health care access, and community resources and policies that support physical activity. The Providence* metro area ranked #31 for "community fitness." *www.americanfitnessindex.org, "ACSM American Fitness Index Health and Community Fitness Status of the 50 Largest Metropolitan Areas," May 2017*

- Providence* was identified as a "2016 Spring Allergy Capital." The area ranked #8 out of 100. Three groups of factors were used to identify the most severe cities for people with allergies during the spring season: annual pollen levels; medicine utilization; access to board-certified allergists. *Asthma and Allergy Foundation of America, "Spring Allergy Capitals 2016"*

- Providence* was identified as a "2016 Fall Allergy Capital." The area ranked #12 out of 100. Three groups of factors were used to identify the most severe cities for people with allergies during the fall season: annual pollen levels; medicine utilization; access to board-certified allergists. *Asthma and Allergy Foundation of America, "Fall Allergy Capitals 2016"*

- Providence* was identified as a "2015 Asthma Capital." The area ranked #14 out of the nation's 100 largest metropolitan areas. Criteria: estimated prevalence; self-reported prevalence; crude death rate for asthma; annual pollen score; annual air quality; public smoking laws; number of board-certified asthma specialists; school inhaler access laws; rescue medication use; controller medication use; ER visits for asthma; uninsured rate; poverty rate. *Asthma and Allergy Foundation of America, "Asthma Capitals 2015"*

- The Providence* metro area ranked #149 out of 189 in The Gallup-Healthways Well-Being Index. Criteria: purpose; social well being; financial health; community and physical health. Results are based on telephone interviews with adults, aged 18 and older, living in metropolitan areas in the 50 U.S. states and the District of Columbia. *Gallup-Healthways, "State of American Well-Being, 2017 Community Well-Being Rankings" March 2018*

Real Estate Rankings

- FitSmallBusiness looked at 50 of the largest metropolitan areas in the U.S. to determine which metro was the best to start a real estate business. Data was compiled from such sources as: Zillow, Trulia, U.S. Census Bureau, and the Bureau of Labor Statistics. Criteria: location; inventory; annual wages; median sales price of homes; days on the market; median price cut percentage; and other factors that would influence real estate professional growth. The Providence* metro area ranked #11. *fitsmallbusiness.com, "The Best Cities to Become a Real Estate Agent in 2018," January 30, 2018*

- The Providence* metro area was identified as one of the 10 worst condo markets in the U.S. in 2017. The area ranked #9 out of 66 markets. Criteria: year-over-year change of median sales price of existing apartment condo-coop homes between the 4th quarter of 2016 and the 4th quarter of 2017. *National Association of Realtors®, Median Sales Price of Existing Apartment Condo-Coop Homes for Metropolitan Areas, 4th Quarter 2017*

- Providence* was ranked #154 out of 238 metro areas in terms of housing affordability in 2017 by the National Association of Home Builders (#1 = most affordable). Criteria: the share of homes sold in that area affordable to a family earning the local median income, based on standard mortgage underwriting criteria. *National Association of Home Builders®, NAHB-Wells Fargo Housing Opportunity Index, 4th Quarter 2017*

Safety Rankings

- South Kingstown was identified as one of the safest cities in America by NeighborhoodScout. The city ranked #58 out of 100 (100 = safest). Criteria: number of violent and property crimes per 1,000 residents. The editors only considered cities with 25,000 or more residents. *NeighborhoodScout, "Top 100 Safest Cities in the U.S. 2018" January 2, 2018*

- The National Insurance Crime Bureau ranked 382 metro areas in the U.S. in terms of per capita rates of vehicle theft. The Providence* metro area ranked #229 (#1 = highest rate). Criteria: number of vehicle theft offenses per 100,000 inhabitants in 2016. *National Insurance Crime Bureau, "Hot Spots 2016," June 8, 2017*

Seniors/Retirement Rankings

- From its Best Cities for Successful Aging indexes, the Milken Institute generated rankings for metropolitan areas, weighing data in nine categories—health care, wellness, living arrangements, transportation and convenience, financial characteristics, education, employment, community engagement, and overall livability. The Providence* metro area was ranked #70 overall in the large metro area category. *Milken Institute, "Best Cities for Successful Aging, 2017" March 14, 2017*

*South Kingstown is located within the Providence-Warwick, RI-MA Metropolitan Statistical Area.

Business Environment

CITY FINANCES

City Government Finances

Component	2015 ($000)	2015 ($ per capita)
Total Revenues	96,766	3,139
Total Expenditures	97,289	3,156
Debt Outstanding	14,256	462
Cash and Securities[1]	66,087	2,144

Note: (1) Cash and security holdings of a government at the close of its fiscal year,, including those of its dependent agencies, utilities, and liquor stores.
Source: U.S Census Bureau, State & Local Government Finances 2015

City Government Revenue by Source

Source	2015 ($000)	2015 ($ per capita)	2015 (%)
General Revenue			
From Federal Government	522	17	0.5
From State Government	12,309	399	12.7
From Local Governments	31	1	0.0
Taxes			
Property	68,282	2,215	70.6
Sales and Gross Receipts	1,311	43	1.4
Personal Income	0	0	0.0
Corporate Income	0	0	0.0
Motor Vehicle License	0	0	0.0
Other Taxes	1,555	50	1.6
Current Charges	6,580	213	6.8
Liquor Store	0	0	0.0
Utility	1,142	37	1.2
Employee Retirement	0	0	0.0

Source: U.S Census Bureau, State & Local Government Finances 2015

City Government Expenditures by Function

Function	2015 ($000)	2015 ($ per capita)	2015 (%)
General Direct Expenditures			
Air Transportation	0	0	0.0
Corrections	0	0	0.0
Education	66,689	2,163	68.5
Employment Security Administration	0	0	0.0
Financial Administration	1,506	48	1.5
Fire Protection	0	0	0.0
General Public Buildings	271	8	0.3
Governmental Administration, Other	1,362	44	1.4
Health	2,176	70	2.2
Highways	3,543	114	3.6
Hospitals	0	0	0.0
Housing and Community Development	493	16	0.5
Interest on General Debt	651	21	0.7
Judicial and Legal	205	6	0.2
Libraries	1,183	38	1.2
Parking	0	0	0.0
Parks and Recreation	3,075	99	3.2
Police Protection	7,959	258	8.2
Public Welfare	953	30	1.0
Sewerage	2,999	97	3.1
Solid Waste Management	405	13	0.4
Veterans' Services	0	0	0.0
Liquor Store	0	0	0.0
Utility	727	23	0.7
Employee Retirement	0	0	0.0

Source: U.S Census Bureau, State & Local Government Finances 2015

DEMOGRAPHICS

Population Growth

Area	1990 Census	2000 Census	2010 Census	2016* Estimate	Population Growth (%)	
					1990-2016	2010-2016
City	24,631	27,921	30,639	30,651	24.4	0.0
MSA[1]	1,509,789	1,582,997	1,600,852	1,609,359	6.6	0.5
U.S.	248,709,873	281,421,906	308,745,538	318,558,162	28.1	3.2

Note: (1) Figures cover the Providence-Warwick, RI-MA Metropolitan Statistical Area—see Appendix B for areas included; (*) 2012-2016 5-year estimated population
Source: U.S. Census Bureau, 1990 Census, Census 2000, Census 2010, 2012-2016 American Community Survey 5-Year Estimates

Household Size

Area	Persons in Household (%)							Average Household Size
	One	Two	Three	Four	Five	Six	Seven or More	
City	28.3	38.1	13.2	12.9	5.9	1.4	0.3	2.40
MSA[1]	29.7	33.2	16.5	13.4	5.0	1.5	0.7	2.50
U.S.	27.7	33.7	15.7	13.1	6.0	2.3	1.5	2.60

Note: (1) Figures cover the Providence-Warwick, RI-MA Metropolitan Statistical Area—see Appendix B for areas included
Source: U.S. Census Bureau, 2012-2016 American Community Survey 5-Year Estimates

Race

Area	White Alone[2] (%)	Black Alone[2] (%)	Asian Alone[2] (%)	AIAN[3] Alone[2] (%)	NHOPI[4] Alone[2] (%)	Other Race Alone[2] (%)	Two or More Races (%)
City	90.7	2.5	1.8	1.4	0.0	1.3	2.3
MSA[1]	82.9	5.6	2.9	0.4	0.1	5.5	2.8
U.S.	73.3	12.6	5.2	0.8	0.2	4.8	3.1

Note: (1) Figures cover the Providence-Warwick, RI-MA Metropolitan Statistical Area—see Appendix B for areas included; (2) Alone is defined as not being in combination with one or more other races; (3) American Indian and Alaska Native; (4) Native Hawaiian and Other Pacific Islander
Source: U.S. Census Bureau, 2012-2016 American Community Survey 5-Year Estimates

Hispanic or Latino Origin

Area	Total (%)	Mexican (%)	Puerto Rican (%)	Cuban (%)	Other (%)
City	5.0	0.4	1.7	0.2	2.7
MSA[1]	11.6	0.8	3.8	0.2	6.9
U.S.	17.3	11.0	1.7	0.7	4.0

Note: Persons of Hispanic or Latino origin can be of any race; (1) Figures cover the Providence-Warwick, RI-MA Metropolitan Statistical Area—see Appendix B for areas included
Source: U.S. Census Bureau, 2012-2016 American Community Survey 5-Year Estimates

Segregation

Type	Segregation Indices[1]				Percent Change		
	1990	2000	2010	2010 Rank[2]	1990-2000	1990-2010	2000-2010
Black/White	60.5	57.2	53.5	57	-3.2	-7.0	-3.8
Asian/White	47.0	44.1	40.1	55	-2.9	-6.9	-4.0
Hispanic/White	57.9	64.5	60.1	4	6.6	2.3	-4.3

Note: All figures cover the Metropolitan Statistical Area—see Appendix B for areas included; Figures are based on an analysis of 1990, 2000, and 2010 Census Decennial Census tract data by William H. Frey, Brookings Institution and the University of Michigan Social Science Data Analysis Network. In this analysis all racial groups (whites, blacks, and asians) are non-Hispanic members of those races. Hispanics are shown as a separate category; (1) Segregation Indices are Dissimilarity Indices that measure the degree to which the minority group is distributed differently than whites across census tracts. They range from 0 (complete integration) to 100 (complete segregation) where the value indicates the percentage of the minority group that needs to move to be distributed exactly like whites; (2) Ranges from 1 (most segregated) to 102 (least segregated); n/a not available.
Source: www.CensusScope.org

Ancestry

Area	German	Irish	English	American	Italian	Polish	French[2]	Scottish	Dutch
City	9.3	22.3	16.6	4.1	18.6	5.5	7.8	2.6	0.6
MSA[1]	4.9	18.3	10.5	3.5	14.8	4.1	10.4	1.7	0.5
U.S.	14.4	10.4	7.7	6.9	5.4	2.9	2.6	1.7	1.3

Note: Figures are the percentage of the total population reporting a particular ancestry. The nine most commonly reported ancestries in the U.S. are shown. Figures include multiple ancestries (e.g. if a person reported being Irish and Italian, they were included in both columns); (1) Figures cover the Providence-Warwick, RI-MA Metropolitan Statistical Area—see Appendix B for areas included; (2) Excludes Basque
Source: U.S. Census Bureau, 2012-2016 American Community Survey 5-Year Estimates

Foreign-Born Population

Area	Percent of Population Born in								
	Any Foreign Country	Asia	Mexico	Europe	Carribean	Central America[2]	South America	Africa	Canada
City	4.9	1.2	0.0	2.0	0.6	0.2	0.4	0.3	0.1
MSA[1]	13.1	2.2	0.2	4.4	2.1	1.4	1.0	1.5	0.2
U.S.	13.2	4.0	3.6	1.5	1.3	1.0	0.9	0.6	0.3

Note: (1) Figures cover the Providence-Warwick, RI-MA Metropolitan Statistical Area—see Appendix B for areas included; (2) Excludes Mexico.
Source: U.S. Census Bureau, 2012-2016 American Community Survey 5-Year Estimates

Marital Status

Area	Never Married	Now Married[2]	Separated	Widowed	Divorced
City	41.8	42.8	0.7	6.1	8.6
MSA[1]	35.4	45.2	1.8	6.4	11.2
U.S.	33.0	48.1	2.1	5.9	11.0

Note: Figures are percentages and cover the population 15 years of age and older; (1) Figures cover the Providence-Warwick, RI-MA Metropolitan Statistical Area—see Appendix B for areas included; (2) Excludes separated
Source: U.S. Census Bureau, 2012-2016 American Community Survey 5-Year Estimates

Disability Status

Area	All Ages	Under 18 Years Old	18 to 64 Years Old	65 Years and Over
City	10.3	3.6	7.3	28.2
MSA[1]	13.5	5.0	11.1	34.8
U.S.	12.5	4.1	10.3	35.7

Note: Figures show percent of the civilian noninstitutionalized population that reported having a disability. Disability status is determined from six types of difficulty: vision, hearing, cognitive, ambulatory, self-care, and independent living. For children under 5 years old, hearing and vision difficulty are used to determine disability status. For children between the ages of 5 and 14, disability status is determined from hearing, vision, cognitive, ambulatory, and self-care difficulties. For people aged 15 years and older, they are considered to have a disability if they have difficulty with any one of the six difficulty types; Note: (1) Figures cover the Providence-Warwick, RI-MA Metropolitan Statistical Area—see Appendix B for areas included
Source: U.S. Census Bureau, 2012-2016 American Community Survey 5-Year Estimates

Age

Area	Percent of Population									Median Age
	Under Age 5	Age 5–19	Age 20–34	Age 35–44	Age 45–54	Age 55–64	Age 65–74	Age 75–84	Age 85+	
City	3.0	27.9	17.5	8.0	12.1	13.8	9.4	5.2	3.0	37.7
MSA[1]	5.2	18.4	20.2	12.2	14.7	13.4	8.6	4.6	2.6	40.2
U.S.	6.2	19.6	20.7	12.7	13.6	12.6	8.3	4.3	1.9	37.7

Note: (1) Figures cover the Providence-Warwick, RI-MA Metropolitan Statistical Area—see Appendix B for areas included
Source: U.S. Census Bureau, 2012-2016 American Community Survey 5-Year Estimates

Gender

Area	Males	Females	Males per 100 Females
City	14,618	16,033	91.2
MSA[1]	780,036	829,323	94.1
U.S.	156,765,322	161,792,840	96.9

Note: (1) Figures cover the Providence-Warwick, RI-MA Metropolitan Statistical Area—see Appendix B for areas included
Source: U.S. Census Bureau, 2012-2016 American Community Survey 5-Year Estimates

Religious Groups by Family

Area	Catholic	Baptist	Non-Den.	Methodist[2]	Lutheran	LDS[3]	Pente-costal	Presby-terian[4]	Muslim[5]	Judaism
MSA[1]	47.0	1.4	1.2	0.8	0.5	0.3	0.6	1.0	0.1	0.7
U.S.	19.1	9.3	4.0	4.0	2.3	2.0	1.9	1.6	0.8	0.7

Note: Figures are the number of adherents as a percentage of the total population; (1) Figures cover the Providence-Warwick, RI-MA Metropolitan Statistical Area—see Appendix B for areas included; (2) Methodist/Pietist; (3) Latter Day Saints; (4) Reformed; (5) Figures are estimates
Source: Association of Statisticians of American Religious Bodies, 2010 U.S. Religion Census: Religious Congregations & Membership Study

Religious Groups by Tradition

Area	Catholic	Evangelical Protestant	Mainline Protestant	Other Tradition	Black Protestant	Orthodox
MSA[1]	47.0	2.8	4.7	1.6	0.1	0.6
U.S.	19.1	16.2	7.3	4.3	1.6	0.3

Note: Figures are the number of adherents as a percentage of the total population; (1) Figures cover the Providence-Warwick, RI-MA Metropolitan Statistical Area—see Appendix B for areas included
Source: Association of Statisticians of American Religious Bodies, 2010 U.S. Religion Census: Religious Congregations & Membership Study

ECONOMY

Gross Metropolitan Product

Area	2014	2015	2016	2017	Rank[2]
MSA[1]	75.7	78.4	80.9	84.2	43

Note: Figures are in billions of dollars; (1) Figures cover the Providence-Warwick, RI-MA Metropolitan Statistical Area—see Appendix B for areas included; (2) Rank is based on 2015 data and ranges from 1 to 381
Source: The U.S. Conference of Mayors, U.S. Metro Economies: GMP and Employment Report, 2015-2017

Economic Growth

Area	2012-14 (%)	2015 (%)	2016 (%)	2017 (%)	Rank[2]
MSA[1]	1.4	1.3	1.4	2.1	164
U.S.	2.0	2.4	1.9	2.6	–

Note: Figures are real gross metropolitan product (GMP) growth rates and represent average annual percent change; (1) Figures cover the Providence-Warwick, RI-MA Metropolitan Statistical Area—see Appendix B for areas included; (2) Rank is based on 2012-2014 average annual percent change and ranges from 1 to 381
Source: The U.S. Conference of Mayors, U.S. Metro Economies: GMP and Employment Report, 2015-2017

Metropolitan Area Exports

Area	2011	2012	2013	2014	2015	2016	Rank[2]
MSA[1]	7,139.1	5,830.8	6,609.0	6,595.1	5,048.8	6,595.7	45

Note: Figures are in millions of dollars; (1) Figures cover the Providence-Warwick, RI-MA Metropolitan Statistical Area—see Appendix B for areas included; (2) Rank is based on 2016 data and ranges from 1 to 385
Source: U.S. Department of Commerce, International Trade Administration, Office of Trade & Industry Information, Manufacturing & Services, data extracted March 15, 2018

Building Permits

Area	Single-Family			Multi-Family			Total		
	2016	2017p	Pct. Chg.	2016	2017p	Pct. Chg.	2016	2017p	Pct. Chg.
City	53	73	37.7	0	0	0.0	53	73	37.7
MSA[1]	1,664	1,740	4.6	883	284	-67.8	2,547	2,024	-20.5
U.S.	750,800	817,300	8.9	455,800	446,800	-2.0	1,206,600	1,264,100	4.8

Note: (1) Figures cover the Providence-Warwick, RI-MA Metropolitan Statistical Area—see Appendix B for areas included; Figures represent new, privately-owned housing units authorized (unadjusted data); All permit data are based on estimates with imputation; (p) preliminary data.
Source: U.S. Census Bureau, Manufacturing, Mining, and Construction Statistics, Building Permits, 2016, 2017

Bankruptcy Filings

Area	Business Filings 2016	Business Filings 2017	Business Filings % Chg.	Nonbusiness Filings 2016	Nonbusiness Filings 2017	Nonbusiness Filings % Chg.
Washington County	14	10	-28.6	163	160	-1.8
U.S.	24,114	23,157	-4.0	770,846	765,863	-0.6

Note: Business filings include Chapter 7, Chapter 11, Chapter 12, and Chapter 13; Nonbusiness filings include Chapter 7, Chapter 11, and Chapter 13
Source: Administrative Office of the U.S. Courts, Business and Nonbusiness Bankruptcy, County Cases Commenced by Chapter of the Bankruptcy Code, During the 12-Month Period Ending December 31, 2016 and Business and Nonbusiness Bankruptcy, County Cases Commenced by Chapter of the Bankruptcy Code, During the 12-Month Period Ending December 31, 2017

Housing Vacancy Rates

Area	Gross Vacancy Rate[2] (%)			Year-Round Vacancy Rate[3] (%)			Rental Vacancy Rate[4] (%)			Homeowner Vacancy Rate[5] (%)		
	2015	2016	2017	2015	2016	2017	2015	2016	2017	2015	2016	2017
MSA[1]	11.0	11.1	11.3	7.8	7.5	8.1	3.3	3.8	4.2	1.7	1.3	1.2
U.S.	12.9	12.8	12.7	10.0	9.9	9.9	7.1	6.9	7.2	1.8	1.7	1.6

Note: (1) Figures cover the Providence-Warwick, RI-MA Metropolitan Statistical Area—see Appendix B for areas included; (2) The percentage of the total housing inventory that is vacant; (3) The percentage of the housing inventory (excluding seasonal units) that is year-round vacant; (4) The percentage of rental inventory that is vacant for rent; (5) The percentage of homeowner inventory that is vacant for sale
Source: U.S. Census Bureau, Housing Vacancies and Homeownership Annual Statistics: 2015, 2016, 2017

INCOME

Income

Area	Per Capita ($)	Median Household ($)	Average Household ($)
City	33,886	73,801	96,207
MSA[1]	31,428	58,699	78,355
U.S.	29,829	55,322	77,866

Note: (1) Figures cover the Providence-Warwick, RI-MA Metropolitan Statistical Area—see Appendix B for areas included
Source: U.S. Census Bureau, 2012-2016 American Community Survey 5-Year Estimates

Household Income Distribution

Area	Percent of Households Earning							
	Under $15,000	$15,000 -$24,999	$25,000 -$34,999	$35,000 -$49,999	$50,000 -$74,999	$75,000 -$99,999	$100,000 -$149,999	$150,000 and up
City	9.4	8.1	7.1	11.0	14.8	11.3	19.9	18.4
MSA[1]	13.2	9.7	8.8	12.0	16.6	12.9	15.3	11.6
U.S.	12.1	10.2	9.9	13.2	17.8	12.2	13.5	11.1

Note: (1) Figures cover the Providence-Warwick, RI-MA Metropolitan Statistical Area—see Appendix B for areas included
Source: U.S. Census Bureau, 2012-2016 American Community Survey 5-Year Estimates

Poverty Rate

Area	All Ages	Under 18 Years Old	18 to 64 Years Old	65 Years and Over
City	10.5	9.6	12.6	5.2
MSA[1]	13.4	18.7	12.5	9.7
U.S.	15.1	21.2	14.2	9.3

Note: Figures are percentage of people whose income during the past 12 months was below the poverty level; (1) Figures cover the Providence-Warwick, RI-MA Metropolitan Statistical Area—see Appendix B for areas included
Source: U.S. Census Bureau, 2012-2016 American Community Survey 5-Year Estimates

EMPLOYMENT

Labor Force and Employment

Area	Civilian Labor Force			Workers Employed		
	Dec. 2016	Dec. 2017	% Chg.	Dec. 2016	Dec. 2017	% Chg.
City	16,403	16,481	0.5	15,804	15,939	0.9
NECTA[1]	680,280	685,055	0.7	651,534	657,109	0.9
U.S.	158,968,000	159,880,000	0.6	151,798,000	153,602,000	1.2

Note: Data is not seasonally adjusted and covers workers 16 years of age and older; (1) Figures cover the Providence-Warwick, RI-MA New England City and Town Area—see Appendix B for areas included
Source: Bureau of Labor Statistics, Local Area Unemployment Statistics

Unemployment Rate

Area	2017											
	Jan.	Feb.	Mar.	Apr.	May	Jun.	Jul.	Aug.	Sep.	Oct.	Nov.	Dec.
City	5.0	4.7	4.9	3.2	3.4	4.1	4.6	4.0	3.2	3.0	3.7	3.3
NECTA[1]	5.6	5.4	5.0	4.1	4.1	4.3	4.7	4.4	4.0	4.0	4.1	4.1
U.S.	5.1	4.9	4.6	4.1	4.1	4.5	4.6	4.5	4.1	3.9	3.9	3.9

Note: Data is not seasonally adjusted and covers workers 16 years of age and older; (1) Figures cover the Providence-Warwick, RI-MA New England City and Town Area—see Appendix B for areas included
Source: Bureau of Labor Statistics, Local Area Unemployment Statistics

Average Wages

Occupation	$/Hr.	Occupation	$/Hr.
Accountants and Auditors	38.50	Maids and Housekeeping Cleaners	13.10
Automotive Mechanics	19.60	Maintenance and Repair Workers	n/a
Bookkeepers	20.30	Marketing Managers	70.10
Carpenters	24.50	Nuclear Medicine Technologists	42.20
Cashiers	11.70	Nurses, Licensed Practical	26.40
Clerks, General Office	17.20	Nurses, Registered	36.70
Clerks, Receptionists/Information	15.50	Nursing Assistants	14.60
Clerks, Shipping/Receiving	17.50	Packers and Packagers, Hand	12.30
Computer Programmers	37.00	Physical Therapists	40.30
Computer Systems Analysts	46.80	Postal Service Mail Carriers	23.80
Computer User Support Specialists	27.30	Real Estate Brokers	45.30
Cooks, Restaurant	13.50	Retail Salespersons	14.70
Dentists	90.20	Sales Reps., Exc. Tech./Scientific	34.50
Electrical Engineers	50.00	Sales Reps., Tech./Scientific	44.00
Electricians	27.20	Secretaries, Exc. Legal/Med./Exec.	19.90
Financial Managers	67.30	Security Guards	14.60
First-Line Supervisors/Managers, Sales	23.40	Surgeons	117.80
Food Preparation Workers	13.10	Teacher Assistants*	14.70
General and Operations Managers	63.80	Teachers, Elementary School*	32.70
Hairdressers/Cosmetologists	13.30	Teachers, Secondary School*	32.60
Internists, General	110.90	Telemarketers	15.90
Janitors and Cleaners	14.50	Truck Drivers, Heavy/Tractor-Trailer	22.40
Landscaping/Groundskeeping Workers	15.90	Truck Drivers, Light/Delivery Svcs.	16.40
Lawyers	61.70	Waiters and Waitresses	12.50

Note: Wage data covers the Providence-Warwick, RI-MA New England City and Town Area—see Appendix B for areas included; (*) Hourly wages for elementary/secondary school teachers and teacher assistants were calculated by the editors from annual wage data based on a 40 hour work week; n/a not available.
Source: Bureau of Labor Statistics, Metro Area Occupational Employment & Wage Estimates, May 2017

Employment by Occupation

Occupation Classification	City (%)	MSA[1] (%)	U.S. (%)
Management, Business, Science, and Arts	47.0	36.8	37.0
Natural Resources, Construction, and Maintenance	5.9	8.0	8.9
Production, Transportation, and Material Moving	6.6	11.8	12.2
Sales and Office	20.4	23.8	23.8
Service	20.1	19.5	18.1

Note: Figures cover employed civilians 16 years of age and older; (1) Figures cover the Providence-Warwick, RI-MA Metropolitan Statistical Area—see Appendix B for areas included
Source: U.S. Census Bureau, 2012-2016 American Community Survey 5-Year Estimates

Employment by Industry

Sector	NECTA[1] Number of Employees	NECTA[1] Percent of Total	U.S. Percent of Total
Construction	23,800	4.0	4.7
Education and Health Services	129,200	21.7	15.9
Financial Activities	39,100	6.6	5.7
Government	72,700	12.2	15.3
Information	7,300	1.2	1.9
Leisure and Hospitality	64,500	10.8	10.7
Manufacturing	52,500	8.8	8.5
Mining and Logging	200	<0.1	0.5
Other Services	27,400	4.6	3.9
Professional and Business Services	75,300	12.6	14.0
Retail Trade	66,000	11.1	11.0
Transportation, Warehousing, and Utilities	18,800	3.2	4.1
Wholesale Trade	19,400	3.3	4.0

Note: Figures are non-farm employment as of December 2017. Figures are not seasonally adjusted and include workers 16 years of age and older; (1) Figures cover the Providence-Warwick, RI-MA New England City and Town Area—see Appendix B for areas included
Source: Bureau of Labor Statistics, Current Employment Statistics, Employment, Hours, and Earnings

Occupations with Greatest Projected Employment Growth: 2017 – 2019

Occupation[1]	2017 Employment	2019 Projected Employment	Numeric Employment Change	Percent Employment Change
Combined Food Preparation and Serving Workers, Including Fast Food	9,890	10,310	420	4.2
Customer Service Representatives	9,960	10,320	360	3.6
Waiters and Waitresses	10,670	10,950	280	2.6
Cooks, Restaurant	5,100	5,350	250	4.9
Nursing Assistants	10,500	10,750	250	2.4
Registered Nurses	12,450	12,650	200	1.5
Retail Salespersons	14,200	14,400	200	1.4
Landscaping and Groundskeeping Workers	6,400	6,590	190	3.0
Accountants and Auditors	5,050	5,220	170	3.3
Bartenders	3,860	4,030	170	4.3

Note: Projections cover Rhode Island; (1) Sorted by numeric employment change
Source: www.projectionscentral.com, State Occupational Projections, 2017–2019 Short-Term Projections

Fastest Growing Occupations: 2017 – 2019

Occupation[1]	2017 Employment	2019 Projected Employment	Numeric Employment Change	Percent Employment Change
Welders, Cutters, Solderers, and Brazers	1,690	1,840	150	8.8
Loan Officers	1,220	1,330	110	8.4
Sheet Metal Workers	550	600	50	8.2
Loan Interviewers and Clerks	1,010	1,080	70	7.3
Plumbers, Pipefitters, and Steamfitters	1,680	1,800	120	7.2
Electricians	2,380	2,540	160	6.5
Computer Systems Analysts	1,960	2,070	110	5.8
Financial Analysts	1,120	1,180	60	5.7
Tellers	1,350	1,430	80	5.4
Computer and Information Systems Managers	1,200	1,260	60	5.3

Note: Projections cover Rhode Island; (1) Sorted by percent employment change and excludes occupations with numeric employment change less than 50
Source: www.projectionscentral.com, State Occupational Projections, 2017–2019 Short-Term Projections

TAXES

State Corporate Income Tax Rates

State	Tax Rate (%)	Income Brackets ($)	Num. of Brackets	Financial Institution Tax Rate (%)[a]	Federal Income Tax Ded.
Rhode Island	7.0 (b)	Flat rate	1	9.0 (b)	No

Note: Tax rates as of January 1, 2018; (a) Rates listed are the corporate income tax rate applied to financial institutions or excise taxes based on income. Some states have other taxes based upon the value of deposits or shares; (b) Minimum tax is $800 in California, $100 in District of Columbia and Arizona, $50 in North Dakota (banks), $500 in Rhode Island, $200 per location in South Dakota (banks), $100 in Utah, $250 in Vermont.
Source: Federation of Tax Administrators, Range of State Corporate Income Tax Rates, January 1, 2018

State Individual Income Tax Rates

State	Tax Rate (%)	Income Brackets ($)	Num. of Brackets	Personal Exempt. ($)[1]		Fed. Inc. Tax Ded.
				Single	Dependents	
Rhode Island (a)	3.75 - 5.99	62,550 - 142,150	3	4,000	4,000	No

Note: Tax rates as of January 1, 2018; Local- and county-level taxes are not included; n/a not applicable; (1) Married joint filers generally receive double the single exemption; (a) 19 states have statutory provision for automatically adjusting to the rate of inflation the dollar values of the income tax brackets, standard deductions, and/or personal exemptions. Massachusetts, Michigan, and Nebraska index the personal exemption only. Oregon does not index the income brackets for $125,000 and over.
Source: Federation of Tax Administrators, State Individual Income Tax Rates, January 1, 2018

Various State Sales and Excise Tax Rates

State	State Sales Tax (%)	Gasoline[1] (¢/gal.)	Cigarette[2] ($/pack)	Spirits[3] ($/gal.)	Wine[4] ($/gal.)	Beer[5] ($/gal.)	Recreational Marijuana (%)
Rhode Island	7.0	34.0	4.25	5.40 (f)	1.40 (l)	0.12 (t)	Not legal

Note: All tax rates as of January 1, 2018; (1) The American Petroleum Institute has developed a methodology for determining the average tax rate on a gallon of fuel. Rates may include any of the following: excise taxes, environmental fees, storage tank fees, other fees or taxes, general sales tax, and local taxes. In states where gasoline is subject to the general sales tax, or where the fuel tax is based on the average sale price, the average rate determined by API is sensitive to changes in the price of gasoline. States that fully or partially apply general sales taxes to gasoline: CA, CO, GA, IL, IN, MI, NY; (2) The federal excise tax of $1.0066 per pack and local taxes are not included; (3) Rates are those applicable to off-premise sales of 40% alcohol by volume (a.b.v.) distilled spirits in 750ml containers. Local excise taxes are excluded; (4) Rates are those applicable to off-premise sales of 11% a.b.v. non-carbonated wine in 750ml containers; (5) Rates are those applicable to off-premise sales of 4.7% a.b.v. beer in 12 ounce containers; (f) Different rates also applicable according to alcohol content, place of production, size of container, or place purchased (on- or off-premise or onboard airlines); (l) Different rates also applicable to alcohol content, place of production, size of container, place purchased (on- or off-premise or on board airlines) or type of wine (carbonated, vermouth, etc.); (t) Includes case fees and/or bottle fees which may vary with the size of container.
Source: Tax Foundation, 2018 Facts & Figures: How Does Your State Compare?

State Business Tax Climate Index Rankings

State	Overall Rank	Corporate Tax Rank	Individual Income Tax Rank	Sales Tax Rank	Unemployment Insurance Tax Rank	Property Tax Rank
Rhode Island	41	30	39	22	23	43

Note: The index is a measure of how each state's tax laws affect economic performance. The lower the rank, the more favorable a state's tax system is for business. States without a given tax are given a ranking of 1. The scores/rankings for the District of Columbia do not affect other states. The 2018 index represents the tax climate as of July 1, 2017.
Source: Tax Foundation, State Business Tax Climate Index 2018

TRANSPORTATION

Means of Transportation to Work

Area	Car/Truck/Van		Public Transportation			Bicycle	Walked	Other Means	Worked at Home
	Drove Alone	Car-pooled	Bus	Subway	Railroad				
City	77.9	6.5	1.0	0.1	0.6	0.2	7.1	1.0	5.6
MSA[1]	80.7	8.5	1.7	0.1	0.9	0.3	3.4	0.9	3.5
U.S.	76.4	9.3	2.6	1.9	0.6	0.6	2.8	1.3	4.6

Note: Figures are percentages and cover workers 16 years of age and older; (1) Figures cover the Providence-Warwick, RI-MA Metropolitan Statistical Area—see Appendix B for areas included
Source: U.S. Census Bureau, 2012-2016 American Community Survey 5-Year Estimates

Travel Time to Work

Area	Less Than 10 Minutes	10 to 19 Minutes	20 to 29 Minutes	30 to 44 Minutes	45 to 59 Minutes	60 to 89 Minutes	90 Minutes or More
City	19.5	28.1	15.5	20.7	8.7	5.1	2.4
MSA[1]	12.6	31.1	22.2	18.7	7.1	5.5	2.9
U.S.	12.9	29.2	20.9	20.4	8.0	6.0	2.7

Note: Note: Figures are percentages and include workers 16 years old and over; (1) Figures cover the Providence-Warwick, RI-MA Metropolitan Statistical Area—see Appendix B for areas included
Source: U.S. Census Bureau, 2012-2016 American Community Survey 5-Year Estimates

Freeway Travel Time Index

Area	1985	1990	1995	2000	2005	2010	2014
Urban Area Rank[1,2]	81	63	59	46	39	39	37
Urban Area Index[1]	1.04	1.08	1.12	1.16	1.19	1.19	1.20
Average Index[3]	1.09	1.11	1.14	1.17	1.20	1.19	1.20

Note: Freeway Travel Time Index—the ratio of travel time in the peak period to the travel time at free-flow conditions. For example, a value of 1.30 indicates a 20-minute free-flow trip takes 26 minutes in the peak (20 minutes x 1.30 = 26 minutes); (1) Covers the Providence RI-MA urban area; (2) Rank is based on 101 urban areas (#1 = highest travel time index); (3) Average of 101 urban areas
Source: Texas Transportation Institute, 2015 Urban Mobility Scorecard, August 2015

Freeway Commuter Stress Index

Area	1985	1990	1995	2000	2005	2010	2014
Urban Area Rank[1,2]	81	71	61	51	47	45	49
Urban Area Index[1]	1.06	1.10	1.14	1.19	1.21	1.22	1.22
Average Index[3]	1.13	1.16	1.19	1.22	1.25	1.24	1.25

Note: The Freeway Commuter Stress Index is the same as the Freeway Travel Time Index (see table above) except that it includes only the travel in the peak directions during the peak periods; the TTI includes travel in all directions during the peak period. Thus, the CSI is more indicative of the work trip experienced by each commuter on a daily basis; (1) Covers the Providence RI-MA urban area; (2) Rank is based on 101 urban areas (#1 = highest travel time index); (3) Average of 101 urban areas
Source: Texas Transportation Institute, 2015 Urban Mobility Scorecard, August 2015

Living Environment

COST OF LIVING

Cost of Living Index

Composite Index	Groceries	Housing	Utilities	Trans- portation	Health Care	Misc. Goods/ Services
123.4	115.0	140.7	126.7	101.5	110.0	119.1

Note: The Cost of Living Index measures regional differences in the cost of consumer goods and services, excluding taxes and non-consumer expenditures, for professional and managerial households in the top income quintile. It is based on more than 50,000 prices covering almost 60 different items for which prices are collected three times a year by chambers of commerce, economic development organizations or university applied economic centers in each participating urban area. The numbers shown should be read as a percentage above or below the national average of 100. For example, a value of 115.4 in the groceries column indicates that grocery prices are 15.4% higher than the national average. Small differences in the index numbers should not be interpreted as significant; Figures cover the Providence RI urban area.
Source: The Council for Community and Economic Research, ACCRA Cost of Living Index, 2017

Grocery Prices

Area[1]	T-Bone Steak ($/pound)	Frying Chicken ($/pound)	Whole Milk ($/half gal.)	Eggs ($/dozen)	Orange Juice ($/64 oz.)	Coffee ($/11.5 oz.)
City[2]	12.39	1.62	2.39	1.99	4.36	4.32
Avg.	11.29	1.40	2.02	1.47	3.55	4.37
Min.	7.71	0.93	1.04	0.70	2.86	3.24
Max.	15.83	2.39	4.03	3.92	6.29	8.16

*Note: (1) Values for the local area are compared with the average, minimum and maximum values for all 294 areas in the Cost of Living Index; (2) Figures cover the Providence RI urban area; **T-Bone Steak** (price per pound); **Frying Chicken** (price per pound, whole fryer); **Whole Milk** (half gallon carton); **Eggs** (price per dozen, Grade A, large); **Orange Juice** (64 oz. Tropicana or Florida Natural); **Coffee** (11.5 oz. can, vacuum-packed, Maxwell House, Hills Bros, or Folgers).*
Source: The Council for Community and Economic Research, ACCRA Cost of Living Index, 2017

Housing and Utility Costs

Area[1]	New Home Price ($)	Apartment Rent ($/month)	All Electric ($/month)	Part Electric ($/month)	Other Energy ($/month)	Telephone ($/month)
City[2]	435,485	1,746	-	110.50	101.89	36.19
Avg.	335,956	1,047	175.01	97.34	67.93	28.71
Min.	187,788	491	109.48	49.33	35.44	12.39
Max.	1,739,087	4,559	432.62	227.09	353.33	44.61

*Note: (1) Values for the local area are compared with the average, minimum and maximum values for all 294 areas in the Cost of Living Index; (2) Figures cover the Providence RI urban area; **New Home Price** (2,400 sf living area, 8,000 sf lot, in urban area with full utilities); **Apartment Rent** (950 sf 2 bedroom/1.5 or 2 bath, unfurnished, excluding all utilities except water); **All Electric** (average monthly cost for an all-electric home); **Part Electric** (average monthly cost for a part-electric home); **Other Energy** (average monthly cost for natural gas, fuel oil, coal, wood, and any other forms of energy except electricity); **Telephone** (price includes basic monthly rate for a private residential line plus additional local usage charges incurred by a family of four).*
Source: The Council for Community and Economic Research, ACCRA Cost of Living Index, 2017

Health Care, Transportation, and Other Costs

Area[1]	Doctor ($/visit)	Dentist ($/visit)	Optometrist ($/visit)	Gasoline ($/gallon)	Beauty Salon ($/visit)	Men's Shirt ($)
City[2]	146.33	91.00	125.67	2.21	55.55	33.33
Avg.	108.00	92.54	101.93	2.25	37.58	30.92
Min.	30.39	60.00	49.75	1.82	16.11	11.20
Max.	193.50	161.94	229.28	3.16	77.35	59.13

*Note: (1) Values for the local area are compared with the average, minimum and maximum values for all 294 areas in the Cost of Living Index; (2) Figures cover the Providence RI urban area; **Doctor** (general practitioners routine exam of an established patient); **Dentist** (adult teeth cleaning and periodic oral examination); **Optometrist** (full vision eye exam for established adult patient); **Gasoline** (one gallon regular unleaded, national brand, including all taxes, cash price at self-service pump if available); **Beauty Salon** (woman's shampoo, trim, and blow-dry); **Men's Shirt** (cotton/polyester dress shirt, pinpoint weave, long sleeves).*
Source: The Council for Community and Economic Research, ACCRA Cost of Living Index, 2017

HOUSING

House Price Index (HPI)

Area	National Ranking[2]	Quarterly Change (%)	One-Year Change (%)	Five-Year Change (%)
MSA[1]	119	0.64	6.36	22.49
U.S.[3]	–	1.61	6.68	34.71

Note: The HPI is a weighted repeat sales index. It measures average price changes in repeat sales or refinancings on the same properties. This information is obtained by reviewing repeat mortgage transactions on single-family properties whose mortgages have been purchased or securitized by Fannie Mae or Freddie Mac in January 1975; (1) Figures cover the Providence-Warwick, RI-MA Metropolitan Statistical Area—see Appendix B for areas included; (2) Rankings are based on annual percentage change for all metro areas containing at least 15,000 transactions over the last 10 years and ranges from 1 to 253; (3) figures based on a weighted average of Census Division estimates using a seasonally adjusted, purchase-only index; all figures are for the period ending December 31, 2017
Source: Federal Housing Finance Agency, House Price Index, February 28, 2018

Median Single-Family Home Prices

Area	2015	2016	2017p	Percent Change 2016 to 2017
MSA[1]	248.8	264.2	278.5	5.4
U.S. Average	223.9	235.5	248.8	5.6

Note: Figures are median sales prices of existing single-family homes in thousands of dollars; (p) preliminary; (1) Figures cover the Providence-Warwick, RI-MA Metropolitan Statistical Area—see Appendix B for areas included
Source: National Association of Realtors, Median Sales Price of Existing Single-Family Homes for Metropolitan Areas, 4th Quarter 2017

Qualifying Income Based on Median Sales Price of Existing Single-Family Homes

Area	With 5% Down ($)	With 10% Down ($)	With 20% Down ($)
MSA[1]	62,516	59,226	52,645
U.S. Average	55,585	52,659	46,808

Note: Figures are preliminary; Qualifying income is based on a mortgage rate of 4.17%. Monthly principal and interest payment is limited to 25% of income; (1) Figures cover the Providence-Warwick, RI-MA Metropolitan Statistical Area—see Appendix B for areas included
Source: National Association of Realtors, Qualifying Income Based on Median Sales Price of Existing Single-Family Homes for Metropolitan Areas, 4th Quarter 2017

Median Apartment Condo-Coop Home Prices

Area	2015	2016	2017p	Percent Change 2016 to 2017
MSA[1]	191.3	195.6	202.7	3.6
U.S. Average	210.7	220.7	234.3	6.2

Note: Figures are median sales prices of existing apartment condo-coop homes in thousands of dollars; (p) preliminary; (1) Figures cover the Providence-Warwick, RI-MA Metropolitan Statistical Area—see Appendix B for areas included
Source: National Association of Realtors, Median Sales Price of Existing Apartment Condo-Coop Homes for Metropolitan Areas, 4th Quarter 2017

Home Value Distribution

Area	Under $50,000	$50,000 -$99,999	$100,000 -$149,999	$150,000 -$199,999	$200,000 -$299,999	$300,000 -$499,999	$500,000 -$999,999	$1,000,000 or more
City	2.1	1.0	3.2	5.7	27.3	45.5	13.8	1.5
MSA[1]	3.2	2.7	8.3	17.8	32.8	26.3	7.5	1.5
U.S.	8.8	14.8	15.3	14.9	18.4	16.4	9.0	2.5

Note: Figures are percentages and cover owner-occupied housing units; (1) Figures cover the Providence-Warwick, RI-MA Metropolitan Statistical Area—see Appendix B for areas included
Source: U.S. Census Bureau, 2012-2016 American Community Survey 5-Year Estimates

Homeownership Rate

Area	2009 (%)	2010 (%)	2011 (%)	2012 (%)	2013 (%)	2014 (%)	2015 (%)	2016 (%)	2017 (%)
MSA[1]	61.7	61.0	61.3	61.7	60.1	61.6	60.0	57.5	58.6
U.S.	67.4	66.9	66.1	65.4	65.1	64.5	63.7	63.4	63.9

Note: (1) Figures cover the Providence-Warwick, RI-MA Metropolitan Statistical Area—see Appendix B for areas included
Source: U.S. Census Bureau, Housing Vacancies and Homeownership Annual Statistics: 2009-2017

Year Housing Structure Built

Area	2010 or Later	2000 -2009	1990 -1999	1980 -1989	1970 -1979	1960 -1969	1950 -1959	1940 -1949	Before 1940	Median Year
City	2.1	12.0	13.7	14.1	15.2	6.6	11.2	5.8	19.3	1975
MSA[1]	0.9	6.6	8.1	10.9	12.3	10.4	11.8	6.7	32.4	1959
U.S.	2.3	14.7	14.0	13.7	15.6	10.9	10.6	5.2	13.0	1977

Note: Figures are percentages except for Median Year; Note: (1) Figures cover the Providence-Warwick, RI-MA Metropolitan Statistical Area—see Appendix B for areas included
Source: U.S. Census Bureau, 2012-2016 American Community Survey 5-Year Estimates

Gross Monthly Rent

Area	Under $500	$500 -$999	$1,000 -$1,499	$1,500 -$1,999	$2,000 -$2,499	$2,500 -$2,999	$3,000 and up	Median ($)
City	19.3	27.5	27.8	16.5	4.5	2.0	2.5	1,038
MSA[1]	16.7	44.7	28.6	7.3	1.7	0.5	0.5	901
U.S.	11.3	43.3	27.7	10.7	4.0	1.6	1.5	949

Note: Figures are percentages except for Median; Gross rent is the contract rent plus the estimated average monthly cost of utilities (electricity, gas, and water and sewer) and fuels (oil, coal, kerosene, wood, etc.) if these are paid by the renter (or paid for the renter by someone else); (1) Figures cover the Providence-Warwick, RI-MA Metropolitan Statistical Area—see Appendix B for areas included
Source: U.S. Census Bureau, 2012-2016 American Community Survey 5-Year Estimates

HEALTH

Health Risk Factors

Category	MSA[1] (%)	U.S. (%)
Adults aged 18–64 who have any kind of health care coverage	90.7	87.7
Adults who reported being in good or excellent health	84.1	83.6
Adults who are current smokers	15.5	17.1
Adults who currently use E-cigarettes	5.2	4.7
Adults who currently use chewing tobacco, snuff, or snus	1.6	4.0
Adults who are heavy drinkers[2]	6.7	6.5
Adults who are binge drinkers[3]	15.8	16.9
Adults who are overweight (BMI 25.0 - 29.9)	36.9	35.3
Adults who are obese (BMI 30.0 - 99.8)	26.8	29.9
Adults who participated in any physical activities in the past month	76.1	76.9
Adults who always or nearly always wears a seat belt	92.2	94.3

Note: (1) Figures cover the Providence-Warwick, RI-MA Metropolitan Statistical Area—see Appendix B for areas included; (2) Heavy drinkers are classified as adult men having more than 14 drinks per week and adult women having more than 7 drinks per week; (3) Binge drinkers are classified as males having five or more drinks on one occasion or females having four or more drinks on one occasion
Source: Centers for Disease Control and Prevention, Behaviorial Risk Factor Surveillance System, SMART: Selected Metropolitan Area Risk Trends, 2016

Health Screening Rates

Category	MSA[1] (%)	U.S. (%)
Adults 50-75 who have had a blood stool test within the past year	10.5	8.0
Adults 50-75 who have had a colonoscopy in the past 10 years	72.9	63.5
Adults aged 65+ who have had flu shot within the past year	58.9	58.6
Adults aged 65+ who have ever had a pneumonia vaccination	75.2	73.4
Adults who have ever been tested for HIV	37.7	35.6
Women aged 21-65 who have had a pap test in the past three years	87.6	79.8
Men aged 40+ who have had a PSA test within the past two years	40.1	39.5
Women aged 40+ who have had a mammogram within the past two years	81.7	72.5

Note: (1) Figures cover the Providence-Warwick, RI-MA Metropolitan Statistical Area—see Appendix B for areas included; Source: Centers for Disease Control and Prevention, Behaviorial Risk Factor Surveillance System, SMART: Selected Metropolitan Area Risk Trends, 2016

Chronic Health Conditions

Category	MSA[1] (%)	U.S. (%)
Adults who have ever been told they had a heart attack	4.4	4.4
Adults who have ever been told they have angina or coronary heart disease	4.2	4.1
Adults who have ever been told they had a stroke	2.3	3.1
Adults who have been told they currently have asthma	10.7	9.3
Adults who have ever been told they have arthritis	28.6	25.8
Adults who have ever been told they have diabetes[2]	10.1	10.5
Adults who have ever been told they had skin cancer	6.6	5.9
Adults who have ever been told they had any other types of cancer	7.9	6.7
Adults who have ever been told they have COPD	7.0	6.3
Adults who have ever been told they have kidney disease	2.5	2.8
Adults who have ever been told they have a form of depression	21.1	17.4

Note: (1) Figures cover the Providence-Warwick, RI-MA Metropolitan Statistical Area—see Appendix B for areas included; (2) Figures do not include pregnancy-related, borderline, or pre-diabetes
Source: Centers for Disease Control and Prevention, Behaviorial Risk Factor Surveillance System, SMART: Selected Metropolitan Area Risk Trends, 2016

Mortality Rates for the Top 10 Causes of Death in the U.S.

ICD-10[a] Sub-Chapter	ICD-10[a] Code	Age-Adjusted Mortality Rate[1] per 100,000 population	
		County[2]	U.S.
Malignant neoplasms	C00-C97	157.3	158.5
Ischaemic heart diseases	I20-I25	92.0	96.8
Other forms of heart disease	I30-I51	35.0	52.4
Chronic lower respiratory diseases	J40-J47	29.0	40.9
Cerebrovascular diseases	I60-I69	23.3	37.2
Organic, including symptomatic, mental disorders	F01-F09	48.9	33.3
Other degenerative diseases of the nervous system	G30-G31	27.0	32.1
Other external causes of accidental injury	W00-X59	44.0	31.2
Diabetes mellitus	E10-E14	14.6	21.1
Hypertensive diseases	I10-I15	18.3	20.8

Note: (a) ICD-10 = International Classification of Diseases 10th Revision; (1) Mortality rates are a three year average covering 2014-2016; (2) Figures cover Washington County.
Source: Centers for Disease Control and Prevention, National Center for Health Statistics. Underlying Cause of Death 1999-2016 on CDC WONDER Online Database, released December 2017

Mortality Rates for Selected Causes of Death

ICD-10[a] Sub-Chapter	ICD-10[a] Code	Age-Adjusted Mortality Rate[1] per 100,000 population	
		County[2]	U.S.
Assault	X85-Y09	Suppressed	5.6
Diseases of the liver	K70-K76	10.6	14.0
Human immunodeficiency virus (HIV) disease	B20-B24	Suppressed	1.9
Influenza and pneumonia	J09-J18	11.8	14.6
Intentional self-harm	X60-X84	9.0	13.2
Malnutrition	E40-E46	Suppressed	1.3
Obesity and other hyperalimentation	E65-E68	Suppressed	2.1
Renal failure	N17-N19	6.2	13.0
Transport accidents	V01-V99	6.7	12.0
Viral hepatitis	B15-B19	Suppressed	1.9

Note: (a) ICD-10 = International Classification of Diseases 10th Revision; (1) Mortality rates are a three year average covering 2014-2016; (2) Figures cover Washington County; Data are Suppressed when the data meet the criteria for confidentiality constraints; Mortality rates are flagged as Unreliable when the rate would be calculated with a numerator of 20 or less.
Source: Centers for Disease Control and Prevention, National Center for Health Statistics. Underlying Cause of Death 1999-2016 on CDC WONDER Online Database, released December 2017

Health Insurance Coverage

Area	With Health Insurance	With Private Health Insurance	With Public Health Insurance	Without Health Insurance	Population Under Age 18 Without Health Insurance
City	94.9	83.8	25.7	5.1	3.3
MSA[1]	93.6	70.2	36.3	6.4	2.8
U.S.	88.3	66.7	33.0	11.7	5.9

Note: Figures are percentages that cover the civilian noninstitutionalized population; (1) Figures cover the Providence-Warwick, RI-MA Metropolitan Statistical Area—see Appendix B for areas included
Source: U.S. Census Bureau, 2012-2016 American Community Survey 5-Year Estimates

Number of Medical Professionals

Area	MDs[3]	DOs[3,4]	Dentists	Podiatrists	Chiropractors	Optometrists
County[1] (number)	285	37	70	8	28	27
County[1] (rate[2])	225.9	29.3	55.6	6.4	22.2	21.4
U.S. (rate[2])	276.5	22.3	67.3	6.0	26.7	15.9

Note: Data as of 2016 unless noted; (1) Data covers Washington County; (2) Rate per 100,000 population; (3) Data as of 2015 and includes all active, non-federal physicians; (4) Doctor of Osteopathic Medicine
Source: U.S. Department of Health and Human Services, Health Resources and Services Administration, Bureau of Health Professions, Area Resource File (ARF) 2016-2017

EDUCATION

Public School District Statistics

District Name	Schls	Pupils	Pupil/ Teacher Ratio	Minority Pupils[1] (%)	Free Lunch Eligible[2] (%)	IEP[3] (%)
South Kingstown	8	3,249	13.2	15.8	19.8	13.2

Note: Table includes school districts with 100 or more students; (1) Percentage of students that are not non-Hispanic white; (2) Percentage of students that are eligible for the free lunch program; (3) Percentage of students that have an Individualized Education Program.
Source: U.S. Department of Education, National Center for Education Statistics, Common Core of Data, Local Education Agency (School District) Universe Survey: School Year 2015-2016; U.S. Department of Education, National Center for Education Statistics, Common Core of Data, Public Elementary/Secondary School Universe Survey: School Year 2015-2016

Highest Level of Education

Area	Less than H.S.	H.S. Diploma	Some College, No Deg.	Associate Degree	Bachelor's Degree	Master's Degree	Prof. School Degree	Doctorate Degree
City	5.6	20.8	16.7	5.4	27.0	15.1	4.2	5.2
MSA[1]	14.2	28.5	18.2	8.7	18.5	8.6	1.8	1.5
U.S.	13.0	27.5	21.0	8.2	18.8	8.2	2.0	1.3

Note: Figures cover persons age 25 and over; (1) Figures cover the Providence-Warwick, RI-MA Metropolitan Statistical Area—see Appendix B for areas included
Source: U.S. Census Bureau, 2012-2016 American Community Survey 5-Year Estimates

Educational Attainment by Race

Area	High School Graduate or Higher (%)					Bachelor's Degree or Higher (%)				
	Total	White	Black	Asian	Hisp.[2]	Total	White	Black	Asian	Hisp.[2]
City	94.4	95.3	74.8	100.0	83.8	51.6	52.8	36.1	85.1	45.1
MSA[1]	85.8	87.6	80.9	82.7	67.2	30.4	31.7	20.9	48.0	12.4
U.S.	87.0	88.9	84.3	86.3	65.7	30.3	31.6	20.0	52.1	14.7

Note: Figures shown cover persons 25 years old and over; (1) Figures cover the Providence-Warwick, RI-MA Metropolitan Statistical Area—see Appendix B for areas included; (2) People of Hispanic origin can be of any race
Source: U.S. Census Bureau, 2012-2016 American Community Survey 5-Year Estimates

School Enrollment by Grade and Control

Area	Preschool (%)		Kindergarten (%)		Grades 1 - 4 (%)		Grades 5 - 8 (%)		Grades 9 - 12 (%)	
	Public	Private	Public	Private	Public	Private	Public	Private	Public	Private
City	55.3	44.7	100.0	0.0	93.1	6.9	97.3	2.7	86.0	14.0
MSA[1]	53.0	47.0	87.5	12.5	89.7	10.3	88.8	11.2	86.8	13.2
U.S.	58.4	41.6	87.7	12.3	89.8	10.2	89.7	10.3	90.4	9.6

Note: Figures shown cover persons 3 years old and over; (1) Figures cover the Providence-Warwick, RI-MA Metropolitan Statistical Area—see Appendix B for areas included
Source: U.S. Census Bureau, 2012-2016 American Community Survey 5-Year Estimates

Average Salaries of Public School Classroom Teachers

Area	2015		2016		Change from 2015 to 2016	
	Dollars	Rank[1]	Dollars	Rank[1]	Percent	Rank[2]
Rhode Island	65,918	8	66,197	9	0.4	39
U.S. Average	57,611	–	58,353	–	1.3	–

Note: (1) Rank ranges from 1 to 51 where 1 indicates highest salary; (2) Rank ranges from 1 to 51 where 1 indicates highest percent change.
Source: National Education Association, Rankings & Estimates: Rankings of the States 2016 and Estimates of School Statistics 2017

Higher Education

Four-Year Colleges			Two-Year Colleges			Medical Schools[1]	Law Schools[2]	Voc/ Tech[3]
Public	Private Non-profit	Private For-profit	Public	Private Non-profit	Private For-profit			
0	0	0	0	0	0	0	0	0

Note: Figures cover institutions located within the city limits and include main campuses only; (1) includes schools accredited by the Liaison Committee on Medical Education and the American Osteopathic Association's Commission on Osteopathic College Accreditation; (2) includes ABA-accredited schools, schools with provisional ABA accreditation, and state accredited schools; (3) includes all schools with programs that are less than 2 years.
Source: National Center for Education Statistics, Integrated Postsecondary Education System (IPEDS), 2016-17; Wikipedia, List of Medical Schools in the United States, accessed April 2, 2018; Wikipedia, List of Law Schools in the United States, accessed April 2, 2018

According to *U.S. News & World Report,* the Providence-Warwick, RI-MA metro area is home to two of the best national universities in the U.S.: **Brown University** (#14 tie); **University of Rhode Island** (#156 tie). The indicators used to capture academic quality fall into a number of categories: assessment by administrators at peer institutions; retention of students; faculty resources; student selectivity; financial resources; alumni giving; high school counselor ratings of colleges; and graduation rate. *U.S. News & World Report, "America's Best Colleges 2018"*

According to *U.S. News & World Report,* the Providence-Warwick, RI-MA metro area is home to two of the best liberal arts colleges in the U.S.: **Wheaton College** (#76 tie); **Stonehill College** (#111). The indicators used to capture academic quality fall into a number of categories: assessment by administrators at peer institutions; retention of students; faculty resources; student selectivity; financial resources; alumni giving; high school counselor ratings of colleges; and graduation rate. *U.S. News & World Report, "America's Best Colleges 2018"*

According to *U.S. News & World Report,* the Providence-Warwick, RI-MA metro area is home to one of the top 75 medical schools for research in the U.S.: **Brown University (Alpert)** (#32 tie). The rankings are based on a weighted average of 11 measures of quality: quality assessment; peer assessment score; assessment score by residency directors; research activity; total research activity; average research activity per faculty member; student selectivity; median MCAT total score; median undergraduate GPA; acceptance rate; and faculty resources. *U.S. News & World Report, "America's Best Graduate Schools, Medical, 2019"*

PRESIDENTIAL ELECTION

2016 Presidential Election Results

Area	Clinton	Trump	Johnson	Stein	Other
Washington County	50.8	41.0	3.8	1.6	2.7
U.S.	48.0	45.9	3.3	1.1	1.7

Note: Results are percentages and may not add to 100% due to rounding
Source: Dave Leip's Atlas of U.S. Presidential Elections

EMPLOYERS

Major Employers

Company Name	Industry
A&M Special Purchasing	Payroll accounting service
Acushnet Company	Sporting & recreation goods
Brown University	Colleges & universities
Charlton Memorial Hospital	General medical & surgical hospitals
City of Fall River	Public elementary & secondary schools
City of Providence	General government administration
CVS Pharmacy	Drug stores
Hasbro	Games, toys, & children's vehicles
Hasbro Managerial Services	Management services
Kent Hospital	General medical & surgical hospitals
Providence School Department	Public elementary & secondary schools
Rhode Island Hospital	General medical & surgical hospitals
Roman Catholic Diocese of Fall River	Catholic church
Saint Luke's Hospital of New Bedford	General medical & surgical hospitals
Samsonite International S.A.	Luggage
Southcoast Hospitals Group	General medical & surgical hospitals
University of Rhode Island	Colleges & universities
US Navy	Navy
Women & Infants Hospital of Rhode Island	Specialty outpatient clinics, nec

Note: Companies shown are located within the Providence-Warwick, RI-MA Metropolitan Statistical Area.
Source: Hoovers.com; Wikipedia

PUBLIC SAFETY

Crime Rate

Area	All Crimes	Violent Crimes				Property Crimes		
		Murder	Rape[3]	Robbery	Aggrav. Assault	Burglary	Larceny -Theft	Motor Vehicle Theft
City	848.7	0.0	6.5	3.2	32.4	204.1	550.7	51.8
Metro[1]	n/a	2.4	38.8	65.7	208.2	367.3	n/a	n/a
U.S.	2,847.8	5.3	40.4	102.8	248.5	468.9	1,745.0	236.9

Note: Figures are crimes per 100,000 population; (1) Figures cover the Providence-Warwick, RI-MA Metropolitan Statistical Area—see Appendix B for areas included; (3) The city and U.S. figures shown were reported using the revised Uniform Crime Reporting (UCR) definition of rape. The metro area figures shown are an aggregate total of the data submitted using both the revised and legacy UCR definitions.
Source: FBI Uniform Crime Reports, 2016

Hate Crimes

Area	Number of Quarters Reported	Number of Incidents per Bias Motivation					
		Race/Ethnicity/ Ancestry	Religion	Sexual Orientation	Disability	Gender	Gender Identity
City	1	0	1	0	0	0	0
U.S.	4	3,489	1,273	1,076	70	31	124

Source: Federal Bureau of Investigation, Hate Crime Statistics 2016

Identity Theft Consumer Reports

Area	Reports	Reports per 100,000 Population	Rank[2]
MSA[1]	1,725	107	78
U.S.	371,061	114	-

Note: (1) Figures cover the Providence-Warwick, RI-MA Metropolitan Statistical Area—see Appendix B for areas included; (2) Rank ranges from 1 to 389 where 1 indicates greatest number of identity theft reports per 100,000 population
Source: Federal Trade Commission, Consumer Sentinel Network Data Book for January–December 2017

Fraud and Other Consumer Reports

Area	Reports	Reports per 100,000 Population	Rank[2]
MSA[1]	6,934	429	210
U.S.	2,304,550	708	-

Note: (1) Figures cover the Providence-Warwick, RI-MA Metropolitan Statistical Area—see Appendix B for areas included; (2) Rank ranges from 1 to 389 where 1 indicates greatest number of fraud and other consumer reports per 100,000 population
Source: Federal Trade Commission, Consumer Sentinel Network Data Book for January–December 2017

SPORTS

Professional Sports Teams

Team Name	League	Year Established
No teams are located in the metro area		

Source: Wikipedia, Major Professional Sports Teams of the United States and Canada, April 5, 2018

CLIMATE

Average and Extreme Temperatures

Temperature	Jan	Feb	Mar	Apr	May	Jun	Jul	Aug	Sep	Oct	Nov	Dec	Yr.
Extreme High (°F)	66	72	80	98	94	97	102	104	100	88	81	70	104
Average High (°F)	37	39	46	58	68	77	82	80	73	63	52	41	60
Average Temp. (°F)	29	30	38	48	58	67	73	71	64	54	44	33	51
Average Low (°F)	20	22	29	39	48	57	63	62	54	43	35	25	42
Extreme Low (°F)	-13	-7	1	14	29	41	48	40	32	20	6	-10	-13

Note: Figures cover the years 1948-1992
Source: National Climatic Data Center, International Station Meteorological Climate Summary, 9/96

Average Precipitation/Snowfall/Humidity

Precip./Humidity	Jan	Feb	Mar	Apr	May	Jun	Jul	Aug	Sep	Oct	Nov	Dec	Yr.
Avg. Precip. (in.)	3.9	3.6	4.2	4.1	3.7	2.9	3.2	4.0	3.5	3.6	4.5	4.3	45.3
Avg. Snowfall (in.)	10	10	7	1	Tr	0	0	0	0	Tr	1	7	35
Avg. Rel. Hum. 7am (%)	71	71	71	70	73	75	78	81	83	81	78	74	75
Avg. Rel. Hum. 4pm (%)	58	56	54	51	55	58	58	60	60	58	60	60	57

Note: Figures cover the years 1948-1992; Tr = Trace amounts (<0.05 in. of rain; <0.5 in. of snow)
Source: National Climatic Data Center, International Station Meteorological Climate Summary, 9/96

Weather Conditions

Temperature			Daytime Sky			Precipitation		
5°F & below	32°F & below	90°F & above	Clear	Partly cloudy	Cloudy	0.01 inch or more precip.	0.1 inch or more snow/ice	Thunder-storms
6	117	9	85	134	146	123	21	21

Note: Figures are average number of days per year and cover the years 1948-1992
Source: National Climatic Data Center, International Station Meteorological Climate Summary, 9/96

HAZARDOUS WASTE

Superfund Sites

The Providence-Warwick, RI-MA metro area is home to 17 sites on the EPA's Superfund National Priorities List: **Atlas Tack Corp.** (final); **Central Landfill** (final); **Centredale Manor Restoration Project** (final); **Davis Liquid Waste** (final); **Davisville Naval Construction Battalion Center** (final); **Landfill & Resource Recovery, Inc.** (final); **New Bedford** (final); **Newport Naval Education & Training Center** (final); **Peterson/Puritan, Inc.** (final); **Picillo Farm** (final); **Re-solve, Inc.** (final); **Rose Hill Regional Landfill** (final); **Stamina Mills, Inc.** (final); **Sullivan's Ledge** (final); **Walton & Lonsbury Inc.** (final); **West Kingston Town Dump/Uri Disposal Area** (final); **Western Sand & Gravel** (final). There are a total of 1,396 Superfund sites with a status of proposed or final on the list in the U.S. *U.S. Environmental Protection Agency, National Priorities List, April 4, 2018*

AIR & WATER QUALITY

Air Quality Trends: Ozone

	1990	1995	2000	2005	2010	2012	2013	2014	2015	2016
MSA[1]	0.106	0.107	0.087	0.090	0.072	0.072	0.073	0.067	0.070	0.075
U.S.	0.087	0.089	0.081	0.079	0.073	0.075	0.069	0.067	0.068	0.069

Note: (1) Data covers the Providence-Warwick, RI-MA Metropolitan Statistical Area—see Appendix B for areas included. The values shown are the composite ozone concentration averages among trend sites based on the highest fourth daily maximum 8-hour concentration in parts per million. These trends are based on sites having an adequate record of monitoring data during the trend period. Data from exceptional events are included.
Source: U.S. Environmental Protection Agency, Air Quality Monitoring Information, "Air Quality Trends by City, 1990-2016"

Air Quality Index

Area	Percent of Days when Air Quality was...[2]					AQI Statistics[2]	
	Good	Moderate	Unhealthy for Sensitive Groups	Unhealthy	Very Unhealthy	Maximum	Median
MSA[1]	73.2	24.9	1.4	0.5	0.0	151	43

Note: (1) Data covers the Providence-Warwick, RI-MA Metropolitan Statistical Area—see Appendix B for areas included; (2) Based on 365 days with AQI data in 2017. Air Quality Index (AQI) is an index for reporting daily air quality. EPA calculates the AQI for five major air pollutants regulated by the Clean Air Act: ground-level ozone, particle pollution (aka particulate matter), carbon monoxide, sulfur dioxide, and nitrogen dioxide. The AQI runs from 0 to 500. The higher the AQI value, the greater the level of air pollution and the greater the health concern. There are six AQI categories: "Good" AQI is between 0 and 50. Air quality is considered satisfactory; "Moderate" AQI is between 51 and 100. Air quality is acceptable; "Unhealthy for Sensitive Groups" When AQI values are between 101 and 150, members of sensitive groups may experience health effects; "Unhealthy" When AQI values are between 151 and 200 everyone may begin to experience health effects; "Very Unhealthy" AQI values between 201 and 300 trigger a health alert; "Hazardous" AQI values over 300 trigger warnings of emergency conditions (not shown).
Source: U.S. Environmental Protection Agency, Air Quality Index Report, 2017

Air Quality Index Pollutants

Area	Percent of Days when AQI Pollutant was...[2]					
	Carbon Monoxide	Nitrogen Dioxide	Ozone	Sulfur Dioxide	Particulate Matter 2.5	Particulate Matter 10
MSA[1]	0.0	3.3	55.9	0.0	40.8	0.0

Note: (1) Data covers the Providence-Warwick, RI-MA Metropolitan Statistical Area—see Appendix B for areas included; (2) Based on 365 days with AQI data in 2017. The Air Quality Index (AQI) is an index for reporting daily air quality. EPA calculates the AQI for five major air pollutants regulated by the Clean Air Act: ground-level ozone, particle pollution (also known as particulate matter), carbon monoxide, sulfur dioxide, and nitrogen dioxide. The AQI runs from 0 to 500. The higher the AQI value, the greater the level of air pollution and the greater the health concern.
Source: U.S. Environmental Protection Agency, Air Quality Index Report, 2017

Maximum Air Pollutant Concentrations: Particulate Matter, Ozone, CO and Lead

	Particulate Matter 10 (ug/m^3)	Particulate Matter 2.5 Wtd AM (ug/m^3)	Particulate Matter 2.5 24-Hr (ug/m^3)	Ozone (ppm)	Carbon Monoxide (ppm)	Lead (ug/m^3)
MSA[1] Level	39	9.3	20	0.076	2	n/a
NAAQS[2]	150	15	35	0.075	9	0.15
Met NAAQS[2]	Yes	Yes	Yes	No	Yes	n/a

Note: (1) Data covers the Providence-Warwick, RI-MA Metropolitan Statistical Area—see Appendix B for areas included; Data from exceptional events are included; (2) National Ambient Air Quality Standards; ppm = parts per million; ug/m^3 = micrograms per cubic meter; n/a not available.
Concentrations: Particulate Matter 10 (coarse particulate)—highest second maximum 24-hour concentration; Particulate Matter 2.5 Wtd AM (fine particulate)—highest weighted annual mean concentration; Particulate Matter 2.5 24-Hour (fine particulate)—highest 98th percentile 24-hour concentration; Ozone—highest fourth daily maximum 8-hour concentration; Carbon Monoxide—highest second maximum non-overlapping 8-hour concentration; Lead—maximum running 3-month average
Source: U.S. Environmental Protection Agency, Air Quality Monitoring Information, "Air Quality Statistics by City, 2016"

Maximum Air Pollutant Concentrations: Nitrogen Dioxide and Sulfur Dioxide

	Nitrogen Dioxide AM (ppb)	Nitrogen Dioxide 1-Hr (ppb)	Sulfur Dioxide AM (ppb)	Sulfur Dioxide 1-Hr (ppb)	Sulfur Dioxide 24-Hr (ppb)
MSA[1] Level	20	56	n/a	7	n/a
NAAQS[2]	53	100	30	75	140
Met NAAQS[2]	Yes	Yes	n/a	Yes	n/a

Note: (1) Data covers the Providence-Warwick, RI-MA Metropolitan Statistical Area—see Appendix B for areas included; Data from exceptional events are included; (2) National Ambient Air Quality Standards; ppm = parts per million; ug/m^3 = micrograms per cubic meter; n/a not available.
Concentrations: Nitrogen Dioxide AM—highest arithmetic mean concentration; Nitrogen Dioxide 1-Hr—highest 98th percentile 1-hour daily maximum concentration; Sulfur Dioxide AM—highest annual mean concentration; Sulfur Dioxide 1-Hr—highest 99th percentile 1-hour daily maximum concentration; Sulfur Dioxide 24-Hr—highest second maximum 24-hour concentration
Source: U.S. Environmental Protection Agency, Air Quality Monitoring Information, "Air Quality Statistics by City, 2016"

Drinking Water

Water System Name	Pop. Served	Primary Water Source Type	Violations[1]	
			Health Based	Monitoring/ Reporting
South Kingstown-South Shore	4,976	Ground	0	2
Suez Water	19,800	Ground	0	0
University of Rhode Island	19,145	Ground	0	0

Note: (1) Based on violation data from January 1, 2017 to December 31, 2017
Source: U.S. Environmental Protection Agency, Office of Ground Water and Drinking Water, Safe Drinking Water Information System (based on data extracted April 5, 2018)

Mount Pleasant, South Carolina

Background

Mount Pleasant is located along the eastern coast of South Carolina, part of the Charleston metro area. It lies northeast of the Cooper River in Charleston County, across the harbor from the City of Charleston, bordered on the west by the Wando River and on the east by the Intracoastal Waterway, Sullivan's Island and the Isle of Palms. A mild climate, excellent public schools, low crime rates, abundant housing, ample opportunities for employment, and access to artistic and cultural amenities are fueling the region's rapid growth.

Originally occupied by the Sewee Indians, Mount Pleasant's first white settlers arrived from England in 1680 under the leadership of Captain Florentia O'Sullivan, who was granted acreage which included not only the island that bears his name, but also the land that was to become Mount Pleasant. A greater part of the area was also called Shipyard Plantation because its deep water and abundance of good timber made it ideal for a prosperous shipbuilding enterprise.

Mount Pleasant played a leading role in the first major military engagement—and victory—of the Revolutionary War. When Charleston finally fell to the British on November 12, 1775, Cornwallis crossed the Cooper River with 2,500 troops and took possession of Haddrell's Point. The British headquarters is said to have been the home of Jacob Motte, later known as Hibben House.

Mount Pleasant was incorporated as a city in 1837. In 1860, a public meeting was held in Mount Pleasant that produced the first secession resolution of the state. The secession convention met in Charleston on December 20, 1860 and seven southern states formed the Confederate States of America.

Twenty years after the Civil War, Mount Pleasant was populated by 783 residents. Four miles of street were laid with shells and the town was known as a pleasure and health resort. Truck farming was a major occupation and Mount Pleasant was the site of a sawmill and brick factory. A steam ferry provided transportation between Charleston and Mount Pleasant until the first Cooper River Bridge was built in 1929.

Today, Mount Pleasant is a proven outstanding location for business, offering a highly desirable lifestyle to attract and retain key employees, while providing a highly skilled regional workforce. A wide range of sites and facilities exist for offices, research and development companies and information/technology intensive operations. The community has an impressive list of companies that have benefited from the mix of essential factors for corporate growth, including an integrated highway system, a growing international airport and the second busiest container port along the Atlantic and Gulf coasts. Businesses located in the Charleston region benefit from highly efficient access to their markets.

Mount Pleasant offers bountiful facilities and natural settings perfect for golf, tennis, boating, kayaking, nature tours, and deep-sea fishing. Practically an island for its expansive waterfront, Mount Pleasant offers quick access to the beaches of Isle of Palms and Sullivan's Island.

Mount Pleasant is home to the most comprehensive collections of naval aircraft and is a tour departure point to Fort Sumter National Monument, and home of the Congressional Medal of Honor Museum. Boone Hall Plantation is one of the few surviving working plantations in the nation and Charles Pinckney National Historic Site is the former residence of one of the framers of the U.S. Constitution.

Mount Pleasant's mild year-round climate is greatly affected by its close proximity to the Atlantic Ocean and the Intracoastal Waterway.

Rankings

General Rankings

- For its "Best Places to Live" rankings (formerly known as Best for Vets: Places to Live), *Military Times* evaluated 577 cities (79 large, 244 medium, 254 small) and compared the locations across three broad categories: veteran and military culture/services; economic indicators; and livability factors such as health, crime, traffic, and school quality. Mount Pleasant ranked #12 out of the top 50, in the small city category (populations of less than 75,000). Data points more specific to veterans and the military weighed more heavily than the rest. *rebootcamp.militarytimes.com, "Military Times Best Places to Live 2017," September 11, 2017*

Business/Finance Rankings

- The personal finance site NerdWallet analyzed 183 American metropolitan areas with populations over 250,000 and more than 15,000 businesses to rank where entrepreneurs find the most success. Criteria included area economy, annual income, housing cost, unemployment rate, and the success rate of area businesses. Charleston* ranked #129. *www.nerdwallet.com, "Best Places to Start a Business," April 27, 2015*
- The Brookings Institution ranked the 100 largest metro areas in the U.S. based on income inequality. Charleston* was ranked #27 (#1 = greatest ineqality). Criteria: the "95/20 ratio," a figure representing the income at which a household earns more than 95 percent of all other households, divided by the income at which a household earns more than only 20 percent of all other households. *Brookings Institution, "Household Income Inequality, 100 Largest U.S. Metro Areas, 2014-2016," February 5, 2018*
- Charleston* was cited as one of America's top metros for new and expanded facility projects in 2017. The area ranked #3 in the mid-sized metro area category (population 200,000 to 1 million). *Site Selection, "Top Metropolitans of 2017," March 2018*
- The Charleston* metro area appeared on the Milken Institute "2017 Best Performing Cities" list. Rank: #22 out of 200 large metro areas. Criteria: job growth; wage and salary growth; high-tech output growth. *Milken Institute, "Best-Performing Cities 2017," January 2018*
- *Forbes* ranked the 200 most populous metro areas to determine the nation's "Best Places for Business and Careers." The Charleston* metro area was ranked #26. Criteria: costs (business and living); job growth (past and projected); income growth; quality of life; educational attainment (college and high school); projected economic growth; cultural and recreational opportunities; net migration patterns; number of highly ranked colleges. *Forbes, "The Best Places for Business and Careers 2017," October 24, 2017*

Education Rankings

- Personal finance website *WalletHub* analyzed the 150 largest U.S. metropolitan statistical areas to determine where the most educated Americans are choosing to settle. Criteria: education quality and attainment gap; education levels; percentage of workers with degrees; public school rankings; quality and size of each metro area's universities. Charleston* was ranked #65 (#1 = most educated city). *www.WalletHub.com, "2017's Most and Least Educated Cities in America, " July 25, 2017*

Environmental Rankings

- Sperling's BestPlaces assessed 379 metropolitan areas of the United States for the likelihood of dangerously extreme weather events or earthquakes. In general the Southeast and South-Central regions have the highest risk of weather extremes and earthquakes, while the Pacific Northwest enjoys the lowest risk. Of the least risky metropolitan areas, the Charleston* metro area was ranked #250. *www.bestplaces.net, "Safest Places from Natural Disasters," April 2011*

- Charleston* was highlighted as one of the cleanest metro areas for ozone air pollution in the U.S. during 2013 through 2015. The list represents cities with no monitored ozone air pollution in unhealthful ranges. *American Lung Association, State of the Air 2017*

Health/Fitness Rankings

- Trulia analyzed the 100 largest U.S. metro areas to identify the nation's best cities for weight loss, based on the percentage of adults who bike or walk to work, sporting goods stores, grocery stores, access to outdoor activities, weight-loss centers, gyms, and average space reserved for parks. Charleston* ranked #6. *Trulia.com, "Where to Live to Get in Shape in the New Year," January 4, 2018*

- Charleston* was identified as a "2016 Spring Allergy Capital." The area ranked #28 out of 100. Three groups of factors were used to identify the most severe cities for people with allergies during the spring season: annual pollen levels; medicine utilization; access to board-certified allergists. *Asthma and Allergy Foundation of America, "Spring Allergy Capitals 2016"*

- Charleston* was identified as a "2016 Fall Allergy Capital." The area ranked #35 out of 100. Three groups of factors were used to identify the most severe cities for people with allergies during the fall season: annual pollen levels; medicine utilization; access to board-certified allergists. *Asthma and Allergy Foundation of America, "Fall Allergy Capitals 2016"*

- Charleston* was identified as a "2015 Asthma Capital." The area ranked #56 out of the nation's 100 largest metropolitan areas. Criteria: estimated prevalence; self-reported prevalence; crude death rate for asthma; annual pollen score; annual air quality; public smoking laws; number of board-certified asthma specialists; school inhaler access laws; rescue medication use; controller medication use; ER visits for asthma; uninsured rate; poverty rate. *Asthma and Allergy Foundation of America, "Asthma Capitals 2015"*

- The Charleston* metro area ranked #33 out of 189 in The Gallup-Healthways Well-Being Index. Criteria: purpose; social well being; financial health; community and physical health. Results are based on telephone interviews with adults, aged 18 and older, living in metropolitan areas in the 50 U.S. states and the District of Columbia. *Gallup-Healthways, "State of American Well-Being, 2017 Community Well-Being Rankings" March 2018*

Real Estate Rankings

- With data from RealtyTrac, Yahoo! Finance researchers listed the housing markets in which housing affordability is improving most, factoring in interest rates as well as median home prices. The Charleston* metro area was among the least affordable housing markets. *news.yahoo.com, "10 Cities Where Ordinary People Can No Longer Afford Homes," March 5, 2014*

- Charleston* was ranked #158 out of 238 metro areas in terms of housing affordability in 2017 by the National Association of Home Builders (#1 = most affordable). Criteria: the share of homes sold in that area affordable to a family earning the local median income, based on standard mortgage underwriting criteria. *National Association of Home Builders®, NAHB-Wells Fargo Housing Opportunity Index, 4th Quarter 2017*

Safety Rankings

- The National Insurance Crime Bureau ranked 382 metro areas in the U.S. in terms of per capita rates of vehicle theft. The Charleston* metro area ranked #51 (#1 = highest rate). Criteria: number of vehicle theft offenses per 100,000 inhabitants in 2016. *National Insurance Crime Bureau, "Hot Spots 2016," June 8, 2017*

Seniors/Retirement Rankings

- From its Best Cities for Successful Aging indexes, the Milken Institute generated rankings for metropolitan areas, weighing data in nine categories—health care, wellness, living arrangements, transportation and convenience, financial characteristics, education, employment, community engagement, and overall livability. The Charleston* metro area was ranked #39 overall in the large metro area category. *Milken Institute, "Best Cities for Successful Aging, 2017" March 14, 2017*

*Mount Pleasant is located within the Charleston-North Charleston, SC Metropolitan Statistical Area.

Business Environment

CITY FINANCES

City Government Finances

Component	2015 ($000)	2015 ($ per capita)
Total Revenues	145,748	1,792
Total Expenditures	117,665	1,447
Debt Outstanding	126,079	1,550
Cash and Securities[1]	160,724	1,977

Note: (1) Cash and security holdings of a government at the close of its fiscal year,, including those of its dependent agencies, utilities, and liquor stores.
Source: U.S Census Bureau, State & Local Government Finances 2015

City Government Revenue by Source

Source	2015 ($000)	2015 ($ per capita)	2015 (%)
General Revenue			
From Federal Government	213	3	0.1
From State Government	3,446	42	2.4
From Local Governments	3,425	42	2.3
Taxes			
Property	30,865	380	21.2
Sales and Gross Receipts	15,412	190	10.6
Personal Income	0	0	0.0
Corporate Income	0	0	0.0
Motor Vehicle License	0	0	0.0
Other Taxes	27,236	335	18.7
Current Charges	42,594	524	29.2
Liquor Store	0	0	0.0
Utility	15,955	196	10.9
Employee Retirement	0	0	0.0

Source: U.S Census Bureau, State & Local Government Finances 2015

City Government Expenditures by Function

Function	2015 ($000)	2015 ($ per capita)	2015 (%)
General Direct Expenditures			
Air Transportation	0	0	0.0
Corrections	0	0	0.0
Education	0	0	0.0
Employment Security Administration	0	0	0.0
Financial Administration	1,467	18	1.2
Fire Protection	8,959	110	7.6
General Public Buildings	2,727	33	2.3
Governmental Administration, Other	5,100	62	4.3
Health	0	0	0.0
Highways	8,183	100	7.0
Hospitals	0	0	0.0
Housing and Community Development	2,059	25	1.7
Interest on General Debt	2,019	24	1.7
Judicial and Legal	1,263	15	1.1
Libraries	0	0	0.0
Parking	0	0	0.0
Parks and Recreation	5,712	70	4.9
Police Protection	11,243	138	9.6
Public Welfare	0	0	0.0
Sewerage	463	5	0.4
Solid Waste Management	8,758	107	7.4
Veterans' Services	0	0	0.0
Liquor Store	0	0	0.0
Utility	18,484	227	15.7
Employee Retirement	0	0	0.0

Source: U.S Census Bureau, State & Local Government Finances 2015

DEMOGRAPHICS

Population Growth

Area	1990 Census	2000 Census	2010 Census	2016* Estimate	Population Growth (%) 1990-2016	2010-2016
City	33,294	47,609	67,843	77,907	134.0	14.8
MSA[1]	506,875	549,033	664,607	728,271	43.7	9.6
U.S.	248,709,873	281,421,906	308,745,538	318,558,162	28.1	3.2

Note: (1) Figures cover the Charleston-North Charleston, SC Metropolitan Statistical Area—see Appendix B for areas included; (*) 2012-2016 5-year estimated population
Source: U.S. Census Bureau, 1990 Census, Census 2000, Census 2010, 2012-2016 American Community Survey 5-Year Estimates

Household Size

Area	Persons in Household (%)							Average Household Size
	One	Two	Three	Four	Five	Six	Seven or More	
City	28.2	34.5	16.7	14.4	4.2	1.4	0.5	2.50
MSA[1]	28.8	35.3	16.6	12.3	4.6	1.5	0.9	2.60
U.S.	27.7	33.7	15.7	13.1	6.0	2.3	1.5	2.60

Note: (1) Figures cover the Charleston-North Charleston, SC Metropolitan Statistical Area—see Appendix B for areas included
Source: U.S. Census Bureau, 2012-2016 American Community Survey 5-Year Estimates

Race

Area	White Alone[2] (%)	Black Alone[2] (%)	Asian Alone[2] (%)	AIAN[3] Alone[2] (%)	NHOPI[4] Alone[2] (%)	Other Race Alone[2] (%)	Two or More Races (%)
City	90.8	5.4	1.5	0.2	0.1	0.1	2.0
MSA[1]	67.5	26.6	1.7	0.3	0.1	1.4	2.4
U.S.	73.3	12.6	5.2	0.8	0.2	4.8	3.1

Note: (1) Figures cover the Charleston-North Charleston, SC Metropolitan Statistical Area—see Appendix B for areas included; (2) Alone is defined as not being in combination with one or more other races; (3) American Indian and Alaska Native; (4) Native Hawaiian and Other Pacific Islander
Source: U.S. Census Bureau, 2012-2016 American Community Survey 5-Year Estimates

Hispanic or Latino Origin

Area	Total (%)	Mexican (%)	Puerto Rican (%)	Cuban (%)	Other (%)
City	3.2	1.1	0.7	0.0	1.3
MSA[1]	5.3	2.7	0.8	0.1	1.6
U.S.	17.3	11.0	1.7	0.7	4.0

Note: Persons of Hispanic or Latino origin can be of any race; (1) Figures cover the Charleston-North Charleston, SC Metropolitan Statistical Area—see Appendix B for areas included
Source: U.S. Census Bureau, 2012-2016 American Community Survey 5-Year Estimates

Segregation

Type	Segregation Indices[1] 1990	2000	2010	2010 Rank[2]	Percent Change 1990-2000	1990-2010	2000-2010
Black/White	47.4	44.2	41.5	88	-3.2	-5.9	-2.7
Asian/White	34.4	34.2	33.4	84	-0.3	-1.1	-0.8
Hispanic/White	26.6	32.2	39.8	66	5.6	13.2	7.6

Note: All figures cover the Metropolitan Statistical Area—see Appendix B for areas included; Figures are based on an analysis of 1990, 2000, and 2010 Census Decennial Census tract data by William H. Frey, Brookings Institution and the University of Michigan Social Science Data Analysis Network. In this analysis all racial groups (whites, blacks, and asians) are non-Hispanic members of those races. Hispanics are shown as a separate category; (1) Segregation Indices are Dissimilarity Indices that measure the degree to which the minority group is distributed differently than whites across census tracts. They range from 0 (complete integration) to 100 (complete segregation) where the value indicates the percentage of the minority group that needs to move to be distributed exactly like whites; (2) Ranges from 1 (most segregated) to 102 (least segregated); n/a not available.
Source: www.CensusScope.org

Ancestry

Area	German	Irish	English	American	Italian	Polish	French[2]	Scottish	Dutch
City	15.3	16.9	13.6	12.3	6.6	3.5	2.7	4.6	1.5
MSA[1]	10.6	10.5	8.5	13.2	3.6	1.7	2.3	2.5	0.9
U.S.	14.4	10.4	7.7	6.9	5.4	2.9	2.6	1.7	1.3

Note: Figures are the percentage of the total population reporting a particular ancestry. The nine most commonly reported ancestries in the U.S. are shown. Figures include multiple ancestries (e.g. if a person reported being Irish and Italian, they were included in both columns); (1) Figures cover the Charleston-North Charleston, SC Metropolitan Statistical Area—see Appendix B for areas included; (2) Excludes Basque
Source: U.S. Census Bureau, 2012-2016 American Community Survey 5-Year Estimates

Foreign-Born Population

Area	Percent of Population Born in								
	Any Foreign Country	Asia	Mexico	Europe	Carribean	Central America[2]	South America	Africa	Canada
City	4.6	1.2	0.6	1.6	0.2	0.1	0.4	0.1	0.2
MSA[1]	4.9	1.3	1.2	1.0	0.3	0.4	0.4	0.2	0.1
U.S.	13.2	4.0	3.6	1.5	1.3	1.0	0.9	0.6	0.3

Note: (1) Figures cover the Charleston-North Charleston, SC Metropolitan Statistical Area—see Appendix B for areas included; (2) Excludes Mexico.
Source: U.S. Census Bureau, 2012-2016 American Community Survey 5-Year Estimates

Marital Status

Area	Never Married	Now Married[2]	Separated	Widowed	Divorced
City	25.2	57.0	2.4	5.0	10.4
MSA[1]	34.1	45.9	2.9	5.6	11.5
U.S.	33.0	48.1	2.1	5.9	11.0

Note: Figures are percentages and cover the population 15 years of age and older; (1) Figures cover the Charleston-North Charleston, SC Metropolitan Statistical Area—see Appendix B for areas included; (2) Excludes separated
Source: U.S. Census Bureau, 2012-2016 American Community Survey 5-Year Estimates

Disability Status

Area	All Ages	Under 18 Years Old	18 to 64 Years Old	65 Years and Over
City	7.5	1.7	5.1	28.1
MSA[1]	11.9	4.1	9.9	35.1
U.S.	12.5	4.1	10.3	35.7

Note: Figures show percent of the civilian noninstitutionalized population that reported having a disability. Disability status is determined from six types of difficulty: vision, hearing, cognitive, ambulatory, self-care, and independent living. For children under 5 years old, hearing and vision difficulty are used to determine disability status. For children between the ages of 5 and 14, disability status is determined from hearing, vision, cognitive, ambulatory, and self-care difficulties. For people aged 15 years and older, they are considered to have a disability if they have difficulty with any one of the six difficulty types; Note: (1) Figures cover the Charleston-North Charleston, SC Metropolitan Statistical Area—see Appendix B for areas included
Source: U.S. Census Bureau, 2012-2016 American Community Survey 5-Year Estimates

Age

Area	Percent of Population									Median Age
	Under Age 5	Age 5–19	Age 20–34	Age 35–44	Age 45–54	Age 55–64	Age 65–74	Age 75–84	Age 85+	
City	6.2	19.3	18.6	14.5	14.7	12.2	8.6	4.0	1.7	39.3
MSA[1]	6.4	18.6	22.9	12.9	13.4	12.4	8.4	3.5	1.4	36.3
U.S.	6.2	19.6	20.7	12.7	13.6	12.6	8.3	4.3	1.9	37.7

Note: (1) Figures cover the Charleston-North Charleston, SC Metropolitan Statistical Area—see Appendix B for areas included
Source: U.S. Census Bureau, 2012-2016 American Community Survey 5-Year Estimates

Gender

Area	Males	Females	Males per 100 Females
City	37,624	40,283	93.4
MSA[1]	355,780	372,491	95.5
U.S.	156,765,322	161,792,840	96.9

Note: (1) Figures cover the Charleston-North Charleston, SC Metropolitan Statistical Area—see Appendix B for areas included
Source: U.S. Census Bureau, 2012-2016 American Community Survey 5-Year Estimates

Religious Groups by Family

Area	Catholic	Baptist	Non-Den.	Methodist[2]	Lutheran	LDS[3]	Pente-costal	Presby-terian[4]	Muslim[5]	Judaism
MSA[1]	6.2	12.4	7.1	10.0	1.1	1.0	2.0	2.4	0.2	0.3
U.S.	19.1	9.3	4.0	4.0	2.3	2.0	1.9	1.6	0.8	0.7

Note: Figures are the number of adherents as a percentage of the total population; (1) Figures cover the Charleston-North Charleston, SC Metropolitan Statistical Area—see Appendix B for areas included; (2) Methodist/Pietist; (3) Latter Day Saints; (4) Reformed; (5) Figures are estimates
Source: Association of Statisticians of American Religious Bodies, 2010 U.S. Religion Census: Religious Congregations & Membership Study

Religious Groups by Tradition

Area	Catholic	Evangelical Protestant	Mainline Protestant	Other Tradition	Black Protestant	Orthodox
MSA[1]	6.2	19.7	11.2	1.9	7.3	0.1
U.S.	19.1	16.2	7.3	4.3	1.6	0.3

Note: Figures are the number of adherents as a percentage of the total population; (1) Figures cover the Charleston-North Charleston, SC Metropolitan Statistical Area—see Appendix B for areas included
Source: Association of Statisticians of American Religious Bodies, 2010 U.S. Religion Census: Religious Congregations & Membership Study

ECONOMY

Gross Metropolitan Product

Area	2014	2015	2016	2017	Rank[2]
MSA[1]	34.2	36.0	37.6	39.8	76

Note: Figures are in billions of dollars; (1) Figures cover the Charleston-North Charleston, SC Metropolitan Statistical Area—see Appendix B for areas included; (2) Rank is based on 2015 data and ranges from 1 to 381
Source: The U.S. Conference of Mayors, U.S. Metro Economies: GMP and Employment Report, 2015-2017

Economic Growth

Area	2012-14 (%)	2015 (%)	2016 (%)	2017 (%)	Rank[2]
MSA[1]	1.8	3.0	2.9	3.9	137
U.S.	2.0	2.4	1.9	2.6	-

Note: Figures are real gross metropolitan product (GMP) growth rates and represent average annual percent change; (1) Figures cover the Charleston-North Charleston, SC Metropolitan Statistical Area—see Appendix B for areas included; (2) Rank is based on 2012-2014 average annual percent change and ranges from 1 to 381
Source: The U.S. Conference of Mayors, U.S. Metro Economies: GMP and Employment Report, 2015-2017

Metropolitan Area Exports

Area	2011	2012	2013	2014	2015	2016	Rank[2]
MSA[1]	2,299.4	2,429.8	3,464.3	5,866.7	6,457.5	9,508.1	31

Note: Figures are in millions of dollars; (1) Figures cover the Charleston-North Charleston, SC Metropolitan Statistical Area—see Appendix B for areas included; (2) Rank is based on 2016 data and ranges from 1 to 385
Source: U.S. Department of Commerce, International Trade Administration, Office of Trade & Industry Information, Manufacturing & Services, data extracted March 15, 2018

Building Permits

Area	Single-Family			Multi-Family			Total		
	2016	2017p	Pct. Chg.	2016	2017p	Pct. Chg.	2016	2017p	Pct. Chg.
City	959	776	-19.1	591	899	52.1	1,550	1,675	8.1
MSA[1]	4,758	4,710	-1.0	2,178	2,663	22.3	6,936	7,373	6.3
U.S.	750,800	817,300	8.9	455,800	446,800	-2.0	1,206,600	1,264,100	4.8

Note: (1) Figures cover the Charleston-North Charleston, SC Metropolitan Statistical Area—see Appendix B for areas included; Figures represent new, privately-owned housing units authorized (unadjusted data); All permit data are based on estimates with imputation; (p) preliminary data.
Source: U.S. Census Bureau, Manufacturing, Mining, and Construction Statistics, Building Permits, 2016, 2017

Bankruptcy Filings

Area	Business Filings			Nonbusiness Filings		
	2016	2017	% Chg.	2016	2017	% Chg.
Charleston County	16	11	-31.3	378	386	2.1
U.S.	24,114	23,157	-4.0	770,846	765,863	-0.6

Note: Business filings include Chapter 7, Chapter 11, Chapter 12, and Chapter 13; Nonbusiness filings include Chapter 7, Chapter 11, and Chapter 13
Source: Administrative Office of the U.S. Courts, Business and Nonbusiness Bankruptcy, County Cases Commenced by Chapter of the Bankruptcy Code, During the 12-Month Period Ending December 31, 2016 and Business and Nonbusiness Bankruptcy, County Cases Commenced by Chapter of the Bankruptcy Code, During the 12-Month Period Ending December 31, 2017

Housing Vacancy Rates

Area	Gross Vacancy Rate² (%)			Year-Round Vacancy Rate³ (%)			Rental Vacancy Rate⁴ (%)			Homeowner Vacancy Rate⁵ (%)		
	2015	2016	2017	2015	2016	2017	2015	2016	2017	2015	2016	2017
MSA[1]	14.3	14.8	16.5	12.4	13.6	16.1	8.7	12.2	17.9	2.2	2.4	1.6
U.S.	12.9	12.8	12.7	10.0	9.9	9.9	7.1	6.9	7.2	1.8	1.7	1.6

Note: (1) Figures cover the Charleston-North Charleston, SC Metropolitan Statistical Area—see Appendix B for areas included; (2) The percentage of the total housing inventory that is vacant; (3) The percentage of the housing inventory (excluding seasonal units) that is year-round vacant; (4) The percentage of rental inventory that is vacant for rent; (5) The percentage of homeowner inventory that is vacant for sale
Source: U.S. Census Bureau, Housing Vacancies and Homeownership Annual Statistics: 2015, 2016, 2017

INCOME

Income

Area	Per Capita ($)	Median Household ($)	Average Household ($)
City	46,622	83,490	114,328
MSA[1]	30,081	55,125	75,938
U.S.	29,829	55,322	77,866

Note: (1) Figures cover the Charleston-North Charleston, SC Metropolitan Statistical Area—see Appendix B for areas included
Source: U.S. Census Bureau, 2012-2016 American Community Survey 5-Year Estimates

Household Income Distribution

Area	Percent of Households Earning							
	Under $15,000	$15,000 -$24,999	$25,000 -$34,999	$35,000 -$49,999	$50,000 -$74,999	$75,000 -$99,999	$100,000 -$149,999	$150,000 and up
City	6.0	4.8	5.4	11.6	17.4	12.9	17.7	24.3
MSA[1]	12.1	9.5	9.6	13.9	19.0	12.6	13.5	9.8
U.S.	12.1	10.2	9.9	13.2	17.8	12.2	13.5	11.1

Note: (1) Figures cover the Charleston-North Charleston, SC Metropolitan Statistical Area—see Appendix B for areas included
Source: U.S. Census Bureau, 2012-2016 American Community Survey 5-Year Estimates

Poverty Rate

Area	All Ages	Under 18 Years Old	18 to 64 Years Old	65 Years and Over
City	6.4	7.0	6.7	4.3
MSA[1]	14.6	21.2	13.4	8.9
U.S.	15.1	21.2	14.2	9.3

Note: Figures are percentage of people whose income during the past 12 months was below the poverty level; (1) Figures cover the Charleston-North Charleston, SC Metropolitan Statistical Area—see Appendix B for areas included
Source: U.S. Census Bureau, 2012-2016 American Community Survey 5-Year Estimates

EMPLOYMENT

Labor Force and Employment

Area	Civilian Labor Force			Workers Employed		
	Dec. 2016	Dec. 2017	% Chg.	Dec. 2016	Dec. 2017	% Chg.
City	45,231	45,696	1.0	43,859	44,392	1.2
MSA[1]	370,074	373,329	0.9	355,988	360,371	1.2
U.S.	158,968,000	159,880,000	0.6	151,798,000	153,602,000	1.2

Note: Data is not seasonally adjusted and covers workers 16 years of age and older; (1) Figures cover the Charleston-North Charleston, SC Metropolitan Statistical Area—see Appendix B for areas included
Source: Bureau of Labor Statistics, Local Area Unemployment Statistics

Unemployment Rate

Area	2017											
	Jan.	Feb.	Mar.	Apr.	May	Jun.	Jul.	Aug.	Sep.	Oct.	Nov.	Dec.
City	3.5	3.2	2.8	2.5	2.7	3.0	2.9	3.2	3.0	2.9	2.8	2.9
MSA[1]	4.2	3.9	3.4	3.2	3.3	3.9	3.8	4.0	3.6	3.5	3.4	3.5
U.S.	5.1	4.9	4.6	4.1	4.1	4.5	4.6	4.5	4.1	3.9	3.9	3.9

Note: Data is not seasonally adjusted and covers workers 16 years of age and older; (1) Figures cover the Charleston-North Charleston, SC Metropolitan Statistical Area—see Appendix B for areas included
Source: Bureau of Labor Statistics, Local Area Unemployment Statistics

Average Wages

Occupation	$/Hr.	Occupation	$/Hr.
Accountants and Auditors	27.80	Maids and Housekeeping Cleaners	10.40
Automotive Mechanics	20.20	Maintenance and Repair Workers	18.90
Bookkeepers	17.40	Marketing Managers	48.00
Carpenters	21.00	Nuclear Medicine Technologists	36.00
Cashiers	9.40	Nurses, Licensed Practical	20.10
Clerks, General Office	13.00	Nurses, Registered	35.60
Clerks, Receptionists/Information	13.80	Nursing Assistants	13.80
Clerks, Shipping/Receiving	19.00	Packers and Packagers, Hand	10.50
Computer Programmers	35.50	Physical Therapists	37.00
Computer Systems Analysts	38.60	Postal Service Mail Carriers	23.60
Computer User Support Specialists	25.30	Real Estate Brokers	29.70
Cooks, Restaurant	11.80	Retail Salespersons	12.20
Dentists	81.20	Sales Reps., Exc. Tech./Scientific	29.50
Electrical Engineers	41.70	Sales Reps., Tech./Scientific	32.90
Electricians	20.70	Secretaries, Exc. Legal/Med./Exec.	17.20
Financial Managers	55.30	Security Guards	14.90
First-Line Supervisors/Managers, Sales	20.30	Surgeons	n/a
Food Preparation Workers	11.60	Teacher Assistants*	10.20
General and Operations Managers	49.00	Teachers, Elementary School*	22.50
Hairdressers/Cosmetologists	10.00	Teachers, Secondary School*	23.70
Internists, General	117.50	Telemarketers	11.90
Janitors and Cleaners	10.50	Truck Drivers, Heavy/Tractor-Trailer	21.90
Landscaping/Groundskeeping Workers	12.90	Truck Drivers, Light/Delivery Svcs.	15.60
Lawyers	39.00	Waiters and Waitresses	10.40

Note: Wage data covers the Charleston-North Charleston, SC Metropolitan Statistical Area—see Appendix B for areas included; (*) Hourly wages for elementary/secondary school teachers and teacher assistants were calculated by the editors from annual wage data based on a 40 hour work week; n/a not available.
Source: Bureau of Labor Statistics, Metro Area Occupational Employment & Wage Estimates, May 2017

Employment by Occupation

Occupation Classification	City (%)	MSA[1] (%)	U.S. (%)
Management, Business, Science, and Arts	53.7	37.8	37.0
Natural Resources, Construction, and Maintenance	3.0	8.9	8.9
Production, Transportation, and Material Moving	5.4	10.9	12.2
Sales and Office	24.3	24.2	23.8
Service	13.5	18.2	18.1

Note: Figures cover employed civilians 16 years of age and older; (1) Figures cover the Charleston-North Charleston, SC Metropolitan Statistical Area—see Appendix B for areas included
Source: U.S. Census Bureau, 2012-2016 American Community Survey 5-Year Estimates

Employment by Industry

Sector	MSA[1] Number of Employees	MSA[1] Percent of Total	U.S. Percent of Total
Construction, Mining, and Logging	20,800	5.8	5.2
Education and Health Services	41,300	11.6	15.9
Financial Activities	14,900	4.2	5.7
Government	66,000	18.6	15.3
Information	6,400	1.8	1.9
Leisure and Hospitality	47,300	13.3	10.7
Manufacturing	26,600	7.5	8.5
Other Services	13,700	3.9	3.9
Professional and Business Services	54,100	15.2	14.0
Retail Trade	40,500	11.4	11.0
Transportation, Warehousing, and Utilities	14,600	4.1	4.1
Wholesale Trade	9,500	2.7	4.0

Note: Figures are non-farm employment as of December 2017. Figures are not seasonally adjusted and include workers 16 years of age and older; (1) Figures cover the Charleston-North Charleston, SC Metropolitan Statistical Area—see Appendix B for areas included
Source: Bureau of Labor Statistics, Current Employment Statistics, Employment, Hours, and Earnings

Occupations with Greatest Projected Employment Growth: 2017 – 2019

Occupation[1]	2017 Employment	2019 Projected Employment	Numeric Employment Change	Percent Employment Change
Combined Food Preparation and Serving Workers, Including Fast Food	51,990	56,220	4,230	8.1
Laborers and Freight, Stock, and Material Movers, Hand	51,700	54,990	3,290	6.4
Construction Laborers	22,210	25,240	3,030	13.7
Retail Salespersons	70,670	73,620	2,950	4.2
Waiters and Waitresses	36,800	39,170	2,370	6.4
Heavy and Tractor-Trailer Truck Drivers	29,890	31,760	1,870	6.3
Cashiers	63,500	65,360	1,860	2.9
General and Operations Managers	34,530	36,370	1,840	5.3
Customer Service Representatives	49,050	50,740	1,690	3.4
Cooks, Restaurant	21,700	23,330	1,630	7.5

Note: Projections cover South Carolina; (1) Sorted by numeric employment change
Source: www.projectionscentral.com, State Occupational Projections, 2017–2019 Short-Term Projections

Fastest Growing Occupations: 2017 – 2019

Occupation[1]	2017 Employment	2019 Projected Employment	Numeric Employment Change	Percent Employment Change
Electrical Power-Line Installers and Repairers	3,280	3,940	660	20.0
Paving, Surfacing, and Tamping Equipment Operators	780	920	140	19.2
Pipelayers	950	1,090	140	14.9
Construction Laborers	22,210	25,240	3,030	13.7
Operating Engineers and Other Construction Equipment Operators	6,150	6,950	800	13.0
Highway Maintenance Workers	450	500	50	11.8
Cabinetmakers and Bench Carpenters	1,470	1,640	170	11.7
First-Line Supervisors of Construction Trades and Extraction Workers	11,430	12,750	1,320	11.6
Captains, Mates, and Pilots of Water Vessels	510	570	60	11.2
Helpers—Pipelayers, Plumbers, Pipefitters, and Steamfitters	1,890	2,100	210	11.2

Note: Projections cover South Carolina; (1) Sorted by percent employment change and excludes occupations with numeric employment change less than 50
Source: www.projectionscentral.com, State Occupational Projections, 2017–2019 Short-Term Projections

TAXES

State Corporate Income Tax Rates

State	Tax Rate (%)	Income Brackets ($)	Num. of Brackets	Financial Institution Tax Rate (%)[a]	Federal Income Tax Ded.
South Carolina	5.0	Flat rate	1	4.5 (v)	No

Note: Tax rates as of January 1, 2018; (a) Rates listed are the corporate income tax rate applied to financial institutions or excise taxes based on income. Some states have other taxes based upon the value of deposits or shares; (v) South Carolina taxes savings and loans at a 6% rate.
Source: Federation of Tax Administrators, Range of State Corporate Income Tax Rates, January 1, 2018

State Individual Income Tax Rates

State	Tax Rate (%)	Income Brackets ($)	Num. of Brackets	Personal Exempt. ($)[1]		Fed. Inc. Tax Ded.
				Single	Dependents	
South Carolina (a)	0.0 - 7.0	2,970 - 14,860	6	4,150 (d)	4,150 (d)	No

Note: Tax rates as of January 1, 2018; Local- and county-level taxes are not included; n/a not applicable; (1) Married joint filers generally receive double the single exemption; (a) 19 states have statutory provision for automatically adjusting to the rate of inflation the dollar values of the income tax brackets, standard deductions, and/or personal exemptions. Massachusetts, Michigan, and Nebraska index the personal exemption only. Oregon does not index the income brackets for $125,000 and over; (d) These states use the personal exemption amounts provided in the federal Internal Revenue Code. Note, the Tax Cut and Reform Act of 2017 has eliminated personal exemptions from the IRC. These states will need to enact legislation to reinstate a personal exemption for tax year 2018. We have reported here the exemption amounts before the federal tax change.
Source: Federation of Tax Administrators, State Individual Income Tax Rates, January 1, 2018

Various State Sales and Excise Tax Rates

State	State Sales Tax (%)	Gasoline[1] (¢/gal.)	Cigarette[2] ($/pack)	Spirits[3] ($/gal.)	Wine[4] ($/gal.)	Beer[5] ($/gal.)	Recreational Marijuana (%)
South Carolina	6.0	20.75	0.57	5.42 (i)	1.08 (l)	0.77	Not legal

Note: All tax rates as of January 1, 2018; (1) The American Petroleum Institute has developed a methodology for determining the average tax rate on a gallon of fuel. Rates may include any of the following: excise taxes, environmental fees, storage tank fees, other fees or taxes, general sales tax, and local taxes. In states where gasoline is subject to the general sales tax, or where the fuel tax is based on the average sale price, the average rate determined by API is sensitive to changes in the price of gasoline. States that fully or partially apply general sales taxes to gasoline: CA, CO, GA, IL, IN, MI, NY; (2) The federal excise tax of $1.0066 per pack and local taxes are not included; (3) Rates are those applicable to off-premise sales of 40% alcohol by volume (a.b.v.) distilled spirits in 750ml containers. Local excise taxes are excluded; (4) Rates are those applicable to off-premise sales of 11% a.b.v. non-carbonated wine in 750ml containers; (5) Rates are those applicable to off-premise sales of 4.7% a.b.v. beer in 12 ounce containers; (i) Includes case fees and/or bottle fees which may vary with size of container; (l) Different rates also applicable to alcohol content, place of production, size of container, place purchased (on- or off-premise or on board airlines) or type of wine (carbonated, vermouth, etc.).
Source: Tax Foundation, 2018 Facts & Figures: How Does Your State Compare?

State Business Tax Climate Index Rankings

State	Overall Rank	Corporate Tax Rank	Individual Income Tax Rank	Sales Tax Rank	Unemployment Insurance Tax Rank	Property Tax Rank
South Carolina	37	15	41	32	29	24

Note: The index is a measure of how each state's tax laws affect economic performance. The lower the rank, the more favorable a state's tax system is for business. States without a given tax are given a ranking of 1. The scores/rankings for the District of Columbia do not affect other states. The 2018 index represents the tax climate as of July 1, 2017.
Source: Tax Foundation, State Business Tax Climate Index 2018

TRANSPORTATION

Means of Transportation to Work

Area	Car/Truck/Van		Public Transportation			Bicycle	Walked	Other Means	Worked at Home
	Drove Alone	Car-pooled	Bus	Subway	Railroad				
City	82.3	5.2	0.4	0.0	0.0	0.6	1.5	0.6	9.5
MSA[1]	81.1	8.5	1.2	0.0	0.0	0.9	2.7	1.0	4.6
U.S.	76.4	9.3	2.6	1.9	0.6	0.6	2.8	1.3	4.6

Note: Figures are percentages and cover workers 16 years of age and older; (1) Figures cover the Charleston-North Charleston, SC Metropolitan Statistical Area—see Appendix B for areas included
Source: U.S. Census Bureau, 2012-2016 American Community Survey 5-Year Estimates

Travel Time to Work

Area	Less Than 10 Minutes	10 to 19 Minutes	20 to 29 Minutes	30 to 44 Minutes	45 to 59 Minutes	60 to 89 Minutes	90 Minutes or More
City	11.3	32.6	28.6	21.6	3.5	1.3	1.3
MSA[1]	10.0	28.1	24.8	23.7	8.3	3.6	1.5
U.S.	12.9	29.2	20.9	20.4	8.0	6.0	2.7

Note: Note: Figures are percentages and include workers 16 years old and over; (1) Figures cover the Charleston-North Charleston, SC Metropolitan Statistical Area—see Appendix B for areas included
Source: U.S. Census Bureau, 2012-2016 American Community Survey 5-Year Estimates

Freeway Travel Time Index

Area	1985	1990	1995	2000	2005	2010	2014
Urban Area Rank[1,2]	26	25	26	28	32	25	29
Urban Area Index[1]	1.10	1.14	1.18	1.20	1.22	1.23	1.23
Average Index[3]	1.09	1.11	1.14	1.17	1.20	1.19	1.20

Note: Freeway Travel Time Index—the ratio of travel time in the peak period to the travel time at free-flow conditions. For example, a value of 1.30 indicates a 20-minute free-flow trip takes 26 minutes in the peak (20 minutes x 1.30 = 26 minutes); (1) Covers the Charleston-North Charleston SC urban area; (2) Rank is based on 101 urban areas (#1 = highest travel time index); (3) Average of 101 urban areas
Source: Texas Transportation Institute, 2015 Urban Mobility Scorecard, August 2015

Freeway Commuter Stress Index

Area	1985	1990	1995	2000	2005	2010	2014
Urban Area Rank[1,2]	33	36	33	36	38	33	33
Urban Area Index[1]	1.14	1.17	1.22	1.24	1.26	1.27	1.27
Average Index[3]	1.13	1.16	1.19	1.22	1.25	1.24	1.25

Note: The Freeway Commuter Stress Index is the same as the Freeway Travel Time Index (see table above) except that it includes only the travel in the peak directions during the peak periods; the TTI includes travel in all directions during the peak period. Thus, the CSI is more indicative of the work trip experienced by each commuter on a daily basis; (1) Covers the Charleston-North Charleston SC urban area; (2) Rank is based on 101 urban areas (#1 = highest travel time index); (3) Average of 101 urban areas
Source: Texas Transportation Institute, 2015 Urban Mobility Scorecard, August 2015

Living Environment

COST OF LIVING

Cost of Living Index

Composite Index	Groceries	Housing	Utilities	Trans-portation	Health Care	Misc. Goods/ Services
103.9	100.9	96.9	118.1	94.8	103.8	108.9

Note: The Cost of Living Index measures regional differences in the cost of consumer goods and services, excluding taxes and non-consumer expenditures, for professional and managerial households in the top income quintile. It is based on more than 50,000 prices covering almost 60 different items for which prices are collected three times a year by chambers of commerce, economic development organizations or university applied economic centers in each participating urban area. The numbers shown should be read as a percentage above or below the national average of 100. For example, a value of 115.4 in the groceries column indicates that grocery prices are 15.4% higher than the national average. Small differences in the index numbers should not be interpreted as significant; Figures cover the Charleston-N Charleston SC urban area.
Source: The Council for Community and Economic Research, ACCRA Cost of Living Index, 2017

Grocery Prices

Area[1]	T-Bone Steak ($/pound)	Frying Chicken ($/pound)	Whole Milk ($/half gal.)	Eggs ($/dozen)	Orange Juice ($/64 oz.)	Coffee ($/11.5 oz.)
City[2]	11.15	1.40	1.98	1.46	3.71	3.78
Avg.	11.29	1.40	2.02	1.47	3.55	4.37
Min.	7.71	0.93	1.04	0.70	2.86	3.24
Max.	15.83	2.39	4.03	3.92	6.29	8.16

*Note: (1) Values for the local area are compared with the average, minimum and maximum values for all 294 areas in the Cost of Living Index; (2) Figures cover the Charleston-N Charleston SC urban area; **T-Bone Steak** (price per pound); **Frying Chicken** (price per pound, whole fryer); **Whole Milk** (half gallon carton); **Eggs** (price per dozen, Grade A, large); **Orange Juice** (64 oz. Tropicana or Florida Natural); **Coffee** (11.5 oz. can, vacuum-packed, Maxwell House, Hills Bros, or Folgers).*
Source: The Council for Community and Economic Research, ACCRA Cost of Living Index, 2017

Housing and Utility Costs

Area[1]	New Home Price ($)	Apartment Rent ($/month)	All Electric ($/month)	Part Electric ($/month)	Other Energy ($/month)	Telephone ($/month)
City[2]	275,736	1,354	260.94	-	-	20.88
Avg.	335,956	1,047	175.01	97.34	67.93	28.71
Min.	187,788	491	109.48	49.33	35.44	12.39
Max.	1,739,087	4,559	432.62	227.09	353.33	44.61

*Note: (1) Values for the local area are compared with the average, minimum and maximum values for all 294 areas in the Cost of Living Index; (2) Figures cover the Charleston-N Charleston SC urban area; **New Home Price** (2,400 sf living area, 8,000 sf lot, in urban area with full utilities); **Apartment Rent** (950 sf 2 bedroom/1.5 or 2 bath, unfurnished, excluding all utilities except water); **All Electric** (average monthly cost for an all-electric home); **Part Electric** (average monthly cost for a part-electric home); **Other Energy** (average monthly cost for natural gas, fuel oil, coal, wood, and any other forms of energy except electricity); **Telephone** (price includes basic monthly rate for a private residential line plus additional local usage charges incurred by a family of four).*
Source: The Council for Community and Economic Research, ACCRA Cost of Living Index, 2017

Health Care, Transportation, and Other Costs

Area[1]	Doctor ($/visit)	Dentist ($/visit)	Optometrist ($/visit)	Gasoline ($/gallon)	Beauty Salon ($/visit)	Men's Shirt ($)
City[2]	114.72	96.39	105.51	2.10	44.38	35.38
Avg.	108.00	92.54	101.93	2.25	37.58	30.92
Min.	30.39	60.00	49.75	1.82	16.11	11.20
Max.	193.50	161.94	229.28	3.16	77.35	59.13

*Note: (1) Values for the local area are compared with the average, minimum and maximum values for all 294 areas in the Cost of Living Index; (2) Figures cover the Charleston-N Charleston SC urban area; **Doctor** (general practitioners routine exam of an established patient); **Dentist** (adult teeth cleaning and periodic oral examination); **Optometrist** (full vision eye exam for established adult patient); **Gasoline** (one gallon regular unleaded, national brand, including all taxes, cash price at self-service pump if available); **Beauty Salon** (woman's shampoo, trim, and blow-dry); **Men's Shirt** (cotton/polyester dress shirt, pinpoint weave, long sleeves).*
Source: The Council for Community and Economic Research, ACCRA Cost of Living Index, 2017

HOUSING

House Price Index (HPI)

Area	National Ranking[2]	Quarterly Change (%)	One-Year Change (%)	Five-Year Change (%)
MSA[1]	53	1.29	9.10	47.71
U.S.[3]	_	1.61	6.68	34.71

Note: The HPI is a weighted repeat sales index. It measures average price changes in repeat sales or refinancings on the same properties. This information is obtained by reviewing repeat mortgage transactions on single-family properties whose mortgages have been purchased or securitized by Fannie Mae or Freddie Mac in January 1975; (1) Figures cover the Charleston-North Charleston, SC Metropolitan Statistical Area—see Appendix B for areas included; (2) Rankings are based on annual percentage change for all metro areas containing at least 15,000 transactions over the last 10 years and ranges from 1 to 253; (3) figures based on a weighted average of Census Division estimates using a seasonally adjusted, purchase-only index; all figures are for the period ending December 31, 2017

Source: Federal Housing Finance Agency, House Price Index, February 28, 2018

Median Single-Family Home Prices

Area	2015	2016	2017p	Percent Change 2016 to 2017
MSA[1]	240.8	252.2	268.8	6.6
U.S. Average	223.9	235.5	248.8	5.6

Note: Figures are median sales prices of existing single-family homes in thousands of dollars; (p) preliminary; (1) Figures cover the Charleston-North Charleston, SC Metropolitan Statistical Area—see Appendix B for areas included

Source: National Association of Realtors, Median Sales Price of Existing Single-Family Homes for Metropolitan Areas, 4th Quarter 2017

Qualifying Income Based on Median Sales Price of Existing Single-Family Homes

Area	With 5% Down ($)	With 10% Down ($)	With 20% Down ($)
MSA[1]	61,170	57,951	51,512
U.S. Average	55,585	52,659	46,808

Note: Figures are preliminary; Qualifying income is based on a mortgage rate of 4.17%. Monthly principal and interest payment is limited to 25% of income; (1) Figures cover the Charleston-North Charleston, SC Metropolitan Statistical Area—see Appendix B for areas included

Source: National Association of Realtors, Qualifying Income Based on Median Sales Price of Existing Single-Family Homes for Metropolitan Areas, 4th Quarter 2017

Median Apartment Condo-Coop Home Prices

Area	2015	2016	2017p	Percent Change 2016 to 2017
MSA[1]	n/a	n/a	n/a	n/a
U.S. Average	210.7	220.7	234.3	6.2

Note: Figures are median sales prices of existing apartment condo-coop homes in thousands of dollars; (p) preliminary; n/a not available; (1) Figures cover the Charleston-North Charleston, SC Metropolitan Statistical Area—see Appendix B for areas included

Source: National Association of Realtors, Median Sales Price of Existing Apartment Condo-Coop Homes for Metropolitan Areas, 4th Quarter 2017

Home Value Distribution

Area	Under $50,000	$50,000 -$99,999	$100,000 -$149,999	$150,000 -$199,999	$200,000 -$299,999	$300,000 -$499,999	$500,000 -$999,999	$1,000,000 or more
City	1.2	1.1	3.7	5.7	16.4	39.8	26.6	5.4
MSA[1]	8.1	10.0	15.3	18.0	20.5	16.0	8.9	3.3
U.S.	8.8	14.8	15.3	14.9	18.4	16.4	9.0	2.5

Note: Figures are percentages and cover owner-occupied housing units; (1) Figures cover the Charleston-North Charleston, SC Metropolitan Statistical Area—see Appendix B for areas included

Source: U.S. Census Bureau, 2012-2016 American Community Survey 5-Year Estimates

Homeownership Rate

Area	2009 (%)	2010 (%)	2011 (%)	2012 (%)	2013 (%)	2014 (%)	2015 (%)	2016 (%)	2017 (%)
MSA[1]	n/a	n/a	n/a	n/a	n/a	n/a	65.8	62.1	67.7
U.S.	67.4	66.9	66.1	65.4	65.1	64.5	63.7	63.4	63.9

Note: (1) Figures cover the Charleston-North Charleston, SC Metropolitan Statistical Area—see Appendix B for areas included

Source: U.S. Census Bureau, Housing Vacancies and Homeownership Annual Statistics: 2009-2017

Year Housing Structure Built

Area	2010 or Later	2000 -2009	1990 -1999	1980 -1989	1970 -1979	1960 -1969	1950 -1959	1940 -1949	Before 1940	Median Year
City	5.9	32.2	24.8	15.3	11.6	5.8	2.9	0.7	0.7	1995
MSA[1]	4.9	24.6	16.5	17.7	15.0	9.1	5.5	2.7	4.0	1988
U.S.	2.3	14.7	14.0	13.7	15.6	10.9	10.6	5.2	13.0	1977

Note: Figures are percentages except for Median Year; Note: (1) Figures cover the Charleston-North Charleston, SC Metropolitan Statistical Area—see Appendix B for areas included
Source: U.S. Census Bureau, 2012-2016 American Community Survey 5-Year Estimates

Gross Monthly Rent

Area	Under $500	$500 -$999	$1,000 -$1,499	$1,500 -$1,999	$2,000 -$2,499	$2,500 -$2,999	$3,000 and up	Median ($)
City	1.3	10.5	46.1	23.0	9.3	4.2	5.5	1,403
MSA[1]	6.9	42.3	34.7	11.1	2.9	1.0	1.1	1,009
U.S.	11.3	43.3	27.7	10.7	4.0	1.6	1.5	949

Note: Figures are percentages except for Median; Gross rent is the contract rent plus the estimated average monthly cost of utilities (electricity, gas, and water and sewer) and fuels (oil, coal, kerosene, wood, etc.) if these are paid by the renter (or paid for the renter by someone else); (1) Figures cover the Charleston-North Charleston, SC Metropolitan Statistical Area—see Appendix B for areas included
Source: U.S. Census Bureau, 2012-2016 American Community Survey 5-Year Estimates

HEALTH

Health Risk Factors

Category	MSA[1] (%)	U.S. (%)
Adults aged 18–64 who have any kind of health care coverage	86.9	87.7
Adults who reported being in good or excellent health	84.5	83.6
Adults who are current smokers	17.6	17.1
Adults who currently use E-cigarettes	6.0	4.7
Adults who currently use chewing tobacco, snuff, or snus	3.0	4.0
Adults who are heavy drinkers[2]	7.9	6.5
Adults who are binge drinkers[3]	20.3	16.9
Adults who are overweight (BMI 25.0 - 29.9)	36.8	35.3
Adults who are obese (BMI 30.0 - 99.8)	30.2	29.9
Adults who participated in any physical activities in the past month	78.9	76.9
Adults who always or nearly always wears a seat belt	96.3	94.3

Note: (1) Figures cover the Charleston-North Charleston, SC Metropolitan Statistical Area—see Appendix B for areas included; (2) Heavy drinkers are classified as adult men having more than 14 drinks per week and adult women having more than 7 drinks per week; (3) Binge drinkers are classified as males having five or more drinks on one occasion or females having four or more drinks on one occasion
Source: Centers for Disease Control and Prevention, Behaviorial Risk Factor Surveillance System, SMART: Selected Metropolitan Area Risk Trends, 2016

Health Screening Rates

Category	MSA[1] (%)	U.S. (%)
Adults 50-75 who have had a blood stool test within the past year	6.9	8.0
Adults 50-75 who have had a colonoscopy in the past 10 years	71.4	63.5
Adults aged 65+ who have had flu shot within the past year	66.1	58.6
Adults aged 65+ who have ever had a pneumonia vaccination	70.6	73.4
Adults who have ever been tested for HIV	40.4	35.6
Women aged 21-65 who have had a pap test in the past three years	81.2	79.8
Men aged 40+ who have had a PSA test within the past two years	45.3	39.5
Women aged 40+ who have had a mammogram within the past two years	69.6	72.5

Note: n/a not available; (1) Figures cover the Charleston-North Charleston, SC Metropolitan Statistical Area—see Appendix B for areas included; Source: Centers for Disease Control and Prevention, Behaviorial Risk Factor Surveillance System, SMART: Selected Metropolitan Area Risk Trends, 2016

Chronic Health Conditions

Category	MSA[1] (%)	U.S. (%)
Adults who have ever been told they had a heart attack	3.7	4.4
Adults who have ever been told they have angina or coronary heart disease	3.2	4.1
Adults who have ever been told they had a stroke	2.6	3.1
Adults who have been told they currently have asthma	9.7	9.3
Adults who have been told they have arthritis	25.3	25.8
Adults who have ever been told they have diabetes[2]	11.1	10.5
Adults who have ever been told they had skin cancer	7.1	5.9
Adults who have ever been told they had any other types of cancer	6.9	6.7
Adults who have ever been told they have COPD	7.3	6.3
Adults who have ever been told they have kidney disease	2.5	2.8
Adults who have ever been told they have a form of depression	18.8	17.4

Note: (1) Figures cover the Charleston-North Charleston, SC Metropolitan Statistical Area—see Appendix B for areas included; (2) Figures do not include pregnancy-related, borderline, or pre-diabetes
Source: Centers for Disease Control and Prevention, Behaviorial Risk Factor Surveillance System, SMART: Selected Metropolitan Area Risk Trends, 2016

Mortality Rates for the Top 10 Causes of Death in the U.S.

ICD-10[a] Sub-Chapter	ICD-10[a] Code	Age-Adjusted Mortality Rate[1] per 100,000 population	
		County[2]	U.S.
Malignant neoplasms	C00-C97	157.7	158.5
Ischaemic heart diseases	I20-I25	76.6	96.8
Other forms of heart disease	I30-I51	52.4	52.4
Chronic lower respiratory diseases	J40-J47	36.9	40.9
Cerebrovascular diseases	I60-I69	40.1	37.2
Organic, including symptomatic, mental disorders	F01-F09	36.4	33.3
Other degenerative diseases of the nervous system	G30-G31	48.6	32.1
Other external causes of accidental injury	W00-X59	29.0	31.2
Diabetes mellitus	E10-E14	18.6	21.1
Hypertensive diseases	I10-I15	12.8	20.8

Note: (a) ICD-10 = International Classification of Diseases 10th Revision; (1) Mortality rates are a three year average covering 2014-2016; (2) Figures cover Charleston County.
Source: Centers for Disease Control and Prevention, National Center for Health Statistics. Underlying Cause of Death 1999-2016 on CDC WONDER Online Database, released December 2017

Mortality Rates for Selected Causes of Death

ICD-10[a] Sub-Chapter	ICD-10[a] Code	Age-Adjusted Mortality Rate[1] per 100,000 population	
		County[2]	U.S.
Assault	X85-Y09	12.2	5.6
Diseases of the liver	K70-K76	13.8	14.0
Human immunodeficiency virus (HIV) disease	B20-B24	3.6	1.9
Influenza and pneumonia	J09-J18	9.1	14.6
Intentional self-harm	X60-X84	14.2	13.2
Malnutrition	E40-E46	1.9	1.3
Obesity and other hyperalimentation	E65-E68	Unreliable	2.1
Renal failure	N17-N19	13.5	13.0
Transport accidents	V01-V99	14.5	12.0
Viral hepatitis	B15-B19	1.9	1.9

Note: (a) ICD-10 = International Classification of Diseases 10th Revision; (1) Mortality rates are a three year average covering 2014-2016; (2) Figures cover Charleston County; Data are Suppressed when the data meet the criteria for confidentiality constraints; Mortality rates are flagged as Unreliable when the rate would be calculated with a numerator of 20 or less.
Source: Centers for Disease Control and Prevention, National Center for Health Statistics. Underlying Cause of Death 1999-2016 on CDC WONDER Online Database, released December 2017

Health Insurance Coverage

Area	With Health Insurance	With Private Health Insurance	With Public Health Insurance	Without Health Insurance	Population Under Age 18 Without Health Insurance
City	92.7	84.3	19.1	7.3	5.6
MSA[1]	87.0	69.0	30.3	13.0	5.7
U.S.	88.3	66.7	33.0	11.7	5.9

Note: Figures are percentages that cover the civilian noninstitutionalized population; (1) Figures cover the Charleston-North Charleston, SC Metropolitan Statistical Area—see Appendix B for areas included
Source: U.S. Census Bureau, 2012-2016 American Community Survey 5-Year Estimates

Number of Medical Professionals

Area	MDs[3]	DOs[3,4]	Dentists	Podiatrists	Chiropractors	Optometrists
County[1] (number)	3,037	108	408	20	182	83
County[1] (rate[2])	780.1	27.7	102.9	5.0	45.9	20.9
U.S. (rate[2])	276.5	22.3	67.3	6.0	26.7	15.9

Note: Data as of 2016 unless noted; (1) Data covers Charleston County; (2) Rate per 100,000 population; (3) Data as of 2015 and includes all active, non-federal physicians; (4) Doctor of Osteopathic Medicine
Source: U.S. Department of Health and Human Services, Health Resources and Services Administration, Bureau of Health Professions, Area Resource File (ARF) 2016-2017

Best Hospitals

According to *U.S. News,* the Charleston-North Charleston, SC metro area is home to one of the best hospitals in the U.S.: **MUSC Health-University Medical Center** (4 adult specialties and 6 pediatric specialties). The hospital listed was nationally ranked in at least one of 16 specialties. Only 152 hospitals nationwide were nationally ranked in one or more specialties. Twenty hospitals in the U.S. made the Honor Roll. The Best Hospitals Honor Roll was revamped last year to take both the national rankings and the procedure and condition ratings into account. Hospitals received points if they were nationally ranked in one of the 16 specialties—the higher they ranked, the more points they got—and how many ratings of "high performing" they earned in the nine procedures and conditions. *U.S. News Online, "America's Best Hospitals 2017-18"*

According to *U.S. News,* the Charleston-North Charleston, SC metro area is home to one of the best children's hospitals in the U.S.: **MUSC Health-Children's Hospital** (6 pediatric specialties). The hospital listed was highly ranked in at least one of 10 pediatric specialties. Eighty-two children's hospitals in the U.S. were nationally ranked in at least one specialty. Hospitals received points for being ranked in a specialty, and the 10 hospitals with the most points across the 10 specialties make up the Honor Roll. *U.S. News Online, "America's Best Children's Hospitals 2017-18"*

EDUCATION

Public School District Statistics

District Name	Schls	Pupils	Pupil/ Teacher Ratio	Minority Pupils[1] (%)	Free Lunch Eligible[2] (%)	IEP[3] (%)
Charleston 01	83	48,084	13.8	52.6	42.2	9.5

Note: Table includes school districts with 100 or more students; (1) Percentage of students that are not non-Hispanic white; (2) Percentage of students that are eligible for the free lunch program; (3) Percentage of students that have an Individualized Education Program.
Source: U.S. Department of Education, National Center for Education Statistics, Common Core of Data, Local Education Agency (School District) Universe Survey: School Year 2015-2016; U.S. Department of Education, National Center for Education Statistics, Common Core of Data, Public Elementary/Secondary School Universe Survey: School Year 2015-2016

Highest Level of Education

Area	Less than H.S.	H.S. Diploma	Some College, No Deg.	Associate Degree	Bachelor's Degree	Master's Degree	Prof. School Degree	Doctorate Degree
City	2.2	13.2	18.1	7.2	38.4	13.6	4.3	3.0
MSA[1]	10.4	25.3	21.8	9.2	21.6	8.3	2.2	1.3
U.S.	13.0	27.5	21.0	8.2	18.8	8.2	2.0	1.3

Note: Figures cover persons age 25 and over; (1) Figures cover the Charleston-North Charleston, SC Metropolitan Statistical Area—see Appendix B for areas included
Source: U.S. Census Bureau, 2012-2016 American Community Survey 5-Year Estimates

Educational Attainment by Race

Area	High School Graduate or Higher (%)					Bachelor's Degree or Higher (%)				
	Total	White	Black	Asian	Hisp.[2]	Total	White	Black	Asian	Hisp.[2]
City	97.8	98.8	86.0	85.2	93.8	59.3	61.9	16.1	55.0	64.1
MSA[1]	89.6	92.7	82.6	86.8	69.4	33.4	40.1	15.4	42.9	22.8
U.S.	87.0	88.9	84.3	86.3	65.7	30.3	31.6	20.0	52.1	14.7

Note: Figures shown cover persons 25 years old and over; (1) Figures cover the Charleston-North Charleston, SC Metropolitan Statistical Area—see Appendix B for areas included; (2) People of Hispanic origin can be of any race
Source: U.S. Census Bureau, 2012-2016 American Community Survey 5-Year Estimates

School Enrollment by Grade and Control

Area	Preschool (%)		Kindergarten (%)		Grades 1 - 4 (%)		Grades 5 - 8 (%)		Grades 9 - 12 (%)	
	Public	Private	Public	Private	Public	Private	Public	Private	Public	Private
City	32.5	67.5	73.3	26.7	89.1	10.9	82.4	17.6	90.7	9.3
MSA[1]	49.7	50.3	86.5	13.5	90.1	9.9	88.8	11.2	88.6	11.4
U.S.	58.4	41.6	87.7	12.3	89.8	10.2	89.7	10.3	90.4	9.6

Note: Figures shown cover persons 3 years old and over; (1) Figures cover the Charleston-North Charleston, SC Metropolitan Statistical Area—see Appendix B for areas included
Source: U.S. Census Bureau, 2012-2016 American Community Survey 5-Year Estimates

Average Salaries of Public School Classroom Teachers

Area	2015		2016		Change from 2015 to 2016	
	Dollars	Rank[1]	Dollars	Rank[1]	Percent	Rank[2]
South Carolina	48,486	37	48,769	36	0.6	28
U.S. Average	57,611	–	58,353	–	1.3	–

Note: (1) Rank ranges from 1 to 51 where 1 indicates highest salary; (2) Rank ranges from 1 to 51 where 1 indicates highest percent change.
Source: National Education Association, Rankings & Estimates: Rankings of the States 2016 and Estimates of School Statistics 2017

Higher Education

Four-Year Colleges			Two-Year Colleges			Medical Schools[1]	Law Schools[2]	Voc/ Tech[3]
Public	Private Non-profit	Private For-profit	Public	Private Non-profit	Private For-profit			
0	0	0	0	0	0	0	0	0

Note: Figures cover institutions located within the city limits and include main campuses only; (1) includes schools accredited by the Liaison Committee on Medical Education and the American Osteopathic Association's Commission on Osteopathic College Accreditation; (2) includes ABA-accredited schools, schools with provisional ABA accreditation, and state accredited schools; (3) includes all schools with programs that are less than 2 years.
Source: National Center for Education Statistics, Integrated Postsecondary Education System (IPEDS), 2016-17; Wikipedia, List of Medical Schools in the United States, accessed April 2, 2018; Wikipedia, List of Law Schools in the United States, accessed April 2, 2018

According to *U.S. News & World Report,* the Charleston-North Charleston, SC metro area is home to one of the top 75 medical schools for research in the U.S.: **Medical University of South Carolina** (#62 tie). The rankings are based on a weighted average of 11 measures of quality: quality assessment; peer assessment score; assessment score by residency directors; research activity; total research activity; average research activity per faculty member; student selectivity; median MCAT total score; median undergraduate GPA; acceptance rate; and faculty resources. *U.S. News & World Report, "America's Best Graduate Schools, Medical, 2019"*

PRESIDENTIAL ELECTION

2016 Presidential Election Results

Area	Clinton	Trump	Johnson	Stein	Other
Charleston County	50.6	42.8	4.1	1.0	1.5
U.S.	48.0	45.9	3.3	1.1	1.7

Note: Results are percentages and may not add to 100% due to rounding
Source: Dave Leip's Atlas of U.S. Presidential Elections

EMPLOYERS

Major Employers

Company Name	Industry
Bi-Lo Stores	Grocery
Boeing South Carolina	Commercial aircraft
Charleston County Government	Local government
Charleston County School District	Public school district
City of Charleston	Local government
College of Charleston	Higher education
Evening Post Publishing Co.	Newspaper publishing
Force Protection	Mine-protected vehicle manufacturing
JEM Restaurant Group	Restaurants/hospitality
Joint Base Charleston	U.S. Air Force & U.S. Navy
Medical University of South Carolina	State's teaching hospital, medical higher education
Piggly Wiggly Carolina Co	Grocery
Roper St. Francis Healthcare	Private hospital system
SAIC	Advanced security
Trident Health System	Hospital system
U.S. Postal Service	Federal mail delivery
Verizon Wireless Call Center	Call center
Wal-Mart Stores	Retail merchandising

Note: Companies shown are located within the Charleston-North Charleston, SC Metropolitan Statistical Area.
Source: Hoovers.com; Wikipedia

PUBLIC SAFETY

Crime Rate

Area	All Crimes	Violent Crimes				Property Crimes		
		Murder	Rape[3]	Robbery	Aggrav. Assault	Burglary	Larceny -Theft	Motor Vehicle Theft
City	1,851.0	0.0	7.1	23.7	119.8	200.5	1,423.9	75.9
Metro[1]	3,264.1	9.4	33.1	87.9	287.8	481.3	2,107.4	257.2
U.S.	2,847.8	5.3	40.4	102.8	248.5	468.9	1,745.0	236.9

Note: Figures are crimes per 100,000 population; (1) Figures cover the Charleston-North Charleston, SC Metropolitan Statistical Area—see Appendix B for areas included; (3) The city and U.S. figures shown were reported using the revised Uniform Crime Reporting (UCR) definition of rape. The metro area figures shown are an aggregate total of the data submitted using both the revised and legacy UCR definitions.
Source: FBI Uniform Crime Reports, 2016

Hate Crimes

Area	Number of Quarters Reported	Number of Incidents per Bias Motivation					
		Race/Ethnicity/ Ancestry	Religion	Sexual Orientation	Disability	Gender	Gender Identity
City	4	0	0	0	0	0	0
U.S.	4	3,489	1,273	1,076	70	31	124

Source: Federal Bureau of Investigation, Hate Crime Statistics 2016

Identity Theft Consumer Reports

Area	Reports	Reports per 100,000 Population	Rank[2]
MSA[1]	704	92	132
U.S.	371,061	114	-

Note: (1) Figures cover the Charleston-North Charleston, SC Metropolitan Statistical Area—see Appendix B for areas included; (2) Rank ranges from 1 to 389 where 1 indicates greatest number of identity theft reports per 100,000 population
Source: Federal Trade Commission, Consumer Sentinel Network Data Book for January–December 2017

Fraud and Other Consumer Reports

Area	Reports	Reports per 100,000 Population	Rank[2]
MSA[1]	4,534	596	42
U.S.	2,304,550	708	-

Note: (1) Figures cover the Charleston-North Charleston, SC Metropolitan Statistical Area—see Appendix B for areas included; (2) Rank ranges from 1 to 389 where 1 indicates greatest number of fraud and other consumer reports per 100,000 population
Source: Federal Trade Commission, Consumer Sentinel Network Data Book for January–December 2017

SPORTS

Professional Sports Teams

Team Name	League	Year Established
No teams are located in the metro area		

Source: Wikipedia, Major Professional Sports Teams of the United States and Canada, April 5, 2018

CLIMATE

Average and Extreme Temperatures

Temperature	Jan	Feb	Mar	Apr	May	Jun	Jul	Aug	Sep	Oct	Nov	Dec	Yr.
Extreme High (°F)	83	87	90	94	98	101	104	102	97	94	88	83	104
Average High (°F)	59	62	68	76	83	88	90	89	85	77	69	61	76
Average Temp. (°F)	49	51	57	65	73	78	81	81	76	67	58	51	66
Average Low (°F)	38	40	46	53	62	69	72	72	67	56	46	39	55
Extreme Low (°F)	6	12	15	30	36	50	58	56	42	27	15	8	6

Note: Figures cover the years 1945-1995
Source: National Climatic Data Center, International Station Meteorological Climate Summary, 9/96

Average Precipitation/Snowfall/Humidity

Precip./Humidity	Jan	Feb	Mar	Apr	May	Jun	Jul	Aug	Sep	Oct	Nov	Dec	Yr.
Avg. Precip. (in.)	3.5	3.1	4.4	2.8	4.1	6.0	7.2	6.9	5.6	3.1	2.5	3.1	52.1
Avg. Snowfall (in.)	Tr	Tr	Tr	0	0	0	0	0	0	0	Tr	Tr	1
Avg. Rel. Hum. 7am (%)	83	81	83	84	85	86	88	90	91	89	86	83	86
Avg. Rel. Hum. 4pm (%)	55	52	51	51	56	62	66	66	65	58	56	55	58

Note: Figures cover the years 1945-1995; Tr = Trace amounts (<0.05 in. of rain; <0.5 in. of snow)
Source: National Climatic Data Center, International Station Meteorological Climate Summary, 9/96

Weather Conditions

Temperature			Daytime Sky			Precipitation		
10°F & below	32°F & below	90°F & above	Clear	Partly cloudy	Cloudy	0.01 inch or more precip.	0.1 inch or more snow/ice	Thunder-storms
< 1	33	53	89	162	114	114	1	59

Note: Figures are average number of days per year and cover the years 1945-1995
Source: National Climatic Data Center, International Station Meteorological Climate Summary, 9/96

HAZARDOUS WASTE

Superfund Sites

The Charleston-North Charleston, SC metro area is home to two sites on the EPA's Superfund National Priorities List: **Koppers Co., Inc. (Charleston Plant)** (final); **Macalloy Corporation** (final). There are a total of 1,396 Superfund sites with a status of proposed or final on the list in the U.S. *U.S. Environmental Protection Agency, National Priorities List, April 4, 2018*

AIR & WATER QUALITY

Air Quality Trends: Ozone

	1990	1995	2000	2005	2010	2012	2013	2014	2015	2016
MSA[1]	0.068	0.071	0.078	0.073	0.067	0.063	0.059	0.060	0.054	0.058
U.S.	0.087	0.089	0.081	0.079	0.073	0.075	0.069	0.067	0.068	0.069

Note: (1) Data covers the Charleston-North Charleston, SC Metropolitan Statistical Area—see Appendix B for areas included. The values shown are the composite ozone concentration averages among trend sites based on the highest fourth daily maximum 8-hour concentration in parts per million. These trends are based on sites having an adequate record of monitoring data during the trend period. Data from exceptional events are included.

Source: U.S. Environmental Protection Agency, Air Quality Monitoring Information, "Air Quality Trends by City, 1990-2016"

Air Quality Index

Area	Percent of Days when Air Quality was...[2]					AQI Statistics[2]	
	Good	Moderate	Unhealthy for Sensitive Groups	Unhealthy	Very Unhealthy	Maximum	Median
MSA[1]	83.6	16.1	0.3	0.0	0.0	101	40

Note: (1) Data covers the Charleston-North Charleston, SC Metropolitan Statistical Area—see Appendix B for areas included; (2) Based on 360 days with AQI data in 2017. Air Quality Index (AQI) is an index for reporting daily air quality. EPA calculates the AQI for five major air pollutants regulated by the Clean Air Act: ground-level ozone, particle pollution (aka particulate matter), carbon monoxide, sulfur dioxide, and nitrogen dioxide. The AQI runs from 0 to 500. The higher the AQI value, the greater the level of air pollution and the greater the health concern. There are six AQI categories: "Good" AQI is between 0 and 50. Air quality is considered satisfactory; "Moderate" AQI is between 51 and 100. Air quality is acceptable; "Unhealthy for Sensitive Groups" When AQI values are between 101 and 150, members of sensitive groups may experience health effects; "Unhealthy" When AQI values are between 151 and 200 everyone may begin to experience health effects; "Very Unhealthy" AQI values between 201 and 300 trigger a health alert; "Hazardous" AQI values over 300 trigger warnings of emergency conditions (not shown).

Source: U.S. Environmental Protection Agency, Air Quality Index Report, 2017

Air Quality Index Pollutants

Area	Percent of Days when AQI Pollutant was...[2]					
	Carbon Monoxide	Nitrogen Dioxide	Ozone	Sulfur Dioxide	Particulate Matter 2.5	Particulate Matter 10
MSA[1]	0.0	1.1	54.2	0.0	43.9	0.8

Note: (1) Data covers the Charleston-North Charleston, SC Metropolitan Statistical Area—see Appendix B for areas included; (2) Based on 360 days with AQI data in 2017. The Air Quality Index (AQI) is an index for reporting daily air quality. EPA calculates the AQI for five major air pollutants regulated by the Clean Air Act: ground-level ozone, particle pollution (also known as particulate matter), carbon monoxide, sulfur dioxide, and nitrogen dioxide. The AQI runs from 0 to 500. The higher the AQI value, the greater the level of air pollution and the greater the health concern.

Source: U.S. Environmental Protection Agency, Air Quality Index Report, 2017

Maximum Air Pollutant Concentrations: Particulate Matter, Ozone, CO and Lead

	Particulate Matter 10 (ug/m^3)	Particulate Matter 2.5 Wtd AM (ug/m^3)	Particulate Matter 2.5 24-Hr (ug/m^3)	Ozone (ppm)	Carbon Monoxide (ppm)	Lead (ug/m^3)
MSA[1] Level	66	7.7	17	0.058	n/a	n/a
NAAQS[2]	150	15	35	0.075	9	0.15
Met NAAQS[2]	Yes	Yes	Yes	Yes	n/a	n/a

Note: (1) Data covers the Charleston-North Charleston, SC Metropolitan Statistical Area—see Appendix B for areas included; Data from exceptional events are included; (2) National Ambient Air Quality Standards; ppm = parts per million; ug/m^3 = micrograms per cubic meter; n/a not available.

Concentrations: Particulate Matter 10 (coarse particulate)—highest second maximum 24-hour concentration; Particulate Matter 2.5 Wtd AM (fine particulate)—highest weighted annual mean concentration; Particulate Matter 2.5 24-Hour (fine particulate)—highest 98th percentile 24-hour concentration; Ozone—highest fourth daily maximum 8-hour concentration; Carbon Monoxide—highest second maximum non-overlapping 8-hour concentration; Lead—maximum running 3-month average

Source: U.S. Environmental Protection Agency, Air Quality Monitoring Information, "Air Quality Statistics by City, 2016"

Maximum Air Pollutant Concentrations: Nitrogen Dioxide and Sulfur Dioxide

	Nitrogen Dioxide AM (ppb)	Nitrogen Dioxide 1-Hr (ppb)	Sulfur Dioxide AM (ppb)	Sulfur Dioxide 1-Hr (ppb)	Sulfur Dioxide 24-Hr (ppb)
MSA[1] Level	n/a	n/a	n/a	10	n/a
NAAQS[2]	53	100	30	75	140
Met NAAQS[2]	n/a	n/a	n/a	Yes	n/a

Note: (1) Data covers the Charleston-North Charleston, SC Metropolitan Statistical Area—see Appendix B for areas included; Data from exceptional events are included; (2) National Ambient Air Quality Standards; ppm = parts per million; ug/m^3 = micrograms per cubic meter; n/a not available.
Concentrations: Nitrogen Dioxide AM—highest arithmetic mean concentration; Nitrogen Dioxide 1-Hr—highest 98th percentile 1-hour daily maximum concentration; Sulfur Dioxide AM—highest annual mean concentration; Sulfur Dioxide 1-Hr—highest 99th percentile 1-hour daily maximum concentration; Sulfur Dioxide 24-Hr—highest second maximum 24-hour concentration
Source: U.S. Environmental Protection Agency, Air Quality Monitoring Information, "Air Quality Statistics by City, 2016"

Drinking Water

Water System Name	Pop. Served	Primary Water Source Type	Violations[1] Health Based	Violations[1] Monitoring/ Reporting
Mount Pleasant Water Works	72,166	Purchased Surface	0	0

Note: (1) Based on violation data from January 1, 2017 to December 31, 2017
Source: U.S. Environmental Protection Agency, Office of Ground Water and Drinking Water, Safe Drinking Water Information System (based on data extracted April 5, 2018)

Aberdeen, South Dakota

Background

Namesake to the Scottish city, Aberdeen is located in the northeast part of South Dakota about an hour's drive south of the North Dakota border. "The Hub City of the Dakotas," as Aberdeen is known for the eight railroad lines that once converged there, is the seat of Brown County.

Today an aggressive promotional and jobs-creation initiative launched in 2001 continues to reap results, including jobs and relatively low unemployment in Aberdeen that also boasts relatively little crime.

The city is located within an agricultural region, with corn, wheat and beef among significant economic drivers. The ethanol business is also in full swing in the region, with plants operated by companies such as Redfield Energy fueled by corn crops. In addition are major employers such as the 3M Company, with a 600-employee manufacturing plant in town. Other notable private employers include Avera St. Luke's, providing Christian health care and 1,500 employees; and Hub City Inc., a power transmission manufacturer. Wyndham Hotel Group operates one of three global operations centers in Aberdeen.

Super 8 Motels was founded in 1972 by Dennis Brown and Ron Rivett as a motel referral system, which was replaced with a franchise operation in 1973. The first Super 8, with 60 rooms, was opened in 1974 in Aberdeen and still operates today as the Super 8 Aberdeen East.

The Aberdeen School District educates the city's youth, with an experienced staff of teachers providing the educational backbone. Institutions of higher education in the city include Northern State University, a small public institution founded in 1901 that was recently named a best regional college in the Midwest by *US News & World Report*. The campus has been watching as a $3.2 million renovation to its Barnett Center athletic facility and a new $6 million Student Center go up. Presentation College, a Catholic-Christian college founded in 1951, has located one of its four bricks-and-mortar campuses in Aberdeen. The school is known as a specialty Health Science Baccalaureate institution.

Aberdeen's old-school downtown provides a cultural anchor for the community, with concerts and other music events in good weather, as well as a farmer's market. The circa-1926 Capitol Theatre is a local landmark and performance venue. Another well-loved local treasure is Storybook Land, a theme park that also includes a nod to one-time Aberdeen resident L. Frank Baum, author of *The Wizard of Oz*.

The Aberdeen Community Theatre was created in 1979 and performs at the Capitol Theatre in downtown Aberdeen. The Capitol Theatre opened in 1927 and donated to the Aberdeen Community Theatre in 1991; since then more than $963,000 has been spent on renovating and preserving the historical aspect of the Capitol Theatre. Today, the Aberdeen Community Theatre performs five mainstage productions and three youth productions per year.

Recreational opportunities include fishing at nearby lakes and hunting; Aberdeen was named #6 in "Best 25 Pheasant Hunting Towns in America" by *Pheasants Forever.*

Average annual snowfall is 36 inches; the city's average high in July is 84 degrees and average low in January is one degree.

Business Environment

CITY FINANCES

City Government Finances

Component	2015 ($000)	2015 ($ per capita)
Total Revenues	52,194	1,857
Total Expenditures	46,285	1,647
Debt Outstanding	60,224	2,143
Cash and Securities[1]	45,474	1,618

Note: (1) Cash and security holdings of a government at the close of its fiscal year,, including those of its dependent agencies, utilities, and liquor stores.
Source: U.S Census Bureau, State & Local Government Finances 2015

City Government Revenue by Source

Source	2015 ($000)	2015 ($ per capita)	2015 (%)
General Revenue			
From Federal Government	2,936	104	5.6
From State Government	2,736	97	5.2
From Local Governments	9	0	0.0
Taxes			
Property	9,754	347	18.7
Sales and Gross Receipts	18,678	665	35.8
Personal Income	0	0	0.0
Corporate Income	0	0	0.0
Motor Vehicle License	0	0	0.0
Other Taxes	482	17	0.9
Current Charges	11,095	395	21.3
Liquor Store	0	0	0.0
Utility	4,953	176	9.5
Employee Retirement	0	0	0.0

Source: U.S Census Bureau, State & Local Government Finances 2015

City Government Expenditures by Function

Function	2015 ($000)	2015 ($ per capita)	2015 (%)
General Direct Expenditures			
Air Transportation	1,026	36	2.2
Corrections	0	0	0.0
Education	0	0	0.0
Employment Security Administration	0	0	0.0
Financial Administration	556	19	1.2
Fire Protection	2,503	89	5.4
General Public Buildings	0	0	0.0
Governmental Administration, Other	523	18	1.1
Health	115	4	0.2
Highways	10,275	365	22.2
Hospitals	0	0	0.0
Housing and Community Development	0	0	0.0
Interest on General Debt	1,934	68	4.2
Judicial and Legal	0	0	0.0
Libraries	1,051	37	2.3
Parking	68	2	0.1
Parks and Recreation	6,007	213	13.0
Police Protection	4,052	144	8.8
Public Welfare	0	0	0.0
Sewerage	4,974	177	10.7
Solid Waste Management	1,247	44	2.7
Veterans' Services	0	0	0.0
Liquor Store	0	0	0.0
Utility	5,103	181	11.0
Employee Retirement	0	0	0.0

Source: U.S Census Bureau, State & Local Government Finances 2015

DEMOGRAPHICS

Population Growth

Area	1990 Census	2000 Census	2010 Census	2016* Estimate	Population Growth (%) 1990-2016	2010-2016
City	25,391	24,658	26,091	27,783	9.4	6.5
MSA[1]	39,936	39,827	40,602	42,430	6.2	4.5
U.S.	248,709,873	281,421,906	308,745,538	318,558,162	28.1	3.2

Note: (1) Figures cover the Aberdeen, SD Micropolitan Statistical Area—see Appendix B for areas included; (*) 2012-2016 5-year estimated population
Source: U.S. Census Bureau, 1990 Census, Census 2000, Census 2010, 2012-2016 American Community Survey 5-Year Estimates

Household Size

Area	Persons in Household (%) One	Two	Three	Four	Five	Six	Seven or More	Average Household Size
City	34.5	33.2	13.6	11.8	3.7	2.2	1.0	2.20
MSA[1]	31.0	35.9	14.2	11.2	4.4	2.3	1.0	2.30
U.S.	27.7	33.7	15.7	13.1	6.0	2.3	1.5	2.60

Note: (1) Figures cover the Aberdeen, SD Micropolitan Statistical Area—see Appendix B for areas included
Source: U.S. Census Bureau, 2012-2016 American Community Survey 5-Year Estimates

Race

Area	White Alone[2] (%)	Black Alone[2] (%)	Asian Alone[2] (%)	AIAN[3] Alone[2] (%)	NHOPI[4] Alone[2] (%)	Other Race Alone[2] (%)	Two or More Races (%)
City	89.9	1.6	3.1	3.9	0.0	0.1	1.5
MSA[1]	91.9	1.4	2.1	3.1	0.0	0.1	1.3
U.S.	73.3	12.6	5.2	0.8	0.2	4.8	3.1

Note: (1) Figures cover the Aberdeen, SD Micropolitan Statistical Area—see Appendix B for areas included; (2) Alone is defined as not being in combination with one or more other races; (3) American Indian and Alaska Native; (4) Native Hawaiian and Other Pacific Islander
Source: U.S. Census Bureau, 2012-2016 American Community Survey 5-Year Estimates

Hispanic or Latino Origin

Area	Total (%)	Mexican (%)	Puerto Rican (%)	Cuban (%)	Other (%)
City	2.5	0.9	0.2	0.7	0.7
MSA[1]	2.3	1.0	0.2	0.5	0.6
U.S.	17.3	11.0	1.7	0.7	4.0

Note: Persons of Hispanic or Latino origin can be of any race; (1) Figures cover the Aberdeen, SD Micropolitan Statistical Area—see Appendix B for areas included
Source: U.S. Census Bureau, 2012-2016 American Community Survey 5-Year Estimates

Segregation

Type	Segregation Indices[1] 1990	2000	2010	2010 Rank[2]	Percent Change 1990-2000	1990-2010	2000-2010
Black/White	n/a	n/a	n/a	n/a	n/a	n/a	n/a
Asian/White	n/a	n/a	n/a	n/a	n/a	n/a	n/a
Hispanic/White	n/a	n/a	n/a	n/a	n/a	n/a	n/a

Note: All figures cover the Metropolitan Statistical Area—see Appendix B for areas included; Figures are based on an analysis of 1990, 2000, and 2010 Census Decennial Census tract data by William H. Frey, Brookings Institution and the University of Michigan Social Science Data Analysis Network. In this analysis all racial groups (whites, blacks, and asians) are non-Hispanic members of those races. Hispanics are shown as a separate category; (1) Segregation Indices are Dissimilarity Indices that measure the degree to which the minority group is distributed differently than whites across census tracts. They range from 0 (complete integration) to 100 (complete segregation) where the value indicates the percentage of the minority group that needs to move to be distributed exactly like whites; (2) Ranges from 1 (most segregated) to 102 (least segregated); n/a not available.
Source: www.CensusScope.org

Ancestry

Area	German	Irish	English	American	Italian	Polish	French[2]	Scottish	Dutch
City	51.8	9.7	5.0	2.6	0.8	2.0	1.8	0.4	2.1
MSA[1]	53.5	9.2	5.3	3.0	0.7	1.6	1.7	0.6	2.1
U.S.	14.4	10.4	7.7	6.9	5.4	2.9	2.6	1.7	1.3

Note: Figures are the percentage of the total population reporting a particular ancestry. The nine most commonly reported ancestries in the U.S. are shown. Figures include multiple ancestries (e.g. if a person reported being Irish and Italian, they were included in both columns); (1) Figures cover the Aberdeen, SD Micropolitan Statistical Area—see Appendix B for areas included; (2) Excludes Basque
Source: U.S. Census Bureau, 2012-2016 American Community Survey 5-Year Estimates

Foreign-Born Population

Area	Percent of Population Born in								
	Any Foreign Country	Asia	Mexico	Europe	Carribean	Central America[2]	South America	Africa	Canada
City	4.2	2.4	0.4	0.1	0.6	0.3	0.0	0.2	0.1
MSA[1]	3.5	1.7	0.3	0.2	0.5	0.3	0.0	0.5	0.1
U.S.	13.2	4.0	3.6	1.5	1.3	1.0	0.9	0.6	0.3

Note: (1) Figures cover the Aberdeen, SD Micropolitan Statistical Area—see Appendix B for areas included; (2) Excludes Mexico.
Source: U.S. Census Bureau, 2012-2016 American Community Survey 5-Year Estimates

Marital Status

Area	Never Married	Now Married[2]	Separated	Widowed	Divorced
City	32.4	48.8	1.0	6.9	10.9
MSA[1]	27.6	54.8	1.0	6.8	9.7
U.S.	33.0	48.1	2.1	5.9	11.0

Note: Figures are percentages and cover the population 15 years of age and older; (1) Figures cover the Aberdeen, SD Micropolitan Statistical Area—see Appendix B for areas included; (2) Excludes separated
Source: U.S. Census Bureau, 2012-2016 American Community Survey 5-Year Estimates

Disability Status

Area	All Ages	Under 18 Years Old	18 to 64 Years Old	65 Years and Over
City	10.5	2.1	7.8	34.9
MSA[1]	10.5	2.8	7.8	33.3
U.S.	12.5	4.1	10.3	35.7

Note: Figures show percent of the civilian noninstitutionalized population that reported having a disability. Disability status is determined from six types of difficulty: vision, hearing, cognitive, ambulatory, self-care, and independent living. For children under 5 years old, hearing and vision difficulty are used to determine disability status. For children between the ages of 5 and 14, disability status is determined from hearing, vision, cognitive, ambulatory, and self-care difficulties. For people aged 15 years and older, they are considered to have a disability if they have difficulty with any one of the six difficulty types; Note: (1) Figures cover the Aberdeen, SD Micropolitan Statistical Area—see Appendix B for areas included
Source: U.S. Census Bureau, 2012-2016 American Community Survey 5-Year Estimates

Age

Area	Percent of Population									Median Age
	Under Age 5	Age 5–19	Age 20–34	Age 35–44	Age 45–54	Age 55–64	Age 65–74	Age 75–84	Age 85+	
City	7.1	19.6	24.0	10.9	10.8	12.1	6.7	5.6	3.3	34.6
MSA[1]	6.4	20.0	20.1	11.1	12.8	13.3	7.7	5.6	2.9	38.2
U.S.	6.2	19.6	20.7	12.7	13.6	12.6	8.3	4.3	1.9	37.7

Note: (1) Figures cover the Aberdeen, SD Micropolitan Statistical Area—see Appendix B for areas included
Source: U.S. Census Bureau, 2012-2016 American Community Survey 5-Year Estimates

Gender

Area	Males	Females	Males per 100 Females
City	13,368	14,415	92.7
MSA[1]	20,717	21,713	95.4
U.S.	156,765,322	161,792,840	96.9

Note: (1) Figures cover the Aberdeen, SD Micropolitan Statistical Area—see Appendix B for areas included
Source: U.S. Census Bureau, 2012-2016 American Community Survey 5-Year Estimates

Religious Groups by Family

Area	Catholic	Baptist	Non-Den.	Methodist[2]	Lutheran	LDS[3]	Pente-costal	Presby-terian[4]	Muslim[5]	Judaism
MSA[1]	n/a	n/a	n/a	n/a	n/a	n/a	n/a	n/a	n/a	n/a
U.S.	19.1	9.3	4.0	4.0	2.3	2.0	1.9	1.6	0.8	0.7

Note: Figures are the number of adherents as a percentage of the total population; (1) Figures cover the Aberdeen, SD Micropolitan Statistical Area—see Appendix B for areas included; (2) Methodist/Pietist; (3) Latter Day Saints; (4) Reformed; (5) Figures are estimates
Source: Association of Statisticians of American Religious Bodies, 2010 U.S. Religion Census: Religious Congregations & Membership Study

Religious Groups by Tradition

Area	Catholic	Evangelical Protestant	Mainline Protestant	Other Tradition	Black Protestant	Orthodox
MSA[1]	n/a	n/a	n/a	n/a	n/a	n/a
U.S.	19.1	16.2	7.3	4.3	1.6	0.3

Note: Figures are the number of adherents as a percentage of the total population; (1) Figures cover the Aberdeen, SD Micropolitan Statistical Area—see Appendix B for areas included
Source: Association of Statisticians of American Religious Bodies, 2010 U.S. Religion Census: Religious Congregations & Membership Study

ECONOMY

Gross Metropolitan Product

Area	2014	2015	2016	2017	Rank[2]
MSA[1]	n/a	n/a	n/a	n/a	n/a

Note: Figures are in billions of dollars; (1) Figures cover the Aberdeen, SD Micropolitan Statistical Area—see Appendix B for areas included; (2) Rank is based on 2015 data and ranges from 1 to 381
Source: The U.S. Conference of Mayors, U.S. Metro Economies: GMP and Employment Report, 2015-2017

Economic Growth

Area	2012-14 (%)	2015 (%)	2016 (%)	2017 (%)	Rank[2]
MSA[1]	n/a	n/a	n/a	n/a	n/a
U.S.	2.0	2.4	1.9	2.6	–

Note: Figures are real gross metropolitan product (GMP) growth rates and represent average annual percent change; (1) Figures cover the Aberdeen, SD Micropolitan Statistical Area—see Appendix B for areas included; (2) Rank is based on 2012-2014 average annual percent change and ranges from 1 to 381
Source: The U.S. Conference of Mayors, U.S. Metro Economies: GMP and Employment Report, 2015-2017

Metropolitan Area Exports

Area	2011	2012	2013	2014	2015	2016	Rank[2]
MSA[1]	n/a	n/a	n/a	n/a	n/a	n/a	n/a

Note: Figures are in millions of dollars; (1) Figures cover the Aberdeen, SD Micropolitan Statistical Area—see Appendix B for areas included; (2) Rank is based on 2016 data and ranges from 1 to 385
Source: U.S. Department of Commerce, International Trade Administration, Office of Trade & Industry Information, Manufacturing & Services, data extracted March 15, 2018

Building Permits

Area	Single-Family			Multi-Family			Total		
	2016	2017p	Pct. Chg.	2016	2017p	Pct. Chg.	2016	2017p	Pct. Chg.
City	83	72	-13.3	0	72	n/a	83	144	73.5
MSA[1]	109	84	-22.9	0	72	n/a	109	156	43.1
U.S.	750,800	817,300	8.9	455,800	446,800	-2.0	1,206,600	1,264,100	4.8

Note: (1) Figures cover the Aberdeen, SD Micropolitan Statistical Area—see Appendix B for areas included; Figures represent new, privately-owned housing units authorized (unadjusted data); All permit data are based on estimates with imputation; (p) preliminary data.
Source: U.S. Census Bureau, Manufacturing, Mining, and Construction Statistics, Building Permits, 2016, 2017

Bankruptcy Filings

Area	Business Filings			Nonbusiness Filings		
	2016	2017	% Chg.	2016	2017	% Chg.
Brown County	3	2	-33.3	65	40	-38.5
U.S.	24,114	23,157	-4.0	770,846	765,863	-0.6

Note: Business filings include Chapter 7, Chapter 11, Chapter 12, and Chapter 13; Nonbusiness filings include Chapter 7, Chapter 11, and Chapter 13
Source: Administrative Office of the U.S. Courts, Business and Nonbusiness Bankruptcy, County Cases Commenced by Chapter of the Bankruptcy Code, During the 12-Month Period Ending December 31, 2016 and Business and Nonbusiness Bankruptcy, County Cases Commenced by Chapter of the Bankruptcy Code, During the 12-Month Period Ending December 31, 2017

Housing Vacancy Rates

Area	Gross Vacancy Rate[2] (%)			Year-Round Vacancy Rate[3] (%)			Rental Vacancy Rate[4] (%)			Homeowner Vacancy Rate[5] (%)		
	2015	2016	2017	2015	2016	2017	2015	2016	2017	2015	2016	2017
MSA[1]	n/a	n/a	n/a	n/a	n/a	n/a	n/a	n/a	n/a	n/a	n/a	n/a
U.S.	12.9	12.8	12.7	10.0	9.9	9.9	7.1	6.9	7.2	1.8	1.7	1.6

Note: (1) Figures cover the Aberdeen, SD Micropolitan Statistical Area—see Appendix B for areas included; (2) The percentage of the total housing inventory that is vacant; (3) The percentage of the housing inventory (excluding seasonal units) that is year-round vacant; (4) The percentage of rental inventory that is vacant for rent; (5) The percentage of homeowner inventory that is vacant for sale; n/a not available
Source: U.S. Census Bureau, Housing Vacancies and Homeownership Annual Statistics: 2015, 2016, 2017

INCOME

Income

Area	Per Capita ($)	Median Household ($)	Average Household ($)
City	26,669	46,330	61,978
MSA[1]	29,525	53,682	70,105
U.S.	29,829	55,322	77,866

Note: (1) Figures cover the Aberdeen, SD Micropolitan Statistical Area—see Appendix B for areas included
Source: U.S. Census Bureau, 2012-2016 American Community Survey 5-Year Estimates

Household Income Distribution

Area	Percent of Households Earning							
	Under $15,000	$15,000 -$24,999	$25,000 -$34,999	$35,000 -$49,999	$50,000 -$74,999	$75,000 -$99,999	$100,000 -$149,999	$150,000 and up
City	11.2	13.3	12.6	15.7	17.6	13.6	11.9	4.1
MSA[1]	9.8	11.0	11.0	14.0	19.3	14.7	13.6	6.5
U.S.	12.1	10.2	9.9	13.2	17.8	12.2	13.5	11.1

Note: (1) Figures cover the Aberdeen, SD Micropolitan Statistical Area—see Appendix B for areas included
Source: U.S. Census Bureau, 2012-2016 American Community Survey 5-Year Estimates

Poverty Rate

Area	All Ages	Under 18 Years Old	18 to 64 Years Old	65 Years and Over
City	13.6	12.5	15.2	9.2
MSA[1]	10.9	9.3	11.7	9.8
U.S.	15.1	21.2	14.2	9.3

Note: Figures are percentage of people whose income during the past 12 months was below the poverty level; (1) Figures cover the Aberdeen, SD Micropolitan Statistical Area—see Appendix B for areas included
Source: U.S. Census Bureau, 2012-2016 American Community Survey 5-Year Estimates

EMPLOYMENT

Labor Force and Employment

Area	Civilian Labor Force			Workers Employed		
	Dec. 2016	Dec. 2017	% Chg.	Dec. 2016	Dec. 2017	% Chg.
City	15,265	15,189	-0.5	14,769	14,666	-0.7
MSA[1]	23,187	23,105	-0.4	22,489	22,345	-0.6
U.S.	158,968,000	159,880,000	0.6	151,798,000	153,602,000	1.2

Note: Data is not seasonally adjusted and covers workers 16 years of age and older; (1) Figures cover the Aberdeen, SD Micropolitan Statistical Area—see Appendix B for areas included
Source: Bureau of Labor Statistics, Local Area Unemployment Statistics

Unemployment Rate

Area	2017											
	Jan.	Feb.	Mar.	Apr.	May	Jun.	Jul.	Aug.	Sep.	Oct.	Nov.	Dec.
City	3.3	3.6	3.5	3.1	2.9	2.9	2.9	3.2	2.6	2.7	2.9	3.4
MSA[1]	3.2	3.4	3.3	3.0	2.8	2.9	2.8	3.1	2.7	2.6	2.9	3.3
U.S.	5.1	4.9	4.6	4.1	4.1	4.5	4.6	4.5	4.1	3.9	3.9	3.9

Note: Data is not seasonally adjusted and covers workers 16 years of age and older; (1) Figures cover the Aberdeen, SD Micropolitan Statistical Area—see Appendix B for areas included
Source: Bureau of Labor Statistics, Local Area Unemployment Statistics

Average Wages

Occupation	$/Hr.	Occupation	$/Hr.
Accountants and Auditors	n/a	Maids and Housekeeping Cleaners	n/a
Automotive Mechanics	n/a	Maintenance and Repair Workers	n/a
Bookkeepers	n/a	Marketing Managers	n/a
Carpenters	n/a	Nuclear Medicine Technologists	n/a
Cashiers	n/a	Nurses, Licensed Practical	n/a
Clerks, General Office	n/a	Nurses, Registered	n/a
Clerks, Receptionists/Information	n/a	Nursing Assistants	n/a
Clerks, Shipping/Receiving	n/a	Packers and Packagers, Hand	n/a
Computer Programmers	n/a	Physical Therapists	n/a
Computer Systems Analysts	n/a	Postal Service Mail Carriers	n/a
Computer User Support Specialists	n/a	Real Estate Brokers	n/a
Cooks, Restaurant	n/a	Retail Salespersons	n/a
Dentists	n/a	Sales Reps., Exc. Tech./Scientific	n/a
Electrical Engineers	n/a	Sales Reps., Tech./Scientific	n/a
Electricians	n/a	Secretaries, Exc. Legal/Med./Exec.	n/a
Financial Managers	n/a	Security Guards	n/a
First-Line Supervisors/Managers, Sales	n/a	Surgeons	n/a
Food Preparation Workers	n/a	Teacher Assistants*	n/a
General and Operations Managers	n/a	Teachers, Elementary School*	n/a
Hairdressers/Cosmetologists	n/a	Teachers, Secondary School*	n/a
Internists, General	n/a	Telemarketers	n/a
Janitors and Cleaners	n/a	Truck Drivers, Heavy/Tractor-Trailer	n/a
Landscaping/Groundskeeping Workers	n/a	Truck Drivers, Light/Delivery Svcs.	n/a
Lawyers	n/a	Waiters and Waitresses	n/a

Note: Wage data was not available.
Source: Bureau of Labor Statistics, Metro Area Occupational Employment & Wage Estimates, May 2017

Employment by Occupation

Occupation Classification	City (%)	MSA[1] (%)	U.S. (%)
Management, Business, Science, and Arts	30.5	33.1	37.0
Natural Resources, Construction, and Maintenance	9.2	10.4	8.9
Production, Transportation, and Material Moving	18.3	16.6	12.2
Sales and Office	24.9	24.5	23.8
Service	17.1	15.4	18.1

Note: Figures cover employed civilians 16 years of age and older; (1) Figures cover the Aberdeen, SD Micropolitan Statistical Area—see Appendix B for areas included
Source: U.S. Census Bureau, 2012-2016 American Community Survey 5-Year Estimates

Employment by Industry

Sector	MSA[1] Number of Employees	MSA[1] Percent of Total	U.S. Percent of Total
Construction, Mining, and Logging	n/a	n/a	5.2
Education and Health Services	n/a	n/a	15.9
Financial Activities	n/a	n/a	5.7
Government	n/a	n/a	15.3
Information	n/a	n/a	1.9
Leisure and Hospitality	n/a	n/a	10.7
Manufacturing	n/a	n/a	8.5
Other Services	n/a	n/a	3.9
Professional and Business Services	n/a	n/a	14.0
Retail Trade	n/a	n/a	11.0
Transportation, Warehousing, and Utilities	n/a	n/a	4.1
Wholesale Trade	n/a	n/a	4.0

Note: Figures are non-farm employment as of December 2017. Figures are not seasonally adjusted and include workers 16 years of age and older; (1) Figures cover the Aberdeen, SD Micropolitan Statistical Area—see Appendix B for areas included; n/a not available
Source: Bureau of Labor Statistics, Current Employment Statistics, Employment, Hours, and Earnings

Occupations with Greatest Projected Employment Growth: 2017 – 2019

Occupation[1]	2017 Employment	2019 Projected Employment	Numeric Employment Change	Percent Employment Change
Registered Nurses	12,650	13,120	470	3.7
Combined Food Preparation and Serving Workers, Including Fast Food	9,700	10,090	390	4.1
Janitors and Cleaners, Except Maids and Housekeeping Cleaners	10,100	10,420	320	3.2
Laborers and Freight, Stock, and Material Movers, Hand	7,240	7,450	210	2.9
Cashiers	13,070	13,260	190	1.5
Personal Care Aides	2,920	3,110	190	6.6
Sales Representatives, Wholesale and Manufacturing, Except Technical and Scientific Products	5,680	5,840	160	2.7
Accountants and Auditors	5,150	5,300	150	3.0
Heavy and Tractor-Trailer Truck Drivers	8,690	8,840	150	1.7
Waiters and Waitresses	7,390	7,540	150	2.0

Note: Projections cover South Dakota; (1) Sorted by numeric employment change
Source: www.projectionscentral.com, State Occupational Projections, 2017–2019 Short-Term Projections

Fastest Growing Occupations: 2017 – 2019

Occupation[1]	2017 Employment	2019 Projected Employment	Numeric Employment Change	Percent Employment Change
Software Developers, Applications	1,240	1,360	120	9.8
Slaughterers and Meat Packers	890	950	60	6.7
Personal Care Aides	2,920	3,110	190	6.6
Emergency Medical Technicians and Paramedics	1,080	1,150	70	6.5
Home Health Aides	1,060	1,130	70	5.8
Residential Advisors	2,500	2,630	130	5.4
Industrial Machinery Mechanics	1,270	1,330	60	5.3
Loan Interviewers and Clerks	2,100	2,210	110	5.1
Medical Assistants	1,070	1,130	60	5.1
Loan Officers	1,640	1,720	80	4.8

Note: Projections cover South Dakota; (1) Sorted by percent employment change and excludes occupations with numeric employment change less than 50
Source: www.projectionscentral.com, State Occupational Projections, 2017–2019 Short-Term Projections

TAXES

State Corporate Income Tax Rates

State	Tax Rate (%)	Income Brackets ($)	Num. of Brackets	Financial Institution Tax Rate (%)[a]	Federal Income Tax Ded.
South Dakota	None	–	–	6.0-0.25 (b)	No

Note: Tax rates as of January 1, 2018; (a) Rates listed are the corporate income tax rate applied to financial institutions or excise taxes based on income. Some states have other taxes based upon the value of deposits or shares; (b) Minimum tax is $800 in California, $100 in District of Columbia and Arizona, $50 in North Dakota (banks), $500 in Rhode Island, $200 per location in South Dakota (banks), $100 in Utah, $250 in Vermont.
Source: Federation of Tax Administrators, Range of State Corporate Income Tax Rates, January 1, 2018

State Individual Income Tax Rates

State	Tax Rate (%)	Income Brackets ($)	Num. of Brackets	Personal Exempt. ($)[1]		Fed. Inc. Tax Ded.
				Single	Dependents	
South Dakota	None	–	–	–	–	–

Note: Tax rates as of January 1, 2018; Local- and county-level taxes are not included; n/a not applicable; (1) Married joint filers generally receive double the single exemption
Source: Federation of Tax Administrators, State Individual Income Tax Rates, January 1, 2018

Various State Sales and Excise Tax Rates

State	State Sales Tax (%)	Gasoline[1] (¢/gal.)	Cigarette[2] ($/pack)	Spirits[3] ($/gal.)	Wine[4] ($/gal.)	Beer[5] ($/gal.)	Recreational Marijuana (%)
South Dakota	4.5 (c)	30.0	1.53	4.67 (f)(j)	1.31 (l)(p)	0.27	Not legal

Note: All tax rates as of January 1, 2018; (1) The American Petroleum Institute has developed a methodology for determining the average tax rate on a gallon of fuel. Rates may include any of the following: excise taxes, environmental fees, storage tank fees, other fees or taxes, general sales tax, and local taxes. In states where gasoline is subject to the general sales tax, or where the fuel tax is based on the average sale price, the average rate determined by API is sensitive to changes in the price of gasoline. States that fully or partially apply general sales taxes to gasoline: CA, CO, GA, IL, IN, MI, NY; (2) The federal excise tax of $1.0066 per pack and local taxes are not included; (3) Rates are those applicable to off-premise sales of 40% alcohol by volume (a.b.v.) distilled spirits in 750ml containers. Local excise taxes are excluded; (4) Rates are those applicable to off-premise sales of 11% a.b.v. non-carbonated wine in 750ml containers; (5) Rates are those applicable to off-premise sales of 4.7% a.b.v. beer in 12 ounce containers; (c) The sales taxes in Hawaii, New Mexico, North Dakota, and South Dakota have broad bases that include many services; (f) Different rates also applicable according to alcohol content, place of production, size of container, or place purchased (on- or off-premise or onboard airlines); (j) Includes sales taxes specific to alcoholic beverages; (l) Different rates also applicable to alcohol content, place of production, size of container, place purchased (on- or off-premise or on board airlines) or type of wine (carbonated, vermouth, etc.); (p) Includes sales taxes specific to alcoholic beverages.
Source: Tax Foundation, 2018 Facts & Figures: How Does Your State Compare?

State Business Tax Climate Index Rankings

State	Overall Rank	Corporate Tax Rank	Individual Income Tax Rank	Sales Tax Rank	Unemployment Insurance Tax Rank	Property Tax Rank
South Dakota	2	1	1	33	39	25

Note: The index is a measure of how each state's tax laws affect economic performance. The lower the rank, the more favorable a state's tax system is for business. States without a given tax are given a ranking of 1. The scores/rankings for the District of Columbia do not affect other states. The 2018 index represents the tax climate as of July 1, 2017.
Source: Tax Foundation, State Business Tax Climate Index 2018

TRANSPORTATION

Means of Transportation to Work

Area	Car/Truck/Van		Public Transportation			Bicycle	Walked	Other Means	Worked at Home
	Drove Alone	Car-pooled	Bus	Subway	Railroad				
City	82.6	8.3	0.3	0.0	0.0	0.8	2.9	2.1	3.0
MSA[1]	81.5	8.7	0.2	0.0	0.0	0.7	3.2	1.5	4.2
U.S.	76.4	9.3	2.6	1.9	0.6	0.6	2.8	1.3	4.6

Note: Figures are percentages and cover workers 16 years of age and older; (1) Figures cover the Aberdeen, SD Micropolitan Statistical Area—see Appendix B for areas included
Source: U.S. Census Bureau, 2012-2016 American Community Survey 5-Year Estimates

Travel Time to Work

Area	Less Than 10 Minutes	10 to 19 Minutes	20 to 29 Minutes	30 to 44 Minutes	45 to 59 Minutes	60 to 89 Minutes	90 Minutes or More
City	43.2	47.9	4.0	2.5	1.1	1.0	0.3
MSA[1]	37.3	43.3	10.1	6.5	1.3	1.0	0.5
U.S.	12.9	29.2	20.9	20.4	8.0	6.0	2.7

Note: Note: Figures are percentages and include workers 16 years old and over; (1) Figures cover the Aberdeen, SD Micropolitan Statistical Area—see Appendix B for areas included
Source: U.S. Census Bureau, 2012-2016 American Community Survey 5-Year Estimates

Freeway Travel Time Index

Area	1985	1990	1995	2000	2005	2010	2014
Urban Area Rank[1,2]	n/a	n/a	n/a	n/a	n/a	n/a	n/a
Urban Area Index[1]	n/a	n/a	n/a	n/a	n/a	n/a	n/a
Average Index[3]	1.09	1.11	1.14	1.17	1.20	1.19	1.20

Note: Freeway Travel Time Index—the ratio of travel time in the peak period to the travel time at free-flow conditions. For example, a value of 1.30 indicates a 20-minute free-flow trip takes 26 minutes in the peak (20 minutes x 1.30 = 26 minutes); (1) Data for the Aberdeen, SD urban area was not available; (2) Rank is based on 101 urban areas (#1 = highest travel time index); (3) Average of 101 urban areas
Source: Texas Transportation Institute, 2015 Urban Mobility Scorecard, August 2015

Freeway Commuter Stress Index

Area	1985	1990	1995	2000	2005	2010	2014
Urban Area Rank[1,2]	n/a	n/a	n/a	n/a	n/a	n/a	n/a
Urban Area Index[1]	n/a	n/a	n/a	n/a	n/a	n/a	n/a
Average Index[3]	1.13	1.16	1.19	1.22	1.25	1.24	1.25

Note: The Freeway Commuter Stress Index is the same as the Freeway Travel Time Index (see table above) except that it includes only the travel in the peak directions during the peak periods; the TTI includes travel in all directions during the peak period. Thus, the CSI is more indicative of the work trip experienced by each commuter on a daily basis; (1) Data for the Aberdeen, SD urban area was not available; (2) Rank is based on 101 urban areas (#1 = highest travel time index); (3) Average of 101 urban areas
Source: Texas Transportation Institute, 2015 Urban Mobility Scorecard, August 2015

Living Environment

COST OF LIVING

Cost of Living Index

Composite Index	Groceries	Housing	Utilities	Trans-portation	Health Care	Misc. Goods/ Services
n/a	n/a	n/a	n/a	n/a	n/a	n/a

Note: The Cost of Living Index measures regional differences in the cost of consumer goods and services, excluding taxes and non-consumer expenditures, for professional and managerial households in the top income quintile. It is based on more than 50,000 prices covering almost 60 different items for which prices are collected three times a year by chambers of commerce, economic development organizations or university applied economic centers in each participating urban area. The numbers shown should be read as a percentage above or below the national average of 100. For example, a value of 115.4 in the groceries column indicates that grocery prices are 15.4% higher than the national average. Small differences in the index numbers should not be interpreted as significant; n/a not available.
Source: The Council for Community and Economic Research, ACCRA Cost of Living Index, 2017

Grocery Prices

Area[1]	T-Bone Steak ($/pound)	Frying Chicken ($/pound)	Whole Milk ($/half gal.)	Eggs ($/dozen)	Orange Juice ($/64 oz.)	Coffee ($/11.5 oz.)
City[2]	n/a	n/a	n/a	n/a	n/a	n/a
Avg.	11.29	1.40	2.02	1.47	3.55	4.37
Min.	7.71	0.93	1.04	0.70	2.86	3.24
Max.	15.83	2.39	4.03	3.92	6.29	8.16

Note: (1) Values for the local area are compared with the average, minimum and maximum values for all 294 areas in the Cost of Living Index; (2) Figures cover the Aberdeen SD urban area; n/a not available; ***T-Bone Steak*** *(price per pound);* ***Frying Chicken*** *(price per pound, whole fryer);* ***Whole Milk*** *(half gallon carton);* ***Eggs*** *(price per dozen, Grade A, large);* ***Orange Juice*** *(64 oz. Tropicana or Florida Natural);* ***Coffee*** *(11.5 oz. can, vacuum-packed, Maxwell House, Hills Bros, or Folgers).*
Source: The Council for Community and Economic Research, ACCRA Cost of Living Index, 2017

Housing and Utility Costs

Area[1]	New Home Price ($)	Apartment Rent ($/month)	All Electric ($/month)	Part Electric ($/month)	Other Energy ($/month)	Telephone ($/month)
City[2]	n/a	n/a	n/a	n/a	n/a	n/a
Avg.	335,956	1,047	175.01	97.34	67.93	28.71
Min.	187,788	491	109.48	49.33	35.44	12.39
Max.	1,739,087	4,559	432.62	227.09	353.33	44.61

Note: (1) Values for the local area are compared with the average, minimum and maximum values for all 294 areas in the Cost of Living Index; (2) Figures cover the Aberdeen SD urban area; n/a not available; ***New Home Price*** *(2,400 sf living area, 8,000 sf lot, in urban area with full utilities);* ***Apartment Rent*** *(950 sf 2 bedroom/1.5 or 2 bath, unfurnished, excluding all utilities except water);* ***All Electric*** *(average monthly cost for an all-electric home);* ***Part Electric*** *(average monthly cost for a part-electric home);* ***Other Energy*** *(average monthly cost for natural gas, fuel oil, coal, wood, and any other forms of energy except electricity);* ***Telephone*** *(price includes basic monthly rate for a private residential line plus additional local usage charges incurred by a family of four).*
Source: The Council for Community and Economic Research, ACCRA Cost of Living Index, 2017

Health Care, Transportation, and Other Costs

Area[1]	Doctor ($/visit)	Dentist ($/visit)	Optometrist ($/visit)	Gasoline ($/gallon)	Beauty Salon ($/visit)	Men's Shirt ($)
City[2]	n/a	n/a	n/a	n/a	n/a	n/a
Avg.	108.00	92.54	101.93	2.25	37.58	30.92
Min.	30.39	60.00	49.75	1.82	16.11	11.20
Max.	193.50	161.94	229.28	3.16	77.35	59.13

Note: (1) Values for the local area are compared with the average, minimum and maximum values for all 294 areas in the Cost of Living Index; (2) Figures cover the Aberdeen SD urban area; n/a not available; ***Doctor*** *(general practitioners routine exam of an established patient);* ***Dentist*** *(adult teeth cleaning and periodic oral examination);* ***Optometrist*** *(full vision eye exam for established adult patient);* ***Gasoline*** *(one gallon regular unleaded, national brand, including all taxes, cash price at self-service pump if available);* ***Beauty Salon*** *(woman's shampoo, trim, and blow-dry);* ***Men's Shirt*** *(cotton/polyester dress shirt, pinpoint weave, long sleeves).*
Source: The Council for Community and Economic Research, ACCRA Cost of Living Index, 2017

HOUSING

House Price Index (HPI)

Area	National Ranking[2]	Quarterly Change (%)	One-Year Change (%)	Five-Year Change (%)
MSA[1]	n/a	n/a	n/a	n/a
U.S.[3]	–	1.61	6.68	34.71

Note: The HPI is a weighted repeat sales index. It measures average price changes in repeat sales or refinancings on the same properties. This information is obtained by reviewing repeat mortgage transactions on single-family properties whose mortgages have been purchased or securitized by Fannie Mae or Freddie Mac in January 1975; (1) Figures cover the , Micropolitan Statistical Area—see Appendix B for areas included; (2) Rankings are based on annual percentage change for all metro areas containing at least 15,000 transactions over the last 10 years and ranges from 1 to 253; (3) figures based on a weighted average of Census Division estimates using a seasonally adjusted, purchase-only index; all figures are for the period ending December 31, 2017; n/a not available
Source: Federal Housing Finance Agency, House Price Index, February 28, 2018

Median Single-Family Home Prices

Area	2015	2016	2017p	Percent Change 2016 to 2017
MSA[1]	n/a	n/a	n/a	n/a
U.S. Average	223.9	235.5	248.8	5.6

Note: Figures are median sales prices of existing single-family homes in thousands of dollars; (p) preliminary; n/a not available; (1) Figures cover the Aberdeen, SD Micropolitan Statistical Area—see Appendix B for areas included
Source: National Association of Realtors, Median Sales Price of Existing Single-Family Homes for Metropolitan Areas, 4th Quarter 2017

Qualifying Income Based on Median Sales Price of Existing Single-Family Homes

Area	With 5% Down ($)	With 10% Down ($)	With 20% Down ($)
MSA[1]	n/a	n/a	n/a
U.S. Average	55,585	52,659	46,808

Note: Figures are preliminary; Qualifying income is based on a mortgage rate of 4.17%. Monthly principal and interest payment is limited to 25% of income; n/a not available; (1) Figures cover the Aberdeen, SD Micropolitan Statistical Area—see Appendix B for areas included
Source: National Association of Realtors, Qualifying Income Based on Median Sales Price of Existing Single-Family Homes for Metropolitan Areas, 4th Quarter 2017

Median Apartment Condo-Coop Home Prices

Area	2015	2016	2017p	Percent Change 2016 to 2017
MSA[1]	n/a	n/a	n/a	n/a
U.S. Average	210.7	220.7	234.3	6.2

Note: Figures are median sales prices of existing apartment condo-coop homes in thousands of dollars; (p) preliminary; n/a not available; (1) Figures cover the Aberdeen, SD Micropolitan Statistical Area—see Appendix B for areas included
Source: National Association of Realtors, Median Sales Price of Existing Apartment Condo-Coop Homes for Metropolitan Areas, 4th Quarter 2017

Home Value Distribution

Area	Under $50,000	$50,000 -$99,999	$100,000 -$149,999	$150,000 -$199,999	$200,000 -$299,999	$300,000 -$499,999	$500,000 -$999,999	$1,000,000 or more
City	9.5	19.3	26.8	20.9	13.1	8.8	1.3	0.3
MSA[1]	13.2	17.8	20.1	19.0	16.0	11.5	2.0	0.4
U.S.	8.8	14.8	15.3	14.9	18.4	16.4	9.0	2.5

Note: Figures are percentages and cover owner-occupied housing units; (1) Figures cover the Aberdeen, SD Micropolitan Statistical Area—see Appendix B for areas included
Source: U.S. Census Bureau, 2012-2016 American Community Survey 5-Year Estimates

Homeownership Rate

Area	2009 (%)	2010 (%)	2011 (%)	2012 (%)	2013 (%)	2014 (%)	2015 (%)	2016 (%)	2017 (%)
MSA[1]	n/a	n/a	n/a	n/a	n/a	n/a	n/a	n/a	n/a
U.S.	67.4	66.9	66.1	65.4	65.1	64.5	63.7	63.4	63.9

Note: (1) Figures cover the Aberdeen, SD Micropolitan Statistical Area—see Appendix B for areas included; n/a not available
Source: U.S. Census Bureau, Housing Vacancies and Homeownership Annual Statistics: 2009-2017

Year Housing Structure Built

Area	2010 or Later	2000 -2009	1990 -1999	1980 -1989	1970 -1979	1960 -1969	1950 -1959	1940 -1949	Before 1940	Median Year
City	5.0	9.0	7.2	8.3	17.4	14.4	9.7	6.8	22.1	1968
MSA[1]	4.5	10.9	10.5	7.2	16.7	12.6	8.7	6.1	22.8	1970
U.S.	2.3	14.7	14.0	13.7	15.6	10.9	10.6	5.2	13.0	1977

Note: Figures are percentages except for Median Year; Note: (1) Figures cover the Aberdeen, SD Micropolitan Statistical Area—see Appendix B for areas included
Source: U.S. Census Bureau, 2012-2016 American Community Survey 5-Year Estimates

Gross Monthly Rent

Area	Under $500	$500 -$999	$1,000 -$1,499	$1,500 -$1,999	$2,000 -$2,499	$2,500 -$2,999	$3,000 and up	Median ($)
City	29.3	60.3	7.2	2.5	0.7	0.0	0.0	616
MSA[1]	29.2	60.3	7.7	2.2	0.6	0.0	0.0	622
U.S.	11.3	43.3	27.7	10.7	4.0	1.6	1.5	949

Note: Figures are percentages except for Median; Gross rent is the contract rent plus the estimated average monthly cost of utilities (electricity, gas, and water and sewer) and fuels (oil, coal, kerosene, wood, etc.) if these are paid by the renter (or paid for the renter by someone else); (1) Figures cover the Aberdeen, SD Micropolitan Statistical Area—see Appendix B for areas included
Source: U.S. Census Bureau, 2012-2016 American Community Survey 5-Year Estimates

HEALTH

Health Risk Factors

Category	MSA[1] (%)	U.S. (%)
Adults aged 18–64 who have any kind of health care coverage	n/a	87.7
Adults who reported being in good or excellent health	n/a	83.6
Adults who are current smokers	n/a	17.1
Adults who currently use E-cigarettes	n/a	4.7
Adults who currently use chewing tobacco, snuff, or snus	n/a	4.0
Adults who are heavy drinkers[2]	n/a	6.5
Adults who are binge drinkers[3]	n/a	16.9
Adults who are overweight (BMI 25.0 - 29.9)	n/a	35.3
Adults who are obese (BMI 30.0 - 99.8)	n/a	29.9
Adults who participated in any physical activities in the past month	n/a	76.9
Adults who always or nearly always wears a seat belt	n/a	94.3

Note: n/a not available; (1) Figures cover the Aberdeen, SD Micropolitan Statistical Area—see Appendix B for areas included; (2) Heavy drinkers are classified as adult men having more than 14 drinks per week and adult women having more than 7 drinks per week; (3) Binge drinkers are classified as males having five or more drinks on one occasion or females having four or more drinks on one occasion
Source: Centers for Disease Control and Prevention, Behaviorial Risk Factor Surveillance System, SMART: Selected Metropolitan Area Risk Trends, 2016

Health Screening Rates

Category	MSA[1] (%)	U.S. (%)
Adults 50-75 who have had a blood stool test within the past year	n/a	8.0
Adults 50-75 who have had a colonoscopy in the past 10 years	n/a	63.5
Adults aged 65+ who have had flu shot within the past year	n/a	58.6
Adults aged 65+ who have ever had a pneumonia vaccination	n/a	73.4
Adults who have ever been tested for HIV	n/a	35.6
Women aged 21-65 who have had a pap test in the past three years	n/a	79.8
Men aged 40+ who have had a PSA test within the past two years	n/a	39.5
Women aged 40+ who have had a mammogram within the past two years	n/a	72.5

Note: n/a not available; (1) Figures cover the Aberdeen, SD Micropolitan Statistical Area—see Appendix B for areas included; Source: Centers for Disease Control and Prevention, Behaviorial Risk Factor Surveillance System, SMART: Selected Metropolitan Area Risk Trends, 2016

Chronic Health Conditions

Category	MSA[1] (%)	U.S. (%)
Adults who have ever been told they had a heart attack	n/a	4.4
Adults who have ever been told they have angina or coronary heart disease	n/a	4.1
Adults who have ever been told they had a stroke	n/a	3.1
Adults who have been told they currently have asthma	n/a	9.3
Adults who have ever been told they have arthritis	n/a	25.8
Adults who have ever been told they have diabetes[2]	n/a	10.5
Adults who have ever been told they had skin cancer	n/a	5.9
Adults who have ever been told they had any other types of cancer	n/a	6.7
Adults who have ever been told they have COPD	n/a	6.3
Adults who have ever been told they have kidney disease	n/a	2.8
Adults who have ever been told they have a form of depression	n/a	17.4

Note: n/a not available; (1) Figures cover the Aberdeen, SD Micropolitan Statistical Area—see Appendix B for areas included; (2) Figures do not include pregnancy-related, borderline, or pre-diabetes
Source: Centers for Disease Control and Prevention, Behaviorial Risk Factor Surveillance System, SMART: Selected Metropolitan Area Risk Trends, 2016

Mortality Rates for the Top 10 Causes of Death in the U.S.

ICD-10[a] Sub-Chapter	ICD-10[a] Code	Age-Adjusted Mortality Rate[1] per 100,000 population	
		County[2]	U.S.
Malignant neoplasms	C00-C97	166.8	158.5
Ischaemic heart diseases	I20-I25	95.6	96.8
Other forms of heart disease	I30-I51	24.8	52.4
Chronic lower respiratory diseases	J40-J47	32.3	40.9
Cerebrovascular diseases	I60-I69	40.9	37.2
Organic, including symptomatic, mental disorders	F01-F09	19.0	33.3
Other degenerative diseases of the nervous system	G30-G31	37.3	32.1
Other external causes of accidental injury	W00-X59	31.5	31.2
Diabetes mellitus	E10-E14	27.3	21.1
Hypertensive diseases	I10-I15	14.5	20.8

Note: (a) ICD-10 = International Classification of Diseases 10th Revision; (1) Mortality rates are a three year average covering 2014-2016; (2) Figures cover Brown County.
Source: Centers for Disease Control and Prevention, National Center for Health Statistics. Underlying Cause of Death 1999-2016 on CDC WONDER Online Database, released December 2017

Mortality Rates for Selected Causes of Death

ICD-10[a] Sub-Chapter	ICD-10[a] Code	Age-Adjusted Mortality Rate[1] per 100,000 population	
		County[2]	U.S.
Assault	X85-Y09	Suppressed	5.6
Diseases of the liver	K70-K76	Unreliable	14.0
Human immunodeficiency virus (HIV) disease	B20-B24	Suppressed	1.9
Influenza and pneumonia	J09-J18	20.6	14.6
Intentional self-harm	X60-X84	Unreliable	13.2
Malnutrition	E40-E46	Suppressed	1.3
Obesity and other hyperalimentation	E65-E68	Suppressed	2.1
Renal failure	N17-N19	Suppressed	13.0
Transport accidents	V01-V99	Unreliable	12.0
Viral hepatitis	B15-B19	Suppressed	1.9

Note: (a) ICD-10 = International Classification of Diseases 10th Revision; (1) Mortality rates are a three year average covering 2014-2016; (2) Figures cover Brown County; Data are Suppressed when the data meet the criteria for confidentiality constraints; Mortality rates are flagged as Unreliable when the rate would be calculated with a numerator of 20 or less.
Source: Centers for Disease Control and Prevention, National Center for Health Statistics. Underlying Cause of Death 1999-2016 on CDC WONDER Online Database, released December 2017

Health Insurance Coverage

Area	With Health Insurance	With Private Health Insurance	With Public Health Insurance	Without Health Insurance	Population Under Age 18 Without Health Insurance
City	90.3	74.5	28.3	9.7	5.9
MSA[1]	92.0	77.5	27.4	8.0	4.3
U.S.	88.3	66.7	33.0	11.7	5.9

Note: Figures are percentages that cover the civilian noninstitutionalized population; (1) Figures cover the Aberdeen, SD Micropolitan Statistical Area—see Appendix B for areas included
Source: U.S. Census Bureau, 2012-2016 American Community Survey 5-Year Estimates

Number of Medical Professionals

Area	MDs[3]	DOs[3,4]	Dentists	Podiatrists	Chiropractors	Optometrists
County[1] (number)	82	7	20	4	20	10
County[1] (rate[2])	213.0	18.2	51.4	10.3	51.4	25.7
U.S. (rate[2])	276.5	22.3	67.3	6.0	26.7	15.9

Note: Data as of 2016 unless noted; (1) Data covers Brown County; (2) Rate per 100,000 population; (3) Data as of 2015 and includes all active, non-federal physicians; (4) Doctor of Osteopathic Medicine
Source: U.S. Department of Health and Human Services, Health Resources and Services Administration, Bureau of Health Professions, Area Resource File (ARF) 2016-2017

EDUCATION

Public School District Statistics

District Name	Schls	Pupils	Pupil/ Teacher Ratio	Minority Pupils[1] (%)	Free Lunch Eligible[2] (%)	IEP[3] (%)
Aberdeen School District 06-1	11	4,491	15.9	17.8	30.8	14.1

Note: Table includes school districts with 100 or more students; (1) Percentage of students that are not non-Hispanic white; (2) Percentage of students that are eligible for the free lunch program; (3) Percentage of students that have an Individualized Education Program.
Source: U.S. Department of Education, National Center for Education Statistics, Common Core of Data, Local Education Agency (School District) Universe Survey: School Year 2015-2016; U.S. Department of Education, National Center for Education Statistics, Common Core of Data, Public Elementary/Secondary School Universe Survey: School Year 2015-2016

Highest Level of Education

Area	Less than H.S.	H.S. Diploma	Some College, No Deg.	Associate Degree	Bachelor's Degree	Master's Degree	Prof. School Degree	Doctorate Degree
City	8.5	32.0	21.0	10.2	20.8	5.2	1.0	1.3
MSA[1]	8.1	32.8	20.8	10.9	19.8	5.2	1.1	1.4
U.S.	13.0	27.5	21.0	8.2	18.8	8.2	2.0	1.3

Note: Figures cover persons age 25 and over; (1) Figures cover the Aberdeen, SD Micropolitan Statistical Area—see Appendix B for areas included
Source: U.S. Census Bureau, 2012-2016 American Community Survey 5-Year Estimates

Educational Attainment by Race

Area	High School Graduate or Higher (%)					Bachelor's Degree or Higher (%)				
	Total	White	Black	Asian	Hisp.[2]	Total	White	Black	Asian	Hisp.[2]
City	91.5	92.4	76.2	60.1	69.7	28.3	28.9	26.7	29.6	23.7
MSA[1]	91.9	92.6	83.2	62.7	73.0	27.4	27.7	36.7	33.6	23.1
U.S.	87.0	88.9	84.3	86.3	65.7	30.3	31.6	20.0	52.1	14.7

Note: Figures shown cover persons 25 years old and over; (1) Figures cover the Aberdeen, SD Micropolitan Statistical Area—see Appendix B for areas included; (2) People of Hispanic origin can be of any race
Source: U.S. Census Bureau, 2012-2016 American Community Survey 5-Year Estimates

School Enrollment by Grade and Control

Area	Preschool (%)		Kindergarten (%)		Grades 1 - 4 (%)		Grades 5 - 8 (%)		Grades 9 - 12 (%)	
	Public	Private	Public	Private	Public	Private	Public	Private	Public	Private
City	69.3	30.7	76.1	23.9	80.8	19.2	78.7	21.3	81.5	18.5
MSA[1]	71.0	29.0	81.2	18.8	85.6	14.4	81.8	18.2	83.1	16.9
U.S.	58.4	41.6	87.7	12.3	89.8	10.2	89.7	10.3	90.4	9.6

Note: Figures shown cover persons 3 years old and over; (1) Figures cover the Aberdeen, SD Micropolitan Statistical Area—see Appendix B for areas included
Source: U.S. Census Bureau, 2012-2016 American Community Survey 5-Year Estimates

Average Salaries of Public School Classroom Teachers

Area	2015		2016		Change from 2015 to 2016	
	Dollars	Rank[1]	Dollars	Rank[1]	Percent	Rank[2]
South Dakota	40,934	51	42,025	51	2.7	6
U.S. Average	57,611	–	58,353	–	1.3	–

Note: (1) Rank ranges from 1 to 51 where 1 indicates highest salary; (2) Rank ranges from 1 to 51 where 1 indicates highest percent change.
Source: National Education Association, Rankings & Estimates: Rankings of the States 2016 and Estimates of School Statistics 2017

Higher Education

Four-Year Colleges			Two-Year Colleges			Medical Schools[1]	Law Schools[2]	Voc/ Tech[3]
Public	Private Non-profit	Private For-profit	Public	Private Non-profit	Private For-profit			
1	1	0	0	0	0	0	0	0

Note: Figures cover institutions located within the city limits and include main campuses only; (1) includes schools accredited by the Liaison Committee on Medical Education and the American Osteopathic Association's Commission on Osteopathic College Accreditation; (2) includes ABA-accredited schools, schools with provisional ABA accreditation, and state accredited schools; (3) includes all schools with programs that are less than 2 years.
Source: National Center for Education Statistics, Integrated Postsecondary Education System (IPEDS), 2016-17; Wikipedia, List of Medical Schools in the United States, accessed April 2, 2018; Wikipedia, List of Law Schools in the United States, accessed April 2, 2018

PRESIDENTIAL ELECTION

2016 Presidential Election Results

Area	Clinton	Trump	Johnson	Stein	Other
Brown County	33.8	59.7	5.7	0.0	0.8
U.S.	48.0	45.9	3.3	1.1	1.7

Note: Results are percentages and may not add to 100% due to rounding
Source: Dave Leip's Atlas of U.S. Presidential Elections

EMPLOYERS

Major Employers

Company Name	Industry
3M Company	Multinational conglomerate
Avera St. Luke's	General medical and surgical hospital
Bethesda Home	Skilled nursing facility
Hub City	Power transmission products
Kessler's	Supermarket chain
Midstates Print & Media Solutions	Printing services
Molded Fiber Glass South Dakota	Composite products and services
Sanford Health	General medical and surgical hospital
WalMart Super Center	Discount retailer
Wells Fargo Bank	Banking
Wyndham Hotel Group	Hospitality services

Note: Companies shown are located within the Aberdeen, SD Micropolitan Statistical Area.
Source: Hoovers.com; Wikipedia

PUBLIC SAFETY

Crime Rate

Area	All Crimes	Violent Crimes				Property Crimes		
		Murder	Rape[3]	Robbery	Aggrav. Assault	Burglary	Larceny -Theft	Motor Vehicle Theft
City	2,649.3	0.0	101.8	17.5	350.9	410.6	1,638.7	129.8
Metro[1]	n/a	n/a	n/a	n/a	n/a	n/a	n/a	n/a
U.S.	2,847.8	5.3	40.4	102.8	248.5	468.9	1,745.0	236.9

Note: Figures are crimes per 100,000 population; (1) Figures cover the Aberdeen, SD Micropolitan Statistical Area—see Appendix B for areas included; n/a not available; (3) The city and U.S. figures shown were reported using the revised Uniform Crime Reporting (UCR) definition of rape. The metro area figures shown are an aggregate total of the data submitted using both the revised and legacy UCR definitions.
Source: FBI Uniform Crime Reports, 2016

Hate Crimes

Area	Number of Quarters Reported	Number of Incidents per Bias Motivation: Race/Ethnicity/ Ancestry	Religion	Sexual Orientation	Disability	Gender	Gender Identity
City	1	0	0	0	0	0	1
U.S.	4	3,489	1,273	1,076	70	31	124

Source: Federal Bureau of Investigation, Hate Crime Statistics 2016

Identity Theft Consumer Reports

Area	Reports	Reports per 100,000 Population	Rank[2]
MSA[1]	n/a	n/a	n/a
U.S.	371,061	114	-

Note: (1) Figures cover the Aberdeen, SD Micropolitan Statistical Area—see Appendix B for areas included; (2) Rank ranges from 1 to 389 where 1 indicates greatest number of identity theft reports per 100,000 population
Source: Federal Trade Commission, Consumer Sentinel Network Data Book for January–December 2017

Fraud and Other Consumer Reports

Area	Reports	Reports per 100,000 Population	Rank[2]
MSA[1]	n/a	n/a	n/a
U.S.	2,304,550	708	-

Note: (1) Figures cover the Aberdeen, SD Micropolitan Statistical Area—see Appendix B for areas included; (2) Rank ranges from 1 to 389 where 1 indicates greatest number of fraud and other consumer reports per 100,000 population
Source: Federal Trade Commission, Consumer Sentinel Network Data Book for January–December 2017

SPORTS

Professional Sports Teams

Team Name	League	Year Established
No teams are located in the metro area		

Source: Wikipedia, Major Professional Sports Teams of the United States and Canada, April 5, 2018

CLIMATE

Average and Extreme Temperatures

Temperature	Jan	Feb	Mar	Apr	May	Jun	Jul	Aug	Sep	Oct	Nov	Dec	Yr.
Extreme High (°F)	62	68	80	93	96	107	109	107	105	95	75	65	109
Average High (°F)	19	26	37	55	68	77	84	83	71	59	39	25	54
Average Temp. (°F)	9	15	27	43	56	65	71	69	58	46	29	15	42
Average Low (°F)	-1	4	17	31	42	52	56	54	43	32	18	4	30
Extreme Low (°F)	-44	-43	-31	-12	15	30	35	33	11	-10	-30	-43	-44

Note: Figures cover the years 1948-1995
Source: National Climatic Data Center, International Station Meteorological Climate Summary, 9/96

Average Precipitation/Snowfall/Humidity

Precip./Humidity	Jan	Feb	Mar	Apr	May	Jun	Jul	Aug	Sep	Oct	Nov	Dec	Yr.
Avg. Precip. (in.)	0.5	0.4	0.8	1.5	2.2	2.9	2.4	1.8	1.4	0.9	0.6	0.5	15.8
Avg. Snowfall (in.)	8	7	9	4	1	0	0	0	Tr	2	7	8	44
Avg. Rel. Hum. 6am (%)	76	78	82	80	79	84	84	84	82	80	81	79	81
Avg. Rel. Hum. 3pm (%)	67	66	59	45	43	47	42	40	42	44	58	67	52

Note: Figures cover the years 1948-1995; Tr = Trace amounts (<0.05 in. of rain; <0.5 in. of snow)
Source: National Climatic Data Center, International Station Meteorological Climate Summary, 9/96

Weather Conditions

Temperature			Daytime Sky			Precipitation		
5°F & below	32°F & below	90°F & above	Clear	Partly cloudy	Cloudy	0.01 inch or more precip.	0.1 inch or more snow/ice	Thunder-storms
61	187	22	84	144	137	96	41	35

Note: Figures are average number of days per year and cover the years 1948-1995
Source: National Climatic Data Center, International Station Meteorological Climate Summary, 9/96

HAZARDOUS WASTE

Superfund Sites

The Aberdeen, SD metro area has no sites on the EPA's Superfund Final National Priorities List. There are a total of 1,396 Superfund sites with a status of proposed or final on the list in the U.S.
U.S. Environmental Protection Agency, National Priorities List, April 4, 2018

AIR & WATER QUALITY

Air Quality Trends: Ozone

	1990	1995	2000	2005	2010	2012	2013	2014	2015	2016
MSA[1]	n/a	n/a	n/a	n/a	n/a	n/a	n/a	n/a	n/a	n/a
U.S.	0.087	0.089	0.081	0.079	0.073	0.075	0.069	0.067	0.068	0.069

Note: (1) Data covers the Aberdeen, SD Micropolitan Statistical Area—see Appendix B for areas included; n/a not available. The values shown are the composite ozone concentration averages among trend sites based on the highest fourth daily maximum 8-hour concentration in parts per million. These trends are based on sites having an adequate record of monitoring data during the trend period. Data from exceptional events are included.
Source: U.S. Environmental Protection Agency, Air Quality Monitoring Information, "Air Quality Trends by City, 1990-2016"

Air Quality Index

Area	Percent of Days when Air Quality was...[2]					AQI Statistics[2]	
	Good	Moderate	Unhealthy for Sensitive Groups	Unhealthy	Very Unhealthy	Maximum	Median
MSA[1]	95.9	4.1	0.0	0.0	0.0	97	23

Note: (1) Data covers the Aberdeen, SD Micropolitan Statistical Area—see Appendix B for areas included; (2) Based on 122 days with AQI data in 2017. Air Quality Index (AQI) is an index for reporting daily air quality. EPA calculates the AQI for five major air pollutants regulated by the Clean Air Act: ground-level ozone, particle pollution (aka particulate matter), carbon monoxide, sulfur dioxide, and nitrogen dioxide. The AQI runs from 0 to 500. The higher the AQI value, the greater the level of air pollution and the greater the health concern. There are six AQI categories: "Good" AQI is between 0 and 50. Air quality is considered satisfactory; "Moderate" AQI is between 51 and 100. Air quality is acceptable; "Unhealthy for Sensitive Groups" When AQI values are between 101 and 150, members of sensitive groups may experience health effects; "Unhealthy" When AQI values are between 151 and 200 everyone may begin to experience health effects; "Very Unhealthy" AQI values between 201 and 300 trigger a health alert; "Hazardous" AQI values over 300 trigger warnings of emergency conditions (not shown).
Source: U.S. Environmental Protection Agency, Air Quality Index Report, 2017

Air Quality Index Pollutants

Area	Percent of Days when AQI Pollutant was...[2]					
	Carbon Monoxide	Nitrogen Dioxide	Ozone	Sulfur Dioxide	Particulate Matter 2.5	Particulate Matter 10
MSA[1]	0.0	0.0	0.0	0.0	91.0	9.0

Note: (1) Data covers the Aberdeen, SD Micropolitan Statistical Area—see Appendix B for areas included; (2) Based on 122 days with AQI data in 2017. The Air Quality Index (AQI) is an index for reporting daily air quality. EPA calculates the AQI for five major air pollutants regulated by the Clean Air Act: ground-level ozone, particle pollution (also known as particulate matter), carbon monoxide, sulfur dioxide, and nitrogen dioxide. The AQI runs from 0 to 500. The higher the AQI value, the greater the level of air pollution and the greater the health concern.
Source: U.S. Environmental Protection Agency, Air Quality Index Report, 2017

Maximum Air Pollutant Concentrations: Particulate Matter, Ozone, CO and Lead

	Particulate Matter 10 (ug/m³)	Particulate Matter 2.5 Wtd AM (ug/m³)	Particulate Matter 2.5 24-Hr (ug/m³)	Ozone (ppm)	Carbon Monoxide (ppm)	Lead (ug/m³)
MSA[1] Level	65	5.4	14	n/a	n/a	n/a
NAAQS[2]	150	15	35	0.075	9	0.15
Met NAAQS[2]	Yes	Yes	Yes	n/a	n/a	n/a

Note: (1) Data covers the Aberdeen, SD Micropolitan Statistical Area—see Appendix B for areas included; Data from exceptional events are included; (2) National Ambient Air Quality Standards; ppm = parts per million; ug/m³ = micrograms per cubic meter; n/a not available.
Concentrations: Particulate Matter 10 (coarse particulate)—highest second maximum 24-hour concentration; Particulate Matter 2.5 Wtd AM (fine particulate)—highest weighted annual mean concentration; Particulate Matter 2.5 24-Hour (fine particulate)—highest 98th percentile 24-hour concentration; Ozone—highest fourth daily maximum 8-hour concentration; Carbon Monoxide—highest second maximum non-overlapping 8-hour concentration; Lead—maximum running 3-month average
Source: U.S. Environmental Protection Agency, Air Quality Monitoring Information, "Air Quality Statistics by City, 2016"

Maximum Air Pollutant Concentrations: Nitrogen Dioxide and Sulfur Dioxide

	Nitrogen Dioxide AM (ppb)	Nitrogen Dioxide 1-Hr (ppb)	Sulfur Dioxide AM (ppb)	Sulfur Dioxide 1-Hr (ppb)	Sulfur Dioxide 24-Hr (ppb)
MSA[1] Level	n/a	n/a	n/a	n/a	n/a
NAAQS[2]	53	100	30	75	140
Met NAAQS[2]	n/a	n/a	n/a	n/a	n/a

Note: (1) Data covers the Aberdeen, SD Micropolitan Statistical Area—see Appendix B for areas included; Data from exceptional events are included; (2) National Ambient Air Quality Standards; ppm = parts per million; ug/m³ = micrograms per cubic meter; n/a not available.
Concentrations: Nitrogen Dioxide AM—highest arithmetic mean concentration; Nitrogen Dioxide 1-Hr—highest 98th percentile 1-hour daily maximum concentration; Sulfur Dioxide AM—highest annual mean concentration; Sulfur Dioxide 1-Hr—highest 99th percentile 1-hour daily maximum concentration; Sulfur Dioxide 24-Hr—highest second maximum 24-hour concentration
Source: U.S. Environmental Protection Agency, Air Quality Monitoring Information, "Air Quality Statistics by City, 2016"

Drinking Water

Water System Name	Pop. Served	Primary Water Source Type	Violations[1]	
			Health Based	Monitoring/ Reporting
Aberdeen	26,091	Surface	0	0

Note: (1) Based on violation data from January 1, 2017 to December 31, 2017
Source: U.S. Environmental Protection Agency, Office of Ground Water and Drinking Water, Safe Drinking Water Information System (based on data extracted April 5, 2018)

Brentwood, Tennessee

Background

Located 10 miles south of Nashville, in Williamson and Davidson Counties, Brentwood is an attractive suburban community that has grown, in part, to major nearby transportation improvements.

According to the city's historian, the Brentwood area first was settled in the late 1700s as Revolutionary War soldiers, granted property by the state of North Carolina, moved into the area. Plantations and beautiful homes flourished by the time of the Civil War, signs of prosperity amid fertile farmland. During the war, both sides of the conflict used these dwellings. However, like much of the South, the war left the town with a broken economy. Improvement came gradually, and as the twentieth century progressed, the city's homes were restored. Starting in the 1960s, the interstate highways arrived.

Today, Brentwood is primarily a residential community with most of its land zoned residential with a minimum one-acre density, and less than 10% zoned for commercial use. Brentwood's largest employers are Comdata Corporation and Tractor Supply Company. The Cool Springs area, situated in Brentwood and nearby Franklin, is home to the Cool Springs Galleria, a shopping center that fills 1.3 million square feet with more than 150 specialty shops.

The city's students attend the Williamson County School System or the many private schools in the area. Upon graduation, they can attend 16 institutions of higher education within easy driving distance, including notable Vanderbilt University in nearby Nashville.

To relax, Brentwood residents can head out to the Deerwood Arboretum and Natural Area. In addition to a nature center with an observation deck and small amphitheater, the area's facilities include nature trails, the Little Harpeth River, and man-made lakes. Brentwood is also home to Crockett Park, more than 164 acres with tennis courts, ball fields, bikeway/jogging trails, an amphitheater, two historic homes, and more. Also in town is the Williamson County Indoor Sports Complex, a facility with tennis courts, and a 50 + meter indoor training pool, fitness equipment and more.

Nearby Nashville offers a multitude of activities befitting "Music City USA," including the fabled Grand Ole Opry, the Carl Van Vechten Gallery at Fisk University, featuring the Alfred Stieglitz Collection.

Brentwood has much the same climate as nearby Nashville. The average relative humidity is moderate, as are temperatures. The city is not in the most common path of storms that cross the country, but it is in a zone of moderate frequency for thunderstorms.

Rankings

General Rankings

- *US News & World Report* conducted a survey of more than 2,000 people and analyzed the 125 largest metropolitan areas to determine what matters the most when selecting the next place to live. Nashville* ranked #11 out of the top 25 as having the best combination of desirable factors. Criteria: cost of living; quality of education; job market, crime rates; and other factors. *realestate.usnews.com, "The 25 Best Places to Live in the U.S. in 2018," April 10, 2018*

- The Nashville* metro area was identified as one of America's fastest-growing areas in terms of population and economy by *Forbes*. The area ranked #7 out of 25. The 100 most populous metro areas in the U.S. were evaluated on the following criteria: estimated population growth; employment; economic output; wages; home values. *Forbes, "America's Fastest-Growing Cities 2018," February 28, 2018*

- Brentwood was selected as one of the best places to live in the United States by *Money* magazine. The city ranked #21 out of 100. This year's list focused on cities with populations of 10,000 to 100,000. Beginning with a pool of over 2,400 candidates, editors looked at 70 data points, from local economy and housing market to schools, crime and healthcare—and then sent reporters to interview residents, search neighborhoods and look for other intangibles. *Money, "Best Places to Live, 2017" September 18, 2017*

Business/Finance Rankings

- According to *Business Insider*, the Nashville* metro area is where startup growth is on the rise. Based on the 2017 Kauffman Index of Growth Entrepreneurship, which measured in-depth national entrepreneurial trends in 40 metro areas, it ranked #4 in highest startup growth. *www.businessinsider.com, "The 21 U.S. Cities with the Highest Startup Growth," October 21, 2017*

- The personal finance site NerdWallet analyzed 183 American metropolitan areas with populations over 250,000 and more than 15,000 businesses to rank where entrepreneurs find the most success. Criteria included area economy, annual income, housing cost, unemployment rate, and the success rate of area businesses. Nashville* ranked #103. *www.nerdwallet.com, "Best Places to Start a Business," April 27, 2015*

- The editors of *Kiplinger's Personal Finance Magazine* named Nashville* to their list of ten of the best metro areas for start-ups. The area ranked #3.Criteria: well-educated workforce; low living costs for self-employed people, as measured by the Council for Community and Economic Research; a strong existing community of small business; low unemployment; low business costs. *www.kiplinger.com, "10 Great Cities for Starting a Business," October 2014*

- Based on metro area social media reviews, the employment opinion group Glassdoor surveyed 50 of the largest U.S. metro areas and equally weighed cost of living, hiring opportunity, and job satisfaction to compose a list of "25 Best Cities for Jobs." Median pay and home value, in-demand jobs and number of current job openings was also factored in. The Nashville* metro area was ranked #20 in overall job satisfaction. *www.glassdoor.com, "Best Cities for Jobs," September 12, 2017*

- In a survey of economic confidence in the nation's 50 largest metropolitan areas conducted January–December 2014, the Nashville* metro area placed #35, according to Gallup's 2014 Economic Confidence Index. *Gallup, "San Jose and San Francisco Lead in Economic Confidence," March 19, 2015*

- The Brookings Institution ranked the 100 largest metro areas in the U.S. based on income inequality. Nashville* was ranked #78 (#1 = greatest ineqality). Criteria: the "95/20 ratio," a figure representing the income at which a household earns more than 95 percent of all other households, divided by the income at which a household earns more than only 20 percent of all other households. *Brookings Institution, "Household Income Inequality, 100 Largest U.S. Metro Areas, 2014-2016," February 5, 2018*

- *Forbes* ranked the 100 largest metro areas in the U.S. in terms of the "Best Cities for Young Professionals." The Nashville* metro area ranked #17 out of 25. (Large metro areas were divided into metro divisions.) Criteria: median rent of a two-bedroom apartment; job growth and unemployment rate; median salary of college graduates with 5 or less years of work experience; networking opportunities; social outlook; percentage of population 25 years of age and older with college degrees. *Forbes.com, "America's 25 Best Cities for Young Professionals in 2017," May 22, 2017*

- Payscale.com ranked the largest metro areas in terms of wage growth. The Nashville* metro area ranked #8. Criteria: private-sector wage growth between the 4th quarter of 2016 and the 4th quarter of 2017. *PayScale, "Wage Trends by Metro Area-4th Quarter," January 17, 2018*

- Nashville* was identified as one of America's most frugal metro areas by *Coupons.com.* The city ranked #9 out of 25. Criteria: digital coupon usage. *Coupons.com, "America's Most Frugal Cities of 2017," March 22, 2018*

- The Nashville* metro area appeared on the Milken Institute "2017 Best Performing Cities" list. Rank: #8 out of 200 large metro areas. Criteria: job growth; wage and salary growth; high-tech output growth. *Milken Institute, "Best-Performing Cities 2017," January 2018*

- *Forbes* ranked the 200 most populous metro areas to determine the nation's "Best Places for Business and Careers." The Nashville* metro area was ranked #12. Criteria: costs (business and living); job growth (past and projected); income growth; quality of life; educational attainment (college and high school); projected economic growth; cultural and recreational opportunities; net migration patterns; number of highly ranked colleges. *Forbes, "The Best Places for Business and Careers 2017," October 24, 2017*

Education Rankings

- Personal finance website *WalletHub* analyzed the 150 largest U.S. metropolitan statistical areas to determine where the most educated Americans are choosing to settle. Criteria: education quality and attainment gap; education levels; percentage of workers with degrees; public school rankings; quality and size of each metro area's universities. Nashville* was ranked #52 (#1 = most educated city). *www.WalletHub.com, "2017's Most and Least Educated Cities in America," July 25, 2017*

Environmental Rankings

- Sperling's BestPlaces assessed 379 metropolitan areas of the United States for the likelihood of dangerously extreme weather events or earthquakes. In general the Southeast and South-Central regions have the highest risk of weather extremes and earthquakes, while the Pacific Northwest enjoys the lowest risk. Of the least risky metropolitan areas, the Nashville* metro area was ranked #234. *www.bestplaces.net, "Safest Places from Natural Disasters," April 2011*

Health/Fitness Rankings

- For each of the 50 most populous metro areas in the United States, the American College of Sports Medicine's American Fitness Index evaluated infrastructure, community assets, and policies that encourage healthy and fit lifestyles, including preventive health behaviors, levels of chronic disease conditions, health care access, and community resources and policies that support physical activity. The Nashville* metro area ranked #42 for "community fitness." *www.americanfitnessindex.org, "ACSM American Fitness Index Health and Community Fitness Status of the 50 Largest Metropolitan Areas," May 2017*

- The Nashville* metro area was identified as one of the worst cities for bed bugs in America by pest control company Orkin. The area ranked #22 out of 50 based on the number of bed bug treatments Orkin performed from December 2016 to November 2017. *Orkin, "Baltimore and Washington D.C. Continue to Hold Top Spots," January 8, 2018*

- Nashville* was identified as a "2016 Spring Allergy Capital." The area ranked #29 out of 100. Three groups of factors were used to identify the most severe cities for people with allergies during the spring season: annual pollen levels; medicine utilization; access to board-certified allergists. *Asthma and Allergy Foundation of America, "Spring Allergy Capitals 2016"*

- Nashville* was identified as a "2016 Fall Allergy Capital." The area ranked #27 out of 100. Three groups of factors were used to identify the most severe cities for people with allergies during the fall season: annual pollen levels; medicine utilization; access to board-certified allergists. *Asthma and Allergy Foundation of America, "Fall Allergy Capitals 2016"*
- Nashville* was identified as a "2015 Asthma Capital." The area ranked #29 out of the nation's 100 largest metropolitan areas. Criteria: estimated prevalence; self-reported prevalence; crude death rate for asthma; annual pollen score; annual air quality; public smoking laws; number of board-certified asthma specialists; school inhaler access laws; rescue medication use; controller medication use; ER visits for asthma; uninsured rate; poverty rate. *Asthma and Allergy Foundation of America, "Asthma Capitals 2015"*
- The Nashville* metro area ranked #46 out of 189 in The Gallup-Healthways Well-Being Index. Criteria: purpose; social well being; financial health; community and physical health. Results are based on telephone interviews with adults, aged 18 and older, living in metropolitan areas in the 50 U.S. states and the District of Columbia. *Gallup-Healthways, "State of American Well-Being, 2017 Community Well-Being Rankings" March 2018*

Real Estate Rankings

- FitSmallBusiness looked at 50 of the largest metropolitan areas in the U.S. to determine which metro was the best to start a real estate business. Data was compiled from such sources as: Zillow, Trulia, U.S. Census Bureau, and the Bureau of Labor Statistics. Criteria: location; inventory; annual wages; median sales price of homes; days on the market; median price cut percentage; and other factors that would influence real estate professional growth. The Nashville* metro area ranked #15. *fitsmallbusiness.com, "The Best Cities to Become a Real Estate Agent in 2018," January 30, 2018*
- The Nashville* metro area was identified as one of the top 20 housing markets to invest in for 2018 by *Forbes*. The area ranked #6. Criteria: strong job and population growth; anticipated home price appreciation; and other factors. *Forbes.com, "Where to Invest in Housing in 2018," February 1, 2018*

Safety Rankings

- Brentwood was identified as one of the safest cities in America by NeighborhoodScout. The city ranked #73 out of 100 (100 = safest). Criteria: number of violent and property crimes per 1,000 residents. The editors only considered cities with 25,000 or more residents. *NeighborhoodScout, "Top 100 Safest Cities in the U.S. 2018" January 2, 2018*
- The National Insurance Crime Bureau ranked 382 metro areas in the U.S. in terms of per capita rates of vehicle theft. The Nashville* metro area ranked #210 (#1 = highest rate). Criteria: number of vehicle theft offenses per 100,000 inhabitants in 2016. *National Insurance Crime Bureau, "Hot Spots 2016," June 8, 2017*

Seniors/Retirement Rankings

- From its Best Cities for Successful Aging indexes, the Milken Institute generated rankings for metropolitan areas, weighing data in nine categories—health care, wellness, living arrangements, transportation and convenience, financial characteristics, education, employment, community engagement, and overall livability. The Nashville* metro area was ranked #30 overall in the large metro area category. *Milken Institute, "Best Cities for Successful Aging, 2017" March 14, 2017*

Miscellaneous Rankings

- The watchdog site Charity Navigator conducts an annual study of charities in the nation's major markets both to analyze statistical differences in their financial, accountability, and transparency practices and to track year-to-year variations in individual philanthropic communities. Charity Navigator's analysis demonstrated that the financial, accountability and transparency behaviors of America's largest charities can be influenced by the metropolitan market within which the charity operates. The Nashville* metro area was ranked #26 among the 30 metro markets in the rating category of Overall Score. *www.charitynavigator.org, "2017 Metro Market Study," May 1, 2017*

  *Brentwood is located within the Nashville-Davidson—Murfreesboro—Franklin, TN Metropolitan Statistical Area.

Business Environment

CITY FINANCES

City Government Finances

Component	2015 ($000)	2015 ($ per capita)
Total Revenues	63,562	1,522
Total Expenditures	53,685	1,285
Debt Outstanding	54,180	1,297
Cash and Securities[1]	90,503	2,167

Note: (1) Cash and security holdings of a government at the close of its fiscal year,, including those of its dependent agencies, utilities, and liquor stores.
Source: U.S Census Bureau, State & Local Government Finances 2015

City Government Revenue by Source

Source	2015 ($000)	2015 ($ per capita)	2015 (%)
General Revenue			
From Federal Government	0	0	0.0
From State Government	9,897	237	15.6
From Local Governments	13,821	331	21.7
Taxes			
Property	11,291	270	17.8
Sales and Gross Receipts	4,350	104	6.8
Personal Income	0	0	0.0
Corporate Income	0	0	0.0
Motor Vehicle License	0	0	0.0
Other Taxes	3,744	90	5.9
Current Charges	8,365	200	13.2
Liquor Store	0	0	0.0
Utility	8,923	214	14.0
Employee Retirement	0	0	0.0

Source: U.S Census Bureau, State & Local Government Finances 2015

City Government Expenditures by Function

Function	2015 ($000)	2015 ($ per capita)	2015 (%)
General Direct Expenditures			
Air Transportation	0	0	0.0
Corrections	0	0	0.0
Education	217	5	0.4
Employment Security Administration	0	0	0.0
Financial Administration	1,935	46	3.6
Fire Protection	6,637	158	12.4
General Public Buildings	781	18	1.5
Governmental Administration, Other	1,533	36	2.9
Health	0	0	0.0
Highways	4,265	102	7.9
Hospitals	0	0	0.0
Housing and Community Development	0	0	0.0
Interest on General Debt	1,689	40	3.1
Judicial and Legal	213	5	0.4
Libraries	2,291	54	4.3
Parking	0	0	0.0
Parks and Recreation	2,004	48	3.7
Police Protection	6,473	155	12.1
Public Welfare	0	0	0.0
Sewerage	9,912	237	18.5
Solid Waste Management	0	0	0.0
Veterans' Services	0	0	0.0
Liquor Store	0	0	0.0
Utility	7,472	178	13.9
Employee Retirement	0	0	0.0

Source: U.S Census Bureau, State & Local Government Finances 2015

DEMOGRAPHICS

Population Growth

Area	1990 Census	2000 Census	2010 Census	2016* Estimate	Population Growth (%) 1990-2016	Population Growth (%) 2010-2016
City	17,287	23,445	37,060	40,873	136.4	10.3
MSA[1]	1,048,218	1,311,789	1,589,934	1,794,570	71.2	12.9
U.S.	248,709,873	281,421,906	308,745,538	318,558,162	28.1	3.2

Note: (1) Figures cover the Nashville-Davidson—Murfreesboro—Franklin, TN Metropolitan Statistical Area—see Appendix B for areas included; (*) 2012-2016 5-year estimated population
Source: U.S. Census Bureau, 1990 Census, Census 2000, Census 2010, 2012-2016 American Community Survey 5-Year Estimates

Household Size

Area	Persons in Household (%) One	Two	Three	Four	Five	Six	Seven or More	Average Household Size
City	10.2	33.1	20.5	23.0	8.8	2.7	1.6	3.10
MSA[1]	27.0	34.1	16.6	13.5	5.6	2.0	1.1	2.60
U.S.	27.7	33.7	15.7	13.1	6.0	2.3	1.5	2.60

Note: (1) Figures cover the Nashville-Davidson—Murfreesboro—Franklin, TN Metropolitan Statistical Area—see Appendix B for areas included
Source: U.S. Census Bureau, 2012-2016 American Community Survey 5-Year Estimates

Race

Area	White Alone[2] (%)	Black Alone[2] (%)	Asian Alone[2] (%)	AIAN[3] Alone[2] (%)	NHOPI[4] Alone[2] (%)	Other Race Alone[2] (%)	Two or More Races (%)
City	87.8	3.0	7.1	0.1	0.0	0.2	1.7
MSA[1]	78.0	15.2	2.5	0.3	0.1	1.8	2.1
U.S.	73.3	12.6	5.2	0.8	0.2	4.8	3.1

Note: (1) Figures cover the Nashville-Davidson—Murfreesboro—Franklin, TN Metropolitan Statistical Area—see Appendix B for areas included; (2) Alone is defined as not being in combination with one or more other races; (3) American Indian and Alaska Native; (4) Native Hawaiian and Other Pacific Islander
Source: U.S. Census Bureau, 2012-2016 American Community Survey 5-Year Estimates

Hispanic or Latino Origin

Area	Total (%)	Mexican (%)	Puerto Rican (%)	Cuban (%)	Other (%)
City	3.4	1.7	0.2	0.2	1.3
MSA[1]	6.8	4.3	0.5	0.2	1.8
U.S.	17.3	11.0	1.7	0.7	4.0

Note: Persons of Hispanic or Latino origin can be of any race; (1) Figures cover the Nashville-Davidson—Murfreesboro—Franklin, TN Metropolitan Statistical Area—see Appendix B for areas included
Source: U.S. Census Bureau, 2012-2016 American Community Survey 5-Year Estimates

Segregation

Type	Segregation Indices[1] 1990	2000	2010	2010 Rank[2]	Percent Change 1990-2000	1990-2010	2000-2010
Black/White	60.7	58.1	56.2	49	-2.6	-4.4	-1.9
Asian/White	45.2	44.4	41.0	51	-0.8	-4.2	-3.4
Hispanic/White	24.3	46.0	47.9	34	21.6	23.5	1.9

Note: All figures cover the Metropolitan Statistical Area—see Appendix B for areas included; Figures are based on an analysis of 1990, 2000, and 2010 Census Decennial Census tract data by William H. Frey, Brookings Institution and the University of Michigan Social Science Data Analysis Network. In this analysis all racial groups (whites, blacks, and asians) are non-Hispanic members of those races. Hispanics are shown as a separate category; (1) Segregation Indices are Dissimilarity Indices that measure the degree to which the minority group is distributed differently than whites across census tracts. They range from 0 (complete integration) to 100 (complete segregation) where the value indicates the percentage of the minority group that needs to move to be distributed exactly like whites; (2) Ranges from 1 (most segregated) to 102 (least segregated); n/a not available.
Source: www.CensusScope.org

Ancestry

Area	German	Irish	English	American	Italian	Polish	French[2]	Scottish	Dutch
City	16.3	12.5	16.8	9.7	3.9	2.2	2.1	4.2	1.1
MSA[1]	10.4	10.4	9.8	13.3	2.7	1.3	2.0	2.3	1.0
U.S.	14.4	10.4	7.7	6.9	5.4	2.9	2.6	1.7	1.3

Note: Figures are the percentage of the total population reporting a particular ancestry. The nine most commonly reported ancestries in the U.S. are shown. Figures include multiple ancestries (e.g. if a person reported being Irish and Italian, they were included in both columns); (1) Figures cover the Nashville-Davidson—Murfreesboro—Franklin, TN Metropolitan Statistical Area—see Appendix B for areas included; (2) Excludes Basque
Source: U.S. Census Bureau, 2012-2016 American Community Survey 5-Year Estimates

Foreign-Born Population

Area	Percent of Population Born in								
	Any Foreign Country	Asia	Mexico	Europe	Carribean	Central America[2]	South America	Africa	Canada
City	8.6	5.3	0.5	1.2	0.1	0.1	0.4	0.4	0.5
MSA[1]	7.6	2.4	2.0	0.6	0.2	0.8	0.3	1.0	0.2
U.S.	13.2	4.0	3.6	1.5	1.3	1.0	0.9	0.6	0.3

Note: (1) Figures cover the Nashville-Davidson—Murfreesboro—Franklin, TN Metropolitan Statistical Area—see Appendix B for areas included; (2) Excludes Mexico.
Source: U.S. Census Bureau, 2012-2016 American Community Survey 5-Year Estimates

Marital Status

Area	Never Married	Now Married[2]	Separated	Widowed	Divorced
City	20.6	70.3	0.7	3.2	5.2
MSA[1]	31.3	49.7	1.9	5.1	11.9
U.S.	33.0	48.1	2.1	5.9	11.0

Note: Figures are percentages and cover the population 15 years of age and older; (1) Figures cover the Nashville-Davidson—Murfreesboro—Franklin, TN Metropolitan Statistical Area—see Appendix B for areas included; (2) Excludes separated
Source: U.S. Census Bureau, 2012-2016 American Community Survey 5-Year Estimates

Disability Status

Area	All Ages	Under 18 Years Old	18 to 64 Years Old	65 Years and Over
City	6.3	1.7	4.9	24.2
MSA[1]	12.0	3.9	10.5	36.5
U.S.	12.5	4.1	10.3	35.7

Note: Figures show percent of the civilian noninstitutionalized population that reported having a disability. Disability status is determined from six types of difficulty: vision, hearing, cognitive, ambulatory, self-care, and independent living. For children under 5 years old, hearing and vision difficulty are used to determine disability status. For children between the ages of 5 and 14, disability status is determined from hearing, vision, cognitive, ambulatory, and self-care difficulties. For people aged 15 years and older, they are considered to have a disability if they have difficulty with any one of the six difficulty types; Note: (1) Figures cover the Nashville-Davidson—Murfreesboro—Franklin, TN Metropolitan Statistical Area—see Appendix B for areas included
Source: U.S. Census Bureau, 2012-2016 American Community Survey 5-Year Estimates

Age

Area	Percent of Population									Median Age
	Under Age 5	Age 5–19	Age 20–34	Age 35–44	Age 45–54	Age 55–64	Age 65–74	Age 75–84	Age 85+	
City	5.6	26.7	9.5	14.8	17.6	13.8	8.1	2.9	1.0	41.4
MSA[1]	6.5	19.7	21.9	13.8	13.9	12.0	7.3	3.5	1.3	36.3
U.S.	6.2	19.6	20.7	12.7	13.6	12.6	8.3	4.3	1.9	37.7

Note: (1) Figures cover the Nashville-Davidson—Murfreesboro—Franklin, TN Metropolitan Statistical Area—see Appendix B for areas included
Source: U.S. Census Bureau, 2012-2016 American Community Survey 5-Year Estimates

Gender

Area	Males	Females	Males per 100 Females
City	20,153	20,720	97.3
MSA[1]	875,099	919,471	95.2
U.S.	156,765,322	161,792,840	96.9

Note: (1) Figures cover the Nashville-Davidson—Murfreesboro—Franklin, TN Metropolitan Statistical Area—see Appendix B for areas included
Source: U.S. Census Bureau, 2012-2016 American Community Survey 5-Year Estimates

Religious Groups by Family

Area	Catholic	Baptist	Non-Den.	Methodist[2]	Lutheran	LDS[3]	Pente-costal	Presby-terian[4]	Muslim[5]	Judaism
MSA[1]	4.1	25.3	5.8	6.1	0.4	0.8	2.2	2.1	0.4	0.2
U.S.	19.1	9.3	4.0	4.0	2.3	2.0	1.9	1.6	0.8	0.7

Note: Figures are the number of adherents as a percentage of the total population; (1) Figures cover the Nashville-Davidson—Murfreesboro—Franklin, TN Metropolitan Statistical Area—see Appendix B for areas included; (2) Methodist/Pietist; (3) Latter Day Saints; (4) Reformed; (5) Figures are estimates
Source: Association of Statisticians of American Religious Bodies, 2010 U.S. Religion Census: Religious Congregations & Membership Study

Religious Groups by Tradition

Area	Catholic	Evangelical Protestant	Mainline Protestant	Other Tradition	Black Protestant	Orthodox
MSA[1]	4.1	33.0	8.0	1.7	3.4	0.5
U.S.	19.1	16.2	7.3	4.3	1.6	0.3

Note: Figures are the number of adherents as a percentage of the total population; (1) Figures cover the Nashville-Davidson—Murfreesboro—Franklin, TN Metropolitan Statistical Area—see Appendix B for areas included
Source: Association of Statisticians of American Religious Bodies, 2010 U.S. Religion Census: Religious Congregations & Membership Study

ECONOMY

Gross Metropolitan Product

Area	2014	2015	2016	2017	Rank[2]
MSA[1]	105.5	110.4	114.6	120.8	34

Note: Figures are in billions of dollars; (1) Figures cover the Nashville-Davidson—Murfreesboro—Franklin, TN Metropolitan Statistical Area—see Appendix B for areas included; (2) Rank is based on 2015 data and ranges from 1 to 381
Source: The U.S. Conference of Mayors, U.S. Metro Economies: GMP and Employment Report, 2015-2017

Economic Growth

Area	2012-14 (%)	2015 (%)	2016 (%)	2017 (%)	Rank[2]
MSA[1]	2.9	2.9	2.4	3.3	66
U.S.	2.0	2.4	1.9	2.6	-

Note: Figures are real gross metropolitan product (GMP) growth rates and represent average annual percent change; (1) Figures cover the Nashville-Davidson—Murfreesboro—Franklin, TN Metropolitan Statistical Area—see Appendix B for areas included; (2) Rank is based on 2012-2014 average annual percent change and ranges from 1 to 381
Source: The U.S. Conference of Mayors, U.S. Metro Economies: GMP and Employment Report, 2015-2017

Metropolitan Area Exports

Area	2011	2012	2013	2014	2015	2016	Rank[2]
MSA[1]	5,878.7	6,402.1	8,702.8	9,620.9	9,353.0	9,460.1	32

Note: Figures are in millions of dollars; (1) Figures cover the Nashville-Davidson—Murfreesboro—Franklin, TN Metropolitan Statistical Area—see Appendix B for areas included; (2) Rank is based on 2016 data and ranges from 1 to 385
Source: U.S. Department of Commerce, International Trade Administration, Office of Trade & Industry Information, Manufacturing & Services, data extracted March 15, 2018

Building Permits

Area	Single-Family			Multi-Family			Total		
	2016	2017p	Pct. Chg.	2016	2017p	Pct. Chg.	2016	2017p	Pct. Chg.
City	175	185	5.7	0	0	0.0	175	185	5.7
MSA[1]	12,014	12,625	5.1	6,543	6,667	1.9	18,557	19,292	4.0
U.S.	750,800	817,300	8.9	455,800	446,800	-2.0	1,206,600	1,264,100	4.8

Note: (1) Figures cover the Nashville-Davidson—Murfreesboro—Franklin, TN Metropolitan Statistical Area—see Appendix B for areas included; Figures represent new, privately-owned housing units authorized (unadjusted data); All permit data are based on estimates with imputation; (p) preliminary data.
Source: U.S. Census Bureau, Manufacturing, Mining, and Construction Statistics, Building Permits, 2016, 2017

Bankruptcy Filings

Area	Business Filings			Nonbusiness Filings		
	2016	2017	% Chg.	2016	2017	% Chg.
Williamson County	35	32	-8.6	289	299	3.5
U.S.	24,114	23,157	-4.0	770,846	765,863	-0.6

Note: Business filings include Chapter 7, Chapter 11, Chapter 12, and Chapter 13; Nonbusiness filings include Chapter 7, Chapter 11, and Chapter 13
Source: Administrative Office of the U.S. Courts, Business and Nonbusiness Bankruptcy, County Cases Commenced by Chapter of the Bankruptcy Code, During the 12-Month Period Ending December 31, 2016 and Business and Nonbusiness Bankruptcy, County Cases Commenced by Chapter of the Bankruptcy Code, During the 12-Month Period Ending December 31, 2017

Housing Vacancy Rates

Area	Gross Vacancy Rate[2] (%)			Year-Round Vacancy Rate[3] (%)			Rental Vacancy Rate[4] (%)			Homeowner Vacancy Rate[5] (%)		
	2015	2016	2017	2015	2016	2017	2015	2016	2017	2015	2016	2017
MSA[1]	8.3	6.6	6.2	8.2	6.4	6.1	4.9	4.8	7.6	3.1	1.5	0.6
U.S.	12.9	12.8	12.7	10.0	9.9	9.9	7.1	6.9	7.2	1.8	1.7	1.6

Note: (1) Figures cover the Nashville-Davidson—Murfreesboro—Franklin, TN Metropolitan Statistical Area—see Appendix B for areas included; (2) The percentage of the total housing inventory that is vacant; (3) The percentage of the housing inventory (excluding seasonal units) that is year-round vacant; (4) The percentage of rental inventory that is vacant for rent; (5) The percentage of homeowner inventory that is vacant for sale
Source: U.S. Census Bureau, Housing Vacancies and Homeownership Annual Statistics: 2015, 2016, 2017

INCOME

Income

Area	Per Capita ($)	Median Household ($)	Average Household ($)
City	64,607	148,340	197,619
MSA[1]	30,269	56,152	77,619
U.S.	29,829	55,322	77,866

Note: (1) Figures cover the Nashville-Davidson—Murfreesboro—Franklin, TN Metropolitan Statistical Area—see Appendix B for areas included
Source: U.S. Census Bureau, 2012-2016 American Community Survey 5-Year Estimates

Household Income Distribution

Area	Percent of Households Earning							
	Under $15,000	$15,000 -$24,999	$25,000 -$34,999	$35,000 -$49,999	$50,000 -$74,999	$75,000 -$99,999	$100,000 -$149,999	$150,000 and up
City	2.5	1.5	3.5	5.6	7.5	9.1	20.8	49.3
MSA[1]	10.3	9.7	10.0	14.6	19.0	13.1	13.2	10.2
U.S.	12.1	10.2	9.9	13.2	17.8	12.2	13.5	11.1

Note: (1) Figures cover the Nashville-Davidson—Murfreesboro—Franklin, TN Metropolitan Statistical Area—see Appendix B for areas included
Source: U.S. Census Bureau, 2012-2016 American Community Survey 5-Year Estimates

Poverty Rate

Area	All Ages	Under 18 Years Old	18 to 64 Years Old	65 Years and Over
City	2.8	2.5	3.0	2.7
MSA[1]	13.5	19.3	12.3	7.8
U.S.	15.1	21.2	14.2	9.3

Note: Figures are percentage of people whose income during the past 12 months was below the poverty level; (1) Figures cover the Nashville-Davidson—Murfreesboro—Franklin, TN Metropolitan Statistical Area—see Appendix B for areas included
Source: U.S. Census Bureau, 2012-2016 American Community Survey 5-Year Estimates

EMPLOYMENT

Labor Force and Employment

Area	Civilian Labor Force			Workers Employed		
	Dec. 2016	Dec. 2017	% Chg.	Dec. 2016	Dec. 2017	% Chg.
City	21,135	21,763	3.0	20,434	21,306	4.3
MSA[1]	985,185	1,015,902	3.1	951,214	991,652	4.3
U.S.	158,968,000	159,880,000	0.6	151,798,000	153,602,000	1.2

Note: Data is not seasonally adjusted and covers workers 16 years of age and older; (1) Figures cover the Nashville-Davidson—Murfreesboro—Franklin, TN Metropolitan Statistical Area—see Appendix B for areas included
Source: Bureau of Labor Statistics, Local Area Unemployment Statistics

Unemployment Rate

Area	2017											
	Jan.	Feb.	Mar.	Apr.	May	Jun.	Jul.	Aug.	Sep.	Oct.	Nov.	Dec.
City	3.5	3.3	3.2	2.6	2.5	3.4	3.2	3.0	2.5	2.4	2.5	2.1
MSA[1]	3.8	3.4	3.1	2.6	2.5	3.2	3.1	2.9	2.6	2.5	2.5	2.4
U.S.	5.1	4.9	4.6	4.1	4.1	4.5	4.6	4.5	4.1	3.9	3.9	3.9

Note: Data is not seasonally adjusted and covers workers 16 years of age and older; (1) Figures cover the Nashville-Davidson—Murfreesboro—Franklin, TN Metropolitan Statistical Area—see Appendix B for areas included
Source: Bureau of Labor Statistics, Local Area Unemployment Statistics

Average Wages

Occupation	$/Hr.	Occupation	$/Hr.
Accountants and Auditors	31.90	Maids and Housekeeping Cleaners	10.70
Automotive Mechanics	21.40	Maintenance and Repair Workers	19.10
Bookkeepers	20.00	Marketing Managers	58.00
Carpenters	20.20	Nuclear Medicine Technologists	35.70
Cashiers	10.30	Nurses, Licensed Practical	20.10
Clerks, General Office	17.80	Nurses, Registered	30.00
Clerks, Receptionists/Information	14.10	Nursing Assistants	12.60
Clerks, Shipping/Receiving	15.00	Packers and Packagers, Hand	11.70
Computer Programmers	38.00	Physical Therapists	40.40
Computer Systems Analysts	36.50	Postal Service Mail Carriers	24.50
Computer User Support Specialists	24.90	Real Estate Brokers	36.90
Cooks, Restaurant	12.40	Retail Salespersons	13.80
Dentists	95.00	Sales Reps., Exc. Tech./Scientific	27.80
Electrical Engineers	41.80	Sales Reps., Tech./Scientific	45.50
Electricians	23.30	Secretaries, Exc. Legal/Med./Exec.	17.00
Financial Managers	n/a	Security Guards	12.40
First-Line Supervisors/Managers, Sales	19.50	Surgeons	117.10
Food Preparation Workers	10.90	Teacher Assistants*	11.70
General and Operations Managers	56.50	Teachers, Elementary School*	23.50
Hairdressers/Cosmetologists	13.90	Teachers, Secondary School*	24.10
Internists, General	128.70	Telemarketers	14.60
Janitors and Cleaners	12.30	Truck Drivers, Heavy/Tractor-Trailer	21.90
Landscaping/Groundskeeping Workers	12.60	Truck Drivers, Light/Delivery Svcs.	17.10
Lawyers	57.00	Waiters and Waitresses	9.50

Note: Wage data covers the Nashville-Davidson—Murfreesboro—Franklin, TN Metropolitan Statistical Area—see Appendix B for areas included; (*) Hourly wages for elementary/secondary school teachers and teacher assistants were calculated by the editors from annual wage data based on a 40 hour work week; n/a not available.
Source: Bureau of Labor Statistics, Metro Area Occupational Employment & Wage Estimates, May 2017

Employment by Occupation

Occupation Classification	City (%)	MSA[1] (%)	U.S. (%)
Management, Business, Science, and Arts	63.7	38.4	37.0
Natural Resources, Construction, and Maintenance	2.5	8.1	8.9
Production, Transportation, and Material Moving	3.1	12.5	12.2
Sales and Office	22.0	25.5	23.8
Service	8.7	15.5	18.1

Note: Figures cover employed civilians 16 years of age and older; (1) Figures cover the Nashville-Davidson—Murfreesboro—Franklin, TN Metropolitan Statistical Area—see Appendix B for areas included
Source: U.S. Census Bureau, 2012-2016 American Community Survey 5-Year Estimates

Employment by Industry

Sector	MSA[1]		U.S.
	Number of Employees	Percent of Total	Percent of Total
Construction, Mining, and Logging	41,700	4.2	5.2
Education and Health Services	151,400	15.2	15.9
Financial Activities	66,600	6.7	5.7
Government	120,500	12.1	15.3
Information	23,000	2.3	1.9
Leisure and Hospitality	113,500	11.4	10.7
Manufacturing	83,200	8.3	8.5
Other Services	40,700	4.1	3.9
Professional and Business Services	165,300	16.5	14.0
Retail Trade	101,300	10.1	11.0
Transportation, Warehousing, and Utilities	51,300	5.1	4.1
Wholesale Trade	40,600	4.1	4.0

Note: Figures are non-farm employment as of December 2017. Figures are not seasonally adjusted and include workers 16 years of age and older; (1) Figures cover the Nashville-Davidson—Murfreesboro—Franklin, TN Metropolitan Statistical Area—see Appendix B for areas included
Source: Bureau of Labor Statistics, Current Employment Statistics, Employment, Hours, and Earnings

Occupations with Greatest Projected Employment Growth: 2017 – 2019

Occupation[1]	2017 Employment	2019 Projected Employment	Numeric Employment Change	Percent Employment Change
Combined Food Preparation and Serving Workers, Including Fast Food	76,930	81,530	4,600	6.0
Laborers and Freight, Stock, and Material Movers, Hand	96,910	100,970	4,060	4.2
Customer Service Representatives	60,280	63,140	2,860	4.7
General and Operations Managers	46,420	48,740	2,320	5.0
Waiters and Waitresses	52,940	55,140	2,200	4.2
Registered Nurses	58,860	61,030	2,170	3.7
Heavy and Tractor-Trailer Truck Drivers	62,960	65,010	2,050	3.3
Personal Care Aides	20,910	22,660	1,750	8.4
Janitors and Cleaners, Except Maids and Housekeeping Cleaners	42,430	44,150	1,720	4.0
Retail Salespersons	94,740	96,460	1,720	1.8

Note: Projections cover Tennessee; (1) Sorted by numeric employment change
Source: www.projectionscentral.com, State Occupational Projections, 2017–2019 Short-Term Projections

Fastest Growing Occupations: 2017 – 2019

Occupation[1]	2017 Employment	2019 Projected Employment	Numeric Employment Change	Percent Employment Change
Dietetic Technicians	660	740	80	12.9
Recreational Vehicle Service Technicians	770	860	90	12.6
Tax Preparers	1,900	2,140	240	12.5
Veterinary Assistants and Laboratory Animal Caretakers	3,170	3,560	390	12.1
Veterinary Technologists and Technicians	1,350	1,510	160	12.0
Material Moving Workers, All Other	880	990	110	11.8
Statisticians	630	710	80	11.7
Veterinarians	1,500	1,670	170	11.6
Insurance Claims and Policy Processing Clerks	4,680	5,190	510	10.9
Medical Appliance Technicians	1,950	2,160	210	10.6

Note: Projections cover Tennessee; (1) Sorted by percent employment change and excludes occupations with numeric employment change less than 50
Source: www.projectionscentral.com, State Occupational Projections, 2017–2019 Short-Term Projections

TAXES

State Corporate Income Tax Rates

State	Tax Rate (%)	Income Brackets ($)	Num. of Brackets	Financial Institution Tax Rate (%)[a]	Federal Income Tax Ded.
Tennessee	6.5	Flat rate	1	6.5	No

Note: Tax rates as of January 1, 2018; (a) Rates listed are the corporate income tax rate applied to financial institutions or excise taxes based on income. Some states have other taxes based upon the value of deposits or shares.
Source: Federation of Tax Administrators, Range of State Corporate Income Tax Rates, January 1, 2018

State Individual Income Tax Rates

State	Tax Rate (%)	Income Brackets ($)	Num. of Brackets	Personal Exempt. ($)[1] Single	Personal Exempt. ($)[1] Dependents	Fed. Inc. Tax Ded.
Tennessee	State income tax of 6% on dividends and interest income only					

Note: Tax rates as of January 1, 2018; Local- and county-level taxes are not included; n/a not applicable; (1) Married joint filers generally receive double the single exemption
Source: Federation of Tax Administrators, State Individual Income Tax Rates, January 1, 2018

Various State Sales and Excise Tax Rates

State	State Sales Tax (%)	Gasoline[1] (¢/gal.)	Cigarette[2] ($/pack)	Spirits[3] ($/gal.)	Wine[4] ($/gal.)	Beer[5] ($/gal.)	Recreational Marijuana (%)
Tennessee	7.0	25.4	0.62	4.46 (i)	1.27 (o)	1.29 (u)	Not legal

Note: All tax rates as of January 1, 2018; (1) The American Petroleum Institute has developed a methodology for determining the average tax rate on a gallon of fuel. Rates may include any of the following: excise taxes, environmental fees, storage tank fees, other fees or taxes, general sales tax, and local taxes. In states where gasoline is subject to the general sales tax, or where the fuel tax is based on the average sale price, the average rate determined by API is sensitive to changes in the price of gasoline. States that fully or partially apply general sales taxes to gasoline: CA, CO, GA, IL, IN, MI, NY; (2) The federal excise tax of $1.0066 per pack and local taxes are not included; (3) Rates are those applicable to off-premise sales of 40% alcohol by volume (a.b.v.) distilled spirits in 750ml containers. Local excise taxes are excluded; (4) Rates are those applicable to off-premise sales of 11% a.b.v. non-carbonated wine in 750ml containers; (5) Rates are those applicable to off-premise sales of 4.7% a.b.v. beer in 12 ounce containers; (i) Includes case fees and/or bottle fees which may vary with size of container; (o) Includes case fees and/or bottle fees which may vary with size of container; (u) Includes the wholesale tax rate in Kentucky (10.5%) and Tennessee (17%), converted into a gallonage excise tax rate.
Source: Tax Foundation, 2018 Facts & Figures: How Does Your State Compare?

State Business Tax Climate Index Rankings

State	Overall Rank	Corporate Tax Rank	Individual Income Tax Rank	Sales Tax Rank	Unemployment Insurance Tax Rank	Property Tax Rank
Tennessee	14	21	8	45	22	29

Note: The index is a measure of how each state's tax laws affect economic performance. The lower the rank, the more favorable a state's tax system is for business. States without a given tax are given a ranking of 1. The scores/rankings for the District of Columbia do not affect other states. The 2018 index represents the tax climate as of July 1, 2017.
Source: Tax Foundation, State Business Tax Climate Index 2018

TRANSPORTATION

Means of Transportation to Work

Area	Car/Truck/Van: Drove Alone	Car/Truck/Van: Car-pooled	Public Transportation: Bus	Public Transportation: Subway	Public Transportation: Railroad	Bicycle	Walked	Other Means	Worked at Home
City	83.9	5.6	0.2	0.0	0.1	0.1	0.5	1.1	8.5
MSA[1]	82.0	9.3	1.0	0.0	0.1	0.2	1.4	1.0	5.0
U.S.	76.4	9.3	2.6	1.9	0.6	0.6	2.8	1.3	4.6

Note: Figures are percentages and cover workers 16 years of age and older; (1) Figures cover the Nashville-Davidson—Murfreesboro—Franklin, TN Metropolitan Statistical Area—see Appendix B for areas included
Source: U.S. Census Bureau, 2012-2016 American Community Survey 5-Year Estimates

Travel Time to Work

Area	Less Than 10 Minutes	10 to 19 Minutes	20 to 29 Minutes	30 to 44 Minutes	45 to 59 Minutes	60 to 89 Minutes	90 Minutes or More
City	6.1	29.3	29.7	26.7	4.9	1.9	1.4
MSA[1]	9.4	27.1	22.4	23.5	9.9	5.9	1.7
U.S.	12.9	29.2	20.9	20.4	8.0	6.0	2.7

Note: Note: Figures are percentages and include workers 16 years old and over; (1) Figures cover the Nashville-Davidson—Murfreesboro—Franklin, TN Metropolitan Statistical Area—see Appendix B for areas included
Source: U.S. Census Bureau, 2012-2016 American Community Survey 5-Year Estimates

Freeway Travel Time Index

Area	1985	1990	1995	2000	2005	2010	2014
Urban Area Rank[1,2]	26	34	36	34	32	39	34
Urban Area Index[1]	1.10	1.12	1.15	1.19	1.22	1.19	1.21
Average Index[3]	1.09	1.11	1.14	1.17	1.20	1.19	1.20

Note: Freeway Travel Time Index—the ratio of travel time in the peak period to the travel time at free-flow conditions. For example, a value of 1.30 indicates a 20-minute free-flow trip takes 26 minutes in the peak (20 minutes x 1.30 = 26 minutes); (1) Covers the Nashville-Davidson TN urban area; (2) Rank is based on 101 urban areas (#1 = highest travel time index); (3) Average of 101 urban areas
Source: Texas Transportation Institute, 2015 Urban Mobility Scorecard, August 2015

Freeway Commuter Stress Index

Area	1985	1990	1995	2000	2005	2010	2014
Urban Area Rank[1,2]	30	33	33	32	30	34	33
Urban Area Index[1]	1.16	1.18	1.22	1.26	1.29	1.26	1.27
Average Index[3]	1.13	1.16	1.19	1.22	1.25	1.24	1.25

Note: The Freeway Commuter Stress Index is the same as the Freeway Travel Time Index (see table above) except that it includes only the travel in the peak directions during the peak periods; the TTI includes travel in all directions during the peak period. Thus, the CSI is more indicative of the work trip experienced by each commuter on a daily basis; (1) Covers the Nashville-Davidson TN urban area; (2) Rank is based on 101 urban areas (#1 = highest travel time index); (3) Average of 101 urban areas
Source: Texas Transportation Institute, 2015 Urban Mobility Scorecard, August 2015

Living Environment

COST OF LIVING

Cost of Living Index

Composite Index	Groceries	Housing	Utilities	Trans-portation	Health Care	Misc. Goods/ Services
96.6	96.9	91.1	89.9	100.3	81.7	103.7

Note: The Cost of Living Index measures regional differences in the cost of consumer goods and services, excluding taxes and non-consumer expenditures, for professional and managerial households in the top income quintile. It is based on more than 50,000 prices covering almost 60 different items for which prices are collected three times a year by chambers of commerce, economic development organizations or university applied economic centers in each participating urban area. The numbers shown should be read as a percentage above or below the national average of 100. For example, a value of 115.4 in the groceries column indicates that grocery prices are 15.4% higher than the national average. Small differences in the index numbers should not be interpreted as significant; Figures cover the Nashville-Murfreesboro TN urban area.
Source: The Council for Community and Economic Research, ACCRA Cost of Living Index, 2017

Grocery Prices

Area[1]	T-Bone Steak ($/pound)	Frying Chicken ($/pound)	Whole Milk ($/half gal.)	Eggs ($/dozen)	Orange Juice ($/64 oz.)	Coffee ($/11.5 oz.)
City[2]	12.68	1.46	1.82	1.31	3.51	4.66
Avg.	11.29	1.40	2.02	1.47	3.55	4.37
Min.	7.71	0.93	1.04	0.70	2.86	3.24
Max.	15.83	2.39	4.03	3.92	6.29	8.16

Note: (1) Values for the local area are compared with the average, minimum and maximum values for all 294 areas in the Cost of Living Index; (2) Figures cover the Nashville-Murfreesboro TN urban area; ***T-Bone Steak*** *(price per pound);* ***Frying Chicken*** *(price per pound, whole fryer);* ***Whole Milk*** *(half gallon carton);* ***Eggs*** *(price per dozen, Grade A, large);* ***Orange Juice*** *(64 oz. Tropicana or Florida Natural);* ***Coffee*** *(11.5 oz. can, vacuum-packed, Maxwell House, Hills Bros, or Folgers).*
Source: The Council for Community and Economic Research, ACCRA Cost of Living Index, 2017

Housing and Utility Costs

Area[1]	New Home Price ($)	Apartment Rent ($/month)	All Electric ($/month)	Part Electric ($/month)	Other Energy ($/month)	Telephone ($/month)
City[2]	295,539	1,009	-	91.73	64.72	24.50
Avg.	335,956	1,047	175.01	97.34	67.93	28.71
Min.	187,788	491	109.48	49.33	35.44	12.39
Max.	1,739,087	4,559	432.62	227.09	353.33	44.61

Note: (1) Values for the local area are compared with the average, minimum and maximum values for all 294 areas in the Cost of Living Index; (2) Figures cover the Nashville-Murfreesboro TN urban area; ***New Home Price*** *(2,400 sf living area, 8,000 sf lot, in urban area with full utilities);* ***Apartment Rent*** *(950 sf 2 bedroom/1.5 or 2 bath, unfurnished, excluding all utilities except water);* ***All Electric*** *(average monthly cost for an all-electric home);* ***Part Electric*** *(average monthly cost for a part-electric home);* ***Other Energy*** *(average monthly cost for natural gas, fuel oil, coal, wood, and any other forms of energy except electricity);* ***Telephone*** *(price includes basic monthly rate for a private residential line plus additional local usage charges incurred by a family of four).*
Source: The Council for Community and Economic Research, ACCRA Cost of Living Index, 2017

Health Care, Transportation, and Other Costs

Area[1]	Doctor ($/visit)	Dentist ($/visit)	Optometrist ($/visit)	Gasoline ($/gallon)	Beauty Salon ($/visit)	Men's Shirt ($)
City[2]	83.40	71.60	77.07	2.11	46.12	32.33
Avg.	108.00	92.54	101.93	2.25	37.58	30.92
Min.	30.39	60.00	49.75	1.82	16.11	11.20
Max.	193.50	161.94	229.28	3.16	77.35	59.13

Note: (1) Values for the local area are compared with the average, minimum and maximum values for all 294 areas in the Cost of Living Index; (2) Figures cover the Nashville-Murfreesboro TN urban area; ***Doctor*** *(general practitioners routine exam of an established patient);* ***Dentist*** *(adult teeth cleaning and periodic oral examination);* ***Optometrist*** *(full vision eye exam for established adult patient);* ***Gasoline*** *(one gallon regular unleaded, national brand, including all taxes, cash price at self-service pump if available);* ***Beauty Salon*** *(woman's shampoo, trim, and blow-dry);* ***Men's Shirt*** *(cotton/polyester dress shirt, pinpoint weave, long sleeves).*
Source: The Council for Community and Economic Research, ACCRA Cost of Living Index, 2017

HOUSING

House Price Index (HPI)

Area	National Ranking[2]	Quarterly Change (%)	One-Year Change (%)	Five-Year Change (%)
MSA[1]	25	1.67	10.32	48.69
U.S.[3]	–	1.61	6.68	34.71

Note: The HPI is a weighted repeat sales index. It measures average price changes in repeat sales or refinancings on the same properties. This information is obtained by reviewing repeat mortgage transactions on single-family properties whose mortgages have been purchased or securitized by Fannie Mae or Freddie Mac in January 1975; (1) Figures cover the Nashville-Davidson—Murfreesboro—Franklin, TN Metropolitan Statistical Area—see Appendix B for areas included; (2) Rankings are based on annual percentage change for all metro areas containing at least 15,000 transactions over the last 10 years and ranges from 1 to 253; (3) figures based on a weighted average of Census Division estimates using a seasonally adjusted, purchase-only index; all figures are for the period ending December 31, 2017

Source: Federal Housing Finance Agency, House Price Index, February 28, 2018

Median Single-Family Home Prices

Area	2015	2016	2017p	Percent Change 2016 to 2017
MSA[1]	204.2	224.5	241.7	7.7
U.S. Average	223.9	235.5	248.8	5.6

Note: Figures are median sales prices of existing single-family homes in thousands of dollars; (p) preliminary; (1) Figures cover the Nashville-Davidson—Murfreesboro—Franklin, TN Metropolitan Statistical Area—see Appendix B for areas included

Source: National Association of Realtors, Median Sales Price of Existing Single-Family Homes for Metropolitan Areas, 4th Quarter 2017

Qualifying Income Based on Median Sales Price of Existing Single-Family Homes

Area	With 5% Down ($)	With 10% Down ($)	With 20% Down ($)
MSA[1]	56,190	53,233	47,318
U.S. Average	55,585	52,659	46,808

Note: Figures are preliminary; Qualifying income is based on a mortgage rate of 4.17%. Monthly principal and interest payment is limited to 25% of income; (1) Figures cover the Nashville-Davidson—Murfreesboro—Franklin, TN Metropolitan Statistical Area—see Appendix B for areas included

Source: National Association of Realtors, Qualifying Income Based on Median Sales Price of Existing Single-Family Homes for Metropolitan Areas, 4th Quarter 2017

Median Apartment Condo-Coop Home Prices

Area	2015	2016	2017p	Percent Change 2016 to 2017
MSA[1]	n/a	n/a	n/a	n/a
U.S. Average	210.7	220.7	234.3	6.2

Note: Figures are median sales prices of existing apartment condo-coop homes in thousands of dollars; (p) preliminary; n/a not available; (1) Figures cover the Nashville-Davidson—Murfreesboro—Franklin, TN Metropolitan Statistical Area—see Appendix B for areas included

Source: National Association of Realtors, Median Sales Price of Existing Apartment Condo-Coop Homes for Metropolitan Areas, 4th Quarter 2017

Home Value Distribution

Area	Under $50,000	$50,000 -$99,999	$100,000 -$149,999	$150,000 -$199,999	$200,000 -$299,999	$300,000 -$499,999	$500,000 -$999,999	$1,000,000 or more
City	1.2	0.6	1.0	2.0	4.4	32.9	49.7	8.2
MSA[1]	4.3	10.1	21.3	19.3	20.8	15.7	7.0	1.5
U.S.	8.8	14.8	15.3	14.9	18.4	16.4	9.0	2.5

Note: Figures are percentages and cover owner-occupied housing units; (1) Figures cover the Nashville-Davidson—Murfreesboro—Franklin, TN Metropolitan Statistical Area—see Appendix B for areas included

Source: U.S. Census Bureau, 2012-2016 American Community Survey 5-Year Estimates

Homeownership Rate

Area	2009 (%)	2010 (%)	2011 (%)	2012 (%)	2013 (%)	2014 (%)	2015 (%)	2016 (%)	2017 (%)
MSA[1]	71.8	70.4	69.6	64.9	63.9	67.1	67.4	65.0	69.4
U.S.	67.4	66.9	66.1	65.4	65.1	64.5	63.7	63.4	63.9

Note: (1) Figures cover the Nashville-Davidson—Murfreesboro—Franklin, TN Metropolitan Statistical Area—see Appendix B for areas included
Source: U.S. Census Bureau, Housing Vacancies and Homeownership Annual Statistics: 2009-2017

Year Housing Structure Built

Area	2010 or Later	2000 -2009	1990 -1999	1980 -1989	1970 -1979	1960 -1969	1950 -1959	1940 -1949	Before 1940	Median Year
City	5.2	27.8	20.3	19.9	17.3	7.7	0.4	0.6	0.8	1992
MSA[1]	4.1	21.2	18.9	15.4	14.4	10.1	7.7	3.3	4.9	1986
U.S.	2.3	14.7	14.0	13.7	15.6	10.9	10.6	5.2	13.0	1977

Note: Figures are percentages except for Median Year; Note: (1) Figures cover the Nashville-Davidson—Murfreesboro—Franklin, TN Metropolitan Statistical Area—see Appendix B for areas included
Source: U.S. Census Bureau, 2012-2016 American Community Survey 5-Year Estimates

Gross Monthly Rent

Area	Under $500	$500 -$999	$1,000 -$1,499	$1,500 -$1,999	$2,000 -$2,499	$2,500 -$2,999	$3,000 and up	Median ($)
City	2.7	5.1	19.4	27.1	13.1	10.0	22.7	1,922
MSA[1]	10.3	51.2	28.6	6.8	1.9	0.6	0.5	899
U.S.	11.3	43.3	27.7	10.7	4.0	1.6	1.5	949

Note: Figures are percentages except for Median; Gross rent is the contract rent plus the estimated average monthly cost of utilities (electricity, gas, and water and sewer) and fuels (oil, coal, kerosene, wood, etc.) if these are paid by the renter (or paid for the renter by someone else); (1) Figures cover the Nashville-Davidson—Murfreesboro—Franklin, TN Metropolitan Statistical Area—see Appendix B for areas included
Source: U.S. Census Bureau, 2012-2016 American Community Survey 5-Year Estimates

HEALTH

Health Risk Factors

Category	MSA[1] (%)	U.S. (%)
Adults aged 18–64 who have any kind of health care coverage	89.7	87.7
Adults who reported being in good or excellent health	83.9	83.6
Adults who are current smokers	20.5	17.1
Adults who currently use E-cigarettes	5.8	4.7
Adults who currently use chewing tobacco, snuff, or snus	4.6	4.0
Adults who are heavy drinkers[2]	7.3	6.5
Adults who are binge drinkers[3]	15.8	16.9
Adults who are overweight (BMI 25.0 - 29.9)	35.0	35.3
Adults who are obese (BMI 30.0 - 99.8)	30.3	29.9
Adults who participated in any physical activities in the past month	75.0	76.9
Adults who always or nearly always wears a seat belt	93.9	94.3

Note: (1) Figures cover the Nashville-Davidson—Murfreesboro—Franklin, TN Metropolitan Statistical Area—see Appendix B for areas included; (2) Heavy drinkers are classified as adult men having more than 14 drinks per week and adult women having more than 7 drinks per week; (3) Binge drinkers are classified as males having five or more drinks on one occasion or females having four or more drinks on one occasion
Source: Centers for Disease Control and Prevention, Behaviorial Risk Factor Surveillance System, SMART: Selected Metropolitan Area Risk Trends, 2016

Health Screening Rates

Category	MSA[1] (%)	U.S. (%)
Adults 50-75 who have had a blood stool test within the past year	6.7	8.0
Adults 50-75 who have had a colonoscopy in the past 10 years	65.3	63.5
Adults aged 65+ who have had flu shot within the past year	62.0	58.6
Adults aged 65+ who have ever had a pneumonia vaccination	78.4	73.4
Adults who have ever been tested for HIV	37.8	35.6
Women aged 21-65 who have had a pap test in the past three years	83.9	79.8
Men aged 40+ who have had a PSA test within the past two years	41.8	39.5
Women aged 40+ who have had a mammogram within the past two years	72.2	72.5

Note: n/a not available; (1) Figures cover the Nashville-Davidson—Murfreesboro—Franklin, TN Metropolitan Statistical Area—see Appendix B for areas included; Source: Centers for Disease Control and Prevention, Behaviorial Risk Factor Surveillance System, SMART: Selected Metropolitan Area Risk Trends, 2016

Chronic Health Conditions

Category	MSA[1] (%)	U.S. (%)
Adults who have ever been told they had a heart attack	4.5	4.4
Adults who have ever been told they have angina or coronary heart disease	4.8	4.1
Adults who have ever been told they had a stroke	3.8	3.1
Adults who have been told they currently have asthma	11.8	9.3
Adults who have ever been told they have arthritis	24.3	25.8
Adults who have ever been told they have diabetes[2]	10.6	10.5
Adults who have ever been told they had skin cancer	6.2	5.9
Adults who have ever been told they had any other types of cancer	6.4	6.7
Adults who have ever been told they have COPD	7.3	6.3
Adults who have ever been told they have kidney disease	2.4	2.8
Adults who have ever been told they have a form of depression	18.1	17.4

Note: (1) Figures cover the Nashville-Davidson—Murfreesboro—Franklin, TN Metropolitan Statistical Area—see Appendix B for areas included; (2) Figures do not include pregnancy-related, borderline, or pre-diabetes
Source: Centers for Disease Control and Prevention, Behaviorial Risk Factor Surveillance System, SMART: Selected Metropolitan Area Risk Trends, 2016

Mortality Rates for the Top 10 Causes of Death in the U.S.

ICD-10[a] Sub-Chapter	ICD-10[a] Code	Age-Adjusted Mortality Rate[1] per 100,000 population	
		County[2]	U.S.
Malignant neoplasms	C00-C97	122.2	158.5
Ischaemic heart diseases	I20-I25	90.4	96.8
Other forms of heart disease	I30-I51	33.9	52.4
Chronic lower respiratory diseases	J40-J47	29.4	40.9
Cerebrovascular diseases	I60-I69	31.6	37.2
Organic, including symptomatic, mental disorders	F01-F09	28.6	33.3
Other degenerative diseases of the nervous system	G30-G31	55.7	32.1
Other external causes of accidental injury	W00-X59	31.6	31.2
Diabetes mellitus	E10-E14	12.0	21.1
Hypertensive diseases	I10-I15	15.0	20.8

Note: (a) ICD-10 = International Classification of Diseases 10th Revision; (1) Mortality rates are a three year average covering 2014-2016; (2) Figures cover Williamson County.
Source: Centers for Disease Control and Prevention, National Center for Health Statistics. Underlying Cause of Death 1999-2016 on CDC WONDER Online Database, released December 2017

Mortality Rates for Selected Causes of Death

ICD-10[a] Sub-Chapter	ICD-10[a] Code	Age-Adjusted Mortality Rate[1] per 100,000 population	
		County[2]	U.S.
Assault	X85-Y09	Suppressed	5.6
Diseases of the liver	K70-K76	6.9	14.0
Human immunodeficiency virus (HIV) disease	B20-B24	Suppressed	1.9
Influenza and pneumonia	J09-J18	11.1	14.6
Intentional self-harm	X60-X84	11.9	13.2
Malnutrition	E40-E46	Suppressed	1.3
Obesity and other hyperalimentation	E65-E68	Suppressed	2.1
Renal failure	N17-N19	8.6	13.0
Transport accidents	V01-V99	9.4	12.0
Viral hepatitis	B15-B19	Suppressed	1.9

Note: (a) ICD-10 = International Classification of Diseases 10th Revision; (1) Mortality rates are a three year average covering 2014-2016; (2) Figures cover Williamson County; Data are Suppressed when the data meet the criteria for confidentiality constraints; Mortality rates are flagged as Unreliable when the rate would be calculated with a numerator of 20 or less.
Source: Centers for Disease Control and Prevention, National Center for Health Statistics. Underlying Cause of Death 1999-2016 on CDC WONDER Online Database, released December 2017

Health Insurance Coverage

Area	With Health Insurance	With Private Health Insurance	With Public Health Insurance	Without Health Insurance	Population Under Age 18 Without Health Insurance
City	96.6	91.2	13.9	3.4	1.7
MSA[1]	88.8	70.3	28.3	11.2	5.0
U.S.	88.3	66.7	33.0	11.7	5.9

Note: Figures are percentages that cover the civilian noninstitutionalized population; (1) Figures cover the Nashville-Davidson—Murfreesboro—Franklin, TN Metropolitan Statistical Area—see Appendix B for areas included

Source: U.S. Census Bureau, 2012-2016 American Community Survey 5-Year Estimates

Number of Medical Professionals

Area	MDs[3]	DOs[3,4]	Dentists	Podiatrists	Chiropractors	Optometrists
County[1] (number)	1,218	51	167	8	101	49
County[1] (rate[2])	576.0	24.1	76.3	3.7	46.1	22.4
U.S. (rate[2])	276.5	22.3	67.3	6.0	26.7	15.9

Note: Data as of 2016 unless noted; (1) Data covers Williamson County; (2) Rate per 100,000 population; (3) Data as of 2015 and includes all active, non-federal physicians; (4) Doctor of Osteopathic Medicine

Source: U.S. Department of Health and Human Services, Health Resources and Services Administration, Bureau of Health Professions, Area Resource File (ARF) 2016-2017

Best Hospitals

According to *U.S. News,* the Nashville-Davidson—Murfreesboro—Franklin, TN metro area is home to one of the best hospitals in the U.S.: **Vanderbilt University Medical Center** (7 adult specialties and 10 pediatric specialties). The hospital listed was nationally ranked in at least one of 16 specialties. Only 152 hospitals nationwide were nationally ranked in one or more specialties. Twenty hospitals in the U.S. made the Honor Roll. The Best Hospitals Honor Roll was revamped last year to take both the national rankings and the procedure and condition ratings into account. Hospitals received points if they were nationally ranked in one of the 16 specialties—the higher they ranked, the more points they got—and how many ratings of "high performing" they earned in the nine procedures and conditions. *U.S. News Online, "America's Best Hospitals 2017-18"*

According to *U.S. News,* the Nashville-Davidson—Murfreesboro—Franklin, TN metro area is home to one of the best children's hospitals in the U.S.: **Monroe Carell Jr. Children's Hospital at Vanderbilt** (10 pediatric specialties). The hospital listed was highly ranked in at least one of 10 pediatric specialties. Eighty-two children's hospitals in the U.S. were nationally ranked in at least one specialty. Hospitals received points for being ranked in a specialty, and the 10 hospitals with the most points across the 10 specialties make up the Honor Roll. *U.S. News Online, "America's Best Children's Hospitals 2017-18"*

EDUCATION

Public School District Statistics

District Name	Schls	Pupils	Pupil/ Teacher Ratio	Minority Pupils[1] (%)	Free Lunch Eligible[2] (%)	IEP[3] (%)
Davidson County	167	85,598	15.5	69.9	n/a	11.5
Williamson County	42	36,874	15.4	17.3	n/a	9.3

Note: Table includes school districts with 100 or more students; (1) Percentage of students that are not non-Hispanic white; (2) Percentage of students that are eligible for the free lunch program; (3) Percentage of students that have an Individualized Education Program.

Source: U.S. Department of Education, National Center for Education Statistics, Common Core of Data, Local Education Agency (School District) Universe Survey: School Year 2015-2016; U.S. Department of Education, National Center for Education Statistics, Common Core of Data, Public Elementary/Secondary School Universe Survey: School Year 2015-2016

Best High Schools

According to *U.S. News,* Brentwood is home to two of the best high schools in the U.S.: **Brentwood High School** (#290); **Ravenwood High School** (#454). More than 22,000 public, magnet and charter schools were ranked based on their performance on state assessments and how well they prepare students for college. Schools with the highest unrounded College Readiness Index values were numerically ranked from 1 to 500 and were classified as gold medal winners. *U.S. News & World Report, "Best High Schools 2017"*

Highest Level of Education

Area	Less than H.S.	H.S. Diploma	Some College, No Deg.	Associate Degree	Bachelor's Degree	Master's Degree	Prof. School Degree	Doctorate Degree
City	2.1	9.6	12.5	4.9	42.3	19.3	5.6	3.7
MSA[1]	11.4	28.1	20.7	6.9	21.4	8.1	2.0	1.4
U.S.	13.0	27.5	21.0	8.2	18.8	8.2	2.0	1.3

Note: Figures cover persons age 25 and over; (1) Figures cover the Nashville-Davidson—Murfreesboro—Franklin, TN Metropolitan Statistical Area—see Appendix B for areas included
Source: U.S. Census Bureau, 2012-2016 American Community Survey 5-Year Estimates

Educational Attainment by Race

Area	High School Graduate or Higher (%)					Bachelor's Degree or Higher (%)				
	Total	White	Black	Asian	Hisp.[2]	Total	White	Black	Asian	Hisp.[2]
City	97.9	98.2	96.8	94.5	88.2	70.9	71.2	45.5	80.9	51.9
MSA[1]	88.6	89.9	86.0	83.6	60.9	33.0	34.3	24.5	49.3	15.0
U.S.	87.0	88.9	84.3	86.3	65.7	30.3	31.6	20.0	52.1	14.7

Note: Figures shown cover persons 25 years old and over; (1) Figures cover the Nashville-Davidson—Murfreesboro—Franklin, TN Metropolitan Statistical Area—see Appendix B for areas included; (2) People of Hispanic origin can be of any race
Source: U.S. Census Bureau, 2012-2016 American Community Survey 5-Year Estimates

School Enrollment by Grade and Control

Area	Preschool (%)		Kindergarten (%)		Grades 1 - 4 (%)		Grades 5 - 8 (%)		Grades 9 - 12 (%)	
	Public	Private	Public	Private	Public	Private	Public	Private	Public	Private
City	31.3	68.8	81.5	18.5	90.4	9.6	81.4	18.6	79.8	20.2
MSA[1]	48.9	51.1	87.9	12.1	88.9	11.1	85.9	14.1	85.1	14.9
U.S.	58.4	41.6	87.7	12.3	89.8	10.2	89.7	10.3	90.4	9.6

Note: Figures shown cover persons 3 years old and over; (1) Figures cover the Nashville-Davidson—Murfreesboro—Franklin, TN Metropolitan Statistical Area—see Appendix B for areas included
Source: U.S. Census Bureau, 2012-2016 American Community Survey 5-Year Estimates

Average Salaries of Public School Classroom Teachers

Area	2015		2016		Change from 2015 to 2016	
	Dollars	Rank[1]	Dollars	Rank[1]	Percent	Rank[2]
Tennessee	47,979	38	48,217	39	0.5	31
U.S. Average	57,611	–	58,353	–	1.3	–

Note: (1) Rank ranges from 1 to 51 where 1 indicates highest salary; (2) Rank ranges from 1 to 51 where 1 indicates highest percent change.
Source: National Education Association, Rankings & Estimates: Rankings of the States 2016 and Estimates of School Statistics 2017

Higher Education

Four-Year Colleges			Two-Year Colleges			Medical Schools[1]	Law Schools[2]	Voc/ Tech[3]
Public	Private Non-profit	Private For-profit	Public	Private Non-profit	Private For-profit			
0	0	0	0	0	0	0	0	1

Note: Figures cover institutions located within the city limits and include main campuses only; (1) includes schools accredited by the Liaison Committee on Medical Education and the American Osteopathic Association's Commission on Osteopathic College Accreditation; (2) includes ABA-accredited schools, schools with provisional ABA accreditation, and state accredited schools; (3) includes all schools with programs that are less than 2 years.
Source: National Center for Education Statistics, Integrated Postsecondary Education System (IPEDS), 2016-17; Wikipedia, List of Medical Schools in the United States, accessed April 2, 2018; Wikipedia, List of Law Schools in the United States, accessed April 2, 2018

According to *U.S. News & World Report,* the Nashville-Davidson—Murfreesboro—Franklin, TN metro area is home to two of the best national universities in the U.S.: **Vanderbilt University** (#14 tie); **Lipscomb University** (#181 tie). The indicators used to capture academic quality fall into a number of categories: assessment by administrators at peer institutions; retention of students; faculty resources; student selectivity; financial resources; alumni giving; high school counselor ratings of colleges; and graduation rate. *U.S. News & World Report, "America's Best Colleges 2018"*

According to *U.S. News & World Report,* the Nashville-Davidson—Murfreesboro—Franklin, TN metro area is home to one of the top 100 law schools in the U.S.: **Vanderbilt University** (#17). The rankings are based on a weighted average of 12 measures of quality: peer assessment score; assessment score by lawyers/judges; median LSAT scores; median undergrad GPA; acceptance rate; employment rates for graduates; placement success; bar passage rate; faculty resources; expenditures per student; student/faculty ratio; and library resources. *U.S. News & World Report, "America's Best Graduate Schools, Law, 2019"*

According to *U.S. News & World Report,* the Nashville-Davidson—Murfreesboro—Franklin, TN metro area is home to one of the top 75 medical schools for research in the U.S.: **Vanderbilt University** (#17). The rankings are based on a weighted average of 11 measures of quality: quality assessment; peer assessment score; assessment score by residency directors; research activity; total research activity; average research activity per faculty member; student selectivity; median MCAT total score; median undergraduate GPA; acceptance rate; and faculty resources. *U.S. News & World Report, "America's Best Graduate Schools, Medical, 2019"*

According to *U.S. News & World Report,* the Nashville-Davidson—Murfreesboro—Franklin, TN metro area is home to one of the top 75 business schools in the U.S.: **Vanderbilt University (Owen)** (#26). The rankings are based on a weighted average of the following nine measures: quality assessment; peer assessment; recruiter assessment; placement success; mean starting salary and bonus; student selectivity; mean GMAT and GRE scores; mean undergraduate GPA; and acceptance rate. *U.S. News & World Report, "America's Best Graduate Schools, Business, 2019"*

PRESIDENTIAL ELECTION

2016 Presidential Election Results

Area	Clinton	Trump	Johnson	Stein	Other
Williamson County	29.2	64.2	4.3	0.5	1.9
U.S.	48.0	45.9	3.3	1.1	1.7

Note: Results are percentages and may not add to 100% due to rounding
Source: Dave Leip's Atlas of U.S. Presidential Elections

EMPLOYERS

Major Employers

Company Name	Industry
AHOM Holdings	Home health care services
Asurion Corporation	Business services nec
Baptist Hospital	General medical & surgical hospitals
Cannon County Knitting Mills	Apparel & outerwear broadwoven fabrics
County of Rutherford	Public elementary & secondary schools
County of Sumner	Executive offices, local government
Gaylord Entertainment Company	Hotels/motels
Gaylord Opryland USA	Hotels
Ingram Book Company	Books, periodicals, & newspapers
International Automotive	Automotive storage garage
LifeWay Christian Resources of the SBC	Religious organizations
Middle Tennessee State University	Colleges/universities
Newspaper Printing Corporation	Newspapers
Nissan North America	Motor vehicles/car bodies
Primus Automotive Financial Services	Automobile loans including insurance
Psychiatric Solutions	Psychiatric clinic
State Industries	Hot water heaters, household
State of Tennessee	Mentally handicapped home
Tennesee Department of Transportation	Regulation, administration of transportation
Vanderbilt Childrens Hospital	General medical & surgical hospitals
Vanderbilt University	Colleges/universities

Note: Companies shown are located within the Nashville-Davidson—Murfreesboro—Franklin, TN Metropolitan Statistical Area.
Source: Hoovers.com; Wikipedia

PUBLIC SAFETY

Crime Rate

Area	All Crimes	Violent Crimes				Property Crimes		
		Murder	Rape[3]	Robbery	Aggrav. Assault	Burglary	Larceny -Theft	Motor Vehicle Theft
City	987.4	2.3	4.7	11.7	39.8	124.0	760.4	44.5
Metro[1]	3,099.9	6.2	45.0	130.7	439.7	446.6	1,865.1	166.6
U.S.	2,847.8	5.3	40.4	102.8	248.5	468.9	1,745.0	236.9

Note: Figures are crimes per 100,000 population; (1) Figures cover the Nashville-Davidson—Murfreesboro—Franklin, TN Metropolitan Statistical Area—see Appendix B for areas included; (3) The city and U.S. figures shown were reported using the revised Uniform Crime Reporting (UCR) definition of rape. The metro area figures shown are an aggregate total of the data submitted using both the revised and legacy UCR definitions.
Source: FBI Uniform Crime Reports, 2016

Hate Crimes

Area	Number of Quarters Reported	Number of Incidents per Bias Motivation					
		Race/Ethnicity/ Ancestry	Religion	Sexual Orientation	Disability	Gender	Gender Identity
City	4	0	0	0	0	0	0
U.S.	4	3,489	1,273	1,076	70	31	124

Source: Federal Bureau of Investigation, Hate Crime Statistics 2016

Identity Theft Consumer Reports

Area	Reports	Reports per 100,000 Population	Rank[2]
MSA[1]	1,793	96	112
U.S.	371,061	114	-

Note: (1) Figures cover the Nashville-Davidson—Murfreesboro—Franklin, TN Metropolitan Statistical Area—see Appendix B for areas included; (2) Rank ranges from 1 to 389 where 1 indicates greatest number of identity theft reports per 100,000 population
Source: Federal Trade Commission, Consumer Sentinel Network Data Book for January–December 2017

Fraud and Other Consumer Reports

Area	Reports	Reports per 100,000 Population	Rank[2]
MSA[1]	10,587	568	54
U.S.	2,304,550	708	-

Note: (1) Figures cover the Nashville-Davidson—Murfreesboro—Franklin, TN Metropolitan Statistical Area—see Appendix B for areas included; (2) Rank ranges from 1 to 389 where 1 indicates greatest number of fraud and other consumer reports per 100,000 population
Source: Federal Trade Commission, Consumer Sentinel Network Data Book for January–December 2017

SPORTS

Professional Sports Teams

Team Name	League	Year Established
Nashville Predators	National Hockey League (NHL)	1998
Tennessee Titans	National Football League (NFL)	1997

Note: Includes teams located in the Nashville-Davidson—Murfreesboro—Franklin, TN Metropolitan Statistical Area.
Source: Wikipedia, Major Professional Sports Teams of the United States and Canada, April 5, 2018

CLIMATE

Average and Extreme Temperatures

Temperature	Jan	Feb	Mar	Apr	May	Jun	Jul	Aug	Sep	Oct	Nov	Dec	Yr.
Extreme High (°F)	78	84	86	91	95	106	107	104	105	94	84	79	107
Average High (°F)	47	51	60	71	79	87	90	89	83	72	60	50	70
Average Temp. (°F)	38	41	50	60	68	76	80	79	72	61	49	41	60
Average Low (°F)	28	31	39	48	57	65	69	68	61	48	39	31	49
Extreme Low (°F)	-17	-13	2	23	34	42	54	49	36	26	-1	-10	-17

Note: Figures cover the years 1948-1990
Source: National Climatic Data Center, International Station Meteorological Climate Summary, 9/96

Average Precipitation/Snowfall/Humidity

Precip./Humidity	Jan	Feb	Mar	Apr	May	Jun	Jul	Aug	Sep	Oct	Nov	Dec	Yr.
Avg. Precip. (in.)	4.4	4.2	5.0	4.1	4.6	3.7	3.8	3.3	3.2	2.6	3.9	4.6	47.4
Avg. Snowfall (in.)	4	3	1	Tr	0	0	0	0	0	Tr	1	1	11
Avg. Rel. Hum. 6am (%)	81	81	80	81	86	86	88	90	90	87	83	82	85
Avg. Rel. Hum. 3pm (%)	61	57	51	48	52	52	54	53	52	49	55	59	54

Note: Figures cover the years 1948-1990; Tr = Trace amounts (<0.05 in. of rain; <0.5 in. of snow)
Source: National Climatic Data Center, International Station Meteorological Climate Summary, 9/96

Weather Conditions

Temperature			Daytime Sky			Precipitation		
10°F & below	32°F & below	90°F & above	Clear	Partly cloudy	Cloudy	0.01 inch or more precip.	0.1 inch or more snow/ice	Thunder-storms
5	76	51	98	135	132	119	8	54

Note: Figures are average number of days per year and cover the years 1948-1990
Source: National Climatic Data Center, International Station Meteorological Climate Summary, 9/96

HAZARDOUS WASTE

Superfund Sites

The Nashville-Davidson—Murfreesboro—Franklin, TN metro area is home to one site on the EPA's Superfund National Priorities List: **Wrigley Charcoal Plant** (final). There are a total of 1,396 Superfund sites with a status of proposed or final on the list in the U.S. *U.S. Environmental Protection Agency, National Priorities List, April 4, 2018*

AIR & WATER QUALITY

Air Quality Trends: Ozone

	1990	1995	2000	2005	2010	2012	2013	2014	2015	2016
MSA[1]	0.089	0.092	0.084	0.078	0.073	0.079	0.065	0.067	0.065	0.068
U.S.	0.087	0.089	0.081	0.079	0.073	0.075	0.069	0.067	0.068	0.069

Note: (1) Data covers the Nashville-Davidson—Murfreesboro—Franklin, TN Metropolitan Statistical Area—see Appendix B for areas included. The values shown are the composite ozone concentration averages among trend sites based on the highest fourth daily maximum 8-hour concentration in parts per million. These trends are based on sites having an adequate record of monitoring data during the trend period. Data from exceptional events are included.
Source: U.S. Environmental Protection Agency, Air Quality Monitoring Information, "Air Quality Trends by City, 1990-2016"

Air Quality Index

Area	Percent of Days when Air Quality was...[2]					AQI Statistics[2]	
	Good	Moderate	Unhealthy for Sensitive Groups	Unhealthy	Very Unhealthy	Maximum	Median
MSA[1]	63.8	35.9	0.3	0.0	0.0	133	45

Note: (1) Data covers the Nashville-Davidson—Murfreesboro—Franklin, TN Metropolitan Statistical Area—see Appendix B for areas included; (2) Based on 365 days with AQI data in 2017. Air Quality Index (AQI) is an index for reporting daily air quality. EPA calculates the AQI for five major air pollutants regulated by the Clean Air Act: ground-level ozone, particle pollution (aka particulate matter), carbon monoxide, sulfur dioxide, and nitrogen dioxide. The AQI runs from 0 to 500. The higher the AQI value, the greater the level of air pollution and the greater the health concern. There are six AQI categories: "Good" AQI is between 0 and 50. Air quality is considered satisfactory; "Moderate" AQI is between 51 and 100. Air quality is acceptable; "Unhealthy for Sensitive Groups" When AQI values are between 101 and 150, members of sensitive groups may experience health effects; "Unhealthy" When AQI values are between 151 and 200 everyone may begin to experience health effects; "Very Unhealthy" AQI values between 201 and 300 trigger a health alert; "Hazardous" AQI values over 300 trigger warnings of emergency conditions (not shown).
Source: U.S. Environmental Protection Agency, Air Quality Index Report, 2017

Air Quality Index Pollutants

Area	Percent of Days when AQI Pollutant was...[2]					
	Carbon Monoxide	Nitrogen Dioxide	Ozone	Sulfur Dioxide	Particulate Matter 2.5	Particulate Matter 10
MSA[1]	0.0	3.8	36.4	0.5	59.2	0.0

Note: (1) Data covers the Nashville-Davidson—Murfreesboro—Franklin, TN Metropolitan Statistical Area—see Appendix B for areas included; (2) Based on 365 days with AQI data in 2017. The Air Quality Index (AQI) is an index for reporting daily air quality. EPA calculates the AQI for five major air pollutants regulated by the Clean Air Act: ground-level ozone, particle pollution (also known as particulate matter), carbon monoxide, sulfur dioxide, and nitrogen dioxide. The AQI runs from 0 to 500. The higher the AQI value, the greater the level of air pollution and the greater the health concern.
Source: U.S. Environmental Protection Agency, Air Quality Index Report, 2017

Maximum Air Pollutant Concentrations: Particulate Matter, Ozone, CO and Lead

	Particulate Matter 10 (ug/m^3)	Particulate Matter 2.5 Wtd AM (ug/m^3)	Particulate Matter 2.5 24-Hr (ug/m^3)	Ozone (ppm)	Carbon Monoxide (ppm)	Lead (ug/m^3)
MSA[1] Level	34	8.9	18	0.068	2	n/a
NAAQS[2]	150	15	35	0.075	9	0.15
Met NAAQS[2]	Yes	Yes	Yes	Yes	Yes	n/a

Note: (1) Data covers the Nashville-Davidson—Murfreesboro—Franklin, TN Metropolitan Statistical Area—see Appendix B for areas included; Data from exceptional events are included; (2) National Ambient Air Quality Standards; ppm = parts per million; ug/m^3 = micrograms per cubic meter; n/a not available.
Concentrations: Particulate Matter 10 (coarse particulate)—highest second maximum 24-hour concentration; Particulate Matter 2.5 Wtd AM (fine particulate)—highest weighted annual mean concentration; Particulate Matter 2.5 24-Hour (fine particulate)—highest 98th percentile 24-hour concentration; Ozone—highest fourth daily maximum 8-hour concentration; Carbon Monoxide—highest second maximum non-overlapping 8-hour concentration; Lead—maximum running 3-month average
Source: U.S. Environmental Protection Agency, Air Quality Monitoring Information, "Air Quality Statistics by City, 2016"

Maximum Air Pollutant Concentrations: Nitrogen Dioxide and Sulfur Dioxide

	Nitrogen Dioxide AM (ppb)	Nitrogen Dioxide 1-Hr (ppb)	Sulfur Dioxide AM (ppb)	Sulfur Dioxide 1-Hr (ppb)	Sulfur Dioxide 24-Hr (ppb)
MSA[1] Level	16	54	n/a	2	n/a
NAAQS[2]	53	100	30	75	140
Met NAAQS[2]	Yes	Yes	n/a	Yes	n/a

Note: (1) Data covers the Nashville-Davidson—Murfreesboro—Franklin, TN Metropolitan Statistical Area—see Appendix B for areas included; Data from exceptional events are included; (2) National Ambient Air Quality Standards; ppm = parts per million; ug/m^3 = micrograms per cubic meter; n/a not available.
Concentrations: Nitrogen Dioxide AM—highest arithmetic mean concentration; Nitrogen Dioxide 1-Hr—highest 98th percentile 1-hour daily maximum concentration; Sulfur Dioxide AM—highest annual mean concentration; Sulfur Dioxide 1-Hr—highest 99th percentile 1-hour daily maximum concentration; Sulfur Dioxide 24-Hr—highest second maximum 24-hour concentration
Source: U.S. Environmental Protection Agency, Air Quality Monitoring Information, "Air Quality Statistics by City, 2016"

Drinking Water

Water System Name	Pop. Served	Primary Water Source Type	Violations[1]	
			Health Based	Monitoring/ Reporting
Brentwood Water Dept	28,950	Purchased Surface	0	0

Note: (1) Based on violation data from January 1, 2017 to December 31, 2017
Source: U.S. Environmental Protection Agency, Office of Ground Water and Drinking Water, Safe Drinking Water Information System (based on data extracted April 5, 2018)

Collierville, Tennessee

Background

Collierville, Tennessee, the second-oldest town in Shelby County, is located southeast of Memphis near the Mississippi state line and is a 30-minute drive from Memphis International Airport.

Named after a pioneer family, Collierville began to develop around 1840 and originally was located to the east of its current site. It was incorporated as a town in 1850, saw four minor battles during the Civil War, and ultimately was burned during Sherman's March to the Sea. The town moved and was incorporated a second time in 1870, and experienced rapid growth in the late nineteenth century. It was incorporated as a city in 1903.

Historically an agricultural center, Collierville first was an important cotton center, then dairy. Industry arrived in the mid-20th century.

Today Collierville is well-known as home to Federal Express's World Tech Center technology center, with its 3,000 workers and 118-acre campus designed to foster collaboration and innovation. When opened, the campus consolidated 20 FedEx divisions. Indeed, Shelby County is a distribution hub that is becoming a logistics center. UPS and the USPS Bulk Mail Facility are here, in addition to five Class 1 intermodal railroads that converge here. The Mississippi River passes through the county, which is located just below the snow line. The Shelby County Economic Development Growth Engine says that from here, truckers reliably reach two-thirds of the American population in two days or less.

The Carrier Corporation, makers of HVAC systems, is a significant Collierville employer and manufacturer.

Collierville's students attend the Shelby County Public Schools; Collierville High School was named one of *US News & World Report's* "Top Performing" high schools in 2012. The high school has similarly been lauded by *Newsweek.* A new Collierville Municipal School district, with 7,600 students, was recently created.

Higher education is easily accessible in Memphis, and The University of Memphis operates the Collier Center in Collierville.

The city's historic Town Square is the hub of the city's community and social activities and dates to the late 1800s. A host of community event are held here, such as the annual Fair on the Square, the Mulberry Fine Arts Festival, and Dickens on the Square. A gazebo centers the site, built in the mid-1960s to replace a predecessor destroyed by a tornado.

The city's parks, recreation and cultural arts department sees to a dozen parks and nature preserves, local museums, numerous classes, and recreation league sports ranging from youth tee ball to adult flag football. The H.W. Cox, Jr. Community Center is a 52,000-square foot facility with basketball courts, racquetball courts, the Harrell Performing Arts Theatre, group fitness studios and more. The center sits amid a 60-acre park with numerous athletic fields and courts.

Collierville is home to many places of worship of various denominations. Among them is Central Church, a non-denominational mega-church of almost 6000 members, the Catholic Church of the Incarnation with nearly 4,500 members, Collierville United Methodist Church with more than 3,400 members, and Collierville First Baptist Church with more than 3,200 members. Collierville is also home to numerous other Baptist churches, three United Methodist churches, one meetinghouse of The Church of Jesus Christ of Latter-day Saints (LDS Church) serving two congregations, a few Presbyterian churches, and a few scattered Lutheran churches. St. Andrew's Episcopal Church has been in existence since 1892. Kirk Christian Church has been around for over a century. Peace Tree is a newly formed church seeking to reach people by meeting in neutral locations such as homes, restaurants, and parks.

Collierville generally experiences mild winters and hot summers. Rainfall is well distributed throughout the year. The town is not in the normal path of winds from the Gulf of Mexico or from Canada, but such winds are occasionally a factor, producing rapid shifts in temperature. Humidity is generally high, but temperatures are seldom extremely high or low.

Rankings

Business/Finance Rankings

- The personal finance site NerdWallet analyzed 183 American metropolitan areas with populations over 250,000 and more than 15,000 businesses to rank where entrepreneurs find the most success. Criteria included area economy, annual income, housing cost, unemployment rate, and the success rate of area businesses. Memphis* ranked #162. *www.nerdwallet.com, "Best Places to Start a Business," April 27, 2015*
- Based on metro area social media reviews, the employment opinion group Glassdoor surveyed 50 of the largest U.S. metro areas and equally weighed cost of living, hiring opportunity, and job satisfaction to compose a list of "25 Best Cities for Jobs." Median pay and home value, in-demand jobs and number of current job openings was also factored in. The Memphis* metro area was ranked #6 in overall job satisfaction. *www.glassdoor.com, "Best Cities for Jobs," September 12, 2017*
- In a survey of economic confidence in the nation's 50 largest metropolitan areas conducted January–December 2014, the Memphis* metro area placed #49, according to Gallup's 2014 Economic Confidence Index. *Gallup, "San Jose and San Francisco Lead in Economic Confidence," March 19, 2015*
- The Brookings Institution ranked the 100 largest metro areas in the U.S. based on income inequality. Memphis* was ranked #14 (#1 = greatest ineqality). Criteria: the "95/20 ratio," a figure representing the income at which a household earns more than 95 percent of all other households, divided by the income at which a household earns more than only 20 percent of all other households. *Brookings Institution, "Household Income Inequality, 100 Largest U.S. Metro Areas, 2014-2016," February 5, 2018*
- The Memphis* metro area was identified as one of the most affordable metropolitan areas in America by *Forbes.* The area ranked #6 out of 20 based on the National Association of Home Builders/Wells Fargo Housing Affordability Index and Sperling's Best Places' cost-of-living index. *Forbes.com, "America's Most Affordable Cities in 2015," March 12, 2015*
- The Memphis* metro area appeared on the Milken Institute "2017 Best Performing Cities" list. Rank: #148 out of 200 large metro areas. Criteria: job growth; wage and salary growth; high-tech output growth. *Milken Institute, "Best-Performing Cities 2017," January 2018*
- *Forbes* ranked the 200 most populous metro areas to determine the nation's "Best Places for Business and Careers." The Memphis* metro area was ranked #106. Criteria: costs (business and living); job growth (past and projected); income growth; quality of life; educational attainment (college and high school); projected economic growth; cultural and recreational opportunities; net migration patterns; number of highly ranked colleges. *Forbes, "The Best Places for Business and Careers 2017," October 24, 2017*

Dating/Romance Rankings

- *Apartment List* conducted its annual survey of renters to compile a list of metros that have the best opportunities for dating. Nearly 11,000 respondents, from February 2017 through January 2018, rated their current city or neighborhood for opportunities to date and make friends. The Memphis* metro area ranked #63 out of 70 where single residents were very satisfied or somewhat satisfied, making it among the ten worst metros for dating opportunities. Other criteria analyzed included gender and education levels of renters. *Apartment List, "Best Metros for Dating 2018," February 6, 2018*

Education Rankings

- Personal finance website *WalletHub* analyzed the 150 largest U.S. metropolitan statistical areas to determine where the most educated Americans are choosing to settle. Criteria: education quality and attainment gap; education levels; percentage of workers with degrees; public school rankings; quality and size of each metro area's universities. Memphis* was ranked #114 (#1 = most educated city). *www.WalletHub.com, "2017's Most and Least Educated Cities in America," July 25, 2017*

Environmental Rankings

- Sperling's BestPlaces assessed 379 metropolitan areas of the United States for the likelihood of dangerously extreme weather events or earthquakes. In general the Southeast and South-Central regions have the highest risk of weather extremes and earthquakes, while the Pacific Northwest enjoys the lowest risk. Of the least risky metropolitan areas, the Memphis* metro area was ranked #360. *www.bestplaces.net, "Safest Places from Natural Disasters," April 2011*

- The U.S. Environmental Protection Agency (EPA) released a list of mid-size U.S. metropolitan areas with the most ENERGY STAR certified buildings in 2016. The Memphis* metro area was ranked #10 out of 10. *U.S. Environmental Protection Agency, "2017 Energy Star Top Cities," June 2017*

Health/Fitness Rankings

- Analysts who tracked obesity rates in the nation's largest metro areas (populations above one million) found that the Memphis* metro area was one of the ten major metros where residents were most likely to be obese, defined as a BMI score of 30 or above. *www.gallup.com, "Boulder, Colo., Residents Still Least Likely to Be Obese," April 4, 2014*

- Analysts who tracked obesity rates in 100 of the nation's most populous areas found that the Memphis* metro area was one of the ten communities where residents were most likely to be obese, defined as a BMI score of 30 or above. *www.gallup.com, "Colorado Springs Residents Least Likely to Be Obese," May 28, 2015*

- For each of the 50 most populous metro areas in the United States, the American College of Sports Medicine's American Fitness Index evaluated infrastructure, community assets, and policies that encourage healthy and fit lifestyles, including preventive health behaviors, levels of chronic disease conditions, health care access, and community resources and policies that support physical activity. The Memphis* metro area ranked #45 for "community fitness." *www.americanfitnessindex.org, "ACSM American Fitness Index Health and Community Fitness Status of the 50 Largest Metropolitan Areas," May 2017*

- Memphis* was identified as a "2016 Spring Allergy Capital." The area ranked #2 out of 100. Three groups of factors were used to identify the most severe cities for people with allergies during the spring season: annual pollen levels; medicine utilization; access to board-certified allergists. *Asthma and Allergy Foundation of America, "Spring Allergy Capitals 2016"*

- Memphis* was identified as a "2016 Fall Allergy Capital." The area ranked #2 out of 100. Three groups of factors were used to identify the most severe cities for people with allergies during the fall season: annual pollen levels; medicine utilization; access to board-certified allergists. *Asthma and Allergy Foundation of America, "Fall Allergy Capitals 2016"*

- Memphis* was identified as a "2015 Asthma Capital." The area ranked #1 out of the nation's 100 largest metropolitan areas. Criteria: estimated prevalence; self-reported prevalence; crude death rate for asthma; annual pollen score; annual air quality; public smoking laws; number of board-certified asthma specialists; school inhaler access laws; rescue medication use; controller medication use; ER visits for asthma; uninsured rate; poverty rate. *Asthma and Allergy Foundation of America, "Asthma Capitals 2015"*

- The Memphis* metro area ranked #176 out of 189 in The Gallup-Healthways Well-Being Index. Criteria: purpose; social well being; financial health; community and physical health. Results are based on telephone interviews with adults, aged 18 and older, living in metropolitan areas in the 50 U.S. states and the District of Columbia. *Gallup-Healthways, "State of American Well-Being, 2017 Community Well-Being Rankings" March 2018*

Real Estate Rankings

- FitSmallBusiness looked at 50 of the largest metropolitan areas in the U.S. to determine which metro was the best to start a real estate business. Data was compiled from such sources as: Zillow, Trulia, U.S. Census Bureau, and the Bureau of Labor Statistics. Criteria: location; inventory; annual wages; median sales price of homes; days on the market; median price cut percentage; and other factors that would influence real estate professional growth. The Memphis* metro area ranked #33. *fitsmallbusiness.com, "The Best Cities to Become a Real Estate Agent in 2018," January 30, 2018*
- The Memphis* metro area was identified as #6 among the ten housing markets with the highest percentage of distressed property sales, based on the findings of the housing data website RealtyTrac. Criteria: short sales; income and poverty figures; and unemployment data. *247wallst.com, "Cities Selling the Most Distressed Homes," January 23, 2014*
- The Memphis* metro area was identified as one of nine best housing markets to invest in. Criteria: single-family rental home investing in the first quarter of 2017 based on first-year returns. The area ranked #4. *The Business Insider, "Here are the 9 Best U.S. Housing Markets for Investment," May 11, 2017*
- Memphis* was ranked #134 out of 238 metro areas in terms of housing affordability in 2017 by the National Association of Home Builders (#1 = most affordable). Criteria: the share of homes sold in that area affordable to a family earning the local median income, based on standard mortgage underwriting criteria. *National Association of Home Builders®, NAHB-Wells Fargo Housing Opportunity Index, 4th Quarter 2017*

Safety Rankings

- The National Insurance Crime Bureau ranked 382 metro areas in the U.S. in terms of per capita rates of vehicle theft. The Memphis* metro area ranked #85 (#1 = highest rate). Criteria: number of vehicle theft offenses per 100,000 inhabitants in 2016. *National Insurance Crime Bureau, "Hot Spots 2016," June 8, 2017*

Seniors/Retirement Rankings

- From its Best Cities for Successful Aging indexes, the Milken Institute generated rankings for metropolitan areas, weighing data in nine categories—health care, wellness, living arrangements, transportation and convenience, financial characteristics, education, employment, community engagement, and overall livability. The Memphis* metro area was ranked #76 overall in the large metro area category. *Milken Institute, "Best Cities for Successful Aging, 2017" March 14, 2017*

*Collierville is located within the Memphis, TN-MS-AR Metropolitan Statistical Area.

Business Environment

CITY FINANCES

City Government Finances

Component	2015 ($000)	2015 ($ per capita)
Total Revenues	n/a	n/a
Total Expenditures	n/a	n/a
Debt Outstanding	n/a	n/a
Cash and Securities[1]	n/a	n/a

Note: (1) Cash and security holdings of a government at the close of its fiscal year,, including those of its dependent agencies, utilities, and liquor stores.
Source: U.S Census Bureau, State & Local Government Finances 2015

City Government Revenue by Source

Source	2015 ($000)	2015 ($ per capita)	2015 (%)
General Revenue			
From Federal Government	n/a	n/a	n/a
From State Government	n/a	n/a	n/a
From Local Governments	n/a	n/a	n/a
Taxes			
Property	n/a	n/a	n/a
Sales and Gross Receipts	n/a	n/a	n/a
Personal Income	n/a	n/a	n/a
Corporate Income	n/a	n/a	n/a
Motor Vehicle License	n/a	n/a	n/a
Other Taxes	n/a	n/a	n/a
Current Charges	n/a	n/a	n/a
Liquor Store	n/a	n/a	n/a
Utility	n/a	n/a	n/a
Employee Retirement	n/a	n/a	n/a

Source: U.S Census Bureau, State & Local Government Finances 2015

City Government Expenditures by Function

Function	2015 ($000)	2015 ($ per capita)	2015 (%)
General Direct Expenditures			
Air Transportation	n/a	n/a	n/a
Corrections	n/a	n/a	n/a
Education	n/a	n/a	n/a
Employment Security Administration	n/a	n/a	n/a
Financial Administration	n/a	n/a	n/a
Fire Protection	n/a	n/a	n/a
General Public Buildings	n/a	n/a	n/a
Governmental Administration, Other	n/a	n/a	n/a
Health	n/a	n/a	n/a
Highways	n/a	n/a	n/a
Hospitals	n/a	n/a	n/a
Housing and Community Development	n/a	n/a	n/a
Interest on General Debt	n/a	n/a	n/a
Judicial and Legal	n/a	n/a	n/a
Libraries	n/a	n/a	n/a
Parking	n/a	n/a	n/a
Parks and Recreation	n/a	n/a	n/a
Police Protection	n/a	n/a	n/a
Public Welfare	n/a	n/a	n/a
Sewerage	n/a	n/a	n/a
Solid Waste Management	n/a	n/a	n/a
Veterans' Services	n/a	n/a	n/a
Liquor Store	n/a	n/a	n/a
Utility	n/a	n/a	n/a
Employee Retirement	n/a	n/a	n/a

Source: U.S Census Bureau, State & Local Government Finances 2015

DEMOGRAPHICS

Population Growth

Area	1990 Census	2000 Census	2010 Census	2016* Estimate	Population Growth (%)	
					1990-2016	2010-2016
City	15,439	31,872	43,965	48,005	210.9	9.2
MSA[1]	1,067,263	1,205,204	1,316,100	1,341,339	25.7	1.9
U.S.	248,709,873	281,421,906	308,745,538	318,558,162	28.1	3.2

Note: (1) Figures cover the Memphis, TN-MS-AR Metropolitan Statistical Area—see Appendix B for areas included; (*) 2012-2016 5-year estimated population
Source: U.S. Census Bureau, 1990 Census, Census 2000, Census 2010, 2012-2016 American Community Survey 5-Year Estimates

Household Size

Area	Persons in Household (%)							Average Household Size
	One	Two	Three	Four	Five	Six	Seven or More	
City	15.4	32.7	22.4	19.6	7.1	2.1	0.8	3.00
MSA[1]	28.6	32.3	16.8	12.8	5.7	2.2	1.5	2.70
U.S.	27.7	33.7	15.7	13.1	6.0	2.3	1.5	2.60

Note: (1) Figures cover the Memphis, TN-MS-AR Metropolitan Statistical Area—see Appendix B for areas included
Source: U.S. Census Bureau, 2012-2016 American Community Survey 5-Year Estimates

Race

Area	White Alone[2] (%)	Black Alone[2] (%)	Asian Alone[2] (%)	AIAN[3] Alone[2] (%)	NHOPI[4] Alone[2] (%)	Other Race Alone[2] (%)	Two or More Races (%)
City	76.3	12.9	7.5	0.9	0.0	0.4	1.9
MSA[1]	47.2	46.6	2.0	0.2	0.0	2.2	1.7
U.S.	73.3	12.6	5.2	0.8	0.2	4.8	3.1

Note: (1) Figures cover the Memphis, TN-MS-AR Metropolitan Statistical Area—see Appendix B for areas included; (2) Alone is defined as not being in combination with one or more other races; (3) American Indian and Alaska Native; (4) Native Hawaiian and Other Pacific Islander
Source: U.S. Census Bureau, 2012-2016 American Community Survey 5-Year Estimates

Hispanic or Latino Origin

Area	Total (%)	Mexican (%)	Puerto Rican (%)	Cuban (%)	Other (%)
City	2.1	1.2	0.1	0.0	0.7
MSA[1]	5.2	3.7	0.3	0.2	1.1
U.S.	17.3	11.0	1.7	0.7	4.0

Note: Persons of Hispanic or Latino origin can be of any race; (1) Figures cover the Memphis, TN-MS-AR Metropolitan Statistical Area—see Appendix B for areas included
Source: U.S. Census Bureau, 2012-2016 American Community Survey 5-Year Estimates

Segregation

Type	Segregation Indices[1]				Percent Change		
	1990	2000	2010	2010 Rank[2]	1990-2000	1990-2010	2000-2010
Black/White	65.5	65.8	62.6	30	0.4	-2.8	-3.2
Asian/White	36.8	40.8	40.1	56	4.0	3.3	-0.7
Hispanic/White	32.3	46.0	50.7	22	13.7	18.4	4.7

Note: All figures cover the Metropolitan Statistical Area—see Appendix B for areas included; Figures are based on an analysis of 1990, 2000, and 2010 Census Decennial Census tract data by William H. Frey, Brookings Institution and the University of Michigan Social Science Data Analysis Network. In this analysis all racial groups (whites, blacks, and asians) are non-Hispanic members of those races. Hispanics are shown as a separate category; (1) Segregation Indices are Dissimilarity Indices that measure the degree to which the minority group is distributed differently than whites across census tracts. They range from 0 (complete integration) to 100 (complete segregation) where the value indicates the percentage of the minority group that needs to move to be distributed exactly like whites; (2) Ranges from 1 (most segregated) to 102 (least segregated); n/a not available.
Source: www.CensusScope.org

Ancestry

Area	German	Irish	English	American	Italian	Polish	French[2]	Scottish	Dutch
City	12.3	11.0	11.5	11.4	4.1	1.4	2.7	2.9	1.8
MSA[1]	6.0	7.1	6.6	6.9	2.1	0.7	1.4	1.6	0.7
U.S.	14.4	10.4	7.7	6.9	5.4	2.9	2.6	1.7	1.3

Note: Figures are the percentage of the total population reporting a particular ancestry. The nine most commonly reported ancestries in the U.S. are shown. Figures include multiple ancestries (e.g. if a person reported being Irish and Italian, they were included in both columns); (1) Figures cover the Memphis, TN-MS-AR Metropolitan Statistical Area—see Appendix B for areas included; (2) Excludes Basque
Source: U.S. Census Bureau, 2012-2016 American Community Survey 5-Year Estimates

Foreign-Born Population

Area	Percent of Population Born in								
	Any Foreign Country	Asia	Mexico	Europe	Carribean	Central America[2]	South America	Africa	Canada
City	7.4	5.3	0.3	0.8	0.0	0.1	0.3	0.2	0.3
MSA[1]	5.0	1.6	1.6	0.4	0.2	0.5	0.2	0.5	0.1
U.S.	13.2	4.0	3.6	1.5	1.3	1.0	0.9	0.6	0.3

Note: (1) Figures cover the Memphis, TN-MS-AR Metropolitan Statistical Area—see Appendix B for areas included; (2) Excludes Mexico.
Source: U.S. Census Bureau, 2012-2016 American Community Survey 5-Year Estimates

Marital Status

Area	Never Married	Now Married[2]	Separated	Widowed	Divorced
City	23.8	64.6	1.3	3.4	6.8
MSA[1]	37.5	42.1	3.3	5.8	11.3
U.S.	33.0	48.1	2.1	5.9	11.0

Note: Figures are percentages and cover the population 15 years of age and older; (1) Figures cover the Memphis, TN-MS-AR Metropolitan Statistical Area—see Appendix B for areas included; (2) Excludes separated
Source: U.S. Census Bureau, 2012-2016 American Community Survey 5-Year Estimates

Disability Status

Area	All Ages	Under 18 Years Old	18 to 64 Years Old	65 Years and Over
City	7.2	3.2	5.2	27.6
MSA[1]	12.9	4.2	11.6	38.4
U.S.	12.5	4.1	10.3	35.7

Note: Figures show percent of the civilian noninstitutionalized population that reported having a disability. Disability status is determined from six types of difficulty: vision, hearing, cognitive, ambulatory, self-care, and independent living. For children under 5 years old, hearing and vision difficulty are used to determine disability status. For children between the ages of 5 and 14, disability status is determined from hearing, vision, cognitive, ambulatory, and self-care difficulties. For people aged 15 years and older, they are considered to have a disability if they have difficulty with any one of the six difficulty types; Note: (1) Figures cover the Memphis, TN-MS-AR Metropolitan Statistical Area—see Appendix B for areas included
Source: U.S. Census Bureau, 2012-2016 American Community Survey 5-Year Estimates

Age

Area	Percent of Population									Median Age
	Under Age 5	Age 5–19	Age 20–34	Age 35–44	Age 45–54	Age 55–64	Age 65–74	Age 75–84	Age 85+	
City	5.2	24.1	14.2	13.9	17.5	13.8	7.1	3.1	1.1	40.2
MSA[1]	7.0	21.3	20.8	13.0	13.5	12.3	7.2	3.5	1.4	35.7
U.S.	6.2	19.6	20.7	12.7	13.6	12.6	8.3	4.3	1.9	37.7

Note: (1) Figures cover the Memphis, TN-MS-AR Metropolitan Statistical Area—see Appendix B for areas included
Source: U.S. Census Bureau, 2012-2016 American Community Survey 5-Year Estimates

Gender

Area	Males	Females	Males per 100 Females
City	22,711	25,294	89.8
MSA[1]	643,139	698,200	92.1
U.S.	156,765,322	161,792,840	96.9

Note: (1) Figures cover the Memphis, TN-MS-AR Metropolitan Statistical Area—see Appendix B for areas included
Source: U.S. Census Bureau, 2012-2016 American Community Survey 5-Year Estimates

Religious Groups by Family

Area	Catholic	Baptist	Non-Den.	Methodist[2]	Lutheran	LDS[3]	Pentecostal	Presbyterian[4]	Muslim[5]	Judaism
MSA[1]	5.3	30.8	5.4	6.2	0.4	0.6	4.8	2.4	0.3	0.6
U.S.	19.1	9.3	4.0	4.0	2.3	2.0	1.9	1.6	0.8	0.7

Note: Figures are the number of adherents as a percentage of the total population; (1) Figures cover the Memphis, TN-MS-AR Metropolitan Statistical Area—see Appendix B for areas included; (2) Methodist/Pietist; (3) Latter Day Saints; (4) Reformed; (5) Figures are estimates
Source: Association of Statisticians of American Religious Bodies, 2010 U.S. Religion Census: Religious Congregations & Membership Study

Religious Groups by Tradition

Area	Catholic	Evangelical Protestant	Mainline Protestant	Other Tradition	Black Protestant	Orthodox
MSA[1]	5.3	29.4	8.4	2.2	13.5	0.1
U.S.	19.1	16.2	7.3	4.3	1.6	0.3

Note: Figures are the number of adherents as a percentage of the total population; (1) Figures cover the Memphis, TN-MS-AR Metropolitan Statistical Area—see Appendix B for areas included
Source: Association of Statisticians of American Religious Bodies, 2010 U.S. Religion Census: Religious Congregations & Membership Study

ECONOMY

Gross Metropolitan Product

Area	2014	2015	2016	2017	Rank[2]
MSA[1]	69.2	71.3	73.1	76.3	47

Note: Figures are in billions of dollars; (1) Figures cover the Memphis, TN-MS-AR Metropolitan Statistical Area—see Appendix B for areas included; (2) Rank is based on 2015 data and ranges from 1 to 381
Source: The U.S. Conference of Mayors, U.S. Metro Economies: GMP and Employment Report, 2015-2017

Economic Growth

Area	2012-14 (%)	2015 (%)	2016 (%)	2017 (%)	Rank[2]
MSA[1]	0.1	1.2	1.3	2.5	281
U.S.	2.0	2.4	1.9	2.6	–

Note: Figures are real gross metropolitan product (GMP) growth rates and represent average annual percent change; (1) Figures cover the Memphis, TN-MS-AR Metropolitan Statistical Area—see Appendix B for areas included; (2) Rank is based on 2012-2014 average annual percent change and ranges from 1 to 381
Source: The U.S. Conference of Mayors, U.S. Metro Economies: GMP and Employment Report, 2015-2017

Metropolitan Area Exports

Area	2011	2012	2013	2014	2015	2016	Rank[2]
MSA[1]	11,978.6	11,360.1	11,276.4	11,002.0	11,819.5	11,628.7	25

Note: Figures are in millions of dollars; (1) Figures cover the Memphis, TN-MS-AR Metropolitan Statistical Area—see Appendix B for areas included; (2) Rank is based on 2016 data and ranges from 1 to 385
Source: U.S. Department of Commerce, International Trade Administration, Office of Trade & Industry Information, Manufacturing & Services, data extracted March 15, 2018

Building Permits

Area	Single-Family			Multi-Family			Total		
	2016	2017p	Pct. Chg.	2016	2017p	Pct. Chg.	2016	2017p	Pct. Chg.
City	177	195	10.2	207	0	-100.0	384	195	-49.2
MSA[1]	3,003	3,210	6.9	1,352	693	-48.7	4,355	3,903	-10.4
U.S.	750,800	817,300	8.9	455,800	446,800	-2.0	1,206,600	1,264,100	4.8

Note: (1) Figures cover the Memphis, TN-MS-AR Metropolitan Statistical Area—see Appendix B for areas included; Figures represent new, privately-owned housing units authorized (unadjusted data); All permit data are based on estimates with imputation; (p) preliminary data.
Source: U.S. Census Bureau, Manufacturing, Mining, and Construction Statistics, Building Permits, 2016, 2017

Bankruptcy Filings

Area	Business Filings 2016	Business Filings 2017	Business Filings % Chg.	Nonbusiness Filings 2016	Nonbusiness Filings 2017	Nonbusiness Filings % Chg.
Shelby County	90	71	-21.1	11,352	10,756	-5.3
U.S.	24,114	23,157	-4.0	770,846	765,863	-0.6

Note: Business filings include Chapter 7, Chapter 11, Chapter 12, and Chapter 13; Nonbusiness filings include Chapter 7, Chapter 11, and Chapter 13
Source: Administrative Office of the U.S. Courts, Business and Nonbusiness Bankruptcy, County Cases Commenced by Chapter of the Bankruptcy Code, During the 12-Month Period Ending December 31, 2016 and Business and Nonbusiness Bankruptcy, County Cases Commenced by Chapter of the Bankruptcy Code, During the 12-Month Period Ending December 31, 2017

Housing Vacancy Rates

Area	Gross Vacancy Rate[2] (%)			Year-Round Vacancy Rate[3] (%)			Rental Vacancy Rate[4] (%)			Homeowner Vacancy Rate[5] (%)		
	2015	2016	2017	2015	2016	2017	2015	2016	2017	2015	2016	2017
MSA[1]	11.2	10.9	12.1	11.0	10.7	12.1	10.7	9.4	10.5	1.4	1.4	1.4
U.S.	12.9	12.8	12.7	10.0	9.9	9.9	7.1	6.9	7.2	1.8	1.7	1.6

Note: (1) Figures cover the Memphis, TN-MS-AR Metropolitan Statistical Area—see Appendix B for areas included; (2) The percentage of the total housing inventory that is vacant; (3) The percentage of the housing inventory (excluding seasonal units) that is year-round vacant; (4) The percentage of rental inventory that is vacant for rent; (5) The percentage of homeowner inventory that is vacant for sale
Source: U.S. Census Bureau, Housing Vacancies and Homeownership Annual Statistics: 2015, 2016, 2017

INCOME

Income

Area	Per Capita ($)	Median Household ($)	Average Household ($)
City	44,410	110,591	129,842
MSA[1]	26,242	48,545	68,581
U.S.	29,829	55,322	77,866

Note: (1) Figures cover the Memphis, TN-MS-AR Metropolitan Statistical Area—see Appendix B for areas included
Source: U.S. Census Bureau, 2012-2016 American Community Survey 5-Year Estimates

Household Income Distribution

Area	Percent of Households Earning: Under $15,000	$15,000 -$24,999	$25,000 -$34,999	$35,000 -$49,999	$50,000 -$74,999	$75,000 -$99,999	$100,000 -$149,999	$150,000 and up
City	1.9	3.5	5.0	8.0	13.4	12.0	24.9	31.1
MSA[1]	14.4	12.0	11.0	13.5	17.7	11.3	11.7	8.3
U.S.	12.1	10.2	9.9	13.2	17.8	12.2	13.5	11.1

Note: (1) Figures cover the Memphis, TN-MS-AR Metropolitan Statistical Area—see Appendix B for areas included
Source: U.S. Census Bureau, 2012-2016 American Community Survey 5-Year Estimates

Poverty Rate

Area	All Ages	Under 18 Years Old	18 to 64 Years Old	65 Years and Over
City	5.4	10.2	4.1	1.8
MSA[1]	19.4	30.1	16.7	10.5
U.S.	15.1	21.2	14.2	9.3

Note: Figures are percentage of people whose income during the past 12 months was below the poverty level; (1) Figures cover the Memphis, TN-MS-AR Metropolitan Statistical Area—see Appendix B for areas included
Source: U.S. Census Bureau, 2012-2016 American Community Survey 5-Year Estimates

EMPLOYMENT

Labor Force and Employment

Area	Civilian Labor Force Dec. 2016	Civilian Labor Force Dec. 2017	Civilian Labor Force % Chg.	Workers Employed Dec. 2016	Workers Employed Dec. 2017	Workers Employed % Chg.
City	25,011	25,465	1.8	24,131	24,839	2.9
MSA[1]	627,910	635,161	1.2	597,226	611,935	2.5
U.S.	158,968,000	159,880,000	0.6	151,798,000	153,602,000	1.2

Note: Data is not seasonally adjusted and covers workers 16 years of age and older; (1) Figures cover the Memphis, TN-MS-AR Metropolitan Statistical Area—see Appendix B for areas included
Source: Bureau of Labor Statistics, Local Area Unemployment Statistics

Unemployment Rate

Area	2017											
	Jan.	Feb.	Mar.	Apr.	May	Jun.	Jul.	Aug.	Sep.	Oct.	Nov.	Dec.
City	4.0	3.6	3.4	2.7	2.5	3.2	3.0	2.9	2.7	2.6	2.7	2.5
MSA[1]	5.4	4.9	4.6	4.0	4.0	4.8	4.5	4.2	3.9	3.8	3.7	3.7
U.S.	5.1	4.9	4.6	4.1	4.1	4.5	4.6	4.5	4.1	3.9	3.9	3.9

Note: Data is not seasonally adjusted and covers workers 16 years of age and older; (1) Figures cover the Memphis, TN-MS-AR Metropolitan Statistical Area—see Appendix B for areas included
Source: Bureau of Labor Statistics, Local Area Unemployment Statistics

Average Wages

Occupation	$/Hr.	Occupation	$/Hr.
Accountants and Auditors	34.30	Maids and Housekeeping Cleaners	10.30
Automotive Mechanics	21.20	Maintenance and Repair Workers	17.90
Bookkeepers	18.80	Marketing Managers	53.30
Carpenters	18.30	Nuclear Medicine Technologists	28.80
Cashiers	9.80	Nurses, Licensed Practical	20.40
Clerks, General Office	15.90	Nurses, Registered	31.50
Clerks, Receptionists/Information	12.90	Nursing Assistants	12.80
Clerks, Shipping/Receiving	14.40	Packers and Packagers, Hand	11.70
Computer Programmers	34.60	Physical Therapists	41.80
Computer Systems Analysts	32.60	Postal Service Mail Carriers	24.10
Computer User Support Specialists	23.90	Real Estate Brokers	29.70
Cooks, Restaurant	10.80	Retail Salespersons	12.70
Dentists	92.20	Sales Reps., Exc. Tech./Scientific	33.60
Electrical Engineers	37.70	Sales Reps., Tech./Scientific	45.70
Electricians	22.50	Secretaries, Exc. Legal/Med./Exec.	17.10
Financial Managers	55.80	Security Guards	13.70
First-Line Supervisors/Managers, Sales	21.50	Surgeons	133.20
Food Preparation Workers	10.20	Teacher Assistants*	12.70
General and Operations Managers	56.00	Teachers, Elementary School*	26.00
Hairdressers/Cosmetologists	13.80	Teachers, Secondary School*	25.90
Internists, General	117.60	Telemarketers	11.90
Janitors and Cleaners	12.50	Truck Drivers, Heavy/Tractor-Trailer	20.30
Landscaping/Groundskeeping Workers	12.80	Truck Drivers, Light/Delivery Svcs.	18.20
Lawyers	61.20	Waiters and Waitresses	9.50

Note: Wage data covers the Memphis, TN-MS-AR Metropolitan Statistical Area—see Appendix B for areas included; (*) Hourly wages for elementary/secondary school teachers and teacher assistants were calculated by the editors from annual wage data based on a 40 hour work week; n/a not available.
Source: Bureau of Labor Statistics, Metro Area Occupational Employment & Wage Estimates, May 2017

Employment by Occupation

Occupation Classification	City (%)	MSA[1] (%)	U.S. (%)
Management, Business, Science, and Arts	53.9	33.9	37.0
Natural Resources, Construction, and Maintenance	3.5	8.0	8.9
Production, Transportation, and Material Moving	8.9	15.8	12.2
Sales and Office	23.0	25.2	23.8
Service	10.7	17.0	18.1

Note: Figures cover employed civilians 16 years of age and older; (1) Figures cover the Memphis, TN-MS-AR Metropolitan Statistical Area—see Appendix B for areas included
Source: U.S. Census Bureau, 2012-2016 American Community Survey 5-Year Estimates

Employment by Industry

Sector	MSA[1] Number of Employees	MSA[1] Percent of Total	U.S. Percent of Total
Construction, Mining, and Logging	22,700	3.5	5.2
Education and Health Services	96,300	14.6	15.9
Financial Activities	29,100	4.4	5.7
Government	84,500	12.8	15.3
Information	5,600	0.9	1.9
Leisure and Hospitality	68,900	10.5	10.7
Manufacturing	45,200	6.9	8.5
Other Services	25,300	3.8	3.9
Professional and Business Services	97,000	14.8	14.0
Retail Trade	70,700	10.8	11.0
Transportation, Warehousing, and Utilities	75,300	11.5	4.1
Wholesale Trade	37,000	5.6	4.0

Note: Figures are non-farm employment as of December 2017. Figures are not seasonally adjusted and include workers 16 years of age and older; (1) Figures cover the Memphis, TN-MS-AR Metropolitan Statistical Area—see Appendix B for areas included
Source: Bureau of Labor Statistics, Current Employment Statistics, Employment, Hours, and Earnings

Occupations with Greatest Projected Employment Growth: 2017 – 2019

Occupation[1]	2017 Employment	2019 Projected Employment	Numeric Employment Change	Percent Employment Change
Combined Food Preparation and Serving Workers, Including Fast Food	76,930	81,530	4,600	6.0
Laborers and Freight, Stock, and Material Movers, Hand	96,910	100,970	4,060	4.2
Customer Service Representatives	60,280	63,140	2,860	4.7
General and Operations Managers	46,420	48,740	2,320	5.0
Waiters and Waitresses	52,940	55,140	2,200	4.2
Registered Nurses	58,860	61,030	2,170	3.7
Heavy and Tractor-Trailer Truck Drivers	62,960	65,010	2,050	3.3
Personal Care Aides	20,910	22,660	1,750	8.4
Janitors and Cleaners, Except Maids and Housekeeping Cleaners	42,430	44,150	1,720	4.0
Retail Salespersons	94,740	96,460	1,720	1.8

Note: Projections cover Tennessee; (1) Sorted by numeric employment change
Source: www.projectionscentral.com, State Occupational Projections, 2017–2019 Short-Term Projections

Fastest Growing Occupations: 2017 – 2019

Occupation[1]	2017 Employment	2019 Projected Employment	Numeric Employment Change	Percent Employment Change
Dietetic Technicians	660	740	80	12.9
Recreational Vehicle Service Technicians	770	860	90	12.6
Tax Preparers	1,900	2,140	240	12.5
Veterinary Assistants and Laboratory Animal Caretakers	3,170	3,560	390	12.1
Veterinary Technologists and Technicians	1,350	1,510	160	12.0
Material Moving Workers, All Other	880	990	110	11.8
Statisticians	630	710	80	11.7
Veterinarians	1,500	1,670	170	11.6
Insurance Claims and Policy Processing Clerks	4,680	5,190	510	10.9
Medical Appliance Technicians	1,950	2,160	210	10.6

Note: Projections cover Tennessee; (1) Sorted by percent employment change and excludes occupations with numeric employment change less than 50
Source: www.projectionscentral.com, State Occupational Projections, 2017–2019 Short-Term Projections

TAXES

State Corporate Income Tax Rates

State	Tax Rate (%)	Income Brackets ($)	Num. of Brackets	Financial Institution Tax Rate (%)[a]	Federal Income Tax Ded.
Tennessee	6.5	Flat rate	1	6.5	No

Note: Tax rates as of January 1, 2018; (a) Rates listed are the corporate income tax rate applied to financial institutions or excise taxes based on income. Some states have other taxes based upon the value of deposits or shares.
Source: Federation of Tax Administrators, Range of State Corporate Income Tax Rates, January 1, 2018

State Individual Income Tax Rates

State	Tax Rate (%)	Income Brackets ($)	Num. of Brackets	Personal Exempt. ($)[1]		Fed. Inc. Tax Ded.
				Single	Dependents	
Tennessee	State income tax of 6% on dividends and interest income only					

Note: Tax rates as of January 1, 2018; Local- and county-level taxes are not included; n/a not applicable; (1) Married joint filers generally receive double the single exemption
Source: Federation of Tax Administrators, State Individual Income Tax Rates, January 1, 2018

Various State Sales and Excise Tax Rates

State	State Sales Tax (%)	Gasoline[1] (¢/gal.)	Cigarette[2] ($/pack)	Spirits[3] ($/gal.)	Wine[4] ($/gal.)	Beer[5] ($/gal.)	Recreational Marijuana (%)
Tennessee	7.0	25.4	0.62	4.46 (i)	1.27 (o)	1.29 (u)	Not legal

Note: All tax rates as of January 1, 2018; (1) The American Petroleum Institute has developed a methodology for determining the average tax rate on a gallon of fuel. Rates may include any of the following: excise taxes, environmental fees, storage tank fees, other fees or taxes, general sales tax, and local taxes. In states where gasoline is subject to the general sales tax, or where the fuel tax is based on the average sale price, the average rate determined by API is sensitive to changes in the price of gasoline. States that fully or partially apply general sales taxes to gasoline: CA, CO, GA, IL, IN, MI, NY; (2) The federal excise tax of $1.0066 per pack and local taxes are not included; (3) Rates are those applicable to off-premise sales of 40% alcohol by volume (a.b.v.) distilled spirits in 750ml containers. Local excise taxes are excluded; (4) Rates are those applicable to off-premise sales of 11% a.b.v. non-carbonated wine in 750ml containers; (5) Rates are those applicable to off-premise sales of 4.7% a.b.v. beer in 12 ounce containers; (i) Includes case fees and/or bottle fees which may vary with size of container; (o) Includes case fees and/or bottle fees which may vary with size of container; (u) Includes the wholesale tax rate in Kentucky (10.5%) and Tennessee (17%), converted into a gallonage excise tax rate.
Source: Tax Foundation, 2018 Facts & Figures: How Does Your State Compare?

State Business Tax Climate Index Rankings

State	Overall Rank	Corporate Tax Rank	Individual Income Tax Rank	Sales Tax Rank	Unemployment Insurance Tax Rank	Property Tax Rank
Tennessee	14	21	8	45	22	29

Note: The index is a measure of how each state's tax laws affect economic performance. The lower the rank, the more favorable a state's tax system is for business. States without a given tax are given a ranking of 1. The scores/rankings for the District of Columbia do not affect other states. The 2018 index represents the tax climate as of July 1, 2017.
Source: Tax Foundation, State Business Tax Climate Index 2018

TRANSPORTATION

Means of Transportation to Work

Area	Car/Truck/Van		Public Transportation			Bicycle	Walked	Other Means	Worked at Home
	Drove Alone	Car-pooled	Bus	Subway	Railroad				
City	88.3	5.3	0.1	0.0	0.0	0.0	0.4	0.6	5.3
MSA[1]	83.9	9.5	1.1	0.0	0.0	0.1	1.2	1.3	2.9
U.S.	76.4	9.3	2.6	1.9	0.6	0.6	2.8	1.3	4.6

Note: Figures are percentages and cover workers 16 years of age and older; (1) Figures cover the Memphis, TN-MS-AR Metropolitan Statistical Area—see Appendix B for areas included
Source: U.S. Census Bureau, 2012-2016 American Community Survey 5-Year Estimates

Travel Time to Work

Area	Less Than 10 Minutes	10 to 19 Minutes	20 to 29 Minutes	30 to 44 Minutes	45 to 59 Minutes	60 to 89 Minutes	90 Minutes or More
City	11.3	23.7	25.2	28.7	8.5	1.4	1.2
MSA[1]	10.5	28.6	25.9	24.0	7.1	2.7	1.2
U.S.	12.9	29.2	20.9	20.4	8.0	6.0	2.7

Note: Note: Figures are percentages and include workers 16 years old and over; (1) Figures cover the Memphis, TN-MS-AR Metropolitan Statistical Area—see Appendix B for areas included
Source: U.S. Census Bureau, 2012-2016 American Community Survey 5-Year Estimates

Freeway Travel Time Index

Area	1985	1990	1995	2000	2005	2010	2014
Urban Area Rank[1,2]	64	41	41	38	42	42	42
Urban Area Index[1]	1.05	1.11	1.14	1.17	1.18	1.18	1.19
Average Index[3]	1.09	1.11	1.14	1.17	1.20	1.19	1.20

Note: Freeway Travel Time Index—the ratio of travel time in the peak period to the travel time at free-flow conditions. For example, a value of 1.30 indicates a 20-minute free-flow trip takes 26 minutes in the peak (20 minutes x 1.30 = 26 minutes); (1) Covers the Memphis TN-MS-AR urban area; (2) Rank is based on 101 urban areas (#1 = highest travel time index); (3) Average of 101 urban areas
Source: Texas Transportation Institute, 2015 Urban Mobility Scorecard, August 2015

Freeway Commuter Stress Index

Area	1985	1990	1995	2000	2005	2010	2014
Urban Area Rank[1,2]	58	47	50	46	47	49	52
Urban Area Index[1]	1.08	1.13	1.16	1.20	1.21	1.21	1.21
Average Index[3]	1.13	1.16	1.19	1.22	1.25	1.24	1.25

Note: The Freeway Commuter Stress Index is the same as the Freeway Travel Time Index (see table above) except that it includes only the travel in the peak directions during the peak periods; the TTI includes travel in all directions during the peak period. Thus, the CSI is more indicative of the work trip experienced by each commuter on a daily basis; (1) Covers the Memphis TN-MS-AR urban area; (2) Rank is based on 101 urban areas (#1 = highest travel time index); (3) Average of 101 urban areas
Source: Texas Transportation Institute, 2015 Urban Mobility Scorecard, August 2015

Living Environment

COST OF LIVING

Cost of Living Index

Composite Index	Groceries	Housing	Utilities	Transportation	Health Care	Misc. Goods/ Services
83.2	91.0	65.8	103.2	89.1	84.8	86.7

Note: The Cost of Living Index measures regional differences in the cost of consumer goods and services, excluding taxes and non-consumer expenditures, for professional and managerial households in the top income quintile. It is based on more than 50,000 prices covering almost 60 different items for which prices are collected three times a year by chambers of commerce, economic development organizations or university applied economic centers in each participating urban area. The numbers shown should be read as a percentage above or below the national average of 100. For example, a value of 115.4 in the groceries column indicates that grocery prices are 15.4% higher than the national average. Small differences in the index numbers should not be interpreted as significant; Figures cover the Memphis TN urban area.
Source: The Council for Community and Economic Research, ACCRA Cost of Living Index, 2017

Grocery Prices

Area[1]	T-Bone Steak ($/pound)	Frying Chicken ($/pound)	Whole Milk ($/half gal.)	Eggs ($/dozen)	Orange Juice ($/64 oz.)	Coffee ($/11.5 oz.)
City[2]	10.52	1.12	1.86	1.14	3.53	4.19
Avg.	11.29	1.40	2.02	1.47	3.55	4.37
Min.	7.71	0.93	1.04	0.70	2.86	3.24
Max.	15.83	2.39	4.03	3.92	6.29	8.16

Note: (1) Values for the local area are compared with the average, minimum and maximum values for all 294 areas in the Cost of Living Index; (2) Figures cover the Memphis TN urban area; ***T-Bone Steak*** *(price per pound);* ***Frying Chicken*** *(price per pound, whole fryer);* ***Whole Milk*** *(half gallon carton);* ***Eggs*** *(price per dozen, Grade A, large);* ***Orange Juice*** *(64 oz. Tropicana or Florida Natural);* ***Coffee*** *(11.5 oz. can, vacuum-packed, Maxwell House, Hills Bros, or Folgers).*
Source: The Council for Community and Economic Research, ACCRA Cost of Living Index, 2017

Housing and Utility Costs

Area[1]	New Home Price ($)	Apartment Rent ($/month)	All Electric ($/month)	Part Electric ($/month)	Other Energy ($/month)	Telephone ($/month)
City[2]	215,913	686	-	113.27	43.60	32.78
Avg.	335,956	1,047	175.01	97.34	67.93	28.71
Min.	187,788	491	109.48	49.33	35.44	12.39
Max.	1,739,087	4,559	432.62	227.09	353.33	44.61

Note: (1) Values for the local area are compared with the average, minimum and maximum values for all 294 areas in the Cost of Living Index; (2) Figures cover the Memphis TN urban area; ***New Home Price*** *(2,400 sf living area, 8,000 sf lot, in urban area with full utilities);* ***Apartment Rent*** *(950 sf 2 bedroom/1.5 or 2 bath, unfurnished, excluding all utilities except water);* ***All Electric*** *(average monthly cost for an all-electric home);* ***Part Electric*** *(average monthly cost for a part-electric home);* ***Other Energy*** *(average monthly cost for natural gas, fuel oil, coal, wood, and any other forms of energy except electricity);* ***Telephone*** *(price includes basic monthly rate for a private residential line plus additional local usage charges incurred by a family of four).*
Source: The Council for Community and Economic Research, ACCRA Cost of Living Index, 2017

Health Care, Transportation, and Other Costs

Area[1]	Doctor ($/visit)	Dentist ($/visit)	Optometrist ($/visit)	Gasoline ($/gallon)	Beauty Salon ($/visit)	Men's Shirt ($)
City[2]	70.43	87.60	64.31	2.08	29.50	25.17
Avg.	108.00	92.54	101.93	2.25	37.58	30.92
Min.	30.39	60.00	49.75	1.82	16.11	11.20
Max.	193.50	161.94	229.28	3.16	77.35	59.13

Note: (1) Values for the local area are compared with the average, minimum and maximum values for all 294 areas in the Cost of Living Index; (2) Figures cover the Memphis TN urban area; ***Doctor*** *(general practitioners routine exam of an established patient);* ***Dentist*** *(adult teeth cleaning and periodic oral examination);* ***Optometrist*** *(full vision eye exam for established adult patient);* ***Gasoline*** *(one gallon regular unleaded, national brand, including all taxes, cash price at self-service pump if available);* ***Beauty Salon*** *(woman's shampoo, trim, and blow-dry);* ***Men's Shirt*** *(cotton/polyester dress shirt, pinpoint weave, long sleeves).*
Source: The Council for Community and Economic Research, ACCRA Cost of Living Index, 2017

HOUSING

House Price Index (HPI)

Area	National Ranking[2]	Quarterly Change (%)	One-Year Change (%)	Five-Year Change (%)
MSA[1]	165	-1.27	4.84	19.45
U.S.[3]	–	1.61	6.68	34.71

Note: The HPI is a weighted repeat sales index. It measures average price changes in repeat sales or refinancings on the same properties. This information is obtained by reviewing repeat mortgage transactions on single-family properties whose mortgages have been purchased or securitized by Fannie Mae or Freddie Mac in January 1975; (1) Figures cover the Memphis, TN-MS-AR Metropolitan Statistical Area—see Appendix B for areas included; (2) Rankings are based on annual percentage change for all metro areas containing at least 15,000 transactions over the last 10 years and ranges from 1 to 253; (3) figures based on a weighted average of Census Division estimates using a seasonally adjusted, purchase-only index; all figures are for the period ending December 31, 2017
Source: Federal Housing Finance Agency, House Price Index, February 28, 2018

Median Single-Family Home Prices

Area	2015	2016	2017p	Percent Change 2016 to 2017
MSA[1]	147.0	155.3	166.9	7.5
U.S. Average	223.9	235.5	248.8	5.6

Note: Figures are median sales prices of existing single-family homes in thousands of dollars; (p) preliminary; (1) Figures cover the Memphis, TN-MS-AR Metropolitan Statistical Area—see Appendix B for areas included
Source: National Association of Realtors, Median Sales Price of Existing Single-Family Homes for Metropolitan Areas, 4th Quarter 2017

Qualifying Income Based on Median Sales Price of Existing Single-Family Homes

Area	With 5% Down ($)	With 10% Down ($)	With 20% Down ($)
MSA[1]	37,752	35,765	31,791
U.S. Average	55,585	52,659	46,808

Note: Figures are preliminary; Qualifying income is based on a mortgage rate of 4.17%. Monthly principal and interest payment is limited to 25% of income; (1) Figures cover the Memphis, TN-MS-AR Metropolitan Statistical Area—see Appendix B for areas included
Source: National Association of Realtors, Qualifying Income Based on Median Sales Price of Existing Single-Family Homes for Metropolitan Areas, 4th Quarter 2017

Median Apartment Condo-Coop Home Prices

Area	2015	2016	2017p	Percent Change 2016 to 2017
MSA[1]	n/a	n/a	n/a	n/a
U.S. Average	210.7	220.7	234.3	6.2

Note: Figures are median sales prices of existing apartment condo-coop homes in thousands of dollars; (p) preliminary; n/a not available; (1) Figures cover the Memphis, TN-MS-AR Metropolitan Statistical Area—see Appendix B for areas included
Source: National Association of Realtors, Median Sales Price of Existing Apartment Condo-Coop Homes for Metropolitan Areas, 4th Quarter 2017

Home Value Distribution

Area	Under $50,000	$50,000 -$99,999	$100,000 -$149,999	$150,000 -$199,999	$200,000 -$299,999	$300,000 -$499,999	$500,000 -$999,999	$1,000,000 or more
City	1.8	2.2	3.4	9.7	40.9	35.5	6.0	0.5
MSA[1]	11.0	25.0	19.6	15.8	16.3	8.7	2.9	0.7
U.S.	8.8	14.8	15.3	14.9	18.4	16.4	9.0	2.5

Note: Figures are percentages and cover owner-occupied housing units; (1) Figures cover the Memphis, TN-MS-AR Metropolitan Statistical Area—see Appendix B for areas included
Source: U.S. Census Bureau, 2012-2016 American Community Survey 5-Year Estimates

Homeownership Rate

Area	2009 (%)	2010 (%)	2011 (%)	2012 (%)	2013 (%)	2014 (%)	2015 (%)	2016 (%)	2017 (%)
MSA[1]	61.5	61.9	60.1	60.5	56.2	57.2	59.6	61.8	62.4
U.S.	67.4	66.9	66.1	65.4	65.1	64.5	63.7	63.4	63.9

Note: (1) Figures cover the Memphis, TN-MS-AR Metropolitan Statistical Area—see Appendix B for areas included
Source: U.S. Census Bureau, Housing Vacancies and Homeownership Annual Statistics: 2009-2017

Year Housing Structure Built

Area	2010 or Later	2000 -2009	1990 -1999	1980 -1989	1970 -1979	1960 -1969	1950 -1959	1940 -1949	Before 1940	Median Year
City	3.5	29.4	38.2	16.6	6.6	2.3	1.2	0.4	1.7	1996
MSA[1]	2.1	16.9	17.0	13.7	16.5	11.2	11.7	5.5	5.5	1980
U.S.	2.3	14.7	14.0	13.7	15.6	10.9	10.6	5.2	13.0	1977

Note: Figures are percentages except for Median Year; Note: (1) Figures cover the Memphis, TN-MS-AR Metropolitan Statistical Area—see Appendix B for areas included
Source: U.S. Census Bureau, 2012-2016 American Community Survey 5-Year Estimates

Gross Monthly Rent

Area	Under $500	$500 -$999	$1,000 -$1,499	$1,500 -$1,999	$2,000 -$2,499	$2,500 -$2,999	$3,000 and up	Median ($)
City	0.9	21.9	56.6	12.1	7.2	0.8	0.5	1,153
MSA[1]	10.0	56.2	27.0	5.1	1.1	0.2	0.5	863
U.S.	11.3	43.3	27.7	10.7	4.0	1.6	1.5	949

Note: Figures are percentages except for Median; Gross rent is the contract rent plus the estimated average monthly cost of utilities (electricity, gas, and water and sewer) and fuels (oil, coal, kerosene, wood, etc.) if these are paid by the renter (or paid for the renter by someone else); (1) Figures cover the Memphis, TN-MS-AR Metropolitan Statistical Area—see Appendix B for areas included
Source: U.S. Census Bureau, 2012-2016 American Community Survey 5-Year Estimates

HEALTH

Health Risk Factors

Category	MSA[1] (%)	U.S. (%)
Adults aged 18–64 who have any kind of health care coverage	82.0	87.7
Adults who reported being in good or excellent health	82.2	83.6
Adults who are current smokers	19.2	17.1
Adults who currently use E-cigarettes	3.8	4.7
Adults who currently use chewing tobacco, snuff, or snus	3.2	4.0
Adults who are heavy drinkers[2]	5.1	6.5
Adults who are binge drinkers[3]	12.8	16.9
Adults who are overweight (BMI 25.0 - 29.9)	30.4	35.3
Adults who are obese (BMI 30.0 - 99.8)	40.5	29.9
Adults who participated in any physical activities in the past month	71.6	76.9
Adults who always or nearly always wears a seat belt	93.4	94.3

Note: (1) Figures cover the Memphis, TN-MS-AR Metropolitan Statistical Area—see Appendix B for areas included; (2) Heavy drinkers are classified as adult men having more than 14 drinks per week and adult women having more than 7 drinks per week; (3) Binge drinkers are classified as males having five or more drinks on one occasion or females having four or more drinks on one occasion
Source: Centers for Disease Control and Prevention, Behaviorial Risk Factor Surveillance System, SMART: Selected Metropolitan Area Risk Trends, 2016

Health Screening Rates

Category	MSA[1] (%)	U.S. (%)
Adults 50-75 who have had a blood stool test within the past year	7.5	8.0
Adults 50-75 who have had a colonoscopy in the past 10 years	63.1	63.5
Adults aged 65+ who have had flu shot within the past year	54.6	58.6
Adults aged 65+ who have ever had a pneumonia vaccination	66.2	73.4
Adults who have ever been tested for HIV	48.9	35.6
Women aged 21-65 who have had a pap test in the past three years	79.0	79.8
Men aged 40+ who have had a PSA test within the past two years	47.5	39.5
Women aged 40+ who have had a mammogram within the past two years	69.7	72.5

Note: n/a not available; (1) Figures cover the Memphis, TN-MS-AR Metropolitan Statistical Area—see Appendix B for areas included; Source: Centers for Disease Control and Prevention, Behaviorial Risk Factor Surveillance System, SMART: Selected Metropolitan Area Risk Trends, 2016

Chronic Health Conditions

Category	MSA[1] (%)	U.S. (%)
Adults who have ever been told they had a heart attack	4.4	4.4
Adults who have ever been told they have angina or coronary heart disease	4.5	4.1
Adults who have ever been told they had a stroke	4.5	3.1
Adults who have been told they currently have asthma	8.5	9.3
Adults who have ever been told they have arthritis	28.4	25.8
Adults who have ever been told they have diabetes[2]	11.5	10.5
Adults who have ever been told they had skin cancer	3.5	5.9
Adults who have ever been told they had any other types of cancer	4.8	6.7
Adults who have ever been told they have COPD	7.7	6.3
Adults who have ever been told they have kidney disease	2.6	2.8
Adults who have ever been told they have a form of depression	20.4	17.4

Note: (1) Figures cover the Memphis, TN-MS-AR Metropolitan Statistical Area—see Appendix B for areas included; (2) Figures do not include pregnancy-related, borderline, or pre-diabetes
Source: Centers for Disease Control and Prevention, Behaviorial Risk Factor Surveillance System, SMART: Selected Metropolitan Area Risk Trends, 2016

Mortality Rates for the Top 10 Causes of Death in the U.S.

ICD-10[a] Sub-Chapter	ICD-10[a] Code	Age-Adjusted Mortality Rate[1] per 100,000 population	
		County[2]	U.S.
Malignant neoplasms	C00-C97	186.7	158.5
Ischaemic heart diseases	I20-I25	113.4	96.8
Other forms of heart disease	I30-I51	55.3	52.4
Chronic lower respiratory diseases	J40-J47	37.6	40.9
Cerebrovascular diseases	I60-I69	51.4	37.2
Organic, including symptomatic, mental disorders	F01-F09	31.1	33.3
Other degenerative diseases of the nervous system	G30-G31	45.3	32.1
Other external causes of accidental injury	W00-X59	36.6	31.2
Diabetes mellitus	E10-E14	26.9	21.1
Hypertensive diseases	I10-I15	37.4	20.8

Note: (a) ICD-10 = International Classification of Diseases 10th Revision; (1) Mortality rates are a three year average covering 2014-2016; (2) Figures cover Shelby County.
Source: Centers for Disease Control and Prevention, National Center for Health Statistics. Underlying Cause of Death 1999-2016 on CDC WONDER Online Database, released December 2017

Mortality Rates for Selected Causes of Death

ICD-10[a] Sub-Chapter	ICD-10[a] Code	Age-Adjusted Mortality Rate[1] per 100,000 population	
		County[2]	U.S.
Assault	X85-Y09	19.9	5.6
Diseases of the liver	K70-K76	12.4	14.0
Human immunodeficiency virus (HIV) disease	B20-B24	6.7	1.9
Influenza and pneumonia	J09-J18	19.3	14.6
Intentional self-harm	X60-X84	9.0	13.2
Malnutrition	E40-E46	2.1	1.3
Obesity and other hyperalimentation	E65-E68	4.0	2.1
Renal failure	N17-N19	14.4	13.0
Transport accidents	V01-V99	15.0	12.0
Viral hepatitis	B15-B19	2.9	1.9

Note: (a) ICD-10 = International Classification of Diseases 10th Revision; (1) Mortality rates are a three year average covering 2014-2016; (2) Figures cover Shelby County; Data are Suppressed when the data meet the criteria for confidentiality constraints; Mortality rates are flagged as Unreliable when the rate would be calculated with a numerator of 20 or less.
Source: Centers for Disease Control and Prevention, National Center for Health Statistics. Underlying Cause of Death 1999-2016 on CDC WONDER Online Database, released December 2017

Health Insurance Coverage

Area	With Health Insurance	With Private Health Insurance	With Public Health Insurance	Without Health Insurance	Population Under Age 18 Without Health Insurance
City	95.4	87.8	16.7	4.6	3.3
MSA[1]	86.8	63.0	33.9	13.2	6.0
U.S.	88.3	66.7	33.0	11.7	5.9

Note: Figures are percentages that cover the civilian noninstitutionalized population; (1) Figures cover the Memphis, TN-MS-AR Metropolitan Statistical Area—see Appendix B for areas included
Source: U.S. Census Bureau, 2012-2016 American Community Survey 5-Year Estimates

Number of Medical Professionals

Area	MDs[3]	DOs[3,4]	Dentists	Podiatrists	Chiropractors	Optometrists
County[1] (number)	3,685	74	662	33	112	278
County[1] (rate[2])	392.9	7.9	70.6	3.5	12.0	29.7
U.S. (rate[2])	276.5	22.3	67.3	6.0	26.7	15.9

Note: Data as of 2016 unless noted; (1) Data covers Shelby County; (2) Rate per 100,000 population; (3) Data as of 2015 and includes all active, non-federal physicians; (4) Doctor of Osteopathic Medicine
Source: U.S. Department of Health and Human Services, Health Resources and Services Administration, Bureau of Health Professions, Area Resource File (ARF) 2016-2017

Best Hospitals

According to *U.S. News,* the Memphis, TN-MS-AR metro area is home to one of the best hospitals in the U.S.: **Methodist Hospitals of Memphis** (8 pediatric specialties). The hospital listed was nationally ranked in at least one of 16 specialties. Only 152 hospitals nationwide were nationally ranked in one or more specialties. Twenty hospitals in the U.S. made the Honor Roll. The Best Hospitals Honor Roll was revamped last year to take both the national rankings and the procedure and condition ratings into account. Hospitals received points if they were nationally ranked in one of the 16 specialties—the higher they ranked, the more points they got—and how many ratings of "high performing" they earned in the nine procedures and conditions. *U.S. News Online, "America's Best Hospitals 2017-18"*

According to *U.S. News,* the Memphis, TN-MS-AR metro area is home to two of the best children's hospitals in the U.S.: **Le Bonheur Children's Hospital** (8 pediatric specialties); **St. Jude Children's Research Hospital** (1 pediatric specialty). The hospitals listed were highly ranked in at least one of 10 pediatric specialties. Eighty-two children's hospitals in the U.S. were nationally ranked in at least one specialty. Hospitals received points for being ranked in a specialty, and the 10 hospitals with the most points across the 10 specialties make up the Honor Roll. *U.S. News Online, "America's Best Children's Hospitals 2017-18"*

EDUCATION

Public School District Statistics

District Name	Schls	Pupils	Pupil/ Teacher Ratio	Minority Pupils[1] (%)	Free Lunch Eligible[2] (%)	IEP[3] (%)
Collierville	8	8,110	16.9	34.6	n/a	12.1

Note: Table includes school districts with 100 or more students; (1) Percentage of students that are not non-Hispanic white; (2) Percentage of students that are eligible for the free lunch program; (3) Percentage of students that have an Individualized Education Program.
Source: U.S. Department of Education, National Center for Education Statistics, Common Core of Data, Local Education Agency (School District) Universe Survey: School Year 2015-2016; U.S. Department of Education, National Center for Education Statistics, Common Core of Data, Public Elementary/Secondary School Universe Survey: School Year 2015-2016

Highest Level of Education

Area	Less than H.S.	H.S. Diploma	Some College, No Deg.	Associate Degree	Bachelor's Degree	Master's Degree	Prof. School Degree	Doctorate Degree
City	3.6	14.8	20.4	6.3	35.5	14.9	2.8	1.8
MSA[1]	13.5	28.7	24.0	6.9	17.0	7.0	1.8	1.1
U.S.	13.0	27.5	21.0	8.2	18.8	8.2	2.0	1.3

Note: Figures cover persons age 25 and over; (1) Figures cover the Memphis, TN-MS-AR Metropolitan Statistical Area—see Appendix B for areas included
Source: U.S. Census Bureau, 2012-2016 American Community Survey 5-Year Estimates

Educational Attainment by Race

Area	High School Graduate or Higher (%)					Bachelor's Degree or Higher (%)				
	Total	White	Black	Asian	Hisp.[2]	Total	White	Black	Asian	Hisp.[2]
City	96.4	97.9	86.2	95.8	97.5	54.9	54.1	51.4	70.0	40.3
MSA[1]	86.5	91.1	82.7	87.7	53.2	26.9	34.1	17.7	54.4	11.8
U.S.	87.0	88.9	84.3	86.3	65.7	30.3	31.6	20.0	52.1	14.7

Note: Figures shown cover persons 25 years old and over; (1) Figures cover the Memphis, TN-MS-AR Metropolitan Statistical Area—see Appendix B for areas included; (2) People of Hispanic origin can be of any race
Source: U.S. Census Bureau, 2012-2016 American Community Survey 5-Year Estimates

School Enrollment by Grade and Control

Area	Preschool (%)		Kindergarten (%)		Grades 1 - 4 (%)		Grades 5 - 8 (%)		Grades 9 - 12 (%)	
	Public	Private	Public	Private	Public	Private	Public	Private	Public	Private
City	22.3	77.7	63.3	36.7	82.7	17.3	81.8	18.2	80.3	19.7
MSA[1]	62.4	37.6	85.1	14.9	86.2	13.8	85.5	14.5	85.3	14.7
U.S.	58.4	41.6	87.7	12.3	89.8	10.2	89.7	10.3	90.4	9.6

Note: Figures shown cover persons 3 years old and over; (1) Figures cover the Memphis, TN-MS-AR Metropolitan Statistical Area—see Appendix B for areas included
Source: U.S. Census Bureau, 2012-2016 American Community Survey 5-Year Estimates

Average Salaries of Public School Classroom Teachers

Area	2015		2016		Change from 2015 to 2016	
	Dollars	Rank[1]	Dollars	Rank[1]	Percent	Rank[2]
Tennessee	47,979	38	48,217	39	0.5	31
U.S. Average	57,611	–	58,353	–	1.3	–

Note: (1) Rank ranges from 1 to 51 where 1 indicates highest salary; (2) Rank ranges from 1 to 51 where 1 indicates highest percent change.
Source: National Education Association, Rankings & Estimates: Rankings of the States 2016 and Estimates of School Statistics 2017

Higher Education

Four-Year Colleges			Two-Year Colleges			Medical Schools[1]	Law Schools[2]	Voc/ Tech[3]
Public	Private Non-profit	Private For-profit	Public	Private Non-profit	Private For-profit			
0	0	0	0	0	0	0	0	0

Note: Figures cover institutions located within the city limits and include main campuses only; (1) includes schools accredited by the Liaison Committee on Medical Education and the American Osteopathic Association's Commission on Osteopathic College Accreditation; (2) includes ABA-accredited schools, schools with provisional ABA accreditation, and state accredited schools; (3) includes all schools with programs that are less than 2 years.
Source: National Center for Education Statistics, Integrated Postsecondary Education System (IPEDS), 2016-17; Wikipedia, List of Medical Schools in the United States, accessed April 2, 2018; Wikipedia, List of Law Schools in the United States, accessed April 2, 2018

According to *U.S. News & World Report,* the Memphis, TN-MS-AR metro area is home to one of the best liberal arts colleges in the U.S.: **Rhodes College** (#51 tie). The indicators used to capture academic quality fall into a number of categories: assessment by administrators at peer institutions; retention of students; faculty resources; student selectivity; financial resources; alumni giving; high school counselor ratings of colleges; and graduation rate. *U.S. News & World Report, "America's Best Colleges 2018"*

According to *U.S. News & World Report,* the Memphis, TN-MS-AR metro area is home to one of the top 75 medical schools for research in the U.S.: **University of Tennessee Health Science Center** (#72 tie). The rankings are based on a weighted average of 11 measures of quality: quality assessment; peer assessment score; assessment score by residency directors; research activity; total research activity; average research activity per faculty member; student selectivity; median MCAT total score; median undergraduate GPA; acceptance rate; and faculty resources. *U.S. News & World Report, "America's Best Graduate Schools, Medical, 2019"*

PRESIDENTIAL ELECTION

2016 Presidential Election Results

Area	Clinton	Trump	Johnson	Stein	Other
Shelby County	61.9	34.5	2.1	0.6	0.9
U.S.	48.0	45.9	3.3	1.1	1.7

Note: Results are percentages and may not add to 100% due to rounding
Source: Dave Leip's Atlas of U.S. Presidential Elections

EMPLOYERS

Major Employers

Company Name	Industry
AutoZone	Auto parts
Baptist Memorial Healthcare	Healthcare
Ducks Unlimited	Food & drug stores
FedEx	Package & delivery services
First Tennessee Bank	Financial services
Horseshoe Casino & Hotel	Gaming & tourism
International Paper	Paper & pulp manufacturing
IRS	Government
Kroger Delta Marketing	Grocery
Memphis City Schools	Education
Methodist Healthcare	Healthcare
Naval Support Activity Mid-South	Military
Park Place Entertainment	Gaming & tourism
ServiceMaster	Diversified outsourcing services
Shelby County Government	Government
Shelby County Schools	Education
St Jude Children's Research	Metals
Tennessee State Government	Government
University of Tennessee Memphis	Education
US Government	Government
US Postal Service	Government

Note: Companies shown are located within the Memphis, TN-MS-AR Metropolitan Statistical Area.
Source: Hoovers.com; Wikipedia

PUBLIC SAFETY

Crime Rate

Area	All Crimes	Violent Crimes				Property Crimes		
		Murder	Rape[3]	Robbery	Aggrav. Assault	Burglary	Larceny -Theft	Motor Vehicle Theft
City	1,655.5	0.0	12.1	20.2	129.2	179.7	1,257.8	56.5
Metro[1]	4,950.3	18.5	54.6	269.4	739.6	934.3	2,623.2	310.6
U.S.	2,847.8	5.3	40.4	102.8	248.5	468.9	1,745.0	236.9

Note: Figures are crimes per 100,000 population; (1) Figures cover the Memphis, TN-MS-AR Metropolitan Statistical Area—see Appendix B for areas included; (3) The city and U.S. figures shown were reported using the revised Uniform Crime Reporting (UCR) definition of rape. The metro area figures shown are an aggregate total of the data submitted using both the revised and legacy UCR definitions.
Source: FBI Uniform Crime Reports, 2016

Hate Crimes

Area	Number of Quarters Reported	Number of Incidents per Bias Motivation					
		Race/Ethnicity/ Ancestry	Religion	Sexual Orientation	Disability	Gender	Gender Identity
City	4	0	0	0	0	0	0
U.S.	4	3,489	1,273	1,076	70	31	124

Source: Federal Bureau of Investigation, Hate Crime Statistics 2016

Identity Theft Consumer Reports

Area	Reports	Reports per 100,000 Population	Rank[2]
MSA[1]	1,492	111	76
U.S.	371,061	114	-

Note: (1) Figures cover the Memphis, TN-MS-AR Metropolitan Statistical Area—see Appendix B for areas included; (2) Rank ranges from 1 to 389 where 1 indicates greatest number of identity theft reports per 100,000 population
Source: Federal Trade Commission, Consumer Sentinel Network Data Book for January–December 2017

Fraud and Other Consumer Reports

Area	Reports	Reports per 100,000 Population	Rank[2]
MSA[1]	8,865	660	18
U.S.	2,304,550	708	-

Note: (1) Figures cover the Memphis, TN-MS-AR Metropolitan Statistical Area—see Appendix B for areas included; (2) Rank ranges from 1 to 389 where 1 indicates greatest number of fraud and other consumer reports per 100,000 population
Source: Federal Trade Commission, Consumer Sentinel Network Data Book for January–December 2017

SPORTS

Professional Sports Teams

Team Name	League	Year Established
Memphis Grizzlies	National Basketball Association (NBA)	2001

Note: Includes teams located in the Memphis, TN-MS-AR Metropolitan Statistical Area.
Source: Wikipedia, Major Professional Sports Teams of the United States and Canada, April 5, 2018

CLIMATE

Average and Extreme Temperatures

Temperature	Jan	Feb	Mar	Apr	May	Jun	Jul	Aug	Sep	Oct	Nov	Dec	Yr.
Extreme High (°F)	83	85	90	95	99	104	107	104	105	97	86	82	107
Average High (°F)	57	62	69	78	84	90	92	92	87	78	68	60	77
Average Temp. (°F)	46	50	57	65	72	79	81	81	76	65	55	48	65
Average Low (°F)	34	37	44	51	59	67	70	69	64	51	42	36	52
Extreme Low (°F)	0	8	15	28	38	42	55	53	34	24	16	2	0

Note: Figures cover the years 1948-1990
Source: National Climatic Data Center, International Station Meteorological Climate Summary, 9/96

Average Precipitation/Snowfall/Humidity

Precip./Humidity	Jan	Feb	Mar	Apr	May	Jun	Jul	Aug	Sep	Oct	Nov	Dec	Yr.
Avg. Precip. (in.)	4.9	5.1	6.6	5.2	4.3	3.7	5.3	3.5	3.6	2.7	4.2	5.6	54.8
Avg. Snowfall (in.)	1	Tr	Tr	Tr	0	0	0	0	0	0	Tr	Tr	1
Avg. Rel. Hum. 6am (%)	87	86	87	90	91	91	93	93	92	91	88	87	90
Avg. Rel. Hum. 3pm (%)	56	51	47	46	50	52	57	54	54	48	49	54	51

Note: Figures cover the years 1948-1990; Tr = Trace amounts (<0.05 in. of rain; <0.5 in. of snow)
Source: National Climatic Data Center, International Station Meteorological Climate Summary, 9/96

Weather Conditions

Temperature			Daytime Sky			Precipitation		
10°F & below	32°F & below	90°F & above	Clear	Partly cloudy	Cloudy	0.01 inch or more precip.	0.1 inch or more snow/ice	Thunder-storms
1	53	86	101	152	112	104	2	59

Note: Figures are average number of days per year and cover the years 1948-1990
Source: National Climatic Data Center, International Station Meteorological Climate Summary, 9/96

HAZARDOUS WASTE

Superfund Sites

The Memphis, TN-MS-AR metro area is home to seven sites on the EPA's Superfund National Priorities List: **Arlington Blending & Packaging** (final); **Carrier Air Conditioning Co.** (final); **Former Custom Cleaners** (final); **Memphis Defense Depot (Dla)** (final); **Ross Metals Inc.** (final); **Smalley-Piper** (final); **Walker Machine Products, Inc.** (final). There are a total of 1,396

Superfund sites with a status of proposed or final on the list in the U.S. *U.S. Environmental Protection Agency, National Priorities List, April 4, 2018*

AIR & WATER QUALITY

Air Quality Trends: Ozone

	1990	1995	2000	2005	2010	2012	2013	2014	2015	2016
MSA[1]	0.088	0.095	0.092	0.086	0.076	0.080	0.066	0.067	0.065	0.069
U.S.	0.087	0.089	0.081	0.079	0.073	0.075	0.069	0.067	0.068	0.069

Note: (1) Data covers the Memphis, TN-MS-AR Metropolitan Statistical Area—see Appendix B for areas included. The values shown are the composite ozone concentration averages among trend sites based on the highest fourth daily maximum 8-hour concentration in parts per million. These trends are based on sites having an adequate record of monitoring data during the trend period. Data from exceptional events are included.
Source: U.S. Environmental Protection Agency, Air Quality Monitoring Information, "Air Quality Trends by City, 1990-2016"

Air Quality Index

Area	Percent of Days when Air Quality was...[2]					AQI Statistics[2]	
	Good	Moderate	Unhealthy for Sensitive Groups	Unhealthy	Very Unhealthy	Maximum	Median
MSA[1]	66.8	32.1	0.8	0.3	0.0	161	44

Note: (1) Data covers the Memphis, TN-MS-AR Metropolitan Statistical Area—see Appendix B for areas included; (2) Based on 365 days with AQI data in 2017. Air Quality Index (AQI) is an index for reporting daily air quality. EPA calculates the AQI for five major air pollutants regulated by the Clean Air Act: ground-level ozone, particle pollution (aka particulate matter), carbon monoxide, sulfur dioxide, and nitrogen dioxide. The AQI runs from 0 to 500. The higher the AQI value, the greater the level of air pollution and the greater the health concern. There are six AQI categories: "Good" AQI is between 0 and 50. Air quality is considered satisfactory; "Moderate" AQI is between 51 and 100. Air quality is acceptable; "Unhealthy for Sensitive Groups" When AQI values are between 101 and 150, members of sensitive groups may experience health effects; "Unhealthy" When AQI values are between 151 and 200 everyone may begin to experience health effects; "Very Unhealthy" AQI values between 201 and 300 trigger a health alert; "Hazardous" AQI values over 300 trigger warnings of emergency conditions (not shown).
Source: U.S. Environmental Protection Agency, Air Quality Index Report, 2017

Air Quality Index Pollutants

Area	Percent of Days when AQI Pollutant was...[2]					
	Carbon Monoxide	Nitrogen Dioxide	Ozone	Sulfur Dioxide	Particulate Matter 2.5	Particulate Matter 10
MSA[1]	0.0	1.4	52.3	0.0	46.3	0.0

Note: (1) Data covers the Memphis, TN-MS-AR Metropolitan Statistical Area—see Appendix B for areas included; (2) Based on 365 days with AQI data in 2017. The Air Quality Index (AQI) is an index for reporting daily air quality. EPA calculates the AQI for five major air pollutants regulated by the Clean Air Act: ground-level ozone, particle pollution (also known as particulate matter), carbon monoxide, sulfur dioxide, and nitrogen dioxide. The AQI runs from 0 to 500. The higher the AQI value, the greater the level of air pollution and the greater the health concern.
Source: U.S. Environmental Protection Agency, Air Quality Index Report, 2017

Maximum Air Pollutant Concentrations: Particulate Matter, Ozone, CO and Lead

	Particulate Matter 10 (ug/m^3)	Particulate Matter 2.5 Wtd AM (ug/m^3)	Particulate Matter 2.5 24-Hr (ug/m^3)	Ozone (ppm)	Carbon Monoxide (ppm)	Lead (ug/m^3)
MSA[1] Level	40	8.4	17	0.071	1	n/a
NAAQS[2]	150	15	35	0.075	9	0.15
Met NAAQS[2]	Yes	Yes	Yes	Yes	Yes	n/a

Note: (1) Data covers the Memphis, TN-MS-AR Metropolitan Statistical Area—see Appendix B for areas included; Data from exceptional events are included; (2) National Ambient Air Quality Standards; ppm = parts per million; ug/m^3 = micrograms per cubic meter; n/a not available.
Concentrations: Particulate Matter 10 (coarse particulate)—highest second maximum 24-hour concentration; Particulate Matter 2.5 Wtd AM (fine particulate)—highest weighted annual mean concentration; Particulate Matter 2.5 24-Hour (fine particulate)—highest 98th percentile 24-hour concentration; Ozone—highest fourth daily maximum 8-hour concentration; Carbon Monoxide—highest second maximum non-overlapping 8-hour concentration; Lead—maximum running 3-month average
Source: U.S. Environmental Protection Agency, Air Quality Monitoring Information, "Air Quality Statistics by City, 2016"

Maximum Air Pollutant Concentrations: Nitrogen Dioxide and Sulfur Dioxide

	Nitrogen Dioxide AM (ppb)	Nitrogen Dioxide 1-Hr (ppb)	Sulfur Dioxide AM (ppb)	Sulfur Dioxide 1-Hr (ppb)	Sulfur Dioxide 24-Hr (ppb)
MSA[1] Level	10	38	n/a	n/a	n/a
NAAQS[2]	53	100	30	75	140
Met NAAQS[2]	Yes	Yes	n/a	n/a	n/a

Note: (1) Data covers the Memphis, TN-MS-AR Metropolitan Statistical Area—see Appendix B for areas included; Data from exceptional events are included; (2) National Ambient Air Quality Standards; ppm = parts per million; ug/m^3 = micrograms per cubic meter; n/a not available.
Concentrations: Nitrogen Dioxide AM—highest arithmetic mean concentration; Nitrogen Dioxide 1-Hr—highest 98th percentile 1-hour daily maximum concentration; Sulfur Dioxide AM—highest annual mean concentration; Sulfur Dioxide 1-Hr—highest 99th percentile 1-hour daily maximum concentration; Sulfur Dioxide 24-Hr—highest second maximum 24-hour concentration
Source: U.S. Environmental Protection Agency, Air Quality Monitoring Information, "Air Quality Statistics by City, 2016"

Drinking Water

Water System Name	Pop. Served	Primary Water Source Type	Violations[1]	
			Health Based	Monitoring/ Reporting
Collierville Water Dept.	46,495	Ground	0	0

Note: (1) Based on violation data from January 1, 2017 to December 31, 2017
Source: U.S. Environmental Protection Agency, Office of Ground Water and Drinking Water, Safe Drinking Water Information System (based on data extracted April 5, 2018)

Allen, Texas

Background

Settlers arrived in the area now known as Allen in the early 1840s in search of free land, traveling the Texas Road and the Central National Road, constructed by the Republic of Texas. The town, located just north of Dallas in northwestern Texas, was officially founded in 1870 as a railroad stop for the Houston Texas railroad, connecting the railway to nearby farms. The town was named after former Texas attorney general and railroad promoter Ebenezer Allen.

It is believed that the first train robbery in Texas took place in Allen on February 22, 1878, when Sam Bass and his associates attacked and stole from a train. The Allen stop was only a short ride from the Bass gang's hideouts in the Elm Trinity brush lands.

The Allen train station closed in 1948 after ownership of the tracks changed several hands, and a devastating fire destroyed most of the business district. When the tracks closed, the population of Allen declined to 400 in a matter of two years. It was only the construction of US highway 75 that finally boosted the city's population. In the 1980s two companies, Developmental Learning Materials and InteCom, Inc. relocated to Allen, leading the way to a healthy and developing corporate environment. Allen continues to attract telecommunications and technology-related companies, with Amphenol Fiber Systems International and PFSweb among the top employers in the area.

The Allen Independent School District has 13 elementary schools, 3 middle schools, 1 freshman center, 1 alternate school, and 1 high school, serving almost all of Allen. The Allen High School was named 2001-2002 Blue Ribbon School by the U.S. Department of Education, a recognition only given to 172 across the nation. In addition to the independent school system, Allen also hosts a campus of the Collin Community College District, located inside Allen High School.

Allen boasts "the goods on everything good." The city has planned parks and recreational areas for the outdoorsman, premium retail outlets for the shopper, and a Civic Ballet and Philharmonic Symphony for the arts enthusiast. Bookworms can visit Allen's public library, which has over 123,000 volumes in its 54,000 square foot facility that includes an auditorium, meeting rooms and an art gallery.

The Texas Health Presbyterian Hospital of Allen operates a 73-bed hospital. The hospital provides top-notch ambulatory and surgical services, diagnostic services and emergency care. The hospital also has two, 60,000 square foot Medical Office Buildings that include a state-of-the-art breast care and sleep disorders center.

Collin County Regional Airport, Dallas/Fort Worth International Airport and Dallas Love Field Airport all serve the Allen and Dallas area.

Rankings

General Rankings

- *US News & World Report* conducted a survey of more than 2,000 people and analyzed the 125 largest metropolitan areas to determine what matters the most when selecting the next place to live. Dallas* ranked #18 out of the top 25 as having the best combination of desirable factors. Criteria: cost of living; quality of education; job market, crime rates; and other factors. *realestate.usnews.com, "The 25 Best Places to Live in the U.S. in 2018," April 10, 2018*
- The Dallas* metro area was identified as one of America's fastest-growing areas in terms of population and economy by *Forbes*. The area ranked #3 out of 25. The 100 most populous metro areas in the U.S. were evaluated on the following criteria: estimated population growth; employment; economic output; wages; home values. *Forbes, "America's Fastest-Growing Cities 2018," February 28, 2018*
- Dallas* was identified as one of America's fastest-growing cities in terms of population growth by CNNMoney.com. The area ranked #8 out of 10. Criteria: population growth between July 2015 and July 2016; cities and towns with populations of 50,000. *CNNMoney, "10 Fastest-Growing Cities," June 2, 2017*
- Allen was selected as one of the best places to live in the United States by *Money* magazine. The city ranked #2 out of 100. This year's list focused on cities with populations of 10,000 to 100,000. Beginning with a pool of over 2,400 candidates, editors looked at 70 data points, from local economy and housing market to schools, crime and healthcare—and then sent reporters to interview residents, search neighborhoods and look for other intangibles. *Money, "Best Places to Live, 2017" September 18, 2017*

Business/Finance Rankings

- According to *Business Insider*, the Dallas* metro area is where startup growth is on the rise. Based on the 2017 Kauffman Index of Growth Entrepreneurship, which measured in-depth national entrepreneurial trends in 40 metro areas, it ranked #11 in highest startup growth. *www.businessinsider.com, "The 21 U.S. Cities with the Highest Startup Growth," October 21, 2017*
- The personal finance site NerdWallet analyzed 183 American metropolitan areas with populations over 250,000 and more than 15,000 businesses to rank where entrepreneurs find the most success. Criteria included area economy, annual income, housing cost, unemployment rate, and the success rate of area businesses. Dallas* ranked #117. *www.nerdwallet.com, "Best Places to Start a Business," April 27, 2015*
- USAA and Hiring Our Heroes worked with Sperlings's BestPlaces and the Institute for Veterans and Military Families at Syracuse University to rank major metropolitan areas where military-skills-related employment is strongest. Criteria for *mid-career* veterans included veteran wage growth; recent job growth; stability; and accessible health resources. Metro areas with a higher than national average crime or unemployment rate were excluded. At #9, the Dallas* metro area made the top ten. *www.usaa.com, "2015 Best Places for Veterans"*
- Based on metro area social media reviews, the employment opinion group Glassdoor surveyed 50 of the largest U.S. metro areas and equally weighed cost of living, hiring opportunity, and job satisfaction to compose a list of "25 Best Cities for Jobs." Median pay and home value, in-demand jobs and number of current job openings was also factored in. The Dallas* metro area was ranked #25 in overall job satisfaction. *www.glassdoor.com, "Best Cities for Jobs," September 12, 2017*
- In a survey of economic confidence in the nation's 50 largest metropolitan areas conducted January–December 2014, the Dallas* metro area placed #14, according to Gallup's 2014 Economic Confidence Index. *Gallup, "San Jose and San Francisco Lead in Economic Confidence," March 19, 2015*

- The Brookings Institution ranked the 100 largest metro areas in the U.S. based on income inequality. Dallas* was ranked #60 (#1 = greatest ineqality). Criteria: the "95/20 ratio," a figure representing the income at which a household earns more than 95 percent of all other households, divided by the income at which a household earns more than only 20 percent of all other households. *Brookings Institution, "Household Income Inequality, 100 Largest U.S. Metro Areas, 2014-2016," February 5, 2018*
- *Forbes* ranked the 100 largest metro areas in the U.S. in terms of the "Best Cities for Young Professionals." The Dallas* metro area ranked #5 out of 25. (Large metro areas were divided into metro divisions.) Criteria: median rent of a two-bedroom apartment; job growth and unemployment rate; median salary of college graduates with 5 or less years of work experience; networking opportunities; social outlook; percentage of population 25 years of age and older with college degrees. *Forbes.com, "America's 25 Best Cities for Young Professionals in 2017," May 22, 2017*
- Payscale.com ranked the largest metro areas in terms of wage growth. The Dallas* metro area ranked #28. Criteria: private-sector wage growth between the 4th quarter of 2016 and the 4th quarter of 2017. *PayScale, "Wage Trends by Metro Area-4th Quarter," January 17, 2018*
- The Dallas* metro area was identified as one of the most debt-ridden places in America by the finance site Credit.com. The metro area was ranked #2. Criteria: residents' average credit card debt as well as median income. *Credit.com, "25 Cities With the Most Credit Card Debt," February 28, 2018*
- Dallas* was identified as one of America's most frugal metro areas by *Coupons.com.* The city ranked #2 out of 25. Criteria: digital coupon usage. *Coupons.com, "America's Most Frugal Cities of 2017," March 22, 2018*
- Dallas* was cited as one of America's top metros for new and expanded facility projects in 2017. The area ranked #3 in the large metro area category (population over 1 million). *Site Selection, "Top Metropolitans of 2017," March 2018*
- The Dallas* metro area appeared on the Milken Institute "2017 Best Performing Cities" list. Rank: #3 out of 200 large metro areas. Criteria: job growth; wage and salary growth; high-tech output growth. *Milken Institute, "Best-Performing Cities 2017," January 2018*
- *Forbes* ranked the 200 most populous metro areas to determine the nation's "Best Places for Business and Careers." The Dallas* metro area was ranked #10. Criteria: costs (business and living); job growth (past and projected); income growth; quality of life; educational attainment (college and high school); projected economic growth; cultural and recreational opportunities; net migration patterns; number of highly ranked colleges. *Forbes, "The Best Places for Business and Careers 2017," October 24, 2017*

Education Rankings

- Personal finance website *WalletHub* analyzed the 150 largest U.S. metropolitan statistical areas to determine where the most educated Americans are choosing to settle. Criteria: education quality and attainment gap; education levels; percentage of workers with degrees; public school rankings; quality and size of each metro area's universities. Dallas* was ranked #70 (#1 = most educated city). *www.WalletHub.com, "2017's Most and Least Educated Cities in America, " July 25, 2017*

Environmental Rankings

- Sperling's BestPlaces assessed 379 metropolitan areas of the United States for the likelihood of dangerously extreme weather events or earthquakes. In general the Southeast and South-Central regions have the highest risk of weather extremes and earthquakes, while the Pacific Northwest enjoys the lowest risk. Of the least risky metropolitan areas, the Dallas* metro area was ranked #379. *www.bestplaces.net, "Safest Places from Natural Disasters," April 2011*

- The U.S. Environmental Protection Agency (EPA) released a list of U.S. metropolitan areas with the most ENERGY STAR certified buildings in 2016. The Dallas* metro area was ranked #6 out of 25. *U.S. Environmental Protection Agency, "2017 Energy Star Top Cities," June 2017*

- Dallas* was highlighted as one of the 25 most ozone-polluted metro areas in the U.S. during 2013 through 2015. The area ranked #13. *American Lung Association, State of the Air 2017*

Health/Fitness Rankings

- For each of the 50 most populous metro areas in the United States, the American College of Sports Medicine's American Fitness Index evaluated infrastructure, community assets, and policies that encourage healthy and fit lifestyles, including preventive health behaviors, levels of chronic disease conditions, health care access, and community resources and policies that support physical activity. The Dallas* metro area ranked #38 for "community fitness." *www.americanfitnessindex.org, "ACSM American Fitness Index Health and Community Fitness Status of the 50 Largest Metropolitan Areas," May 2017*

- The Dallas* metro area was identified as one of the worst cities for bed bugs in America by pest control company Orkin. The area ranked #10 out of 50 based on the number of bed bug treatments Orkin performed from December 2016 to November 2017. *Orkin, "Baltimore and Washington D.C. Continue to Hold Top Spots," January 8, 2018*

- Dallas* was identified as a "2016 Spring Allergy Capital." The area ranked #27 out of 100. Three groups of factors were used to identify the most severe cities for people with allergies during the spring season: annual pollen levels; medicine utilization; access to board-certified allergists. *Asthma and Allergy Foundation of America, "Spring Allergy Capitals 2016"*

- Dallas* was identified as a "2016 Fall Allergy Capital." The area ranked #23 out of 100. Three groups of factors were used to identify the most severe cities for people with allergies during the fall season: annual pollen levels; medicine utilization; access to board-certified allergists. *Asthma and Allergy Foundation of America, "Fall Allergy Capitals 2016"*

- Dallas* was identified as a "2015 Asthma Capital." The area ranked #39 out of the nation's 100 largest metropolitan areas. Criteria: estimated prevalence; self-reported prevalence; crude death rate for asthma; annual pollen score; annual air quality; public smoking laws; number of board-certified asthma specialists; school inhaler access laws; rescue medication use; controller medication use; ER visits for asthma; uninsured rate; poverty rate. *Asthma and Allergy Foundation of America, "Asthma Capitals 2015"*

- The Dallas* metro area ranked #47 out of 189 in The Gallup-Healthways Well-Being Index. Criteria: purpose; social well being; financial health; community and physical health. Results are based on telephone interviews with adults, aged 18 and older, living in metropolitan areas in the 50 U.S. states and the District of Columbia. *Gallup-Healthways, "State of American Well-Being, 2017 Community Well-Being Rankings" March 2018*

Real Estate Rankings

- FitSmallBusiness looked at 50 of the largest metropolitan areas in the U.S. to determine which metro was the best to start a real estate business. Data was compiled from such sources as: Zillow, Trulia, U.S. Census Bureau, and the Bureau of Labor Statistics. Criteria: location; inventory; annual wages; median sales price of homes; days on the market; median price cut percentage; and other factors that would influence real estate professional growth. The Dallas* metro area ranked #19. *fitsmallbusiness.com, "The Best Cities to Become a Real Estate Agent in 2018," January 30, 2018*

- According to Penske Truck Rental, the Dallas* metro area was named the #3 moving destination in 2017, based on one-way consumer truck rental reservations made through Penske's website, rental locations, and reservations call center. *blog.gopenske.com, "Penske Truck Rental's 2017 Top Moving Destinations List," January 22, 2018*

- The Dallas* metro area appeared on Realtor.com's list of the hottest housing markets to watch in 2018. The area ranked #2. Criteria: existing homes inventory and price; new home construction; median household incomes; local economy/population trends. *Realtor.com®, "The 6 Hottest Real Estate Markets to Watch in 2018," January 5, 2018*
- The Dallas* metro area was identified as one of the nations's 20 hottest housing markets in 2018. Criteria: listing views as an indicator of demand and median days on the market as an indicator of supply. The area ranked #12. *Realtor.com, "The 20 Hottest Real Estate Markets for February 2018," March 1, 2018*
- Dallas* was ranked #20 in the top 20 out of 265 metro areas in terms of house price appreciation in 2017 (#1 = highest rate). *Federal Housing Finance Agency, House Price Index, 4th Quarter 2017. February 27, 2018*
- Dallas* was ranked #195 out of 238 metro areas in terms of housing affordability in 2017 by the National Association of Home Builders (#1 = most affordable). Criteria: the share of homes sold in that area affordable to a family earning the local median income, based on standard mortgage underwriting criteria. *National Association of Home Builders®, NAHB-Wells Fargo Housing Opportunity Index, 4th Quarter 2017*

Safety Rankings

- The National Insurance Crime Bureau ranked 382 metro areas in the U.S. in terms of per capita rates of vehicle theft. The Dallas* metro area ranked #87 (#1 = highest rate). Criteria: number of vehicle theft offenses per 100,000 inhabitants in 2016. *National Insurance Crime Bureau, "Hot Spots 2016," June 8, 2017*

Seniors/Retirement Rankings

- From its Best Cities for Successful Aging indexes, the Milken Institute generated rankings for metropolitan areas, weighing data in nine categories—health care, wellness, living arrangements, transportation and convenience, financial characteristics, education, employment, community engagement, and overall livability. The Dallas* metro area was ranked #25 overall in the large metro area category. *Milken Institute, "Best Cities for Successful Aging, 2017" March 14, 2017*

Sports/Recreation Rankings

- According to the personal finance website NerdWallet, the Dallas* metro area, at #1, is one of the nation's top dozen metro areas for sports fans. Criteria included the presence of all four major sports—MLB, NFL, NHL, and NBA, fan enthusiasm (as measured by game attendance), ticket affordability, and "sports culture," that is, number of sports bars. *www.nerdwallet.com, "Best Cities for Sports Fans," May 5, 2013*

Women/Minorities Rankings

- The *Houston Chronicle* listed the Dallas* metro area as #7 in top places for young Latinos to live in the U.S. Research was largely based on housing and occupational data from the largest metropolitan areas performed by *Forbes* and NBC Universo. Criteria: percentage of 18-34 year-olds; Latino college grad rates; and diversity. *blog.chron.com, "The 15 Best Big Cities for Latino Millenials," January 26, 2016*

Miscellaneous Rankings

- Allen was selected as a 2017 Digital Cities Survey winner. The city ranked #7 in the small city (75,000 to 124,999 population) category. The survey examined and assessed how city governments are utilizing technology to improve citizen services, enhance inclusion, and solve social challenges. Survey questions focused on ten characteristics: engaged, mobile, open, secure, staffed/supported, efficient, connected, resilient, best practices, and use of innovation. *Center for Digital Government, "2017 Digital Cities Survey," November 9, 2017*

- The watchdog site Charity Navigator conducts an annual study of charities in the nation's major markets both to analyze statistical differences in their financial, accountability, and transparency practices and to track year-to-year variations in individual philanthropic communities. Charity Navigator's analysis demonstrated that the financial, accountability and transparency behaviors of America's largest charities can be influenced by the metropolitan market within which the charity operates. The Dallas* metro area was ranked #5 among the 30 metro markets in the rating category of Overall Score. *www.charitynavigator.org, "2017 Metro Market Study," May 1, 2017*

- The Harris Poll's Happiness Index survey revealed that of the top ten U.S. markets, the Dallas* metro area residents ranked #1 in happiness. Criteria included strong assent to positive statements and strong disagreement with negative ones, and degree of agreement with a series of statements about respondents' personal relationships and general outlook. *www.theharrispoll.com, "Dallas/Fort Worth Is "Happiest" City among America's Top Ten Markets," September 4, 2013*

- The National Alliance to End Homelessness listed the 25 most populous metro areas with the highest rate of homelessness. The Dallas* metro area had a high rate of homelessness. Criteria: number of homeless people per 10,000 population in 2016. *National Alliance to End Homelessness, "Homelessness in the 25 Most Populous U.S. Metro Areas," September 1, 2017*

*Allen is located within the Dallas-Fort Worth-Arlington, TX Metropolitan Statistical Area and the Dallas-Plano-Irving, TX Metropolitan Division.

Business Environment

CITY FINANCES

City Government Finances

Component	2015 ($000)	2015 ($ per capita)
Total Revenues	150,048	1,529
Total Expenditures	132,571	1,351
Debt Outstanding	157,855	1,608
Cash and Securities[1]	115,027	1,172

Note: (1) Cash and security holdings of a government at the close of its fiscal year,, including those of its dependent agencies, utilities, and liquor stores.
Source: U.S Census Bureau, State & Local Government Finances 2015

City Government Revenue by Source

Source	2015 ($000)	2015 ($ per capita)	2015 (%)
General Revenue			
From Federal Government	0	0	0.0
From State Government	339	3	0.2
From Local Governments	151	2	0.1
Taxes			
Property	46,142	470	30.8
Sales and Gross Receipts	43,805	446	29.2
Personal Income	0	0	0.0
Corporate Income	0	0	0.0
Motor Vehicle License	0	0	0.0
Other Taxes	2,863	29	1.9
Current Charges	34,045	347	22.7
Liquor Store	0	0	0.0
Utility	15,475	158	10.3
Employee Retirement	0	0	0.0

Source: U.S Census Bureau, State & Local Government Finances 2015

City Government Expenditures by Function

Function	2015 ($000)	2015 ($ per capita)	2015 (%)
General Direct Expenditures			
Air Transportation	0	0	0.0
Corrections	0	0	0.0
Education	0	0	0.0
Employment Security Administration	0	0	0.0
Financial Administration	4,818	49	3.6
Fire Protection	12,384	126	9.3
General Public Buildings	1,644	16	1.2
Governmental Administration, Other	3,009	30	2.3
Health	141	1	0.1
Highways	8,418	85	6.3
Hospitals	0	0	0.0
Housing and Community Development	3,778	38	2.8
Interest on General Debt	6,568	66	5.0
Judicial and Legal	686	7	0.5
Libraries	2,486	25	1.9
Parking	0	0	0.0
Parks and Recreation	22,035	224	16.6
Police Protection	16,634	169	12.5
Public Welfare	0	0	0.0
Sewerage	3,736	38	2.8
Solid Waste Management	3,757	38	2.8
Veterans' Services	0	0	0.0
Liquor Store	0	0	0.0
Utility	17,215	175	13.0
Employee Retirement	0	0	0.0

Source: U.S Census Bureau, State & Local Government Finances 2015

DEMOGRAPHICS

Population Growth

Area	1990 Census	2000 Census	2010 Census	2016* Estimate	Population Growth (%) 1990-2016	Population Growth (%) 2010-2016
City	19,208	43,554	84,246	94,710	393.1	12.4
MSA[1]	3,989,294	5,161,544	6,371,773	6,957,123	74.4	9.2
U.S.	248,709,873	281,421,906	308,745,538	318,558,162	28.1	3.2

Note: (1) Figures cover the Dallas-Fort Worth-Arlington, TX Metropolitan Statistical Area—see Appendix B for areas included; (*) 2012-2016 5-year estimated population
Source: U.S. Census Bureau, 1990 Census, Census 2000, Census 2010, 2012-2016 American Community Survey 5-Year Estimates

Household Size

Area	Persons in Household (%) One	Two	Three	Four	Five	Six	Seven or More	Average Household Size
City	14.8	28.4	18.8	24.8	8.6	3.2	1.5	3.10
MSA[1]	24.9	30.8	16.7	15.3	7.5	3.0	1.8	2.80
U.S.	27.7	33.7	15.7	13.1	6.0	2.3	1.5	2.60

Note: (1) Figures cover the Dallas-Fort Worth-Arlington, TX Metropolitan Statistical Area—see Appendix B for areas included
Source: U.S. Census Bureau, 2012-2016 American Community Survey 5-Year Estimates

Race

Area	White Alone[2] (%)	Black Alone[2] (%)	Asian Alone[2] (%)	AIAN[3] Alone[2] (%)	NHOPI[4] Alone[2] (%)	Other Race Alone[2] (%)	Two or More Races (%)
City	70.6	9.8	14.2	0.5	0.0	1.5	3.4
MSA[1]	69.7	15.3	6.1	0.4	0.1	5.5	2.9
U.S.	73.3	12.6	5.2	0.8	0.2	4.8	3.1

Note: (1) Figures cover the Dallas-Fort Worth-Arlington, TX Metropolitan Statistical Area—see Appendix B for areas included; (2) Alone is defined as not being in combination with one or more other races; (3) American Indian and Alaska Native; (4) Native Hawaiian and Other Pacific Islander
Source: U.S. Census Bureau, 2012-2016 American Community Survey 5-Year Estimates

Hispanic or Latino Origin

Area	Total (%)	Mexican (%)	Puerto Rican (%)	Cuban (%)	Other (%)
City	10.6	7.3	1.1	0.2	2.0
MSA[1]	28.2	23.8	0.7	0.2	3.5
U.S.	17.3	11.0	1.7	0.7	4.0

Note: Persons of Hispanic or Latino origin can be of any race; (1) Figures cover the Dallas-Fort Worth-Arlington, TX Metropolitan Statistical Area—see Appendix B for areas included
Source: U.S. Census Bureau, 2012-2016 American Community Survey 5-Year Estimates

Segregation

Type	Segregation Indices[1] 1990	2000	2010	2010 Rank[2]	Percent Change 1990-2000	1990-2010	2000-2010
Black/White	62.8	59.8	56.6	48	-3.1	-6.2	-3.2
Asian/White	41.8	45.6	46.6	19	3.8	4.8	1.0
Hispanic/White	48.8	52.3	50.3	24	3.5	1.5	-2.0

Note: All figures cover the Metropolitan Statistical Area—see Appendix B for areas included; Figures are based on an analysis of 1990, 2000, and 2010 Census Decennial Census tract data by William H. Frey, Brookings Institution and the University of Michigan Social Science Data Analysis Network. In this analysis all racial groups (whites, blacks, and asians) are non-Hispanic members of those races. Hispanics are shown as a separate category; (1) Segregation Indices are Dissimilarity Indices that measure the degree to which the minority group is distributed differently than whites across census tracts. They range from 0 (complete integration) to 100 (complete segregation) where the value indicates the percentage of the minority group that needs to move to be distributed exactly like whites; (2) Ranges from 1 (most segregated) to 102 (least segregated); n/a not available.
Source: www.CensusScope.org

Ancestry

Area	German	Irish	English	American	Italian	Polish	French[2]	Scottish	Dutch
City	14.5	9.7	9.7	5.9	3.2	2.1	2.0	2.1	1.2
MSA[1]	9.8	7.6	7.3	6.6	2.2	1.1	1.9	1.7	0.9
U.S.	14.4	10.4	7.7	6.9	5.4	2.9	2.6	1.7	1.3

Note: Figures are the percentage of the total population reporting a particular ancestry. The nine most commonly reported ancestries in the U.S. are shown. Figures include multiple ancestries (e.g. if a person reported being Irish and Italian, they were included in both columns); (1) Figures cover the Dallas-Fort Worth-Arlington, TX Metropolitan Statistical Area—see Appendix B for areas included; (2) Excludes Basque
Source: U.S. Census Bureau, 2012-2016 American Community Survey 5-Year Estimates

Foreign-Born Population

Area	Percent of Population Born in								
	Any Foreign Country	Asia	Mexico	Europe	Carribean	Central America[2]	South America	Africa	Canada
City	18.3	10.1	2.2	1.7	0.2	0.4	0.5	2.8	0.4
MSA[1]	17.8	4.7	8.8	0.8	0.2	1.3	0.5	1.2	0.2
U.S.	13.2	4.0	3.6	1.5	1.3	1.0	0.9	0.6	0.3

Note: (1) Figures cover the Dallas-Fort Worth-Arlington, TX Metropolitan Statistical Area—see Appendix B for areas included; (2) Excludes Mexico.
Source: U.S. Census Bureau, 2012-2016 American Community Survey 5-Year Estimates

Marital Status

Area	Never Married	Now Married[2]	Separated	Widowed	Divorced
City	26.0	61.5	0.9	2.4	9.1
MSA[1]	31.9	50.5	2.3	4.5	10.9
U.S.	33.0	48.1	2.1	5.9	11.0

Note: Figures are percentages and cover the population 15 years of age and older; (1) Figures cover the Dallas-Fort Worth-Arlington, TX Metropolitan Statistical Area—see Appendix B for areas included; (2) Excludes separated
Source: U.S. Census Bureau, 2012-2016 American Community Survey 5-Year Estimates

Disability Status

Area	All Ages	Under 18 Years Old	18 to 64 Years Old	65 Years and Over
City	6.0	2.6	4.9	30.3
MSA[1]	9.6	3.4	8.2	35.2
U.S.	12.5	4.1	10.3	35.7

Note: Figures show percent of the civilian noninstitutionalized population that reported having a disability. Disability status is determined from six types of difficulty: vision, hearing, cognitive, ambulatory, self-care, and independent living. For children under 5 years old, hearing and vision difficulty are used to determine disability status. For children between the ages of 5 and 14, disability status is determined from hearing, vision, cognitive, ambulatory, and self-care difficulties. For people aged 15 years and older, they are considered to have a disability if they have difficulty with any one of the six difficulty types; Note: (1) Figures cover the Dallas-Fort Worth-Arlington, TX Metropolitan Statistical Area—see Appendix B for areas included
Source: U.S. Census Bureau, 2012-2016 American Community Survey 5-Year Estimates

Age

Area	Percent of Population									Median Age
	Under Age 5	Age 5–19	Age 20–34	Age 35–44	Age 45–54	Age 55–64	Age 65–74	Age 75–84	Age 85+	
City	6.8	25.7	16.5	17.4	16.6	9.7	4.6	2.3	0.5	35.6
MSA[1]	7.2	22.2	21.4	14.4	13.8	10.9	6.2	2.9	1.1	34.5
U.S.	6.2	19.6	20.7	12.7	13.6	12.6	8.3	4.3	1.9	37.7

Note: (1) Figures cover the Dallas-Fort Worth-Arlington, TX Metropolitan Statistical Area—see Appendix B for areas included
Source: U.S. Census Bureau, 2012-2016 American Community Survey 5-Year Estimates

Gender

Area	Males	Females	Males per 100 Females
City	47,398	47,312	100.2
MSA[1]	3,421,036	3,536,087	96.7
U.S.	156,765,322	161,792,840	96.9

Note: (1) Figures cover the Dallas-Fort Worth-Arlington, TX Metropolitan Statistical Area—see Appendix B for areas included
Source: U.S. Census Bureau, 2012-2016 American Community Survey 5-Year Estimates

Religious Groups by Family

Area	Catholic	Baptist	Non-Den.	Methodist[2]	Lutheran	LDS[3]	Pente-costal	Presby-terian[4]	Muslim[5]	Judaism
MSA[1]	13.3	18.7	7.8	5.3	0.8	1.2	2.2	1.0	2.4	0.4
U.S.	19.1	9.3	4.0	4.0	2.3	2.0	1.9	1.6	0.8	0.7

Note: Figures are the number of adherents as a percentage of the total population; (1) Figures cover the Dallas-Fort Worth-Arlington, TX Metropolitan Statistical Area—see Appendix B for areas included; (2) Methodist/Pietist; (3) Latter Day Saints; (4) Reformed; (5) Figures are estimates
Source: Association of Statisticians of American Religious Bodies, 2010 U.S. Religion Census: Religious Congregations & Membership Study

Religious Groups by Tradition

Area	Catholic	Evangelical Protestant	Mainline Protestant	Other Tradition	Black Protestant	Orthodox
MSA[1]	13.3	28.3	7.0	4.8	1.8	0.2
U.S.	19.1	16.2	7.3	4.3	1.6	0.3

Note: Figures are the number of adherents as a percentage of the total population; (1) Figures cover the Dallas-Fort Worth-Arlington, TX Metropolitan Statistical Area—see Appendix B for areas included
Source: Association of Statisticians of American Religious Bodies, 2010 U.S. Religion Census: Religious Congregations & Membership Study

ECONOMY

Gross Metropolitan Product

Area	2014	2015	2016	2017	Rank[2]
MSA[1]	502.3	524.8	545.3	577.5	4

Note: Figures are in billions of dollars; (1) Figures cover the Dallas-Fort Worth-Arlington, TX Metropolitan Statistical Area—see Appendix B for areas included; (2) Rank is based on 2015 data and ranges from 1 to 381
Source: The U.S. Conference of Mayors, U.S. Metro Economies: GMP and Employment Report, 2015-2017

Economic Growth

Area	2012-14 (%)	2015 (%)	2016 (%)	2017 (%)	Rank[2]
MSA[1]	6.7	7.1	2.4	3.4	7
U.S.	2.0	2.4	1.9	2.6	–

Note: Figures are real gross metropolitan product (GMP) growth rates and represent average annual percent change; (1) Figures cover the Dallas-Fort Worth-Arlington, TX Metropolitan Statistical Area—see Appendix B for areas included; (2) Rank is based on 2012-2014 average annual percent change and ranges from 1 to 381
Source: The U.S. Conference of Mayors, U.S. Metro Economies: GMP and Employment Report, 2015-2017

Metropolitan Area Exports

Area	2011	2012	2013	2014	2015	2016	Rank[2]
MSA[1]	26,648.7	27,820.9	27,596.0	28,669.4	27,372.9	27,187.8	9

Note: Figures are in millions of dollars; (1) Figures cover the Dallas-Fort Worth-Arlington, TX Metropolitan Statistical Area—see Appendix B for areas included; (2) Rank is based on 2016 data and ranges from 1 to 385
Source: U.S. Department of Commerce, International Trade Administration, Office of Trade & Industry Information, Manufacturing & Services, data extracted March 15, 2018

Building Permits

Area	Single-Family			Multi-Family			Total		
	2016	2017p	Pct. Chg.	2016	2017p	Pct. Chg.	2016	2017p	Pct. Chg.
City	447	435	-2.7	243	1,044	329.6	690	1,479	114.3
MSA[1]	29,846	34,210	14.6	25,772	27,499	6.7	55,618	61,709	11.0
U.S.	750,800	817,300	8.9	455,800	446,800	-2.0	1,206,600	1,264,100	4.8

Note: (1) Figures cover the Dallas-Fort Worth-Arlington, TX Metropolitan Statistical Area—see Appendix B for areas included; Figures represent new, privately-owned housing units authorized (unadjusted data); All permit data are based on estimates with imputation; (p) preliminary data.
Source: U.S. Census Bureau, Manufacturing, Mining, and Construction Statistics, Building Permits, 2016, 2017

Bankruptcy Filings

Area	Business Filings			Nonbusiness Filings		
	2016	2017	% Chg.	2016	2017	% Chg.
Collin County	135	151	11.9	1,204	1,408	16.9
U.S.	24,114	23,157	-4.0	770,846	765,863	-0.6

Note: Business filings include Chapter 7, Chapter 11, Chapter 12, and Chapter 13; Nonbusiness filings include Chapter 7, Chapter 11, and Chapter 13
Source: Administrative Office of the U.S. Courts, Business and Nonbusiness Bankruptcy, County Cases Commenced by Chapter of the Bankruptcy Code, During the 12-Month Period Ending December 31, 2016 and Business and Nonbusiness Bankruptcy, County Cases Commenced by Chapter of the Bankruptcy Code, During the 12-Month Period Ending December 31, 2017

Housing Vacancy Rates

Area	Gross Vacancy Rate[2] (%)			Year-Round Vacancy Rate[3] (%)			Rental Vacancy Rate[4] (%)			Homeowner Vacancy Rate[5] (%)		
	2015	2016	2017	2015	2016	2017	2015	2016	2017	2015	2016	2017
MSA[1]	8.0	7.9	7.8	7.8	7.7	7.6	8.3	6.8	7.1	1.4	1.4	0.8
U.S.	12.9	12.8	12.7	10.0	9.9	9.9	7.1	6.9	7.2	1.8	1.7	1.6

Note: (1) Figures cover the Dallas-Fort Worth-Arlington, TX Metropolitan Statistical Area—see Appendix B for areas included; (2) The percentage of the total housing inventory that is vacant; (3) The percentage of the housing inventory (excluding seasonal units) that is year-round vacant; (4) The percentage of rental inventory that is vacant for rent; (5) The percentage of homeowner inventory that is vacant for sale
Source: U.S. Census Bureau, Housing Vacancies and Homeownership Annual Statistics: 2015, 2016, 2017

INCOME

Income

Area	Per Capita ($)	Median Household ($)	Average Household ($)
City	40,563	102,215	122,963
MSA[1]	31,143	61,330	85,693
U.S.	29,829	55,322	77,866

Note: (1) Figures cover the Dallas-Fort Worth-Arlington, TX Metropolitan Statistical Area—see Appendix B for areas included
Source: U.S. Census Bureau, 2012-2016 American Community Survey 5-Year Estimates

Household Income Distribution

Area	Percent of Households Earning							
	Under $15,000	$15,000 -$24,999	$25,000 -$34,999	$35,000 -$49,999	$50,000 -$74,999	$75,000 -$99,999	$100,000 -$149,999	$150,000 and up
City	3.1	3.2	5.2	8.8	15.2	12.6	24.2	27.8
MSA[1]	9.5	8.9	9.5	13.0	18.2	12.4	15.1	13.4
U.S.	12.1	10.2	9.9	13.2	17.8	12.2	13.5	11.1

Note: (1) Figures cover the Dallas-Fort Worth-Arlington, TX Metropolitan Statistical Area—see Appendix B for areas included
Source: U.S. Census Bureau, 2012-2016 American Community Survey 5-Year Estimates

Poverty Rate

Area	All Ages	Under 18 Years Old	18 to 64 Years Old	65 Years and Over
City	5.1	6.9	4.8	1.2
MSA[1]	14.0	20.3	12.3	8.5
U.S.	15.1	21.2	14.2	9.3

Note: Figures are percentage of people whose income during the past 12 months was below the poverty level; (1) Figures cover the Dallas-Fort Worth-Arlington, TX Metropolitan Statistical Area—see Appendix B for areas included
Source: U.S. Census Bureau, 2012-2016 American Community Survey 5-Year Estimates

EMPLOYMENT

Labor Force and Employment

Area	Civilian Labor Force			Workers Employed		
	Dec. 2016	Dec. 2017	% Chg.	Dec. 2016	Dec. 2017	% Chg.
City	54,579	56,018	2.6	52,825	54,349	2.9
MD[1]	2,526,544	2,585,893	2.3	2,434,063	2,504,449	2.9
U.S.	158,968,000	159,880,000	0.6	151,798,000	153,602,000	1.2

Note: Data is not seasonally adjusted and covers workers 16 years of age and older; (1) Figures cover the Dallas-Plano-Irving, TX Metropolitan Division—see Appendix B for areas included
Source: Bureau of Labor Statistics, Local Area Unemployment Statistics

Unemployment Rate

Area	2017											
	Jan.	Feb.	Mar.	Apr.	May	Jun.	Jul.	Aug.	Sep.	Oct.	Nov.	Dec.
City	3.5	3.7	3.5	3.3	3.3	3.5	3.4	3.5	3.1	3.0	3.1	3.0
MD[1]	4.0	4.1	3.9	3.5	3.6	3.9	3.8	3.8	3.4	3.2	3.2	3.1
U.S.	5.1	4.9	4.6	4.1	4.1	4.5	4.6	4.5	4.1	3.9	3.9	3.9

Note: Data is not seasonally adjusted and covers workers 16 years of age and older; (1) Figures cover the Dallas-Plano-Irving, TX Metropolitan Division—see Appendix B for areas included
Source: Bureau of Labor Statistics, Local Area Unemployment Statistics

Average Wages

Occupation	$/Hr.	Occupation	$/Hr.
Accountants and Auditors	39.90	Maids and Housekeeping Cleaners	10.20
Automotive Mechanics	20.50	Maintenance and Repair Workers	18.80
Bookkeepers	21.60	Marketing Managers	68.60
Carpenters	18.80	Nuclear Medicine Technologists	38.30
Cashiers	10.10	Nurses, Licensed Practical	23.10
Clerks, General Office	17.20	Nurses, Registered	35.80
Clerks, Receptionists/Information	13.60	Nursing Assistants	12.90
Clerks, Shipping/Receiving	14.70	Packers and Packagers, Hand	11.50
Computer Programmers	41.60	Physical Therapists	46.50
Computer Systems Analysts	47.10	Postal Service Mail Carriers	24.50
Computer User Support Specialists	25.80	Real Estate Brokers	38.70
Cooks, Restaurant	13.10	Retail Salespersons	12.90
Dentists	83.10	Sales Reps., Exc. Tech./Scientific	35.50
Electrical Engineers	50.70	Sales Reps., Tech./Scientific	46.30
Electricians	22.40	Secretaries, Exc. Legal/Med./Exec.	18.50
Financial Managers	75.80	Security Guards	14.50
First-Line Supervisors/Managers, Sales	22.60	Surgeons	95.40
Food Preparation Workers	10.80	Teacher Assistants*	12.40
General and Operations Managers	70.00	Teachers, Elementary School*	29.00
Hairdressers/Cosmetologists	12.60	Teachers, Secondary School*	30.00
Internists, General	56.10	Telemarketers	14.70
Janitors and Cleaners	11.60	Truck Drivers, Heavy/Tractor-Trailer	22.60
Landscaping/Groundskeeping Workers	13.90	Truck Drivers, Light/Delivery Svcs.	18.40
Lawyers	74.30	Waiters and Waitresses	13.50

Note: Wage data covers the Dallas-Plano-Irving, TX Metropolitan Division—see Appendix B for areas included; (*) Hourly wages for elementary/secondary school teachers and teacher assistants were calculated by the editors from annual wage data based on a 40 hour work week; n/a not available.
Source: Bureau of Labor Statistics, Metro Area Occupational Employment & Wage Estimates, May 2017

Employment by Occupation

Occupation Classification	City (%)	MSA[1] (%)	U.S. (%)
Management, Business, Science, and Arts	54.9	38.2	37.0
Natural Resources, Construction, and Maintenance	4.3	9.3	8.9
Production, Transportation, and Material Moving	5.4	11.6	12.2
Sales and Office	24.4	24.9	23.8
Service	11.0	15.9	18.1

Note: Figures cover employed civilians 16 years of age and older; (1) Figures cover the Dallas-Fort Worth-Arlington, TX Metropolitan Statistical Area—see Appendix B for areas included
Source: U.S. Census Bureau, 2012-2016 American Community Survey 5-Year Estimates

Employment by Industry

Sector	MD[1] Number of Employees	MD[1] Percent of Total	U.S. Percent of Total
Construction, Mining, and Logging	141,400	5.4	5.2
Education and Health Services	313,000	12.0	15.9
Financial Activities	235,200	9.0	5.7
Government	304,800	11.6	15.3
Information	72,900	2.8	1.9
Leisure and Hospitality	262,800	10.0	10.7
Manufacturing	179,300	6.8	8.5
Other Services	85,200	3.3	3.9
Professional and Business Services	488,500	18.7	14.0
Retail Trade	266,600	10.2	11.0
Transportation, Warehousing, and Utilities	121,000	4.6	4.1
Wholesale Trade	147,700	5.6	4.0

Note: Figures are non-farm employment as of December 2017. Figures are not seasonally adjusted and include workers 16 years of age and older; (1) Figures cover the Dallas-Plano-Irving, TX Metropolitan Division—see Appendix B for areas included

Source: Bureau of Labor Statistics, Current Employment Statistics, Employment, Hours, and Earnings

Occupations with Greatest Projected Employment Growth: 2017 – 2019

Occupation[1]	2017 Employment	2019 Projected Employment	Numeric Employment Change	Percent Employment Change
Combined Food Preparation and Serving Workers, Including Fast Food	335,660	354,370	18,710	5.6
Personal Care Aides	212,280	230,990	18,710	8.8
Retail Salespersons	393,950	406,100	12,150	3.1
Customer Service Representatives	261,530	273,600	12,070	4.6
Janitors and Cleaners, Except Maids and Housekeeping Cleaners	180,710	192,060	11,350	6.3
Laborers and Freight, Stock, and Material Movers, Hand	185,140	196,200	11,060	6.0
Registered Nurses	214,500	224,450	9,950	4.6
Office Clerks, General	379,860	389,540	9,680	2.6
Heavy and Tractor-Trailer Truck Drivers	192,710	201,560	8,850	4.6
Waiters and Waitresses	222,630	231,020	8,390	3.8

Note: Projections cover Texas; (1) Sorted by numeric employment change

Source: www.projectionscentral.com, State Occupational Projections, 2017–2019 Short-Term Projections

Fastest Growing Occupations: 2017 – 2019

Occupation[1]	2017 Employment	2019 Projected Employment	Numeric Employment Change	Percent Employment Change
Wind Turbine Service Technicians	1,740	2,090	350	20.7
Home Health Aides	72,760	80,000	7,240	10.0
Security and Fire Alarm Systems Installers	8,190	8,930	740	8.9
Personal Care Aides	212,280	230,990	18,710	8.8
Statisticians	1,760	1,910	150	8.2
Tree Trimmers and Pruners	5,980	6,480	500	8.2
Physician Assistants	6,860	7,400	540	7.9
Nurse Practitioners	9,230	9,950	720	7.7
Elevator Installers and Repairers	2,190	2,350	160	7.4
Helpers—Roofers	800	850	50	7.4

Note: Projections cover Texas; (1) Sorted by percent employment change and excludes occupations with numeric employment change less than 50

Source: www.projectionscentral.com, State Occupational Projections, 2017–2019 Short-Term Projections

TAXES

State Corporate Income Tax Rates

State	Tax Rate (%)	Income Brackets ($)	Num. of Brackets	Financial Institution Tax Rate (%)[a]	Federal Income Tax Ded.
Texas	(w)	–	–	(w)	No

Note: Tax rates as of January 1, 2018; (a) Rates listed are the corporate income tax rate applied to financial institutions or excise taxes based on income. Some states have other taxes based upon the value of deposits or shares; (w) Texas imposes a Franchise Tax, otherwise known as margin tax, imposed on entities with more than $1,110,000 total revenues at rate of 0.75%, or 0.375% for entities primarily engaged in retail or wholesale trade, on lesser of 70% of total revenues or 100% of gross receipts after deductions for either compensation or cost of goods sold.
Source: Federation of Tax Administrators, Range of State Corporate Income Tax Rates, January 1, 2018

State Individual Income Tax Rates

State	Tax Rate (%)	Income Brackets ($)	Num. of Brackets	Personal Exempt. ($)[1] Single	Personal Exempt. ($)[1] Dependents	Fed. Inc. Tax Ded.
Texas	None	–	–	–	–	–

Note: Tax rates as of January 1, 2018; Local- and county-level taxes are not included; n/a not applicable; (1) Married joint filers generally receive double the single exemption
Source: Federation of Tax Administrators, State Individual Income Tax Rates, January 1, 2018

Various State Sales and Excise Tax Rates

State	State Sales Tax (%)	Gasoline[1] (¢/gal.)	Cigarette[2] ($/pack)	Spirits[3] ($/gal.)	Wine[4] ($/gal.)	Beer[5] ($/gal.)	Recreational Marijuana (%)
Texas	6.25	20.0	1.41	2.40 (f)	0.20 (l)	0.20 (q)	Not legal

Note: All tax rates as of January 1, 2018; (1) The American Petroleum Institute has developed a methodology for determining the average tax rate on a gallon of fuel. Rates may include any of the following: excise taxes, environmental fees, storage tank fees, other fees or taxes, general sales tax, and local taxes. In states where gasoline is subject to the general sales tax, or where the fuel tax is based on the average sale price, the average rate determined by API is sensitive to changes in the price of gasoline. States that fully or partially apply general sales taxes to gasoline: CA, CO, GA, IL, IN, MI, NY; (2) The federal excise tax of $1.0066 per pack and local taxes are not included; (3) Rates are those applicable to off-premise sales of 40% alcohol by volume (a.b.v.) distilled spirits in 750ml containers. Local excise taxes are excluded; (4) Rates are those applicable to off-premise sales of 11% a.b.v. non-carbonated wine in 750ml containers; (5) Rates are those applicable to off-premise sales of 4.7% a.b.v. beer in 12 ounce containers; (f) Different rates also applicable according to alcohol content, place of production, size of container, or place purchased (on- or off-premise or onboard airlines); (l) Different rates also applicable to alcohol content, place of production, size of container, place purchased (on- or off-premise or on board airlines) or type of wine (carbonated, vermouth, etc.); (q) Different rates also applicable according to alcohol content, place of production, size of container, or place purchased (on- or off-premise or onboard airlines).
Source: Tax Foundation, 2018 Facts & Figures: How Does Your State Compare?

State Business Tax Climate Index Rankings

State	Overall Rank	Corporate Tax Rank	Individual Income Tax Rank	Sales Tax Rank	Unemployment Insurance Tax Rank	Property Tax Rank
Texas	13	49	6	37	26	37

Note: The index is a measure of how each state's tax laws affect economic performance. The lower the rank, the more favorable a state's tax system is for business. States without a given tax are given a ranking of 1. The scores/rankings for the District of Columbia do not affect other states. The 2018 index represents the tax climate as of July 1, 2017.
Source: Tax Foundation, State Business Tax Climate Index 2018

TRANSPORTATION

Means of Transportation to Work

Area	Car/Truck/Van: Drove Alone	Car/Truck/Van: Car-pooled	Public Transportation: Bus	Public Transportation: Subway	Public Transportation: Railroad	Bicycle	Walked	Other Means	Worked at Home
City	81.6	7.0	0.1	0.4	0.9	0.0	0.9	1.1	7.9
MSA[1]	80.7	9.9	1.0	0.2	0.3	0.2	1.2	1.5	5.0
U.S.	76.4	9.3	2.6	1.9	0.6	0.6	2.8	1.3	4.6

Note: Figures are percentages and cover workers 16 years of age and older; (1) Figures cover the Dallas-Fort Worth-Arlington, TX Metropolitan Statistical Area—see Appendix B for areas included
Source: U.S. Census Bureau, 2012-2016 American Community Survey 5-Year Estimates

Travel Time to Work

Area	Less Than 10 Minutes	10 to 19 Minutes	20 to 29 Minutes	30 to 44 Minutes	45 to 59 Minutes	60 to 89 Minutes	90 Minutes or More
City	10.9	23.3	23.8	22.8	11.1	7.2	0.9
MSA[1]	9.4	25.8	21.1	25.0	10.3	6.3	2.0
U.S.	12.9	29.2	20.9	20.4	8.0	6.0	2.7

Note: Note: Figures are percentages and include workers 16 years old and over; (1) Figures cover the Dallas-Fort Worth-Arlington, TX Metropolitan Statistical Area—see Appendix B for areas included
Source: U.S. Census Bureau, 2012-2016 American Community Survey 5-Year Estimates

Freeway Travel Time Index

Area	1985	1990	1995	2000	2005	2010	2014
Urban Area Rank[1,2]	6	9	10	19	21	22	19
Urban Area Index[1]	1.19	1.20	1.23	1.24	1.26	1.24	1.27
Average Index[3]	1.09	1.11	1.14	1.17	1.20	1.19	1.20

Note: Freeway Travel Time Index—the ratio of travel time in the peak period to the travel time at free-flow conditions. For example, a value of 1.30 indicates a 20-minute free-flow trip takes 26 minutes in the peak (20 minutes x 1.30 = 26 minutes); (1) Covers the Dallas-Fort Worth-Arlington TX urban area; (2) Rank is based on 101 urban areas (#1 = highest travel time index); (3) Average of 101 urban areas
Source: Texas Transportation Institute, 2015 Urban Mobility Scorecard, August 2015

Freeway Commuter Stress Index

Area	1985	1990	1995	2000	2005	2010	2014
Urban Area Rank[1,2]	12	15	13	20	22	25	20
Urban Area Index[1]	1.25	1.26	1.29	1.30	1.32	1.30	1.33
Average Index[3]	1.13	1.16	1.19	1.22	1.25	1.24	1.25

Note: The Freeway Commuter Stress Index is the same as the Freeway Travel Time Index (see table above) except that it includes only the travel in the peak directions during the peak periods; the TTI includes travel in all directions during the peak period. Thus, the CSI is more indicative of the work trip experienced by each commuter on a daily basis; (1) Covers the Dallas-Fort Worth-Arlington TX urban area; (2) Rank is based on 101 urban areas (#1 = highest travel time index); (3) Average of 101 urban areas
Source: Texas Transportation Institute, 2015 Urban Mobility Scorecard, August 2015

Living Environment

COST OF LIVING

Cost of Living Index

Composite Index	Groceries	Housing	Utilities	Trans- portation	Health Care	Misc. Goods/ Services
107.2	99.6	120.8	97.9	103.9	85.0	105.6

Note: The Cost of Living Index measures regional differences in the cost of consumer goods and services, excluding taxes and non-consumer expenditures, for professional and managerial households in the top income quintile. It is based on more than 50,000 prices covering almost 60 different items for which prices are collected three times a year by chambers of commerce, economic development organizations or university applied economic centers in each participating urban area. The numbers shown should be read as a percentage above or below the national average of 100. For example, a value of 115.4 in the groceries column indicates that grocery prices are 15.4% higher than the national average. Small differences in the index numbers should not be interpreted as significant; Figures cover the Plano TX urban area.
Source: The Council for Community and Economic Research, ACCRA Cost of Living Index, 2017

Grocery Prices

Area[1]	T-Bone Steak ($/pound)	Frying Chicken ($/pound)	Whole Milk ($/half gal.)	Eggs ($/dozen)	Orange Juice ($/64 oz.)	Coffee ($/11.5 oz.)
City[2]	11.99	1.19	1.82	1.82	3.99	4.43
Avg.	11.29	1.40	2.02	1.47	3.55	4.37
Min.	7.71	0.93	1.04	0.70	2.86	3.24
Max.	15.83	2.39	4.03	3.92	6.29	8.16

*Note: (1) Values for the local area are compared with the average, minimum and maximum values for all 294 areas in the Cost of Living Index; (2) Figures cover the Plano TX urban area; **T-Bone Steak** (price per pound); **Frying Chicken** (price per pound, whole fryer); **Whole Milk** (half gallon carton); **Eggs** (price per dozen, Grade A, large); **Orange Juice** (64 oz. Tropicana or Florida Natural); **Coffee** (11.5 oz. can, vacuum-packed, Maxwell House, Hills Bros, or Folgers).*
Source: The Council for Community and Economic Research, ACCRA Cost of Living Index, 2017

Housing and Utility Costs

Area[1]	New Home Price ($)	Apartment Rent ($/month)	All Electric ($/month)	Part Electric ($/month)	Other Energy ($/month)	Telephone ($/month)
City[2]	387,838	1,300	-	110.21	55.03	27.72
Avg.	335,956	1,047	175.01	97.34	67.93	28.71
Min.	187,788	491	109.48	49.33	35.44	12.39
Max.	1,739,087	4,559	432.62	227.09	353.33	44.61

*Note: (1) Values for the local area are compared with the average, minimum and maximum values for all 294 areas in the Cost of Living Index; (2) Figures cover the Plano TX urban area; **New Home Price** (2,400 sf living area, 8,000 sf lot, in urban area with full utilities); **Apartment Rent** (950 sf 2 bedroom/1.5 or 2 bath, unfurnished, excluding all utilities except water); **All Electric** (average monthly cost for an all-electric home); **Part Electric** (average monthly cost for a part-electric home); **Other Energy** (average monthly cost for natural gas, fuel oil, coal, wood, and any other forms of energy except electricity); **Telephone** (price includes basic monthly rate for a private residential line plus additional local usage charges incurred by a family of four).*
Source: The Council for Community and Economic Research, ACCRA Cost of Living Index, 2017

Health Care, Transportation, and Other Costs

Area[1]	Doctor ($/visit)	Dentist ($/visit)	Optometrist ($/visit)	Gasoline ($/gallon)	Beauty Salon ($/visit)	Men's Shirt ($)
City[2]	80.02	73.81	108.39	2.18	48.10	29.06
Avg.	108.00	92.54	101.93	2.25	37.58	30.92
Min.	30.39	60.00	49.75	1.82	16.11	11.20
Max.	193.50	161.94	229.28	3.16	77.35	59.13

*Note: (1) Values for the local area are compared with the average, minimum and maximum values for all 294 areas in the Cost of Living Index; (2) Figures cover the Plano TX urban area; **Doctor** (general practitioners routine exam of an established patient); **Dentist** (adult teeth cleaning and periodic oral examination); **Optometrist** (full vision eye exam for established adult patient); **Gasoline** (one gallon regular unleaded, national brand, including all taxes, cash price at self-service pump if available); **Beauty Salon** (woman's shampoo, trim, and blow-dry); **Men's Shirt** (cotton/polyester dress shirt, pinpoint weave, long sleeves).*
Source: The Council for Community and Economic Research, ACCRA Cost of Living Index, 2017

HOUSING

House Price Index (HPI)

Area	National Ranking[2]	Quarterly Change (%)	One-Year Change (%)	Five-Year Change (%)
MD[1]	20	1.01	10.57	57.15
U.S.[3]	–	1.61	6.68	34.71

Note: The HPI is a weighted repeat sales index. It measures average price changes in repeat sales or refinancings on the same properties. This information is obtained by reviewing repeat mortgage transactions on single-family properties whose mortgages have been purchased or securitized by Fannie Mae or Freddie Mac in January 1975; (1) Figures cover the Dallas-Plano-Irving, TX Metropolitan Division—see Appendix B for areas included; (2) Rankings are based on annual percentage change for all metro areas containing at least 15,000 transactions over the last 10 years and ranges from 1 to 253; (3) figures based on a weighted average of Census Division estimates using a seasonally adjusted, purchase-only index; all figures are for the period ending December 31, 2017
Source: Federal Housing Finance Agency, House Price Index, February 28, 2018

Median Single-Family Home Prices

Area	2015	2016	2017[p]	Percent Change 2016 to 2017
MSA[1]	207.2	227.1	247.4	8.9
U.S. Average	223.9	235.5	248.8	5.6

Note: Figures are median sales prices of existing single-family homes in thousands of dollars; (p) preliminary; (1) Figures cover the Dallas-Fort Worth-Arlington, TX Metropolitan Statistical Area—see Appendix B for areas included
Source: National Association of Realtors, Median Sales Price of Existing Single-Family Homes for Metropolitan Areas, 4th Quarter 2017

Qualifying Income Based on Median Sales Price of Existing Single-Family Homes

Area	With 5% Down ($)	With 10% Down ($)	With 20% Down ($)
MSA[1]	55,203	52,298	46,487
U.S. Average	55,585	52,659	46,808

Note: Figures are preliminary; Qualifying income is based on a mortgage rate of 4.17%. Monthly principal and interest payment is limited to 25% of income; (1) Figures cover the Dallas-Fort Worth-Arlington, TX Metropolitan Statistical Area—see Appendix B for areas included
Source: National Association of Realtors, Qualifying Income Based on Median Sales Price of Existing Single-Family Homes for Metropolitan Areas, 4th Quarter 2017

Median Apartment Condo-Coop Home Prices

Area	2015	2016	2017[p]	Percent Change 2016 to 2017
MSA[1]	148.7	167.7	185.7	10.7
U.S. Average	210.7	220.7	234.3	6.2

Note: Figures are median sales prices of existing apartment condo-coop homes in thousands of dollars; (p) preliminary; (1) Figures cover the Dallas-Fort Worth-Arlington, TX Metropolitan Statistical Area—see Appendix B for areas included
Source: National Association of Realtors, Median Sales Price of Existing Apartment Condo-Coop Homes for Metropolitan Areas, 4th Quarter 2017

Home Value Distribution

Area	Under $50,000	$50,000 -$99,999	$100,000 -$149,999	$150,000 -$199,999	$200,000 -$299,999	$300,000 -$499,999	$500,000 -$999,999	$1,000,000 or more
City	1.1	3.5	12.1	21.3	30.2	24.2	7.0	0.8
MSA[1]	6.4	17.3	20.6	17.5	18.4	13.4	4.9	1.5
U.S.	8.8	14.8	15.3	14.9	18.4	16.4	9.0	2.5

Note: Figures are percentages and cover owner-occupied housing units; (1) Figures cover the Dallas-Fort Worth-Arlington, TX Metropolitan Statistical Area—see Appendix B for areas included
Source: U.S. Census Bureau, 2012-2016 American Community Survey 5-Year Estimates

Homeownership Rate

Area	2009 (%)	2010 (%)	2011 (%)	2012 (%)	2013 (%)	2014 (%)	2015 (%)	2016 (%)	2017 (%)
MSA[1]	61.6	63.8	62.6	61.8	59.9	57.7	57.8	59.7	61.8
U.S.	67.4	66.9	66.1	65.4	65.1	64.5	63.7	63.4	63.9

Note: (1) Figures cover the Dallas-Fort Worth-Arlington, TX Metropolitan Statistical Area—see Appendix B for areas included
Source: U.S. Census Bureau, Housing Vacancies and Homeownership Annual Statistics: 2009-2017

Year Housing Structure Built

Area	2010 or Later	2000 -2009	1990 -1999	1980 -1989	1970 -1979	1960 -1969	1950 -1959	1940 -1949	Before 1940	Median Year
City	9.7	40.1	26.3	13.7	7.3	1.4	0.9	0.3	0.3	2000
MSA[1]	4.5	22.2	16.8	19.1	14.9	9.0	7.7	2.9	2.9	1987
U.S.	2.3	14.7	14.0	13.7	15.6	10.9	10.6	5.2	13.0	1977

Note: Figures are percentages except for Median Year; Note: (1) Figures cover the Dallas-Fort Worth-Arlington, TX Metropolitan Statistical Area—see Appendix B for areas included
Source: U.S. Census Bureau, 2012-2016 American Community Survey 5-Year Estimates

Gross Monthly Rent

Area	Under $500	$500 -$999	$1,000 -$1,499	$1,500 -$1,999	$2,000 -$2,499	$2,500 -$2,999	$3,000 and up	Median ($)
City	1.4	18.1	49.1	19.1	8.4	2.5	1.5	1,299
MSA[1]	4.6	49.0	32.4	10.0	2.5	0.8	0.7	969
U.S.	11.3	43.3	27.7	10.7	4.0	1.6	1.5	949

Note: Figures are percentages except for Median; Gross rent is the contract rent plus the estimated average monthly cost of utilities (electricity, gas, and water and sewer) and fuels (oil, coal, kerosene, wood, etc.) if these are paid by the renter (or paid for the renter by someone else); (1) Figures cover the Dallas-Fort Worth-Arlington, TX Metropolitan Statistical Area—see Appendix B for areas included
Source: U.S. Census Bureau, 2012-2016 American Community Survey 5-Year Estimates

HEALTH

Health Risk Factors

Category	MD[1] (%)	U.S. (%)
Adults aged 18–64 who have any kind of health care coverage	79.8	87.7
Adults who reported being in good or excellent health	86.4	83.6
Adults who are current smokers	13.2	17.1
Adults who currently use E-cigarettes	5.3	4.7
Adults who currently use chewing tobacco, snuff, or snus	3.3	4.0
Adults who are heavy drinkers[2]	5.8	6.5
Adults who are binge drinkers[3]	15.0	16.9
Adults who are overweight (BMI 25.0 - 29.9)	34.7	35.3
Adults who are obese (BMI 30.0 - 99.8)	34.6	29.9
Adults who participated in any physical activities in the past month	77.4	76.9
Adults who always or nearly always wears a seat belt	96.2	94.3

Note: (1) Figures cover the Dallas-Plano-Irving, TX Metropolitan Division—see Appendix B for areas included; (2) Heavy drinkers are classified as adult men having more than 14 drinks per week and adult women having more than 7 drinks per week; (3) Binge drinkers are classified as males having five or more drinks on one occasion or females having four or more drinks on one occasion
Source: Centers for Disease Control and Prevention, Behaviorial Risk Factor Surveillance System, SMART: Selected Metropolitan Area Risk Trends, 2016

Health Screening Rates

Category	MD[1] (%)	U.S. (%)
Adults 50-75 who have had a blood stool test within the past year	n/a	8.0
Adults 50-75 who have had a colonoscopy in the past 10 years	60.9	63.5
Adults aged 65+ who have had flu shot within the past year	61.1	58.6
Adults aged 65+ who have ever had a pneumonia vaccination	72.6	73.4
Adults who have ever been tested for HIV	41.3	35.6
Women aged 21-65 who have had a pap test in the past three years	72.4	79.8
Men aged 40+ who have had a PSA test within the past two years	42.0	39.5
Women aged 40+ who have had a mammogram within the past two years	58.5	72.5

Note: n/a not available; (1) Figures cover the Dallas-Plano-Irving, TX Metropolitan Division—see Appendix B for areas included; Source: Centers for Disease Control and Prevention, Behaviorial Risk Factor Surveillance System, SMART: Selected Metropolitan Area Risk Trends, 2016

Chronic Health Conditions

Category	MD[1] (%)	U.S. (%)
Adults who have ever been told they had a heart attack	2.5	4.4
Adults who have ever been told they have angina or coronary heart disease	2.6	4.1
Adults who have ever been told they had a stroke	n/a	3.1
Adults who have been told they currently have asthma	6.4	9.3
Adults who have ever been told they have arthritis	20.7	25.8
Adults who have ever been told they have diabetes[2]	8.8	10.5
Adults who have ever been told they had skin cancer	6.0	5.9
Adults who have ever been told they had any other types of cancer	6.7	6.7
Adults who have ever been told they have COPD	3.1	6.3
Adults who have ever been told they have kidney disease	n/a	2.8
Adults who have ever been told they have a form of depression	11.7	17.4

Note: n/a not available; (1) Figures cover the Dallas-Plano-Irving, TX Metropolitan Division—see Appendix B for areas included; (2) Figures do not include pregnancy-related, borderline, or pre-diabetes
Source: Centers for Disease Control and Prevention, Behaviorial Risk Factor Surveillance System, SMART: Selected Metropolitan Area Risk Trends, 2016

Mortality Rates for the Top 10 Causes of Death in the U.S.

ICD-10[a] Sub-Chapter	ICD-10[a] Code	Age-Adjusted Mortality Rate[1] per 100,000 population	
		County[2]	U.S.
Malignant neoplasms	C00-C97	122.7	158.5
Ischaemic heart diseases	I20-I25	69.2	96.8
Other forms of heart disease	I30-I51	42.2	52.4
Chronic lower respiratory diseases	J40-J47	29.9	40.9
Cerebrovascular diseases	I60-I69	35.7	37.2
Organic, including symptomatic, mental disorders	F01-F09	37.4	33.3
Other degenerative diseases of the nervous system	G30-G31	45.2	32.1
Other external causes of accidental injury	W00-X59	22.3	31.2
Diabetes mellitus	E10-E14	8.7	21.1
Hypertensive diseases	I10-I15	11.5	20.8

Note: (a) ICD-10 = International Classification of Diseases 10th Revision; (1) Mortality rates are a three year average covering 2014-2016; (2) Figures cover Collin County.
Source: Centers for Disease Control and Prevention, National Center for Health Statistics. Underlying Cause of Death 1999-2016 on CDC WONDER Online Database, released December 2017

Mortality Rates for Selected Causes of Death

ICD-10[a] Sub-Chapter	ICD-10[a] Code	Age-Adjusted Mortality Rate[1] per 100,000 population	
		County[2]	U.S.
Assault	X85-Y09	2.2	5.6
Diseases of the liver	K70-K76	8.5	14.0
Human immunodeficiency virus (HIV) disease	B20-B24	0.7	1.9
Influenza and pneumonia	J09-J18	9.5	14.6
Intentional self-harm	X60-X84	10.2	13.2
Malnutrition	E40-E46	1.1	1.3
Obesity and other hyperalimentation	E65-E68	1.2	2.1
Renal failure	N17-N19	12.1	13.0
Transport accidents	V01-V99	6.9	12.0
Viral hepatitis	B15-B19	Unreliable	1.9

Note: (a) ICD-10 = International Classification of Diseases 10th Revision; (1) Mortality rates are a three year average covering 2014-2016; (2) Figures cover Collin County; Data are Suppressed when the data meet the criteria for confidentiality constraints; Mortality rates are flagged as Unreliable when the rate would be calculated with a numerator of 20 or less.
Source: Centers for Disease Control and Prevention, National Center for Health Statistics. Underlying Cause of Death 1999-2016 on CDC WONDER Online Database, released December 2017

Health Insurance Coverage

Area	With Health Insurance	With Private Health Insurance	With Public Health Insurance	Without Health Insurance	Population Under Age 18 Without Health Insurance
City	90.2	81.5	14.8	9.8	6.6
MSA[1]	81.5	63.6	25.2	18.5	10.8
U.S.	88.3	66.7	33.0	11.7	5.9

Note: Figures are percentages that cover the civilian noninstitutionalized population; (1) Figures cover the Dallas-Fort Worth-Arlington, TX Metropolitan Statistical Area—see Appendix B for areas included
Source: U.S. Census Bureau, 2012-2016 American Community Survey 5-Year Estimates

Number of Medical Professionals

Area	MDs[3]	DOs[3,4]	Dentists	Podiatrists	Chiropractors	Optometrists
County[1] (number)	2,455	171	627	38	303	154
County[1] (rate[2])	268.4	18.7	66.5	4.0	32.2	16.3
U.S. (rate[2])	276.5	22.3	67.3	6.0	26.7	15.9

Note: Data as of 2016 unless noted; (1) Data covers Collin County; (2) Rate per 100,000 population; (3) Data as of 2015 and includes all active, non-federal physicians; (4) Doctor of Osteopathic Medicine
Source: U.S. Department of Health and Human Services, Health Resources and Services Administration, Bureau of Health Professions, Area Resource File (ARF) 2016-2017

Best Hospitals

According to *U.S. News,* the Dallas-Plano-Irving, TX metro area is home to three of the best hospitals in the U.S.: **Baylor University Medical Center** (2 adult specialties); **Medical City Dallas Hospital** (1 adult specialty); **UT Southwestern Medical Center** (6 adult specialties). The hospitals listed were nationally ranked in at least one of 16 specialties. Only 152 hospitals nationwide were nationally ranked in one or more specialties. Twenty hospitals in the U.S. made the Honor Roll. The Best Hospitals Honor Roll was revamped last year to take both the national rankings and the procedure and condition ratings into account. Hospitals received points if they were nationally ranked in one of the 16 specialties—the higher they ranked, the more points they got—and how many ratings of "high performing" they earned in the nine procedures and conditions. *U.S. News Online, "America's Best Hospitals 2017-18"*

According to *U.S. News,* the Dallas-Plano-Irving, TX metro area is home to two of the best children's hospitals in the U.S.: **Children's Medical Center Dallas** (9 pediatric specialties); **Texas Scottish Rite Hospital for Children** (1 pediatric specialty). The hospitals listed were highly ranked in at least one of 10 pediatric specialties. Eighty-two children's hospitals in the U.S. were nationally ranked in at least one specialty. Hospitals received points for being ranked in a specialty, and the 10 hospitals with the most points across the 10 specialties make up the Honor Roll. *U.S. News Online, "America's Best Children's Hospitals 2017-18"*

EDUCATION

Public School District Statistics

District Name	Schls	Pupils	Pupil/ Teacher Ratio	Minority Pupils[1] (%)	Free Lunch Eligible[2] (%)	IEP[3] (%)
Allen ISD	24	20,822	15.9	46.9	11.8	10.4
Lovejoy ISD	8	3,946	14.0	20.7	2.2	7.3
Plano ISD	86	54,570	14.0	62.5	23.9	10.6

Note: Table includes school districts with 100 or more students; (1) Percentage of students that are not non-Hispanic white; (2) Percentage of students that are eligible for the free lunch program; (3) Percentage of students that have an Individualized Education Program.
Source: U.S. Department of Education, National Center for Education Statistics, Common Core of Data, Local Education Agency (School District) Universe Survey: School Year 2015-2016; U.S. Department of Education, National Center for Education Statistics, Common Core of Data, Public Elementary/Secondary School Universe Survey: School Year 2015-2016

Highest Level of Education

Area	Less than H.S.	H.S. Diploma	Some College, No Deg.	Associate Degree	Bachelor's Degree	Master's Degree	Prof. School Degree	Doctorate Degree
City	4.8	13.7	21.2	7.2	34.7	14.3	2.4	1.8
MSA[1]	15.4	22.5	22.2	6.7	21.9	8.5	1.7	1.0
U.S.	13.0	27.5	21.0	8.2	18.8	8.2	2.0	1.3

Note: Figures cover persons age 25 and over; (1) Figures cover the Dallas-Fort Worth-Arlington, TX Metropolitan Statistical Area—see Appendix B for areas included
Source: U.S. Census Bureau, 2012-2016 American Community Survey 5-Year Estimates

Educational Attainment by Race

Area	High School Graduate or Higher (%)					Bachelor's Degree or Higher (%)				
	Total	White	Black	Asian	Hisp.[2]	Total	White	Black	Asian	Hisp.[2]
City	95.2	95.5	98.9	91.7	77.9	53.1	51.4	52.1	68.7	30.8
MSA[1]	84.6	85.2	89.6	88.0	56.8	33.1	34.1	24.8	58.8	12.0
U.S.	87.0	88.9	84.3	86.3	65.7	30.3	31.6	20.0	52.1	14.7

Note: Figures shown cover persons 25 years old and over; (1) Figures cover the Dallas-Fort Worth-Arlington, TX Metropolitan Statistical Area—see Appendix B for areas included; (2) People of Hispanic origin can be of any race
Source: U.S. Census Bureau, 2012-2016 American Community Survey 5-Year Estimates

School Enrollment by Grade and Control

Area	Preschool (%)		Kindergarten (%)		Grades 1 - 4 (%)		Grades 5 - 8 (%)		Grades 9 - 12 (%)	
	Public	Private	Public	Private	Public	Private	Public	Private	Public	Private
City	33.8	66.2	86.6	13.4	92.9	7.1	93.3	6.7	95.7	4.3
MSA[1]	57.4	42.6	89.3	10.7	92.6	7.4	92.0	8.0	92.3	7.7
U.S.	58.4	41.6	87.7	12.3	89.8	10.2	89.7	10.3	90.4	9.6

Note: Figures shown cover persons 3 years old and over; (1) Figures cover the Dallas-Fort Worth-Arlington, TX Metropolitan Statistical Area—see Appendix B for areas included
Source: U.S. Census Bureau, 2012-2016 American Community Survey 5-Year Estimates

Average Salaries of Public School Classroom Teachers

Area	2015		2016		Change from 2015 to 2016	
	Dollars	Rank[1]	Dollars	Rank[1]	Percent	Rank[2]
Texas	50,713	28	51,890	27	2.3	8
U.S. Average	57,611	–	58,353	–	1.3	–

Note: (1) Rank ranges from 1 to 51 where 1 indicates highest salary; (2) Rank ranges from 1 to 51 where 1 indicates highest percent change.
Source: National Education Association, Rankings & Estimates: Rankings of the States 2016 and Estimates of School Statistics 2017

Higher Education

Four-Year Colleges			Two-Year Colleges			Medical Schools[1]	Law Schools[2]	Voc/ Tech[3]
Public	Private Non-profit	Private For-profit	Public	Private Non-profit	Private For-profit			
0	0	0	0	0	0	0	0	0

Note: Figures cover institutions located within the city limits and include main campuses only; (1) includes schools accredited by the Liaison Committee on Medical Education and the American Osteopathic Association's Commission on Osteopathic College Accreditation; (2) includes ABA-accredited schools, schools with provisional ABA accreditation, and state accredited schools; (3) includes all schools with programs that are less than 2 years.
Source: National Center for Education Statistics, Integrated Postsecondary Education System (IPEDS), 2016-17; Wikipedia, List of Medical Schools in the United States, accessed April 2, 2018; Wikipedia, List of Law Schools in the United States, accessed April 2, 2018

According to *U.S. News & World Report,* the Dallas-Plano-Irving, TX metro division is home to three of the best national universities in the U.S.: **Southern Methodist University** (#61 tie); **University of Texas—Dallas** (#145 tie); **Dallas Baptist University** (#202 tie). The indicators used to capture academic quality fall into a number of categories: assessment by administrators at peer institutions; retention of students; faculty resources; student selectivity; financial resources; alumni giving; high school counselor ratings of colleges; and graduation rate. *U.S. News & World Report, "America's Best Colleges 2018"*

According to *U.S. News & World Report,* the Dallas-Plano-Irving, TX metro division is home to one of the top 100 law schools in the U.S.: **Southern Methodist University (Dedman)** (#50 tie). The rankings are based on a weighted average of 12 measures of quality: peer assessment score;

assessment score by lawyers/judges; median LSAT scores; median undergrad GPA; acceptance rate; employment rates for graduates; placement success; bar passage rate; faculty resources; expenditures per student; student/faculty ratio; and library resources. *U.S. News & World Report, "America's Best Graduate Schools, Law, 2019"*

According to *U.S. News & World Report,* the Dallas-Plano-Irving, TX metro division is home to one of the top 75 medical schools for research in the U.S.: **University of Texas Southwestern Medical Center** (#26 tie). The rankings are based on a weighted average of 11 measures of quality: quality assessment; peer assessment score; assessment score by residency directors; research activity; total research activity; average research activity per faculty member; student selectivity; median MCAT total score; median undergraduate GPA; acceptance rate; and faculty resources. *U.S. News & World Report, "America's Best Graduate Schools, Medical, 2019"*

According to *U.S. News & World Report,* the Dallas-Plano-Irving, TX metro division is home to two of the top 75 business schools in the U.S.: **University of Texas—Dallas** (#40 tie); **Southern Methodist University (Cox)** (#48 tie). The rankings are based on a weighted average of the following nine measures: quality assessment; peer assessment; recruiter assessment; placement success; mean starting salary and bonus; student selectivity; mean GMAT and GRE scores; mean undergraduate GPA; and acceptance rate. *U.S. News & World Report, "America's Best Graduate Schools, Business, 2019"*

PRESIDENTIAL ELECTION

2016 Presidential Election Results

Area	Clinton	Trump	Johnson	Stein	Other
Collin County	38.6	55.2	3.8	0.7	1.8
U.S.	48.0	45.9	3.3	1.1	1.7

Note: Results are percentages and may not add to 100% due to rounding
Source: Dave Leip's Atlas of U.S. Presidential Elections

EMPLOYERS

Major Employers

Company Name	Industry
AMR Corporation	Air transportation, scheduled
Associates First Capital Corporation	Mortgage bankers
Baylor University Medical Center	General medical & surgical hospitals
Children's Medical Center Dallas	Specialty hospitals, except psychiatric
Combat Support Associates	Engineering services
County of Dallas	County supervisors' & executives' offices
Dallas County Hospital District	General medical & surgical hospitals
Fort Worth Independent School District	Public elementary & secondary schools
Housewares Holding Company	Toasters, electric: household
HP Enterprise Services	Computer integrated systems design
J.C. Penney Company	Department stores
JCP Publications Corp.	Department stores
L-3 Communications Corporation	Business economic service
Odyssey HealthCare	Home health care services
Romano's Macaroni Grill	Italian restaurant
SFG Management Limited Liability	Milk processing (pasteurizing, homogenizing, bottling)
Texas Instruments Incorporated	Semiconductors & related devices
University of North Texas	Colleges & universities
University of Texas SW Medical Center	Accident & health insurance
Verizon Business Global	Telephone communication, except radio

Note: Companies shown are located within the Dallas-Fort Worth-Arlington, TX Metropolitan Statistical Area.
Source: Hoovers.com; Wikipedia

PUBLIC SAFETY

Crime Rate

Area	All Crimes	Violent Crimes				Property Crimes		
		Murder	Rape[3]	Robbery	Aggrav. Assault	Burglary	Larceny -Theft	Motor Vehicle Theft
City	1,210.7	0.0	24.7	10.9	43.6	151.5	927.5	52.5
Metro[1]	2,776.8	5.2	40.2	141.3	170.0	488.1	1,640.0	292.0
U.S.	2,847.8	5.3	40.4	102.8	248.5	468.9	1,745.0	236.9

Note: Figures are crimes per 100,000 population; (1) Figures cover the Dallas-Plano-Irving, TX Metropolitan Division—see Appendix B for areas included; (3) The city and U.S. figures shown were reported using the revised Uniform Crime Reporting (UCR) definition of rape. The metro area figures shown are an aggregate total of the data submitted using both the revised and legacy UCR definitions.
Source: FBI Uniform Crime Reports, 2016

Hate Crimes

Area	Number of Quarters Reported	Number of Incidents per Bias Motivation					
		Race/Ethnicity/ Ancestry	Religion	Sexual Orientation	Disability	Gender	Gender Identity
City	4	0	0	0	0	0	0
U.S.	4	3,489	1,273	1,076	70	31	124

Source: Federal Bureau of Investigation, Hate Crime Statistics 2016

Identity Theft Consumer Reports

Area	Reports	Reports per 100,000 Population	Rank[2]
MSA[1]	11,506	159	11
U.S.	371,061	114	-

Note: (1) Figures cover the Dallas-Fort Worth-Arlington, TX Metropolitan Statistical Area—see Appendix B for areas included; (2) Rank ranges from 1 to 389 where 1 indicates greatest number of identity theft reports per 100,000 population
Source: Federal Trade Commission, Consumer Sentinel Network Data Book for January–December 2017

Fraud and Other Consumer Reports

Area	Reports	Reports per 100,000 Population	Rank[2]
MSA[1]	55,938	773	8
U.S.	2,304,550	708	-

Note: (1) Figures cover the Dallas-Fort Worth-Arlington, TX Metropolitan Statistical Area—see Appendix B for areas included; (2) Rank ranges from 1 to 389 where 1 indicates greatest number of fraud and other consumer reports per 100,000 population
Source: Federal Trade Commission, Consumer Sentinel Network Data Book for January–December 2017

SPORTS

Professional Sports Teams

Team Name	League	Year Established
Dallas Cowboys	National Football League (NFL)	1960
Dallas Mavericks	National Basketball Association (NBA)	1980
Dallas Stars	National Hockey League (NHL)	1993
FC Dallas	Major League Soccer (MLS)	1996
Texas Rangers	Major League Baseball (MLB)	1972

Note: Includes teams located in the Dallas-Fort Worth-Arlington, TX Metropolitan Statistical Area.
Source: Wikipedia, Major Professional Sports Teams of the United States and Canada, April 5, 2018

CLIMATE

Average and Extreme Temperatures

Temperature	Jan	Feb	Mar	Apr	May	Jun	Jul	Aug	Sep	Oct	Nov	Dec	Yr.
Extreme High (°F)	85	90	100	100	101	112	111	109	107	101	91	87	112
Average High (°F)	55	60	68	76	84	92	96	96	89	79	67	58	77
Average Temp. (°F)	45	50	57	66	74	82	86	86	79	68	56	48	67
Average Low (°F)	35	39	47	56	64	72	76	75	68	57	46	38	56
Extreme Low (°F)	-2	9	12	30	39	53	58	58	42	24	16	0	-2

Note: Figures cover the years 1945-1993
Source: National Climatic Data Center, International Station Meteorological Climate Summary, 9/96

Average Precipitation/Snowfall/Humidity

Precip./Humidity	Jan	Feb	Mar	Apr	May	Jun	Jul	Aug	Sep	Oct	Nov	Dec	Yr.
Avg. Precip. (in.)	1.9	2.3	2.6	3.8	4.9	3.4	2.1	2.3	2.9	3.3	2.3	2.1	33.9
Avg. Snowfall (in.)	1	1	Tr	Tr	0	0	0	0	0	Tr	Tr	Tr	3
Avg. Rel. Hum. 6am (%)	78	77	75	77	82	81	77	76	80	79	78	77	78
Avg. Rel. Hum. 3pm (%)	53	51	47	49	51	48	43	41	46	46	48	51	48

Note: Figures cover the years 1945-1993; Tr = Trace amounts (<0.05 in. of rain; <0.5 in. of snow)
Source: National Climatic Data Center, International Station Meteorological Climate Summary, 9/96

Weather Conditions

Temperature			Daytime Sky			Precipitation		
10°F & below	32°F & below	90°F & above	Clear	Partly cloudy	Cloudy	0.01 inch or more precip.	0.1 inch or more snow/ice	Thunderstorms
1	34	102	108	160	97	78	2	49

Note: Figures are average number of days per year and cover the years 1945-1993
Source: National Climatic Data Center, International Station Meteorological Climate Summary, 9/96

HAZARDOUS WASTE

Superfund Sites

The Dallas-Plano-Irving, TX metro division is home to four sites on the EPA's Superfund National Priorities List: **Lane Plating Works, Inc** (proposed); **Old Esco Manufacturing** (final); **RSR Corporation** (final); **Van Der Horst Usa Corporation** (final). There are a total of 1,396 Superfund sites with a status of proposed or final on the list in the U.S. *U.S. Environmental Protection Agency, National Priorities List, April 4, 2018*

AIR & WATER QUALITY

Air Quality Trends: Ozone

	1990	1995	2000	2005	2010	2012	2013	2014	2015	2016
MSA[1]	0.095	0.105	0.096	0.097	0.080	0.080	0.081	0.076	0.077	0.070
U.S.	0.087	0.089	0.081	0.079	0.073	0.075	0.069	0.067	0.068	0.069

Note: (1) Data covers the Dallas-Fort Worth-Arlington, TX Metropolitan Statistical Area—see Appendix B for areas included. The values shown are the composite ozone concentration averages among trend sites based on the highest fourth daily maximum 8-hour concentration in parts per million. These trends are based on sites having an adequate record of monitoring data during the trend period. Data from exceptional events are included.
Source: U.S. Environmental Protection Agency, Air Quality Monitoring Information, "Air Quality Trends by City, 1990-2016"

Air Quality Index

Area	Percent of Days when Air Quality was...[2]					AQI Statistics[2]	
	Good	Moderate	Unhealthy for Sensitive Groups	Unhealthy	Very Unhealthy	Maximum	Median
MSA[1]	52.6	40.8	6.6	0.0	0.0	147	50

Note: (1) Data covers the Dallas-Fort Worth-Arlington, TX Metropolitan Statistical Area—see Appendix B for areas included; (2) Based on 365 days with AQI data in 2017. Air Quality Index (AQI) is an index for reporting daily air quality. EPA calculates the AQI for five major air pollutants regulated by the Clean Air Act: ground-level ozone, particle pollution (aka particulate matter), carbon monoxide, sulfur dioxide, and nitrogen dioxide. The AQI runs from 0 to 500. The higher the AQI value, the greater the level of air pollution and the greater the health concern. There are six AQI categories: "Good" AQI is between 0 and 50. Air quality is considered satisfactory; "Moderate" AQI is between 51 and 100. Air quality is acceptable; "Unhealthy for Sensitive Groups" When AQI values are between 101 and 150, members of sensitive groups may experience health effects; "Unhealthy" When AQI values are between 151 and 200 everyone may begin to experience health effects; "Very Unhealthy" AQI values between 201 and 300 trigger a health alert; "Hazardous" AQI values over 300 trigger warnings of emergency conditions (not shown).
Source: U.S. Environmental Protection Agency, Air Quality Index Report, 2017

Air Quality Index Pollutants

Area	Percent of Days when AQI Pollutant was...[2]					
	Carbon Monoxide	Nitrogen Dioxide	Ozone	Sulfur Dioxide	Particulate Matter 2.5	Particulate Matter 10
MSA[1]	0.0	2.7	57.0	0.0	40.3	0.0

Note: (1) Data covers the Dallas-Fort Worth-Arlington, TX Metropolitan Statistical Area—see Appendix B for areas included; (2) Based on 365 days with AQI data in 2017. The Air Quality Index (AQI) is an index for reporting daily air quality. EPA calculates the AQI for five major air pollutants regulated by the Clean Air Act: ground-level ozone, particle pollution (also known as particulate matter), carbon monoxide, sulfur dioxide, and nitrogen dioxide. The AQI runs from 0 to 500. The higher the AQI value, the greater the level of air pollution and the greater the health concern.
Source: U.S. Environmental Protection Agency, Air Quality Index Report, 2017

Maximum Air Pollutant Concentrations: Particulate Matter, Ozone, CO and Lead

	Particulate Matter 10 (ug/m^3)	Particulate Matter 2.5 Wtd AM (ug/m^3)	Particulate Matter 2.5 24-Hr (ug/m^3)	Ozone (ppm)	Carbon Monoxide (ppm)	Lead (ug/m^3)
MSA[1] Level	52	8.5	19	0.076	1	0.06
NAAQS[2]	150	15	35	0.075	9	0.15
Met NAAQS[2]	Yes	Yes	Yes	No	Yes	Yes

Note: (1) Data covers the Dallas-Fort Worth-Arlington, TX Metropolitan Statistical Area—see Appendix B for areas included; Data from exceptional events are included; (2) National Ambient Air Quality Standards; ppm = parts per million; ug/m^3 = micrograms per cubic meter; n/a not available.
Concentrations: Particulate Matter 10 (coarse particulate)—highest second maximum 24-hour concentration; Particulate Matter 2.5 Wtd AM (fine particulate)—highest weighted annual mean concentration; Particulate Matter 2.5 24-Hour (fine particulate)—highest 98th percentile 24-hour concentration; Ozone—highest fourth daily maximum 8-hour concentration; Carbon Monoxide—highest second maximum non-overlapping 8-hour concentration; Lead—maximum running 3-month average
Source: U.S. Environmental Protection Agency, Air Quality Monitoring Information, "Air Quality Statistics by City, 2016"

Maximum Air Pollutant Concentrations: Nitrogen Dioxide and Sulfur Dioxide

	Nitrogen Dioxide AM (ppb)	Nitrogen Dioxide 1-Hr (ppb)	Sulfur Dioxide AM (ppb)	Sulfur Dioxide 1-Hr (ppb)	Sulfur Dioxide 24-Hr (ppb)
MSA[1] Level	12	45	n/a	8	n/a
NAAQS[2]	53	100	30	75	140
Met NAAQS[2]	Yes	Yes	n/a	Yes	n/a

Note: (1) Data covers the Dallas-Fort Worth-Arlington, TX Metropolitan Statistical Area—see Appendix B for areas included; Data from exceptional events are included; (2) National Ambient Air Quality Standards; ppm = parts per million; ug/m^3 = micrograms per cubic meter; n/a not available.
Concentrations: Nitrogen Dioxide AM—highest arithmetic mean concentration; Nitrogen Dioxide 1-Hr—highest 98th percentile 1-hour daily maximum concentration; Sulfur Dioxide AM—highest annual mean concentration; Sulfur Dioxide 1-Hr—highest 99th percentile 1-hour daily maximum concentration; Sulfur Dioxide 24-Hr—highest second maximum 24-hour concentration
Source: U.S. Environmental Protection Agency, Air Quality Monitoring Information, "Air Quality Statistics by City, 2016"

Drinking Water

Water System Name	Pop. Served	Primary Water Source Type	Violations[1]	
			Health Based	Monitoring/ Reporting
City of Allen	93,528	Purchased Surface	0	0

Note: (1) Based on violation data from January 1, 2017 to December 31, 2017
Source: U.S. Environmental Protection Agency, Office of Ground Water and Drinking Water, Safe Drinking Water Information System (based on data extracted April 5, 2018)

Cedar Park, Texas

Background

Cedar Park straddles Williamson and Travis Counties in "Hill Country," central Texas, roughly 16 miles northwest of Austin.

Prior to European settlement, the area was populated with several Native American tribes, the Comanche among them. An archeological site in Cedar Park suggests that the area was populated since 5000 BC.

In the 1830s, the area was settled by ranchers George and Harriet Cluck, and the community was known as Running Brushy, named after a nearby spring and running creek. The Austin & Northwest Railroad came through Running Brushy several years later, and the area was renamed Bruggerhoff, for an executive with the railroad. Both hard to spell and hard to pronounce, the name did not stick. The son of its earliest ranchers, Emmett Cluck, renamed the community Cedar Park, and this one stuck.

As nearby Austin grew, so did Cedar Park. But, growth was slow, up until recently. Cedar Park had a population of just over 5,000 in 1990. In the last decade it has grown by 400%. It has the third largest population in the Austin metro area. With small town roots, and easy access to Austin's nearby attractions, Cedar Park has much to offer its residents. It's no wonder the city is growing by leaps and bounds.

Residents can take advantage of the city's many parks, baseball or softball complexes and sports parks. Additional outdoor attractions include several Cave Preserves for exploration and two top-notch golf courses.

Heritage Oak Tree, a majestic 400 year old majestic and still living, is decorated with over 30,000 lights each year in December. It is fifty-seven feet tall with a spread of eighty feet. The tree is located in the median on Quest Blvd in Cedar Park.

The H-E-B Center at Cedar Park, formerly the Cedar Park Center, was completed in 2009 and is home to the Texas Stars Hockey Club, an AHL affiliate of the Dallas Stars. In 2011 it also became the home of the Austin Toros, the NBA Development League affiliate for the San Antonio Spurs. The Center is also a popular venue for live music, rodeos, trade shows and conferences. Cedar Park is also home to Schlitterbahn Water Park, with a new boutique hotel and conference center in the works.

The Cedar Park Regional Medical Center opened its doors in 2007 and offers residents state of the art medical care, close to home.

Most of Cedar Park is served by the Leander Independent School District, while one neighborhood is part of the Round Rock Independent School District. The city is also home to the Cypress Creek campus of Austin Community College.

The climate in Cedar Park consists of hot summers and cool winters. Average temperatures in July and August exceed 95 degrees, winter months average around 60 degrees. Flooding is common in river valleys and low lying areas in April and May.

Rankings

General Rankings

- *US News & World Report* conducted a survey of more than 2,000 people and analyzed the 125 largest metropolitan areas to determine what matters the most when selecting the next place to live. Austin* ranked #1 out of the top 25 as having the best combination of desirable factors. Criteria: cost of living; quality of education; job market, crime rates; and other factors. *realestate.usnews.com, "The 25 Best Places to Live in the U.S. in 2018," April 10, 2018*
- The Austin* metro area was identified as one of America's fastest-growing areas in terms of population and economy by *Forbes*. The area ranked #8 out of 25. The 100 most populous metro areas in the U.S. were evaluated on the following criteria: estimated population growth; employment; economic output; wages; home values. *Forbes, "America's Fastest-Growing Cities 2018," February 28, 2018*
- Austin* was identified as one of America's fastest-growing cities in terms of population growth by CNNMoney.com. The area ranked #4 out of 10. Criteria: population growth between July 2015 and July 2016; cities and towns with populations of 50,000. *CNNMoney, "10 Fastest-Growing Cities," June 2, 2017*

Business/Finance Rankings

- According to *Business Insider*, the Austin* metro area is where startup growth is on the rise. Based on the 2017 Kauffman Index of Growth Entrepreneurship, which measured in-depth national entrepreneurial trends in 40 metro areas, it ranked #2 in highest startup growth. *www.businessinsider.com, "The 21 U.S. Cities with the Highest Startup Growth," October 21, 2017*
- The personal finance site NerdWallet analyzed 183 American metropolitan areas with populations over 250,000 and more than 15,000 businesses to rank where entrepreneurs find the most success. Criteria included area economy, annual income, housing cost, unemployment rate, and the success rate of area businesses. Austin* ranked #89. *www.nerdwallet.com, "Best Places to Start a Business," April 27, 2015*
- The editors of *Kiplinger's Personal Finance Magazine* named Austin* to their list of ten of the best metro areas for start-ups. The area ranked #5.Criteria: well-educated workforce; low living costs for self-employed people, as measured by the Council for Community and Economic Research; a strong existing community of small business; low unemployment; low business costs. *www.kiplinger.com, "10 Great Cities for Starting a Business," October 2014*
- 24/7 Wall Street used Brookings Institution research on 50 advanced industries to identify the proportion of workers in the nation's largest metropolitan areas that were employed in jobs requiring knowledge in the science, technology, engineering, or math (STEM) fields and where there was heavy investment in research and development (R&D). The Austin* metro area was #9. *247wallst.com, "15 Cities with the Most High-Tech Jobs," February 23, 2017*
- In a survey of economic confidence in the nation's 50 largest metropolitan areas conducted January–December 2014, the Austin* metro area placed #9, according to Gallup's 2014 Economic Confidence Index. *Gallup, "San Jose and San Francisco Lead in Economic Confidence," March 19, 2015*
- The Brookings Institution ranked the 100 largest metro areas in the U.S. based on income inequality. Austin* was ranked #37 (#1 = greatest ineqality). Criteria: the "95/20 ratio," a figure representing the income at which a household earns more than 95 percent of all other households, divided by the income at which a household earns more than only 20 percent of all other households. *Brookings Institution, "Household Income Inequality, 100 Largest U.S. Metro Areas, 2014-2016," February 5, 2018*

- *Forbes* ranked the 100 largest metro areas in the U.S. in terms of the "Best Cities for Young Professionals." The Austin* metro area ranked #2 out of 25. (Large metro areas were divided into metro divisions.) Criteria: median rent of a two-bedroom apartment; job growth and unemployment rate; median salary of college graduates with 5 or less years of work experience; networking opportunities; social outlook; percentage of population 25 years of age and older with college degrees. *Forbes.com, "America's 25 Best Cities for Young Professionals in 2017," May 22, 2017*

- Payscale.com ranked the largest metro areas in terms of wage growth. The Austin* metro area ranked #16. Criteria: private-sector wage growth between the 4th quarter of 2016 and the 4th quarter of 2017. *PayScale, "Wage Trends by Metro Area-4th Quarter," January 17, 2018*

- The Austin* metro area was identified as one of the most affordable metropolitan areas in America by *Forbes.* The area ranked #19 out of 20 based on the National Association of Home Builders/Wells Fargo Housing Affordability Index and Sperling's Best Places' cost-of-living index. *Forbes.com, "America's Most Affordable Cities in 2015," March 12, 2015*

- The Austin* metro area appeared on the Milken Institute "2017 Best Performing Cities" list. Rank: #9 out of 200 large metro areas. Criteria: job growth; wage and salary growth; high-tech output growth. *Milken Institute, "Best-Performing Cities 2017," January 2018*

- *Forbes* ranked the 200 most populous metro areas to determine the nation's "Best Places for Business and Careers." The Austin* metro area was ranked #8. Criteria: costs (business and living); job growth (past and projected); income growth; quality of life; educational attainment (college and high school); projected economic growth; cultural and recreational opportunities; net migration patterns; number of highly ranked colleges. *Forbes, "The Best Places for Business and Careers 2017," October 24, 2017*

Children/Family Rankings

- *Forbes* analyzed data on the 100 largest metropolitan areas in the United States to compile its 2016 ranking of the best cities for raising a family. The Austin* metro area was ranked #14. Criteria: median income; childcare costs; percent of population under 18; commuting delays; crime rate; percentage of families owning homes; education quality (mainly test scores). Overall cost of living and housing affordability was also unofficially considered. *Forbes, "America's Best Cities for Raising a Family 2016," August 30, 2016*

Dating/Romance Rankings

- *Apartment List* conducted its annual survey of renters to compile a list of metros that have the best opportunities for dating. Nearly 11,000 respondents, from February 2017 through January 2018, rated their current city or neighborhood for opportunities to date and make friends. The Austin* metro area ranked #6 out of 70 where single residents were very satisfied or somewhat satisfied, making it among the ten best metros for dating opportunities. Other criteria analyzed included gender and education levels of renters. *Apartment List, "Best Metros for Dating 2018," February 6, 2018*

Education Rankings

- Personal finance website *WalletHub* analyzed the 150 largest U.S. metropolitan statistical areas to determine where the most educated Americans are choosing to settle. Criteria: education quality and attainment gap; education levels; percentage of workers with degrees; public school rankings; quality and size of each metro area's universities. Austin* was ranked #9 (#1 = most educated city). *www.WalletHub.com, "2017's Most and Least Educated Cities in America," July 25, 2017*

Environmental Rankings

- Sperling's BestPlaces assessed 379 metropolitan areas of the United States for the likelihood of dangerously extreme weather events or earthquakes. In general the Southeast and South-Central regions have the highest risk of weather extremes and earthquakes, while the Pacific Northwest enjoys the lowest risk. Of the least risky metropolitan areas, the Austin* metro area was ranked #373. *www.bestplaces.net, "Safest Places from Natural Disasters," April 2011*

- The U.S. Environmental Protection Agency (EPA) released a list of U.S. metropolitan areas with the most ENERGY STAR certified buildings in 2016. The Austin* metro area was ranked #13 out of 25. *U.S. Environmental Protection Agency, "2017 Energy Star Top Cities," June 2017*

- Austin* was highlighted as one of the top 99 cleanest metro areas for short-term particle pollution (24-hour PM 2.5) in the U.S. during 2013 through 2015. Monitors in these cities reported no days with unhealthful PM 2.5 levels. *American Lung Association, State of the Air 2017*

Health/Fitness Rankings

- For each of the 50 most populous metro areas in the United States, the American College of Sports Medicine's American Fitness Index evaluated infrastructure, community assets, and policies that encourage healthy and fit lifestyles, including preventive health behaviors, levels of chronic disease conditions, health care access, and community resources and policies that support physical activity. The Austin* metro area ranked #12 for "community fitness." *www.americanfitnessindex.org, "ACSM American Fitness Index Health and Community Fitness Status of the 50 Largest Metropolitan Areas," May 2017*

- Austin* was identified as a "2016 Spring Allergy Capital." The area ranked #58 out of 100. Three groups of factors were used to identify the most severe cities for people with allergies during the spring season: annual pollen levels; medicine utilization; access to board-certified allergists. *Asthma and Allergy Foundation of America, "Spring Allergy Capitals 2016"*

- Austin* was identified as a "2016 Fall Allergy Capital." The area ranked #46 out of 100. Three groups of factors were used to identify the most severe cities for people with allergies during the fall season: annual pollen levels; medicine utilization; access to board-certified allergists. *Asthma and Allergy Foundation of America, "Fall Allergy Capitals 2016"*

- Austin* was identified as a "2015 Asthma Capital." The area ranked #91 out of the nation's 100 largest metropolitan areas. Criteria: estimated prevalence; self-reported prevalence; crude death rate for asthma; annual pollen score; annual air quality; public smoking laws; number of board-certified asthma specialists; school inhaler access laws; rescue medication use; controller medication use; ER visits for asthma; uninsured rate; poverty rate. *Asthma and Allergy Foundation of America, "Asthma Capitals 2015"*

- The Austin* metro area ranked #49 out of 189 in The Gallup-Healthways Well-Being Index. Criteria: purpose; social well being; financial health; community and physical health. Results are based on telephone interviews with adults, aged 18 and older, living in metropolitan areas in the 50 U.S. states and the District of Columbia. *Gallup-Healthways, "State of American Well-Being, 2017 Community Well-Being Rankings" March 2018*

Real Estate Rankings

- FitSmallBusiness looked at 50 of the largest metropolitan areas in the U.S. to determine which metro was the best to start a real estate business. Data was compiled from such sources as: Zillow, Trulia, U.S. Census Bureau, and the Bureau of Labor Statistics. Criteria: location; inventory; annual wages; median sales price of homes; days on the market; median price cut percentage; and other factors that would influence real estate professional growth. The Austin* metro area ranked #13. *fitsmallbusiness.com, "The Best Cities to Become a Real Estate Agent in 2018," January 30, 2018*

- Austin* was ranked #169 out of 238 metro areas in terms of housing affordability in 2017 by the National Association of Home Builders (#1 = most affordable). Criteria: the share of homes sold in that area affordable to a family earning the local median income, based on standard mortgage underwriting criteria. *National Association of Home Builders®, NAHB-Wells Fargo Housing Opportunity Index, 4th Quarter 2017*

Safety Rankings

- The National Insurance Crime Bureau ranked 382 metro areas in the U.S. in terms of per capita rates of vehicle theft. The Austin* metro area ranked #167 (#1 = highest rate). Criteria: number of vehicle theft offenses per 100,000 inhabitants in 2016. *National Insurance Crime Bureau, "Hot Spots 2016," June 8, 2017*

Seniors/Retirement Rankings

- From its Best Cities for Successful Aging indexes, the Milken Institute generated rankings for metropolitan areas, weighing data in nine categories—health care, wellness, living arrangements, transportation and convenience, financial characteristics, education, employment, community engagement, and overall livability. The Austin* metro area was ranked #6 overall in the large metro area category. *Milken Institute, "Best Cities for Successful Aging, 2017" March 14, 2017*

Women/Minorities Rankings

- The *Houston Chronicle* listed the Austin* metro area as #2 in top places for young Latinos to live in the U.S. Research was largely based on housing and occupational data from the largest metropolitan areas performed by *Forbes* and NBC Universo. Criteria: percentage of 18-34 year-olds; Latino college grad rates; and diversity. *blog.chron.com, "The 15 Best Big Cities for Latino Millenials," January 26, 2016*

*Cedar Park is located within the Austin-Round Rock, TX Metropolitan Statistical Area.

Business Environment

CITY FINANCES

City Government Finances

Component	2015 ($000)	2015 ($ per capita)
Total Revenues	105,833	1,605
Total Expenditures	93,857	1,423
Debt Outstanding	135,592	2,056
Cash and Securities[1]	103,610	1,571

Note: (1) Cash and security holdings of a government at the close of its fiscal year,, including those of its dependent agencies, utilities, and liquor stores.
Source: U.S Census Bureau, State & Local Government Finances 2015

City Government Revenue by Source

Source	2015 ($000)	2015 ($ per capita)	2015 (%)
General Revenue			
From Federal Government	0	0	0.0
From State Government	6,337	96	6.0
From Local Governments	0	0	0.0
Taxes			
Property	23,260	353	22.0
Sales and Gross Receipts	21,972	333	20.8
Personal Income	0	0	0.0
Corporate Income	0	0	0.0
Motor Vehicle License	0	0	0.0
Other Taxes	6,238	95	5.9
Current Charges	18,348	278	17.3
Liquor Store	0	0	0.0
Utility	18,328	278	17.3
Employee Retirement	0	0	0.0

Source: U.S Census Bureau, State & Local Government Finances 2015

City Government Expenditures by Function

Function	2015 ($000)	2015 ($ per capita)	2015 (%)
General Direct Expenditures			
Air Transportation	0	0	0.0
Corrections	0	0	0.0
Education	0	0	0.0
Employment Security Administration	0	0	0.0
Financial Administration	1,651	25	1.8
Fire Protection	7,163	108	7.6
General Public Buildings	5,040	76	5.4
Governmental Administration, Other	2,069	31	2.2
Health	294	4	0.3
Highways	13,355	202	14.2
Hospitals	0	0	0.0
Housing and Community Development	0	0	0.0
Interest on General Debt	6,910	104	7.4
Judicial and Legal	1,053	16	1.1
Libraries	1,099	16	1.2
Parking	0	0	0.0
Parks and Recreation	3,108	47	3.3
Police Protection	9,120	138	9.7
Public Welfare	0	0	0.0
Sewerage	9,071	137	9.7
Solid Waste Management	3,183	48	3.4
Veterans' Services	0	0	0.0
Liquor Store	0	0	0.0
Utility	19,776	299	21.1
Employee Retirement	0	0	0.0

Source: U.S Census Bureau, State & Local Government Finances 2015

DEMOGRAPHICS

Population Growth

Area	1990 Census	2000 Census	2010 Census	2016* Estimate	Population Growth (%)	
					1990-2016	2010-2016
City	9,798	26,049	48,937	63,551	548.6	29.9
MSA[1]	846,217	1,249,763	1,716,289	1,942,615	129.6	13.2
U.S.	248,709,873	281,421,906	308,745,538	318,558,162	28.1	3.2

Note: (1) Figures cover the Austin-Round Rock, TX Metropolitan Statistical Area—see Appendix B for areas included; (*) 2012-2016 5-year estimated population
Source: U.S. Census Bureau, 1990 Census, Census 2000, Census 2010, 2012-2016 American Community Survey 5-Year Estimates

Household Size

Area	Persons in Household (%)							Average Household Size
	One	Two	Three	Four	Five	Six	Seven or More	
City	20.2	29.5	17.5	21.9	6.8	2.8	1.2	3.10
MSA[1]	28.0	33.3	15.6	13.8	5.8	2.1	1.4	2.70
U.S.	27.7	33.7	15.7	13.1	6.0	2.3	1.5	2.60

Note: (1) Figures cover the Austin-Round Rock, TX Metropolitan Statistical Area—see Appendix B for areas included
Source: U.S. Census Bureau, 2012-2016 American Community Survey 5-Year Estimates

Race

Area	White Alone[2] (%)	Black Alone[2] (%)	Asian Alone[2] (%)	AIAN[3] Alone[2] (%)	NHOPI[4] Alone[2] (%)	Other Race Alone[2] (%)	Two or More Races (%)
City	81.7	3.7	9.0	0.5	0.0	1.6	3.4
MSA[1]	78.7	7.3	5.3	0.4	0.1	5.1	3.2
U.S.	73.3	12.6	5.2	0.8	0.2	4.8	3.1

Note: (1) Figures cover the Austin-Round Rock, TX Metropolitan Statistical Area—see Appendix B for areas included; (2) Alone is defined as not being in combination with one or more other races; (3) American Indian and Alaska Native; (4) Native Hawaiian and Other Pacific Islander
Source: U.S. Census Bureau, 2012-2016 American Community Survey 5-Year Estimates

Hispanic or Latino Origin

Area	Total (%)	Mexican (%)	Puerto Rican (%)	Cuban (%)	Other (%)
City	18.9	15.7	0.4	0.3	2.5
MSA[1]	31.9	26.9	0.7	0.5	3.9
U.S.	17.3	11.0	1.7	0.7	4.0

Note: Persons of Hispanic or Latino origin can be of any race; (1) Figures cover the Austin-Round Rock, TX Metropolitan Statistical Area—see Appendix B for areas included
Source: U.S. Census Bureau, 2012-2016 American Community Survey 5-Year Estimates

Segregation

Type	Segregation Indices[1]				Percent Change		
	1990	2000	2010	2010 Rank[2]	1990-2000	1990-2010	2000-2010
Black/White	54.1	52.1	50.1	70	-1.9	-4.0	-2.1
Asian/White	39.4	42.3	41.2	49	2.9	1.8	-1.2
Hispanic/White	41.7	45.6	43.2	51	3.9	1.5	-2.4

Note: All figures cover the Metropolitan Statistical Area—see Appendix B for areas included; Figures are based on an analysis of 1990, 2000, and 2010 Census Decennial Census tract data by William H. Frey, Brookings Institution and the University of Michigan Social Science Data Analysis Network. In this analysis all racial groups (whites, blacks, and asians) are non-Hispanic members of those races. Hispanics are shown as a separate category; (1) Segregation Indices are Dissimilarity Indices that measure the degree to which the minority group is distributed differently than whites across census tracts. They range from 0 (complete integration) to 100 (complete segregation) where the value indicates the percentage of the minority group that needs to move to be distributed exactly like whites; (2) Ranges from 1 (most segregated) to 102 (least segregated); n/a not available.
Source: www.CensusScope.org

Ancestry

Area	German	Irish	English	American	Italian	Polish	French[2]	Scottish	Dutch
City	16.6	10.0	9.9	6.8	3.8	1.9	2.8	2.4	1.8
MSA[1]	13.5	8.0	8.2	4.5	2.8	1.7	2.6	2.2	1.0
U.S.	14.4	10.4	7.7	6.9	5.4	2.9	2.6	1.7	1.3

Note: Figures are the percentage of the total population reporting a particular ancestry. The nine most commonly reported ancestries in the U.S. are shown. Figures include multiple ancestries (e.g. if a person reported being Irish and Italian, they were included in both columns); (1) Figures cover the Austin-Round Rock, TX Metropolitan Statistical Area—see Appendix B for areas included; (2) Excludes Basque
Source: U.S. Census Bureau, 2012-2016 American Community Survey 5-Year Estimates

Foreign-Born Population

Area	Percent of Population Born in								
	Any Foreign Country	Asia	Mexico	Europe	Carribean	Central America[2]	South America	Africa	Canada
City	13.1	6.2	3.1	1.0	0.7	0.3	0.8	0.6	0.3
MSA[1]	14.6	4.0	6.8	1.0	0.4	1.1	0.5	0.5	0.3
U.S.	13.2	4.0	3.6	1.5	1.3	1.0	0.9	0.6	0.3

Note: (1) Figures cover the Austin-Round Rock, TX Metropolitan Statistical Area—see Appendix B for areas included; (2) Excludes Mexico.
Source: U.S. Census Bureau, 2012-2016 American Community Survey 5-Year Estimates

Marital Status

Area	Never Married	Now Married[2]	Separated	Widowed	Divorced
City	25.5	57.8	1.6	3.7	11.4
MSA[1]	36.1	47.4	1.9	3.7	10.9
U.S.	33.0	48.1	2.1	5.9	11.0

Note: Figures are percentages and cover the population 15 years of age and older; (1) Figures cover the Austin-Round Rock, TX Metropolitan Statistical Area—see Appendix B for areas included; (2) Excludes separated
Source: U.S. Census Bureau, 2012-2016 American Community Survey 5-Year Estimates

Disability Status

Area	All Ages	Under 18 Years Old	18 to 64 Years Old	65 Years and Over
City	7.6	3.6	6.3	33.3
MSA[1]	9.3	3.9	7.9	33.1
U.S.	12.5	4.1	10.3	35.7

Note: Figures show percent of the civilian noninstitutionalized population that reported having a disability. Disability status is determined from six types of difficulty: vision, hearing, cognitive, ambulatory, self-care, and independent living. For children under 5 years old, hearing and vision difficulty are used to determine disability status. For children between the ages of 5 and 14, disability status is determined from hearing, vision, cognitive, ambulatory, and self-care difficulties. For people aged 15 years and older, they are considered to have a disability if they have difficulty with any one of the six difficulty types; Note: (1) Figures cover the Austin-Round Rock, TX Metropolitan Statistical Area—see Appendix B for areas included
Source: U.S. Census Bureau, 2012-2016 American Community Survey 5-Year Estimates

Age

Area	Percent of Population									Median Age
	Under Age 5	Age 5–19	Age 20–34	Age 35–44	Age 45–54	Age 55–64	Age 65–74	Age 75–84	Age 85+	
City	7.4	24.8	19.1	18.2	13.8	8.8	4.9	2.1	0.9	34.3
MSA[1]	6.8	20.3	24.7	15.4	12.9	10.4	5.9	2.6	1.0	33.9
U.S.	6.2	19.6	20.7	12.7	13.6	12.6	8.3	4.3	1.9	37.7

Note: (1) Figures cover the Austin-Round Rock, TX Metropolitan Statistical Area—see Appendix B for areas included
Source: U.S. Census Bureau, 2012-2016 American Community Survey 5-Year Estimates

Gender

Area	Males	Females	Males per 100 Females
City	30,804	32,747	94.1
MSA[1]	971,489	971,126	100.0
U.S.	156,765,322	161,792,840	96.9

Note: (1) Figures cover the Austin-Round Rock, TX Metropolitan Statistical Area—see Appendix B for areas included
Source: U.S. Census Bureau, 2012-2016 American Community Survey 5-Year Estimates

Religious Groups by Family

Area	Catholic	Baptist	Non-Den.	Methodist[2]	Lutheran	LDS[3]	Pente-costal	Presby-terian[4]	Muslim[5]	Judaism
MSA[1]	16.0	10.3	4.5	3.6	2.0	1.2	0.8	1.1	1.2	0.3
U.S.	19.1	9.3	4.0	4.0	2.3	2.0	1.9	1.6	0.8	0.7

Note: Figures are the number of adherents as a percentage of the total population; (1) Figures cover the Austin-Round Rock, TX Metropolitan Statistical Area—see Appendix B for areas included; (2) Methodist/Pietist; (3) Latter Day Saints; (4) Reformed; (5) Figures are estimates
Source: Association of Statisticians of American Religious Bodies, 2010 U.S. Religion Census: Religious Congregations & Membership Study

Religious Groups by Tradition

Area	Catholic	Evangelical Protestant	Mainline Protestant	Other Tradition	Black Protestant	Orthodox
MSA[1]	16.0	16.1	6.3	3.9	1.4	0.1
U.S.	19.1	16.2	7.3	4.3	1.6	0.3

Note: Figures are the number of adherents as a percentage of the total population; (1) Figures cover the Austin-Round Rock, TX Metropolitan Statistical Area—see Appendix B for areas included
Source: Association of Statisticians of American Religious Bodies, 2010 U.S. Religion Census: Religious Congregations & Membership Study

ECONOMY

Gross Metropolitan Product

Area	2014	2015	2016	2017	Rank[2]
MSA[1]	114.8	119.5	125.3	133.1	32

Note: Figures are in billions of dollars; (1) Figures cover the Austin-Round Rock, TX Metropolitan Statistical Area—see Appendix B for areas included; (2) Rank is based on 2015 data and ranges from 1 to 381
Source: The U.S. Conference of Mayors, U.S. Metro Economies: GMP and Employment Report, 2015-2017

Economic Growth

Area	2012-14 (%)	2015 (%)	2016 (%)	2017 (%)	Rank[2]
MSA[1]	5.2	5.8	3.3	3.9	14
U.S.	2.0	2.4	1.9	2.6	–

Note: Figures are real gross metropolitan product (GMP) growth rates and represent average annual percent change; (1) Figures cover the Austin-Round Rock, TX Metropolitan Statistical Area—see Appendix B for areas included; (2) Rank is based on 2012-2014 average annual percent change and ranges from 1 to 381
Source: The U.S. Conference of Mayors, U.S. Metro Economies: GMP and Employment Report, 2015-2017

Metropolitan Area Exports

Area	2011	2012	2013	2014	2015	2016	Rank[2]
MSA[1]	8,626.3	8,976.6	8,870.8	9,400.0	10,094.5	10,682.7	26

Note: Figures are in millions of dollars; (1) Figures cover the Austin-Round Rock, TX Metropolitan Statistical Area—see Appendix B for areas included; (2) Rank is based on 2016 data and ranges from 1 to 385
Source: U.S. Department of Commerce, International Trade Administration, Office of Trade & Industry Information, Manufacturing & Services, data extracted March 15, 2018

Building Permits

Area	Single-Family			Multi-Family			Total		
	2016	2017p	Pct. Chg.	2016	2017p	Pct. Chg.	2016	2017p	Pct. Chg.
City	535	399	-25.4	411	31	-92.5	946	430	-54.5
MSA[1]	13,609	15,206	11.7	8,633	10,597	22.7	22,242	25,803	16.0
U.S.	750,800	817,300	8.9	455,800	446,800	-2.0	1,206,600	1,264,100	4.8

Note: (1) Figures cover the Austin-Round Rock, TX Metropolitan Statistical Area—see Appendix B for areas included; Figures represent new, privately-owned housing units authorized (unadjusted data); All permit data are based on estimates with imputation; (p) preliminary data.
Source: U.S. Census Bureau, Manufacturing, Mining, and Construction Statistics, Building Permits, 2016, 2017

Bankruptcy Filings

Area	Business Filings			Nonbusiness Filings		
	2016	2017	% Chg.	2016	2017	% Chg.
Williamson County	42	46	9.5	469	468	-0.2
U.S.	24,114	23,157	-4.0	770,846	765,863	-0.6

Note: Business filings include Chapter 7, Chapter 11, Chapter 12, and Chapter 13; Nonbusiness filings include Chapter 7, Chapter 11, and Chapter 13
Source: Administrative Office of the U.S. Courts, Business and Nonbusiness Bankruptcy, County Cases Commenced by Chapter of the Bankruptcy Code, During the 12-Month Period Ending December 31, 2016 and Business and Nonbusiness Bankruptcy, County Cases Commenced by Chapter of the Bankruptcy Code, During the 12-Month Period Ending December 31, 2017

Housing Vacancy Rates

Area	Gross Vacancy Rate[2] (%)			Year-Round Vacancy Rate[3] (%)			Rental Vacancy Rate[4] (%)			Homeowner Vacancy Rate[5] (%)		
	2015	2016	2017	2015	2016	2017	2015	2016	2017	2015	2016	2017
MSA[1]	9.2	8.2	10.4	8.5	7.6	9.3	6.0	5.5	6.1	1.3	1.0	2.0
U.S.	12.9	12.8	12.7	10.0	9.9	9.9	7.1	6.9	7.2	1.8	1.7	1.6

Note: (1) Figures cover the Austin-Round Rock, TX Metropolitan Statistical Area—see Appendix B for areas included; (2) The percentage of the total housing inventory that is vacant; (3) The percentage of the housing inventory (excluding seasonal units) that is year-round vacant; (4) The percentage of rental inventory that is vacant for rent; (5) The percentage of homeowner inventory that is vacant for sale
Source: U.S. Census Bureau, Housing Vacancies and Homeownership Annual Statistics: 2015, 2016, 2017

INCOME

Income

Area	Per Capita ($)	Median Household ($)	Average Household ($)
City	34,534	87,466	101,888
MSA[1]	34,093	66,093	89,787
U.S.	29,829	55,322	77,866

Note: (1) Figures cover the Austin-Round Rock, TX Metropolitan Statistical Area—see Appendix B for areas included
Source: U.S. Census Bureau, 2012-2016 American Community Survey 5-Year Estimates

Household Income Distribution

Area	Percent of Households Earning							
	Under $15,000	$15,000 -$24,999	$25,000 -$34,999	$35,000 -$49,999	$50,000 -$74,999	$75,000 -$99,999	$100,000 -$149,999	$150,000 and up
City	4.0	4.1	6.2	10.0	17.2	16.0	23.3	19.2
MSA[1]	8.9	8.0	8.3	12.5	18.2	13.3	16.2	14.5
U.S.	12.1	10.2	9.9	13.2	17.8	12.2	13.5	11.1

Note: (1) Figures cover the Austin-Round Rock, TX Metropolitan Statistical Area—see Appendix B for areas included
Source: U.S. Census Bureau, 2012-2016 American Community Survey 5-Year Estimates

Poverty Rate

Area	All Ages	Under 18 Years Old	18 to 64 Years Old	65 Years and Over
City	4.5	4.7	4.2	5.8
MSA[1]	13.3	17.3	12.6	7.3
U.S.	15.1	21.2	14.2	9.3

Note: Figures are percentage of people whose income during the past 12 months was below the poverty level; (1) Figures cover the Austin-Round Rock, TX Metropolitan Statistical Area—see Appendix B for areas included
Source: U.S. Census Bureau, 2012-2016 American Community Survey 5-Year Estimates

EMPLOYMENT

Labor Force and Employment

Area	Civilian Labor Force			Workers Employed		
	Dec. 2016	Dec. 2017	% Chg.	Dec. 2016	Dec. 2017	% Chg.
City	37,261	38,371	3.0	36,034	37,322	3.6
MSA[1]	1,129,840	1,164,240	3.0	1,093,771	1,133,101	3.6
U.S.	158,968,000	159,880,000	0.6	151,798,000	153,602,000	1.2

Note: Data is not seasonally adjusted and covers workers 16 years of age and older; (1) Figures cover the Austin-Round Rock, TX Metropolitan Statistical Area—see Appendix B for areas included
Source: Bureau of Labor Statistics, Local Area Unemployment Statistics

Unemployment Rate

Area	2017											
	Jan.	Feb.	Mar.	Apr.	May	Jun.	Jul.	Aug.	Sep.	Oct.	Nov.	Dec.
City	3.6	3.7	3.3	3.0	3.1	3.3	3.3	3.4	3.0	2.8	2.9	2.7
MSA[1]	3.5	3.5	3.3	2.9	3.0	3.3	3.3	3.3	2.9	2.7	2.8	2.7
U.S.	5.1	4.9	4.6	4.1	4.1	4.5	4.6	4.5	4.1	3.9	3.9	3.9

Note: Data is not seasonally adjusted and covers workers 16 years of age and older; (1) Figures cover the Austin-Round Rock, TX Metropolitan Statistical Area—see Appendix B for areas included
Source: Bureau of Labor Statistics, Local Area Unemployment Statistics

Average Wages

Occupation	$/Hr.	Occupation	$/Hr.
Accountants and Auditors	35.40	Maids and Housekeeping Cleaners	10.40
Automotive Mechanics	23.90	Maintenance and Repair Workers	18.20
Bookkeepers	20.40	Marketing Managers	71.30
Carpenters	19.10	Nuclear Medicine Technologists	36.20
Cashiers	10.90	Nurses, Licensed Practical	22.10
Clerks, General Office	17.40	Nurses, Registered	33.10
Clerks, Receptionists/Information	13.30	Nursing Assistants	13.20
Clerks, Shipping/Receiving	15.20	Packers and Packagers, Hand	11.80
Computer Programmers	43.40	Physical Therapists	47.00
Computer Systems Analysts	44.70	Postal Service Mail Carriers	24.00
Computer User Support Specialists	24.30	Real Estate Brokers	n/a
Cooks, Restaurant	12.10	Retail Salespersons	13.50
Dentists	76.40	Sales Reps., Exc. Tech./Scientific	31.30
Electrical Engineers	56.20	Sales Reps., Tech./Scientific	58.20
Electricians	24.30	Secretaries, Exc. Legal/Med./Exec.	17.10
Financial Managers	67.00	Security Guards	15.40
First-Line Supervisors/Managers, Sales	21.50	Surgeons	n/a
Food Preparation Workers	12.30	Teacher Assistants*	12.30
General and Operations Managers	62.90	Teachers, Elementary School*	26.90
Hairdressers/Cosmetologists	14.80	Teachers, Secondary School*	26.60
Internists, General	73.80	Telemarketers	17.70
Janitors and Cleaners	11.60	Truck Drivers, Heavy/Tractor-Trailer	19.00
Landscaping/Groundskeeping Workers	13.90	Truck Drivers, Light/Delivery Svcs.	17.90
Lawyers	62.40	Waiters and Waitresses	12.10

Note: Wage data covers the Austin-Round Rock, TX Metropolitan Statistical Area—see Appendix B for areas included; (*) Hourly wages for elementary/secondary school teachers and teacher assistants were calculated by the editors from annual wage data based on a 40 hour work week; n/a not available.
Source: Bureau of Labor Statistics, Metro Area Occupational Employment & Wage Estimates, May 2017

Employment by Occupation

Occupation Classification	City (%)	MSA[1] (%)	U.S. (%)
Management, Business, Science, and Arts	50.8	44.7	37.0
Natural Resources, Construction, and Maintenance	4.9	8.5	8.9
Production, Transportation, and Material Moving	5.5	7.2	12.2
Sales and Office	26.0	23.6	23.8
Service	12.8	16.0	18.1

Note: Figures cover employed civilians 16 years of age and older; (1) Figures cover the Austin-Round Rock, TX Metropolitan Statistical Area—see Appendix B for areas included
Source: U.S. Census Bureau, 2012-2016 American Community Survey 5-Year Estimates

Employment by Industry

Sector	MSA[1] Number of Employees	MSA[1] Percent of Total	U.S. Percent of Total
Construction, Mining, and Logging	62,100	5.9	5.2
Education and Health Services	121,100	11.5	15.9
Financial Activities	60,700	5.8	5.7
Government	178,400	16.9	15.3
Information	30,900	2.9	1.9
Leisure and Hospitality	129,800	12.3	10.7
Manufacturing	57,700	5.5	8.5
Other Services	45,300	4.3	3.9
Professional and Business Services	183,000	17.4	14.0
Retail Trade	108,400	10.3	11.0
Transportation, Warehousing, and Utilities	22,200	2.1	4.1
Wholesale Trade	53,900	5.1	4.0

Note: Figures are non-farm employment as of December 2017. Figures are not seasonally adjusted and include workers 16 years of age and older; (1) Figures cover the Austin-Round Rock, TX Metropolitan Statistical Area—see Appendix B for areas included
Source: Bureau of Labor Statistics, Current Employment Statistics, Employment, Hours, and Earnings

Occupations with Greatest Projected Employment Growth: 2017 – 2019

Occupation[1]	2017 Employment	2019 Projected Employment	Numeric Employment Change	Percent Employment Change
Combined Food Preparation and Serving Workers, Including Fast Food	335,660	354,370	18,710	5.6
Personal Care Aides	212,280	230,990	18,710	8.8
Retail Salespersons	393,950	406,100	12,150	3.1
Customer Service Representatives	261,530	273,600	12,070	4.6
Janitors and Cleaners, Except Maids and Housekeeping Cleaners	180,710	192,060	11,350	6.3
Laborers and Freight, Stock, and Material Movers, Hand	185,140	196,200	11,060	6.0
Registered Nurses	214,500	224,450	9,950	4.6
Office Clerks, General	379,860	389,540	9,680	2.6
Heavy and Tractor-Trailer Truck Drivers	192,710	201,560	8,850	4.6
Waiters and Waitresses	222,630	231,020	8,390	3.8

Note: Projections cover Texas; (1) Sorted by numeric employment change
Source: www.projectionscentral.com, State Occupational Projections, 2017–2019 Short-Term Projections

Fastest Growing Occupations: 2017 – 2019

Occupation[1]	2017 Employment	2019 Projected Employment	Numeric Employment Change	Percent Employment Change
Wind Turbine Service Technicians	1,740	2,090	350	20.7
Home Health Aides	72,760	80,000	7,240	10.0
Security and Fire Alarm Systems Installers	8,190	8,930	740	8.9
Personal Care Aides	212,280	230,990	18,710	8.8
Statisticians	1,760	1,910	150	8.2
Tree Trimmers and Pruners	5,980	6,480	500	8.2
Physician Assistants	6,860	7,400	540	7.9
Nurse Practitioners	9,230	9,950	720	7.7
Elevator Installers and Repairers	2,190	2,350	160	7.4
Helpers—Roofers	800	850	50	7.4

Note: Projections cover Texas; (1) Sorted by percent employment change and excludes occupations with numeric employment change less than 50
Source: www.projectionscentral.com, State Occupational Projections, 2017–2019 Short-Term Projections

TAXES

State Corporate Income Tax Rates

State	Tax Rate (%)	Income Brackets ($)	Num. of Brackets	Financial Institution Tax Rate (%)[a]	Federal Income Tax Ded.
Texas	(w)	–	–	(w)	No

Note: Tax rates as of January 1, 2018; (a) Rates listed are the corporate income tax rate applied to financial institutions or excise taxes based on income. Some states have other taxes based upon the value of deposits or shares; (w) Texas imposes a Franchise Tax, otherwise known as margin tax, imposed on entities with more than $1,110,000 total revenues at rate of 0.75%, or 0.375% for entities primarily engaged in retail or wholesale trade, on lesser of 70% of total revenues or 100% of gross receipts after deductions for either compensation or cost of goods sold.
Source: Federation of Tax Administrators, Range of State Corporate Income Tax Rates, January 1, 2018

State Individual Income Tax Rates

State	Tax Rate (%)	Income Brackets ($)	Num. of Brackets	Personal Exempt. ($)[1] Single	Personal Exempt. ($)[1] Dependents	Fed. Inc. Tax Ded.
Texas	None	–	–	–	–	–

Note: Tax rates as of January 1, 2018; Local- and county-level taxes are not included; n/a not applicable; (1) Married joint filers generally receive double the single exemption
Source: Federation of Tax Administrators, State Individual Income Tax Rates, January 1, 2018

Various State Sales and Excise Tax Rates

State	State Sales Tax (%)	Gasoline[1] (¢/gal.)	Cigarette[2] ($/pack)	Spirits[3] ($/gal.)	Wine[4] ($/gal.)	Beer[5] ($/gal.)	Recreational Marijuana (%)
Texas	6.25	20.0	1.41	2.40 (f)	0.20 (l)	0.20 (q)	Not legal

Note: All tax rates as of January 1, 2018; (1) The American Petroleum Institute has developed a methodology for determining the average tax rate on a gallon of fuel. Rates may include any of the following: excise taxes, environmental fees, storage tank fees, other fees or taxes, general sales tax, and local taxes. In states where gasoline is subject to the general sales tax, or where the fuel tax is based on the average sale price, the average rate determined by API is sensitive to changes in the price of gasoline. States that fully or partially apply general sales taxes to gasoline: CA, CO, GA, IL, IN, MI, NY; (2) The federal excise tax of $1.0066 per pack and local taxes are not included; (3) Rates are those applicable to off-premise sales of 40% alcohol by volume (a.b.v.) distilled spirits in 750ml containers. Local excise taxes are excluded; (4) Rates are those applicable to off-premise sales of 11% a.b.v. non-carbonated wine in 750ml containers; (5) Rates are those applicable to off-premise sales of 4.7% a.b.v. beer in 12 ounce containers; (f) Different rates also applicable according to alcohol content, place of production, size of container, or place purchased (on- or off-premise or onboard airlines); (l) Different rates also applicable to alcohol content, place of production, size of container, place purchased (on- or off-premise or on board airlines) or type of wine (carbonated, vermouth, etc.); (q) Different rates also applicable according to alcohol content, place of production, size of container, or place purchased (on- or off-premise or onboard airlines).
Source: Tax Foundation, 2018 Facts & Figures: How Does Your State Compare?

State Business Tax Climate Index Rankings

State	Overall Rank	Corporate Tax Rank	Individual Income Tax Rank	Sales Tax Rank	Unemployment Insurance Tax Rank	Property Tax Rank
Texas	13	49	6	37	26	37

Note: The index is a measure of how each state's tax laws affect economic performance. The lower the rank, the more favorable a state's tax system is for business. States without a given tax are given a ranking of 1. The scores/rankings for the District of Columbia do not affect other states. The 2018 index represents the tax climate as of July 1, 2017.
Source: Tax Foundation, State Business Tax Climate Index 2018

TRANSPORTATION

Means of Transportation to Work

Area	Car/Truck/Van		Public Transportation			Bicycle	Walked	Other Means	Worked at Home
	Drove Alone	Car-pooled	Bus	Subway	Railroad				
City	81.9	7.6	0.4	0.0	0.3	0.4	0.8	0.7	8.0
MSA[1]	76.5	9.9	2.2	0.0	0.1	0.8	1.7	1.3	7.4
U.S.	76.4	9.3	2.6	1.9	0.6	0.6	2.8	1.3	4.6

Note: Figures are percentages and cover workers 16 years of age and older; (1) Figures cover the Austin-Round Rock, TX Metropolitan Statistical Area—see Appendix B for areas included
Source: U.S. Census Bureau, 2012-2016 American Community Survey 5-Year Estimates

Travel Time to Work

Area	Less Than 10 Minutes	10 to 19 Minutes	20 to 29 Minutes	30 to 44 Minutes	45 to 59 Minutes	60 to 89 Minutes	90 Minutes or More
City	10.5	22.3	23.3	24.2	12.3	6.6	0.8
MSA[1]	10.2	28.3	22.3	22.7	9.2	5.5	1.9
U.S.	12.9	29.2	20.9	20.4	8.0	6.0	2.7

Note: Note: Figures are percentages and include workers 16 years old and over; (1) Figures cover the Austin-Round Rock, TX Metropolitan Statistical Area—see Appendix B for areas included
Source: U.S. Census Bureau, 2012-2016 American Community Survey 5-Year Estimates

Freeway Travel Time Index

Area	1985	1990	1995	2000	2005	2010	2014
Urban Area Rank[1,2]	20	21	23	15	12	12	10
Urban Area Index[1]	1.12	1.15	1.19	1.26	1.31	1.29	1.33
Average Index[3]	1.09	1.11	1.14	1.17	1.20	1.19	1.20

Note: Freeway Travel Time Index—the ratio of travel time in the peak period to the travel time at free-flow conditions. For example, a value of 1.30 indicates a 20-minute free-flow trip takes 26 minutes in the peak (20 minutes x 1.30 = 26 minutes); (1) Covers the Austin TX urban area; (2) Rank is based on 101 urban areas (#1 = highest travel time index); (3) Average of 101 urban areas
Source: Texas Transportation Institute, 2015 Urban Mobility Scorecard, August 2015

Freeway Commuter Stress Index

Area	1985	1990	1995	2000	2005	2010	2014
Urban Area Rank[1,2]	18	17	11	8	7	9	7
Urban Area Index[1]	1.22	1.25	1.30	1.37	1.43	1.40	1.44
Average Index[3]	1.13	1.16	1.19	1.22	1.25	1.24	1.25

Note: The Freeway Commuter Stress Index is the same as the Freeway Travel Time Index (see table above) except that it includes only the travel in the peak directions during the peak periods; the TTI includes travel in all directions during the peak period. Thus, the CSI is more indicative of the work trip experienced by each commuter on a daily basis; (1) Covers the Austin TX urban area; (2) Rank is based on 101 urban areas (#1 = highest travel time index); (3) Average of 101 urban areas
Source: Texas Transportation Institute, 2015 Urban Mobility Scorecard, August 2015

Living Environment

COST OF LIVING

Cost of Living Index

Composite Index	Groceries	Housing	Utilities	Trans-portation	Health Care	Misc. Goods/ Services
97.3	87.7	101.8	87.7	93.3	99.4	100.8

Note: The Cost of Living Index measures regional differences in the cost of consumer goods and services, excluding taxes and non-consumer expenditures, for professional and managerial households in the top income quintile. It is based on more than 50,000 prices covering almost 60 different items for which prices are collected three times a year by chambers of commerce, economic development organizations or university applied economic centers in each participating urban area. The numbers shown should be read as a percentage above or below the national average of 100. For example, a value of 115.4 in the groceries column indicates that grocery prices are 15.4% higher than the national average. Small differences in the index numbers should not be interpreted as significant; Figures cover the Austin TX urban area.
Source: The Council for Community and Economic Research, ACCRA Cost of Living Index, 2017

Grocery Prices

Area[1]	T-Bone Steak ($/pound)	Frying Chicken ($/pound)	Whole Milk ($/half gal.)	Eggs ($/dozen)	Orange Juice ($/64 oz.)	Coffee ($/11.5 oz.)
City[2]	9.91	1.15	1.81	1.34	3.14	3.97
Avg.	11.29	1.40	2.02	1.47	3.55	4.37
Min.	7.71	0.93	1.04	0.70	2.86	3.24
Max.	15.83	2.39	4.03	3.92	6.29	8.16

Note: (1) Values for the local area are compared with the average, minimum and maximum values for all 294 areas in the Cost of Living Index; (2) Figures cover the Austin TX urban area; ***T-Bone Steak*** *(price per pound);* ***Frying Chicken*** *(price per pound, whole fryer);* ***Whole Milk*** *(half gallon carton);* ***Eggs*** *(price per dozen, Grade A, large);* ***Orange Juice*** *(64 oz. Tropicana or Florida Natural);* ***Coffee*** *(11.5 oz. can, vacuum-packed, Maxwell House, Hills Bros, or Folgers).*
Source: The Council for Community and Economic Research, ACCRA Cost of Living Index, 2017

Housing and Utility Costs

Area[1]	New Home Price ($)	Apartment Rent ($/month)	All Electric ($/month)	Part Electric ($/month)	Other Energy ($/month)	Telephone ($/month)
City[2]	301,734	1,305	-	103.67	53.64	22.94
Avg.	335,956	1,047	175.01	97.34	67.93	28.71
Min.	187,788	491	109.48	49.33	35.44	12.39
Max.	1,739,087	4,559	432.62	227.09	353.33	44.61

Note: (1) Values for the local area are compared with the average, minimum and maximum values for all 294 areas in the Cost of Living Index; (2) Figures cover the Austin TX urban area; ***New Home Price*** *(2,400 sf living area, 8,000 sf lot, in urban area with full utilities);* ***Apartment Rent*** *(950 sf 2 bedroom/1.5 or 2 bath, unfurnished, excluding all utilities except water);* ***All Electric*** *(average monthly cost for an all-electric home);* ***Part Electric*** *(average monthly cost for a part-electric home);* ***Other Energy*** *(average monthly cost for natural gas, fuel oil, coal, wood, and any other forms of energy except electricity);* ***Telephone*** *(price includes basic monthly rate for a private residential line plus additional local usage charges incurred by a family of four).*
Source: The Council for Community and Economic Research, ACCRA Cost of Living Index, 2017

Health Care, Transportation, and Other Costs

Area[1]	Doctor ($/visit)	Dentist ($/visit)	Optometrist ($/visit)	Gasoline ($/gallon)	Beauty Salon ($/visit)	Men's Shirt ($)
City[2]	98.76	99.00	109.83	2.11	46.34	29.05
Avg.	108.00	92.54	101.93	2.25	37.58	30.92
Min.	30.39	60.00	49.75	1.82	16.11	11.20
Max.	193.50	161.94	229.28	3.16	77.35	59.13

Note: (1) Values for the local area are compared with the average, minimum and maximum values for all 294 areas in the Cost of Living Index; (2) Figures cover the Austin TX urban area; ***Doctor*** *(general practitioners routine exam of an established patient);* ***Dentist*** *(adult teeth cleaning and periodic oral examination);* ***Optometrist*** *(full vision eye exam for established adult patient);* ***Gasoline*** *(one gallon regular unleaded, national brand, including all taxes, cash price at self-service pump if available);* ***Beauty Salon*** *(woman's shampoo, trim, and blow-dry);* ***Men's Shirt*** *(cotton/polyester dress shirt, pinpoint weave, long sleeves).*
Source: The Council for Community and Economic Research, ACCRA Cost of Living Index, 2017

HOUSING

House Price Index (HPI)

Area	National Ranking[2]	Quarterly Change (%)	One-Year Change (%)	Five-Year Change (%)
MSA[1]	85	0.63	7.61	55.90
U.S.[3]	–	1.61	6.68	34.71

Note: The HPI is a weighted repeat sales index. It measures average price changes in repeat sales or refinancings on the same properties. This information is obtained by reviewing repeat mortgage transactions on single-family properties whose mortgages have been purchased or securitized by Fannie Mae or Freddie Mac in January 1975; (1) Figures cover the Austin-Round Rock, TX Metropolitan Statistical Area—see Appendix B for areas included; (2) Rankings are based on annual percentage change for all metro areas containing at least 15,000 transactions over the last 10 years and ranges from 1 to 253; (3) figures based on a weighted average of Census Division estimates using a seasonally adjusted, purchase-only index; all figures are for the period ending December 31, 2017
Source: Federal Housing Finance Agency, House Price Index, February 28, 2018

Median Single-Family Home Prices

Area	2015	2016	2017p	Percent Change 2016 to 2017
MSA[1]	263.3	284.0	295.8	4.2
U.S. Average	223.9	235.5	248.8	5.6

Note: Figures are median sales prices of existing single-family homes in thousands of dollars; (p) preliminary; (1) Figures cover the Austin-Round Rock, TX Metropolitan Statistical Area—see Appendix B for areas included
Source: National Association of Realtors, Median Sales Price of Existing Single-Family Homes for Metropolitan Areas, 4th Quarter 2017

Qualifying Income Based on Median Sales Price of Existing Single-Family Homes

Area	With 5% Down ($)	With 10% Down ($)	With 20% Down ($)
MSA[1]	65,769	62,307	55,384
U.S. Average	55,585	52,659	46,808

Note: Figures are preliminary; Qualifying income is based on a mortgage rate of 4.17%. Monthly principal and interest payment is limited to 25% of income; (1) Figures cover the Austin-Round Rock, TX Metropolitan Statistical Area—see Appendix B for areas included
Source: National Association of Realtors, Qualifying Income Based on Median Sales Price of Existing Single-Family Homes for Metropolitan Areas, 4th Quarter 2017

Median Apartment Condo-Coop Home Prices

Area	2015	2016	2017p	Percent Change 2016 to 2017
MSA[1]	227.5	228.0	241.8	6.1
U.S. Average	210.7	220.7	234.3	6.2

Note: Figures are median sales prices of existing apartment condo-coop homes in thousands of dollars; (p) preliminary; (1) Figures cover the Austin-Round Rock, TX Metropolitan Statistical Area—see Appendix B for areas included
Source: National Association of Realtors, Median Sales Price of Existing Apartment Condo-Coop Homes for Metropolitan Areas, 4th Quarter 2017

Home Value Distribution

Area	Under $50,000	$50,000 -$99,999	$100,000 -$149,999	$150,000 -$199,999	$200,000 -$299,999	$300,000 -$499,999	$500,000 -$999,999	$1,000,000 or more
City	2.2	1.6	10.3	21.8	37.9	23.5	2.5	0.2
MSA[1]	4.5	6.2	14.1	18.3	24.9	20.4	9.3	2.2
U.S.	8.8	14.8	15.3	14.9	18.4	16.4	9.0	2.5

Note: Figures are percentages and cover owner-occupied housing units; (1) Figures cover the Austin-Round Rock, TX Metropolitan Statistical Area—see Appendix B for areas included
Source: U.S. Census Bureau, 2012-2016 American Community Survey 5-Year Estimates

Homeownership Rate

Area	2009 (%)	2010 (%)	2011 (%)	2012 (%)	2013 (%)	2014 (%)	2015 (%)	2016 (%)	2017 (%)
MSA[1]	64.0	65.8	58.4	60.1	59.6	61.1	57.5	56.5	55.6
U.S.	67.4	66.9	66.1	65.4	65.1	64.5	63.7	63.4	63.9

Note: (1) Figures cover the Austin-Round Rock, TX Metropolitan Statistical Area—see Appendix B for areas included
Source: U.S. Census Bureau, Housing Vacancies and Homeownership Annual Statistics: 2009-2017

Year Housing Structure Built

Area	2010 or Later	2000 -2009	1990 -1999	1980 -1989	1970 -1979	1960 -1969	1950 -1959	1940 -1949	Before 1940	Median Year
City	12.4	43.7	27.9	11.3	3.5	0.7	0.2	0.1	0.3	2001
MSA[1]	7.0	28.6	19.4	18.2	13.1	5.4	3.7	2.0	2.5	1993
U.S.	2.3	14.7	14.0	13.7	15.6	10.9	10.6	5.2	13.0	1977

Note: Figures are percentages except for Median Year; Note: (1) Figures cover the Austin-Round Rock, TX Metropolitan Statistical Area—see Appendix B for areas included
Source: U.S. Census Bureau, 2012-2016 American Community Survey 5-Year Estimates

Gross Monthly Rent

Area	Under $500	$500 -$999	$1,000 -$1,499	$1,500 -$1,999	$2,000 -$2,499	$2,500 -$2,999	$3,000 and up	Median ($)
City	0.6	30.6	40.8	20.3	5.9	0.9	0.7	1,195
MSA[1]	3.7	36.9	38.9	15.0	3.5	1.0	0.9	1,098
U.S.	11.3	43.3	27.7	10.7	4.0	1.6	1.5	949

Note: Figures are percentages except for Median; Gross rent is the contract rent plus the estimated average monthly cost of utilities (electricity, gas, and water and sewer) and fuels (oil, coal, kerosene, wood, etc.) if these are paid by the renter (or paid for the renter by someone else); (1) Figures cover the Austin-Round Rock, TX Metropolitan Statistical Area—see Appendix B for areas included
Source: U.S. Census Bureau, 2012-2016 American Community Survey 5-Year Estimates

HEALTH

Health Risk Factors

Category	MSA[1] (%)	U.S. (%)
Adults aged 18–64 who have any kind of health care coverage	78.8	87.7
Adults who reported being in good or excellent health	85.7	83.6
Adults who are current smokers	14.6	17.1
Adults who currently use E-cigarettes	6.1	4.7
Adults who currently use chewing tobacco, snuff, or snus	3.2	4.0
Adults who are heavy drinkers[2]	9.1	6.5
Adults who are binge drinkers[3]	22.7	16.9
Adults who are overweight (BMI 25.0 - 29.9)	32.9	35.3
Adults who are obese (BMI 30.0 - 99.8)	29.4	29.9
Adults who participated in any physical activities in the past month	81.2	76.9
Adults who always or nearly always wears a seat belt	96.6	94.3

Note: (1) Figures cover the Austin-Round Rock, TX Metropolitan Statistical Area—see Appendix B for areas included; (2) Heavy drinkers are classified as adult men having more than 14 drinks per week and adult women having more than 7 drinks per week; (3) Binge drinkers are classified as males having five or more drinks on one occasion or females having four or more drinks on one occasion
Source: Centers for Disease Control and Prevention, Behaviorial Risk Factor Surveillance System, SMART: Selected Metropolitan Area Risk Trends, 2016

Health Screening Rates

Category	MSA[1] (%)	U.S. (%)
Adults 50-75 who have had a blood stool test within the past year	7.2	8.0
Adults 50-75 who have had a colonoscopy in the past 10 years	66.0	63.5
Adults aged 65+ who have had flu shot within the past year	53.3	58.6
Adults aged 65+ who have ever had a pneumonia vaccination	80.1	73.4
Adults who have ever been tested for HIV	46.4	35.6
Women aged 21-65 who have had a pap test in the past three years	79.0	79.8
Men aged 40+ who have had a PSA test within the past two years	36.8	39.5
Women aged 40+ who have had a mammogram within the past two years	70.1	72.5

Note: n/a not available; (1) Figures cover the Austin-Round Rock, TX Metropolitan Statistical Area—see Appendix B for areas included; Source: Centers for Disease Control and Prevention, Behaviorial Risk Factor Surveillance System, SMART: Selected Metropolitan Area Risk Trends, 2016

Chronic Health Conditions

Category	MSA[1] (%)	U.S. (%)
Adults who have ever been told they had a heart attack	3.1	4.4
Adults who have ever been told they have angina or coronary heart disease	3.5	4.1
Adults who have ever been told they had a stroke	2.3	3.1
Adults who have been told they currently have asthma	8.6	9.3
Adults who have ever been told they have arthritis	18.4	25.8
Adults who have ever been told they have diabetes[2]	10.4	10.5
Adults who have ever been told they had skin cancer	6.8	5.9
Adults who have ever been told they had any other types of cancer	5.5	6.7
Adults who have ever been told they have COPD	3.6	6.3
Adults who have ever been told they have kidney disease	2.6	2.8
Adults who have ever been told they have a form of depression	13.7	17.4

Note: (1) Figures cover the Austin-Round Rock, TX Metropolitan Statistical Area—see Appendix B for areas included; (2) Figures do not include pregnancy-related, borderline, or pre-diabetes
Source: Centers for Disease Control and Prevention, Behaviorial Risk Factor Surveillance System, SMART: Selected Metropolitan Area Risk Trends, 2016

Mortality Rates for the Top 10 Causes of Death in the U.S.

ICD-10[a] Sub-Chapter	ICD-10[a] Code	Age-Adjusted Mortality Rate[1] per 100,000 population	
		County[2]	U.S.
Malignant neoplasms	C00-C97	129.1	158.5
Ischaemic heart diseases	I20-I25	66.9	96.8
Other forms of heart disease	I30-I51	35.7	52.4
Chronic lower respiratory diseases	J40-J47	31.4	40.9
Cerebrovascular diseases	I60-I69	34.8	37.2
Organic, including symptomatic, mental disorders	F01-F09	40.1	33.3
Other degenerative diseases of the nervous system	G30-G31	43.6	32.1
Other external causes of accidental injury	W00-X59	17.2	31.2
Diabetes mellitus	E10-E14	10.8	21.1
Hypertensive diseases	I10-I15	16.1	20.8

Note: (a) ICD-10 = International Classification of Diseases 10th Revision; (1) Mortality rates are a three year average covering 2014-2016; (2) Figures cover Williamson County.
Source: Centers for Disease Control and Prevention, National Center for Health Statistics. Underlying Cause of Death 1999-2016 on CDC WONDER Online Database, released December 2017

Mortality Rates for Selected Causes of Death

ICD-10[a] Sub-Chapter	ICD-10[a] Code	Age-Adjusted Mortality Rate[1] per 100,000 population	
		County[2]	U.S.
Assault	X85-Y09	1.5	5.6
Diseases of the liver	K70-K76	12.8	14.0
Human immunodeficiency virus (HIV) disease	B20-B24	Suppressed	1.9
Influenza and pneumonia	J09-J18	9.4	14.6
Intentional self-harm	X60-X84	14.0	13.2
Malnutrition	E40-E46	Unreliable	1.3
Obesity and other hyperalimentation	E65-E68	Suppressed	2.1
Renal failure	N17-N19	10.6	13.0
Transport accidents	V01-V99	11.0	12.0
Viral hepatitis	B15-B19	Unreliable	1.9

Note: (a) ICD-10 = International Classification of Diseases 10th Revision; (1) Mortality rates are a three year average covering 2014-2016; (2) Figures cover Williamson County; Data are Suppressed when the data meet the criteria for confidentiality constraints; Mortality rates are flagged as Unreliable when the rate would be calculated with a numerator of 20 or less.
Source: Centers for Disease Control and Prevention, National Center for Health Statistics. Underlying Cause of Death 1999-2016 on CDC WONDER Online Database, released December 2017

Health Insurance Coverage

Area	With Health Insurance	With Private Health Insurance	With Public Health Insurance	Without Health Insurance	Population Under Age 18 Without Health Insurance
City	90.1	83.0	13.7	9.9	6.3
MSA[1]	85.1	71.7	21.8	14.9	8.7
U.S.	88.3	66.7	33.0	11.7	5.9

Note: Figures are percentages that cover the civilian noninstitutionalized population; (1) Figures cover the Austin-Round Rock, TX Metropolitan Statistical Area—see Appendix B for areas included
Source: U.S. Census Bureau, 2012-2016 American Community Survey 5-Year Estimates

Number of Medical Professionals

Area	MDs[3]	DOs[3,4]	Dentists	Podiatrists	Chiropractors	Optometrists
County[1] (number)	874	90	286	22	142	92
County[1] (rate[2])	172.2	17.7	54.2	4.2	26.9	17.4
U.S. (rate[2])	276.5	22.3	67.3	6.0	26.7	15.9

Note: Data as of 2016 unless noted; (1) Data covers Williamson County; (2) Rate per 100,000 population; (3) Data as of 2015 and includes all active, non-federal physicians; (4) Doctor of Osteopathic Medicine
Source: U.S. Department of Health and Human Services, Health Resources and Services Administration, Bureau of Health Professions, Area Resource File (ARF) 2016-2017

Best Hospitals

According to *U.S. News,* the Austin-Round Rock, TX metro area is home to one of the best children's hospitals in the U.S.: **Dell Children's Medical Center of Central Texas** (1 pediatric specialty). The hospital listed was highly ranked in at least one of 10 pediatric specialties. Eighty-two children's hospitals in the U.S. were nationally ranked in at least one specialty. Hospitals received points for being ranked in a specialty, and the 10 hospitals with the most points across the 10 specialties make up the Honor Roll. *U.S. News Online, "America's Best Children's Hospitals 2017-18"*

EDUCATION

Public School District Statistics

District Name	Schls	Pupils	Pupil/ Teacher Ratio	Minority Pupils[1] (%)	Free Lunch Eligible[2] (%)	IEP[3] (%)
Leander ISD	42	37,158	15.2	39.3	14.2	10.3

Note: Table includes school districts with 100 or more students; (1) Percentage of students that are not non-Hispanic white; (2) Percentage of students that are eligible for the free lunch program; (3) Percentage of students that have an Individualized Education Program.
Source: U.S. Department of Education, National Center for Education Statistics, Common Core of Data, Local Education Agency (School District) Universe Survey: School Year 2015-2016; U.S. Department of Education, National Center for Education Statistics, Common Core of Data, Public Elementary/Secondary School Universe Survey: School Year 2015-2016

Highest Level of Education

Area	Less than H.S.	H.S. Diploma	Some College, No Deg.	Associate Degree	Bachelor's Degree	Master's Degree	Prof. School Degree	Doctorate Degree
City	4.4	17.1	25.6	8.4	30.7	11.2	1.5	1.0
MSA[1]	11.1	19.2	21.3	6.4	27.4	10.6	2.3	1.8
U.S.	13.0	27.5	21.0	8.2	18.8	8.2	2.0	1.3

Note: Figures cover persons age 25 and over; (1) Figures cover the Austin-Round Rock, TX Metropolitan Statistical Area—see Appendix B for areas included
Source: U.S. Census Bureau, 2012-2016 American Community Survey 5-Year Estimates

Educational Attainment by Race

Area	High School Graduate or Higher (%)					Bachelor's Degree or Higher (%)				
	Total	White	Black	Asian	Hisp.[2]	Total	White	Black	Asian	Hisp.[2]
City	95.6	95.7	92.6	96.2	89.5	44.5	42.8	23.9	70.9	29.0
MSA[1]	88.9	90.1	89.6	91.8	70.4	42.0	43.6	25.5	67.7	20.2
U.S.	87.0	88.9	84.3	86.3	65.7	30.3	31.6	20.0	52.1	14.7

Note: Figures shown cover persons 25 years old and over; (1) Figures cover the Austin-Round Rock, TX Metropolitan Statistical Area—see Appendix B for areas included; (2) People of Hispanic origin can be of any race
Source: U.S. Census Bureau, 2012-2016 American Community Survey 5-Year Estimates

School Enrollment by Grade and Control

Area	Preschool (%)		Kindergarten (%)		Grades 1 - 4 (%)		Grades 5 - 8 (%)		Grades 9 - 12 (%)	
	Public	Private	Public	Private	Public	Private	Public	Private	Public	Private
City	31.5	68.5	87.0	13.0	95.1	4.9	90.2	9.8	93.9	6.1
MSA[1]	50.0	50.0	88.8	11.2	91.4	8.6	91.6	8.4	93.5	6.5
U.S.	58.4	41.6	87.7	12.3	89.8	10.2	89.7	10.3	90.4	9.6

Note: Figures shown cover persons 3 years old and over; (1) Figures cover the Austin-Round Rock, TX Metropolitan Statistical Area—see Appendix B for areas included
Source: U.S. Census Bureau, 2012-2016 American Community Survey 5-Year Estimates

Average Salaries of Public School Classroom Teachers

Area	2015		2016		Change from 2015 to 2016	
	Dollars	Rank[1]	Dollars	Rank[1]	Percent	Rank[2]
Texas	50,713	28	51,890	27	2.3	8
U.S. Average	57,611	–	58,353	–	1.3	–

Note: (1) Rank ranges from 1 to 51 where 1 indicates highest salary; (2) Rank ranges from 1 to 51 where 1 indicates highest percent change.
Source: National Education Association, Rankings & Estimates: Rankings of the States 2016 and Estimates of School Statistics 2017

Higher Education

Four-Year Colleges			Two-Year Colleges			Medical Schools[1]	Law Schools[2]	Voc/ Tech[3]
Public	Private Non-profit	Private For-profit	Public	Private Non-profit	Private For-profit			
0	0	1	0	0	0	0	0	0

Note: Figures cover institutions located within the city limits and include main campuses only; (1) includes schools accredited by the Liaison Committee on Medical Education and the American Osteopathic Association's Commission on Osteopathic College Accreditation; (2) includes ABA-accredited schools, schools with provisional ABA accreditation, and state accredited schools; (3) includes all schools with programs that are less than 2 years.
Source: National Center for Education Statistics, Integrated Postsecondary Education System (IPEDS), 2016-17; Wikipedia, List of Medical Schools in the United States, accessed April 2, 2018; Wikipedia, List of Law Schools in the United States, accessed April 2, 2018

According to *U.S. News & World Report,* the Austin-Round Rock, TX metro area is home to one of the best national universities in the U.S.: **University of Texas—Austin** (#56 tie). The indicators used to capture academic quality fall into a number of categories: assessment by administrators at peer institutions; retention of students; faculty resources; student selectivity; financial resources; alumni giving; high school counselor ratings of colleges; and graduation rate. *U.S. News & World Report, "America's Best Colleges 2018"*

According to *U.S. News & World Report,* the Austin-Round Rock, TX metro area is home to one of the best liberal arts colleges in the U.S.: **Southwestern University** (#96 tie). The indicators used to capture academic quality fall into a number of categories: assessment by administrators at peer institutions; retention of students; faculty resources; student selectivity; financial resources; alumni giving; high school counselor ratings of colleges; and graduation rate. *U.S. News & World Report, "America's Best Colleges 2018"*

According to *U.S. News & World Report,* the Austin-Round Rock, TX metro area is home to one of the top 100 law schools in the U.S.: **University of Texas—Austin** (#15). The rankings are based on a weighted average of 12 measures of quality: peer assessment score; assessment score by lawyers/judges; median LSAT scores; median undergrad GPA; acceptance rate; employment rates for graduates; placement success; bar passage rate; faculty resources; expenditures per student; student/faculty ratio; and library resources. *U.S. News & World Report, "America's Best Graduate Schools, Law, 2019"*

According to *U.S. News & World Report,* the Austin-Round Rock, TX metro area is home to one of the top 75 business schools in the U.S.: **University of Texas—Austin (McCombs)** (#17 tie). The rankings are based on a weighted average of the following nine measures: quality assessment; peer assessment; recruiter assessment; placement success; mean starting salary and bonus; student selectivity; mean GMAT and GRE scores; mean undergraduate GPA; and acceptance rate. *U.S. News & World Report, "America's Best Graduate Schools, Business, 2019"*

PRESIDENTIAL ELECTION

2016 Presidential Election Results

Area	Clinton	Trump	Johnson	Stein	Other
Williamson County	41.3	50.9	5.0	1.0	1.8
U.S.	48.0	45.9	3.3	1.1	1.7

Note: Results are percentages and may not add to 100% due to rounding
Source: Dave Leip's Atlas of U.S. Presidential Elections

EMPLOYERS

Major Employers

Company Name	Industry
Accenture	Management consulting & software development center
Apple	Computer maker's tech & admin support center
Applied Materials	Semiconductor production equipment mfg. & r&d
AT&T	Telecommunications (hdq. of texas ops.)
Austin Community College	Higher education, public
Austin School Independent District	Public education
City of Austin	Government
Dell	Computer technology solutions & equipment mfg./sales
Federal Government	Government
Flextronics	Contract electronics mfg. & integrated supply chain svcs
Hays Consolidated ISD	Public education
IBM Corp.	Computer systems, hardware, software, & chip r&d
Keller Williams Realty	Residential real estate
Leander Independent School District	Public education
National Instruments	Virtual instrumentation software & hardware mfg.
NXP Semiconductors	Semiconductor chip design & mfg.
Pflugerville Independent School District	Public education
Round Rock Independent School District	Public education
Samsung Austin Semiconductor	Semiconductor chip mfg., R&D
Seton Healthcare Family	Healthcare
St. David's Healthcare Partnership	Healthcare
State of Texas	Government
Texas State University-San Marcos	Higher education, public
Travis County	Government
U.S. Internal Revenue Service	Government (regional call & processing center)
University of Texas at Austin	Higher education, public
Whole Foods Market	Grocery stores

Note: Companies shown are located within the Austin-Round Rock, TX Metropolitan Statistical Area.
Source: Hoovers.com; Wikipedia

PUBLIC SAFETY

Crime Rate

Area	All Crimes	Violent Crimes				Property Crimes		
		Murder	Rape[3]	Robbery	Aggrav. Assault	Burglary	Larceny -Theft	Motor Vehicle Theft
City	1,564.1	0.0	59.4	24.6	84.0	220.1	1,125.3	50.7
Metro[1]	2,872.1	3.4	57.4	68.7	187.4	421.9	1,968.3	165.1
U.S.	2,847.8	5.3	40.4	102.8	248.5	468.9	1,745.0	236.9

Note: Figures are crimes per 100,000 population; (1) Figures cover the Austin-Round Rock, TX Metropolitan Statistical Area—see Appendix B for areas included; (3) The city and U.S. figures shown were reported using the revised Uniform Crime Reporting (UCR) definition of rape. The metro area figures shown are an aggregate total of the data submitted using both the revised and legacy UCR definitions.
Source: FBI Uniform Crime Reports, 2016

Hate Crimes

Area	Number of Quarters Reported	Number of Incidents per Bias Motivation: Race/Ethnicity/ Ancestry	Religion	Sexual Orientation	Disability	Gender	Gender Identity
City	1	1	0	1	0	0	0
U.S.	4	3,489	1,273	1,076	70	31	124

Source: Federal Bureau of Investigation, Hate Crime Statistics 2016

Identity Theft Consumer Reports

Area	Reports	Reports per 100,000 Population	Rank[2]
MSA[1]	2,485	121	53
U.S.	371,061	114	-

Note: (1) Figures cover the Austin-Round Rock, TX Metropolitan Statistical Area—see Appendix B for areas included; (2) Rank ranges from 1 to 389 where 1 indicates greatest number of identity theft reports per 100,000 population
Source: Federal Trade Commission, Consumer Sentinel Network Data Book for January–December 2017

Fraud and Other Consumer Reports

Area	Reports	Reports per 100,000 Population	Rank[2]
MSA[1]	10,984	534	84
U.S.	2,304,550	708	-

Note: (1) Figures cover the Austin-Round Rock, TX Metropolitan Statistical Area—see Appendix B for areas included; (2) Rank ranges from 1 to 389 where 1 indicates greatest number of fraud and other consumer reports per 100,000 population
Source: Federal Trade Commission, Consumer Sentinel Network Data Book for January–December 2017

SPORTS

Professional Sports Teams

Team Name	League	Year Established
No teams are located in the metro area		

Source: Wikipedia, Major Professional Sports Teams of the United States and Canada, April 5, 2018

CLIMATE

Average and Extreme Temperatures

Temperature	Jan	Feb	Mar	Apr	May	Jun	Jul	Aug	Sep	Oct	Nov	Dec	Yr.
Extreme High (°F)	90	97	98	98	100	105	109	106	104	98	91	90	109
Average High (°F)	60	64	72	79	85	91	95	96	90	81	70	63	79
Average Temp. (°F)	50	53	61	69	75	82	85	85	80	70	60	52	69
Average Low (°F)	39	43	50	58	65	72	74	74	69	59	49	41	58
Extreme Low (°F)	-2	7	18	35	43	53	64	61	47	32	20	4	-2

Note: Figures cover the years 1948-1990
Source: National Climatic Data Center, International Station Meteorological Climate Summary, 9/96

Average Precipitation/Snowfall/Humidity

Precip./Humidity	Jan	Feb	Mar	Apr	May	Jun	Jul	Aug	Sep	Oct	Nov	Dec	Yr.
Avg. Precip. (in.)	1.6	2.3	1.8	2.9	4.3	3.5	1.9	1.9	3.3	3.5	2.1	1.9	31.1
Avg. Snowfall (in.)	1	Tr	Tr	0	0	0	0	0	0	0	Tr	Tr	1
Avg. Rel. Hum. 6am (%)	79	80	79	83	88	89	88	87	86	84	81	79	84
Avg. Rel. Hum. 3pm (%)	53	51	47	50	53	49	43	42	47	47	49	51	48

Note: Figures cover the years 1948-1990; Tr = Trace amounts (<0.05 in. of rain; <0.5 in. of snow)
Source: National Climatic Data Center, International Station Meteorological Climate Summary, 9/96

Weather Conditions

Temperature: 10°F & below	32°F & below	90°F & above	Daytime Sky: Clear	Partly cloudy	Cloudy	Precipitation: 0.01 inch or more precip.	0.1 inch or more snow/ice	Thunder-storms
< 1	20	111	105	148	112	83	1	41

Note: Figures are average number of days per year and cover the years 1948-1990
Source: National Climatic Data Center, International Station Meteorological Climate Summary, 9/96

HAZARDOUS WASTE

Superfund Sites

The Austin-Round Rock, TX metro area has no sites on the EPA's Superfund Final National Priorities List. There are a total of 1,396 Superfund sites with a status of proposed or final on the list in the U.S. *U.S. Environmental Protection Agency, National Priorities List, April 4, 2018*

AIR & WATER QUALITY

Air Quality Trends: Ozone

	1990	1995	2000	2005	2010	2012	2013	2014	2015	2016
MSA[1]	0.088	0.089	0.088	0.082	0.074	0.074	0.069	0.062	0.073	0.064
U.S.	0.087	0.089	0.081	0.079	0.073	0.075	0.069	0.067	0.068	0.069

Note: (1) Data covers the Austin-Round Rock, TX Metropolitan Statistical Area—see Appendix B for areas included. The values shown are the composite ozone concentration averages among trend sites based on the highest fourth daily maximum 8-hour concentration in parts per million. These trends are based on sites having an adequate record of monitoring data during the trend period. Data from exceptional events are included.
Source: U.S. Environmental Protection Agency, Air Quality Monitoring Information, "Air Quality Trends by City, 1990-2016"

Air Quality Index

Area	Percent of Days when Air Quality was...[2]					AQI Statistics[2]	
	Good	Moderate	Unhealthy for Sensitive Groups	Unhealthy	Very Unhealthy	Maximum	Median
MSA[1]	71.8	27.1	1.1	0.0	0.0	130	43

Note: (1) Data covers the Austin-Round Rock, TX Metropolitan Statistical Area—see Appendix B for areas included; (2) Based on 365 days with AQI data in 2017. Air Quality Index (AQI) is an index for reporting daily air quality. EPA calculates the AQI for five major air pollutants regulated by the Clean Air Act: ground-level ozone, particle pollution (aka particulate matter), carbon monoxide, sulfur dioxide, and nitrogen dioxide. The AQI runs from 0 to 500. The higher the AQI value, the greater the level of air pollution and the greater the health concern. There are six AQI categories: "Good" AQI is between 0 and 50. Air quality is considered satisfactory; "Moderate" AQI is between 51 and 100. Air quality is acceptable; "Unhealthy for Sensitive Groups" When AQI values are between 101 and 150, members of sensitive groups may experience health effects; "Unhealthy" When AQI values are between 151 and 200 everyone may begin to experience health effects; "Very Unhealthy" AQI values between 201 and 300 trigger a health alert; "Hazardous" AQI values over 300 trigger warnings of emergency conditions (not shown).
Source: U.S. Environmental Protection Agency, Air Quality Index Report, 2017

Air Quality Index Pollutants

Area	Percent of Days when AQI Pollutant was...[2]					
	Carbon Monoxide	Nitrogen Dioxide	Ozone	Sulfur Dioxide	Particulate Matter 2.5	Particulate Matter 10
MSA[1]	0.0	3.8	49.9	0.0	46.3	0.0

Note: (1) Data covers the Austin-Round Rock, TX Metropolitan Statistical Area—see Appendix B for areas included; (2) Based on 365 days with AQI data in 2017. The Air Quality Index (AQI) is an index for reporting daily air quality. EPA calculates the AQI for five major air pollutants regulated by the Clean Air Act: ground-level ozone, particle pollution (also known as particulate matter), carbon monoxide, sulfur dioxide, and nitrogen dioxide. The AQI runs from 0 to 500. The higher the AQI value, the greater the level of air pollution and the greater the health concern.
Source: U.S. Environmental Protection Agency, Air Quality Index Report, 2017

Maximum Air Pollutant Concentrations: Particulate Matter, Ozone, CO and Lead

	Particulate Matter 10 (ug/m³)	Particulate Matter 2.5 Wtd AM (ug/m³)	Particulate Matter 2.5 24-Hr (ug/m³)	Ozone (ppm)	Carbon Monoxide (ppm)	Lead (ug/m³)
MSA[1] Level	72	n/a	n/a	0.064	n/a	n/a
NAAQS[2]	150	15	35	0.075	9	0.15
Met NAAQS[2]	Yes	n/a	n/a	Yes	n/a	n/a

Note: (1) Data covers the Austin-Round Rock, TX Metropolitan Statistical Area—see Appendix B for areas included; Data from exceptional events are included; (2) National Ambient Air Quality Standards; ppm = parts per million; ug/m³ = micrograms per cubic meter; n/a not available.
Concentrations: Particulate Matter 10 (coarse particulate)—highest second maximum 24-hour concentration; Particulate Matter 2.5 Wtd AM (fine particulate)—highest weighted annual mean concentration; Particulate Matter 2.5 24-Hour (fine particulate)—highest 98th percentile 24-hour concentration; Ozone—highest fourth daily maximum 8-hour concentration; Carbon Monoxide—highest second maximum non-overlapping 8-hour concentration; Lead—maximum running 3-month average
Source: U.S. Environmental Protection Agency, Air Quality Monitoring Information, "Air Quality Statistics by City, 2016"

Maximum Air Pollutant Concentrations: Nitrogen Dioxide and Sulfur Dioxide

	Nitrogen Dioxide AM (ppb)	Nitrogen Dioxide 1-Hr (ppb)	Sulfur Dioxide AM (ppb)	Sulfur Dioxide 1-Hr (ppb)	Sulfur Dioxide 24-Hr (ppb)
MSA[1] Level	14	47	n/a	4	n/a
NAAQS[2]	53	100	30	75	140
Met NAAQS[2]	Yes	Yes	n/a	Yes	n/a

Note: (1) Data covers the Austin-Round Rock, TX Metropolitan Statistical Area—see Appendix B for areas included; Data from exceptional events are included; (2) National Ambient Air Quality Standards; ppm = parts per million; ug/m³ = micrograms per cubic meter; n/a not available.
Concentrations: Nitrogen Dioxide AM—highest arithmetic mean concentration; Nitrogen Dioxide 1-Hr—highest 98th percentile 1-hour daily maximum concentration; Sulfur Dioxide AM—highest annual mean concentration; Sulfur Dioxide 1-Hr—highest 99th percentile 1-hour daily maximum concentration; Sulfur Dioxide 24-Hr—highest second maximum 24-hour concentration
Source: U.S. Environmental Protection Agency, Air Quality Monitoring Information, "Air Quality Statistics by City, 2016"

Drinking Water

Water System Name	Pop. Served	Primary Water Source Type	Violations[1] Health Based	Violations[1] Monitoring/ Reporting
City of Cedar Park	65,627	Surface	0	1

Note: (1) Based on violation data from January 1, 2017 to December 31, 2017
Source: U.S. Environmental Protection Agency, Office of Ground Water and Drinking Water, Safe Drinking Water Information System (based on data extracted April 5, 2018)

Cibolo, Texas

Background

Cibolo is a city in two counties, Guadalupe County and Bexar County. In 1876, the Southern Pacific Railroad was created to pass through Cibolo and connect with the larger cities of Texas, including Houston and San Antonio. Prior to the first German settlers arriving, Native American tribes including the Comanche Nation roamed the land. Cibolo is a Native American word meaning "buffalo." It became an independent township in 1965. More recently, Cibolo has been experiencing high levels of growth, with its population increasing 733 percent since 2000.

To the east, Cibolo is bordered by Santa Clara and Marion, while New Berlin, Zuehl, and St. Hedwig border Cibolo to the south. To the north and west, Schertz borders Cibolo.

Cibolo is served by the Schertz-Cibolo-Universal City Independent School District. Within Cibolo are one high school, one junior high school, two intermediate schools, and three elementary schools.

Community activities and programs within Cibolo include the CiboloFest, held in October to coincide with the city's anniversary of independence. Other activities include a Christmas Parade and the Cibolo BBQ Cook-Off. Residents and tourists enjoy the city's numerous parks, including Al Rich Park, Niemetz Park, Schlather Park, and Veteran's Park.

Cibolo is served by the Austin-Bergstrom International Airport in Austin, Texas for regional flights and by the San Antonio International Airport in San Antonio, Texas for international ventures.

Rankings

General Rankings

- *US News & World Report* conducted a survey of more than 2,000 people and analyzed the 125 largest metropolitan areas to determine what matters the most when selecting the next place to live. San Antonio* ranked #14 out of the top 25 as having the best combination of desirable factors. Criteria: cost of living; quality of education; job market, crime rates; and other factors. *realestate.usnews.com, "The 25 Best Places to Live in the U.S. in 2018," April 10, 2018*

- The San Antonio* metro area was identified as one of America's fastest-growing areas in terms of population and economy by *Forbes.* The area ranked #21 out of 25. The 100 most populous metro areas in the U.S. were evaluated on the following criteria: estimated population growth; employment; economic output; wages; home values. *Forbes, "America's Fastest-Growing Cities 2018," February 28, 2018*

- San Antonio* was identified as one of America's fastest-growing cities in terms of population growth by CNNMoney.com. The area ranked #5 out of 10. Criteria: population growth between July 2015 and July 2016; cities and towns with populations of 50,000. *CNNMoney, "10 Fastest-Growing Cities," June 2, 2017*

Business/Finance Rankings

- According to *Business Insider,* the San Antonio* metro area is where startup growth is on the rise. Based on the 2017 Kauffman Index of Growth Entrepreneurship, which measured in-depth national entrepreneurial trends in 40 metro areas, it ranked #14 in highest startup growth. *www.businessinsider.com, "The 21 U.S. Cities with the Highest Startup Growth," October 21, 2017*

- The personal finance site NerdWallet analyzed 183 American metropolitan areas with populations over 250,000 and more than 15,000 businesses to rank where entrepreneurs find the most success. Criteria included area economy, annual income, housing cost, unemployment rate, and the success rate of area businesses. San Antonio* ranked #158. *www.nerdwallet.com, "Best Places to Start a Business," April 27, 2015*

- USAA and Hiring Our Heroes worked with Sperlings's BestPlaces and the Institute for Veterans and Military Families at Syracuse University to rank major metropolitan areas where military-skills-related employment is strongest. Criteria for *mid-career* veterans included veteran wage growth; recent job growth; stability; and accessible health resources. Metro areas with a higher than national average crime or unemployment rate were excluded. At #10, the San Antonio* metro area made the top ten. *www.usaa.com, "2015 Best Places for Veterans"*

- In a survey of economic confidence in the nation's 50 largest metropolitan areas conducted January–December 2014, the San Antonio* metro area placed #24, according to Gallup's 2014 Economic Confidence Index. *Gallup, "San Jose and San Francisco Lead in Economic Confidence," March 19, 2015*

- The Brookings Institution ranked the 100 largest metro areas in the U.S. based on income inequality. San Antonio* was ranked #56 (#1 = greatest ineqality). Criteria: the "95/20 ratio," a figure representing the income at which a household earns more than 95 percent of all other households, divided by the income at which a household earns more than only 20 percent of all other households. *Brookings Institution, "Household Income Inequality, 100 Largest U.S. Metro Areas, 2014-2016," February 5, 2018*

- The San Antonio* metro area was identified as one of the most debt-ridden places in America by the finance site Credit.com. The metro area was ranked #5. Criteria: residents' average credit card debt as well as median income. *Credit.com, "25 Cities With the Most Credit Card Debt," February 28, 2018*

- The San Antonio* metro area was identified as one of the most affordable metropolitan areas in America by *Forbes.* The area ranked #20 out of 20 based on the National Association of Home Builders/Wells Fargo Housing Affordability Index and Sperling's Best Places' cost-of-living index. *Forbes.com, "America's Most Affordable Cities in 2015," March 12, 2015*

- The San Antonio* metro area appeared on the Milken Institute "2017 Best Performing Cities" list. Rank: #19 out of 200 large metro areas. Criteria: job growth; wage and salary growth; high-tech output growth. *Milken Institute, "Best-Performing Cities 2017," January 2018*
- *Forbes* ranked the 200 most populous metro areas to determine the nation's "Best Places for Business and Careers." The San Antonio* metro area was ranked #42. Criteria: costs (business and living); job growth (past and projected); income growth; quality of life; educational attainment (college and high school); projected economic growth; cultural and recreational opportunities; net migration patterns; number of highly ranked colleges. *Forbes, "The Best Places for Business and Careers 2017," October 24, 2017*

Dating/Romance Rankings

- *Apartment List* conducted its annual survey of renters to compile a list of metros that have the best opportunities for dating. Nearly 11,000 respondents, from February 2017 through January 2018, rated their current city or neighborhood for opportunities to date and make friends. The San Antonio* metro area ranked #2 out of 70 where single residents were very satisfied or somewhat satisfied, making it among the ten best metros for dating opportunities. Other criteria analyzed included gender and education levels of renters. *Apartment List, "Best Metros for Dating 2018," February 6, 2018*

Education Rankings

- Personal finance website *WalletHub* analyzed the 150 largest U.S. metropolitan statistical areas to determine where the most educated Americans are choosing to settle. Criteria: education quality and attainment gap; education levels; percentage of workers with degrees; public school rankings; quality and size of each metro area's universities. San Antonio* was ranked #109 (#1 = most educated city). *www.WalletHub.com, "2017's Most and Least Educated Cities in America," July 25, 2017*

Environmental Rankings

- Sperling's BestPlaces assessed 379 metropolitan areas of the United States for the likelihood of dangerously extreme weather events or earthquakes. In general the Southeast and South-Central regions have the highest risk of weather extremes and earthquakes, while the Pacific Northwest enjoys the lowest risk. Of the least risky metropolitan areas, the San Antonio* metro area was ranked #356. *www.bestplaces.net, "Safest Places from Natural Disasters," April 2011*
- San Antonio* was highlighted as one of the 25 most ozone-polluted metro areas in the U.S. during 2013 through 2015. The area ranked #19. *American Lung Association, State of the Air 2017*
- San Antonio* was highlighted as one of the top 99 cleanest metro areas for short-term particle pollution (24-hour PM 2.5) in the U.S. during 2013 through 2015. Monitors in these cities reported no days with unhealthful PM 2.5 levels. *American Lung Association, State of the Air 2017*

Health/Fitness Rankings

- Analysts who tracked obesity rates in the nation's largest metro areas (populations above one million) found that the San Antonio* metro area was one of the ten major metros where residents were most likely to be obese, defined as a BMI score of 30 or above. *www.gallup.com, "Boulder, Colo., Residents Still Least Likely to Be Obese," April 4, 2014*
- For each of the 50 most populous metro areas in the United States, the American College of Sports Medicine's American Fitness Index evaluated infrastructure, community assets, and policies that encourage healthy and fit lifestyles, including preventive health behaviors, levels of chronic disease conditions, health care access, and community resources and policies that support physical activity. The San Antonio* metro area ranked #44 for "community fitness." *www.americanfitnessindex.org, "ACSM American Fitness Index Health and Community Fitness Status of the 50 Largest Metropolitan Areas," May 2017*

- San Antonio* was identified as a "2016 Spring Allergy Capital." The area ranked #22 out of 100. Three groups of factors were used to identify the most severe cities for people with allergies during the spring season: annual pollen levels; medicine utilization; access to board-certified allergists. *Asthma and Allergy Foundation of America, "Spring Allergy Capitals 2016"*
- San Antonio* was identified as a "2016 Fall Allergy Capital." The area ranked #16 out of 100. Three groups of factors were used to identify the most severe cities for people with allergies during the fall season: annual pollen levels; medicine utilization; access to board-certified allergists. *Asthma and Allergy Foundation of America, "Fall Allergy Capitals 2016"*
- San Antonio* was identified as a "2015 Asthma Capital." The area ranked #65 out of the nation's 100 largest metropolitan areas. Criteria: estimated prevalence; self-reported prevalence; crude death rate for asthma; annual pollen score; annual air quality; public smoking laws; number of board-certified asthma specialists; school inhaler access laws; rescue medication use; controller medication use; ER visits for asthma; uninsured rate; poverty rate. *Asthma and Allergy Foundation of America, "Asthma Capitals 2015"*
- The San Antonio* metro area ranked #44 out of 189 in The Gallup-Healthways Well-Being Index. Criteria: purpose; social well being; financial health; community and physical health. Results are based on telephone interviews with adults, aged 18 and older, living in metropolitan areas in the 50 U.S. states and the District of Columbia. *Gallup-Healthways, "State of American Well-Being, 2017 Community Well-Being Rankings" March 2018*

Real Estate Rankings

- FitSmallBusiness looked at 50 of the largest metropolitan areas in the U.S. to determine which metro was the best to start a real estate business. Data was compiled from such sources as: Zillow, Trulia, U.S. Census Bureau, and the Bureau of Labor Statistics. Criteria: location; inventory; annual wages; median sales price of homes; days on the market; median price cut percentage; and other factors that would influence real estate professional growth. The San Antonio* metro area ranked #12. *fitsmallbusiness.com, "The Best Cities to Become a Real Estate Agent in 2018," January 30, 2018*
- The San Antonio* metro area was identified as one of the top 20 housing markets to invest in for 2018 by *Forbes*. The area ranked #12. Criteria: strong job and population growth; anticipated home price appreciation; and other factors. *Forbes.com, "Where to Invest in Housing in 2018," February 1, 2018*
- San Antonio* was ranked #161 out of 238 metro areas in terms of housing affordability in 2017 by the National Association of Home Builders (#1 = most affordable). Criteria: the share of homes sold in that area affordable to a family earning the local median income, based on standard mortgage underwriting criteria. *National Association of Home Builders®, NAHB-Wells Fargo Housing Opportunity Index, 4th Quarter 2017*

Safety Rankings

- The National Insurance Crime Bureau ranked 382 metro areas in the U.S. in terms of per capita rates of vehicle theft. The San Antonio* metro area ranked #38 (#1 = highest rate). Criteria: number of vehicle theft offenses per 100,000 inhabitants in 2016. *National Insurance Crime Bureau, "Hot Spots 2016," June 8, 2017*

Seniors/Retirement Rankings

- From its Best Cities for Successful Aging indexes, the Milken Institute generated rankings for metropolitan areas, weighing data in nine categories—health care, wellness, living arrangements, transportation and convenience, financial characteristics, education, employment, community engagement, and overall livability. The San Antonio* metro area was ranked #64 overall in the large metro area category. *Milken Institute, "Best Cities for Successful Aging, 2017" March 14, 2017*

Women/Minorities Rankings

- The *Houston Chronicle* listed the San Antonio* metro area as #13 in top places for young Latinos to live in the U.S. Research was largely based on housing and occupational data from the largest metropolitan areas performed by *Forbes* and NBC Universo. Criteria: percentage of 18-34 year-olds; Latino college grad rates; and diversity. *blog.chron.com, "The 15 Best Big Cities for Latino Millenials," January 26, 2016*

Miscellaneous Rankings

- The National Alliance to End Homelessness listed the 25 most populous metro areas with the highest rate of homelessness. The San Antonio* metro area had a high rate of homelessness. Criteria: number of homeless people per 10,000 population in 2016. *National Alliance to End Homelessness, "Homelessness in the 25 Most Populous U.S. Metro Areas," September 1, 2017*

*Cibolo is located within the San Antonio-New Braunfels, TX Metropolitan Statistical Area.

Business Environment

CITY FINANCES

City Government Finances

Component	2015 ($000)	2015 ($ per capita)
Total Revenues	n/a	n/a
Total Expenditures	n/a	n/a
Debt Outstanding	n/a	n/a
Cash and Securities[1]	n/a	n/a

Note: (1) Cash and security holdings of a government at the close of its fiscal year,, including those of its dependent agencies, utilities, and liquor stores.
Source: U.S Census Bureau, State & Local Government Finances 2015

City Government Revenue by Source

Source	2015 ($000)	2015 ($ per capita)	2015 (%)
General Revenue			
From Federal Government	n/a	n/a	n/a
From State Government	n/a	n/a	n/a
From Local Governments	n/a	n/a	n/a
Taxes			
Property	n/a	n/a	n/a
Sales and Gross Receipts	n/a	n/a	n/a
Personal Income	n/a	n/a	n/a
Corporate Income	n/a	n/a	n/a
Motor Vehicle License	n/a	n/a	n/a
Other Taxes	n/a	n/a	n/a
Current Charges	n/a	n/a	n/a
Liquor Store	n/a	n/a	n/a
Utility	n/a	n/a	n/a
Employee Retirement	n/a	n/a	n/a

Source: U.S Census Bureau, State & Local Government Finances 2015

City Government Expenditures by Function

Function	2015 ($000)	2015 ($ per capita)	2015 (%)
General Direct Expenditures			
Air Transportation	n/a	n/a	n/a
Corrections	n/a	n/a	n/a
Education	n/a	n/a	n/a
Employment Security Administration	n/a	n/a	n/a
Financial Administration	n/a	n/a	n/a
Fire Protection	n/a	n/a	n/a
General Public Buildings	n/a	n/a	n/a
Governmental Administration, Other	n/a	n/a	n/a
Health	n/a	n/a	n/a
Highways	n/a	n/a	n/a
Hospitals	n/a	n/a	n/a
Housing and Community Development	n/a	n/a	n/a
Interest on General Debt	n/a	n/a	n/a
Judicial and Legal	n/a	n/a	n/a
Libraries	n/a	n/a	n/a
Parking	n/a	n/a	n/a
Parks and Recreation	n/a	n/a	n/a
Police Protection	n/a	n/a	n/a
Public Welfare	n/a	n/a	n/a
Sewerage	n/a	n/a	n/a
Solid Waste Management	n/a	n/a	n/a
Veterans' Services	n/a	n/a	n/a
Liquor Store	n/a	n/a	n/a
Utility	n/a	n/a	n/a
Employee Retirement	n/a	n/a	n/a

Source: U.S Census Bureau, State & Local Government Finances 2015

DEMOGRAPHICS

Population Growth

Area	1990 Census	2000 Census	2010 Census	2016* Estimate	Population Growth (%) 1990-2016	Population Growth (%) 2010-2016
City	1,879	3,035	15,349	25,256	***.*	64.5
MSA[1]	1,407,745	1,711,703	2,142,508	2,332,345	65.7	8.9
U.S.	248,709,873	281,421,906	308,745,538	318,558,162	28.1	3.2

Note: (1) Figures cover the San Antonio-New Braunfels, TX Metropolitan Statistical Area—see Appendix B for areas included; (*) 2012-2016 5-year estimated population
Source: U.S. Census Bureau, 1990 Census, Census 2000, Census 2010, 2012-2016 American Community Survey 5-Year Estimates

Household Size

Area	Persons in Household (%)							Average Household Size
	One	Two	Three	Four	Five	Six	Seven or More	
City	13.3	27.1	20.3	24.4	8.7	5.4	0.9	3.30
MSA[1]	25.5	31.0	17.0	14.2	7.4	3.0	1.9	2.90
U.S.	27.7	33.7	15.7	13.1	6.0	2.3	1.5	2.60

Note: (1) Figures cover the San Antonio-New Braunfels, TX Metropolitan Statistical Area—see Appendix B for areas included
Source: U.S. Census Bureau, 2012-2016 American Community Survey 5-Year Estimates

Race

Area	White Alone[2] (%)	Black Alone[2] (%)	Asian Alone[2] (%)	AIAN[3] Alone[2] (%)	NHOPI[4] Alone[2] (%)	Other Race Alone[2] (%)	Two or More Races (%)
City	71.1	11.9	2.1	0.4	0.1	9.9	4.5
MSA[1]	80.1	6.7	2.4	0.6	0.1	7.2	2.9
U.S.	73.3	12.6	5.2	0.8	0.2	4.8	3.1

Note: (1) Figures cover the San Antonio-New Braunfels, TX Metropolitan Statistical Area—see Appendix B for areas included; (2) Alone is defined as not being in combination with one or more other races; (3) American Indian and Alaska Native; (4) Native Hawaiian and Other Pacific Islander
Source: U.S. Census Bureau, 2012-2016 American Community Survey 5-Year Estimates

Hispanic or Latino Origin

Area	Total (%)	Mexican (%)	Puerto Rican (%)	Cuban (%)	Other (%)
City	30.1	23.4	2.2	0.1	4.4
MSA[1]	54.8	49.0	1.2	0.2	4.4
U.S.	17.3	11.0	1.7	0.7	4.0

Note: Persons of Hispanic or Latino origin can be of any race; (1) Figures cover the San Antonio-New Braunfels, TX Metropolitan Statistical Area—see Appendix B for areas included
Source: U.S. Census Bureau, 2012-2016 American Community Survey 5-Year Estimates

Segregation

Type	Segregation Indices[1]				Percent Change		
	1990	2000	2010	2010 Rank[2]	1990-2000	1990-2010	2000-2010
Black/White	56.1	52.8	49.0	73	-3.3	-7.1	-3.8
Asian/White	33.8	35.4	38.3	66	1.6	4.5	2.9
Hispanic/White	52.1	49.7	46.1	43	-2.4	-6.0	-3.6

Note: All figures cover the Metropolitan Statistical Area—see Appendix B for areas included; Figures are based on an analysis of 1990, 2000, and 2010 Census Decennial Census tract data by William H. Frey, Brookings Institution and the University of Michigan Social Science Data Analysis Network. In this analysis all racial groups (whites, blacks, and asians) are non-Hispanic members of those races. Hispanics are shown as a separate category; (1) Segregation Indices are Dissimilarity Indices that measure the degree to which the minority group is distributed differently than whites across census tracts. They range from 0 (complete integration) to 100 (complete segregation) where the value indicates the percentage of the minority group that needs to move to be distributed exactly like whites; (2) Ranges from 1 (most segregated) to 102 (least segregated); n/a not available.
Source: www.CensusScope.org

Ancestry

Area	German	Irish	English	American	Italian	Polish	French[2]	Scottish	Dutch
City	14.9	7.5	6.4	5.5	2.9	1.9	2.6	1.2	1.2
MSA[1]	11.2	5.8	5.4	3.7	2.1	1.5	1.8	1.2	0.7
U.S.	14.4	10.4	7.7	6.9	5.4	2.9	2.6	1.7	1.3

Note: Figures are the percentage of the total population reporting a particular ancestry. The nine most commonly reported ancestries in the U.S. are shown. Figures include multiple ancestries (e.g. if a person reported being Irish and Italian, they were included in both columns); (1) Figures cover the San Antonio-New Braunfels, TX Metropolitan Statistical Area—see Appendix B for areas included; (2) Excludes Basque
Source: U.S. Census Bureau, 2012-2016 American Community Survey 5-Year Estimates

Foreign-Born Population

Area	Percent of Population Born in								
	Any Foreign Country	Asia	Mexico	Europe	Carribean	Central America[2]	South America	Africa	Canada
City	8.8	1.9	3.1	1.2	0.6	0.7	0.7	0.2	0.3
MSA[1]	11.8	2.0	7.6	0.7	0.2	0.6	0.3	0.3	0.1
U.S.	13.2	4.0	3.6	1.5	1.3	1.0	0.9	0.6	0.3

Note: (1) Figures cover the San Antonio-New Braunfels, TX Metropolitan Statistical Area—see Appendix B for areas included; (2) Excludes Mexico.
Source: U.S. Census Bureau, 2012-2016 American Community Survey 5-Year Estimates

Marital Status

Area	Never Married	Now Married[2]	Separated	Widowed	Divorced
City	26.4	62.4	0.4	3.1	7.6
MSA[1]	33.5	46.8	2.8	5.2	11.7
U.S.	33.0	48.1	2.1	5.9	11.0

Note: Figures are percentages and cover the population 15 years of age and older; (1) Figures cover the San Antonio-New Braunfels, TX Metropolitan Statistical Area—see Appendix B for areas included; (2) Excludes separated
Source: U.S. Census Bureau, 2012-2016 American Community Survey 5-Year Estimates

Disability Status

Area	All Ages	Under 18 Years Old	18 to 64 Years Old	65 Years and Over
City	7.9	2.7	6.7	39.4
MSA[1]	13.5	5.0	11.9	40.6
U.S.	12.5	4.1	10.3	35.7

Note: Figures show percent of the civilian noninstitutionalized population that reported having a disability. Disability status is determined from six types of difficulty: vision, hearing, cognitive, ambulatory, self-care, and independent living. For children under 5 years old, hearing and vision difficulty are used to determine disability status. For children between the ages of 5 and 14, disability status is determined from hearing, vision, cognitive, ambulatory, and self-care difficulties. For people aged 15 years and older, they are considered to have a disability if they have difficulty with any one of the six difficulty types; Note: (1) Figures cover the San Antonio-New Braunfels, TX Metropolitan Statistical Area—see Appendix B for areas included
Source: U.S. Census Bureau, 2012-2016 American Community Survey 5-Year Estimates

Age

Area	Percent of Population									Median Age
	Under Age 5	Age 5–19	Age 20–34	Age 35–44	Age 45–54	Age 55–64	Age 65–74	Age 75–84	Age 85+	
City	7.5	26.6	16.7	18.1	16.5	7.4	5.2	1.5	0.6	34.4
MSA[1]	7.0	21.8	22.1	13.1	12.8	11.0	7.1	3.6	1.4	34.4
U.S.	6.2	19.6	20.7	12.7	13.6	12.6	8.3	4.3	1.9	37.7

Note: (1) Figures cover the San Antonio-New Braunfels, TX Metropolitan Statistical Area—see Appendix B for areas included
Source: U.S. Census Bureau, 2012-2016 American Community Survey 5-Year Estimates

Gender

Area	Males	Females	Males per 100 Females
City	11,898	13,358	89.1
MSA[1]	1,150,424	1,181,921	97.3
U.S.	156,765,322	161,792,840	96.9

Note: (1) Figures cover the San Antonio-New Braunfels, TX Metropolitan Statistical Area—see Appendix B for areas included
Source: U.S. Census Bureau, 2012-2016 American Community Survey 5-Year Estimates

Religious Groups by Family

Area	Catholic	Baptist	Non-Den.	Methodist[2]	Lutheran	LDS[3]	Pente-costal	Presby-terian[4]	Muslim[5]	Judaism
MSA[1]	28.4	8.5	6.0	3.1	1.7	1.4	1.3	0.8	1.0	0.2
U.S.	19.1	9.3	4.0	4.0	2.3	2.0	1.9	1.6	0.8	0.7

Note: Figures are the number of adherents as a percentage of the total population; (1) Figures cover the San Antonio-New Braunfels, TX Metropolitan Statistical Area—see Appendix B for areas included; (2) Methodist/Pietist; (3) Latter Day Saints; (4) Reformed; (5) Figures are estimates
Source: Association of Statisticians of American Religious Bodies, 2010 U.S. Religion Census: Religious Congregations & Membership Study

Religious Groups by Tradition

Area	Catholic	Evangelical Protestant	Mainline Protestant	Other Tradition	Black Protestant	Orthodox
MSA[1]	28.4	17.0	5.0	3.2	0.4	0.1
U.S.	19.1	16.2	7.3	4.3	1.6	0.3

Note: Figures are the number of adherents as a percentage of the total population; (1) Figures cover the San Antonio-New Braunfels, TX Metropolitan Statistical Area—see Appendix B for areas included
Source: Association of Statisticians of American Religious Bodies, 2010 U.S. Religion Census: Religious Congregations & Membership Study

ECONOMY

Gross Metropolitan Product

Area	2014	2015	2016	2017	Rank[2]
MSA[1]	104.3	108.3	112.7	118.9	35

Note: Figures are in billions of dollars; (1) Figures cover the San Antonio-New Braunfels, TX Metropolitan Statistical Area—see Appendix B for areas included; (2) Rank is based on 2015 data and ranges from 1 to 381
Source: The U.S. Conference of Mayors, U.S. Metro Economies: GMP and Employment Report, 2015-2017

Economic Growth

Area	2012-14 (%)	2015 (%)	2016 (%)	2017 (%)	Rank[2]
MSA[1]	4.0	5.5	2.3	3.1	27
U.S.	2.0	2.4	1.9	2.6	–

Note: Figures are real gross metropolitan product (GMP) growth rates and represent average annual percent change; (1) Figures cover the San Antonio-New Braunfels, TX Metropolitan Statistical Area—see Appendix B for areas included; (2) Rank is based on 2012-2014 average annual percent change and ranges from 1 to 381
Source: The U.S. Conference of Mayors, U.S. Metro Economies: GMP and Employment Report, 2015-2017

Metropolitan Area Exports

Area	2011	2012	2013	2014	2015	2016	Rank[2]
MSA[1]	10,506.5	14,010.2	19,287.6	25,781.8	15,919.2	5,621.2	49

Note: Figures are in millions of dollars; (1) Figures cover the San Antonio-New Braunfels, TX Metropolitan Statistical Area—see Appendix B for areas included; (2) Rank is based on 2016 data and ranges from 1 to 385
Source: U.S. Department of Commerce, International Trade Administration, Office of Trade & Industry Information, Manufacturing & Services, data extracted March 15, 2018

Building Permits

Area	Single-Family			Multi-Family			Total		
	2016	2017p	Pct. Chg.	2016	2017p	Pct. Chg.	2016	2017p	Pct. Chg.
City	377	308	-18.3	0	136	n/a	377	444	17.8
MSA[1]	6,441	7,513	16.6	3,344	4,996	49.4	9,785	12,509	27.8
U.S.	750,800	817,300	8.9	455,800	446,800	-2.0	1,206,600	1,264,100	4.8

Note: (1) Figures cover the San Antonio-New Braunfels, TX Metropolitan Statistical Area—see Appendix B for areas included; Figures represent new, privately-owned housing units authorized (unadjusted data); All permit data are based on estimates with imputation; (p) preliminary data.
Source: U.S. Census Bureau, Manufacturing, Mining, and Construction Statistics, Building Permits, 2016, 2017

Bankruptcy Filings

Area	Business Filings			Nonbusiness Filings		
	2016	2017	% Chg.	2016	2017	% Chg.
Guadalupe County	7	10	42.9	153	177	15.7
U.S.	24,114	23,157	-4.0	770,846	765,863	-0.6

Note: Business filings include Chapter 7, Chapter 11, Chapter 12, and Chapter 13; Nonbusiness filings include Chapter 7, Chapter 11, and Chapter 13
Source: Administrative Office of the U.S. Courts, Business and Nonbusiness Bankruptcy, County Cases Commenced by Chapter of the Bankruptcy Code, During the 12-Month Period Ending December 31, 2016 and Business and Nonbusiness Bankruptcy, County Cases Commenced by Chapter of the Bankruptcy Code, During the 12-Month Period Ending December 31, 2017

Housing Vacancy Rates

Area	Gross Vacancy Rate[2] (%)			Year-Round Vacancy Rate[3] (%)			Rental Vacancy Rate[4] (%)			Homeowner Vacancy Rate[5] (%)		
	2015	2016	2017	2015	2016	2017	2015	2016	2017	2015	2016	2017
MSA[1]	9.0	9.9	9.9	7.8	8.6	8.8	9.6	10.3	11.5	0.8	1.9	1.8
U.S.	12.9	12.8	12.7	10.0	9.9	9.9	7.1	6.9	7.2	1.8	1.7	1.6

Note: (1) Figures cover the San Antonio-New Braunfels, TX Metropolitan Statistical Area—see Appendix B for areas included; (2) The percentage of the total housing inventory that is vacant; (3) The percentage of the housing inventory (excluding seasonal units) that is year-round vacant; (4) The percentage of rental inventory that is vacant for rent; (5) The percentage of homeowner inventory that is vacant for sale
Source: U.S. Census Bureau, Housing Vacancies and Homeownership Annual Statistics: 2015, 2016, 2017

INCOME

Income

Area	Per Capita ($)	Median Household ($)	Average Household ($)
City	30,753	91,827	98,016
MSA[1]	26,192	54,638	73,360
U.S.	29,829	55,322	77,866

Note: (1) Figures cover the San Antonio-New Braunfels, TX Metropolitan Statistical Area—see Appendix B for areas included
Source: U.S. Census Bureau, 2012-2016 American Community Survey 5-Year Estimates

Household Income Distribution

Area	Percent of Households Earning							
	Under $15,000	$15,000 -$24,999	$25,000 -$34,999	$35,000 -$49,999	$50,000 -$74,999	$75,000 -$99,999	$100,000 -$149,999	$150,000 and up
City	3.8	3.9	4.3	7.9	17.5	18.4	28.4	15.8
MSA[1]	11.7	10.2	10.0	13.8	18.9	12.5	13.7	9.3
U.S.	12.1	10.2	9.9	13.2	17.8	12.2	13.5	11.1

Note: (1) Figures cover the San Antonio-New Braunfels, TX Metropolitan Statistical Area—see Appendix B for areas included
Source: U.S. Census Bureau, 2012-2016 American Community Survey 5-Year Estimates

Poverty Rate

Area	All Ages	Under 18 Years Old	18 to 64 Years Old	65 Years and Over
City	5.1	4.9	4.7	9.9
MSA[1]	15.9	22.7	14.1	10.7
U.S.	15.1	21.2	14.2	9.3

Note: Figures are percentage of people whose income during the past 12 months was below the poverty level; (1) Figures cover the San Antonio-New Braunfels, TX Metropolitan Statistical Area—see Appendix B for areas included
Source: U.S. Census Bureau, 2012-2016 American Community Survey 5-Year Estimates

EMPLOYMENT

Labor Force and Employment

Area	Civilian Labor Force			Workers Employed		
	Dec. 2016	Dec. 2017	% Chg.	Dec. 2016	Dec. 2017	% Chg.
City	13,507	13,722	1.6	13,060	13,381	2.5
MSA[1]	1,151,068	1,171,978	1.8	1,109,096	1,136,835	2.5
U.S.	158,968,000	159,880,000	0.6	151,798,000	153,602,000	1.2

Note: Data is not seasonally adjusted and covers workers 16 years of age and older; (1) Figures cover the San Antonio-New Braunfels, TX Metropolitan Statistical Area—see Appendix B for areas included
Source: Bureau of Labor Statistics, Local Area Unemployment Statistics

Unemployment Rate

Area	2017											
	Jan.	Feb.	Mar.	Apr.	May	Jun.	Jul.	Aug.	Sep.	Oct.	Nov.	Dec.
City	3.5	3.7	3.4	3.0	3.1	3.3	3.3	3.3	2.9	2.5	2.6	2.5
MSA[1]	4.0	3.9	3.7	3.3	3.4	3.7	3.7	3.7	3.2	3.0	3.1	3.0
U.S.	5.1	4.9	4.6	4.1	4.1	4.5	4.6	4.5	4.1	3.9	3.9	3.9

Note: Data is not seasonally adjusted and covers workers 16 years of age and older; (1) Figures cover the San Antonio-New Braunfels, TX Metropolitan Statistical Area—see Appendix B for areas included
Source: Bureau of Labor Statistics, Local Area Unemployment Statistics

Average Wages

Occupation	$/Hr.	Occupation	$/Hr.
Accountants and Auditors	36.40	Maids and Housekeeping Cleaners	10.30
Automotive Mechanics	21.10	Maintenance and Repair Workers	16.70
Bookkeepers	18.50	Marketing Managers	79.50
Carpenters	19.10	Nuclear Medicine Technologists	32.80
Cashiers	10.30	Nurses, Licensed Practical	21.80
Clerks, General Office	17.00	Nurses, Registered	32.70
Clerks, Receptionists/Information	12.40	Nursing Assistants	12.40
Clerks, Shipping/Receiving	14.70	Packers and Packagers, Hand	10.70
Computer Programmers	47.10	Physical Therapists	44.10
Computer Systems Analysts	46.40	Postal Service Mail Carriers	24.00
Computer User Support Specialists	25.30	Real Estate Brokers	27.40
Cooks, Restaurant	11.80	Retail Salespersons	13.70
Dentists	75.90	Sales Reps., Exc. Tech./Scientific	31.70
Electrical Engineers	50.50	Sales Reps., Tech./Scientific	40.00
Electricians	22.50	Secretaries, Exc. Legal/Med./Exec.	16.60
Financial Managers	75.80	Security Guards	13.70
First-Line Supervisors/Managers, Sales	22.40	Surgeons	101.10
Food Preparation Workers	12.10	Teacher Assistants*	12.10
General and Operations Managers	59.90	Teachers, Elementary School*	27.50
Hairdressers/Cosmetologists	11.40	Teachers, Secondary School*	27.60
Internists, General	122.50	Telemarketers	13.80
Janitors and Cleaners	11.80	Truck Drivers, Heavy/Tractor-Trailer	22.10
Landscaping/Groundskeeping Workers	13.00	Truck Drivers, Light/Delivery Svcs.	14.50
Lawyers	53.90	Waiters and Waitresses	11.80

Note: Wage data covers the San Antonio-New Braunfels, TX Metropolitan Statistical Area—see Appendix B for areas included; (*) Hourly wages for elementary/secondary school teachers and teacher assistants were calculated by the editors from annual wage data based on a 40 hour work week; n/a not available.
Source: Bureau of Labor Statistics, Metro Area Occupational Employment & Wage Estimates, May 2017

Employment by Occupation

Occupation Classification	City (%)	MSA[1] (%)	U.S. (%)
Management, Business, Science, and Arts	41.1	34.5	37.0
Natural Resources, Construction, and Maintenance	7.4	10.2	8.9
Production, Transportation, and Material Moving	10.1	10.2	12.2
Sales and Office	26.6	25.8	23.8
Service	14.7	19.2	18.1

Note: Figures cover employed civilians 16 years of age and older; (1) Figures cover the San Antonio-New Braunfels, TX Metropolitan Statistical Area—see Appendix B for areas included
Source: U.S. Census Bureau, 2012-2016 American Community Survey 5-Year Estimates

Employment by Industry

Sector	MSA[1] Number of Employees	MSA[1] Percent of Total	U.S. Percent of Total
Construction	55,000	5.2	4.7
Education and Health Services	163,100	15.4	15.9
Financial Activities	90,100	8.5	5.7
Government	174,100	16.5	15.3
Information	20,500	1.9	1.9
Leisure and Hospitality	134,000	12.7	10.7
Manufacturing	48,300	4.6	8.5
Mining and Logging	8,100	0.8	0.5
Other Services	38,000	3.6	3.9
Professional and Business Services	138,000	13.1	14.0
Retail Trade	117,300	11.1	11.0
Transportation, Warehousing, and Utilities	33,800	3.2	4.1
Wholesale Trade	36,000	3.4	4.0

Note: Figures are non-farm employment as of December 2017. Figures are not seasonally adjusted and include workers 16 years of age and older; (1) Figures cover the San Antonio-New Braunfels, TX Metropolitan Statistical Area—see Appendix B for areas included
Source: Bureau of Labor Statistics, Current Employment Statistics, Employment, Hours, and Earnings

Occupations with Greatest Projected Employment Growth: 2017 – 2019

Occupation[1]	2017 Employment	2019 Projected Employment	Numeric Employment Change	Percent Employment Change
Combined Food Preparation and Serving Workers, Including Fast Food	335,660	354,370	18,710	5.6
Personal Care Aides	212,280	230,990	18,710	8.8
Retail Salespersons	393,950	406,100	12,150	3.1
Customer Service Representatives	261,530	273,600	12,070	4.6
Janitors and Cleaners, Except Maids and Housekeeping Cleaners	180,710	192,060	11,350	6.3
Laborers and Freight, Stock, and Material Movers, Hand	185,140	196,200	11,060	6.0
Registered Nurses	214,500	224,450	9,950	4.6
Office Clerks, General	379,860	389,540	9,680	2.6
Heavy and Tractor-Trailer Truck Drivers	192,710	201,560	8,850	4.6
Waiters and Waitresses	222,630	231,020	8,390	3.8

Note: Projections cover Texas; (1) Sorted by numeric employment change
Source: www.projectionscentral.com, State Occupational Projections, 2017–2019 Short-Term Projections

Fastest Growing Occupations: 2017 – 2019

Occupation[1]	2017 Employment	2019 Projected Employment	Numeric Employment Change	Percent Employment Change
Wind Turbine Service Technicians	1,740	2,090	350	20.7
Home Health Aides	72,760	80,000	7,240	10.0
Security and Fire Alarm Systems Installers	8,190	8,930	740	8.9
Personal Care Aides	212,280	230,990	18,710	8.8
Statisticians	1,760	1,910	150	8.2
Tree Trimmers and Pruners	5,980	6,480	500	8.2
Physician Assistants	6,860	7,400	540	7.9
Nurse Practitioners	9,230	9,950	720	7.7
Elevator Installers and Repairers	2,190	2,350	160	7.4
Helpers—Roofers	800	850	50	7.4

Note: Projections cover Texas; (1) Sorted by percent employment change and excludes occupations with numeric employment change less than 50
Source: www.projectionscentral.com, State Occupational Projections, 2017–2019 Short-Term Projections

TAXES

State Corporate Income Tax Rates

State	Tax Rate (%)	Income Brackets ($)	Num. of Brackets	Financial Institution Tax Rate (%)[a]	Federal Income Tax Ded.
Texas	(w)	–	–	(w)	No

Note: Tax rates as of January 1, 2018; (a) Rates listed are the corporate income tax rate applied to financial institutions or excise taxes based on income. Some states have other taxes based upon the value of deposits or shares; (w) Texas imposes a Franchise Tax, otherwise known as margin tax, imposed on entities with more than $1,110,000 total revenues at rate of 0.75%, or 0.375% for entities primarily engaged in retail or wholesale trade, on lesser of 70% of total revenues or 100% of gross receipts after deductions for either compensation or cost of goods sold.
Source: Federation of Tax Administrators, Range of State Corporate Income Tax Rates, January 1, 2018

State Individual Income Tax Rates

State	Tax Rate (%)	Income Brackets ($)	Num. of Brackets	Personal Exempt. ($)[1]		Fed. Inc. Tax Ded.
				Single	Dependents	
Texas	None	–	–	–	–	–

Note: Tax rates as of January 1, 2018; Local- and county-level taxes are not included; n/a not applicable; (1) Married joint filers generally receive double the single exemption
Source: Federation of Tax Administrators, State Individual Income Tax Rates, January 1, 2018

Various State Sales and Excise Tax Rates

State	State Sales Tax (%)	Gasoline[1] (¢/gal.)	Cigarette[2] ($/pack)	Spirits[3] ($/gal.)	Wine[4] ($/gal.)	Beer[5] ($/gal.)	Recreational Marijuana (%)
Texas	6.25	20.0	1.41	2.40 (f)	0.20 (l)	0.20 (q)	Not legal

Note: All tax rates as of January 1, 2018; (1) The American Petroleum Institute has developed a methodology for determining the average tax rate on a gallon of fuel. Rates may include any of the following: excise taxes, environmental fees, storage tank fees, other fees or taxes, general sales tax, and local taxes. In states where gasoline is subject to the general sales tax, or where the fuel tax is based on the average sale price, the average rate determined by API is sensitive to changes in the price of gasoline. States that fully or partially apply general sales taxes to gasoline: CA, CO, GA, IL, IN, MI, NY; (2) The federal excise tax of $1.0066 per pack and local taxes are not included; (3) Rates are those applicable to off-premise sales of 40% alcohol by volume (a.b.v.) distilled spirits in 750ml containers. Local excise taxes are excluded; (4) Rates are those applicable to off-premise sales of 11% a.b.v. non-carbonated wine in 750ml containers; (5) Rates are those applicable to off-premise sales of 4.7% a.b.v. beer in 12 ounce containers; (f) Different rates also applicable according to alcohol content, place of production, size of container, or place purchased (on- or off-premise or onboard airlines); (l) Different rates also applicable to alcohol content, place of production, size of container, place purchased (on- or off-premise or on board airlines) or type of wine (carbonated, vermouth, etc.); (q) Different rates also applicable according to alcohol content, place of production, size of container, or place purchased (on- or off-premise or onboard airlines).
Source: Tax Foundation, 2018 Facts & Figures: How Does Your State Compare?

State Business Tax Climate Index Rankings

State	Overall Rank	Corporate Tax Rank	Individual Income Tax Rank	Sales Tax Rank	Unemployment Insurance Tax Rank	Property Tax Rank
Texas	13	49	6	37	26	37

Note: The index is a measure of how each state's tax laws affect economic performance. The lower the rank, the more favorable a state's tax system is for business. States without a given tax are given a ranking of 1. The scores/rankings for the District of Columbia do not affect other states. The 2018 index represents the tax climate as of July 1, 2017.
Source: Tax Foundation, State Business Tax Climate Index 2018

TRANSPORTATION

Means of Transportation to Work

Area	Car/Truck/Van		Public Transportation			Bicycle	Walked	Other Means	Worked at Home
	Drove Alone	Car-pooled	Bus	Subway	Railroad				
City	85.8	7.6	0.1	0.0	0.0	0.1	0.8	1.7	4.0
MSA[1]	79.6	10.9	2.2	0.0	0.0	0.2	1.7	1.1	4.4
U.S.	76.4	9.3	2.6	1.9	0.6	0.6	2.8	1.3	4.6

Note: Figures are percentages and cover workers 16 years of age and older; (1) Figures cover the San Antonio-New Braunfels, TX Metropolitan Statistical Area—see Appendix B for areas included
Source: U.S. Census Bureau, 2012-2016 American Community Survey 5-Year Estimates

Travel Time to Work

Area	Less Than 10 Minutes	10 to 19 Minutes	20 to 29 Minutes	30 to 44 Minutes	45 to 59 Minutes	60 to 89 Minutes	90 Minutes or More
City	6.0	25.1	21.9	28.0	12.7	4.4	1.9
MSA[1]	10.0	28.8	24.7	22.6	7.7	4.1	2.1
U.S.	12.9	29.2	20.9	20.4	8.0	6.0	2.7

Note: Note: Figures are percentages and include workers 16 years old and over; (1) Figures cover the San Antonio-New Braunfels, TX Metropolitan Statistical Area—see Appendix B for areas included
Source: U.S. Census Bureau, 2012-2016 American Community Survey 5-Year Estimates

Freeway Travel Time Index

Area	1985	1990	1995	2000	2005	2010	2014
Urban Area Rank[1,2]	24	34	23	24	26	25	24
Urban Area Index[1]	1.11	1.12	1.19	1.22	1.24	1.23	1.25
Average Index[3]	1.09	1.11	1.14	1.17	1.20	1.19	1.20

Note: Freeway Travel Time Index—the ratio of travel time in the peak period to the travel time at free-flow conditions. For example, a value of 1.30 indicates a 20-minute free-flow trip takes 26 minutes in the peak (20 minutes x 1.30 = 26 minutes); (1) Covers the San Antonio TX urban area; (2) Rank is based on 101 urban areas (#1 = highest travel time index); (3) Average of 101 urban areas
Source: Texas Transportation Institute, 2015 Urban Mobility Scorecard, August 2015

Freeway Commuter Stress Index

Area	1985	1990	1995	2000	2005	2010	2014
Urban Area Rank[1,2]	22	26	19	17	22	22	20
Urban Area Index[1]	1.19	1.20	1.27	1.31	1.32	1.31	1.33
Average Index[3]	1.13	1.16	1.19	1.22	1.25	1.24	1.25

Note: The Freeway Commuter Stress Index is the same as the Freeway Travel Time Index (see table above) except that it includes only the travel in the peak directions during the peak periods; the TTI includes travel in all directions during the peak period. Thus, the CSI is more indicative of the work trip experienced by each commuter on a daily basis; (1) Covers the San Antonio TX urban area; (2) Rank is based on 101 urban areas (#1 = highest travel time index); (3) Average of 101 urban areas
Source: Texas Transportation Institute, 2015 Urban Mobility Scorecard, August 2015

Living Environment

COST OF LIVING

Cost of Living Index

Composite Index	Groceries	Housing	Utilities	Trans-portation	Health Care	Misc. Goods/ Services
88.6	92.1	75.9	115.7	83.5	92.5	90.5

Note: The Cost of Living Index measures regional differences in the cost of consumer goods and services, excluding taxes and non-consumer expenditures, for professional and managerial households in the top income quintile. It is based on more than 50,000 prices covering almost 60 different items for which prices are collected three times a year by chambers of commerce, economic development organizations or university applied economic centers in each participating urban area. The numbers shown should be read as a percentage above or below the national average of 100. For example, a value of 115.4 in the groceries column indicates that grocery prices are 15.4% higher than the national average. Small differences in the index numbers should not be interpreted as significant; Figures cover the Seguin TX urban area.
Source: The Council for Community and Economic Research, ACCRA Cost of Living Index, 2017

Grocery Prices

Area[1]	T-Bone Steak ($/pound)	Frying Chicken ($/pound)	Whole Milk ($/half gal.)	Eggs ($/dozen)	Orange Juice ($/64 oz.)	Coffee ($/11.5 oz.)
City[2]	10.48	1.18	2.07	1.49	3.96	4.12
Avg.	11.29	1.40	2.02	1.47	3.55	4.37
Min.	7.71	0.93	1.04	0.70	2.86	3.24
Max.	15.83	2.39	4.03	3.92	6.29	8.16

*Note: (1) Values for the local area are compared with the average, minimum and maximum values for all 294 areas in the Cost of Living Index; (2) Figures cover the Seguin TX urban area; **T-Bone Steak** (price per pound); **Frying Chicken** (price per pound, whole fryer); **Whole Milk** (half gallon carton); **Eggs** (price per dozen, Grade A, large); **Orange Juice** (64 oz. Tropicana or Florida Natural); **Coffee** (11.5 oz. can, vacuum-packed, Maxwell House, Hills Bros, or Folgers).*
Source: The Council for Community and Economic Research, ACCRA Cost of Living Index, 2017

Housing and Utility Costs

Area[1]	New Home Price ($)	Apartment Rent ($/month)	All Electric ($/month)	Part Electric ($/month)	Other Energy ($/month)	Telephone ($/month)
City[2]	249,814	816	156.37	-	-	40.74
Avg.	335,956	1,047	175.01	97.34	67.93	28.71
Min.	187,788	491	109.48	49.33	35.44	12.39
Max.	1,739,087	4,559	432.62	227.09	353.33	44.61

*Note: (1) Values for the local area are compared with the average, minimum and maximum values for all 294 areas in the Cost of Living Index; (2) Figures cover the Seguin TX urban area; **New Home Price** (2,400 sf living area, 8,000 sf lot, in urban area with full utilities); **Apartment Rent** (950 sf 2 bedroom/1.5 or 2 bath, unfurnished, excluding all utilities except water); **All Electric** (average monthly cost for an all-electric home); **Part Electric** (average monthly cost for a part-electric home); **Other Energy** (average monthly cost for natural gas, fuel oil, coal, wood, and any other forms of energy except electricity); **Telephone** (price includes basic monthly rate for a private residential line plus additional local usage charges incurred by a family of four).*
Source: The Council for Community and Economic Research, ACCRA Cost of Living Index, 2017

Health Care, Transportation, and Other Costs

Area[1]	Doctor ($/visit)	Dentist ($/visit)	Optometrist ($/visit)	Gasoline ($/gallon)	Beauty Salon ($/visit)	Men's Shirt ($)
City[2]	94.61	85.54	98.68	1.99	26.70	26.28
Avg.	108.00	92.54	101.93	2.25	37.58	30.92
Min.	30.39	60.00	49.75	1.82	16.11	11.20
Max.	193.50	161.94	229.28	3.16	77.35	59.13

*Note: (1) Values for the local area are compared with the average, minimum and maximum values for all 294 areas in the Cost of Living Index; (2) Figures cover the Seguin TX urban area; **Doctor** (general practitioners routine exam of an established patient); **Dentist** (adult teeth cleaning and periodic oral examination); **Optometrist** (full vision eye exam for established adult patient); **Gasoline** (one gallon regular unleaded, national brand, including all taxes, cash price at self-service pump if available); **Beauty Salon** (woman's shampoo, trim, and blow-dry); **Men's Shirt** (cotton/polyester dress shirt, pinpoint weave, long sleeves).*
Source: The Council for Community and Economic Research, ACCRA Cost of Living Index, 2017

HOUSING

House Price Index (HPI)

Area	National Ranking[2]	Quarterly Change (%)	One-Year Change (%)	Five-Year Change (%)
MSA[1]	81	1.04	7.81	34.40
U.S.[3]	–	1.61	6.68	34.71

Note: The HPI is a weighted repeat sales index. It measures average price changes in repeat sales or refinancings on the same properties. This information is obtained by reviewing repeat mortgage transactions on single-family properties whose mortgages have been purchased or securitized by Fannie Mae or Freddie Mac in January 1975; (1) Figures cover the San Antonio-New Braunfels, TX Metropolitan Statistical Area—see Appendix B for areas included; (2) Rankings are based on annual percentage change for all metro areas containing at least 15,000 transactions over the last 10 years and ranges from 1 to 253; (3) figures based on a weighted average of Census Division estimates using a seasonally adjusted, purchase-only index; all figures are for the period ending December 31, 2017
Source: Federal Housing Finance Agency, House Price Index, February 28, 2018

Median Single-Family Home Prices

Area	2015	2016	2017p	Percent Change 2016 to 2017
MSA[1]	195.0	206.9	217.2	5.0
U.S. Average	223.9	235.5	248.8	5.6

Note: Figures are median sales prices of existing single-family homes in thousands of dollars; (p) preliminary; (1) Figures cover the San Antonio-New Braunfels, TX Metropolitan Statistical Area—see Appendix B for areas included
Source: National Association of Realtors, Median Sales Price of Existing Single-Family Homes for Metropolitan Areas, 4th Quarter 2017

Qualifying Income Based on Median Sales Price of Existing Single-Family Homes

Area	With 5% Down ($)	With 10% Down ($)	With 20% Down ($)
MSA[1]	48,855	46,284	41,141
U.S. Average	55,585	52,659	46,808

Note: Figures are preliminary; Qualifying income is based on a mortgage rate of 4.17%. Monthly principal and interest payment is limited to 25% of income; (1) Figures cover the San Antonio-New Braunfels, TX Metropolitan Statistical Area—see Appendix B for areas included
Source: National Association of Realtors, Qualifying Income Based on Median Sales Price of Existing Single-Family Homes for Metropolitan Areas, 4th Quarter 2017

Median Apartment Condo-Coop Home Prices

Area	2015	2016	2017p	Percent Change 2016 to 2017
MSA[1]	n/a	n/a	n/a	n/a
U.S. Average	210.7	220.7	234.3	6.2

Note: Figures are median sales prices of existing apartment condo-coop homes in thousands of dollars; (p) preliminary; n/a not available; (1) Figures cover the San Antonio-New Braunfels, TX Metropolitan Statistical Area—see Appendix B for areas included
Source: National Association of Realtors, Median Sales Price of Existing Apartment Condo-Coop Homes for Metropolitan Areas, 4th Quarter 2017

Home Value Distribution

Area	Under $50,000	$50,000 -$99,999	$100,000 -$149,999	$150,000 -$199,999	$200,000 -$299,999	$300,000 -$499,999	$500,000 -$999,999	$1,000,000 or more
City	2.6	3.8	9.3	30.3	45.3	8.1	0.6	0.0
MSA[1]	9.3	23.2	19.7	17.1	16.1	10.0	3.6	0.9
U.S.	8.8	14.8	15.3	14.9	18.4	16.4	9.0	2.5

Note: Figures are percentages and cover owner-occupied housing units; (1) Figures cover the San Antonio-New Braunfels, TX Metropolitan Statistical Area—see Appendix B for areas included
Source: U.S. Census Bureau, 2012-2016 American Community Survey 5-Year Estimates

Homeownership Rate

Area	2009 (%)	2010 (%)	2011 (%)	2012 (%)	2013 (%)	2014 (%)	2015 (%)	2016 (%)	2017 (%)
MSA[1]	69.8	70.1	66.5	67.5	70.1	70.2	66.0	61.6	62.5
U.S.	67.4	66.9	66.1	65.4	65.1	64.5	63.7	63.4	63.9

Note: (1) Figures cover the San Antonio-New Braunfels, TX Metropolitan Statistical Area—see Appendix B for areas included
Source: U.S. Census Bureau, Housing Vacancies and Homeownership Annual Statistics: 2009-2017

Year Housing Structure Built

Area	2010 or Later	2000 -2009	1990 -1999	1980 -1989	1970 -1979	1960 -1969	1950 -1959	1940 -1949	Before 1940	Median Year
City	15.5	60.2	9.3	7.4	4.5	0.6	1.2	0.4	1.1	2004
MSA[1]	5.5	22.7	14.9	16.2	14.5	9.0	8.0	4.4	4.8	1986
U.S.	2.3	14.7	14.0	13.7	15.6	10.9	10.6	5.2	13.0	1977

Note: Figures are percentages except for Median Year; Note: (1) Figures cover the San Antonio-New Braunfels, TX Metropolitan Statistical Area—see Appendix B for areas included
Source: U.S. Census Bureau, 2012-2016 American Community Survey 5-Year Estimates

Gross Monthly Rent

Area	Under $500	$500 -$999	$1,000 -$1,499	$1,500 -$1,999	$2,000 -$2,499	$2,500 -$2,999	$3,000 and up	Median ($)
City	4.3	11.2	33.5	41.8	9.2	0.0	0.0	1,512
MSA[1]	9.1	51.0	29.6	7.5	1.7	0.5	0.5	909
U.S.	11.3	43.3	27.7	10.7	4.0	1.6	1.5	949

Note: Figures are percentages except for Median; Gross rent is the contract rent plus the estimated average monthly cost of utilities (electricity, gas, and water and sewer) and fuels (oil, coal, kerosene, wood, etc.) if these are paid by the renter (or paid for the renter by someone else); (1) Figures cover the San Antonio-New Braunfels, TX Metropolitan Statistical Area—see Appendix B for areas included
Source: U.S. Census Bureau, 2012-2016 American Community Survey 5-Year Estimates

HEALTH

Health Risk Factors

Category	MSA[1] (%)	U.S. (%)
Adults aged 18–64 who have any kind of health care coverage	78.1	87.7
Adults who reported being in good or excellent health	78.0	83.6
Adults who are current smokers	10.9	17.1
Adults who currently use E-cigarettes	3.7	4.7
Adults who currently use chewing tobacco, snuff, or snus	5.1	4.0
Adults who are heavy drinkers[2]	5.9	6.5
Adults who are binge drinkers[3]	19.1	16.9
Adults who are overweight (BMI 25.0 - 29.9)	32.4	35.3
Adults who are obese (BMI 30.0 - 99.8)	39.1	29.9
Adults who participated in any physical activities in the past month	74.0	76.9
Adults who always or nearly always wears a seat belt	97.0	94.3

Note: (1) Figures cover the San Antonio-New Braunfels, TX Metropolitan Statistical Area—see Appendix B for areas included; (2) Heavy drinkers are classified as adult men having more than 14 drinks per week and adult women having more than 7 drinks per week; (3) Binge drinkers are classified as males having five or more drinks on one occasion or females having four or more drinks on one occasion
Source: Centers for Disease Control and Prevention, Behaviorial Risk Factor Surveillance System, SMART: Selected Metropolitan Area Risk Trends, 2016

Health Screening Rates

Category	MSA[1] (%)	U.S. (%)
Adults 50-75 who have had a blood stool test within the past year	10.5	8.0
Adults 50-75 who have had a colonoscopy in the past 10 years	58.1	63.5
Adults aged 65+ who have had flu shot within the past year	62.3	58.6
Adults aged 65+ who have ever had a pneumonia vaccination	76.7	73.4
Adults who have ever been tested for HIV	42.8	35.6
Women aged 21-65 who have had a pap test in the past three years	75.7	79.8
Men aged 40+ who have had a PSA test within the past two years	39.6	39.5
Women aged 40+ who have had a mammogram within the past two years	72.2	72.5

Note: n/a not available; (1) Figures cover the San Antonio-New Braunfels, TX Metropolitan Statistical Area—see Appendix B for areas included; Source: Centers for Disease Control and Prevention, Behaviorial Risk Factor Surveillance System, SMART: Selected Metropolitan Area Risk Trends, 2016

Chronic Health Conditions

Category	MSA[1] (%)	U.S. (%)
Adults who have ever been told they had a heart attack	4.2	4.4
Adults who have ever been told they have angina or coronary heart disease	3.6	4.1
Adults who have ever been told they had a stroke	3.6	3.1
Adults who have been told they currently have asthma	7.4	9.3
Adults who have ever been told they have arthritis	25.4	25.8
Adults who have ever been told they have diabetes[2]	10.7	10.5
Adults who have ever been told they had skin cancer	4.1	5.9
Adults who have ever been told they had any other types of cancer	5.0	6.7
Adults who have ever been told they have COPD	5.8	6.3
Adults who have ever been told they have kidney disease	4.3	2.8
Adults who have ever been told they have a form of depression	13.6	17.4

Note: (1) Figures cover the San Antonio-New Braunfels, TX Metropolitan Statistical Area—see Appendix B for areas included; (2) Figures do not include pregnancy-related, borderline, or pre-diabetes
Source: Centers for Disease Control and Prevention, Behaviorial Risk Factor Surveillance System, SMART: Selected Metropolitan Area Risk Trends, 2016

Mortality Rates for the Top 10 Causes of Death in the U.S.

ICD-10[a] Sub-Chapter	ICD-10[a] Code	Age-Adjusted Mortality Rate[1] per 100,000 population	
		County[2]	U.S.
Malignant neoplasms	C00-C97	148.6	158.5
Ischaemic heart diseases	I20-I25	117.2	96.8
Other forms of heart disease	I30-I51	42.6	52.4
Chronic lower respiratory diseases	J40-J47	36.4	40.9
Cerebrovascular diseases	I60-I69	33.5	37.2
Organic, including symptomatic, mental disorders	F01-F09	25.4	33.3
Other degenerative diseases of the nervous system	G30-G31	52.0	32.1
Other external causes of accidental injury	W00-X59	18.7	31.2
Diabetes mellitus	E10-E14	16.1	21.1
Hypertensive diseases	I10-I15	12.5	20.8

Note: (a) ICD-10 = International Classification of Diseases 10th Revision; (1) Mortality rates are a three year average covering 2014-2016; (2) Figures cover Guadalupe County.
Source: Centers for Disease Control and Prevention, National Center for Health Statistics. Underlying Cause of Death 1999-2016 on CDC WONDER Online Database, released December 2017

Mortality Rates for Selected Causes of Death

ICD-10[a] Sub-Chapter	ICD-10[a] Code	Age-Adjusted Mortality Rate[1] per 100,000 population	
		County[2]	U.S.
Assault	X85-Y09	Unreliable	5.6
Diseases of the liver	K70-K76	17.5	14.0
Human immunodeficiency virus (HIV) disease	B20-B24	Suppressed	1.9
Influenza and pneumonia	J09-J18	11.0	14.6
Intentional self-harm	X60-X84	12.9	13.2
Malnutrition	E40-E46	Suppressed	1.3
Obesity and other hyperalimentation	E65-E68	Suppressed	2.1
Renal failure	N17-N19	8.9	13.0
Transport accidents	V01-V99	15.0	12.0
Viral hepatitis	B15-B19	Unreliable	1.9

Note: (a) ICD-10 = International Classification of Diseases 10th Revision; (1) Mortality rates are a three year average covering 2014-2016; (2) Figures cover Guadalupe County; Data are Suppressed when the data meet the criteria for confidentiality constraints; Mortality rates are flagged as Unreliable when the rate would be calculated with a numerator of 20 or less.
Source: Centers for Disease Control and Prevention, National Center for Health Statistics. Underlying Cause of Death 1999-2016 on CDC WONDER Online Database, released December 2017

Health Insurance Coverage

Area	With Health Insurance	With Private Health Insurance	With Public Health Insurance	Without Health Insurance	Population Under Age 18 Without Health Insurance
City	91.8	84.6	19.0	8.2	4.6
MSA[1]	83.7	63.6	30.7	16.3	8.3
U.S.	88.3	66.7	33.0	11.7	5.9

Note: Figures are percentages that cover the civilian noninstitutionalized population; (1) Figures cover the San Antonio-New Braunfels, TX Metropolitan Statistical Area—see Appendix B for areas included
Source: U.S. Census Bureau, 2012-2016 American Community Survey 5-Year Estimates

Number of Medical Professionals

Area	MDs[3]	DOs[3,4]	Dentists	Podiatrists	Chiropractors	Optometrists
County[1] (number)	135	19	49	2	16	15
County[1] (rate[2])	89.7	12.6	31.7	1.3	10.3	9.7
U.S. (rate[2])	276.5	22.3	67.3	6.0	26.7	15.9

Note: Data as of 2016 unless noted; (1) Data covers Guadalupe County; (2) Rate per 100,000 population; (3) Data as of 2015 and includes all active, non-federal physicians; (4) Doctor of Osteopathic Medicine
Source: U.S. Department of Health and Human Services, Health Resources and Services Administration, Bureau of Health Professions, Area Resource File (ARF) 2016-2017

Best Hospitals

According to *U.S. News,* the San Antonio-New Braunfels, TX metro area is home to one of the best hospitals in the U.S.: **University Hospital** (1 adult specialty). The hospital listed was nationally ranked in at least one of 16 specialties. Only 152 hospitals nationwide were nationally ranked in one or more specialties. Twenty hospitals in the U.S. made the Honor Roll. The Best Hospitals Honor Roll was revamped last year to take both the national rankings and the procedure and condition ratings into account. Hospitals received points if they were nationally ranked in one of the 16 specialties—the higher they ranked, the more points they got—and how many ratings of "high performing" they earned in the nine procedures and conditions. *U.S. News Online, "America's Best Hospitals 2017-18"*

EDUCATION

Public School District Statistics

District Name	Schls	Pupils	Pupil/ Teacher Ratio	Minority Pupils[1] (%)	Free Lunch Eligible[2] (%)	IEP[3] (%)
Schertz-Cibolo-Universal City ISD	17	15,118	17.0	59.0	22.4	8.2

Note: Table includes school districts with 100 or more students; (1) Percentage of students that are not non-Hispanic white; (2) Percentage of students that are eligible for the free lunch program; (3) Percentage of students that have an Individualized Education Program.
Source: U.S. Department of Education, National Center for Education Statistics, Common Core of Data, Local Education Agency (School District) Universe Survey: School Year 2015-2016; U.S. Department of Education, National Center for Education Statistics, Common Core of Data, Public Elementary/Secondary School Universe Survey: School Year 2015-2016

Highest Level of Education

Area	Less than H.S.	H.S. Diploma	Some College, No Deg.	Associate Degree	Bachelor's Degree	Master's Degree	Prof. School Degree	Doctorate Degree
City	4.4	19.0	24.3	13.7	23.4	13.3	1.3	0.6
MSA[1]	15.7	26.2	23.3	7.8	17.4	7.0	1.6	1.0
U.S.	13.0	27.5	21.0	8.2	18.8	8.2	2.0	1.3

Note: Figures cover persons age 25 and over; (1) Figures cover the San Antonio-New Braunfels, TX Metropolitan Statistical Area—see Appendix B for areas included
Source: U.S. Census Bureau, 2012-2016 American Community Survey 5-Year Estimates

Educational Attainment by Race

Area	High School Graduate or Higher (%)					Bachelor's Degree or Higher (%)				
	Total	White	Black	Asian	Hisp.[2]	Total	White	Black	Asian	Hisp.[2]
City	95.6	95.7	96.4	88.5	91.8	38.6	38.7	46.8	31.3	38.6
MSA[1]	84.3	85.0	90.4	86.4	74.6	27.0	27.7	26.1	51.4	15.8
U.S.	87.0	88.9	84.3	86.3	65.7	30.3	31.6	20.0	52.1	14.7

Note: Figures shown cover persons 25 years old and over; (1) Figures cover the San Antonio-New Braunfels, TX Metropolitan Statistical Area—see Appendix B for areas included; (2) People of Hispanic origin can be of any race
Source: U.S. Census Bureau, 2012-2016 American Community Survey 5-Year Estimates

School Enrollment by Grade and Control

Area	Preschool (%)		Kindergarten (%)		Grades 1 - 4 (%)		Grades 5 - 8 (%)		Grades 9 - 12 (%)	
	Public	Private	Public	Private	Public	Private	Public	Private	Public	Private
City	60.7	39.3	76.2	23.8	89.8	10.2	96.4	3.6	96.8	3.2
MSA[1]	67.1	32.9	90.9	9.1	93.1	6.9	92.4	7.6	93.6	6.4
U.S.	58.4	41.6	87.7	12.3	89.8	10.2	89.7	10.3	90.4	9.6

Note: Figures shown cover persons 3 years old and over; (1) Figures cover the San Antonio-New Braunfels, TX Metropolitan Statistical Area—see Appendix B for areas included
Source: U.S. Census Bureau, 2012-2016 American Community Survey 5-Year Estimates

Average Salaries of Public School Classroom Teachers

Area	2015		2016		Change from 2015 to 2016	
	Dollars	Rank[1]	Dollars	Rank[1]	Percent	Rank[2]
Texas	50,713	28	51,890	27	2.3	8
U.S. Average	57,611	–	58,353	–	1.3	–

Note: (1) Rank ranges from 1 to 51 where 1 indicates highest salary; (2) Rank ranges from 1 to 51 where 1 indicates highest percent change.
Source: National Education Association, Rankings & Estimates: Rankings of the States 2016 and Estimates of School Statistics 2017

Higher Education

Four-Year Colleges			Two-Year Colleges			Medical Schools[1]	Law Schools[2]	Voc/ Tech[3]
Public	Private Non-profit	Private For-profit	Public	Private Non-profit	Private For-profit			
0	0	0	0	0	0	0	0	0

Note: Figures cover institutions located within the city limits and include main campuses only; (1) includes schools accredited by the Liaison Committee on Medical Education and the American Osteopathic Association's Commission on Osteopathic College Accreditation; (2) includes ABA-accredited schools, schools with provisional ABA accreditation, and state accredited schools; (3) includes all schools with programs that are less than 2 years.
Source: National Center for Education Statistics, Integrated Postsecondary Education System (IPEDS), 2016-17; Wikipedia, List of Medical Schools in the United States, accessed April 2, 2018; Wikipedia, List of Law Schools in the United States, accessed April 2, 2018

According to *U.S. News & World Report,* the San Antonio-New Braunfels, TX metro area is home to one of the top 75 medical schools for research in the U.S.: **University of Texas Health Science Center—San Antonio** (#62 tie). The rankings are based on a weighted average of 11 measures of quality: quality assessment; peer assessment score; assessment score by residency directors; research activity; total research activity; average research activity per faculty member; student selectivity; median MCAT total score; median undergraduate GPA; acceptance rate; and faculty resources. *U.S. News & World Report, "America's Best Graduate Schools, Medical, 2019"*

PRESIDENTIAL ELECTION

2016 Presidential Election Results

Area	Clinton	Trump	Johnson	Stein	Other
Guadalupe County	31.6	63.0	3.5	0.7	1.1
U.S.	48.0	45.9	3.3	1.1	1.7

Note: Results are percentages and may not add to 100% due to rounding
Source: Dave Leip's Atlas of U.S. Presidential Elections

EMPLOYERS

Major Employers

Company Name	Industry
AT&T	Phone, wireless & internet services
Baptist Health System	Health care services
Bill Miller BBQ	Restaurant chain
Christus Santa Rosa Health Care	Health care services
City of San Antonio	San antonio
Clear Channel Communications	TV & radio stations, outdoor ads
CPS Energy	Utilities
Fort Sam Houston-U.S. Army	Military
H-E-B	Super market chain
JP Morgan Chase	Financial services
Lackland Air Force Base	Military
Methodist Healthcare System	Health care services
North East I.S.D.	School district
Northside ISD	School district
Rackspace	IT managed hosting solutions
Randolph Air Force Base	Military
San Antonio I.S.D.	School district
Toyota Motor Manufacturing	Manufacturing
USAA	Financial services & insurance
Wells Fargo	Financial services

Note: Companies shown are located within the San Antonio-New Braunfels, TX Metropolitan Statistical Area.
Source: Hoovers.com; Wikipedia

PUBLIC SAFETY

Crime Rate

Area	All Crimes	Violent Crimes				Property Crimes		
		Murder	Rape[3]	Robbery	Aggrav. Assault	Burglary	Larceny -Theft	Motor Vehicle Theft
City	1,161.1	0.0	10.7	14.2	60.5	110.4	901.1	64.1
Metro[1]	4,608.3	7.7	65.8	104.9	348.0	663.3	3,055.2	363.3
U.S.	2,847.8	5.3	40.4	102.8	248.5	468.9	1,745.0	236.9

Note: Figures are crimes per 100,000 population; (1) Figures cover the San Antonio-New Braunfels, TX Metropolitan Statistical Area—see Appendix B for areas included; (3) The city and U.S. figures shown were reported using the revised Uniform Crime Reporting (UCR) definition of rape. The metro area figures shown are an aggregate total of the data submitted using both the revised and legacy UCR definitions.
Source: FBI Uniform Crime Reports, 2016

Hate Crimes

Area	Number of Quarters Reported	Number of Incidents per Bias Motivation					
		Race/Ethnicity/ Ancestry	Religion	Sexual Orientation	Disability	Gender	Gender Identity
City	4	0	0	0	0	0	0
U.S.	4	3,489	1,273	1,076	70	31	124

Source: Federal Bureau of Investigation, Hate Crime Statistics 2016

Identity Theft Consumer Reports

Area	Reports	Reports per 100,000 Population	Rank[2]
MSA[1]	2,811	116	66
U.S.	371,061	114	-

Note: (1) Figures cover the San Antonio-New Braunfels, TX Metropolitan Statistical Area—see Appendix B for areas included; (2) Rank ranges from 1 to 389 where 1 indicates greatest number of identity theft reports per 100,000 population
Source: Federal Trade Commission, Consumer Sentinel Network Data Book for January–December 2017

Fraud and Other Consumer Reports

Area	Reports	Reports per 100,000 Population	Rank[2]
MSA[1]	10,979	452	172
U.S.	2,304,550	708	-

Note: (1) Figures cover the San Antonio-New Braunfels, TX Metropolitan Statistical Area—see Appendix B for areas included; (2) Rank ranges from 1 to 389 where 1 indicates greatest number of fraud and other consumer reports per 100,000 population
Source: Federal Trade Commission, Consumer Sentinel Network Data Book for January–December 2017

SPORTS

Professional Sports Teams

Team Name	League	Year Established
San Antonio Spurs	National Basketball Association (NBA)	1973

Note: Includes teams located in the San Antonio-New Braunfels, TX Metropolitan Statistical Area.
Source: Wikipedia, Major Professional Sports Teams of the United States and Canada, April 5, 2018

CLIMATE

Average and Extreme Temperatures

Temperature	Jan	Feb	Mar	Apr	May	Jun	Jul	Aug	Sep	Oct	Nov	Dec	Yr.
Extreme High (°F)	89	97	100	100	103	105	106	108	103	98	94	90	108
Average High (°F)	62	66	74	80	86	92	95	95	90	82	71	64	80
Average Temp. (°F)	51	55	62	70	76	82	85	85	80	71	60	53	69
Average Low (°F)	39	43	50	58	66	72	74	74	69	59	49	41	58
Extreme Low (°F)	0	6	19	31	43	53	62	61	46	33	21	6	0

Note: Figures cover the years 1948-1990
Source: National Climatic Data Center, International Station Meteorological Climate Summary, 9/96

Average Precipitation/Snowfall/Humidity

Precip./Humidity	Jan	Feb	Mar	Apr	May	Jun	Jul	Aug	Sep	Oct	Nov	Dec	Yr.
Avg. Precip. (in.)	1.5	1.8	1.5	2.6	3.8	3.6	2.0	2.5	3.3	3.2	2.3	1.4	29.6
Avg. Snowfall (in.)	1	Tr	Tr	0	0	0	0	0	0	0	Tr	Tr	1
Avg. Rel. Hum. 6am (%)	79	80	79	82	87	87	87	86	85	83	81	79	83
Avg. Rel. Hum. 3pm (%)	51	48	45	48	51	48	43	42	47	46	48	49	47

Note: Figures cover the years 1948-1990; Tr = Trace amounts (<0.05 in. of rain; <0.5 in. of snow)
Source: National Climatic Data Center, International Station Meteorological Climate Summary, 9/96

Weather Conditions

Temperature			Daytime Sky			Precipitation		
32°F & below	45°F & below	90°F & above	Clear	Partly cloudy	Cloudy	0.01 inch or more precip.	0.1 inch or more snow/ice	Thunder-storms
23	91	112	97	153	115	81	1	36

Note: Figures are average number of days per year and cover the years 1948-1990
Source: National Climatic Data Center, International Station Meteorological Climate Summary, 9/96

HAZARDOUS WASTE

Superfund Sites

The San Antonio-New Braunfels, TX metro area is home to four sites on the EPA's Superfund National Priorities List: **Bandera Road Ground Water Plume** (final); **Eldorado Chemical Co., Inc.** (final); **R & H Oil/Tropicana** (proposed); **River City Metal Finishing** (proposed). There are a total of 1,396 Superfund sites with a status of proposed or final on the list in the U.S. *U.S. Environmental Protection Agency, National Priorities List, April 4, 2018*

AIR & WATER QUALITY

Air Quality Trends: Ozone

	1990	1995	2000	2005	2010	2012	2013	2014	2015	2016
MSA[1]	0.090	0.095	0.078	0.084	0.072	0.081	0.076	0.069	0.079	0.071
U.S.	0.087	0.089	0.081	0.079	0.073	0.075	0.069	0.067	0.068	0.069

Note: (1) Data covers the San Antonio-New Braunfels, TX Metropolitan Statistical Area—see Appendix B for areas included. The values shown are the composite ozone concentration averages among trend sites based on the highest fourth daily maximum 8-hour concentration in parts per million. These trends are based on sites having an adequate record of monitoring data during the trend period. Data from exceptional events are included.
Source: U.S. Environmental Protection Agency, Air Quality Monitoring Information, "Air Quality Trends by City, 1990-2016"

Air Quality Index

Area	Percent of Days when Air Quality was...[2]					AQI Statistics[2]	
	Good	Moderate	Unhealthy for Sensitive Groups	Unhealthy	Very Unhealthy	Maximum	Median
MSA[1]	72.4	26.0	1.1	0.6	0.0	188	43

Note: (1) Data covers the San Antonio-New Braunfels, TX Metropolitan Statistical Area—see Appendix B for areas included; (2) Based on 362 days with AQI data in 2017. Air Quality Index (AQI) is an index for reporting daily air quality. EPA calculates the AQI for five major air pollutants regulated by the Clean Air Act: ground-level ozone, particle pollution (aka particulate matter), carbon monoxide, sulfur dioxide, and nitrogen dioxide. The AQI runs from 0 to 500. The higher the AQI value, the greater the level of air pollution and the greater the health concern. There are six AQI categories: "Good" AQI is between 0 and 50. Air quality is considered satisfactory; "Moderate" AQI is between 51 and 100. Air quality is acceptable; "Unhealthy for Sensitive Groups" When AQI values are between 101 and 150, members of sensitive groups may experience health effects; "Unhealthy" When AQI values are between 151 and 200 everyone may begin to experience health effects; "Very Unhealthy" AQI values between 201 and 300 trigger a health alert; "Hazardous" AQI values over 300 trigger warnings of emergency conditions (not shown).
Source: U.S. Environmental Protection Agency, Air Quality Index Report, 2017

Air Quality Index Pollutants

Area	Percent of Days when AQI Pollutant was...[2]					
	Carbon Monoxide	Nitrogen Dioxide	Ozone	Sulfur Dioxide	Particulate Matter 2.5	Particulate Matter 10
MSA[1]	0.0	1.7	55.0	0.6	42.8	0.0

Note: (1) Data covers the San Antonio-New Braunfels, TX Metropolitan Statistical Area—see Appendix B for areas included; (2) Based on 362 days with AQI data in 2017. The Air Quality Index (AQI) is an index for reporting daily air quality. EPA calculates the AQI for five major air pollutants regulated by the Clean Air Act: ground-level ozone, particle pollution (also known as particulate matter), carbon monoxide, sulfur dioxide, and nitrogen dioxide. The AQI runs from 0 to 500. The higher the AQI value, the greater the level of air pollution and the greater the health concern.
Source: U.S. Environmental Protection Agency, Air Quality Index Report, 2017

Maximum Air Pollutant Concentrations: Particulate Matter, Ozone, CO and Lead

	Particulate Matter 10 (ug/m^3)	Particulate Matter 2.5 Wtd AM (ug/m^3)	Particulate Matter 2.5 24-Hr (ug/m^3)	Ozone (ppm)	Carbon Monoxide (ppm)	Lead (ug/m^3)
MSA[1] Level	47	7.9	16	0.071	n/a	n/a
NAAQS[2]	150	15	35	0.075	9	0.15
Met NAAQS[2]	Yes	Yes	Yes	Yes	n/a	n/a

Note: (1) Data covers the San Antonio-New Braunfels, TX Metropolitan Statistical Area—see Appendix B for areas included; Data from exceptional events are included; (2) National Ambient Air Quality Standards; ppm = parts per million; ug/m^3 = micrograms per cubic meter; n/a not available.
Concentrations: Particulate Matter 10 (coarse particulate)—highest second maximum 24-hour concentration; Particulate Matter 2.5 Wtd AM (fine particulate)—highest weighted annual mean concentration; Particulate Matter 2.5 24-Hour (fine particulate)—highest 98th percentile 24-hour concentration; Ozone—highest fourth daily maximum 8-hour concentration; Carbon Monoxide—highest second maximum non-overlapping 8-hour concentration; Lead—maximum running 3-month average
Source: U.S. Environmental Protection Agency, Air Quality Monitoring Information, "Air Quality Statistics by City, 2016"

Maximum Air Pollutant Concentrations: Nitrogen Dioxide and Sulfur Dioxide

	Nitrogen Dioxide AM (ppb)	Nitrogen Dioxide 1-Hr (ppb)	Sulfur Dioxide AM (ppb)	Sulfur Dioxide 1-Hr (ppb)	Sulfur Dioxide 24-Hr (ppb)
MSA[1] Level	8	42	n/a	7	n/a
NAAQS[2]	53	100	30	75	140
Met NAAQS[2]	Yes	Yes	n/a	Yes	n/a

Note: (1) Data covers the San Antonio-New Braunfels, TX Metropolitan Statistical Area—see Appendix B for areas included; Data from exceptional events are included; (2) National Ambient Air Quality Standards; ppm = parts per million; ug/m^3 = micrograms per cubic meter; n/a not available.
Concentrations: Nitrogen Dioxide AM—highest arithmetic mean concentration; Nitrogen Dioxide 1-Hr—highest 98th percentile 1-hour daily maximum concentration; Sulfur Dioxide AM—highest annual mean concentration; Sulfur Dioxide 1-Hr—highest 99th percentile 1-hour daily maximum concentration; Sulfur Dioxide 24-Hr—highest second maximum 24-hour concentration
Source: U.S. Environmental Protection Agency, Air Quality Monitoring Information, "Air Quality Statistics by City, 2016"

Drinking Water

Water System Name	Pop. Served	Primary Water Source Type	Violations[1]	
			Health Based	Monitoring/ Reporting
City of Cibolo	16,242	Purchased Surface	0	1

Note: (1) Based on violation data from January 1, 2017 to December 31, 2017
Source: U.S. Environmental Protection Agency, Office of Ground Water and Drinking Water, Safe Drinking Water Information System (based on data extracted April 5, 2018)

Coppell, Texas

Background

Located in Dallas County, Coppell lies northwest of Dallas, just minutes from Dallas/Fort Worth International Airport (DFW). Due to its close proximity to DFW, several large corporations have shifted their distribution facilities to Coppell, including CiCi's Pizza, Lucent, Mohawk Industries and Samsung. STMicroelectronics, a French-Italian multinational electronics and semi-conductor manufacturer also recently moved its corporate headquarters, with over 300 employees, to Coppell.

In the early nineteenth century, Coppell was a farming community called Grapevine Springs. By 1873, it was known as Gibbs, after the former Texas senator and lieutenant governor, Barnett Gibbs. Finally, in 1890, the city became Coppell in honor of George Coppell, the engineer credited with bringing the railroad to the community.

Transportation has played a key role in the history of this city on the move. In 1889, the Cotton Belt Railroad served the area's farms until the 1920s, when paved roads and automobiles became the preferred mode of transport. Coppell was incorporated in 1955, and waited only until the 1960s to reap the benefits of the newly constructed Interstate Highway system that runs close by the city.

At the time the DFW International Airport opened in 1974, it was the world's largest airport, with approximately 18,000 acres. It is still one of the world's largest international airports, with almost 60 million passengers annually, bringing to Coppell opportunities for new development.

The city maintains a commitment to education. Among its achievements, the Coppell Independent School District boasts four national Blue Ribbon Schools of Excellence. With more than 20 colleges and universities close by, the city's focus on education is easy to maintain.

Seven medical facilities in the area, along with readily available professional, full-service daycare, make Coppell a great place to raise children. In addition to its schools, the city has educational resources such as the William T. Cozby Public Library.

Recreation in Coppell includes 480 acres of park land, a public golf course, and facilities for tennis, swimming, and team sports. For fishing, boating, and water sports, Lewisville Lake and Grapevine Lake are only a few minutes away, with other area lakes located within close driving distance. Coppell is not far from Grapevine Mills shopping mall and Vista Ridge Mall in Lewisville.

One of the city's important historical attractions is Bethel Cemetery. Established in 1853 by the Parrish family, it is home to the graves of several early Texas pioneers, one Revolutionary War veteran, Civil War veterans, Indians and black slaves.

Coppell's climate is similar to that of the Dallas-Fort Worth area in general, that is, both continental and humid-subtropical, with wide annual swings in temperatures. One can expect mild winters and hot summers. There are occasionally very cold days in winter and extreme high temperatures in summer, but these spells generally do not last for extended periods.

Rankings

General Rankings

- *US News & World Report* conducted a survey of more than 2,000 people and analyzed the 125 largest metropolitan areas to determine what matters the most when selecting the next place to live. Dallas* ranked #18 out of the top 25 as having the best combination of desirable factors. Criteria: cost of living; quality of education; job market, crime rates; and other factors. *realestate.usnews.com, "The 25 Best Places to Live in the U.S. in 2018," April 10, 2018*

- The Dallas* metro area was identified as one of America's fastest-growing areas in terms of population and economy by *Forbes*. The area ranked #3 out of 25. The 100 most populous metro areas in the U.S. were evaluated on the following criteria: estimated population growth; employment; economic output; wages; home values. *Forbes, "America's Fastest-Growing Cities 2018," February 28, 2018*

- Dallas* was identified as one of America's fastest-growing cities in terms of population growth by CNNMoney.com. The area ranked #8 out of 10. Criteria: population growth between July 2015 and July 2016; cities and towns with populations of 50,000. *CNNMoney, "10 Fastest-Growing Cities," June 2, 2017*

Business/Finance Rankings

- According to *Business Insider*, the Dallas* metro area is where startup growth is on the rise. Based on the 2017 Kauffman Index of Growth Entrepreneurship, which measured in-depth national entrepreneurial trends in 40 metro areas, it ranked #11 in highest startup growth. *www.businessinsider.com, "The 21 U.S. Cities with the Highest Startup Growth," October 21, 2017*

- The personal finance site NerdWallet analyzed 183 American metropolitan areas with populations over 250,000 and more than 15,000 businesses to rank where entrepreneurs find the most success. Criteria included area economy, annual income, housing cost, unemployment rate, and the success rate of area businesses. Dallas* ranked #117. *www.nerdwallet.com, "Best Places to Start a Business," April 27, 2015*

- USAA and Hiring Our Heroes worked with Sperlings's BestPlaces and the Institute for Veterans and Military Families at Syracuse University to rank major metropolitan areas where military-skills-related employment is strongest. Criteria for *mid-career* veterans included veteran wage growth; recent job growth; stability; and accessible health resources. Metro areas with a higher than national average crime or unemployment rate were excluded. At #9, the Dallas* metro area made the top ten. *www.usaa.com, "2015 Best Places for Veterans"*

- Based on metro area social media reviews, the employment opinion group Glassdoor surveyed 50 of the largest U.S. metro areas and equally weighed cost of living, hiring opportunity, and job satisfaction to compose a list of "25 Best Cities for Jobs." Median pay and home value, in-demand jobs and number of current job openings was also factored in. The Dallas* metro area was ranked #25 in overall job satisfaction. *www.glassdoor.com, "Best Cities for Jobs," September 12, 2017*

- In a survey of economic confidence in the nation's 50 largest metropolitan areas conducted January–December 2014, the Dallas* metro area placed #14, according to Gallup's 2014 Economic Confidence Index. *Gallup, "San Jose and San Francisco Lead in Economic Confidence," March 19, 2015*

- The Brookings Institution ranked the 100 largest metro areas in the U.S. based on income inequality. Dallas* was ranked #60 (#1 = greatest ineqality). Criteria: the "95/20 ratio," a figure representing the income at which a household earns more than 95 percent of all other households, divided by the income at which a household earns more than only 20 percent of all other households. *Brookings Institution, "Household Income Inequality, 100 Largest U.S. Metro Areas, 2014-2016," February 5, 2018*

- *Forbes* ranked the 100 largest metro areas in the U.S. in terms of the "Best Cities for Young Professionals." The Dallas* metro area ranked #5 out of 25. (Large metro areas were divided into metro divisions.) Criteria: median rent of a two-bedroom apartment; job growth and unemployment rate; median salary of college graduates with 5 or less years of work experience; networking opportunities; social outlook; percentage of population 25 years of age and older with college degrees. *Forbes.com, "America's 25 Best Cities for Young Professionals in 2017," May 22, 2017*
- Payscale.com ranked the largest metro areas in terms of wage growth. The Dallas* metro area ranked #28. Criteria: private-sector wage growth between the 4th quarter of 2016 and the 4th quarter of 2017. *PayScale, "Wage Trends by Metro Area-4th Quarter," January 17, 2018*
- The Dallas* metro area was identified as one of the most debt-ridden places in America by the finance site Credit.com. The metro area was ranked #2. Criteria: residents' average credit card debt as well as median income. *Credit.com, "25 Cities With the Most Credit Card Debt," February 28, 2018*
- Dallas* was identified as one of America's most frugal metro areas by *Coupons.com.* The city ranked #2 out of 25. Criteria: digital coupon usage. *Coupons.com, "America's Most Frugal Cities of 2017," March 22, 2018*
- Dallas* was cited as one of America's top metros for new and expanded facility projects in 2017. The area ranked #3 in the large metro area category (population over 1 million). *Site Selection, "Top Metropolitans of 2017," March 2018*
- The Dallas* metro area appeared on the Milken Institute "2017 Best Performing Cities" list. Rank: #3 out of 200 large metro areas. Criteria: job growth; wage and salary growth; high-tech output growth. *Milken Institute, "Best-Performing Cities 2017," January 2018*
- *Forbes* ranked the 200 most populous metro areas to determine the nation's "Best Places for Business and Careers." The Dallas* metro area was ranked #10. Criteria: costs (business and living); job growth (past and projected); income growth; quality of life; educational attainment (college and high school); projected economic growth; cultural and recreational opportunities; net migration patterns; number of highly ranked colleges. *Forbes, "The Best Places for Business and Careers 2017," October 24, 2017*

Education Rankings

- Personal finance website *WalletHub* analyzed the 150 largest U.S. metropolitan statistical areas to determine where the most educated Americans are choosing to settle. Criteria: education quality and attainment gap; education levels; percentage of workers with degrees; public school rankings; quality and size of each metro area's universities. Dallas* was ranked #70 (#1 = most educated city). *www.WalletHub.com, "2017's Most and Least Educated Cities in America," July 25, 2017*

Environmental Rankings

- Sperling's BestPlaces assessed 379 metropolitan areas of the United States for the likelihood of dangerously extreme weather events or earthquakes. In general the Southeast and South-Central regions have the highest risk of weather extremes and earthquakes, while the Pacific Northwest enjoys the lowest risk. Of the least risky metropolitan areas, the Dallas* metro area was ranked #379. *www.bestplaces.net, "Safest Places from Natural Disasters," April 2011*
- The U.S. Environmental Protection Agency (EPA) released a list of U.S. metropolitan areas with the most ENERGY STAR certified buildings in 2016. The Dallas* metro area was ranked #6 out of 25. *U.S. Environmental Protection Agency, "2017 Energy Star Top Cities," June 2017*
- Dallas* was highlighted as one of the 25 most ozone-polluted metro areas in the U.S. during 2013 through 2015. The area ranked #13. *American Lung Association, State of the Air 2017*

Health/Fitness Rankings

- For each of the 50 most populous metro areas in the United States, the American College of Sports Medicine's American Fitness Index evaluated infrastructure, community assets, and policies that encourage healthy and fit lifestyles, including preventive health behaviors, levels of chronic disease conditions, health care access, and community resources and policies that support physical activity. The Dallas* metro area ranked #38 for "community fitness." *www.americanfitnessindex.org, "ACSM American Fitness Index Health and Community Fitness Status of the 50 Largest Metropolitan Areas," May 2017*
- The Dallas* metro area was identified as one of the worst cities for bed bugs in America by pest control company Orkin. The area ranked #10 out of 50 based on the number of bed bug treatments Orkin performed from December 2016 to November 2017. *Orkin, "Baltimore and Washington D.C. Continue to Hold Top Spots," January 8, 2018*
- Dallas* was identified as a "2016 Spring Allergy Capital." The area ranked #27 out of 100. Three groups of factors were used to identify the most severe cities for people with allergies during the spring season: annual pollen levels; medicine utilization; access to board-certified allergists. *Asthma and Allergy Foundation of America, "Spring Allergy Capitals 2016"*
- Dallas* was identified as a "2016 Fall Allergy Capital." The area ranked #23 out of 100. Three groups of factors were used to identify the most severe cities for people with allergies during the fall season: annual pollen levels; medicine utilization; access to board-certified allergists. *Asthma and Allergy Foundation of America, "Fall Allergy Capitals 2016"*
- Dallas* was identified as a "2015 Asthma Capital." The area ranked #39 out of the nation's 100 largest metropolitan areas. Criteria: estimated prevalence; self-reported prevalence; crude death rate for asthma; annual pollen score; annual air quality; public smoking laws; number of board-certified asthma specialists; school inhaler access laws; rescue medication use; controller medication use; ER visits for asthma; uninsured rate; poverty rate. *Asthma and Allergy Foundation of America, "Asthma Capitals 2015"*
- The Dallas* metro area ranked #47 out of 189 in The Gallup-Healthways Well-Being Index. Criteria: purpose; social well being; financial health; community and physical health. Results are based on telephone interviews with adults, aged 18 and older, living in metropolitan areas in the 50 U.S. states and the District of Columbia. *Gallup-Healthways, "State of American Well-Being, 2017 Community Well-Being Rankings" March 2018*

Real Estate Rankings

- FitSmallBusiness looked at 50 of the largest metropolitan areas in the U.S. to determine which metro was the best to start a real estate business. Data was compiled from such sources as: Zillow, Trulia, U.S. Census Bureau, and the Bureau of Labor Statistics. Criteria: location; inventory; annual wages; median sales price of homes; days on the market; median price cut percentage; and other factors that would influence real estate professional growth. The Dallas* metro area ranked #19. *fitsmallbusiness.com, "The Best Cities to Become a Real Estate Agent in 2018," January 30, 2018*
- According to Penske Truck Rental, the Dallas* metro area was named the #3 moving destination in 2017, based on one-way consumer truck rental reservations made through Penske's website, rental locations, and reservations call center. *blog.gopenske.com, "Penske Truck Rental's 2017 Top Moving Destinations List," January 22, 2018*
- The Dallas* metro area appeared on Realtor.com's list of the hottest housing markets to watch in 2018. The area ranked #2. Criteria: existing homes inventory and price; new home construction; median household incomes; local economy/population trends. *Realtor.com®, "The 6 Hottest Real Estate Markets to Watch in 2018," January 5, 2018*
- The Dallas* metro area was identified as one of the nations's 20 hottest housing markets in 2018. Criteria: listing views as an indicator of demand and median days on the market as an indicator of supply. The area ranked #12. *Realtor.com, "The 20 Hottest Real Estate Markets for February 2018," March 1, 2018*

- Dallas* was ranked #20 in the top 20 out of 265 metro areas in terms of house price appreciation in 2017 (#1 = highest rate). *Federal Housing Finance Agency, House Price Index, 4th Quarter 2017. February 27, 2018*
- Dallas* was ranked #195 out of 238 metro areas in terms of housing affordability in 2017 by the National Association of Home Builders (#1 = most affordable). Criteria: the share of homes sold in that area affordable to a family earning the local median income, based on standard mortgage underwriting criteria. *National Association of Home Builders®, NAHB-Wells Fargo Housing Opportunity Index, 4th Quarter 2017*

Safety Rankings

- The National Insurance Crime Bureau ranked 382 metro areas in the U.S. in terms of per capita rates of vehicle theft. The Dallas* metro area ranked #87 (#1 = highest rate). Criteria: number of vehicle theft offenses per 100,000 inhabitants in 2016. *National Insurance Crime Bureau, "Hot Spots 2016," June 8, 2017*

Seniors/Retirement Rankings

- From its Best Cities for Successful Aging indexes, the Milken Institute generated rankings for metropolitan areas, weighing data in nine categories—health care, wellness, living arrangements, transportation and convenience, financial characteristics, education, employment, community engagement, and overall livability. The Dallas* metro area was ranked #25 overall in the large metro area category. *Milken Institute, "Best Cities for Successful Aging, 2017" March 14, 2017*

Sports/Recreation Rankings

- According to the personal finance website NerdWallet, the Dallas* metro area, at #1, is one of the nation's top dozen metro areas for sports fans. Criteria included the presence of all four major sports—MLB, NFL, NHL, and NBA, fan enthusiasm (as measured by game attendance), ticket affordability, and "sports culture," that is, number of sports bars. *www.nerdwallet.com, "Best Cities for Sports Fans," May 5, 2013*

Women/Minorities Rankings

- The *Houston Chronicle* listed the Dallas* metro area as #7 in top places for young Latinos to live in the U.S. Research was largely based on housing and occupational data from the largest metropolitan areas performed by *Forbes* and NBC Universo. Criteria: percentage of 18-34 year-olds; Latino college grad rates; and diversity. *blog.chron.com, "The 15 Best Big Cities for Latino Millenials," January 26, 2016*

Miscellaneous Rankings

- The watchdog site Charity Navigator conducts an annual study of charities in the nation's major markets both to analyze statistical differences in their financial, accountability, and transparency practices and to track year-to-year variations in individual philanthropic communities. Charity Navigator's analysis demonstrated that the financial, accountability and transparency behaviors of America's largest charities can be influenced by the metropolitan market within which the charity operates. The Dallas* metro area was ranked #5 among the 30 metro markets in the rating category of Overall Score. *www.charitynavigator.org, "2017 Metro Market Study," May 1, 2017*
- The Harris Poll's Happiness Index survey revealed that of the top ten U.S. markets, the Dallas* metro area residents ranked #1 in happiness. Criteria included strong assent to positive statements and strong disagreement with negative ones, and degree of agreement with a series of statements about respondents' personal relationships and general outlook. *www.theharrispoll.com, "Dallas/Fort Worth Is "Happiest" City among America's Top Ten Markets," September 4, 2013*

- The National Alliance to End Homelessness listed the 25 most populous metro areas with the highest rate of homelessness. The Dallas* metro area had a high rate of homelessness. Criteria: number of homeless people per 10,000 population in 2016. *National Alliance to End Homelessness, "Homelessness in the 25 Most Populous U.S. Metro Areas," September 1, 2017*

*Coppell is located within the Dallas-Fort Worth-Arlington, TX Metropolitan Statistical Area and the Dallas-Plano-Irving, TX Metropolitan Division.

Business Environment

CITY FINANCES

City Government Finances

Component	2015 ($000)	2015 ($ per capita)
Total Revenues	n/a	n/a
Total Expenditures	n/a	n/a
Debt Outstanding	n/a	n/a
Cash and Securities[1]	n/a	n/a

Note: (1) Cash and security holdings of a government at the close of its fiscal year,, including those of its dependent agencies, utilities, and liquor stores.
Source: U.S Census Bureau, State & Local Government Finances 2015

City Government Revenue by Source

Source	2015 ($000)	2015 ($ per capita)	2015 (%)
General Revenue			
From Federal Government	n/a	n/a	n/a
From State Government	n/a	n/a	n/a
From Local Governments	n/a	n/a	n/a
Taxes			
Property	n/a	n/a	n/a
Sales and Gross Receipts	n/a	n/a	n/a
Personal Income	n/a	n/a	n/a
Corporate Income	n/a	n/a	n/a
Motor Vehicle License	n/a	n/a	n/a
Other Taxes	n/a	n/a	n/a
Current Charges	n/a	n/a	n/a
Liquor Store	n/a	n/a	n/a
Utility	n/a	n/a	n/a
Employee Retirement	n/a	n/a	n/a

Source: U.S Census Bureau, State & Local Government Finances 2015

City Government Expenditures by Function

Function	2015 ($000)	2015 ($ per capita)	2015 (%)
General Direct Expenditures			
Air Transportation	n/a	n/a	n/a
Corrections	n/a	n/a	n/a
Education	n/a	n/a	n/a
Employment Security Administration	n/a	n/a	n/a
Financial Administration	n/a	n/a	n/a
Fire Protection	n/a	n/a	n/a
General Public Buildings	n/a	n/a	n/a
Governmental Administration, Other	n/a	n/a	n/a
Health	n/a	n/a	n/a
Highways	n/a	n/a	n/a
Hospitals	n/a	n/a	n/a
Housing and Community Development	n/a	n/a	n/a
Interest on General Debt	n/a	n/a	n/a
Judicial and Legal	n/a	n/a	n/a
Libraries	n/a	n/a	n/a
Parking	n/a	n/a	n/a
Parks and Recreation	n/a	n/a	n/a
Police Protection	n/a	n/a	n/a
Public Welfare	n/a	n/a	n/a
Sewerage	n/a	n/a	n/a
Solid Waste Management	n/a	n/a	n/a
Veterans' Services	n/a	n/a	n/a
Liquor Store	n/a	n/a	n/a
Utility	n/a	n/a	n/a
Employee Retirement	n/a	n/a	n/a

Source: U.S Census Bureau, State & Local Government Finances 2015

DEMOGRAPHICS

Population Growth

Area	1990 Census	2000 Census	2010 Census	2016* Estimate	Population Growth (%) 1990-2016	Population Growth (%) 2010-2016
City	16,881	35,958	38,659	40,631	140.7	5.1
MSA[1]	3,989,294	5,161,544	6,371,773	6,957,123	74.4	9.2
U.S.	248,709,873	281,421,906	308,745,538	318,558,162	28.1	3.2

Note: (1) Figures cover the Dallas-Fort Worth-Arlington, TX Metropolitan Statistical Area—see Appendix B for areas included; (*) 2012-2016 5-year estimated population
Source: U.S. Census Bureau, 1990 Census, Census 2000, Census 2010, 2012-2016 American Community Survey 5-Year Estimates

Household Size

Area	Persons in Household (%)							Average Household Size
	One	Two	Three	Four	Five	Six	Seven or More	
City	19.0	29.5	21.9	20.6	6.5	2.2	0.2	2.80
MSA[1]	24.9	30.8	16.7	15.3	7.5	3.0	1.8	2.80
U.S.	27.7	33.7	15.7	13.1	6.0	2.3	1.5	2.60

Note: (1) Figures cover the Dallas-Fort Worth-Arlington, TX Metropolitan Statistical Area—see Appendix B for areas included
Source: U.S. Census Bureau, 2012-2016 American Community Survey 5-Year Estimates

Race

Area	White Alone[2] (%)	Black Alone[2] (%)	Asian Alone[2] (%)	AIAN[3] Alone[2] (%)	NHOPI[4] Alone[2] (%)	Other Race Alone[2] (%)	Two or More Races (%)
City	70.5	4.5	21.0	0.3	0.0	1.2	2.4
MSA[1]	69.7	15.3	6.1	0.4	0.1	5.5	2.9
U.S.	73.3	12.6	5.2	0.8	0.2	4.8	3.1

Note: (1) Figures cover the Dallas-Fort Worth-Arlington, TX Metropolitan Statistical Area—see Appendix B for areas included; (2) Alone is defined as not being in combination with one or more other races; (3) American Indian and Alaska Native; (4) Native Hawaiian and Other Pacific Islander
Source: U.S. Census Bureau, 2012-2016 American Community Survey 5-Year Estimates

Hispanic or Latino Origin

Area	Total (%)	Mexican (%)	Puerto Rican (%)	Cuban (%)	Other (%)
City	11.2	8.8	0.4	0.3	1.6
MSA[1]	28.2	23.8	0.7	0.2	3.5
U.S.	17.3	11.0	1.7	0.7	4.0

Note: Persons of Hispanic or Latino origin can be of any race; (1) Figures cover the Dallas-Fort Worth-Arlington, TX Metropolitan Statistical Area—see Appendix B for areas included
Source: U.S. Census Bureau, 2012-2016 American Community Survey 5-Year Estimates

Segregation

Type	Segregation Indices[1]				Percent Change		
	1990	2000	2010	2010 Rank[2]	1990-2000	1990-2010	2000-2010
Black/White	62.8	59.8	56.6	48	-3.1	-6.2	-3.2
Asian/White	41.8	45.6	46.6	19	3.8	4.8	1.0
Hispanic/White	48.8	52.3	50.3	24	3.5	1.5	-2.0

Note: All figures cover the Metropolitan Statistical Area—see Appendix B for areas included; Figures are based on an analysis of 1990, 2000, and 2010 Census Decennial Census tract data by William H. Frey, Brookings Institution and the University of Michigan Social Science Data Analysis Network. In this analysis all racial groups (whites, blacks, and asians) are non-Hispanic members of those races. Hispanics are shown as a separate category; (1) Segregation Indices are Dissimilarity Indices that measure the degree to which the minority group is distributed differently than whites across census tracts. They range from 0 (complete integration) to 100 (complete segregation) where the value indicates the percentage of the minority group that needs to move to be distributed exactly like whites; (2) Ranges from 1 (most segregated) to 102 (least segregated); n/a not available.
Source: www.CensusScope.org

Ancestry

Area	German	Irish	English	American	Italian	Polish	French[2]	Scottish	Dutch
City	14.6	9.0	13.9	5.8	3.7	1.5	3.1	2.3	1.2
MSA[1]	9.8	7.6	7.3	6.6	2.2	1.1	1.9	1.7	0.9
U.S.	14.4	10.4	7.7	6.9	5.4	2.9	2.6	1.7	1.3

Note: Figures are the percentage of the total population reporting a particular ancestry. The nine most commonly reported ancestries in the U.S. are shown. Figures include multiple ancestries (e.g. if a person reported being Irish and Italian, they were included in both columns); (1) Figures cover the Dallas-Fort Worth-Arlington, TX Metropolitan Statistical Area—see Appendix B for areas included; (2) Excludes Basque
Source: U.S. Census Bureau, 2012-2016 American Community Survey 5-Year Estimates

Foreign-Born Population

Area	Percent of Population Born in								
	Any Foreign Country	Asia	Mexico	Europe	Carribean	Central America[2]	South America	Africa	Canada
City	20.7	14.6	2.6	0.9	0.2	0.2	0.6	1.1	0.3
MSA[1]	17.8	4.7	8.8	0.8	0.2	1.3	0.5	1.2	0.2
U.S.	13.2	4.0	3.6	1.5	1.3	1.0	0.9	0.6	0.3

Note: (1) Figures cover the Dallas-Fort Worth-Arlington, TX Metropolitan Statistical Area—see Appendix B for areas included; (2) Excludes Mexico.
Source: U.S. Census Bureau, 2012-2016 American Community Survey 5-Year Estimates

Marital Status

Area	Never Married	Now Married[2]	Separated	Widowed	Divorced
City	23.3	64.9	1.0	2.7	8.0
MSA[1]	31.9	50.5	2.3	4.5	10.9
U.S.	33.0	48.1	2.1	5.9	11.0

Note: Figures are percentages and cover the population 15 years of age and older; (1) Figures cover the Dallas-Fort Worth-Arlington, TX Metropolitan Statistical Area—see Appendix B for areas included; (2) Excludes separated
Source: U.S. Census Bureau, 2012-2016 American Community Survey 5-Year Estimates

Disability Status

Area	All Ages	Under 18 Years Old	18 to 64 Years Old	65 Years and Over
City	4.6	1.7	3.3	27.7
MSA[1]	9.6	3.4	8.2	35.2
U.S.	12.5	4.1	10.3	35.7

Note: Figures show percent of the civilian noninstitutionalized population that reported having a disability. Disability status is determined from six types of difficulty: vision, hearing, cognitive, ambulatory, self-care, and independent living. For children under 5 years old, hearing and vision difficulty are used to determine disability status. For children between the ages of 5 and 14, disability status is determined from hearing, vision, cognitive, ambulatory, and self-care difficulties. For people aged 15 years and older, they are considered to have a disability if they have difficulty with any one of the six difficulty types; Note: (1) Figures cover the Dallas-Fort Worth-Arlington, TX Metropolitan Statistical Area—see Appendix B for areas included
Source: U.S. Census Bureau, 2012-2016 American Community Survey 5-Year Estimates

Age

Area	Percent of Population									Median Age
	Under Age 5	Age 5–19	Age 20–34	Age 35–44	Age 45–54	Age 55–64	Age 65–74	Age 75–84	Age 85+	
City	5.4	24.4	13.0	15.4	20.2	14.3	4.7	2.0	0.5	40.0
MSA[1]	7.2	22.2	21.4	14.4	13.8	10.9	6.2	2.9	1.1	34.5
U.S.	6.2	19.6	20.7	12.7	13.6	12.6	8.3	4.3	1.9	37.7

Note: (1) Figures cover the Dallas-Fort Worth-Arlington, TX Metropolitan Statistical Area—see Appendix B for areas included
Source: U.S. Census Bureau, 2012-2016 American Community Survey 5-Year Estimates

Gender

Area	Males	Females	Males per 100 Females
City	20,310	20,321	99.9
MSA[1]	3,421,036	3,536,087	96.7
U.S.	156,765,322	161,792,840	96.9

Note: (1) Figures cover the Dallas-Fort Worth-Arlington, TX Metropolitan Statistical Area—see Appendix B for areas included
Source: U.S. Census Bureau, 2012-2016 American Community Survey 5-Year Estimates

Religious Groups by Family

Area	Catholic	Baptist	Non-Den.	Methodist[2]	Lutheran	LDS[3]	Pente-costal	Presby-terian[4]	Muslim[5]	Judaism
MSA[1]	13.3	18.7	7.8	5.3	0.8	1.2	2.2	1.0	2.4	0.4
U.S.	19.1	9.3	4.0	4.0	2.3	2.0	1.9	1.6	0.8	0.7

Note: Figures are the number of adherents as a percentage of the total population; (1) Figures cover the Dallas-Fort Worth-Arlington, TX Metropolitan Statistical Area—see Appendix B for areas included; (2) Methodist/Pietist; (3) Latter Day Saints; (4) Reformed; (5) Figures are estimates
Source: Association of Statisticians of American Religious Bodies, 2010 U.S. Religion Census: Religious Congregations & Membership Study

Religious Groups by Tradition

Area	Catholic	Evangelical Protestant	Mainline Protestant	Other Tradition	Black Protestant	Orthodox
MSA[1]	13.3	28.3	7.0	4.8	1.8	0.2
U.S.	19.1	16.2	7.3	4.3	1.6	0.3

Note: Figures are the number of adherents as a percentage of the total population; (1) Figures cover the Dallas-Fort Worth-Arlington, TX Metropolitan Statistical Area—see Appendix B for areas included
Source: Association of Statisticians of American Religious Bodies, 2010 U.S. Religion Census: Religious Congregations & Membership Study

ECONOMY

Gross Metropolitan Product

Area	2014	2015	2016	2017	Rank[2]
MSA[1]	502.3	524.8	545.3	577.5	4

Note: Figures are in billions of dollars; (1) Figures cover the Dallas-Fort Worth-Arlington, TX Metropolitan Statistical Area—see Appendix B for areas included; (2) Rank is based on 2015 data and ranges from 1 to 381
Source: The U.S. Conference of Mayors, U.S. Metro Economies: GMP and Employment Report, 2015-2017

Economic Growth

Area	2012-14 (%)	2015 (%)	2016 (%)	2017 (%)	Rank[2]
MSA[1]	6.7	7.1	2.4	3.4	7
U.S.	2.0	2.4	1.9	2.6	-

Note: Figures are real gross metropolitan product (GMP) growth rates and represent average annual percent change; (1) Figures cover the Dallas-Fort Worth-Arlington, TX Metropolitan Statistical Area—see Appendix B for areas included; (2) Rank is based on 2012-2014 average annual percent change and ranges from 1 to 381
Source: The U.S. Conference of Mayors, U.S. Metro Economies: GMP and Employment Report, 2015-2017

Metropolitan Area Exports

Area	2011	2012	2013	2014	2015	2016	Rank[2]
MSA[1]	26,648.7	27,820.9	27,596.0	28,669.4	27,372.9	27,187.8	9

Note: Figures are in millions of dollars; (1) Figures cover the Dallas-Fort Worth-Arlington, TX Metropolitan Statistical Area—see Appendix B for areas included; (2) Rank is based on 2016 data and ranges from 1 to 385
Source: U.S. Department of Commerce, International Trade Administration, Office of Trade & Industry Information, Manufacturing & Services, data extracted March 15, 2018

Building Permits

Area	Single-Family			Multi-Family			Total		
	2016	2017p	Pct. Chg.	2016	2017p	Pct. Chg.	2016	2017p	Pct. Chg.
City	140	95	-32.1	0	0	0.0	140	95	-32.1
MSA[1]	29,846	34,210	14.6	25,772	27,499	6.7	55,618	61,709	11.0
U.S.	750,800	817,300	8.9	455,800	446,800	-2.0	1,206,600	1,264,100	4.8

Note: (1) Figures cover the Dallas-Fort Worth-Arlington, TX Metropolitan Statistical Area—see Appendix B for areas included; Figures represent new, privately-owned housing units authorized (unadjusted data); All permit data are based on estimates with imputation; (p) preliminary data.
Source: U.S. Census Bureau, Manufacturing, Mining, and Construction Statistics, Building Permits, 2016, 2017

Bankruptcy Filings

Area	Business Filings			Nonbusiness Filings		
	2016	2017	% Chg.	2016	2017	% Chg.
Dallas County	332	306	-7.8	3,955	3,997	1.1
U.S.	24,114	23,157	-4.0	770,846	765,863	-0.6

Note: Business filings include Chapter 7, Chapter 11, Chapter 12, and Chapter 13; Nonbusiness filings include Chapter 7, Chapter 11, and Chapter 13
Source: Administrative Office of the U.S. Courts, Business and Nonbusiness Bankruptcy, County Cases Commenced by Chapter of the Bankruptcy Code, During the 12-Month Period Ending December 31, 2016 and Business and Nonbusiness Bankruptcy, County Cases Commenced by Chapter of the Bankruptcy Code, During the 12-Month Period Ending December 31, 2017

Housing Vacancy Rates

Area	Gross Vacancy Rate[2] (%)			Year-Round Vacancy Rate[3] (%)			Rental Vacancy Rate[4] (%)			Homeowner Vacancy Rate[5] (%)		
	2015	2016	2017	2015	2016	2017	2015	2016	2017	2015	2016	2017
MSA[1]	8.0	7.9	7.8	7.8	7.7	7.6	8.3	6.8	7.1	1.4	1.4	0.8
U.S.	12.9	12.8	12.7	10.0	9.9	9.9	7.1	6.9	7.2	1.8	1.7	1.6

Note: (1) Figures cover the Dallas-Fort Worth-Arlington, TX Metropolitan Statistical Area—see Appendix B for areas included; (2) The percentage of the total housing inventory that is vacant; (3) The percentage of the housing inventory (excluding seasonal units) that is year-round vacant; (4) The percentage of rental inventory that is vacant for rent; (5) The percentage of homeowner inventory that is vacant for sale
Source: U.S. Census Bureau, Housing Vacancies and Homeownership Annual Statistics: 2015, 2016, 2017

INCOME

Income

Area	Per Capita ($)	Median Household ($)	Average Household ($)
City	52,509	114,839	142,951
MSA[1]	31,143	61,330	85,693
U.S.	29,829	55,322	77,866

Note: (1) Figures cover the Dallas-Fort Worth-Arlington, TX Metropolitan Statistical Area—see Appendix B for areas included
Source: U.S. Census Bureau, 2012-2016 American Community Survey 5-Year Estimates

Household Income Distribution

Area	Percent of Households Earning							
	Under $15,000	$15,000 -$24,999	$25,000 -$34,999	$35,000 -$49,999	$50,000 -$74,999	$75,000 -$99,999	$100,000 -$149,999	$150,000 and up
City	3.2	3.8	4.0	8.2	11.2	11.8	22.0	35.8
MSA[1]	9.5	8.9	9.5	13.0	18.2	12.4	15.1	13.4
U.S.	12.1	10.2	9.9	13.2	17.8	12.2	13.5	11.1

Note: (1) Figures cover the Dallas-Fort Worth-Arlington, TX Metropolitan Statistical Area—see Appendix B for areas included
Source: U.S. Census Bureau, 2012-2016 American Community Survey 5-Year Estimates

Poverty Rate

Area	All Ages	Under 18 Years Old	18 to 64 Years Old	65 Years and Over
City	4.6	6.4	4.1	2.4
MSA[1]	14.0	20.3	12.3	8.5
U.S.	15.1	21.2	14.2	9.3

Note: Figures are percentage of people whose income during the past 12 months was below the poverty level; (1) Figures cover the Dallas-Fort Worth-Arlington, TX Metropolitan Statistical Area—see Appendix B for areas included
Source: U.S. Census Bureau, 2012-2016 American Community Survey 5-Year Estimates

EMPLOYMENT

Labor Force and Employment

Area	Civilian Labor Force			Workers Employed		
	Dec. 2016	Dec. 2017	% Chg.	Dec. 2016	Dec. 2017	% Chg.
City	23,538	24,111	2.4	22,763	23,425	2.9
MD[1]	2,526,544	2,585,893	2.3	2,434,063	2,504,449	2.9
U.S.	158,968,000	159,880,000	0.6	151,798,000	153,602,000	1.2

Note: Data is not seasonally adjusted and covers workers 16 years of age and older; (1) Figures cover the Dallas-Plano-Irving, TX Metropolitan Division—see Appendix B for areas included
Source: Bureau of Labor Statistics, Local Area Unemployment Statistics

Unemployment Rate

Area	2017											
	Jan.	Feb.	Mar.	Apr.	May	Jun.	Jul.	Aug.	Sep.	Oct.	Nov.	Dec.
City	3.7	3.7	3.7	3.4	3.3	3.5	3.5	3.6	3.1	3.0	3.0	2.8
MD[1]	4.0	4.1	3.9	3.5	3.6	3.9	3.8	3.8	3.4	3.2	3.2	3.1
U.S.	5.1	4.9	4.6	4.1	4.1	4.5	4.6	4.5	4.1	3.9	3.9	3.9

Note: Data is not seasonally adjusted and covers workers 16 years of age and older; (1) Figures cover the Dallas-Plano-Irving, TX Metropolitan Division—see Appendix B for areas included
Source: Bureau of Labor Statistics, Local Area Unemployment Statistics

Average Wages

Occupation	$/Hr.	Occupation	$/Hr.
Accountants and Auditors	39.90	Maids and Housekeeping Cleaners	10.20
Automotive Mechanics	20.50	Maintenance and Repair Workers	18.80
Bookkeepers	21.60	Marketing Managers	68.60
Carpenters	18.80	Nuclear Medicine Technologists	38.30
Cashiers	10.10	Nurses, Licensed Practical	23.10
Clerks, General Office	17.20	Nurses, Registered	35.80
Clerks, Receptionists/Information	13.60	Nursing Assistants	12.90
Clerks, Shipping/Receiving	14.70	Packers and Packagers, Hand	11.50
Computer Programmers	41.60	Physical Therapists	46.50
Computer Systems Analysts	47.10	Postal Service Mail Carriers	24.50
Computer User Support Specialists	25.80	Real Estate Brokers	38.70
Cooks, Restaurant	13.10	Retail Salespersons	12.90
Dentists	83.10	Sales Reps., Exc. Tech./Scientific	35.50
Electrical Engineers	50.70	Sales Reps., Tech./Scientific	46.30
Electricians	22.40	Secretaries, Exc. Legal/Med./Exec.	18.50
Financial Managers	75.80	Security Guards	14.50
First-Line Supervisors/Managers, Sales	22.60	Surgeons	95.40
Food Preparation Workers	10.80	Teacher Assistants*	12.40
General and Operations Managers	70.00	Teachers, Elementary School*	29.00
Hairdressers/Cosmetologists	12.60	Teachers, Secondary School*	30.00
Internists, General	56.10	Telemarketers	14.70
Janitors and Cleaners	11.60	Truck Drivers, Heavy/Tractor-Trailer	22.60
Landscaping/Groundskeeping Workers	13.90	Truck Drivers, Light/Delivery Svcs.	18.40
Lawyers	74.30	Waiters and Waitresses	13.50

Note: Wage data covers the Dallas-Plano-Irving, TX Metropolitan Division—see Appendix B for areas included; (*) Hourly wages for elementary/secondary school teachers and teacher assistants were calculated by the editors from annual wage data based on a 40 hour work week; n/a not available.
Source: Bureau of Labor Statistics, Metro Area Occupational Employment & Wage Estimates, May 2017

Employment by Occupation

Occupation Classification	City (%)	MSA[1] (%)	U.S. (%)
Management, Business, Science, and Arts	61.7	38.2	37.0
Natural Resources, Construction, and Maintenance	2.7	9.3	8.9
Production, Transportation, and Material Moving	5.0	11.6	12.2
Sales and Office	22.2	24.9	23.8
Service	8.4	15.9	18.1

Note: Figures cover employed civilians 16 years of age and older; (1) Figures cover the Dallas-Fort Worth-Arlington, TX Metropolitan Statistical Area—see Appendix B for areas included
Source: U.S. Census Bureau, 2012-2016 American Community Survey 5-Year Estimates

Employment by Industry

Sector	MD[1] Number of Employees	MD[1] Percent of Total	U.S. Percent of Total
Construction, Mining, and Logging	141,400	5.4	5.2
Education and Health Services	313,000	12.0	15.9
Financial Activities	235,200	9.0	5.7
Government	304,800	11.6	15.3
Information	72,900	2.8	1.9
Leisure and Hospitality	262,800	10.0	10.7
Manufacturing	179,300	6.8	8.5
Other Services	85,200	3.3	3.9
Professional and Business Services	488,500	18.7	14.0
Retail Trade	266,600	10.2	11.0
Transportation, Warehousing, and Utilities	121,000	4.6	4.1
Wholesale Trade	147,700	5.6	4.0

Note: Figures are non-farm employment as of December 2017. Figures are not seasonally adjusted and include workers 16 years of age and older; (1) Figures cover the Dallas-Plano-Irving, TX Metropolitan Division—see Appendix B for areas included
Source: Bureau of Labor Statistics, Current Employment Statistics, Employment, Hours, and Earnings

Occupations with Greatest Projected Employment Growth: 2017 – 2019

Occupation[1]	2017 Employment	2019 Projected Employment	Numeric Employment Change	Percent Employment Change
Combined Food Preparation and Serving Workers, Including Fast Food	335,660	354,370	18,710	5.6
Personal Care Aides	212,280	230,990	18,710	8.8
Retail Salespersons	393,950	406,100	12,150	3.1
Customer Service Representatives	261,530	273,600	12,070	4.6
Janitors and Cleaners, Except Maids and Housekeeping Cleaners	180,710	192,060	11,350	6.3
Laborers and Freight, Stock, and Material Movers, Hand	185,140	196,200	11,060	6.0
Registered Nurses	214,500	224,450	9,950	4.6
Office Clerks, General	379,860	389,540	9,680	2.6
Heavy and Tractor-Trailer Truck Drivers	192,710	201,560	8,850	4.6
Waiters and Waitresses	222,630	231,020	8,390	3.8

Note: Projections cover Texas; (1) Sorted by numeric employment change
Source: www.projectionscentral.com, State Occupational Projections, 2017–2019 Short-Term Projections

Fastest Growing Occupations: 2017 – 2019

Occupation[1]	2017 Employment	2019 Projected Employment	Numeric Employment Change	Percent Employment Change
Wind Turbine Service Technicians	1,740	2,090	350	20.7
Home Health Aides	72,760	80,000	7,240	10.0
Security and Fire Alarm Systems Installers	8,190	8,930	740	8.9
Personal Care Aides	212,280	230,990	18,710	8.8
Statisticians	1,760	1,910	150	8.2
Tree Trimmers and Pruners	5,980	6,480	500	8.2
Physician Assistants	6,860	7,400	540	7.9
Nurse Practitioners	9,230	9,950	720	7.7
Elevator Installers and Repairers	2,190	2,350	160	7.4
Helpers—Roofers	800	850	50	7.4

Note: Projections cover Texas; (1) Sorted by percent employment change and excludes occupations with numeric employment change less than 50
Source: www.projectionscentral.com, State Occupational Projections, 2017–2019 Short-Term Projections

TAXES

State Corporate Income Tax Rates

State	Tax Rate (%)	Income Brackets ($)	Num. of Brackets	Financial Institution Tax Rate (%)[a]	Federal Income Tax Ded.
Texas	(w)	–	–	(w)	No

Note: Tax rates as of January 1, 2018; (a) Rates listed are the corporate income tax rate applied to financial institutions or excise taxes based on income. Some states have other taxes based upon the value of deposits or shares; (w) Texas imposes a Franchise Tax, otherwise known as margin tax, imposed on entities with more than $1,110,000 total revenues at rate of 0.75%, or 0.375% for entities primarily engaged in retail or wholesale trade, on lesser of 70% of total revenues or 100% of gross receipts after deductions for either compensation or cost of goods sold.
Source: Federation of Tax Administrators, Range of State Corporate Income Tax Rates, January 1, 2018

State Individual Income Tax Rates

State	Tax Rate (%)	Income Brackets ($)	Num. of Brackets	Personal Exempt. ($)[1] Single	Personal Exempt. ($)[1] Dependents	Fed. Inc. Tax Ded.
Texas	None	–	–	–	–	–

Note: Tax rates as of January 1, 2018; Local- and county-level taxes are not included; n/a not applicable; (1) Married joint filers generally receive double the single exemption
Source: Federation of Tax Administrators, State Individual Income Tax Rates, January 1, 2018

Various State Sales and Excise Tax Rates

State	State Sales Tax (%)	Gasoline[1] (¢/gal.)	Cigarette[2] ($/pack)	Spirits[3] ($/gal.)	Wine[4] ($/gal.)	Beer[5] ($/gal.)	Recreational Marijuana (%)
Texas	6.25	20.0	1.41	2.40 (f)	0.20 (l)	0.20 (q)	Not legal

Note: All tax rates as of January 1, 2018; (1) The American Petroleum Institute has developed a methodology for determining the average tax rate on a gallon of fuel. Rates may include any of the following: excise taxes, environmental fees, storage tank fees, other fees or taxes, general sales tax, and local taxes. In states where gasoline is subject to the general sales tax, or where the fuel tax is based on the average sale price, the average rate determined by API is sensitive to changes in the price of gasoline. States that fully or partially apply general sales taxes to gasoline: CA, CO, GA, IL, IN, MI, NY; (2) The federal excise tax of $1.0066 per pack and local taxes are not included; (3) Rates are those applicable to off-premise sales of 40% alcohol by volume (a.b.v.) distilled spirits in 750ml containers. Local excise taxes are excluded; (4) Rates are those applicable to off-premise sales of 11% a.b.v. non-carbonated wine in 750ml containers; (5) Rates are those applicable to off-premise sales of 4.7% a.b.v. beer in 12 ounce containers; (f) Different rates also applicable according to alcohol content, place of production, size of container, or place purchased (on- or off-premise or onboard airlines); (l) Different rates also applicable to alcohol content, place of production, size of container, place purchased (on- or off-premise or on board airlines) or type of wine (carbonated, vermouth, etc.); (q) Different rates also applicable according to alcohol content, place of production, size of container, or place purchased (on- or off-premise or onboard airlines).
Source: Tax Foundation, 2018 Facts & Figures: How Does Your State Compare?

State Business Tax Climate Index Rankings

State	Overall Rank	Corporate Tax Rank	Individual Income Tax Rank	Sales Tax Rank	Unemployment Insurance Tax Rank	Property Tax Rank
Texas	13	49	6	37	26	37

Note: The index is a measure of how each state's tax laws affect economic performance. The lower the rank, the more favorable a state's tax system is for business. States without a given tax are given a ranking of 1. The scores/rankings for the District of Columbia do not affect other states. The 2018 index represents the tax climate as of July 1, 2017.
Source: Tax Foundation, State Business Tax Climate Index 2018

TRANSPORTATION

Means of Transportation to Work

Area	Car/Truck/Van: Drove Alone	Car/Truck/Van: Car-pooled	Public Transportation: Bus	Public Transportation: Subway	Public Transportation: Railroad	Bicycle	Walked	Other Means	Worked at Home
City	81.2	6.0	0.1	0.4	0.4	0.1	0.5	1.4	9.8
MSA[1]	80.7	9.9	1.0	0.2	0.3	0.2	1.2	1.5	5.0
U.S.	76.4	9.3	2.6	1.9	0.6	0.6	2.8	1.3	4.6

Note: Figures are percentages and cover workers 16 years of age and older; (1) Figures cover the Dallas-Fort Worth-Arlington, TX Metropolitan Statistical Area—see Appendix B for areas included
Source: U.S. Census Bureau, 2012-2016 American Community Survey 5-Year Estimates

Travel Time to Work

Area	Less Than 10 Minutes	10 to 19 Minutes	20 to 29 Minutes	30 to 44 Minutes	45 to 59 Minutes	60 to 89 Minutes	90 Minutes or More
City	8.4	27.8	25.2	26.9	8.2	2.2	1.3
MSA[1]	9.4	25.8	21.1	25.0	10.3	6.3	2.0
U.S.	12.9	29.2	20.9	20.4	8.0	6.0	2.7

Note: Note: Figures are percentages and include workers 16 years old and over; (1) Figures cover the Dallas-Fort Worth-Arlington, TX Metropolitan Statistical Area—see Appendix B for areas included
Source: U.S. Census Bureau, 2012-2016 American Community Survey 5-Year Estimates

Freeway Travel Time Index

Area	1985	1990	1995	2000	2005	2010	2014
Urban Area Rank[1,2]	6	9	10	19	21	22	19
Urban Area Index[1]	1.19	1.20	1.23	1.24	1.26	1.24	1.27
Average Index[3]	1.09	1.11	1.14	1.17	1.20	1.19	1.20

Note: Freeway Travel Time Index—the ratio of travel time in the peak period to the travel time at free-flow conditions. For example, a value of 1.30 indicates a 20-minute free-flow trip takes 26 minutes in the peak (20 minutes x 1.30 = 26 minutes); (1) Covers the Dallas-Fort Worth-Arlington TX urban area; (2) Rank is based on 101 urban areas (#1 = highest travel time index); (3) Average of 101 urban areas
Source: Texas Transportation Institute, 2015 Urban Mobility Scorecard, August 2015

Freeway Commuter Stress Index

Area	1985	1990	1995	2000	2005	2010	2014
Urban Area Rank[1,2]	12	15	13	20	22	25	20
Urban Area Index[1]	1.25	1.26	1.29	1.30	1.32	1.30	1.33
Average Index[3]	1.13	1.16	1.19	1.22	1.25	1.24	1.25

Note: The Freeway Commuter Stress Index is the same as the Freeway Travel Time Index (see table above) except that it includes only the travel in the peak directions during the peak periods; the TTI includes travel in all directions during the peak period. Thus, the CSI is more indicative of the work trip experienced by each commuter on a daily basis; (1) Covers the Dallas-Fort Worth-Arlington TX urban area; (2) Rank is based on 101 urban areas (#1 = highest travel time index); (3) Average of 101 urban areas
Source: Texas Transportation Institute, 2015 Urban Mobility Scorecard, August 2015

Living Environment

COST OF LIVING

Cost of Living Index

Composite Index	Groceries	Housing	Utilities	Transportation	Health Care	Misc. Goods/ Services
107.2	99.6	120.8	97.9	103.9	85.0	105.6

Note: The Cost of Living Index measures regional differences in the cost of consumer goods and services, excluding taxes and non-consumer expenditures, for professional and managerial households in the top income quintile. It is based on more than 50,000 prices covering almost 60 different items for which prices are collected three times a year by chambers of commerce, economic development organizations or university applied economic centers in each participating urban area. The numbers shown should be read as a percentage above or below the national average of 100. For example, a value of 115.4 in the groceries column indicates that grocery prices are 15.4% higher than the national average. Small differences in the index numbers should not be interpreted as significant; Figures cover the Plano TX urban area.
Source: The Council for Community and Economic Research, ACCRA Cost of Living Index, 2017

Grocery Prices

Area[1]	T-Bone Steak ($/pound)	Frying Chicken ($/pound)	Whole Milk ($/half gal.)	Eggs ($/dozen)	Orange Juice ($/64 oz.)	Coffee ($/11.5 oz.)
City[2]	11.99	1.19	1.82	1.82	3.99	4.43
Avg.	11.29	1.40	2.02	1.47	3.55	4.37
Min.	7.71	0.93	1.04	0.70	2.86	3.24
Max.	15.83	2.39	4.03	3.92	6.29	8.16

*Note: (1) Values for the local area are compared with the average, minimum and maximum values for all 294 areas in the Cost of Living Index; (2) Figures cover the Plano TX urban area; **T-Bone Steak** (price per pound); **Frying Chicken** (price per pound, whole fryer); **Whole Milk** (half gallon carton); **Eggs** (price per dozen, Grade A, large); **Orange Juice** (64 oz. Tropicana or Florida Natural); **Coffee** (11.5 oz. can, vacuum-packed, Maxwell House, Hills Bros, or Folgers).*
Source: The Council for Community and Economic Research, ACCRA Cost of Living Index, 2017

Housing and Utility Costs

Area[1]	New Home Price ($)	Apartment Rent ($/month)	All Electric ($/month)	Part Electric ($/month)	Other Energy ($/month)	Telephone ($/month)
City[2]	387,838	1,300	-	110.21	55.03	27.72
Avg.	335,956	1,047	175.01	97.34	67.93	28.71
Min.	187,788	491	109.48	49.33	35.44	12.39
Max.	1,739,087	4,559	432.62	227.09	353.33	44.61

*Note: (1) Values for the local area are compared with the average, minimum and maximum values for all 294 areas in the Cost of Living Index; (2) Figures cover the Plano TX urban area; **New Home Price** (2,400 sf living area, 8,000 sf lot, in urban area with full utilities); **Apartment Rent** (950 sf 2 bedroom/1.5 or 2 bath, unfurnished, excluding all utilities except water); **All Electric** (average monthly cost for an all-electric home); **Part Electric** (average monthly cost for a part-electric home); **Other Energy** (average monthly cost for natural gas, fuel oil, coal, wood, and any other forms of energy except electricity); **Telephone** (price includes basic monthly rate for a private residential line plus additional local usage charges incurred by a family of four).*
Source: The Council for Community and Economic Research, ACCRA Cost of Living Index, 2017

Health Care, Transportation, and Other Costs

Area[1]	Doctor ($/visit)	Dentist ($/visit)	Optometrist ($/visit)	Gasoline ($/gallon)	Beauty Salon ($/visit)	Men's Shirt ($)
City[2]	80.02	73.81	108.39	2.18	48.10	29.06
Avg.	108.00	92.54	101.93	2.25	37.58	30.92
Min.	30.39	60.00	49.75	1.82	16.11	11.20
Max.	193.50	161.94	229.28	3.16	77.35	59.13

*Note: (1) Values for the local area are compared with the average, minimum and maximum values for all 294 areas in the Cost of Living Index; (2) Figures cover the Plano TX urban area; **Doctor** (general practitioners routine exam of an established patient); **Dentist** (adult teeth cleaning and periodic oral examination); **Optometrist** (full vision eye exam for established adult patient); **Gasoline** (one gallon regular unleaded, national brand, including all taxes, cash price at self-service pump if available); **Beauty Salon** (woman's shampoo, trim, and blow-dry); **Men's Shirt** (cotton/polyester dress shirt, pinpoint weave, long sleeves).*
Source: The Council for Community and Economic Research, ACCRA Cost of Living Index, 2017

HOUSING

House Price Index (HPI)

Area	National Ranking[2]	Quarterly Change (%)	One-Year Change (%)	Five-Year Change (%)
MD[1]	20	1.01	10.57	57.15
U.S.[3]	–	1.61	6.68	34.71

Note: The HPI is a weighted repeat sales index. It measures average price changes in repeat sales or refinancings on the same properties. This information is obtained by reviewing repeat mortgage transactions on single-family properties whose mortgages have been purchased or securitized by Fannie Mae or Freddie Mac in January 1975; (1) Figures cover the Dallas-Plano-Irving, TX Metropolitan Division—see Appendix B for areas included; (2) Rankings are based on annual percentage change for all metro areas containing at least 15,000 transactions over the last 10 years and ranges from 1 to 253; (3) figures based on a weighted average of Census Division estimates using a seasonally adjusted, purchase-only index; all figures are for the period ending December 31, 2017
Source: Federal Housing Finance Agency, House Price Index, February 28, 2018

Median Single-Family Home Prices

Area	2015	2016	2017p	Percent Change 2016 to 2017
MSA[1]	207.2	227.1	247.4	8.9
U.S. Average	223.9	235.5	248.8	5.6

Note: Figures are median sales prices of existing single-family homes in thousands of dollars; (p) preliminary; (1) Figures cover the Dallas-Fort Worth-Arlington, TX Metropolitan Statistical Area—see Appendix B for areas included
Source: National Association of Realtors, Median Sales Price of Existing Single-Family Homes for Metropolitan Areas, 4th Quarter 2017

Qualifying Income Based on Median Sales Price of Existing Single-Family Homes

Area	With 5% Down ($)	With 10% Down ($)	With 20% Down ($)
MSA[1]	55,203	52,298	46,487
U.S. Average	55,585	52,659	46,808

Note: Figures are preliminary; Qualifying income is based on a mortgage rate of 4.17%. Monthly principal and interest payment is limited to 25% of income; (1) Figures cover the Dallas-Fort Worth-Arlington, TX Metropolitan Statistical Area—see Appendix B for areas included
Source: National Association of Realtors, Qualifying Income Based on Median Sales Price of Existing Single-Family Homes for Metropolitan Areas, 4th Quarter 2017

Median Apartment Condo-Coop Home Prices

Area	2015	2016	2017p	Percent Change 2016 to 2017
MSA[1]	148.7	167.7	185.7	10.7
U.S. Average	210.7	220.7	234.3	6.2

Note: Figures are median sales prices of existing apartment condo-coop homes in thousands of dollars; (p) preliminary; (1) Figures cover the Dallas-Fort Worth-Arlington, TX Metropolitan Statistical Area—see Appendix B for areas included
Source: National Association of Realtors, Median Sales Price of Existing Apartment Condo-Coop Homes for Metropolitan Areas, 4th Quarter 2017

Home Value Distribution

Area	Under $50,000	$50,000 -$99,999	$100,000 -$149,999	$150,000 -$199,999	$200,000 -$299,999	$300,000 -$499,999	$500,000 -$999,999	$1,000,000 or more
City	3.9	0.7	3.6	10.2	27.4	39.2	13.6	1.6
MSA[1]	6.4	17.3	20.6	17.5	18.4	13.4	4.9	1.5
U.S.	8.8	14.8	15.3	14.9	18.4	16.4	9.0	2.5

Note: Figures are percentages and cover owner-occupied housing units; (1) Figures cover the Dallas-Fort Worth-Arlington, TX Metropolitan Statistical Area—see Appendix B for areas included
Source: U.S. Census Bureau, 2012-2016 American Community Survey 5-Year Estimates

Homeownership Rate

Area	2009 (%)	2010 (%)	2011 (%)	2012 (%)	2013 (%)	2014 (%)	2015 (%)	2016 (%)	2017 (%)
MSA[1]	61.6	63.8	62.6	61.8	59.9	57.7	57.8	59.7	61.8
U.S.	67.4	66.9	66.1	65.4	65.1	64.5	63.7	63.4	63.9

Note: (1) Figures cover the Dallas-Fort Worth-Arlington, TX Metropolitan Statistical Area—see Appendix B for areas included
Source: U.S. Census Bureau, Housing Vacancies and Homeownership Annual Statistics: 2009-2017

Year Housing Structure Built

Area	2010 or Later	2000 -2009	1990 -1999	1980 -1989	1970 -1979	1960 -1969	1950 -1959	1940 -1949	Before 1940	Median Year
City	3.8	12.9	40.4	34.1	5.7	1.2	0.9	0.5	0.4	1992
MSA[1]	4.5	22.2	16.8	19.1	14.9	9.0	7.7	2.9	2.9	1987
U.S.	2.3	14.7	14.0	13.7	15.6	10.9	10.6	5.2	13.0	1977

Note: Figures are percentages except for Median Year; Note: (1) Figures cover the Dallas-Fort Worth-Arlington, TX Metropolitan Statistical Area—see Appendix B for areas included
Source: U.S. Census Bureau, 2012-2016 American Community Survey 5-Year Estimates

Gross Monthly Rent

Area	Under $500	$500 -$999	$1,000 -$1,499	$1,500 -$1,999	$2,000 -$2,499	$2,500 -$2,999	$3,000 and up	Median ($)
City	0.2	25.5	44.3	18.5	4.5	3.9	3.2	1,225
MSA[1]	4.6	49.0	32.4	10.0	2.5	0.8	0.7	969
U.S.	11.3	43.3	27.7	10.7	4.0	1.6	1.5	949

Note: Figures are percentages except for Median; Gross rent is the contract rent plus the estimated average monthly cost of utilities (electricity, gas, and water and sewer) and fuels (oil, coal, kerosene, wood, etc.) if these are paid by the renter (or paid for the renter by someone else); (1) Figures cover the Dallas-Fort Worth-Arlington, TX Metropolitan Statistical Area—see Appendix B for areas included
Source: U.S. Census Bureau, 2012-2016 American Community Survey 5-Year Estimates

HEALTH

Health Risk Factors

Category	MD[1] (%)	U.S. (%)
Adults aged 18–64 who have any kind of health care coverage	79.8	87.7
Adults who reported being in good or excellent health	86.4	83.6
Adults who are current smokers	13.2	17.1
Adults who currently use E-cigarettes	5.3	4.7
Adults who currently use chewing tobacco, snuff, or snus	3.3	4.0
Adults who are heavy drinkers[2]	5.8	6.5
Adults who are binge drinkers[3]	15.0	16.9
Adults who are overweight (BMI 25.0 - 29.9)	34.7	35.3
Adults who are obese (BMI 30.0 - 99.8)	34.6	29.9
Adults who participated in any physical activities in the past month	77.4	76.9
Adults who always or nearly always wears a seat belt	96.2	94.3

Note: (1) Figures cover the Dallas-Plano-Irving, TX Metropolitan Division—see Appendix B for areas included; (2) Heavy drinkers are classified as adult men having more than 14 drinks per week and adult women having more than 7 drinks per week; (3) Binge drinkers are classified as males having five or more drinks on one occasion or females having four or more drinks on one occasion
Source: Centers for Disease Control and Prevention, Behaviorial Risk Factor Surveillance System, SMART: Selected Metropolitan Area Risk Trends, 2016

Health Screening Rates

Category	MD[1] (%)	U.S. (%)
Adults 50-75 who have had a blood stool test within the past year	n/a	8.0
Adults 50-75 who have had a colonoscopy in the past 10 years	60.9	63.5
Adults aged 65+ who have had flu shot within the past year	61.1	58.6
Adults aged 65+ who have ever had a pneumonia vaccination	72.6	73.4
Adults who have ever been tested for HIV	41.3	35.6
Women aged 21-65 who have had a pap test in the past three years	72.4	79.8
Men aged 40+ who have had a PSA test within the past two years	42.0	39.5
Women aged 40+ who have had a mammogram within the past two years	58.5	72.5

Note: n/a not available; (1) Figures cover the Dallas-Plano-Irving, TX Metropolitan Division—see Appendix B for areas included; Source: Centers for Disease Control and Prevention, Behaviorial Risk Factor Surveillance System, SMART: Selected Metropolitan Area Risk Trends, 2016

Chronic Health Conditions

Category	MD[1] (%)	U.S. (%)
Adults who have ever been told they had a heart attack	2.5	4.4
Adults who have ever been told they have angina or coronary heart disease	2.6	4.1
Adults who have ever been told they had a stroke	n/a	3.1
Adults who have been told they currently have asthma	6.4	9.3
Adults who have ever been told they have arthritis	20.7	25.8
Adults who have ever been told they have diabetes[2]	8.8	10.5
Adults who have ever been told they had skin cancer	6.0	5.9
Adults who have ever been told they had any other types of cancer	6.7	6.7
Adults who have ever been told they have COPD	3.1	6.3
Adults who have ever been told they have kidney disease	n/a	2.8
Adults who have ever been told they have a form of depression	11.7	17.4

Note: n/a not available; (1) Figures cover the Dallas-Plano-Irving, TX Metropolitan Division—see Appendix B for areas included; (2) Figures do not include pregnancy-related, borderline, or pre-diabetes
Source: Centers for Disease Control and Prevention, Behaviorial Risk Factor Surveillance System, SMART: Selected Metropolitan Area Risk Trends, 2016

Mortality Rates for the Top 10 Causes of Death in the U.S.

ICD-10[a] Sub-Chapter	ICD-10[a] Code	Age-Adjusted Mortality Rate[1] per 100,000 population	
		County[2]	U.S.
Malignant neoplasms	C00-C97	151.4	158.5
Ischaemic heart diseases	I20-I25	90.5	96.8
Other forms of heart disease	I30-I51	52.2	52.4
Chronic lower respiratory diseases	J40-J47	35.5	40.9
Cerebrovascular diseases	I60-I69	48.2	37.2
Organic, including symptomatic, mental disorders	F01-F09	35.8	33.3
Other degenerative diseases of the nervous system	G30-G31	44.5	32.1
Other external causes of accidental injury	W00-X59	25.0	31.2
Diabetes mellitus	E10-E14	18.1	21.1
Hypertensive diseases	I10-I15	31.3	20.8

Note: (a) ICD-10 = International Classification of Diseases 10th Revision; (1) Mortality rates are a three year average covering 2014-2016; (2) Figures cover Dallas County.
Source: Centers for Disease Control and Prevention, National Center for Health Statistics. Underlying Cause of Death 1999-2016 on CDC WONDER Online Database, released December 2017

Mortality Rates for Selected Causes of Death

ICD-10[a] Sub-Chapter	ICD-10[a] Code	Age-Adjusted Mortality Rate[1] per 100,000 population	
		County[2]	U.S.
Assault	X85-Y09	7.3	5.6
Diseases of the liver	K70-K76	14.5	14.0
Human immunodeficiency virus (HIV) disease	B20-B24	3.7	1.9
Influenza and pneumonia	J09-J18	12.9	14.6
Intentional self-harm	X60-X84	10.1	13.2
Malnutrition	E40-E46	1.6	1.3
Obesity and other hyperalimentation	E65-E68	2.3	2.1
Renal failure	N17-N19	19.3	13.0
Transport accidents	V01-V99	12.2	12.0
Viral hepatitis	B15-B19	2.0	1.9

Note: (a) ICD-10 = International Classification of Diseases 10th Revision; (1) Mortality rates are a three year average covering 2014-2016; (2) Figures cover Dallas County; Data are Suppressed when the data meet the criteria for confidentiality constraints; Mortality rates are flagged as Unreliable when the rate would be calculated with a numerator of 20 or less.
Source: Centers for Disease Control and Prevention, National Center for Health Statistics. Underlying Cause of Death 1999-2016 on CDC WONDER Online Database, released December 2017

Health Insurance Coverage

Area	With Health Insurance	With Private Health Insurance	With Public Health Insurance	Without Health Insurance	Population Under Age 18 Without Health Insurance
City	91.8	86.2	10.3	8.2	6.7
MSA[1]	81.5	63.6	25.2	18.5	10.8
U.S.	88.3	66.7	33.0	11.7	5.9

Note: Figures are percentages that cover the civilian noninstitutionalized population; (1) Figures cover the Dallas-Fort Worth-Arlington, TX Metropolitan Statistical Area—see Appendix B for areas included
Source: U.S. Census Bureau, 2012-2016 American Community Survey 5-Year Estimates

Number of Medical Professionals

Area	MDs[3]	DOs[3,4]	Dentists	Podiatrists	Chiropractors	Optometrists
County[1] (number)	8,299	529	2,076	102	886	336
County[1] (rate[2])	324.9	20.7	80.2	3.9	34.2	13.0
U.S. (rate[2])	276.5	22.3	67.3	6.0	26.7	15.9

Note: Data as of 2016 unless noted; (1) Data covers Dallas County; (2) Rate per 100,000 population; (3) Data as of 2015 and includes all active, non-federal physicians; (4) Doctor of Osteopathic Medicine
Source: U.S. Department of Health and Human Services, Health Resources and Services Administration, Bureau of Health Professions, Area Resource File (ARF) 2016-2017

Best Hospitals

According to *U.S. News,* the Dallas-Plano-Irving, TX metro area is home to three of the best hospitals in the U.S.: **Baylor University Medical Center** (2 adult specialties); **Medical City Dallas Hospital** (1 adult specialty); **UT Southwestern Medical Center** (6 adult specialties). The hospitals listed were nationally ranked in at least one of 16 specialties. Only 152 hospitals nationwide were nationally ranked in one or more specialties. Twenty hospitals in the U.S. made the Honor Roll. The Best Hospitals Honor Roll was revamped last year to take both the national rankings and the procedure and condition ratings into account. Hospitals received points if they were nationally ranked in one of the 16 specialties—the higher they ranked, the more points they got—and how many ratings of "high performing" they earned in the nine procedures and conditions. *U.S. News Online, "America's Best Hospitals 2017-18"*

According to *U.S. News,* the Dallas-Plano-Irving, TX metro area is home to two of the best children's hospitals in the U.S.: **Children's Medical Center Dallas** (9 pediatric specialties); **Texas Scottish Rite Hospital for Children** (1 pediatric specialty). The hospitals listed were highly ranked in at least one of 10 pediatric specialties. Eighty-two children's hospitals in the U.S. were nationally ranked in at least one specialty. Hospitals received points for being ranked in a specialty, and the 10 hospitals with the most points across the 10 specialties make up the Honor Roll. *U.S. News Online, "America's Best Children's Hospitals 2017-18"*

EDUCATION

Public School District Statistics

District Name	Schls	Pupils	Pupil/ Teacher Ratio	Minority Pupils[1] (%)	Free Lunch Eligible[2] (%)	IEP[3] (%)
Carrollton-farmers Branch ISD	41	25,796	15.5	85.7	54.5	10.1
Coppell Isd	17	11,881	15.6	61.7	6.4	5.4
Texas College Preparatory Academies	38	12,778	20.2	56.3	33.3	6.9
Universal Academy	3	1,985	17.5	98.2	29.6	1.9

Note: Table includes school districts with 100 or more students; (1) Percentage of students that are not non-Hispanic white; (2) Percentage of students that are eligible for the free lunch program; (3) Percentage of students that have an Individualized Education Program.
Source: U.S. Department of Education, National Center for Education Statistics, Common Core of Data, Local Education Agency (School District) Universe Survey: School Year 2015-2016; U.S. Department of Education, National Center for Education Statistics, Common Core of Data, Public Elementary/Secondary School Universe Survey: School Year 2015-2016

Best High Schools

According to *U.S. News,* Coppell is home to one of the best high schools in the U.S.: **Coppell High School** (#463). More than 22,000 public, magnet and charter schools were ranked based on their performance on state assessments and how well they prepare students for college. Schools with the highest unrounded College Readiness Index values were numerically ranked from 1 to 500 and were classified as gold medal winners. *U.S. News & World Report, "Best High Schools 2017"*

Highest Level of Education

Area	Less than H.S.	H.S. Diploma	Some College, No Deg.	Associate Degree	Bachelor's Degree	Master's Degree	Prof. School Degree	Doctorate Degree
City	3.3	10.4	15.8	5.7	38.5	19.8	4.3	2.1
MSA[1]	15.4	22.5	22.2	6.7	21.9	8.5	1.7	1.0
U.S.	13.0	27.5	21.0	8.2	18.8	8.2	2.0	1.3

Note: Figures cover persons age 25 and over; (1) Figures cover the Dallas-Fort Worth-Arlington, TX Metropolitan Statistical Area—see Appendix B for areas included
Source: U.S. Census Bureau, 2012-2016 American Community Survey 5-Year Estimates

Educational Attainment by Race

Area	High School Graduate or Higher (%)					Bachelor's Degree or Higher (%)				
	Total	White	Black	Asian	Hisp.[2]	Total	White	Black	Asian	Hisp.[2]
City	96.7	97.2	99.3	95.4	84.8	64.7	63.1	56.5	75.1	43.8
MSA[1]	84.6	85.2	89.6	88.0	56.8	33.1	34.1	24.8	58.8	12.0
U.S.	87.0	88.9	84.3	86.3	65.7	30.3	31.6	20.0	52.1	14.7

Note: Figures shown cover persons 25 years old and over; (1) Figures cover the Dallas-Fort Worth-Arlington, TX Metropolitan Statistical Area—see Appendix B for areas included; (2) People of Hispanic origin can be of any race
Source: U.S. Census Bureau, 2012-2016 American Community Survey 5-Year Estimates

School Enrollment by Grade and Control

Area	Preschool (%)		Kindergarten (%)		Grades 1 - 4 (%)		Grades 5 - 8 (%)		Grades 9 - 12 (%)	
	Public	Private	Public	Private	Public	Private	Public	Private	Public	Private
City	31.0	69.0	84.5	15.5	90.5	9.5	87.3	12.7	91.6	8.4
MSA[1]	57.4	42.6	89.3	10.7	92.6	7.4	92.0	8.0	92.3	7.7
U.S.	58.4	41.6	87.7	12.3	89.8	10.2	89.7	10.3	90.4	9.6

Note: Figures shown cover persons 3 years old and over; (1) Figures cover the Dallas-Fort Worth-Arlington, TX Metropolitan Statistical Area—see Appendix B for areas included
Source: U.S. Census Bureau, 2012-2016 American Community Survey 5-Year Estimates

Average Salaries of Public School Classroom Teachers

Area	2015		2016		Change from 2015 to 2016	
	Dollars	Rank[1]	Dollars	Rank[1]	Percent	Rank[2]
Texas	50,713	28	51,890	27	2.3	8
U.S. Average	57,611	–	58,353	–	1.3	–

Note: (1) Rank ranges from 1 to 51 where 1 indicates highest salary; (2) Rank ranges from 1 to 51 where 1 indicates highest percent change.
Source: National Education Association, Rankings & Estimates: Rankings of the States 2016 and Estimates of School Statistics 2017

Higher Education

Four-Year Colleges			Two-Year Colleges			Medical Schools[1]	Law Schools[2]	Voc/ Tech[3]
Public	Private Non-profit	Private For-profit	Public	Private Non-profit	Private For-profit			
0	0	0	0	0	0	0	0	0

Note: Figures cover institutions located within the city limits and include main campuses only; (1) includes schools accredited by the Liaison Committee on Medical Education and the American Osteopathic Association's Commission on Osteopathic College Accreditation; (2) includes ABA-accredited schools, schools with provisional ABA accreditation, and state accredited schools; (3) includes all schools with programs that are less than 2 years.
Source: National Center for Education Statistics, Integrated Postsecondary Education System (IPEDS), 2016-17; Wikipedia, List of Medical Schools in the United States, accessed April 2, 2018; Wikipedia, List of Law Schools in the United States, accessed April 2, 2018

According to *U.S. News & World Report,* the Dallas-Plano-Irving, TX metro division is home to three of the best national universities in the U.S.: **Southern Methodist University** (#61 tie); **University of Texas—Dallas** (#145 tie); **Dallas Baptist University** (#202 tie). The indicators used to capture academic quality fall into a number of categories: assessment by administrators at peer institutions; retention of students; faculty resources; student selectivity; financial resources; alumni giving; high school counselor ratings of colleges; and graduation rate. *U.S. News & World Report, "America's Best Colleges 2018"*

According to *U.S. News & World Report,* the Dallas-Plano-Irving, TX metro division is home to one of the top 100 law schools in the U.S.: **Southern Methodist University (Dedman)** (#50 tie). The rankings are based on a weighted average of 12 measures of quality: peer assessment score;

assessment score by lawyers/judges; median LSAT scores; median undergrad GPA; acceptance rate; employment rates for graduates; placement success; bar passage rate; faculty resources; expenditures per student; student/faculty ratio; and library resources. *U.S. News & World Report, "America's Best Graduate Schools, Law, 2019"*

According to *U.S. News & World Report,* the Dallas-Plano-Irving, TX metro division is home to one of the top 75 medical schools for research in the U.S.: **University of Texas Southwestern Medical Center** (#26 tie). The rankings are based on a weighted average of 11 measures of quality: quality assessment; peer assessment score; assessment score by residency directors; research activity; total research activity; average research activity per faculty member; student selectivity; median MCAT total score; median undergraduate GPA; acceptance rate; and faculty resources. *U.S. News & World Report, "America's Best Graduate Schools, Medical, 2019"*

According to *U.S. News & World Report,* the Dallas-Plano-Irving, TX metro division is home to two of the top 75 business schools in the U.S.: **University of Texas—Dallas** (#40 tie); **Southern Methodist University (Cox)** (#48 tie). The rankings are based on a weighted average of the following nine measures: quality assessment; peer assessment; recruiter assessment; placement success; mean starting salary and bonus; student selectivity; mean GMAT and GRE scores; mean undergraduate GPA; and acceptance rate. *U.S. News & World Report, "America's Best Graduate Schools, Business, 2019"*

PRESIDENTIAL ELECTION

2016 Presidential Election Results

Area	Clinton	Trump	Johnson	Stein	Other
Dallas County	60.2	34.3	3.1	0.8	1.5
U.S.	48.0	45.9	3.3	1.1	1.7

Note: Results are percentages and may not add to 100% due to rounding
Source: Dave Leip's Atlas of U.S. Presidential Elections

EMPLOYERS

Major Employers

Company Name	Industry
AMR Corporation	Air transportation, scheduled
Associates First Capital Corporation	Mortgage bankers
Baylor University Medical Center	General medical & surgical hospitals
Children's Medical Center Dallas	Specialty hospitals, except psychiatric
Combat Support Associates	Engineering services
County of Dallas	County supervisors' & executives' offices
Dallas County Hospital District	General medical & surgical hospitals
Fort Worth Independent School District	Public elementary & secondary schools
Housewares Holding Company	Toasters, electric: household
HP Enterprise Services	Computer integrated systems design
J.C. Penney Company	Department stores
JCP Publications Corp.	Department stores
L-3 Communications Corporation	Business economic service
Odyssey HealthCare	Home health care services
Romano's Macaroni Grill	Italian restaurant
SFG Management Limited Liability	Milk processing (pasteurizing, homogenizing, bottling)
Texas Instruments Incorporated	Semiconductors & related devices
University of North Texas	Colleges & universities
University of Texas SW Medical Center	Accident & health insurance
Verizon Business Global	Telephone communication, except radio

Note: Companies shown are located within the Dallas-Fort Worth-Arlington, TX Metropolitan Statistical Area.
Source: Hoovers.com; Wikipedia

PUBLIC SAFETY

Crime Rate

Area	All Crimes	Violent Crimes				Property Crimes		
		Murder	Rape[3]	Robbery	Aggrav. Assault	Burglary	Larceny -Theft	Motor Vehicle Theft
City	1,303.6	0.0	19.2	9.6	36.0	177.7	998.7	62.4
Metro[1]	2,776.8	5.2	40.2	141.3	170.0	488.1	1,640.0	292.0
U.S.	2,847.8	5.3	40.4	102.8	248.5	468.9	1,745.0	236.9

Note: Figures are crimes per 100,000 population; (1) Figures cover the Dallas-Plano-Irving, TX Metropolitan Division—see Appendix B for areas included; (3) The city and U.S. figures shown were reported using the revised Uniform Crime Reporting (UCR) definition of rape. The metro area figures shown are an aggregate total of the data submitted using both the revised and legacy UCR definitions.
Source: FBI Uniform Crime Reports, 2016

Hate Crimes

Area	Number of Quarters Reported	Number of Incidents per Bias Motivation					
		Race/Ethnicity/ Ancestry	Religion	Sexual Orientation	Disability	Gender	Gender Identity
City	4	0	0	0	0	0	0
U.S.	4	3,489	1,273	1,076	70	31	124

Source: Federal Bureau of Investigation, Hate Crime Statistics 2016

Identity Theft Consumer Reports

Area	Reports	Reports per 100,000 Population	Rank[2]
MSA[1]	11,506	159	11
U.S.	371,061	114	-

Note: (1) Figures cover the Dallas-Fort Worth-Arlington, TX Metropolitan Statistical Area—see Appendix B for areas included; (2) Rank ranges from 1 to 389 where 1 indicates greatest number of identity theft reports per 100,000 population
Source: Federal Trade Commission, Consumer Sentinel Network Data Book for January–December 2017

Fraud and Other Consumer Reports

Area	Reports	Reports per 100,000 Population	Rank[2]
MSA[1]	55,938	773	8
U.S.	2,304,550	708	-

Note: (1) Figures cover the Dallas-Fort Worth-Arlington, TX Metropolitan Statistical Area—see Appendix B for areas included; (2) Rank ranges from 1 to 389 where 1 indicates greatest number of fraud and other consumer reports per 100,000 population
Source: Federal Trade Commission, Consumer Sentinel Network Data Book for January–December 2017

SPORTS

Professional Sports Teams

Team Name	League	Year Established
Dallas Cowboys	National Football League (NFL)	1960
Dallas Mavericks	National Basketball Association (NBA)	1980
Dallas Stars	National Hockey League (NHL)	1993
FC Dallas	Major League Soccer (MLS)	1996
Texas Rangers	Major League Baseball (MLB)	1972

Note: Includes teams located in the Dallas-Fort Worth-Arlington, TX Metropolitan Statistical Area.
Source: Wikipedia, Major Professional Sports Teams of the United States and Canada, April 5, 2018

CLIMATE

Average and Extreme Temperatures

Temperature	Jan	Feb	Mar	Apr	May	Jun	Jul	Aug	Sep	Oct	Nov	Dec	Yr.
Extreme High (°F)	85	90	100	100	101	112	111	109	107	101	91	87	112
Average High (°F)	55	60	68	76	84	92	96	96	89	79	67	58	77
Average Temp. (°F)	45	50	57	66	74	82	86	86	79	68	56	48	67
Average Low (°F)	35	39	47	56	64	72	76	75	68	57	46	38	56
Extreme Low (°F)	-2	9	12	30	39	53	58	58	42	24	16	0	-2

Note: Figures cover the years 1945-1993
Source: National Climatic Data Center, International Station Meteorological Climate Summary, 9/96

Average Precipitation/Snowfall/Humidity

Precip./Humidity	Jan	Feb	Mar	Apr	May	Jun	Jul	Aug	Sep	Oct	Nov	Dec	Yr.
Avg. Precip. (in.)	1.9	2.3	2.6	3.8	4.9	3.4	2.1	2.3	2.9	3.3	2.3	2.1	33.9
Avg. Snowfall (in.)	1	1	Tr	Tr	0	0	0	0	0	Tr	Tr	Tr	3
Avg. Rel. Hum. 6am (%)	78	77	75	77	82	81	77	76	80	79	78	77	78
Avg. Rel. Hum. 3pm (%)	53	51	47	49	51	48	43	41	46	46	48	51	48

Note: Figures cover the years 1945-1993; Tr = Trace amounts (<0.05 in. of rain; <0.5 in. of snow)
Source: National Climatic Data Center, International Station Meteorological Climate Summary, 9/96

Weather Conditions

Temperature			Daytime Sky			Precipitation		
10°F & below	32°F & below	90°F & above	Clear	Partly cloudy	Cloudy	0.01 inch or more precip.	0.1 inch or more snow/ice	Thunder-storms
1	34	102	108	160	97	78	2	49

Note: Figures are average number of days per year and cover the years 1945-1993
Source: National Climatic Data Center, International Station Meteorological Climate Summary, 9/96

HAZARDOUS WASTE

Superfund Sites

The Dallas-Plano-Irving, TX metro division is home to four sites on the EPA's Superfund National Priorities List: **Lane Plating Works, Inc** (proposed); **Old Esco Manufacturing** (final); **RSR Corporation** (final); **Van Der Horst Usa Corporation** (final). There are a total of 1,396 Superfund sites with a status of proposed or final on the list in the U.S. *U.S. Environmental Protection Agency, National Priorities List, April 4, 2018*

AIR & WATER QUALITY

Air Quality Trends: Ozone

	1990	1995	2000	2005	2010	2012	2013	2014	2015	2016
MSA[1]	0.095	0.105	0.096	0.097	0.080	0.080	0.081	0.076	0.077	0.070
U.S.	0.087	0.089	0.081	0.079	0.073	0.075	0.069	0.067	0.068	0.069

Note: (1) Data covers the Dallas-Fort Worth-Arlington, TX Metropolitan Statistical Area—see Appendix B for areas included. The values shown are the composite ozone concentration averages among trend sites based on the highest fourth daily maximum 8-hour concentration in parts per million. These trends are based on sites having an adequate record of monitoring data during the trend period. Data from exceptional events are included.
Source: U.S. Environmental Protection Agency, Air Quality Monitoring Information, "Air Quality Trends by City, 1990-2016"

Air Quality Index

Area	Percent of Days when Air Quality was...[2]					AQI Statistics[2]	
	Good	Moderate	Unhealthy for Sensitive Groups	Unhealthy	Very Unhealthy	Maximum	Median
MSA[1]	52.6	40.8	6.6	0.0	0.0	147	50

Note: (1) Data covers the Dallas-Fort Worth-Arlington, TX Metropolitan Statistical Area—see Appendix B for areas included; (2) Based on 365 days with AQI data in 2017. Air Quality Index (AQI) is an index for reporting daily air quality. EPA calculates the AQI for five major air pollutants regulated by the Clean Air Act: ground-level ozone, particle pollution (aka particulate matter), carbon monoxide, sulfur dioxide, and nitrogen dioxide. The AQI runs from 0 to 500. The higher the AQI value, the greater the level of air pollution and the greater the health concern. There are six AQI categories: "Good" AQI is between 0 and 50. Air quality is considered satisfactory; "Moderate" AQI is between 51 and 100. Air quality is acceptable; "Unhealthy for Sensitive Groups" When AQI values are between 101 and 150, members of sensitive groups may experience health effects; "Unhealthy" When AQI values are between 151 and 200 everyone may begin to experience health effects; "Very Unhealthy" AQI values between 201 and 300 trigger a health alert; "Hazardous" AQI values over 300 trigger warnings of emergency conditions (not shown).
Source: U.S. Environmental Protection Agency, Air Quality Index Report, 2017

Air Quality Index Pollutants

Area	Percent of Days when AQI Pollutant was...[2]					
	Carbon Monoxide	Nitrogen Dioxide	Ozone	Sulfur Dioxide	Particulate Matter 2.5	Particulate Matter 10
MSA[1]	0.0	2.7	57.0	0.0	40.3	0.0

Note: (1) Data covers the Dallas-Fort Worth-Arlington, TX Metropolitan Statistical Area—see Appendix B for areas included; (2) Based on 365 days with AQI data in 2017. The Air Quality Index (AQI) is an index for reporting daily air quality. EPA calculates the AQI for five major air pollutants regulated by the Clean Air Act: ground-level ozone, particle pollution (also known as particulate matter), carbon monoxide, sulfur dioxide, and nitrogen dioxide. The AQI runs from 0 to 500. The higher the AQI value, the greater the level of air pollution and the greater the health concern.
Source: U.S. Environmental Protection Agency, Air Quality Index Report, 2017

Maximum Air Pollutant Concentrations: Particulate Matter, Ozone, CO and Lead

	Particulate Matter 10 (ug/m³)	Particulate Matter 2.5 Wtd AM (ug/m³)	Particulate Matter 2.5 24-Hr (ug/m³)	Ozone (ppm)	Carbon Monoxide (ppm)	Lead (ug/m³)
MSA[1] Level	52	8.5	19	0.076	1	0.06
NAAQS[2]	150	15	35	0.075	9	0.15
Met NAAQS[2]	Yes	Yes	Yes	No	Yes	Yes

Note: (1) Data covers the Dallas-Fort Worth-Arlington, TX Metropolitan Statistical Area—see Appendix B for areas included; Data from exceptional events are included; (2) National Ambient Air Quality Standards; ppm = parts per million; ug/m³ = micrograms per cubic meter; n/a not available.
Concentrations: Particulate Matter 10 (coarse particulate)—highest second maximum 24-hour concentration; Particulate Matter 2.5 Wtd AM (fine particulate)—highest weighted annual mean concentration; Particulate Matter 2.5 24-Hour (fine particulate)—highest 98th percentile 24-hour concentration; Ozone—highest fourth daily maximum 8-hour concentration; Carbon Monoxide—highest second maximum non-overlapping 8-hour concentration; Lead—maximum running 3-month average
Source: U.S. Environmental Protection Agency, Air Quality Monitoring Information, "Air Quality Statistics by City, 2016"

Maximum Air Pollutant Concentrations: Nitrogen Dioxide and Sulfur Dioxide

	Nitrogen Dioxide AM (ppb)	Nitrogen Dioxide 1-Hr (ppb)	Sulfur Dioxide AM (ppb)	Sulfur Dioxide 1-Hr (ppb)	Sulfur Dioxide 24-Hr (ppb)
MSA[1] Level	12	45	n/a	8	n/a
NAAQS[2]	53	100	30	75	140
Met NAAQS[2]	Yes	Yes	n/a	Yes	n/a

Note: (1) Data covers the Dallas-Fort Worth-Arlington, TX Metropolitan Statistical Area—see Appendix B for areas included; Data from exceptional events are included; (2) National Ambient Air Quality Standards; ppm = parts per million; ug/m³ = micrograms per cubic meter; n/a not available.
Concentrations: Nitrogen Dioxide AM—highest arithmetic mean concentration; Nitrogen Dioxide 1-Hr—highest 98th percentile 1-hour daily maximum concentration; Sulfur Dioxide AM—highest annual mean concentration; Sulfur Dioxide 1-Hr—highest 99th percentile 1-hour daily maximum concentration; Sulfur Dioxide 24-Hr—highest second maximum 24-hour concentration
Source: U.S. Environmental Protection Agency, Air Quality Monitoring Information, "Air Quality Statistics by City, 2016"

Drinking Water

Water System Name	Pop. Served	Primary Water Source Type	Violations[1]	
			Health Based	Monitoring/ Reporting
City of Coppell	39,880	Purchased Surface	0	1

Note: (1) Based on violation data from January 1, 2017 to December 31, 2017
Source: U.S. Environmental Protection Agency, Office of Ground Water and Drinking Water, Safe Drinking Water Information System (based on data extracted April 5, 2018)

Flower Mound, Texas

Background

Situated at the southern edge of Denton County, Flower Mound is 23 miles northwest of Dallas and five miles north of DFW International Airport. The city is a rapidly growing community of highly-educated, affluent residents.

A prime location for business development, Flower Mound has good schools, a low tax rate, and significant recreational attractions. Its proximity to Dallas and Fort Worth offers cultural activities, dining, and shopping, as well as several excellent colleges and universities.

Located on the shore of Grapevine Lake, Flower Mound was established soon after Sam Houston settled a tribal dispute in 1844, leading to the cessation of Indian raids in the area. Permanent settlers arrived, attracted by the quality of the soil, which was suitable for growing cotton, corn, and wheat. The town was named for a 50-foot-high mound covered with Indian paintbrush and blue stem grasses. Historians believe the mound was once used by the Wichita Indians as a sacred ceremonial ground dating back to the early 1800s.

During the first half of the twentieth century, Flower Mound was a substantial farming and cattle-raising community. In the mid-1950s the town really began to grow, thanks to construction by the United States Corps of Engineers of Grapevine Lake, which stimulated the town's economy and attracted workers who preferred to live outside the central Dallas area. Flower Mound was incorporated as a city in February 1961.

The Flower Mound school system, part of the Lewisville Independent School District, has received several awards, including the Texas Successful Schools and the National Blue Ribbon Schools of Excellence awards. The city's schools all have been rated "exemplary" by the Texas Education Agency. Area universities include the Southern Methodist University, University of Dallas, University of North Texas, and Texas Women's University.

Located only minutes from Flower Mound are two hospitals—Medical Center of Lewisville and Baylor Regional Medical Center at Grapevine.

Unsurpassed recreational facilities thrive in Flower Mound, with its heavily wooded hills, panoramic views, and the creeks and shorelines provided by Grapevine Lake and Lewisville Lake. The city maintains baseball and softball fields, soccer fields, public tennis courts, and some 680 acres of parkland, with more than 30 miles of multi-purpose trail linking parks, neighborhoods, schools, and businesses. The parks host a range of facilities; including playgrounds, picnic kiosks and grills, and basketball play pads. Two notable golf courses, Tour 18 and Bridlewood, are open to the public.

The town encourages conservation development projects to protect and preserve existing open space, vistas, and natural habitats while allowing for controlled growth. Much of the town is located on the Barnett Shale, and drilling for shale gas in close proximity to residential neighborhoods has sharply divided parts of the community.In 1994, amateur fossil collector Gary Byrd discovered a fossilized example of a Hadrosaurid dinosaur among black shale rock formations in the southwest edge of the town near Grapevine Lake. The fossilized creature from the Cenomanian age was named "Protohadros byrdi" in Byrd's honor.

Nearby Grapevine Mills Mall houses over 200 outlet stores, an aquarium, Legoland Discovery Center, and a 30-screen theater, while the Dallas Metroplex offers the Texas Motor Speedway, Six Flags and Hurricane Harbor, and Cowboys Stadium, as well as the symphony halls and art museums of Dallas and Fort Worth.

Flower Mound is a four-season city, with mild winters, and hot, humid summers. The town's location on the shores of Grapevine Lake provides welcome respite during the summer. Look for bluebonnets in spring.

Rankings

General Rankings

- For its "Best Places to Live" rankings (formerly known as Best for Vets: Places to Live), *Military Times* evaluated 577 cities (79 large, 244 medium, 254 small) and compared the locations across three broad categories: veteran and military culture/services; economic indicators; and livability factors such as health, crime, traffic, and school quality. Flower Mound ranked #17 out of the top 50, in the small city category (populations of less than 75,000). Data points more specific to veterans and the military weighed more heavily than the rest. *rebootcamp.militarytimes.com, "Military Times Best Places to Live 2017," September 11, 2017*
- *US News & World Report* conducted a survey of more than 2,000 people and analyzed the 125 largest metropolitan areas to determine what matters the most when selecting the next place to live. Dallas* ranked #18 out of the top 25 as having the best combination of desirable factors. Criteria: cost of living; quality of education; job market, crime rates; and other factors. *realestate.usnews.com, "The 25 Best Places to Live in the U.S. in 2018," April 10, 2018*
- The Dallas* metro area was identified as one of America's fastest-growing areas in terms of population and economy by *Forbes*. The area ranked #3 out of 25. The 100 most populous metro areas in the U.S. were evaluated on the following criteria: estimated population growth; employment; economic output; wages; home values. *Forbes, "America's Fastest-Growing Cities 2018," February 28, 2018*
- Dallas* was identified as one of America's fastest-growing cities in terms of population growth by CNNMoney.com. The area ranked #8 out of 10. Criteria: population growth between July 2015 and July 2016; cities and towns with populations of 50,000. *CNNMoney, "10 Fastest-Growing Cities," June 2, 2017*

Business/Finance Rankings

- According to *Business Insider*, the Dallas* metro area is where startup growth is on the rise. Based on the 2017 Kauffman Index of Growth Entrepreneurship, which measured in-depth national entrepreneurial trends in 40 metro areas, it ranked #11 in highest startup growth. *www.businessinsider.com, "The 21 U.S. Cities with the Highest Startup Growth," October 21, 2017*
- The personal finance site NerdWallet analyzed 183 American metropolitan areas with populations over 250,000 and more than 15,000 businesses to rank where entrepreneurs find the most success. Criteria included area economy, annual income, housing cost, unemployment rate, and the success rate of area businesses. Dallas* ranked #117. *www.nerdwallet.com, "Best Places to Start a Business," April 27, 2015*
- USAA and Hiring Our Heroes worked with Sperlings's BestPlaces and the Institute for Veterans and Military Families at Syracuse University to rank major metropolitan areas where military-skills-related employment is strongest. Criteria for *mid-career* veterans included veteran wage growth; recent job growth; stability; and accessible health resources. Metro areas with a higher than national average crime or unemployment rate were excluded. At #9, the Dallas* metro area made the top ten. *www.usaa.com, "2015 Best Places for Veterans"*
- Based on metro area social media reviews, the employment opinion group Glassdoor surveyed 50 of the largest U.S. metro areas and equally weighed cost of living, hiring opportunity, and job satisfaction to compose a list of "25 Best Cities for Jobs." Median pay and home value, in-demand jobs and number of current job openings was also factored in. The Dallas* metro area was ranked #25 in overall job satisfaction. *www.glassdoor.com, "Best Cities for Jobs," September 12, 2017*
- In a survey of economic confidence in the nation's 50 largest metropolitan areas conducted January–December 2014, the Dallas* metro area placed #14, according to Gallup's 2014 Economic Confidence Index. *Gallup, "San Jose and San Francisco Lead in Economic Confidence," March 19, 2015*

- The Brookings Institution ranked the 100 largest metro areas in the U.S. based on income inequality. Dallas* was ranked #60 (#1 = greatest ineqality). Criteria: the "95/20 ratio," a figure representing the income at which a household earns more than 95 percent of all other households, divided by the income at which a household earns more than only 20 percent of all other households. *Brookings Institution, "Household Income Inequality, 100 Largest U.S. Metro Areas, 2014-2016," February 5, 2018*
- *Forbes* ranked the 100 largest metro areas in the U.S. in terms of the "Best Cities for Young Professionals." The Dallas* metro area ranked #5 out of 25. (Large metro areas were divided into metro divisions.) Criteria: median rent of a two-bedroom apartment; job growth and unemployment rate; median salary of college graduates with 5 or less years of work experience; networking opportunities; social outlook; percentage of population 25 years of age and older with college degrees. *Forbes.com, "America's 25 Best Cities for Young Professionals in 2017," May 22, 2017*
- Payscale.com ranked the largest metro areas in terms of wage growth. The Dallas* metro area ranked #28. Criteria: private-sector wage growth between the 4th quarter of 2016 and the 4th quarter of 2017. *PayScale, "Wage Trends by Metro Area-4th Quarter," January 17, 2018*
- The Dallas* metro area was identified as one of the most debt-ridden places in America by the finance site Credit.com. The metro area was ranked #2. Criteria: residents' average credit card debt as well as median income. *Credit.com, "25 Cities With the Most Credit Card Debt," February 28, 2018*
- Dallas* was identified as one of America's most frugal metro areas by *Coupons.com.* The city ranked #2 out of 25. Criteria: digital coupon usage. *Coupons.com, "America's Most Frugal Cities of 2017," March 22, 2018*
- Dallas* was cited as one of America's top metros for new and expanded facility projects in 2017. The area ranked #3 in the large metro area category (population over 1 million). *Site Selection, "Top Metropolitans of 2017," March 2018*
- The Dallas* metro area appeared on the Milken Institute "2017 Best Performing Cities" list. Rank: #3 out of 200 large metro areas. Criteria: job growth; wage and salary growth; high-tech output growth. *Milken Institute, "Best-Performing Cities 2017," January 2018*
- *Forbes* ranked the 200 most populous metro areas to determine the nation's "Best Places for Business and Careers." The Dallas* metro area was ranked #10. Criteria: costs (business and living); job growth (past and projected); income growth; quality of life; educational attainment (college and high school); projected economic growth; cultural and recreational opportunities; net migration patterns; number of highly ranked colleges. *Forbes, "The Best Places for Business and Careers 2017," October 24, 2017*

Education Rankings

- Personal finance website *WalletHub* analyzed the 150 largest U.S. metropolitan statistical areas to determine where the most educated Americans are choosing to settle. Criteria: education quality and attainment gap; education levels; percentage of workers with degrees; public school rankings; quality and size of each metro area's universities. Dallas* was ranked #70 (#1 = most educated city). *www.WalletHub.com, "2017's Most and Least Educated Cities in America," July 25, 2017*

Environmental Rankings

- Sperling's BestPlaces assessed 379 metropolitan areas of the United States for the likelihood of dangerously extreme weather events or earthquakes. In general the Southeast and South-Central regions have the highest risk of weather extremes and earthquakes, while the Pacific Northwest enjoys the lowest risk. Of the least risky metropolitan areas, the Dallas* metro area was ranked #379. *www.bestplaces.net, "Safest Places from Natural Disasters," April 2011*

- The U.S. Environmental Protection Agency (EPA) released a list of U.S. metropolitan areas with the most ENERGY STAR certified buildings in 2016. The Dallas* metro area was ranked #6 out of 25. *U.S. Environmental Protection Agency, "2017 Energy Star Top Cities," June 2017*

- Dallas* was highlighted as one of the 25 most ozone-polluted metro areas in the U.S. during 2013 through 2015. The area ranked #13. *American Lung Association, State of the Air 2017*

Health/Fitness Rankings

- For each of the 50 most populous metro areas in the United States, the American College of Sports Medicine's American Fitness Index evaluated infrastructure, community assets, and policies that encourage healthy and fit lifestyles, including preventive health behaviors, levels of chronic disease conditions, health care access, and community resources and policies that support physical activity. The Dallas* metro area ranked #38 for "community fitness." *www.americanfitnessindex.org, "ACSM American Fitness Index Health and Community Fitness Status of the 50 Largest Metropolitan Areas," May 2017*

- The Dallas* metro area was identified as one of the worst cities for bed bugs in America by pest control company Orkin. The area ranked #10 out of 50 based on the number of bed bug treatments Orkin performed from December 2016 to November 2017. *Orkin, "Baltimore and Washington D.C. Continue to Hold Top Spots," January 8, 2018*

- Dallas* was identified as a "2016 Spring Allergy Capital." The area ranked #27 out of 100. Three groups of factors were used to identify the most severe cities for people with allergies during the spring season: annual pollen levels; medicine utilization; access to board-certified allergists. *Asthma and Allergy Foundation of America, "Spring Allergy Capitals 2016"*

- Dallas* was identified as a "2016 Fall Allergy Capital." The area ranked #23 out of 100. Three groups of factors were used to identify the most severe cities for people with allergies during the fall season: annual pollen levels; medicine utilization; access to board-certified allergists. *Asthma and Allergy Foundation of America, "Fall Allergy Capitals 2016"*

- Dallas* was identified as a "2015 Asthma Capital." The area ranked #39 out of the nation's 100 largest metropolitan areas. Criteria: estimated prevalence; self-reported prevalence; crude death rate for asthma; annual pollen score; annual air quality; public smoking laws; number of board-certified asthma specialists; school inhaler access laws; rescue medication use; controller medication use; ER visits for asthma; uninsured rate; poverty rate. *Asthma and Allergy Foundation of America, "Asthma Capitals 2015"*

- The Dallas* metro area ranked #47 out of 189 in The Gallup-Healthways Well-Being Index. Criteria: purpose; social well being; financial health; community and physical health. Results are based on telephone interviews with adults, aged 18 and older, living in metropolitan areas in the 50 U.S. states and the District of Columbia. *Gallup-Healthways, "State of American Well-Being, 2017 Community Well-Being Rankings" March 2018*

Real Estate Rankings

- FitSmallBusiness looked at 50 of the largest metropolitan areas in the U.S. to determine which metro was the best to start a real estate business. Data was compiled from such sources as: Zillow, Trulia, U.S. Census Bureau, and the Bureau of Labor Statistics. Criteria: location; inventory; annual wages; median sales price of homes; days on the market; median price cut percentage; and other factors that would influence real estate professional growth. The Dallas* metro area ranked #19. *fitsmallbusiness.com, "The Best Cities to Become a Real Estate Agent in 2018," January 30, 2018*

- According to Penske Truck Rental, the Dallas* metro area was named the #3 moving destination in 2017, based on one-way consumer truck rental reservations made through Penske's website, rental locations, and reservations call center. *blog.gopenske.com, "Penske Truck Rental's 2017 Top Moving Destinations List," January 22, 2018*

- The Dallas* metro area appeared on Realtor.com's list of the hottest housing markets to watch in 2018. The area ranked #2. Criteria: existing homes inventory and price; new home construction; median household incomes; local economy/population trends. *Realtor.com®, "The 6 Hottest Real Estate Markets to Watch in 2018," January 5, 2018*
- The Dallas* metro area was identified as one of the nations's 20 hottest housing markets in 2018. Criteria: listing views as an indicator of demand and median days on the market as an indicator of supply. The area ranked #12. *Realtor.com, "The 20 Hottest Real Estate Markets for February 2018," March 1, 2018*
- Dallas* was ranked #20 in the top 20 out of 265 metro areas in terms of house price appreciation in 2017 (#1 = highest rate). *Federal Housing Finance Agency, House Price Index, 4th Quarter 2017. February 27, 2018*
- Dallas* was ranked #195 out of 238 metro areas in terms of housing affordability in 2017 by the National Association of Home Builders (#1 = most affordable). Criteria: the share of homes sold in that area affordable to a family earning the local median income, based on standard mortgage underwriting criteria. *National Association of Home Builders®, NAHB-Wells Fargo Housing Opportunity Index, 4th Quarter 2017*

Safety Rankings

- Flower Mound was identified as one of the safest cities in America by NeighborhoodScout. The city ranked #54 out of 100 (100 = safest). Criteria: number of violent and property crimes per 1,000 residents. The editors only considered cities with 25,000 or more residents. *NeighborhoodScout, "Top 100 Safest Cities in the U.S. 2018" January 2, 2018*
- The National Insurance Crime Bureau ranked 382 metro areas in the U.S. in terms of per capita rates of vehicle theft. The Dallas* metro area ranked #87 (#1 = highest rate). Criteria: number of vehicle theft offenses per 100,000 inhabitants in 2016. *National Insurance Crime Bureau, "Hot Spots 2016," June 8, 2017*

Seniors/Retirement Rankings

- From its Best Cities for Successful Aging indexes, the Milken Institute generated rankings for metropolitan areas, weighing data in nine categories—health care, wellness, living arrangements, transportation and convenience, financial characteristics, education, employment, community engagement, and overall livability. The Dallas* metro area was ranked #25 overall in the large metro area category. *Milken Institute, "Best Cities for Successful Aging, 2017" March 14, 2017*

Sports/Recreation Rankings

- According to the personal finance website NerdWallet, the Dallas* metro area, at #1, is one of the nation's top dozen metro areas for sports fans. Criteria included the presence of all four major sports—MLB, NFL, NHL, and NBA, fan enthusiasm (as measured by game attendance), ticket affordability, and "sports culture," that is, number of sports bars. *www.nerdwallet.com, "Best Cities for Sports Fans," May 5, 2013*

Women/Minorities Rankings

- The *Houston Chronicle* listed the Dallas* metro area as #7 in top places for young Latinos to live in the U.S. Research was largely based on housing and occupational data from the largest metropolitan areas performed by *Forbes* and NBC Universo. Criteria: percentage of 18-34 year-olds; Latino college grad rates; and diversity. *blog.chron.com, "The 15 Best Big Cities for Latino Millenials," January 26, 2016*

Miscellaneous Rankings

- The watchdog site Charity Navigator conducts an annual study of charities in the nation's major markets both to analyze statistical differences in their financial, accountability, and transparency practices and to track year-to-year variations in individual philanthropic communities. Charity Navigator's analysis demonstrated that the financial, accountability and transparency behaviors of America's largest charities can be influenced by the metropolitan market within which the charity operates. The Dallas* metro area was ranked #5 among the 30 metro markets in the rating category of Overall Score. *www.charitynavigator.org, "2017 Metro Market Study," May 1, 2017*
- The Harris Poll's Happiness Index survey revealed that of the top ten U.S. markets, the Dallas* metro area residents ranked #1 in happiness. Criteria included strong assent to positive statements and strong disagreement with negative ones, and degree of agreement with a series of statements about respondents' personal relationships and general outlook. *www.theharrispoll.com, "Dallas/Fort Worth Is "Happiest" City among America's Top Ten Markets," September 4, 2013*
- The National Alliance to End Homelessness listed the 25 most populous metro areas with the highest rate of homelessness. The Dallas* metro area had a high rate of homelessness. Criteria: number of homeless people per 10,000 population in 2016. *National Alliance to End Homelessness, "Homelessness in the 25 Most Populous U.S. Metro Areas," September 1, 2017*

*Flower Mound is located within the Dallas-Fort Worth-Arlington, TX Metropolitan Statistical Area and the Dallas-Plano-Irving, TX Metropolitan Division.

Business Environment

CITY FINANCES

City Government Finances

Component	2015 ($000)	2015 ($ per capita)
Total Revenues	115,566	1,622
Total Expenditures	101,055	1,418
Debt Outstanding	95,140	1,335
Cash and Securities[1]	62,707	880

Note: (1) Cash and security holdings of a government at the close of its fiscal year,, including those of its dependent agencies, utilities, and liquor stores.
Source: U.S Census Bureau, State & Local Government Finances 2015

City Government Revenue by Source

Source	2015 ($000)	2015 ($ per capita)	2015 (%)
General Revenue			
From Federal Government	1,265	18	1.1
From State Government	6,839	96	5.9
From Local Governments	319	4	0.3
Taxes			
Property	35,038	492	30.3
Sales and Gross Receipts	22,997	323	19.9
Personal Income	0	0	0.0
Corporate Income	0	0	0.0
Motor Vehicle License	0	0	0.0
Other Taxes	4,561	64	3.9
Current Charges	13,648	192	11.8
Liquor Store	0	0	0.0
Utility	25,800	362	22.3
Employee Retirement	0	0	0.0

Source: U.S Census Bureau, State & Local Government Finances 2015

City Government Expenditures by Function

Function	2015 ($000)	2015 ($ per capita)	2015 (%)
General Direct Expenditures			
Air Transportation	0	0	0.0
Corrections	0	0	0.0
Education	0	0	0.0
Employment Security Administration	0	0	0.0
Financial Administration	3,368	47	3.3
Fire Protection	7,873	110	7.8
General Public Buildings	2,478	34	2.5
Governmental Administration, Other	2,562	36	2.5
Health	434	6	0.4
Highways	12,984	182	12.8
Hospitals	0	0	0.0
Housing and Community Development	396	5	0.4
Interest on General Debt	3,640	51	3.6
Judicial and Legal	682	9	0.7
Libraries	1,472	20	1.5
Parking	0	0	0.0
Parks and Recreation	8,311	116	8.2
Police Protection	14,731	206	14.6
Public Welfare	0	0	0.0
Sewerage	8,719	122	8.6
Solid Waste Management	98	1	0.1
Veterans' Services	0	0	0.0
Liquor Store	0	0	0.0
Utility	28,426	398	28.1
Employee Retirement	0	0	0.0

Source: U.S Census Bureau, State & Local Government Finances 2015

DEMOGRAPHICS

Population Growth

Area	1990 Census	2000 Census	2010 Census	2016* Estimate	Population Growth (%)	
					1990-2016	2010-2016
City	15,788	50,702	64,669	69,966	343.2	8.2
MSA[1]	3,989,294	5,161,544	6,371,773	6,957,123	74.4	9.2
U.S.	248,709,873	281,421,906	308,745,538	318,558,162	28.1	3.2

Note: (1) Figures cover the Dallas-Fort Worth-Arlington, TX Metropolitan Statistical Area—see Appendix B for areas included; (*) 2012-2016 5-year estimated population
Source: U.S. Census Bureau, 1990 Census, Census 2000, Census 2010, 2012-2016 American Community Survey 5-Year Estimates

Household Size

Area	Persons in Household (%)							Average Household Size
	One	Two	Three	Four	Five	Six	Seven or More	
City	11.0	30.6	22.3	24.5	8.6	2.4	0.5	3.10
MSA[1]	24.9	30.8	16.7	15.3	7.5	3.0	1.8	2.80
U.S.	27.7	33.7	15.7	13.1	6.0	2.3	1.5	2.60

Note: (1) Figures cover the Dallas-Fort Worth-Arlington, TX Metropolitan Statistical Area—see Appendix B for areas included
Source: U.S. Census Bureau, 2012-2016 American Community Survey 5-Year Estimates

Race

Area	White Alone[2] (%)	Black Alone[2] (%)	Asian Alone[2] (%)	AIAN[3] Alone[2] (%)	NHOPI[4] Alone[2] (%)	Other Race Alone[2] (%)	Two or More Races (%)
City	82.5	3.7	9.5	0.4	0.0	1.0	2.9
MSA[1]	69.7	15.3	6.1	0.4	0.1	5.5	2.9
U.S.	73.3	12.6	5.2	0.8	0.2	4.8	3.1

Note: (1) Figures cover the Dallas-Fort Worth-Arlington, TX Metropolitan Statistical Area—see Appendix B for areas included; (2) Alone is defined as not being in combination with one or more other races; (3) American Indian and Alaska Native; (4) Native Hawaiian and Other Pacific Islander
Source: U.S. Census Bureau, 2012-2016 American Community Survey 5-Year Estimates

Hispanic or Latino Origin

Area	Total (%)	Mexican (%)	Puerto Rican (%)	Cuban (%)	Other (%)
City	9.5	6.5	0.5	0.3	2.3
MSA[1]	28.2	23.8	0.7	0.2	3.5
U.S.	17.3	11.0	1.7	0.7	4.0

Note: Persons of Hispanic or Latino origin can be of any race; (1) Figures cover the Dallas-Fort Worth-Arlington, TX Metropolitan Statistical Area—see Appendix B for areas included
Source: U.S. Census Bureau, 2012-2016 American Community Survey 5-Year Estimates

Segregation

Type	Segregation Indices[1]				Percent Change		
	1990	2000	2010	2010 Rank[2]	1990-2000	1990-2010	2000-2010
Black/White	62.8	59.8	56.6	48	-3.1	-6.2	-3.2
Asian/White	41.8	45.6	46.6	19	3.8	4.8	1.0
Hispanic/White	48.8	52.3	50.3	24	3.5	1.5	-2.0

Note: All figures cover the Metropolitan Statistical Area—see Appendix B for areas included; Figures are based on an analysis of 1990, 2000, and 2010 Census Decennial Census tract data by William H. Frey, Brookings Institution and the University of Michigan Social Science Data Analysis Network. In this analysis all racial groups (whites, blacks, and asians) are non-Hispanic members of those races. Hispanics are shown as a separate category; (1) Segregation Indices are Dissimilarity Indices that measure the degree to which the minority group is distributed differently than whites across census tracts. They range from 0 (complete integration) to 100 (complete segregation) where the value indicates the percentage of the minority group that needs to move to be distributed exactly like whites; (2) Ranges from 1 (most segregated) to 102 (least segregated); n/a not available.
Source: www.CensusScope.org

Ancestry

Area	German	Irish	English	American	Italian	Polish	French[2]	Scottish	Dutch
City	18.9	12.8	13.7	7.3	4.3	2.3	3.6	2.7	1.6
MSA[1]	9.8	7.6	7.3	6.6	2.2	1.1	1.9	1.7	0.9
U.S.	14.4	10.4	7.7	6.9	5.4	2.9	2.6	1.7	1.3

Note: Figures are the percentage of the total population reporting a particular ancestry. The nine most commonly reported ancestries in the U.S. are shown. Figures include multiple ancestries (e.g. if a person reported being Irish and Italian, they were included in both columns); (1) Figures cover the Dallas-Fort Worth-Arlington, TX Metropolitan Statistical Area—see Appendix B for areas included; (2) Excludes Basque
Source: U.S. Census Bureau, 2012-2016 American Community Survey 5-Year Estimates

Foreign-Born Population

Area	Percent of Population Born in								
	Any Foreign Country	Asia	Mexico	Europe	Carribean	Central America[2]	South America	Africa	Canada
City	11.7	6.8	1.3	1.2	0.2	0.3	0.7	0.6	0.5
MSA[1]	17.8	4.7	8.8	0.8	0.2	1.3	0.5	1.2	0.2
U.S.	13.2	4.0	3.6	1.5	1.3	1.0	0.9	0.6	0.3

Note: (1) Figures cover the Dallas-Fort Worth-Arlington, TX Metropolitan Statistical Area—see Appendix B for areas included; (2) Excludes Mexico.
Source: U.S. Census Bureau, 2012-2016 American Community Survey 5-Year Estimates

Marital Status

Area	Never Married	Now Married[2]	Separated	Widowed	Divorced
City	23.3	65.3	0.9	2.8	7.6
MSA[1]	31.9	50.5	2.3	4.5	10.9
U.S.	33.0	48.1	2.1	5.9	11.0

Note: Figures are percentages and cover the population 15 years of age and older; (1) Figures cover the Dallas-Fort Worth-Arlington, TX Metropolitan Statistical Area—see Appendix B for areas included; (2) Excludes separated
Source: U.S. Census Bureau, 2012-2016 American Community Survey 5-Year Estimates

Disability Status

Area	All Ages	Under 18 Years Old	18 to 64 Years Old	65 Years and Over
City	6.7	2.6	6.0	29.2
MSA[1]	9.6	3.4	8.2	35.2
U.S.	12.5	4.1	10.3	35.7

Note: Figures show percent of the civilian noninstitutionalized population that reported having a disability. Disability status is determined from six types of difficulty: vision, hearing, cognitive, ambulatory, self-care, and independent living. For children under 5 years old, hearing and vision difficulty are used to determine disability status. For children between the ages of 5 and 14, disability status is determined from hearing, vision, cognitive, ambulatory, and self-care difficulties. For people aged 15 years and older, they are considered to have a disability if they have difficulty with any one of the six difficulty types; Note: (1) Figures cover the Dallas-Fort Worth-Arlington, TX Metropolitan Statistical Area—see Appendix B for areas included
Source: U.S. Census Bureau, 2012-2016 American Community Survey 5-Year Estimates

Age

Area	Percent of Population									Median Age
	Under Age 5	Age 5–19	Age 20–34	Age 35–44	Age 45–54	Age 55–64	Age 65–74	Age 75–84	Age 85+	
City	5.9	25.5	12.8	16.1	20.4	12.0	5.0	1.8	0.6	39.6
MSA[1]	7.2	22.2	21.4	14.4	13.8	10.9	6.2	2.9	1.1	34.5
U.S.	6.2	19.6	20.7	12.7	13.6	12.6	8.3	4.3	1.9	37.7

Note: (1) Figures cover the Dallas-Fort Worth-Arlington, TX Metropolitan Statistical Area—see Appendix B for areas included
Source: U.S. Census Bureau, 2012-2016 American Community Survey 5-Year Estimates

ECONOMY

Gender

Area	Males	Females	Males per 100 Females
City	34,344	35,622	96.4
MSA[1]	3,421,036	3,536,087	96.7
U.S.	156,765,322	161,792,840	96.9

Note: (1) Figures cover the Dallas-Fort Worth-Arlington, TX Metropolitan Statistical Area—see Appendix B for areas included
Source: U.S. Census Bureau, 2012-2016 American Community Survey 5-Year Estimates

Religious Groups by Family

Area	Catholic	Baptist	Non-Den.	Methodist[2]	Lutheran	LDS[3]	Pente-costal	Presby-terian[4]	Muslim[5]	Judaism
MSA[1]	13.3	18.7	7.8	5.3	0.8	1.2	2.2	1.0	2.4	0.4
U.S.	19.1	9.3	4.0	4.0	2.3	2.0	1.9	1.6	0.8	0.7

Note: Figures are the number of adherents as a percentage of the total population; (1) Figures cover the Dallas-Fort Worth-Arlington, TX Metropolitan Statistical Area—see Appendix B for areas included; (2) Methodist/Pietist; (3) Latter Day Saints; (4) Reformed; (5) Figures are estimates
Source: Association of Statisticians of American Religious Bodies, 2010 U.S. Religion Census: Religious Congregations & Membership Study

Religious Groups by Tradition

Area	Catholic	Evangelical Protestant	Mainline Protestant	Other Tradition	Black Protestant	Orthodox
MSA[1]	13.3	28.3	7.0	4.8	1.8	0.2
U.S.	19.1	16.2	7.3	4.3	1.6	0.3

Note: Figures are the number of adherents as a percentage of the total population; (1) Figures cover the Dallas-Fort Worth-Arlington, TX Metropolitan Statistical Area—see Appendix B for areas included
Source: Association of Statisticians of American Religious Bodies, 2010 U.S. Religion Census: Religious Congregations & Membership Study

Gross Metropolitan Product

Area	2014	2015	2016	2017	Rank[2]
MSA[1]	502.3	524.8	545.3	577.5	4

Note: Figures are in billions of dollars; (1) Figures cover the Dallas-Fort Worth-Arlington, TX Metropolitan Statistical Area—see Appendix B for areas included; (2) Rank is based on 2015 data and ranges from 1 to 381
Source: The U.S. Conference of Mayors, U.S. Metro Economies: GMP and Employment Report, 2015-2017

Economic Growth

Area	2012-14 (%)	2015 (%)	2016 (%)	2017 (%)	Rank[2]
MSA[1]	6.7	7.1	2.4	3.4	7
U.S.	2.0	2.4	1.9	2.6	–

Note: Figures are real gross metropolitan product (GMP) growth rates and represent average annual percent change; (1) Figures cover the Dallas-Fort Worth-Arlington, TX Metropolitan Statistical Area—see Appendix B for areas included; (2) Rank is based on 2012-2014 average annual percent change and ranges from 1 to 381
Source: The U.S. Conference of Mayors, U.S. Metro Economies: GMP and Employment Report, 2015-2017

Metropolitan Area Exports

Area	2011	2012	2013	2014	2015	2016	Rank[2]
MSA[1]	26,648.7	27,820.9	27,596.0	28,669.4	27,372.9	27,187.8	9

Note: Figures are in millions of dollars; (1) Figures cover the Dallas-Fort Worth-Arlington, TX Metropolitan Statistical Area—see Appendix B for areas included; (2) Rank is based on 2016 data and ranges from 1 to 385
Source: U.S. Department of Commerce, International Trade Administration, Office of Trade & Industry Information, Manufacturing & Services, data extracted March 15, 2018

Building Permits

Area	Single-Family			Multi-Family			Total		
	2016	2017p	Pct. Chg.	2016	2017p	Pct. Chg.	2016	2017p	Pct. Chg.
City	397	467	17.6	670	0	-100.0	1,067	467	-56.2
MSA[1]	29,846	34,210	14.6	25,772	27,499	6.7	55,618	61,709	11.0
U.S.	750,800	817,300	8.9	455,800	446,800	-2.0	1,206,600	1,264,100	4.8

Note: (1) Figures cover the Dallas-Fort Worth-Arlington, TX Metropolitan Statistical Area—see Appendix B for areas included; Figures represent new, privately-owned housing units authorized (unadjusted data); All permit data are based on estimates with imputation; (p) preliminary data.
Source: U.S. Census Bureau, Manufacturing, Mining, and Construction Statistics, Building Permits, 2016, 2017

Bankruptcy Filings

Area	Business Filings			Nonbusiness Filings		
	2016	2017	% Chg.	2016	2017	% Chg.
Denton County	78	231	196.2	1,037	1,117	7.7
U.S.	24,114	23,157	-4.0	770,846	765,863	-0.6

Note: Business filings include Chapter 7, Chapter 11, Chapter 12, and Chapter 13; Nonbusiness filings include Chapter 7, Chapter 11, and Chapter 13
Source: Administrative Office of the U.S. Courts, Business and Nonbusiness Bankruptcy, County Cases Commenced by Chapter of the Bankruptcy Code, During the 12-Month Period Ending December 31, 2016 and Business and Nonbusiness Bankruptcy, County Cases Commenced by Chapter of the Bankruptcy Code, During the 12-Month Period Ending December 31, 2017

Housing Vacancy Rates

Area	Gross Vacancy Rate[2] (%)			Year-Round Vacancy Rate[3] (%)			Rental Vacancy Rate[4] (%)			Homeowner Vacancy Rate[5] (%)		
	2015	2016	2017	2015	2016	2017	2015	2016	2017	2015	2016	2017
MSA[1]	8.0	7.9	7.8	7.8	7.7	7.6	8.3	6.8	7.1	1.4	1.4	0.8
U.S.	12.9	12.8	12.7	10.0	9.9	9.9	7.1	6.9	7.2	1.8	1.7	1.6

Note: (1) Figures cover the Dallas-Fort Worth-Arlington, TX Metropolitan Statistical Area—see Appendix B for areas included; (2) The percentage of the total housing inventory that is vacant; (3) The percentage of the housing inventory (excluding seasonal units) that is year-round vacant; (4) The percentage of rental inventory that is vacant for rent; (5) The percentage of homeowner inventory that is vacant for sale
Source: U.S. Census Bureau, Housing Vacancies and Homeownership Annual Statistics: 2015, 2016, 2017

INCOME

Income

Area	Per Capita ($)	Median Household ($)	Average Household ($)
City	47,857	123,492	144,467
MSA[1]	31,143	61,330	85,693
U.S.	29,829	55,322	77,866

Note: (1) Figures cover the Dallas-Fort Worth-Arlington, TX Metropolitan Statistical Area—see Appendix B for areas included
Source: U.S. Census Bureau, 2012-2016 American Community Survey 5-Year Estimates

Household Income Distribution

Area	Percent of Households Earning							
	Under $15,000	$15,000 -$24,999	$25,000 -$34,999	$35,000 -$49,999	$50,000 -$74,999	$75,000 -$99,999	$100,000 -$149,999	$150,000 and up
City	2.1	2.6	3.2	5.0	11.0	13.2	26.6	36.2
MSA[1]	9.5	8.9	9.5	13.0	18.2	12.4	15.1	13.4
U.S.	12.1	10.2	9.9	13.2	17.8	12.2	13.5	11.1

Note: (1) Figures cover the Dallas-Fort Worth-Arlington, TX Metropolitan Statistical Area—see Appendix B for areas included
Source: U.S. Census Bureau, 2012-2016 American Community Survey 5-Year Estimates

Poverty Rate

Area	All Ages	Under 18 Years Old	18 to 64 Years Old	65 Years and Over
City	3.2	4.3	2.7	3.4
MSA[1]	14.0	20.3	12.3	8.5
U.S.	15.1	21.2	14.2	9.3

Note: Figures are percentage of people whose income during the past 12 months was below the poverty level; (1) Figures cover the Dallas-Fort Worth-Arlington, TX Metropolitan Statistical Area—see Appendix B for areas included
Source: U.S. Census Bureau, 2012-2016 American Community Survey 5-Year Estimates

EMPLOYMENT

Labor Force and Employment

Area	Civilian Labor Force			Workers Employed		
	Dec. 2016	Dec. 2017	% Chg.	Dec. 2016	Dec. 2017	% Chg.
City	40,860	41,705	2.1	39,554	40,688	2.9
MD[1]	2,526,544	2,585,893	2.3	2,434,063	2,504,449	2.9
U.S.	158,968,000	159,880,000	0.6	151,798,000	153,602,000	1.2

Note: Data is not seasonally adjusted and covers workers 16 years of age and older; (1) Figures cover the Dallas-Plano-Irving, TX Metropolitan Division—see Appendix B for areas included
Source: Bureau of Labor Statistics, Local Area Unemployment Statistics

Unemployment Rate

Area	2017											
	Jan.	Feb.	Mar.	Apr.	May	Jun.	Jul.	Aug.	Sep.	Oct.	Nov.	Dec.
City	3.5	3.6	3.3	3.0	3.1	3.4	3.2	3.2	2.8	2.6	2.6	2.4
MD[1]	4.0	4.1	3.9	3.5	3.6	3.9	3.8	3.8	3.4	3.2	3.2	3.1
U.S.	5.1	4.9	4.6	4.1	4.1	4.5	4.6	4.5	4.1	3.9	3.9	3.9

Note: Data is not seasonally adjusted and covers workers 16 years of age and older; (1) Figures cover the Dallas-Plano-Irving, TX Metropolitan Division—see Appendix B for areas included
Source: Bureau of Labor Statistics, Local Area Unemployment Statistics

Average Wages

Occupation	$/Hr.	Occupation	$/Hr.
Accountants and Auditors	39.90	Maids and Housekeeping Cleaners	10.20
Automotive Mechanics	20.50	Maintenance and Repair Workers	18.80
Bookkeepers	21.60	Marketing Managers	68.60
Carpenters	18.80	Nuclear Medicine Technologists	38.30
Cashiers	10.10	Nurses, Licensed Practical	23.10
Clerks, General Office	17.20	Nurses, Registered	35.80
Clerks, Receptionists/Information	13.60	Nursing Assistants	12.90
Clerks, Shipping/Receiving	14.70	Packers and Packagers, Hand	11.50
Computer Programmers	41.60	Physical Therapists	46.50
Computer Systems Analysts	47.10	Postal Service Mail Carriers	24.50
Computer User Support Specialists	25.80	Real Estate Brokers	38.70
Cooks, Restaurant	13.10	Retail Salespersons	12.90
Dentists	83.10	Sales Reps., Exc. Tech./Scientific	35.50
Electrical Engineers	50.70	Sales Reps., Tech./Scientific	46.30
Electricians	22.40	Secretaries, Exc. Legal/Med./Exec.	18.50
Financial Managers	75.80	Security Guards	14.50
First-Line Supervisors/Managers, Sales	22.60	Surgeons	95.40
Food Preparation Workers	10.80	Teacher Assistants*	12.40
General and Operations Managers	70.00	Teachers, Elementary School*	29.00
Hairdressers/Cosmetologists	12.60	Teachers, Secondary School*	30.00
Internists, General	56.10	Telemarketers	14.70
Janitors and Cleaners	11.60	Truck Drivers, Heavy/Tractor-Trailer	22.60
Landscaping/Groundskeeping Workers	13.90	Truck Drivers, Light/Delivery Svcs.	18.40
Lawyers	74.30	Waiters and Waitresses	13.50

Note: Wage data covers the Dallas-Plano-Irving, TX Metropolitan Division—see Appendix B for areas included; (*) Hourly wages for elementary/secondary school teachers and teacher assistants were calculated by the editors from annual wage data based on a 40 hour work week; n/a not available.
Source: Bureau of Labor Statistics, Metro Area Occupational Employment & Wage Estimates, May 2017

Employment by Occupation

Occupation Classification	City (%)	MSA[1] (%)	U.S. (%)
Management, Business, Science, and Arts	57.3	38.2	37.0
Natural Resources, Construction, and Maintenance	3.2	9.3	8.9
Production, Transportation, and Material Moving	5.1	11.6	12.2
Sales and Office	24.9	24.9	23.8
Service	9.5	15.9	18.1

Note: Figures cover employed civilians 16 years of age and older; (1) Figures cover the Dallas-Fort Worth-Arlington, TX Metropolitan Statistical Area—see Appendix B for areas included
Source: U.S. Census Bureau, 2012-2016 American Community Survey 5-Year Estimates

Employment by Industry

Sector	MD[1] Number of Employees	MD[1] Percent of Total	U.S. Percent of Total
Construction, Mining, and Logging	141,400	5.4	5.2
Education and Health Services	313,000	12.0	15.9
Financial Activities	235,200	9.0	5.7
Government	304,800	11.6	15.3
Information	72,900	2.8	1.9
Leisure and Hospitality	262,800	10.0	10.7
Manufacturing	179,300	6.8	8.5
Other Services	85,200	3.3	3.9
Professional and Business Services	488,500	18.7	14.0
Retail Trade	266,600	10.2	11.0
Transportation, Warehousing, and Utilities	121,000	4.6	4.1
Wholesale Trade	147,700	5.6	4.0

Note: Figures are non-farm employment as of December 2017. Figures are not seasonally adjusted and include workers 16 years of age and older; (1) Figures cover the Dallas-Plano-Irving, TX Metropolitan Division—see Appendix B for areas included
Source: Bureau of Labor Statistics, Current Employment Statistics, Employment, Hours, and Earnings

Occupations with Greatest Projected Employment Growth: 2017 – 2019

Occupation[1]	2017 Employment	2019 Projected Employment	Numeric Employment Change	Percent Employment Change
Combined Food Preparation and Serving Workers, Including Fast Food	335,660	354,370	18,710	5.6
Personal Care Aides	212,280	230,990	18,710	8.8
Retail Salespersons	393,950	406,100	12,150	3.1
Customer Service Representatives	261,530	273,600	12,070	4.6
Janitors and Cleaners, Except Maids and Housekeeping Cleaners	180,710	192,060	11,350	6.3
Laborers and Freight, Stock, and Material Movers, Hand	185,140	196,200	11,060	6.0
Registered Nurses	214,500	224,450	9,950	4.6
Office Clerks, General	379,860	389,540	9,680	2.6
Heavy and Tractor-Trailer Truck Drivers	192,710	201,560	8,850	4.6
Waiters and Waitresses	222,630	231,020	8,390	3.8

Note: Projections cover Texas; (1) Sorted by numeric employment change
Source: www.projectionscentral.com, State Occupational Projections, 2017–2019 Short-Term Projections

Fastest Growing Occupations: 2017 – 2019

Occupation[1]	2017 Employment	2019 Projected Employment	Numeric Employment Change	Percent Employment Change
Wind Turbine Service Technicians	1,740	2,090	350	20.7
Home Health Aides	72,760	80,000	7,240	10.0
Security and Fire Alarm Systems Installers	8,190	8,930	740	8.9
Personal Care Aides	212,280	230,990	18,710	8.8
Statisticians	1,760	1,910	150	8.2
Tree Trimmers and Pruners	5,980	6,480	500	8.2
Physician Assistants	6,860	7,400	540	7.9
Nurse Practitioners	9,230	9,950	720	7.7
Elevator Installers and Repairers	2,190	2,350	160	7.4
Helpers—Roofers	800	850	50	7.4

Note: Projections cover Texas; (1) Sorted by percent employment change and excludes occupations with numeric employment change less than 50
Source: www.projectionscentral.com, State Occupational Projections, 2017–2019 Short-Term Projections

TAXES

State Corporate Income Tax Rates

State	Tax Rate (%)	Income Brackets ($)	Num. of Brackets	Financial Institution Tax Rate (%)[a]	Federal Income Tax Ded.
Texas	(w)	–	–	(w)	No

Note: Tax rates as of January 1, 2018; (a) Rates listed are the corporate income tax rate applied to financial institutions or excise taxes based on income. Some states have other taxes based upon the value of deposits or shares; (w) Texas imposes a Franchise Tax, otherwise known as margin tax, imposed on entities with more than $1,110,000 total revenues at rate of 0.75%, or 0.375% for entities primarily engaged in retail or wholesale trade, on lesser of 70% of total revenues or 100% of gross receipts after deductions for either compensation or cost of goods sold.
Source: Federation of Tax Administrators, Range of State Corporate Income Tax Rates, January 1, 2018

State Individual Income Tax Rates

State	Tax Rate (%)	Income Brackets ($)	Num. of Brackets	Personal Exempt. ($)[1] Single	Personal Exempt. ($)[1] Dependents	Fed. Inc. Tax Ded.
Texas	None	–	–	–	–	–

Note: Tax rates as of January 1, 2018; Local- and county-level taxes are not included; n/a not applicable; (1) Married joint filers generally receive double the single exemption
Source: Federation of Tax Administrators, State Individual Income Tax Rates, January 1, 2018

Various State Sales and Excise Tax Rates

State	State Sales Tax (%)	Gasoline[1] (¢/gal.)	Cigarette[2] ($/pack)	Spirits[3] ($/gal.)	Wine[4] ($/gal.)	Beer[5] ($/gal.)	Recreational Marijuana (%)
Texas	6.25	20.0	1.41	2.40 (f)	0.20 (l)	0.20 (q)	Not legal

Note: All tax rates as of January 1, 2018; (1) The American Petroleum Institute has developed a methodology for determining the average tax rate on a gallon of fuel. Rates may include any of the following: excise taxes, environmental fees, storage tank fees, other fees or taxes, general sales tax, and local taxes. In states where gasoline is subject to the general sales tax, or where the fuel tax is based on the average sale price, the average rate determined by API is sensitive to changes in the price of gasoline. States that fully or partially apply general sales taxes to gasoline: CA, CO, GA, IL, IN, MI, NY; (2) The federal excise tax of $1.0066 per pack and local taxes are not included; (3) Rates are those applicable to off-premise sales of 40% alcohol by volume (a.b.v.) distilled spirits in 750ml containers. Local excise taxes are excluded; (4) Rates are those applicable to off-premise sales of 11% a.b.v. non-carbonated wine in 750ml containers; (5) Rates are those applicable to off-premise sales of 4.7% a.b.v. beer in 12 ounce containers; (f) Different rates also applicable according to alcohol content, place of production, size of container, or place purchased (on- or off-premise or onboard airlines); (l) Different rates also applicable to alcohol content, place of production, size of container, place purchased (on- or off-premise or on board airlines) or type of wine (carbonated, vermouth, etc.); (q) Different rates also applicable according to alcohol content, place of production, size of container, or place purchased (on- or off-premise or onboard airlines).
Source: Tax Foundation, 2018 Facts & Figures: How Does Your State Compare?

State Business Tax Climate Index Rankings

State	Overall Rank	Corporate Tax Rank	Individual Income Tax Rank	Sales Tax Rank	Unemployment Insurance Tax Rank	Property Tax Rank
Texas	13	49	6	37	26	37

Note: The index is a measure of how each state's tax laws affect economic performance. The lower the rank, the more favorable a state's tax system is for business. States without a given tax are given a ranking of 1. The scores/rankings for the District of Columbia do not affect other states. The 2018 index represents the tax climate as of July 1, 2017.
Source: Tax Foundation, State Business Tax Climate Index 2018

TRANSPORTATION

Means of Transportation to Work

Area	Car/Truck/Van: Drove Alone	Car/Truck/Van: Car-pooled	Public Transportation: Bus	Public Transportation: Subway	Public Transportation: Railroad	Bicycle	Walked	Other Means	Worked at Home
City	82.1	5.2	0.1	0.1	0.3	0.0	0.8	1.1	10.4
MSA[1]	80.7	9.9	1.0	0.2	0.3	0.2	1.2	1.5	5.0
U.S.	76.4	9.3	2.6	1.9	0.6	0.6	2.8	1.3	4.6

Note: Figures are percentages and cover workers 16 years of age and older; (1) Figures cover the Dallas-Fort Worth-Arlington, TX Metropolitan Statistical Area—see Appendix B for areas included
Source: U.S. Census Bureau, 2012-2016 American Community Survey 5-Year Estimates

Travel Time to Work

Area	Less Than 10 Minutes	10 to 19 Minutes	20 to 29 Minutes	30 to 44 Minutes	45 to 59 Minutes	60 to 89 Minutes	90 Minutes or More
City	10.1	20.6	20.0	29.4	13.1	5.2	1.5
MSA[1]	9.4	25.8	21.1	25.0	10.3	6.3	2.0
U.S.	12.9	29.2	20.9	20.4	8.0	6.0	2.7

Note: Note: Figures are percentages and include workers 16 years old and over; (1) Figures cover the Dallas-Fort Worth-Arlington, TX Metropolitan Statistical Area—see Appendix B for areas included
Source: U.S. Census Bureau, 2012-2016 American Community Survey 5-Year Estimates

Freeway Travel Time Index

Area	1985	1990	1995	2000	2005	2010	2014
Urban Area Rank[1,2]	6	9	10	19	21	22	19
Urban Area Index[1]	1.19	1.20	1.23	1.24	1.26	1.24	1.27
Average Index[3]	1.09	1.11	1.14	1.17	1.20	1.19	1.20

Note: Freeway Travel Time Index—the ratio of travel time in the peak period to the travel time at free-flow conditions. For example, a value of 1.30 indicates a 20-minute free-flow trip takes 26 minutes in the peak (20 minutes x 1.30 = 26 minutes); (1) Covers the Dallas-Fort Worth-Arlington TX urban area; (2) Rank is based on 101 urban areas (#1 = highest travel time index); (3) Average of 101 urban areas
Source: Texas Transportation Institute, 2015 Urban Mobility Scorecard, August 2015

Freeway Commuter Stress Index

Area	1985	1990	1995	2000	2005	2010	2014
Urban Area Rank[1,2]	12	15	13	20	22	25	20
Urban Area Index[1]	1.25	1.26	1.29	1.30	1.32	1.30	1.33
Average Index[3]	1.13	1.16	1.19	1.22	1.25	1.24	1.25

Note: The Freeway Commuter Stress Index is the same as the Freeway Travel Time Index (see table above) except that it includes only the travel in the peak directions during the peak periods; the TTI includes travel in all directions during the peak period. Thus, the CSI is more indicative of the work trip experienced by each commuter on a daily basis; (1) Covers the Dallas-Fort Worth-Arlington TX urban area; (2) Rank is based on 101 urban areas (#1 = highest travel time index); (3) Average of 101 urban areas
Source: Texas Transportation Institute, 2015 Urban Mobility Scorecard, August 2015

Living Environment

COST OF LIVING

Cost of Living Index

Composite Index	Groceries	Housing	Utilities	Trans-portation	Health Care	Misc. Goods/ Services
107.2	99.6	120.8	97.9	103.9	85.0	105.6

Note: The Cost of Living Index measures regional differences in the cost of consumer goods and services, excluding taxes and non-consumer expenditures, for professional and managerial households in the top income quintile. It is based on more than 50,000 prices covering almost 60 different items for which prices are collected three times a year by chambers of commerce, economic development organizations or university applied economic centers in each participating urban area. The numbers shown should be read as a percentage above or below the national average of 100. For example, a value of 115.4 in the groceries column indicates that grocery prices are 15.4% higher than the national average. Small differences in the index numbers should not be interpreted as significant; Figures cover the Plano TX urban area.
Source: The Council for Community and Economic Research, ACCRA Cost of Living Index, 2017

Grocery Prices

Area[1]	T-Bone Steak ($/pound)	Frying Chicken ($/pound)	Whole Milk ($/half gal.)	Eggs ($/dozen)	Orange Juice ($/64 oz.)	Coffee ($/11.5 oz.)
City[2]	11.99	1.19	1.82	1.82	3.99	4.43
Avg.	11.29	1.40	2.02	1.47	3.55	4.37
Min.	7.71	0.93	1.04	0.70	2.86	3.24
Max.	15.83	2.39	4.03	3.92	6.29	8.16

Note: (1) Values for the local area are compared with the average, minimum and maximum values for all 294 areas in the Cost of Living Index; (2) Figures cover the Plano TX urban area; ***T-Bone Steak*** *(price per pound);* ***Frying Chicken*** *(price per pound, whole fryer);* ***Whole Milk*** *(half gallon carton);* ***Eggs*** *(price per dozen, Grade A, large);* ***Orange Juice*** *(64 oz. Tropicana or Florida Natural);* ***Coffee*** *(11.5 oz. can, vacuum-packed, Maxwell House, Hills Bros, or Folgers).*
Source: The Council for Community and Economic Research, ACCRA Cost of Living Index, 2017

Housing and Utility Costs

Area[1]	New Home Price ($)	Apartment Rent ($/month)	All Electric ($/month)	Part Electric ($/month)	Other Energy ($/month)	Telephone ($/month)
City[2]	387,838	1,300	-	110.21	55.03	27.72
Avg.	335,956	1,047	175.01	97.34	67.93	28.71
Min.	187,788	491	109.48	49.33	35.44	12.39
Max.	1,739,087	4,559	432.62	227.09	353.33	44.61

Note: (1) Values for the local area are compared with the average, minimum and maximum values for all 294 areas in the Cost of Living Index; (2) Figures cover the Plano TX urban area; ***New Home Price*** *(2,400 sf living area, 8,000 sf lot, in urban area with full utilities);* ***Apartment Rent*** *(950 sf 2 bedroom/1.5 or 2 bath, unfurnished, excluding all utilities except water);* ***All Electric*** *(average monthly cost for an all-electric home);* ***Part Electric*** *(average monthly cost for a part-electric home);* ***Other Energy*** *(average monthly cost for natural gas, fuel oil, coal, wood, and any other forms of energy except electricity);* ***Telephone*** *(price includes basic monthly rate for a private residential line plus additional local usage charges incurred by a family of four).*
Source: The Council for Community and Economic Research, ACCRA Cost of Living Index, 2017

Health Care, Transportation, and Other Costs

Area[1]	Doctor ($/visit)	Dentist ($/visit)	Optometrist ($/visit)	Gasoline ($/gallon)	Beauty Salon ($/visit)	Men's Shirt ($)
City[2]	80.02	73.81	108.39	2.18	48.10	29.06
Avg.	108.00	92.54	101.93	2.25	37.58	30.92
Min.	30.39	60.00	49.75	1.82	16.11	11.20
Max.	193.50	161.94	229.28	3.16	77.35	59.13

Note: (1) Values for the local area are compared with the average, minimum and maximum values for all 294 areas in the Cost of Living Index; (2) Figures cover the Plano TX urban area; ***Doctor*** *(general practitioners routine exam of an established patient);* ***Dentist*** *(adult teeth cleaning and periodic oral examination);* ***Optometrist*** *(full vision eye exam for established adult patient);* ***Gasoline*** *(one gallon regular unleaded, national brand, including all taxes, cash price at self-service pump if available);* ***Beauty Salon*** *(woman's shampoo, trim, and blow-dry);* ***Men's Shirt*** *(cotton/polyester dress shirt, pinpoint weave, long sleeves).*
Source: The Council for Community and Economic Research, ACCRA Cost of Living Index, 2017

HOUSING

House Price Index (HPI)

Area	National Ranking[2]	Quarterly Change (%)	One-Year Change (%)	Five-Year Change (%)
MD[1]	20	1.01	10.57	57.15
U.S.[3]	–	1.61	6.68	34.71

Note: The HPI is a weighted repeat sales index. It measures average price changes in repeat sales or refinancings on the same properties. This information is obtained by reviewing repeat mortgage transactions on single-family properties whose mortgages have been purchased or securitized by Fannie Mae or Freddie Mac in January 1975; (1) Figures cover the Dallas-Plano-Irving, TX Metropolitan Division—see Appendix B for areas included; (2) Rankings are based on annual percentage change for all metro areas containing at least 15,000 transactions over the last 10 years and ranges from 1 to 253; (3) figures based on a weighted average of Census Division estimates using a seasonally adjusted, purchase-only index; all figures are for the period ending December 31, 2017

Source: Federal Housing Finance Agency, House Price Index, February 28, 2018

Median Single-Family Home Prices

Area	2015	2016	2017p	Percent Change 2016 to 2017
MSA[1]	207.2	227.1	247.4	8.9
U.S. Average	223.9	235.5	248.8	5.6

Note: Figures are median sales prices of existing single-family homes in thousands of dollars; (p) preliminary; (1) Figures cover the Dallas-Fort Worth-Arlington, TX Metropolitan Statistical Area—see Appendix B for areas included

Source: National Association of Realtors, Median Sales Price of Existing Single-Family Homes for Metropolitan Areas, 4th Quarter 2017

Qualifying Income Based on Median Sales Price of Existing Single-Family Homes

Area	With 5% Down ($)	With 10% Down ($)	With 20% Down ($)
MSA[1]	55,203	52,298	46,487
U.S. Average	55,585	52,659	46,808

Note: Figures are preliminary; Qualifying income is based on a mortgage rate of 4.17%. Monthly principal and interest payment is limited to 25% of income; (1) Figures cover the Dallas-Fort Worth-Arlington, TX Metropolitan Statistical Area—see Appendix B for areas included

Source: National Association of Realtors, Qualifying Income Based on Median Sales Price of Existing Single-Family Homes for Metropolitan Areas, 4th Quarter 2017

Median Apartment Condo-Coop Home Prices

Area	2015	2016	2017p	Percent Change 2016 to 2017
MSA[1]	148.7	167.7	185.7	10.7
U.S. Average	210.7	220.7	234.3	6.2

Note: Figures are median sales prices of existing apartment condo-coop homes in thousands of dollars; (p) preliminary; (1) Figures cover the Dallas-Fort Worth-Arlington, TX Metropolitan Statistical Area—see Appendix B for areas included

Source: National Association of Realtors, Median Sales Price of Existing Apartment Condo-Coop Homes for Metropolitan Areas, 4th Quarter 2017

Home Value Distribution

Area	Under $50,000	$50,000 -$99,999	$100,000 -$149,999	$150,000 -$199,999	$200,000 -$299,999	$300,000 -$499,999	$500,000 -$999,999	$1,000,000 or more
City	1.6	1.0	4.7	12.8	32.4	35.9	10.6	1.0
MSA[1]	6.4	17.3	20.6	17.5	18.4	13.4	4.9	1.5
U.S.	8.8	14.8	15.3	14.9	18.4	16.4	9.0	2.5

Note: Figures are percentages and cover owner-occupied housing units; (1) Figures cover the Dallas-Fort Worth-Arlington, TX Metropolitan Statistical Area—see Appendix B for areas included

Source: U.S. Census Bureau, 2012-2016 American Community Survey 5-Year Estimates

Homeownership Rate

Area	2009 (%)	2010 (%)	2011 (%)	2012 (%)	2013 (%)	2014 (%)	2015 (%)	2016 (%)	2017 (%)
MSA[1]	61.6	63.8	62.6	61.8	59.9	57.7	57.8	59.7	61.8
U.S.	67.4	66.9	66.1	65.4	65.1	64.5	63.7	63.4	63.9

Note: (1) Figures cover the Dallas-Fort Worth-Arlington, TX Metropolitan Statistical Area—see Appendix B for areas included

Source: U.S. Census Bureau, Housing Vacancies and Homeownership Annual Statistics: 2009-2017

Year Housing Structure Built

Area	2010 or Later	2000 -2009	1990 -1999	1980 -1989	1970 -1979	1960 -1969	1950 -1959	1940 -1949	Before 1940	Median Year
City	3.7	21.9	50.4	16.8	4.8	1.2	0.7	0.4	0.2	1995
MSA[1]	4.5	22.2	16.8	19.1	14.9	9.0	7.7	2.9	2.9	1987
U.S.	2.3	14.7	14.0	13.7	15.6	10.9	10.6	5.2	13.0	1977

Note: Figures are percentages except for Median Year; Note: (1) Figures cover the Dallas-Fort Worth-Arlington, TX Metropolitan Statistical Area—see Appendix B for areas included
Source: U.S. Census Bureau, 2012-2016 American Community Survey 5-Year Estimates

Gross Monthly Rent

Area	Under $500	$500 -$999	$1,000 -$1,499	$1,500 -$1,999	$2,000 -$2,499	$2,500 -$2,999	$3,000 and up	Median ($)
City	0.7	12.5	28.4	37.7	11.9	6.3	2.4	1,611
MSA[1]	4.6	49.0	32.4	10.0	2.5	0.8	0.7	969
U.S.	11.3	43.3	27.7	10.7	4.0	1.6	1.5	949

Note: Figures are percentages except for Median; Gross rent is the contract rent plus the estimated average monthly cost of utilities (electricity, gas, and water and sewer) and fuels (oil, coal, kerosene, wood, etc.) if these are paid by the renter (or paid for the renter by someone else); (1) Figures cover the Dallas-Fort Worth-Arlington, TX Metropolitan Statistical Area—see Appendix B for areas included
Source: U.S. Census Bureau, 2012-2016 American Community Survey 5-Year Estimates

HEALTH

Health Risk Factors

Category	MD[1] (%)	U.S. (%)
Adults aged 18–64 who have any kind of health care coverage	79.8	87.7
Adults who reported being in good or excellent health	86.4	83.6
Adults who are current smokers	13.2	17.1
Adults who currently use E-cigarettes	5.3	4.7
Adults who currently use chewing tobacco, snuff, or snus	3.3	4.0
Adults who are heavy drinkers[2]	5.8	6.5
Adults who are binge drinkers[3]	15.0	16.9
Adults who are overweight (BMI 25.0 - 29.9)	34.7	35.3
Adults who are obese (BMI 30.0 - 99.8)	34.6	29.9
Adults who participated in any physical activities in the past month	77.4	76.9
Adults who always or nearly always wears a seat belt	96.2	94.3

Note: (1) Figures cover the Dallas-Plano-Irving, TX Metropolitan Division—see Appendix B for areas included; (2) Heavy drinkers are classified as adult men having more than 14 drinks per week and adult women having more than 7 drinks per week; (3) Binge drinkers are classified as males having five or more drinks on one occasion or females having four or more drinks on one occasion
Source: Centers for Disease Control and Prevention, Behaviorial Risk Factor Surveillance System, SMART: Selected Metropolitan Area Risk Trends, 2016

Health Screening Rates

Category	MD[1] (%)	U.S. (%)
Adults 50-75 who have had a blood stool test within the past year	n/a	8.0
Adults 50-75 who have had a colonoscopy in the past 10 years	60.9	63.5
Adults aged 65+ who have had flu shot within the past year	61.1	58.6
Adults aged 65+ who have ever had a pneumonia vaccination	72.6	73.4
Adults who have ever been tested for HIV	41.3	35.6
Women aged 21-65 who have had a pap test in the past three years	72.4	79.8
Men aged 40+ who have had a PSA test within the past two years	42.0	39.5
Women aged 40+ who have had a mammogram within the past two years	58.5	72.5

Note: n/a not available; (1) Figures cover the Dallas-Plano-Irving, TX Metropolitan Division—see Appendix B for areas included; Source: Centers for Disease Control and Prevention, Behaviorial Risk Factor Surveillance System, SMART: Selected Metropolitan Area Risk Trends, 2016

Chronic Health Conditions

Category	MD[1] (%)	U.S. (%)
Adults who have ever been told they had a heart attack	2.5	4.4
Adults who have ever been told they have angina or coronary heart disease	2.6	4.1
Adults who have ever been told they had a stroke	n/a	3.1
Adults who have been told they currently have asthma	6.4	9.3
Adults who have ever been told they have arthritis	20.7	25.8
Adults who have ever been told they have diabetes[2]	8.8	10.5
Adults who have ever been told they had skin cancer	6.0	5.9
Adults who have ever been told they had any other types of cancer	6.7	6.7
Adults who have ever been told they have COPD	3.1	6.3
Adults who have ever been told they have kidney disease	n/a	2.8
Adults who have ever been told they have a form of depression	11.7	17.4

Note: n/a not available; (1) Figures cover the Dallas-Plano-Irving, TX Metropolitan Division—see Appendix B for areas included; (2) Figures do not include pregnancy-related, borderline, or pre-diabetes
Source: Centers for Disease Control and Prevention, Behaviorial Risk Factor Surveillance System, SMART: Selected Metropolitan Area Risk Trends, 2016

Mortality Rates for the Top 10 Causes of Death in the U.S.

ICD-10[a] Sub-Chapter	ICD-10[a] Code	Age-Adjusted Mortality Rate[1] per 100,000 population	
		County[2]	U.S.
Malignant neoplasms	C00-C97	132.9	158.5
Ischaemic heart diseases	I20-I25	63.8	96.8
Other forms of heart disease	I30-I51	48.2	52.4
Chronic lower respiratory diseases	J40-J47	44.2	40.9
Cerebrovascular diseases	I60-I69	39.6	37.2
Organic, including symptomatic, mental disorders	F01-F09	35.2	33.3
Other degenerative diseases of the nervous system	G30-G31	45.3	32.1
Other external causes of accidental injury	W00-X59	16.9	31.2
Diabetes mellitus	E10-E14	16.9	21.1
Hypertensive diseases	I10-I15	18.5	20.8

Note: (a) ICD-10 = International Classification of Diseases 10th Revision; (1) Mortality rates are a three year average covering 2014-2016; (2) Figures cover Denton County.
Source: Centers for Disease Control and Prevention, National Center for Health Statistics. Underlying Cause of Death 1999-2016 on CDC WONDER Online Database, released December 2017

Mortality Rates for Selected Causes of Death

ICD-10[a] Sub-Chapter	ICD-10[a] Code	Age-Adjusted Mortality Rate[1] per 100,000 population	
		County[2]	U.S.
Assault	X85-Y09	1.2	5.6
Diseases of the liver	K70-K76	10.1	14.0
Human immunodeficiency virus (HIV) disease	B20-B24	0.9	1.9
Influenza and pneumonia	J09-J18	17.3	14.6
Intentional self-harm	X60-X84	10.0	13.2
Malnutrition	E40-E46	1.8	1.3
Obesity and other hyperalimentation	E65-E68	0.9	2.1
Renal failure	N17-N19	15.0	13.0
Transport accidents	V01-V99	8.2	12.0
Viral hepatitis	B15-B19	1.0	1.9

Note: (a) ICD-10 = International Classification of Diseases 10th Revision; (1) Mortality rates are a three year average covering 2014-2016; (2) Figures cover Denton County; Data are Suppressed when the data meet the criteria for confidentiality constraints; Mortality rates are flagged as Unreliable when the rate would be calculated with a numerator of 20 or less.
Source: Centers for Disease Control and Prevention, National Center for Health Statistics. Underlying Cause of Death 1999-2016 on CDC WONDER Online Database, released December 2017

Health Insurance Coverage

Area	With Health Insurance	With Private Health Insurance	With Public Health Insurance	Without Health Insurance	Population Under Age 18 Without Health Insurance
City	95.1	90.4	10.7	4.9	3.5
MSA[1]	81.5	63.6	25.2	18.5	10.8
U.S.	88.3	66.7	33.0	11.7	5.9

Note: Figures are percentages that cover the civilian noninstitutionalized population; (1) Figures cover the Dallas-Fort Worth-Arlington, TX Metropolitan Statistical Area—see Appendix B for areas included
Source: U.S. Census Bureau, 2012-2016 American Community Survey 5-Year Estimates

Number of Medical Professionals

Area	MDs[3]	DOs[3,4]	Dentists	Podiatrists	Chiropractors	Optometrists
County[1] (number)	1,362	146	431	29	295	136
County[1] (rate[2])	174.7	18.7	53.3	3.6	36.5	16.8
U.S. (rate[2])	276.5	22.3	67.3	6.0	26.7	15.9

Note: Data as of 2016 unless noted; (1) Data covers Denton County; (2) Rate per 100,000 population; (3) Data as of 2015 and includes all active, non-federal physicians; (4) Doctor of Osteopathic Medicine
Source: U.S. Department of Health and Human Services, Health Resources and Services Administration, Bureau of Health Professions, Area Resource File (ARF) 2016-2017

Best Hospitals

According to *U.S. News,* the Dallas-Plano-Irving, TX metro area is home to three of the best hospitals in the U.S.: **Baylor University Medical Center** (2 adult specialties); **Medical City Dallas Hospital** (1 adult specialty); **UT Southwestern Medical Center** (6 adult specialties). The hospitals listed were nationally ranked in at least one of 16 specialties. Only 152 hospitals nationwide were nationally ranked in one or more specialties. Twenty hospitals in the U.S. made the Honor Roll. The Best Hospitals Honor Roll was revamped last year to take both the national rankings and the procedure and condition ratings into account. Hospitals received points if they were nationally ranked in one of the 16 specialties—the higher they ranked, the more points they got—and how many ratings of "high performing" they earned in the nine procedures and conditions. *U.S. News Online, "America's Best Hospitals 2017-18"*

According to *U.S. News,* the Dallas-Plano-Irving, TX metro area is home to two of the best children's hospitals in the U.S.: **Children's Medical Center Dallas** (9 pediatric specialties); **Texas Scottish Rite Hospital for Children** (1 pediatric specialty). The hospitals listed were highly ranked in at least one of 10 pediatric specialties. Eighty-two children's hospitals in the U.S. were nationally ranked in at least one specialty. Hospitals received points for being ranked in a specialty, and the 10 hospitals with the most points across the 10 specialties make up the Honor Roll. *U.S. News Online, "America's Best Children's Hospitals 2017-18"*

EDUCATION

Public School District Statistics

District Name	Schls	Pupils	Pupil/ Teacher Ratio	Minority Pupils[1] (%)	Free Lunch Eligible[2] (%)	IEP[3] (%)
Lewisville ISD	72	53,490	14.1	55.4	26.9	10.3
Texas College Preparatory Academies	38	12,778	20.2	56.3	33.3	6.9

Note: Table includes school districts with 100 or more students; (1) Percentage of students that are not non-Hispanic white; (2) Percentage of students that are eligible for the free lunch program; (3) Percentage of students that have an Individualized Education Program.
Source: U.S. Department of Education, National Center for Education Statistics, Common Core of Data, Local Education Agency (School District) Universe Survey: School Year 2015-2016; U.S. Department of Education, National Center for Education Statistics, Common Core of Data, Public Elementary/Secondary School Universe Survey: School Year 2015-2016

Highest Level of Education

Area	Less than H.S.	H.S. Diploma	Some College, No Deg.	Associate Degree	Bachelor's Degree	Master's Degree	Prof. School Degree	Doctorate Degree
City	3.4	11.6	18.3	6.9	40.7	15.3	2.4	1.3
MSA[1]	15.4	22.5	22.2	6.7	21.9	8.5	1.7	1.0
U.S.	13.0	27.5	21.0	8.2	18.8	8.2	2.0	1.3

Note: Figures cover persons age 25 and over; (1) Figures cover the Dallas-Fort Worth-Arlington, TX Metropolitan Statistical Area—see Appendix B for areas included
Source: U.S. Census Bureau, 2012-2016 American Community Survey 5-Year Estimates

Educational Attainment by Race

Area	High School Graduate or Higher (%)					Bachelor's Degree or Higher (%)				
	Total	White	Black	Asian	Hisp.[2]	Total	White	Black	Asian	Hisp.[2]
City	96.6	97.0	96.7	95.9	87.7	59.8	58.6	53.7	78.8	47.3
MSA[1]	84.6	85.2	89.6	88.0	56.8	33.1	34.1	24.8	58.8	12.0
U.S.	87.0	88.9	84.3	86.3	65.7	30.3	31.6	20.0	52.1	14.7

Note: Figures shown cover persons 25 years old and over; (1) Figures cover the Dallas-Fort Worth-Arlington, TX Metropolitan Statistical Area—see Appendix B for areas included; (2) People of Hispanic origin can be of any race
Source: U.S. Census Bureau, 2012-2016 American Community Survey 5-Year Estimates

School Enrollment by Grade and Control

Area	Preschool (%)		Kindergarten (%)		Grades 1 - 4 (%)		Grades 5 - 8 (%)		Grades 9 - 12 (%)	
	Public	Private	Public	Private	Public	Private	Public	Private	Public	Private
City	29.3	70.7	77.7	22.3	91.7	8.3	93.6	6.4	92.2	7.8
MSA[1]	57.4	42.6	89.3	10.7	92.6	7.4	92.0	8.0	92.3	7.7
U.S.	58.4	41.6	87.7	12.3	89.8	10.2	89.7	10.3	90.4	9.6

Note: Figures shown cover persons 3 years old and over; (1) Figures cover the Dallas-Fort Worth-Arlington, TX Metropolitan Statistical Area—see Appendix B for areas included
Source: U.S. Census Bureau, 2012-2016 American Community Survey 5-Year Estimates

Average Salaries of Public School Classroom Teachers

Area	2015		2016		Change from 2015 to 2016	
	Dollars	Rank[1]	Dollars	Rank[1]	Percent	Rank[2]
Texas	50,713	28	51,890	27	2.3	8
U.S. Average	57,611	–	58,353	–	1.3	–

Note: (1) Rank ranges from 1 to 51 where 1 indicates highest salary; (2) Rank ranges from 1 to 51 where 1 indicates highest percent change.
Source: National Education Association, Rankings & Estimates: Rankings of the States 2016 and Estimates of School Statistics 2017

Higher Education

Four-Year Colleges			Two-Year Colleges			Medical Schools[1]	Law Schools[2]	Voc/ Tech[3]
Public	Private Non-profit	Private For-profit	Public	Private Non-profit	Private For-profit			
0	0	0	0	0	0	0	0	0

Note: Figures cover institutions located within the city limits and include main campuses only; (1) includes schools accredited by the Liaison Committee on Medical Education and the American Osteopathic Association's Commission on Osteopathic College Accreditation; (2) includes ABA-accredited schools, schools with provisional ABA accreditation, and state accredited schools; (3) includes all schools with programs that are less than 2 years.
Source: National Center for Education Statistics, Integrated Postsecondary Education System (IPEDS), 2016-17; Wikipedia, List of Medical Schools in the United States, accessed April 2, 2018; Wikipedia, List of Law Schools in the United States, accessed April 2, 2018

According to *U.S. News & World Report,* the Dallas-Plano-Irving, TX metro division is home to three of the best national universities in the U.S.: **Southern Methodist University** (#61 tie); **University of Texas—Dallas** (#145 tie); **Dallas Baptist University** (#202 tie). The indicators used to capture academic quality fall into a number of categories: assessment by administrators at peer institutions; retention of students; faculty resources; student selectivity; financial resources; alumni giving; high school counselor ratings of colleges; and graduation rate. *U.S. News & World Report, "America's Best Colleges 2018"*

According to *U.S. News & World Report,* the Dallas-Plano-Irving, TX metro division is home to one of the top 100 law schools in the U.S.: **Southern Methodist University (Dedman)** (#50 tie). The rankings are based on a weighted average of 12 measures of quality: peer assessment score; assessment score by lawyers/judges; median LSAT scores; median undergrad GPA; acceptance rate; employment rates for graduates; placement success; bar passage rate; faculty resources; expenditures per student; student/faculty ratio; and library resources. *U.S. News & World Report, "America's Best Graduate Schools, Law, 2019"*

According to *U.S. News & World Report,* the Dallas-Plano-Irving, TX metro division is home to one of the top 75 medical schools for research in the U.S.: **University of Texas Southwestern Medical Center** (#26 tie). The rankings are based on a weighted average of 11 measures of quality: quality assessment; peer assessment score; assessment score by residency directors; research activity; total research activity; average research activity per faculty member; student selectivity; median MCAT total score; median undergraduate GPA; acceptance rate; and faculty resources. *U.S. News & World Report, "America's Best Graduate Schools, Medical, 2019"*

According to *U.S. News & World Report,* the Dallas-Plano-Irving, TX metro division is home to two of the top 75 business schools in the U.S.: **University of Texas—Dallas** (#40 tie); **Southern Methodist University (Cox)** (#48 tie). The rankings are based on a weighted average of the following nine measures: quality assessment; peer assessment; recruiter assessment; placement success; mean starting salary and bonus; student selectivity; mean GMAT and GRE scores; mean undergraduate GPA; and acceptance rate. *U.S. News & World Report, "America's Best Graduate Schools, Business, 2019"*

PRESIDENTIAL ELECTION

2016 Presidential Election Results

Area	Clinton	Trump	Johnson	Stein	Other
Denton County	37.1	57.1	3.9	0.9	1.0
U.S.	48.0	45.9	3.3	1.1	1.7

Note: Results are percentages and may not add to 100% due to rounding
Source: Dave Leip's Atlas of U.S. Presidential Elections

EMPLOYERS

Major Employers

Company Name	Industry
AMR Corporation	Air transportation, scheduled
Associates First Capital Corporation	Mortgage bankers
Baylor University Medical Center	General medical & surgical hospitals
Children's Medical Center Dallas	Specialty hospitals, except psychiatric
Combat Support Associates	Engineering services
County of Dallas	County supervisors' & executives' offices
Dallas County Hospital District	General medical & surgical hospitals
Fort Worth Independent School District	Public elementary & secondary schools
Housewares Holding Company	Toasters, electric: household
HP Enterprise Services	Computer integrated systems design
J.C. Penney Company	Department stores
JCP Publications Corp.	Department stores
L-3 Communications Corporation	Business economic service
Odyssey HealthCare	Home health care services
Romano's Macaroni Grill	Italian restaurant
SFG Management Limited Liability	Milk processing (pasteurizing, homogenizing, bottling)
Texas Instruments Incorporated	Semiconductors & related devices
University of North Texas	Colleges & universities
University of Texas SW Medical Center	Accident & health insurance
Verizon Business Global	Telephone communication, except radio

Note: Companies shown are located within the Dallas-Fort Worth-Arlington, TX Metropolitan Statistical Area.
Source: Hoovers.com; Wikipedia

PUBLIC SAFETY

Crime Rate

Area	All Crimes	Violent Crimes				Property Crimes		
		Murder	Rape[3]	Robbery	Aggrav. Assault	Burglary	Larceny -Theft	Motor Vehicle Theft
City	873.3	0.0	9.6	5.5	30.3	88.2	698.3	41.3
Metro[1]	2,776.8	5.2	40.2	141.3	170.0	488.1	1,640.0	292.0
U.S.	2,847.8	5.3	40.4	102.8	248.5	468.9	1,745.0	236.9

Note: Figures are crimes per 100,000 population; (1) Figures cover the Dallas-Plano-Irving, TX Metropolitan Division—see Appendix B for areas included; (3) The city and U.S. figures shown were reported using the revised Uniform Crime Reporting (UCR) definition of rape. The metro area figures shown are an aggregate total of the data submitted using both the revised and legacy UCR definitions.
Source: FBI Uniform Crime Reports, 2016

Hate Crimes

Area	Number of Quarters Reported	Number of Incidents per Bias Motivation					
		Race/Ethnicity/ Ancestry	Religion	Sexual Orientation	Disability	Gender	Gender Identity
City	4	0	0	0	0	0	0
U.S.	4	3,489	1,273	1,076	70	31	124

Source: Federal Bureau of Investigation, Hate Crime Statistics 2016

Identity Theft Consumer Reports

Area	Reports	Reports per 100,000 Population	Rank[2]
MSA[1]	11,506	159	11
U.S.	371,061	114	-

Note: (1) Figures cover the Dallas-Fort Worth-Arlington, TX Metropolitan Statistical Area—see Appendix B for areas included; (2) Rank ranges from 1 to 389 where 1 indicates greatest number of identity theft reports per 100,000 population
Source: Federal Trade Commission, Consumer Sentinel Network Data Book for January–December 2017

Fraud and Other Consumer Reports

Area	Reports	Reports per 100,000 Population	Rank[2]
MSA[1]	55,938	773	8
U.S.	2,304,550	708	-

Note: (1) Figures cover the Dallas-Fort Worth-Arlington, TX Metropolitan Statistical Area—see Appendix B for areas included; (2) Rank ranges from 1 to 389 where 1 indicates greatest number of fraud and other consumer reports per 100,000 population
Source: Federal Trade Commission, Consumer Sentinel Network Data Book for January–December 2017

SPORTS

Professional Sports Teams

Team Name	League	Year Established
Dallas Cowboys	National Football League (NFL)	1960
Dallas Mavericks	National Basketball Association (NBA)	1980
Dallas Stars	National Hockey League (NHL)	1993
FC Dallas	Major League Soccer (MLS)	1996
Texas Rangers	Major League Baseball (MLB)	1972

Note: Includes teams located in the Dallas-Fort Worth-Arlington, TX Metropolitan Statistical Area.
Source: Wikipedia, Major Professional Sports Teams of the United States and Canada, April 5, 2018

CLIMATE

Average and Extreme Temperatures

Temperature	Jan	Feb	Mar	Apr	May	Jun	Jul	Aug	Sep	Oct	Nov	Dec	Yr.
Extreme High (°F)	85	90	100	100	101	112	111	109	107	101	91	87	112
Average High (°F)	55	60	68	76	84	92	96	96	89	79	67	58	77
Average Temp. (°F)	45	50	57	66	74	82	86	86	79	68	56	48	67
Average Low (°F)	35	39	47	56	64	72	76	75	68	57	46	38	56
Extreme Low (°F)	-2	9	12	30	39	53	58	58	42	24	16	0	-2

Note: Figures cover the years 1945-1993
Source: National Climatic Data Center, International Station Meteorological Climate Summary, 9/96

Average Precipitation/Snowfall/Humidity

Precip./Humidity	Jan	Feb	Mar	Apr	May	Jun	Jul	Aug	Sep	Oct	Nov	Dec	Yr.
Avg. Precip. (in.)	1.9	2.3	2.6	3.8	4.9	3.4	2.1	2.3	2.9	3.3	2.3	2.1	33.9
Avg. Snowfall (in.)	1	1	Tr	Tr	0	0	0	0	0	Tr	Tr	Tr	3
Avg. Rel. Hum. 6am (%)	78	77	75	77	82	81	77	76	80	79	78	77	78
Avg. Rel. Hum. 3pm (%)	53	51	47	49	51	48	43	41	46	46	48	51	48

Note: Figures cover the years 1945-1993; Tr = Trace amounts (<0.05 in. of rain; <0.5 in. of snow)
Source: National Climatic Data Center, International Station Meteorological Climate Summary, 9/96

Weather Conditions

Temperature			Daytime Sky			Precipitation		
10°F & below	32°F & below	90°F & above	Clear	Partly cloudy	Cloudy	0.01 inch or more precip.	0.1 inch or more snow/ice	Thunder-storms
1	34	102	108	160	97	78	2	49

Note: Figures are average number of days per year and cover the years 1945-1993
Source: National Climatic Data Center, International Station Meteorological Climate Summary, 9/96

HAZARDOUS WASTE

Superfund Sites

The Dallas-Plano-Irving, TX metro division is home to four sites on the EPA's Superfund National Priorities List: **Lane Plating Works, Inc** (proposed); **Old Esco Manufacturing** (final); **RSR Corporation** (final); **Van Der Horst Usa Corporation** (final). There are a total of 1,396 Superfund sites with a status of proposed or final on the list in the U.S. *U.S. Environmental Protection Agency, National Priorities List, April 4, 2018*

AIR & WATER QUALITY

Air Quality Trends: Ozone

	1990	1995	2000	2005	2010	2012	2013	2014	2015	2016
MSA[1]	0.095	0.105	0.096	0.097	0.080	0.080	0.081	0.076	0.077	0.070
U.S.	0.087	0.089	0.081	0.079	0.073	0.075	0.069	0.067	0.068	0.069

Note: (1) Data covers the Dallas-Fort Worth-Arlington, TX Metropolitan Statistical Area—see Appendix B for areas included. The values shown are the composite ozone concentration averages among trend sites based on the highest fourth daily maximum 8-hour concentration in parts per million. These trends are based on sites having an adequate record of monitoring data during the trend period. Data from exceptional events are included.
Source: U.S. Environmental Protection Agency, Air Quality Monitoring Information, "Air Quality Trends by City, 1990-2016"

Air Quality Index

Area	Percent of Days when Air Quality was...[2]					AQI Statistics[2]	
	Good	Moderate	Unhealthy for Sensitive Groups	Unhealthy	Very Unhealthy	Maximum	Median
MSA[1]	52.6	40.8	6.6	0.0	0.0	147	50

Note: (1) Data covers the Dallas-Fort Worth-Arlington, TX Metropolitan Statistical Area—see Appendix B for areas included; (2) Based on 365 days with AQI data in 2017. Air Quality Index (AQI) is an index for reporting daily air quality. EPA calculates the AQI for five major air pollutants regulated by the Clean Air Act: ground-level ozone, particle pollution (aka particulate matter), carbon monoxide, sulfur dioxide, and nitrogen dioxide. The AQI runs from 0 to 500. The higher the AQI value, the greater the level of air pollution and the greater the health concern. There are six AQI categories: "Good" AQI is between 0 and 50. Air quality is considered satisfactory; "Moderate" AQI is between 51 and 100. Air quality is acceptable; "Unhealthy for Sensitive Groups" When AQI values are between 101 and 150, members of sensitive groups may experience health effects; "Unhealthy" When AQI values are between 151 and 200 everyone may begin to experience health effects; "Very Unhealthy" AQI values between 201 and 300 trigger a health alert; "Hazardous" AQI values over 300 trigger warnings of emergency conditions (not shown).
Source: U.S. Environmental Protection Agency, Air Quality Index Report, 2017

Air Quality Index Pollutants

Area	Percent of Days when AQI Pollutant was...[2]					
	Carbon Monoxide	Nitrogen Dioxide	Ozone	Sulfur Dioxide	Particulate Matter 2.5	Particulate Matter 10
MSA[1]	0.0	2.7	57.0	0.0	40.3	0.0

Note: (1) Data covers the Dallas-Fort Worth-Arlington, TX Metropolitan Statistical Area—see Appendix B for areas included; (2) Based on 365 days with AQI data in 2017. The Air Quality Index (AQI) is an index for reporting daily air quality. EPA calculates the AQI for five major air pollutants regulated by the Clean Air Act: ground-level ozone, particle pollution (also known as particulate matter), carbon monoxide, sulfur dioxide, and nitrogen dioxide. The AQI runs from 0 to 500. The higher the AQI value, the greater the level of air pollution and the greater the health concern.
Source: U.S. Environmental Protection Agency, Air Quality Index Report, 2017

Maximum Air Pollutant Concentrations: Particulate Matter, Ozone, CO and Lead

	Particulate Matter 10 (ug/m^3)	Particulate Matter 2.5 Wtd AM (ug/m^3)	Particulate Matter 2.5 24-Hr (ug/m^3)	Ozone (ppm)	Carbon Monoxide (ppm)	Lead (ug/m^3)
MSA[1] Level	52	8.5	19	0.076	1	0.06
NAAQS[2]	150	15	35	0.075	9	0.15
Met NAAQS[2]	Yes	Yes	Yes	No	Yes	Yes

Note: (1) Data covers the Dallas-Fort Worth-Arlington, TX Metropolitan Statistical Area—see Appendix B for areas included; Data from exceptional events are included; (2) National Ambient Air Quality Standards; ppm = parts per million; ug/m^3 = micrograms per cubic meter; n/a not available.
Concentrations: Particulate Matter 10 (coarse particulate)—highest second maximum 24-hour concentration; Particulate Matter 2.5 Wtd AM (fine particulate)—highest weighted annual mean concentration; Particulate Matter 2.5 24-Hour (fine particulate)—highest 98th percentile 24-hour concentration; Ozone—highest fourth daily maximum 8-hour concentration; Carbon Monoxide—highest second maximum non-overlapping 8-hour concentration; Lead—maximum running 3-month average
Source: U.S. Environmental Protection Agency, Air Quality Monitoring Information, "Air Quality Statistics by City, 2016"

Maximum Air Pollutant Concentrations: Nitrogen Dioxide and Sulfur Dioxide

	Nitrogen Dioxide AM (ppb)	Nitrogen Dioxide 1-Hr (ppb)	Sulfur Dioxide AM (ppb)	Sulfur Dioxide 1-Hr (ppb)	Sulfur Dioxide 24-Hr (ppb)
MSA[1] Level	12	45	n/a	8	n/a
NAAQS[2]	53	100	30	75	140
Met NAAQS[2]	Yes	Yes	n/a	Yes	n/a

Note: (1) Data covers the Dallas-Fort Worth-Arlington, TX Metropolitan Statistical Area—see Appendix B for areas included; Data from exceptional events are included; (2) National Ambient Air Quality Standards; ppm = parts per million; ug/m^3 = micrograms per cubic meter; n/a not available.
Concentrations: Nitrogen Dioxide AM—highest arithmetic mean concentration; Nitrogen Dioxide 1-Hr—highest 98th percentile 1-hour daily maximum concentration; Sulfur Dioxide AM—highest annual mean concentration; Sulfur Dioxide 1-Hr—highest 99th percentile 1-hour daily maximum concentration; Sulfur Dioxide 24-Hr—highest second maximum 24-hour concentration
Source: U.S. Environmental Protection Agency, Air Quality Monitoring Information, "Air Quality Statistics by City, 2016"

Drinking Water

Water System Name	Pop. Served	Primary Water Source Type	Violations[1]	
			Health Based	Monitoring/ Reporting
Town of Flower Mound	73,547	Purchased Surface	0	2

Note: (1) Based on violation data from January 1, 2017 to December 31, 2017
Source: U.S. Environmental Protection Agency, Office of Ground Water and Drinking Water, Safe Drinking Water Information System (based on data extracted April 5, 2018)

Friendswood, Texas

Background

Friendswood is conveniently located between downtown Houston and Galveston. The city boasts a low crime rate, beautiful parks, abundant trees, and recreational and sports facilities, including Timbera championship golf course. The "friends" in the city's name refers to Quakers. In 1895, Frank Jacob Brown and Thomas Hadley Lewis came to the area to establish a Quaker colony, and purchased 1,538 acres of prairie framed by dense woods and called the colony "Friendswood." More than a dozen Quaker families joined them.

Friendswood developed as a farming community characterized by Quaker ideals of hard work and clean living. Houston developers advertised the Gulf Coast as a Garden of Eden, with figs and oranges growing everywhere. Farmers were drawn to the area in large numbers through 1920. Later, in the 1930s, newly developing oil fields near Friendswood attracted newcomers. But Friendswood remained a largely rural area, with few stores, even as young families from Houston moved in during the 1950s. It wasn't until 1960 that the town elected its first mayor and city council. Soon after, the town started to grow rapidly as NASA employees moved in. In the 1970s and 1980s, it grew into a suburb.

Friendswood is located in two counties—northern Galveston County and southern Harris County, along the upper Texas Gulf Coast. In 2011, *Family Circle Magazine* named it one of the Best Towns for Families. In 2009, *Business Week Magazine* named it one of Best Affordable Suburbs in the United States.

The predominant industries in the surrounding area are aerospace and defense, software and computing, biotechnology, and communication services. Friendswood offers economic incentives for business expansion, including grants and property tax abatements. All fees are waived for new development or renovation in the Downtown Neighborhood Empowerment Zone.

William P. Hobby Airport is about nine miles away, while the George Bush Intercontinental Airport is about 33 miles away.

Friendswood is served by two schools districts, Friendswood Independent School District and, for residents of Harris County, Clear Creek Independent School District. In 2010, Clear Creek received an "Exemplary" rating from the state. The University of Houston Clear Lake and San Jinto College are nearby, as are several community colleges. Friendswood has acres of green space and parks, as well as a city pool.

Located in the Sunbelt, Friendswood has a subtropical climate. Plenty of rain means the growing season lasts more than 290 days. January is the coldest month, with an average temperature of 52, while August, at 83 degrees on average, is the hottest month.

Rankings

General Rankings

- Houston* was identified as one of America's fastest-growing cities in terms of population growth by CNNMoney.com. The area ranked #2 out of 10. Criteria: population growth between July 2015 and July 2016; cities and towns with populations of 50,000. *CNNMoney, "10 Fastest-Growing Cities," June 2, 2017*

Business/Finance Rankings

- According to *Business Insider*, the Houston* metro area is where startup growth is on the rise. Based on the 2017 Kauffman Index of Growth Entrepreneurship, which measured in-depth national entrepreneurial trends in 40 metro areas, it ranked #19 in highest startup growth. *www.businessinsider.com, "The 21 U.S. Cities with the Highest Startup Growth," October 21, 2017*
- The personal finance site NerdWallet analyzed 183 American metropolitan areas with populations over 250,000 and more than 15,000 businesses to rank where entrepreneurs find the most success. Criteria included area economy, annual income, housing cost, unemployment rate, and the success rate of area businesses. Houston* ranked #80. *www.nerdwallet.com, "Best Places to Start a Business," April 27, 2015*
- USAA and Hiring Our Heroes worked with Sperlings's BestPlaces and the Institute for Veterans and Military Families at Syracuse University to rank major metropolitan areas where military-skills-related employment is strongest. Criteria for *mid-career* veterans included veteran wage growth; recent job growth; stability; and accessible health resources. Metro areas with a higher than national average crime or unemployment rate were excluded. At #3, the Houston* metro area made the top ten. *www.usaa.com, "2015 Best Places for Veterans"*
- 24/7 Wall Street used Brookings Institution research on 50 advanced industries to identify the proportion of workers in the nation's largest metropolitan areas that were employed in jobs requiring knowledge in the science, technology, engineering, or math (STEM) fields and where there was heavy investment in research and development (R&D). The Houston* metro area was #13. *247wallst.com, "15 Cities with the Most High-Tech Jobs," February 23, 2017*
- In a survey of economic confidence in the nation's 50 largest metropolitan areas conducted January–December 2014, the Houston* metro area placed #10, according to Gallup's 2014 Economic Confidence Index. *Gallup, "San Jose and San Francisco Lead in Economic Confidence," March 19, 2015*
- The Brookings Institution ranked the 100 largest metro areas in the U.S. based on income inequality. Houston* was ranked #8 (#1 = greatest ineqality). Criteria: the "95/20 ratio," a figure representing the income at which a household earns more than 95 percent of all other households, divided by the income at which a household earns more than only 20 percent of all other households. *Brookings Institution, "Household Income Inequality, 100 Largest U.S. Metro Areas, 2014-2016," February 5, 2018*
- Payscale.com ranked the largest metro areas in terms of wage growth. The Houston* metro area ranked #13. Criteria: private-sector wage growth between the 4th quarter of 2016 and the 4th quarter of 2017. *PayScale, "Wage Trends by Metro Area-4th Quarter," January 17, 2018*
- The Houston* metro area was identified as one of the most debt-ridden places in America by the finance site Credit.com. The metro area was ranked #4. Criteria: residents' average credit card debt as well as median income. *Credit.com, "25 Cities With the Most Credit Card Debt," February 28, 2018*
- Houston* was identified as one of America's most frugal metro areas by *Coupons.com*. The city ranked #19 out of 25. Criteria: digital coupon usage. *Coupons.com, "America's Most Frugal Cities of 2017," March 22, 2018*
- Houston* was cited as one of America's top metros for new and expanded facility projects in 2017. The area ranked #2 in the large metro area category (population over 1 million). *Site Selection, "Top Metropolitans of 2017," March 2018*

- The Houston* metro area appeared on the Milken Institute "2017 Best Performing Cities" list. Rank: #113 out of 200 large metro areas. Criteria: job growth; wage and salary growth; high-tech output growth. *Milken Institute, "Best-Performing Cities 2017," January 2018*
- *Forbes* ranked the 200 most populous metro areas to determine the nation's "Best Places for Business and Careers." The Houston* metro area was ranked #43. Criteria: costs (business and living); job growth (past and projected); income growth; quality of life; educational attainment (college and high school); projected economic growth; cultural and recreational opportunities; net migration patterns; number of highly ranked colleges. *Forbes, "The Best Places for Business and Careers 2017," October 24, 2017*

Dating/Romance Rankings

- *Apartment List* conducted its annual survey of renters to compile a list of metros that have the best opportunities for dating. Nearly 11,000 respondents, from February 2017 through January 2018, rated their current city or neighborhood for opportunities to date and make friends. The Houston* metro area ranked #9 out of 70 where single residents were very satisfied or somewhat satisfied, making it among the ten best metros for dating opportunities. Other criteria analyzed included gender and education levels of renters. *Apartment List, "Best Metros for Dating 2018," February 6, 2018*

Education Rankings

- Personal finance website *WalletHub* analyzed the 150 largest U.S. metropolitan statistical areas to determine where the most educated Americans are choosing to settle. Criteria: education quality and attainment gap; education levels; percentage of workers with degrees; public school rankings; quality and size of each metro area's universities. Houston* was ranked #79 (#1 = most educated city). *www.WalletHub.com, "2017's Most and Least Educated Cities in America, " July 25, 2017*

Environmental Rankings

- Sperling's BestPlaces assessed 379 metropolitan areas of the United States for the likelihood of dangerously extreme weather events or earthquakes. In general the Southeast and South-Central regions have the highest risk of weather extremes and earthquakes, while the Pacific Northwest enjoys the lowest risk. Of the least risky metropolitan areas, the Houston* metro area was ranked #376. *www.bestplaces.net, "Safest Places from Natural Disasters," April 2011*
- The U.S. Environmental Protection Agency (EPA) released a list of U.S. metropolitan areas with the most ENERGY STAR certified buildings in 2016. The Houston* metro area was ranked #8 out of 25. *U.S. Environmental Protection Agency, "2017 Energy Star Top Cities," June 2017*
- Houston* was highlighted as one of the 25 most ozone-polluted metro areas in the U.S. during 2013 through 2015. The area ranked #12. *American Lung Association, State of the Air 2017*
- Houston* was highlighted as one of the 25 metro areas most polluted by year-round particle pollution (Annual PM 2.5) in the U.S. during 2013 through 2015. The area ranked #16. *American Lung Association, State of the Air 2017*

Health/Fitness Rankings

- For each of the 50 most populous metro areas in the United States, the American College of Sports Medicine's American Fitness Index evaluated infrastructure, community assets, and policies that encourage healthy and fit lifestyles, including preventive health behaviors, levels of chronic disease conditions, health care access, and community resources and policies that support physical activity. The Houston* metro area ranked #40 for "community fitness." *www.americanfitnessindex.org, "ACSM American Fitness Index Health and Community Fitness Status of the 50 Largest Metropolitan Areas," May 2017*

- The Houston* metro area was identified as one of the worst cities for bed bugs in America by pest control company Orkin. The area ranked #17 out of 50 based on the number of bed bug treatments Orkin performed from December 2016 to November 2017. *Orkin, "Baltimore and Washington D.C. Continue to Hold Top Spots," January 8, 2018*
- Houston* was identified as a "2016 Spring Allergy Capital." The area ranked #60 out of 100. Three groups of factors were used to identify the most severe cities for people with allergies during the spring season: annual pollen levels; medicine utilization; access to board-certified allergists. *Asthma and Allergy Foundation of America, "Spring Allergy Capitals 2016"*
- Houston* was identified as a "2016 Fall Allergy Capital." The area ranked #41 out of 100. Three groups of factors were used to identify the most severe cities for people with allergies during the fall season: annual pollen levels; medicine utilization; access to board-certified allergists. *Asthma and Allergy Foundation of America, "Fall Allergy Capitals 2016"*
- Houston* was identified as a "2015 Asthma Capital." The area ranked #82 out of the nation's 100 largest metropolitan areas. Criteria: estimated prevalence; self-reported prevalence; crude death rate for asthma; annual pollen score; annual air quality; public smoking laws; number of board-certified asthma specialists; school inhaler access laws; rescue medication use; controller medication use; ER visits for asthma; uninsured rate; poverty rate. *Asthma and Allergy Foundation of America, "Asthma Capitals 2015"*
- The Houston* metro area ranked #57 out of 189 in The Gallup-Healthways Well-Being Index. Criteria: purpose; social well being; financial health; community and physical health. Results are based on telephone interviews with adults, aged 18 and older, living in metropolitan areas in the 50 U.S. states and the District of Columbia. *Gallup-Healthways, "State of American Well-Being, 2017 Community Well-Being Rankings" March 2018*

Real Estate Rankings

- FitSmallBusiness looked at 50 of the largest metropolitan areas in the U.S. to determine which metro was the best to start a real estate business. Data was compiled from such sources as: Zillow, Trulia, U.S. Census Bureau, and the Bureau of Labor Statistics. Criteria: location; inventory; annual wages; median sales price of homes; days on the market; median price cut percentage; and other factors that would influence real estate professional growth. The Houston* metro area ranked #38. *fitsmallbusiness.com, "The Best Cities to Become a Real Estate Agent in 2018," January 30, 2018*
- According to Penske Truck Rental, the Houston* metro area was named the #4 moving destination in 2017, based on one-way consumer truck rental reservations made through Penske's website, rental locations, and reservations call center. *blog.gopenske.com, "Penske Truck Rental's 2017 Top Moving Destinations List," January 22, 2018*
- The Houston* metro area was identified as one of the 10 worst condo markets in the U.S. in 2017. The area ranked #2 out of 66 markets. Criteria: year-over-year change of median sales price of existing apartment condo-coop homes between the 4th quarter of 2016 and the 4th quarter of 2017. *National Association of Realtors®, Median Sales Price of Existing Apartment Condo-Coop Homes for Metropolitan Areas, 4th Quarter 2017*
- Houston* was ranked #159 out of 238 metro areas in terms of housing affordability in 2017 by the National Association of Home Builders (#1 = most affordable). Criteria: the share of homes sold in that area affordable to a family earning the local median income, based on standard mortgage underwriting criteria. *National Association of Home Builders®, NAHB-Wells Fargo Housing Opportunity Index, 4th Quarter 2017*

Safety Rankings

- Friendswood was identified as one of the safest cities in America by NeighborhoodScout. The city ranked #43 out of 100 (100 = safest). Criteria: number of violent and property crimes per 1,000 residents. The editors only considered cities with 25,000 or more residents. *NeighborhoodScout, "Top 100 Safest Cities in the U.S. 2018" January 2, 2018*

- The National Insurance Crime Bureau ranked 382 metro areas in the U.S. in terms of per capita rates of vehicle theft. The Houston* metro area ranked #45 (#1 = highest rate). Criteria: number of vehicle theft offenses per 100,000 inhabitants in 2016. *National Insurance Crime Bureau, "Hot Spots 2016," June 8, 2017*

Seniors/Retirement Rankings

- From its Best Cities for Successful Aging indexes, the Milken Institute generated rankings for metropolitan areas, weighing data in nine categories—health care, wellness, living arrangements, transportation and convenience, financial characteristics, education, employment, community engagement, and overall livability. The Houston* metro area was ranked #35 overall in the large metro area category. *Milken Institute, "Best Cities for Successful Aging, 2017" March 14, 2017*

Transportation Rankings

- Houston* was identified as one of the most congested metro areas in the U.S. The area ranked #8 out of 10. Criteria: yearly delay per auto commuter in hours. *Texas A&M Transportation Institute, "2015 Urban Mobility Scorecard," August 2015*

Women/Minorities Rankings

- The *Houston Chronicle* listed the Houston* metro area as #11 in top places for young Latinos to live in the U.S. Research was largely based on housing and occupational data from the largest metropolitan areas performed by *Forbes* and NBC Universo. Criteria: percentage of 18-34 year-olds; Latino college grad rates; and diversity. *blog.chron.com, "The 15 Best Big Cities for Latino Millenials," January 26, 2016*

Miscellaneous Rankings

- The watchdog site Charity Navigator conducts an annual study of charities in the nation's major markets both to analyze statistical differences in their financial, accountability, and transparency practices and to track year-to-year variations in individual philanthropic communities. Charity Navigator's analysis demonstrated that the financial, accountability and transparency behaviors of America's largest charities can be influenced by the metropolitan market within which the charity operates. The Houston* metro area was ranked #2 among the 30 metro markets in the rating category of Overall Score. *www.charitynavigator.org, "2017 Metro Market Study," May 1, 2017*
- The Harris Poll's Happiness Index survey revealed that of the top ten U.S. markets, the Houston* metro area residents ranked #2 in happiness. Criteria included strong assent to positive statements and strong disagreement with negative ones, and degree of agreement with a series of statements about respondents' personal relationships and general outlook. *www.theharrispoll.com, "Dallas/Fort Worth Is "Happiest" City among America's Top Ten Markets," September 4, 2013*
- Energizer Personal Care, the makers of Edge® shave gel, in partnership with Sperling's BestPlaces, ranked 50 major metro areas in terms of everyday irritations. The Houston* metro area ranked #8 the 50 metro area most irritating to guys. Criteria: high male-to-female ratio; poor sports team performance and high ticket prices; slow traffic; lack of job availability; unaffordable housing; extreme weather; lack of nightlife and fitness options. *Energizer Personal Care, "Most Irritating Cities for Guys," August 26, 2013*
- The National Alliance to End Homelessness listed the 25 most populous metro areas with the highest rate of homelessness. The Houston* metro area had a high rate of homelessness. Criteria: number of homeless people per 10,000 population in 2016. *National Alliance to End Homelessness, "Homelessness in the 25 Most Populous U.S. Metro Areas," September 1, 2017*

*Friendswood is located within the Houston-The Woodlands-Sugar Land, TX Metropolitan Statistical Area.

Business Environment

CITY FINANCES

City Government Finances

Component	2015 ($000)	2015 ($ per capita)
Total Revenues	n/a	n/a
Total Expenditures	n/a	n/a
Debt Outstanding	n/a	n/a
Cash and Securities[1]	n/a	n/a

Note: (1) Cash and security holdings of a government at the close of its fiscal year,, including those of its dependent agencies, utilities, and liquor stores.
Source: U.S Census Bureau, State & Local Government Finances 2015

City Government Revenue by Source

Source	2015 ($000)	2015 ($ per capita)	2015 (%)
General Revenue			
From Federal Government	n/a	n/a	n/a
From State Government	n/a	n/a	n/a
From Local Governments	n/a	n/a	n/a
Taxes			
Property	n/a	n/a	n/a
Sales and Gross Receipts	n/a	n/a	n/a
Personal Income	n/a	n/a	n/a
Corporate Income	n/a	n/a	n/a
Motor Vehicle License	n/a	n/a	n/a
Other Taxes	n/a	n/a	n/a
Current Charges	n/a	n/a	n/a
Liquor Store	n/a	n/a	n/a
Utility	n/a	n/a	n/a
Employee Retirement	n/a	n/a	n/a

Source: U.S Census Bureau, State & Local Government Finances 2015

City Government Expenditures by Function

Function	2015 ($000)	2015 ($ per capita)	2015 (%)
General Direct Expenditures			
Air Transportation	n/a	n/a	n/a
Corrections	n/a	n/a	n/a
Education	n/a	n/a	n/a
Employment Security Administration	n/a	n/a	n/a
Financial Administration	n/a	n/a	n/a
Fire Protection	n/a	n/a	n/a
General Public Buildings	n/a	n/a	n/a
Governmental Administration, Other	n/a	n/a	n/a
Health	n/a	n/a	n/a
Highways	n/a	n/a	n/a
Hospitals	n/a	n/a	n/a
Housing and Community Development	n/a	n/a	n/a
Interest on General Debt	n/a	n/a	n/a
Judicial and Legal	n/a	n/a	n/a
Libraries	n/a	n/a	n/a
Parking	n/a	n/a	n/a
Parks and Recreation	n/a	n/a	n/a
Police Protection	n/a	n/a	n/a
Public Welfare	n/a	n/a	n/a
Sewerage	n/a	n/a	n/a
Solid Waste Management	n/a	n/a	n/a
Veterans' Services	n/a	n/a	n/a
Liquor Store	n/a	n/a	n/a
Utility	n/a	n/a	n/a
Employee Retirement	n/a	n/a	n/a

Source: U.S Census Bureau, State & Local Government Finances 2015

DEMOGRAPHICS

Population Growth

Area	1990 Census	2000 Census	2010 Census	2016* Estimate	Population Growth (%) 1990-2016	Population Growth (%) 2010-2016
City	23,020	29,037	35,805	38,272	66.3	6.9
MSA[1]	3,767,335	4,715,407	5,946,800	6,482,592	72.1	9.0
U.S.	248,709,873	281,421,906	308,745,538	318,558,162	28.1	3.2

Note: (1) Figures cover the Houston-The Woodlands-Sugar Land, TX Metropolitan Statistical Area—see Appendix B for areas included; (*) 2012-2016 5-year estimated population
Source: U.S. Census Bureau, 1990 Census, Census 2000, Census 2010, 2012-2016 American Community Survey 5-Year Estimates

Household Size

Area	Persons in Household (%) One	Two	Three	Four	Five	Six	Seven or More	Average Household Size
City	19.1	32.9	17.6	20.0	5.5	3.5	1.5	2.90
MSA[1]	24.5	29.6	17.0	15.4	8.2	3.2	2.1	2.90
U.S.	27.7	33.7	15.7	13.1	6.0	2.3	1.5	2.60

Note: (1) Figures cover the Houston-The Woodlands-Sugar Land, TX Metropolitan Statistical Area—see Appendix B for areas included
Source: U.S. Census Bureau, 2012-2016 American Community Survey 5-Year Estimates

Race

Area	White Alone[2] (%)	Black Alone[2] (%)	Asian Alone[2] (%)	AIAN[3] Alone[2] (%)	NHOPI[4] Alone[2] (%)	Other Race Alone[2] (%)	Two or More Races (%)
City	87.6	2.6	6.3	0.4	0.0	1.0	2.0
MSA[1]	65.7	17.2	7.3	0.4	0.1	7.1	2.3
U.S.	73.3	12.6	5.2	0.8	0.2	4.8	3.1

Note: (1) Figures cover the Houston-The Woodlands-Sugar Land, TX Metropolitan Statistical Area—see Appendix B for areas included; (2) Alone is defined as not being in combination with one or more other races; (3) American Indian and Alaska Native; (4) Native Hawaiian and Other Pacific Islander
Source: U.S. Census Bureau, 2012-2016 American Community Survey 5-Year Estimates

Hispanic or Latino Origin

Area	Total (%)	Mexican (%)	Puerto Rican (%)	Cuban (%)	Other (%)
City	15.8	12.3	0.5	0.7	2.2
MSA[1]	36.3	27.8	0.6	0.4	7.4
U.S.	17.3	11.0	1.7	0.7	4.0

Note: Persons of Hispanic or Latino origin can be of any race; (1) Figures cover the Houston-The Woodlands-Sugar Land, TX Metropolitan Statistical Area—see Appendix B for areas included
Source: U.S. Census Bureau, 2012-2016 American Community Survey 5-Year Estimates

Segregation

Type	Segregation Indices[1] 1990	2000	2010	2010 Rank[2]	Percent Change 1990-2000	1990-2010	2000-2010
Black/White	65.5	65.7	61.4	36	0.1	-4.1	-4.2
Asian/White	48.0	51.4	50.4	7	3.4	2.4	-1.0
Hispanic/White	47.8	53.4	52.5	18	5.6	4.7	-0.9

Note: All figures cover the Metropolitan Statistical Area—see Appendix B for areas included; Figures are based on an analysis of 1990, 2000, and 2010 Census Decennial Census tract data by William H. Frey, Brookings Institution and the University of Michigan Social Science Data Analysis Network. In this analysis all racial groups (whites, blacks, and asians) are non-Hispanic members of those races. Hispanics are shown as a separate category; (1) Segregation Indices are Dissimilarity Indices that measure the degree to which the minority group is distributed differently than whites across census tracts. They range from 0 (complete integration) to 100 (complete segregation) where the value indicates the percentage of the minority group that needs to move to be distributed exactly like whites; (2) Ranges from 1 (most segregated) to 102 (least segregated); n/a not available.
Source: www.CensusScope.org

Ancestry

Area	German	Irish	English	American	Italian	Polish	French[2]	Scottish	Dutch
City	16.3	10.9	11.9	8.6	3.6	1.0	3.1	1.8	0.9
MSA[1]	8.5	5.8	5.4	4.7	2.1	1.2	2.3	1.2	0.6
U.S.	14.4	10.4	7.7	6.9	5.4	2.9	2.6	1.7	1.3

Note: Figures are the percentage of the total population reporting a particular ancestry. The nine most commonly reported ancestries in the U.S. are shown. Figures include multiple ancestries (e.g. if a person reported being Irish and Italian, they were included in both columns); (1) Figures cover the Houston-The Woodlands-Sugar Land, TX Metropolitan Statistical Area—see Appendix B for areas included; (2) Excludes Basque
Source: U.S. Census Bureau, 2012-2016 American Community Survey 5-Year Estimates

Foreign-Born Population

Area	Percent of Population Born in								
	Any Foreign Country	Asia	Mexico	Europe	Carribean	Central America[2]	South America	Africa	Canada
City	9.4	4.2	1.9	1.3	0.3	0.3	0.8	0.4	0.3
MSA[1]	22.9	5.7	9.6	1.0	0.6	3.4	1.1	1.2	0.3
U.S.	13.2	4.0	3.6	1.5	1.3	1.0	0.9	0.6	0.3

Note: (1) Figures cover the Houston-The Woodlands-Sugar Land, TX Metropolitan Statistical Area—see Appendix B for areas included; (2) Excludes Mexico.
Source: U.S. Census Bureau, 2012-2016 American Community Survey 5-Year Estimates

Marital Status

Area	Never Married	Now Married[2]	Separated	Widowed	Divorced
City	21.7	62.4	1.4	5.5	9.1
MSA[1]	33.1	49.9	2.6	4.5	9.8
U.S.	33.0	48.1	2.1	5.9	11.0

Note: Figures are percentages and cover the population 15 years of age and older; (1) Figures cover the Houston-The Woodlands-Sugar Land, TX Metropolitan Statistical Area—see Appendix B for areas included; (2) Excludes separated
Source: U.S. Census Bureau, 2012-2016 American Community Survey 5-Year Estimates

Disability Status

Area	All Ages	Under 18 Years Old	18 to 64 Years Old	65 Years and Over
City	8.6	3.9	6.1	28.5
MSA[1]	9.6	3.5	8.2	36.2
U.S.	12.5	4.1	10.3	35.7

Note: Figures show percent of the civilian noninstitutionalized population that reported having a disability. Disability status is determined from six types of difficulty: vision, hearing, cognitive, ambulatory, self-care, and independent living. For children under 5 years old, hearing and vision difficulty are used to determine disability status. For children between the ages of 5 and 14, disability status is determined from hearing, vision, cognitive, ambulatory, and self-care difficulties. For people aged 15 years and older, they are considered to have a disability if they have difficulty with any one of the six difficulty types; Note: (1) Figures cover the Houston-The Woodlands-Sugar Land, TX Metropolitan Statistical Area—see Appendix B for areas included
Source: U.S. Census Bureau, 2012-2016 American Community Survey 5-Year Estimates

Age

Area	Percent of Population									Median Age
	Under Age 5	Age 5–19	Age 20–34	Age 35–44	Age 45–54	Age 55–64	Age 65–74	Age 75–84	Age 85+	
City	5.5	23.3	15.2	12.2	17.0	12.7	9.2	3.2	1.7	40.4
MSA[1]	7.6	22.2	22.0	14.2	13.2	11.0	6.1	2.7	1.0	33.9
U.S.	6.2	19.6	20.7	12.7	13.6	12.6	8.3	4.3	1.9	37.7

Note: (1) Figures cover the Houston-The Woodlands-Sugar Land, TX Metropolitan Statistical Area—see Appendix B for areas included
Source: U.S. Census Bureau, 2012-2016 American Community Survey 5-Year Estimates

Gender

Area	Males	Females	Males per 100 Females
City	18,961	19,311	98.2
MSA[1]	3,220,604	3,261,988	98.7
U.S.	156,765,322	161,792,840	96.9

Note: (1) Figures cover the Houston-The Woodlands-Sugar Land, TX Metropolitan Statistical Area—see Appendix B for areas included
Source: U.S. Census Bureau, 2012-2016 American Community Survey 5-Year Estimates

Religious Groups by Family

Area	Catholic	Baptist	Non-Den.	Methodist[2]	Lutheran	LDS[3]	Pente-costal	Presby-terian[4]	Muslim[5]	Judaism
MSA[1]	17.1	16.0	7.3	4.9	1.1	1.1	1.5	0.9	2.7	0.4
U.S.	19.1	9.3	4.0	4.0	2.3	2.0	1.9	1.6	0.8	0.7

Note: Figures are the number of adherents as a percentage of the total population; (1) Figures cover the Houston-The Woodlands-Sugar Land, TX Metropolitan Statistical Area—see Appendix B for areas included; (2) Methodist/Pietist; (3) Latter Day Saints; (4) Reformed; (5) Figures are estimates
Source: Association of Statisticians of American Religious Bodies, 2010 U.S. Religion Census: Religious Congregations & Membership Study

Religious Groups by Tradition

Area	Catholic	Evangelical Protestant	Mainline Protestant	Other Tradition	Black Protestant	Orthodox
MSA[1]	17.1	24.9	6.7	4.9	1.3	0.2
U.S.	19.1	16.2	7.3	4.3	1.6	0.3

Note: Figures are the number of adherents as a percentage of the total population; (1) Figures cover the Houston-The Woodlands-Sugar Land, TX Metropolitan Statistical Area—see Appendix B for areas included
Source: Association of Statisticians of American Religious Bodies, 2010 U.S. Religion Census: Religious Congregations & Membership Study

ECONOMY

Gross Metropolitan Product

Area	2014	2015	2016	2017	Rank[2]
MSA[1]	523.1	498.5	491.3	526.0	5

Note: Figures are in billions of dollars; (1) Figures cover the Houston-The Woodlands-Sugar Land, TX Metropolitan Statistical Area—see Appendix B for areas included; (2) Rank is based on 2015 data and ranges from 1 to 381
Source: The U.S. Conference of Mayors, U.S. Metro Economies: GMP and Employment Report, 2015-2017

Economic Growth

Area	2012-14 (%)	2015 (%)	2016 (%)	2017 (%)	Rank[2]
MSA[1]	3.9	0.3	-2.0	3.9	33
U.S.	2.0	2.4	1.9	2.6	–

Note: Figures are real gross metropolitan product (GMP) growth rates and represent average annual percent change; (1) Figures cover the Houston-The Woodlands-Sugar Land, TX Metropolitan Statistical Area—see Appendix B for areas included; (2) Rank is based on 2012-2014 average annual percent change and ranges from 1 to 381
Source: The U.S. Conference of Mayors, U.S. Metro Economies: GMP and Employment Report, 2015-2017

Metropolitan Area Exports

Area	2011	2012	2013	2014	2015	2016	Rank[2]
MSA[1]	104,457.3	110,297.8	114,962.6	118,966.0	97,054.3	84,105.5	2

Note: Figures are in millions of dollars; (1) Figures cover the Houston-The Woodlands-Sugar Land, TX Metropolitan Statistical Area—see Appendix B for areas included; (2) Rank is based on 2016 data and ranges from 1 to 385
Source: U.S. Department of Commerce, International Trade Administration, Office of Trade & Industry Information, Manufacturing & Services, data extracted March 15, 2018

Building Permits

Area	Single-Family			Multi-Family			Total		
	2016	2017p	Pct. Chg.	2016	2017p	Pct. Chg.	2016	2017p	Pct. Chg.
City	173	182	5.2	0	0	0.0	173	182	5.2
MSA[1]	35,397	36,601	3.4	9,246	6,072	-34.3	44,643	42,673	-4.4
U.S.	750,800	817,300	8.9	455,800	446,800	-2.0	1,206,600	1,264,100	4.8

Note: (1) Figures cover the Houston-The Woodlands-Sugar Land, TX Metropolitan Statistical Area—see Appendix B for areas included; Figures represent new, privately-owned housing units authorized (unadjusted data); All permit data are based on estimates with imputation; (p) preliminary data.
Source: U.S. Census Bureau, Manufacturing, Mining, and Construction Statistics, Building Permits, 2016, 2017

Bankruptcy Filings

Area	Business Filings			Nonbusiness Filings		
	2016	2017	% Chg.	2016	2017	% Chg.
Galveston County	22	26	18.2	328	283	-13.7
U.S.	24,114	23,157	-4.0	770,846	765,863	-0.6

Note: Business filings include Chapter 7, Chapter 11, Chapter 12, and Chapter 13; Nonbusiness filings include Chapter 7, Chapter 11, and Chapter 13
Source: Administrative Office of the U.S. Courts, Business and Nonbusiness Bankruptcy, County Cases Commenced by Chapter of the Bankruptcy Code, During the 12-Month Period Ending December 31, 2016 and Business and Nonbusiness Bankruptcy, County Cases Commenced by Chapter of the Bankruptcy Code, During the 12-Month Period Ending December 31, 2017

Housing Vacancy Rates

Area	Gross Vacancy Rate[2] (%)			Year-Round Vacancy Rate[3] (%)			Rental Vacancy Rate[4] (%)			Homeowner Vacancy Rate[5] (%)		
	2015	2016	2017	2015	2016	2017	2015	2016	2017	2015	2016	2017
MSA[1]	9.2	8.6	9.3	8.7	8.0	8.9	9.6	9.3	9.9	1.5	1.8	1.5
U.S.	12.9	12.8	12.7	10.0	9.9	9.9	7.1	6.9	7.2	1.8	1.7	1.6

Note: (1) Figures cover the Houston-The Woodlands-Sugar Land, TX Metropolitan Statistical Area—see Appendix B for areas included; (2) The percentage of the total housing inventory that is vacant; (3) The percentage of the housing inventory (excluding seasonal units) that is year-round vacant; (4) The percentage of rental inventory that is vacant for rent; (5) The percentage of homeowner inventory that is vacant for sale
Source: U.S. Census Bureau, Housing Vacancies and Homeownership Annual Statistics: 2015, 2016, 2017

INCOME

Income

Area	Per Capita ($)	Median Household ($)	Average Household ($)
City	45,954	95,241	130,636
MSA[1]	31,165	60,902	87,925
U.S.	29,829	55,322	77,866

Note: (1) Figures cover the Houston-The Woodlands-Sugar Land, TX Metropolitan Statistical Area—see Appendix B for areas included
Source: U.S. Census Bureau, 2012-2016 American Community Survey 5-Year Estimates

Household Income Distribution

Area	Percent of Households Earning							
	Under $15,000	$15,000 -$24,999	$25,000 -$34,999	$35,000 -$49,999	$50,000 -$74,999	$75,000 -$99,999	$100,000 -$149,999	$150,000 and up
City	5.2	4.5	5.9	9.4	15.2	11.4	16.6	31.8
MSA[1]	10.2	9.5	9.5	12.6	17.1	11.7	14.6	14.8
U.S.	12.1	10.2	9.9	13.2	17.8	12.2	13.5	11.1

Note: (1) Figures cover the Houston-The Woodlands-Sugar Land, TX Metropolitan Statistical Area—see Appendix B for areas included
Source: U.S. Census Bureau, 2012-2016 American Community Survey 5-Year Estimates

Poverty Rate

Area	All Ages	Under 18 Years Old	18 to 64 Years Old	65 Years and Over
City	5.8	7.4	5.4	4.3
MSA[1]	15.3	22.4	13.1	10.1
U.S.	15.1	21.2	14.2	9.3

Note: Figures are percentage of people whose income during the past 12 months was below the poverty level; (1) Figures cover the Houston-The Woodlands-Sugar Land, TX Metropolitan Statistical Area—see Appendix B for areas included
Source: U.S. Census Bureau, 2012-2016 American Community Survey 5-Year Estimates

EMPLOYMENT

Labor Force and Employment

Area	Civilian Labor Force			Workers Employed		
	Dec. 2016	Dec. 2017	% Chg.	Dec. 2016	Dec. 2017	% Chg.
City	19,542	19,766	1.1	18,620	19,081	2.5
MSA[1]	3,297,292	3,343,410	1.4	3,121,317	3,199,215	2.5
U.S.	158,968,000	159,880,000	0.6	151,798,000	153,602,000	1.2

Note: Data is not seasonally adjusted and covers workers 16 years of age and older; (1) Figures cover the Houston-The Woodlands-Sugar Land, TX Metropolitan Statistical Area—see Appendix B for areas included
Source: Bureau of Labor Statistics, Local Area Unemployment Statistics

Unemployment Rate

Area	2017											
	Jan.	Feb.	Mar.	Apr.	May	Jun.	Jul.	Aug.	Sep.	Oct.	Nov.	Dec.
City	5.0	4.9	4.5	4.2	4.0	4.3	4.1	4.0	3.9	3.5	3.6	3.5
MSA[1]	5.8	5.6	5.2	4.8	4.8	5.1	5.1	5.1	4.8	4.4	4.4	4.3
U.S.	5.1	4.9	4.6	4.1	4.1	4.5	4.6	4.5	4.1	3.9	3.9	3.9

Note: Data is not seasonally adjusted and covers workers 16 years of age and older; (1) Figures cover the Houston-The Woodlands-Sugar Land, TX Metropolitan Statistical Area—see Appendix B for areas included
Source: Bureau of Labor Statistics, Local Area Unemployment Statistics

Average Wages

Occupation	$/Hr.	Occupation	$/Hr.
Accountants and Auditors	42.90	Maids and Housekeeping Cleaners	10.00
Automotive Mechanics	22.70	Maintenance and Repair Workers	18.70
Bookkeepers	20.80	Marketing Managers	87.10
Carpenters	20.50	Nuclear Medicine Technologists	38.30
Cashiers	10.10	Nurses, Licensed Practical	23.50
Clerks, General Office	18.70	Nurses, Registered	38.00
Clerks, Receptionists/Information	13.00	Nursing Assistants	13.30
Clerks, Shipping/Receiving	15.70	Packers and Packagers, Hand	11.50
Computer Programmers	42.20	Physical Therapists	44.70
Computer Systems Analysts	48.60	Postal Service Mail Carriers	24.00
Computer User Support Specialists	30.10	Real Estate Brokers	38.00
Cooks, Restaurant	12.60	Retail Salespersons	12.60
Dentists	91.10	Sales Reps., Exc. Tech./Scientific	35.50
Electrical Engineers	50.10	Sales Reps., Tech./Scientific	50.20
Electricians	26.60	Secretaries, Exc. Legal/Med./Exec.	18.10
Financial Managers	79.10	Security Guards	14.70
First-Line Supervisors/Managers, Sales	21.20	Surgeons	111.20
Food Preparation Workers	11.40	Teacher Assistants*	11.30
General and Operations Managers	72.40	Teachers, Elementary School*	30.20
Hairdressers/Cosmetologists	16.50	Teachers, Secondary School*	29.90
Internists, General	64.80	Telemarketers	13.60
Janitors and Cleaners	11.30	Truck Drivers, Heavy/Tractor-Trailer	20.80
Landscaping/Groundskeeping Workers	13.40	Truck Drivers, Light/Delivery Svcs.	17.10
Lawyers	84.10	Waiters and Waitresses	11.70

Note: Wage data covers the Houston-The Woodlands-Sugar Land, TX Metropolitan Statistical Area—see Appendix B for areas included; (*) Hourly wages for elementary/secondary school teachers and teacher assistants were calculated by the editors from annual wage data based on a 40 hour work week; n/a not available.
Source: Bureau of Labor Statistics, Metro Area Occupational Employment & Wage Estimates, May 2017

Employment by Occupation

Occupation Classification	City (%)	MSA[1] (%)	U.S. (%)
Management, Business, Science, and Arts	53.3	37.3	37.0
Natural Resources, Construction, and Maintenance	6.3	10.9	8.9
Production, Transportation, and Material Moving	7.6	12.2	12.2
Sales and Office	22.8	23.0	23.8
Service	10.1	16.6	18.1

Note: Figures cover employed civilians 16 years of age and older; (1) Figures cover the Houston-The Woodlands-Sugar Land, TX Metropolitan Statistical Area—see Appendix B for areas included
Source: U.S. Census Bureau, 2012-2016 American Community Survey 5-Year Estimates

Employment by Industry

Sector	MSA[1] Number of Employees	MSA[1] Percent of Total	U.S. Percent of Total
Construction	221,400	7.2	4.7
Education and Health Services	383,900	12.5	15.9
Financial Activities	160,400	5.2	5.7
Government	416,100	13.5	15.3
Information	31,900	1.0	1.9
Leisure and Hospitality	318,500	10.4	10.7
Manufacturing	221,100	7.2	8.5
Mining and Logging	77,900	2.5	0.5
Other Services	109,200	3.6	3.9
Professional and Business Services	492,800	16.0	14.0
Retail Trade	324,500	10.6	11.0
Transportation, Warehousing, and Utilities	147,700	4.8	4.1
Wholesale Trade	168,000	5.5	4.0

Note: Figures are non-farm employment as of December 2017. Figures are not seasonally adjusted and include workers 16 years of age and older; (1) Figures cover the Houston-The Woodlands-Sugar Land, TX Metropolitan Statistical Area—see Appendix B for areas included
Source: Bureau of Labor Statistics, Current Employment Statistics, Employment, Hours, and Earnings

Occupations with Greatest Projected Employment Growth: 2017 – 2019

Occupation[1]	2017 Employment	2019 Projected Employment	Numeric Employment Change	Percent Employment Change
Combined Food Preparation and Serving Workers, Including Fast Food	335,660	354,370	18,710	5.6
Personal Care Aides	212,280	230,990	18,710	8.8
Retail Salespersons	393,950	406,100	12,150	3.1
Customer Service Representatives	261,530	273,600	12,070	4.6
Janitors and Cleaners, Except Maids and Housekeeping Cleaners	180,710	192,060	11,350	6.3
Laborers and Freight, Stock, and Material Movers, Hand	185,140	196,200	11,060	6.0
Registered Nurses	214,500	224,450	9,950	4.6
Office Clerks, General	379,860	389,540	9,680	2.6
Heavy and Tractor-Trailer Truck Drivers	192,710	201,560	8,850	4.6
Waiters and Waitresses	222,630	231,020	8,390	3.8

Note: Projections cover Texas; (1) Sorted by numeric employment change
Source: www.projectionscentral.com, State Occupational Projections, 2017–2019 Short-Term Projections

Fastest Growing Occupations: 2017 – 2019

Occupation[1]	2017 Employment	2019 Projected Employment	Numeric Employment Change	Percent Employment Change
Wind Turbine Service Technicians	1,740	2,090	350	20.7
Home Health Aides	72,760	80,000	7,240	10.0
Security and Fire Alarm Systems Installers	8,190	8,930	740	8.9
Personal Care Aides	212,280	230,990	18,710	8.8
Statisticians	1,760	1,910	150	8.2
Tree Trimmers and Pruners	5,980	6,480	500	8.2
Physician Assistants	6,860	7,400	540	7.9
Nurse Practitioners	9,230	9,950	720	7.7
Elevator Installers and Repairers	2,190	2,350	160	7.4
Helpers—Roofers	800	850	50	7.4

Note: Projections cover Texas; (1) Sorted by percent employment change and excludes occupations with numeric employment change less than 50

Source: www.projectionscentral.com, State Occupational Projections, 2017–2019 Short-Term Projections

TAXES

State Corporate Income Tax Rates

State	Tax Rate (%)	Income Brackets ($)	Num. of Brackets	Financial Institution Tax Rate (%)[a]	Federal Income Tax Ded.
Texas	(w)	–	–	(w)	No

Note: Tax rates as of January 1, 2018; (a) Rates listed are the corporate income tax rate applied to financial institutions or excise taxes based on income. Some states have other taxes based upon the value of deposits or shares; (w) Texas imposes a Franchise Tax, otherwise known as margin tax, imposed on entities with more than $1,110,000 total revenues at rate of 0.75%, or 0.375% for entities primarily engaged in retail or wholesale trade, on lesser of 70% of total revenues or 100% of gross receipts after deductions for either compensation or cost of goods sold.

Source: Federation of Tax Administrators, Range of State Corporate Income Tax Rates, January 1, 2018

State Individual Income Tax Rates

State	Tax Rate (%)	Income Brackets ($)	Num. of Brackets	Personal Exempt. ($)[1] Single	Personal Exempt. ($)[1] Dependents	Fed. Inc. Tax Ded.
Texas	None	–	–	–	–	–

Note: Tax rates as of January 1, 2018; Local- and county-level taxes are not included; n/a not applicable; (1) Married joint filers generally receive double the single exemption

Source: Federation of Tax Administrators, State Individual Income Tax Rates, January 1, 2018

Various State Sales and Excise Tax Rates

State	State Sales Tax (%)	Gasoline[1] (¢/gal.)	Cigarette[2] ($/pack)	Spirits[3] ($/gal.)	Wine[4] ($/gal.)	Beer[5] ($/gal.)	Recreational Marijuana (%)
Texas	6.25	20.0	1.41	2.40 (f)	0.20 (l)	0.20 (q)	Not legal

Note: All tax rates as of January 1, 2018; (1) The American Petroleum Institute has developed a methodology for determining the average tax rate on a gallon of fuel. Rates may include any of the following: excise taxes, environmental fees, storage tank fees, other fees or taxes, general sales tax, and local taxes. In states where gasoline is subject to the general sales tax, or where the fuel tax is based on the average sale price, the average rate determined by API is sensitive to changes in the price of gasoline. States that fully or partially apply general sales taxes to gasoline: CA, CO, GA, IL, IN, MI, NY; (2) The federal excise tax of $1.0066 per pack and local taxes are not included; (3) Rates are those applicable to off-premise sales of 40% alcohol by volume (a.b.v.) distilled spirits in 750ml containers. Local excise taxes are excluded; (4) Rates are those applicable to off-premise sales of 11% a.b.v. non-carbonated wine in 750ml containers; (5) Rates are those applicable to off-premise sales of 4.7% a.b.v. beer in 12 ounce containers; (f) Different rates also applicable according to alcohol content, place of production, size of container, or place purchased (on- or off-premise or onboard airlines); (l) Different rates also applicable to alcohol content, place of production, size of container, place purchased (on- or off-premise or on board airlines) or type of wine (carbonated, vermouth, etc.); (q) Different rates also applicable according to alcohol content, place of production, size of container, or place purchased (on- or off-premise or onboard airlines).

Source: Tax Foundation, 2018 Facts & Figures: How Does Your State Compare?

TRANSPORTATION

State Business Tax Climate Index Rankings

State	Overall Rank	Corporate Tax Rank	Individual Income Tax Rank	Sales Tax Rank	Unemployment Insurance Tax Rank	Property Tax Rank
Texas	13	49	6	37	26	37

Note: The index is a measure of how each state's tax laws affect economic performance. The lower the rank, the more favorable a state's tax system is for business. States without a given tax are given a ranking of 1. The scores/rankings for the District of Columbia do not affect other states. The 2018 index represents the tax climate as of July 1, 2017.
Source: Tax Foundation, State Business Tax Climate Index 2018

Means of Transportation to Work

Area	Car/Truck/Van		Public Transportation			Bicycle	Walked	Other Means	Worked at Home
	Drove Alone	Car-pooled	Bus	Subway	Railroad				
City	86.3	5.9	0.8	0.0	0.0	0.2	0.9	0.7	5.3
MSA[1]	80.2	10.7	2.2	0.0	0.0	0.3	1.4	1.5	3.7
U.S.	76.4	9.3	2.6	1.9	0.6	0.6	2.8	1.3	4.6

Note: Figures are percentages and cover workers 16 years of age and older; (1) Figures cover the Houston-The Woodlands-Sugar Land, TX Metropolitan Statistical Area—see Appendix B for areas included
Source: U.S. Census Bureau, 2012-2016 American Community Survey 5-Year Estimates

Travel Time to Work

Area	Less Than 10 Minutes	10 to 19 Minutes	20 to 29 Minutes	30 to 44 Minutes	45 to 59 Minutes	60 to 89 Minutes	90 Minutes or More
City	9.9	20.4	18.5	23.6	13.9	10.5	3.2
MSA[1]	8.3	24.1	19.6	25.8	11.3	8.5	2.4
U.S.	12.9	29.2	20.9	20.4	8.0	6.0	2.7

Note: Note: Figures are percentages and include workers 16 years old and over; (1) Figures cover the Houston-The Woodlands-Sugar Land, TX Metropolitan Statistical Area—see Appendix B for areas included
Source: U.S. Census Bureau, 2012-2016 American Community Survey 5-Year Estimates

Freeway Travel Time Index

Area	1985	1990	1995	2000	2005	2010	2014
Urban Area Rank[1,2]	3	5	13	22	17	14	10
Urban Area Index[1]	1.25	1.22	1.22	1.23	1.28	1.28	1.33
Average Index[3]	1.09	1.11	1.14	1.17	1.20	1.19	1.20

Note: Freeway Travel Time Index—the ratio of travel time in the peak period to the travel time at free-flow conditions. For example, a value of 1.30 indicates a 20-minute free-flow trip takes 26 minutes in the peak (20 minutes x 1.30 = 26 minutes); (1) Covers the Houston TX urban area; (2) Rank is based on 101 urban areas (#1 = highest travel time index); (3) Average of 101 urban areas
Source: Texas Transportation Institute, 2015 Urban Mobility Scorecard, August 2015

Freeway Commuter Stress Index

Area	1985	1990	1995	2000	2005	2010	2014
Urban Area Rank[1,2]	4	12	18	23	16	17	12
Urban Area Index[1]	1.30	1.27	1.28	1.29	1.34	1.34	1.39
Average Index[3]	1.13	1.16	1.19	1.22	1.25	1.24	1.25

Note: The Freeway Commuter Stress Index is the same as the Freeway Travel Time Index (see table above) except that it includes only the travel in the peak directions during the peak periods; the TTI includes travel in all directions during the peak period. Thus, the CSI is more indicative of the work trip experienced by each commuter on a daily basis; (1) Covers the Houston TX urban area; (2) Rank is based on 101 urban areas (#1 = highest travel time index); (3) Average of 101 urban areas
Source: Texas Transportation Institute, 2015 Urban Mobility Scorecard, August 2015

Living Environment

COST OF LIVING

Cost of Living Index

Composite Index	Groceries	Housing	Utilities	Trans-portation	Health Care	Misc. Goods/ Services
86.6	83.2	89.3	72.0	93.4	101.4	86.2

Note: The Cost of Living Index measures regional differences in the cost of consumer goods and services, excluding taxes and non-consumer expenditures, for professional and managerial households in the top income quintile. It is based on more than 50,000 prices covering almost 60 different items for which prices are collected three times a year by chambers of commerce, economic development organizations or university applied economic centers in each participating urban area. The numbers shown should be read as a percentage above or below the national average of 100. For example, a value of 115.4 in the groceries column indicates that grocery prices are 15.4% higher than the national average. Small differences in the index numbers should not be interpreted as significant; Figures cover the Brazoria County TX urban area.
Source: The Council for Community and Economic Research, ACCRA Cost of Living Index, 2017

Grocery Prices

Area[1]	T-Bone Steak ($/pound)	Frying Chicken ($/pound)	Whole Milk ($/half gal.)	Eggs ($/dozen)	Orange Juice ($/64 oz.)	Coffee ($/11.5 oz.)
City[2]	9.80	0.99	1.47	1.26	3.06	4.41
Avg.	11.29	1.40	2.02	1.47	3.55	4.37
Min.	7.71	0.93	1.04	0.70	2.86	3.24
Max.	15.83	2.39	4.03	3.92	6.29	8.16

*Note: (1) Values for the local area are compared with the average, minimum and maximum values for all 294 areas in the Cost of Living Index; (2) Figures cover the Brazoria County TX urban area; **T-Bone Steak** (price per pound); **Frying Chicken** (price per pound, whole fryer); **Whole Milk** (half gallon carton); **Eggs** (price per dozen, Grade A, large); **Orange Juice** (64 oz. Tropicana or Florida Natural); **Coffee** (11.5 oz. can, vacuum-packed, Maxwell House, Hills Bros, or Folgers).*
Source: The Council for Community and Economic Research, ACCRA Cost of Living Index, 2017

Housing and Utility Costs

Area[1]	New Home Price ($)	Apartment Rent ($/month)	All Electric ($/month)	Part Electric ($/month)	Other Energy ($/month)	Telephone ($/month)
City[2]	279,516	1,054	-	93.44	38.40	18.33
Avg.	335,956	1,047	175.01	97.34	67.93	28.71
Min.	187,788	491	109.48	49.33	35.44	12.39
Max.	1,739,087	4,559	432.62	227.09	353.33	44.61

*Note: (1) Values for the local area are compared with the average, minimum and maximum values for all 294 areas in the Cost of Living Index; (2) Figures cover the Brazoria County TX urban area; **New Home Price** (2,400 sf living area, 8,000 sf lot, in urban area with full utilities); **Apartment Rent** (950 sf 2 bedroom/1.5 or 2 bath, unfurnished, excluding all utilities except water); **All Electric** (average monthly cost for an all-electric home); **Part Electric** (average monthly cost for a part-electric home); **Other Energy** (average monthly cost for natural gas, fuel oil, coal, wood, and any other forms of energy except electricity); **Telephone** (price includes basic monthly rate for a private residential line plus additional local usage charges incurred by a family of four).*
Source: The Council for Community and Economic Research, ACCRA Cost of Living Index, 2017

Health Care, Transportation, and Other Costs

Area[1]	Doctor ($/visit)	Dentist ($/visit)	Optometrist ($/visit)	Gasoline ($/gallon)	Beauty Salon ($/visit)	Men's Shirt ($)
City[2]	110.52	96.61	102.00	2.02	33.50	37.83
Avg.	108.00	92.54	101.93	2.25	37.58	30.92
Min.	30.39	60.00	49.75	1.82	16.11	11.20
Max.	193.50	161.94	229.28	3.16	77.35	59.13

*Note: (1) Values for the local area are compared with the average, minimum and maximum values for all 294 areas in the Cost of Living Index; (2) Figures cover the Brazoria County TX urban area; **Doctor** (general practitioners routine exam of an established patient); **Dentist** (adult teeth cleaning and periodic oral examination); **Optometrist** (full vision eye exam for established adult patient); **Gasoline** (one gallon regular unleaded, national brand, including all taxes, cash price at self-service pump if available); **Beauty Salon** (woman's shampoo, trim, and blow-dry); **Men's Shirt** (cotton/polyester dress shirt, pinpoint weave, long sleeves).*
Source: The Council for Community and Economic Research, ACCRA Cost of Living Index, 2017

HOUSING

House Price Index (HPI)

Area	National Ranking[2]	Quarterly Change (%)	One-Year Change (%)	Five-Year Change (%)
MSA[1]	149	1.74	5.34	40.98
U.S.[3]	–	1.61	6.68	34.71

Note: The HPI is a weighted repeat sales index. It measures average price changes in repeat sales or refinancings on the same properties. This information is obtained by reviewing repeat mortgage transactions on single-family properties whose mortgages have been purchased or securitized by Fannie Mae or Freddie Mac in January 1975; (1) Figures cover the Houston-The Woodlands-Sugar Land, TX Metropolitan Statistical Area—see Appendix B for areas included; (2) Rankings are based on annual percentage change for all metro areas containing at least 15,000 transactions over the last 10 years and ranges from 1 to 253; (3) figures based on a weighted average of Census Division estimates using a seasonally adjusted, purchase-only index; all figures are for the period ending December 31, 2017
Source: Federal Housing Finance Agency, House Price Index, February 28, 2018

Median Single-Family Home Prices

Area	2015	2016	2017p	Percent Change 2016 to 2017
MSA[1]	213.4	217.4	231.1	6.3
U.S. Average	223.9	235.5	248.8	5.6

Note: Figures are median sales prices of existing single-family homes in thousands of dollars; (p) preliminary; (1) Figures cover the Houston-The Woodlands-Sugar Land, TX Metropolitan Statistical Area—see Appendix B for areas included
Source: National Association of Realtors, Median Sales Price of Existing Single-Family Homes for Metropolitan Areas, 4th Quarter 2017

Qualifying Income Based on Median Sales Price of Existing Single-Family Homes

Area	With 5% Down ($)	With 10% Down ($)	With 20% Down ($)
MSA[1]	51,547	48,834	43,408
U.S. Average	55,585	52,659	46,808

Note: Figures are preliminary; Qualifying income is based on a mortgage rate of 4.17%. Monthly principal and interest payment is limited to 25% of income; (1) Figures cover the Houston-The Woodlands-Sugar Land, TX Metropolitan Statistical Area—see Appendix B for areas included
Source: National Association of Realtors, Qualifying Income Based on Median Sales Price of Existing Single-Family Homes for Metropolitan Areas, 4th Quarter 2017

Median Apartment Condo-Coop Home Prices

Area	2015	2016	2017p	Percent Change 2016 to 2017
MSA[1]	149.6	150.8	160.3	6.3
U.S. Average	210.7	220.7	234.3	6.2

Note: Figures are median sales prices of existing apartment condo-coop homes in thousands of dollars; (p) preliminary; (1) Figures cover the Houston-The Woodlands-Sugar Land, TX Metropolitan Statistical Area—see Appendix B for areas included
Source: National Association of Realtors, Median Sales Price of Existing Apartment Condo-Coop Homes for Metropolitan Areas, 4th Quarter 2017

Home Value Distribution

Area	Under $50,000	$50,000 -$99,999	$100,000 -$149,999	$150,000 -$199,999	$200,000 -$299,999	$300,000 -$499,999	$500,000 -$999,999	$1,000,000 or more
City	2.6	4.6	20.2	13.1	21.2	28.8	8.3	1.2
MSA[1]	7.0	18.8	21.1	17.1	16.9	12.1	5.3	1.7
U.S.	8.8	14.8	15.3	14.9	18.4	16.4	9.0	2.5

Note: Figures are percentages and cover owner-occupied housing units; (1) Figures cover the Houston-The Woodlands-Sugar Land, TX Metropolitan Statistical Area—see Appendix B for areas included
Source: U.S. Census Bureau, 2012-2016 American Community Survey 5-Year Estimates

Homeownership Rate

Area	2009 (%)	2010 (%)	2011 (%)	2012 (%)	2013 (%)	2014 (%)	2015 (%)	2016 (%)	2017 (%)
MSA[1]	63.6	61.4	61.3	62.1	60.5	60.4	60.3	59.0	58.9
U.S.	67.4	66.9	66.1	65.4	65.1	64.5	63.7	63.4	63.9

Note: (1) Figures cover the Houston-The Woodlands-Sugar Land, TX Metropolitan Statistical Area—see Appendix B for areas included
Source: U.S. Census Bureau, Housing Vacancies and Homeownership Annual Statistics: 2009-2017

Year Housing Structure Built

Area	2010 or Later	2000 -2009	1990 -1999	1980 -1989	1970 -1979	1960 -1969	1950 -1959	1940 -1949	Before 1940	Median Year
City	5.1	22.6	18.9	14.8	27.1	10.4	0.9	0.1	0.1	1988
MSA[1]	5.6	23.9	14.8	15.7	18.8	9.1	6.7	2.8	2.7	1986
U.S.	2.3	14.7	14.0	13.7	15.6	10.9	10.6	5.2	13.0	1977

Note: Figures are percentages except for Median Year; Note: (1) Figures cover the Houston-The Woodlands-Sugar Land, TX Metropolitan Statistical Area—see Appendix B for areas included
Source: U.S. Census Bureau, 2012-2016 American Community Survey 5-Year Estimates

Gross Monthly Rent

Area	Under $500	$500 -$999	$1,000 -$1,499	$1,500 -$1,999	$2,000 -$2,499	$2,500 -$2,999	$3,000 and up	Median ($)
City	0.0	39.6	38.7	15.2	4.2	1.9	0.4	1,097
MSA[1]	5.2	49.7	30.4	10.1	2.7	1.0	1.0	955
U.S.	11.3	43.3	27.7	10.7	4.0	1.6	1.5	949

Note: Figures are percentages except for Median; Gross rent is the contract rent plus the estimated average monthly cost of utilities (electricity, gas, and water and sewer) and fuels (oil, coal, kerosene, wood, etc.) if these are paid by the renter (or paid for the renter by someone else); (1) Figures cover the Houston-The Woodlands-Sugar Land, TX Metropolitan Statistical Area—see Appendix B for areas included
Source: U.S. Census Bureau, 2012-2016 American Community Survey 5-Year Estimates

HEALTH

Health Risk Factors

Category	MSA[1] (%)	U.S. (%)
Adults aged 18–64 who have any kind of health care coverage	71.3	87.7
Adults who reported being in good or excellent health	82.6	83.6
Adults who are current smokers	12.6	17.1
Adults who currently use E-cigarettes	5.6	4.7
Adults who currently use chewing tobacco, snuff, or snus	3.5	4.0
Adults who are heavy drinkers[2]	6.1	6.5
Adults who are binge drinkers[3]	17.7	16.9
Adults who are overweight (BMI 25.0 - 29.9)	36.0	35.3
Adults who are obese (BMI 30.0 - 99.8)	29.5	29.9
Adults who participated in any physical activities in the past month	77.6	76.9
Adults who always or nearly always wears a seat belt	96.5	94.3

Note: (1) Figures cover the Houston-The Woodlands-Sugar Land, TX Metropolitan Statistical Area—see Appendix B for areas included; (2) Heavy drinkers are classified as adult men having more than 14 drinks per week and adult women having more than 7 drinks per week; (3) Binge drinkers are classified as males having five or more drinks on one occasion or females having four or more drinks on one occasion
Source: Centers for Disease Control and Prevention, Behaviorial Risk Factor Surveillance System, SMART: Selected Metropolitan Area Risk Trends, 2016

Health Screening Rates

Category	MSA[1] (%)	U.S. (%)
Adults 50-75 who have had a blood stool test within the past year	8.4	8.0
Adults 50-75 who have had a colonoscopy in the past 10 years	51.6	63.5
Adults aged 65+ who have had flu shot within the past year	55.0	58.6
Adults aged 65+ who have ever had a pneumonia vaccination	73.7	73.4
Adults who have ever been tested for HIV	42.3	35.6
Women aged 21-65 who have had a pap test in the past three years	76.8	79.8
Men aged 40+ who have had a PSA test within the past two years	40.9	39.5
Women aged 40+ who have had a mammogram within the past two years	67.7	72.5

Note: n/a not available; (1) Figures cover the Houston-The Woodlands-Sugar Land, TX Metropolitan Statistical Area—see Appendix B for areas included; Source: Centers for Disease Control and Prevention, Behaviorial Risk Factor Surveillance System, SMART: Selected Metropolitan Area Risk Trends, 2016

Chronic Health Conditions

Category	MSA[1] (%)	U.S. (%)
Adults who have ever been told they had a heart attack	3.8	4.4
Adults who have ever been told they have angina or coronary heart disease	4.3	4.1
Adults who have ever been told they had a stroke	n/a	3.1
Adults who have been told they currently have asthma	6.8	9.3
Adults who have ever been told they have arthritis	17.2	25.8
Adults who have ever been told they have diabetes[2]	9.6	10.5
Adults who have ever been told they had skin cancer	3.3	5.9
Adults who have ever been told they had any other types of cancer	6.6	6.7
Adults who have ever been told they have COPD	5.3	6.3
Adults who have ever been told they have kidney disease	3.5	2.8
Adults who have ever been told they have a form of depression	12.0	17.4

Note: n/a not available; (1) Figures cover the Houston-The Woodlands-Sugar Land, TX Metropolitan Statistical Area—see Appendix B for areas included; (2) Figures do not include pregnancy-related, borderline, or pre-diabetes
Source: Centers for Disease Control and Prevention, Behaviorial Risk Factor Surveillance System, SMART: Selected Metropolitan Area Risk Trends, 2016

Mortality Rates for the Top 10 Causes of Death in the U.S.

ICD-10[a] Sub-Chapter	ICD-10[a] Code	Age-Adjusted Mortality Rate[1] per 100,000 population	
		County[2]	U.S.
Malignant neoplasms	C00-C97	186.6	158.5
Ischaemic heart diseases	I20-I25	78.1	96.8
Other forms of heart disease	I30-I51	78.3	52.4
Chronic lower respiratory diseases	J40-J47	36.0	40.9
Cerebrovascular diseases	I60-I69	43.0	37.2
Organic, including symptomatic, mental disorders	F01-F09	45.9	33.3
Other degenerative diseases of the nervous system	G30-G31	33.1	32.1
Other external causes of accidental injury	W00-X59	25.6	31.2
Diabetes mellitus	E10-E14	14.3	21.1
Hypertensive diseases	I10-I15	22.6	20.8

Note: (a) ICD-10 = International Classification of Diseases 10th Revision; (1) Mortality rates are a three year average covering 2014-2016; (2) Figures cover Galveston County.
Source: Centers for Disease Control and Prevention, National Center for Health Statistics. Underlying Cause of Death 1999-2016 on CDC WONDER Online Database, released December 2017

Mortality Rates for Selected Causes of Death

ICD-10[a] Sub-Chapter	ICD-10[a] Code	Age-Adjusted Mortality Rate[1] per 100,000 population	
		County[2]	U.S.
Assault	X85-Y09	5.5	5.6
Diseases of the liver	K70-K76	19.9	14.0
Human immunodeficiency virus (HIV) disease	B20-B24	3.3	1.9
Influenza and pneumonia	J09-J18	11.8	14.6
Intentional self-harm	X60-X84	15.8	13.2
Malnutrition	E40-E46	Suppressed	1.3
Obesity and other hyperalimentation	E65-E68	Unreliable	2.1
Renal failure	N17-N19	20.5	13.0
Transport accidents	V01-V99	16.5	12.0
Viral hepatitis	B15-B19	3.0	1.9

Note: (a) ICD-10 = International Classification of Diseases 10th Revision; (1) Mortality rates are a three year average covering 2014-2016; (2) Figures cover Galveston County; Data are Suppressed when the data meet the criteria for confidentiality constraints; Mortality rates are flagged as Unreliable when the rate would be calculated with a numerator of 20 or less.
Source: Centers for Disease Control and Prevention, National Center for Health Statistics. Underlying Cause of Death 1999-2016 on CDC WONDER Online Database, released December 2017

Health Insurance Coverage

Area	With Health Insurance	With Private Health Insurance	With Public Health Insurance	Without Health Insurance	Population Under Age 18 Without Health Insurance
City	90.8	83.3	18.4	9.2	5.8
MSA[1]	80.1	60.5	26.1	19.9	11.0
U.S.	88.3	66.7	33.0	11.7	5.9

Note: Figures are percentages that cover the civilian noninstitutionalized population; (1) Figures cover the Houston-The Woodlands-Sugar Land, TX Metropolitan Statistical Area—see Appendix B for areas included
Source: U.S. Census Bureau, 2012-2016 American Community Survey 5-Year Estimates

Number of Medical Professionals

Area	MDs[3]	DOs[3,4]	Dentists	Podiatrists	Chiropractors	Optometrists
County[1] (number)	1,519	57	141	12	94	57
County[1] (rate[2])	472.8	17.7	42.8	3.6	28.5	17.3
U.S. (rate[2])	276.5	22.3	67.3	6.0	26.7	15.9

Note: Data as of 2016 unless noted; (1) Data covers Galveston County; (2) Rate per 100,000 population; (3) Data as of 2015 and includes all active, non-federal physicians; (4) Doctor of Osteopathic Medicine
Source: U.S. Department of Health and Human Services, Health Resources and Services Administration, Bureau of Health Professions, Area Resource File (ARF) 2016-2017

Best Hospitals

According to *U.S. News,* the Houston-The Woodlands-Sugar Land, TX metro area is home to six of the best hospitals in the U.S.: **Baylor St. Luke's Medical Center** (2 adult specialties); **Houston Methodist Hospital** (8 adult specialties); **Memorial Hermann-Texas Medical Center** (2 adult specialties and 1 pediatric specialty); **Menninger Clinic** (1 adult specialty); **TIRR Memorial Hermann** (1 adult specialty); **University of Texas MD Anderson Cancer Center** (3 adult specialties and 1 pediatric specialty). The hospitals listed were nationally ranked in at least one of 16 specialties. Only 152 hospitals nationwide were nationally ranked in one or more specialties. Twenty hospitals in the U.S. made the Honor Roll. The Best Hospitals Honor Roll was revamped last year to take both the national rankings and the procedure and condition ratings into account. Hospitals received points if they were nationally ranked in one of the 16 specialties—the higher they ranked, the more points they got—and how many ratings of "high performing" they earned in the nine procedures and conditions. *U.S. News Online, "America's Best Hospitals 2017-18"*

According to *U.S. News,* the Houston-The Woodlands-Sugar Land, TX metro area is home to three of the best children's hospitals in the U.S.: **Children's Memorial Hermann Hospital** (1 pediatric specialty); **Texas Children's Hospital** (Honor Roll/10 pediatric specialties); **Children's Cancer Hospital-University of Texas M.D. Anderson Cancer Center** (1 pediatric specialty). The hospitals listed were highly ranked in at least one of 10 pediatric specialties. Eighty-two children's hospitals in the U.S. were nationally ranked in at least one specialty. Hospitals received points for being ranked in a specialty, and the 10 hospitals with the most points across the 10 specialties make up the Honor Roll. *U.S. News Online, "America's Best Children's Hospitals 2017-18"*

EDUCATION

Public School District Statistics

District Name	Schls	Pupils	Pupil/ Teacher Ratio	Minority Pupils[1] (%)	Free Lunch Eligible[2] (%)	IEP[3] (%)
Clear Creek ISD	47	41,226	16.9	51.9	23.2	9.7
Friendswood ISD	7	6,133	16.6	26.3	6.9	9.0

Note: Table includes school districts with 100 or more students; (1) Percentage of students that are not non-Hispanic white; (2) Percentage of students that are eligible for the free lunch program; (3) Percentage of students that have an Individualized Education Program.
Source: U.S. Department of Education, National Center for Education Statistics, Common Core of Data, Local Education Agency (School District) Universe Survey: School Year 2015-2016; U.S. Department of Education, National Center for Education Statistics, Common Core of Data, Public Elementary/Secondary School Universe Survey: School Year 2015-2016

Highest Level of Education

Area	Less than H.S.	H.S. Diploma	Some College, No Deg.	Associate Degree	Bachelor's Degree	Master's Degree	Prof. School Degree	Doctorate Degree
City	4.9	16.0	21.9	9.2	31.5	12.0	2.7	1.7
MSA[1]	17.7	23.3	21.3	6.5	20.1	7.8	1.9	1.4
U.S.	13.0	27.5	21.0	8.2	18.8	8.2	2.0	1.3

Note: Figures cover persons age 25 and over; (1) Figures cover the Houston-The Woodlands-Sugar Land, TX Metropolitan Statistical Area—see Appendix B for areas included
Source: U.S. Census Bureau, 2012-2016 American Community Survey 5-Year Estimates

Educational Attainment by Race

Area	High School Graduate or Higher (%)					Bachelor's Degree or Higher (%)				
	Total	White	Black	Asian	Hisp.[2]	Total	White	Black	Asian	Hisp.[2]
City	95.1	96.0	97.0	86.6	89.2	48.0	47.8	54.5	56.6	43.8
MSA[1]	82.3	82.5	89.4	86.7	60.6	31.3	31.9	25.9	56.2	13.1
U.S.	87.0	88.9	84.3	86.3	65.7	30.3	31.6	20.0	52.1	14.7

Note: Figures shown cover persons 25 years old and over; (1) Figures cover the Houston-The Woodlands-Sugar Land, TX Metropolitan Statistical Area—see Appendix B for areas included; (2) People of Hispanic origin can be of any race
Source: U.S. Census Bureau, 2012-2016 American Community Survey 5-Year Estimates

School Enrollment by Grade and Control

Area	Preschool (%)		Kindergarten (%)		Grades 1 - 4 (%)		Grades 5 - 8 (%)		Grades 9 - 12 (%)	
	Public	Private	Public	Private	Public	Private	Public	Private	Public	Private
City	31.6	68.4	89.5	10.5	92.2	7.8	92.9	7.1	95.9	4.1
MSA[1]	58.9	41.1	90.0	10.0	92.8	7.2	93.4	6.6	93.4	6.6
U.S.	58.4	41.6	87.7	12.3	89.8	10.2	89.7	10.3	90.4	9.6

Note: Figures shown cover persons 3 years old and over; (1) Figures cover the Houston-The Woodlands-Sugar Land, TX Metropolitan Statistical Area—see Appendix B for areas included
Source: U.S. Census Bureau, 2012-2016 American Community Survey 5-Year Estimates

Average Salaries of Public School Classroom Teachers

Area	2015		2016		Change from 2015 to 2016	
	Dollars	Rank[1]	Dollars	Rank[1]	Percent	Rank[2]
Texas	50,713	28	51,890	27	2.3	8
U.S. Average	57,611	–	58,353	–	1.3	–

Note: (1) Rank ranges from 1 to 51 where 1 indicates highest salary; (2) Rank ranges from 1 to 51 where 1 indicates highest percent change.
Source: National Education Association, Rankings & Estimates: Rankings of the States 2016 and Estimates of School Statistics 2017

Higher Education

Four-Year Colleges			Two-Year Colleges			Medical Schools[1]	Law Schools[2]	Voc/ Tech[3]
Public	Private Non-profit	Private For-profit	Public	Private Non-profit	Private For-profit			
0	0	0	0	0	1	0	0	0

Note: Figures cover institutions located within the city limits and include main campuses only; (1) includes schools accredited by the Liaison Committee on Medical Education and the American Osteopathic Association's Commission on Osteopathic College Accreditation; (2) includes ABA-accredited schools, schools with provisional ABA accreditation, and state accredited schools; (3) includes all schools with programs that are less than 2 years.
Source: National Center for Education Statistics, Integrated Postsecondary Education System (IPEDS), 2016-17; Wikipedia, List of Medical Schools in the United States, accessed April 2, 2018; Wikipedia, List of Law Schools in the United States, accessed April 2, 2018

According to *U.S. News & World Report,* the Houston-The Woodlands-Sugar Land, TX metro area is home to two of the best national universities in the U.S.: **Rice University** (#14 tie); **University of Houston** (#192 tie). The indicators used to capture academic quality fall into a number of categories: assessment by administrators at peer institutions; retention of students; faculty resources; student selectivity; financial resources; alumni giving; high school counselor ratings of colleges; and graduation rate. *U.S. News & World Report, "America's Best Colleges 2018"*

According to *U.S. News & World Report,* the Houston-The Woodlands-Sugar Land, TX metro area is home to one of the top 100 law schools in the U.S.: **University of Houston** (#56 tie). The rankings are based on a weighted average of 12 measures of quality: peer assessment score; assessment score by lawyers/judges; median LSAT scores; median undergrad GPA; acceptance rate; employment rates for graduates; placement success; bar passage rate; faculty resources; expenditures per student; student/faculty ratio; and library resources. *U.S. News & World Report, "America's Best Graduate Schools, Law, 2019"*

According to *U.S. News & World Report,* the Houston-The Woodlands-Sugar Land, TX metro area is home to three of the top 75 medical schools for research in the U.S.: **Baylor College of Medicine** (#16); **University of Texas Health Science Center—Houston (McGovern)** (#52 tie); **University of Texas Medical Branch—Galveston** (#66 tie). The rankings are based on a weighted average of 11 measures of quality: quality assessment; peer assessment score; assessment score by residency directors; research activity; total research activity; average research activity per faculty member; student selectivity; median MCAT total score; median undergraduate GPA; acceptance rate; and faculty resources. *U.S. News & World Report, "America's Best Graduate Schools, Medical, 2019"*

According to *U.S. News & World Report,* the Houston-The Woodlands-Sugar Land, TX metro area is home to one of the top 75 business schools in the U.S.: **Rice University (Jones)** (#23 tie). The rankings are based on a weighted average of the following nine measures: quality assessment; peer assessment; recruiter assessment; placement success; mean starting salary and bonus; student selectivity; mean GMAT and GRE scores; mean undergraduate GPA; and acceptance rate. *U.S. News & World Report, "America's Best Graduate Schools, Business, 2019"*

PRESIDENTIAL ELECTION

2016 Presidential Election Results

Area	Clinton	Trump	Johnson	Stein	Other
Galveston County	35.5	60.0	3.3	0.7	0.5
U.S.	48.0	45.9	3.3	1.1	1.7

Note: Results are percentages and may not add to 100% due to rounding
Source: Dave Leip's Atlas of U.S. Presidential Elections

EMPLOYERS

Major Employers

Company Name	Industry
Christus Health Gulf Coast	Management consulting services
Conoco Phillips	Petroleum refining
Continental Airlines	Air trans scheduled
Dibellos Dynamic Orthotics & Prosthetics	Surgical appliances & supplies
El Paso E&P Company	Petroleum refining
F Charles Brunicardi MD	Accounting
Grey Wolf	Drilling oil & gas wells
Kellogg Brown &Root	Industrial plant construction
Mustang Engineers and Constructors	Construction management consultant
Philip Industrial Services	Environmental consultant
Philips Petroleum Company	Oil & gas exploration services
Quaker State Corp	Lubricating oils & greases
St Lukes Episcopal Health System	General medical & surgical hospitals
Texas Childrens Hospital	Specialty hosp, except psychiatric
The Methodist Hospital	General medical & surgical hospitals
Tracer Industries	Plumbing
Univ of Texas Medical Branch at Galveston	Accident & health insurance
University of Houston System	University
University of Texas System	General medical & surgical hospitals
US Dept of Veteran Affairs	Administration of veterans' affairs
Veterans Health Administration	Administration of veterans' affairs

Note: Companies shown are located within the Houston-The Woodlands-Sugar Land, TX Metropolitan Statistical Area.
Source: Hoovers.com; Wikipedia

PUBLIC SAFETY

Crime Rate

Area	All Crimes	Violent Crimes: Murder	Rape[3]	Robbery	Aggrav. Assault	Property Crimes: Burglary	Larceny -Theft	Motor Vehicle Theft
City	835.0	0.0	27.9	15.2	25.4	91.4	634.5	40.6
Metro[1]	3,502.0	7.2	39.9	215.5	315.6	548.2	2,035.1	340.5
U.S.	2,847.8	5.3	40.4	102.8	248.5	468.9	1,745.0	236.9

Note: Figures are crimes per 100,000 population; (1) Figures cover the Houston-The Woodlands-Sugar Land, TX Metropolitan Statistical Area—see Appendix B for areas included; (3) The city and U.S. figures shown were reported using the revised Uniform Crime Reporting (UCR) definition of rape. The metro area figures shown are an aggregate total of the data submitted using both the revised and legacy UCR definitions.
Source: FBI Uniform Crime Reports, 2016

Hate Crimes

Area	Number of Quarters Reported	Number of Incidents per Bias Motivation: Race/Ethnicity/ Ancestry	Religion	Sexual Orientation	Disability	Gender	Gender Identity
City	4	0	0	0	0	0	0
U.S.	4	3,489	1,273	1,076	70	31	124

Source: Federal Bureau of Investigation, Hate Crime Statistics 2016

Identity Theft Consumer Reports

Area	Reports	Reports per 100,000 Population	Rank[2]
MSA[1]	9,180	136	31
U.S.	371,061	114	-

Note: (1) Figures cover the Houston-The Woodlands-Sugar Land, TX Metropolitan Statistical Area—see Appendix B for areas included; (2) Rank ranges from 1 to 389 where 1 indicates greatest number of identity theft reports per 100,000 population
Source: Federal Trade Commission, Consumer Sentinel Network Data Book for January–December 2017

Fraud and Other Consumer Reports

Area	Reports	Reports per 100,000 Population	Rank[2]
MSA[1]	34,244	506	110
U.S.	2,304,550	708	-

Note: (1) Figures cover the Houston-The Woodlands-Sugar Land, TX Metropolitan Statistical Area—see Appendix B for areas included; (2) Rank ranges from 1 to 389 where 1 indicates greatest number of fraud and other consumer reports per 100,000 population
Source: Federal Trade Commission, Consumer Sentinel Network Data Book for January–December 2017

SPORTS

Professional Sports Teams

Team Name	League	Year Established
Houston Astros	Major League Baseball (MLB)	1962
Houston Dynamo	Major League Soccer (MLS)	2006
Houston Rockets	National Basketball Association (NBA)	1971
Houston Texans	National Football League (NFL)	2002

Note: Includes teams located in the Houston-The Woodlands-Sugar Land, TX Metropolitan Statistical Area.
Source: Wikipedia, Major Professional Sports Teams of the United States and Canada, April 5, 2018

CLIMATE

Average and Extreme Temperatures

Temperature	Jan	Feb	Mar	Apr	May	Jun	Jul	Aug	Sep	Oct	Nov	Dec	Yr.
Extreme High (°F)	84	91	91	95	97	103	104	107	102	94	89	83	107
Average High (°F)	61	65	73	79	85	91	93	93	89	81	72	65	79
Average Temp. (°F)	51	54	62	69	75	81	83	83	79	70	61	54	69
Average Low (°F)	41	43	51	58	65	71	73	73	68	58	50	43	58
Extreme Low (°F)	12	20	22	31	44	52	62	62	48	32	19	7	7

Note: Figures cover the years 1969-1990
Source: National Climatic Data Center, International Station Meteorological Climate Summary, 9/96

Average Precipitation/Snowfall/Humidity

Precip./Humidity	Jan	Feb	Mar	Apr	May	Jun	Jul	Aug	Sep	Oct	Nov	Dec	Yr.
Avg. Precip. (in.)	3.3	2.7	3.3	3.3	5.6	4.9	3.7	3.7	4.8	4.7	3.7	3.3	46.9
Avg. Snowfall (in.)	Tr	Tr	0	0	0	0	0	0	0	0	Tr	Tr	Tr
Avg. Rel. Hum. 6am (%)	85	86	87	89	91	92	93	93	93	91	89	86	90
Avg. Rel. Hum. 3pm (%)	58	55	54	54	57	56	55	55	57	53	55	57	55

Note: Figures cover the years 1969-1990; Tr = Trace amounts (<0.05 in. of rain; <0.5 in. of snow)
Source: National Climatic Data Center, International Station Meteorological Climate Summary, 9/96

Weather Conditions

Temperature			Daytime Sky			Precipitation		
32°F & below	45°F & below	90°F & above	Clear	Partly cloudy	Cloudy	0.01 inch or more precip.	0.1 inch or more snow/ice	Thunder-storms
21	87	96	83	167	115	101	1	62

Note: Figures are average number of days per year and cover the years 1969-1990
Source: National Climatic Data Center, International Station Meteorological Climate Summary, 9/96

HAZARDOUS WASTE

Superfund Sites

The Houston-The Woodlands-Sugar Land, TX metro area is home to 21 sites on the EPA's Superfund National Priorities List: **Conroe Creosoting Co.** (final); **Crystal Chemical Co.** (final); **French, Ltd.** (final); **Geneva Industries/Fuhrmann Energy** (final); **Gulfco Marine Maintenance** (final); **Highlands Acid Pit** (final); **Jones Road Ground Water Plume** (final); **Malone Service Co - Swan Lake Plant** (final); **Many Diversified Interests, Inc.** (final); **Motco, Inc.** (final); **North Cavalcade Street** (final); **Patrick Bayou** (final); **Petro-chemical Systems, Inc. (Turtle Bayou)** (final); **San Jacinto River Waste Pits** (final); **Sheridan Disposal Services** (final); **Sikes Disposal Pits** (final); **Sol Lynn/Industrial Transformers** (final); **South Cavalcade Street** (final); **Tex-tin Corp.** (final); **United Creosoting Co.** (final); **US Oil Recovery** (final). There are a total of 1,396 Superfund sites with a status of proposed or final on the list in the U.S.
U.S. Environmental Protection Agency, National Priorities List, April 4, 2018

AIR & WATER QUALITY

Air Quality Trends: Ozone

	1990	1995	2000	2005	2010	2012	2013	2014	2015	2016
MSA[1]	0.119	0.114	0.102	0.087	0.079	0.080	0.075	0.064	0.083	0.066
U.S.	0.087	0.089	0.081	0.079	0.073	0.075	0.069	0.067	0.068	0.069

Note: (1) Data covers the Houston-The Woodlands-Sugar Land, TX Metropolitan Statistical Area—see Appendix B for areas included. The values shown are the composite ozone concentration averages among trend sites based on the highest fourth daily maximum 8-hour concentration in parts per million. These trends are based on sites having an adequate record of monitoring data during the trend period. Data from exceptional events are included.
Source: U.S. Environmental Protection Agency, Air Quality Monitoring Information, "Air Quality Trends by City, 1990-2016"

Air Quality Index

Area	Percent of Days when Air Quality was...[2]					AQI Statistics[2]	
	Good	Moderate	Unhealthy for Sensitive Groups	Unhealthy	Very Unhealthy	Maximum	Median
MSA[1]	50.4	42.7	6.0	0.8	0.0	177	50

Note: (1) Data covers the Houston-The Woodlands-Sugar Land, TX Metropolitan Statistical Area—see Appendix B for areas included; (2) Based on 365 days with AQI data in 2017. Air Quality Index (AQI) is an index for reporting daily air quality. EPA calculates the AQI for five major air pollutants regulated by the Clean Air Act: ground-level ozone, particle pollution (aka particulate matter), carbon monoxide, sulfur dioxide, and nitrogen dioxide. The AQI runs from 0 to 500. The higher the AQI value, the greater the level of air pollution and the greater the health concern. There are six AQI categories: "Good" AQI is between 0 and 50. Air quality is considered satisfactory; "Moderate" AQI is between 51 and 100. Air quality is acceptable; "Unhealthy for Sensitive Groups" When AQI values are between 101 and 150, members of sensitive groups may experience health effects; "Unhealthy" When AQI values are between 151 and 200 everyone may begin to experience health effects; "Very Unhealthy" AQI values between 201 and 300 trigger a health alert; "Hazardous" AQI values over 300 trigger warnings of emergency conditions (not shown).
Source: U.S. Environmental Protection Agency, Air Quality Index Report, 2017

Air Quality Index Pollutants

Area	Percent of Days when AQI Pollutant was...[2]					
	Carbon Monoxide	Nitrogen Dioxide	Ozone	Sulfur Dioxide	Particulate Matter 2.5	Particulate Matter 10
MSA[1]	0.0	4.4	47.4	0.0	47.9	0.3

Note: (1) Data covers the Houston-The Woodlands-Sugar Land, TX Metropolitan Statistical Area—see Appendix B for areas included; (2) Based on 365 days with AQI data in 2017. The Air Quality Index (AQI) is an index for reporting daily air quality. EPA calculates the AQI for five major air pollutants regulated by the Clean Air Act: ground-level ozone, particle pollution (also known as particulate matter), carbon monoxide, sulfur dioxide, and nitrogen dioxide. The AQI runs from 0 to 500. The higher the AQI value, the greater the level of air pollution and the greater the health concern.
Source: U.S. Environmental Protection Agency, Air Quality Index Report, 2017

Maximum Air Pollutant Concentrations: Particulate Matter, Ozone, CO and Lead

	Particulate Matter 10 (ug/m^3)	Particulate Matter 2.5 Wtd AM (ug/m^3)	Particulate Matter 2.5 24-Hr (ug/m^3)	Ozone (ppm)	Carbon Monoxide (ppm)	Lead (ug/m^3)
MSA[1] Level	81	10.1	23	0.079	2	0
NAAQS[2]	150	15	35	0.075	9	0.15
Met NAAQS[2]	Yes	Yes	Yes	No	Yes	Yes

Note: (1) Data covers the Houston-The Woodlands-Sugar Land, TX Metropolitan Statistical Area—see Appendix B for areas included; Data from exceptional events are included; (2) National Ambient Air Quality Standards; ppm = parts per million; ug/m^3 = micrograms per cubic meter; n/a not available.
Concentrations: Particulate Matter 10 (coarse particulate)—highest second maximum 24-hour concentration; Particulate Matter 2.5 Wtd AM (fine particulate)—highest weighted annual mean concentration; Particulate Matter 2.5 24-Hour (fine particulate)—highest 98th percentile 24-hour concentration; Ozone—highest fourth daily maximum 8-hour concentration; Carbon Monoxide—highest second maximum non-overlapping 8-hour concentration; Lead—maximum running 3-month average
Source: U.S. Environmental Protection Agency, Air Quality Monitoring Information, "Air Quality Statistics by City, 2016"

Maximum Air Pollutant Concentrations: Nitrogen Dioxide and Sulfur Dioxide

	Nitrogen Dioxide AM (ppb)	Nitrogen Dioxide 1-Hr (ppb)	Sulfur Dioxide AM (ppb)	Sulfur Dioxide 1-Hr (ppb)	Sulfur Dioxide 24-Hr (ppb)
MSA[1] Level	14	54	n/a	23	n/a
NAAQS[2]	53	100	30	75	140
Met NAAQS[2]	Yes	Yes	n/a	Yes	n/a

Note: (1) Data covers the Houston-The Woodlands-Sugar Land, TX Metropolitan Statistical Area—see Appendix B for areas included; Data from exceptional events are included; (2) National Ambient Air Quality Standards; ppm = parts per million; ug/m^3 = micrograms per cubic meter; n/a not available.
Concentrations: Nitrogen Dioxide AM—highest arithmetic mean concentration; Nitrogen Dioxide 1-Hr—highest 98th percentile 1-hour daily maximum concentration; Sulfur Dioxide AM—highest annual mean concentration; Sulfur Dioxide 1-Hr—highest 99th percentile 1-hour daily maximum concentration; Sulfur Dioxide 24-Hr—highest second maximum 24-hour concentration
Source: U.S. Environmental Protection Agency, Air Quality Monitoring Information, "Air Quality Statistics by City, 2016"

Drinking Water

Water System Name	Pop. Served	Primary Water Source Type	Violations[1]	
			Health Based	Monitoring/ Reporting
City of Friendswood	37,921	Purchased Surface	0	0

Note: (1) Based on violation data from January 1, 2017 to December 31, 2017
Source: U.S. Environmental Protection Agency, Office of Ground Water and Drinking Water, Safe Drinking Water Information System (based on data extracted April 5, 2018)

Keller, Texas

Background

Located in north Central Texas, Keller retains its country feel while located only a short commute from both Dallas and Fort Worth. The town was established in 1881 during the rapid development of the railroad service through the area, and was named after John C. Keller, a foreman on the railroad.

While Keller's residents were originally farmers, the arrival of the railroad helped develop the city into a successful trade center where a number of businesses flourished. Many of the buildings housing those original businesses still stand today in the Old Town Keller area of the city. The city has improved the historic area with pedestrian walkways, landscaping, lighting areas, and renovated facades. The renovations continue to attract local business such as tea rooms, specialty shops, and cafes, creating a vibrant historic district.

In addition to Old Town, there is the Keller Town Center, which is located in a park-like setting of lakes, walking paths, and open green land. The Town Center's infrastructure was created through a public-private partnership between the City of Keller and TriWest Enterprises. Through the partnership, the Keller Town Hall, Town Hall Plaza and Keller Independent School District's Natatorium are incorporated with private businesses and homes in the form of detached villas, luxury rental housing, ground floor retail with office lofts above, restaurants, and an entertainment venue, all combining to create a bustling downtown.

The forward-looking city has also gone high-tech. Keller was the first city in the country to receive Verizon's new Fiber to the Premises (FTTP) technology which was made available to individual homeowners and businesses through the community. The FTTP wiring, in its most basic form, is three-times faster than the fastest broadband technology offered today.

The technology is not only found in the businesses and the homes of the residents of Keller, but also in the Keller Public Library, where there is wireless Internet access for patrons throughout the 22,000-foot facility.

If residents are looking to enjoy the warm Texas climate, with summer temperatures hovering in the high 80s, they can visit any number of the 11 park sites and 16 miles of hike and bike trails that meander throughout the city. The city's Keller Point is a 87,000-square foot fitness, aquatic and recreation center, with indoor and outdoor pools, fitness facilities, and meeting rooms for all residents.

The city is part of the Keller Independent School District, which encompasses six cities with campuses including: four high schools, six intermediate schools, six middle schools and 23 elementary schools, which serve more than 31,000 students. Due to its proximity to two major Texas cities, Keller is also close to some of the top universities in the state, including Southern Methodist University, Texas Christian University, University of North Texas and University of Texas at Dallas.

The city is served by the Dallas/Fort Worth Airport, which is about 15 miles away.

Rankings

General Rankings

- *US News & World Report* conducted a survey of more than 2,000 people and analyzed the 125 largest metropolitan areas to determine what matters the most when selecting the next place to live. Dallas* ranked #18 out of the top 25 as having the best combination of desirable factors. Criteria: cost of living; quality of education; job market, crime rates; and other factors. *realestate.usnews.com, "The 25 Best Places to Live in the U.S. in 2018," April 10, 2018*

- The Fort Worth* metro area was identified as one of America's fastest-growing areas in terms of population and economy by *Forbes*. The area ranked #5 out of 25. The 100 most populous metro areas in the U.S. were evaluated on the following criteria: estimated population growth; employment; economic output; wages; home values. *Forbes, "America's Fastest-Growing Cities 2018," February 28, 2018*

- Fort Worth* was identified as one of America's fastest-growing cities in terms of population growth by CNNMoney.com. The area ranked #9 out of 10. Criteria: population growth between July 2015 and July 2016; cities and towns with populations of 50,000. *CNNMoney, "10 Fastest-Growing Cities," June 2, 2017*

Business/Finance Rankings

- According to *Business Insider*, the Dallas* metro area is where startup growth is on the rise. Based on the 2017 Kauffman Index of Growth Entrepreneurship, which measured in-depth national entrepreneurial trends in 40 metro areas, it ranked #11 in highest startup growth. *www.businessinsider.com, "The 21 U.S. Cities with the Highest Startup Growth," October 21, 2017*

- The personal finance site NerdWallet analyzed 183 American metropolitan areas with populations over 250,000 and more than 15,000 businesses to rank where entrepreneurs find the most success. Criteria included area economy, annual income, housing cost, unemployment rate, and the success rate of area businesses. Fort Worth* ranked #117. *www.nerdwallet.com, "Best Places to Start a Business," April 27, 2015*

- USAA and Hiring Our Heroes worked with Sperlings's BestPlaces and the Institute for Veterans and Military Families at Syracuse University to rank major metropolitan areas where military-skills-related employment is strongest. Criteria for *mid-career* veterans included veteran wage growth; recent job growth; stability; and accessible health resources. Metro areas with a higher than national average crime or unemployment rate were excluded. At #9, the Dallas* metro area made the top ten. *www.usaa.com, "2015 Best Places for Veterans"*

- Based on metro area social media reviews, the employment opinion group Glassdoor surveyed 50 of the largest U.S. metro areas and equally weighed cost of living, hiring opportunity, and job satisfaction to compose a list of "25 Best Cities for Jobs." Median pay and home value, in-demand jobs and number of current job openings was also factored in. The Dallas* metro area was ranked #25 in overall job satisfaction. *www.glassdoor.com, "Best Cities for Jobs," September 12, 2017*

- In a survey of economic confidence in the nation's 50 largest metropolitan areas conducted January–December 2014, the Dallas* metro area placed #14, according to Gallup's 2014 Economic Confidence Index. *Gallup, "San Jose and San Francisco Lead in Economic Confidence," March 19, 2015*

- The Brookings Institution ranked the 100 largest metro areas in the U.S. based on income inequality. Dallas* was ranked #60 (#1 = greatest ineqality). Criteria: the "95/20 ratio," a figure representing the income at which a household earns more than 95 percent of all other households, divided by the income at which a household earns more than only 20 percent of all other households. *Brookings Institution, "Household Income Inequality, 100 Largest U.S. Metro Areas, 2014-2016," February 5, 2018*

- *Forbes* ranked the 100 largest metro areas in the U.S. in terms of the "Best Cities for Young Professionals." The Dallas* metro area ranked #5 out of 25. (Large metro areas were divided into metro divisions.) Criteria: median rent of a two-bedroom apartment; job growth and unemployment rate; median salary of college graduates with 5 or less years of work experience; networking opportunities; social outlook; percentage of population 25 years of age and older with college degrees. *Forbes.com, "America's 25 Best Cities for Young Professionals in 2017," May 22, 2017*
- Payscale.com ranked the largest metro areas in terms of wage growth. The Dallas* metro area ranked #28. Criteria: private-sector wage growth between the 4th quarter of 2016 and the 4th quarter of 2017. *PayScale, "Wage Trends by Metro Area-4th Quarter," January 17, 2018*
- The Dallas* metro area was identified as one of the most debt-ridden places in America by the finance site Credit.com. The metro area was ranked #2. Criteria: residents' average credit card debt as well as median income. *Credit.com, "25 Cities With the Most Credit Card Debt," February 28, 2018*
- Dallas* was identified as one of America's most frugal metro areas by *Coupons.com.* The city ranked #2 out of 25. Criteria: digital coupon usage. *Coupons.com, "America's Most Frugal Cities of 2017," March 22, 2018*
- Dallas* was cited as one of America's top metros for new and expanded facility projects in 2017. The area ranked #3 in the large metro area category (population over 1 million). *Site Selection, "Top Metropolitans of 2017," March 2018*
- The Fort Worth* metro area appeared on the Milken Institute "2017 Best Performing Cities" list. Rank: #60 out of 200 large metro areas. Criteria: job growth; wage and salary growth; high-tech output growth. *Milken Institute, "Best-Performing Cities 2017," January 2018*
- *Forbes* ranked the 200 most populous metro areas to determine the nation's "Best Places for Business and Careers." The Fort Worth* metro area was ranked #38. Criteria: costs (business and living); job growth (past and projected); income growth; quality of life; educational attainment (college and high school); projected economic growth; cultural and recreational opportunities; net migration patterns; number of highly ranked colleges. *Forbes, "The Best Places for Business and Careers 2017," October 24, 2017*

Education Rankings

- Personal finance website *WalletHub* analyzed the 150 largest U.S. metropolitan statistical areas to determine where the most educated Americans are choosing to settle. Criteria: education quality and attainment gap; education levels; percentage of workers with degrees; public school rankings; quality and size of each metro area's universities. Dallas* was ranked #70 (#1 = most educated city). *www.WalletHub.com, "2017's Most and Least Educated Cities in America, " July 25, 2017*

Environmental Rankings

- Sperling's BestPlaces assessed 379 metropolitan areas of the United States for the likelihood of dangerously extreme weather events or earthquakes. In general the Southeast and South-Central regions have the highest risk of weather extremes and earthquakes, while the Pacific Northwest enjoys the lowest risk. Of the least risky metropolitan areas, the Fort Worth* metro area was ranked #371. *www.bestplaces.net, "Safest Places from Natural Disasters," April 2011*
- The U.S. Environmental Protection Agency (EPA) released a list of U.S. metropolitan areas with the most ENERGY STAR certified buildings in 2016. The Dallas* metro area was ranked #6 out of 25. *U.S. Environmental Protection Agency, "2017 Energy Star Top Cities," June 2017*
- Dallas* was highlighted as one of the 25 most ozone-polluted metro areas in the U.S. during 2013 through 2015. The area ranked #13. *American Lung Association, State of the Air 2017*

Health/Fitness Rankings

- For each of the 50 most populous metro areas in the United States, the American College of Sports Medicine's American Fitness Index evaluated infrastructure, community assets, and policies that encourage healthy and fit lifestyles, including preventive health behaviors, levels of chronic disease conditions, health care access, and community resources and policies that support physical activity. The Dallas* metro area ranked #38 for "community fitness." *www.americanfitnessindex.org, "ACSM American Fitness Index Health and Community Fitness Status of the 50 Largest Metropolitan Areas," May 2017*
- The Dallas* metro area was identified as one of the worst cities for bed bugs in America by pest control company Orkin. The area ranked #10 out of 50 based on the number of bed bug treatments Orkin performed from December 2016 to November 2017. *Orkin, "Baltimore and Washington D.C. Continue to Hold Top Spots," January 8, 2018*
- Dallas* was identified as a "2016 Spring Allergy Capital." The area ranked #27 out of 100. Three groups of factors were used to identify the most severe cities for people with allergies during the spring season: annual pollen levels; medicine utilization; access to board-certified allergists. *Asthma and Allergy Foundation of America, "Spring Allergy Capitals 2016"*
- Dallas* was identified as a "2016 Fall Allergy Capital." The area ranked #23 out of 100. Three groups of factors were used to identify the most severe cities for people with allergies during the fall season: annual pollen levels; medicine utilization; access to board-certified allergists. *Asthma and Allergy Foundation of America, "Fall Allergy Capitals 2016"*
- Dallas* was identified as a "2015 Asthma Capital." The area ranked #39 out of the nation's 100 largest metropolitan areas. Criteria: estimated prevalence; self-reported prevalence; crude death rate for asthma; annual pollen score; annual air quality; public smoking laws; number of board-certified asthma specialists; school inhaler access laws; rescue medication use; controller medication use; ER visits for asthma; uninsured rate; poverty rate. *Asthma and Allergy Foundation of America, "Asthma Capitals 2015"*
- The Dallas* metro area ranked #47 out of 189 in The Gallup-Healthways Well-Being Index. Criteria: purpose; social well being; financial health; community and physical health. Results are based on telephone interviews with adults, aged 18 and older, living in metropolitan areas in the 50 U.S. states and the District of Columbia. *Gallup-Healthways, "State of American Well-Being, 2017 Community Well-Being Rankings" March 2018*

Real Estate Rankings

- FitSmallBusiness looked at 50 of the largest metropolitan areas in the U.S. to determine which metro was the best to start a real estate business. Data was compiled from such sources as: Zillow, Trulia, U.S. Census Bureau, and the Bureau of Labor Statistics. Criteria: location; inventory; annual wages; median sales price of homes; days on the market; median price cut percentage; and other factors that would influence real estate professional growth. The Dallas* metro area ranked #19. *fitsmallbusiness.com, "The Best Cities to Become a Real Estate Agent in 2018," January 30, 2018*
- According to Penske Truck Rental, the Dallas* metro area was named the #3 moving destination in 2017, based on one-way consumer truck rental reservations made through Penske's website, rental locations, and reservations call center. *blog.gopenske.com, "Penske Truck Rental's 2017 Top Moving Destinations List," January 22, 2018*
- The Dallas* metro area appeared on Realtor.com's list of the hottest housing markets to watch in 2018. The area ranked #2. Criteria: existing homes inventory and price; new home construction; median household incomes; local economy/population trends. *Realtor.com®, "The 6 Hottest Real Estate Markets to Watch in 2018," January 5, 2018*
- The Dallas* metro area was identified as one of the nations's 20 hottest housing markets in 2018. Criteria: listing views as an indicator of demand and median days on the market as an indicator of supply. The area ranked #12. *Realtor.com, "The 20 Hottest Real Estate Markets for February 2018," March 1, 2018*

- The Fort Worth* metro area was identified as one of the top 20 housing markets to invest in for 2018 by *Forbes*. The area ranked #9. Criteria: strong job and population growth; anticipated home price appreciation; and other factors. *Forbes.com, "Where to Invest in Housing in 2018," February 1, 2018*

- Fort Worth* was ranked #15 in the top 20 out of 265 metro areas in terms of house price appreciation in 2017 (#1 = highest rate). *Federal Housing Finance Agency, House Price Index, 4th Quarter 2017. February 27, 2018*

- Fort Worth* was ranked #157 out of 238 metro areas in terms of housing affordability in 2017 by the National Association of Home Builders (#1 = most affordable). Criteria: the share of homes sold in that area affordable to a family earning the local median income, based on standard mortgage underwriting criteria. *National Association of Home Builders®, NAHB-Wells Fargo Housing Opportunity Index, 4th Quarter 2017*

Safety Rankings

- Keller was identified as one of the safest cities in America by NeighborhoodScout. The city ranked #16 out of 100 (100 = safest). Criteria: number of violent and property crimes per 1,000 residents. The editors only considered cities with 25,000 or more residents. *NeighborhoodScout, "Top 100 Safest Cities in the U.S. 2018" January 2, 2018*

- The National Insurance Crime Bureau ranked 382 metro areas in the U.S. in terms of per capita rates of vehicle theft. The Dallas* metro area ranked #87 (#1 = highest rate). Criteria: number of vehicle theft offenses per 100,000 inhabitants in 2016. *National Insurance Crime Bureau, "Hot Spots 2016," June 8, 2017*

Seniors/Retirement Rankings

- From its Best Cities for Successful Aging indexes, the Milken Institute generated rankings for metropolitan areas, weighing data in nine categories—health care, wellness, living arrangements, transportation and convenience, financial characteristics, education, employment, community engagement, and overall livability. The Dallas* metro area was ranked #25 overall in the large metro area category. *Milken Institute, "Best Cities for Successful Aging, 2017" March 14, 2017*

Sports/Recreation Rankings

- According to the personal finance website NerdWallet, the Dallas* metro area, at #1, is one of the nation's top dozen metro areas for sports fans. Criteria included the presence of all four major sports—MLB, NFL, NHL, and NBA, fan enthusiasm (as measured by game attendance), ticket affordability, and "sports culture," that is, number of sports bars. *www.nerdwallet.com, "Best Cities for Sports Fans," May 5, 2013*

Women/Minorities Rankings

- The *Houston Chronicle* listed the Dallas* metro area as #7 in top places for young Latinos to live in the U.S. Research was largely based on housing and occupational data from the largest metropolitan areas performed by *Forbes* and NBC Universo. Criteria: percentage of 18-34 year-olds; Latino college grad rates; and diversity. *blog.chron.com, "The 15 Best Big Cities for Latino Millenials," January 26, 2016*

Miscellaneous Rankings

- The watchdog site Charity Navigator conducts an annual study of charities in the nation's major markets both to analyze statistical differences in their financial, accountability, and transparency practices and to track year-to-year variations in individual philanthropic communities. Charity Navigator's analysis demonstrated that the financial, accountability and transparency behaviors of America's largest charities can be influenced by the metropolitan market within which the charity operates. The Dallas* metro area was ranked #5 among the 30 metro markets in the rating category of Overall Score. *www.charitynavigator.org, "2017 Metro Market Study," May 1, 2017*

- The Harris Poll's Happiness Index survey revealed that of the top ten U.S. markets, the Fort Worth* metro area residents ranked #1 in happiness. Criteria included strong assent to positive statements and strong disagreement with negative ones, and degree of agreement with a series of statements about respondents' personal relationships and general outlook. *www.theharrispoll.com, "Dallas/Fort Worth Is "Happiest" City among America's Top Ten Markets," September 4, 2013*
- The National Alliance to End Homelessness listed the 25 most populous metro areas with the highest rate of homelessness. The Dallas* metro area had a high rate of homelessness. Criteria: number of homeless people per 10,000 population in 2016. *National Alliance to End Homelessness, "Homelessness in the 25 Most Populous U.S. Metro Areas," September 1, 2017*

*Keller is located within the Dallas-Fort Worth-Arlington, TX Metropolitan Statistical Area and the Fort Worth-Arlington, TX Metropolitan Division.

Business Environment

CITY FINANCES

City Government Finances

Component	2015 ($000)	2015 ($ per capita)
Total Revenues	73,407	1,604
Total Expenditures	61,723	1,349
Debt Outstanding	101,666	2,222
Cash and Securities[1]	85,477	1,868

Note: (1) Cash and security holdings of a government at the close of its fiscal year,, including those of its dependent agencies, utilities, and liquor stores.
Source: U.S Census Bureau, State & Local Government Finances 2015

City Government Revenue by Source

Source	2015 ($000)	2015 ($ per capita)	2015 (%)
General Revenue			
From Federal Government	0	0	0.0
From State Government	3,422	75	4.7
From Local Governments	2,199	48	3.0
Taxes			
Property	22,726	497	31.0
Sales and Gross Receipts	12,727	278	17.3
Personal Income	0	0	0.0
Corporate Income	0	0	0.0
Motor Vehicle License	0	0	0.0
Other Taxes	1,462	32	2.0
Current Charges	11,914	260	16.2
Liquor Store	0	0	0.0
Utility	15,792	345	21.5
Employee Retirement	0	0	0.0

Source: U.S Census Bureau, State & Local Government Finances 2015

City Government Expenditures by Function

Function	2015 ($000)	2015 ($ per capita)	2015 (%)
General Direct Expenditures			
Air Transportation	0	0	0.0
Corrections	0	0	0.0
Education	0	0	0.0
Employment Security Administration	0	0	0.0
Financial Administration	2,442	53	4.0
Fire Protection	7,489	163	12.1
General Public Buildings	589	12	1.0
Governmental Administration, Other	1,493	32	2.4
Health	0	0	0.0
Highways	7,848	171	12.7
Hospitals	0	0	0.0
Housing and Community Development	0	0	0.0
Interest on General Debt	4,351	95	7.0
Judicial and Legal	596	13	1.0
Libraries	1,440	31	2.3
Parking	0	0	0.0
Parks and Recreation	6,126	133	9.9
Police Protection	8,816	192	14.3
Public Welfare	0	0	0.0
Sewerage	3,600	78	5.8
Solid Waste Management	0	0	0.0
Veterans' Services	0	0	0.0
Liquor Store	0	0	0.0
Utility	12,430	271	20.1
Employee Retirement	0	0	0.0

Source: U.S Census Bureau, State & Local Government Finances 2015

DEMOGRAPHICS

Population Growth

Area	1990 Census	2000 Census	2010 Census	2016* Estimate	Population Growth (%)	
					1990-2016	2010-2016
City	13,683	27,345	39,627	44,250	223.4	11.7
MSA[1]	3,989,294	5,161,544	6,371,773	6,957,123	74.4	9.2
U.S.	248,709,873	281,421,906	308,745,538	318,558,162	28.1	3.2

Note: (1) Figures cover the Dallas-Fort Worth-Arlington, TX Metropolitan Statistical Area—see Appendix B for areas included; (*) 2012-2016 5-year estimated population
Source: U.S. Census Bureau, 1990 Census, Census 2000, Census 2010, 2012-2016 American Community Survey 5-Year Estimates

Household Size

Area	Persons in Household (%)							Average Household Size
	One	Two	Three	Four	Five	Six	Seven or More	
City	14.8	32.7	19.3	20.2	9.9	2.2	0.9	3.00
MSA[1]	24.9	30.8	16.7	15.3	7.5	3.0	1.8	2.80
U.S.	27.7	33.7	15.7	13.1	6.0	2.3	1.5	2.60

Note: (1) Figures cover the Dallas-Fort Worth-Arlington, TX Metropolitan Statistical Area—see Appendix B for areas included
Source: U.S. Census Bureau, 2012-2016 American Community Survey 5-Year Estimates

Race

Area	White Alone[2] (%)	Black Alone[2] (%)	Asian Alone[2] (%)	AIAN[3] Alone[2] (%)	NHOPI[4] Alone[2] (%)	Other Race Alone[2] (%)	Two or More Races (%)
City	88.0	1.6	4.6	0.2	0.0	2.2	3.2
MSA[1]	69.7	15.3	6.1	0.4	0.1	5.5	2.9
U.S.	73.3	12.6	5.2	0.8	0.2	4.8	3.1

Note: (1) Figures cover the Dallas-Fort Worth-Arlington, TX Metropolitan Statistical Area—see Appendix B for areas included; (2) Alone is defined as not being in combination with one or more other races; (3) American Indian and Alaska Native; (4) Native Hawaiian and Other Pacific Islander
Source: U.S. Census Bureau, 2012-2016 American Community Survey 5-Year Estimates

Hispanic or Latino Origin

Area	Total (%)	Mexican (%)	Puerto Rican (%)	Cuban (%)	Other (%)
City	8.5	5.8	0.7	0.2	1.8
MSA[1]	28.2	23.8	0.7	0.2	3.5
U.S.	17.3	11.0	1.7	0.7	4.0

Note: Persons of Hispanic or Latino origin can be of any race; (1) Figures cover the Dallas-Fort Worth-Arlington, TX Metropolitan Statistical Area—see Appendix B for areas included
Source: U.S. Census Bureau, 2012-2016 American Community Survey 5-Year Estimates

Segregation

Type	Segregation Indices[1]				Percent Change		
	1990	2000	2010	2010 Rank[2]	1990-2000	1990-2010	2000-2010
Black/White	62.8	59.8	56.6	48	-3.1	-6.2	-3.2
Asian/White	41.8	45.6	46.6	19	3.8	4.8	1.0
Hispanic/White	48.8	52.3	50.3	24	3.5	1.5	-2.0

Note: All figures cover the Metropolitan Statistical Area—see Appendix B for areas included; Figures are based on an analysis of 1990, 2000, and 2010 Census Decennial Census tract data by William H. Frey, Brookings Institution and the University of Michigan Social Science Data Analysis Network. In this analysis all racial groups (whites, blacks, and asians) are non-Hispanic members of those races. Hispanics are shown as a separate category; (1) Segregation Indices are Dissimilarity Indices that measure the degree to which the minority group is distributed differently than whites across census tracts. They range from 0 (complete integration) to 100 (complete segregation) where the value indicates the percentage of the minority group that needs to move to be distributed exactly like whites; (2) Ranges from 1 (most segregated) to 102 (least segregated); n/a not available.
Source: www.CensusScope.org

Ancestry

Area	German	Irish	English	American	Italian	Polish	French[2]	Scottish	Dutch
City	19.2	13.2	13.0	9.0	4.3	2.6	3.7	3.1	1.3
MSA[1]	9.8	7.6	7.3	6.6	2.2	1.1	1.9	1.7	0.9
U.S.	14.4	10.4	7.7	6.9	5.4	2.9	2.6	1.7	1.3

Note: Figures are the percentage of the total population reporting a particular ancestry. The nine most commonly reported ancestries in the U.S. are shown. Figures include multiple ancestries (e.g. if a person reported being Irish and Italian, they were included in both columns); (1) Figures cover the Dallas-Fort Worth-Arlington, TX Metropolitan Statistical Area—see Appendix B for areas included; (2) Excludes Basque
Source: U.S. Census Bureau, 2012-2016 American Community Survey 5-Year Estimates

Foreign-Born Population

Area	Percent of Population Born in								
	Any Foreign Country	Asia	Mexico	Europe	Carribean	Central America[2]	South America	Africa	Canada
City	7.9	3.2	1.0	1.5	0.3	0.7	0.4	0.5	0.4
MSA[1]	17.8	4.7	8.8	0.8	0.2	1.3	0.5	1.2	0.2
U.S.	13.2	4.0	3.6	1.5	1.3	1.0	0.9	0.6	0.3

Note: (1) Figures cover the Dallas-Fort Worth-Arlington, TX Metropolitan Statistical Area—see Appendix B for areas included; (2) Excludes Mexico.
Source: U.S. Census Bureau, 2012-2016 American Community Survey 5-Year Estimates

Marital Status

Area	Never Married	Now Married[2]	Separated	Widowed	Divorced
City	21.0	66.1	1.0	4.9	6.9
MSA[1]	31.9	50.5	2.3	4.5	10.9
U.S.	33.0	48.1	2.1	5.9	11.0

Note: Figures are percentages and cover the population 15 years of age and older; (1) Figures cover the Dallas-Fort Worth-Arlington, TX Metropolitan Statistical Area—see Appendix B for areas included; (2) Excludes separated
Source: U.S. Census Bureau, 2012-2016 American Community Survey 5-Year Estimates

Disability Status

Area	All Ages	Under 18 Years Old	18 to 64 Years Old	65 Years and Over
City	8.4	3.4	5.3	37.4
MSA[1]	9.6	3.4	8.2	35.2
U.S.	12.5	4.1	10.3	35.7

Note: Figures show percent of the civilian noninstitutionalized population that reported having a disability. Disability status is determined from six types of difficulty: vision, hearing, cognitive, ambulatory, self-care, and independent living. For children under 5 years old, hearing and vision difficulty are used to determine disability status. For children between the ages of 5 and 14, disability status is determined from hearing, vision, cognitive, ambulatory, and self-care difficulties. For people aged 15 years and older, they are considered to have a disability if they have difficulty with any one of the six difficulty types; Note: (1) Figures cover the Dallas-Fort Worth-Arlington, TX Metropolitan Statistical Area—see Appendix B for areas included
Source: U.S. Census Bureau, 2012-2016 American Community Survey 5-Year Estimates

Age

Area	Percent of Population									Median Age
	Under Age 5	Age 5–19	Age 20–34	Age 35–44	Age 45–54	Age 55–64	Age 65–74	Age 75–84	Age 85+	
City	5.5	25.3	12.1	14.6	18.0	12.9	6.6	3.5	1.5	40.7
MSA[1]	7.2	22.2	21.4	14.4	13.8	10.9	6.2	2.9	1.1	34.5
U.S.	6.2	19.6	20.7	12.7	13.6	12.6	8.3	4.3	1.9	37.7

Note: (1) Figures cover the Dallas-Fort Worth-Arlington, TX Metropolitan Statistical Area—see Appendix B for areas included
Source: U.S. Census Bureau, 2012-2016 American Community Survey 5-Year Estimates

Gender

Area	Males	Females	Males per 100 Females
City	21,815	22,435	97.2
MSA[1]	3,421,036	3,536,087	96.7
U.S.	156,765,322	161,792,840	96.9

Note: (1) Figures cover the Dallas-Fort Worth-Arlington, TX Metropolitan Statistical Area—see Appendix B for areas included
Source: U.S. Census Bureau, 2012-2016 American Community Survey 5-Year Estimates

Religious Groups by Family

Area	Catholic	Baptist	Non-Den.	Methodist[2]	Lutheran	LDS[3]	Pente-costal	Presby-terian[4]	Muslim[5]	Judaism
MSA[1]	13.3	18.7	7.8	5.3	0.8	1.2	2.2	1.0	2.4	0.4
U.S.	19.1	9.3	4.0	4.0	2.3	2.0	1.9	1.6	0.8	0.7

Note: Figures are the number of adherents as a percentage of the total population; (1) Figures cover the Dallas-Fort Worth-Arlington, TX Metropolitan Statistical Area—see Appendix B for areas included; (2) Methodist/Pietist; (3) Latter Day Saints; (4) Reformed; (5) Figures are estimates
Source: Association of Statisticians of American Religious Bodies, 2010 U.S. Religion Census: Religious Congregations & Membership Study

Religious Groups by Tradition

Area	Catholic	Evangelical Protestant	Mainline Protestant	Other Tradition	Black Protestant	Orthodox
MSA[1]	13.3	28.3	7.0	4.8	1.8	0.2
U.S.	19.1	16.2	7.3	4.3	1.6	0.3

Note: Figures are the number of adherents as a percentage of the total population; (1) Figures cover the Dallas-Fort Worth-Arlington, TX Metropolitan Statistical Area—see Appendix B for areas included
Source: Association of Statisticians of American Religious Bodies, 2010 U.S. Religion Census: Religious Congregations & Membership Study

ECONOMY

Gross Metropolitan Product

Area	2014	2015	2016	2017	Rank[2]
MSA[1]	502.3	524.8	545.3	577.5	4

Note: Figures are in billions of dollars; (1) Figures cover the Dallas-Fort Worth-Arlington, TX Metropolitan Statistical Area—see Appendix B for areas included; (2) Rank is based on 2015 data and ranges from 1 to 381
Source: The U.S. Conference of Mayors, U.S. Metro Economies: GMP and Employment Report, 2015-2017

Economic Growth

Area	2012-14 (%)	2015 (%)	2016 (%)	2017 (%)	Rank[2]
MSA[1]	6.7	7.1	2.4	3.4	7
U.S.	2.0	2.4	1.9	2.6	–

Note: Figures are real gross metropolitan product (GMP) growth rates and represent average annual percent change; (1) Figures cover the Dallas-Fort Worth-Arlington, TX Metropolitan Statistical Area—see Appendix B for areas included; (2) Rank is based on 2012-2014 average annual percent change and ranges from 1 to 381
Source: The U.S. Conference of Mayors, U.S. Metro Economies: GMP and Employment Report, 2015-2017

Metropolitan Area Exports

Area	2011	2012	2013	2014	2015	2016	Rank[2]
MSA[1]	26,648.7	27,820.9	27,596.0	28,669.4	27,372.9	27,187.8	9

Note: Figures are in millions of dollars; (1) Figures cover the Dallas-Fort Worth-Arlington, TX Metropolitan Statistical Area—see Appendix B for areas included; (2) Rank is based on 2016 data and ranges from 1 to 385
Source: U.S. Department of Commerce, International Trade Administration, Office of Trade & Industry Information, Manufacturing & Services, data extracted March 15, 2018

Building Permits

Area	Single-Family			Multi-Family			Total		
	2016	2017p	Pct. Chg.	2016	2017p	Pct. Chg.	2016	2017p	Pct. Chg.
City	138	105	-23.9	0	0	0.0	138	105	-23.9
MSA[1]	29,846	34,210	14.6	25,772	27,499	6.7	55,618	61,709	11.0
U.S.	750,800	817,300	8.9	455,800	446,800	-2.0	1,206,600	1,264,100	4.8

Note: (1) Figures cover the Dallas-Fort Worth-Arlington, TX Metropolitan Statistical Area—see Appendix B for areas included; Figures represent new, privately-owned housing units authorized (unadjusted data); All permit data are based on estimates with imputation; (p) preliminary data.
Source: U.S. Census Bureau, Manufacturing, Mining, and Construction Statistics, Building Permits, 2016, 2017

Bankruptcy Filings

Area	Business Filings			Nonbusiness Filings		
	2016	2017	% Chg.	2016	2017	% Chg.
Tarrant County	231	204	-11.7	4,050	3,983	-1.7
U.S.	24,114	23,157	-4.0	770,846	765,863	-0.6

Note: Business filings include Chapter 7, Chapter 11, Chapter 12, and Chapter 13; Nonbusiness filings include Chapter 7, Chapter 11, and Chapter 13
Source: Administrative Office of the U.S. Courts, Business and Nonbusiness Bankruptcy, County Cases Commenced by Chapter of the Bankruptcy Code, During the 12-Month Period Ending December 31, 2016 and Business and Nonbusiness Bankruptcy, County Cases Commenced by Chapter of the Bankruptcy Code, During the 12-Month Period Ending December 31, 2017

Housing Vacancy Rates

Area	Gross Vacancy Rate[2] (%)			Year-Round Vacancy Rate[3] (%)			Rental Vacancy Rate[4] (%)			Homeowner Vacancy Rate[5] (%)		
	2015	2016	2017	2015	2016	2017	2015	2016	2017	2015	2016	2017
MSA[1]	8.0	7.9	7.8	7.8	7.7	7.6	8.3	6.8	7.1	1.4	1.4	0.8
U.S.	12.9	12.8	12.7	10.0	9.9	9.9	7.1	6.9	7.2	1.8	1.7	1.6

Note: (1) Figures cover the Dallas-Fort Worth-Arlington, TX Metropolitan Statistical Area—see Appendix B for areas included; (2) The percentage of the total housing inventory that is vacant; (3) The percentage of the housing inventory (excluding seasonal units) that is year-round vacant; (4) The percentage of rental inventory that is vacant for rent; (5) The percentage of homeowner inventory that is vacant for sale
Source: U.S. Census Bureau, Housing Vacancies and Homeownership Annual Statistics: 2015, 2016, 2017

INCOME

Income

Area	Per Capita ($)	Median Household ($)	Average Household ($)
City	49,916	122,292	147,606
MSA[1]	31,143	61,330	85,693
U.S.	29,829	55,322	77,866

Note: (1) Figures cover the Dallas-Fort Worth-Arlington, TX Metropolitan Statistical Area—see Appendix B for areas included
Source: U.S. Census Bureau, 2012-2016 American Community Survey 5-Year Estimates

Household Income Distribution

Area	Percent of Households Earning							
	Under $15,000	$15,000 -$24,999	$25,000 -$34,999	$35,000 -$49,999	$50,000 -$74,999	$75,000 -$99,999	$100,000 -$149,999	$150,000 and up
City	4.9	3.6	4.8	5.8	10.0	11.9	20.2	38.8
MSA[1]	9.5	8.9	9.5	13.0	18.2	12.4	15.1	13.4
U.S.	12.1	10.2	9.9	13.2	17.8	12.2	13.5	11.1

Note: (1) Figures cover the Dallas-Fort Worth-Arlington, TX Metropolitan Statistical Area—see Appendix B for areas included
Source: U.S. Census Bureau, 2012-2016 American Community Survey 5-Year Estimates

Poverty Rate

Area	All Ages	Under 18 Years Old	18 to 64 Years Old	65 Years and Over
City	3.7	3.9	3.3	5.5
MSA[1]	14.0	20.3	12.3	8.5
U.S.	15.1	21.2	14.2	9.3

Note: Figures are percentage of people whose income during the past 12 months was below the poverty level; (1) Figures cover the Dallas-Fort Worth-Arlington, TX Metropolitan Statistical Area—see Appendix B for areas included
Source: U.S. Census Bureau, 2012-2016 American Community Survey 5-Year Estimates

EMPLOYMENT

Labor Force and Employment

Area	Civilian Labor Force			Workers Employed		
	Dec. 2016	Dec. 2017	% Chg.	Dec. 2016	Dec. 2017	% Chg.
City	23,633	24,151	2.2	22,846	23,475	2.8
MD[1]	1,216,491	1,241,227	2.0	1,169,689	1,201,876	2.8
U.S.	158,968,000	159,880,000	0.6	151,798,000	153,602,000	1.2

Note: Data is not seasonally adjusted and covers workers 16 years of age and older; (1) Figures cover the Fort Worth-Arlington, TX Metropolitan Division—see Appendix B for areas included
Source: Bureau of Labor Statistics, Local Area Unemployment Statistics

Unemployment Rate

Area	2017											
	Jan.	Feb.	Mar.	Apr.	May	Jun.	Jul.	Aug.	Sep.	Oct.	Nov.	Dec.
City	3.5	3.7	3.5	3.1	3.2	3.5	3.6	3.6	3.2	2.9	3.0	2.8
MD[1]	4.2	4.2	4.0	3.5	3.6	3.9	3.9	3.9	3.4	3.2	3.3	3.2
U.S.	5.1	4.9	4.6	4.1	4.1	4.5	4.6	4.5	4.1	3.9	3.9	3.9

Note: Data is not seasonally adjusted and covers workers 16 years of age and older; (1) Figures cover the Fort Worth-Arlington, TX Metropolitan Division—see Appendix B for areas included
Source: Bureau of Labor Statistics, Local Area Unemployment Statistics

Average Wages

Occupation	$/Hr.	Occupation	$/Hr.
Accountants and Auditors	39.70	Maids and Housekeeping Cleaners	10.60
Automotive Mechanics	19.80	Maintenance and Repair Workers	20.20
Bookkeepers	19.70	Marketing Managers	64.80
Carpenters	18.40	Nuclear Medicine Technologists	41.30
Cashiers	10.30	Nurses, Licensed Practical	24.10
Clerks, General Office	17.50	Nurses, Registered	36.10
Clerks, Receptionists/Information	12.70	Nursing Assistants	12.90
Clerks, Shipping/Receiving	15.80	Packers and Packagers, Hand	13.20
Computer Programmers	38.30	Physical Therapists	45.00
Computer Systems Analysts	44.40	Postal Service Mail Carriers	24.30
Computer User Support Specialists	23.90	Real Estate Brokers	n/a
Cooks, Restaurant	11.50	Retail Salespersons	12.80
Dentists	80.10	Sales Reps., Exc. Tech./Scientific	34.20
Electrical Engineers	45.90	Sales Reps., Tech./Scientific	43.10
Electricians	22.10	Secretaries, Exc. Legal/Med./Exec.	16.50
Financial Managers	62.30	Security Guards	14.00
First-Line Supervisors/Managers, Sales	21.60	Surgeons	134.40
Food Preparation Workers	11.00	Teacher Assistants*	10.20
General and Operations Managers	64.30	Teachers, Elementary School*	28.00
Hairdressers/Cosmetologists	14.40	Teachers, Secondary School*	28.90
Internists, General	56.70	Telemarketers	12.10
Janitors and Cleaners	12.30	Truck Drivers, Heavy/Tractor-Trailer	23.10
Landscaping/Groundskeeping Workers	12.40	Truck Drivers, Light/Delivery Svcs.	17.10
Lawyers	61.40	Waiters and Waitresses	10.50

Note: Wage data covers the Fort Worth-Arlington, TX Metropolitan Division—see Appendix B for areas included; (*) Hourly wages for elementary/secondary school teachers and teacher assistants were calculated by the editors from annual wage data based on a 40 hour work week; n/a not available.
Source: Bureau of Labor Statistics, Metro Area Occupational Employment & Wage Estimates, May 2017

Employment by Occupation

Occupation Classification	City (%)	MSA[1] (%)	U.S. (%)
Management, Business, Science, and Arts	55.4	38.2	37.0
Natural Resources, Construction, and Maintenance	5.2	9.3	8.9
Production, Transportation, and Material Moving	5.5	11.6	12.2
Sales and Office	25.1	24.9	23.8
Service	8.8	15.9	18.1

Note: Figures cover employed civilians 16 years of age and older; (1) Figures cover the Dallas-Fort Worth-Arlington, TX Metropolitan Statistical Area—see Appendix B for areas included
Source: U.S. Census Bureau, 2012-2016 American Community Survey 5-Year Estimates

Employment by Industry

Sector	MD[1] Number of Employees	MD[1] Percent of Total	U.S. Percent of Total
Construction, Mining, and Logging	70,500	6.7	5.2
Education and Health Services	137,400	13.1	15.9
Financial Activities	60,300	5.8	5.7
Government	140,700	13.4	15.3
Information	11,300	1.1	1.9
Leisure and Hospitality	120,300	11.5	10.7
Manufacturing	95,300	9.1	8.5
Other Services	38,100	3.6	3.9
Professional and Business Services	113,800	10.9	14.0
Retail Trade	121,400	11.6	11.0
Transportation, Warehousing, and Utilities	86,800	8.3	4.1
Wholesale Trade	52,500	5.0	4.0

Note: Figures are non-farm employment as of December 2017. Figures are not seasonally adjusted and include workers 16 years of age and older; (1) Figures cover the Fort Worth-Arlington, TX Metropolitan Division—see Appendix B for areas included
Source: Bureau of Labor Statistics, Current Employment Statistics, Employment, Hours, and Earnings

Occupations with Greatest Projected Employment Growth: 2017 – 2019

Occupation[1]	2017 Employment	2019 Projected Employment	Numeric Employment Change	Percent Employment Change
Combined Food Preparation and Serving Workers, Including Fast Food	335,660	354,370	18,710	5.6
Personal Care Aides	212,280	230,990	18,710	8.8
Retail Salespersons	393,950	406,100	12,150	3.1
Customer Service Representatives	261,530	273,600	12,070	4.6
Janitors and Cleaners, Except Maids and Housekeeping Cleaners	180,710	192,060	11,350	6.3
Laborers and Freight, Stock, and Material Movers, Hand	185,140	196,200	11,060	6.0
Registered Nurses	214,500	224,450	9,950	4.6
Office Clerks, General	379,860	389,540	9,680	2.6
Heavy and Tractor-Trailer Truck Drivers	192,710	201,560	8,850	4.6
Waiters and Waitresses	222,630	231,020	8,390	3.8

Note: Projections cover Texas; (1) Sorted by numeric employment change
Source: www.projectionscentral.com, State Occupational Projections, 2017–2019 Short-Term Projections

Fastest Growing Occupations: 2017 – 2019

Occupation[1]	2017 Employment	2019 Projected Employment	Numeric Employment Change	Percent Employment Change
Wind Turbine Service Technicians	1,740	2,090	350	20.7
Home Health Aides	72,760	80,000	7,240	10.0
Security and Fire Alarm Systems Installers	8,190	8,930	740	8.9
Personal Care Aides	212,280	230,990	18,710	8.8
Statisticians	1,760	1,910	150	8.2
Tree Trimmers and Pruners	5,980	6,480	500	8.2
Physician Assistants	6,860	7,400	540	7.9
Nurse Practitioners	9,230	9,950	720	7.7
Elevator Installers and Repairers	2,190	2,350	160	7.4
Helpers—Roofers	800	850	50	7.4

Note: Projections cover Texas; (1) Sorted by percent employment change and excludes occupations with numeric employment change less than 50
Source: www.projectionscentral.com, State Occupational Projections, 2017–2019 Short-Term Projections

TAXES

State Corporate Income Tax Rates

State	Tax Rate (%)	Income Brackets ($)	Num. of Brackets	Financial Institution Tax Rate (%)[a]	Federal Income Tax Ded.
Texas	(w)	–	–	(w)	No

Note: Tax rates as of January 1, 2018; (a) Rates listed are the corporate income tax rate applied to financial institutions or excise taxes based on income. Some states have other taxes based upon the value of deposits or shares; (w) Texas imposes a Franchise Tax, otherwise known as margin tax, imposed on entities with more than $1,110,000 total revenues at rate of 0.75%, or 0.375% for entities primarily engaged in retail or wholesale trade, on lesser of 70% of total revenues or 100% of gross receipts after deductions for either compensation or cost of goods sold.
Source: Federation of Tax Administrators, Range of State Corporate Income Tax Rates, January 1, 2018

State Individual Income Tax Rates

State	Tax Rate (%)	Income Brackets ($)	Num. of Brackets	Personal Exempt. ($)[1] Single	Personal Exempt. ($)[1] Dependents	Fed. Inc. Tax Ded.
Texas	None	–	–	–	–	–

Note: Tax rates as of January 1, 2018; Local- and county-level taxes are not included; n/a not applicable; (1) Married joint filers generally receive double the single exemption
Source: Federation of Tax Administrators, State Individual Income Tax Rates, January 1, 2018

Various State Sales and Excise Tax Rates

State	State Sales Tax (%)	Gasoline[1] (¢/gal.)	Cigarette[2] ($/pack)	Spirits[3] ($/gal.)	Wine[4] ($/gal.)	Beer[5] ($/gal.)	Recreational Marijuana (%)
Texas	6.25	20.0	1.41	2.40 (f)	0.20 (l)	0.20 (q)	Not legal

Note: All tax rates as of January 1, 2018; (1) The American Petroleum Institute has developed a methodology for determining the average tax rate on a gallon of fuel. Rates may include any of the following: excise taxes, environmental fees, storage tank fees, other fees or taxes, general sales tax, and local taxes. In states where gasoline is subject to the general sales tax, or where the fuel tax is based on the average sale price, the average rate determined by API is sensitive to changes in the price of gasoline. States that fully or partially apply general sales taxes to gasoline: CA, CO, GA, IL, IN, MI, NY; (2) The federal excise tax of $1.0066 per pack and local taxes are not included; (3) Rates are those applicable to off-premise sales of 40% alcohol by volume (a.b.v.) distilled spirits in 750ml containers. Local excise taxes are excluded; (4) Rates are those applicable to off-premise sales of 11% a.b.v. non-carbonated wine in 750ml containers; (5) Rates are those applicable to off-premise sales of 4.7% a.b.v. beer in 12 ounce containers; (f) Different rates also applicable according to alcohol content, place of production, size of container, or place purchased (on- or off-premise or onboard airlines); (l) Different rates also applicable to alcohol content, place of production, size of container, place purchased (on- or off-premise or on board airlines) or type of wine (carbonated, vermouth, etc.); (q) Different rates also applicable according to alcohol content, place of production, size of container, or place purchased (on- or off-premise or onboard airlines).
Source: Tax Foundation, 2018 Facts & Figures: How Does Your State Compare?

State Business Tax Climate Index Rankings

State	Overall Rank	Corporate Tax Rank	Individual Income Tax Rank	Sales Tax Rank	Unemployment Insurance Tax Rank	Property Tax Rank
Texas	13	49	6	37	26	37

Note: The index is a measure of how each state's tax laws affect economic performance. The lower the rank, the more favorable a state's tax system is for business. States without a given tax are given a ranking of 1. The scores/rankings for the District of Columbia do not affect other states. The 2018 index represents the tax climate as of July 1, 2017.
Source: Tax Foundation, State Business Tax Climate Index 2018

TRANSPORTATION

Means of Transportation to Work

Area	Car/Truck/Van: Drove Alone	Car/Truck/Van: Car-pooled	Public Transportation: Bus	Public Transportation: Subway	Public Transportation: Railroad	Bicycle	Walked	Other Means	Worked at Home
City	83.2	5.7	0.0	0.1	0.1	0.2	0.6	0.9	9.4
MSA[1]	80.7	9.9	1.0	0.2	0.3	0.2	1.2	1.5	5.0
U.S.	76.4	9.3	2.6	1.9	0.6	0.6	2.8	1.3	4.6

Note: Figures are percentages and cover workers 16 years of age and older; (1) Figures cover the Dallas-Fort Worth-Arlington, TX Metropolitan Statistical Area—see Appendix B for areas included
Source: U.S. Census Bureau, 2012-2016 American Community Survey 5-Year Estimates

Travel Time to Work

Area	Less Than 10 Minutes	10 to 19 Minutes	20 to 29 Minutes	30 to 44 Minutes	45 to 59 Minutes	60 to 89 Minutes	90 Minutes or More
City	8.1	19.5	19.9	29.8	14.4	6.5	1.8
MSA[1]	9.4	25.8	21.1	25.0	10.3	6.3	2.0
U.S.	12.9	29.2	20.9	20.4	8.0	6.0	2.7

Note: Note: Figures are percentages and include workers 16 years old and over; (1) Figures cover the Dallas-Fort Worth-Arlington, TX Metropolitan Statistical Area—see Appendix B for areas included
Source: U.S. Census Bureau, 2012-2016 American Community Survey 5-Year Estimates

Freeway Travel Time Index

Area	1985	1990	1995	2000	2005	2010	2014
Urban Area Rank[1,2]	6	9	10	19	21	22	19
Urban Area Index[1]	1.19	1.20	1.23	1.24	1.26	1.24	1.27
Average Index[3]	1.09	1.11	1.14	1.17	1.20	1.19	1.20

Note: Freeway Travel Time Index—the ratio of travel time in the peak period to the travel time at free-flow conditions. For example, a value of 1.30 indicates a 20-minute free-flow trip takes 26 minutes in the peak (20 minutes x 1.30 = 26 minutes); (1) Covers the Dallas-Fort Worth-Arlington TX urban area; (2) Rank is based on 101 urban areas (#1 = highest travel time index); (3) Average of 101 urban areas
Source: Texas Transportation Institute, 2015 Urban Mobility Scorecard, August 2015

Freeway Commuter Stress Index

Area	1985	1990	1995	2000	2005	2010	2014
Urban Area Rank[1,2]	12	15	13	20	22	25	20
Urban Area Index[1]	1.25	1.26	1.29	1.30	1.32	1.30	1.33
Average Index[3]	1.13	1.16	1.19	1.22	1.25	1.24	1.25

Note: The Freeway Commuter Stress Index is the same as the Freeway Travel Time Index (see table above) except that it includes only the travel in the peak directions during the peak periods; the TTI includes travel in all directions during the peak period. Thus, the CSI is more indicative of the work trip experienced by each commuter on a daily basis; (1) Covers the Dallas-Fort Worth-Arlington TX urban area; (2) Rank is based on 101 urban areas (#1 = highest travel time index); (3) Average of 101 urban areas
Source: Texas Transportation Institute, 2015 Urban Mobility Scorecard, August 2015

Living Environment

COST OF LIVING

Cost of Living Index

Composite Index	Groceries	Housing	Utilities	Trans- portation	Health Care	Misc. Goods/ Services
99.1	101.2	90.0	108.7	102.9	103.8	101.4

Note: The Cost of Living Index measures regional differences in the cost of consumer goods and services, excluding taxes and non-consumer expenditures, for professional and managerial households in the top income quintile. It is based on more than 50,000 prices covering almost 60 different items for which prices are collected three times a year by chambers of commerce, economic development organizations or university applied economic centers in each participating urban area. The numbers shown should be read as a percentage above or below the national average of 100. For example, a value of 115.4 in the groceries column indicates that grocery prices are 15.4% higher than the national average. Small differences in the index numbers should not be interpreted as significant; Figures cover the Fort Worth TX urban area.
Source: The Council for Community and Economic Research, ACCRA Cost of Living Index, 2017

Grocery Prices

Area[1]	T-Bone Steak ($/pound)	Frying Chicken ($/pound)	Whole Milk ($/half gal.)	Eggs ($/dozen)	Orange Juice ($/64 oz.)	Coffee ($/11.5 oz.)
City[2]	12.84	1.09	1.67	1.47	3.93	4.76
Avg.	11.29	1.40	2.02	1.47	3.55	4.37
Min.	7.71	0.93	1.04	0.70	2.86	3.24
Max.	15.83	2.39	4.03	3.92	6.29	8.16

*Note: (1) Values for the local area are compared with the average, minimum and maximum values for all 294 areas in the Cost of Living Index; (2) Figures cover the Fort Worth TX urban area; **T-Bone Steak** (price per pound); **Frying Chicken** (price per pound, whole fryer); **Whole Milk** (half gallon carton); **Eggs** (price per dozen, Grade A, large); **Orange Juice** (64 oz. Tropicana or Florida Natural); **Coffee** (11.5 oz. can, vacuum-packed, Maxwell House, Hills Bros, or Folgers).*
Source: The Council for Community and Economic Research, ACCRA Cost of Living Index, 2017

Housing and Utility Costs

Area[1]	New Home Price ($)	Apartment Rent ($/month)	All Electric ($/month)	Part Electric ($/month)	Other Energy ($/month)	Telephone ($/month)
City[2]	267,887	1,164	-	128.21	57.85	30.25
Avg.	335,956	1,047	175.01	97.34	67.93	28.71
Min.	187,788	491	109.48	49.33	35.44	12.39
Max.	1,739,087	4,559	432.62	227.09	353.33	44.61

*Note: (1) Values for the local area are compared with the average, minimum and maximum values for all 294 areas in the Cost of Living Index; (2) Figures cover the Fort Worth TX urban area; **New Home Price** (2,400 sf living area, 8,000 sf lot, in urban area with full utilities); **Apartment Rent** (950 sf 2 bedroom/1.5 or 2 bath, unfurnished, excluding all utilities except water); **All Electric** (average monthly cost for an all-electric home); **Part Electric** (average monthly cost for a part-electric home); **Other Energy** (average monthly cost for natural gas, fuel oil, coal, wood, and any other forms of energy except electricity); **Telephone** (price includes basic monthly rate for a private residential line plus additional local usage charges incurred by a family of four).*
Source: The Council for Community and Economic Research, ACCRA Cost of Living Index, 2017

Health Care, Transportation, and Other Costs

Area[1]	Doctor ($/visit)	Dentist ($/visit)	Optometrist ($/visit)	Gasoline ($/gallon)	Beauty Salon ($/visit)	Men's Shirt ($)
City[2]	120.46	93.52	96.19	2.19	57.67	42.84
Avg.	108.00	92.54	101.93	2.25	37.58	30.92
Min.	30.39	60.00	49.75	1.82	16.11	11.20
Max.	193.50	161.94	229.28	3.16	77.35	59.13

*Note: (1) Values for the local area are compared with the average, minimum and maximum values for all 294 areas in the Cost of Living Index; (2) Figures cover the Fort Worth TX urban area; **Doctor** (general practitioners routine exam of an established patient); **Dentist** (adult teeth cleaning and periodic oral examination); **Optometrist** (full vision eye exam for established adult patient); **Gasoline** (one gallon regular unleaded, national brand, including all taxes, cash price at self-service pump if available); **Beauty Salon** (woman's shampoo, trim, and blow-dry); **Men's Shirt** (cotton/polyester dress shirt, pinpoint weave, long sleeves).*
Source: The Council for Community and Economic Research, ACCRA Cost of Living Index, 2017

HOUSING

House Price Index (HPI)

Area	National Ranking[2]	Quarterly Change (%)	One-Year Change (%)	Five-Year Change (%)
MD[1]	15	1.36	11.00	48.21
U.S.[3]	–	1.61	6.68	34.71

Note: The HPI is a weighted repeat sales index. It measures average price changes in repeat sales or refinancings on the same properties. This information is obtained by reviewing repeat mortgage transactions on single-family properties whose mortgages have been purchased or securitized by Fannie Mae or Freddie Mac in January 1975; (1) Figures cover the Fort Worth-Arlington, TX Metropolitan Division—see Appendix B for areas included; (2) Rankings are based on annual percentage change for all metro areas containing at least 15,000 transactions over the last 10 years and ranges from 1 to 253; (3) figures based on a weighted average of Census Division estimates using a seasonally adjusted, purchase-only index; all figures are for the period ending December 31, 2017
Source: Federal Housing Finance Agency, House Price Index, February 28, 2018

Median Single-Family Home Prices

Area	2015	2016	2017[p]	Percent Change 2016 to 2017
MSA[1]	207.2	227.1	247.4	8.9
U.S. Average	223.9	235.5	248.8	5.6

Note: Figures are median sales prices of existing single-family homes in thousands of dollars; (p) preliminary; (1) Figures cover the Dallas-Fort Worth-Arlington, TX Metropolitan Statistical Area—see Appendix B for areas included
Source: National Association of Realtors, Median Sales Price of Existing Single-Family Homes for Metropolitan Areas, 4th Quarter 2017

Qualifying Income Based on Median Sales Price of Existing Single-Family Homes

Area	With 5% Down ($)	With 10% Down ($)	With 20% Down ($)
MSA[1]	55,203	52,298	46,487
U.S. Average	55,585	52,659	46,808

Note: Figures are preliminary; Qualifying income is based on a mortgage rate of 4.17%. Monthly principal and interest payment is limited to 25% of income; (1) Figures cover the Dallas-Fort Worth-Arlington, TX Metropolitan Statistical Area—see Appendix B for areas included
Source: National Association of Realtors, Qualifying Income Based on Median Sales Price of Existing Single-Family Homes for Metropolitan Areas, 4th Quarter 2017

Median Apartment Condo-Coop Home Prices

Area	2015	2016	2017[p]	Percent Change 2016 to 2017
MSA[1]	148.7	167.7	185.7	10.7
U.S. Average	210.7	220.7	234.3	6.2

Note: Figures are median sales prices of existing apartment condo-coop homes in thousands of dollars; (p) preliminary; (1) Figures cover the Dallas-Fort Worth-Arlington, TX Metropolitan Statistical Area—see Appendix B for areas included
Source: National Association of Realtors, Median Sales Price of Existing Apartment Condo-Coop Homes for Metropolitan Areas, 4th Quarter 2017

Home Value Distribution

Area	Under $50,000	$50,000 -$99,999	$100,000 -$149,999	$150,000 -$199,999	$200,000 -$299,999	$300,000 -$499,999	$500,000 -$999,999	$1,000,000 or more
City	2.0	2.6	8.3	7.4	26.8	37.3	14.4	1.1
MSA[1]	6.4	17.3	20.6	17.5	18.4	13.4	4.9	1.5
U.S.	8.8	14.8	15.3	14.9	18.4	16.4	9.0	2.5

Note: Figures are percentages and cover owner-occupied housing units; (1) Figures cover the Dallas-Fort Worth-Arlington, TX Metropolitan Statistical Area—see Appendix B for areas included
Source: U.S. Census Bureau, 2012-2016 American Community Survey 5-Year Estimates

Homeownership Rate

Area	2009 (%)	2010 (%)	2011 (%)	2012 (%)	2013 (%)	2014 (%)	2015 (%)	2016 (%)	2017 (%)
MSA[1]	61.6	63.8	62.6	61.8	59.9	57.7	57.8	59.7	61.8
U.S.	67.4	66.9	66.1	65.4	65.1	64.5	63.7	63.4	63.9

Note: (1) Figures cover the Dallas-Fort Worth-Arlington, TX Metropolitan Statistical Area—see Appendix B for areas included
Source: U.S. Census Bureau, Housing Vacancies and Homeownership Annual Statistics: 2009-2017

Year Housing Structure Built

Area	2010 or Later	2000 -2009	1990 -1999	1980 -1989	1970 -1979	1960 -1969	1950 -1959	1940 -1949	Before 1940	Median Year
City	6.4	33.0	31.0	19.0	7.8	1.8	0.6	0.3	0.1	1997
MSA[1]	4.5	22.2	16.8	19.1	14.9	9.0	7.7	2.9	2.9	1987
U.S.	2.3	14.7	14.0	13.7	15.6	10.9	10.6	5.2	13.0	1977

Note: Figures are percentages except for Median Year; Note: (1) Figures cover the Dallas-Fort Worth-Arlington, TX Metropolitan Statistical Area—see Appendix B for areas included
Source: U.S. Census Bureau, 2012-2016 American Community Survey 5-Year Estimates

Gross Monthly Rent

Area	Under $500	$500 -$999	$1,000 -$1,499	$1,500 -$1,999	$2,000 -$2,499	$2,500 -$2,999	$3,000 and up	Median ($)
City	0.0	23.1	56.2	9.9	3.0	4.5	3.3	1,207
MSA[1]	4.6	49.0	32.4	10.0	2.5	0.8	0.7	969
U.S.	11.3	43.3	27.7	10.7	4.0	1.6	1.5	949

Note: Figures are percentages except for Median; Gross rent is the contract rent plus the estimated average monthly cost of utilities (electricity, gas, and water and sewer) and fuels (oil, coal, kerosene, wood, etc.) if these are paid by the renter (or paid for the renter by someone else); (1) Figures cover the Dallas-Fort Worth-Arlington, TX Metropolitan Statistical Area—see Appendix B for areas included
Source: U.S. Census Bureau, 2012-2016 American Community Survey 5-Year Estimates

HEALTH

Health Risk Factors

Category	MD[1] (%)	U.S. (%)
Adults aged 18–64 who have any kind of health care coverage	79.9	87.7
Adults who reported being in good or excellent health	87.0	83.6
Adults who are current smokers	15.3	17.1
Adults who currently use E-cigarettes	n/a	4.7
Adults who currently use chewing tobacco, snuff, or snus	3.1	4.0
Adults who are heavy drinkers[2]	9.7	6.5
Adults who are binge drinkers[3]	19.1	16.9
Adults who are overweight (BMI 25.0 - 29.9)	33.0	35.3
Adults who are obese (BMI 30.0 - 99.8)	30.6	29.9
Adults who participated in any physical activities in the past month	73.0	76.9
Adults who always or nearly always wears a seat belt	97.2	94.3

Note: n/a not available; (1) Figures cover the Fort Worth-Arlington, TX Metropolitan Division—see Appendix B for areas included; (2) Heavy drinkers are classified as adult men having more than 14 drinks per week and adult women having more than 7 drinks per week; (3) Binge drinkers are classified as males having five or more drinks on one occasion or females having four or more drinks on one occasion
Source: Centers for Disease Control and Prevention, Behaviorial Risk Factor Surveillance System, SMART: Selected Metropolitan Area Risk Trends, 2016

Health Screening Rates

Category	MD[1] (%)	U.S. (%)
Adults 50-75 who have had a blood stool test within the past year	9.1	8.0
Adults 50-75 who have had a colonoscopy in the past 10 years	54.7	63.5
Adults aged 65+ who have had flu shot within the past year	57.0	58.6
Adults aged 65+ who have ever had a pneumonia vaccination	65.3	73.4
Adults who have ever been tested for HIV	40.8	35.6
Women aged 21-65 who have had a pap test in the past three years	76.4	79.8
Men aged 40+ who have had a PSA test within the past two years	29.5	39.5
Women aged 40+ who have had a mammogram within the past two years	78.8	72.5

Note: n/a not available; (1) Figures cover the Fort Worth-Arlington, TX Metropolitan Division—see Appendix B for areas included; Source: Centers for Disease Control and Prevention, Behaviorial Risk Factor Surveillance System, SMART: Selected Metropolitan Area Risk Trends, 2016

Chronic Health Conditions

Category	MD[1] (%)	U.S. (%)
Adults who have ever been told they had a heart attack	4.4	4.4
Adults who have ever been told they have angina or coronary heart disease	2.8	4.1
Adults who have ever been told they had a stroke	n/a	3.1
Adults who have been told they currently have asthma	9.1	9.3
Adults who have ever been told they have arthritis	19.8	25.8
Adults who have ever been told they have diabetes[2]	10.9	10.5
Adults who have ever been told they had skin cancer	5.2	5.9
Adults who have ever been told they had any other types of cancer	4.8	6.7
Adults who have ever been told they have COPD	5.2	6.3
Adults who have ever been told they have kidney disease	n/a	2.8
Adults who have ever been told they have a form of depression	13.1	17.4

Note: n/a not available; (1) Figures cover the Fort Worth-Arlington, TX Metropolitan Division—see Appendix B for areas included; (2) Figures do not include pregnancy-related, borderline, or pre-diabetes
Source: Centers for Disease Control and Prevention, Behaviorial Risk Factor Surveillance System, SMART: Selected Metropolitan Area Risk Trends, 2016

Mortality Rates for the Top 10 Causes of Death in the U.S.

ICD-10[a] Sub-Chapter	ICD-10[a] Code	Age-Adjusted Mortality Rate[1] per 100,000 population	
		County[2]	U.S.
Malignant neoplasms	C00-C97	153.1	158.5
Ischaemic heart diseases	I20-I25	83.9	96.8
Other forms of heart disease	I30-I51	48.2	52.4
Chronic lower respiratory diseases	J40-J47	44.0	40.9
Cerebrovascular diseases	I60-I69	46.0	37.2
Organic, including symptomatic, mental disorders	F01-F09	37.9	33.3
Other degenerative diseases of the nervous system	G30-G31	47.0	32.1
Other external causes of accidental injury	W00-X59	20.1	31.2
Diabetes mellitus	E10-E14	22.6	21.1
Hypertensive diseases	I10-I15	33.2	20.8

Note: (a) ICD-10 = International Classification of Diseases 10th Revision; (1) Mortality rates are a three year average covering 2014-2016; (2) Figures cover Tarrant County.
Source: Centers for Disease Control and Prevention, National Center for Health Statistics. Underlying Cause of Death 1999-2016 on CDC WONDER Online Database, released December 2017

Mortality Rates for Selected Causes of Death

ICD-10[a] Sub-Chapter	ICD-10[a] Code	Age-Adjusted Mortality Rate[1] per 100,000 population	
		County[2]	U.S.
Assault	X85-Y09	5.1	5.6
Diseases of the liver	K70-K76	15.2	14.0
Human immunodeficiency virus (HIV) disease	B20-B24	1.7	1.9
Influenza and pneumonia	J09-J18	11.1	14.6
Intentional self-harm	X60-X84	12.1	13.2
Malnutrition	E40-E46	2.6	1.3
Obesity and other hyperalimentation	E65-E68	1.4	2.1
Renal failure	N17-N19	15.1	13.0
Transport accidents	V01-V99	10.6	12.0
Viral hepatitis	B15-B19	1.9	1.9

Note: (a) ICD-10 = International Classification of Diseases 10th Revision; (1) Mortality rates are a three year average covering 2014-2016; (2) Figures cover Tarrant County; Data are Suppressed when the data meet the criteria for confidentiality constraints; Mortality rates are flagged as Unreliable when the rate would be calculated with a numerator of 20 or less.
Source: Centers for Disease Control and Prevention, National Center for Health Statistics. Underlying Cause of Death 1999-2016 on CDC WONDER Online Database, released December 2017

EDUCATION

Health Insurance Coverage

Area	With Health Insurance	With Private Health Insurance	With Public Health Insurance	Without Health Insurance	Population Under Age 18 Without Health Insurance
City	94.2	88.0	14.9	5.8	3.0
MSA[1]	81.5	63.6	25.2	18.5	10.8
U.S.	88.3	66.7	33.0	11.7	5.9

Note: Figures are percentages that cover the civilian noninstitutionalized population; (1) Figures cover the Dallas-Fort Worth-Arlington, TX Metropolitan Statistical Area—see Appendix B for areas included
Source: U.S. Census Bureau, 2012-2016 American Community Survey 5-Year Estimates

Number of Medical Professionals

Area	MDs[3]	DOs[3,4]	Dentists	Podiatrists	Chiropractors	Optometrists
County[1] (number)	3,497	759	1,160	84	497	292
County[1] (rate[2])	176.3	38.3	57.4	4.2	24.6	14.4
U.S. (rate[2])	276.5	22.3	67.3	6.0	26.7	15.9

Note: Data as of 2016 unless noted; (1) Data covers Tarrant County; (2) Rate per 100,000 population; (3) Data as of 2015 and includes all active, non-federal physicians; (4) Doctor of Osteopathic Medicine
Source: U.S. Department of Health and Human Services, Health Resources and Services Administration, Bureau of Health Professions, Area Resource File (ARF) 2016-2017

Best Hospitals

According to *U.S. News,* the Fort Worth-Arlington, TX metro area is home to one of the best hospitals in the U.S.: **Baylor Scott and White All Saints Medical Center-Fort Worth** (1 adult specialty). The hospital listed was nationally ranked in at least one of 16 specialties. Only 152 hospitals nationwide were nationally ranked in one or more specialties. Twenty hospitals in the U.S. made the Honor Roll. The Best Hospitals Honor Roll was revamped last year to take both the national rankings and the procedure and condition ratings into account. Hospitals received points if they were nationally ranked in one of the 16 specialties—the higher they ranked, the more points they got—and how many ratings of "high performing" they earned in the nine procedures and conditions. *U.S. News Online, "America's Best Hospitals 2017-18"*

According to *U.S. News,* the Fort Worth-Arlington, TX metro area is home to one of the best children's hospitals in the U.S.: **Cook Children's Medical Center** (4 pediatric specialties). The hospital listed was highly ranked in at least one of 10 pediatric specialties. Eighty-two children's hospitals in the U.S. were nationally ranked in at least one specialty. Hospitals received points for being ranked in a specialty, and the 10 hospitals with the most points across the 10 specialties make up the Honor Roll. *U.S. News Online, "America's Best Children's Hospitals 2017-18"*

Public School District Statistics

District Name	Schls	Pupils	Pupil/ Teacher Ratio	Minority Pupils[1] (%)	Free Lunch Eligible[2] (%)	IEP[3] (%)
Keller Isd	43	34,180	15.4	43.1	19.1	9.1
Northwest ISD	29	20,976	15.5	34.1	14.4	8.4

Note: Table includes school districts with 100 or more students; (1) Percentage of students that are not non-Hispanic white; (2) Percentage of students that are eligible for the free lunch program; (3) Percentage of students that have an Individualized Education Program.
Source: U.S. Department of Education, National Center for Education Statistics, Common Core of Data, Local Education Agency (School District) Universe Survey: School Year 2015-2016; U.S. Department of Education, National Center for Education Statistics, Common Core of Data, Public Elementary/Secondary School Universe Survey: School Year 2015-2016

Highest Level of Education

Area	Less than H.S.	H.S. Diploma	Some College, No Deg.	Associate Degree	Bachelor's Degree	Master's Degree	Prof. School Degree	Doctorate Degree
City	3.5	13.1	20.0	6.4	37.9	14.3	3.3	1.5
MSA[1]	15.4	22.5	22.2	6.7	21.9	8.5	1.7	1.0
U.S.	13.0	27.5	21.0	8.2	18.8	8.2	2.0	1.3

Note: Figures cover persons age 25 and over; (1) Figures cover the Dallas-Fort Worth-Arlington, TX Metropolitan Statistical Area—see Appendix B for areas included
Source: U.S. Census Bureau, 2012-2016 American Community Survey 5-Year Estimates

Educational Attainment by Race

Area	High School Graduate or Higher (%)					Bachelor's Degree or Higher (%)				
	Total	White	Black	Asian	Hisp.[2]	Total	White	Black	Asian	Hisp.[2]
City	96.5	97.2	98.9	97.6	80.7	57.0	56.3	72.5	78.4	38.4
MSA[1]	84.6	85.2	89.6	88.0	56.8	33.1	34.1	24.8	58.8	12.0
U.S.	87.0	88.9	84.3	86.3	65.7	30.3	31.6	20.0	52.1	14.7

Note: Figures shown cover persons 25 years old and over; (1) Figures cover the Dallas-Fort Worth-Arlington, TX Metropolitan Statistical Area—see Appendix B for areas included; (2) People of Hispanic origin can be of any race
Source: U.S. Census Bureau, 2012-2016 American Community Survey 5-Year Estimates

School Enrollment by Grade and Control

Area	Preschool (%)		Kindergarten (%)		Grades 1 - 4 (%)		Grades 5 - 8 (%)		Grades 9 - 12 (%)	
	Public	Private	Public	Private	Public	Private	Public	Private	Public	Private
City	27.6	72.4	85.0	15.0	83.7	16.3	85.2	14.8	82.1	17.9
MSA[1]	57.4	42.6	89.3	10.7	92.6	7.4	92.0	8.0	92.3	7.7
U.S.	58.4	41.6	87.7	12.3	89.8	10.2	89.7	10.3	90.4	9.6

Note: Figures shown cover persons 3 years old and over; (1) Figures cover the Dallas-Fort Worth-Arlington, TX Metropolitan Statistical Area—see Appendix B for areas included
Source: U.S. Census Bureau, 2012-2016 American Community Survey 5-Year Estimates

Average Salaries of Public School Classroom Teachers

Area	2015		2016		Change from 2015 to 2016	
	Dollars	Rank[1]	Dollars	Rank[1]	Percent	Rank[2]
Texas	50,713	28	51,890	27	2.3	8
U.S. Average	57,611	–	58,353	–	1.3	–

Note: (1) Rank ranges from 1 to 51 where 1 indicates highest salary; (2) Rank ranges from 1 to 51 where 1 indicates highest percent change.
Source: National Education Association, Rankings & Estimates: Rankings of the States 2016 and Estimates of School Statistics 2017

Higher Education

Four-Year Colleges			Two-Year Colleges			Medical Schools[1]	Law Schools[2]	Voc/ Tech[3]
Public	Private Non-profit	Private For-profit	Public	Private Non-profit	Private For-profit			
0	0	0	0	0	0	0	0	0

Note: Figures cover institutions located within the city limits and include main campuses only; (1) includes schools accredited by the Liaison Committee on Medical Education and the American Osteopathic Association's Commission on Osteopathic College Accreditation; (2) includes ABA-accredited schools, schools with provisional ABA accreditation, and state accredited schools; (3) includes all schools with programs that are less than 2 years.
Source: National Center for Education Statistics, Integrated Postsecondary Education System (IPEDS), 2016-17; Wikipedia, List of Medical Schools in the United States, accessed April 2, 2018; Wikipedia, List of Law Schools in the United States, accessed April 2, 2018

According to *U.S. News & World Report,* the Fort Worth-Arlington, TX metro division is home to one of the best national universities in the U.S.: **Texas Christian University** (#78 tie). The indicators used to capture academic quality fall into a number of categories: assessment by administrators at peer institutions; retention of students; faculty resources; student selectivity; financial resources; alumni giving; high school counselor ratings of colleges; and graduation rate. *U.S. News & World Report, "America's Best Colleges 2018"*

According to *U.S. News & World Report,* the Fort Worth-Arlington, TX metro division is home to one of the top 100 law schools in the U.S.: **Texas A&M University** (#80 tie). The rankings are based on a weighted average of 12 measures of quality: peer assessment score; assessment score by lawyers/judges; median LSAT scores; median undergrad GPA; acceptance rate; employment rates for graduates; placement success; bar passage rate; faculty resources; expenditures per student; student/faculty ratio; and library resources. *U.S. News & World Report, "America's Best Graduate Schools, Law, 2019"*

According to *U.S. News & World Report,* the Fort Worth-Arlington, TX metro division is home to one of the top 75 business schools in the U.S.: **Texas Christian University (Neeley)** (#54). The rankings are based on a weighted average of the following nine measures: quality assessment; peer assessment; recruiter assessment; placement success; mean starting salary and bonus; student selectivity; mean GMAT and GRE scores; mean undergraduate GPA; and acceptance rate. *U.S. News & World Report, "America's Best Graduate Schools, Business, 2019"*

PRESIDENTIAL ELECTION

2016 Presidential Election Results

Area	Clinton	Trump	Johnson	Stein	Other
Tarrant County	43.1	51.7	3.6	0.8	0.7
U.S.	48.0	45.9	3.3	1.1	1.7

Note: Results are percentages and may not add to 100% due to rounding
Source: Dave Leip's Atlas of U.S. Presidential Elections

EMPLOYERS

Major Employers

Company Name	Industry
AMR Corporation	Air transportation, scheduled
Associates First Capital Corporation	Mortgage bankers
Baylor University Medical Center	General medical & surgical hospitals
Children's Medical Center Dallas	Specialty hospitals, except psychiatric
Combat Support Associates	Engineering services
County of Dallas	County supervisors' & executives' offices
Dallas County Hospital District	General medical & surgical hospitals
Fort Worth Independent School District	Public elementary & secondary schools
Housewares Holding Company	Toasters, electric: household
HP Enterprise Services	Computer integrated systems design
J.C. Penney Company	Department stores
JCP Publications Corp.	Department stores
L-3 Communications Corporation	Business economic service
Odyssey HealthCare	Home health care services
Romano's Macaroni Grill	Italian restaurant
SFG Management Limited Liability	Milk processing (pasteurizing, homogenizing, bottling)
Texas Instruments Incorporated	Semiconductors & related devices
University of North Texas	Colleges & universities
University of Texas SW Medical Center	Accident & health insurance
Verizon Business Global	Telephone communication, except radio

Note: Companies shown are located within the Dallas-Fort Worth-Arlington, TX Metropolitan Statistical Area.
Source: Hoovers.com; Wikipedia

PUBLIC SAFETY

Crime Rate

Area	All Crimes	Violent Crimes				Property Crimes		
		Murder	Rape[3]	Robbery	Aggrav. Assault	Burglary	Larceny -Theft	Motor Vehicle Theft
City	627.0	0.0	17.0	6.4	40.4	102.0	446.4	14.9
Metro[1]	2,952.5	4.9	50.8	90.6	219.3	467.5	1,910.3	209.1
U.S.	2,847.8	5.3	40.4	102.8	248.5	468.9	1,745.0	236.9

Note: Figures are crimes per 100,000 population; (1) Figures cover the Fort Worth-Arlington, TX Metropolitan Division—see Appendix B for areas included; (3) The city and U.S. figures shown were reported using the revised Uniform Crime Reporting (UCR) definition of rape. The metro area figures shown are an aggregate total of the data submitted using both the revised and legacy UCR definitions.
Source: FBI Uniform Crime Reports, 2016

Hate Crimes

Area	Number of Quarters Reported	Number of Incidents per Bias Motivation					
		Race/Ethnicity/ Ancestry	Religion	Sexual Orientation	Disability	Gender	Gender Identity
City	4	0	0	0	0	0	0
U.S.	4	3,489	1,273	1,076	70	31	124

Source: Federal Bureau of Investigation, Hate Crime Statistics 2016

Identity Theft Consumer Reports

Area	Reports	Reports per 100,000 Population	Rank[2]
MSA[1]	11,506	159	11
U.S.	371,061	114	-

Note: (1) Figures cover the Dallas-Fort Worth-Arlington, TX Metropolitan Statistical Area—see Appendix B for areas included; (2) Rank ranges from 1 to 389 where 1 indicates greatest number of identity theft reports per 100,000 population
Source: Federal Trade Commission, Consumer Sentinel Network Data Book for January–December 2017

Fraud and Other Consumer Reports

Area	Reports	Reports per 100,000 Population	Rank[2]
MSA[1]	55,938	773	8
U.S.	2,304,550	708	-

Note: (1) Figures cover the Dallas-Fort Worth-Arlington, TX Metropolitan Statistical Area—see Appendix B for areas included; (2) Rank ranges from 1 to 389 where 1 indicates greatest number of fraud and other consumer reports per 100,000 population
Source: Federal Trade Commission, Consumer Sentinel Network Data Book for January–December 2017

SPORTS

Professional Sports Teams

Team Name	League	Year Established
Dallas Cowboys	National Football League (NFL)	1960
Dallas Mavericks	National Basketball Association (NBA)	1980
Dallas Stars	National Hockey League (NHL)	1993
FC Dallas	Major League Soccer (MLS)	1996
Texas Rangers	Major League Baseball (MLB)	1972

Note: Includes teams located in the Dallas-Fort Worth-Arlington, TX Metropolitan Statistical Area.
Source: Wikipedia, Major Professional Sports Teams of the United States and Canada, April 5, 2018

CLIMATE

Average and Extreme Temperatures

Temperature	Jan	Feb	Mar	Apr	May	Jun	Jul	Aug	Sep	Oct	Nov	Dec	Yr.
Extreme High (°F)	85	90	100	100	101	112	111	109	107	101	91	87	112
Average High (°F)	55	60	68	76	84	92	96	96	89	79	67	58	77
Average Temp. (°F)	45	50	57	66	74	82	86	86	79	68	56	48	67
Average Low (°F)	35	39	47	56	64	72	76	75	68	57	46	38	56
Extreme Low (°F)	-2	9	12	30	39	53	58	58	42	24	16	0	-2

Note: Figures cover the years 1945-1993
Source: National Climatic Data Center, International Station Meteorological Climate Summary, 9/96

Average Precipitation/Snowfall/Humidity

Precip./Humidity	Jan	Feb	Mar	Apr	May	Jun	Jul	Aug	Sep	Oct	Nov	Dec	Yr.
Avg. Precip. (in.)	1.9	2.3	2.6	3.8	4.9	3.4	2.1	2.3	2.9	3.3	2.3	2.1	33.9
Avg. Snowfall (in.)	1	1	Tr	Tr	0	0	0	0	0	Tr	Tr	Tr	3
Avg. Rel. Hum. 6am (%)	78	77	75	77	82	81	77	76	80	79	78	77	78
Avg. Rel. Hum. 3pm (%)	53	51	47	49	51	48	43	41	46	46	48	51	48

Note: Figures cover the years 1945-1993; Tr = Trace amounts (<0.05 in. of rain; <0.5 in. of snow)
Source: National Climatic Data Center, International Station Meteorological Climate Summary, 9/96

Weather Conditions

Temperature			Daytime Sky			Precipitation		
10°F & below	32°F & below	90°F & above	Clear	Partly cloudy	Cloudy	0.01 inch or more precip.	0.1 inch or more snow/ice	Thunder-storms
1	34	102	108	160	97	78	2	49

Note: Figures are average number of days per year and cover the years 1945-1993
Source: National Climatic Data Center, International Station Meteorological Climate Summary, 9/96

HAZARDOUS WASTE

Superfund Sites

The Fort Worth-Arlington, TX metro division is home to three sites on the EPA's Superfund National Priorities List: **Air Force Plant #4 (General Dynamics)** (final); **Circle Court Ground Water Plume** (final); **Sandy Beach Road Ground Water Plume** (final). There are a total of 1,396 Superfund sites with a status of proposed or final on the list in the U.S. *U.S. Environmental Protection Agency, National Priorities List, April 4, 2018*

AIR & WATER QUALITY

Air Quality Trends: Ozone

	1990	1995	2000	2005	2010	2012	2013	2014	2015	2016
MSA[1]	0.095	0.105	0.096	0.097	0.080	0.080	0.081	0.076	0.077	0.070
U.S.	0.087	0.089	0.081	0.079	0.073	0.075	0.069	0.067	0.068	0.069

Note: (1) Data covers the Dallas-Fort Worth-Arlington, TX Metropolitan Statistical Area—see Appendix B for areas included. The values shown are the composite ozone concentration averages among trend sites based on the highest fourth daily maximum 8-hour concentration in parts per million. These trends are based on sites having an adequate record of monitoring data during the trend period. Data from exceptional events are included.
Source: U.S. Environmental Protection Agency, Air Quality Monitoring Information, "Air Quality Trends by City, 1990-2016"

Air Quality Index

Area	Percent of Days when Air Quality was...[2]					AQI Statistics[2]	
	Good	Moderate	Unhealthy for Sensitive Groups	Unhealthy	Very Unhealthy	Maximum	Median
MSA[1]	52.6	40.8	6.6	0.0	0.0	147	50

Note: (1) Data covers the Dallas-Fort Worth-Arlington, TX Metropolitan Statistical Area—see Appendix B for areas included; (2) Based on 365 days with AQI data in 2017. Air Quality Index (AQI) is an index for reporting daily air quality. EPA calculates the AQI for five major air pollutants regulated by the Clean Air Act: ground-level ozone, particle pollution (aka particulate matter), carbon monoxide, sulfur dioxide, and nitrogen dioxide. The AQI runs from 0 to 500. The higher the AQI value, the greater the level of air pollution and the greater the health concern. There are six AQI categories: "Good" AQI is between 0 and 50. Air quality is considered satisfactory; "Moderate" AQI is between 51 and 100. Air quality is acceptable; "Unhealthy for Sensitive Groups" When AQI values are between 101 and 150, members of sensitive groups may experience health effects; "Unhealthy" When AQI values are between 151 and 200 everyone may begin to experience health effects; "Very Unhealthy" AQI values between 201 and 300 trigger a health alert; "Hazardous" AQI values over 300 trigger warnings of emergency conditions (not shown).
Source: U.S. Environmental Protection Agency, Air Quality Index Report, 2017

Air Quality Index Pollutants

Area	Percent of Days when AQI Pollutant was...[2]					
	Carbon Monoxide	Nitrogen Dioxide	Ozone	Sulfur Dioxide	Particulate Matter 2.5	Particulate Matter 10
MSA[1]	0.0	2.7	57.0	0.0	40.3	0.0

Note: (1) Data covers the Dallas-Fort Worth-Arlington, TX Metropolitan Statistical Area—see Appendix B for areas included; (2) Based on 365 days with AQI data in 2017. The Air Quality Index (AQI) is an index for reporting daily air quality. EPA calculates the AQI for five major air pollutants regulated by the Clean Air Act: ground-level ozone, particle pollution (also known as particulate matter), carbon monoxide, sulfur dioxide, and nitrogen dioxide. The AQI runs from 0 to 500. The higher the AQI value, the greater the level of air pollution and the greater the health concern.
Source: U.S. Environmental Protection Agency, Air Quality Index Report, 2017

Maximum Air Pollutant Concentrations: Particulate Matter, Ozone, CO and Lead

	Particulate Matter 10 (ug/m³)	Particulate Matter 2.5 Wtd AM (ug/m³)	Particulate Matter 2.5 24-Hr (ug/m³)	Ozone (ppm)	Carbon Monoxide (ppm)	Lead (ug/m³)
MSA[1] Level	52	8.5	19	0.076	1	0.06
NAAQS[2]	150	15	35	0.075	9	0.15
Met NAAQS[2]	Yes	Yes	Yes	No	Yes	Yes

Note: (1) Data covers the Dallas-Fort Worth-Arlington, TX Metropolitan Statistical Area—see Appendix B for areas included; Data from exceptional events are included; (2) National Ambient Air Quality Standards; ppm = parts per million; ug/m³ = micrograms per cubic meter; n/a not available.
Concentrations: Particulate Matter 10 (coarse particulate)—highest second maximum 24-hour concentration; Particulate Matter 2.5 Wtd AM (fine particulate)—highest weighted annual mean concentration; Particulate Matter 2.5 24-Hour (fine particulate)—highest 98th percentile 24-hour concentration; Ozone—highest fourth daily maximum 8-hour concentration; Carbon Monoxide—highest second maximum non-overlapping 8-hour concentration; Lead—maximum running 3-month average
Source: U.S. Environmental Protection Agency, Air Quality Monitoring Information, "Air Quality Statistics by City, 2016"

Maximum Air Pollutant Concentrations: Nitrogen Dioxide and Sulfur Dioxide

	Nitrogen Dioxide AM (ppb)	Nitrogen Dioxide 1-Hr (ppb)	Sulfur Dioxide AM (ppb)	Sulfur Dioxide 1-Hr (ppb)	Sulfur Dioxide 24-Hr (ppb)
MSA[1] Level	12	45	n/a	8	n/a
NAAQS[2]	53	100	30	75	140
Met NAAQS[2]	Yes	Yes	n/a	Yes	n/a

Note: (1) Data covers the Dallas-Fort Worth-Arlington, TX Metropolitan Statistical Area—see Appendix B for areas included; Data from exceptional events are included; (2) National Ambient Air Quality Standards; ppm = parts per million; ug/m³ = micrograms per cubic meter; n/a not available.
Concentrations: Nitrogen Dioxide AM—highest arithmetic mean concentration; Nitrogen Dioxide 1-Hr—highest 98th percentile 1-hour daily maximum concentration; Sulfur Dioxide AM—highest annual mean concentration; Sulfur Dioxide 1-Hr—highest 99th percentile 1-hour daily maximum concentration; Sulfur Dioxide 24-Hr—highest second maximum 24-hour concentration
Source: U.S. Environmental Protection Agency, Air Quality Monitoring Information, "Air Quality Statistics by City, 2016"

Drinking Water

Water System Name	Pop. Served	Primary Water Source Type	Violations[1]	
			Health Based	Monitoring/ Reporting
City of Keller	42,500	Purchased Surface	0	0

Note: (1) Based on violation data from January 1, 2017 to December 31, 2017
Source: U.S. Environmental Protection Agency, Office of Ground Water and Drinking Water, Safe Drinking Water Information System (based on data extracted April 5, 2018)

Leander, Texas

Background

Leander lies within the boundaries of both Williamson County and Travis County. It is a suburb of Austin and part of the Greater Austin metropolitan area. Leander, a hill-country city, is the fourth-fastest-growing city in Texas.

In the 1880s, as settlers of what was then known as Bagdad enjoyed their first school, hotel, and church socials, the railroad industry threatened to build tracks directly through Bagdad's downtown. Due to community opposition, the railroad was built one mile east of the city. After realizing that business would boom near the railroad, however, original settlers of Bagdad began to move their businesses and other activity closer to the railroad. As the town shifted east, the new incarnation of this community would be called Leander, after Leander "Catfish" Brown, who was one of the railroad officials responsible for the completion of the tracks. In 1978, Leander was incorporated as a city. Despite its growth, Leander still remains a relatively rural community.

Today, Leander prospers, with the Leander Independent School District having grown into the largest school district in Williamson County and being the fastest growing district in Texas. Leander is the center of this school district, which also serves the cities of Cedar Park, Jonestown, and parts of northwest Austin. Leander Independent School District contains five high schools, eight middle schools, and twenty-three elementary schools.

A significant historical find near Leander was the Leanderthal lady, one of the oldest and most complete human skeletal finds in North America. Discovered in 1983 in the nearby city of Cedar Park, the remains are also known as "Leanne"—both names in reference to Leander.

A highlight of recreation in Leander is the Crystal Falls Municipal Golf Course, which is one of the most challenging and breath-taking golf courses in the region. Another highlight is the Leander Public Library, founded in 1987. Leander's Parks & Recreation team also manages 14 city-owned parks. Annual events in Leander include the 4th of July Liberty Fest and the Leander Bluegrass Festival.

Leander is a jurisdiction member of the Capital Metropolitan Transportation Authority, regularly referred to as Capital Metro. Leander Station, where the Capital MetroRail's Red Line has its northern terminus, also provides access to several express bus lines, and includes a Park & Ride amenity.

Rankings

General Rankings

- *US News & World Report* conducted a survey of more than 2,000 people and analyzed the 125 largest metropolitan areas to determine what matters the most when selecting the next place to live. Austin* ranked #1 out of the top 25 as having the best combination of desirable factors. Criteria: cost of living; quality of education; job market, crime rates; and other factors. *realestate.usnews.com, "The 25 Best Places to Live in the U.S. in 2018," April 10, 2018*
- The Austin* metro area was identified as one of America's fastest-growing areas in terms of population and economy by *Forbes*. The area ranked #8 out of 25. The 100 most populous metro areas in the U.S. were evaluated on the following criteria: estimated population growth; employment; economic output; wages; home values. *Forbes, "America's Fastest-Growing Cities 2018," February 28, 2018*
- Austin* was identified as one of America's fastest-growing cities in terms of population growth by CNNMoney.com. The area ranked #4 out of 10. Criteria: population growth between July 2015 and July 2016; cities and towns with populations of 50,000. *CNNMoney, "10 Fastest-Growing Cities," June 2, 2017*

Business/Finance Rankings

- According to *Business Insider*, the Austin* metro area is where startup growth is on the rise. Based on the 2017 Kauffman Index of Growth Entrepreneurship, which measured in-depth national entrepreneurial trends in 40 metro areas, it ranked #2 in highest startup growth. *www.businessinsider.com, "The 21 U.S. Cities with the Highest Startup Growth," October 21, 2017*
- The personal finance site NerdWallet analyzed 183 American metropolitan areas with populations over 250,000 and more than 15,000 businesses to rank where entrepreneurs find the most success. Criteria included area economy, annual income, housing cost, unemployment rate, and the success rate of area businesses. Austin* ranked #89. *www.nerdwallet.com, "Best Places to Start a Business," April 27, 2015*
- The editors of *Kiplinger's Personal Finance Magazine* named Austin* to their list of ten of the best metro areas for start-ups. The area ranked #5.Criteria: well-educated workforce; low living costs for self-employed people, as measured by the Council for Community and Economic Research; a strong existing community of small business; low unemployment; low business costs. *www.kiplinger.com, "10 Great Cities for Starting a Business," October 2014*
- 24/7 Wall Street used Brookings Institution research on 50 advanced industries to identify the proportion of workers in the nation's largest metropolitan areas that were employed in jobs requiring knowledge in the science, technology, engineering, or math (STEM) fields and where there was heavy investment in research and development (R&D). The Austin* metro area was #9. *247wallst.com, "15 Cities with the Most High-Tech Jobs," February 23, 2017*
- In a survey of economic confidence in the nation's 50 largest metropolitan areas conducted January–December 2014, the Austin* metro area placed #9, according to Gallup's 2014 Economic Confidence Index. *Gallup, "San Jose and San Francisco Lead in Economic Confidence," March 19, 2015*
- The Brookings Institution ranked the 100 largest metro areas in the U.S. based on income inequality. Austin* was ranked #37 (#1 = greatest ineqality). Criteria: the "95/20 ratio," a figure representing the income at which a household earns more than 95 percent of all other households, divided by the income at which a household earns more than only 20 percent of all other households. *Brookings Institution, "Household Income Inequality, 100 Largest U.S. Metro Areas, 2014-2016," February 5, 2018*

- *Forbes* ranked the 100 largest metro areas in the U.S. in terms of the "Best Cities for Young Professionals." The Austin* metro area ranked #2 out of 25. (Large metro areas were divided into metro divisions.) Criteria: median rent of a two-bedroom apartment; job growth and unemployment rate; median salary of college graduates with 5 or less years of work experience; networking opportunities; social outlook; percentage of population 25 years of age and older with college degrees. *Forbes.com, "America's 25 Best Cities for Young Professionals in 2017," May 22, 2017*

- Payscale.com ranked the largest metro areas in terms of wage growth. The Austin* metro area ranked #16. Criteria: private-sector wage growth between the 4th quarter of 2016 and the 4th quarter of 2017. *PayScale, "Wage Trends by Metro Area-4th Quarter," January 17, 2018*

- The Austin* metro area was identified as one of the most affordable metropolitan areas in America by *Forbes.* The area ranked #19 out of 20 based on the National Association of Home Builders/Wells Fargo Housing Affordability Index and Sperling's Best Places' cost-of-living index. *Forbes.com, "America's Most Affordable Cities in 2015," March 12, 2015*

- The Austin* metro area appeared on the Milken Institute "2017 Best Performing Cities" list. Rank: #9 out of 200 large metro areas. Criteria: job growth; wage and salary growth; high-tech output growth. *Milken Institute, "Best-Performing Cities 2017," January 2018*

- *Forbes* ranked the 200 most populous metro areas to determine the nation's "Best Places for Business and Careers." The Austin* metro area was ranked #8. Criteria: costs (business and living); job growth (past and projected); income growth; quality of life; educational attainment (college and high school); projected economic growth; cultural and recreational opportunities; net migration patterns; number of highly ranked colleges. *Forbes, "The Best Places for Business and Careers 2017," October 24, 2017*

Children/Family Rankings

- *Forbes* analyzed data on the 100 largest metropolitan areas in the United States to compile its 2016 ranking of the best cities for raising a family. The Austin* metro area was ranked #14. Criteria: median income; childcare costs; percent of population under 18; commuting delays; crime rate; percentage of families owning homes; education quality (mainly test scores). Overall cost of living and housing affordability was also unofficially considered. *Forbes, "America's Best Cities for Raising a Family 2016," August 30, 2016*

Dating/Romance Rankings

- *Apartment List* conducted its annual survey of renters to compile a list of metros that have the best opportunities for dating. Nearly 11,000 respondents, from February 2017 through January 2018, rated their current city or neighborhood for opportunities to date and make friends. The Austin* metro area ranked #6 out of 70 where single residents were very satisfied or somewhat satisfied, making it among the ten best metros for dating opportunities. Other criteria analyzed included gender and education levels of renters. *Apartment List, "Best Metros for Dating 2018," February 6, 2018*

Education Rankings

- Personal finance website *WalletHub* analyzed the 150 largest U.S. metropolitan statistical areas to determine where the most educated Americans are choosing to settle. Criteria: education quality and attainment gap; education levels; percentage of workers with degrees; public school rankings; quality and size of each metro area's universities. Austin* was ranked #9 (#1 = most educated city). *www.WalletHub.com, "2017's Most and Least Educated Cities in America," July 25, 2017*

Environmental Rankings

- Sperling's BestPlaces assessed 379 metropolitan areas of the United States for the likelihood of dangerously extreme weather events or earthquakes. In general the Southeast and South-Central regions have the highest risk of weather extremes and earthquakes, while the Pacific Northwest enjoys the lowest risk. Of the least risky metropolitan areas, the Austin* metro area was ranked #373. *www.bestplaces.net, "Safest Places from Natural Disasters," April 2011*

- The U.S. Environmental Protection Agency (EPA) released a list of U.S. metropolitan areas with the most ENERGY STAR certified buildings in 2016. The Austin* metro area was ranked #13 out of 25. *U.S. Environmental Protection Agency, "2017 Energy Star Top Cities," June 2017*

- Austin* was highlighted as one of the top 99 cleanest metro areas for short-term particle pollution (24-hour PM 2.5) in the U.S. during 2013 through 2015. Monitors in these cities reported no days with unhealthful PM 2.5 levels. *American Lung Association, State of the Air 2017*

Health/Fitness Rankings

- For each of the 50 most populous metro areas in the United States, the American College of Sports Medicine's American Fitness Index evaluated infrastructure, community assets, and policies that encourage healthy and fit lifestyles, including preventive health behaviors, levels of chronic disease conditions, health care access, and community resources and policies that support physical activity. The Austin* metro area ranked #12 for "community fitness." *www.americanfitnessindex.org, "ACSM American Fitness Index Health and Community Fitness Status of the 50 Largest Metropolitan Areas," May 2017*

- Austin* was identified as a "2016 Spring Allergy Capital." The area ranked #58 out of 100. Three groups of factors were used to identify the most severe cities for people with allergies during the spring season: annual pollen levels; medicine utilization; access to board-certified allergists. *Asthma and Allergy Foundation of America, "Spring Allergy Capitals 2016"*

- Austin* was identified as a "2016 Fall Allergy Capital." The area ranked #46 out of 100. Three groups of factors were used to identify the most severe cities for people with allergies during the fall season: annual pollen levels; medicine utilization; access to board-certified allergists. *Asthma and Allergy Foundation of America, "Fall Allergy Capitals 2016"*

- Austin* was identified as a "2015 Asthma Capital." The area ranked #91 out of the nation's 100 largest metropolitan areas. Criteria: estimated prevalence; self-reported prevalence; crude death rate for asthma; annual pollen score; annual air quality; public smoking laws; number of board-certified asthma specialists; school inhaler access laws; rescue medication use; controller medication use; ER visits for asthma; uninsured rate; poverty rate. *Asthma and Allergy Foundation of America, "Asthma Capitals 2015"*

- The Austin* metro area ranked #49 out of 189 in The Gallup-Healthways Well-Being Index. Criteria: purpose; social well being; financial health; community and physical health. Results are based on telephone interviews with adults, aged 18 and older, living in metropolitan areas in the 50 U.S. states and the District of Columbia. *Gallup-Healthways, "State of American Well-Being, 2017 Community Well-Being Rankings" March 2018*

Real Estate Rankings

- FitSmallBusiness looked at 50 of the largest metropolitan areas in the U.S. to determine which metro was the best to start a real estate business. Data was compiled from such sources as: Zillow, Trulia, U.S. Census Bureau, and the Bureau of Labor Statistics. Criteria: location; inventory; annual wages; median sales price of homes; days on the market; median price cut percentage; and other factors that would influence real estate professional growth. The Austin* metro area ranked #13. *fitsmallbusiness.com, "The Best Cities to Become a Real Estate Agent in 2018," January 30, 2018*

- Austin* was ranked #169 out of 238 metro areas in terms of housing affordability in 2017 by the National Association of Home Builders (#1 = most affordable). Criteria: the share of homes sold in that area affordable to a family earning the local median income, based on standard mortgage underwriting criteria. *National Association of Home Builders®, NAHB-Wells Fargo Housing Opportunity Index, 4th Quarter 2017*

Safety Rankings

- The National Insurance Crime Bureau ranked 382 metro areas in the U.S. in terms of per capita rates of vehicle theft. The Austin* metro area ranked #167 (#1 = highest rate). Criteria: number of vehicle theft offenses per 100,000 inhabitants in 2016. *National Insurance Crime Bureau, "Hot Spots 2016," June 8, 2017*

Seniors/Retirement Rankings

- From its Best Cities for Successful Aging indexes, the Milken Institute generated rankings for metropolitan areas, weighing data in nine categories—health care, wellness, living arrangements, transportation and convenience, financial characteristics, education, employment, community engagement, and overall livability. The Austin* metro area was ranked #6 overall in the large metro area category. *Milken Institute, "Best Cities for Successful Aging, 2017" March 14, 2017*

Women/Minorities Rankings

- The *Houston Chronicle* listed the Austin* metro area as #2 in top places for young Latinos to live in the U.S. Research was largely based on housing and occupational data from the largest metropolitan areas performed by *Forbes* and NBC Universo. Criteria: percentage of 18-34 year-olds; Latino college grad rates; and diversity. *blog.chron.com, "The 15 Best Big Cities for Latino Millenials," January 26, 2016*

*Leander is located within the Austin-Round Rock, TX Metropolitan Statistical Area.

Business Environment

CITY FINANCES

City Government Finances

Component	2015 ($000)	2015 ($ per capita)
Total Revenues	n/a	n/a
Total Expenditures	n/a	n/a
Debt Outstanding	n/a	n/a
Cash and Securities[1]	n/a	n/a

Note: (1) Cash and security holdings of a government at the close of its fiscal year,, including those of its dependent agencies, utilities, and liquor stores.
Source: U.S Census Bureau, State & Local Government Finances 2015

City Government Revenue by Source

Source	2015 ($000)	2015 ($ per capita)	2015 (%)
General Revenue			
From Federal Government	n/a	n/a	n/a
From State Government	n/a	n/a	n/a
From Local Governments	n/a	n/a	n/a
Taxes			
Property	n/a	n/a	n/a
Sales and Gross Receipts	n/a	n/a	n/a
Personal Income	n/a	n/a	n/a
Corporate Income	n/a	n/a	n/a
Motor Vehicle License	n/a	n/a	n/a
Other Taxes	n/a	n/a	n/a
Current Charges	n/a	n/a	n/a
Liquor Store	n/a	n/a	n/a
Utility	n/a	n/a	n/a
Employee Retirement	n/a	n/a	n/a

Source: U.S Census Bureau, State & Local Government Finances 2015

City Government Expenditures by Function

Function	2015 ($000)	2015 ($ per capita)	2015 (%)
General Direct Expenditures			
Air Transportation	n/a	n/a	n/a
Corrections	n/a	n/a	n/a
Education	n/a	n/a	n/a
Employment Security Administration	n/a	n/a	n/a
Financial Administration	n/a	n/a	n/a
Fire Protection	n/a	n/a	n/a
General Public Buildings	n/a	n/a	n/a
Governmental Administration, Other	n/a	n/a	n/a
Health	n/a	n/a	n/a
Highways	n/a	n/a	n/a
Hospitals	n/a	n/a	n/a
Housing and Community Development	n/a	n/a	n/a
Interest on General Debt	n/a	n/a	n/a
Judicial and Legal	n/a	n/a	n/a
Libraries	n/a	n/a	n/a
Parking	n/a	n/a	n/a
Parks and Recreation	n/a	n/a	n/a
Police Protection	n/a	n/a	n/a
Public Welfare	n/a	n/a	n/a
Sewerage	n/a	n/a	n/a
Solid Waste Management	n/a	n/a	n/a
Veterans' Services	n/a	n/a	n/a
Liquor Store	n/a	n/a	n/a
Utility	n/a	n/a	n/a
Employee Retirement	n/a	n/a	n/a

Source: U.S Census Bureau, State & Local Government Finances 2015

DEMOGRAPHICS

Population Growth

Area	1990 Census	2000 Census	2010 Census	2016* Estimate	Population Growth (%) 1990-2016	2010-2016
City	3,661	7,596	26,521	36,204	888.9	36.5
MSA[1]	846,217	1,249,763	1,716,289	1,942,615	129.6	13.2
U.S.	248,709,873	281,421,906	308,745,538	318,558,162	28.1	3.2

Note: (1) Figures cover the Austin-Round Rock, TX Metropolitan Statistical Area—see Appendix B for areas included; (*) 2012-2016 5-year estimated population
Source: U.S. Census Bureau, 1990 Census, Census 2000, Census 2010, 2012-2016 American Community Survey 5-Year Estimates

Household Size

Area	Persons in Household (%) One	Two	Three	Four	Five	Six	Seven or More	Average Household Size
City	16.4	23.9	22.3	22.3	9.6	3.8	1.6	3.40
MSA[1]	28.0	33.3	15.6	13.8	5.8	2.1	1.4	2.70
U.S.	27.7	33.7	15.7	13.1	6.0	2.3	1.5	2.60

Note: (1) Figures cover the Austin-Round Rock, TX Metropolitan Statistical Area—see Appendix B for areas included
Source: U.S. Census Bureau, 2012-2016 American Community Survey 5-Year Estimates

Race

Area	White Alone[2] (%)	Black Alone[2] (%)	Asian Alone[2] (%)	AIAN[3] Alone[2] (%)	NHOPI[4] Alone[2] (%)	Other Race Alone[2] (%)	Two or More Races (%)
City	86.2	4.4	2.4	0.2	0.0	2.7	4.2
MSA[1]	78.7	7.3	5.3	0.4	0.1	5.1	3.2
U.S.	73.3	12.6	5.2	0.8	0.2	4.8	3.1

Note: (1) Figures cover the Austin-Round Rock, TX Metropolitan Statistical Area—see Appendix B for areas included; (2) Alone is defined as not being in combination with one or more other races; (3) American Indian and Alaska Native; (4) Native Hawaiian and Other Pacific Islander
Source: U.S. Census Bureau, 2012-2016 American Community Survey 5-Year Estimates

Hispanic or Latino Origin

Area	Total (%)	Mexican (%)	Puerto Rican (%)	Cuban (%)	Other (%)
City	26.3	23.5	0.6	0.2	2.0
MSA[1]	31.9	26.9	0.7	0.5	3.9
U.S.	17.3	11.0	1.7	0.7	4.0

Note: Persons of Hispanic or Latino origin can be of any race; (1) Figures cover the Austin-Round Rock, TX Metropolitan Statistical Area—see Appendix B for areas included
Source: U.S. Census Bureau, 2012-2016 American Community Survey 5-Year Estimates

Segregation

Type	Segregation Indices[1] 1990	2000	2010	2010 Rank[2]	Percent Change 1990-2000	1990-2010	2000-2010
Black/White	54.1	52.1	50.1	70	-1.9	-4.0	-2.1
Asian/White	39.4	42.3	41.2	49	2.9	1.8	-1.2
Hispanic/White	41.7	45.6	43.2	51	3.9	1.5	-2.4

Note: All figures cover the Metropolitan Statistical Area—see Appendix B for areas included; Figures are based on an analysis of 1990, 2000, and 2010 Census Decennial Census tract data by William H. Frey, Brookings Institution and the University of Michigan Social Science Data Analysis Network. In this analysis all racial groups (whites, blacks, and asians) are non-Hispanic members of those races. Hispanics are shown as a separate category; (1) Segregation Indices are Dissimilarity Indices that measure the degree to which the minority group is distributed differently than whites across census tracts. They range from 0 (complete integration) to 100 (complete segregation) where the value indicates the percentage of the minority group that needs to move to be distributed exactly like whites; (2) Ranges from 1 (most segregated) to 102 (least segregated); n/a not available.
Source: www.CensusScope.org

Ancestry

Area	German	Irish	English	American	Italian	Polish	French[2]	Scottish	Dutch
City	17.6	9.0	7.8	6.0	4.8	2.3	2.4	1.8	0.9
MSA[1]	13.5	8.0	8.2	4.5	2.8	1.7	2.6	2.2	1.0
U.S.	14.4	10.4	7.7	6.9	5.4	2.9	2.6	1.7	1.3

Note: Figures are the percentage of the total population reporting a particular ancestry. The nine most commonly reported ancestries in the U.S. are shown. Figures include multiple ancestries (e.g. if a person reported being Irish and Italian, they were included in both columns); (1) Figures cover the Austin-Round Rock, TX Metropolitan Statistical Area—see Appendix B for areas included; (2) Excludes Basque
Source: U.S. Census Bureau, 2012-2016 American Community Survey 5-Year Estimates

Foreign-Born Population

Area	Percent of Population Born in								
	Any Foreign Country	Asia	Mexico	Europe	Carribean	Central America[2]	South America	Africa	Canada
City	7.9	1.6	4.2	0.7	0.1	0.6	0.1	0.5	0.1
MSA[1]	14.6	4.0	6.8	1.0	0.4	1.1	0.5	0.5	0.3
U.S.	13.2	4.0	3.6	1.5	1.3	1.0	0.9	0.6	0.3

Note: (1) Figures cover the Austin-Round Rock, TX Metropolitan Statistical Area—see Appendix B for areas included; (2) Excludes Mexico.
Source: U.S. Census Bureau, 2012-2016 American Community Survey 5-Year Estimates

Marital Status

Area	Never Married	Now Married[2]	Separated	Widowed	Divorced
City	24.2	60.0	1.2	4.0	10.6
MSA[1]	36.1	47.4	1.9	3.7	10.9
U.S.	33.0	48.1	2.1	5.9	11.0

Note: Figures are percentages and cover the population 15 years of age and older; (1) Figures cover the Austin-Round Rock, TX Metropolitan Statistical Area—see Appendix B for areas included; (2) Excludes separated
Source: U.S. Census Bureau, 2012-2016 American Community Survey 5-Year Estimates

Disability Status

Area	All Ages	Under 18 Years Old	18 to 64 Years Old	65 Years and Over
City	8.4	4.7	7.6	32.7
MSA[1]	9.3	3.9	7.9	33.1
U.S.	12.5	4.1	10.3	35.7

Note: Figures show percent of the civilian noninstitutionalized population that reported having a disability. Disability status is determined from six types of difficulty: vision, hearing, cognitive, ambulatory, self-care, and independent living. For children under 5 years old, hearing and vision difficulty are used to determine disability status. For children between the ages of 5 and 14, disability status is determined from hearing, vision, cognitive, ambulatory, and self-care difficulties. For people aged 15 years and older, they are considered to have a disability if they have difficulty with any one of the six difficulty types; Note: (1) Figures cover the Austin-Round Rock, TX Metropolitan Statistical Area—see Appendix B for areas included
Source: U.S. Census Bureau, 2012-2016 American Community Survey 5-Year Estimates

Age

Area	Percent of Population									Median Age
	Under Age 5	Age 5–19	Age 20–34	Age 35–44	Age 45–54	Age 55–64	Age 65–74	Age 75–84	Age 85+	
City	9.7	24.9	19.2	17.5	13.7	8.0	4.8	1.5	0.7	33.1
MSA[1]	6.8	20.3	24.7	15.4	12.9	10.4	5.9	2.6	1.0	33.9
U.S.	6.2	19.6	20.7	12.7	13.6	12.6	8.3	4.3	1.9	37.7

Note: (1) Figures cover the Austin-Round Rock, TX Metropolitan Statistical Area—see Appendix B for areas included
Source: U.S. Census Bureau, 2012-2016 American Community Survey 5-Year Estimates

Gender

Area	Males	Females	Males per 100 Females
City	17,803	18,401	96.8
MSA[1]	971,489	971,126	100.0
U.S.	156,765,322	161,792,840	96.9

Note: (1) Figures cover the Austin-Round Rock, TX Metropolitan Statistical Area—see Appendix B for areas included
Source: U.S. Census Bureau, 2012-2016 American Community Survey 5-Year Estimates

Religious Groups by Family

Area	Catholic	Baptist	Non-Den.	Methodist[2]	Lutheran	LDS[3]	Pente-costal	Presby-terian[4]	Muslim[5]	Judaism
MSA[1]	16.0	10.3	4.5	3.6	2.0	1.2	0.8	1.1	1.2	0.3
U.S.	19.1	9.3	4.0	4.0	2.3	2.0	1.9	1.6	0.8	0.7

Note: Figures are the number of adherents as a percentage of the total population; (1) Figures cover the Austin-Round Rock, TX Metropolitan Statistical Area—see Appendix B for areas included; (2) Methodist/Pietist; (3) Latter Day Saints; (4) Reformed; (5) Figures are estimates
Source: Association of Statisticians of American Religious Bodies, 2010 U.S. Religion Census: Religious Congregations & Membership Study

Religious Groups by Tradition

Area	Catholic	Evangelical Protestant	Mainline Protestant	Other Tradition	Black Protestant	Orthodox
MSA[1]	16.0	16.1	6.3	3.9	1.4	0.1
U.S.	19.1	16.2	7.3	4.3	1.6	0.3

Note: Figures are the number of adherents as a percentage of the total population; (1) Figures cover the Austin-Round Rock, TX Metropolitan Statistical Area—see Appendix B for areas included
Source: Association of Statisticians of American Religious Bodies, 2010 U.S. Religion Census: Religious Congregations & Membership Study

ECONOMY

Gross Metropolitan Product

Area	2014	2015	2016	2017	Rank[2]
MSA[1]	114.8	119.5	125.3	133.1	32

Note: Figures are in billions of dollars; (1) Figures cover the Austin-Round Rock, TX Metropolitan Statistical Area—see Appendix B for areas included; (2) Rank is based on 2015 data and ranges from 1 to 381
Source: The U.S. Conference of Mayors, U.S. Metro Economies: GMP and Employment Report, 2015-2017

Economic Growth

Area	2012-14 (%)	2015 (%)	2016 (%)	2017 (%)	Rank[2]
MSA[1]	5.2	5.8	3.3	3.9	14
U.S.	2.0	2.4	1.9	2.6	–

Note: Figures are real gross metropolitan product (GMP) growth rates and represent average annual percent change; (1) Figures cover the Austin-Round Rock, TX Metropolitan Statistical Area—see Appendix B for areas included; (2) Rank is based on 2012-2014 average annual percent change and ranges from 1 to 381
Source: The U.S. Conference of Mayors, U.S. Metro Economies: GMP and Employment Report, 2015-2017

Metropolitan Area Exports

Area	2011	2012	2013	2014	2015	2016	Rank[2]
MSA[1]	8,626.3	8,976.6	8,870.8	9,400.0	10,094.5	10,682.7	26

Note: Figures are in millions of dollars; (1) Figures cover the Austin-Round Rock, TX Metropolitan Statistical Area—see Appendix B for areas included; (2) Rank is based on 2016 data and ranges from 1 to 385
Source: U.S. Department of Commerce, International Trade Administration, Office of Trade & Industry Information, Manufacturing & Services, data extracted March 15, 2018

Building Permits

Area	Single-Family			Multi-Family			Total		
	2016	2017p	Pct. Chg.	2016	2017p	Pct. Chg.	2016	2017p	Pct. Chg.
City	1,551	1,608	3.7	255	270	5.9	1,806	1,878	4.0
MSA[1]	13,609	15,206	11.7	8,633	10,597	22.7	22,242	25,803	16.0
U.S.	750,800	817,300	8.9	455,800	446,800	-2.0	1,206,600	1,264,100	4.8

Note: (1) Figures cover the Austin-Round Rock, TX Metropolitan Statistical Area—see Appendix B for areas included; Figures represent new, privately-owned housing units authorized (unadjusted data); All permit data are based on estimates with imputation; (p) preliminary data.
Source: U.S. Census Bureau, Manufacturing, Mining, and Construction Statistics, Building Permits, 2016, 2017

Bankruptcy Filings

Area	Business Filings			Nonbusiness Filings		
	2016	2017	% Chg.	2016	2017	% Chg.
Williamson County	42	46	9.5	469	468	-0.2
U.S.	24,114	23,157	-4.0	770,846	765,863	-0.6

Note: Business filings include Chapter 7, Chapter 11, Chapter 12, and Chapter 13; Nonbusiness filings include Chapter 7, Chapter 11, and Chapter 13
Source: Administrative Office of the U.S. Courts, Business and Nonbusiness Bankruptcy, County Cases Commenced by Chapter of the Bankruptcy Code, During the 12-Month Period Ending December 31, 2016 and Business and Nonbusiness Bankruptcy, County Cases Commenced by Chapter of the Bankruptcy Code, During the 12-Month Period Ending December 31, 2017

Housing Vacancy Rates

Area	Gross Vacancy Rate[2] (%)			Year-Round Vacancy Rate[3] (%)			Rental Vacancy Rate[4] (%)			Homeowner Vacancy Rate[5] (%)		
	2015	2016	2017	2015	2016	2017	2015	2016	2017	2015	2016	2017
MSA[1]	9.2	8.2	10.4	8.5	7.6	9.3	6.0	5.5	6.1	1.3	1.0	2.0
U.S.	12.9	12.8	12.7	10.0	9.9	9.9	7.1	6.9	7.2	1.8	1.7	1.6

Note: (1) Figures cover the Austin-Round Rock, TX Metropolitan Statistical Area—see Appendix B for areas included; (2) The percentage of the total housing inventory that is vacant; (3) The percentage of the housing inventory (excluding seasonal units) that is year-round vacant; (4) The percentage of rental inventory that is vacant for rent; (5) The percentage of homeowner inventory that is vacant for sale
Source: U.S. Census Bureau, Housing Vacancies and Homeownership Annual Statistics: 2015, 2016, 2017

INCOME

Income

Area	Per Capita ($)	Median Household ($)	Average Household ($)
City	30,521	83,550	97,976
MSA[1]	34,093	66,093	89,787
U.S.	29,829	55,322	77,866

Note: (1) Figures cover the Austin-Round Rock, TX Metropolitan Statistical Area—see Appendix B for areas included
Source: U.S. Census Bureau, 2012-2016 American Community Survey 5-Year Estimates

Household Income Distribution

Area	Percent of Households Earning							
	Under $15,000	$15,000 -$24,999	$25,000 -$34,999	$35,000 -$49,999	$50,000 -$74,999	$75,000 -$99,999	$100,000 -$149,999	$150,000 and up
City	3.3	2.8	6.1	10.9	22.0	16.2	23.9	14.7
MSA[1]	8.9	8.0	8.3	12.5	18.2	13.3	16.2	14.5
U.S.	12.1	10.2	9.9	13.2	17.8	12.2	13.5	11.1

Note: (1) Figures cover the Austin-Round Rock, TX Metropolitan Statistical Area—see Appendix B for areas included
Source: U.S. Census Bureau, 2012-2016 American Community Survey 5-Year Estimates

Poverty Rate

Area	All Ages	Under 18 Years Old	18 to 64 Years Old	65 Years and Over
City	4.8	5.5	4.5	4.4
MSA[1]	13.3	17.3	12.6	7.3
U.S.	15.1	21.2	14.2	9.3

Note: Figures are percentage of people whose income during the past 12 months was below the poverty level; (1) Figures cover the Austin-Round Rock, TX Metropolitan Statistical Area—see Appendix B for areas included
Source: U.S. Census Bureau, 2012-2016 American Community Survey 5-Year Estimates

EMPLOYMENT

Labor Force and Employment

Area	Civilian Labor Force			Workers Employed		
	Dec. 2016	Dec. 2017	% Chg.	Dec. 2016	Dec. 2017	% Chg.
City	22,019	22,777	3.4	21,327	22,089	3.6
MSA[1]	1,129,840	1,164,240	3.0	1,093,771	1,133,101	3.6
U.S.	158,968,000	159,880,000	0.6	151,798,000	153,602,000	1.2

Note: Data is not seasonally adjusted and covers workers 16 years of age and older; (1) Figures cover the Austin-Round Rock, TX Metropolitan Statistical Area—see Appendix B for areas included
Source: Bureau of Labor Statistics, Local Area Unemployment Statistics

Unemployment Rate

Area	2017											
	Jan.	Feb.	Mar.	Apr.	May	Jun.	Jul.	Aug.	Sep.	Oct.	Nov.	Dec.
City	3.5	3.6	3.4	3.2	3.1	3.5	3.5	3.5	3.1	2.9	3.2	3.0
MSA[1]	3.5	3.5	3.3	2.9	3.0	3.3	3.3	3.3	2.9	2.7	2.8	2.7
U.S.	5.1	4.9	4.6	4.1	4.1	4.5	4.6	4.5	4.1	3.9	3.9	3.9

Note: Data is not seasonally adjusted and covers workers 16 years of age and older; (1) Figures cover the Austin-Round Rock, TX Metropolitan Statistical Area—see Appendix B for areas included
Source: Bureau of Labor Statistics, Local Area Unemployment Statistics

Average Wages

Occupation	$/Hr.	Occupation	$/Hr.
Accountants and Auditors	35.40	Maids and Housekeeping Cleaners	10.40
Automotive Mechanics	23.90	Maintenance and Repair Workers	18.20
Bookkeepers	20.40	Marketing Managers	71.30
Carpenters	19.10	Nuclear Medicine Technologists	36.20
Cashiers	10.90	Nurses, Licensed Practical	22.10
Clerks, General Office	17.40	Nurses, Registered	33.10
Clerks, Receptionists/Information	13.30	Nursing Assistants	13.20
Clerks, Shipping/Receiving	15.20	Packers and Packagers, Hand	11.80
Computer Programmers	43.40	Physical Therapists	47.00
Computer Systems Analysts	44.70	Postal Service Mail Carriers	24.00
Computer User Support Specialists	24.30	Real Estate Brokers	n/a
Cooks, Restaurant	12.10	Retail Salespersons	13.50
Dentists	76.40	Sales Reps., Exc. Tech./Scientific	31.30
Electrical Engineers	56.20	Sales Reps., Tech./Scientific	58.20
Electricians	24.30	Secretaries, Exc. Legal/Med./Exec.	17.10
Financial Managers	67.00	Security Guards	15.40
First-Line Supervisors/Managers, Sales	21.50	Surgeons	n/a
Food Preparation Workers	12.30	Teacher Assistants*	12.30
General and Operations Managers	62.90	Teachers, Elementary School*	26.90
Hairdressers/Cosmetologists	14.80	Teachers, Secondary School*	26.60
Internists, General	73.80	Telemarketers	17.70
Janitors and Cleaners	11.60	Truck Drivers, Heavy/Tractor-Trailer	19.00
Landscaping/Groundskeeping Workers	13.90	Truck Drivers, Light/Delivery Svcs.	17.90
Lawyers	62.40	Waiters and Waitresses	12.10

Note: Wage data covers the Austin-Round Rock, TX Metropolitan Statistical Area—see Appendix B for areas included; (*) Hourly wages for elementary/secondary school teachers and teacher assistants were calculated by the editors from annual wage data based on a 40 hour work week; n/a not available.
Source: Bureau of Labor Statistics, Metro Area Occupational Employment & Wage Estimates, May 2017

Employment by Occupation

Occupation Classification	City (%)	MSA[1] (%)	U.S. (%)
Management, Business, Science, and Arts	44.6	44.7	37.0
Natural Resources, Construction, and Maintenance	8.6	8.5	8.9
Production, Transportation, and Material Moving	6.2	7.2	12.2
Sales and Office	27.2	23.6	23.8
Service	13.4	16.0	18.1

Note: Figures cover employed civilians 16 years of age and older; (1) Figures cover the Austin-Round Rock, TX Metropolitan Statistical Area—see Appendix B for areas included
Source: U.S. Census Bureau, 2012-2016 American Community Survey 5-Year Estimates

Employment by Industry

Sector	MSA[1] Number of Employees	MSA[1] Percent of Total	U.S. Percent of Total
Construction, Mining, and Logging	62,100	5.9	5.2
Education and Health Services	121,100	11.5	15.9
Financial Activities	60,700	5.8	5.7
Government	178,400	16.9	15.3
Information	30,900	2.9	1.9
Leisure and Hospitality	129,800	12.3	10.7
Manufacturing	57,700	5.5	8.5
Other Services	45,300	4.3	3.9
Professional and Business Services	183,000	17.4	14.0
Retail Trade	108,400	10.3	11.0
Transportation, Warehousing, and Utilities	22,200	2.1	4.1
Wholesale Trade	53,900	5.1	4.0

Note: Figures are non-farm employment as of December 2017. Figures are not seasonally adjusted and include workers 16 years of age and older; (1) Figures cover the Austin-Round Rock, TX Metropolitan Statistical Area—see Appendix B for areas included
Source: Bureau of Labor Statistics, Current Employment Statistics, Employment, Hours, and Earnings

Occupations with Greatest Projected Employment Growth: 2017 – 2019

Occupation[1]	2017 Employment	2019 Projected Employment	Numeric Employment Change	Percent Employment Change
Combined Food Preparation and Serving Workers, Including Fast Food	335,660	354,370	18,710	5.6
Personal Care Aides	212,280	230,990	18,710	8.8
Retail Salespersons	393,950	406,100	12,150	3.1
Customer Service Representatives	261,530	273,600	12,070	4.6
Janitors and Cleaners, Except Maids and Housekeeping Cleaners	180,710	192,060	11,350	6.3
Laborers and Freight, Stock, and Material Movers, Hand	185,140	196,200	11,060	6.0
Registered Nurses	214,500	224,450	9,950	4.6
Office Clerks, General	379,860	389,540	9,680	2.6
Heavy and Tractor-Trailer Truck Drivers	192,710	201,560	8,850	4.6
Waiters and Waitresses	222,630	231,020	8,390	3.8

Note: Projections cover Texas; (1) Sorted by numeric employment change
Source: www.projectionscentral.com, State Occupational Projections, 2017–2019 Short-Term Projections

Fastest Growing Occupations: 2017 – 2019

Occupation[1]	2017 Employment	2019 Projected Employment	Numeric Employment Change	Percent Employment Change
Wind Turbine Service Technicians	1,740	2,090	350	20.7
Home Health Aides	72,760	80,000	7,240	10.0
Security and Fire Alarm Systems Installers	8,190	8,930	740	8.9
Personal Care Aides	212,280	230,990	18,710	8.8
Statisticians	1,760	1,910	150	8.2
Tree Trimmers and Pruners	5,980	6,480	500	8.2
Physician Assistants	6,860	7,400	540	7.9
Nurse Practitioners	9,230	9,950	720	7.7
Elevator Installers and Repairers	2,190	2,350	160	7.4
Helpers—Roofers	800	850	50	7.4

Note: Projections cover Texas; (1) Sorted by percent employment change and excludes occupations with numeric employment change less than 50
Source: www.projectionscentral.com, State Occupational Projections, 2017–2019 Short-Term Projections

TAXES

State Corporate Income Tax Rates

State	Tax Rate (%)	Income Brackets ($)	Num. of Brackets	Financial Institution Tax Rate (%)[a]	Federal Income Tax Ded.
Texas	(w)	–	–	(w)	No

Note: Tax rates as of January 1, 2018; (a) Rates listed are the corporate income tax rate applied to financial institutions or excise taxes based on income. Some states have other taxes based upon the value of deposits or shares; (w) Texas imposes a Franchise Tax, otherwise known as margin tax, imposed on entities with more than $1,110,000 total revenues at rate of 0.75%, or 0.375% for entities primarily engaged in retail or wholesale trade, on lesser of 70% of total revenues or 100% of gross receipts after deductions for either compensation or cost of goods sold.
Source: Federation of Tax Administrators, Range of State Corporate Income Tax Rates, January 1, 2018

State Individual Income Tax Rates

State	Tax Rate (%)	Income Brackets ($)	Num. of Brackets	Personal Exempt. ($)[1] Single	Personal Exempt. ($)[1] Dependents	Fed. Inc. Tax Ded.
Texas	None	–	–	–	–	–

Note: Tax rates as of January 1, 2018; Local- and county-level taxes are not included; n/a not applicable; (1) Married joint filers generally receive double the single exemption
Source: Federation of Tax Administrators, State Individual Income Tax Rates, January 1, 2018

Various State Sales and Excise Tax Rates

State	State Sales Tax (%)	Gasoline[1] (¢/gal.)	Cigarette[2] ($/pack)	Spirits[3] ($/gal.)	Wine[4] ($/gal.)	Beer[5] ($/gal.)	Recreational Marijuana (%)
Texas	6.25	20.0	1.41	2.40 (f)	0.20 (l)	0.20 (q)	Not legal

Note: All tax rates as of January 1, 2018; (1) The American Petroleum Institute has developed a methodology for determining the average tax rate on a gallon of fuel. Rates may include any of the following: excise taxes, environmental fees, storage tank fees, other fees or taxes, general sales tax, and local taxes. In states where gasoline is subject to the general sales tax, or where the fuel tax is based on the average sale price, the average rate determined by API is sensitive to changes in the price of gasoline. States that fully or partially apply general sales taxes to gasoline: CA, CO, GA, IL, IN, MI, NY; (2) The federal excise tax of $1.0066 per pack and local taxes are not included; (3) Rates are those applicable to off-premise sales of 40% alcohol by volume (a.b.v.) distilled spirits in 750ml containers. Local excise taxes are excluded; (4) Rates are those applicable to off-premise sales of 11% a.b.v. non-carbonated wine in 750ml containers; (5) Rates are those applicable to off-premise sales of 4.7% a.b.v. beer in 12 ounce containers; (f) Different rates also applicable according to alcohol content, place of production, size of container, or place purchased (on- or off-premise or onboard airlines); (l) Different rates also applicable to alcohol content, place of production, size of container, place purchased (on- or off-premise or on board airlines) or type of wine (carbonated, vermouth, etc.); (q) Different rates also applicable according to alcohol content, place of production, size of container, or place purchased (on- or off-premise or onboard airlines).
Source: Tax Foundation, 2018 Facts & Figures: How Does Your State Compare?

State Business Tax Climate Index Rankings

State	Overall Rank	Corporate Tax Rank	Individual Income Tax Rank	Sales Tax Rank	Unemployment Insurance Tax Rank	Property Tax Rank
Texas	13	49	6	37	26	37

Note: The index is a measure of how each state's tax laws affect economic performance. The lower the rank, the more favorable a state's tax system is for business. States without a given tax are given a ranking of 1. The scores/rankings for the District of Columbia do not affect other states. The 2018 index represents the tax climate as of July 1, 2017.
Source: Tax Foundation, State Business Tax Climate Index 2018

TRANSPORTATION

Means of Transportation to Work

Area	Car/Truck/Van		Public Transportation			Bicycle	Walked	Other Means	Worked at Home
	Drove Alone	Car-pooled	Bus	Subway	Railroad				
City	78.9	10.2	0.7	0.0	0.3	0.3	0.3	0.9	8.4
MSA[1]	76.5	9.9	2.2	0.0	0.1	0.8	1.7	1.3	7.4
U.S.	76.4	9.3	2.6	1.9	0.6	0.6	2.8	1.3	4.6

Note: Figures are percentages and cover workers 16 years of age and older; (1) Figures cover the Austin-Round Rock, TX Metropolitan Statistical Area—see Appendix B for areas included
Source: U.S. Census Bureau, 2012-2016 American Community Survey 5-Year Estimates

Travel Time to Work

Area	Less Than 10 Minutes	10 to 19 Minutes	20 to 29 Minutes	30 to 44 Minutes	45 to 59 Minutes	60 to 89 Minutes	90 Minutes or More
City	7.5	20.5	20.5	27.5	14.8	7.4	1.8
MSA[1]	10.2	28.3	22.3	22.7	9.2	5.5	1.9
U.S.	12.9	29.2	20.9	20.4	8.0	6.0	2.7

Note: Note: Figures are percentages and include workers 16 years old and over; (1) Figures cover the Austin-Round Rock, TX Metropolitan Statistical Area—see Appendix B for areas included
Source: U.S. Census Bureau, 2012-2016 American Community Survey 5-Year Estimates

Freeway Travel Time Index

Area	1985	1990	1995	2000	2005	2010	2014
Urban Area Rank[1,2]	20	21	23	15	12	12	10
Urban Area Index[1]	1.12	1.15	1.19	1.26	1.31	1.29	1.33
Average Index[3]	1.09	1.11	1.14	1.17	1.20	1.19	1.20

Note: Freeway Travel Time Index—the ratio of travel time in the peak period to the travel time at free-flow conditions. For example, a value of 1.30 indicates a 20-minute free-flow trip takes 26 minutes in the peak (20 minutes x 1.30 = 26 minutes); (1) Covers the Austin TX urban area; (2) Rank is based on 101 urban areas (#1 = highest travel time index); (3) Average of 101 urban areas
Source: Texas Transportation Institute, 2015 Urban Mobility Scorecard, August 2015

Freeway Commuter Stress Index

Area	1985	1990	1995	2000	2005	2010	2014
Urban Area Rank[1,2]	18	17	11	8	7	9	7
Urban Area Index[1]	1.22	1.25	1.30	1.37	1.43	1.40	1.44
Average Index[3]	1.13	1.16	1.19	1.22	1.25	1.24	1.25

Note: The Freeway Commuter Stress Index is the same as the Freeway Travel Time Index (see table above) except that it includes only the travel in the peak directions during the peak periods; the TTI includes travel in all directions during the peak period. Thus, the CSI is more indicative of the work trip experienced by each commuter on a daily basis; (1) Covers the Austin TX urban area; (2) Rank is based on 101 urban areas (#1 = highest travel time index); (3) Average of 101 urban areas
Source: Texas Transportation Institute, 2015 Urban Mobility Scorecard, August 2015

Living Environment

COST OF LIVING

Cost of Living Index

Composite Index	Groceries	Housing	Utilities	Transportation	Health Care	Misc. Goods/ Services
97.3	87.7	101.8	87.7	93.3	99.4	100.8

Note: The Cost of Living Index measures regional differences in the cost of consumer goods and services, excluding taxes and non-consumer expenditures, for professional and managerial households in the top income quintile. It is based on more than 50,000 prices covering almost 60 different items for which prices are collected three times a year by chambers of commerce, economic development organizations or university applied economic centers in each participating urban area. The numbers shown should be read as a percentage above or below the national average of 100. For example, a value of 115.4 in the groceries column indicates that grocery prices are 15.4% higher than the national average. Small differences in the index numbers should not be interpreted as significant; Figures cover the Austin TX urban area.
Source: The Council for Community and Economic Research, ACCRA Cost of Living Index, 2017

Grocery Prices

Area[1]	T-Bone Steak ($/pound)	Frying Chicken ($/pound)	Whole Milk ($/half gal.)	Eggs ($/dozen)	Orange Juice ($/64 oz.)	Coffee ($/11.5 oz.)
City[2]	9.91	1.15	1.81	1.34	3.14	3.97
Avg.	11.29	1.40	2.02	1.47	3.55	4.37
Min.	7.71	0.93	1.04	0.70	2.86	3.24
Max.	15.83	2.39	4.03	3.92	6.29	8.16

Note: (1) Values for the local area are compared with the average, minimum and maximum values for all 294 areas in the Cost of Living Index; (2) Figures cover the Austin TX urban area; ***T-Bone Steak*** *(price per pound);* ***Frying Chicken*** *(price per pound, whole fryer);* ***Whole Milk*** *(half gallon carton);* ***Eggs*** *(price per dozen, Grade A, large);* ***Orange Juice*** *(64 oz. Tropicana or Florida Natural);* ***Coffee*** *(11.5 oz. can, vacuum-packed, Maxwell House, Hills Bros, or Folgers).*
Source: The Council for Community and Economic Research, ACCRA Cost of Living Index, 2017

Housing and Utility Costs

Area[1]	New Home Price ($)	Apartment Rent ($/month)	All Electric ($/month)	Part Electric ($/month)	Other Energy ($/month)	Telephone ($/month)
City[2]	301,734	1,305	-	103.67	53.64	22.94
Avg.	335,956	1,047	175.01	97.34	67.93	28.71
Min.	187,788	491	109.48	49.33	35.44	12.39
Max.	1,739,087	4,559	432.62	227.09	353.33	44.61

Note: (1) Values for the local area are compared with the average, minimum and maximum values for all 294 areas in the Cost of Living Index; (2) Figures cover the Austin TX urban area; ***New Home Price*** *(2,400 sf living area, 8,000 sf lot, in urban area with full utilities);* ***Apartment Rent*** *(950 sf 2 bedroom/1.5 or 2 bath, unfurnished, excluding all utilities except water);* ***All Electric*** *(average monthly cost for an all-electric home);* ***Part Electric*** *(average monthly cost for a part-electric home);* ***Other Energy*** *(average monthly cost for natural gas, fuel oil, coal, wood, and any other forms of energy except electricity);* ***Telephone*** *(price includes basic monthly rate for a private residential line plus additional local usage charges incurred by a family of four).*
Source: The Council for Community and Economic Research, ACCRA Cost of Living Index, 2017

Health Care, Transportation, and Other Costs

Area[1]	Doctor ($/visit)	Dentist ($/visit)	Optometrist ($/visit)	Gasoline ($/gallon)	Beauty Salon ($/visit)	Men's Shirt ($)
City[2]	98.76	99.00	109.83	2.11	46.34	29.05
Avg.	108.00	92.54	101.93	2.25	37.58	30.92
Min.	30.39	60.00	49.75	1.82	16.11	11.20
Max.	193.50	161.94	229.28	3.16	77.35	59.13

Note: (1) Values for the local area are compared with the average, minimum and maximum values for all 294 areas in the Cost of Living Index; (2) Figures cover the Austin TX urban area; ***Doctor*** *(general practitioners routine exam of an established patient);* ***Dentist*** *(adult teeth cleaning and periodic oral examination);* ***Optometrist*** *(full vision eye exam for established adult patient);* ***Gasoline*** *(one gallon regular unleaded, national brand, including all taxes, cash price at self-service pump if available);* ***Beauty Salon*** *(woman's shampoo, trim, and blow-dry);* ***Men's Shirt*** *(cotton/polyester dress shirt, pinpoint weave, long sleeves).*
Source: The Council for Community and Economic Research, ACCRA Cost of Living Index, 2017

HOUSING

House Price Index (HPI)

Area	National Ranking[2]	Quarterly Change (%)	One-Year Change (%)	Five-Year Change (%)
MSA[1]	85	0.63	7.61	55.90
U.S.[3]	–	1.61	6.68	34.71

Note: The HPI is a weighted repeat sales index. It measures average price changes in repeat sales or refinancings on the same properties. This information is obtained by reviewing repeat mortgage transactions on single-family properties whose mortgages have been purchased or securitized by Fannie Mae or Freddie Mac in January 1975; (1) Figures cover the Austin-Round Rock, TX Metropolitan Statistical Area—see Appendix B for areas included; (2) Rankings are based on annual percentage change for all metro areas containing at least 15,000 transactions over the last 10 years and ranges from 1 to 253; (3) figures based on a weighted average of Census Division estimates using a seasonally adjusted, purchase-only index; all figures are for the period ending December 31, 2017
Source: Federal Housing Finance Agency, House Price Index, February 28, 2018

Median Single-Family Home Prices

Area	2015	2016	2017[p]	Percent Change 2016 to 2017
MSA[1]	263.3	284.0	295.8	4.2
U.S. Average	223.9	235.5	248.8	5.6

Note: Figures are median sales prices of existing single-family homes in thousands of dollars; (p) preliminary; (1) Figures cover the Austin-Round Rock, TX Metropolitan Statistical Area—see Appendix B for areas included
Source: National Association of Realtors, Median Sales Price of Existing Single-Family Homes for Metropolitan Areas, 4th Quarter 2017

Qualifying Income Based on Median Sales Price of Existing Single-Family Homes

Area	With 5% Down ($)	With 10% Down ($)	With 20% Down ($)
MSA[1]	65,769	62,307	55,384
U.S. Average	55,585	52,659	46,808

Note: Figures are preliminary; Qualifying income is based on a mortgage rate of 4.17%. Monthly principal and interest payment is limited to 25% of income; (1) Figures cover the Austin-Round Rock, TX Metropolitan Statistical Area—see Appendix B for areas included
Source: National Association of Realtors, Qualifying Income Based on Median Sales Price of Existing Single-Family Homes for Metropolitan Areas, 4th Quarter 2017

Median Apartment Condo-Coop Home Prices

Area	2015	2016	2017[p]	Percent Change 2016 to 2017
MSA[1]	227.5	228.0	241.8	6.1
U.S. Average	210.7	220.7	234.3	6.2

Note: Figures are median sales prices of existing apartment condo-coop homes in thousands of dollars; (p) preliminary; (1) Figures cover the Austin-Round Rock, TX Metropolitan Statistical Area—see Appendix B for areas included
Source: National Association of Realtors, Median Sales Price of Existing Apartment Condo-Coop Homes for Metropolitan Areas, 4th Quarter 2017

Home Value Distribution

Area	Under $50,000	$50,000 -$99,999	$100,000 -$149,999	$150,000 -$199,999	$200,000 -$299,999	$300,000 -$499,999	$500,000 -$999,999	$1,000,000 or more
City	2.7	2.5	26.1	25.3	21.8	15.2	6.0	0.3
MSA[1]	4.5	6.2	14.1	18.3	24.9	20.4	9.3	2.2
U.S.	8.8	14.8	15.3	14.9	18.4	16.4	9.0	2.5

Note: Figures are percentages and cover owner-occupied housing units; (1) Figures cover the Austin-Round Rock, TX Metropolitan Statistical Area—see Appendix B for areas included
Source: U.S. Census Bureau, 2012-2016 American Community Survey 5-Year Estimates

Homeownership Rate

Area	2009 (%)	2010 (%)	2011 (%)	2012 (%)	2013 (%)	2014 (%)	2015 (%)	2016 (%)	2017 (%)
MSA[1]	64.0	65.8	58.4	60.1	59.6	61.1	57.5	56.5	55.6
U.S.	67.4	66.9	66.1	65.4	65.1	64.5	63.7	63.4	63.9

Note: (1) Figures cover the Austin-Round Rock, TX Metropolitan Statistical Area—see Appendix B for areas included
Source: U.S. Census Bureau, Housing Vacancies and Homeownership Annual Statistics: 2009-2017

Year Housing Structure Built

Area	2010 or Later	2000 -2009	1990 -1999	1980 -1989	1970 -1979	1960 -1969	1950 -1959	1940 -1949	Before 1940	Median Year
City	14.5	51.2	17.0	11.0	3.8	0.8	0.0	0.4	1.3	2003
MSA[1]	7.0	28.6	19.4	18.2	13.1	5.4	3.7	2.0	2.5	1993
U.S.	2.3	14.7	14.0	13.7	15.6	10.9	10.6	5.2	13.0	1977

Note: Figures are percentages except for Median Year; Note: (1) Figures cover the Austin-Round Rock, TX Metropolitan Statistical Area—see Appendix B for areas included
Source: U.S. Census Bureau, 2012-2016 American Community Survey 5-Year Estimates

Gross Monthly Rent

Area	Under $500	$500 -$999	$1,000 -$1,499	$1,500 -$1,999	$2,000 -$2,499	$2,500 -$2,999	$3,000 and up	Median ($)
City	0.8	19.9	31.6	40.7	6.4	0.5	0.0	1,461
MSA[1]	3.7	36.9	38.9	15.0	3.5	1.0	0.9	1,098
U.S.	11.3	43.3	27.7	10.7	4.0	1.6	1.5	949

Note: Figures are percentages except for Median; Gross rent is the contract rent plus the estimated average monthly cost of utilities (electricity, gas, and water and sewer) and fuels (oil, coal, kerosene, wood, etc.) if these are paid by the renter (or paid for the renter by someone else); (1) Figures cover the Austin-Round Rock, TX Metropolitan Statistical Area—see Appendix B for areas included
Source: U.S. Census Bureau, 2012-2016 American Community Survey 5-Year Estimates

HEALTH

Health Risk Factors

Category	MSA[1] (%)	U.S. (%)
Adults aged 18–64 who have any kind of health care coverage	78.8	87.7
Adults who reported being in good or excellent health	85.7	83.6
Adults who are current smokers	14.6	17.1
Adults who currently use E-cigarettes	6.1	4.7
Adults who currently use chewing tobacco, snuff, or snus	3.2	4.0
Adults who are heavy drinkers[2]	9.1	6.5
Adults who are binge drinkers[3]	22.7	16.9
Adults who are overweight (BMI 25.0 - 29.9)	32.9	35.3
Adults who are obese (BMI 30.0 - 99.8)	29.4	29.9
Adults who participated in any physical activities in the past month	81.2	76.9
Adults who always or nearly always wears a seat belt	96.6	94.3

Note: (1) Figures cover the Austin-Round Rock, TX Metropolitan Statistical Area—see Appendix B for areas included; (2) Heavy drinkers are classified as adult men having more than 14 drinks per week and adult women having more than 7 drinks per week; (3) Binge drinkers are classified as males having five or more drinks on one occasion or females having four or more drinks on one occasion
Source: Centers for Disease Control and Prevention, Behaviorial Risk Factor Surveillance System, SMART: Selected Metropolitan Area Risk Trends, 2016

Health Screening Rates

Category	MSA[1] (%)	U.S. (%)
Adults 50-75 who have had a blood stool test within the past year	7.2	8.0
Adults 50-75 who have had a colonoscopy in the past 10 years	66.0	63.5
Adults aged 65+ who have had flu shot within the past year	53.3	58.6
Adults aged 65+ who have ever had a pneumonia vaccination	80.1	73.4
Adults who have ever been tested for HIV	46.4	35.6
Women aged 21-65 who have had a pap test in the past three years	79.0	79.8
Men aged 40+ who have had a PSA test within the past two years	36.8	39.5
Women aged 40+ who have had a mammogram within the past two years	70.1	72.5

Note: n/a not available; (1) Figures cover the Austin-Round Rock, TX Metropolitan Statistical Area—see Appendix B for areas included; Source: Centers for Disease Control and Prevention, Behaviorial Risk Factor Surveillance System, SMART: Selected Metropolitan Area Risk Trends, 2016

Chronic Health Conditions

Category	MSA[1] (%)	U.S. (%)
Adults who have ever been told they had a heart attack	3.1	4.4
Adults who have ever been told they have angina or coronary heart disease	3.5	4.1
Adults who have ever been told they had a stroke	2.3	3.1
Adults who have been told they currently have asthma	8.6	9.3
Adults who have ever been told they have arthritis	18.4	25.8
Adults who have ever been told they have diabetes[2]	10.4	10.5
Adults who have ever been told they had skin cancer	6.8	5.9
Adults who have ever been told they had any other types of cancer	5.5	6.7
Adults who have ever been told they have COPD	3.6	6.3
Adults who have ever been told they have kidney disease	2.6	2.8
Adults who have ever been told they have a form of depression	13.7	17.4

Note: (1) Figures cover the Austin-Round Rock, TX Metropolitan Statistical Area—see Appendix B for areas included; (2) Figures do not include pregnancy-related, borderline, or pre-diabetes
Source: Centers for Disease Control and Prevention, Behaviorial Risk Factor Surveillance System, SMART: Selected Metropolitan Area Risk Trends, 2016

Mortality Rates for the Top 10 Causes of Death in the U.S.

ICD-10[a] Sub-Chapter	ICD-10[a] Code	Age-Adjusted Mortality Rate[1] per 100,000 population	
		County[2]	U.S.
Malignant neoplasms	C00-C97	129.1	158.5
Ischaemic heart diseases	I20-I25	66.9	96.8
Other forms of heart disease	I30-I51	35.7	52.4
Chronic lower respiratory diseases	J40-J47	31.4	40.9
Cerebrovascular diseases	I60-I69	34.8	37.2
Organic, including symptomatic, mental disorders	F01-F09	40.1	33.3
Other degenerative diseases of the nervous system	G30-G31	43.6	32.1
Other external causes of accidental injury	W00-X59	17.2	31.2
Diabetes mellitus	E10-E14	10.8	21.1
Hypertensive diseases	I10-I15	16.1	20.8

Note: (a) ICD-10 = International Classification of Diseases 10th Revision; (1) Mortality rates are a three year average covering 2014-2016; (2) Figures cover Williamson County.
Source: Centers for Disease Control and Prevention, National Center for Health Statistics. Underlying Cause of Death 1999-2016 on CDC WONDER Online Database, released December 2017

Mortality Rates for Selected Causes of Death

ICD-10[a] Sub-Chapter	ICD-10[a] Code	Age-Adjusted Mortality Rate[1] per 100,000 population	
		County[2]	U.S.
Assault	X85-Y09	1.5	5.6
Diseases of the liver	K70-K76	12.8	14.0
Human immunodeficiency virus (HIV) disease	B20-B24	Suppressed	1.9
Influenza and pneumonia	J09-J18	9.4	14.6
Intentional self-harm	X60-X84	14.0	13.2
Malnutrition	E40-E46	Unreliable	1.3
Obesity and other hyperalimentation	E65-E68	Suppressed	2.1
Renal failure	N17-N19	10.6	13.0
Transport accidents	V01-V99	11.0	12.0
Viral hepatitis	B15-B19	Unreliable	1.9

Note: (a) ICD-10 = International Classification of Diseases 10th Revision; (1) Mortality rates are a three year average covering 2014-2016; (2) Figures cover Williamson County; Data are Suppressed when the data meet the criteria for confidentiality constraints; Mortality rates are flagged as Unreliable when the rate would be calculated with a numerator of 20 or less.
Source: Centers for Disease Control and Prevention, National Center for Health Statistics. Underlying Cause of Death 1999-2016 on CDC WONDER Online Database, released December 2017

Health Insurance Coverage

Area	With Health Insurance	With Private Health Insurance	With Public Health Insurance	Without Health Insurance	Population Under Age 18 Without Health Insurance
City	89.5	78.8	19.0	10.5	6.9
MSA[1]	85.1	71.7	21.8	14.9	8.7
U.S.	88.3	66.7	33.0	11.7	5.9

Note: Figures are percentages that cover the civilian noninstitutionalized population; (1) Figures cover the Austin-Round Rock, TX Metropolitan Statistical Area—see Appendix B for areas included
Source: U.S. Census Bureau, 2012-2016 American Community Survey 5-Year Estimates

Number of Medical Professionals

Area	MDs[3]	DOs[3,4]	Dentists	Podiatrists	Chiropractors	Optometrists
County[1] (number)	874	90	286	22	142	92
County[1] (rate[2])	172.2	17.7	54.2	4.2	26.9	17.4
U.S. (rate[2])	276.5	22.3	67.3	6.0	26.7	15.9

Note: Data as of 2016 unless noted; (1) Data covers Williamson County; (2) Rate per 100,000 population; (3) Data as of 2015 and includes all active, non-federal physicians; (4) Doctor of Osteopathic Medicine
Source: U.S. Department of Health and Human Services, Health Resources and Services Administration, Bureau of Health Professions, Area Resource File (ARF) 2016-2017

Best Hospitals

According to *U.S. News,* the Austin-Round Rock, TX metro area is home to one of the best children's hospitals in the U.S.: **Dell Children's Medical Center of Central Texas** (1 pediatric specialty). The hospital listed was highly ranked in at least one of 10 pediatric specialties. Eighty-two children's hospitals in the U.S. were nationally ranked in at least one specialty. Hospitals received points for being ranked in a specialty, and the 10 hospitals with the most points across the 10 specialties make up the Honor Roll. *U.S. News Online, "America's Best Children's Hospitals 2017-18"*

EDUCATION

Public School District Statistics

District Name	Schls	Pupils	Pupil/ Teacher Ratio	Minority Pupils[1] (%)	Free Lunch Eligible[2] (%)	IEP[3] (%)
Leander ISD	42	37,158	15.2	39.3	14.2	10.3
Priority Charter Schools	5	1,030	16.2	52.9	42.0	9.4
Texas College Preparatory Academies	38	12,778	20.2	56.3	33.3	6.9

Note: Table includes school districts with 100 or more students; (1) Percentage of students that are not non-Hispanic white; (2) Percentage of students that are eligible for the free lunch program; (3) Percentage of students that have an Individualized Education Program.
Source: U.S. Department of Education, National Center for Education Statistics, Common Core of Data, Local Education Agency (School District) Universe Survey: School Year 2015-2016; U.S. Department of Education, National Center for Education Statistics, Common Core of Data, Public Elementary/Secondary School Universe Survey: School Year 2015-2016

Highest Level of Education

Area	Less than H.S.	H.S. Diploma	Some College, No Deg.	Associate Degree	Bachelor's Degree	Master's Degree	Prof. School Degree	Doctorate Degree
City	7.4	19.8	25.9	11.2	24.4	8.6	1.4	1.3
MSA[1]	11.1	19.2	21.3	6.4	27.4	10.6	2.3	1.8
U.S.	13.0	27.5	21.0	8.2	18.8	8.2	2.0	1.3

Note: Figures cover persons age 25 and over; (1) Figures cover the Austin-Round Rock, TX Metropolitan Statistical Area—see Appendix B for areas included
Source: U.S. Census Bureau, 2012-2016 American Community Survey 5-Year Estimates

Educational Attainment by Race

Area	High School Graduate or Higher (%)					Bachelor's Degree or Higher (%)				
	Total	White	Black	Asian	Hisp.[2]	Total	White	Black	Asian	Hisp.[2]
City	92.6	93.7	89.5	81.6	81.0	35.7	36.2	34.5	63.9	17.8
MSA[1]	88.9	90.1	89.6	91.8	70.4	42.0	43.6	25.5	67.7	20.2
U.S.	87.0	88.9	84.3	86.3	65.7	30.3	31.6	20.0	52.1	14.7

Note: Figures shown cover persons 25 years old and over; (1) Figures cover the Austin-Round Rock, TX Metropolitan Statistical Area—see Appendix B for areas included; (2) People of Hispanic origin can be of any race
Source: U.S. Census Bureau, 2012-2016 American Community Survey 5-Year Estimates

School Enrollment by Grade and Control

Area	Preschool (%)		Kindergarten (%)		Grades 1 - 4 (%)		Grades 5 - 8 (%)		Grades 9 - 12 (%)	
	Public	Private	Public	Private	Public	Private	Public	Private	Public	Private
City	52.2	47.8	82.8	17.2	98.0	2.0	94.8	5.2	97.2	2.8
MSA[1]	50.0	50.0	88.8	11.2	91.4	8.6	91.6	8.4	93.5	6.5
U.S.	58.4	41.6	87.7	12.3	89.8	10.2	89.7	10.3	90.4	9.6

Note: Figures shown cover persons 3 years old and over; (1) Figures cover the Austin-Round Rock, TX Metropolitan Statistical Area—see Appendix B for areas included
Source: U.S. Census Bureau, 2012-2016 American Community Survey 5-Year Estimates

Average Salaries of Public School Classroom Teachers

Area	2015		2016		Change from 2015 to 2016	
	Dollars	Rank[1]	Dollars	Rank[1]	Percent	Rank[2]
Texas	50,713	28	51,890	27	2.3	8
U.S. Average	57,611	–	58,353	–	1.3	–

Note: (1) Rank ranges from 1 to 51 where 1 indicates highest salary; (2) Rank ranges from 1 to 51 where 1 indicates highest percent change.
Source: National Education Association, Rankings & Estimates: Rankings of the States 2016 and Estimates of School Statistics 2017

Higher Education

Four-Year Colleges			Two-Year Colleges			Medical Schools[1]	Law Schools[2]	Voc/ Tech[3]
Public	Private Non-profit	Private For-profit	Public	Private Non-profit	Private For-profit			
0	0	0	0	0	0	0	0	0

Note: Figures cover institutions located within the city limits and include main campuses only; (1) includes schools accredited by the Liaison Committee on Medical Education and the American Osteopathic Association's Commission on Osteopathic College Accreditation; (2) includes ABA-accredited schools, schools with provisional ABA accreditation, and state accredited schools; (3) includes all schools with programs that are less than 2 years.
Source: National Center for Education Statistics, Integrated Postsecondary Education System (IPEDS), 2016-17; Wikipedia, List of Medical Schools in the United States, accessed April 2, 2018; Wikipedia, List of Law Schools in the United States, accessed April 2, 2018

According to *U.S. News & World Report,* the Austin-Round Rock, TX metro area is home to one of the best national universities in the U.S.: **University of Texas—Austin** (#56 tie). The indicators used to capture academic quality fall into a number of categories: assessment by administrators at peer institutions; retention of students; faculty resources; student selectivity; financial resources; alumni giving; high school counselor ratings of colleges; and graduation rate. *U.S. News & World Report, "America's Best Colleges 2018"*

According to *U.S. News & World Report,* the Austin-Round Rock, TX metro area is home to one of the best liberal arts colleges in the U.S.: **Southwestern University** (#96 tie). The indicators used to capture academic quality fall into a number of categories: assessment by administrators at peer institutions; retention of students; faculty resources; student selectivity; financial resources; alumni giving; high school counselor ratings of colleges; and graduation rate. *U.S. News & World Report, "America's Best Colleges 2018"*

According to *U.S. News & World Report,* the Austin-Round Rock, TX metro area is home to one of the top 100 law schools in the U.S.: **University of Texas—Austin** (#15). The rankings are based on a weighted average of 12 measures of quality: peer assessment score; assessment score by lawyers/judges; median LSAT scores; median undergrad GPA; acceptance rate; employment rates for graduates; placement success; bar passage rate; faculty resources; expenditures per student; student/faculty ratio; and library resources. *U.S. News & World Report, "America's Best Graduate Schools, Law, 2019"*

According to *U.S. News & World Report,* the Austin-Round Rock, TX metro area is home to one of the top 75 business schools in the U.S.: **University of Texas—Austin (McCombs)** (#17 tie). The rankings are based on a weighted average of the following nine measures: quality assessment; peer assessment; recruiter assessment; placement success; mean starting salary and bonus; student selectivity; mean GMAT and GRE scores; mean undergraduate GPA; and acceptance rate. *U.S. News & World Report, "America's Best Graduate Schools, Business, 2019"*

PRESIDENTIAL ELECTION

2016 Presidential Election Results

Area	Clinton	Trump	Johnson	Stein	Other
Williamson County	41.3	50.9	5.0	1.0	1.8
U.S.	48.0	45.9	3.3	1.1	1.7

Note: Results are percentages and may not add to 100% due to rounding
Source: Dave Leip's Atlas of U.S. Presidential Elections

EMPLOYERS

Major Employers

Company Name	Industry
Accenture	Management consulting & software development center
Apple	Computer maker's tech & admin support center
Applied Materials	Semiconductor production equipment mfg. & r&d
AT&T	Telecommunications (hdq. of texas ops.)
Austin Community College	Higher education, public
Austin School Independent District	Public education
City of Austin	Government
Dell	Computer technology solutions & equipment mfg./sales
Federal Government	Government
Flextronics	Contract electronics mfg. & integrated supply chain svcs
Hays Consolidated ISD	Public education
IBM Corp.	Computer systems, hardware, software, & chip r&d
Keller Williams Realty	Residential real estate
Leander Independent School District	Public education
National Instruments	Virtual instrumentation software & hardware mfg.
NXP Semiconductors	Semiconductor chip design & mfg.
Pflugerville Independent School District	Public education
Round Rock Independent School District	Public education
Samsung Austin Semiconductor	Semiconductor chip mfg., R&D
Seton Healthcare Family	Healthcare
St. David's Healthcare Partnership	Healthcare
State of Texas	Government
Texas State University-San Marcos	Higher education, public
Travis County	Government
U.S. Internal Revenue Service	Government (regional call & processing center)
University of Texas at Austin	Higher education, public
Whole Foods Market	Grocery stores

Note: Companies shown are located within the Austin-Round Rock, TX Metropolitan Statistical Area.
Source: Hoovers.com; Wikipedia

PUBLIC SAFETY

Crime Rate

Area	All Crimes	Violent Crimes				Property Crimes		
		Murder	Rape[3]	Robbery	Aggrav. Assault	Burglary	Larceny -Theft	Motor Vehicle Theft
City	1,232.5	0.0	46.7	9.8	56.6	140.2	927.4	51.7
Metro[1]	2,872.1	3.4	57.4	68.7	187.4	421.9	1,968.3	165.1
U.S.	2,847.8	5.3	40.4	102.8	248.5	468.9	1,745.0	236.9

Note: Figures are crimes per 100,000 population; (1) Figures cover the Austin-Round Rock, TX Metropolitan Statistical Area—see Appendix B for areas included; (3) The city and U.S. figures shown were reported using the revised Uniform Crime Reporting (UCR) definition of rape. The metro area figures shown are an aggregate total of the data submitted using both the revised and legacy UCR definitions.
Source: FBI Uniform Crime Reports, 2016

Hate Crimes

Area	Number of Quarters Reported	Number of Incidents per Bias Motivation: Race/Ethnicity/Ancestry	Religion	Sexual Orientation	Disability	Gender	Gender Identity
City	4	0	0	0	0	0	0
U.S.	4	3,489	1,273	1,076	70	31	124

Source: Federal Bureau of Investigation, Hate Crime Statistics 2016

Identity Theft Consumer Reports

Area	Reports	Reports per 100,000 Population	Rank[2]
MSA[1]	2,485	121	53
U.S.	371,061	114	-

Note: (1) Figures cover the Austin-Round Rock, TX Metropolitan Statistical Area—see Appendix B for areas included; (2) Rank ranges from 1 to 389 where 1 indicates greatest number of identity theft reports per 100,000 population
Source: Federal Trade Commission, Consumer Sentinel Network Data Book for January–December 2017

Fraud and Other Consumer Reports

Area	Reports	Reports per 100,000 Population	Rank[2]
MSA[1]	10,984	534	84
U.S.	2,304,550	708	-

Note: (1) Figures cover the Austin-Round Rock, TX Metropolitan Statistical Area—see Appendix B for areas included; (2) Rank ranges from 1 to 389 where 1 indicates greatest number of fraud and other consumer reports per 100,000 population
Source: Federal Trade Commission, Consumer Sentinel Network Data Book for January–December 2017

SPORTS

Professional Sports Teams

Team Name	League	Year Established
No teams are located in the metro area		

Source: Wikipedia, Major Professional Sports Teams of the United States and Canada, April 5, 2018

CLIMATE

Average and Extreme Temperatures

Temperature	Jan	Feb	Mar	Apr	May	Jun	Jul	Aug	Sep	Oct	Nov	Dec	Yr.
Extreme High (°F)	90	97	98	98	100	105	109	106	104	98	91	90	109
Average High (°F)	60	64	72	79	85	91	95	96	90	81	70	63	79
Average Temp. (°F)	50	53	61	69	75	82	85	85	80	70	60	52	69
Average Low (°F)	39	43	50	58	65	72	74	74	69	59	49	41	58
Extreme Low (°F)	-2	7	18	35	43	53	64	61	47	32	20	4	-2

Note: Figures cover the years 1948-1990
Source: National Climatic Data Center, International Station Meteorological Climate Summary, 9/96

Average Precipitation/Snowfall/Humidity

Precip./Humidity	Jan	Feb	Mar	Apr	May	Jun	Jul	Aug	Sep	Oct	Nov	Dec	Yr.
Avg. Precip. (in.)	1.6	2.3	1.8	2.9	4.3	3.5	1.9	1.9	3.3	3.5	2.1	1.9	31.1
Avg. Snowfall (in.)	1	Tr	Tr	0	0	0	0	0	0	0	Tr	Tr	1
Avg. Rel. Hum. 6am (%)	79	80	79	83	88	89	88	87	86	84	81	79	84
Avg. Rel. Hum. 3pm (%)	53	51	47	50	53	49	43	42	47	47	49	51	48

Note: Figures cover the years 1948-1990; Tr = Trace amounts (<0.05 in. of rain; <0.5 in. of snow)
Source: National Climatic Data Center, International Station Meteorological Climate Summary, 9/96

Weather Conditions

Temperature: 10°F & below	32°F & below	90°F & above	Daytime Sky: Clear	Partly cloudy	Cloudy	Precipitation: 0.01 inch or more precip.	0.1 inch or more snow/ice	Thunder-storms
< 1	20	111	105	148	112	83	1	41

Note: Figures are average number of days per year and cover the years 1948-1990
Source: National Climatic Data Center, International Station Meteorological Climate Summary, 9/96

HAZARDOUS WASTE

Superfund Sites

The Austin-Round Rock, TX metro area has no sites on the EPA's Superfund Final National Priorities List. There are a total of 1,396 Superfund sites with a status of proposed or final on the list in the U.S. *U.S. Environmental Protection Agency, National Priorities List, April 4, 2018*

AIR & WATER QUALITY

Air Quality Trends: Ozone

	1990	1995	2000	2005	2010	2012	2013	2014	2015	2016
MSA[1]	0.088	0.089	0.088	0.082	0.074	0.074	0.069	0.062	0.073	0.064
U.S.	0.087	0.089	0.081	0.079	0.073	0.075	0.069	0.067	0.068	0.069

Note: (1) Data covers the Austin-Round Rock, TX Metropolitan Statistical Area—see Appendix B for areas included. The values shown are the composite ozone concentration averages among trend sites based on the highest fourth daily maximum 8-hour concentration in parts per million. These trends are based on sites having an adequate record of monitoring data during the trend period. Data from exceptional events are included.
Source: U.S. Environmental Protection Agency, Air Quality Monitoring Information, "Air Quality Trends by City, 1990-2016"

Air Quality Index

Area	Percent of Days when Air Quality was...[2]					AQI Statistics[2]	
	Good	Moderate	Unhealthy for Sensitive Groups	Unhealthy	Very Unhealthy	Maximum	Median
MSA[1]	71.8	27.1	1.1	0.0	0.0	130	43

Note: (1) Data covers the Austin-Round Rock, TX Metropolitan Statistical Area—see Appendix B for areas included; (2) Based on 365 days with AQI data in 2017. Air Quality Index (AQI) is an index for reporting daily air quality. EPA calculates the AQI for five major air pollutants regulated by the Clean Air Act: ground-level ozone, particle pollution (aka particulate matter), carbon monoxide, sulfur dioxide, and nitrogen dioxide. The AQI runs from 0 to 500. The higher the AQI value, the greater the level of air pollution and the greater the health concern. There are six AQI categories: "Good" AQI is between 0 and 50. Air quality is considered satisfactory; "Moderate" AQI is between 51 and 100. Air quality is acceptable; "Unhealthy for Sensitive Groups" When AQI values are between 101 and 150, members of sensitive groups may experience health effects; "Unhealthy" When AQI values are between 151 and 200 everyone may begin to experience health effects; "Very Unhealthy" AQI values between 201 and 300 trigger a health alert; "Hazardous" AQI values over 300 trigger warnings of emergency conditions (not shown).
Source: U.S. Environmental Protection Agency, Air Quality Index Report, 2017

Air Quality Index Pollutants

Area	Percent of Days when AQI Pollutant was...[2]					
	Carbon Monoxide	Nitrogen Dioxide	Ozone	Sulfur Dioxide	Particulate Matter 2.5	Particulate Matter 10
MSA[1]	0.0	3.8	49.9	0.0	46.3	0.0

Note: (1) Data covers the Austin-Round Rock, TX Metropolitan Statistical Area—see Appendix B for areas included; (2) Based on 365 days with AQI data in 2017. The Air Quality Index (AQI) is an index for reporting daily air quality. EPA calculates the AQI for five major air pollutants regulated by the Clean Air Act: ground-level ozone, particle pollution (also known as particulate matter), carbon monoxide, sulfur dioxide, and nitrogen dioxide. The AQI runs from 0 to 500. The higher the AQI value, the greater the level of air pollution and the greater the health concern.
Source: U.S. Environmental Protection Agency, Air Quality Index Report, 2017

Maximum Air Pollutant Concentrations: Particulate Matter, Ozone, CO and Lead

	Particulate Matter 10 (ug/m^3)	Particulate Matter 2.5 Wtd AM (ug/m^3)	Particulate Matter 2.5 24-Hr (ug/m^3)	Ozone (ppm)	Carbon Monoxide (ppm)	Lead (ug/m^3)
MSA[1] Level	72	n/a	n/a	0.064	n/a	n/a
NAAQS[2]	150	15	35	0.075	9	0.15
Met NAAQS[2]	Yes	n/a	n/a	Yes	n/a	n/a

Note: (1) Data covers the Austin-Round Rock, TX Metropolitan Statistical Area—see Appendix B for areas included; Data from exceptional events are included; (2) National Ambient Air Quality Standards; ppm = parts per million; ug/m^3 = micrograms per cubic meter; n/a not available.

Concentrations: Particulate Matter 10 (coarse particulate)—highest second maximum 24-hour concentration; Particulate Matter 2.5 Wtd AM (fine particulate)—highest weighted annual mean concentration; Particulate Matter 2.5 24-Hour (fine particulate)—highest 98th percentile 24-hour concentration; Ozone—highest fourth daily maximum 8-hour concentration; Carbon Monoxide—highest second maximum non-overlapping 8-hour concentration; Lead—maximum running 3-month average

Source: U.S. Environmental Protection Agency, Air Quality Monitoring Information, "Air Quality Statistics by City, 2016"

Maximum Air Pollutant Concentrations: Nitrogen Dioxide and Sulfur Dioxide

	Nitrogen Dioxide AM (ppb)	Nitrogen Dioxide 1-Hr (ppb)	Sulfur Dioxide AM (ppb)	Sulfur Dioxide 1-Hr (ppb)	Sulfur Dioxide 24-Hr (ppb)
MSA[1] Level	14	47	n/a	4	n/a
NAAQS[2]	53	100	30	75	140
Met NAAQS[2]	Yes	Yes	n/a	Yes	n/a

Note: (1) Data covers the Austin-Round Rock, TX Metropolitan Statistical Area—see Appendix B for areas included; Data from exceptional events are included; (2) National Ambient Air Quality Standards; ppm = parts per million; ug/m^3 = micrograms per cubic meter; n/a not available.

Concentrations: Nitrogen Dioxide AM—highest arithmetic mean concentration; Nitrogen Dioxide 1-Hr—highest 98th percentile 1-hour daily maximum concentration; Sulfur Dioxide AM—highest annual mean concentration; Sulfur Dioxide 1-Hr—highest 99th percentile 1-hour daily maximum concentration; Sulfur Dioxide 24-Hr—highest second maximum 24-hour concentration

Source: U.S. Environmental Protection Agency, Air Quality Monitoring Information, "Air Quality Statistics by City, 2016"

Drinking Water

Water System Name	Pop. Served	Primary Water Source Type	Violations[1]	
			Health Based	Monitoring/ Reporting
City of Leander	43,764	Surface	0	0

Note: (1) Based on violation data from January 1, 2017 to December 31, 2017

Source: U.S. Environmental Protection Agency, Office of Ground Water and Drinking Water, Safe Drinking Water Information System (based on data extracted April 5, 2018)

Sugar Land, Texas

Background

Sugar Land is located in northeast Fort Bend County, 25 miles southwest of Houston, along the Gulf Coast of Texas. The Brazos River and Oyster Creek run through the city. Sugar Land also has many natural and man-made lakes.

Sugar Land's history dates back to the original Mexican land grant to Stephen F. Austin. Early settler Samuel M. Williams, called it Oakland Plantation because of the different oak varieties—Willow, Post, Water, Southern Red, and Live—that survived there. Williams' brother, Nathaniel, purchased the land in 1838 and together they grew cotton, corn, and sugarcane. In 1853, Benjamin Terry and William J. Kyle purchased the Oakland Plantation from the Williams family. Terry is known for organizing Terry's Texas Rangers during the Civil War, and is believed to have introduced the name Sugar Land. Shortly after the war, Colonel E. H. Cunningham bought the land and developed a town around his sugar refining plant.

In 1906, Isaac H. Kempner and William T. Eldridge purchased nearby Ellis Plantation and, in 1908, purchased the Cunningham Plantation with its raw sugar mill and cane-sugar refinery—Imperial Sugar Company was born. The oldest railroad in Texas went right through the middle of the town, by the sugar refinery. Until 1959, Sugar Land was virtually self-contained. Imperial Sugar Company provided housing, a school, a hospital, and businesses to meet the workers' needs. Many of the original homes built by Imperial remain today.

In the 1950s, Imperial Sugar expanded the town with the creation of Venetian Estates, featuring waterfront home sites. In the early 1960s Covington Woods was built. In 1968, the 1,200-acre Imperial Cattle Ranch became Sugar Creek, introducing country club living, golf courses, swimming pools, and security. Sugar Land annexed Sugar Creek in 1986, First Colony (another small independent nearby community) in 1997, with 5 more annexations completed in 2004.

The city is still home to Imperial Sugar headquarters although Sugar Land today is considered more an affluent Houston suburb than the blue-collar, agriculture-dependent town it was a generation ago. It has become the largest economic center of Fort Bend County, supplying a large percentage of the labor for Houston's renowned energy industry.

Sugar Land Town Square is a pedestrian-oriented business district in walking distance of stores, services, mid-rise office buildings, restaurants, entertainment and a Marriott Hotel/Conference Center. The area boasts a wide range of recreational activities including golf courses, country clubs and the Sugar Land Ice & Sports Center, the home practice facility for the Houston Aeros.

Coca-Cola's Minute Maid headquarters is now in Sugar Land Town Square, and the development of a master planned, mixed-use community, that will total 651 acres, in is progress.

In May 2016, two sculptures in the Town Square's public plaza were installed as part of a 10-piece collection donated by a Sugar Land resident to the city through the Sugar Land Legacy Foundation. One of the statues, which depicts two girls taking a selfie, has received both criticism and acclaim from the media and general public.

A portion of the 1974 movie, The Sugarland Express, takes place in Sugar Land. Many of the movie's earliest scenes were filmed at the nearby Beauford H. Jester prison pre-release center. Other parts of the set were filmed in and around Sugar Land. The film was the first theatrical feature film directed by Steven Spielberg.

Sugar Land's School District includes a Technical Education Center, the M. R. Wood Alternative Education Center, and the Progressive High School, serving a variety of vocational interests as well as special learning needs. Individual high schools have garnered exemplary awards. In 2002, the University of Houston System at Fort Bend relocated to what became the University of Houston System at Sugar Land.

The climate is humid subtropical. Prevailing winds, from the south/southeast, bring heat from the deserts of Mexico and moisture from the Gulf of Mexico nearly year round. High temperatures dominate throughout much of July and August, with extremely high humidity. Summer thunderstorms sometimes bring tornadoes to the area. Afternoon rains are not uncommon. Winters are cool and temperate. The coldest period is usually in January, when north winds bring winter rains. Snow is almost unheard of.

Rankings

General Rankings

- For its "Best Places to Live" rankings (formerly known as Best for Vets: Places to Live), *Military Times* evaluated 577 cities (79 large, 244 medium, 254 small) and compared the locations across three broad categories: veteran and military culture/services; economic indicators; and livability factors such as health, crime, traffic, and school quality. Sugar Land ranked #10 out of the top 50, in the small city category (populations of less than 75,000). Data points more specific to veterans and the military weighed more heavily than the rest. *rebootcamp.militarytimes.com, "Military Times Best Places to Live 2017," September 11, 2017*
- Houston* was identified as one of America's fastest-growing cities in terms of population growth by CNNMoney.com. The area ranked #2 out of 10. Criteria: population growth between July 2015 and July 2016; cities and towns with populations of 50,000. *CNNMoney, "10 Fastest-Growing Cities," June 2, 2017*

Business/Finance Rankings

- According to *Business Insider*, the Houston* metro area is where startup growth is on the rise. Based on the 2017 Kauffman Index of Growth Entrepreneurship, which measured in-depth national entrepreneurial trends in 40 metro areas, it ranked #19 in highest startup growth. *www.businessinsider.com, "The 21 U.S. Cities with the Highest Startup Growth," October 21, 2017*
- The personal finance site NerdWallet analyzed 183 American metropolitan areas with populations over 250,000 and more than 15,000 businesses to rank where entrepreneurs find the most success. Criteria included area economy, annual income, housing cost, unemployment rate, and the success rate of area businesses. Houston* ranked #80. *www.nerdwallet.com, "Best Places to Start a Business," April 27, 2015*
- USAA and Hiring Our Heroes worked with Sperlings's BestPlaces and the Institute for Veterans and Military Families at Syracuse University to rank major metropolitan areas where military-skills-related employment is strongest. Criteria for *mid-career* veterans included veteran wage growth; recent job growth; stability; and accessible health resources. Metro areas with a higher than national average crime or unemployment rate were excluded. At #3, the Houston* metro area made the top ten. *www.usaa.com, "2015 Best Places for Veterans"*
- 24/7 Wall Street used Brookings Institution research on 50 advanced industries to identify the proportion of workers in the nation's largest metropolitan areas that were employed in jobs requiring knowledge in the science, technology, engineering, or math (STEM) fields and where there was heavy investment in research and development (R&D). The Houston* metro area was #13. *247wallst.com, "15 Cities with the Most High-Tech Jobs," February 23, 2017*
- In a survey of economic confidence in the nation's 50 largest metropolitan areas conducted January–December 2014, the Houston* metro area placed #10, according to Gallup's 2014 Economic Confidence Index. *Gallup, "San Jose and San Francisco Lead in Economic Confidence," March 19, 2015*
- The Brookings Institution ranked the 100 largest metro areas in the U.S. based on income inequality. Houston* was ranked #8 (#1 = greatest ineqality). Criteria: the "95/20 ratio," a figure representing the income at which a household earns more than 95 percent of all other households, divided by the income at which a household earns more than only 20 percent of all other households. *Brookings Institution, "Household Income Inequality, 100 Largest U.S. Metro Areas, 2014-2016," February 5, 2018*
- Payscale.com ranked the largest metro areas in terms of wage growth. The Houston* metro area ranked #13. Criteria: private-sector wage growth between the 4th quarter of 2016 and the 4th quarter of 2017. *PayScale, "Wage Trends by Metro Area-4th Quarter," January 17, 2018*

- The Houston* metro area was identified as one of the most debt-ridden places in America by the finance site Credit.com. The metro area was ranked #4. Criteria: residents' average credit card debt as well as median income. *Credit.com, "25 Cities With the Most Credit Card Debt," February 28, 2018*
- Houston* was identified as one of America's most frugal metro areas by *Coupons.com.* The city ranked #19 out of 25. Criteria: digital coupon usage. *Coupons.com, "America's Most Frugal Cities of 2017," March 22, 2018*
- Houston* was cited as one of America's top metros for new and expanded facility projects in 2017. The area ranked #2 in the large metro area category (population over 1 million). *Site Selection, "Top Metropolitans of 2017," March 2018*
- The Houston* metro area appeared on the Milken Institute "2017 Best Performing Cities" list. Rank: #113 out of 200 large metro areas. Criteria: job growth; wage and salary growth; high-tech output growth. *Milken Institute, "Best-Performing Cities 2017," January 2018*
- *Forbes* ranked the 200 most populous metro areas to determine the nation's "Best Places for Business and Careers." The Houston* metro area was ranked #43. Criteria: costs (business and living); job growth (past and projected); income growth; quality of life; educational attainment (college and high school); projected economic growth; cultural and recreational opportunities; net migration patterns; number of highly ranked colleges. *Forbes, "The Best Places for Business and Careers 2017," October 24, 2017*

Dating/Romance Rankings

- *Apartment List* conducted its annual survey of renters to compile a list of metros that have the best opportunities for dating. Nearly 11,000 respondents, from February 2017 through January 2018, rated their current city or neighborhood for opportunities to date and make friends. The Houston* metro area ranked #9 out of 70 where single residents were very satisfied or somewhat satisfied, making it among the ten best metros for dating opportunities. Other criteria analyzed included gender and education levels of renters. *Apartment List, "Best Metros for Dating 2018," February 6, 2018*

Education Rankings

- Personal finance website *WalletHub* analyzed the 150 largest U.S. metropolitan statistical areas to determine where the most educated Americans are choosing to settle. Criteria: education quality and attainment gap; education levels; percentage of workers with degrees; public school rankings; quality and size of each metro area's universities. Houston* was ranked #79 (#1 = most educated city). *www.WalletHub.com, "2017's Most and Least Educated Cities in America, " July 25, 2017*

Environmental Rankings

- Sperling's BestPlaces assessed 379 metropolitan areas of the United States for the likelihood of dangerously extreme weather events or earthquakes. In general the Southeast and South-Central regions have the highest risk of weather extremes and earthquakes, while the Pacific Northwest enjoys the lowest risk. Of the least risky metropolitan areas, the Houston* metro area was ranked #376. *www.bestplaces.net, "Safest Places from Natural Disasters," April 2011*
- The U.S. Environmental Protection Agency (EPA) released a list of U.S. metropolitan areas with the most ENERGY STAR certified buildings in 2016. The Houston* metro area was ranked #8 out of 25. *U.S. Environmental Protection Agency, "2017 Energy Star Top Cities," June 2017*
- Houston* was highlighted as one of the 25 most ozone-polluted metro areas in the U.S. during 2013 through 2015. The area ranked #12. *American Lung Association, State of the Air 2017*
- Houston* was highlighted as one of the 25 metro areas most polluted by year-round particle pollution (Annual PM 2.5) in the U.S. during 2013 through 2015. The area ranked #16. *American Lung Association, State of the Air 2017*

Health/Fitness Rankings

- For each of the 50 most populous metro areas in the United States, the American College of Sports Medicine's American Fitness Index evaluated infrastructure, community assets, and policies that encourage healthy and fit lifestyles, including preventive health behaviors, levels of chronic disease conditions, health care access, and community resources and policies that support physical activity. The Houston* metro area ranked #40 for "community fitness." *www.americanfitnessindex.org, "ACSM American Fitness Index Health and Community Fitness Status of the 50 Largest Metropolitan Areas," May 2017*
- The Houston* metro area was identified as one of the worst cities for bed bugs in America by pest control company Orkin. The area ranked #17 out of 50 based on the number of bed bug treatments Orkin performed from December 2016 to November 2017. *Orkin, "Baltimore and Washington D.C. Continue to Hold Top Spots," January 8, 2018*
- Houston* was identified as a "2016 Spring Allergy Capital." The area ranked #60 out of 100. Three groups of factors were used to identify the most severe cities for people with allergies during the spring season: annual pollen levels; medicine utilization; access to board-certified allergists. *Asthma and Allergy Foundation of America, "Spring Allergy Capitals 2016"*
- Houston* was identified as a "2016 Fall Allergy Capital." The area ranked #41 out of 100. Three groups of factors were used to identify the most severe cities for people with allergies during the fall season: annual pollen levels; medicine utilization; access to board-certified allergists. *Asthma and Allergy Foundation of America, "Fall Allergy Capitals 2016"*
- Houston* was identified as a "2015 Asthma Capital." The area ranked #82 out of the nation's 100 largest metropolitan areas. Criteria: estimated prevalence; self-reported prevalence; crude death rate for asthma; annual pollen score; annual air quality; public smoking laws; number of board-certified asthma specialists; school inhaler access laws; rescue medication use; controller medication use; ER visits for asthma; uninsured rate; poverty rate. *Asthma and Allergy Foundation of America, "Asthma Capitals 2015"*
- The Houston* metro area ranked #57 out of 189 in The Gallup-Healthways Well-Being Index. Criteria: purpose; social well being; financial health; community and physical health. Results are based on telephone interviews with adults, aged 18 and older, living in metropolitan areas in the 50 U.S. states and the District of Columbia. *Gallup-Healthways, "State of American Well-Being, 2017 Community Well-Being Rankings" March 2018*

Real Estate Rankings

- FitSmallBusiness looked at 50 of the largest metropolitan areas in the U.S. to determine which metro was the best to start a real estate business. Data was compiled from such sources as: Zillow, Trulia, U.S. Census Bureau, and the Bureau of Labor Statistics. Criteria: location; inventory; annual wages; median sales price of homes; days on the market; median price cut percentage; and other factors that would influence real estate professional growth. The Houston* metro area ranked #38. *fitsmallbusiness.com, "The Best Cities to Become a Real Estate Agent in 2018," January 30, 2018*
- According to Penske Truck Rental, the Houston* metro area was named the #4 moving destination in 2017, based on one-way consumer truck rental reservations made through Penske's website, rental locations, and reservations call center. *blog.gopenske.com, "Penske Truck Rental's 2017 Top Moving Destinations List," January 22, 2018*
- The Houston* metro area was identified as one of the 10 worst condo markets in the U.S. in 2017. The area ranked #2 out of 66 markets. Criteria: year-over-year change of median sales price of existing apartment condo-coop homes between the 4th quarter of 2016 and the 4th quarter of 2017. *National Association of Realtors®, Median Sales Price of Existing Apartment Condo-Coop Homes for Metropolitan Areas, 4th Quarter 2017*
- Houston* was ranked #159 out of 238 metro areas in terms of housing affordability in 2017 by the National Association of Home Builders (#1 = most affordable). Criteria: the share of homes sold in that area affordable to a family earning the local median income, based on standard mortgage underwriting criteria. *National Association of Home Builders®, NAHB-Wells Fargo Housing Opportunity Index, 4th Quarter 2017*

Safety Rankings

- The National Insurance Crime Bureau ranked 382 metro areas in the U.S. in terms of per capita rates of vehicle theft. The Houston* metro area ranked #45 (#1 = highest rate). Criteria: number of vehicle theft offenses per 100,000 inhabitants in 2016. *National Insurance Crime Bureau, "Hot Spots 2016," June 8, 2017*

Seniors/Retirement Rankings

- From its Best Cities for Successful Aging indexes, the Milken Institute generated rankings for metropolitan areas, weighing data in nine categories—health care, wellness, living arrangements, transportation and convenience, financial characteristics, education, employment, community engagement, and overall livability. The Houston* metro area was ranked #35 overall in the large metro area category. *Milken Institute, "Best Cities for Successful Aging, 2017" March 14, 2017*

Transportation Rankings

- Houston* was identified as one of the most congested metro areas in the U.S. The area ranked #8 out of 10. Criteria: yearly delay per auto commuter in hours. *Texas A&M Transportation Institute, "2015 Urban Mobility Scorecard," August 2015*

Women/Minorities Rankings

- The *Houston Chronicle* listed the Houston* metro area as #11 in top places for young Latinos to live in the U.S. Research was largely based on housing and occupational data from the largest metropolitan areas performed by *Forbes* and NBC Universo. Criteria: percentage of 18-34 year-olds; Latino college grad rates; and diversity. *blog.chron.com, "The 15 Best Big Cities for Latino Millenials," January 26, 2016*

Miscellaneous Rankings

- Sugar Land was selected as a 2017 Digital Cities Survey winner. The city ranked #5 in the small city (75,000 to 124,999 population) category. The survey examined and assessed how city governments are utilizing technology to improve citizen services, enhance inclusion, and solve social challenges. Survey questions focused on ten characteristics: engaged, mobile, open, secure, staffed/supported, efficient, connected, resilient, best practices, and use of innovation. *Center for Digital Government, "2017 Digital Cities Survey," November 9, 2017*

- The watchdog site Charity Navigator conducts an annual study of charities in the nation's major markets both to analyze statistical differences in their financial, accountability, and transparency practices and to track year-to-year variations in individual philanthropic communities. Charity Navigator's analysis demonstrated that the financial, accountability and transparency behaviors of America's largest charities can be influenced by the metropolitan market within which the charity operates. The Houston* metro area was ranked #2 among the 30 metro markets in the rating category of Overall Score. *www.charitynavigator.org, "2017 Metro Market Study," May 1, 2017*

- The Harris Poll's Happiness Index survey revealed that of the top ten U.S. markets, the Houston* metro area residents ranked #2 in happiness. Criteria included strong assent to positive statements and strong disagreement with negative ones, and degree of agreement with a series of statements about respondents' personal relationships and general outlook. *www.theharrispoll.com, "Dallas/Fort Worth Is "Happiest" City among America's Top Ten Markets," September 4, 2013*

- Energizer Personal Care, the makers of Edge® shave gel, in partnership with Sperling's BestPlaces, ranked 50 major metro areas in terms of everyday irritations. The Houston* metro area ranked #8 the 50 metro area most irritating to guys. Criteria: high male-to-female ratio; poor sports team performance and high ticket prices; slow traffic; lack of job availability; unaffordable housing; extreme weather; lack of nightlife and fitness options. *Energizer Personal Care, "Most Irritating Cities for Guys," August 26, 2013*

- The National Alliance to End Homelessness listed the 25 most populous metro areas with the highest rate of homelessness. The Houston* metro area had a high rate of homelessness. Criteria: number of homeless people per 10,000 population in 2016. *National Alliance to End Homelessness, "Homelessness in the 25 Most Populous U.S. Metro Areas," September 1, 2017*

  *Sugar Land is located within the Houston-The Woodlands-Sugar Land, TX Metropolitan Statistical Area.

Business Environment

CITY FINANCES

City Government Finances

Component	2015 ($000)	2015 ($ per capita)
Total Revenues	207,511	2,354
Total Expenditures	223,225	2,532
Debt Outstanding	302,220	3,428
Cash and Securities[1]	191,164	2,168

Note: (1) Cash and security holdings of a government at the close of its fiscal year,, including those of its dependent agencies, utilities, and liquor stores.
Source: U.S Census Bureau, State & Local Government Finances 2015

City Government Revenue by Source

Source	2015 ($000)	2015 ($ per capita)	2015 (%)
General Revenue			
From Federal Government	2,164	25	1.0
From State Government	29,462	334	14.2
From Local Governments	6,711	76	3.2
Taxes			
Property	30,966	351	14.9
Sales and Gross Receipts	55,562	630	26.8
Personal Income	0	0	0.0
Corporate Income	0	0	0.0
Motor Vehicle License	0	0	0.0
Other Taxes	2,590	29	1.2
Current Charges	45,687	518	22.0
Liquor Store	0	0	0.0
Utility	21,331	242	10.3
Employee Retirement	0	0	0.0

Source: U.S Census Bureau, State & Local Government Finances 2015

City Government Expenditures by Function

Function	2015 ($000)	2015 ($ per capita)	2015 (%)
General Direct Expenditures			
Air Transportation	15,883	180	7.1
Corrections	378	4	0.2
Education	0	0	0.0
Employment Security Administration	0	0	0.0
Financial Administration	5,555	63	2.5
Fire Protection	10,906	123	4.9
General Public Buildings	2,433	27	1.1
Governmental Administration, Other	5,301	60	2.4
Health	698	7	0.3
Highways	23,596	267	10.6
Hospitals	0	0	0.0
Housing and Community Development	654	7	0.3
Interest on General Debt	10,052	114	4.5
Judicial and Legal	1,431	16	0.6
Libraries	0	0	0.0
Parking	0	0	0.0
Parks and Recreation	30,100	341	13.5
Police Protection	19,583	222	8.8
Public Welfare	0	0	0.0
Sewerage	9,777	110	4.4
Solid Waste Management	5,417	61	2.4
Veterans' Services	0	0	0.0
Liquor Store	0	0	0.0
Utility	64,412	730	28.9
Employee Retirement	0	0	0.0

Source: U.S Census Bureau, State & Local Government Finances 2015

DEMOGRAPHICS

Population Growth

Area	1990 Census	2000 Census	2010 Census	2016* Estimate	Population Growth (%)	
					1990-2016	2010-2016
City	44,150	63,328	78,817	85,681	94.1	8.7
MSA[1]	3,767,335	4,715,407	5,946,800	6,482,592	72.1	9.0
U.S.	248,709,873	281,421,906	308,745,538	318,558,162	28.1	3.2

Note: (1) Figures cover the Houston-The Woodlands-Sugar Land, TX Metropolitan Statistical Area—see Appendix B for areas included; (*) 2012-2016 5-year estimated population
Source: U.S. Census Bureau, 1990 Census, Census 2000, Census 2010, 2012-2016 American Community Survey 5-Year Estimates

Household Size

Area	Persons in Household (%)							Average Household Size
	One	Two	Three	Four	Five	Six	Seven or More	
City	16.2	32.9	20.6	17.4	8.1	2.8	2.0	3.00
MSA[1]	24.5	29.6	17.0	15.4	8.2	3.2	2.1	2.90
U.S.	27.7	33.7	15.7	13.1	6.0	2.3	1.5	2.60

Note: (1) Figures cover the Houston-The Woodlands-Sugar Land, TX Metropolitan Statistical Area—see Appendix B for areas included
Source: U.S. Census Bureau, 2012-2016 American Community Survey 5-Year Estimates

Race

Area	White Alone[2] (%)	Black Alone[2] (%)	Asian Alone[2] (%)	AIAN[3] Alone[2] (%)	NHOPI[4] Alone[2] (%)	Other Race Alone[2] (%)	Two or More Races (%)
City	50.0	7.2	38.6	0.1	0.0	1.5	2.5
MSA[1]	65.7	17.2	7.3	0.4	0.1	7.1	2.3
U.S.	73.3	12.6	5.2	0.8	0.2	4.8	3.1

Note: (1) Figures cover the Houston-The Woodlands-Sugar Land, TX Metropolitan Statistical Area—see Appendix B for areas included; (2) Alone is defined as not being in combination with one or more other races; (3) American Indian and Alaska Native; (4) Native Hawaiian and Other Pacific Islander
Source: U.S. Census Bureau, 2012-2016 American Community Survey 5-Year Estimates

Hispanic or Latino Origin

Area	Total (%)	Mexican (%)	Puerto Rican (%)	Cuban (%)	Other (%)
City	9.3	6.6	0.6	0.3	1.8
MSA[1]	36.3	27.8	0.6	0.4	7.4
U.S.	17.3	11.0	1.7	0.7	4.0

Note: Persons of Hispanic or Latino origin can be of any race; (1) Figures cover the Houston-The Woodlands-Sugar Land, TX Metropolitan Statistical Area—see Appendix B for areas included
Source: U.S. Census Bureau, 2012-2016 American Community Survey 5-Year Estimates

Segregation

Type	Segregation Indices[1]				Percent Change		
	1990	2000	2010	2010 Rank[2]	1990-2000	1990-2010	2000-2010
Black/White	65.5	65.7	61.4	36	0.1	-4.1	-4.2
Asian/White	48.0	51.4	50.4	7	3.4	2.4	-1.0
Hispanic/White	47.8	53.4	52.5	18	5.6	4.7	-0.9

Note: All figures cover the Metropolitan Statistical Area—see Appendix B for areas included; Figures are based on an analysis of 1990, 2000, and 2010 Census Decennial Census tract data by William H. Frey, Brookings Institution and the University of Michigan Social Science Data Analysis Network. In this analysis all racial groups (whites, blacks, and asians) are non-Hispanic members of those races. Hispanics are shown as a separate category; (1) Segregation Indices are Dissimilarity Indices that measure the degree to which the minority group is distributed differently than whites across census tracts. They range from 0 (complete integration) to 100 (complete segregation) where the value indicates the percentage of the minority group that needs to move to be distributed exactly like whites; (2) Ranges from 1 (most segregated) to 102 (least segregated); n/a not available.
Source: www.CensusScope.org

Ancestry

Area	German	Irish	English	American	Italian	Polish	French[2]	Scottish	Dutch
City	9.1	5.4	6.6	4.0	2.3	1.2	2.0	1.7	0.5
MSA[1]	8.5	5.8	5.4	4.7	2.1	1.2	2.3	1.2	0.6
U.S.	14.4	10.4	7.7	6.9	5.4	2.9	2.6	1.7	1.3

Note: Figures are the percentage of the total population reporting a particular ancestry. The nine most commonly reported ancestries in the U.S. are shown. Figures include multiple ancestries (e.g. if a person reported being Irish and Italian, they were included in both columns); (1) Figures cover the Houston-The Woodlands-Sugar Land, TX Metropolitan Statistical Area—see Appendix B for areas included; (2) Excludes Basque
Source: U.S. Census Bureau, 2012-2016 American Community Survey 5-Year Estimates

Foreign-Born Population

Area	Percent of Population Born in								
	Any Foreign Country	Asia	Mexico	Europe	Carribean	Central America[2]	South America	Africa	Canada
City	35.2	27.6	1.3	1.8	0.2	0.3	1.0	2.0	0.7
MSA[1]	22.9	5.7	9.6	1.0	0.6	3.4	1.1	1.2	0.3
U.S.	13.2	4.0	3.6	1.5	1.3	1.0	0.9	0.6	0.3

Note: (1) Figures cover the Houston-The Woodlands-Sugar Land, TX Metropolitan Statistical Area—see Appendix B for areas included; (2) Excludes Mexico.
Source: U.S. Census Bureau, 2012-2016 American Community Survey 5-Year Estimates

Marital Status

Area	Never Married	Now Married[2]	Separated	Widowed	Divorced
City	24.3	64.3	0.9	4.5	5.9
MSA[1]	33.1	49.9	2.6	4.5	9.8
U.S.	33.0	48.1	2.1	5.9	11.0

Note: Figures are percentages and cover the population 15 years of age and older; (1) Figures cover the Houston-The Woodlands-Sugar Land, TX Metropolitan Statistical Area—see Appendix B for areas included; (2) Excludes separated
Source: U.S. Census Bureau, 2012-2016 American Community Survey 5-Year Estimates

Disability Status

Area	All Ages	Under 18 Years Old	18 to 64 Years Old	65 Years and Over
City	6.6	3.3	4.0	24.7
MSA[1]	9.6	3.5	8.2	36.2
U.S.	12.5	4.1	10.3	35.7

Note: Figures show percent of the civilian noninstitutionalized population that reported having a disability. Disability status is determined from six types of difficulty: vision, hearing, cognitive, ambulatory, self-care, and independent living. For children under 5 years old, hearing and vision difficulty are used to determine disability status. For children between the ages of 5 and 14, disability status is determined from hearing, vision, cognitive, ambulatory, and self-care difficulties. For people aged 15 years and older, they are considered to have a disability if they have difficulty with any one of the six difficulty types; Note: (1) Figures cover the Houston-The Woodlands-Sugar Land, TX Metropolitan Statistical Area—see Appendix B for areas included
Source: U.S. Census Bureau, 2012-2016 American Community Survey 5-Year Estimates

Age

Area	Percent of Population									Median Age
	Under Age 5	Age 5–19	Age 20–34	Age 35–44	Age 45–54	Age 55–64	Age 65–74	Age 75–84	Age 85+	
City	5.3	19.8	16.4	12.6	16.3	16.1	8.4	3.7	1.6	41.8
MSA[1]	7.6	22.2	22.0	14.2	13.2	11.0	6.1	2.7	1.0	33.9
U.S.	6.2	19.6	20.7	12.7	13.6	12.6	8.3	4.3	1.9	37.7

Note: (1) Figures cover the Houston-The Woodlands-Sugar Land, TX Metropolitan Statistical Area—see Appendix B for areas included
Source: U.S. Census Bureau, 2012-2016 American Community Survey 5-Year Estimates

Gender

Area	Males	Females	Males per 100 Females
City	42,590	43,091	98.8
MSA[1]	3,220,604	3,261,988	98.7
U.S.	156,765,322	161,792,840	96.9

Note: (1) Figures cover the Houston-The Woodlands-Sugar Land, TX Metropolitan Statistical Area—see Appendix B for areas included
Source: U.S. Census Bureau, 2012-2016 American Community Survey 5-Year Estimates

Religious Groups by Family

Area	Catholic	Baptist	Non-Den.	Methodist[2]	Lutheran	LDS[3]	Pente-costal	Presby-terian[4]	Muslim[5]	Judaism
MSA[1]	17.1	16.0	7.3	4.9	1.1	1.1	1.5	0.9	2.7	0.4
U.S.	19.1	9.3	4.0	4.0	2.3	2.0	1.9	1.6	0.8	0.7

Note: Figures are the number of adherents as a percentage of the total population; (1) Figures cover the Houston-The Woodlands-Sugar Land, TX Metropolitan Statistical Area—see Appendix B for areas included; (2) Methodist/Pietist; (3) Latter Day Saints; (4) Reformed; (5) Figures are estimates
Source: Association of Statisticians of American Religious Bodies, 2010 U.S. Religion Census: Religious Congregations & Membership Study

Religious Groups by Tradition

Area	Catholic	Evangelical Protestant	Mainline Protestant	Other Tradition	Black Protestant	Orthodox
MSA[1]	17.1	24.9	6.7	4.9	1.3	0.2
U.S.	19.1	16.2	7.3	4.3	1.6	0.3

Note: Figures are the number of adherents as a percentage of the total population; (1) Figures cover the Houston-The Woodlands-Sugar Land, TX Metropolitan Statistical Area—see Appendix B for areas included
Source: Association of Statisticians of American Religious Bodies, 2010 U.S. Religion Census: Religious Congregations & Membership Study

ECONOMY

Gross Metropolitan Product

Area	2014	2015	2016	2017	Rank[2]
MSA[1]	523.1	498.5	491.3	526.0	5

Note: Figures are in billions of dollars; (1) Figures cover the Houston-The Woodlands-Sugar Land, TX Metropolitan Statistical Area—see Appendix B for areas included; (2) Rank is based on 2015 data and ranges from 1 to 381
Source: The U.S. Conference of Mayors, U.S. Metro Economies: GMP and Employment Report, 2015-2017

Economic Growth

Area	2012-14 (%)	2015 (%)	2016 (%)	2017 (%)	Rank[2]
MSA[1]	3.9	0.3	-2.0	3.9	33
U.S.	2.0	2.4	1.9	2.6	–

Note: Figures are real gross metropolitan product (GMP) growth rates and represent average annual percent change; (1) Figures cover the Houston-The Woodlands-Sugar Land, TX Metropolitan Statistical Area—see Appendix B for areas included; (2) Rank is based on 2012-2014 average annual percent change and ranges from 1 to 381
Source: The U.S. Conference of Mayors, U.S. Metro Economies: GMP and Employment Report, 2015-2017

Metropolitan Area Exports

Area	2011	2012	2013	2014	2015	2016	Rank[2]
MSA[1]	104,457.3	110,297.8	114,962.6	118,966.0	97,054.3	84,105.5	2

Note: Figures are in millions of dollars; (1) Figures cover the Houston-The Woodlands-Sugar Land, TX Metropolitan Statistical Area—see Appendix B for areas included; (2) Rank is based on 2016 data and ranges from 1 to 385
Source: U.S. Department of Commerce, International Trade Administration, Office of Trade & Industry Information, Manufacturing & Services, data extracted March 15, 2018

Building Permits

Area	Single-Family 2016	Single-Family 2017p	Single-Family Pct. Chg.	Multi-Family 2016	Multi-Family 2017p	Multi-Family Pct. Chg.	Total 2016	Total 2017p	Total Pct. Chg.
City	162	158	-2.5	351	0	-100.0	513	158	-69.2
MSA[1]	35,397	36,601	3.4	9,246	6,072	-34.3	44,643	42,673	-4.4
U.S.	750,800	817,300	8.9	455,800	446,800	-2.0	1,206,600	1,264,100	4.8

Note: (1) Figures cover the Houston-The Woodlands-Sugar Land, TX Metropolitan Statistical Area—see Appendix B for areas included; Figures represent new, privately-owned housing units authorized (unadjusted data); All permit data are based on estimates with imputation; (p) preliminary data.
Source: U.S. Census Bureau, Manufacturing, Mining, and Construction Statistics, Building Permits, 2016, 2017

Bankruptcy Filings

Area	Business Filings 2016	Business Filings 2017	Business Filings % Chg.	Nonbusiness Filings 2016	Nonbusiness Filings 2017	Nonbusiness Filings % Chg.
Fort Bend County	59	47	-20.3	788	742	-5.8
U.S.	24,114	23,157	-4.0	770,846	765,863	-0.6

Note: Business filings include Chapter 7, Chapter 11, Chapter 12, and Chapter 13; Nonbusiness filings include Chapter 7, Chapter 11, and Chapter 13
Source: Administrative Office of the U.S. Courts, Business and Nonbusiness Bankruptcy, County Cases Commenced by Chapter of the Bankruptcy Code, During the 12-Month Period Ending December 31, 2016 and Business and Nonbusiness Bankruptcy, County Cases Commenced by Chapter of the Bankruptcy Code, During the 12-Month Period Ending December 31, 2017

Housing Vacancy Rates

Area	Gross Vacancy Rate[2] (%) 2015	2016	2017	Year-Round Vacancy Rate[3] (%) 2015	2016	2017	Rental Vacancy Rate[4] (%) 2015	2016	2017	Homeowner Vacancy Rate[5] (%) 2015	2016	2017
MSA[1]	9.2	8.6	9.3	8.7	8.0	8.9	9.6	9.3	9.9	1.5	1.8	1.5
U.S.	12.9	12.8	12.7	10.0	9.9	9.9	7.1	6.9	7.2	1.8	1.7	1.6

Note: (1) Figures cover the Houston-The Woodlands-Sugar Land, TX Metropolitan Statistical Area—see Appendix B for areas included; (2) The percentage of the total housing inventory that is vacant; (3) The percentage of the housing inventory (excluding seasonal units) that is year-round vacant; (4) The percentage of rental inventory that is vacant for rent; (5) The percentage of homeowner inventory that is vacant for sale
Source: U.S. Census Bureau, Housing Vacancies and Homeownership Annual Statistics: 2015, 2016, 2017

INCOME

Income

Area	Per Capita ($)	Median Household ($)	Average Household ($)
City	48,793	108,504	146,270
MSA[1]	31,165	60,902	87,925
U.S.	29,829	55,322	77,866

Note: (1) Figures cover the Houston-The Woodlands-Sugar Land, TX Metropolitan Statistical Area—see Appendix B for areas included
Source: U.S. Census Bureau, 2012-2016 American Community Survey 5-Year Estimates

Household Income Distribution

Area	Percent of Households Earning: Under $15,000	$15,000 -$24,999	$25,000 -$34,999	$35,000 -$49,999	$50,000 -$74,999	$75,000 -$99,999	$100,000 -$149,999	$150,000 and up
City	4.5	3.7	4.5	7.6	12.9	12.9	19.4	34.5
MSA[1]	10.2	9.5	9.5	12.6	17.1	11.7	14.6	14.8
U.S.	12.1	10.2	9.9	13.2	17.8	12.2	13.5	11.1

Note: (1) Figures cover the Houston-The Woodlands-Sugar Land, TX Metropolitan Statistical Area—see Appendix B for areas included
Source: U.S. Census Bureau, 2012-2016 American Community Survey 5-Year Estimates

Poverty Rate

Area	All Ages	Under 18 Years Old	18 to 64 Years Old	65 Years and Over
City	5.1	6.0	5.0	4.4
MSA[1]	15.3	22.4	13.1	10.1
U.S.	15.1	21.2	14.2	9.3

Note: Figures are percentage of people whose income during the past 12 months was below the poverty level; (1) Figures cover the Houston-The Woodlands-Sugar Land, TX Metropolitan Statistical Area—see Appendix B for areas included
Source: U.S. Census Bureau, 2012-2016 American Community Survey 5-Year Estimates

EMPLOYMENT

Labor Force and Employment

Area	Civilian Labor Force			Workers Employed		
	Dec. 2016	Dec. 2017	% Chg.	Dec. 2016	Dec. 2017	% Chg.
City	45,075	45,569	1.1	42,917	43,981	2.5
MSA[1]	3,297,292	3,343,410	1.4	3,121,317	3,199,215	2.5
U.S.	158,968,000	159,880,000	0.6	151,798,000	153,602,000	1.2

Note: Data is not seasonally adjusted and covers workers 16 years of age and older; (1) Figures cover the Houston-The Woodlands-Sugar Land, TX Metropolitan Statistical Area—see Appendix B for areas included
Source: Bureau of Labor Statistics, Local Area Unemployment Statistics

Unemployment Rate

Area	2017											
	Jan.	Feb.	Mar.	Apr.	May	Jun.	Jul.	Aug.	Sep.	Oct.	Nov.	Dec.
City	5.1	5.0	4.6	4.1	4.1	4.4	4.4	4.6	3.9	3.6	3.6	3.5
MSA[1]	5.8	5.6	5.2	4.8	4.8	5.1	5.1	5.1	4.8	4.4	4.4	4.3
U.S.	5.1	4.9	4.6	4.1	4.1	4.5	4.6	4.5	4.1	3.9	3.9	3.9

Note: Data is not seasonally adjusted and covers workers 16 years of age and older; (1) Figures cover the Houston-The Woodlands-Sugar Land, TX Metropolitan Statistical Area—see Appendix B for areas included
Source: Bureau of Labor Statistics, Local Area Unemployment Statistics

Average Wages

Occupation	$/Hr.	Occupation	$/Hr.
Accountants and Auditors	42.90	Maids and Housekeeping Cleaners	10.00
Automotive Mechanics	22.70	Maintenance and Repair Workers	18.70
Bookkeepers	20.80	Marketing Managers	87.10
Carpenters	20.50	Nuclear Medicine Technologists	38.30
Cashiers	10.10	Nurses, Licensed Practical	23.50
Clerks, General Office	18.70	Nurses, Registered	38.00
Clerks, Receptionists/Information	13.00	Nursing Assistants	13.30
Clerks, Shipping/Receiving	15.70	Packers and Packagers, Hand	11.50
Computer Programmers	42.20	Physical Therapists	44.70
Computer Systems Analysts	48.60	Postal Service Mail Carriers	24.00
Computer User Support Specialists	30.10	Real Estate Brokers	38.00
Cooks, Restaurant	12.60	Retail Salespersons	12.60
Dentists	91.10	Sales Reps., Exc. Tech./Scientific	35.50
Electrical Engineers	50.10	Sales Reps., Tech./Scientific	50.20
Electricians	26.60	Secretaries, Exc. Legal/Med./Exec.	18.10
Financial Managers	79.10	Security Guards	14.70
First-Line Supervisors/Managers, Sales	21.20	Surgeons	111.20
Food Preparation Workers	11.40	Teacher Assistants*	11.30
General and Operations Managers	72.40	Teachers, Elementary School*	30.20
Hairdressers/Cosmetologists	16.50	Teachers, Secondary School*	29.90
Internists, General	64.80	Telemarketers	13.60
Janitors and Cleaners	11.30	Truck Drivers, Heavy/Tractor-Trailer	20.80
Landscaping/Groundskeeping Workers	13.40	Truck Drivers, Light/Delivery Svcs.	17.10
Lawyers	84.10	Waiters and Waitresses	11.70

Note: Wage data covers the Houston-The Woodlands-Sugar Land, TX Metropolitan Statistical Area—see Appendix B for areas included; (*) Hourly wages for elementary/secondary school teachers and teacher assistants were calculated by the editors from annual wage data based on a 40 hour work week; n/a not available.
Source: Bureau of Labor Statistics, Metro Area Occupational Employment & Wage Estimates, May 2017

Employment by Occupation

Occupation Classification	City (%)	MSA[1] (%)	U.S. (%)
Management, Business, Science, and Arts	59.5	37.3	37.0
Natural Resources, Construction, and Maintenance	3.5	10.9	8.9
Production, Transportation, and Material Moving	4.2	12.2	12.2
Sales and Office	25.1	23.0	23.8
Service	7.7	16.6	18.1

Note: Figures cover employed civilians 16 years of age and older; (1) Figures cover the Houston-The Woodlands-Sugar Land, TX Metropolitan Statistical Area—see Appendix B for areas included
Source: U.S. Census Bureau, 2012-2016 American Community Survey 5-Year Estimates

Employment by Industry

Sector	MSA[1]		U.S.
	Number of Employees	Percent of Total	Percent of Total
Construction	221,400	7.2	4.7
Education and Health Services	383,900	12.5	15.9
Financial Activities	160,400	5.2	5.7
Government	416,100	13.5	15.3
Information	31,900	1.0	1.9
Leisure and Hospitality	318,500	10.4	10.7
Manufacturing	221,100	7.2	8.5
Mining and Logging	77,900	2.5	0.5
Other Services	109,200	3.6	3.9
Professional and Business Services	492,800	16.0	14.0
Retail Trade	324,500	10.6	11.0
Transportation, Warehousing, and Utilities	147,700	4.8	4.1
Wholesale Trade	168,000	5.5	4.0

Note: Figures are non-farm employment as of December 2017. Figures are not seasonally adjusted and include workers 16 years of age and older; (1) Figures cover the Houston-The Woodlands-Sugar Land, TX Metropolitan Statistical Area—see Appendix B for areas included
Source: Bureau of Labor Statistics, Current Employment Statistics, Employment, Hours, and Earnings

Occupations with Greatest Projected Employment Growth: 2017 – 2019

Occupation[1]	2017 Employment	2019 Projected Employment	Numeric Employment Change	Percent Employment Change
Combined Food Preparation and Serving Workers, Including Fast Food	335,660	354,370	18,710	5.6
Personal Care Aides	212,280	230,990	18,710	8.8
Retail Salespersons	393,950	406,100	12,150	3.1
Customer Service Representatives	261,530	273,600	12,070	4.6
Janitors and Cleaners, Except Maids and Housekeeping Cleaners	180,710	192,060	11,350	6.3
Laborers and Freight, Stock, and Material Movers, Hand	185,140	196,200	11,060	6.0
Registered Nurses	214,500	224,450	9,950	4.6
Office Clerks, General	379,860	389,540	9,680	2.6
Heavy and Tractor-Trailer Truck Drivers	192,710	201,560	8,850	4.6
Waiters and Waitresses	222,630	231,020	8,390	3.8

Note: Projections cover Texas; (1) Sorted by numeric employment change
Source: www.projectionscentral.com, State Occupational Projections, 2017–2019 Short-Term Projections

Fastest Growing Occupations: 2017 – 2019

Occupation[1]	2017 Employment	2019 Projected Employment	Numeric Employment Change	Percent Employment Change
Wind Turbine Service Technicians	1,740	2,090	350	20.7
Home Health Aides	72,760	80,000	7,240	10.0
Security and Fire Alarm Systems Installers	8,190	8,930	740	8.9
Personal Care Aides	212,280	230,990	18,710	8.8
Statisticians	1,760	1,910	150	8.2
Tree Trimmers and Pruners	5,980	6,480	500	8.2
Physician Assistants	6,860	7,400	540	7.9
Nurse Practitioners	9,230	9,950	720	7.7
Elevator Installers and Repairers	2,190	2,350	160	7.4
Helpers—Roofers	800	850	50	7.4

Note: Projections cover Texas; (1) Sorted by percent employment change and excludes occupations with numeric employment change less than 50
Source: www.projectionscentral.com, State Occupational Projections, 2017–2019 Short-Term Projections

TAXES

State Corporate Income Tax Rates

State	Tax Rate (%)	Income Brackets ($)	Num. of Brackets	Financial Institution Tax Rate (%)[a]	Federal Income Tax Ded.
Texas	(w)	–	–	(w)	No

Note: Tax rates as of January 1, 2018; (a) Rates listed are the corporate income tax rate applied to financial institutions or excise taxes based on income. Some states have other taxes based upon the value of deposits or shares; (w) Texas imposes a Franchise Tax, otherwise known as margin tax, imposed on entities with more than $1,110,000 total revenues at rate of 0.75%, or 0.375% for entities primarily engaged in retail or wholesale trade, on lesser of 70% of total revenues or 100% of gross receipts after deductions for either compensation or cost of goods sold.
Source: Federation of Tax Administrators, Range of State Corporate Income Tax Rates, January 1, 2018

State Individual Income Tax Rates

State	Tax Rate (%)	Income Brackets ($)	Num. of Brackets	Personal Exempt. ($)[1]		Fed. Inc. Tax Ded.
				Single	Dependents	
Texas	None	–	–	–	–	–

Note: Tax rates as of January 1, 2018; Local- and county-level taxes are not included; n/a not applicable; (1) Married joint filers generally receive double the single exemption
Source: Federation of Tax Administrators, State Individual Income Tax Rates, January 1, 2018

Various State Sales and Excise Tax Rates

State	State Sales Tax (%)	Gasoline[1] (¢/gal.)	Cigarette[2] ($/pack)	Spirits[3] ($/gal.)	Wine[4] ($/gal.)	Beer[5] ($/gal.)	Recreational Marijuana (%)
Texas	6.25	20.0	1.41	2.40 (f)	0.20 (l)	0.20 (q)	Not legal

Note: All tax rates as of January 1, 2018; (1) The American Petroleum Institute has developed a methodology for determining the average tax rate on a gallon of fuel. Rates may include any of the following: excise taxes, environmental fees, storage tank fees, other fees or taxes, general sales tax, and local taxes. In states where gasoline is subject to the general sales tax, or where the fuel tax is based on the average sale price, the average rate determined by API is sensitive to changes in the price of gasoline. States that fully or partially apply general sales taxes to gasoline: CA, CO, GA, IL, IN, MI, NY; (2) The federal excise tax of $1.0066 per pack and local taxes are not included; (3) Rates are those applicable to off-premise sales of 40% alcohol by volume (a.b.v.) distilled spirits in 750ml containers. Local excise taxes are excluded; (4) Rates are those applicable to off-premise sales of 11% a.b.v. non-carbonated wine in 750ml containers; (5) Rates are those applicable to off-premise sales of 4.7% a.b.v. beer in 12 ounce containers; (f) Different rates also applicable according to alcohol content, place of production, size of container, or place purchased (on- or off-premise or onboard airlines); (l) Different rates also applicable to alcohol content, place of production, size of container, place purchased (on- or off-premise or on board airlines) or type of wine (carbonated, vermouth, etc.); (q) Different rates also applicable according to alcohol content, place of production, size of container, or place purchased (on- or off-premise or onboard airlines).
Source: Tax Foundation, 2018 Facts & Figures: How Does Your State Compare?

State Business Tax Climate Index Rankings

State	Overall Rank	Corporate Tax Rank	Individual Income Tax Rank	Sales Tax Rank	Unemployment Insurance Tax Rank	Property Tax Rank
Texas	13	49	6	37	26	37

Note: The index is a measure of how each state's tax laws affect economic performance. The lower the rank, the more favorable a state's tax system is for business. States without a given tax are given a ranking of 1. The scores/rankings for the District of Columbia do not affect other states. The 2018 index represents the tax climate as of July 1, 2017.
Source: Tax Foundation, State Business Tax Climate Index 2018

TRANSPORTATION

Means of Transportation to Work

Area	Car/Truck/Van		Public Transportation			Bicycle	Walked	Other Means	Worked at Home
	Drove Alone	Car-pooled	Bus	Subway	Railroad				
City	80.3	9.6	2.3	0.0	0.0	0.0	0.6	0.8	6.3
MSA[1]	80.2	10.7	2.2	0.0	0.0	0.3	1.4	1.5	3.7
U.S.	76.4	9.3	2.6	1.9	0.6	0.6	2.8	1.3	4.6

Note: Figures are percentages and cover workers 16 years of age and older; (1) Figures cover the Houston-The Woodlands-Sugar Land, TX Metropolitan Statistical Area—see Appendix B for areas included
Source: U.S. Census Bureau, 2012-2016 American Community Survey 5-Year Estimates

Travel Time to Work

Area	Less Than 10 Minutes	10 to 19 Minutes	20 to 29 Minutes	30 to 44 Minutes	45 to 59 Minutes	60 to 89 Minutes	90 Minutes or More
City	7.7	20.9	18.2	29.6	14.9	6.4	2.4
MSA[1]	8.3	24.1	19.6	25.8	11.3	8.5	2.4
U.S.	12.9	29.2	20.9	20.4	8.0	6.0	2.7

Note: Note: Figures are percentages and include workers 16 years old and over; (1) Figures cover the Houston-The Woodlands-Sugar Land, TX Metropolitan Statistical Area—see Appendix B for areas included
Source: U.S. Census Bureau, 2012-2016 American Community Survey 5-Year Estimates

Freeway Travel Time Index

Area	1985	1990	1995	2000	2005	2010	2014
Urban Area Rank[1,2]	3	5	13	22	17	14	10
Urban Area Index[1]	1.25	1.22	1.22	1.23	1.28	1.28	1.33
Average Index[3]	1.09	1.11	1.14	1.17	1.20	1.19	1.20

Note: Freeway Travel Time Index—the ratio of travel time in the peak period to the travel time at free-flow conditions. For example, a value of 1.30 indicates a 20-minute free-flow trip takes 26 minutes in the peak (20 minutes x 1.30 = 26 minutes); (1) Covers the Houston TX urban area; (2) Rank is based on 101 urban areas (#1 = highest travel time index); (3) Average of 101 urban areas
Source: Texas Transportation Institute, 2015 Urban Mobility Scorecard, August 2015

Freeway Commuter Stress Index

Area	1985	1990	1995	2000	2005	2010	2014
Urban Area Rank[1,2]	4	12	18	23	16	17	12
Urban Area Index[1]	1.30	1.27	1.28	1.29	1.34	1.34	1.39
Average Index[3]	1.13	1.16	1.19	1.22	1.25	1.24	1.25

Note: The Freeway Commuter Stress Index is the same as the Freeway Travel Time Index (see table above) except that it includes only the travel in the peak directions during the peak periods; the TTI includes travel in all directions during the peak period. Thus, the CSI is more indicative of the work trip experienced by each commuter on a daily basis; (1) Covers the Houston TX urban area; (2) Rank is based on 101 urban areas (#1 = highest travel time index); (3) Average of 101 urban areas
Source: Texas Transportation Institute, 2015 Urban Mobility Scorecard, August 2015

Living Environment

COST OF LIVING

Cost of Living Index

Composite Index	Groceries	Housing	Utilities	Transportation	Health Care	Misc. Goods/ Services
98.1	86.8	104.8	110.6	97.4	91.2	94.5

Note: The Cost of Living Index measures regional differences in the cost of consumer goods and services, excluding taxes and non-consumer expenditures, for professional and managerial households in the top income quintile. It is based on more than 50,000 prices covering almost 60 different items for which prices are collected three times a year by chambers of commerce, economic development organizations or university applied economic centers in each participating urban area. The numbers shown should be read as a percentage above or below the national average of 100. For example, a value of 115.4 in the groceries column indicates that grocery prices are 15.4% higher than the national average. Small differences in the index numbers should not be interpreted as significant; Figures cover the Houston TX urban area.
Source: The Council for Community and Economic Research, ACCRA Cost of Living Index, 2017

Grocery Prices

Area[1]	T-Bone Steak ($/pound)	Frying Chicken ($/pound)	Whole Milk ($/half gal.)	Eggs ($/dozen)	Orange Juice ($/64 oz.)	Coffee ($/11.5 oz.)
City[2]	10.13	1.04	1.55	1.50	3.07	4.05
Avg.	11.29	1.40	2.02	1.47	3.55	4.37
Min.	7.71	0.93	1.04	0.70	2.86	3.24
Max.	15.83	2.39	4.03	3.92	6.29	8.16

*Note: (1) Values for the local area are compared with the average, minimum and maximum values for all 294 areas in the Cost of Living Index; (2) Figures cover the Houston TX urban area; **T-Bone Steak** (price per pound); **Frying Chicken** (price per pound, whole fryer); **Whole Milk** (half gallon carton); **Eggs** (price per dozen, Grade A, large); **Orange Juice** (64 oz. Tropicana or Florida Natural); **Coffee** (11.5 oz. can, vacuum-packed, Maxwell House, Hills Bros, or Folgers).*
Source: The Council for Community and Economic Research, ACCRA Cost of Living Index, 2017

Housing and Utility Costs

Area[1]	New Home Price ($)	Apartment Rent ($/month)	All Electric ($/month)	Part Electric ($/month)	Other Energy ($/month)	Telephone ($/month)
City[2]	307,633	1,337	-	147.08	37.96	31.67
Avg.	335,956	1,047	175.01	97.34	67.93	28.71
Min.	187,788	491	109.48	49.33	35.44	12.39
Max.	1,739,087	4,559	432.62	227.09	353.33	44.61

*Note: (1) Values for the local area are compared with the average, minimum and maximum values for all 294 areas in the Cost of Living Index; (2) Figures cover the Houston TX urban area; **New Home Price** (2,400 sf living area, 8,000 sf lot, in urban area with full utilities); **Apartment Rent** (950 sf 2 bedroom/1.5 or 2 bath, unfurnished, excluding all utilities except water); **All Electric** (average monthly cost for an all-electric home); **Part Electric** (average monthly cost for a part-electric home); **Other Energy** (average monthly cost for natural gas, fuel oil, coal, wood, and any other forms of energy except electricity); **Telephone** (price includes basic monthly rate for a private residential line plus additional local usage charges incurred by a family of four).*
Source: The Council for Community and Economic Research, ACCRA Cost of Living Index, 2017

Health Care, Transportation, and Other Costs

Area[1]	Doctor ($/visit)	Dentist ($/visit)	Optometrist ($/visit)	Gasoline ($/gallon)	Beauty Salon ($/visit)	Men's Shirt ($)
City[2]	80.33	92.07	106.05	2.09	49.70	25.00
Avg.	108.00	92.54	101.93	2.25	37.58	30.92
Min.	30.39	60.00	49.75	1.82	16.11	11.20
Max.	193.50	161.94	229.28	3.16	77.35	59.13

*Note: (1) Values for the local area are compared with the average, minimum and maximum values for all 294 areas in the Cost of Living Index; (2) Figures cover the Houston TX urban area; **Doctor** (general practitioners routine exam of an established patient); **Dentist** (adult teeth cleaning and periodic oral examination); **Optometrist** (full vision eye exam for established adult patient); **Gasoline** (one gallon regular unleaded, national brand, including all taxes, cash price at self-service pump if available); **Beauty Salon** (woman's shampoo, trim, and blow-dry); **Men's Shirt** (cotton/polyester dress shirt, pinpoint weave, long sleeves).*
Source: The Council for Community and Economic Research, ACCRA Cost of Living Index, 2017

HOUSING

House Price Index (HPI)

Area	National Ranking[2]	Quarterly Change (%)	One-Year Change (%)	Five-Year Change (%)
MSA[1]	149	1.74	5.34	40.98
U.S.[3]	–	1.61	6.68	34.71

Note: The HPI is a weighted repeat sales index. It measures average price changes in repeat sales or refinancings on the same properties. This information is obtained by reviewing repeat mortgage transactions on single-family properties whose mortgages have been purchased or securitized by Fannie Mae or Freddie Mac in January 1975; (1) Figures cover the Houston-The Woodlands-Sugar Land, TX Metropolitan Statistical Area—see Appendix B for areas included; (2) Rankings are based on annual percentage change for all metro areas containing at least 15,000 transactions over the last 10 years and ranges from 1 to 253; (3) figures based on a weighted average of Census Division estimates using a seasonally adjusted, purchase-only index; all figures are for the period ending December 31, 2017
Source: Federal Housing Finance Agency, House Price Index, February 28, 2018

Median Single-Family Home Prices

Area	2015	2016	2017p	Percent Change 2016 to 2017
MSA[1]	213.4	217.4	231.1	6.3
U.S. Average	223.9	235.5	248.8	5.6

Note: Figures are median sales prices of existing single-family homes in thousands of dollars; (p) preliminary; (1) Figures cover the Houston-The Woodlands-Sugar Land, TX Metropolitan Statistical Area—see Appendix B for areas included
Source: National Association of Realtors, Median Sales Price of Existing Single-Family Homes for Metropolitan Areas, 4th Quarter 2017

Qualifying Income Based on Median Sales Price of Existing Single-Family Homes

Area	With 5% Down ($)	With 10% Down ($)	With 20% Down ($)
MSA[1]	51,547	48,834	43,408
U.S. Average	55,585	52,659	46,808

Note: Figures are preliminary; Qualifying income is based on a mortgage rate of 4.17%. Monthly principal and interest payment is limited to 25% of income; (1) Figures cover the Houston-The Woodlands-Sugar Land, TX Metropolitan Statistical Area—see Appendix B for areas included
Source: National Association of Realtors, Qualifying Income Based on Median Sales Price of Existing Single-Family Homes for Metropolitan Areas, 4th Quarter 2017

Median Apartment Condo-Coop Home Prices

Area	2015	2016	2017p	Percent Change 2016 to 2017
MSA[1]	149.6	150.8	160.3	6.3
U.S. Average	210.7	220.7	234.3	6.2

Note: Figures are median sales prices of existing apartment condo-coop homes in thousands of dollars; (p) preliminary; (1) Figures cover the Houston-The Woodlands-Sugar Land, TX Metropolitan Statistical Area—see Appendix B for areas included
Source: National Association of Realtors, Median Sales Price of Existing Apartment Condo-Coop Homes for Metropolitan Areas, 4th Quarter 2017

Home Value Distribution

Area	Under $50,000	$50,000 -$99,999	$100,000 -$149,999	$150,000 -$199,999	$200,000 -$299,999	$300,000 -$499,999	$500,000 -$999,999	$1,000,000 or more
City	1.3	1.2	10.6	14.6	26.9	30.5	13.0	1.9
MSA[1]	7.0	18.8	21.1	17.1	16.9	12.1	5.3	1.7
U.S.	8.8	14.8	15.3	14.9	18.4	16.4	9.0	2.5

Note: Figures are percentages and cover owner-occupied housing units; (1) Figures cover the Houston-The Woodlands-Sugar Land, TX Metropolitan Statistical Area—see Appendix B for areas included
Source: U.S. Census Bureau, 2012-2016 American Community Survey 5-Year Estimates

Homeownership Rate

Area	2009 (%)	2010 (%)	2011 (%)	2012 (%)	2013 (%)	2014 (%)	2015 (%)	2016 (%)	2017 (%)
MSA[1]	63.6	61.4	61.3	62.1	60.5	60.4	60.3	59.0	58.9
U.S.	67.4	66.9	66.1	65.4	65.1	64.5	63.7	63.4	63.9

Note: (1) Figures cover the Houston-The Woodlands-Sugar Land, TX Metropolitan Statistical Area—see Appendix B for areas included
Source: U.S. Census Bureau, Housing Vacancies and Homeownership Annual Statistics: 2009-2017

Year Housing Structure Built

Area	2010 or Later	2000 -2009	1990 -1999	1980 -1989	1970 -1979	1960 -1969	1950 -1959	1940 -1949	Before 1940	Median Year
City	6.4	19.8	22.2	32.3	15.6	1.7	0.7	0.4	0.9	1990
MSA[1]	5.6	23.9	14.8	15.7	18.8	9.1	6.7	2.8	2.7	1986
U.S.	2.3	14.7	14.0	13.7	15.6	10.9	10.6	5.2	13.0	1977

Note: Figures are percentages except for Median Year; Note: (1) Figures cover the Houston-The Woodlands-Sugar Land, TX Metropolitan Statistical Area—see Appendix B for areas included
Source: U.S. Census Bureau, 2012-2016 American Community Survey 5-Year Estimates

Gross Monthly Rent

Area	Under $500	$500 -$999	$1,000 -$1,499	$1,500 -$1,999	$2,000 -$2,499	$2,500 -$2,999	$3,000 and up	Median ($)
City	0.0	3.7	39.5	29.2	13.2	7.5	6.9	1,617
MSA[1]	5.2	49.7	30.4	10.1	2.7	1.0	1.0	955
U.S.	11.3	43.3	27.7	10.7	4.0	1.6	1.5	949

Note: Figures are percentages except for Median; Gross rent is the contract rent plus the estimated average monthly cost of utilities (electricity, gas, and water and sewer) and fuels (oil, coal, kerosene, wood, etc.) if these are paid by the renter (or paid for the renter by someone else); (1) Figures cover the Houston-The Woodlands-Sugar Land, TX Metropolitan Statistical Area—see Appendix B for areas included
Source: U.S. Census Bureau, 2012-2016 American Community Survey 5-Year Estimates

HEALTH

Health Risk Factors

Category	MSA[1] (%)	U.S. (%)
Adults aged 18–64 who have any kind of health care coverage	71.3	87.7
Adults who reported being in good or excellent health	82.6	83.6
Adults who are current smokers	12.6	17.1
Adults who currently use E-cigarettes	5.6	4.7
Adults who currently use chewing tobacco, snuff, or snus	3.5	4.0
Adults who are heavy drinkers[2]	6.1	6.5
Adults who are binge drinkers[3]	17.7	16.9
Adults who are overweight (BMI 25.0 - 29.9)	36.0	35.3
Adults who are obese (BMI 30.0 - 99.8)	29.5	29.9
Adults who participated in any physical activities in the past month	77.6	76.9
Adults who always or nearly always wears a seat belt	96.5	94.3

Note: (1) Figures cover the Houston-The Woodlands-Sugar Land, TX Metropolitan Statistical Area—see Appendix B for areas included; (2) Heavy drinkers are classified as adult men having more than 14 drinks per week and adult women having more than 7 drinks per week; (3) Binge drinkers are classified as males having five or more drinks on one occasion or females having four or more drinks on one occasion
Source: Centers for Disease Control and Prevention, Behaviorial Risk Factor Surveillance System, SMART: Selected Metropolitan Area Risk Trends, 2016

Health Screening Rates

Category	MSA[1] (%)	U.S. (%)
Adults 50-75 who have had a blood stool test within the past year	8.4	8.0
Adults 50-75 who have had a colonoscopy in the past 10 years	51.6	63.5
Adults aged 65+ who have had flu shot within the past year	55.0	58.6
Adults aged 65+ who have ever had a pneumonia vaccination	73.7	73.4
Adults who have ever been tested for HIV	42.3	35.6
Women aged 21-65 who have had a pap test in the past three years	76.8	79.8
Men aged 40+ who have had a PSA test within the past two years	40.9	39.5
Women aged 40+ who have had a mammogram within the past two years	67.7	72.5

Note: n/a not available; (1) Figures cover the Houston-The Woodlands-Sugar Land, TX Metropolitan Statistical Area—see Appendix B for areas included; Source: Centers for Disease Control and Prevention, Behaviorial Risk Factor Surveillance System, SMART: Selected Metropolitan Area Risk Trends, 2016

Chronic Health Conditions

Category	MSA[1] (%)	U.S. (%)
Adults who have ever been told they had a heart attack	3.8	4.4
Adults who have ever been told they have angina or coronary heart disease	4.3	4.1
Adults who have ever been told they had a stroke	n/a	3.1
Adults who have been told they currently have asthma	6.8	9.3
Adults who have ever been told they have arthritis	17.2	25.8
Adults who have ever been told they have diabetes[2]	9.6	10.5
Adults who have ever been told they had skin cancer	3.3	5.9
Adults who have ever been told they had any other types of cancer	6.6	6.7
Adults who have ever been told they have COPD	5.3	6.3
Adults who have ever been told they have kidney disease	3.5	2.8
Adults who have ever been told they have a form of depression	12.0	17.4

Note: n/a not available; (1) Figures cover the Houston-The Woodlands-Sugar Land, TX Metropolitan Statistical Area—see Appendix B for areas included; (2) Figures do not include pregnancy-related, borderline, or pre-diabetes
Source: Centers for Disease Control and Prevention, Behaviorial Risk Factor Surveillance System, SMART: Selected Metropolitan Area Risk Trends, 2016

Mortality Rates for the Top 10 Causes of Death in the U.S.

ICD-10[a] Sub-Chapter	ICD-10[a] Code	Age-Adjusted Mortality Rate[1] per 100,000 population	
		County[2]	U.S.
Malignant neoplasms	C00-C97	118.1	158.5
Ischaemic heart diseases	I20-I25	67.1	96.8
Other forms of heart disease	I30-I51	39.7	52.4
Chronic lower respiratory diseases	J40-J47	20.5	40.9
Cerebrovascular diseases	I60-I69	33.9	37.2
Organic, including symptomatic, mental disorders	F01-F09	27.7	33.3
Other degenerative diseases of the nervous system	G30-G31	34.5	32.1
Other external causes of accidental injury	W00-X59	15.0	31.2
Diabetes mellitus	E10-E14	13.1	21.1
Hypertensive diseases	I10-I15	14.7	20.8

Note: (a) ICD-10 = International Classification of Diseases 10th Revision; (1) Mortality rates are a three year average covering 2014-2016; (2) Figures cover Fort Bend County.
Source: Centers for Disease Control and Prevention, National Center for Health Statistics. Underlying Cause of Death 1999-2016 on CDC WONDER Online Database, released December 2017

Mortality Rates for Selected Causes of Death

ICD-10[a] Sub-Chapter	ICD-10[a] Code	Age-Adjusted Mortality Rate[1] per 100,000 population	
		County[2]	U.S.
Assault	X85-Y09	4.3	5.6
Diseases of the liver	K70-K76	8.4	14.0
Human immunodeficiency virus (HIV) disease	B20-B24	1.0	1.9
Influenza and pneumonia	J09-J18	12.9	14.6
Intentional self-harm	X60-X84	9.4	13.2
Malnutrition	E40-E46	1.7	1.3
Obesity and other hyperalimentation	E65-E68	1.0	2.1
Renal failure	N17-N19	11.2	13.0
Transport accidents	V01-V99	7.9	12.0
Viral hepatitis	B15-B19	1.2	1.9

Note: (a) ICD-10 = International Classification of Diseases 10th Revision; (1) Mortality rates are a three year average covering 2014-2016; (2) Figures cover Fort Bend County; Data are Suppressed when the data meet the criteria for confidentiality constraints; Mortality rates are flagged as Unreliable when the rate would be calculated with a numerator of 20 or less.
Source: Centers for Disease Control and Prevention, National Center for Health Statistics. Underlying Cause of Death 1999-2016 on CDC WONDER Online Database, released December 2017

Health Insurance Coverage

Area	With Health Insurance	With Private Health Insurance	With Public Health Insurance	Without Health Insurance	Population Under Age 18 Without Health Insurance
City	89.9	79.7	17.8	10.1	8.4
MSA[1]	80.1	60.5	26.1	19.9	11.0
U.S.	88.3	66.7	33.0	11.7	5.9

Note: Figures are percentages that cover the civilian noninstitutionalized population; (1) Figures cover the Houston-The Woodlands-Sugar Land, TX Metropolitan Statistical Area—see Appendix B for areas included
Source: U.S. Census Bureau, 2012-2016 American Community Survey 5-Year Estimates

Number of Medical Professionals

Area	MDs[3]	DOs[3,4]	Dentists	Podiatrists	Chiropractors	Optometrists
County[1] (number)	1,804	123	384	23	96	109
County[1] (rate[2])	252.7	17.2	51.8	3.1	12.9	14.7
U.S. (rate[2])	276.5	22.3	67.3	6.0	26.7	15.9

Note: Data as of 2016 unless noted; (1) Data covers Fort Bend County; (2) Rate per 100,000 population; (3) Data as of 2015 and includes all active, non-federal physicians; (4) Doctor of Osteopathic Medicine
Source: U.S. Department of Health and Human Services, Health Resources and Services Administration, Bureau of Health Professions, Area Resource File (ARF) 2016-2017

Best Hospitals

According to *U.S. News,* the Houston-The Woodlands-Sugar Land, TX metro area is home to six of the best hospitals in the U.S.: **Baylor St. Luke's Medical Center** (2 adult specialties); **Houston Methodist Hospital** (8 adult specialties); **Memorial Hermann-Texas Medical Center** (2 adult specialties and 1 pediatric specialty); **Menninger Clinic** (1 adult specialty); **TIRR Memorial Hermann** (1 adult specialty); **University of Texas MD Anderson Cancer Center** (3 adult specialties and 1 pediatric specialty). The hospitals listed were nationally ranked in at least one of 16 specialties. Only 152 hospitals nationwide were nationally ranked in one or more specialties. Twenty hospitals in the U.S. made the Honor Roll. The Best Hospitals Honor Roll was revamped last year to take both the national rankings and the procedure and condition ratings into account. Hospitals received points if they were nationally ranked in one of the 16 specialties—the higher they ranked, the more points they got—and how many ratings of "high performing" they earned in the nine procedures and conditions. *U.S. News Online, "America's Best Hospitals 2017-18"*

According to *U.S. News,* the Houston-The Woodlands-Sugar Land, TX metro area is home to three of the best children's hospitals in the U.S.: **Children's Memorial Hermann Hospital** (1 pediatric specialty); **Texas Children's Hospital** (Honor Roll/10 pediatric specialties); **Children's Cancer Hospital-University of Texas M.D. Anderson Cancer Center** (1 pediatric specialty). The hospitals listed were highly ranked in at least one of 10 pediatric specialties. Eighty-two children's hospitals in the U.S. were nationally ranked in at least one specialty. Hospitals received points for being ranked in a specialty, and the 10 hospitals with the most points across the 10 specialties make up the Honor Roll. *U.S. News Online, "America's Best Children's Hospitals 2017-18"*

EDUCATION

Public School District Statistics

District Name	Schls	Pupils	Pupil/ Teacher Ratio	Minority Pupils[1] (%)	Free Lunch Eligible[2] (%)	IEP[3] (%)
Fort Bend ISD	79	73,115	16.2	82.6	29.0	6.4
Harmony School of Science - Houston	4	3,074	17.0	79.0	37.6	5.4
Lamar CISD	40	29,692	17.1	72.2	39.6	8.3

Note: Table includes school districts with 100 or more students; (1) Percentage of students that are not non-Hispanic white; (2) Percentage of students that are eligible for the free lunch program; (3) Percentage of students that have an Individualized Education Program.
Source: U.S. Department of Education, National Center for Education Statistics, Common Core of Data, Local Education Agency (School District) Universe Survey: School Year 2015-2016; U.S. Department of Education, National Center for Education Statistics, Common Core of Data, Public Elementary/Secondary School Universe Survey: School Year 2015-2016

Best High Schools

According to *U.S. News,* Sugar Land is home to one of the best high schools in the U.S.: **Harmony School Of Science - Houston High** (#158). More than 22,000 public, magnet and charter schools were ranked based on their performance on state assessments and how well they prepare students for college. Schools with the highest unrounded College Readiness Index values were numerically ranked from 1 to 500 and were classified as gold medal winners. *U.S. News & World Report, "Best High Schools 2017"*

Highest Level of Education

Area	Less than H.S.	H.S. Diploma	Some College, No Deg.	Associate Degree	Bachelor's Degree	Master's Degree	Prof. School Degree	Doctorate Degree
City	7.1	12.4	17.9	6.0	33.4	16.2	3.4	3.5
MSA[1]	17.7	23.3	21.3	6.5	20.1	7.8	1.9	1.4
U.S.	13.0	27.5	21.0	8.2	18.8	8.2	2.0	1.3

Note: Figures cover persons age 25 and over; (1) Figures cover the Houston-The Woodlands-Sugar Land, TX Metropolitan Statistical Area—see Appendix B for areas included
Source: U.S. Census Bureau, 2012-2016 American Community Survey 5-Year Estimates

Educational Attainment by Race

Area	High School Graduate or Higher (%)					Bachelor's Degree or Higher (%)				
	Total	White	Black	Asian	Hisp.[2]	Total	White	Black	Asian	Hisp.[2]
City	92.9	95.5	96.8	89.6	86.9	56.5	53.0	59.9	62.7	37.2
MSA[1]	82.3	82.5	89.4	86.7	60.6	31.3	31.9	25.9	56.2	13.1
U.S.	87.0	88.9	84.3	86.3	65.7	30.3	31.6	20.0	52.1	14.7

Note: Figures shown cover persons 25 years old and over; (1) Figures cover the Houston-The Woodlands-Sugar Land, TX Metropolitan Statistical Area—see Appendix B for areas included; (2) People of Hispanic origin can be of any race
Source: U.S. Census Bureau, 2012-2016 American Community Survey 5-Year Estimates

School Enrollment by Grade and Control

Area	Preschool (%)		Kindergarten (%)		Grades 1 - 4 (%)		Grades 5 - 8 (%)		Grades 9 - 12 (%)	
	Public	Private	Public	Private	Public	Private	Public	Private	Public	Private
City	28.4	71.6	80.5	19.5	83.8	16.2	89.2	10.8	91.6	8.4
MSA[1]	58.9	41.1	90.0	10.0	92.8	7.2	93.4	6.6	93.4	6.6
U.S.	58.4	41.6	87.7	12.3	89.8	10.2	89.7	10.3	90.4	9.6

Note: Figures shown cover persons 3 years old and over; (1) Figures cover the Houston-The Woodlands-Sugar Land, TX Metropolitan Statistical Area—see Appendix B for areas included
Source: U.S. Census Bureau, 2012-2016 American Community Survey 5-Year Estimates

Average Salaries of Public School Classroom Teachers

Area	2015		2016		Change from 2015 to 2016	
	Dollars	Rank[1]	Dollars	Rank[1]	Percent	Rank[2]
Texas	50,713	28	51,890	27	2.3	8
U.S. Average	57,611	–	58,353	–	1.3	–

Note: (1) Rank ranges from 1 to 51 where 1 indicates highest salary; (2) Rank ranges from 1 to 51 where 1 indicates highest percent change.
Source: National Education Association, Rankings & Estimates: Rankings of the States 2016 and Estimates of School Statistics 2017

Higher Education

Four-Year Colleges			Two-Year Colleges			Medical Schools[1]	Law Schools[2]	Voc/ Tech[3]
Public	Private Non-profit	Private For-profit	Public	Private Non-profit	Private For-profit			
0	0	0	0	0	0	0	0	0

Note: Figures cover institutions located within the city limits and include main campuses only; (1) includes schools accredited by the Liaison Committee on Medical Education and the American Osteopathic Association's Commission on Osteopathic College Accreditation; (2) includes ABA-accredited schools, schools with provisional ABA accreditation, and state accredited schools; (3) includes all schools with programs that are less than 2 years.
Source: National Center for Education Statistics, Integrated Postsecondary Education System (IPEDS), 2016-17; Wikipedia, List of Medical Schools in the United States, accessed April 2, 2018; Wikipedia, List of Law Schools in the United States, accessed April 2, 2018

According to *U.S. News & World Report,* the Houston-The Woodlands-Sugar Land, TX metro area is home to two of the best national universities in the U.S.: **Rice University** (#14 tie); **University of Houston** (#192 tie). The indicators used to capture academic quality fall into a number of categories: assessment by administrators at peer institutions; retention of students; faculty resources; student selectivity; financial resources; alumni giving; high school counselor ratings of colleges; and graduation rate. *U.S. News & World Report, "America's Best Colleges 2018"*

According to *U.S. News & World Report,* the Houston-The Woodlands-Sugar Land, TX metro area is home to one of the top 100 law schools in the U.S.: **University of Houston** (#56 tie). The rankings are based on a weighted average of 12 measures of quality: peer assessment score; assessment score by lawyers/judges; median LSAT scores; median undergrad GPA; acceptance rate; employment rates for graduates; placement success; bar passage rate; faculty resources; expenditures per student; student/faculty ratio; and library resources. *U.S. News & World Report, "America's Best Graduate Schools, Law, 2019"*

According to *U.S. News & World Report,* the Houston-The Woodlands-Sugar Land, TX metro area is home to three of the top 75 medical schools for research in the U.S.: **Baylor College of Medicine** (#16); **University of Texas Health Science Center—Houston (McGovern)** (#52 tie); **University of Texas Medical Branch—Galveston** (#66 tie). The rankings are based on a weighted average of 11 measures of quality: quality assessment; peer assessment score; assessment score by residency directors; research activity; total research activity; average research activity per faculty member; student selectivity; median MCAT total score; median undergraduate GPA; acceptance rate; and faculty resources. *U.S. News & World Report, "America's Best Graduate Schools, Medical, 2019"*

According to *U.S. News & World Report,* the Houston-The Woodlands-Sugar Land, TX metro area is home to one of the top 75 business schools in the U.S.: **Rice University (Jones)** (#23 tie). The rankings are based on a weighted average of the following nine measures: quality assessment; peer assessment; recruiter assessment; placement success; mean starting salary and bonus; student selectivity; mean GMAT and GRE scores; mean undergraduate GPA; and acceptance rate. *U.S. News & World Report, "America's Best Graduate Schools, Business, 2019"*

PRESIDENTIAL ELECTION

2016 Presidential Election Results

Area	Clinton	Trump	Johnson	Stein	Other
Fort Bend County	51.4	44.8	2.6	0.7	0.5
U.S.	48.0	45.9	3.3	1.1	1.7

Note: Results are percentages and may not add to 100% due to rounding
Source: Dave Leip's Atlas of U.S. Presidential Elections

EMPLOYERS

Major Employers

Company Name	Industry
Christus Health Gulf Coast	Management consulting services
Conoco Phillips	Petroleum refining
Continental Airlines	Air trans scheduled
Dibellos Dynamic Orthotics & Prosthetics	Surgical appliances & supplies
El Paso E&P Company	Petroleum refining
F Charles Brunicardi MD	Accounting
Grey Wolf	Drilling oil & gas wells
Kellogg Brown &Root	Industrial plant construction
Mustang Engineers and Constructors	Construction management consultant
Philip Industrial Services	Environmental consultant
Philips Petroleum Company	Oil & gas exploration services
Quaker State Corp	Lubricating oils & greases
St Lukes Episcopal Health System	General medical & surgical hospitals
Texas Childrens Hospital	Specialty hosp, except psychiatric
The Methodist Hospital	General medical & surgical hospitals
Tracer Industries	Plumbing
Univ of Texas Medical Branch at Galveston	Accident & health insurance
University of Houston System	University
University of Texas System	General medical & surgical hospitals
US Dept of Veteran Affairs	Administration of veterans' affairs
Veterans Health Administration	Administration of veterans' affairs

Note: Companies shown are located within the Houston-The Woodlands-Sugar Land, TX Metropolitan Statistical Area.
Source: Hoovers.com; Wikipedia

PUBLIC SAFETY

Crime Rate

Area	All Crimes	Violent Crimes				Property Crimes		
		Murder	Rape[3]	Robbery	Aggrav. Assault	Burglary	Larceny -Theft	Motor Vehicle Theft
City	1,706.1	0.0	17.8	47.7	20.0	277.5	1,289.8	53.3
Metro[1]	3,502.0	7.2	39.9	215.5	315.6	548.2	2,035.1	340.5
U.S.	2,847.8	5.3	40.4	102.8	248.5	468.9	1,745.0	236.9

Note: Figures are crimes per 100,000 population; (1) Figures cover the Houston-The Woodlands-Sugar Land, TX Metropolitan Statistical Area—see Appendix B for areas included; (3) The city and U.S. figures shown were reported using the revised Uniform Crime Reporting (UCR) definition of rape. The metro area figures shown are an aggregate total of the data submitted using both the revised and legacy UCR definitions.
Source: FBI Uniform Crime Reports, 2016

Hate Crimes

Area	Number of Quarters Reported	Number of Incidents per Bias Motivation					
		Race/Ethnicity/ Ancestry	Religion	Sexual Orientation	Disability	Gender	Gender Identity
City	1	1	0	0	0	0	0
U.S.	4	3,489	1,273	1,076	70	31	124

Source: Federal Bureau of Investigation, Hate Crime Statistics 2016

Identity Theft Consumer Reports

Area	Reports	Reports per 100,000 Population	Rank[2]
MSA[1]	9,180	136	31
U.S.	371,061	114	-

Note: (1) Figures cover the Houston-The Woodlands-Sugar Land, TX Metropolitan Statistical Area—see Appendix B for areas included; (2) Rank ranges from 1 to 389 where 1 indicates greatest number of identity theft reports per 100,000 population
Source: Federal Trade Commission, Consumer Sentinel Network Data Book for January–December 2017

Fraud and Other Consumer Reports

Area	Reports	Reports per 100,000 Population	Rank[2]
MSA[1]	34,244	506	110
U.S.	2,304,550	708	-

Note: (1) Figures cover the Houston-The Woodlands-Sugar Land, TX Metropolitan Statistical Area—see Appendix B for areas included; (2) Rank ranges from 1 to 389 where 1 indicates greatest number of fraud and other consumer reports per 100,000 population
Source: Federal Trade Commission, Consumer Sentinel Network Data Book for January–December 2017

SPORTS

Professional Sports Teams

Team Name	League	Year Established
Houston Astros	Major League Baseball (MLB)	1962
Houston Dynamo	Major League Soccer (MLS)	2006
Houston Rockets	National Basketball Association (NBA)	1971
Houston Texans	National Football League (NFL)	2002

Note: Includes teams located in the Houston-The Woodlands-Sugar Land, TX Metropolitan Statistical Area.
Source: Wikipedia, Major Professional Sports Teams of the United States and Canada, April 5, 2018

CLIMATE

Average and Extreme Temperatures

Temperature	Jan	Feb	Mar	Apr	May	Jun	Jul	Aug	Sep	Oct	Nov	Dec	Yr.
Extreme High (°F)	84	91	91	95	97	103	104	107	102	94	89	83	107
Average High (°F)	61	65	73	79	85	91	93	93	89	81	72	65	79
Average Temp. (°F)	51	54	62	69	75	81	83	83	79	70	61	54	69
Average Low (°F)	41	43	51	58	65	71	73	73	68	58	50	43	58
Extreme Low (°F)	12	20	22	31	44	52	62	62	48	32	19	7	7

Note: Figures cover the years 1969-1990
Source: National Climatic Data Center, International Station Meteorological Climate Summary, 9/96

Average Precipitation/Snowfall/Humidity

Precip./Humidity	Jan	Feb	Mar	Apr	May	Jun	Jul	Aug	Sep	Oct	Nov	Dec	Yr.
Avg. Precip. (in.)	3.3	2.7	3.3	3.3	5.6	4.9	3.7	3.7	4.8	4.7	3.7	3.3	46.9
Avg. Snowfall (in.)	Tr	Tr	0	0	0	0	0	0	0	0	Tr	Tr	Tr
Avg. Rel. Hum. 6am (%)	85	86	87	89	91	92	93	93	93	91	89	86	90
Avg. Rel. Hum. 3pm (%)	58	55	54	54	57	56	55	55	57	53	55	57	55

Note: Figures cover the years 1969-1990; Tr = Trace amounts (<0.05 in. of rain; <0.5 in. of snow)
Source: National Climatic Data Center, International Station Meteorological Climate Summary, 9/96

Weather Conditions

Temperature			Daytime Sky			Precipitation		
32°F & below	45°F & below	90°F & above	Clear	Partly cloudy	Cloudy	0.01 inch or more precip.	0.1 inch or more snow/ice	Thunder-storms
21	87	96	83	167	115	101	1	62

Note: Figures are average number of days per year and cover the years 1969-1990
Source: National Climatic Data Center, International Station Meteorological Climate Summary, 9/96

HAZARDOUS WASTE

Superfund Sites

The Houston-The Woodlands-Sugar Land, TX metro area is home to 21 sites on the EPA's Superfund National Priorities List: **Conroe Creosoting Co.** (final); **Crystal Chemical Co.** (final); **French, Ltd.** (final); **Geneva Industries/Fuhrmann Energy** (final); **Gulfco Marine Maintenance** (final); **Highlands Acid Pit** (final); **Jones Road Ground Water Plume** (final); **Malone Service Co - Swan Lake Plant** (final); **Many Diversified Interests, Inc.** (final); **Motco, Inc.** (final); **North Cavalcade Street** (final); **Patrick Bayou** (final); **Petro-chemical Systems, Inc. (Turtle Bayou)** (final); **San Jacinto River Waste Pits** (final); **Sheridan Disposal Services** (final); **Sikes Disposal Pits** (final); **Sol Lynn/Industrial Transformers** (final); **South Cavalcade Street** (final); **Tex-tin Corp.** (final); **United Creosoting Co.** (final); **US Oil Recovery** (final). There are a total of 1,396 Superfund sites with a status of proposed or final on the list in the U.S.
U.S. Environmental Protection Agency, National Priorities List, April 4, 2018

AIR & WATER QUALITY

Air Quality Trends: Ozone

	1990	1995	2000	2005	2010	2012	2013	2014	2015	2016
MSA[1]	0.119	0.114	0.102	0.087	0.079	0.080	0.075	0.064	0.083	0.066
U.S.	0.087	0.089	0.081	0.079	0.073	0.075	0.069	0.067	0.068	0.069

Note: (1) Data covers the Houston-The Woodlands-Sugar Land, TX Metropolitan Statistical Area—see Appendix B for areas included. The values shown are the composite ozone concentration averages among trend sites based on the highest fourth daily maximum 8-hour concentration in parts per million. These trends are based on sites having an adequate record of monitoring data during the trend period. Data from exceptional events are included.
Source: U.S. Environmental Protection Agency, Air Quality Monitoring Information, "Air Quality Trends by City, 1990-2016"

Air Quality Index

Area	Percent of Days when Air Quality was...[2]					AQI Statistics[2]	
	Good	Moderate	Unhealthy for Sensitive Groups	Unhealthy	Very Unhealthy	Maximum	Median
MSA[1]	50.4	42.7	6.0	0.8	0.0	177	50

Note: (1) Data covers the Houston-The Woodlands-Sugar Land, TX Metropolitan Statistical Area—see Appendix B for areas included; (2) Based on 365 days with AQI data in 2017. Air Quality Index (AQI) is an index for reporting daily air quality. EPA calculates the AQI for five major air pollutants regulated by the Clean Air Act: ground-level ozone, particle pollution (aka particulate matter), carbon monoxide, sulfur dioxide, and nitrogen dioxide. The AQI runs from 0 to 500. The higher the AQI value, the greater the level of air pollution and the greater the health concern. There are six AQI categories: "Good" AQI is between 0 and 50. Air quality is considered satisfactory; "Moderate" AQI is between 51 and 100. Air quality is acceptable; "Unhealthy for Sensitive Groups" When AQI values are between 101 and 150, members of sensitive groups may experience health effects; "Unhealthy" When AQI values are between 151 and 200 everyone may begin to experience health effects; "Very Unhealthy" AQI values between 201 and 300 trigger a health alert; "Hazardous" AQI values over 300 trigger warnings of emergency conditions (not shown).
Source: U.S. Environmental Protection Agency, Air Quality Index Report, 2017

Air Quality Index Pollutants

Area	Percent of Days when AQI Pollutant was...[2]					
	Carbon Monoxide	Nitrogen Dioxide	Ozone	Sulfur Dioxide	Particulate Matter 2.5	Particulate Matter 10
MSA[1]	0.0	4.4	47.4	0.0	47.9	0.3

Note: (1) Data covers the Houston-The Woodlands-Sugar Land, TX Metropolitan Statistical Area—see Appendix B for areas included; (2) Based on 365 days with AQI data in 2017. The Air Quality Index (AQI) is an index for reporting daily air quality. EPA calculates the AQI for five major air pollutants regulated by the Clean Air Act: ground-level ozone, particle pollution (also known as particulate matter), carbon monoxide, sulfur dioxide, and nitrogen dioxide. The AQI runs from 0 to 500. The higher the AQI value, the greater the level of air pollution and the greater the health concern.
Source: U.S. Environmental Protection Agency, Air Quality Index Report, 2017

Maximum Air Pollutant Concentrations: Particulate Matter, Ozone, CO and Lead

	Particulate Matter 10 (ug/m^3)	Particulate Matter 2.5 Wtd AM (ug/m^3)	Particulate Matter 2.5 24-Hr (ug/m^3)	Ozone (ppm)	Carbon Monoxide (ppm)	Lead (ug/m^3)
MSA[1] Level	81	10.1	23	0.079	2	0
NAAQS[2]	150	15	35	0.075	9	0.15
Met NAAQS[2]	Yes	Yes	Yes	No	Yes	Yes

Note: (1) Data covers the Houston-The Woodlands-Sugar Land, TX Metropolitan Statistical Area—see Appendix B for areas included; Data from exceptional events are included; (2) National Ambient Air Quality Standards; ppm = parts per million; ug/m^3 = micrograms per cubic meter; n/a not available.
Concentrations: Particulate Matter 10 (coarse particulate)—highest second maximum 24-hour concentration; Particulate Matter 2.5 Wtd AM (fine particulate)—highest weighted annual mean concentration; Particulate Matter 2.5 24-Hour (fine particulate)—highest 98th percentile 24-hour concentration; Ozone—highest fourth daily maximum 8-hour concentration; Carbon Monoxide—highest second maximum non-overlapping 8-hour concentration; Lead—maximum running 3-month average
Source: U.S. Environmental Protection Agency, Air Quality Monitoring Information, "Air Quality Statistics by City, 2016"

Maximum Air Pollutant Concentrations: Nitrogen Dioxide and Sulfur Dioxide

	Nitrogen Dioxide AM (ppb)	Nitrogen Dioxide 1-Hr (ppb)	Sulfur Dioxide AM (ppb)	Sulfur Dioxide 1-Hr (ppb)	Sulfur Dioxide 24-Hr (ppb)
MSA[1] Level	14	54	n/a	23	n/a
NAAQS[2]	53	100	30	75	140
Met NAAQS[2]	Yes	Yes	n/a	Yes	n/a

Note: (1) Data covers the Houston-The Woodlands-Sugar Land, TX Metropolitan Statistical Area—see Appendix B for areas included; Data from exceptional events are included; (2) National Ambient Air Quality Standards; ppm = parts per million; ug/m^3 = micrograms per cubic meter; n/a not available.
Concentrations: Nitrogen Dioxide AM—highest arithmetic mean concentration; Nitrogen Dioxide 1-Hr—highest 98th percentile 1-hour daily maximum concentration; Sulfur Dioxide AM—highest annual mean concentration; Sulfur Dioxide 1-Hr—highest 99th percentile 1-hour daily maximum concentration; Sulfur Dioxide 24-Hr—highest second maximum 24-hour concentration
Source: U.S. Environmental Protection Agency, Air Quality Monitoring Information, "Air Quality Statistics by City, 2016"

Drinking Water

Water System Name	Pop. Served	Primary Water Source Type	Violations[1]	
			Health Based	Monitoring/ Reporting
City of Sugar Land	83,886	Surface	0	0

Note: (1) Based on violation data from January 1, 2017 to December 31, 2017
Source: U.S. Environmental Protection Agency, Office of Ground Water and Drinking Water, Safe Drinking Water Information System (based on data extracted April 5, 2018)

Kaysville, Utah

Background

Kaysville is located in northern Utah, in Davis County. At an elevation of 4,400 feet, Kaysville is 25 miles north of Salt Lake City and 15 miles south of Ogden.

Kaysville's name changed as it expanded and grew. The first settlers in the area included Hector Haight, in 1847, along with the families of Samuel Holmes, Edward Philips, John Green and William Kay just two years later. Shortly after, more families, mostly Mormons descending from Salt Lake, arrived in droves. In 1851, Brigham Young, then head of the Mormon Church, suggested that the city form a ward (similar to that of a congregation). William Kay was appointed the city's first Bishop and it took the name "Kay's Ward." Just three years later, fearing Indian attacks, the settlers built a fort in the town square and the city took the name, "Kay's Fort." The city was then incorporated as "Kaysville" in 1868, the first city to incorporate in Davis County and the 27th to incorporate in the Utah territory.

Kaysville strives to maintain its quiet, rural setting, with much of the city devoted to residential areas. Filled with beautiful vistas, Kaysville offers its residents a calm, serene atmosphere, without the hustle and bustle of the big city.

Tucked between the Rocky Mountains and the Great Salt Lake, Kaysville offers the best of both worlds. Residents and visitors are just minutes from mountain hiking or camping, with easy access to lakeside swimming, boating and fishing. For wintertime recreation, some of Utah's most popular ski areas are just a short drive away.

The Mormon faith has maintained its roots in Kaysville, with seven Mormon stakes still in operation. The Kaysville Tabernacle, built in 1913, still stands today and is unique among area Mormon meetinghouses, for its colorful stained-glass windows and early 20th century architecture.

Kaysville is part of the Davis School District. Kaysville's public schools include eight elementary schools, three middle schools and one high school, some of which are in operation year-round. Two alternative high schools, one for new parents, are also located in Kaysville. Institutions of higher education include Kaysville's Davis Applied Technology College along with several colleges and universities in nearby Salt Lake City.

The climate in Kaysville is characterized by hot and dry summers with relative low humidity. Winters are typically cold, with a significant amount of snowfall annually.

Kaysville is served primarily by the Salt Lake City International Airport. Additional airports include Ogden-Hinckley Airport and Brigham City Airport.

Rankings

Business/Finance Rankings

- The personal finance site NerdWallet analyzed 183 American metropolitan areas with populations over 250,000 and more than 15,000 businesses to rank where entrepreneurs find the most success. Criteria included area economy, annual income, housing cost, unemployment rate, and the success rate of area businesses. Ogden* ranked #120. *www.nerdwallet.com, "Best Places to Start a Business," April 27, 2015*
- 24/7 Wall Street used Brookings Institution research on 50 advanced industries to identify the proportion of workers in the nation's largest metropolitan areas that were employed in jobs requiring knowledge in the science, technology, engineering, or math (STEM) fields and where there was heavy investment in research and development (R&D). The Ogden* metro area was #14. *247wallst.com, "15 Cities with the Most High-Tech Jobs," February 23, 2017*
- The Brookings Institution ranked the 100 largest metro areas in the U.S. based on income inequality. Ogden* was ranked #100 (#1 = greatest ineqality). Criteria: the "95/20 ratio," a figure representing the income at which a household earns more than 95 percent of all other households, divided by the income at which a household earns more than only 20 percent of all other households. *Brookings Institution, "Household Income Inequality, 100 Largest U.S. Metro Areas, 2014-2016," February 5, 2018*
- The Ogden* metro area appeared on the Milken Institute "2017 Best Performing Cities" list. Rank: #28 out of 200 large metro areas. Criteria: job growth; wage and salary growth; high-tech output growth. *Milken Institute, "Best-Performing Cities 2017," January 2018*
- *Forbes* ranked the 200 most populous metro areas to determine the nation's "Best Places for Business and Careers." The Ogden* metro area was ranked #33. Criteria: costs (business and living); job growth (past and projected); income growth; quality of life; educational attainment (college and high school); projected economic growth; cultural and recreational opportunities; net migration patterns; number of highly ranked colleges. *Forbes, "The Best Places for Business and Careers 2017," October 24, 2017*

Children/Family Rankings

- *Forbes* analyzed data on the 100 largest metropolitan areas in the United States to compile its 2016 ranking of the best cities for raising a family. The Ogden* metro area was ranked #2. Criteria: median income; childcare costs; percent of population under 18; commuting delays; crime rate; percentage of families owning homes; education quality (mainly test scores). Overall cost of living and housing affordability was also unofficially considered. *Forbes, "America's Best Cities for Raising a Family 2016," August 30, 2016*

Education Rankings

- Personal finance website *WalletHub* analyzed the 150 largest U.S. metropolitan statistical areas to determine where the most educated Americans are choosing to settle. Criteria: education quality and attainment gap; education levels; percentage of workers with degrees; public school rankings; quality and size of each metro area's universities. Ogden* was ranked #68 (#1 = most educated city). *www.WalletHub.com, "2017's Most and Least Educated Cities in America," July 25, 2017*

Environmental Rankings

- Sperling's BestPlaces assessed 379 metropolitan areas of the United States for the likelihood of dangerously extreme weather events or earthquakes. In general the Southeast and South-Central regions have the highest risk of weather extremes and earthquakes, while the Pacific Northwest enjoys the lowest risk. Of the least risky metropolitan areas, the Ogden* metro area was ranked #39. *www.bestplaces.net, "Safest Places from Natural Disasters," April 2011*

Food/Drink Rankings

- For the Gallup-Healthways Well-Being Index, researchers interviewed at least 300 adults in each of 189 metropolitan areas on residents' access to affordable fresh produce. The Ogden* metro area was found to be among the top ten communities for accessibility to affordable produce. *www.gallup.com, "In Anchorage, Access to Fruits and Vegetables Remains Lowest," April 8, 2014*

Health/Fitness Rankings

- Ogden* was identified as a "2016 Spring Allergy Capital." The area ranked #90 out of 100. Three groups of factors were used to identify the most severe cities for people with allergies during the spring season: annual pollen levels; medicine utilization; access to board-certified allergists. *Asthma and Allergy Foundation of America, "Spring Allergy Capitals 2016"*
- Ogden* was identified as a "2016 Fall Allergy Capital." The area ranked #84 out of 100. Three groups of factors were used to identify the most severe cities for people with allergies during the fall season: annual pollen levels; medicine utilization; access to board-certified allergists. *Asthma and Allergy Foundation of America, "Fall Allergy Capitals 2016"*
- Ogden* was identified as a "2015 Asthma Capital." The area ranked #69 out of the nation's 100 largest metropolitan areas. Criteria: estimated prevalence; self-reported prevalence; crude death rate for asthma; annual pollen score; annual air quality; public smoking laws; number of board-certified asthma specialists; school inhaler access laws; rescue medication use; controller medication use; ER visits for asthma; uninsured rate; poverty rate. *Asthma and Allergy Foundation of America, "Asthma Capitals 2015"*
- The Ogden* metro area ranked #51 out of 189 in The Gallup-Healthways Well-Being Index. Criteria: purpose; social well being; financial health; community and physical health. Results are based on telephone interviews with adults, aged 18 and older, living in metropolitan areas in the 50 U.S. states and the District of Columbia. *Gallup-Healthways, "State of American Well-Being, 2017 Community Well-Being Rankings" March 2018*

Real Estate Rankings

- The Ogden* metro area was identified as one of the top 20 housing markets to invest in for 2018 by *Forbes*. The area ranked #5. Criteria: strong job and population growth; anticipated home price appreciation; and other factors. *Forbes.com, "Where to Invest in Housing in 2018," February 1, 2018*
- Ogden* was ranked #18 in the top 20 out of 265 metro areas in terms of house price appreciation in 2017 (#1 = highest rate). *Federal Housing Finance Agency, House Price Index, 4th Quarter 2017. February 27, 2018*
- Ogden* was ranked #90 out of 238 metro areas in terms of housing affordability in 2017 by the National Association of Home Builders (#1 = most affordable). Criteria: the share of homes sold in that area affordable to a family earning the local median income, based on standard mortgage underwriting criteria. *National Association of Home Builders®, NAHB-Wells Fargo Housing Opportunity Index, 4th Quarter 2017*

Safety Rankings

- The National Insurance Crime Bureau ranked 382 metro areas in the U.S. in terms of per capita rates of vehicle theft. The Ogden* metro area ranked #233 (#1 = highest rate). Criteria: number of vehicle theft offenses per 100,000 inhabitants in 2016. *National Insurance Crime Bureau, "Hot Spots 2016," June 8, 2017*

Seniors/Retirement Rankings

- From its Best Cities for Successful Aging indexes, the Milken Institute generated rankings for metropolitan areas, weighing data in nine categories—health care, wellness, living arrangements, transportation and convenience, financial characteristics, education, employment, community engagement, and overall livability. The Ogden* metro area was ranked #38 overall in the large metro area category. *Milken Institute, "Best Cities for Successful Aging, 2017" March 14, 2017*

Women/Minorities Rankings

- *24/7 Wall St.* compared median earnings over a 12-month period for men and women who worked full-time, year-round, and employment composition by sector to identify the worst-paying cities for women. Of the largest 100 U.S. metropolitan areas, Ogden* was ranked #5 in pay disparity. *24/7 Wall St., "The Best (and Worst) Paying Cities for Women," March 27, 2017*

Miscellaneous Rankings

- The finance and lifestyle site NerdWallet looked for the U.S. cities that topped the list in donating money and time to good causes. The Ogden* metro area proved to be the #2-ranked metro area, judged by culture of volunteerism, depth of commitment in terms of volunteer hours per year, and monetary contributions. *www.nerdwallet.com, "Most Generous Cities," September 22, 2013*

*Kaysville is located within the Ogden-Clearfield, UT Metropolitan Statistical Area.

Business Environment

CITY FINANCES

City Government Finances

Component	2015 ($000)	2015 ($ per capita)
Total Revenues	37,723	1,238
Total Expenditures	37,727	1,238
Debt Outstanding	5,733	188
Cash and Securities[1]	16,509	542

Note: (1) Cash and security holdings of a government at the close of its fiscal year,, including those of its dependent agencies, utilities, and liquor stores.
Source: U.S Census Bureau, State & Local Government Finances 2015

City Government Revenue by Source

Source	2015 ($000)	2015 ($ per capita)	2015 (%)
General Revenue			
From Federal Government	0	0	0.0
From State Government	1,576	52	4.2
From Local Governments	0	0	0.0
Taxes			
Property	3,003	99	8.0
Sales and Gross Receipts	5,360	176	14.2
Personal Income	0	0	0.0
Corporate Income	0	0	0.0
Motor Vehicle License	0	0	0.0
Other Taxes	594	19	1.6
Current Charges	8,577	281	22.7
Liquor Store	0	0	0.0
Utility	16,353	537	43.4
Employee Retirement	0	0	0.0

Source: U.S Census Bureau, State & Local Government Finances 2015

City Government Expenditures by Function

Function	2015 ($000)	2015 ($ per capita)	2015 (%)
General Direct Expenditures			
Air Transportation	0	0	0.0
Corrections	0	0	0.0
Education	0	0	0.0
Employment Security Administration	0	0	0.0
Financial Administration	0	0	0.0
Fire Protection	726	23	1.9
General Public Buildings	4,419	145	11.7
Governmental Administration, Other	1,685	55	4.5
Health	47	1	0.1
Highways	752	24	2.0
Hospitals	0	0	0.0
Housing and Community Development	0	0	0.0
Interest on General Debt	247	8	0.7
Judicial and Legal	119	3	0.3
Libraries	50	1	0.1
Parking	0	0	0.0
Parks and Recreation	1,950	64	5.2
Police Protection	3,926	128	10.4
Public Welfare	0	0	0.0
Sewerage	2,708	88	7.2
Solid Waste Management	1,624	53	4.3
Veterans' Services	0	0	0.0
Liquor Store	0	0	0.0
Utility	14,703	482	39.0
Employee Retirement	0	0	0.0

Source: U.S Census Bureau, State & Local Government Finances 2015

DEMOGRAPHICS

Population Growth

Area	1990 Census	2000 Census	2010 Census	2016* Estimate	Population Growth (%) 1990-2016	Population Growth (%) 2010-2016
City	14,224	20,351	27,300	29,799	109.5	9.2
MSA[1]	351,799	442,656	547,184	632,793	79.9	15.6
U.S.	248,709,873	281,421,906	308,745,538	318,558,162	28.1	3.2

Note: (1) Figures cover the Ogden-Clearfield, UT Metropolitan Statistical Area—see Appendix B for areas included; (*) 2012-2016 5-year estimated population
Source: U.S. Census Bureau, 1990 Census, Census 2000, Census 2010, 2012-2016 American Community Survey 5-Year Estimates

Household Size

Area	Persons in Household (%)							Average Household Size
	One	Two	Three	Four	Five	Six	Seven or More	
City	11.6	26.8	14.9	15.2	17.8	8.4	5.3	3.60
MSA[1]	18.2	30.7	15.1	15.5	10.6	6.3	3.6	3.20
U.S.	27.7	33.7	15.7	13.1	6.0	2.3	1.5	2.60

Note: (1) Figures cover the Ogden-Clearfield, UT Metropolitan Statistical Area—see Appendix B for areas included
Source: U.S. Census Bureau, 2012-2016 American Community Survey 5-Year Estimates

Race

Area	White Alone[2] (%)	Black Alone[2] (%)	Asian Alone[2] (%)	AIAN[3] Alone[2] (%)	NHOPI[4] Alone[2] (%)	Other Race Alone[2] (%)	Two or More Races (%)
City	96.3	0.4	1.0	0.3	0.3	0.2	1.5
MSA[1]	89.8	1.1	1.5	0.6	0.4	3.6	2.9
U.S.	73.3	12.6	5.2	0.8	0.2	4.8	3.1

Note: (1) Figures cover the Ogden-Clearfield, UT Metropolitan Statistical Area—see Appendix B for areas included; (2) Alone is defined as not being in combination with one or more other races; (3) American Indian and Alaska Native; (4) Native Hawaiian and Other Pacific Islander
Source: U.S. Census Bureau, 2012-2016 American Community Survey 5-Year Estimates

Hispanic or Latino Origin

Area	Total (%)	Mexican (%)	Puerto Rican (%)	Cuban (%)	Other (%)
City	3.1	1.6	0.0	0.0	1.5
MSA[1]	12.2	8.8	0.3	0.0	3.0
U.S.	17.3	11.0	1.7	0.7	4.0

Note: Persons of Hispanic or Latino origin can be of any race; (1) Figures cover the Ogden-Clearfield, UT Metropolitan Statistical Area—see Appendix B for areas included
Source: U.S. Census Bureau, 2012-2016 American Community Survey 5-Year Estimates

Segregation

Type	Segregation Indices[1]				Percent Change		
	1990	2000	2010	2010 Rank[2]	1990-2000	1990-2010	2000-2010
Black/White	49.8	42.0	32.0	98	-7.8	-17.9	-10.0
Asian/White	25.9	23.1	20.5	102	-2.9	-5.4	-2.6
Hispanic/White	35.5	39.7	35.8	81	4.2	0.3	-3.9

Note: All figures cover the Metropolitan Statistical Area—see Appendix B for areas included; Figures are based on an analysis of 1990, 2000, and 2010 Census Decennial Census tract data by William H. Frey, Brookings Institution and the University of Michigan Social Science Data Analysis Network. In this analysis all racial groups (whites, blacks, and asians) are non-Hispanic members of those races. Hispanics are shown as a separate category; (1) Segregation Indices are Dissimilarity Indices that measure the degree to which the minority group is distributed differently than whites across census tracts. They range from 0 (complete integration) to 100 (complete segregation) where the value indicates the percentage of the minority group that needs to move to be distributed exactly like whites; (2) Ranges from 1 (most segregated) to 102 (least segregated); n/a not available.
Source: www.CensusScope.org

Ancestry

Area	German	Irish	English	American	Italian	Polish	French[2]	Scottish	Dutch
City	9.8	4.2	34.7	6.3	1.3	0.7	2.4	7.3	2.1
MSA[1]	11.3	5.5	25.0	7.8	2.7	0.7	1.8	4.6	2.8
U.S.	14.4	10.4	7.7	6.9	5.4	2.9	2.6	1.7	1.3

Note: Figures are the percentage of the total population reporting a particular ancestry. The nine most commonly reported ancestries in the U.S. are shown. Figures include multiple ancestries (e.g. if a person reported being Irish and Italian, they were included in both columns); (1) Figures cover the Ogden-Clearfield, UT Metropolitan Statistical Area—see Appendix B for areas included; (2) Excludes Basque
Source: U.S. Census Bureau, 2012-2016 American Community Survey 5-Year Estimates

Foreign-Born Population

Area	Percent of Population Born in								
	Any Foreign Country	Asia	Mexico	Europe	Carribean	Central America[2]	South America	Africa	Canada
City	2.4	0.9	0.1	1.0	0.0	0.1	0.2	0.0	0.1
MSA[1]	5.5	1.0	2.5	0.6	0.0	0.4	0.5	0.1	0.2
U.S.	13.2	4.0	3.6	1.5	1.3	1.0	0.9	0.6	0.3

Note: (1) Figures cover the Ogden-Clearfield, UT Metropolitan Statistical Area—see Appendix B for areas included; (2) Excludes Mexico.
Source: U.S. Census Bureau, 2012-2016 American Community Survey 5-Year Estimates

Marital Status

Area	Never Married	Now Married[2]	Separated	Widowed	Divorced
City	24.1	65.8	0.9	2.4	6.7
MSA[1]	26.1	58.9	1.6	3.5	9.9
U.S.	33.0	48.1	2.1	5.9	11.0

Note: Figures are percentages and cover the population 15 years of age and older; (1) Figures cover the Ogden-Clearfield, UT Metropolitan Statistical Area—see Appendix B for areas included; (2) Excludes separated
Source: U.S. Census Bureau, 2012-2016 American Community Survey 5-Year Estimates

Disability Status

Area	All Ages	Under 18 Years Old	18 to 64 Years Old	65 Years and Over
City	9.3	3.7	8.3	40.5
MSA[1]	10.3	3.7	9.6	35.3
U.S.	12.5	4.1	10.3	35.7

Note: Figures show percent of the civilian noninstitutionalized population that reported having a disability. Disability status is determined from six types of difficulty: vision, hearing, cognitive, ambulatory, self-care, and independent living. For children under 5 years old, hearing and vision difficulty are used to determine disability status. For children between the ages of 5 and 14, disability status is determined from hearing, vision, cognitive, ambulatory, and self-care difficulties. For people aged 15 years and older, they are considered to have a disability if they have difficulty with any one of the six difficulty types; Note: (1) Figures cover the Ogden-Clearfield, UT Metropolitan Statistical Area—see Appendix B for areas included
Source: U.S. Census Bureau, 2012-2016 American Community Survey 5-Year Estimates

Age

Area	Percent of Population									Median Age
	Under Age 5	Age 5–19	Age 20–34	Age 35–44	Age 45–54	Age 55–64	Age 65–74	Age 75–84	Age 85+	
City	10.3	29.5	18.1	13.1	12.3	8.4	4.7	3.2	0.5	28.9
MSA[1]	8.7	25.7	21.5	13.4	10.9	9.8	5.8	3.2	1.2	31.2
U.S.	6.2	19.6	20.7	12.7	13.6	12.6	8.3	4.3	1.9	37.7

Note: (1) Figures cover the Ogden-Clearfield, UT Metropolitan Statistical Area—see Appendix B for areas included
Source: U.S. Census Bureau, 2012-2016 American Community Survey 5-Year Estimates

Gender

Area	Males	Females	Males per 100 Females
City	14,857	14,942	99.4
MSA[1]	318,228	314,565	101.2
U.S.	156,765,322	161,792,840	96.9

Note: (1) Figures cover the Ogden-Clearfield, UT Metropolitan Statistical Area—see Appendix B for areas included
Source: U.S. Census Bureau, 2012-2016 American Community Survey 5-Year Estimates

Religious Groups by Family

Area	Catholic	Baptist	Non-Den.	Methodist[2]	Lutheran	LDS[3]	Pente-costal	Presby-terian[4]	Muslim[5]	Judaism
MSA[1]	5.8	1.0	0.9	0.2	0.5	68.7	1.2	0.2	<0.1	<0.1
U.S.	19.1	9.3	4.0	4.0	2.3	2.0	1.9	1.6	0.8	0.7

Note: Figures are the number of adherents as a percentage of the total population; (1) Figures cover the Ogden-Clearfield, UT Metropolitan Statistical Area—see Appendix B for areas included; (2) Methodist/Pietist; (3) Latter Day Saints; (4) Reformed; (5) Figures are estimates
Source: Association of Statisticians of American Religious Bodies, 2010 U.S. Religion Census: Religious Congregations & Membership Study

Religious Groups by Tradition

Area	Catholic	Evangelical Protestant	Mainline Protestant	Other Tradition	Black Protestant	Orthodox
MSA[1]	5.8	3.4	0.7	69.3	0.2	0.1
U.S.	19.1	16.2	7.3	4.3	1.6	0.3

Note: Figures are the number of adherents as a percentage of the total population; (1) Figures cover the Ogden-Clearfield, UT Metropolitan Statistical Area—see Appendix B for areas included
Source: Association of Statisticians of American Religious Bodies, 2010 U.S. Religion Census: Religious Congregations & Membership Study

ECONOMY

Gross Metropolitan Product

Area	2014	2015	2016	2017	Rank[2]
MSA[1]	23.6	24.8	25.9	27.5	100

Note: Figures are in billions of dollars; (1) Figures cover the Ogden-Clearfield, UT Metropolitan Statistical Area—see Appendix B for areas included; (2) Rank is based on 2015 data and ranges from 1 to 381
Source: The U.S. Conference of Mayors, U.S. Metro Economies: GMP and Employment Report, 2015-2017

Economic Growth

Area	2012-14 (%)	2015 (%)	2016 (%)	2017 (%)	Rank[2]
MSA[1]	3.7	4.1	2.5	3.7	35
U.S.	2.0	2.4	1.9	2.6	–

Note: Figures are real gross metropolitan product (GMP) growth rates and represent average annual percent change; (1) Figures cover the Ogden-Clearfield, UT Metropolitan Statistical Area—see Appendix B for areas included; (2) Rank is based on 2012-2014 average annual percent change and ranges from 1 to 381
Source: The U.S. Conference of Mayors, U.S. Metro Economies: GMP and Employment Report, 2015-2017

Metropolitan Area Exports

Area	2011	2012	2013	2014	2015	2016	Rank[2]
MSA[1]	896.5	855.5	1,310.0	1,363.6	1,415.6	1,602.2	110

Note: Figures are in millions of dollars; (1) Figures cover the Ogden-Clearfield, UT Metropolitan Statistical Area—see Appendix B for areas included; (2) Rank is based on 2016 data and ranges from 1 to 385
Source: U.S. Department of Commerce, International Trade Administration, Office of Trade & Industry Information, Manufacturing & Services, data extracted March 15, 2018

Building Permits

Area	Single-Family			Multi-Family			Total		
	2016	2017p	Pct. Chg.	2016	2017p	Pct. Chg.	2016	2017p	Pct. Chg.
City	170	132	-22.4	0	0	0.0	170	132	-22.4
MSA[1]	2,198	2,300	4.6	1,237	960	-22.4	3,435	3,260	-5.1
U.S.	750,800	817,300	8.9	455,800	446,800	-2.0	1,206,600	1,264,100	4.8

Note: (1) Figures cover the Ogden-Clearfield, UT Metropolitan Statistical Area—see Appendix B for areas included; Figures represent new, privately-owned housing units authorized (unadjusted data); All permit data are based on estimates with imputation; (p) preliminary data.
Source: U.S. Census Bureau, Manufacturing, Mining, and Construction Statistics, Building Permits, 2016, 2017

Bankruptcy Filings

Area	Business Filings			Nonbusiness Filings		
	2016	2017	% Chg.	2016	2017	% Chg.
Davis County	25	12	-52.0	1,218	1,264	3.8
U.S.	24,114	23,157	-4.0	770,846	765,863	-0.6

Note: Business filings include Chapter 7, Chapter 11, Chapter 12, and Chapter 13; Nonbusiness filings include Chapter 7, Chapter 11, and Chapter 13
Source: Administrative Office of the U.S. Courts, Business and Nonbusiness Bankruptcy, County Cases Commenced by Chapter of the Bankruptcy Code, During the 12-Month Period Ending December 31, 2016 and Business and Nonbusiness Bankruptcy, County Cases Commenced by Chapter of the Bankruptcy Code, During the 12-Month Period Ending December 31, 2017

Housing Vacancy Rates

Area	Gross Vacancy Rate[2] (%)			Year-Round Vacancy Rate[3] (%)			Rental Vacancy Rate[4] (%)			Homeowner Vacancy Rate[5] (%)		
	2015	2016	2017	2015	2016	2017	2015	2016	2017	2015	2016	2017
MSA[1]	n/a	n/a	n/a	n/a	n/a	n/a	n/a	n/a	n/a	n/a	n/a	n/a
U.S.	12.9	12.8	12.7	10.0	9.9	9.9	7.1	6.9	7.2	1.8	1.7	1.6

Note: (1) Figures cover the Ogden-Clearfield, UT Metropolitan Statistical Area—see Appendix B for areas included; (2) The percentage of the total housing inventory that is vacant; (3) The percentage of the housing inventory (excluding seasonal units) that is year-round vacant; (4) The percentage of rental inventory that is vacant for rent; (5) The percentage of homeowner inventory that is vacant for sale; n/a not available
Source: U.S. Census Bureau, Housing Vacancies and Homeownership Annual Statistics: 2015, 2016, 2017

INCOME

Income

Area	Per Capita ($)	Median Household ($)	Average Household ($)
City	28,324	87,975	100,483
MSA[1]	25,568	65,687	78,987
U.S.	29,829	55,322	77,866

Note: (1) Figures cover the Ogden-Clearfield, UT Metropolitan Statistical Area—see Appendix B for areas included
Source: U.S. Census Bureau, 2012-2016 American Community Survey 5-Year Estimates

Household Income Distribution

Area	Percent of Households Earning							
	Under $15,000	$15,000 -$24,999	$25,000 -$34,999	$35,000 -$49,999	$50,000 -$74,999	$75,000 -$99,999	$100,000 -$149,999	$150,000 and up
City	4.6	4.7	4.8	11.5	17.3	15.8	23.8	17.5
MSA[1]	7.4	6.8	7.9	13.6	22.1	16.4	16.6	9.2
U.S.	12.1	10.2	9.9	13.2	17.8	12.2	13.5	11.1

Note: (1) Figures cover the Ogden-Clearfield, UT Metropolitan Statistical Area—see Appendix B for areas included
Source: U.S. Census Bureau, 2012-2016 American Community Survey 5-Year Estimates

Poverty Rate

Area	All Ages	Under 18 Years Old	18 to 64 Years Old	65 Years and Over
City	4.8	6.8	3.4	4.3
MSA[1]	9.3	11.4	8.7	6.8
U.S.	15.1	21.2	14.2	9.3

Note: Figures are percentage of people whose income during the past 12 months was below the poverty level; (1) Figures cover the Ogden-Clearfield, UT Metropolitan Statistical Area—see Appendix B for areas included
Source: U.S. Census Bureau, 2012-2016 American Community Survey 5-Year Estimates

EMPLOYMENT

Labor Force and Employment

Area	Civilian Labor Force			Workers Employed		
	Dec. 2016	Dec. 2017	% Chg.	Dec. 2016	Dec. 2017	% Chg.
City	14,309	14,649	2.4	13,972	14,311	2.4
MSA[1]	318,562	326,295	2.4	308,975	316,612	2.5
U.S.	158,968,000	159,880,000	0.6	151,798,000	153,602,000	1.2

Note: Data is not seasonally adjusted and covers workers 16 years of age and older; (1) Figures cover the Ogden-Clearfield, UT Metropolitan Statistical Area—see Appendix B for areas included
Source: Bureau of Labor Statistics, Local Area Unemployment Statistics

Unemployment Rate

Area	2017											
	Jan.	Feb.	Mar.	Apr.	May	Jun.	Jul.	Aug.	Sep.	Oct.	Nov.	Dec.
City	2.5	2.7	2.8	2.6	2.8	3.3	3.1	3.1	2.9	2.8	2.5	2.3
MSA[1]	3.6	3.7	3.5	3.2	3.1	3.6	3.4	3.4	3.1	3.2	2.9	3.0
U.S.	5.1	4.9	4.6	4.1	4.1	4.5	4.6	4.5	4.1	3.9	3.9	3.9

Note: Data is not seasonally adjusted and covers workers 16 years of age and older; (1) Figures cover the Ogden-Clearfield, UT Metropolitan Statistical Area—see Appendix B for areas included
Source: Bureau of Labor Statistics, Local Area Unemployment Statistics

Average Wages

Occupation	$/Hr.	Occupation	$/Hr.
Accountants and Auditors	33.50	Maids and Housekeeping Cleaners	11.30
Automotive Mechanics	21.20	Maintenance and Repair Workers	18.60
Bookkeepers	18.30	Marketing Managers	57.80
Carpenters	20.20	Nuclear Medicine Technologists	n/a
Cashiers	10.70	Nurses, Licensed Practical	23.10
Clerks, General Office	15.20	Nurses, Registered	29.70
Clerks, Receptionists/Information	12.40	Nursing Assistants	11.70
Clerks, Shipping/Receiving	16.80	Packers and Packagers, Hand	11.60
Computer Programmers	36.40	Physical Therapists	47.20
Computer Systems Analysts	39.70	Postal Service Mail Carriers	23.70
Computer User Support Specialists	26.80	Real Estate Brokers	n/a
Cooks, Restaurant	12.90	Retail Salespersons	12.70
Dentists	58.00	Sales Reps., Exc. Tech./Scientific	33.50
Electrical Engineers	43.40	Sales Reps., Tech./Scientific	42.10
Electricians	24.30	Secretaries, Exc. Legal/Med./Exec.	15.70
Financial Managers	47.30	Security Guards	15.70
First-Line Supervisors/Managers, Sales	19.10	Surgeons	132.40
Food Preparation Workers	10.00	Teacher Assistants*	12.60
General and Operations Managers	37.10	Teachers, Elementary School*	24.80
Hairdressers/Cosmetologists	10.30	Teachers, Secondary School*	26.90
Internists, General	121.20	Telemarketers	11.70
Janitors and Cleaners	12.90	Truck Drivers, Heavy/Tractor-Trailer	20.70
Landscaping/Groundskeeping Workers	13.50	Truck Drivers, Light/Delivery Svcs.	14.40
Lawyers	37.30	Waiters and Waitresses	12.20

Note: Wage data covers the Ogden-Clearfield, UT Metropolitan Statistical Area—see Appendix B for areas included; (*) Hourly wages for elementary/secondary school teachers and teacher assistants were calculated by the editors from annual wage data based on a 40 hour work week; n/a not available.
Source: Bureau of Labor Statistics, Metro Area Occupational Employment & Wage Estimates, May 2017

Employment by Occupation

Occupation Classification	City (%)	MSA[1] (%)	U.S. (%)
Management, Business, Science, and Arts	48.7	36.5	37.0
Natural Resources, Construction, and Maintenance	5.9	8.8	8.9
Production, Transportation, and Material Moving	7.0	14.5	12.2
Sales and Office	24.8	25.9	23.8
Service	13.7	14.3	18.1

Note: Figures cover employed civilians 16 years of age and older; (1) Figures cover the Ogden-Clearfield, UT Metropolitan Statistical Area—see Appendix B for areas included
Source: U.S. Census Bureau, 2012-2016 American Community Survey 5-Year Estimates

Employment by Industry

Sector	MSA[1] Number of Employees	MSA[1] Percent of Total	U.S. Percent of Total
Construction, Mining, and Logging	17,500	6.8	5.2
Education and Health Services	32,400	12.7	15.9
Financial Activities	10,000	3.9	5.7
Government	53,100	20.7	15.3
Information	2,200	0.9	1.9
Leisure and Hospitality	23,600	9.2	10.7
Manufacturing	33,100	12.9	8.5
Other Services	6,700	2.6	3.9
Professional and Business Services	30,100	11.8	14.0
Retail Trade	31,000	12.1	11.0
Transportation, Warehousing, and Utilities	9,300	3.6	4.1
Wholesale Trade	7,000	2.7	4.0

Note: Figures are non-farm employment as of December 2017. Figures are not seasonally adjusted and include workers 16 years of age and older; (1) Figures cover the Ogden-Clearfield, UT Metropolitan Statistical Area—see Appendix B for areas included
Source: Bureau of Labor Statistics, Current Employment Statistics, Employment, Hours, and Earnings

Occupations with Greatest Projected Employment Growth: 2017 – 2019

Occupation[1]	2017 Employment	2019 Projected Employment	Numeric Employment Change	Percent Employment Change
Combined Food Preparation and Serving Workers, Including Fast Food	40,810	43,640	2,830	6.9
Customer Service Representatives	44,760	46,800	2,040	4.6
Construction Laborers	17,940	19,780	1,840	10.3
General and Operations Managers	29,140	30,980	1,840	6.3
Carpenters	15,870	17,610	1,740	10.9
Heavy and Tractor-Trailer Truck Drivers	24,080	25,570	1,490	6.2
Janitors and Cleaners, Except Maids and Housekeeping Cleaners	22,610	23,970	1,360	6.0
Retail Salespersons	47,280	48,580	1,300	2.7
Laborers and Freight, Stock, and Material Movers, Hand	19,560	20,850	1,290	6.6
Registered Nurses	22,690	23,950	1,260	5.6

Note: Projections cover Utah; (1) Sorted by numeric employment change
Source: www.projectionscentral.com, State Occupational Projections, 2017–2019 Short-Term Projections

Fastest Growing Occupations: 2017 – 2019

Occupation[1]	2017 Employment	2019 Projected Employment	Numeric Employment Change	Percent Employment Change
Roofers	2,300	2,640	340	14.7
Brickmasons and Blockmasons	2,310	2,650	340	14.6
Plasterers and Stucco Masons	660	750	90	13.9
Roustabouts, Oil and Gas	1,170	1,330	160	13.8
Cement Masons and Concrete Finishers	3,470	3,930	460	13.2
Helpers—Brickmasons, Blockmasons, Stonemasons, and Tile and Marble Setters	690	780	90	13.0
Stonemasons	360	410	50	12.8
Helpers—Pipelayers, Plumbers, Pipefitters, and Steamfitters	570	640	70	12.6
Plumbers, Pipefitters, and Steamfitters	6,750	7,590	840	12.5
Software Developers, Applications	8,310	9,330	1,020	12.3

Note: Projections cover Utah; (1) Sorted by percent employment change and excludes occupations with numeric employment change less than 50
Source: www.projectionscentral.com, State Occupational Projections, 2017–2019 Short-Term Projections

TAXES

State Corporate Income Tax Rates

State	Tax Rate (%)	Income Brackets ($)	Num. of Brackets	Financial Institution Tax Rate (%)[a]	Federal Income Tax Ded.
Utah	5.0 (b)	Flat rate	–	5.0 (b)	No

Note: Tax rates as of January 1, 2018; (a) Rates listed are the corporate income tax rate applied to financial institutions or excise taxes based on income. Some states have other taxes based upon the value of deposits or shares; (b) Minimum tax is $800 in California, $100 in District of Columbia and Arizona, $50 in North Dakota (banks), $500 in Rhode Island, $200 per location in South Dakota (banks), $100 in Utah, $250 in Vermont.
Source: Federation of Tax Administrators, Range of State Corporate Income Tax Rates, January 1, 2018

State Individual Income Tax Rates

State	Tax Rate (%)	Income Brackets ($)	Num. of Brackets	Personal Exempt. ($)[1]		Fed. Inc. Tax Ded.
				Single	Dependents	
Utah	5.0	Flat rate	1	(v)	(v)	No

Note: Tax rates as of January 1, 2018; Local- and county-level taxes are not included; n/a not applicable; (1) Married joint filers generally receive double the single exemption; (v) Utah provides a tax credit equal to 6% of the federal personal exemption amounts (and applicable standard deduction). Note, the Tax Cut and Reform Act of 2017 has eliminated personal exemptions and increased the standard deduction in the IRC. Utah will need to enact legislation to reinstate a personal credit for tax year 2018.
Source: Federation of Tax Administrators, State Individual Income Tax Rates, January 1, 2018

Various State Sales and Excise Tax Rates

State	State Sales Tax (%)	Gasoline[1] (¢/gal.)	Cigarette[2] ($/pack)	Spirits[3] ($/gal.)	Wine[4] ($/gal.)	Beer[5] ($/gal.)	Recreational Marijuana (%)
Utah	5.95 (b)	29.41	1.70	15.38 (g)	(m)	0.41 (q)	Not legal

Note: All tax rates as of January 1, 2018; (1) The American Petroleum Institute has developed a methodology for determining the average tax rate on a gallon of fuel. Rates may include any of the following: excise taxes, environmental fees, storage tank fees, other fees or taxes, general sales tax, and local taxes. In states where gasoline is subject to the general sales tax, or where the fuel tax is based on the average sale price, the average rate determined by API is sensitive to changes in the price of gasoline. States that fully or partially apply general sales taxes to gasoline: CA, CO, GA, IL, IN, MI, NY; (2) The federal excise tax of $1.0066 per pack and local taxes are not included; (3) Rates are those applicable to off-premise sales of 40% alcohol by volume (a.b.v.) distilled spirits in 750ml containers. Local excise taxes are excluded; (4) Rates are those applicable to off-premise sales of 11% a.b.v. non-carbonated wine in 750ml containers; (5) Rates are those applicable to off-premise sales of 4.7% a.b.v. beer in 12 ounce containers; (b) Three states levy mandatory, statewide, local add-on sales taxes at the state level: California (1.25%), Utah (1.25%), Virginia (1%), we include these in their state sales tax; (g) Control states, where the government controls all sales. Products can be subject to ad valorem mark-up as well as excise taxes; (m) Control states, where the government controls all sales. Products can be subject to ad valorem mark-up as well as excise taxes; (q) Different rates also applicable according to alcohol content, place of production, size of container, or place purchased (on- or off-premise or onboard airlines).
Source: Tax Foundation, 2018 Facts & Figures: How Does Your State Compare?

State Business Tax Climate Index Rankings

State	Overall Rank	Corporate Tax Rank	Individual Income Tax Rank	Sales Tax Rank	Unemployment Insurance Tax Rank	Property Tax Rank
Utah	8	4	11	17	21	5

Note: The index is a measure of how each state's tax laws affect economic performance. The lower the rank, the more favorable a state's tax system is for business. States without a given tax are given a ranking of 1. The scores/rankings for the District of Columbia do not affect other states. The 2018 index represents the tax climate as of July 1, 2017.
Source: Tax Foundation, State Business Tax Climate Index 2018

TRANSPORTATION

Means of Transportation to Work

Area	Car/Truck/Van		Public Transportation			Bicycle	Walked	Other Means	Worked at Home
	Drove Alone	Car-pooled	Bus	Subway	Railroad				
City	76.3	8.9	2.7	0.4	1.3	0.0	1.0	1.7	7.6
MSA[1]	79.5	10.7	1.4	0.1	0.6	0.5	1.5	1.1	4.7
U.S.	76.4	9.3	2.6	1.9	0.6	0.6	2.8	1.3	4.6

Note: Figures are percentages and cover workers 16 years of age and older; (1) Figures cover the Ogden-Clearfield, UT Metropolitan Statistical Area—see Appendix B for areas included
Source: U.S. Census Bureau, 2012-2016 American Community Survey 5-Year Estimates

Travel Time to Work

Area	Less Than 10 Minutes	10 to 19 Minutes	20 to 29 Minutes	30 to 44 Minutes	45 to 59 Minutes	60 to 89 Minutes	90 Minutes or More
City	14.3	30.8	20.8	22.9	5.2	5.6	0.5
MSA[1]	16.0	33.7	22.3	16.3	6.2	3.9	1.6
U.S.	12.9	29.2	20.9	20.4	8.0	6.0	2.7

Note: Note: Figures are percentages and include workers 16 years old and over; (1) Figures cover the Ogden-Clearfield, UT Metropolitan Statistical Area—see Appendix B for areas included
Source: U.S. Census Bureau, 2012-2016 American Community Survey 5-Year Estimates

Freeway Travel Time Index

Area	1985	1990	1995	2000	2005	2010	2014
Urban Area Rank[1,2]	n/a	n/a	n/a	n/a	n/a	n/a	n/a
Urban Area Index[1]	n/a	n/a	n/a	n/a	n/a	n/a	n/a
Average Index[3]	1.09	1.11	1.14	1.17	1.20	1.19	1.20

Note: Freeway Travel Time Index—the ratio of travel time in the peak period to the travel time at free-flow conditions. For example, a value of 1.30 indicates a 20-minute free-flow trip takes 26 minutes in the peak (20 minutes x 1.30 = 26 minutes); (1) Data for the Ogden-Clearfield, UT urban area was not available; (2) Rank is based on 101 urban areas (#1 = highest travel time index); (3) Average of 101 urban areas
Source: Texas Transportation Institute, 2015 Urban Mobility Scorecard, August 2015

Freeway Commuter Stress Index

Area	1985	1990	1995	2000	2005	2010	2014
Urban Area Rank[1,2]	n/a	n/a	n/a	n/a	n/a	n/a	n/a
Urban Area Index[1]	n/a	n/a	n/a	n/a	n/a	n/a	n/a
Average Index[3]	1.13	1.16	1.19	1.22	1.25	1.24	1.25

Note: The Freeway Commuter Stress Index is the same as the Freeway Travel Time Index (see table above) except that it includes only the travel in the peak directions during the peak periods; the TTI includes travel in all directions during the peak period. Thus, the CSI is more indicative of the work trip experienced by each commuter on a daily basis; (1) Data for the Ogden-Clearfield, UT urban area was not available; (2) Rank is based on 101 urban areas (#1 = highest travel time index); (3) Average of 101 urban areas
Source: Texas Transportation Institute, 2015 Urban Mobility Scorecard, August 2015

Living Environment

COST OF LIVING

Cost of Living Index

Composite Index	Groceries	Housing	Utilities	Trans-portation	Health Care	Misc. Goods/ Services
100.1	103.9	105.5	76.0	101.8	113.4	99.0

Note: The Cost of Living Index measures regional differences in the cost of consumer goods and services, excluding taxes and non-consumer expenditures, for professional and managerial households in the top income quintile. It is based on more than 50,000 prices covering almost 60 different items for which prices are collected three times a year by chambers of commerce, economic development organizations or university applied economic centers in each participating urban area. The numbers shown should be read as a percentage above or below the national average of 100. For example, a value of 115.4 in the groceries column indicates that grocery prices are 15.4% higher than the national average. Small differences in the index numbers should not be interpreted as significant; Figures cover the Ogden UT urban area.
Source: The Council for Community and Economic Research, ACCRA Cost of Living Index, 2017

Grocery Prices

Area[1]	T-Bone Steak ($/pound)	Frying Chicken ($/pound)	Whole Milk ($/half gal.)	Eggs ($/dozen)	Orange Juice ($/64 oz.)	Coffee ($/11.5 oz.)
City[2]	10.69	1.86	1.87	2.61	3.76	4.32
Avg.	11.29	1.40	2.02	1.47	3.55	4.37
Min.	7.71	0.93	1.04	0.70	2.86	3.24
Max.	15.83	2.39	4.03	3.92	6.29	8.16

*Note: (1) Values for the local area are compared with the average, minimum and maximum values for all 294 areas in the Cost of Living Index; (2) Figures cover the Ogden UT urban area; **T-Bone Steak** (price per pound); **Frying Chicken** (price per pound, whole fryer); **Whole Milk** (half gallon carton); **Eggs** (price per dozen, Grade A, large); **Orange Juice** (64 oz. Tropicana or Florida Natural); **Coffee** (11.5 oz. can, vacuum-packed, Maxwell House, Hills Bros, or Folgers).*
Source: The Council for Community and Economic Research, ACCRA Cost of Living Index, 2017

Housing and Utility Costs

Area[1]	New Home Price ($)	Apartment Rent ($/month)	All Electric ($/month)	Part Electric ($/month)	Other Energy ($/month)	Telephone ($/month)
City[2]	393,127	890	-	69.29	68.50	19.62
Avg.	335,956	1,047	175.01	97.34	67.93	28.71
Min.	187,788	491	109.48	49.33	35.44	12.39
Max.	1,739,087	4,559	432.62	227.09	353.33	44.61

*Note: (1) Values for the local area are compared with the average, minimum and maximum values for all 294 areas in the Cost of Living Index; (2) Figures cover the Ogden UT urban area; **New Home Price** (2,400 sf living area, 8,000 sf lot, in urban area with full utilities); **Apartment Rent** (950 sf 2 bedroom/1.5 or 2 bath, unfurnished, excluding all utilities except water); **All Electric** (average monthly cost for an all-electric home); **Part Electric** (average monthly cost for a part-electric home); **Other Energy** (average monthly cost for natural gas, fuel oil, coal, wood, and any other forms of energy except electricity); **Telephone** (price includes basic monthly rate for a private residential line plus additional local usage charges incurred by a family of four).*
Source: The Council for Community and Economic Research, ACCRA Cost of Living Index, 2017

Health Care, Transportation, and Other Costs

Area[1]	Doctor ($/visit)	Dentist ($/visit)	Optometrist ($/visit)	Gasoline ($/gallon)	Beauty Salon ($/visit)	Men's Shirt ($)
City[2]	103.34	124.99	109.34	2.32	30.34	26.97
Avg.	108.00	92.54	101.93	2.25	37.58	30.92
Min.	30.39	60.00	49.75	1.82	16.11	11.20
Max.	193.50	161.94	229.28	3.16	77.35	59.13

*Note: (1) Values for the local area are compared with the average, minimum and maximum values for all 294 areas in the Cost of Living Index; (2) Figures cover the Ogden UT urban area; **Doctor** (general practitioners routine exam of an established patient); **Dentist** (adult teeth cleaning and periodic oral examination); **Optometrist** (full vision eye exam for established adult patient); **Gasoline** (one gallon regular unleaded, national brand, including all taxes, cash price at self-service pump if available); **Beauty Salon** (woman's shampoo, trim, and blow-dry); **Men's Shirt** (cotton/polyester dress shirt, pinpoint weave, long sleeves).*
Source: The Council for Community and Economic Research, ACCRA Cost of Living Index, 2017

HOUSING

House Price Index (HPI)

Area	National Ranking[2]	Quarterly Change (%)	One-Year Change (%)	Five-Year Change (%)
MSA[1]	18	1.67	10.80	39.80
U.S.[3]	–	1.61	6.68	34.71

Note: The HPI is a weighted repeat sales index. It measures average price changes in repeat sales or refinancings on the same properties. This information is obtained by reviewing repeat mortgage transactions on single-family properties whose mortgages have been purchased or securitized by Fannie Mae or Freddie Mac in January 1975; (1) Figures cover the Ogden-Clearfield, UT Metropolitan Statistical Area—see Appendix B for areas included; (2) Rankings are based on annual percentage change for all metro areas containing at least 15,000 transactions over the last 10 years and ranges from 1 to 253; (3) figures based on a weighted average of Census Division estimates using a seasonally adjusted, purchase-only index; all figures are for the period ending December 31, 2017

Source: Federal Housing Finance Agency, House Price Index, February 28, 2018

Median Single-Family Home Prices

Area	2015	2016	2017p	Percent Change 2016 to 2017
MSA[1]	n/a	n/a	n/a	n/a
U.S. Average	223.9	235.5	248.8	5.6

Note: Figures are median sales prices of existing single-family homes in thousands of dollars; (p) preliminary; n/a not available; (1) Figures cover the Ogden-Clearfield, UT Metropolitan Statistical Area—see Appendix B for areas included

Source: National Association of Realtors, Median Sales Price of Existing Single-Family Homes for Metropolitan Areas, 4th Quarter 2017

Qualifying Income Based on Median Sales Price of Existing Single-Family Homes

Area	With 5% Down ($)	With 10% Down ($)	With 20% Down ($)
MSA[1]	n/a	n/a	n/a
U.S. Average	55,585	52,659	46,808

Note: Figures are preliminary; Qualifying income is based on a mortgage rate of 4.17%. Monthly principal and interest payment is limited to 25% of income; n/a not available; (1) Figures cover the Ogden-Clearfield, UT Metropolitan Statistical Area—see Appendix B for areas included

Source: National Association of Realtors, Qualifying Income Based on Median Sales Price of Existing Single-Family Homes for Metropolitan Areas, 4th Quarter 2017

Median Apartment Condo-Coop Home Prices

Area	2015	2016	2017p	Percent Change 2016 to 2017
MSA[1]	n/a	n/a	n/a	n/a
U.S. Average	210.7	220.7	234.3	6.2

Note: Figures are median sales prices of existing apartment condo-coop homes in thousands of dollars; (p) preliminary; n/a not available; (1) Figures cover the Ogden-Clearfield, UT Metropolitan Statistical Area—see Appendix B for areas included

Source: National Association of Realtors, Median Sales Price of Existing Apartment Condo-Coop Homes for Metropolitan Areas, 4th Quarter 2017

Home Value Distribution

Area	Under $50,000	$50,000 -$99,999	$100,000 -$149,999	$150,000 -$199,999	$200,000 -$299,999	$300,000 -$499,999	$500,000 -$999,999	$1,000,000 or more
City	3.1	0.4	4.1	12.9	35.4	34.9	7.1	2.1
MSA[1]	4.6	4.2	16.5	22.3	29.1	18.7	3.7	0.8
U.S.	8.8	14.8	15.3	14.9	18.4	16.4	9.0	2.5

Note: Figures are percentages and cover owner-occupied housing units; (1) Figures cover the Ogden-Clearfield, UT Metropolitan Statistical Area—see Appendix B for areas included

Source: U.S. Census Bureau, 2012-2016 American Community Survey 5-Year Estimates

Homeownership Rate

Area	2009 (%)	2010 (%)	2011 (%)	2012 (%)	2013 (%)	2014 (%)	2015 (%)	2016 (%)	2017 (%)
MSA[1]	n/a	n/a	n/a	n/a	n/a	n/a	n/a	n/a	n/a
U.S.	67.4	66.9	66.1	65.4	65.1	64.5	63.7	63.4	63.9

Note: (1) Figures cover the Ogden-Clearfield, UT Metropolitan Statistical Area—see Appendix B for areas included; n/a not available

Source: U.S. Census Bureau, Housing Vacancies and Homeownership Annual Statistics: 2009-2017

Year Housing Structure Built

Area	2010 or Later	2000 -2009	1990 -1999	1980 -1989	1970 -1979	1960 -1969	1950 -1959	1940 -1949	Before 1940	Median Year
City	4.6	25.0	22.4	15.9	15.0	8.2	3.2	2.3	3.4	1991
MSA[1]	4.5	21.9	17.1	12.8	15.6	8.5	8.8	4.3	6.4	1985
U.S.	2.3	14.7	14.0	13.7	15.6	10.9	10.6	5.2	13.0	1977

Note: Figures are percentages except for Median Year; Note: (1) Figures cover the Ogden-Clearfield, UT Metropolitan Statistical Area—see Appendix B for areas included
Source: U.S. Census Bureau, 2012-2016 American Community Survey 5-Year Estimates

Gross Monthly Rent

Area	Under $500	$500 -$999	$1,000 -$1,499	$1,500 -$1,999	$2,000 -$2,499	$2,500 -$2,999	$3,000 and up	Median ($)
City	18.9	52.8	12.4	14.3	1.6	0.0	0.0	760
MSA[1]	10.6	55.4	25.7	6.6	1.0	0.3	0.4	856
U.S.	11.3	43.3	27.7	10.7	4.0	1.6	1.5	949

Note: Figures are percentages except for Median; Gross rent is the contract rent plus the estimated average monthly cost of utilities (electricity, gas, and water and sewer) and fuels (oil, coal, kerosene, wood, etc.) if these are paid by the renter (or paid for the renter by someone else); (1) Figures cover the Ogden-Clearfield, UT Metropolitan Statistical Area—see Appendix B for areas included
Source: U.S. Census Bureau, 2012-2016 American Community Survey 5-Year Estimates

HEALTH

Health Risk Factors

Category	MSA[1] (%)	U.S. (%)
Adults aged 18–64 who have any kind of health care coverage	89.3	87.7
Adults who reported being in good or excellent health	88.4	83.6
Adults who are current smokers	8.2	17.1
Adults who currently use E-cigarettes	6.3	4.7
Adults who currently use chewing tobacco, snuff, or snus	3.7	4.0
Adults who are heavy drinkers[2]	4.5	6.5
Adults who are binge drinkers[3]	10.8	16.9
Adults who are overweight (BMI 25.0 - 29.9)	33.5	35.3
Adults who are obese (BMI 30.0 - 99.8)	29.8	29.9
Adults who participated in any physical activities in the past month	81.0	76.9
Adults who always or nearly always wears a seat belt	95.2	94.3

Note: (1) Figures cover the Ogden-Clearfield, UT Metropolitan Statistical Area—see Appendix B for areas included; (2) Heavy drinkers are classified as adult men having more than 14 drinks per week and adult women having more than 7 drinks per week; (3) Binge drinkers are classified as males having five or more drinks on one occasion or females having four or more drinks on one occasion
Source: Centers for Disease Control and Prevention, Behaviorial Risk Factor Surveillance System, SMART: Selected Metropolitan Area Risk Trends, 2016

Health Screening Rates

Category	MSA[1] (%)	U.S. (%)
Adults 50-75 who have had a blood stool test within the past year	3.0	8.0
Adults 50-75 who have had a colonoscopy in the past 10 years	74.5	63.5
Adults aged 65+ who have had flu shot within the past year	60.3	58.6
Adults aged 65+ who have ever had a pneumonia vaccination	78.3	73.4
Adults who have ever been tested for HIV	23.0	35.6
Women aged 21-65 who have had a pap test in the past three years	78.9	79.8
Men aged 40+ who have had a PSA test within the past two years	36.4	39.5
Women aged 40+ who have had a mammogram within the past two years	70.1	72.5

Note: n/a not available; (1) Figures cover the Ogden-Clearfield, UT Metropolitan Statistical Area—see Appendix B for areas included; Source: Centers for Disease Control and Prevention, Behaviorial Risk Factor Surveillance System, SMART: Selected Metropolitan Area Risk Trends, 2016

Chronic Health Conditions

Category	MSA[1] (%)	U.S. (%)
Adults who have ever been told they had a heart attack	3.3	4.4
Adults who have ever been told they have angina or coronary heart disease	2.6	4.1
Adults who have ever been told they had a stroke	2.4	3.1
Adults who have been told they currently have asthma	9.0	9.3
Adults who have ever been told they have arthritis	21.7	25.8
Adults who have ever been told they have diabetes[2]	8.3	10.5
Adults who have ever been told they had skin cancer	8.1	5.9
Adults who have ever been told they had any other types of cancer	6.2	6.7
Adults who have ever been told they have COPD	3.8	6.3
Adults who have ever been told they have kidney disease	2.5	2.8
Adults who have ever been told they have a form of depression	21.9	17.4

Note: (1) Figures cover the Ogden-Clearfield, UT Metropolitan Statistical Area—see Appendix B for areas included; (2) Figures do not include pregnancy-related, borderline, or pre-diabetes
Source: Centers for Disease Control and Prevention, Behaviorial Risk Factor Surveillance System, SMART: Selected Metropolitan Area Risk Trends, 2016

Mortality Rates for the Top 10 Causes of Death in the U.S.

ICD-10[a] Sub-Chapter	ICD-10[a] Code	Age-Adjusted Mortality Rate[1] per 100,000 population	
		County[2]	U.S.
Malignant neoplasms	C00-C97	115.4	158.5
Ischaemic heart diseases	I20-I25	74.4	96.8
Other forms of heart disease	I30-I51	70.4	52.4
Chronic lower respiratory diseases	J40-J47	28.7	40.9
Cerebrovascular diseases	I60-I69	36.4	37.2
Organic, including symptomatic, mental disorders	F01-F09	35.6	33.3
Other degenerative diseases of the nervous system	G30-G31	43.7	32.1
Other external causes of accidental injury	W00-X59	29.3	31.2
Diabetes mellitus	E10-E14	23.9	21.1
Hypertensive diseases	I10-I15	11.0	20.8

Note: (a) ICD-10 = International Classification of Diseases 10th Revision; (1) Mortality rates are a three year average covering 2014-2016; (2) Figures cover Davis County.
Source: Centers for Disease Control and Prevention, National Center for Health Statistics. Underlying Cause of Death 1999-2016 on CDC WONDER Online Database, released December 2017

Mortality Rates for Selected Causes of Death

ICD-10[a] Sub-Chapter	ICD-10[a] Code	Age-Adjusted Mortality Rate[1] per 100,000 population	
		County[2]	U.S.
Assault	X85-Y09	Unreliable	5.6
Diseases of the liver	K70-K76	10.9	14.0
Human immunodeficiency virus (HIV) disease	B20-B24	Suppressed	1.9
Influenza and pneumonia	J09-J18	16.0	14.6
Intentional self-harm	X60-X84	15.9	13.2
Malnutrition	E40-E46	2.8	1.3
Obesity and other hyperalimentation	E65-E68	Unreliable	2.1
Renal failure	N17-N19	14.2	13.0
Transport accidents	V01-V99	10.6	12.0
Viral hepatitis	B15-B19	Suppressed	1.9

Note: (a) ICD-10 = International Classification of Diseases 10th Revision; (1) Mortality rates are a three year average covering 2014-2016; (2) Figures cover Davis County; Data are Suppressed when the data meet the criteria for confidentiality constraints; Mortality rates are flagged as Unreliable when the rate would be calculated with a numerator of 20 or less.
Source: Centers for Disease Control and Prevention, National Center for Health Statistics. Underlying Cause of Death 1999-2016 on CDC WONDER Online Database, released December 2017

Health Insurance Coverage

Area	With Health Insurance	With Private Health Insurance	With Public Health Insurance	Without Health Insurance	Population Under Age 18 Without Health Insurance
City	94.1	87.4	13.5	5.9	4.6
MSA[1]	90.5	79.0	21.0	9.5	5.8
U.S.	88.3	66.7	33.0	11.7	5.9

Note: Figures are percentages that cover the civilian noninstitutionalized population; (1) Figures cover the Ogden-Clearfield, UT Metropolitan Statistical Area—see Appendix B for areas included
Source: U.S. Census Bureau, 2012-2016 American Community Survey 5-Year Estimates

Number of Medical Professionals

Area	MDs[3]	DOs[3,4]	Dentists	Podiatrists	Chiropractors	Optometrists
County[1] (number)	482	55	219	16	89	37
County[1] (rate[2])	144.0	16.4	64.2	4.7	26.1	10.8
U.S. (rate[2])	276.5	22.3	67.3	6.0	26.7	15.9

Note: Data as of 2016 unless noted; (1) Data covers Davis County; (2) Rate per 100,000 population; (3) Data as of 2015 and includes all active, non-federal physicians; (4) Doctor of Osteopathic Medicine
Source: U.S. Department of Health and Human Services, Health Resources and Services Administration, Bureau of Health Professions, Area Resource File (ARF) 2016-2017

EDUCATION

Public School District Statistics

District Name	Schls	Pupils	Pupil/ Teacher Ratio	Minority Pupils[1] (%)	Free Lunch Eligible[2] (%)	IEP[3] (%)
Davis District	91	71,721	n/a	15.9	17.3	11.9
Jefferson Academy	1	553	n/a	14.8	14.1	8.9
Utah Career Path High School	1	179	n/a	11.7	13.4	16.2

Note: Table includes school districts with 100 or more students; (1) Percentage of students that are not non-Hispanic white; (2) Percentage of students that are eligible for the free lunch program; (3) Percentage of students that have an Individualized Education Program.
Source: U.S. Department of Education, National Center for Education Statistics, Common Core of Data, Local Education Agency (School District) Universe Survey: School Year 2015-2016; U.S. Department of Education, National Center for Education Statistics, Common Core of Data, Public Elementary/Secondary School Universe Survey: School Year 2015-2016

Highest Level of Education

Area	Less than H.S.	H.S. Diploma	Some College, No Deg.	Associate Degree	Bachelor's Degree	Master's Degree	Prof. School Degree	Doctorate Degree
City	2.3	14.5	25.5	9.9	32.7	12.5	2.2	0.6
MSA[1]	6.8	25.3	28.2	10.2	20.4	7.1	1.2	0.8
U.S.	13.0	27.5	21.0	8.2	18.8	8.2	2.0	1.3

Note: Figures cover persons age 25 and over; (1) Figures cover the Ogden-Clearfield, UT Metropolitan Statistical Area—see Appendix B for areas included
Source: U.S. Census Bureau, 2012-2016 American Community Survey 5-Year Estimates

Educational Attainment by Race

Area	High School Graduate or Higher (%)					Bachelor's Degree or Higher (%)				
	Total	White	Black	Asian	Hisp.[2]	Total	White	Black	Asian	Hisp.[2]
City	97.7	98.0	83.3	100.0	76.4	47.9	48.8	19.7	27.6	14.5
MSA[1]	93.2	94.3	92.6	88.9	71.4	29.5	30.5	19.9	33.0	10.9
U.S.	87.0	88.9	84.3	86.3	65.7	30.3	31.6	20.0	52.1	14.7

Note: Figures shown cover persons 25 years old and over; (1) Figures cover the Ogden-Clearfield, UT Metropolitan Statistical Area—see Appendix B for areas included; (2) People of Hispanic origin can be of any race
Source: U.S. Census Bureau, 2012-2016 American Community Survey 5-Year Estimates

School Enrollment by Grade and Control

Area	Preschool (%)		Kindergarten (%)		Grades 1 - 4 (%)		Grades 5 - 8 (%)		Grades 9 - 12 (%)	
	Public	Private	Public	Private	Public	Private	Public	Private	Public	Private
City	38.9	61.1	92.7	7.3	98.0	2.0	96.8	3.2	99.5	0.5
MSA[1]	55.7	44.3	93.2	6.8	96.6	3.4	96.6	3.4	96.9	3.1
U.S.	58.4	41.6	87.7	12.3	89.8	10.2	89.7	10.3	90.4	9.6

Note: Figures shown cover persons 3 years old and over; (1) Figures cover the Ogden-Clearfield, UT Metropolitan Statistical Area—see Appendix B for areas included
Source: U.S. Census Bureau, 2012-2016 American Community Survey 5-Year Estimates

Average Salaries of Public School Classroom Teachers

Area	2015		2016		Change from 2015 to 2016	
	Dollars	Rank[1]	Dollars	Rank[1]	Percent	Rank[2]
Utah	46,689	44	46,887	45	0.4	33
U.S. Average	57,611	–	58,353	–	1.3	–

Note: (1) Rank ranges from 1 to 51 where 1 indicates highest salary; (2) Rank ranges from 1 to 51 where 1 indicates highest percent change.
Source: National Education Association, Rankings & Estimates: Rankings of the States 2016 and Estimates of School Statistics 2017

Higher Education

Four-Year Colleges			Two-Year Colleges			Medical Schools[1]	Law Schools[2]	Voc/ Tech[3]
Public	Private Non-profit	Private For-profit	Public	Private Non-profit	Private For-profit			
0	0	0	1	0	0	0	0	0

Note: Figures cover institutions located within the city limits and include main campuses only; (1) includes schools accredited by the Liaison Committee on Medical Education and the American Osteopathic Association's Commission on Osteopathic College Accreditation; (2) includes ABA-accredited schools, schools with provisional ABA accreditation, and state accredited schools; (3) includes all schools with programs that are less than 2 years.
Source: National Center for Education Statistics, Integrated Postsecondary Education System (IPEDS), 2016-17; Wikipedia, List of Medical Schools in the United States, accessed April 2, 2018; Wikipedia, List of Law Schools in the United States, accessed April 2, 2018

PRESIDENTIAL ELECTION

2016 Presidential Election Results

Area	Clinton	Trump	Johnson	Stein	Other
Davis County	20.5	44.4	3.8	0.6	30.7
U.S.	48.0	45.9	3.3	1.1	1.7

Note: Results are percentages and may not add to 100% due to rounding
Source: Dave Leip's Atlas of U.S. Presidential Elections

EMPLOYERS

Major Employers

Company Name	Industry
ATK	Manufacturing
Autoliv Inc.	Manufacturing
Bourns Sensors and Controls	Manufacturing
Chromalox	Manufacturing
Fresenius USA Manufacturing	Manufacturing
Great Salt Lake Minerals	Manufacturing
GSC Foundries	Manufacturing
Hill Air Force Base	Government
IRS	Government
JBT Aerotech	Manufacturing
Kimberly-Clark Corp.	Manufacturing
Lagoon Corp.	Leisure & hospitality
Levelor	Manufacturing
Lifetime Products, Inc.	Manufacturing
McKay-Dee Hospital Center	Education & health services
Odgen School District	Education
Ogden City	Government
Ogden Regional Medical Center	Healthcare
Parker Hannifin	Manufacturing
Smith's Marketplace	Wholesale & retail trade
US Forest Service	Government
Wal-Mart	Retail grocery
Weber County	Government
Weber School District	Education
Weber State University	Education & health services

Note: Companies shown are located within the Ogden-Clearfield, UT Metropolitan Statistical Area.
Source: Hoovers.com; Wikipedia

PUBLIC SAFETY

Crime Rate

Area	All Crimes	Violent Crimes				Property Crimes		
		Murder	Rape[3]	Robbery	Aggrav. Assault	Burglary	Larceny -Theft	Motor Vehicle Theft
City	937.0	0.0	22.5	12.9	22.5	173.9	679.4	25.8
Metro[1]	2,374.8	1.4	41.5	27.2	85.5	377.4	1,686.1	155.7
U.S.	2,847.8	5.3	40.4	102.8	248.5	468.9	1,745.0	236.9

Note: Figures are crimes per 100,000 population; (1) Figures cover the Ogden-Clearfield, UT Metropolitan Statistical Area—see Appendix B for areas included; (3) The city and U.S. figures shown were reported using the revised Uniform Crime Reporting (UCR) definition of rape. The metro area figures shown are an aggregate total of the data submitted using both the revised and legacy UCR definitions.
Source: FBI Uniform Crime Reports, 2016

Hate Crimes

Area	Number of Quarters Reported	Number of Incidents per Bias Motivation					
		Race/Ethnicity/ Ancestry	Religion	Sexual Orientation	Disability	Gender	Gender Identity
City	4	0	0	0	0	0	0
U.S.	4	3,489	1,273	1,076	70	31	124

Source: Federal Bureau of Investigation, Hate Crime Statistics 2016

Identity Theft Consumer Reports

Area	Reports	Reports per 100,000 Population	Rank[2]
MSA[1]	492	75	223
U.S.	371,061	114	-

Note: (1) Figures cover the Ogden-Clearfield, UT Metropolitan Statistical Area—see Appendix B for areas included; (2) Rank ranges from 1 to 389 where 1 indicates greatest number of identity theft reports per 100,000 population
Source: Federal Trade Commission, Consumer Sentinel Network Data Book for January–December 2017

Fraud and Other Consumer Reports

Area	Reports	Reports per 100,000 Population	Rank[2]
MSA[1]	2,405	368	306
U.S.	2,304,550	708	-

Note: (1) Figures cover the Ogden-Clearfield, UT Metropolitan Statistical Area—see Appendix B for areas included; (2) Rank ranges from 1 to 389 where 1 indicates greatest number of fraud and other consumer reports per 100,000 population
Source: Federal Trade Commission, Consumer Sentinel Network Data Book for January–December 2017

SPORTS

Professional Sports Teams

Team Name	League	Year Established
No teams are located in the metro area		

Source: Wikipedia, Major Professional Sports Teams of the United States and Canada, April 5, 2018

CLIMATE

Average and Extreme Temperatures

Temperature	Jan	Feb	Mar	Apr	May	Jun	Jul	Aug	Sep	Oct	Nov	Dec	Yr.
Extreme High (°F)	62	69	78	85	93	104	107	104	100	89	75	67	107
Average High (°F)	37	43	52	62	72	83	93	90	80	66	50	38	64
Average Temp. (°F)	28	34	41	50	59	69	78	76	65	53	40	30	52
Average Low (°F)	19	24	31	38	46	54	62	61	51	40	30	22	40
Extreme Low (°F)	-22	-14	2	15	25	35	40	37	27	16	-14	-15	-22

Note: Figures cover the years 1948-1990
Source: National Climatic Data Center, International Station Meteorological Climate Summary, 9/96

Average Precipitation/Snowfall/Humidity

Precip./Humidity	Jan	Feb	Mar	Apr	May	Jun	Jul	Aug	Sep	Oct	Nov	Dec	Yr.
Avg. Precip. (in.)	1.3	1.2	1.8	2.0	1.7	0.9	0.8	0.9	1.1	1.3	1.3	1.4	15.6
Avg. Snowfall (in.)	13	10	11	6	1	Tr	0	0	Tr	2	6	13	63
Avg. Rel. Hum. 5am (%)	79	77	71	67	66	60	53	54	60	68	75	79	67
Avg. Rel. Hum. 5pm (%)	69	59	47	38	33	26	22	23	28	40	59	71	43

Note: Figures cover the years 1948-1990; Tr = Trace amounts (<0.05 in. of rain; <0.5 in. of snow)
Source: National Climatic Data Center, International Station Meteorological Climate Summary, 9/96

Weather Conditions

Temperature			Daytime Sky			Precipitation		
5°F & below	32°F & below	90°F & above	Clear	Partly cloudy	Cloudy	0.01 inch or more precip.	0.1 inch or more snow/ice	Thunder-storms
7	128	56	94	152	119	92	38	38

Note: Figures are average number of days per year and cover the years 1948-1990
Source: National Climatic Data Center, International Station Meteorological Climate Summary, 9/96

HAZARDOUS WASTE

Superfund Sites

The Ogden-Clearfield, UT metro area is home to five sites on the EPA's Superfund National Priorities List: **Bountiful/Woods Cross 5th S. Pce Plume** (final); **Five Points Pce Plume** (final); **Hill Air Force Base** (final); **Intermountain Waste Oil Refinery** (final); **Ogden Defense Depot (Dla)** (final). There are a total of 1,396 Superfund sites with a status of proposed or final on the list in the U.S. *U.S. Environmental Protection Agency, National Priorities List, April 4, 2018*

AIR & WATER QUALITY

Air Quality Trends: Ozone

	1990	1995	2000	2005	2010	2012	2013	2014	2015	2016
MSA[1]	n/a	n/a	n/a	n/a	n/a	n/a	n/a	n/a	n/a	n/a
U.S.	0.087	0.089	0.081	0.079	0.073	0.075	0.069	0.067	0.068	0.069

Note: (1) Data covers the Ogden-Clearfield, UT Metropolitan Statistical Area—see Appendix B for areas included; n/a not available. The values shown are the composite ozone concentration averages among trend sites based on the highest fourth daily maximum 8-hour concentration in parts per million. These trends are based on sites having an adequate record of monitoring data during the trend period. Data from exceptional events are included.
Source: U.S. Environmental Protection Agency, Air Quality Monitoring Information, "Air Quality Trends by City, 1990-2016"

Air Quality Index

Area	Percent of Days when Air Quality was...[2]					AQI Statistics[2]	
	Good	Moderate	Unhealthy for Sensitive Groups	Unhealthy	Very Unhealthy	Maximum	Median
MSA[1]	48.8	41.1	9.6	0.5	0.0	162	51

Note: (1) Data covers the Ogden-Clearfield, UT Metropolitan Statistical Area—see Appendix B for areas included; (2) Based on 365 days with AQI data in 2017. Air Quality Index (AQI) is an index for reporting daily air quality. EPA calculates the AQI for five major air pollutants regulated by the Clean Air Act: ground-level ozone, particle pollution (aka particulate matter), carbon monoxide, sulfur dioxide, and nitrogen dioxide. The AQI runs from 0 to 500. The higher the AQI value, the greater the level of air pollution and the greater the health concern. There are six AQI categories: "Good" AQI is between 0 and 50. Air quality is considered satisfactory; "Moderate" AQI is between 51 and 100. Air quality is acceptable; "Unhealthy for Sensitive Groups" When AQI values are between 101 and 150, members of sensitive groups may experience health effects; "Unhealthy" When AQI values are between 151 and 200 everyone may begin to experience health effects; "Very Unhealthy" AQI values between 201 and 300 trigger a health alert; "Hazardous" AQI values over 300 trigger warnings of emergency conditions (not shown).
Source: U.S. Environmental Protection Agency, Air Quality Index Report, 2017

Air Quality Index Pollutants

Area	Percent of Days when AQI Pollutant was...[2]					
	Carbon Monoxide	Nitrogen Dioxide	Ozone	Sulfur Dioxide	Particulate Matter 2.5	Particulate Matter 10
MSA[1]	0.0	8.5	69.0	0.0	21.6	0.8

Note: (1) Data covers the Ogden-Clearfield, UT Metropolitan Statistical Area—see Appendix B for areas included; (2) Based on 365 days with AQI data in 2017. The Air Quality Index (AQI) is an index for reporting daily air quality. EPA calculates the AQI for five major air pollutants regulated by the Clean Air Act: ground-level ozone, particle pollution (also known as particulate matter), carbon monoxide, sulfur dioxide, and nitrogen dioxide. The AQI runs from 0 to 500. The higher the AQI value, the greater the level of air pollution and the greater the health concern.
Source: U.S. Environmental Protection Agency, Air Quality Index Report, 2017

Maximum Air Pollutant Concentrations: Particulate Matter, Ozone, CO and Lead

	Particulate Matter 10 (ug/m^3)	Particulate Matter 2.5 Wtd AM (ug/m^3)	Particulate Matter 2.5 24-Hr (ug/m^3)	Ozone (ppm)	Carbon Monoxide (ppm)	Lead (ug/m^3)
MSA[1] Level	62	9	39	0.076	3	n/a
NAAQS[2]	150	15	35	0.075	9	0.15
Met NAAQS[2]	Yes	Yes	No	No	Yes	n/a

Note: (1) Data covers the Ogden-Clearfield, UT Metropolitan Statistical Area—see Appendix B for areas included; Data from exceptional events are included; (2) National Ambient Air Quality Standards; ppm = parts per million; ug/m^3 = micrograms per cubic meter; n/a not available.
Concentrations: Particulate Matter 10 (coarse particulate)—highest second maximum 24-hour concentration; Particulate Matter 2.5 Wtd AM (fine particulate)—highest weighted annual mean concentration; Particulate Matter 2.5 24-Hour (fine particulate)—highest 98th percentile 24-hour concentration; Ozone—highest fourth daily maximum 8-hour concentration; Carbon Monoxide—highest second maximum non-overlapping 8-hour concentration; Lead—maximum running 3-month average
Source: U.S. Environmental Protection Agency, Air Quality Monitoring Information, "Air Quality Statistics by City, 2016"

Maximum Air Pollutant Concentrations: Nitrogen Dioxide and Sulfur Dioxide

	Nitrogen Dioxide AM (ppb)	Nitrogen Dioxide 1-Hr (ppb)	Sulfur Dioxide AM (ppb)	Sulfur Dioxide 1-Hr (ppb)	Sulfur Dioxide 24-Hr (ppb)
MSA[1] Level	15	n/a	n/a	n/a	n/a
NAAQS[2]	53	100	30	75	140
Met NAAQS[2]	Yes	n/a	n/a	n/a	n/a

Note: (1) Data covers the Ogden-Clearfield, UT Metropolitan Statistical Area—see Appendix B for areas included; Data from exceptional events are included; (2) National Ambient Air Quality Standards; ppm = parts per million; ug/m³ = micrograms per cubic meter; n/a not available.
Concentrations: Nitrogen Dioxide AM—highest arithmetic mean concentration; Nitrogen Dioxide 1-Hr—highest 98th percentile 1-hour daily maximum concentration; Sulfur Dioxide AM—highest annual mean concentration; Sulfur Dioxide 1-Hr—highest 99th percentile 1-hour daily maximum concentration; Sulfur Dioxide 24-Hr—highest second maximum 24-hour concentration
Source: U.S. Environmental Protection Agency, Air Quality Monitoring Information, "Air Quality Statistics by City, 2016"

Drinking Water

Water System Name	Pop. Served	Primary Water Source Type	Violations[1]	
			Health Based	Monitoring/ Reporting
Kaysville City Water System	27,300	Purchased Surface	0	3

Note: (1) Based on violation data from January 1, 2017 to December 31, 2017
Source: U.S. Environmental Protection Agency, Office of Ground Water and Drinking Water, Safe Drinking Water Information System (based on data extracted April 5, 2018)

Lehi, Utah

Background

Lehi occupies 21 square miles in the northern part of Utah County. Part of the Provo-Orem metropolitan area, the city proudly proclaims its official slogan, "Lehi is a good place to live." First settled by Mormon pioneers in 1850, the area of Lehi was known as Sulphur Springs, Dry Creek, and Evansville before finally being named after a prophet from the Book of Mormon. In 1852, Lehi received its current name and was incorporated, making the city one of the oldest cities in Utah.

The Overland Stage Coach Route, the Pony Express Trail, and the Transcontinental Telegraph Line impacted the city's early development. Lehi's early economy was driven primarily by industry related to agriculture and animals. Currently the city's economic growth rate is strong and driven by its largest businesses including Cabela's, Costco Wholesale, IM Flash Technologies, Jack B. Parsons, Lehi Block, and others.

This historically small city has grown more than 86 percent since the 2000 Census. In 2010 the population increased to over 47,000. Despite its recent growth spurt, the city remains a welcoming place for families due to its low crime rate, high employment rate, and low cost of living. The city's school system, attractions, temperate climate, and available services are just a few additional reasons Lehi is a great place to live.

In keeping with the high literacy and high school graduation rates in the state of Utah, Lehi schools boast more than a 90 percent high school graduation rate. Brigham Young University, Utah Valley State College and the University of Utah are just a few of the institutions of higher education within 30 miles of Lehi.

Outdoor attractions abound in the Lehi area, including more than twenty parks, a scenic paved path along the Jordan River, Utah Lake and the Wasatch Mountains. The Saratoga Hot Springs in Lehi offer a way for people to simultaneously enjoy nature and relax.

Nature is not the only thing that attracts residents and visitors to Lehi. Thanksgiving Point, a more than 700-acre area housing a golf course, restaurant, gardens, shops, and more, features a popular open-air Farmer's Market in the summer, where residents shop for fresh local produce, snack at the food vendors, and purchase local crafts. For more fun in the summer, Lehi's annual festival, known as the Lehi Roundup rodeo, is celebrated every June.

The John Hutchings Museum of Natural History, Railroad Depot Museum, Legacy Center, Roller Mill, the city sports complex, and local movie theaters and stores offer opportunities for entertainment. Also notable is that Lehi 's flourmill was featured in the 1984 movie "Footloose."

Provo, Utah, made famous by "Butch Cassidy and the Sundance Kid," offers many additional opportunities for employment and entertainment for Lehi residents. Bridal Veil Falls, Sundance Ski Resort, and the McCurdy Doll Museum are a few examples of Provo's attractions. In addition, Lehi's proximity to Salt Lake City opens up another world of opportunity.

The mild weather in Lehi is one of its most attractive features. The mountains surrounding the city keep the air dry. While the weather varies, as one would expect with the changing seasons, the city does not experience the extreme heat, cold, or precipitation associated with other parts of the country. Average rainfall is around 15 inches while the average annual snowfall is less than 27 inches.

Travel in and out of Lehi is facilitated by two conveniently located airports. Provo Airport is 17 miles away and Salt Lake City International Airport is 28 miles away.

Rankings

General Rankings

- Lehi was selected as one of the best places to live in the United States by *Money* magazine. The city ranked #74 out of 100. This year's list focused on cities with populations of 10,000 to 100,000. Beginning with a pool of over 2,400 candidates, editors looked at 70 data points, from local economy and housing market to schools, crime and healthcare—and then sent reporters to interview residents, search neighborhoods and look for other intangibles. *Money, "Best Places to Live, 2017" September 18, 2017*

Business/Finance Rankings

- The personal finance site NerdWallet analyzed 183 American metropolitan areas with populations over 250,000 and more than 15,000 businesses to rank where entrepreneurs find the most success. Criteria included area economy, annual income, housing cost, unemployment rate, and the success rate of area businesses. Provo* ranked #131. *www.nerdwallet.com, "Best Places to Start a Business," April 27, 2015*
- According to data by the Bureau of Economic Analysis (BEA) and the Bureau of Labor Statistics (BLS), the Provo* metro area has the fastest-growing GDP (gross domestic product) and positive employment trends, at #4. *247wallst.com, "Cities With the Fastest Growing (and Shrinking) Economies," September 26, 2016*
- 24/7 Wall Street used Brookings Institution research on 50 advanced industries to identify the proportion of workers in the nation's largest metropolitan areas that were employed in jobs requiring knowledge in the science, technology, engineering, or math (STEM) fields and where there was heavy investment in research and development (R&D). The Provo* metro area was #12. *247wallst.com, "15 Cities with the Most High-Tech Jobs," February 23, 2017*
- The Brookings Institution ranked the 100 largest metro areas in the U.S. based on income inequality. Provo* was ranked #99 (#1 = greatest ineqality). Criteria: the "95/20 ratio," a figure representing the income at which a household earns more than 95 percent of all other households, divided by the income at which a household earns more than only 20 percent of all other households. *Brookings Institution, "Household Income Inequality, 100 Largest U.S. Metro Areas, 2014-2016," February 5, 2018*
- The Provo* metro area appeared on the Milken Institute "2017 Best Performing Cities" list. Rank: #1 out of 200 large metro areas. Criteria: job growth; wage and salary growth; high-tech output growth. *Milken Institute, "Best-Performing Cities 2017," January 2018*
- *Forbes* ranked the 200 most populous metro areas to determine the nation's "Best Places for Business and Careers." The Provo* metro area was ranked #6. Criteria: costs (business and living); job growth (past and projected); income growth; quality of life; educational attainment (college and high school); projected economic growth; cultural and recreational opportunities; net migration patterns; number of highly ranked colleges. *Forbes, "The Best Places for Business and Careers 2017," October 24, 2017*

Children/Family Rankings

- *Forbes* analyzed data on the 100 largest metropolitan areas in the United States to compile its 2016 ranking of the best cities for raising a family. The Provo* metro area was ranked #1. Criteria: median income; childcare costs; percent of population under 18; commuting delays; crime rate; percentage of families owning homes; education quality (mainly test scores). Overall cost of living and housing affordability was also unofficially considered. *Forbes, "America's Best Cities for Raising a Family 2016," August 30, 2016*

Education Rankings

- Personal finance website *WalletHub* analyzed the 150 largest U.S. metropolitan statistical areas to determine where the most educated Americans are choosing to settle. Criteria: education quality and attainment gap; education levels; percentage of workers with degrees; public school rankings; quality and size of each metro area's universities. Provo* was ranked #7 (#1 = most educated city). *www.WalletHub.com, "2017's Most and Least Educated Cities in America," July 25, 2017*

Environmental Rankings

- Sperling's BestPlaces assessed 379 metropolitan areas of the United States for the likelihood of dangerously extreme weather events or earthquakes. In general the Southeast and South-Central regions have the highest risk of weather extremes and earthquakes, while the Pacific Northwest enjoys the lowest risk. Of the least risky metropolitan areas, the Provo* metro area was ranked #29. *www.bestplaces.net, "Safest Places from Natural Disasters," April 2011*

Food/Drink Rankings

- For the Gallup-Healthways Well-Being Index, researchers interviewed at least 300 adults in each of 189 metropolitan areas on residents' access to affordable fresh produce. The Provo* metro area was found to be among the top ten communities for accessibility to affordable produce. *www.gallup.com, "In Anchorage, Access to Fruits and Vegetables Remains Lowest," April 8, 2014*

Health/Fitness Rankings

- Analysts who tracked obesity rates in 100 of the nation's most populous areas found that the Provo* metro area was one of the ten communities where residents were least likely to be obese, defined as a BMI score of 30 or above. *www.gallup.com, "Colorado Springs Residents Least Likely to Be Obese," May 28, 2015*

- Provo* was identified as a "2016 Spring Allergy Capital." The area ranked #98 out of 100. Three groups of factors were used to identify the most severe cities for people with allergies during the spring season: annual pollen levels; medicine utilization; access to board-certified allergists. *Asthma and Allergy Foundation of America, "Spring Allergy Capitals 2016"*

- Provo* was identified as a "2016 Fall Allergy Capital." The area ranked #91 out of 100. Three groups of factors were used to identify the most severe cities for people with allergies during the fall season: annual pollen levels; medicine utilization; access to board-certified allergists. *Asthma and Allergy Foundation of America, "Fall Allergy Capitals 2016"*

- Provo* was identified as a "2015 Asthma Capital." The area ranked #84 out of the nation's 100 largest metropolitan areas. Criteria: estimated prevalence; self-reported prevalence; crude death rate for asthma; annual pollen score; annual air quality; public smoking laws; number of board-certified asthma specialists; school inhaler access laws; rescue medication use; controller medication use; ER visits for asthma; uninsured rate; poverty rate. *Asthma and Allergy Foundation of America, "Asthma Capitals 2015"*

- The Provo* metro area ranked #29 out of 189 in The Gallup-Healthways Well-Being Index. Criteria: purpose; social well being; financial health; community and physical health. Results are based on telephone interviews with adults, aged 18 and older, living in metropolitan areas in the 50 U.S. states and the District of Columbia. *Gallup-Healthways, "State of American Well-Being, 2017 Community Well-Being Rankings" March 2018*

Real Estate Rankings

- The Provo* metro area was identified as one of the top 20 housing markets to invest in for 2018 by *Forbes*. The area ranked #2. Criteria: strong job and population growth; anticipated home price appreciation; and other factors. *Forbes.com, "Where to Invest in Housing in 2018," February 1, 2018*

- Provo* was ranked #170 out of 238 metro areas in terms of housing affordability in 2017 by the National Association of Home Builders (#1 = most affordable). Criteria: the share of homes sold in that area affordable to a family earning the local median income, based on standard mortgage underwriting criteria. *National Association of Home Builders®, NAHB-Wells Fargo Housing Opportunity Index, 4th Quarter 2017*

Safety Rankings

- The National Insurance Crime Bureau ranked 382 metro areas in the U.S. in terms of per capita rates of vehicle theft. The Provo* metro area ranked #280 (#1 = highest rate). Criteria: number of vehicle theft offenses per 100,000 inhabitants in 2016. *National Insurance Crime Bureau, "Hot Spots 2016," June 8, 2017*

Seniors/Retirement Rankings

- From its Best Cities for Successful Aging indexes, the Milken Institute generated rankings for metropolitan areas, weighing data in nine categories—health care, wellness, living arrangements, transportation and convenience, financial characteristics, education, employment, community engagement, and overall livability. The Provo* metro area was ranked #1 overall in the large metro area category. *Milken Institute, "Best Cities for Successful Aging, 2017" March 14, 2017*

Women/Minorities Rankings

- *24/7 Wall St.* compared median earnings over a 12-month period for men and women who worked full-time, year-round, and employment composition by sector to identify the worst-paying cities for women. Of the largest 100 U.S. metropolitan areas, Provo* was ranked #1 in pay disparity. *24/7 Wall St., "The Best (and Worst) Paying Cities for Women," March 27, 2017*

Miscellaneous Rankings

- The finance and lifestyle site NerdWallet looked for the U.S. cities that topped the list in donating money and time to good causes. The Provo* metro area proved to be the #1-ranked metro area, judged by culture of volunteerism, depth of commitment in terms of volunteer hours per year, and monetary contributions. *www.nerdwallet.com, "Most Generous Cities," September 22, 2013*

*Lehi is located within the Provo-Orem, UT Metropolitan Statistical Area.

Business Environment

CITY FINANCES

City Government Finances

Component	2015 ($000)	2015 ($ per capita)
Total Revenues	89,294	1,527
Total Expenditures	104,011	1,778
Debt Outstanding	133,283	2,279
Cash and Securities[1]	37,159	635

Note: (1) Cash and security holdings of a government at the close of its fiscal year,, including those of its dependent agencies, utilities, and liquor stores.
Source: U.S Census Bureau, State & Local Government Finances 2015

City Government Revenue by Source

Source	2015 ($000)	2015 ($ per capita)	2015 (%)
General Revenue			
From Federal Government	0	0	0.0
From State Government	380	6	0.4
From Local Governments	2,065	35	2.3
Taxes			
Property	7,494	128	8.4
Sales and Gross Receipts	11,893	203	13.3
Personal Income	0	0	0.0
Corporate Income	0	0	0.0
Motor Vehicle License	0	0	0.0
Other Taxes	2,299	39	2.6
Current Charges	23,614	404	26.4
Liquor Store	0	0	0.0
Utility	35,118	600	39.3
Employee Retirement	0	0	0.0

Source: U.S Census Bureau, State & Local Government Finances 2015

City Government Expenditures by Function

Function	2015 ($000)	2015 ($ per capita)	2015 (%)
General Direct Expenditures			
Air Transportation	0	0	0.0
Corrections	0	0	0.0
Education	69	1	0.1
Employment Security Administration	0	0	0.0
Financial Administration	1,028	17	1.0
Fire Protection	3,733	63	3.6
General Public Buildings	439	7	0.4
Governmental Administration, Other	3,969	67	3.8
Health	148	2	0.1
Highways	11,972	204	11.5
Hospitals	0	0	0.0
Housing and Community Development	431	7	0.4
Interest on General Debt	378	6	0.4
Judicial and Legal	1,079	18	1.0
Libraries	1,027	17	1.0
Parking	0	0	0.0
Parks and Recreation	11,717	200	11.3
Police Protection	5,088	87	4.9
Public Welfare	130	2	0.1
Sewerage	8,674	148	8.3
Solid Waste Management	2,402	41	2.3
Veterans' Services	0	0	0.0
Liquor Store	0	0	0.0
Utility	41,863	715	40.2
Employee Retirement	0	0	0.0

Source: U.S Census Bureau, State & Local Government Finances 2015

DEMOGRAPHICS

Population Growth

Area	1990 Census	2000 Census	2010 Census	2016* Estimate	Population Growth (%)	
					1990-2016	2010-2016
City	9,766	19,028	47,407	56,314	476.6	18.8
MSA[1]	269,407	376,774	526,810	574,684	113.3	9.1
U.S.	248,709,873	281,421,906	308,745,538	318,558,162	28.1	3.2

Note: (1) Figures cover the Provo-Orem, UT Metropolitan Statistical Area—see Appendix B for areas included; (*) 2012-2016 5-year estimated population
Source: U.S. Census Bureau, 1990 Census, Census 2000, Census 2010, 2012-2016 American Community Survey 5-Year Estimates

Household Size

Area	Persons in Household (%)							Average Household Size
	One	Two	Three	Four	Five	Six	Seven or More	
City	8.8	21.8	13.4	19.5	18.2	12.1	6.0	3.90
MSA[1]	11.9	27.3	15.6	16.5	12.7	9.4	6.7	3.60
U.S.	27.7	33.7	15.7	13.1	6.0	2.3	1.5	2.60

Note: (1) Figures cover the Provo-Orem, UT Metropolitan Statistical Area—see Appendix B for areas included
Source: U.S. Census Bureau, 2012-2016 American Community Survey 5-Year Estimates

Race

Area	White Alone[2] (%)	Black Alone[2] (%)	Asian Alone[2] (%)	AIAN[3] Alone[2] (%)	NHOPI[4] Alone[2] (%)	Other Race Alone[2] (%)	Two or More Races (%)
City	94.6	0.1	1.2	0.5	0.2	1.3	2.1
MSA[1]	92.2	0.6	1.4	0.5	0.7	1.8	2.7
U.S.	73.3	12.6	5.2	0.8	0.2	4.8	3.1

Note: (1) Figures cover the Provo-Orem, UT Metropolitan Statistical Area—see Appendix B for areas included; (2) Alone is defined as not being in combination with one or more other races; (3) American Indian and Alaska Native; (4) Native Hawaiian and Other Pacific Islander
Source: U.S. Census Bureau, 2012-2016 American Community Survey 5-Year Estimates

Hispanic or Latino Origin

Area	Total (%)	Mexican (%)	Puerto Rican (%)	Cuban (%)	Other (%)
City	6.5	3.7	0.1	0.0	2.7
MSA[1]	11.0	7.5	0.2	0.1	3.3
U.S.	17.3	11.0	1.7	0.7	4.0

Note: Persons of Hispanic or Latino origin can be of any race; (1) Figures cover the Provo-Orem, UT Metropolitan Statistical Area—see Appendix B for areas included
Source: U.S. Census Bureau, 2012-2016 American Community Survey 5-Year Estimates

Segregation

Type	Segregation Indices[1]				Percent Change		
	1990	2000	2010	2010 Rank[2]	1990-2000	1990-2010	2000-2010
Black/White	38.6	29.4	21.9	102	-9.2	-16.7	-7.5
Asian/White	32.3	31.5	28.2	94	-0.8	-4.1	-3.3
Hispanic/White	20.9	33.3	30.9	93	12.4	10.0	-2.4

Note: All figures cover the Metropolitan Statistical Area—see Appendix B for areas included; Figures are based on an analysis of 1990, 2000, and 2010 Census Decennial Census tract data by William H. Frey, Brookings Institution and the University of Michigan Social Science Data Analysis Network. In this analysis all racial groups (whites, blacks, and asians) are non-Hispanic members of those races. Hispanics are shown as a separate category; (1) Segregation Indices are Dissimilarity Indices that measure the degree to which the minority group is distributed differently than whites across census tracts. They range from 0 (complete integration) to 100 (complete segregation) where the value indicates the percentage of the minority group that needs to move to be distributed exactly like whites; (2) Ranges from 1 (most segregated) to 102 (least segregated); n/a not available.
Source: www.CensusScope.org

Ancestry

Area	German	Irish	English	American	Italian	Polish	French[2]	Scottish	Dutch
City	11.4	6.4	30.9	6.0	3.1	0.4	1.7	6.2	1.7
MSA[1]	11.1	5.1	28.7	5.2	2.4	0.7	2.1	5.4	1.9
U.S.	14.4	10.4	7.7	6.9	5.4	2.9	2.6	1.7	1.3

Note: Figures are the percentage of the total population reporting a particular ancestry. The nine most commonly reported ancestries in the U.S. are shown. Figures include multiple ancestries (e.g. if a person reported being Irish and Italian, they were included in both columns); (1) Figures cover the Provo-Orem, UT Metropolitan Statistical Area—see Appendix B for areas included; (2) Excludes Basque
Source: U.S. Census Bureau, 2012-2016 American Community Survey 5-Year Estimates

Foreign-Born Population

Area	Percent of Population Born in								
	Any Foreign Country	Asia	Mexico	Europe	Carribean	Central America[2]	South America	Africa	Canada
City	4.0	0.8	1.1	0.5	0.1	0.1	1.0	0.0	0.3
MSA[1]	6.9	1.1	2.8	0.5	0.1	0.5	1.2	0.1	0.3
U.S.	13.2	4.0	3.6	1.5	1.3	1.0	0.9	0.6	0.3

Note: (1) Figures cover the Provo-Orem, UT Metropolitan Statistical Area—see Appendix B for areas included; (2) Excludes Mexico.
Source: U.S. Census Bureau, 2012-2016 American Community Survey 5-Year Estimates

Marital Status

Area	Never Married	Now Married[2]	Separated	Widowed	Divorced
City	24.2	67.8	0.7	1.8	5.5
MSA[1]	32.0	58.5	1.0	2.6	5.9
U.S.	33.0	48.1	2.1	5.9	11.0

Note: Figures are percentages and cover the population 15 years of age and older; (1) Figures cover the Provo-Orem, UT Metropolitan Statistical Area—see Appendix B for areas included; (2) Excludes separated
Source: U.S. Census Bureau, 2012-2016 American Community Survey 5-Year Estimates

Disability Status

Area	All Ages	Under 18 Years Old	18 to 64 Years Old	65 Years and Over
City	6.4	3.0	6.2	35.0
MSA[1]	7.6	3.0	7.0	34.6
U.S.	12.5	4.1	10.3	35.7

Note: Figures show percent of the civilian noninstitutionalized population that reported having a disability. Disability status is determined from six types of difficulty: vision, hearing, cognitive, ambulatory, self-care, and independent living. For children under 5 years old, hearing and vision difficulty are used to determine disability status. For children between the ages of 5 and 14, disability status is determined from hearing, vision, cognitive, ambulatory, and self-care difficulties. For people aged 15 years and older, they are considered to have a disability if they have difficulty with any one of the six difficulty types; Note: (1) Figures cover the Provo-Orem, UT Metropolitan Statistical Area—see Appendix B for areas included
Source: U.S. Census Bureau, 2012-2016 American Community Survey 5-Year Estimates

Age

Area	Percent of Population									Median Age
	Under Age 5	Age 5–19	Age 20–34	Age 35–44	Age 45–54	Age 55–64	Age 65–74	Age 75–84	Age 85+	
City	13.0	32.4	20.8	15.0	7.7	5.5	3.4	1.7	0.5	24.7
MSA[1]	10.1	28.7	27.0	12.1	8.3	6.6	4.2	2.3	0.8	24.5
U.S.	6.2	19.6	20.7	12.7	13.6	12.6	8.3	4.3	1.9	37.7

Note: (1) Figures cover the Provo-Orem, UT Metropolitan Statistical Area—see Appendix B for areas included
Source: U.S. Census Bureau, 2012-2016 American Community Survey 5-Year Estimates

Gender

Area	Males	Females	Males per 100 Females
City	28,828	27,486	104.9
MSA[1]	289,878	284,806	101.8
U.S.	156,765,322	161,792,840	96.9

Note: (1) Figures cover the Provo-Orem, UT Metropolitan Statistical Area—see Appendix B for areas included
Source: U.S. Census Bureau, 2012-2016 American Community Survey 5-Year Estimates

Religious Groups by Family

Area	Catholic	Baptist	Non-Den.	Methodist[2]	Lutheran	LDS[3]	Pente-costal	Presby-terian[4]	Muslim[5]	Judaism
MSA[1]	1.3	0.1	0.1	0.2	<0.1	88.6	0.1	0.1	<0.1	<0.1
U.S.	19.1	9.3	4.0	4.0	2.3	2.0	1.9	1.6	0.8	0.7

Note: Figures are the number of adherents as a percentage of the total population; (1) Figures cover the Provo-Orem, UT Metropolitan Statistical Area—see Appendix B for areas included; (2) Methodist/Pietist; (3) Latter Day Saints; (4) Reformed; (5) Figures are estimates
Source: Association of Statisticians of American Religious Bodies, 2010 U.S. Religion Census: Religious Congregations & Membership Study

Religious Groups by Tradition

Area	Catholic	Evangelical Protestant	Mainline Protestant	Other Tradition	Black Protestant	Orthodox
MSA[1]	1.3	0.5	0.1	88.9	<0.1	<0.1
U.S.	19.1	16.2	7.3	4.3	1.6	0.3

Note: Figures are the number of adherents as a percentage of the total population; (1) Figures cover the Provo-Orem, UT Metropolitan Statistical Area—see Appendix B for areas included
Source: Association of Statisticians of American Religious Bodies, 2010 U.S. Religion Census: Religious Congregations & Membership Study

ECONOMY

Gross Metropolitan Product

Area	2014	2015	2016	2017	Rank[2]
MSA[1]	19.3	20.7	21.9	23.5	119

Note: Figures are in billions of dollars; (1) Figures cover the Provo-Orem, UT Metropolitan Statistical Area—see Appendix B for areas included; (2) Rank is based on 2015 data and ranges from 1 to 381
Source: The U.S. Conference of Mayors, U.S. Metro Economies: GMP and Employment Report, 2015-2017

Economic Growth

Area	2012-14 (%)	2015 (%)	2016 (%)	2017 (%)	Rank[2]
MSA[1]	3.9	6.6	3.9	5.1	30
U.S.	2.0	2.4	1.9	2.6	–

Note: Figures are real gross metropolitan product (GMP) growth rates and represent average annual percent change; (1) Figures cover the Provo-Orem, UT Metropolitan Statistical Area—see Appendix B for areas included; (2) Rank is based on 2012-2014 average annual percent change and ranges from 1 to 381
Source: The U.S. Conference of Mayors, U.S. Metro Economies: GMP and Employment Report, 2015-2017

Metropolitan Area Exports

Area	2011	2012	2013	2014	2015	2016	Rank[2]
MSA[1]	2,056.4	2,058.1	2,789.2	2,533.4	2,216.4	1,894.8	98

Note: Figures are in millions of dollars; (1) Figures cover the Provo-Orem, UT Metropolitan Statistical Area—see Appendix B for areas included; (2) Rank is based on 2016 data and ranges from 1 to 385
Source: U.S. Department of Commerce, International Trade Administration, Office of Trade & Industry Information, Manufacturing & Services, data extracted March 15, 2018

Building Permits

Area	Single-Family			Multi-Family			Total		
	2016	2017p	Pct. Chg.	2016	2017p	Pct. Chg.	2016	2017p	Pct. Chg.
City	616	934	51.6	0	0	0.0	616	934	51.6
MSA[1]	4,417	5,082	15.1	888	2,155	142.7	5,305	7,237	36.4
U.S.	750,800	817,300	8.9	455,800	446,800	-2.0	1,206,600	1,264,100	4.8

Note: (1) Figures cover the Provo-Orem, UT Metropolitan Statistical Area—see Appendix B for areas included; Figures represent new, privately-owned housing units authorized (unadjusted data); All permit data are based on estimates with imputation; (p) preliminary data.
Source: U.S. Census Bureau, Manufacturing, Mining, and Construction Statistics, Building Permits, 2016, 2017

Bankruptcy Filings

Area	Business Filings 2016	Business Filings 2017	Business Filings % Chg.	Nonbusiness Filings 2016	Nonbusiness Filings 2017	Nonbusiness Filings % Chg.
Utah County	41	36	-12.2	1,588	1,598	0.6
U.S.	24,114	23,157	-4.0	770,846	765,863	-0.6

Note: Business filings include Chapter 7, Chapter 11, Chapter 12, and Chapter 13; Nonbusiness filings include Chapter 7, Chapter 11, and Chapter 13
Source: Administrative Office of the U.S. Courts, Business and Nonbusiness Bankruptcy, County Cases Commenced by Chapter of the Bankruptcy Code, During the 12-Month Period Ending December 31, 2016 and Business and Nonbusiness Bankruptcy, County Cases Commenced by Chapter of the Bankruptcy Code, During the 12-Month Period Ending December 31, 2017

Housing Vacancy Rates

Area	Gross Vacancy Rate[2] (%) 2015	2016	2017	Year-Round Vacancy Rate[3] (%) 2015	2016	2017	Rental Vacancy Rate[4] (%) 2015	2016	2017	Homeowner Vacancy Rate[5] (%) 2015	2016	2017
MSA[1]	n/a	n/a	n/a	n/a	n/a	n/a	n/a	n/a	n/a	n/a	n/a	n/a
U.S.	12.9	12.8	12.7	10.0	9.9	9.9	7.1	6.9	7.2	1.8	1.7	1.6

Note: (1) Figures cover the Provo-Orem, UT Metropolitan Statistical Area—see Appendix B for areas included; (2) The percentage of the total housing inventory that is vacant; (3) The percentage of the housing inventory (excluding seasonal units) that is year-round vacant; (4) The percentage of rental inventory that is vacant for rent; (5) The percentage of homeowner inventory that is vacant for sale; n/a not available
Source: U.S. Census Bureau, Housing Vacancies and Homeownership Annual Statistics: 2015, 2016, 2017

INCOME

Income

Area	Per Capita ($)	Median Household ($)	Average Household ($)
City	24,478	81,013	95,108
MSA[1]	22,035	63,994	79,701
U.S.	29,829	55,322	77,866

Note: (1) Figures cover the Provo-Orem, UT Metropolitan Statistical Area—see Appendix B for areas included
Source: U.S. Census Bureau, 2012-2016 American Community Survey 5-Year Estimates

Household Income Distribution

Area	Under $15,000	$15,000 -$24,999	$25,000 -$34,999	$35,000 -$49,999	$50,000 -$74,999	$75,000 -$99,999	$100,000 -$149,999	$150,000 and up
	Percent of Households Earning							
City	3.7	4.3	4.5	9.7	22.0	20.7	22.6	12.5
MSA[1]	7.8	7.9	8.3	13.4	21.3	15.5	16.1	9.6
U.S.	12.1	10.2	9.9	13.2	17.8	12.2	13.5	11.1

Note: (1) Figures cover the Provo-Orem, UT Metropolitan Statistical Area—see Appendix B for areas included
Source: U.S. Census Bureau, 2012-2016 American Community Survey 5-Year Estimates

Poverty Rate

Area	All Ages	Under 18 Years Old	18 to 64 Years Old	65 Years and Over
City	5.9	7.0	5.3	3.3
MSA[1]	12.6	11.4	14.1	5.8
U.S.	15.1	21.2	14.2	9.3

Note: Figures are percentage of people whose income during the past 12 months was below the poverty level; (1) Figures cover the Provo-Orem, UT Metropolitan Statistical Area—see Appendix B for areas included
Source: U.S. Census Bureau, 2012-2016 American Community Survey 5-Year Estimates

EMPLOYMENT

Labor Force and Employment

Area	Civilian Labor Force Dec. 2016	Civilian Labor Force Dec. 2017	Civilian Labor Force % Chg.	Workers Employed Dec. 2016	Workers Employed Dec. 2017	Workers Employed % Chg.
City	26,175	27,443	4.8	25,516	26,729	4.8
MSA[1]	290,826	304,146	4.6	283,195	296,661	4.8
U.S.	158,968,000	159,880,000	0.6	151,798,000	153,602,000	1.2

Note: Data is not seasonally adjusted and covers workers 16 years of age and older; (1) Figures cover the Provo-Orem, UT Metropolitan Statistical Area—see Appendix B for areas included
Source: Bureau of Labor Statistics, Local Area Unemployment Statistics

Unemployment Rate

Area	2017											
	Jan.	Feb.	Mar.	Apr.	May	Jun.	Jul.	Aug.	Sep.	Oct.	Nov.	Dec.
City	3.0	3.3	3.3	3.0	2.9	3.3	3.1	3.1	2.7	2.8	2.6	2.6
MSA[1]	3.1	3.2	3.1	2.8	2.9	3.4	3.2	3.1	2.7	2.6	2.4	2.5
U.S.	5.1	4.9	4.6	4.1	4.1	4.5	4.6	4.5	4.1	3.9	3.9	3.9

Note: Data is not seasonally adjusted and covers workers 16 years of age and older; (1) Figures cover the Provo-Orem, UT Metropolitan Statistical Area—see Appendix B for areas included
Source: Bureau of Labor Statistics, Local Area Unemployment Statistics

Average Wages

Occupation	$/Hr.	Occupation	$/Hr.
Accountants and Auditors	32.70	Maids and Housekeeping Cleaners	10.60
Automotive Mechanics	19.70	Maintenance and Repair Workers	18.60
Bookkeepers	17.90	Marketing Managers	51.90
Carpenters	19.00	Nuclear Medicine Technologists	n/a
Cashiers	10.30	Nurses, Licensed Practical	19.60
Clerks, General Office	14.60	Nurses, Registered	29.60
Clerks, Receptionists/Information	13.00	Nursing Assistants	12.20
Clerks, Shipping/Receiving	14.30	Packers and Packagers, Hand	11.40
Computer Programmers	42.60	Physical Therapists	42.50
Computer Systems Analysts	46.20	Postal Service Mail Carriers	23.60
Computer User Support Specialists	22.40	Real Estate Brokers	28.10
Cooks, Restaurant	12.50	Retail Salespersons	12.20
Dentists	n/a	Sales Reps., Exc. Tech./Scientific	28.30
Electrical Engineers	39.90	Sales Reps., Tech./Scientific	33.80
Electricians	26.10	Secretaries, Exc. Legal/Med./Exec.	15.30
Financial Managers	50.20	Security Guards	14.50
First-Line Supervisors/Managers, Sales	17.90	Surgeons	n/a
Food Preparation Workers	11.30	Teacher Assistants*	12.10
General and Operations Managers	38.90	Teachers, Elementary School*	30.60
Hairdressers/Cosmetologists	11.20	Teachers, Secondary School*	30.60
Internists, General	n/a	Telemarketers	17.40
Janitors and Cleaners	9.90	Truck Drivers, Heavy/Tractor-Trailer	19.70
Landscaping/Groundskeeping Workers	13.50	Truck Drivers, Light/Delivery Svcs.	16.10
Lawyers	59.00	Waiters and Waitresses	10.90

Note: Wage data covers the Provo-Orem, UT Metropolitan Statistical Area—see Appendix B for areas included; (*) Hourly wages for elementary/secondary school teachers and teacher assistants were calculated by the editors from annual wage data based on a 40 hour work week; n/a not available.
Source: Bureau of Labor Statistics, Metro Area Occupational Employment & Wage Estimates, May 2017

Employment by Occupation

Occupation Classification	City (%)	MSA[1] (%)	U.S. (%)
Management, Business, Science, and Arts	45.2	40.3	37.0
Natural Resources, Construction, and Maintenance	7.2	7.6	8.9
Production, Transportation, and Material Moving	6.8	10.2	12.2
Sales and Office	25.6	26.4	23.8
Service	15.2	15.4	18.1

Note: Figures cover employed civilians 16 years of age and older; (1) Figures cover the Provo-Orem, UT Metropolitan Statistical Area—see Appendix B for areas included
Source: U.S. Census Bureau, 2012-2016 American Community Survey 5-Year Estimates

Employment by Industry

Sector	MSA[1] Number of Employees	MSA[1] Percent of Total	U.S. Percent of Total
Construction, Mining, and Logging	25,000	9.8	5.2
Education and Health Services	54,500	21.3	15.9
Financial Activities	8,600	3.4	5.7
Government	32,100	12.5	15.3
Information	12,200	4.8	1.9
Leisure and Hospitality	20,200	7.9	10.7
Manufacturing	19,400	7.6	8.5
Other Services	5,400	2.1	3.9
Professional and Business Services	34,000	13.3	14.0
Retail Trade	34,200	13.3	11.0
Transportation, Warehousing, and Utilities	3,800	1.5	4.1
Wholesale Trade	6,800	2.7	4.0

Note: Figures are non-farm employment as of December 2017. Figures are not seasonally adjusted and include workers 16 years of age and older; (1) Figures cover the Provo-Orem, UT Metropolitan Statistical Area—see Appendix B for areas included
Source: Bureau of Labor Statistics, Current Employment Statistics, Employment, Hours, and Earnings

Occupations with Greatest Projected Employment Growth: 2017 – 2019

Occupation[1]	2017 Employment	2019 Projected Employment	Numeric Employment Change	Percent Employment Change
Combined Food Preparation and Serving Workers, Including Fast Food	40,810	43,640	2,830	6.9
Customer Service Representatives	44,760	46,800	2,040	4.6
Construction Laborers	17,940	19,780	1,840	10.3
General and Operations Managers	29,140	30,980	1,840	6.3
Carpenters	15,870	17,610	1,740	10.9
Heavy and Tractor-Trailer Truck Drivers	24,080	25,570	1,490	6.2
Janitors and Cleaners, Except Maids and Housekeeping Cleaners	22,610	23,970	1,360	6.0
Retail Salespersons	47,280	48,580	1,300	2.7
Laborers and Freight, Stock, and Material Movers, Hand	19,560	20,850	1,290	6.6
Registered Nurses	22,690	23,950	1,260	5.6

Note: Projections cover Utah; (1) Sorted by numeric employment change
Source: www.projectionscentral.com, State Occupational Projections, 2017–2019 Short-Term Projections

Fastest Growing Occupations: 2017 – 2019

Occupation[1]	2017 Employment	2019 Projected Employment	Numeric Employment Change	Percent Employment Change
Roofers	2,300	2,640	340	14.7
Brickmasons and Blockmasons	2,310	2,650	340	14.6
Plasterers and Stucco Masons	660	750	90	13.9
Roustabouts, Oil and Gas	1,170	1,330	160	13.8
Cement Masons and Concrete Finishers	3,470	3,930	460	13.2
Helpers—Brickmasons, Blockmasons, Stonemasons, and Tile and Marble Setters	690	780	90	13.0
Stonemasons	360	410	50	12.8
Helpers—Pipelayers, Plumbers, Pipefitters, and Steamfitters	570	640	70	12.6
Plumbers, Pipefitters, and Steamfitters	6,750	7,590	840	12.5
Software Developers, Applications	8,310	9,330	1,020	12.3

Note: Projections cover Utah; (1) Sorted by percent employment change and excludes occupations with numeric employment change less than 50
Source: www.projectionscentral.com, State Occupational Projections, 2017–2019 Short-Term Projections

TAXES

State Corporate Income Tax Rates

State	Tax Rate (%)	Income Brackets ($)	Num. of Brackets	Financial Institution Tax Rate (%)[a]	Federal Income Tax Ded.
Utah	5.0 (b)	Flat rate	–	5.0 (b)	No

Note: Tax rates as of January 1, 2018; (a) Rates listed are the corporate income tax rate applied to financial institutions or excise taxes based on income. Some states have other taxes based upon the value of deposits or shares; (b) Minimum tax is $800 in California, $100 in District of Columbia and Arizona, $50 in North Dakota (banks), $500 in Rhode Island, $200 per location in South Dakota (banks), $100 in Utah, $250 in Vermont.
Source: Federation of Tax Administrators, Range of State Corporate Income Tax Rates, January 1, 2018

State Individual Income Tax Rates

State	Tax Rate (%)	Income Brackets ($)	Num. of Brackets	Personal Exempt. ($)[1]		Fed. Inc. Tax Ded.
				Single	Dependents	
Utah	5.0	Flat rate	1	(v)	(v)	No

Note: Tax rates as of January 1, 2018; Local- and county-level taxes are not included; n/a not applicable; (1) Married joint filers generally receive double the single exemption; (v) Utah provides a tax credit equal to 6% of the federal personal exemption amounts (and applicable standard deduction). Note, the Tax Cut and Reform Act of 2017 has eliminated personal exemptions and increased the standard deduction in the IRC. Utah will need to enact legislation to reinstate a personal credit for tax year 2018.
Source: Federation of Tax Administrators, State Individual Income Tax Rates, January 1, 2018

Various State Sales and Excise Tax Rates

State	State Sales Tax (%)	Gasoline[1] (¢/gal.)	Cigarette[2] ($/pack)	Spirits[3] ($/gal.)	Wine[4] ($/gal.)	Beer[5] ($/gal.)	Recreational Marijuana (%)
Utah	5.95 (b)	29.41	1.70	15.38 (g)	(m)	0.41 (q)	Not legal

Note: All tax rates as of January 1, 2018; (1) The American Petroleum Institute has developed a methodology for determining the average tax rate on a gallon of fuel. Rates may include any of the following: excise taxes, environmental fees, storage tank fees, other fees or taxes, general sales tax, and local taxes. In states where gasoline is subject to the general sales tax, or where the fuel tax is based on the average sale price, the average rate determined by API is sensitive to changes in the price of gasoline. States that fully or partially apply general sales taxes to gasoline: CA, CO, GA, IL, IN, MI, NY; (2) The federal excise tax of $1.0066 per pack and local taxes are not included; (3) Rates are those applicable to off-premise sales of 40% alcohol by volume (a.b.v.) distilled spirits in 750ml containers. Local excise taxes are excluded; (4) Rates are those applicable to off-premise sales of 11% a.b.v. non-carbonated wine in 750ml containers; (5) Rates are those applicable to off-premise sales of 4.7% a.b.v. beer in 12 ounce containers; (b) Three states levy mandatory, statewide, local add-on sales taxes at the state level: California (1.25%), Utah (1.25%), Virginia (1%), we include these in their state sales tax; (g) Control states, where the government controls all sales. Products can be subject to ad valorem mark-up as well as excise taxes; (m) Control states, where the government controls all sales. Products can be subject to ad valorem mark-up as well as excise taxes; (q) Different rates also applicable according to alcohol content, place of production, size of container, or place purchased (on- or off-premise or onboard airlines).
Source: Tax Foundation, 2018 Facts & Figures: How Does Your State Compare?

State Business Tax Climate Index Rankings

State	Overall Rank	Corporate Tax Rank	Individual Income Tax Rank	Sales Tax Rank	Unemployment Insurance Tax Rank	Property Tax Rank
Utah	8	4	11	17	21	5

Note: The index is a measure of how each state's tax laws affect economic performance. The lower the rank, the more favorable a state's tax system is for business. States without a given tax are given a ranking of 1. The scores/rankings for the District of Columbia do not affect other states. The 2018 index represents the tax climate as of July 1, 2017.
Source: Tax Foundation, State Business Tax Climate Index 2018

TRANSPORTATION

Means of Transportation to Work

Area	Car/Truck/Van		Public Transportation			Bicycle	Walked	Other Means	Worked at Home
	Drove Alone	Car-pooled	Bus	Subway	Railroad				
City	76.2	10.6	0.6	0.2	1.3	0.4	1.0	1.7	7.9
MSA[1]	73.1	12.1	0.9	0.2	0.7	1.1	4.1	1.4	6.3
U.S.	76.4	9.3	2.6	1.9	0.6	0.6	2.8	1.3	4.6

Note: Figures are percentages and cover workers 16 years of age and older; (1) Figures cover the Provo-Orem, UT Metropolitan Statistical Area—see Appendix B for areas included
Source: U.S. Census Bureau, 2012-2016 American Community Survey 5-Year Estimates

Travel Time to Work

Area	Less Than 10 Minutes	10 to 19 Minutes	20 to 29 Minutes	30 to 44 Minutes	45 to 59 Minutes	60 to 89 Minutes	90 Minutes or More
City	16.6	27.6	22.2	22.0	7.1	3.1	1.3
MSA[1]	19.1	35.9	19.7	14.6	5.3	3.6	1.6
U.S.	12.9	29.2	20.9	20.4	8.0	6.0	2.7

Note: Note: Figures are percentages and include workers 16 years old and over; (1) Figures cover the Provo-Orem, UT Metropolitan Statistical Area—see Appendix B for areas included
Source: U.S. Census Bureau, 2012-2016 American Community Survey 5-Year Estimates

Freeway Travel Time Index

Area	1985	1990	1995	2000	2005	2010	2014
Urban Area Rank[1,2]	64	76	84	86	86	92	91
Urban Area Index[1]	1.05	1.07	1.08	1.10	1.12	1.11	1.12
Average Index[3]	1.09	1.11	1.14	1.17	1.20	1.19	1.20

Note: Freeway Travel Time Index—the ratio of travel time in the peak period to the travel time at free-flow conditions. For example, a value of 1.30 indicates a 20-minute free-flow trip takes 26 minutes in the peak (20 minutes x 1.30 = 26 minutes); (1) Covers the Provo-Orem UT urban area; (2) Rank is based on 101 urban areas (#1 = highest travel time index); (3) Average of 101 urban areas
Source: Texas Transportation Institute, 2015 Urban Mobility Scorecard, August 2015

Freeway Commuter Stress Index

Area	1985	1990	1995	2000	2005	2010	2014
Urban Area Rank[1,2]	81	94	93	94	94	96	94
Urban Area Index[1]	1.06	1.07	1.09	1.11	1.13	1.12	1.13
Average Index[3]	1.13	1.16	1.19	1.22	1.25	1.24	1.25

Note: The Freeway Commuter Stress Index is the same as the Freeway Travel Time Index (see table above) except that it includes only the travel in the peak directions during the peak periods; the TTI includes travel in all directions during the peak period. Thus, the CSI is more indicative of the work trip experienced by each commuter on a daily basis; (1) Covers the Provo-Orem UT urban area; (2) Rank is based on 101 urban areas (#1 = highest travel time index); (3) Average of 101 urban areas
Source: Texas Transportation Institute, 2015 Urban Mobility Scorecard, August 2015

Living Environment

COST OF LIVING

Cost of Living Index

Composite Index	Groceries	Housing	Utilities	Trans-portation	Health Care	Misc. Goods/ Services
98.0	100.0	100.4	72.6	101.9	110.9	99.8

Note: The Cost of Living Index measures regional differences in the cost of consumer goods and services, excluding taxes and non-consumer expenditures, for professional and managerial households in the top income quintile. It is based on more than 50,000 prices covering almost 60 different items for which prices are collected three times a year by chambers of commerce, economic development organizations or university applied economic centers in each participating urban area. The numbers shown should be read as a percentage above or below the national average of 100. For example, a value of 115.4 in the groceries column indicates that grocery prices are 15.4% higher than the national average. Small differences in the index numbers should not be interpreted as significant; Figures cover the Provo-Orem UT urban area.
Source: The Council for Community and Economic Research, ACCRA Cost of Living Index, 2017

Grocery Prices

Area[1]	T-Bone Steak ($/pound)	Frying Chicken ($/pound)	Whole Milk ($/half gal.)	Eggs ($/dozen)	Orange Juice ($/64 oz.)	Coffee ($/11.5 oz.)
City[2]	10.90	1.47	1.57	1.89	3.84	4.40
Avg.	11.29	1.40	2.02	1.47	3.55	4.37
Min.	7.71	0.93	1.04	0.70	2.86	3.24
Max.	15.83	2.39	4.03	3.92	6.29	8.16

*Note: (1) Values for the local area are compared with the average, minimum and maximum values for all 294 areas in the Cost of Living Index; (2) Figures cover the Provo-Orem UT urban area; **T-Bone Steak** (price per pound); **Frying Chicken** (price per pound, whole fryer); **Whole Milk** (half gallon carton); **Eggs** (price per dozen, Grade A, large); **Orange Juice** (64 oz. Tropicana or Florida Natural); **Coffee** (11.5 oz. can, vacuum-packed, Maxwell House, Hills Bros, or Folgers).*
Source: The Council for Community and Economic Research, ACCRA Cost of Living Index, 2017

Housing and Utility Costs

Area[1]	New Home Price ($)	Apartment Rent ($/month)	All Electric ($/month)	Part Electric ($/month)	Other Energy ($/month)	Telephone ($/month)
City[2]	353,645	992	-	67.76	62.38	19.00
Avg.	335,956	1,047	175.01	97.34	67.93	28.71
Min.	187,788	491	109.48	49.33	35.44	12.39
Max.	1,739,087	4,559	432.62	227.09	353.33	44.61

*Note: (1) Values for the local area are compared with the average, minimum and maximum values for all 294 areas in the Cost of Living Index; (2) Figures cover the Provo-Orem UT urban area; **New Home Price** (2,400 sf living area, 8,000 sf lot, in urban area with full utilities); **Apartment Rent** (950 sf 2 bedroom/1.5 or 2 bath, unfurnished, excluding all utilities except water); **All Electric** (average monthly cost for an all-electric home); **Part Electric** (average monthly cost for a part-electric home); **Other Energy** (average monthly cost for natural gas, fuel oil, coal, wood, and any other forms of energy except electricity); **Telephone** (price includes basic monthly rate for a private residential line plus additional local usage charges incurred by a family of four).*
Source: The Council for Community and Economic Research, ACCRA Cost of Living Index, 2017

Health Care, Transportation, and Other Costs

Area[1]	Doctor ($/visit)	Dentist ($/visit)	Optometrist ($/visit)	Gasoline ($/gallon)	Beauty Salon ($/visit)	Men's Shirt ($)
City[2]	105.68	119.67	92.59	2.23	33.57	31.19
Avg.	108.00	92.54	101.93	2.25	37.58	30.92
Min.	30.39	60.00	49.75	1.82	16.11	11.20
Max.	193.50	161.94	229.28	3.16	77.35	59.13

*Note: (1) Values for the local area are compared with the average, minimum and maximum values for all 294 areas in the Cost of Living Index; (2) Figures cover the Provo-Orem UT urban area; **Doctor** (general practitioners routine exam of an established patient); **Dentist** (adult teeth cleaning and periodic oral examination); **Optometrist** (full vision eye exam for established adult patient); **Gasoline** (one gallon regular unleaded, national brand, including all taxes, cash price at self-service pump if available); **Beauty Salon** (woman's shampoo, trim, and blow-dry); **Men's Shirt** (cotton/polyester dress shirt, pinpoint weave, long sleeves).*
Source: The Council for Community and Economic Research, ACCRA Cost of Living Index, 2017

HOUSING

House Price Index (HPI)

Area	National Ranking[2]	Quarterly Change (%)	One-Year Change (%)	Five-Year Change (%)
MSA[1]	41	0.30	9.55	45.03
U.S.[3]	–	1.61	6.68	34.71

Note: The HPI is a weighted repeat sales index. It measures average price changes in repeat sales or refinancings on the same properties. This information is obtained by reviewing repeat mortgage transactions on single-family properties whose mortgages have been purchased or securitized by Fannie Mae or Freddie Mac in January 1975; (1) Figures cover the Provo-Orem, UT Metropolitan Statistical Area—see Appendix B for areas included; (2) Rankings are based on annual percentage change for all metro areas containing at least 15,000 transactions over the last 10 years and ranges from 1 to 253; (3) figures based on a weighted average of Census Division estimates using a seasonally adjusted, purchase-only index; all figures are for the period ending December 31, 2017
Source: Federal Housing Finance Agency, House Price Index, February 28, 2018

Median Single-Family Home Prices

Area	2015	2016	2017p	Percent Change 2016 to 2017
MSA[1]	n/a	n/a	n/a	n/a
U.S. Average	223.9	235.5	248.8	5.6

Note: Figures are median sales prices of existing single-family homes in thousands of dollars; (p) preliminary; n/a not available; (1) Figures cover the Provo-Orem, UT Metropolitan Statistical Area—see Appendix B for areas included
Source: National Association of Realtors, Median Sales Price of Existing Single-Family Homes for Metropolitan Areas, 4th Quarter 2017

Qualifying Income Based on Median Sales Price of Existing Single-Family Homes

Area	With 5% Down ($)	With 10% Down ($)	With 20% Down ($)
MSA[1]	n/a	n/a	n/a
U.S. Average	55,585	52,659	46,808

Note: Figures are preliminary; Qualifying income is based on a mortgage rate of 4.17%. Monthly principal and interest payment is limited to 25% of income; n/a not available; (1) Figures cover the Provo-Orem, UT Metropolitan Statistical Area—see Appendix B for areas included
Source: National Association of Realtors, Qualifying Income Based on Median Sales Price of Existing Single-Family Homes for Metropolitan Areas, 4th Quarter 2017

Median Apartment Condo-Coop Home Prices

Area	2015	2016	2017p	Percent Change 2016 to 2017
MSA[1]	n/a	n/a	n/a	n/a
U.S. Average	210.7	220.7	234.3	6.2

Note: Figures are median sales prices of existing apartment condo-coop homes in thousands of dollars; (p) preliminary; n/a not available; (1) Figures cover the Provo-Orem, UT Metropolitan Statistical Area—see Appendix B for areas included
Source: National Association of Realtors, Median Sales Price of Existing Apartment Condo-Coop Homes for Metropolitan Areas, 4th Quarter 2017

Home Value Distribution

Area	Under $50,000	$50,000 -$99,999	$100,000 -$149,999	$150,000 -$199,999	$200,000 -$299,999	$300,000 -$499,999	$500,000 -$999,999	$1,000,000 or more
City	1.9	1.0	3.0	14.9	42.3	31.5	4.9	0.5
MSA[1]	3.3	1.5	9.8	20.0	34.6	23.1	6.7	1.0
U.S.	8.8	14.8	15.3	14.9	18.4	16.4	9.0	2.5

Note: Figures are percentages and cover owner-occupied housing units; (1) Figures cover the Provo-Orem, UT Metropolitan Statistical Area—see Appendix B for areas included
Source: U.S. Census Bureau, 2012-2016 American Community Survey 5-Year Estimates

Homeownership Rate

Area	2009 (%)	2010 (%)	2011 (%)	2012 (%)	2013 (%)	2014 (%)	2015 (%)	2016 (%)	2017 (%)
MSA[1]	n/a	n/a	n/a	n/a	n/a	n/a	n/a	n/a	n/a
U.S.	67.4	66.9	66.1	65.4	65.1	64.5	63.7	63.4	63.9

Note: (1) Figures cover the Provo-Orem, UT Metropolitan Statistical Area—see Appendix B for areas included; n/a not available
Source: U.S. Census Bureau, Housing Vacancies and Homeownership Annual Statistics: 2009-2017

Year Housing Structure Built

Area	2010 or Later	2000 -2009	1990 -1999	1980 -1989	1970 -1979	1960 -1969	1950 -1959	1940 -1949	Before 1940	Median Year
City	11.7	51.8	17.1	4.2	5.1	1.8	1.9	2.6	3.9	2003
MSA[1]	5.5	29.0	20.6	9.6	15.7	5.4	5.2	3.5	5.4	1992
U.S.	2.3	14.7	14.0	13.7	15.6	10.9	10.6	5.2	13.0	1977

Note: Figures are percentages except for Median Year; Note: (1) Figures cover the Provo-Orem, UT Metropolitan Statistical Area—see Appendix B for areas included
Source: U.S. Census Bureau, 2012-2016 American Community Survey 5-Year Estimates

Gross Monthly Rent

Area	Under $500	$500 -$999	$1,000 -$1,499	$1,500 -$1,999	$2,000 -$2,499	$2,500 -$2,999	$3,000 and up	Median ($)
City	2.4	21.9	37.8	32.5	5.1	0.3	0.0	1,306
MSA[1]	8.3	49.5	28.3	10.3	2.6	0.6	0.3	916
U.S.	11.3	43.3	27.7	10.7	4.0	1.6	1.5	949

Note: Figures are percentages except for Median; Gross rent is the contract rent plus the estimated average monthly cost of utilities (electricity, gas, and water and sewer) and fuels (oil, coal, kerosene, wood, etc.) if these are paid by the renter (or paid for the renter by someone else); (1) Figures cover the Provo-Orem, UT Metropolitan Statistical Area—see Appendix B for areas included
Source: U.S. Census Bureau, 2012-2016 American Community Survey 5-Year Estimates

HEALTH

Health Risk Factors

Category	MSA[1] (%)	U.S. (%)
Adults aged 18–64 who have any kind of health care coverage	87.9	87.7
Adults who reported being in good or excellent health	90.0	83.6
Adults who are current smokers	5.2	17.1
Adults who currently use E-cigarettes	3.9	4.7
Adults who currently use chewing tobacco, snuff, or snus	2.2	4.0
Adults who are heavy drinkers[2]	3.4	6.5
Adults who are binge drinkers[3]	7.2	16.9
Adults who are overweight (BMI 25.0 - 29.9)	34.2	35.3
Adults who are obese (BMI 30.0 - 99.8)	22.5	29.9
Adults who participated in any physical activities in the past month	87.4	76.9
Adults who always or nearly always wears a seat belt	95.7	94.3

Note: (1) Figures cover the Provo-Orem, UT Metropolitan Statistical Area—see Appendix B for areas included; (2) Heavy drinkers are classified as adult men having more than 14 drinks per week and adult women having more than 7 drinks per week; (3) Binge drinkers are classified as males having five or more drinks on one occasion or females having four or more drinks on one occasion
Source: Centers for Disease Control and Prevention, Behaviorial Risk Factor Surveillance System, SMART: Selected Metropolitan Area Risk Trends, 2016

Health Screening Rates

Category	MSA[1] (%)	U.S. (%)
Adults 50-75 who have had a blood stool test within the past year	n/a	8.0
Adults 50-75 who have had a colonoscopy in the past 10 years	69.6	63.5
Adults aged 65+ who have had flu shot within the past year	52.9	58.6
Adults aged 65+ who have ever had a pneumonia vaccination	66.2	73.4
Adults who have ever been tested for HIV	18.6	35.6
Women aged 21-65 who have had a pap test in the past three years	72.7	79.8
Men aged 40+ who have had a PSA test within the past two years	36.0	39.5
Women aged 40+ who have had a mammogram within the past two years	64.3	72.5

Note: n/a not available; (1) Figures cover the Provo-Orem, UT Metropolitan Statistical Area—see Appendix B for areas included; Source: Centers for Disease Control and Prevention, Behaviorial Risk Factor Surveillance System, SMART: Selected Metropolitan Area Risk Trends, 2016

Chronic Health Conditions

Category	MSA[1] (%)	U.S. (%)
Adults who have ever been told they had a heart attack	2.0	4.4
Adults who have ever been told they have angina or coronary heart disease	2.0	4.1
Adults who have ever been told they had a stroke	1.7	3.1
Adults who have been told they currently have asthma	7.0	9.3
Adults who have ever been told they have arthritis	15.5	25.8
Adults who have ever been told they have diabetes[2]	6.3	10.5
Adults who have ever been told they had skin cancer	5.7	5.9
Adults who have ever been told they had any other types of cancer	4.3	6.7
Adults who have ever been told they have COPD	3.3	6.3
Adults who have ever been told they have kidney disease	2.7	2.8
Adults who have ever been told they have a form of depression	23.8	17.4

Note: (1) Figures cover the Provo-Orem, UT Metropolitan Statistical Area—see Appendix B for areas included; (2) Figures do not include pregnancy-related, borderline, or pre-diabetes
Source: Centers for Disease Control and Prevention, Behaviorial Risk Factor Surveillance System, SMART: Selected Metropolitan Area Risk Trends, 2016

Mortality Rates for the Top 10 Causes of Death in the U.S.

ICD-10[a] Sub-Chapter	ICD-10[a] Code	Age-Adjusted Mortality Rate[1] per 100,000 population	
		County[2]	U.S.
Malignant neoplasms	C00-C97	118.1	158.5
Ischaemic heart diseases	I20-I25	62.5	96.8
Other forms of heart disease	I30-I51	85.4	52.4
Chronic lower respiratory diseases	J40-J47	27.9	40.9
Cerebrovascular diseases	I60-I69	41.0	37.2
Organic, including symptomatic, mental disorders	F01-F09	42.2	33.3
Other degenerative diseases of the nervous system	G30-G31	37.6	32.1
Other external causes of accidental injury	W00-X59	31.4	31.2
Diabetes mellitus	E10-E14	23.6	21.1
Hypertensive diseases	I10-I15	10.7	20.8

Note: (a) ICD-10 = International Classification of Diseases 10th Revision; (1) Mortality rates are a three year average covering 2014-2016; (2) Figures cover Utah County.
Source: Centers for Disease Control and Prevention, National Center for Health Statistics. Underlying Cause of Death 1999-2016 on CDC WONDER Online Database, released December 2017

Mortality Rates for Selected Causes of Death

ICD-10[a] Sub-Chapter	ICD-10[a] Code	Age-Adjusted Mortality Rate[1] per 100,000 population	
		County[2]	U.S.
Assault	X85-Y09	1.4	5.6
Diseases of the liver	K70-K76	9.7	14.0
Human immunodeficiency virus (HIV) disease	B20-B24	Suppressed	1.9
Influenza and pneumonia	J09-J18	15.3	14.6
Intentional self-harm	X60-X84	16.4	13.2
Malnutrition	E40-E46	2.8	1.3
Obesity and other hyperalimentation	E65-E68	1.9	2.1
Renal failure	N17-N19	19.9	13.0
Transport accidents	V01-V99	7.1	12.0
Viral hepatitis	B15-B19	Unreliable	1.9

Note: (a) ICD-10 = International Classification of Diseases 10th Revision; (1) Mortality rates are a three year average covering 2014-2016; (2) Figures cover Utah County; Data are Suppressed when the data meet the criteria for confidentiality constraints; Mortality rates are flagged as Unreliable when the rate would be calculated with a numerator of 20 or less.
Source: Centers for Disease Control and Prevention, National Center for Health Statistics. Underlying Cause of Death 1999-2016 on CDC WONDER Online Database, released December 2017

Health Insurance Coverage

Area	With Health Insurance	With Private Health Insurance	With Public Health Insurance	Without Health Insurance	Population Under Age 18 Without Health Insurance
City	93.4	86.1	13.0	6.6	4.1
MSA[1]	89.7	79.5	17.2	10.3	7.2
U.S.	88.3	66.7	33.0	11.7	5.9

Note: Figures are percentages that cover the civilian noninstitutionalized population; (1) Figures cover the Provo-Orem, UT Metropolitan Statistical Area—see Appendix B for areas included
Source: U.S. Census Bureau, 2012-2016 American Community Survey 5-Year Estimates

Number of Medical Professionals

Area	MDs[3]	DOs[3,4]	Dentists	Podiatrists	Chiropractors	Optometrists
County[1] (number)	681	103	361	24	141	61
County[1] (rate[2])	118.8	18.0	61.1	4.1	23.9	10.3
U.S. (rate[2])	276.5	22.3	67.3	6.0	26.7	15.9

Note: Data as of 2016 unless noted; (1) Data covers Utah County; (2) Rate per 100,000 population; (3) Data as of 2015 and includes all active, non-federal physicians; (4) Doctor of Osteopathic Medicine
Source: U.S. Department of Health and Human Services, Health Resources and Services Administration, Bureau of Health Professions, Area Resource File (ARF) 2016-2017

EDUCATION

Public School District Statistics

District Name	Schls	Pupils	Pupil/ Teacher Ratio	Minority Pupils[1] (%)	Free Lunch Eligible[2] (%)	IEP[3] (%)
Alpine District	86	76,938	n/a	16.6	16.7	10.8
Ascent Academies of Utah	3	1,907	n/a	16.5	17.5	13.0
Renaissance Academy	1	749	n/a	20.0	10.3	8.0

Note: Table includes school districts with 100 or more students; (1) Percentage of students that are not non-Hispanic white; (2) Percentage of students that are eligible for the free lunch program; (3) Percentage of students that have an Individualized Education Program.
Source: U.S. Department of Education, National Center for Education Statistics, Common Core of Data, Local Education Agency (School District) Universe Survey: School Year 2015-2016; U.S. Department of Education, National Center for Education Statistics, Common Core of Data, Public Elementary/Secondary School Universe Survey: School Year 2015-2016

Highest Level of Education

Area	Less than H.S.	H.S. Diploma	Some College, No Deg.	Associate Degree	Bachelor's Degree	Master's Degree	Prof. School Degree	Doctorate Degree
City	3.1	16.1	27.3	12.7	29.4	9.1	1.3	1.1
MSA[1]	6.4	17.0	27.8	11.1	26.0	8.3	1.6	1.8
U.S.	13.0	27.5	21.0	8.2	18.8	8.2	2.0	1.3

Note: Figures cover persons age 25 and over; (1) Figures cover the Provo-Orem, UT Metropolitan Statistical Area—see Appendix B for areas included
Source: U.S. Census Bureau, 2012-2016 American Community Survey 5-Year Estimates

Educational Attainment by Race

Area	High School Graduate or Higher (%)					Bachelor's Degree or Higher (%)				
	Total	White	Black	Asian	Hisp.[2]	Total	White	Black	Asian	Hisp.[2]
City	96.9	96.9	100.0	96.5	85.7	40.8	40.5	27.3	67.7	23.2
MSA[1]	93.6	94.2	90.6	92.0	70.5	37.7	37.9	37.1	57.1	18.1
U.S.	87.0	88.9	84.3	86.3	65.7	30.3	31.6	20.0	52.1	14.7

Note: Figures shown cover persons 25 years old and over; (1) Figures cover the Provo-Orem, UT Metropolitan Statistical Area—see Appendix B for areas included; (2) People of Hispanic origin can be of any race
Source: U.S. Census Bureau, 2012-2016 American Community Survey 5-Year Estimates

School Enrollment by Grade and Control

Area	Preschool (%)		Kindergarten (%)		Grades 1 - 4 (%)		Grades 5 - 8 (%)		Grades 9 - 12 (%)	
	Public	Private	Public	Private	Public	Private	Public	Private	Public	Private
City	42.4	57.6	96.3	3.7	96.3	3.7	97.1	2.9	96.9	3.1
MSA[1]	46.7	53.3	91.9	8.1	94.6	5.4	95.0	5.0	95.0	5.0
U.S.	58.4	41.6	87.7	12.3	89.8	10.2	89.7	10.3	90.4	9.6

Note: Figures shown cover persons 3 years old and over; (1) Figures cover the Provo-Orem, UT Metropolitan Statistical Area—see Appendix B for areas included
Source: U.S. Census Bureau, 2012-2016 American Community Survey 5-Year Estimates

Average Salaries of Public School Classroom Teachers

Area	2015		2016		Change from 2015 to 2016	
	Dollars	Rank[1]	Dollars	Rank[1]	Percent	Rank[2]
Utah	46,689	44	46,887	45	0.4	33
U.S. Average	57,611	–	58,353	–	1.3	–

Note: (1) Rank ranges from 1 to 51 where 1 indicates highest salary; (2) Rank ranges from 1 to 51 where 1 indicates highest percent change.
Source: National Education Association, Rankings & Estimates: Rankings of the States 2016 and Estimates of School Statistics 2017

Higher Education

Four-Year Colleges			Two-Year Colleges			Medical Schools[1]	Law Schools[2]	Voc/ Tech[3]
Public	Private Non-profit	Private For-profit	Public	Private Non-profit	Private For-profit			
0	0	0	1	0	0	0	0	0

Note: Figures cover institutions located within the city limits and include main campuses only; (1) includes schools accredited by the Liaison Committee on Medical Education and the American Osteopathic Association's Commission on Osteopathic College Accreditation; (2) includes ABA-accredited schools, schools with provisional ABA accreditation, and state accredited schools; (3) includes all schools with programs that are less than 2 years.
Source: National Center for Education Statistics, Integrated Postsecondary Education System (IPEDS), 2016-17; Wikipedia, List of Medical Schools in the United States, accessed April 2, 2018; Wikipedia, List of Law Schools in the United States, accessed April 2, 2018

According to *U.S. News & World Report,* the Provo-Orem, UT metro area is home to one of the best national universities in the U.S.: **Brigham Young University—Provo** (#61 tie). The indicators used to capture academic quality fall into a number of categories: assessment by administrators at peer institutions; retention of students; faculty resources; student selectivity; financial resources; alumni giving; high school counselor ratings of colleges; and graduation rate. *U.S. News & World Report, "America's Best Colleges 2018"*

According to *U.S. News & World Report,* the Provo-Orem, UT metro area is home to one of the top 100 law schools in the U.S.: **Brigham Young University (Clark)** (#41 tie). The rankings are based on a weighted average of 12 measures of quality: peer assessment score; assessment score by lawyers/judges; median LSAT scores; median undergrad GPA; acceptance rate; employment rates for graduates; placement success; bar passage rate; faculty resources; expenditures per student; student/faculty ratio; and library resources. *U.S. News & World Report, "America's Best Graduate Schools, Law, 2019"*

According to *U.S. News & World Report,* the Provo-Orem, UT metro area is home to one of the top 75 business schools in the U.S.: **Brigham Young University (Marriott)** (#35). The rankings are based on a weighted average of the following nine measures: quality assessment; peer assessment; recruiter assessment; placement success; mean starting salary and bonus; student selectivity; mean GMAT and GRE scores; mean undergraduate GPA; and acceptance rate. *U.S. News & World Report, "America's Best Graduate Schools, Business, 2019"*

PRESIDENTIAL ELECTION

2016 Presidential Election Results

Area	Clinton	Trump	Johnson	Stein	Other
Utah County	14.0	50.2	3.2	0.5	32.2
U.S.	48.0	45.9	3.3	1.1	1.7

Note: Results are percentages and may not add to 100% due to rounding
Source: Dave Leip's Atlas of U.S. Presidential Elections

EMPLOYERS

Major Employers

Company Name	Industry
About Time Technologies	Movements, clock or watch
Ancestry.com	Communication services, nec
Brigham Young University	Colleges & universities
City of Provo	Mayors' office
Intermountain Health Care	General medical & surgical hospitals
Morinda Holdings	Bottled & canned soft drinks
Novell	Prepackaged software
Nu Skin Enterprises United States	Drugs, proprietaries, & sundries
Nu Skin International	Toilet preparations
Phone Directories Company	Directories, phone: publish only, not printed on site
Rbm Services	Building cleaning service
TPUSA	Telemarketing services
Utah Dept of Human Services	Mental hospital, except for the mentally retarded
Utah Valley University	Colleges, except junior
Wal-Mart Stores	Department stores, discount
Wasatch Summit	Management consulting services
Xango	Drugs, proprietaries, & sundries

Note: Companies shown are located within the Provo-Orem, UT Metropolitan Statistical Area.
Source: Hoovers.com; Wikipedia

PUBLIC SAFETY

Crime Rate

Area	All Crimes	Violent Crimes				Property Crimes		
		Murder	Rape[3]	Robbery	Aggrav. Assault	Burglary	Larceny -Theft	Motor Vehicle Theft
City	1,391.3	0.0	59.2	13.2	54.3	213.8	985.1	65.8
Metro[1]	1,838.9	0.8	27.4	10.7	38.7	207.1	1,462.7	91.6
U.S.	2,847.8	5.3	40.4	102.8	248.5	468.9	1,745.0	236.9

Note: Figures are crimes per 100,000 population; (1) Figures cover the Provo-Orem, UT Metropolitan Statistical Area—see Appendix B for areas included; (3) The city and U.S. figures shown were reported using the revised Uniform Crime Reporting (UCR) definition of rape. The metro area figures shown are an aggregate total of the data submitted using both the revised and legacy UCR definitions.
Source: FBI Uniform Crime Reports, 2016

Hate Crimes

Area	Number of Quarters Reported	Number of Incidents per Bias Motivation					
		Race/Ethnicity/ Ancestry	Religion	Sexual Orientation	Disability	Gender	Gender Identity
City	4	0	0	0	0	0	0
U.S.	4	3,489	1,273	1,076	70	31	124

Source: Federal Bureau of Investigation, Hate Crime Statistics 2016

Identity Theft Consumer Reports

Area	Reports	Reports per 100,000 Population	Rank[2]
MSA[1]	421	70	254
U.S.	371,061	114	-

Note: (1) Figures cover the Provo-Orem, UT Metropolitan Statistical Area—see Appendix B for areas included; (2) Rank ranges from 1 to 389 where 1 indicates greatest number of identity theft reports per 100,000 population
Source: Federal Trade Commission, Consumer Sentinel Network Data Book for January–December 2017

Fraud and Other Consumer Reports

Area	Reports	Reports per 100,000 Population	Rank[2]
MSA[1]	1,694	281	367
U.S.	2,304,550	708	-

Note: (1) Figures cover the Provo-Orem, UT Metropolitan Statistical Area—see Appendix B for areas included; (2) Rank ranges from 1 to 389 where 1 indicates greatest number of fraud and other consumer reports per 100,000 population
Source: Federal Trade Commission, Consumer Sentinel Network Data Book for January–December 2017

SPORTS

Professional Sports Teams

Team Name	League	Year Established
No teams are located in the metro area		

Source: Wikipedia, Major Professional Sports Teams of the United States and Canada, April 5, 2018

CLIMATE

Average and Extreme Temperatures

Temperature	Jan	Feb	Mar	Apr	May	Jun	Jul	Aug	Sep	Oct	Nov	Dec	Yr.
Extreme High (°F)	62	69	78	85	93	104	107	104	100	89	75	67	107
Average High (°F)	37	43	52	62	72	83	93	90	80	66	50	38	64
Average Temp. (°F)	28	34	41	50	59	69	78	76	65	53	40	30	52
Average Low (°F)	19	24	31	38	46	54	62	61	51	40	30	22	40
Extreme Low (°F)	-22	-14	2	15	25	35	40	37	27	16	-14	-15	-22

Note: Figures cover the years 1948-1990
Source: National Climatic Data Center, International Station Meteorological Climate Summary, 9/96

Average Precipitation/Snowfall/Humidity

Precip./Humidity	Jan	Feb	Mar	Apr	May	Jun	Jul	Aug	Sep	Oct	Nov	Dec	Yr.
Avg. Precip. (in.)	1.3	1.2	1.8	2.0	1.7	0.9	0.8	0.9	1.1	1.3	1.3	1.4	15.6
Avg. Snowfall (in.)	13	10	11	6	1	Tr	0	0	Tr	2	6	13	63
Avg. Rel. Hum. 5am (%)	79	77	71	67	66	60	53	54	60	68	75	79	67
Avg. Rel. Hum. 5pm (%)	69	59	47	38	33	26	22	23	28	40	59	71	43

Note: Figures cover the years 1948-1990; Tr = Trace amounts (<0.05 in. of rain; <0.5 in. of snow)
Source: National Climatic Data Center, International Station Meteorological Climate Summary, 9/96

Weather Conditions

Temperature			Daytime Sky			Precipitation		
5°F & below	32°F & below	90°F & above	Clear	Partly cloudy	Cloudy	0.01 inch or more precip.	0.1 inch or more snow/ice	Thunderstorms
7	128	56	94	152	119	92	38	38

Note: Figures are average number of days per year and cover the years 1948-1990
Source: National Climatic Data Center, International Station Meteorological Climate Summary, 9/96

HAZARDOUS WASTE

Superfund Sites

The Provo-Orem, UT metro area is home to one site on the EPA's Superfund National Priorities List: **Eureka Mills** (final). There are a total of 1,396 Superfund sites with a status of proposed or final on the list in the U.S. *U.S. Environmental Protection Agency, National Priorities List, April 4, 2018*

AIR & WATER QUALITY

Air Quality Trends: Ozone

	1990	1995	2000	2005	2010	2012	2013	2014	2015	2016
MSA[1]	0.070	0.068	0.083	0.078	0.070	0.077	0.077	0.068	0.073	0.072
U.S.	0.087	0.089	0.081	0.079	0.073	0.075	0.069	0.067	0.068	0.069

Note: (1) Data covers the Provo-Orem, UT Metropolitan Statistical Area—see Appendix B for areas included. The values shown are the composite ozone concentration averages among trend sites based on the highest fourth daily maximum 8-hour concentration in parts per million. These trends are based on sites having an adequate record of monitoring data during the trend period. Data from exceptional events are included.
Source: U.S. Environmental Protection Agency, Air Quality Monitoring Information, "Air Quality Trends by City, 1990-2016"

Air Quality Index

Area	Percent of Days when Air Quality was...[2]					AQI Statistics[2]	
	Good	Moderate	Unhealthy for Sensitive Groups	Unhealthy	Very Unhealthy	Maximum	Median
MSA[1]	50.1	46.0	3.0	0.8	0.0	161	50

Note: (1) Data covers the Provo-Orem, UT Metropolitan Statistical Area—see Appendix B for areas included; (2) Based on 365 days with AQI data in 2017. Air Quality Index (AQI) is an index for reporting daily air quality. EPA calculates the AQI for five major air pollutants regulated by the Clean Air Act: ground-level ozone, particle pollution (aka particulate matter), carbon monoxide, sulfur dioxide, and nitrogen dioxide. The AQI runs from 0 to 500. The higher the AQI value, the greater the level of air pollution and the greater the health concern. There are six AQI categories: "Good" AQI is between 0 and 50. Air quality is considered satisfactory; "Moderate" AQI is between 51 and 100. Air quality is acceptable; "Unhealthy for Sensitive Groups" When AQI values are between 101 and 150, members of sensitive groups may experience health effects; "Unhealthy" When AQI values are between 151 and 200 everyone may begin to experience health effects; "Very Unhealthy" AQI values between 201 and 300 trigger a health alert; "Hazardous" AQI values over 300 trigger warnings of emergency conditions (not shown).
Source: U.S. Environmental Protection Agency, Air Quality Index Report, 2017

Air Quality Index Pollutants

Area	Percent of Days when AQI Pollutant was...[2]					
	Carbon Monoxide	Nitrogen Dioxide	Ozone	Sulfur Dioxide	Particulate Matter 2.5	Particulate Matter 10
MSA[1]	0.0	6.8	70.1	0.0	21.6	1.4

Note: (1) Data covers the Provo-Orem, UT Metropolitan Statistical Area—see Appendix B for areas included; (2) Based on 365 days with AQI data in 2017. The Air Quality Index (AQI) is an index for reporting daily air quality. EPA calculates the AQI for five major air pollutants regulated by the Clean Air Act: ground-level ozone, particle pollution (also known as particulate matter), carbon monoxide, sulfur dioxide, and nitrogen dioxide. The AQI runs from 0 to 500. The higher the AQI value, the greater the level of air pollution and the greater the health concern.
Source: U.S. Environmental Protection Agency, Air Quality Index Report, 2017

Maximum Air Pollutant Concentrations: Particulate Matter, Ozone, CO and Lead

	Particulate Matter 10 (ug/m³)	Particulate Matter 2.5 Wtd AM (ug/m³)	Particulate Matter 2.5 24-Hr (ug/m³)	Ozone (ppm)	Carbon Monoxide (ppm)	Lead (ug/m³)
MSA[1] Level	66	8.8	37	0.072	1	n/a
NAAQS[2]	150	15	35	0.075	9	0.15
Met NAAQS[2]	Yes	Yes	No	Yes	Yes	n/a

Note: (1) Data covers the Provo-Orem, UT Metropolitan Statistical Area—see Appendix B for areas included; Data from exceptional events are included; (2) National Ambient Air Quality Standards; ppm = parts per million; ug/m³ = micrograms per cubic meter; n/a not available.
Concentrations: Particulate Matter 10 (coarse particulate)—highest second maximum 24-hour concentration; Particulate Matter 2.5 Wtd AM (fine particulate)—highest weighted annual mean concentration; Particulate Matter 2.5 24-Hour (fine particulate)—highest 98th percentile 24-hour concentration; Ozone—highest fourth daily maximum 8-hour concentration; Carbon Monoxide—highest second maximum non-overlapping 8-hour concentration; Lead—maximum running 3-month average
Source: U.S. Environmental Protection Agency, Air Quality Monitoring Information, "Air Quality Statistics by City, 2016"

Maximum Air Pollutant Concentrations: Nitrogen Dioxide and Sulfur Dioxide

	Nitrogen Dioxide AM (ppb)	Nitrogen Dioxide 1-Hr (ppb)	Sulfur Dioxide AM (ppb)	Sulfur Dioxide 1-Hr (ppb)	Sulfur Dioxide 24-Hr (ppb)
MSA[1] Level	15	60	n/a	n/a	n/a
NAAQS[2]	53	100	30	75	140
Met NAAQS[2]	Yes	Yes	n/a	n/a	n/a

Note: (1) Data covers the Provo-Orem, UT Metropolitan Statistical Area—see Appendix B for areas included; Data from exceptional events are included; (2) National Ambient Air Quality Standards; ppm = parts per million; ug/m^3 = micrograms per cubic meter; n/a not available.
Concentrations: Nitrogen Dioxide AM—highest arithmetic mean concentration; Nitrogen Dioxide 1-Hr—highest 98th percentile 1-hour daily maximum concentration; Sulfur Dioxide AM—highest annual mean concentration; Sulfur Dioxide 1-Hr—highest 99th percentile 1-hour daily maximum concentration; Sulfur Dioxide 24-Hr—highest second maximum 24-hour concentration
Source: U.S. Environmental Protection Agency, Air Quality Monitoring Information, "Air Quality Statistics by City, 2016"

Drinking Water

Water System Name	Pop. Served	Primary Water Source Type	Violations[1] Health Based	Monitoring/ Reporting
Lehi City	54,382	Purchased Surface	0	0

Note: (1) Based on violation data from January 1, 2017 to December 31, 2017
Source: U.S. Environmental Protection Agency, Office of Ground Water and Drinking Water, Safe Drinking Water Information System (based on data extracted April 5, 2018)

Pleasant Grove, Utah

Background

Part of the Provo-Orem metro area, Pleasant Grove is located east of Utah Lake and south of Salt Lake City. The majestic Wasatch Mountains stretch to the west of Pleasant Grove, known as "Utah's City of Trees."

This was the site of a significant 1849 battle between the Mormons and the resident Timpanogos Ute Indians. When pioneers sent by Brigham Young came to make a settlement here in 1850, they marked this skirmish by calling their settlement Battle Creek. A grove of cottonwood trees drew the settlers. Pleasant Grove was incorporated in 1855.

Today, the city welcomes summer with its Strawberry Days celebration, a nod to the city's former status as the nation's highest-producing strawberry locale. The event, which began in June 1921, is replete with a rodeo, a parade, and a carnival—and is the state's longest continually running event.

With its easy access to the cultural and higher education offerings in the area, Pleasant Grove is seeing growth of its own. More than 800 high tech firms call Pleasant Grove home, more than 25 office and retail buildings are under construction, and hundreds of residential units are either under construction or on the drawing board. doTERRA International "a world leader in the sourcing, testing, manufacturing and distribution of pure, therapeutic-grade essential oils" plans to build its global corporate campus in Pleasant Grove, which is anticipated to house more than 750 workers when the $60 million project is finished. Also in the works is a Walmart Neighborhood Market, and a 45-acre Evermore Adventure Park, an interactive park, where visitors can choose their own adventure.

Local students attend the Alpine School District schools; district schools located in Pleasant Grove include three charter schools for grades K-8: John Hancock Charter School, the Lincoln Academy and Quail Run Primary School. Older students attend junior high and high school in town, and kids interested in an "ed-venture" in space can enjoy programs at the Christa McAuliffe Space Center. Nearby universities include Brigham Young University in Provo and Utah Valley University in Orem.

Recreation in the region can't be beat, with hiking and biking trails in the nearby canyons and mountains. The Uinta-Wasatch-Cache National Forest and Battle Creek Falls are close by. The city operates 13 parks that include a pool, sports fields, tennis courts, and picnic tables. There's also the Pleasant Grove Recreation Center, a 77,000-square foot facility that offers a range of fitness classes and equipment, as well as classes and programs ranging from a chef class to a youth fishing club.

Pleasant Grove's climate means snowy winters that appeal to skiers with 44 average inches of snowfall annually, and hot, dry summers that average in the low 90s come July. Spring and fall are pleasant and mild.

Rankings

Business/Finance Rankings

- The personal finance site NerdWallet analyzed 183 American metropolitan areas with populations over 250,000 and more than 15,000 businesses to rank where entrepreneurs find the most success. Criteria included area economy, annual income, housing cost, unemployment rate, and the success rate of area businesses. Provo* ranked #131. *www.nerdwallet.com, "Best Places to Start a Business," April 27, 2015*
- According to data by the Bureau of Economic Analysis (BEA) and the Bureau of Labor Statistics (BLS), the Provo* metro area has the fastest-growing GDP (gross domestic product) and positive employment trends, at #4. *247wallst.com, "Cities With the Fastest Growing (and Shrinking) Economies," September 26, 2016*
- 24/7 Wall Street used Brookings Institution research on 50 advanced industries to identify the proportion of workers in the nation's largest metropolitan areas that were employed in jobs requiring knowledge in the science, technology, engineering, or math (STEM) fields and where there was heavy investment in research and development (R&D). The Provo* metro area was #12. *247wallst.com, "15 Cities with the Most High-Tech Jobs," February 23, 2017*
- The Brookings Institution ranked the 100 largest metro areas in the U.S. based on income inequality. Provo* was ranked #99 (#1 = greatest ineqality). Criteria: the "95/20 ratio," a figure representing the income at which a household earns more than 95 percent of all other households, divided by the income at which a household earns more than only 20 percent of all other households. *Brookings Institution, "Household Income Inequality, 100 Largest U.S. Metro Areas, 2014-2016," February 5, 2018*
- The Provo* metro area appeared on the Milken Institute "2017 Best Performing Cities" list. Rank: #1 out of 200 large metro areas. Criteria: job growth; wage and salary growth; high-tech output growth. *Milken Institute, "Best-Performing Cities 2017," January 2018*
- *Forbes* ranked the 200 most populous metro areas to determine the nation's "Best Places for Business and Careers." The Provo* metro area was ranked #6. Criteria: costs (business and living); job growth (past and projected); income growth; quality of life; educational attainment (college and high school); projected economic growth; cultural and recreational opportunities; net migration patterns; number of highly ranked colleges. *Forbes, "The Best Places for Business and Careers 2017," October 24, 2017*

Children/Family Rankings

- *Forbes* analyzed data on the 100 largest metropolitan areas in the United States to compile its 2016 ranking of the best cities for raising a family. The Provo* metro area was ranked #1. Criteria: median income; childcare costs; percent of population under 18; commuting delays; crime rate; percentage of families owning homes; education quality (mainly test scores). Overall cost of living and housing affordability was also unofficially considered. *Forbes, "America's Best Cities for Raising a Family 2016," August 30, 2016*

Education Rankings

- Personal finance website *WalletHub* analyzed the 150 largest U.S. metropolitan statistical areas to determine where the most educated Americans are choosing to settle. Criteria: education quality and attainment gap; education levels; percentage of workers with degrees; public school rankings; quality and size of each metro area's universities. Provo* was ranked #7 (#1 = most educated city). *www.WalletHub.com, "2017's Most and Least Educated Cities in America, " July 25, 2017*

Environmental Rankings

- Sperling's BestPlaces assessed 379 metropolitan areas of the United States for the likelihood of dangerously extreme weather events or earthquakes. In general the Southeast and South-Central regions have the highest risk of weather extremes and earthquakes, while the Pacific Northwest enjoys the lowest risk. Of the least risky metropolitan areas, the Provo* metro area was ranked #29. *www.bestplaces.net, "Safest Places from Natural Disasters," April 2011*

Food/Drink Rankings

- For the Gallup-Healthways Well-Being Index, researchers interviewed at least 300 adults in each of 189 metropolitan areas on residents' access to affordable fresh produce. The Provo* metro area was found to be among the top ten communities for accessibility to affordable produce. *www.gallup.com, "In Anchorage, Access to Fruits and Vegetables Remains Lowest," April 8, 2014*

Health/Fitness Rankings

- Analysts who tracked obesity rates in 100 of the nation's most populous areas found that the Provo* metro area was one of the ten communities where residents were least likely to be obese, defined as a BMI score of 30 or above. *www.gallup.com, "Colorado Springs Residents Least Likely to Be Obese," May 28, 2015*

- Provo* was identified as a "2016 Spring Allergy Capital." The area ranked #98 out of 100. Three groups of factors were used to identify the most severe cities for people with allergies during the spring season: annual pollen levels; medicine utilization; access to board-certified allergists. *Asthma and Allergy Foundation of America, "Spring Allergy Capitals 2016"*

- Provo* was identified as a "2016 Fall Allergy Capital." The area ranked #91 out of 100. Three groups of factors were used to identify the most severe cities for people with allergies during the fall season: annual pollen levels; medicine utilization; access to board-certified allergists. *Asthma and Allergy Foundation of America, "Fall Allergy Capitals 2016"*

- Provo* was identified as a "2015 Asthma Capital." The area ranked #84 out of the nation's 100 largest metropolitan areas. Criteria: estimated prevalence; self-reported prevalence; crude death rate for asthma; annual pollen score; annual air quality; public smoking laws; number of board-certified asthma specialists; school inhaler access laws; rescue medication use; controller medication use; ER visits for asthma; uninsured rate; poverty rate. *Asthma and Allergy Foundation of America, "Asthma Capitals 2015"*

- The Provo* metro area ranked #29 out of 189 in The Gallup-Healthways Well-Being Index. Criteria: purpose; social well being; financial health; community and physical health. Results are based on telephone interviews with adults, aged 18 and older, living in metropolitan areas in the 50 U.S. states and the District of Columbia. *Gallup-Healthways, "State of American Well-Being, 2017 Community Well-Being Rankings" March 2018*

Real Estate Rankings

- The Provo* metro area was identified as one of the top 20 housing markets to invest in for 2018 by *Forbes*. The area ranked #2. Criteria: strong job and population growth; anticipated home price appreciation; and other factors. *Forbes.com, "Where to Invest in Housing in 2018," February 1, 2018*

- Provo* was ranked #170 out of 238 metro areas in terms of housing affordability in 2017 by the National Association of Home Builders (#1 = most affordable). Criteria: the share of homes sold in that area affordable to a family earning the local median income, based on standard mortgage underwriting criteria. *National Association of Home Builders®, NAHB-Wells Fargo Housing Opportunity Index, 4th Quarter 2017*

Safety Rankings

- The National Insurance Crime Bureau ranked 382 metro areas in the U.S. in terms of per capita rates of vehicle theft. The Provo* metro area ranked #280 (#1 = highest rate). Criteria: number of vehicle theft offenses per 100,000 inhabitants in 2016. *National Insurance Crime Bureau, "Hot Spots 2016," June 8, 2017*

Seniors/Retirement Rankings

- From its Best Cities for Successful Aging indexes, the Milken Institute generated rankings for metropolitan areas, weighing data in nine categories—health care, wellness, living arrangements, transportation and convenience, financial characteristics, education, employment, community engagement, and overall livability. The Provo* metro area was ranked #1 overall in the large metro area category. *Milken Institute, "Best Cities for Successful Aging, 2017" March 14, 2017*

Women/Minorities Rankings

- *24/7 Wall St.* compared median earnings over a 12-month period for men and women who worked full-time, year-round, and employment composition by sector to identify the worst-paying cities for women. Of the largest 100 U.S. metropolitan areas, Provo* was ranked #1 in pay disparity. *24/7 Wall St., "The Best (and Worst) Paying Cities for Women," March 27, 2017*

Miscellaneous Rankings

- The finance and lifestyle site NerdWallet looked for the U.S. cities that topped the list in donating money and time to good causes. The Provo* metro area proved to be the #1-ranked metro area, judged by culture of volunteerism, depth of commitment in terms of volunteer hours per year, and monetary contributions. *www.nerdwallet.com, "Most Generous Cities," September 22, 2013*

*Pleasant Grove is located within the Provo-Orem, UT Metropolitan Statistical Area.

Business Environment

CITY FINANCES

City Government Finances

Component	2015 ($000)	2015 ($ per capita)
Total Revenues	33,818	889
Total Expenditures	27,807	731
Debt Outstanding	61,734	1,622
Cash and Securities[1]	22,292	586

Note: (1) Cash and security holdings of a government at the close of its fiscal year,, including those of its dependent agencies, utilities, and liquor stores.
Source: U.S Census Bureau, State & Local Government Finances 2015

City Government Revenue by Source

Source	2015 ($000)	2015 ($ per capita)	2015 (%)
General Revenue			
From Federal Government	0	0	0.0
From State Government	1,408	37	4.2
From Local Governments	0	0	0.0
Taxes			
Property	3,077	81	9.1
Sales and Gross Receipts	6,427	169	19.0
Personal Income	0	0	0.0
Corporate Income	0	0	0.0
Motor Vehicle License	0	0	0.0
Other Taxes	979	26	2.9
Current Charges	10,134	266	30.0
Liquor Store	0	0	0.0
Utility	6,096	160	18.0
Employee Retirement	0	0	0.0

Source: U.S Census Bureau, State & Local Government Finances 2015

City Government Expenditures by Function

Function	2015 ($000)	2015 ($ per capita)	2015 (%)
General Direct Expenditures			
Air Transportation	0	0	0.0
Corrections	0	0	0.0
Education	0	0	0.0
Employment Security Administration	0	0	0.0
Financial Administration	0	0	0.0
Fire Protection	1,849	48	6.6
General Public Buildings	384	10	1.4
Governmental Administration, Other	1,016	26	3.7
Health	0	0	0.0
Highways	812	21	2.9
Hospitals	0	0	0.0
Housing and Community Development	1,325	34	4.8
Interest on General Debt	2,493	65	9.0
Judicial and Legal	317	8	1.1
Libraries	608	16	2.2
Parking	0	0	0.0
Parks and Recreation	3,359	88	12.1
Police Protection	4,228	111	15.2
Public Welfare	0	0	0.0
Sewerage	4,784	125	17.2
Solid Waste Management	1,361	35	4.9
Veterans' Services	0	0	0.0
Liquor Store	0	0	0.0
Utility	2,948	77	10.6
Employee Retirement	0	0	0.0

Source: U.S Census Bureau, State & Local Government Finances 2015

DEMOGRAPHICS

Population Growth

Area	1990 Census	2000 Census	2010 Census	2016* Estimate	Population Growth (%) 1990-2016	Population Growth (%) 2010-2016
City	14,047	23,468	33,509	36,678	161.1	9.5
MSA[1]	269,407	376,774	526,810	574,684	113.3	9.1
U.S.	248,709,873	281,421,906	308,745,538	318,558,162	28.1	3.2

Note: (1) Figures cover the Provo-Orem, UT Metropolitan Statistical Area—see Appendix B for areas included; (*) 2012-2016 5-year estimated population
Source: U.S. Census Bureau, 1990 Census, Census 2000, Census 2010, 2012-2016 American Community Survey 5-Year Estimates

Household Size

Area	Persons in Household (%) One	Two	Three	Four	Five	Six	Seven or More	Average Household Size
City	13.0	26.0	16.1	15.0	12.5	9.6	7.7	3.60
MSA[1]	11.9	27.3	15.6	16.5	12.7	9.4	6.7	3.60
U.S.	27.7	33.7	15.7	13.1	6.0	2.3	1.5	2.60

Note: (1) Figures cover the Provo-Orem, UT Metropolitan Statistical Area—see Appendix B for areas included
Source: U.S. Census Bureau, 2012-2016 American Community Survey 5-Year Estimates

Race

Area	White Alone[2] (%)	Black Alone[2] (%)	Asian Alone[2] (%)	AIAN[3] Alone[2] (%)	NHOPI[4] Alone[2] (%)	Other Race Alone[2] (%)	Two or More Races (%)
City	94.8	0.5	1.7	0.3	0.3	0.4	2.1
MSA[1]	92.2	0.6	1.4	0.5	0.7	1.8	2.7
U.S.	73.3	12.6	5.2	0.8	0.2	4.8	3.1

Note: (1) Figures cover the Provo-Orem, UT Metropolitan Statistical Area—see Appendix B for areas included; (2) Alone is defined as not being in combination with one or more other races; (3) American Indian and Alaska Native; (4) Native Hawaiian and Other Pacific Islander
Source: U.S. Census Bureau, 2012-2016 American Community Survey 5-Year Estimates

Hispanic or Latino Origin

Area	Total (%)	Mexican (%)	Puerto Rican (%)	Cuban (%)	Other (%)
City	7.3	4.5	0.5	0.0	2.2
MSA[1]	11.0	7.5	0.2	0.1	3.3
U.S.	17.3	11.0	1.7	0.7	4.0

Note: Persons of Hispanic or Latino origin can be of any race; (1) Figures cover the Provo-Orem, UT Metropolitan Statistical Area—see Appendix B for areas included
Source: U.S. Census Bureau, 2012-2016 American Community Survey 5-Year Estimates

Segregation

Type	Segregation Indices[1] 1990	2000	2010	2010 Rank[2]	Percent Change 1990-2000	1990-2010	2000-2010
Black/White	38.6	29.4	21.9	102	-9.2	-16.7	-7.5
Asian/White	32.3	31.5	28.2	94	-0.8	-4.1	-3.3
Hispanic/White	20.9	33.3	30.9	93	12.4	10.0	-2.4

Note: All figures cover the Metropolitan Statistical Area—see Appendix B for areas included; Figures are based on an analysis of 1990, 2000, and 2010 Census Decennial Census tract data by William H. Frey, Brookings Institution and the University of Michigan Social Science Data Analysis Network. In this analysis all racial groups (whites, blacks, and asians) are non-Hispanic members of those races. Hispanics are shown as a separate category; (1) Segregation Indices are Dissimilarity Indices that measure the degree to which the minority group is distributed differently than whites across census tracts. They range from 0 (complete integration) to 100 (complete segregation) where the value indicates the percentage of the minority group that needs to move to be distributed exactly like whites; (2) Ranges from 1 (most segregated) to 102 (least segregated); n/a not available.
Source: www.CensusScope.org

Ancestry

Area	German	Irish	English	American	Italian	Polish	French[2]	Scottish	Dutch
City	8.2	5.6	30.7	5.2	3.3	1.0	2.2	5.8	2.8
MSA[1]	11.1	5.1	28.7	5.2	2.4	0.7	2.1	5.4	1.9
U.S.	14.4	10.4	7.7	6.9	5.4	2.9	2.6	1.7	1.3

Note: Figures are the percentage of the total population reporting a particular ancestry. The nine most commonly reported ancestries in the U.S. are shown. Figures include multiple ancestries (e.g. if a person reported being Irish and Italian, they were included in both columns); (1) Figures cover the Provo-Orem, UT Metropolitan Statistical Area—see Appendix B for areas included; (2) Excludes Basque
Source: U.S. Census Bureau, 2012-2016 American Community Survey 5-Year Estimates

Foreign-Born Population

Area	Percent of Population Born in								
	Any Foreign Country	Asia	Mexico	Europe	Carribean	Central America[2]	South America	Africa	Canada
City	4.1	1.3	0.9	0.5	0.0	0.2	0.5	0.0	0.5
MSA[1]	6.9	1.1	2.8	0.5	0.1	0.5	1.2	0.1	0.3
U.S.	13.2	4.0	3.6	1.5	1.3	1.0	0.9	0.6	0.3

Note: (1) Figures cover the Provo-Orem, UT Metropolitan Statistical Area—see Appendix B for areas included; (2) Excludes Mexico.
Source: U.S. Census Bureau, 2012-2016 American Community Survey 5-Year Estimates

Marital Status

Area	Never Married	Now Married[2]	Separated	Widowed	Divorced
City	27.9	60.7	1.4	3.2	6.8
MSA[1]	32.0	58.5	1.0	2.6	5.9
U.S.	33.0	48.1	2.1	5.9	11.0

Note: Figures are percentages and cover the population 15 years of age and older; (1) Figures cover the Provo-Orem, UT Metropolitan Statistical Area—see Appendix B for areas included; (2) Excludes separated
Source: U.S. Census Bureau, 2012-2016 American Community Survey 5-Year Estimates

Disability Status

Area	All Ages	Under 18 Years Old	18 to 64 Years Old	65 Years and Over
City	8.5	2.9	7.9	40.8
MSA[1]	7.6	3.0	7.0	34.6
U.S.	12.5	4.1	10.3	35.7

Note: Figures show percent of the civilian noninstitutionalized population that reported having a disability. Disability status is determined from six types of difficulty: vision, hearing, cognitive, ambulatory, self-care, and independent living. For children under 5 years old, hearing and vision difficulty are used to determine disability status. For children between the ages of 5 and 14, disability status is determined from hearing, vision, cognitive, ambulatory, and self-care difficulties. For people aged 15 years and older, they are considered to have a disability if they have difficulty with any one of the six difficulty types; Note: (1) Figures cover the Provo-Orem, UT Metropolitan Statistical Area—see Appendix B for areas included
Source: U.S. Census Bureau, 2012-2016 American Community Survey 5-Year Estimates

Age

Area	Percent of Population									Median Age
	Under Age 5	Age 5–19	Age 20–34	Age 35–44	Age 45–54	Age 55–64	Age 65–74	Age 75–84	Age 85+	
City	10.6	29.4	24.8	12.2	8.8	7.1	4.6	1.9	0.7	26.0
MSA[1]	10.1	28.7	27.0	12.1	8.3	6.6	4.2	2.3	0.8	24.5
U.S.	6.2	19.6	20.7	12.7	13.6	12.6	8.3	4.3	1.9	37.7

Note: (1) Figures cover the Provo-Orem, UT Metropolitan Statistical Area—see Appendix B for areas included
Source: U.S. Census Bureau, 2012-2016 American Community Survey 5-Year Estimates

Gender

Area	Males	Females	Males per 100 Females
City	18,102	18,576	97.4
MSA[1]	289,878	284,806	101.8
U.S.	156,765,322	161,792,840	96.9

Note: (1) Figures cover the Provo-Orem, UT Metropolitan Statistical Area—see Appendix B for areas included
Source: U.S. Census Bureau, 2012-2016 American Community Survey 5-Year Estimates

Religious Groups by Family

Area	Catholic	Baptist	Non-Den.	Methodist[2]	Lutheran	LDS[3]	Pentecostal	Presbyterian[4]	Muslim[5]	Judaism
MSA[1]	1.3	0.1	0.1	0.2	<0.1	88.6	0.1	0.1	<0.1	<0.1
U.S.	19.1	9.3	4.0	4.0	2.3	2.0	1.9	1.6	0.8	0.7

Note: Figures are the number of adherents as a percentage of the total population; (1) Figures cover the Provo-Orem, UT Metropolitan Statistical Area—see Appendix B for areas included; (2) Methodist/Pietist; (3) Latter Day Saints; (4) Reformed; (5) Figures are estimates
Source: Association of Statisticians of American Religious Bodies, 2010 U.S. Religion Census: Religious Congregations & Membership Study

Religious Groups by Tradition

Area	Catholic	Evangelical Protestant	Mainline Protestant	Other Tradition	Black Protestant	Orthodox
MSA[1]	1.3	0.5	0.1	88.9	<0.1	<0.1
U.S.	19.1	16.2	7.3	4.3	1.6	0.3

Note: Figures are the number of adherents as a percentage of the total population; (1) Figures cover the Provo-Orem, UT Metropolitan Statistical Area—see Appendix B for areas included
Source: Association of Statisticians of American Religious Bodies, 2010 U.S. Religion Census: Religious Congregations & Membership Study

ECONOMY

Gross Metropolitan Product

Area	2014	2015	2016	2017	Rank[2]
MSA[1]	19.3	20.7	21.9	23.5	119

Note: Figures are in billions of dollars; (1) Figures cover the Provo-Orem, UT Metropolitan Statistical Area—see Appendix B for areas included; (2) Rank is based on 2015 data and ranges from 1 to 381
Source: The U.S. Conference of Mayors, U.S. Metro Economies: GMP and Employment Report, 2015-2017

Economic Growth

Area	2012-14 (%)	2015 (%)	2016 (%)	2017 (%)	Rank[2]
MSA[1]	3.9	6.6	3.9	5.1	30
U.S.	2.0	2.4	1.9	2.6	–

Note: Figures are real gross metropolitan product (GMP) growth rates and represent average annual percent change; (1) Figures cover the Provo-Orem, UT Metropolitan Statistical Area—see Appendix B for areas included; (2) Rank is based on 2012-2014 average annual percent change and ranges from 1 to 381
Source: The U.S. Conference of Mayors, U.S. Metro Economies: GMP and Employment Report, 2015-2017

Metropolitan Area Exports

Area	2011	2012	2013	2014	2015	2016	Rank[2]
MSA[1]	2,056.4	2,058.1	2,789.2	2,533.4	2,216.4	1,894.8	98

Note: Figures are in millions of dollars; (1) Figures cover the Provo-Orem, UT Metropolitan Statistical Area—see Appendix B for areas included; (2) Rank is based on 2016 data and ranges from 1 to 385
Source: U.S. Department of Commerce, International Trade Administration, Office of Trade & Industry Information, Manufacturing & Services, data extracted March 15, 2018

Building Permits

Area	Single-Family			Multi-Family			Total		
	2016	2017p	Pct. Chg.	2016	2017p	Pct. Chg.	2016	2017p	Pct. Chg.
City	114	66	-42.1	10	5	-50.0	124	71	-42.7
MSA[1]	4,417	5,082	15.1	888	2,155	142.7	5,305	7,237	36.4
U.S.	750,800	817,300	8.9	455,800	446,800	-2.0	1,206,600	1,264,100	4.8

Note: (1) Figures cover the Provo-Orem, UT Metropolitan Statistical Area—see Appendix B for areas included; Figures represent new, privately-owned housing units authorized (unadjusted data); All permit data are based on estimates with imputation; (p) preliminary data.
Source: U.S. Census Bureau, Manufacturing, Mining, and Construction Statistics, Building Permits, 2016, 2017

Bankruptcy Filings

Area	Business Filings 2016	Business Filings 2017	Business Filings % Chg.	Nonbusiness Filings 2016	Nonbusiness Filings 2017	Nonbusiness Filings % Chg.
Utah County	41	36	-12.2	1,588	1,598	0.6
U.S.	24,114	23,157	-4.0	770,846	765,863	-0.6

Note: Business filings include Chapter 7, Chapter 11, Chapter 12, and Chapter 13; Nonbusiness filings include Chapter 7, Chapter 11, and Chapter 13
Source: Administrative Office of the U.S. Courts, Business and Nonbusiness Bankruptcy, County Cases Commenced by Chapter of the Bankruptcy Code, During the 12-Month Period Ending December 31, 2016 and Business and Nonbusiness Bankruptcy, County Cases Commenced by Chapter of the Bankruptcy Code, During the 12-Month Period Ending December 31, 2017

Housing Vacancy Rates

Area	Gross Vacancy Rate[2] (%)			Year-Round Vacancy Rate[3] (%)			Rental Vacancy Rate[4] (%)			Homeowner Vacancy Rate[5] (%)		
	2015	2016	2017	2015	2016	2017	2015	2016	2017	2015	2016	2017
MSA[1]	n/a	n/a	n/a	n/a	n/a	n/a	n/a	n/a	n/a	n/a	n/a	n/a
U.S.	12.9	12.8	12.7	10.0	9.9	9.9	7.1	6.9	7.2	1.8	1.7	1.6

Note: (1) Figures cover the Provo-Orem, UT Metropolitan Statistical Area—see Appendix B for areas included; (2) The percentage of the total housing inventory that is vacant; (3) The percentage of the housing inventory (excluding seasonal units) that is year-round vacant; (4) The percentage of rental inventory that is vacant for rent; (5) The percentage of homeowner inventory that is vacant for sale; n/a not available
Source: U.S. Census Bureau, Housing Vacancies and Homeownership Annual Statistics: 2015, 2016, 2017

INCOME

Income

Area	Per Capita ($)	Median Household ($)	Average Household ($)
City	21,768	64,124	77,670
MSA[1]	22,035	63,994	79,701
U.S.	29,829	55,322	77,866

Note: (1) Figures cover the Provo-Orem, UT Metropolitan Statistical Area—see Appendix B for areas included
Source: U.S. Census Bureau, 2012-2016 American Community Survey 5-Year Estimates

Household Income Distribution

Area	Percent of Households Earning							
	Under $15,000	$15,000 -$24,999	$25,000 -$34,999	$35,000 -$49,999	$50,000 -$74,999	$75,000 -$99,999	$100,000 -$149,999	$150,000 and up
City	7.5	6.8	6.1	14.4	23.7	16.8	15.5	9.2
MSA[1]	7.8	7.9	8.3	13.4	21.3	15.5	16.1	9.6
U.S.	12.1	10.2	9.9	13.2	17.8	12.2	13.5	11.1

Note: (1) Figures cover the Provo-Orem, UT Metropolitan Statistical Area—see Appendix B for areas included
Source: U.S. Census Bureau, 2012-2016 American Community Survey 5-Year Estimates

Poverty Rate

Area	All Ages	Under 18 Years Old	18 to 64 Years Old	65 Years and Over
City	12.1	12.9	12.2	7.5
MSA[1]	12.6	11.4	14.1	5.8
U.S.	15.1	21.2	14.2	9.3

Note: Figures are percentage of people whose income during the past 12 months was below the poverty level; (1) Figures cover the Provo-Orem, UT Metropolitan Statistical Area—see Appendix B for areas included
Source: U.S. Census Bureau, 2012-2016 American Community Survey 5-Year Estimates

EMPLOYMENT

Labor Force and Employment

Area	Civilian Labor Force Dec. 2016	Civilian Labor Force Dec. 2017	Civilian Labor Force % Chg.	Workers Employed Dec. 2016	Workers Employed Dec. 2017	Workers Employed % Chg.
City	18,762	19,613	4.5	18,269	19,138	4.8
MSA[1]	290,826	304,146	4.6	283,195	296,661	4.8
U.S.	158,968,000	159,880,000	0.6	151,798,000	153,602,000	1.2

Note: Data is not seasonally adjusted and covers workers 16 years of age and older; (1) Figures cover the Provo-Orem, UT Metropolitan Statistical Area—see Appendix B for areas included
Source: Bureau of Labor Statistics, Local Area Unemployment Statistics

Unemployment Rate

Area	2017											
	Jan.	Feb.	Mar.	Apr.	May	Jun.	Jul.	Aug.	Sep.	Oct.	Nov.	Dec.
City	3.0	3.2	2.9	2.8	2.9	3.4	3.3	3.3	2.8	2.8	2.5	2.4
MSA[1]	3.1	3.2	3.1	2.8	2.9	3.4	3.2	3.1	2.7	2.6	2.4	2.5
U.S.	5.1	4.9	4.6	4.1	4.1	4.5	4.6	4.5	4.1	3.9	3.9	3.9

Note: Data is not seasonally adjusted and covers workers 16 years of age and older; (1) Figures cover the Provo-Orem, UT Metropolitan Statistical Area—see Appendix B for areas included
Source: Bureau of Labor Statistics, Local Area Unemployment Statistics

Average Wages

Occupation	$/Hr.	Occupation	$/Hr.
Accountants and Auditors	32.70	Maids and Housekeeping Cleaners	10.60
Automotive Mechanics	19.70	Maintenance and Repair Workers	18.60
Bookkeepers	17.90	Marketing Managers	51.90
Carpenters	19.00	Nuclear Medicine Technologists	n/a
Cashiers	10.30	Nurses, Licensed Practical	19.60
Clerks, General Office	14.60	Nurses, Registered	29.60
Clerks, Receptionists/Information	13.00	Nursing Assistants	12.20
Clerks, Shipping/Receiving	14.30	Packers and Packagers, Hand	11.40
Computer Programmers	42.60	Physical Therapists	42.50
Computer Systems Analysts	46.20	Postal Service Mail Carriers	23.60
Computer User Support Specialists	22.40	Real Estate Brokers	28.10
Cooks, Restaurant	12.50	Retail Salespersons	12.20
Dentists	n/a	Sales Reps., Exc. Tech./Scientific	28.30
Electrical Engineers	39.90	Sales Reps., Tech./Scientific	33.80
Electricians	26.10	Secretaries, Exc. Legal/Med./Exec.	15.30
Financial Managers	50.20	Security Guards	14.50
First-Line Supervisors/Managers, Sales	17.90	Surgeons	n/a
Food Preparation Workers	11.30	Teacher Assistants*	12.10
General and Operations Managers	38.90	Teachers, Elementary School*	30.60
Hairdressers/Cosmetologists	11.20	Teachers, Secondary School*	30.60
Internists, General	n/a	Telemarketers	17.40
Janitors and Cleaners	9.90	Truck Drivers, Heavy/Tractor-Trailer	19.70
Landscaping/Groundskeeping Workers	13.50	Truck Drivers, Light/Delivery Svcs.	16.10
Lawyers	59.00	Waiters and Waitresses	10.90

Note: Wage data covers the Provo-Orem, UT Metropolitan Statistical Area—see Appendix B for areas included; (*) Hourly wages for elementary/secondary school teachers and teacher assistants were calculated by the editors from annual wage data based on a 40 hour work week; n/a not available.
Source: Bureau of Labor Statistics, Metro Area Occupational Employment & Wage Estimates, May 2017

Employment by Occupation

Occupation Classification	City (%)	MSA[1] (%)	U.S. (%)
Management, Business, Science, and Arts	40.3	40.3	37.0
Natural Resources, Construction, and Maintenance	6.5	7.6	8.9
Production, Transportation, and Material Moving	10.7	10.2	12.2
Sales and Office	28.6	26.4	23.8
Service	13.9	15.4	18.1

Note: Figures cover employed civilians 16 years of age and older; (1) Figures cover the Provo-Orem, UT Metropolitan Statistical Area—see Appendix B for areas included
Source: U.S. Census Bureau, 2012-2016 American Community Survey 5-Year Estimates

Employment by Industry

Sector	MSA[1] Number of Employees	MSA[1] Percent of Total	U.S. Percent of Total
Construction, Mining, and Logging	25,000	9.8	5.2
Education and Health Services	54,500	21.3	15.9
Financial Activities	8,600	3.4	5.7
Government	32,100	12.5	15.3
Information	12,200	4.8	1.9
Leisure and Hospitality	20,200	7.9	10.7
Manufacturing	19,400	7.6	8.5
Other Services	5,400	2.1	3.9
Professional and Business Services	34,000	13.3	14.0
Retail Trade	34,200	13.3	11.0
Transportation, Warehousing, and Utilities	3,800	1.5	4.1
Wholesale Trade	6,800	2.7	4.0

Note: Figures are non-farm employment as of December 2017. Figures are not seasonally adjusted and include workers 16 years of age and older; (1) Figures cover the Provo-Orem, UT Metropolitan Statistical Area—see Appendix B for areas included
Source: Bureau of Labor Statistics, Current Employment Statistics, Employment, Hours, and Earnings

Occupations with Greatest Projected Employment Growth: 2017 – 2019

Occupation[1]	2017 Employment	2019 Projected Employment	Numeric Employment Change	Percent Employment Change
Combined Food Preparation and Serving Workers, Including Fast Food	40,810	43,640	2,830	6.9
Customer Service Representatives	44,760	46,800	2,040	4.6
Construction Laborers	17,940	19,780	1,840	10.3
General and Operations Managers	29,140	30,980	1,840	6.3
Carpenters	15,870	17,610	1,740	10.9
Heavy and Tractor-Trailer Truck Drivers	24,080	25,570	1,490	6.2
Janitors and Cleaners, Except Maids and Housekeeping Cleaners	22,610	23,970	1,360	6.0
Retail Salespersons	47,280	48,580	1,300	2.7
Laborers and Freight, Stock, and Material Movers, Hand	19,560	20,850	1,290	6.6
Registered Nurses	22,690	23,950	1,260	5.6

Note: Projections cover Utah; (1) Sorted by numeric employment change
Source: www.projectionscentral.com, State Occupational Projections, 2017–2019 Short-Term Projections

Fastest Growing Occupations: 2017 – 2019

Occupation[1]	2017 Employment	2019 Projected Employment	Numeric Employment Change	Percent Employment Change
Roofers	2,300	2,640	340	14.7
Brickmasons and Blockmasons	2,310	2,650	340	14.6
Plasterers and Stucco Masons	660	750	90	13.9
Roustabouts, Oil and Gas	1,170	1,330	160	13.8
Cement Masons and Concrete Finishers	3,470	3,930	460	13.2
Helpers—Brickmasons, Blockmasons, Stonemasons, and Tile and Marble Setters	690	780	90	13.0
Stonemasons	360	410	50	12.8
Helpers—Pipelayers, Plumbers, Pipefitters, and Steamfitters	570	640	70	12.6
Plumbers, Pipefitters, and Steamfitters	6,750	7,590	840	12.5
Software Developers, Applications	8,310	9,330	1,020	12.3

Note: Projections cover Utah; (1) Sorted by percent employment change and excludes occupations with numeric employment change less than 50
Source: www.projectionscentral.com, State Occupational Projections, 2017–2019 Short-Term Projections

TAXES

State Corporate Income Tax Rates

State	Tax Rate (%)	Income Brackets ($)	Num. of Brackets	Financial Institution Tax Rate (%)[a]	Federal Income Tax Ded.
Utah	5.0 (b)	Flat rate	–	5.0 (b)	No

Note: Tax rates as of January 1, 2018; (a) Rates listed are the corporate income tax rate applied to financial institutions or excise taxes based on income. Some states have other taxes based upon the value of deposits or shares; (b) Minimum tax is $800 in California, $100 in District of Columbia and Arizona, $50 in North Dakota (banks), $500 in Rhode Island, $200 per location in South Dakota (banks), $100 in Utah, $250 in Vermont.
Source: Federation of Tax Administrators, Range of State Corporate Income Tax Rates, January 1, 2018

State Individual Income Tax Rates

State	Tax Rate (%)	Income Brackets ($)	Num. of Brackets	Personal Exempt. ($)[1]		Fed. Inc. Tax Ded.
				Single	Dependents	
Utah	5.0	Flat rate	1	(v)	(v)	No

Note: Tax rates as of January 1, 2018; Local- and county-level taxes are not included; n/a not applicable; (1) Married joint filers generally receive double the single exemption; (v) Utah provides a tax credit equal to 6% of the federal personal exemption amounts (and applicable standard deduction). Note, the Tax Cut and Reform Act of 2017 has eliminated personal exemptions and increased the standard deduction in the IRC. Utah will need to enact legislation to reinstate a personal credit for tax year 2018.
Source: Federation of Tax Administrators, State Individual Income Tax Rates, January 1, 2018

Various State Sales and Excise Tax Rates

State	State Sales Tax (%)	Gasoline[1] (¢/gal.)	Cigarette[2] ($/pack)	Spirits[3] ($/gal.)	Wine[4] ($/gal.)	Beer[5] ($/gal.)	Recreational Marijuana (%)
Utah	5.95 (b)	29.41	1.70	15.38 (g)	(m)	0.41 (q)	Not legal

Note: All tax rates as of January 1, 2018; (1) The American Petroleum Institute has developed a methodology for determining the average tax rate on a gallon of fuel. Rates may include any of the following: excise taxes, environmental fees, storage tank fees, other fees or taxes, general sales tax, and local taxes. In states where gasoline is subject to the general sales tax, or where the fuel tax is based on the average sale price, the average rate determined by API is sensitive to changes in the price of gasoline. States that fully or partially apply general sales taxes to gasoline: CA, CO, GA, IL, IN, MI, NY; (2) The federal excise tax of $1.0066 per pack and local taxes are not included; (3) Rates are those applicable to off-premise sales of 40% alcohol by volume (a.b.v.) distilled spirits in 750ml containers. Local excise taxes are excluded; (4) Rates are those applicable to off-premise sales of 11% a.b.v. non-carbonated wine in 750ml containers; (5) Rates are those applicable to off-premise sales of 4.7% a.b.v. beer in 12 ounce containers; (b) Three states levy mandatory, statewide, local add-on sales taxes at the state level: California (1.25%), Utah (1.25%), Virginia (1%), we include these in their state sales tax; (g) Control states, where the government controls all sales. Products can be subject to ad valorem mark-up as well as excise taxes; (m) Control states, where the government controls all sales. Products can be subject to ad valorem mark-up as well as excise taxes; (q) Different rates also applicable according to alcohol content, place of production, size of container, or place purchased (on- or off-premise or onboard airlines).
Source: Tax Foundation, 2018 Facts & Figures: How Does Your State Compare?

State Business Tax Climate Index Rankings

State	Overall Rank	Corporate Tax Rank	Individual Income Tax Rank	Sales Tax Rank	Unemployment Insurance Tax Rank	Property Tax Rank
Utah	8	4	11	17	21	5

Note: The index is a measure of how each state's tax laws affect economic performance. The lower the rank, the more favorable a state's tax system is for business. States without a given tax are given a ranking of 1. The scores/rankings for the District of Columbia do not affect other states. The 2018 index represents the tax climate as of July 1, 2017.
Source: Tax Foundation, State Business Tax Climate Index 2018

TRANSPORTATION

Means of Transportation to Work

Area	Car/Truck/Van		Public Transportation			Bicycle	Walked	Other Means	Worked at Home
	Drove Alone	Car-pooled	Bus	Subway	Railroad				
City	77.5	10.8	1.6	0.0	0.3	0.6	1.1	1.7	6.5
MSA[1]	73.1	12.1	0.9	0.2	0.7	1.1	4.1	1.4	6.3
U.S.	76.4	9.3	2.6	1.9	0.6	0.6	2.8	1.3	4.6

Note: Figures are percentages and cover workers 16 years of age and older; (1) Figures cover the Provo-Orem, UT Metropolitan Statistical Area—see Appendix B for areas included
Source: U.S. Census Bureau, 2012-2016 American Community Survey 5-Year Estimates

Travel Time to Work

Area	Less Than 10 Minutes	10 to 19 Minutes	20 to 29 Minutes	30 to 44 Minutes	45 to 59 Minutes	60 to 89 Minutes	90 Minutes or More
City	17.2	34.4	23.5	13.9	6.1	3.2	1.6
MSA[1]	19.1	35.9	19.7	14.6	5.3	3.6	1.6
U.S.	12.9	29.2	20.9	20.4	8.0	6.0	2.7

Note: Note: Figures are percentages and include workers 16 years old and over; (1) Figures cover the Provo-Orem, UT Metropolitan Statistical Area—see Appendix B for areas included
Source: U.S. Census Bureau, 2012-2016 American Community Survey 5-Year Estimates

Freeway Travel Time Index

Area	1985	1990	1995	2000	2005	2010	2014
Urban Area Rank[1,2]	64	76	84	86	86	92	91
Urban Area Index[1]	1.05	1.07	1.08	1.10	1.12	1.11	1.12
Average Index[3]	1.09	1.11	1.14	1.17	1.20	1.19	1.20

Note: Freeway Travel Time Index—the ratio of travel time in the peak period to the travel time at free-flow conditions. For example, a value of 1.30 indicates a 20-minute free-flow trip takes 26 minutes in the peak (20 minutes x 1.30 = 26 minutes); (1) Covers the Provo-Orem UT urban area; (2) Rank is based on 101 urban areas (#1 = highest travel time index); (3) Average of 101 urban areas
Source: Texas Transportation Institute, 2015 Urban Mobility Scorecard, August 2015

Freeway Commuter Stress Index

Area	1985	1990	1995	2000	2005	2010	2014
Urban Area Rank[1,2]	81	94	93	94	94	96	94
Urban Area Index[1]	1.06	1.07	1.09	1.11	1.13	1.12	1.13
Average Index[3]	1.13	1.16	1.19	1.22	1.25	1.24	1.25

Note: The Freeway Commuter Stress Index is the same as the Freeway Travel Time Index (see table above) except that it includes only the travel in the peak directions during the peak periods; the TTI includes travel in all directions during the peak period. Thus, the CSI is more indicative of the work trip experienced by each commuter on a daily basis; (1) Covers the Provo-Orem UT urban area; (2) Rank is based on 101 urban areas (#1 = highest travel time index); (3) Average of 101 urban areas
Source: Texas Transportation Institute, 2015 Urban Mobility Scorecard, August 2015

Living Environment

COST OF LIVING

Cost of Living Index

Composite Index	Groceries	Housing	Utilities	Trans-portation	Health Care	Misc. Goods/ Services
98.0	100.0	100.4	72.6	101.9	110.9	99.8

Note: The Cost of Living Index measures regional differences in the cost of consumer goods and services, excluding taxes and non-consumer expenditures, for professional and managerial households in the top income quintile. It is based on more than 50,000 prices covering almost 60 different items for which prices are collected three times a year by chambers of commerce, economic development organizations or university applied economic centers in each participating urban area. The numbers shown should be read as a percentage above or below the national average of 100. For example, a value of 115.4 in the groceries column indicates that grocery prices are 15.4% higher than the national average. Small differences in the index numbers should not be interpreted as significant; Figures cover the Provo-Orem UT urban area.
Source: The Council for Community and Economic Research, ACCRA Cost of Living Index, 2017

Grocery Prices

Area[1]	T-Bone Steak ($/pound)	Frying Chicken ($/pound)	Whole Milk ($/half gal.)	Eggs ($/dozen)	Orange Juice ($/64 oz.)	Coffee ($/11.5 oz.)
City[2]	10.90	1.47	1.57	1.89	3.84	4.40
Avg.	11.29	1.40	2.02	1.47	3.55	4.37
Min.	7.71	0.93	1.04	0.70	2.86	3.24
Max.	15.83	2.39	4.03	3.92	6.29	8.16

Note: (1) Values for the local area are compared with the average, minimum and maximum values for all 294 areas in the Cost of Living Index; (2) Figures cover the Provo-Orem UT urban area; ***T-Bone Steak*** *(price per pound);* ***Frying Chicken*** *(price per pound, whole fryer);* ***Whole Milk*** *(half gallon carton);* ***Eggs*** *(price per dozen, Grade A, large);* ***Orange Juice*** *(64 oz. Tropicana or Florida Natural);* ***Coffee*** *(11.5 oz. can, vacuum-packed, Maxwell House, Hills Bros, or Folgers).*
Source: The Council for Community and Economic Research, ACCRA Cost of Living Index, 2017

Housing and Utility Costs

Area[1]	New Home Price ($)	Apartment Rent ($/month)	All Electric ($/month)	Part Electric ($/month)	Other Energy ($/month)	Telephone ($/month)
City[2]	353,645	992	-	67.76	62.38	19.00
Avg.	335,956	1,047	175.01	97.34	67.93	28.71
Min.	187,788	491	109.48	49.33	35.44	12.39
Max.	1,739,087	4,559	432.62	227.09	353.33	44.61

Note: (1) Values for the local area are compared with the average, minimum and maximum values for all 294 areas in the Cost of Living Index; (2) Figures cover the Provo-Orem UT urban area; ***New Home Price*** *(2,400 sf living area, 8,000 sf lot, in urban area with full utilities);* ***Apartment Rent*** *(950 sf 2 bedroom/1.5 or 2 bath, unfurnished, excluding all utilities except water);* ***All Electric*** *(average monthly cost for an all-electric home);* ***Part Electric*** *(average monthly cost for a part-electric home);* ***Other Energy*** *(average monthly cost for natural gas, fuel oil, coal, wood, and any other forms of energy except electricity);* ***Telephone*** *(price includes basic monthly rate for a private residential line plus additional local usage charges incurred by a family of four).*
Source: The Council for Community and Economic Research, ACCRA Cost of Living Index, 2017

Health Care, Transportation, and Other Costs

Area[1]	Doctor ($/visit)	Dentist ($/visit)	Optometrist ($/visit)	Gasoline ($/gallon)	Beauty Salon ($/visit)	Men's Shirt ($)
City[2]	105.68	119.67	92.59	2.23	33.57	31.19
Avg.	108.00	92.54	101.93	2.25	37.58	30.92
Min.	30.39	60.00	49.75	1.82	16.11	11.20
Max.	193.50	161.94	229.28	3.16	77.35	59.13

Note: (1) Values for the local area are compared with the average, minimum and maximum values for all 294 areas in the Cost of Living Index; (2) Figures cover the Provo-Orem UT urban area; ***Doctor*** *(general practitioners routine exam of an established patient);* ***Dentist*** *(adult teeth cleaning and periodic oral examination);* ***Optometrist*** *(full vision eye exam for established adult patient);* ***Gasoline*** *(one gallon regular unleaded, national brand, including all taxes, cash price at self-service pump if available);* ***Beauty Salon*** *(woman's shampoo, trim, and blow-dry);* ***Men's Shirt*** *(cotton/polyester dress shirt, pinpoint weave, long sleeves).*
Source: The Council for Community and Economic Research, ACCRA Cost of Living Index, 2017

HOUSING

House Price Index (HPI)

Area	National Ranking[2]	Quarterly Change (%)	One-Year Change (%)	Five-Year Change (%)
MSA[1]	41	0.30	9.55	45.03
U.S.[3]	–	1.61	6.68	34.71

Note: The HPI is a weighted repeat sales index. It measures average price changes in repeat sales or refinancings on the same properties. This information is obtained by reviewing repeat mortgage transactions on single-family properties whose mortgages have been purchased or securitized by Fannie Mae or Freddie Mac in January 1975; (1) Figures cover the Provo-Orem, UT Metropolitan Statistical Area—see Appendix B for areas included; (2) Rankings are based on annual percentage change for all metro areas containing at least 15,000 transactions over the last 10 years and ranges from 1 to 253; (3) figures based on a weighted average of Census Division estimates using a seasonally adjusted, purchase-only index; all figures are for the period ending December 31, 2017
Source: Federal Housing Finance Agency, House Price Index, February 28, 2018

Median Single-Family Home Prices

Area	2015	2016	2017p	Percent Change 2016 to 2017
MSA[1]	n/a	n/a	n/a	n/a
U.S. Average	223.9	235.5	248.8	5.6

Note: Figures are median sales prices of existing single-family homes in thousands of dollars; (p) preliminary; n/a not available; (1) Figures cover the Provo-Orem, UT Metropolitan Statistical Area—see Appendix B for areas included
Source: National Association of Realtors, Median Sales Price of Existing Single-Family Homes for Metropolitan Areas, 4th Quarter 2017

Qualifying Income Based on Median Sales Price of Existing Single-Family Homes

Area	With 5% Down ($)	With 10% Down ($)	With 20% Down ($)
MSA[1]	n/a	n/a	n/a
U.S. Average	55,585	52,659	46,808

Note: Figures are preliminary; Qualifying income is based on a mortgage rate of 4.17%. Monthly principal and interest payment is limited to 25% of income; n/a not available; (1) Figures cover the Provo-Orem, UT Metropolitan Statistical Area—see Appendix B for areas included
Source: National Association of Realtors, Qualifying Income Based on Median Sales Price of Existing Single-Family Homes for Metropolitan Areas, 4th Quarter 2017

Median Apartment Condo-Coop Home Prices

Area	2015	2016	2017p	Percent Change 2016 to 2017
MSA[1]	n/a	n/a	n/a	n/a
U.S. Average	210.7	220.7	234.3	6.2

Note: Figures are median sales prices of existing apartment condo-coop homes in thousands of dollars; (p) preliminary; n/a not available; (1) Figures cover the Provo-Orem, UT Metropolitan Statistical Area—see Appendix B for areas included
Source: National Association of Realtors, Median Sales Price of Existing Apartment Condo-Coop Homes for Metropolitan Areas, 4th Quarter 2017

Home Value Distribution

Area	Under $50,000	$50,000 -$99,999	$100,000 -$149,999	$150,000 -$199,999	$200,000 -$299,999	$300,000 -$499,999	$500,000 -$999,999	$1,000,000 or more
City	2.9	2.0	11.6	20.8	33.3	23.0	5.9	0.5
MSA[1]	3.3	1.5	9.8	20.0	34.6	23.1	6.7	1.0
U.S.	8.8	14.8	15.3	14.9	18.4	16.4	9.0	2.5

Note: Figures are percentages and cover owner-occupied housing units; (1) Figures cover the Provo-Orem, UT Metropolitan Statistical Area—see Appendix B for areas included
Source: U.S. Census Bureau, 2012-2016 American Community Survey 5-Year Estimates

Homeownership Rate

Area	2009 (%)	2010 (%)	2011 (%)	2012 (%)	2013 (%)	2014 (%)	2015 (%)	2016 (%)	2017 (%)
MSA[1]	n/a	n/a	n/a	n/a	n/a	n/a	n/a	n/a	n/a
U.S.	67.4	66.9	66.1	65.4	65.1	64.5	63.7	63.4	63.9

Note: (1) Figures cover the Provo-Orem, UT Metropolitan Statistical Area—see Appendix B for areas included; n/a not available
Source: U.S. Census Bureau, Housing Vacancies and Homeownership Annual Statistics: 2009-2017

Year Housing Structure Built

Area	2010 or Later	2000 -2009	1990 -1999	1980 -1989	1970 -1979	1960 -1969	1950 -1959	1940 -1949	Before 1940	Median Year
City	6.0	33.0	23.2	7.1	16.7	2.1	4.4	2.8	4.7	1995
MSA[1]	5.5	29.0	20.6	9.6	15.7	5.4	5.2	3.5	5.4	1992
U.S.	2.3	14.7	14.0	13.7	15.6	10.9	10.6	5.2	13.0	1977

Note: Figures are percentages except for Median Year; Note: (1) Figures cover the Provo-Orem, UT Metropolitan Statistical Area—see Appendix B for areas included
Source: U.S. Census Bureau, 2012-2016 American Community Survey 5-Year Estimates

Gross Monthly Rent

Area	Under $500	$500 -$999	$1,000 -$1,499	$1,500 -$1,999	$2,000 -$2,499	$2,500 -$2,999	$3,000 and up	Median ($)
City	3.7	39.2	46.4	7.3	2.9	0.2	0.3	1,051
MSA[1]	8.3	49.5	28.3	10.3	2.6	0.6	0.3	916
U.S.	11.3	43.3	27.7	10.7	4.0	1.6	1.5	949

Note: Figures are percentages except for Median; Gross rent is the contract rent plus the estimated average monthly cost of utilities (electricity, gas, and water and sewer) and fuels (oil, coal, kerosene, wood, etc.) if these are paid by the renter (or paid for the renter by someone else); (1) Figures cover the Provo-Orem, UT Metropolitan Statistical Area—see Appendix B for areas included
Source: U.S. Census Bureau, 2012-2016 American Community Survey 5-Year Estimates

HEALTH

Health Risk Factors

Category	MSA[1] (%)	U.S. (%)
Adults aged 18–64 who have any kind of health care coverage	87.9	87.7
Adults who reported being in good or excellent health	90.0	83.6
Adults who are current smokers	5.2	17.1
Adults who currently use E-cigarettes	3.9	4.7
Adults who currently use chewing tobacco, snuff, or snus	2.2	4.0
Adults who are heavy drinkers[2]	3.4	6.5
Adults who are binge drinkers[3]	7.2	16.9
Adults who are overweight (BMI 25.0 - 29.9)	34.2	35.3
Adults who are obese (BMI 30.0 - 99.8)	22.5	29.9
Adults who participated in any physical activities in the past month	87.4	76.9
Adults who always or nearly always wears a seat belt	95.7	94.3

Note: (1) Figures cover the Provo-Orem, UT Metropolitan Statistical Area—see Appendix B for areas included; (2) Heavy drinkers are classified as adult men having more than 14 drinks per week and adult women having more than 7 drinks per week; (3) Binge drinkers are classified as males having five or more drinks on one occasion or females having four or more drinks on one occasion
Source: Centers for Disease Control and Prevention, Behaviorial Risk Factor Surveillance System, SMART: Selected Metropolitan Area Risk Trends, 2016

Health Screening Rates

Category	MSA[1] (%)	U.S. (%)
Adults 50-75 who have had a blood stool test within the past year	n/a	8.0
Adults 50-75 who have had a colonoscopy in the past 10 years	69.6	63.5
Adults aged 65+ who have had flu shot within the past year	52.9	58.6
Adults aged 65+ who have ever had a pneumonia vaccination	66.2	73.4
Adults who have ever been tested for HIV	18.6	35.6
Women aged 21-65 who have had a pap test in the past three years	72.7	79.8
Men aged 40+ who have had a PSA test within the past two years	36.0	39.5
Women aged 40+ who have had a mammogram within the past two years	64.3	72.5

Note: n/a not available; (1) Figures cover the Provo-Orem, UT Metropolitan Statistical Area—see Appendix B for areas included; Source: Centers for Disease Control and Prevention, Behaviorial Risk Factor Surveillance System, SMART: Selected Metropolitan Area Risk Trends, 2016

Chronic Health Conditions

Category	MSA[1] (%)	U.S. (%)
Adults who have ever been told they had a heart attack	2.0	4.4
Adults who have ever been told they have angina or coronary heart disease	2.0	4.1
Adults who have ever been told they had a stroke	1.7	3.1
Adults who have been told they currently have asthma	7.0	9.3
Adults who have ever been told they have arthritis	15.5	25.8
Adults who have ever been told they have diabetes[2]	6.3	10.5
Adults who have ever been told they had skin cancer	5.7	5.9
Adults who have ever been told they had any other types of cancer	4.3	6.7
Adults who have ever been told they have COPD	3.3	6.3
Adults who have ever been told they have kidney disease	2.7	2.8
Adults who have ever been told they have a form of depression	23.8	17.4

Note: (1) Figures cover the Provo-Orem, UT Metropolitan Statistical Area—see Appendix B for areas included; (2) Figures do not include pregnancy-related, borderline, or pre-diabetes
Source: Centers for Disease Control and Prevention, Behaviorial Risk Factor Surveillance System, SMART: Selected Metropolitan Area Risk Trends, 2016

Mortality Rates for the Top 10 Causes of Death in the U.S.

ICD-10[a] Sub-Chapter	ICD-10[a] Code	Age-Adjusted Mortality Rate[1] per 100,000 population	
		County[2]	U.S.
Malignant neoplasms	C00-C97	118.1	158.5
Ischaemic heart diseases	I20-I25	62.5	96.8
Other forms of heart disease	I30-I51	85.4	52.4
Chronic lower respiratory diseases	J40-J47	27.9	40.9
Cerebrovascular diseases	I60-I69	41.0	37.2
Organic, including symptomatic, mental disorders	F01-F09	42.2	33.3
Other degenerative diseases of the nervous system	G30-G31	37.6	32.1
Other external causes of accidental injury	W00-X59	31.4	31.2
Diabetes mellitus	E10-E14	23.6	21.1
Hypertensive diseases	I10-I15	10.7	20.8

Note: (a) ICD-10 = International Classification of Diseases 10th Revision; (1) Mortality rates are a three year average covering 2014-2016; (2) Figures cover Utah County.
Source: Centers for Disease Control and Prevention, National Center for Health Statistics. Underlying Cause of Death 1999-2016 on CDC WONDER Online Database, released December 2017

Mortality Rates for Selected Causes of Death

ICD-10[a] Sub-Chapter	ICD-10[a] Code	Age-Adjusted Mortality Rate[1] per 100,000 population	
		County[2]	U.S.
Assault	X85-Y09	1.4	5.6
Diseases of the liver	K70-K76	9.7	14.0
Human immunodeficiency virus (HIV) disease	B20-B24	Suppressed	1.9
Influenza and pneumonia	J09-J18	15.3	14.6
Intentional self-harm	X60-X84	16.4	13.2
Malnutrition	E40-E46	2.8	1.3
Obesity and other hyperalimentation	E65-E68	1.9	2.1
Renal failure	N17-N19	19.9	13.0
Transport accidents	V01-V99	7.1	12.0
Viral hepatitis	B15-B19	Unreliable	1.9

Note: (a) ICD-10 = International Classification of Diseases 10th Revision; (1) Mortality rates are a three year average covering 2014-2016; (2) Figures cover Utah County; Data are Suppressed when the data meet the criteria for confidentiality constraints; Mortality rates are flagged as Unreliable when the rate would be calculated with a numerator of 20 or less.
Source: Centers for Disease Control and Prevention, National Center for Health Statistics. Underlying Cause of Death 1999-2016 on CDC WONDER Online Database, released December 2017

Health Insurance Coverage

Area	With Health Insurance	With Private Health Insurance	With Public Health Insurance	Without Health Insurance	Population Under Age 18 Without Health Insurance
City	90.0	79.9	16.2	10.0	7.6
MSA[1]	89.7	79.5	17.2	10.3	7.2
U.S.	88.3	66.7	33.0	11.7	5.9

Note: Figures are percentages that cover the civilian noninstitutionalized population; (1) Figures cover the Provo-Orem, UT Metropolitan Statistical Area—see Appendix B for areas included
Source: U.S. Census Bureau, 2012-2016 American Community Survey 5-Year Estimates

Number of Medical Professionals

Area	MDs[3]	DOs[3,4]	Dentists	Podiatrists	Chiropractors	Optometrists
County[1] (number)	681	103	361	24	141	61
County[1] (rate[2])	118.8	18.0	61.1	4.1	23.9	10.3
U.S. (rate[2])	276.5	22.3	67.3	6.0	26.7	15.9

Note: Data as of 2016 unless noted; (1) Data covers Utah County; (2) Rate per 100,000 population; (3) Data as of 2015 and includes all active, non-federal physicians; (4) Doctor of Osteopathic Medicine
Source: U.S. Department of Health and Human Services, Health Resources and Services Administration, Bureau of Health Professions, Area Resource File (ARF) 2016-2017

EDUCATION

Public School District Statistics

District Name	Schls	Pupils	Pupil/ Teacher Ratio	Minority Pupils[1] (%)	Free Lunch Eligible[2] (%)	IEP[3] (%)
Alpine District	86	76,938	n/a	16.6	16.7	10.8
Canyon Grove Academy	1	380	n/a	26.1	32.6	15.3
John Hancock Charter School	1	189	n/a	18.0	22.8	7.9
Lincoln Academy	1	863	n/a	12.2	10.1	10.7
Spectrum Academy	2	1,030	n/a	11.8	26.6	81.7

Note: Table includes school districts with 100 or more students; (1) Percentage of students that are not non-Hispanic white; (2) Percentage of students that are eligible for the free lunch program; (3) Percentage of students that have an Individualized Education Program.
Source: U.S. Department of Education, National Center for Education Statistics, Common Core of Data, Local Education Agency (School District) Universe Survey: School Year 2015-2016; U.S. Department of Education, National Center for Education Statistics, Common Core of Data, Public Elementary/Secondary School Universe Survey: School Year 2015-2016

Highest Level of Education

Area	Less than H.S.	H.S. Diploma	Some College, No Deg.	Associate Degree	Bachelor's Degree	Master's Degree	Prof. School Degree	Doctorate Degree
City	5.3	17.6	27.8	12.5	26.7	8.5	0.6	1.0
MSA[1]	6.4	17.0	27.8	11.1	26.0	8.3	1.6	1.8
U.S.	13.0	27.5	21.0	8.2	18.8	8.2	2.0	1.3

Note: Figures cover persons age 25 and over; (1) Figures cover the Provo-Orem, UT Metropolitan Statistical Area—see Appendix B for areas included
Source: U.S. Census Bureau, 2012-2016 American Community Survey 5-Year Estimates

Educational Attainment by Race

Area	High School Graduate or Higher (%)					Bachelor's Degree or Higher (%)				
	Total	White	Black	Asian	Hisp.[2]	Total	White	Black	Asian	Hisp.[2]
City	94.7	95.0	100.0	96.1	74.0	36.8	37.1	0.0	37.4	30.5
MSA[1]	93.6	94.2	90.6	92.0	70.5	37.7	37.9	37.1	57.1	18.1
U.S.	87.0	88.9	84.3	86.3	65.7	30.3	31.6	20.0	52.1	14.7

Note: Figures shown cover persons 25 years old and over; (1) Figures cover the Provo-Orem, UT Metropolitan Statistical Area—see Appendix B for areas included; (2) People of Hispanic origin can be of any race
Source: U.S. Census Bureau, 2012-2016 American Community Survey 5-Year Estimates

School Enrollment by Grade and Control

Area	Preschool (%)		Kindergarten (%)		Grades 1 - 4 (%)		Grades 5 - 8 (%)		Grades 9 - 12 (%)	
	Public	Private	Public	Private	Public	Private	Public	Private	Public	Private
City	57.0	43.0	89.1	10.9	93.9	6.1	92.7	7.3	97.7	2.3
MSA[1]	46.7	53.3	91.9	8.1	94.6	5.4	95.0	5.0	95.0	5.0
U.S.	58.4	41.6	87.7	12.3	89.8	10.2	89.7	10.3	90.4	9.6

Note: Figures shown cover persons 3 years old and over; (1) Figures cover the Provo-Orem, UT Metropolitan Statistical Area—see Appendix B for areas included
Source: U.S. Census Bureau, 2012-2016 American Community Survey 5-Year Estimates

Average Salaries of Public School Classroom Teachers

Area	2015		2016		Change from 2015 to 2016	
	Dollars	Rank[1]	Dollars	Rank[1]	Percent	Rank[2]
Utah	46,689	44	46,887	45	0.4	33
U.S. Average	57,611	–	58,353	–	1.3	–

Note: (1) Rank ranges from 1 to 51 where 1 indicates highest salary; (2) Rank ranges from 1 to 51 where 1 indicates highest percent change.
Source: National Education Association, Rankings & Estimates: Rankings of the States 2016 and Estimates of School Statistics 2017

Higher Education

Four-Year Colleges			Two-Year Colleges			Medical Schools[1]	Law Schools[2]	Voc/ Tech[3]
Public	Private Non-profit	Private For-profit	Public	Private Non-profit	Private For-profit			
0	0	0	0	0	0	0	0	0

Note: Figures cover institutions located within the city limits and include main campuses only; (1) includes schools accredited by the Liaison Committee on Medical Education and the American Osteopathic Association's Commission on Osteopathic College Accreditation; (2) includes ABA-accredited schools, schools with provisional ABA accreditation, and state accredited schools; (3) includes all schools with programs that are less than 2 years.
Source: National Center for Education Statistics, Integrated Postsecondary Education System (IPEDS), 2016-17; Wikipedia, List of Medical Schools in the United States, accessed April 2, 2018; Wikipedia, List of Law Schools in the United States, accessed April 2, 2018

According to *U.S. News & World Report,* the Provo-Orem, UT metro area is home to one of the best national universities in the U.S.: **Brigham Young University—Provo** (#61 tie). The indicators used to capture academic quality fall into a number of categories: assessment by administrators at peer institutions; retention of students; faculty resources; student selectivity; financial resources; alumni giving; high school counselor ratings of colleges; and graduation rate. *U.S. News & World Report, "America's Best Colleges 2018"*

According to *U.S. News & World Report,* the Provo-Orem, UT metro area is home to one of the top 100 law schools in the U.S.: **Brigham Young University (Clark)** (#41 tie). The rankings are based on a weighted average of 12 measures of quality: peer assessment score; assessment score by lawyers/judges; median LSAT scores; median undergrad GPA; acceptance rate; employment rates for graduates; placement success; bar passage rate; faculty resources; expenditures per student; student/faculty ratio; and library resources. *U.S. News & World Report, "America's Best Graduate Schools, Law, 2019"*

According to *U.S. News & World Report,* the Provo-Orem, UT metro area is home to one of the top 75 business schools in the U.S.: **Brigham Young University (Marriott)** (#35). The rankings are based on a weighted average of the following nine measures: quality assessment; peer assessment; recruiter assessment; placement success; mean starting salary and bonus; student selectivity; mean GMAT and GRE scores; mean undergraduate GPA; and acceptance rate. *U.S. News & World Report, "America's Best Graduate Schools, Business, 2019"*

PRESIDENTIAL ELECTION

2016 Presidential Election Results

Area	Clinton	Trump	Johnson	Stein	Other
Utah County	14.0	50.2	3.2	0.5	32.2
U.S.	48.0	45.9	3.3	1.1	1.7

Note: Results are percentages and may not add to 100% due to rounding
Source: Dave Leip's Atlas of U.S. Presidential Elections

EMPLOYERS

Major Employers

Company Name	Industry
About Time Technologies	Movements, clock or watch
Ancestry.com	Communication services, nec
Brigham Young University	Colleges & universities
City of Provo	Mayors' office
Intermountain Health Care	General medical & surgical hospitals
Morinda Holdings	Bottled & canned soft drinks
Novell	Prepackaged software
Nu Skin Enterprises United States	Drugs, proprietaries, & sundries
Nu Skin International	Toilet preparations
Phone Directories Company	Directories, phone: publish only, not printed on site
Rbm Services	Building cleaning service
TPUSA	Telemarketing services
Utah Dept of Human Services	Mental hospital, except for the mentally retarded
Utah Valley University	Colleges, except junior
Wal-Mart Stores	Department stores, discount
Wasatch Summit	Management consulting services
Xango	Drugs, proprietaries, & sundries

Note: Companies shown are located within the Provo-Orem, UT Metropolitan Statistical Area.
Source: Hoovers.com; Wikipedia

PUBLIC SAFETY

Crime Rate

Area	All Crimes	Violent Crimes				Property Crimes		
		Murder	Rape[3]	Robbery	Aggrav. Assault	Burglary	Larceny -Theft	Motor Vehicle Theft
City	677.2	2.6	2.6	0.0	25.7	105.2	520.7	20.5
Metro[1]	1,838.9	0.8	27.4	10.7	38.7	207.1	1,462.7	91.6
U.S.	2,847.8	5.3	40.4	102.8	248.5	468.9	1,745.0	236.9

Note: Figures are crimes per 100,000 population; (1) Figures cover the Provo-Orem, UT Metropolitan Statistical Area—see Appendix B for areas included; (3) The city and U.S. figures shown were reported using the revised Uniform Crime Reporting (UCR) definition of rape. The metro area figures shown are an aggregate total of the data submitted using both the revised and legacy UCR definitions.
Source: FBI Uniform Crime Reports, 2016

Hate Crimes

Area	Number of Quarters Reported	Number of Incidents per Bias Motivation					
		Race/Ethnicity/ Ancestry	Religion	Sexual Orientation	Disability	Gender	Gender Identity
City	4	0	0	0	0	0	0
U.S.	4	3,489	1,273	1,076	70	31	124

Source: Federal Bureau of Investigation, Hate Crime Statistics 2016

Identity Theft Consumer Reports

Area	Reports	Reports per 100,000 Population	Rank[2]
MSA[1]	421	70	254
U.S.	371,061	114	-

Note: (1) Figures cover the Provo-Orem, UT Metropolitan Statistical Area—see Appendix B for areas included; (2) Rank ranges from 1 to 389 where 1 indicates greatest number of identity theft reports per 100,000 population
Source: Federal Trade Commission, Consumer Sentinel Network Data Book for January–December 2017

Fraud and Other Consumer Reports

Area	Reports	Reports per 100,000 Population	Rank[2]
MSA[1]	1,694	281	367
U.S.	2,304,550	708	-

Note: (1) Figures cover the Provo-Orem, UT Metropolitan Statistical Area—see Appendix B for areas included; (2) Rank ranges from 1 to 389 where 1 indicates greatest number of fraud and other consumer reports per 100,000 population
Source: Federal Trade Commission, Consumer Sentinel Network Data Book for January–December 2017

SPORTS

Professional Sports Teams

Team Name	League	Year Established

No teams are located in the metro area
Source: Wikipedia, Major Professional Sports Teams of the United States and Canada, April 5, 2018

CLIMATE

Average and Extreme Temperatures

Temperature	Jan	Feb	Mar	Apr	May	Jun	Jul	Aug	Sep	Oct	Nov	Dec	Yr.
Extreme High (°F)	62	69	78	85	93	104	107	104	100	89	75	67	107
Average High (°F)	37	43	52	62	72	83	93	90	80	66	50	38	64
Average Temp. (°F)	28	34	41	50	59	69	78	76	65	53	40	30	52
Average Low (°F)	19	24	31	38	46	54	62	61	51	40	30	22	40
Extreme Low (°F)	-22	-14	2	15	25	35	40	37	27	16	-14	-15	-22

Note: Figures cover the years 1948-1990
Source: National Climatic Data Center, International Station Meteorological Climate Summary, 9/96

Average Precipitation/Snowfall/Humidity

Precip./Humidity	Jan	Feb	Mar	Apr	May	Jun	Jul	Aug	Sep	Oct	Nov	Dec	Yr.
Avg. Precip. (in.)	1.3	1.2	1.8	2.0	1.7	0.9	0.8	0.9	1.1	1.3	1.3	1.4	15.6
Avg. Snowfall (in.)	13	10	11	6	1	Tr	0	0	Tr	2	6	13	63
Avg. Rel. Hum. 5am (%)	79	77	71	67	66	60	53	54	60	68	75	79	67
Avg. Rel. Hum. 5pm (%)	69	59	47	38	33	26	22	23	28	40	59	71	43

Note: Figures cover the years 1948-1990; Tr = Trace amounts (<0.05 in. of rain; <0.5 in. of snow)
Source: National Climatic Data Center, International Station Meteorological Climate Summary, 9/96

Weather Conditions

Temperature			Daytime Sky			Precipitation		
5°F & below	32°F & below	90°F & above	Clear	Partly cloudy	Cloudy	0.01 inch or more precip.	0.1 inch or more snow/ice	Thunder-storms
7	128	56	94	152	119	92	38	38

Note: Figures are average number of days per year and cover the years 1948-1990
Source: National Climatic Data Center, International Station Meteorological Climate Summary, 9/96

HAZARDOUS WASTE

Superfund Sites

The Provo-Orem, UT metro area is home to one site on the EPA's Superfund National Priorities List: **Eureka Mills** (final). There are a total of 1,396 Superfund sites with a status of proposed or final on the list in the U.S. *U.S. Environmental Protection Agency, National Priorities List, April 4, 2018*

AIR & WATER QUALITY

Air Quality Trends: Ozone

	1990	1995	2000	2005	2010	2012	2013	2014	2015	2016
MSA[1]	0.070	0.068	0.083	0.078	0.070	0.077	0.077	0.068	0.073	0.072
U.S.	0.087	0.089	0.081	0.079	0.073	0.075	0.069	0.067	0.068	0.069

Note: (1) Data covers the Provo-Orem, UT Metropolitan Statistical Area—see Appendix B for areas included. The values shown are the composite ozone concentration averages among trend sites based on the highest fourth daily maximum 8-hour concentration in parts per million. These trends are based on sites having an adequate record of monitoring data during the trend period. Data from exceptional events are included.
Source: U.S. Environmental Protection Agency, Air Quality Monitoring Information, "Air Quality Trends by City, 1990-2016"

Air Quality Index

Area	Percent of Days when Air Quality was...[2]					AQI Statistics[2]	
	Good	Moderate	Unhealthy for Sensitive Groups	Unhealthy	Very Unhealthy	Maximum	Median
MSA[1]	50.1	46.0	3.0	0.8	0.0	161	50

Note: (1) Data covers the Provo-Orem, UT Metropolitan Statistical Area—see Appendix B for areas included; (2) Based on 365 days with AQI data in 2017. Air Quality Index (AQI) is an index for reporting daily air quality. EPA calculates the AQI for five major air pollutants regulated by the Clean Air Act: ground-level ozone, particle pollution (aka particulate matter), carbon monoxide, sulfur dioxide, and nitrogen dioxide. The AQI runs from 0 to 500. The higher the AQI value, the greater the level of air pollution and the greater the health concern. There are six AQI categories: "Good" AQI is between 0 and 50. Air quality is considered satisfactory; "Moderate" AQI is between 51 and 100. Air quality is acceptable; "Unhealthy for Sensitive Groups" When AQI values are between 101 and 150, members of sensitive groups may experience health effects; "Unhealthy" When AQI values are between 151 and 200 everyone may begin to experience health effects; "Very Unhealthy" AQI values between 201 and 300 trigger a health alert; "Hazardous" AQI values over 300 trigger warnings of emergency conditions (not shown).
Source: U.S. Environmental Protection Agency, Air Quality Index Report, 2017

Air Quality Index Pollutants

Area	Percent of Days when AQI Pollutant was...[2]					
	Carbon Monoxide	Nitrogen Dioxide	Ozone	Sulfur Dioxide	Particulate Matter 2.5	Particulate Matter 10
MSA[1]	0.0	6.8	70.1	0.0	21.6	1.4

Note: (1) Data covers the Provo-Orem, UT Metropolitan Statistical Area—see Appendix B for areas included; (2) Based on 365 days with AQI data in 2017. The Air Quality Index (AQI) is an index for reporting daily air quality. EPA calculates the AQI for five major air pollutants regulated by the Clean Air Act: ground-level ozone, particle pollution (also known as particulate matter), carbon monoxide, sulfur dioxide, and nitrogen dioxide. The AQI runs from 0 to 500. The higher the AQI value, the greater the level of air pollution and the greater the health concern.
Source: U.S. Environmental Protection Agency, Air Quality Index Report, 2017

Maximum Air Pollutant Concentrations: Particulate Matter, Ozone, CO and Lead

	Particulate Matter 10 (ug/m^3)	Particulate Matter 2.5 Wtd AM (ug/m^3)	Particulate Matter 2.5 24-Hr (ug/m^3)	Ozone (ppm)	Carbon Monoxide (ppm)	Lead (ug/m^3)
MSA[1] Level	66	8.8	37	0.072	1	n/a
NAAQS[2]	150	15	35	0.075	9	0.15
Met NAAQS[2]	Yes	Yes	No	Yes	Yes	n/a

Note: (1) Data covers the Provo-Orem, UT Metropolitan Statistical Area—see Appendix B for areas included; Data from exceptional events are included; (2) National Ambient Air Quality Standards; ppm = parts per million; ug/m^3 = micrograms per cubic meter; n/a not available.
Concentrations: Particulate Matter 10 (coarse particulate)—highest second maximum 24-hour concentration; Particulate Matter 2.5 Wtd AM (fine particulate)—highest weighted annual mean concentration; Particulate Matter 2.5 24-Hour (fine particulate)—highest 98th percentile 24-hour concentration; Ozone—highest fourth daily maximum 8-hour concentration; Carbon Monoxide—highest second maximum non-overlapping 8-hour concentration; Lead—maximum running 3-month average
Source: U.S. Environmental Protection Agency, Air Quality Monitoring Information, "Air Quality Statistics by City, 2016"

Maximum Air Pollutant Concentrations: Nitrogen Dioxide and Sulfur Dioxide

	Nitrogen Dioxide AM (ppb)	Nitrogen Dioxide 1-Hr (ppb)	Sulfur Dioxide AM (ppb)	Sulfur Dioxide 1-Hr (ppb)	Sulfur Dioxide 24-Hr (ppb)
MSA[1] Level	15	60	n/a	n/a	n/a
NAAQS[2]	53	100	30	75	140
Met NAAQS[2]	Yes	Yes	n/a	n/a	n/a

Note: (1) Data covers the Provo-Orem, UT Metropolitan Statistical Area—see Appendix B for areas included; Data from exceptional events are included; (2) National Ambient Air Quality Standards; ppm = parts per million; ug/m^3 = micrograms per cubic meter; n/a not available.

Concentrations: Nitrogen Dioxide AM—highest arithmetic mean concentration; Nitrogen Dioxide 1-Hr—highest 98th percentile 1-hour daily maximum concentration; Sulfur Dioxide AM—highest annual mean concentration; Sulfur Dioxide 1-Hr—highest 99th percentile 1-hour daily maximum concentration; Sulfur Dioxide 24-Hr—highest second maximum 24-hour concentration

Source: U.S. Environmental Protection Agency, Air Quality Monitoring Information, "Air Quality Statistics by City, 2016"

Drinking Water

Water System Name	Pop. Served	Primary Water Source Type	Violations[1]	
			Health Based	Monitoring/ Reporting
Pleasant Grove City	40,000	Ground	0	6

Note: (1) Based on violation data from January 1, 2017 to December 31, 2017

Source: U.S. Environmental Protection Agency, Office of Ground Water and Drinking Water, Safe Drinking Water Information System (based on data extracted April 5, 2018)

South Jordan, Utah

Background

South Jordan, in southern Salt Lake County, is located 15 miles from Salt Lake City. The city adjoins West Jordan to the north, Sandy to the east, and Riverton to the south. South Jordan is one of the fastest growing cities in Utah and is carefully planning for controlled future development in order to preserve the unique quality of life enjoyed by its citizens.

The region's first inhabitants were the Ute Indians. Mormon pioneers began immigrating to the area in July 1847, and within two years, several communities emerged throughout the valley. A small number of settlers traveled across the Jordan River to establish homes and farms, raise livestock, and grow grain and alfalfa. South Jordan itself was settled in 1857 by Alexander and Catherine Lince Beckstead. After digging their first home out of a cave in the riverbank, the Beckstead family built the "Beckstead Ditch," bringing water from the Jordan River to irrigate crops.

South Jordan was primarily a rural farming community in its earliest years. During most of the twentieth century, the area's major crop was sugar beets, but today, only grain and hay are grown to feed horses and cattle. South Jordan was incorporated in 1935.

The state of Utah experienced a tremendous growth spurt during the 1990s, upon which South Jordan is capitalizing as it clears and zones substantial tracts of land for business development. Close proximity to Salt Lake City International Airport also favorably positions South Jordan for growth. To meet future transportation needs of this growing population, the Mountain View Corridor (MVC), a planned freeway servicing 13 municipalities, including South Jordan, was recently completed.

The city has seven elementary schools, two middle schools, three high schools and several other/private schools. In Salt Lake City, higher learning is represented by the University of Utah, Westminster College, L.D.S. Business College, and Salt Lake Community College, among others.

South Jordan lies in an extraordinarily beautiful region. The Bingham open-pit copper mine and the Oquirrh Mountains are visible several miles to the west. The city boasts more than 25 municipal parks and playgrounds of varying sizes and there are over 10 golf courses in the area, including a private golf course within the city, as well as a county-operated equestrian complex and racetrack. The ski resorts closest to South Jordan have an average annual snowfall of nearly 42 feet covering a wide variety of terrain from gentle runs and winding cross-country trails to helicopter-accessed peaks.

A wealth of cultural and recreational attractions can be pursued in nearby Salt Lake City, including the Utah Museum of Fine Arts, the Clark Planetarium, Red Butte Garden at the University of Utah, the Tracy Aviary, the new Natural History Museum of Utah at Rio Tinto Center, and the Hogle Zoo. In South Jordan there is the Gale Center of History & Culture which promotes the city's history and culture and is open six days a week with free admission.

The climate of South Jordan, like that of Salt Lake City and other nearby communities, is semi-arid and continental, with some moderating of temperatures by the Great Salt Lake. Summers are generally hot and dry; winters are cold but not severe. Mountains act as a barrier to frequent invasions of cold air. Temperature inversions can occur in winter, when heavy fog at ground level is held down by warmer air aloft.

Rankings

General Rankings

- *US News & World Report* conducted a survey of more than 2,000 people and analyzed the 125 largest metropolitan areas to determine what matters the most when selecting the next place to live. Salt Lake City* ranked #15 out of the top 25 as having the best combination of desirable factors. Criteria: cost of living; quality of education; job market, crime rates; and other factors. *realestate.usnews.com, "The 25 Best Places to Live in the U.S. in 2018," April 10, 2018*

- The Salt Lake City* metro area was identified as one of America's fastest-growing areas in terms of population and economy by *Forbes*. The area ranked #24 out of 25. The 100 most populous metro areas in the U.S. were evaluated on the following criteria: estimated population growth; employment; economic output; wages; home values. *Forbes, "America's Fastest-Growing Cities 2018," February 28, 2018*

Business/Finance Rankings

- The personal finance site NerdWallet analyzed 183 American metropolitan areas with populations over 250,000 and more than 15,000 businesses to rank where entrepreneurs find the most success. Criteria included area economy, annual income, housing cost, unemployment rate, and the success rate of area businesses. Salt Lake City* ranked #15. *www.nerdwallet.com, "Best Places to Start a Business," April 27, 2015*

- The editors of *Kiplinger's Personal Finance Magazine* named Salt Lake City* to their list of ten of the best metro areas for start-ups. The area ranked #6.Criteria: well-educated workforce; low living costs for self-employed people, as measured by the Council for Community and Economic Research; a strong existing community of small business; low unemployment; low business costs. *www.kiplinger.com, "10 Great Cities for Starting a Business," October 2014*

- The Brookings Institution ranked the 100 largest metro areas in the U.S. based on income inequality. Salt Lake City* was ranked #98 (#1 = greatest ineqality). Criteria: the "95/20 ratio," a figure representing the income at which a household earns more than 95 percent of all other households, divided by the income at which a household earns more than only 20 percent of all other households. *Brookings Institution, "Household Income Inequality, 100 Largest U.S. Metro Areas, 2014-2016," February 5, 2018*

- *Forbes* ranked the 100 largest metro areas in the U.S. in terms of the "Best Cities for Young Professionals." The Salt Lake City* metro area ranked #3 out of 25. (Large metro areas were divided into metro divisions.) Criteria: median rent of a two-bedroom apartment; job growth and unemployment rate; median salary of college graduates with 5 or less years of work experience; networking opportunities; social outlook; percentage of population 25 years of age and older with college degrees. *Forbes.com, "America's 25 Best Cities for Young Professionals in 2017," May 22, 2017*

- The Salt Lake City* metro area appeared on the Milken Institute "2017 Best Performing Cities" list. Rank: #10 out of 200 large metro areas. Criteria: job growth; wage and salary growth; high-tech output growth. *Milken Institute, "Best-Performing Cities 2017," January 2018*

- *Forbes* ranked the 200 most populous metro areas to determine the nation's "Best Places for Business and Careers." The Salt Lake City* metro area was ranked #14. Criteria: costs (business and living); job growth (past and projected); income growth; quality of life; educational attainment (college and high school); projected economic growth; cultural and recreational opportunities; net migration patterns; number of highly ranked colleges. *Forbes, "The Best Places for Business and Careers 2017," October 24, 2017*

Children/Family Rankings

- *Forbes* analyzed data on the 100 largest metropolitan areas in the United States to compile its 2016 ranking of the best cities for raising a family. The Salt Lake City* metro area was ranked #17. Criteria: median income; childcare costs; percent of population under 18; commuting delays; crime rate; percentage of families owning homes; education quality (mainly test scores). Overall cost of living and housing affordability was also unofficially considered. *Forbes, "America's Best Cities for Raising a Family 2016," August 30, 2016*

Education Rankings

- Personal finance website *WalletHub* analyzed the 150 largest U.S. metropolitan statistical areas to determine where the most educated Americans are choosing to settle. Criteria: education quality and attainment gap; education levels; percentage of workers with degrees; public school rankings; quality and size of each metro area's universities. Salt Lake City* was ranked #32 (#1 = most educated city). *www.WalletHub.com, "2017's Most and Least Educated Cities in America," July 25, 2017*

Environmental Rankings

- Sperling's BestPlaces assessed 379 metropolitan areas of the United States for the likelihood of dangerously extreme weather events or earthquakes. In general the Southeast and South-Central regions have the highest risk of weather extremes and earthquakes, while the Pacific Northwest enjoys the lowest risk. Of the least risky metropolitan areas, the Salt Lake City* metro area was ranked #56. *www.bestplaces.net, "Safest Places from Natural Disasters," April 2011*
- Salt Lake City* was highlighted as one of the 25 most ozone-polluted metro areas in the U.S. during 2013 through 2015. The area ranked #20. *American Lung Association, State of the Air 2017*
- Salt Lake City* was highlighted as one of the 25 metro areas most polluted by short-term particle pollution (24-hour PM 2.5) in the U.S. during 2013 through 2015. The area ranked #7. *American Lung Association, State of the Air 2017*

Health/Fitness Rankings

- For each of the 50 most populous metro areas in the United States, the American College of Sports Medicine's American Fitness Index evaluated infrastructure, community assets, and policies that encourage healthy and fit lifestyles, including preventive health behaviors, levels of chronic disease conditions, health care access, and community resources and policies that support physical activity. The Salt Lake City* metro area ranked #9 for "community fitness." *www.americanfitnessindex.org, "ACSM American Fitness Index Health and Community Fitness Status of the 50 Largest Metropolitan Areas," May 2017*
- Trulia analyzed the 100 largest U.S. metro areas to identify the nation's best cities for weight loss, based on the percentage of adults who bike or walk to work, sporting goods stores, grocery stores, access to outdoor activities, weight-loss centers, gyms, and average space reserved for parks. Salt Lake City* ranked #1. *Trulia.com, "Where to Live to Get in Shape in the New Year," January 4, 2018*
- Salt Lake City* was identified as a "2016 Spring Allergy Capital." The area ranked #88 out of 100. Three groups of factors were used to identify the most severe cities for people with allergies during the spring season: annual pollen levels; medicine utilization; access to board-certified allergists. *Asthma and Allergy Foundation of America, "Spring Allergy Capitals 2016"*
- Salt Lake City* was identified as a "2016 Fall Allergy Capital." The area ranked #83 out of 100. Three groups of factors were used to identify the most severe cities for people with allergies during the fall season: annual pollen levels; medicine utilization; access to board-certified allergists. *Asthma and Allergy Foundation of America, "Fall Allergy Capitals 2016"*

- Salt Lake City* was identified as a "2015 Asthma Capital." The area ranked #51 out of the nation's 100 largest metropolitan areas. Criteria: estimated prevalence; self-reported prevalence; crude death rate for asthma; annual pollen score; annual air quality; public smoking laws; number of board-certified asthma specialists; school inhaler access laws; rescue medication use; controller medication use; ER visits for asthma; uninsured rate; poverty rate. *Asthma and Allergy Foundation of America, "Asthma Capitals 2015"*
- The Salt Lake City* metro area ranked #86 out of 189 in The Gallup-Healthways Well-Being Index. Criteria: purpose; social well being; financial health; community and physical health. Results are based on telephone interviews with adults, aged 18 and older, living in metropolitan areas in the 50 U.S. states and the District of Columbia. *Gallup-Healthways, "State of American Well-Being, 2017 Community Well-Being Rankings" March 2018*

Real Estate Rankings

- FitSmallBusiness looked at 50 of the largest metropolitan areas in the U.S. to determine which metro was the best to start a real estate business. Data was compiled from such sources as: Zillow, Trulia, U.S. Census Bureau, and the Bureau of Labor Statistics. Criteria: location; inventory; annual wages; median sales price of homes; days on the market; median price cut percentage; and other factors that would influence real estate professional growth. The Salt Lake City* metro area ranked #36. *fitsmallbusiness.com, "The Best Cities to Become a Real Estate Agent in 2018," January 30, 2018*
- The Salt Lake City* metro area appeared on Realtor.com's list of the hottest housing markets to watch in 2018. The area ranked #6. Criteria: existing homes inventory and price; new home construction; median household incomes; local economy/population trends. *Realtor.com®, "The 6 Hottest Real Estate Markets to Watch in 2018," January 5, 2018*
- The Salt Lake City* metro area was identified as one of the 10 worst housing markets to invest in. Criteria: single-family rental home investing in the first quarter of 2017 based on first-year returns. The area ranked #8. *The Business Insider, "Here Are the 10 Worst U.S. Housing Markets for Investment," May 12, 2017*
- The Salt Lake City* metro area was identified as one of the 20 best housing markets in the U.S. in 2017. The area ranked #13 out of 180 markets. Criteria: year-over-year change of median sales price of existing single-family homes between the 4th quarter of 2016 and the 4th quarter of 2017. *National Association of Realtors®, Median Sales Price of Existing Single-Family Homes for Metropolitan Areas, 4th Quarter 2017*
- Salt Lake City* was ranked #152 out of 238 metro areas in terms of housing affordability in 2017 by the National Association of Home Builders (#1 = most affordable). Criteria: the share of homes sold in that area affordable to a family earning the local median income, based on standard mortgage underwriting criteria. *National Association of Home Builders®, NAHB-Wells Fargo Housing Opportunity Index, 4th Quarter 2017*

Safety Rankings

- The National Insurance Crime Bureau ranked 382 metro areas in the U.S. in terms of per capita rates of vehicle theft. The Salt Lake City* metro area ranked #15 (#1 = highest rate). Criteria: number of vehicle theft offenses per 100,000 inhabitants in 2016. *National Insurance Crime Bureau, "Hot Spots 2016," June 8, 2017*

Seniors/Retirement Rankings

- From its Best Cities for Successful Aging indexes, the Milken Institute generated rankings for metropolitan areas, weighing data in nine categories—health care, wellness, living arrangements, transportation and convenience, financial characteristics, education, employment, community engagement, and overall livability. The Salt Lake City* metro area was ranked #4 overall in the large metro area category. *Milken Institute, "Best Cities for Successful Aging, 2017" March 14, 2017*

Women/Minorities Rankings

- *24/7 Wall St.* compared median earnings over a 12-month period for men and women who worked full-time, year-round, and employment composition by sector to identify the worst-paying cities for women. Of the largest 100 U.S. metropolitan areas, Salt Lake City* was ranked #9 in pay disparity. *24/7 Wall St., "The Best (and Worst) Paying Cities for Women," March 27, 2017*

Miscellaneous Rankings

- The finance and lifestyle site NerdWallet looked for the U.S. cities that topped the list in donating money and time to good causes. The Salt Lake City* metro area proved to be the #3-ranked metro area, judged by culture of volunteerism, depth of commitment in terms of volunteer hours per year, and monetary contributions. *www.nerdwallet.com, "Most Generous Cities," September 22, 2013*

*South Jordan is located within the Salt Lake City, UT Metropolitan Statistical Area.

Business Environment

CITY FINANCES

City Government Finances

Component	2015 ($000)	2015 ($ per capita)
Total Revenues	61,970	930
Total Expenditures	17,706	266
Debt Outstanding	53,701	806
Cash and Securities[1]	92,978	1,395

Note: (1) Cash and security holdings of a government at the close of its fiscal year,, including those of its dependent agencies, utilities, and liquor stores.
Source: U.S Census Bureau, State & Local Government Finances 2015

City Government Revenue by Source

Source	2015 ($000)	2015 ($ per capita)	2015 (%)
General Revenue			
From Federal Government	0	0	0.0
From State Government	643	10	1.0
From Local Governments	0	0	0.0
Taxes			
Property	21,701	326	35.0
Sales and Gross Receipts	14,476	217	23.4
Personal Income	0	0	0.0
Corporate Income	0	0	0.0
Motor Vehicle License	0	0	0.0
Other Taxes	2,246	34	3.6
Current Charges	4,816	72	7.8
Liquor Store	0	0	0.0
Utility	18,088	271	29.2
Employee Retirement	0	0	0.0

Source: U.S Census Bureau, State & Local Government Finances 2015

City Government Expenditures by Function

Function	2015 ($000)	2015 ($ per capita)	2015 (%)
General Direct Expenditures			
Air Transportation	0	0	0.0
Corrections	0	0	0.0
Education	0	0	0.0
Employment Security Administration	0	0	0.0
Financial Administration	527	7	3.0
Fire Protection	0	0	0.0
General Public Buildings	0	0	0.0
Governmental Administration, Other	0	0	0.0
Health	0	0	0.0
Highways	120	1	0.7
Hospitals	0	0	0.0
Housing and Community Development	0	0	0.0
Interest on General Debt	88	1	0.5
Judicial and Legal	711	10	4.0
Libraries	0	0	0.0
Parking	0	0	0.0
Parks and Recreation	182	2	1.0
Police Protection	5,886	88	33.2
Public Welfare	0	0	0.0
Sewerage	0	0	0.0
Solid Waste Management	712	10	4.0
Veterans' Services	0	0	0.0
Liquor Store	0	0	0.0
Utility	7,773	116	43.9
Employee Retirement	0	0	0.0

Source: U.S Census Bureau, State & Local Government Finances 2015

DEMOGRAPHICS

Population Growth

Area	1990 Census	2000 Census	2010 Census	2016* Estimate	Population Growth (%) 1990-2016	Population Growth (%) 2010-2016
City	12,183	29,437	50,418	62,751	415.1	24.5
MSA[1]	768,075	968,858	1,124,197	1,154,504	50.3	2.7
U.S.	248,709,873	281,421,906	308,745,538	318,558,162	28.1	3.2

Note: (1) Figures cover the Salt Lake City, UT Metropolitan Statistical Area—see Appendix B for areas included; (*) 2012-2016 5-year estimated population
Source: U.S. Census Bureau, 1990 Census, Census 2000, Census 2010, 2012-2016 American Community Survey 5-Year Estimates

Household Size

Area	Persons in Household (%)							Average Household Size
	One	Two	Three	Four	Five	Six	Seven or More	
City	14.3	29.0	14.8	16.7	11.8	8.9	4.6	3.50
MSA[1]	22.3	29.6	16.2	14.7	8.7	5.0	3.4	3.00
U.S.	27.7	33.7	15.7	13.1	6.0	2.3	1.5	2.60

Note: (1) Figures cover the Salt Lake City, UT Metropolitan Statistical Area—see Appendix B for areas included
Source: U.S. Census Bureau, 2012-2016 American Community Survey 5-Year Estimates

Race

Area	White Alone[2] (%)	Black Alone[2] (%)	Asian Alone[2] (%)	AIAN[3] Alone[2] (%)	NHOPI[4] Alone[2] (%)	Other Race Alone[2] (%)	Two or More Races (%)
City	90.9	0.8	2.7	0.1	0.5	2.6	2.4
MSA[1]	81.7	1.6	3.6	0.7	1.5	8.0	2.8
U.S.	73.3	12.6	5.2	0.8	0.2	4.8	3.1

Note: (1) Figures cover the Salt Lake City, UT Metropolitan Statistical Area—see Appendix B for areas included; (2) Alone is defined as not being in combination with one or more other races; (3) American Indian and Alaska Native; (4) Native Hawaiian and Other Pacific Islander
Source: U.S. Census Bureau, 2012-2016 American Community Survey 5-Year Estimates

Hispanic or Latino Origin

Area	Total (%)	Mexican (%)	Puerto Rican (%)	Cuban (%)	Other (%)
City	5.4	3.1	0.2	0.0	2.0
MSA[1]	17.4	13.1	0.4	0.1	3.9
U.S.	17.3	11.0	1.7	0.7	4.0

Note: Persons of Hispanic or Latino origin can be of any race; (1) Figures cover the Salt Lake City, UT Metropolitan Statistical Area—see Appendix B for areas included
Source: U.S. Census Bureau, 2012-2016 American Community Survey 5-Year Estimates

Segregation

Type	Segregation Indices[1]				Percent Change		
	1990	2000	2010	2010 Rank[2]	1990-2000	1990-2010	2000-2010
Black/White	44.0	38.1	39.3	93	-5.9	-4.8	1.2
Asian/White	32.0	33.3	31.0	88	1.3	-1.0	-2.3
Hispanic/White	31.4	41.2	42.9	53	9.8	11.5	1.7

Note: All figures cover the Metropolitan Statistical Area—see Appendix B for areas included; Figures are based on an analysis of 1990, 2000, and 2010 Census Decennial Census tract data by William H. Frey, Brookings Institution and the University of Michigan Social Science Data Analysis Network. In this analysis all racial groups (whites, blacks, and asians) are non-Hispanic members of those races. Hispanics are shown as a separate category; (1) Segregation Indices are Dissimilarity Indices that measure the degree to which the minority group is distributed differently than whites across census tracts. They range from 0 (complete integration) to 100 (complete segregation) where the value indicates the percentage of the minority group that needs to move to be distributed exactly like whites; (2) Ranges from 1 (most segregated) to 102 (least segregated); n/a not available.
Source: www.CensusScope.org

Ancestry

Area	German	Irish	English	American	Italian	Polish	French[2]	Scottish	Dutch
City	12.5	6.7	30.8	5.5	4.7	0.8	1.1	5.3	2.5
MSA[1]	10.9	5.9	21.4	4.8	3.0	0.9	1.9	4.0	2.4
U.S.	14.4	10.4	7.7	6.9	5.4	2.9	2.6	1.7	1.3

Note: Figures are the percentage of the total population reporting a particular ancestry. The nine most commonly reported ancestries in the U.S. are shown. Figures include multiple ancestries (e.g. if a person reported being Irish and Italian, they were included in both columns); (1) Figures cover the Salt Lake City, UT Metropolitan Statistical Area—see Appendix B for areas included; (2) Excludes Basque
Source: U.S. Census Bureau, 2012-2016 American Community Survey 5-Year Estimates

Foreign-Born Population

Area	Percent of Population Born in								
	Any Foreign Country	Asia	Mexico	Europe	Carribean	Central America[2]	South America	Africa	Canada
City	5.4	2.0	0.9	0.8	0.3	0.2	0.5	0.0	0.4
MSA[1]	12.0	2.9	4.8	1.3	0.2	0.6	1.0	0.5	0.3
U.S.	13.2	4.0	3.6	1.5	1.3	1.0	0.9	0.6	0.3

Note: (1) Figures cover the Salt Lake City, UT Metropolitan Statistical Area—see Appendix B for areas included; (2) Excludes Mexico.
Source: U.S. Census Bureau, 2012-2016 American Community Survey 5-Year Estimates

Marital Status

Area	Never Married	Now Married[2]	Separated	Widowed	Divorced
City	25.7	63.1	1.1	2.4	7.6
MSA[1]	31.4	52.3	1.9	3.9	10.5
U.S.	33.0	48.1	2.1	5.9	11.0

Note: Figures are percentages and cover the population 15 years of age and older; (1) Figures cover the Salt Lake City, UT Metropolitan Statistical Area—see Appendix B for areas included; (2) Excludes separated
Source: U.S. Census Bureau, 2012-2016 American Community Survey 5-Year Estimates

Disability Status

Area	All Ages	Under 18 Years Old	18 to 64 Years Old	65 Years and Over
City	7.6	2.7	6.6	32.8
MSA[1]	9.3	3.3	8.2	34.9
U.S.	12.5	4.1	10.3	35.7

Note: Figures show percent of the civilian noninstitutionalized population that reported having a disability. Disability status is determined from six types of difficulty: vision, hearing, cognitive, ambulatory, self-care, and independent living. For children under 5 years old, hearing and vision difficulty are used to determine disability status. For children between the ages of 5 and 14, disability status is determined from hearing, vision, cognitive, ambulatory, and self-care difficulties. For people aged 15 years and older, they are considered to have a disability if they have difficulty with any one of the six difficulty types; Note: (1) Figures cover the Salt Lake City, UT Metropolitan Statistical Area—see Appendix B for areas included
Source: U.S. Census Bureau, 2012-2016 American Community Survey 5-Year Estimates

Age

Area	Percent of Population									Median Age
	Under Age 5	Age 5–19	Age 20–34	Age 35–44	Age 45–54	Age 55–64	Age 65–74	Age 75–84	Age 85+	
City	8.3	27.2	18.8	15.7	12.0	9.3	5.6	2.5	0.7	32.4
MSA[1]	8.1	23.0	23.7	14.2	11.4	10.0	5.7	2.8	1.1	32.1
U.S.	6.2	19.6	20.7	12.7	13.6	12.6	8.3	4.3	1.9	37.7

Note: (1) Figures cover the Salt Lake City, UT Metropolitan Statistical Area—see Appendix B for areas included
Source: U.S. Census Bureau, 2012-2016 American Community Survey 5-Year Estimates

Gender

Area	Males	Females	Males per 100 Females
City	31,638	31,113	101.7
MSA[1]	580,157	574,347	101.0
U.S.	156,765,322	161,792,840	96.9

Note: (1) Figures cover the Salt Lake City, UT Metropolitan Statistical Area—see Appendix B for areas included
Source: U.S. Census Bureau, 2012-2016 American Community Survey 5-Year Estimates

Religious Groups by Family

Area	Catholic	Baptist	Non-Den.	Methodist[2]	Lutheran	LDS[3]	Pente-costal	Presby-terian[4]	Muslim[5]	Judaism
MSA[1]	8.9	0.8	0.5	0.5	0.5	58.9	0.7	0.4	0.4	0.1
U.S.	19.1	9.3	4.0	4.0	2.3	2.0	1.9	1.6	0.8	0.7

Note: Figures are the number of adherents as a percentage of the total population; (1) Figures cover the Salt Lake City, UT Metropolitan Statistical Area—see Appendix B for areas included; (2) Methodist/Pietist; (3) Latter Day Saints; (4) Reformed; (5) Figures are estimates
Source: Association of Statisticians of American Religious Bodies, 2010 U.S. Religion Census: Religious Congregations & Membership Study

Religious Groups by Tradition

Area	Catholic	Evangelical Protestant	Mainline Protestant	Other Tradition	Black Protestant	Orthodox
MSA[1]	8.9	2.6	1.3	60.1	0.1	0.5
U.S.	19.1	16.2	7.3	4.3	1.6	0.3

Note: Figures are the number of adherents as a percentage of the total population; (1) Figures cover the Salt Lake City, UT Metropolitan Statistical Area—see Appendix B for areas included
Source: Association of Statisticians of American Religious Bodies, 2010 U.S. Religion Census: Religious Congregations & Membership Study

ECONOMY

Gross Metropolitan Product

Area	2014	2015	2016	2017	Rank[2]
MSA[1]	74.9	78.6	81.5	86.5	42

Note: Figures are in billions of dollars; (1) Figures cover the Salt Lake City, UT Metropolitan Statistical Area—see Appendix B for areas included; (2) Rank is based on 2015 data and ranges from 1 to 381
Source: The U.S. Conference of Mayors, U.S. Metro Economies: GMP and Employment Report, 2015-2017

Economic Growth

Area	2012-14 (%)	2015 (%)	2016 (%)	2017 (%)	Rank[2]
MSA[1]	2.4	3.8	1.9	3.8	102
U.S.	2.0	2.4	1.9	2.6	–

Note: Figures are real gross metropolitan product (GMP) growth rates and represent average annual percent change; (1) Figures cover the Salt Lake City, UT Metropolitan Statistical Area—see Appendix B for areas included; (2) Rank is based on 2012-2014 average annual percent change and ranges from 1 to 381
Source: The U.S. Conference of Mayors, U.S. Metro Economies: GMP and Employment Report, 2015-2017

Metropolitan Area Exports

Area	2011	2012	2013	2014	2015	2016	Rank[2]
MSA[1]	15,579.2	15,990.0	11,867.2	8,361.5	10,380.5	8,653.7	36

Note: Figures are in millions of dollars; (1) Figures cover the Salt Lake City, UT Metropolitan Statistical Area—see Appendix B for areas included; (2) Rank is based on 2016 data and ranges from 1 to 385
Source: U.S. Department of Commerce, International Trade Administration, Office of Trade & Industry Information, Manufacturing & Services, data extracted March 15, 2018

Building Permits

Area	Single-Family			Multi-Family			Total		
	2016	2017p	Pct. Chg.	2016	2017p	Pct. Chg.	2016	2017p	Pct. Chg.
City	850	843	-0.8	9	212	2,255.6	859	1,055	22.8
MSA[1]	4,311	4,954	14.9	4,489	2,469	-45.0	8,800	7,423	-15.6
U.S.	750,800	817,300	8.9	455,800	446,800	-2.0	1,206,600	1,264,100	4.8

Note: (1) Figures cover the Salt Lake City, UT Metropolitan Statistical Area—see Appendix B for areas included; Figures represent new, privately-owned housing units authorized (unadjusted data); All permit data are based on estimates with imputation; (p) preliminary data.
Source: U.S. Census Bureau, Manufacturing, Mining, and Construction Statistics, Building Permits, 2016, 2017

Bankruptcy Filings

Area	Business Filings			Nonbusiness Filings		
	2016	2017	% Chg.	2016	2017	% Chg.
Salt Lake County	70	94	34.3	5,045	4,775	-5.4
U.S.	24,114	23,157	-4.0	770,846	765,863	-0.6

Note: Business filings include Chapter 7, Chapter 11, Chapter 12, and Chapter 13; Nonbusiness filings include Chapter 7, Chapter 11, and Chapter 13
Source: Administrative Office of the U.S. Courts, Business and Nonbusiness Bankruptcy, County Cases Commenced by Chapter of the Bankruptcy Code, During the 12-Month Period Ending December 31, 2016 and Business and Nonbusiness Bankruptcy, County Cases Commenced by Chapter of the Bankruptcy Code, During the 12-Month Period Ending December 31, 2017

Housing Vacancy Rates

Area	Gross Vacancy Rate[2] (%)			Year-Round Vacancy Rate[3] (%)			Rental Vacancy Rate[4] (%)			Homeowner Vacancy Rate[5] (%)		
	2015	2016	2017	2015	2016	2017	2015	2016	2017	2015	2016	2017
MSA[1]	5.2	5.4	5.0	5.1	5.0	4.8	5.8	6.4	6.2	1.3	0.5	0.6
U.S.	12.9	12.8	12.7	10.0	9.9	9.9	7.1	6.9	7.2	1.8	1.7	1.6

Note: (1) Figures cover the Salt Lake City, UT Metropolitan Statistical Area—see Appendix B for areas included; (2) The percentage of the total housing inventory that is vacant; (3) The percentage of the housing inventory (excluding seasonal units) that is year-round vacant; (4) The percentage of rental inventory that is vacant for rent; (5) The percentage of homeowner inventory that is vacant for sale
Source: U.S. Census Bureau, Housing Vacancies and Homeownership Annual Statistics: 2015, 2016, 2017

INCOME

Income

Area	Per Capita ($)	Median Household ($)	Average Household ($)
City	33,620	95,858	113,234
MSA[1]	28,277	64,564	83,633
U.S.	29,829	55,322	77,866

Note: (1) Figures cover the Salt Lake City, UT Metropolitan Statistical Area—see Appendix B for areas included
Source: U.S. Census Bureau, 2012-2016 American Community Survey 5-Year Estimates

Household Income Distribution

Area	Percent of Households Earning							
	Under $15,000	$15,000 -$24,999	$25,000 -$34,999	$35,000 -$49,999	$50,000 -$74,999	$75,000 -$99,999	$100,000 -$149,999	$150,000 and up
City	3.1	2.4	4.5	6.9	17.2	19.6	23.2	23.1
MSA[1]	7.8	7.8	8.7	13.0	20.3	15.0	16.1	11.3
U.S.	12.1	10.2	9.9	13.2	17.8	12.2	13.5	11.1

Note: (1) Figures cover the Salt Lake City, UT Metropolitan Statistical Area—see Appendix B for areas included
Source: U.S. Census Bureau, 2012-2016 American Community Survey 5-Year Estimates

Poverty Rate

Area	All Ages	Under 18 Years Old	18 to 64 Years Old	65 Years and Over
City	3.5	3.0	3.5	5.1
MSA[1]	11.1	14.1	10.4	7.1
U.S.	15.1	21.2	14.2	9.3

Note: Figures are percentage of people whose income during the past 12 months was below the poverty level; (1) Figures cover the Salt Lake City, UT Metropolitan Statistical Area—see Appendix B for areas included
Source: U.S. Census Bureau, 2012-2016 American Community Survey 5-Year Estimates

EMPLOYMENT

Labor Force and Employment

Area	Civilian Labor Force			Workers Employed		
	Dec. 2016	Dec. 2017	% Chg.	Dec. 2016	Dec. 2017	% Chg.
City	35,042	36,066	2.9	34,163	35,157	2.9
MSA[1]	643,054	661,109	2.8	624,955	643,138	2.9
U.S.	158,968,000	159,880,000	0.6	151,798,000	153,602,000	1.2

Note: Data is not seasonally adjusted and covers workers 16 years of age and older; (1) Figures cover the Salt Lake City, UT Metropolitan Statistical Area—see Appendix B for areas included
Source: Bureau of Labor Statistics, Local Area Unemployment Statistics

Unemployment Rate

Area	2017											
	Jan.	Feb.	Mar.	Apr.	May	Jun.	Jul.	Aug.	Sep.	Oct.	Nov.	Dec.
City	2.9	3.2	3.1	2.9	2.9	3.3	3.1	3.1	2.8	2.8	2.6	2.5
MSA[1]	3.2	3.4	3.4	3.2	3.1	3.5	3.2	3.3	2.9	2.8	2.6	2.7
U.S.	5.1	4.9	4.6	4.1	4.1	4.5	4.6	4.5	4.1	3.9	3.9	3.9

Note: Data is not seasonally adjusted and covers workers 16 years of age and older; (1) Figures cover the Salt Lake City, UT Metropolitan Statistical Area—see Appendix B for areas included
Source: Bureau of Labor Statistics, Local Area Unemployment Statistics

Average Wages

Occupation	$/Hr.	Occupation	$/Hr.
Accountants and Auditors	35.30	Maids and Housekeeping Cleaners	11.80
Automotive Mechanics	21.10	Maintenance and Repair Workers	19.70
Bookkeepers	19.60	Marketing Managers	56.20
Carpenters	18.70	Nuclear Medicine Technologists	35.10
Cashiers	10.80	Nurses, Licensed Practical	26.50
Clerks, General Office	15.10	Nurses, Registered	31.20
Clerks, Receptionists/Information	13.60	Nursing Assistants	13.10
Clerks, Shipping/Receiving	14.70	Packers and Packagers, Hand	11.80
Computer Programmers	38.90	Physical Therapists	41.00
Computer Systems Analysts	37.90	Postal Service Mail Carriers	24.20
Computer User Support Specialists	25.00	Real Estate Brokers	29.40
Cooks, Restaurant	13.10	Retail Salespersons	12.80
Dentists	79.50	Sales Reps., Exc. Tech./Scientific	31.20
Electrical Engineers	42.60	Sales Reps., Tech./Scientific	49.80
Electricians	26.00	Secretaries, Exc. Legal/Med./Exec.	16.50
Financial Managers	57.80	Security Guards	15.00
First-Line Supervisors/Managers, Sales	19.70	Surgeons	n/a
Food Preparation Workers	11.70	Teacher Assistants*	11.60
General and Operations Managers	45.10	Teachers, Elementary School*	26.20
Hairdressers/Cosmetologists	11.90	Teachers, Secondary School*	26.60
Internists, General	117.20	Telemarketers	13.90
Janitors and Cleaners	11.10	Truck Drivers, Heavy/Tractor-Trailer	21.30
Landscaping/Groundskeeping Workers	13.70	Truck Drivers, Light/Delivery Svcs.	16.80
Lawyers	54.10	Waiters and Waitresses	11.70

Note: Wage data covers the Salt Lake City, UT Metropolitan Statistical Area—see Appendix B for areas included; (*) Hourly wages for elementary/secondary school teachers and teacher assistants were calculated by the editors from annual wage data based on a 40 hour work week; n/a not available.
Source: Bureau of Labor Statistics, Metro Area Occupational Employment & Wage Estimates, May 2017

Employment by Occupation

Occupation Classification	City (%)	MSA[1] (%)	U.S. (%)
Management, Business, Science, and Arts	50.0	37.9	37.0
Natural Resources, Construction, and Maintenance	5.8	8.0	8.9
Production, Transportation, and Material Moving	7.4	12.0	12.2
Sales and Office	27.4	27.2	23.8
Service	9.4	15.0	18.1

Note: Figures cover employed civilians 16 years of age and older; (1) Figures cover the Salt Lake City, UT Metropolitan Statistical Area—see Appendix B for areas included
Source: U.S. Census Bureau, 2012-2016 American Community Survey 5-Year Estimates

Employment by Industry

Sector	MSA[1] Number of Employees	MSA[1] Percent of Total	U.S. Percent of Total
Construction, Mining, and Logging	42,400	5.8	5.2
Education and Health Services	83,300	11.4	15.9
Financial Activities	58,400	8.0	5.7
Government	110,500	15.1	15.3
Information	21,400	2.9	1.9
Leisure and Hospitality	64,300	8.8	10.7
Manufacturing	58,600	8.0	8.5
Other Services	20,500	2.8	3.9
Professional and Business Services	122,100	16.7	14.0
Retail Trade	77,000	10.5	11.0
Transportation, Warehousing, and Utilities	38,700	5.3	4.1
Wholesale Trade	32,900	4.5	4.0

Note: Figures are non-farm employment as of December 2017. Figures are not seasonally adjusted and include workers 16 years of age and older; (1) Figures cover the Salt Lake City, UT Metropolitan Statistical Area—see Appendix B for areas included
Source: Bureau of Labor Statistics, Current Employment Statistics, Employment, Hours, and Earnings

Occupations with Greatest Projected Employment Growth: 2017 – 2019

Occupation[1]	2017 Employment	2019 Projected Employment	Numeric Employment Change	Percent Employment Change
Combined Food Preparation and Serving Workers, Including Fast Food	40,810	43,640	2,830	6.9
Customer Service Representatives	44,760	46,800	2,040	4.6
Construction Laborers	17,940	19,780	1,840	10.3
General and Operations Managers	29,140	30,980	1,840	6.3
Carpenters	15,870	17,610	1,740	10.9
Heavy and Tractor-Trailer Truck Drivers	24,080	25,570	1,490	6.2
Janitors and Cleaners, Except Maids and Housekeeping Cleaners	22,610	23,970	1,360	6.0
Retail Salespersons	47,280	48,580	1,300	2.7
Laborers and Freight, Stock, and Material Movers, Hand	19,560	20,850	1,290	6.6
Registered Nurses	22,690	23,950	1,260	5.6

Note: Projections cover Utah; (1) Sorted by numeric employment change
Source: www.projectionscentral.com, State Occupational Projections, 2017–2019 Short-Term Projections

Fastest Growing Occupations: 2017 – 2019

Occupation[1]	2017 Employment	2019 Projected Employment	Numeric Employment Change	Percent Employment Change
Roofers	2,300	2,640	340	14.7
Brickmasons and Blockmasons	2,310	2,650	340	14.6
Plasterers and Stucco Masons	660	750	90	13.9
Roustabouts, Oil and Gas	1,170	1,330	160	13.8
Cement Masons and Concrete Finishers	3,470	3,930	460	13.2
Helpers—Brickmasons, Blockmasons, Stonemasons, and Tile and Marble Setters	690	780	90	13.0
Stonemasons	360	410	50	12.8
Helpers—Pipelayers, Plumbers, Pipefitters, and Steamfitters	570	640	70	12.6
Plumbers, Pipefitters, and Steamfitters	6,750	7,590	840	12.5
Software Developers, Applications	8,310	9,330	1,020	12.3

Note: Projections cover Utah; (1) Sorted by percent employment change and excludes occupations with numeric employment change less than 50
Source: www.projectionscentral.com, State Occupational Projections, 2017–2019 Short-Term Projections

TAXES

State Corporate Income Tax Rates

State	Tax Rate (%)	Income Brackets ($)	Num. of Brackets	Financial Institution Tax Rate (%)[a]	Federal Income Tax Ded.
Utah	5.0 (b)	Flat rate	–	5.0 (b)	No

Note: Tax rates as of January 1, 2018; (a) Rates listed are the corporate income tax rate applied to financial institutions or excise taxes based on income. Some states have other taxes based upon the value of deposits or shares; (b) Minimum tax is $800 in California, $100 in District of Columbia and Arizona, $50 in North Dakota (banks), $500 in Rhode Island, $200 per location in South Dakota (banks), $100 in Utah, $250 in Vermont.
Source: Federation of Tax Administrators, Range of State Corporate Income Tax Rates, January 1, 2018

State Individual Income Tax Rates

State	Tax Rate (%)	Income Brackets ($)	Num. of Brackets	Personal Exempt. ($)[1]		Fed. Inc. Tax Ded.
				Single	Dependents	
Utah	5.0	Flat rate	1	(v)	(v)	No

Note: Tax rates as of January 1, 2018; Local- and county-level taxes are not included; n/a not applicable; (1) Married joint filers generally receive double the single exemption; (v) Utah provides a tax credit equal to 6% of the federal personal exemption amounts (and applicable standard deduction). Note, the Tax Cut and Reform Act of 2017 has eliminated personal exemptions and increased the standard deduction in the IRC. Utah will need to enact legislation to reinstate a personal credit for tax year 2018.
Source: Federation of Tax Administrators, State Individual Income Tax Rates, January 1, 2018

Various State Sales and Excise Tax Rates

State	State Sales Tax (%)	Gasoline[1] (¢/gal.)	Cigarette[2] ($/pack)	Spirits[3] ($/gal.)	Wine[4] ($/gal.)	Beer[5] ($/gal.)	Recreational Marijuana (%)
Utah	5.95 (b)	29.41	1.70	15.38 (g)	(m)	0.41 (q)	Not legal

Note: All tax rates as of January 1, 2018; (1) The American Petroleum Institute has developed a methodology for determining the average tax rate on a gallon of fuel. Rates may include any of the following: excise taxes, environmental fees, storage tank fees, other fees or taxes, general sales tax, and local taxes. In states where gasoline is subject to the general sales tax, or where the fuel tax is based on the average sale price, the average rate determined by API is sensitive to changes in the price of gasoline. States that fully or partially apply general sales taxes to gasoline: CA, CO, GA, IL, IN, MI, NY; (2) The federal excise tax of $1.0066 per pack and local taxes are not included; (3) Rates are those applicable to off-premise sales of 40% alcohol by volume (a.b.v.) distilled spirits in 750ml containers. Local excise taxes are excluded; (4) Rates are those applicable to off-premise sales of 11% a.b.v. non-carbonated wine in 750ml containers; (5) Rates are those applicable to off-premise sales of 4.7% a.b.v. beer in 12 ounce containers; (b) Three states levy mandatory, statewide, local add-on sales taxes at the state level: California (1.25%), Utah (1.25%), Virginia (1%), we include these in their state sales tax; (g) Control states, where the government controls all sales. Products can be subject to ad valorem mark-up as well as excise taxes; (m) Control states, where the government controls all sales. Products can be subject to ad valorem mark-up as well as excise taxes; (q) Different rates also applicable according to alcohol content, place of production, size of container, or place purchased (on- or off-premise or onboard airlines).
Source: Tax Foundation, 2018 Facts & Figures: How Does Your State Compare?

State Business Tax Climate Index Rankings

State	Overall Rank	Corporate Tax Rank	Individual Income Tax Rank	Sales Tax Rank	Unemployment Insurance Tax Rank	Property Tax Rank
Utah	8	4	11	17	21	5

Note: The index is a measure of how each state's tax laws affect economic performance. The lower the rank, the more favorable a state's tax system is for business. States without a given tax are given a ranking of 1. The scores/rankings for the District of Columbia do not affect other states. The 2018 index represents the tax climate as of July 1, 2017.
Source: Tax Foundation, State Business Tax Climate Index 2018

TRANSPORTATION

Means of Transportation to Work

Area	Car/Truck/Van		Public Transportation			Bicycle	Walked	Other Means	Worked at Home
	Drove Alone	Car-pooled	Bus	Subway	Railroad				
City	75.6	9.5	0.5	1.2	1.6	0.7	1.8	1.0	8.1
MSA[1]	75.0	12.0	2.4	0.4	0.6	0.8	2.2	1.6	5.1
U.S.	76.4	9.3	2.6	1.9	0.6	0.6	2.8	1.3	4.6

Note: Figures are percentages and cover workers 16 years of age and older; (1) Figures cover the Salt Lake City, UT Metropolitan Statistical Area—see Appendix B for areas included
Source: U.S. Census Bureau, 2012-2016 American Community Survey 5-Year Estimates

Travel Time to Work

Area	Less Than 10 Minutes	10 to 19 Minutes	20 to 29 Minutes	30 to 44 Minutes	45 to 59 Minutes	60 to 89 Minutes	90 Minutes or More
City	9.5	25.2	26.6	28.5	6.1	3.1	1.1
MSA[1]	10.8	32.8	27.7	19.8	5.2	2.5	1.2
U.S.	12.9	29.2	20.9	20.4	8.0	6.0	2.7

Note: Note: Figures are percentages and include workers 16 years old and over; (1) Figures cover the Salt Lake City, UT Metropolitan Statistical Area—see Appendix B for areas included
Source: U.S. Census Bureau, 2012-2016 American Community Survey 5-Year Estimates

Freeway Travel Time Index

Area	1985	1990	1995	2000	2005	2010	2014
Urban Area Rank[1,2]	54	76	73	65	51	48	46
Urban Area Index[1]	1.06	1.07	1.10	1.14	1.17	1.17	1.18
Average Index[3]	1.09	1.11	1.14	1.17	1.20	1.19	1.20

Note: Freeway Travel Time Index—the ratio of travel time in the peak period to the travel time at free-flow conditions. For example, a value of 1.30 indicates a 20-minute free-flow trip takes 26 minutes in the peak (20 minutes x 1.30 = 26 minutes); (1) Covers the Salt Lake City-West Valley City UT urban area; (2) Rank is based on 101 urban areas (#1 = highest travel time index); (3) Average of 101 urban areas
Source: Texas Transportation Institute, 2015 Urban Mobility Scorecard, August 2015

Freeway Commuter Stress Index

Area	1985	1990	1995	2000	2005	2010	2014
Urban Area Rank[1,2]	48	59	61	54	47	49	43
Urban Area Index[1]	1.10	1.11	1.14	1.18	1.21	1.21	1.23
Average Index[3]	1.13	1.16	1.19	1.22	1.25	1.24	1.25

Note: The Freeway Commuter Stress Index is the same as the Freeway Travel Time Index (see table above) except that it includes only the travel in the peak directions during the peak periods; the TTI includes travel in all directions during the peak period. Thus, the CSI is more indicative of the work trip experienced by each commuter on a daily basis; (1) Covers the Salt Lake City-West Valley City UT urban area; (2) Rank is based on 101 urban areas (#1 = highest travel time index); (3) Average of 101 urban areas
Source: Texas Transportation Institute, 2015 Urban Mobility Scorecard, August 2015

Living Environment

COST OF LIVING

Cost of Living Index

Composite Index	Groceries	Housing	Utilities	Trans-portation	Health Care	Misc. Goods/ Services
96.9	106.8	94.1	75.2	103.5	98.6	99.5

Note: The Cost of Living Index measures regional differences in the cost of consumer goods and services, excluding taxes and non-consumer expenditures, for professional and managerial households in the top income quintile. It is based on more than 50,000 prices covering almost 60 different items for which prices are collected three times a year by chambers of commerce, economic development organizations or university applied economic centers in each participating urban area. The numbers shown should be read as a percentage above or below the national average of 100. For example, a value of 115.4 in the groceries column indicates that grocery prices are 15.4% higher than the national average. Small differences in the index numbers should not be interpreted as significant; Figures cover the Salt Lake City UT urban area.
Source: The Council for Community and Economic Research, ACCRA Cost of Living Index, 2017

Grocery Prices

Area[1]	T-Bone Steak ($/pound)	Frying Chicken ($/pound)	Whole Milk ($/half gal.)	Eggs ($/dozen)	Orange Juice ($/64 oz.)	Coffee ($/11.5 oz.)
City[2]	10.77	1.50	1.74	2.60	3.85	4.39
Avg.	11.29	1.40	2.02	1.47	3.55	4.37
Min.	7.71	0.93	1.04	0.70	2.86	3.24
Max.	15.83	2.39	4.03	3.92	6.29	8.16

*Note: (1) Values for the local area are compared with the average, minimum and maximum values for all 294 areas in the Cost of Living Index; (2) Figures cover the Salt Lake City UT urban area; **T-Bone Steak** (price per pound); **Frying Chicken** (price per pound, whole fryer); **Whole Milk** (half gallon carton); **Eggs** (price per dozen, Grade A, large); **Orange Juice** (64 oz. Tropicana or Florida Natural); **Coffee** (11.5 oz. can, vacuum-packed, Maxwell House, Hills Bros, or Folgers).*
Source: The Council for Community and Economic Research, ACCRA Cost of Living Index, 2017

Housing and Utility Costs

Area[1]	New Home Price ($)	Apartment Rent ($/month)	All Electric ($/month)	Part Electric ($/month)	Other Energy ($/month)	Telephone ($/month)
City[2]	317,989	1,010	-	74.59	63.74	19.00
Avg.	335,956	1,047	175.01	97.34	67.93	28.71
Min.	187,788	491	109.48	49.33	35.44	12.39
Max.	1,739,087	4,559	432.62	227.09	353.33	44.61

*Note: (1) Values for the local area are compared with the average, minimum and maximum values for all 294 areas in the Cost of Living Index; (2) Figures cover the Salt Lake City UT urban area; **New Home Price** (2,400 sf living area, 8,000 sf lot, in urban area with full utilities); **Apartment Rent** (950 sf 2 bedroom/1.5 or 2 bath, unfurnished, excluding all utilities except water); **All Electric** (average monthly cost for an all-electric home); **Part Electric** (average monthly cost for a part-electric home); **Other Energy** (average monthly cost for natural gas, fuel oil, coal, wood, and any other forms of energy except electricity); **Telephone** (price includes basic monthly rate for a private residential line plus additional local usage charges incurred by a family of four).*
Source: The Council for Community and Economic Research, ACCRA Cost of Living Index, 2017

Health Care, Transportation, and Other Costs

Area[1]	Doctor ($/visit)	Dentist ($/visit)	Optometrist ($/visit)	Gasoline ($/gallon)	Beauty Salon ($/visit)	Men's Shirt ($)
City[2]	107.86	86.24	89.33	2.23	31.67	27.18
Avg.	108.00	92.54	101.93	2.25	37.58	30.92
Min.	30.39	60.00	49.75	1.82	16.11	11.20
Max.	193.50	161.94	229.28	3.16	77.35	59.13

*Note: (1) Values for the local area are compared with the average, minimum and maximum values for all 294 areas in the Cost of Living Index; (2) Figures cover the Salt Lake City UT urban area; **Doctor** (general practitioners routine exam of an established patient); **Dentist** (adult teeth cleaning and periodic oral examination); **Optometrist** (full vision eye exam for established adult patient); **Gasoline** (one gallon regular unleaded, national brand, including all taxes, cash price at self-service pump if available); **Beauty Salon** (woman's shampoo, trim, and blow-dry); **Men's Shirt** (cotton/polyester dress shirt, pinpoint weave, long sleeves).*
Source: The Council for Community and Economic Research, ACCRA Cost of Living Index, 2017

HOUSING

House Price Index (HPI)

Area	National Ranking[2]	Quarterly Change (%)	One-Year Change (%)	Five-Year Change (%)
MSA[1]	22	1.27	10.46	45.01
U.S.[3]	–	1.61	6.68	34.71

Note: The HPI is a weighted repeat sales index. It measures average price changes in repeat sales or refinancings on the same properties. This information is obtained by reviewing repeat mortgage transactions on single-family properties whose mortgages have been purchased or securitized by Fannie Mae or Freddie Mac in January 1975; (1) Figures cover the Salt Lake City, UT Metropolitan Statistical Area—see Appendix B for areas included; (2) Rankings are based on annual percentage change for all metro areas containing at least 15,000 transactions over the last 10 years and ranges from 1 to 253; (3) figures based on a weighted average of Census Division estimates using a seasonally adjusted, purchase-only index; all figures are for the period ending December 31, 2017
Source: Federal Housing Finance Agency, House Price Index, February 28, 2018

Median Single-Family Home Prices

Area	2015	2016	2017[p]	Percent Change 2016 to 2017
MSA[1]	255.0	272.5	300.1	10.1
U.S. Average	223.9	235.5	248.8	5.6

Note: Figures are median sales prices of existing single-family homes in thousands of dollars; (p) preliminary; (1) Figures cover the Salt Lake City, UT Metropolitan Statistical Area—see Appendix B for areas included
Source: National Association of Realtors, Median Sales Price of Existing Single-Family Homes for Metropolitan Areas, 4th Quarter 2017

Qualifying Income Based on Median Sales Price of Existing Single-Family Homes

Area	With 5% Down ($)	With 10% Down ($)	With 20% Down ($)
MSA[1]	70,681	66,961	59,521
U.S. Average	55,585	52,659	46,808

Note: Figures are preliminary; Qualifying income is based on a mortgage rate of 4.17%. Monthly principal and interest payment is limited to 25% of income; (1) Figures cover the Salt Lake City, UT Metropolitan Statistical Area—see Appendix B for areas included
Source: National Association of Realtors, Qualifying Income Based on Median Sales Price of Existing Single-Family Homes for Metropolitan Areas, 4th Quarter 2017

Median Apartment Condo-Coop Home Prices

Area	2015	2016	2017[p]	Percent Change 2016 to 2017
MSA[1]	178.9	193.0	214.2	11.0
U.S. Average	210.7	220.7	234.3	6.2

Note: Figures are median sales prices of existing apartment condo-coop homes in thousands of dollars; (p) preliminary; (1) Figures cover the Salt Lake City, UT Metropolitan Statistical Area—see Appendix B for areas included
Source: National Association of Realtors, Median Sales Price of Existing Apartment Condo-Coop Homes for Metropolitan Areas, 4th Quarter 2017

Home Value Distribution

Area	Under $50,000	$50,000 -$99,999	$100,000 -$149,999	$150,000 -$199,999	$200,000 -$299,999	$300,000 -$499,999	$500,000 -$999,999	$1,000,000 or more
City	1.6	0.0	0.7	5.7	25.9	53.0	12.9	0.2
MSA[1]	4.3	2.1	11.1	18.7	30.7	23.9	8.1	1.1
U.S.	8.8	14.8	15.3	14.9	18.4	16.4	9.0	2.5

Note: Figures are percentages and cover owner-occupied housing units; (1) Figures cover the Salt Lake City, UT Metropolitan Statistical Area—see Appendix B for areas included
Source: U.S. Census Bureau, 2012-2016 American Community Survey 5-Year Estimates

Homeownership Rate

Area	2009 (%)	2010 (%)	2011 (%)	2012 (%)	2013 (%)	2014 (%)	2015 (%)	2016 (%)	2017 (%)
MSA[1]	68.8	65.5	66.4	66.9	66.8	68.2	69.1	69.2	68.1
U.S.	67.4	66.9	66.1	65.4	65.1	64.5	63.7	63.4	63.9

Note: (1) Figures cover the Salt Lake City, UT Metropolitan Statistical Area—see Appendix B for areas included
Source: U.S. Census Bureau, Housing Vacancies and Homeownership Annual Statistics: 2009-2017

Year Housing Structure Built

Area	2010 or Later	2000 -2009	1990 -1999	1980 -1989	1970 -1979	1960 -1969	1950 -1959	1940 -1949	Before 1940	Median Year
City	16.8	41.4	25.6	6.6	6.3	1.7	0.5	0.4	0.8	2002
MSA[1]	3.9	16.5	16.3	13.2	19.4	9.0	9.3	3.9	8.4	1980
U.S.	2.3	14.7	14.0	13.7	15.6	10.9	10.6	5.2	13.0	1977

Note: Figures are percentages except for Median Year; Note: (1) Figures cover the Salt Lake City, UT Metropolitan Statistical Area—see Appendix B for areas included
Source: U.S. Census Bureau, 2012-2016 American Community Survey 5-Year Estimates

Gross Monthly Rent

Area	Under $500	$500 -$999	$1,000 -$1,499	$1,500 -$1,999	$2,000 -$2,499	$2,500 -$2,999	$3,000 and up	Median ($)
City	2.5	7.5	50.7	23.8	13.0	2.5	0.0	1,399
MSA[1]	6.8	47.1	33.6	9.7	1.8	0.5	0.5	967
U.S.	11.3	43.3	27.7	10.7	4.0	1.6	1.5	949

Note: Figures are percentages except for Median; Gross rent is the contract rent plus the estimated average monthly cost of utilities (electricity, gas, and water and sewer) and fuels (oil, coal, kerosene, wood, etc.) if these are paid by the renter (or paid for the renter by someone else); (1) Figures cover the Salt Lake City, UT Metropolitan Statistical Area—see Appendix B for areas included
Source: U.S. Census Bureau, 2012-2016 American Community Survey 5-Year Estimates

HEALTH

Health Risk Factors

Category	MSA[1] (%)	U.S. (%)
Adults aged 18–64 who have any kind of health care coverage	86.0	87.7
Adults who reported being in good or excellent health	87.4	83.6
Adults who are current smokers	10.9	17.1
Adults who currently use E-cigarettes	5.5	4.7
Adults who currently use chewing tobacco, snuff, or snus	3.5	4.0
Adults who are heavy drinkers[2]	5.9	6.5
Adults who are binge drinkers[3]	17.1	16.9
Adults who are overweight (BMI 25.0 - 29.9)	35.5	35.3
Adults who are obese (BMI 30.0 - 99.8)	25.0	29.9
Adults who participated in any physical activities in the past month	84.6	76.9
Adults who always or nearly always wears a seat belt	95.5	94.3

Note: (1) Figures cover the Salt Lake City, UT Metropolitan Statistical Area—see Appendix B for areas included; (2) Heavy drinkers are classified as adult men having more than 14 drinks per week and adult women having more than 7 drinks per week; (3) Binge drinkers are classified as males having five or more drinks on one occasion or females having four or more drinks on one occasion
Source: Centers for Disease Control and Prevention, Behaviorial Risk Factor Surveillance System, SMART: Selected Metropolitan Area Risk Trends, 2016

Health Screening Rates

Category	MSA[1] (%)	U.S. (%)
Adults 50-75 who have had a blood stool test within the past year	2.5	8.0
Adults 50-75 who have had a colonoscopy in the past 10 years	69.6	63.5
Adults aged 65+ who have had flu shot within the past year	54.9	58.6
Adults aged 65+ who have ever had a pneumonia vaccination	78.8	73.4
Adults who have ever been tested for HIV	26.6	35.6
Women aged 21-65 who have had a pap test in the past three years	76.5	79.8
Men aged 40+ who have had a PSA test within the past two years	32.8	39.5
Women aged 40+ who have had a mammogram within the past two years	69.2	72.5

Note: n/a not available; (1) Figures cover the Salt Lake City, UT Metropolitan Statistical Area—see Appendix B for areas included; Source: Centers for Disease Control and Prevention, Behaviorial Risk Factor Surveillance System, SMART: Selected Metropolitan Area Risk Trends, 2016

Chronic Health Conditions

Category	MSA[1] (%)	U.S. (%)
Adults who have ever been told they had a heart attack	2.3	4.4
Adults who have ever been told they have angina or coronary heart disease	2.1	4.1
Adults who have ever been told they had a stroke	2.1	3.1
Adults who have been told they currently have asthma	9.0	9.3
Adults who have ever been told they have arthritis	19.6	25.8
Adults who have ever been told they have diabetes[2]	6.6	10.5
Adults who have ever been told they had skin cancer	6.6	5.9
Adults who have ever been told they had any other types of cancer	5.5	6.7
Adults who have ever been told they have COPD	3.9	6.3
Adults who have ever been told they have kidney disease	2.2	2.8
Adults who have ever been told they have a form of depression	21.4	17.4

Note: (1) Figures cover the Salt Lake City, UT Metropolitan Statistical Area—see Appendix B for areas included; (2) Figures do not include pregnancy-related, borderline, or pre-diabetes
Source: Centers for Disease Control and Prevention, Behaviorial Risk Factor Surveillance System, SMART: Selected Metropolitan Area Risk Trends, 2016

Mortality Rates for the Top 10 Causes of Death in the U.S.

ICD-10[a] Sub-Chapter	ICD-10[a] Code	Age-Adjusted Mortality Rate[1] per 100,000 population	
		County[2]	U.S.
Malignant neoplasms	C00-C97	134.1	158.5
Ischaemic heart diseases	I20-I25	66.7	96.8
Other forms of heart disease	I30-I51	71.6	52.4
Chronic lower respiratory diseases	J40-J47	35.1	40.9
Cerebrovascular diseases	I60-I69	38.5	37.2
Organic, including symptomatic, mental disorders	F01-F09	38.9	33.3
Other degenerative diseases of the nervous system	G30-G31	41.7	32.1
Other external causes of accidental injury	W00-X59	34.9	31.2
Diabetes mellitus	E10-E14	26.5	21.1
Hypertensive diseases	I10-I15	12.3	20.8

Note: (a) ICD-10 = International Classification of Diseases 10th Revision; (1) Mortality rates are a three year average covering 2014-2016; (2) Figures cover Salt Lake County.
Source: Centers for Disease Control and Prevention, National Center for Health Statistics. Underlying Cause of Death 1999-2016 on CDC WONDER Online Database, released December 2017

Mortality Rates for Selected Causes of Death

ICD-10[a] Sub-Chapter	ICD-10[a] Code	Age-Adjusted Mortality Rate[1] per 100,000 population	
		County[2]	U.S.
Assault	X85-Y09	2.9	5.6
Diseases of the liver	K70-K76	13.7	14.0
Human immunodeficiency virus (HIV) disease	B20-B24	0.7	1.9
Influenza and pneumonia	J09-J18	13.3	14.6
Intentional self-harm	X60-X84	22.8	13.2
Malnutrition	E40-E46	3.4	1.3
Obesity and other hyperalimentation	E65-E68	2.6	2.1
Renal failure	N17-N19	14.0	13.0
Transport accidents	V01-V99	9.6	12.0
Viral hepatitis	B15-B19	1.8	1.9

Note: (a) ICD-10 = International Classification of Diseases 10th Revision; (1) Mortality rates are a three year average covering 2014-2016; (2) Figures cover Salt Lake County; Data are Suppressed when the data meet the criteria for confidentiality constraints; Mortality rates are flagged as Unreliable when the rate would be calculated with a numerator of 20 or less.
Source: Centers for Disease Control and Prevention, National Center for Health Statistics. Underlying Cause of Death 1999-2016 on CDC WONDER Online Database, released December 2017

Health Insurance Coverage

Area	With Health Insurance	With Private Health Insurance	With Public Health Insurance	Without Health Insurance	Population Under Age 18 Without Health Insurance
City	93.4	86.5	13.9	6.6	5.5
MSA[1]	86.8	74.5	20.2	13.2	9.8
U.S.	88.3	66.7	33.0	11.7	5.9

Note: Figures are percentages that cover the civilian noninstitutionalized population; (1) Figures cover the Salt Lake City, UT Metropolitan Statistical Area—see Appendix B for areas included
Source: U.S. Census Bureau, 2012-2016 American Community Survey 5-Year Estimates

Number of Medical Professionals

Area	MDs[3]	DOs[3,4]	Dentists	Podiatrists	Chiropractors	Optometrists
County[1] (number)	3,970	159	843	66	298	149
County[1] (rate[2])	359.5	14.4	75.2	5.9	26.6	13.3
U.S. (rate[2])	276.5	22.3	67.3	6.0	26.7	15.9

Note: Data as of 2016 unless noted; (1) Data covers Salt Lake County; (2) Rate per 100,000 population; (3) Data as of 2015 and includes all active, non-federal physicians; (4) Doctor of Osteopathic Medicine
Source: U.S. Department of Health and Human Services, Health Resources and Services Administration, Bureau of Health Professions, Area Resource File (ARF) 2016-2017

Best Hospitals

According to *U.S. News,* the Salt Lake City, UT metro area is home to two of the best hospitals in the U.S.: **Intermountain Medical Center** (1 adult specialty); **University of Utah Health Care-Hospital and Clinics** (2 adult specialties). The hospitals listed were nationally ranked in at least one of 16 specialties. Only 152 hospitals nationwide were nationally ranked in one or more specialties. Twenty hospitals in the U.S. made the Honor Roll. The Best Hospitals Honor Roll was revamped last year to take both the national rankings and the procedure and condition ratings into account. Hospitals received points if they were nationally ranked in one of the 16 specialties—the higher they ranked, the more points they got—and how many ratings of "high performing" they earned in the nine procedures and conditions. *U.S. News Online, "America's Best Hospitals 2017-18"*

According to *U.S. News,* the Salt Lake City, UT metro area is home to two of the best children's hospitals in the U.S.: **Primary Children's Hospital** (10 pediatric specialties); **Shriners Hospitals for Children-Salt Lake City** (1 pediatric specialty). The hospitals listed were highly ranked in at least one of 10 pediatric specialties. Eighty-two children's hospitals in the U.S. were nationally ranked in at least one specialty. Hospitals received points for being ranked in a specialty, and the 10 hospitals with the most points across the 10 specialties make up the Honor Roll. *U.S. News Online, "America's Best Children's Hospitals 2017-18"*

EDUCATION

Public School District Statistics

District Name	Schls	Pupils	Pupil/ Teacher Ratio	Minority Pupils[1] (%)	Free Lunch Eligible[2] (%)	IEP[3] (%)
Early Light Academy at Daybreak	1	998	n/a	14.6	13.4	11.7
Hawthorn Academy	2	1,464	n/a	26.3	20.1	10.4
Jordan District	59	52,985	n/a	21.7	17.3	12.0
Mountain West Montessori Academy	1	492	n/a	14.6	7.7	13.8
Paradigm High School	1	584	n/a	12.0	22.1	14.4

Note: Table includes school districts with 100 or more students; (1) Percentage of students that are not non-Hispanic white; (2) Percentage of students that are eligible for the free lunch program; (3) Percentage of students that have an Individualized Education Program.
Source: U.S. Department of Education, National Center for Education Statistics, Common Core of Data, Local Education Agency (School District) Universe Survey: School Year 2015-2016; U.S. Department of Education, National Center for Education Statistics, Common Core of Data, Public Elementary/Secondary School Universe Survey: School Year 2015-2016

Highest Level of Education

Area	Less than H.S.	H.S. Diploma	Some College, No Deg.	Associate Degree	Bachelor's Degree	Master's Degree	Prof. School Degree	Doctorate Degree
City	3.3	16.7	28.3	11.7	25.7	10.7	2.1	1.4
MSA[1]	10.1	23.1	25.6	8.9	20.7	7.9	2.1	1.6
U.S.	13.0	27.5	21.0	8.2	18.8	8.2	2.0	1.3

Note: Figures cover persons age 25 and over; (1) Figures cover the Salt Lake City, UT Metropolitan Statistical Area—see Appendix B for areas included
Source: U.S. Census Bureau, 2012-2016 American Community Survey 5-Year Estimates

Educational Attainment by Race

Area	High School Graduate or Higher (%)					Bachelor's Degree or Higher (%)				
	Total	White	Black	Asian	Hisp.[2]	Total	White	Black	Asian	Hisp.[2]
City	96.7	97.6	83.2	93.3	86.1	40.1	39.7	37.1	56.1	40.0
MSA[1]	89.9	93.1	84.8	83.8	64.8	32.2	33.8	25.0	49.5	12.7
U.S.	87.0	88.9	84.3	86.3	65.7	30.3	31.6	20.0	52.1	14.7

Note: Figures shown cover persons 25 years old and over; (1) Figures cover the Salt Lake City, UT Metropolitan Statistical Area—see Appendix B for areas included; (2) People of Hispanic origin can be of any race
Source: U.S. Census Bureau, 2012-2016 American Community Survey 5-Year Estimates

School Enrollment by Grade and Control

Area	Preschool (%)		Kindergarten (%)		Grades 1 - 4 (%)		Grades 5 - 8 (%)		Grades 9 - 12 (%)	
	Public	Private	Public	Private	Public	Private	Public	Private	Public	Private
City	51.9	48.1	97.5	2.5	95.5	4.5	96.8	3.2	96.3	3.7
MSA[1]	54.4	45.6	91.1	8.9	93.1	6.9	92.8	7.2	93.8	6.2
U.S.	58.4	41.6	87.7	12.3	89.8	10.2	89.7	10.3	90.4	9.6

Note: Figures shown cover persons 3 years old and over; (1) Figures cover the Salt Lake City, UT Metropolitan Statistical Area—see Appendix B for areas included
Source: U.S. Census Bureau, 2012-2016 American Community Survey 5-Year Estimates

Average Salaries of Public School Classroom Teachers

Area	2015		2016		Change from 2015 to 2016	
	Dollars	Rank[1]	Dollars	Rank[1]	Percent	Rank[2]
Utah	46,689	44	46,887	45	0.4	33
U.S. Average	57,611	–	58,353	–	1.3	–

Note: (1) Rank ranges from 1 to 51 where 1 indicates highest salary; (2) Rank ranges from 1 to 51 where 1 indicates highest percent change.
Source: National Education Association, Rankings & Estimates: Rankings of the States 2016 and Estimates of School Statistics 2017

Higher Education

Four-Year Colleges			Two-Year Colleges			Medical Schools[1]	Law Schools[2]	Voc/Tech[3]
Public	Private Non-profit	Private For-profit	Public	Private Non-profit	Private For-profit			
0	0	0	0	0	0	0	0	1

Note: Figures cover institutions located within the city limits and include main campuses only; (1) includes schools accredited by the Liaison Committee on Medical Education and the American Osteopathic Association's Commission on Osteopathic College Accreditation; (2) includes ABA-accredited schools, schools with provisional ABA accreditation, and state accredited schools; (3) includes all schools with programs that are less than 2 years.
Source: National Center for Education Statistics, Integrated Postsecondary Education System (IPEDS), 2016-17; Wikipedia, List of Medical Schools in the United States, accessed April 2, 2018; Wikipedia, List of Law Schools in the United States, accessed April 2, 2018

According to *U.S. News & World Report,* the Salt Lake City, UT metro area is home to one of the best national universities in the U.S.: **University of Utah** (#110 tie). The indicators used to capture academic quality fall into a number of categories: assessment by administrators at peer institutions; retention of students; faculty resources; student selectivity; financial resources; alumni giving; high school counselor ratings of colleges; and graduation rate. *U.S. News & World Report, "America's Best Colleges 2018"*

According to *U.S. News & World Report,* the Salt Lake City, UT metro area is home to one of the top 100 law schools in the U.S.: **University of Utah (Quinney)** (#54 tie). The rankings are based on a weighted average of 12 measures of quality: peer assessment score; assessment score by lawyers/judges; median LSAT scores; median undergrad GPA; acceptance rate; employment rates for graduates; placement success; bar passage rate; faculty resources; expenditures per student; student/faculty ratio; and library resources. *U.S. News & World Report, "America's Best Graduate Schools, Law, 2019"*

According to *U.S. News & World Report,* the Salt Lake City, UT metro area is home to one of the top 75 medical schools for research in the U.S.: **University of Utah** (#41 tie). The rankings are based on a weighted average of 11 measures of quality: quality assessment; peer assessment score; assessment score by residency directors; research activity; total research activity; average research activity per faculty member; student selectivity; median MCAT total score; median undergraduate GPA; acceptance rate; and faculty resources. *U.S. News & World Report, "America's Best Graduate Schools, Medical, 2019"*

According to *U.S. News & World Report,* the Salt Lake City, UT metro area is home to one of the top 75 business schools in the U.S.: **University of Utah (Eccles)** (#44 tie). The rankings are based on a weighted average of the following nine measures: quality assessment; peer assessment; recruiter assessment; placement success; mean starting salary and bonus; student selectivity; mean GMAT and GRE scores; mean undergraduate GPA; and acceptance rate. *U.S. News & World Report, "America's Best Graduate Schools, Business, 2019"*

PRESIDENTIAL ELECTION

2016 Presidential Election Results

Area	Clinton	Trump	Johnson	Stein	Other
Salt Lake County	41.5	32.6	3.8	1.2	20.9
U.S.	48.0	45.9	3.3	1.1	1.7

Note: Results are percentages and may not add to 100% due to rounding
Source: Dave Leip's Atlas of U.S. Presidential Elections

EMPLOYERS

Major Employers

Company Name	Industry
ACS Commercial Solutions	Data entry service
Alsco	Laundry & garment services, nec
Boart Longyear Company	Test boring for nonmetallic minerals
Church of Jesus Christ of LDS	Mormon church
Comenity Capital Bank	State commercial banks
County of Salt Lake	Executive offices
EnergySolutions	Nonresidential construction, nec
Executive Office of the State of Utah	Executive offices
Granite School District Aid Association	Public elementary & secondary schools
Huntsman Corporation	Plastics materials & resins
Huntsman Holdings	Polystyrene resins
Intermountain Health Care	General medical & surgical hospitals
Jordan School District	Public elementary & secondary schools
Longyear Holdings	Test boring for nonmetallic minerals
Sinclair Oil Corporation	Petroleum refining
Smith's Food & Drug Centers	Grocery stores
Sportsman's Warehouse Holdings	Hunting equipment
State of Utah	Governor's office
The University of Utah	Colleges & universities
TPUSA	Telemarketing services
University of Utah Hospitals & Clinics	General medical & surgical hospitals
Utah Department of Human Services	Administration of social & manpower programs
Zions Bancorporation	Bank holding companies

Note: Companies shown are located within the Salt Lake City, UT Metropolitan Statistical Area.
Source: Hoovers.com; Wikipedia

PUBLIC SAFETY

Crime Rate

Area	All Crimes	Violent Crimes: Murder	Violent Crimes: Rape[3]	Violent Crimes: Robbery	Violent Crimes: Aggrav. Assault	Property Crimes: Burglary	Property Crimes: Larceny -Theft	Property Crimes: Motor Vehicle Theft
City	2,276.9	0.0	27.1	10.0	38.4	280.5	1,775.7	145.2
Metro[1]	5,009.9	3.9	69.5	103.9	233.2	612.4	3,396.6	590.4
U.S.	2,847.8	5.3	40.4	102.8	248.5	468.9	1,745.0	236.9

Note: Figures are crimes per 100,000 population; (1) Figures cover the Salt Lake City, UT Metropolitan Statistical Area—see Appendix B for areas included; (3) The city and U.S. figures shown were reported using the revised Uniform Crime Reporting (UCR) definition of rape. The metro area figures shown are an aggregate total of the data submitted using both the revised and legacy UCR definitions.
Source: FBI Uniform Crime Reports, 2016

Hate Crimes

Area	Number of Quarters Reported	Race/Ethnicity/ Ancestry	Religion	Sexual Orientation	Disability	Gender	Gender Identity
		Number of Incidents per Bias Motivation					
City	1	1	0	0	0	0	0
U.S.	4	3,489	1,273	1,076	70	31	124

Source: Federal Bureau of Investigation, Hate Crime Statistics 2016

Identity Theft Consumer Reports

Area	Reports	Reports per 100,000 Population	Rank[2]
MSA[1]	1,150	97	107
U.S.	371,061	114	-

Note: (1) Figures cover the Salt Lake City, UT Metropolitan Statistical Area—see Appendix B for areas included; (2) Rank ranges from 1 to 389 where 1 indicates greatest number of identity theft reports per 100,000 population
Source: Federal Trade Commission, Consumer Sentinel Network Data Book for January–December 2017

Fraud and Other Consumer Reports

Area	Reports	Reports per 100,000 Population	Rank[2]
MSA[1]	4,974	419	232
U.S.	2,304,550	708	-

Note: (1) Figures cover the Salt Lake City, UT Metropolitan Statistical Area—see Appendix B for areas included; (2) Rank ranges from 1 to 389 where 1 indicates greatest number of fraud and other consumer reports per 100,000 population
Source: Federal Trade Commission, Consumer Sentinel Network Data Book for January–December 2017

SPORTS

Professional Sports Teams

Team Name	League	Year Established
Real Salt Lake	Major League Soccer (MLS)	2005
Utah Jazz	National Basketball Association (NBA)	1979

Note: Includes teams located in the Salt Lake City, UT Metropolitan Statistical Area.
Source: Wikipedia, Major Professional Sports Teams of the United States and Canada, April 5, 2018

CLIMATE

Average and Extreme Temperatures

Temperature	Jan	Feb	Mar	Apr	May	Jun	Jul	Aug	Sep	Oct	Nov	Dec	Yr.
Extreme High (°F)	62	69	78	85	93	104	107	104	100	89	75	67	107
Average High (°F)	37	43	52	62	72	83	93	90	80	66	50	38	64
Average Temp. (°F)	28	34	41	50	59	69	78	76	65	53	40	30	52
Average Low (°F)	19	24	31	38	46	54	62	61	51	40	30	22	40
Extreme Low (°F)	-22	-14	2	15	25	35	40	37	27	16	-14	-15	-22

Note: Figures cover the years 1948-1990
Source: National Climatic Data Center, International Station Meteorological Climate Summary, 9/96

Average Precipitation/Snowfall/Humidity

Precip./Humidity	Jan	Feb	Mar	Apr	May	Jun	Jul	Aug	Sep	Oct	Nov	Dec	Yr.
Avg. Precip. (in.)	1.3	1.2	1.8	2.0	1.7	0.9	0.8	0.9	1.1	1.3	1.3	1.4	15.6
Avg. Snowfall (in.)	13	10	11	6	1	Tr	0	0	Tr	2	6	13	63
Avg. Rel. Hum. 5am (%)	79	77	71	67	66	60	53	54	60	68	75	79	67
Avg. Rel. Hum. 5pm (%)	69	59	47	38	33	26	22	23	28	40	59	71	43

Note: Figures cover the years 1948-1990; Tr = Trace amounts (<0.05 in. of rain; <0.5 in. of snow)
Source: National Climatic Data Center, International Station Meteorological Climate Summary, 9/96

Weather Conditions

Temperature			Daytime Sky			Precipitation		
5°F & below	32°F & below	90°F & above	Clear	Partly cloudy	Cloudy	0.01 inch or more precip.	0.1 inch or more snow/ice	Thunder-storms
7	128	56	94	152	119	92	38	38

Note: Figures are average number of days per year and cover the years 1948-1990
Source: National Climatic Data Center, International Station Meteorological Climate Summary, 9/96

HAZARDOUS WASTE

Superfund Sites

The Salt Lake City, UT metro area is home to 10 sites on the EPA's Superfund National Priorities List: **700 South 1600 East PCE Plume** (final); **Davenport and Flagstaff Smelters** (final); **Jacobs Smelter** (final); **Kennecott (North Zone)** (proposed); **Murray Smelter** (proposed); **Portland Cement (Kiln Dust 2 & 3)** (final); **Tooele Army Depot (North Area)** (final); **Us Magnesium** (final); **Utah Power & Light/American Barrel Co.** (final); **Wasatch Chemical Co. (Lot 6)** (final). There are a total of 1,396 Superfund sites with a status of proposed or final on the list in the U.S. *U.S. Environmental Protection Agency, National Priorities List, April 4, 2018*

AIR & WATER QUALITY

Air Quality Trends: Ozone

	1990	1995	2000	2005	2010	2012	2013	2014	2015	2016
MSA[1]	n/a	n/a	n/a	n/a	n/a	n/a	n/a	n/a	n/a	n/a
U.S.	0.087	0.089	0.081	0.079	0.073	0.075	0.069	0.067	0.068	0.069

Note: (1) Data covers the Salt Lake City, UT Metropolitan Statistical Area—see Appendix B for areas included; n/a not available. The values shown are the composite ozone concentration averages among trend sites based on the highest fourth daily maximum 8-hour concentration in parts per million. These trends are based on sites having an adequate record of monitoring data during the trend period. Data from exceptional events are included.
Source: U.S. Environmental Protection Agency, Air Quality Monitoring Information, "Air Quality Trends by City, 1990-2016"

Air Quality Index

Area	Percent of Days when Air Quality was...[2]					AQI Statistics[2]	
	Good	Moderate	Unhealthy for Sensitive Groups	Unhealthy	Very Unhealthy	Maximum	Median
MSA[1]	44.7	43.0	12.1	0.3	0.0	155	53

Note: (1) Data covers the Salt Lake City, UT Metropolitan Statistical Area—see Appendix B for areas included; (2) Based on 365 days with AQI data in 2017. Air Quality Index (AQI) is an index for reporting daily air quality. EPA calculates the AQI for five major air pollutants regulated by the Clean Air Act: ground-level ozone, particle pollution (aka particulate matter), carbon monoxide, sulfur dioxide, and nitrogen dioxide. The AQI runs from 0 to 500. The higher the AQI value, the greater the level of air pollution and the greater the health concern. There are six AQI categories: "Good" AQI is between 0 and 50. Air quality is considered satisfactory; "Moderate" AQI is between 51 and 100. Air quality is acceptable; "Unhealthy for Sensitive Groups" When AQI values are between 101 and 150, members of sensitive groups may experience health effects; "Unhealthy" When AQI values are between 151 and 200 everyone may begin to experience health effects; "Very Unhealthy" AQI values between 201 and 300 trigger a health alert; "Hazardous" AQI values over 300 trigger warnings of emergency conditions (not shown).
Source: U.S. Environmental Protection Agency, Air Quality Index Report, 2017

Air Quality Index Pollutants

Area	Percent of Days when AQI Pollutant was...[2]					
	Carbon Monoxide	Nitrogen Dioxide	Ozone	Sulfur Dioxide	Particulate Matter 2.5	Particulate Matter 10
MSA[1]	0.0	3.0	69.3	0.0	26.8	0.8

Note: (1) Data covers the Salt Lake City, UT Metropolitan Statistical Area—see Appendix B for areas included; (2) Based on 365 days with AQI data in 2017. The Air Quality Index (AQI) is an index for reporting daily air quality. EPA calculates the AQI for five major air pollutants regulated by the Clean Air Act: ground-level ozone, particle pollution (also known as particulate matter), carbon monoxide, sulfur dioxide, and nitrogen dioxide. The AQI runs from 0 to 500. The higher the AQI value, the greater the level of air pollution and the greater the health concern.
Source: U.S. Environmental Protection Agency, Air Quality Index Report, 2017

Maximum Air Pollutant Concentrations: Particulate Matter, Ozone, CO and Lead

	Particulate Matter 10 (ug/m^3)	Particulate Matter 2.5 Wtd AM (ug/m^3)	Particulate Matter 2.5 24-Hr (ug/m^3)	Ozone (ppm)	Carbon Monoxide (ppm)	Lead (ug/m^3)
MSA[1] Level	78	9.4	43	0.076	n/a	0.05
NAAQS[2]	150	15	35	0.075	9	0.15
Met NAAQS[2]	Yes	Yes	No	No	n/a	Yes

Note: (1) Data covers the Salt Lake City, UT Metropolitan Statistical Area—see Appendix B for areas included; Data from exceptional events are included; (2) National Ambient Air Quality Standards; ppm = parts per million; ug/m^3 = micrograms per cubic meter; n/a not available.
Concentrations: Particulate Matter 10 (coarse particulate)—highest second maximum 24-hour concentration; Particulate Matter 2.5 Wtd AM (fine particulate)—highest weighted annual mean concentration; Particulate Matter 2.5 24-Hour (fine particulate)—highest 98th percentile 24-hour concentration; Ozone—highest fourth daily maximum 8-hour concentration; Carbon Monoxide—highest second maximum non-overlapping 8-hour concentration; Lead—maximum running 3-month average
Source: U.S. Environmental Protection Agency, Air Quality Monitoring Information, "Air Quality Statistics by City, 2016"

Maximum Air Pollutant Concentrations: Nitrogen Dioxide and Sulfur Dioxide

	Nitrogen Dioxide AM (ppb)	Nitrogen Dioxide 1-Hr (ppb)	Sulfur Dioxide AM (ppb)	Sulfur Dioxide 1-Hr (ppb)	Sulfur Dioxide 24-Hr (ppb)
MSA[1] Level	7	48	n/a	n/a	n/a
NAAQS[2]	53	100	30	75	140
Met NAAQS[2]	Yes	Yes	n/a	n/a	n/a

Note: (1) Data covers the Salt Lake City, UT Metropolitan Statistical Area—see Appendix B for areas included; Data from exceptional events are included; (2) National Ambient Air Quality Standards; ppm = parts per million; ug/m^3 = micrograms per cubic meter; n/a not available.
Concentrations: Nitrogen Dioxide AM—highest arithmetic mean concentration; Nitrogen Dioxide 1-Hr—highest 98th percentile 1-hour daily maximum concentration; Sulfur Dioxide AM—highest annual mean concentration; Sulfur Dioxide 1-Hr—highest 99th percentile 1-hour daily maximum concentration; Sulfur Dioxide 24-Hr—highest second maximum 24-hour concentration
Source: U.S. Environmental Protection Agency, Air Quality Monitoring Information, "Air Quality Statistics by City, 2016"

Drinking Water

Water System Name	Pop. Served	Primary Water Source Type	Violations[1]	
			Health Based	Monitoring/ Reporting
South Jordan City	57,067	Purchased Surface	0	0

Note: (1) Based on violation data from January 1, 2017 to December 31, 2017
Source: U.S. Environmental Protection Agency, Office of Ground Water and Drinking Water, Safe Drinking Water Information System (based on data extracted April 5, 2018)

Syracuse, Utah

Background

Syracuse is a vibrant city in Davis County, situated between the Great Salt Lake and Interstate 15, about 30 miles north of Salt Lake City. The city is bordered to the north by West Point, to the northeast by Clearfield, and to the southeast by Layton. Syracuse covers a total area of about 9.6 square miles.

The Homestead Act of 1862 made the land that is now Syracuse available for settlement. David Cook is thought to be the first person to work the land, ploughing in the spring of 1876, and harvesting the first grain that fall. The land was fertile but was slow to produce due to the lack of water in the desert environment. This changed when the Hooper Canal was extended to bring fresh water from the Weber River. With access to water, homesteads were established quite quickly and efficiently and, within 20 years of the first settlers, most of the land was being cultivated. The farmers soon realized the land was well suited for fruit farming and by the turn of the 20th century, the Syracuse area was the largest producer of fruit in Davis County.

The name Syracuse comes from the influence of William Galbraith, a salt maker on the Great Salt Lake. He printed the name Syracuse on his salt bags, inspired from a salt company he knew of in Syracuse, New York. The name was also used by the Syracuse Bathing Resort, built in 1887 on the shores of the Great Salt Lake. When the Union Pacific Railroad constructed the Ogden and Syracuse Railway in 1887, the railway linked the Syracuse Resort to the main line between Ogden and Salt Lake City. At this time, the name Syracuse was adopted as the official name of the city.

Today, Syracuse is a vibrant small city of about 27,000 residents who enjoy a high quality life in a safe, family oriented area. The city is nestled between the towering Wasatch Mountains and the Great Salt Lake and is known as the 'Gateway to Antelope Island,' the massive national park island in the Great Salt Lake. The park offers many recreation activities and facilities including beaches, showers, grills, hiking trails and bike paths, horse riding trails, a visitor's center, and art displays and exhibits. Syracuse is surrounded by natural beauty and offers many ways to explore the wilderness.

The beautiful natural setting along with its diverse economy and friendly people make Syracuse an ideal place to raise a family and conduct business. With the growth of the city in recent years, there has been ongoing commercial development, including a new Town Center within walking distance to city offices, police and fire stations, and community center. The Town Center includes expanding retail offerings, new restaurants, and housing opportunities. The city benefits from a well-managed city government and services, and well-planned and maintained public spaces. Syracuse also boasts a number of excellent public schools that consistently rank high within the state.

Syracuse has a distinct arts community supported by the Syracuse City Arts Council. The Arts Council prides itself on its commitment to providing learning experiences, as well as opportunities to express and display the creative endeavors of Syracuse residents and visitors. Performing arts in music and theatre also contribute to the vibrant arts scene in the city. The Syracuse Museum and Cultural Center works to celebrate and preserve the local history of the city. The main building is a site of curated collections of personal belongings from the pioneer days of Utah, as well as family histories and memorabilia. The center also houses items related to the agricultural history of Syracuse in the 1900s.

Syracuse sees about 18 inches of rain per year and an average of 36 inches of snowfall. The city has an average of 230 days of sunshine and four distinct seasons. The mountainous setting makes for glorious summers with little humidity and temperatures in the upper 80s. Winters are cold and temperatures can drop into the teens.

Rankings

Business/Finance Rankings

- The personal finance site NerdWallet analyzed 183 American metropolitan areas with populations over 250,000 and more than 15,000 businesses to rank where entrepreneurs find the most success. Criteria included area economy, annual income, housing cost, unemployment rate, and the success rate of area businesses. Ogden* ranked #120. *www.nerdwallet.com, "Best Places to Start a Business," April 27, 2015*

- 24/7 Wall Street used Brookings Institution research on 50 advanced industries to identify the proportion of workers in the nation's largest metropolitan areas that were employed in jobs requiring knowledge in the science, technology, engineering, or math (STEM) fields and where there was heavy investment in research and development (R&D). The Ogden* metro area was #14. *247wallst.com, "15 Cities with the Most High-Tech Jobs," February 23, 2017*

- The Brookings Institution ranked the 100 largest metro areas in the U.S. based on income inequality. Ogden* was ranked #100 (#1 = greatest ineqality). Criteria: the "95/20 ratio," a figure representing the income at which a household earns more than 95 percent of all other households, divided by the income at which a household earns more than only 20 percent of all other households. *Brookings Institution, "Household Income Inequality, 100 Largest U.S. Metro Areas, 2014-2016," February 5, 2018*

- The Ogden* metro area appeared on the Milken Institute "2017 Best Performing Cities" list. Rank: #28 out of 200 large metro areas. Criteria: job growth; wage and salary growth; high-tech output growth. *Milken Institute, "Best-Performing Cities 2017," January 2018*

- *Forbes* ranked the 200 most populous metro areas to determine the nation's "Best Places for Business and Careers." The Ogden* metro area was ranked #33. Criteria: costs (business and living); job growth (past and projected); income growth; quality of life; educational attainment (college and high school); projected economic growth; cultural and recreational opportunities; net migration patterns; number of highly ranked colleges. *Forbes, "The Best Places for Business and Careers 2017," October 24, 2017*

Children/Family Rankings

- *Forbes* analyzed data on the 100 largest metropolitan areas in the United States to compile its 2016 ranking of the best cities for raising a family. The Ogden* metro area was ranked #2. Criteria: median income; childcare costs; percent of population under 18; commuting delays; crime rate; percentage of families owning homes; education quality (mainly test scores). Overall cost of living and housing affordability was also unofficially considered. *Forbes, "America's Best Cities for Raising a Family 2016," August 30, 2016*

Education Rankings

- Personal finance website *WalletHub* analyzed the 150 largest U.S. metropolitan statistical areas to determine where the most educated Americans are choosing to settle. Criteria: education quality and attainment gap; education levels; percentage of workers with degrees; public school rankings; quality and size of each metro area's universities. Ogden* was ranked #68 (#1 = most educated city). *www.WalletHub.com, "2017's Most and Least Educated Cities in America," July 25, 2017*

Environmental Rankings

- Sperling's BestPlaces assessed 379 metropolitan areas of the United States for the likelihood of dangerously extreme weather events or earthquakes. In general the Southeast and South-Central regions have the highest risk of weather extremes and earthquakes, while the Pacific Northwest enjoys the lowest risk. Of the least risky metropolitan areas, the Ogden* metro area was ranked #39. *www.bestplaces.net, "Safest Places from Natural Disasters," April 2011*

Food/Drink Rankings

- For the Gallup-Healthways Well-Being Index, researchers interviewed at least 300 adults in each of 189 metropolitan areas on residents' access to affordable fresh produce. The Ogden* metro area was found to be among the top ten communities for accessibility to affordable produce. *www.gallup.com, "In Anchorage, Access to Fruits and Vegetables Remains Lowest," April 8, 2014*

Health/Fitness Rankings

- Ogden* was identified as a "2016 Spring Allergy Capital." The area ranked #90 out of 100. Three groups of factors were used to identify the most severe cities for people with allergies during the spring season: annual pollen levels; medicine utilization; access to board-certified allergists. *Asthma and Allergy Foundation of America, "Spring Allergy Capitals 2016"*
- Ogden* was identified as a "2016 Fall Allergy Capital." The area ranked #84 out of 100. Three groups of factors were used to identify the most severe cities for people with allergies during the fall season: annual pollen levels; medicine utilization; access to board-certified allergists. *Asthma and Allergy Foundation of America, "Fall Allergy Capitals 2016"*
- Ogden* was identified as a "2015 Asthma Capital." The area ranked #69 out of the nation's 100 largest metropolitan areas. Criteria: estimated prevalence; self-reported prevalence; crude death rate for asthma; annual pollen score; annual air quality; public smoking laws; number of board-certified asthma specialists; school inhaler access laws; rescue medication use; controller medication use; ER visits for asthma; uninsured rate; poverty rate. *Asthma and Allergy Foundation of America, "Asthma Capitals 2015"*
- The Ogden* metro area ranked #51 out of 189 in The Gallup-Healthways Well-Being Index. Criteria: purpose; social well being; financial health; community and physical health. Results are based on telephone interviews with adults, aged 18 and older, living in metropolitan areas in the 50 U.S. states and the District of Columbia. *Gallup-Healthways, "State of American Well-Being, 2017 Community Well-Being Rankings" March 2018*

Real Estate Rankings

- The Ogden* metro area was identified as one of the top 20 housing markets to invest in for 2018 by *Forbes*. The area ranked #5. Criteria: strong job and population growth; anticipated home price appreciation; and other factors. *Forbes.com, "Where to Invest in Housing in 2018," February 1, 2018*
- Ogden* was ranked #18 in the top 20 out of 265 metro areas in terms of house price appreciation in 2017 (#1 = highest rate). *Federal Housing Finance Agency, House Price Index, 4th Quarter 2017. February 27, 2018*
- Ogden* was ranked #90 out of 238 metro areas in terms of housing affordability in 2017 by the National Association of Home Builders (#1 = most affordable). Criteria: the share of homes sold in that area affordable to a family earning the local median income, based on standard mortgage underwriting criteria. *National Association of Home Builders®, NAHB-Wells Fargo Housing Opportunity Index, 4th Quarter 2017*

Safety Rankings

- The National Insurance Crime Bureau ranked 382 metro areas in the U.S. in terms of per capita rates of vehicle theft. The Ogden* metro area ranked #233 (#1 = highest rate). Criteria: number of vehicle theft offenses per 100,000 inhabitants in 2016. *National Insurance Crime Bureau, "Hot Spots 2016," June 8, 2017*

Seniors/Retirement Rankings

- From its Best Cities for Successful Aging indexes, the Milken Institute generated rankings for metropolitan areas, weighing data in nine categories—health care, wellness, living arrangements, transportation and convenience, financial characteristics, education, employment, community engagement, and overall livability. The Ogden* metro area was ranked #38 overall in the large metro area category. *Milken Institute, "Best Cities for Successful Aging, 2017" March 14, 2017*

Women/Minorities Rankings

- *24/7 Wall St.* compared median earnings over a 12-month period for men and women who worked full-time, year-round, and employment composition by sector to identify the worst-paying cities for women. Of the largest 100 U.S. metropolitan areas, Ogden* was ranked #5 in pay disparity. *24/7 Wall St., "The Best (and Worst) Paying Cities for Women," March 27, 2017*

Miscellaneous Rankings

- The finance and lifestyle site NerdWallet looked for the U.S. cities that topped the list in donating money and time to good causes. The Ogden* metro area proved to be the #2-ranked metro area, judged by culture of volunteerism, depth of commitment in terms of volunteer hours per year, and monetary contributions. *www.nerdwallet.com, "Most Generous Cities," September 22, 2013*

*Syracuse is located within the Ogden-Clearfield, UT Metropolitan Statistical Area.

Business Environment

CITY FINANCES

City Government Finances

Component	2015 ($000)	2015 ($ per capita)
Total Revenues	23,176	846
Total Expenditures	18,705	683
Debt Outstanding	6,481	237
Cash and Securities[1]	12,597	460

Note: (1) Cash and security holdings of a government at the close of its fiscal year,, including those of its dependent agencies, utilities, and liquor stores.
Source: U.S Census Bureau, State & Local Government Finances 2015

City Government Revenue by Source

Source	2015 ($000)	2015 ($ per capita)	2015 (%)
General Revenue			
From Federal Government	1,264	46	5.5
From State Government	916	33	4.0
From Local Governments	16	1	0.1
Taxes			
Property	1,923	70	8.3
Sales and Gross Receipts	4,677	171	20.2
Personal Income	0	0	0.0
Corporate Income	0	0	0.0
Motor Vehicle License	0	0	0.0
Other Taxes	580	21	2.5
Current Charges	7,084	259	30.6
Liquor Store	0	0	0.0
Utility	1,890	69	8.2
Employee Retirement	0	0	0.0

Source: U.S Census Bureau, State & Local Government Finances 2015

City Government Expenditures by Function

Function	2015 ($000)	2015 ($ per capita)	2015 (%)
General Direct Expenditures			
Air Transportation	0	0	0.0
Corrections	0	0	0.0
Education	0	0	0.0
Employment Security Administration	0	0	0.0
Financial Administration	0	0	0.0
Fire Protection	1,173	42	6.3
General Public Buildings	419	15	2.2
Governmental Administration, Other	3,038	110	16.2
Health	0	0	0.0
Highways	3,515	128	18.8
Hospitals	0	0	0.0
Housing and Community Development	0	0	0.0
Interest on General Debt	416	15	2.2
Judicial and Legal	190	6	1.0
Libraries	0	0	0.0
Parking	0	0	0.0
Parks and Recreation	1,136	41	6.1
Police Protection	2,247	82	12.0
Public Welfare	0	0	0.0
Sewerage	1,512	55	8.1
Solid Waste Management	0	0	0.0
Veterans' Services	0	0	0.0
Liquor Store	0	0	0.0
Utility	1,037	37	5.5
Employee Retirement	0	0	0.0

Source: U.S Census Bureau, State & Local Government Finances 2015

DEMOGRAPHICS

Population Growth

Area	1990 Census	2000 Census	2010 Census	2016* Estimate	Population Growth (%) 1990-2016	2010-2016
City	4,977	9,398	24,331	26,668	435.8	9.6
MSA[1]	351,799	442,656	547,184	632,793	79.9	15.6
U.S.	248,709,873	281,421,906	308,745,538	318,558,162	28.1	3.2

Note: (1) Figures cover the Ogden-Clearfield, UT Metropolitan Statistical Area—see Appendix B for areas included; (*) 2012-2016 5-year estimated population
Source: U.S. Census Bureau, 1990 Census, Census 2000, Census 2010, 2012-2016 American Community Survey 5-Year Estimates

Household Size

Area	Persons in Household (%) One	Two	Three	Four	Five	Six	Seven or More	Average Household Size
City	7.0	25.1	13.8	20.4	15.5	11.4	6.9	3.90
MSA[1]	18.2	30.7	15.1	15.5	10.6	6.3	3.6	3.20
U.S.	27.7	33.7	15.7	13.1	6.0	2.3	1.5	2.60

Note: (1) Figures cover the Ogden-Clearfield, UT Metropolitan Statistical Area—see Appendix B for areas included
Source: U.S. Census Bureau, 2012-2016 American Community Survey 5-Year Estimates

Race

Area	White Alone[2] (%)	Black Alone[2] (%)	Asian Alone[2] (%)	AIAN[3] Alone[2] (%)	NHOPI[4] Alone[2] (%)	Other Race Alone[2] (%)	Two or More Races (%)
City	92.3	1.7	1.0	0.1	0.0	1.4	3.6
MSA[1]	89.8	1.1	1.5	0.6	0.4	3.6	2.9
U.S.	73.3	12.6	5.2	0.8	0.2	4.8	3.1

Note: (1) Figures cover the Ogden-Clearfield, UT Metropolitan Statistical Area—see Appendix B for areas included; (2) Alone is defined as not being in combination with one or more other races; (3) American Indian and Alaska Native; (4) Native Hawaiian and Other Pacific Islander
Source: U.S. Census Bureau, 2012-2016 American Community Survey 5-Year Estimates

Hispanic or Latino Origin

Area	Total (%)	Mexican (%)	Puerto Rican (%)	Cuban (%)	Other (%)
City	5.9	3.7	0.0	0.0	2.2
MSA[1]	12.2	8.8	0.3	0.0	3.0
U.S.	17.3	11.0	1.7	0.7	4.0

Note: Persons of Hispanic or Latino origin can be of any race; (1) Figures cover the Ogden-Clearfield, UT Metropolitan Statistical Area—see Appendix B for areas included
Source: U.S. Census Bureau, 2012-2016 American Community Survey 5-Year Estimates

Segregation

Type	Segregation Indices[1] 1990	2000	2010	2010 Rank[2]	Percent Change 1990-2000	1990-2010	2000-2010
Black/White	49.8	42.0	32.0	98	-7.8	-17.9	-10.0
Asian/White	25.9	23.1	20.5	102	-2.9	-5.4	-2.6
Hispanic/White	35.5	39.7	35.8	81	4.2	0.3	-3.9

Note: All figures cover the Metropolitan Statistical Area—see Appendix B for areas included; Figures are based on an analysis of 1990, 2000, and 2010 Census Decennial Census tract data by William H. Frey, Brookings Institution and the University of Michigan Social Science Data Analysis Network. In this analysis all racial groups (whites, blacks, and asians) are non-Hispanic members of those races. Hispanics are shown as a separate category; (1) Segregation Indices are Dissimilarity Indices that measure the degree to which the minority group is distributed differently than whites across census tracts. They range from 0 (complete integration) to 100 (complete segregation) where the value indicates the percentage of the minority group that needs to move to be distributed exactly like whites; (2) Ranges from 1 (most segregated) to 102 (least segregated); n/a not available.
Source: www.CensusScope.org

Ancestry

Area	German	Irish	English	American	Italian	Polish	French[2]	Scottish	Dutch
City	9.2	5.8	27.8	9.8	2.5	1.6	2.4	5.4	1.6
MSA[1]	11.3	5.5	25.0	7.8	2.7	0.7	1.8	4.6	2.8
U.S.	14.4	10.4	7.7	6.9	5.4	2.9	2.6	1.7	1.3

Note: Figures are the percentage of the total population reporting a particular ancestry. The nine most commonly reported ancestries in the U.S. are shown. Figures include multiple ancestries (e.g. if a person reported being Irish and Italian, they were included in both columns); (1) Figures cover the Ogden-Clearfield, UT Metropolitan Statistical Area—see Appendix B for areas included; (2) Excludes Basque
Source: U.S. Census Bureau, 2012-2016 American Community Survey 5-Year Estimates

Foreign-Born Population

Area	Percent of Population Born in								
	Any Foreign Country	Asia	Mexico	Europe	Carribean	Central America[2]	South America	Africa	Canada
City	2.5	0.4	0.3	0.7	0.1	0.1	0.6	0.3	0.2
MSA[1]	5.5	1.0	2.5	0.6	0.0	0.4	0.5	0.1	0.2
U.S.	13.2	4.0	3.6	1.5	1.3	1.0	0.9	0.6	0.3

Note: (1) Figures cover the Ogden-Clearfield, UT Metropolitan Statistical Area—see Appendix B for areas included; (2) Excludes Mexico.
Source: U.S. Census Bureau, 2012-2016 American Community Survey 5-Year Estimates

Marital Status

Area	Never Married	Now Married[2]	Separated	Widowed	Divorced
City	24.0	66.6	0.9	1.4	7.2
MSA[1]	26.1	58.9	1.6	3.5	9.9
U.S.	33.0	48.1	2.1	5.9	11.0

Note: Figures are percentages and cover the population 15 years of age and older; (1) Figures cover the Ogden-Clearfield, UT Metropolitan Statistical Area—see Appendix B for areas included; (2) Excludes separated
Source: U.S. Census Bureau, 2012-2016 American Community Survey 5-Year Estimates

Disability Status

Area	All Ages	Under 18 Years Old	18 to 64 Years Old	65 Years and Over
City	7.0	2.7	8.3	24.9
MSA[1]	10.3	3.7	9.6	35.3
U.S.	12.5	4.1	10.3	35.7

Note: Figures show percent of the civilian noninstitutionalized population that reported having a disability. Disability status is determined from six types of difficulty: vision, hearing, cognitive, ambulatory, self-care, and independent living. For children under 5 years old, hearing and vision difficulty are used to determine disability status. For children between the ages of 5 and 14, disability status is determined from hearing, vision, cognitive, ambulatory, and self-care difficulties. For people aged 15 years and older, they are considered to have a disability if they have difficulty with any one of the six difficulty types; Note: (1) Figures cover the Ogden-Clearfield, UT Metropolitan Statistical Area—see Appendix B for areas included
Source: U.S. Census Bureau, 2012-2016 American Community Survey 5-Year Estimates

Age

Area	Percent of Population									Median Age
	Under Age 5	Age 5–19	Age 20–34	Age 35–44	Age 45–54	Age 55–64	Age 65–74	Age 75–84	Age 85+	
City	8.4	35.5	14.7	16.9	11.4	7.1	3.6	2.1	0.3	27.8
MSA[1]	8.7	25.7	21.5	13.4	10.9	9.8	5.8	3.2	1.2	31.2
U.S.	6.2	19.6	20.7	12.7	13.6	12.6	8.3	4.3	1.9	37.7

Note: (1) Figures cover the Ogden-Clearfield, UT Metropolitan Statistical Area—see Appendix B for areas included
Source: U.S. Census Bureau, 2012-2016 American Community Survey 5-Year Estimates

Gender

Area	Males	Females	Males per 100 Females
City	13,673	12,995	105.2
MSA[1]	318,228	314,565	101.2
U.S.	156,765,322	161,792,840	96.9

Note: (1) Figures cover the Ogden-Clearfield, UT Metropolitan Statistical Area—see Appendix B for areas included
Source: U.S. Census Bureau, 2012-2016 American Community Survey 5-Year Estimates

Religious Groups by Family

Area	Catholic	Baptist	Non-Den.	Methodist[2]	Lutheran	LDS[3]	Pente-costal	Presby-terian[4]	Muslim[5]	Judaism
MSA[1]	5.8	1.0	0.9	0.2	0.5	68.7	1.2	0.2	<0.1	<0.1
U.S.	19.1	9.3	4.0	4.0	2.3	2.0	1.9	1.6	0.8	0.7

Note: Figures are the number of adherents as a percentage of the total population; (1) Figures cover the Ogden-Clearfield, UT Metropolitan Statistical Area—see Appendix B for areas included; (2) Methodist/Pietist; (3) Latter Day Saints; (4) Reformed; (5) Figures are estimates
Source: Association of Statisticians of American Religious Bodies, 2010 U.S. Religion Census: Religious Congregations & Membership Study

Religious Groups by Tradition

Area	Catholic	Evangelical Protestant	Mainline Protestant	Other Tradition	Black Protestant	Orthodox
MSA[1]	5.8	3.4	0.7	69.3	0.2	0.1
U.S.	19.1	16.2	7.3	4.3	1.6	0.3

Note: Figures are the number of adherents as a percentage of the total population; (1) Figures cover the Ogden-Clearfield, UT Metropolitan Statistical Area—see Appendix B for areas included
Source: Association of Statisticians of American Religious Bodies, 2010 U.S. Religion Census: Religious Congregations & Membership Study

ECONOMY

Gross Metropolitan Product

Area	2014	2015	2016	2017	Rank[2]
MSA[1]	23.6	24.8	25.9	27.5	100

Note: Figures are in billions of dollars; (1) Figures cover the Ogden-Clearfield, UT Metropolitan Statistical Area—see Appendix B for areas included; (2) Rank is based on 2015 data and ranges from 1 to 381
Source: The U.S. Conference of Mayors, U.S. Metro Economies: GMP and Employment Report, 2015-2017

Economic Growth

Area	2012-14 (%)	2015 (%)	2016 (%)	2017 (%)	Rank[2]
MSA[1]	3.7	4.1	2.5	3.7	35
U.S.	2.0	2.4	1.9	2.6	–

Note: Figures are real gross metropolitan product (GMP) growth rates and represent average annual percent change; (1) Figures cover the Ogden-Clearfield, UT Metropolitan Statistical Area—see Appendix B for areas included; (2) Rank is based on 2012-2014 average annual percent change and ranges from 1 to 381
Source: The U.S. Conference of Mayors, U.S. Metro Economies: GMP and Employment Report, 2015-2017

Metropolitan Area Exports

Area	2011	2012	2013	2014	2015	2016	Rank[2]
MSA[1]	896.5	855.5	1,310.0	1,363.6	1,415.6	1,602.2	110

Note: Figures are in millions of dollars; (1) Figures cover the Ogden-Clearfield, UT Metropolitan Statistical Area—see Appendix B for areas included; (2) Rank is based on 2016 data and ranges from 1 to 385
Source: U.S. Department of Commerce, International Trade Administration, Office of Trade & Industry Information, Manufacturing & Services, data extracted March 15, 2018

Building Permits

Area	Single-Family			Multi-Family			Total		
	2016	2017p	Pct. Chg.	2016	2017p	Pct. Chg.	2016	2017p	Pct. Chg.
City	324	270	-16.7	0	0	0.0	324	270	-16.7
MSA[1]	2,198	2,300	4.6	1,237	960	-22.4	3,435	3,260	-5.1
U.S.	750,800	817,300	8.9	455,800	446,800	-2.0	1,206,600	1,264,100	4.8

Note: (1) Figures cover the Ogden-Clearfield, UT Metropolitan Statistical Area—see Appendix B for areas included; Figures represent new, privately-owned housing units authorized (unadjusted data); All permit data are based on estimates with imputation; (p) preliminary data.
Source: U.S. Census Bureau, Manufacturing, Mining, and Construction Statistics, Building Permits, 2016, 2017

Bankruptcy Filings

Area	Business Filings			Nonbusiness Filings		
	2016	2017	% Chg.	2016	2017	% Chg.
Davis County	25	12	-52.0	1,218	1,264	3.8
U.S.	24,114	23,157	-4.0	770,846	765,863	-0.6

Note: Business filings include Chapter 7, Chapter 11, Chapter 12, and Chapter 13; Nonbusiness filings include Chapter 7, Chapter 11, and Chapter 13
Source: Administrative Office of the U.S. Courts, Business and Nonbusiness Bankruptcy, County Cases Commenced by Chapter of the Bankruptcy Code, During the 12-Month Period Ending December 31, 2016 and Business and Nonbusiness Bankruptcy, County Cases Commenced by Chapter of the Bankruptcy Code, During the 12-Month Period Ending December 31, 2017

Housing Vacancy Rates

Area	Gross Vacancy Rate[2] (%)			Year-Round Vacancy Rate[3] (%)			Rental Vacancy Rate[4] (%)			Homeowner Vacancy Rate[5] (%)		
	2015	2016	2017	2015	2016	2017	2015	2016	2017	2015	2016	2017
MSA[1]	n/a	n/a	n/a	n/a	n/a	n/a	n/a	n/a	n/a	n/a	n/a	n/a
U.S.	12.9	12.8	12.7	10.0	9.9	9.9	7.1	6.9	7.2	1.8	1.7	1.6

Note: (1) Figures cover the Ogden-Clearfield, UT Metropolitan Statistical Area—see Appendix B for areas included; (2) The percentage of the total housing inventory that is vacant; (3) The percentage of the housing inventory (excluding seasonal units) that is year-round vacant; (4) The percentage of rental inventory that is vacant for rent; (5) The percentage of homeowner inventory that is vacant for sale; n/a not available
Source: U.S. Census Bureau, Housing Vacancies and Homeownership Annual Statistics: 2015, 2016, 2017

INCOME

Income

Area	Per Capita ($)	Median Household ($)	Average Household ($)
City	26,867	88,284	102,218
MSA[1]	25,568	65,687	78,987
U.S.	29,829	55,322	77,866

Note: (1) Figures cover the Ogden-Clearfield, UT Metropolitan Statistical Area—see Appendix B for areas included
Source: U.S. Census Bureau, 2012-2016 American Community Survey 5-Year Estimates

Household Income Distribution

Area	Percent of Households Earning							
	Under $15,000	$15,000 -$24,999	$25,000 -$34,999	$35,000 -$49,999	$50,000 -$74,999	$75,000 -$99,999	$100,000 -$149,999	$150,000 and up
City	2.9	3.2	4.5	7.2	20.6	22.1	24.6	14.9
MSA[1]	7.4	6.8	7.9	13.6	22.1	16.4	16.6	9.2
U.S.	12.1	10.2	9.9	13.2	17.8	12.2	13.5	11.1

Note: (1) Figures cover the Ogden-Clearfield, UT Metropolitan Statistical Area—see Appendix B for areas included
Source: U.S. Census Bureau, 2012-2016 American Community Survey 5-Year Estimates

Poverty Rate

Area	All Ages	Under 18 Years Old	18 to 64 Years Old	65 Years and Over
City	4.2	5.7	3.2	2.5
MSA[1]	9.3	11.4	8.7	6.8
U.S.	15.1	21.2	14.2	9.3

Note: Figures are percentage of people whose income during the past 12 months was below the poverty level; (1) Figures cover the Ogden-Clearfield, UT Metropolitan Statistical Area—see Appendix B for areas included
Source: U.S. Census Bureau, 2012-2016 American Community Survey 5-Year Estimates

EMPLOYMENT

Labor Force and Employment

Area	Civilian Labor Force			Workers Employed		
	Dec. 2016	Dec. 2017	% Chg.	Dec. 2016	Dec. 2017	% Chg.
City	13,663	13,990	2.4	13,367	13,692	2.4
MSA[1]	318,562	326,295	2.4	308,975	316,612	2.5
U.S.	158,968,000	159,880,000	0.6	151,798,000	153,602,000	1.2

Note: Data is not seasonally adjusted and covers workers 16 years of age and older; (1) Figures cover the Ogden-Clearfield, UT Metropolitan Statistical Area—see Appendix B for areas included
Source: Bureau of Labor Statistics, Local Area Unemployment Statistics

Unemployment Rate

Area	2017											
	Jan.	Feb.	Mar.	Apr.	May	Jun.	Jul.	Aug.	Sep.	Oct.	Nov.	Dec.
City	2.6	2.7	2.8	2.7	2.7	3.2	3.0	3.0	2.6	2.6	2.4	2.1
MSA[1]	3.6	3.7	3.5	3.2	3.1	3.6	3.4	3.4	3.1	3.2	2.9	3.0
U.S.	5.1	4.9	4.6	4.1	4.1	4.5	4.6	4.5	4.1	3.9	3.9	3.9

Note: Data is not seasonally adjusted and covers workers 16 years of age and older; (1) Figures cover the Ogden-Clearfield, UT Metropolitan Statistical Area—see Appendix B for areas included
Source: Bureau of Labor Statistics, Local Area Unemployment Statistics

Average Wages

Occupation	$/Hr.	Occupation	$/Hr.
Accountants and Auditors	33.50	Maids and Housekeeping Cleaners	11.30
Automotive Mechanics	21.20	Maintenance and Repair Workers	18.60
Bookkeepers	18.30	Marketing Managers	57.80
Carpenters	20.20	Nuclear Medicine Technologists	n/a
Cashiers	10.70	Nurses, Licensed Practical	23.10
Clerks, General Office	15.20	Nurses, Registered	29.70
Clerks, Receptionists/Information	12.40	Nursing Assistants	11.70
Clerks, Shipping/Receiving	16.80	Packers and Packagers, Hand	11.60
Computer Programmers	36.40	Physical Therapists	47.20
Computer Systems Analysts	39.70	Postal Service Mail Carriers	23.70
Computer User Support Specialists	26.80	Real Estate Brokers	n/a
Cooks, Restaurant	12.90	Retail Salespersons	12.70
Dentists	58.00	Sales Reps., Exc. Tech./Scientific	33.50
Electrical Engineers	43.40	Sales Reps., Tech./Scientific	42.10
Electricians	24.30	Secretaries, Exc. Legal/Med./Exec.	15.70
Financial Managers	47.30	Security Guards	15.70
First-Line Supervisors/Managers, Sales	19.10	Surgeons	132.40
Food Preparation Workers	10.00	Teacher Assistants*	12.60
General and Operations Managers	37.10	Teachers, Elementary School*	24.80
Hairdressers/Cosmetologists	10.30	Teachers, Secondary School*	26.90
Internists, General	121.20	Telemarketers	11.70
Janitors and Cleaners	12.90	Truck Drivers, Heavy/Tractor-Trailer	20.70
Landscaping/Groundskeeping Workers	13.50	Truck Drivers, Light/Delivery Svcs.	14.40
Lawyers	37.30	Waiters and Waitresses	12.20

Note: Wage data covers the Ogden-Clearfield, UT Metropolitan Statistical Area—see Appendix B for areas included; (*) Hourly wages for elementary/secondary school teachers and teacher assistants were calculated by the editors from annual wage data based on a 40 hour work week; n/a not available.
Source: Bureau of Labor Statistics, Metro Area Occupational Employment & Wage Estimates, May 2017

Employment by Occupation

Occupation Classification	City (%)	MSA[1] (%)	U.S. (%)
Management, Business, Science, and Arts	40.4	36.5	37.0
Natural Resources, Construction, and Maintenance	7.8	8.8	8.9
Production, Transportation, and Material Moving	12.7	14.5	12.2
Sales and Office	25.3	25.9	23.8
Service	13.8	14.3	18.1

Note: Figures cover employed civilians 16 years of age and older; (1) Figures cover the Ogden-Clearfield, UT Metropolitan Statistical Area—see Appendix B for areas included
Source: U.S. Census Bureau, 2012-2016 American Community Survey 5-Year Estimates

Employment by Industry

Sector	MSA[1] Number of Employees	MSA[1] Percent of Total	U.S. Percent of Total
Construction, Mining, and Logging	17,500	6.8	5.2
Education and Health Services	32,400	12.7	15.9
Financial Activities	10,000	3.9	5.7
Government	53,100	20.7	15.3
Information	2,200	0.9	1.9
Leisure and Hospitality	23,600	9.2	10.7
Manufacturing	33,100	12.9	8.5
Other Services	6,700	2.6	3.9
Professional and Business Services	30,100	11.8	14.0
Retail Trade	31,000	12.1	11.0
Transportation, Warehousing, and Utilities	9,300	3.6	4.1
Wholesale Trade	7,000	2.7	4.0

Note: Figures are non-farm employment as of December 2017. Figures are not seasonally adjusted and include workers 16 years of age and older; (1) Figures cover the Ogden-Clearfield, UT Metropolitan Statistical Area—see Appendix B for areas included
Source: Bureau of Labor Statistics, Current Employment Statistics, Employment, Hours, and Earnings

Occupations with Greatest Projected Employment Growth: 2017 – 2019

Occupation[1]	2017 Employment	2019 Projected Employment	Numeric Employment Change	Percent Employment Change
Combined Food Preparation and Serving Workers, Including Fast Food	40,810	43,640	2,830	6.9
Customer Service Representatives	44,760	46,800	2,040	4.6
Construction Laborers	17,940	19,780	1,840	10.3
General and Operations Managers	29,140	30,980	1,840	6.3
Carpenters	15,870	17,610	1,740	10.9
Heavy and Tractor-Trailer Truck Drivers	24,080	25,570	1,490	6.2
Janitors and Cleaners, Except Maids and Housekeeping Cleaners	22,610	23,970	1,360	6.0
Retail Salespersons	47,280	48,580	1,300	2.7
Laborers and Freight, Stock, and Material Movers, Hand	19,560	20,850	1,290	6.6
Registered Nurses	22,690	23,950	1,260	5.6

Note: Projections cover Utah; (1) Sorted by numeric employment change
Source: www.projectionscentral.com, State Occupational Projections, 2017–2019 Short-Term Projections

Fastest Growing Occupations: 2017 – 2019

Occupation[1]	2017 Employment	2019 Projected Employment	Numeric Employment Change	Percent Employment Change
Roofers	2,300	2,640	340	14.7
Brickmasons and Blockmasons	2,310	2,650	340	14.6
Plasterers and Stucco Masons	660	750	90	13.9
Roustabouts, Oil and Gas	1,170	1,330	160	13.8
Cement Masons and Concrete Finishers	3,470	3,930	460	13.2
Helpers—Brickmasons, Blockmasons, Stonemasons, and Tile and Marble Setters	690	780	90	13.0
Stonemasons	360	410	50	12.8
Helpers—Pipelayers, Plumbers, Pipefitters, and Steamfitters	570	640	70	12.6
Plumbers, Pipefitters, and Steamfitters	6,750	7,590	840	12.5
Software Developers, Applications	8,310	9,330	1,020	12.3

Note: Projections cover Utah; (1) Sorted by percent employment change and excludes occupations with numeric employment change less than 50
Source: www.projectionscentral.com, State Occupational Projections, 2017–2019 Short-Term Projections

TAXES

State Corporate Income Tax Rates

State	Tax Rate (%)	Income Brackets ($)	Num. of Brackets	Financial Institution Tax Rate (%)[a]	Federal Income Tax Ded.
Utah	5.0 (b)	Flat rate	–	5.0 (b)	No

Note: Tax rates as of January 1, 2018; (a) Rates listed are the corporate income tax rate applied to financial institutions or excise taxes based on income. Some states have other taxes based upon the value of deposits or shares; (b) Minimum tax is $800 in California, $100 in District of Columbia and Arizona, $50 in North Dakota (banks), $500 in Rhode Island, $200 per location in South Dakota (banks), $100 in Utah, $250 in Vermont.
Source: Federation of Tax Administrators, Range of State Corporate Income Tax Rates, January 1, 2018

State Individual Income Tax Rates

State	Tax Rate (%)	Income Brackets ($)	Num. of Brackets	Personal Exempt. ($)[1]		Fed. Inc. Tax Ded.
				Single	Dependents	
Utah	5.0	Flat rate	1	(v)	(v)	No

Note: Tax rates as of January 1, 2018; Local- and county-level taxes are not included; n/a not applicable; (1) Married joint filers generally receive double the single exemption; (v) Utah provides a tax credit equal to 6% of the federal personal exemption amounts (and applicable standard deduction). Note, the Tax Cut and Reform Act of 2017 has eliminated personal exemptions and increased the standard deduction in the IRC. Utah will need to enact legislation to reinstate a personal credit for tax year 2018.
Source: Federation of Tax Administrators, State Individual Income Tax Rates, January 1, 2018

Various State Sales and Excise Tax Rates

State	State Sales Tax (%)	Gasoline[1] (¢/gal.)	Cigarette[2] ($/pack)	Spirits[3] ($/gal.)	Wine[4] ($/gal.)	Beer[5] ($/gal.)	Recreational Marijuana (%)
Utah	5.95 (b)	29.41	1.70	15.38 (g)	(m)	0.41 (q)	Not legal

Note: All tax rates as of January 1, 2018; (1) The American Petroleum Institute has developed a methodology for determining the average tax rate on a gallon of fuel. Rates may include any of the following: excise taxes, environmental fees, storage tank fees, other fees or taxes, general sales tax, and local taxes. In states where gasoline is subject to the general sales tax, or where the fuel tax is based on the average sale price, the average rate determined by API is sensitive to changes in the price of gasoline. States that fully or partially apply general sales taxes to gasoline: CA, CO, GA, IL, IN, MI, NY; (2) The federal excise tax of $1.0066 per pack and local taxes are not included; (3) Rates are those applicable to off-premise sales of 40% alcohol by volume (a.b.v.) distilled spirits in 750ml containers. Local excise taxes are excluded; (4) Rates are those applicable to off-premise sales of 11% a.b.v. non-carbonated wine in 750ml containers; (5) Rates are those applicable to off-premise sales of 4.7% a.b.v. beer in 12 ounce containers; (b) Three states levy mandatory, statewide, local add-on sales taxes at the state level: California (1.25%), Utah (1.25%), Virginia (1%), we include these in their state sales tax; (g) Control states, where the government controls all sales. Products can be subject to ad valorem mark-up as well as excise taxes; (m) Control states, where the government controls all sales. Products can be subject to ad valorem mark-up as well as excise taxes; (q) Different rates also applicable according to alcohol content, place of production, size of container, or place purchased (on- or off-premise or onboard airlines).
Source: Tax Foundation, 2018 Facts & Figures: How Does Your State Compare?

State Business Tax Climate Index Rankings

State	Overall Rank	Corporate Tax Rank	Individual Income Tax Rank	Sales Tax Rank	Unemployment Insurance Tax Rank	Property Tax Rank
Utah	8	4	11	17	21	5

Note: The index is a measure of how each state's tax laws affect economic performance. The lower the rank, the more favorable a state's tax system is for business. States without a given tax are given a ranking of 1. The scores/rankings for the District of Columbia do not affect other states. The 2018 index represents the tax climate as of July 1, 2017.
Source: Tax Foundation, State Business Tax Climate Index 2018

TRANSPORTATION

Means of Transportation to Work

Area	Car/Truck/Van		Public Transportation			Bicycle	Walked	Other Means	Worked at Home
	Drove Alone	Car-pooled	Bus	Subway	Railroad				
City	80.0	11.0	0.3	0.0	1.2	0.2	1.8	0.9	4.6
MSA[1]	79.5	10.7	1.4	0.1	0.6	0.5	1.5	1.1	4.7
U.S.	76.4	9.3	2.6	1.9	0.6	0.6	2.8	1.3	4.6

Note: Figures are percentages and cover workers 16 years of age and older; (1) Figures cover the Ogden-Clearfield, UT Metropolitan Statistical Area—see Appendix B for areas included
Source: U.S. Census Bureau, 2012-2016 American Community Survey 5-Year Estimates

Travel Time to Work

Area	Less Than 10 Minutes	10 to 19 Minutes	20 to 29 Minutes	30 to 44 Minutes	45 to 59 Minutes	60 to 89 Minutes	90 Minutes or More
City	10.2	30.4	17.1	23.9	10.8	4.8	2.7
MSA[1]	16.0	33.7	22.3	16.3	6.2	3.9	1.6
U.S.	12.9	29.2	20.9	20.4	8.0	6.0	2.7

Note: Note: Figures are percentages and include workers 16 years old and over; (1) Figures cover the Ogden-Clearfield, UT Metropolitan Statistical Area—see Appendix B for areas included
Source: U.S. Census Bureau, 2012-2016 American Community Survey 5-Year Estimates

Freeway Travel Time Index

Area	1985	1990	1995	2000	2005	2010	2014
Urban Area Rank[1,2]	n/a	n/a	n/a	n/a	n/a	n/a	n/a
Urban Area Index[1]	n/a	n/a	n/a	n/a	n/a	n/a	n/a
Average Index[3]	1.09	1.11	1.14	1.17	1.20	1.19	1.20

Note: Freeway Travel Time Index—the ratio of travel time in the peak period to the travel time at free-flow conditions. For example, a value of 1.30 indicates a 20-minute free-flow trip takes 26 minutes in the peak (20 minutes x 1.30 = 26 minutes); (1) Data for the Ogden-Clearfield, UT urban area was not available; (2) Rank is based on 101 urban areas (#1 = highest travel time index); (3) Average of 101 urban areas
Source: Texas Transportation Institute, 2015 Urban Mobility Scorecard, August 2015

Freeway Commuter Stress Index

Area	1985	1990	1995	2000	2005	2010	2014
Urban Area Rank[1,2]	n/a	n/a	n/a	n/a	n/a	n/a	n/a
Urban Area Index[1]	n/a	n/a	n/a	n/a	n/a	n/a	n/a
Average Index[3]	1.13	1.16	1.19	1.22	1.25	1.24	1.25

Note: The Freeway Commuter Stress Index is the same as the Freeway Travel Time Index (see table above) except that it includes only the travel in the peak directions during the peak periods; the TTI includes travel in all directions during the peak period. Thus, the CSI is more indicative of the work trip experienced by each commuter on a daily basis; (1) Data for the Ogden-Clearfield, UT urban area was not available; (2) Rank is based on 101 urban areas (#1 = highest travel time index); (3) Average of 101 urban areas
Source: Texas Transportation Institute, 2015 Urban Mobility Scorecard, August 2015

Living Environment

COST OF LIVING

Cost of Living Index

Composite Index	Groceries	Housing	Utilities	Trans-portation	Health Care	Misc. Goods/ Services
100.1	103.9	105.5	76.0	101.8	113.4	99.0

Note: The Cost of Living Index measures regional differences in the cost of consumer goods and services, excluding taxes and non-consumer expenditures, for professional and managerial households in the top income quintile. It is based on more than 50,000 prices covering almost 60 different items for which prices are collected three times a year by chambers of commerce, economic development organizations or university applied economic centers in each participating urban area. The numbers shown should be read as a percentage above or below the national average of 100. For example, a value of 115.4 in the groceries column indicates that grocery prices are 15.4% higher than the national average. Small differences in the index numbers should not be interpreted as significant; Figures cover the Ogden UT urban area.
Source: The Council for Community and Economic Research, ACCRA Cost of Living Index, 2017

Grocery Prices

Area[1]	T-Bone Steak ($/pound)	Frying Chicken ($/pound)	Whole Milk ($/half gal.)	Eggs ($/dozen)	Orange Juice ($/64 oz.)	Coffee ($/11.5 oz.)
City[2]	10.69	1.86	1.87	2.61	3.76	4.32
Avg.	11.29	1.40	2.02	1.47	3.55	4.37
Min.	7.71	0.93	1.04	0.70	2.86	3.24
Max.	15.83	2.39	4.03	3.92	6.29	8.16

*Note: (1) Values for the local area are compared with the average, minimum and maximum values for all 294 areas in the Cost of Living Index; (2) Figures cover the Ogden UT urban area; **T-Bone Steak** (price per pound); **Frying Chicken** (price per pound, whole fryer); **Whole Milk** (half gallon carton); **Eggs** (price per dozen, Grade A, large); **Orange Juice** (64 oz. Tropicana or Florida Natural); **Coffee** (11.5 oz. can, vacuum-packed, Maxwell House, Hills Bros, or Folgers).*
Source: The Council for Community and Economic Research, ACCRA Cost of Living Index, 2017

Housing and Utility Costs

Area[1]	New Home Price ($)	Apartment Rent ($/month)	All Electric ($/month)	Part Electric ($/month)	Other Energy ($/month)	Telephone ($/month)
City[2]	393,127	890	-	69.29	68.50	19.62
Avg.	335,956	1,047	175.01	97.34	67.93	28.71
Min.	187,788	491	109.48	49.33	35.44	12.39
Max.	1,739,087	4,559	432.62	227.09	353.33	44.61

*Note: (1) Values for the local area are compared with the average, minimum and maximum values for all 294 areas in the Cost of Living Index; (2) Figures cover the Ogden UT urban area; **New Home Price** (2,400 sf living area, 8,000 sf lot, in urban area with full utilities); **Apartment Rent** (950 sf 2 bedroom/1.5 or 2 bath, unfurnished, excluding all utilities except water); **All Electric** (average monthly cost for an all-electric home); **Part Electric** (average monthly cost for a part-electric home); **Other Energy** (average monthly cost for natural gas, fuel oil, coal, wood, and any other forms of energy except electricity); **Telephone** (price includes basic monthly rate for a private residential line plus additional local usage charges incurred by a family of four).*
Source: The Council for Community and Economic Research, ACCRA Cost of Living Index, 2017

Health Care, Transportation, and Other Costs

Area[1]	Doctor ($/visit)	Dentist ($/visit)	Optometrist ($/visit)	Gasoline ($/gallon)	Beauty Salon ($/visit)	Men's Shirt ($)
City[2]	103.34	124.99	109.34	2.32	30.34	26.97
Avg.	108.00	92.54	101.93	2.25	37.58	30.92
Min.	30.39	60.00	49.75	1.82	16.11	11.20
Max.	193.50	161.94	229.28	3.16	77.35	59.13

*Note: (1) Values for the local area are compared with the average, minimum and maximum values for all 294 areas in the Cost of Living Index; (2) Figures cover the Ogden UT urban area; **Doctor** (general practitioners routine exam of an established patient); **Dentist** (adult teeth cleaning and periodic oral examination); **Optometrist** (full vision eye exam for established adult patient); **Gasoline** (one gallon regular unleaded, national brand, including all taxes, cash price at self-service pump if available); **Beauty Salon** (woman's shampoo, trim, and blow-dry); **Men's Shirt** (cotton/polyester dress shirt, pinpoint weave, long sleeves).*
Source: The Council for Community and Economic Research, ACCRA Cost of Living Index, 2017

HOUSING

House Price Index (HPI)

Area	National Ranking[2]	Quarterly Change (%)	One-Year Change (%)	Five-Year Change (%)
MSA[1]	18	1.67	10.80	39.80
U.S.[3]	–	1.61	6.68	34.71

Note: The HPI is a weighted repeat sales index. It measures average price changes in repeat sales or refinancings on the same properties. This information is obtained by reviewing repeat mortgage transactions on single-family properties whose mortgages have been purchased or securitized by Fannie Mae or Freddie Mac in January 1975; (1) Figures cover the Ogden-Clearfield, UT Metropolitan Statistical Area—see Appendix B for areas included; (2) Rankings are based on annual percentage change for all metro areas containing at least 15,000 transactions over the last 10 years and ranges from 1 to 253; (3) figures based on a weighted average of Census Division estimates using a seasonally adjusted, purchase-only index; all figures are for the period ending December 31, 2017

Source: Federal Housing Finance Agency, House Price Index, February 28, 2018

Median Single-Family Home Prices

Area	2015	2016	2017p	Percent Change 2016 to 2017
MSA[1]	n/a	n/a	n/a	n/a
U.S. Average	223.9	235.5	248.8	5.6

Note: Figures are median sales prices of existing single-family homes in thousands of dollars; (p) preliminary; n/a not available; (1) Figures cover the Ogden-Clearfield, UT Metropolitan Statistical Area—see Appendix B for areas included

Source: National Association of Realtors, Median Sales Price of Existing Single-Family Homes for Metropolitan Areas, 4th Quarter 2017

Qualifying Income Based on Median Sales Price of Existing Single-Family Homes

Area	With 5% Down ($)	With 10% Down ($)	With 20% Down ($)
MSA[1]	n/a	n/a	n/a
U.S. Average	55,585	52,659	46,808

Note: Figures are preliminary; Qualifying income is based on a mortgage rate of 4.17%. Monthly principal and interest payment is limited to 25% of income; n/a not available; (1) Figures cover the Ogden-Clearfield, UT Metropolitan Statistical Area—see Appendix B for areas included

Source: National Association of Realtors, Qualifying Income Based on Median Sales Price of Existing Single-Family Homes for Metropolitan Areas, 4th Quarter 2017

Median Apartment Condo-Coop Home Prices

Area	2015	2016	2017p	Percent Change 2016 to 2017
MSA[1]	n/a	n/a	n/a	n/a
U.S. Average	210.7	220.7	234.3	6.2

Note: Figures are median sales prices of existing apartment condo-coop homes in thousands of dollars; (p) preliminary; n/a not available; (1) Figures cover the Ogden-Clearfield, UT Metropolitan Statistical Area—see Appendix B for areas included

Source: National Association of Realtors, Median Sales Price of Existing Apartment Condo-Coop Homes for Metropolitan Areas, 4th Quarter 2017

Home Value Distribution

Area	Under $50,000	$50,000 -$99,999	$100,000 -$149,999	$150,000 -$199,999	$200,000 -$299,999	$300,000 -$499,999	$500,000 -$999,999	$1,000,000 or more
City	2.9	0.5	5.3	16.4	44.8	28.3	1.3	0.5
MSA[1]	4.6	4.2	16.5	22.3	29.1	18.7	3.7	0.8
U.S.	8.8	14.8	15.3	14.9	18.4	16.4	9.0	2.5

Note: Figures are percentages and cover owner-occupied housing units; (1) Figures cover the Ogden-Clearfield, UT Metropolitan Statistical Area—see Appendix B for areas included

Source: U.S. Census Bureau, 2012-2016 American Community Survey 5-Year Estimates

Homeownership Rate

Area	2009 (%)	2010 (%)	2011 (%)	2012 (%)	2013 (%)	2014 (%)	2015 (%)	2016 (%)	2017 (%)
MSA[1]	n/a	n/a	n/a	n/a	n/a	n/a	n/a	n/a	n/a
U.S.	67.4	66.9	66.1	65.4	65.1	64.5	63.7	63.4	63.9

Note: (1) Figures cover the Ogden-Clearfield, UT Metropolitan Statistical Area—see Appendix B for areas included; n/a not available

Source: U.S. Census Bureau, Housing Vacancies and Homeownership Annual Statistics: 2009-2017

Year Housing Structure Built

Area	2010 or Later	2000 -2009	1990 -1999	1980 -1989	1970 -1979	1960 -1969	1950 -1959	1940 -1949	Before 1940	Median Year
City	8.5	56.2	17.3	3.5	7.6	3.2	1.6	0.6	1.4	2003
MSA[1]	4.5	21.9	17.1	12.8	15.6	8.5	8.8	4.3	6.4	1985
U.S.	2.3	14.7	14.0	13.7	15.6	10.9	10.6	5.2	13.0	1977

Note: Figures are percentages except for Median Year; Note: (1) Figures cover the Ogden-Clearfield, UT Metropolitan Statistical Area—see Appendix B for areas included
Source: U.S. Census Bureau, 2012-2016 American Community Survey 5-Year Estimates

Gross Monthly Rent

Area	Under $500	$500 -$999	$1,000 -$1,499	$1,500 -$1,999	$2,000 -$2,499	$2,500 -$2,999	$3,000 and up	Median ($)
City	4.2	22.7	24.3	33.5	15.4	0.0	0.0	1,478
MSA[1]	10.6	55.4	25.7	6.6	1.0	0.3	0.4	856
U.S.	11.3	43.3	27.7	10.7	4.0	1.6	1.5	949

Note: Figures are percentages except for Median; Gross rent is the contract rent plus the estimated average monthly cost of utilities (electricity, gas, and water and sewer) and fuels (oil, coal, kerosene, wood, etc.) if these are paid by the renter (or paid for the renter by someone else); (1) Figures cover the Ogden-Clearfield, UT Metropolitan Statistical Area—see Appendix B for areas included
Source: U.S. Census Bureau, 2012-2016 American Community Survey 5-Year Estimates

HEALTH

Health Risk Factors

Category	MSA[1] (%)	U.S. (%)
Adults aged 18–64 who have any kind of health care coverage	89.3	87.7
Adults who reported being in good or excellent health	88.4	83.6
Adults who are current smokers	8.2	17.1
Adults who currently use E-cigarettes	6.3	4.7
Adults who currently use chewing tobacco, snuff, or snus	3.7	4.0
Adults who are heavy drinkers[2]	4.5	6.5
Adults who are binge drinkers[3]	10.8	16.9
Adults who are overweight (BMI 25.0 - 29.9)	33.5	35.3
Adults who are obese (BMI 30.0 - 99.8)	29.8	29.9
Adults who participated in any physical activities in the past month	81.0	76.9
Adults who always or nearly always wears a seat belt	95.2	94.3

Note: (1) Figures cover the Ogden-Clearfield, UT Metropolitan Statistical Area—see Appendix B for areas included; (2) Heavy drinkers are classified as adult men having more than 14 drinks per week and adult women having more than 7 drinks per week; (3) Binge drinkers are classified as males having five or more drinks on one occasion or females having four or more drinks on one occasion
Source: Centers for Disease Control and Prevention, Behaviorial Risk Factor Surveillance System, SMART: Selected Metropolitan Area Risk Trends, 2016

Health Screening Rates

Category	MSA[1] (%)	U.S. (%)
Adults 50-75 who have had a blood stool test within the past year	3.0	8.0
Adults 50-75 who have had a colonoscopy in the past 10 years	74.5	63.5
Adults aged 65+ who have had flu shot within the past year	60.3	58.6
Adults aged 65+ who have ever had a pneumonia vaccination	78.3	73.4
Adults who have ever been tested for HIV	23.0	35.6
Women aged 21-65 who have had a pap test in the past three years	78.9	79.8
Men aged 40+ who have had a PSA test within the past two years	36.4	39.5
Women aged 40+ who have had a mammogram within the past two years	70.1	72.5

Note: n/a not available; (1) Figures cover the Ogden-Clearfield, UT Metropolitan Statistical Area—see Appendix B for areas included; Source: Centers for Disease Control and Prevention, Behaviorial Risk Factor Surveillance System, SMART: Selected Metropolitan Area Risk Trends, 2016

Chronic Health Conditions

Category	MSA[1] (%)	U.S. (%)
Adults who have ever been told they had a heart attack	3.3	4.4
Adults who have ever been told they have angina or coronary heart disease	2.6	4.1
Adults who have ever been told they had a stroke	2.4	3.1
Adults who have been told they currently have asthma	9.0	9.3
Adults who have ever been told they have arthritis	21.7	25.8
Adults who have ever been told they have diabetes[2]	8.3	10.5
Adults who have ever been told they had skin cancer	8.1	5.9
Adults who have ever been told they had any other types of cancer	6.2	6.7
Adults who have ever been told they have COPD	3.8	6.3
Adults who have ever been told they have kidney disease	2.5	2.8
Adults who have ever been told they have a form of depression	21.9	17.4

Note: (1) Figures cover the Ogden-Clearfield, UT Metropolitan Statistical Area—see Appendix B for areas included; (2) Figures do not include pregnancy-related, borderline, or pre-diabetes
Source: Centers for Disease Control and Prevention, Behaviorial Risk Factor Surveillance System, SMART: Selected Metropolitan Area Risk Trends, 2016

Mortality Rates for the Top 10 Causes of Death in the U.S.

ICD-10[a] Sub-Chapter	ICD-10[a] Code	Age-Adjusted Mortality Rate[1] per 100,000 population	
		County[2]	U.S.
Malignant neoplasms	C00-C97	115.4	158.5
Ischaemic heart diseases	I20-I25	74.4	96.8
Other forms of heart disease	I30-I51	70.4	52.4
Chronic lower respiratory diseases	J40-J47	28.7	40.9
Cerebrovascular diseases	I60-I69	36.4	37.2
Organic, including symptomatic, mental disorders	F01-F09	35.6	33.3
Other degenerative diseases of the nervous system	G30-G31	43.7	32.1
Other external causes of accidental injury	W00-X59	29.3	31.2
Diabetes mellitus	E10-E14	23.9	21.1
Hypertensive diseases	I10-I15	11.0	20.8

Note: (a) ICD-10 = International Classification of Diseases 10th Revision; (1) Mortality rates are a three year average covering 2014-2016; (2) Figures cover Davis County.
Source: Centers for Disease Control and Prevention, National Center for Health Statistics. Underlying Cause of Death 1999-2016 on CDC WONDER Online Database, released December 2017

Mortality Rates for Selected Causes of Death

ICD-10[a] Sub-Chapter	ICD-10[a] Code	Age-Adjusted Mortality Rate[1] per 100,000 population	
		County[2]	U.S.
Assault	X85-Y09	Unreliable	5.6
Diseases of the liver	K70-K76	10.9	14.0
Human immunodeficiency virus (HIV) disease	B20-B24	Suppressed	1.9
Influenza and pneumonia	J09-J18	16.0	14.6
Intentional self-harm	X60-X84	15.9	13.2
Malnutrition	E40-E46	2.8	1.3
Obesity and other hyperalimentation	E65-E68	Unreliable	2.1
Renal failure	N17-N19	14.2	13.0
Transport accidents	V01-V99	10.6	12.0
Viral hepatitis	B15-B19	Suppressed	1.9

Note: (a) ICD-10 = International Classification of Diseases 10th Revision; (1) Mortality rates are a three year average covering 2014-2016; (2) Figures cover Davis County; Data are Suppressed when the data meet the criteria for confidentiality constraints; Mortality rates are flagged as Unreliable when the rate would be calculated with a numerator of 20 or less.
Source: Centers for Disease Control and Prevention, National Center for Health Statistics. Underlying Cause of Death 1999-2016 on CDC WONDER Online Database, released December 2017

Health Insurance Coverage

Area	With Health Insurance	With Private Health Insurance	With Public Health Insurance	Without Health Insurance	Population Under Age 18 Without Health Insurance
City	95.3	87.4	14.4	4.7	2.5
MSA[1]	90.5	79.0	21.0	9.5	5.8
U.S.	88.3	66.7	33.0	11.7	5.9

Note: Figures are percentages that cover the civilian noninstitutionalized population; (1) Figures cover the Ogden-Clearfield, UT Metropolitan Statistical Area—see Appendix B for areas included
Source: U.S. Census Bureau, 2012-2016 American Community Survey 5-Year Estimates

Number of Medical Professionals

Area	MDs[3]	DOs[3,4]	Dentists	Podiatrists	Chiropractors	Optometrists
County[1] (number)	482	55	219	16	89	37
County[1] (rate[2])	144.0	16.4	64.2	4.7	26.1	10.8
U.S. (rate[2])	276.5	22.3	67.3	6.0	26.7	15.9

Note: Data as of 2016 unless noted; (1) Data covers Davis County; (2) Rate per 100,000 population; (3) Data as of 2015 and includes all active, non-federal physicians; (4) Doctor of Osteopathic Medicine
Source: U.S. Department of Health and Human Services, Health Resources and Services Administration, Bureau of Health Professions, Area Resource File (ARF) 2016-2017

EDUCATION

Public School District Statistics

District Name	Schls	Pupils	Pupil/ Teacher Ratio	Minority Pupils[1] (%)	Free Lunch Eligible[2] (%)	IEP[3] (%)
Davis District	91	71,721	n/a	15.9	17.3	11.9
Syracuse Arts Academy	2	1,662	n/a	17.0	23.3	10.3

Note: Table includes school districts with 100 or more students; (1) Percentage of students that are not non-Hispanic white; (2) Percentage of students that are eligible for the free lunch program; (3) Percentage of students that have an Individualized Education Program.
Source: U.S. Department of Education, National Center for Education Statistics, Common Core of Data, Local Education Agency (School District) Universe Survey: School Year 2015-2016; U.S. Department of Education, National Center for Education Statistics, Common Core of Data, Public Elementary/Secondary School Universe Survey: School Year 2015-2016

Highest Level of Education

Area	Less than H.S.	H.S. Diploma	Some College, No Deg.	Associate Degree	Bachelor's Degree	Master's Degree	Prof. School Degree	Doctorate Degree
City	2.7	20.6	27.4	12.6	25.3	9.4	1.2	0.8
MSA[1]	6.8	25.3	28.2	10.2	20.4	7.1	1.2	0.8
U.S.	13.0	27.5	21.0	8.2	18.8	8.2	2.0	1.3

Note: Figures cover persons age 25 and over; (1) Figures cover the Ogden-Clearfield, UT Metropolitan Statistical Area—see Appendix B for areas included
Source: U.S. Census Bureau, 2012-2016 American Community Survey 5-Year Estimates

Educational Attainment by Race

Area	High School Graduate or Higher (%)					Bachelor's Degree or Higher (%)				
	Total	White	Black	Asian	Hisp.[2]	Total	White	Black	Asian	Hisp.[2]
City	97.3	97.2	100.0	93.8	91.0	36.7	37.9	33.0	0.0	16.1
MSA[1]	93.2	94.3	92.6	88.9	71.4	29.5	30.5	19.9	33.0	10.9
U.S.	87.0	88.9	84.3	86.3	65.7	30.3	31.6	20.0	52.1	14.7

Note: Figures shown cover persons 25 years old and over; (1) Figures cover the Ogden-Clearfield, UT Metropolitan Statistical Area—see Appendix B for areas included; (2) People of Hispanic origin can be of any race
Source: U.S. Census Bureau, 2012-2016 American Community Survey 5-Year Estimates

School Enrollment by Grade and Control

Area	Preschool (%)		Kindergarten (%)		Grades 1 - 4 (%)		Grades 5 - 8 (%)		Grades 9 - 12 (%)	
	Public	Private	Public	Private	Public	Private	Public	Private	Public	Private
City	58.1	41.9	98.5	1.5	95.6	4.4	96.3	3.7	94.9	5.1
MSA[1]	55.7	44.3	93.2	6.8	96.6	3.4	96.6	3.4	96.9	3.1
U.S.	58.4	41.6	87.7	12.3	89.8	10.2	89.7	10.3	90.4	9.6

Note: Figures shown cover persons 3 years old and over; (1) Figures cover the Ogden-Clearfield, UT Metropolitan Statistical Area—see Appendix B for areas included
Source: U.S. Census Bureau, 2012-2016 American Community Survey 5-Year Estimates

Average Salaries of Public School Classroom Teachers

Area	2015		2016		Change from 2015 to 2016	
	Dollars	Rank[1]	Dollars	Rank[1]	Percent	Rank[2]
Utah	46,689	44	46,887	45	0.4	33
U.S. Average	57,611	–	58,353	–	1.3	–

Note: (1) Rank ranges from 1 to 51 where 1 indicates highest salary; (2) Rank ranges from 1 to 51 where 1 indicates highest percent change.
Source: National Education Association, Rankings & Estimates: Rankings of the States 2016 and Estimates of School Statistics 2017

Higher Education

Four-Year Colleges			Two-Year Colleges			Medical Schools[1]	Law Schools[2]	Voc/ Tech[3]
Public	Private Non-profit	Private For-profit	Public	Private Non-profit	Private For-profit			
0	0	0	0	0	0	0	0	0

Note: Figures cover institutions located within the city limits and include main campuses only; (1) includes schools accredited by the Liaison Committee on Medical Education and the American Osteopathic Association's Commission on Osteopathic College Accreditation; (2) includes ABA-accredited schools, schools with provisional ABA accreditation, and state accredited schools; (3) includes all schools with programs that are less than 2 years.
Source: National Center for Education Statistics, Integrated Postsecondary Education System (IPEDS), 2016-17; Wikipedia, List of Medical Schools in the United States, accessed April 2, 2018; Wikipedia, List of Law Schools in the United States, accessed April 2, 2018

PRESIDENTIAL ELECTION

2016 Presidential Election Results

Area	Clinton	Trump	Johnson	Stein	Other
Davis County	20.5	44.4	3.8	0.6	30.7
U.S.	48.0	45.9	3.3	1.1	1.7

Note: Results are percentages and may not add to 100% due to rounding
Source: Dave Leip's Atlas of U.S. Presidential Elections

EMPLOYERS

Major Employers

Company Name	Industry
ATK	Manufacturing
Autoliv Inc.	Manufacturing
Bourns Sensors and Controls	Manufacturing
Chromalox	Manufacturing
Fresenius USA Manufacturing	Manufacturing
Great Salt Lake Minerals	Manufacturing
GSC Foundries	Manufacturing
Hill Air Force Base	Government
IRS	Government
JBT Aerotech	Manufacturing
Kimberly-Clark Corp.	Manufacturing
Lagoon Corp.	Leisure & hospitality
Levelor	Manufacturing
Lifetime Products, Inc.	Manufacturing
McKay-Dee Hospital Center	Education & health services
Odgen School District	Education
Ogden City	Government
Ogden Regional Medical Center	Healthcare
Parker Hannifin	Manufacturing
Smith's Marketplace	Wholesale & retail trade
US Forest Service	Government
Wal-Mart	Retail grocery
Weber County	Government
Weber School District	Education
Weber State University	Education & health services

Note: Companies shown are located within the Ogden-Clearfield, UT Metropolitan Statistical Area.
Source: Hoovers.com; Wikipedia

PUBLIC SAFETY

Crime Rate

Area	All Crimes	Violent Crimes				Property Crimes		
		Murder	Rape[3]	Robbery	Aggrav. Assault	Burglary	Larceny -Theft	Motor Vehicle Theft
City	1,135.3	0.0	17.9	3.6	21.4	153.5	917.5	21.4
Metro[1]	2,374.8	1.4	41.5	27.2	85.5	377.4	1,686.1	155.7
U.S.	2,847.8	5.3	40.4	102.8	248.5	468.9	1,745.0	236.9

Note: Figures are crimes per 100,000 population; (1) Figures cover the Ogden-Clearfield, UT Metropolitan Statistical Area—see Appendix B for areas included; (3) The city and U.S. figures shown were reported using the revised Uniform Crime Reporting (UCR) definition of rape. The metro area figures shown are an aggregate total of the data submitted using both the revised and legacy UCR definitions.
Source: FBI Uniform Crime Reports, 2016

Hate Crimes

Area	Number of Quarters Reported	Number of Incidents per Bias Motivation					
		Race/Ethnicity/ Ancestry	Religion	Sexual Orientation	Disability	Gender	Gender Identity
City	4	0	0	0	0	0	0
U.S.	4	3,489	1,273	1,076	70	31	124

Source: Federal Bureau of Investigation, Hate Crime Statistics 2016

Identity Theft Consumer Reports

Area	Reports	Reports per 100,000 Population	Rank[2]
MSA[1]	492	75	223
U.S.	371,061	114	-

Note: (1) Figures cover the Ogden-Clearfield, UT Metropolitan Statistical Area—see Appendix B for areas included; (2) Rank ranges from 1 to 389 where 1 indicates greatest number of identity theft reports per 100,000 population
Source: Federal Trade Commission, Consumer Sentinel Network Data Book for January–December 2017

Fraud and Other Consumer Reports

Area	Reports	Reports per 100,000 Population	Rank[2]
MSA[1]	2,405	368	306
U.S.	2,304,550	708	-

Note: (1) Figures cover the Ogden-Clearfield, UT Metropolitan Statistical Area—see Appendix B for areas included; (2) Rank ranges from 1 to 389 where 1 indicates greatest number of fraud and other consumer reports per 100,000 population

Source: Federal Trade Commission, Consumer Sentinel Network Data Book for January–December 2017

SPORTS

Professional Sports Teams

Team Name	League	Year Established
No teams are located in the metro area		

Source: Wikipedia, Major Professional Sports Teams of the United States and Canada, April 5, 2018

CLIMATE

Average and Extreme Temperatures

Temperature	Jan	Feb	Mar	Apr	May	Jun	Jul	Aug	Sep	Oct	Nov	Dec	Yr.
Extreme High (°F)	62	69	78	85	93	104	107	104	100	89	75	67	107
Average High (°F)	37	43	52	62	72	83	93	90	80	66	50	38	64
Average Temp. (°F)	28	34	41	50	59	69	78	76	65	53	40	30	52
Average Low (°F)	19	24	31	38	46	54	62	61	51	40	30	22	40
Extreme Low (°F)	-22	-14	2	15	25	35	40	37	27	16	-14	-15	-22

Note: Figures cover the years 1948-1990

Source: National Climatic Data Center, International Station Meteorological Climate Summary, 9/96

Average Precipitation/Snowfall/Humidity

Precip./Humidity	Jan	Feb	Mar	Apr	May	Jun	Jul	Aug	Sep	Oct	Nov	Dec	Yr.
Avg. Precip. (in.)	1.3	1.2	1.8	2.0	1.7	0.9	0.8	0.9	1.1	1.3	1.3	1.4	15.6
Avg. Snowfall (in.)	13	10	11	6	1	Tr	0	0	Tr	2	6	13	63
Avg. Rel. Hum. 5am (%)	79	77	71	67	66	60	53	54	60	68	75	79	67
Avg. Rel. Hum. 5pm (%)	69	59	47	38	33	26	22	23	28	40	59	71	43

Note: Figures cover the years 1948-1990; Tr = Trace amounts (<0.05 in. of rain; <0.5 in. of snow)

Source: National Climatic Data Center, International Station Meteorological Climate Summary, 9/96

Weather Conditions

Temperature			Daytime Sky			Precipitation		
5°F & below	32°F & below	90°F & above	Clear	Partly cloudy	Cloudy	0.01 inch or more precip.	0.1 inch or more snow/ice	Thunder-storms
7	128	56	94	152	119	92	38	38

Note: Figures are average number of days per year and cover the years 1948-1990

Source: National Climatic Data Center, International Station Meteorological Climate Summary, 9/96

HAZARDOUS WASTE

Superfund Sites

The Ogden-Clearfield, UT metro area is home to five sites on the EPA's Superfund National Priorities List: **Bountiful/Woods Cross 5th S. Pce Plume** (final); **Five Points Pce Plume** (final); **Hill Air Force Base** (final); **Intermountain Waste Oil Refinery** (final); **Ogden Defense Depot (Dla)** (final). There are a total of 1,396 Superfund sites with a status of proposed or final on the list in the U.S. *U.S. Environmental Protection Agency, National Priorities List, April 4, 2018*

AIR & WATER QUALITY

Air Quality Trends: Ozone

	1990	1995	2000	2005	2010	2012	2013	2014	2015	2016
MSA[1]	n/a	n/a	n/a	n/a	n/a	n/a	n/a	n/a	n/a	n/a
U.S.	0.087	0.089	0.081	0.079	0.073	0.075	0.069	0.067	0.068	0.069

Note: (1) Data covers the Ogden-Clearfield, UT Metropolitan Statistical Area—see Appendix B for areas included; n/a not available. The values shown are the composite ozone concentration averages among trend sites based on the highest fourth daily maximum 8-hour concentration in parts per million. These trends are based on sites having an adequate record of monitoring data during the trend period. Data from exceptional events are included.
Source: U.S. Environmental Protection Agency, Air Quality Monitoring Information, "Air Quality Trends by City, 1990-2016"

Air Quality Index

Area	Percent of Days when Air Quality was...[2]					AQI Statistics[2]	
	Good	Moderate	Unhealthy for Sensitive Groups	Unhealthy	Very Unhealthy	Maximum	Median
MSA[1]	48.8	41.1	9.6	0.5	0.0	162	51

Note: (1) Data covers the Ogden-Clearfield, UT Metropolitan Statistical Area—see Appendix B for areas included; (2) Based on 365 days with AQI data in 2017. Air Quality Index (AQI) is an index for reporting daily air quality. EPA calculates the AQI for five major air pollutants regulated by the Clean Air Act: ground-level ozone, particle pollution (aka particulate matter), carbon monoxide, sulfur dioxide, and nitrogen dioxide. The AQI runs from 0 to 500. The higher the AQI value, the greater the level of air pollution and the greater the health concern. There are six AQI categories: "Good" AQI is between 0 and 50. Air quality is considered satisfactory; "Moderate" AQI is between 51 and 100. Air quality is acceptable; "Unhealthy for Sensitive Groups" When AQI values are between 101 and 150, members of sensitive groups may experience health effects; "Unhealthy" When AQI values are between 151 and 200 everyone may begin to experience health effects; "Very Unhealthy" AQI values between 201 and 300 trigger a health alert; "Hazardous" AQI values over 300 trigger warnings of emergency conditions (not shown).
Source: U.S. Environmental Protection Agency, Air Quality Index Report, 2017

Air Quality Index Pollutants

Area	Percent of Days when AQI Pollutant was...[2]					
	Carbon Monoxide	Nitrogen Dioxide	Ozone	Sulfur Dioxide	Particulate Matter 2.5	Particulate Matter 10
MSA[1]	0.0	8.5	69.0	0.0	21.6	0.8

Note: (1) Data covers the Ogden-Clearfield, UT Metropolitan Statistical Area—see Appendix B for areas included; (2) Based on 365 days with AQI data in 2017. The Air Quality Index (AQI) is an index for reporting daily air quality. EPA calculates the AQI for five major air pollutants regulated by the Clean Air Act: ground-level ozone, particle pollution (also known as particulate matter), carbon monoxide, sulfur dioxide, and nitrogen dioxide. The AQI runs from 0 to 500. The higher the AQI value, the greater the level of air pollution and the greater the health concern.
Source: U.S. Environmental Protection Agency, Air Quality Index Report, 2017

Maximum Air Pollutant Concentrations: Particulate Matter, Ozone, CO and Lead

	Particulate Matter 10 (ug/m^3)	Particulate Matter 2.5 Wtd AM (ug/m^3)	Particulate Matter 2.5 24-Hr (ug/m^3)	Ozone (ppm)	Carbon Monoxide (ppm)	Lead (ug/m^3)
MSA[1] Level	62	9	39	0.076	3	n/a
NAAQS[2]	150	15	35	0.075	9	0.15
Met NAAQS[2]	Yes	Yes	No	No	Yes	n/a

Note: (1) Data covers the Ogden-Clearfield, UT Metropolitan Statistical Area—see Appendix B for areas included; Data from exceptional events are included; (2) National Ambient Air Quality Standards; ppm = parts per million; ug/m^3 = micrograms per cubic meter; n/a not available.
Concentrations: Particulate Matter 10 (coarse particulate)—highest second maximum 24-hour concentration; Particulate Matter 2.5 Wtd AM (fine particulate)—highest weighted annual mean concentration; Particulate Matter 2.5 24-Hour (fine particulate)—highest 98th percentile 24-hour concentration; Ozone—highest fourth daily maximum 8-hour concentration; Carbon Monoxide—highest second maximum non-overlapping 8-hour concentration; Lead—maximum running 3-month average
Source: U.S. Environmental Protection Agency, Air Quality Monitoring Information, "Air Quality Statistics by City, 2016"

Maximum Air Pollutant Concentrations: Nitrogen Dioxide and Sulfur Dioxide

	Nitrogen Dioxide AM (ppb)	Nitrogen Dioxide 1-Hr (ppb)	Sulfur Dioxide AM (ppb)	Sulfur Dioxide 1-Hr (ppb)	Sulfur Dioxide 24-Hr (ppb)
MSA[1] Level	15	n/a	n/a	n/a	n/a
NAAQS[2]	53	100	30	75	140
Met NAAQS[2]	Yes	n/a	n/a	n/a	n/a

Note: (1) Data covers the Ogden-Clearfield, UT Metropolitan Statistical Area—see Appendix B for areas included; Data from exceptional events are included; (2) National Ambient Air Quality Standards; ppm = parts per million; ug/m^3 = micrograms per cubic meter; n/a not available.
Concentrations: Nitrogen Dioxide AM—highest arithmetic mean concentration; Nitrogen Dioxide 1-Hr—highest 98th percentile 1-hour daily maximum concentration; Sulfur Dioxide AM—highest annual mean concentration; Sulfur Dioxide 1-Hr—highest 99th percentile 1-hour daily maximum concentration; Sulfur Dioxide 24-Hr—highest second maximum 24-hour concentration
Source: U.S. Environmental Protection Agency, Air Quality Monitoring Information, "Air Quality Statistics by City, 2016"

Drinking Water

Water System Name	Pop. Served	Primary Water Source Type	Violations[1]	
			Health Based	Monitoring/ Reporting
Syracuse City Water System	26,693	Purchased Surface	0	0

Note: (1) Based on violation data from January 1, 2017 to December 31, 2017
Source: U.S. Environmental Protection Agency, Office of Ground Water and Drinking Water, Safe Drinking Water Information System (based on data extracted April 5, 2018)

Burlington, Vermont

Background

The most populous city in the state of Vermont, Burlington holds the county seat of Chittenden County and is a regional college town.

Originating as a land grant from colonial governor Benning Wentworth as a part of the New Hampshire grants in 1763, Burlington was officially organized after the Revolutionary War, in 1785. The War of 1812 put a strain on its resources, but prosperity grew with the completion of the Champlain Canal in 1823, the Erie Canal in 1825, and the Chambly Canal in 1843. The city became an important port of entry and center for trade on Lake Champlain, and a center for lumbering and manufacturing.

Burlington was incorporated in 1865 and, in 1870, the Pine Street Barge Canal was constructed, as the city continued to flourish. In 1978, Ben & Jerry's Ice Cream was founded in a renovated gas station within the city, an event that continues to draw national attention.

Burlington is located 45 miles south of the Canada-United States border, and sits on the eastern shore of Lake Champlain, north of Shelburne Bay. It is divided into six neighborhoods: Downtown, Hill Section, New North End, Old North End, South End, and the University District. The Intervale is a large area within Burlington as well, though is not considered a neighborhood.

A bustling college town, Burlington is home to the University of Vermont and Champlain College. The University of Vermont Medical Center houses one of the ten most selective medical schools in the US, the UVM College of Medicine. The Community College of Vermont has its campus in the adjacent city of Winooski, while Saint Michael's College and a satellite campus of South New Hampshire University are in the nearby town of Colchester. Neighboring town Williston also houses a satellite campus of Vermont Technical College. The public schools of Burlington are operated by Burlington School District.

Many Burlington areas of interest include historic buildings and sites on the National Register of Historic Places, including The Ethan Allen Homestead, Follett House, and Old Ohavi Zedek Synagogue. Other areas of interest include the Ethan Allen Homestead Museum, the ECHO Lake Aquarium and Science Center, and the Flynn Center for the Performing Arts. Burlington also contains the world's shortest "tallest building" in the US, Decker Towers. Local art and music culture make up much of Burlington's activities and events, and a number of local bands have made it to national fame. The annual "South End Art Hop" is hosted by the South End Arts and Business Association, and the Burlington City Arts organizes events such as Art from the Heart in collaboration with UVM Medical Center. Dragon boat races are held on Lake Champlain for charity every year, and the drag troupe, House of LeMay, performs around the city raising funds for various charities as well.

In 2015, Burlington became the first US city to run entirely on renewable energy.

Burlington owns Vermont's largest airport, Burlington National Airport, providing major regional and international services.

The city has a humid continental climate, with warm, humid summers and cold winters. Between the years of 2000 and 2009, there were six documented heat waves in Burlington. Due to its location east of Lake Champlain, the city occasionally experiences localized snow squalls.

Rankings

General Rankings

- Burlington appeared on *Business Insider's* list of the "13 Hottest American Cities for 2016." Criteria: job and population growth; demographics; affordability; livability; residents' health and welfare; technological innovation; sustainability; burgeoning art and food scenes. *www.businessinsider.com, "The Thirteen Hottest American Cities for 2016," December 4, 2015*
- In their fifth annual survey, Livability.com looked at data for nearly 2,300 U.S. cities to determine the rankings for Livability's "Top 100 Best Places to Live" in 2018. Burlington ranked #24. Criteria: vibrant economy; low cost of living; education, demographics, health care options; transportation & infrastructure; abundant lifestyle amenities. *Livability.com, "Top 100 Best Places to Live 2018" January 16, 2018*

Business/Finance Rankings

- The Burlington metro area appeared on the Milken Institute "2017 Best Performing Cities" list. Rank: #125 out of 201 small metro areas. Criteria: job growth; wage and salary growth; high-tech output growth. *Milken Institute, "Best-Performing Cities 2017," January 2018*
- *Forbes* ranked 200 smaller metro areas (population under 265,400) to determine the nation's "Best Small Places for Business and Careers." The Burlington metro area was ranked #86. Criteria: costs (business and living); job growth (past and projected); income growth; quality of life; educational attainment (college and high school); projected economic growth; cultural and recreational opportunities; net migration patterns; number of highly ranked colleges. *Forbes, "The Best Small Cities for Business and Careers 2017," November, 6 2017*

Environmental Rankings

- Sperling's BestPlaces assessed 379 metropolitan areas of the United States for the likelihood of dangerously extreme weather events or earthquakes. In general the Southeast and South-Central regions have the highest risk of weather extremes and earthquakes, while the Pacific Northwest enjoys the lowest risk. Of the least risky metropolitan areas, the Burlington metro area was ranked #80. *www.bestplaces.net, "Safest Places from Natural Disasters," April 2011*
- Burlington was highlighted as one of the cleanest metro areas for ozone air pollution in the U.S. during 2013 through 2015. The list represents cities with no monitored ozone air pollution in unhealthful ranges. *American Lung Association, State of the Air 2017*
- Burlington was highlighted as one of the top 25 cleanest metro areas for year-round particle pollution (Annual PM 2.5) in the U.S. during 2013 through 2015. The area ranked #17. *American Lung Association, State of the Air 2017*
- Burlington was highlighted as one of the top 99 cleanest metro areas for short-term particle pollution (24-hour PM 2.5) in the U.S. during 2013 through 2015. Monitors in these cities reported no days with unhealthful PM 2.5 levels. *American Lung Association, State of the Air 2017*

Food/Drink Rankings

- In compiling its list of "Top 10 Best Foodie Cities, 2015," the lifestyle website Livability analyzed data for cities with high concentrations of restaurants and bars. Looking at access to healthy food and farmers' markets, adult obesity rates, and other factors like Yelp reviews and James Beard Award winners, Livability chose Burlington as the #9 American foodie town. *livability.com, "Top 10 Best Foodie Cities, 2015," July 6, 2015*
- *Men's Health* ranked 100 major U.S. cities in terms of alcohol intoxication. Burlington ranked #46 (#1 = most sober).Criteria: binge drinking; alcohol-related traffic accidents, arrests, and fatalities. *Men's Health, "America's Drunkest Cities," March 9, 2015*

Health/Fitness Rankings

- *Men's Health* ranked 100 major U.S. cities in terms of the best cities for men. Burlington ranked #5. Criteria: health; fitness; quality of life. *Men's Health, "The Best & Worst Cities for Men Who Want to Be Fit and Happy," January 1, 2016*
- The Burlington metro area ranked #37 out of 189 in The Gallup-Healthways Well-Being Index. Criteria: purpose; social well being; financial health; community and physical health. Results are based on telephone interviews with adults, aged 18 and older, living in metropolitan areas in the 50 U.S. states and the District of Columbia. *Gallup-Healthways, "State of American Well-Being, 2017 Community Well-Being Rankings" March 2018*

Real Estate Rankings

- *WalletHub* compared the most populated U.S. cities, as well as at least two of the most populated cities in each state, for a total of 179, to determine which had the best markets for real estate agents. Burlington ranked #125 where demand was high and pay was the best. Criteria: sales per agent; annual median wage for real-estate agents; monthly average starting salary for real estate agents; real estate job density and competition; unemployment rate; housing-market health index; and other relevant metrics. *www.WalletHub.com, "2018's Best Places to Be a Real Estate Agent,"April 25, 2018*
- Burlington was ranked #122 out of 238 metro areas in terms of housing affordability in 2017 by the National Association of Home Builders (#1 = most affordable). Criteria: the share of homes sold in that area affordable to a family earning the local median income, based on standard mortgage underwriting criteria. *National Association of Home Builders®, NAHB-Wells Fargo Housing Opportunity Index, 4th Quarter 2017*

Safety Rankings

- The National Insurance Crime Bureau ranked 382 metro areas in the U.S. in terms of per capita rates of vehicle theft. The Burlington metro area ranked #342 (#1 = highest rate). Criteria: number of vehicle theft offenses per 100,000 inhabitants in 2016. *National Insurance Crime Bureau, "Hot Spots 2016," June 8, 2017*

Seniors/Retirement Rankings

- From its Best Cities for Successful Aging indexes, the Milken Institute generated rankings for metropolitan areas, weighing data in nine categories—health care, wellness, living arrangements, transportation and convenience, financial characteristics, education, employment, community engagement, and overall livability. The Burlington metro area was ranked #20 overall in the small metro area category. *Milken Institute, "Best Cities for Successful Aging, 2017" March 14, 2017*

Miscellaneous Rankings

- Of the American metro areas that allow medical or recreational use of marijuana, the Burlington metro area was identified by CNBC editors as one of the most livable for marijuana lovers. Criteria included the Sperling's BestPlaces assessment of marijuana-friendly cities in terms of sound economy, cultural diversity, and a healthy population, plus cost-of-living index and high-quality schools. *www.cnbc.com, "The Best Cities to Live for Marijuana Lovers," February 5, 2014*

Business Environment

CITY FINANCES

City Government Finances

Component	2015 ($000)	2015 ($ per capita)
Total Revenues	213,884	5,038
Total Expenditures	208,497	4,911
Debt Outstanding	182,392	4,296
Cash and Securities[1]	248,894	5,863

Note: (1) Cash and security holdings of a government at the close of its fiscal year,, including those of its dependent agencies, utilities, and liquor stores.
Source: U.S Census Bureau, State & Local Government Finances 2015

City Government Revenue by Source

Source	2015 ($000)	2015 ($ per capita)	2015 (%)
General Revenue			
From Federal Government	8,343	197	3.9
From State Government	10,415	245	4.9
From Local Governments	0	0	0.0
Taxes			
Property	33,226	783	15.5
Sales and Gross Receipts	7,973	188	3.7
Personal Income	0	0	0.0
Corporate Income	0	0	0.0
Motor Vehicle License	0	0	0.0
Other Taxes	3,867	91	1.8
Current Charges	56,325	1,327	26.3
Liquor Store	0	0	0.0
Utility	68,413	1,612	32.0
Employee Retirement	16,741	394	7.8

Source: U.S Census Bureau, State & Local Government Finances 2015

City Government Expenditures by Function

Function	2015 ($000)	2015 ($ per capita)	2015 (%)
General Direct Expenditures			
Air Transportation	19,805	466	9.5
Corrections	0	0	0.0
Education	6	< 1	< 0.1
Employment Security Administration	0	0	0.0
Financial Administration	1,876	44	0.9
Fire Protection	9,214	217	4.4
General Public Buildings	0	0	0.0
Governmental Administration, Other	3,529	83	1.7
Health	113	2	0.1
Highways	12,882	303	6.2
Hospitals	0	0	0.0
Housing and Community Development	4,113	96	2.0
Interest on General Debt	4,614	108	2.2
Judicial and Legal	1,094	25	0.5
Libraries	1,849	43	0.9
Parking	3,916	92	1.9
Parks and Recreation	9,934	234	4.8
Police Protection	14,574	343	7.0
Public Welfare	34	< 1	< 0.1
Sewerage	5,464	128	2.6
Solid Waste Management	350	8	0.2
Veterans' Services	0	0	0.0
Liquor Store	0	0	0.0
Utility	86,061	2,027	41.3
Employee Retirement	12,349	290	5.9

Source: U.S Census Bureau, State & Local Government Finances 2015

DEMOGRAPHICS

Population Growth

Area	1990 Census	2000 Census	2010 Census	2016* Estimate	Population Growth (%) 1990-2016	Population Growth (%) 2010-2016
City	39,127	38,889	42,417	42,556	8.8	0.3
MSA[1]	177,059	198,889	211,261	216,080	22.0	2.3
U.S.	248,709,873	281,421,906	308,745,538	318,558,162	28.1	3.2

Note: (1) Figures cover the Burlington-South Burlington, VT Metropolitan Statistical Area—see Appendix B for areas included; (*) 2012-2016 5-year estimated population
Source: U.S. Census Bureau, 1990 Census, Census 2000, Census 2010, 2012-2016 American Community Survey 5-Year Estimates

Household Size

Area	Persons in Household (%) One	Two	Three	Four	Five	Six	Seven or More	Average Household Size
City	36.2	35.2	12.9	9.9	3.6	0.8	1.3	2.20
MSA[1]	27.2	38.3	14.8	13.1	4.4	1.4	0.8	2.40
U.S.	27.7	33.7	15.7	13.1	6.0	2.3	1.5	2.60

Note: (1) Figures cover the Burlington-South Burlington, VT Metropolitan Statistical Area—see Appendix B for areas included
Source: U.S. Census Bureau, 2012-2016 American Community Survey 5-Year Estimates

Race

Area	White Alone[2] (%)	Black Alone[2] (%)	Asian Alone[2] (%)	AIAN[3] Alone[2] (%)	NHOPI[4] Alone[2] (%)	Other Race Alone[2] (%)	Two or More Races (%)
City	85.7	4.9	6.0	0.4	0.0	0.5	2.5
MSA[1]	92.2	2.0	2.7	0.4	0.0	0.5	2.2
U.S.	73.3	12.6	5.2	0.8	0.2	4.8	3.1

Note: (1) Figures cover the Burlington-South Burlington, VT Metropolitan Statistical Area—see Appendix B for areas included; (2) Alone is defined as not being in combination with one or more other races; (3) American Indian and Alaska Native; (4) Native Hawaiian and Other Pacific Islander
Source: U.S. Census Bureau, 2012-2016 American Community Survey 5-Year Estimates

Hispanic or Latino Origin

Area	Total (%)	Mexican (%)	Puerto Rican (%)	Cuban (%)	Other (%)
City	2.6	0.4	0.7	0.2	1.3
MSA[1]	2.0	0.6	0.4	0.1	0.8
U.S.	17.3	11.0	1.7	0.7	4.0

Note: Persons of Hispanic or Latino origin can be of any race; (1) Figures cover the Burlington-South Burlington, VT Metropolitan Statistical Area—see Appendix B for areas included
Source: U.S. Census Bureau, 2012-2016 American Community Survey 5-Year Estimates

Segregation

Type	Segregation Indices[1] 1990	2000	2010	2010 Rank[2]	Percent Change 1990-2000	1990-2010	2000-2010
Black/White	n/a	n/a	n/a	n/a	n/a	n/a	n/a
Asian/White	n/a	n/a	n/a	n/a	n/a	n/a	n/a
Hispanic/White	n/a	n/a	n/a	n/a	n/a	n/a	n/a

Note: All figures cover the Metropolitan Statistical Area—see Appendix B for areas included; Figures are based on an analysis of 1990, 2000, and 2010 Census Decennial Census tract data by William H. Frey, Brookings Institution and the University of Michigan Social Science Data Analysis Network. In this analysis all racial groups (whites, blacks, and asians) are non-Hispanic members of those races. Hispanics are shown as a separate category; (1) Segregation Indices are Dissimilarity Indices that measure the degree to which the minority group is distributed differently than whites across census tracts. They range from 0 (complete integration) to 100 (complete segregation) where the value indicates the percentage of the minority group that needs to move to be distributed exactly like whites; (2) Ranges from 1 (most segregated) to 102 (least segregated); n/a not available.
Source: www.CensusScope.org

Ancestry

Area	German	Irish	English	American	Italian	Polish	French[2]	Scottish	Dutch
City	12.8	19.6	13.7	4.6	9.6	4.8	8.9	4.1	1.1
MSA[1]	10.8	18.1	14.3	8.8	7.3	3.4	13.3	4.0	1.3
U.S.	14.4	10.4	7.7	6.9	5.4	2.9	2.6	1.7	1.3

Note: Figures are the percentage of the total population reporting a particular ancestry. The nine most commonly reported ancestries in the U.S. are shown. Figures include multiple ancestries (e.g. if a person reported being Irish and Italian, they were included in both columns); (1) Figures cover the Burlington-South Burlington, VT Metropolitan Statistical Area—see Appendix B for areas included; (2) Excludes Basque
Source: U.S. Census Bureau, 2012-2016 American Community Survey 5-Year Estimates

Foreign-Born Population

Area	Percent of Population Born in								
	Any Foreign Country	Asia	Mexico	Europe	Carribean	Central America[2]	South America	Africa	Canada
City	11.9	5.5	0.0	2.9	0.3	0.3	0.2	2.3	0.4
MSA[1]	6.9	2.5	0.2	1.8	0.1	0.1	0.3	0.9	1.0
U.S.	13.2	4.0	3.6	1.5	1.3	1.0	0.9	0.6	0.3

Note: (1) Figures cover the Burlington-South Burlington, VT Metropolitan Statistical Area—see Appendix B for areas included; (2) Excludes Mexico.
Source: U.S. Census Bureau, 2012-2016 American Community Survey 5-Year Estimates

Marital Status

Area	Never Married	Now Married[2]	Separated	Widowed	Divorced
City	60.0	27.0	1.0	4.3	7.7
MSA[1]	36.2	47.4	1.1	5.0	10.3
U.S.	33.0	48.1	2.1	5.9	11.0

Note: Figures are percentages and cover the population 15 years of age and older; (1) Figures cover the Burlington-South Burlington, VT Metropolitan Statistical Area—see Appendix B for areas included; (2) Excludes separated
Source: U.S. Census Bureau, 2012-2016 American Community Survey 5-Year Estimates

Disability Status

Area	All Ages	Under 18 Years Old	18 to 64 Years Old	65 Years and Over
City	11.9	5.3	9.7	38.1
MSA[1]	11.4	5.1	9.3	32.1
U.S.	12.5	4.1	10.3	35.7

Note: Figures show percent of the civilian noninstitutionalized population that reported having a disability. Disability status is determined from six types of difficulty: vision, hearing, cognitive, ambulatory, self-care, and independent living. For children under 5 years old, hearing and vision difficulty are used to determine disability status. For children between the ages of 5 and 14, disability status is determined from hearing, vision, cognitive, ambulatory, and self-care difficulties. For people aged 15 years and older, they are considered to have a disability if they have difficulty with any one of the six difficulty types; Note: (1) Figures cover the Burlington-South Burlington, VT Metropolitan Statistical Area—see Appendix B for areas included
Source: U.S. Census Bureau, 2012-2016 American Community Survey 5-Year Estimates

Age

Area	Percent of Population									Median Age
	Under Age 5	Age 5–19	Age 20–34	Age 35–44	Age 45–54	Age 55–64	Age 65–74	Age 75–84	Age 85+	
City	3.2	21.3	37.8	9.4	8.6	9.0	5.6	3.1	2.1	26.7
MSA[1]	5.1	19.1	22.8	12.0	14.3	13.4	7.8	3.7	1.9	37.6
U.S.	6.2	19.6	20.7	12.7	13.6	12.6	8.3	4.3	1.9	37.7

Note: (1) Figures cover the Burlington-South Burlington, VT Metropolitan Statistical Area—see Appendix B for areas included
Source: U.S. Census Bureau, 2012-2016 American Community Survey 5-Year Estimates

Gender

Area	Males	Females	Males per 100 Females
City	20,881	21,675	96.3
MSA[1]	106,131	109,949	96.5
U.S.	156,765,322	161,792,840	96.9

Note: (1) Figures cover the Burlington-South Burlington, VT Metropolitan Statistical Area—see Appendix B for areas included
Source: U.S. Census Bureau, 2012-2016 American Community Survey 5-Year Estimates

Religious Groups by Family

Area	Catholic	Baptist	Non-Den.	Methodist[2]	Lutheran	LDS[3]	Pente-costal	Presby-terian[4]	Muslim[5]	Judaism
MSA[1]	27.6	1.3	1.0	2.5	0.3	0.5	0.5	2.0	0.1	0.7
U.S.	19.1	9.3	4.0	4.0	2.3	2.0	1.9	1.6	0.8	0.7

Note: Figures are the number of adherents as a percentage of the total population; (1) Figures cover the Burlington-South Burlington, VT Metropolitan Statistical Area—see Appendix B for areas included; (2) Methodist/Pietist; (3) Latter Day Saints; (4) Reformed; (5) Figures are estimates
Source: Association of Statisticians of American Religious Bodies, 2010 U.S. Religion Census: Religious Congregations & Membership Study

Religious Groups by Tradition

Area	Catholic	Evangelical Protestant	Mainline Protestant	Other Tradition	Black Protestant	Orthodox
MSA[1]	27.6	4.5	6.2	1.9	<0.1	<0.1
U.S.	19.1	16.2	7.3	4.3	1.6	0.3

Note: Figures are the number of adherents as a percentage of the total population; (1) Figures cover the Burlington-South Burlington, VT Metropolitan Statistical Area—see Appendix B for areas included
Source: Association of Statisticians of American Religious Bodies, 2010 U.S. Religion Census: Religious Congregations & Membership Study

ECONOMY

Gross Metropolitan Product

Area	2014	2015	2016	2017	Rank[2]
MSA[1]	12.6	12.9	13.3	13.8	170

Note: Figures are in billions of dollars; (1) Figures cover the Burlington-South Burlington, VT Metropolitan Statistical Area—see Appendix B for areas included; (2) Rank is based on 2015 data and ranges from 1 to 381
Source: The U.S. Conference of Mayors, U.S. Metro Economies: GMP and Employment Report, 2015-2017

Economic Growth

Area	2012-14 (%)	2015 (%)	2016 (%)	2017 (%)	Rank[2]
MSA[1]	-0.9	1.0	1.5	2.2	339
U.S.	2.0	2.4	1.9	2.6	–

Note: Figures are real gross metropolitan product (GMP) growth rates and represent average annual percent change; (1) Figures cover the Burlington-South Burlington, VT Metropolitan Statistical Area—see Appendix B for areas included; (2) Rank is based on 2012-2014 average annual percent change and ranges from 1 to 381
Source: The U.S. Conference of Mayors, U.S. Metro Economies: GMP and Employment Report, 2015-2017

Metropolitan Area Exports

Area	2011	2012	2013	2014	2015	2016	Rank[2]
MSA[1]	3,656.8	3,572.0	3,434.5	3,012.6	2,089.4	1,404.7	120

Note: Figures are in millions of dollars; (1) Figures cover the Burlington-South Burlington, VT Metropolitan Statistical Area—see Appendix B for areas included; (2) Rank is based on 2016 data and ranges from 1 to 385
Source: U.S. Department of Commerce, International Trade Administration, Office of Trade & Industry Information, Manufacturing & Services, data extracted March 15, 2018

Building Permits

Area	Single-Family			Multi-Family			Total		
	2016	2017p	Pct. Chg.	2016	2017p	Pct. Chg.	2016	2017p	Pct. Chg.
City	n/a	n/a	n/a	n/a	n/a	n/a	n/a	n/a	n/a
MSA[1]	255	250	-2.0	388	379	-2.3	643	629	-2.2
U.S.	750,800	817,300	8.9	455,800	446,800	-2.0	1,206,600	1,264,100	4.8

Note: (1) Figures cover the Burlington-South Burlington, VT Metropolitan Statistical Area—see Appendix B for areas included; Figures represent new, privately-owned housing units authorized (unadjusted data); All permit data are based on estimates with imputation; (p) preliminary data.
Source: U.S. Census Bureau, Manufacturing, Mining, and Construction Statistics, Building Permits, 2016, 2017

Bankruptcy Filings

Area	Business Filings			Nonbusiness Filings		
	2016	2017	% Chg.	2016	2017	% Chg.
Chittenden County	7	6	-14.3	88	126	43.2
U.S.	24,114	23,157	-4.0	770,846	765,863	-0.6

Note: Business filings include Chapter 7, Chapter 11, Chapter 12, and Chapter 13; Nonbusiness filings include Chapter 7, Chapter 11, and Chapter 13
Source: Administrative Office of the U.S. Courts, Business and Nonbusiness Bankruptcy, County Cases Commenced by Chapter of the Bankruptcy Code, During the 12-Month Period Ending December 31, 2016 and Business and Nonbusiness Bankruptcy, County Cases Commenced by Chapter of the Bankruptcy Code, During the 12-Month Period Ending December 31, 2017

Housing Vacancy Rates

Area	Gross Vacancy Rate[2] (%)			Year-Round Vacancy Rate[3] (%)			Rental Vacancy Rate[4] (%)			Homeowner Vacancy Rate[5] (%)		
	2015	2016	2017	2015	2016	2017	2015	2016	2017	2015	2016	2017
MSA[1]	n/a	n/a	n/a	n/a	n/a	n/a	n/a	n/a	n/a	n/a	n/a	n/a
U.S.	12.9	12.8	12.7	10.0	9.9	9.9	7.1	6.9	7.2	1.8	1.7	1.6

Note: (1) Figures cover the Burlington-South Burlington, VT Metropolitan Statistical Area—see Appendix B for areas included; (2) The percentage of the total housing inventory that is vacant; (3) The percentage of the housing inventory (excluding seasonal units) that is year-round vacant; (4) The percentage of rental inventory that is vacant for rent; (5) The percentage of homeowner inventory that is vacant for sale; n/a not available
Source: U.S. Census Bureau, Housing Vacancies and Homeownership Annual Statistics: 2015, 2016, 2017

INCOME

Income

Area	Per Capita ($)	Median Household ($)	Average Household ($)
City	25,231	46,754	63,415
MSA[1]	33,391	64,127	82,667
U.S.	29,829	55,322	77,866

Note: (1) Figures cover the Burlington-South Burlington, VT Metropolitan Statistical Area—see Appendix B for areas included
Source: U.S. Census Bureau, 2012-2016 American Community Survey 5-Year Estimates

Household Income Distribution

Area	Percent of Households Earning							
	Under $15,000	$15,000 -$24,999	$25,000 -$34,999	$35,000 -$49,999	$50,000 -$74,999	$75,000 -$99,999	$100,000 -$149,999	$150,000 and up
City	16.9	13.8	8.8	13.0	15.6	13.5	11.7	6.6
MSA[1]	9.8	8.3	8.2	12.2	18.6	14.7	17.3	10.9
U.S.	12.1	10.2	9.9	13.2	17.8	12.2	13.5	11.1

Note: (1) Figures cover the Burlington-South Burlington, VT Metropolitan Statistical Area—see Appendix B for areas included
Source: U.S. Census Bureau, 2012-2016 American Community Survey 5-Year Estimates

Poverty Rate

Area	All Ages	Under 18 Years Old	18 to 64 Years Old	65 Years and Over
City	25.1	25.3	27.2	11.4
MSA[1]	10.7	11.9	11.0	7.3
U.S.	15.1	21.2	14.2	9.3

Note: Figures are percentage of people whose income during the past 12 months was below the poverty level; (1) Figures cover the Burlington-South Burlington, VT Metropolitan Statistical Area—see Appendix B for areas included
Source: U.S. Census Bureau, 2012-2016 American Community Survey 5-Year Estimates

EMPLOYMENT

Labor Force and Employment

Area	Civilian Labor Force			Workers Employed		
	Dec. 2016	Dec. 2017	% Chg.	Dec. 2016	Dec. 2017	% Chg.
City	23,865	23,774	-0.4	23,335	23,334	0.0
NECTA[1]	123,888	123,521	-0.3	121,124	121,119	0.0
U.S.	158,968,000	159,880,000	0.6	151,798,000	153,602,000	1.2

Note: Data is not seasonally adjusted and covers workers 16 years of age and older; (1) Figures cover the Burlington-South Burlington, VT New England City and Town Area—see Appendix B for areas included
Source: Bureau of Labor Statistics, Local Area Unemployment Statistics

Unemployment Rate

Area	2017											
	Jan.	Feb.	Mar.	Apr.	May	Jun.	Jul.	Aug.	Sep.	Oct.	Nov.	Dec.
City	2.6	2.1	2.5	2.0	2.2	3.2	3.1	3.0	2.8	2.1	2.2	1.9
NECTA[1]	2.8	2.5	2.7	2.3	2.2	2.6	2.6	2.6	2.5	1.9	2.2	1.9
U.S.	5.1	4.9	4.6	4.1	4.1	4.5	4.6	4.5	4.1	3.9	3.9	3.9

Note: Data is not seasonally adjusted and covers workers 16 years of age and older; (1) Figures cover the Burlington-South Burlington, VT New England City and Town Area—see Appendix B for areas included
Source: Bureau of Labor Statistics, Local Area Unemployment Statistics

Average Wages

Occupation	$/Hr.	Occupation	$/Hr.
Accountants and Auditors	38.30	Maids and Housekeeping Cleaners	11.70
Automotive Mechanics	18.20	Maintenance and Repair Workers	19.40
Bookkeepers	20.60	Marketing Managers	59.10
Carpenters	22.20	Nuclear Medicine Technologists	n/a
Cashiers	11.90	Nurses, Licensed Practical	25.10
Clerks, General Office	16.20	Nurses, Registered	34.00
Clerks, Receptionists/Information	16.30	Nursing Assistants	14.30
Clerks, Shipping/Receiving	16.50	Packers and Packagers, Hand	13.10
Computer Programmers	34.30	Physical Therapists	37.10
Computer Systems Analysts	39.60	Postal Service Mail Carriers	24.60
Computer User Support Specialists	26.00	Real Estate Brokers	n/a
Cooks, Restaurant	13.80	Retail Salespersons	13.90
Dentists	n/a	Sales Reps., Exc. Tech./Scientific	33.20
Electrical Engineers	46.40	Sales Reps., Tech./Scientific	48.00
Electricians	25.60	Secretaries, Exc. Legal/Med./Exec.	17.40
Financial Managers	65.90	Security Guards	16.90
First-Line Supervisors/Managers, Sales	23.30	Surgeons	132.30
Food Preparation Workers	12.90	Teacher Assistants*	15.50
General and Operations Managers	53.90	Teachers, Elementary School*	29.70
Hairdressers/Cosmetologists	18.20	Teachers, Secondary School*	31.60
Internists, General	88.80	Telemarketers	11.90
Janitors and Cleaners	14.40	Truck Drivers, Heavy/Tractor-Trailer	22.20
Landscaping/Groundskeeping Workers	16.70	Truck Drivers, Light/Delivery Svcs.	18.80
Lawyers	54.70	Waiters and Waitresses	14.90

Note: Wage data covers the Burlington-South Burlington, VT New England City and Town Area—see Appendix B for areas included; (*) Hourly wages for elementary/secondary school teachers and teacher assistants were calculated by the editors from annual wage data based on a 40 hour work week; n/a not available.
Source: Bureau of Labor Statistics, Metro Area Occupational Employment & Wage Estimates, May 2017

Employment by Occupation

Occupation Classification	City (%)	MSA[1] (%)	U.S. (%)
Management, Business, Science, and Arts	43.6	44.8	37.0
Natural Resources, Construction, and Maintenance	4.0	7.7	8.9
Production, Transportation, and Material Moving	7.3	9.7	12.2
Sales and Office	23.0	21.6	23.8
Service	22.0	16.2	18.1

Note: Figures cover employed civilians 16 years of age and older; (1) Figures cover the Burlington-South Burlington, VT Metropolitan Statistical Area—see Appendix B for areas included
Source: U.S. Census Bureau, 2012-2016 American Community Survey 5-Year Estimates

Employment by Industry

Sector	NECTA[1] Number of Employees	NECTA[1] Percent of Total	U.S. Percent of Total
Construction, Mining, and Logging	6,000	4.8	5.2
Education and Health Services	22,400	17.9	15.9
Financial Activities	4,700	3.7	5.7
Government	23,600	18.8	15.3
Information	2,200	1.8	1.9
Leisure and Hospitality	12,600	10.0	10.7
Manufacturing	12,700	10.1	8.5
Other Services	4,200	3.3	3.9
Professional and Business Services	14,200	11.3	14.0
Retail Trade	15,300	12.2	11.0
Transportation, Warehousing, and Utilities	3,500	2.8	4.1
Wholesale Trade	4,000	3.2	4.0

Note: Figures are non-farm employment as of December 2017. Figures are not seasonally adjusted and include workers 16 years of age and older; (1) Figures cover the Burlington-South Burlington, VT New England City and Town Area—see Appendix B for areas included
Source: Bureau of Labor Statistics, Current Employment Statistics, Employment, Hours, and Earnings

Occupations with Greatest Projected Employment Growth: 2017 – 2019

Occupation[1]	2017 Employment	2019 Projected Employment	Numeric Employment Change	Percent Employment Change
Personal Care Aides	7,440	7,860	420	5.6
Registered Nurses	6,060	6,330	270	4.5
Combined Food Preparation and Serving Workers, Including Fast Food	6,260	6,450	190	3.1
Janitors and Cleaners, Except Maids and Housekeeping Cleaners	5,560	5,700	140	2.5
Landscaping and Groundskeeping Workers	4,950	5,080	130	2.7
Waiters and Waitresses	5,730	5,840	110	2.0
Accountants and Auditors	3,690	3,770	80	2.3
Market Research Analysts and Marketing Specialists	1,680	1,760	80	4.9
Nursing Assistants	3,530	3,610	80	2.2
Compliance Officers	2,210	2,280	70	3.1

Note: Projections cover Vermont; (1) Sorted by numeric employment change
Source: www.projectionscentral.com, State Occupational Projections, 2017–2019 Short-Term Projections

Fastest Growing Occupations: 2017 – 2019

Occupation[1]	2017 Employment	2019 Projected Employment	Numeric Employment Change	Percent Employment Change
Software Developers, Applications	1,100	1,170	70	6.7
Personal Care Aides	7,440	7,860	420	5.6
Market Research Analysts and Marketing Specialists	1,680	1,760	80	4.9
Registered Nurses	6,060	6,330	270	4.5
Medical Secretaries	1,000	1,050	50	4.3
Combined Food Preparation and Serving Workers, Including Fast Food	6,260	6,450	190	3.1
Compliance Officers	2,210	2,280	70	3.1
Landscaping and Groundskeeping Workers	4,950	5,080	130	2.7
Social and Human Service Assistants	2,540	2,600	60	2.7
Cooks, Restaurant	2,620	2,690	70	2.6

Note: Projections cover Vermont; (1) Sorted by percent employment change and excludes occupations with numeric employment change less than 50
Source: www.projectionscentral.com, State Occupational Projections, 2017–2019 Short-Term Projections

TAXES

State Corporate Income Tax Rates

State	Tax Rate (%)	Income Brackets ($)	Num. of Brackets	Financial Institution Tax Rate (%)[a]	Federal Income Tax Ded.
Vermont	6.0 - 8.5 (b)	10,000 - 25,000	3	(a)	No

Note: Tax rates as of January 1, 2018; (a) Rates listed are the corporate income tax rate applied to financial institutions or excise taxes based on income. Some states have other taxes based upon the value of deposits or shares; (b) Minimum tax is $800 in California, $100 in District of Columbia and Arizona, $50 in North Dakota (banks), $500 in Rhode Island, $200 per location in South Dakota (banks), $100 in Utah, $250 in Vermont.
Source: Federation of Tax Administrators, Range of State Corporate Income Tax Rates, January 1, 2018

State Individual Income Tax Rates

State	Tax Rate (%)	Income Brackets ($)	Num. of Brackets	Personal Exempt. ($)[1]		Fed. Inc. Tax Ded.
				Single	Dependents	
Vermont (a)	3.55 - 8.95	37,950 - 416,700 (w)	5	4,150 (d)	4,150 (d)	No

Note: Tax rates as of January 1, 2018; Local- and county-level taxes are not included; n/a not applicable; (1) Married joint filers generally receive double the single exemption; (a) 19 states have statutory provision for automatically adjusting to the rate of inflation the dollar values of the income tax brackets, standard deductions, and/or personal exemptions. Massachusetts, Michigan, and Nebraska index the personal exemption only. Oregon does not index the income brackets for $125,000 and over; (d) These states use the personal exemption amounts provided in the federal Internal Revenue Code. Note, the Tax Cut and Reform Act of 2017 has eliminated personal exemptions from the IRC. These states will need to enact legislation to reinstate a personal exemption for tax year 2018. We have reported here the exemption amounts before the federal tax change; (w) Vermont's income brackets reported are for single individuals. For married taxpayers filing jointly, the same tax rates apply to income brackets ranging from $63,350 to $416,700.
Source: Federation of Tax Administrators, State Individual Income Tax Rates, January 1, 2018

Various State Sales and Excise Tax Rates

State	State Sales Tax (%)	Gasoline[1] (¢/gal.)	Cigarette[2] ($/pack)	Spirits[3] ($/gal.)	Wine[4] ($/gal.)	Beer[5] ($/gal.)	Recreational Marijuana (%)
Vermont	6.0	30.72	3.08	7.72 (g)	0.55 (l)	0.27	Not legal

Note: All tax rates as of January 1, 2018; (1) The American Petroleum Institute has developed a methodology for determining the average tax rate on a gallon of fuel. Rates may include any of the following: excise taxes, environmental fees, storage tank fees, other fees or taxes, general sales tax, and local taxes. In states where gasoline is subject to the general sales tax, or where the fuel tax is based on the average sale price, the average rate determined by API is sensitive to changes in the price of gasoline. States that fully or partially apply general sales taxes to gasoline: CA, CO, GA, IL, IN, MI, NY; (2) The federal excise tax of $1.0066 per pack and local taxes are not included; (3) Rates are those applicable to off-premise sales of 40% alcohol by volume (a.b.v.) distilled spirits in 750ml containers. Local excise taxes are excluded; (4) Rates are those applicable to off-premise sales of 11% a.b.v. non-carbonated wine in 750ml containers; (5) Rates are those applicable to off-premise sales of 4.7% a.b.v. beer in 12 ounce containers; (g) Control states, where the government controls all sales. Products can be subject to ad valorem mark-up as well as excise taxes; (l) Different rates also applicable to alcohol content, place of production, size of container, place purchased (on- or off-premise or on board airlines) or type of wine (carbonated, vermouth, etc.).
Source: Tax Foundation, 2018 Facts & Figures: How Does Your State Compare?

State Business Tax Climate Index Rankings

State	Overall Rank	Corporate Tax Rank	Individual Income Tax Rank	Sales Tax Rank	Unemployment Insurance Tax Rank	Property Tax Rank
Vermont	47	37	44	16	18	48

Note: The index is a measure of how each state's tax laws affect economic performance. The lower the rank, the more favorable a state's tax system is for business. States without a given tax are given a ranking of 1. The scores/rankings for the District of Columbia do not affect other states. The 2018 index represents the tax climate as of July 1, 2017.
Source: Tax Foundation, State Business Tax Climate Index 2018

TRANSPORTATION

Means of Transportation to Work

Area	Car/Truck/Van		Public Transportation			Bicycle	Walked	Other Means	Worked at Home
	Drove Alone	Car-pooled	Bus	Subway	Railroad				
City	52.9	8.3	5.2	0.0	0.0	5.6	21.7	0.8	5.3
MSA[1]	74.7	8.7	2.0	0.0	0.0	1.6	6.6	0.8	5.6
U.S.	76.4	9.3	2.6	1.9	0.6	0.6	2.8	1.3	4.6

Note: Figures are percentages and cover workers 16 years of age and older; (1) Figures cover the Burlington-South Burlington, VT Metropolitan Statistical Area—see Appendix B for areas included
Source: U.S. Census Bureau, 2012-2016 American Community Survey 5-Year Estimates

Travel Time to Work

Area	Less Than 10 Minutes	10 to 19 Minutes	20 to 29 Minutes	30 to 44 Minutes	45 to 59 Minutes	60 to 89 Minutes	90 Minutes or More
City	18.4	43.1	19.7	12.5	3.8	2.0	0.5
MSA[1]	14.7	33.4	22.7	18.8	6.3	2.9	1.1
U.S.	12.9	29.2	20.9	20.4	8.0	6.0	2.7

Note: Note: Figures are percentages and include workers 16 years old and over; (1) Figures cover the Burlington-South Burlington, VT Metropolitan Statistical Area—see Appendix B for areas included
Source: U.S. Census Bureau, 2012-2016 American Community Survey 5-Year Estimates

Freeway Travel Time Index

Area	1985	1990	1995	2000	2005	2010	2014
Urban Area Rank[1,2]	n/a	n/a	n/a	n/a	n/a	n/a	n/a
Urban Area Index[1]	n/a	n/a	n/a	n/a	n/a	n/a	n/a
Average Index[3]	1.09	1.11	1.14	1.17	1.20	1.19	1.20

Note: Freeway Travel Time Index—the ratio of travel time in the peak period to the travel time at free-flow conditions. For example, a value of 1.30 indicates a 20-minute free-flow trip takes 26 minutes in the peak (20 minutes x 1.30 = 26 minutes); (1) Data for the Burlington-South Burlington, VT urban area was not available; (2) Rank is based on 101 urban areas (#1 = highest travel time index); (3) Average of 101 urban areas
Source: Texas Transportation Institute, 2015 Urban Mobility Scorecard, August 2015

Freeway Commuter Stress Index

Area	1985	1990	1995	2000	2005	2010	2014
Urban Area Rank[1,2]	n/a	n/a	n/a	n/a	n/a	n/a	n/a
Urban Area Index[1]	n/a	n/a	n/a	n/a	n/a	n/a	n/a
Average Index[3]	1.13	1.16	1.19	1.22	1.25	1.24	1.25

Note: The Freeway Commuter Stress Index is the same as the Freeway Travel Time Index (see table above) except that it includes only the travel in the peak directions during the peak periods; the TTI includes travel in all directions during the peak period. Thus, the CSI is more indicative of the work trip experienced by each commuter on a daily basis; (1) Data for the Burlington-South Burlington, VT urban area was not available; (2) Rank is based on 101 urban areas (#1 = highest travel time index); (3) Average of 101 urban areas
Source: Texas Transportation Institute, 2015 Urban Mobility Scorecard, August 2015

Living Environment

COST OF LIVING

Cost of Living Index

Composite Index	Groceries	Housing	Utilities	Transportation	Health Care	Misc. Goods/ Services
120.5	111.9	146.9	119.1	111.7	104.5	107.2

Note: The Cost of Living Index measures regional differences in the cost of consumer goods and services, excluding taxes and non-consumer expenditures, for professional and managerial households in the top income quintile. It is based on more than 50,000 prices covering almost 60 different items for which prices are collected three times a year by chambers of commerce, economic development organizations or university applied economic centers in each participating urban area. The numbers shown should be read as a percentage above or below the national average of 100. For example, a value of 115.4 in the groceries column indicates that grocery prices are 15.4% higher than the national average. Small differences in the index numbers should not be interpreted as significant; Figures cover the Burlington-Chittenden County VT urban area.
Source: The Council for Community and Economic Research, ACCRA Cost of Living Index, 2017

Grocery Prices

Area[1]	T-Bone Steak ($/pound)	Frying Chicken ($/pound)	Whole Milk ($/half gal.)	Eggs ($/dozen)	Orange Juice ($/64 oz.)	Coffee ($/11.5 oz.)
City[2]	11.60	1.37	2.67	2.43	3.36	4.14
Avg.	11.29	1.40	2.02	1.47	3.55	4.37
Min.	7.71	0.93	1.04	0.70	2.86	3.24
Max.	15.83	2.39	4.03	3.92	6.29	8.16

Note: (1) Values for the local area are compared with the average, minimum and maximum values for all 294 areas in the Cost of Living Index; (2) Figures cover the Burlington-Chittenden County VT urban area; ***T-Bone Steak*** *(price per pound);* ***Frying Chicken*** *(price per pound, whole fryer);* ***Whole Milk*** *(half gallon carton);* ***Eggs*** *(price per dozen, Grade A, large);* ***Orange Juice*** *(64 oz. Tropicana or Florida Natural);* ***Coffee*** *(11.5 oz. can, vacuum-packed, Maxwell House, Hills Bros, or Folgers).*
Source: The Council for Community and Economic Research, ACCRA Cost of Living Index, 2017

Housing and Utility Costs

Area[1]	New Home Price ($)	Apartment Rent ($/month)	All Electric ($/month)	Part Electric ($/month)	Other Energy ($/month)	Telephone ($/month)
City[2]	500,962	1,489	-	100.24	128.91	28.00
Avg.	335,956	1,047	175.01	97.34	67.93	28.71
Min.	187,788	491	109.48	49.33	35.44	12.39
Max.	1,739,087	4,559	432.62	227.09	353.33	44.61

Note: (1) Values for the local area are compared with the average, minimum and maximum values for all 294 areas in the Cost of Living Index; (2) Figures cover the Burlington-Chittenden County VT urban area; ***New Home Price*** *(2,400 sf living area, 8,000 sf lot, in urban area with full utilities);* ***Apartment Rent*** *(950 sf 2 bedroom/1.5 or 2 bath, unfurnished, excluding all utilities except water);* ***All Electric*** *(average monthly cost for an all-electric home);* ***Part Electric*** *(average monthly cost for a part-electric home);* ***Other Energy*** *(average monthly cost for natural gas, fuel oil, coal, wood, and any other forms of energy except electricity);* ***Telephone*** *(price includes basic monthly rate for a private residential line plus additional local usage charges incurred by a family of four).*
Source: The Council for Community and Economic Research, ACCRA Cost of Living Index, 2017

Health Care, Transportation, and Other Costs

Area[1]	Doctor ($/visit)	Dentist ($/visit)	Optometrist ($/visit)	Gasoline ($/gallon)	Beauty Salon ($/visit)	Men's Shirt ($)
City[2]	113.28	94.00	130.00	2.32	49.11	29.00
Avg.	108.00	92.54	101.93	2.25	37.58	30.92
Min.	30.39	60.00	49.75	1.82	16.11	11.20
Max.	193.50	161.94	229.28	3.16	77.35	59.13

Note: (1) Values for the local area are compared with the average, minimum and maximum values for all 294 areas in the Cost of Living Index; (2) Figures cover the Burlington-Chittenden County VT urban area; ***Doctor*** *(general practitioners routine exam of an established patient);* ***Dentist*** *(adult teeth cleaning and periodic oral examination);* ***Optometrist*** *(full vision eye exam for established adult patient);* ***Gasoline*** *(one gallon regular unleaded, national brand, including all taxes, cash price at self-service pump if available);* ***Beauty Salon*** *(woman's shampoo, trim, and blow-dry);* ***Men's Shirt*** *(cotton/polyester dress shirt, pinpoint weave, long sleeves).*
Source: The Council for Community and Economic Research, ACCRA Cost of Living Index, 2017

HOUSING

House Price Index (HPI)

Area	National Ranking[2]	Quarterly Change (%)	One-Year Change (%)	Five-Year Change (%)
MSA[1]	200	1.29	3.69	12.41
U.S.[3]	–	1.61	6.68	34.71

Note: The HPI is a weighted repeat sales index. It measures average price changes in repeat sales or refinancings on the same properties. This information is obtained by reviewing repeat mortgage transactions on single-family properties whose mortgages have been purchased or securitized by Fannie Mae or Freddie Mac in January 1975; (1) Figures cover the Burlington-South Burlington, VT Metropolitan Statistical Area—see Appendix B for areas included; (2) Rankings are based on annual percentage change for all metro areas containing at least 15,000 transactions over the last 10 years and ranges from 1 to 253; (3) figures based on a weighted average of Census Division estimates using a seasonally adjusted, purchase-only index; all figures are for the period ending December 31, 2017
Source: Federal Housing Finance Agency, House Price Index, February 28, 2018

Median Single-Family Home Prices

Area	2015	2016	2017p	Percent Change 2016 to 2017
MSA[1]	258.2	266.0	280.1	5.3
U.S. Average	223.9	235.5	248.8	5.6

Note: Figures are median sales prices of existing single-family homes in thousands of dollars; (p) preliminary; (1) Figures cover the Burlington-South Burlington, VT Metropolitan Statistical Area—see Appendix B for areas included
Source: National Association of Realtors, Median Sales Price of Existing Single-Family Homes for Metropolitan Areas, 4th Quarter 2017

Qualifying Income Based on Median Sales Price of Existing Single-Family Homes

Area	With 5% Down ($)	With 10% Down ($)	With 20% Down ($)
MSA[1]	64,176	60,798	54,043
U.S. Average	55,585	52,659	46,808

Note: Figures are preliminary; Qualifying income is based on a mortgage rate of 4.17%. Monthly principal and interest payment is limited to 25% of income; (1) Figures cover the Burlington-South Burlington, VT Metropolitan Statistical Area—see Appendix B for areas included
Source: National Association of Realtors, Qualifying Income Based on Median Sales Price of Existing Single-Family Homes for Metropolitan Areas, 4th Quarter 2017

Median Apartment Condo-Coop Home Prices

Area	2015	2016	2017p	Percent Change 2016 to 2017
MSA[1]	n/a	n/a	n/a	n/a
U.S. Average	210.7	220.7	234.3	6.2

Note: Figures are median sales prices of existing apartment condo-coop homes in thousands of dollars; (p) preliminary; n/a not available; (1) Figures cover the Burlington-South Burlington, VT Metropolitan Statistical Area—see Appendix B for areas included
Source: National Association of Realtors, Median Sales Price of Existing Apartment Condo-Coop Homes for Metropolitan Areas, 4th Quarter 2017

Home Value Distribution

Area	Under $50,000	$50,000 -$99,999	$100,000 -$149,999	$150,000 -$199,999	$200,000 -$299,999	$300,000 -$499,999	$500,000 -$999,999	$1,000,000 or more
City	3.1	1.4	3.1	15.4	37.5	29.0	9.5	0.9
MSA[1]	4.6	2.5	6.3	14.9	36.8	26.1	7.7	1.1
U.S.	8.8	14.8	15.3	14.9	18.4	16.4	9.0	2.5

Note: Figures are percentages and cover owner-occupied housing units; (1) Figures cover the Burlington-South Burlington, VT Metropolitan Statistical Area—see Appendix B for areas included
Source: U.S. Census Bureau, 2012-2016 American Community Survey 5-Year Estimates

Homeownership Rate

Area	2009 (%)	2010 (%)	2011 (%)	2012 (%)	2013 (%)	2014 (%)	2015 (%)	2016 (%)	2017 (%)
MSA[1]	n/a	n/a	n/a	n/a	n/a	n/a	n/a	n/a	n/a
U.S.	67.4	66.9	66.1	65.4	65.1	64.5	63.7	63.4	63.9

Note: (1) Figures cover the Burlington-South Burlington, VT Metropolitan Statistical Area—see Appendix B for areas included; n/a not available
Source: U.S. Census Bureau, Housing Vacancies and Homeownership Annual Statistics: 2009-2017

Year Housing Structure Built

Area	2010 or Later	2000 -2009	1990 -1999	1980 -1989	1970 -1979	1960 -1969	1950 -1959	1940 -1949	Before 1940	Median Year
City	1.3	3.5	8.0	9.5	10.5	9.6	11.9	4.6	41.2	1954
MSA[1]	2.6	12.7	13.3	16.2	14.7	9.3	7.1	3.1	21.0	1976
U.S.	2.3	14.7	14.0	13.7	15.6	10.9	10.6	5.2	13.0	1977

Note: Figures are percentages except for Median Year; Note: (1) Figures cover the Burlington-South Burlington, VT Metropolitan Statistical Area—see Appendix B for areas included
Source: U.S. Census Bureau, 2012-2016 American Community Survey 5-Year Estimates

Gross Monthly Rent

Area	Under $500	$500 -$999	$1,000 -$1,499	$1,500 -$1,999	$2,000 -$2,499	$2,500 -$2,999	$3,000 and up	Median ($)
City	11.8	32.0	36.5	14.4	4.0	1.0	0.4	1,071
MSA[1]	10.8	31.5	37.2	15.2	3.5	1.0	0.7	1,089
U.S.	11.3	43.3	27.7	10.7	4.0	1.6	1.5	949

Note: Figures are percentages except for Median; Gross rent is the contract rent plus the estimated average monthly cost of utilities (electricity, gas, and water and sewer) and fuels (oil, coal, kerosene, wood, etc.) if these are paid by the renter (or paid for the renter by someone else); (1) Figures cover the Burlington-South Burlington, VT Metropolitan Statistical Area—see Appendix B for areas included
Source: U.S. Census Bureau, 2012-2016 American Community Survey 5-Year Estimates

HEALTH

Health Risk Factors

Category	MSA[1] (%)	U.S. (%)
Adults aged 18–64 who have any kind of health care coverage	94.7	87.7
Adults who reported being in good or excellent health	88.7	83.6
Adults who are current smokers	14.2	17.1
Adults who currently use E-cigarettes	2.9	4.7
Adults who currently use chewing tobacco, snuff, or snus	2.6	4.0
Adults who are heavy drinkers[2]	9.5	6.5
Adults who are binge drinkers[3]	20.6	16.9
Adults who are overweight (BMI 25.0 - 29.9)	34.9	35.3
Adults who are obese (BMI 30.0 - 99.8)	24.0	29.9
Adults who participated in any physical activities in the past month	83.1	76.9
Adults who always or nearly always wears a seat belt	95.0	94.3

Note: (1) Figures cover the Burlington-South Burlington, VT Metropolitan Statistical Area—see Appendix B for areas included; (2) Heavy drinkers are classified as adult men having more than 14 drinks per week and adult women having more than 7 drinks per week; (3) Binge drinkers are classified as males having five or more drinks on one occasion or females having four or more drinks on one occasion
Source: Centers for Disease Control and Prevention, Behaviorial Risk Factor Surveillance System, SMART: Selected Metropolitan Area Risk Trends, 2016

Health Screening Rates

Category	MSA[1] (%)	U.S. (%)
Adults 50-75 who have had a blood stool test within the past year	5.6	8.0
Adults 50-75 who have had a colonoscopy in the past 10 years	73.3	63.5
Adults aged 65+ who have had flu shot within the past year	60.8	58.6
Adults aged 65+ who have ever had a pneumonia vaccination	79.0	73.4
Adults who have ever been tested for HIV	40.0	35.6
Women aged 21-65 who have had a pap test in the past three years	n/a	79.8
Men aged 40+ who have had a PSA test within the past two years	32.7	39.5
Women aged 40+ who have had a mammogram within the past two years	72.1	72.5

Note: n/a not available; (1) Figures cover the Burlington-South Burlington, VT Metropolitan Statistical Area—see Appendix B for areas included; Source: Centers for Disease Control and Prevention, Behaviorial Risk Factor Surveillance System, SMART: Selected Metropolitan Area Risk Trends, 2016

Chronic Health Conditions

Category	MSA[1] (%)	U.S. (%)
Adults who have ever been told they had a heart attack	3.8	4.4
Adults who have ever been told they have angina or coronary heart disease	2.9	4.1
Adults who have ever been told they had a stroke	1.9	3.1
Adults who have been told they currently have asthma	9.6	9.3
Adults who have ever been told they have arthritis	23.2	25.8
Adults who have ever been told they have diabetes[2]	7.0	10.5
Adults who have ever been told they had skin cancer	6.6	5.9
Adults who have ever been told they had any other types of cancer	7.3	6.7
Adults who have ever been told they have COPD	4.4	6.3
Adults who have ever been told they have kidney disease	2.4	2.8
Adults who have ever been told they have a form of depression	20.0	17.4

Note: (1) Figures cover the Burlington-South Burlington, VT Metropolitan Statistical Area—see Appendix B for areas included; (2) Figures do not include pregnancy-related, borderline, or pre-diabetes
Source: Centers for Disease Control and Prevention, Behaviorial Risk Factor Surveillance System, SMART: Selected Metropolitan Area Risk Trends, 2016

Mortality Rates for the Top 10 Causes of Death in the U.S.

ICD-10[a] Sub-Chapter	ICD-10[a] Code	Age-Adjusted Mortality Rate[1] per 100,000 population	
		County[2]	U.S.
Malignant neoplasms	C00-C97	150.3	158.5
Ischaemic heart diseases	I20-I25	82.5	96.8
Other forms of heart disease	I30-I51	24.6	52.4
Chronic lower respiratory diseases	J40-J47	34.8	40.9
Cerebrovascular diseases	I60-I69	27.2	37.2
Organic, including symptomatic, mental disorders	F01-F09	25.6	33.3
Other degenerative diseases of the nervous system	G30-G31	40.9	32.1
Other external causes of accidental injury	W00-X59	37.2	31.2
Diabetes mellitus	E10-E14	15.6	21.1
Hypertensive diseases	I10-I15	21.2	20.8

Note: (a) ICD-10 = International Classification of Diseases 10th Revision; (1) Mortality rates are a three year average covering 2014-2016; (2) Figures cover Chittenden County.
Source: Centers for Disease Control and Prevention, National Center for Health Statistics. Underlying Cause of Death 1999-2016 on CDC WONDER Online Database, released December 2017

Mortality Rates for Selected Causes of Death

ICD-10[a] Sub-Chapter	ICD-10[a] Code	Age-Adjusted Mortality Rate[1] per 100,000 population	
		County[2]	U.S.
Assault	X85-Y09	Unreliable	5.6
Diseases of the liver	K70-K76	11.6	14.0
Human immunodeficiency virus (HIV) disease	B20-B24	Suppressed	1.9
Influenza and pneumonia	J09-J18	6.4	14.6
Intentional self-harm	X60-X84	14.2	13.2
Malnutrition	E40-E46	Suppressed	1.3
Obesity and other hyperalimentation	E65-E68	4.1	2.1
Renal failure	N17-N19	Unreliable	13.0
Transport accidents	V01-V99	4.6	12.0
Viral hepatitis	B15-B19	Suppressed	1.9

Note: (a) ICD-10 = International Classification of Diseases 10th Revision; (1) Mortality rates are a three year average covering 2014-2016; (2) Figures cover Chittenden County; Data are Suppressed when the data meet the criteria for confidentiality constraints; Mortality rates are flagged as Unreliable when the rate would be calculated with a numerator of 20 or less.
Source: Centers for Disease Control and Prevention, National Center for Health Statistics. Underlying Cause of Death 1999-2016 on CDC WONDER Online Database, released December 2017

Health Insurance Coverage

Area	With Health Insurance	With Private Health Insurance	With Public Health Insurance	Without Health Insurance	Population Under Age 18 Without Health Insurance
City	95.4	73.3	30.6	4.6	1.8
MSA[1]	95.7	75.2	32.3	4.3	1.9
U.S.	88.3	66.7	33.0	11.7	5.9

Note: Figures are percentages that cover the civilian noninstitutionalized population; (1) Figures cover the Burlington-South Burlington, VT Metropolitan Statistical Area—see Appendix B for areas included
Source: U.S. Census Bureau, 2012-2016 American Community Survey 5-Year Estimates

Number of Medical Professionals

Area	MDs[3]	DOs[3,4]	Dentists	Podiatrists	Chiropractors	Optometrists
County[1] (number)	1,327	32	148	6	76	33
County[1] (rate[2])	824.2	19.9	91.6	3.7	47.1	20.4
U.S. (rate[2])	276.5	22.3	67.3	6.0	26.7	15.9

Note: Data as of 2016 unless noted; (1) Data covers Chittenden County; (2) Rate per 100,000 population; (3) Data as of 2015 and includes all active, non-federal physicians; (4) Doctor of Osteopathic Medicine
Source: U.S. Department of Health and Human Services, Health Resources and Services Administration, Bureau of Health Professions, Area Resource File (ARF) 2016-2017

EDUCATION

Public School District Statistics

District Name	Schls	Pupils	Pupil/ Teacher Ratio	Minority Pupils[1] (%)	Free Lunch Eligible[2] (%)	IEP[3] (%)
Burlington School District	10	3,942	11.1	34.8	41.2	10.8

Note: Table includes school districts with 100 or more students; (1) Percentage of students that are not non-Hispanic white; (2) Percentage of students that are eligible for the free lunch program; (3) Percentage of students that have an Individualized Education Program.
Source: U.S. Department of Education, National Center for Education Statistics, Common Core of Data, Local Education Agency (School District) Universe Survey: School Year 2015-2016; U.S. Department of Education, National Center for Education Statistics, Common Core of Data, Public Elementary/Secondary School Universe Survey: School Year 2015-2016

Highest Level of Education

Area	Less than H.S.	H.S. Diploma	Some College, No Deg.	Associate Degree	Bachelor's Degree	Master's Degree	Prof. School Degree	Doctorate Degree
City	10.2	17.8	16.2	4.8	29.7	14.2	4.0	3.0
MSA[1]	7.1	24.7	16.7	8.7	25.8	11.6	3.2	2.1
U.S.	13.0	27.5	21.0	8.2	18.8	8.2	2.0	1.3

Note: Figures cover persons age 25 and over; (1) Figures cover the Burlington-South Burlington, VT Metropolitan Statistical Area—see Appendix B for areas included
Source: U.S. Census Bureau, 2012-2016 American Community Survey 5-Year Estimates

Educational Attainment by Race

Area	High School Graduate or Higher (%)					Bachelor's Degree or Higher (%)				
	Total	White	Black	Asian	Hisp.[2]	Total	White	Black	Asian	Hisp.[2]
City	89.8	93.1	75.5	52.4	88.8	50.9	54.1	21.7	28.9	42.5
MSA[1]	92.9	93.8	85.0	70.3	87.3	42.8	43.1	39.6	42.6	43.7
U.S.	87.0	88.9	84.3	86.3	65.7	30.3	31.6	20.0	52.1	14.7

Note: Figures shown cover persons 25 years old and over; (1) Figures cover the Burlington-South Burlington, VT Metropolitan Statistical Area—see Appendix B for areas included; (2) People of Hispanic origin can be of any race
Source: U.S. Census Bureau, 2012-2016 American Community Survey 5-Year Estimates

School Enrollment by Grade and Control

Area	Preschool (%)		Kindergarten (%)		Grades 1 - 4 (%)		Grades 5 - 8 (%)		Grades 9 - 12 (%)	
	Public	Private	Public	Private	Public	Private	Public	Private	Public	Private
City	47.2	52.8	89.8	10.2	93.0	7.0	94.3	5.7	91.9	8.1
MSA[1]	49.8	50.2	93.5	6.5	94.3	5.7	92.6	7.4	93.9	6.1
U.S.	58.4	41.6	87.7	12.3	89.8	10.2	89.7	10.3	90.4	9.6

Note: Figures shown cover persons 3 years old and over; (1) Figures cover the Burlington-South Burlington, VT Metropolitan Statistical Area—see Appendix B for areas included
Source: U.S. Census Bureau, 2012-2016 American Community Survey 5-Year Estimates

Average Salaries of Public School Classroom Teachers

Area	2015		2016		Change from 2015 to 2016	
	Dollars	Rank[1]	Dollars	Rank[1]	Percent	Rank[2]
Vermont	57,642	15	58,901	15	2.2	9
U.S. Average	57,611	–	58,353	–	1.3	–

Note: (1) Rank ranges from 1 to 51 where 1 indicates highest salary; (2) Rank ranges from 1 to 51 where 1 indicates highest percent change.
Source: National Education Association, Rankings & Estimates: Rankings of the States 2016 and Estimates of School Statistics 2017

Higher Education

Four-Year Colleges			Two-Year Colleges			Medical Schools[1]	Law Schools[2]	Voc/ Tech[3]
Public	Private Non-profit	Private For-profit	Public	Private Non-profit	Private For-profit			
1	1	0	0	0	0	1	0	0

Note: Figures cover institutions located within the city limits and include main campuses only; (1) includes schools accredited by the Liaison Committee on Medical Education and the American Osteopathic Association's Commission on Osteopathic College Accreditation; (2) includes ABA-accredited schools, schools with provisional ABA accreditation, and state accredited schools; (3) includes all schools with programs that are less than 2 years.
Source: National Center for Education Statistics, Integrated Postsecondary Education System (IPEDS), 2016-17; Wikipedia, List of Medical Schools in the United States, accessed April 2, 2018; Wikipedia, List of Law Schools in the United States, accessed April 2, 2018

According to *U.S. News & World Report,* the Burlington-South Burlington, VT metro area is home to one of the best national universities in the U.S.: **University of Vermont** (#97 tie). The indicators used to capture academic quality fall into a number of categories: assessment by administrators at peer institutions; retention of students; faculty resources; student selectivity; financial resources; alumni giving; high school counselor ratings of colleges; and graduation rate. *U.S. News & World Report, "America's Best Colleges 2018"*

According to *U.S. News & World Report,* the Burlington-South Burlington, VT metro area is home to one of the best liberal arts colleges in the U.S.: **Saint Michael's College** (#106 tie). The indicators used to capture academic quality fall into a number of categories: assessment by administrators at peer institutions; retention of students; faculty resources; student selectivity; financial resources; alumni giving; high school counselor ratings of colleges; and graduation rate. *U.S. News & World Report, "America's Best Colleges 2018"*

According to *U.S. News & World Report,* the Burlington-South Burlington, VT metro area is home to one of the top 75 medical schools for research in the U.S.: **University of Vermont** (#66 tie). The rankings are based on a weighted average of 11 measures of quality: quality assessment; peer assessment score; assessment score by residency directors; research activity; total research activity; average research activity per faculty member; student selectivity; median MCAT total score; median undergraduate GPA; acceptance rate; and faculty resources. *U.S. News & World Report, "America's Best Graduate Schools, Medical, 2019"*

PRESIDENTIAL ELECTION

2016 Presidential Election Results

Area	Clinton	Trump	Johnson	Stein	Other
Chittenden County	65.7	22.3	3.0	2.2	6.9
U.S.	48.0	45.9	3.3	1.1	1.7

Note: Results are percentages and may not add to 100% due to rounding
Source: Dave Leip's Atlas of U.S. Presidential Elections

EMPLOYERS

Major Employers

Company Name	Industry
Ben & Jerry's	Ice cream manufacturing
Dealer.com	Automotive internet marketing
G.S. Blodgett Company	Commercial oven manufacturer
General Dynamics Armament & Tech Prods	Weapon and platform systems
General Electric	Healthcare industry software
University of Vermont	public university
University of Vermont Medical Center	Health care
Vermont Teddy Bear Company	Custom teddy bear manufacturing

Note: Companies shown are located within the Burlington-South Burlington, VT Metropolitan Statistical Area.
Source: Hoovers.com; Wikipedia

PUBLIC SAFETY

Crime Rate

Area	All Crimes	Violent Crimes				Property Crimes		
		Murder	Rape[3]	Robbery	Aggrav. Assault	Burglary	Larceny -Theft	Motor Vehicle Theft
City	3,674.1	2.4	35.6	42.7	154.2	540.8	2,898.5	0.0
Metro[1]	n/a	n/a	n/a	n/a	n/a	n/a	n/a	n/a
U.S.	2,870.2	4.9	39.3	102.2	238.1	494.7	1,783.6	222.2

Note: Figures are crimes per 100,000 population; (1) Figures cover the Burlington-South Burlington, VT Metropolitan Statistical Area—see Appendix B for areas included; n/a not available; (3) The city and U.S. figures shown were reported using the revised Uniform Crime Reporting (UCR) definition of rape. The metro area figures shown are an aggregate total of the data submitted using both the revised and legacy UCR definitions.
Source: FBI Uniform Crime Reports, 2015 (data for 2016 was not available)

Hate Crimes

Area	Number of Quarters Reported	Number of Incidents per Bias Motivation					
		Race/Ethnicity/ Ancestry	Religion	Sexual Orientation	Disability	Gender	Gender Identity
City	3	2	1	2	0	0	0
U.S.	4	3,489	1,273	1,076	70	31	124

Source: Federal Bureau of Investigation, Hate Crime Statistics 2016

Identity Theft Consumer Reports

Area	Reports	Reports per 100,000 Population	Rank[2]
MSA[1]	127	58	322
U.S.	371,061	114	-

Note: (1) Figures cover the Burlington-South Burlington, VT Metropolitan Statistical Area—see Appendix B for areas included; (2) Rank ranges from 1 to 389 where 1 indicates greatest number of identity theft reports per 100,000 population
Source: Federal Trade Commission, Consumer Sentinel Network Data Book for January–December 2017

Fraud and Other Consumer Reports

Area	Reports	Reports per 100,000 Population	Rank[2]
MSA[1]	733	337	334
U.S.	2,304,550	708	-

Note: (1) Figures cover the Burlington-South Burlington, VT Metropolitan Statistical Area—see Appendix B for areas included; (2) Rank ranges from 1 to 389 where 1 indicates greatest number of fraud and other consumer reports per 100,000 population
Source: Federal Trade Commission, Consumer Sentinel Network Data Book for January–December 2017

SPORTS

Professional Sports Teams

Team Name	League	Year Established
No teams are located in the metro area		

Source: Wikipedia, Major Professional Sports Teams of the United States and Canada, April 5, 2018

CLIMATE

Average and Extreme Temperatures

Temperature	Jan	Feb	Mar	Apr	May	Jun	Jul	Aug	Sep	Oct	Nov	Dec	Yr.
Extreme High (°F)	66	62	80	91	93	100	100	99	92	85	75	65	100
Average High (°F)	26	28	38	53	67	76	81	78	69	57	44	31	54
Average Temp. (°F)	18	19	30	44	56	65	70	68	59	48	37	24	45
Average Low (°F)	8	10	21	33	44	54	59	57	49	39	30	16	35
Extreme Low (°F)	-30	-30	-20	2	24	33	39	35	25	15	-2	-26	-30

Note: Figures cover the years 1948-1995
Source: National Climatic Data Center, International Station Meteorological Climate Summary, 9/96

Average Precipitation/Snowfall/Humidity

Precip./Humidity	Jan	Feb	Mar	Apr	May	Jun	Jul	Aug	Sep	Oct	Nov	Dec	Yr.
Avg. Precip. (in.)	1.8	1.7	2.2	2.8	3.0	3.3	3.6	4.0	3.3	3.0	3.0	2.3	34.0
Avg. Snowfall (in.)	19	17	13	4	Tr	0	0	0	Tr	Tr	7	19	79
Avg. Rel. Hum. 7am (%)	73	74	75	74	73	76	78	83	85	82	78	76	77
Avg. Rel. Hum. 4pm (%)	65	61	58	52	51	54	53	56	60	61	67	69	59

Note: Figures cover the years 1948-1995; Tr = Trace amounts (<0.05 in. of rain; <0.5 in. of snow)
Source: National Climatic Data Center, International Station Meteorological Climate Summary, 9/96

Weather Conditions

Temperature			Daytime Sky			Precipitation		
5°F & below	32°F & below	90°F & above	Clear	Partly cloudy	Cloudy	0.01 inch or more precip.	0.1 inch or more snow/ice	Thunder-storms
36	156	7	49	146	170	154	55	22

Note: Figures are average number of days per year and cover the years 1948-1995
Source: National Climatic Data Center, International Station Meteorological Climate Summary, 9/96

HAZARDOUS WASTE

Superfund Sites

The Burlington-South Burlington, VT metro area is home to two sites on the EPA's Superfund National Priorities List: **Commerce Street Plume** (final); **Pine Street Canal** (final). There are a total of 1,396 Superfund sites with a status of proposed or final on the list in the U.S. *U.S. Environmental Protection Agency, National Priorities List, April 4, 2018*

AIR & WATER QUALITY

Air Quality Trends: Ozone

	1990	1995	2000	2005	2010	2012	2013	2014	2015	2016
MSA[1]	0.072	0.074	0.071	0.069	0.063	0.065	0.062	0.059	0.066	0.063
U.S.	0.087	0.089	0.081	0.079	0.073	0.075	0.069	0.067	0.068	0.069

Note: (1) Data covers the Burlington-South Burlington, VT Metropolitan Statistical Area—see Appendix B for areas included. The values shown are the composite ozone concentration averages among trend sites based on the highest fourth daily maximum 8-hour concentration in parts per million. These trends are based on sites having an adequate record of monitoring data during the trend period. Data from exceptional events are included.
Source: U.S. Environmental Protection Agency, Air Quality Monitoring Information, "Air Quality Trends by City, 1990-2016"

Air Quality Index

Area	Percent of Days when Air Quality was...[2]					AQI Statistics[2]	
	Good	Moderate	Unhealthy for Sensitive Groups	Unhealthy	Very Unhealthy	Maximum	Median
MSA[1]	93.7	6.3	0.0	0.0	0.0	74	35

Note: (1) Data covers the Burlington-South Burlington, VT Metropolitan Statistical Area—see Appendix B for areas included; (2) Based on 365 days with AQI data in 2017. Air Quality Index (AQI) is an index for reporting daily air quality. EPA calculates the AQI for five major air pollutants regulated by the Clean Air Act: ground-level ozone, particle pollution (aka particulate matter), carbon monoxide, sulfur dioxide, and nitrogen dioxide. The AQI runs from 0 to 500. The higher the AQI value, the greater the level of air pollution and the greater the health concern. There are six AQI categories: "Good" AQI is between 0 and 50. Air quality is considered satisfactory; "Moderate" AQI is between 51 and 100. Air quality is acceptable; "Unhealthy for Sensitive Groups" When AQI values are between 101 and 150, members of sensitive groups may experience health effects; "Unhealthy" When AQI values are between 151 and 200 everyone may begin to experience health effects; "Very Unhealthy" AQI values between 201 and 300 trigger a health alert; "Hazardous" AQI values over 300 trigger warnings of emergency conditions (not shown).
Source: U.S. Environmental Protection Agency, Air Quality Index Report, 2017

Air Quality Index Pollutants

Area	Percent of Days when AQI Pollutant was...[2]					
	Carbon Monoxide	Nitrogen Dioxide	Ozone	Sulfur Dioxide	Particulate Matter 2.5	Particulate Matter 10
MSA[1]	0.0	1.4	77.3	0.0	21.1	0.3

Note: (1) Data covers the Burlington-South Burlington, VT Metropolitan Statistical Area—see Appendix B for areas included; (2) Based on 365 days with AQI data in 2017. The Air Quality Index (AQI) is an index for reporting daily air quality. EPA calculates the AQI for five major air pollutants regulated by the Clean Air Act: ground-level ozone, particle pollution (also known as particulate matter), carbon monoxide, sulfur dioxide, and nitrogen dioxide. The AQI runs from 0 to 500. The higher the AQI value, the greater the level of air pollution and the greater the health concern.
Source: U.S. Environmental Protection Agency, Air Quality Index Report, 2017

Maximum Air Pollutant Concentrations: Particulate Matter, Ozone, CO and Lead

	Particulate Matter 10 (ug/m^3)	Particulate Matter 2.5 Wtd AM (ug/m^3)	Particulate Matter 2.5 24-Hr (ug/m^3)	Ozone (ppm)	Carbon Monoxide (ppm)	Lead (ug/m^3)
MSA[1] Level	33	5.4	13	0.063	1	n/a
NAAQS[2]	150	15	35	0.075	9	0.15
Met NAAQS[2]	Yes	Yes	Yes	Yes	Yes	n/a

Note: (1) Data covers the Burlington-South Burlington, VT Metropolitan Statistical Area—see Appendix B for areas included; Data from exceptional events are included; (2) National Ambient Air Quality Standards; ppm = parts per million; ug/m^3 = micrograms per cubic meter; n/a not available.
Concentrations: Particulate Matter 10 (coarse particulate)—highest second maximum 24-hour concentration; Particulate Matter 2.5 Wtd AM (fine particulate)—highest weighted annual mean concentration; Particulate Matter 2.5 24-Hour (fine particulate)—highest 98th percentile 24-hour concentration; Ozone—highest fourth daily maximum 8-hour concentration; Carbon Monoxide—highest second maximum non-overlapping 8-hour concentration; Lead—maximum running 3-month average
Source: U.S. Environmental Protection Agency, Air Quality Monitoring Information, "Air Quality Statistics by City, 2016"

Maximum Air Pollutant Concentrations: Nitrogen Dioxide and Sulfur Dioxide

	Nitrogen Dioxide AM (ppb)	Nitrogen Dioxide 1-Hr (ppb)	Sulfur Dioxide AM (ppb)	Sulfur Dioxide 1-Hr (ppb)	Sulfur Dioxide 24-Hr (ppb)
MSA[1] Level	6	n/a	n/a	2	n/a
NAAQS[2]	53	100	30	75	140
Met NAAQS[2]	Yes	n/a	n/a	Yes	n/a

Note: (1) Data covers the Burlington-South Burlington, VT Metropolitan Statistical Area—see Appendix B for areas included; Data from exceptional events are included; (2) National Ambient Air Quality Standards; ppm = parts per million; ug/m^3 = micrograms per cubic meter; n/a not available.
Concentrations: Nitrogen Dioxide AM—highest arithmetic mean concentration; Nitrogen Dioxide 1-Hr—highest 98th percentile 1-hour daily maximum concentration; Sulfur Dioxide AM—highest annual mean concentration; Sulfur Dioxide 1-Hr—highest 99th percentile 1-hour daily maximum concentration; Sulfur Dioxide 24-Hr—highest second maximum 24-hour concentration
Source: U.S. Environmental Protection Agency, Air Quality Monitoring Information, "Air Quality Statistics by City, 2016"

Drinking Water

Water System Name	Pop. Served	Primary Water Source Type	Violations[1]	
			Health Based	Monitoring/ Reporting
Burlington Dept of Public Works	42,000	Surface	0	0

Note: (1) Based on violation data from January 1, 2017 to December 31, 2017
Source: U.S. Environmental Protection Agency, Office of Ground Water and Drinking Water, Safe Drinking Water Information System (based on data extracted April 5, 2018)

Blacksburg, Virginia

Background

Blacksburg is located on a plateau between the Blue Ridge and Allegheny Mountains, in Montgomery County, within Southwest Virginia's New River Valley.

Led by Abraham Wood, European explorers first reached the area in 1671, claiming all lands surrounding the newly-named Wood's River for King Charles II. Seventy years later, the land was divided into Montgomery County and Pulaski County. With both fertile soil and adequate irrigation from neighboring springs, the area was ideal for settlement. The Draper family was one of the original settlers in the region, and the area was known as Draper's Meadow.

As the Great Migration reached the Allegheny Ridge, known also as the Eastern Continental Divide, in the 1750s, the terrain proved incredibly difficult to negotiate. Settlers looking for the best and safest route over the Ridge found themselves at Draper's Meadow.

The French and Indian War took a devastating toll on the area. The Draper's Meadow massacre occurred in July 1755, where 5 settlers were killed by local Shawnee Indians, and an additional five were taken as captives. With little protection on the frontier, the area was completely abandoned by the end of the war.

Twenty years later, Samuel Black purchased the 600-acre lot at Draper's Meadow for his sons John and William. In William's plot, 38 acres were set aside to establish a village. In this village, William laid out a small, square grid of streets now known as "The Old Sixteen Squares," where visitors can still go to catch a glimpse of the past. The village was officially established and founded in 1798 and was named in the Blacks' honor, Blacksburg.

The town of Blacksburg, and surrounding Montgomery County, have grown steadily in the past several decades. With a county-wide population of over 90,000 people, over 68 percent live in either the towns of Blacksburg or Christiansburg, with only 32 percent living in areas outside the two towns.

Blacksburg is part of the Montgomery County School System, with five elementary schools, one middle school and one high school. Residents can also choose from one of the many private schools in the area. Blacksburg is home to the campus of Virginia Polytechnic Institute & State University, commonly known as Virginia Tech. With over 25,000 full time students, the University is an important part of the community.

With Virginia Tech in its backyard, and easy access to nearby Radnor University and Edward Via School of Osteopathic Medicine, over 85 percent of Blacksburg residents have a college education. With is highly-educated population, Blacksburg is an area well-suited for the development of technology companies. The Corporate Research Center and Blacksburg's Industrial Park are home to some of the country's top technology companies.

Blacksburg can be found at the top of surveys for good places to raise a family, with good educational opportunities. Its public transportation system, Blacksburg Transit, which also connects to the neighboring town of Christiansburg, has repeatedly been recognized for the quality of its service. Blacksburg High School is often ranked among the top schools in the nation for its academics. Its soccer, track, and cross-country teams are also among the top in the state.

Montgomery Regional Hospital provides medical, surgical, obstetrical, pediatric, emergency, orthopedic and outpatient services to the area. Additional area hospitals, less than 25 miles from Blacksburg, include Carilion New River Valley Medical Center in Christianburg; Carilion Giles Memorial Hospital in Pearisburg, Catawba Hospital in Catawba and Pulaski Community Hospital in Pulaski.

The climate in Blacksburg consists of humid and warm summers, with cooler temperatures in the lower lying areas. Winters are cool to cold, with some warm periods throughout the winter months.

Rankings

General Rankings

- In their fifth annual survey, Livability.com looked at data for nearly 2,300 U.S. cities to determine the rankings for Livability's "Top 100 Best Places to Live" in 2018. Blacksburg ranked #63. Criteria: vibrant economy; low cost of living; education, demographics, health care options; transportation & infrastructure; abundant lifestyle amenities. *Livability.com, "Top 100 Best Places to Live 2018" January 16, 2018*

Business/Finance Rankings

- The Blacksburg metro area appeared on the Milken Institute "2017 Best Performing Cities" list. Rank: #65 out of 201 small metro areas. Criteria: job growth; wage and salary growth; high-tech output growth. *Milken Institute, "Best-Performing Cities 2017," January 2018*
- *Forbes* ranked 200 smaller metro areas (population under 265,400) to determine the nation's "Best Small Places for Business and Careers." The Blacksburg metro area was ranked #54. Criteria: costs (business and living); job growth (past and projected); income growth; quality of life; educational attainment (college and high school); projected economic growth; cultural and recreational opportunities; net migration patterns; number of highly ranked colleges. *Forbes, "The Best Small Cities for Business and Careers 2017," November, 6 2017*

Environmental Rankings

- Sperling's BestPlaces assessed 379 metropolitan areas of the United States for the likelihood of dangerously extreme weather events or earthquakes. In general the Southeast and South-Central regions have the highest risk of weather extremes and earthquakes, while the Pacific Northwest enjoys the lowest risk. Of the least risky metropolitan areas, the Blacksburg metro area was ranked #91. *www.bestplaces.net, "Safest Places from Natural Disasters," April 2011*
- Blacksburg was highlighted as one of the cleanest metro areas for ozone air pollution in the U.S. during 2013 through 2015. The list represents cities with no monitored ozone air pollution in unhealthful ranges. *American Lung Association, State of the Air 2017*

Safety Rankings

- The National Insurance Crime Bureau ranked 382 metro areas in the U.S. in terms of per capita rates of vehicle theft. The Blacksburg metro area ranked #374 (#1 = highest rate). Criteria: number of vehicle theft offenses per 100,000 inhabitants in 2016. *National Insurance Crime Bureau, "Hot Spots 2016," June 8, 2017*

Seniors/Retirement Rankings

- From its Best Cities for Successful Aging indexes, the Milken Institute generated rankings for metropolitan areas, weighing data in nine categories—health care, wellness, living arrangements, transportation and convenience, financial characteristics, education, employment, community engagement, and overall livability. The Blacksburg metro area was ranked #168 overall in the small metro area category. *Milken Institute, "Best Cities for Successful Aging, 2017" March 14, 2017*

Business Environment

CITY FINANCES

City Government Finances

Component	2015 ($000)	2015 ($ per capita)
Total Revenues	49,084	1,110
Total Expenditures	49,540	1,120
Debt Outstanding	0	0
Cash and Securities[1]	25,404	575

Note: (1) Cash and security holdings of a government at the close of its fiscal year,, including those of its dependent agencies, utilities, and liquor stores.
Source: U.S Census Bureau, State & Local Government Finances 2015

City Government Revenue by Source

Source	2015 ($000)	2015 ($ per capita)	2015 (%)
General Revenue			
From Federal Government	2,632	60	5.4
From State Government	6,733	152	13.7
From Local Governments	4,789	108	9.8
Taxes			
Property	6,092	138	12.4
Sales and Gross Receipts	9,089	206	18.5
Personal Income	0	0	0.0
Corporate Income	0	0	0.0
Motor Vehicle License	256	6	0.5
Other Taxes	2,497	56	5.1
Current Charges	7,383	167	15.0
Liquor Store	0	0	0.0
Utility	7,906	179	16.1
Employee Retirement	0	0	0.0

Source: U.S Census Bureau, State & Local Government Finances 2015

City Government Expenditures by Function

Function	2015 ($000)	2015 ($ per capita)	2015 (%)
General Direct Expenditures			
Air Transportation	0	0	0.0
Corrections	0	0	0.0
Education	0	0	0.0
Employment Security Administration	0	0	0.0
Financial Administration	2,063	46	4.2
Fire Protection	497	11	1.0
General Public Buildings	1,279	28	2.6
Governmental Administration, Other	2,169	49	4.4
Health	529	12	1.1
Highways	7,480	169	15.1
Hospitals	0	0	0.0
Housing and Community Development	2,256	51	4.6
Interest on General Debt	31	< 1	< 0.1
Judicial and Legal	286	6	0.6
Libraries	12	< 1	< 0.1
Parking	0	0	0.0
Parks and Recreation	2,206	49	4.5
Police Protection	7,243	163	14.6
Public Welfare	0	0	0.0
Sewerage	4,402	99	8.9
Solid Waste Management	1,514	34	3.1
Veterans' Services	0	0	0.0
Liquor Store	0	0	0.0
Utility	15,111	341	30.5
Employee Retirement	0	0	0.0

Source: U.S Census Bureau, State & Local Government Finances 2015

DEMOGRAPHICS

Population Growth

Area	1990 Census	2000 Census	2010 Census	2016* Estimate	Population Growth (%) 1990-2016	2010-2016
City	34,649	39,573	42,620	43,973	26.9	3.2
MSA[1]	140,690	151,272	162,958	181,288	28.9	11.2
U.S.	248,709,873	281,421,906	308,745,538	318,558,162	28.1	3.2

Note: (1) Figures cover the Blacksburg-Christiansburg-Radford, VA Metropolitan Statistical Area—see Appendix B for areas included; (*) 2012-2016 5-year estimated population
Source: U.S. Census Bureau, 1990 Census, Census 2000, Census 2010, 2012-2016 American Community Survey 5-Year Estimates

Household Size

Area	Persons in Household (%) One	Two	Three	Four	Five	Six	Seven or More	Average Household Size
City	26.7	36.5	18.5	15.6	1.8	0.5	0.4	2.50
MSA[1]	27.7	38.0	15.9	12.8	3.8	1.0	0.9	2.40
U.S.	27.7	33.7	15.7	13.1	6.0	2.3	1.5	2.60

Note: (1) Figures cover the Blacksburg-Christiansburg-Radford, VA Metropolitan Statistical Area—see Appendix B for areas included
Source: U.S. Census Bureau, 2012-2016 American Community Survey 5-Year Estimates

Race

Area	White Alone[2] (%)	Black Alone[2] (%)	Asian Alone[2] (%)	AIAN[3] Alone[2] (%)	NHOPI[4] Alone[2] (%)	Other Race Alone[2] (%)	Two or More Races (%)
City	78.4	4.9	11.6	0.3	0.1	1.4	3.2
MSA[1]	89.0	4.7	3.6	0.2	0.0	0.6	1.8
U.S.	73.3	12.6	5.2	0.8	0.2	4.8	3.1

Note: (1) Figures cover the Blacksburg-Christiansburg-Radford, VA Metropolitan Statistical Area—see Appendix B for areas included; (2) Alone is defined as not being in combination with one or more other races; (3) American Indian and Alaska Native; (4) Native Hawaiian and Other Pacific Islander
Source: U.S. Census Bureau, 2012-2016 American Community Survey 5-Year Estimates

Hispanic or Latino Origin

Area	Total (%)	Mexican (%)	Puerto Rican (%)	Cuban (%)	Other (%)
City	4.3	1.0	0.7	0.3	2.3
MSA[1]	2.6	0.9	0.5	0.1	1.1
U.S.	17.3	11.0	1.7	0.7	4.0

Note: Persons of Hispanic or Latino origin can be of any race; (1) Figures cover the Blacksburg-Christiansburg-Radford, VA Metropolitan Statistical Area—see Appendix B for areas included
Source: U.S. Census Bureau, 2012-2016 American Community Survey 5-Year Estimates

Segregation

Type	Segregation Indices[1] 1990	2000	2010	2010 Rank[2]	Percent Change 1990-2000	1990-2010	2000-2010
Black/White	n/a	n/a	n/a	n/a	n/a	n/a	n/a
Asian/White	n/a	n/a	n/a	n/a	n/a	n/a	n/a
Hispanic/White	n/a	n/a	n/a	n/a	n/a	n/a	n/a

Note: All figures cover the Metropolitan Statistical Area—see Appendix B for areas included; Figures are based on an analysis of 1990, 2000, and 2010 Census Decennial Census tract data by William H. Frey, Brookings Institution and the University of Michigan Social Science Data Analysis Network. In this analysis all racial groups (whites, blacks, and asians) are non-Hispanic members of those races. Hispanics are shown as a separate category; (1) Segregation Indices are Dissimilarity Indices that measure the degree to which the minority group is distributed differently than whites across census tracts. They range from 0 (complete integration) to 100 (complete segregation) where the value indicates the percentage of the minority group that needs to move to be distributed exactly like whites; (2) Ranges from 1 (most segregated) to 102 (least segregated); n/a not available.
Source: www.CensusScope.org

Ancestry

Area	German	Irish	English	American	Italian	Polish	French[2]	Scottish	Dutch
City	14.4	9.9	8.0	6.8	5.1	2.5	1.6	2.0	1.0
MSA[1]	13.3	10.6	9.2	16.3	3.3	1.5	1.7	2.1	1.1
U.S.	14.4	10.4	7.7	6.9	5.4	2.9	2.6	1.7	1.3

Note: Figures are the percentage of the total population reporting a particular ancestry. The nine most commonly reported ancestries in the U.S. are shown. Figures include multiple ancestries (e.g. if a person reported being Irish and Italian, they were included in both columns); (1) Figures cover the Blacksburg-Christiansburg-Radford, VA Metropolitan Statistical Area—see Appendix B for areas included; (2) Excludes Basque
Source: U.S. Census Bureau, 2012-2016 American Community Survey 5-Year Estimates

Foreign-Born Population

Area	Percent of Population Born in								
	Any Foreign Country	Asia	Mexico	Europe	Carribean	Central America[2]	South America	Africa	Canada
City	14.6	9.1	0.5	1.9	0.4	0.4	0.9	1.1	0.3
MSA[1]	5.4	3.0	0.3	0.8	0.2	0.2	0.3	0.4	0.2
U.S.	13.2	4.0	3.6	1.5	1.3	1.0	0.9	0.6	0.3

Note: (1) Figures cover the Blacksburg-Christiansburg-Radford, VA Metropolitan Statistical Area—see Appendix B for areas included; (2) Excludes Mexico.
Source: U.S. Census Bureau, 2012-2016 American Community Survey 5-Year Estimates

Marital Status

Area	Never Married	Now Married[2]	Separated	Widowed	Divorced
City	71.8	22.1	0.5	2.1	3.4
MSA[1]	39.2	43.5	2.1	5.4	9.7
U.S.	33.0	48.1	2.1	5.9	11.0

Note: Figures are percentages and cover the population 15 years of age and older; (1) Figures cover the Blacksburg-Christiansburg-Radford, VA Metropolitan Statistical Area—see Appendix B for areas included; (2) Excludes separated
Source: U.S. Census Bureau, 2012-2016 American Community Survey 5-Year Estimates

Disability Status

Area	All Ages	Under 18 Years Old	18 to 64 Years Old	65 Years and Over
City	5.6	2.3	4.5	33.0
MSA[1]	12.7	4.6	10.2	35.2
U.S.	12.5	4.1	10.3	35.7

Note: Figures show percent of the civilian noninstitutionalized population that reported having a disability. Disability status is determined from six types of difficulty: vision, hearing, cognitive, ambulatory, self-care, and independent living. For children under 5 years old, hearing and vision difficulty are used to determine disability status. For children between the ages of 5 and 14, disability status is determined from hearing, vision, cognitive, ambulatory, and self-care difficulties. For people aged 15 years and older, they are considered to have a disability if they have difficulty with any one of the six difficulty types; Note: (1) Figures cover the Blacksburg-Christiansburg-Radford, VA Metropolitan Statistical Area—see Appendix B for areas included
Source: U.S. Census Bureau, 2012-2016 American Community Survey 5-Year Estimates

Age

Area	Percent of Population									Median Age
	Under Age 5	Age 5–19	Age 20–34	Age 35–44	Age 45–54	Age 55–64	Age 65–74	Age 75–84	Age 85+	
City	3.1	26.3	48.7	6.4	6.1	4.5	3.2	0.9	0.8	22.0
MSA[1]	4.5	19.9	27.2	11.0	11.9	11.4	8.4	4.0	1.8	33.5
U.S.	6.2	19.6	20.7	12.7	13.6	12.6	8.3	4.3	1.9	37.7

Note: (1) Figures cover the Blacksburg-Christiansburg-Radford, VA Metropolitan Statistical Area—see Appendix B for areas included
Source: U.S. Census Bureau, 2012-2016 American Community Survey 5-Year Estimates

Gender

Area	Males	Females	Males per 100 Females
City	23,820	20,153	118.2
MSA[1]	91,970	89,318	103.0
U.S.	156,765,322	161,792,840	96.9

Note: (1) Figures cover the Blacksburg-Christiansburg-Radford, VA Metropolitan Statistical Area—see Appendix B for areas included
Source: U.S. Census Bureau, 2012-2016 American Community Survey 5-Year Estimates

Religious Groups by Family

Area	Catholic	Baptist	Non-Den.	Methodist[2]	Lutheran	LDS[3]	Pente-costal	Presby-terian[4]	Muslim[5]	Judaism
MSA[1]	2.1	9.6	4.3	8.6	0.9	1.0	5.9	1.7	2.3	<0.1
U.S.	19.1	9.3	4.0	4.0	2.3	2.0	1.9	1.6	0.8	0.7

Note: Figures are the number of adherents as a percentage of the total population; (1) Figures cover the Blacksburg-Christiansburg-Radford, VA Metropolitan Statistical Area—see Appendix B for areas included; (2) Methodist/Pietist; (3) Latter Day Saints; (4) Reformed; (5) Figures are estimates
Source: Association of Statisticians of American Religious Bodies, 2010 U.S. Religion Census: Religious Congregations & Membership Study

Religious Groups by Tradition

Area	Catholic	Evangelical Protestant	Mainline Protestant	Other Tradition	Black Protestant	Orthodox
MSA[1]	2.1	19.8	12.7	3.5	0.4	<0.1
U.S.	19.1	16.2	7.3	4.3	1.6	0.3

Note: Figures are the number of adherents as a percentage of the total population; (1) Figures cover the Blacksburg-Christiansburg-Radford, VA Metropolitan Statistical Area—see Appendix B for areas included
Source: Association of Statisticians of American Religious Bodies, 2010 U.S. Religion Census: Religious Congregations & Membership Study

ECONOMY

Gross Metropolitan Product

Area	2014	2015	2016	2017	Rank[2]
MSA[1]	6.6	6.9	7.0	7.2	246

Note: Figures are in billions of dollars; (1) Figures cover the Blacksburg-Christiansburg-Radford, VA Metropolitan Statistical Area—see Appendix B for areas included; (2) Rank is based on 2015 data and ranges from 1 to 381
Source: The U.S. Conference of Mayors, U.S. Metro Economies: GMP and Employment Report, 2015-2017

Economic Growth

Area	2012-14 (%)	2015 (%)	2016 (%)	2017 (%)	Rank[2]
MSA[1]	0.0	2.2	0.1	1.2	286
U.S.	2.0	2.4	1.9	2.6	–

Note: Figures are real gross metropolitan product (GMP) growth rates and represent average annual percent change; (1) Figures cover the Blacksburg-Christiansburg-Radford, VA Metropolitan Statistical Area—see Appendix B for areas included; (2) Rank is based on 2012-2014 average annual percent change and ranges from 1 to 381
Source: The U.S. Conference of Mayors, U.S. Metro Economies: GMP and Employment Report, 2015-2017

Metropolitan Area Exports

Area	2011	2012	2013	2014	2015	2016	Rank[2]
MSA[1]	994.0	844.3	753.4	1,042.5	1,070.3	794.6	176

Note: Figures are in millions of dollars; (1) Figures cover the Blacksburg-Christiansburg-Radford, VA Metropolitan Statistical Area—see Appendix B for areas included; (2) Rank is based on 2016 data and ranges from 1 to 385
Source: U.S. Department of Commerce, International Trade Administration, Office of Trade & Industry Information, Manufacturing & Services, data extracted March 15, 2018

Building Permits

Area	Single-Family			Multi-Family			Total		
	2016	2017p	Pct. Chg.	2016	2017p	Pct. Chg.	2016	2017p	Pct. Chg.
City	132	98	-25.8	84	0	-100.0	216	98	-54.6
MSA[1]	132	98	-25.8	84	0	-100.0	216	98	-54.6
U.S.	750,800	817,300	8.9	455,800	446,800	-2.0	1,206,600	1,264,100	4.8

Note: (1) Figures cover the Blacksburg-Christiansburg-Radford, VA Metropolitan Statistical Area—see Appendix B for areas included; Figures represent new, privately-owned housing units authorized (unadjusted data); All permit data are based on estimates with imputation; (p) preliminary data.
Source: U.S. Census Bureau, Manufacturing, Mining, and Construction Statistics, Building Permits, 2016, 2017

Bankruptcy Filings

Area	Business Filings			Nonbusiness Filings		
	2016	2017	% Chg.	2016	2017	% Chg.
Montgomery County	1	1	0.0	106	104	-1.9
U.S.	24,114	23,157	-4.0	770,846	765,863	-0.6

Note: Business filings include Chapter 7, Chapter 11, Chapter 12, and Chapter 13; Nonbusiness filings include Chapter 7, Chapter 11, and Chapter 13
Source: Administrative Office of the U.S. Courts, Business and Nonbusiness Bankruptcy, County Cases Commenced by Chapter of the Bankruptcy Code, During the 12-Month Period Ending December 31, 2016 and Business and Nonbusiness Bankruptcy, County Cases Commenced by Chapter of the Bankruptcy Code, During the 12-Month Period Ending December 31, 2017

Housing Vacancy Rates

Area	Gross Vacancy Rate[2] (%)			Year-Round Vacancy Rate[3] (%)			Rental Vacancy Rate[4] (%)			Homeowner Vacancy Rate[5] (%)		
	2015	2016	2017	2015	2016	2017	2015	2016	2017	2015	2016	2017
MSA[1]	n/a	n/a	n/a	n/a	n/a	n/a	n/a	n/a	n/a	n/a	n/a	n/a
U.S.	12.9	12.8	12.7	10.0	9.9	9.9	7.1	6.9	7.2	1.8	1.7	1.6

Note: (1) Figures cover the Blacksburg-Christiansburg-Radford, VA Metropolitan Statistical Area—see Appendix B for areas included; (2) The percentage of the total housing inventory that is vacant; (3) The percentage of the housing inventory (excluding seasonal units) that is year-round vacant; (4) The percentage of rental inventory that is vacant for rent; (5) The percentage of homeowner inventory that is vacant for sale; n/a not available
Source: U.S. Census Bureau, Housing Vacancies and Homeownership Annual Statistics: 2015, 2016, 2017

INCOME

Income

Area	Per Capita ($)	Median Household ($)	Average Household ($)
City	20,141	34,863	58,960
MSA[1]	25,417	47,456	64,012
U.S.	29,829	55,322	77,866

Note: (1) Figures cover the Blacksburg-Christiansburg-Radford, VA Metropolitan Statistical Area—see Appendix B for areas included
Source: U.S. Census Bureau, 2012-2016 American Community Survey 5-Year Estimates

Household Income Distribution

Area	Percent of Households Earning							
	Under $15,000	$15,000 -$24,999	$25,000 -$34,999	$35,000 -$49,999	$50,000 -$74,999	$75,000 -$99,999	$100,000 -$149,999	$150,000 and up
City	31.5	12.2	6.4	11.8	12.9	7.1	10.1	8.0
MSA[1]	16.7	11.8	8.5	15.3	19.1	11.3	10.7	6.6
U.S.	12.1	10.2	9.9	13.2	17.8	12.2	13.5	11.1

Note: (1) Figures cover the Blacksburg-Christiansburg-Radford, VA Metropolitan Statistical Area—see Appendix B for areas included
Source: U.S. Census Bureau, 2012-2016 American Community Survey 5-Year Estimates

Poverty Rate

Area	All Ages	Under 18 Years Old	18 to 64 Years Old	65 Years and Over
City	44.7	19.9	50.9	6.7
MSA[1]	20.9	16.0	25.2	7.7
U.S.	15.1	21.2	14.2	9.3

Note: Figures are percentage of people whose income during the past 12 months was below the poverty level; (1) Figures cover the Blacksburg-Christiansburg-Radford, VA Metropolitan Statistical Area—see Appendix B for areas included
Source: U.S. Census Bureau, 2012-2016 American Community Survey 5-Year Estimates

EMPLOYMENT

Labor Force and Employment

Area	Civilian Labor Force			Workers Employed		
	Dec. 2016	Dec. 2017	% Chg.	Dec. 2016	Dec. 2017	% Chg.
City	20,447	20,343	-0.5	19,529	19,607	0.4
MSA[1]	89,969	89,477	-0.5	86,145	86,419	0.3
U.S.	158,968,000	159,880,000	0.6	151,798,000	153,602,000	1.2

Note: Data is not seasonally adjusted and covers workers 16 years of age and older; (1) Figures cover the Blacksburg-Christiansburg-Radford, VA Metropolitan Statistical Area—see Appendix B for areas included
Source: Bureau of Labor Statistics, Local Area Unemployment Statistics

Unemployment Rate

Area	2017											
	Jan.	Feb.	Mar.	Apr.	May	Jun.	Jul.	Aug.	Sep.	Oct.	Nov.	Dec.
City	4.9	5.0	4.8	4.3	4.6	5.8	5.4	5.2	4.8	4.2	4.7	3.6
MSA[1]	6.0	4.5	5.1	3.7	4.0	4.5	4.4	4.5	3.9	3.6	3.7	3.4
U.S.	5.1	4.9	4.6	4.1	4.1	4.5	4.6	4.5	4.1	3.9	3.9	3.9

Note: Data is not seasonally adjusted and covers workers 16 years of age and older; (1) Figures cover the Blacksburg-Christiansburg-Radford, VA Metropolitan Statistical Area—see Appendix B for areas included
Source: Bureau of Labor Statistics, Local Area Unemployment Statistics

Average Wages

Occupation	$/Hr.	Occupation	$/Hr.
Accountants and Auditors	33.20	Maids and Housekeeping Cleaners	9.40
Automotive Mechanics	19.50	Maintenance and Repair Workers	17.20
Bookkeepers	17.10	Marketing Managers	n/a
Carpenters	18.00	Nuclear Medicine Technologists	n/a
Cashiers	9.30	Nurses, Licensed Practical	18.30
Clerks, General Office	14.10	Nurses, Registered	26.90
Clerks, Receptionists/Information	12.90	Nursing Assistants	12.30
Clerks, Shipping/Receiving	14.50	Packers and Packagers, Hand	10.30
Computer Programmers	40.20	Physical Therapists	41.70
Computer Systems Analysts	38.70	Postal Service Mail Carriers	24.60
Computer User Support Specialists	21.30	Real Estate Brokers	n/a
Cooks, Restaurant	11.80	Retail Salespersons	12.30
Dentists	96.60	Sales Reps., Exc. Tech./Scientific	26.70
Electrical Engineers	46.40	Sales Reps., Tech./Scientific	46.30
Electricians	22.20	Secretaries, Exc. Legal/Med./Exec.	16.00
Financial Managers	60.70	Security Guards	16.80
First-Line Supervisors/Managers, Sales	20.20	Surgeons	n/a
Food Preparation Workers	9.80	Teacher Assistants*	10.80
General and Operations Managers	51.20	Teachers, Elementary School*	22.00
Hairdressers/Cosmetologists	n/a	Teachers, Secondary School*	22.10
Internists, General	n/a	Telemarketers	17.30
Janitors and Cleaners	13.30	Truck Drivers, Heavy/Tractor-Trailer	18.50
Landscaping/Groundskeeping Workers	12.90	Truck Drivers, Light/Delivery Svcs.	13.10
Lawyers	48.70	Waiters and Waitresses	12.10

Note: Wage data covers the Blacksburg-Christiansburg-Radford, VA Metropolitan Statistical Area—see Appendix B for areas included; (*) Hourly wages for elementary/secondary school teachers and teacher assistants were calculated by the editors from annual wage data based on a 40 hour work week; n/a not available.
Source: Bureau of Labor Statistics, Metro Area Occupational Employment & Wage Estimates, May 2017

Employment by Occupation

Occupation Classification	City (%)	MSA[1] (%)	U.S. (%)
Management, Business, Science, and Arts	51.7	38.2	37.0
Natural Resources, Construction, and Maintenance	1.5	7.2	8.9
Production, Transportation, and Material Moving	4.1	13.6	12.2
Sales and Office	19.1	21.6	23.8
Service	23.6	19.5	18.1

Note: Figures cover employed civilians 16 years of age and older; (1) Figures cover the Blacksburg-Christiansburg-Radford, VA Metropolitan Statistical Area—see Appendix B for areas included
Source: U.S. Census Bureau, 2012-2016 American Community Survey 5-Year Estimates

Employment by Industry

Sector	MSA[1]		U.S.
	Number of Employees	Percent of Total	Percent of Total
Construction, Mining, and Logging	n/a	n/a	5.2
Education and Health Services	n/a	n/a	15.9
Financial Activities	n/a	n/a	5.7
Government	24,900	32.1	15.3
Information	n/a	n/a	1.9
Leisure and Hospitality	n/a	n/a	10.7
Manufacturing	n/a	n/a	8.5
Other Services	n/a	n/a	3.9
Professional and Business Services	n/a	n/a	14.0
Retail Trade	n/a	n/a	11.0
Transportation, Warehousing, and Utilities	n/a	n/a	4.1
Wholesale Trade	n/a	n/a	4.0

Note: Figures are non-farm employment as of December 2017. Figures are not seasonally adjusted and include workers 16 years of age and older; (1) Figures cover the Blacksburg-Christiansburg-Radford, VA Metropolitan Statistical Area—see Appendix B for areas included; n/a not available
Source: Bureau of Labor Statistics, Current Employment Statistics, Employment, Hours, and Earnings

Occupations with Greatest Projected Employment Growth: 2017 – 2019

Occupation[1]	2017 Employment	2019 Projected Employment	Numeric Employment Change	Percent Employment Change
Combined Food Preparation and Serving Workers, Including Fast Food	91,620	97,950	6,330	6.9
Waiters and Waitresses	69,000	72,910	3,910	5.7
Personal Care Aides	44,180	46,820	2,640	6.0
Management Analysts	58,220	60,700	2,480	4.3
Software Developers, Applications	36,000	38,380	2,380	6.6
Cooks, Restaurant	32,340	34,500	2,160	6.7
Janitors and Cleaners, Except Maids and Housekeeping Cleaners	63,140	65,290	2,150	3.4
Cashiers	107,100	109,180	2,080	1.9
Customer Service Representatives	63,140	65,140	2,000	3.2
Laborers and Freight, Stock, and Material Movers, Hand	49,100	51,080	1,980	4.0

Note: Projections cover Virginia; (1) Sorted by numeric employment change
Source: www.projectionscentral.com, State Occupational Projections, 2017–2019 Short-Term Projections

Fastest Growing Occupations: 2017 – 2019

Occupation[1]	2017 Employment	2019 Projected Employment	Numeric Employment Change	Percent Employment Change
Information Security Analysts	11,770	12,750	980	8.3
Dental Laboratory Technicians	980	1,060	80	8.0
Statisticians	1,170	1,260	90	7.6
Operations Research Analysts	8,130	8,740	610	7.5
Nurse Practitioners	4,720	5,060	340	7.4
Physician Assistants	2,480	2,650	170	7.1
Combined Food Preparation and Serving Workers, Including Fast Food	91,620	97,950	6,330	6.9
Home Health Aides	11,620	12,410	790	6.8
Cooks, Restaurant	32,340	34,500	2,160	6.7
Software Developers, Applications	36,000	38,380	2,380	6.6

Note: Projections cover Virginia; (1) Sorted by percent employment change and excludes occupations with numeric employment change less than 50
Source: www.projectionscentral.com, State Occupational Projections, 2017–2019 Short-Term Projections

TAXES

State Corporate Income Tax Rates

State	Tax Rate (%)	Income Brackets ($)	Num. of Brackets	Financial Institution Tax Rate (%)[a]	Federal Income Tax Ded.
Virginia	6.0	Flat rate	1	6.0	No

Note: Tax rates as of January 1, 2018; (a) Rates listed are the corporate income tax rate applied to financial institutions or excise taxes based on income. Some states have other taxes based upon the value of deposits or shares.
Source: Federation of Tax Administrators, Range of State Corporate Income Tax Rates, January 1, 2018

State Individual Income Tax Rates

State	Tax Rate (%)	Income Brackets ($)	Num. of Brackets	Personal Exempt. ($)[1]		Fed. Inc. Tax Ded.
				Single	Dependents	
Virginia	2.0 - 5.75	3,000 - 17,001	4	930	930	No

Note: Tax rates as of January 1, 2018; Local- and county-level taxes are not included; n/a not applicable; (1) Married joint filers generally receive double the single exemption
Source: Federation of Tax Administrators, State Individual Income Tax Rates, January 1, 2018

Various State Sales and Excise Tax Rates

State	State Sales Tax (%)	Gasoline[1] (¢/gal.)	Cigarette[2] ($/pack)	Spirits[3] ($/gal.)	Wine[4] ($/gal.)	Beer[5] ($/gal.)	Recreational Marijuana (%)
Virginia	5.3 (b)	22.4	0.30	19.93 (g)	1.51 (l)	0.26 (q)	Not legal

Note: All tax rates as of January 1, 2018; (1) The American Petroleum Institute has developed a methodology for determining the average tax rate on a gallon of fuel. Rates may include any of the following: excise taxes, environmental fees, storage tank fees, other fees or taxes, general sales tax, and local taxes. In states where gasoline is subject to the general sales tax, or where the fuel tax is based on the average sale price, the average rate determined by API is sensitive to changes in the price of gasoline. States that fully or partially apply general sales taxes to gasoline: CA, CO, GA, IL, IN, MI, NY; (2) The federal excise tax of $1.0066 per pack and local taxes are not included; (3) Rates are those applicable to off-premise sales of 40% alcohol by volume (a.b.v.) distilled spirits in 750ml containers. Local excise taxes are excluded; (4) Rates are those applicable to off-premise sales of 11% a.b.v. non-carbonated wine in 750ml containers; (5) Rates are those applicable to off-premise sales of 4.7% a.b.v. beer in 12 ounce containers; (b) Three states levy mandatory, statewide, local add-on sales taxes at the state level: California (1.25%), Utah (1.25%), Virginia (1%), we include these in their state sales tax; (g) Control states, where the government controls all sales. Products can be subject to ad valorem mark-up as well as excise taxes; (l) Different rates also applicable to alcohol content, place of production, size of container, place purchased (on- or off-premise or on board airlines) or type of wine (carbonated, vermouth, etc.); (q) Different rates also applicable according to alcohol content, place of production, size of container, or place purchased (on- or off-premise or onboard airlines).
Source: Tax Foundation, 2018 Facts & Figures: How Does Your State Compare?

State Business Tax Climate Index Rankings

State	Overall Rank	Corporate Tax Rank	Individual Income Tax Rank	Sales Tax Rank	Unemployment Insurance Tax Rank	Property Tax Rank
Virginia	31	6	40	10	41	31

Note: The index is a measure of how each state's tax laws affect economic performance. The lower the rank, the more favorable a state's tax system is for business. States without a given tax are given a ranking of 1. The scores/rankings for the District of Columbia do not affect other states. The 2018 index represents the tax climate as of July 1, 2017.
Source: Tax Foundation, State Business Tax Climate Index 2018

TRANSPORTATION

Means of Transportation to Work

Area	Car/Truck/Van		Public Transportation			Bicycle	Walked	Other Means	Worked at Home
	Drove Alone	Car-pooled	Bus	Subway	Railroad				
City	62.7	5.9	11.0	0.6	0.0	2.8	11.3	1.5	4.2
MSA[1]	78.1	9.2	2.7	0.1	0.0	0.9	4.2	1.4	3.3
U.S.	76.4	9.3	2.6	1.9	0.6	0.6	2.8	1.3	4.6

Note: Figures are percentages and cover workers 16 years of age and older; (1) Figures cover the Blacksburg-Christiansburg-Radford, VA Metropolitan Statistical Area—see Appendix B for areas included
Source: U.S. Census Bureau, 2012-2016 American Community Survey 5-Year Estimates

Travel Time to Work

Area	Less Than 10 Minutes	10 to 19 Minutes	20 to 29 Minutes	30 to 44 Minutes	45 to 59 Minutes	60 to 89 Minutes	90 Minutes or More
City	33.6	46.4	9.8	6.6	2.0	1.3	0.4
MSA[1]	20.2	36.3	18.5	14.6	5.3	3.5	1.5
U.S.	12.9	29.2	20.9	20.4	8.0	6.0	2.7

Note: Note: Figures are percentages and include workers 16 years old and over; (1) Figures cover the Blacksburg-Christiansburg-Radford, VA Metropolitan Statistical Area—see Appendix B for areas included
Source: U.S. Census Bureau, 2012-2016 American Community Survey 5-Year Estimates

Freeway Travel Time Index

Area	1985	1990	1995	2000	2005	2010	2014
Urban Area Rank[1,2]	n/a	n/a	n/a	n/a	n/a	n/a	n/a
Urban Area Index[1]	n/a	n/a	n/a	n/a	n/a	n/a	n/a
Average Index[3]	1.09	1.11	1.14	1.17	1.20	1.19	1.20

Note: Freeway Travel Time Index—the ratio of travel time in the peak period to the travel time at free-flow conditions. For example, a value of 1.30 indicates a 20-minute free-flow trip takes 26 minutes in the peak (20 minutes x 1.30 = 26 minutes); (1) Data for the Blacksburg-Christiansburg-Radford, VA urban area was not available; (2) Rank is based on 101 urban areas (#1 = highest travel time index); (3) Average of 101 urban areas
Source: Texas Transportation Institute, 2015 Urban Mobility Scorecard, August 2015

Freeway Commuter Stress Index

Area	1985	1990	1995	2000	2005	2010	2014
Urban Area Rank[1,2]	n/a	n/a	n/a	n/a	n/a	n/a	n/a
Urban Area Index[1]	n/a	n/a	n/a	n/a	n/a	n/a	n/a
Average Index[3]	1.13	1.16	1.19	1.22	1.25	1.24	1.25

Note: The Freeway Commuter Stress Index is the same as the Freeway Travel Time Index (see table above) except that it includes only the travel in the peak directions during the peak periods; the TTI includes travel in all directions during the peak period. Thus, the CSI is more indicative of the work trip experienced by each commuter on a daily basis; (1) Data for the Blacksburg-Christiansburg-Radford, VA urban area was not available; (2) Rank is based on 101 urban areas (#1 = highest travel time index); (3) Average of 101 urban areas
Source: Texas Transportation Institute, 2015 Urban Mobility Scorecard, August 2015

Living Environment

COST OF LIVING

Cost of Living Index

Composite Index	Groceries	Housing	Utilities	Transportation	Health Care	Misc. Goods/ Services
90.4	88.2	66.2	117.7	88.2	111.1	100.9

Note: The Cost of Living Index measures regional differences in the cost of consumer goods and services, excluding taxes and non-consumer expenditures, for professional and managerial households in the top income quintile. It is based on more than 50,000 prices covering almost 60 different items for which prices are collected three times a year by chambers of commerce, economic development organizations or university applied economic centers in each participating urban area. The numbers shown should be read as a percentage above or below the national average of 100. For example, a value of 115.4 in the groceries column indicates that grocery prices are 15.4% higher than the national average. Small differences in the index numbers should not be interpreted as significant; Figures cover the Blacksburg VA urban area.
Source: The Council for Community and Economic Research, ACCRA Cost of Living Index, 2017

Grocery Prices

Area[1]	T-Bone Steak ($/pound)	Frying Chicken ($/pound)	Whole Milk ($/half gal.)	Eggs ($/dozen)	Orange Juice ($/64 oz.)	Coffee ($/11.5 oz.)
City[2]	10.99	1.06	1.88	1.12	3.23	4.01
Avg.	11.29	1.40	2.02	1.47	3.55	4.37
Min.	7.71	0.93	1.04	0.70	2.86	3.24
Max.	15.83	2.39	4.03	3.92	6.29	8.16

Note: (1) Values for the local area are compared with the average, minimum and maximum values for all 294 areas in the Cost of Living Index; (2) Figures cover the Blacksburg VA urban area; ***T-Bone Steak*** *(price per pound);* ***Frying Chicken*** *(price per pound, whole fryer);* ***Whole Milk*** *(half gallon carton);* ***Eggs*** *(price per dozen, Grade A, large);* ***Orange Juice*** *(64 oz. Tropicana or Florida Natural);* ***Coffee*** *(11.5 oz. can, vacuum-packed, Maxwell House, Hills Bros, or Folgers).*
Source: The Council for Community and Economic Research, ACCRA Cost of Living Index, 2017

Housing and Utility Costs

Area[1]	New Home Price ($)	Apartment Rent ($/month)	All Electric ($/month)	Part Electric ($/month)	Other Energy ($/month)	Telephone ($/month)
City[2]	202,531	859	-	84.93	58.72	44.61
Avg.	335,956	1,047	175.01	97.34	67.93	28.71
Min.	187,788	491	109.48	49.33	35.44	12.39
Max.	1,739,087	4,559	432.62	227.09	353.33	44.61

Note: (1) Values for the local area are compared with the average, minimum and maximum values for all 294 areas in the Cost of Living Index; (2) Figures cover the Blacksburg VA urban area; ***New Home Price*** *(2,400 sf living area, 8,000 sf lot, in urban area with full utilities);* ***Apartment Rent*** *(950 sf 2 bedroom/1.5 or 2 bath, unfurnished, excluding all utilities except water);* ***All Electric*** *(average monthly cost for an all-electric home);* ***Part Electric*** *(average monthly cost for a part-electric home);* ***Other Energy*** *(average monthly cost for natural gas, fuel oil, coal, wood, and any other forms of energy except electricity);* ***Telephone*** *(price includes basic monthly rate for a private residential line plus additional local usage charges incurred by a family of four).*
Source: The Council for Community and Economic Research, ACCRA Cost of Living Index, 2017

Health Care, Transportation, and Other Costs

Area[1]	Doctor ($/visit)	Dentist ($/visit)	Optometrist ($/visit)	Gasoline ($/gallon)	Beauty Salon ($/visit)	Men's Shirt ($)
City[2]	120.31	111.97	102.22	2.02	33.44	37.57
Avg.	108.00	92.54	101.93	2.25	37.58	30.92
Min.	30.39	60.00	49.75	1.82	16.11	11.20
Max.	193.50	161.94	229.28	3.16	77.35	59.13

Note: (1) Values for the local area are compared with the average, minimum and maximum values for all 294 areas in the Cost of Living Index; (2) Figures cover the Blacksburg VA urban area; ***Doctor*** *(general practitioners routine exam of an established patient);* ***Dentist*** *(adult teeth cleaning and periodic oral examination);* ***Optometrist*** *(full vision eye exam for established adult patient);* ***Gasoline*** *(one gallon regular unleaded, national brand, including all taxes, cash price at self-service pump if available);* ***Beauty Salon*** *(woman's shampoo, trim, and blow-dry);* ***Men's Shirt*** *(cotton/polyester dress shirt, pinpoint weave, long sleeves).*
Source: The Council for Community and Economic Research, ACCRA Cost of Living Index, 2017

HOUSING

House Price Index (HPI)

Area	National Ranking[2]	Quarterly Change (%)	One-Year Change (%)	Five-Year Change (%)
MSA[1]	179	1.46	4.26	10.88
U.S.[3]	–	1.61	6.68	34.71

Note: The HPI is a weighted repeat sales index. It measures average price changes in repeat sales or refinancings on the same properties. This information is obtained by reviewing repeat mortgage transactions on single-family properties whose mortgages have been purchased or securitized by Fannie Mae or Freddie Mac in January 1975; (1) Figures cover the Blacksburg-Christiansburg-Radford, VA Metropolitan Statistical Area—see Appendix B for areas included; (2) Rankings are based on annual percentage change for all metro areas containing at least 15,000 transactions over the last 10 years and ranges from 1 to 253; (3) figures based on a weighted average of Census Division estimates using a seasonally adjusted, purchase-only index; all figures are for the period ending December 31, 2017
Source: Federal Housing Finance Agency, House Price Index, February 28, 2018

Median Single-Family Home Prices

Area	2015	2016	2017p	Percent Change 2016 to 2017
MSA[1]	n/a	n/a	n/a	n/a
U.S. Average	223.9	235.5	248.8	5.6

Note: Figures are median sales prices of existing single-family homes in thousands of dollars; (p) preliminary; n/a not available; (1) Figures cover the Blacksburg-Christiansburg-Radford, VA Metropolitan Statistical Area—see Appendix B for areas included
Source: National Association of Realtors, Median Sales Price of Existing Single-Family Homes for Metropolitan Areas, 4th Quarter 2017

Qualifying Income Based on Median Sales Price of Existing Single-Family Homes

Area	With 5% Down ($)	With 10% Down ($)	With 20% Down ($)
MSA[1]	n/a	n/a	n/a
U.S. Average	55,585	52,659	46,808

Note: Figures are preliminary; Qualifying income is based on a mortgage rate of 4.17%. Monthly principal and interest payment is limited to 25% of income; n/a not available; (1) Figures cover the Blacksburg-Christiansburg-Radford, VA Metropolitan Statistical Area—see Appendix B for areas included
Source: National Association of Realtors, Qualifying Income Based on Median Sales Price of Existing Single-Family Homes for Metropolitan Areas, 4th Quarter 2017

Median Apartment Condo-Coop Home Prices

Area	2015	2016	2017p	Percent Change 2016 to 2017
MSA[1]	n/a	n/a	n/a	n/a
U.S. Average	210.7	220.7	234.3	6.2

Note: Figures are median sales prices of existing apartment condo-coop homes in thousands of dollars; (p) preliminary; n/a not available; (1) Figures cover the Blacksburg-Christiansburg-Radford, VA Metropolitan Statistical Area—see Appendix B for areas included
Source: National Association of Realtors, Median Sales Price of Existing Apartment Condo-Coop Homes for Metropolitan Areas, 4th Quarter 2017

Home Value Distribution

Area	Under $50,000	$50,000 -$99,999	$100,000 -$149,999	$150,000 -$199,999	$200,000 -$299,999	$300,000 -$499,999	$500,000 -$999,999	$1,000,000 or more
City	5.8	1.3	3.7	10.8	36.7	31.5	9.6	0.7
MSA[1]	9.6	15.7	18.1	19.8	19.3	12.5	4.2	0.7
U.S.	8.8	14.8	15.3	14.9	18.4	16.4	9.0	2.5

Note: Figures are percentages and cover owner-occupied housing units; (1) Figures cover the Blacksburg-Christiansburg-Radford, VA Metropolitan Statistical Area—see Appendix B for areas included
Source: U.S. Census Bureau, 2012-2016 American Community Survey 5-Year Estimates

Homeownership Rate

Area	2009 (%)	2010 (%)	2011 (%)	2012 (%)	2013 (%)	2014 (%)	2015 (%)	2016 (%)	2017 (%)
MSA[1]	n/a	n/a	n/a	n/a	n/a	n/a	n/a	n/a	n/a
U.S.	67.4	66.9	66.1	65.4	65.1	64.5	63.7	63.4	63.9

Note: (1) Figures cover the Blacksburg-Christiansburg-Radford, VA Metropolitan Statistical Area—see Appendix B for areas included; n/a not available
Source: U.S. Census Bureau, Housing Vacancies and Homeownership Annual Statistics: 2009-2017

Year Housing Structure Built

Area	2010 or Later	2000 -2009	1990 -1999	1980 -1989	1970 -1979	1960 -1969	1950 -1959	1940 -1949	Before 1940	Median Year
City	2.8	14.2	18.7	19.9	21.7	8.3	7.6	3.4	3.4	1983
MSA[1]	2.2	14.9	16.2	15.4	18.4	10.4	8.0	6.4	8.2	1979
U.S.	2.3	14.7	14.0	13.7	15.6	10.9	10.6	5.2	13.0	1977

Note: Figures are percentages except for Median Year; Note: (1) Figures cover the Blacksburg-Christiansburg-Radford, VA Metropolitan Statistical Area—see Appendix B for areas included
Source: U.S. Census Bureau, 2012-2016 American Community Survey 5-Year Estimates

Gross Monthly Rent

Area	Under $500	$500 -$999	$1,000 -$1,499	$1,500 -$1,999	$2,000 -$2,499	$2,500 -$2,999	$3,000 and up	Median ($)
City	5.1	48.9	34.2	8.6	3.1	0.0	0.0	964
MSA[1]	14.8	56.3	21.5	5.4	1.6	0.2	0.3	797
U.S.	11.3	43.3	27.7	10.7	4.0	1.6	1.5	949

Note: Figures are percentages except for Median; Gross rent is the contract rent plus the estimated average monthly cost of utilities (electricity, gas, and water and sewer) and fuels (oil, coal, kerosene, wood, etc.) if these are paid by the renter (or paid for the renter by someone else); (1) Figures cover the Blacksburg-Christiansburg-Radford, VA Metropolitan Statistical Area—see Appendix B for areas included
Source: U.S. Census Bureau, 2012-2016 American Community Survey 5-Year Estimates

HEALTH

Health Risk Factors

Category	MSA[1] (%)	U.S. (%)
Adults aged 18–64 who have any kind of health care coverage	n/a	87.7
Adults who reported being in good or excellent health	n/a	83.6
Adults who are current smokers	n/a	17.1
Adults who currently use E-cigarettes	n/a	4.7
Adults who currently use chewing tobacco, snuff, or snus	n/a	4.0
Adults who are heavy drinkers[2]	n/a	6.5
Adults who are binge drinkers[3]	n/a	16.9
Adults who are overweight (BMI 25.0 - 29.9)	n/a	35.3
Adults who are obese (BMI 30.0 - 99.8)	n/a	29.9
Adults who participated in any physical activities in the past month	n/a	76.9
Adults who always or nearly always wears a seat belt	n/a	94.3

Note: n/a not available; (1) Figures cover the Blacksburg-Christiansburg-Radford, VA Metropolitan Statistical Area—see Appendix B for areas included; (2) Heavy drinkers are classified as adult men having more than 14 drinks per week and adult women having more than 7 drinks per week; (3) Binge drinkers are classified as males having five or more drinks on one occasion or females having four or more drinks on one occasion
Source: Centers for Disease Control and Prevention, Behaviorial Risk Factor Surveillance System, SMART: Selected Metropolitan Area Risk Trends, 2016

Health Screening Rates

Category	MSA[1] (%)	U.S. (%)
Adults 50-75 who have had a blood stool test within the past year	n/a	8.0
Adults 50-75 who have had a colonoscopy in the past 10 years	n/a	63.5
Adults aged 65+ who have had flu shot within the past year	n/a	58.6
Adults aged 65+ who have ever had a pneumonia vaccination	n/a	73.4
Adults who have ever been tested for HIV	n/a	35.6
Women aged 21-65 who have had a pap test in the past three years	n/a	79.8
Men aged 40+ who have had a PSA test within the past two years	n/a	39.5
Women aged 40+ who have had a mammogram within the past two years	n/a	72.5

Note: n/a not available; (1) Figures cover the Blacksburg-Christiansburg-Radford, VA Metropolitan Statistical Area—see Appendix B for areas included; Source: Centers for Disease Control and Prevention, Behaviorial Risk Factor Surveillance System, SMART: Selected Metropolitan Area Risk Trends, 2016

Chronic Health Conditions

Category	MSA[1] (%)	U.S. (%)
Adults who have ever been told they had a heart attack	n/a	4.4
Adults who have ever been told they have angina or coronary heart disease	n/a	4.1
Adults who have ever been told they had a stroke	n/a	3.1
Adults who have been told they currently have asthma	n/a	9.3
Adults who have ever been told they have arthritis	n/a	25.8
Adults who have ever been told they have diabetes[2]	n/a	10.5
Adults who have ever been told they had skin cancer	n/a	5.9
Adults who have ever been told they had any other types of cancer	n/a	6.7
Adults who have ever been told they have COPD	n/a	6.3
Adults who have ever been told they have kidney disease	n/a	2.8
Adults who have ever been told they have a form of depression	n/a	17.4

Note: n/a not available; (1) Figures cover the Blacksburg-Christiansburg-Radford, VA Metropolitan Statistical Area—see Appendix B for areas included; (2) Figures do not include pregnancy-related, borderline, or pre-diabetes
Source: Centers for Disease Control and Prevention, Behaviorial Risk Factor Surveillance System, SMART: Selected Metropolitan Area Risk Trends, 2016

Mortality Rates for the Top 10 Causes of Death in the U.S.

ICD-10[a] Sub-Chapter	ICD-10[a] Code	Age-Adjusted Mortality Rate[1] per 100,000 population	
		County[2]	U.S.
Malignant neoplasms	C00-C97	139.8	158.5
Ischaemic heart diseases	I20-I25	97.9	96.8
Other forms of heart disease	I30-I51	48.2	52.4
Chronic lower respiratory diseases	J40-J47	41.7	40.9
Cerebrovascular diseases	I60-I69	36.6	37.2
Organic, including symptomatic, mental disorders	F01-F09	47.9	33.3
Other degenerative diseases of the nervous system	G30-G31	17.5	32.1
Other external causes of accidental injury	W00-X59	24.7	31.2
Diabetes mellitus	E10-E14	23.9	21.1
Hypertensive diseases	I10-I15	13.2	20.8

Note: (a) ICD-10 = International Classification of Diseases 10th Revision; (1) Mortality rates are a three year average covering 2014-2016; (2) Figures cover Montgomery County.
Source: Centers for Disease Control and Prevention, National Center for Health Statistics. Underlying Cause of Death 1999-2016 on CDC WONDER Online Database, released December 2017

Mortality Rates for Selected Causes of Death

ICD-10[a] Sub-Chapter	ICD-10[a] Code	Age-Adjusted Mortality Rate[1] per 100,000 population	
		County[2]	U.S.
Assault	X85-Y09	Suppressed	5.6
Diseases of the liver	K70-K76	14.4	14.0
Human immunodeficiency virus (HIV) disease	B20-B24	Suppressed	1.9
Influenza and pneumonia	J09-J18	21.4	14.6
Intentional self-harm	X60-X84	13.3	13.2
Malnutrition	E40-E46	Suppressed	1.3
Obesity and other hyperalimentation	E65-E68	Suppressed	2.1
Renal failure	N17-N19	15.3	13.0
Transport accidents	V01-V99	Unreliable	12.0
Viral hepatitis	B15-B19	Suppressed	1.9

Note: (a) ICD-10 = International Classification of Diseases 10th Revision; (1) Mortality rates are a three year average covering 2014-2016; (2) Figures cover Montgomery County; Data are Suppressed when the data meet the criteria for confidentiality constraints; Mortality rates are flagged as Unreliable when the rate would be calculated with a numerator of 20 or less.
Source: Centers for Disease Control and Prevention, National Center for Health Statistics. Underlying Cause of Death 1999-2016 on CDC WONDER Online Database, released December 2017

Health Insurance Coverage

Area	With Health Insurance	With Private Health Insurance	With Public Health Insurance	Without Health Insurance	Population Under Age 18 Without Health Insurance
City	94.5	89.9	9.8	5.5	2.5
MSA[1]	91.5	77.4	26.2	8.5	4.3
U.S.	88.3	66.7	33.0	11.7	5.9

Note: Figures are percentages that cover the civilian noninstitutionalized population; (1) Figures cover the Blacksburg-Christiansburg-Radford, VA Metropolitan Statistical Area—see Appendix B for areas included
Source: U.S. Census Bureau, 2012-2016 American Community Survey 5-Year Estimates

Number of Medical Professionals

Area	MDs[3]	DOs[3,4]	Dentists	Podiatrists	Chiropractors	Optometrists
County[1] (number)	156	93	43	1	21	8
County[1] (rate[2])	160.0	95.4	43.7	1.0	21.3	8.1
U.S. (rate[2])	276.5	22.3	67.3	6.0	26.7	15.9

Note: Data as of 2016 unless noted; (1) Data covers Montgomery County; (2) Rate per 100,000 population; (3) Data as of 2015 and includes all active, non-federal physicians; (4) Doctor of Osteopathic Medicine
Source: U.S. Department of Health and Human Services, Health Resources and Services Administration, Bureau of Health Professions, Area Resource File (ARF) 2016-2017

EDUCATION

Public School District Statistics

District Name	Schls	Pupils	Pupil/ Teacher Ratio	Minority Pupils[1] (%)	Free Lunch Eligible[2] (%)	IEP[3] (%)
Montgomery Co Public Schools	21	9,775	12.6	17.1	29.3	9.1

Note: Table includes school districts with 100 or more students; (1) Percentage of students that are not non-Hispanic white; (2) Percentage of students that are eligible for the free lunch program; (3) Percentage of students that have an Individualized Education Program.
Source: U.S. Department of Education, National Center for Education Statistics, Common Core of Data, Local Education Agency (School District) Universe Survey: School Year 2015-2016; U.S. Department of Education, National Center for Education Statistics, Common Core of Data, Public Elementary/Secondary School Universe Survey: School Year 2015-2016

Highest Level of Education

Area	Less than H.S.	H.S. Diploma	Some College, No Deg.	Associate Degree	Bachelor's Degree	Master's Degree	Prof. School Degree	Doctorate Degree
City	5.1	9.5	9.7	4.3	31.1	21.4	4.4	14.4
MSA[1]	11.9	28.2	18.9	8.4	17.2	9.4	1.8	4.1
U.S.	13.0	27.5	21.0	8.2	18.8	8.2	2.0	1.3

Note: Figures cover persons age 25 and over; (1) Figures cover the Blacksburg-Christiansburg-Radford, VA Metropolitan Statistical Area—see Appendix B for areas included
Source: U.S. Census Bureau, 2012-2016 American Community Survey 5-Year Estimates

Educational Attainment by Race

Area	High School Graduate or Higher (%)					Bachelor's Degree or Higher (%)				
	Total	White	Black	Asian	Hisp.[2]	Total	White	Black	Asian	Hisp.[2]
City	94.9	95.0	84.9	97.5	88.3	71.3	70.5	54.1	89.9	63.5
MSA[1]	88.1	88.0	84.8	95.3	74.8	32.5	31.1	27.2	85.3	38.7
U.S.	87.0	88.9	84.3	86.3	65.7	30.3	31.6	20.0	52.1	14.7

Note: Figures shown cover persons 25 years old and over; (1) Figures cover the Blacksburg-Christiansburg-Radford, VA Metropolitan Statistical Area—see Appendix B for areas included; (2) People of Hispanic origin can be of any race
Source: U.S. Census Bureau, 2012-2016 American Community Survey 5-Year Estimates

School Enrollment by Grade and Control

Area	Preschool (%)		Kindergarten (%)		Grades 1 - 4 (%)		Grades 5 - 8 (%)		Grades 9 - 12 (%)	
	Public	Private	Public	Private	Public	Private	Public	Private	Public	Private
City	11.7	88.3	81.4	18.6	84.8	15.2	90.5	9.5	89.8	10.2
MSA[1]	48.1	51.9	89.6	10.4	91.0	9.0	88.7	11.3	90.5	9.5
U.S.	58.4	41.6	87.7	12.3	89.8	10.2	89.7	10.3	90.4	9.6

Note: Figures shown cover persons 3 years old and over; (1) Figures cover the Blacksburg-Christiansburg-Radford, VA Metropolitan Statistical Area—see Appendix B for areas included
Source: U.S. Census Bureau, 2012-2016 American Community Survey 5-Year Estimates

Average Salaries of Public School Classroom Teachers

Area	2015		2016		Change from 2015 to 2016	
	Dollars	Rank[1]	Dollars	Rank[1]	Percent	Rank[2]
Virginia	50,544	30	50,834	30	0.6	29
U.S. Average	57,611	–	58,353	–	1.3	–

Note: (1) Rank ranges from 1 to 51 where 1 indicates highest salary; (2) Rank ranges from 1 to 51 where 1 indicates highest percent change.
Source: National Education Association, Rankings & Estimates: Rankings of the States 2016 and Estimates of School Statistics 2017

Higher Education

Four-Year Colleges			Two-Year Colleges			Medical Schools[1]	Law Schools[2]	Voc/ Tech[3]
Public	Private Non-profit	Private For-profit	Public	Private Non-profit	Private For-profit			
1	1	0	0	0	0	1	0	0

Note: Figures cover institutions located within the city limits and include main campuses only; (1) includes schools accredited by the Liaison Committee on Medical Education and the American Osteopathic Association's Commission on Osteopathic College Accreditation; (2) includes ABA-accredited schools, schools with provisional ABA accreditation, and state accredited schools; (3) includes all schools with programs that are less than 2 years.
Source: National Center for Education Statistics, Integrated Postsecondary Education System (IPEDS), 2016-17; Wikipedia, List of Medical Schools in the United States, accessed April 2, 2018; Wikipedia, List of Law Schools in the United States, accessed April 2, 2018

According to *U.S. News & World Report,* the Blacksburg-Christiansburg-Radford, VA metro area is home to one of the best national universities in the U.S.: **Virginia Tech** (#69 tie). The indicators used to capture academic quality fall into a number of categories: assessment by administrators at peer institutions; retention of students; faculty resources; student selectivity; financial resources; alumni giving; high school counselor ratings of colleges; and graduation rate. *U.S. News & World Report, "America's Best Colleges 2018"*

PRESIDENTIAL ELECTION

2016 Presidential Election Results

Area	Clinton	Trump	Johnson	Stein	Other
Montgomery County	46.5	45.2	4.7	0.9	2.6
U.S.	48.0	45.9	3.3	1.1	1.7

Note: Results are percentages and may not add to 100% due to rounding
Source: Dave Leip's Atlas of U.S. Presidential Elections

EMPLOYERS

Major Employers

Company Name	Industry
Bae Systems Ordnance Systems	International defense, aerospace and security products
Carilion New River Valley Medical Center	Health care
HCA Virginia Health System	Health care
Montgomery County School Board	School district
Moog Inc	Motion control technology
Pulaski County School Board	School district
Radford University	public university
Virginia Polytechnic Institute	public, land-grant, research university
Volvo Group North America	Automotive manufacturing
Wal Mart	Discount retailer

Note: Companies shown are located within the Blacksburg-Christiansburg-Radford, VA Metropolitan Statistical Area.
Source: Hoovers.com; Wikipedia

PUBLIC SAFETY

Crime Rate

Area	All Crimes	Violent Crimes: Murder	Violent Crimes: Rape[3]	Violent Crimes: Robbery	Violent Crimes: Aggrav. Assault	Property Crimes: Burglary	Property Crimes: Larceny -Theft	Property Crimes: Motor Vehicle Theft
City	1,015.1	0.0	42.7	6.7	47.2	139.2	747.8	31.4
Metro[1]	1,879.8	2.8	63.4	14.9	116.9	259.1	1,363.8	59.0
U.S.	2,847.8	5.3	40.4	102.8	248.5	468.9	1,745.0	236.9

Note: Figures are crimes per 100,000 population; (1) Figures cover the Blacksburg-Christiansburg-Radford, VA Metropolitan Statistical Area—see Appendix B for areas included; (3) The city and U.S. figures shown were reported using the revised Uniform Crime Reporting (UCR) definition of rape. The metro area figures shown are an aggregate total of the data submitted using both the revised and legacy UCR definitions.
Source: FBI Uniform Crime Reports, 2016

Hate Crimes

Area	Number of Quarters Reported	Race/Ethnicity/ Ancestry	Religion	Sexual Orientation	Disability	Gender	Gender Identity
		Number of Incidents per Bias Motivation					
City	4	0	0	0	0	0	0
U.S.	4	3,489	1,273	1,076	70	31	124

Source: Federal Bureau of Investigation, Hate Crime Statistics 2016

Identity Theft Consumer Reports

Area	Reports	Reports per 100,000 Population	Rank[2]
MSA[1]	65	36	383
U.S.	371,061	114	-

Note: (1) Figures cover the Blacksburg-Christiansburg-Radford, VA Metropolitan Statistical Area—see Appendix B for areas included; (2) Rank ranges from 1 to 389 where 1 indicates greatest number of identity theft reports per 100,000 population
Source: Federal Trade Commission, Consumer Sentinel Network Data Book for January–December 2017

Fraud and Other Consumer Reports

Area	Reports	Reports per 100,000 Population	Rank[2]
MSA[1]	583	319	348
U.S.	2,304,550	708	-

Note: (1) Figures cover the Blacksburg-Christiansburg-Radford, VA Metropolitan Statistical Area—see Appendix B for areas included; (2) Rank ranges from 1 to 389 where 1 indicates greatest number of fraud and other consumer reports per 100,000 population
Source: Federal Trade Commission, Consumer Sentinel Network Data Book for January–December 2017

SPORTS

Professional Sports Teams

Team Name	League	Year Established

No teams are located in the metro area
Source: Wikipedia, Major Professional Sports Teams of the United States and Canada, April 5, 2018

CLIMATE

Average and Extreme Temperatures

Temperature	Jan	Feb	Mar	Apr	May	Jun	Jul	Aug	Sep	Oct	Nov	Dec	Yr.
Extreme High (°F)	78	80	87	95	96	100	104	105	101	93	83	76	105
Average High (°F)	45	48	57	68	76	84	87	86	79	69	57	48	67
Average Temp. (°F)	36	39	46	56	65	72	77	75	68	57	47	39	57
Average Low (°F)	27	28	35	45	53	61	65	64	57	46	37	29	46
Extreme Low (°F)	-11	1	9	20	31	39	47	42	34	22	9	-4	-11

Note: Figures cover the years 1948-1995
Source: National Climatic Data Center, International Station Meteorological Climate Summary, 9/96

Average Precipitation/Snowfall/Humidity

Precip./Humidity	Jan	Feb	Mar	Apr	May	Jun	Jul	Aug	Sep	Oct	Nov	Dec	Yr.
Avg. Precip. (in.)	2.9	3.2	3.7	3.3	3.9	3.5	3.8	4.0	3.3	3.4	3.0	3.1	40.8
Avg. Snowfall (in.)	6	7	4	Tr	Tr	0	0	0	0	Tr	1	4	23
Avg. Rel. Hum. 7am (%)	70	70	70	71	79	81	83	86	88	83	75	72	77
Avg. Rel. Hum. 4pm (%)	51	48	45	44	51	53	54	54	54	49	50	52	51

Note: Figures cover the years 1948-1995; Tr = Trace amounts (<0.05 in. of rain; <0.5 in. of snow)
Source: National Climatic Data Center, International Station Meteorological Climate Summary, 9/96

Weather Conditions

Temperature			Daytime Sky			Precipitation		
10°F & below	32°F & below	90°F & above	Clear	Partly cloudy	Cloudy	0.01 inch or more precip.	0.1 inch or more snow/ice	Thunder-storms
4	89	31	90	152	123	119	11	35

Note: Figures are average number of days per year and cover the years 1948-1995
Source: National Climatic Data Center, International Station Meteorological Climate Summary, 9/96

HAZARDOUS WASTE

Superfund Sites

The Blacksburg-Christiansburg-Radford, VA metro area has no sites on the EPA's Superfund Final National Priorities List. There are a total of 1,396 Superfund sites with a status of proposed or final on the list in the U.S. *U.S. Environmental Protection Agency, National Priorities List, April 4, 2018*

AIR & WATER QUALITY

Air Quality Trends: Ozone

	1990	1995	2000	2005	2010	2012	2013	2014	2015	2016
MSA[1]	n/a	n/a	n/a	n/a	n/a	n/a	n/a	n/a	n/a	n/a
U.S.	0.087	0.089	0.081	0.079	0.073	0.075	0.069	0.067	0.068	0.069

Note: (1) Data covers the Blacksburg-Christiansburg-Radford, VA Metropolitan Statistical Area—see Appendix B for areas included; n/a not available. The values shown are the composite ozone concentration averages among trend sites based on the highest fourth daily maximum 8-hour concentration in parts per million. These trends are based on sites having an adequate record of monitoring data during the trend period. Data from exceptional events are included.
Source: U.S. Environmental Protection Agency, Air Quality Monitoring Information, "Air Quality Trends by City, 1990-2016"

Air Quality Index

Area	Percent of Days when Air Quality was...[2]					AQI Statistics[2]	
	Good	Moderate	Unhealthy for Sensitive Groups	Unhealthy	Very Unhealthy	Maximum	Median
MSA[1]	59.2	20.8	12.6	7.4	0.0	200	44

Note: (1) Data covers the Blacksburg-Christiansburg-Radford, VA Metropolitan Statistical Area—see Appendix B for areas included; (2) Based on 365 days with AQI data in 2017. Air Quality Index (AQI) is an index for reporting daily air quality. EPA calculates the AQI for five major air pollutants regulated by the Clean Air Act: ground-level ozone, particle pollution (aka particulate matter), carbon monoxide, sulfur dioxide, and nitrogen dioxide. The AQI runs from 0 to 500. The higher the AQI value, the greater the level of air pollution and the greater the health concern. There are six AQI categories: "Good" AQI is between 0 and 50. Air quality is considered satisfactory; "Moderate" AQI is between 51 and 100. Air quality is acceptable; "Unhealthy for Sensitive Groups" When AQI values are between 101 and 150, members of sensitive groups may experience health effects; "Unhealthy" When AQI values are between 151 and 200 everyone may begin to experience health effects; "Very Unhealthy" AQI values between 201 and 300 trigger a health alert; "Hazardous" AQI values over 300 trigger warnings of emergency conditions (not shown).
Source: U.S. Environmental Protection Agency, Air Quality Index Report, 2017

Air Quality Index Pollutants

Area	Percent of Days when AQI Pollutant was...[2]					
	Carbon Monoxide	Nitrogen Dioxide	Ozone	Sulfur Dioxide	Particulate Matter 2.5	Particulate Matter 10
MSA[1]	0.0	0.0	54.8	45.2	0.0	0.0

Note: (1) Data covers the Blacksburg-Christiansburg-Radford, VA Metropolitan Statistical Area—see Appendix B for areas included; (2) Based on 365 days with AQI data in 2017. The Air Quality Index (AQI) is an index for reporting daily air quality. EPA calculates the AQI for five major air pollutants regulated by the Clean Air Act: ground-level ozone, particle pollution (also known as particulate matter), carbon monoxide, sulfur dioxide, and nitrogen dioxide. The AQI runs from 0 to 500. The higher the AQI value, the greater the level of air pollution and the greater the health concern.
Source: U.S. Environmental Protection Agency, Air Quality Index Report, 2017

Maximum Air Pollutant Concentrations: Particulate Matter, Ozone, CO and Lead

	Particulate Matter 10 (ug/m^3)	Particulate Matter 2.5 Wtd AM (ug/m^3)	Particulate Matter 2.5 24-Hr (ug/m^3)	Ozone (ppm)	Carbon Monoxide (ppm)	Lead (ug/m^3)
MSA[1] Level	n/a	n/a	n/a	0.064	n/a	n/a
NAAQS[2]	150	15	35	0.075	9	0.15
Met NAAQS[2]	n/a	n/a	n/a	Yes	n/a	n/a

Note: (1) Data covers the Blacksburg-Christiansburg-Radford, VA Metropolitan Statistical Area—see Appendix B for areas included; Data from exceptional events are included; (2) National Ambient Air Quality Standards; ppm = parts per million; ug/m^3 = micrograms per cubic meter; n/a not available.
Concentrations: Particulate Matter 10 (coarse particulate)—highest second maximum 24-hour concentration; Particulate Matter 2.5 Wtd AM (fine particulate)—highest weighted annual mean concentration; Particulate Matter 2.5 24-Hour (fine particulate)—highest 98th percentile 24-hour concentration; Ozone—highest fourth daily maximum 8-hour concentration; Carbon Monoxide—highest second maximum non-overlapping 8-hour concentration; Lead—maximum running 3-month average
Source: U.S. Environmental Protection Agency, Air Quality Monitoring Information, "Air Quality Statistics by City, 2016"

Maximum Air Pollutant Concentrations: Nitrogen Dioxide and Sulfur Dioxide

	Nitrogen Dioxide AM (ppb)	Nitrogen Dioxide 1-Hr (ppb)	Sulfur Dioxide AM (ppb)	Sulfur Dioxide 1-Hr (ppb)	Sulfur Dioxide 24-Hr (ppb)
MSA[1] Level	n/a	n/a	n/a	n/a	n/a
NAAQS[2]	53	100	30	75	140
Met NAAQS[2]	n/a	n/a	n/a	n/a	n/a

Note: (1) Data covers the Blacksburg-Christiansburg-Radford, VA Metropolitan Statistical Area—see Appendix B for areas included; Data from exceptional events are included; (2) National Ambient Air Quality Standards; ppm = parts per million; ug/m^3 = micrograms per cubic meter; n/a not available.
Concentrations: Nitrogen Dioxide AM—highest arithmetic mean concentration; Nitrogen Dioxide 1-Hr—highest 98th percentile 1-hour daily maximum concentration; Sulfur Dioxide AM—highest annual mean concentration; Sulfur Dioxide 1-Hr—highest 99th percentile 1-hour daily maximum concentration; Sulfur Dioxide 24-Hr—highest second maximum 24-hour concentration
Source: U.S. Environmental Protection Agency, Air Quality Monitoring Information, "Air Quality Statistics by City, 2016"

Drinking Water

Water System Name	Pop. Served	Primary Water Source Type	Violations[1]	
			Health Based	Monitoring/ Reporting
Town of Blacksburg	34,578	Purchased Surface	0	0

Note: (1) Based on violation data from January 1, 2017 to December 31, 2017
Source: U.S. Environmental Protection Agency, Office of Ground Water and Drinking Water, Safe Drinking Water Information System (based on data extracted April 5, 2018)

Leesburg, Virginia

Background

Leesburg, located 35 miles northwest of Washington, DC, was established in 1758, and is the government seat of Loudon County. Home to Leesburg Executive Airport (Godrey Field), it is also within 15 miles of Washington Dulles International Airport. Set in Virginia's Piedmont Region, between the Potomac River and the Blue Ridge Mountain foothills, the original Leesburg settlement was named George Town, to honor Britain's George II. It was later renamed for the area's prominent Lee family, in particular Thomas Lee, who served as Virginia's governor in 1749.

Leesburg played a role in both the French and Indian War and the Revolutionary War. It served as temporary capital of the nation during the War of 1812, and it was the site of the Battle of Ball's Bluff during the Civil War. The town's historic district has been placed on the National Register of Historic Places as one of Virginia's most picturesque downtown areas. Visitors can explore the town's rich history at The Loudon Museum or Thomas Balch Library and visit the national cemetery at the Ball's Bluff Battlefield.

In recent years, growth in the city has been rapid, in part due to the Dulles Greenway Toll Road, which has cut down traveling time to the District of Columbia and Dulles Airport. Major employers in Loudon County include the County itself and the Federal Aviation Administration.

Nearby Washington, DC offers a multitude of attractions, most notably the White House, Capitol Building, Washington Monument, the National Gallery of Art, and the Smithsonian Institute museums, which include the National Air & Space Museum and the Steven F. Udvar-Hazy Center near Dulles International Airport that showcases the history of aviation and space flight. Activities available in Leesburg include the Leesburg Flower & Garden Festival, the Bluemont Concert Series, the Waterford Homes Tour & Crafts Exhibit and the Holidays in Leesburg Fine Arts & Crafts Show.

The Leesburg Parks and Recreation Department operates 16 public parks with more than 250 acres of land. The largest is Ida Lee Park, with a full service recreation center including two indoor pools, spa, gym, weight room and child care center.

The Leesburg area hosts the George Washington University's Virginia campus, Marymount University's Loudon Center, Northern Virginia Community College, the School of Islamic and Social Sciences, Shenandoah University's Loudon campus and Strayer University.

The weather in Leesburg is typical of northern Virginia: moderately cold winters, pleasant springs, and long summers. Temperatures average about freezing in January; snowfall is moderate and large snowstorms are rare. The long summer shades gradually into fall, with summer-like weather lasting well into October.

Rankings

General Rankings

- *US News & World Report* conducted a survey of more than 2,000 people and analyzed the 125 largest metropolitan areas to determine what matters the most when selecting the next place to live. Washington* ranked #8 out of the top 25 as having the best combination of desirable factors. Criteria: cost of living; quality of education; job market, crime rates; and other factors. *realestate.usnews.com, "The 25 Best Places to Live in the U.S. in 2018," April 10, 2018*

Business/Finance Rankings

- According to *Business Insider*, the Washington* metro area is where startup growth is on the rise. Based on the 2017 Kauffman Index of Growth Entrepreneurship, which measured in-depth national entrepreneurial trends in 40 metro areas, it ranked #1 in highest startup growth. *www.businessinsider.com, "The 21 U.S. Cities with the Highest Startup Growth," October 21, 2017*

- The personal finance site NerdWallet analyzed 183 American metropolitan areas with populations over 250,000 and more than 15,000 businesses to rank where entrepreneurs find the most success. Criteria included area economy, annual income, housing cost, unemployment rate, and the success rate of area businesses. Washington* ranked #81. *www.nerdwallet.com, "Best Places to Start a Business," April 27, 2015*

- 24/7 Wall Street used Brookings Institution research on 50 advanced industries to identify the proportion of workers in the nation's largest metropolitan areas that were employed in jobs requiring knowledge in the science, technology, engineering, or math (STEM) fields and where there was heavy investment in research and development (R&D). The Washington* metro area was #7. *247wallst.com, "15 Cities with the Most High-Tech Jobs," February 23, 2017*

- Based on metro area social media reviews, the employment opinion group Glassdoor surveyed 50 of the largest U.S. metro areas and equally weighed cost of living, hiring opportunity, and job satisfaction to compose a list of "25 Best Cities for Jobs." Median pay and home value, in-demand jobs and number of current job openings was also factored in. The Washington* metro area was ranked #16 in overall job satisfaction. *www.glassdoor.com, "Best Cities for Jobs," September 12, 2017*

- In a survey of economic confidence in the nation's 50 largest metropolitan areas conducted January–December 2014, the Washington* metro area placed #3, according to Gallup's 2014 Economic Confidence Index. *Gallup, "San Jose and San Francisco Lead in Economic Confidence," March 19, 2015*

- The Brookings Institution ranked the 100 largest metro areas in the U.S. based on income inequality. Washington* was ranked #70 (#1 = greatest ineqality). Criteria: the "95/20 ratio," a figure representing the income at which a household earns more than 95 percent of all other households, divided by the income at which a household earns more than only 20 percent of all other households. *Brookings Institution, "Household Income Inequality, 100 Largest U.S. Metro Areas, 2014-2016," February 5, 2018*

- *Forbes* ranked the 100 largest metro areas in the U.S. in terms of the "Best Cities for Young Professionals." The Washington* metro area ranked #7 out of 25. (Large metro areas were divided into metro divisions.) Criteria: median rent of a two-bedroom apartment; job growth and unemployment rate; median salary of college graduates with 5 or less years of work experience; networking opportunities; social outlook; percentage of population 25 years of age and older with college degrees. *Forbes.com, "America's 25 Best Cities for Young Professionals in 2017," May 22, 2017*

- Payscale.com ranked the largest metro areas in terms of wage growth. The Washington* metro area ranked #11. Criteria: private-sector wage growth between the 4th quarter of 2016 and the 4th quarter of 2017. *PayScale, "Wage Trends by Metro Area-4th Quarter," January 17, 2018*

- The Washington* metro area was identified as one of the most debt-ridden places in America by the finance site Credit.com. The metro area was ranked #1. Criteria: residents' average credit card debt as well as median income. *Credit.com, "25 Cities With the Most Credit Card Debt," February 28, 2018*
- Washington* was identified as one of America's most frugal metro areas by *Coupons.com.* The city ranked #1 out of 25. Criteria: digital coupon usage. *Coupons.com, "America's Most Frugal Cities of 2017," March 22, 2018*
- Washington* was cited as one of America's top metros for new and expanded facility projects in 2017. The area ranked #8 in the large metro area category (population over 1 million). *Site Selection, "Top Metropolitans of 2017," March 2018*
- The Washington* metro area appeared on the Milken Institute "2017 Best Performing Cities" list. Rank: #118 out of 200 large metro areas. Criteria: job growth; wage and salary growth; high-tech output growth. *Milken Institute, "Best-Performing Cities 2017," January 2018*
- *Forbes* ranked the 200 most populous metro areas to determine the nation's "Best Places for Business and Careers." The Washington* metro area was ranked #57. Criteria: costs (business and living); job growth (past and projected); income growth; quality of life; educational attainment (college and high school); projected economic growth; cultural and recreational opportunities; net migration patterns; number of highly ranked colleges. *Forbes, "The Best Places for Business and Careers 2017," October 24, 2017*

Dating/Romance Rankings

- *Apartment List* conducted its annual survey of renters to compile a list of metros that have the best opportunities for dating. Nearly 11,000 respondents, from February 2017 through January 2018, rated their current city or neighborhood for opportunities to date and make friends. The Washington* metro area ranked #5 out of 70 where single residents were very satisfied or somewhat satisfied, making it among the ten best metros for dating opportunities. Other criteria analyzed included gender and education levels of renters. *Apartment List, "Best Metros for Dating 2018," February 6, 2018*

Education Rankings

- Washington* was identified as one of America's "smartest" metropolitan areas by *The Business Journals*. The area ranked #1 out of 10. Criteria: percentage of adults (25 and older) with high school diplomas, bachelor's degrees and graduate degrees. *The Business Journals, "Where the Brainpower Is: Exclusive U.S. Rankings, Insights," February 27, 2014*
- Personal finance website *WalletHub* analyzed the 150 largest U.S. metropolitan statistical areas to determine where the most educated Americans are choosing to settle. Criteria: education quality and attainment gap; education levels; percentage of workers with degrees; public school rankings; quality and size of each metro area's universities. Washington* was ranked #2 (#1 = most educated city). *www.WalletHub.com, "2017's Most and Least Educated Cities in America, " July 25, 2017*

Environmental Rankings

- Sperling's BestPlaces assessed 379 metropolitan areas of the United States for the likelihood of dangerously extreme weather events or earthquakes. In general the Southeast and South-Central regions have the highest risk of weather extremes and earthquakes, while the Pacific Northwest enjoys the lowest risk. Of the least risky metropolitan areas, the Washington* metro area was ranked #212. *www.bestplaces.net, "Safest Places from Natural Disasters," April 2011*
- The U.S. Environmental Protection Agency (EPA) released a list of U.S. metropolitan areas with the most ENERGY STAR certified buildings in 2016. The Washington* metro area was ranked #1 out of 25. *U.S. Environmental Protection Agency, "2017 Energy Star Top Cities," June 2017*

Health/Fitness Rankings

- Analysts who tracked obesity rates in the nation's largest metro areas (populations above one million) found that the Washington* metro area was one of the ten major metros where residents were least likely to be obese, defined as a BMI score of 30 or above. *www.gallup.com, "Boulder, Colo., Residents Still Least Likely to Be Obese," April 4, 2014*
- For each of the 50 most populous metro areas in the United States, the American College of Sports Medicine's American Fitness Index evaluated infrastructure, community assets, and policies that encourage healthy and fit lifestyles, including preventive health behaviors, levels of chronic disease conditions, health care access, and community resources and policies that support physical activity. The Washington* metro area ranked #2 for "community fitness." *www.americanfitnessindex.org, "ACSM American Fitness Index Health and Community Fitness Status of the 50 Largest Metropolitan Areas," May 2017*
- The Washington* metro area was identified as one of the worst cities for bed bugs in America by pest control company Orkin. The area ranked #2 out of 50 based on the number of bed bug treatments Orkin performed from December 2016 to November 2017. *Orkin, "Baltimore and Washington D.C. Continue to Hold Top Spots," January 8, 2018*
- Washington* was identified as a "2016 Spring Allergy Capital." The area ranked #84 out of 100. Three groups of factors were used to identify the most severe cities for people with allergies during the spring season: annual pollen levels; medicine utilization; access to board-certified allergists. *Asthma and Allergy Foundation of America, "Spring Allergy Capitals 2016"*
- Washington* was identified as a "2016 Fall Allergy Capital." The area ranked #87 out of 100. Three groups of factors were used to identify the most severe cities for people with allergies during the fall season: annual pollen levels; medicine utilization; access to board-certified allergists. *Asthma and Allergy Foundation of America, "Fall Allergy Capitals 2016"*
- Washington* was identified as a "2015 Asthma Capital." The area ranked #48 out of the nation's 100 largest metropolitan areas. Criteria: estimated prevalence; self-reported prevalence; crude death rate for asthma; annual pollen score; annual air quality; public smoking laws; number of board-certified asthma specialists; school inhaler access laws; rescue medication use; controller medication use; ER visits for asthma; uninsured rate; poverty rate. *Asthma and Allergy Foundation of America, "Asthma Capitals 2015"*
- The Washington* metro area ranked #36 out of 189 in The Gallup-Healthways Well-Being Index. Criteria: purpose; social well being; financial health; community and physical health. Results are based on telephone interviews with adults, aged 18 and older, living in metropolitan areas in the 50 U.S. states and the District of Columbia. *Gallup-Healthways, "State of American Well-Being, 2017 Community Well-Being Rankings" March 2018*

Real Estate Rankings

- FitSmallBusiness looked at 50 of the largest metropolitan areas in the U.S. to determine which metro was the best to start a real estate business. Data was compiled from such sources as: Zillow, Trulia, U.S. Census Bureau, and the Bureau of Labor Statistics. Criteria: location; inventory; annual wages; median sales price of homes; days on the market; median price cut percentage; and other factors that would influence real estate professional growth. The Washington* metro area ranked #5. *fitsmallbusiness.com, "The Best Cities to Become a Real Estate Agent in 2018," January 30, 2018*
- The Washington* metro area was identified as one of the top 20 housing markets to invest in for 2018 by *Forbes*. The area ranked #17. Criteria: strong job and population growth; anticipated home price appreciation; and other factors. *Forbes.com, "Where to Invest in Housing in 2018," February 1, 2018*
- Washington* was ranked #128 out of 238 metro areas in terms of housing affordability in 2017 by the National Association of Home Builders (#1 = most affordable). Criteria: the share of homes sold in that area affordable to a family earning the local median income, based on standard mortgage underwriting criteria. *National Association of Home Builders®, NAHB-Wells Fargo Housing Opportunity Index, 4th Quarter 2017*

Safety Rankings

- The National Insurance Crime Bureau ranked 382 metro areas in the U.S. in terms of per capita rates of vehicle theft. The Washington* metro area ranked #174 (#1 = highest rate). Criteria: number of vehicle theft offenses per 100,000 inhabitants in 2016. *National Insurance Crime Bureau, "Hot Spots 2016," June 8, 2017*

Seniors/Retirement Rankings

- Leesburg made *Southern Living's* list of charming and unique southern places to retire or dream of retiring to. The favorite places focused on the following: presence of unique amenities; opportunities to volunteer; low cost of living; continued learning opportunities; stable housing market; access to medical care; availability of part-time work; and ease of travel. *Southern Living, "Best Places to Retire"*
- From its Best Cities for Successful Aging indexes, the Milken Institute generated rankings for metropolitan areas, weighing data in nine categories—health care, wellness, living arrangements, transportation and convenience, financial characteristics, education, employment, community engagement, and overall livability. The Washington* metro area was ranked #19 overall in the large metro area category. *Milken Institute, "Best Cities for Successful Aging, 2017" March 14, 2017*

Sports/Recreation Rankings

- According to the personal finance website NerdWallet, the Washington* metro area, at #12, is one of the nation's top dozen metro areas for sports fans. Criteria included the presence of all four major sports—MLB, NFL, NHL, and NBA, fan enthusiasm (as measured by game attendance), ticket affordability, and "sports culture," that is, number of sports bars. *www.nerdwallet.com, "Best Cities for Sports Fans," May 5, 2013*

Transportation Rankings

- Washington* was identified as one of the most congested metro areas in the U.S. The area ranked #1 out of 10. Criteria: yearly delay per auto commuter in hours. *Texas A&M Transportation Institute, "2015 Urban Mobility Scorecard," August 2015*
- The Washington* metro area appeared on *Forbes* list of places with the most extreme commutes. The metro area ranked #3 out of 10. Criteria: average travel time; percentage of mega commuters. Mega-commuters travel more than 90 minutes and 50 miles each way to work. *Forbes.com, "The Cities with the Most Extreme Commutes," March 5, 2013*

Miscellaneous Rankings

- The watchdog site Charity Navigator conducts an annual study of charities in the nation's major markets both to analyze statistical differences in their financial, accountability, and transparency practices and to track year-to-year variations in individual philanthropic communities. Charity Navigator's analysis demonstrated that the financial, accountability and transparency behaviors of America's largest charities can be influenced by the metropolitan market within which the charity operates. The Washington* metro area was ranked #24 among the 30 metro markets in the rating category of Overall Score. *www.charitynavigator.org, "2017 Metro Market Study," May 1, 2017*
- The finance and lifestyle site NerdWallet looked for the U.S. cities that topped the list in donating money and time to good causes. The Washington* metro area proved to be the #17-ranked metro area, judged by culture of volunteerism, depth of commitment in terms of volunteer hours per year, and monetary contributions. *www.nerdwallet.com, "Most Generous Cities," September 22, 2013*

- The Harris Poll's Happiness Index survey revealed that of the top ten U.S. markets, the Washington* metro area residents ranked #7 in happiness. Criteria included strong assent to positive statements and strong disagreement with negative ones, and degree of agreement with a series of statements about respondents' personal relationships and general outlook. *www.theharrispoll.com, "Dallas/Fort Worth Is "Happiest" City among America's Top Ten Markets," September 4, 2013*

- Energizer Personal Care, the makers of Edge® shave gel, in partnership with Sperling's BestPlaces, ranked 50 major metro areas in terms of everyday irritations. The Washington* metro area ranked #9 the 50 metro area most irritating to guys. Criteria: high male-to-female ratio; poor sports team performance and high ticket prices; slow traffic; lack of job availability; unaffordable housing; extreme weather; lack of nightlife and fitness options. *Energizer Personal Care, "Most Irritating Cities for Guys," August 26, 2013*

- The National Alliance to End Homelessness listed the 25 most populous metro areas with the highest rate of homelessness. The Washington* metro area had a high rate of homelessness. Criteria: number of homeless people per 10,000 population in 2016. *National Alliance to End Homelessness, "Homelessness in the 25 Most Populous U.S. Metro Areas," September 1, 2017*

*Leesburg is located within the Washington-Arlington-Alexandria, DC-VA-MD-WV Metropolitan Statistical Area and the Washington-Arlington-Alexandria, DC-VA-MD-WV Metropolitan Division.

Business Environment

CITY FINANCES

City Government Finances

Component	2015 ($000)	2015 ($ per capita)
Total Revenues	63,946	1,249
Total Expenditures	68,646	1,341
Debt Outstanding	135,882	2,653
Cash and Securities[1]	62,584	1,222

Note: (1) Cash and security holdings of a government at the close of its fiscal year,, including those of its dependent agencies, utilities, and liquor stores.
Source: U.S Census Bureau, State & Local Government Finances 2015

City Government Revenue by Source

Source	2015 ($000)	2015 ($ per capita)	2015 (%)
General Revenue			
From Federal Government	48	1	0.1
From State Government	13,429	262	21.0
From Local Governments	0	0	0.0
Taxes			
Property	13,569	265	21.2
Sales and Gross Receipts	8,746	171	13.7
Personal Income	0	0	0.0
Corporate Income	0	0	0.0
Motor Vehicle License	843	16	1.3
Other Taxes	4,240	83	6.6
Current Charges	5,117	100	8.0
Liquor Store	0	0	0.0
Utility	15,620	305	24.4
Employee Retirement	0	0	0.0

Source: U.S Census Bureau, State & Local Government Finances 2015

City Government Expenditures by Function

Function	2015 ($000)	2015 ($ per capita)	2015 (%)
General Direct Expenditures			
Air Transportation	660	12	1.0
Corrections	0	0	0.0
Education	0	0	0.0
Employment Security Administration	0	0	0.0
Financial Administration	4,460	87	6.5
Fire Protection	645	12	0.9
General Public Buildings	1,104	21	1.6
Governmental Administration, Other	2,774	54	4.0
Health	0	0	0.0
Highways	0	0	0.0
Hospitals	0	0	0.0
Housing and Community Development	0	0	0.0
Interest on General Debt	4,824	94	7.0
Judicial and Legal	0	0	0.0
Libraries	451	8	0.7
Parking	0	0	0.0
Parks and Recreation	8,061	157	11.7
Police Protection	13,488	263	19.6
Public Welfare	0	0	0.0
Sewerage	6,539	127	9.5
Solid Waste Management	2,542	49	3.7
Veterans' Services	0	0	0.0
Liquor Store	0	0	0.0
Utility	14,780	288	21.5
Employee Retirement	0	0	0.0

Source: U.S Census Bureau, State & Local Government Finances 2015

DEMOGRAPHICS

Population Growth

Area	1990 Census	2000 Census	2010 Census	2016* Estimate	Population Growth (%)	
					1990-2016	2010-2016
City	16,240	28,311	42,616	49,401	204.2	15.9
MSA[1]	4,122,914	4,796,183	5,582,170	6,011,752	45.8	7.7
U.S.	248,709,873	281,421,906	308,745,538	318,558,162	28.1	3.2

Note: (1) Figures cover the Washington-Arlington-Alexandria, DC-VA-MD-WV Metropolitan Statistical Area—see Appendix B for areas included; (*) 2012-2016 5-year estimated population
Source: U.S. Census Bureau, 1990 Census, Census 2000, Census 2010, 2012-2016 American Community Survey 5-Year Estimates

Household Size

Area	Persons in Household (%)							Average Household Size
	One	Two	Three	Four	Five	Six	Seven or More	
City	19.1	28.0	19.3	18.9	9.4	3.9	1.4	3.00
MSA[1]	27.0	30.5	16.8	14.8	6.6	2.7	1.6	2.70
U.S.	27.7	33.7	15.7	13.1	6.0	2.3	1.5	2.60

Note: (1) Figures cover the Washington-Arlington-Alexandria, DC-VA-MD-WV Metropolitan Statistical Area—see Appendix B for areas included
Source: U.S. Census Bureau, 2012-2016 American Community Survey 5-Year Estimates

Race

Area	White Alone[2] (%)	Black Alone[2] (%)	Asian Alone[2] (%)	AIAN[3] Alone[2] (%)	NHOPI[4] Alone[2] (%)	Other Race Alone[2] (%)	Two or More Races (%)
City	74.3	8.0	9.1	0.1	0.3	5.0	3.2
MSA[1]	55.1	25.4	9.8	0.3	0.1	5.5	3.9
U.S.	73.3	12.6	5.2	0.8	0.2	4.8	3.1

Note: (1) Figures cover the Washington-Arlington-Alexandria, DC-VA-MD-WV Metropolitan Statistical Area—see Appendix B for areas included; (2) Alone is defined as not being in combination with one or more other races; (3) American Indian and Alaska Native; (4) Native Hawaiian and Other Pacific Islander
Source: U.S. Census Bureau, 2012-2016 American Community Survey 5-Year Estimates

Hispanic or Latino Origin

Area	Total (%)	Mexican (%)	Puerto Rican (%)	Cuban (%)	Other (%)
City	16.8	2.2	1.6	0.1	13.0
MSA[1]	14.9	2.2	1.0	0.3	11.4
U.S.	17.3	11.0	1.7	0.7	4.0

Note: Persons of Hispanic or Latino origin can be of any race; (1) Figures cover the Washington-Arlington-Alexandria, DC-VA-MD-WV Metropolitan Statistical Area—see Appendix B for areas included
Source: U.S. Census Bureau, 2012-2016 American Community Survey 5-Year Estimates

Segregation

Type	Segregation Indices[1]				Percent Change		
	1990	2000	2010	2010 Rank[2]	1990-2000	1990-2010	2000-2010
Black/White	65.5	63.8	62.3	32	-1.7	-3.2	-1.5
Asian/White	34.5	38.7	38.9	64	4.2	4.4	0.2
Hispanic/White	41.8	47.4	48.3	32	5.6	6.5	0.9

Note: All figures cover the Metropolitan Statistical Area—see Appendix B for areas included; Figures are based on an analysis of 1990, 2000, and 2010 Census Decennial Census tract data by William H. Frey, Brookings Institution and the University of Michigan Social Science Data Analysis Network. In this analysis all racial groups (whites, blacks, and asians) are non-Hispanic members of those races. Hispanics are shown as a separate category; (1) Segregation Indices are Dissimilarity Indices that measure the degree to which the minority group is distributed differently than whites across census tracts. They range from 0 (complete integration) to 100 (complete segregation) where the value indicates the percentage of the minority group that needs to move to be distributed exactly like whites; (2) Ranges from 1 (most segregated) to 102 (least segregated); n/a not available.
Source: www.CensusScope.org

Ancestry

Area	German	Irish	English	American	Italian	Polish	French[2]	Scottish	Dutch
City	13.8	9.6	10.1	5.8	7.0	2.5	3.1	2.7	1.4
MSA[1]	10.3	9.0	7.2	4.5	4.5	2.3	1.7	1.7	0.8
U.S.	14.4	10.4	7.7	6.9	5.4	2.9	2.6	1.7	1.3

Note: Figures are the percentage of the total population reporting a particular ancestry. The nine most commonly reported ancestries in the U.S. are shown. Figures include multiple ancestries (e.g. if a person reported being Irish and Italian, they were included in both columns); (1) Figures cover the Washington-Arlington-Alexandria, DC-VA-MD-WV Metropolitan Statistical Area—see Appendix B for areas included; (2) Excludes Basque
Source: U.S. Census Bureau, 2012-2016 American Community Survey 5-Year Estimates

Foreign-Born Population

Area	Percent of Population Born in								
	Any Foreign Country	Asia	Mexico	Europe	Carribean	Central America[2]	South America	Africa	Canada
City	22.0	8.9	0.9	2.4	0.2	5.8	1.6	1.7	0.3
MSA[1]	22.3	8.0	0.8	1.9	1.1	4.8	2.2	3.2	0.2
U.S.	13.2	4.0	3.6	1.5	1.3	1.0	0.9	0.6	0.3

Note: (1) Figures cover the Washington-Arlington-Alexandria, DC-VA-MD-WV Metropolitan Statistical Area—see Appendix B for areas included; (2) Excludes Mexico.
Source: U.S. Census Bureau, 2012-2016 American Community Survey 5-Year Estimates

Marital Status

Area	Never Married	Now Married[2]	Separated	Widowed	Divorced
City	30.1	56.1	2.1	3.4	8.3
MSA[1]	36.1	48.5	2.1	4.3	8.9
U.S.	33.0	48.1	2.1	5.9	11.0

Note: Figures are percentages and cover the population 15 years of age and older; (1) Figures cover the Washington-Arlington-Alexandria, DC-VA-MD-WV Metropolitan Statistical Area—see Appendix B for areas included; (2) Excludes separated
Source: U.S. Census Bureau, 2012-2016 American Community Survey 5-Year Estimates

Disability Status

Area	All Ages	Under 18 Years Old	18 to 64 Years Old	65 Years and Over
City	6.8	2.9	5.5	35.7
MSA[1]	8.3	2.9	6.5	29.7
U.S.	12.5	4.1	10.3	35.7

Note: Figures show percent of the civilian noninstitutionalized population that reported having a disability. Disability status is determined from six types of difficulty: vision, hearing, cognitive, ambulatory, self-care, and independent living. For children under 5 years old, hearing and vision difficulty are used to determine disability status. For children between the ages of 5 and 14, disability status is determined from hearing, vision, cognitive, ambulatory, and self-care difficulties. For people aged 15 years and older, they are considered to have a disability if they have difficulty with any one of the six difficulty types; Note: (1) Figures cover the Washington-Arlington-Alexandria, DC-VA-MD-WV Metropolitan Statistical Area—see Appendix B for areas included
Source: U.S. Census Bureau, 2012-2016 American Community Survey 5-Year Estimates

Age

Area	Percent of Population									Median Age
	Under Age 5	Age 5–19	Age 20–34	Age 35–44	Age 45–54	Age 55–64	Age 65–74	Age 75–84	Age 85+	
City	6.7	24.0	19.9	15.9	17.0	9.1	4.1	2.1	1.2	34.6
MSA[1]	6.6	19.3	21.8	14.5	14.6	11.8	6.9	3.2	1.4	36.5
U.S.	6.2	19.6	20.7	12.7	13.6	12.6	8.3	4.3	1.9	37.7

Note: (1) Figures cover the Washington-Arlington-Alexandria, DC-VA-MD-WV Metropolitan Statistical Area—see Appendix B for areas included
Source: U.S. Census Bureau, 2012-2016 American Community Survey 5-Year Estimates

Gender

Area	Males	Females	Males per 100 Females
City	24,225	25,176	96.2
MSA[1]	2,934,987	3,076,765	95.4
U.S.	156,765,322	161,792,840	96.9

Note: (1) Figures cover the Washington-Arlington-Alexandria, DC-VA-MD-WV Metropolitan Statistical Area—see Appendix B for areas included
Source: U.S. Census Bureau, 2012-2016 American Community Survey 5-Year Estimates

Religious Groups by Family

Area	Catholic	Baptist	Non-Den.	Methodist[2]	Lutheran	LDS[3]	Pente-costal	Presby-terian[4]	Muslim[5]	Judaism
MSA[1]	14.5	7.3	4.9	4.5	1.3	1.2	1.1	1.4	2.4	1.2
U.S.	19.1	9.3	4.0	4.0	2.3	2.0	1.9	1.6	0.8	0.7

Note: Figures are the number of adherents as a percentage of the total population; (1) Figures cover the Washington-Arlington-Alexandria, DC-VA-MD-WV Metropolitan Statistical Area—see Appendix B for areas included; (2) Methodist/Pietist; (3) Latter Day Saints; (4) Reformed; (5) Figures are estimates
Source: Association of Statisticians of American Religious Bodies, 2010 U.S. Religion Census: Religious Congregations & Membership Study

Religious Groups by Tradition

Area	Catholic	Evangelical Protestant	Mainline Protestant	Other Tradition	Black Protestant	Orthodox
MSA[1]	14.5	12.4	8.8	5.9	2.3	0.6
U.S.	19.1	16.2	7.3	4.3	1.6	0.3

Note: Figures are the number of adherents as a percentage of the total population; (1) Figures cover the Washington-Arlington-Alexandria, DC-VA-MD-WV Metropolitan Statistical Area—see Appendix B for areas included
Source: Association of Statisticians of American Religious Bodies, 2010 U.S. Religion Census: Religious Congregations & Membership Study

ECONOMY

Gross Metropolitan Product

Area	2014	2015	2016	2017	Rank[2]
MSA[1]	470.5	489.8	506.6	531.3	6

Note: Figures are in billions of dollars; (1) Figures cover the Washington-Arlington-Alexandria, DC-VA-MD-WV Metropolitan Statistical Area—see Appendix B for areas included; (2) Rank is based on 2015 data and ranges from 1 to 381
Source: The U.S. Conference of Mayors, U.S. Metro Economies: GMP and Employment Report, 2015-2017

Economic Growth

Area	2012-14 (%)	2015 (%)	2016 (%)	2017 (%)	Rank[2]
MSA[1]	0.0	2.2	1.9	2.7	285
U.S.	2.0	2.4	1.9	2.6	–

Note: Figures are real gross metropolitan product (GMP) growth rates and represent average annual percent change; (1) Figures cover the Washington-Arlington-Alexandria, DC-VA-MD-WV Metropolitan Statistical Area—see Appendix B for areas included; (2) Rank is based on 2012-2014 average annual percent change and ranges from 1 to 381
Source: The U.S. Conference of Mayors, U.S. Metro Economies: GMP and Employment Report, 2015-2017

Metropolitan Area Exports

Area	2011	2012	2013	2014	2015	2016	Rank[2]
MSA[1]	10,237.9	14,609.7	16,225.0	13,053.6	13,900.4	13,582.4	22

Note: Figures are in millions of dollars; (1) Figures cover the Washington-Arlington-Alexandria, DC-VA-MD-WV Metropolitan Statistical Area—see Appendix B for areas included; (2) Rank is based on 2016 data and ranges from 1 to 385
Source: U.S. Department of Commerce, International Trade Administration, Office of Trade & Industry Information, Manufacturing & Services, data extracted March 15, 2018

Building Permits

Area	Single-Family			Multi-Family			Total		
	2016	2017p	Pct. Chg.	2016	2017p	Pct. Chg.	2016	2017p	Pct. Chg.
City	n/a	22	n/a	0	0	0.0	n/a	22	n/a
MSA[1]	12,974	13,968	7.7	11,970	12,461	4.1	24,944	26,429	6.0
U.S.	750,800	817,300	8.9	455,800	446,800	-2.0	1,206,600	1,264,100	4.8

Note: (1) Figures cover the Washington-Arlington-Alexandria, DC-VA-MD-WV Metropolitan Statistical Area—see Appendix B for areas included; Figures represent new, privately-owned housing units authorized (unadjusted data); All permit data are based on estimates with imputation; (p) preliminary data.
Source: U.S. Census Bureau, Manufacturing, Mining, and Construction Statistics, Building Permits, 2016, 2017

Bankruptcy Filings

Area	Business Filings			Nonbusiness Filings		
	2016	2017	% Chg.	2016	2017	% Chg.
Loudoun County	40	41	2.5	557	558	0.2
U.S.	24,114	23,157	-4.0	770,846	765,863	-0.6

Note: Business filings include Chapter 7, Chapter 11, Chapter 12, and Chapter 13; Nonbusiness filings include Chapter 7, Chapter 11, and Chapter 13
Source: Administrative Office of the U.S. Courts, Business and Nonbusiness Bankruptcy, County Cases Commenced by Chapter of the Bankruptcy Code, During the 12-Month Period Ending December 31, 2016 and Business and Nonbusiness Bankruptcy, County Cases Commenced by Chapter of the Bankruptcy Code, During the 12-Month Period Ending December 31, 2017

Housing Vacancy Rates

Area	Gross Vacancy Rate[2] (%)			Year-Round Vacancy Rate[3] (%)			Rental Vacancy Rate[4] (%)			Homeowner Vacancy Rate[5] (%)		
	2015	2016	2017	2015	2016	2017	2015	2016	2017	2015	2016	2017
MSA[1]	7.7	8.2	7.4	7.4	7.9	7.1	5.7	6.0	6.2	0.9	1.7	1.2
U.S.	12.9	12.8	12.7	10.0	9.9	9.9	7.1	6.9	7.2	1.8	1.7	1.6

Note: (1) Figures cover the Washington-Arlington-Alexandria, DC-VA-MD-WV Metropolitan Statistical Area—see Appendix B for areas included; (2) The percentage of the total housing inventory that is vacant; (3) The percentage of the housing inventory (excluding seasonal units) that is year-round vacant; (4) The percentage of rental inventory that is vacant for rent; (5) The percentage of homeowner inventory that is vacant for sale
Source: U.S. Census Bureau, Housing Vacancies and Homeownership Annual Statistics: 2015, 2016, 2017

INCOME

Income

Area	Per Capita ($)	Median Household ($)	Average Household ($)
City	41,184	102,132	121,286
MSA[1]	44,862	93,804	121,079
U.S.	29,829	55,322	77,866

Note: (1) Figures cover the Washington-Arlington-Alexandria, DC-VA-MD-WV Metropolitan Statistical Area—see Appendix B for areas included
Source: U.S. Census Bureau, 2012-2016 American Community Survey 5-Year Estimates

Household Income Distribution

Area	Percent of Households Earning							
	Under $15,000	$15,000 -$24,999	$25,000 -$34,999	$35,000 -$49,999	$50,000 -$74,999	$75,000 -$99,999	$100,000 -$149,999	$150,000 and up
City	2.9	4.0	5.3	9.6	14.7	12.4	22.3	28.8
MSA[1]	6.4	4.8	5.4	8.5	15.0	12.9	20.1	26.9
U.S.	12.1	10.2	9.9	13.2	17.8	12.2	13.5	11.1

Note: (1) Figures cover the Washington-Arlington-Alexandria, DC-VA-MD-WV Metropolitan Statistical Area—see Appendix B for areas included
Source: U.S. Census Bureau, 2012-2016 American Community Survey 5-Year Estimates

Poverty Rate

Area	All Ages	Under 18 Years Old	18 to 64 Years Old	65 Years and Over
City	5.7	6.0	5.4	6.8
MSA[1]	8.4	10.8	7.8	7.2
U.S.	15.1	21.2	14.2	9.3

Note: Figures are percentage of people whose income during the past 12 months was below the poverty level; (1) Figures cover the Washington-Arlington-Alexandria, DC-VA-MD-WV Metropolitan Statistical Area—see Appendix B for areas included
Source: U.S. Census Bureau, 2012-2016 American Community Survey 5-Year Estimates

EMPLOYMENT

Labor Force and Employment

Area	Civilian Labor Force			Workers Employed		
	Dec. 2016	Dec. 2017	% Chg.	Dec. 2016	Dec. 2017	% Chg.
City	28,243	28,758	1.8	27,412	28,049	2.3
MD[1]	2,655,258	2,688,714	1.3	2,556,370	2,597,010	1.6
U.S.	158,968,000	159,880,000	0.6	151,798,000	153,602,000	1.2

Note: Data is not seasonally adjusted and covers workers 16 years of age and older; (1) Figures cover the Washington-Arlington-Alexandria, DC-VA-MD-WV Metropolitan Division—see Appendix B for areas included
Source: Bureau of Labor Statistics, Local Area Unemployment Statistics

Unemployment Rate

Area	2017											
	Jan.	Feb.	Mar.	Apr.	May	Jun.	Jul.	Aug.	Sep.	Oct.	Nov.	Dec.
City	3.3	3.2	3.0	2.6	2.8	2.9	3.0	3.0	2.8	2.6	2.6	2.5
MD[1]	4.2	4.1	3.8	3.5	3.7	4.0	4.0	4.0	3.7	3.6	3.6	3.4
U.S.	5.1	4.9	4.6	4.1	4.1	4.5	4.6	4.5	4.1	3.9	3.9	3.9

Note: Data is not seasonally adjusted and covers workers 16 years of age and older; (1) Figures cover the Washington-Arlington-Alexandria, DC-VA-MD-WV Metropolitan Division—see Appendix B for areas included
Source: Bureau of Labor Statistics, Local Area Unemployment Statistics

Average Wages

Occupation	$/Hr.	Occupation	$/Hr.
Accountants and Auditors	45.10	Maids and Housekeeping Cleaners	13.60
Automotive Mechanics	24.10	Maintenance and Repair Workers	22.50
Bookkeepers	24.00	Marketing Managers	80.60
Carpenters	23.20	Nuclear Medicine Technologists	40.50
Cashiers	11.40	Nurses, Licensed Practical	23.80
Clerks, General Office	19.40	Nurses, Registered	39.20
Clerks, Receptionists/Information	16.30	Nursing Assistants	14.90
Clerks, Shipping/Receiving	18.40	Packers and Packagers, Hand	12.30
Computer Programmers	47.80	Physical Therapists	44.20
Computer Systems Analysts	50.10	Postal Service Mail Carriers	23.70
Computer User Support Specialists	30.90	Real Estate Brokers	34.10
Cooks, Restaurant	13.50	Retail Salespersons	13.50
Dentists	96.40	Sales Reps., Exc. Tech./Scientific	38.70
Electrical Engineers	57.20	Sales Reps., Tech./Scientific	44.60
Electricians	29.20	Secretaries, Exc. Legal/Med./Exec.	21.80
Financial Managers	79.60	Security Guards	20.00
First-Line Supervisors/Managers, Sales	23.30	Surgeons	121.00
Food Preparation Workers	12.00	Teacher Assistants*	16.30
General and Operations Managers	73.10	Teachers, Elementary School*	37.60
Hairdressers/Cosmetologists	17.60	Teachers, Secondary School*	37.60
Internists, General	66.30	Telemarketers	14.20
Janitors and Cleaners	14.10	Truck Drivers, Heavy/Tractor-Trailer	21.50
Landscaping/Groundskeeping Workers	15.40	Truck Drivers, Light/Delivery Svcs.	18.10
Lawyers	85.60	Waiters and Waitresses	13.20

Note: Wage data covers the Washington-Arlington-Alexandria, DC-VA-MD-WV Metropolitan Division—see Appendix B for areas included; (*) Hourly wages for elementary/secondary school teachers and teacher assistants were calculated by the editors from annual wage data based on a 40 hour work week; n/a not available.
Source: Bureau of Labor Statistics, Metro Area Occupational Employment & Wage Estimates, May 2017

Employment by Occupation

Occupation Classification	City (%)	MSA[1] (%)	U.S. (%)
Management, Business, Science, and Arts	50.0	51.4	37.0
Natural Resources, Construction, and Maintenance	6.0	6.8	8.9
Production, Transportation, and Material Moving	6.6	5.7	12.2
Sales and Office	22.0	20.0	23.8
Service	15.4	16.1	18.1

Note: Figures cover employed civilians 16 years of age and older; (1) Figures cover the Washington-Arlington-Alexandria, DC-VA-MD-WV Metropolitan Statistical Area—see Appendix B for areas included

Source: U.S. Census Bureau, 2012-2016 American Community Survey 5-Year Estimates

Employment by Industry

Sector	MD[1]		U.S.
	Number of Employees	Percent of Total	Percent of Total
Construction, Mining, and Logging	124,100	4.6	5.2
Education and Health Services	356,300	13.1	15.9
Financial Activities	121,100	4.5	5.7
Government	595,700	21.9	15.3
Information	62,100	2.3	1.9
Leisure and Hospitality	272,000	10.0	10.7
Manufacturing	36,700	1.4	8.5
Other Services	185,700	6.8	3.9
Professional and Business Services	619,800	22.8	14.0
Retail Trade	226,100	8.3	11.0
Transportation, Warehousing, and Utilities	64,400	2.4	4.1
Wholesale Trade	50,700	1.9	4.0

Note: Figures are non-farm employment as of December 2017. Figures are not seasonally adjusted and include workers 16 years of age and older; (1) Figures cover the Washington-Arlington-Alexandria, DC-VA-MD-WV Metropolitan Division—see Appendix B for areas included

Source: Bureau of Labor Statistics, Current Employment Statistics, Employment, Hours, and Earnings

Occupations with Greatest Projected Employment Growth: 2017 – 2019

Occupation[1]	2017 Employment	2019 Projected Employment	Numeric Employment Change	Percent Employment Change
Combined Food Preparation and Serving Workers, Including Fast Food	91,620	97,950	6,330	6.9
Waiters and Waitresses	69,000	72,910	3,910	5.7
Personal Care Aides	44,180	46,820	2,640	6.0
Management Analysts	58,220	60,700	2,480	4.3
Software Developers, Applications	36,000	38,380	2,380	6.6
Cooks, Restaurant	32,340	34,500	2,160	6.7
Janitors and Cleaners, Except Maids and Housekeeping Cleaners	63,140	65,290	2,150	3.4
Cashiers	107,100	109,180	2,080	1.9
Customer Service Representatives	63,140	65,140	2,000	3.2
Laborers and Freight, Stock, and Material Movers, Hand	49,100	51,080	1,980	4.0

Note: Projections cover Virginia; (1) Sorted by numeric employment change

Source: www.projectionscentral.com, State Occupational Projections, 2017–2019 Short-Term Projections

Fastest Growing Occupations: 2017 – 2019

Occupation[1]	2017 Employment	2019 Projected Employment	Numeric Employment Change	Percent Employment Change
Information Security Analysts	11,770	12,750	980	8.3
Dental Laboratory Technicians	980	1,060	80	8.0
Statisticians	1,170	1,260	90	7.6
Operations Research Analysts	8,130	8,740	610	7.5
Nurse Practitioners	4,720	5,060	340	7.4
Physician Assistants	2,480	2,650	170	7.1
Combined Food Preparation and Serving Workers, Including Fast Food	91,620	97,950	6,330	6.9
Home Health Aides	11,620	12,410	790	6.8
Cooks, Restaurant	32,340	34,500	2,160	6.7
Software Developers, Applications	36,000	38,380	2,380	6.6

Note: Projections cover Virginia; (1) Sorted by percent employment change and excludes occupations with numeric employment change less than 50
Source: www.projectionscentral.com, State Occupational Projections, 2017–2019 Short-Term Projections

TAXES

State Corporate Income Tax Rates

State	Tax Rate (%)	Income Brackets ($)	Num. of Brackets	Financial Institution Tax Rate (%)[a]	Federal Income Tax Ded.
Virginia	6.0	Flat rate	1	6.0	No

Note: Tax rates as of January 1, 2018; (a) Rates listed are the corporate income tax rate applied to financial institutions or excise taxes based on income. Some states have other taxes based upon the value of deposits or shares.
Source: Federation of Tax Administrators, Range of State Corporate Income Tax Rates, January 1, 2018

State Individual Income Tax Rates

State	Tax Rate (%)	Income Brackets ($)	Num. of Brackets	Personal Exempt. ($)[1] Single	Personal Exempt. ($)[1] Dependents	Fed. Inc. Tax Ded.
Virginia	2.0 - 5.75	3,000 - 17,001	4	930	930	No

Note: Tax rates as of January 1, 2018; Local- and county-level taxes are not included; n/a not applicable; (1) Married joint filers generally receive double the single exemption
Source: Federation of Tax Administrators, State Individual Income Tax Rates, January 1, 2018

Various State Sales and Excise Tax Rates

State	State Sales Tax (%)	Gasoline[1] (¢/gal.)	Cigarette[2] ($/pack)	Spirits[3] ($/gal.)	Wine[4] ($/gal.)	Beer[5] ($/gal.)	Recreational Marijuana (%)
Virginia	5.3 (b)	22.4	0.30	19.93 (g)	1.51 (l)	0.26 (q)	Not legal

Note: All tax rates as of January 1, 2018; (1) The American Petroleum Institute has developed a methodology for determining the average tax rate on a gallon of fuel. Rates may include any of the following: excise taxes, environmental fees, storage tank fees, other fees or taxes, general sales tax, and local taxes. In states where gasoline is subject to the general sales tax, or where the fuel tax is based on the average sale price, the average rate determined by API is sensitive to changes in the price of gasoline. States that fully or partially apply general sales taxes to gasoline: CA, CO, GA, IL, IN, MI, NY; (2) The federal excise tax of $1.0066 per pack and local taxes are not included; (3) Rates are those applicable to off-premise sales of 40% alcohol by volume (a.b.v.) distilled spirits in 750ml containers. Local excise taxes are excluded; (4) Rates are those applicable to off-premise sales of 11% a.b.v. non-carbonated wine in 750ml containers; (5) Rates are those applicable to off-premise sales of 4.7% a.b.v. beer in 12 ounce containers; (b) Three states levy mandatory, statewide, local add-on sales taxes at the state level: California (1.25%), Utah (1.25%), Virginia (1%), we include these in their state sales tax; (g) Control states, where the government controls all sales. Products can be subject to ad valorem mark-up as well as excise taxes; (l) Different rates also applicable to alcohol content, place of production, size of container, place purchased (on- or off-premise or on board airlines) or type of wine (carbonated, vermouth, etc.); (q) Different rates also applicable according to alcohol content, place of production, size of container, or place purchased (on- or off-premise or onboard airlines).
Source: Tax Foundation, 2018 Facts & Figures: How Does Your State Compare?

State Business Tax Climate Index Rankings

State	Overall Rank	Corporate Tax Rank	Individual Income Tax Rank	Sales Tax Rank	Unemployment Insurance Tax Rank	Property Tax Rank
Virginia	31	6	40	10	41	31

Note: The index is a measure of how each state's tax laws affect economic performance. The lower the rank, the more favorable a state's tax system is for business. States without a given tax are given a ranking of 1. The scores/rankings for the District of Columbia do not affect other states. The 2018 index represents the tax climate as of July 1, 2017.
Source: Tax Foundation, State Business Tax Climate Index 2018

TRANSPORTATION

Means of Transportation to Work

Area	Car/Truck/Van		Public Transportation			Bicycle	Walked	Other Means	Worked at Home
	Drove Alone	Car-pooled	Bus	Subway	Railroad				
City	77.2	10.5	3.3	0.3	0.1	0.3	2.1	0.9	5.2
MSA[1]	65.9	9.7	5.2	8.0	0.8	0.8	3.3	1.1	5.2
U.S.	76.4	9.3	2.6	1.9	0.6	0.6	2.8	1.3	4.6

Note: Figures are percentages and cover workers 16 years of age and older; (1) Figures cover the Washington-Arlington-Alexandria, DC-VA-MD-WV Metropolitan Statistical Area—see Appendix B for areas included
Source: U.S. Census Bureau, 2012-2016 American Community Survey 5-Year Estimates

Travel Time to Work

Area	Less Than 10 Minutes	10 to 19 Minutes	20 to 29 Minutes	30 to 44 Minutes	45 to 59 Minutes	60 to 89 Minutes	90 Minutes or More
City	13.0	23.3	15.8	22.8	10.7	9.5	4.9
MSA[1]	6.1	19.2	18.0	25.8	13.7	12.8	4.4
U.S.	12.9	29.2	20.9	20.4	8.0	6.0	2.7

Note: Note: Figures are percentages and include workers 16 years old and over; (1) Figures cover the Washington-Arlington-Alexandria, DC-VA-MD-WV Metropolitan Statistical Area—see Appendix B for areas included
Source: U.S. Census Bureau, 2012-2016 American Community Survey 5-Year Estimates

Freeway Travel Time Index

Area	1985	1990	1995	2000	2005	2010	2014
Urban Area Rank[1,2]	6	5	5	7	6	5	8
Urban Area Index[1]	1.19	1.22	1.27	1.29	1.34	1.35	1.34
Average Index[3]	1.09	1.11	1.14	1.17	1.20	1.19	1.20

Note: Freeway Travel Time Index—the ratio of travel time in the peak period to the travel time at free-flow conditions. For example, a value of 1.30 indicates a 20-minute free-flow trip takes 26 minutes in the peak (20 minutes x 1.30 = 26 minutes); (1) Covers the Washington DC-VA-MD urban area; (2) Rank is based on 101 urban areas (#1 = highest travel time index); (3) Average of 101 urban areas
Source: Texas Transportation Institute, 2015 Urban Mobility Scorecard, August 2015

Freeway Commuter Stress Index

Area	1985	1990	1995	2000	2005	2010	2014
Urban Area Rank[1,2]	8	8	6	8	9	7	9
Urban Area Index[1]	1.26	1.30	1.35	1.37	1.42	1.44	1.43
Average Index[3]	1.13	1.16	1.19	1.22	1.25	1.24	1.25

Note: The Freeway Commuter Stress Index is the same as the Freeway Travel Time Index (see table above) except that it includes only the travel in the peak directions during the peak periods; the TTI includes travel in all directions during the peak period. Thus, the CSI is more indicative of the work trip experienced by each commuter on a daily basis; (1) Covers the Washington DC-VA-MD urban area; (2) Rank is based on 101 urban areas (#1 = highest travel time index); (3) Average of 101 urban areas
Source: Texas Transportation Institute, 2015 Urban Mobility Scorecard, August 2015

Living Environment

COST OF LIVING

Cost of Living Index

Composite Index	Groceries	Housing	Utilities	Transportation	Health Care	Misc. Goods/ Services
144.0	114.4	233.7	89.4	105.5	97.8	114.6

Note: The Cost of Living Index measures regional differences in the cost of consumer goods and services, excluding taxes and non-consumer expenditures, for professional and managerial households in the top income quintile. It is based on more than 50,000 prices covering almost 60 different items for which prices are collected three times a year by chambers of commerce, economic development organizations or university applied economic centers in each participating urban area. The numbers shown should be read as a percentage above or below the national average of 100. For example, a value of 115.4 in the groceries column indicates that grocery prices are 15.4% higher than the national average. Small differences in the index numbers should not be interpreted as significant; Figures cover the Arlington VA urban area.
Source: The Council for Community and Economic Research, ACCRA Cost of Living Index, 2017

Grocery Prices

Area[1]	T-Bone Steak ($/pound)	Frying Chicken ($/pound)	Whole Milk ($/half gal.)	Eggs ($/dozen)	Orange Juice ($/64 oz.)	Coffee ($/11.5 oz.)
City[2]	10.29	1.98	2.53	1.62	3.35	4.55
Avg.	11.29	1.40	2.02	1.47	3.55	4.37
Min.	7.71	0.93	1.04	0.70	2.86	3.24
Max.	15.83	2.39	4.03	3.92	6.29	8.16

Note: (1) Values for the local area are compared with the average, minimum and maximum values for all 294 areas in the Cost of Living Index; (2) Figures cover the Arlington VA urban area; ***T-Bone Steak*** *(price per pound);* ***Frying Chicken*** *(price per pound, whole fryer);* ***Whole Milk*** *(half gallon carton);* ***Eggs*** *(price per dozen, Grade A, large);* ***Orange Juice*** *(64 oz. Tropicana or Florida Natural);* ***Coffee*** *(11.5 oz. can, vacuum-packed, Maxwell House, Hills Bros, or Folgers).*
Source: The Council for Community and Economic Research, ACCRA Cost of Living Index, 2017

Housing and Utility Costs

Area[1]	New Home Price ($)	Apartment Rent ($/month)	All Electric ($/month)	Part Electric ($/month)	Other Energy ($/month)	Telephone ($/month)
City[2]	799,297	2,344	-	77.90	63.27	27.32
Avg.	335,956	1,047	175.01	97.34	67.93	28.71
Min.	187,788	491	109.48	49.33	35.44	12.39
Max.	1,739,087	4,559	432.62	227.09	353.33	44.61

Note: (1) Values for the local area are compared with the average, minimum and maximum values for all 294 areas in the Cost of Living Index; (2) Figures cover the Arlington VA urban area; ***New Home Price*** *(2,400 sf living area, 8,000 sf lot, in urban area with full utilities);* ***Apartment Rent*** *(950 sf 2 bedroom/1.5 or 2 bath, unfurnished, excluding all utilities except water);* ***All Electric*** *(average monthly cost for an all-electric home);* ***Part Electric*** *(average monthly cost for a part-electric home);* ***Other Energy*** *(average monthly cost for natural gas, fuel oil, coal, wood, and any other forms of energy except electricity);* ***Telephone*** *(price includes basic monthly rate for a private residential line plus additional local usage charges incurred by a family of four).*
Source: The Council for Community and Economic Research, ACCRA Cost of Living Index, 2017

Health Care, Transportation, and Other Costs

Area[1]	Doctor ($/visit)	Dentist ($/visit)	Optometrist ($/visit)	Gasoline ($/gallon)	Beauty Salon ($/visit)	Men's Shirt ($)
City[2]	97.42	95.33	77.00	2.44	56.89	37.78
Avg.	108.00	92.54	101.93	2.25	37.58	30.92
Min.	30.39	60.00	49.75	1.82	16.11	11.20
Max.	193.50	161.94	229.28	3.16	77.35	59.13

Note: (1) Values for the local area are compared with the average, minimum and maximum values for all 294 areas in the Cost of Living Index; (2) Figures cover the Arlington VA urban area; ***Doctor*** *(general practitioners routine exam of an established patient);* ***Dentist*** *(adult teeth cleaning and periodic oral examination);* ***Optometrist*** *(full vision eye exam for established adult patient);* ***Gasoline*** *(one gallon regular unleaded, national brand, including all taxes, cash price at self-service pump if available);* ***Beauty Salon*** *(woman's shampoo, trim, and blow-dry);* ***Men's Shirt*** *(cotton/polyester dress shirt, pinpoint weave, long sleeves).*
Source: The Council for Community and Economic Research, ACCRA Cost of Living Index, 2017

HOUSING

House Price Index (HPI)

Area	National Ranking[2]	Quarterly Change (%)	One-Year Change (%)	Five-Year Change (%)
MD[1]	178	0.59	4.26	24.94
U.S.[3]	–	1.61	6.68	34.71

Note: The HPI is a weighted repeat sales index. It measures average price changes in repeat sales or refinancings on the same properties. This information is obtained by reviewing repeat mortgage transactions on single-family properties whose mortgages have been purchased or securitized by Fannie Mae or Freddie Mac in January 1975; (1) Figures cover the Washington-Arlington-Alexandria, DC-VA-MD-WV Metropolitan Division—see Appendix B for areas included; (2) Rankings are based on annual percentage change for all metro areas containing at least 15,000 transactions over the last 10 years and ranges from 1 to 253; (3) figures based on a weighted average of Census Division estimates using a seasonally adjusted, purchase-only index; all figures are for the period ending December 31, 2017
Source: Federal Housing Finance Agency, House Price Index, February 28, 2018

Median Single-Family Home Prices

Area	2015	2016	2017p	Percent Change 2016 to 2017
MSA[1]	383.4	390.6	406.7	4.1
U.S. Average	223.9	235.5	248.8	5.6

Note: Figures are median sales prices of existing single-family homes in thousands of dollars; (p) preliminary; (1) Figures cover the Washington-Arlington-Alexandria, DC-VA-MD-WV Metropolitan Statistical Area—see Appendix B for areas included
Source: National Association of Realtors, Median Sales Price of Existing Single-Family Homes for Metropolitan Areas, 4th Quarter 2017

Qualifying Income Based on Median Sales Price of Existing Single-Family Homes

Area	With 5% Down ($)	With 10% Down ($)	With 20% Down ($)
MSA[1]	89,075	84,386	75,010
U.S. Average	55,585	52,659	46,808

Note: Figures are preliminary; Qualifying income is based on a mortgage rate of 4.17%. Monthly principal and interest payment is limited to 25% of income; (1) Figures cover the Washington-Arlington-Alexandria, DC-VA-MD-WV Metropolitan Statistical Area—see Appendix B for areas included
Source: National Association of Realtors, Qualifying Income Based on Median Sales Price of Existing Single-Family Homes for Metropolitan Areas, 4th Quarter 2017

Median Apartment Condo-Coop Home Prices

Area	2015	2016	2017p	Percent Change 2016 to 2017
MSA[1]	274.8	273.6	280.3	2.4
U.S. Average	210.7	220.7	234.3	6.2

Note: Figures are median sales prices of existing apartment condo-coop homes in thousands of dollars; (p) preliminary; (1) Figures cover the Washington-Arlington-Alexandria, DC-VA-MD-WV Metropolitan Statistical Area—see Appendix B for areas included
Source: National Association of Realtors, Median Sales Price of Existing Apartment Condo-Coop Homes for Metropolitan Areas, 4th Quarter 2017

Home Value Distribution

Area	Under $50,000	$50,000 -$99,999	$100,000 -$149,999	$150,000 -$199,999	$200,000 -$299,999	$300,000 -$499,999	$500,000 -$999,999	$1,000,000 or more
City	2.4	1.1	1.7	4.5	17.6	46.0	26.4	0.3
MSA[1]	2.2	1.4	3.2	6.9	19.4	33.8	27.5	5.6
U.S.	8.8	14.8	15.3	14.9	18.4	16.4	9.0	2.5

Note: Figures are percentages and cover owner-occupied housing units; (1) Figures cover the Washington-Arlington-Alexandria, DC-VA-MD-WV Metropolitan Statistical Area—see Appendix B for areas included
Source: U.S. Census Bureau, 2012-2016 American Community Survey 5-Year Estimates

Homeownership Rate

Area	2009 (%)	2010 (%)	2011 (%)	2012 (%)	2013 (%)	2014 (%)	2015 (%)	2016 (%)	2017 (%)
MSA[1]	67.2	67.3	67.6	66.9	66.0	65.0	64.6	63.1	63.3
U.S.	67.4	66.9	66.1	65.4	65.1	64.5	63.7	63.4	63.9

Note: (1) Figures cover the Washington-Arlington-Alexandria, DC-VA-MD-WV Metropolitan Statistical Area—see Appendix B for areas included
Source: U.S. Census Bureau, Housing Vacancies and Homeownership Annual Statistics: 2009-2017

Year Housing Structure Built

Area	2010 or Later	2000 -2009	1990 -1999	1980 -1989	1970 -1979	1960 -1969	1950 -1959	1940 -1949	Before 1940	Median Year
City	2.7	25.6	29.6	20.4	10.2	5.0	3.2	0.6	2.7	1993
MSA[1]	3.0	15.3	14.5	16.3	14.8	12.5	9.8	5.2	8.6	1979
U.S.	2.3	14.7	14.0	13.7	15.6	10.9	10.6	5.2	13.0	1977

Note: Figures are percentages except for Median Year; Note: (1) Figures cover the Washington-Arlington-Alexandria, DC-VA-MD-WV Metropolitan Statistical Area—see Appendix B for areas included
Source: U.S. Census Bureau, 2012-2016 American Community Survey 5-Year Estimates

Gross Monthly Rent

Area	Under $500	$500 -$999	$1,000 -$1,499	$1,500 -$1,999	$2,000 -$2,499	$2,500 -$2,999	$3,000 and up	Median ($)
City	4.7	14.1	36.8	33.8	8.5	1.6	0.5	1,446
MSA[1]	5.0	11.2	31.5	28.0	14.1	5.7	4.5	1,541
U.S.	11.3	43.3	27.7	10.7	4.0	1.6	1.5	949

Note: Figures are percentages except for Median; Gross rent is the contract rent plus the estimated average monthly cost of utilities (electricity, gas, and water and sewer) and fuels (oil, coal, kerosene, wood, etc.) if these are paid by the renter (or paid for the renter by someone else); (1) Figures cover the Washington-Arlington-Alexandria, DC-VA-MD-WV Metropolitan Statistical Area—see Appendix B for areas included
Source: U.S. Census Bureau, 2012-2016 American Community Survey 5-Year Estimates

HEALTH

Health Risk Factors

Category	MD[1] (%)	U.S. (%)
Adults aged 18–64 who have any kind of health care coverage	87.6	87.7
Adults who reported being in good or excellent health	86.9	83.6
Adults who are current smokers	11.8	17.1
Adults who currently use E-cigarettes	3.8	4.7
Adults who currently use chewing tobacco, snuff, or snus	2.1	4.0
Adults who are heavy drinkers[2]	6.3	6.5
Adults who are binge drinkers[3]	17.2	16.9
Adults who are overweight (BMI 25.0 - 29.9)	36.1	35.3
Adults who are obese (BMI 30.0 - 99.8)	26.4	29.9
Adults who participated in any physical activities in the past month	79.8	76.9
Adults who always or nearly always wears a seat belt	96.4	94.3

Note: (1) Figures cover the Washington-Arlington-Alexandria, DC-VA-MD-WV Metropolitan Division—see Appendix B for areas included; (2) Heavy drinkers are classified as adult men having more than 14 drinks per week and adult women having more than 7 drinks per week; (3) Binge drinkers are classified as males having five or more drinks on one occasion or females having four or more drinks on one occasion
Source: Centers for Disease Control and Prevention, Behaviorial Risk Factor Surveillance System, SMART: Selected Metropolitan Area Risk Trends, 2016

Health Screening Rates

Category	MD[1] (%)	U.S. (%)
Adults 50-75 who have had a blood stool test within the past year	10.0	8.0
Adults 50-75 who have had a colonoscopy in the past 10 years	66.4	63.5
Adults aged 65+ who have had flu shot within the past year	60.0	58.6
Adults aged 65+ who have ever had a pneumonia vaccination	72.5	73.4
Adults who have ever been tested for HIV	53.1	35.6
Women aged 21-65 who have had a pap test in the past three years	83.2	79.8
Men aged 40+ who have had a PSA test within the past two years	39.5	39.5
Women aged 40+ who have had a mammogram within the past two years	77.5	72.5

Note: (1) Figures cover the Washington-Arlington-Alexandria, DC-VA-MD-WV Metropolitan Division—see Appendix B for areas included; Source: Centers for Disease Control and Prevention, Behaviorial Risk Factor Surveillance System, SMART: Selected Metropolitan Area Risk Trends, 2016

Chronic Health Conditions

Category	MD[1] (%)	U.S. (%)
Adults who have ever been told they had a heart attack	3.3	4.4
Adults who have ever been told they have angina or coronary heart disease	2.6	4.1
Adults who have ever been told they had a stroke	2.2	3.1
Adults who have been told they currently have asthma	8.6	9.3
Adults who have ever been told they have arthritis	20.0	25.8
Adults who have ever been told they have diabetes[2]	8.7	10.5
Adults who have ever been told they had skin cancer	4.3	5.9
Adults who have ever been told they had any other types of cancer	5.0	6.7
Adults who have ever been told they have COPD	4.1	6.3
Adults who have ever been told they have kidney disease	2.1	2.8
Adults who have ever been told they have a form of depression	14.4	17.4

Note: (1) Figures cover the Washington-Arlington-Alexandria, DC-VA-MD-WV Metropolitan Division—see Appendix B for areas included; (2) Figures do not include pregnancy-related, borderline, or pre-diabetes
Source: Centers for Disease Control and Prevention, Behaviorial Risk Factor Surveillance System, SMART: Selected Metropolitan Area Risk Trends, 2016

Mortality Rates for the Top 10 Causes of Death in the U.S.

ICD-10[a] Sub-Chapter	ICD-10[a] Code	Age-Adjusted Mortality Rate[1] per 100,000 population	
		County[2]	U.S.
Malignant neoplasms	C00-C97	120.7	158.5
Ischaemic heart diseases	I20-I25	60.8	96.8
Other forms of heart disease	I30-I51	36.6	52.4
Chronic lower respiratory diseases	J40-J47	22.2	40.9
Cerebrovascular diseases	I60-I69	27.5	37.2
Organic, including symptomatic, mental disorders	F01-F09	26.6	33.3
Other degenerative diseases of the nervous system	G30-G31	27.8	32.1
Other external causes of accidental injury	W00-X59	20.4	31.2
Diabetes mellitus	E10-E14	13.3	21.1
Hypertensive diseases	I10-I15	8.6	20.8

Note: (a) ICD-10 = International Classification of Diseases 10th Revision; (1) Mortality rates are a three year average covering 2014-2016; (2) Figures cover Loudoun County.
Source: Centers for Disease Control and Prevention, National Center for Health Statistics. Underlying Cause of Death 1999-2016 on CDC WONDER Online Database, released December 2017

Mortality Rates for Selected Causes of Death

ICD-10[a] Sub-Chapter	ICD-10[a] Code	Age-Adjusted Mortality Rate[1] per 100,000 population	
		County[2]	U.S.
Assault	X85-Y09	Unreliable	5.6
Diseases of the liver	K70-K76	6.4	14.0
Human immunodeficiency virus (HIV) disease	B20-B24	Suppressed	1.9
Influenza and pneumonia	J09-J18	9.2	14.6
Intentional self-harm	X60-X84	12.1	13.2
Malnutrition	E40-E46	Suppressed	1.3
Obesity and other hyperalimentation	E65-E68	Unreliable	2.1
Renal failure	N17-N19	8.9	13.0
Transport accidents	V01-V99	5.2	12.0
Viral hepatitis	B15-B19	Suppressed	1.9

Note: (a) ICD-10 = International Classification of Diseases 10th Revision; (1) Mortality rates are a three year average covering 2014-2016; (2) Figures cover Loudoun County; Data are Suppressed when the data meet the criteria for confidentiality constraints; Mortality rates are flagged as Unreliable when the rate would be calculated with a numerator of 20 or less.
Source: Centers for Disease Control and Prevention, National Center for Health Statistics. Underlying Cause of Death 1999-2016 on CDC WONDER Online Database, released December 2017

Health Insurance Coverage

Area	With Health Insurance	With Private Health Insurance	With Public Health Insurance	Without Health Insurance	Population Under Age 18 Without Health Insurance
City	89.3	82.9	12.5	10.7	7.1
MSA[1]	90.4	77.4	23.2	9.6	4.7
U.S.	88.3	66.7	33.0	11.7	5.9

Note: Figures are percentages that cover the civilian noninstitutionalized population; (1) Figures cover the Washington-Arlington-Alexandria, DC-VA-MD-WV Metropolitan Statistical Area—see Appendix B for areas included
Source: U.S. Census Bureau, 2012-2016 American Community Survey 5-Year Estimates

Number of Medical Professionals

Area	MDs[3]	DOs[3,4]	Dentists	Podiatrists	Chiropractors	Optometrists
County[1] (number)	720	30	233	13	86	65
County[1] (rate[2])	192.2	8.0	60.3	3.4	22.3	16.8
U.S. (rate[2])	276.5	22.3	67.3	6.0	26.7	15.9

Note: Data as of 2016 unless noted; (1) Data covers Loudoun County; (2) Rate per 100,000 population; (3) Data as of 2015 and includes all active, non-federal physicians; (4) Doctor of Osteopathic Medicine
Source: U.S. Department of Health and Human Services, Health Resources and Services Administration, Bureau of Health Professions, Area Resource File (ARF) 2016-2017

Best Hospitals

According to *U.S. News,* the Washington-Arlington-Alexandria, DC-VA-MD-WV metro area is home to three of the best hospitals in the U.S.: **Inova Fairfax Hospital** (1 pediatric specialty); **MedStar Georgetown University Hospital** (1 adult specialty); **MedStar Washington Hospital Center** (1 adult specialty). The hospitals listed were nationally ranked in at least one of 16 specialties. Only 152 hospitals nationwide were nationally ranked in one or more specialties. Twenty hospitals in the U.S. made the Honor Roll. The Best Hospitals Honor Roll was revamped last year to take both the national rankings and the procedure and condition ratings into account. Hospitals received points if they were nationally ranked in one of the 16 specialties—the higher they ranked, the more points they got—and how many ratings of "high performing" they earned in the nine procedures and conditions. *U.S. News Online, "America's Best Hospitals 2017-18"*

According to *U.S. News,* the Washington-Arlington-Alexandria, DC-VA-MD-WV metro area is home to two of the best children's hospitals in the U.S.: **Children's National Medical Center** (Honor Roll/10 pediatric specialties); **Inova Children's Hospital** (1 pediatric specialty). The hospitals listed were highly ranked in at least one of 10 pediatric specialties. Eighty-two children's hospitals in the U.S. were nationally ranked in at least one specialty. Hospitals received points for being ranked in a specialty, and the 10 hospitals with the most points across the 10 specialties make up the Honor Roll. *U.S. News Online, "America's Best Children's Hospitals 2017-18"*

EDUCATION

Public School District Statistics

District Name	Schls	Pupils	Pupil/ Teacher Ratio	Minority Pupils[1] (%)	Free Lunch Eligible[2] (%)	IEP[3] (%)
Loudoun Co Public Schools	93	76,202	13.6	48.2	13.2	11.2

Note: Table includes school districts with 100 or more students; (1) Percentage of students that are not non-Hispanic white; (2) Percentage of students that are eligible for the free lunch program; (3) Percentage of students that have an Individualized Education Program.
Source: U.S. Department of Education, National Center for Education Statistics, Common Core of Data, Local Education Agency (School District) Universe Survey: School Year 2015-2016; U.S. Department of Education, National Center for Education Statistics, Common Core of Data, Public Elementary/Secondary School Universe Survey: School Year 2015-2016

Highest Level of Education

Area	Less than H.S.	H.S. Diploma	Some College, No Deg.	Associate Degree	Bachelor's Degree	Master's Degree	Prof. School Degree	Doctorate Degree
City	9.8	16.0	15.8	7.3	32.1	15.3	1.7	2.1
MSA[1]	9.6	18.7	16.8	5.6	25.3	16.8	4.2	3.1
U.S.	13.0	27.5	21.0	8.2	18.8	8.2	2.0	1.3

Note: Figures cover persons age 25 and over; (1) Figures cover the Washington-Arlington-Alexandria, DC-VA-MD-WV Metropolitan Statistical Area—see Appendix B for areas included
Source: U.S. Census Bureau, 2012-2016 American Community Survey 5-Year Estimates

Educational Attainment by Race

Area	High School Graduate or Higher (%)					Bachelor's Degree or Higher (%)				
	Total	White	Black	Asian	Hisp.[2]	Total	White	Black	Asian	Hisp.[2]
City	90.2	92.1	90.4	81.9	64.1	51.2	54.1	33.9	52.1	19.4
MSA[1]	90.4	93.2	90.5	90.7	66.0	49.4	57.0	32.7	63.4	24.4
U.S.	87.0	88.9	84.3	86.3	65.7	30.3	31.6	20.0	52.1	14.7

Note: Figures shown cover persons 25 years old and over; (1) Figures cover the Washington-Arlington-Alexandria, DC-VA-MD-WV Metropolitan Statistical Area—see Appendix B for areas included; (2) People of Hispanic origin can be of any race
Source: U.S. Census Bureau, 2012-2016 American Community Survey 5-Year Estimates

School Enrollment by Grade and Control

Area	Preschool (%)		Kindergarten (%)		Grades 1 - 4 (%)		Grades 5 - 8 (%)		Grades 9 - 12 (%)	
	Public	Private	Public	Private	Public	Private	Public	Private	Public	Private
City	31.5	68.5	93.0	7.0	93.9	6.1	94.6	5.4	96.0	4.0
MSA[1]	43.0	57.0	85.5	14.5	88.7	11.3	88.1	11.9	88.6	11.4
U.S.	58.4	41.6	87.7	12.3	89.8	10.2	89.7	10.3	90.4	9.6

Note: Figures shown cover persons 3 years old and over; (1) Figures cover the Washington-Arlington-Alexandria, DC-VA-MD-WV Metropolitan Statistical Area—see Appendix B for areas included
Source: U.S. Census Bureau, 2012-2016 American Community Survey 5-Year Estimates

Average Salaries of Public School Classroom Teachers

Area	2015		2016		Change from 2015 to 2016	
	Dollars	Rank[1]	Dollars	Rank[1]	Percent	Rank[2]
Virginia	50,544	30	50,834	30	0.6	29
U.S. Average	57,611	–	58,353	–	1.3	–

Note: (1) Rank ranges from 1 to 51 where 1 indicates highest salary; (2) Rank ranges from 1 to 51 where 1 indicates highest percent change.
Source: National Education Association, Rankings & Estimates: Rankings of the States 2016 and Estimates of School Statistics 2017

Higher Education

Four-Year Colleges			Two-Year Colleges			Medical Schools[1]	Law Schools[2]	Voc/ Tech[3]
Public	Private Non-profit	Private For-profit	Public	Private Non-profit	Private For-profit			
0	0	0	0	0	0	0	0	0

Note: Figures cover institutions located within the city limits and include main campuses only; (1) includes schools accredited by the Liaison Committee on Medical Education and the American Osteopathic Association's Commission on Osteopathic College Accreditation; (2) includes ABA-accredited schools, schools with provisional ABA accreditation, and state accredited schools; (3) includes all schools with programs that are less than 2 years.
Source: National Center for Education Statistics, Integrated Postsecondary Education System (IPEDS), 2016-17; Wikipedia, List of Medical Schools in the United States, accessed April 2, 2018; Wikipedia, List of Law Schools in the United States, accessed April 2, 2018

According to *U.S. News & World Report,* the Washington-Arlington-Alexandria, DC-VA-MD-WV metro division is home to seven of the best national universities in the U.S.: **Georgetown University** (#20); **George Washington University** (#56 tie); **University of Maryland—College Park** (#61 tie); **American University** (#69 tie); **Howard University** (#110 tie); **The Catholic University of America** (#120 tie); **George Mason University** (#140 tie). The indicators used to capture academic quality fall into a number of categories: assessment by administrators at peer institutions; retention of students; faculty resources; student selectivity; financial resources; alumni giving; high school counselor ratings of colleges; and graduation rate. *U.S. News & World Report, "America's Best Colleges 2018"*

According to *U.S. News & World Report,* the Washington-Arlington-Alexandria, DC-VA-MD-WV metro division is home to four of the top 100 law schools in the U.S.: **Georgetown University** (#14); **George Washington University** (#24 tie); **George Mason University** (#41 tie); **American University (Washington)** (#80 tie). The rankings are based on a weighted average of 12 measures of quality: peer assessment score; assessment score by lawyers/judges; median LSAT scores; median undergrad GPA; acceptance rate; employment rates for graduates; placement success; bar passage rate; faculty resources; expenditures per student; student/faculty ratio; and library resources. *U.S. News & World Report, "America's Best Graduate Schools, Law, 2019"*

According to *U.S. News & World Report,* the Washington-Arlington-Alexandria, DC-VA-MD-WV metro division is home to two of the top 75 medical schools for research in the U.S.: **Georgetown**

University (#46 tie); **George Washington University** (#62 tie). The rankings are based on a weighted average of 11 measures of quality: quality assessment; peer assessment score; assessment score by residency directors; research activity; total research activity; average research activity per faculty member; student selectivity; median MCAT total score; median undergraduate GPA; acceptance rate; and faculty resources. *U.S. News & World Report, "America's Best Graduate Schools, Medical, 2019"*

According to *U.S. News & World Report,* the Washington-Arlington-Alexandria, DC-VA-MD-WV metro division is home to three of the top 75 business schools in the U.S.: **Georgetown University (McDonough)** (#25); **University of Maryland—College Park (Smith)** (#48 tie); **George Washington University** (#59 tie). The rankings are based on a weighted average of the following nine measures: quality assessment; peer assessment; recruiter assessment; placement success; mean starting salary and bonus; student selectivity; mean GMAT and GRE scores; mean undergraduate GPA; and acceptance rate. *U.S. News & World Report, "America's Best Graduate Schools, Business, 2019"*

PRESIDENTIAL ELECTION

2016 Presidential Election Results

Area	Clinton	Trump	Johnson	Stein	Other
Loudoun County	55.1	38.2	3.1	0.7	2.9
U.S.	48.0	45.9	3.3	1.1	1.7

Note: Results are percentages and may not add to 100% due to rounding
Source: Dave Leip's Atlas of U.S. Presidential Elections

EMPLOYERS

Major Employers

Company Name	Industry
Adventist HealthCare	General medical & surgical hospitals
Bechtel National	Engineering services
Computer Sciences Corporation	Computer related consulting services
Federal Aviation Administration	Air traffic control operations, government
Federal Bureau of Investigation	Police protection
Fish and Wildlife Service, United States	Fish & wildlife conservation agency, government
Howard University	Colleges & universities
HR Solutions	Human resource consulting services
Internal Revenue Service	Finance, taxation, & monetary policy
Intl Bank for Recons. & Dev.	Foreign trade & international banks
Natl Inst of Standards & Technology	Administration of general economic programs
Office of the Secretary of Defense	National security
US Department of Agriculture	Regulation of agricultural marketing
US Department of Commerce	Regulation, miscellaneous commercial sectors
US Department of Labor	Administration of social & manpower programs
US Department of the Army	National security
US Department of the Navy	National security
US Department of Transportation	Regulation, administration of transportation
US Environmental Protection Agency	Land, mineral, & wildlife conservation
Washington Hospital Center Corporation	General medical & surgical hospitals

Note: Companies shown are located within the Washington-Arlington-Alexandria, DC-VA-MD-WV Metropolitan Statistical Area.
Source: Hoovers.com; Wikipedia

PUBLIC SAFETY

Crime Rate

Area	All Crimes	Violent Crimes				Property Crimes		
		Murder	Rape[3]	Robbery	Aggrav. Assault	Burglary	Larceny -Theft	Motor Vehicle Theft
City	1,752.3	5.7	54.7	22.6	122.6	34.0	1,452.4	60.4
Metro[1]	2,278.3	5.3	31.2	120.4	174.4	183.0	1,624.9	139.2
U.S.	2,847.8	5.3	40.4	102.8	248.5	468.9	1,745.0	236.9

Note: Figures are crimes per 100,000 population; (1) Figures cover the Washington-Arlington-Alexandria, DC-VA-MD-WV Metropolitan Division—see Appendix B for areas included; (3) The city and U.S. figures shown were reported using the revised Uniform Crime Reporting (UCR) definition of rape. The metro area figures shown are an aggregate total of the data submitted using both the revised and legacy UCR definitions.
Source: FBI Uniform Crime Reports, 2016

Hate Crimes

Area	Number of Quarters Reported	Number of Incidents per Bias Motivation					
		Race/Ethnicity/ Ancestry	Religion	Sexual Orientation	Disability	Gender	Gender Identity
City	4	0	0	0	0	0	0
U.S.	4	3,489	1,273	1,076	70	31	124

Source: Federal Bureau of Investigation, Hate Crime Statistics 2016

Identity Theft Consumer Reports

Area	Reports	Reports per 100,000 Population	Rank[2]
MSA[1]	6,428	105	87
U.S.	371,061	114	-

Note: (1) Figures cover the Washington-Arlington-Alexandria, DC-VA-MD-WV Metropolitan Statistical Area—see Appendix B for areas included; (2) Rank ranges from 1 to 389 where 1 indicates greatest number of identity theft reports per 100,000 population
Source: Federal Trade Commission, Consumer Sentinel Network Data Book for January–December 2017

Fraud and Other Consumer Reports

Area	Reports	Reports per 100,000 Population	Rank[2]
MSA[1]	29,839	487	127
U.S.	2,304,550	708	-

Note: (1) Figures cover the Washington-Arlington-Alexandria, DC-VA-MD-WV Metropolitan Statistical Area—see Appendix B for areas included; (2) Rank ranges from 1 to 389 where 1 indicates greatest number of fraud and other consumer reports per 100,000 population
Source: Federal Trade Commission, Consumer Sentinel Network Data Book for January–December 2017

SPORTS

Professional Sports Teams

Team Name	League	Year Established
D.C. United	Major League Soccer (MLS)	1996
Washington Capitals	National Hockey League (NHL)	1974
Washington Nationals	Major League Baseball (MLB)	2005
Washington Redskins	National Football League (NFL)	1937
Washington Wizards	National Basketball Association (NBA)	1973

Note: Includes teams located in the Washington-Arlington-Alexandria, DC-VA-MD-WV Metropolitan Statistical Area.
Source: Wikipedia, Major Professional Sports Teams of the United States and Canada, April 5, 2018

CLIMATE

Average and Extreme Temperatures

Temperature	Jan	Feb	Mar	Apr	May	Jun	Jul	Aug	Sep	Oct	Nov	Dec	Yr.
Extreme High (°F)	79	82	89	95	97	101	104	103	101	94	86	75	104
Average High (°F)	43	46	55	67	76	84	88	86	80	69	58	47	67
Average Temp. (°F)	36	38	46	57	66	75	79	78	71	60	49	39	58
Average Low (°F)	28	30	37	46	56	65	70	69	62	50	40	31	49
Extreme Low (°F)	-5	4	14	24	34	47	54	49	39	29	16	3	-5

Note: Figures cover the years 1945-1990
Source: National Climatic Data Center, International Station Meteorological Climate Summary, 9/96

Average Precipitation/Snowfall/Humidity

Precip./Humidity	Jan	Feb	Mar	Apr	May	Jun	Jul	Aug	Sep	Oct	Nov	Dec	Yr.
Avg. Precip. (in.)	2.8	2.6	3.3	2.9	4.0	3.4	4.1	4.2	3.3	2.9	3.0	3.1	39.5
Avg. Snowfall (in.)	6	6	2	Tr	0	0	0	0	0	Tr	1	3	18
Avg. Rel. Hum. 7am (%)	71	70	70	70	74	75	77	80	82	80	76	72	75
Avg. Rel. Hum. 4pm (%)	54	50	46	45	51	52	53	54	54	53	53	55	52

Note: Figures cover the years 1945-1990; Tr = Trace amounts (<0.05 in. of rain; <0.5 in. of snow)
Source: National Climatic Data Center, International Station Meteorological Climate Summary, 9/96

Weather Conditions

Temperature			Daytime Sky			Precipitation		
10°F & below	32°F & below	90°F & above	Clear	Partly cloudy	Cloudy	0.01 inch or more precip.	0.1 inch or more snow/ice	Thunder-storms
2	71	34	84	143	138	112	9	30

Note: Figures are average number of days per year and cover the years 1945-1990
Source: National Climatic Data Center, International Station Meteorological Climate Summary, 9/96

HAZARDOUS WASTE

Superfund Sites

The Washington-Arlington-Alexandria, DC-VA-MD-WV metro division is home to 10 sites on the EPA's Superfund National Priorities List: **Andrews Air Force Base** (final); **Avtex Fibers, Inc.** (final); **Beltsville Agricultural Research Center (USDA)** (final); **Brandywine Drmo** (final); **Culpeper Wood Preservers, Inc.** (final); **Hidden Lane Landfill** (final); **Indian Head Naval Surface Warfare Center** (final); **L.A. Clarke & Son** (final); **Marine Corps Combat Development Command** (final); **Washington Navy Yard** (final). There are a total of 1,396 Superfund sites with a status of proposed or final on the list in the U.S. *U.S. Environmental Protection Agency, National Priorities List, April 4, 2018*

AIR & WATER QUALITY

Air Quality Trends: Ozone

	1990	1995	2000	2005	2010	2012	2013	2014	2015	2016
MSA[1]	0.088	0.093	0.082	0.081	0.077	0.075	0.065	0.065	0.067	0.068
U.S.	0.087	0.089	0.081	0.079	0.073	0.075	0.069	0.067	0.068	0.069

Note: (1) Data covers the Washington-Arlington-Alexandria, DC-VA-MD-WV Metropolitan Statistical Area—see Appendix B for areas included. The values shown are the composite ozone concentration averages among trend sites based on the highest fourth daily maximum 8-hour concentration in parts per million. These trends are based on sites having an adequate record of monitoring data during the trend period. Data from exceptional events are included.
Source: U.S. Environmental Protection Agency, Air Quality Monitoring Information, "Air Quality Trends by City, 1990-2016"

Air Quality Index

Area	Percent of Days when Air Quality was...[2]					AQI Statistics[2]	
	Good	Moderate	Unhealthy for Sensitive Groups	Unhealthy	Very Unhealthy	Maximum	Median
MSA[1]	40.0	57.8	2.2	0.0	0.0	133	53

Note: (1) Data covers the Washington-Arlington-Alexandria, DC-VA-MD-WV Metropolitan Statistical Area—see Appendix B for areas included; (2) Based on 365 days with AQI data in 2017. Air Quality Index (AQI) is an index for reporting daily air quality. EPA calculates the AQI for five major air pollutants regulated by the Clean Air Act: ground-level ozone, particle pollution (aka particulate matter), carbon monoxide, sulfur dioxide, and nitrogen dioxide. The AQI runs from 0 to 500. The higher the AQI value, the greater the level of air pollution and the greater the health concern. There are six AQI categories: "Good" AQI is between 0 and 50. Air quality is considered satisfactory; "Moderate" AQI is between 51 and 100. Air quality is acceptable; "Unhealthy for Sensitive Groups" When AQI values are between 101 and 150, members of sensitive groups may experience health effects; "Unhealthy" When AQI values are between 151 and 200 everyone may begin to experience health effects; "Very Unhealthy" AQI values between 201 and 300 trigger a health alert; "Hazardous" AQI values over 300 trigger warnings of emergency conditions (not shown).
Source: U.S. Environmental Protection Agency, Air Quality Index Report, 2017

Air Quality Index Pollutants

Area	Percent of Days when AQI Pollutant was...[2]					
	Carbon Monoxide	Nitrogen Dioxide	Ozone	Sulfur Dioxide	Particulate Matter 2.5	Particulate Matter 10
MSA[1]	0.0	5.8	44.1	0.0	50.1	0.0

Note: (1) Data covers the Washington-Arlington-Alexandria, DC-VA-MD-WV Metropolitan Statistical Area—see Appendix B for areas included; (2) Based on 365 days with AQI data in 2017. The Air Quality Index (AQI) is an index for reporting daily air quality. EPA calculates the AQI for five major air pollutants regulated by the Clean Air Act: ground-level ozone, particle pollution (also known as particulate matter), carbon monoxide, sulfur dioxide, and nitrogen dioxide. The AQI runs from 0 to 500. The higher the AQI value, the greater the level of air pollution and the greater the health concern.
Source: U.S. Environmental Protection Agency, Air Quality Index Report, 2017

Maximum Air Pollutant Concentrations: Particulate Matter, Ozone, CO and Lead

	Particulate Matter 10 (ug/m^3)	Particulate Matter 2.5 Wtd AM (ug/m^3)	Particulate Matter 2.5 24-Hr (ug/m^3)	Ozone (ppm)	Carbon Monoxide (ppm)	Lead (ug/m^3)
MSA[1] Level	41	8.5	20	0.076	2	0.01
NAAQS[2]	150	15	35	0.075	9	0.15
Met NAAQS[2]	Yes	Yes	Yes	No	Yes	Yes

Note: (1) Data covers the Washington-Arlington-Alexandria, DC-VA-MD-WV Metropolitan Statistical Area—see Appendix B for areas included; Data from exceptional events are included; (2) National Ambient Air Quality Standards; ppm = parts per million; ug/m^3 = micrograms per cubic meter; n/a not available.
Concentrations: Particulate Matter 10 (coarse particulate)—highest second maximum 24-hour concentration; Particulate Matter 2.5 Wtd AM (fine particulate)—highest weighted annual mean concentration; Particulate Matter 2.5 24-Hour (fine particulate)—highest 98th percentile 24-hour concentration; Ozone—highest fourth daily maximum 8-hour concentration; Carbon Monoxide—highest second maximum non-overlapping 8-hour concentration; Lead—maximum running 3-month average
Source: U.S. Environmental Protection Agency, Air Quality Monitoring Information, "Air Quality Statistics by City, 2016"

Maximum Air Pollutant Concentrations: Nitrogen Dioxide and Sulfur Dioxide

	Nitrogen Dioxide AM (ppb)	Nitrogen Dioxide 1-Hr (ppb)	Sulfur Dioxide AM (ppb)	Sulfur Dioxide 1-Hr (ppb)	Sulfur Dioxide 24-Hr (ppb)
MSA[1] Level	18	59	n/a	8	n/a
NAAQS[2]	53	100	30	75	140
Met NAAQS[2]	Yes	Yes	n/a	Yes	n/a

Note: (1) Data covers the Washington-Arlington-Alexandria, DC-VA-MD-WV Metropolitan Statistical Area—see Appendix B for areas included; Data from exceptional events are included; (2) National Ambient Air Quality Standards; ppm = parts per million; ug/m^3 = micrograms per cubic meter; n/a not available.
Concentrations: Nitrogen Dioxide AM—highest arithmetic mean concentration; Nitrogen Dioxide 1-Hr—highest 98th percentile 1-hour daily maximum concentration; Sulfur Dioxide AM—highest annual mean concentration; Sulfur Dioxide 1-Hr—highest 99th percentile 1-hour daily maximum concentration; Sulfur Dioxide 24-Hr—highest second maximum 24-hour concentration
Source: U.S. Environmental Protection Agency, Air Quality Monitoring Information, "Air Quality Statistics by City, 2016"

Drinking Water

Water System Name	Pop. Served	Primary Water Source Type	Violations[1]	
			Health Based	Monitoring/ Reporting
Town of Leesburg	61,540	Surface	0	0

Note: (1) Based on violation data from January 1, 2017 to December 31, 2017
Source: U.S. Environmental Protection Agency, Office of Ground Water and Drinking Water, Safe Drinking Water Information System (based on data extracted April 5, 2018)

Maple Valley, Washington

Background

In 1879, when a name for a future community was proposed, Vine Maple Valley and Maple Ridge were suggested, and Vine Maple Valley made the cut. "Vine" was later removed by the post office due to the name being too long, and the name Maple Valley stuck.

Coal mining, lumber, and the railroad defined the community as it grew, with blacksmith shops, hotels, schools, and stores populating the city in the 1910s and 1920s. Tahoma High School, a three-story brick school built in 1927, was named by the students as a combination of three local town names: Taylor, Hobart, and Maple Valley. The school still serves the Tahoma School District to this day as Tahoma Elementary School, while a newly renovated Tahoma High School was opened in 2017. Recently, the city has experienced new growth in the south side of Maple Valley where the new school is situated. The city was officially incorporated in 1997.

Maple Valley has a total area of 5.90 square miles. The Cedar River passes very close to the northeastern border of the city, through unincorporated King County. The main bodies of water within Maple Valley are Lake Wilderness, Lake Lucerne, Rock Creek, and part of Pipe Lake.

The city is served by the Tahoma School District, which encompasses six elementary schools, two middle schools, and one high school. Private schools in Maple Valley include Rainier Christian School, Renton Christian School, and the Russell Ridge Center.

Maple Valley is a city filled with lush, beautiful greenery and many city parks and outdoor recreational areas. These include Take-A-Break Park, Skate Park, Cedar River Trail, Lake Wilderness Park, and the Lake Wilderness Arboretum. The city boasts a year-around schedule of adult and children's activities and programs, including the Maple Valley Creative Arts Council's Arts Fest, and the annual Maple Valley Farmers' Market, held once each week during summer. Other events include the Annual Fishing Derby at Lake Wilderness, Music in the Park, Maple Valley Days, and Make a Difference Day. The Maple Valley Historical Society manages the Fire Engine Museum and the Gibbon Store and Gaffney's Grove, a popular resort on Lake Wilderness which closed in 1964 but reopened as Lake Wilderness Park.

The Greater Maple Valley Veterans Memorial Foundation is currently fundraising for a Maple Valley Veterans Memorial, with a projected 2018 dedication.

Rankings

General Rankings

- *US News & World Report* conducted a survey of more than 2,000 people and analyzed the 125 largest metropolitan areas to determine what matters the most when selecting the next place to live. Seattle* ranked #10 out of the top 25 as having the best combination of desirable factors. Criteria: cost of living; quality of education; job market, crime rates; and other factors. *realestate.usnews.com, "The 25 Best Places to Live in the U.S. in 2018," April 10, 2018*
- The Seattle* metro area was identified as one of America's fastest-growing areas in terms of population and economy by *Forbes.* The area ranked #2 out of 25. The 100 most populous metro areas in the U.S. were evaluated on the following criteria: estimated population growth; employment; economic output; wages; home values. *Forbes, "America's Fastest-Growing Cities 2018," February 28, 2018*

Business/Finance Rankings

- According to *Business Insider,* the Seattle* metro area is where startup growth is on the rise. Based on the 2017 Kauffman Index of Growth Entrepreneurship, which measured in-depth national entrepreneurial trends in 40 metro areas, it ranked #20 in highest startup growth. *www.businessinsider.com, "The 21 U.S. Cities with the Highest Startup Growth," October 21, 2017*
- The personal finance site NerdWallet analyzed 183 American metropolitan areas with populations over 250,000 and more than 15,000 businesses to rank where entrepreneurs find the most success. Criteria included area economy, annual income, housing cost, unemployment rate, and the success rate of area businesses. Seattle* ranked #18. *www.nerdwallet.com, "Best Places to Start a Business," April 27, 2015*
- 24/7 Wall Street used Brookings Institution research on 50 advanced industries to identify the proportion of workers in the nation's largest metropolitan areas that were employed in jobs requiring knowledge in the science, technology, engineering, or math (STEM) fields and where there was heavy investment in research and development (R&D). The Seattle* metro area was #2. *247wallst.com, "15 Cities with the Most High-Tech Jobs," February 23, 2017*
- Based on metro area social media reviews, the employment opinion group Glassdoor surveyed 50 of the largest U.S. metro areas and equally weighed cost of living, hiring opportunity, and job satisfaction to compose a list of "25 Best Cities for Jobs." Median pay and home value, in-demand jobs and number of current job openings was also factored in. The Seattle* metro area was ranked #17 in overall job satisfaction. *www.glassdoor.com, "Best Cities for Jobs," September 12, 2017*
- In a survey of economic confidence in the nation's 50 largest metropolitan areas conducted January–December 2014, the Seattle* metro area placed #7, according to Gallup's 2014 Economic Confidence Index. *Gallup, "San Jose and San Francisco Lead in Economic Confidence," March 19, 2015*
- The Brookings Institution ranked the 100 largest metro areas in the U.S. based on income inequality. Seattle* was ranked #71 (#1 = greatest ineqality). Criteria: the "95/20 ratio," a figure representing the income at which a household earns more than 95 percent of all other households, divided by the income at which a household earns more than only 20 percent of all other households. *Brookings Institution, "Household Income Inequality, 100 Largest U.S. Metro Areas, 2014-2016," February 5, 2018*
- *Forbes* ranked the 100 largest metro areas in the U.S. in terms of the "Best Cities for Young Professionals." The Seattle* metro area ranked #1 out of 25. (Large metro areas were divided into metro divisions.) Criteria: median rent of a two-bedroom apartment; job growth and unemployment rate; median salary of college graduates with 5 or less years of work experience; networking opportunities; social outlook; percentage of population 25 years of age and older with college degrees. *Forbes.com, "America's 25 Best Cities for Young Professionals in 2017," May 22, 2017*

- Payscale.com ranked the largest metro areas in terms of wage growth. The Seattle* metro area ranked #4. Criteria: private-sector wage growth between the 4th quarter of 2016 and the 4th quarter of 2017. *PayScale, "Wage Trends by Metro Area-4th Quarter," January 17, 2018*

- The Seattle* metro area was identified as one of the most debt-ridden places in America by the finance site Credit.com. The metro area was ranked #9. Criteria: residents' average credit card debt as well as median income. *Credit.com, "25 Cities With the Most Credit Card Debt," February 28, 2018*

- The Seattle* metro area appeared on the Milken Institute "2017 Best Performing Cities" list. Rank: #17 out of 200 large metro areas. Criteria: job growth; wage and salary growth; high-tech output growth. *Milken Institute, "Best-Performing Cities 2017," January 2018*

- *Forbes* ranked the 200 most populous metro areas to determine the nation's "Best Places for Business and Careers." The Seattle* metro area was ranked #3. Criteria: costs (business and living); job growth (past and projected); income growth; quality of life; educational attainment (college and high school); projected economic growth; cultural and recreational opportunities; net migration patterns; number of highly ranked colleges. *Forbes, "The Best Places for Business and Careers 2017," October 24, 2017*

Education Rankings

- Personal finance website *WalletHub* analyzed the 150 largest U.S. metropolitan statistical areas to determine where the most educated Americans are choosing to settle. Criteria: education quality and attainment gap; education levels; percentage of workers with degrees; public school rankings; quality and size of each metro area's universities. Seattle* was ranked #11 (#1 = most educated city). *www.WalletHub.com, "2017's Most and Least Educated Cities in America," July 25, 2017*

Environmental Rankings

- Sperling's BestPlaces assessed 379 metropolitan areas of the United States for the likelihood of dangerously extreme weather events or earthquakes. In general the Southeast and South-Central regions have the highest risk of weather extremes and earthquakes, while the Pacific Northwest enjoys the lowest risk. Of the least risky metropolitan areas, the Seattle* metro area was ranked #8. *www.bestplaces.net, "Safest Places from Natural Disasters," April 2011*

- The U.S. Environmental Protection Agency (EPA) released a list of U.S. metropolitan areas with the most ENERGY STAR certified buildings in 2016. The Seattle* metro area was ranked #15 out of 25. *U.S. Environmental Protection Agency, "2017 Energy Star Top Cities," June 2017*

- Seattle* was highlighted as one of the 25 metro areas most polluted by short-term particle pollution (24-hour PM 2.5) in the U.S. during 2013 through 2015. The area ranked #17. *American Lung Association, State of the Air 2017*

Health/Fitness Rankings

- Analysts who tracked obesity rates in the nation's largest metro areas (populations above one million) found that the Seattle* metro area was one of the ten major metros where residents were least likely to be obese, defined as a BMI score of 30 or above. *www.gallup.com, "Boulder, Colo., Residents Still Least Likely to Be Obese," April 4, 2014*

- For each of the 50 most populous metro areas in the United States, the American College of Sports Medicine's American Fitness Index evaluated infrastructure, community assets, and policies that encourage healthy and fit lifestyles, including preventive health behaviors, levels of chronic disease conditions, health care access, and community resources and policies that support physical activity. The Seattle* metro area ranked #4 for "community fitness." *www.americanfitnessindex.org, "ACSM American Fitness Index Health and Community Fitness Status of the 50 Largest Metropolitan Areas," May 2017*

- Trulia analyzed the 100 largest U.S. metro areas to identify the nation's best cities for weight loss, based on the percentage of adults who bike or walk to work, sporting goods stores, grocery stores, access to outdoor activities, weight-loss centers, gyms, and average space reserved for parks. Seattle* ranked #4. *Trulia.com, "Where to Live to Get in Shape in the New Year," January 4, 2018*
- The Seattle* metro area was identified as one of the worst cities for bed bugs in America by pest control company Orkin. The area ranked #36 out of 50 based on the number of bed bug treatments Orkin performed from December 2016 to November 2017. *Orkin, "Baltimore and Washington D.C. Continue to Hold Top Spots," January 8, 2018*
- Seattle* was identified as a "2016 Spring Allergy Capital." The area ranked #82 out of 100. Three groups of factors were used to identify the most severe cities for people with allergies during the spring season: annual pollen levels; medicine utilization; access to board-certified allergists. *Asthma and Allergy Foundation of America, "Spring Allergy Capitals 2016"*
- Seattle* was identified as a "2016 Fall Allergy Capital." The area ranked #89 out of 100. Three groups of factors were used to identify the most severe cities for people with allergies during the fall season: annual pollen levels; medicine utilization; access to board-certified allergists. *Asthma and Allergy Foundation of America, "Fall Allergy Capitals 2016"*
- Seattle* was identified as a "2015 Asthma Capital." The area ranked #98 out of the nation's 100 largest metropolitan areas. Criteria: estimated prevalence; self-reported prevalence; crude death rate for asthma; annual pollen score; annual air quality; public smoking laws; number of board-certified asthma specialists; school inhaler access laws; rescue medication use; controller medication use; ER visits for asthma; uninsured rate; poverty rate. *Asthma and Allergy Foundation of America, "Asthma Capitals 2015"*
- The Seattle* metro area ranked #85 out of 189 in The Gallup-Healthways Well-Being Index. Criteria: purpose; social well being; financial health; community and physical health. Results are based on telephone interviews with adults, aged 18 and older, living in metropolitan areas in the 50 U.S. states and the District of Columbia. *Gallup-Healthways, "State of American Well-Being, 2017 Community Well-Being Rankings" March 2018*

Real Estate Rankings

- FitSmallBusiness looked at 50 of the largest metropolitan areas in the U.S. to determine which metro was the best to start a real estate business. Data was compiled from such sources as: Zillow, Trulia, U.S. Census Bureau, and the Bureau of Labor Statistics. Criteria: location; inventory; annual wages; median sales price of homes; days on the market; median price cut percentage; and other factors that would influence real estate professional growth. The Seattle* metro area ranked #27. *fitsmallbusiness.com, "The Best Cities to Become a Real Estate Agent in 2018," January 30, 2018*
- With data from RealtyTrac, Yahoo! Finance researchers listed the housing markets in which housing affordability is improving most, factoring in interest rates as well as median home prices. The Seattle* metro area was among the least affordable housing markets. *news.yahoo.com, "10 Cities Where Ordinary People Can No Longer Afford Homes," March 5, 2014*
- Seattle* was ranked #2 in the top 20 out of 265 metro areas in terms of house price appreciation in 2017 (#1 = highest rate). *Federal Housing Finance Agency, House Price Index, 4th Quarter 2017. February 27, 2018*
- The Seattle* metro area was identified as one of the 10 worst housing markets to invest in. Criteria: single-family rental home investing in the first quarter of 2017 based on first-year returns. The area ranked #6. *The Business Insider, "Here Are the 10 Worst U.S. Housing Markets for Investment," May 12, 2017*
- The Seattle* metro area was identified as one of the 20 best housing markets in the U.S. in 2017. The area ranked #14 out of 180 markets. Criteria: year-over-year change of median sales price of existing single-family homes between the 4th quarter of 2016 and the 4th quarter of 2017. *National Association of Realtors®, Median Sales Price of Existing Single-Family Homes for Metropolitan Areas, 4th Quarter 2017*

- The Seattle* metro area was identified as one of the 20 least affordable housing markets in the U.S. in 2017. The area ranked #13 out of 180 markets. Criteria: qualification for a mortgage loan on a typical home. *National Association of Realtors®, Affordability Index of Existing Single-Family Homes for Metropolitan Areas, 2017*
- Seattle* was ranked #210 out of 238 metro areas in terms of housing affordability in 2017 by the National Association of Home Builders (#1 = most affordable). Criteria: the share of homes sold in that area affordable to a family earning the local median income, based on standard mortgage underwriting criteria. *National Association of Home Builders®, NAHB-Wells Fargo Housing Opportunity Index, 4th Quarter 2017*

Safety Rankings

- The National Insurance Crime Bureau ranked 382 metro areas in the U.S. in terms of per capita rates of vehicle theft. The Seattle* metro area ranked #22 (#1 = highest rate). Criteria: number of vehicle theft offenses per 100,000 inhabitants in 2016. *National Insurance Crime Bureau, "Hot Spots 2016," June 8, 2017*

Seniors/Retirement Rankings

- From its Best Cities for Successful Aging indexes, the Milken Institute generated rankings for metropolitan areas, weighing data in nine categories—health care, wellness, living arrangements, transportation and convenience, financial characteristics, education, employment, community engagement, and overall livability. The Seattle* metro area was ranked #43 overall in the large metro area category. *Milken Institute, "Best Cities for Successful Aging, 2017" March 14, 2017*

Transportation Rankings

- Seattle* was identified as one of the most congested metro areas in the U.S. The area ranked #7 out of 10. Criteria: yearly delay per auto commuter in hours. *Texas A&M Transportation Institute, "2015 Urban Mobility Scorecard," August 2015*
- The Seattle* metro area appeared on *Forbes* list of places with the most extreme commutes. The metro area ranked #10 out of 10. Criteria: average travel time; percentage of mega commuters. Mega-commuters travel more than 90 minutes and 50 miles each way to work. *Forbes.com, "The Cities with the Most Extreme Commutes," March 5, 2013*

Miscellaneous Rankings

- Of the American metro areas that allow medical or recreational use of marijuana, the Seattle* metro area was identified by CNBC editors as one of the most livable for marijuana lovers. Criteria included the Sperling's BestPlaces assessment of marijuana-friendly cities in terms of sound economy, cultural diversity, and a healthy population, plus cost-of-living index and high-quality schools. *www.cnbc.com, "The Best Cities to Live for Marijuana Lovers," February 5, 2014*
- The watchdog site Charity Navigator conducts an annual study of charities in the nation's major markets both to analyze statistical differences in their financial, accountability, and transparency practices and to track year-to-year variations in individual philanthropic communities. Charity Navigator's analysis demonstrated that the financial, accountability and transparency behaviors of America's largest charities can be influenced by the metropolitan market within which the charity operates. The Seattle* metro area was ranked #25 among the 30 metro markets in the rating category of Overall Score. *www.charitynavigator.org, "2017 Metro Market Study," May 1, 2017*
- The National Alliance to End Homelessness listed the 25 most populous metro areas with the highest rate of homelessness. The Seattle* metro area had a high rate of homelessness. Criteria: number of homeless people per 10,000 population in 2016. *National Alliance to End Homelessness, "Homelessness in the 25 Most Populous U.S. Metro Areas," September 1, 2017*

*Maple Valley is located within the Seattle-Tacoma-Bellevue, WA Metropolitan Statistical Area and the Seattle-Bellevue-Everett, WA Metropolitan Division.

Business Environment

CITY FINANCES

City Government Finances

Component	2015 ($000)	2015 ($ per capita)
Total Revenues	n/a	n/a
Total Expenditures	n/a	n/a
Debt Outstanding	n/a	n/a
Cash and Securities[1]	n/a	n/a

Note: (1) Cash and security holdings of a government at the close of its fiscal year,, including those of its dependent agencies, utilities, and liquor stores.
Source: U.S Census Bureau, State & Local Government Finances 2015

City Government Revenue by Source

Source	2015 ($000)	2015 ($ per capita)	2015 (%)
General Revenue			
From Federal Government	n/a	n/a	n/a
From State Government	n/a	n/a	n/a
From Local Governments	n/a	n/a	n/a
Taxes			
Property	n/a	n/a	n/a
Sales and Gross Receipts	n/a	n/a	n/a
Personal Income	n/a	n/a	n/a
Corporate Income	n/a	n/a	n/a
Motor Vehicle License	n/a	n/a	n/a
Other Taxes	n/a	n/a	n/a
Current Charges	n/a	n/a	n/a
Liquor Store	n/a	n/a	n/a
Utility	n/a	n/a	n/a
Employee Retirement	n/a	n/a	n/a

Source: U.S Census Bureau, State & Local Government Finances 2015

City Government Expenditures by Function

Function	2015 ($000)	2015 ($ per capita)	2015 (%)
General Direct Expenditures			
Air Transportation	n/a	n/a	n/a
Corrections	n/a	n/a	n/a
Education	n/a	n/a	n/a
Employment Security Administration	n/a	n/a	n/a
Financial Administration	n/a	n/a	n/a
Fire Protection	n/a	n/a	n/a
General Public Buildings	n/a	n/a	n/a
Governmental Administration, Other	n/a	n/a	n/a
Health	n/a	n/a	n/a
Highways	n/a	n/a	n/a
Hospitals	n/a	n/a	n/a
Housing and Community Development	n/a	n/a	n/a
Interest on General Debt	n/a	n/a	n/a
Judicial and Legal	n/a	n/a	n/a
Libraries	n/a	n/a	n/a
Parking	n/a	n/a	n/a
Parks and Recreation	n/a	n/a	n/a
Police Protection	n/a	n/a	n/a
Public Welfare	n/a	n/a	n/a
Sewerage	n/a	n/a	n/a
Solid Waste Management	n/a	n/a	n/a
Veterans' Services	n/a	n/a	n/a
Liquor Store	n/a	n/a	n/a
Utility	n/a	n/a	n/a
Employee Retirement	n/a	n/a	n/a

Source: U.S Census Bureau, State & Local Government Finances 2015

DEMOGRAPHICS

Population Growth

Area	1990 Census	2000 Census	2010 Census	2016* Estimate	Population Growth (%)	
					1990-2016	2010-2016
City	6,490	14,209	22,684	25,093	286.6	10.6
MSA[1]	2,559,164	3,043,878	3,439,809	3,671,095	43.4	6.7
U.S.	248,709,873	281,421,906	308,745,538	318,558,162	28.1	3.2

Note: (1) Figures cover the Seattle-Tacoma-Bellevue, WA Metropolitan Statistical Area—see Appendix B for areas included; (*) 2012-2016 5-year estimated population
Source: U.S. Census Bureau, 1990 Census, Census 2000, Census 2010, 2012-2016 American Community Survey 5-Year Estimates

Household Size

Area	Persons in Household (%)							Average Household Size
	One	Two	Three	Four	Five	Six	Seven or More	
City	17.6	30.0	15.7	22.9	10.5	2.6	0.7	2.90
MSA[1]	28.3	34.1	15.9	13.3	5.3	2.0	1.2	2.50
U.S.	27.7	33.7	15.7	13.1	6.0	2.3	1.5	2.60

Note: (1) Figures cover the Seattle-Tacoma-Bellevue, WA Metropolitan Statistical Area—see Appendix B for areas included
Source: U.S. Census Bureau, 2012-2016 American Community Survey 5-Year Estimates

Race

Area	White Alone[2] (%)	Black Alone[2] (%)	Asian Alone[2] (%)	AIAN[3] Alone[2] (%)	NHOPI[4] Alone[2] (%)	Other Race Alone[2] (%)	Two or More Races (%)
City	82.9	2.4	6.2	0.4	0.0	1.3	6.8
MSA[1]	71.1	5.6	12.4	0.9	0.9	3.0	6.3
U.S.	73.3	12.6	5.2	0.8	0.2	4.8	3.1

Note: (1) Figures cover the Seattle-Tacoma-Bellevue, WA Metropolitan Statistical Area—see Appendix B for areas included; (2) Alone is defined as not being in combination with one or more other races; (3) American Indian and Alaska Native; (4) Native Hawaiian and Other Pacific Islander
Source: U.S. Census Bureau, 2012-2016 American Community Survey 5-Year Estimates

Hispanic or Latino Origin

Area	Total (%)	Mexican (%)	Puerto Rican (%)	Cuban (%)	Other (%)
City	5.9	4.1	0.1	0.0	1.6
MSA[1]	9.6	6.8	0.5	0.1	2.1
U.S.	17.3	11.0	1.7	0.7	4.0

Note: Persons of Hispanic or Latino origin can be of any race; (1) Figures cover the Seattle-Tacoma-Bellevue, WA Metropolitan Statistical Area—see Appendix B for areas included
Source: U.S. Census Bureau, 2012-2016 American Community Survey 5-Year Estimates

Segregation

Type	Segregation Indices[1]				Percent Change		
	1990	2000	2010	2010 Rank[2]	1990-2000	1990-2010	2000-2010
Black/White	56.5	52.4	49.1	72	-4.1	-7.4	-3.3
Asian/White	36.8	37.6	37.6	69	0.8	0.8	0.0
Hispanic/White	22.3	30.4	32.8	87	8.1	10.5	2.4

Note: All figures cover the Metropolitan Statistical Area—see Appendix B for areas included; Figures are based on an analysis of 1990, 2000, and 2010 Census Decennial Census tract data by William H. Frey, Brookings Institution and the University of Michigan Social Science Data Analysis Network. In this analysis all racial groups (whites, blacks, and asians) are non-Hispanic members of those races. Hispanics are shown as a separate category; (1) Segregation Indices are Dissimilarity Indices that measure the degree to which the minority group is distributed differently than whites across census tracts. They range from 0 (complete integration) to 100 (complete segregation) where the value indicates the percentage of the minority group that needs to move to be distributed exactly like whites; (2) Ranges from 1 (most segregated) to 102 (least segregated); n/a not available.
Source: www.CensusScope.org

Ancestry

Area	German	Irish	English	American	Italian	Polish	French[2]	Scottish	Dutch
City	19.9	13.3	14.9	4.6	6.0	2.2	3.2	2.3	2.5
MSA[1]	16.2	10.3	10.1	3.7	3.7	2.0	3.0	2.8	1.7
U.S.	14.4	10.4	7.7	6.9	5.4	2.9	2.6	1.7	1.3

Note: Figures are the percentage of the total population reporting a particular ancestry. The nine most commonly reported ancestries in the U.S. are shown. Figures include multiple ancestries (e.g. if a person reported being Irish and Italian, they were included in both columns); (1) Figures cover the Seattle-Tacoma-Bellevue, WA Metropolitan Statistical Area—see Appendix B for areas included; (2) Excludes Basque
Source: U.S. Census Bureau, 2012-2016 American Community Survey 5-Year Estimates

Foreign-Born Population

Area	Percent of Population Born in								
	Any Foreign Country	Asia	Mexico	Europe	Carribean	Central America[2]	South America	Africa	Canada
City	7.0	3.8	0.7	1.5	0.0	0.2	0.1	0.3	0.3
MSA[1]	17.5	8.9	2.4	2.7	0.1	0.5	0.4	1.3	0.7
U.S.	13.2	4.0	3.6	1.5	1.3	1.0	0.9	0.6	0.3

Note: (1) Figures cover the Seattle-Tacoma-Bellevue, WA Metropolitan Statistical Area—see Appendix B for areas included; (2) Excludes Mexico.
Source: U.S. Census Bureau, 2012-2016 American Community Survey 5-Year Estimates

Marital Status

Area	Never Married	Now Married[2]	Separated	Widowed	Divorced
City	20.1	64.0	0.9	3.8	11.1
MSA[1]	32.5	50.2	1.5	4.4	11.5
U.S.	33.0	48.1	2.1	5.9	11.0

Note: Figures are percentages and cover the population 15 years of age and older; (1) Figures cover the Seattle-Tacoma-Bellevue, WA Metropolitan Statistical Area—see Appendix B for areas included; (2) Excludes separated
Source: U.S. Census Bureau, 2012-2016 American Community Survey 5-Year Estimates

Disability Status

Area	All Ages	Under 18 Years Old	18 to 64 Years Old	65 Years and Over
City	7.7	5.6	5.6	33.1
MSA[1]	11.0	3.5	9.1	34.7
U.S.	12.5	4.1	10.3	35.7

Note: Figures show percent of the civilian noninstitutionalized population that reported having a disability. Disability status is determined from six types of difficulty: vision, hearing, cognitive, ambulatory, self-care, and independent living. For children under 5 years old, hearing and vision difficulty are used to determine disability status. For children between the ages of 5 and 14, disability status is determined from hearing, vision, cognitive, ambulatory, and self-care difficulties. For people aged 15 years and older, they are considered to have a disability if they have difficulty with any one of the six difficulty types; Note: (1) Figures cover the Seattle-Tacoma-Bellevue, WA Metropolitan Statistical Area—see Appendix B for areas included
Source: U.S. Census Bureau, 2012-2016 American Community Survey 5-Year Estimates

Age

Area	Percent of Population									Median Age
	Under Age 5	Age 5–19	Age 20–34	Age 35–44	Age 45–54	Age 55–64	Age 65–74	Age 75–84	Age 85+	
City	8.3	25.5	15.0	17.8	16.0	9.8	4.8	2.0	0.7	35.6
MSA[1]	6.3	18.1	22.6	14.2	14.2	12.5	7.2	3.4	1.6	37.1
U.S.	6.2	19.6	20.7	12.7	13.6	12.6	8.3	4.3	1.9	37.7

Note: (1) Figures cover the Seattle-Tacoma-Bellevue, WA Metropolitan Statistical Area—see Appendix B for areas included
Source: U.S. Census Bureau, 2012-2016 American Community Survey 5-Year Estimates

Gender

Area	Males	Females	Males per 100 Females
City	12,067	13,026	92.6
MSA[1]	1,831,699	1,839,396	99.6
U.S.	156,765,322	161,792,840	96.9

Note: (1) Figures cover the Seattle-Tacoma-Bellevue, WA Metropolitan Statistical Area—see Appendix B for areas included
Source: U.S. Census Bureau, 2012-2016 American Community Survey 5-Year Estimates

Religious Groups by Family

Area	Catholic	Baptist	Non-Den.	Methodist[2]	Lutheran	LDS[3]	Pente-costal	Presby-terian[4]	Muslim[5]	Judaism
MSA[1]	12.3	2.2	5.0	1.2	2.1	3.3	2.8	1.4	0.5	0.5
U.S.	19.1	9.3	4.0	4.0	2.3	2.0	1.9	1.6	0.8	0.7

Note: Figures are the number of adherents as a percentage of the total population; (1) Figures cover the Seattle-Tacoma-Bellevue, WA Metropolitan Statistical Area—see Appendix B for areas included; (2) Methodist/Pietist; (3) Latter Day Saints; (4) Reformed; (5) Figures are estimates
Source: Association of Statisticians of American Religious Bodies, 2010 U.S. Religion Census: Religious Congregations & Membership Study

Religious Groups by Tradition

Area	Catholic	Evangelical Protestant	Mainline Protestant	Other Tradition	Black Protestant	Orthodox
MSA[1]	12.3	11.9	4.7	5.9	0.4	0.4
U.S.	19.1	16.2	7.3	4.3	1.6	0.3

Note: Figures are the number of adherents as a percentage of the total population; (1) Figures cover the Seattle-Tacoma-Bellevue, WA Metropolitan Statistical Area—see Appendix B for areas included
Source: Association of Statisticians of American Religious Bodies, 2010 U.S. Religion Census: Religious Congregations & Membership Study

ECONOMY

Gross Metropolitan Product

Area	2014	2015	2016	2017	Rank[2]
MSA[1]	297.9	314.1	324.1	339.1	12

Note: Figures are in billions of dollars; (1) Figures cover the Seattle-Tacoma-Bellevue, WA Metropolitan Statistical Area—see Appendix B for areas included; (2) Rank is based on 2015 data and ranges from 1 to 381
Source: The U.S. Conference of Mayors, U.S. Metro Economies: GMP and Employment Report, 2015-2017

Economic Growth

Area	2012-14 (%)	2015 (%)	2016 (%)	2017 (%)	Rank[2]
MSA[1]	2.5	3.8	1.9	2.8	93
U.S.	2.0	2.4	1.9	2.6	–

Note: Figures are real gross metropolitan product (GMP) growth rates and represent average annual percent change; (1) Figures cover the Seattle-Tacoma-Bellevue, WA Metropolitan Statistical Area—see Appendix B for areas included; (2) Rank is based on 2012-2014 average annual percent change and ranges from 1 to 381
Source: The U.S. Conference of Mayors, U.S. Metro Economies: GMP and Employment Report, 2015-2017

Metropolitan Area Exports

Area	2011	2012	2013	2014	2015	2016	Rank[2]
MSA[1]	41,117.5	50,301.7	56,686.4	61,938.4	67,226.4	61,881.0	3

Note: Figures are in millions of dollars; (1) Figures cover the Seattle-Tacoma-Bellevue, WA Metropolitan Statistical Area—see Appendix B for areas included; (2) Rank is based on 2016 data and ranges from 1 to 385
Source: U.S. Department of Commerce, International Trade Administration, Office of Trade & Industry Information, Manufacturing & Services, data extracted March 15, 2018

Building Permits

Area	Single-Family			Multi-Family			Total		
	2016	2017p	Pct. Chg.	2016	2017p	Pct. Chg.	2016	2017p	Pct. Chg.
City	51	117	129.4	0	326	n/a	51	443	768.6
MSA[1]	9,396	9,943	5.8	16,120	17,428	8.1	25,516	27,371	7.3
U.S.	750,800	817,300	8.9	455,800	446,800	-2.0	1,206,600	1,264,100	4.8

Note: (1) Figures cover the Seattle-Tacoma-Bellevue, WA Metropolitan Statistical Area—see Appendix B for areas included; Figures represent new, privately-owned housing units authorized (unadjusted data); All permit data are based on estimates with imputation; (p) preliminary data.
Source: U.S. Census Bureau, Manufacturing, Mining, and Construction Statistics, Building Permits, 2016, 2017

Bankruptcy Filings

Area	Business Filings			Nonbusiness Filings		
	2016	2017	% Chg.	2016	2017	% Chg.
King County	129	142	10.1	3,161	2,633	-16.7
U.S.	24,114	23,157	-4.0	770,846	765,863	-0.6

Note: Business filings include Chapter 7, Chapter 11, Chapter 12, and Chapter 13; Nonbusiness filings include Chapter 7, Chapter 11, and Chapter 13
Source: Administrative Office of the U.S. Courts, Business and Nonbusiness Bankruptcy, County Cases Commenced by Chapter of the Bankruptcy Code, During the 12-Month Period Ending December 31, 2016 and Business and Nonbusiness Bankruptcy, County Cases Commenced by Chapter of the Bankruptcy Code, During the 12-Month Period Ending December 31, 2017

Housing Vacancy Rates

Area	Gross Vacancy Rate[2] (%)			Year-Round Vacancy Rate[3] (%)			Rental Vacancy Rate[4] (%)			Homeowner Vacancy Rate[5] (%)		
	2015	2016	2017	2015	2016	2017	2015	2016	2017	2015	2016	2017
MSA[1]	5.6	5.6	6.0	5.4	5.3	5.4	3.8	3.3	3.4	1.1	0.9	0.5
U.S.	12.9	12.8	12.7	10.0	9.9	9.9	7.1	6.9	7.2	1.8	1.7	1.6

Note: (1) Figures cover the Seattle-Tacoma-Bellevue, WA Metropolitan Statistical Area—see Appendix B for areas included; (2) The percentage of the total housing inventory that is vacant; (3) The percentage of the housing inventory (excluding seasonal units) that is year-round vacant; (4) The percentage of rental inventory that is vacant for rent; (5) The percentage of homeowner inventory that is vacant for sale
Source: U.S. Census Bureau, Housing Vacancies and Homeownership Annual Statistics: 2015, 2016, 2017

INCOME

Income

Area	Per Capita ($)	Median Household ($)	Average Household ($)
City	38,227	98,925	111,352
MSA[1]	38,466	73,044	97,001
U.S.	29,829	55,322	77,866

Note: (1) Figures cover the Seattle-Tacoma-Bellevue, WA Metropolitan Statistical Area—see Appendix B for areas included
Source: U.S. Census Bureau, 2012-2016 American Community Survey 5-Year Estimates

Household Income Distribution

Area	Percent of Households Earning							
	Under $15,000	$15,000 -$24,999	$25,000 -$34,999	$35,000 -$49,999	$50,000 -$74,999	$75,000 -$99,999	$100,000 -$149,999	$150,000 and up
City	2.8	4.2	2.9	6.4	17.9	16.5	27.4	21.9
MSA[1]	8.5	6.8	7.3	11.4	17.3	13.6	17.8	17.4
U.S.	12.1	10.2	9.9	13.2	17.8	12.2	13.5	11.1

Note: (1) Figures cover the Seattle-Tacoma-Bellevue, WA Metropolitan Statistical Area—see Appendix B for areas included
Source: U.S. Census Bureau, 2012-2016 American Community Survey 5-Year Estimates

Poverty Rate

Area	All Ages	Under 18 Years Old	18 to 64 Years Old	65 Years and Over
City	4.2	5.2	3.6	5.0
MSA[1]	10.9	13.7	10.4	8.2
U.S.	15.1	21.2	14.2	9.3

Note: Figures are percentage of people whose income during the past 12 months was below the poverty level; (1) Figures cover the Seattle-Tacoma-Bellevue, WA Metropolitan Statistical Area—see Appendix B for areas included
Source: U.S. Census Bureau, 2012-2016 American Community Survey 5-Year Estimates

EMPLOYMENT

Labor Force and Employment

Area	Civilian Labor Force			Workers Employed		
	Dec. 2016	Dec. 2017	% Chg.	Dec. 2016	Dec. 2017	% Chg.
City	13,317	13,764	3.4	12,898	13,267	2.9
MD[1]	1,613,459	1,663,045	3.1	1,557,412	1,602,109	2.9
U.S.	158,968,000	159,880,000	0.6	151,798,000	153,602,000	1.2

Note: Data is not seasonally adjusted and covers workers 16 years of age and older; (1) Figures cover the Seattle-Bellevue-Everett, WA Metropolitan Division—see Appendix B for areas included
Source: Bureau of Labor Statistics, Local Area Unemployment Statistics

Unemployment Rate

Area	2017											
	Jan.	Feb.	Mar.	Apr.	May	Jun.	Jul.	Aug.	Sep.	Oct.	Nov.	Dec.
City	3.7	3.6	3.5	3.1	3.4	3.7	3.7	3.9	3.8	3.5	3.9	3.6
MD[1]	3.8	3.8	3.6	3.2	3.5	4.0	4.1	4.1	4.0	3.9	4.1	3.7
U.S.	5.1	4.9	4.6	4.1	4.1	4.5	4.6	4.5	4.1	3.9	3.9	3.9

Note: Data is not seasonally adjusted and covers workers 16 years of age and older; (1) Figures cover the Seattle-Bellevue-Everett, WA Metropolitan Division—see Appendix B for areas included
Source: Bureau of Labor Statistics, Local Area Unemployment Statistics

Average Wages

Occupation	$/Hr.	Occupation	$/Hr.
Accountants and Auditors	38.60	Maids and Housekeeping Cleaners	13.80
Automotive Mechanics	24.00	Maintenance and Repair Workers	22.80
Bookkeepers	22.40	Marketing Managers	75.80
Carpenters	29.80	Nuclear Medicine Technologists	44.70
Cashiers	14.30	Nurses, Licensed Practical	27.60
Clerks, General Office	19.70	Nurses, Registered	39.40
Clerks, Receptionists/Information	16.80	Nursing Assistants	15.20
Clerks, Shipping/Receiving	18.50	Packers and Packagers, Hand	14.10
Computer Programmers	60.00	Physical Therapists	43.20
Computer Systems Analysts	48.00	Postal Service Mail Carriers	24.20
Computer User Support Specialists	32.00	Real Estate Brokers	32.20
Cooks, Restaurant	15.40	Retail Salespersons	17.30
Dentists	88.40	Sales Reps., Exc. Tech./Scientific	35.60
Electrical Engineers	55.20	Sales Reps., Tech./Scientific	43.90
Electricians	33.40	Secretaries, Exc. Legal/Med./Exec.	21.40
Financial Managers	71.10	Security Guards	17.30
First-Line Supervisors/Managers, Sales	25.90	Surgeons	120.50
Food Preparation Workers	15.00	Teacher Assistants*	17.40
General and Operations Managers	67.80	Teachers, Elementary School*	30.90
Hairdressers/Cosmetologists	21.30	Teachers, Secondary School*	31.90
Internists, General	116.90	Telemarketers	17.50
Janitors and Cleaners	16.00	Truck Drivers, Heavy/Tractor-Trailer	23.90
Landscaping/Groundskeeping Workers	17.90	Truck Drivers, Light/Delivery Svcs.	19.50
Lawyers	68.30	Waiters and Waitresses	18.10

Note: Wage data covers the Seattle-Bellevue-Everett, WA Metropolitan Division—see Appendix B for areas included; (*) Hourly wages for elementary/secondary school teachers and teacher assistants were calculated by the editors from annual wage data based on a 40 hour work week; n/a not available.
Source: Bureau of Labor Statistics, Metro Area Occupational Employment & Wage Estimates, May 2017

Employment by Occupation

Occupation Classification	City (%)	MSA[1] (%)	U.S. (%)
Management, Business, Science, and Arts	47.4	44.2	37.0
Natural Resources, Construction, and Maintenance	6.4	7.5	8.9
Production, Transportation, and Material Moving	8.7	10.2	12.2
Sales and Office	27.1	21.8	23.8
Service	10.4	16.2	18.1

Note: Figures cover employed civilians 16 years of age and older; (1) Figures cover the Seattle-Tacoma-Bellevue, WA Metropolitan Statistical Area—see Appendix B for areas included
Source: U.S. Census Bureau, 2012-2016 American Community Survey 5-Year Estimates

Employment by Industry

Sector	MD[1] Number of Employees	MD[1] Percent of Total	U.S. Percent of Total
Construction	101,300	5.9	4.7
Education and Health Services	218,600	12.7	15.9
Financial Activities	86,200	5.0	5.7
Government	222,800	13.0	15.3
Information	111,000	6.5	1.9
Leisure and Hospitality	170,700	9.9	10.7
Manufacturing	157,600	9.2	8.5
Mining and Logging	800	<0.1	0.5
Other Services	59,100	3.4	3.9
Professional and Business Services	260,700	15.2	14.0
Retail Trade	197,300	11.5	11.0
Transportation, Warehousing, and Utilities	59,400	3.5	4.1
Wholesale Trade	73,100	4.3	4.0

Note: Figures are non-farm employment as of December 2017. Figures are not seasonally adjusted and include workers 16 years of age and older; (1) Figures cover the Seattle-Bellevue-Everett, WA Metropolitan Division—see Appendix B for areas included
Source: Bureau of Labor Statistics, Current Employment Statistics, Employment, Hours, and Earnings

Occupations with Greatest Projected Employment Growth: 2017 – 2019

Occupation[1]	2017 Employment	2019 Projected Employment	Numeric Employment Change	Percent Employment Change
Software Developers, Applications	71,590	80,750	9,160	12.8
Combined Food Preparation and Serving Workers, Including Fast Food	89,540	95,300	5,760	6.4
Waiters and Waitresses	49,520	52,940	3,420	6.9
Carpenters	50,500	53,840	3,340	6.6
Office Clerks, General	73,340	76,280	2,940	4.0
Janitors and Cleaners, Except Maids and Housekeeping Cleaners	50,690	53,370	2,680	5.3
Customer Service Representatives	53,140	55,500	2,360	4.4
Retail Salespersons	105,870	108,230	2,360	2.2
Registered Nurses	59,730	62,060	2,330	3.9
Construction Laborers	38,500	40,790	2,290	5.9

Note: Projections cover Washington; (1) Sorted by numeric employment change
Source: www.projectionscentral.com, State Occupational Projections, 2017–2019 Short-Term Projections

Fastest Growing Occupations: 2017 – 2019

Occupation[1]	2017 Employment	2019 Projected Employment	Numeric Employment Change	Percent Employment Change
Psychiatric Technicians	750	850	100	12.8
Software Developers, Applications	71,590	80,750	9,160	12.8
Travel Agents	1,720	1,930	210	11.9
Computer Operators	870	970	100	11.3
Computer Programmers	15,710	17,310	1,600	10.2
Multimedia Artists and Animators	4,550	5,020	470	10.2
Web Developers	7,050	7,750	700	10.0
Computer and Information Systems Managers	13,190	14,420	1,230	9.3
Editors	2,910	3,170	260	9.0
Database Administrators	2,670	2,900	230	8.6

Note: Projections cover Washington; (1) Sorted by percent employment change and excludes occupations with numeric employment change less than 50
Source: www.projectionscentral.com, State Occupational Projections, 2017–2019 Short-Term Projections

TAXES

State Corporate Income Tax Rates

State	Tax Rate (%)	Income Brackets ($)	Num. of Brackets	Financial Institution Tax Rate (%)[a]	Federal Income Tax Ded.
Washington	None	–	–	–	–

Note: Tax rates as of January 1, 2018; (a) Rates listed are the corporate income tax rate applied to financial institutions or excise taxes based on income. Some states have other taxes based upon the value of deposits or shares.
Source: Federation of Tax Administrators, Range of State Corporate Income Tax Rates, January 1, 2018

State Individual Income Tax Rates

State	Tax Rate (%)	Income Brackets ($)	Num. of Brackets	Personal Exempt. ($)[1]		Fed. Inc. Tax Ded.
				Single	Dependents	
Washington	None	–	–	–	–	–

Note: Tax rates as of January 1, 2018; Local- and county-level taxes are not included; n/a not applicable; (1) Married joint filers generally receive double the single exemption
Source: Federation of Tax Administrators, State Individual Income Tax Rates, January 1, 2018

Various State Sales and Excise Tax Rates

State	State Sales Tax (%)	Gasoline[1] (¢/gal.)	Cigarette[2] ($/pack)	Spirits[3] ($/gal.)	Wine[4] ($/gal.)	Beer[5] ($/gal.)	Recreational Marijuana (%)
Washington	6.5	49.4	3.025	32.52 (j)(k)	0.87 (l)	0.26 (q)	37.0

Note: All tax rates as of January 1, 2018; (1) The American Petroleum Institute has developed a methodology for determining the average tax rate on a gallon of fuel. Rates may include any of the following: excise taxes, environmental fees, storage tank fees, other fees or taxes, general sales tax, and local taxes. In states where gasoline is subject to the general sales tax, or where the fuel tax is based on the average sale price, the average rate determined by API is sensitive to changes in the price of gasoline. States that fully or partially apply general sales taxes to gasoline: CA, CO, GA, IL, IN, MI, NY; (2) The federal excise tax of $1.0066 per pack and local taxes are not included; (3) Rates are those applicable to off-premise sales of 40% alcohol by volume (a.b.v.) distilled spirits in 750ml containers. Local excise taxes are excluded; (4) Rates are those applicable to off-premise sales of 11% a.b.v. non-carbonated wine in 750ml containers; (5) Rates are those applicable to off-premise sales of 4.7% a.b.v. beer in 12 ounce containers; (j) Includes sales taxes specific to alcoholic beverages; (k) Includes the retail (17%) and distributor (5/10%) license fees, converted into a gallonage excise tax rate; (l) Different rates also applicable to alcohol content, place of production, size of container, place purchased (on- or off-premise or on board airlines) or type of wine (carbonated, vermouth, etc.); (q) Different rates also applicable according to alcohol content, place of production, size of container, or place purchased (on- or off-premise or onboard airlines).
Source: Tax Foundation, 2018 Facts & Figures: How Does Your State Compare?

State Business Tax Climate Index Rankings

State	Overall Rank	Corporate Tax Rank	Individual Income Tax Rank	Sales Tax Rank	Unemployment Insurance Tax Rank	Property Tax Rank
Washington	17	46	6	48	17	27

Note: The index is a measure of how each state's tax laws affect economic performance. The lower the rank, the more favorable a state's tax system is for business. States without a given tax are given a ranking of 1. The scores/rankings for the District of Columbia do not affect other states. The 2018 index represents the tax climate as of July 1, 2017.
Source: Tax Foundation, State Business Tax Climate Index 2018

TRANSPORTATION

Means of Transportation to Work

Area	Car/Truck/Van		Public Transportation			Bicycle	Walked	Other Means	Worked at Home
	Drove Alone	Car-pooled	Bus	Subway	Railroad				
City	77.4	9.6	2.5	0.5	0.8	0.2	0.9	1.2	7.0
MSA[1]	69.1	10.0	8.4	0.2	0.4	1.1	3.8	1.3	5.7
U.S.	76.4	9.3	2.6	1.9	0.6	0.6	2.8	1.3	4.6

Note: Figures are percentages and cover workers 16 years of age and older; (1) Figures cover the Seattle-Tacoma-Bellevue, WA Metropolitan Statistical Area—see Appendix B for areas included
Source: U.S. Census Bureau, 2012-2016 American Community Survey 5-Year Estimates

Travel Time to Work

Area	Less Than 10 Minutes	10 to 19 Minutes	20 to 29 Minutes	30 to 44 Minutes	45 to 59 Minutes	60 to 89 Minutes	90 Minutes or More
City	7.4	11.3	12.5	31.9	17.2	14.2	5.4
MSA[1]	8.2	23.9	21.5	25.1	10.5	7.9	2.9
U.S.	12.9	29.2	20.9	20.4	8.0	6.0	2.7

Note: Note: Figures are percentages and include workers 16 years old and over; (1) Figures cover the Seattle-Tacoma-Bellevue, WA Metropolitan Statistical Area—see Appendix B for areas included
Source: U.S. Census Bureau, 2012-2016 American Community Survey 5-Year Estimates

Freeway Travel Time Index

Area	1985	1990	1995	2000	2005	2010	2014
Urban Area Rank[1,2]	4	3	3	3	3	4	3
Urban Area Index[1]	1.22	1.26	1.29	1.33	1.37	1.36	1.38
Average Index[3]	1.09	1.11	1.14	1.17	1.20	1.19	1.20

Note: Freeway Travel Time Index—the ratio of travel time in the peak period to the travel time at free-flow conditions. For example, a value of 1.30 indicates a 20-minute free-flow trip takes 26 minutes in the peak (20 minutes x 1.30 = 26 minutes); (1) Covers the Seattle WA urban area; (2) Rank is based on 101 urban areas (#1 = highest travel time index); (3) Average of 101 urban areas
Source: Texas Transportation Institute, 2015 Urban Mobility Scorecard, August 2015

Freeway Commuter Stress Index

Area	1985	1990	1995	2000	2005	2010	2014
Urban Area Rank[1,2]	5	4	4	5	5	5	6
Urban Area Index[1]	1.29	1.33	1.37	1.41	1.45	1.45	1.46
Average Index[3]	1.13	1.16	1.19	1.22	1.25	1.24	1.25

Note: The Freeway Commuter Stress Index is the same as the Freeway Travel Time Index (see table above) except that it includes only the travel in the peak directions during the peak periods; the TTI includes travel in all directions during the peak period. Thus, the CSI is more indicative of the work trip experienced by each commuter on a daily basis; (1) Covers the Seattle WA urban area; (2) Rank is based on 101 urban areas (#1 = highest travel time index); (3) Average of 101 urban areas
Source: Texas Transportation Institute, 2015 Urban Mobility Scorecard, August 2015

Living Environment

COST OF LIVING

Cost of Living Index

Composite Index	Groceries	Housing	Utilities	Trans-portation	Health Care	Misc. Goods/ Services
148.8	126.7	194.2	123.1	133.1	124.2	135.3

Note: The Cost of Living Index measures regional differences in the cost of consumer goods and services, excluding taxes and non-consumer expenditures, for professional and managerial households in the top income quintile. It is based on more than 50,000 prices covering almost 60 different items for which prices are collected three times a year by chambers of commerce, economic development organizations or university applied economic centers in each participating urban area. The numbers shown should be read as a percentage above or below the national average of 100. For example, a value of 115.4 in the groceries column indicates that grocery prices are 15.4% higher than the national average. Small differences in the index numbers should not be interpreted as significant; Figures cover the Seattle WA urban area.
Source: The Council for Community and Economic Research, ACCRA Cost of Living Index, 2017

Grocery Prices

Area[1]	T-Bone Steak ($/pound)	Frying Chicken ($/pound)	Whole Milk ($/half gal.)	Eggs ($/dozen)	Orange Juice ($/64 oz.)	Coffee ($/11.5 oz.)
City[2]	15.36	1.88	2.03	1.68	4.11	5.76
Avg.	11.29	1.40	2.02	1.47	3.55	4.37
Min.	7.71	0.93	1.04	0.70	2.86	3.24
Max.	15.83	2.39	4.03	3.92	6.29	8.16

*Note: (1) Values for the local area are compared with the average, minimum and maximum values for all 294 areas in the Cost of Living Index; (2) Figures cover the Seattle WA urban area; **T-Bone Steak** (price per pound); **Frying Chicken** (price per pound, whole fryer); **Whole Milk** (half gallon carton); **Eggs** (price per dozen, Grade A, large); **Orange Juice** (64 oz. Tropicana or Florida Natural); **Coffee** (11.5 oz. can, vacuum-packed, Maxwell House, Hills Bros, or Folgers).*
Source: The Council for Community and Economic Research, ACCRA Cost of Living Index, 2017

Housing and Utility Costs

Area[1]	New Home Price ($)	Apartment Rent ($/month)	All Electric ($/month)	Part Electric ($/month)	Other Energy ($/month)	Telephone ($/month)
City[2]	649,370	2,366	190.91	-	-	38.34
Avg.	335,956	1,047	175.01	97.34	67.93	28.71
Min.	187,788	491	109.48	49.33	35.44	12.39
Max.	1,739,087	4,559	432.62	227.09	353.33	44.61

*Note: (1) Values for the local area are compared with the average, minimum and maximum values for all 294 areas in the Cost of Living Index; (2) Figures cover the Seattle WA urban area; **New Home Price** (2,400 sf living area, 8,000 sf lot, in urban area with full utilities); **Apartment Rent** (950 sf 2 bedroom/1.5 or 2 bath, unfurnished, excluding all utilities except water); **All Electric** (average monthly cost for an all-electric home); **Part Electric** (average monthly cost for a part-electric home); **Other Energy** (average monthly cost for natural gas, fuel oil, coal, wood, and any other forms of energy except electricity); **Telephone** (price includes basic monthly rate for a private residential line plus additional local usage charges incurred by a family of four).*
Source: The Council for Community and Economic Research, ACCRA Cost of Living Index, 2017

Health Care, Transportation, and Other Costs

Area[1]	Doctor ($/visit)	Dentist ($/visit)	Optometrist ($/visit)	Gasoline ($/gallon)	Beauty Salon ($/visit)	Men's Shirt ($)
City[2]	124.00	132.64	145.72	2.88	43.43	45.00
Avg.	108.00	92.54	101.93	2.25	37.58	30.92
Min.	30.39	60.00	49.75	1.82	16.11	11.20
Max.	193.50	161.94	229.28	3.16	77.35	59.13

*Note: (1) Values for the local area are compared with the average, minimum and maximum values for all 294 areas in the Cost of Living Index; (2) Figures cover the Seattle WA urban area; **Doctor** (general practitioners routine exam of an established patient); **Dentist** (adult teeth cleaning and periodic oral examination); **Optometrist** (full vision eye exam for established adult patient); **Gasoline** (one gallon regular unleaded, national brand, including all taxes, cash price at self-service pump if available); **Beauty Salon** (woman's shampoo, trim, and blow-dry); **Men's Shirt** (cotton/polyester dress shirt, pinpoint weave, long sleeves).*
Source: The Council for Community and Economic Research, ACCRA Cost of Living Index, 2017

HOUSING

House Price Index (HPI)

Area	National Ranking[2]	Quarterly Change (%)	One-Year Change (%)	Five-Year Change (%)
MD[1]	2	1.73	14.34	69.01
U.S.[3]	–	1.61	6.68	34.71

Note: The HPI is a weighted repeat sales index. It measures average price changes in repeat sales or refinancings on the same properties. This information is obtained by reviewing repeat mortgage transactions on single-family properties whose mortgages have been purchased or securitized by Fannie Mae or Freddie Mac in January 1975; (1) Figures cover the Seattle-Bellevue-Everett, WA Metropolitan Division—see Appendix B for areas included; (2) Rankings are based on annual percentage change for all metro areas containing at least 15,000 transactions over the last 10 years and ranges from 1 to 253; (3) figures based on a weighted average of Census Division estimates using a seasonally adjusted, purchase-only index; all figures are for the period ending December 31, 2017
Source: Federal Housing Finance Agency, House Price Index, February 28, 2018

Median Single-Family Home Prices

Area	2015	2016	2017p	Percent Change 2016 to 2017
MSA[1]	379.7	414.5	465.8	12.4
U.S. Average	223.9	235.5	248.8	5.6

Note: Figures are median sales prices of existing single-family homes in thousands of dollars; (p) preliminary; (1) Figures cover the Seattle-Tacoma-Bellevue, WA Metropolitan Statistical Area—see Appendix B for areas included
Source: National Association of Realtors, Median Sales Price of Existing Single-Family Homes for Metropolitan Areas, 4th Quarter 2017

Qualifying Income Based on Median Sales Price of Existing Single-Family Homes

Area	With 5% Down ($)	With 10% Down ($)	With 20% Down ($)
MSA[1]	n/a	n/a	n/a
U.S. Average	55,585	52,659	46,808

Note: Figures are preliminary; Qualifying income is based on a mortgage rate of 4.17%. Monthly principal and interest payment is limited to 25% of income; n/a not available; (1) Figures cover the Seattle-Tacoma-Bellevue, WA Metropolitan Statistical Area—see Appendix B for areas included
Source: National Association of Realtors, Qualifying Income Based on Median Sales Price of Existing Single-Family Homes for Metropolitan Areas, 4th Quarter 2017

Median Apartment Condo-Coop Home Prices

Area	2015	2016	2017p	Percent Change 2016 to 2017
MSA[1]	n/a	n/a	n/a	n/a
U.S. Average	210.7	220.7	234.3	6.2

Note: Figures are median sales prices of existing apartment condo-coop homes in thousands of dollars; (p) preliminary; n/a not available; (1) Figures cover the Seattle-Tacoma-Bellevue, WA Metropolitan Statistical Area—see Appendix B for areas included
Source: National Association of Realtors, Median Sales Price of Existing Apartment Condo-Coop Homes for Metropolitan Areas, 4th Quarter 2017

Home Value Distribution

Area	Under $50,000	$50,000 -$99,999	$100,000 -$149,999	$150,000 -$199,999	$200,000 -$299,999	$300,000 -$499,999	$500,000 -$999,999	$1,000,000 or more
City	1.6	0.3	1.7	7.8	34.6	46.5	6.8	0.6
MSA[1]	3.8	1.8	4.3	9.1	23.4	32.3	21.1	4.2
U.S.	8.8	14.8	15.3	14.9	18.4	16.4	9.0	2.5

Note: Figures are percentages and cover owner-occupied housing units; (1) Figures cover the Seattle-Tacoma-Bellevue, WA Metropolitan Statistical Area—see Appendix B for areas included
Source: U.S. Census Bureau, 2012-2016 American Community Survey 5-Year Estimates

Homeownership Rate

Area	2009 (%)	2010 (%)	2011 (%)	2012 (%)	2013 (%)	2014 (%)	2015 (%)	2016 (%)	2017 (%)
MSA[1]	61.2	60.9	60.7	60.4	61.0	61.3	59.5	57.7	59.5
U.S.	67.4	66.9	66.1	65.4	65.1	64.5	63.7	63.4	63.9

Note: (1) Figures cover the Seattle-Tacoma-Bellevue, WA Metropolitan Statistical Area—see Appendix B for areas included
Source: U.S. Census Bureau, Housing Vacancies and Homeownership Annual Statistics: 2009-2017

Year Housing Structure Built

Area	2010 or Later	2000 -2009	1990 -1999	1980 -1989	1970 -1979	1960 -1969	1950 -1959	1940 -1949	Before 1940	Median Year
City	5.5	34.9	29.3	16.4	8.3	2.9	0.2	0.6	1.8	1997
MSA[1]	3.4	16.1	16.1	15.1	15.1	11.2	7.8	4.5	10.7	1980
U.S.	2.3	14.7	14.0	13.7	15.6	10.9	10.6	5.2	13.0	1977

Note: Figures are percentages except for Median Year; Note: (1) Figures cover the Seattle-Tacoma-Bellevue, WA Metropolitan Statistical Area—see Appendix B for areas included
Source: U.S. Census Bureau, 2012-2016 American Community Survey 5-Year Estimates

Gross Monthly Rent

Area	Under $500	$500 -$999	$1,000 -$1,499	$1,500 -$1,999	$2,000 -$2,499	$2,500 -$2,999	$3,000 and up	Median ($)
City	5.3	12.6	22.7	25.6	27.5	5.6	0.7	1,684
MSA[1]	6.1	27.3	35.9	19.6	6.9	2.5	1.8	1,212
U.S.	11.3	43.3	27.7	10.7	4.0	1.6	1.5	949

Note: Figures are percentages except for Median; Gross rent is the contract rent plus the estimated average monthly cost of utilities (electricity, gas, and water and sewer) and fuels (oil, coal, kerosene, wood, etc.) if these are paid by the renter (or paid for the renter by someone else); (1) Figures cover the Seattle-Tacoma-Bellevue, WA Metropolitan Statistical Area—see Appendix B for areas included
Source: U.S. Census Bureau, 2012-2016 American Community Survey 5-Year Estimates

HEALTH

Health Risk Factors

Category	MD[1] (%)	U.S. (%)
Adults aged 18–64 who have any kind of health care coverage	89.8	87.7
Adults who reported being in good or excellent health	87.1	83.6
Adults who are current smokers	11.2	17.1
Adults who currently use E-cigarettes	4.9	4.7
Adults who currently use chewing tobacco, snuff, or snus	2.6	4.0
Adults who are heavy drinkers[2]	7.3	6.5
Adults who are binge drinkers[3]	16.3	16.9
Adults who are overweight (BMI 25.0 - 29.9)	35.3	35.3
Adults who are obese (BMI 30.0 - 99.8)	24.1	29.9
Adults who participated in any physical activities in the past month	84.8	76.9
Adults who always or nearly always wears a seat belt	97.1	94.3

Note: (1) Figures cover the Seattle-Bellevue-Everett, WA Metropolitan Division—see Appendix B for areas included; (2) Heavy drinkers are classified as adult men having more than 14 drinks per week and adult women having more than 7 drinks per week; (3) Binge drinkers are classified as males having five or more drinks on one occasion or females having four or more drinks on one occasion
Source: Centers for Disease Control and Prevention, Behaviorial Risk Factor Surveillance System, SMART: Selected Metropolitan Area Risk Trends, 2016

Health Screening Rates

Category	MD[1] (%)	U.S. (%)
Adults 50-75 who have had a blood stool test within the past year	11.8	8.0
Adults 50-75 who have had a colonoscopy in the past 10 years	64.4	63.5
Adults aged 65+ who have had flu shot within the past year	61.0	58.6
Adults aged 65+ who have ever had a pneumonia vaccination	78.4	73.4
Adults who have ever been tested for HIV	37.2	35.6
Women aged 21-65 who have had a pap test in the past three years	n/a	79.8
Men aged 40+ who have had a PSA test within the past two years	29.0	39.5
Women aged 40+ who have had a mammogram within the past two years	68.7	72.5

Note: n/a not available; (1) Figures cover the Seattle-Bellevue-Everett, WA Metropolitan Division—see Appendix B for areas included; Source: Centers for Disease Control and Prevention, Behaviorial Risk Factor Surveillance System, SMART: Selected Metropolitan Area Risk Trends, 2016

Chronic Health Conditions

Category	MD[1] (%)	U.S. (%)
Adults who have ever been told they had a heart attack	2.9	4.4
Adults who have ever been told they have angina or coronary heart disease	3.2	4.1
Adults who have ever been told they had a stroke	2.4	3.1
Adults who have been told they currently have asthma	8.5	9.3
Adults who have ever been told they have arthritis	21.1	25.8
Adults who have ever been told they have diabetes[2]	8.1	10.5
Adults who have ever been told they had skin cancer	5.5	5.9
Adults who have ever been told they had any other types of cancer	6.1	6.7
Adults who have ever been told they have COPD	4.6	6.3
Adults who have ever been told they have kidney disease	3.0	2.8
Adults who have ever been told they have a form of depression	19.5	17.4

Note: (1) Figures cover the Seattle-Bellevue-Everett, WA Metropolitan Division—see Appendix B for areas included; (2) Figures do not include pregnancy-related, borderline, or pre-diabetes
Source: Centers for Disease Control and Prevention, Behaviorial Risk Factor Surveillance System, SMART: Selected Metropolitan Area Risk Trends, 2016

Mortality Rates for the Top 10 Causes of Death in the U.S.

ICD-10[a] Sub-Chapter	ICD-10[a] Code	Age-Adjusted Mortality Rate[1] per 100,000 population	
		County[2]	U.S.
Malignant neoplasms	C00-C97	137.5	158.5
Ischaemic heart diseases	I20-I25	71.3	96.8
Other forms of heart disease	I30-I51	33.2	52.4
Chronic lower respiratory diseases	J40-J47	25.9	40.9
Cerebrovascular diseases	I60-I69	29.5	37.2
Organic, including symptomatic, mental disorders	F01-F09	23.8	33.3
Other degenerative diseases of the nervous system	G30-G31	44.9	32.1
Other external causes of accidental injury	W00-X59	26.6	31.2
Diabetes mellitus	E10-E14	17.5	21.1
Hypertensive diseases	I10-I15	16.8	20.8

Note: (a) ICD-10 = International Classification of Diseases 10th Revision; (1) Mortality rates are a three year average covering 2014-2016; (2) Figures cover King County.
Source: Centers for Disease Control and Prevention, National Center for Health Statistics. Underlying Cause of Death 1999-2016 on CDC WONDER Online Database, released December 2017

Mortality Rates for Selected Causes of Death

ICD-10[a] Sub-Chapter	ICD-10[a] Code	Age-Adjusted Mortality Rate[1] per 100,000 population	
		County[2]	U.S.
Assault	X85-Y09	2.6	5.6
Diseases of the liver	K70-K76	10.9	14.0
Human immunodeficiency virus (HIV) disease	B20-B24	1.3	1.9
Influenza and pneumonia	J09-J18	8.6	14.6
Intentional self-harm	X60-X84	11.6	13.2
Malnutrition	E40-E46	0.9	1.3
Obesity and other hyperalimentation	E65-E68	1.9	2.1
Renal failure	N17-N19	5.9	13.0
Transport accidents	V01-V99	5.8	12.0
Viral hepatitis	B15-B19	2.5	1.9

Note: (a) ICD-10 = International Classification of Diseases 10th Revision; (1) Mortality rates are a three year average covering 2014-2016; (2) Figures cover King County; Data are Suppressed when the data meet the criteria for confidentiality constraints; Mortality rates are flagged as Unreliable when the rate would be calculated with a numerator of 20 or less.
Source: Centers for Disease Control and Prevention, National Center for Health Statistics. Underlying Cause of Death 1999-2016 on CDC WONDER Online Database, released December 2017

Health Insurance Coverage

Area	With Health Insurance	With Private Health Insurance	With Public Health Insurance	Without Health Insurance	Population Under Age 18 Without Health Insurance
City	95.4	85.8	17.4	4.6	4.0
MSA[1]	91.2	74.6	27.0	8.8	3.8
U.S.	88.3	66.7	33.0	11.7	5.9

Note: Figures are percentages that cover the civilian noninstitutionalized population; (1) Figures cover the Seattle-Tacoma-Bellevue, WA Metropolitan Statistical Area—see Appendix B for areas included
Source: U.S. Census Bureau, 2012-2016 American Community Survey 5-Year Estimates

Number of Medical Professionals

Area	MDs[3]	DOs[3,4]	Dentists	Podiatrists	Chiropractors	Optometrists
County[1] (number)	10,017	320	2,270	138	988	459
County[1] (rate[2])	473.0	15.1	105.3	6.4	45.8	21.3
U.S. (rate[2])	276.5	22.3	67.3	6.0	26.7	15.9

Note: Data as of 2016 unless noted; (1) Data covers King County; (2) Rate per 100,000 population; (3) Data as of 2015 and includes all active, non-federal physicians; (4) Doctor of Osteopathic Medicine
Source: U.S. Department of Health and Human Services, Health Resources and Services Administration, Bureau of Health Professions, Area Resource File (ARF) 2016-2017

Best Hospitals

According to *U.S. News,* the Seattle-Bellevue-Everett, WA metro area is home to three of the best hospitals in the U.S.: **Seattle Cancer Care Alliance** (1 adult specialty); **UW Medicine/Harborview Medical Center** (1 adult specialty); **University of Washington Medical Center** (10 adult specialties). The hospitals listed were nationally ranked in at least one of 16 specialties. Only 152 hospitals nationwide were nationally ranked in one or more specialties. Twenty hospitals in the U.S. made the Honor Roll. The Best Hospitals Honor Roll was revamped last year to take both the national rankings and the procedure and condition ratings into account. Hospitals received points if they were nationally ranked in one of the 16 specialties—the higher they ranked, the more points they got—and how many ratings of "high performing" they earned in the nine procedures and conditions. *U.S. News Online, "America's Best Hospitals 2017-18"*

According to *U.S. News,* the Seattle-Bellevue-Everett, WA metro area is home to one of the best children's hospitals in the U.S.: **Seattle Children's Hospital** (10 pediatric specialties). The hospital listed was highly ranked in at least one of 10 pediatric specialties. Eighty-two children's hospitals in the U.S. were nationally ranked in at least one specialty. Hospitals received points for being ranked in a specialty, and the 10 hospitals with the most points across the 10 specialties make up the Honor Roll. *U.S. News Online, "America's Best Children's Hospitals 2017-18"*

EDUCATION

Public School District Statistics

District Name	Schls	Pupils	Pupil/ Teacher Ratio	Minority Pupils[1] (%)	Free Lunch Eligible[2] (%)	IEP[3] (%)
Tahoma School District	9	8,191	22.8	25.0	12.0	11.5

Note: Table includes school districts with 100 or more students; (1) Percentage of students that are not non-Hispanic white; (2) Percentage of students that are eligible for the free lunch program; (3) Percentage of students that have an Individualized Education Program.
Source: U.S. Department of Education, National Center for Education Statistics, Common Core of Data, Local Education Agency (School District) Universe Survey: School Year 2015-2016; U.S. Department of Education, National Center for Education Statistics, Common Core of Data, Public Elementary/Secondary School Universe Survey: School Year 2015-2016

Highest Level of Education

Area	Less than H.S.	H.S. Diploma	Some College, No Deg.	Associate Degree	Bachelor's Degree	Master's Degree	Prof. School Degree	Doctorate Degree
City	2.4	18.8	27.9	10.2	27.9	11.1	0.8	0.9
MSA[1]	8.0	20.3	22.3	9.2	25.4	10.4	2.5	1.8
U.S.	13.0	27.5	21.0	8.2	18.8	8.2	2.0	1.3

Note: Figures cover persons age 25 and over; (1) Figures cover the Seattle-Tacoma-Bellevue, WA Metropolitan Statistical Area—see Appendix B for areas included
Source: U.S. Census Bureau, 2012-2016 American Community Survey 5-Year Estimates

Educational Attainment by Race

Area	High School Graduate or Higher (%)					Bachelor's Degree or Higher (%)				
	Total	White	Black	Asian	Hisp.[2]	Total	White	Black	Asian	Hisp.[2]
City	97.6	97.5	94.4	100.0	96.2	40.7	40.2	43.6	45.2	44.5
MSA[1]	92.0	94.2	88.2	87.2	71.5	40.1	41.0	22.2	52.0	20.3
U.S.	87.0	88.9	84.3	86.3	65.7	30.3	31.6	20.0	52.1	14.7

Note: Figures shown cover persons 25 years old and over; (1) Figures cover the Seattle-Tacoma-Bellevue, WA Metropolitan Statistical Area—see Appendix B for areas included; (2) People of Hispanic origin can be of any race
Source: U.S. Census Bureau, 2012-2016 American Community Survey 5-Year Estimates

School Enrollment by Grade and Control

Area	Preschool (%)		Kindergarten (%)		Grades 1 - 4 (%)		Grades 5 - 8 (%)		Grades 9 - 12 (%)	
	Public	Private	Public	Private	Public	Private	Public	Private	Public	Private
City	31.4	68.6	79.9	20.1	91.9	8.1	94.2	5.8	97.1	2.9
MSA[1]	40.4	59.6	83.9	16.1	88.6	11.4	88.5	11.5	90.7	9.3
U.S.	58.4	41.6	87.7	12.3	89.8	10.2	89.7	10.3	90.4	9.6

Note: Figures shown cover persons 3 years old and over; (1) Figures cover the Seattle-Tacoma-Bellevue, WA Metropolitan Statistical Area—see Appendix B for areas included
Source: U.S. Census Bureau, 2012-2016 American Community Survey 5-Year Estimates

Average Salaries of Public School Classroom Teachers

Area	2015		2016		Change from 2015 to 2016	
	Dollars	Rank[1]	Dollars	Rank[1]	Percent	Rank[2]
Washington	52,502	24	53,738	25	2.4	7
U.S. Average	57,611	–	58,353	–	1.3	–

Note: (1) Rank ranges from 1 to 51 where 1 indicates highest salary; (2) Rank ranges from 1 to 51 where 1 indicates highest percent change.
Source: National Education Association, Rankings & Estimates: Rankings of the States 2016 and Estimates of School Statistics 2017

Higher Education

Four-Year Colleges			Two-Year Colleges			Medical Schools[1]	Law Schools[2]	Voc/ Tech[3]
Public	Private Non-profit	Private For-profit	Public	Private Non-profit	Private For-profit			
0	0	0	0	0	0	0	0	0

Note: Figures cover institutions located within the city limits and include main campuses only; (1) includes schools accredited by the Liaison Committee on Medical Education and the American Osteopathic Association's Commission on Osteopathic College Accreditation; (2) includes ABA-accredited schools, schools with provisional ABA accreditation, and state accredited schools; (3) includes all schools with programs that are less than 2 years.
Source: National Center for Education Statistics, Integrated Postsecondary Education System (IPEDS), 2016-17; Wikipedia, List of Medical Schools in the United States, accessed April 2, 2018; Wikipedia, List of Law Schools in the United States, accessed April 2, 2018

According to *U.S. News & World Report,* the Seattle-Bellevue-Everett, WA metro division is home to two of the best national universities in the U.S.: **University of Washington** (#56 tie); **Seattle Pacific University** (#151 tie). The indicators used to capture academic quality fall into a number of categories: assessment by administrators at peer institutions; retention of students; faculty resources; student selectivity; financial resources; alumni giving; high school counselor ratings of colleges; and graduation rate. *U.S. News & World Report, "America's Best Colleges 2018"*

According to *U.S. News & World Report,* the Seattle-Bellevue-Everett, WA metro division is home to one of the top 100 law schools in the U.S.: **University of Washington** (#32 tie). The rankings are based on a weighted average of 12 measures of quality: peer assessment score; assessment score by lawyers/judges; median LSAT scores; median undergrad GPA; acceptance rate; employment rates for graduates; placement success; bar passage rate; faculty resources; expenditures per student; student/faculty ratio; and library resources. *U.S. News & World Report, "America's Best Graduate Schools, Law, 2019"*

According to *U.S. News & World Report,* the Seattle-Bellevue-Everett, WA metro division is home to one of the top 75 medical schools for research in the U.S.: **University of Washington** (#11 tie). The rankings are based on a weighted average of 11 measures of quality: quality assessment; peer assessment score; assessment score by residency directors; research activity; total research activity; average research activity per faculty member; student selectivity; median MCAT total score; median undergraduate GPA; acceptance rate; and faculty resources. *U.S. News & World Report, "America's Best Graduate Schools, Medical, 2019"*

According to *U.S. News & World Report,* the Seattle-Bellevue-Everett, WA metro division is home to one of the top 75 business schools in the U.S.: **University of Washington (Foster)** (#22). The rankings are based on a weighted average of the following nine measures: quality assessment; peer assessment; recruiter assessment; placement success; mean starting salary and bonus; student selectivity; mean GMAT and GRE scores; mean undergraduate GPA; and acceptance rate. *U.S. News & World Report, "America's Best Graduate Schools, Business, 2019"*

PRESIDENTIAL ELECTION

2016 Presidential Election Results

Area	Clinton	Trump	Johnson	Stein	Other
King County	69.8	21.0	4.0	1.7	3.4
U.S.	48.0	45.9	3.3	1.1	1.7

Note: Results are percentages and may not add to 100% due to rounding
Source: Dave Leip's Atlas of U.S. Presidential Elections

EMPLOYERS

Major Employers

Company Name	Industry
City of Tacoma	Switching & terminal services
Costco Wholesale Corporation	Miscellaneous general merchandise stores
County of Snohomish	Bureau of public roads
Evergreen Healthcare	General medical & surgical hospitals
Harborview Medical Center	General medical & surgical hospitals
King County Public Hospital Dist No. 2	Hospital & health services consultant
Microsoft Corporation	Prepackaged software
Prologix Distribution Services (West)	General merchandise, non-durable
R U Corporation	American restaurant
SNC-Lavalin Constructors	Heavy construction, nec
Social & Health Svcs, Washington Dept of	General medical & surgical hospitals
Swedish Health Services	General medical & surgical hospitals
T-Mobile USA	Radio, telephone communication
The Boeing Company	Airplanes, fixed or rotary wing
Tulalip Resort Casino	Casino hotels
United States Department of the Army	Medical centers
University of Washington	Colleges & universities
Virginia Mason Medical Center	General medical & surgical hospitals
Virginia Mason Seattle Main Clinic	Clinic, operated by physicians

Note: Companies shown are located within the Seattle-Tacoma-Bellevue, WA Metropolitan Statistical Area.
Source: Hoovers.com; Wikipedia

PUBLIC SAFETY

Crime Rate

Area	All Crimes	Violent Crimes: Murder	Violent Crimes: Rape[3]	Violent Crimes: Robbery	Violent Crimes: Aggrav. Assault	Property Crimes: Burglary	Property Crimes: Larceny -Theft	Property Crimes: Motor Vehicle Theft
City	1,452.3	0.0	19.0	38.0	22.8	330.7	821.2	220.5
Metro[1]	4,169.6	2.4	36.9	105.6	168.5	697.7	2,632.0	526.5
U.S.	2,837.0	5.3	29.6	102.8	248.5	468.9	1,745.0	236.9

Note: Figures are crimes per 100,000 population; (1) Figures cover the Seattle-Bellevue-Everett, WA Metropolitan Division—see Appendix B for areas included; (3) The city and U.S. figures shown were reported using the legacy Uniform Crime Reporting (UCR) definition of rape. The metro area figures shown are an aggregate total of the data submitted using both the revised and legacy UCR definitions.
Source: FBI Uniform Crime Reports, 2016

Hate Crimes

Area	Number of Quarters Reported	Race/Ethnicity/ Ancestry	Religion	Sexual Orientation	Disability	Gender	Gender Identity
		Number of Incidents per Bias Motivation					
City	4	0	0	0	0	0	0
U.S.	4	3,489	1,273	1,076	70	31	124

Source: Federal Bureau of Investigation, Hate Crime Statistics 2016

Identity Theft Consumer Reports

Area	Reports	Reports per 100,000 Population	Rank[2]
MSA[1]	4,497	118	59
U.S.	371,061	114	-

Note: (1) Figures cover the Seattle-Tacoma-Bellevue, WA Metropolitan Statistical Area—see Appendix B for areas included; (2) Rank ranges from 1 to 389 where 1 indicates greatest number of identity theft reports per 100,000 population
Source: Federal Trade Commission, Consumer Sentinel Network Data Book for January–December 2017

Fraud and Other Consumer Reports

Area	Reports	Reports per 100,000 Population	Rank[2]
MSA[1]	18,825	496	117
U.S.	2,304,550	708	-

Note: (1) Figures cover the Seattle-Tacoma-Bellevue, WA Metropolitan Statistical Area—see Appendix B for areas included; (2) Rank ranges from 1 to 389 where 1 indicates greatest number of fraud and other consumer reports per 100,000 population
Source: Federal Trade Commission, Consumer Sentinel Network Data Book for January–December 2017

SPORTS

Professional Sports Teams

Team Name	League	Year Established
Seattle Mariners	Major League Baseball (MLB)	1977
Seattle Seahawks	National Football League (NFL)	1976
Seattle Sounders FC	Major League Soccer (MLS)	2009

Note: Includes teams located in the Seattle-Tacoma-Bellevue, WA Metropolitan Statistical Area.
Source: Wikipedia, Major Professional Sports Teams of the United States and Canada, April 5, 2018

CLIMATE

Average and Extreme Temperatures

Temperature	Jan	Feb	Mar	Apr	May	Jun	Jul	Aug	Sep	Oct	Nov	Dec	Yr.
Extreme High (°F)	64	70	75	85	93	96	98	99	98	89	74	63	99
Average High (°F)	44	48	52	57	64	69	75	74	69	59	50	45	59
Average Temp. (°F)	39	43	45	49	55	61	65	65	60	52	45	41	52
Average Low (°F)	34	36	38	41	46	51	54	55	51	45	39	36	44
Extreme Low (°F)	0	1	11	29	28	38	43	44	35	28	6	6	0

Note: Figures cover the years 1948-1990
Source: National Climatic Data Center, International Station Meteorological Climate Summary, 9/96

Average Precipitation/Snowfall/Humidity

Precip./Humidity	Jan	Feb	Mar	Apr	May	Jun	Jul	Aug	Sep	Oct	Nov	Dec	Yr.
Avg. Precip. (in.)	5.7	4.2	3.7	2.4	1.7	1.4	0.8	1.1	1.9	3.5	5.9	5.9	38.4
Avg. Snowfall (in.)	5	2	1	Tr	Tr	0	0	0	0	Tr	1	3	13
Avg. Rel. Hum. 7am (%)	83	83	84	83	80	79	79	84	87	88	85	85	83
Avg. Rel. Hum. 4pm (%)	76	69	63	57	54	54	49	51	57	68	76	79	63

Note: Figures cover the years 1948-1990; Tr = Trace amounts (<0.05 in. of rain; <0.5 in. of snow)
Source: National Climatic Data Center, International Station Meteorological Climate Summary, 9/96

Weather Conditions

Temperature			Daytime Sky			Precipitation		
5°F & below	32°F & below	90°F & above	Clear	Partly cloudy	Cloudy	0.01 inch or more precip.	0.1 inch or more snow/ice	Thunder-storms
< 1	38	3	57	120	188	157	8	8

Note: Figures are average number of days per year and cover the years 1948-1990
Source: National Climatic Data Center, International Station Meteorological Climate Summary, 9/96

HAZARDOUS WASTE

Superfund Sites

The Seattle-Bellevue-Everett, WA metro division is home to 10 sites on the EPA's Superfund National Priorities List: **Harbor Island (Lead)** (final); **Lockheed West Seattle** (final); **Lower Duwamish Waterway** (final); **Midway Landfill** (final); **Pacific Car & Foundry Co.** (final);

Pacific Sound Resources (final); **Queen City Farms** (final); **Quendall Terminal** (final); **Seattle Municipal Landfill (Kent Highlands)** (final); **Western Processing Co., Inc.** (final). There are a total of 1,396 Superfund sites with a status of proposed or final on the list in the U.S. *U.S. Environmental Protection Agency, National Priorities List, April 4, 2018*

AIR & WATER QUALITY

Air Quality Trends: Ozone

	1990	1995	2000	2005	2010	2012	2013	2014	2015	2016
MSA[1]	0.082	0.062	0.056	0.053	0.053	0.059	0.048	0.052	0.059	0.054
U.S.	0.087	0.089	0.081	0.079	0.073	0.075	0.069	0.067	0.068	0.069

Note: (1) Data covers the Seattle-Tacoma-Bellevue, WA Metropolitan Statistical Area—see Appendix B for areas included. The values shown are the composite ozone concentration averages among trend sites based on the highest fourth daily maximum 8-hour concentration in parts per million. These trends are based on sites having an adequate record of monitoring data during the trend period. Data from exceptional events are included.
Source: U.S. Environmental Protection Agency, Air Quality Monitoring Information, "Air Quality Trends by City, 1990-2016"

Air Quality Index

Area	Percent of Days when Air Quality was...[2]					AQI Statistics[2]	
	Good	Moderate	Unhealthy for Sensitive Groups	Unhealthy	Very Unhealthy	Maximum	Median
MSA[1]	60.8	32.6	3.6	2.7	0.3	202	47

Note: (1) Data covers the Seattle-Tacoma-Bellevue, WA Metropolitan Statistical Area—see Appendix B for areas included; (2) Based on 365 days with AQI data in 2017. Air Quality Index (AQI) is an index for reporting daily air quality. EPA calculates the AQI for five major air pollutants regulated by the Clean Air Act: ground-level ozone, particle pollution (aka particulate matter), carbon monoxide, sulfur dioxide, and nitrogen dioxide. The AQI runs from 0 to 500. The higher the AQI value, the greater the level of air pollution and the greater the health concern. There are six AQI categories: "Good" AQI is between 0 and 50. Air quality is considered satisfactory; "Moderate" AQI is between 51 and 100. Air quality is acceptable; "Unhealthy for Sensitive Groups" When AQI values are between 101 and 150, members of sensitive groups may experience health effects; "Unhealthy" When AQI values are between 151 and 200 everyone may begin to experience health effects; "Very Unhealthy" AQI values between 201 and 300 trigger a health alert; "Hazardous" AQI values over 300 trigger warnings of emergency conditions (not shown).
Source: U.S. Environmental Protection Agency, Air Quality Index Report, 2017

Air Quality Index Pollutants

Area	Percent of Days when AQI Pollutant was...[2]					
	Carbon Monoxide	Nitrogen Dioxide	Ozone	Sulfur Dioxide	Particulate Matter 2.5	Particulate Matter 10
MSA[1]	0.0	5.8	49.0	0.0	45.2	0.0

Note: (1) Data covers the Seattle-Tacoma-Bellevue, WA Metropolitan Statistical Area—see Appendix B for areas included; (2) Based on 365 days with AQI data in 2017. The Air Quality Index (AQI) is an index for reporting daily air quality. EPA calculates the AQI for five major air pollutants regulated by the Clean Air Act: ground-level ozone, particle pollution (also known as particulate matter), carbon monoxide, sulfur dioxide, and nitrogen dioxide. The AQI runs from 0 to 500. The higher the AQI value, the greater the level of air pollution and the greater the health concern.
Source: U.S. Environmental Protection Agency, Air Quality Index Report, 2017

Maximum Air Pollutant Concentrations: Particulate Matter, Ozone, CO and Lead

	Particulate Matter 10 (ug/m^3)	Particulate Matter 2.5 Wtd AM (ug/m^3)	Particulate Matter 2.5 24-Hr (ug/m^3)	Ozone (ppm)	Carbon Monoxide (ppm)	Lead (ug/m^3)
MSA[1] Level	n/a	6.9	31	0.061	1	n/a
NAAQS[2]	150	15	35	0.075	9	0.15
Met NAAQS[2]	n/a	Yes	Yes	Yes	Yes	n/a

Note: (1) Data covers the Seattle-Tacoma-Bellevue, WA Metropolitan Statistical Area—see Appendix B for areas included; Data from exceptional events are included; (2) National Ambient Air Quality Standards; ppm = parts per million; ug/m^3 = micrograms per cubic meter; n/a not available.
Concentrations: Particulate Matter 10 (coarse particulate)—highest second maximum 24-hour concentration; Particulate Matter 2.5 Wtd AM (fine particulate)—highest weighted annual mean concentration; Particulate Matter 2.5 24-Hour (fine particulate)—highest 98th percentile 24-hour concentration; Ozone—highest fourth daily maximum 8-hour concentration; Carbon Monoxide—highest second maximum non-overlapping 8-hour concentration; Lead—maximum running 3-month average
Source: U.S. Environmental Protection Agency, Air Quality Monitoring Information, "Air Quality Statistics by City, 2016"

Maximum Air Pollutant Concentrations: Nitrogen Dioxide and Sulfur Dioxide

	Nitrogen Dioxide AM (ppb)	Nitrogen Dioxide 1-Hr (ppb)	Sulfur Dioxide AM (ppb)	Sulfur Dioxide 1-Hr (ppb)	Sulfur Dioxide 24-Hr (ppb)
MSA[1] Level	21	49	n/a	n/a	n/a
NAAQS[2]	53	100	30	75	140
Met NAAQS[2]	Yes	Yes	n/a	n/a	n/a

Note: (1) Data covers the Seattle-Tacoma-Bellevue, WA Metropolitan Statistical Area—see Appendix B for areas included; Data from exceptional events are included; (2) National Ambient Air Quality Standards; ppm = parts per million; ug/m^3 = micrograms per cubic meter; n/a not available.

Concentrations: Nitrogen Dioxide AM—highest arithmetic mean concentration; Nitrogen Dioxide 1-Hr—highest 98th percentile 1-hour daily maximum concentration; Sulfur Dioxide AM—highest annual mean concentration; Sulfur Dioxide 1-Hr—highest 99th percentile 1-hour daily maximum concentration; Sulfur Dioxide 24-Hr—highest second maximum 24-hour concentration

Source: U.S. Environmental Protection Agency, Air Quality Monitoring Information, "Air Quality Statistics by City, 2016"

Drinking Water

Water System Name	Pop. Served	Primary Water Source Type	Violations[1]	
			Health Based	Monitoring/ Reporting
Cedar River Water & Sewer District	25,065	Purchased Surface	0	0
Covington Water District	49,993	Purchased Surface	0	0

Note: (1) Based on violation data from January 1, 2017 to December 31, 2017

Source: U.S. Environmental Protection Agency, Office of Ground Water and Drinking Water, Safe Drinking Water Information System (based on data extracted April 5, 2018)

Sammamish, Washington

Background

Sammamish is a young city—incorporated in 1999—situated in Washington state's famously beautiful Olympic Mountains, with the Seattle skyline to its west, and the Cascade range to its east. Less than ten miles away from the larger city of Bellevue, and twenty miles from Seattle, Sammamish is intent on retaining the best of its small town atmosphere and rural character, embarking on new plans to develop and modernize the city while maintaining its rich natural resources.

Generally recognized as one of the most desirable residential communities in the Puget Sound region, median household income in Sammamish is well above the state average, and more than a fifth of its residents hold either graduate or professional degrees.

The name Sammamish is derived from two Native American words: Samena, which means "hunter," and mish, which means "people," and this area, not surprisingly, was inhabited by Native American hunter-gatherers for centuries prior to the arrival of white settlers. The town was originally named Monohon, after Martin Monohon, who arrived in 1877. Shortly thereafter, the first of several lumber industry firms was established and, by the early 1900s, the town hosted a major shingle company. Economic growth was strong enough to support a school (K – 8), churches, various craft businesses dependent on lumber, such as a boat and canoe company, and a wood-turning shop.

There are a number of homes and artifacts remaining from the earlier era in the town's history, including the Reard/Freed House, considered the best remaining example of a frontier farmhouse in the area. Such sites, and the natural environment, are considered prime resources for the town and are carefully preserved and protected.

The Puget Sound area is widely noted for its natural beauty and recreational opportunities, and the town itself owns and operates nearly forty acres of Puget Sound parkland. Sammamish has embarked on an ambitious twenty-year plan to further enhance its already extensive system of trails, and is particularly interested in establishing new non-motorized trail systems to encourage pedestrian and bicycle alternatives to automobiles.

Medical facilities convenient to Sammamish include three hospitals in nearby Redmond, Bellevue or Kirkland, all less than a half-hour away. Sammamish is about twenty miles away from two major international airports, King County International/Boeing Field, and Seattle-Tacoma International.

Schools in Sammamish are in the highly-rated Issaquah School District. The town is also convenient to many institutions of higher learning, including Bellevue Community College, City University, Renton Technical College, Lake Washington Technical College, Seattle University, the University of Washington at Seattle, and Seattle Community College-Central Campus.

Sammamish is governed by a seven member City Council, including a mayor and deputy-mayor. Day to day administrative details are overseen by a city manager, who is selected by the City Council.

Rankings

General Rankings

- *US News & World Report* conducted a survey of more than 2,000 people and analyzed the 125 largest metropolitan areas to determine what matters the most when selecting the next place to live. Seattle* ranked #10 out of the top 25 as having the best combination of desirable factors. Criteria: cost of living; quality of education; job market, crime rates; and other factors. *realestate.usnews.com, "The 25 Best Places to Live in the U.S. in 2018," April 10, 2018*

- The Seattle* metro area was identified as one of America's fastest-growing areas in terms of population and economy by *Forbes.* The area ranked #2 out of 25. The 100 most populous metro areas in the U.S. were evaluated on the following criteria: estimated population growth; employment; economic output; wages; home values. *Forbes, "America's Fastest-Growing Cities 2018," February 28, 2018*

Business/Finance Rankings

- According to *Business Insider*, the Seattle* metro area is where startup growth is on the rise. Based on the 2017 Kauffman Index of Growth Entrepreneurship, which measured in-depth national entrepreneurial trends in 40 metro areas, it ranked #20 in highest startup growth. *www.businessinsider.com, "The 21 U.S. Cities with the Highest Startup Growth," October 21, 2017*

- The personal finance site NerdWallet analyzed 183 American metropolitan areas with populations over 250,000 and more than 15,000 businesses to rank where entrepreneurs find the most success. Criteria included area economy, annual income, housing cost, unemployment rate, and the success rate of area businesses. Seattle* ranked #18. *www.nerdwallet.com, "Best Places to Start a Business," April 27, 2015*

- 24/7 Wall Street used Brookings Institution research on 50 advanced industries to identify the proportion of workers in the nation's largest metropolitan areas that were employed in jobs requiring knowledge in the science, technology, engineering, or math (STEM) fields and where there was heavy investment in research and development (R&D). The Seattle* metro area was #2. *247wallst.com, "15 Cities with the Most High-Tech Jobs," February 23, 2017*

- Based on metro area social media reviews, the employment opinion group Glassdoor surveyed 50 of the largest U.S. metro areas and equally weighed cost of living, hiring opportunity, and job satisfaction to compose a list of "25 Best Cities for Jobs." Median pay and home value, in-demand jobs and number of current job openings was also factored in. The Seattle* metro area was ranked #17 in overall job satisfaction. *www.glassdoor.com, "Best Cities for Jobs," September 12, 2017*

- In a survey of economic confidence in the nation's 50 largest metropolitan areas conducted January–December 2014, the Seattle* metro area placed #7, according to Gallup's 2014 Economic Confidence Index. *Gallup, "San Jose and San Francisco Lead in Economic Confidence," March 19, 2015*

- The Brookings Institution ranked the 100 largest metro areas in the U.S. based on income inequality. Seattle* was ranked #71 (#1 = greatest ineqality). Criteria: the "95/20 ratio," a figure representing the income at which a household earns more than 95 percent of all other households, divided by the income at which a household earns more than only 20 percent of all other households. *Brookings Institution, "Household Income Inequality, 100 Largest U.S. Metro Areas, 2014-2016," February 5, 2018*

- *Forbes* ranked the 100 largest metro areas in the U.S. in terms of the "Best Cities for Young Professionals." The Seattle* metro area ranked #1 out of 25. (Large metro areas were divided into metro divisions.) Criteria: median rent of a two-bedroom apartment; job growth and unemployment rate; median salary of college graduates with 5 or less years of work experience; networking opportunities; social outlook; percentage of population 25 years of age and older with college degrees. *Forbes.com, "America's 25 Best Cities for Young Professionals in 2017," May 22, 2017*

- Payscale.com ranked the largest metro areas in terms of wage growth. The Seattle* metro area ranked #4. Criteria: private-sector wage growth between the 4th quarter of 2016 and the 4th quarter of 2017. *PayScale, "Wage Trends by Metro Area-4th Quarter," January 17, 2018*

- The Seattle* metro area was identified as one of the most debt-ridden places in America by the finance site Credit.com. The metro area was ranked #9. Criteria: residents' average credit card debt as well as median income. *Credit.com, "25 Cities With the Most Credit Card Debt," February 28, 2018*

- The Seattle* metro area appeared on the Milken Institute "2017 Best Performing Cities" list. Rank: #17 out of 200 large metro areas. Criteria: job growth; wage and salary growth; high-tech output growth. *Milken Institute, "Best-Performing Cities 2017," January 2018*

- *Forbes* ranked the 200 most populous metro areas to determine the nation's "Best Places for Business and Careers." The Seattle* metro area was ranked #3. Criteria: costs (business and living); job growth (past and projected); income growth; quality of life; educational attainment (college and high school); projected economic growth; cultural and recreational opportunities; net migration patterns; number of highly ranked colleges. *Forbes, "The Best Places for Business and Careers 2017," October 24, 2017*

Education Rankings

- Personal finance website *WalletHub* analyzed the 150 largest U.S. metropolitan statistical areas to determine where the most educated Americans are choosing to settle. Criteria: education quality and attainment gap; education levels; percentage of workers with degrees; public school rankings; quality and size of each metro area's universities. Seattle* was ranked #11 (#1 = most educated city). *www.WalletHub.com, "2017's Most and Least Educated Cities in America," July 25, 2017*

Environmental Rankings

- Sperling's BestPlaces assessed 379 metropolitan areas of the United States for the likelihood of dangerously extreme weather events or earthquakes. In general the Southeast and South-Central regions have the highest risk of weather extremes and earthquakes, while the Pacific Northwest enjoys the lowest risk. Of the least risky metropolitan areas, the Seattle* metro area was ranked #8. *www.bestplaces.net, "Safest Places from Natural Disasters," April 2011*

- The U.S. Environmental Protection Agency (EPA) released a list of U.S. metropolitan areas with the most ENERGY STAR certified buildings in 2016. The Seattle* metro area was ranked #15 out of 25. *U.S. Environmental Protection Agency, "2017 Energy Star Top Cities," June 2017*

- Seattle* was highlighted as one of the 25 metro areas most polluted by short-term particle pollution (24-hour PM 2.5) in the U.S. during 2013 through 2015. The area ranked #17. *American Lung Association, State of the Air 2017*

Health/Fitness Rankings

- Analysts who tracked obesity rates in the nation's largest metro areas (populations above one million) found that the Seattle* metro area was one of the ten major metros where residents were least likely to be obese, defined as a BMI score of 30 or above. *www.gallup.com, "Boulder, Colo., Residents Still Least Likely to Be Obese," April 4, 2014*

- For each of the 50 most populous metro areas in the United States, the American College of Sports Medicine's American Fitness Index evaluated infrastructure, community assets, and policies that encourage healthy and fit lifestyles, including preventive health behaviors, levels of chronic disease conditions, health care access, and community resources and policies that support physical activity. The Seattle* metro area ranked #4 for "community fitness." *www.americanfitnessindex.org, "ACSM American Fitness Index Health and Community Fitness Status of the 50 Largest Metropolitan Areas," May 2017*

- Trulia analyzed the 100 largest U.S. metro areas to identify the nation's best cities for weight loss, based on the percentage of adults who bike or walk to work, sporting goods stores, grocery stores, access to outdoor activities, weight-loss centers, gyms, and average space reserved for parks. Seattle* ranked #4. *Trulia.com, "Where to Live to Get in Shape in the New Year," January 4, 2018*
- The Seattle* metro area was identified as one of the worst cities for bed bugs in America by pest control company Orkin. The area ranked #36 out of 50 based on the number of bed bug treatments Orkin performed from December 2016 to November 2017. *Orkin, "Baltimore and Washington D.C. Continue to Hold Top Spots," January 8, 2018*
- Seattle* was identified as a "2016 Spring Allergy Capital." The area ranked #82 out of 100. Three groups of factors were used to identify the most severe cities for people with allergies during the spring season: annual pollen levels; medicine utilization; access to board-certified allergists. *Asthma and Allergy Foundation of America, "Spring Allergy Capitals 2016"*
- Seattle* was identified as a "2016 Fall Allergy Capital." The area ranked #89 out of 100. Three groups of factors were used to identify the most severe cities for people with allergies during the fall season: annual pollen levels; medicine utilization; access to board-certified allergists. *Asthma and Allergy Foundation of America, "Fall Allergy Capitals 2016"*
- Seattle* was identified as a "2015 Asthma Capital." The area ranked #98 out of the nation's 100 largest metropolitan areas. Criteria: estimated prevalence; self-reported prevalence; crude death rate for asthma; annual pollen score; annual air quality; public smoking laws; number of board-certified asthma specialists; school inhaler access laws; rescue medication use; controller medication use; ER visits for asthma; uninsured rate; poverty rate. *Asthma and Allergy Foundation of America, "Asthma Capitals 2015"*
- The Seattle* metro area ranked #85 out of 189 in The Gallup-Healthways Well-Being Index. Criteria: purpose; social well being; financial health; community and physical health. Results are based on telephone interviews with adults, aged 18 and older, living in metropolitan areas in the 50 U.S. states and the District of Columbia. *Gallup-Healthways, "State of American Well-Being, 2017 Community Well-Being Rankings" March 2018*

Real Estate Rankings

- FitSmallBusiness looked at 50 of the largest metropolitan areas in the U.S. to determine which metro was the best to start a real estate business. Data was compiled from such sources as: Zillow, Trulia, U.S. Census Bureau, and the Bureau of Labor Statistics. Criteria: location; inventory; annual wages; median sales price of homes; days on the market; median price cut percentage; and other factors that would influence real estate professional growth. The Seattle* metro area ranked #27. *fitsmallbusiness.com, "The Best Cities to Become a Real Estate Agent in 2018," January 30, 2018*
- With data from RealtyTrac, Yahoo! Finance researchers listed the housing markets in which housing affordability is improving most, factoring in interest rates as well as median home prices. The Seattle* metro area was among the least affordable housing markets. *news.yahoo.com, "10 Cities Where Ordinary People Can No Longer Afford Homes," March 5, 2014*
- Seattle* was ranked #2 in the top 20 out of 265 metro areas in terms of house price appreciation in 2017 (#1 = highest rate). *Federal Housing Finance Agency, House Price Index, 4th Quarter 2017. February 27, 2018*
- The Seattle* metro area was identified as one of the 10 worst housing markets to invest in. Criteria: single-family rental home investing in the first quarter of 2017 based on first-year returns. The area ranked #6. *The Business Insider, "Here Are the 10 Worst U.S. Housing Markets for Investment," May 12, 2017*
- The Seattle* metro area was identified as one of the 20 best housing markets in the U.S. in 2017. The area ranked #14 out of 180 markets. Criteria: year-over-year change of median sales price of existing single-family homes between the 4th quarter of 2016 and the 4th quarter of 2017. *National Association of Realtors®, Median Sales Price of Existing Single-Family Homes for Metropolitan Areas, 4th Quarter 2017*

- The Seattle* metro area was identified as one of the 20 least affordable housing markets in the U.S. in 2017. The area ranked #13 out of 180 markets. Criteria: qualification for a mortgage loan on a typical home. *National Association of Realtors®, Affordability Index of Existing Single-Family Homes for Metropolitan Areas, 2017*

- Seattle* was ranked #210 out of 238 metro areas in terms of housing affordability in 2017 by the National Association of Home Builders (#1 = most affordable). Criteria: the share of homes sold in that area affordable to a family earning the local median income, based on standard mortgage underwriting criteria. *National Association of Home Builders®, NAHB-Wells Fargo Housing Opportunity Index, 4th Quarter 2017*

Safety Rankings

- Sammamish was identified as one of the safest cities in America by NeighborhoodScout. The city ranked #30 out of 100 (100 = safest). Criteria: number of violent and property crimes per 1,000 residents. The editors only considered cities with 25,000 or more residents. *NeighborhoodScout, "Top 100 Safest Cities in the U.S. 2018" January 2, 2018*

- The National Insurance Crime Bureau ranked 382 metro areas in the U.S. in terms of per capita rates of vehicle theft. The Seattle* metro area ranked #22 (#1 = highest rate). Criteria: number of vehicle theft offenses per 100,000 inhabitants in 2016. *National Insurance Crime Bureau, "Hot Spots 2016," June 8, 2017*

Seniors/Retirement Rankings

- From its Best Cities for Successful Aging indexes, the Milken Institute generated rankings for metropolitan areas, weighing data in nine categories—health care, wellness, living arrangements, transportation and convenience, financial characteristics, education, employment, community engagement, and overall livability. The Seattle* metro area was ranked #43 overall in the large metro area category. *Milken Institute, "Best Cities for Successful Aging, 2017" March 14, 2017*

Transportation Rankings

- Seattle* was identified as one of the most congested metro areas in the U.S. The area ranked #7 out of 10. Criteria: yearly delay per auto commuter in hours. *Texas A&M Transportation Institute, "2015 Urban Mobility Scorecard," August 2015*

- The Seattle* metro area appeared on *Forbes* list of places with the most extreme commutes. The metro area ranked #10 out of 10. Criteria: average travel time; percentage of mega commuters. Mega-commuters travel more than 90 minutes and 50 miles each way to work. *Forbes.com, "The Cities with the Most Extreme Commutes," March 5, 2013*

Miscellaneous Rankings

- Of the American metro areas that allow medical or recreational use of marijuana, the Seattle* metro area was identified by CNBC editors as one of the most livable for marijuana lovers. Criteria included the Sperling's BestPlaces assessment of marijuana-friendly cities in terms of sound economy, cultural diversity, and a healthy population, plus cost-of-living index and high-quality schools. *www.cnbc.com, "The Best Cities to Live for Marijuana Lovers," February 5, 2014*

- The watchdog site Charity Navigator conducts an annual study of charities in the nation's major markets both to analyze statistical differences in their financial, accountability, and transparency practices and to track year-to-year variations in individual philanthropic communities. Charity Navigator's analysis demonstrated that the financial, accountability and transparency behaviors of America's largest charities can be influenced by the metropolitan market within which the charity operates. The Seattle* metro area was ranked #25 among the 30 metro markets in the rating category of Overall Score. *www.charitynavigator.org, "2017 Metro Market Study," May 1, 2017*

- The National Alliance to End Homelessness listed the 25 most populous metro areas with the highest rate of homelessness. The Seattle* metro area had a high rate of homelessness. Criteria: number of homeless people per 10,000 population in 2016. *National Alliance to End Homelessness, "Homelessness in the 25 Most Populous U.S. Metro Areas," September 1, 2017*

*Sammamish is located within the Seattle-Tacoma-Bellevue, WA Metropolitan Statistical Area and the Seattle-Bellevue-Everett, WA Metropolitan Division.

Business Environment

CITY FINANCES

City Government Finances

Component	2015 ($000)	2015 ($ per capita)
Total Revenues	n/a	n/a
Total Expenditures	n/a	n/a
Debt Outstanding	n/a	n/a
Cash and Securities[1]	n/a	n/a

Note: (1) Cash and security holdings of a government at the close of its fiscal year,, including those of its dependent agencies, utilities, and liquor stores.
Source: U.S Census Bureau, State & Local Government Finances 2015

City Government Revenue by Source

Source	2015 ($000)	2015 ($ per capita)	2015 (%)
General Revenue			
From Federal Government	n/a	n/a	n/a
From State Government	n/a	n/a	n/a
From Local Governments	n/a	n/a	n/a
Taxes			
Property	n/a	n/a	n/a
Sales and Gross Receipts	n/a	n/a	n/a
Personal Income	n/a	n/a	n/a
Corporate Income	n/a	n/a	n/a
Motor Vehicle License	n/a	n/a	n/a
Other Taxes	n/a	n/a	n/a
Current Charges	n/a	n/a	n/a
Liquor Store	n/a	n/a	n/a
Utility	n/a	n/a	n/a
Employee Retirement	n/a	n/a	n/a

Source: U.S Census Bureau, State & Local Government Finances 2015

City Government Expenditures by Function

Function	2015 ($000)	2015 ($ per capita)	2015 (%)
General Direct Expenditures			
Air Transportation	n/a	n/a	n/a
Corrections	n/a	n/a	n/a
Education	n/a	n/a	n/a
Employment Security Administration	n/a	n/a	n/a
Financial Administration	n/a	n/a	n/a
Fire Protection	n/a	n/a	n/a
General Public Buildings	n/a	n/a	n/a
Governmental Administration, Other	n/a	n/a	n/a
Health	n/a	n/a	n/a
Highways	n/a	n/a	n/a
Hospitals	n/a	n/a	n/a
Housing and Community Development	n/a	n/a	n/a
Interest on General Debt	n/a	n/a	n/a
Judicial and Legal	n/a	n/a	n/a
Libraries	n/a	n/a	n/a
Parking	n/a	n/a	n/a
Parks and Recreation	n/a	n/a	n/a
Police Protection	n/a	n/a	n/a
Public Welfare	n/a	n/a	n/a
Sewerage	n/a	n/a	n/a
Solid Waste Management	n/a	n/a	n/a
Veterans' Services	n/a	n/a	n/a
Liquor Store	n/a	n/a	n/a
Utility	n/a	n/a	n/a
Employee Retirement	n/a	n/a	n/a

Source: U.S Census Bureau, State & Local Government Finances 2015

DEMOGRAPHICS

Population Growth

Area	1990 Census	2000 Census	2010 Census	2016* Estimate	Population Growth (%) 1990-2016	2010-2016
City	23,254	34,104	45,780	62,136	167.2	35.7
MSA[1]	2,559,164	3,043,878	3,439,809	3,671,095	43.4	6.7
U.S.	248,709,873	281,421,906	308,745,538	318,558,162	28.1	3.2

Note: (1) Figures cover the Seattle-Tacoma-Bellevue, WA Metropolitan Statistical Area—see Appendix B for areas included; (*) 2012-2016 5-year estimated population
Source: U.S. Census Bureau, 1990 Census, Census 2000, Census 2010, 2012-2016 American Community Survey 5-Year Estimates

Household Size

Area	Persons in Household (%) One	Two	Three	Four	Five	Six	Seven or More	Average Household Size
City	10.2	29.7	22.0	27.5	7.3	2.4	1.0	3.00
MSA[1]	28.3	34.1	15.9	13.3	5.3	2.0	1.2	2.50
U.S.	27.7	33.7	15.7	13.1	6.0	2.3	1.5	2.60

Note: (1) Figures cover the Seattle-Tacoma-Bellevue, WA Metropolitan Statistical Area—see Appendix B for areas included
Source: U.S. Census Bureau, 2012-2016 American Community Survey 5-Year Estimates

Race

Area	White Alone[2] (%)	Black Alone[2] (%)	Asian Alone[2] (%)	AIAN[3] Alone[2] (%)	NHOPI[4] Alone[2] (%)	Other Race Alone[2] (%)	Two or More Races (%)
City	69.2	1.0	25.2	0.0	0.1	0.5	4.1
MSA[1]	71.1	5.6	12.4	0.9	0.9	3.0	6.3
U.S.	73.3	12.6	5.2	0.8	0.2	4.8	3.1

Note: (1) Figures cover the Seattle-Tacoma-Bellevue, WA Metropolitan Statistical Area—see Appendix B for areas included; (2) Alone is defined as not being in combination with one or more other races; (3) American Indian and Alaska Native; (4) Native Hawaiian and Other Pacific Islander
Source: U.S. Census Bureau, 2012-2016 American Community Survey 5-Year Estimates

Hispanic or Latino Origin

Area	Total (%)	Mexican (%)	Puerto Rican (%)	Cuban (%)	Other (%)
City	4.0	2.4	0.2	0.0	1.4
MSA[1]	9.6	6.8	0.5	0.1	2.1
U.S.	17.3	11.0	1.7	0.7	4.0

Note: Persons of Hispanic or Latino origin can be of any race; (1) Figures cover the Seattle-Tacoma-Bellevue, WA Metropolitan Statistical Area—see Appendix B for areas included
Source: U.S. Census Bureau, 2012-2016 American Community Survey 5-Year Estimates

Segregation

Type	Segregation Indices[1] 1990	2000	2010	2010 Rank[2]	Percent Change 1990-2000	1990-2010	2000-2010
Black/White	56.5	52.4	49.1	72	-4.1	-7.4	-3.3
Asian/White	36.8	37.6	37.6	69	0.8	0.8	0.0
Hispanic/White	22.3	30.4	32.8	87	8.1	10.5	2.4

Note: All figures cover the Metropolitan Statistical Area—see Appendix B for areas included; Figures are based on an analysis of 1990, 2000, and 2010 Census Decennial Census tract data by William H. Frey, Brookings Institution and the University of Michigan Social Science Data Analysis Network. In this analysis all racial groups (whites, blacks, and asians) are non-Hispanic members of those races. Hispanics are shown as a separate category; (1) Segregation Indices are Dissimilarity Indices that measure the degree to which the minority group is distributed differently than whites across census tracts. They range from 0 (complete integration) to 100 (complete segregation) where the value indicates the percentage of the minority group that needs to move to be distributed exactly like whites; (2) Ranges from 1 (most segregated) to 102 (least segregated); n/a not available.
Source: www.CensusScope.org

Ancestry

Area	German	Irish	English	American	Italian	Polish	French[2]	Scottish	Dutch
City	14.3	9.2	11.4	4.9	3.9	2.2	2.4	2.6	1.3
MSA[1]	16.2	10.3	10.1	3.7	3.7	2.0	3.0	2.8	1.7
U.S.	14.4	10.4	7.7	6.9	5.4	2.9	2.6	1.7	1.3

Note: Figures are the percentage of the total population reporting a particular ancestry. The nine most commonly reported ancestries in the U.S. are shown. Figures include multiple ancestries (e.g. if a person reported being Irish and Italian, they were included in both columns); (1) Figures cover the Seattle-Tacoma-Bellevue, WA Metropolitan Statistical Area—see Appendix B for areas included; (2) Excludes Basque
Source: U.S. Census Bureau, 2012-2016 American Community Survey 5-Year Estimates

Foreign-Born Population

Area	Percent of Population Born in								
	Any Foreign Country	Asia	Mexico	Europe	Carribean	Central America[2]	South America	Africa	Canada
City	25.1	17.2	0.6	3.8	0.0	0.0	0.7	0.8	1.8
MSA[1]	17.5	8.9	2.4	2.7	0.1	0.5	0.4	1.3	0.7
U.S.	13.2	4.0	3.6	1.5	1.3	1.0	0.9	0.6	0.3

Note: (1) Figures cover the Seattle-Tacoma-Bellevue, WA Metropolitan Statistical Area—see Appendix B for areas included; (2) Excludes Mexico.
Source: U.S. Census Bureau, 2012-2016 American Community Survey 5-Year Estimates

Marital Status

Area	Never Married	Now Married[2]	Separated	Widowed	Divorced
City	19.1	74.0	0.4	2.0	4.6
MSA[1]	32.5	50.2	1.5	4.4	11.5
U.S.	33.0	48.1	2.1	5.9	11.0

Note: Figures are percentages and cover the population 15 years of age and older; (1) Figures cover the Seattle-Tacoma-Bellevue, WA Metropolitan Statistical Area—see Appendix B for areas included; (2) Excludes separated
Source: U.S. Census Bureau, 2012-2016 American Community Survey 5-Year Estimates

Disability Status

Area	All Ages	Under 18 Years Old	18 to 64 Years Old	65 Years and Over
City	4.2	2.1	3.3	21.6
MSA[1]	11.0	3.5	9.1	34.7
U.S.	12.5	4.1	10.3	35.7

Note: Figures show percent of the civilian noninstitutionalized population that reported having a disability. Disability status is determined from six types of difficulty: vision, hearing, cognitive, ambulatory, self-care, and independent living. For children under 5 years old, hearing and vision difficulty are used to determine disability status. For children between the ages of 5 and 14, disability status is determined from hearing, vision, cognitive, ambulatory, and self-care difficulties. For people aged 15 years and older, they are considered to have a disability if they have difficulty with any one of the six difficulty types; Note: (1) Figures cover the Seattle-Tacoma-Bellevue, WA Metropolitan Statistical Area—see Appendix B for areas included
Source: U.S. Census Bureau, 2012-2016 American Community Survey 5-Year Estimates

Age

Area	Percent of Population									Median Age
	Under Age 5	Age 5–19	Age 20–34	Age 35–44	Age 45–54	Age 55–64	Age 65–74	Age 75–84	Age 85+	
City	6.6	26.1	11.8	18.6	18.4	11.3	4.9	1.5	0.7	38.3
MSA[1]	6.3	18.1	22.6	14.2	14.2	12.5	7.2	3.4	1.6	37.1
U.S.	6.2	19.6	20.7	12.7	13.6	12.6	8.3	4.3	1.9	37.7

Note: (1) Figures cover the Seattle-Tacoma-Bellevue, WA Metropolitan Statistical Area—see Appendix B for areas included
Source: U.S. Census Bureau, 2012-2016 American Community Survey 5-Year Estimates

Gender

Area	Males	Females	Males per 100 Females
City	30,801	31,335	98.3
MSA[1]	1,831,699	1,839,396	99.6
U.S.	156,765,322	161,792,840	96.9

Note: (1) Figures cover the Seattle-Tacoma-Bellevue, WA Metropolitan Statistical Area—see Appendix B for areas included
Source: U.S. Census Bureau, 2012-2016 American Community Survey 5-Year Estimates

Religious Groups by Family

Area	Catholic	Baptist	Non-Den.	Methodist[2]	Lutheran	LDS[3]	Pente-costal	Presby-terian[4]	Muslim[5]	Judaism
MSA[1]	12.3	2.2	5.0	1.2	2.1	3.3	2.8	1.4	0.5	0.5
U.S.	19.1	9.3	4.0	4.0	2.3	2.0	1.9	1.6	0.8	0.7

Note: Figures are the number of adherents as a percentage of the total population; (1) Figures cover the Seattle-Tacoma-Bellevue, WA Metropolitan Statistical Area—see Appendix B for areas included; (2) Methodist/Pietist; (3) Latter Day Saints; (4) Reformed; (5) Figures are estimates
Source: Association of Statisticians of American Religious Bodies, 2010 U.S. Religion Census: Religious Congregations & Membership Study

Religious Groups by Tradition

Area	Catholic	Evangelical Protestant	Mainline Protestant	Other Tradition	Black Protestant	Orthodox
MSA[1]	12.3	11.9	4.7	5.9	0.4	0.4
U.S.	19.1	16.2	7.3	4.3	1.6	0.3

Note: Figures are the number of adherents as a percentage of the total population; (1) Figures cover the Seattle-Tacoma-Bellevue, WA Metropolitan Statistical Area—see Appendix B for areas included
Source: Association of Statisticians of American Religious Bodies, 2010 U.S. Religion Census: Religious Congregations & Membership Study

ECONOMY

Gross Metropolitan Product

Area	2014	2015	2016	2017	Rank[2]
MSA[1]	297.9	314.1	324.1	339.1	12

Note: Figures are in billions of dollars; (1) Figures cover the Seattle-Tacoma-Bellevue, WA Metropolitan Statistical Area—see Appendix B for areas included; (2) Rank is based on 2015 data and ranges from 1 to 381
Source: The U.S. Conference of Mayors, U.S. Metro Economies: GMP and Employment Report, 2015-2017

Economic Growth

Area	2012-14 (%)	2015 (%)	2016 (%)	2017 (%)	Rank[2]
MSA[1]	2.5	3.8	1.9	2.8	93
U.S.	2.0	2.4	1.9	2.6	–

Note: Figures are real gross metropolitan product (GMP) growth rates and represent average annual percent change; (1) Figures cover the Seattle-Tacoma-Bellevue, WA Metropolitan Statistical Area—see Appendix B for areas included; (2) Rank is based on 2012-2014 average annual percent change and ranges from 1 to 381
Source: The U.S. Conference of Mayors, U.S. Metro Economies: GMP and Employment Report, 2015-2017

Metropolitan Area Exports

Area	2011	2012	2013	2014	2015	2016	Rank[2]
MSA[1]	41,117.5	50,301.7	56,686.4	61,938.4	67,226.4	61,881.0	3

Note: Figures are in millions of dollars; (1) Figures cover the Seattle-Tacoma-Bellevue, WA Metropolitan Statistical Area—see Appendix B for areas included; (2) Rank is based on 2016 data and ranges from 1 to 385
Source: U.S. Department of Commerce, International Trade Administration, Office of Trade & Industry Information, Manufacturing & Services, data extracted March 15, 2018

Building Permits

Area	Single-Family			Multi-Family			Total		
	2016	2017p	Pct. Chg.	2016	2017p	Pct. Chg.	2016	2017p	Pct. Chg.
City	289	367	27.0	96	0	-100.0	385	367	-4.7
MSA[1]	9,396	9,943	5.8	16,120	17,428	8.1	25,516	27,371	7.3
U.S.	750,800	817,300	8.9	455,800	446,800	-2.0	1,206,600	1,264,100	4.8

Note: (1) Figures cover the Seattle-Tacoma-Bellevue, WA Metropolitan Statistical Area—see Appendix B for areas included; Figures represent new, privately-owned housing units authorized (unadjusted data); All permit data are based on estimates with imputation; (p) preliminary data.
Source: U.S. Census Bureau, Manufacturing, Mining, and Construction Statistics, Building Permits, 2016, 2017

Bankruptcy Filings

Area	Business Filings			Nonbusiness Filings		
	2016	2017	% Chg.	2016	2017	% Chg.
King County	129	142	10.1	3,161	2,633	-16.7
U.S.	24,114	23,157	-4.0	770,846	765,863	-0.6

Note: Business filings include Chapter 7, Chapter 11, Chapter 12, and Chapter 13; Nonbusiness filings include Chapter 7, Chapter 11, and Chapter 13
Source: Administrative Office of the U.S. Courts, Business and Nonbusiness Bankruptcy, County Cases Commenced by Chapter of the Bankruptcy Code, During the 12-Month Period Ending December 31, 2016 and Business and Nonbusiness Bankruptcy, County Cases Commenced by Chapter of the Bankruptcy Code, During the 12-Month Period Ending December 31, 2017

Housing Vacancy Rates

Area	Gross Vacancy Rate[2] (%)			Year-Round Vacancy Rate[3] (%)			Rental Vacancy Rate[4] (%)			Homeowner Vacancy Rate[5] (%)		
	2015	2016	2017	2015	2016	2017	2015	2016	2017	2015	2016	2017
MSA[1]	5.6	5.6	6.0	5.4	5.3	5.4	3.8	3.3	3.4	1.1	0.9	0.5
U.S.	12.9	12.8	12.7	10.0	9.9	9.9	7.1	6.9	7.2	1.8	1.7	1.6

Note: (1) Figures cover the Seattle-Tacoma-Bellevue, WA Metropolitan Statistical Area—see Appendix B for areas included; (2) The percentage of the total housing inventory that is vacant; (3) The percentage of the housing inventory (excluding seasonal units) that is year-round vacant; (4) The percentage of rental inventory that is vacant for rent; (5) The percentage of homeowner inventory that is vacant for sale
Source: U.S. Census Bureau, Housing Vacancies and Homeownership Annual Statistics: 2015, 2016, 2017

INCOME

Income

Area	Per Capita ($)	Median Household ($)	Average Household ($)
City	58,567	153,253	177,471
MSA[1]	38,466	73,044	97,001
U.S.	29,829	55,322	77,866

Note: (1) Figures cover the Seattle-Tacoma-Bellevue, WA Metropolitan Statistical Area—see Appendix B for areas included
Source: U.S. Census Bureau, 2012-2016 American Community Survey 5-Year Estimates

Household Income Distribution

Area	Percent of Households Earning							
	Under $15,000	$15,000 -$24,999	$25,000 -$34,999	$35,000 -$49,999	$50,000 -$74,999	$75,000 -$99,999	$100,000 -$149,999	$150,000 and up
City	2.8	1.5	2.2	3.5	7.6	8.6	22.8	51.2
MSA[1]	8.5	6.8	7.3	11.4	17.3	13.6	17.8	17.4
U.S.	12.1	10.2	9.9	13.2	17.8	12.2	13.5	11.1

Note: (1) Figures cover the Seattle-Tacoma-Bellevue, WA Metropolitan Statistical Area—see Appendix B for areas included
Source: U.S. Census Bureau, 2012-2016 American Community Survey 5-Year Estimates

Poverty Rate

Area	All Ages	Under 18 Years Old	18 to 64 Years Old	65 Years and Over
City	2.7	3.1	2.2	4.7
MSA[1]	10.9	13.7	10.4	8.2
U.S.	15.1	21.2	14.2	9.3

Note: Figures are percentage of people whose income during the past 12 months was below the poverty level; (1) Figures cover the Seattle-Tacoma-Bellevue, WA Metropolitan Statistical Area—see Appendix B for areas included
Source: U.S. Census Bureau, 2012-2016 American Community Survey 5-Year Estimates

EMPLOYMENT

Labor Force and Employment

Area	Civilian Labor Force			Workers Employed		
	Dec. 2016	Dec. 2017	% Chg.	Dec. 2016	Dec. 2017	% Chg.
City	32,056	33,015	3.0	31,062	31,952	2.9
MD[1]	1,613,459	1,663,045	3.1	1,557,412	1,602,109	2.9
U.S.	158,968,000	159,880,000	0.6	151,798,000	153,602,000	1.2

Note: Data is not seasonally adjusted and covers workers 16 years of age and older; (1) Figures cover the Seattle-Bellevue-Everett, WA Metropolitan Division—see Appendix B for areas included
Source: Bureau of Labor Statistics, Local Area Unemployment Statistics

Unemployment Rate

Area	2017											
	Jan.	Feb.	Mar.	Apr.	May	Jun.	Jul.	Aug.	Sep.	Oct.	Nov.	Dec.
City	3.6	3.5	3.4	2.9	3.1	3.7	3.6	3.6	3.6	3.5	3.6	3.2
MD[1]	3.8	3.8	3.6	3.2	3.5	4.0	4.1	4.1	4.0	3.9	4.1	3.7
U.S.	5.1	4.9	4.6	4.1	4.1	4.5	4.6	4.5	4.1	3.9	3.9	3.9

Note: Data is not seasonally adjusted and covers workers 16 years of age and older; (1) Figures cover the Seattle-Bellevue-Everett, WA Metropolitan Division—see Appendix B for areas included
Source: Bureau of Labor Statistics, Local Area Unemployment Statistics

Average Wages

Occupation	$/Hr.	Occupation	$/Hr.
Accountants and Auditors	38.60	Maids and Housekeeping Cleaners	13.80
Automotive Mechanics	24.00	Maintenance and Repair Workers	22.80
Bookkeepers	22.40	Marketing Managers	75.80
Carpenters	29.80	Nuclear Medicine Technologists	44.70
Cashiers	14.30	Nurses, Licensed Practical	27.60
Clerks, General Office	19.70	Nurses, Registered	39.40
Clerks, Receptionists/Information	16.80	Nursing Assistants	15.20
Clerks, Shipping/Receiving	18.50	Packers and Packagers, Hand	14.10
Computer Programmers	60.00	Physical Therapists	43.20
Computer Systems Analysts	48.00	Postal Service Mail Carriers	24.20
Computer User Support Specialists	32.00	Real Estate Brokers	32.20
Cooks, Restaurant	15.40	Retail Salespersons	17.30
Dentists	88.40	Sales Reps., Exc. Tech./Scientific	35.60
Electrical Engineers	55.20	Sales Reps., Tech./Scientific	43.90
Electricians	33.40	Secretaries, Exc. Legal/Med./Exec.	21.40
Financial Managers	71.10	Security Guards	17.30
First-Line Supervisors/Managers, Sales	25.90	Surgeons	120.50
Food Preparation Workers	15.00	Teacher Assistants*	17.40
General and Operations Managers	67.80	Teachers, Elementary School*	30.90
Hairdressers/Cosmetologists	21.30	Teachers, Secondary School*	31.90
Internists, General	116.90	Telemarketers	17.50
Janitors and Cleaners	16.00	Truck Drivers, Heavy/Tractor-Trailer	23.90
Landscaping/Groundskeeping Workers	17.90	Truck Drivers, Light/Delivery Svcs.	19.50
Lawyers	68.30	Waiters and Waitresses	18.10

Note: Wage data covers the Seattle-Bellevue-Everett, WA Metropolitan Division—see Appendix B for areas included; (*) Hourly wages for elementary/secondary school teachers and teacher assistants were calculated by the editors from annual wage data based on a 40 hour work week; n/a not available.
Source: Bureau of Labor Statistics, Metro Area Occupational Employment & Wage Estimates, May 2017

Employment by Occupation

Occupation Classification	City (%)	MSA[1] (%)	U.S. (%)
Management, Business, Science, and Arts	67.1	44.2	37.0
Natural Resources, Construction, and Maintenance	1.9	7.5	8.9
Production, Transportation, and Material Moving	3.7	10.2	12.2
Sales and Office	19.8	21.8	23.8
Service	7.6	16.2	18.1

Note: Figures cover employed civilians 16 years of age and older; (1) Figures cover the Seattle-Tacoma-Bellevue, WA Metropolitan Statistical Area—see Appendix B for areas included
Source: U.S. Census Bureau, 2012-2016 American Community Survey 5-Year Estimates

Employment by Industry

Sector	MD[1] Number of Employees	MD[1] Percent of Total	U.S. Percent of Total
Construction	101,300	5.9	4.7
Education and Health Services	218,600	12.7	15.9
Financial Activities	86,200	5.0	5.7
Government	222,800	13.0	15.3
Information	111,000	6.5	1.9
Leisure and Hospitality	170,700	9.9	10.7
Manufacturing	157,600	9.2	8.5
Mining and Logging	800	<0.1	0.5
Other Services	59,100	3.4	3.9
Professional and Business Services	260,700	15.2	14.0
Retail Trade	197,300	11.5	11.0
Transportation, Warehousing, and Utilities	59,400	3.5	4.1
Wholesale Trade	73,100	4.3	4.0

Note: Figures are non-farm employment as of December 2017. Figures are not seasonally adjusted and include workers 16 years of age and older; (1) Figures cover the Seattle-Bellevue-Everett, WA Metropolitan Division—see Appendix B for areas included
Source: Bureau of Labor Statistics, Current Employment Statistics, Employment, Hours, and Earnings

Occupations with Greatest Projected Employment Growth: 2017 – 2019

Occupation[1]	2017 Employment	2019 Projected Employment	Numeric Employment Change	Percent Employment Change
Software Developers, Applications	71,590	80,750	9,160	12.8
Combined Food Preparation and Serving Workers, Including Fast Food	89,540	95,300	5,760	6.4
Waiters and Waitresses	49,520	52,940	3,420	6.9
Carpenters	50,500	53,840	3,340	6.6
Office Clerks, General	73,340	76,280	2,940	4.0
Janitors and Cleaners, Except Maids and Housekeeping Cleaners	50,690	53,370	2,680	5.3
Customer Service Representatives	53,140	55,500	2,360	4.4
Retail Salespersons	105,870	108,230	2,360	2.2
Registered Nurses	59,730	62,060	2,330	3.9
Construction Laborers	38,500	40,790	2,290	5.9

Note: Projections cover Washington; (1) Sorted by numeric employment change
Source: www.projectionscentral.com, State Occupational Projections, 2017–2019 Short-Term Projections

Fastest Growing Occupations: 2017 – 2019

Occupation[1]	2017 Employment	2019 Projected Employment	Numeric Employment Change	Percent Employment Change
Psychiatric Technicians	750	850	100	12.8
Software Developers, Applications	71,590	80,750	9,160	12.8
Travel Agents	1,720	1,930	210	11.9
Computer Operators	870	970	100	11.3
Computer Programmers	15,710	17,310	1,600	10.2
Multimedia Artists and Animators	4,550	5,020	470	10.2
Web Developers	7,050	7,750	700	10.0
Computer and Information Systems Managers	13,190	14,420	1,230	9.3
Editors	2,910	3,170	260	9.0
Database Administrators	2,670	2,900	230	8.6

Note: Projections cover Washington; (1) Sorted by percent employment change and excludes occupations with numeric employment change less than 50
Source: www.projectionscentral.com, State Occupational Projections, 2017–2019 Short-Term Projections

TAXES

State Corporate Income Tax Rates

State	Tax Rate (%)	Income Brackets ($)	Num. of Brackets	Financial Institution Tax Rate (%)[a]	Federal Income Tax Ded.
Washington	None	–	–	–	–

Note: Tax rates as of January 1, 2018; (a) Rates listed are the corporate income tax rate applied to financial institutions or excise taxes based on income. Some states have other taxes based upon the value of deposits or shares.
Source: Federation of Tax Administrators, Range of State Corporate Income Tax Rates, January 1, 2018

State Individual Income Tax Rates

State	Tax Rate (%)	Income Brackets ($)	Num. of Brackets	Personal Exempt. ($)[1]		Fed. Inc. Tax Ded.
				Single	Dependents	
Washington	None	–	–	–	–	–

Note: Tax rates as of January 1, 2018; Local- and county-level taxes are not included; n/a not applicable; (1) Married joint filers generally receive double the single exemption
Source: Federation of Tax Administrators, State Individual Income Tax Rates, January 1, 2018

Various State Sales and Excise Tax Rates

State	State Sales Tax (%)	Gasoline[1] (¢/gal.)	Cigarette[2] ($/pack)	Spirits[3] ($/gal.)	Wine[4] ($/gal.)	Beer[5] ($/gal.)	Recreational Marijuana (%)
Washington	6.5	49.4	3.025	32.52 (j)(k)	0.87 (l)	0.26 (q)	37.0

Note: All tax rates as of January 1, 2018; (1) The American Petroleum Institute has developed a methodology for determining the average tax rate on a gallon of fuel. Rates may include any of the following: excise taxes, environmental fees, storage tank fees, other fees or taxes, general sales tax, and local taxes. In states where gasoline is subject to the general sales tax, or where the fuel tax is based on the average sale price, the average rate determined by API is sensitive to changes in the price of gasoline. States that fully or partially apply general sales taxes to gasoline: CA, CO, GA, IL, IN, MI, NY; (2) The federal excise tax of $1.0066 per pack and local taxes are not included; (3) Rates are those applicable to off-premise sales of 40% alcohol by volume (a.b.v.) distilled spirits in 750ml containers. Local excise taxes are excluded; (4) Rates are those applicable to off-premise sales of 11% a.b.v. non-carbonated wine in 750ml containers; (5) Rates are those applicable to off-premise sales of 4.7% a.b.v. beer in 12 ounce containers; (j) Includes sales taxes specific to alcoholic beverages; (k) Includes the retail (17%) and distributor (5/10%) license fees, converted into a gallonage excise tax rate; (l) Different rates also applicable to alcohol content, place of production, size of container, place purchased (on- or off-premise or on board airlines) or type of wine (carbonated, vermouth, etc.); (q) Different rates also applicable according to alcohol content, place of production, size of container, or place purchased (on- or off-premise or onboard airlines).
Source: Tax Foundation, 2018 Facts & Figures: How Does Your State Compare?

State Business Tax Climate Index Rankings

State	Overall Rank	Corporate Tax Rank	Individual Income Tax Rank	Sales Tax Rank	Unemployment Insurance Tax Rank	Property Tax Rank
Washington	17	46	6	48	17	27

Note: The index is a measure of how each state's tax laws affect economic performance. The lower the rank, the more favorable a state's tax system is for business. States without a given tax are given a ranking of 1. The scores/rankings for the District of Columbia do not affect other states. The 2018 index represents the tax climate as of July 1, 2017.
Source: Tax Foundation, State Business Tax Climate Index 2018

TRANSPORTATION

Means of Transportation to Work

Area	Car/Truck/Van		Public Transportation			Bicycle	Walked	Other Means	Worked at Home
	Drove Alone	Car-pooled	Bus	Subway	Railroad				
City	69.0	11.8	6.9	0.0	0.0	0.5	0.9	0.6	10.4
MSA[1]	69.1	10.0	8.4	0.2	0.4	1.1	3.8	1.3	5.7
U.S.	76.4	9.3	2.6	1.9	0.6	0.6	2.8	1.3	4.6

Note: Figures are percentages and cover workers 16 years of age and older; (1) Figures cover the Seattle-Tacoma-Bellevue, WA Metropolitan Statistical Area—see Appendix B for areas included
Source: U.S. Census Bureau, 2012-2016 American Community Survey 5-Year Estimates

Travel Time to Work

Area	Less Than 10 Minutes	10 to 19 Minutes	20 to 29 Minutes	30 to 44 Minutes	45 to 59 Minutes	60 to 89 Minutes	90 Minutes or More
City	5.5	14.5	22.1	35.8	13.9	6.7	1.7
MSA[1]	8.2	23.9	21.5	25.1	10.5	7.9	2.9
U.S.	12.9	29.2	20.9	20.4	8.0	6.0	2.7

Note: Note: Figures are percentages and include workers 16 years old and over; (1) Figures cover the Seattle-Tacoma-Bellevue, WA Metropolitan Statistical Area—see Appendix B for areas included
Source: U.S. Census Bureau, 2012-2016 American Community Survey 5-Year Estimates

Freeway Travel Time Index

Area	1985	1990	1995	2000	2005	2010	2014
Urban Area Rank[1,2]	4	3	3	3	3	4	3
Urban Area Index[1]	1.22	1.26	1.29	1.33	1.37	1.36	1.38
Average Index[3]	1.09	1.11	1.14	1.17	1.20	1.19	1.20

Note: Freeway Travel Time Index—the ratio of travel time in the peak period to the travel time at free-flow conditions. For example, a value of 1.30 indicates a 20-minute free-flow trip takes 26 minutes in the peak (20 minutes x 1.30 = 26 minutes); (1) Covers the Seattle WA urban area; (2) Rank is based on 101 urban areas (#1 = highest travel time index); (3) Average of 101 urban areas
Source: Texas Transportation Institute, 2015 Urban Mobility Scorecard, August 2015

Freeway Commuter Stress Index

Area	1985	1990	1995	2000	2005	2010	2014
Urban Area Rank[1,2]	5	4	4	5	5	5	6
Urban Area Index[1]	1.29	1.33	1.37	1.41	1.45	1.45	1.46
Average Index[3]	1.13	1.16	1.19	1.22	1.25	1.24	1.25

Note: The Freeway Commuter Stress Index is the same as the Freeway Travel Time Index (see table above) except that it includes only the travel in the peak directions during the peak periods; the TTI includes travel in all directions during the peak period. Thus, the CSI is more indicative of the work trip experienced by each commuter on a daily basis; (1) Covers the Seattle WA urban area; (2) Rank is based on 101 urban areas (#1 = highest travel time index); (3) Average of 101 urban areas
Source: Texas Transportation Institute, 2015 Urban Mobility Scorecard, August 2015

Living Environment

COST OF LIVING

Cost of Living Index

Composite Index	Groceries	Housing	Utilities	Transportation	Health Care	Misc. Goods/ Services
148.8	126.7	194.2	123.1	133.1	124.2	135.3

Note: The Cost of Living Index measures regional differences in the cost of consumer goods and services, excluding taxes and non-consumer expenditures, for professional and managerial households in the top income quintile. It is based on more than 50,000 prices covering almost 60 different items for which prices are collected three times a year by chambers of commerce, economic development organizations or university applied economic centers in each participating urban area. The numbers shown should be read as a percentage above or below the national average of 100. For example, a value of 115.4 in the groceries column indicates that grocery prices are 15.4% higher than the national average. Small differences in the index numbers should not be interpreted as significant; Figures cover the Seattle WA urban area.
Source: The Council for Community and Economic Research, ACCRA Cost of Living Index, 2017

Grocery Prices

Area[1]	T-Bone Steak ($/pound)	Frying Chicken ($/pound)	Whole Milk ($/half gal.)	Eggs ($/dozen)	Orange Juice ($/64 oz.)	Coffee ($/11.5 oz.)
City[2]	15.36	1.88	2.03	1.68	4.11	5.76
Avg.	11.29	1.40	2.02	1.47	3.55	4.37
Min.	7.71	0.93	1.04	0.70	2.86	3.24
Max.	15.83	2.39	4.03	3.92	6.29	8.16

*Note: (1) Values for the local area are compared with the average, minimum and maximum values for all 294 areas in the Cost of Living Index; (2) Figures cover the Seattle WA urban area; **T-Bone Steak** (price per pound); **Frying Chicken** (price per pound, whole fryer); **Whole Milk** (half gallon carton); **Eggs** (price per dozen, Grade A, large); **Orange Juice** (64 oz. Tropicana or Florida Natural); **Coffee** (11.5 oz. can, vacuum-packed, Maxwell House, Hills Bros, or Folgers).*
Source: The Council for Community and Economic Research, ACCRA Cost of Living Index, 2017

Housing and Utility Costs

Area[1]	New Home Price ($)	Apartment Rent ($/month)	All Electric ($/month)	Part Electric ($/month)	Other Energy ($/month)	Telephone ($/month)
City[2]	649,370	2,366	190.91	-	-	38.34
Avg.	335,956	1,047	175.01	97.34	67.93	28.71
Min.	187,788	491	109.48	49.33	35.44	12.39
Max.	1,739,087	4,559	432.62	227.09	353.33	44.61

*Note: (1) Values for the local area are compared with the average, minimum and maximum values for all 294 areas in the Cost of Living Index; (2) Figures cover the Seattle WA urban area; **New Home Price** (2,400 sf living area, 8,000 sf lot, in urban area with full utilities); **Apartment Rent** (950 sf 2 bedroom/1.5 or 2 bath, unfurnished, excluding all utilities except water); **All Electric** (average monthly cost for an all-electric home); **Part Electric** (average monthly cost for a part-electric home); **Other Energy** (average monthly cost for natural gas, fuel oil, coal, wood, and any other forms of energy except electricity); **Telephone** (price includes basic monthly rate for a private residential line plus additional local usage charges incurred by a family of four).*
Source: The Council for Community and Economic Research, ACCRA Cost of Living Index, 2017

Health Care, Transportation, and Other Costs

Area[1]	Doctor ($/visit)	Dentist ($/visit)	Optometrist ($/visit)	Gasoline ($/gallon)	Beauty Salon ($/visit)	Men's Shirt ($)
City[2]	124.00	132.64	145.72	2.88	43.43	45.00
Avg.	108.00	92.54	101.93	2.25	37.58	30.92
Min.	30.39	60.00	49.75	1.82	16.11	11.20
Max.	193.50	161.94	229.28	3.16	77.35	59.13

*Note: (1) Values for the local area are compared with the average, minimum and maximum values for all 294 areas in the Cost of Living Index; (2) Figures cover the Seattle WA urban area; **Doctor** (general practitioners routine exam of an established patient); **Dentist** (adult teeth cleaning and periodic oral examination); **Optometrist** (full vision eye exam for established adult patient); **Gasoline** (one gallon regular unleaded, national brand, including all taxes, cash price at self-service pump if available); **Beauty Salon** (woman's shampoo, trim, and blow-dry); **Men's Shirt** (cotton/polyester dress shirt, pinpoint weave, long sleeves).*
Source: The Council for Community and Economic Research, ACCRA Cost of Living Index, 2017

HOUSING

House Price Index (HPI)

Area	National Ranking[2]	Quarterly Change (%)	One-Year Change (%)	Five-Year Change (%)
MD[1]	2	1.73	14.34	69.01
U.S.[3]	–	1.61	6.68	34.71

Note: The HPI is a weighted repeat sales index. It measures average price changes in repeat sales or refinancings on the same properties. This information is obtained by reviewing repeat mortgage transactions on single-family properties whose mortgages have been purchased or securitized by Fannie Mae or Freddie Mac in January 1975; (1) Figures cover the Seattle-Bellevue-Everett, WA Metropolitan Division—see Appendix B for areas included; (2) Rankings are based on annual percentage change for all metro areas containing at least 15,000 transactions over the last 10 years and ranges from 1 to 253; (3) figures based on a weighted average of Census Division estimates using a seasonally adjusted, purchase-only index; all figures are for the period ending December 31, 2017

Source: Federal Housing Finance Agency, House Price Index, February 28, 2018

Median Single-Family Home Prices

Area	2015	2016	2017p	Percent Change 2016 to 2017
MSA[1]	379.7	414.5	465.8	12.4
U.S. Average	223.9	235.5	248.8	5.6

Note: Figures are median sales prices of existing single-family homes in thousands of dollars; (p) preliminary; (1) Figures cover the Seattle-Tacoma-Bellevue, WA Metropolitan Statistical Area—see Appendix B for areas included

Source: National Association of Realtors, Median Sales Price of Existing Single-Family Homes for Metropolitan Areas, 4th Quarter 2017

Qualifying Income Based on Median Sales Price of Existing Single-Family Homes

Area	With 5% Down ($)	With 10% Down ($)	With 20% Down ($)
MSA[1]	n/a	n/a	n/a
U.S. Average	55,585	52,659	46,808

Note: Figures are preliminary; Qualifying income is based on a mortgage rate of 4.17%. Monthly principal and interest payment is limited to 25% of income; n/a not available; (1) Figures cover the Seattle-Tacoma-Bellevue, WA Metropolitan Statistical Area—see Appendix B for areas included

Source: National Association of Realtors, Qualifying Income Based on Median Sales Price of Existing Single-Family Homes for Metropolitan Areas, 4th Quarter 2017

Median Apartment Condo-Coop Home Prices

Area	2015	2016	2017p	Percent Change 2016 to 2017
MSA[1]	n/a	n/a	n/a	n/a
U.S. Average	210.7	220.7	234.3	6.2

Note: Figures are median sales prices of existing apartment condo-coop homes in thousands of dollars; (p) preliminary; n/a not available; (1) Figures cover the Seattle-Tacoma-Bellevue, WA Metropolitan Statistical Area—see Appendix B for areas included

Source: National Association of Realtors, Median Sales Price of Existing Apartment Condo-Coop Homes for Metropolitan Areas, 4th Quarter 2017

Home Value Distribution

Area	Under $50,000	$50,000 -$99,999	$100,000 -$149,999	$150,000 -$199,999	$200,000 -$299,999	$300,000 -$499,999	$500,000 -$999,999	$1,000,000 or more
City	0.7	0.1	0.4	1.3	5.1	21.4	62.3	8.7
MSA[1]	3.8	1.8	4.3	9.1	23.4	32.3	21.1	4.2
U.S.	8.8	14.8	15.3	14.9	18.4	16.4	9.0	2.5

Note: Figures are percentages and cover owner-occupied housing units; (1) Figures cover the Seattle-Tacoma-Bellevue, WA Metropolitan Statistical Area—see Appendix B for areas included

Source: U.S. Census Bureau, 2012-2016 American Community Survey 5-Year Estimates

Homeownership Rate

Area	2009 (%)	2010 (%)	2011 (%)	2012 (%)	2013 (%)	2014 (%)	2015 (%)	2016 (%)	2017 (%)
MSA[1]	61.2	60.9	60.7	60.4	61.0	61.3	59.5	57.7	59.5
U.S.	67.4	66.9	66.1	65.4	65.1	64.5	63.7	63.4	63.9

Note: (1) Figures cover the Seattle-Tacoma-Bellevue, WA Metropolitan Statistical Area—see Appendix B for areas included

Source: U.S. Census Bureau, Housing Vacancies and Homeownership Annual Statistics: 2009-2017

Year Housing Structure Built

Area	2010 or Later	2000 -2009	1990 -1999	1980 -1989	1970 -1979	1960 -1969	1950 -1959	1940 -1949	Before 1940	Median Year
City	4.4	21.9	29.3	28.7	10.5	2.5	1.2	0.5	1.0	1992
MSA[1]	3.4	16.1	16.1	15.1	15.1	11.2	7.8	4.5	10.7	1980
U.S.	2.3	14.7	14.0	13.7	15.6	10.9	10.6	5.2	13.0	1977

Note: Figures are percentages except for Median Year; Note: (1) Figures cover the Seattle-Tacoma-Bellevue, WA Metropolitan Statistical Area—see Appendix B for areas included
Source: U.S. Census Bureau, 2012-2016 American Community Survey 5-Year Estimates

Gross Monthly Rent

Area	Under $500	$500 -$999	$1,000 -$1,499	$1,500 -$1,999	$2,000 -$2,499	$2,500 -$2,999	$3,000 and up	Median ($)
City	0.7	7.9	15.9	26.5	21.1	14.5	13.4	1,982
MSA[1]	6.1	27.3	35.9	19.6	6.9	2.5	1.8	1,212
U.S.	11.3	43.3	27.7	10.7	4.0	1.6	1.5	949

Note: Figures are percentages except for Median; Gross rent is the contract rent plus the estimated average monthly cost of utilities (electricity, gas, and water and sewer) and fuels (oil, coal, kerosene, wood, etc.) if these are paid by the renter (or paid for the renter by someone else); (1) Figures cover the Seattle-Tacoma-Bellevue, WA Metropolitan Statistical Area—see Appendix B for areas included
Source: U.S. Census Bureau, 2012-2016 American Community Survey 5-Year Estimates

HEALTH

Health Risk Factors

Category	MD[1] (%)	U.S. (%)
Adults aged 18–64 who have any kind of health care coverage	89.8	87.7
Adults who reported being in good or excellent health	87.1	83.6
Adults who are current smokers	11.2	17.1
Adults who currently use E-cigarettes	4.9	4.7
Adults who currently use chewing tobacco, snuff, or snus	2.6	4.0
Adults who are heavy drinkers[2]	7.3	6.5
Adults who are binge drinkers[3]	16.3	16.9
Adults who are overweight (BMI 25.0 - 29.9)	35.3	35.3
Adults who are obese (BMI 30.0 - 99.8)	24.1	29.9
Adults who participated in any physical activities in the past month	84.8	76.9
Adults who always or nearly always wears a seat belt	97.1	94.3

Note: (1) Figures cover the Seattle-Bellevue-Everett, WA Metropolitan Division—see Appendix B for areas included; (2) Heavy drinkers are classified as adult men having more than 14 drinks per week and adult women having more than 7 drinks per week; (3) Binge drinkers are classified as males having five or more drinks on one occasion or females having four or more drinks on one occasion
Source: Centers for Disease Control and Prevention, Behaviorial Risk Factor Surveillance System, SMART: Selected Metropolitan Area Risk Trends, 2016

Health Screening Rates

Category	MD[1] (%)	U.S. (%)
Adults 50-75 who have had a blood stool test within the past year	11.8	8.0
Adults 50-75 who have had a colonoscopy in the past 10 years	64.4	63.5
Adults aged 65+ who have had flu shot within the past year	61.0	58.6
Adults aged 65+ who have ever had a pneumonia vaccination	78.4	73.4
Adults who have ever been tested for HIV	37.2	35.6
Women aged 21-65 who have had a pap test in the past three years	n/a	79.8
Men aged 40+ who have had a PSA test within the past two years	29.0	39.5
Women aged 40+ who have had a mammogram within the past two years	68.7	72.5

Note: n/a not available; (1) Figures cover the Seattle-Bellevue-Everett, WA Metropolitan Division—see Appendix B for areas included; Source: Centers for Disease Control and Prevention, Behaviorial Risk Factor Surveillance System, SMART: Selected Metropolitan Area Risk Trends, 2016

Chronic Health Conditions

Category	MD[1] (%)	U.S. (%)
Adults who have ever been told they had a heart attack	2.9	4.4
Adults who have ever been told they have angina or coronary heart disease	3.2	4.1
Adults who have ever been told they had a stroke	2.4	3.1
Adults who have been told they currently have asthma	8.5	9.3
Adults who have ever been told they have arthritis	21.1	25.8
Adults who have ever been told they have diabetes[2]	8.1	10.5
Adults who have ever been told they had skin cancer	5.5	5.9
Adults who have ever been told they had any other types of cancer	6.1	6.7
Adults who have ever been told they have COPD	4.6	6.3
Adults who have ever been told they have kidney disease	3.0	2.8
Adults who have ever been told they have a form of depression	19.5	17.4

Note: (1) Figures cover the Seattle-Bellevue-Everett, WA Metropolitan Division—see Appendix B for areas included; (2) Figures do not include pregnancy-related, borderline, or pre-diabetes
Source: Centers for Disease Control and Prevention, Behaviorial Risk Factor Surveillance System, SMART: Selected Metropolitan Area Risk Trends, 2016

Mortality Rates for the Top 10 Causes of Death in the U.S.

ICD-10[a] Sub-Chapter	ICD-10[a] Code	Age-Adjusted Mortality Rate[1] per 100,000 population	
		County[2]	U.S.
Malignant neoplasms	C00-C97	137.5	158.5
Ischaemic heart diseases	I20-I25	71.3	96.8
Other forms of heart disease	I30-I51	33.2	52.4
Chronic lower respiratory diseases	J40-J47	25.9	40.9
Cerebrovascular diseases	I60-I69	29.5	37.2
Organic, including symptomatic, mental disorders	F01-F09	23.8	33.3
Other degenerative diseases of the nervous system	G30-G31	44.9	32.1
Other external causes of accidental injury	W00-X59	26.6	31.2
Diabetes mellitus	E10-E14	17.5	21.1
Hypertensive diseases	I10-I15	16.8	20.8

Note: (a) ICD-10 = International Classification of Diseases 10th Revision; (1) Mortality rates are a three year average covering 2014-2016; (2) Figures cover King County.
Source: Centers for Disease Control and Prevention, National Center for Health Statistics. Underlying Cause of Death 1999-2016 on CDC WONDER Online Database, released December 2017

Mortality Rates for Selected Causes of Death

ICD-10[a] Sub-Chapter	ICD-10[a] Code	Age-Adjusted Mortality Rate[1] per 100,000 population	
		County[2]	U.S.
Assault	X85-Y09	2.6	5.6
Diseases of the liver	K70-K76	10.9	14.0
Human immunodeficiency virus (HIV) disease	B20-B24	1.3	1.9
Influenza and pneumonia	J09-J18	8.6	14.6
Intentional self-harm	X60-X84	11.6	13.2
Malnutrition	E40-E46	0.9	1.3
Obesity and other hyperalimentation	E65-E68	1.9	2.1
Renal failure	N17-N19	5.9	13.0
Transport accidents	V01-V99	5.8	12.0
Viral hepatitis	B15-B19	2.5	1.9

Note: (a) ICD-10 = International Classification of Diseases 10th Revision; (1) Mortality rates are a three year average covering 2014-2016; (2) Figures cover King County; Data are Suppressed when the data meet the criteria for confidentiality constraints; Mortality rates are flagged as Unreliable when the rate would be calculated with a numerator of 20 or less.
Source: Centers for Disease Control and Prevention, National Center for Health Statistics. Underlying Cause of Death 1999-2016 on CDC WONDER Online Database, released December 2017

Health Insurance Coverage

Area	With Health Insurance	With Private Health Insurance	With Public Health Insurance	Without Health Insurance	Population Under Age 18 Without Health Insurance
City	97.8	94.1	9.3	2.2	1.5
MSA[1]	91.2	74.6	27.0	8.8	3.8
U.S.	88.3	66.7	33.0	11.7	5.9

Note: Figures are percentages that cover the civilian noninstitutionalized population; (1) Figures cover the Seattle-Tacoma-Bellevue, WA Metropolitan Statistical Area—see Appendix B for areas included
Source: U.S. Census Bureau, 2012-2016 American Community Survey 5-Year Estimates

Number of Medical Professionals

Area	MDs[3]	DOs[3,4]	Dentists	Podiatrists	Chiropractors	Optometrists
County[1] (number)	10,017	320	2,270	138	988	459
County[1] (rate[2])	473.0	15.1	105.3	6.4	45.8	21.3
U.S. (rate[2])	276.5	22.3	67.3	6.0	26.7	15.9

Note: Data as of 2016 unless noted; (1) Data covers King County; (2) Rate per 100,000 population; (3) Data as of 2015 and includes all active, non-federal physicians; (4) Doctor of Osteopathic Medicine
Source: U.S. Department of Health and Human Services, Health Resources and Services Administration, Bureau of Health Professions, Area Resource File (ARF) 2016-2017

Best Hospitals

According to *U.S. News,* the Seattle-Bellevue-Everett, WA metro area is home to three of the best hospitals in the U.S.: **Seattle Cancer Care Alliance** (1 adult specialty); **UW Medicine/Harborview Medical Center** (1 adult specialty); **University of Washington Medical Center** (10 adult specialties). The hospitals listed were nationally ranked in at least one of 16 specialties. Only 152 hospitals nationwide were nationally ranked in one or more specialties. Twenty hospitals in the U.S. made the Honor Roll. The Best Hospitals Honor Roll was revamped last year to take both the national rankings and the procedure and condition ratings into account. Hospitals received points if they were nationally ranked in one of the 16 specialties—the higher they ranked, the more points they got—and how many ratings of "high performing" they earned in the nine procedures and conditions. *U.S. News Online, "America's Best Hospitals 2017-18"*

According to *U.S. News,* the Seattle-Bellevue-Everett, WA metro area is home to one of the best children's hospitals in the U.S.: **Seattle Children's Hospital** (10 pediatric specialties). The hospital listed was highly ranked in at least one of 10 pediatric specialties. Eighty-two children's hospitals in the U.S. were nationally ranked in at least one specialty. Hospitals received points for being ranked in a specialty, and the 10 hospitals with the most points across the 10 specialties make up the Honor Roll. *U.S. News Online, "America's Best Children's Hospitals 2017-18"*

EDUCATION

Public School District Statistics

District Name	Schls	Pupils	Pupil/ Teacher Ratio	Minority Pupils[1] (%)	Free Lunch Eligible[2] (%)	IEP[3] (%)
Issaquah School District	28	19,951	20.8	42.7	7.3	8.1
Lake Washington School District	53	27,886	19.1	43.2	10.1	11.4

Note: Table includes school districts with 100 or more students; (1) Percentage of students that are not non-Hispanic white; (2) Percentage of students that are eligible for the free lunch program; (3) Percentage of students that have an Individualized Education Program.
Source: U.S. Department of Education, National Center for Education Statistics, Common Core of Data, Local Education Agency (School District) Universe Survey: School Year 2015-2016; U.S. Department of Education, National Center for Education Statistics, Common Core of Data, Public Elementary/Secondary School Universe Survey: School Year 2015-2016

Highest Level of Education

Area	Less than H.S.	H.S. Diploma	Some College, No Deg.	Associate Degree	Bachelor's Degree	Master's Degree	Prof. School Degree	Doctorate Degree
City	1.8	6.2	11.7	7.4	43.5	22.6	3.0	3.7
MSA[1]	8.0	20.3	22.3	9.2	25.4	10.4	2.5	1.8
U.S.	13.0	27.5	21.0	8.2	18.8	8.2	2.0	1.3

Note: Figures cover persons age 25 and over; (1) Figures cover the Seattle-Tacoma-Bellevue, WA Metropolitan Statistical Area—see Appendix B for areas included
Source: U.S. Census Bureau, 2012-2016 American Community Survey 5-Year Estimates

Educational Attainment by Race

Area	High School Graduate or Higher (%)					Bachelor's Degree or Higher (%)				
	Total	White	Black	Asian	Hisp.[2]	Total	White	Black	Asian	Hisp.[2]
City	98.2	98.6	89.7	97.2	95.9	72.9	69.4	63.7	83.4	65.7
MSA[1]	92.0	94.2	88.2	87.2	71.5	40.1	41.0	22.2	52.0	20.3
U.S.	87.0	88.9	84.3	86.3	65.7	30.3	31.6	20.0	52.1	14.7

Note: Figures shown cover persons 25 years old and over; (1) Figures cover the Seattle-Tacoma-Bellevue, WA Metropolitan Statistical Area—see Appendix B for areas included; (2) People of Hispanic origin can be of any race
Source: U.S. Census Bureau, 2012-2016 American Community Survey 5-Year Estimates

School Enrollment by Grade and Control

Area	Preschool (%)		Kindergarten (%)		Grades 1 - 4 (%)		Grades 5 - 8 (%)		Grades 9 - 12 (%)	
	Public	Private	Public	Private	Public	Private	Public	Private	Public	Private
City	24.0	76.0	74.8	25.2	89.5	10.5	91.8	8.2	89.2	10.8
MSA[1]	40.4	59.6	83.9	16.1	88.6	11.4	88.5	11.5	90.7	9.3
U.S.	58.4	41.6	87.7	12.3	89.8	10.2	89.7	10.3	90.4	9.6

Note: Figures shown cover persons 3 years old and over; (1) Figures cover the Seattle-Tacoma-Bellevue, WA Metropolitan Statistical Area—see Appendix B for areas included
Source: U.S. Census Bureau, 2012-2016 American Community Survey 5-Year Estimates

Average Salaries of Public School Classroom Teachers

Area	2015		2016		Change from 2015 to 2016	
	Dollars	Rank[1]	Dollars	Rank[1]	Percent	Rank[2]
Washington	52,502	24	53,738	25	2.4	7
U.S. Average	57,611	–	58,353	–	1.3	–

Note: (1) Rank ranges from 1 to 51 where 1 indicates highest salary; (2) Rank ranges from 1 to 51 where 1 indicates highest percent change.
Source: National Education Association, Rankings & Estimates: Rankings of the States 2016 and Estimates of School Statistics 2017

Higher Education

Four-Year Colleges			Two-Year Colleges			Medical Schools[1]	Law Schools[2]	Voc/ Tech[3]
Public	Private Non-profit	Private For-profit	Public	Private Non-profit	Private For-profit			
0	0	0	0	0	0	0	0	0

Note: Figures cover institutions located within the city limits and include main campuses only; (1) includes schools accredited by the Liaison Committee on Medical Education and the American Osteopathic Association's Commission on Osteopathic College Accreditation; (2) includes ABA-accredited schools, schools with provisional ABA accreditation, and state accredited schools; (3) includes all schools with programs that are less than 2 years.
Source: National Center for Education Statistics, Integrated Postsecondary Education System (IPEDS), 2016-17; Wikipedia, List of Medical Schools in the United States, accessed April 2, 2018; Wikipedia, List of Law Schools in the United States, accessed April 2, 2018

According to *U.S. News & World Report,* the Seattle-Bellevue-Everett, WA metro division is home to two of the best national universities in the U.S.: **University of Washington** (#56 tie); **Seattle Pacific University** (#151 tie). The indicators used to capture academic quality fall into a number of categories: assessment by administrators at peer institutions; retention of students; faculty resources; student selectivity; financial resources; alumni giving; high school counselor ratings of colleges; and graduation rate. *U.S. News & World Report, "America's Best Colleges 2018"*

According to *U.S. News & World Report,* the Seattle-Bellevue-Everett, WA metro division is home to one of the top 100 law schools in the U.S.: **University of Washington** (#32 tie). The rankings are based on a weighted average of 12 measures of quality: peer assessment score; assessment score by lawyers/judges; median LSAT scores; median undergrad GPA; acceptance rate; employment rates for graduates; placement success; bar passage rate; faculty resources; expenditures per student; student/faculty ratio; and library resources. *U.S. News & World Report, "America's Best Graduate Schools, Law, 2019"*

According to *U.S. News & World Report,* the Seattle-Bellevue-Everett, WA metro division is home to one of the top 75 medical schools for research in the U.S.: **University of Washington** (#11 tie). The rankings are based on a weighted average of 11 measures of quality: quality assessment; peer assessment score; assessment score by residency directors; research activity; total research activity; average research activity per faculty member; student selectivity; median MCAT total score; median undergraduate GPA; acceptance rate; and faculty resources. *U.S. News & World Report, "America's Best Graduate Schools, Medical, 2019"*

According to *U.S. News & World Report,* the Seattle-Bellevue-Everett, WA metro division is home to one of the top 75 business schools in the U.S.: **University of Washington (Foster)** (#22). The rankings are based on a weighted average of the following nine measures: quality assessment; peer assessment; recruiter assessment; placement success; mean starting salary and bonus; student selectivity; mean GMAT and GRE scores; mean undergraduate GPA; and acceptance rate. *U.S. News & World Report, "America's Best Graduate Schools, Business, 2019"*

PRESIDENTIAL ELECTION

2016 Presidential Election Results

Area	Clinton	Trump	Johnson	Stein	Other
King County	69.8	21.0	4.0	1.7	3.4
U.S.	48.0	45.9	3.3	1.1	1.7

Note: Results are percentages and may not add to 100% due to rounding
Source: Dave Leip's Atlas of U.S. Presidential Elections

EMPLOYERS

Major Employers

Company Name	Industry
City of Tacoma	Switching & terminal services
Costco Wholesale Corporation	Miscellaneous general merchandise stores
County of Snohomish	Bureau of public roads
Evergreen Healthcare	General medical & surgical hospitals
Harborview Medical Center	General medical & surgical hospitals
King County Public Hospital Dist No. 2	Hospital & health services consultant
Microsoft Corporation	Prepackaged software
Prologix Distribution Services (West)	General merchandise, non-durable
R U Corporation	American restaurant
SNC-Lavalin Constructors	Heavy construction, nec
Social & Health Svcs, Washington Dept of	General medical & surgical hospitals
Swedish Health Services	General medical & surgical hospitals
T-Mobile USA	Radio, telephone communication
The Boeing Company	Airplanes, fixed or rotary wing
Tulalip Resort Casino	Casino hotels
United States Department of the Army	Medical centers
University of Washington	Colleges & universities
Virginia Mason Medical Center	General medical & surgical hospitals
Virginia Mason Seattle Main Clinic	Clinic, operated by physicians

Note: Companies shown are located within the Seattle-Tacoma-Bellevue, WA Metropolitan Statistical Area.
Source: Hoovers.com; Wikipedia

PUBLIC SAFETY

Crime Rate

Area	All Crimes	Violent Crimes				Property Crimes		
		Murder	Rape[3]	Robbery	Aggrav. Assault	Burglary	Larceny -Theft	Motor Vehicle Theft
City	865.4	0.0	16.9	3.7	15.0	157.3	612.5	59.9
Metro[1]	4,169.6	2.4	36.9	105.6	168.5	697.7	2,632.0	526.5
U.S.	2,837.0	5.3	29.6	102.8	248.5	468.9	1,745.0	236.9

Note: Figures are crimes per 100,000 population; (1) Figures cover the Seattle-Bellevue-Everett, WA Metropolitan Division—see Appendix B for areas included; (3) The city and U.S. figures shown were reported using the legacy Uniform Crime Reporting (UCR) definition of rape. The metro area figures shown are an aggregate total of the data submitted using both the revised and legacy UCR definitions.
Source: FBI Uniform Crime Reports, 2016

Hate Crimes

Area	Number of Quarters Reported	Number of Incidents per Bias Motivation					
		Race/Ethnicity/ Ancestry	Religion	Sexual Orientation	Disability	Gender	Gender Identity
City	2	5	1	0	0	1	0
U.S.	4	3,489	1,273	1,076	70	31	124

Source: Federal Bureau of Investigation, Hate Crime Statistics 2016

Identity Theft Consumer Reports

Area	Reports	Reports per 100,000 Population	Rank[2]
MSA[1]	4,497	118	59
U.S.	371,061	114	-

Note: (1) Figures cover the Seattle-Tacoma-Bellevue, WA Metropolitan Statistical Area—see Appendix B for areas included; (2) Rank ranges from 1 to 389 where 1 indicates greatest number of identity theft reports per 100,000 population
Source: Federal Trade Commission, Consumer Sentinel Network Data Book for January–December 2017

Fraud and Other Consumer Reports

Area	Reports	Reports per 100,000 Population	Rank[2]
MSA[1]	18,825	496	117
U.S.	2,304,550	708	-

Note: (1) Figures cover the Seattle-Tacoma-Bellevue, WA Metropolitan Statistical Area—see Appendix B for areas included; (2) Rank ranges from 1 to 389 where 1 indicates greatest number of fraud and other consumer reports per 100,000 population
Source: Federal Trade Commission, Consumer Sentinel Network Data Book for January–December 2017

SPORTS

Professional Sports Teams

Team Name	League	Year Established
Seattle Mariners	Major League Baseball (MLB)	1977
Seattle Seahawks	National Football League (NFL)	1976
Seattle Sounders FC	Major League Soccer (MLS)	2009

Note: Includes teams located in the Seattle-Tacoma-Bellevue, WA Metropolitan Statistical Area.
Source: Wikipedia, Major Professional Sports Teams of the United States and Canada, April 5, 2018

CLIMATE

Average and Extreme Temperatures

Temperature	Jan	Feb	Mar	Apr	May	Jun	Jul	Aug	Sep	Oct	Nov	Dec	Yr.
Extreme High (°F)	64	70	75	85	93	96	98	99	98	89	74	63	99
Average High (°F)	44	48	52	57	64	69	75	74	69	59	50	45	59
Average Temp. (°F)	39	43	45	49	55	61	65	65	60	52	45	41	52
Average Low (°F)	34	36	38	41	46	51	54	55	51	45	39	36	44
Extreme Low (°F)	0	1	11	29	28	38	43	44	35	28	6	6	0

Note: Figures cover the years 1948-1990
Source: National Climatic Data Center, International Station Meteorological Climate Summary, 9/96

Average Precipitation/Snowfall/Humidity

Precip./Humidity	Jan	Feb	Mar	Apr	May	Jun	Jul	Aug	Sep	Oct	Nov	Dec	Yr.
Avg. Precip. (in.)	5.7	4.2	3.7	2.4	1.7	1.4	0.8	1.1	1.9	3.5	5.9	5.9	38.4
Avg. Snowfall (in.)	5	2	1	Tr	Tr	0	0	0	0	Tr	1	3	13
Avg. Rel. Hum. 7am (%)	83	83	84	83	80	79	79	84	87	88	85	85	83
Avg. Rel. Hum. 4pm (%)	76	69	63	57	54	54	49	51	57	68	76	79	63

Note: Figures cover the years 1948-1990; Tr = Trace amounts (<0.05 in. of rain; <0.5 in. of snow)
Source: National Climatic Data Center, International Station Meteorological Climate Summary, 9/96

Weather Conditions

Temperature			Daytime Sky			Precipitation		
5°F & below	32°F & below	90°F & above	Clear	Partly cloudy	Cloudy	0.01 inch or more precip.	0.1 inch or more snow/ice	Thunder-storms
< 1	38	3	57	120	188	157	8	8

Note: Figures are average number of days per year and cover the years 1948-1990
Source: National Climatic Data Center, International Station Meteorological Climate Summary, 9/96

HAZARDOUS WASTE

Superfund Sites

The Seattle-Bellevue-Everett, WA metro division is home to 10 sites on the EPA's Superfund National Priorities List: **Harbor Island (Lead)** (final); **Lockheed West Seattle** (final); **Lower Duwamish Waterway** (final); **Midway Landfill** (final); **Pacific Car & Foundry Co.** (final);

Pacific Sound Resources (final); **Queen City Farms** (final); **Quendall Terminal** (final); **Seattle Municipal Landfill (Kent Highlands)** (final); **Western Processing Co., Inc.** (final). There are a total of 1,396 Superfund sites with a status of proposed or final on the list in the U.S. *U.S. Environmental Protection Agency, National Priorities List, April 4, 2018*

AIR & WATER QUALITY

Air Quality Trends: Ozone

	1990	1995	2000	2005	2010	2012	2013	2014	2015	2016
MSA[1]	0.082	0.062	0.056	0.053	0.053	0.059	0.048	0.052	0.059	0.054
U.S.	0.087	0.089	0.081	0.079	0.073	0.075	0.069	0.067	0.068	0.069

Note: (1) Data covers the Seattle-Tacoma-Bellevue, WA Metropolitan Statistical Area—see Appendix B for areas included. The values shown are the composite ozone concentration averages among trend sites based on the highest fourth daily maximum 8-hour concentration in parts per million. These trends are based on sites having an adequate record of monitoring data during the trend period. Data from exceptional events are included.
Source: U.S. Environmental Protection Agency, Air Quality Monitoring Information, "Air Quality Trends by City, 1990-2016"

Air Quality Index

Area	Percent of Days when Air Quality was...[2]					AQI Statistics[2]	
	Good	Moderate	Unhealthy for Sensitive Groups	Unhealthy	Very Unhealthy	Maximum	Median
MSA[1]	60.8	32.6	3.6	2.7	0.3	202	47

Note: (1) Data covers the Seattle-Tacoma-Bellevue, WA Metropolitan Statistical Area—see Appendix B for areas included; (2) Based on 365 days with AQI data in 2017. Air Quality Index (AQI) is an index for reporting daily air quality. EPA calculates the AQI for five major air pollutants regulated by the Clean Air Act: ground-level ozone, particle pollution (aka particulate matter), carbon monoxide, sulfur dioxide, and nitrogen dioxide. The AQI runs from 0 to 500. The higher the AQI value, the greater the level of air pollution and the greater the health concern. There are six AQI categories: "Good" AQI is between 0 and 50. Air quality is considered satisfactory; "Moderate" AQI is between 51 and 100. Air quality is acceptable; "Unhealthy for Sensitive Groups" When AQI values are between 101 and 150, members of sensitive groups may experience health effects; "Unhealthy" When AQI values are between 151 and 200 everyone may begin to experience health effects; "Very Unhealthy" AQI values between 201 and 300 trigger a health alert; "Hazardous" AQI values over 300 trigger warnings of emergency conditions (not shown).
Source: U.S. Environmental Protection Agency, Air Quality Index Report, 2017

Air Quality Index Pollutants

Area	Percent of Days when AQI Pollutant was...[2]					
	Carbon Monoxide	Nitrogen Dioxide	Ozone	Sulfur Dioxide	Particulate Matter 2.5	Particulate Matter 10
MSA[1]	0.0	5.8	49.0	0.0	45.2	0.0

Note: (1) Data covers the Seattle-Tacoma-Bellevue, WA Metropolitan Statistical Area—see Appendix B for areas included; (2) Based on 365 days with AQI data in 2017. The Air Quality Index (AQI) is an index for reporting daily air quality. EPA calculates the AQI for five major air pollutants regulated by the Clean Air Act: ground-level ozone, particle pollution (also known as particulate matter), carbon monoxide, sulfur dioxide, and nitrogen dioxide. The AQI runs from 0 to 500. The higher the AQI value, the greater the level of air pollution and the greater the health concern.
Source: U.S. Environmental Protection Agency, Air Quality Index Report, 2017

Maximum Air Pollutant Concentrations: Particulate Matter, Ozone, CO and Lead

	Particulate Matter 10 (ug/m³)	Particulate Matter 2.5 Wtd AM (ug/m³)	Particulate Matter 2.5 24-Hr (ug/m³)	Ozone (ppm)	Carbon Monoxide (ppm)	Lead (ug/m³)
MSA[1] Level	n/a	6.9	31	0.061	1	n/a
NAAQS[2]	150	15	35	0.075	9	0.15
Met NAAQS[2]	n/a	Yes	Yes	Yes	Yes	n/a

Note: (1) Data covers the Seattle-Tacoma-Bellevue, WA Metropolitan Statistical Area—see Appendix B for areas included; Data from exceptional events are included; (2) National Ambient Air Quality Standards; ppm = parts per million; ug/m³ = micrograms per cubic meter; n/a not available.
Concentrations: Particulate Matter 10 (coarse particulate)—highest second maximum 24-hour concentration; Particulate Matter 2.5 Wtd AM (fine particulate)—highest weighted annual mean concentration; Particulate Matter 2.5 24-Hour (fine particulate)—highest 98th percentile 24-hour concentration; Ozone—highest fourth daily maximum 8-hour concentration; Carbon Monoxide—highest second maximum non-overlapping 8-hour concentration; Lead—maximum running 3-month average
Source: U.S. Environmental Protection Agency, Air Quality Monitoring Information, "Air Quality Statistics by City, 2016"

Maximum Air Pollutant Concentrations: Nitrogen Dioxide and Sulfur Dioxide

	Nitrogen Dioxide AM (ppb)	Nitrogen Dioxide 1-Hr (ppb)	Sulfur Dioxide AM (ppb)	Sulfur Dioxide 1-Hr (ppb)	Sulfur Dioxide 24-Hr (ppb)
MSA[1] Level	21	49	n/a	n/a	n/a
NAAQS[2]	53	100	30	75	140
Met NAAQS[2]	Yes	Yes	n/a	n/a	n/a

Note: (1) Data covers the Seattle-Tacoma-Bellevue, WA Metropolitan Statistical Area—see Appendix B for areas included; Data from exceptional events are included; (2) National Ambient Air Quality Standards; ppm = parts per million; ug/m^3 = micrograms per cubic meter; n/a not available.
Concentrations: Nitrogen Dioxide AM—highest arithmetic mean concentration; Nitrogen Dioxide 1-Hr—highest 98th percentile 1-hour daily maximum concentration; Sulfur Dioxide AM—highest annual mean concentration; Sulfur Dioxide 1-Hr—highest 99th percentile 1-hour daily maximum concentration; Sulfur Dioxide 24-Hr—highest second maximum 24-hour concentration
Source: U.S. Environmental Protection Agency, Air Quality Monitoring Information, "Air Quality Statistics by City, 2016"

Drinking Water

Water System Name	Pop. Served	Primary Water Source Type	Violations[1]	
			Health Based	Monitoring/ Reporting
Sammamish Plateau Water & Sewer	54,468	Ground	0	0

Note: (1) Based on violation data from January 1, 2017 to December 31, 2017
Source: U.S. Environmental Protection Agency, Office of Ground Water and Drinking Water, Safe Drinking Water Information System (based on data extracted April 5, 2018)

Morgantown, West Virginia

Background

Morgantown is the county seat of Monongalia County, located along the Pennsylvania border in the north central part of West Virginia. Until the Treaty of Paris in 1763, what is now known as Morgantown was greatly contested among French and English settlers and native Indians. In 1772 Morgantown was settled by Zaquill Morgan and the Virginia Assembly chartered the territory in 1785. The direct result of the Virginia Charter is the present city of Morgantown.

Through most of the nineteenth century, Morgantown was a quiet place with one and two-story houses and stores on tree-lined High Street and its connecting streets down to the river. When the railroad came in 1886 and gas and oil production began nearby, industries sprang up in the outlying areas and Morgantown experienced an economic and population boom. From 1890 to 1900, the population more than doubled and, while more people lived in the industrial areas of Seneca and Sabraton, downtown was booming as a commercial district.

Architecturally, Morgantown's builders preferred traditional forms to high style. This gives High Street the eclectic charm characteristic of Main Street, U.S.A. Elmer F. Jacobs who came to Morgantown by way of Pittsburgh in 1894, renovated High Street and its environs, replacing the modest buildings of an earlier era with Romanesque and Queen Anne Revival structures. By the early 1900s he had designed over 400 buildings, many of which may still be seen in the downtown area.

Downtown Morgantown is a mixture of small retail businesses, professional services, restaurants, and residential units, and boasts an award winning Mainstreet Organization.

In the Wharf District, next to the Monongahela River, unused warehouses were revitalized into commercial and residential use. Public and private investments have combined to include street improvements, restaurants, retail, professional offices, and high-end loft apartments in the Wharf District, with a 16-story Radisson Hotel, a Public Theater and Public Piers.

Morgantown is well known for sporting events at Mountaineer Field and the Coliseum, performing arts at the Creative Arts Center (CAC), and an excellent parks system, including the newly developed Pedestrian Walking and Recreational Trails System. Two main trails traverse Morgantown: The Caperton Trail and the Decker's Creek Trail that, together, provide nearly 10 miles of paved fun and connect into an additional 17 miles of packed sand ways. Just north of Caperton Trail is the Historic B&O Train Depot and the Riverfront Amphitheater which hosts the Wheeling Symphony Orchestra and the Arts and River Festival. Cooper's Rock State Forest provides a popular area for hiking, biking, camping, skiing and white-water rafting.

Morgantown is home to West Virginia University, the largest institution of higher education in the State. WV University's medical center and school of medicine draw a high number of doctors and health care professionals to the city, where the ratio of medical specialists is nearly 3 times the national average.

Along with the University, other major employers in the area include the National Institute of Occupational Safety and Health (NIOSH), Mylan Pharmaceuticals and two large health-care systems serving parts of West Virginia and Pennsylvania.

Rankings

General Rankings

- In their fifth annual survey, Livability.com looked at data for nearly 2,300 U.S. cities to determine the rankings for Livability's "Top 100 Best Places to Live" in 2018. Morgantown ranked #43. Criteria: vibrant economy; low cost of living; education, demographics, health care options; transportation & infrastructure; abundant lifestyle amenities. *Livability.com, "Top 100 Best Places to Live 2018" January 16, 2018*

Business/Finance Rankings

- The Morgantown metro area appeared on the Milken Institute "2017 Best Performing Cities" list. Rank: #49 out of 201 small metro areas. Criteria: job growth; wage and salary growth; high-tech output growth. *Milken Institute, "Best-Performing Cities 2017," January 2018*

- *Forbes* ranked 200 smaller metro areas (population under 265,400) to determine the nation's "Best Small Places for Business and Careers." The Morgantown metro area was ranked #58. Criteria: costs (business and living); job growth (past and projected); income growth; quality of life; educational attainment (college and high school); projected economic growth; cultural and recreational opportunities; net migration patterns; number of highly ranked colleges. *Forbes, "The Best Small Cities for Business and Careers 2017," November, 6 2017*

Environmental Rankings

- Sperling's BestPlaces assessed 379 metropolitan areas of the United States for the likelihood of dangerously extreme weather events or earthquakes. In general the Southeast and South-Central regions have the highest risk of weather extremes and earthquakes, while the Pacific Northwest enjoys the lowest risk. Of the least risky metropolitan areas, the Morgantown metro area was ranked #32. *www.bestplaces.net, "Safest Places from Natural Disasters," April 2011*

- Morgantown was highlighted as one of the top 99 cleanest metro areas for short-term particle pollution (24-hour PM 2.5) in the U.S. during 2013 through 2015. Monitors in these cities reported no days with unhealthful PM 2.5 levels. *American Lung Association, State of the Air 2017*

Safety Rankings

- The National Insurance Crime Bureau ranked 382 metro areas in the U.S. in terms of per capita rates of vehicle theft. The Morgantown metro area ranked #287 (#1 = highest rate). Criteria: number of vehicle theft offenses per 100,000 inhabitants in 2016. *National Insurance Crime Bureau, "Hot Spots 2016," June 8, 2017*

Seniors/Retirement Rankings

- Morgantown made *Southern Living's* list of charming and unique southern places to retire or dream of retiring to. The favorite places focused on the following: presence of unique amenities; opportunities to volunteer; low cost of living; continued learning opportunities; stable housing market; access to medical care; availability of part-time work; and ease of travel. *Southern Living, "Best Places to Retire"*

- From its Best Cities for Successful Aging indexes, the Milken Institute generated rankings for metropolitan areas, weighing data in nine categories—health care, wellness, living arrangements, transportation and convenience, financial characteristics, education, employment, community engagement, and overall livability. The Morgantown metro area was ranked #18 overall in the small metro area category. *Milken Institute, "Best Cities for Successful Aging, 2017" March 14, 2017*

Business Environment

CITY FINANCES

City Government Finances

Component	2015 ($000)	2015 ($ per capita)
Total Revenues	71,854	2,340
Total Expenditures	90,008	2,931
Debt Outstanding	124,965	4,069
Cash and Securities[1]	102,674	3,344

Note: (1) Cash and security holdings of a government at the close of its fiscal year,, including those of its dependent agencies, utilities, and liquor stores.
Source: U.S Census Bureau, State & Local Government Finances 2015

City Government Revenue by Source

Source	2015 ($000)	2015 ($ per capita)	2015 (%)
General Revenue			
From Federal Government	651	21	0.9
From State Government	1,936	63	2.7
From Local Governments	92	3	0.1
Taxes			
Property	5,219	170	7.3
Sales and Gross Receipts	2,878	94	4.0
Personal Income	0	0	0.0
Corporate Income	0	0	0.0
Motor Vehicle License	0	0	0.0
Other Taxes	17,923	584	24.9
Current Charges	21,679	706	30.2
Liquor Store	0	0	0.0
Utility	10,416	339	14.5
Employee Retirement	8,374	273	11.7

Source: U.S Census Bureau, State & Local Government Finances 2015

City Government Expenditures by Function

Function	2015 ($000)	2015 ($ per capita)	2015 (%)
General Direct Expenditures			
Air Transportation	2,890	94	3.2
Corrections	0	0	0.0
Education	0	0	0.0
Employment Security Administration	0	0	0.0
Financial Administration	1,465	47	1.6
Fire Protection	4,231	137	4.7
General Public Buildings	1,073	34	1.2
Governmental Administration, Other	2,033	66	2.3
Health	0	0	0.0
Highways	4,160	135	4.6
Hospitals	0	0	0.0
Housing and Community Development	2,006	65	2.2
Interest on General Debt	1,259	41	1.4
Judicial and Legal	1,130	36	1.3
Libraries	1,696	55	1.9
Parking	2,160	70	2.4
Parks and Recreation	4,190	136	4.7
Police Protection	6,364	207	7.1
Public Welfare	147	4	0.2
Sewerage	27,951	910	31.1
Solid Waste Management	0	0	0.0
Veterans' Services	0	0	0.0
Liquor Store	0	0	0.0
Utility	13,984	455	15.5
Employee Retirement	6,173	201	6.9

Source: U.S Census Bureau, State & Local Government Finances 2015

DEMOGRAPHICS

Population Growth

Area	1990 Census	2000 Census	2010 Census	2016* Estimate	Population Growth (%) 1990-2016	Population Growth (%) 2010-2016
City	26,814	26,809	29,660	30,364	13.2	2.4
MSA[1]	104,546	111,200	129,709	136,620	30.7	5.3
U.S.	248,709,873	281,421,906	308,745,538	318,558,162	28.1	3.2

Note: (1) Figures cover the Morgantown, WV Metropolitan Statistical Area—see Appendix B for areas included; (*) 2012-2016 5-year estimated population
Source: U.S. Census Bureau, 1990 Census, Census 2000, Census 2010, 2012-2016 American Community Survey 5-Year Estimates

Household Size

Area	Persons in Household (%)							Average Household Size
	One	Two	Three	Four	Five	Six	Seven or More	
City	42.4	33.6	14.0	6.7	2.2	0.7	0.4	2.40
MSA[1]	32.8	36.5	14.7	10.7	3.7	1.0	0.6	2.50
U.S.	27.7	33.7	15.7	13.1	6.0	2.3	1.5	2.60

Note: (1) Figures cover the Morgantown, WV Metropolitan Statistical Area—see Appendix B for areas included
Source: U.S. Census Bureau, 2012-2016 American Community Survey 5-Year Estimates

Race

Area	White Alone[2] (%)	Black Alone[2] (%)	Asian Alone[2] (%)	AIAN[3] Alone[2] (%)	NHOPI[4] Alone[2] (%)	Other Race Alone[2] (%)	Two or More Races (%)
City	86.6	6.2	4.8	0.2	0.0	0.4	1.9
MSA[1]	91.0	4.1	2.5	0.2	0.0	0.5	1.7
U.S.	73.3	12.6	5.2	0.8	0.2	4.8	3.1

Note: (1) Figures cover the Morgantown, WV Metropolitan Statistical Area—see Appendix B for areas included; (2) Alone is defined as not being in combination with one or more other races; (3) American Indian and Alaska Native; (4) Native Hawaiian and Other Pacific Islander
Source: U.S. Census Bureau, 2012-2016 American Community Survey 5-Year Estimates

Hispanic or Latino Origin

Area	Total (%)	Mexican (%)	Puerto Rican (%)	Cuban (%)	Other (%)
City	2.9	0.5	0.8	0.0	1.6
MSA[1]	2.0	0.7	0.6	0.0	0.6
U.S.	17.3	11.0	1.7	0.7	4.0

Note: Persons of Hispanic or Latino origin can be of any race; (1) Figures cover the Morgantown, WV Metropolitan Statistical Area—see Appendix B for areas included
Source: U.S. Census Bureau, 2012-2016 American Community Survey 5-Year Estimates

Segregation

Type	Segregation Indices[1]				Percent Change		
	1990	2000	2010	2010 Rank[2]	1990-2000	1990-2010	2000-2010
Black/White	n/a	n/a	n/a	n/a	n/a	n/a	n/a
Asian/White	n/a	n/a	n/a	n/a	n/a	n/a	n/a
Hispanic/White	n/a	n/a	n/a	n/a	n/a	n/a	n/a

Note: All figures cover the Metropolitan Statistical Area—see Appendix B for areas included; Figures are based on an analysis of 1990, 2000, and 2010 Census Decennial Census tract data by William H. Frey, Brookings Institution and the University of Michigan Social Science Data Analysis Network. In this analysis all racial groups (whites, blacks, and asians) are non-Hispanic members of those races. Hispanics are shown as a separate category; (1) Segregation Indices are Dissimilarity Indices that measure the degree to which the minority group is distributed differently than whites across census tracts. They range from 0 (complete integration) to 100 (complete segregation) where the value indicates the percentage of the minority group that needs to move to be distributed exactly like whites; (2) Ranges from 1 (most segregated) to 102 (least segregated); n/a not available.
Source: www.CensusScope.org

Ancestry

Area	German	Irish	English	American	Italian	Polish	French[2]	Scottish	Dutch
City	19.4	15.3	9.4	4.1	11.6	5.6	2.5	2.8	1.5
MSA[1]	19.5	14.2	10.0	12.4	8.2	3.7	1.6	2.1	2.0
U.S.	14.4	10.4	7.7	6.9	5.4	2.9	2.6	1.7	1.3

Note: Figures are the percentage of the total population reporting a particular ancestry. The nine most commonly reported ancestries in the U.S. are shown. Figures include multiple ancestries (e.g. if a person reported being Irish and Italian, they were included in both columns); (1) Figures cover the Morgantown, WV Metropolitan Statistical Area—see Appendix B for areas included; (2) Excludes Basque
Source: U.S. Census Bureau, 2012-2016 American Community Survey 5-Year Estimates

Foreign-Born Population

Area	Percent of Population Born in								
	Any Foreign Country	Asia	Mexico	Europe	Carribean	Central America[2]	South America	Africa	Canada
City	7.0	4.9	0.2	0.7	0.5	0.1	0.1	0.3	0.2
MSA[1]	4.3	2.8	0.2	0.4	0.2	0.1	0.1	0.3	0.1
U.S.	13.2	4.0	3.6	1.5	1.3	1.0	0.9	0.6	0.3

Note: (1) Figures cover the Morgantown, WV Metropolitan Statistical Area—see Appendix B for areas included; (2) Excludes Mexico.
Source: U.S. Census Bureau, 2012-2016 American Community Survey 5-Year Estimates

Marital Status

Area	Never Married	Now Married[2]	Separated	Widowed	Divorced
City	65.0	24.1	0.6	2.8	7.4
MSA[1]	42.8	41.5	1.1	5.0	9.5
U.S.	33.0	48.1	2.1	5.9	11.0

Note: Figures are percentages and cover the population 15 years of age and older; (1) Figures cover the Morgantown, WV Metropolitan Statistical Area—see Appendix B for areas included; (2) Excludes separated
Source: U.S. Census Bureau, 2012-2016 American Community Survey 5-Year Estimates

Disability Status

Area	All Ages	Under 18 Years Old	18 to 64 Years Old	65 Years and Over
City	8.9	2.9	6.2	39.2
MSA[1]	13.0	3.5	10.6	39.4
U.S.	12.5	4.1	10.3	35.7

Note: Figures show percent of the civilian noninstitutionalized population that reported having a disability. Disability status is determined from six types of difficulty: vision, hearing, cognitive, ambulatory, self-care, and independent living. For children under 5 years old, hearing and vision difficulty are used to determine disability status. For children between the ages of 5 and 14, disability status is determined from hearing, vision, cognitive, ambulatory, and self-care difficulties. For people aged 15 years and older, they are considered to have a disability if they have difficulty with any one of the six difficulty types; Note: (1) Figures cover the Morgantown, WV Metropolitan Statistical Area—see Appendix B for areas included
Source: U.S. Census Bureau, 2012-2016 American Community Survey 5-Year Estimates

Age

Area	Percent of Population									Median Age
	Under Age 5	Age 5–19	Age 20–34	Age 35–44	Age 45–54	Age 55–64	Age 65–74	Age 75–84	Age 85+	
City	2.3	23.5	43.2	7.7	7.2	7.0	4.6	2.9	1.6	24.0
MSA[1]	5.0	16.9	30.5	11.6	11.7	11.7	7.4	3.6	1.6	33.2
U.S.	6.2	19.6	20.7	12.7	13.6	12.6	8.3	4.3	1.9	37.7

Note: (1) Figures cover the Morgantown, WV Metropolitan Statistical Area—see Appendix B for areas included
Source: U.S. Census Bureau, 2012-2016 American Community Survey 5-Year Estimates

Gender

Area	Males	Females	Males per 100 Females
City	16,986	13,378	127.0
MSA[1]	70,643	65,977	107.1
U.S.	156,765,322	161,792,840	96.9

Note: (1) Figures cover the Morgantown, WV Metropolitan Statistical Area—see Appendix B for areas included
Source: U.S. Census Bureau, 2012-2016 American Community Survey 5-Year Estimates

Religious Groups by Family

Area	Catholic	Baptist	Non-Den.	Methodist[2]	Lutheran	LDS[3]	Pente-costal	Presby-terian[4]	Muslim[5]	Judaism
MSA[1]	7.1	3.0	3.1	7.6	0.7	1.2	0.7	0.5	0.2	0.2
U.S.	19.1	9.3	4.0	4.0	2.3	2.0	1.9	1.6	0.8	0.7

Note: Figures are the number of adherents as a percentage of the total population; (1) Figures cover the Morgantown, WV Metropolitan Statistical Area—see Appendix B for areas included; (2) Methodist/Pietist; (3) Latter Day Saints; (4) Reformed; (5) Figures are estimates
Source: Association of Statisticians of American Religious Bodies, 2010 U.S. Religion Census: Religious Congregations & Membership Study

Religious Groups by Tradition

Area	Catholic	Evangelical Protestant	Mainline Protestant	Other Tradition	Black Protestant	Orthodox
MSA[1]	7.1	7.6	10.8	1.7	0.1	0.2
U.S.	19.1	16.2	7.3	4.3	1.6	0.3

Note: Figures are the number of adherents as a percentage of the total population; (1) Figures cover the Morgantown, WV Metropolitan Statistical Area—see Appendix B for areas included
Source: Association of Statisticians of American Religious Bodies, 2010 U.S. Religion Census: Religious Congregations & Membership Study

ECONOMY

Gross Metropolitan Product

Area	2014	2015	2016	2017	Rank[2]
MSA[1]	7.1	6.7	6.9	7.3	249

Note: Figures are in billions of dollars; (1) Figures cover the Morgantown, WV Metropolitan Statistical Area—see Appendix B for areas included; (2) Rank is based on 2015 data and ranges from 1 to 381
Source: The U.S. Conference of Mayors, U.S. Metro Economies: GMP and Employment Report, 2015-2017

Economic Growth

Area	2012-14 (%)	2015 (%)	2016 (%)	2017 (%)	Rank[2]
MSA[1]	3.3	4.3	0.0	2.9	51
U.S.	2.0	2.4	1.9	2.6	–

Note: Figures are real gross metropolitan product (GMP) growth rates and represent average annual percent change; (1) Figures cover the Morgantown, WV Metropolitan Statistical Area—see Appendix B for areas included; (2) Rank is based on 2012-2014 average annual percent change and ranges from 1 to 381
Source: The U.S. Conference of Mayors, U.S. Metro Economies: GMP and Employment Report, 2015-2017

Metropolitan Area Exports

Area	2011	2012	2013	2014	2015	2016	Rank[2]
MSA[1]	58.7	75.9	53.9	61.4	71.6	59.4	356

Note: Figures are in millions of dollars; (1) Figures cover the Morgantown, WV Metropolitan Statistical Area—see Appendix B for areas included; (2) Rank is based on 2016 data and ranges from 1 to 385
Source: U.S. Department of Commerce, International Trade Administration, Office of Trade & Industry Information, Manufacturing & Services, data extracted March 15, 2018

Building Permits

Area	Single-Family			Multi-Family			Total		
	2016	2017p	Pct. Chg.	2016	2017p	Pct. Chg.	2016	2017p	Pct. Chg.
City	11	11	0.0	2	52	2,500.0	13	63	384.6
MSA[1]	12	12	0.0	2	52	2,500.0	14	64	357.1
U.S.	750,800	817,300	8.9	455,800	446,800	-2.0	1,206,600	1,264,100	4.8

Note: (1) Figures cover the Morgantown, WV Metropolitan Statistical Area—see Appendix B for areas included; Figures represent new, privately-owned housing units authorized (unadjusted data); All permit data are based on estimates with imputation; (p) preliminary data.
Source: U.S. Census Bureau, Manufacturing, Mining, and Construction Statistics, Building Permits, 2016, 2017

Bankruptcy Filings

Area	Business Filings 2016	Business Filings 2017	Business Filings % Chg.	Nonbusiness Filings 2016	Nonbusiness Filings 2017	Nonbusiness Filings % Chg.
Monongalia County	14	10	-28.6	92	100	8.7
U.S.	24,114	23,157	-4.0	770,846	765,863	-0.6

Note: Business filings include Chapter 7, Chapter 11, Chapter 12, and Chapter 13; Nonbusiness filings include Chapter 7, Chapter 11, and Chapter 13
Source: Administrative Office of the U.S. Courts, Business and Nonbusiness Bankruptcy, County Cases Commenced by Chapter of the Bankruptcy Code, During the 12-Month Period Ending December 31, 2016 and Business and Nonbusiness Bankruptcy, County Cases Commenced by Chapter of the Bankruptcy Code, During the 12-Month Period Ending December 31, 2017

Housing Vacancy Rates

Area	Gross Vacancy Rate[2] (%)			Year-Round Vacancy Rate[3] (%)			Rental Vacancy Rate[4] (%)			Homeowner Vacancy Rate[5] (%)		
	2015	2016	2017	2015	2016	2017	2015	2016	2017	2015	2016	2017
MSA[1]	n/a	n/a	n/a	n/a	n/a	n/a	n/a	n/a	n/a	n/a	n/a	n/a
U.S.	12.9	12.8	12.7	10.0	9.9	9.9	7.1	6.9	7.2	1.8	1.7	1.6

Note: (1) Figures cover the Morgantown, WV Metropolitan Statistical Area—see Appendix B for areas included; (2) The percentage of the total housing inventory that is vacant; (3) The percentage of the housing inventory (excluding seasonal units) that is year-round vacant; (4) The percentage of rental inventory that is vacant for rent; (5) The percentage of homeowner inventory that is vacant for sale; n/a not available
Source: U.S. Census Bureau, Housing Vacancies and Homeownership Annual Statistics: 2015, 2016, 2017

INCOME

Income

Area	Per Capita ($)	Median Household ($)	Average Household ($)
City	23,209	35,502	60,934
MSA[1]	26,477	46,484	66,161
U.S.	29,829	55,322	77,866

Note: (1) Figures cover the Morgantown, WV Metropolitan Statistical Area—see Appendix B for areas included
Source: U.S. Census Bureau, 2012-2016 American Community Survey 5-Year Estimates

Household Income Distribution

Area	Percent of Households Earning							
	Under $15,000	$15,000 -$24,999	$25,000 -$34,999	$35,000 -$49,999	$50,000 -$74,999	$75,000 -$99,999	$100,000 -$149,999	$150,000 and up
City	28.0	13.2	8.2	10.6	13.7	8.7	9.1	8.3
MSA[1]	18.2	11.5	9.8	13.2	17.7	10.4	11.1	8.1
U.S.	12.1	10.2	9.9	13.2	17.8	12.2	13.5	11.1

Note: (1) Figures cover the Morgantown, WV Metropolitan Statistical Area—see Appendix B for areas included
Source: U.S. Census Bureau, 2012-2016 American Community Survey 5-Year Estimates

Poverty Rate

Area	All Ages	Under 18 Years Old	18 to 64 Years Old	65 Years and Over
City	35.3	27.3	40.2	9.0
MSA[1]	20.5	18.8	23.3	8.0
U.S.	15.1	21.2	14.2	9.3

Note: Figures are percentage of people whose income during the past 12 months was below the poverty level; (1) Figures cover the Morgantown, WV Metropolitan Statistical Area—see Appendix B for areas included
Source: U.S. Census Bureau, 2012-2016 American Community Survey 5-Year Estimates

EMPLOYMENT

Labor Force and Employment

Area	Civilian Labor Force Dec. 2016	Civilian Labor Force Dec. 2017	Civilian Labor Force % Chg.	Workers Employed Dec. 2016	Workers Employed Dec. 2017	Workers Employed % Chg.
City	14,270	14,659	2.7	13,789	14,151	2.6
MSA[1]	66,036	67,848	2.7	63,618	65,203	2.5
U.S.	158,968,000	159,880,000	0.6	151,798,000	153,602,000	1.2

Note: Data is not seasonally adjusted and covers workers 16 years of age and older; (1) Figures cover the Morgantown, WV Metropolitan Statistical Area—see Appendix B for areas included
Source: Bureau of Labor Statistics, Local Area Unemployment Statistics

Unemployment Rate

Area	2017											
	Jan.	Feb.	Mar.	Apr.	May	Jun.	Jul.	Aug.	Sep.	Oct.	Nov.	Dec.
City	4.4	4.4	4.0	3.6	3.7	5.3	4.5	4.9	3.6	3.6	3.5	3.5
MSA[1]	4.7	4.6	4.2	3.6	3.4	4.3	4.0	4.4	3.6	3.6	3.7	3.9
U.S.	5.1	4.9	4.6	4.1	4.1	4.5	4.6	4.5	4.1	3.9	3.9	3.9

Note: Data is not seasonally adjusted and covers workers 16 years of age and older; (1) Figures cover the Morgantown, WV Metropolitan Statistical Area—see Appendix B for areas included
Source: Bureau of Labor Statistics, Local Area Unemployment Statistics

Average Wages

Occupation	$/Hr.	Occupation	$/Hr.
Accountants and Auditors	32.00	Maids and Housekeeping Cleaners	10.70
Automotive Mechanics	14.60	Maintenance and Repair Workers	17.20
Bookkeepers	16.60	Marketing Managers	n/a
Carpenters	22.70	Nuclear Medicine Technologists	n/a
Cashiers	10.00	Nurses, Licensed Practical	18.30
Clerks, General Office	15.10	Nurses, Registered	31.10
Clerks, Receptionists/Information	12.60	Nursing Assistants	13.10
Clerks, Shipping/Receiving	21.70	Packers and Packagers, Hand	n/a
Computer Programmers	44.10	Physical Therapists	44.90
Computer Systems Analysts	35.20	Postal Service Mail Carriers	24.20
Computer User Support Specialists	20.10	Real Estate Brokers	n/a
Cooks, Restaurant	11.60	Retail Salespersons	12.00
Dentists	102.10	Sales Reps., Exc. Tech./Scientific	24.40
Electrical Engineers	47.30	Sales Reps., Tech./Scientific	38.60
Electricians	26.10	Secretaries, Exc. Legal/Med./Exec.	15.70
Financial Managers	64.40	Security Guards	16.30
First-Line Supervisors/Managers, Sales	15.70	Surgeons	n/a
Food Preparation Workers	10.50	Teacher Assistants*	11.90
General and Operations Managers	48.60	Teachers, Elementary School*	n/a
Hairdressers/Cosmetologists	n/a	Teachers, Secondary School*	n/a
Internists, General	n/a	Telemarketers	n/a
Janitors and Cleaners	13.10	Truck Drivers, Heavy/Tractor-Trailer	20.00
Landscaping/Groundskeeping Workers	12.30	Truck Drivers, Light/Delivery Svcs.	13.70
Lawyers	49.60	Waiters and Waitresses	11.50

Note: Wage data covers the Morgantown, WV Metropolitan Statistical Area—see Appendix B for areas included; (*) Hourly wages for elementary/secondary school teachers and teacher assistants were calculated by the editors from annual wage data based on a 40 hour work week; n/a not available.
Source: Bureau of Labor Statistics, Metro Area Occupational Employment & Wage Estimates, May 2017

Employment by Occupation

Occupation Classification	City (%)	MSA[1] (%)	U.S. (%)
Management, Business, Science, and Arts	46.7	40.0	37.0
Natural Resources, Construction, and Maintenance	3.6	10.4	8.9
Production, Transportation, and Material Moving	6.1	9.6	12.2
Sales and Office	22.1	22.0	23.8
Service	21.5	18.1	18.1

Note: Figures cover employed civilians 16 years of age and older; (1) Figures cover the Morgantown, WV Metropolitan Statistical Area—see Appendix B for areas included
Source: U.S. Census Bureau, 2012-2016 American Community Survey 5-Year Estimates

Employment by Industry

Sector	MSA[1] Number of Employees	MSA[1] Percent of Total	U.S. Percent of Total
Construction, Mining, and Logging	n/a	n/a	5.2
Education and Health Services	15,300	20.9	15.9
Financial Activities	n/a	n/a	5.7
Government	19,200	26.2	15.3
Information	n/a	n/a	1.9
Leisure and Hospitality	7,500	10.2	10.7
Manufacturing	4,400	6.0	8.5
Other Services	n/a	n/a	3.9
Professional and Business Services	7,000	9.6	14.0
Retail Trade	7,000	9.6	11.0
Transportation, Warehousing, and Utilities	n/a	n/a	4.1
Wholesale Trade	n/a	n/a	4.0

Note: Figures are non-farm employment as of December 2017. Figures are not seasonally adjusted and include workers 16 years of age and older; (1) Figures cover the Morgantown, WV Metropolitan Statistical Area—see Appendix B for areas included; n/a not available
Source: Bureau of Labor Statistics, Current Employment Statistics, Employment, Hours, and Earnings

Occupations with Greatest Projected Employment Growth: 2017 – 2019

Occupation[1]	2017 Employment	2019 Projected Employment	Numeric Employment Change	Percent Employment Change
Registered Nurses	22,360	22,970	610	2.7
Personal Care Aides	11,640	12,240	600	5.2
Customer Service Representatives	12,110	12,400	290	2.4
Heavy and Tractor-Trailer Truck Drivers	11,940	12,220	280	2.3
Maids and Housekeeping Cleaners	9,090	9,330	240	2.7
Childcare Workers	5,460	5,690	230	4.2
Home Health Aides	3,950	4,170	220	5.6
Janitors and Cleaners, Except Maids and Housekeeping Cleaners	8,970	9,150	180	2.0
Maintenance and Repair Workers, General	10,570	10,750	180	1.7
Nursing Assistants	7,950	8,130	180	2.2

Note: Projections cover West Virginia; (1) Sorted by numeric employment change
Source: www.projectionscentral.com, State Occupational Projections, 2017–2019 Short-Term Projections

Fastest Growing Occupations: 2017 – 2019

Occupation[1]	2017 Employment	2019 Projected Employment	Numeric Employment Change	Percent Employment Change
Fundraisers	820	870	50	6.5
Clergy	760	810	50	6.0
Home Health Aides	3,950	4,170	220	5.6
Public Relations Specialists	1,390	1,470	80	5.4
Personal Care Aides	11,640	12,240	600	5.2
Computer Systems Analysts	920	970	50	5.1
Market Research Analysts and Marketing Specialists	1,150	1,210	60	5.0
Self-Enrichment Education Teachers	1,190	1,250	60	4.9
Lifeguards, Ski Patrol, and Other Recreational Protective Service Workers	1,050	1,100	50	4.6
Fitness Trainers and Aerobics Instructors	1,870	1,950	80	4.4

Note: Projections cover West Virginia; (1) Sorted by percent employment change and excludes occupations with numeric employment change less than 50
Source: www.projectionscentral.com, State Occupational Projections, 2017–2019 Short-Term Projections

TAXES

State Corporate Income Tax Rates

State	Tax Rate (%)	Income Brackets ($)	Num. of Brackets	Financial Institution Tax Rate (%)[a]	Federal Income Tax Ded.
West Virginia	6.5	Flat rate	1	6.5	No

Note: Tax rates as of January 1, 2018; (a) Rates listed are the corporate income tax rate applied to financial institutions or excise taxes based on income. Some states have other taxes based upon the value of deposits or shares.
Source: Federation of Tax Administrators, Range of State Corporate Income Tax Rates, January 1, 2018

State Individual Income Tax Rates

State	Tax Rate (%)	Income Brackets ($)	Num. of Brackets	Personal Exempt. ($)[1]		Fed. Inc. Tax Ded.
				Single	Dependents	
West Virginia	3.0 - 6.5	10,000 - 60,000	5	2,000	2,000	No

Note: Tax rates as of January 1, 2018; Local- and county-level taxes are not included; n/a not applicable; (1) Married joint filers generally receive double the single exemption
Source: Federation of Tax Administrators, State Individual Income Tax Rates, January 1, 2018

Various State Sales and Excise Tax Rates

State	State Sales Tax (%)	Gasoline[1] (¢/gal.)	Cigarette[2] ($/pack)	Spirits[3] ($/gal.)	Wine[4] ($/gal.)	Beer[5] ($/gal.)	Recreational Marijuana (%)
West Virginia	6.0	35.7	1.20	7.67 (g)	1.00 (l)	0.18	Not legal

Note: All tax rates as of January 1, 2018; (1) The American Petroleum Institute has developed a methodology for determining the average tax rate on a gallon of fuel. Rates may include any of the following: excise taxes, environmental fees, storage tank fees, other fees or taxes, general sales tax, and local taxes. In states where gasoline is subject to the general sales tax, or where the fuel tax is based on the average sale price, the average rate determined by API is sensitive to changes in the price of gasoline. States that fully or partially apply general sales taxes to gasoline: CA, CO, GA, IL, IN, MI, NY; (2) The federal excise tax of $1.0066 per pack and local taxes are not included; (3) Rates are those applicable to off-premise sales of 40% alcohol by volume (a.b.v.) distilled spirits in 750ml containers. Local excise taxes are excluded; (4) Rates are those applicable to off-premise sales of 11% a.b.v. non-carbonated wine in 750ml containers; (5) Rates are those applicable to off-premise sales of 4.7% a.b.v. beer in 12 ounce containers; (g) Control states, where the government controls all sales. Products can be subject to ad valorem mark-up as well as excise taxes; (l) Different rates also applicable to alcohol content, place of production, size of container, place purchased (on- or off-premise or on board airlines) or type of wine (carbonated, vermouth, etc.).
Source: Tax Foundation, 2018 Facts & Figures: How Does Your State Compare?

State Business Tax Climate Index Rankings

State	Overall Rank	Corporate Tax Rank	Individual Income Tax Rank	Sales Tax Rank	Unemployment Insurance Tax Rank	Property Tax Rank
West Virginia	19	17	25	15	28	17

Note: The index is a measure of how each state's tax laws affect economic performance. The lower the rank, the more favorable a state's tax system is for business. States without a given tax are given a ranking of 1. The scores/rankings for the District of Columbia do not affect other states. The 2018 index represents the tax climate as of July 1, 2017.
Source: Tax Foundation, State Business Tax Climate Index 2018

TRANSPORTATION

Means of Transportation to Work

Area	Car/Truck/Van		Public Transportation			Bicycle	Walked	Other Means	Worked at Home
	Drove Alone	Car-pooled	Bus	Subway	Railroad				
City	63.6	7.2	3.0	0.8	0.0	0.9	16.4	0.8	7.3
MSA[1]	76.6	10.0	1.7	0.2	0.0	0.5	5.4	0.7	4.9
U.S.	76.4	9.3	2.6	1.9	0.6	0.6	2.8	1.3	4.6

Note: Figures are percentages and cover workers 16 years of age and older; (1) Figures cover the Morgantown, WV Metropolitan Statistical Area—see Appendix B for areas included
Source: U.S. Census Bureau, 2012-2016 American Community Survey 5-Year Estimates

Travel Time to Work

Area	Less Than 10 Minutes	10 to 19 Minutes	20 to 29 Minutes	30 to 44 Minutes	45 to 59 Minutes	60 to 89 Minutes	90 Minutes or More
City	21.2	52.0	13.7	6.7	2.7	3.2	0.5
MSA[1]	13.0	37.1	22.3	15.4	5.9	4.2	2.1
U.S.	12.9	29.2	20.9	20.4	8.0	6.0	2.7

Note: Note: Figures are percentages and include workers 16 years old and over; (1) Figures cover the Morgantown, WV Metropolitan Statistical Area—see Appendix B for areas included
Source: U.S. Census Bureau, 2012-2016 American Community Survey 5-Year Estimates

Freeway Travel Time Index

Area	1985	1990	1995	2000	2005	2010	2014
Urban Area Rank[1,2]	n/a	n/a	n/a	n/a	n/a	n/a	n/a
Urban Area Index[1]	n/a	n/a	n/a	n/a	n/a	n/a	n/a
Average Index[3]	1.09	1.11	1.14	1.17	1.20	1.19	1.20

Note: Freeway Travel Time Index—the ratio of travel time in the peak period to the travel time at free-flow conditions. For example, a value of 1.30 indicates a 20-minute free-flow trip takes 26 minutes in the peak (20 minutes x 1.30 = 26 minutes); (1) Data for the Morgantown, WV urban area was not available; (2) Rank is based on 101 urban areas (#1 = highest travel time index); (3) Average of 101 urban areas
Source: Texas Transportation Institute, 2015 Urban Mobility Scorecard, August 2015

Freeway Commuter Stress Index

Area	1985	1990	1995	2000	2005	2010	2014
Urban Area Rank[1,2]	n/a	n/a	n/a	n/a	n/a	n/a	n/a
Urban Area Index[1]	n/a	n/a	n/a	n/a	n/a	n/a	n/a
Average Index[3]	1.13	1.16	1.19	1.22	1.25	1.24	1.25

Note: The Freeway Commuter Stress Index is the same as the Freeway Travel Time Index (see table above) except that it includes only the travel in the peak directions during the peak periods; the TTI includes travel in all directions during the peak period. Thus, the CSI is more indicative of the work trip experienced by each commuter on a daily basis; (1) Data for the Morgantown, WV urban area was not available; (2) Rank is based on 101 urban areas (#1 = highest travel time index); (3) Average of 101 urban areas
Source: Texas Transportation Institute, 2015 Urban Mobility Scorecard, August 2015

Living Environment

COST OF LIVING

Cost of Living Index

Composite Index	Groceries	Housing	Utilities	Trans-portation	Health Care	Misc. Goods/ Services
95.7	103.1	87.3	88.3	97.7	91.4	101.8

Note: The Cost of Living Index measures regional differences in the cost of consumer goods and services, excluding taxes and non-consumer expenditures, for professional and managerial households in the top income quintile. It is based on more than 50,000 prices covering almost 60 different items for which prices are collected three times a year by chambers of commerce, economic development organizations or university applied economic centers in each participating urban area. The numbers shown should be read as a percentage above or below the national average of 100. For example, a value of 115.4 in the groceries column indicates that grocery prices are 15.4% higher than the national average. Small differences in the index numbers should not be interpreted as significant; Figures cover the Morgantown WV urban area.
Source: The Council for Community and Economic Research, ACCRA Cost of Living Index, 2017

Grocery Prices

Area[1]	T-Bone Steak ($/pound)	Frying Chicken ($/pound)	Whole Milk ($/half gal.)	Eggs ($/dozen)	Orange Juice ($/64 oz.)	Coffee ($/11.5 oz.)
City[2]	11.00	1.33	1.55	1.75	3.55	4.73
Avg.	11.29	1.40	2.02	1.47	3.55	4.37
Min.	7.71	0.93	1.04	0.70	2.86	3.24
Max.	15.83	2.39	4.03	3.92	6.29	8.16

*Note: (1) Values for the local area are compared with the average, minimum and maximum values for all 294 areas in the Cost of Living Index; (2) Figures cover the Morgantown WV urban area; **T-Bone Steak** (price per pound); **Frying Chicken** (price per pound, whole fryer); **Whole Milk** (half gallon carton); **Eggs** (price per dozen, Grade A, large); **Orange Juice** (64 oz. Tropicana or Florida Natural); **Coffee** (11.5 oz. can, vacuum-packed, Maxwell House, Hills Bros, or Folgers).*
Source: The Council for Community and Economic Research, ACCRA Cost of Living Index, 2017

Housing and Utility Costs

Area[1]	New Home Price ($)	Apartment Rent ($/month)	All Electric ($/month)	Part Electric ($/month)	Other Energy ($/month)	Telephone ($/month)
City[2]	311,942	785	-	74.32	58.69	28.31
Avg.	335,956	1,047	175.01	97.34	67.93	28.71
Min.	187,788	491	109.48	49.33	35.44	12.39
Max.	1,739,087	4,559	432.62	227.09	353.33	44.61

*Note: (1) Values for the local area are compared with the average, minimum and maximum values for all 294 areas in the Cost of Living Index; (2) Figures cover the Morgantown WV urban area; **New Home Price** (2,400 sf living area, 8,000 sf lot, in urban area with full utilities); **Apartment Rent** (950 sf 2 bedroom/1.5 or 2 bath, unfurnished, excluding all utilities except water); **All Electric** (average monthly cost for an all-electric home); **Part Electric** (average monthly cost for a part-electric home); **Other Energy** (average monthly cost for natural gas, fuel oil, coal, wood, and any other forms of energy except electricity); **Telephone** (price includes basic monthly rate for a private residential line plus additional local usage charges incurred by a family of four).*
Source: The Council for Community and Economic Research, ACCRA Cost of Living Index, 2017

Health Care, Transportation, and Other Costs

Area[1]	Doctor ($/visit)	Dentist ($/visit)	Optometrist ($/visit)	Gasoline ($/gallon)	Beauty Salon ($/visit)	Men's Shirt ($)
City[2]	91.50	82.50	94.75	2.41	35.37	45.75
Avg.	108.00	92.54	101.93	2.25	37.58	30.92
Min.	30.39	60.00	49.75	1.82	16.11	11.20
Max.	193.50	161.94	229.28	3.16	77.35	59.13

*Note: (1) Values for the local area are compared with the average, minimum and maximum values for all 294 areas in the Cost of Living Index; (2) Figures cover the Morgantown WV urban area; **Doctor** (general practitioners routine exam of an established patient); **Dentist** (adult teeth cleaning and periodic oral examination); **Optometrist** (full vision eye exam for established adult patient); **Gasoline** (one gallon regular unleaded, national brand, including all taxes, cash price at self-service pump if available); **Beauty Salon** (woman's shampoo, trim, and blow-dry); **Men's Shirt** (cotton/polyester dress shirt, pinpoint weave, long sleeves).*
Source: The Council for Community and Economic Research, ACCRA Cost of Living Index, 2017

HOUSING

House Price Index (HPI)

Area	National Ranking[2]	Quarterly Change (%)	One-Year Change (%)	Five-Year Change (%)
MSA[1]	(a)	n/a	-0.30	13.09
U.S.[3]	–	1.61	6.68	34.71

Note: The HPI is a weighted repeat sales index. It measures average price changes in repeat sales or refinancings on the same properties. This information is obtained by reviewing repeat mortgage transactions on single-family properties whose mortgages have been purchased or securitized by Fannie Mae or Freddie Mac in January 1975; (1) Figures cover the Morgantown, WV Metropolitan Statistical Area—see Appendix B for areas included; (2) Rankings are based on annual percentage change for all metro areas containing at least 15,000 transactions over the last 10 years and ranges from 1 to 253; (3) figures based on a weighted average of Census Division estimates using a seasonally adjusted, purchase-only index; all figures are for the period ending December 31, 2017; n/a not available; (a) Not ranked because of increased index variability due to smaller sample size
Source: Federal Housing Finance Agency, House Price Index, February 28, 2018

Median Single-Family Home Prices

Area	2015	2016	2017p	Percent Change 2016 to 2017
MSA[1]	n/a	n/a	n/a	n/a
U.S. Average	223.9	235.5	248.8	5.6

Note: Figures are median sales prices of existing single-family homes in thousands of dollars; (p) preliminary; n/a not available; (1) Figures cover the Morgantown, WV Metropolitan Statistical Area—see Appendix B for areas included
Source: National Association of Realtors, Median Sales Price of Existing Single-Family Homes for Metropolitan Areas, 4th Quarter 2017

Qualifying Income Based on Median Sales Price of Existing Single-Family Homes

Area	With 5% Down ($)	With 10% Down ($)	With 20% Down ($)
MSA[1]	n/a	n/a	n/a
U.S. Average	55,585	52,659	46,808

Note: Figures are preliminary; Qualifying income is based on a mortgage rate of 4.17%. Monthly principal and interest payment is limited to 25% of income; n/a not available; (1) Figures cover the Morgantown, WV Metropolitan Statistical Area—see Appendix B for areas included
Source: National Association of Realtors, Qualifying Income Based on Median Sales Price of Existing Single-Family Homes for Metropolitan Areas, 4th Quarter 2017

Median Apartment Condo-Coop Home Prices

Area	2015	2016	2017p	Percent Change 2016 to 2017
MSA[1]	n/a	n/a	n/a	n/a
U.S. Average	210.7	220.7	234.3	6.2

Note: Figures are median sales prices of existing apartment condo-coop homes in thousands of dollars; (p) preliminary; n/a not available; (1) Figures cover the Morgantown, WV Metropolitan Statistical Area—see Appendix B for areas included
Source: National Association of Realtors, Median Sales Price of Existing Apartment Condo-Coop Homes for Metropolitan Areas, 4th Quarter 2017

Home Value Distribution

Area	Under $50,000	$50,000 -$99,999	$100,000 -$149,999	$150,000 -$199,999	$200,000 -$299,999	$300,000 -$499,999	$500,000 -$999,999	$1,000,000 or more
City	8.0	9.1	15.6	26.8	21.6	12.7	5.5	0.6
MSA[1]	17.3	15.5	16.6	17.4	18.4	10.0	4.3	0.5
U.S.	8.8	14.8	15.3	14.9	18.4	16.4	9.0	2.5

Note: Figures are percentages and cover owner-occupied housing units; (1) Figures cover the Morgantown, WV Metropolitan Statistical Area—see Appendix B for areas included
Source: U.S. Census Bureau, 2012-2016 American Community Survey 5-Year Estimates

Homeownership Rate

Area	2009 (%)	2010 (%)	2011 (%)	2012 (%)	2013 (%)	2014 (%)	2015 (%)	2016 (%)	2017 (%)
MSA[1]	n/a	n/a	n/a	n/a	n/a	n/a	n/a	n/a	n/a
U.S.	67.4	66.9	66.1	65.4	65.1	64.5	63.7	63.4	63.9

Note: (1) Figures cover the Morgantown, WV Metropolitan Statistical Area—see Appendix B for areas included; n/a not available
Source: U.S. Census Bureau, Housing Vacancies and Homeownership Annual Statistics: 2009-2017

Year Housing Structure Built

Area	2010 or Later	2000 -2009	1990 -1999	1980 -1989	1970 -1979	1960 -1969	1950 -1959	1940 -1949	Before 1940	Median Year
City	3.1	9.9	10.6	7.3	9.8	12.8	13.3	7.6	25.5	1963
MSA[1]	3.8	17.6	15.9	13.0	14.7	7.5	6.9	5.1	15.5	1980
U.S.	2.3	14.7	14.0	13.7	15.6	10.9	10.6	5.2	13.0	1977

Note: Figures are percentages except for Median Year; Note: (1) Figures cover the Morgantown, WV Metropolitan Statistical Area—see Appendix B for areas included
Source: U.S. Census Bureau, 2012-2016 American Community Survey 5-Year Estimates

Gross Monthly Rent

Area	Under $500	$500 -$999	$1,000 -$1,499	$1,500 -$1,999	$2,000 -$2,499	$2,500 -$2,999	$3,000 and up	Median ($)
City	18.0	52.7	23.7	4.4	1.2	0.0	0.0	742
MSA[1]	16.4	56.5	19.8	6.3	0.7	0.1	0.1	743
U.S.	11.3	43.3	27.7	10.7	4.0	1.6	1.5	949

Note: Figures are percentages except for Median; Gross rent is the contract rent plus the estimated average monthly cost of utilities (electricity, gas, and water and sewer) and fuels (oil, coal, kerosene, wood, etc.) if these are paid by the renter (or paid for the renter by someone else); (1) Figures cover the Morgantown, WV Metropolitan Statistical Area—see Appendix B for areas included
Source: U.S. Census Bureau, 2012-2016 American Community Survey 5-Year Estimates

HEALTH

Health Risk Factors

Category	MSA[1] (%)	U.S. (%)
Adults aged 18–64 who have any kind of health care coverage	n/a	87.7
Adults who reported being in good or excellent health	n/a	83.6
Adults who are current smokers	n/a	17.1
Adults who currently use E-cigarettes	n/a	4.7
Adults who currently use chewing tobacco, snuff, or snus	n/a	4.0
Adults who are heavy drinkers[2]	n/a	6.5
Adults who are binge drinkers[3]	n/a	16.9
Adults who are overweight (BMI 25.0 - 29.9)	n/a	35.3
Adults who are obese (BMI 30.0 - 99.8)	n/a	29.9
Adults who participated in any physical activities in the past month	n/a	76.9
Adults who always or nearly always wears a seat belt	n/a	94.3

Note: n/a not available; (1) Figures cover the Morgantown, WV Metropolitan Statistical Area—see Appendix B for areas included; (2) Heavy drinkers are classified as adult men having more than 14 drinks per week and adult women having more than 7 drinks per week; (3) Binge drinkers are classified as males having five or more drinks on one occasion or females having four or more drinks on one occasion
Source: Centers for Disease Control and Prevention, Behaviorial Risk Factor Surveillance System, SMART: Selected Metropolitan Area Risk Trends, 2016

Health Screening Rates

Category	MSA[1] (%)	U.S. (%)
Adults 50-75 who have had a blood stool test within the past year	n/a	8.0
Adults 50-75 who have had a colonoscopy in the past 10 years	n/a	63.5
Adults aged 65+ who have had flu shot within the past year	n/a	58.6
Adults aged 65+ who have ever had a pneumonia vaccination	n/a	73.4
Adults who have ever been tested for HIV	n/a	35.6
Women aged 21-65 who have had a pap test in the past three years	n/a	79.8
Men aged 40+ who have had a PSA test within the past two years	n/a	39.5
Women aged 40+ who have had a mammogram within the past two years	n/a	72.5

Note: n/a not available; (1) Figures cover the Morgantown, WV Metropolitan Statistical Area—see Appendix B for areas included; Source: Centers for Disease Control and Prevention, Behaviorial Risk Factor Surveillance System, SMART: Selected Metropolitan Area Risk Trends, 2016

Chronic Health Conditions

Category	MSA[1] (%)	U.S. (%)
Adults who have ever been told they had a heart attack	n/a	4.4
Adults who have ever been told they have angina or coronary heart disease	n/a	4.1
Adults who have ever been told they had a stroke	n/a	3.1
Adults who have been told they currently have asthma	n/a	9.3
Adults who have ever been told they have arthritis	n/a	25.8
Adults who have ever been told they have diabetes[2]	n/a	10.5
Adults who have ever been told they had skin cancer	n/a	5.9
Adults who have ever been told they had any other types of cancer	n/a	6.7
Adults who have ever been told they have COPD	n/a	6.3
Adults who have ever been told they have kidney disease	n/a	2.8
Adults who have ever been told they have a form of depression	n/a	17.4

Note: n/a not available; (1) Figures cover the Morgantown, WV Metropolitan Statistical Area—see Appendix B for areas included; (2) Figures do not include pregnancy-related, borderline, or pre-diabetes
Source: Centers for Disease Control and Prevention, Behaviorial Risk Factor Surveillance System, SMART: Selected Metropolitan Area Risk Trends, 2016

Mortality Rates for the Top 10 Causes of Death in the U.S.

ICD-10[a] Sub-Chapter	ICD-10[a] Code	Age-Adjusted Mortality Rate[1] per 100,000 population	
		County[2]	U.S.
Malignant neoplasms	C00-C97	153.7	158.5
Ischaemic heart diseases	I20-I25	110.5	96.8
Other forms of heart disease	I30-I51	49.6	52.4
Chronic lower respiratory diseases	J40-J47	53.4	40.9
Cerebrovascular diseases	I60-I69	37.7	37.2
Organic, including symptomatic, mental disorders	F01-F09	29.5	33.3
Other degenerative diseases of the nervous system	G30-G31	27.7	32.1
Other external causes of accidental injury	W00-X59	39.4	31.2
Diabetes mellitus	E10-E14	23.4	21.1
Hypertensive diseases	I10-I15	18.8	20.8

Note: (a) ICD-10 = International Classification of Diseases 10th Revision; (1) Mortality rates are a three year average covering 2014-2016; (2) Figures cover Monongalia County.
Source: Centers for Disease Control and Prevention, National Center for Health Statistics. Underlying Cause of Death 1999-2016 on CDC WONDER Online Database, released December 2017

Mortality Rates for Selected Causes of Death

ICD-10[a] Sub-Chapter	ICD-10[a] Code	Age-Adjusted Mortality Rate[1] per 100,000 population	
		County[2]	U.S.
Assault	X85-Y09	Unreliable	5.6
Diseases of the liver	K70-K76	12.3	14.0
Human immunodeficiency virus (HIV) disease	B20-B24	Suppressed	1.9
Influenza and pneumonia	J09-J18	13.3	14.6
Intentional self-harm	X60-X84	13.1	13.2
Malnutrition	E40-E46	Suppressed	1.3
Obesity and other hyperalimentation	E65-E68	Unreliable	2.1
Renal failure	N17-N19	15.3	13.0
Transport accidents	V01-V99	11.0	12.0
Viral hepatitis	B15-B19	Suppressed	1.9

Note: (a) ICD-10 = International Classification of Diseases 10th Revision; (1) Mortality rates are a three year average covering 2014-2016; (2) Figures cover Monongalia County; Data are Suppressed when the data meet the criteria for confidentiality constraints; Mortality rates are flagged as Unreliable when the rate would be calculated with a numerator of 20 or less.
Source: Centers for Disease Control and Prevention, National Center for Health Statistics. Underlying Cause of Death 1999-2016 on CDC WONDER Online Database, released December 2017

Health Insurance Coverage

Area	With Health Insurance	With Private Health Insurance	With Public Health Insurance	Without Health Insurance	Population Under Age 18 Without Health Insurance
City	91.5	80.4	20.1	8.5	3.6
MSA[1]	90.8	73.0	28.5	9.2	3.2
U.S.	88.3	66.7	33.0	11.7	5.9

Note: Figures are percentages that cover the civilian noninstitutionalized population; (1) Figures cover the Morgantown, WV Metropolitan Statistical Area—see Appendix B for areas included
Source: U.S. Census Bureau, 2012-2016 American Community Survey 5-Year Estimates

Number of Medical Professionals

Area	MDs[3]	DOs[3,4]	Dentists	Podiatrists	Chiropractors	Optometrists
County[1] (number)	986	53	121	7	18	16
County[1] (rate[2])	948.6	51.0	115.5	6.7	17.2	15.3
U.S. (rate[2])	276.5	22.3	67.3	6.0	26.7	15.9

Note: Data as of 2016 unless noted; (1) Data covers Monongalia County; (2) Rate per 100,000 population; (3) Data as of 2015 and includes all active, non-federal physicians; (4) Doctor of Osteopathic Medicine
Source: U.S. Department of Health and Human Services, Health Resources and Services Administration, Bureau of Health Professions, Area Resource File (ARF) 2016-2017

Best Hospitals

According to *U.S. News,* the Morgantown, WV metro area is home to one of the best hospitals in the U.S.: **West Virginia University Hospitals** (1 adult specialty). The hospital listed was nationally ranked in at least one of 16 specialties. Only 152 hospitals nationwide were nationally ranked in one or more specialties. Twenty hospitals in the U.S. made the Honor Roll. The Best Hospitals Honor Roll was revamped last year to take both the national rankings and the procedure and condition ratings into account. Hospitals received points if they were nationally ranked in one of the 16 specialties—the higher they ranked, the more points they got—and how many ratings of "high performing" they earned in the nine procedures and conditions. *U.S. News Online, "America's Best Hospitals 2017-18"*

EDUCATION

Public School District Statistics

District Name	Schls	Pupils	Pupil/ Teacher Ratio	Minority Pupils[1] (%)	Free Lunch Eligible[2] (%)	IEP[3] (%)
Monongalia County Schools	19	11,414	15.1	13.5	32.0	12.9

Note: Table includes school districts with 100 or more students; (1) Percentage of students that are not non-Hispanic white; (2) Percentage of students that are eligible for the free lunch program; (3) Percentage of students that have an Individualized Education Program.
Source: U.S. Department of Education, National Center for Education Statistics, Common Core of Data, Local Education Agency (School District) Universe Survey: School Year 2015-2016; U.S. Department of Education, National Center for Education Statistics, Common Core of Data, Public Elementary/Secondary School Universe Survey: School Year 2015-2016

Highest Level of Education

Area	Less than H.S.	H.S. Diploma	Some College, No Deg.	Associate Degree	Bachelor's Degree	Master's Degree	Prof. School Degree	Doctorate Degree
City	7.1	20.9	17.6	5.7	24.9	13.5	4.6	5.8
MSA[1]	10.7	35.5	16.4	5.3	16.7	9.5	2.9	3.1
U.S.	13.0	27.5	21.0	8.2	18.8	8.2	2.0	1.3

Note: Figures cover persons age 25 and over; (1) Figures cover the Morgantown, WV Metropolitan Statistical Area—see Appendix B for areas included
Source: U.S. Census Bureau, 2012-2016 American Community Survey 5-Year Estimates

Educational Attainment by Race

Area	High School Graduate or Higher (%)					Bachelor's Degree or Higher (%)				
	Total	White	Black	Asian	Hisp.[2]	Total	White	Black	Asian	Hisp.[2]
City	92.9	92.9	89.1	100.0	50.1	48.7	49.4	21.4	74.5	23.4
MSA[1]	89.3	89.4	84.4	98.0	66.5	32.2	31.4	20.6	76.4	29.2
U.S.	87.0	88.9	84.3	86.3	65.7	30.3	31.6	20.0	52.1	14.7

Note: Figures shown cover persons 25 years old and over; (1) Figures cover the Morgantown, WV Metropolitan Statistical Area—see Appendix B for areas included; (2) People of Hispanic origin can be of any race
Source: U.S. Census Bureau, 2012-2016 American Community Survey 5-Year Estimates

School Enrollment by Grade and Control

Area	Preschool (%)		Kindergarten (%)		Grades 1 - 4 (%)		Grades 5 - 8 (%)		Grades 9 - 12 (%)	
	Public	Private	Public	Private	Public	Private	Public	Private	Public	Private
City	54.2	45.8	93.3	6.7	78.4	21.6	86.4	13.6	94.0	6.0
MSA[1]	70.3	29.7	92.1	7.9	89.7	10.3	90.2	9.8	91.1	8.9
U.S.	58.4	41.6	87.7	12.3	89.8	10.2	89.7	10.3	90.4	9.6

Note: Figures shown cover persons 3 years old and over; (1) Figures cover the Morgantown, WV Metropolitan Statistical Area—see Appendix B for areas included
Source: U.S. Census Bureau, 2012-2016 American Community Survey 5-Year Estimates

Average Salaries of Public School Classroom Teachers

Area	2015		2016		Change from 2015 to 2016	
	Dollars	Rank[1]	Dollars	Rank[1]	Percent	Rank[2]
West Virginia	45,783	46	45,622	48	-0.4	50
U.S. Average	57,611	–	58,353	–	1.3	–

Note: (1) Rank ranges from 1 to 51 where 1 indicates highest salary; (2) Rank ranges from 1 to 51 where 1 indicates highest percent change.
Source: National Education Association, Rankings & Estimates: Rankings of the States 2016 and Estimates of School Statistics 2017

Higher Education

Four-Year Colleges			Two-Year Colleges			Medical Schools[1]	Law Schools[2]	Voc/ Tech[3]
Public	Private Non-profit	Private For-profit	Public	Private Non-profit	Private For-profit			
1	1	0	0	0	2	1	1	2

Note: Figures cover institutions located within the city limits and include main campuses only; (1) includes schools accredited by the Liaison Committee on Medical Education and the American Osteopathic Association's Commission on Osteopathic College Accreditation; (2) includes ABA-accredited schools, schools with provisional ABA accreditation, and state accredited schools; (3) includes all schools with programs that are less than 2 years.
Source: National Center for Education Statistics, Integrated Postsecondary Education System (IPEDS), 2016-17; Wikipedia, List of Medical Schools in the United States, accessed April 2, 2018; Wikipedia, List of Law Schools in the United States, accessed April 2, 2018

According to *U.S. News & World Report,* the Morgantown, WV metro area is home to one of the best national universities in the U.S.: **West Virginia University** (#187 tie). The indicators used to capture academic quality fall into a number of categories: assessment by administrators at peer institutions; retention of students; faculty resources; student selectivity; financial resources; alumni giving; high school counselor ratings of colleges; and graduation rate. *U.S. News & World Report, "America's Best Colleges 2018"*

PRESIDENTIAL ELECTION

2016 Presidential Election Results

Area	Clinton	Trump	Johnson	Stein	Other
Monongalia County	40.0	50.1	5.0	2.2	2.7
U.S.	48.0	45.9	3.3	1.1	1.7

Note: Results are percentages and may not add to 100% due to rounding
Source: Dave Leip's Atlas of U.S. Presidential Elections

EMPLOYERS

Major Employers

Company Name	Industry
Greer Industries	Producer of limestone and steel
Monongalia County Board of Education	School district
Monongalia County Government	County government
Monongalia General Hospital	Healthcare
Morgantown Energy Technology Center	Energy and environmental research and development
Mylan Pharmaceuticals	Pharmaceutical manufacturing
TeleTech	Customer experience consulting
US Centers for Disease Control	Federal government agency
West Virginia University	Public university
WVU Medicine	Healthcare

Note: Companies shown are located within the Morgantown, WV Metropolitan Statistical Area.
Source: Hoovers.com; Wikipedia

PUBLIC SAFETY

Crime Rate

Area	All Crimes	Violent Crimes				Property Crimes		
		Murder	Rape[3]	Robbery	Aggrav. Assault	Burglary	Larceny -Theft	Motor Vehicle Theft
City	2,452.7	6.4	38.6	61.1	180.0	414.7	1,661.9	90.0
Metro[1]	1,879.0	2.2	46.8	24.5	190.0	361.3	1,168.0	86.4
U.S.	2,847.8	5.3	40.4	102.8	248.5	468.9	1,745.0	236.9

Note: Figures are crimes per 100,000 population; (1) Figures cover the Morgantown, WV Metropolitan Statistical Area—see Appendix B for areas included; (3) The city and U.S. figures shown were reported using the revised Uniform Crime Reporting (UCR) definition of rape. The metro area figures shown are an aggregate total of the data submitted using both the revised and legacy UCR definitions.
Source: FBI Uniform Crime Reports, 2016

Hate Crimes

Area	Number of Quarters Reported	Number of Incidents per Bias Motivation					
		Race/Ethnicity/ Ancestry	Religion	Sexual Orientation	Disability	Gender	Gender Identity
City	4	0	0	0	0	0	0
U.S.	4	3,489	1,273	1,076	70	31	124

Source: Federal Bureau of Investigation, Hate Crime Statistics 2016

Identity Theft Consumer Reports

Area	Reports	Reports per 100,000 Population	Rank[2]
MSA[1]	87	63	297
U.S.	371,061	114	-

Note: (1) Figures cover the Morgantown, WV Metropolitan Statistical Area—see Appendix B for areas included; (2) Rank ranges from 1 to 389 where 1 indicates greatest number of identity theft reports per 100,000 population
Source: Federal Trade Commission, Consumer Sentinel Network Data Book for January–December 2017

Fraud and Other Consumer Reports

Area	Reports	Reports per 100,000 Population	Rank[2]
MSA[1]	521	376	295
U.S.	2,304,550	708	-

Note: (1) Figures cover the Morgantown, WV Metropolitan Statistical Area—see Appendix B for areas included; (2) Rank ranges from 1 to 389 where 1 indicates greatest number of fraud and other consumer reports per 100,000 population
Source: Federal Trade Commission, Consumer Sentinel Network Data Book for January–December 2017

SPORTS

Professional Sports Teams

Team Name	League	Year Established
No teams are located in the metro area		

Source: Wikipedia, Major Professional Sports Teams of the United States and Canada, April 5, 2018

CLIMATE

Average and Extreme Temperatures

Temperature	Jan	Feb	Mar	Apr	May	Jun	Jul	Aug	Sep	Oct	Nov	Dec	Yr.
Extreme High (°F)	75	69	83	89	91	98	103	100	97	89	82	74	103
Average High (°F)	35	38	48	61	71	79	83	81	75	63	50	39	60
Average Temp. (°F)	28	30	39	50	60	68	73	71	64	53	42	32	51
Average Low (°F)	20	22	29	39	49	57	62	61	54	43	34	25	41
Extreme Low (°F)	-18	-12	-1	14	26	34	42	39	31	16	-1	-12	-18

Note: Figures cover the years 1948-1990
Source: National Climatic Data Center, International Station Meteorological Climate Summary, 9/96

Average Precipitation/Snowfall/Humidity

Precip./Humidity	Jan	Feb	Mar	Apr	May	Jun	Jul	Aug	Sep	Oct	Nov	Dec	Yr.
Avg. Precip. (in.)	2.8	2.4	3.4	3.3	3.6	3.9	3.8	3.2	2.8	2.4	2.7	2.8	37.1
Avg. Snowfall (in.)	11	9	8	2	Tr	0	0	0	0	Tr	4	8	43
Avg. Rel. Hum. 7am (%)	76	75	75	73	76	79	82	86	85	81	78	77	79
Avg. Rel. Hum. 4pm (%)	64	60	54	49	50	51	53	54	55	53	60	66	56

Note: Figures cover the years 1948-1990; Tr = Trace amounts (<0.05 in. of rain; <0.5 in. of snow)
Source: National Climatic Data Center, International Station Meteorological Climate Summary, 9/96

Weather Conditions

Temperature			Daytime Sky			Precipitation		
5°F & below	32°F & below	90°F & above	Clear	Partly cloudy	Cloudy	0.01 inch or more precip.	0.1 inch or more snow/ice	Thunder-storms
9	121	8	62	137	166	154	42	35

Note: Figures are average number of days per year and cover the years 1948-1990
Source: National Climatic Data Center, International Station Meteorological Climate Summary, 9/96

HAZARDOUS WASTE

Superfund Sites

The Morgantown, WV metro area is home to one site on the EPA's Superfund National Priorities List: **Ordnance Works Disposal Areas** (final). There are a total of 1,396 Superfund sites with a status of proposed or final on the list in the U.S. *U.S. Environmental Protection Agency, National Priorities List, April 4, 2018*

AIR & WATER QUALITY

Air Quality Trends: Ozone

	1990	1995	2000	2005	2010	2012	2013	2014	2015	2016
MSA[1]	n/a	n/a	n/a	n/a	n/a	n/a	n/a	n/a	n/a	n/a
U.S.	0.087	0.089	0.081	0.079	0.073	0.075	0.069	0.067	0.068	0.069

Note: (1) Data covers the Morgantown, WV Metropolitan Statistical Area—see Appendix B for areas included; n/a not available. The values shown are the composite ozone concentration averages among trend sites based on the highest fourth daily maximum 8-hour concentration in parts per million. These trends are based on sites having an adequate record of monitoring data during the trend period. Data from exceptional events are included.
Source: U.S. Environmental Protection Agency, Air Quality Monitoring Information, "Air Quality Trends by City, 1990-2016"

Air Quality Index

Area	Percent of Days when Air Quality was...[2]					AQI Statistics[2]	
	Good	Moderate	Unhealthy for Sensitive Groups	Unhealthy	Very Unhealthy	Maximum	Median
MSA[1]	92.8	7.2	0.0	0.0	0.0	90	35

Note: (1) Data covers the Morgantown, WV Metropolitan Statistical Area—see Appendix B for areas included; (2) Based on 362 days with AQI data in 2017. Air Quality Index (AQI) is an index for reporting daily air quality. EPA calculates the AQI for five major air pollutants regulated by the Clean Air Act: ground-level ozone, particle pollution (aka particulate matter), carbon monoxide, sulfur dioxide, and nitrogen dioxide. The AQI runs from 0 to 500. The higher the AQI value, the greater the level of air pollution and the greater the health concern. There are six AQI categories: "Good" AQI is between 0 and 50. Air quality is considered satisfactory; "Moderate" AQI is between 51 and 100. Air quality is acceptable; "Unhealthy for Sensitive Groups" When AQI values are between 101 and 150, members of sensitive groups may experience health effects; "Unhealthy" When AQI values are between 151 and 200 everyone may begin to experience health effects; "Very Unhealthy" AQI values between 201 and 300 trigger a health alert; "Hazardous" AQI values over 300 trigger warnings of emergency conditions (not shown).
Source: U.S. Environmental Protection Agency, Air Quality Index Report, 2017

Air Quality Index Pollutants

Area	Percent of Days when AQI Pollutant was...[2]					
	Carbon Monoxide	Nitrogen Dioxide	Ozone	Sulfur Dioxide	Particulate Matter 2.5	Particulate Matter 10
MSA[1]	0.0	0.0	61.0	22.1	16.9	0.0

Note: (1) Data covers the Morgantown, WV Metropolitan Statistical Area—see Appendix B for areas included; (2) Based on 362 days with AQI data in 2017. The Air Quality Index (AQI) is an index for reporting daily air quality. EPA calculates the AQI for five major air pollutants regulated by the Clean Air Act: ground-level ozone, particle pollution (also known as particulate matter), carbon monoxide, sulfur dioxide, and nitrogen dioxide. The AQI runs from 0 to 500. The higher the AQI value, the greater the level of air pollution and the greater the health concern.
Source: U.S. Environmental Protection Agency, Air Quality Index Report, 2017

Maximum Air Pollutant Concentrations: Particulate Matter, Ozone, CO and Lead

	Particulate Matter 10 (ug/m^3)	Particulate Matter 2.5 Wtd AM (ug/m^3)	Particulate Matter 2.5 24-Hr (ug/m^3)	Ozone (ppm)	Carbon Monoxide (ppm)	Lead (ug/m^3)
MSA[1] Level	n/a	7.4	16	0.059	n/a	n/a
NAAQS[2]	150	15	35	0.075	9	0.15
Met NAAQS[2]	n/a	Yes	Yes	Yes	n/a	n/a

Note: (1) Data covers the Morgantown, WV Metropolitan Statistical Area—see Appendix B for areas included; Data from exceptional events are included; (2) National Ambient Air Quality Standards; ppm = parts per million; ug/m^3 = micrograms per cubic meter; n/a not available.
Concentrations: Particulate Matter 10 (coarse particulate)—highest second maximum 24-hour concentration; Particulate Matter 2.5 Wtd AM (fine particulate)—highest weighted annual mean concentration; Particulate Matter 2.5 24-Hour (fine particulate)—highest 98th percentile 24-hour concentration; Ozone—highest fourth daily maximum 8-hour concentration; Carbon Monoxide—highest second maximum non-overlapping 8-hour concentration; Lead—maximum running 3-month average
Source: U.S. Environmental Protection Agency, Air Quality Monitoring Information, "Air Quality Statistics by City, 2016"

Maximum Air Pollutant Concentrations: Nitrogen Dioxide and Sulfur Dioxide

	Nitrogen Dioxide AM (ppb)	Nitrogen Dioxide 1-Hr (ppb)	Sulfur Dioxide AM (ppb)	Sulfur Dioxide 1-Hr (ppb)	Sulfur Dioxide 24-Hr (ppb)
MSA[1] Level	n/a	n/a	n/a	9	n/a
NAAQS[2]	53	100	30	75	140
Met NAAQS[2]	n/a	n/a	n/a	Yes	n/a

Note: (1) Data covers the Morgantown, WV Metropolitan Statistical Area—see Appendix B for areas included; Data from exceptional events are included; (2) National Ambient Air Quality Standards; ppm = parts per million; ug/m^3 = micrograms per cubic meter; n/a not available.
Concentrations: Nitrogen Dioxide AM—highest arithmetic mean concentration; Nitrogen Dioxide 1-Hr—highest 98th percentile 1-hour daily maximum concentration; Sulfur Dioxide AM—highest annual mean concentration; Sulfur Dioxide 1-Hr—highest 99th percentile 1-hour daily maximum concentration; Sulfur Dioxide 24-Hr—highest second maximum 24-hour concentration
Source: U.S. Environmental Protection Agency, Air Quality Monitoring Information, "Air Quality Statistics by City, 2016"

Drinking Water

Water System Name	Pop. Served	Primary Water Source Type	Violations[1]	
			Health Based	Monitoring/ Reporting
Morgantown Utility Board	57,134	Surface	0	0

Note: (1) Based on violation data from January 1, 2017 to December 31, 2017
Source: U.S. Environmental Protection Agency, Office of Ground Water and Drinking Water, Safe Drinking Water Information System (based on data extracted April 5, 2018)

Menomonee Falls, Wisconsin

Background

Menomonee Falls sits on Milwaukee's northwest border in Waukesha County. It is a bedroom community that has gained much of its population from Milwaukee, as people moved to Menomonee Falls for its suburban charm and relative tranquility. The convenience of the Milwaukee Airport is minutes away.

Menomonee Falls has kept its designation as a village despite its population growth. Its logo—Menomonee Falls—more than a village—expresses its small-town feel as well as the multitude of resources it offers. The village began as a 36-square-mile tract resulting from an 1839 act of Wisconsin's Territorial Legislature. The area that is presently the Tamarack Swamp was home to seasonal encampments of the Chippewa Indian Tribe until the 1840s. Public sales of land first occurred in 1839, and the first permanent settler was reported to have been an Irishman named Peter Rafferty. Early Irish and Yankee settlers were soon outnumbered by large numbers of German immigrants. Much of the town's history can be seen at the Old Falls Village Museum in town.

A major employer in town is Harley-Davidson, which operates a large plant in the village. In 2003 the company put on a huge celebration of its 100th anniversary, which included a road tour and culminated in a huge party in Menomonee Falls. Kohl's Department Stores and Wells Fargo are among the area's top employers.

Due to close proximity to Milwaukee, educational and cultural opportunities abound. The area is home to Marquette University, and the University of Wisconsin's Green Bay, Madison, Milwaukee and Parkside campuses. Residents and visitors enjoy Green Bay Packers football, the Florentine Opera Company, and the Boerner Botanical Gardens. Children look forward to the Milwaukee County Zoo, the Great Circus Parade, and the Schlitz Audubon Center.

The village hosts the renowned Vince Lombardi Golf Tournament and boasts its own symphony orchestra. Its recreational facilities include 13 municipal parks. The Waukesha County Park system also operates golf courses, bike trails, ice arenas, boat launches and events and programs, as well as nature and expo centers. The Waukesha Expo Center has over 40,000 square feet of exhibit and meeting space and grounds covering 135 acres. It has hosted presidential campaigns, trade shows, corporate events, meetings, banquets and concerts.

The Menomonee Falls Historical Society celebrates its 49th year in 2014, and supports the Old Falls Village Museum.

The climate is typically continental, with some moderation due to the proximity of the Great Lakes. In late autumn, cold air often passes over the lakes and is warmed before reaching the region. Winters are moist, with precipitation of relatively long duration and low intensity; occasional periods of strong cold can occur, as arctic air reaches the region. Spring and summer are cooler than expected, again owing to the lakes; in summer precipitation usually comes in the form of brief, sharp thunderstorms.

Rankings

Business/Finance Rankings

- The personal finance site NerdWallet analyzed 183 American metropolitan areas with populations over 250,000 and more than 15,000 businesses to rank where entrepreneurs find the most success. Criteria included area economy, annual income, housing cost, unemployment rate, and the success rate of area businesses. Milwaukee* ranked #21. *www.nerdwallet.com, "Best Places to Start a Business," April 27, 2015*
- Based on metro area social media reviews, the employment opinion group Glassdoor surveyed 50 of the largest U.S. metro areas and equally weighed cost of living, hiring opportunity, and job satisfaction to compose a list of "25 Best Cities for Jobs." Median pay and home value, in-demand jobs and number of current job openings was also factored in. The Milwaukee* metro area was ranked #21 in overall job satisfaction. *www.glassdoor.com, "Best Cities for Jobs," September 12, 2017*
- In a survey of economic confidence in the nation's 50 largest metropolitan areas conducted January–December 2014, the Milwaukee* metro area placed #27, according to Gallup's 2014 Economic Confidence Index. *Gallup, "San Jose and San Francisco Lead in Economic Confidence," March 19, 2015*
- The Brookings Institution ranked the 100 largest metro areas in the U.S. based on income inequality. Milwaukee* was ranked #17 (#1 = greatest ineqality). Criteria: the "95/20 ratio," a figure representing the income at which a household earns more than 95 percent of all other households, divided by the income at which a household earns more than only 20 percent of all other households. *Brookings Institution, "Household Income Inequality, 100 Largest U.S. Metro Areas, 2014-2016," February 5, 2018*
- Payscale.com ranked the largest metro areas in terms of wage growth. The Milwaukee* metro area ranked #29. Criteria: private-sector wage growth between the 4th quarter of 2016 and the 4th quarter of 2017. *PayScale, "Wage Trends by Metro Area-4th Quarter," January 17, 2018*
- The Milwaukee* metro area appeared on the Milken Institute "2017 Best Performing Cities" list. Rank: #164 out of 200 large metro areas. Criteria: job growth; wage and salary growth; high-tech output growth. *Milken Institute, "Best-Performing Cities 2017," January 2018*
- *Forbes* ranked the 200 most populous metro areas to determine the nation's "Best Places for Business and Careers." The Milwaukee* metro area was ranked #98. Criteria: costs (business and living); job growth (past and projected); income growth; quality of life; educational attainment (college and high school); projected economic growth; cultural and recreational opportunities; net migration patterns; number of highly ranked colleges. *Forbes, "The Best Places for Business and Careers 2017," October 24, 2017*

Education Rankings

- Personal finance website *WalletHub* analyzed the 150 largest U.S. metropolitan statistical areas to determine where the most educated Americans are choosing to settle. Criteria: education quality and attainment gap; education levels; percentage of workers with degrees; public school rankings; quality and size of each metro area's universities. Milwaukee* was ranked #42 (#1 = most educated city). *www.WalletHub.com, "2017's Most and Least Educated Cities in America," July 25, 2017*

Environmental Rankings

- Sperling's BestPlaces assessed 379 metropolitan areas of the United States for the likelihood of dangerously extreme weather events or earthquakes. In general the Southeast and South-Central regions have the highest risk of weather extremes and earthquakes, while the Pacific Northwest enjoys the lowest risk. Of the least risky metropolitan areas, the Milwaukee* metro area was ranked #167. *www.bestplaces.net, "Safest Places from Natural Disasters," April 2011*

- Milwaukee* was highlighted as one of the top 99 cleanest metro areas for short-term particle pollution (24-hour PM 2.5) in the U.S. during 2013 through 2015. Monitors in these cities reported no days with unhealthful PM 2.5 levels. *American Lung Association, State of the Air 2017*

Health/Fitness Rankings

- For each of the 50 most populous metro areas in the United States, the American College of Sports Medicine's American Fitness Index evaluated infrastructure, community assets, and policies that encourage healthy and fit lifestyles, including preventive health behaviors, levels of chronic disease conditions, health care access, and community resources and policies that support physical activity. The Milwaukee* metro area ranked #21 for "community fitness." *www.americanfitnessindex.org, "ACSM American Fitness Index Health and Community Fitness Status of the 50 Largest Metropolitan Areas," May 2017*
- The Milwaukee* metro area was identified as one of the worst cities for bed bugs in America by pest control company Orkin. The area ranked #29 out of 50 based on the number of bed bug treatments Orkin performed from December 2016 to November 2017. *Orkin, "Baltimore and Washington D.C. Continue to Hold Top Spots," January 8, 2018*
- Milwaukee* was identified as a "2016 Spring Allergy Capital." The area ranked #73 out of 100. Three groups of factors were used to identify the most severe cities for people with allergies during the spring season: annual pollen levels; medicine utilization; access to board-certified allergists. *Asthma and Allergy Foundation of America, "Spring Allergy Capitals 2016"*
- Milwaukee* was identified as a "2016 Fall Allergy Capital." The area ranked #60 out of 100. Three groups of factors were used to identify the most severe cities for people with allergies during the fall season: annual pollen levels; medicine utilization; access to board-certified allergists. *Asthma and Allergy Foundation of America, "Fall Allergy Capitals 2016"*
- Milwaukee* was identified as a "2015 Asthma Capital." The area ranked #22 out of the nation's 100 largest metropolitan areas. Criteria: estimated prevalence; self-reported prevalence; crude death rate for asthma; annual pollen score; annual air quality; public smoking laws; number of board-certified asthma specialists; school inhaler access laws; rescue medication use; controller medication use; ER visits for asthma; uninsured rate; poverty rate. *Asthma and Allergy Foundation of America, "Asthma Capitals 2015"*
- The Milwaukee* metro area ranked #102 out of 189 in The Gallup-Healthways Well-Being Index. Criteria: purpose; social well being; financial health; community and physical health. Results are based on telephone interviews with adults, aged 18 and older, living in metropolitan areas in the 50 U.S. states and the District of Columbia. *Gallup-Healthways, "State of American Well-Being, 2017 Community Well-Being Rankings" March 2018*

Real Estate Rankings

- FitSmallBusiness looked at 50 of the largest metropolitan areas in the U.S. to determine which metro was the best to start a real estate business. Data was compiled from such sources as: Zillow, Trulia, U.S. Census Bureau, and the Bureau of Labor Statistics. Criteria: location; inventory; annual wages; median sales price of homes; days on the market; median price cut percentage; and other factors that would influence real estate professional growth. The Milwaukee* metro area ranked #43. *fitsmallbusiness.com, "The Best Cities to Become a Real Estate Agent in 2018," January 30, 2018*
- Milwaukee* was ranked #98 out of 238 metro areas in terms of housing affordability in 2017 by the National Association of Home Builders (#1 = most affordable). Criteria: the share of homes sold in that area affordable to a family earning the local median income, based on standard mortgage underwriting criteria. *National Association of Home Builders®, NAHB-Wells Fargo Housing Opportunity Index, 4th Quarter 2017*

Safety Rankings

- The National Insurance Crime Bureau ranked 382 metro areas in the U.S. in terms of per capita rates of vehicle theft. The Milwaukee* metro area ranked #44 (#1 = highest rate). Criteria: number of vehicle theft offenses per 100,000 inhabitants in 2016. *National Insurance Crime Bureau, "Hot Spots 2016," June 8, 2017*

Seniors/Retirement Rankings

- From its Best Cities for Successful Aging indexes, the Milken Institute generated rankings for metropolitan areas, weighing data in nine categories—health care, wellness, living arrangements, transportation and convenience, financial characteristics, education, employment, community engagement, and overall livability. The Milwaukee* metro area was ranked #33 overall in the large metro area category. *Milken Institute, "Best Cities for Successful Aging, 2017" March 14, 2017*

Miscellaneous Rankings

- The watchdog site Charity Navigator conducts an annual study of charities in the nation's major markets both to analyze statistical differences in their financial, accountability, and transparency practices and to track year-to-year variations in individual philanthropic communities. Charity Navigator's analysis demonstrated that the financial, accountability and transparency behaviors of America's largest charities can be influenced by the metropolitan market within which the charity operates. The Milwaukee* metro area was ranked #12 among the 30 metro markets in the rating category of Overall Score. *www.charitynavigator.org, "2017 Metro Market Study," May 1, 2017*

*Menomonee Falls is located within the Milwaukee-Waukesha-West Allis, WI Metropolitan Statistical Area.

Business Environment

CITY FINANCES

City Government Finances

Component	2015 ($000)	2015 ($ per capita)
Total Revenues	57,332	1,587
Total Expenditures	76,612	2,121
Debt Outstanding	97,223	2,692
Cash and Securities[1]	69,417	1,922

Note: (1) Cash and security holdings of a government at the close of its fiscal year,, including those of its dependent agencies, utilities, and liquor stores.
Source: U.S Census Bureau, State & Local Government Finances 2015

City Government Revenue by Source

Source	2015 ($000)	2015 ($ per capita)	2015 (%)
General Revenue			
From Federal Government	7	0	0.0
From State Government	5,299	147	9.2
From Local Governments	308	9	0.5
Taxes			
Property	26,190	725	45.7
Sales and Gross Receipts	228	6	0.4
Personal Income	0	0	0.0
Corporate Income	0	0	0.0
Motor Vehicle License	0	0	0.0
Other Taxes	4,529	125	7.9
Current Charges	13,767	381	24.0
Liquor Store	0	0	0.0
Utility	5,264	146	9.2
Employee Retirement	0	0	0.0

Source: U.S Census Bureau, State & Local Government Finances 2015

City Government Expenditures by Function

Function	2015 ($000)	2015 ($ per capita)	2015 (%)
General Direct Expenditures			
Air Transportation	0	0	0.0
Corrections	0	0	0.0
Education	0	0	0.0
Employment Security Administration	0	0	0.0
Financial Administration	392	10	0.5
Fire Protection	7,888	218	10.3
General Public Buildings	277	7	0.4
Governmental Administration, Other	2,315	64	3.0
Health	144	4	0.2
Highways	16,023	443	20.9
Hospitals	0	0	0.0
Housing and Community Development	0	0	0.0
Interest on General Debt	2,418	66	3.2
Judicial and Legal	713	19	0.9
Libraries	1,728	47	2.3
Parking	0	0	0.0
Parks and Recreation	1,071	29	1.4
Police Protection	8,979	248	11.7
Public Welfare	0	0	0.0
Sewerage	10,233	283	13.4
Solid Waste Management	1,832	50	2.4
Veterans' Services	0	0	0.0
Liquor Store	0	0	0.0
Utility	6,480	179	8.5
Employee Retirement	0	0	0.0

Source: U.S Census Bureau, State & Local Government Finances 2015

DEMOGRAPHICS

Population Growth

Area	1990 Census	2000 Census	2010 Census	2016* Estimate	Population Growth (%) 1990-2016	2010-2016
City	26,840	32,647	35,626	36,118	34.6	1.4
MSA[1]	1,432,149	1,500,741	1,555,908	1,571,730	9.7	1.0
U.S.	248,709,873	281,421,906	308,745,538	318,558,162	28.1	3.2

Note: (1) Figures cover the Milwaukee-Waukesha-West Allis, WI Metropolitan Statistical Area—see Appendix B for areas included; (*) 2012-2016 5-year estimated population
Source: U.S. Census Bureau, 1990 Census, Census 2000, Census 2010, 2012-2016 American Community Survey 5-Year Estimates

Household Size

Area	Persons in Household (%) One	Two	Three	Four	Five	Six	Seven or More	Average Household Size
City	28.9	35.5	14.5	14.5	4.7	1.3	0.7	2.40
MSA[1]	31.0	33.8	14.6	12.3	5.4	1.8	1.0	2.50
U.S.	27.7	33.7	15.7	13.1	6.0	2.3	1.5	2.60

Note: (1) Figures cover the Milwaukee-Waukesha-West Allis, WI Metropolitan Statistical Area—see Appendix B for areas included
Source: U.S. Census Bureau, 2012-2016 American Community Survey 5-Year Estimates

Race

Area	White Alone[2] (%)	Black Alone[2] (%)	Asian Alone[2] (%)	AIAN[3] Alone[2] (%)	NHOPI[4] Alone[2] (%)	Other Race Alone[2] (%)	Two or More Races (%)
City	91.3	1.6	5.3	0.2	0.0	0.4	1.2
MSA[1]	73.8	16.6	3.4	0.4	0.0	3.2	2.6
U.S.	73.3	12.6	5.2	0.8	0.2	4.8	3.1

Note: (1) Figures cover the Milwaukee-Waukesha-West Allis, WI Metropolitan Statistical Area—see Appendix B for areas included; (2) Alone is defined as not being in combination with one or more other races; (3) American Indian and Alaska Native; (4) Native Hawaiian and Other Pacific Islander
Source: U.S. Census Bureau, 2012-2016 American Community Survey 5-Year Estimates

Hispanic or Latino Origin

Area	Total (%)	Mexican (%)	Puerto Rican (%)	Cuban (%)	Other (%)
City	2.5	1.2	0.4	0.0	0.9
MSA[1]	10.2	6.9	2.3	0.1	0.9
U.S.	17.3	11.0	1.7	0.7	4.0

Note: Persons of Hispanic or Latino origin can be of any race; (1) Figures cover the Milwaukee-Waukesha-West Allis, WI Metropolitan Statistical Area—see Appendix B for areas included
Source: U.S. Census Bureau, 2012-2016 American Community Survey 5-Year Estimates

Segregation

Type	Segregation Indices[1] 1990	2000	2010	2010 Rank[2]	Percent Change 1990-2000	1990-2010	2000-2010
Black/White	82.8	83.3	81.5	1	0.6	-1.2	-1.8
Asian/White	42.2	43.4	40.7	52	1.2	-1.5	-2.7
Hispanic/White	56.4	59.5	57.0	9	3.2	0.7	-2.5

Note: All figures cover the Metropolitan Statistical Area—see Appendix B for areas included; Figures are based on an analysis of 1990, 2000, and 2010 Census Decennial Census tract data by William H. Frey, Brookings Institution and the University of Michigan Social Science Data Analysis Network. In this analysis all racial groups (whites, blacks, and asians) are non-Hispanic members of those races. Hispanics are shown as a separate category; (1) Segregation Indices are Dissimilarity Indices that measure the degree to which the minority group is distributed differently than whites across census tracts. They range from 0 (complete integration) to 100 (complete segregation) where the value indicates the percentage of the minority group that needs to move to be distributed exactly like whites; (2) Ranges from 1 (most segregated) to 102 (least segregated); n/a not available.
Source: www.CensusScope.org

Ancestry

Area	German	Irish	English	American	Italian	Polish	French[2]	Scottish	Dutch
City	50.3	12.0	7.3	2.9	4.7	11.2	3.4	1.5	1.5
MSA[1]	34.6	9.9	4.4	2.4	4.4	11.2	2.6	0.9	1.3
U.S.	14.4	10.4	7.7	6.9	5.4	2.9	2.6	1.7	1.3

Note: Figures are the percentage of the total population reporting a particular ancestry. The nine most commonly reported ancestries in the U.S. are shown. Figures include multiple ancestries (e.g. if a person reported being Irish and Italian, they were included in both columns); (1) Figures cover the Milwaukee-Waukesha-West Allis, WI Metropolitan Statistical Area—see Appendix B for areas included; (2) Excludes Basque
Source: U.S. Census Bureau, 2012-2016 American Community Survey 5-Year Estimates

Foreign-Born Population

Area	Percent of Population Born in								
	Any Foreign Country	Asia	Mexico	Europe	Carribean	Central America[2]	South America	Africa	Canada
City	5.7	3.4	0.1	1.7	0.0	0.0	0.2	0.1	0.1
MSA[1]	7.1	2.4	2.4	1.3	0.2	0.2	0.2	0.3	0.1
U.S.	13.2	4.0	3.6	1.5	1.3	1.0	0.9	0.6	0.3

Note: (1) Figures cover the Milwaukee-Waukesha-West Allis, WI Metropolitan Statistical Area—see Appendix B for areas included; (2) Excludes Mexico.
Source: U.S. Census Bureau, 2012-2016 American Community Survey 5-Year Estimates

Marital Status

Area	Never Married	Now Married[2]	Separated	Widowed	Divorced
City	24.2	58.0	0.5	8.1	9.3
MSA[1]	36.4	46.5	1.3	5.6	10.2
U.S.	33.0	48.1	2.1	5.9	11.0

Note: Figures are percentages and cover the population 15 years of age and older; (1) Figures cover the Milwaukee-Waukesha-West Allis, WI Metropolitan Statistical Area—see Appendix B for areas included; (2) Excludes separated
Source: U.S. Census Bureau, 2012-2016 American Community Survey 5-Year Estimates

Disability Status

Area	All Ages	Under 18 Years Old	18 to 64 Years Old	65 Years and Over
City	10.3	2.9	6.3	31.5
MSA[1]	11.9	4.8	10.0	33.5
U.S.	12.5	4.1	10.3	35.7

Note: Figures show percent of the civilian noninstitutionalized population that reported having a disability. Disability status is determined from six types of difficulty: vision, hearing, cognitive, ambulatory, self-care, and independent living. For children under 5 years old, hearing and vision difficulty are used to determine disability status. For children between the ages of 5 and 14, disability status is determined from hearing, vision, cognitive, ambulatory, and self-care difficulties. For people aged 15 years and older, they are considered to have a disability if they have difficulty with any one of the six difficulty types; Note: (1) Figures cover the Milwaukee-Waukesha-West Allis, WI Metropolitan Statistical Area—see Appendix B for areas included
Source: U.S. Census Bureau, 2012-2016 American Community Survey 5-Year Estimates

Age

Area	Percent of Population									Median Age
	Under Age 5	Age 5–19	Age 20–34	Age 35–44	Age 45–54	Age 55–64	Age 65–74	Age 75–84	Age 85+	
City	6.1	17.5	16.1	11.5	14.3	15.5	9.1	6.5	3.5	44.1
MSA[1]	6.4	19.9	20.5	12.4	13.8	13.0	7.5	4.1	2.2	37.4
U.S.	6.2	19.6	20.7	12.7	13.6	12.6	8.3	4.3	1.9	37.7

Note: (1) Figures cover the Milwaukee-Waukesha-West Allis, WI Metropolitan Statistical Area—see Appendix B for areas included
Source: U.S. Census Bureau, 2012-2016 American Community Survey 5-Year Estimates

Gender

Area	Males	Females	Males per 100 Females
City	17,318	18,800	92.1
MSA[1]	765,346	806,384	94.9
U.S.	156,765,322	161,792,840	96.9

Note: (1) Figures cover the Milwaukee-Waukesha-West Allis, WI Metropolitan Statistical Area—see Appendix B for areas included
Source: U.S. Census Bureau, 2012-2016 American Community Survey 5-Year Estimates

Religious Groups by Family

Area	Catholic	Baptist	Non-Den.	Methodist[2]	Lutheran	LDS[3]	Pentecostal	Presbyterian[4]	Muslim[5]	Judaism
MSA[1]	24.6	3.1	3.9	1.6	10.8	0.4	2.0	1.6	0.6	0.6
U.S.	19.1	9.3	4.0	4.0	2.3	2.0	1.9	1.6	0.8	0.7

Note: Figures are the number of adherents as a percentage of the total population; (1) Figures cover the Milwaukee-Waukesha-West Allis, WI Metropolitan Statistical Area—see Appendix B for areas included; (2) Methodist/Pietist; (3) Latter Day Saints; (4) Reformed; (5) Figures are estimates
Source: Association of Statisticians of American Religious Bodies, 2010 U.S. Religion Census: Religious Congregations & Membership Study

Religious Groups by Tradition

Area	Catholic	Evangelical Protestant	Mainline Protestant	Other Tradition	Black Protestant	Orthodox
MSA[1]	24.6	14.6	7.2	2.3	2.5	0.6
U.S.	19.1	16.2	7.3	4.3	1.6	0.3

Note: Figures are the number of adherents as a percentage of the total population; (1) Figures cover the Milwaukee-Waukesha-West Allis, WI Metropolitan Statistical Area—see Appendix B for areas included
Source: Association of Statisticians of American Religious Bodies, 2010 U.S. Religion Census: Religious Congregations & Membership Study

ECONOMY

Gross Metropolitan Product

Area	2014	2015	2016	2017	Rank[2]
MSA[1]	96.2	99.0	101.8	106.2	38

Note: Figures are in billions of dollars; (1) Figures cover the Milwaukee-Waukesha-West Allis, WI Metropolitan Statistical Area—see Appendix B for areas included; (2) Rank is based on 2015 data and ranges from 1 to 381
Source: The U.S. Conference of Mayors, U.S. Metro Economies: GMP and Employment Report, 2015-2017

Economic Growth

Area	2012-14 (%)	2015 (%)	2016 (%)	2017 (%)	Rank[2]
MSA[1]	0.5	1.1	1.4	2.3	246
U.S.	2.0	2.4	1.9	2.6	–

Note: Figures are real gross metropolitan product (GMP) growth rates and represent average annual percent change; (1) Figures cover the Milwaukee-Waukesha-West Allis, WI Metropolitan Statistical Area—see Appendix B for areas included; (2) Rank is based on 2012-2014 average annual percent change and ranges from 1 to 381
Source: The U.S. Conference of Mayors, U.S. Metro Economies: GMP and Employment Report, 2015-2017

Metropolitan Area Exports

Area	2011	2012	2013	2014	2015	2016	Rank[2]
MSA[1]	8,826.3	9,175.6	8,874.6	8,696.0	7,953.6	7,256.2	42

Note: Figures are in millions of dollars; (1) Figures cover the Milwaukee-Waukesha-West Allis, WI Metropolitan Statistical Area—see Appendix B for areas included; (2) Rank is based on 2016 data and ranges from 1 to 385
Source: U.S. Department of Commerce, International Trade Administration, Office of Trade & Industry Information, Manufacturing & Services, data extracted March 15, 2018

Building Permits

Area	Single-Family			Multi-Family			Total		
	2016	2017p	Pct. Chg.	2016	2017p	Pct. Chg.	2016	2017p	Pct. Chg.
City	121	139	14.9	210	0	-100.0	331	139	-58.0
MSA[1]	1,634	1,537	-5.9	2,195	2,024	-7.8	3,829	3,561	-7.0
U.S.	750,800	817,300	8.9	455,800	446,800	-2.0	1,206,600	1,264,100	4.8

Note: (1) Figures cover the Milwaukee-Waukesha-West Allis, WI Metropolitan Statistical Area—see Appendix B for areas included; Figures represent new, privately-owned housing units authorized (unadjusted data); All permit data are based on estimates with imputation; (p) preliminary data.
Source: U.S. Census Bureau, Manufacturing, Mining, and Construction Statistics, Building Permits, 2016, 2017

Bankruptcy Filings

Area	Business Filings			Nonbusiness Filings		
	2016	2017	% Chg.	2016	2017	% Chg.
Waukesha County	29	19	-34.5	827	827	0.0
U.S.	24,114	23,157	-4.0	770,846	765,863	-0.6

Note: Business filings include Chapter 7, Chapter 11, Chapter 12, and Chapter 13; Nonbusiness filings include Chapter 7, Chapter 11, and Chapter 13
Source: Administrative Office of the U.S. Courts, Business and Nonbusiness Bankruptcy, County Cases Commenced by Chapter of the Bankruptcy Code, During the 12-Month Period Ending December 31, 2016 and Business and Nonbusiness Bankruptcy, County Cases Commenced by Chapter of the Bankruptcy Code, During the 12-Month Period Ending December 31, 2017

Housing Vacancy Rates

Area	Gross Vacancy Rate[2] (%)			Year-Round Vacancy Rate[3] (%)			Rental Vacancy Rate[4] (%)			Homeowner Vacancy Rate[5] (%)		
	2015	2016	2017	2015	2016	2017	2015	2016	2017	2015	2016	2017
MSA[1]	8.0	6.5	7.9	7.3	5.9	7.0	4.5	5.2	6.5	0.8	1.3	0.9
U.S.	12.9	12.8	12.7	10.0	9.9	9.9	7.1	6.9	7.2	1.8	1.7	1.6

Note: (1) Figures cover the Milwaukee-Waukesha-West Allis, WI Metropolitan Statistical Area—see Appendix B for areas included; (2) The percentage of the total housing inventory that is vacant; (3) The percentage of the housing inventory (excluding seasonal units) that is year-round vacant; (4) The percentage of rental inventory that is vacant for rent; (5) The percentage of homeowner inventory that is vacant for sale
Source: U.S. Census Bureau, Housing Vacancies and Homeownership Annual Statistics: 2015, 2016, 2017

INCOME

Income

Area	Per Capita ($)	Median Household ($)	Average Household ($)
City	38,219	74,266	92,245
MSA[1]	31,258	55,625	76,646
U.S.	29,829	55,322	77,866

Note: (1) Figures cover the Milwaukee-Waukesha-West Allis, WI Metropolitan Statistical Area—see Appendix B for areas included
Source: U.S. Census Bureau, 2012-2016 American Community Survey 5-Year Estimates

Household Income Distribution

Area	Percent of Households Earning							
	Under $15,000	$15,000 -$24,999	$25,000 -$34,999	$35,000 -$49,999	$50,000 -$74,999	$75,000 -$99,999	$100,000 -$149,999	$150,000 and up
City	5.2	9.0	8.3	12.5	15.6	16.6	17.2	15.7
MSA[1]	12.1	10.5	9.6	12.9	17.8	12.9	14.1	10.0
U.S.	12.1	10.2	9.9	13.2	17.8	12.2	13.5	11.1

Note: (1) Figures cover the Milwaukee-Waukesha-West Allis, WI Metropolitan Statistical Area—see Appendix B for areas included
Source: U.S. Census Bureau, 2012-2016 American Community Survey 5-Year Estimates

Poverty Rate

Area	All Ages	Under 18 Years Old	18 to 64 Years Old	65 Years and Over
City	4.0	4.7	2.8	6.6
MSA[1]	15.0	22.1	13.7	8.2
U.S.	15.1	21.2	14.2	9.3

Note: Figures are percentage of people whose income during the past 12 months was below the poverty level; (1) Figures cover the Milwaukee-Waukesha-West Allis, WI Metropolitan Statistical Area—see Appendix B for areas included
Source: U.S. Census Bureau, 2012-2016 American Community Survey 5-Year Estimates

EMPLOYMENT

Labor Force and Employment

Area	Civilian Labor Force			Workers Employed		
	Dec. 2016	Dec. 2017	% Chg.	Dec. 2016	Dec. 2017	% Chg.
City	20,339	20,358	0.1	19,767	19,893	0.6
MSA[1]	823,210	822,220	-0.1	794,650	799,577	0.6
U.S.	158,968,000	159,880,000	0.6	151,798,000	153,602,000	1.2

Note: Data is not seasonally adjusted and covers workers 16 years of age and older; (1) Figures cover the Milwaukee-Waukesha-West Allis, WI Metropolitan Statistical Area—see Appendix B for areas included
Source: Bureau of Labor Statistics, Local Area Unemployment Statistics

Unemployment Rate

Area	2017											
	Jan.	Feb.	Mar.	Apr.	May	Jun.	Jul.	Aug.	Sep.	Oct.	Nov.	Dec.
City	3.4	3.5	2.8	2.6	2.8	3.4	3.0	2.9	2.7	2.5	2.6	2.3
MSA[1]	4.0	4.1	3.6	3.3	3.4	4.1	3.9	3.9	3.3	3.1	3.1	2.8
U.S.	5.1	4.9	4.6	4.1	4.1	4.5	4.6	4.5	4.1	3.9	3.9	3.9

Note: Data is not seasonally adjusted and covers workers 16 years of age and older; (1) Figures cover the Milwaukee-Waukesha-West Allis, WI Metropolitan Statistical Area—see Appendix B for areas included
Source: Bureau of Labor Statistics, Local Area Unemployment Statistics

Average Wages

Occupation	$/Hr.	Occupation	$/Hr.
Accountants and Auditors	33.60	Maids and Housekeeping Cleaners	11.20
Automotive Mechanics	20.60	Maintenance and Repair Workers	20.00
Bookkeepers	18.60	Marketing Managers	60.40
Carpenters	25.70	Nuclear Medicine Technologists	37.00
Cashiers	10.20	Nurses, Licensed Practical	22.40
Clerks, General Office	17.50	Nurses, Registered	33.60
Clerks, Receptionists/Information	13.80	Nursing Assistants	13.70
Clerks, Shipping/Receiving	18.30	Packers and Packagers, Hand	12.90
Computer Programmers	39.90	Physical Therapists	38.10
Computer Systems Analysts	38.00	Postal Service Mail Carriers	24.10
Computer User Support Specialists	25.40	Real Estate Brokers	n/a
Cooks, Restaurant	12.60	Retail Salespersons	12.30
Dentists	109.20	Sales Reps., Exc. Tech./Scientific	37.40
Electrical Engineers	39.00	Sales Reps., Tech./Scientific	44.20
Electricians	29.70	Secretaries, Exc. Legal/Med./Exec.	18.40
Financial Managers	70.40	Security Guards	13.20
First-Line Supervisors/Managers, Sales	19.80	Surgeons	132.60
Food Preparation Workers	10.60	Teacher Assistants*	14.70
General and Operations Managers	67.90	Teachers, Elementary School*	28.70
Hairdressers/Cosmetologists	13.40	Teachers, Secondary School*	30.70
Internists, General	114.70	Telemarketers	15.40
Janitors and Cleaners	12.60	Truck Drivers, Heavy/Tractor-Trailer	22.10
Landscaping/Groundskeeping Workers	14.50	Truck Drivers, Light/Delivery Svcs.	16.90
Lawyers	n/a	Waiters and Waitresses	9.90

Note: Wage data covers the Milwaukee-Waukesha-West Allis, WI Metropolitan Statistical Area—see Appendix B for areas included; (*) Hourly wages for elementary/secondary school teachers and teacher assistants were calculated by the editors from annual wage data based on a 40 hour work week; n/a not available.
Source: Bureau of Labor Statistics, Metro Area Occupational Employment & Wage Estimates, May 2017

Employment by Occupation

Occupation Classification	City (%)	MSA[1] (%)	U.S. (%)
Management, Business, Science, and Arts	46.9	38.9	37.0
Natural Resources, Construction, and Maintenance	4.9	6.3	8.9
Production, Transportation, and Material Moving	12.4	14.0	12.2
Sales and Office	27.0	23.6	23.8
Service	8.8	17.2	18.1

Note: Figures cover employed civilians 16 years of age and older; (1) Figures cover the Milwaukee-Waukesha-West Allis, WI Metropolitan Statistical Area—see Appendix B for areas included
Source: U.S. Census Bureau, 2012-2016 American Community Survey 5-Year Estimates

Employment by Industry

Sector	MSA[1]		U.S.
	Number of Employees	Percent of Total	Percent of Total
Construction	28,700	3.3	4.7
Education and Health Services	171,100	19.7	15.9
Financial Activities	50,600	5.8	5.7
Government	88,500	10.2	15.3
Information	13,200	1.5	1.9
Leisure and Hospitality	76,600	8.8	10.7
Manufacturing	118,500	13.6	8.5
Mining and Logging	400	<0.1	0.5
Other Services	46,100	5.3	3.9
Professional and Business Services	129,300	14.9	14.0
Retail Trade	81,100	9.3	11.0
Transportation, Warehousing, and Utilities	27,600	3.2	4.1
Wholesale Trade	38,700	4.4	4.0

Note: Figures are non-farm employment as of December 2017. Figures are not seasonally adjusted and include workers 16 years of age and older; (1) Figures cover the Milwaukee-Waukesha-West Allis, WI Metropolitan Statistical Area—see Appendix B for areas included
Source: Bureau of Labor Statistics, Current Employment Statistics, Employment, Hours, and Earnings

Occupations with Greatest Projected Employment Growth: 2017 – 2019

Occupation[1]	2017 Employment	2019 Projected Employment	Numeric Employment Change	Percent Employment Change
Personal Care Aides	67,040	71,960	4,920	7.3
Combined Food Preparation and Serving Workers, Including Fast Food	67,080	69,290	2,210	3.3
Janitors and Cleaners, Except Maids and Housekeeping Cleaners	48,250	49,690	1,440	3.0
Laborers and Freight, Stock, and Material Movers, Hand	57,070	58,260	1,190	2.1
Sales Representatives, Wholesale and Manufacturing, Except Technical and Scientific Products	43,060	44,250	1,190	2.8
Registered Nurses	57,240	58,170	930	1.6
Maintenance and Repair Workers, General	33,060	33,980	920	2.8
General and Operations Managers	37,020	37,900	880	2.4
Elementary School Teachers, Except Special Education	34,520	35,260	740	2.2
Software Developers, Applications	12,140	12,870	730	6.1

Note: Projections cover Wisconsin; (1) Sorted by numeric employment change
Source: www.projectionscentral.com, State Occupational Projections, 2017–2019 Short-Term Projections

Fastest Growing Occupations: 2017 – 2019

Occupation[1]	2017 Employment	2019 Projected Employment	Numeric Employment Change	Percent Employment Change
Septic Tank Servicers and Sewer Pipe Cleaners	700	760	60	8.2
Personal Care Aides	67,040	71,960	4,920	7.3
Musicians and Singers	850	900	50	6.5
Appraisers and Assessors of Real Estate	1,250	1,330	80	6.3
Software Developers, Applications	12,140	12,870	730	6.1
Home Health Aides	7,640	8,090	450	6.0
Computer Numerically Controlled Machine Tool Programmers, Metal and Plastic	1,470	1,560	90	5.8
Health Specialties Teachers, Postsecondary	6,570	6,940	370	5.7
Fundraisers	2,370	2,500	130	5.3
Nursing Instructors and Teachers, Postsecondary	1,670	1,760	90	5.3

Note: Projections cover Wisconsin; (1) Sorted by percent employment change and excludes occupations with numeric employment change less than 50
Source: www.projectionscentral.com, State Occupational Projections, 2017–2019 Short-Term Projections

TAXES

State Corporate Income Tax Rates

State	Tax Rate (%)	Income Brackets ($)	Num. of Brackets	Financial Institution Tax Rate (%)[a]	Federal Income Tax Ded.
Wisconsin	7.9	Flat rate	1	7.9	No

Note: Tax rates as of January 1, 2018; (a) Rates listed are the corporate income tax rate applied to financial institutions or excise taxes based on income. Some states have other taxes based upon the value of deposits or shares.
Source: Federation of Tax Administrators, Range of State Corporate Income Tax Rates, January 1, 2018

State Individual Income Tax Rates

State	Tax Rate (%)	Income Brackets ($)	Num. of Brackets	Personal Exempt. ($)[1] Single	Personal Exempt. ($)[1] Dependents	Fed. Inc. Tax Ded.
Wisconsin (a)	4.0 - 7.65	11,450 - 252,150 (x)	4	700	700	No

Note: Tax rates as of January 1, 2018; Local- and county-level taxes are not included; n/a not applicable; (1) Married joint filers generally receive double the single exemption; (a) 19 states have statutory provision for automatically adjusting to the rate of inflation the dollar values of the income tax brackets, standard deductions, and/or personal exemptions. Massachusetts, Michigan, and Nebraska index the personal exemption only. Oregon does not index the income brackets for $125,000 and over; (x) The Wisconsin income brackets reported are for single individuals. For married taxpayers filing jointly, the same tax rates apply income brackets ranging from $15,270, to $336,200.
Source: Federation of Tax Administrators, State Individual Income Tax Rates, January 1, 2018

Various State Sales and Excise Tax Rates

State	State Sales Tax (%)	Gasoline[1] (¢/gal.)	Cigarette[2] ($/pack)	Spirits[3] ($/gal.)	Wine[4] ($/gal.)	Beer[5] ($/gal.)	Recreational Marijuana (%)
Wisconsin	5.0	32.9	2.52	3.25	0.25 (l)	0.06 (q)	Not legal

Note: All tax rates as of January 1, 2018; (1) The American Petroleum Institute has developed a methodology for determining the average tax rate on a gallon of fuel. Rates may include any of the following: excise taxes, environmental fees, storage tank fees, other fees or taxes, general sales tax, and local taxes. In states where gasoline is subject to the general sales tax, or where the fuel tax is based on the average sale price, the average rate determined by API is sensitive to changes in the price of gasoline. States that fully or partially apply general sales taxes to gasoline: CA, CO, GA, IL, IN, MI, NY; (2) The federal excise tax of $1.0066 per pack and local taxes are not included; (3) Rates are those applicable to off-premise sales of 40% alcohol by volume (a.b.v.) distilled spirits in 750ml containers. Local excise taxes are excluded; (4) Rates are those applicable to off-premise sales of 11% a.b.v. non-carbonated wine in 750ml containers; (5) Rates are those applicable to off-premise sales of 4.7% a.b.v. beer in 12 ounce containers; (l) Different rates also applicable to alcohol content, place of production, size of container, place purchased (on- or off-premise or on board airlines) or type of wine (carbonated, vermouth, etc.); (q) Different rates also applicable according to alcohol content, place of production, size of container, or place purchased (on- or off-premise or onboard airlines).
Source: Tax Foundation, 2018 Facts & Figures: How Does Your State Compare?

State Business Tax Climate Index Rankings

State	Overall Rank	Corporate Tax Rank	Individual Income Tax Rank	Sales Tax Rank	Unemployment Insurance Tax Rank	Property Tax Rank
Wisconsin	38	29	43	7	40	26

Note: The index is a measure of how each state's tax laws affect economic performance. The lower the rank, the more favorable a state's tax system is for business. States without a given tax are given a ranking of 1. The scores/rankings for the District of Columbia do not affect other states. The 2018 index represents the tax climate as of July 1, 2017.
Source: Tax Foundation, State Business Tax Climate Index 2018

TRANSPORTATION

Means of Transportation to Work

Area	Car/Truck/Van		Public Transportation			Bicycle	Walked	Other Means	Worked at Home
	Drove Alone	Car-pooled	Bus	Subway	Railroad				
City	87.7	6.6	0.3	0.0	0.1	0.1	0.9	0.3	3.9
MSA[1]	80.5	8.2	3.6	0.0	0.1	0.6	2.8	0.8	3.6
U.S.	76.4	9.3	2.6	1.9	0.6	0.6	2.8	1.3	4.6

Note: Figures are percentages and cover workers 16 years of age and older; (1) Figures cover the Milwaukee-Waukesha-West Allis, WI Metropolitan Statistical Area—see Appendix B for areas included
Source: U.S. Census Bureau, 2012-2016 American Community Survey 5-Year Estimates

Travel Time to Work

Area	Less Than 10 Minutes	10 to 19 Minutes	20 to 29 Minutes	30 to 44 Minutes	45 to 59 Minutes	60 to 89 Minutes	90 Minutes or More
City	14.7	29.5	31.0	18.5	3.2	2.0	1.3
MSA[1]	12.2	31.5	25.8	20.7	5.6	2.7	1.5
U.S.	12.9	29.2	20.9	20.4	8.0	6.0	2.7

Note: Note: Figures are percentages and include workers 16 years old and over; (1) Figures cover the Milwaukee-Waukesha-West Allis, WI Metropolitan Statistical Area—see Appendix B for areas included
Source: U.S. Census Bureau, 2012-2016 American Community Survey 5-Year Estimates

Freeway Travel Time Index

Area	1985	1990	1995	2000	2005	2010	2014
Urban Area Rank[1,2]	39	34	41	57	61	57	54
Urban Area Index[1]	1.08	1.12	1.14	1.15	1.16	1.16	1.17
Average Index[3]	1.09	1.11	1.14	1.17	1.20	1.19	1.20

Note: Freeway Travel Time Index—the ratio of travel time in the peak period to the travel time at free-flow conditions. For example, a value of 1.30 indicates a 20-minute free-flow trip takes 26 minutes in the peak (20 minutes x 1.30 = 26 minutes); (1) Covers the Milwaukee WI urban area; (2) Rank is based on 101 urban areas (#1 = highest travel time index); (3) Average of 101 urban areas
Source: Texas Transportation Institute, 2015 Urban Mobility Scorecard, August 2015

Freeway Commuter Stress Index

Area	1985	1990	1995	2000	2005	2010	2014
Urban Area Rank[1,2]	42	42	43	54	53	53	57
Urban Area Index[1]	1.11	1.15	1.18	1.18	1.20	1.20	1.20
Average Index[3]	1.13	1.16	1.19	1.22	1.25	1.24	1.25

Note: The Freeway Commuter Stress Index is the same as the Freeway Travel Time Index (see table above) except that it includes only the travel in the peak directions during the peak periods; the TTI includes travel in all directions during the peak period. Thus, the CSI is more indicative of the work trip experienced by each commuter on a daily basis; (1) Covers the Milwaukee WI urban area; (2) Rank is based on 101 urban areas (#1 = highest travel time index); (3) Average of 101 urban areas
Source: Texas Transportation Institute, 2015 Urban Mobility Scorecard, August 2015

Living Environment

COST OF LIVING

Cost of Living Index

Composite Index	Groceries	Housing	Utilities	Transportation	Health Care	Misc. Goods/ Services
97.1	97.9	93.9	107.2	95.5	113.4	94.7

Note: The Cost of Living Index measures regional differences in the cost of consumer goods and services, excluding taxes and non-consumer expenditures, for professional and managerial households in the top income quintile. It is based on more than 50,000 prices covering almost 60 different items for which prices are collected three times a year by chambers of commerce, economic development organizations or university applied economic centers in each participating urban area. The numbers shown should be read as a percentage above or below the national average of 100. For example, a value of 115.4 in the groceries column indicates that grocery prices are 15.4% higher than the national average. Small differences in the index numbers should not be interpreted as significant; Figures cover the Milwaukee-Waukesha WI urban area.
Source: The Council for Community and Economic Research, ACCRA Cost of Living Index, 2017

Grocery Prices

Area[1]	T-Bone Steak ($/pound)	Frying Chicken ($/pound)	Whole Milk ($/half gal.)	Eggs ($/dozen)	Orange Juice ($/64 oz.)	Coffee ($/11.5 oz.)
City[2]	12.83	1.95	1.85	1.00	3.68	4.46
Avg.	11.29	1.40	2.02	1.47	3.55	4.37
Min.	7.71	0.93	1.04	0.70	2.86	3.24
Max.	15.83	2.39	4.03	3.92	6.29	8.16

Note: (1) Values for the local area are compared with the average, minimum and maximum values for all 294 areas in the Cost of Living Index; (2) Figures cover the Milwaukee-Waukesha WI urban area; ***T-Bone Steak*** *(price per pound);* ***Frying Chicken*** *(price per pound, whole fryer);* ***Whole Milk*** *(half gallon carton);* ***Eggs*** *(price per dozen, Grade A, large);* ***Orange Juice*** *(64 oz. Tropicana or Florida Natural);* ***Coffee*** *(11.5 oz. can, vacuum-packed, Maxwell House, Hills Bros, or Folgers).*
Source: The Council for Community and Economic Research, ACCRA Cost of Living Index, 2017

Housing and Utility Costs

Area[1]	New Home Price ($)	Apartment Rent ($/month)	All Electric ($/month)	Part Electric ($/month)	Other Energy ($/month)	Telephone ($/month)
City[2]	324,408	977	-	98.69	61.89	34.53
Avg.	335,956	1,047	175.01	97.34	67.93	28.71
Min.	187,788	491	109.48	49.33	35.44	12.39
Max.	1,739,087	4,559	432.62	227.09	353.33	44.61

Note: (1) Values for the local area are compared with the average, minimum and maximum values for all 294 areas in the Cost of Living Index; (2) Figures cover the Milwaukee-Waukesha WI urban area; ***New Home Price*** *(2,400 sf living area, 8,000 sf lot, in urban area with full utilities);* ***Apartment Rent*** *(950 sf 2 bedroom/1.5 or 2 bath, unfurnished, excluding all utilities except water);* ***All Electric*** *(average monthly cost for an all-electric home);* ***Part Electric*** *(average monthly cost for a part-electric home);* ***Other Energy*** *(average monthly cost for natural gas, fuel oil, coal, wood, and any other forms of energy except electricity);* ***Telephone*** *(price includes basic monthly rate for a private residential line plus additional local usage charges incurred by a family of four).*
Source: The Council for Community and Economic Research, ACCRA Cost of Living Index, 2017

Health Care, Transportation, and Other Costs

Area[1]	Doctor ($/visit)	Dentist ($/visit)	Optometrist ($/visit)	Gasoline ($/gallon)	Beauty Salon ($/visit)	Men's Shirt ($)
City[2]	163.66	98.09	53.85	2.27	34.01	35.41
Avg.	108.00	92.54	101.93	2.25	37.58	30.92
Min.	30.39	60.00	49.75	1.82	16.11	11.20
Max.	193.50	161.94	229.28	3.16	77.35	59.13

Note: (1) Values for the local area are compared with the average, minimum and maximum values for all 294 areas in the Cost of Living Index; (2) Figures cover the Milwaukee-Waukesha WI urban area; ***Doctor*** *(general practitioners routine exam of an established patient);* ***Dentist*** *(adult teeth cleaning and periodic oral examination);* ***Optometrist*** *(full vision eye exam for established adult patient);* ***Gasoline*** *(one gallon regular unleaded, national brand, including all taxes, cash price at self-service pump if available);* ***Beauty Salon*** *(woman's shampoo, trim, and blow-dry);* ***Men's Shirt*** *(cotton/polyester dress shirt, pinpoint weave, long sleeves).*
Source: The Council for Community and Economic Research, ACCRA Cost of Living Index, 2017

HOUSING

House Price Index (HPI)

Area	National Ranking[2]	Quarterly Change (%)	One-Year Change (%)	Five-Year Change (%)
MSA[1]	157	0.11	5.20	17.25
U.S.[3]	–	1.61	6.68	34.71

Note: The HPI is a weighted repeat sales index. It measures average price changes in repeat sales or refinancings on the same properties. This information is obtained by reviewing repeat mortgage transactions on single-family properties whose mortgages have been purchased or securitized by Fannie Mae or Freddie Mac in January 1975; (1) Figures cover the Milwaukee-Waukesha-West Allis, WI Metropolitan Statistical Area—see Appendix B for areas included; (2) Rankings are based on annual percentage change for all metro areas containing at least 15,000 transactions over the last 10 years and ranges from 1 to 253; (3) figures based on a weighted average of Census Division estimates using a seasonally adjusted, purchase-only index; all figures are for the period ending December 31, 2017
Source: Federal Housing Finance Agency, House Price Index, February 28, 2018

Median Single-Family Home Prices

Area	2015	2016	2017p	Percent Change 2016 to 2017
MSA[1]	220.4	228.2	239.6	5.0
U.S. Average	223.9	235.5	248.8	5.6

Note: Figures are median sales prices of existing single-family homes in thousands of dollars; (p) preliminary; (1) Figures cover the Milwaukee-Waukesha-West Allis, WI Metropolitan Statistical Area—see Appendix B for areas included
Source: National Association of Realtors, Median Sales Price of Existing Single-Family Homes for Metropolitan Areas, 4th Quarter 2017

Qualifying Income Based on Median Sales Price of Existing Single-Family Homes

Area	With 5% Down ($)	With 10% Down ($)	With 20% Down ($)
MSA[1]	52,556	49,790	44,258
U.S. Average	55,585	52,659	46,808

Note: Figures are preliminary; Qualifying income is based on a mortgage rate of 4.17%. Monthly principal and interest payment is limited to 25% of income; (1) Figures cover the Milwaukee-Waukesha-West Allis, WI Metropolitan Statistical Area—see Appendix B for areas included
Source: National Association of Realtors, Qualifying Income Based on Median Sales Price of Existing Single-Family Homes for Metropolitan Areas, 4th Quarter 2017

Median Apartment Condo-Coop Home Prices

Area	2015	2016	2017p	Percent Change 2016 to 2017
MSA[1]	150.1	159.4	169.0	6.0
U.S. Average	210.7	220.7	234.3	6.2

Note: Figures are median sales prices of existing apartment condo-coop homes in thousands of dollars; (p) preliminary; (1) Figures cover the Milwaukee-Waukesha-West Allis, WI Metropolitan Statistical Area—see Appendix B for areas included
Source: National Association of Realtors, Median Sales Price of Existing Apartment Condo-Coop Homes for Metropolitan Areas, 4th Quarter 2017

Home Value Distribution

Area	Under $50,000	$50,000 -$99,999	$100,000 -$149,999	$150,000 -$199,999	$200,000 -$299,999	$300,000 -$499,999	$500,000 -$999,999	$1,000,000 or more
City	2.1	1.9	5.1	28.1	35.7	23.2	3.7	0.3
MSA[1]	4.5	10.3	16.9	20.3	26.6	15.8	4.7	0.9
U.S.	8.8	14.8	15.3	14.9	18.4	16.4	9.0	2.5

Note: Figures are percentages and cover owner-occupied housing units; (1) Figures cover the Milwaukee-Waukesha-West Allis, WI Metropolitan Statistical Area—see Appendix B for areas included
Source: U.S. Census Bureau, 2012-2016 American Community Survey 5-Year Estimates

Homeownership Rate

Area	2009 (%)	2010 (%)	2011 (%)	2012 (%)	2013 (%)	2014 (%)	2015 (%)	2016 (%)	2017 (%)
MSA[1]	61.6	62.4	62.3	61.9	60.0	55.9	57.0	60.4	63.9
U.S.	67.4	66.9	66.1	65.4	65.1	64.5	63.7	63.4	63.9

Note: (1) Figures cover the Milwaukee-Waukesha-West Allis, WI Metropolitan Statistical Area—see Appendix B for areas included
Source: U.S. Census Bureau, Housing Vacancies and Homeownership Annual Statistics: 2009-2017

Year Housing Structure Built

Area	2010 or Later	2000 -2009	1990 -1999	1980 -1989	1970 -1979	1960 -1969	1950 -1959	1940 -1949	Before 1940	Median Year
City	2.6	12.2	21.5	8.7	8.5	21.1	19.1	2.7	3.6	1974
MSA[1]	1.1	8.3	10.7	7.8	13.2	11.4	17.3	7.5	22.6	1962
U.S.	2.3	14.7	14.0	13.7	15.6	10.9	10.6	5.2	13.0	1977

Note: Figures are percentages except for Median Year; Note: (1) Figures cover the Milwaukee-Waukesha-West Allis, WI Metropolitan Statistical Area—see Appendix B for areas included
Source: U.S. Census Bureau, 2012-2016 American Community Survey 5-Year Estimates

Gross Monthly Rent

Area	Under $500	$500 -$999	$1,000 -$1,499	$1,500 -$1,999	$2,000 -$2,499	$2,500 -$2,999	$3,000 and up	Median ($)
City	4.0	52.2	34.2	5.2	3.4	0.7	0.3	946
MSA[1]	9.2	60.9	23.5	4.5	1.3	0.2	0.3	841
U.S.	11.3	43.3	27.7	10.7	4.0	1.6	1.5	949

Note: Figures are percentages except for Median; Gross rent is the contract rent plus the estimated average monthly cost of utilities (electricity, gas, and water and sewer) and fuels (oil, coal, kerosene, wood, etc.) if these are paid by the renter (or paid for the renter by someone else); (1) Figures cover the Milwaukee-Waukesha-West Allis, WI Metropolitan Statistical Area—see Appendix B for areas included
Source: U.S. Census Bureau, 2012-2016 American Community Survey 5-Year Estimates

HEALTH

Health Risk Factors

Category	MSA[1] (%)	U.S. (%)
Adults aged 18–64 who have any kind of health care coverage	89.5	87.7
Adults who reported being in good or excellent health	82.4	83.6
Adults who are current smokers	16.1	17.1
Adults who currently use E-cigarettes	6.7	4.7
Adults who currently use chewing tobacco, snuff, or snus	2.8	4.0
Adults who are heavy drinkers[2]	9.3	6.5
Adults who are binge drinkers[3]	24.9	16.9
Adults who are overweight (BMI 25.0 - 29.9)	34.2	35.3
Adults who are obese (BMI 30.0 - 99.8)	30.2	29.9
Adults who participated in any physical activities in the past month	81.2	76.9
Adults who always or nearly always wears a seat belt	89.2	94.3

Note: (1) Figures cover the Milwaukee-Waukesha-West Allis, WI Metropolitan Statistical Area—see Appendix B for areas included; (2) Heavy drinkers are classified as adult men having more than 14 drinks per week and adult women having more than 7 drinks per week; (3) Binge drinkers are classified as males having five or more drinks on one occasion or females having four or more drinks on one occasion
Source: Centers for Disease Control and Prevention, Behaviorial Risk Factor Surveillance System, SMART: Selected Metropolitan Area Risk Trends, 2016

Health Screening Rates

Category	MSA[1] (%)	U.S. (%)
Adults 50-75 who have had a blood stool test within the past year	6.7	8.0
Adults 50-75 who have had a colonoscopy in the past 10 years	69.4	63.5
Adults aged 65+ who have had flu shot within the past year	50.4	58.6
Adults aged 65+ who have ever had a pneumonia vaccination	84.6	73.4
Adults who have ever been tested for HIV	33.6	35.6
Women aged 21-65 who have had a pap test in the past three years	83.5	79.8
Men aged 40+ who have had a PSA test within the past two years	45.3	39.5
Women aged 40+ who have had a mammogram within the past two years	77.8	72.5

Note: n/a not available; (1) Figures cover the Milwaukee-Waukesha-West Allis, WI Metropolitan Statistical Area—see Appendix B for areas included; Source: Centers for Disease Control and Prevention, Behaviorial Risk Factor Surveillance System, SMART: Selected Metropolitan Area Risk Trends, 2016

Chronic Health Conditions

Category	MSA[1] (%)	U.S. (%)
Adults who have ever been told they had a heart attack	3.3	4.4
Adults who have ever been told they have angina or coronary heart disease	3.4	4.1
Adults who have ever been told they had a stroke	3.1	3.1
Adults who have been told they currently have asthma	8.8	9.3
Adults who have ever been told they have arthritis	25.2	25.8
Adults who have ever been told they have diabetes[2]	9.3	10.5
Adults who have ever been told they had skin cancer	5.4	5.9
Adults who have ever been told they had any other types of cancer	6.7	6.7
Adults who have ever been told they have COPD	4.7	6.3
Adults who have ever been told they have kidney disease	3.2	2.8
Adults who have ever been told they have a form of depression	16.4	17.4

Note: (1) Figures cover the Milwaukee-Waukesha-West Allis, WI Metropolitan Statistical Area—see Appendix B for areas included; (2) Figures do not include pregnancy-related, borderline, or pre-diabetes
Source: Centers for Disease Control and Prevention, Behaviorial Risk Factor Surveillance System, SMART: Selected Metropolitan Area Risk Trends, 2016

Mortality Rates for the Top 10 Causes of Death in the U.S.

ICD-10[a] Sub-Chapter	ICD-10[a] Code	Age-Adjusted Mortality Rate[1] per 100,000 population	
		County[2]	U.S.
Malignant neoplasms	C00-C97	143.8	158.5
Ischaemic heart diseases	I20-I25	67.7	96.8
Other forms of heart disease	I30-I51	42.2	52.4
Chronic lower respiratory diseases	J40-J47	31.1	40.9
Cerebrovascular diseases	I60-I69	28.7	37.2
Organic, including symptomatic, mental disorders	F01-F09	39.2	33.3
Other degenerative diseases of the nervous system	G30-G31	28.9	32.1
Other external causes of accidental injury	W00-X59	39.8	31.2
Diabetes mellitus	E10-E14	15.7	21.1
Hypertensive diseases	I10-I15	15.2	20.8

Note: (a) ICD-10 = International Classification of Diseases 10th Revision; (1) Mortality rates are a three year average covering 2014-2016; (2) Figures cover Waukesha County.
Source: Centers for Disease Control and Prevention, National Center for Health Statistics. Underlying Cause of Death 1999-2016 on CDC WONDER Online Database, released December 2017

Mortality Rates for Selected Causes of Death

ICD-10[a] Sub-Chapter	ICD-10[a] Code	Age-Adjusted Mortality Rate[1] per 100,000 population	
		County[2]	U.S.
Assault	X85-Y09	Unreliable	5.6
Diseases of the liver	K70-K76	9.8	14.0
Human immunodeficiency virus (HIV) disease	B20-B24	Suppressed	1.9
Influenza and pneumonia	J09-J18	14.3	14.6
Intentional self-harm	X60-X84	12.9	13.2
Malnutrition	E40-E46	1.5	1.3
Obesity and other hyperalimentation	E65-E68	Suppressed	2.1
Renal failure	N17-N19	11.9	13.0
Transport accidents	V01-V99	6.8	12.0
Viral hepatitis	B15-B19	Suppressed	1.9

Note: (a) ICD-10 = International Classification of Diseases 10th Revision; (1) Mortality rates are a three year average covering 2014-2016; (2) Figures cover Waukesha County; Data are Suppressed when the data meet the criteria for confidentiality constraints; Mortality rates are flagged as Unreliable when the rate would be calculated with a numerator of 20 or less.
Source: Centers for Disease Control and Prevention, National Center for Health Statistics. Underlying Cause of Death 1999-2016 on CDC WONDER Online Database, released December 2017

Health Insurance Coverage

Area	With Health Insurance	With Private Health Insurance	With Public Health Insurance	Without Health Insurance	Population Under Age 18 Without Health Insurance
City	96.9	85.5	26.1	3.1	2.0
MSA[1]	92.5	70.3	33.3	7.5	2.9
U.S.	88.3	66.7	33.0	11.7	5.9

Note: Figures are percentages that cover the civilian noninstitutionalized population; (1) Figures cover the Milwaukee-Waukesha-West Allis, WI Metropolitan Statistical Area—see Appendix B for areas included
Source: U.S. Census Bureau, 2012-2016 American Community Survey 5-Year Estimates

Number of Medical Professionals

Area	MDs[3]	DOs[3,4]	Dentists	Podiatrists	Chiropractors	Optometrists
County[1] (number)	1,858	109	360	23	181	88
County[1] (rate[2])	469.4	27.5	90.4	5.8	45.5	22.1
U.S. (rate[2])	276.5	22.3	67.3	6.0	26.7	15.9

Note: Data as of 2016 unless noted; (1) Data covers Waukesha County; (2) Rate per 100,000 population; (3) Data as of 2015 and includes all active, non-federal physicians; (4) Doctor of Osteopathic Medicine
Source: U.S. Department of Health and Human Services, Health Resources and Services Administration, Bureau of Health Professions, Area Resource File (ARF) 2016-2017

Best Hospitals

According to *U.S. News,* the Milwaukee-Waukesha-West Allis, WI metro area is home to two of the best hospitals in the U.S.: **Aurora St. Luke's Medical Center** (5 adult specialties); **Froedtert Hospital and the Medical College of Wisconsin** (4 adult specialties). The hospitals listed were nationally ranked in at least one of 16 specialties. Only 152 hospitals nationwide were nationally ranked in one or more specialties. Twenty hospitals in the U.S. made the Honor Roll. The Best Hospitals Honor Roll was revamped last year to take both the national rankings and the procedure and condition ratings into account. Hospitals received points if they were nationally ranked in one of the 16 specialties—the higher they ranked, the more points they got—and how many ratings of "high performing" they earned in the nine procedures and conditions. *U.S. News Online, "America's Best Hospitals 2017-18"*

According to *U.S. News,* the Milwaukee-Waukesha-West Allis, WI metro area is home to one of the best children's hospitals in the U.S.: **Children's Hospital of Wisconsin** (10 pediatric specialties). The hospital listed was highly ranked in at least one of 10 pediatric specialties. Eighty-two children's hospitals in the U.S. were nationally ranked in at least one specialty. Hospitals received points for being ranked in a specialty, and the 10 hospitals with the most points across the 10 specialties make up the Honor Roll. *U.S. News Online, "America's Best Children's Hospitals 2017-18"*

EDUCATION

Public School District Statistics

District Name	Schls	Pupils	Pupil/ Teacher Ratio	Minority Pupils[1] (%)	Free Lunch Eligible[2] (%)	IEP[3] (%)
Hamilton School District	7	4,711	17.6	16.8	12.1	9.5
Menomonee Falls School District	6	4,041	15.1	24.6	13.5	12.6

Note: Table includes school districts with 100 or more students; (1) Percentage of students that are not non-Hispanic white; (2) Percentage of students that are eligible for the free lunch program; (3) Percentage of students that have an Individualized Education Program.
Source: U.S. Department of Education, National Center for Education Statistics, Common Core of Data, Local Education Agency (School District) Universe Survey: School Year 2015-2016; U.S. Department of Education, National Center for Education Statistics, Common Core of Data, Public Elementary/Secondary School Universe Survey: School Year 2015-2016

Highest Level of Education

Area	Less than H.S.	H.S. Diploma	Some College, No Deg.	Associate Degree	Bachelor's Degree	Master's Degree	Prof. School Degree	Doctorate Degree
City	4.5	25.8	19.1	9.6	26.8	10.9	2.0	1.3
MSA[1]	9.6	26.8	21.2	8.6	22.1	8.4	2.1	1.1
U.S.	13.0	27.5	21.0	8.2	18.8	8.2	2.0	1.3

Note: Figures cover persons age 25 and over; (1) Figures cover the Milwaukee-Waukesha-West Allis, WI Metropolitan Statistical Area—see Appendix B for areas included
Source: U.S. Census Bureau, 2012-2016 American Community Survey 5-Year Estimates

Educational Attainment by Race

Area	High School Graduate or Higher (%)					Bachelor's Degree or Higher (%)				
	Total	White	Black	Asian	Hisp.[2]	Total	White	Black	Asian	Hisp.[2]
City	95.5	95.7	87.2	96.3	93.7	41.1	39.3	41.8	77.7	34.0
MSA[1]	90.4	93.5	80.9	83.6	66.0	33.8	37.6	13.6	51.3	12.9
U.S.	87.0	88.9	84.3	86.3	65.7	30.3	31.6	20.0	52.1	14.7

Note: Figures shown cover persons 25 years old and over; (1) Figures cover the Milwaukee-Waukesha-West Allis, WI Metropolitan Statistical Area—see Appendix B for areas included; (2) People of Hispanic origin can be of any race
Source: U.S. Census Bureau, 2012-2016 American Community Survey 5-Year Estimates

School Enrollment by Grade and Control

Area	Preschool (%)		Kindergarten (%)		Grades 1 - 4 (%)		Grades 5 - 8 (%)		Grades 9 - 12 (%)	
	Public	Private	Public	Private	Public	Private	Public	Private	Public	Private
City	41.3	58.7	88.1	11.9	77.9	22.1	81.3	18.7	86.9	13.1
MSA[1]	53.5	46.5	77.3	22.7	80.4	19.6	79.7	20.3	85.4	14.6
U.S.	58.4	41.6	87.7	12.3	89.8	10.2	89.7	10.3	90.4	9.6

Note: Figures shown cover persons 3 years old and over; (1) Figures cover the Milwaukee-Waukesha-West Allis, WI Metropolitan Statistical Area—see Appendix B for areas included
Source: U.S. Census Bureau, 2012-2016 American Community Survey 5-Year Estimates

Average Salaries of Public School Classroom Teachers

Area	2015		2016		Change from 2015 to 2016	
	Dollars	Rank[1]	Dollars	Rank[1]	Percent	Rank[2]
Wisconsin	52,264	25	54,115	24	3.5	3
U.S. Average	57,611	–	58,353	–	1.3	–

Note: (1) Rank ranges from 1 to 51 where 1 indicates highest salary; (2) Rank ranges from 1 to 51 where 1 indicates highest percent change.
Source: National Education Association, Rankings & Estimates: Rankings of the States 2016 and Estimates of School Statistics 2017

Higher Education

Four-Year Colleges			Two-Year Colleges			Medical Schools[1]	Law Schools[2]	Voc/ Tech[3]
Public	Private Non-profit	Private For-profit	Public	Private Non-profit	Private For-profit			
0	0	0	0	0	0	0	0	0

Note: Figures cover institutions located within the city limits and include main campuses only; (1) includes schools accredited by the Liaison Committee on Medical Education and the American Osteopathic Association's Commission on Osteopathic College Accreditation; (2) includes ABA-accredited schools, schools with provisional ABA accreditation, and state accredited schools; (3) includes all schools with programs that are less than 2 years.
Source: National Center for Education Statistics, Integrated Postsecondary Education System (IPEDS), 2016-17; Wikipedia, List of Medical Schools in the United States, accessed April 2, 2018; Wikipedia, List of Law Schools in the United States, accessed April 2, 2018

According to *U.S. News & World Report,* the Milwaukee-Waukesha-West Allis, WI metro area is home to one of the best national universities in the U.S.: **Marquette University** (#90 tie). The indicators used to capture academic quality fall into a number of categories: assessment by administrators at peer institutions; retention of students; faculty resources; student selectivity; financial resources; alumni giving; high school counselor ratings of colleges; and graduation rate. *U.S. News & World Report, "America's Best Colleges 2018"*

According to *U.S. News & World Report,* the Milwaukee-Waukesha-West Allis, WI metro area is home to one of the top 100 law schools in the U.S.: **Marquette University** (#95 tie). The rankings are based on a weighted average of 12 measures of quality: peer assessment score; assessment score by lawyers/judges; median LSAT scores; median undergrad GPA; acceptance rate; employment rates for graduates; placement success; bar passage rate; faculty resources; expenditures per student; student/faculty ratio; and library resources. *U.S. News & World Report, "America's Best Graduate Schools, Law, 2019"*

According to *U.S. News & World Report,* the Milwaukee-Waukesha-West Allis, WI metro area is home to one of the top 75 medical schools for research in the U.S.: **Medical College of Wisconsin** (#72 tie). The rankings are based on a weighted average of 11 measures of quality: quality assessment; peer assessment score; assessment score by residency directors; research activity; total research activity; average research activity per faculty member; student selectivity; median MCAT total score; median undergraduate GPA; acceptance rate; and faculty resources. *U.S. News & World Report, "America's Best Graduate Schools, Medical, 2019"*

PRESIDENTIAL ELECTION

2016 Presidential Election Results

Area	Clinton	Trump	Johnson	Stein	Other
Waukesha County	33.3	60.0	3.7	0.7	2.2
U.S.	48.0	45.9	3.3	1.1	1.7

Note: Results are percentages and may not add to 100% due to rounding
Source: Dave Leip's Atlas of U.S. Presidential Elections

EMPLOYERS

Major Employers

Company Name	Industry
AT&T Wisconsin	Telecommunications
Aurora Health Care	Health care system
BMO Harris	Financial services
Briggs & Stratton Corp.	Manufacturer
Columbia St. Mary's	Health care system
Cooper Power Systems	Utilities
Froedtert Health	Health care
GE Healthcare	Diagnostic imaging, clinical info systems
Harley Davidson	Motorcycle manufacturing
Johnson Controls	Automotive
Kohl's Department Stores	Retail
Medical College of Wisconsin	Medical school
Northwestern Mutual	Insurance
Potawatomi Bingo Casino	Gaming & tourism
ProHealth Care, Inc.	Health care system
Quad/Graphics	Printer
Rockwell Automation	Info technologies
Roundy's Supermarkets, Inc.	Retail
SC Johnson	Manufacturer
U.S. Bank	Financial services
We Energies	Utilities
Wheaton Franciscan Healthcare	Health care system

Note: Companies shown are located within the Milwaukee-Waukesha-West Allis, WI Metropolitan Statistical Area.
Source: Hoovers.com; Wikipedia

PUBLIC SAFETY

Crime Rate

Area	All Crimes	Violent Crimes: Murder	Violent Crimes: Rape[3]	Violent Crimes: Robbery	Violent Crimes: Aggrav. Assault	Property Crimes: Burglary	Property Crimes: Larceny-Theft	Property Crimes: Motor Vehicle Theft
City	1,248.0	0.0	0.0	22.1	22.1	69.0	1,054.7	80.1
Metro[1]	3,373.6	9.9	40.5	232.1	373.5	512.0	1,746.6	459.0
U.S.	2,847.8	5.3	40.4	102.8	248.5	468.9	1,745.0	236.9

Note: Figures are crimes per 100,000 population; (1) Figures cover the Milwaukee-Waukesha-West Allis, WI Metropolitan Statistical Area—see Appendix B for areas included; (3) The city and U.S. figures shown were reported using the revised Uniform Crime Reporting (UCR) definition of rape. The metro area figures shown are an aggregate total of the data submitted using both the revised and legacy UCR definitions.
Source: FBI Uniform Crime Reports, 2016

Hate Crimes

Area	Number of Quarters Reported	Race/Ethnicity/Ancestry	Religion	Sexual Orientation	Disability	Gender	Gender Identity
		Number of Incidents per Bias Motivation					
City	4	0	0	0	0	0	0
U.S.	4	3,489	1,273	1,076	70	31	124

Source: Federal Bureau of Investigation, Hate Crime Statistics 2016

Identity Theft Consumer Reports

Area	Reports	Reports per 100,000 Population	Rank[2]
MSA[1]	1,322	84	171
U.S.	371,061	114	-

Note: (1) Figures cover the Milwaukee-Waukesha-West Allis, WI Metropolitan Statistical Area—see Appendix B for areas included; (2) Rank ranges from 1 to 389 where 1 indicates greatest number of identity theft reports per 100,000 population
Source: Federal Trade Commission, Consumer Sentinel Network Data Book for January–December 2017

Fraud and Other Consumer Reports

Area	Reports	Reports per 100,000 Population	Rank[2]
MSA[1]	8,076	514	97
U.S.	2,304,550	708	-

Note: (1) Figures cover the Milwaukee-Waukesha-West Allis, WI Metropolitan Statistical Area—see Appendix B for areas included; (2) Rank ranges from 1 to 389 where 1 indicates greatest number of fraud and other consumer reports per 100,000 population
Source: Federal Trade Commission, Consumer Sentinel Network Data Book for January–December 2017

SPORTS

Professional Sports Teams

Team Name	League	Year Established
Milwaukee Brewers	Major League Baseball (MLB)	1970
Milwaukee Bucks	National Basketball Association (NBA)	1968

Note: Includes teams located in the Milwaukee-Waukesha-West Allis, WI Metropolitan Statistical Area.
Source: Wikipedia, Major Professional Sports Teams of the United States and Canada, April 5, 2018

CLIMATE

Average and Extreme Temperatures

Temperature	Jan	Feb	Mar	Apr	May	Jun	Jul	Aug	Sep	Oct	Nov	Dec	Yr.
Extreme High (°F)	60	65	82	91	92	101	101	103	98	89	77	63	103
Average High (°F)	27	31	40	54	65	76	80	79	71	60	45	32	55
Average Temp. (°F)	20	24	33	45	55	66	71	70	62	51	38	25	47
Average Low (°F)	12	16	26	36	45	55	62	61	53	42	30	18	38
Extreme Low (°F)	-26	-19	-10	12	21	36	40	44	28	18	-5	-20	-26

Note: Figures cover the years 1948-1990
Source: National Climatic Data Center, International Station Meteorological Climate Summary, 9/96

Average Precipitation/Snowfall/Humidity

Precip./Humidity	Jan	Feb	Mar	Apr	May	Jun	Jul	Aug	Sep	Oct	Nov	Dec	Yr.
Avg. Precip. (in.)	1.6	1.4	2.6	3.3	2.9	3.4	3.6	3.4	2.9	2.3	2.3	2.2	32.0
Avg. Snowfall (in.)	13	10	9	2	Tr	0	0	0	0	Tr	3	11	49
Avg. Rel. Hum. 6am (%)	76	77	78	78	77	79	82	86	86	82	80	80	80
Avg. Rel. Hum. 3pm (%)	68	66	64	58	58	58	59	62	61	61	66	70	63

Note: Figures cover the years 1948-1990; Tr = Trace amounts (<0.05 in. of rain; <0.5 in. of snow)
Source: National Climatic Data Center, International Station Meteorological Climate Summary, 9/96

Weather Conditions

Temperature			Daytime Sky			Precipitation		
5°F & below	32°F & below	90°F & above	Clear	Partly cloudy	Cloudy	0.01 inch or more precip.	0.1 inch or more snow/ice	Thunder-storms
22	141	10	90	118	157	126	38	35

Note: Figures are average number of days per year and cover the years 1948-1990
Source: National Climatic Data Center, International Station Meteorological Climate Summary, 9/96

HAZARDOUS WASTE

Superfund Sites

The Milwaukee-Waukesha-West Allis, WI metro area is home to six sites on the EPA's Superfund National Priorities List: **Amcast Industrial Corporation** (final); **Lauer I Sanitary Landfill** (final); **Master Disposal Service Landfill** (final); **Moss-American Co., Inc. (Kerr-Mcgee Oil Co.)** (final); **Muskego Sanitary Landfill** (final); **Waste Management of Wisconsin, Inc.**

(Brookfield Sanitary Landfill) (final). There are a total of 1,396 Superfund sites with a status of proposed or final on the list in the U.S. *U.S. Environmental Protection Agency, National Priorities List, April 4, 2018*

AIR & WATER QUALITY

Air Quality Trends: Ozone

	1990	1995	2000	2005	2010	2012	2013	2014	2015	2016
MSA[1]	0.095	0.106	0.082	0.092	0.079	0.092	0.069	0.072	0.069	0.074
U.S.	0.087	0.089	0.081	0.079	0.073	0.075	0.069	0.067	0.068	0.069

Note: (1) Data covers the Milwaukee-Waukesha-West Allis, WI Metropolitan Statistical Area—see Appendix B for areas included. The values shown are the composite ozone concentration averages among trend sites based on the highest fourth daily maximum 8-hour concentration in parts per million. These trends are based on sites having an adequate record of monitoring data during the trend period. Data from exceptional events are included.
Source: U.S. Environmental Protection Agency, Air Quality Monitoring Information, "Air Quality Trends by City, 1990-2016"

Air Quality Index

Area	Percent of Days when Air Quality was...[2]					AQI Statistics[2]	
	Good	Moderate	Unhealthy for Sensitive Groups	Unhealthy	Very Unhealthy	Maximum	Median
MSA[1]	72.1	25.8	2.2	0.0	0.0	136	42

Note: (1) Data covers the Milwaukee-Waukesha-West Allis, WI Metropolitan Statistical Area—see Appendix B for areas included; (2) Based on 365 days with AQI data in 2017. Air Quality Index (AQI) is an index for reporting daily air quality. EPA calculates the AQI for five major air pollutants regulated by the Clean Air Act: ground-level ozone, particle pollution (aka particulate matter), carbon monoxide, sulfur dioxide, and nitrogen dioxide. The AQI runs from 0 to 500. The higher the AQI value, the greater the level of air pollution and the greater the health concern. There are six AQI categories: "Good" AQI is between 0 and 50. Air quality is considered satisfactory; "Moderate" AQI is between 51 and 100. Air quality is acceptable; "Unhealthy for Sensitive Groups" When AQI values are between 101 and 150, members of sensitive groups may experience health effects; "Unhealthy" When AQI values are between 151 and 200 everyone may begin to experience health effects; "Very Unhealthy" AQI values between 201 and 300 trigger a health alert; "Hazardous" AQI values over 300 trigger warnings of emergency conditions (not shown).
Source: U.S. Environmental Protection Agency, Air Quality Index Report, 2017

Air Quality Index Pollutants

Area	Percent of Days when AQI Pollutant was...[2]					
	Carbon Monoxide	Nitrogen Dioxide	Ozone	Sulfur Dioxide	Particulate Matter 2.5	Particulate Matter 10
MSA[1]	0.0	1.9	58.4	0.0	39.7	0.0

Note: (1) Data covers the Milwaukee-Waukesha-West Allis, WI Metropolitan Statistical Area—see Appendix B for areas included; (2) Based on 365 days with AQI data in 2017. The Air Quality Index (AQI) is an index for reporting daily air quality. EPA calculates the AQI for five major air pollutants regulated by the Clean Air Act: ground-level ozone, particle pollution (also known as particulate matter), carbon monoxide, sulfur dioxide, and nitrogen dioxide. The AQI runs from 0 to 500. The higher the AQI value, the greater the level of air pollution and the greater the health concern.
Source: U.S. Environmental Protection Agency, Air Quality Index Report, 2017

Maximum Air Pollutant Concentrations: Particulate Matter, Ozone, CO and Lead

	Particulate Matter 10 (ug/m^3)	Particulate Matter 2.5 Wtd AM (ug/m^3)	Particulate Matter 2.5 24-Hr (ug/m^3)	Ozone (ppm)	Carbon Monoxide (ppm)	Lead (ug/m^3)
MSA[1] Level	48	8.3	20	0.079	1	n/a
NAAQS[2]	150	15	35	0.075	9	0.15
Met NAAQS[2]	Yes	Yes	Yes	No	Yes	n/a

Note: (1) Data covers the Milwaukee-Waukesha-West Allis, WI Metropolitan Statistical Area—see Appendix B for areas included; Data from exceptional events are included; (2) National Ambient Air Quality Standards; ppm = parts per million; ug/m^3 = micrograms per cubic meter; n/a not available.
Concentrations: Particulate Matter 10 (coarse particulate)—highest second maximum 24-hour concentration; Particulate Matter 2.5 Wtd AM (fine particulate)—highest weighted annual mean concentration; Particulate Matter 2.5 24-Hour (fine particulate)—highest 98th percentile 24-hour concentration; Ozone—highest fourth daily maximum 8-hour concentration; Carbon Monoxide—highest second maximum non-overlapping 8-hour concentration; Lead—maximum running 3-month average
Source: U.S. Environmental Protection Agency, Air Quality Monitoring Information, "Air Quality Statistics by City, 2016"

Maximum Air Pollutant Concentrations: Nitrogen Dioxide and Sulfur Dioxide

	Nitrogen Dioxide AM (ppb)	Nitrogen Dioxide 1-Hr (ppb)	Sulfur Dioxide AM (ppb)	Sulfur Dioxide 1-Hr (ppb)	Sulfur Dioxide 24-Hr (ppb)
MSA[1] Level	14	49	n/a	6	n/a
NAAQS[2]	53	100	30	75	140
Met NAAQS[2]	Yes	Yes	n/a	Yes	n/a

Note: (1) Data covers the Milwaukee-Waukesha-West Allis, WI Metropolitan Statistical Area—see Appendix B for areas included; Data from exceptional events are included; (2) National Ambient Air Quality Standards; ppm = parts per million; ug/m^3 = micrograms per cubic meter; n/a not available.
Concentrations: Nitrogen Dioxide AM—highest arithmetic mean concentration; Nitrogen Dioxide 1-Hr—highest 98th percentile 1-hour daily maximum concentration; Sulfur Dioxide AM—highest annual mean concentration; Sulfur Dioxide 1-Hr—highest 99th percentile 1-hour daily maximum concentration; Sulfur Dioxide 24-Hr—highest second maximum 24-hour concentration
Source: U.S. Environmental Protection Agency, Air Quality Monitoring Information, "Air Quality Statistics by City, 2016"

Drinking Water

Water System Name	Pop. Served	Primary Water Source Type	Violations[1]	
			Health Based	Monitoring/ Reporting
Menomonee Falls WW-Groundwater	1,796	Ground	0	0
Menomonee Falls WW-Surface Water	23,867	Purchased Surface	0	2

Note: (1) Based on violation data from January 1, 2017 to December 31, 2017
Source: U.S. Environmental Protection Agency, Office of Ground Water and Drinking Water, Safe Drinking Water Information System (based on data extracted April 5, 2018)

Sun Prairie, Wisconsin

Background

Sun Prairie prides itself on being a small town with big city advantages. The community is located outside of Madison: far enough to still have a rural community feel but close enough to take advantage of all the amenities the city has to offer. However, as one of the fastest growing cities in the state of Wisconsin, Sun Prairie won't be able to call itself a "small town" for much longer.

The name "Sun Prairie" predates its actual settlement. In May of 1837 President Van Buren commissioned a company of over forty men to build a state capitol building in Madison, Wisconsin. Before reaching their destination, the group traveled for days in the pouring rain. Finally, on the 9th of June, as the clouds dissipated, the men came upon an open prairie with rays of sun shining up from the horizon. At this, one of the men carved the words "sun prairie" into a tree. It was not until years later that Charles Bird returned to the land and began its settlement.

Today, visitors and residents alike will find much to do and see in Sun Prairie. Angell Park Speedway offers midget auto racing. From spring through fall the city hosts a bustling farmers market. Sun Prairie Public Library and Sun Prairie Historical Museum both offer a stimulating educational experience. The streets of historic downtown are lined with specialty shopping boutiques and unique dining experiences. Sun Prairie is also the birthplace of world-renowned artist, Georgia O'Keeffe. The farmstead on which she was raised is open to the public for tours.

The Sun Prairie park system consists of more than 30 parks, a 13-diamond baseball complex, four soccer fields, 11 skating rinks, two sledding hills, a public golf course, and a YMCA. In addition, Sun Prairie has a fantastic family aquatic facility that features waterslides, a sandy play area, and a zero depth pool for swimming. Patrick Marsh, a natural wetland area on the northeast side of Sun Prairie, provides the opportunity for a scenic nature walk and offers a tranquil escape from busy city life. There are several attractions in the area, just a short drive from Sun Prairie. These include House on the Rock, the Wisconsin Dells, and the recreation sites of Lake Mendota and Lake Monona.

The city's claim to fame is that the quality of life its residents experience is unparalleled in excellence. To start, Sun Prairie offers residents a small town atmosphere without depriving them of any of the amenities and conveniences of a larger metropolis. The array of housing opportunities range from reasonably priced, affordable starter homes to more expensive, luxury houses built for executives and professionals.

The city is also known for its exceptional educational system, comprised of schools that consistently perform well above the state average. The nearness to the University of Wisconsin-Madison is an added educational bonus. Access to quality health care is provided by two clinics in Sun Prairie and is served by three regional hospitals. Finding qualified child care providers is easy with over 40 licensed daycare facilities in the area. As a community, Sun Prairie has made a commitment to providing superior care to its senior citizens and is home to 13 senior living facilities.

The Sun Prairie Area School District serves nearly 6,000 students annually. Their vision is that by working together to provide high quality education for all students, they will build a community of life-long learners, prepared for both higher education and their roles as citizens. The district is comprised of six elementary schools, two middle schools, one senior high school, an alternative high school, and four parochial schools. Nearby is world-class University of Wisconsin-Madison, internationally acclaimed for its academic excellence.

As Sun Prairie continues to expand, the city emphasizes diversification of its economic resources. By balancing the rate at which commercial, residential, and industrial development takes place, the city ensures a high quality of life for its residents. Sun Prairie relies on its location, exponential growth, unparalleled transportation access, affordable utilities, and access to a skilled labor force to attract new business to the area. A downtown revitalization project was recently completed.

Sun Prairie is located only minutes away from Dane County Regional Airport.

Sun Prairie is in the warm summer humid continental climate zone. Summers tend to be hot and humid. The warmest month of the year is July and the coldest month of the year is January. The city of Sun Prairie encounters occasional flooding because of the presence of hydric soils, spring melting and its proximity to the Koshkonong Creek. This condition is compounded by storm water runoff from development and urbanization in the upper reaches of the watershed. Many residents of the city believe that the problems with flooding are worsening, becoming more frequent over the last 14 years.

Rankings

General Rankings

- *US News & World Report* conducted a survey of more than 2,000 people and analyzed the 125 largest metropolitan areas to determine what matters the most when selecting the next place to live. Madison* ranked #16 out of the top 25 as having the best combination of desirable factors. Criteria: cost of living; quality of education; job market, crime rates; and other factors. *realestate.usnews.com, "The 25 Best Places to Live in the U.S. in 2018," April 10, 2018*

Business/Finance Rankings

- The personal finance site NerdWallet analyzed 183 American metropolitan areas with populations over 250,000 and more than 15,000 businesses to rank where entrepreneurs find the most success. Criteria included area economy, annual income, housing cost, unemployment rate, and the success rate of area businesses. Madison* ranked #40. *www.nerdwallet.com, "Best Places to Start a Business," April 27, 2015*
- The Brookings Institution ranked the 100 largest metro areas in the U.S. based on income inequality. Madison* was ranked #95 (#1 = greatest ineqality). Criteria: the "95/20 ratio," a figure representing the income at which a household earns more than 95 percent of all other households, divided by the income at which a household earns more than only 20 percent of all other households. *Brookings Institution, "Household Income Inequality, 100 Largest U.S. Metro Areas, 2014-2016," February 5, 2018*
- The Madison* metro area appeared on the Milken Institute "2017 Best Performing Cities" list. Rank: #58 out of 200 large metro areas. Criteria: job growth; wage and salary growth; high-tech output growth. *Milken Institute, "Best-Performing Cities 2017," January 2018*
- *Forbes* ranked the 200 most populous metro areas to determine the nation's "Best Places for Business and Careers." The Madison* metro area was ranked #49. Criteria: costs (business and living); job growth (past and projected); income growth; quality of life; educational attainment (college and high school); projected economic growth; cultural and recreational opportunities; net migration patterns; number of highly ranked colleges. *Forbes, "The Best Places for Business and Careers 2017," October 24, 2017*

Children/Family Rankings

- *Forbes* analyzed data on the 100 largest metropolitan areas in the United States to compile its 2016 ranking of the best cities for raising a family. The Madison* metro area was ranked #12. Criteria: median income; childcare costs; percent of population under 18; commuting delays; crime rate; percentage of families owning homes; education quality (mainly test scores). Overall cost of living and housing affordability was also unofficially considered. *Forbes, "America's Best Cities for Raising a Family 2016," August 30, 2016*

Education Rankings

- Madison* was identified as one of America's "smartest" metropolitan areas by *The Business Journals*. The area ranked #2 out of 10. Criteria: percentage of adults (25 and older) with high school diplomas, bachelor's degrees and graduate degrees. *The Business Journals, "Where the Brainpower Is: Exclusive U.S. Rankings, Insights," February 27, 2014*
- Personal finance website *WalletHub* analyzed the 150 largest U.S. metropolitan statistical areas to determine where the most educated Americans are choosing to settle. Criteria: education quality and attainment gap; education levels; percentage of workers with degrees; public school rankings; quality and size of each metro area's universities. Madison* was ranked #5 (#1 = most educated city). *www.WalletHub.com, "2017's Most and Least Educated Cities in America," July 25, 2017*

Environmental Rankings

- Sperling's BestPlaces assessed 379 metropolitan areas of the United States for the likelihood of dangerously extreme weather events or earthquakes. In general the Southeast and South-Central regions have the highest risk of weather extremes and earthquakes, while the Pacific Northwest enjoys the lowest risk. Of the least risky metropolitan areas, the Madison* metro area was ranked #185. *www.bestplaces.net, "Safest Places from Natural Disasters," April 2011*

Health/Fitness Rankings

- Madison* was identified as a "2016 Spring Allergy Capital." The area ranked #26 out of 100. Three groups of factors were used to identify the most severe cities for people with allergies during the spring season: annual pollen levels; medicine utilization; access to board-certified allergists. *Asthma and Allergy Foundation of America, "Spring Allergy Capitals 2016"*
- Madison* was identified as a "2016 Fall Allergy Capital." The area ranked #25 out of 100. Three groups of factors were used to identify the most severe cities for people with allergies during the fall season: annual pollen levels; medicine utilization; access to board-certified allergists. *Asthma and Allergy Foundation of America, "Fall Allergy Capitals 2016"*
- Madison* was identified as a "2015 Asthma Capital." The area ranked #81 out of the nation's 100 largest metropolitan areas. Criteria: estimated prevalence; self-reported prevalence; crude death rate for asthma; annual pollen score; annual air quality; public smoking laws; number of board-certified asthma specialists; school inhaler access laws; rescue medication use; controller medication use; ER visits for asthma; uninsured rate; poverty rate. *Asthma and Allergy Foundation of America, "Asthma Capitals 2015"*
- The Madison* metro area ranked #61 out of 189 in The Gallup-Healthways Well-Being Index. Criteria: purpose; social well being; financial health; community and physical health. Results are based on telephone interviews with adults, aged 18 and older, living in metropolitan areas in the 50 U.S. states and the District of Columbia. *Gallup-Healthways, "State of American Well-Being, 2017 Community Well-Being Rankings" March 2018*

Real Estate Rankings

- Madison* was ranked #116 out of 238 metro areas in terms of housing affordability in 2017 by the National Association of Home Builders (#1 = most affordable). Criteria: the share of homes sold in that area affordable to a family earning the local median income, based on standard mortgage underwriting criteria. *National Association of Home Builders®, NAHB-Wells Fargo Housing Opportunity Index, 4th Quarter 2017*

Safety Rankings

- The National Insurance Crime Bureau ranked 382 metro areas in the U.S. in terms of per capita rates of vehicle theft. The Madison* metro area ranked #318 (#1 = highest rate). Criteria: number of vehicle theft offenses per 100,000 inhabitants in 2016. *National Insurance Crime Bureau, "Hot Spots 2016," June 8, 2017*

Seniors/Retirement Rankings

- From its Best Cities for Successful Aging indexes, the Milken Institute generated rankings for metropolitan areas, weighing data in nine categories—health care, wellness, living arrangements, transportation and convenience, financial characteristics, education, employment, community engagement, and overall livability. The Madison* metro area was ranked #2 overall in the large metro area category. *Milken Institute, "Best Cities for Successful Aging, 2017" March 14, 2017*

Miscellaneous Rankings

- Of the American metro areas that allow medical or recreational use of marijuana, the Madison* metro area was identified by CNBC editors as one of the most livable for marijuana lovers. Criteria included the Sperling's BestPlaces assessment of marijuana-friendly cities in terms of sound economy, cultural diversity, and a healthy population, plus cost-of-living index and high-quality schools. *www.cnbc.com, "The Best Cities to Live for Marijuana Lovers," February 5, 2014*

  *Sun Prairie is located within the Madison, WI Metropolitan Statistical Area.

Business Environment

CITY FINANCES

City Government Finances

Component	2015 ($000)	2015 ($ per capita)
Total Revenues	69,663	2,152
Total Expenditures	63,169	1,952
Debt Outstanding	62,130	1,920
Cash and Securities[1]	68,965	2,131

Note: (1) Cash and security holdings of a government at the close of its fiscal year,, including those of its dependent agencies, utilities, and liquor stores.
Source: U.S Census Bureau, State & Local Government Finances 2015

City Government Revenue by Source

Source	2015 ($000)	2015 ($ per capita)	2015 (%)
General Revenue			
From Federal Government	3	0	0.0
From State Government	5,024	155	7.2
From Local Governments	626	19	0.9
Taxes			
Property	21,566	666	31.0
Sales and Gross Receipts	73	2	0.1
Personal Income	0	0	0.0
Corporate Income	0	0	0.0
Motor Vehicle License	0	0	0.0
Other Taxes	1,518	47	2.2
Current Charges	8,876	274	12.7
Liquor Store	0	0	0.0
Utility	30,198	933	43.3
Employee Retirement	0	0	0.0

Source: U.S Census Bureau, State & Local Government Finances 2015

City Government Expenditures by Function

Function	2015 ($000)	2015 ($ per capita)	2015 (%)
General Direct Expenditures			
Air Transportation	0	0	0.0
Corrections	0	0	0.0
Education	0	0	0.0
Employment Security Administration	0	0	0.0
Financial Administration	882	27	1.4
Fire Protection	807	24	1.3
General Public Buildings	281	8	0.4
Governmental Administration, Other	1,587	49	2.5
Health	1,570	48	2.5
Highways	7,896	244	12.5
Hospitals	0	0	0.0
Housing and Community Development	3	< 1	< 0.1
Interest on General Debt	2,014	62	3.2
Judicial and Legal	341	10	0.5
Libraries	1,729	53	2.7
Parking	0	0	0.0
Parks and Recreation	2,228	68	3.5
Police Protection	7,350	227	11.6
Public Welfare	0	0	0.0
Sewerage	3,205	99	5.1
Solid Waste Management	1,417	43	2.2
Veterans' Services	0	0	0.0
Liquor Store	0	0	0.0
Utility	29,685	917	47.0
Employee Retirement	0	0	0.0

Source: U.S Census Bureau, State & Local Government Finances 2015

DEMOGRAPHICS

Population Growth

Area	1990 Census	2000 Census	2010 Census	2016* Estimate	Population Growth (%) 1990-2016	2010-2016
City	15,836	20,369	29,364	31,721	100.3	8.0
MSA[1]	432,323	501,774	568,593	634,269	46.7	11.6
U.S.	248,709,873	281,421,906	308,745,538	318,558,162	28.1	3.2

Note: (1) Figures cover the Madison, WI Metropolitan Statistical Area—see Appendix B for areas included; (*) 2012-2016 5-year estimated population
Source: U.S. Census Bureau, 1990 Census, Census 2000, Census 2010, 2012-2016 American Community Survey 5-Year Estimates

Household Size

Area	Persons in Household (%) One	Two	Three	Four	Five	Six	Seven or More	Average Household Size
City	28.9	32.4	15.3	13.5	6.2	2.0	1.6	2.50
MSA[1]	29.6	36.9	14.3	12.1	4.8	1.5	0.8	2.40
U.S.	27.7	33.7	15.7	13.1	6.0	2.3	1.5	2.60

Note: (1) Figures cover the Madison, WI Metropolitan Statistical Area—see Appendix B for areas included
Source: U.S. Census Bureau, 2012-2016 American Community Survey 5-Year Estimates

Race

Area	White Alone[2] (%)	Black Alone[2] (%)	Asian Alone[2] (%)	AIAN[3] Alone[2] (%)	NHOPI[4] Alone[2] (%)	Other Race Alone[2] (%)	Two or More Races (%)
City	83.8	7.0	4.5	0.1	0.0	1.4	3.1
MSA[1]	86.4	4.4	4.6	0.3	0.0	1.7	2.6
U.S.	73.3	12.6	5.2	0.8	0.2	4.8	3.1

Note: (1) Figures cover the Madison, WI Metropolitan Statistical Area—see Appendix B for areas included; (2) Alone is defined as not being in combination with one or more other races; (3) American Indian and Alaska Native; (4) Native Hawaiian and Other Pacific Islander
Source: U.S. Census Bureau, 2012-2016 American Community Survey 5-Year Estimates

Hispanic or Latino Origin

Area	Total (%)	Mexican (%)	Puerto Rican (%)	Cuban (%)	Other (%)
City	5.0	3.1	0.2	0.4	1.3
MSA[1]	5.6	3.9	0.4	0.1	1.1
U.S.	17.3	11.0	1.7	0.7	4.0

Note: Persons of Hispanic or Latino origin can be of any race; (1) Figures cover the Madison, WI Metropolitan Statistical Area—see Appendix B for areas included
Source: U.S. Census Bureau, 2012-2016 American Community Survey 5-Year Estimates

Segregation

Type	Segregation Indices[1] 1990	2000	2010	2010 Rank[2]	Percent Change 1990-2000	1990-2010	2000-2010
Black/White	52.1	49.9	49.6	71	-2.2	-2.6	-0.3
Asian/White	54.5	49.5	44.2	29	-5.0	-10.3	-5.3
Hispanic/White	31.1	38.7	40.1	65	7.7	9.1	1.4

Note: All figures cover the Metropolitan Statistical Area—see Appendix B for areas included; Figures are based on an analysis of 1990, 2000, and 2010 Census Decennial Census tract data by William H. Frey, Brookings Institution and the University of Michigan Social Science Data Analysis Network. In this analysis all racial groups (whites, blacks, and asians) are non-Hispanic members of those races. Hispanics are shown as a separate category; (1) Segregation Indices are Dissimilarity Indices that measure the degree to which the minority group is distributed differently than whites across census tracts. They range from 0 (complete integration) to 100 (complete segregation) where the value indicates the percentage of the minority group that needs to move to be distributed exactly like whites; (2) Ranges from 1 (most segregated) to 102 (least segregated); n/a not available.
Source: www.CensusScope.org

Ancestry

Area	German	Irish	English	American	Italian	Polish	French[2]	Scottish	Dutch
City	40.9	13.1	7.1	4.3	3.1	6.5	1.9	0.9	3.1
MSA[1]	39.5	13.8	8.9	3.2	3.6	5.3	2.9	1.5	2.1
U.S.	14.4	10.4	7.7	6.9	5.4	2.9	2.6	1.7	1.3

Note: Figures are the percentage of the total population reporting a particular ancestry. The nine most commonly reported ancestries in the U.S. are shown. Figures include multiple ancestries (e.g. if a person reported being Irish and Italian, they were included in both columns); (1) Figures cover the Madison, WI Metropolitan Statistical Area—see Appendix B for areas included; (2) Excludes Basque
Source: U.S. Census Bureau, 2012-2016 American Community Survey 5-Year Estimates

Foreign-Born Population

Area	Percent of Population Born in								
	Any Foreign Country	Asia	Mexico	Europe	Carribean	Central America[2]	South America	Africa	Canada
City	6.1	2.6	1.0	0.9	0.0	0.3	0.1	0.9	0.3
MSA[1]	7.1	3.2	1.6	1.0	0.1	0.2	0.3	0.4	0.2
U.S.	13.2	4.0	3.6	1.5	1.3	1.0	0.9	0.6	0.3

Note: (1) Figures cover the Madison, WI Metropolitan Statistical Area—see Appendix B for areas included; (2) Excludes Mexico.
Source: U.S. Census Bureau, 2012-2016 American Community Survey 5-Year Estimates

Marital Status

Area	Never Married	Now Married[2]	Separated	Widowed	Divorced
City	31.5	51.2	1.7	5.2	10.5
MSA[1]	35.7	49.2	1.1	4.3	9.7
U.S.	33.0	48.1	2.1	5.9	11.0

Note: Figures are percentages and cover the population 15 years of age and older; (1) Figures cover the Madison, WI Metropolitan Statistical Area—see Appendix B for areas included; (2) Excludes separated
Source: U.S. Census Bureau, 2012-2016 American Community Survey 5-Year Estimates

Disability Status

Area	All Ages	Under 18 Years Old	18 to 64 Years Old	65 Years and Over
City	10.4	3.9	9.0	35.8
MSA[1]	9.3	3.6	7.4	29.4
U.S.	12.5	4.1	10.3	35.7

Note: Figures show percent of the civilian noninstitutionalized population that reported having a disability. Disability status is determined from six types of difficulty: vision, hearing, cognitive, ambulatory, self-care, and independent living. For children under 5 years old, hearing and vision difficulty are used to determine disability status. For children between the ages of 5 and 14, disability status is determined from hearing, vision, cognitive, ambulatory, and self-care difficulties. For people aged 15 years and older, they are considered to have a disability if they have difficulty with any one of the six difficulty types; Note: (1) Figures cover the Madison, WI Metropolitan Statistical Area—see Appendix B for areas included
Source: U.S. Census Bureau, 2012-2016 American Community Survey 5-Year Estimates

Age

Area	Percent of Population									Median Age
	Under Age 5	Age 5–19	Age 20–34	Age 35–44	Age 45–54	Age 55–64	Age 65–74	Age 75–84	Age 85+	
City	7.4	21.6	22.1	14.5	13.0	10.4	6.9	2.7	1.3	34.3
MSA[1]	5.9	18.6	24.2	12.7	13.3	12.4	7.4	3.6	1.8	35.9
U.S.	6.2	19.6	20.7	12.7	13.6	12.6	8.3	4.3	1.9	37.7

Note: (1) Figures cover the Madison, WI Metropolitan Statistical Area—see Appendix B for areas included
Source: U.S. Census Bureau, 2012-2016 American Community Survey 5-Year Estimates

Gender

Area	Males	Females	Males per 100 Females
City	15,350	16,371	93.8
MSA[1]	315,443	318,826	98.9
U.S.	156,765,322	161,792,840	96.9

Note: (1) Figures cover the Madison, WI Metropolitan Statistical Area—see Appendix B for areas included
Source: U.S. Census Bureau, 2012-2016 American Community Survey 5-Year Estimates

Religious Groups by Family

Area	Catholic	Baptist	Non-Den.	Methodist[2]	Lutheran	LDS[3]	Pentecostal	Presbyterian[4]	Muslim[5]	Judaism
MSA[1]	21.8	1.1	1.6	3.7	12.8	0.5	0.4	2.2	0.5	0.5
U.S.	19.1	9.3	4.0	4.0	2.3	2.0	1.9	1.6	0.8	0.7

Note: Figures are the number of adherents as a percentage of the total population; (1) Figures cover the Madison, WI Metropolitan Statistical Area—see Appendix B for areas included; (2) Methodist/Pietist; (3) Latter Day Saints; (4) Reformed; (5) Figures are estimates
Source: Association of Statisticians of American Religious Bodies, 2010 U.S. Religion Census: Religious Congregations & Membership Study

Religious Groups by Tradition

Area	Catholic	Evangelical Protestant	Mainline Protestant	Other Tradition	Black Protestant	Orthodox
MSA[1]	21.8	7.3	15.4	2.3	0.1	0.1
U.S.	19.1	16.2	7.3	4.3	1.6	0.3

Note: Figures are the number of adherents as a percentage of the total population; (1) Figures cover the Madison, WI Metropolitan Statistical Area—see Appendix B for areas included
Source: Association of Statisticians of American Religious Bodies, 2010 U.S. Religion Census: Religious Congregations & Membership Study

ECONOMY

Gross Metropolitan Product

Area	2014	2015	2016	2017	Rank[2]
MSA[1]	43.6	45.3	47.1	49.5	62

Note: Figures are in billions of dollars; (1) Figures cover the Madison, WI Metropolitan Statistical Area—see Appendix B for areas included; (2) Rank is based on 2015 data and ranges from 1 to 381
Source: The U.S. Conference of Mayors, U.S. Metro Economies: GMP and Employment Report, 2015-2017

Economic Growth

Area	2012-14 (%)	2015 (%)	2016 (%)	2017 (%)	Rank[2]
MSA[1]	1.7	2.6	2.4	3.1	143
U.S.	2.0	2.4	1.9	2.6	–

Note: Figures are real gross metropolitan product (GMP) growth rates and represent average annual percent change; (1) Figures cover the Madison, WI Metropolitan Statistical Area—see Appendix B for areas included; (2) Rank is based on 2012-2014 average annual percent change and ranges from 1 to 381
Source: The U.S. Conference of Mayors, U.S. Metro Economies: GMP and Employment Report, 2015-2017

Metropolitan Area Exports

Area	2011	2012	2013	2014	2015	2016	Rank[2]
MSA[1]	1,958.1	2,168.7	2,292.1	2,369.5	2,280.4	2,204.8	91

Note: Figures are in millions of dollars; (1) Figures cover the Madison, WI Metropolitan Statistical Area—see Appendix B for areas included; (2) Rank is based on 2016 data and ranges from 1 to 385
Source: U.S. Department of Commerce, International Trade Administration, Office of Trade & Industry Information, Manufacturing & Services, data extracted March 15, 2018

Building Permits

Area	Single-Family			Multi-Family			Total		
	2016	2017p	Pct. Chg.	2016	2017p	Pct. Chg.	2016	2017p	Pct. Chg.
City	149	138	-7.4	20	416	1,980.0	169	554	227.8
MSA[1]	1,598	1,645	2.9	3,332	3,025	-9.2	4,930	4,670	-5.3
U.S.	750,800	817,300	8.9	455,800	446,800	-2.0	1,206,600	1,264,100	4.8

Note: (1) Figures cover the Madison, WI Metropolitan Statistical Area—see Appendix B for areas included; Figures represent new, privately-owned housing units authorized (unadjusted data); All permit data are based on estimates with imputation; (p) preliminary data.
Source: U.S. Census Bureau, Manufacturing, Mining, and Construction Statistics, Building Permits, 2016, 2017

Bankruptcy Filings

Area	Business Filings			Nonbusiness Filings		
	2016	2017	% Chg.	2016	2017	% Chg.
Dane County	28	26	-7.1	748	774	3.5
U.S.	24,114	23,157	-4.0	770,846	765,863	-0.6

Note: Business filings include Chapter 7, Chapter 11, Chapter 12, and Chapter 13; Nonbusiness filings include Chapter 7, Chapter 11, and Chapter 13
Source: Administrative Office of the U.S. Courts, Business and Nonbusiness Bankruptcy, County Cases Commenced by Chapter of the Bankruptcy Code, During the 12-Month Period Ending December 31, 2016 and Business and Nonbusiness Bankruptcy, County Cases Commenced by Chapter of the Bankruptcy Code, During the 12-Month Period Ending December 31, 2017

Housing Vacancy Rates

Area	Gross Vacancy Rate[2] (%)			Year-Round Vacancy Rate[3] (%)			Rental Vacancy Rate[4] (%)			Homeowner Vacancy Rate[5] (%)		
	2015	2016	2017	2015	2016	2017	2015	2016	2017	2015	2016	2017
MSA[1]	n/a	n/a	n/a	n/a	n/a	n/a	n/a	n/a	n/a	n/a	n/a	n/a
U.S.	12.9	12.8	12.7	10.0	9.9	9.9	7.1	6.9	7.2	1.8	1.7	1.6

Note: (1) Figures cover the Madison, WI Metropolitan Statistical Area—see Appendix B for areas included; (2) The percentage of the total housing inventory that is vacant; (3) The percentage of the housing inventory (excluding seasonal units) that is year-round vacant; (4) The percentage of rental inventory that is vacant for rent; (5) The percentage of homeowner inventory that is vacant for sale; n/a not available
Source: U.S. Census Bureau, Housing Vacancies and Homeownership Annual Statistics: 2015, 2016, 2017

INCOME

Income

Area	Per Capita ($)	Median Household ($)	Average Household ($)
City	30,373	65,203	76,418
MSA[1]	34,548	63,642	82,875
U.S.	29,829	55,322	77,866

Note: (1) Figures cover the Madison, WI Metropolitan Statistical Area—see Appendix B for areas included
Source: U.S. Census Bureau, 2012-2016 American Community Survey 5-Year Estimates

Household Income Distribution

Area	Percent of Households Earning							
	Under $15,000	$15,000 -$24,999	$25,000 -$34,999	$35,000 -$49,999	$50,000 -$74,999	$75,000 -$99,999	$100,000 -$149,999	$150,000 and up
City	6.4	7.7	8.9	14.3	20.9	15.0	17.5	9.5
MSA[1]	9.1	8.0	9.2	12.8	18.8	14.3	16.2	11.6
U.S.	12.1	10.2	9.9	13.2	17.8	12.2	13.5	11.1

Note: (1) Figures cover the Madison, WI Metropolitan Statistical Area—see Appendix B for areas included
Source: U.S. Census Bureau, 2012-2016 American Community Survey 5-Year Estimates

Poverty Rate

Area	All Ages	Under 18 Years Old	18 to 64 Years Old	65 Years and Over
City	9.5	14.4	8.0	5.9
MSA[1]	12.0	12.8	12.9	5.6
U.S.	15.1	21.2	14.2	9.3

Note: Figures are percentage of people whose income during the past 12 months was below the poverty level; (1) Figures cover the Madison, WI Metropolitan Statistical Area—see Appendix B for areas included
Source: U.S. Census Bureau, 2012-2016 American Community Survey 5-Year Estimates

EMPLOYMENT

Labor Force and Employment

Area	Civilian Labor Force			Workers Employed		
	Dec. 2016	Dec. 2017	% Chg.	Dec. 2016	Dec. 2017	% Chg.
City	19,617	19,856	1.2	19,165	19,455	1.5
MSA[1]	385,845	390,310	1.2	376,538	382,618	1.6
U.S.	158,968,000	159,880,000	0.6	151,798,000	153,602,000	1.2

Note: Data is not seasonally adjusted and covers workers 16 years of age and older; (1) Figures cover the Madison, WI Metropolitan Statistical Area—see Appendix B for areas included
Source: Bureau of Labor Statistics, Local Area Unemployment Statistics

Unemployment Rate

Area	2017											
	Jan.	Feb.	Mar.	Apr.	May	Jun.	Jul.	Aug.	Sep.	Oct.	Nov.	Dec.
City	2.8	2.9	2.4	2.2	2.3	2.8	2.6	2.6	2.3	2.2	2.2	2.0
MSA[1]	3.0	3.1	2.6	2.3	2.4	2.8	2.6	2.4	2.3	2.2	2.1	2.0
U.S.	5.1	4.9	4.6	4.1	4.1	4.5	4.6	4.5	4.1	3.9	3.9	3.9

Note: Data is not seasonally adjusted and covers workers 16 years of age and older; (1) Figures cover the Madison, WI Metropolitan Statistical Area—see Appendix B for areas included
Source: Bureau of Labor Statistics, Local Area Unemployment Statistics

Average Wages

Occupation	$/Hr.	Occupation	$/Hr.
Accountants and Auditors	32.70	Maids and Housekeeping Cleaners	11.10
Automotive Mechanics	20.40	Maintenance and Repair Workers	19.90
Bookkeepers	19.10	Marketing Managers	58.80
Carpenters	27.60	Nuclear Medicine Technologists	n/a
Cashiers	10.30	Nurses, Licensed Practical	22.30
Clerks, General Office	17.50	Nurses, Registered	37.90
Clerks, Receptionists/Information	14.00	Nursing Assistants	15.30
Clerks, Shipping/Receiving	16.90	Packers and Packagers, Hand	16.40
Computer Programmers	36.30	Physical Therapists	38.60
Computer Systems Analysts	42.30	Postal Service Mail Carriers	23.80
Computer User Support Specialists	26.40	Real Estate Brokers	n/a
Cooks, Restaurant	12.70	Retail Salespersons	12.20
Dentists	102.30	Sales Reps., Exc. Tech./Scientific	32.50
Electrical Engineers	45.60	Sales Reps., Tech./Scientific	35.00
Electricians	26.40	Secretaries, Exc. Legal/Med./Exec.	18.70
Financial Managers	62.80	Security Guards	14.20
First-Line Supervisors/Managers, Sales	21.00	Surgeons	136.50
Food Preparation Workers	11.50	Teacher Assistants*	14.10
General and Operations Managers	60.40	Teachers, Elementary School*	27.80
Hairdressers/Cosmetologists	17.20	Teachers, Secondary School*	26.70
Internists, General	108.90	Telemarketers	14.30
Janitors and Cleaners	13.40	Truck Drivers, Heavy/Tractor-Trailer	23.10
Landscaping/Groundskeeping Workers	15.00	Truck Drivers, Light/Delivery Svcs.	18.40
Lawyers	60.30	Waiters and Waitresses	14.10

Note: Wage data covers the Madison, WI Metropolitan Statistical Area—see Appendix B for areas included; (*) Hourly wages for elementary/secondary school teachers and teacher assistants were calculated by the editors from annual wage data based on a 40 hour work week; n/a not available.
Source: Bureau of Labor Statistics, Metro Area Occupational Employment & Wage Estimates, May 2017

Employment by Occupation

Occupation Classification	City (%)	MSA[1] (%)	U.S. (%)
Management, Business, Science, and Arts	43.0	46.4	37.0
Natural Resources, Construction, and Maintenance	5.6	6.6	8.9
Production, Transportation, and Material Moving	10.2	9.8	12.2
Sales and Office	25.5	21.7	23.8
Service	15.7	15.4	18.1

Note: Figures cover employed civilians 16 years of age and older; (1) Figures cover the Madison, WI Metropolitan Statistical Area—see Appendix B for areas included
Source: U.S. Census Bureau, 2012-2016 American Community Survey 5-Year Estimates

Employment by Industry

Sector	MSA[1] Number of Employees	MSA[1] Percent of Total	U.S. Percent of Total
Construction, Mining, and Logging	17,300	4.3	5.2
Education and Health Services	48,700	12.0	15.9
Financial Activities	23,300	5.7	5.7
Government	86,600	21.3	15.3
Information	17,300	4.3	1.9
Leisure and Hospitality	37,900	9.3	10.7
Manufacturing	34,800	8.6	8.5
Other Services	20,300	5.0	3.9
Professional and Business Services	52,000	12.8	14.0
Retail Trade	43,100	10.6	11.0
Transportation, Warehousing, and Utilities	9,900	2.4	4.1
Wholesale Trade	14,800	3.6	4.0

Note: Figures are non-farm employment as of December 2017. Figures are not seasonally adjusted and include workers 16 years of age and older; (1) Figures cover the Madison, WI Metropolitan Statistical Area—see Appendix B for areas included
Source: Bureau of Labor Statistics, Current Employment Statistics, Employment, Hours, and Earnings

Occupations with Greatest Projected Employment Growth: 2017 – 2019

Occupation[1]	2017 Employment	2019 Projected Employment	Numeric Employment Change	Percent Employment Change
Personal Care Aides	67,040	71,960	4,920	7.3
Combined Food Preparation and Serving Workers, Including Fast Food	67,080	69,290	2,210	3.3
Janitors and Cleaners, Except Maids and Housekeeping Cleaners	48,250	49,690	1,440	3.0
Laborers and Freight, Stock, and Material Movers, Hand	57,070	58,260	1,190	2.1
Sales Representatives, Wholesale and Manufacturing, Except Technical and Scientific Products	43,060	44,250	1,190	2.8
Registered Nurses	57,240	58,170	930	1.6
Maintenance and Repair Workers, General	33,060	33,980	920	2.8
General and Operations Managers	37,020	37,900	880	2.4
Elementary School Teachers, Except Special Education	34,520	35,260	740	2.2
Software Developers, Applications	12,140	12,870	730	6.1

Note: Projections cover Wisconsin; (1) Sorted by numeric employment change
Source: www.projectionscentral.com, State Occupational Projections, 2017–2019 Short-Term Projections

Fastest Growing Occupations: 2017 – 2019

Occupation[1]	2017 Employment	2019 Projected Employment	Numeric Employment Change	Percent Employment Change
Septic Tank Servicers and Sewer Pipe Cleaners	700	760	60	8.2
Personal Care Aides	67,040	71,960	4,920	7.3
Musicians and Singers	850	900	50	6.5
Appraisers and Assessors of Real Estate	1,250	1,330	80	6.3
Software Developers, Applications	12,140	12,870	730	6.1
Home Health Aides	7,640	8,090	450	6.0
Computer Numerically Controlled Machine Tool Programmers, Metal and Plastic	1,470	1,560	90	5.8
Health Specialties Teachers, Postsecondary	6,570	6,940	370	5.7
Fundraisers	2,370	2,500	130	5.3
Nursing Instructors and Teachers, Postsecondary	1,670	1,760	90	5.3

Note: Projections cover Wisconsin; (1) Sorted by percent employment change and excludes occupations with numeric employment change less than 50
Source: www.projectionscentral.com, State Occupational Projections, 2017–2019 Short-Term Projections

TAXES

State Corporate Income Tax Rates

State	Tax Rate (%)	Income Brackets ($)	Num. of Brackets	Financial Institution Tax Rate (%)[a]	Federal Income Tax Ded.
Wisconsin	7.9	Flat rate	1	7.9	No

Note: Tax rates as of January 1, 2018; (a) Rates listed are the corporate income tax rate applied to financial institutions or excise taxes based on income. Some states have other taxes based upon the value of deposits or shares.
Source: Federation of Tax Administrators, Range of State Corporate Income Tax Rates, January 1, 2018

State Individual Income Tax Rates

State	Tax Rate (%)	Income Brackets ($)	Num. of Brackets	Personal Exempt. ($)[1]		Fed. Inc. Tax Ded.
				Single	Dependents	
Wisconsin (a)	4.0 - 7.65	11,450 - 252,150 (x)	4	700	700	No

Note: Tax rates as of January 1, 2018; Local- and county-level taxes are not included; n/a not applicable; (1) Married joint filers generally receive double the single exemption; (a) 19 states have statutory provision for automatically adjusting to the rate of inflation the dollar values of the income tax brackets, standard deductions, and/or personal exemptions. Massachusetts, Michigan, and Nebraska index the personal exemption only. Oregon does not index the income brackets for $125,000 and over; (x) The Wisconsin income brackets reported are for single individuals. For married taxpayers filing jointly, the same tax rates apply income brackets ranging from $15,270, to $336,200.
Source: Federation of Tax Administrators, State Individual Income Tax Rates, January 1, 2018

Various State Sales and Excise Tax Rates

State	State Sales Tax (%)	Gasoline[1] (¢/gal.)	Cigarette[2] ($/pack)	Spirits[3] ($/gal.)	Wine[4] ($/gal.)	Beer[5] ($/gal.)	Recreational Marijuana (%)
Wisconsin	5.0	32.9	2.52	3.25	0.25 (l)	0.06 (q)	Not legal

Note: All tax rates as of January 1, 2018; (1) The American Petroleum Institute has developed a methodology for determining the average tax rate on a gallon of fuel. Rates may include any of the following: excise taxes, environmental fees, storage tank fees, other fees or taxes, general sales tax, and local taxes. In states where gasoline is subject to the general sales tax, or where the fuel tax is based on the average sale price, the average rate determined by API is sensitive to changes in the price of gasoline. States that fully or partially apply general sales taxes to gasoline: CA, CO, GA, IL, IN, MI, NY; (2) The federal excise tax of $1.0066 per pack and local taxes are not included; (3) Rates are those applicable to off-premise sales of 40% alcohol by volume (a.b.v.) distilled spirits in 750ml containers. Local excise taxes are excluded; (4) Rates are those applicable to off-premise sales of 11% a.b.v. non-carbonated wine in 750ml containers; (5) Rates are those applicable to off-premise sales of 4.7% a.b.v. beer in 12 ounce containers; (l) Different rates also applicable to alcohol content, place of production, size of container, place purchased (on- or off-premise or on board airlines) or type of wine (carbonated, vermouth, etc.); (q) Different rates also applicable according to alcohol content, place of production, size of container, or place purchased (on- or off-premise or onboard airlines).
Source: Tax Foundation, 2018 Facts & Figures: How Does Your State Compare?

State Business Tax Climate Index Rankings

State	Overall Rank	Corporate Tax Rank	Individual Income Tax Rank	Sales Tax Rank	Unemployment Insurance Tax Rank	Property Tax Rank
Wisconsin	38	29	43	7	40	26

Note: The index is a measure of how each state's tax laws affect economic performance. The lower the rank, the more favorable a state's tax system is for business. States without a given tax are given a ranking of 1. The scores/rankings for the District of Columbia do not affect other states. The 2018 index represents the tax climate as of July 1, 2017.
Source: Tax Foundation, State Business Tax Climate Index 2018

TRANSPORTATION

Means of Transportation to Work

Area	Car/Truck/Van		Public Transportation			Bicycle	Walked	Other Means	Worked at Home
	Drove Alone	Car-pooled	Bus	Subway	Railroad				
City	83.4	8.9	0.3	0.0	0.0	0.5	1.9	0.7	4.3
MSA[1]	74.2	8.3	4.4	0.0	0.0	2.4	5.2	0.9	4.7
U.S.	76.4	9.3	2.6	1.9	0.6	0.6	2.8	1.3	4.6

Note: Figures are percentages and cover workers 16 years of age and older; (1) Figures cover the Madison, WI Metropolitan Statistical Area—see Appendix B for areas included
Source: U.S. Census Bureau, 2012-2016 American Community Survey 5-Year Estimates

Travel Time to Work

Area	Less Than 10 Minutes	10 to 19 Minutes	20 to 29 Minutes	30 to 44 Minutes	45 to 59 Minutes	60 to 89 Minutes	90 Minutes or More
City	18.3	35.3	21.7	18.2	3.5	1.9	1.0
MSA[1]	16.3	33.1	24.2	17.9	4.8	2.5	1.2
U.S.	12.9	29.2	20.9	20.4	8.0	6.0	2.7

Note: Note: Figures are percentages and include workers 16 years old and over; (1) Figures cover the Madison, WI Metropolitan Statistical Area—see Appendix B for areas included
Source: U.S. Census Bureau, 2012-2016 American Community Survey 5-Year Estimates

Freeway Travel Time Index

Area	1985	1990	1995	2000	2005	2010	2014
Urban Area Rank[1,2]	39	63	77	80	72	48	46
Urban Area Index[1]	1.08	1.08	1.09	1.11	1.15	1.17	1.18
Average Index[3]	1.09	1.11	1.14	1.17	1.20	1.19	1.20

Note: Freeway Travel Time Index—the ratio of travel time in the peak period to the travel time at free-flow conditions. For example, a value of 1.30 indicates a 20-minute free-flow trip takes 26 minutes in the peak (20 minutes x 1.30 = 26 minutes); (1) Covers the Madison WI urban area; (2) Rank is based on 101 urban areas (#1 = highest travel time index); (3) Average of 101 urban areas
Source: Texas Transportation Institute, 2015 Urban Mobility Scorecard, August 2015

Freeway Commuter Stress Index

Area	1985	1990	1995	2000	2005	2010	2014
Urban Area Rank[1,2]	42	59	76	81	68	53	52
Urban Area Index[1]	1.11	1.11	1.12	1.14	1.18	1.20	1.21
Average Index[3]	1.13	1.16	1.19	1.22	1.25	1.24	1.25

Note: The Freeway Commuter Stress Index is the same as the Freeway Travel Time Index (see table above) except that it includes only the travel in the peak directions during the peak periods; the TTI includes travel in all directions during the peak period. Thus, the CSI is more indicative of the work trip experienced by each commuter on a daily basis; (1) Covers the Madison WI urban area; (2) Rank is based on 101 urban areas (#1 = highest travel time index); (3) Average of 101 urban areas
Source: Texas Transportation Institute, 2015 Urban Mobility Scorecard, August 2015

Living Environment

COST OF LIVING

Cost of Living Index

Composite Index	Groceries	Housing	Utilities	Trans-portation	Health Care	Misc. Goods/ Services
107.4	102.9	109.4	105.2	107.3	122.4	106.1

Note: The Cost of Living Index measures regional differences in the cost of consumer goods and services, excluding taxes and non-consumer expenditures, for professional and managerial households in the top income quintile. It is based on more than 50,000 prices covering almost 60 different items for which prices are collected three times a year by chambers of commerce, economic development organizations or university applied economic centers in each participating urban area. The numbers shown should be read as a percentage above or below the national average of 100. For example, a value of 115.4 in the groceries column indicates that grocery prices are 15.4% higher than the national average. Small differences in the index numbers should not be interpreted as significant; Figures cover the Madison WI urban area.
Source: The Council for Community and Economic Research, ACCRA Cost of Living Index, 2017

Grocery Prices

Area[1]	T-Bone Steak ($/pound)	Frying Chicken ($/pound)	Whole Milk ($/half gal.)	Eggs ($/dozen)	Orange Juice ($/64 oz.)	Coffee ($/11.5 oz.)
City[2]	12.91	1.77	1.97	1.21	3.58	4.65
Avg.	11.29	1.40	2.02	1.47	3.55	4.37
Min.	7.71	0.93	1.04	0.70	2.86	3.24
Max.	15.83	2.39	4.03	3.92	6.29	8.16

*Note: (1) Values for the local area are compared with the average, minimum and maximum values for all 294 areas in the Cost of Living Index; (2) Figures cover the Madison WI urban area; **T-Bone Steak** (price per pound); **Frying Chicken** (price per pound, whole fryer); **Whole Milk** (half gallon carton); **Eggs** (price per dozen, Grade A, large); **Orange Juice** (64 oz. Tropicana or Florida Natural); **Coffee** (11.5 oz. can, vacuum-packed, Maxwell House, Hills Bros, or Folgers).*
Source: The Council for Community and Economic Research, ACCRA Cost of Living Index, 2017

Housing and Utility Costs

Area[1]	New Home Price ($)	Apartment Rent ($/month)	All Electric ($/month)	Part Electric ($/month)	Other Energy ($/month)	Telephone ($/month)
City[2]	388,298	1,048	-	105.90	70.78	29.99
Avg.	335,956	1,047	175.01	97.34	67.93	28.71
Min.	187,788	491	109.48	49.33	35.44	12.39
Max.	1,739,087	4,559	432.62	227.09	353.33	44.61

*Note: (1) Values for the local area are compared with the average, minimum and maximum values for all 294 areas in the Cost of Living Index; (2) Figures cover the Madison WI urban area; **New Home Price** (2,400 sf living area, 8,000 sf lot, in urban area with full utilities); **Apartment Rent** (950 sf 2 bedroom/1.5 or 2 bath, unfurnished, excluding all utilities except water); **All Electric** (average monthly cost for an all-electric home); **Part Electric** (average monthly cost for a part-electric home); **Other Energy** (average monthly cost for natural gas, fuel oil, coal, wood, and any other forms of energy except electricity); **Telephone** (price includes basic monthly rate for a private residential line plus additional local usage charges incurred by a family of four).*
Source: The Council for Community and Economic Research, ACCRA Cost of Living Index, 2017

Health Care, Transportation, and Other Costs

Area[1]	Doctor ($/visit)	Dentist ($/visit)	Optometrist ($/visit)	Gasoline ($/gallon)	Beauty Salon ($/visit)	Men's Shirt ($)
City[2]	182.00	101.89	60.83	2.21	41.66	33.66
Avg.	108.00	92.54	101.93	2.25	37.58	30.92
Min.	30.39	60.00	49.75	1.82	16.11	11.20
Max.	193.50	161.94	229.28	3.16	77.35	59.13

*Note: (1) Values for the local area are compared with the average, minimum and maximum values for all 294 areas in the Cost of Living Index; (2) Figures cover the Madison WI urban area; **Doctor** (general practitioners routine exam of an established patient); **Dentist** (adult teeth cleaning and periodic oral examination); **Optometrist** (full vision eye exam for established adult patient); **Gasoline** (one gallon regular unleaded, national brand, including all taxes, cash price at self-service pump if available); **Beauty Salon** (woman's shampoo, trim, and blow-dry); **Men's Shirt** (cotton/polyester dress shirt, pinpoint weave, long sleeves).*
Source: The Council for Community and Economic Research, ACCRA Cost of Living Index, 2017

HOUSING

House Price Index (HPI)

Area	National Ranking[2]	Quarterly Change (%)	One-Year Change (%)	Five-Year Change (%)
MSA[1]	131	-0.22	5.95	20.83
U.S.[3]	–	1.61	6.68	34.71

Note: The HPI is a weighted repeat sales index. It measures average price changes in repeat sales or refinancings on the same properties. This information is obtained by reviewing repeat mortgage transactions on single-family properties whose mortgages have been purchased or securitized by Fannie Mae or Freddie Mac in January 1975; (1) Figures cover the Madison, WI Metropolitan Statistical Area—see Appendix B for areas included; (2) Rankings are based on annual percentage change for all metro areas containing at least 15,000 transactions over the last 10 years and ranges from 1 to 253; (3) figures based on a weighted average of Census Division estimates using a seasonally adjusted, purchase-only index; all figures are for the period ending December 31, 2017

Source: Federal Housing Finance Agency, House Price Index, February 28, 2018

Median Single-Family Home Prices

Area	2015	2016	2017p	Percent Change 2016 to 2017
MSA[1]	238.0	247.3	267.9	8.3
U.S. Average	223.9	235.5	248.8	5.6

Note: Figures are median sales prices of existing single-family homes in thousands of dollars; (p) preliminary; (1) Figures cover the Madison, WI Metropolitan Statistical Area—see Appendix B for areas included

Source: National Association of Realtors, Median Sales Price of Existing Single-Family Homes for Metropolitan Areas, 4th Quarter 2017

Qualifying Income Based on Median Sales Price of Existing Single-Family Homes

Area	With 5% Down ($)	With 10% Down ($)	With 20% Down ($)
MSA[1]	58,815	55,719	49,528
U.S. Average	55,585	52,659	46,808

Note: Figures are preliminary; Qualifying income is based on a mortgage rate of 4.17%. Monthly principal and interest payment is limited to 25% of income; (1) Figures cover the Madison, WI Metropolitan Statistical Area—see Appendix B for areas included

Source: National Association of Realtors, Qualifying Income Based on Median Sales Price of Existing Single-Family Homes for Metropolitan Areas, 4th Quarter 2017

Median Apartment Condo-Coop Home Prices

Area	2015	2016	2017p	Percent Change 2016 to 2017
MSA[1]	156.0	169.2	183.1	8.2
U.S. Average	210.7	220.7	234.3	6.2

Note: Figures are median sales prices of existing apartment condo-coop homes in thousands of dollars; (p) preliminary; (1) Figures cover the Madison, WI Metropolitan Statistical Area—see Appendix B for areas included

Source: National Association of Realtors, Median Sales Price of Existing Apartment Condo-Coop Homes for Metropolitan Areas, 4th Quarter 2017

Home Value Distribution

Area	Under $50,000	$50,000 -$99,999	$100,000 -$149,999	$150,000 -$199,999	$200,000 -$299,999	$300,000 -$499,999	$500,000 -$999,999	$1,000,000 or more
City	1.6	0.9	12.5	32.4	38.3	13.4	0.6	0.2
MSA[1]	3.0	4.5	11.8	21.3	32.2	20.4	5.8	0.9
U.S.	8.8	14.8	15.3	14.9	18.4	16.4	9.0	2.5

Note: Figures are percentages and cover owner-occupied housing units; (1) Figures cover the Madison, WI Metropolitan Statistical Area—see Appendix B for areas included

Source: U.S. Census Bureau, 2012-2016 American Community Survey 5-Year Estimates

Homeownership Rate

Area	2009 (%)	2010 (%)	2011 (%)	2012 (%)	2013 (%)	2014 (%)	2015 (%)	2016 (%)	2017 (%)
MSA[1]	n/a	n/a	n/a	n/a	n/a	n/a	n/a	n/a	n/a
U.S.	67.4	66.9	66.1	65.4	65.1	64.5	63.7	63.4	63.9

Note: (1) Figures cover the Madison, WI Metropolitan Statistical Area—see Appendix B for areas included; n/a not available

Source: U.S. Census Bureau, Housing Vacancies and Homeownership Annual Statistics: 2009-2017

Year Housing Structure Built

Area	2010 or Later	2000 -2009	1990 -1999	1980 -1989	1970 -1979	1960 -1969	1950 -1959	1940 -1949	Before 1940	Median Year
City	3.3	32.0	19.0	9.2	12.7	10.6	5.6	2.1	5.5	1992
MSA[1]	2.6	17.6	16.1	11.3	16.3	9.6	8.5	3.7	14.4	1978
U.S.	2.3	14.7	14.0	13.7	15.6	10.9	10.6	5.2	13.0	1977

Note: Figures are percentages except for Median Year; Note: (1) Figures cover the Madison, WI Metropolitan Statistical Area—see Appendix B for areas included
Source: U.S. Census Bureau, 2012-2016 American Community Survey 5-Year Estimates

Gross Monthly Rent

Area	Under $500	$500 -$999	$1,000 -$1,499	$1,500 -$1,999	$2,000 -$2,499	$2,500 -$2,999	$3,000 and up	Median ($)
City	3.2	50.5	38.4	6.8	1.0	0.0	0.0	976
MSA[1]	6.3	54.2	29.0	7.4	2.1	0.5	0.5	919
U.S.	11.3	43.3	27.7	10.7	4.0	1.6	1.5	949

Note: Figures are percentages except for Median; Gross rent is the contract rent plus the estimated average monthly cost of utilities (electricity, gas, and water and sewer) and fuels (oil, coal, kerosene, wood, etc.) if these are paid by the renter (or paid for the renter by someone else); (1) Figures cover the Madison, WI Metropolitan Statistical Area—see Appendix B for areas included
Source: U.S. Census Bureau, 2012-2016 American Community Survey 5-Year Estimates

HEALTH

Health Risk Factors

Category	MSA[1] (%)	U.S. (%)
Adults aged 18–64 who have any kind of health care coverage	n/a	87.7
Adults who reported being in good or excellent health	n/a	83.6
Adults who are current smokers	n/a	17.1
Adults who currently use E-cigarettes	n/a	4.7
Adults who currently use chewing tobacco, snuff, or snus	n/a	4.0
Adults who are heavy drinkers[2]	n/a	6.5
Adults who are binge drinkers[3]	n/a	16.9
Adults who are overweight (BMI 25.0 - 29.9)	n/a	35.3
Adults who are obese (BMI 30.0 - 99.8)	n/a	29.9
Adults who participated in any physical activities in the past month	n/a	76.9
Adults who always or nearly always wears a seat belt	n/a	94.3

Note: n/a not available; (1) Figures cover the Madison, WI Metropolitan Statistical Area—see Appendix B for areas included; (2) Heavy drinkers are classified as adult men having more than 14 drinks per week and adult women having more than 7 drinks per week; (3) Binge drinkers are classified as males having five or more drinks on one occasion or females having four or more drinks on one occasion
Source: Centers for Disease Control and Prevention, Behaviorial Risk Factor Surveillance System, SMART: Selected Metropolitan Area Risk Trends, 2016

Health Screening Rates

Category	MSA[1] (%)	U.S. (%)
Adults 50-75 who have had a blood stool test within the past year	n/a	8.0
Adults 50-75 who have had a colonoscopy in the past 10 years	n/a	63.5
Adults aged 65+ who have had flu shot within the past year	n/a	58.6
Adults aged 65+ who have ever had a pneumonia vaccination	n/a	73.4
Adults who have ever been tested for HIV	n/a	35.6
Women aged 21-65 who have had a pap test in the past three years	n/a	79.8
Men aged 40+ who have had a PSA test within the past two years	n/a	39.5
Women aged 40+ who have had a mammogram within the past two years	n/a	72.5

Note: n/a not available; (1) Figures cover the Madison, WI Metropolitan Statistical Area—see Appendix B for areas included; Source: Centers for Disease Control and Prevention, Behaviorial Risk Factor Surveillance System, SMART: Selected Metropolitan Area Risk Trends, 2016

Chronic Health Conditions

Category	MSA[1] (%)	U.S. (%)
Adults who have ever been told they had a heart attack	n/a	4.4
Adults who have ever been told they have angina or coronary heart disease	n/a	4.1
Adults who have ever been told they had a stroke	n/a	3.1
Adults who have been told they currently have asthma	n/a	9.3
Adults who have ever been told they have arthritis	n/a	25.8
Adults who have ever been told they have diabetes[2]	n/a	10.5
Adults who have ever been told they had skin cancer	n/a	5.9
Adults who have ever been told they had any other types of cancer	n/a	6.7
Adults who have ever been told they have COPD	n/a	6.3
Adults who have ever been told they have kidney disease	n/a	2.8
Adults who have ever been told they have a form of depression	n/a	17.4

Note: n/a not available; (1) Figures cover the Madison, WI Metropolitan Statistical Area—see Appendix B for areas included; (2) Figures do not include pregnancy-related, borderline, or pre-diabetes
Source: Centers for Disease Control and Prevention, Behaviorial Risk Factor Surveillance System, SMART: Selected Metropolitan Area Risk Trends, 2016

Mortality Rates for the Top 10 Causes of Death in the U.S.

ICD-10[a] Sub-Chapter	ICD-10[a] Code	Age-Adjusted Mortality Rate[1] per 100,000 population	
		County[2]	U.S.
Malignant neoplasms	C00-C97	142.3	158.5
Ischaemic heart diseases	I20-I25	67.8	96.8
Other forms of heart disease	I30-I51	41.5	52.4
Chronic lower respiratory diseases	J40-J47	26.9	40.9
Cerebrovascular diseases	I60-I69	29.6	37.2
Organic, including symptomatic, mental disorders	F01-F09	38.1	33.3
Other degenerative diseases of the nervous system	G30-G31	41.5	32.1
Other external causes of accidental injury	W00-X59	42.2	31.2
Diabetes mellitus	E10-E14	14.7	21.1
Hypertensive diseases	I10-I15	13.6	20.8

Note: (a) ICD-10 = International Classification of Diseases 10th Revision; (1) Mortality rates are a three year average covering 2014-2016; (2) Figures cover Dane County.
Source: Centers for Disease Control and Prevention, National Center for Health Statistics. Underlying Cause of Death 1999-2016 on CDC WONDER Online Database, released December 2017

Mortality Rates for Selected Causes of Death

ICD-10[a] Sub-Chapter	ICD-10[a] Code	Age-Adjusted Mortality Rate[1] per 100,000 population	
		County[2]	U.S.
Assault	X85-Y09	1.8	5.6
Diseases of the liver	K70-K76	6.9	14.0
Human immunodeficiency virus (HIV) disease	B20-B24	Suppressed	1.9
Influenza and pneumonia	J09-J18	9.8	14.6
Intentional self-harm	X60-X84	12.6	13.2
Malnutrition	E40-E46	Suppressed	1.3
Obesity and other hyperalimentation	E65-E68	1.3	2.1
Renal failure	N17-N19	7.5	13.0
Transport accidents	V01-V99	7.2	12.0
Viral hepatitis	B15-B19	Unreliable	1.9

Note: (a) ICD-10 = International Classification of Diseases 10th Revision; (1) Mortality rates are a three year average covering 2014-2016; (2) Figures cover Dane County; Data are Suppressed when the data meet the criteria for confidentiality constraints; Mortality rates are flagged as Unreliable when the rate would be calculated with a numerator of 20 or less.
Source: Centers for Disease Control and Prevention, National Center for Health Statistics. Underlying Cause of Death 1999-2016 on CDC WONDER Online Database, released December 2017

Health Insurance Coverage

Area	With Health Insurance	With Private Health Insurance	With Public Health Insurance	Without Health Insurance	Population Under Age 18 Without Health Insurance
City	93.5	79.6	26.5	6.5	1.7
MSA[1]	94.5	82.3	24.1	5.5	2.8
U.S.	88.3	66.7	33.0	11.7	5.9

Note: Figures are percentages that cover the civilian noninstitutionalized population; (1) Figures cover the Madison, WI Metropolitan Statistical Area—see Appendix B for areas included
Source: U.S. Census Bureau, 2012-2016 American Community Survey 5-Year Estimates

Number of Medical Professionals

Area	MDs[3]	DOs[3,4]	Dentists	Podiatrists	Chiropractors	Optometrists
County[1] (number)	3,037	104	360	27	219	118
County[1] (rate[2])	581.7	19.9	67.9	5.1	41.3	22.3
U.S. (rate[2])	276.5	22.3	67.3	6.0	26.7	15.9

Note: Data as of 2016 unless noted; (1) Data covers Dane County; (2) Rate per 100,000 population; (3) Data as of 2015 and includes all active, non-federal physicians; (4) Doctor of Osteopathic Medicine
Source: U.S. Department of Health and Human Services, Health Resources and Services Administration, Bureau of Health Professions, Area Resource File (ARF) 2016-2017

Best Hospitals

According to *U.S. News,* the Madison, WI metro area is home to one of the best hospitals in the U.S.: **University of Wisconsin Hospitals** (9 adult specialties and 6 pediatric specialties). The hospital listed was nationally ranked in at least one of 16 specialties. Only 152 hospitals nationwide were nationally ranked in one or more specialties. Twenty hospitals in the U.S. made the Honor Roll. The Best Hospitals Honor Roll was revamped last year to take both the national rankings and the procedure and condition ratings into account. Hospitals received points if they were nationally ranked in one of the 16 specialties—the higher they ranked, the more points they got—and how many ratings of "high performing" they earned in the nine procedures and conditions. *U.S. News Online, "America's Best Hospitals 2017-18"*

According to *U.S. News,* the Madison, WI metro area is home to one of the best children's hospitals in the U.S.: **American Family Children's Hospital** (6 pediatric specialties). The hospital listed was highly ranked in at least one of 10 pediatric specialties. Eighty-two children's hospitals in the U.S. were nationally ranked in at least one specialty. Hospitals received points for being ranked in a specialty, and the 10 hospitals with the most points across the 10 specialties make up the Honor Roll. *U.S. News Online, "America's Best Children's Hospitals 2017-18"*

EDUCATION

Public School District Statistics

District Name	Schls	Pupils	Pupil/ Teacher Ratio	Minority Pupils[1] (%)	Free Lunch Eligible[2] (%)	IEP[3] (%)
Sun Prairie Area School District	13	8,107	14.5	34.2	21.3	11.3

Note: Table includes school districts with 100 or more students; (1) Percentage of students that are not non-Hispanic white; (2) Percentage of students that are eligible for the free lunch program; (3) Percentage of students that have an Individualized Education Program.
Source: U.S. Department of Education, National Center for Education Statistics, Common Core of Data, Local Education Agency (School District) Universe Survey: School Year 2015-2016; U.S. Department of Education, National Center for Education Statistics, Common Core of Data, Public Elementary/Secondary School Universe Survey: School Year 2015-2016

Highest Level of Education

Area	Less than H.S.	H.S. Diploma	Some College, No Deg.	Associate Degree	Bachelor's Degree	Master's Degree	Prof. School Degree	Doctorate Degree
City	4.0	19.8	22.7	12.4	27.3	10.4	2.2	1.1
MSA[1]	5.2	21.8	18.8	10.2	26.6	11.3	2.9	3.0
U.S.	13.0	27.5	21.0	8.2	18.8	8.2	2.0	1.3

Note: Figures cover persons age 25 and over; (1) Figures cover the Madison, WI Metropolitan Statistical Area—see Appendix B for areas included
Source: U.S. Census Bureau, 2012-2016 American Community Survey 5-Year Estimates

Educational Attainment by Race

Area	High School Graduate or Higher (%)					Bachelor's Degree or Higher (%)				
	Total	White	Black	Asian	Hisp.[2]	Total	White	Black	Asian	Hisp.[2]
City	96.0	96.6	94.5	93.3	80.7	41.1	41.7	20.5	62.1	28.3
MSA[1]	94.8	95.9	88.0	87.7	70.9	43.9	44.4	20.9	65.8	24.5
U.S.	87.0	88.9	84.3	86.3	65.7	30.3	31.6	20.0	52.1	14.7

Note: Figures shown cover persons 25 years old and over; (1) Figures cover the Madison, WI Metropolitan Statistical Area—see Appendix B for areas included; (2) People of Hispanic origin can be of any race
Source: U.S. Census Bureau, 2012-2016 American Community Survey 5-Year Estimates

School Enrollment by Grade and Control

Area	Preschool (%)		Kindergarten (%)		Grades 1 - 4 (%)		Grades 5 - 8 (%)		Grades 9 - 12 (%)	
	Public	Private	Public	Private	Public	Private	Public	Private	Public	Private
City	52.1	47.9	84.8	15.2	93.0	7.0	93.2	6.8	96.1	3.9
MSA[1]	61.1	38.9	89.5	10.5	89.9	10.1	90.3	9.7	94.8	5.2
U.S.	58.4	41.6	87.7	12.3	89.8	10.2	89.7	10.3	90.4	9.6

Note: Figures shown cover persons 3 years old and over; (1) Figures cover the Madison, WI Metropolitan Statistical Area—see Appendix B for areas included
Source: U.S. Census Bureau, 2012-2016 American Community Survey 5-Year Estimates

Average Salaries of Public School Classroom Teachers

Area	2015		2016		Change from 2015 to 2016	
	Dollars	Rank[1]	Dollars	Rank[1]	Percent	Rank[2]
Wisconsin	52,264	25	54,115	24	3.5	3
U.S. Average	57,611	–	58,353	–	1.3	–

Note: (1) Rank ranges from 1 to 51 where 1 indicates highest salary; (2) Rank ranges from 1 to 51 where 1 indicates highest percent change.
Source: National Education Association, Rankings & Estimates: Rankings of the States 2016 and Estimates of School Statistics 2017

Higher Education

Four-Year Colleges			Two-Year Colleges			Medical Schools[1]	Law Schools[2]	Voc/ Tech[3]
Public	Private Non-profit	Private For-profit	Public	Private Non-profit	Private For-profit			
0	0	0	0	0	0	0	0	0

Note: Figures cover institutions located within the city limits and include main campuses only; (1) includes schools accredited by the Liaison Committee on Medical Education and the American Osteopathic Association's Commission on Osteopathic College Accreditation; (2) includes ABA-accredited schools, schools with provisional ABA accreditation, and state accredited schools; (3) includes all schools with programs that are less than 2 years.
Source: National Center for Education Statistics, Integrated Postsecondary Education System (IPEDS), 2016-17; Wikipedia, List of Medical Schools in the United States, accessed April 2, 2018; Wikipedia, List of Law Schools in the United States, accessed April 2, 2018

According to *U.S. News & World Report,* the Madison, WI metro area is home to two of the best national universities in the U.S.: **University of Wisconsin—Madison** (#46 tie); **Edgewood College** (#181 tie). The indicators used to capture academic quality fall into a number of categories: assessment by administrators at peer institutions; retention of students; faculty resources; student selectivity; financial resources; alumni giving; high school counselor ratings of colleges; and graduation rate. *U.S. News & World Report, "America's Best Colleges 2018"*

According to *U.S. News & World Report,* the Madison, WI metro area is home to one of the top 100 law schools in the U.S.: **University of Wisconsin—Madison** (#27 tie). The rankings are based on a weighted average of 12 measures of quality: peer assessment score; assessment score by lawyers/judges; median LSAT scores; median undergrad GPA; acceptance rate; employment rates for graduates; placement success; bar passage rate; faculty resources; expenditures per student; student/faculty ratio; and library resources. *U.S. News & World Report, "America's Best Graduate Schools, Law, 2019"*

According to *U.S. News & World Report,* the Madison, WI metro area is home to one of the top 75 medical schools for research in the U.S.: **University of Wisconsin—Madison** (#28). The rankings are based on a weighted average of 11 measures of quality: quality assessment; peer assessment score; assessment score by residency directors; research activity; total research activity; average research activity per faculty member; student selectivity; median MCAT total score; median undergraduate GPA; acceptance rate; and faculty resources. *U.S. News & World Report, "America's Best Graduate Schools, Medical, 2019"*

According to *U.S. News & World Report,* the Madison, WI metro area is home to one of the top 75 business schools in the U.S.: **University of Wisconsin—Madison** (#37 tie). The rankings are based on a weighted average of the following nine measures: quality assessment; peer assessment; recruiter assessment; placement success; mean starting salary and bonus; student selectivity; mean GMAT and GRE scores; mean undergraduate GPA; and acceptance rate. *U.S. News & World Report, "America's Best Graduate Schools, Business, 2019"*

PRESIDENTIAL ELECTION

2016 Presidential Election Results

Area	Clinton	Trump	Johnson	Stein	Other
Dane County	70.4	23.0	3.4	1.4	1.8
U.S.	48.0	45.9	3.3	1.1	1.7

Note: Results are percentages and may not add to 100% due to rounding
Source: Dave Leip's Atlas of U.S. Presidential Elections

EMPLOYERS

Major Employers

Company Name	Industry
American Family Mutual Insurance Company	Fire, marine, & casualty insurance
Community Living Alliance	Social services for the handicapped
Covence Laboratories	Druggists preparations
CUNA Mutual Insurance Society	Telephone communication except radio
Kraft Foods Global	Luncheon meat from purchased meat
University of Wisconsin Hospitals	General medical & surgical hospitals
Veterans Health Administration	General medical & surgical hospitals
WI Dept of Workforce Development	Administration of social & manpower programs
Wisconsin Department of Administration	Administration of general economic programs
Wisconsin Department of Health Services	Administration of public health programs
Wisconsin Department of Natural Resources	Land, mineral, & wildlife conservation
Wisconsin Department of Transportation	State highway patrol
Wisconsin Dept of Natural Resources	Land, mineral, & wildlife conservation
Wisconsin Dept of Transportation	Regulation, administration of transportation
Wisconsin Physicians Srvc Ins Corp	Hospital & medical services plans

Note: Companies shown are located within the Madison, WI Metropolitan Statistical Area.
Source: Hoovers.com; Wikipedia

PUBLIC SAFETY

Crime Rate

Area	All Crimes	Violent Crimes				Property Crimes		
		Murder	Rape[3]	Robbery	Aggrav. Assault	Burglary	Larceny -Theft	Motor Vehicle Theft
City	1,885.1	0.0	15.2	18.2	72.9	109.3	1,602.8	66.8
Metro[1]	2,118.5	2.0	30.7	48.0	122.0	268.1	1,556.5	91.1
U.S.	2,837.0	5.3	29.6	102.8	248.5	468.9	1,745.0	236.9

Note: Figures are crimes per 100,000 population; (1) Figures cover the Madison, WI Metropolitan Statistical Area—see Appendix B for areas included; (3) The city and U.S. figures shown were reported using the legacy Uniform Crime Reporting (UCR) definition of rape. The metro area figures shown are an aggregate total of the data submitted using both the revised and legacy UCR definitions.
Source: FBI Uniform Crime Reports, 2016

Hate Crimes

Area	Number of Quarters Reported	Number of Incidents per Bias Motivation					
		Race/Ethnicity/ Ancestry	Religion	Sexual Orientation	Disability	Gender	Gender Identity
City	4	0	0	0	0	0	0
U.S.	4	3,489	1,273	1,076	70	31	124

Source: Federal Bureau of Investigation, Hate Crime Statistics 2016

Identity Theft Consumer Reports

Area	Reports	Reports per 100,000 Population	Rank[2]
MSA[1]	519	80	196
U.S.	371,061	114	-

Note: (1) Figures cover the Madison, WI Metropolitan Statistical Area—see Appendix B for areas included; (2) Rank ranges from 1 to 389 where 1 indicates greatest number of identity theft reports per 100,000 population
Source: Federal Trade Commission, Consumer Sentinel Network Data Book for January–December 2017

Fraud and Other Consumer Reports

Area	Reports	Reports per 100,000 Population	Rank[2]
MSA[1]	2,637	406	251
U.S.	2,304,550	708	-

Note: (1) Figures cover the Madison, WI Metropolitan Statistical Area—see Appendix B for areas included; (2) Rank ranges from 1 to 389 where 1 indicates greatest number of fraud and other consumer reports per 100,000 population
Source: Federal Trade Commission, Consumer Sentinel Network Data Book for January–December 2017

SPORTS

Professional Sports Teams

Team Name	League	Year Established
No teams are located in the metro area		

Source: Wikipedia, Major Professional Sports Teams of the United States and Canada, April 5, 2018

CLIMATE

Average and Extreme Temperatures

Temperature	Jan	Feb	Mar	Apr	May	Jun	Jul	Aug	Sep	Oct	Nov	Dec	Yr.
Extreme High (°F)	56	61	82	94	93	101	104	102	99	90	76	62	104
Average High (°F)	26	30	42	58	70	79	84	81	72	61	44	30	57
Average Temp. (°F)	17	21	32	46	57	67	72	69	61	50	36	23	46
Average Low (°F)	8	12	22	35	45	54	59	57	49	38	27	14	35
Extreme Low (°F)	-37	-28	-29	0	19	31	36	35	25	13	-8	-25	-37

Note: Figures cover the years 1948-1990
Source: National Climatic Data Center, International Station Meteorological Climate Summary, 9/96

Average Precipitation/Snowfall/Humidity

Precip./Humidity	Jan	Feb	Mar	Apr	May	Jun	Jul	Aug	Sep	Oct	Nov	Dec	Yr.
Avg. Precip. (in.)	1.1	1.1	2.1	2.9	3.2	3.8	3.9	3.9	3.0	2.3	2.0	1.7	31.1
Avg. Snowfall (in.)	10	7	9	2	Tr	0	0	0	Tr	Tr	4	11	42
Avg. Rel. Hum. 6am (%)	78	80	81	80	79	81	85	89	90	85	84	82	83
Avg. Rel. Hum. 3pm (%)	66	63	59	50	50	51	53	55	55	54	64	69	57

Note: Figures cover the years 1948-1990; Tr = Trace amounts (<0.05 in. of rain; <0.5 in. of snow)
Source: National Climatic Data Center, International Station Meteorological Climate Summary, 9/96

Weather Conditions

Temperature			Daytime Sky			Precipitation		
5°F & below	32°F & below	90°F & above	Clear	Partly cloudy	Cloudy	0.01 inch or more precip.	0.1 inch or more snow/ice	Thunder-storms
35	161	14	88	119	158	118	38	40

Note: Figures are average number of days per year and cover the years 1948-1990
Source: National Climatic Data Center, International Station Meteorological Climate Summary, 9/96

HAZARDOUS WASTE

Superfund Sites

The Madison, WI metro area is home to five sites on the EPA's Superfund National Priorities List: **City Disposal Corp. Landfill** (final); **Hagen Farm** (final); **Madison Metropolitan Sewerage District Lagoons** (final); **Refuse Hideaway Landfill** (final); **Stoughton City Landfill** (final). There are a total of 1,396 Superfund sites with a status of proposed or final on the list in the U.S.
U.S. Environmental Protection Agency, National Priorities List, April 4, 2018

AIR & WATER QUALITY

Air Quality Trends: Ozone

	1990	1995	2000	2005	2010	2012	2013	2014	2015	2016
MSA[1]	0.077	0.084	0.072	0.079	0.062	0.074	0.067	0.068	0.064	0.068
U.S.	0.087	0.089	0.081	0.079	0.073	0.075	0.069	0.067	0.068	0.069

Note: (1) Data covers the Madison, WI Metropolitan Statistical Area—see Appendix B for areas included. The values shown are the composite ozone concentration averages among trend sites based on the highest fourth daily maximum 8-hour concentration in parts per million. These trends are based on sites having an adequate record of monitoring data during the trend period. Data from exceptional events are included.
Source: U.S. Environmental Protection Agency, Air Quality Monitoring Information, "Air Quality Trends by City, 1990-2016"

Air Quality Index

Area	Percent of Days when Air Quality was...[2]					AQI Statistics[2]	
	Good	Moderate	Unhealthy for Sensitive Groups	Unhealthy	Very Unhealthy	Maximum	Median
MSA[1]	80.5	19.5	0.0	0.0	0.0	93	39

Note: (1) Data covers the Madison, WI Metropolitan Statistical Area—see Appendix B for areas included; (2) Based on 365 days with AQI data in 2017. Air Quality Index (AQI) is an index for reporting daily air quality. EPA calculates the AQI for five major air pollutants regulated by the Clean Air Act: ground-level ozone, particle pollution (aka particulate matter), carbon monoxide, sulfur dioxide, and nitrogen dioxide. The AQI runs from 0 to 500. The higher the AQI value, the greater the level of air pollution and the greater the health concern. There are six AQI categories: "Good" AQI is between 0 and 50. Air quality is considered satisfactory; "Moderate" AQI is between 51 and 100. Air quality is acceptable; "Unhealthy for Sensitive Groups" When AQI values are between 101 and 150, members of sensitive groups may experience health effects; "Unhealthy" When AQI values are between 151 and 200 everyone may begin to experience health effects; "Very Unhealthy" AQI values between 201 and 300 trigger a health alert; "Hazardous" AQI values over 300 trigger warnings of emergency conditions (not shown).
Source: U.S. Environmental Protection Agency, Air Quality Index Report, 2017

Air Quality Index Pollutants

Area	Percent of Days when AQI Pollutant was...[2]					
	Carbon Monoxide	Nitrogen Dioxide	Ozone	Sulfur Dioxide	Particulate Matter 2.5	Particulate Matter 10
MSA[1]	0.0	0.0	53.2	1.9	44.9	0.0

Note: (1) Data covers the Madison, WI Metropolitan Statistical Area—see Appendix B for areas included; (2) Based on 365 days with AQI data in 2017. The Air Quality Index (AQI) is an index for reporting daily air quality. EPA calculates the AQI for five major air pollutants regulated by the Clean Air Act: ground-level ozone, particle pollution (also known as particulate matter), carbon monoxide, sulfur dioxide, and nitrogen dioxide. The AQI runs from 0 to 500. The higher the AQI value, the greater the level of air pollution and the greater the health concern.
Source: U.S. Environmental Protection Agency, Air Quality Index Report, 2017

Maximum Air Pollutant Concentrations: Particulate Matter, Ozone, CO and Lead

	Particulate Matter 10 (ug/m^3)	Particulate Matter 2.5 Wtd AM (ug/m^3)	Particulate Matter 2.5 24-Hr (ug/m^3)	Ozone (ppm)	Carbon Monoxide (ppm)	Lead (ug/m^3)
MSA[1] Level	34	8.1	19	0.07	n/a	n/a
NAAQS[2]	150	15	35	0.075	9	0.15
Met NAAQS[2]	Yes	Yes	Yes	Yes	n/a	n/a

Note: (1) Data covers the Madison, WI Metropolitan Statistical Area—see Appendix B for areas included; Data from exceptional events are included; (2) National Ambient Air Quality Standards; ppm = parts per million; ug/m^3 = micrograms per cubic meter; n/a not available.
Concentrations: Particulate Matter 10 (coarse particulate)—highest second maximum 24-hour concentration; Particulate Matter 2.5 Wtd AM (fine particulate)—highest weighted annual mean concentration; Particulate Matter 2.5 24-Hour (fine particulate)—highest 98th percentile 24-hour concentration; Ozone—highest fourth daily maximum 8-hour concentration; Carbon Monoxide—highest second maximum non-overlapping 8-hour concentration; Lead—maximum running 3-month average
Source: U.S. Environmental Protection Agency, Air Quality Monitoring Information, "Air Quality Statistics by City, 2016"

Maximum Air Pollutant Concentrations: Nitrogen Dioxide and Sulfur Dioxide

	Nitrogen Dioxide AM (ppb)	Nitrogen Dioxide 1-Hr (ppb)	Sulfur Dioxide AM (ppb)	Sulfur Dioxide 1-Hr (ppb)	Sulfur Dioxide 24-Hr (ppb)
MSA[1] Level	n/a	n/a	n/a	1	n/a
NAAQS[2]	53	100	30	75	140
Met NAAQS[2]	n/a	n/a	n/a	Yes	n/a

Note: (1) Data covers the Madison, WI Metropolitan Statistical Area—see Appendix B for areas included; Data from exceptional events are included; (2) National Ambient Air Quality Standards; ppm = parts per million; ug/m^3 = micrograms per cubic meter; n/a not available.
Concentrations: Nitrogen Dioxide AM—highest arithmetic mean concentration; Nitrogen Dioxide 1-Hr—highest 98th percentile 1-hour daily maximum concentration; Sulfur Dioxide AM—highest annual mean concentration; Sulfur Dioxide 1-Hr—highest 99th percentile 1-hour daily maximum concentration; Sulfur Dioxide 24-Hr—highest second maximum 24-hour concentration
Source: U.S. Environmental Protection Agency, Air Quality Monitoring Information, "Air Quality Statistics by City, 2016"

Drinking Water

Water System Name	Pop. Served	Primary Water Source Type	Violations[1]	
			Health Based	Monitoring/ Reporting
Sun Prairie Utiities	32,613	Ground	0	0

Note: (1) Based on violation data from January 1, 2017 to December 31, 2017
Source: U.S. Environmental Protection Agency, Office of Ground Water and Drinking Water, Safe Drinking Water Information System (based on data extracted April 5, 2018)

Laramie, Wyoming

Background

Laramie is located in southeastern Wyoming, in Albany County, on the Laramie River. The city is roughly 49 miles west of the state capital of Cheyenne and 130 miles north of Denver. The city sits on a high plateau, Laramie Plains, at an elevation of 7,200 feet.

Laramie took its name from Jacques LaRamie, a trapper who disappeared into the Laramie Mountains in the late 1810s, never to be heard from again. His name was also lent to a county, US Army fort, river, mountain range and mountain peak.

Laramie was founded near the Union Pacific railroad and the Overland Stage Line.

By 1868, the town had stores, houses, a school and a church. At that time, however, Laramie was more like a scene from an old western movie rather than a bustling little town. Stories are told of rowdy saloon brawls, gun-slingers bullying settlers for the deeds of their property, gunfights, all ending with the local sheriff battling the bad guys and winning the day. Law and order reigned and life in Laramie continued unfettered.

The Wyoming Territory was organized in 1869. Just a year later, Laramie was the site where Louisa Swain cast the first legal US female vote. A statue honoring the event is located in downtown Laramie. Also that year, five Laramie residents became the first females to serve on a jury.

The University of Wyoming was opened in Laramie in 1887. By 1901, Laramie was a bustling urban center and the home to the Laramie, North Park & Pacific Railroad & Telegraph Company, the Laramie, North Park & Western Railroad, alongside several other local manufacturers, plants and mills.

Now, with a population topping 28,000, the city of Laramie is noted for its neighborly atmosphere and striking natural beauty.

Given its location in between the Snowy Range and the Laramie Range of the Rocky Mountains, Laramie attracts outdoor enthusiasts from miles around. The area has much to offer in the way of downhill and cross-country skiing, snowboarding, snowmobiling, hiking, rock climbing, hunting, fishing, rafting and biking.

Headquartered in Laramie, Albany County School District #1 covers 4,000 square miles, where 3,400 students attend 19 public schools. Laramie schools include seven elementary schools, two middle schools and two high schools, along with a K-7 charter school and K-6 Catholic school.

Institutions of higher learning in Laramie include the University of Wyoming and Laramie County Community College. The WyoTech campus in Larmie closed in 2016. In addition to bringing in students and faculty and serving as some of Laramie's largest employers, the local Universities bring cultural and educational opportunities to the city's residents as well. The University of Wyoming's Geological Museum, Art Museum and Fine Arts Concert Hall attract both students and residents. Additional cultural attractions include the Laramie Plains Museum and the Wyoming Children's Museum & Nature Center.

In 2004, Laramie became the first city in Wyoming to pass a law to prohibit smoking in enclosed workplaces, including bars, restaurants and private clubs. Opponents of the clean indoor air ordinance, funded in part by the R.J. Reynolds Tobacco Company, immediately petitioned to have the ordinance repealed. However, the voters upheld the ordinance in a citywide referendum which was conducted concurrently with the 2004 general election.

In 2015, Laramie passed an LGBT anti-discrimination bill. The ordinance bans discrimination against LGBT people in employment, housing and public accommodations such as bars and restaurants.

Laramie is served by Laramie Regional Airport, with regional service to Denver provided by Great Lakes Airlines.

Summers in Laramie are short and relatively cool, with an average high temperature of 79 in July. Winters are long, with average temperatures in the 20s and 30s from November through April.

Rankings

General Rankings

- In their fifth annual survey, Livability.com looked at data for nearly 2,300 U.S. cities to determine the rankings for Livability's "Top 100 Best Places to Live" in 2018. Laramie ranked #69. Criteria: vibrant economy; low cost of living; education, demographics, health care options; transportation & infrastructure; abundant lifestyle amenities. *Livability.com, "Top 100 Best Places to Live 2018" January 16, 2018*

Business Environment

CITY FINANCES

City Government Finances

Component	2015 ($000)	2015 ($ per capita)
Total Revenues	67,405	2,096
Total Expenditures	51,419	1,599
Debt Outstanding	29,249	910
Cash and Securities[1]	95,345	2,965

Note: (1) Cash and security holdings of a government at the close of its fiscal year,, including those of its dependent agencies, utilities, and liquor stores.
Source: U.S Census Bureau, State & Local Government Finances 2015

City Government Revenue by Source

Source	2015 ($000)	2015 ($ per capita)	2015 (%)
General Revenue			
From Federal Government	1,126	35	1.7
From State Government	24,150	751	35.8
From Local Governments	10,409	324	15.4
Taxes			
Property	2,256	70	3.3
Sales and Gross Receipts	1,638	51	2.4
Personal Income	0	0	0.0
Corporate Income	0	0	0.0
Motor Vehicle License	0	0	0.0
Other Taxes	900	28	1.3
Current Charges	11,503	358	17.1
Liquor Store	0	0	0.0
Utility	8,625	268	12.8
Employee Retirement	0	0	0.0

Source: U.S Census Bureau, State & Local Government Finances 2015

City Government Expenditures by Function

Function	2015 ($000)	2015 ($ per capita)	2015 (%)
General Direct Expenditures			
Air Transportation	0	0	0.0
Corrections	0	0	0.0
Education	0	0	0.0
Employment Security Administration	0	0	0.0
Financial Administration	928	28	1.8
Fire Protection	5,641	175	11.0
General Public Buildings	967	30	1.9
Governmental Administration, Other	3,512	109	6.8
Health	643	20	1.3
Highways	4,470	139	8.7
Hospitals	0	0	0.0
Housing and Community Development	536	16	1.0
Interest on General Debt	428	13	0.8
Judicial and Legal	851	26	1.7
Libraries	0	0	0.0
Parking	0	0	0.0
Parks and Recreation	5,565	173	10.8
Police Protection	7,957	247	15.5
Public Welfare	0	0	0.0
Sewerage	3,067	95	6.0
Solid Waste Management	2,894	90	5.6
Veterans' Services	0	0	0.0
Liquor Store	0	0	0.0
Utility	6,205	193	12.1
Employee Retirement	0	0	0.0

Source: U.S Census Bureau, State & Local Government Finances 2015

DEMOGRAPHICS

Population Growth

Area	1990 Census	2000 Census	2010 Census	2016* Estimate	Population Growth (%) 1990-2016	Population Growth (%) 2010-2016
City	26,768	27,204	30,816	32,096	19.9	4.2
MSA[1]	30,797	32,014	36,299	37,836	22.9	4.2
U.S.	248,709,873	281,421,906	308,745,538	318,558,162	28.1	3.2

Note: (1) Figures cover the Laramie, WY Micropolitan Statistical Area—see Appendix B for areas included; (*) 2012-2016 5-year estimated population
Source: U.S. Census Bureau, 1990 Census, Census 2000, Census 2010, 2012-2016 American Community Survey 5-Year Estimates

Household Size

Area	Persons in Household (%) One	Two	Three	Four	Five	Six	Seven or More	Average Household Size
City	33.1	34.1	16.3	11.4	2.9	1.2	1.0	2.30
MSA[1]	32.4	35.3	15.8	11.5	2.8	1.3	0.9	2.30
U.S.	27.7	33.7	15.7	13.1	6.0	2.3	1.5	2.60

Note: (1) Figures cover the Laramie, WY Micropolitan Statistical Area—see Appendix B for areas included
Source: U.S. Census Bureau, 2012-2016 American Community Survey 5-Year Estimates

Race

Area	White Alone[2] (%)	Black Alone[2] (%)	Asian Alone[2] (%)	AIAN[3] Alone[2] (%)	NHOPI[4] Alone[2] (%)	Other Race Alone[2] (%)	Two or More Races (%)
City	88.8	1.7	3.2	0.8	0.0	2.3	3.1
MSA[1]	89.8	1.5	3.0	0.7	0.0	2.2	2.8
U.S.	73.3	12.6	5.2	0.8	0.2	4.8	3.1

Note: (1) Figures cover the Laramie, WY Micropolitan Statistical Area—see Appendix B for areas included; (2) Alone is defined as not being in combination with one or more other races; (3) American Indian and Alaska Native; (4) Native Hawaiian and Other Pacific Islander
Source: U.S. Census Bureau, 2012-2016 American Community Survey 5-Year Estimates

Hispanic or Latino Origin

Area	Total (%)	Mexican (%)	Puerto Rican (%)	Cuban (%)	Other (%)
City	10.3	7.7	0.2	0.1	2.3
MSA[1]	9.2	6.9	0.2	0.1	2.0
U.S.	17.3	11.0	1.7	0.7	4.0

Note: Persons of Hispanic or Latino origin can be of any race; (1) Figures cover the Laramie, WY Micropolitan Statistical Area—see Appendix B for areas included
Source: U.S. Census Bureau, 2012-2016 American Community Survey 5-Year Estimates

Segregation

Type	Segregation Indices[1] 1990	2000	2010	2010 Rank[2]	Percent Change 1990-2000	1990-2010	2000-2010
Black/White	n/a	n/a	n/a	n/a	n/a	n/a	n/a
Asian/White	n/a	n/a	n/a	n/a	n/a	n/a	n/a
Hispanic/White	n/a	n/a	n/a	n/a	n/a	n/a	n/a

Note: All figures cover the Metropolitan Statistical Area—see Appendix B for areas included; Figures are based on an analysis of 1990, 2000, and 2010 Census Decennial Census tract data by William H. Frey, Brookings Institution and the University of Michigan Social Science Data Analysis Network. In this analysis all racial groups (whites, blacks, and asians) are non-Hispanic members of those races. Hispanics are shown as a separate category; (1) Segregation Indices are Dissimilarity Indices that measure the degree to which the minority group is distributed differently than whites across census tracts. They range from 0 (complete integration) to 100 (complete segregation) where the value indicates the percentage of the minority group that needs to move to be distributed exactly like whites; (2) Ranges from 1 (most segregated) to 102 (least segregated); n/a not available.
Source: www.CensusScope.org

Ancestry

Area	German	Irish	English	American	Italian	Polish	French[2]	Scottish	Dutch
City	27.3	11.9	11.6	4.0	5.1	2.5	4.1	3.6	1.1
MSA[1]	27.1	12.1	11.9	4.8	4.6	2.4	3.7	3.8	1.3
U.S.	14.4	10.4	7.7	6.9	5.4	2.9	2.6	1.7	1.3

Note: Figures are the percentage of the total population reporting a particular ancestry. The nine most commonly reported ancestries in the U.S. are shown. Figures include multiple ancestries (e.g. if a person reported being Irish and Italian, they were included in both columns); (1) Figures cover the Laramie, WY Micropolitan Statistical Area—see Appendix B for areas included; (2) Excludes Basque
Source: U.S. Census Bureau, 2012-2016 American Community Survey 5-Year Estimates

Foreign-Born Population

Area	Percent of Population Born in								
	Any Foreign Country	Asia	Mexico	Europe	Carribean	Central America[2]	South America	Africa	Canada
City	6.7	3.0	0.9	0.9	0.0	0.2	0.2	0.9	0.2
MSA[1]	6.1	2.8	0.9	0.8	0.0	0.2	0.2	0.8	0.2
U.S.	13.2	4.0	3.6	1.5	1.3	1.0	0.9	0.6	0.3

Note: (1) Figures cover the Laramie, WY Micropolitan Statistical Area—see Appendix B for areas included; (2) Excludes Mexico.
Source: U.S. Census Bureau, 2012-2016 American Community Survey 5-Year Estimates

Marital Status

Area	Never Married	Now Married[2]	Separated	Widowed	Divorced
City	53.4	35.6	0.8	2.5	7.7
MSA[1]	48.5	39.5	0.8	3.1	8.1
U.S.	33.0	48.1	2.1	5.9	11.0

Note: Figures are percentages and cover the population 15 years of age and older; (1) Figures cover the Laramie, WY Micropolitan Statistical Area—see Appendix B for areas included; (2) Excludes separated
Source: U.S. Census Bureau, 2012-2016 American Community Survey 5-Year Estimates

Disability Status

Area	All Ages	Under 18 Years Old	18 to 64 Years Old	65 Years and Over
City	8.8	2.5	7.4	38.2
MSA[1]	9.5	2.3	7.6	36.5
U.S.	12.5	4.1	10.3	35.7

Note: Figures show percent of the civilian noninstitutionalized population that reported having a disability. Disability status is determined from six types of difficulty: vision, hearing, cognitive, ambulatory, self-care, and independent living. For children under 5 years old, hearing and vision difficulty are used to determine disability status. For children between the ages of 5 and 14, disability status is determined from hearing, vision, cognitive, ambulatory, and self-care difficulties. For people aged 15 years and older, they are considered to have a disability if they have difficulty with any one of the six difficulty types; Note: (1) Figures cover the Laramie, WY Micropolitan Statistical Area—see Appendix B for areas included
Source: U.S. Census Bureau, 2012-2016 American Community Survey 5-Year Estimates

Age

Area	Percent of Population									Median Age
	Under Age 5	Age 5–19	Age 20–34	Age 35–44	Age 45–54	Age 55–64	Age 65–74	Age 75–84	Age 85+	
City	5.4	18.5	43.1	9.4	7.6	8.8	4.0	2.2	1.0	25.2
MSA[1]	5.3	17.8	39.1	9.4	8.8	10.1	5.7	2.6	1.2	26.6
U.S.	6.2	19.6	20.7	12.7	13.6	12.6	8.3	4.3	1.9	37.7

Note: (1) Figures cover the Laramie, WY Micropolitan Statistical Area—see Appendix B for areas included
Source: U.S. Census Bureau, 2012-2016 American Community Survey 5-Year Estimates

Gender

Area	Males	Females	Males per 100 Females
City	16,675	15,421	108.1
MSA[1]	19,767	18,069	109.4
U.S.	156,765,322	161,792,840	96.9

Note: (1) Figures cover the Laramie, WY Micropolitan Statistical Area—see Appendix B for areas included
Source: U.S. Census Bureau, 2012-2016 American Community Survey 5-Year Estimates

Religious Groups by Family

Area	Catholic	Baptist	Non-Den.	Methodist[2]	Lutheran	LDS[3]	Pentecostal	Presbyterian[4]	Muslim[5]	Judaism
MSA[1]	n/a	n/a	n/a	n/a	n/a	n/a	n/a	n/a	n/a	n/a
U.S.	19.1	9.3	4.0	4.0	2.3	2.0	1.9	1.6	0.8	0.7

Note: Figures are the number of adherents as a percentage of the total population; (1) Figures cover the Laramie, WY Micropolitan Statistical Area—see Appendix B for areas included; (2) Methodist/Pietist; (3) Latter Day Saints; (4) Reformed; (5) Figures are estimates
Source: Association of Statisticians of American Religious Bodies, 2010 U.S. Religion Census: Religious Congregations & Membership Study

Religious Groups by Tradition

Area	Catholic	Evangelical Protestant	Mainline Protestant	Other Tradition	Black Protestant	Orthodox
MSA[1]	n/a	n/a	n/a	n/a	n/a	n/a
U.S.	19.1	16.2	7.3	4.3	1.6	0.3

Note: Figures are the number of adherents as a percentage of the total population; (1) Figures cover the Laramie, WY Micropolitan Statistical Area—see Appendix B for areas included
Source: Association of Statisticians of American Religious Bodies, 2010 U.S. Religion Census: Religious Congregations & Membership Study

ECONOMY

Gross Metropolitan Product

Area	2014	2015	2016	2017	Rank[2]
MSA[1]	n/a	n/a	n/a	n/a	n/a

Note: Figures are in billions of dollars; (1) Figures cover the Laramie, WY Micropolitan Statistical Area—see Appendix B for areas included; (2) Rank is based on 2015 data and ranges from 1 to 381
Source: The U.S. Conference of Mayors, U.S. Metro Economies: GMP and Employment Report, 2015-2017

Economic Growth

Area	2012-14 (%)	2015 (%)	2016 (%)	2017 (%)	Rank[2]
MSA[1]	n/a	n/a	n/a	n/a	n/a
U.S.	2.0	2.4	1.9	2.6	–

Note: Figures are real gross metropolitan product (GMP) growth rates and represent average annual percent change; (1) Figures cover the Laramie, WY Micropolitan Statistical Area—see Appendix B for areas included; (2) Rank is based on 2012-2014 average annual percent change and ranges from 1 to 381
Source: The U.S. Conference of Mayors, U.S. Metro Economies: GMP and Employment Report, 2015-2017

Metropolitan Area Exports

Area	2011	2012	2013	2014	2015	2016	Rank[2]
MSA[1]	n/a	n/a	n/a	n/a	n/a	n/a	n/a

Note: Figures are in millions of dollars; (1) Figures cover the Laramie, WY Micropolitan Statistical Area—see Appendix B for areas included; (2) Rank is based on 2016 data and ranges from 1 to 385
Source: U.S. Department of Commerce, International Trade Administration, Office of Trade & Industry Information, Manufacturing & Services, data extracted March 15, 2018

Building Permits

Area	Single-Family			Multi-Family			Total		
	2016	2017p	Pct. Chg.	2016	2017p	Pct. Chg.	2016	2017p	Pct. Chg.
City	60	40	-33.3	28	8	-71.4	88	48	-45.5
MSA[1]	123	97	-21.1	28	28	0.0	151	125	-17.2
U.S.	750,800	817,300	8.9	455,800	446,800	-2.0	1,206,600	1,264,100	4.8

Note: (1) Figures cover the Laramie, WY Micropolitan Statistical Area—see Appendix B for areas included; Figures represent new, privately-owned housing units authorized (unadjusted data); All permit data are based on estimates with imputation; (p) preliminary data.
Source: U.S. Census Bureau, Manufacturing, Mining, and Construction Statistics, Building Permits, 2016, 2017

Bankruptcy Filings

Area	Business Filings			Nonbusiness Filings		
	2016	2017	% Chg.	2016	2017	% Chg.
Albany County	2	1	-50.0	28	26	-7.1
U.S.	24,114	23,157	-4.0	770,846	765,863	-0.6

Note: Business filings include Chapter 7, Chapter 11, Chapter 12, and Chapter 13; Nonbusiness filings include Chapter 7, Chapter 11, and Chapter 13
Source: Administrative Office of the U.S. Courts, Business and Nonbusiness Bankruptcy, County Cases Commenced by Chapter of the Bankruptcy Code, During the 12-Month Period Ending December 31, 2016 and Business and Nonbusiness Bankruptcy, County Cases Commenced by Chapter of the Bankruptcy Code, During the 12-Month Period Ending December 31, 2017

Housing Vacancy Rates

Area	Gross Vacancy Rate[2] (%)			Year-Round Vacancy Rate[3] (%)			Rental Vacancy Rate[4] (%)			Homeowner Vacancy Rate[5] (%)		
	2015	2016	2017	2015	2016	2017	2015	2016	2017	2015	2016	2017
MSA[1]	n/a	n/a	n/a	n/a	n/a	n/a	n/a	n/a	n/a	n/a	n/a	n/a
U.S.	12.9	12.8	12.7	10.0	9.9	9.9	7.1	6.9	7.2	1.8	1.7	1.6

Note: (1) Figures cover the Laramie, WY Micropolitan Statistical Area—see Appendix B for areas included; (2) The percentage of the total housing inventory that is vacant; (3) The percentage of the housing inventory (excluding seasonal units) that is year-round vacant; (4) The percentage of rental inventory that is vacant for rent; (5) The percentage of homeowner inventory that is vacant for sale; n/a not available
Source: U.S. Census Bureau, Housing Vacancies and Homeownership Annual Statistics: 2015, 2016, 2017

INCOME

Income

Area	Per Capita ($)	Median Household ($)	Average Household ($)
City	22,404	40,240	53,432
MSA[1]	25,227	43,043	59,866
U.S.	29,829	55,322	77,866

Note: (1) Figures cover the Laramie, WY Micropolitan Statistical Area—see Appendix B for areas included
Source: U.S. Census Bureau, 2012-2016 American Community Survey 5-Year Estimates

Household Income Distribution

Area	Percent of Households Earning							
	Under $15,000	$15,000 -$24,999	$25,000 -$34,999	$35,000 -$49,999	$50,000 -$74,999	$75,000 -$99,999	$100,000 -$149,999	$150,000 and up
City	21.1	14.3	11.5	12.6	16.8	9.1	9.7	4.9
MSA[1]	19.1	13.1	12.1	12.4	16.8	10.1	10.4	6.0
U.S.	12.1	10.2	9.9	13.2	17.8	12.2	13.5	11.1

Note: (1) Figures cover the Laramie, WY Micropolitan Statistical Area—see Appendix B for areas included
Source: U.S. Census Bureau, 2012-2016 American Community Survey 5-Year Estimates

Poverty Rate

Area	All Ages	Under 18 Years Old	18 to 64 Years Old	65 Years and Over
City	28.8	18.8	33.2	8.3
MSA[1]	25.5	17.6	29.8	8.0
U.S.	15.1	21.2	14.2	9.3

Note: Figures are percentage of people whose income during the past 12 months was below the poverty level; (1) Figures cover the Laramie, WY Micropolitan Statistical Area—see Appendix B for areas included
Source: U.S. Census Bureau, 2012-2016 American Community Survey 5-Year Estimates

EMPLOYMENT

Labor Force and Employment

Area	Civilian Labor Force			Workers Employed		
	Dec. 2016	Dec. 2017	% Chg.	Dec. 2016	Dec. 2017	% Chg.
City	17,845	17,448	-2.2	17,337	16,997	-2.0
MSA[1]	21,286	20,808	-2.2	20,655	20,249	-2.0
U.S.	158,968,000	159,880,000	0.6	151,798,000	153,602,000	1.2

Note: Data is not seasonally adjusted and covers workers 16 years of age and older; (1) Figures cover the Laramie, WY Micropolitan Statistical Area—see Appendix B for areas included
Source: Bureau of Labor Statistics, Local Area Unemployment Statistics

Unemployment Rate

Area	2017											
	Jan.	Feb.	Mar.	Apr.	May	Jun.	Jul.	Aug.	Sep.	Oct.	Nov.	Dec.
City	3.3	2.6	2.9	2.4	2.6	3.1	2.8	2.6	2.4	2.6	2.7	2.6
MSA[1]	3.5	2.9	3.1	2.5	2.6	3.2	2.9	2.8	2.6	2.7	2.7	2.7
U.S.	5.1	4.9	4.6	4.1	4.1	4.5	4.6	4.5	4.1	3.9	3.9	3.9

Note: Data is not seasonally adjusted and covers workers 16 years of age and older; (1) Figures cover the Laramie, WY Micropolitan Statistical Area—see Appendix B for areas included
Source: Bureau of Labor Statistics, Local Area Unemployment Statistics

Average Wages

Occupation	$/Hr.	Occupation	$/Hr.
Accountants and Auditors	n/a	Maids and Housekeeping Cleaners	n/a
Automotive Mechanics	n/a	Maintenance and Repair Workers	n/a
Bookkeepers	n/a	Marketing Managers	n/a
Carpenters	n/a	Nuclear Medicine Technologists	n/a
Cashiers	n/a	Nurses, Licensed Practical	n/a
Clerks, General Office	n/a	Nurses, Registered	n/a
Clerks, Receptionists/Information	n/a	Nursing Assistants	n/a
Clerks, Shipping/Receiving	n/a	Packers and Packagers, Hand	n/a
Computer Programmers	n/a	Physical Therapists	n/a
Computer Systems Analysts	n/a	Postal Service Mail Carriers	n/a
Computer User Support Specialists	n/a	Real Estate Brokers	n/a
Cooks, Restaurant	n/a	Retail Salespersons	n/a
Dentists	n/a	Sales Reps., Exc. Tech./Scientific	n/a
Electrical Engineers	n/a	Sales Reps., Tech./Scientific	n/a
Electricians	n/a	Secretaries, Exc. Legal/Med./Exec.	n/a
Financial Managers	n/a	Security Guards	n/a
First-Line Supervisors/Managers, Sales	n/a	Surgeons	n/a
Food Preparation Workers	n/a	Teacher Assistants*	n/a
General and Operations Managers	n/a	Teachers, Elementary School*	n/a
Hairdressers/Cosmetologists	n/a	Teachers, Secondary School*	n/a
Internists, General	n/a	Telemarketers	n/a
Janitors and Cleaners	n/a	Truck Drivers, Heavy/Tractor-Trailer	n/a
Landscaping/Groundskeeping Workers	n/a	Truck Drivers, Light/Delivery Svcs.	n/a
Lawyers	n/a	Waiters and Waitresses	n/a

Note: Wage data was not available.
Source: Bureau of Labor Statistics, Metro Area Occupational Employment & Wage Estimates, May 2017

Employment by Occupation

Occupation Classification	City (%)	MSA[1] (%)	U.S. (%)
Management, Business, Science, and Arts	40.5	41.3	37.0
Natural Resources, Construction, and Maintenance	7.9	8.9	8.9
Production, Transportation, and Material Moving	7.1	7.5	12.2
Sales and Office	19.9	19.1	23.8
Service	24.5	23.2	18.1

Note: Figures cover employed civilians 16 years of age and older; (1) Figures cover the Laramie, WY Micropolitan Statistical Area—see Appendix B for areas included
Source: U.S. Census Bureau, 2012-2016 American Community Survey 5-Year Estimates

Employment by Industry

Sector	MSA[1] Number of Employees	MSA[1] Percent of Total	U.S. Percent of Total
Construction, Mining, and Logging	n/a	n/a	5.2
Education and Health Services	n/a	n/a	15.9
Financial Activities	n/a	n/a	5.7
Government	n/a	n/a	15.3
Information	n/a	n/a	1.9
Leisure and Hospitality	n/a	n/a	10.7
Manufacturing	n/a	n/a	8.5
Other Services	n/a	n/a	3.9
Professional and Business Services	n/a	n/a	14.0
Retail Trade	n/a	n/a	11.0
Transportation, Warehousing, and Utilities	n/a	n/a	4.1
Wholesale Trade	n/a	n/a	4.0

Note: Figures are non-farm employment as of December 2017. Figures are not seasonally adjusted and include workers 16 years of age and older; (1) Figures cover the Laramie, WY Micropolitan Statistical Area—see Appendix B for areas included; n/a not available
Source: Bureau of Labor Statistics, Current Employment Statistics, Employment, Hours, and Earnings

Occupations with Greatest Projected Employment Growth: 2017 – 2019

Occupation[1]	2017 Employment	2019 Projected Employment	Numeric Employment Change	Percent Employment Change
Service Unit Operators, Oil, Gas, and Mining	1,590	2,010	420	26.2
Roustabouts, Oil and Gas	1,470	1,860	390	26.1
Combined Food Preparation and Serving Workers, Including Fast Food	4,760	5,010	250	5.4
Heavy and Tractor-Trailer Truck Drivers	6,280	6,530	250	4.0
Waiters and Waitresses	5,520	5,730	210	3.8
General and Operations Managers	4,740	4,930	190	4.0
Industrial Machinery Mechanics	2,140	2,310	170	8.1
Janitors and Cleaners, Except Maids and Housekeeping Cleaners	5,340	5,510	170	3.3
Retail Salespersons	8,450	8,620	170	2.0
First-Line Supervisors of Construction Trades and Extraction Workers	2,730	2,890	160	5.9

Note: Projections cover Wyoming; (1) Sorted by numeric employment change
Source: www.projectionscentral.com, State Occupational Projections, 2017–2019 Short-Term Projections

Fastest Growing Occupations: 2017 – 2019

Occupation[1]	2017 Employment	2019 Projected Employment	Numeric Employment Change	Percent Employment Change
Extraction Workers, All Other	130	180	50	30.6
Rotary Drill Operators, Oil and Gas	290	370	80	27.2
Derrick Operators, Oil and Gas	340	430	90	26.8
Helpers—Extraction Workers	230	290	60	26.7
Service Unit Operators, Oil, Gas, and Mining	1,590	2,010	420	26.2
Roustabouts, Oil and Gas	1,470	1,860	390	26.1
Geological and Petroleum Technicians	310	380	70	22.8
Petroleum Engineers	540	620	80	15.4
Wellhead Pumpers	510	580	70	13.7
Industrial Machinery Mechanics	2,140	2,310	170	8.1

Note: Projections cover Wyoming; (1) Sorted by percent employment change and excludes occupations with numeric employment change less than 50
Source: www.projectionscentral.com, State Occupational Projections, 2017–2019 Short-Term Projections

TAXES

State Corporate Income Tax Rates

State	Tax Rate (%)	Income Brackets ($)	Num. of Brackets	Financial Institution Tax Rate (%)[a]	Federal Income Tax Ded.
Wyoming	None	–	–	–	–

Note: Tax rates as of January 1, 2018; (a) Rates listed are the corporate income tax rate applied to financial institutions or excise taxes based on income. Some states have other taxes based upon the value of deposits or shares.
Source: Federation of Tax Administrators, Range of State Corporate Income Tax Rates, January 1, 2018

State Individual Income Tax Rates

State	Tax Rate (%)	Income Brackets ($)	Num. of Brackets	Personal Exempt. ($)[1]		Fed. Inc. Tax Ded.
				Single	Dependents	
Wyoming	None	–	–	–	–	–

Note: Tax rates as of January 1, 2018; Local- and county-level taxes are not included; n/a not applicable; (1) Married joint filers generally receive double the single exemption
Source: Federation of Tax Administrators, State Individual Income Tax Rates, January 1, 2018

Various State Sales and Excise Tax Rates

State	State Sales Tax (%)	Gasoline[1] (¢/gal.)	Cigarette[2] ($/pack)	Spirits[3] ($/gal.)	Wine[4] ($/gal.)	Beer[5] ($/gal.)	Recreational Marijuana (%)
Wyoming	4.0	24.0	0.60	0 (g)	(m)	0.02	Not legal

Note: All tax rates as of January 1, 2018; (1) The American Petroleum Institute has developed a methodology for determining the average tax rate on a gallon of fuel. Rates may include any of the following: excise taxes, environmental fees, storage tank fees, other fees or taxes, general sales tax, and local taxes. In states where gasoline is subject to the general sales tax, or where the fuel tax is based on the average sale price, the average rate determined by API is sensitive to changes in the price of gasoline. States that fully or partially apply general sales taxes to gasoline: CA, CO, GA, IL, IN, MI, NY; (2) The federal excise tax of $1.0066 per pack and local taxes are not included; (3) Rates are those applicable to off-premise sales of 40% alcohol by volume (a.b.v.) distilled spirits in 750ml containers. Local excise taxes are excluded; (4) Rates are those applicable to off-premise sales of 11% a.b.v. non-carbonated wine in 750ml containers; (5) Rates are those applicable to off-premise sales of 4.7% a.b.v. beer in 12 ounce containers; (g) Control states, where the government controls all sales. Products can be subject to ad valorem mark-up as well as excise taxes; (m) Control states, where the government controls all sales. Products can be subject to ad valorem mark-up as well as excise taxes.
Source: Tax Foundation, 2018 Facts & Figures: How Does Your State Compare?

State Business Tax Climate Index Rankings

State	Overall Rank	Corporate Tax Rank	Individual Income Tax Rank	Sales Tax Rank	Unemployment Insurance Tax Rank	Property Tax Rank
Wyoming	1	1	1	6	33	34

Note: The index is a measure of how each state's tax laws affect economic performance. The lower the rank, the more favorable a state's tax system is for business. States without a given tax are given a ranking of 1. The scores/rankings for the District of Columbia do not affect other states. The 2018 index represents the tax climate as of July 1, 2017.
Source: Tax Foundation, State Business Tax Climate Index 2018

TRANSPORTATION

Means of Transportation to Work

Area	Car/Truck/Van		Public Transportation			Bicycle	Walked	Other Means	Worked at Home
	Drove Alone	Car-pooled	Bus	Subway	Railroad				
City	65.3	10.6	2.9	0.0	0.0	5.1	10.8	0.7	4.6
MSA[1]	66.6	10.4	2.5	0.0	0.0	4.4	9.8	0.7	5.5
U.S.	76.4	9.3	2.6	1.9	0.6	0.6	2.8	1.3	4.6

Note: Figures are percentages and cover workers 16 years of age and older; (1) Figures cover the Laramie, WY Micropolitan Statistical Area—see Appendix B for areas included
Source: U.S. Census Bureau, 2012-2016 American Community Survey 5-Year Estimates

Travel Time to Work

Area	Less Than 10 Minutes	10 to 19 Minutes	20 to 29 Minutes	30 to 44 Minutes	45 to 59 Minutes	60 to 89 Minutes	90 Minutes or More
City	50.7	38.3	4.5	1.7	2.2	1.8	0.8
MSA[1]	46.1	39.3	6.3	2.9	2.7	1.8	0.9
U.S.	12.9	29.2	20.9	20.4	8.0	6.0	2.7

Note: Note: Figures are percentages and include workers 16 years old and over; (1) Figures cover the Laramie, WY Micropolitan Statistical Area—see Appendix B for areas included
Source: U.S. Census Bureau, 2012-2016 American Community Survey 5-Year Estimates

Freeway Travel Time Index

Area	1985	1990	1995	2000	2005	2010	2014
Urban Area Rank[1,2]	n/a	n/a	n/a	n/a	n/a	n/a	n/a
Urban Area Index[1]	n/a	n/a	n/a	n/a	n/a	n/a	n/a
Average Index[3]	1.09	1.11	1.14	1.17	1.20	1.19	1.20

Note: Freeway Travel Time Index—the ratio of travel time in the peak period to the travel time at free-flow conditions. For example, a value of 1.30 indicates a 20-minute free-flow trip takes 26 minutes in the peak (20 minutes x 1.30 = 26 minutes); (1) Data for the Laramie, WY urban area was not available; (2) Rank is based on 101 urban areas (#1 = highest travel time index); (3) Average of 101 urban areas
Source: Texas Transportation Institute, 2015 Urban Mobility Scorecard, August 2015

Freeway Commuter Stress Index

Area	1985	1990	1995	2000	2005	2010	2014
Urban Area Rank[1,2]	n/a	n/a	n/a	n/a	n/a	n/a	n/a
Urban Area Index[1]	n/a	n/a	n/a	n/a	n/a	n/a	n/a
Average Index[3]	1.13	1.16	1.19	1.22	1.25	1.24	1.25

Note: The Freeway Commuter Stress Index is the same as the Freeway Travel Time Index (see table above) except that it includes only the travel in the peak directions during the peak periods; the TTI includes travel in all directions during the peak period. Thus, the CSI is more indicative of the work trip experienced by each commuter on a daily basis; (1) Data for the Laramie, WY urban area was not available; (2) Rank is based on 101 urban areas (#1 = highest travel time index); (3) Average of 101 urban areas
Source: Texas Transportation Institute, 2015 Urban Mobility Scorecard, August 2015

Living Environment

COST OF LIVING

Cost of Living Index

Composite Index	Groceries	Housing	Utilities	Transportation	Health Care	Misc. Goods/ Services
95.3	109.3	81.9	109.3	94.6	98.6	96.6

Note: The Cost of Living Index measures regional differences in the cost of consumer goods and services, excluding taxes and non-consumer expenditures, for professional and managerial households in the top income quintile. It is based on more than 50,000 prices covering almost 60 different items for which prices are collected three times a year by chambers of commerce, economic development organizations or university applied economic centers in each participating urban area. The numbers shown should be read as a percentage above or below the national average of 100. For example, a value of 115.4 in the groceries column indicates that grocery prices are 15.4% higher than the national average. Small differences in the index numbers should not be interpreted as significant; Figures cover the Laramie WY urban area.
Source: The Council for Community and Economic Research, ACCRA Cost of Living Index, 2017

Grocery Prices

Area[1]	T-Bone Steak ($/pound)	Frying Chicken ($/pound)	Whole Milk ($/half gal.)	Eggs ($/dozen)	Orange Juice ($/64 oz.)	Coffee ($/11.5 oz.)
City[2]	12.92	1.28	2.56	1.57	3.85	4.95
Avg.	11.29	1.40	2.02	1.47	3.55	4.37
Min.	7.71	0.93	1.04	0.70	2.86	3.24
Max.	15.83	2.39	4.03	3.92	6.29	8.16

*Note: (1) Values for the local area are compared with the average, minimum and maximum values for all 294 areas in the Cost of Living Index; (2) Figures cover the Laramie WY urban area; **T-Bone Steak** (price per pound); **Frying Chicken** (price per pound, whole fryer); **Whole Milk** (half gallon carton); **Eggs** (price per dozen, Grade A, large); **Orange Juice** (64 oz. Tropicana or Florida Natural); **Coffee** (11.5 oz. can, vacuum-packed, Maxwell House, Hills Bros, or Folgers).*
Source: The Council for Community and Economic Research, ACCRA Cost of Living Index, 2017

Housing and Utility Costs

Area[1]	New Home Price ($)	Apartment Rent ($/month)	All Electric ($/month)	Part Electric ($/month)	Other Energy ($/month)	Telephone ($/month)
City[2]	276,055	858	-	65.31	66.99	41.62
Avg.	335,956	1,047	175.01	97.34	67.93	28.71
Min.	187,788	491	109.48	49.33	35.44	12.39
Max.	1,739,087	4,559	432.62	227.09	353.33	44.61

*Note: (1) Values for the local area are compared with the average, minimum and maximum values for all 294 areas in the Cost of Living Index; (2) Figures cover the Laramie WY urban area; **New Home Price** (2,400 sf living area, 8,000 sf lot, in urban area with full utilities); **Apartment Rent** (950 sf 2 bedroom/1.5 or 2 bath, unfurnished, excluding all utilities except water); **All Electric** (average monthly cost for an all-electric home); **Part Electric** (average monthly cost for a part-electric home); **Other Energy** (average monthly cost for natural gas, fuel oil, coal, wood, and any other forms of energy except electricity); **Telephone** (price includes basic monthly rate for a private residential line plus additional local usage charges incurred by a family of four).*
Source: The Council for Community and Economic Research, ACCRA Cost of Living Index, 2017

Health Care, Transportation, and Other Costs

Area[1]	Doctor ($/visit)	Dentist ($/visit)	Optometrist ($/visit)	Gasoline ($/gallon)	Beauty Salon ($/visit)	Men's Shirt ($)
City[2]	104.92	86.92	140.76	2.16	30.00	50.83
Avg.	108.00	92.54	101.93	2.25	37.58	30.92
Min.	30.39	60.00	49.75	1.82	16.11	11.20
Max.	193.50	161.94	229.28	3.16	77.35	59.13

*Note: (1) Values for the local area are compared with the average, minimum and maximum values for all 294 areas in the Cost of Living Index; (2) Figures cover the Laramie WY urban area; **Doctor** (general practitioners routine exam of an established patient); **Dentist** (adult teeth cleaning and periodic oral examination); **Optometrist** (full vision eye exam for established adult patient); **Gasoline** (one gallon regular unleaded, national brand, including all taxes, cash price at self-service pump if available); **Beauty Salon** (woman's shampoo, trim, and blow-dry); **Men's Shirt** (cotton/polyester dress shirt, pinpoint weave, long sleeves).*
Source: The Council for Community and Economic Research, ACCRA Cost of Living Index, 2017

HOUSING

House Price Index (HPI)

Area	National Ranking[2]	Quarterly Change (%)	One-Year Change (%)	Five-Year Change (%)
MSA[1]	n/a	n/a	n/a	n/a
U.S.[3]	-	1.61	6.68	34.71

Note: The HPI is a weighted repeat sales index. It measures average price changes in repeat sales or refinancings on the same properties. This information is obtained by reviewing repeat mortgage transactions on single-family properties whose mortgages have been purchased or securitized by Fannie Mae or Freddie Mac in January 1975; (1) Figures cover the , Micropolitan Statistical Area—see Appendix B for areas included; (2) Rankings are based on annual percentage change for all metro areas containing at least 15,000 transactions over the last 10 years and ranges from 1 to 253; (3) figures based on a weighted average of Census Division estimates using a seasonally adjusted, purchase-only index; all figures are for the period ending December 31, 2017; n/a not available
Source: Federal Housing Finance Agency, House Price Index, February 28, 2018

Median Single-Family Home Prices

Area	2015	2016	2017p	Percent Change 2016 to 2017
MSA[1]	n/a	n/a	n/a	n/a
U.S. Average	223.9	235.5	248.8	5.6

Note: Figures are median sales prices of existing single-family homes in thousands of dollars; (p) preliminary; n/a not available; (1) Figures cover the Laramie, WY Micropolitan Statistical Area—see Appendix B for areas included
Source: National Association of Realtors, Median Sales Price of Existing Single-Family Homes for Metropolitan Areas, 4th Quarter 2017

Qualifying Income Based on Median Sales Price of Existing Single-Family Homes

Area	With 5% Down ($)	With 10% Down ($)	With 20% Down ($)
MSA[1]	n/a	n/a	n/a
U.S. Average	55,585	52,659	46,808

Note: Figures are preliminary; Qualifying income is based on a mortgage rate of 4.17%. Monthly principal and interest payment is limited to 25% of income; n/a not available; (1) Figures cover the Laramie, WY Micropolitan Statistical Area—see Appendix B for areas included
Source: National Association of Realtors, Qualifying Income Based on Median Sales Price of Existing Single-Family Homes for Metropolitan Areas, 4th Quarter 2017

Median Apartment Condo-Coop Home Prices

Area	2015	2016	2017p	Percent Change 2016 to 2017
MSA[1]	n/a	n/a	n/a	n/a
U.S. Average	210.7	220.7	234.3	6.2

Note: Figures are median sales prices of existing apartment condo-coop homes in thousands of dollars; (p) preliminary; n/a not available; (1) Figures cover the Laramie, WY Micropolitan Statistical Area—see Appendix B for areas included
Source: National Association of Realtors, Median Sales Price of Existing Apartment Condo-Coop Homes for Metropolitan Areas, 4th Quarter 2017

Home Value Distribution

Area	Under $50,000	$50,000 -$99,999	$100,000 -$149,999	$150,000 -$199,999	$200,000 -$299,999	$300,000 -$499,999	$500,000 -$999,999	$1,000,000 or more
City	11.9	3.1	10.6	22.0	31.6	19.2	1.3	0.3
MSA[1]	11.0	3.5	10.7	17.8	30.4	20.5	4.0	2.2
U.S.	8.8	14.8	15.3	14.9	18.4	16.4	9.0	2.5

Note: Figures are percentages and cover owner-occupied housing units; (1) Figures cover the Laramie, WY Micropolitan Statistical Area—see Appendix B for areas included
Source: U.S. Census Bureau, 2012-2016 American Community Survey 5-Year Estimates

Homeownership Rate

Area	2009 (%)	2010 (%)	2011 (%)	2012 (%)	2013 (%)	2014 (%)	2015 (%)	2016 (%)	2017 (%)
MSA[1]	n/a	n/a	n/a	n/a	n/a	n/a	n/a	n/a	n/a
U.S.	67.4	66.9	66.1	65.4	65.1	64.5	63.7	63.4	63.9

Note: (1) Figures cover the Laramie, WY Micropolitan Statistical Area—see Appendix B for areas included; n/a not available
Source: U.S. Census Bureau, Housing Vacancies and Homeownership Annual Statistics: 2009-2017

Year Housing Structure Built

Area	2010 or Later	2000 -2009	1990 -1999	1980 -1989	1970 -1979	1960 -1969	1950 -1959	1940 -1949	Before 1940	Median Year
City	3.9	19.5	12.3	9.1	14.7	9.9	10.0	3.9	16.7	1976
MSA[1]	3.7	19.3	13.0	9.1	17.0	9.8	9.3	3.9	15.0	1977
U.S.	2.3	14.7	14.0	13.7	15.6	10.9	10.6	5.2	13.0	1977

Note: Figures are percentages except for Median Year; Note: (1) Figures cover the Laramie, WY Micropolitan Statistical Area—see Appendix B for areas included
Source: U.S. Census Bureau, 2012-2016 American Community Survey 5-Year Estimates

Gross Monthly Rent

Area	Under $500	$500 -$999	$1,000 -$1,499	$1,500 -$1,999	$2,000 -$2,499	$2,500 -$2,999	$3,000 and up	Median ($)
City	16.8	56.6	21.4	4.9	0.2	0.0	0.0	728
MSA[1]	17.4	56.4	21.3	4.7	0.2	0.0	0.0	729
U.S.	11.3	43.3	27.7	10.7	4.0	1.6	1.5	949

Note: Figures are percentages except for Median; Gross rent is the contract rent plus the estimated average monthly cost of utilities (electricity, gas, and water and sewer) and fuels (oil, coal, kerosene, wood, etc.) if these are paid by the renter (or paid for the renter by someone else); (1) Figures cover the Laramie, WY Micropolitan Statistical Area—see Appendix B for areas included
Source: U.S. Census Bureau, 2012-2016 American Community Survey 5-Year Estimates

HEALTH

Health Risk Factors

Category	MSA[1] (%)	U.S. (%)
Adults aged 18–64 who have any kind of health care coverage	n/a	87.7
Adults who reported being in good or excellent health	n/a	83.6
Adults who are current smokers	n/a	17.1
Adults who currently use E-cigarettes	n/a	4.7
Adults who currently use chewing tobacco, snuff, or snus	n/a	4.0
Adults who are heavy drinkers[2]	n/a	6.5
Adults who are binge drinkers[3]	n/a	16.9
Adults who are overweight (BMI 25.0 - 29.9)	n/a	35.3
Adults who are obese (BMI 30.0 - 99.8)	n/a	29.9
Adults who participated in any physical activities in the past month	n/a	76.9
Adults who always or nearly always wears a seat belt	n/a	94.3

Note: n/a not available; (1) Figures cover the Laramie, WY Micropolitan Statistical Area—see Appendix B for areas included; (2) Heavy drinkers are classified as adult men having more than 14 drinks per week and adult women having more than 7 drinks per week; (3) Binge drinkers are classified as males having five or more drinks on one occasion or females having four or more drinks on one occasion
Source: Centers for Disease Control and Prevention, Behaviorial Risk Factor Surveillance System, SMART: Selected Metropolitan Area Risk Trends, 2016

Health Screening Rates

Category	MSA[1] (%)	U.S. (%)
Adults 50-75 who have had a blood stool test within the past year	n/a	8.0
Adults 50-75 who have had a colonoscopy in the past 10 years	n/a	63.5
Adults aged 65+ who have had flu shot within the past year	n/a	58.6
Adults aged 65+ who have ever had a pneumonia vaccination	n/a	73.4
Adults who have ever been tested for HIV	n/a	35.6
Women aged 21-65 who have had a pap test in the past three years	n/a	79.8
Men aged 40+ who have had a PSA test within the past two years	n/a	39.5
Women aged 40+ who have had a mammogram within the past two years	n/a	72.5

Note: n/a not available; (1) Figures cover the Laramie, WY Micropolitan Statistical Area—see Appendix B for areas included; Source: Centers for Disease Control and Prevention, Behaviorial Risk Factor Surveillance System, SMART: Selected Metropolitan Area Risk Trends, 2016

Chronic Health Conditions

Category	MSA[1] (%)	U.S. (%)
Adults who have ever been told they had a heart attack	n/a	4.4
Adults who have ever been told they have angina or coronary heart disease	n/a	4.1
Adults who have ever been told they had a stroke	n/a	3.1
Adults who have been told they currently have asthma	n/a	9.3
Adults who have ever been told they have arthritis	n/a	25.8
Adults who have ever been told they have diabetes[2]	n/a	10.5
Adults who have ever been told they had skin cancer	n/a	5.9
Adults who have ever been told they had any other types of cancer	n/a	6.7
Adults who have ever been told they have COPD	n/a	6.3
Adults who have ever been told they have kidney disease	n/a	2.8
Adults who have ever been told they have a form of depression	n/a	17.4

Note: n/a not available; (1) Figures cover the Laramie, WY Micropolitan Statistical Area—see Appendix B for areas included; (2) Figures do not include pregnancy-related, borderline, or pre-diabetes
Source: Centers for Disease Control and Prevention, Behaviorial Risk Factor Surveillance System, SMART: Selected Metropolitan Area Risk Trends, 2016

Mortality Rates for the Top 10 Causes of Death in the U.S.

ICD-10[a] Sub-Chapter	ICD-10[a] Code	Age-Adjusted Mortality Rate[1] per 100,000 population	
		County[2]	U.S.
Malignant neoplasms	C00-C97	95.0	158.5
Ischaemic heart diseases	I20-I25	71.7	96.8
Other forms of heart disease	I30-I51	49.7	52.4
Chronic lower respiratory diseases	J40-J47	47.8	40.9
Cerebrovascular diseases	I60-I69	27.0	37.2
Organic, including symptomatic, mental disorders	F01-F09	Unreliable	33.3
Other degenerative diseases of the nervous system	G30-G31	25.7	32.1
Other external causes of accidental injury	W00-X59	31.1	31.2
Diabetes mellitus	E10-E14	Unreliable	21.1
Hypertensive diseases	I10-I15	Suppressed	20.8

Note: (a) ICD-10 = International Classification of Diseases 10th Revision; (1) Mortality rates are a three year average covering 2014-2016; (2) Figures cover Albany County.
Source: Centers for Disease Control and Prevention, National Center for Health Statistics. Underlying Cause of Death 1999-2016 on CDC WONDER Online Database, released December 2017

Mortality Rates for Selected Causes of Death

ICD-10[a] Sub-Chapter	ICD-10[a] Code	Age-Adjusted Mortality Rate[1] per 100,000 population	
		County[2]	U.S.
Assault	X85-Y09	Suppressed	5.6
Diseases of the liver	K70-K76	Unreliable	14.0
Human immunodeficiency virus (HIV) disease	B20-B24	Suppressed	1.9
Influenza and pneumonia	J09-J18	Unreliable	14.6
Intentional self-harm	X60-X84	Unreliable	13.2
Malnutrition	E40-E46	Suppressed	1.3
Obesity and other hyperalimentation	E65-E68	Suppressed	2.1
Renal failure	N17-N19	Suppressed	13.0
Transport accidents	V01-V99	Unreliable	12.0
Viral hepatitis	B15-B19	Suppressed	1.9

Note: (a) ICD-10 = International Classification of Diseases 10th Revision; (1) Mortality rates are a three year average covering 2014-2016; (2) Figures cover Albany County; Data are Suppressed when the data meet the criteria for confidentiality constraints; Mortality rates are flagged as Unreliable when the rate would be calculated with a numerator of 20 or less.
Source: Centers for Disease Control and Prevention, National Center for Health Statistics. Underlying Cause of Death 1999-2016 on CDC WONDER Online Database, released December 2017

Health Insurance Coverage

Area	With Health Insurance	With Private Health Insurance	With Public Health Insurance	Without Health Insurance	Population Under Age 18 Without Health Insurance
City	91.2	81.2	17.3	8.8	3.8
MSA[1]	91.3	80.5	19.3	8.7	3.8
U.S.	88.3	66.7	33.0	11.7	5.9

Note: Figures are percentages that cover the civilian noninstitutionalized population; (1) Figures cover the Laramie, WY Micropolitan Statistical Area—see Appendix B for areas included
Source: U.S. Census Bureau, 2012-2016 American Community Survey 5-Year Estimates

Number of Medical Professionals

Area	MDs[3]	DOs[3,4]	Dentists	Podiatrists	Chiropractors	Optometrists
County[1] (number)	62	8	20	1	8	10
County[1] (rate[2])	163.0	21.0	52.6	2.6	21.1	26.3
U.S. (rate[2])	276.5	22.3	67.3	6.0	26.7	15.9

Note: Data as of 2016 unless noted; (1) Data covers Albany County; (2) Rate per 100,000 population; (3) Data as of 2015 and includes all active, non-federal physicians; (4) Doctor of Osteopathic Medicine
Source: U.S. Department of Health and Human Services, Health Resources and Services Administration, Bureau of Health Professions, Area Resource File (ARF) 2016-2017

EDUCATION

Public School District Statistics

District Name	Schls	Pupils	Pupil/ Teacher Ratio	Minority Pupils[1] (%)	Free Lunch Eligible[2] (%)	IEP[3] (%)
Albany County School District #1	18	3,965	n/a	23.6	20.5	12.4

Note: Table includes school districts with 100 or more students; (1) Percentage of students that are not non-Hispanic white; (2) Percentage of students that are eligible for the free lunch program; (3) Percentage of students that have an Individualized Education Program.
Source: U.S. Department of Education, National Center for Education Statistics, Common Core of Data, Local Education Agency (School District) Universe Survey: School Year 2015-2016; U.S. Department of Education, National Center for Education Statistics, Common Core of Data, Public Elementary/Secondary School Universe Survey: School Year 2015-2016

Highest Level of Education

Area	Less than H.S.	H.S. Diploma	Some College, No Deg.	Associate Degree	Bachelor's Degree	Master's Degree	Prof. School Degree	Doctorate Degree
City	4.3	15.1	22.5	8.6	28.4	11.8	2.6	6.7
MSA[1]	4.2	16.8	22.2	8.9	27.4	11.6	2.5	6.3
U.S.	13.0	27.5	21.0	8.2	18.8	8.2	2.0	1.3

Note: Figures cover persons age 25 and over; (1) Figures cover the Laramie, WY Micropolitan Statistical Area—see Appendix B for areas included
Source: U.S. Census Bureau, 2012-2016 American Community Survey 5-Year Estimates

Educational Attainment by Race

Area	High School Graduate or Higher (%)					Bachelor's Degree or Higher (%)				
	Total	White	Black	Asian	Hisp.[2]	Total	White	Black	Asian	Hisp.[2]
City	95.7	96.1	100.0	100.0	77.3	49.5	49.2	80.7	85.9	20.6
MSA[1]	95.8	96.2	100.0	100.0	77.9	47.9	47.5	79.5	81.8	23.3
U.S.	87.0	88.9	84.3	86.3	65.7	30.3	31.6	20.0	52.1	14.7

Note: Figures shown cover persons 25 years old and over; (1) Figures cover the Laramie, WY Micropolitan Statistical Area—see Appendix B for areas included; (2) People of Hispanic origin can be of any race
Source: U.S. Census Bureau, 2012-2016 American Community Survey 5-Year Estimates

School Enrollment by Grade and Control

Area	Preschool (%)		Kindergarten (%)		Grades 1 - 4 (%)		Grades 5 - 8 (%)		Grades 9 - 12 (%)	
	Public	Private	Public	Private	Public	Private	Public	Private	Public	Private
City	62.5	37.5	100.0	0.0	89.8	10.2	93.4	6.6	92.4	7.6
MSA[1]	65.9	34.1	100.0	0.0	90.4	9.6	92.7	7.3	90.6	9.4
U.S.	58.4	41.6	87.7	12.3	89.8	10.2	89.7	10.3	90.4	9.6

Note: Figures shown cover persons 3 years old and over; (1) Figures cover the Laramie, WY Micropolitan Statistical Area—see Appendix B for areas included
Source: U.S. Census Bureau, 2012-2016 American Community Survey 5-Year Estimates

Average Salaries of Public School Classroom Teachers

Area	2015 Dollars	2015 Rank[1]	2016 Dollars	2016 Rank[1]	Change from 2015 to 2016 Percent	Change from 2015 to 2016 Rank[2]
Wyoming	57,414	16	58,140	16	1.3	19
U.S. Average	57,611	–	58,353	–	1.3	–

Note: (1) Rank ranges from 1 to 51 where 1 indicates highest salary; (2) Rank ranges from 1 to 51 where 1 indicates highest percent change.
Source: National Education Association, Rankings & Estimates: Rankings of the States 2016 and Estimates of School Statistics 2017

Higher Education

Four-Year Colleges			Two-Year Colleges			Medical Schools[1]	Law Schools[2]	Voc/ Tech[3]
Public	Private Non-profit	Private For-profit	Public	Private Non-profit	Private For-profit			
1	0	0	0	1	0	0	1	0

Note: Figures cover institutions located within the city limits and include main campuses only; (1) includes schools accredited by the Liaison Committee on Medical Education and the American Osteopathic Association's Commission on Osteopathic College Accreditation; (2) includes ABA-accredited schools, schools with provisional ABA accreditation, and state accredited schools; (3) includes all schools with programs that are less than 2 years.
Source: National Center for Education Statistics, Integrated Postsecondary Education System (IPEDS), 2016-17; Wikipedia, List of Medical Schools in the United States, accessed April 2, 2018; Wikipedia, List of Law Schools in the United States, accessed April 2, 2018

According to *U.S. News & World Report,* the Laramie, WY metro area is home to one of the best national universities in the U.S.: **University of Wyoming** (#181 tie). The indicators used to capture academic quality fall into a number of categories: assessment by administrators at peer institutions; retention of students; faculty resources; student selectivity; financial resources; alumni giving; high school counselor ratings of colleges; and graduation rate. *U.S. News & World Report, "America's Best Colleges 2018"*

PRESIDENTIAL ELECTION

2016 Presidential Election Results

Area	Clinton	Trump	Johnson	Stein	Other
Albany County	40.4	44.6	8.2	2.0	4.9
U.S.	48.0	45.9	3.3	1.1	1.7

Note: Results are percentages and may not add to 100% due to rounding
Source: Dave Leip's Atlas of U.S. Presidential Elections

EMPLOYERS

Major Employers

Company Name	Industry
Behavioral Health Services-Ivinson	Healthcare
City of Laramie	Local government
Laramie Regional Airport	Airport
Trihydro Corp	Environmental engineering
University of Wyoming	Public university
WyoTech	Education

Note: Companies shown are located within the Laramie, WY Micropolitan Statistical Area.
Source: Hoovers.com; Wikipedia

PUBLIC SAFETY

Crime Rate

Area	All Crimes	Violent Crimes: Murder	Violent Crimes: Rape[3]	Violent Crimes: Robbery	Violent Crimes: Aggrav. Assault	Property Crimes: Burglary	Property Crimes: Larceny -Theft	Property Crimes: Motor Vehicle Theft
City	1,382.2	0.0	37.0	6.2	74.0	175.9	1,036.7	52.5
Metro[1]	n/a	n/a	n/a	n/a	n/a	n/a	n/a	n/a
U.S.	2,847.8	5.3	40.4	102.8	248.5	468.9	1,745.0	236.9

Note: Figures are crimes per 100,000 population; (1) Figures cover the Laramie, WY Micropolitan Statistical Area—see Appendix B for areas included; n/a not available; (3) The city and U.S. figures shown were reported using the revised Uniform Crime Reporting (UCR) definition of rape. The metro area figures shown are an aggregate total of the data submitted using both the revised and legacy UCR definitions.
Source: FBI Uniform Crime Reports, 2016

Hate Crimes

Area	Number of Quarters Reported	Race/Ethnicity/ Ancestry	Religion	Sexual Orientation	Disability	Gender	Gender Identity
		Number of Incidents per Bias Motivation					
City	4	0	0	0	0	0	0
U.S.	4	3,489	1,273	1,076	70	31	124

Source: Federal Bureau of Investigation, Hate Crime Statistics 2016

Identity Theft Consumer Reports

Area	Reports	Reports per 100,000 Population	Rank[2]
MSA[1]	n/a	n/a	n/a
U.S.	371,061	114	-

Note: (1) Figures cover the Laramie, WY Micropolitan Statistical Area—see Appendix B for areas included; (2) Rank ranges from 1 to 389 where 1 indicates greatest number of identity theft reports per 100,000 population
Source: Federal Trade Commission, Consumer Sentinel Network Data Book for January–December 2017

Fraud and Other Consumer Reports

Area	Reports	Reports per 100,000 Population	Rank[2]
MSA[1]	n/a	n/a	n/a
U.S.	2,304,550	708	-

Note: (1) Figures cover the Laramie, WY Micropolitan Statistical Area—see Appendix B for areas included; (2) Rank ranges from 1 to 389 where 1 indicates greatest number of fraud and other consumer reports per 100,000 population
Source: Federal Trade Commission, Consumer Sentinel Network Data Book for January–December 2017

SPORTS

Professional Sports Teams

Team Name	League	Year Established

No teams are located in the metro area
Source: Wikipedia, Major Professional Sports Teams of the United States and Canada, April 5, 2018

CLIMATE

Average and Extreme Temperatures

Temperature	Jan	Feb	Mar	Apr	May	Jun	Jul	Aug	Sep	Oct	Nov	Dec	Yr.
Extreme High (°F)	66	71	74	83	90	100	98	96	95	83	73	66	100
Average High (°F)	38	41	45	55	64	75	82	81	72	60	46	40	58
Average Temp. (°F)	27	29	33	42	52	62	69	67	58	47	35	29	46
Average Low (°F)	15	18	22	30	40	48	54	53	44	34	23	18	33
Extreme Low (°F)	-29	-25	-19	-8	17	25	38	36	8	-1	-16	-28	-29

Note: Figures cover the years 1948-1995
Source: National Climatic Data Center, International Station Meteorological Climate Summary, 9/96

Average Precipitation/Snowfall/Humidity

Precip./Humidity	Jan	Feb	Mar	Apr	May	Jun	Jul	Aug	Sep	Oct	Nov	Dec	Yr.
Avg. Precip. (in.)	0.4	0.4	1.0	1.4	2.5	2.2	2.0	1.6	1.2	0.8	0.6	0.4	14.6
Avg. Snowfall (in.)	6	6	11	8	3	Tr	Tr	0	1	4	7	6	53
Avg. Rel. Hum. 5am (%)	58	62	66	69	74	73	71	70	66	61	61	59	66
Avg. Rel. Hum. 5pm (%)	51	49	48	43	46	41	38	38	38	41	51	53	45

Note: Figures cover the years 1948-1995; Tr = Trace amounts (<0.05 in. of rain; <0.5 in. of snow)
Source: National Climatic Data Center, International Station Meteorological Climate Summary, 9/96

Weather Conditions

Temperature			Daytime Sky			Precipitation		
5°F & below	32°F & below	90°F & above	Clear	Partly cloudy	Cloudy	0.01 inch or more precip.	0.1 inch or more snow/ice	Thunder-storms
19	173	9	94	172	99	99	44	51

Note: Figures are average number of days per year and cover the years 1948-1995
Source: National Climatic Data Center, International Station Meteorological Climate Summary, 9/96

HAZARDOUS WASTE

Superfund Sites

The Laramie, WY metro area has no sites on the EPA's Superfund Final National Priorities List. There are a total of 1,396 Superfund sites with a status of proposed or final on the list in the U.S.
U.S. Environmental Protection Agency, National Priorities List, April 4, 2018

AIR & WATER QUALITY

Air Quality Trends: Ozone

	1990	1995	2000	2005	2010	2012	2013	2014	2015	2016
MSA[1]	n/a	n/a	n/a	n/a	n/a	n/a	n/a	n/a	n/a	n/a
U.S.	0.087	0.089	0.081	0.079	0.073	0.075	0.069	0.067	0.068	0.069

Note: (1) Data covers the Laramie, WY Micropolitan Statistical Area—see Appendix B for areas included; n/a not available. The values shown are the composite ozone concentration averages among trend sites based on the highest fourth daily maximum 8-hour concentration in parts per million. These trends are based on sites having an adequate record of monitoring data during the trend period. Data from exceptional events are included.
Source: U.S. Environmental Protection Agency, Air Quality Monitoring Information, "Air Quality Trends by City, 1990-2016"

Air Quality Index

Area	Percent of Days when Air Quality was...[2]					AQI Statistics[2]	
	Good	Moderate	Unhealthy for Sensitive Groups	Unhealthy	Very Unhealthy	Maximum	Median
MSA[1]	61.6	37.5	0.5	0.3	0.0	153	48

Note: (1) Data covers the Laramie, WY Micropolitan Statistical Area—see Appendix B for areas included; (2) Based on 365 days with AQI data in 2017. Air Quality Index (AQI) is an index for reporting daily air quality. EPA calculates the AQI for five major air pollutants regulated by the Clean Air Act: ground-level ozone, particle pollution (aka particulate matter), carbon monoxide, sulfur dioxide, and nitrogen dioxide. The AQI runs from 0 to 500. The higher the AQI value, the greater the level of air pollution and the greater the health concern. There are six AQI categories: "Good" AQI is between 0 and 50. Air quality is considered satisfactory; "Moderate" AQI is between 51 and 100. Air quality is acceptable; "Unhealthy for Sensitive Groups" When AQI values are between 101 and 150, members of sensitive groups may experience health effects; "Unhealthy" When AQI values are between 151 and 200 everyone may begin to experience health effects; "Very Unhealthy" AQI values between 201 and 300 trigger a health alert; "Hazardous" AQI values over 300 trigger warnings of emergency conditions (not shown).
Source: U.S. Environmental Protection Agency, Air Quality Index Report, 2017

Air Quality Index Pollutants

Area	Percent of Days when AQI Pollutant was...[2]					
	Carbon Monoxide	Nitrogen Dioxide	Ozone	Sulfur Dioxide	Particulate Matter 2.5	Particulate Matter 10
MSA[1]	0.0	0.5	88.5	0.0	2.2	8.8

Note: (1) Data covers the Laramie, WY Micropolitan Statistical Area—see Appendix B for areas included; (2) Based on 365 days with AQI data in 2017. The Air Quality Index (AQI) is an index for reporting daily air quality. EPA calculates the AQI for five major air pollutants regulated by the Clean Air Act: ground-level ozone, particle pollution (also known as particulate matter), carbon monoxide, sulfur dioxide, and nitrogen dioxide. The AQI runs from 0 to 500. The higher the AQI value, the greater the level of air pollution and the greater the health concern.
Source: U.S. Environmental Protection Agency, Air Quality Index Report, 2017

Maximum Air Pollutant Concentrations: Particulate Matter, Ozone, CO and Lead

	Particulate Matter 10 (ug/m^3)	Particulate Matter 2.5 Wtd AM (ug/m^3)	Particulate Matter 2.5 24-Hr (ug/m^3)	Ozone (ppm)	Carbon Monoxide (ppm)	Lead (ug/m^3)
MSA[1] Level	114	3.9	11	0.064	n/a	n/a
NAAQS[2]	150	15	35	0.075	9	0.15
Met NAAQS[2]	Yes	Yes	Yes	Yes	n/a	n/a

Note: (1) Data covers the Laramie, WY Micropolitan Statistical Area—see Appendix B for areas included; Data from exceptional events are included; (2) National Ambient Air Quality Standards; ppm = parts per million; ug/m^3 = micrograms per cubic meter; n/a not available.
Concentrations: Particulate Matter 10 (coarse particulate)—highest second maximum 24-hour concentration; Particulate Matter 2.5 Wtd AM (fine particulate)—highest weighted annual mean concentration; Particulate Matter 2.5 24-Hour (fine particulate)—highest 98th percentile 24-hour concentration; Ozone—highest fourth daily maximum 8-hour concentration; Carbon Monoxide—highest second maximum non-overlapping 8-hour concentration; Lead—maximum running 3-month average
Source: U.S. Environmental Protection Agency, Air Quality Monitoring Information, "Air Quality Statistics by City, 2016"

Maximum Air Pollutant Concentrations: Nitrogen Dioxide and Sulfur Dioxide

	Nitrogen Dioxide AM (ppb)	Nitrogen Dioxide 1-Hr (ppb)	Sulfur Dioxide AM (ppb)	Sulfur Dioxide 1-Hr (ppb)	Sulfur Dioxide 24-Hr (ppb)
MSA[1] Level	n/a	n/a	n/a	n/a	n/a
NAAQS[2]	53	100	30	75	140
Met NAAQS[2]	n/a	n/a	n/a	n/a	n/a

Note: (1) Data covers the Laramie, WY Micropolitan Statistical Area—see Appendix B for areas included; Data from exceptional events are included; (2) National Ambient Air Quality Standards; ppm = parts per million; ug/m^3 = micrograms per cubic meter; n/a not available.
Concentrations: Nitrogen Dioxide AM—highest arithmetic mean concentration; Nitrogen Dioxide 1-Hr—highest 98th percentile 1-hour daily maximum concentration; Sulfur Dioxide AM—highest annual mean concentration; Sulfur Dioxide 1-Hr—highest 99th percentile 1-hour daily maximum concentration; Sulfur Dioxide 24-Hr—highest second maximum 24-hour concentration
Source: U.S. Environmental Protection Agency, Air Quality Monitoring Information, "Air Quality Statistics by City, 2016"

Drinking Water

Water System Name	Pop. Served	Primary Water Source Type	Violations[1]	
			Health Based	Monitoring/ Reporting
City of Laramie	28,000	Surface	0	0

Note: (1) Based on violation data from January 1, 2017 to December 31, 2017
Source: U.S. Environmental Protection Agency, Office of Ground Water and Drinking Water, Safe Drinking Water Information System (based on data extracted April 5, 2018)

Appendix A: Comparative Statistics

Population Growth: City

Area	1990 Census	2000 Census	2010 Census	2016* Estimate	Population Growth (%) 1990-2016	2010-2016
Aberdeen, SD	25,391	24,658	26,091	27,783	9.4	6.5
Aliso Viejo, CA	8,963	40,166	47,823	50,219	460.3	5.0
Allen, TX	19,208	43,554	84,246	94,710	393.1	12.4
Ames, IA	48,062	50,731	58,965	64,073	33.3	8.7
Amherst, MA	35,228	34,874	37,819	39,724	12.8	5.0
Apex, NC	7,092	20,212	37,476	43,893	518.9	17.1
Beavercreek, OH	33,946	37,984	45,193	46,086	35.8	2.0
Bellevue, NE	43,698	44,382	50,137	52,993	21.3	5.7
Bend, OR	34,266	52,029	76,639	84,416	146.4	10.1
Benicia, CA	24,566	26,865	26,997	27,780	13.1	2.9
Bentonville, AR	12,010	19,730	35,301	42,499	253.9	20.4
Bethlehem, NY	27,552	31,304	33,656	34,709	26.0	3.1
Blacksburg, VA	34,649	39,573	42,620	43,973	26.9	3.2
Bowie, MD	39,831	50,269	54,727	57,633	44.7	5.3
Bozeman, MT	23,499	27,509	37,280	41,761	77.7	12.0
Brentwood, TN	17,287	23,445	37,060	40,873	136.4	10.3
Burlington, VT	39,127	38,889	42,417	42,556	8.8	0.3
Cabot, AR	9,576	15,261	23,776	25,407	165.3	6.9
Carmel, IN	27,705	37,733	79,191	86,940	213.8	9.8
Cedar Falls, IA	34,298	36,145	39,260	40,828	19.0	4.0
Cedar Park, TX	9,798	26,049	48,937	63,551	548.6	29.9
Central, LA	n/a	n/a	26,864	28,017	n/a	4.3
Chapel Hill, NC	39,674	48,715	57,233	59,005	48.7	3.1
Cheshire, CT	25,684	28,543	29,261	29,254	13.9	0.0
Chino Hills, CA	38,388	66,787	74,799	77,266	101.3	3.3
Cibolo, TX	1,879	3,035	15,349	25,256	1,244.1	64.5
Cicero, NY	25,560	27,982	31,632	31,495	23.2	-0.4
Collierville, TN	15,439	31,872	43,965	48,005	210.9	9.2
Coppell, TX	16,881	35,958	38,659	40,631	140.7	5.1
Cornelius, NC	5,815	11,969	24,866	27,426	371.6	10.3
Cranberry, PA	14,764	23,625	28,098	29,914	102.6	6.5
Crown Point, IN	18,540	19,806	27,317	28,743	55.0	5.2
Dublin, OH	17,231	31,392	41,751	43,874	154.6	5.1
East Fishkill, NY	22,101	25,589	29,029	29,282	32.5	0.9
Eden Prairie, MN	39,311	54,901	60,797	63,206	60.8	4.0
Edmond, OK	52,239	68,315	81,405	88,342	69.1	8.5
Edwardsville, IL	17,105	21,491	24,293	25,044	46.4	3.1
Evesham, NJ	35,309	42,275	45,538	45,578	29.1	0.1
Flower Mound, TX	15,788	50,702	64,669	69,966	343.2	8.2
Folsom, CA	29,701	51,884	72,203	74,960	152.4	3.8
Friendswood, TX	23,020	29,037	35,805	38,272	66.3	6.9
Gaines, MI	14,533	20,112	25,146	26,122	79.7	3.9
Glastonbury, CT	27,901	31,876	34,427	34,677	24.3	0.7
Grand Blanc, MI	25,180	29,827	37,508	36,771	46.0	-2.0
Hampden, PA	20,384	24,135	28,044	28,962	42.1	3.3
Hilliard, OH	12,516	24,230	28,435	33,108	164.5	16.4
Hillsborough, NJ	28,842	36,634	38,303	39,517	37.0	3.2
Holly Springs, NC	2,351	9,192	24,661	30,126	1,181.4	22.2
Independence, KY	10,645	14,982	24,757	26,317	147.2	6.3
Juneau, AK	26,751	30,711	31,275	32,524	21.6	4.0
Kaysville, UT	14,224	20,351	27,300	29,799	109.5	9.2
Keller, TX	13,683	27,345	39,627	44,250	223.4	11.7
Lafayette, CA	23,604	23,908	23,893	25,381	7.5	6.2
Lafayette, CO	15,609	23,197	24,453	27,053	73.3	10.6
Lake Oswego, OR	32,216	35,278	36,619	38,065	18.2	3.9
Laramie, WY	26,768	27,204	30,816	32,096	19.9	4.2
Leander, TX	3,661	7,596	26,521	36,204	888.9	36.5
Leawood, KS	19,683	27,656	31,867	33,763	71.5	5.9
Lee's Summit, MO	46,585	70,700	91,364	94,257	102.3	3.2
Leesburg, VA	16,240	28,311	42,616	49,401	204.2	15.9
Lehi, UT	9,766	19,028	47,407	56,314	476.6	18.8
Lexington, MA	28,974	30,355	31,394	32,936	13.7	4.9
Los Altos, CA	26,400	27,693	28,976	30,238	14.5	4.4
Loveland, CO	37,805	50,608	66,859	73,360	94.0	9.7
Lower Macungie, PA	16,832	19,220	30,633	31,662	88.1	3.4
Madison, AL	16,813	29,329	42,938	46,396	176.0	8.1
Madison, MS	8,104	14,692	24,149	25,473	214.3	5.5
Maple Valley, WA	6,490	14,209	22,684	25,093	286.6	10.6

Table continued on next page.

Area	1990 Census	2000 Census	2010 Census	2016* Estimate	Population Growth (%) 1990-2016	Population Growth (%) 2010-2016
Marion, IA	21,274	26,294	34,768	37,198	74.9	7.0
Marlboro, NJ	27,974	36,398	40,191	40,416	44.5	0.6
Mason, OH	12,046	22,016	30,712	32,025	165.9	4.3
Menomonee Falls, WI	26,840	32,647	35,626	36,118	34.6	1.4
Meridian, ID	12,266	34,919	75,092	88,247	619.4	17.5
Meridian, MI	35,198	39,116	39,688	41,501	17.9	4.6
Merrimack, NH	22,156	25,119	25,494	25,580	15.5	0.3
Milton, GA	n/a	n/a	32,661	36,755	n/a	12.5
Moon, PA	19,638	22,290	24,185	25,435	29.5	5.2
Moorpark, CA	25,494	31,415	34,421	35,594	39.6	3.4
Morgantown, WV	26,814	26,809	29,660	30,364	13.2	2.4
Mount Pleasant, SC	33,294	47,609	67,843	77,907	134.0	14.8
Newark, DE	25,693	28,547	31,454	32,941	28.2	4.7
Newtown, CT	20,779	25,031	27,560	27,990	34.7	1.6
North Attleborough, MA	25,038	27,143	28,712	28,945	15.6	0.8
North Port, FL	11,987	22,797	57,357	60,871	407.8	6.1
North Ridgeville, OH	21,564	22,338	29,465	31,832	47.6	8.0
Northville, MI	17,300	21,036	28,497	28,724	66.0	0.8
O'Fallon, MO	21,851	46,169	79,329	84,018	284.5	5.9
Orchard Park, NY	24,632	27,637	29,054	29,521	19.8	1.6
Oro Valley, AZ	9,492	29,700	41,011	42,379	346.5	3.3
Oviedo, FL	11,588	26,316	33,342	37,545	224.0	12.6
Parker, CO	5,562	23,558	45,297	48,442	770.9	6.9
Parkland, FL	4,201	13,835	23,962	28,354	574.9	18.3
Peachtree City, GA	18,908	31,580	34,364	34,988	85.0	1.8
Pittsfield, MI	17,408	30,167	34,663	37,225	113.8	7.4
Plainfield, IL	6,409	13,038	39,581	41,881	553.5	5.8
Pleasant Grove, UT	14,047	23,468	33,509	36,678	161.1	9.5
Poway, CA	42,908	48,044	47,811	49,675	15.8	3.9
Princeton, NJ	12,064	14,203	12,307	30,168	150.1	145.1
Queen Creek, AZ	2,860	4,316	26,361	30,849	978.6	17.0
Radnor, PA	28,710	30,878	31,531	31,616	10.1	0.3
Randolph, NJ	19,974	24,847	25,734	25,916	29.7	0.7
Rexburg, ID	14,510	17,257	25,484	27,114	86.9	6.4
Rio Rancho, NM	32,674	51,765	87,521	92,966	184.5	6.2
Rye, NY	39,524	43,880	45,928	46,676	18.1	1.6
Sammamish, WA	23,254	34,104	45,780	62,136	167.2	35.7
San Ramon, CA	35,463	44,722	72,148	74,366	109.7	3.1
Saratoga, CA	28,177	29,843	29,926	30,830	9.4	3.0
Shrewsbury, MA	24,146	31,640	35,608	36,494	51.1	2.5
South Brunswick, NJ	25,792	37,734	43,417	45,097	74.8	3.9
South Jordan, UT	12,183	29,437	50,418	62,751	415.1	24.5
South Kingstown, RI	24,631	27,921	30,639	30,651	24.4	0.0
South Portland, ME	23,372	23,324	25,002	25,397	8.7	1.6
Sparks, NV	54,716	66,346	90,264	94,718	73.1	4.9
State College, PA	38,933	38,420	42,034	42,074	8.1	0.1
Sugar Land, TX	44,150	63,328	78,817	85,681	94.1	8.7
Sun Prairie, WI	15,836	20,369	29,364	31,721	100.3	8.0
Syracuse, UT	4,977	9,398	24,331	26,668	435.8	9.6
Tredyffrin, PA	28,021	29,062	29,332	29,491	5.2	0.5
Upper Dublin, PA	24,028	25,878	25,569	26,181	9.0	2.4
Urbandale, IA	23,943	29,072	39,463	41,578	73.7	5.4
Vestal, NY	26,733	26,535	28,043	28,267	5.7	0.8
Vestavia Hills, AL	22,183	24,476	34,033	34,243	54.4	0.6
Webster, NY	31,639	37,926	42,641	44,084	39.3	3.4
Wellesley, MA	26,615	26,613	27,982	28,909	8.6	3.3
West Fargo, ND	12,276	14,940	25,830	31,557	157.1	22.2
West Lafayette, IN	26,691	28,778	29,596	44,543	66.9	50.5
Weston, FL	10,099	49,286	65,333	68,893	582.2	5.4
Wilmette, IL	26,685	27,651	27,087	27,367	2.6	1.0
Yorba Linda, CA	52,827	58,918	64,234	67,362	27.5	4.9
Zionsville, IN	7,014	8,775	14,160	25,709	266.5	81.6
U.S.	248,709,873	281,421,906	308,745,538	318,558,162	28.1	3.2

Note: (*) 2012-2016 5-year estimated population
Source: U.S. Census Bureau, 1990 Census, Census 2000, Census 2010, 2012-2016 American Community Survey 5-Year Estimates

Population Growth: Metro Area

Area	1990 Census	2000 Census	2010 Census	2016* Estimate	Population Growth (%) 1990-2016	2010-2016
Aberdeen, SD	39,936	39,827	40,602	42,430	6.2	4.5
Aliso Viejo, CA	11,273,720	12,365,627	12,828,837	13,189,366	17.0	2.8
Allen, TX	3,989,294	5,161,544	6,371,773	6,957,123	74.4	9.2
Ames, IA	74,252	79,981	89,542	94,834	27.7	5.9
Amherst, MA	672,947	680,014	692,942	629,107	-6.5	-9.2
Apex, NC	541,081	797,071	1,130,490	1,243,720	129.9	10.0
Beavercreek, OH	843,857	848,153	841,502	800,950	-5.1	-4.8
Bellevue, NE	685,797	767,041	865,350	904,834	31.9	4.6
Bend, OR	74,958	115,367	157,733	170,813	127.9	8.3
Benicia, CA	340,397	394,542	413,344	429,596	26.2	3.9
Bentonville, AR	239,474	347,045	463,204	503,642	110.3	8.7
Bethlehem, NY	809,443	825,875	870,716	879,291	8.6	1.0
Blacksburg, VA	140,690	151,272	162,958	181,288	28.9	11.2
Bowie, MD	4,122,914	4,796,183	5,582,170	6,011,752	45.8	7.7
Bozeman, MT	50,491	67,831	89,513	97,958	94.0	9.4
Brentwood, TN	1,048,218	1,311,789	1,589,934	1,794,570	71.2	12.9
Burlington, VT	177,059	198,889	211,261	216,080	22.0	2.3
Cabot, AR	535,034	610,518	699,757	727,371	35.9	3.9
Carmel, IN	1,294,217	1,525,104	1,756,241	1,968,768	52.1	12.1
Cedar Falls, IA	158,640	163,706	167,819	169,857	7.1	1.2
Cedar Park, TX	846,217	1,249,763	1,716,289	1,942,615	129.6	13.2
Central, LA	623,853	705,973	802,484	824,667	32.2	2.8
Chapel Hill, NC	344,646	426,493	504,357	542,399	57.4	7.5
Cheshire, CT	804,219	824,008	862,477	860,874	7.0	-0.2
Chino Hills, CA	2,588,793	3,254,821	4,224,851	4,430,646	71.1	4.9
Cibolo, TX	1,407,745	1,711,703	2,142,508	2,332,345	65.7	8.9
Cicero, NY	659,864	650,154	662,577	660,652	0.1	-0.3
Collierville, TN	1,067,263	1,205,204	1,316,100	1,341,339	25.7	1.9
Coppell, TX	3,989,294	5,161,544	6,371,773	6,957,123	74.4	9.2
Cornelius, NC	1,024,331	1,330,448	1,758,038	2,381,152	132.5	35.4
Cranberry, PA	2,468,289	2,431,087	2,356,285	2,354,926	-4.6	-0.1
Crown Point, IN	8,182,076	9,098,316	9,461,105	9,528,396	16.5	0.7
Dublin, OH	1,405,176	1,612,694	1,836,536	1,995,004	42.0	8.6
East Fishkill, NY	16,845,992	18,323,002	18,897,109	20,031,443	18.9	6.0
Eden Prairie, MN	2,538,834	2,968,806	3,279,833	3,488,436	37.4	6.4
Edmond, OK	971,042	1,095,421	1,252,987	1,337,075	37.7	6.7
Edwardsville, IL	2,580,897	2,698,687	2,812,896	2,803,449	8.6	-0.3
Evesham, NJ	5,435,470	5,687,147	5,965,343	6,047,721	11.3	1.4
Flower Mound, TX	3,989,294	5,161,544	6,371,773	6,957,123	74.4	9.2
Folsom, CA	1,481,126	1,796,857	2,149,127	2,242,542	51.4	4.3
Friendswood, TX	3,767,335	4,715,407	5,946,800	6,482,592	72.1	9.0
Gaines, MI	645,914	740,482	774,160	1,028,173	59.2	32.8
Glastonbury, CT	1,123,706	1,148,618	1,212,381	1,211,826	7.8	0.0
Grand Blanc, MI	430,459	436,141	425,790	413,090	-4.0	-3.0
Hampden, PA	474,242	509,074	549,475	561,447	18.4	2.2
Hilliard, OH	1,405,176	1,612,694	1,836,536	1,995,004	42.0	8.6
Hillsborough, NJ	16,845,992	18,323,002	18,897,109	20,031,443	18.9	6.0
Holly Springs, NC	541,081	797,071	1,130,490	1,243,720	129.9	10.0
Independence, KY	1,844,917	2,009,632	2,130,151	2,146,410	16.3	0.8
Juneau, AK	26,751	30,711	31,275	32,524	21.6	4.0
Kaysville, UT	351,799	442,656	547,184	632,793	79.9	15.6
Keller, TX	3,989,294	5,161,544	6,371,773	6,957,123	74.4	9.2
Lafayette, CA	3,686,592	4,123,740	4,335,391	4,577,530	24.2	5.6
Lafayette, CO	208,898	269,758	294,567	313,961	50.3	6.6
Lake Oswego, OR	1,523,741	1,927,881	2,226,009	2,351,319	54.3	5.6
Laramie, WY	30,797	32,014	36,299	37,836	22.9	4.2
Leander, TX	846,217	1,249,763	1,716,289	1,942,615	129.6	13.2
Leawood, KS	1,636,528	1,836,038	2,035,334	2,070,147	26.5	1.7
Lee's Summit, MO	1,636,528	1,836,038	2,035,334	2,070,147	26.5	1.7
Leesburg, VA	4,122,914	4,796,183	5,582,170	6,011,752	45.8	7.7
Lehi, UT	269,407	376,774	526,810	574,684	113.3	9.1
Lexington, MA	4,133,895	4,391,344	4,552,402	4,728,844	14.4	3.9
Los Altos, CA	1,534,280	1,735,819	1,836,911	1,943,107	26.6	5.8
Loveland, CO	186,136	251,494	299,630	325,228	74.7	8.5
Lower Macungie, PA	686,666	740,395	821,173	830,737	21.0	1.2
Madison, AL	293,047	342,376	417,593	440,230	50.2	5.4
Madison, MS	446,941	497,197	539,057	578,095	29.3	7.2
Maple Valley, WA	2,559,164	3,043,878	3,439,809	3,671,095	43.4	6.7

Table continued on next page.

Area	1990 Census	2000 Census	2010 Census	2016* Estimate	Population Growth (%) 1990-2016	2010-2016
Marion, IA	210,640	237,230	257,940	264,277	25.5	2.5
Marlboro, NJ	16,845,992	18,323,002	18,897,109	20,031,443	18.9	6.0
Mason, OH	1,844,917	2,009,632	2,130,151	2,146,410	16.3	0.8
Menomonee Falls, WI	1,432,149	1,500,741	1,555,908	1,571,730	9.7	1.0
Meridian, ID	319,596	464,840	616,561	663,680	107.7	7.6
Meridian, MI	432,674	447,728	464,036	470,348	8.7	1.4
Merrimack, NH	336,073	380,841	400,721	404,948	20.5	1.1
Milton, GA	3,069,411	4,247,981	5,268,860	5,612,777	82.9	6.5
Moon, PA	2,468,289	2,431,087	2,356,285	2,354,926	-4.6	-0.1
Moorpark, CA	669,016	753,197	823,318	843,110	26.0	2.4
Morgantown, WV	104,546	111,200	129,709	136,620	30.7	5.3
Mount Pleasant, SC	506,875	549,033	664,607	728,271	43.7	9.6
Newark, DE	5,435,470	5,687,147	5,965,343	6,047,721	11.3	1.4
Newtown, CT	827,645	882,567	916,829	941,618	13.8	2.7
North Attleborough, MA	1,509,789	1,582,997	1,600,852	1,609,359	6.6	0.5
North Port, FL	489,483	589,959	702,281	751,422	53.5	7.0
North Ridgeville, OH	2,102,219	2,148,143	2,077,240	2,061,630	-1.9	-0.8
Northville, MI	4,248,699	4,452,557	4,296,250	4,296,731	1.1	0.0
O'Fallon, MO	2,580,897	2,698,687	2,812,896	2,803,449	8.6	-0.3
Orchard Park, NY	1,189,288	1,170,111	1,135,509	1,135,503	-4.5	0.0
Oro Valley, AZ	666,880	843,746	980,263	1,003,338	50.5	2.4
Oviedo, FL	1,224,852	1,644,561	2,134,411	2,328,508	90.1	9.1
Parker, CO	1,666,935	2,179,296	2,543,482	2,752,056	65.1	8.2
Parkland, FL	4,056,100	5,007,564	5,564,635	5,926,955	46.1	6.5
Peachtree City, GA	3,069,411	4,247,981	5,268,860	5,612,777	82.9	6.5
Pittsfield, MI	282,937	322,895	344,791	358,082	26.6	3.9
Plainfield, IL	8,182,076	9,098,316	9,461,105	9,528,396	16.5	0.7
Pleasant Grove, UT	269,407	376,774	526,810	574,684	113.3	9.1
Poway, CA	2,498,016	2,813,833	3,095,313	3,253,356	30.2	5.1
Princeton, NJ	325,804	350,761	366,513	371,101	13.9	1.3
Queen Creek, AZ	2,238,480	3,251,876	4,192,887	4,486,153	100.4	7.0
Radnor, PA	5,435,470	5,687,147	5,965,343	6,047,721	11.3	1.4
Randolph, NJ	16,845,992	18,323,002	18,897,109	20,031,443	18.9	6.0
Rexburg, ID	34,611	39,286	50,778	51,010	47.4	0.5
Rio Rancho, NM	599,416	729,649	887,077	904,486	50.9	2.0
Rye, NY	16,845,992	18,323,002	18,897,109	20,031,443	18.9	6.0
Sammamish, WA	2,559,164	3,043,878	3,439,809	3,671,095	43.4	6.7
San Ramon, CA	3,686,592	4,123,740	4,335,391	4,577,530	24.2	5.6
Saratoga, CA	1,534,280	1,735,819	1,836,911	1,943,107	26.6	5.8
Shrewsbury, MA	709,728	750,963	798,552	930,667	31.1	16.5
South Brunswick, NJ	16,845,992	18,323,002	18,897,109	20,031,443	18.9	6.0
South Jordan, UT	768,075	968,858	1,124,197	1,154,504	50.3	2.7
South Kingstown, RI	1,509,789	1,582,997	1,600,852	1,609,359	6.6	0.5
South Portland, ME	441,257	487,568	514,098	523,874	18.7	1.9
Sparks, NV	257,193	342,885	425,417	443,855	72.6	4.3
State College, PA	123,786	135,758	153,990	159,178	28.6	3.4
Sugar Land, TX	3,767,335	4,715,407	5,946,800	6,482,592	72.1	9.0
Sun Prairie, WI	432,323	501,774	568,593	634,269	46.7	11.6
Syracuse, UT	351,799	442,656	547,184	632,793	79.9	15.6
Tredyffrin, PA	5,435,470	5,687,147	5,965,343	6,047,721	11.3	1.4
Upper Dublin, PA	5,435,470	5,687,147	5,965,343	6,047,721	11.3	1.4
Urbandale, IA	416,346	481,394	569,633	611,755	46.9	7.4
Vestal, NY	264,497	252,320	251,725	247,030	-6.6	-1.9
Vestavia Hills, AL	956,894	1,052,238	1,128,047	1,141,309	19.3	1.2
Webster, NY	1,002,410	1,037,831	1,054,323	1,082,226	8.0	2.6
Wellesley, MA	4,133,895	4,391,344	4,552,402	4,728,844	14.4	3.9
West Fargo, ND	153,296	174,367	208,777	228,254	48.9	9.3
West Lafayette, IN	158,848	178,541	201,789	212,113	33.5	5.1
Weston, FL	4,056,100	5,007,564	5,564,635	5,926,955	46.1	6.5
Wilmette, IL	8,182,076	9,098,316	9,461,105	9,528,396	16.5	0.7
Yorba Linda, CA	11,273,720	12,365,627	12,828,837	13,189,366	17.0	2.8
Zionsville, IN	1,294,217	1,525,104	1,756,241	1,968,768	52.1	12.1
U.S.	248,709,873	281,421,906	308,745,538	318,558,162	28.1	3.2

Note: (*) 2012-2016 5-year estimated population; Figures cover the Metropolitan Statistical Area (MSA)—see Appendix B for areas included

Source: U.S. Census Bureau, 1990 Census, Census 2000, Census 2010, 2012-2016 American Community Survey 5-Year Estimates

Household Size: City

City	Persons in Household (%)							Average Household Size
	One	Two	Three	Four	Five	Six	Seven or More	
Aberdeen, SD	34.5	33.2	13.6	11.7	3.7	2.1	0.9	2.24
Aliso Viejo, CA	24.0	31.1	19.4	17.6	5.0	1.8	0.8	2.68
Allen, TX	14.8	28.3	18.7	24.7	8.5	3.2	1.4	3.09
Ames, IA	29.4	37.8	16.3	12.8	2.3	0.9	0.1	2.24
Amherst, MA	28.4	30.1	15.3	19.8	4.4	0.8	0.9	2.59
Apex, NC	19.0	26.5	21.2	21.1	9.4	1.9	0.5	2.89
Beavercreek, OH	25.0	37.4	17.4	12.2	5.1	2.0	0.6	2.45
Bellevue, NE	25.1	33.8	15.1	13.6	7.9	2.6	1.7	2.64
Bend, OR	28.3	39.1	14.6	11.8	3.9	1.1	0.8	2.46
Benicia, CA	24.4	37.2	18.1	13.5	4.9	1.3	0.3	2.52
Bentonville, AR	20.6	33.6	17.4	17.9	6.8	2.3	1.0	2.75
Bethlehem, NY	28.2	34.7	15.3	15.1	4.5	1.7	0.1	2.53
Blacksburg, VA	26.6	36.4	18.5	15.5	1.7	0.5	0.4	2.53
Bowie, MD	25.1	30.8	18.3	13.2	7.6	3.3	1.3	2.82
Bozeman, MT	33.0	38.5	15.5	9.0	2.8	0.8	0.1	2.24
Brentwood, TN	10.2	33.1	20.5	23.0	8.7	2.7	1.6	3.09
Burlington, VT	36.2	35.2	12.8	9.8	3.5	0.8	1.3	2.20
Cabot, AR	22.3	31.1	20.4	15.0	8.4	1.9	0.6	2.71
Carmel, IN	20.7	35.8	16.3	17.3	7.7	1.4	0.5	2.67
Cedar Falls, IA	28.0	38.9	14.8	11.1	4.5	2.4	0.0	2.51
Cedar Park, TX	20.1	29.5	17.5	21.8	6.8	2.8	1.1	3.08
Central, LA	18.8	44.0	14.3	13.8	4.9	2.4	1.4	2.74
Chapel Hill, NC	31.0	34.9	15.0	13.3	4.4	0.8	0.3	2.44
Cheshire, CT	22.3	37.4	17.2	16.0	4.7	1.7	0.4	2.65
Chino Hills, CA	13.8	28.6	20.8	24.7	7.8	2.2	1.7	3.21
Cibolo, TX	13.2	27.0	20.2	24.4	8.6	5.3	0.8	3.31
Cicero, NY	24.4	33.2	18.3	16.3	5.3	1.5	0.7	2.60
Collierville, TN	15.3	32.6	22.4	19.5	7.0	2.0	0.8	2.95
Coppell, TX	18.9	29.5	21.9	20.6	6.5	2.2	0.1	2.75
Cornelius, NC	28.7	39.9	16.1	8.4	5.4	1.0	0.0	2.32
Cranberry, PA	19.8	32.8	16.8	19.8	7.9	2.0	0.6	2.72
Crown Point, IN	27.7	37.2	13.7	12.5	7.1	0.8	0.7	2.47
Dublin, OH	18.6	31.1	18.0	21.6	8.3	1.7	0.2	2.80
East Fishkill, NY	13.5	34.0	18.4	20.1	9.6	2.2	1.9	3.08
Eden Prairie, MN	24.5	34.9	17.1	14.9	5.5	2.3	0.5	2.55
Edmond, OK	23.2	35.6	17.8	14.3	6.2	1.8	0.7	2.65
Edwardsville, IL	25.1	33.2	17.4	16.8	5.7	1.2	0.3	2.58
Evesham, NJ	25.7	32.7	17.7	15.8	6.3	1.1	0.4	2.59
Flower Mound, TX	11.0	30.6	22.2	24.4	8.5	2.4	0.5	3.06
Folsom, CA	24.4	32.9	17.1	17.1	5.8	1.9	0.4	2.61
Friendswood, TX	19.0	32.8	17.6	20.0	5.4	3.4	1.4	2.88
Gaines, MI	21.4	37.3	17.8	11.2	7.5	3.1	1.4	2.69
Glastonbury, CT	25.1	34.4	15.9	15.6	6.6	1.3	0.7	2.57
Grand Blanc, MI	25.5	35.3	15.2	14.3	6.2	2.2	0.9	2.53
Hampden, PA	27.9	37.7	12.7	13.4	6.2	1.4	0.4	2.44
Hilliard, OH	22.8	29.5	17.8	19.2	7.9	0.7	1.7	2.75
Hillsborough, NJ	18.9	31.3	19.9	20.0	6.6	2.3	0.6	2.91
Holly Springs, NC	13.1	28.4	21.1	23.5	10.1	2.7	0.6	3.05
Independence, KY	16.2	31.7	21.6	17.1	9.4	1.2	2.3	3.00
Juneau, AK	25.0	37.1	15.4	13.2	5.2	2.9	0.9	2.62
Kaysville, UT	11.6	26.8	14.9	15.1	17.7	8.3	5.3	3.63
Keller, TX	14.8	32.6	19.3	20.1	9.9	2.1	0.8	2.99
Lafayette, CA	18.7	37.2	19.0	16.1	7.3	1.0	0.4	2.67
Lafayette, CO	26.8	34.6	18.7	12.8	5.5	0.5	0.8	2.49
Lake Oswego, OR	29.8	36.3	14.9	13.0	4.5	1.2	0.1	2.34
Laramie, WY	33.1	34.0	16.2	11.4	2.8	1.1	1.0	2.28
Leander, TX	16.3	23.9	22.2	22.3	9.6	3.8	1.6	3.41
Leawood, KS	18.3	39.7	12.9	18.1	7.3	2.2	1.2	2.72
Lee's Summit, MO	20.9	36.2	17.2	16.3	6.5	1.5	1.1	2.70
Leesburg, VA	19.0	28.0	19.3	18.9	9.3	3.8	1.4	3.02
Lehi, UT	8.8	21.8	13.4	19.5	18.2	12.1	6.0	3.91
Lexington, MA	19.9	30.2	18.6	20.4	8.3	1.3	0.8	2.79
Los Altos, CA	18.1	34.7	16.2	21.9	8.0	0.6	0.1	2.75
Loveland, CO	27.7	38.2	14.2	12.6	4.7	1.6	0.5	2.41
Lower Macungie, PA	23.8	36.0	15.4	17.2	5.1	1.7	0.6	2.56
Madison, AL	24.3	34.3	16.0	16.7	5.1	2.4	0.8	2.67
Madison, MS	20.3	33.8	19.4	17.6	6.9	1.0	0.6	2.76

Table continued on next page.

City	Persons in Household (%)							Average Household Size
	One	Two	Three	Four	Five	Six	Seven or More	
Maple Valley, WA	17.5	29.9	15.7	22.9	10.5	2.5	0.7	2.94
Marion, IA	26.1	34.9	17.0	14.4	5.4	1.4	0.4	2.49
Marlboro, NJ	12.6	30.1	17.7	26.4	9.0	2.3	1.6	3.16
Mason, OH	26.1	29.6	16.5	18.4	7.3	1.3	0.3	2.65
Menomonee Falls, WI	28.8	35.4	14.5	14.4	4.7	1.2	0.6	2.43
Meridian, ID	23.8	33.9	13.2	15.7	8.1	3.1	1.9	2.82
Meridian, MI	32.3	38.0	13.0	10.4	4.2	1.2	0.7	2.30
Merrimack, NH	20.7	38.9	17.4	13.8	6.1	2.0	0.7	2.63
Milton, GA	15.9	33.9	18.4	21.8	7.9	1.7	0.1	2.95
Moon, PA	29.4	32.5	18.4	11.6	5.5	1.1	1.2	2.45
Moorpark, CA	12.7	30.8	19.0	21.7	8.1	4.8	2.7	3.29
Morgantown, WV	42.4	33.6	14.0	6.6	2.1	0.7	0.3	2.42
Mount Pleasant, SC	28.1	34.5	16.7	14.4	4.2	1.4	0.5	2.50
Newark, DE	30.0	36.9	13.8	11.6	5.1	2.0	0.3	2.57
Newtown, CT	20.4	33.1	19.2	15.9	8.5	1.9	0.8	2.79
North Attleborough, MA	24.9	28.8	18.2	17.1	7.2	2.2	1.3	2.75
North Port, FL	23.3	42.8	11.9	12.1	6.4	2.1	0.9	2.65
North Ridgeville, OH	24.6	36.8	15.2	13.9	6.6	2.0	0.5	2.58
Northville, MI	26.1	32.4	14.8	17.7	6.7	1.7	0.2	2.60
O'Fallon, MO	20.7	31.3	17.5	19.3	7.9	2.2	0.8	2.76
Orchard Park, NY	25.9	34.7	15.9	15.1	5.9	1.5	0.6	2.53
Oro Valley, AZ	24.9	46.6	13.7	8.8	3.7	1.3	0.7	2.35
Oviedo, FL	14.6	31.7	22.5	20.6	6.9	2.1	1.1	3.40
Parker, CO	18.4	29.3	18.1	21.5	7.9	2.6	1.8	2.85
Parkland, FL	9.3	30.2	23.2	26.7	8.0	2.0	0.3	3.21
Peachtree City, GA	22.3	35.3	15.1	16.0	7.8	2.0	1.1	2.76
Pittsfield, MI	28.7	33.9	14.9	14.2	4.7	2.5	0.7	2.49
Plainfield, IL	13.3	21.9	18.9	28.8	12.4	2.6	1.8	3.37
Pleasant Grove, UT	12.9	26.0	16.1	15.0	12.4	9.6	7.7	3.63
Poway, CA	14.6	35.3	17.9	18.4	9.1	3.0	1.4	3.10
Princeton, NJ	26.5	37.7	15.5	12.6	6.1	0.8	0.4	2.48
Queen Creek, AZ	16.2	25.9	15.0	20.5	11.9	8.1	2.1	3.37
Radnor, PA	30.8	30.9	14.7	13.5	7.3	1.8	0.8	2.55
Randolph, NJ	20.6	27.4	20.1	21.2	8.2	1.6	0.6	2.86
Rexburg, ID	12.4	41.0	16.1	10.2	7.7	10.2	2.1	3.47
Rio Rancho, NM	23.0	34.5	15.1	14.9	7.2	3.8	1.1	2.82
Rye, NY	22.5	26.8	18.7	18.5	6.4	3.3	3.4	3.02
Sammamish, WA	10.1	29.7	21.9	27.4	7.2	2.3	1.0	3.04
San Ramon, CA	17.6	25.1	20.3	26.2	7.1	2.6	0.8	2.97
Saratoga, CA	14.4	35.2	21.1	20.4	6.0	1.7	0.9	2.85
Shrewsbury, MA	21.1	32.4	16.0	21.3	6.4	1.4	0.9	2.79
South Brunswick, NJ	18.9	26.3	21.2	22.6	7.1	2.8	0.8	2.90
South Jordan, UT	14.2	28.9	14.7	16.7	11.7	8.9	4.5	3.45
South Kingstown, RI	28.2	38.0	13.1	12.8	5.8	1.4	0.2	2.40
South Portland, ME	29.6	36.3	21.5	8.0	2.2	1.6	0.4	2.33
Sparks, NV	27.9	33.2	15.3	14.1	6.2	2.0	0.9	2.63
State College, PA	38.2	30.6	15.4	10.4	4.2	0.6	0.3	2.45
Sugar Land, TX	16.2	32.8	20.6	17.3	8.1	2.8	1.9	3.03
Sun Prairie, WI	28.9	32.3	15.3	13.5	6.2	2.0	1.6	2.53
Syracuse, UT	6.9	25.1	13.7	20.4	15.4	11.3	6.8	3.87
Tredyffrin, PA	28.9	32.2	15.4	15.8	5.8	1.3	0.3	2.46
Upper Dublin, PA	19.0	33.8	19.3	18.0	7.6	1.6	0.3	2.74
Urbandale, IA	24.9	37.6	13.8	14.0	7.0	1.9	0.5	2.52
Vestal, NY	26.3	39.4	11.8	15.8	4.2	1.5	0.6	2.47
Vestavia Hills, AL	28.1	31.8	16.2	16.5	5.7	1.0	0.4	2.53
Webster, NY	26.5	36.8	14.6	14.7	4.9	1.3	1.0	2.51
Wellesley, MA	19.9	32.2	13.4	20.8	10.6	2.4	0.2	2.84
West Fargo, ND	23.7	36.3	17.7	13.0	7.2	0.9	0.9	2.55
West Lafayette, IN	36.7	29.4	17.0	11.4	3.8	0.6	0.6	2.34
Weston, FL	11.7	28.1	20.4	28.3	8.8	2.3	0.1	3.26
Wilmette, IL	20.8	31.7	15.5	19.4	8.4	3.2	0.5	2.83
Yorba Linda, CA	13.0	32.2	20.9	20.3	8.6	3.8	0.7	3.07
Zionsville, IN	19.4	31.3	16.0	19.8	9.7	2.7	0.9	2.83
U.S.	27.6	33.7	15.7	13.0	6.0	2.3	1.4	2.64

U.S. Census Bureau, 2012-2016 American Community Survey 5-Year Estimates

Household Size: Metro Area

Metro Area	Persons in Household (%)							Average Household Size
	One	Two	Three	Four	Five	Six	Seven or More	
Aberdeen, SD	30.9	35.8	14.1	11.2	4.4	2.2	1.0	2.30
Aliso Viejo, CA	24.5	28.3	16.8	15.4	8.1	3.6	2.9	3.02
Allen, TX	24.9	30.8	16.6	15.2	7.5	2.9	1.8	2.80
Ames, IA	26.9	38.3	15.9	13.0	4.3	1.0	0.3	2.34
Amherst, MA	29.3	32.6	16.6	13.5	4.9	1.6	1.1	2.51
Apex, NC	25.5	32.6	17.5	15.2	5.8	2.0	0.9	2.65
Beavercreek, OH	32.0	34.2	14.8	11.3	4.9	1.6	0.8	2.36
Bellevue, NE	28.4	33.4	14.6	13.1	6.3	2.4	1.3	2.55
Bend, OR	25.3	42.5	14.4	11.5	3.9	1.3	0.8	2.50
Benicia, CA	21.7	32.6	17.7	15.0	7.7	2.9	2.0	2.88
Bentonville, AR	24.4	34.7	15.4	14.4	6.6	2.5	1.6	2.65
Bethlehem, NY	31.9	34.9	15.3	11.6	4.2	1.3	0.5	2.45
Blacksburg, VA	27.6	38.0	15.8	12.8	3.7	0.9	0.8	2.42
Bowie, MD	27.0	30.4	16.7	14.8	6.6	2.6	1.6	2.74
Bozeman, MT	27.8	38.0	15.4	12.0	4.2	1.4	0.7	2.43
Brentwood, TN	27.0	34.1	16.6	13.5	5.5	2.0	1.1	2.60
Burlington, VT	27.1	38.2	14.7	13.1	4.3	1.4	0.8	2.41
Cabot, AR	29.8	34.9	16.1	11.2	5.1	1.6	0.8	2.57
Carmel, IN	29.1	33.2	15.4	13.2	5.8	2.0	0.9	2.57
Cedar Falls, IA	30.4	37.9	13.4	10.8	4.7	2.1	0.4	2.42
Cedar Park, TX	27.9	33.3	15.6	13.8	5.8	2.0	1.3	2.69
Central, LA	28.2	33.6	16.9	12.2	5.6	2.0	1.1	2.66
Chapel Hill, NC	30.7	35.9	15.1	11.5	4.3	1.5	0.6	2.42
Cheshire, CT	31.1	32.5	15.9	12.8	5.0	1.7	0.6	2.55
Chino Hills, CA	20.2	27.9	16.2	16.3	10.3	4.9	3.8	3.28
Cibolo, TX	25.4	30.9	17.0	14.2	7.3	2.9	1.9	2.92
Cicero, NY	30.1	34.3	15.8	11.9	4.9	1.7	1.0	2.46
Collierville, TN	28.6	32.3	16.8	12.7	5.7	2.2	1.5	2.66
Coppell, TX	24.9	30.8	16.6	15.2	7.5	2.9	1.8	2.80
Cornelius, NC	26.5	33.8	16.9	13.7	5.7	1.9	1.0	2.65
Cranberry, PA	32.5	35.4	14.8	11.2	4.1	1.2	0.5	2.31
Crown Point, IN	28.4	30.3	15.7	14.1	6.9	2.6	1.6	2.70
Dublin, OH	28.6	33.5	15.9	13.1	5.7	1.9	1.0	2.54
East Fishkill, NY	27.9	29.0	17.0	14.7	6.7	2.5	1.9	2.75
Eden Prairie, MN	27.7	34.0	15.0	13.7	5.9	2.1	1.3	2.55
Edmond, OK	28.3	34.0	15.6	12.7	5.7	2.2	1.2	2.61
Edwardsville, IL	29.5	33.9	15.7	12.9	5.3	1.6	0.8	2.48
Evesham, NJ	29.2	31.7	16.3	13.4	5.9	2.0	1.1	2.63
Flower Mound, TX	24.9	30.8	16.6	15.2	7.5	2.9	1.8	2.80
Folsom, CA	25.8	32.7	15.8	14.2	6.5	2.8	1.9	2.74
Friendswood, TX	24.5	29.6	16.9	15.4	8.1	3.1	2.0	2.88
Gaines, MI	24.5	35.0	15.2	14.2	6.9	2.5	1.4	2.66
Glastonbury, CT	28.4	34.1	16.1	13.5	5.5	1.4	0.6	2.48
Grand Blanc, MI	29.8	33.4	15.6	12.4	5.6	1.9	0.9	2.45
Hampden, PA	29.7	35.6	15.4	12.0	4.3	1.6	1.0	2.41
Hilliard, OH	28.6	33.5	15.9	13.1	5.7	1.9	1.0	2.54
Hillsborough, NJ	27.9	29.0	17.0	14.7	6.7	2.5	1.9	2.75
Holly Springs, NC	25.5	32.6	17.5	15.2	5.8	2.0	0.9	2.65
Independence, KY	28.5	34.3	15.2	13.0	5.8	1.9	1.0	2.53
Juneau, AK	25.0	37.1	15.4	13.2	5.2	2.9	0.9	2.62
Kaysville, UT	18.1	30.7	15.1	15.5	10.5	6.2	3.6	3.15
Keller, TX	24.9	30.8	16.6	15.2	7.5	2.9	1.8	2.80
Lafayette, CA	27.2	31.5	16.7	14.2	6.0	2.3	1.7	2.69
Lafayette, CO	27.9	36.6	15.6	12.6	4.8	1.5	0.6	2.45
Lake Oswego, OR	27.1	34.6	15.7	13.2	5.6	2.1	1.3	2.58
Laramie, WY	32.4	35.2	15.8	11.4	2.8	1.2	0.9	2.29
Leander, TX	27.9	33.3	15.6	13.8	5.8	2.0	1.3	2.69
Leawood, KS	28.9	33.7	15.3	12.9	5.8	2.0	1.0	2.53
Lee's Summit, MO	28.9	33.7	15.3	12.9	5.8	2.0	1.0	2.53
Leesburg, VA	27.0	30.4	16.7	14.8	6.6	2.6	1.6	2.74
Lehi, UT	11.9	27.2	15.5	16.4	12.6	9.3	6.6	3.62
Lexington, MA	27.9	32.5	16.6	14.4	5.6	1.7	0.8	2.56
Los Altos, CA	20.8	29.7	18.4	17.8	7.5	2.9	2.5	2.96
Loveland, CO	24.3	39.5	16.1	12.6	4.9	1.5	0.7	2.49
Lower Macungie, PA	26.0	34.8	16.4	13.5	6.0	1.9	1.0	2.56
Madison, AL	30.0	34.3	15.7	12.8	4.8	1.6	0.6	2.49
Madison, MS	27.0	32.5	17.2	13.2	6.5	2.3	1.1	2.66

Table continued on next page.

Metro Area	Persons in Household (%)							Average Household Size
	One	Two	Three	Four	Five	Six	Seven or More	
Maple Valley, WA	28.2	34.0	15.8	13.2	5.2	2.0	1.2	2.54
Marion, IA	28.5	36.7	14.1	12.8	4.9	1.8	0.8	2.42
Marlboro, NJ	27.9	29.0	17.0	14.7	6.7	2.5	1.9	2.75
Mason, OH	28.5	34.3	15.2	13.0	5.8	1.9	1.0	2.53
Menomonee Falls, WI	30.9	33.7	14.6	12.3	5.3	1.8	1.0	2.46
Meridian, ID	26.7	34.4	14.4	13.3	6.7	2.4	1.8	2.71
Meridian, MI	30.6	35.5	14.0	11.8	5.1	1.6	0.9	2.44
Merrimack, NH	24.6	36.5	16.7	14.0	5.3	1.5	1.0	2.54
Milton, GA	26.6	31.2	17.0	14.5	6.6	2.5	1.4	2.77
Moon, PA	32.5	35.4	14.8	11.2	4.1	1.2	0.5	2.31
Moorpark, CA	20.8	30.2	17.4	16.3	8.1	3.6	3.2	3.09
Morgantown, WV	32.7	36.5	14.7	10.6	3.6	0.9	0.5	2.54
Mount Pleasant, SC	28.7	35.2	16.6	12.3	4.5	1.5	0.8	2.59
Newark, DE	29.2	31.7	16.3	13.4	5.9	2.0	1.1	2.63
Newtown, CT	24.5	31.4	17.2	16.4	7.1	2.1	1.1	2.75
North Attleborough, MA	29.6	33.1	16.4	13.4	4.9	1.5	0.7	2.49
North Port, FL	30.8	44.1	11.2	8.2	3.4	1.3	0.6	2.38
North Ridgeville, OH	33.2	33.2	14.7	11.1	4.8	1.7	0.9	2.38
Northville, MI	30.1	32.2	15.5	13.0	5.6	2.0	1.2	2.54
O'Fallon, MO	29.5	33.9	15.7	12.9	5.3	1.6	0.8	2.48
Orchard Park, NY	33.3	33.4	14.9	11.3	4.5	1.6	0.7	2.35
Oro Valley, AZ	30.7	35.6	13.9	10.9	5.2	2.1	1.3	2.47
Oviedo, FL	25.9	34.5	17.0	13.4	5.7	2.0	1.1	2.80
Parker, CO	28.4	33.6	15.1	13.3	5.7	2.2	1.3	2.57
Parkland, FL	28.4	32.1	16.6	13.5	5.7	2.1	1.2	2.83
Peachtree City, GA	26.6	31.2	17.0	14.5	6.6	2.5	1.4	2.77
Pittsfield, MI	29.9	35.5	14.0	12.7	4.9	1.6	1.0	2.44
Plainfield, IL	28.4	30.3	15.7	14.1	6.9	2.6	1.6	2.70
Pleasant Grove, UT	11.9	27.2	15.5	16.4	12.6	9.3	6.6	3.62
Poway, CA	24.2	32.4	17.0	14.6	6.8	2.8	1.8	2.87
Princeton, NJ	26.8	31.0	16.9	15.2	6.4	2.1	1.2	2.71
Queen Creek, AZ	26.7	34.5	14.3	12.6	6.5	3.1	2.0	2.76
Radnor, PA	29.2	31.7	16.3	13.4	5.9	2.0	1.1	2.63
Randolph, NJ	27.9	29.0	17.0	14.7	6.7	2.5	1.9	2.75
Rexburg, ID	15.2	38.0	13.9	10.9	8.3	8.7	4.7	3.32
Rio Rancho, NM	30.2	34.0	14.7	11.8	5.6	2.2	1.2	2.60
Rye, NY	27.9	29.0	17.0	14.7	6.7	2.5	1.9	2.75
Sammamish, WA	28.2	34.0	15.8	13.2	5.2	2.0	1.2	2.54
San Ramon, CA	27.2	31.5	16.7	14.2	6.0	2.3	1.7	2.69
Saratoga, CA	20.8	29.7	18.4	17.8	7.5	2.9	2.5	2.96
Shrewsbury, MA	26.9	33.4	16.7	14.4	5.6	1.7	0.8	2.58
South Brunswick, NJ	27.9	29.0	17.0	14.7	6.7	2.5	1.9	2.75
South Jordan, UT	22.3	29.5	16.2	14.7	8.7	5.0	3.4	3.04
South Kingstown, RI	29.6	33.1	16.4	13.4	4.9	1.5	0.7	2.49
South Portland, ME	28.6	38.2	15.1	11.9	3.9	1.4	0.6	2.37
Sparks, NV	29.2	34.9	15.0	11.8	5.0	2.4	1.3	2.56
State College, PA	28.1	36.7	16.7	12.1	4.2	1.0	0.9	2.49
Sugar Land, TX	24.5	29.6	16.9	15.4	8.1	3.1	2.0	2.88
Sun Prairie, WI	29.6	36.9	14.2	12.1	4.7	1.4	0.7	2.37
Syracuse, UT	18.1	30.7	15.1	15.5	10.5	6.2	3.6	3.15
Tredyffrin, PA	29.2	31.7	16.3	13.4	5.9	2.0	1.1	2.63
Upper Dublin, PA	29.2	31.7	16.3	13.4	5.9	2.0	1.1	2.63
Urbandale, IA	27.4	34.0	15.2	13.4	6.4	2.3	1.0	2.53
Vestal, NY	30.6	35.7	14.4	11.8	4.7	1.7	0.9	2.40
Vestavia Hills, AL	28.7	34.2	16.7	12.6	4.9	1.7	0.7	2.54
Webster, NY	30.7	35.2	15.0	11.8	4.7	1.5	0.9	2.41
Wellesley, MA	27.9	32.5	16.6	14.4	5.6	1.7	0.8	2.56
West Fargo, ND	31.6	34.3	15.1	11.8	4.9	1.4	0.6	2.34
West Lafayette, IN	29.2	34.1	16.1	12.1	5.2	1.9	1.1	2.47
Weston, FL	28.4	32.1	16.6	13.5	5.7	2.1	1.2	2.83
Wilmette, IL	28.4	30.3	15.7	14.1	6.9	2.6	1.6	2.70
Yorba Linda, CA	24.5	28.3	16.8	15.4	8.1	3.6	2.9	3.02
Zionsville, IN	29.1	33.2	15.4	13.2	5.8	2.0	0.9	2.57
U.S.	27.6	33.7	15.7	13.0	6.0	2.3	1.4	2.64

Note: Figures cover the Metropolitan Statistical Area (MSA)—see Appendix B for areas included
Source: U.S. Census Bureau, 2012-2016 American Community Survey 5-Year Estimates

Race: City

City	White Alone[1] (%)	Black Alone[1] (%)	Asian Alone[1] (%)	AIAN[2] Alone[1] (%)	NHOPI[3] Alone[1] (%)	Other Race Alone[1] (%)	Two or More Races (%)
Aberdeen, SD	89.9	1.6	3.1	3.9	0.0	0.1	1.5
Aliso Viejo, CA	70.1	2.1	15.9	0.5	0.0	4.9	6.5
Allen, TX	70.6	9.8	14.2	0.5	0.0	1.5	3.4
Ames, IA	83.5	3.1	9.6	0.2	0.0	0.4	3.1
Amherst, MA	77.3	5.9	12.7	0.4	0.0	0.9	2.8
Apex, NC	79.7	8.5	7.0	0.3	0.0	1.6	2.9
Beavercreek, OH	87.4	3.0	5.3	0.2	0.0	0.5	3.6
Bellevue, NE	84.3	6.4	2.6	0.6	0.3	1.9	3.9
Bend, OR	93.1	0.5	1.6	0.2	0.1	1.7	2.9
Benicia, CA	71.6	5.8	12.5	0.4	0.2	2.4	7.1
Bentonville, AR	81.6	2.7	10.2	1.0	0.1	1.7	2.7
Bethlehem, NY	91.6	2.1	3.9	0.0	0.0	0.5	1.9
Blacksburg, VA	78.4	4.9	11.6	0.3	0.1	1.4	3.2
Bowie, MD	38.4	51.3	4.7	0.1	0.0	1.4	4.0
Bozeman, MT	92.6	0.6	2.5	1.5	0.0	0.5	2.2
Brentwood, TN	87.8	3.0	7.1	0.1	0.0	0.2	1.7
Burlington, VT	85.7	4.9	6.0	0.4	0.0	0.5	2.5
Cabot, AR	92.4	1.2	1.6	0.2	0.0	2.1	2.6
Carmel, IN	84.6	2.6	9.7	0.1	0.0	0.8	2.1
Cedar Falls, IA	92.9	2.3	2.9	0.3	0.1	0.4	1.1
Cedar Park, TX	81.7	3.7	9.0	0.5	0.0	1.6	3.4
Central, LA	86.1	10.2	0.7	0.2	0.1	0.8	1.9
Chapel Hill, NC	72.8	9.9	12.6	0.4	0.0	1.1	3.2
Cheshire, CT	83.1	4.3	6.9	0.1	0.0	2.6	3.0
Chino Hills, CA	48.1	4.1	33.2	0.3	0.2	9.0	5.0
Cibolo, TX	71.1	11.9	2.1	0.4	0.1	9.9	4.5
Cicero, NY	94.8	1.6	1.2	0.5	0.0	0.2	1.7
Collierville, TN	76.3	12.9	7.5	0.9	0.0	0.4	1.9
Coppell, TX	70.5	4.5	21.0	0.3	0.0	1.2	2.4
Cornelius, NC	89.3	5.8	2.2	0.1	0.0	1.0	1.6
Cranberry, PA	93.4	1.3	3.1	0.0	0.1	0.7	1.4
Crown Point, IN	87.1	5.7	2.7	0.1	0.0	3.0	1.5
Dublin, OH	76.4	2.3	16.9	0.3	0.0	0.8	3.3
East Fishkill, NY	88.0	2.3	3.5	0.2	0.0	2.7	3.3
Eden Prairie, MN	79.5	5.9	10.5	0.4	0.1	0.8	2.7
Edmond, OK	80.6	5.7	3.3	2.4	0.3	0.9	6.9
Edwardsville, IL	84.4	10.2	2.6	0.3	0.0	0.1	2.4
Evesham, NJ	86.1	4.7	5.9	0.0	0.0	1.6	1.6
Flower Mound, TX	82.5	3.7	9.5	0.4	0.0	1.0	2.9
Folsom, CA	70.6	4.6	15.6	0.5	0.4	3.0	5.4
Friendswood, TX	87.6	2.6	6.3	0.4	0.0	1.0	2.0
Gaines, MI	82.2	9.3	3.2	1.0	0.0	1.1	3.3
Glastonbury, CT	87.5	1.3	8.1	0.0	0.0	1.4	1.7
Grand Blanc, MI	82.8	10.0	4.4	0.1	0.0	0.3	2.4
Hampden, PA	84.0	1.9	11.1	0.2	0.0	0.6	2.2
Hilliard, OH	88.2	3.4	6.5	0.1	0.1	0.2	1.4
Hillsborough, NJ	75.5	5.1	15.8	0.2	0.0	1.2	2.3
Holly Springs, NC	79.3	12.4	2.6	0.3	0.0	1.7	3.6
Independence, KY	95.6	0.8	1.5	0.0	0.2	0.4	1.5
Juneau, AK	69.4	1.2	7.2	12.3	1.0	0.8	8.2
Kaysville, UT	96.3	0.4	1.0	0.3	0.3	0.2	1.5
Keller, TX	88.0	1.6	4.6	0.2	0.0	2.2	3.2
Lafayette, CA	82.7	1.1	9.9	0.1	0.0	0.6	5.5
Lafayette, CO	86.9	0.4	5.0	0.5	0.0	3.6	3.5
Lake Oswego, OR	88.9	0.4	6.2	0.1	0.1	0.9	3.4
Laramie, WY	88.8	1.7	3.2	0.8	0.0	2.3	3.1
Leander, TX	86.2	4.4	2.4	0.2	0.0	2.7	4.2
Leawood, KS	92.5	1.2	4.2	0.1	0.1	0.0	1.9
Lee's Summit, MO	84.7	8.4	2.1	0.4	0.5	1.6	2.3
Leesburg, VA	74.3	8.0	9.1	0.1	0.3	5.0	3.2
Lehi, UT	94.6	0.1	1.2	0.5	0.2	1.3	2.1
Lexington, MA	70.0	1.0	25.5	0.1	0.0	0.3	3.1
Los Altos, CA	65.9	0.2	27.3	0.1	0.0	0.8	5.7
Loveland, CO	92.1	0.4	1.0	0.5	0.1	2.7	3.2
Lower Macungie, PA	85.9	3.6	5.2	0.0	0.0	1.9	3.4
Madison, AL	75.1	14.3	5.6	0.9	0.0	0.8	3.4

Table continued on next page.

City	White Alone[1] (%)	Black Alone[1] (%)	Asian Alone[1] (%)	AIAN[2] Alone[1] (%)	NHOPI[3] Alone[1] (%)	Other Race Alone[1] (%)	Two or More Races (%)
Madison, MS	86.4	9.0	3.0	0.2	0.0	0.7	0.8
Maple Valley, WA	82.9	2.4	6.2	0.4	0.0	1.3	6.8
Marion, IA	93.5	2.3	1.6	0.1	0.0	0.5	2.1
Marlboro, NJ	76.9	2.3	18.5	0.1	0.0	0.7	1.6
Mason, OH	84.6	3.9	8.8	0.0	0.0	1.0	1.8
Menomonee Falls, WI	91.3	1.6	5.3	0.2	0.0	0.4	1.2
Meridian, ID	93.7	1.0	2.0	0.2	0.2	1.0	1.9
Meridian, MI	78.3	3.5	12.5	0.6	0.0	0.9	4.2
Merrimack, NH	95.2	0.4	2.1	0.1	0.1	0.6	1.5
Milton, GA	76.0	11.6	8.8	0.1	0.1	1.1	2.3
Moon, PA	88.6	4.4	4.3	0.2	0.0	0.5	1.9
Moorpark, CA	80.0	1.1	7.5	0.4	0.6	7.1	3.2
Morgantown, WV	86.6	6.2	4.8	0.2	0.0	0.4	1.9
Mount Pleasant, SC	90.8	5.4	1.5	0.2	0.1	0.1	2.0
Newark, DE	79.2	8.6	8.4	0.1	0.0	1.8	1.8
Newtown, CT	92.9	1.3	2.3	0.1	0.0	1.3	2.1
North Attleborough, MA	89.5	3.0	4.2	0.1	0.0	1.1	2.1
North Port, FL	86.4	7.7	1.6	0.1	0.0	1.2	2.9
North Ridgeville, OH	92.9	1.6	1.7	0.1	0.0	0.7	3.0
Northville, MI	79.5	3.4	14.5	0.1	0.0	0.5	1.9
O'Fallon, MO	90.0	4.1	3.7	0.1	0.0	0.3	1.9
Orchard Park, NY	96.2	1.0	1.7	0.1	0.0	0.4	0.7
Oro Valley, AZ	88.7	1.3	3.2	0.4	0.0	2.6	3.7
Oviedo, FL	79.4	9.5	4.7	0.3	0.1	3.3	2.5
Parker, CO	90.2	1.6	3.4	0.2	0.1	0.9	3.7
Parkland, FL	83.7	7.3	6.6	0.5	0.0	0.7	1.2
Peachtree City, GA	82.8	7.1	6.3	0.4	0.1	1.0	2.3
Pittsfield, MI	66.8	13.8	13.2	0.3	0.1	0.7	5.0
Plainfield, IL	81.1	5.9	7.1	0.0	0.0	3.3	2.4
Pleasant Grove, UT	94.8	0.5	1.7	0.3	0.3	0.4	2.1
Poway, CA	77.6	1.6	11.8	1.2	0.1	2.2	5.6
Princeton, NJ	74.6	6.1	15.4	0.1	0.0	1.3	2.5
Queen Creek, AZ	87.8	2.6	2.5	0.9	0.1	3.9	2.1
Radnor, PA	82.9	6.5	7.4	0.0	0.0	1.2	2.0
Randolph, NJ	81.6	3.5	10.3	0.0	0.1	1.7	2.8
Rexburg, ID	93.4	0.9	1.4	0.0	0.3	1.6	2.4
Rio Rancho, NM	79.6	2.9	1.5	2.4	0.1	8.6	4.9
Rye, NY	63.7	5.5	2.8	0.7	0.0	25.0	2.2
Sammamish, WA	69.2	1.0	25.2	0.0	0.1	0.5	4.1
San Ramon, CA	47.6	2.3	42.3	0.3	0.3	1.3	5.8
Saratoga, CA	49.4	0.7	45.8	0.4	0.0	0.7	3.1
Shrewsbury, MA	76.1	3.8	16.6	0.1	0.0	0.8	2.6
South Brunswick, NJ	46.8	8.6	41.0	0.1	0.0	1.8	1.7
South Jordan, UT	90.9	0.8	2.7	0.1	0.5	2.6	2.4
South Kingstown, RI	90.7	2.5	1.8	1.4	0.0	1.3	2.3
South Portland, ME	93.2	0.9	2.7	0.4	0.0	0.1	2.7
Sparks, NV	78.4	2.8	5.8	1.5	0.4	6.8	4.4
State College, PA	82.0	4.2	10.8	0.1	0.1	0.7	2.1
Sugar Land, TX	50.0	7.2	38.6	0.1	0.0	1.5	2.5
Sun Prairie, WI	83.8	7.0	4.5	0.1	0.0	1.4	3.1
Syracuse, UT	92.3	1.7	1.0	0.1	0.0	1.4	3.6
Tredyffrin, PA	80.7	3.7	12.7	0.0	0.0	0.7	2.2
Upper Dublin, PA	85.3	5.4	7.9	0.0	0.0	0.0	1.4
Urbandale, IA	89.7	3.8	3.5	0.0	0.3	0.4	2.3
Vestal, NY	80.3	5.0	11.7	0.2	0.0	0.9	1.9
Vestavia Hills, AL	91.1	2.4	4.5	0.1	0.0	1.2	0.8
Webster, NY	92.4	1.7	3.7	0.0	0.0	0.4	1.8
Wellesley, MA	82.5	2.4	11.0	0.1	0.1	0.9	3.0
West Fargo, ND	92.5	2.6	2.0	1.2	0.0	0.0	1.8
West Lafayette, IN	70.9	3.0	22.8	0.1	0.1	0.4	2.6
Weston, FL	84.2	4.6	5.2	0.5	0.0	2.4	3.1
Wilmette, IL	82.9	0.9	13.5	0.1	0.0	0.3	2.3
Yorba Linda, CA	73.8	1.1	17.8	0.1	0.1	1.7	5.4
Zionsville, IN	91.3	1.5	5.3	0.2	0.0	0.3	1.4
U.S.	73.3	12.6	5.2	0.8	0.2	4.8	3.1

Note: (1) Alone is defined as not being in combination with one or more other races; (2) American Indian and Alaska Native; (3) Native Hawaiian and Other Pacific Islander

Source: U.S. Census Bureau, 2012-2016 American Community Survey 5-Year Estimates

Race: Metro Area

Metro Area	White Alone[1] (%)	Black Alone[1] (%)	Asian Alone[1] (%)	AIAN[2] Alone[1] (%)	NHOPI[3] Alone[1] (%)	Other Race Alone[1] (%)	Two or More Races (%)
Aberdeen, SD	91.9	1.4	2.1	3.1	0.0	0.1	1.3
Aliso Viejo, CA	55.0	6.7	15.4	0.6	0.3	18.1	3.9
Allen, TX	69.7	15.3	6.1	0.4	0.1	5.5	2.9
Ames, IA	87.6	2.3	6.9	0.2	0.0	0.3	2.7
Amherst, MA	82.1	7.1	2.9	0.3	0.0	5.1	2.5
Apex, NC	68.7	20.1	5.1	0.4	0.0	3.0	2.7
Beavercreek, OH	78.8	15.5	2.1	0.2	0.0	0.6	2.9
Bellevue, NE	84.6	7.7	2.5	0.5	0.1	2.1	2.7
Bend, OR	93.4	0.5	1.0	0.5	0.1	1.5	2.9
Benicia, CA	52.9	14.1	15.2	0.5	0.8	9.0	7.4
Bentonville, AR	84.2	2.3	2.9	1.2	1.2	5.3	2.9
Bethlehem, NY	83.7	7.7	4.1	0.2	0.0	1.4	2.9
Blacksburg, VA	89.0	4.7	3.6	0.2	0.0	0.6	1.8
Bowie, MD	55.1	25.4	9.8	0.3	0.1	5.5	3.9
Bozeman, MT	94.8	0.4	1.3	0.9	0.0	0.6	2.0
Brentwood, TN	78.0	15.2	2.5	0.3	0.1	1.8	2.1
Burlington, VT	92.2	2.0	2.7	0.4	0.0	0.5	2.2
Cabot, AR	71.7	22.9	1.6	0.3	0.1	1.1	2.3
Carmel, IN	77.4	14.9	2.7	0.2	0.0	2.5	2.3
Cedar Falls, IA	87.7	7.1	1.7	0.3	0.2	1.2	1.8
Cedar Park, TX	78.7	7.3	5.3	0.4	0.1	5.1	3.2
Central, LA	59.8	35.5	2.0	0.2	0.0	0.9	1.7
Chapel Hill, NC	62.2	26.8	4.6	0.4	0.0	3.0	2.8
Cheshire, CT	74.9	12.9	3.9	0.2	0.0	5.4	2.7
Chino Hills, CA	62.7	7.4	6.4	0.9	0.3	17.9	4.5
Cibolo, TX	80.1	6.7	2.4	0.6	0.1	7.2	2.9
Cicero, NY	84.6	8.3	2.8	0.5	0.0	0.9	2.9
Collierville, TN	47.2	46.6	2.0	0.2	0.0	2.2	1.7
Coppell, TX	69.7	15.3	6.1	0.4	0.1	5.5	2.9
Cornelius, NC	68.4	22.2	3.3	0.4	0.0	3.4	2.3
Cranberry, PA	87.1	8.2	2.1	0.1	0.0	0.3	2.1
Crown Point, IN	66.3	16.9	6.2	0.2	0.0	8.0	2.4
Dublin, OH	77.2	14.8	3.6	0.2	0.0	1.0	3.1
East Fishkill, NY	58.7	17.1	10.6	0.3	0.0	10.3	2.9
Eden Prairie, MN	80.3	7.8	6.2	0.6	0.0	2.0	3.2
Edmond, OK	74.1	10.2	3.1	3.5	0.1	2.6	6.4
Edwardsville, IL	76.3	18.3	2.4	0.2	0.0	0.6	2.2
Evesham, NJ	67.5	20.9	5.6	0.2	0.0	3.2	2.6
Flower Mound, TX	69.7	15.3	6.1	0.4	0.1	5.5	2.9
Folsom, CA	66.2	7.1	12.7	0.7	0.8	6.4	6.1
Friendswood, TX	65.7	17.2	7.3	0.4	0.1	7.1	2.3
Gaines, MI	85.1	6.5	2.4	0.5	0.0	2.5	3.0
Glastonbury, CT	76.7	11.0	4.5	0.2	0.0	4.4	3.1
Grand Blanc, MI	74.8	20.2	1.0	0.4	0.0	0.5	3.0
Hampden, PA	81.4	10.5	3.5	0.2	0.0	1.8	2.7
Hilliard, OH	77.2	14.8	3.6	0.2	0.0	1.0	3.1
Hillsborough, NJ	58.7	17.1	10.6	0.3	0.0	10.3	2.9
Holly Springs, NC	68.7	20.1	5.1	0.4	0.0	3.0	2.7
Independence, KY	82.3	12.2	2.2	0.1	0.0	0.9	2.1
Juneau, AK	69.4	1.2	7.2	12.3	1.0	0.8	8.2
Kaysville, UT	89.8	1.1	1.5	0.6	0.4	3.6	2.9
Keller, TX	69.7	15.3	6.1	0.4	0.1	5.5	2.9
Lafayette, CA	52.1	7.6	24.7	0.5	0.7	8.6	5.8
Lafayette, CO	88.6	0.9	4.5	0.5	0.1	2.7	2.7
Lake Oswego, OR	81.9	2.8	6.2	0.7	0.5	3.3	4.6
Laramie, WY	89.8	1.5	3.0	0.7	0.0	2.2	2.8
Leander, TX	78.7	7.3	5.3	0.4	0.1	5.1	3.2
Leawood, KS	78.8	12.5	2.6	0.4	0.1	2.5	3.0
Lee's Summit, MO	78.8	12.5	2.6	0.4	0.1	2.5	3.0
Leesburg, VA	55.1	25.4	9.8	0.3	0.1	5.5	3.9
Lehi, UT	92.2	0.6	1.4	0.5	0.7	1.8	2.7
Lexington, MA	77.3	8.0	7.3	0.2	0.0	4.1	3.1
Los Altos, CA	48.0	2.5	33.4	0.5	0.4	10.4	4.8
Loveland, CO	91.0	0.9	2.0	0.5	0.1	2.1	3.3
Lower Macungie, PA	84.2	5.4	2.8	0.3	0.0	4.6	2.7
Madison, AL	71.4	21.8	2.2	0.6	0.1	1.1	2.8

Table continued on next page.

Metro Area	White Alone[1] (%)	Black Alone[1] (%)	Asian Alone[1] (%)	AIAN[2] Alone[1] (%)	NHOPI[3] Alone[1] (%)	Other Race Alone[1] (%)	Two or More Races (%)
Madison, MS	47.9	49.1	1.1	0.1	0.0	0.9	0.8
Maple Valley, WA	71.1	5.6	12.4	0.9	0.9	3.0	6.3
Marion, IA	90.8	4.1	1.8	0.2	0.0	0.7	2.4
Marlboro, NJ	58.7	17.1	10.6	0.3	0.0	10.3	2.9
Mason, OH	82.3	12.2	2.2	0.1	0.0	0.9	2.1
Menomonee Falls, WI	73.8	16.6	3.4	0.4	0.0	3.2	2.6
Meridian, ID	90.6	0.9	1.9	0.8	0.2	2.8	2.9
Meridian, MI	81.0	8.4	4.2	0.4	0.0	1.5	4.5
Merrimack, NH	90.7	2.4	3.7	0.1	0.0	0.9	2.2
Milton, GA	55.1	33.5	5.5	0.3	0.0	3.3	2.3
Moon, PA	87.1	8.2	2.1	0.1	0.0	0.3	2.1
Moorpark, CA	79.4	1.8	7.1	0.7	0.2	6.5	4.3
Morgantown, WV	91.0	4.1	2.5	0.2	0.0	0.5	1.7
Mount Pleasant, SC	67.5	26.6	1.7	0.3	0.1	1.4	2.4
Newark, DE	67.5	20.9	5.6	0.2	0.0	3.2	2.6
Newtown, CT	73.8	11.4	5.1	0.3	0.0	6.7	2.8
North Attleborough, MA	82.9	5.6	2.9	0.4	0.1	5.5	2.8
North Port, FL	88.6	6.6	1.7	0.3	0.0	1.2	1.7
North Ridgeville, OH	74.0	20.0	2.1	0.2	0.0	1.1	2.5
Northville, MI	69.9	22.4	3.9	0.3	0.0	1.1	2.4
O'Fallon, MO	76.3	18.3	2.4	0.2	0.0	0.6	2.2
Orchard Park, NY	80.2	12.2	2.9	0.6	0.0	1.9	2.2
Oro Valley, AZ	77.3	3.5	2.7	3.2	0.1	8.9	4.1
Oviedo, FL	71.2	16.3	4.2	0.2	0.1	4.8	3.1
Parker, CO	81.9	5.6	3.9	0.8	0.1	4.2	3.4
Parkland, FL	71.1	21.4	2.4	0.2	0.0	2.8	2.1
Peachtree City, GA	55.1	33.5	5.5	0.3	0.0	3.3	2.3
Pittsfield, MI	74.0	12.0	8.5	0.3	0.0	0.9	4.3
Plainfield, IL	66.3	16.9	6.2	0.2	0.0	8.0	2.4
Pleasant Grove, UT	92.2	0.6	1.4	0.5	0.7	1.8	2.7
Poway, CA	71.0	5.0	11.6	0.7	0.5	6.4	4.9
Princeton, NJ	63.4	20.5	10.4	0.1	0.0	3.7	1.9
Queen Creek, AZ	78.7	5.2	3.7	2.2	0.2	6.7	3.3
Radnor, PA	67.5	20.9	5.6	0.2	0.0	3.2	2.6
Randolph, NJ	58.7	17.1	10.6	0.3	0.0	10.3	2.9
Rexburg, ID	94.4	0.5	0.8	0.1	0.2	1.9	2.1
Rio Rancho, NM	72.7	2.6	2.1	5.7	0.1	12.8	4.1
Rye, NY	58.7	17.1	10.6	0.3	0.0	10.3	2.9
Sammamish, WA	71.1	5.6	12.4	0.9	0.9	3.0	6.3
San Ramon, CA	52.1	7.6	24.7	0.5	0.7	8.6	5.8
Saratoga, CA	48.0	2.5	33.4	0.5	0.4	10.4	4.8
Shrewsbury, MA	85.4	4.5	4.1	0.2	0.0	3.0	2.8
South Brunswick, NJ	58.7	17.1	10.6	0.3	0.0	10.3	2.9
South Jordan, UT	81.7	1.6	3.6	0.7	1.5	8.0	2.8
South Kingstown, RI	82.9	5.6	2.9	0.4	0.1	5.5	2.8
South Portland, ME	93.9	1.9	1.6	0.3	0.0	0.3	2.0
Sparks, NV	80.6	2.3	5.4	1.6	0.6	5.6	4.0
State College, PA	88.0	3.8	5.8	0.2	0.0	0.5	1.7
Sugar Land, TX	65.7	17.2	7.3	0.4	0.1	7.1	2.3
Sun Prairie, WI	86.4	4.4	4.6	0.3	0.0	1.7	2.6
Syracuse, UT	89.8	1.1	1.5	0.6	0.4	3.6	2.9
Tredyffrin, PA	67.5	20.9	5.6	0.2	0.0	3.2	2.6
Upper Dublin, PA	67.5	20.9	5.6	0.2	0.0	3.2	2.6
Urbandale, IA	87.3	5.0	3.6	0.2	0.1	1.3	2.5
Vestal, NY	88.5	4.6	3.4	0.2	0.0	0.9	2.4
Vestavia Hills, AL	66.4	28.6	1.3	0.2	0.0	2.0	1.5
Webster, NY	81.3	11.5	2.8	0.4	0.0	1.6	2.4
Wellesley, MA	77.3	8.0	7.3	0.2	0.0	4.1	3.1
West Fargo, ND	90.1	3.3	2.3	1.1	0.0	0.5	2.6
West Lafayette, IN	85.8	4.1	6.6	0.1	0.0	1.4	1.9
Weston, FL	71.1	21.4	2.4	0.2	0.0	2.8	2.1
Wilmette, IL	66.3	16.9	6.2	0.2	0.0	8.0	2.4
Yorba Linda, CA	55.0	6.7	15.4	0.6	0.3	18.1	3.9
Zionsville, IN	77.4	14.9	2.7	0.2	0.0	2.5	2.3
U.S.	73.3	12.6	5.2	0.8	0.2	4.8	3.1

Note: (1) Figures cover the Metropolitan Statistical Area (MSA)—see Appendix B for areas included; (1) Alone is defined as not being in combination with one or more other races; (2) American Indian and Alaska Native; (3) Native Hawaiian & Other Pacific Islander
Source: U.S. Census Bureau, 2012-2016 American Community Survey 5-Year Estimates

Hispanic Origin: City

City	Hispanic or Latino (%)	Mexican (%)	Puerto Rican (%)	Cuban (%)	Other Hispanic or Latino (%)
Aberdeen, SD	2.5	0.9	0.2	0.7	0.7
Aliso Viejo, CA	16.2	11.6	0.6	0.4	3.6
Allen, TX	10.6	7.3	1.1	0.2	2.0
Ames, IA	3.2	1.7	0.3	0.1	1.1
Amherst, MA	5.8	0.8	1.3	0.3	3.3
Apex, NC	7.8	3.5	1.2	0.3	2.8
Beavercreek, OH	2.8	1.5	0.7	0.1	0.5
Bellevue, NE	14.6	11.3	0.4	0.1	2.7
Bend, OR	8.7	6.6	0.5	0.4	1.2
Benicia, CA	15.6	11.3	0.3	0.0	3.9
Bentonville, AR	9.2	6.3	0.3	0.0	2.6
Bethlehem, NY	1.9	0.4	0.8	0.1	0.5
Blacksburg, VA	4.3	1.0	0.7	0.3	2.3
Bowie, MD	6.4	1.4	1.0	0.5	3.5
Bozeman, MT	3.0	1.8	0.0	0.1	1.1
Brentwood, TN	3.4	1.7	0.2	0.2	1.3
Burlington, VT	2.6	0.4	0.7	0.2	1.3
Cabot, AR	4.9	2.3	0.3	0.2	2.1
Carmel, IN	3.3	1.7	0.0	0.2	1.2
Cedar Falls, IA	2.0	1.2	0.0	0.0	0.8
Cedar Park, TX	18.9	15.7	0.4	0.3	2.5
Central, LA	2.1	1.1	0.0	0.0	1.0
Chapel Hill, NC	5.9	2.2	0.4	0.3	3.0
Cheshire, CT	5.3	0.4	3.3	0.4	1.2
Chino Hills, CA	27.6	22.6	0.4	0.2	4.4
Cibolo, TX	30.1	23.4	2.2	0.1	4.4
Cicero, NY	1.5	0.7	0.3	0.0	0.5
Collierville, TN	2.1	1.2	0.1	0.0	0.7
Coppell, TX	11.2	8.8	0.4	0.3	1.6
Cornelius, NC	5.2	0.9	2.0	0.4	1.8
Cranberry, PA	2.2	1.3	0.3	0.0	0.6
Crown Point, IN	8.2	5.7	1.2	0.1	1.2
Dublin, OH	5.5	1.8	0.7	0.2	2.8
East Fishkill, NY	7.4	1.0	3.1	0.4	2.9
Eden Prairie, MN	4.5	2.5	0.2	0.0	1.7
Edmond, OK	5.6	4.2	0.2	0.2	1.0
Edwardsville, IL	2.5	1.4	0.3	0.4	0.3
Evesham, NJ	4.9	1.0	2.0	0.3	1.6
Flower Mound, TX	9.5	6.5	0.5	0.3	2.3
Folsom, CA	11.0	8.2	0.4	0.1	2.2
Friendswood, TX	15.8	12.3	0.5	0.7	2.2
Gaines, MI	5.9	4.4	0.7	0.5	0.4
Glastonbury, CT	4.3	0.5	1.7	0.2	2.0
Grand Blanc, MI	2.2	1.4	0.4	0.3	0.1
Hampden, PA	2.6	1.3	0.9	0.0	0.5
Hilliard, OH	2.6	1.8	0.2	0.1	0.7
Hillsborough, NJ	7.5	0.9	2.8	0.2	3.6
Holly Springs, NC	5.1	1.9	1.1	0.8	1.3
Independence, KY	1.0	0.2	0.1	0.0	0.7
Juneau, AK	6.3	3.5	0.9	0.1	1.9
Kaysville, UT	3.1	1.6	0.0	0.0	1.5
Keller, TX	8.5	5.8	0.7	0.2	1.8
Lafayette, CA	7.1	4.6	0.2	0.2	2.1
Lafayette, CO	14.8	12.4	0.1	0.1	2.3
Lake Oswego, OR	4.2	1.7	0.3	0.5	1.7
Laramie, WY	10.3	7.7	0.2	0.1	2.3
Leander, TX	26.3	23.5	0.6	0.2	2.0
Leawood, KS	2.2	0.8	0.2	0.3	0.8
Lee's Summit, MO	4.5	3.2	0.3	0.1	0.9
Leesburg, VA	16.8	2.2	1.6	0.1	13.0
Lehi, UT	6.5	3.7	0.1	0.0	2.7
Lexington, MA	1.8	0.6	0.2	0.1	0.8
Los Altos, CA	3.3	1.6	0.0	0.1	1.5
Loveland, CO	11.8	9.2	0.3	0.0	2.4
Lower Macungie, PA	7.1	1.6	3.0	0.1	2.4
Madison, AL	4.9	2.2	1.7	0.1	0.9
Madison, MS	1.0	0.2	0.1	0.2	0.5

Table continued on next page.

City	Hispanic or Latino (%)	Mexican (%)	Puerto Rican (%)	Cuban (%)	Other Hispanic or Latino (%)
Maple Valley, WA	5.9	4.1	0.1	0.0	1.6
Marion, IA	1.8	1.4	0.0	0.0	0.3
Marlboro, NJ	4.3	0.1	2.2	0.5	1.5
Mason, OH	3.4	0.2	0.2	0.9	2.1
Menomonee Falls, WI	2.5	1.2	0.4	0.0	0.9
Meridian, ID	7.0	5.3	0.3	0.1	1.3
Meridian, MI	4.0	2.2	0.6	0.0	1.2
Merrimack, NH	2.6	0.8	0.8	0.1	0.9
Milton, GA	8.6	3.7	0.7	0.9	3.3
Moon, PA	2.6	0.4	0.3	0.1	1.9
Moorpark, CA	30.4	26.1	0.5	0.5	3.2
Morgantown, WV	2.9	0.5	0.8	0.0	1.6
Mount Pleasant, SC	3.2	1.1	0.7	0.0	1.3
Newark, DE	6.7	1.8	1.5	0.4	2.9
Newtown, CT	6.2	0.7	2.0	0.7	2.8
North Attleborough, MA	4.2	1.5	0.5	0.0	2.2
North Port, FL	6.5	2.8	1.9	0.4	1.4
North Ridgeville, OH	3.8	0.9	2.1	0.1	0.7
Northville, MI	4.9	3.4	0.6	0.1	0.8
O'Fallon, MO	2.4	1.2	0.1	0.1	1.0
Orchard Park, NY	2.0	0.2	0.3	0.0	1.5
Oro Valley, AZ	12.6	9.8	1.0	0.4	1.4
Oviedo, FL	20.5	1.6	10.5	1.8	6.7
Parker, CO	8.9	5.3	0.6	0.0	3.0
Parkland, FL	19.1	1.9	3.1	3.9	10.1
Peachtree City, GA	7.2	3.0	0.7	0.3	3.1
Pittsfield, MI	4.9	2.3	0.4	0.1	2.1
Plainfield, IL	11.5	8.7	0.9	0.2	1.6
Pleasant Grove, UT	7.3	4.5	0.5	0.0	2.2
Poway, CA	18.1	14.2	0.4	0.1	3.3
Princeton, NJ	8.4	1.5	0.8	0.4	5.7
Queen Creek, AZ	16.4	10.9	1.6	0.1	3.8
Radnor, PA	4.0	0.8	1.1	0.2	1.9
Randolph, NJ	9.5	0.9	2.3	0.2	6.1
Rexburg, ID	6.2	3.2	0.4	0.1	2.6
Rio Rancho, NM	40.3	21.3	0.5	0.2	18.2
Rye, NY	44.3	10.3	2.7	0.8	30.5
Sammamish, WA	4.0	2.4	0.2	0.0	1.4
San Ramon, CA	7.9	4.3	0.4	0.1	3.1
Saratoga, CA	3.7	2.0	0.3	0.1	1.3
Shrewsbury, MA	3.7	0.0	2.2	0.1	1.4
South Brunswick, NJ	6.2	0.4	2.5	0.2	3.0
South Jordan, UT	5.4	3.1	0.2	0.0	2.0
South Kingstown, RI	5.0	0.4	1.7	0.2	2.7
South Portland, ME	1.7	0.2	0.8	0.1	0.6
Sparks, NV	27.6	22.8	0.4	0.1	4.3
State College, PA	4.2	1.2	0.9	0.2	1.9
Sugar Land, TX	9.3	6.6	0.6	0.3	1.8
Sun Prairie, WI	5.0	3.1	0.2	0.4	1.3
Syracuse, UT	5.9	3.7	0.0	0.0	2.2
Tredyffrin, PA	2.5	0.8	0.4	0.2	1.1
Upper Dublin, PA	2.0	0.6	0.3	0.0	1.1
Urbandale, IA	3.2	1.7	0.4	0.0	1.2
Vestal, NY	4.8	0.6	1.4	0.2	2.5
Vestavia Hills, AL	2.9	1.7	0.2	0.1	0.9
Webster, NY	2.7	0.3	1.9	0.0	0.5
Wellesley, MA	4.8	1.1	0.5	0.4	2.8
West Fargo, ND	1.0	0.8	0.0	0.0	0.2
West Lafayette, IN	4.1	2.0	0.2	0.1	1.8
Weston, FL	50.9	1.7	3.4	4.1	41.7
Wilmette, IL	3.6	0.9	0.6	0.7	1.4
Yorba Linda, CA	16.5	12.5	0.3	0.5	3.2
Zionsville, IN	1.6	0.5	0.3	0.0	0.8
U.S.	17.3	11.0	1.7	0.7	4.0

Note: Persons of Hispanic or Latino origin can be of any race
Source: U.S. Census Bureau, 2012-2016 American Community Survey 5-Year Estimates

Age: City

City	Percent of Population							
	Under Age 5	Age 5–19	Age 20–34	Age 35–44	Age 45–54	Age 55–64	Age 65–74	Age 75–84
Aberdeen, SD	7.1	19.6	24.0	10.9	10.8	12.1	6.7	5.6
Aliso Viejo, CA	7.1	21.1	19.6	16.9	17.1	10.1	5.5	1.6
Allen, TX	6.8	25.7	16.5	17.4	16.6	9.7	4.6	2.3
Ames, IA	3.9	22.9	43.0	7.4	6.9	6.6	4.7	3.3
Amherst, MA	2.0	30.6	44.3	4.8	5.3	5.9	4.0	2.3
Apex, NC	7.4	25.6	15.5	19.3	16.5	8.7	4.5	1.5
Beavercreek, OH	5.0	17.1	21.6	11.2	14.5	14.1	9.8	4.8
Bellevue, NE	7.3	21.4	22.9	11.7	12.6	11.1	7.7	4.2
Bend, OR	6.1	18.8	20.1	14.4	12.7	12.4	8.7	4.2
Benicia, CA	5.3	18.5	16.1	11.2	16.4	16.1	10.4	4.9
Bentonville, AR	7.7	22.6	25.0	17.2	11.8	8.6	4.0	1.9
Bethlehem, NY	5.3	20.3	13.9	12.6	15.3	15.9	9.7	4.1
Blacksburg, VA	3.1	26.3	48.7	6.4	6.1	4.5	3.2	0.9
Bowie, MD	6.1	19.0	16.8	14.4	17.8	12.5	7.4	4.0
Bozeman, MT	5.2	17.3	39.7	12.5	8.1	8.8	4.5	2.5
Brentwood, TN	5.6	26.7	9.5	14.8	17.6	13.8	8.1	2.9
Burlington, VT	3.2	21.3	37.8	9.4	8.6	9.0	5.6	3.1
Cabot, AR	7.3	24.0	19.2	14.7	13.3	10.1	6.6	3.8
Carmel, IN	6.0	23.5	14.4	14.3	15.7	13.4	7.6	3.2
Cedar Falls, IA	5.7	20.0	33.3	9.5	8.2	10.4	6.2	4.0
Cedar Park, TX	7.4	24.8	19.1	18.2	13.8	8.8	4.9	2.1
Central, LA	6.2	19.4	17.3	12.9	12.7	14.8	10.4	5.1
Chapel Hill, NC	3.0	24.0	33.3	9.8	10.7	8.9	5.5	3.4
Cheshire, CT	3.5	20.5	14.3	11.6	18.8	14.8	9.2	4.4
Chino Hills, CA	5.5	21.0	19.5	13.9	17.0	13.7	5.4	2.7
Cibolo, TX	7.5	26.6	16.7	18.1	16.5	7.4	5.2	1.5
Cicero, NY	6.3	19.6	17.3	13.3	16.6	13.7	8.2	3.6
Collierville, TN	5.2	24.1	14.2	13.9	17.5	13.8	7.1	3.1
Coppell, TX	5.4	24.4	13.0	15.4	20.2	14.3	4.7	2.0
Cornelius, NC	4.8	20.6	16.6	16.0	16.8	12.1	8.3	3.6
Cranberry, PA	6.6	22.6	14.3	15.9	17.6	12.7	6.1	2.9
Crown Point, IN	5.3	17.5	19.3	12.8	14.9	11.6	9.6	5.7
Dublin, OH	6.2	25.4	11.5	17.2	16.6	13.7	5.3	2.7
East Fishkill, NY	4.6	22.4	14.5	11.7	19.0	14.1	8.3	3.9
Eden Prairie, MN	6.2	20.6	18.0	12.8	17.0	14.6	6.7	2.6
Edmond, OK	7.2	22.1	21.2	12.0	12.5	12.1	7.4	3.7
Edwardsville, IL	4.7	23.2	26.6	11.6	11.7	10.8	6.8	3.1
Evesham, NJ	4.7	18.0	19.0	12.4	16.9	13.3	8.3	4.7
Flower Mound, TX	5.9	25.5	12.8	16.1	20.4	12.0	5.0	1.8
Folsom, CA	6.2	20.1	16.1	16.0	17.6	12.1	6.7	3.6
Friendswood, TX	5.5	23.3	15.2	12.2	17.0	12.7	9.2	3.2
Gaines, MI	6.8	21.3	20.1	13.3	14.5	12.8	6.5	3.5
Glastonbury, CT	4.2	21.7	10.9	13.1	18.3	15.1	9.5	4.7
Grand Blanc, MI	5.5	21.7	19.1	14.2	14.1	11.8	7.5	4.0
Hampden, PA	4.9	19.8	13.3	14.1	14.5	15.5	10.2	5.4
Hilliard, OH	6.8	23.6	18.2	14.5	15.9	10.8	5.8	3.0
Hillsborough, NJ	6.6	20.2	15.4	14.5	18.3	14.2	6.7	3.0
Holly Springs, NC	8.1	26.3	15.4	19.2	16.5	7.5	4.9	1.8
Independence, KY	8.7	21.5	20.5	14.6	13.4	12.5	6.2	1.9
Juneau, AK	6.0	18.7	21.4	13.6	15.0	14.9	7.2	2.0
Kaysville, UT	10.3	29.5	18.1	13.1	12.3	8.4	4.7	3.2
Keller, TX	5.5	25.3	12.1	14.6	18.0	12.9	6.6	3.5
Lafayette, CA	4.6	22.1	12.0	11.7	17.6	13.6	10.8	4.9
Lafayette, CO	6.2	19.4	19.1	16.0	14.3	14.5	6.5	3.3
Lake Oswego, OR	4.5	19.4	12.4	13.4	14.6	17.1	10.9	4.4
Laramie, WY	5.4	18.5	43.1	9.4	7.6	8.8	4.0	2.2
Leander, TX	9.7	24.9	19.2	17.5	13.7	8.0	4.8	1.5
Leawood, KS	5.4	23.8	7.8	12.7	16.6	16.8	10.1	4.7
Lee's Summit, MO	6.8	22.3	17.1	13.2	14.7	12.6	7.6	3.7
Leesburg, VA	6.7	24.0	19.9	15.9	17.0	9.1	4.1	2.1
Lehi, UT	13.0	32.4	20.8	15.0	7.7	5.5	3.4	1.7
Lexington, MA	5.0	23.7	8.5	13.3	18.0	13.4	9.0	5.4
Los Altos, CA	5.1	23.0	6.9	13.9	16.0	15.5	9.5	6.8
Loveland, CO	5.6	18.8	18.8	12.9	12.9	13.8	9.7	5.3
Lower Macungie, PA	5.5	20.1	13.9	13.6	15.2	12.3	10.7	6.4
Madison, AL	5.1	22.2	19.4	13.7	16.6	13.2	6.5	2.3
Madison, MS	5.3	24.9	12.8	13.6	17.1	13.3	8.0	3.3

Table continued on next page.

City	Percent of Population							
	Under Age 5	Age 5–19	Age 20–34	Age 35–44	Age 45–54	Age 55–64	Age 65–74	Age 75–84
Maple Valley, WA	8.3	25.5	15.0	17.8	16.0	9.8	4.8	2.0
Marion, IA	6.4	21.0	19.1	13.6	14.7	10.5	8.1	4.7
Marlboro, NJ	4.3	24.0	13.0	12.2	19.0	14.3	8.5	3.6
Mason, OH	4.3	25.8	11.5	14.1	17.7	12.1	7.9	4.5
Menomonee Falls, WI	6.1	17.5	16.1	11.5	14.3	15.5	9.1	6.5
Meridian, ID	7.2	24.8	17.4	15.0	13.5	10.3	7.2	3.6
Meridian, MI	5.2	15.8	25.5	10.9	12.5	14.4	8.8	4.3
Merrimack, NH	4.5	19.1	15.5	14.3	18.5	15.6	8.5	3.0
Milton, GA	6.1	27.2	10.4	17.1	18.5	12.4	5.6	2.2
Moon, PA	5.6	20.6	18.8	12.8	15.5	13.5	7.6	3.8
Moorpark, CA	5.6	21.8	20.2	12.4	16.6	13.4	6.1	2.5
Morgantown, WV	2.3	23.5	43.2	7.7	7.2	7.0	4.6	2.9
Mount Pleasant, SC	6.2	19.3	18.6	14.5	14.7	12.2	8.6	4.0
Newark, DE	3.1	26.7	34.6	7.5	7.8	8.5	6.2	4.0
Newtown, CT	3.9	23.6	12.1	11.3	20.7	12.9	7.6	5.2
North Attleborough, MA	4.1	23.1	17.0	15.1	15.9	13.3	7.0	3.3
North Port, FL	4.5	18.7	14.4	11.0	12.5	15.1	14.4	7.2
North Ridgeville, OH	7.3	17.2	16.2	13.1	14.0	12.7	12.3	5.2
Northville, MI	4.3	21.2	12.6	14.2	16.8	12.8	9.8	5.8
O'Fallon, MO	6.8	23.3	17.8	16.0	14.9	10.3	6.1	3.5
Orchard Park, NY	4.1	20.2	12.6	11.0	17.6	15.0	10.9	5.6
Oro Valley, AZ	4.0	15.8	12.0	9.6	12.7	16.5	16.2	9.9
Oviedo, FL	5.5	23.6	20.2	14.0	16.9	10.9	5.1	3.0
Parker, CO	7.0	26.2	16.7	19.2	15.3	9.3	4.4	1.6
Parkland, FL	6.4	26.2	11.8	13.7	17.6	13.8	6.6	2.5
Peachtree City, GA	4.4	24.6	12.9	12.6	16.6	13.7	10.2	3.4
Pittsfield, MI	5.8	17.6	26.4	14.8	14.4	11.1	5.7	3.1
Plainfield, IL	6.9	28.2	16.0	16.5	16.4	9.3	4.6	1.6
Pleasant Grove, UT	10.6	29.4	24.8	12.2	8.8	7.1	4.6	1.9
Poway, CA	6.7	20.4	16.7	12.7	15.0	13.9	8.8	4.1
Princeton, NJ	3.7	23.3	25.0	9.2	12.6	11.2	8.0	4.9
Queen Creek, AZ	9.3	31.1	13.6	18.3	12.0	8.8	5.2	1.5
Radnor, PA	4.7	29.1	22.2	9.1	12.1	10.5	6.7	3.7
Randolph, NJ	6.1	21.4	16.0	12.4	18.0	14.3	6.8	3.7
Rexburg, ID	11.1	22.3	48.1	5.0	4.5	4.2	2.9	0.9
Rio Rancho, NM	6.2	22.3	18.6	13.9	13.7	12.3	7.9	3.5
Rye, NY	6.0	19.9	18.5	15.7	13.9	12.7	6.9	4.0
Sammamish, WA	6.6	26.1	11.8	18.6	18.4	11.3	4.9	1.5
San Ramon, CA	6.2	25.3	13.2	19.1	17.2	9.8	5.8	2.7
Saratoga, CA	3.1	21.1	8.5	11.1	19.9	15.3	9.9	7.7
Shrewsbury, MA	5.3	22.3	15.3	14.3	17.1	11.1	8.2	4.2
South Brunswick, NJ	4.6	23.3	14.7	15.5	17.6	12.4	6.8	3.1
South Jordan, UT	8.3	27.2	18.8	15.7	12.0	9.3	5.6	2.5
South Kingstown, RI	3.0	27.9	17.5	8.0	12.1	13.8	9.4	5.2
South Portland, ME	3.9	19.2	19.5	13.8	16.0	12.9	8.3	4.5
Sparks, NV	6.4	19.9	20.2	13.3	13.2	12.9	9.0	3.4
State College, PA	1.8	26.6	53.9	4.3	4.3	3.9	2.7	1.6
Sugar Land, TX	5.3	19.8	16.4	12.6	16.3	16.1	8.4	3.7
Sun Prairie, WI	7.4	21.6	22.1	14.5	13.0	10.4	6.9	2.7
Syracuse, UT	8.4	35.5	14.7	16.9	11.4	7.1	3.6	2.1
Tredyffrin, PA	4.8	20.2	14.6	11.8	16.2	15.0	9.7	5.6
Upper Dublin, PA	4.9	20.5	12.6	12.4	16.7	15.2	10.3	4.8
Urbandale, IA	7.0	20.4	17.9	13.6	15.2	12.5	7.9	4.0
Vestal, NY	3.0	27.8	23.6	7.2	10.3	11.9	8.0	5.6
Vestavia Hills, AL	6.0	21.8	15.7	14.8	13.4	12.9	6.8	5.0
Webster, NY	6.0	18.0	16.7	11.8	15.7	14.2	9.5	5.1
Wellesley, MA	5.0	30.1	13.5	10.8	14.9	11.5	7.3	4.8
West Fargo, ND	8.4	20.1	24.5	14.3	13.4	10.6	5.6	2.3
West Lafayette, IN	2.8	27.3	48.7	5.2	5.3	4.2	2.6	2.2
Weston, FL	4.9	27.0	13.2	14.6	19.2	11.3	5.7	3.0
Wilmette, IL	5.5	25.9	7.3	12.7	17.2	13.7	9.5	5.0
Yorba Linda, CA	5.0	21.1	15.5	11.5	16.1	15.0	10.1	3.9
Zionsville, IN	7.3	25.9	12.8	15.1	18.2	10.7	6.0	2.5
U.S.	6.2	19.6	20.7	12.7	13.6	12.6	8.3	4.3

Source: U.S. Census Bureau, 2012-2016 American Community Survey 5-Year Estimates

Age: Metro Area

Metro Area	Percent of Population							
	Under Age 5	Age 5–19	Age 20–34	Age 35–44	Age 45–54	Age 55–64	Age 65–74	Age 75–84
Aberdeen, SD	6.4	20.0	20.1	11.1	12.8	13.3	7.7	5.6
Aliso Viejo, CA	6.3	19.4	22.7	13.8	13.9	11.4	6.9	3.8
Allen, TX	7.2	22.2	21.4	14.4	13.8	10.9	6.2	2.9
Ames, IA	4.9	22.5	34.3	9.2	9.0	9.3	5.6	3.5
Amherst, MA	5.2	20.1	21.6	11.2	13.7	13.2	8.4	4.4
Apex, NC	6.5	21.4	20.5	15.4	14.6	11.1	6.5	2.9
Beavercreek, OH	6.0	19.0	20.1	11.5	13.5	13.5	9.1	5.1
Bellevue, NE	7.4	21.1	21.3	12.9	13.2	11.9	7.0	3.6
Bend, OR	5.4	18.0	17.5	13.0	13.1	14.7	11.5	4.6
Benicia, CA	6.2	19.3	21.4	12.4	14.0	13.3	8.1	3.9
Bentonville, AR	7.2	22.1	22.5	13.4	12.3	10.4	7.1	3.6
Bethlehem, NY	5.3	18.4	20.5	12.0	14.5	13.7	8.7	4.4
Blacksburg, VA	4.5	19.9	27.2	11.0	11.9	11.4	8.4	4.0
Bowie, MD	6.6	19.3	21.8	14.5	14.6	11.8	6.9	3.2
Bozeman, MT	6.0	18.5	28.2	12.8	11.6	11.8	6.8	3.1
Brentwood, TN	6.5	19.7	21.9	13.8	13.9	12.0	7.3	3.5
Burlington, VT	5.1	19.1	22.8	12.0	14.3	13.4	7.8	3.7
Cabot, AR	6.6	19.9	21.6	13.0	12.9	12.1	8.1	4.0
Carmel, IN	6.8	20.8	20.7	13.5	13.9	12.0	7.2	3.6
Cedar Falls, IA	6.2	19.3	23.3	11.1	11.7	12.7	8.3	5.0
Cedar Park, TX	6.8	20.3	24.7	15.4	12.9	10.4	5.9	2.6
Central, LA	6.6	20.4	23.3	12.5	12.8	11.9	7.5	3.6
Chapel Hill, NC	6.0	19.0	23.1	13.4	13.0	12.3	7.8	3.7
Cheshire, CT	5.3	19.0	20.1	12.1	14.6	13.4	8.5	4.5
Chino Hills, CA	7.0	22.9	21.8	12.8	13.0	10.7	6.9	3.6
Cibolo, TX	7.0	21.8	22.1	13.1	12.8	11.0	7.1	3.6
Cicero, NY	5.6	19.9	19.9	11.2	14.6	13.6	8.4	4.5
Collierville, TN	7.0	21.3	20.8	13.0	13.5	12.3	7.2	3.5
Coppell, TX	7.2	22.2	21.4	14.4	13.8	10.9	6.2	2.9
Cornelius, NC	6.4	20.7	20.0	14.5	14.4	11.6	7.5	3.5
Cranberry, PA	5.1	16.9	19.1	11.5	14.2	14.9	9.7	5.7
Crown Point, IN	6.3	20.2	21.2	13.5	13.9	12.2	7.3	3.8
Dublin, OH	6.8	20.0	22.2	13.6	13.6	11.8	7.1	3.4
East Fishkill, NY	6.1	18.4	21.3	13.3	14.3	12.3	7.8	4.2
Eden Prairie, MN	6.6	20.1	21.0	13.2	14.4	12.5	7.1	3.5
Edmond, OK	7.1	20.5	22.7	12.7	12.5	11.8	7.4	3.8
Edwardsville, IL	6.1	19.2	20.0	12.3	14.1	13.5	8.2	4.5
Evesham, NJ	6.0	19.1	20.8	12.4	14.3	13.0	8.0	4.4
Flower Mound, TX	7.2	22.2	21.4	14.4	13.8	10.9	6.2	2.9
Folsom, CA	6.2	20.1	21.3	12.7	13.5	12.4	7.9	4.1
Friendswood, TX	7.6	22.2	22.0	14.2	13.2	11.0	6.1	2.7
Gaines, MI	6.7	21.2	21.3	12.1	13.4	12.2	7.3	3.8
Glastonbury, CT	5.1	19.0	19.4	12.1	15.0	13.6	8.6	4.6
Grand Blanc, MI	6.0	20.0	18.3	12.2	14.2	13.7	8.8	4.9
Hampden, PA	5.8	18.4	19.5	12.2	14.2	13.8	9.0	4.9
Hilliard, OH	6.8	20.0	22.2	13.6	13.6	11.8	7.1	3.4
Hillsborough, NJ	6.1	18.4	21.3	13.3	14.3	12.3	7.8	4.2
Holly Springs, NC	6.5	21.4	20.5	15.4	14.6	11.1	6.5	2.9
Independence, KY	6.4	20.4	19.9	12.5	14.1	13.0	7.8	4.0
Juneau, AK	6.0	18.7	21.4	13.6	15.0	14.9	7.2	2.0
Kaysville, UT	8.7	25.7	21.5	13.4	10.9	9.8	5.8	3.2
Keller, TX	7.2	22.2	21.4	14.4	13.8	10.9	6.2	2.9
Lafayette, CA	5.7	16.9	21.9	14.6	14.4	12.6	7.9	4.1
Lafayette, CO	5.0	19.7	24.0	12.9	13.5	12.7	7.3	3.4
Lake Oswego, OR	6.1	18.6	21.2	14.5	13.6	12.7	8.0	3.5
Laramie, WY	5.3	17.8	39.1	9.4	8.8	10.1	5.7	2.6
Leander, TX	6.8	20.3	24.7	15.4	12.9	10.4	5.9	2.6
Leawood, KS	6.7	20.5	20.0	13.2	13.7	12.5	7.6	3.9
Lee's Summit, MO	6.7	20.5	20.0	13.2	13.7	12.5	7.6	3.9
Leesburg, VA	6.6	19.3	21.8	14.5	14.6	11.8	6.9	3.2
Lehi, UT	10.1	28.7	27.0	12.1	8.3	6.6	4.2	2.3
Lexington, MA	5.5	18.2	21.8	12.7	14.7	12.8	8.0	4.2
Los Altos, CA	6.4	19.2	21.7	14.9	14.3	11.3	6.8	3.7
Loveland, CO	5.4	18.8	25.0	12.0	12.1	12.9	8.3	3.9
Lower Macungie, PA	5.4	19.0	18.3	12.2	14.8	13.7	9.0	5.0
Madison, AL	5.9	19.5	20.3	12.6	15.3	12.7	7.9	4.3
Madison, MS	6.5	21.1	21.3	12.9	13.1	12.2	7.5	3.7

Table continued on next page.

Metro Area	Percent of Population							
	Under Age 5	Age 5–19	Age 20–34	Age 35–44	Age 45–54	Age 55–64	Age 65–74	Age 75–84
Maple Valley, WA	6.3	18.1	22.6	14.2	14.2	12.5	7.2	3.4
Marion, IA	6.3	19.9	19.9	12.7	13.8	12.7	8.1	4.7
Marlboro, NJ	6.1	18.4	21.3	13.3	14.3	12.3	7.8	4.2
Mason, OH	6.4	20.4	19.9	12.5	14.1	13.0	7.8	4.0
Menomonee Falls, WI	6.4	19.9	20.5	12.4	13.8	13.0	7.5	4.1
Meridian, ID	6.7	22.3	20.1	13.5	12.8	11.6	7.9	3.6
Meridian, MI	5.6	20.3	24.0	11.3	12.7	12.7	8.0	3.8
Merrimack, NH	5.5	18.8	19.2	12.8	16.2	13.8	8.0	4.0
Milton, GA	6.6	21.5	20.6	14.7	14.6	11.4	6.8	2.9
Moon, PA	5.1	16.9	19.1	11.5	14.2	14.9	9.7	5.7
Moorpark, CA	6.3	20.6	20.2	12.7	14.2	12.5	7.7	3.9
Morgantown, WV	5.0	16.9	30.5	11.6	11.7	11.7	7.4	3.6
Mount Pleasant, SC	6.4	18.6	22.9	12.9	13.4	12.4	8.4	3.5
Newark, DE	6.0	19.1	20.8	12.4	14.3	13.0	8.0	4.4
Newtown, CT	5.7	20.7	17.6	13.0	15.7	13.0	7.7	4.4
North Attleborough, MA	5.2	18.4	20.2	12.2	14.7	13.4	8.6	4.6
North Port, FL	4.4	14.5	13.9	9.7	12.6	14.9	15.7	9.9
North Ridgeville, OH	5.6	18.8	18.5	11.9	14.3	14.2	9.0	5.0
Northville, MI	5.9	19.4	18.8	12.6	14.8	13.7	8.4	4.3
O'Fallon, MO	6.1	19.2	20.0	12.3	14.1	13.5	8.2	4.5
Orchard Park, NY	5.3	18.1	20.3	11.2	14.3	14.1	8.9	5.1
Oro Valley, AZ	5.9	19.1	21.2	11.4	11.9	12.6	10.0	5.6
Oviedo, FL	6.0	19.1	22.3	13.5	13.8	11.5	8.0	4.1
Parker, CO	6.4	19.6	22.1	14.5	13.7	12.1	7.0	3.2
Parkland, FL	5.7	17.4	19.7	13.4	14.7	12.2	8.9	5.5
Peachtree City, GA	6.6	21.5	20.6	14.7	14.6	11.4	6.8	2.9
Pittsfield, MI	5.2	19.8	27.1	11.7	12.5	11.6	7.2	3.3
Plainfield, IL	6.3	20.2	21.2	13.5	13.9	12.2	7.3	3.8
Pleasant Grove, UT	10.1	28.7	27.0	12.1	8.3	6.6	4.2	2.3
Poway, CA	6.5	18.7	24.4	13.2	13.1	11.4	7.1	3.8
Princeton, NJ	5.7	19.6	20.5	13.2	14.6	12.6	7.5	4.1
Queen Creek, AZ	6.7	20.9	20.9	13.3	12.8	11.2	8.3	4.2
Radnor, PA	6.0	19.1	20.8	12.4	14.3	13.0	8.0	4.4
Randolph, NJ	6.1	18.4	21.3	13.3	14.3	12.3	7.8	4.2
Rexburg, ID	9.3	25.0	33.2	8.4	7.9	7.4	5.2	2.5
Rio Rancho, NM	6.1	19.8	21.0	12.5	13.2	13.1	8.6	4.3
Rye, NY	6.1	18.4	21.3	13.3	14.3	12.3	7.8	4.2
Sammamish, WA	6.3	18.1	22.6	14.2	14.2	12.5	7.2	3.4
San Ramon, CA	5.7	16.9	21.9	14.6	14.4	12.6	7.9	4.1
Saratoga, CA	6.4	19.2	21.7	14.9	14.3	11.3	6.8	3.7
Shrewsbury, MA	5.5	19.4	19.3	12.6	15.6	13.5	7.9	4.1
South Brunswick, NJ	6.1	18.4	21.3	13.3	14.3	12.3	7.8	4.2
South Jordan, UT	8.1	23.0	23.7	14.2	11.4	10.0	5.7	2.8
South Kingstown, RI	5.2	18.4	20.2	12.2	14.7	13.4	8.6	4.6
South Portland, ME	4.9	17.3	18.1	12.2	15.4	15.1	9.8	5.0
Sparks, NV	6.1	18.7	21.3	12.3	13.6	13.3	9.3	3.9
State College, PA	4.1	18.8	32.0	10.4	11.5	10.8	6.9	4.0
Sugar Land, TX	7.6	22.2	22.0	14.2	13.2	11.0	6.1	2.7
Sun Prairie, WI	5.9	18.6	24.2	12.7	13.3	12.4	7.4	3.6
Syracuse, UT	8.7	25.7	21.5	13.4	10.9	9.8	5.8	3.2
Tredyffrin, PA	6.0	19.1	20.8	12.4	14.3	13.0	8.0	4.4
Upper Dublin, PA	6.0	19.1	20.8	12.4	14.3	13.0	8.0	4.4
Urbandale, IA	7.3	20.8	21.1	13.6	13.4	11.6	7.0	3.5
Vestal, NY	5.2	18.8	20.0	10.4	13.9	14.0	9.2	5.7
Vestavia Hills, AL	6.3	19.4	19.9	13.1	13.6	13.1	8.4	4.4
Webster, NY	5.5	19.0	20.2	11.3	14.4	13.6	8.9	4.6
Wellesley, MA	5.5	18.2	21.8	12.7	14.7	12.8	8.0	4.2
West Fargo, ND	7.1	19.4	28.1	11.9	11.5	10.8	5.9	3.5
West Lafayette, IN	6.0	20.7	30.2	10.9	10.7	10.3	6.3	3.3
Weston, FL	5.7	17.4	19.7	13.4	14.7	12.2	8.9	5.5
Wilmette, IL	6.3	20.2	21.2	13.5	13.9	12.2	7.3	3.8
Yorba Linda, CA	6.3	19.4	22.7	13.8	13.9	11.4	6.9	3.8
Zionsville, IN	6.8	20.8	20.7	13.5	13.9	12.0	7.2	3.6
U.S.	6.2	19.6	20.7	12.7	13.6	12.6	8.3	4.3

Note: Figures cover the Metropolitan Statistical Area (MSA)—see Appendix B for areas included
Source: U.S. Census Bureau, 2012-2016 American Community Survey 5-Year Estimates

Segregation

Metro Area	Black/White		Asian/White		Hispanic/White	
	Index[1]	Rank[2]	Index[1]	Rank[2]	Index[1]	Rank[2]
Aberdeen, SD	n/a	n/a	n/a	n/a	n/a	n/a
Aliso Viejo, CA	67.8	10	48.4	12	62.2	2
Allen, TX	56.6	48	46.6	19	50.3	24
Ames, IA	n/a	n/a	n/a	n/a	n/a	n/a
Amherst, MA	65.3	22	39.9	57	63.4	1
Apex, NC	42.1	87	46.7	16	37.1	76
Beavercreek, OH	66.4	14	39.8	58	27.3	99
Bellevue, NE	61.3	38	36.3	74	48.8	30
Bend, OR	n/a	n/a	n/a	n/a	n/a	n/a
Benicia, CA	n/a	n/a	n/a	n/a	n/a	n/a
Bentonville, AR	n/a	n/a	n/a	n/a	n/a	n/a
Bethlehem, NY	61.3	37	43.1	38	38.9	70
Blacksburg, VA	n/a	n/a	n/a	n/a	n/a	n/a
Bowie, MD	62.3	32	38.9	64	48.3	32
Bozeman, MT	n/a	n/a	n/a	n/a	n/a	n/a
Brentwood, TN	56.2	49	41.0	51	47.9	34
Burlington, VT	n/a	n/a	n/a	n/a	n/a	n/a
Cabot, AR	58.8	42	39.7	59	39.7	68
Carmel, IN	66.4	15	41.6	47	47.3	37
Cedar Falls, IA	n/a	n/a	n/a	n/a	n/a	n/a
Cedar Park, TX	50.1	70	41.2	49	43.2	51
Central, LA	57.5	45	50.8	5	32.7	88
Chapel Hill, NC	48.1	75	44.0	30	48.0	33
Cheshire, CT	63.7	29	29.7	90	54.4	14
Chino Hills, CA	45.7	82	40.7	53	42.4	55
Cibolo, TX	49.0	73	38.3	66	46.1	43
Cicero, NY	67.8	11	51.5	4	42.2	57
Collierville, TN	62.6	30	40.1	56	50.7	22
Coppell, TX	56.6	48	46.6	19	50.3	24
Cornelius, NC	53.8	56	43.6	34	47.6	35
Cranberry, PA	65.8	17	52.4	2	28.6	97
Crown Point, IN	76.4	3	44.9	26	56.3	10
Dublin, OH	62.2	33	43.3	35	41.5	59
East Fishkill, NY	78.0	2	51.9	3	62.0	3
Eden Prairie, MN	52.9	60	42.8	39	42.5	54
Edmond, OK	51.4	67	39.2	60	47.0	38
Edwardsville, IL	72.3	7	44.3	28	30.7	94
Evesham, NJ	68.4	9	42.3	42	55.1	12
Flower Mound, TX	56.6	48	46.6	19	50.3	24
Folsom, CA	56.9	46	49.9	8	38.9	71
Friendswood, TX	61.4	36	50.4	7	52.5	18
Gaines, MI	64.3	26	43.2	37	50.4	23
Glastonbury, CT	64.8	24	36.9	73	58.4	7
Grand Blanc, MI	n/a	n/a	n/a	n/a	n/a	n/a
Hampden, PA	65.7	18	41.1	50	47.0	39
Hilliard, OH	62.2	33	43.3	35	41.5	59
Hillsborough, NJ	78.0	2	51.9	3	62.0	3
Holly Springs, NC	42.1	87	46.7	16	37.1	76
Independence, KY	69.4	8	46.0	21	36.9	77
Juneau, AK	n/a	n/a	n/a	n/a	n/a	n/a
Kaysville, UT	32.0	98	20.5	102	35.8	81
Keller, TX	56.6	48	46.6	19	50.3	24
Lafayette, CA	62.0	34	46.6	18	49.6	26
Lafayette, CO	n/a	n/a	n/a	n/a	n/a	n/a
Lake Oswego, OR	46.0	81	35.8	75	34.3	83
Laramie, WY	n/a	n/a	n/a	n/a	n/a	n/a
Leander, TX	50.1	70	41.2	49	43.2	51
Leawood, KS	61.2	39	38.4	65	44.4	48
Lee's Summit, MO	61.2	39	38.4	65	44.4	48
Leesburg, VA	62.3	32	38.9	64	48.3	32
Lehi, UT	21.9	102	28.2	94	30.9	93
Lexington, MA	64.0	27	45.4	23	59.6	5
Los Altos, CA	40.9	89	45.0	25	47.6	36
Loveland, CO	n/a	n/a	n/a	n/a	n/a	n/a
Lower Macungie, PA	47.2	78	38.0	67	55.4	11
Madison, AL	n/a	n/a	n/a	n/a	n/a	n/a
Madison, MS	56.0	51	38.9	63	42.9	52
Maple Valley, WA	49.1	72	37.6	69	32.8	87

Table continued on next page.

Metro Area	Black/White		Asian/White		Hispanic/White	
	Index[1]	Rank[2]	Index[1]	Rank[2]	Index[1]	Rank[2]
Marion, IA	n/a	n/a	n/a	n/a	n/a	n/a
Marlboro, NJ	78.0	2	51.9	3	62.0	3
Mason, OH	69.4	8	46.0	21	36.9	77
Menomonee Falls, WI	81.5	1	40.7	52	57.0	9
Meridian, ID	30.2	101	27.6	95	36.2	80
Meridian, MI	n/a	n/a	n/a	n/a	n/a	n/a
Merrimack, NH	n/a	n/a	n/a	n/a	n/a	n/a
Milton, GA	59.0	41	48.5	10	49.5	27
Moon, PA	65.8	17	52.4	2	28.6	97
Moorpark, CA	39.9	91	31.2	87	54.6	13
Morgantown, WV	n/a	n/a	n/a	n/a	n/a	n/a
Mount Pleasant, SC	41.5	88	33.4	84	39.8	66
Newark, DE	68.4	9	42.3	42	55.1	12
Newtown, CT	67.5	12	31.4	86	59.2	6
North Attleborough, MA	53.5	57	40.1	55	60.1	4
North Port, FL	55.2	52	23.4	99	41.2	60
North Ridgeville, OH	74.1	5	41.3	48	52.3	20
Northville, MI	75.3	4	50.6	6	43.3	49
O'Fallon, MO	72.3	7	44.3	28	30.7	94
Orchard Park, NY	73.2	6	54.4	1	50.7	21
Oro Valley, AZ	36.9	96	24.8	97	46.2	42
Oviedo, FL	50.7	69	33.9	81	40.2	64
Parker, CO	62.6	31	33.4	83	48.8	31
Parkland, FL	64.8	23	34.2	80	57.4	8
Peachtree City, GA	59.0	41	48.5	10	49.5	27
Pittsfield, MI	n/a	n/a	n/a	n/a	n/a	n/a
Plainfield, IL	76.4	3	44.9	26	56.3	10
Pleasant Grove, UT	21.9	102	28.2	94	30.9	93
Poway, CA	51.2	68	48.2	13	49.6	25
Princeton, NJ	n/a	n/a	n/a	n/a	n/a	n/a
Queen Creek, AZ	43.6	86	32.7	85	49.3	28
Radnor, PA	68.4	9	42.3	42	55.1	12
Randolph, NJ	78.0	2	51.9	3	62.0	3
Rexburg, ID	n/a	n/a	n/a	n/a	n/a	n/a
Rio Rancho, NM	30.9	99	28.5	93	36.4	79
Rye, NY	78.0	2	51.9	3	62.0	3
Sammamish, WA	49.1	72	37.6	69	32.8	87
San Ramon, CA	62.0	34	46.6	18	49.6	26
Saratoga, CA	40.9	89	45.0	25	47.6	36
Shrewsbury, MA	52.6	61	45.8	22	52.7	17
South Brunswick, NJ	78.0	2	51.9	3	62.0	3
South Jordan, UT	39.3	93	31.0	88	42.9	53
South Kingstown, RI	53.5	57	40.1	55	60.1	4
South Portland, ME	52.2	64	33.9	82	23.8	102
Sparks, NV	n/a	n/a	n/a	n/a	n/a	n/a
State College, PA	n/a	n/a	n/a	n/a	n/a	n/a
Sugar Land, TX	61.4	36	50.4	7	52.5	18
Sun Prairie, WI	49.6	71	44.2	29	40.1	65
Syracuse, UT	32.0	98	20.5	102	35.8	81
Tredyffrin, PA	68.4	9	42.3	42	55.1	12
Upper Dublin, PA	68.4	9	42.3	42	55.1	12
Urbandale, IA	51.6	66	35.5	76	46.7	40
Vestal, NY	n/a	n/a	n/a	n/a	n/a	n/a
Vestavia Hills, AL	65.8	16	47.1	15	44.5	47
Webster, NY	65.3	21	45.1	24	48.9	29
Wellesley, MA	64.0	27	45.4	23	59.6	5
West Fargo, ND	n/a	n/a	n/a	n/a	n/a	n/a
West Lafayette, IN	n/a	n/a	n/a	n/a	n/a	n/a
Weston, FL	64.8	23	34.2	80	57.4	8
Wilmette, IL	76.4	3	44.9	26	56.3	10
Yorba Linda, CA	67.8	10	48.4	12	62.2	2
Zionsville, IN	66.4	15	41.6	47	47.3	37

Note: Figures are based on an analysis of 1990, 2000, and 2010 Census Decennial Census tract data by William H. Frey, Brookings Institution and the University of Michigan Social Science Data Analysis Network. In this analysis all racial groups (whites, blacks, and asians) are non-Hispanic members of those races. Hispanics are shown as a separate category; All figures cover the Metropolitan Statistical Area (see Appendix B for areas included); (1) Segregation Indices are Dissimilarity Indices that measure the degree to which the minority group is distributed differently than whites across census tracts. They range from 0 (complete integration) to 100 (complete [segregation) where the value indicates the percentage of the minority group that needs to move to be distributed exactly like whites; (2) Ranges from 1 (most segregated) to 102 (least segregated); n/a not available.
Source: www.CensusScope.org

Religious Groups by Family

Area[1]	Catholic	Baptist	Non-Den.	Methodist[2]	Lutheran	LDS[3]	Pente-costal	Presby-terian[4]	Muslim[5]	Judaism
Aberdeen, SD	n/a	n/a	n/a	n/a	n/a	n/a	n/a	n/a	n/a	n/a
Aliso Viejo, CA	33.8	2.7	3.6	1.0	0.6	1.7	1.7	0.9	0.7	0.9
Allen, TX	13.3	18.7	7.7	5.2	0.7	1.1	2.1	0.9	2.4	0.3
Ames, IA	9.8	2.4	6.4	9.3	14.7	1.2	0.9	2.1	0.3	0.1
Amherst, MA	41.9	1.5	1.2	0.9	0.5	0.3	1.1	2.1	0.1	0.8
Apex, NC	9.1	12.1	5.9	6.7	0.9	0.8	2.2	2.2	0.9	0.3
Beavercreek, OH	12.4	9.6	4.2	4.4	2.0	0.8	1.4	2.1	0.2	0.3
Bellevue, NE	21.6	4.5	1.8	3.9	7.8	1.7	1.2	2.2	0.5	0.4
Bend, OR	7.3	1.7	3.4	0.6	1.7	3.4	3.1	0.8	<0.1	0.1
Benicia, CA	19.6	4.9	4.5	0.9	0.6	2.5	1.3	0.5	0.8	<0.1
Bentonville, AR	9.1	22.9	5.7	4.8	0.8	1.7	2.2	0.9	0.1	<0.1
Bethlehem, NY	26.8	1.2	2.2	2.9	1.5	0.3	0.5	2.1	1.2	1.0
Blacksburg, VA	2.1	9.5	4.2	8.6	0.9	0.9	5.8	1.7	2.2	<0.1
Bowie, MD	14.5	7.3	4.8	4.5	1.2	1.1	1.0	1.3	2.3	1.1
Bozeman, MT	n/a	n/a	n/a	n/a	n/a	n/a	n/a	n/a	n/a	n/a
Brentwood, TN	4.1	25.2	5.8	6.1	0.3	0.7	2.1	2.1	0.3	0.1
Burlington, VT	27.5	1.2	0.9	2.4	0.3	0.5	0.5	2.0	0.1	0.6
Cabot, AR	4.5	25.9	6.0	7.3	0.5	0.9	2.8	0.8	0.1	0.1
Carmel, IN	10.5	10.2	7.1	4.9	1.6	0.7	1.6	1.6	0.2	0.3
Cedar Falls, IA	14.1	7.7	1.1	6.1	14.3	0.7	3.2	6.6	0.5	<0.1
Cedar Park, TX	16.0	10.3	4.5	3.6	1.9	1.1	0.8	1.0	1.2	0.2
Central, LA	22.5	18.2	9.6	4.6	0.2	0.7	1.1	0.6	0.2	0.1
Chapel Hill, NC	5.0	13.8	5.6	8.1	0.4	0.7	1.3	2.5	0.4	0.5
Cheshire, CT	35.3	1.4	1.9	1.5	0.6	0.3	1.0	2.2	0.5	1.2
Chino Hills, CA	24.8	2.6	5.5	0.6	0.5	2.4	1.5	0.6	0.5	<0.1
Cibolo, TX	28.4	8.5	6.0	3.0	1.6	1.4	1.3	0.7	0.9	0.2
Cicero, NY	30.1	2.1	1.9	4.8	1.3	0.4	1.1	1.3	0.9	0.6
Collierville, TN	5.2	30.8	5.4	6.2	0.3	0.6	4.7	2.4	0.3	0.6
Coppell, TX	13.3	18.7	7.7	5.2	0.7	1.1	2.1	0.9	2.4	0.3
Cornelius, NC	5.9	17.2	6.7	8.6	1.3	0.7	3.2	4.5	0.2	0.3
Cranberry, PA	32.8	2.3	2.8	5.6	3.3	0.3	1.1	4.6	0.3	0.7
Crown Point, IN	34.2	3.2	4.4	1.9	3.0	0.3	1.2	1.9	3.2	0.8
Dublin, OH	11.7	5.3	3.5	4.7	2.4	0.7	1.9	2.0	0.8	0.5
East Fishkill, NY	36.9	1.8	1.7	1.3	0.7	0.3	0.8	1.0	2.3	4.7
Eden Prairie, MN	21.7	2.4	2.9	2.7	14.4	0.6	1.7	1.8	0.4	0.7
Edmond, OK	6.3	25.3	7.0	10.6	0.7	1.2	3.1	0.9	0.2	0.1
Edwardsville, IL	19.8	10.0	3.8	3.4	4.1	0.6	1.2	3.0	0.4	0.7
Evesham, NJ	33.4	3.9	2.8	2.9	1.8	0.3	0.8	2.1	1.2	1.3
Flower Mound, TX	13.3	18.7	7.7	5.2	0.7	1.1	2.1	0.9	2.4	0.3
Folsom, CA	16.1	3.1	4.0	1.7	0.7	3.3	2.0	0.8	0.8	0.2
Friendswood, TX	17.0	16.0	7.2	4.8	1.0	1.1	1.5	0.8	2.6	0.3
Gaines, MI	17.1	1.7	8.3	3.0	2.1	0.5	1.1	9.9	1.0	0.1
Glastonbury, CT	30.3	1.9	2.1	1.9	1.3	0.3	0.9	3.6	0.2	1.2
Grand Blanc, MI	10.7	6.9	3.4	3.0	3.2	0.5	2.9	1.4	2.5	0.1
Hampden, PA	14.1	1.6	3.2	9.8	5.5	0.6	2.0	5.1	0.8	0.7
Hilliard, OH	11.7	5.3	3.5	4.7	2.4	0.7	1.9	2.0	0.8	0.5
Hillsborough, NJ	36.9	1.8	1.7	1.3	0.7	0.3	0.8	1.0	2.3	4.7
Holly Springs, NC	9.1	12.1	5.9	6.7	0.9	0.8	2.2	2.2	0.9	0.3
Independence, KY	19.0	9.5	3.6	3.8	1.1	0.5	2.2	1.5	0.2	0.5
Juneau, AK	n/a	n/a	n/a	n/a	n/a	n/a	n/a	n/a	n/a	n/a
Kaysville, UT	5.7	0.9	0.9	0.2	0.4	68.7	1.2	0.1	<0.1	<0.1
Keller, TX	13.3	18.7	7.7	5.2	0.7	1.1	2.1	0.9	2.4	0.3
Lafayette, CA	20.7	2.5	2.4	1.9	0.5	1.5	1.2	1.1	1.2	0.8
Lafayette, CO	20.1	2.3	4.7	1.7	3.0	2.9	0.4	2.0	0.1	0.7
Lake Oswego, OR	10.5	2.3	4.5	1.0	1.6	3.7	2.0	0.9	0.1	0.3
Laramie, WY	n/a	n/a	n/a	n/a	n/a	n/a	n/a	n/a	n/a	n/a
Leander, TX	16.0	10.3	4.5	3.6	1.9	1.1	0.8	1.0	1.2	0.2
Leawood, KS	12.6	13.1	5.2	5.8	2.2	2.4	2.6	1.6	0.3	0.4
Lee's Summit, MO	12.6	13.1	5.2	5.8	2.2	2.4	2.6	1.6	0.3	0.4
Leesburg, VA	14.5	7.3	4.8	4.5	1.2	1.1	1.0	1.3	2.3	1.1
Lehi, UT	1.3	<0.1	<0.1	0.1	<0.1	88.5	0.1	<0.1	<0.1	<0.1
Lexington, MA	44.3	1.1	1.0	0.9	0.3	0.4	0.6	1.6	0.4	1.4
Los Altos, CA	26.0	1.3	4.2	1.0	0.5	1.4	1.1	0.7	1.0	0.6
Loveland, CO	11.8	2.2	6.3	4.3	3.4	2.9	4.7	1.9	0.1	<0.1
Lower Macungie, PA	23.1	0.4	1.9	3.9	7.9	0.3	0.4	6.2	0.6	0.6
Madison, AL	3.9	27.6	3.1	7.5	0.7	1.1	1.2	1.7	0.2	0.1
Madison, MS	3.1	34.4	7.6	10.5	0.2	0.7	2.1	2.0	0.2	0.1
Maple Valley, WA	12.3	2.1	5.0	1.2	2.0	3.3	2.8	1.4	0.4	0.4

Table continued on next page.

Area[1]	Catholic	Baptist	Non-Den.	Methodist[2]	Lutheran	LDS[3]	Pente-costal	Presby-terian[4]	Muslim[5]	Judaism
Marion, IA	18.8	2.3	3.0	7.3	11.3	0.8	1.8	3.2	0.5	0.1
Marlboro, NJ	36.9	1.8	1.7	1.3	0.7	0.3	0.8	1.0	2.3	4.7
Mason, OH	19.0	9.5	3.6	3.8	1.1	0.5	2.2	1.5	0.2	0.5
Menomonee Falls, WI	24.6	3.1	3.8	1.5	10.7	0.4	1.9	1.5	0.5	0.5
Meridian, ID	8.0	2.9	4.1	2.1	1.1	15.8	2.3	0.6	0.1	0.1
Meridian, MI	13.9	2.0	3.8	3.6	2.7	0.7	4.4	2.2	0.8	0.2
Merrimack, NH	31.1	1.3	2.3	1.1	0.5	0.6	0.4	2.0	0.3	0.5
Milton, GA	7.4	17.4	6.8	7.8	0.5	0.7	2.6	1.8	0.7	0.5
Moon, PA	32.8	2.3	2.8	5.6	3.3	0.3	1.1	4.6	0.3	0.7
Moorpark, CA	28.2	1.9	4.1	1.0	1.4	2.4	1.2	0.7	0.4	0.6
Morgantown, WV	7.0	3.0	3.0	7.5	0.6	1.1	0.6	0.5	0.2	0.2
Mount Pleasant, SC	6.1	12.4	7.0	10.0	1.1	0.9	2.0	2.3	0.1	0.3
Newark, DE	33.4	3.9	2.8	2.9	1.8	0.3	0.8	2.1	1.2	1.3
Newtown, CT	44.1	1.9	2.3	2.0	0.8	0.5	1.1	3.0	0.5	1.9
North Attleborough, MA	47.0	1.4	1.2	0.8	0.5	0.3	0.5	1.0	0.1	0.7
North Port, FL	18.0	5.6	4.3	3.6	1.0	0.4	1.4	2.1	0.1	0.7
North Ridgeville, OH	28.8	4.3	3.3	2.8	2.5	0.3	1.1	2.0	0.1	1.4
Northville, MI	21.3	4.5	4.9	2.1	3.1	0.3	1.2	1.3	1.8	0.8
O'Fallon, MO	19.8	10.0	3.8	3.4	4.1	0.6	1.2	3.0	0.4	0.7
Orchard Park, NY	35.6	2.7	2.0	2.3	3.3	0.3	1.0	1.9	1.6	0.7
Oro Valley, AZ	20.7	3.3	3.7	1.3	1.5	2.9	1.5	1.0	<0.1	0.5
Oviedo, FL	13.2	6.9	5.6	2.9	0.9	0.9	3.2	1.3	1.3	0.2
Parker, CO	16.0	2.9	4.6	1.7	2.1	2.4	1.2	1.5	0.5	0.6
Parkland, FL	18.5	5.3	4.1	1.2	0.4	0.5	1.7	0.6	0.9	1.5
Peachtree City, GA	7.4	17.4	6.8	7.8	0.5	0.7	2.6	1.8	0.7	0.5
Pittsfield, MI	12.3	2.2	1.5	3.0	2.8	0.8	1.9	2.9	1.2	0.9
Plainfield, IL	34.2	3.2	4.4	1.9	3.0	0.3	1.2	1.9	3.2	0.8
Pleasant Grove, UT	1.3	<0.1	<0.1	0.1	<0.1	88.5	0.1	<0.1	<0.1	<0.1
Poway, CA	25.9	2.0	4.8	1.1	0.9	2.3	1.0	0.9	0.7	0.5
Princeton, NJ	33.1	2.7	2.2	2.1	1.1	0.4	1.2	2.2	1.3	2.1
Queen Creek, AZ	13.3	3.4	5.1	1.0	1.6	6.1	2.9	0.6	0.1	0.3
Radnor, PA	33.4	3.9	2.8	2.9	1.8	0.3	0.8	2.1	1.2	1.3
Randolph, NJ	36.9	1.8	1.7	1.3	0.7	0.3	0.8	1.0	2.3	4.7
Rexburg, ID	n/a	n/a	n/a	n/a	n/a	n/a	n/a	n/a	n/a	n/a
Rio Rancho, NM	27.1	3.7	4.2	1.4	0.9	2.3	1.4	1.0	0.2	0.2
Rye, NY	36.9	1.8	1.7	1.3	0.7	0.3	0.8	1.0	2.3	4.7
Sammamish, WA	12.3	2.1	5.0	1.2	2.0	3.3	2.8	1.4	0.4	0.4
San Ramon, CA	20.7	2.5	2.4	1.9	0.5	1.5	1.2	1.1	1.2	0.8
Saratoga, CA	26.0	1.3	4.2	1.0	0.5	1.4	1.1	0.7	1.0	0.6
Shrewsbury, MA	38.4	1.1	1.7	0.9	0.9	0.3	1.0	2.0	<0.1	0.5
South Brunswick, NJ	36.9	1.8	1.7	1.3	0.7	0.3	0.8	1.0	2.3	4.7
South Jordan, UT	8.9	0.8	0.5	0.5	0.5	58.9	0.6	0.3	0.4	0.1
South Kingstown, RI	47.0	1.4	1.2	0.8	0.5	0.3	0.5	1.0	0.1	0.7
South Portland, ME	15.8	1.6	1.5	1.5	0.4	0.6	0.7	2.7	0.1	0.4
Sparks, NV	14.3	1.5	3.1	0.9	0.7	4.6	1.9	0.4	<0.1	0.1
State College, PA	12.4	2.3	0.8	7.4	4.3	0.7	1.0	2.7	0.2	0.3
Sugar Land, TX	17.0	16.0	7.2	4.8	1.0	1.1	1.5	0.8	2.6	0.3
Sun Prairie, WI	21.8	1.1	1.5	3.6	12.7	0.5	0.3	2.1	0.4	0.4
Syracuse, UT	5.7	0.9	0.9	0.2	0.4	68.7	1.2	0.1	<0.1	<0.1
Tredyffrin, PA	33.4	3.9	2.8	2.9	1.8	0.3	0.8	2.1	1.2	1.3
Upper Dublin, PA	33.4	3.9	2.8	2.9	1.8	0.3	0.8	2.1	1.2	1.3
Urbandale, IA	13.6	4.7	3.3	6.9	8.2	0.9	2.3	2.9	0.3	0.3
Vestal, NY	27.0	1.1	2.8	7.7	1.1	0.5	0.9	1.5	0.3	0.7
Vestavia Hills, AL	5.7	39.0	7.0	7.8	0.3	0.6	4.8	2.1	0.3	0.3
Webster, NY	24.0	2.7	4.0	3.2	1.8	0.6	0.6	2.3	0.8	0.9
Wellesley, MA	44.3	1.1	1.0	0.9	0.3	0.4	0.6	1.6	0.4	1.4
West Fargo, ND	17.4	0.4	0.4	3.3	32.5	0.6	1.5	1.8	0.1	<0.1
West Lafayette, IN	12.1	4.2	2.2	6.3	2.6	0.9	2.0	2.7	0.1	0.2
Weston, FL	18.5	5.3	4.1	1.2	0.4	0.5	1.7	0.6	0.9	1.5
Wilmette, IL	34.2	3.2	4.4	1.9	3.0	0.3	1.2	1.9	3.2	0.8
Yorba Linda, CA	33.8	2.7	3.6	1.0	0.6	1.7	1.7	0.9	0.7	0.9
Zionsville, IN	10.5	10.2	7.1	4.9	1.6	0.7	1.6	1.6	0.2	0.3
U.S.	19.1	9.3	4.0	4.0	2.3	2.0	1.9	1.6	0.8	0.7

Note: Figures are the number of adherents as a percentage of the total population; (1) Figures cover the Metropolitan Statistical Area—see Appendix B for areas included; (2) Methodist/Pietist; (3) Latter Day Saints; (4) Reformed; (5) Figures are estimates

Source: Association of Statisticians of American Religious Bodies, 2010 U.S. Religion Census: Religious Congregations & Membership Study

Religious Groups by Tradition

Area	Catholic	Evangelical Protestant	Mainline Protestant	Other Tradition	Black Protestant	Orthodox
Aberdeen, SD	n/a	n/a	n/a	n/a	n/a	n/a
Aliso Viejo, CA	33.8	9.0	2.3	4.6	0.8	0.6
Allen, TX	13.3	28.3	6.9	4.7	1.7	0.1
Ames, IA	9.8	15.8	21.0	2.3	<0.1	<0.1
Amherst, MA	41.9	3.5	5.0	2.2	0.3	0.4
Apex, NC	9.1	19.9	10.1	3.2	1.7	0.2
Beavercreek, OH	12.4	16.0	9.5	2.5	2.7	0.5
Bellevue, NE	21.6	12.1	10.7	3.2	1.4	0.1
Bend, OR	7.3	10.9	3.1	4.0	<0.1	<0.1
Benicia, CA	19.6	11.3	2.1	3.6	0.6	0.1
Bentonville, AR	9.1	32.6	7.0	2.1	0.1	<0.1
Bethlehem, NY	26.8	4.5	7.3	3.1	0.5	0.3
Blacksburg, VA	2.1	19.7	12.6	3.4	0.3	<0.1
Bowie, MD	14.5	12.4	8.7	5.9	2.3	0.6
Bozeman, MT	n/a	n/a	n/a	n/a	n/a	n/a
Brentwood, TN	4.1	32.9	8.0	1.7	3.3	0.4
Burlington, VT	27.5	4.5	6.2	1.9	<0.1	<0.1
Cabot, AR	4.5	33.9	8.1	1.7	3.4	<0.1
Carmel, IN	10.5	18.2	9.6	1.6	1.8	0.2
Cedar Falls, IA	14.1	11.5	24.4	1.5	5.4	<0.1
Cedar Park, TX	16.0	16.1	6.3	3.9	1.3	0.1
Central, LA	22.5	24.8	5.6	1.5	5.1	<0.1
Chapel Hill, NC	5.0	19.3	11.7	2.9	3.1	<0.1
Cheshire, CT	35.3	3.8	6.1	2.3	0.7	0.4
Chino Hills, CA	24.8	11.4	1.3	3.7	0.8	0.1
Cibolo, TX	28.4	16.9	5.0	3.1	0.4	<0.1
Cicero, NY	30.1	5.0	9.1	2.9	0.8	0.6
Collierville, TN	5.2	29.4	8.3	2.1	13.4	<0.1
Coppell, TX	13.3	28.3	6.9	4.7	1.7	0.1
Cornelius, NC	5.9	27.5	13.3	1.6	2.7	0.4
Cranberry, PA	32.8	7.3	13.8	2.0	0.8	0.6
Crown Point, IN	34.2	9.7	5.1	5.0	2.0	0.9
Dublin, OH	11.7	11.8	9.5	3.1	1.1	0.2
East Fishkill, NY	36.9	3.9	4.1	8.3	1.2	0.9
Eden Prairie, MN	21.7	12.8	14.5	2.2	0.4	0.2
Edmond, OK	6.3	39.0	9.8	2.7	1.9	0.1
Edwardsville, IL	19.8	17.4	7.3	2.3	2.1	0.2
Evesham, NJ	33.4	6.3	8.9	3.7	1.7	0.4
Flower Mound, TX	13.3	28.3	6.9	4.7	1.7	0.1
Folsom, CA	16.1	11.3	2.2	5.8	0.5	0.3
Friendswood, TX	17.0	24.9	6.6	4.9	1.3	0.2
Gaines, MI	17.1	20.7	7.5	2.1	1.0	0.2
Glastonbury, CT	30.3	4.8	8.2	2.6	0.7	0.3
Grand Blanc, MI	10.7	14.0	5.3	4.1	4.8	0.3
Hampden, PA	14.1	11.4	17.7	4.0	1.2	0.3
Hilliard, OH	11.7	11.8	9.5	3.1	1.1	0.2
Hillsborough, NJ	36.9	3.9	4.1	8.3	1.2	0.9
Holly Springs, NC	9.1	19.9	10.1	3.2	1.7	0.2
Independence, KY	19.0	15.5	7.1	1.5	1.1	0.1
Juneau, AK	n/a	n/a	n/a	n/a	n/a	n/a
Kaysville, UT	5.7	3.4	0.7	69.3	0.1	<0.1
Keller, TX	13.3	28.3	6.9	4.7	1.7	0.1
Lafayette, CA	20.7	6.1	3.8	5.2	1.0	0.6
Lafayette, CO	20.1	9.7	6.4	4.8	<0.1	0.2
Lake Oswego, OR	10.5	11.6	3.6	5.2	0.1	0.3
Laramie, WY	n/a	n/a	n/a	n/a	n/a	n/a
Leander, TX	16.0	16.1	6.3	3.9	1.3	0.1
Leawood, KS	12.6	20.5	9.9	3.6	2.6	0.1
Lee's Summit, MO	12.6	20.5	9.9	3.6	2.6	0.1
Leesburg, VA	14.5	12.4	8.7	5.9	2.3	0.6
Lehi, UT	1.3	0.4	<0.1	88.8	<0.1	<0.1
Lexington, MA	44.3	3.2	4.5	3.4	0.1	1.0
Los Altos, CA	26.0	8.2	2.4	6.8	0.1	0.4
Loveland, CO	11.8	18.8	5.9	3.9	<0.1	0.1
Lower Macungie, PA	23.1	5.3	17.7	3.0	0.1	0.6
Madison, AL	3.9	33.3	9.6	1.8	1.8	<0.1
Madison, MS	3.1	41.3	9.6	1.6	8.1	0.1
Maple Valley, WA	12.3	11.9	4.6	5.9	0.3	0.4

Table continued on next page.

Area	Catholic	Evangelical Protestant	Mainline Protestant	Other Tradition	Black Protestant	Orthodox
Marion, IA	18.8	13.7	17.5	1.9	0.1	0.2
Marlboro, NJ	36.9	3.9	4.1	8.3	1.2	0.9
Mason, OH	19.0	15.5	7.1	1.5	1.1	0.1
Menomonee Falls, WI	24.6	14.6	7.1	2.3	2.4	0.6
Meridian, ID	8.0	12.9	4.3	16.7	<0.1	<0.1
Meridian, MI	13.9	13.1	7.4	2.1	0.7	0.1
Merrimack, NH	31.1	5.1	4.4	1.8	<0.1	0.7
Milton, GA	7.4	26.0	9.8	2.9	3.1	0.2
Moon, PA	32.8	7.3	13.8	2.0	0.8	0.6
Moorpark, CA	28.2	8.9	2.6	4.5	0.2	0.2
Morgantown, WV	7.0	7.6	10.8	1.6	<0.1	0.1
Mount Pleasant, SC	6.1	19.6	11.1	1.8	7.3	0.1
Newark, DE	33.4	6.3	8.9	3.7	1.7	0.4
Newtown, CT	44.1	5.1	9.0	3.5	0.4	1.0
North Attleborough, MA	47.0	2.8	4.7	1.6	<0.1	0.5
North Port, FL	18.0	13.4	6.8	1.6	0.6	0.2
North Ridgeville, OH	28.8	9.0	7.5	2.6	2.1	0.8
Northville, MI	21.3	10.6	4.7	3.5	3.3	0.9
O'Fallon, MO	19.8	17.4	7.3	2.3	2.1	0.2
Orchard Park, NY	35.6	5.8	7.1	3.2	2.2	0.4
Oro Valley, AZ	20.7	10.0	3.7	4.5	0.4	0.2
Oviedo, FL	13.2	17.8	4.7	3.2	1.2	0.3
Parker, CO	16.0	11.0	4.5	4.6	0.3	0.3
Parkland, FL	18.5	11.4	2.4	3.5	1.7	0.2
Peachtree City, GA	7.4	26.0	9.8	2.9	3.1	0.2
Pittsfield, MI	12.3	7.3	7.5	3.7	1.5	0.2
Plainfield, IL	34.2	9.7	5.1	5.0	2.0	0.9
Pleasant Grove, UT	1.3	0.4	<0.1	88.8	<0.1	<0.1
Poway, CA	25.9	9.7	2.4	5.2	0.3	0.2
Princeton, NJ	33.1	4.7	8.0	4.6	1.4	0.5
Queen Creek, AZ	13.3	13.2	2.6	7.8	0.1	0.3
Radnor, PA	33.4	6.3	8.9	3.7	1.7	0.4
Randolph, NJ	36.9	3.9	4.1	8.3	1.2	0.9
Rexburg, ID	n/a	n/a	n/a	n/a	n/a	n/a
Rio Rancho, NM	27.1	11.2	3.2	3.9	0.2	0.1
Rye, NY	36.9	3.9	4.1	8.3	1.2	0.9
Sammamish, WA	12.3	11.9	4.6	5.9	0.3	0.4
San Ramon, CA	20.7	6.1	3.8	5.2	1.0	0.6
Saratoga, CA	26.0	8.2	2.4	6.8	0.1	0.4
Shrewsbury, MA	38.4	4.6	5.4	2.3	<0.1	0.9
South Brunswick, NJ	36.9	3.9	4.1	8.3	1.2	0.9
South Jordan, UT	8.9	2.6	1.2	60.0	0.1	0.4
South Kingstown, RI	47.0	2.8	4.7	1.6	<0.1	0.5
South Portland, ME	15.8	3.9	7.0	1.8	<0.1	0.2
Sparks, NV	14.3	7.6	1.9	5.1	0.2	0.1
State College, PA	12.4	7.5	15.5	1.6	0.1	0.1
Sugar Land, TX	17.0	24.9	6.6	4.9	1.3	0.2
Sun Prairie, WI	21.8	7.2	15.3	2.2	0.1	<0.1
Syracuse, UT	5.7	3.4	0.7	69.3	0.1	<0.1
Tredyffrin, PA	33.4	6.3	8.9	3.7	1.7	0.4
Upper Dublin, PA	33.4	6.3	8.9	3.7	1.7	0.4
Urbandale, IA	13.6	12.3	16.8	1.8	0.9	0.1
Vestal, NY	27.0	6.4	11.4	2.0	0.1	0.9
Vestavia Hills, AL	5.7	45.2	8.3	1.4	10.1	0.1
Webster, NY	24.0	7.3	8.5	2.9	0.9	0.2
Wellesley, MA	44.3	3.2	4.5	3.4	0.1	1.0
West Fargo, ND	17.4	10.7	30.8	0.8	<0.1	<0.1
West Lafayette, IN	12.1	11.6	9.8	1.4	<0.1	<0.1
Weston, FL	18.5	11.4	2.4	3.5	1.7	0.2
Wilmette, IL	34.2	9.7	5.1	5.0	2.0	0.9
Yorba Linda, CA	33.8	9.0	2.3	4.6	0.8	0.6
Zionsville, IN	10.5	18.2	9.6	1.6	1.8	0.2
U.S.	19.1	16.2	7.3	4.3	1.6	0.3

Note: Figures are the number of adherents as a percentage of the total population; (1) Figures cover the Metropolitan Statistical Area—see Appendix B for areas included

Source: Association of Statisticians of American Religious Bodies, 2010 U.S. Religion Census: Religious Congregations & Membership Study

Ancestry: City

City	German	Irish	English	American	Italian	Polish	French[1]	Scottish	Dutch
Aberdeen, SD	51.8	9.7	5.0	2.6	0.8	2.0	1.8	0.4	2.1
Aliso Viejo, CA	13.3	10.8	8.6	3.4	6.2	2.2	2.6	1.6	1.6
Allen, TX	14.5	9.7	9.7	5.9	3.2	2.1	2.0	2.1	1.2
Ames, IA	33.2	12.7	7.0	2.9	3.3	1.9	2.3	2.2	3.0
Amherst, MA	7.9	16.4	9.0	1.5	11.2	6.4	4.1	2.0	0.9
Apex, NC	18.5	14.5	14.2	5.5	8.4	3.5	1.9	3.6	1.9
Beavercreek, OH	24.5	13.2	10.6	10.0	4.8	3.8	2.8	2.1	1.7
Bellevue, NE	27.1	15.6	10.5	3.3	4.3	4.9	2.9	1.2	1.4
Bend, OR	21.4	13.5	11.9	6.3	4.5	2.8	2.8	3.4	2.1
Benicia, CA	13.7	13.3	11.6	2.9	7.1	2.7	4.0	1.8	2.3
Bentonville, AR	11.3	6.7	8.1	6.4	1.9	1.5	1.3	1.0	1.3
Bethlehem, NY	18.8	27.3	13.0	6.4	16.9	6.4	4.7	2.1	3.4
Blacksburg, VA	14.4	9.9	8.0	6.8	5.1	2.5	1.6	2.0	1.0
Bowie, MD	8.4	7.6	5.2	3.8	4.2	2.3	1.1	1.6	0.5
Bozeman, MT	26.4	14.5	13.1	3.1	5.7	2.8	3.7	3.7	3.2
Brentwood, TN	16.3	12.5	16.8	9.7	3.9	2.2	2.1	4.2	1.1
Burlington, VT	12.8	19.6	13.7	4.6	9.6	4.8	8.9	4.1	1.1
Cabot, AR	16.2	13.4	13.7	12.4	1.9	1.5	1.7	3.2	1.8
Carmel, IN	25.4	14.1	12.4	8.8	4.0	3.1	2.2	3.2	1.9
Cedar Falls, IA	39.3	13.1	8.6	9.2	1.9	1.1	2.2	1.4	3.2
Cedar Park, TX	16.6	10.0	9.9	6.8	3.8	1.9	2.8	2.4	1.8
Central, LA	6.4	11.2	9.5	17.4	6.7	0.7	14.4	2.1	0.2
Chapel Hill, NC	13.8	9.9	12.3	3.6	5.2	3.5	2.7	3.4	1.3
Cheshire, CT	11.2	21.8	9.9	2.5	24.8	8.7	4.0	2.9	0.4
Chino Hills, CA	8.0	5.3	4.5	2.7	4.3	1.2	2.1	1.2	0.9
Cibolo, TX	14.9	7.5	6.4	5.5	2.9	1.9	2.6	1.2	1.2
Cicero, NY	20.8	24.7	11.3	3.5	23.2	8.4	5.8	2.1	2.0
Collierville, TN	12.3	11.0	11.5	11.4	4.1	1.4	2.7	2.9	1.8
Coppell, TX	14.6	9.0	13.9	5.8	3.7	1.5	3.1	2.3	1.2
Cornelius, NC	19.1	12.0	11.3	8.8	8.8	3.6	3.8	4.0	1.7
Cranberry, PA	36.1	22.0	9.5	3.7	17.5	8.9	2.5	1.6	1.0
Crown Point, IN	24.4	13.6	6.2	4.5	7.1	12.1	2.4	1.8	3.5
Dublin, OH	27.3	14.1	10.7	6.3	7.2	4.5	3.2	2.0	1.2
East Fishkill, NY	13.6	23.3	6.8	4.3	30.5	5.5	2.1	1.3	1.7
Eden Prairie, MN	30.3	10.9	7.1	3.1	2.7	3.2	2.8	1.6	1.7
Edmond, OK	17.7	11.5	10.5	7.9	3.0	1.6	2.8	2.4	1.5
Edwardsville, IL	31.1	13.3	11.6	5.3	5.2	3.5	3.6	1.9	1.5
Evesham, NJ	18.5	25.7	9.0	3.2	23.8	8.5	2.0	2.0	1.3
Flower Mound, TX	18.9	12.8	13.7	7.3	4.3	2.3	3.6	2.7	1.6
Folsom, CA	15.7	11.4	10.3	4.4	8.2	2.2	2.6	2.1	1.2
Friendswood, TX	16.3	10.9	11.9	8.6	3.6	1.0	3.1	1.8	0.9
Gaines, MI	19.7	9.6	7.0	3.7	2.1	6.8	2.8	1.4	25.7
Glastonbury, CT	12.6	21.7	12.4	5.0	20.3	9.9	6.2	2.6	0.9
Grand Blanc, MI	16.9	9.4	9.4	13.2	3.0	7.8	3.3	2.8	1.9
Hampden, PA	28.9	13.7	8.7	4.8	9.5	4.7	2.6	2.1	1.7
Hilliard, OH	28.6	14.5	11.2	5.8	8.4	3.6	3.0	2.7	1.6
Hillsborough, NJ	12.6	14.3	5.3	5.1	18.0	9.6	1.6	1.7	1.3
Holly Springs, NC	16.6	13.3	10.9	7.7	9.9	3.8	2.4	4.5	0.9
Independence, KY	36.7	18.1	10.9	9.4	5.2	2.8	1.9	2.2	1.2
Juneau, AK	14.8	11.6	9.8	2.9	2.6	2.5	2.7	2.8	1.2
Kaysville, UT	9.8	4.2	34.7	6.3	1.3	0.7	2.4	7.3	2.1
Keller, TX	19.2	13.2	13.0	9.0	4.3	2.6	3.7	3.1	1.3
Lafayette, CA	15.9	15.8	15.0	4.3	9.7	3.3	3.4	3.9	1.5
Lafayette, CO	20.7	15.1	13.8	5.8	5.8	3.7	3.9	3.4	2.2
Lake Oswego, OR	21.2	14.0	14.7	5.1	5.4	3.0	3.3	6.4	2.1
Laramie, WY	27.3	11.9	11.6	4.0	5.1	2.5	4.1	3.6	1.1
Leander, TX	17.6	9.0	7.8	6.0	4.8	2.3	2.4	1.8	0.9
Leawood, KS	30.2	19.1	15.2	5.9	6.4	2.5	2.5	3.9	1.3
Lee's Summit, MO	23.4	12.1	11.3	6.5	4.4	1.5	2.4	1.8	1.4
Leesburg, VA	13.8	9.6	10.1	5.8	7.0	2.5	3.1	2.7	1.4
Lehi, UT	11.4	6.4	30.9	6.0	3.1	0.4	1.7	6.2	1.7
Lexington, MA	7.5	13.3	10.6	3.1	10.3	3.2	2.3	2.5	0.5
Los Altos, CA	12.5	10.6	12.5	2.9	5.4	1.9	3.0	2.7	1.5
Loveland, CO	28.3	14.3	12.0	5.2	4.8	2.5	5.0	3.0	2.1
Lower Macungie, PA	30.2	16.3	7.6	5.7	11.8	5.2	2.3	1.3	2.3
Madison, AL	13.9	10.7	11.7	10.1	2.8	1.8	2.0	2.2	1.0
Madison, MS	10.3	11.7	21.1	10.0	4.5	0.9	3.6	3.4	0.5
Maple Valley, WA	19.9	13.3	14.9	4.6	6.0	2.2	3.2	2.3	2.5
Marion, IA	38.1	16.3	10.1	5.9	1.6	1.8	2.0	2.0	2.0

Table continued on next page.

City	German	Irish	English	American	Italian	Polish	French[1]	Scottish	Dutch
Marlboro, NJ	6.7	8.2	2.3	5.1	24.7	8.1	0.6	0.4	0.3
Mason, OH	29.0	11.8	9.4	5.7	6.1	2.2	2.1	1.9	2.2
Menomonee Falls, WI	50.3	12.0	7.3	2.9	4.7	11.2	3.4	1.5	1.5
Meridian, ID	16.1	8.0	19.6	5.9	3.6	1.9	2.0	2.2	2.1
Meridian, MI	24.3	12.6	11.7	4.1	4.4	5.7	3.2	3.2	3.0
Merrimack, NH	8.2	22.5	17.1	4.0	10.9	5.3	15.2	4.1	0.7
Milton, GA	15.5	10.9	11.0	7.4	6.0	2.9	1.9	2.6	0.8
Moon, PA	28.5	19.0	7.7	2.8	19.7	8.8	2.0	1.7	0.8
Moorpark, CA	13.7	10.9	11.0	5.1	6.5	2.2	3.2	2.6	1.2
Morgantown, WV	19.4	15.3	9.4	4.1	11.6	5.6	2.5	2.8	1.5
Mount Pleasant, SC	15.3	16.9	13.6	12.3	6.6	3.5	2.7	4.6	1.5
Newark, DE	16.6	17.9	10.5	5.2	13.5	5.9	1.9	2.7	1.2
Newtown, CT	16.4	21.2	14.5	4.6	24.1	6.8	3.8	3.1	1.4
North Attleborough, MA	7.5	26.8	13.8	3.3	16.2	3.2	10.3	2.7	0.5
North Port, FL	19.0	14.5	8.7	13.9	8.5	4.2	3.3	2.0	1.1
North Ridgeville, OH	28.4	20.6	9.3	5.5	11.4	9.8	2.0	2.4	1.3
Northville, MI	17.2	10.7	8.7	7.9	7.6	12.1	3.0	3.2	1.1
O'Fallon, MO	36.4	17.2	8.8	6.7	6.4	4.0	4.7	1.7	2.0
Orchard Park, NY	28.4	25.5	9.3	2.7	18.0	20.2	1.7	2.9	0.9
Oro Valley, AZ	22.2	15.3	16.5	5.1	7.0	4.4	4.5	3.1	1.5
Oviedo, FL	13.5	10.3	8.4	8.5	7.6	3.2	2.8	2.1	1.1
Parker, CO	26.9	16.1	13.0	4.7	6.0	2.2	3.0	4.0	1.9
Parkland, FL	8.6	10.5	5.5	5.9	12.2	7.6	2.4	1.0	0.4
Peachtree City, GA	15.6	13.5	11.5	12.6	5.0	2.7	1.8	2.7	1.5
Pittsfield, MI	18.3	10.3	8.8	6.7	3.8	6.0	2.6	2.5	1.6
Plainfield, IL	24.5	18.4	6.0	2.9	11.9	14.5	1.7	1.5	1.2
Pleasant Grove, UT	8.2	5.6	30.7	5.2	3.3	1.0	2.2	5.8	2.8
Poway, CA	17.0	12.4	10.2	3.8	6.3	2.9	4.1	2.3	1.6
Princeton, NJ	12.2	12.5	10.4	2.8	8.3	5.5	2.6	2.6	2.4
Queen Creek, AZ	19.1	9.3	11.5	5.7	4.2	3.0	3.1	3.2	1.3
Radnor, PA	15.0	25.5	9.4	4.1	16.5	4.4	2.3	1.7	0.8
Randolph, NJ	14.2	16.1	6.3	4.2	20.6	8.2	1.7	1.5	0.8
Rexburg, ID	11.0	5.3	27.2	10.3	3.1	0.3	3.3	4.0	2.2
Rio Rancho, NM	12.6	9.1	8.1	4.7	4.0	2.5	2.1	2.5	1.4
Rye, NY	3.7	7.3	2.4	8.2	16.9	2.8	0.8	0.5	0.2
Sammamish, WA	14.3	9.2	11.4	4.9	3.9	2.2	2.4	2.6	1.3
San Ramon, CA	7.8	7.2	6.4	3.7	6.0	1.5	1.4	1.3	0.7
Saratoga, CA	8.2	6.5	7.6	1.8	5.9	1.4	1.8	2.1	1.1
Shrewsbury, MA	5.6	22.1	9.5	3.5	17.3	5.4	7.9	2.0	0.5
South Brunswick, NJ	6.6	8.0	2.5	7.0	9.9	3.6	0.5	0.7	0.6
South Jordan, UT	12.5	6.7	30.8	5.5	4.7	0.8	1.1	5.3	2.5
South Kingstown, RI	9.3	22.3	16.6	4.1	18.6	5.5	7.8	2.6	0.6
South Portland, ME	8.9	25.4	23.2	5.0	9.5	3.2	12.7	5.3	1.9
Sparks, NV	13.4	11.0	8.9	5.5	6.8	2.1	2.7	2.4	1.3
State College, PA	18.5	11.6	5.6	1.8	10.0	5.7	2.1	1.5	1.1
Sugar Land, TX	9.1	5.4	6.6	4.0	2.3	1.2	2.0	1.7	0.5
Sun Prairie, WI	40.9	13.1	7.1	4.3	3.1	6.5	1.9	0.9	3.1
Syracuse, UT	9.2	5.8	27.8	9.8	2.5	1.6	2.4	5.4	1.6
Tredyffrin, PA	21.3	21.7	11.9	3.7	12.8	5.2	2.4	3.0	1.1
Upper Dublin, PA	20.4	23.6	8.2	4.9	16.1	8.1	1.4	1.8	0.8
Urbandale, IA	30.4	15.5	8.2	3.7	3.2	1.4	1.9	1.8	3.5
Vestal, NY	14.7	15.4	10.4	4.5	11.8	4.9	3.0	1.0	2.0
Vestavia Hills, AL	11.3	10.9	15.9	14.9	4.6	1.1	2.4	4.8	1.0
Webster, NY	22.9	18.6	12.1	3.9	27.2	6.3	2.7	2.3	3.3
Wellesley, MA	10.8	22.1	13.5	4.0	12.8	4.7	2.6	2.1	1.3
West Fargo, ND	45.1	5.8	5.1	1.5	1.7	2.7	3.0	2.1	1.5
West Lafayette, IN	24.4	11.3	7.7	3.4	4.5	5.1	2.2	2.1	1.6
Weston, FL	6.6	5.4	2.8	6.1	8.3	3.2	1.8	0.5	0.6
Wilmette, IL	22.2	16.0	10.0	4.8	6.0	8.2	3.3	1.8	1.0
Yorba Linda, CA	14.7	9.8	10.8	6.7	6.0	2.3	3.1	2.0	1.7
Zionsville, IN	27.7	11.9	13.6	8.2	5.6	3.7	2.7	2.5	3.5
U.S.	14.4	10.4	7.7	6.9	5.4	2.9	2.6	1.7	1.3

Note: Figures are the percentage of the total population reporting a particular ancestry. The nine most commonly reported ancestries in the U.S. are shown. Figures include multiple ancestries (e.g. if a person reported being Irish and Italian, they were included in both columns); (1) Excludes Basque
Source: U.S. Census Bureau, 2012-2016 American Community Survey 5-Year Estimates

Ancestry: Metro Area

Metro Area	German	Irish	English	American	Italian	Polish	French[1]	Scottish	Dutch
Aberdeen, SD	53.5	9.2	5.3	3.0	0.7	1.6	1.7	0.6	2.1
Aliso Viejo, CA	5.7	4.6	4.1	3.3	3.0	1.3	1.3	0.9	0.7
Allen, TX	9.8	7.6	7.3	6.6	2.2	1.1	1.9	1.7	0.9
Ames, IA	35.1	12.9	7.6	3.6	3.0	1.6	2.4	2.3	3.4
Amherst, MA	6.4	17.2	9.0	3.2	10.3	10.5	11.3	2.2	0.6
Apex, NC	11.2	9.9	10.6	11.3	4.8	2.1	1.9	2.7	1.0
Beavercreek, OH	24.3	12.7	8.6	7.9	3.5	2.0	2.3	2.0	1.5
Bellevue, NE	30.9	14.8	8.1	3.9	4.1	3.9	2.4	1.4	1.7
Bend, OR	21.4	13.2	12.5	6.6	3.8	2.1	2.9	3.4	2.3
Benicia, CA	8.3	6.7	5.3	3.0	4.1	1.1	1.7	1.3	1.0
Bentonville, AR	11.9	9.6	8.6	7.9	2.1	1.2	1.9	1.8	1.2
Bethlehem, NY	16.1	22.4	9.6	4.7	17.2	6.7	6.5	1.9	3.3
Blacksburg, VA	13.3	10.6	9.2	16.3	3.3	1.5	1.7	2.1	1.1
Bowie, MD	10.3	9.0	7.2	4.5	4.5	2.3	1.7	1.7	0.8
Bozeman, MT	28.2	14.5	13.1	4.3	5.0	2.3	3.9	3.8	4.3
Brentwood, TN	10.4	10.4	9.8	13.3	2.7	1.3	2.0	2.3	1.0
Burlington, VT	10.8	18.1	14.3	8.8	7.3	3.4	13.3	4.0	1.3
Cabot, AR	10.8	9.9	9.6	8.9	1.6	1.0	2.1	2.1	1.1
Carmel, IN	20.0	11.2	8.4	9.8	2.7	2.0	2.0	1.9	1.6
Cedar Falls, IA	38.9	11.7	7.5	8.5	1.3	0.9	1.8	1.3	2.7
Cedar Park, TX	13.5	8.0	8.2	4.5	2.8	1.7	2.6	2.2	1.0
Central, LA	7.5	7.6	6.0	8.4	4.9	0.6	13.6	1.1	0.5
Chapel Hill, NC	9.5	7.6	9.8	6.5	3.2	1.9	1.8	2.5	0.9
Cheshire, CT	8.0	15.3	7.0	2.9	21.4	6.8	3.8	1.3	0.6
Chino Hills, CA	8.1	5.9	5.0	4.0	3.3	1.1	1.8	1.1	1.0
Cibolo, TX	11.2	5.8	5.4	3.7	2.1	1.5	1.8	1.2	0.7
Cicero, NY	17.3	21.1	11.3	7.1	15.6	6.2	4.9	1.9	2.1
Collierville, TN	6.0	7.1	6.6	6.9	2.1	0.7	1.4	1.6	0.7
Coppell, TX	9.8	7.6	7.3	6.6	2.2	1.1	1.9	1.7	0.9
Cornelius, NC	12.1	9.1	8.2	9.3	3.8	1.7	1.7	2.3	1.1
Cranberry, PA	27.8	18.4	8.1	4.2	16.3	8.7	1.8	1.9	1.2
Crown Point, IN	15.2	11.2	4.3	2.9	6.9	9.2	1.5	1.0	1.2
Dublin, OH	24.4	13.5	9.0	6.9	5.5	2.3	2.2	2.2	1.5
East Fishkill, NY	6.8	10.0	2.9	4.8	13.1	4.0	1.0	0.7	0.7
Eden Prairie, MN	31.4	11.4	5.7	3.2	2.7	4.6	3.5	1.3	1.5
Edmond, OK	13.6	10.3	7.8	8.0	1.9	1.0	2.0	1.8	1.4
Edwardsville, IL	28.7	13.5	7.7	7.1	4.9	2.6	3.5	1.5	1.2
Evesham, NJ	15.7	19.2	7.1	3.6	13.7	5.2	1.5	1.3	0.9
Flower Mound, TX	9.8	7.6	7.3	6.6	2.2	1.1	1.9	1.7	0.9
Folsom, CA	12.5	9.2	8.4	3.4	5.2	1.4	2.6	1.9	1.2
Friendswood, TX	8.5	5.8	5.4	4.7	2.1	1.2	2.3	1.2	0.6
Gaines, MI	21.2	10.5	9.3	4.5	3.1	6.8	3.4	1.9	20.4
Glastonbury, CT	8.8	15.6	9.0	4.1	16.5	9.7	6.8	1.8	0.6
Grand Blanc, MI	16.5	10.4	8.9	8.9	3.0	5.7	4.3	2.2	1.8
Hampden, PA	30.6	12.5	6.8	5.7	7.2	3.8	1.7	1.7	1.7
Hilliard, OH	24.4	13.5	9.0	6.9	5.5	2.3	2.2	2.2	1.5
Hillsborough, NJ	6.8	10.0	2.9	4.8	13.1	4.0	1.0	0.7	0.7
Holly Springs, NC	11.2	9.9	10.6	11.3	4.8	2.1	1.9	2.7	1.0
Independence, KY	29.1	14.0	8.6	9.0	4.1	1.6	1.9	1.7	1.2
Juneau, AK	14.8	11.6	9.8	2.9	2.6	2.5	2.7	2.8	1.2
Kaysville, UT	11.3	5.5	25.0	7.8	2.7	0.7	1.8	4.6	2.8
Keller, TX	9.8	7.6	7.3	6.6	2.2	1.1	1.9	1.7	0.9
Lafayette, CA	8.3	7.7	6.0	2.7	5.2	1.5	2.0	1.6	0.9
Lafayette, CO	21.2	12.5	12.5	4.8	5.8	3.5	3.4	3.5	1.9
Lake Oswego, OR	19.3	11.2	11.0	5.0	4.0	1.9	3.1	3.2	2.0
Laramie, WY	27.1	12.1	11.9	4.8	4.6	2.4	3.7	3.8	1.3
Leander, TX	13.5	8.0	8.2	4.5	2.8	1.7	2.6	2.2	1.0
Leawood, KS	22.6	13.0	9.9	6.8	3.4	1.6	2.4	1.9	1.6
Lee's Summit, MO	22.6	13.0	9.9	6.8	3.4	1.6	2.4	1.9	1.6
Leesburg, VA	10.3	9.0	7.2	4.5	4.5	2.3	1.7	1.7	0.8
Lehi, UT	11.1	5.1	28.7	5.2	2.4	0.7	2.1	5.4	1.9
Lexington, MA	6.2	22.3	9.9	4.2	14.1	3.6	5.3	2.5	0.6
Los Altos, CA	6.8	5.3	4.9	1.9	4.0	1.2	1.6	1.1	0.7
Loveland, CO	27.1	13.8	12.2	4.8	5.2	2.9	3.9	3.0	2.1
Lower Macungie, PA	25.8	13.6	6.1	5.2	12.7	5.6	1.6	1.1	2.6
Madison, AL	9.9	9.8	10.1	12.0	2.2	1.0	1.9	2.2	0.9
Madison, MS	4.0	6.4	6.6	8.9	1.4	0.3	1.5	1.5	0.4
Maple Valley, WA	16.2	10.3	10.1	3.7	3.7	2.0	3.0	2.8	1.7
Marion, IA	38.0	15.7	8.4	5.9	1.7	1.5	2.2	1.5	2.2

Table continued on next page.

Metro Area	German	Irish	English	American	Italian	Polish	French[1]	Scottish	Dutch
Marlboro, NJ	6.8	10.0	2.9	4.8	13.1	4.0	1.0	0.7	0.7
Mason, OH	29.1	14.0	8.6	9.0	4.1	1.6	1.9	1.7	1.2
Menomonee Falls, WI	34.6	9.9	4.4	2.4	4.4	11.2	2.6	0.9	1.3
Meridian, ID	17.0	9.1	17.0	6.7	3.1	1.4	2.3	3.1	2.0
Meridian, MI	24.9	12.7	11.6	5.6	3.8	5.1	3.6	2.4	3.4
Merrimack, NH	8.2	20.7	13.1	4.3	10.3	4.7	14.4	3.2	0.8
Milton, GA	7.1	7.4	7.4	9.6	2.5	1.3	1.5	1.8	0.7
Moon, PA	27.8	18.4	8.1	4.2	16.3	8.7	1.8	1.9	1.2
Moorpark, CA	11.1	8.3	7.4	4.0	5.0	2.0	2.4	1.8	1.0
Morgantown, WV	19.5	14.2	10.0	12.4	8.2	3.7	1.6	2.1	2.0
Mount Pleasant, SC	10.6	10.5	8.5	13.2	3.6	1.7	2.3	2.5	0.9
Newark, DE	15.7	19.2	7.1	3.6	13.7	5.2	1.5	1.3	0.9
Newtown, CT	9.0	14.5	7.7	4.7	16.9	5.2	2.2	1.7	0.8
North Attleborough, MA	4.9	18.3	10.5	3.5	14.8	4.1	10.4	1.7	0.5
North Port, FL	16.5	12.2	10.7	11.0	7.4	3.7	3.2	2.4	1.6
North Ridgeville, OH	19.9	14.1	7.4	3.8	9.9	7.8	1.6	1.6	1.0
Northville, MI	16.1	9.9	6.9	5.7	6.3	10.3	3.5	2.2	1.2
O'Fallon, MO	28.7	13.5	7.7	7.1	4.9	2.6	3.5	1.5	1.2
Orchard Park, NY	24.7	16.7	7.5	4.3	16.6	16.5	2.4	1.7	0.9
Oro Valley, AZ	14.2	10.0	8.5	3.3	4.4	2.3	2.6	1.9	1.3
Oviedo, FL	9.5	8.2	6.5	7.9	5.1	2.1	2.1	1.5	0.9
Parker, CO	19.0	11.3	9.7	4.8	5.1	2.6	2.6	2.4	1.6
Parkland, FL	4.9	4.7	3.1	6.1	5.3	2.0	1.3	0.7	0.4
Peachtree City, GA	7.1	7.4	7.4	9.6	2.5	1.3	1.5	1.8	0.7
Pittsfield, MI	20.3	10.9	10.2	7.2	5.0	6.8	3.2	2.6	2.1
Plainfield, IL	15.2	11.2	4.3	2.9	6.9	9.2	1.5	1.0	1.2
Pleasant Grove, UT	11.1	5.1	28.7	5.2	2.4	0.7	2.1	5.4	1.9
Poway, CA	10.5	8.2	7.5	2.9	4.3	1.8	2.2	1.6	1.0
Princeton, NJ	10.5	11.5	5.7	2.6	13.2	6.2	1.5	1.4	0.9
Queen Creek, AZ	13.8	8.9	8.0	4.8	4.5	2.6	2.2	1.7	1.2
Radnor, PA	15.7	19.2	7.1	3.6	13.7	5.2	1.5	1.3	0.9
Randolph, NJ	6.8	10.0	2.9	4.8	13.1	4.0	1.0	0.7	0.7
Rexburg, ID	12.1	5.1	26.5	12.2	2.1	0.7	2.3	3.9	1.7
Rio Rancho, NM	9.9	7.1	6.4	4.4	3.0	1.4	1.8	1.7	0.9
Rye, NY	6.8	10.0	2.9	4.8	13.1	4.0	1.0	0.7	0.7
Sammamish, WA	16.2	10.3	10.1	3.7	3.7	2.0	3.0	2.8	1.7
San Ramon, CA	8.3	7.7	6.0	2.7	5.2	1.5	2.0	1.6	0.9
Saratoga, CA	6.8	5.3	4.9	1.9	4.0	1.2	1.6	1.1	0.7
Shrewsbury, MA	6.1	19.4	10.1	4.6	13.2	6.3	12.9	2.1	0.8
South Brunswick, NJ	6.8	10.0	2.9	4.8	13.1	4.0	1.0	0.7	0.7
South Jordan, UT	10.9	5.9	21.4	4.8	3.0	0.9	1.9	4.0	2.4
South Kingstown, RI	4.9	18.3	10.5	3.5	14.8	4.1	10.4	1.7	0.5
South Portland, ME	9.2	19.5	21.2	6.3	7.8	2.9	14.6	5.5	1.0
Sparks, NV	14.5	11.8	9.4	5.5	6.7	1.9	2.8	2.5	1.5
State College, PA	25.1	11.9	7.5	5.1	7.4	5.2	1.9	1.8	1.6
Sugar Land, TX	8.5	5.8	5.4	4.7	2.1	1.2	2.3	1.2	0.6
Sun Prairie, WI	39.5	13.8	8.9	3.2	3.6	5.3	2.9	1.5	2.1
Syracuse, UT	11.3	5.5	25.0	7.8	2.7	0.7	1.8	4.6	2.8
Tredyffrin, PA	15.7	19.2	7.1	3.6	13.7	5.2	1.5	1.3	0.9
Upper Dublin, PA	15.7	19.2	7.1	3.6	13.7	5.2	1.5	1.3	0.9
Urbandale, IA	28.2	13.3	8.8	4.9	3.3	1.3	2.1	1.8	3.5
Vestal, NY	16.3	18.1	12.5	5.8	11.9	5.8	2.6	2.0	2.5
Vestavia Hills, AL	6.9	9.6	8.6	14.6	2.3	0.7	1.5	2.1	0.8
Webster, NY	20.4	16.0	12.0	4.9	16.4	5.0	3.1	2.0	3.6
Wellesley, MA	6.2	22.3	9.9	4.2	14.1	3.6	5.3	2.5	0.6
West Fargo, ND	39.9	8.0	4.2	2.1	1.2	2.9	3.4	1.4	1.2
West Lafayette, IN	26.3	13.6	9.1	6.9	2.7	3.2	2.6	2.2	2.7
Weston, FL	4.9	4.7	3.1	6.1	5.3	2.0	1.3	0.7	0.4
Wilmette, IL	15.2	11.2	4.3	2.9	6.9	9.2	1.5	1.0	1.2
Yorba Linda, CA	5.7	4.6	4.1	3.3	3.0	1.3	1.3	0.9	0.7
Zionsville, IN	20.0	11.2	8.4	9.8	2.7	2.0	2.0	1.9	1.6
U.S.	14.4	10.4	7.7	6.9	5.4	2.9	2.6	1.7	1.3

Note: Figures are the percentage of the total population reporting a particular ancestry. The nine most commonly reported ancestries in the U.S. are shown. Figures include multiple ancestries (e.g. if a person reported being Irish and Italian, they were included in both columns); Figures cover the Metropolitan Statistical Area—see Appendix B for areas included; (1) Excludes Basque
Source: U.S. Census Bureau, 2012-2016 American Community Survey 5-Year Estimates

Foreign-Born Population: City

City	Percent of Population Born in								
	Any Foreign Country	Asia	Mexico	Europe	Carribean	Central America[1]	South America	Africa	Canada
Aberdeen, SD	4.2	2.4	0.4	0.1	0.6	0.3	0.0	0.2	0.1
Aliso Viejo, CA	21.4	13.7	2.3	2.4	0.2	0.3	1.3	0.5	0.5
Allen, TX	18.3	10.1	2.2	1.7	0.2	0.4	0.5	2.8	0.4
Ames, IA	12.3	9.2	0.2	0.9	0.2	0.0	0.5	0.8	0.4
Amherst, MA	15.2	8.4	0.2	2.3	1.0	0.6	1.0	1.1	0.4
Apex, NC	11.4	4.7	1.9	1.4	0.4	0.5	0.7	1.3	0.4
Beavercreek, OH	7.9	5.7	0.1	0.9	0.1	0.0	0.4	0.5	0.2
Bellevue, NE	8.7	2.0	3.6	1.3	0.1	0.9	0.3	0.6	0.0
Bend, OR	4.8	1.0	1.5	1.1	0.0	0.3	0.1	0.1	0.5
Benicia, CA	12.3	6.6	1.7	1.7	0.1	1.0	0.5	0.1	0.5
Bentonville, AR	13.9	9.6	1.7	0.9	0.1	0.8	0.4	0.2	0.1
Bethlehem, NY	6.2	3.3	0.0	2.0	0.1	0.0	0.4	0.2	0.2
Blacksburg, VA	14.6	9.1	0.5	1.9	0.4	0.4	0.9	1.1	0.3
Bowie, MD	13.7	3.6	0.3	1.1	1.7	1.1	0.7	4.9	0.2
Bozeman, MT	4.3	2.1	0.2	0.8	0.1	0.1	0.1	0.4	0.5
Brentwood, TN	8.6	5.3	0.5	1.2	0.1	0.1	0.4	0.4	0.5
Burlington, VT	11.9	5.5	0.0	2.9	0.3	0.3	0.2	2.3	0.4
Cabot, AR	2.7	1.1	0.1	0.6	0.0	0.4	0.0	0.1	0.2
Carmel, IN	11.6	7.5	0.5	1.8	0.2	0.3	0.3	0.7	0.3
Cedar Falls, IA	4.8	2.8	0.0	1.2	0.0	0.0	0.3	0.4	0.1
Cedar Park, TX	13.1	6.2	3.1	1.0	0.7	0.3	0.8	0.6	0.3
Central, LA	1.6	0.7	0.0	0.1	0.1	0.4	0.3	0.0	0.0
Chapel Hill, NC	16.4	8.8	0.8	3.5	0.2	0.4	1.1	0.9	0.5
Cheshire, CT	10.0	4.9	0.2	3.6	0.3	0.0	0.4	0.3	0.4
Chino Hills, CA	29.0	20.1	4.5	0.9	0.1	0.7	0.8	1.4	0.4
Cibolo, TX	8.8	1.9	3.1	1.2	0.6	0.7	0.7	0.2	0.3
Cicero, NY	2.9	1.0	0.0	1.2	0.0	0.1	0.2	0.0	0.4
Collierville, TN	7.4	5.3	0.3	0.8	0.0	0.1	0.3	0.2	0.3
Coppell, TX	20.7	14.6	2.6	0.9	0.2	0.2	0.6	1.1	0.3
Cornelius, NC	6.9	1.9	0.4	2.7	0.2	0.4	0.6	0.4	0.2
Cranberry, PA	4.9	2.4	0.4	0.7	0.1	0.1	0.7	0.1	0.3
Crown Point, IN	9.1	2.3	1.2	4.8	0.0	0.1	0.3	0.0	0.3
Dublin, OH	16.5	12.7	0.3	1.9	0.3	0.1	0.4	0.3	0.5
East Fishkill, NY	9.9	3.6	0.6	2.9	0.7	0.1	1.5	0.4	0.1
Eden Prairie, MN	14.8	8.3	0.8	1.6	0.1	0.6	0.5	2.3	0.4
Edmond, OK	6.4	3.0	1.5	0.5	0.1	0.1	0.3	0.6	0.2
Edwardsville, IL	4.7	2.9	0.2	0.7	0.1	0.0	0.1	0.8	0.1
Evesham, NJ	8.3	4.3	0.5	1.3	0.6	0.1	0.6	0.7	0.1
Flower Mound, TX	11.7	6.8	1.3	1.2	0.2	0.3	0.7	0.6	0.5
Folsom, CA	15.9	11.0	1.1	1.9	0.1	0.4	0.4	0.2	0.6
Friendswood, TX	9.4	4.2	1.9	1.3	0.3	0.3	0.8	0.4	0.3
Gaines, MI	7.1	2.4	1.0	2.4	0.2	0.1	0.0	0.8	0.1
Glastonbury, CT	11.5	5.0	0.0	4.0	0.3	0.2	1.2	0.2	0.7
Grand Blanc, MI	6.0	4.8	0.1	0.6	0.1	0.0	0.0	0.1	0.3
Hampden, PA	12.3	8.0	0.2	2.3	0.0	0.0	0.2	1.2	0.2
Hilliard, OH	6.2	4.7	0.3	0.6	0.0	0.0	0.1	0.4	0.0
Hillsborough, NJ	17.9	9.9	0.2	3.8	1.0	0.5	1.2	1.2	0.2
Holly Springs, NC	6.9	2.3	0.5	1.2	0.5	0.1	0.4	1.3	0.6
Independence, KY	2.2	1.1	0.0	0.2	0.1	0.1	0.5	0.1	0.2
Juneau, AK	8.2	4.5	0.6	1.3	0.0	0.4	0.3	0.1	0.4
Kaysville, UT	2.4	0.9	0.1	1.0	0.0	0.1	0.2	0.0	0.1
Keller, TX	7.9	3.2	1.0	1.5	0.3	0.7	0.4	0.5	0.4
Lafayette, CA	13.5	6.3	1.2	3.4	0.2	0.3	0.3	0.8	0.8
Lafayette, CO	10.6	3.0	3.7	2.0	0.0	0.7	0.7	0.1	0.4
Lake Oswego, OR	10.5	5.6	0.4	2.6	0.2	0.1	0.2	0.2	1.0
Laramie, WY	6.7	3.0	0.9	0.9	0.0	0.2	0.2	0.9	0.2
Leander, TX	7.9	1.6	4.2	0.7	0.1	0.6	0.1	0.5	0.1
Leawood, KS	5.2	3.0	0.1	1.2	0.1	0.0	0.4	0.1	0.3
Lee's Summit, MO	4.2	1.6	0.7	0.8	0.0	0.2	0.3	0.3	0.1
Leesburg, VA	22.0	8.9	0.9	2.4	0.2	5.8	1.6	1.7	0.3
Lehi, UT	4.0	0.8	1.1	0.5	0.1	0.1	1.0	0.0	0.3
Lexington, MA	26.2	19.0	0.2	4.9	0.1	0.0	0.5	0.6	0.8
Los Altos, CA	25.4	16.5	0.2	6.2	0.0	0.3	0.5	0.3	1.3
Loveland, CO	4.0	0.8	1.4	0.9	0.0	0.1	0.4	0.2	0.2
Lower Macungie, PA	9.2	4.3	0.2	2.3	0.7	0.0	1.1	0.4	0.1
Madison, AL	7.9	4.6	0.4	1.6	0.0	0.1	0.5	0.4	0.2

Table continued on next page.

City	Percent of Population Born in: Any Foreign Country	Asia	Mexico	Europe	Carribean	Central America[1]	South America	Africa	Canada
Madison, MS	3.4	2.4	0.0	0.6	0.0	0.0	0.2	0.1	0.0
Maple Valley, WA	7.0	3.8	0.7	1.5	0.0	0.2	0.1	0.3	0.3
Marion, IA	2.9	1.5	0.2	0.3	0.2	0.0	0.1	0.3	0.3
Marlboro, NJ	21.2	12.9	0.1	5.3	1.0	0.1	0.7	1.1	0.1
Mason, OH	11.3	6.8	0.0	1.5	0.2	0.1	1.7	0.6	0.1
Menomonee Falls, WI	5.7	3.4	0.1	1.7	0.0	0.0	0.2	0.1	0.1
Meridian, ID	5.7	1.3	1.1	1.8	0.0	0.0	0.5	0.3	0.5
Meridian, MI	14.9	11.3	0.3	1.5	0.0	0.0	0.3	0.7	0.7
Merrimack, NH	4.6	1.6	0.0	1.6	0.0	0.0	0.5	0.2	0.3
Milton, GA	14.7	6.5	1.1	2.8	1.7	0.5	0.7	0.5	0.7
Moon, PA	8.3	3.9	0.4	1.4	0.8	0.8	0.4	0.4	0.1
Moorpark, CA	17.7	4.5	8.2	1.8	0.2	0.8	1.0	0.6	0.2
Morgantown, WV	7.0	4.9	0.2	0.7	0.5	0.1	0.1	0.3	0.2
Mount Pleasant, SC	4.6	1.2	0.6	1.6	0.2	0.1	0.4	0.1	0.2
Newark, DE	11.8	7.1	0.5	2.3	0.4	0.1	0.5	0.7	0.1
Newtown, CT	8.0	2.5	0.3	3.0	0.3	0.2	1.1	0.2	0.2
North Attleborough, MA	7.7	3.4	0.6	1.4	0.3	0.7	0.3	0.6	0.3
North Port, FL	10.3	1.2	0.9	3.9	1.6	0.6	1.0	0.0	1.1
North Ridgeville, OH	4.7	2.0	0.3	2.1	0.0	0.0	0.1	0.1	0.1
Northville, MI	16.6	11.5	0.5	2.4	0.0	0.1	0.7	0.1	1.3
O'Fallon, MO	4.4	2.9	0.1	0.7	0.0	0.0	0.4	0.1	0.1
Orchard Park, NY	4.3	1.4	0.0	1.3	0.3	0.2	0.2	0.1	0.9
Oro Valley, AZ	6.9	2.1	1.3	2.0	0.2	0.0	0.2	0.1	0.9
Oviedo, FL	12.2	2.6	0.3	1.8	2.7	0.6	2.7	1.1	0.4
Parker, CO	6.4	2.8	1.1	1.1	0.0	0.4	0.3	0.4	0.3
Parkland, FL	20.4	5.5	0.3	3.3	4.1	0.6	5.0	0.2	1.3
Peachtree City, GA	11.4	4.7	1.9	1.9	0.5	0.1	1.3	0.6	0.4
Pittsfield, MI	18.6	11.9	0.9	2.2	0.3	0.7	0.6	1.4	0.6
Plainfield, IL	9.5	4.6	2.1	1.6	0.0	0.1	0.5	0.4	0.3
Pleasant Grove, UT	4.1	1.3	0.9	0.5	0.0	0.2	0.5	0.0	0.5
Poway, CA	18.2	9.5	4.3	2.4	0.1	0.7	0.2	0.5	0.3
Princeton, NJ	26.2	10.9	0.1	8.1	0.3	3.4	1.1	1.3	0.9
Queen Creek, AZ	5.9	1.8	1.6	0.9	0.0	0.1	0.3	0.3	0.7
Radnor, PA	10.7	5.3	0.2	2.6	0.5	0.2	0.6	0.9	0.1
Randolph, NJ	18.7	8.1	0.7	3.7	0.9	0.6	3.2	1.2	0.3
Rexburg, ID	5.0	0.9	0.7	0.4	0.0	0.2	1.2	0.4	1.1
Rio Rancho, NM	5.6	1.1	2.7	0.8	0.1	0.2	0.4	0.1	0.2
Rye, NY	36.6	2.2	6.7	4.0	2.0	7.6	13.0	0.6	0.4
Sammamish, WA	25.1	17.2	0.6	3.8	0.0	0.0	0.7	0.8	1.8
San Ramon, CA	34.2	27.8	0.8	3.0	0.1	0.5	0.7	0.5	0.5
Saratoga, CA	37.4	30.8	0.3	4.2	0.1	0.1	0.4	0.7	0.7
Shrewsbury, MA	20.6	12.5	0.0	3.4	0.4	0.3	1.6	1.9	0.4
South Brunswick, NJ	37.0	28.5	0.2	2.3	1.3	0.8	1.5	1.9	0.3
South Jordan, UT	5.4	2.0	0.9	0.8	0.3	0.2	0.5	0.0	0.4
South Kingstown, RI	4.9	1.2	0.0	2.0	0.6	0.2	0.4	0.3	0.1
South Portland, ME	6.1	2.4	0.1	1.9	0.2	0.1	0.0	1.0	0.5
Sparks, NV	16.3	3.8	8.6	0.8	0.1	1.7	0.5	0.4	0.2
State College, PA	13.5	9.1	0.2	1.9	0.4	0.2	0.5	0.3	0.7
Sugar Land, TX	35.2	27.6	1.3	1.8	0.2	0.3	1.0	2.0	0.7
Sun Prairie, WI	6.1	2.6	1.0	0.9	0.0	0.3	0.1	0.9	0.3
Syracuse, UT	2.5	0.4	0.3	0.7	0.1	0.1	0.6	0.3	0.2
Tredyffrin, PA	15.0	9.4	0.2	3.7	0.2	0.0	0.5	0.6	0.4
Upper Dublin, PA	9.8	6.4	0.3	1.9	0.1	0.1	0.6	0.3	0.0
Urbandale, IA	8.4	2.7	0.4	3.2	0.0	0.0	0.6	1.3	0.2
Vestal, NY	11.1	7.6	0.1	1.4	1.2	0.1	0.3	0.1	0.3
Vestavia Hills, AL	6.4	3.7	1.2	0.9	0.1	0.1	0.1	0.2	0.1
Webster, NY	10.1	4.2	0.1	4.7	0.1	0.1	0.3	0.1	0.5
Wellesley, MA	14.8	7.0	0.2	4.4	0.3	0.2	0.8	0.8	0.9
West Fargo, ND	4.0	1.5	0.0	0.4	0.3	0.0	0.0	1.3	0.5
West Lafayette, IN	23.9	19.8	0.1	1.8	0.0	0.1	0.8	0.9	0.2
Weston, FL	43.6	3.6	1.2	2.7	4.8	1.4	28.9	0.3	0.7
Wilmette, IL	18.0	9.9	0.1	5.9	0.2	0.1	0.5	0.4	0.5
Yorba Linda, CA	19.0	12.7	2.2	2.0	0.2	0.3	0.5	0.5	0.6
Zionsville, IN	6.3	3.4	0.0	1.5	0.0	0.1	0.5	0.2	0.3
U.S.	13.2	4.0	3.6	1.5	1.3	1.0	0.9	0.6	0.3

Note: (1) Excludes Mexico

Source: U.S. Census Bureau, 2012-2016 American Community Survey 5-Year Estimates

Foreign-Born Population: Metro Area

Metro Area	Percent of Population Born in								
	Any Foreign Country	Asia	Mexico	Europe	Carribean	Central America[1]	South America	Africa	Canada
Aberdeen, SD	3.5	1.7	0.3	0.2	0.5	0.3	0.0	0.5	0.1
Aliso Viejo, CA	33.6	12.5	12.9	1.7	0.3	4.2	0.9	0.5	0.3
Allen, TX	17.8	4.7	8.8	0.8	0.2	1.3	0.5	1.2	0.2
Ames, IA	9.2	6.6	0.5	0.8	0.1	0.0	0.4	0.6	0.3
Amherst, MA	8.7	2.5	0.2	2.9	1.2	0.3	0.5	0.7	0.4
Apex, NC	11.8	4.1	3.0	1.2	0.6	1.0	0.6	1.0	0.4
Beavercreek, OH	4.1	2.2	0.3	0.7	0.1	0.1	0.1	0.4	0.1
Bellevue, NE	7.0	2.1	2.7	0.6	0.1	0.6	0.2	0.6	0.1
Bend, OR	4.1	0.8	1.5	1.0	0.0	0.2	0.2	0.0	0.4
Benicia, CA	20.1	9.8	6.4	1.2	0.2	1.3	0.4	0.3	0.2
Bentonville, AR	10.9	2.1	5.0	0.5	0.1	1.8	0.3	0.2	0.1
Bethlehem, NY	7.3	3.1	0.2	1.7	0.6	0.1	1.0	0.4	0.2
Blacksburg, VA	5.4	3.0	0.3	0.8	0.2	0.2	0.3	0.4	0.2
Bowie, MD	22.3	8.0	0.8	1.9	1.1	4.8	2.2	3.2	0.2
Bozeman, MT	3.1	1.1	0.4	0.9	0.1	0.1	0.1	0.2	0.3
Brentwood, TN	7.6	2.4	2.0	0.6	0.2	0.8	0.3	1.0	0.2
Burlington, VT	6.9	2.5	0.2	1.8	0.1	0.1	0.3	0.9	1.0
Cabot, AR	3.9	1.4	1.3	0.4	0.0	0.5	0.2	0.1	0.1
Carmel, IN	6.4	2.2	1.9	0.6	0.2	0.5	0.2	0.7	0.1
Cedar Falls, IA	4.5	1.4	0.7	1.5	0.0	0.1	0.1	0.5	0.1
Cedar Park, TX	14.6	4.0	6.8	1.0	0.4	1.1	0.5	0.5	0.3
Central, LA	3.7	1.6	0.6	0.3	0.2	0.6	0.2	0.1	0.1
Chapel Hill, NC	12.0	3.5	3.2	1.3	0.4	1.7	0.6	0.8	0.4
Cheshire, CT	12.1	3.2	1.0	3.1	1.6	0.5	1.6	0.8	0.3
Chino Hills, CA	21.6	4.7	12.7	0.9	0.2	1.7	0.5	0.5	0.4
Cibolo, TX	11.8	2.0	7.6	0.7	0.2	0.6	0.3	0.3	0.1
Cicero, NY	5.8	2.4	0.1	1.5	0.6	0.1	0.3	0.6	0.3
Collierville, TN	5.0	1.6	1.6	0.4	0.2	0.5	0.2	0.5	0.1
Coppell, TX	17.8	4.7	8.8	0.8	0.2	1.3	0.5	1.2	0.2
Cornelius, NC	9.6	2.6	2.3	1.0	0.6	1.3	0.9	0.8	0.2
Cranberry, PA	3.7	1.8	0.1	1.0	0.1	0.1	0.2	0.2	0.1
Crown Point, IN	17.7	4.9	6.8	3.8	0.3	0.5	0.6	0.6	0.2
Dublin, OH	7.3	3.0	0.8	0.8	0.2	0.2	0.2	1.8	0.1
East Fishkill, NY	28.7	8.3	1.6	4.5	6.6	1.9	4.2	1.2	0.2
Eden Prairie, MN	10.0	4.0	1.4	1.1	0.1	0.4	0.5	2.2	0.2
Edmond, OK	8.1	2.5	3.7	0.4	0.1	0.6	0.2	0.4	0.1
Edwardsville, IL	4.5	2.0	0.5	1.1	0.1	0.1	0.1	0.3	0.1
Evesham, NJ	10.3	4.2	0.9	1.9	1.2	0.4	0.6	0.9	0.1
Flower Mound, TX	17.8	4.7	8.8	0.8	0.2	1.3	0.5	1.2	0.2
Folsom, CA	18.1	8.2	4.9	2.7	0.1	0.6	0.3	0.4	0.3
Friendswood, TX	22.9	5.7	9.6	1.0	0.6	3.4	1.1	1.2	0.3
Gaines, MI	6.5	1.9	1.9	1.1	0.3	0.5	0.1	0.3	0.3
Glastonbury, CT	13.0	3.5	0.3	3.9	2.4	0.3	1.4	0.6	0.5
Grand Blanc, MI	2.4	1.3	0.1	0.5	0.1	0.0	0.0	0.1	0.2
Hampden, PA	6.1	3.0	0.3	1.1	0.4	0.1	0.4	0.6	0.2
Hilliard, OH	7.3	3.0	0.8	0.8	0.2	0.2	0.2	1.8	0.1
Hillsborough, NJ	28.7	8.3	1.6	4.5	6.6	1.9	4.2	1.2	0.2
Holly Springs, NC	11.8	4.1	3.0	1.2	0.6	1.0	0.6	1.0	0.4
Independence, KY	4.3	1.9	0.4	0.7	0.1	0.3	0.2	0.5	0.1
Juneau, AK	8.2	4.5	0.6	1.3	0.0	0.4	0.3	0.1	0.4
Kaysville, UT	5.5	1.0	2.5	0.6	0.0	0.4	0.5	0.1	0.2
Keller, TX	17.8	4.7	8.8	0.8	0.2	1.3	0.5	1.2	0.2
Lafayette, CA	30.2	16.7	5.4	2.9	0.2	2.5	0.9	0.7	0.5
Lafayette, CO	10.7	3.4	3.2	2.2	0.1	0.3	0.6	0.3	0.4
Lake Oswego, OR	12.5	4.6	3.5	2.4	0.1	0.4	0.3	0.5	0.5
Laramie, WY	6.1	2.8	0.9	0.8	0.0	0.2	0.2	0.8	0.2
Leander, TX	14.6	4.0	6.8	1.0	0.4	1.1	0.5	0.5	0.3
Leawood, KS	6.4	2.1	2.0	0.6	0.2	0.5	0.2	0.6	0.1
Lee's Summit, MO	6.4	2.1	2.0	0.6	0.2	0.5	0.2	0.6	0.1
Leesburg, VA	22.3	8.0	0.8	1.9	1.1	4.8	2.2	3.2	0.2
Lehi, UT	6.9	1.1	2.8	0.5	0.1	0.5	1.2	0.1	0.3
Lexington, MA	17.7	5.6	0.2	3.3	3.1	1.5	1.9	1.5	0.5
Los Altos, CA	37.5	23.9	7.8	2.9	0.1	0.9	0.7	0.6	0.5
Loveland, CO	5.1	1.7	1.3	1.1	0.0	0.1	0.4	0.2	0.2
Lower Macungie, PA	8.7	2.6	0.4	1.7	1.7	0.5	1.2	0.4	0.1
Madison, AL	5.3	1.9	1.3	0.8	0.3	0.3	0.1	0.3	0.2

Table continued on next page.

Metro Area	Percent of Population Born in								
	Any Foreign Country	Asia	Mexico	Europe	Carribean	Central America[1]	South America	Africa	Canada
Madison, MS	2.4	0.9	0.6	0.3	0.0	0.3	0.1	0.2	0.1
Maple Valley, WA	17.5	8.9	2.4	2.7	0.1	0.5	0.4	1.3	0.7
Marion, IA	3.1	1.4	0.4	0.4	0.1	0.1	0.1	0.4	0.1
Marlboro, NJ	28.7	8.3	1.6	4.5	6.6	1.9	4.2	1.2	0.2
Mason, OH	4.3	1.9	0.4	0.7	0.1	0.3	0.2	0.5	0.1
Menomonee Falls, WI	7.1	2.4	2.4	1.3	0.2	0.2	0.2	0.3	0.1
Meridian, ID	6.5	1.6	2.8	1.0	0.0	0.2	0.2	0.3	0.3
Meridian, MI	6.6	4.0	0.5	0.7	0.3	0.1	0.2	0.5	0.3
Merrimack, NH	9.1	3.1	0.6	1.8	0.7	0.4	0.8	0.7	1.0
Milton, GA	13.4	4.2	2.9	1.2	1.4	1.1	0.9	1.5	0.2
Moon, PA	3.7	1.8	0.1	1.0	0.1	0.1	0.2	0.2	0.1
Moorpark, CA	22.8	5.4	13.3	1.5	0.1	1.2	0.7	0.2	0.4
Morgantown, WV	4.3	2.8	0.2	0.4	0.2	0.1	0.1	0.3	0.1
Mount Pleasant, SC	4.9	1.3	1.2	1.0	0.3	0.4	0.4	0.2	0.1
Newark, DE	10.3	4.2	0.9	1.9	1.2	0.4	0.6	0.9	0.1
Newtown, CT	21.2	4.2	1.4	4.6	3.4	2.2	4.3	0.6	0.4
North Attleborough, MA	13.1	2.2	0.2	4.4	2.1	1.4	1.0	1.5	0.2
North Port, FL	12.2	1.5	2.2	3.4	1.6	0.7	1.4	0.2	1.2
North Ridgeville, OH	5.6	2.1	0.3	2.2	0.2	0.2	0.2	0.3	0.2
Northville, MI	9.3	5.0	0.9	2.1	0.1	0.1	0.2	0.3	0.6
O'Fallon, MO	4.5	2.0	0.5	1.1	0.1	0.1	0.1	0.3	0.1
Orchard Park, NY	6.1	2.6	0.1	1.5	0.4	0.1	0.3	0.5	0.6
Oro Valley, AZ	12.9	2.3	7.8	1.2	0.1	0.3	0.2	0.5	0.4
Oviedo, FL	16.9	2.9	1.2	1.4	5.2	1.1	4.1	0.6	0.3
Parker, CO	12.2	3.0	5.3	1.5	0.1	0.5	0.4	0.9	0.3
Parkland, FL	39.4	2.1	1.1	2.3	20.7	4.2	8.0	0.4	0.6
Peachtree City, GA	13.4	4.2	2.9	1.2	1.4	1.1	0.9	1.5	0.2
Pittsfield, MI	11.7	6.8	0.5	1.9	0.2	0.4	0.5	0.7	0.5
Plainfield, IL	17.7	4.9	6.8	3.8	0.3	0.5	0.6	0.6	0.2
Pleasant Grove, UT	6.9	1.1	2.8	0.5	0.1	0.5	1.2	0.1	0.3
Poway, CA	23.5	8.9	10.4	1.9	0.2	0.5	0.6	0.5	0.4
Princeton, NJ	21.8	7.3	0.9	3.7	2.7	3.9	1.6	1.5	0.3
Queen Creek, AZ	14.3	3.1	7.6	1.3	0.2	0.5	0.3	0.5	0.7
Radnor, PA	10.3	4.2	0.9	1.9	1.2	0.4	0.6	0.9	0.1
Randolph, NJ	28.7	8.3	1.6	4.5	6.6	1.9	4.2	1.2	0.2
Rexburg, ID	4.6	0.5	2.0	0.2	0.0	0.1	0.7	0.2	0.7
Rio Rancho, NM	9.5	1.7	5.9	0.8	0.2	0.2	0.3	0.2	0.2
Rye, NY	28.7	8.3	1.6	4.5	6.6	1.9	4.2	1.2	0.2
Sammamish, WA	17.5	8.9	2.4	2.7	0.1	0.5	0.4	1.3	0.7
San Ramon, CA	30.2	16.7	5.4	2.9	0.2	2.5	0.9	0.7	0.5
Saratoga, CA	37.5	23.9	7.8	2.9	0.1	0.9	0.7	0.6	0.5
Shrewsbury, MA	10.8	3.4	0.3	2.1	1.0	0.4	1.5	1.4	0.5
South Brunswick, NJ	28.7	8.3	1.6	4.5	6.6	1.9	4.2	1.2	0.2
South Jordan, UT	12.0	2.9	4.8	1.3	0.2	0.6	1.0	0.5	0.3
South Kingstown, RI	13.1	2.2	0.2	4.4	2.1	1.4	1.0	1.5	0.2
South Portland, ME	4.8	1.6	0.1	1.1	0.2	0.1	0.2	0.9	0.6
Sparks, NV	14.7	3.9	6.8	1.2	0.1	1.6	0.4	0.2	0.3
State College, PA	8.1	5.6	0.1	1.1	0.2	0.1	0.2	0.4	0.3
Sugar Land, TX	22.9	5.7	9.6	1.0	0.6	3.4	1.1	1.2	0.3
Sun Prairie, WI	7.1	3.2	1.6	1.0	0.1	0.2	0.3	0.4	0.2
Syracuse, UT	5.5	1.0	2.5	0.6	0.0	0.4	0.5	0.1	0.2
Tredyffrin, PA	10.3	4.2	0.9	1.9	1.2	0.4	0.6	0.9	0.1
Upper Dublin, PA	10.3	4.2	0.9	1.9	1.2	0.4	0.6	0.9	0.1
Urbandale, IA	7.7	2.8	1.7	1.3	0.0	0.5	0.2	1.0	0.1
Vestal, NY	5.7	2.8	0.1	1.5	0.6	0.1	0.2	0.2	0.1
Vestavia Hills, AL	3.9	1.1	1.6	0.3	0.1	0.3	0.1	0.3	0.1
Webster, NY	6.9	2.5	0.2	2.0	0.9	0.2	0.3	0.5	0.4
Wellesley, MA	17.7	5.6	0.2	3.3	3.1	1.5	1.9	1.5	0.5
West Fargo, ND	5.7	2.5	0.1	0.9	0.1	0.1	0.1	1.6	0.3
West Lafayette, IN	9.9	5.8	2.0	0.8	0.1	0.4	0.3	0.2	0.1
Weston, FL	39.4	2.1	1.1	2.3	20.7	4.2	8.0	0.4	0.6
Wilmette, IL	17.7	4.9	6.8	3.8	0.3	0.5	0.6	0.6	0.2
Yorba Linda, CA	33.6	12.5	12.9	1.7	0.3	4.2	0.9	0.5	0.3
Zionsville, IN	6.4	2.2	1.9	0.6	0.2	0.5	0.2	0.7	0.1
U.S.	13.2	4.0	3.6	1.5	1.3	1.0	0.9	0.6	0.3

Note: Figures cover the Metropolitan Statistical Area—see Appendix B for areas included; (1) Excludes Mexico
Source: U.S. Census Bureau, 2012-2016 American Community Survey 5-Year Estimates

Marital Status: City

City	Never Married	Now Married[1]	Separated	Widowed	Divorced
Aberdeen, SD	32.4	48.8	1.0	6.9	10.9
Aliso Viejo, CA	28.7	55.2	1.0	3.7	11.5
Allen, TX	26.0	61.5	0.9	2.4	9.1
Ames, IA	60.2	32.4	0.5	2.2	4.7
Amherst, MA	74.3	18.5	0.7	2.1	4.3
Apex, NC	25.6	61.6	1.3	2.9	8.5
Beavercreek, OH	26.4	59.7	0.8	4.9	8.2
Bellevue, NE	31.6	51.0	1.1	5.4	11.0
Bend, OR	27.6	51.2	1.6	5.1	14.4
Benicia, CA	27.5	53.2	1.9	4.4	13.0
Bentonville, AR	25.7	57.7	1.3	3.7	11.6
Bethlehem, NY	28.1	56.2	0.8	6.7	8.1
Blacksburg, VA	71.8	22.1	0.5	2.1	3.4
Bowie, MD	32.5	47.7	2.0	6.5	11.3
Bozeman, MT	54.1	33.8	0.9	3.2	8.1
Brentwood, TN	20.6	70.3	0.7	3.2	5.2
Burlington, VT	60.0	27.0	1.0	4.3	7.7
Cabot, AR	21.0	57.7	1.2	6.0	14.1
Carmel, IN	23.3	64.7	0.5	3.8	7.7
Cedar Falls, IA	47.5	40.4	0.7	4.5	6.9
Cedar Park, TX	25.5	57.8	1.6	3.7	11.4
Central, LA	21.6	59.6	1.1	6.1	11.6
Chapel Hill, NC	52.6	37.1	0.8	2.6	7.0
Cheshire, CT	28.9	55.4	0.4	6.1	9.1
Chino Hills, CA	30.7	56.6	1.3	4.2	7.1
Cibolo, TX	26.4	62.4	0.4	3.1	7.6
Cicero, NY	27.4	55.3	2.0	5.4	9.8
Collierville, TN	23.8	64.6	1.3	3.4	6.8
Coppell, TX	23.3	64.9	1.0	2.7	8.0
Cornelius, NC	24.7	55.2	1.1	4.4	14.6
Cranberry, PA	23.0	65.8	1.2	4.3	5.6
Crown Point, IN	28.3	52.3	0.7	7.9	10.8
Dublin, OH	21.6	67.7	0.4	3.0	7.2
East Fishkill, NY	26.0	60.7	1.3	4.5	7.5
Eden Prairie, MN	25.1	62.1	1.1	3.4	8.4
Edmond, OK	28.0	56.5	1.2	5.1	9.1
Edwardsville, IL	43.9	42.6	1.0	4.2	8.2
Evesham, NJ	28.8	54.3	1.6	6.0	9.3
Flower Mound, TX	23.3	65.3	0.9	2.8	7.6
Folsom, CA	26.4	55.4	1.6	4.8	11.8
Friendswood, TX	21.7	62.4	1.4	5.5	9.1
Gaines, MI	29.3	53.2	2.0	4.3	11.1
Glastonbury, CT	24.5	57.9	1.0	5.6	10.9
Grand Blanc, MI	27.4	56.7	1.7	4.8	9.4
Hampden, PA	21.5	62.5	1.2	6.9	8.0
Hilliard, OH	26.7	59.1	1.3	5.0	8.0
Hillsborough, NJ	26.7	61.3	0.4	4.7	7.0
Holly Springs, NC	22.5	64.3	2.0	3.4	7.8
Independence, KY	23.9	59.1	1.8	3.8	11.3
Juneau, AK	33.1	50.1	1.9	3.4	11.5
Kaysville, UT	24.1	65.8	0.9	2.4	6.7
Keller, TX	21.0	66.1	1.0	4.9	6.9
Lafayette, CA	24.7	62.1	1.2	4.1	7.9
Lafayette, CO	28.9	53.3	0.8	3.7	13.2
Lake Oswego, OR	21.8	59.0	1.4	5.9	11.9
Laramie, WY	53.4	35.6	0.8	2.5	7.7
Leander, TX	24.2	60.0	1.2	4.0	10.6
Leawood, KS	17.9	70.5	0.3	5.0	6.3
Lee's Summit, MO	24.5	59.3	1.1	5.0	10.2
Leesburg, VA	30.1	56.1	2.1	3.4	8.3
Lehi, UT	24.2	67.8	0.7	1.8	5.5
Lexington, MA	23.3	64.7	0.5	5.6	5.8
Los Altos, CA	18.7	68.9	0.6	5.6	6.1
Loveland, CO	26.4	53.7	1.3	5.7	13.0
Lower Macungie, PA	21.1	63.5	1.4	6.5	7.5
Madison, AL	28.7	57.3	1.0	3.7	9.3
Madison, MS	20.9	65.4	0.6	5.5	7.6
Maple Valley, WA	20.1	64.0	0.9	3.8	11.1
Marion, IA	24.2	56.0	1.5	5.1	13.3

Table continued on next page.

City	Never Married	Now Married[1]	Separated	Widowed	Divorced
Marlboro, NJ	25.7	64.6	0.5	4.5	4.8
Mason, OH	24.4	59.8	1.4	5.5	8.9
Menomonee Falls, WI	24.2	58.0	0.5	8.1	9.3
Meridian, ID	24.7	59.6	1.0	4.3	10.5
Meridian, MI	35.1	48.7	0.5	5.9	9.8
Merrimack, NH	26.9	55.6	0.9	4.5	12.0
Milton, GA	24.4	62.7	1.2	2.7	9.1
Moon, PA	34.2	50.2	1.3	5.8	8.6
Moorpark, CA	30.6	57.7	1.0	3.0	7.7
Morgantown, WV	65.0	24.1	0.6	2.8	7.4
Mount Pleasant, SC	25.2	57.0	2.4	5.0	10.4
Newark, DE	61.1	29.3	0.8	3.0	5.7
Newtown, CT	26.2	59.0	0.6	5.4	8.7
North Attleborough, MA	31.8	50.2	1.5	4.8	11.7
North Port, FL	25.0	54.5	2.1	7.0	11.4
North Ridgeville, OH	21.7	60.7	1.3	6.7	9.6
Northville, MI	23.9	62.2	0.7	5.2	8.0
O'Fallon, MO	26.0	57.9	1.1	4.5	10.5
Orchard Park, NY	26.6	58.2	1.4	5.9	7.9
Oro Valley, AZ	22.5	60.3	1.1	6.5	9.5
Oviedo, FL	33.8	53.5	1.2	3.5	8.0
Parker, CO	24.1	63.9	0.6	2.0	9.4
Parkland, FL	23.2	65.0	0.5	4.1	7.2
Peachtree City, GA	23.6	62.6	0.9	5.1	7.8
Pittsfield, MI	37.8	49.1	0.8	3.4	8.9
Plainfield, IL	26.7	61.6	0.7	3.2	7.9
Pleasant Grove, UT	27.9	60.7	1.4	3.2	6.8
Poway, CA	25.1	59.2	1.6	5.2	8.9
Princeton, NJ	43.5	47.0	0.7	2.8	6.1
Queen Creek, AZ	23.7	64.0	1.0	2.8	8.5
Radnor, PA	48.8	40.1	1.0	3.9	6.2
Randolph, NJ	26.2	63.3	1.0	3.6	5.9
Rexburg, ID	40.9	53.7	0.3	2.6	2.5
Rio Rancho, NM	29.6	51.0	1.2	5.3	12.9
Rye, NY	35.2	49.5	3.3	4.9	7.1
Sammamish, WA	19.1	74.0	0.4	2.0	4.6
San Ramon, CA	22.9	66.2	1.1	3.2	6.6
Saratoga, CA	19.2	68.7	0.9	6.2	4.9
Shrewsbury, MA	28.6	57.0	1.2	5.5	7.8
South Brunswick, NJ	27.2	61.1	0.7	4.5	6.5
South Jordan, UT	25.7	63.1	1.1	2.4	7.6
South Kingstown, RI	41.8	42.8	0.7	6.1	8.6
South Portland, ME	36.5	42.1	1.4	5.6	14.4
Sparks, NV	29.1	49.2	1.9	5.4	14.4
State College, PA	79.7	15.5	0.5	1.5	2.8
Sugar Land, TX	24.3	64.3	0.9	4.5	5.9
Sun Prairie, WI	31.5	51.2	1.7	5.2	10.5
Syracuse, UT	24.0	66.6	0.9	1.4	7.2
Tredyffrin, PA	23.9	59.7	1.7	5.4	9.3
Upper Dublin, PA	25.3	62.6	1.3	5.1	5.8
Urbandale, IA	24.2	61.7	1.0	5.1	8.1
Vestal, NY	46.5	41.2	0.6	5.0	6.7
Vestavia Hills, AL	20.9	62.3	1.0	5.6	10.2
Webster, NY	24.6	58.1	1.5	6.5	9.3
Wellesley, MA	34.9	55.4	0.5	3.9	5.3
West Fargo, ND	27.8	56.6	0.9	4.1	10.6
West Lafayette, IN	73.2	20.9	0.2	2.5	3.1
Weston, FL	26.6	59.1	1.2	3.9	9.3
Wilmette, IL	21.1	65.8	0.8	5.4	6.9
Yorba Linda, CA	24.9	62.7	0.9	5.0	6.6
Zionsville, IN	21.1	66.5	0.5	4.2	7.7
U.S.	33.0	48.1	2.1	5.9	11.0

Note: Figures are percentages and cover the population 15 years of age and older; (1) Excludes separated
Source: U.S. Census Bureau, 2012-2016 American Community Survey 5-Year Estimates

Marital Status: Metro Area

Metro Area	Never Married	Now Married[1]	Separated	Widowed	Divorced
Aberdeen, SD	27.6	54.8	1.0	6.8	9.7
Aliso Viejo, CA	39.8	44.4	2.4	5.0	8.5
Allen, TX	31.9	50.5	2.3	4.5	10.9
Ames, IA	48.7	41.3	0.6	3.2	6.2
Amherst, MA	39.9	41.1	2.2	6.1	10.8
Apex, NC	31.7	51.7	2.5	4.4	9.7
Beavercreek, OH	31.9	46.6	1.7	6.8	13.0
Bellevue, NE	31.3	51.1	1.4	5.1	11.0
Bend, OR	25.1	53.7	1.5	5.3	14.4
Benicia, CA	33.9	46.7	2.5	5.3	11.6
Bentonville, AR	28.1	54.5	1.4	5.2	10.8
Bethlehem, NY	36.3	45.9	2.0	6.2	9.7
Blacksburg, VA	39.2	43.5	2.1	5.4	9.7
Bowie, MD	36.1	48.5	2.1	4.3	8.9
Bozeman, MT	37.8	48.4	0.9	3.4	9.5
Brentwood, TN	31.3	49.7	1.9	5.1	11.9
Burlington, VT	36.2	47.4	1.1	5.0	10.3
Cabot, AR	30.6	47.8	2.3	6.0	13.3
Carmel, IN	32.1	48.3	1.7	5.2	12.7
Cedar Falls, IA	34.1	48.6	1.0	6.1	10.2
Cedar Park, TX	36.1	47.4	1.9	3.7	10.9
Central, LA	36.4	43.1	2.3	6.2	12.1
Chapel Hill, NC	37.1	45.5	2.3	5.0	10.2
Cheshire, CT	37.3	44.5	1.3	6.2	10.8
Chino Hills, CA	35.6	46.8	2.6	5.0	10.0
Cibolo, TX	33.5	46.8	2.8	5.2	11.7
Cicero, NY	36.0	45.1	2.3	6.0	10.6
Collierville, TN	37.5	42.1	3.3	5.8	11.3
Coppell, TX	31.9	50.5	2.3	4.5	10.9
Cornelius, NC	31.8	49.7	2.7	5.4	10.4
Cranberry, PA	31.8	48.9	1.8	7.7	9.8
Crown Point, IN	36.8	46.9	1.8	5.5	9.0
Dublin, OH	34.0	47.5	1.9	4.9	11.7
East Fishkill, NY	38.1	45.7	2.4	5.8	7.9
Eden Prairie, MN	32.9	51.4	1.2	4.4	10.0
Edmond, OK	30.6	48.8	2.2	5.7	12.7
Edwardsville, IL	32.3	48.4	1.8	6.2	11.3
Evesham, NJ	37.4	45.1	2.2	6.2	9.1
Flower Mound, TX	31.9	50.5	2.3	4.5	10.9
Folsom, CA	33.3	47.6	2.3	5.4	11.4
Friendswood, TX	33.1	49.9	2.6	4.5	9.8
Gaines, MI	32.3	51.7	1.2	4.9	9.9
Glastonbury, CT	34.9	47.2	1.3	5.8	10.8
Grand Blanc, MI	33.1	45.1	1.9	6.2	13.7
Hampden, PA	31.1	50.3	2.1	6.4	10.1
Hilliard, OH	34.0	47.5	1.9	4.9	11.7
Hillsborough, NJ	38.1	45.7	2.4	5.8	7.9
Holly Springs, NC	31.7	51.7	2.5	4.4	9.7
Independence, KY	31.8	49.2	1.8	5.7	11.5
Juneau, AK	33.1	50.1	1.9	3.4	11.5
Kaysville, UT	26.1	58.9	1.6	3.5	9.9
Keller, TX	31.9	50.5	2.3	4.5	10.9
Lafayette, CA	36.0	48.1	1.7	5.0	9.1
Lafayette, CO	37.3	47.3	0.9	3.5	11.1
Lake Oswego, OR	31.5	49.7	1.8	4.7	12.4
Laramie, WY	48.5	39.5	0.8	3.1	8.1
Leander, TX	36.1	47.4	1.9	3.7	10.9
Leawood, KS	30.1	50.4	1.7	5.5	12.3
Lee's Summit, MO	30.1	50.4	1.7	5.5	12.3
Leesburg, VA	36.1	48.5	2.1	4.3	8.9
Lehi, UT	32.0	58.5	1.0	2.6	5.9
Lexington, MA	37.0	47.1	1.7	5.3	8.9
Los Altos, CA	32.9	53.2	1.6	4.3	7.9
Loveland, CO	34.4	50.1	1.1	3.9	10.4
Lower Macungie, PA	30.9	50.2	2.3	6.7	9.9
Madison, AL	30.2	50.3	1.8	5.8	11.9
Madison, MS	35.9	43.6	2.8	6.4	11.3
Maple Valley, WA	32.5	50.2	1.5	4.4	11.5
Marion, IA	28.7	53.1	1.3	5.6	11.3

Table continued on next page.

Metro Area	Never Married	Now Married[1]	Separated	Widowed	Divorced
Marlboro, NJ	38.1	45.7	2.4	5.8	7.9
Mason, OH	31.8	49.2	1.8	5.7	11.5
Menomonee Falls, WI	36.4	46.5	1.3	5.6	10.2
Meridian, ID	28.8	52.9	1.3	4.7	12.3
Meridian, MI	38.5	44.3	1.1	4.9	11.2
Merrimack, NH	30.2	51.5	1.4	5.3	11.7
Milton, GA	34.7	47.4	2.1	4.7	11.0
Moon, PA	31.8	48.9	1.8	7.7	9.8
Moorpark, CA	32.8	50.4	1.8	5.0	10.1
Morgantown, WV	42.8	41.5	1.1	5.0	9.5
Mount Pleasant, SC	34.1	45.9	2.9	5.6	11.5
Newark, DE	37.4	45.1	2.2	6.2	9.1
Newtown, CT	32.8	50.9	1.3	5.6	9.4
North Attleborough, MA	35.4	45.2	1.8	6.4	11.2
North Port, FL	23.6	52.3	1.7	9.1	13.3
North Ridgeville, OH	34.3	45.3	1.8	6.8	11.9
Northville, MI	34.5	46.3	1.5	6.3	11.4
O'Fallon, MO	32.3	48.4	1.8	6.2	11.3
Orchard Park, NY	35.8	44.7	1.9	7.0	10.6
Oro Valley, AZ	33.9	45.1	2.0	6.0	13.1
Oviedo, FL	34.9	45.5	2.4	5.3	11.9
Parker, CO	32.2	49.9	1.6	4.2	12.1
Parkland, FL	34.5	43.0	3.0	6.7	12.8
Peachtree City, GA	34.7	47.4	2.1	4.7	11.0
Pittsfield, MI	42.4	44.0	0.9	3.9	8.8
Plainfield, IL	36.8	46.9	1.8	5.5	9.0
Pleasant Grove, UT	32.0	58.5	1.0	2.6	5.9
Poway, CA	35.6	47.3	1.8	4.9	10.4
Princeton, NJ	37.4	47.0	1.8	5.7	8.1
Queen Creek, AZ	33.7	47.2	1.7	5.1	12.3
Radnor, PA	37.4	45.1	2.2	6.2	9.1
Randolph, NJ	38.1	45.7	2.4	5.8	7.9
Rexburg, ID	33.5	57.9	0.4	3.5	4.7
Rio Rancho, NM	34.4	44.9	1.7	5.6	13.4
Rye, NY	38.1	45.7	2.4	5.8	7.9
Sammamish, WA	32.5	50.2	1.5	4.4	11.5
San Ramon, CA	36.0	48.1	1.7	5.0	9.1
Saratoga, CA	32.9	53.2	1.6	4.3	7.9
Shrewsbury, MA	33.7	47.9	1.8	5.7	11.0
South Brunswick, NJ	38.1	45.7	2.4	5.8	7.9
South Jordan, UT	31.4	52.3	1.9	3.9	10.5
South Kingstown, RI	35.4	45.2	1.8	6.4	11.2
South Portland, ME	28.8	51.0	1.0	5.7	13.5
Sparks, NV	31.2	47.4	1.9	5.1	14.5
State College, PA	47.0	40.7	1.0	4.2	7.1
Sugar Land, TX	33.1	49.9	2.6	4.5	9.8
Sun Prairie, WI	35.7	49.2	1.1	4.3	9.7
Syracuse, UT	26.1	58.9	1.6	3.5	9.9
Tredyffrin, PA	37.4	45.1	2.2	6.2	9.1
Upper Dublin, PA	37.4	45.1	2.2	6.2	9.1
Urbandale, IA	29.2	52.7	1.4	5.0	11.7
Vestal, NY	34.5	46.0	2.1	6.6	10.7
Vestavia Hills, AL	29.8	48.4	2.3	6.8	12.7
Webster, NY	35.2	45.8	2.3	6.2	10.6
Wellesley, MA	37.0	47.1	1.7	5.3	8.9
West Fargo, ND	37.8	47.8	0.9	4.5	9.0
West Lafayette, IN	41.9	42.4	0.8	4.2	10.6
Weston, FL	34.5	43.0	3.0	6.7	12.8
Wilmette, IL	36.8	46.9	1.8	5.5	9.0
Yorba Linda, CA	39.8	44.4	2.4	5.0	8.5
Zionsville, IN	32.1	48.3	1.7	5.2	12.7
U.S.	33.0	48.1	2.1	5.9	11.0

Note: Figures are percentages and cover the population 15 years of age and older; Figures cover the Metropolitan Statistical Area—see Appendix B for areas included; (1) Excludes separated
Source: U.S. Census Bureau, 2012-2016 American Community Survey 5-Year Estimates

Disability Status: City

City	All Ages	Under 18 Years Old	18 to 64 Years Old	65 Years and Over
Aberdeen, SD	10.5	2.1	7.8	34.9
Aliso Viejo, CA	5.6	3.7	3.9	25.1
Allen, TX	6.0	2.6	4.9	30.3
Ames, IA	5.6	1.9	4.0	25.6
Amherst, MA	5.9	7.1	4.2	25.2
Apex, NC	5.9	3.0	5.3	25.6
Beavercreek, OH	9.6	4.0	6.6	28.2
Bellevue, NE	11.7	3.8	10.3	33.2
Bend, OR	10.5	3.4	7.8	31.8
Benicia, CA	10.1	2.3	8.1	28.2
Bentonville, AR	7.0	2.4	6.3	33.5
Bethlehem, NY	9.7	4.2	6.2	30.0
Blacksburg, VA	5.6	2.3	4.5	33.0
Bowie, MD	9.3	3.1	7.1	31.2
Bozeman, MT	7.1	3.2	5.6	27.7
Brentwood, TN	6.3	1.7	4.9	24.2
Burlington, VT	11.9	5.3	9.7	38.1
Cabot, AR	13.0	5.0	10.5	47.0
Carmel, IN	5.9	1.1	3.7	27.6
Cedar Falls, IA	8.3	3.0	5.7	30.2
Cedar Park, TX	7.6	3.6	6.3	33.3
Central, LA	15.0	4.3	12.5	39.4
Chapel Hill, NC	6.6	3.1	4.7	25.5
Cheshire, CT	8.8	2.3	5.7	28.2
Chino Hills, CA	6.9	1.6	4.9	34.1
Cibolo, TX	7.9	2.7	6.7	39.4
Cicero, NY	10.3	3.8	9.3	26.8
Collierville, TN	7.2	3.2	5.2	27.6
Coppell, TX	4.6	1.7	3.3	27.7
Cornelius, NC	7.6	2.3	5.7	26.4
Cranberry, PA	6.9	4.1	4.6	30.1
Crown Point, IN	11.2	2.2	6.9	36.5
Dublin, OH	5.7	3.1	4.0	25.1
East Fishkill, NY	10.9	4.1	7.5	38.5
Eden Prairie, MN	6.5	3.2	4.7	24.5
Edmond, OK	9.5	3.7	7.0	33.4
Edwardsville, IL	8.2	4.6	6.0	29.2
Evesham, NJ	9.0	2.6	5.5	32.1
Flower Mound, TX	6.7	2.6	6.0	29.2
Folsom, CA	7.9	2.9	5.0	32.9
Friendswood, TX	8.6	3.9	6.1	28.5
Gaines, MI	11.5	5.6	10.2	32.3
Glastonbury, CT	7.6	1.5	5.5	24.9
Grand Blanc, MI	9.5	2.7	6.7	34.8
Hampden, PA	9.0	2.5	4.8	31.0
Hilliard, OH	7.7	4.4	5.2	33.1
Hillsborough, NJ	7.8	2.1	5.3	35.9
Holly Springs, NC	6.4	3.7	5.3	28.2
Independence, KY	11.0	3.8	10.7	36.5
Juneau, AK	9.8	3.4	8.8	30.3
Kaysville, UT	9.3	3.7	8.3	40.5
Keller, TX	8.4	3.4	5.3	37.4
Lafayette, CA	6.2	1.9	3.8	19.8
Lafayette, CO	9.8	4.5	8.8	27.8
Lake Oswego, OR	8.1	2.6	4.4	26.7
Laramie, WY	8.8	2.5	7.4	38.2
Leander, TX	8.4	4.7	7.6	32.7
Leawood, KS	6.9	1.2	4.3	24.4
Lee's Summit, MO	9.2	2.7	7.0	32.9
Leesburg, VA	6.8	2.9	5.5	35.7
Lehi, UT	6.4	3.0	6.2	35.0
Lexington, MA	7.1	2.2	4.2	23.9
Los Altos, CA	6.0	1.5	2.4	22.7
Loveland, CO	11.8	4.9	10.0	27.7
Lower Macungie, PA	10.7	6.4	6.8	27.9
Madison, AL	9.5	3.7	8.0	34.6
Madison, MS	7.3	2.9	5.1	27.3
Maple Valley, WA	7.7	5.6	5.6	33.1

Table continued on next page.

City	All Ages	Under 18 Years Old	18 to 64 Years Old	65 Years and Over
Marion, IA	10.2	5.1	8.1	28.5
Marlboro, NJ	7.0	1.4	4.5	29.9
Mason, OH	8.3	3.2	4.2	34.9
Menomonee Falls, WI	10.3	2.9	6.3	31.5
Meridian, ID	7.9	2.6	6.7	26.9
Meridian, MI	9.2	2.9	6.5	29.7
Merrimack, NH	8.8	3.8	7.5	24.2
Milton, GA	4.9	1.8	3.8	23.9
Moon, PA	9.3	2.7	7.7	27.3
Moorpark, CA	7.2	3.1	5.2	30.9
Morgantown, WV	8.9	2.9	6.2	39.2
Mount Pleasant, SC	7.5	1.7	5.1	28.1
Newark, DE	7.5	5.1	4.6	28.7
Newtown, CT	10.4	3.5	6.3	37.7
North Attleborough, MA	9.8	3.7	9.0	28.2
North Port, FL	16.1	4.1	13.9	32.0
North Ridgeville, OH	10.7	4.0	7.8	27.7
Northville, MI	8.4	2.3	5.4	26.2
O'Fallon, MO	8.6	3.9	6.2	35.5
Orchard Park, NY	8.7	2.9	4.9	27.7
Oro Valley, AZ	11.3	3.6	7.8	22.2
Oviedo, FL	8.9	3.5	8.4	29.8
Parker, CO	6.4	2.9	5.8	27.8
Parkland, FL	6.9	2.7	4.6	32.0
Peachtree City, GA	7.6	3.6	4.7	26.1
Pittsfield, MI	7.6	2.0	5.7	31.7
Plainfield, IL	6.0	3.2	4.2	38.0
Pleasant Grove, UT	8.5	2.9	7.9	40.8
Poway, CA	9.6	1.9	6.7	35.0
Princeton, NJ	6.0	2.9	4.3	17.9
Queen Creek, AZ	5.7	2.2	5.2	28.8
Radnor, PA	5.9	2.2	3.6	25.7
Randolph, NJ	5.9	2.1	3.9	24.6
Rexburg, ID	6.3	3.7	5.3	35.0
Rio Rancho, NM	12.8	3.8	11.2	38.7
Rye, NY	9.0	2.1	6.8	32.1
Sammamish, WA	4.2	2.1	3.3	21.6
San Ramon, CA	4.8	1.7	3.3	24.7
Saratoga, CA	6.8	2.4	2.5	23.3
Shrewsbury, MA	9.0	4.5	5.3	32.5
South Brunswick, NJ	7.4	3.0	5.3	28.0
South Jordan, UT	7.6	2.7	6.6	32.8
South Kingstown, RI	10.3	3.6	7.3	28.2
South Portland, ME	12.0	5.4	9.8	30.9
Sparks, NV	12.0	4.1	9.9	34.6
State College, PA	5.6	2.3	4.6	28.4
Sugar Land, TX	6.6	3.3	4.0	24.7
Sun Prairie, WI	10.4	3.9	9.0	35.8
Syracuse, UT	7.0	2.7	8.3	24.9
Tredyffrin, PA	6.8	0.4	3.9	25.0
Upper Dublin, PA	7.7	2.3	5.4	22.6
Urbandale, IA	6.6	1.7	5.5	21.2
Vestal, NY	8.7	5.0	5.5	27.2
Vestavia Hills, AL	8.7	2.2	4.6	35.7
Webster, NY	10.2	2.3	7.0	30.9
Wellesley, MA	6.2	1.8	3.8	24.9
West Fargo, ND	9.8	3.5	8.5	38.6
West Lafayette, IN	5.8	2.7	4.0	35.7
Weston, FL	5.1	1.5	4.1	22.1
Wilmette, IL	7.9	1.4	4.9	27.9
Yorba Linda, CA	7.5	2.0	4.7	26.8
Zionsville, IN	5.3	1.8	3.8	25.2
U.S.	12.5	4.1	10.3	35.7

Note: Figures show percent of the civilian noninstitutionalized population that reported having a disability. Disability status is determined from from six types of difficulty: vision, hearing, cognitive, ambulatory, self-care, and independent living. For children under 5 years old, hearing and vision difficulty are used to determine disability status. For children between the ages of 5 and 14, disability status is determined from hearing, vision, cognitive, ambulatory, and self-care difficulties. For people aged 15 years and older, they are considered to have a disability if they have difficulty with any one of the six difficulty types.
Source: U.S. Census Bureau, 2012-2016 American Community Survey 5-Year Estimates

Disability Status: Metro Area

Metro Area	All Ages	Under 18 Years Old	18 to 64 Years Old	65 Years and Over
Aberdeen, SD	10.5	2.8	7.8	33.3
Aliso Viejo, CA	9.5	2.9	7.0	35.6
Allen, TX	9.6	3.4	8.2	35.2
Ames, IA	7.1	2.8	5.1	28.4
Amherst, MA	14.4	6.8	11.8	37.0
Apex, NC	9.4	3.7	7.8	33.0
Beavercreek, OH	14.4	4.8	12.4	35.5
Bellevue, NE	10.7	3.5	9.4	33.4
Bend, OR	12.8	3.9	10.2	32.1
Benicia, CA	12.1	3.7	10.0	36.1
Bentonville, AR	10.4	3.4	8.7	35.1
Bethlehem, NY	12.0	4.4	9.8	32.0
Blacksburg, VA	12.7	4.6	10.2	35.2
Bowie, MD	8.3	2.9	6.5	29.7
Bozeman, MT	8.0	2.8	6.4	27.4
Brentwood, TN	12.0	3.9	10.5	36.5
Burlington, VT	11.4	5.1	9.3	32.1
Cabot, AR	14.4	5.7	12.3	39.3
Carmel, IN	12.4	4.7	10.9	36.8
Cedar Falls, IA	10.8	3.2	8.9	29.4
Cedar Park, TX	9.3	3.9	7.9	33.1
Central, LA	14.1	6.1	12.0	40.8
Chapel Hill, NC	10.9	3.5	9.0	32.9
Cheshire, CT	11.4	4.0	8.7	32.8
Chino Hills, CA	11.1	3.4	9.4	37.6
Cibolo, TX	13.5	5.0	11.9	40.6
Cicero, NY	12.7	5.0	10.7	32.4
Collierville, TN	12.9	4.2	11.6	38.4
Coppell, TX	9.6	3.4	8.2	35.2
Cornelius, NC	11.1	3.6	9.5	34.7
Cranberry, PA	14.0	5.0	11.0	34.2
Crown Point, IN	9.9	3.1	7.7	34.2
Dublin, OH	11.8	4.6	10.3	35.1
East Fishkill, NY	10.0	3.2	7.4	33.3
Eden Prairie, MN	9.6	3.6	7.9	31.0
Edmond, OK	13.6	4.4	12.0	40.0
Edwardsville, IL	12.5	4.4	10.4	34.5
Evesham, NJ	12.3	4.6	10.2	34.0
Flower Mound, TX	9.6	3.4	8.2	35.2
Folsom, CA	12.2	3.9	9.9	37.0
Friendswood, TX	9.6	3.5	8.2	36.2
Gaines, MI	11.8	4.4	10.2	33.7
Glastonbury, CT	11.4	4.1	8.7	32.5
Grand Blanc, MI	16.5	6.1	15.3	37.3
Hampden, PA	12.4	4.4	10.1	32.5
Hilliard, OH	11.8	4.6	10.3	35.1
Hillsborough, NJ	10.0	3.2	7.4	33.3
Holly Springs, NC	9.4	3.7	7.8	33.0
Independence, KY	12.2	4.5	10.7	33.9
Juneau, AK	9.8	3.4	8.8	30.3
Kaysville, UT	10.3	3.7	9.6	35.3
Keller, TX	9.6	3.4	8.2	35.2
Lafayette, CA	9.9	2.9	7.2	33.1
Lafayette, CO	8.3	2.8	6.7	26.5
Lake Oswego, OR	12.3	4.0	10.4	36.0
Laramie, WY	9.5	2.3	7.6	36.5
Leander, TX	9.3	3.9	7.9	33.1
Leawood, KS	12.1	3.9	10.7	34.9
Lee's Summit, MO	12.1	3.9	10.7	34.9
Leesburg, VA	8.3	2.9	6.5	29.7
Lehi, UT	7.6	3.0	7.0	34.6
Lexington, MA	10.6	4.0	8.0	32.4
Los Altos, CA	7.9	2.3	5.3	32.4
Loveland, CO	9.7	3.3	7.6	29.3
Lower Macungie, PA	13.4	5.8	10.9	33.5
Madison, AL	13.3	4.6	11.1	37.7
Madison, MS	13.1	4.1	11.6	38.6
Maple Valley, WA	11.0	3.5	9.1	34.7

Table continued on next page.

Metro Area	All Ages	Under 18 Years Old	18 to 64 Years Old	65 Years and Over
Marion, IA	10.6	4.3	8.6	29.5
Marlboro, NJ	10.0	3.2	7.4	33.3
Mason, OH	12.2	4.5	10.7	33.9
Menomonee Falls, WI	11.9	4.8	10.0	33.5
Meridian, ID	11.6	4.0	10.2	33.7
Meridian, MI	12.9	5.3	10.9	34.9
Merrimack, NH	11.1	4.7	8.9	32.1
Milton, GA	10.0	3.4	8.7	34.1
Moon, PA	14.0	5.0	11.0	34.2
Moorpark, CA	10.5	3.5	7.9	35.0
Morgantown, WV	13.0	3.5	10.6	39.4
Mount Pleasant, SC	11.9	4.1	9.9	35.1
Newark, DE	12.3	4.6	10.2	34.0
Newtown, CT	9.0	3.2	6.6	29.6
North Attleborough, MA	13.5	5.0	11.1	34.8
North Port, FL	14.9	4.2	10.4	29.2
North Ridgeville, OH	14.0	5.3	11.7	34.9
Northville, MI	14.1	4.8	12.3	36.8
O'Fallon, MO	12.5	4.4	10.4	34.5
Orchard Park, NY	13.1	4.7	10.8	32.6
Oro Valley, AZ	14.7	4.8	12.2	35.2
Oviedo, FL	11.7	4.6	9.4	34.3
Parker, CO	9.2	2.9	7.6	31.8
Parkland, FL	11.0	3.2	7.4	33.6
Peachtree City, GA	10.0	3.4	8.7	34.1
Pittsfield, MI	8.6	2.9	6.7	29.1
Plainfield, IL	9.9	3.1	7.7	34.2
Pleasant Grove, UT	7.6	3.0	7.0	34.6
Poway, CA	9.9	2.9	7.2	35.4
Princeton, NJ	10.0	3.4	7.9	31.0
Queen Creek, AZ	11.1	3.6	9.0	33.2
Radnor, PA	12.3	4.6	10.2	34.0
Randolph, NJ	10.0	3.2	7.4	33.3
Rexburg, ID	7.9	2.7	6.4	35.2
Rio Rancho, NM	13.8	3.8	12.0	37.8
Rye, NY	10.0	3.2	7.4	33.3
Sammamish, WA	11.0	3.5	9.1	34.7
San Ramon, CA	9.9	2.9	7.2	33.1
Saratoga, CA	7.9	2.3	5.3	32.4
Shrewsbury, MA	12.1	4.9	10.0	33.7
South Brunswick, NJ	10.0	3.2	7.4	33.3
South Jordan, UT	9.3	3.3	8.2	34.9
South Kingstown, RI	13.5	5.0	11.1	34.8
South Portland, ME	12.9	5.1	10.4	31.4
Sparks, NV	12.3	4.4	10.4	32.3
State College, PA	9.9	4.0	7.4	32.3
Sugar Land, TX	9.6	3.5	8.2	36.2
Sun Prairie, WI	9.3	3.6	7.4	29.4
Syracuse, UT	10.3	3.7	9.6	35.3
Tredyffrin, PA	12.3	4.6	10.2	34.0
Upper Dublin, PA	12.3	4.6	10.2	34.0
Urbandale, IA	10.5	3.6	9.3	31.9
Vestal, NY	14.9	6.5	12.1	35.1
Vestavia Hills, AL	15.2	4.3	13.6	39.6
Webster, NY	13.2	5.6	11.0	32.6
Wellesley, MA	10.6	4.0	8.0	32.4
West Fargo, ND	10.1	2.9	8.4	35.6
West Lafayette, IN	10.8	4.8	8.7	35.1
Weston, FL	11.0	3.2	7.4	33.6
Wilmette, IL	9.9	3.1	7.7	34.2
Yorba Linda, CA	9.5	2.9	7.0	35.6
Zionsville, IN	12.4	4.7	10.9	36.8
U.S.	12.5	4.1	10.3	35.7

Note: Figures show percent of the civilian noninstitutionalized population that reported having a disability. Disability status is determined from from six types of difficulty: vision, hearing, cognitive, ambulatory, self-care, and independent living. For children under 5 years old, hearing and vision difficulty are used to determine disability status. For children between the ages of 5 and 14, disability status is determined from hearing, vision, cognitive, ambulatory, and self-care difficulties. For people aged 15 years and older, they are considered to have a disability if they have difficulty with any one of the six difficulty types; Figures cover the Metropolitan Statistical Area—see Appendix B for areas included

Source: U.S. Census Bureau, 2012-2016 American Community Survey 5-Year Estimates

Male/Female Ratio: City

City	Males	Females	Males per 100 Females
Aberdeen, SD	13,368	14,415	92.7
Aliso Viejo, CA	23,597	26,622	88.6
Allen, TX	47,398	47,312	100.2
Ames, IA	33,845	30,228	112.0
Amherst, MA	19,533	20,191	96.7
Apex, NC	20,739	23,154	89.6
Beavercreek, OH	23,536	22,550	104.4
Bellevue, NE	26,482	26,511	99.9
Bend, OR	40,755	43,661	93.3
Benicia, CA	13,548	14,232	95.2
Bentonville, AR	21,830	20,669	105.6
Bethlehem, NY	16,704	18,005	92.8
Blacksburg, VA	23,820	20,153	118.2
Bowie, MD	27,289	30,344	89.9
Bozeman, MT	22,115	19,646	112.6
Brentwood, TN	20,153	20,720	97.3
Burlington, VT	20,881	21,675	96.3
Cabot, AR	12,390	13,017	95.2
Carmel, IN	41,991	44,949	93.4
Cedar Falls, IA	19,325	21,503	89.9
Cedar Park, TX	30,804	32,747	94.1
Central, LA	13,232	14,785	89.5
Chapel Hill, NC	27,334	31,671	86.3
Cheshire, CT	14,985	14,269	105.0
Chino Hills, CA	38,024	39,242	96.9
Cibolo, TX	11,898	13,358	89.1
Cicero, NY	15,357	16,138	95.2
Collierville, TN	22,711	25,294	89.8
Coppell, TX	20,310	20,321	99.9
Cornelius, NC	13,389	14,037	95.4
Cranberry, PA	15,057	14,857	101.3
Crown Point, IN	13,882	14,861	93.4
Dublin, OH	21,682	22,192	97.7
East Fishkill, NY	14,789	14,493	102.0
Eden Prairie, MN	31,739	31,467	100.9
Edmond, OK	43,050	45,292	95.0
Edwardsville, IL	12,001	13,043	92.0
Evesham, NJ	22,116	23,462	94.3
Flower Mound, TX	34,344	35,622	96.4
Folsom, CA	40,135	34,825	115.2
Friendswood, TX	18,961	19,311	98.2
Gaines, MI	12,876	13,246	97.2
Glastonbury, CT	16,783	17,894	93.8
Grand Blanc, MI	18,086	18,685	96.8
Hampden, PA	13,588	15,374	88.4
Hilliard, OH	16,438	16,670	98.6
Hillsborough, NJ	19,167	20,350	94.2
Holly Springs, NC	14,853	15,273	97.3
Independence, KY	12,971	13,346	97.2
Juneau, AK	16,648	15,876	104.9
Kaysville, UT	14,857	14,942	99.4
Keller, TX	21,815	22,435	97.2
Lafayette, CA	12,073	13,308	90.7
Lafayette, CO	12,995	14,058	92.4
Lake Oswego, OR	17,591	20,474	85.9
Laramie, WY	16,675	15,421	108.1
Leander, TX	17,803	18,401	96.8
Leawood, KS	16,907	16,856	100.3
Lee's Summit, MO	45,563	48,694	93.6
Leesburg, VA	24,225	25,176	96.2
Lehi, UT	28,828	27,486	104.9
Lexington, MA	15,866	17,070	92.9
Los Altos, CA	14,343	15,895	90.2
Loveland, CO	35,978	37,382	96.2
Lower Macungie, PA	15,474	16,188	95.6
Madison, AL	22,695	23,701	95.8
Madison, MS	12,267	13,206	92.9
Maple Valley, WA	12,067	13,026	92.6

Table continued on next page.

City	Males	Females	Males per 100 Females
Marion, IA	18,609	18,589	100.1
Marlboro, NJ	19,361	21,055	92.0
Mason, OH	15,348	16,677	92.0
Menomonee Falls, WI	17,318	18,800	92.1
Meridian, ID	43,121	45,126	95.6
Meridian, MI	19,435	22,066	88.1
Merrimack, NH	12,878	12,702	101.4
Milton, GA	17,562	19,193	91.5
Moon, PA	12,821	12,614	101.6
Moorpark, CA	17,146	18,448	92.9
Morgantown, WV	16,986	13,378	127.0
Mount Pleasant, SC	37,624	40,283	93.4
Newark, DE	15,466	17,475	88.5
Newtown, CT	13,911	14,079	98.8
North Attleborough, MA	14,407	14,538	99.1
North Port, FL	29,201	31,670	92.2
North Ridgeville, OH	16,071	15,761	102.0
Northville, MI	13,689	15,035	91.0
O'Fallon, MO	41,358	42,660	96.9
Orchard Park, NY	14,192	15,329	92.6
Oro Valley, AZ	20,371	22,008	92.6
Oviedo, FL	18,084	19,461	92.9
Parker, CO	24,354	24,088	101.1
Parkland, FL	13,689	14,665	93.3
Peachtree City, GA	17,059	17,929	95.1
Pittsfield, MI	17,796	19,429	91.6
Plainfield, IL	20,162	21,719	92.8
Pleasant Grove, UT	18,102	18,576	97.4
Poway, CA	24,280	25,395	95.6
Princeton, NJ	15,544	14,624	106.3
Queen Creek, AZ	15,679	15,170	103.4
Radnor, PA	14,888	16,728	89.0
Randolph, NJ	12,428	13,488	92.1
Rexburg, ID	13,366	13,748	97.2
Rio Rancho, NM	45,469	47,497	95.7
Rye, NY	23,127	23,549	98.2
Sammamish, WA	30,801	31,335	98.3
San Ramon, CA	37,252	37,114	100.4
Saratoga, CA	15,047	15,783	95.3
Shrewsbury, MA	18,071	18,423	98.1
South Brunswick, NJ	21,787	23,310	93.5
South Jordan, UT	31,638	31,113	101.7
South Kingstown, RI	14,618	16,033	91.2
South Portland, ME	11,735	13,662	85.9
Sparks, NV	46,253	48,465	95.4
State College, PA	22,705	19,369	117.2
Sugar Land, TX	42,590	43,091	98.8
Sun Prairie, WI	15,350	16,371	93.8
Syracuse, UT	13,673	12,995	105.2
Tredyffrin, PA	14,052	15,439	91.0
Upper Dublin, PA	12,469	13,712	90.9
Urbandale, IA	20,389	21,189	96.2
Vestal, NY	13,814	14,453	95.6
Vestavia Hills, AL	16,702	17,541	95.2
Webster, NY	20,994	23,090	90.9
Wellesley, MA	12,601	16,308	77.3
West Fargo, ND	15,877	15,680	101.3
West Lafayette, IN	24,014	20,529	117.0
Weston, FL	33,278	35,615	93.4
Wilmette, IL	13,349	14,018	95.2
Yorba Linda, CA	33,159	34,203	96.9
Zionsville, IN	12,606	13,103	96.2
U.S.	156,765,322	161,792,840	96.9

Source: U.S. Census Bureau, 2012-2016 American Community Survey 5-Year Estimates

Male/Female Ratio: Metro Area

Metro Area	Males	Females	Males per 100 Females
Aberdeen, SD	20,717	21,713	95.4
Aliso Viejo, CA	6,501,303	6,688,063	97.2
Allen, TX	3,421,036	3,536,087	96.7
Ames, IA	49,349	45,485	108.5
Amherst, MA	301,223	327,884	91.9
Apex, NC	605,735	637,985	94.9
Beavercreek, OH	388,398	412,552	94.1
Bellevue, NE	447,762	457,072	98.0
Bend, OR	84,267	86,546	97.4
Benicia, CA	213,518	216,078	98.8
Bentonville, AR	250,778	252,864	99.2
Bethlehem, NY	430,051	449,240	95.7
Blacksburg, VA	91,970	89,318	103.0
Bowie, MD	2,934,987	3,076,765	95.4
Bozeman, MT	50,509	47,449	106.4
Brentwood, TN	875,099	919,471	95.2
Burlington, VT	106,131	109,949	96.5
Cabot, AR	352,647	374,724	94.1
Carmel, IN	961,597	1,007,171	95.5
Cedar Falls, IA	83,296	86,561	96.2
Cedar Park, TX	971,489	971,126	100.0
Central, LA	403,322	421,345	95.7
Chapel Hill, NC	259,801	282,598	91.9
Cheshire, CT	415,286	445,588	93.2
Chino Hills, CA	2,204,051	2,226,595	99.0
Cibolo, TX	1,150,424	1,181,921	97.3
Cicero, NY	321,835	338,817	95.0
Collierville, TN	643,139	698,200	92.1
Coppell, TX	3,421,036	3,536,087	96.7
Cornelius, NC	1,154,769	1,226,383	94.2
Cranberry, PA	1,144,208	1,210,718	94.5
Crown Point, IN	4,660,614	4,867,782	95.7
Dublin, OH	981,638	1,013,366	96.9
East Fishkill, NY	9,684,087	10,347,356	93.6
Eden Prairie, MN	1,726,228	1,762,208	98.0
Edmond, OK	659,180	677,895	97.2
Edwardsville, IL	1,359,236	1,444,213	94.1
Evesham, NJ	2,923,439	3,124,282	93.6
Flower Mound, TX	3,421,036	3,536,087	96.7
Folsom, CA	1,097,362	1,145,180	95.8
Friendswood, TX	3,220,604	3,261,988	98.7
Gaines, MI	508,020	520,153	97.7
Glastonbury, CT	590,791	621,035	95.1
Grand Blanc, MI	199,181	213,909	93.1
Hampden, PA	275,187	286,260	96.1
Hilliard, OH	981,638	1,013,366	96.9
Hillsborough, NJ	9,684,087	10,347,356	93.6
Holly Springs, NC	605,735	637,985	94.9
Independence, KY	1,050,706	1,095,704	95.9
Juneau, AK	16,648	15,876	104.9
Kaysville, UT	318,228	314,565	101.2
Keller, TX	3,421,036	3,536,087	96.7
Lafayette, CA	2,258,917	2,318,613	97.4
Lafayette, CO	157,617	156,344	100.8
Lake Oswego, OR	1,161,988	1,189,331	97.7
Laramie, WY	19,767	18,069	109.4
Leander, TX	971,489	971,126	100.0
Leawood, KS	1,014,663	1,055,484	96.1
Lee's Summit, MO	1,014,663	1,055,484	96.1
Leesburg, VA	2,934,987	3,076,765	95.4
Lehi, UT	289,878	284,806	101.8
Lexington, MA	2,294,912	2,433,932	94.3
Los Altos, CA	978,285	964,822	101.4
Loveland, CO	161,828	163,400	99.0
Lower Macungie, PA	406,498	424,239	95.8
Madison, AL	216,231	223,999	96.5
Madison, MS	276,773	301,322	91.9
Maple Valley, WA	1,831,699	1,839,396	99.6

Table continued on next page.

Metro Area	Males	Females	Males per 100 Females
Marion, IA	131,160	133,117	98.5
Marlboro, NJ	9,684,087	10,347,356	93.6
Mason, OH	1,050,706	1,095,704	95.9
Menomonee Falls, WI	765,346	806,384	94.9
Meridian, ID	331,630	332,050	99.9
Meridian, MI	229,414	240,934	95.2
Merrimack, NH	200,979	203,969	98.5
Milton, GA	2,719,100	2,893,677	94.0
Moon, PA	1,144,208	1,210,718	94.5
Moorpark, CA	417,442	425,668	98.1
Morgantown, WV	70,643	65,977	107.1
Mount Pleasant, SC	355,780	372,491	95.5
Newark, DE	2,923,439	3,124,282	93.6
Newtown, CT	458,490	483,128	94.9
North Attleborough, MA	780,036	829,323	94.1
North Port, FL	360,749	390,673	92.3
North Ridgeville, OH	994,214	1,067,416	93.1
Northville, MI	2,086,284	2,210,447	94.4
O'Fallon, MO	1,359,236	1,444,213	94.1
Orchard Park, NY	550,057	585,446	94.0
Oro Valley, AZ	493,568	509,770	96.8
Oviedo, FL	1,138,560	1,189,948	95.7
Parker, CO	1,370,467	1,381,589	99.2
Parkland, FL	2,875,505	3,051,450	94.2
Peachtree City, GA	2,719,100	2,893,677	94.0
Pittsfield, MI	177,102	180,980	97.9
Plainfield, IL	4,660,614	4,867,782	95.7
Pleasant Grove, UT	289,878	284,806	101.8
Poway, CA	1,635,137	1,618,219	101.0
Princeton, NJ	181,642	189,459	95.9
Queen Creek, AZ	2,229,288	2,256,865	98.8
Radnor, PA	2,923,439	3,124,282	93.6
Randolph, NJ	9,684,087	10,347,356	93.6
Rexburg, ID	25,884	25,126	103.0
Rio Rancho, NM	444,849	459,637	96.8
Rye, NY	9,684,087	10,347,356	93.6
Sammamish, WA	1,831,699	1,839,396	99.6
San Ramon, CA	2,258,917	2,318,613	97.4
Saratoga, CA	978,285	964,822	101.4
Shrewsbury, MA	459,364	471,303	97.5
South Brunswick, NJ	9,684,087	10,347,356	93.6
South Jordan, UT	580,157	574,347	101.0
South Kingstown, RI	780,036	829,323	94.1
South Portland, ME	255,131	268,743	94.9
Sparks, NV	223,053	220,802	101.0
State College, PA	83,558	75,620	110.5
Sugar Land, TX	3,220,604	3,261,988	98.7
Sun Prairie, WI	315,443	318,826	98.9
Syracuse, UT	318,228	314,565	101.2
Tredyffrin, PA	2,923,439	3,124,282	93.6
Upper Dublin, PA	2,923,439	3,124,282	93.6
Urbandale, IA	301,158	310,597	97.0
Vestal, NY	121,540	125,490	96.9
Vestavia Hills, AL	549,726	591,583	92.9
Webster, NY	526,580	555,646	94.8
Wellesley, MA	2,294,912	2,433,932	94.3
West Fargo, ND	114,611	113,643	100.9
West Lafayette, IN	108,074	104,039	103.9
Weston, FL	2,875,505	3,051,450	94.2
Wilmette, IL	4,660,614	4,867,782	95.7
Yorba Linda, CA	6,501,303	6,688,063	97.2
Zionsville, IN	961,597	1,007,171	95.5
U.S.	156,765,322	161,792,840	96.9

Note: Figures cover the Metropolitan Statistical Area (MSA)—see Appendix B for areas included
Source: U.S. Census Bureau, 2012-2016 American Community Survey 5-Year Estimates

Gross Metropolitan Product

MSA[1]	2014	2015	2016	2017	Rank[2]
Aberdeen, SD	n/a	n/a	n/a	n/a	n/a
Aliso Viejo, CA	864.6	905.9	934.3	978.2	2
Allen, TX	502.3	524.8	545.3	577.5	4
Ames, IA	4.7	4.9	5.0	5.2	318
Amherst, MA	24.7	25.5	26.1	27.0	95
Apex, NC	71.4	75.9	79.7	84.8	44
Beavercreek, OH	37.7	38.9	40.1	41.7	69
Bellevue, NE	57.3	58.4	60.6	63.5	52
Bend, OR	7.0	7.6	7.9	8.3	230
Benicia, CA	18.0	18.8	19.5	20.5	126
Bentonville, AR	24.8	26.1	27.3	29.0	94
Bethlehem, NY	49.2	50.8	52.0	54.0	58
Blacksburg, VA	6.6	6.9	7.0	7.2	246
Bowie, MD	470.5	489.8	506.6	531.3	6
Bozeman, MT	n/a	n/a	n/a	n/a	n/a
Brentwood, TN	105.5	110.4	114.6	120.8	34
Burlington, VT	12.6	12.9	13.3	13.8	170
Cabot, AR	38.2	39.0	40.2	42.3	68
Carmel, IN	126.0	130.8	135.5	142.0	26
Cedar Falls, IA	9.5	9.4	9.6	10.0	206
Cedar Park, TX	114.8	119.5	125.3	133.1	32
Central, LA	51.2	52.8	54.6	57.4	57
Chapel Hill, NC	43.4	45.5	47.3	50.2	61
Cheshire, CT	44.4	45.9	47.1	49.0	60
Chino Hills, CA	133.6	142.4	147.1	155.0	23
Cibolo, TX	104.3	108.3	112.7	118.9	35
Cicero, NY	31.1	31.7	32.4	33.5	80
Collierville, TN	69.2	71.3	73.1	76.3	47
Coppell, TX	502.3	524.8	545.3	577.5	4
Cornelius, NC	143.2	151.6	157.9	167.4	22
Cranberry, PA	134.7	138.6	142.1	147.9	24
Crown Point, IN	603.1	629.4	644.1	670.5	3
Dublin, OH	116.4	121.8	126.5	132.9	31
East Fishkill, NY	1,551.3	1,613.8	1,664.0	1,735.1	1
Eden Prairie, MN	236.4	248.1	256.9	268.8	13
Edmond, OK	72.5	72.7	73.8	77.6	46
Edwardsville, IL	147.6	152.2	156.4	162.5	21
Evesham, NJ	389.2	403.6	416.4	433.9	8
Flower Mound, TX	502.3	524.8	545.3	577.5	4
Folsom, CA	112.4	119.0	123.2	130.0	33
Friendswood, TX	523.1	498.5	491.3	526.0	5
Gaines, MI	51.5	53.8	55.1	57.1	56
Glastonbury, CT	84.7	87.8	89.7	93.0	40
Grand Blanc, MI	13.1	13.4	13.6	14.1	168
Hampden, PA	32.0	33.3	34.2	35.5	78
Hilliard, OH	116.4	121.8	126.5	132.9	31
Hillsborough, NJ	1,551.3	1,613.8	1,664.0	1,735.1	1
Holly Springs, NC	71.4	75.9	79.7	84.8	44
Independence, KY	120.1	124.7	128.8	134.7	28
Juneau, AK	n/a	n/a	n/a	n/a	n/a
Kaysville, UT	23.6	24.8	25.9	27.5	100
Keller, TX	502.3	524.8	545.3	577.5	4
Lafayette, CA	411.0	438.2	456.5	481.4	7
Lafayette, CO	22.3	22.8	23.5	24.6	109
Lake Oswego, OR	157.3	167.7	173.9	183.9	20
Laramie, WY	n/a	n/a	n/a	n/a	n/a
Leander, TX	114.8	119.5	125.3	133.1	32
Leawood, KS	119.6	123.6	128.1	134.2	29
Lee's Summit, MO	119.6	123.6	128.1	134.2	29
Leesburg, VA	470.5	489.8	506.6	531.3	6
Lehi, UT	19.3	20.7	21.9	23.5	119
Lexington, MA	378.8	395.4	408.9	428.2	9
Los Altos, CA	213.3	227.0	236.7	250.9	15
Loveland, CO	14.3	15.2	16.0	17.1	149
Lower Macungie, PA	35.2	36.5	37.5	39.0	75
Madison, AL	23.9	24.8	25.7	27.0	101
Madison, MS	28.6	29.6	30.6	32.2	85
Maple Valley, WA	297.9	314.1	324.1	339.1	12
Marion, IA	17.6	17.9	18.5	19.2	131

Table continued on next page.

MSA[1]	2014	2015	2016	2017	Rank[2]
Marlboro, NJ	1,551.3	1,613.8	1,664.0	1,735.1	1
Mason, OH	120.1	124.7	128.8	134.7	28
Menomonee Falls, WI	96.2	99.0	101.8	106.2	38
Meridian, ID	29.0	30.2	31.4	33.1	84
Meridian, MI	20.9	21.7	22.4	23.1	114
Merrimack, NH	24.5	25.0	25.8	27.0	98
Milton, GA	323.7	340.7	353.3	371.2	10
Moon, PA	134.7	138.6	142.1	147.9	24
Moorpark, CA	46.8	48.4	49.7	52.1	59
Morgantown, WV	7.1	6.7	6.9	7.3	249
Mount Pleasant, SC	34.2	36.0	37.6	39.8	76
Newark, DE	389.2	403.6	416.4	433.9	8
Newtown, CT	96.3	100.4	103.6	108.2	37
North Attleborough, MA	75.7	78.4	80.9	84.2	43
North Port, FL	27.2	29.0	30.2	31.9	87
North Ridgeville, OH	123.1	126.3	129.3	134.6	27
Northville, MI	234.8	243.5	249.8	258.6	14
O'Fallon, MO	147.6	152.2	156.4	162.5	21
Orchard Park, NY	54.6	56.2	57.5	59.7	53
Oro Valley, AZ	36.0	36.8	38.0	40.1	74
Oviedo, FL	115.8	123.3	129.4	137.2	30
Parker, CO	186.6	194.3	201.7	213.9	18
Parkland, FL	298.8	316.4	328.9	345.9	11
Peachtree City, GA	323.7	340.7	353.3	371.2	10
Pittsfield, MI	20.3	21.0	21.8	22.7	116
Plainfield, IL	603.1	629.4	644.1	670.5	3
Pleasant Grove, UT	19.3	20.7	21.9	23.5	119
Poway, CA	206.3	217.0	224.2	235.8	17
Princeton, NJ	29.8	31.4	32.5	33.9	81
Queen Creek, AZ	217.0	225.4	234.6	249.2	16
Radnor, PA	389.2	403.6	416.4	433.9	8
Randolph, NJ	1,551.3	1,613.8	1,664.0	1,735.1	1
Rexburg, ID	n/a	n/a	n/a	n/a	n/a
Rio Rancho, NM	41.6	41.3	42.4	44.3	64
Rye, NY	1,551.3	1,613.8	1,664.0	1,735.1	1
Sammamish, WA	297.9	314.1	324.1	339.1	12
San Ramon, CA	411.0	438.2	456.5	481.4	7
Saratoga, CA	213.3	227.0	236.7	250.9	15
Shrewsbury, MA	37.6	38.9	39.8	41.5	70
South Brunswick, NJ	1,551.3	1,613.8	1,664.0	1,735.1	1
South Jordan, UT	74.9	78.6	81.5	86.5	42
South Kingstown, RI	75.7	78.4	80.9	84.2	43
South Portland, ME	27.2	27.9	28.6	29.8	90
Sparks, NV	21.0	21.8	22.6	24.1	112
State College, PA	7.7	8.0	8.2	8.5	225
Sugar Land, TX	523.1	498.5	491.3	526.0	5
Sun Prairie, WI	43.6	45.3	47.1	49.5	62
Syracuse, UT	23.6	24.8	25.9	27.5	100
Tredyffrin, PA	389.2	403.6	416.4	433.9	8
Upper Dublin, PA	389.2	403.6	416.4	433.9	8
Urbandale, IA	45.0	45.2	46.8	49.1	63
Vestal, NY	9.1	9.1	9.2	9.5	211
Vestavia Hills, AL	62.5	64.9	66.7	69.5	50
Webster, NY	52.9	54.4	55.5	57.4	55
Wellesley, MA	378.8	395.4	408.9	428.2	9
West Fargo, ND	15.2	15.8	16.3	17.1	145
West Lafayette, IN	9.7	10.0	10.4	10.9	200
Weston, FL	298.8	316.4	328.9	345.9	11
Wilmette, IL	603.1	629.4	644.1	670.5	3
Yorba Linda, CA	864.6	905.9	934.3	978.2	2
Zionsville, IN	126.0	130.8	135.5	142.0	26

Note: Figures are in billions of dollars; (1) Metropolitan Statistical Area—see Appendix B for areas included; (2) Rank is based on 2015 data and ranges from 1 to 381.

Source: The U.S. Conference of Mayors, U.S. Metro Economies: GMP and Employment Report 2015-2017

Economic Growth

Area	2012-14 (%)	2015 (%)	2016 (%)	2017 (%)	Rank[2]
Aberdeen, SD	n/a	n/a	n/a	n/a	n/a
Aliso Viejo, CA	1.8	3.3	1.8	2.8	134
Allen, TX	6.7	7.1	2.4	3.4	7
Ames, IA	1.3	2.6	1.5	2.3	176
Amherst, MA	0.3	0.9	0.1	1.5	270
Apex, NC	3.5	4.5	3.5	4.4	41
Beavercreek, OH	-0.6	1.5	1.4	1.9	318
Bellevue, NE	2.2	0.3	2.5	2.8	111
Bend, OR	4.8	6.8	3.2	4.0	19
Benicia, CA	3.1	3.1	2.2	3.7	58
Bentonville, AR	4.4	4.1	3.2	4.5	24
Bethlehem, NY	1.8	1.1	0.8	1.7	139
Blacksburg, VA	0.0	2.2	0.1	1.2	286
Bowie, MD	0.0	2.2	1.9	2.7	285
Bozeman, MT	n/a	n/a	n/a	n/a	n/a
Brentwood, TN	2.9	2.9	2.4	3.3	66
Burlington, VT	-0.9	1.0	1.5	2.2	339
Cabot, AR	0.7	1.6	1.8	3.2	235
Carmel, IN	2.2	1.7	2.2	2.9	110
Cedar Falls, IA	-0.9	-2.4	1.1	2.5	337
Cedar Park, TX	5.2	5.8	3.3	3.9	14
Central, LA	1.2	4.1	2.0	2.9	182
Chapel Hill, NC	4.3	3.1	2.5	4.0	25
Cheshire, CT	0.6	1.1	1.0	2.0	238
Chino Hills, CA	2.7	4.9	1.9	3.4	72
Cibolo, TX	4.0	5.5	2.3	3.1	27
Cicero, NY	-0.5	-0.1	0.5	1.6	311
Collierville, TN	0.1	1.2	1.3	2.5	281
Coppell, TX	6.7	7.1	2.4	3.4	7
Cornelius, NC	3.3	3.8	2.7	4.0	48
Cranberry, PA	2.0	1.7	0.9	2.0	125
Crown Point, IN	0.4	2.3	0.9	2.1	256
Dublin, OH	1.6	2.6	2.3	3.0	155
East Fishkill, NY	1.6	1.9	1.6	2.2	151
Eden Prairie, MN	2.7	3.1	2.1	2.6	77
Edmond, OK	2.6	3.4	-0.4	2.3	81
Edwardsville, IL	0.5	1.3	1.3	1.9	253
Evesham, NJ	0.9	2.2	1.6	2.1	216
Flower Mound, TX	6.7	7.1	2.4	3.4	7
Folsom, CA	1.6	4.3	2.1	3.4	149
Friendswood, TX	3.9	0.3	-2.0	3.9	33
Gaines, MI	3.9	2.1	1.1	1.7	32
Glastonbury, CT	0.5	1.3	0.7	1.8	249
Grand Blanc, MI	0.9	0.7	0.0	1.6	212
Hampden, PA	0.3	2.5	1.3	1.8	269
Hilliard, OH	1.6	2.6	2.3	3.0	155
Hillsborough, NJ	1.6	1.9	1.6	2.2	151
Holly Springs, NC	3.5	4.5	3.5	4.4	41
Independence, KY	1.3	2.0	1.8	2.6	174
Juneau, AK	n/a	n/a	n/a	n/a	n/a
Kaysville, UT	3.7	4.1	2.5	3.7	35
Keller, TX	6.7	7.1	2.4	3.4	7
Lafayette, CA	3.6	5.2	2.8	3.5	39
Lafayette, CO	3.9	1.6	1.2	2.9	29
Lake Oswego, OR	0.5	4.0	2.0	3.5	247
Laramie, WY	n/a	n/a	n/a	n/a	n/a
Leander, TX	5.2	5.8	3.3	3.9	14
Leawood, KS	0.8	1.7	2.1	2.7	218
Lee's Summit, MO	0.8	1.7	2.1	2.7	218
Leesburg, VA	0.0	2.2	1.9	2.7	285
Lehi, UT	3.9	6.6	3.9	5.1	30
Lexington, MA	1.2	2.1	1.4	2.6	185
Los Altos, CA	6.5	5.2	3.1	4.2	8
Loveland, CO	4.7	6.3	3.5	4.9	20
Lower Macungie, PA	1.7	2.1	1.3	2.0	148
Madison, AL	1.9	2.6	1.9	2.9	129
Madison, MS	1.1	2.0	2.2	3.1	198
Maple Valley, WA	2.5	3.8	1.9	2.8	93
Marion, IA	1.5	0.3	1.8	2.6	161

Table continued on next page.

Area	2012-14 (%)	2015 (%)	2016 (%)	2017 (%)	Rank[2]
Marlboro, NJ	1.6	1.9	1.6	2.2	151
Mason, OH	1.3	2.0	1.8	2.6	174
Menomonee Falls, WI	0.5	1.1	1.4	2.3	246
Meridian, ID	2.8	2.8	2.5	3.1	67
Meridian, MI	2.4	1.5	1.6	1.6	97
Merrimack, NH	1.1	0.0	2.0	2.8	200
Milton, GA	2.8	3.2	2.3	3.1	71
Moon, PA	2.0	1.7	0.9	2.0	125
Moorpark, CA	1.1	2.3	1.3	2.9	201
Morgantown, WV	3.3	4.3	0.0	2.9	51
Mount Pleasant, SC	1.8	3.0	2.9	3.9	137
Newark, DE	0.9	2.2	1.6	2.1	216
Newtown, CT	0.7	1.9	1.8	2.5	234
North Attleborough, MA	1.4	1.3	1.4	2.1	164
North Port, FL	3.8	4.6	2.6	3.6	34
North Ridgeville, OH	0.3	0.7	0.9	2.1	273
Northville, MI	2.1	1.5	1.2	1.6	115
O'Fallon, MO	0.5	1.3	1.3	1.9	253
Orchard Park, NY	0.7	0.7	0.9	1.8	229
Oro Valley, AZ	0.4	0.9	1.8	3.3	258
Oviedo, FL	2.8	4.2	3.4	4.0	70
Parker, CO	3.7	4.0	2.3	3.7	36
Parkland, FL	2.9	3.6	2.5	3.2	63
Peachtree City, GA	2.8	3.2	2.3	3.1	71
Pittsfield, MI	1.3	1.8	2.6	2.0	180
Plainfield, IL	0.4	2.3	0.9	2.1	256
Pleasant Grove, UT	3.9	6.6	3.9	5.1	30
Poway, CA	1.5	3.7	1.8	3.1	162
Princeton, NJ	1.3	3.4	2.1	2.1	178
Queen Creek, AZ	1.9	2.4	2.5	4.1	127
Radnor, PA	0.9	2.2	1.6	2.1	216
Randolph, NJ	1.6	1.9	1.6	2.2	151
Rexburg, ID	n/a	n/a	n/a	n/a	n/a
Rio Rancho, NM	-0.7	0.5	1.0	2.1	321
Rye, NY	1.6	1.9	1.6	2.2	151
Sammamish, WA	2.5	3.8	1.9	2.8	93
San Ramon, CA	3.6	5.2	2.8	3.5	39
Saratoga, CA	6.5	5.2	3.1	4.2	8
Shrewsbury, MA	1.1	1.0	0.4	2.0	194
South Brunswick, NJ	1.6	1.9	1.6	2.2	151
South Jordan, UT	2.4	3.8	1.9	3.8	102
South Kingstown, RI	1.4	1.3	1.4	2.1	164
South Portland, ME	-0.6	0.4	1.2	2.1	316
Sparks, NV	2.6	3.1	1.9	4.4	86
State College, PA	3.1	3.2	1.2	2.3	57
Sugar Land, TX	3.9	0.3	-2.0	3.9	33
Sun Prairie, WI	1.7	2.6	2.4	3.1	143
Syracuse, UT	3.7	4.1	2.5	3.7	35
Tredyffrin, PA	0.9	2.2	1.6	2.1	216
Upper Dublin, PA	0.9	2.2	1.6	2.1	216
Urbandale, IA	1.8	-1.1	2.2	2.9	138
Vestal, NY	-0.9	-1.2	-0.2	1.5	340
Vestavia Hills, AL	1.5	2.2	1.3	2.2	159
Webster, NY	-0.5	0.8	0.4	1.5	314
Wellesley, MA	1.2	2.1	1.4	2.6	185
West Fargo, ND	2.6	4.1	1.5	3.1	79
West Lafayette, IN	2.1	2.4	2.0	2.6	117
Weston, FL	2.9	3.6	2.5	3.2	63
Wilmette, IL	0.4	2.3	0.9	2.1	256
Yorba Linda, CA	1.8	3.3	1.8	2.8	134
Zionsville, IN	2.2	1.7	2.2	2.9	110
U.S.	2.0	2.4	1.9	2.6	–

Note: Figures are real gross metropolitan product (GMP) growth rates and represent annual average percent change; (1) Metropolitan Statistical Area—see Appendix B for areas included; (2) Rank is based on 2012-2014 average annual percent change and ranges from 1 to 381

Source: The U.S. Conference of Mayors, U.S. Metro Economies: GMP and Employment Report 2015-2017

Metropolitan Area Exports

Area	2011	2012	2013	2014	2015	2016	Rank[2]
Aberdeen, SD	n/a	n/a	n/a	n/a	n/a	n/a	n/a
Aliso Viejo, CA	72,688.9	75,007.5	76,305.7	75,471.2	61,758.7	61,245.7	4
Allen, TX	26,648.7	27,820.9	27,596.0	28,669.4	27,372.9	27,187.8	9
Ames, IA	256.0	251.2	253.3	274.9	261.7	316.7	244
Amherst, MA	949.1	928.8	816.9	914.0	868.9	820.0	170
Apex, NC	2,254.4	2,308.1	2,280.6	2,713.1	2,553.4	2,620.4	81
Beavercreek, OH	2,749.2	2,790.4	2,740.1	3,026.1	2,991.1	2,874.5	78
Bellevue, NE	2,658.0	3,529.3	4,255.9	4,528.5	3,753.4	3,509.7	68
Bend, OR	87.3	93.5	119.0	114.9	149.3	214.8	292
Benicia, CA	484.1	721.4	564.3	516.3	564.6	574.7	196
Bentonville, AR	568.2	667.6	699.1	786.9	710.1	682.8	184
Bethlehem, NY	3,525.1	3,420.1	3,946.1	4,547.0	4,470.3	4,135.0	59
Blacksburg, VA	994.0	844.3	753.4	1,042.5	1,070.3	794.6	176
Bowie, MD	10,237.9	14,609.7	16,225.0	13,053.6	13,900.4	13,582.4	22
Bozeman, MT	n/a	n/a	n/a	n/a	n/a	n/a	n/a
Brentwood, TN	5,878.7	6,402.1	8,702.8	9,620.9	9,353.0	9,460.1	32
Burlington, VT	3,656.8	3,572.0	3,434.5	3,012.6	2,089.4	1,404.7	120
Cabot, AR	892.4	2,418.9	2,497.5	2,463.5	1,777.5	1,871.0	99
Carmel, IN	9,560.7	10,436.0	9,747.5	9,539.4	9,809.4	9,655.4	30
Cedar Falls, IA	220.4	371.9	300.3	361.5	305.8	276.3	268
Cedar Park, TX	8,626.3	8,976.6	8,870.8	9,400.0	10,094.5	10,682.7	26
Central, LA	4,864.6	5,820.2	6,261.5	7,528.3	6,505.4	6,580.5	46
Chapel Hill, NC	2,640.3	2,723.2	2,971.7	2,934.0	2,807.2	2,937.4	77
Cheshire, CT	1,856.7	1,965.3	1,903.9	1,834.5	1,756.3	1,819.8	107
Chino Hills, CA	7,070.4	7,986.4	9,569.0	9,134.8	8,970.0	10,211.6	28
Cibolo, TX	10,506.5	14,010.2	19,287.6	25,781.8	15,919.2	5,621.2	49
Cicero, NY	2,054.1	1,915.5	1,753.3	1,922.5	1,930.3	1,853.1	103
Collierville, TN	11,978.6	11,360.1	11,276.4	11,002.0	11,819.5	11,628.7	25
Coppell, TX	26,648.7	27,820.9	27,596.0	28,669.4	27,372.9	27,187.8	9
Cornelius, NC	6,253.3	6,322.6	10,684.1	12,885.3	13,985.8	11,944.1	24
Cranberry, PA	15,165.5	14,134.7	10,444.4	10,015.8	9,137.1	7,971.0	39
Crown Point, IN	39,522.4	40,568.0	44,910.6	47,340.1	44,820.9	43,932.7	5
Dublin, OH	4,327.5	5,488.6	5,731.4	6,245.6	6,201.6	5,675.4	48
East Fishkill, NY	105,102.0	102,298.0	106,922.8	105,266.6	95,645.4	89,649.5	1
Eden Prairie, MN	26,189.1	25,155.7	23,747.5	21,198.2	19,608.6	18,329.2	19
Edmond, OK	1,592.8	1,574.6	1,581.7	1,622.0	1,353.1	1,260.0	130
Edwardsville, IL	12,307.6	14,642.3	12,393.6	10,359.8	8,913.7	8,346.5	38
Evesham, NJ	26,155.8	22,991.6	24,929.2	26,321.3	24,236.1	21,359.9	14
Flower Mound, TX	26,648.7	27,820.9	27,596.0	28,669.4	27,372.9	27,187.8	9
Folsom, CA	4,686.0	5,194.6	5,777.1	7,143.9	8,101.2	7,032.1	43
Friendswood, TX	104,457.3	110,297.8	114,962.6	118,966.0	97,054.3	84,105.5	2
Gaines, MI	2,791.9	3,156.4	5,314.8	5,244.5	5,143.0	5,168.5	52
Glastonbury, CT	9,321.6	9,680.4	10,152.2	10,463.9	10,092.4	10,412.4	27
Grand Blanc, MI	367.6	399.2	474.6	561.3	582.8	611.9	192
Hampden, PA	2,595.7	2,894.4	3,030.4	3,052.8	2,926.2	2,252.5	89
Hilliard, OH	4,327.5	5,488.6	5,731.4	6,245.6	6,201.6	5,675.4	48
Hillsborough, NJ	105,102.0	102,298.0	106,922.8	105,266.6	95,645.4	89,649.5	1
Holly Springs, NC	2,254.4	2,308.1	2,280.6	2,713.1	2,553.4	2,620.4	81
Independence, KY	18,744.2	19,966.8	20,976.4	22,280.7	24,127.0	26,326.2	11
Juneau, AK	n/a	n/a	n/a	n/a	n/a	n/a	n/a
Kaysville, UT	896.5	855.5	1,310.0	1,363.6	1,415.6	1,602.2	110
Keller, TX	26,648.7	27,820.9	27,596.0	28,669.4	27,372.9	27,187.8	9
Lafayette, CA	23,573.8	23,031.7	25,305.3	26,863.7	25,061.1	24,506.3	12
Lafayette, CO	946.7	1,128.0	1,046.0	1,016.1	1,039.1	956.3	158
Lake Oswego, OR	20,875.7	20,337.7	17,606.8	18,667.2	18,847.8	20,256.8	17
Laramie, WY	n/a	n/a	n/a	n/a	n/a	n/a	n/a
Leander, TX	8,626.3	8,976.6	8,870.8	9,400.0	10,094.5	10,682.7	26
Leawood, KS	7,958.9	7,880.8	8,012.1	8,262.9	6,723.2	6,709.8	44
Lee's Summit, MO	7,958.9	7,880.8	8,012.1	8,262.9	6,723.2	6,709.8	44
Leesburg, VA	10,237.9	14,609.7	16,225.0	13,053.6	13,900.4	13,582.4	22
Lehi, UT	2,056.4	2,058.1	2,789.2	2,533.4	2,216.4	1,894.8	98
Lexington, MA	22,292.8	21,234.8	22,212.8	23,378.5	21,329.5	21,168.0	15
Los Altos, CA	26,712.1	26,687.7	23,413.1	21,128.8	19,827.2	21,716.8	13
Loveland, CO	812.7	861.7	986.1	1,037.4	990.7	993.8	155
Lower Macungie, PA	2,955.2	2,939.0	2,949.9	3,152.5	3,439.9	3,657.2	65
Madison, AL	1,293.3	1,491.5	1,518.7	1,440.4	1,344.7	1,827.3	106
Madison, MS	829.9	942.8	1,252.8	1,229.0	1,336.1	1,261.6	129
Maple Valley, WA	41,117.5	50,301.7	56,686.4	61,938.4	67,226.4	61,881.0	3
Marion, IA	880.8	889.1	930.2	879.0	873.5	945.0	159

Table continued on next page.

Area	2011	2012	2013	2014	2015	2016	Rank[2]
Marlboro, NJ	105,102.0	102,298.0	106,922.8	105,266.6	95,645.4	89,649.5	1
Mason, OH	18,744.2	19,966.8	20,976.4	22,280.7	24,127.0	26,326.2	11
Menomonee Falls, WI	8,826.3	9,175.6	8,874.6	8,696.0	7,953.6	7,256.2	42
Meridian, ID	4,131.5	4,088.2	3,657.9	3,143.4	2,668.0	3,021.7	76
Meridian, MI	863.1	756.0	864.9	936.0	852.5	936.3	162
Merrimack, NH	2,494.1	1,634.9	1,445.8	1,575.4	1,556.6	1,465.2	117
Milton, GA	17,229.1	18,169.1	18,827.9	19,870.3	19,163.9	20,480.1	16
Moon, PA	15,165.5	14,134.7	10,444.4	10,015.8	9,137.1	7,971.0	39
Moorpark, CA	2,919.8	2,854.6	2,893.9	2,882.4	2,991.7	3,300.6	71
Morgantown, WV	58.7	75.9	53.9	61.4	71.6	59.4	356
Mount Pleasant, SC	2,299.4	2,429.8	3,464.3	5,866.7	6,457.5	9,508.1	31
Newark, DE	26,155.8	22,991.6	24,929.2	26,321.3	24,236.1	21,359.9	14
Newtown, CT	11,250.4	10,332.6	11,055.2	12,103.0	9,207.5	8,556.2	37
North Attleborough, MA	7,139.1	5,830.8	6,609.0	6,595.1	5,048.8	6,595.7	45
North Port, FL	804.3	804.5	869.7	837.9	760.0	624.5	189
North Ridgeville, OH	11,276.1	11,063.7	11,137.9	10,706.5	9,629.7	8,752.9	34
Northville, MI	49,422.8	55,387.3	53,906.5	50,279.3	44,348.6	42,131.7	6
O'Fallon, MO	12,307.6	14,642.3	12,393.6	10,359.8	8,913.7	8,346.5	38
Orchard Park, NY	4,179.7	4,305.1	4,376.6	4,798.7	4,684.6	4,783.4	55
Oro Valley, AZ	2,310.0	2,508.3	2,589.9	2,277.4	2,485.9	2,563.9	82
Oviedo, FL	3,230.0	3,850.6	3,227.7	3,134.8	3,082.7	3,363.9	70
Parker, CO	3,771.3	3,355.8	3,618.4	4,958.6	3,909.5	3,649.3	66
Parkland, FL	43,129.9	47,858.7	41,771.5	37,969.5	33,258.5	32,734.5	7
Peachtree City, GA	17,229.1	18,169.1	18,827.9	19,870.3	19,163.9	20,480.1	16
Pittsfield, MI	1,129.5	1,053.4	1,156.2	1,213.6	1,053.0	1,207.9	134
Plainfield, IL	39,522.4	40,568.0	44,910.6	47,340.1	44,820.9	43,932.7	5
Pleasant Grove, UT	2,056.4	2,058.1	2,789.2	2,533.4	2,216.4	1,894.8	98
Poway, CA	17,410.5	17,183.3	17,885.5	18,585.7	17,439.7	18,086.6	20
Princeton, NJ	754.1	713.0	879.2	947.1	812.9	969.6	156
Queen Creek, AZ	10,914.4	10,834.3	11,473.5	12,764.4	13,821.5	12,838.2	23
Radnor, PA	26,155.8	22,991.6	24,929.2	26,321.3	24,236.1	21,359.9	14
Randolph, NJ	105,102.0	102,298.0	106,922.8	105,266.6	95,645.4	89,649.5	1
Rexburg, ID	n/a	n/a	n/a	n/a	n/a	n/a	n/a
Rio Rancho, NM	951.9	1,790.6	1,389.6	1,564.0	1,761.2	999.7	153
Rye, NY	105,102.0	102,298.0	106,922.8	105,266.6	95,645.4	89,649.5	1
Sammamish, WA	41,117.5	50,301.7	56,686.4	61,938.4	67,226.4	61,881.0	3
San Ramon, CA	23,573.8	23,031.7	25,305.3	26,863.7	25,061.1	24,506.3	12
Saratoga, CA	26,712.1	26,687.7	23,413.1	21,128.8	19,827.2	21,716.8	13
Shrewsbury, MA	2,397.0	2,966.2	3,393.6	3,126.6	3,144.1	3,093.5	73
South Brunswick, NJ	105,102.0	102,298.0	106,922.8	105,266.6	95,645.4	89,649.5	1
South Jordan, UT	15,579.2	15,990.0	11,867.2	8,361.5	10,380.5	8,653.7	36
South Kingstown, RI	7,139.1	5,830.8	6,609.0	6,595.1	5,048.8	6,595.7	45
South Portland, ME	1,670.8	1,200.6	881.0	1,053.1	1,140.9	1,248.2	131
Sparks, NV	1,687.4	2,019.0	2,117.4	2,138.9	1,943.3	2,382.1	86
State College, PA	225.1	234.8	218.0	232.0	225.4	221.6	291
Sugar Land, TX	104,457.3	110,297.8	114,962.6	118,966.0	97,054.3	84,105.5	2
Sun Prairie, WI	1,958.1	2,168.7	2,292.1	2,369.5	2,280.4	2,204.8	91
Syracuse, UT	896.5	855.5	1,310.0	1,363.6	1,415.6	1,602.2	110
Tredyffrin, PA	26,155.8	22,991.6	24,929.2	26,321.3	24,236.1	21,359.9	14
Upper Dublin, PA	26,155.8	22,991.6	24,929.2	26,321.3	24,236.1	21,359.9	14
Urbandale, IA	970.1	1,183.2	1,279.4	1,361.8	1,047.8	1,052.2	147
Vestal, NY	605.6	508.3	388.5	471.0	431.4	404.8	226
Vestavia Hills, AL	2,383.3	1,939.2	1,865.3	1,803.5	1,791.2	1,870.2	100
Webster, NY	5,492.9	5,329.8	5,092.0	5,150.2	5,038.4	4,627.5	56
Wellesley, MA	22,292.8	21,234.8	22,212.8	23,378.5	21,329.5	21,168.0	15
West Fargo, ND	730.8	785.9	817.9	782.8	543.2	474.5	211
West Lafayette, IN	655.5	711.5	659.1	653.7	630.7	713.4	180
Weston, FL	43,129.9	47,858.7	41,771.5	37,969.5	33,258.5	32,734.5	7
Wilmette, IL	39,522.4	40,568.0	44,910.6	47,340.1	44,820.9	43,932.7	5
Yorba Linda, CA	72,688.9	75,007.5	76,305.7	75,471.2	61,758.7	61,245.7	4
Zionsville, IN	9,560.7	10,436.0	9,747.5	9,539.4	9,809.4	9,655.4	30

Note: Figures are in millions of dollars; (1) Metropolitan Statistical Area—see Appendix B for areas included; (2) Rank is based on 2016 data and ranges from 1 to 385; n/a not available

Source: U.S. Department of Commerce, International Trade Administration, Office of Trade & Industry Information, Manufacturing & Services, data extracted March 15, 2018

Building Permits: City

City	Single-Family			Multi-Family			Total		
	2016	2017	Pct. Chg.	2016	2017	Pct. Chg.	2016	2017	Pct. Chg.
Aberdeen, SD	83	72	-13.3	0	72	-	83	144	73.5
Aliso Viejo, CA	0	0	0.0	69	286	314.5	69	286	314.5
Allen, TX	447	435	-2.7	243	1,044	329.6	690	1,479	114.3
Ames, IA	110	125	13.6	459	625	36.2	569	750	31.8
Amherst, MA	n/a	n/a	n/a	n/a	n/a	n/a	n/a	n/a	n/a
Apex, NC	959	1,388	44.7	212	0	-100.0	1,171	1,388	18.5
Beavercreek, OH	n/a	n/a	n/a	n/a	n/a	n/a	n/a	n/a	n/a
Bellevue, NE	133	162	21.8	4	0	-100.0	137	162	18.2
Bend, OR	1,014	946	-6.7	457	266	-41.8	1,471	1,212	-17.6
Benicia, CA	10	4	-60.0	0	0	0.0	10	4	-60.0
Bentonville, AR	594	459	-22.7	314	444	41.4	908	903	-0.6
Bethlehem, NY	94	67	-28.7	46	0	-100.0	140	67	-52.1
Blacksburg, VA	132	98	-25.8	84	0	-100.0	216	98	-54.6
Bowie, MD	n/a	n/a	n/a	n/a	n/a	n/a	n/a	n/a	n/a
Bozeman, MT	373	403	8.0	365	419	14.8	738	822	11.4
Brentwood, TN	175	185	5.7	0	0	0.0	175	185	5.7
Burlington, VT	n/a	n/a	n/a	n/a	n/a	n/a	n/a	n/a	n/a
Cabot, AR	86	96	11.6	0	16	-	86	112	30.2
Carmel, IN	423	452	6.9	8	305	3,712.5	431	757	75.6
Cedar Falls, IA	151	121	-19.9	78	7	-91.0	229	128	-44.1
Cedar Park, TX	535	399	-25.4	411	31	-92.5	946	430	-54.5
Central, LA	175	146	-16.6	0	0	0.0	175	146	-16.6
Chapel Hill, NC	38	71	86.8	88	477	442.0	126	548	334.9
Cheshire, CT	29	22	-24.1	0	0	0.0	29	22	-24.1
Chino Hills, CA	119	377	216.8	331	656	98.2	450	1,033	129.6
Cibolo, TX	377	308	-18.3	0	136	-	377	444	17.8
Cicero, NY	36	46	27.8	0	0	0.0	36	46	27.8
Collierville, TN	177	195	10.2	207	0	-100.0	384	195	-49.2
Coppell, TX	140	95	-32.1	0	0	0.0	140	95	-32.1
Cornelius, NC	n/a	n/a	n/a	n/a	n/a	n/a	n/a	n/a	n/a
Cranberry, PA	132	157	18.9	48	310	545.8	180	467	159.4
Crown Point, IN	218	279	28.0	42	27	-35.7	260	306	17.7
Dublin, OH	148	258	74.3	482	30	-93.8	630	288	-54.3
East Fishkill, NY	62	69	11.3	0	0	0.0	62	69	11.3
Eden Prairie, MN	50	60	20.0	0	0	0.0	50	60	20.0
Edmond, OK	394	526	33.5	6	74	1,133.3	400	600	50.0
Edwardsville, IL	31	31	0.0	0	5	-	31	36	16.1
Evesham, NJ	13	49	276.9	64	18	-71.9	77	67	-13.0
Flower Mound, TX	397	467	17.6	670	0	-100.0	1,067	467	-56.2
Folsom, CA	157	139	-11.5	4	355	8,775.0	161	494	206.8
Friendswood, TX	173	182	5.2	0	0	0.0	173	182	5.2
Gaines, MI	n/a	n/a	n/a	n/a	n/a	n/a	n/a	n/a	n/a
Glastonbury, CT	30	38	26.7	4	0	-100.0	34	38	11.8
Grand Blanc, MI	1	60	5,900.0	0	0	0.0	1	60	5,900.0
Hampden, PA	129	127	-1.6	120	52	-56.7	249	179	-28.1
Hilliard, OH	74	98	32.4	122	2	-98.4	196	100	-49.0
Hillsborough, NJ	63	73	15.9	48	116	141.7	111	189	70.3
Holly Springs, NC	683	633	-7.3	0	0	0.0	683	633	-7.3
Independence, KY	156	130	-16.7	41	32	-22.0	197	162	-17.8
Juneau, AK	50	46	-8.0	103	18	-82.5	153	64	-58.2
Kaysville, UT	170	132	-22.4	0	0	0.0	170	132	-22.4
Keller, TX	138	105	-23.9	0	0	0.0	138	105	-23.9
Lafayette, CA	n/a	n/a	n/a	n/a	n/a	n/a	n/a	n/a	n/a
Lafayette, CO	166	193	16.3	77	78	1.3	243	271	11.5
Lake Oswego, OR	94	101	7.4	200	93	-53.5	294	194	-34.0
Laramie, WY	60	40	-33.3	28	8	-71.4	88	48	-45.5
Leander, TX	1,551	1,608	3.7	255	270	5.9	1,806	1,878	4.0
Leawood, KS	45	54	20.0	18	0	-100.0	63	54	-14.3
Lee's Summit, MO	333	396	18.9	194	379	95.4	527	775	47.1
Leesburg, VA	n/a	n/a	n/a	n/a	n/a	n/a	n/a	n/a	n/a
Lehi, UT	616	934	51.6	0	0	0.0	616	934	51.6
Lexington, MA	87	86	-1.1	0	0	0.0	87	86	-1.1
Los Altos, CA	52	41	-21.2	0	4	0.0	52	45	-13.5
Loveland, CO	392	283	-27.8	180	175	-2.8	572	458	-19.9
Lower Macungie, PA	n/a	n/a	n/a	n/a	n/a	n/a	n/a	n/a	n/a
Madison, AL	490	558	13.9	0	0	0.0	490	558	13.9
Madison, MS	115	118	2.6	0	0	0.0	115	118	2.6

Table continued on next page.

City	Single-Family			Multi-Family			Total		
	2016	2017	Pct. Chg.	2016	2017	Pct. Chg.	2016	2017	Pct. Chg.
Maple Valley, WA	51	117	129.4	0	326	-	51	443	768.6
Marion, IA	161	170	5.6	72	99	37.5	233	269	15.5
Marlboro, NJ	9	87	866.7	0	0	0.0	9	87	866.7
Mason, OH	144	170	18.1	0	0	0.0	144	170	18.1
Menomonee Falls, WI	121	139	14.9	210	0	-100.0	331	139	-58.0
Meridian, ID	1,481	1,594	7.6	88	820	831.8	1,569	2,414	53.9
Meridian, MI	62	66	6.5	74	60	-18.9	136	126	-7.4
Merrimack, NH	n/a	n/a	n/a	n/a	n/a	n/a	n/a	n/a	n/a
Milton, GA	216	207	-4.2	0	0	0.0	216	207	-4.2
Moon, PA	n/a	n/a	n/a	n/a	n/a	n/a	n/a	n/a	n/a
Moorpark, CA	n/a	n/a	n/a	n/a	n/a	n/a	n/a	n/a	n/a
Morgantown, WV	11	11	0.0	2	52	2,500.0	13	63	384.6
Mount Pleasant, SC	959	776	-19.1	591	899	52.1	1,550	1,675	8.1
Newark, DE	21	10	-52.4	224	53	-76.3	245	63	-74.3
Newtown, CT	22	20	-9.1	20	30	50.0	42	50	19.0
North Attleborough, MA	29	42	44.8	0	30	-	29	72	148.3
North Port, FL	890	1,064	19.6	8	24	200.0	898	1,088	21.2
North Ridgeville, OH	193	207	7.3	8	8	0.0	201	215	7.0
Northville, MI	42	90	114.3	19	0	-100.0	61	90	47.5
O'Fallon, MO	383	223	-41.8	126	210	66.7	509	433	-14.9
Orchard Park, NY	56	55	-1.8	0	0	0.0	56	55	-1.8
Oro Valley, AZ	176	217	23.3	0	0	0.0	176	217	23.3
Oviedo, FL	220	273	24.1	281	2	-99.3	501	275	-45.1
Parker, CO	309	414	34.0	380	358	-5.8	689	772	12.0
Parkland, FL	444	436	-1.8	0	0	0.0	444	436	-1.8
Peachtree City, GA	87	282	224.1	0	0	0.0	87	282	224.1
Pittsfield, MI	59	62	5.1	0	0	0.0	59	62	5.1
Plainfield, IL	143	144	0.7	200	0	-100.0	343	144	-58.0
Pleasant Grove, UT	114	66	-42.1	10	5	-50.0	124	71	-42.7
Poway, CA	18	14	-22.2	0	0	0.0	18	14	-22.2
Princeton, NJ	28	41	46.4	0	0	0.0	28	41	46.4
Queen Creek, AZ	1,096	1,076	-1.8	0	0	0.0	1,096	1,076	-1.8
Radnor, PA	18	17	-5.6	3	0	-100.0	21	17	-19.0
Randolph, NJ	37	93	151.4	5	0	-100.0	42	93	121.4
Rexburg, ID	49	63	28.6	293	363	23.9	342	426	24.6
Rio Rancho, NM	698	530	-24.1	32	5	-84.4	730	535	-26.7
Rye, NY	n/a	n/a	n/a	n/a	n/a	n/a	n/a	n/a	n/a
Sammamish, WA	289	367	27.0	96	0	-100.0	385	367	-4.7
San Ramon, CA	2	2	0.0	27	33	22.2	29	35	20.7
Saratoga, CA	21	21	0.0	0	0	0.0	21	21	0.0
Shrewsbury, MA	n/a	n/a	n/a	n/a	n/a	n/a	n/a	n/a	n/a
South Brunswick, NJ	217	72	-66.8	0	0	0.0	217	72	-66.8
South Jordan, UT	850	843	-0.8	9	212	2,255.6	859	1,055	22.8
South Kingstown, RI	53	73	37.7	0	0	0.0	53	73	37.7
South Portland, ME	13	40	207.7	26	96	269.2	39	136	248.7
Sparks, NV	490	602	22.9	417	1,242	197.8	907	1,844	103.3
State College, PA	n/a	n/a	n/a	n/a	n/a	n/a	n/a	n/a	n/a
Sugar Land, TX	162	158	-2.5	351	0	-100.0	513	158	-69.2
Sun Prairie, WI	149	138	-7.4	20	416	1,980.0	169	554	227.8
Syracuse, UT	324	270	-16.7	0	0	0.0	324	270	-16.7
Tredyffrin, PA	63	0	-100.0	0	0	0.0	63	0	-100.0
Upper Dublin, PA	72	69	-4.2	0	20	-	72	89	23.6
Urbandale, IA	159	168	5.7	0	4	-	159	172	8.2
Vestal, NY	n/a	n/a	n/a	n/a	n/a	n/a	n/a	n/a	n/a
Vestavia Hills, AL	104	112	7.7	0	0	0.0	104	112	7.7
Webster, NY	102	90	-11.8	6	123	1,950.0	108	213	97.2
Wellesley, MA	88	57	-35.2	0	0	0.0	88	57	-35.2
West Fargo, ND	409	341	-16.6	65	0	-100.0	474	341	-28.1
West Lafayette, IN	51	36	-29.4	80	362	352.5	131	398	203.8
Weston, FL	20	14	-30.0	0	0	0.0	20	14	-30.0
Wilmette, IL	35	48	37.1	75	14	-81.3	110	62	-43.6
Yorba Linda, CA	126	79	-37.3	0	0	0.0	126	79	-37.3
Zionsville, IN	122	176	44.3	2	28	1,300.0	124	204	64.5
U.S.	750,800	817,300	8.9	455,800	446,800	-2.0	1,206,600	1,264,100	4.8

Note: Figures represent new, privately-owned housing units authorized (unadjusted data); All permit data are based on estimates with imputation

Source: U.S. Census Bureau, Manufacturing, Mining, and Construction Statistics, Building Permits, 2016, 2017

Building Permits: Metro Area

Metro Area	Single-Family			Multi-Family			Total		
	2016	2017	Pct. Chg.	2016	2017	Pct. Chg.	2016	2017	Pct. Chg.
Aberdeen, SD	109	84	-22.9	0	72	-	109	156	43.1
Aliso Viejo, CA	9,307	10,612	14.0	22,701	20,586	-9.3	32,008	31,198	-2.5
Allen, TX	29,846	34,210	14.6	25,772	27,499	6.7	55,618	61,709	11.0
Ames, IA	112	126	12.5	459	625	36.2	571	751	31.5
Amherst, MA	31	42	35.5	2	0	-100.0	33	42	27.3
Apex, NC	9,435	10,785	14.3	4,072	3,428	-15.8	13,507	14,213	5.2
Beavercreek, OH	901	994	10.3	323	176	-45.5	1,224	1,170	-4.4
Bellevue, NE	2,903	3,172	9.3	1,341	1,802	34.4	4,244	4,974	17.2
Bend, OR	1,761	1,741	-1.1	457	320	-30.0	2,218	2,061	-7.1
Benicia, CA	618	615	-0.5	63	0	-100.0	681	615	-9.7
Bentonville, AR	3,414	3,469	1.6	919	1,135	23.5	4,333	4,604	6.3
Bethlehem, NY	1,353	1,200	-11.3	1,437	1,255	-12.7	2,790	2,455	-12.0
Blacksburg, VA	132	98	-25.8	84	0	-100.0	216	98	-54.6
Bowie, MD	12,974	13,968	7.7	11,970	12,461	4.1	24,944	26,429	6.0
Bozeman, MT	1,072	1,045	-2.5	478	567	18.6	1,550	1,612	4.0
Brentwood, TN	12,014	12,625	5.1	6,543	6,667	1.9	18,557	19,292	4.0
Burlington, VT	255	250	-2.0	388	379	-2.3	643	629	-2.2
Cabot, AR	1,624	2,014	24.0	678	1,121	65.3	2,302	3,135	36.2
Carmel, IN	5,643	6,205	10.0	1,911	1,909	-0.1	7,554	8,114	7.4
Cedar Falls, IA	151	121	-19.9	78	7	-91.0	229	128	-44.1
Cedar Park, TX	13,609	15,206	11.7	8,633	10,597	22.7	22,242	25,803	16.0
Central, LA	3,395	3,560	4.9	24	43	79.2	3,419	3,603	5.4
Chapel Hill, NC	2,957	3,268	10.5	1,431	1,656	15.7	4,388	4,924	12.2
Cheshire, CT	189	286	51.3	378	181	-52.1	567	467	-17.6
Chino Hills, CA	7,930	10,089	27.2	2,089	3,890	86.2	10,019	13,979	39.5
Cibolo, TX	6,441	7,513	16.6	3,344	4,996	49.4	9,785	12,509	27.8
Cicero, NY	375	307	-18.1	441	518	17.5	816	825	1.1
Collierville, TN	3,003	3,210	6.9	1,352	693	-48.7	4,355	3,903	-10.4
Coppell, TX	29,846	34,210	14.6	25,772	27,499	6.7	55,618	61,709	11.0
Cornelius, NC	12,989	13,974	7.6	6,364	7,451	17.1	19,353	21,425	10.7
Cranberry, PA	999	1,053	5.4	510	815	59.8	1,509	1,868	23.8
Crown Point, IN	8,118	8,299	2.2	11,351	13,570	19.5	19,469	21,869	12.3
Dublin, OH	4,040	4,166	3.1	4,209	4,593	9.1	8,249	8,759	6.2
East Fishkill, NY	9,987	10,549	5.6	32,479	39,344	21.1	42,466	49,893	17.5
Eden Prairie, MN	7,761	8,673	11.8	6,372	6,004	-5.8	14,133	14,677	3.8
Edmond, OK	5,039	5,167	2.5	1,731	292	-83.1	6,770	5,459	-19.4
Edwardsville, IL	5,340	5,538	3.7	2,603	1,653	-36.5	7,943	7,191	-9.5
Evesham, NJ	6,820	7,278	6.7	5,295	6,021	13.7	12,115	13,299	9.8
Flower Mound, TX	29,846	34,210	14.6	25,772	27,499	6.7	55,618	61,709	11.0
Folsom, CA	6,148	6,816	10.9	1,069	2,613	144.4	7,217	9,429	30.6
Friendswood, TX	35,397	36,601	3.4	9,246	6,072	-34.3	44,643	42,673	-4.4
Gaines, MI	1,644	1,797	9.3	2,011	1,694	-15.8	3,655	3,491	-4.5
Glastonbury, CT	841	762	-9.4	1,213	748	-38.3	2,054	1,510	-26.5
Grand Blanc, MI	126	184	46.0	48	0	-100.0	174	184	5.7
Hampden, PA	1,162	1,253	7.8	393	305	-22.4	1,555	1,558	0.2
Hilliard, OH	4,040	4,166	3.1	4,209	4,593	9.1	8,249	8,759	6.2
Hillsborough, NJ	9,987	10,549	5.6	32,479	39,344	21.1	42,466	49,893	17.5
Holly Springs, NC	9,435	10,785	14.3	4,072	3,428	-15.8	13,507	14,213	5.2
Independence, KY	3,932	4,425	12.5	1,927	1,886	-2.1	5,859	6,311	7.7
Juneau, AK	50	46	-8.0	103	18	-82.5	153	64	-58.2
Kaysville, UT	2,198	2,300	4.6	1,237	960	-22.4	3,435	3,260	-5.1
Keller, TX	29,846	34,210	14.6	25,772	27,499	6.7	55,618	61,709	11.0
Lafayette, CA	4,927	4,756	-3.5	10,062	12,221	21.5	14,989	16,977	13.3
Lafayette, CO	669	708	5.8	1,144	846	-26.0	1,813	1,554	-14.3
Lake Oswego, OR	7,344	6,684	-9.0	7,379	10,350	40.3	14,723	17,034	15.7
Laramie, WY	123	97	-21.1	28	28	0.0	151	125	-17.2
Leander, TX	13,609	15,206	11.7	8,633	10,597	22.7	22,242	25,803	16.0
Leawood, KS	5,248	5,932	13.0	4,815	4,095	-15.0	10,063	10,027	-0.4
Lee's Summit, MO	5,248	5,932	13.0	4,815	4,095	-15.0	10,063	10,027	-0.4
Leesburg, VA	12,974	13,968	7.7	11,970	12,461	4.1	24,944	26,429	6.0
Lehi, UT	4,417	5,082	15.1	888	2,155	142.7	5,305	7,237	36.4
Lexington, MA	5,268	5,093	-3.3	7,749	9,726	25.5	13,017	14,819	13.8
Los Altos, CA	2,057	2,618	27.3	4,070	5,947	46.1	6,127	8,565	39.8
Loveland, CO	1,614	2,020	25.2	1,910	908	-52.5	3,524	2,928	-16.9
Lower Macungie, PA	329	298	-9.4	153	110	-28.1	482	408	-15.4
Madison, AL	2,320	2,578	11.1	672	382	-43.2	2,992	2,960	-1.1
Madison, MS	1,636	1,643	0.4	4	32	700.0	1,640	1,675	2.1

Table continued on next page.

Metro Area	Single-Family			Multi-Family			Total		
	2016	2017	Pct. Chg.	2016	2017	Pct. Chg.	2016	2017	Pct. Chg.
Maple Valley, WA	9,396	9,943	5.8	16,120	17,428	8.1	25,516	27,371	7.3
Marion, IA	451	422	-6.4	199	412	107.0	650	834	28.3
Marlboro, NJ	9,987	10,549	5.6	32,479	39,344	21.1	42,466	49,893	17.5
Mason, OH	3,932	4,425	12.5	1,927	1,886	-2.1	5,859	6,311	7.7
Menomonee Falls, WI	1,634	1,537	-5.9	2,195	2,024	-7.8	3,829	3,561	-7.0
Meridian, ID	5,396	6,250	15.8	1,344	1,639	21.9	6,740	7,889	17.0
Meridian, MI	197	162	-17.8	167	107	-35.9	364	269	-26.1
Merrimack, NH	435	453	4.1	394	150	-61.9	829	603	-27.3
Milton, GA	22,931	24,849	8.4	13,190	8,041	-39.0	36,121	32,890	-8.9
Moon, PA	999	1,053	5.4	510	815	59.8	1,509	1,868	23.8
Moorpark, CA	274	762	178.1	802	1,414	76.3	1,076	2,176	102.2
Morgantown, WV	12	12	0.0	2	52	2,500.0	14	64	357.1
Mount Pleasant, SC	4,758	4,710	-1.0	2,178	2,663	22.3	6,936	7,373	6.3
Newark, DE	6,820	7,278	6.7	5,295	6,021	13.7	12,115	13,299	9.8
Newtown, CT	714	775	8.5	1,203	974	-19.0	1,917	1,749	-8.8
North Attleborough, MA	1,664	1,740	4.6	883	284	-67.8	2,547	2,024	-20.5
North Port, FL	5,821	5,981	2.7	2,290	2,190	-4.4	8,111	8,171	0.7
North Ridgeville, OH	2,653	2,706	2.0	302	506	67.5	2,955	3,212	8.7
Northville, MI	5,728	6,771	18.2	1,808	3,240	79.2	7,536	10,011	32.8
O'Fallon, MO	5,340	5,538	3.7	2,603	1,653	-36.5	7,943	7,191	-9.5
Orchard Park, NY	935	958	2.5	1,057	678	-35.9	1,992	1,636	-17.9
Oro Valley, AZ	2,164	2,758	27.4	421	348	-17.3	2,585	3,106	20.2
Oviedo, FL	14,208	14,766	3.9	9,043	4,666	-48.4	23,251	19,432	-16.4
Parker, CO	10,211	10,937	7.1	11,111	11,610	4.5	21,322	22,547	5.7
Parkland, FL	6,688	6,642	-0.7	12,006	12,654	5.4	18,694	19,296	3.2
Peachtree City, GA	22,931	24,849	8.4	13,190	8,041	-39.0	36,121	32,890	-8.9
Pittsfield, MI	216	315	45.8	0	42	-	216	357	65.3
Plainfield, IL	8,118	8,299	2.2	11,351	13,570	19.5	19,469	21,869	12.3
Pleasant Grove, UT	4,417	5,082	15.1	888	2,155	142.7	5,305	7,237	36.4
Poway, CA	2,341	4,058	73.3	8,328	6,357	-23.7	10,669	10,415	-2.4
Princeton, NJ	180	144	-20.0	525	463	-11.8	705	607	-13.9
Queen Creek, AZ	18,577	20,551	10.6	9,965	9,102	-8.7	28,542	29,653	3.9
Radnor, PA	6,820	7,278	6.7	5,295	6,021	13.7	12,115	13,299	9.8
Randolph, NJ	9,987	10,549	5.6	32,479	39,344	21.1	42,466	49,893	17.5
Rexburg, ID	221	209	-5.4	293	363	23.9	514	572	11.3
Rio Rancho, NM	1,927	1,996	3.6	534	260	-51.3	2,461	2,256	-8.3
Rye, NY	9,987	10,549	5.6	32,479	39,344	21.1	42,466	49,893	17.5
Sammamish, WA	9,396	9,943	5.8	16,120	17,428	8.1	25,516	27,371	7.3
San Ramon, CA	4,927	4,756	-3.5	10,062	12,221	21.5	14,989	16,977	13.3
Saratoga, CA	2,057	2,618	27.3	4,070	5,947	46.1	6,127	8,565	39.8
Shrewsbury, MA	164	221	34.8	7	126	1,700.0	171	347	102.9
South Brunswick, NJ	9,987	10,549	5.6	32,479	39,344	21.1	42,466	49,893	17.5
South Jordan, UT	4,311	4,954	14.9	4,489	2,469	-45.0	8,800	7,423	-15.6
South Kingstown, RI	1,664	1,740	4.6	883	284	-67.8	2,547	2,024	-20.5
South Portland, ME	1,272	1,463	15.0	358	581	62.3	1,630	2,044	25.4
Sparks, NV	1,867	2,091	12.0	1,732	2,473	42.8	3,599	4,564	26.8
State College, PA	72	73	1.4	0	74	-	72	147	104.2
Sugar Land, TX	35,397	36,601	3.4	9,246	6,072	-34.3	44,643	42,673	-4.4
Sun Prairie, WI	1,598	1,645	2.9	3,332	3,025	-9.2	4,930	4,670	-5.3
Syracuse, UT	2,198	2,300	4.6	1,237	960	-22.4	3,435	3,260	-5.1
Tredyffrin, PA	6,820	7,278	6.7	5,295	6,021	13.7	12,115	13,299	9.8
Upper Dublin, PA	6,820	7,278	6.7	5,295	6,021	13.7	12,115	13,299	9.8
Urbandale, IA	3,758	3,704	-1.4	2,962	2,405	-18.8	6,720	6,109	-9.1
Vestal, NY	1	5	400.0	0	0	0.0	1	5	400.0
Vestavia Hills, AL	2,701	2,720	0.7	762	219	-71.3	3,463	2,939	-15.1
Webster, NY	1,282	1,089	-15.1	718	606	-15.6	2,000	1,695	-15.3
Wellesley, MA	5,268	5,093	-3.3	7,749	9,726	25.5	13,017	14,819	13.8
West Fargo, ND	1,197	1,062	-11.3	1,287	826	-35.8	2,484	1,888	-24.0
West Lafayette, IN	437	490	12.1	132	409	209.8	569	899	58.0
Weston, FL	6,688	6,642	-0.7	12,006	12,654	5.4	18,694	19,296	3.2
Wilmette, IL	8,118	8,299	2.2	11,351	13,570	19.5	19,469	21,869	12.3
Yorba Linda, CA	9,307	10,612	14.0	22,701	20,586	-9.3	32,008	31,198	-2.5
Zionsville, IN	5,643	6,205	10.0	1,911	1,909	-0.1	7,554	8,114	7.4
U.S.	750,800	817,300	8.9	455,800	446,800	-2.0	1,206,600	1,264,100	4.8

Note: Figures cover the Metropolitan Statistical Area—see Appendix B for areas included; Figures represent new, privately-owned housing units authorized (unadjusted data); All permit data are based on estimates with imputation
Source: U.S. Census Bureau, Manufacturing, Mining, and Construction Statistics, Building Permits, 2016, 2017

Housing Vacancy Rates

Metro Area[1]	Gross Vacancy Rate[2] (%)			Year-Round Vacancy Rate[3] (%)			Rental Vacancy Rate[4] (%)			Homeowner Vacancy Rate[5] (%)		
	2015	2016	2017	2015	2016	2017	2015	2016	2017	2015	2016	2017
Aberdeen, SD	n/a	n/a	n/a	n/a	n/a	n/a	n/a	n/a	n/a	n/a	n/a	n/a
Aliso Viejo, CA	5.4	5.0	6.3	5.0	4.7	5.9	3.3	2.9	4.1	0.8	0.8	0.9
Allen, TX	8.0	7.9	7.8	7.8	7.7	7.6	8.3	6.8	7.1	1.4	1.4	0.8
Ames, IA	n/a	n/a	n/a	n/a	n/a	n/a	n/a	n/a	n/a	n/a	n/a	n/a
Amherst, MA	n/a	n/a	n/a	n/a	n/a	n/a	n/a	n/a	n/a	n/a	n/a	n/a
Apex, NC	6.8	6.8	8.0	6.7	6.7	7.8	6.6	4.3	5.8	1.7	1.9	1.7
Beavercreek, OH	11.4	12.0	11.1	11.4	11.9	11.1	9.4	10.5	6.9	2.3	3.3	3.7
Bellevue, NE	9.0	6.9	5.9	8.5	6.2	5.4	6.4	6.7	4.7	1.5	0.7	0.9
Bend, OR	n/a	n/a	n/a	n/a	n/a	n/a	n/a	n/a	n/a	n/a	n/a	n/a
Benicia, CA	n/a	n/a	n/a	n/a	n/a	n/a	n/a	n/a	n/a	n/a	n/a	n/a
Bentonville, AR	n/a	n/a	n/a	n/a	n/a	n/a	n/a	n/a	n/a	n/a	n/a	n/a
Bethlehem, NY	13.2	11.8	10.5	8.9	8.7	8.3	6.5	3.8	8.5	1.8	2.1	2.1
Blacksburg, VA	n/a	n/a	n/a	n/a	n/a	n/a	n/a	n/a	n/a	n/a	n/a	n/a
Bowie, MD	7.7	8.2	7.4	7.4	7.9	7.1	5.7	6.0	6.2	0.9	1.7	1.2
Bozeman, MT	n/a	n/a	n/a	n/a	n/a	n/a	n/a	n/a	n/a	n/a	n/a	n/a
Brentwood, TN	8.3	6.6	6.2	8.2	6.4	6.1	4.9	4.8	7.6	3.1	1.5	0.6
Burlington, VT	n/a	n/a	n/a	n/a	n/a	n/a	n/a	n/a	n/a	n/a	n/a	n/a
Cabot, AR	12.0	11.8	10.3	11.7	11.8	10.0	12.8	12.2	11.3	3.0	2.4	2.0
Carmel, IN	7.4	9.1	10.9	7.4	9.0	10.8	8.4	9.2	11.9	1.0	1.4	1.5
Cedar Falls, IA	n/a	n/a	n/a	n/a	n/a	n/a	n/a	n/a	n/a	n/a	n/a	n/a
Cedar Park, TX	9.2	8.2	10.4	8.5	7.6	9.3	6.0	5.5	6.1	1.3	1.0	2.0
Central, LA	11.8	12.3	13.6	11.6	12.0	13.0	7.8	7.4	8.7	1.6	1.5	1.0
Chapel Hill, NC	n/a	n/a	n/a	n/a	n/a	n/a	n/a	n/a	n/a	n/a	n/a	n/a
Cheshire, CT	8.7	10.0	10.0	8.6	9.7	9.8	5.8	7.3	6.9	2.1	2.5	2.1
Chino Hills, CA	14.7	14.8	16.2	12.1	10.3	9.4	7.0	5.6	5.6	2.0	1.8	1.6
Cibolo, TX	9.0	9.9	9.9	7.8	8.6	8.8	9.6	10.3	11.5	0.8	1.9	1.8
Cicero, NY	11.1	12.0	13.0	10.4	10.2	11.1	9.2	6.5	6.5	2.3	2.3	1.8
Collierville, TN	11.2	10.9	12.1	11.0	10.7	12.1	10.7	9.4	10.5	1.4	1.4	1.4
Coppell, TX	8.0	7.9	7.8	7.8	7.7	7.6	8.3	6.8	7.1	1.4	1.4	0.8
Cornelius, NC	8.2	7.7	6.9	7.8	7.5	6.8	6.4	7.4	5.4	1.8	1.1	0.8
Cranberry, PA	13.5	17.7	13.6	13.2	17.4	13.4	7.1	7.4	9.7	1.5	1.8	2.2
Crown Point, IN	9.7	8.6	8.4	9.4	8.5	8.3	7.4	6.4	7.0	2.3	2.3	1.8
Dublin, OH	9.6	8.0	6.6	9.2	7.8	6.0	6.5	6.1	6.3	1.5	1.0	1.1
East Fishkill, NY	9.8	10.3	10.7	8.6	9.1	9.6	4.2	4.7	4.6	2.1	2.2	1.9
Eden Prairie, MN	6.4	5.3	4.5	6.0	4.7	4.1	4.9	3.8	4.2	0.8	0.8	0.9
Edmond, OK	11.9	11.9	11.1	11.1	11.6	10.8	7.6	10.9	9.9	2.0	1.6	1.9
Edwardsville, IL	10.7	9.5	9.2	10.3	9.2	8.9	9.7	8.5	7.9	3.1	2.9	1.4
Evesham, NJ	10.7	9.3	8.6	10.2	8.6	8.3	7.6	6.8	7.3	2.4	1.4	1.6
Flower Mound, TX	8.0	7.9	7.8	7.8	7.7	7.6	8.3	6.8	7.1	1.4	1.4	0.8
Folsom, CA	8.8	8.6	7.5	6.0	6.7	6.0	5.3	5.9	4.2	1.4	0.6	1.0
Friendswood, TX	9.2	8.6	9.3	8.7	8.0	8.9	9.6	9.3	9.9	1.5	1.8	1.5
Gaines, MI	9.2	7.1	8.5	5.5	4.4	6.3	4.4	5.1	4.0	0.9	0.5	1.1
Glastonbury, CT	10.5	13.4	10.1	9.7	11.9	9.2	6.1	6.8	5.4	1.5	1.7	1.4
Grand Blanc, MI	n/a	n/a	n/a	n/a	n/a	n/a	n/a	n/a	n/a	n/a	n/a	n/a
Hampden, PA	n/a	n/a	n/a	n/a	n/a	n/a	n/a	n/a	n/a	n/a	n/a	n/a
Hilliard, OH	9.6	8.0	6.6	9.2	7.8	6.0	6.5	6.1	6.3	1.5	1.0	1.1
Hillsborough, NJ	9.8	10.3	10.7	8.6	9.1	9.6	4.2	4.7	4.6	2.1	2.2	1.9
Holly Springs, NC	6.8	6.8	8.0	6.7	6.7	7.8	6.6	4.3	5.8	1.7	1.9	1.7
Independence, KY	10.5	9.2	8.4	10.0	8.3	7.5	10.1	5.8	7.5	2.2	1.4	1.9
Juneau, AK	n/a	n/a	n/a	n/a	n/a	n/a	n/a	n/a	n/a	n/a	n/a	n/a
Kaysville, UT	n/a	n/a	n/a	n/a	n/a	n/a	n/a	n/a	n/a	n/a	n/a	n/a
Keller, TX	8.0	7.9	7.8	7.8	7.7	7.6	8.3	6.8	7.1	1.4	1.4	0.8
Lafayette, CA	5.7	6.0	6.0	5.7	5.9	5.9	3.6	3.6	4.2	0.7	0.7	0.7
Lafayette, CO	n/a	n/a	n/a	n/a	n/a	n/a	n/a	n/a	n/a	n/a	n/a	n/a
Lake Oswego, OR	6.0	6.7	6.4	5.5	6.2	6.1	3.4	5.0	4.8	1.0	1.0	1.1
Laramie, WY	n/a	n/a	n/a	n/a	n/a	n/a	n/a	n/a	n/a	n/a	n/a	n/a
Leander, TX	9.2	8.2	10.4	8.5	7.6	9.3	6.0	5.5	6.1	1.3	1.0	2.0
Leawood, KS	7.3	8.1	8.1	7.1	8.0	7.9	7.9	9.2	9.4	1.3	0.8	0.8
Lee's Summit, MO	7.3	8.1	8.1	7.1	8.0	7.9	7.9	9.2	9.4	1.3	0.8	0.8
Leesburg, VA	7.7	8.2	7.4	7.4	7.9	7.1	5.7	6.0	6.2	0.9	1.7	1.2
Lehi, UT	n/a	n/a	n/a	n/a	n/a	n/a	n/a	n/a	n/a	n/a	n/a	n/a
Lexington, MA	9.9	7.8	7.6	6.3	6.5	6.5	3.3	3.7	4.8	1.1	0.9	0.6
Los Altos, CA	5.7	6.1	6.0	5.6	5.8	5.9	3.5	4.5	3.2	0.9	0.8	0.7
Loveland, CO	n/a	n/a	n/a	n/a	n/a	n/a	n/a	n/a	n/a	n/a	n/a	n/a
Lower Macungie, PA	9.1	7.4	9.5	6.5	5.2	8.5	3.7	4.2	5.3	1.7	1.1	1.7
Madison, AL	n/a	n/a	n/a	n/a	n/a	n/a	n/a	n/a	n/a	n/a	n/a	n/a
Madison, MS	n/a	n/a	n/a	n/a	n/a	n/a	n/a	n/a	n/a	n/a	n/a	n/a

Table continued on next page.

Metro Area[1]	Gross Vacancy Rate[2] (%)			Year-Round Vacancy Rate[3] (%)			Rental Vacancy Rate[4] (%)			Homeowner Vacancy Rate[5] (%)		
	2015	2016	2017	2015	2016	2017	2015	2016	2017	2015	2016	2017
Maple Valley, WA	5.6	5.6	6.0	5.4	5.3	5.4	3.8	3.3	3.4	1.1	0.9	0.5
Marion, IA	n/a	n/a	n/a	n/a	n/a	n/a	n/a	n/a	n/a	n/a	n/a	n/a
Marlboro, NJ	9.8	10.3	10.7	8.6	9.1	9.6	4.2	4.7	4.6	2.1	2.2	1.9
Mason, OH	10.5	9.2	8.4	10.0	8.3	7.5	10.1	5.8	7.5	2.2	1.4	1.9
Menomonee Falls, WI	8.0	6.5	7.9	7.3	5.9	7.0	4.5	5.2	6.5	0.8	1.3	0.9
Meridian, ID	n/a	n/a	n/a	n/a	n/a	n/a	n/a	n/a	n/a	n/a	n/a	n/a
Meridian, MI	n/a	n/a	n/a	n/a	n/a	n/a	n/a	n/a	n/a	n/a	n/a	n/a
Merrimack, NH	n/a	n/a	n/a	n/a	n/a	n/a	n/a	n/a	n/a	n/a	n/a	n/a
Milton, GA	11.0	9.7	8.9	10.7	9.4	8.4	8.2	6.2	7.0	2.2	1.6	1.0
Moon, PA	13.5	17.7	13.6	13.2	17.4	13.4	7.1	7.4	9.7	1.5	1.8	2.2
Moorpark, CA	n/a	n/a	n/a	n/a	n/a	n/a	n/a	n/a	n/a	n/a	n/a	n/a
Morgantown, WV	n/a	n/a	n/a	n/a	n/a	n/a	n/a	n/a	n/a	n/a	n/a	n/a
Mount Pleasant, SC	14.3	14.8	16.5	12.4	13.6	16.1	8.7	12.2	17.9	2.2	2.4	1.6
Newark, DE	10.7	9.3	8.6	10.2	8.6	8.3	7.6	6.8	7.3	2.4	1.4	1.6
Newtown, CT	11.3	8.6	9.3	10.1	7.9	8.8	7.1	7.9	9.1	1.8	2.3	1.0
North Attleborough, MA	11.0	11.1	11.3	7.8	7.5	8.1	3.3	3.8	4.2	1.7	1.3	1.2
North Port, FL	34.2	27.9	28.3	18.6	15.7	13.7	8.3	9.8	5.7	3.3	1.2	2.5
North Ridgeville, OH	11.0	11.1	9.2	10.9	10.9	9.2	7.4	7.1	8.0	1.4	1.7	1.2
Northville, MI	9.7	8.3	8.1	9.5	8.2	7.8	6.8	7.1	8.1	1.1	0.6	0.4
O'Fallon, MO	10.7	9.5	9.2	10.3	9.2	8.9	9.7	8.5	7.9	3.1	2.9	1.4
Orchard Park, NY	12.3	11.6	12.4	11.8	10.1	11.2	11.9	9.3	6.4	2.5	1.2	3.3
Oro Valley, AZ	11.8	15.6	13.8	9.8	12.5	9.2	10.1	9.8	6.9	1.7	1.6	1.1
Oviedo, FL	14.3	13.2	14.3	11.3	10.3	10.5	8.0	6.6	6.9	4.1	2.1	1.5
Parker, CO	7.4	6.4	7.8	5.6	5.2	6.9	4.8	4.5	5.9	0.7	1.1	0.7
Parkland, FL	16.9	17.9	17.8	8.5	9.5	9.2	6.4	7.2	7.0	1.4	1.4	1.9
Peachtree City, GA	11.0	9.7	8.9	10.7	9.4	8.4	8.2	6.2	7.0	2.2	1.6	1.0
Pittsfield, MI	n/a	n/a	n/a	n/a	n/a	n/a	n/a	n/a	n/a	n/a	n/a	n/a
Plainfield, IL	9.7	8.6	8.4	9.4	8.5	8.3	7.4	6.4	7.0	2.3	2.3	1.8
Pleasant Grove, UT	n/a	n/a	n/a	n/a	n/a	n/a	n/a	n/a	n/a	n/a	n/a	n/a
Poway, CA	7.7	7.5	6.4	6.9	6.9	6.0	3.4	2.9	3.9	1.0	1.2	0.6
Princeton, NJ	n/a	n/a	n/a	n/a	n/a	n/a	n/a	n/a	n/a	n/a	n/a	n/a
Queen Creek, AZ	15.3	13.9	13.7	9.5	8.8	8.1	6.3	5.8	6.0	2.0	1.6	1.5
Radnor, PA	10.7	9.3	8.6	10.2	8.6	8.3	7.6	6.8	7.3	2.4	1.4	1.6
Randolph, NJ	9.8	10.3	10.7	8.6	9.1	9.6	4.2	4.7	4.6	2.1	2.2	1.9
Rexburg, ID	n/a	n/a	n/a	n/a	n/a	n/a	n/a	n/a	n/a	n/a	n/a	n/a
Rio Rancho, NM	9.3	9.2	8.9	8.3	8.9	8.6	7.2	8.1	9.0	2.7	1.9	2.1
Rye, NY	9.8	10.3	10.7	8.6	9.1	9.6	4.2	4.7	4.6	2.1	2.2	1.9
Sammamish, WA	5.6	5.6	6.0	5.4	5.3	5.4	3.8	3.3	3.4	1.1	0.9	0.5
San Ramon, CA	5.7	6.0	6.0	5.7	5.9	5.9	3.6	3.6	4.2	0.7	0.7	0.7
Saratoga, CA	5.7	6.1	6.0	5.6	5.8	5.9	3.5	4.5	3.2	0.9	0.8	0.7
Shrewsbury, MA	10.1	8.6	8.2	7.8	6.6	7.3	2.9	3.7	3.9	1.9	1.2	2.0
South Brunswick, NJ	9.8	10.3	10.7	8.6	9.1	9.6	4.2	4.7	4.6	2.1	2.2	1.9
South Jordan, UT	5.2	5.4	5.0	5.1	5.0	4.8	5.8	6.4	6.2	1.3	0.5	0.6
South Kingstown, RI	11.0	11.1	11.3	7.8	7.5	8.1	3.3	3.8	4.2	1.7	1.3	1.2
South Portland, ME	n/a	n/a	n/a	n/a	n/a	n/a	n/a	n/a	n/a	n/a	n/a	n/a
Sparks, NV	n/a	n/a	n/a	n/a	n/a	n/a	n/a	n/a	n/a	n/a	n/a	n/a
State College, PA	n/a	n/a	n/a	n/a	n/a	n/a	n/a	n/a	n/a	n/a	n/a	n/a
Sugar Land, TX	9.2	8.6	9.3	8.7	8.0	8.9	9.6	9.3	9.9	1.5	1.8	1.5
Sun Prairie, WI	n/a	n/a	n/a	n/a	n/a	n/a	n/a	n/a	n/a	n/a	n/a	n/a
Syracuse, UT	n/a	n/a	n/a	n/a	n/a	n/a	n/a	n/a	n/a	n/a	n/a	n/a
Tredyffrin, PA	10.7	9.3	8.6	10.2	8.6	8.3	7.6	6.8	7.3	2.4	1.4	1.6
Upper Dublin, PA	10.7	9.3	8.6	10.2	8.6	8.3	7.6	6.8	7.3	2.4	1.4	1.6
Urbandale, IA	n/a	n/a	n/a	n/a	n/a	n/a	n/a	n/a	n/a	n/a	n/a	n/a
Vestal, NY	n/a	n/a	n/a	n/a	n/a	n/a	n/a	n/a	n/a	n/a	n/a	n/a
Vestavia Hills, AL	16.0	16.7	15.6	15.6	15.7	13.8	17.7	15.1	15.7	2.2	2.1	2.0
Webster, NY	8.0	7.9	8.5	6.2	7.2	8.1	6.5	6.4	6.5	0.8	1.4	2.0
Wellesley, MA	9.9	7.8	7.6	6.3	6.5	6.5	3.3	3.7	4.8	1.1	0.9	0.6
West Fargo, ND	n/a	n/a	n/a	n/a	n/a	n/a	n/a	n/a	n/a	n/a	n/a	n/a
West Lafayette, IN	n/a	n/a	n/a	n/a	n/a	n/a	n/a	n/a	n/a	n/a	n/a	n/a
Weston, FL	16.9	17.9	17.8	8.5	9.5	9.2	6.4	7.2	7.0	1.4	1.4	1.9
Wilmette, IL	9.7	8.6	8.4	9.4	8.5	8.3	7.4	6.4	7.0	2.3	2.3	1.8
Yorba Linda, CA	5.4	5.0	6.3	5.0	4.7	5.9	3.3	2.9	4.1	0.8	0.8	0.9
Zionsville, IN	7.4	9.1	10.9	7.4	9.0	10.8	8.4	9.2	11.9	1.0	1.4	1.5
U.S.	12.9	12.8	12.7	10.0	9.9	9.9	7.1	6.9	7.2	1.8	1.7	1.6

Note: (1) Metropolitan Statistical Area—see Appendix B for areas included; (2) The percentage of the total housing inventory that is vacant; (3) The percentage of the housing inventory (excluding seasonal units) that is year-round vacant; (4) The percentage of rental inventory that is vacant for rent; (5) The percentage of homeowner inventory that is vacant for sale; n/a not available
Source: U.S. Census Bureau, Housing Vacancies and Homeownership Annual Statistics: 2015, 2016, 2017

Bankruptcy Filings

City	Area Covered	Business Filings 2016	Business Filings 2017	Business Filings % Chg.	Nonbusiness Filings 2016	Nonbusiness Filings 2017	Nonbusiness Filings % Chg.
Aberdeen, SD	Brown County	3	2	-33.3	65	40	-38.5
Aliso Viejo, CA	Orange County	339	344	1.5	5,151	4,839	-6.1
Allen, TX	Collin County	135	151	11.9	1,204	1,408	16.9
Ames, IA	Story County	4	3	-25.0	56	58	3.6
Amherst, MA	Hampshire County	10	6	-40.0	165	143	-13.3
Apex, NC	Wake County	76	79	3.9	1,539	1,458	-5.3
Beavercreek, OH	Greene County	7	2	-71.4	323	376	16.4
Bellevue, NE	Sarpy County	7	5	-28.6	418	395	-5.5
Bend, OR	Deschutes County	17	15	-11.8	514	459	-10.7
Benicia, CA	Solano County	31	27	-12.9	961	858	-10.7
Bentonville, AR	Benton County	24	28	16.7	523	516	-1.3
Bethlehem, NY	Albany County	14	12	-14.3	505	513	1.6
Blacksburg, VA	Montgomery County	1	1	0.0	106	104	-1.9
Bowie, MD	Prince George's County	61	67	9.8	3,752	3,727	-0.7
Bozeman, MT	Gallatin County	6	5	-16.7	120	134	11.7
Brentwood, TN	Williamson County	35	32	-8.6	289	299	3.5
Burlington, VT	Chittenden County	7	6	-14.3	88	126	43.2
Cabot, AR	Lonoke County	8	12	50.0	305	369	21.0
Carmel, IN	Hamilton County	34	29	-14.7	664	617	-7.1
Cedar Falls, IA	Black Hawk County	6	6	0.0	193	177	-8.3
Cedar Park, TX	Williamson County	42	46	9.5	469	468	-0.2
Central, LA	East Baton Rouge Parish	22	21	-4.5	728	616	-15.4
Chapel Hill, NC	Orange County	7	4	-42.9	103	115	11.7
Cheshire, CT	New Haven County	54	49	-9.3	1,704	1,698	-0.4
Chino Hills, CA	San Bernardino County	111	90	-18.9	5,510	4,974	-9.7
Cibolo, TX	Guadalupe County	7	10	42.9	153	177	15.7
Cicero, NY	Onondaga County	30	13	-56.7	933	886	-5.0
Collierville, TN	Shelby County	90	71	-21.1	11,352	10,756	-5.3
Coppell, TX	Dallas County	332	306	-7.8	3,955	3,997	1.1
Cornelius, NC	Mecklenburg County	49	81	65.3	1,312	1,262	-3.8
Cranberry, PA	Butler County	16	34	112.5	265	308	16.2
Crown Point, IN	Lake County	40	40	0.0	2,822	2,882	2.1
Dublin, OH	Franklin County	58	70	20.7	4,463	4,479	0.4
East Fishkill, NY	Dutchess County	29	22	-24.1	643	665	3.4
Eden Prairie, MN	Hennepin County	84	83	-1.2	2,025	2,112	4.3
Edmond, OK	Oklahoma County	110	59	-46.4	2,113	2,098	-0.7
Edwardsville, IL	Madison County	17	17	0.0	761	787	3.4
Evesham, NJ	Burlington County	49	40	-18.4	1,598	1,764	10.4
Flower Mound, TX	Denton County	78	231	196.2	1,037	1,117	7.7
Folsom, CA	Sacramento County	110	115	4.5	3,541	3,622	2.3
Friendswood, TX	Galveston County	22	26	18.2	328	283	-13.7
Gaines, MI	Kent County	38	32	-15.8	1,249	1,072	-14.2
Glastonbury, CT	Hartford County	57	46	-19.3	1,323	1,316	-0.5
Grand Blanc, MI	Genesee County	32	28	-12.5	2,294	2,342	2.1
Hampden, PA	Cumberland County	19	22	15.8	361	374	3.6
Hilliard, OH	Franklin County	58	70	20.7	4,463	4,479	0.4
Hillsborough, NJ	Somerset County	29	25	-13.8	568	596	4.9
Holly Springs, NC	Wake County	76	79	3.9	1,539	1,458	-5.3
Independence, KY	Kenton County	6	10	66.7	651	653	0.3
Juneau, AK	Juneau Borough	1	1	0.0	9	16	77.8
Kaysville, UT	Davis County	25	12	-52.0	1,218	1,264	3.8
Keller, TX	Tarrant County	231	204	-11.7	4,050	3,983	-1.7
Lafayette, CA	Contra Costa County	77	74	-3.9	1,778	1,527	-14.1
Lafayette, CO	Boulder County	27	23	-14.8	407	392	-3.7
Lake Oswego, OR	Clackamas County	22	35	59.1	834	898	7.7
Laramie, WY	Albany County	2	1	-50.0	28	26	-7.1
Leander, TX	Williamson County	42	46	9.5	469	468	-0.2
Leawood, KS	Johnson County	51	46	-9.8	1,121	1,122	0.1
Lee's Summit, MO	Jackson County	45	31	-31.1	2,457	2,373	-3.4
Leesburg, VA	Loudoun County	40	41	2.5	557	558	0.2
Lehi, UT	Utah County	41	36	-12.2	1,588	1,598	0.6
Lexington, MA	Middlesex County	100	72	-28.0	1,187	1,249	5.2
Los Altos, CA	Santa Clara County	92	99	7.6	2,067	1,843	-10.8
Loveland, CO	Larimer County	17	32	88.2	630	605	-4.0
Lower Macungie, PA	Lehigh County	25	27	8.0	603	585	-3.0
Madison, AL	Madison County	33	21	-36.4	1,397	1,432	2.5
Madison, MS	Madison County	16	13	-18.8	406	491	20.9
Maple Valley, WA	King County	129	142	10.1	3,161	2,633	-16.7

Table continued on next page.

City	Area Covered	Business Filings 2016	Business Filings 2017	Business Filings % Chg.	Nonbusiness Filings 2016	Nonbusiness Filings 2017	Nonbusiness Filings % Chg.
Marion, IA	Linn County	7	9	28.6	283	289	2.1
Marlboro, NJ	Monmouth County	66	54	-18.2	1,587	1,697	6.9
Mason, OH	Warren County	12	22	83.3	479	459	-4.2
Menomonee Falls, WI	Waukesha County	29	19	-34.5	827	827	0.0
Meridian, ID	Ada County	27	35	29.6	861	946	9.9
Meridian, MI	Ingham County	15	4	-73.3	776	784	1.0
Merrimack, NH	Hillsborough County	47	30	-36.2	545	591	8.4
Milton, GA	Fulton County	145	108	-25.5	4,655	4,600	-1.2
Moon, PA	Allegheny County	131	120	-8.4	2,299	2,583	12.4
Moorpark, CA	Ventura County	78	65	-16.7	1,543	1,508	-2.3
Morgantown, WV	Monongalia County	14	10	-28.6	92	100	8.7
Mount Pleasant, SC	Charleston County	16	11	-31.3	378	386	2.1
Newark, DE	New Castle County	56	46	-17.9	1,282	1,344	4.8
Newtown, CT	Fairfield County	87	51	-41.4	1,335	1,202	-10.0
North Attleborough, MA	Bristol County	47	32	-31.9	1,032	1,039	0.7
North Port, FL	Sarasota County	28	38	35.7	617	650	5.3
North Ridgeville, OH	Lorain County	14	11	-21.4	934	1,001	7.2
Northville, MI	Wayne County	85	64	-24.7	8,815	9,208	4.5
O'Fallon, MO	Saint Charles County	23	19	-17.4	1,170	1,198	2.4
Orchard Park, NY	Erie County	86	67	-22.1	1,639	1,858	13.4
Oro Valley, AZ	Pima County	50	68	36.0	2,120	2,306	8.8
Oviedo, FL	Seminole County	48	43	-10.4	1,034	1,041	0.7
Parker, CO	Douglas County	39	43	10.3	586	540	-7.8
Parkland, FL	Broward County	171	181	5.8	5,097	4,265	-16.3
Peachtree City, GA	Fayette County	12	11	-8.3	331	363	9.7
Pittsfield, MI	Washtenaw County	15	18	20.0	650	645	-0.8
Plainfield, IL	Will County	66	101	53.0	2,798	2,703	-3.4
Pleasant Grove, UT	Utah County	41	36	-12.2	1,588	1,598	0.6
Poway, CA	San Diego County	290	296	2.1	7,553	7,405	-2.0
Princeton, NJ	Mercer County	43	81	88.4	910	961	5.6
Queen Creek, AZ	Maricopa County	413	385	-6.8	10,064	10,423	3.6
Radnor, PA	Delaware County	44	25	-43.2	908	888	-2.2
Randolph, NJ	Morris County	53	61	15.1	799	801	0.3
Rexburg, ID	Madison County	2	3	50.0	31	37	19.4
Rio Rancho, NM	Sandoval County	16	13	-18.8	284	298	4.9
Rye, NY	Westchester County	101	102	1.0	1,191	1,243	4.4
Sammamish, WA	King County	129	142	10.1	3,161	2,633	-16.7
San Ramon, CA	Contra Costa County	77	74	-3.9	1,778	1,527	-14.1
Saratoga, CA	Santa Clara County	92	99	7.6	2,067	1,843	-10.8
Shrewsbury, MA	Worcester County	44	36	-18.2	1,194	1,222	2.3
South Brunswick, NJ	Middlesex County	62	55	-11.3	1,895	1,945	2.6
South Jordan, UT	Salt Lake County	70	94	34.3	5,045	4,775	-5.4
South Kingstown, RI	Washington County	14	10	-28.6	163	160	-1.8
South Portland, ME	Cumberland County	23	23	0.0	271	235	-13.3
Sparks, NV	Washoe County	32	43	34.4	1,037	920	-11.3
State College, PA	Centre County	6	6	0.0	83	69	-16.9
Sugar Land, TX	Fort Bend County	59	47	-20.3	788	742	-5.8
Sun Prairie, WI	Dane County	28	26	-7.1	748	774	3.5
Syracuse, UT	Davis County	25	12	-52.0	1,218	1,264	3.8
Tredyffrin, PA	Chester County	51	25	-51.0	562	556	-1.1
Upper Dublin, PA	Montgomery County	65	59	-9.2	1,057	1,038	-1.8
Urbandale, IA	Polk County	34	20	-41.2	807	820	1.6
Vestal, NY	Broome County	9	9	0.0	326	329	0.9
Vestavia Hills, AL	Jefferson County	68	41	-39.7	4,468	4,394	-1.7
Webster, NY	Monroe County	39	44	12.8	902	854	-5.3
Wellesley, MA	Norfolk County	49	40	-18.4	715	661	-7.6
West Fargo, ND	Cass County	7	14	100.0	188	177	-5.9
West Lafayette, IN	Tippecanoe County	5	6	20.0	282	313	11.0
Weston, FL	Broward County	171	181	5.8	5,097	4,265	-16.3
Wilmette, IL	Cook County	424	435	2.6	31,634	29,321	-7.3
Yorba Linda, CA	Orange County	339	344	1.5	5,151	4,839	-6.1
Zionsville, IN	Boone County	4	4	0.0	151	131	-13.2
U.S.	U.S.	24,114	23,157	-4.0	770,846	765,863	-0.6

Note: Business filings include Chapter 7, Chapter 11, Chapter 12, and Chapter 13; Nonbusiness filings include Chapter 7, Chapter 11, and Chapter 13

Source: Administrative Office of the U.S. Courts, Business and Nonbusiness Bankruptcy, County Cases Commenced by Chapter of the Bankruptcy Code, During the 12- Month Period Ending December 31, 2016 and Business and Nonbusiness Bankruptcy, County Cases Commenced by Chapter of the Bankruptcy Code, During the 12- Month Period Ending December 31, 2017

Income: City

City	Per Capita ($)	Median Household ($)	Average Household ($)
Aberdeen, SD	26,669	46,330	61,978
Aliso Viejo, CA	46,026	103,261	122,345
Allen, TX	40,563	102,215	122,963
Ames, IA	23,519	41,278	59,378
Amherst, MA	18,856	45,999	73,901
Apex, NC	38,886	95,283	111,252
Beavercreek, OH	40,639	82,956	99,010
Bellevue, NE	27,155	58,053	70,671
Bend, OR	32,162	55,625	77,559
Benicia, CA	44,572	87,011	110,507
Bentonville, AR	35,753	76,447	98,239
Bethlehem, NY	47,364	92,708	120,094
Blacksburg, VA	20,141	34,863	58,960
Bowie, MD	44,488	106,098	121,760
Bozeman, MT	28,748	48,612	67,350
Brentwood, TN	64,607	148,340	197,619
Burlington, VT	25,231	46,754	63,415
Cabot, AR	24,902	58,711	66,332
Carmel, IN	54,178	106,546	144,480
Cedar Falls, IA	29,181	58,544	78,763
Cedar Park, TX	34,534	87,466	101,888
Central, LA	31,539	70,618	83,604
Chapel Hill, NC	38,854	65,373	110,561
Cheshire, CT	45,164	108,559	127,386
Chino Hills, CA	36,145	97,222	113,249
Cibolo, TX	30,753	91,827	98,016
Cicero, NY	33,296	69,949	85,060
Collierville, TN	44,410	110,591	129,842
Coppell, TX	52,509	114,839	142,951
Cornelius, NC	49,391	86,355	113,221
Cranberry, PA	46,315	103,276	125,734
Crown Point, IN	32,402	65,968	81,989
Dublin, OH	58,698	125,540	163,872
East Fishkill, NY	41,074	104,980	123,722
Eden Prairie, MN	54,601	101,094	138,218
Edmond, OK	39,643	74,632	105,799
Edwardsville, IL	32,733	68,454	92,663
Evesham, NJ	43,130	90,315	110,180
Flower Mound, TX	47,857	123,492	144,467
Folsom, CA	41,732	102,692	117,158
Friendswood, TX	45,954	95,241	130,636
Gaines, MI	27,655	60,519	73,965
Glastonbury, CT	58,216	108,600	149,545
Grand Blanc, MI	32,316	63,501	81,896
Hampden, PA	44,012	82,967	106,351
Hilliard, OH	40,964	92,727	111,490
Hillsborough, NJ	48,515	114,731	138,347
Holly Springs, NC	36,369	98,041	109,757
Independence, KY	26,939	73,038	78,245
Juneau, AK	40,592	87,436	104,005
Kaysville, UT	28,324	87,975	100,483
Keller, TX	49,916	122,292	147,606
Lafayette, CA	76,726	142,977	202,914
Lafayette, CO	39,220	72,895	96,407
Lake Oswego, OR	59,953	89,979	138,952
Laramie, WY	22,404	40,240	53,432
Leander, TX	30,521	83,550	97,976
Leawood, KS	82,350	147,722	222,429
Lee's Summit, MO	35,722	80,494	95,165
Leesburg, VA	41,184	102,132	121,286
Lehi, UT	24,478	81,013	95,108
Lexington, MA	70,005	152,872	197,029
Los Altos, CA	96,464	187,656	265,087
Loveland, CO	30,521	59,353	73,069
Lower Macungie, PA	41,369	81,929	105,584
Madison, AL	42,487	95,423	111,800
Madison, MS	46,999	100,978	128,848
Maple Valley, WA	38,227	98,925	111,352
Marion, IA	32,034	67,308	78,856

Table continued on next page.

City	Per Capita ($)	Median Household ($)	Average Household ($)
Marlboro, NJ	55,618	140,403	173,465
Mason, OH	46,005	92,819	121,969
Menomonee Falls, WI	38,219	74,266	92,245
Meridian, ID	28,872	64,337	79,379
Meridian, MI	39,707	65,414	91,041
Merrimack, NH	40,980	93,798	106,535
Milton, GA	56,635	109,784	162,851
Moon, PA	39,428	75,553	100,794
Moorpark, CA	39,247	100,457	125,013
Morgantown, WV	23,209	35,502	60,934
Mount Pleasant, SC	46,622	83,490	114,328
Newark, DE	25,326	55,256	76,183
Newtown, CT	49,603	110,036	138,713
North Attleborough, MA	39,288	83,735	105,932
North Port, FL	27,070	53,815	68,268
North Ridgeville, OH	31,399	68,778	80,662
Northville, MI	55,484	106,288	142,353
O'Fallon, MO	34,448	81,004	94,566
Orchard Park, NY	45,686	88,467	115,420
Oro Valley, AZ	41,615	75,966	96,705
Oviedo, FL	31,251	82,402	99,254
Parker, CO	39,869	101,969	113,806
Parkland, FL	54,337	128,292	170,480
Peachtree City, GA	43,017	90,051	117,212
Pittsfield, MI	37,302	70,463	97,513
Plainfield, IL	39,106	116,896	129,365
Pleasant Grove, UT	21,768	64,124	77,670
Poway, CA	41,399	98,859	125,789
Princeton, NJ	67,660	118,467	200,430
Queen Creek, AZ	33,087	90,687	109,131
Radnor, PA	53,456	106,209	170,904
Randolph, NJ	57,054	121,334	162,062
Rexburg, ID	12,747	26,445	41,759
Rio Rancho, NM	27,537	62,637	75,295
Rye, NY	38,754	73,773	114,413
Sammamish, WA	58,567	153,253	177,471
San Ramon, CA	53,732	134,188	157,855
Saratoga, CA	79,870	169,579	226,400
Shrewsbury, MA	44,093	98,790	122,218
South Brunswick, NJ	46,504	109,893	133,824
South Jordan, UT	33,620	95,858	113,234
South Kingstown, RI	33,886	73,801	96,207
South Portland, ME	32,272	56,250	74,386
Sparks, NV	27,039	54,196	68,455
State College, PA	17,472	31,618	54,784
Sugar Land, TX	48,793	108,504	146,270
Sun Prairie, WI	30,373	65,203	76,418
Syracuse, UT	26,867	88,284	102,218
Tredyffrin, PA	63,030	118,462	154,327
Upper Dublin, PA	55,003	111,516	150,599
Urbandale, IA	42,880	81,862	107,291
Vestal, NY	26,831	61,627	82,711
Vestavia Hills, AL	51,797	93,178	130,483
Webster, NY	34,792	70,745	85,670
Wellesley, MA	79,631	171,719	264,145
West Fargo, ND	33,489	71,516	84,689
West Lafayette, IN	17,762	28,793	54,860
Weston, FL	39,844	93,883	125,525
Wilmette, IL	73,832	138,651	207,371
Yorba Linda, CA	48,249	119,697	145,867
Zionsville, IN	56,105	118,190	158,653
U.S.	29,829	55,322	77,866

Source: U.S. Census Bureau, 2012-2016 American Community Survey 5-Year Estimates

Income: Metro Area

Metro Area	Per Capita ($)	Median Household ($)	Average Household ($)
Aberdeen, SD	29,525	53,682	70,105
Aliso Viejo, CA	30,877	62,216	90,585
Allen, TX	31,143	61,330	85,693
Ames, IA	26,032	51,201	66,278
Amherst, MA	28,080	53,609	72,280
Apex, NC	33,233	65,834	87,616
Beavercreek, OH	27,628	49,223	65,799
Bellevue, NE	30,506	59,803	77,649
Bend, OR	30,177	54,211	73,597
Benicia, CA	30,251	69,227	86,345
Bentonville, AR	26,699	50,651	71,135
Bethlehem, NY	33,284	63,758	81,749
Blacksburg, VA	25,417	47,456	64,012
Bowie, MD	44,862	93,804	121,079
Bozeman, MT	31,909	57,021	78,101
Brentwood, TN	30,269	56,152	77,619
Burlington, VT	33,391	64,127	82,667
Cabot, AR	27,031	50,252	67,597
Carmel, IN	29,244	54,261	74,522
Cedar Falls, IA	27,679	52,469	67,838
Cedar Park, TX	34,093	66,093	89,787
Central, LA	27,999	53,004	73,010
Chapel Hill, NC	32,704	54,842	80,993
Cheshire, CT	33,706	62,715	85,132
Chino Hills, CA	23,213	56,295	73,661
Cibolo, TX	26,192	54,638	73,360
Cicero, NY	28,770	54,581	71,507
Collierville, TN	26,242	48,545	68,581
Coppell, TX	31,143	61,330	85,693
Cornelius, NC	29,969	55,191	77,959
Cranberry, PA	31,728	54,020	73,756
Crown Point, IN	33,101	63,327	88,235
Dublin, OH	30,399	57,440	77,221
East Fishkill, NY	37,510	69,211	101,617
Eden Prairie, MN	36,242	70,915	92,296
Edmond, OK	27,964	52,825	72,006
Edwardsville, IL	31,332	56,726	77,549
Evesham, NJ	34,118	63,952	88,881
Flower Mound, TX	31,143	61,330	85,693
Folsom, CA	30,666	61,686	82,859
Friendswood, TX	31,165	60,902	87,925
Gaines, MI	27,382	55,675	72,810
Glastonbury, CT	37,359	71,379	94,209
Grand Blanc, MI	23,755	43,246	58,131
Hampden, PA	31,179	58,774	75,966
Hilliard, OH	30,399	57,440	77,221
Hillsborough, NJ	37,510	69,211	101,617
Holly Springs, NC	33,233	65,834	87,616
Independence, KY	30,431	56,861	76,908
Juneau, AK	40,592	87,436	104,005
Kaysville, UT	25,568	65,687	78,987
Keller, TX	31,143	61,330	85,693
Lafayette, CA	45,777	85,947	121,370
Lafayette, CO	40,097	72,282	99,755
Lake Oswego, OR	32,654	62,772	83,175
Laramie, WY	25,227	43,043	59,866
Leander, TX	34,093	66,093	89,787
Leawood, KS	31,528	59,344	78,907
Lee's Summit, MO	31,528	59,344	78,907
Leesburg, VA	44,862	93,804	121,079
Lehi, UT	22,035	63,994	79,701
Lexington, MA	41,329	77,809	106,402
Los Altos, CA	45,490	100,469	133,546
Loveland, CO	32,433	61,942	81,601
Lower Macungie, PA	30,579	60,441	78,662
Madison, AL	31,793	58,084	79,060
Madison, MS	25,110	46,972	66,544
Maple Valley, WA	38,466	73,044	97,001
Marion, IA	31,452	60,537	76,624

Table continued on next page.

Metro Area	Per Capita ($)	Median Household ($)	Average Household ($)
Marlboro, NJ	37,510	69,211	101,617
Mason, OH	30,431	56,861	76,908
Menomonee Falls, WI	31,258	55,625	76,646
Meridian, ID	26,077	52,377	69,449
Meridian, MI	27,505	51,562	68,222
Merrimack, NH	36,012	73,189	91,648
Milton, GA	30,292	59,183	82,033
Moon, PA	31,728	54,020	73,756
Moorpark, CA	34,331	78,593	103,512
Morgantown, WV	26,477	46,484	66,161
Mount Pleasant, SC	30,081	55,125	75,938
Newark, DE	34,118	63,952	88,881
Newtown, CT	51,719	86,670	141,494
North Attleborough, MA	31,428	58,699	78,355
North Port, FL	32,355	52,235	74,329
North Ridgeville, OH	29,822	51,001	70,884
Northville, MI	29,690	54,037	74,518
O'Fallon, MO	31,332	56,726	77,549
Orchard Park, NY	29,479	52,303	69,343
Oro Valley, AZ	26,204	46,764	64,779
Oviedo, FL	25,850	50,183	69,146
Parker, CO	36,162	68,173	91,685
Parkland, FL	28,360	50,064	75,483
Peachtree City, GA	30,292	59,183	82,033
Pittsfield, MI	35,888	62,484	88,161
Plainfield, IL	33,101	63,327	88,235
Pleasant Grove, UT	22,035	63,994	79,701
Poway, CA	32,482	66,529	90,685
Princeton, NJ	38,652	73,966	106,676
Queen Creek, AZ	28,188	55,227	75,829
Radnor, PA	34,118	63,952	88,881
Randolph, NJ	37,510	69,211	101,617
Rexburg, ID	16,644	39,184	53,793
Rio Rancho, NM	26,569	49,711	66,762
Rye, NY	37,510	69,211	101,617
Sammamish, WA	38,466	73,044	97,001
San Ramon, CA	45,777	85,947	121,370
Saratoga, CA	45,490	100,469	133,546
Shrewsbury, MA	32,692	65,973	85,177
South Brunswick, NJ	37,510	69,211	101,617
South Jordan, UT	28,277	64,564	83,633
South Kingstown, RI	31,428	58,699	78,355
South Portland, ME	33,463	60,486	79,546
Sparks, NV	29,987	55,103	75,030
State College, PA	27,584	54,407	73,047
Sugar Land, TX	31,165	60,902	87,925
Sun Prairie, WI	34,548	63,642	82,875
Syracuse, UT	25,568	65,687	78,987
Tredyffrin, PA	34,118	63,952	88,881
Upper Dublin, PA	34,118	63,952	88,881
Urbandale, IA	33,115	63,534	83,275
Vestal, NY	26,638	49,707	65,240
Vestavia Hills, AL	27,735	50,529	69,844
Webster, NY	29,293	53,480	71,174
Wellesley, MA	41,329	77,809	106,402
West Fargo, ND	31,054	55,941	74,460
West Lafayette, IN	24,313	48,143	63,164
Weston, FL	28,360	50,064	75,483
Wilmette, IL	33,101	63,327	88,235
Yorba Linda, CA	30,877	62,216	90,585
Zionsville, IN	29,244	54,261	74,522
U.S.	29,829	55,322	77,866

Note: Figures cover the Metropolitan Statistical Area (MSA)—see Appendix B for areas included
Source: U.S. Census Bureau, 2012-2016 American Community Survey 5-Year Estimates

Household Income Distribution: City

City	Percent of Households Earning							
	Under $15,000	$15,000 -$24,999	$25,000 -$34,999	$35,000 -$49,999	$50,000 -$74,999	$75,000 -$99,999	$100,000 -$149,999	$150,000 and up
Aberdeen, SD	11.2	13.3	12.6	15.7	17.6	13.6	11.9	4.1
Aliso Viejo, CA	4.4	3.3	3.5	6.7	14.1	15.5	23.0	29.4
Allen, TX	3.1	3.2	5.2	8.8	15.2	12.6	24.2	27.8
Ames, IA	20.8	14.0	9.3	12.1	14.8	10.7	11.8	6.4
Amherst, MA	20.5	10.4	11.2	10.9	11.0	10.3	11.8	13.8
Apex, NC	5.9	3.9	5.6	7.9	13.5	16.1	24.2	23.0
Beavercreek, OH	4.8	5.6	5.4	10.6	18.6	15.4	21.9	17.8
Bellevue, NE	8.4	8.1	11.2	14.8	21.5	14.6	15.3	6.0
Bend, OR	9.9	10.5	10.6	14.6	18.9	12.8	13.3	9.4
Benicia, CA	6.9	4.9	5.3	10.3	16.4	12.1	19.9	24.3
Bentonville, AR	7.5	7.0	7.5	10.8	16.6	14.6	19.2	16.8
Bethlehem, NY	4.5	5.3	5.5	8.2	16.1	14.9	20.8	24.8
Blacksburg, VA	31.5	12.2	6.4	11.8	12.9	7.1	10.1	8.0
Bowie, MD	3.3	3.4	3.5	7.1	13.8	14.0	27.6	27.3
Bozeman, MT	15.1	10.6	9.6	15.6	19.8	11.6	11.0	6.8
Brentwood, TN	2.5	1.5	3.5	5.6	7.5	9.1	20.8	49.3
Burlington, VT	16.9	13.8	8.8	13.0	15.6	13.5	11.7	6.6
Cabot, AR	11.5	7.9	11.0	10.6	22.3	14.7	17.0	5.1
Carmel, IN	3.3	4.0	5.2	7.5	13.9	12.2	22.3	31.6
Cedar Falls, IA	12.2	8.4	10.9	12.4	18.2	13.7	15.4	8.8
Cedar Park, TX	4.0	4.1	6.2	10.0	17.2	16.0	23.3	19.2
Central, LA	5.4	9.5	9.2	11.1	17.8	14.8	20.0	12.3
Chapel Hill, NC	15.0	7.0	7.3	12.6	12.1	8.5	13.4	24.2
Cheshire, CT	2.6	4.3	4.8	7.7	12.4	14.1	24.2	29.7
Chino Hills, CA	5.6	4.0	4.9	7.7	15.6	13.8	24.6	23.7
Cibolo, TX	3.8	3.9	4.3	7.9	17.5	18.4	28.4	15.8
Cicero, NY	8.4	7.7	8.2	11.4	17.1	16.7	18.8	11.6
Collierville, TN	1.9	3.5	5.0	8.0	13.4	12.0	24.9	31.1
Coppell, TX	3.2	3.8	4.0	8.2	11.2	11.8	22.0	35.8
Cornelius, NC	5.4	8.2	5.5	11.4	12.9	14.2	20.1	22.4
Cranberry, PA	3.4	4.2	4.2	6.7	16.2	13.9	21.8	29.6
Crown Point, IN	6.5	7.7	7.7	14.1	19.9	15.9	17.7	10.4
Dublin, OH	3.2	2.3	2.0	5.3	12.3	13.0	22.2	39.7
East Fishkill, NY	3.2	4.8	5.7	7.3	14.1	12.1	23.3	29.5
Eden Prairie, MN	4.5	4.5	4.7	7.1	15.8	12.7	20.0	30.6
Edmond, OK	8.5	7.0	6.3	12.3	16.1	12.2	18.3	19.4
Edwardsville, IL	10.1	7.0	8.4	9.6	20.5	12.7	17.3	14.5
Evesham, NJ	5.7	5.1	6.3	7.6	15.7	14.2	21.1	24.4
Flower Mound, TX	2.1	2.6	3.2	5.0	11.0	13.2	26.6	36.2
Folsom, CA	5.0	4.0	5.2	8.2	13.7	11.6	24.6	27.7
Friendswood, TX	5.2	4.5	5.9	9.4	15.2	11.4	16.6	31.8
Gaines, MI	7.4	7.0	12.1	12.6	24.0	14.0	15.8	7.0
Glastonbury, CT	5.0	4.1	3.6	7.6	12.4	12.7	20.3	34.4
Grand Blanc, MI	8.3	7.0	9.8	15.6	16.1	14.5	16.5	12.1
Hampden, PA	4.0	6.2	9.5	8.7	16.2	14.1	21.1	20.2
Hilliard, OH	4.9	4.9	7.5	7.7	15.6	13.3	21.3	24.8
Hillsborough, NJ	3.3	3.6	3.3	8.6	10.0	14.3	20.6	36.3
Holly Springs, NC	4.1	2.8	3.9	7.5	15.4	17.7	27.3	21.3
Independence, KY	5.8	4.2	6.4	12.1	23.3	21.6	19.1	7.4
Juneau, AK	5.1	3.9	4.4	9.2	18.2	17.2	25.2	16.9
Kaysville, UT	4.6	4.7	4.8	11.5	17.3	15.8	23.8	17.5
Keller, TX	4.9	3.6	4.8	5.8	10.0	11.9	20.2	38.8
Lafayette, CA	4.7	3.7	3.3	8.8	7.5	10.3	13.1	48.6
Lafayette, CO	6.5	6.9	6.6	14.5	17.2	13.1	17.8	17.4
Lake Oswego, OR	6.2	7.5	6.7	7.2	13.9	12.6	14.0	31.8
Laramie, WY	21.1	14.3	11.5	12.6	16.8	9.1	9.7	4.9
Leander, TX	3.3	2.8	6.1	10.9	22.0	16.2	23.9	14.7
Leawood, KS	3.2	3.7	4.8	5.5	8.1	7.4	17.7	49.6
Lee's Summit, MO	5.8	6.5	6.1	10.6	17.0	16.6	21.1	16.3
Leesburg, VA	2.9	4.0	5.3	9.6	14.7	12.4	22.3	28.8
Lehi, UT	3.7	4.3	4.5	9.7	22.0	20.7	22.6	12.5
Lexington, MA	5.4	3.7	3.9	5.1	7.1	8.2	15.6	51.0
Los Altos, CA	3.8	3.4	3.6	3.8	6.8	7.3	13.9	57.5
Loveland, CO	7.8	10.1	10.5	14.0	20.3	15.2	13.9	8.2
Lower Macungie, PA	4.0	6.1	8.4	11.4	16.6	13.7	20.9	18.9
Madison, AL	3.4	5.5	6.8	10.3	14.4	11.3	24.1	24.1
Madison, MS	4.7	3.8	3.4	9.7	13.4	14.1	23.3	27.6

Table continued on next page.

City	Percent of Households Earning							
	Under $15,000	$15,000 -$24,999	$25,000 -$34,999	$35,000 -$49,999	$50,000 -$74,999	$75,000 -$99,999	$100,000 -$149,999	$150,000 and up
Maple Valley, WA	2.8	4.2	2.9	6.4	17.9	16.5	27.4	21.9
Marion, IA	6.6	10.3	9.0	10.9	19.0	18.2	16.5	9.4
Marlboro, NJ	2.9	3.0	3.6	4.9	9.4	9.5	21.0	45.7
Mason, OH	3.7	5.2	6.9	9.8	15.0	12.9	19.0	27.5
Menomonee Falls, WI	5.2	9.0	8.3	12.5	15.6	16.6	17.2	15.7
Meridian, ID	8.0	6.7	9.2	13.8	23.1	14.4	14.5	10.2
Meridian, MI	11.4	9.1	8.9	10.3	15.7	11.5	16.3	16.6
Merrimack, NH	4.3	3.8	4.0	10.1	15.6	16.9	22.7	22.7
Milton, GA	3.9	4.8	2.8	6.4	15.0	12.3	16.1	38.7
Moon, PA	5.8	7.8	7.5	11.0	17.7	10.2	20.8	19.3
Moorpark, CA	2.9	3.4	5.3	7.5	15.4	15.2	21.5	28.8
Morgantown, WV	28.0	13.2	8.2	10.6	13.7	8.7	9.1	8.3
Mount Pleasant, SC	6.0	4.8	5.4	11.6	17.4	12.9	17.7	24.3
Newark, DE	17.6	10.4	7.1	11.3	14.6	13.0	14.5	11.4
Newtown, CT	4.7	3.2	5.5	9.1	11.2	11.4	20.4	34.4
North Attleborough, MA	5.0	6.2	6.8	11.1	14.4	15.5	21.1	20.0
North Port, FL	8.0	11.9	9.8	16.3	25.0	12.6	9.0	7.4
North Ridgeville, OH	4.3	5.3	9.5	13.6	22.1	16.9	18.5	9.9
Northville, MI	4.1	5.8	6.5	7.5	12.8	10.8	17.9	34.6
O'Fallon, MO	4.6	5.8	6.0	10.0	18.9	16.9	22.6	15.0
Orchard Park, NY	4.0	6.1	7.9	11.2	14.6	11.9	23.0	21.4
Oro Valley, AZ	5.5	6.7	7.9	13.1	16.6	14.7	19.4	16.3
Oviedo, FL	6.1	3.9	6.6	9.2	18.7	16.5	19.9	19.0
Parker, CO	4.2	3.6	4.5	7.2	15.0	14.1	25.9	25.5
Parkland, FL	2.4	3.2	4.7	5.3	9.9	11.9	19.6	43.1
Peachtree City, GA	4.0	4.9	4.7	9.9	17.6	12.6	20.4	25.8
Pittsfield, MI	8.8	6.7	8.5	13.1	14.7	12.4	17.5	18.2
Plainfield, IL	2.7	2.6	2.8	6.1	13.8	12.6	27.4	32.0
Pleasant Grove, UT	7.5	6.8	6.1	14.4	23.7	16.8	15.5	9.2
Poway, CA	5.0	5.4	6.1	7.5	13.9	12.4	22.4	27.2
Princeton, NJ	5.7	4.7	7.0	7.1	11.0	8.4	13.2	42.9
Queen Creek, AZ	5.6	4.8	6.0	8.7	13.2	15.7	22.8	23.3
Radnor, PA	9.4	6.1	4.6	7.7	11.7	7.8	17.5	35.1
Randolph, NJ	3.9	2.8	3.4	5.3	11.4	12.0	21.2	39.9
Rexburg, ID	28.7	18.3	14.7	10.8	12.0	7.6	5.6	2.3
Rio Rancho, NM	8.4	8.7	7.4	14.0	21.6	14.6	16.2	9.1
Rye, NY	7.3	8.9	8.6	10.1	15.7	11.6	14.2	23.5
Sammamish, WA	2.8	1.5	2.2	3.5	7.6	8.6	22.8	51.2
San Ramon, CA	3.2	2.4	3.4	5.3	9.1	9.9	22.9	43.8
Saratoga, CA	4.3	2.9	2.7	5.7	6.5	8.2	12.4	57.3
Shrewsbury, MA	4.4	5.0	6.8	7.8	12.5	13.8	20.7	29.0
South Brunswick, NJ	4.8	4.1	3.3	7.1	12.8	12.4	22.6	32.8
South Jordan, UT	3.1	2.4	4.5	6.9	17.2	19.6	23.2	23.1
South Kingstown, RI	9.4	8.1	7.1	11.0	14.8	11.3	19.9	18.4
South Portland, ME	11.3	8.6	8.6	13.8	21.1	13.7	13.7	9.3
Sparks, NV	9.3	10.9	10.1	15.1	21.1	12.7	13.7	7.1
State College, PA	29.5	12.9	10.3	12.0	12.8	6.6	9.2	6.6
Sugar Land, TX	4.5	3.7	4.5	7.6	12.9	12.9	19.4	34.5
Sun Prairie, WI	6.4	7.7	8.9	14.3	20.9	15.0	17.5	9.5
Syracuse, UT	2.9	3.2	4.5	7.2	20.6	22.1	24.6	14.9
Tredyffrin, PA	3.8	5.6	3.7	6.3	11.5	10.1	20.9	38.1
Upper Dublin, PA	3.5	4.9	4.2	6.3	12.3	13.3	21.9	33.7
Urbandale, IA	4.6	5.9	6.9	11.2	17.3	14.8	19.5	19.6
Vestal, NY	9.4	8.0	9.0	14.2	20.4	13.6	14.2	11.3
Vestavia Hills, AL	5.0	6.9	7.2	9.8	13.4	11.5	17.3	28.9
Webster, NY	7.3	7.0	8.4	12.0	17.4	16.9	18.0	13.1
Wellesley, MA	2.9	4.3	2.9	4.0	6.4	8.3	13.6	57.6
West Fargo, ND	5.0	8.0	7.9	11.8	20.8	17.6	17.2	11.7
West Lafayette, IN	30.2	15.2	9.6	9.6	12.7	7.1	7.4	8.2
Weston, FL	6.0	4.1	6.0	8.7	15.5	12.2	19.3	28.2
Wilmette, IL	4.3	3.2	4.6	6.5	9.1	10.3	14.4	47.6
Yorba Linda, CA	3.0	4.2	4.2	7.2	10.6	12.6	20.9	37.2
Zionsville, IN	2.6	3.0	3.9	9.6	12.1	10.7	19.4	38.8
U.S.	12.1	10.2	9.9	13.2	17.8	12.2	13.5	11.1

Source: U.S. Census Bureau, 2012-2016 American Community Survey 5-Year Estimates

Household Income Distribution: Metro Area

Metro Area	Percent of Households Earning							
	Under $15,000	$15,000 -$24,999	$25,000 -$34,999	$35,000 -$49,999	$50,000 -$74,999	$75,000 -$99,999	$100,000 -$149,999	$150,000 and up
Aberdeen, SD	9.8	11.0	11.0	14.0	19.3	14.7	13.6	6.5
Aliso Viejo, CA	11.1	9.4	8.8	11.9	16.4	11.9	14.9	15.6
Allen, TX	9.5	8.9	9.5	13.0	18.2	12.4	15.1	13.4
Ames, IA	16.6	11.6	8.3	12.4	17.5	12.6	13.4	7.5
Amherst, MA	14.4	10.6	9.7	12.4	16.4	12.6	14.5	9.4
Apex, NC	8.4	7.7	9.0	13.0	17.7	13.6	16.4	14.2
Beavercreek, OH	14.0	11.4	10.7	14.5	18.2	11.7	12.1	7.3
Bellevue, NE	9.9	9.0	9.3	13.9	18.7	13.6	15.3	10.2
Bend, OR	10.8	10.7	10.4	14.8	18.7	13.2	13.4	8.1
Benicia, CA	9.1	7.5	7.8	11.4	17.7	14.7	17.8	14.0
Bentonville, AR	12.0	10.8	11.1	15.4	19.1	10.8	12.0	8.8
Bethlehem, NY	9.7	8.8	8.6	12.1	18.3	13.9	16.8	11.7
Blacksburg, VA	16.7	11.8	8.5	15.3	19.1	11.3	10.7	6.6
Bowie, MD	6.4	4.8	5.4	8.5	15.0	12.9	20.1	26.9
Bozeman, MT	11.2	8.8	9.4	14.5	20.3	12.6	13.7	9.5
Brentwood, TN	10.3	9.7	10.0	14.6	19.0	13.1	13.2	10.2
Burlington, VT	9.8	8.3	8.2	12.2	18.6	14.7	17.3	10.9
Cabot, AR	12.8	11.3	10.9	14.8	18.8	11.8	12.2	7.4
Carmel, IN	11.3	10.2	10.2	14.4	18.3	12.6	13.5	9.4
Cedar Falls, IA	11.7	10.2	11.3	14.0	20.4	13.5	12.7	6.1
Cedar Park, TX	8.9	8.0	8.3	12.5	18.2	13.3	16.2	14.5
Central, LA	14.2	10.4	9.6	13.1	17.1	11.8	14.3	9.5
Chapel Hill, NC	12.2	10.0	9.7	13.7	17.4	11.5	12.9	12.7
Cheshire, CT	11.4	9.2	8.3	11.9	16.5	12.2	16.1	14.4
Chino Hills, CA	11.2	10.2	9.8	13.4	18.4	12.9	14.2	9.9
Cibolo, TX	11.7	10.2	10.0	13.8	18.9	12.5	13.7	9.3
Cicero, NY	12.7	9.9	9.7	13.7	18.6	12.8	14.0	8.6
Collierville, TN	14.4	12.0	11.0	13.5	17.7	11.3	11.7	8.3
Coppell, TX	9.5	8.9	9.5	13.0	18.2	12.4	15.1	13.4
Cornelius, NC	11.1	9.8	10.3	14.1	18.1	12.5	13.2	10.8
Cranberry, PA	12.2	11.0	10.1	13.1	18.2	12.5	13.6	9.4
Crown Point, IN	10.8	8.9	8.5	11.9	17.0	12.8	15.6	14.4
Dublin, OH	11.3	9.4	9.6	13.4	18.7	12.9	14.3	10.5
East Fishkill, NY	11.7	8.5	7.7	10.2	15.0	11.7	15.9	19.3
Eden Prairie, MN	8.0	7.6	7.7	11.7	17.8	14.2	18.0	15.0
Edmond, OK	11.7	10.2	10.8	14.4	19.1	12.5	12.5	8.7
Edwardsville, IL	11.2	9.7	9.7	13.5	18.3	12.8	14.2	10.5
Evesham, NJ	11.3	8.8	8.4	11.6	16.4	12.3	16.0	15.2
Flower Mound, TX	9.5	8.9	9.5	13.0	18.2	12.4	15.1	13.4
Folsom, CA	11.1	9.0	8.9	12.2	17.4	12.5	15.6	13.3
Friendswood, TX	10.2	9.5	9.5	12.6	17.1	11.7	14.6	14.8
Gaines, MI	9.8	10.0	10.5	14.5	20.6	13.5	13.2	8.0
Glastonbury, CT	9.4	8.1	7.6	10.8	16.4	13.4	17.6	16.8
Grand Blanc, MI	16.0	12.4	12.2	16.0	17.8	10.8	9.6	5.2
Hampden, PA	9.0	9.1	10.0	14.0	20.2	13.8	14.5	9.3
Hilliard, OH	11.3	9.4	9.6	13.4	18.7	12.9	14.3	10.5
Hillsborough, NJ	11.7	8.5	7.7	10.2	15.0	11.7	15.9	19.3
Holly Springs, NC	8.4	7.7	9.0	13.0	17.7	13.6	16.4	14.2
Independence, KY	12.2	9.8	9.4	12.9	18.3	12.6	14.0	10.8
Juneau, AK	5.1	3.9	4.4	9.2	18.2	17.2	25.2	16.9
Kaysville, UT	7.4	6.8	7.9	13.6	22.1	16.4	16.6	9.2
Keller, TX	9.5	8.9	9.5	13.0	18.2	12.4	15.1	13.4
Lafayette, CA	8.7	6.7	6.1	8.9	14.0	11.6	17.7	26.2
Lafayette, CO	10.1	7.2	7.7	11.0	15.6	12.0	16.7	19.7
Lake Oswego, OR	9.5	8.6	8.9	12.8	18.3	13.9	15.9	12.1
Laramie, WY	19.1	13.1	12.1	12.4	16.8	10.1	10.4	6.0
Leander, TX	8.9	8.0	8.3	12.5	18.2	13.3	16.2	14.5
Leawood, KS	10.3	9.0	9.6	13.7	18.5	13.6	14.8	10.6
Lee's Summit, MO	10.3	9.0	9.6	13.7	18.5	13.6	14.8	10.6
Leesburg, VA	6.4	4.8	5.4	8.5	15.0	12.9	20.1	26.9
Lehi, UT	7.8	7.9	8.3	13.4	21.3	15.5	16.1	9.6
Lexington, MA	10.0	7.3	6.7	9.5	15.1	12.3	18.0	21.2
Los Altos, CA	6.7	5.5	5.6	8.0	12.8	11.1	18.7	31.5
Loveland, CO	9.1	9.7	9.0	13.4	17.6	14.5	15.0	11.7
Lower Macungie, PA	9.1	9.4	9.3	13.3	19.1	13.7	15.3	10.7
Madison, AL	12.1	9.4	9.5	12.7	16.6	12.2	15.5	11.9
Madison, MS	15.9	11.5	10.9	14.2	17.0	11.0	11.6	7.9

Table continued on next page.

Metro Area	Percent of Households Earning							
	Under $15,000	$15,000 -$24,999	$25,000 -$34,999	$35,000 -$49,999	$50,000 -$74,999	$75,000 -$99,999	$100,000 -$149,999	$150,000 and up
Maple Valley, WA	8.5	6.8	7.3	11.4	17.3	13.6	17.8	17.4
Marion, IA	8.9	9.3	10.0	13.1	19.2	15.4	15.3	8.9
Marlboro, NJ	11.7	8.5	7.7	10.2	15.0	11.7	15.9	19.3
Mason, OH	12.2	9.8	9.4	12.9	18.3	12.6	14.0	10.8
Menomonee Falls, WI	12.1	10.5	9.6	12.9	17.8	12.9	14.1	10.0
Meridian, ID	11.7	10.2	10.9	14.7	20.2	12.4	12.1	7.8
Meridian, MI	12.9	10.7	10.5	14.3	19.2	12.3	12.6	7.5
Merrimack, NH	7.1	7.4	7.8	11.4	17.3	14.6	18.7	15.6
Milton, GA	10.5	9.1	9.4	13.4	18.4	12.6	14.2	12.4
Moon, PA	12.2	11.0	10.1	13.1	18.2	12.5	13.6	9.4
Moorpark, CA	6.5	6.8	7.2	10.5	16.8	13.8	18.5	19.9
Morgantown, WV	18.2	11.5	9.8	13.2	17.7	10.4	11.1	8.1
Mount Pleasant, SC	12.1	9.5	9.6	13.9	19.0	12.6	13.5	9.8
Newark, DE	11.3	8.8	8.4	11.6	16.4	12.3	16.0	15.2
Newtown, CT	8.0	6.9	6.5	9.3	13.8	11.3	16.4	27.9
North Attleborough, MA	13.2	9.7	8.8	12.0	16.6	12.9	15.3	11.6
North Port, FL	10.5	11.2	11.4	14.7	19.0	11.8	12.0	9.5
North Ridgeville, OH	14.2	11.0	10.4	13.5	17.6	11.9	12.7	8.7
Northville, MI	13.2	10.4	9.7	13.1	17.4	12.1	13.7	10.3
O'Fallon, MO	11.2	9.7	9.7	13.5	18.3	12.8	14.2	10.5
Orchard Park, NY	13.7	10.9	10.2	13.2	17.7	12.8	13.7	7.9
Oro Valley, AZ	14.3	12.4	11.4	14.7	17.9	11.3	10.8	7.1
Oviedo, FL	11.9	11.2	11.4	15.3	19.2	11.5	11.3	8.2
Parker, CO	8.4	7.4	8.3	12.3	18.0	13.6	16.8	15.1
Parkland, FL	13.6	11.7	10.6	14.0	17.1	10.9	11.8	10.2
Peachtree City, GA	10.5	9.1	9.4	13.4	18.4	12.6	14.2	12.4
Pittsfield, MI	11.2	8.6	9.0	12.3	16.0	11.8	15.7	15.4
Plainfield, IL	10.8	8.9	8.5	11.9	17.0	12.8	15.6	14.4
Pleasant Grove, UT	7.8	7.9	8.3	13.4	21.3	15.5	16.1	9.6
Poway, CA	9.5	8.1	8.4	11.9	17.0	12.8	16.4	15.8
Princeton, NJ	9.6	7.7	7.3	9.6	16.4	12.0	16.5	20.9
Queen Creek, AZ	11.2	9.6	10.1	14.2	18.7	12.5	13.6	10.1
Radnor, PA	11.3	8.8	8.4	11.6	16.4	12.3	16.0	15.2
Randolph, NJ	11.7	8.5	7.7	10.2	15.0	11.7	15.9	19.3
Rexburg, ID	18.5	14.2	13.0	14.2	16.1	11.8	8.4	3.6
Rio Rancho, NM	14.1	11.9	10.6	13.6	18.0	11.8	12.1	7.9
Rye, NY	11.7	8.5	7.7	10.2	15.0	11.7	15.9	19.3
Sammamish, WA	8.5	6.8	7.3	11.4	17.3	13.6	17.8	17.4
San Ramon, CA	8.7	6.7	6.1	8.9	14.0	11.6	17.7	26.2
Saratoga, CA	6.7	5.5	5.6	8.0	12.8	11.1	18.7	31.5
Shrewsbury, MA	10.4	9.0	8.3	11.0	16.8	13.2	17.4	14.0
South Brunswick, NJ	11.7	8.5	7.7	10.2	15.0	11.7	15.9	19.3
South Jordan, UT	7.8	7.8	8.7	13.0	20.3	15.0	16.1	11.3
South Kingstown, RI	13.2	9.7	8.8	12.0	16.6	12.9	15.3	11.6
South Portland, ME	10.0	8.9	9.5	13.2	18.8	14.0	15.0	10.5
Sparks, NV	11.2	10.9	9.8	13.9	18.5	12.5	13.6	9.6
State College, PA	13.7	9.9	10.3	12.5	17.7	11.7	14.0	10.1
Sugar Land, TX	10.2	9.5	9.5	12.6	17.1	11.7	14.6	14.8
Sun Prairie, WI	9.1	8.0	9.2	12.8	18.8	14.3	16.2	11.6
Syracuse, UT	7.4	6.8	7.9	13.6	22.1	16.4	16.6	9.2
Tredyffrin, PA	11.3	8.8	8.4	11.6	16.4	12.3	16.0	15.2
Upper Dublin, PA	11.3	8.8	8.4	11.6	16.4	12.3	16.0	15.2
Urbandale, IA	8.9	8.0	8.9	12.7	19.8	14.3	15.9	11.5
Vestal, NY	13.3	12.5	10.8	13.6	18.6	12.1	12.2	6.8
Vestavia Hills, AL	14.2	11.2	10.7	13.3	17.8	12.0	12.2	8.5
Webster, NY	12.0	10.5	10.4	13.8	18.4	12.8	13.6	8.4
Wellesley, MA	10.0	7.3	6.7	9.5	15.1	12.3	18.0	21.2
West Fargo, ND	10.5	9.4	10.9	14.1	18.8	14.0	13.3	9.0
West Lafayette, IN	14.8	11.5	10.5	14.5	19.5	11.7	11.5	5.9
Weston, FL	13.6	11.7	10.6	14.0	17.1	10.9	11.8	10.2
Wilmette, IL	10.8	8.9	8.5	11.9	17.0	12.8	15.6	14.4
Yorba Linda, CA	11.1	9.4	8.8	11.9	16.4	11.9	14.9	15.6
Zionsville, IN	11.3	10.2	10.2	14.4	18.3	12.6	13.5	9.4
U.S.	12.1	10.2	9.9	13.2	17.8	12.2	13.5	11.1

Note: Figures cover the Metropolitan Statistical Area (MSA)—see Appendix B for areas included
Source: Source: U.S. Census Bureau, 2012-2016 American Community Survey 5-Year Estimates

Poverty Rate: City

City	All Ages	Under 18 Years Old	18 to 64 Years Old	65 Years and Over
Aberdeen, SD	13.6	12.5	15.2	9.2
Aliso Viejo, CA	4.8	4.6	4.5	8.0
Allen, TX	5.1	6.9	4.8	1.2
Ames, IA	30.1	9.8	37.3	3.8
Amherst, MA	35.7	19.5	43.5	6.7
Apex, NC	4.6	3.8	4.3	11.3
Beavercreek, OH	4.8	3.0	5.6	4.2
Bellevue, NE	11.0	16.4	10.0	5.8
Bend, OR	12.4	15.0	12.3	9.2
Benicia, CA	7.1	7.6	7.4	5.4
Bentonville, AR	7.8	7.9	7.4	11.2
Bethlehem, NY	4.5	4.0	4.6	4.9
Blacksburg, VA	44.7	19.9	50.9	6.7
Bowie, MD	3.3	2.3	3.4	4.5
Bozeman, MT	20.7	10.1	24.6	7.5
Brentwood, TN	2.8	2.5	3.0	2.7
Burlington, VT	25.1	25.3	27.2	11.4
Cabot, AR	12.8	19.2	9.9	12.0
Carmel, IN	3.6	4.3	3.6	1.8
Cedar Falls, IA	18.5	11.9	23.5	3.9
Cedar Park, TX	4.5	4.7	4.2	5.8
Central, LA	6.0	7.9	5.9	3.9
Chapel Hill, NC	20.1	5.2	26.9	3.8
Cheshire, CT	2.4	2.0	2.3	3.3
Chino Hills, CA	6.7	7.4	6.9	4.1
Cibolo, TX	5.1	4.9	4.7	9.9
Cicero, NY	7.9	9.6	6.9	9.3
Collierville, TN	5.4	10.2	4.1	1.8
Coppell, TX	4.6	6.4	4.1	2.4
Cornelius, NC	4.8	4.5	5.2	3.9
Cranberry, PA	3.1	3.4	2.6	5.0
Crown Point, IN	7.2	10.7	6.6	5.3
Dublin, OH	2.7	2.9	2.2	5.8
East Fishkill, NY	3.4	4.8	3.0	2.9
Eden Prairie, MN	4.4	5.2	4.1	4.1
Edmond, OK	10.0	11.1	10.7	4.4
Edwardsville, IL	13.7	5.8	18.1	3.7
Evesham, NJ	4.8	6.1	4.0	6.3
Flower Mound, TX	3.2	4.3	2.7	3.4
Folsom, CA	4.7	4.5	4.2	7.7
Friendswood, TX	5.8	7.4	5.4	4.3
Gaines, MI	11.2	13.8	11.7	2.6
Glastonbury, CT	3.8	2.4	3.6	6.4
Grand Blanc, MI	10.0	10.7	10.7	5.3
Hampden, PA	3.0	2.7	2.7	4.4
Hilliard, OH	4.0	6.3	2.8	4.4
Hillsborough, NJ	3.6	3.0	4.0	2.3
Holly Springs, NC	3.9	3.3	4.0	5.9
Independence, KY	6.9	11.5	5.1	5.3
Juneau, AK	7.4	13.4	6.4	1.3
Kaysville, UT	4.8	6.8	3.4	4.3
Keller, TX	3.7	3.9	3.3	5.5
Lafayette, CA	5.3	2.3	7.7	2.2
Lafayette, CO	8.2	11.1	7.7	4.8
Lake Oswego, OR	7.2	9.9	6.8	5.1
Laramie, WY	28.8	18.8	33.2	8.3
Leander, TX	4.8	5.5	4.5	4.4
Leawood, KS	2.6	2.4	2.4	3.4
Lee's Summit, MO	5.9	7.2	5.5	4.7
Leesburg, VA	5.7	6.0	5.4	6.8
Lehi, UT	5.9	7.0	5.3	3.3
Lexington, MA	3.5	2.5	3.9	3.9
Los Altos, CA	3.3	2.8	3.2	4.2
Loveland, CO	9.4	13.6	8.7	6.3
Lower Macungie, PA	2.8	2.5	3.2	2.1
Madison, AL	5.7	6.9	5.3	5.3
Madison, MS	3.1	1.5	3.8	3.1
Maple Valley, WA	4.2	5.2	3.6	5.0

Table continued on next page.

City	All Ages	Under 18 Years Old	18 to 64 Years Old	65 Years and Over
Marion, IA	7.0	9.1	7.0	3.4
Marlboro, NJ	1.6	0.9	1.7	2.4
Mason, OH	2.6	1.8	2.4	4.6
Menomonee Falls, WI	4.0	4.7	2.8	6.6
Meridian, ID	9.3	10.9	8.5	9.7
Meridian, MI	12.1	6.9	15.1	5.7
Merrimack, NH	4.6	4.8	4.7	3.3
Milton, GA	5.5	6.7	4.9	5.9
Moon, PA	6.5	5.5	7.5	3.7
Moorpark, CA	5.9	7.6	5.6	3.2
Morgantown, WV	35.3	27.3	40.2	9.0
Mount Pleasant, SC	6.4	7.0	6.7	4.3
Newark, DE	24.8	11.7	31.2	6.5
Newtown, CT	4.5	3.4	4.9	5.0
North Attleborough, MA	6.3	6.9	6.2	4.9
North Port, FL	12.3	14.7	14.3	5.6
North Ridgeville, OH	4.9	5.8	5.0	3.4
Northville, MI	2.7	1.9	2.7	3.6
O'Fallon, MO	4.6	4.8	4.5	4.3
Orchard Park, NY	2.8	2.5	3.5	1.1
Oro Valley, AZ	7.4	12.4	7.0	5.2
Oviedo, FL	5.9	4.7	6.2	7.2
Parker, CO	4.8	5.8	4.2	6.6
Parkland, FL	3.5	5.0	2.7	3.9
Peachtree City, GA	5.8	8.1	5.2	4.4
Pittsfield, MI	10.8	9.0	12.2	5.5
Plainfield, IL	1.9	1.5	1.8	5.4
Pleasant Grove, UT	12.1	12.9	12.2	7.5
Poway, CA	5.9	6.2	5.8	5.9
Princeton, NJ	6.6	4.5	8.0	4.4
Queen Creek, AZ	7.8	9.5	6.8	7.2
Radnor, PA	8.9	7.3	10.0	7.6
Randolph, NJ	3.0	2.5	2.9	5.0
Rexburg, ID	43.2	30.2	50.0	9.0
Rio Rancho, NM	11.7	15.8	10.8	8.4
Rye, NY	10.5	12.1	10.4	8.3
Sammamish, WA	2.7	3.1	2.2	4.7
San Ramon, CA	3.9	3.9	3.5	6.6
Saratoga, CA	4.5	5.5	4.0	4.9
Shrewsbury, MA	4.5	3.7	4.5	5.5
South Brunswick, NJ	4.3	5.5	4.0	3.4
South Jordan, UT	3.5	3.0	3.5	5.1
South Kingstown, RI	10.5	9.6	12.6	5.2
South Portland, ME	12.3	18.4	11.4	8.9
Sparks, NV	12.3	18.1	11.1	7.5
State College, PA	44.8	14.1	50.7	3.8
Sugar Land, TX	5.1	6.0	5.0	4.4
Sun Prairie, WI	9.5	14.4	8.0	5.9
Syracuse, UT	4.2	5.7	3.2	2.5
Tredyffrin, PA	4.5	7.4	4.1	2.1
Upper Dublin, PA	3.0	3.9	2.5	3.7
Urbandale, IA	6.2	8.6	5.7	4.3
Vestal, NY	11.1	11.6	13.5	3.0
Vestavia Hills, AL	4.9	4.7	5.3	3.3
Webster, NY	6.7	9.4	6.5	3.8
Wellesley, MA	3.3	3.1	3.7	2.2
West Fargo, ND	6.8	8.4	6.4	5.2
West Lafayette, IN	41.0	15.2	50.3	3.7
Weston, FL	7.9	8.2	7.7	7.4
Wilmette, IL	3.3	2.2	2.7	7.0
Yorba Linda, CA	3.8	4.9	3.3	4.3
Zionsville, IN	2.7	4.1	2.0	2.8
U.S.	15.1	21.2	14.2	9.3

Note: Figures are percentage of people whose income during the past 12 months was below the poverty level; Source: U.S. Census Bureau, 2012-2016 American Community Survey 5-Year Estimates

Poverty Rate: Metro Area

Metro Area	All Ages	Under 18 Years Old	18 to 64 Years Old	65 Years and Over
Aberdeen, SD	10.9	9.3	11.7	9.8
Aliso Viejo, CA	16.5	23.3	14.9	12.3
Allen, TX	14.0	20.3	12.3	8.5
Ames, IA	22.3	10.1	28.4	4.8
Amherst, MA	17.0	25.1	16.1	9.2
Apex, NC	11.6	15.7	10.8	6.9
Beavercreek, OH	16.4	24.8	15.5	8.1
Bellevue, NE	11.8	16.1	10.9	7.3
Bend, OR	13.9	18.3	14.0	8.3
Benicia, CA	12.7	18.1	11.9	7.4
Bentonville, AR	15.3	19.5	14.8	8.8
Bethlehem, NY	11.0	15.0	10.8	6.5
Blacksburg, VA	20.9	16.0	25.2	7.7
Bowie, MD	8.4	10.8	7.8	7.2
Bozeman, MT	13.5	10.4	15.8	5.3
Brentwood, TN	13.5	19.3	12.3	7.8
Burlington, VT	10.7	11.9	11.0	7.3
Cabot, AR	15.5	21.8	14.7	7.9
Carmel, IN	14.2	20.3	13.1	7.1
Cedar Falls, IA	13.6	15.4	14.9	5.6
Cedar Park, TX	13.3	17.3	12.6	7.3
Central, LA	17.5	23.6	16.4	10.9
Chapel Hill, NC	16.2	21.4	16.2	7.8
Cheshire, CT	12.8	18.9	11.9	8.0
Chino Hills, CA	17.7	24.8	16.0	10.3
Cibolo, TX	15.9	22.7	14.1	10.7
Cicero, NY	15.4	22.4	14.6	8.4
Collierville, TN	19.4	30.1	16.7	10.5
Coppell, TX	14.0	20.3	12.3	8.5
Cornelius, NC	14.1	19.4	13.0	8.8
Cranberry, PA	12.0	16.9	11.7	7.9
Crown Point, IN	13.6	19.5	12.3	9.3
Dublin, OH	14.4	20.3	13.5	7.7
East Fishkill, NY	14.2	20.0	12.7	11.7
Eden Prairie, MN	9.8	12.9	9.3	6.6
Edmond, OK	15.0	21.2	14.1	7.3
Edwardsville, IL	12.7	18.3	12.0	7.4
Evesham, NJ	13.1	18.1	12.3	8.9
Flower Mound, TX	14.0	20.3	12.3	8.5
Folsom, CA	15.8	20.7	15.5	9.0
Friendswood, TX	15.3	22.4	13.1	10.1
Gaines, MI	13.4	17.6	13.1	6.6
Glastonbury, CT	10.4	14.1	9.9	7.3
Grand Blanc, MI	20.9	31.4	20.3	7.7
Hampden, PA	11.0	16.3	10.5	5.8
Hilliard, OH	14.4	20.3	13.5	7.7
Hillsborough, NJ	14.2	20.0	12.7	11.7
Holly Springs, NC	11.6	15.7	10.8	6.9
Independence, KY	13.8	19.4	12.9	7.7
Juneau, AK	7.4	13.4	6.4	1.3
Kaysville, UT	9.3	11.4	8.7	6.8
Keller, TX	14.0	20.3	12.3	8.5
Lafayette, CA	10.7	12.6	10.5	8.8
Lafayette, CO	13.4	12.0	15.1	6.4
Lake Oswego, OR	12.8	16.3	12.7	7.6
Laramie, WY	25.5	17.6	29.8	8.0
Leander, TX	13.3	17.3	12.6	7.3
Leawood, KS	12.2	17.4	11.2	6.9
Lee's Summit, MO	12.2	17.4	11.2	6.9
Leesburg, VA	8.4	10.8	7.8	7.2
Lehi, UT	12.6	11.4	14.1	5.8
Lexington, MA	10.2	12.6	9.7	8.9
Los Altos, CA	9.3	10.7	8.9	8.9
Loveland, CO	13.2	11.8	15.3	5.4
Lower Macungie, PA	10.9	16.9	10.0	5.9
Madison, AL	13.4	18.4	12.7	8.5
Madison, MS	19.7	27.7	18.0	12.2
Maple Valley, WA	10.9	13.7	10.4	8.2

Table continued on next page.

Metro Area	All Ages	Under 18 Years Old	18 to 64 Years Old	65 Years and Over
Marion, IA	9.4	10.8	9.7	6.2
Marlboro, NJ	14.2	20.0	12.7	11.7
Mason, OH	13.8	19.4	12.9	7.7
Menomonee Falls, WI	15.0	22.1	13.7	8.2
Meridian, ID	14.7	18.4	14.0	10.2
Meridian, MI	17.7	21.5	18.9	6.4
Merrimack, NH	8.6	11.3	8.3	6.1
Milton, GA	14.9	21.6	13.2	9.0
Moon, PA	12.0	16.9	11.7	7.9
Moorpark, CA	10.6	15.2	9.7	6.8
Morgantown, WV	20.5	18.8	23.3	8.0
Mount Pleasant, SC	14.6	21.2	13.4	8.9
Newark, DE	13.1	18.1	12.3	8.9
Newtown, CT	8.8	10.8	8.5	7.0
North Attleborough, MA	13.4	18.7	12.5	9.7
North Port, FL	12.6	21.1	13.1	6.8
North Ridgeville, OH	15.2	22.0	14.3	9.1
Northville, MI	16.2	23.8	15.1	9.0
O'Fallon, MO	12.7	18.3	12.0	7.4
Orchard Park, NY	14.5	21.7	13.7	8.4
Oro Valley, AZ	19.1	27.4	19.1	8.8
Oviedo, FL	16.1	23.4	14.8	10.0
Parker, CO	10.9	14.9	10.2	6.9
Parkland, FL	16.7	23.3	15.0	15.0
Peachtree City, GA	14.9	21.6	13.2	9.0
Pittsfield, MI	15.2	13.7	17.3	6.0
Plainfield, IL	13.6	19.5	12.3	9.3
Pleasant Grove, UT	12.6	11.4	14.1	5.8
Poway, CA	14.0	18.0	13.6	9.1
Princeton, NJ	11.2	15.6	10.4	7.5
Queen Creek, AZ	16.5	23.8	15.4	8.3
Radnor, PA	13.1	18.1	12.3	8.9
Randolph, NJ	14.2	20.0	12.7	11.7
Rexburg, ID	27.6	20.9	33.4	6.8
Rio Rancho, NM	18.6	26.3	17.6	10.6
Rye, NY	14.2	20.0	12.7	11.7
Sammamish, WA	10.9	13.7	10.4	8.2
San Ramon, CA	10.7	12.6	10.5	8.8
Saratoga, CA	9.3	10.7	8.9	8.9
Shrewsbury, MA	11.4	14.7	10.9	8.6
South Brunswick, NJ	14.2	20.0	12.7	11.7
South Jordan, UT	11.1	14.1	10.4	7.1
South Kingstown, RI	13.4	18.7	12.5	9.7
South Portland, ME	10.4	13.1	10.3	7.7
Sparks, NV	14.9	20.0	14.8	7.5
State College, PA	19.1	13.6	23.1	5.7
Sugar Land, TX	15.3	22.4	13.1	10.1
Sun Prairie, WI	12.0	12.8	12.9	5.6
Syracuse, UT	9.3	11.4	8.7	6.8
Tredyffrin, PA	13.1	18.1	12.3	8.9
Upper Dublin, PA	13.1	18.1	12.3	8.9
Urbandale, IA	11.0	14.6	10.2	7.4
Vestal, NY	16.1	22.1	16.6	7.1
Vestavia Hills, AL	16.2	23.3	15.1	9.5
Webster, NY	14.1	20.9	13.7	6.8
Wellesley, MA	10.2	12.6	9.7	8.9
West Fargo, ND	11.8	11.9	12.6	6.9
West Lafayette, IN	20.3	19.4	23.3	4.8
Weston, FL	16.7	23.3	15.0	15.0
Wilmette, IL	13.6	19.5	12.3	9.3
Yorba Linda, CA	16.5	23.3	14.9	12.3
Zionsville, IN	14.2	20.3	13.1	7.1
U.S.	15.1	21.2	14.2	9.3

Note: Figures are percentage of people whose income during the past 12 months was below the poverty level; Figures cover the Metropolitan Statistical Area—see Appendix B for areas included
Source: U.S. Census Bureau, 2012-2016 American Community Survey 5-Year Estimates

Employment by Industry

Metro Area[1]	(A)	(B)	(C)	(D)	(E)	(F)	(G)	(H)	(I)	(J)	(K)	(L)	(M)	(N)
Aberdeen, SD	n/a	n/a	n/a	n/a	n/a	n/a	n/a	n/a	n/a	n/a	n/a	n/a	n/a	n/a
Aliso Viejo, CA[2]	6.3	6.3	13.4	7.2	9.9	1.6	13.3	9.5	<0.1	3.1	18.9	9.7	1.7	4.9
Allen, TX[2]	5.4	n/a	11.9	8.9	11.6	2.7	10.0	6.8	n/a	3.2	18.6	10.1	4.6	5.6
Ames, IA	n/a	n/a	n/a	n/a	41.6	n/a	n/a	n/a	n/a	n/a	n/a	n/a	n/a	n/a
Amherst, MA[3]	3.3	n/a	24.6	4.8	18.8	0.9	8.8	8.5	n/a	3.8	7.9	10.4	4.1	3.5
Apex, NC	6.0	n/a	12.0	5.1	15.7	3.5	11.1	5.6	n/a	3.7	18.8	11.4	2.2	4.4
Beavercreek, OH	3.1	n/a	19.5	4.6	15.8	2.0	10.3	10.8	n/a	3.6	12.9	10.4	3.3	3.3
Bellevue, NE	5.4	n/a	16.0	8.6	13.2	2.2	9.7	6.7	n/a	3.5	14.3	11.3	5.3	3.3
Bend, OR	8.1	n/a	15.9	5.8	12.1	2.0	14.6	6.8	n/a	3.4	11.8	14.1	2.5	2.4
Benicia, CA	8.4	8.2	19.1	3.7	17.9	0.7	10.5	8.8	0.2	3.0	7.1	14.0	3.3	3.0
Bentonville, AR	4.4	n/a	11.3	3.1	14.1	0.7	9.7	11.4	n/a	3.5	19.2	10.5	6.5	5.1
Bethlehem, NY	3.9	n/a	20.4	5.4	21.7	1.7	8.7	5.6	n/a	4.0	11.9	10.5	2.9	2.8
Blacksburg, VA	n/a	n/a	n/a	n/a	32.1	n/a	n/a	n/a	n/a	n/a	n/a	n/a	n/a	n/a
Bowie, MD[2]	4.5	n/a	13.1	4.4	21.9	2.2	10.0	1.3	n/a	6.8	22.8	8.3	2.3	1.8
Bozeman, MT	n/a	n/a	n/a	n/a	n/a	n/a	n/a	n/a	n/a	n/a	n/a	n/a	n/a	n/a
Brentwood, TN	4.1	n/a	15.1	6.6	12.0	2.3	11.3	8.3	n/a	4.0	16.5	10.1	5.1	4.0
Burlington, VT[3]	4.7	n/a	17.8	3.7	18.8	1.7	10.0	10.1	n/a	3.3	11.3	12.2	2.7	3.1
Cabot, AR	4.8	n/a	15.8	5.8	19.6	1.6	9.3	5.5	n/a	4.2	13.4	10.9	4.5	4.1
Carmel, IN	4.7	4.6	15.0	6.3	12.5	1.3	9.7	8.6	<0.1	4.1	16.2	10.5	6.1	4.5
Cedar Falls, IA	n/a	n/a	15.2	5.2	16.5	n/a	8.2	17.9	n/a	n/a	8.1	11.9	n/a	n/a
Cedar Park, TX	5.8	n/a	11.5	5.7	16.9	2.9	12.3	5.4	n/a	4.3	17.3	10.2	2.1	5.1
Central, LA	12.0	11.7	13.0	4.7	18.4	1.2	10.1	7.1	0.2	4.0	11.7	10.8	3.4	3.2
Chapel Hill, NC	2.5	n/a	21.3	4.8	22.8	1.4	8.9	8.9	n/a	3.5	13.5	8.0	1.4	2.5
Cheshire, CT[3]	3.6	n/a	28.5	4.3	12.4	1.2	8.1	8.4	n/a	3.7	10.5	11.0	3.6	4.1
Chino Hills, CA	6.7	6.6	15.3	2.9	17.0	0.7	11.2	6.5	<0.1	3.0	10.2	12.8	8.7	4.3
Cibolo, TX	5.9	5.2	15.4	8.5	16.4	1.9	12.6	4.5	0.7	3.6	13.0	11.1	3.2	3.4
Cicero, NY	3.7	n/a	20.1	4.5	18.3	1.4	9.1	7.9	n/a	3.8	10.8	11.3	4.2	4.5
Collierville, TN	3.4	n/a	14.6	4.4	12.8	0.8	10.4	6.8	n/a	3.8	14.7	10.7	11.4	5.6
Coppell, TX[2]	5.4	n/a	11.9	8.9	11.6	2.7	10.0	6.8	n/a	3.2	18.6	10.1	4.6	5.6
Cornelius, NC	5.1	n/a	10.2	7.7	13.4	2.3	11.3	8.7	n/a	3.4	16.7	10.8	4.8	5.0
Cranberry, PA	5.8	5.0	21.3	6.0	9.8	1.5	10.0	7.2	0.8	4.3	15.3	10.6	4.0	3.6
Crown Point, IN[2]	6.1	6.0	18.9	3.1	12.7	0.7	11.0	12.7	<0.1	4.8	8.3	12.3	5.6	3.4
Dublin, OH	3.5	n/a	14.7	7.8	16.2	1.5	9.5	6.7	n/a	3.6	16.4	10.4	5.3	3.8
East Fishkill, NY[2]	5.2	n/a	27.0	3.1	17.5	1.2	9.8	6.3	n/a	4.7	8.3	11.5	2.9	1.9
Eden Prairie, MN	3.8	n/a	16.8	7.2	12.7	1.8	8.9	9.7	n/a	4.0	16.1	9.8	3.8	4.9
Edmond, OK	7.7	4.5	14.4	5.1	20.4	1.1	11.1	5.2	3.1	4.3	12.7	10.4	3.4	3.7
Edwardsville, IL	4.7	n/a	18.4	6.3	11.2	2.0	10.5	8.3	n/a	3.7	15.4	10.5	3.8	4.7
Evesham, NJ[2]	3.9	n/a	18.0	5.2	14.6	1.1	8.8	7.0	n/a	3.4	14.6	12.6	4.7	5.3
Flower Mound, TX[2]	5.4	n/a	11.9	8.9	11.6	2.7	10.0	6.8	n/a	3.2	18.6	10.1	4.6	5.6
Folsom, CA	6.1	6.1	15.8	5.2	24.3	1.2	10.6	3.5	<0.1	3.2	13.3	10.8	2.8	2.7
Friendswood, TX	9.7	7.2	12.4	5.2	13.5	1.0	10.3	7.1	2.5	3.5	16.0	10.5	4.8	5.4
Gaines, MI	4.2	n/a	16.4	4.6	8.7	0.9	8.5	20.6	n/a	3.9	14.4	8.9	2.7	5.6
Glastonbury, CT[3]	3.1	n/a	18.8	9.7	14.8	1.7	8.1	10.2	n/a	3.7	13.1	9.7	3.4	3.1
Grand Blanc, MI	3.6	n/a	20.3	4.2	13.6	2.8	10.6	8.7	n/a	3.8	10.8	14.2	2.8	4.0
Hampden, PA	3.4	n/a	16.8	6.2	17.0	1.0	8.9	6.3	n/a	4.3	14.0	9.6	8.6	3.4
Hilliard, OH	3.5	n/a	14.7	7.8	16.2	1.5	9.5	6.7	n/a	3.6	16.4	10.4	5.3	3.8
Hillsborough, NJ[2]	3.6	n/a	15.7	6.2	14.6	1.6	7.8	6.1	n/a	4.5	18.4	10.1	5.6	5.2
Holly Springs, NC	6.0	n/a	12.0	5.1	15.7	3.5	11.1	5.6	n/a	3.7	18.8	11.4	2.2	4.4
Independence, KY	4.2	n/a	14.9	6.7	12.0	1.2	10.6	10.6	n/a	3.9	15.1	10.2	4.5	5.7
Juneau, AK	n/a	n/a	n/a	n/a	n/a	n/a	n/a	n/a	n/a	n/a	n/a	n/a	n/a	n/a
Kaysville, UT	6.8	n/a	12.6	3.9	20.7	0.8	9.2	12.9	n/a	2.6	11.7	12.1	3.6	2.7
Keller, TX[2]	6.7	n/a	13.1	5.7	13.4	1.0	11.4	9.0	n/a	3.6	10.8	11.5	8.2	5.0
Lafayette, CA[2]	6.2	6.1	16.5	4.8	14.9	2.2	9.7	8.2	<0.1	3.3	15.7	10.2	3.7	4.2
Lafayette, CO	3.0	n/a	13.4	3.7	19.8	4.2	11.0	9.6	n/a	3.1	18.1	9.5	0.8	3.2
Lake Oswego, OR	5.7	5.6	14.6	5.9	13.3	2.1	10.2	10.4	0.1	3.5	15.2	10.3	3.5	4.8
Laramie, WY	n/a	n/a	n/a	n/a	n/a	n/a	n/a	n/a	n/a	n/a	n/a	n/a	n/a	n/a
Leander, TX	5.8	n/a	11.5	5.7	16.9	2.9	12.3	5.4	n/a	4.3	17.3	10.2	2.1	5.1
Leawood, KS	4.6	n/a	13.9	7.2	13.9	1.6	9.5	6.9	n/a	3.9	17.9	10.4	4.9	4.7
Lee's Summit, MO	4.6	n/a	13.9	7.2	13.9	1.6	9.5	6.9	n/a	3.9	17.9	10.4	4.9	4.7
Leesburg, VA[2]	4.5	n/a	13.1	4.4	21.9	2.2	10.0	1.3	n/a	6.8	22.8	8.3	2.3	1.8
Lehi, UT	9.7	n/a	21.2	3.3	12.5	4.7	7.8	7.5	n/a	2.1	13.2	13.3	1.4	2.6
Lexington, MA[4]	3.6	n/a	22.7	8.2	10.6	3.1	10.0	4.3	n/a	3.6	19.7	8.0	2.4	3.2
Los Altos, CA	4.6	4.6	15.4	3.2	8.8	7.8	9.3	15.1	<0.1	2.5	20.3	8.1	1.4	3.0
Loveland, CO	6.7	n/a	10.5	4.1	24.1	1.7	11.9	8.3	n/a	3.6	12.1	11.8	2.0	2.8
Lower Macungie, PA	3.5	n/a	20.7	3.8	10.9	1.4	9.4	9.8	n/a	3.8	13.0	10.8	8.4	3.9
Madison, AL	3.6	n/a	9.1	2.8	21.4	1.1	9.5	10.6	n/a	3.3	23.6	10.7	1.3	2.5
Madison, MS	4.0	3.5	15.7	5.5	20.0	1.3	9.4	7.2	0.4	4.8	12.6	10.9	4.5	3.7
Maple Valley, WA[2]	5.9	5.8	12.7	5.0	12.9	6.4	9.9	9.1	<0.1	3.4	15.1	11.4	3.4	4.2
Marion, IA	5.3	n/a	14.3	7.3	11.8	2.7	8.2	13.5	n/a	3.5	10.2	10.8	7.7	4.0

Table continued on next page.

Metro Area[1]	(A)	(B)	(C)	(D)	(E)	(F)	(G)	(H)	(I)	(J)	(K)	(L)	(M)	(N)
Marlboro, NJ[2]	3.7	n/a	20.8	8.8	12.8	3.4	9.4	2.9	n/a	4.2	16.1	9.6	3.8	4.0
Mason, OH	4.2	n/a	14.9	6.7	12.0	1.2	10.6	10.6	n/a	3.9	15.1	10.2	4.5	5.7
Menomonee Falls, WI	3.3	3.3	19.6	5.8	10.1	1.5	8.8	13.6	<0.1	5.3	14.8	9.3	3.1	4.4
Meridian, ID	6.8	n/a	14.8	5.7	15.0	1.4	9.7	8.8	n/a	3.5	14.4	11.6	3.2	4.6
Meridian, MI	3.0	n/a	13.6	6.9	28.3	1.0	7.8	8.5	n/a	4.2	9.8	9.6	4.3	2.4
Merrimack, NH[4]	4.1	n/a	14.8	5.9	10.5	1.3	8.7	15.8	n/a	4.0	11.5	15.9	2.7	4.2
Milton, GA	4.6	4.5	12.6	6.1	12.1	3.6	10.4	6.1	<0.1	3.6	18.1	10.8	5.8	5.8
Moon, PA	5.8	5.0	21.3	6.0	9.8	1.5	10.0	7.2	0.8	4.3	15.3	10.6	4.0	3.6
Moorpark, CA	5.6	5.3	14.8	5.4	15.6	1.6	12.3	9.8	0.2	3.0	11.6	13.5	2.0	4.3
Morgantown, WV	n/a	n/a	20.9	n/a	26.2	n/a	10.2	6.0	n/a	n/a	9.5	9.5	n/a	n/a
Mount Pleasant, SC	5.8	n/a	11.6	4.1	18.5	1.8	13.3	7.4	n/a	3.8	15.2	11.3	4.1	2.6
Newark, DE[2]	4.9	n/a	17.3	12.2	13.5	1.0	8.5	4.7	n/a	3.9	15.3	10.3	5.5	2.4
Newtown, CT[3]	n/a	n/a	n/a	n/a	12.9	n/a	9.6	n/a	n/a	n/a	12.5	16.8	n/a	n/a
North Attleborough, MA[3]	4.0	3.9	21.6	6.5	12.1	1.2	10.8	8.8	<0.1	4.6	12.6	11.0	3.1	3.2
North Port, FL	7.7	n/a	17.1	5.0	9.0	1.1	14.9	5.5	n/a	4.3	15.6	15.0	1.7	2.7
North Ridgeville, OH	3.2	n/a	19.0	6.3	12.9	1.3	9.7	11.6	n/a	3.7	14.2	9.6	3.0	5.0
Northville, MI[2]	2.8	n/a	17.3	4.9	11.4	0.9	10.7	12.2	n/a	3.7	16.5	9.1	5.8	4.1
O'Fallon, MO	4.7	n/a	18.4	6.3	11.2	2.0	10.5	8.3	n/a	3.7	15.4	10.5	3.8	4.7
Orchard Park, NY	3.3	n/a	17.6	6.5	16.2	1.2	10.7	9.1	n/a	4.6	12.3	11.1	3.2	3.8
Oro Valley, AZ	4.7	4.2	17.0	4.6	20.9	1.3	11.8	6.3	0.4	3.3	13.5	11.2	3.0	1.9
Oviedo, FL	5.9	5.8	12.0	6.0	9.9	1.8	20.4	3.6	<0.1	3.4	17.6	12.2	3.2	3.4
Parker, CO	7.0	n/a	12.5	7.3	13.3	3.2	11.3	4.7	n/a	3.8	17.9	9.6	4.0	4.9
Parkland, FL[2]	n/a	5.7	13.1	6.8	12.4	2.4	10.9	3.2	n/a	4.6	18.1	13.2	3.5	5.7
Peachtree City, GA	4.6	4.5	12.6	6.1	12.1	3.6	10.4	6.1	<0.1	3.6	18.1	10.8	5.8	5.8
Pittsfield, MI	1.8	n/a	12.3	3.1	38.0	2.3	7.7	6.6	n/a	2.8	13.2	7.4	1.6	2.7
Plainfield, IL[2]	3.3	3.3	15.7	6.9	11.2	1.8	9.9	7.6	<0.1	4.1	18.4	9.6	5.4	5.4
Pleasant Grove, UT	9.7	n/a	21.2	3.3	12.5	4.7	7.8	7.5	n/a	2.1	13.2	13.3	1.4	2.6
Poway, CA	5.5	5.5	14.0	5.0	17.1	1.6	13.1	7.5	<0.1	3.6	16.1	10.5	2.2	3.3
Princeton, NJ	1.9	n/a	17.9	6.9	27.5	1.8	5.9	3.1	n/a	3.8	15.7	7.7	4.6	2.7
Queen Creek, AZ	5.8	5.6	15.1	9.0	11.6	1.7	10.8	6.1	0.1	3.1	16.9	11.9	3.8	3.8
Radnor, PA[2]	2.4	n/a	30.9	6.1	13.3	1.4	10.0	3.5	n/a	4.1	13.3	8.0	4.0	2.4
Randolph, NJ[2]	3.6	n/a	15.7	6.2	14.6	1.6	7.8	6.1	n/a	4.5	18.4	10.1	5.6	5.2
Rexburg, ID	n/a	n/a	n/a	n/a	n/a	n/a	n/a	n/a	n/a	n/a	n/a	n/a	n/a	n/a
Rio Rancho, NM	5.9	n/a	16.2	4.9	21.3	1.8	10.7	4.0	n/a	3.0	15.4	10.8	2.6	2.9
Rye, NY[2]	3.7	n/a	20.8	8.8	12.8	3.4	9.4	2.9	n/a	4.2	16.1	9.6	3.8	4.0
Sammamish, WA[2]	5.9	5.8	12.7	5.0	12.9	6.4	9.9	9.1	<0.1	3.4	15.1	11.4	3.4	4.2
San Ramon, CA[2]	6.2	6.1	16.5	4.8	14.9	2.2	9.7	8.2	<0.1	3.3	15.7	10.2	3.7	4.2
Saratoga, CA	4.6	4.6	15.4	3.2	8.8	7.8	9.3	15.1	<0.1	2.5	20.3	8.1	1.4	3.0
Shrewsbury, MA[3]	3.9	n/a	23.5	5.0	15.3	1.2	8.6	9.5	n/a	3.7	10.1	10.5	4.6	3.5
South Brunswick, NJ[2]	3.7	n/a	20.8	8.8	12.8	3.4	9.4	2.9	n/a	4.2	16.1	9.6	3.8	4.0
South Jordan, UT	5.8	n/a	11.4	8.0	15.1	2.9	8.8	8.0	n/a	2.8	16.7	10.5	5.3	4.5
South Kingstown, RI[3]	4.0	3.9	21.6	6.5	12.1	1.2	10.8	8.8	<0.1	4.6	12.6	11.0	3.1	3.2
South Portland, ME[3]	4.6	n/a	21.1	7.7	11.4	1.4	9.9	6.5	n/a	3.7	13.5	12.2	3.4	3.9
Sparks, NV	7.0	6.9	11.1	4.4	13.4	0.9	15.7	8.0	0.1	2.6	13.4	10.0	8.7	4.1
State College, PA	n/a	n/a	12.4	n/a	41.1	n/a	9.0	4.9	n/a	n/a	8.4	9.7	n/a	n/a
Sugar Land, TX	9.7	7.2	12.4	5.2	13.5	1.0	10.3	7.1	2.5	3.5	16.0	10.5	4.8	5.4
Sun Prairie, WI	4.2	n/a	12.0	5.7	21.3	4.2	9.3	8.5	n/a	5.0	12.8	10.6	2.4	3.6
Syracuse, UT	6.8	n/a	12.6	3.9	20.7	0.8	9.2	12.9	n/a	2.6	11.7	12.1	3.6	2.7
Tredyffrin, PA[2]	4.6	n/a	18.3	7.7	7.9	1.9	7.8	8.5	n/a	4.4	19.2	11.3	2.7	5.3
Upper Dublin, PA[2]	4.6	n/a	18.3	7.7	7.9	1.9	7.8	8.5	n/a	4.4	19.2	11.3	2.7	5.3
Urbandale, IA	5.1	n/a	14.1	15.5	12.1	1.7	9.4	5.6	n/a	3.4	13.1	11.6	3.1	4.8
Vestal, NY	3.9	n/a	16.2	3.4	22.0	1.4	10.1	10.7	n/a	5.3	8.0	11.6	2.5	4.3
Vestavia Hills, AL	5.3	4.8	13.7	7.8	15.8	1.3	9.6	7.1	0.4	5.5	12.6	11.1	4.4	5.3
Webster, NY	3.7	3.6	24.5	3.9	15.0	1.4	8.2	10.6	0.1	3.8	12.5	10.4	2.1	3.2
Wellesley, MA[4]	3.6	n/a	22.7	8.2	10.6	3.1	10.0	4.3	n/a	3.6	19.7	8.0	2.4	3.2
West Fargo, ND	5.7	n/a	17.3	7.9	14.1	2.1	9.4	7.0	n/a	3.8	10.8	11.1	4.1	6.2
West Lafayette, IN	3.3	n/a	11.9	3.4	27.1	0.7	9.6	17.7	n/a	3.6	7.5	9.6	2.6	2.4
Weston, FL[2]	n/a	5.7	13.1	6.8	12.4	2.4	10.9	3.2	n/a	4.6	18.1	13.2	3.5	5.7
Wilmette, IL[2]	3.3	3.3	15.7	6.9	11.2	1.8	9.9	7.6	<0.1	4.1	18.4	9.6	5.4	5.4
Yorba Linda, CA[2]	6.3	6.3	13.4	7.2	9.9	1.6	13.3	9.5	<0.1	3.1	18.9	9.7	1.7	4.9
Zionsville, IN	4.7	4.6	15.0	6.3	12.5	1.3	9.7	8.6	<0.1	4.1	16.2	10.5	6.1	4.5
U.S.	5.2	4.7	15.9	5.7	15.3	1.9	10.7	8.5	0.5	3.9	14.0	11.0	4.1	4.0

Note: All figures are percentages covering non-farm employment as of December 2017 and are not seasonally adjusted; (1) Figures cover the Metropolitan Statistical Area (MSA) except where noted. See Appendix B for areas included; (2) Metropolitan Division; (3) New England City and Town Area; (4) New England City and Town Area Division; (A) Construction, Mining, and Logging (some areas report Construction separate from Mining and Logging); (B) Construction; (C) Education and Health Services; (D) Financial Activities; (E) Government; (F) Information; (G) Leisure and Hospitality; (H) Manufacturing; (I) Mining and Logging; (J) Other Services; (K) Professional and Business Services; (L) Retail Trade; (M) Transportation and Utilities; (N) Wholesale Trade; n/a not available
Source: Bureau of Labor Statistics, Current Employment Statistics, Employment, Hours, and Earnings, December 2017

Labor Force, Employment and Job Growth: City

City	Civilian Labor Force			Workers Employed		
	Dec. 2016	Dec. 2017	% Chg.	Dec. 2016	Dec. 2017	% Chg.
Aberdeen, SD	15,265	15,189	-0.5	14,769	14,666	-0.7
Aliso Viejo, CA	30,171	30,569	1.3	29,180	29,767	2.0
Allen, TX	54,579	56,018	2.6	52,825	54,349	2.8
Ames, IA	39,504	40,044	1.3	38,781	39,508	1.8
Amherst, MA	18,848	18,857	0.0	18,336	18,455	0.6
Apex, NC	25,251	25,875	2.4	24,330	25,039	2.9
Beavercreek, OH	23,178	23,733	2.3	22,326	22,906	2.6
Bellevue, NE	26,724	26,678	-0.1	25,890	25,882	0.0
Bend, OR	49,242	51,296	4.1	47,749	49,402	3.4
Benicia, CA	14,847	14,982	0.9	14,324	14,526	1.4
Bentonville, AR	24,631	25,168	2.1	24,102	24,477	1.5
Bethlehem, NY	18,059	18,061	0.0	17,527	17,524	0.0
Blacksburg, VA	20,447	20,343	-0.5	19,529	19,607	0.4
Bowie, MD	34,546	34,489	-0.1	33,422	33,422	0.0
Bozeman, MT	27,860	28,801	3.3	27,182	28,023	3.0
Brentwood, TN	21,135	21,763	2.9	20,434	21,306	4.2
Burlington, VT	23,865	23,774	-0.3	23,335	23,334	0.0
Cabot, AR	11,679	11,871	1.6	11,358	11,444	0.7
Carmel, IN	48,927	49,069	0.2	47,585	47,985	0.8
Cedar Falls, IA	22,498	21,923	-2.5	21,863	21,473	-1.7
Cedar Park, TX	37,261	38,371	2.9	36,034	37,322	3.5
Central, LA	15,104	15,357	1.6	14,524	14,926	2.7
Chapel Hill, NC	29,418	29,861	1.5	28,033	28,608	2.0
Cheshire, CT	15,856	15,738	-0.7	15,354	15,264	-0.5
Chino Hills, CA	42,240	43,588	3.1	40,865	42,367	3.6
Cibolo, TX	13,507	13,722	1.5	13,060	13,381	2.4
Cicero, NY	15,929	15,828	-0.6	15,278	15,143	-0.8
Collierville, TN	25,011	25,465	1.8	24,131	24,839	2.9
Coppell, TX	23,538	24,111	2.4	22,763	23,425	2.9
Cornelius, NC	16,784	17,459	4.0	16,187	16,818	3.9
Cranberry, PA	17,082	17,184	0.6	16,486	16,661	1.0
Crown Point, IN	14,955	14,697	-1.7	14,261	14,117	-1.0
Dublin, OH	24,862	25,161	1.2	24,005	24,405	1.6
East Fishkill, NY	14,146	14,264	0.8	13,564	13,656	0.6
Eden Prairie, MN	36,101	36,554	1.2	35,143	35,663	1.4
Edmond, OK	46,484	47,372	1.9	45,132	46,033	2.0
Edwardsville, IL	13,425	13,265	-1.1	12,863	12,870	0.0
Evesham, NJ	26,177	26,122	-0.2	25,374	25,372	0.0
Flower Mound, TX	40,860	41,705	2.0	39,554	40,688	2.8
Folsom, CA	36,301	36,859	1.5	34,907	35,840	2.6
Friendswood, TX	19,542	19,766	1.1	18,620	19,081	2.4
Gaines, MI	14,944	15,191	1.6	14,539	14,752	1.4
Glastonbury, CT	19,006	19,088	0.4	18,414	18,565	0.8
Grand Blanc, MI	18,522	18,519	0.0	17,891	17,852	-0.2
Hampden, PA	16,481	16,347	-0.8	16,037	15,912	-0.7
Hilliard, OH	19,044	19,326	1.4	18,435	18,752	1.7
Hillsborough, NJ	21,747	21,597	-0.6	21,108	20,912	-0.9
Holly Springs, NC	16,639	17,065	2.5	16,025	16,493	2.9
Independence, KY	14,166	14,262	0.6	13,659	13,811	1.1
Juneau, AK	16,835	17,042	1.2	16,030	16,199	1.0
Kaysville, UT	14,309	14,649	2.3	13,972	14,311	2.4
Keller, TX	23,633	24,151	2.1	22,846	23,475	2.7
Lafayette, CA	12,517	12,672	1.2	12,113	12,387	2.2
Lafayette, CO	16,378	16,941	3.4	16,060	16,560	3.1
Lake Oswego, OR	20,705	21,403	3.3	20,064	20,734	3.3
Laramie, WY	17,845	17,448	-2.2	17,337	16,997	-1.9
Leander, TX	22,019	22,777	3.4	21,327	22,089	3.5
Leawood, KS	17,407	17,504	0.5	16,929	17,089	0.9
Lee's Summit, MO	54,435	54,530	0.1	52,704	53,130	0.8
Leesburg, VA	28,243	28,758	1.8	27,412	28,049	2.3
Lehi, UT	26,175	27,443	4.8	25,516	26,729	4.7
Lexington, MA	16,105	16,179	0.4	15,689	15,812	0.7
Los Altos, CA	14,536	14,932	2.7	14,074	14,542	3.3
Loveland, CO	40,750	42,477	4.2	39,703	41,328	4.0
Lower Macungie, PA	16,533	16,308	-1.3	15,908	15,766	-0.8
Madison, AL	24,429	24,534	0.4	23,368	23,881	2.2
Madison, MS	13,580	13,717	1.0	13,089	13,307	1.6
Maple Valley, WA	13,317	13,764	3.3	12,898	13,267	2.8

Table continued on next page.

City	Civilian Labor Force			Workers Employed		
	Dec. 2016	Dec. 2017	% Chg.	Dec. 2016	Dec. 2017	% Chg.
Marion, IA	20,159	20,040	-0.5	19,616	19,463	-0.7
Marlboro, NJ	20,177	19,993	-0.9	19,545	19,459	-0.4
Mason, OH	16,880	17,007	0.7	16,244	16,389	0.8
Menomonee Falls, WI	20,339	20,358	0.0	19,767	19,893	0.6
Meridian, ID	46,620	48,572	4.1	45,275	47,431	4.7
Meridian, MI	23,658	23,821	0.6	23,088	23,199	0.4
Merrimack, NH	15,718	15,680	-0.2	15,292	15,311	0.1
Milton, GA	19,575	20,041	2.3	18,767	19,364	3.1
Moon, PA	14,166	14,249	0.5	13,641	13,767	0.9
Moorpark, CA	19,458	19,519	0.3	18,773	18,975	1.0
Morgantown, WV	14,270	14,659	2.7	13,789	14,151	2.6
Mount Pleasant, SC	45,231	45,696	1.0	43,859	44,392	1.2
Newark, DE	16,362	16,309	-0.3	15,694	15,758	0.4
Newtown, CT	14,294	14,244	-0.3	13,784	13,790	0.0
North Attleborough, MA	16,054	16,133	0.4	15,528	15,660	0.8
North Port, FL	27,880	28,482	2.1	26,695	27,486	2.9
North Ridgeville, OH	17,341	17,173	-0.9	16,450	16,444	0.0
Northville, MI	15,352	15,571	1.4	15,111	15,352	1.5
O'Fallon, MO	48,105	47,896	-0.4	46,729	46,711	0.0
Orchard Park, NY	15,140	15,134	0.0	14,549	14,516	-0.2
Oro Valley, AZ	19,059	19,308	1.3	18,216	18,528	1.7
Oviedo, FL	21,128	21,899	3.6	20,364	21,287	4.5
Parker, CO	28,671	29,768	3.8	27,986	28,985	3.5
Parkland, FL	16,663	16,918	1.5	16,106	16,472	2.2
Peachtree City, GA	18,122	18,517	2.1	17,365	17,918	3.1
Pittsfield, MI	21,153	21,358	0.9	20,560	20,743	0.8
Plainfield, IL	22,279	22,379	0.4	21,367	21,566	0.9
Pleasant Grove, UT	18,762	19,613	4.5	18,269	19,138	4.7
Poway, CA	25,669	25,924	0.9	24,805	25,238	1.7
Princeton, NJ	16,595	16,474	-0.7	16,233	16,156	-0.4
Queen Creek, AZ	17,426	18,047	3.5	16,838	17,409	3.3
Radnor, PA	15,629	15,570	-0.3	15,109	15,102	0.0
Randolph, NJ	13,705	13,538	-1.2	13,267	13,145	-0.9
Rexburg, ID	14,452	15,285	5.7	14,175	15,077	6.3
Rio Rancho, NM	44,746	45,369	1.3	42,172	42,932	1.8
Rye, NY	24,797	24,782	0.0	23,952	23,838	-0.4
Sammamish, WA	32,056	33,015	2.9	31,062	31,952	2.8
San Ramon, CA	39,817	40,453	1.6	38,440	39,309	2.2
Saratoga, CA	14,674	15,047	2.5	14,156	14,626	3.3
Shrewsbury, MA	19,934	20,137	1.0	19,380	19,616	1.2
South Brunswick, NJ	25,125	24,981	-0.5	24,354	24,216	-0.5
South Jordan, UT	35,042	36,066	2.9	34,163	35,157	2.9
South Kingstown, RI	16,403	16,481	0.4	15,804	15,939	0.8
South Portland, ME	14,701	14,767	0.4	14,329	14,491	1.1
Sparks, NV	50,706	52,900	4.3	48,480	50,951	5.1
State College, PA	16,383	16,351	-0.2	15,746	15,798	0.3
Sugar Land, TX	45,075	45,569	1.1	42,917	43,981	2.4
Sun Prairie, WI	19,617	19,856	1.2	19,165	19,455	1.5
Syracuse, UT	13,663	13,990	2.3	13,367	13,692	2.4
Tredyffrin, PA	15,841	15,877	0.2	15,373	15,452	0.5
Upper Dublin, PA	14,108	14,076	-0.2	13,657	13,646	0.0
Urbandale, IA	24,509	24,463	-0.1	23,980	23,975	0.0
Vestal, NY	11,354	11,223	-1.1	10,795	10,649	-1.3
Vestavia Hills, AL	17,696	17,582	-0.6	17,076	17,215	0.8
Webster, NY	22,250	22,146	-0.4	21,348	21,234	-0.5
Wellesley, MA	13,241	13,290	0.3	12,885	12,986	0.7
West Fargo, ND	20,940	20,950	0.0	20,480	20,492	0.0
West Lafayette, IN	20,797	20,731	-0.3	20,183	20,227	0.2
Weston, FL	35,894	36,382	1.3	34,545	35,330	2.2
Wilmette, IL	12,742	12,829	0.6	12,293	12,423	1.0
Yorba Linda, CA	35,110	35,638	1.5	33,945	34,628	2.0
Zionsville, IN	13,939	13,997	0.4	13,550	13,689	1.0
U.S.	158,968,000	159,880,000	0.6	151,798,000	153,602,000	1.2

Note: Data is not seasonally adjusted and covers workers 16 years of age and older
Source: Bureau of Labor Statistics, Local Area Unemployment Statistics

Labor Force, Employment and Job Growth: Metro Area

Metro Area[1]	Civilian Labor Force			Workers Employed		
	Dec. 2016	Dec. 2017	% Chg.	Dec. 2016	Dec. 2017	% Chg.
Aberdeen, SD	23,187	23,105	-0.3	22,489	22,345	-0.6
Aliso Viejo, CA[2]	1,608,205	1,628,598	1.2	1,550,152	1,581,334	2.0
Allen, TX[2]	2,526,544	2,585,893	2.3	2,434,063	2,504,449	2.8
Ames, IA	57,316	58,060	1.3	56,105	57,157	1.8
Amherst, MA[3]	367,837	368,225	0.1	352,296	354,704	0.6
Apex, NC	679,166	696,216	2.5	650,915	669,860	2.9
Beavercreek, OH	385,769	394,624	2.3	367,844	377,877	2.7
Bellevue, NE	479,056	478,265	-0.1	464,340	464,636	0.0
Bend, OR	90,518	93,692	3.5	86,682	89,684	3.4
Benicia, CA	208,389	208,826	0.2	197,459	200,238	1.4
Bentonville, AR	266,049	270,541	1.6	259,319	263,215	1.5
Bethlehem, NY	444,458	445,967	0.3	426,777	427,121	0.0
Blacksburg, VA	89,969	89,477	-0.5	86,145	86,419	0.3
Bowie, MD[2]	2,655,258	2,688,714	1.2	2,556,370	2,597,010	1.5
Bozeman, MT	62,360	64,392	3.2	60,568	62,443	3.1
Brentwood, TN	985,185	1,015,902	3.1	951,214	991,652	4.2
Burlington, VT[3]	123,888	123,521	-0.3	121,124	121,119	0.0
Cabot, AR	349,466	353,050	1.0	338,473	341,315	0.8
Carmel, IN	1,028,186	1,029,258	0.1	991,552	999,968	0.8
Cedar Falls, IA	89,592	87,387	-2.4	85,819	84,556	-1.4
Cedar Park, TX	1,129,840	1,164,240	3.0	1,093,771	1,133,101	3.6
Central, LA	411,843	418,468	1.6	393,017	403,814	2.7
Chapel Hill, NC	288,945	293,411	1.5	276,804	282,262	1.9
Cheshire, CT[3]	327,357	324,271	-0.9	313,549	311,593	-0.6
Chino Hills, CA	2,000,221	2,050,338	2.5	1,893,621	1,964,133	3.7
Cibolo, TX	1,151,068	1,171,978	1.8	1,109,096	1,136,835	2.5
Cicero, NY	304,859	303,285	-0.5	289,509	287,500	-0.6
Collierville, TN	627,910	635,161	1.1	597,226	611,935	2.4
Coppell, TX[2]	2,526,544	2,585,893	2.3	2,434,063	2,504,449	2.8
Cornelius, NC	1,284,384	1,325,794	3.2	1,225,922	1,271,766	3.7
Cranberry, PA	1,197,241	1,200,452	0.2	1,135,886	1,146,911	0.9
Crown Point, IN[2]	338,051	331,165	-2.0	319,491	316,454	-0.9
Dublin, OH	1,066,787	1,080,007	1.2	1,023,273	1,039,735	1.6
East Fishkill, NY[2]	192,703	194,103	0.7	185,083	186,184	0.5
Eden Prairie, MN	1,967,019	1,983,313	0.8	1,897,339	1,924,623	1.4
Edmond, OK	663,581	674,115	1.5	637,645	650,461	2.0
Edwardsville, IL	1,453,575	1,444,413	-0.6	1,396,917	1,395,979	0.0
Evesham, NJ[2]	641,023	640,625	0.0	614,203	613,865	0.0
Flower Mound, TX[2]	2,526,544	2,585,893	2.3	2,434,063	2,504,449	2.8
Folsom, CA	1,067,080	1,083,040	1.5	1,013,762	1,041,760	2.7
Friendswood, TX	3,297,292	3,343,410	1.4	3,121,317	3,199,215	2.5
Gaines, MI	563,496	573,055	1.7	544,944	552,982	1.4
Glastonbury, CT[3]	620,001	622,822	0.4	593,154	597,962	0.8
Grand Blanc, MI	182,246	182,447	0.1	172,382	172,013	-0.2
Hampden, PA	293,946	291,194	-0.9	282,533	280,229	-0.8
Hilliard, OH	1,066,787	1,080,007	1.2	1,023,273	1,039,735	1.6
Hillsborough, NJ[2]	1,240,075	1,228,255	-0.9	1,188,742	1,178,033	-0.9
Holly Springs, NC	679,166	696,216	2.5	650,915	669,860	2.9
Independence, KY	1,094,195	1,099,941	0.5	1,048,073	1,057,790	0.9
Juneau, AK	16,835	17,042	1.2	16,030	16,199	1.0
Kaysville, UT	318,562	326,295	2.4	308,975	316,612	2.4
Keller, TX[2]	1,216,491	1,241,227	2.0	1,169,689	1,201,876	2.7
Lafayette, CA[2]	1,396,442	1,415,371	1.3	1,341,574	1,371,935	2.2
Lafayette, CO	182,589	189,048	3.5	178,685	184,248	3.1
Lake Oswego, OR	1,283,618	1,324,396	3.1	1,234,956	1,276,346	3.3
Laramie, WY	21,286	20,808	-2.2	20,655	20,249	-1.9
Leander, TX	1,129,840	1,164,240	3.0	1,093,771	1,133,101	3.6
Leawood, KS	1,118,057	1,123,293	0.4	1,077,438	1,086,716	0.8
Lee's Summit, MO	1,118,057	1,123,293	0.4	1,077,438	1,086,716	0.8
Leesburg, VA[2]	2,655,258	2,688,714	1.2	2,556,370	2,597,010	1.5
Lehi, UT	290,826	304,146	4.5	283,195	296,661	4.7
Lexington, MA[4]	1,590,065	1,597,698	0.4	1,543,977	1,556,045	0.7
Los Altos, CA	1,052,822	1,078,824	2.4	1,015,537	1,049,364	3.3
Loveland, CO	188,248	196,349	4.3	183,925	191,451	4.0
Lower Macungie, PA	434,946	429,942	-1.1	415,241	411,484	-0.9
Madison, AL	215,744	216,297	0.2	205,426	209,920	2.1
Madison, MS	271,163	273,189	0.7	258,752	262,991	1.6
Maple Valley, WA[2]	1,613,459	1,663,045	3.0	1,557,412	1,602,109	2.8

Table continued on next page.

Metro Area[1]	Civilian Labor Force			Workers Employed		
	Dec. 2016	Dec. 2017	% Chg.	Dec. 2016	Dec. 2017	% Chg.
Marion, IA	142,692	141,463	-0.8	137,678	136,902	-0.5
Marlboro, NJ[2]	7,114,448	7,115,615	0.0	6,809,258	6,832,994	0.3
Mason, OH	1,094,195	1,099,941	0.5	1,048,073	1,057,790	0.9
Menomonee Falls, WI	823,210	822,220	-0.1	794,650	799,577	0.6
Meridian, ID	337,940	351,551	4.0	326,932	342,090	4.6
Meridian, MI	247,095	249,000	0.7	238,137	239,290	0.4
Merrimack, NH[4]	169,304	169,049	-0.1	164,446	164,679	0.1
Milton, GA	2,986,185	3,056,722	2.3	2,840,901	2,931,140	3.1
Moon, PA	1,197,241	1,200,452	0.2	1,135,886	1,146,911	0.9
Moorpark, CA	425,110	425,256	0.0	403,870	408,220	1.0
Morgantown, WV	66,036	67,848	2.7	63,618	65,203	2.4
Mount Pleasant, SC	370,074	373,329	0.8	355,988	360,371	1.2
Newark, DE[2]	380,873	381,566	0.1	365,102	366,089	0.2
Newtown, CT[3]	107,729	107,260	-0.4	103,847	103,893	0.0
North Attleborough, MA[3]	680,280	685,055	0.7	651,534	657,109	0.8
North Port, FL	355,007	361,817	1.9	340,092	349,860	2.8
North Ridgeville, OH	1,013,960	1,005,220	-0.8	956,780	957,181	0.0
Northville, MI[2]	781,033	788,952	1.0	738,407	750,189	1.6
O'Fallon, MO	1,453,575	1,444,413	-0.6	1,396,917	1,395,979	0.0
Orchard Park, NY	541,721	542,119	0.0	513,281	512,388	-0.1
Oro Valley, AZ	472,148	478,935	1.4	450,886	458,610	1.7
Oviedo, FL	1,266,187	1,312,511	3.6	1,214,206	1,269,679	4.5
Parker, CO	1,546,944	1,607,274	3.9	1,507,045	1,561,361	3.6
Parkland, FL[2]	1,007,810	1,022,607	1.4	965,939	987,871	2.2
Peachtree City, GA	2,986,185	3,056,722	2.3	2,840,901	2,931,140	3.1
Pittsfield, MI	192,398	194,270	0.9	186,599	188,260	0.8
Plainfield, IL[2]	3,752,535	3,782,099	0.7	3,560,698	3,597,700	1.0
Pleasant Grove, UT	290,826	304,146	4.5	283,195	296,661	4.7
Poway, CA	1,571,067	1,583,042	0.7	1,503,893	1,530,168	1.7
Princeton, NJ	198,967	198,071	-0.4	191,840	190,927	-0.4
Queen Creek, AZ	2,260,824	2,333,423	3.2	2,165,247	2,239,985	3.4
Radnor, PA[2]	995,008	992,557	-0.2	941,604	941,721	0.0
Randolph, NJ[2]	1,240,075	1,228,255	-0.9	1,188,742	1,178,033	-0.9
Rexburg, ID	27,408	28,952	5.6	26,746	28,421	6.2
Rio Rancho, NM	425,294	430,911	1.3	401,812	408,815	1.7
Rye, NY[2]	7,114,448	7,115,615	0.0	6,809,258	6,832,994	0.3
Sammamish, WA[2]	1,613,459	1,663,045	3.0	1,557,412	1,602,109	2.8
San Ramon, CA[2]	1,396,442	1,415,371	1.3	1,341,574	1,371,935	2.2
Saratoga, CA	1,052,822	1,078,824	2.4	1,015,537	1,049,364	3.3
Shrewsbury, MA[3]	349,514	352,220	0.7	336,659	340,797	1.2
South Brunswick, NJ[2]	7,114,448	7,115,615	0.0	6,809,258	6,832,994	0.3
South Jordan, UT	643,054	661,109	2.8	624,955	643,138	2.9
South Kingstown, RI[3]	680,280	685,055	0.7	651,534	657,109	0.8
South Portland, ME[3]	205,865	206,896	0.5	200,537	202,804	1.1
Sparks, NV	235,149	245,311	4.3	224,830	236,289	5.1
State College, PA	79,179	79,021	-0.2	76,212	76,466	0.3
Sugar Land, TX	3,297,292	3,343,410	1.4	3,121,317	3,199,215	2.5
Sun Prairie, WI	385,845	390,310	1.1	376,538	382,618	1.6
Syracuse, UT	318,562	326,295	2.4	308,975	316,612	2.4
Tredyffrin, PA[2]	1,060,053	1,058,151	-0.1	1,021,300	1,022,167	0.0
Upper Dublin, PA[2]	1,060,053	1,058,151	-0.1	1,021,300	1,022,167	0.0
Urbandale, IA	345,840	344,073	-0.5	335,123	335,149	0.0
Vestal, NY	108,011	106,915	-1.0	102,292	101,009	-1.2
Vestavia Hills, AL	537,402	530,515	-1.2	510,132	514,316	0.8
Webster, NY	517,289	518,223	0.1	492,682	492,345	0.0
Wellesley, MA[4]	1,590,065	1,597,698	0.4	1,543,977	1,556,045	0.7
West Fargo, ND	137,322	137,092	-0.1	133,698	133,678	0.0
West Lafayette, IN	107,776	107,356	-0.3	104,009	104,391	0.3
Weston, FL[2]	1,007,810	1,022,607	1.4	965,939	987,871	2.2
Wilmette, IL[2]	3,752,535	3,782,099	0.7	3,560,698	3,597,700	1.0
Yorba Linda, CA[2]	1,608,205	1,628,598	1.2	1,550,152	1,581,334	2.0
Zionsville, IN	1,028,186	1,029,258	0.1	991,552	999,968	0.8
U.S.	158,968,000	159,880,000	0.6	151,798,000	153,602,000	1.2

Note: Data is not seasonally adjusted and covers workers 16 years of age and older; (1) Figures cover the Metropolitan Statistical Area (MSA) except where noted. See Appendix B for areas included; (2) Metropolitan Division; (3) New England City and Town Area; (4) New England City and Town Area Division

Source: Bureau of Labor Statistics, Local Area Unemployment Statistics

Unemployment Rate: City

City	2017 Jan.	Feb.	Mar.	Apr.	May	Jun.	Jul.	Aug.	Sep.	Oct.	Nov.	Dec.
Aberdeen, SD	3.3	3.6	3.5	3.1	2.9	2.9	2.9	3.2	2.6	2.7	2.9	3.4
Aliso Viejo, CA	3.6	3.4	3.3	3.1	3.0	3.3	3.5	3.4	2.9	2.8	2.7	2.6
Allen, TX	3.5	3.7	3.5	3.3	3.3	3.5	3.4	3.5	3.1	3.0	3.1	3.0
Ames, IA	2.1	2.1	1.9	1.5	1.7	2.6	2.3	2.4	1.8	1.3	1.3	1.3
Amherst, MA	3.3	3.3	3.5	3.3	3.4	4.8	5.2	3.6	3.1	2.6	2.3	2.1
Apex, NC	3.8	3.7	3.5	3.0	3.3	3.5	3.7	3.7	3.2	3.2	3.5	3.2
Beavercreek, OH	4.4	4.2	3.7	3.4	3.6	4.0	4.0	4.0	3.8	3.6	3.6	3.5
Bellevue, NE	3.8	3.7	3.3	2.9	3.0	3.4	3.4	3.1	3.0	2.7	2.7	3.0
Bend, OR	4.1	4.0	3.8	3.2	3.1	3.7	3.7	3.6	3.5	3.6	3.6	3.7
Benicia, CA	3.9	4.0	3.8	3.6	3.5	4.1	4.3	4.1	3.3	3.4	3.2	3.0
Bentonville, AR	2.6	2.9	2.6	2.6	3.0	3.4	3.6	3.4	2.9	2.7	2.6	2.7
Bethlehem, NY	3.6	3.8	3.3	3.1	3.3	3.3	3.5	3.4	3.4	3.1	3.1	3.0
Blacksburg, VA	4.9	5.0	4.8	4.3	4.6	5.8	5.4	5.2	4.8	4.2	4.7	3.6
Bowie, MD	3.7	3.6	3.3	3.3	3.5	3.7	3.6	3.6	3.3	3.4	3.3	3.1
Bozeman, MT	2.9	2.7	3.0	2.5	2.4	2.7	2.5	2.3	2.4	2.8	2.7	2.7
Brentwood, TN	3.5	3.3	3.2	2.6	2.5	3.4	3.2	3.0	2.5	2.4	2.5	2.1
Burlington, VT	2.6	2.1	2.5	2.0	2.2	3.2	3.1	3.0	2.8	2.1	2.2	1.9
Cabot, AR	3.5	3.4	3.0	2.6	2.9	3.3	3.4	3.4	3.2	2.9	2.8	3.6
Carmel, IN	3.1	3.0	2.7	2.2	2.5	2.8	2.9	3.3	2.6	2.4	2.5	2.2
Cedar Falls, IA	3.3	3.1	2.8	2.4	2.3	2.8	2.5	2.7	2.4	1.9	1.9	2.1
Cedar Park, TX	3.6	3.7	3.3	3.0	3.1	3.3	3.3	3.4	3.0	2.8	2.9	2.7
Central, LA	4.8	3.7	3.6	3.6	3.7	4.5	4.3	4.3	3.6	3.1	3.0	2.8
Chapel Hill, NC	5.0	4.8	4.8	4.0	4.4	4.9	5.2	5.3	4.0	4.0	4.2	4.2
Cheshire, CT	3.8	3.6	3.2	3.3	3.4	3.5	3.5	3.2	3.1	3.0	3.1	3.0
Chino Hills, CA	3.6	3.5	3.4	3.2	3.1	3.5	3.9	3.8	3.2	3.0	2.9	2.8
Cibolo, TX	3.5	3.7	3.4	3.0	3.1	3.3	3.3	3.3	2.9	2.5	2.6	2.5
Cicero, NY	5.1	5.1	4.3	4.0	4.3	4.3	4.2	4.2	4.2	3.9	4.1	4.3
Collierville, TN	4.0	3.6	3.4	2.7	2.5	3.2	3.0	2.9	2.7	2.6	2.7	2.5
Coppell, TX	3.7	3.7	3.7	3.4	3.3	3.5	3.5	3.6	3.1	3.0	3.0	2.8
Cornelius, NC	3.8	3.9	3.2	3.0	3.2	3.3	3.7	3.5	3.2	3.3	3.7	3.7
Cranberry, PA	3.8	3.9	3.4	3.2	3.6	3.6	3.7	3.8	3.4	3.3	3.2	3.0
Crown Point, IN	5.5	5.6	4.5	3.5	3.7	4.1	4.5	4.6	4.2	3.7	3.5	3.9
Dublin, OH	4.0	3.7	3.3	3.1	3.3	3.7	3.6	3.7	3.4	3.3	3.2	3.0
East Fishkill, NY	4.6	4.5	4.0	3.9	4.0	4.4	4.3	4.3	4.5	4.5	4.4	4.3
Eden Prairie, MN	2.8	2.8	2.5	2.4	2.5	3.0	3.0	3.1	2.6	2.2	2.3	2.4
Edmond, OK	3.5	3.7	3.3	2.9	3.5	3.6	3.3	3.3	3.1	2.9	2.9	2.8
Edwardsville, IL	4.4	4.0	3.6	3.1	3.2	3.6	3.6	3.8	3.3	3.4	3.4	3.0
Evesham, NJ	3.5	3.4	3.0	2.9	3.2	3.2	3.7	3.6	3.5	3.2	3.2	2.9
Flower Mound, TX	3.5	3.6	3.3	3.0	3.1	3.4	3.2	3.2	2.8	2.6	2.6	2.4
Folsom, CA	4.1	3.9	3.7	3.4	3.3	3.7	3.9	3.7	3.2	3.0	2.9	2.8
Friendswood, TX	5.0	4.9	4.5	4.2	4.0	4.3	4.1	4.0	3.9	3.5	3.6	3.5
Gaines, MI	3.3	3.1	2.8	2.3	2.6	3.0	3.8	3.4	2.9	2.7	2.8	2.9
Glastonbury, CT	3.9	3.7	3.3	3.0	3.4	3.7	3.4	3.0	3.0	2.9	2.8	2.7
Grand Blanc, MI	4.2	4.2	3.7	3.1	3.2	3.5	4.4	3.9	3.4	3.1	3.2	3.6
Hampden, PA	3.2	3.2	2.8	2.7	3.1	3.1	3.3	3.3	2.9	2.6	2.7	2.7
Hilliard, OH	3.9	3.6	3.3	2.9	3.1	3.8	3.7	3.7	3.3	3.1	3.1	3.0
Hillsborough, NJ	3.6	3.6	3.2	3.1	3.3	3.5	3.9	4.0	3.7	3.4	3.2	3.2
Holly Springs, NC	3.9	3.9	3.7	3.4	3.5	3.5	3.6	3.8	3.3	3.3	3.4	3.4
Independence, KY	4.6	4.5	4.1	3.5	3.7	4.3	4.0	3.8	3.6	3.7	3.5	3.2
Juneau, AK	5.4	5.4	5.2	4.7	4.2	4.7	4.5	4.1	4.5	4.6	4.8	4.9
Kaysville, UT	2.5	2.7	2.8	2.6	2.8	3.3	3.1	3.1	2.9	2.8	2.5	2.3
Keller, TX	3.5	3.7	3.5	3.1	3.2	3.5	3.6	3.6	3.2	2.9	3.0	2.8
Lafayette, CA	3.9	3.7	3.3	3.1	3.0	3.5	3.7	3.5	2.8	2.7	2.4	2.2
Lafayette, CO	2.4	2.4	2.3	2.2	2.1	2.5	2.4	2.4	2.2	2.2	2.2	2.2
Lake Oswego, OR	3.3	3.2	3.3	3.1	3.1	3.7	3.7	3.6	3.3	3.3	3.3	3.1
Laramie, WY	3.3	2.6	2.9	2.4	2.6	3.1	2.8	2.6	2.4	2.6	2.7	2.6
Leander, TX	3.5	3.6	3.4	3.2	3.1	3.5	3.5	3.5	3.1	2.9	3.2	3.0
Leawood, KS	2.9	2.8	2.6	2.8	2.9	3.1	3.3	3.1	2.7	2.4	2.6	2.4
Lee's Summit, MO	3.3	3.6	3.3	2.9	3.0	2.8	3.0	3.2	2.6	2.3	2.5	2.6
Leesburg, VA	3.3	3.2	3.0	2.6	2.8	2.9	3.0	3.0	2.8	2.6	2.6	2.5
Lehi, UT	3.0	3.3	3.3	3.0	2.9	3.3	3.1	3.1	2.7	2.8	2.6	2.6
Lexington, MA	3.0	2.9	2.7	2.6	2.9	3.3	3.2	2.9	2.9	2.7	2.5	2.3
Los Altos, CA	3.5	3.3	3.2	2.9	2.8	3.2	3.4	3.1	2.8	2.8	2.6	2.6
Loveland, CO	3.1	3.0	2.6	2.4	2.3	2.7	2.6	2.7	2.5	2.6	2.7	2.7
Lower Macungie, PA	4.1	4.3	3.9	3.6	3.8	3.9	4.2	4.5	3.5	3.3	3.4	3.3
Madison, AL	4.7	4.5	4.0	3.3	3.2	3.9	3.7	3.5	2.9	2.8	2.7	2.7
Madison, MS	3.7	3.1	3.3	3.0	3.6	3.9	3.6	3.2	3.1	2.9	3.0	3.0
Maple Valley, WA	3.7	3.6	3.5	3.1	3.4	3.7	3.7	3.9	3.8	3.5	3.9	3.6

Table continued on next page.

City	2017											
	Jan.	Feb.	Mar.	Apr.	May	Jun.	Jul.	Aug.	Sep.	Oct.	Nov.	Dec.
Marion, IA	4.0	3.6	3.2	2.8	2.8	2.9	2.7	2.8	2.6	2.3	2.5	2.9
Marlboro, NJ	3.5	3.5	3.1	3.1	3.5	3.6	4.1	3.9	3.7	3.4	3.1	2.7
Mason, OH	4.5	4.2	3.8	3.6	3.7	4.4	4.5	4.4	4.0	3.8	3.6	3.6
Menomonee Falls, WI	3.4	3.5	2.8	2.6	2.8	3.4	3.0	2.9	2.7	2.5	2.6	2.3
Meridian, ID	3.5	3.2	3.1	2.7	2.4	2.8	2.9	2.8	2.5	2.4	2.6	2.3
Meridian, MI	3.0	2.9	2.6	2.2	2.5	3.4	3.9	3.4	2.8	2.6	2.5	2.6
Merrimack, NH	3.2	3.0	2.8	2.5	2.5	2.4	2.5	2.5	2.4	2.3	2.5	2.4
Milton, GA	4.2	4.2	4.0	3.8	3.9	4.1	4.0	3.9	3.5	3.7	3.5	3.4
Moon, PA	4.3	4.3	3.9	3.5	3.9	4.2	4.3	4.1	3.6	3.7	3.4	3.4
Moorpark, CA	3.9	3.9	3.9	3.7	3.4	4.1	4.1	3.9	3.3	3.2	3.0	2.8
Morgantown, WV	4.4	4.4	4.0	3.6	3.7	5.3	4.5	4.9	3.6	3.6	3.5	3.5
Mount Pleasant, SC	3.5	3.2	2.8	2.5	2.7	3.0	2.9	3.2	3.0	2.9	2.8	2.9
Newark, DE	4.6	4.6	4.9	4.8	4.1	5.4	5.3	4.9	4.2	4.4	3.9	3.4
Newtown, CT	4.5	4.6	4.2	4.0	3.8	4.0	3.9	3.7	3.4	3.2	3.2	3.2
North Attleborough, MA	4.2	4.4	4.1	3.2	3.5	3.8	3.7	3.5	3.3	3.0	3.1	2.9
North Port, FL	4.9	4.5	4.1	3.8	3.8	4.2	4.2	4.2	4.1	3.8	3.7	3.5
North Ridgeville, OH	6.0	6.6	5.7	4.9	4.8	5.4	5.3	5.3	4.7	4.2	4.0	4.2
Northville, MI	1.9	1.8	1.6	1.2	1.2	1.4	1.8	1.8	1.7	1.5	1.3	1.4
O'Fallon, MO	3.1	3.4	2.9	2.6	2.8	2.8	3.0	3.1	2.6	1.9	2.4	2.5
Orchard Park, NY	4.7	4.7	4.2	3.9	3.9	3.9	4.2	4.2	4.0	3.8	3.9	4.1
Oro Valley, AZ	4.9	4.6	4.4	4.1	4.0	4.4	4.4	4.6	4.2	4.1	4.1	4.0
Oviedo, FL	4.1	3.6	3.4	3.2	3.2	3.6	3.5	3.5	3.1	2.9	3.1	2.8
Parker, CO	2.6	2.6	2.4	2.3	2.3	2.6	2.7	2.5	2.5	2.5	2.6	2.6
Parkland, FL	3.6	3.1	3.0	2.8	2.7	3.2	3.2	3.1	2.8	2.8	2.8	2.6
Peachtree City, GA	4.2	3.9	3.6	3.5	3.6	3.9	4.0	3.6	3.5	3.4	3.3	3.2
Pittsfield, MI	3.5	3.4	2.9	2.5	3.1	3.6	4.6	4.0	3.6	3.2	3.0	2.9
Plainfield, IL	4.5	4.3	3.8	3.6	3.6	4.5	4.3	4.3	3.7	3.9	3.9	3.6
Pleasant Grove, UT	3.0	3.2	2.9	2.8	2.9	3.4	3.3	3.3	2.8	2.8	2.5	2.4
Poway, CA	3.9	3.5	3.3	2.9	2.9	3.4	3.7	3.5	3.0	2.9	2.8	2.6
Princeton, NJ	2.9	2.8	2.3	2.1	2.7	2.6	3.2	3.1	2.8	2.7	2.4	1.9
Queen Creek, AZ	3.9	3.8	3.6	3.4	3.2	3.5	3.4	3.6	3.4	3.4	3.4	3.5
Radnor, PA	3.7	3.8	3.6	3.6	4.3	4.0	4.4	4.3	3.9	3.5	3.6	3.0
Randolph, NJ	3.7	3.6	3.4	3.2	3.4	3.5	3.9	3.8	3.5	3.2	3.0	2.9
Rexburg, ID	2.3	2.2	1.9	1.7	1.8	2.1	1.9	2.0	1.8	1.5	1.8	1.4
Rio Rancho, NM	6.3	6.2	5.9	5.5	5.7	6.6	6.5	6.2	6.0	5.8	5.6	5.4
Rye, NY	4.5	4.5	3.9	3.2	3.1	3.4	3.8	3.8	3.5	3.4	3.5	3.8
Sammamish, WA	3.6	3.5	3.4	2.9	3.1	3.7	3.6	3.6	3.6	3.5	3.6	3.2
San Ramon, CA	3.7	3.5	3.3	3.0	2.9	3.2	3.4	3.4	3.1	3.0	2.9	2.8
Saratoga, CA	3.8	3.8	3.6	3.5	3.3	3.7	3.7	3.6	3.1	3.1	3.0	2.8
Shrewsbury, MA	3.6	3.5	3.4	3.1	3.3	3.5	3.4	3.2	3.0	2.7	2.8	2.6
South Brunswick, NJ	3.4	3.5	3.3	3.1	3.2	3.4	4.0	3.8	3.7	3.5	3.4	3.1
South Jordan, UT	2.9	3.2	3.1	2.9	2.9	3.3	3.1	3.1	2.8	2.8	2.6	2.5
South Kingstown, RI	5.0	4.7	4.9	3.2	3.4	4.1	4.6	4.0	3.2	3.0	3.7	3.3
South Portland, ME	2.9	2.9	2.8	2.5	2.6	2.8	2.7	2.4	2.4	2.3	2.3	1.9
Sparks, NV	5.3	4.8	4.6	4.3	4.1	4.3	4.0	3.8	3.8	3.7	3.6	3.7
State College, PA	4.5	4.3	3.9	4.2	5.5	5.3	6.0	5.2	4.6	4.2	4.1	3.4
Sugar Land, TX	5.1	5.0	4.6	4.1	4.1	4.4	4.4	4.6	3.9	3.6	3.6	3.5
Sun Prairie, WI	2.8	2.9	2.4	2.2	2.3	2.8	2.6	2.6	2.3	2.2	2.2	2.0
Syracuse, UT	2.6	2.7	2.8	2.7	2.7	3.2	3.0	3.0	2.6	2.6	2.4	2.1
Tredyffrin, PA	3.4	3.5	3.0	3.0	3.4	3.3	3.4	3.3	3.0	3.0	2.8	2.7
Upper Dublin, PA	3.3	3.5	3.2	2.9	3.5	3.5	4.0	4.0	3.5	3.2	3.2	3.1
Urbandale, IA	2.8	2.6	2.5	2.2	2.3	2.5	2.5	2.5	2.2	2.0	2.0	2.0
Vestal, NY	6.1	6.3	5.4	5.4	5.5	6.6	6.5	5.8	6.0	5.7	6.0	5.1
Vestavia Hills, AL	3.8	3.7	3.2	2.7	2.6	3.0	2.8	2.8	2.4	2.5	2.3	2.1
Webster, NY	4.6	4.6	3.9	3.6	3.8	3.9	3.9	3.8	4.0	3.9	4.0	4.1
Wellesley, MA	3.0	3.0	2.9	2.8	3.2	3.8	3.7	3.0	3.0	2.6	2.4	2.3
West Fargo, ND	2.9	2.8	2.6	1.9	1.5	2.0	1.6	1.7	1.4	1.4	1.8	2.2
West Lafayette, IN	3.3	3.1	2.8	2.2	2.7	3.2	3.2	3.5	2.6	2.5	2.7	2.4
Weston, FL	4.2	3.8	3.6	3.3	3.3	3.6	3.6	3.4	3.2	3.1	3.3	2.9
Wilmette, IL	3.7	3.5	3.1	3.2	3.2	4.0	3.7	4.0	3.7	3.8	3.6	3.2
Yorba Linda, CA	3.7	3.5	3.4	3.1	2.9	3.5	3.7	3.6	3.1	3.0	2.9	2.8
Zionsville, IN	3.0	3.0	2.7	2.1	2.4	2.8	2.8	3.2	2.6	2.4	2.4	2.2
U.S.	5.3	5.2	5.1	4.7	4.5	5.1	5.1	5.0	4.8	4.7	4.4	4.5

Note: Data is not seasonally adjusted and covers workers 16 years of age and older; All figures are percentages
Source: Bureau of Labor Statistics, Local Area Unemployment Statistics

Unemployment Rate: Metro Area

Metro Area[1]	2017											
	Jan.	Feb.	Mar.	Apr.	May	Jun.	Jul.	Aug.	Sep.	Oct.	Nov.	Dec.
Aberdeen, SD	3.2	3.4	3.3	3.0	2.8	2.9	2.8	3.1	2.7	2.6	2.9	3.3
Aliso Viejo, CA[2]	4.0	3.8	3.7	3.4	3.2	3.7	3.9	3.8	3.3	3.2	3.1	2.9
Allen, TX[2]	4.0	4.1	3.9	3.5	3.6	3.9	3.8	3.8	3.4	3.2	3.2	3.1
Ames, IA	2.4	2.4	2.1	1.7	1.9	2.6	2.3	2.4	1.9	1.4	1.4	1.6
Amherst, MA[3]	5.5	5.3	5.0	4.3	4.4	4.9	5.0	4.6	4.2	3.7	3.6	3.7
Apex, NC	4.5	4.3	4.0	3.6	3.8	4.0	4.2	4.3	3.8	3.7	3.9	3.8
Beavercreek, OH	5.7	5.3	4.7	4.2	4.3	4.9	4.9	4.9	4.4	4.2	4.2	4.2
Bellevue, NE	3.6	3.4	3.2	2.9	2.9	3.2	3.3	3.0	2.8	2.6	2.6	2.8
Bend, OR	5.1	4.8	4.5	3.8	3.6	4.1	4.2	4.1	3.8	4.0	4.1	4.3
Benicia, CA	5.8	5.5	5.2	4.7	4.4	4.8	5.1	4.9	4.2	4.2	4.1	4.1
Bentonville, AR	2.9	3.0	2.5	2.3	2.7	3.0	3.2	2.9	2.7	2.5	2.5	2.7
Bethlehem, NY	4.9	4.8	4.2	4.0	4.1	4.3	4.4	4.3	4.3	4.1	4.2	4.2
Blacksburg, VA	6.0	4.5	5.1	3.7	4.0	4.5	4.4	4.5	3.9	3.6	3.7	3.4
Bowie, MD[2]	4.2	4.1	3.8	3.5	3.7	4.0	4.0	4.0	3.7	3.6	3.6	3.4
Bozeman, MT	3.1	2.9	2.9	2.6	2.8	2.6	2.3	2.2	2.3	3.0	3.4	3.0
Brentwood, TN	3.8	3.4	3.1	2.6	2.5	3.2	3.1	2.9	2.6	2.5	2.5	2.4
Burlington, VT[3]	2.8	2.5	2.7	2.3	2.2	2.6	2.6	2.6	2.5	1.9	2.2	1.9
Cabot, AR	3.7	3.7	3.2	2.9	3.2	3.5	3.6	3.4	3.2	2.9	2.9	3.3
Carmel, IN	4.0	3.9	3.4	2.8	3.0	3.3	3.4	3.7	3.1	3.0	3.0	2.8
Cedar Falls, IA	5.3	4.4	4.1	3.5	3.3	3.7	3.4	3.6	3.1	2.6	2.8	3.2
Cedar Park, TX	3.5	3.5	3.3	2.9	3.0	3.3	3.3	3.3	2.9	2.7	2.8	2.7
Central, LA	5.4	4.6	4.5	4.4	4.4	5.2	5.0	4.9	4.3	3.8	3.7	3.5
Chapel Hill, NC	4.5	4.3	4.0	3.6	3.8	4.1	4.3	4.4	3.8	3.8	3.9	3.8
Cheshire, CT[3]	5.4	5.2	5.0	4.6	4.7	4.9	4.9	4.7	4.2	4.1	4.1	3.9
Chino Hills, CA	5.8	5.6	5.4	4.9	4.6	5.3	5.7	5.6	4.9	4.7	4.4	4.2
Cibolo, TX	4.0	3.9	3.7	3.3	3.4	3.7	3.7	3.7	3.2	3.0	3.1	3.0
Cicero, NY	5.8	5.9	5.2	4.8	4.8	5.0	5.1	5.0	5.0	4.7	5.0	5.2
Collierville, TN	5.4	4.9	4.6	4.0	4.0	4.8	4.5	4.2	3.9	3.8	3.7	3.7
Coppell, TX[2]	4.0	4.1	3.9	3.5	3.6	3.9	3.8	3.8	3.4	3.2	3.2	3.1
Cornelius, NC	4.9	4.7	4.2	3.9	4.1	4.3	4.5	4.6	4.1	4.1	4.2	4.1
Cranberry, PA	6.1	6.0	5.5	4.6	4.9	5.2	5.3	5.4	4.4	4.3	4.4	4.5
Crown Point, IN[2]	6.1	6.0	5.1	4.3	4.2	4.5	4.8	5.1	4.5	4.2	4.2	4.4
Dublin, OH	4.9	4.6	4.1	3.7	3.7	4.3	4.3	4.2	3.9	3.7	3.7	3.7
East Fishkill, NY[2]	4.7	4.8	4.1	4.0	4.1	4.4	4.4	4.4	4.4	4.2	4.2	4.1
Eden Prairie, MN	4.0	3.9	3.6	3.1	3.0	3.3	3.2	3.3	2.8	2.4	2.5	3.0
Edmond, OK	4.2	4.3	3.9	3.6	4.0	4.3	3.9	3.9	3.7	3.6	3.5	3.5
Edwardsville, IL	4.4	4.4	4.0	3.6	3.6	3.8	4.1	4.1	3.4	2.9	3.3	3.4
Evesham, NJ[2]	4.9	4.9	4.5	4.1	4.4	4.7	5.3	5.1	4.7	4.5	4.4	4.2
Flower Mound, TX[2]	4.0	4.1	3.9	3.5	3.6	3.9	3.8	3.8	3.4	3.2	3.2	3.1
Folsom, CA	5.5	5.3	5.0	4.5	4.2	4.6	4.8	4.7	4.0	4.0	3.9	3.8
Friendswood, TX	5.8	5.6	5.2	4.8	4.8	5.1	5.1	5.1	4.8	4.4	4.4	4.3
Gaines, MI	4.0	3.8	3.4	2.8	3.1	3.6	4.6	4.1	3.5	3.3	3.3	3.5
Glastonbury, CT[3]	5.5	5.3	5.0	4.7	4.6	4.8	5.0	4.8	4.3	4.1	4.1	4.0
Grand Blanc, MI	6.6	6.6	5.9	4.9	5.0	5.6	7.0	6.1	5.4	5.0	5.1	5.7
Hampden, PA	4.6	4.6	4.3	3.8	4.2	4.4	4.6	4.6	3.9	3.7	3.8	3.8
Hilliard, OH	4.9	4.6	4.1	3.7	3.7	4.3	4.3	4.2	3.9	3.7	3.7	3.7
Hillsborough, NJ[2]	4.9	4.9	4.5	4.2	4.4	4.6	5.1	5.0	4.7	4.4	4.3	4.1
Holly Springs, NC	4.5	4.3	4.0	3.6	3.8	4.0	4.2	4.3	3.8	3.7	3.9	3.8
Independence, KY	5.2	4.8	4.3	3.9	4.0	4.6	4.6	4.5	4.0	3.9	3.8	3.8
Juneau, AK	5.4	5.4	5.2	4.7	4.2	4.7	4.5	4.1	4.5	4.6	4.8	4.9
Kaysville, UT	3.6	3.7	3.5	3.2	3.1	3.6	3.4	3.4	3.1	3.2	2.9	3.0
Keller, TX[2]	4.2	4.2	4.0	3.5	3.6	3.9	3.9	3.9	3.4	3.2	3.3	3.2
Lafayette, CA[2]	4.3	4.1	3.9	3.6	3.4	3.9	4.1	4.0	3.4	3.3	3.2	3.1
Lafayette, CO	2.6	2.6	2.3	2.2	2.2	2.6	2.5	2.4	2.3	2.4	2.5	2.5
Lake Oswego, OR	4.2	4.1	4.0	3.6	3.6	4.1	4.2	4.3	3.9	3.8	3.7	3.6
Laramie, WY	3.5	2.9	3.1	2.5	2.6	3.2	2.9	2.8	2.6	2.7	2.7	2.7
Leander, TX	3.5	3.5	3.3	2.9	3.0	3.3	3.3	3.3	2.9	2.7	2.8	2.7
Leawood, KS	4.5	4.3	4.2	3.4	3.6	3.8	4.3	4.4	3.3	3.4	3.2	3.3
Lee's Summit, MO	4.5	4.3	4.2	3.4	3.6	3.8	4.3	4.4	3.3	3.4	3.2	3.3
Leesburg, VA[2]	4.2	4.1	3.8	3.5	3.7	4.0	4.0	4.0	3.7	3.6	3.6	3.4
Lehi, UT	3.1	3.2	3.1	2.8	2.9	3.4	3.2	3.1	2.7	2.6	2.4	2.5
Lexington, MA[4]	3.6	3.5	3.3	3.0	3.3	3.6	3.5	3.2	3.1	2.7	2.7	2.6
Los Altos, CA	3.9	3.7	3.5	3.2	3.1	3.4	3.6	3.5	3.0	2.9	2.8	2.7
Loveland, CO	2.8	2.8	2.4	2.2	2.2	2.5	2.3	2.4	2.3	2.4	2.5	2.5
Lower Macungie, PA	5.5	5.6	5.2	4.5	4.9	4.9	5.3	5.4	4.5	4.4	4.4	4.3
Madison, AL	5.3	5.0	4.5	3.6	3.6	4.3	4.0	3.8	3.3	3.2	3.0	2.9
Madison, MS	5.0	4.2	4.3	3.9	4.7	5.3	5.0	4.3	4.1	3.9	3.7	3.7
Maple Valley, WA[2]	3.8	3.8	3.6	3.2	3.5	4.0	4.1	4.1	4.0	3.9	4.1	3.7

Table continued on next page.

Metro Area[1]	2017											
	Jan.	Feb.	Mar.	Apr.	May	Jun.	Jul.	Aug.	Sep.	Oct.	Nov.	Dec.
Marion, IA	4.4	4.1	3.7	3.3	3.2	3.4	3.2	3.4	3.1	2.6	2.8	3.2
Marlboro, NJ[2]	4.9	4.9	4.4	4.1	4.3	4.5	4.9	4.9	4.5	4.3	4.1	4.0
Mason, OH	5.2	4.8	4.3	3.9	4.0	4.6	4.6	4.5	4.0	3.9	3.8	3.8
Menomonee Falls, WI	4.0	4.1	3.6	3.3	3.4	4.1	3.9	3.9	3.3	3.1	3.1	2.8
Meridian, ID	4.1	3.8	3.4	3.0	2.7	3.0	3.0	2.9	2.7	2.6	2.9	2.7
Meridian, MI	4.6	4.4	4.0	3.3	3.7	4.9	5.6	4.9	4.2	3.8	3.7	3.9
Merrimack, NH[4]	3.6	3.6	3.4	3.0	2.8	3.0	3.0	3.0	2.8	2.7	2.7	2.6
Milton, GA	5.2	5.0	4.7	4.4	4.4	4.8	4.8	4.7	4.2	4.2	4.1	4.1
Moon, PA	6.1	6.0	5.5	4.6	4.9	5.2	5.3	5.4	4.4	4.3	4.4	4.5
Moorpark, CA	5.4	5.0	4.7	4.2	3.9	4.4	4.8	4.8	4.3	4.1	4.1	4.0
Morgantown, WV	4.7	4.6	4.2	3.6	3.4	4.3	4.0	4.4	3.6	3.6	3.7	3.9
Mount Pleasant, SC	4.2	3.9	3.4	3.2	3.3	3.9	3.8	4.0	3.6	3.5	3.4	3.5
Newark, DE[2]	5.0	5.0	4.7	4.5	4.4	5.1	5.1	5.0	4.6	4.4	4.1	4.1
Newtown, CT[3]	4.8	4.8	4.4	4.0	3.8	4.0	4.0	3.8	3.4	3.3	3.2	3.1
North Attleborough, MA[3]	5.6	5.4	5.0	4.1	4.1	4.3	4.7	4.4	4.0	4.0	4.1	4.1
North Port, FL	4.6	4.2	3.8	3.7	3.8	4.0	4.1	4.1	3.7	3.6	3.5	3.3
North Ridgeville, OH	6.6	7.1	6.1	5.4	5.5	6.1	6.0	5.9	5.1	4.7	4.5	4.8
Northville, MI[2]	6.7	6.2	5.4	4.1	4.1	5.0	6.3	6.3	5.8	5.3	4.7	4.9
O'Fallon, MO	4.4	4.4	4.0	3.6	3.6	3.8	4.1	4.1	3.4	2.9	3.3	3.4
Orchard Park, NY	6.2	6.2	5.5	5.1	5.0	5.2	5.4	5.4	5.0	4.9	5.2	5.5
Oro Valley, AZ	4.9	4.7	4.6	4.3	4.3	4.7	4.6	4.7	4.4	4.3	4.2	4.2
Oviedo, FL	4.5	4.1	3.8	3.6	3.7	4.0	4.0	3.9	3.6	3.4	3.5	3.3
Parker, CO	3.0	2.9	2.7	2.5	2.4	2.8	2.7	2.7	2.7	2.7	2.8	2.9
Parkland, FL[2]	4.5	4.2	3.9	3.7	3.8	4.0	4.1	4.0	3.7	3.6	3.6	3.4
Peachtree City, GA	5.2	5.0	4.7	4.4	4.4	4.8	4.8	4.7	4.2	4.2	4.1	4.1
Pittsfield, MI	3.7	3.6	3.1	2.6	3.3	3.9	5.0	4.3	3.9	3.4	3.3	3.1
Plainfield, IL[2]	5.7	5.3	4.7	4.6	4.5	5.4	5.3	5.6	4.9	4.8	4.8	4.9
Pleasant Grove, UT	3.1	3.2	3.1	2.8	2.9	3.4	3.2	3.1	2.7	2.6	2.4	2.5
Poway, CA	4.7	4.4	4.2	3.9	3.7	4.2	4.4	4.3	3.7	3.6	3.5	3.3
Princeton, NJ	4.4	4.4	4.0	3.7	3.9	4.1	4.7	4.6	4.2	3.9	3.8	3.6
Queen Creek, AZ	4.6	4.4	4.4	4.1	4.1	4.4	4.3	4.4	4.2	4.0	4.0	4.0
Radnor, PA[2]	6.1	6.1	5.7	5.3	5.8	5.8	6.3	6.4	5.5	5.4	5.3	5.1
Randolph, NJ[2]	4.9	4.9	4.5	4.2	4.4	4.6	5.1	5.0	4.7	4.4	4.3	4.1
Rexburg, ID	3.0	2.7	2.4	2.1	1.9	2.0	1.9	2.0	1.8	1.6	2.0	1.8
Rio Rancho, NM	6.0	5.9	5.7	5.3	5.4	6.3	6.3	6.0	5.7	5.5	5.3	5.1
Rye, NY[2]	4.9	4.9	4.4	4.1	4.3	4.5	4.9	4.9	4.5	4.3	4.1	4.0
Sammamish, WA[2]	3.8	3.8	3.6	3.2	3.5	4.0	4.1	4.1	4.0	3.9	4.1	3.7
San Ramon, CA[2]	4.3	4.1	3.9	3.6	3.4	3.9	4.1	4.0	3.4	3.3	3.2	3.1
Saratoga, CA	3.9	3.7	3.5	3.2	3.1	3.4	3.6	3.5	3.0	2.9	2.8	2.7
Shrewsbury, MA[3]	4.7	4.6	4.3	3.8	3.9	4.2	4.3	4.0	3.7	3.3	3.2	3.2
South Brunswick, NJ[2]	4.9	4.9	4.4	4.1	4.3	4.5	4.9	4.9	4.5	4.3	4.1	4.0
South Jordan, UT	3.2	3.4	3.4	3.2	3.1	3.5	3.2	3.3	2.9	2.8	2.6	2.7
South Kingstown, RI[3]	5.6	5.4	5.0	4.1	4.1	4.3	4.7	4.4	4.0	4.0	4.1	4.1
South Portland, ME[3]	3.0	3.1	2.9	2.7	2.7	2.8	2.6	2.3	2.3	2.3	2.4	2.0
Sparks, NV	5.2	4.8	4.6	4.3	4.1	4.3	4.1	4.0	3.9	3.7	3.7	3.7
State College, PA	4.4	4.2	3.7	3.2	4.0	3.9	4.2	3.9	3.3	3.1	3.2	3.2
Sugar Land, TX	5.8	5.6	5.2	4.8	4.8	5.1	5.1	5.1	4.8	4.4	4.4	4.3
Sun Prairie, WI	3.0	3.1	2.6	2.3	2.4	2.8	2.6	2.4	2.3	2.2	2.1	2.0
Syracuse, UT	3.6	3.7	3.5	3.2	3.1	3.6	3.4	3.4	3.1	3.2	2.9	3.0
Tredyffrin, PA[2]	4.3	4.4	4.0	3.6	3.9	4.0	4.3	4.3	3.7	3.5	3.6	3.4
Upper Dublin, PA[2]	4.3	4.4	4.0	3.6	3.9	4.0	4.3	4.3	3.7	3.5	3.6	3.4
Urbandale, IA	3.9	3.6	3.3	2.9	2.8	3.1	2.9	2.9	2.7	2.2	2.4	2.6
Vestal, NY	6.6	6.5	5.8	5.3	5.1	5.5	5.5	5.3	5.1	4.9	5.3	5.5
Vestavia Hills, AL	5.6	5.3	4.6	3.8	3.7	4.4	4.1	3.9	3.4	3.3	3.1	3.1
Webster, NY	5.5	5.6	5.0	4.6	4.7	4.9	5.1	5.0	4.8	4.7	4.9	5.0
Wellesley, MA[4]	3.6	3.5	3.3	3.0	3.3	3.6	3.5	3.2	3.1	2.7	2.7	2.6
West Fargo, ND	3.3	3.2	3.0	2.3	2.0	2.4	2.1	2.1	1.9	1.6	2.1	2.5
West Lafayette, IN	4.0	3.8	3.4	2.6	3.0	3.4	3.5	3.7	2.9	2.8	3.0	2.8
Weston, FL[2]	4.5	4.2	3.9	3.7	3.8	4.0	4.1	4.0	3.7	3.6	3.6	3.4
Wilmette, IL[2]	5.7	5.3	4.7	4.6	4.5	5.4	5.3	5.6	4.9	4.8	4.8	4.9
Yorba Linda, CA[2]	4.0	3.8	3.7	3.4	3.2	3.7	3.9	3.8	3.3	3.2	3.1	2.9
Zionsville, IN	4.0	3.9	3.4	2.8	3.0	3.3	3.4	3.7	3.1	3.0	3.0	2.8
U.S.	5.1	4.9	4.6	4.1	4.1	4.5	4.6	4.5	4.1	3.9	3.9	3.9

Note: Data is not seasonally adjusted and covers workers 16 years of age and older; All figures are percentages; (1) Figures cover the Metropolitan Statistical Area (MSA) except where noted. See Appendix B for areas included; (2) Metropolitan Division; (3) New England City and Town Area; (4) New England City and Town Area Division
Source: Bureau of Labor Statistics, Local Area Unemployment Statistics

Average Hourly Wages: Occupations A – C

Metro Area[1]	Accountants/ Auditors	Automotive Mechanics	Book-keepers	Carpenters	Cashiers	Clerks, Gen. Office	Clerks, Recep./Info.
Aberdeen, SD	n/a	n/a	n/a	n/a	n/a	n/a	n/a
Aliso Viejo, CA[2]	37.88	24.19	22.86	28.35	12.00	16.92	15.74
Allen, TX[2]	39.94	20.46	21.57	18.75	10.12	17.18	13.64
Ames, IA	34.41	18.98	19.61	18.38	10.08	17.24	13.78
Amherst, MA[3]	31.96	21.13	20.00	24.12	12.13	17.74	15.56
Apex, NC	34.71	21.30	19.94	18.97	9.75	15.48	13.89
Beavercreek, OH	36.70	17.78	19.17	22.19	9.99	16.55	12.85
Bellevue, NE	32.77	21.76	18.51	20.17	10.63	15.61	13.57
Bend, OR	30.74	22.11	19.17	19.51	12.48	15.95	15.14
Benicia, CA	39.70	18.96	22.50	28.98	12.63	18.05	17.12
Bentonville, AR	36.12	18.68	17.81	18.47	9.85	14.35	12.27
Bethlehem, NY	36.35	19.24	19.85	24.57	11.09	16.70	15.34
Blacksburg, VA	33.19	19.52	17.06	18.01	9.33	14.13	12.85
Bowie, MD[2]	45.14	24.06	24.04	23.16	11.38	19.40	16.27
Bozeman, MT	n/a	n/a	n/a	n/a	n/a	n/a	n/a
Brentwood, TN	31.90	21.40	20.01	20.16	10.25	17.75	14.07
Burlington, VT[3]	38.27	18.24	20.56	22.23	11.92	16.21	16.28
Cabot, AR	31.13	18.49	18.13	16.87	9.96	14.22	12.88
Carmel, IN	34.48	21.02	19.34	22.81	9.61	16.21	14.04
Cedar Falls, IA	25.95	18.53	16.47	19.32	10.08	17.05	13.13
Cedar Park, TX	35.35	23.90	20.35	19.06	10.85	17.43	13.34
Central, LA	31.29	19.57	18.03	20.29	9.19	12.38	11.73
Chapel Hill, NC	38.72	21.36	20.69	17.42	10.21	16.69	13.61
Cheshire, CT[3]	37.59	21.40	22.58	25.46	11.54	18.93	15.73
Chino Hills, CA	34.32	22.37	20.16	24.69	12.36	16.92	14.51
Cibolo, TX	36.39	21.06	18.51	19.13	10.28	17.01	12.36
Cicero, NY	35.16	18.39	19.24	21.13	10.88	15.62	14.73
Collierville, TN	34.25	21.22	18.76	18.33	9.78	15.94	12.87
Coppell, TX[2]	39.94	20.46	21.57	18.75	10.12	17.18	13.64
Cornelius, NC	38.27	20.98	19.03	17.33	9.60	15.52	13.68
Cranberry, PA	34.61	18.82	18.47	25.97	9.40	15.92	12.80
Crown Point, IN[2]	31.31	20.49	18.87	25.13	9.62	15.82	13.20
Dublin, OH	35.88	20.00	19.71	22.26	10.21	16.82	13.31
East Fishkill, NY[2]	41.35	24.65	20.46	25.05	10.89	15.91	15.80
Eden Prairie, MN	35.44	21.44	21.64	25.83	11.35	17.91	15.04
Edmond, OK	33.51	19.95	18.70	19.84	10.14	13.87	13.22
Edwardsville, IL	36.95	21.76	19.44	28.62	10.67	15.77	12.90
Evesham, NJ[2]	40.53	23.80	20.60	26.65	10.48	16.75	14.71
Flower Mound, TX[2]	39.94	20.46	21.57	18.75	10.12	17.18	13.64
Folsom, CA	34.68	22.18	21.48	25.79	12.60	16.78	15.56
Friendswood, TX	42.92	22.73	20.76	20.46	10.10	18.68	13.02
Gaines, MI	32.40	19.93	17.93	19.19	10.82	17.56	14.01
Glastonbury, CT[3]	37.85	23.07	22.21	26.38	11.64	18.74	16.76
Grand Blanc, MI	28.29	17.04	17.92	21.98	10.59	16.01	12.96
Hampden, PA	33.60	18.76	19.15	22.83	9.73	16.76	13.48
Hilliard, OH	35.88	20.00	19.71	22.26	10.21	16.82	13.31
Hillsborough, NJ[2]	45.07	23.47	22.72	32.97	10.84	17.64	16.02
Holly Springs, NC	34.71	21.30	19.94	18.97	9.75	15.48	13.89
Independence, KY	33.99	19.84	19.25	21.49	10.18	16.21	13.27
Juneau, AK	n/a	n/a	n/a	n/a	n/a	n/a	n/a
Kaysville, UT	33.54	21.20	18.30	20.22	10.69	15.19	12.44
Keller, TX[2]	39.66	19.82	19.65	18.39	10.34	17.49	12.69
Lafayette, CA[2]	43.07	25.07	25.15	32.45	13.38	19.02	16.97
Lafayette, CO	40.29	22.17	22.56	21.06	12.35	19.40	14.89
Lake Oswego, OR	33.82	24.65	20.42	25.33	12.47	17.79	15.44
Laramie, WY	n/a	n/a	n/a	n/a	n/a	n/a	n/a
Leander, TX	35.35	23.90	20.35	19.06	10.85	17.43	13.34
Leawood, KS	32.92	20.92	19.42	25.50	10.49	15.66	13.84
Lee's Summit, MO	32.92	20.92	19.42	25.50	10.49	15.66	13.84
Leesburg, VA[2]	45.14	24.06	24.04	23.16	11.38	19.40	16.27
Lehi, UT	32.67	19.67	17.87	19.04	10.33	14.60	13.00
Lexington, MA[4]	39.62	21.87	22.91	30.93	12.52	19.95	16.01
Los Altos, CA	47.07	25.47	23.97	30.41	13.08	22.21	17.16
Loveland, CO	33.05	25.03	19.23	22.61	11.47	17.22	14.61
Lower Macungie, PA	37.01	20.88	18.26	23.81	9.80	16.49	13.93
Madison, AL	37.18	19.12	18.00	17.68	9.83	12.16	12.49
Madison, MS	27.27	19.49	18.19	16.92	9.20	13.38	13.18
Maple Valley, WA[2]	38.64	23.95	22.35	29.80	14.34	19.73	16.79

Table continued on next page.

Metro Area[1]	Accountants/ Auditors	Automotive Mechanics	Book-keepers	Carpenters	Cashiers	Clerks, Gen. Office	Clerks, Recep./Info.
Marion, IA	32.87	20.58	18.81	20.74	10.01	16.64	14.19
Marlboro, NJ[2]	48.81	21.74	22.51	33.01	11.51	16.57	16.16
Mason, OH	33.99	19.84	19.25	21.49	10.18	16.21	13.27
Menomonee Falls, WI	33.56	20.60	18.57	25.65	10.18	17.54	13.80
Meridian, ID	31.91	20.13	18.69	15.97	10.29	15.04	13.16
Meridian, MI	33.48	20.13	18.81	20.99	10.26	16.45	14.32
Merrimack, NH[4]	36.09	20.92	20.45	23.73	10.74	19.64	13.74
Milton, GA	37.20	19.40	19.95	23.50	9.64	14.70	14.32
Moon, PA	34.61	18.82	18.47	25.97	9.40	15.92	12.80
Moorpark, CA	43.68	20.31	23.18	25.81	13.01	18.24	15.87
Morgantown, WV	32.02	14.64	16.55	22.74	9.96	15.12	12.55
Mount Pleasant, SC	27.79	20.15	17.44	21.03	9.40	12.97	13.82
Newark, DE[2]	39.15	21.32	21.94	24.38	10.22	14.91	13.19
Newtown, CT[3]	41.72	24.08	21.45	25.29	12.15	17.08	17.20
North Attleborough, MA[3]	38.50	19.57	20.31	24.46	11.71	17.15	15.48
North Port, FL	34.36	19.18	18.96	19.39	10.42	15.47	13.53
North Ridgeville, OH	36.46	21.19	19.43	25.94	10.62	16.44	13.34
Northville, MI[2]	36.91	20.40	19.96	28.32	11.34	17.46	13.87
O'Fallon, MO	36.95	21.76	19.44	28.62	10.67	15.77	12.90
Orchard Park, NY	34.80	19.53	18.66	22.01	10.88	15.15	14.78
Oro Valley, AZ	30.10	18.45	18.76	16.89	11.44	16.06	14.04
Oviedo, FL	34.34	17.68	17.59	19.99	10.14	14.53	13.41
Parker, CO	39.25	22.72	20.47	22.13	11.40	19.71	15.43
Parkland, FL[2]	34.71	21.08	19.92	19.64	10.23	15.36	14.73
Peachtree City, GA	37.20	19.40	19.95	23.50	9.64	14.70	14.32
Pittsfield, MI	36.51	26.52	19.28	28.90	10.81	16.26	14.43
Plainfield, IL[2]	39.74	22.81	20.35	33.34	10.93	18.20	14.93
Pleasant Grove, UT	32.67	19.67	17.87	19.04	10.33	14.60	13.00
Poway, CA	38.99	21.93	21.86	25.07	12.37	16.13	15.62
Princeton, NJ	40.80	24.03	22.66	30.32	10.78	19.17	16.07
Queen Creek, AZ	34.28	21.15	19.37	21.48	11.41	17.50	14.34
Radnor, PA[2]	40.79	18.98	21.31	31.19	10.55	18.04	14.11
Randolph, NJ[2]	45.07	23.47	22.72	32.97	10.84	17.64	16.02
Rexburg, ID	n/a	n/a	n/a	n/a	n/a	n/a	n/a
Rio Rancho, NM	33.76	19.25	17.45	17.64	10.30	12.44	13.56
Rye, NY[2]	48.81	21.74	22.51	33.01	11.51	16.57	16.16
Sammamish, WA[2]	38.64	23.95	22.35	29.80	14.34	19.73	16.79
San Ramon, CA[2]	43.07	25.07	25.15	32.45	13.38	19.02	16.97
Saratoga, CA	47.07	25.47	23.97	30.41	13.08	22.21	17.16
Shrewsbury, MA[3]	35.60	21.98	21.25	26.55	12.20	16.38	14.36
South Brunswick, NJ[2]	48.81	21.74	22.51	33.01	11.51	16.57	16.16
South Jordan, UT	35.33	21.12	19.63	18.65	10.78	15.13	13.61
South Kingstown, RI[3]	38.50	19.57	20.31	24.46	11.71	17.15	15.48
South Portland, ME[3]	36.26	20.85	19.63	18.82	11.24	16.88	15.43
Sparks, NV	33.90	22.18	20.43	24.95	10.51	18.16	14.26
State College, PA	31.36	18.25	17.59	21.73	9.36	15.85	11.57
Sugar Land, TX	42.92	22.73	20.76	20.46	10.10	18.68	13.02
Sun Prairie, WI	32.71	20.42	19.05	27.59	10.30	17.52	14.04
Syracuse, UT	33.54	21.20	18.30	20.22	10.69	15.19	12.44
Tredyffrin, PA[2]	38.57	21.89	21.03	28.22	10.18	17.31	14.41
Upper Dublin, PA[2]	38.57	21.89	21.03	28.22	10.18	17.31	14.41
Urbandale, IA	34.51	21.23	20.17	22.55	10.47	17.75	15.01
Vestal, NY	34.64	18.26	17.61	22.03	10.61	13.99	13.74
Vestavia Hills, AL	35.13	21.76	19.75	20.26	9.42	13.21	13.12
Webster, NY	35.07	18.72	19.06	21.23	10.63	15.62	14.10
Wellesley, MA[4]	39.62	21.87	22.91	30.93	12.52	19.95	16.01
West Fargo, ND	28.83	20.17	18.66	19.12	10.72	16.27	13.38
West Lafayette, IN	29.57	17.73	16.14	21.08	9.16	14.94	12.06
Weston, FL[2]	34.71	21.08	19.92	19.64	10.23	15.36	14.73
Wilmette, IL[2]	39.74	22.81	20.35	33.34	10.93	18.20	14.93
Yorba Linda, CA[2]	37.88	24.19	22.86	28.35	12.00	16.92	15.74
Zionsville, IN	34.48	21.02	19.34	22.81	9.61	16.21	14.04

Notes: (1) Figures cover the Metropolitan Statistical Area (MSA) except where noted. See Appendix B for areas included; (2) Metropolitan Division; (3) New England City and Town Area; (4) New England City and Town Area Division; n/a not available
Source: Bureau of Labor Statistics, May 2017 Metro Area Occupational Employment and Wage Estimates

Average Hourly Wages: Occupations C – E

Metro Area	Clerks, Ship./Rec.	Computer Program-mers	Computer Systems Analysts	Comp. User Support Specialists	Cooks, Restaurant	Dentists	Electrical Engineers
Aberdeen, SD	n/a	n/a	n/a	n/a	n/a	n/a	n/a
Aliso Viejo, CA[2]	16.10	43.06	46.39	28.61	14.72	78.65	49.24
Allen, TX[2]	14.70	41.55	47.06	25.83	13.08	83.05	50.73
Ames, IA	17.09	34.54	33.70	21.91	11.27	n/a	n/a
Amherst, MA[3]	17.97	40.14	41.69	25.03	13.27	91.10	45.16
Apex, NC	15.06	47.15	44.69	28.10	11.95	114.16	53.49
Beavercreek, OH	15.72	37.84	43.29	22.36	11.24	94.50	41.74
Bellevue, NE	16.09	38.98	38.21	24.42	12.99	79.19	42.83
Bend, OR	17.41	31.90	40.16	23.44	13.64	107.95	41.09
Benicia, CA	17.94	48.79	44.61	26.43	13.98	85.33	52.69
Bentonville, AR	16.40	31.69	34.25	20.52	11.41	84.64	39.53
Bethlehem, NY	16.76	37.32	38.33	24.97	13.21	89.57	50.17
Blacksburg, VA	14.46	40.19	38.69	21.33	11.75	96.58	46.41
Bowie, MD[2]	18.44	47.77	50.09	30.85	13.52	96.40	57.22
Bozeman, MT	n/a	n/a	n/a	n/a	n/a	n/a	n/a
Brentwood, TN	14.97	38.01	36.47	24.85	12.38	95.04	41.78
Burlington, VT[3]	16.45	34.31	39.63	26.03	13.79	n/a	46.42
Cabot, AR	14.87	34.74	33.32	21.42	11.83	65.57	43.19
Carmel, IN	14.16	37.69	41.11	23.71	11.91	72.41	39.42
Cedar Falls, IA	16.73	31.51	36.87	23.00	10.61	n/a	45.66
Cedar Park, TX	15.17	43.36	44.69	24.28	12.11	76.41	56.24
Central, LA	17.34	31.97	36.49	22.61	11.20	81.70	44.57
Chapel Hill, NC	15.11	44.44	41.23	26.13	11.89	99.18	50.82
Cheshire, CT[3]	17.05	38.87	40.69	27.09	13.91	121.97	44.33
Chino Hills, CA	17.06	37.89	38.42	26.12	13.23	75.81	41.66
Cibolo, TX	14.69	47.14	46.43	25.27	11.81	75.88	50.53
Cicero, NY	16.41	37.18	39.05	28.05	12.54	88.46	46.92
Collierville, TN	14.37	34.62	32.60	23.85	10.84	92.16	37.70
Coppell, TX[2]	14.70	41.55	47.06	25.83	13.08	83.05	50.73
Cornelius, NC	16.52	45.47	45.29	27.52	11.37	118.73	49.93
Cranberry, PA	16.90	35.09	44.75	23.58	11.65	41.18	46.80
Crown Point, IN[2]	15.23	39.31	42.24	18.01	10.46	101.44	41.57
Dublin, OH	15.14	36.38	47.08	24.99	13.01	100.73	38.45
East Fishkill, NY[2]	17.17	33.66	48.16	27.42	14.25	96.45	45.16
Eden Prairie, MN	17.71	43.16	44.79	27.72	13.31	103.13	45.94
Edmond, OK	16.24	38.18	34.00	21.87	12.38	68.39	45.36
Edwardsville, IL	17.34	40.89	44.52	23.56	11.71	83.75	48.27
Evesham, NJ[2]	18.02	39.71	45.97	24.12	14.85	75.94	60.31
Flower Mound, TX[2]	14.70	41.55	47.06	25.83	13.08	83.05	50.73
Folsom, CA	17.41	39.50	40.25	27.13	13.29	62.94	58.89
Friendswood, TX	15.68	42.18	48.63	30.13	12.57	91.06	50.09
Gaines, MI	15.37	37.40	36.83	22.63	11.49	84.11	36.15
Glastonbury, CT[3]	17.53	44.78	45.39	29.31	13.28	95.67	45.09
Grand Blanc, MI	14.48	n/a	32.89	19.92	11.64	99.86	48.61
Hampden, PA	16.01	36.85	42.09	24.35	12.05	67.95	43.76
Hilliard, OH	15.14	36.38	47.08	24.99	13.01	100.73	38.45
Hillsborough, NJ[2]	16.71	42.91	48.12	34.60	15.38	n/a	49.81
Holly Springs, NC	15.06	47.15	44.69	28.10	11.95	114.16	53.49
Independence, KY	16.29	31.90	42.77	23.88	11.17	96.35	40.26
Juneau, AK	n/a	n/a	n/a	n/a	n/a	n/a	n/a
Kaysville, UT	16.80	36.39	39.69	26.76	12.90	58.01	43.38
Keller, TX[2]	15.83	38.29	44.41	23.85	11.54	80.13	45.92
Lafayette, CA[2]	18.74	n/a	49.27	30.73	14.62	75.83	52.00
Lafayette, CO	17.80	44.98	46.57	28.44	14.49	94.33	45.85
Lake Oswego, OR	17.98	40.83	44.76	26.45	13.55	87.84	46.42
Laramie, WY	n/a	n/a	n/a	n/a	n/a	n/a	n/a
Leander, TX	15.17	43.36	44.69	24.28	12.11	76.41	56.24
Leawood, KS	16.68	38.22	40.73	23.18	12.19	88.92	43.32
Lee's Summit, MO	16.68	38.22	40.73	23.18	12.19	88.92	43.32
Leesburg, VA[2]	18.44	47.77	50.09	30.85	13.52	96.40	57.22
Lehi, UT	14.30	42.56	46.21	22.39	12.54	n/a	39.89
Lexington, MA[4]	18.68	47.59	44.79	30.74	15.38	75.42	55.85
Los Altos, CA	18.21	50.22	56.74	38.29	14.90	89.35	60.37
Loveland, CO	15.57	46.43	43.84	27.53	13.10	108.87	49.57
Lower Macungie, PA	17.32	33.02	42.55	25.17	12.97	94.69	39.43
Madison, AL	14.88	50.18	43.98	22.30	10.97	n/a	49.01
Madison, MS	16.34	37.58	30.30	22.92	10.89	88.91	45.27

Table continued on next page.

Metro Area	Clerks, Ship./Rec.	Computer Programmers	Computer Systems Analysts	Comp. User Support Specialists	Cooks, Restaurant	Dentists	Electrical Engineers
Maple Valley, WA[2]	18.46	59.98	48.02	31.95	15.42	88.44	55.24
Marion, IA	17.35	36.00	39.89	22.28	11.35	117.65	43.41
Marlboro, NJ[2]	17.41	46.79	55.18	30.38	14.34	77.98	51.97
Mason, OH	16.29	31.90	42.77	23.88	11.17	96.35	40.26
Menomonee Falls, WI	18.30	39.92	38.01	25.41	12.62	109.15	39.04
Meridian, ID	14.52	34.44	38.75	20.70	11.40	114.31	42.20
Meridian, MI	16.53	35.87	35.81	25.97	11.55	80.71	38.24
Merrimack, NH[4]	17.12	31.86	46.10	26.90	13.14	106.66	53.59
Milton, GA	15.71	42.12	43.46	26.22	11.31	84.34	44.59
Moon, PA	16.90	35.09	44.75	23.58	11.65	41.18	46.80
Moorpark, CA	16.47	38.58	53.82	24.84	14.16	68.06	48.12
Morgantown, WV	21.71	44.08	35.20	20.14	11.55	102.14	47.29
Mount Pleasant, SC	18.99	35.46	38.58	25.30	11.83	81.24	41.67
Newark, DE[2]	14.65	38.13	46.84	28.43	13.05	121.32	48.29
Newtown, CT[3]	17.89	40.25	52.55	26.17	15.10	n/a	46.33
North Attleborough, MA[3]	17.53	36.96	46.80	27.29	13.46	90.23	50.00
North Port, FL	15.20	35.12	38.75	22.43	12.53	68.93	48.51
North Ridgeville, OH	16.44	31.20	39.37	22.84	12.68	79.11	41.49
Northville, MI[2]	19.14	36.99	40.81	24.13	13.34	93.82	44.61
O'Fallon, MO	17.34	40.89	44.52	23.56	11.71	83.75	48.27
Orchard Park, NY	16.36	35.14	36.83	23.28	12.98	96.38	38.04
Oro Valley, AZ	16.23	42.49	37.96	24.63	12.23	68.66	52.48
Oviedo, FL	15.10	43.67	40.82	23.03	13.33	90.97	43.29
Parker, CO	16.31	46.52	47.12	30.15	13.21	80.93	44.33
Parkland, FL[2]	15.82	34.23	40.55	22.22	13.59	55.72	37.36
Peachtree City, GA	15.71	42.12	43.46	26.22	11.31	84.34	44.59
Pittsfield, MI	17.54	35.36	40.37	23.06	12.91	90.76	41.69
Plainfield, IL[2]	16.88	44.41	43.53	26.58	13.03	69.75	43.83
Pleasant Grove, UT	14.30	42.56	46.21	22.39	12.54	n/a	39.89
Poway, CA	16.66	46.71	48.55	28.48	14.17	89.58	50.12
Princeton, NJ	18.87	41.80	48.30	30.78	13.71	n/a	53.67
Queen Creek, AZ	16.04	43.32	43.03	24.39	13.34	87.57	49.98
Radnor, PA[2]	17.75	42.09	47.67	27.69	12.92	67.88	48.32
Randolph, NJ[2]	16.71	42.91	48.12	34.60	15.38	n/a	49.81
Rexburg, ID	n/a	n/a	n/a	n/a	n/a	n/a	n/a
Rio Rancho, NM	14.55	39.11	40.60	20.74	11.26	79.68	48.92
Rye, NY[2]	17.41	46.79	55.18	30.38	14.34	77.98	51.97
Sammamish, WA[2]	18.46	59.98	48.02	31.95	15.42	88.44	55.24
San Ramon, CA[2]	18.74	n/a	49.27	30.73	14.62	75.83	52.00
Saratoga, CA	18.21	50.22	56.74	38.29	14.90	89.35	60.37
Shrewsbury, MA[3]	17.72	45.52	43.81	24.68	14.00	103.76	n/a
South Brunswick, NJ[2]	17.41	46.79	55.18	30.38	14.34	77.98	51.97
South Jordan, UT	14.65	38.86	37.92	25.00	13.13	79.45	42.63
South Kingstown, RI[3]	17.53	36.96	46.80	27.29	13.46	90.23	50.00
South Portland, ME[3]	16.13	38.54	40.43	26.17	13.25	87.12	41.16
Sparks, NV	17.67	39.90	34.36	22.11	12.86	126.87	44.04
State College, PA	16.00	37.02	41.49	25.80	11.70	94.34	48.73
Sugar Land, TX	15.68	42.18	48.63	30.13	12.57	91.06	50.09
Sun Prairie, WI	16.88	36.34	42.31	26.36	12.65	102.25	45.59
Syracuse, UT	16.80	36.39	39.69	26.76	12.90	58.01	43.38
Tredyffrin, PA[2]	17.02	41.78	47.43	25.42	14.52	68.04	47.81
Upper Dublin, PA[2]	17.02	41.78	47.43	25.42	14.52	68.04	47.81
Urbandale, IA	17.78	37.43	41.94	24.93	12.52	100.97	40.89
Vestal, NY	15.71	43.44	42.74	23.40	12.45	97.88	37.73
Vestavia Hills, AL	14.91	39.28	36.63	24.59	11.38	97.17	45.87
Webster, NY	16.26	38.88	37.98	23.36	12.69	86.80	44.56
Wellesley, MA[4]	18.68	47.59	44.79	30.74	15.38	75.42	55.85
West Fargo, ND	16.22	32.41	39.10	27.76	14.23	107.04	37.63
West Lafayette, IN	18.31	31.39	33.24	21.66	12.22	77.37	37.70
Weston, FL[2]	15.82	34.23	40.55	22.22	13.59	55.72	37.36
Wilmette, IL[2]	16.88	44.41	43.53	26.58	13.03	69.75	43.83
Yorba Linda, CA[2]	16.10	43.06	46.39	28.61	14.72	78.65	49.24
Zionsville, IN	14.16	37.69	41.11	23.71	11.91	72.41	39.42

Notes: (1) Figures cover the Metropolitan Statistical Area (MSA) except where noted. See Appendix B for areas included; (2) Metropolitan Division; (3) New England City and Town Area; (4) New England City and Town Area Division; n/a not available

Source: Bureau of Labor Statistics, May 2017 Metro Area Occupational Employment and Wage Estimates

Average Hourly Wages: Occupations E – I

Metro Area	Electricians	Financial Managers	First-Line Supervisors/ Mgrs., Sales	Food Preparation Workers	General/ Operations Managers	Hairdressers/ Cosmetologists	Internists
Aberdeen, SD	n/a	n/a	n/a	n/a	n/a	n/a	n/a
Aliso Viejo, CA[2]	28.42	69.46	21.56	12.55	70.39	13.36	108.07
Allen, TX[2]	22.38	75.75	22.64	10.78	70.03	12.62	56.09
Ames, IA	24.44	45.88	18.81	11.77	46.14	13.53	n/a
Amherst, MA[3]	28.48	51.44	20.78	13.74	48.32	15.79	111.38
Apex, NC	19.75	67.15	21.24	10.81	67.89	15.59	n/a
Beavercreek, OH	23.74	62.85	20.94	10.96	53.97	11.56	115.04
Bellevue, NE	24.23	58.97	21.06	11.22	48.77	17.63	108.35
Bend, OR	28.28	47.33	19.40	12.22	43.46	12.74	n/a
Benicia, CA	32.35	64.43	20.37	11.45	52.58	12.14	n/a
Bentonville, AR	19.57	68.09	19.02	10.08	49.30	15.55	n/a
Bethlehem, NY	29.46	67.46	20.39	12.63	60.12	14.40	122.55
Blacksburg, VA	22.24	60.72	20.20	9.81	51.18	n/a	n/a
Bowie, MD[2]	29.20	79.63	23.27	11.96	73.09	17.57	66.30
Bozeman, MT	n/a	n/a	n/a	n/a	n/a	n/a	n/a
Brentwood, TN	23.26	n/a	19.52	10.88	56.45	13.87	128.69
Burlington, VT[3]	25.62	65.89	23.28	12.89	53.94	18.15	88.78
Cabot, AR	20.74	43.32	20.19	10.82	45.38	11.74	n/a
Carmel, IN	27.93	64.87	19.38	10.77	53.29	13.03	124.42
Cedar Falls, IA	23.07	49.59	16.48	10.55	47.56	11.76	n/a
Cedar Park, TX	24.27	67.04	21.52	12.25	62.93	14.78	73.84
Central, LA	25.83	50.47	17.82	8.98	59.75	12.18	104.05
Chapel Hill, NC	21.41	72.44	21.15	11.48	69.65	21.37	n/a
Cheshire, CT[3]	28.39	62.81	23.75	13.64	69.09	18.71	132.90
Chino Hills, CA	27.30	55.30	20.37	12.40	56.82	15.06	59.49
Cibolo, TX	22.50	75.83	22.43	12.11	59.91	11.35	122.46
Cicero, NY	27.13	70.02	22.56	11.89	55.75	14.01	107.49
Collierville, TN	22.53	55.80	21.45	10.15	56.01	13.82	117.56
Coppell, TX[2]	22.38	75.75	22.64	10.78	70.03	12.62	56.09
Cornelius, NC	21.74	74.58	22.28	11.00	67.30	16.10	125.09
Cranberry, PA	31.65	74.73	21.12	11.19	61.83	12.14	n/a
Crown Point, IN[2]	37.03	48.34	18.19	9.63	42.96	11.26	n/a
Dublin, OH	22.13	66.61	20.96	10.68	59.14	13.24	122.29
East Fishkill, NY[2]	26.83	66.80	22.41	12.73	62.13	13.93	n/a
Eden Prairie, MN	36.14	68.09	21.62	12.77	58.07	16.29	126.54
Edmond, OK	21.63	52.29	20.77	9.62	51.74	12.63	89.69
Edwardsville, IL	33.20	67.70	20.54	10.66	56.81	14.86	105.16
Evesham, NJ[2]	34.91	80.47	24.38	11.41	72.95	15.61	94.81
Flower Mound, TX[2]	22.38	75.75	22.64	10.78	70.03	12.62	56.09
Folsom, CA	34.00	61.25	20.33	12.48	55.08	14.46	101.39
Friendswood, TX	26.60	79.13	21.23	11.38	72.37	16.50	64.84
Gaines, MI	24.18	57.74	20.84	12.58	61.07	14.23	97.39
Glastonbury, CT[3]	25.36	70.60	22.05	12.56	63.09	16.05	130.70
Grand Blanc, MI	28.64	53.99	19.26	11.27	56.42	11.91	n/a
Hampden, PA	25.14	60.82	22.87	10.68	58.89	12.07	n/a
Hilliard, OH	22.13	66.61	20.96	10.68	59.14	13.24	122.29
Hillsborough, NJ[2]	33.76	85.56	23.37	11.27	82.52	18.60	98.44
Holly Springs, NC	19.75	67.15	21.24	10.81	67.89	15.59	n/a
Independence, KY	22.88	64.84	20.24	10.91	58.92	13.41	80.35
Juneau, AK	n/a	n/a	n/a	n/a	n/a	n/a	n/a
Kaysville, UT	24.32	47.30	19.13	10.04	37.10	10.30	121.23
Keller, TX[2]	22.06	62.27	21.55	11.01	64.25	14.35	56.70
Lafayette, CA[2]	41.84	75.56	23.31	13.08	71.42	16.33	n/a
Lafayette, CO	27.78	74.68	25.23	12.11	66.19	21.69	109.67
Lake Oswego, OR	33.87	60.25	21.04	12.55	57.07	15.84	100.74
Laramie, WY	n/a	n/a	n/a	n/a	n/a	n/a	n/a
Leander, TX	24.27	67.04	21.52	12.25	62.93	14.78	73.84
Leawood, KS	30.13	65.63	19.38	10.27	54.34	13.95	n/a
Lee's Summit, MO	30.13	65.63	19.38	10.27	54.34	13.95	n/a
Leesburg, VA[2]	29.20	79.63	23.27	11.96	73.09	17.57	66.30
Lehi, UT	26.08	50.24	17.85	11.29	38.87	11.15	n/a
Lexington, MA[4]	33.06	73.25	22.73	14.24	71.68	18.96	117.53
Los Altos, CA	37.50	83.75	24.67	13.30	76.91	14.05	100.79
Loveland, CO	27.97	66.21	23.55	11.29	50.84	16.54	n/a
Lower Macungie, PA	28.68	72.56	22.37	11.52	61.13	14.03	n/a
Madison, AL	20.26	64.38	20.54	10.07	64.98	14.14	n/a
Madison, MS	21.03	53.52	17.79	9.30	41.71	11.82	n/a

Table continued on next page.

Metro Area	Electricians	Financial Managers	First-Line Supervisors/ Mgrs., Sales	Food Preparation Workers	General/ Operations Managers	Hairdressers/ Cosmetologists	Internists
Maple Valley, WA[2]	33.41	71.14	25.89	15.01	67.78	21.28	116.93
Marion, IA	27.28	56.38	19.10	12.06	50.49	11.89	n/a
Marlboro, NJ[2]	40.29	102.01	25.05	12.50	82.38	18.07	99.14
Mason, OH	22.88	64.84	20.24	10.91	58.92	13.41	80.35
Menomonee Falls, WI	29.73	70.36	19.79	10.58	67.86	13.44	114.74
Meridian, ID	22.63	52.39	19.69	11.36	41.01	13.09	n/a
Meridian, MI	31.12	54.73	24.66	11.44	55.38	14.58	123.42
Merrimack, NH[4]	26.61	60.44	24.96	10.69	67.35	14.20	123.22
Milton, GA	23.80	71.92	21.35	10.16	58.86	13.81	n/a
Moon, PA	31.65	74.73	21.12	11.19	61.83	12.14	n/a
Moorpark, CA	27.78	66.43	21.24	12.41	63.64	15.21	83.43
Morgantown, WV	26.09	64.36	15.71	10.45	48.62	n/a	n/a
Mount Pleasant, SC	20.66	55.33	20.27	11.62	48.99	10.01	117.50
Newark, DE[2]	30.35	79.77	21.70	11.06	73.13	16.57	n/a
Newtown, CT[3]	29.91	66.50	23.05	12.42	70.82	16.05	n/a
North Attleborough, MA[3]	27.18	67.30	23.44	13.06	63.80	13.31	110.91
North Port, FL	22.95	63.53	20.76	11.35	55.69	15.64	127.36
North Ridgeville, OH	24.94	66.79	18.79	11.33	58.08	13.85	100.22
Northville, MI[2]	29.92	65.38	20.38	11.78	63.40	13.80	95.44
O'Fallon, MO	33.20	67.70	20.54	10.66	56.81	14.86	105.16
Orchard Park, NY	27.51	73.88	21.82	11.43	55.65	12.68	39.76
Oro Valley, AZ	21.50	45.99	20.67	12.09	40.05	14.29	n/a
Oviedo, FL	20.90	62.58	21.29	11.20	54.61	13.14	n/a
Parker, CO	25.13	80.03	24.59	12.32	67.71	14.42	94.76
Parkland, FL[2]	22.76	66.88	22.64	11.58	59.24	15.47	85.80
Peachtree City, GA	23.80	71.92	21.35	10.16	58.86	13.81	n/a
Pittsfield, MI	34.71	58.46	21.08	12.71	65.72	12.49	n/a
Plainfield, IL[2]	38.07	69.07	21.43	11.77	64.78	13.83	104.71
Pleasant Grove, UT	26.08	50.24	17.85	11.29	38.87	11.15	n/a
Poway, CA	30.45	69.31	23.48	12.26	62.30	15.07	101.87
Princeton, NJ	36.53	83.29	22.70	11.44	84.82	16.82	112.50
Queen Creek, AZ	23.78	56.09	20.07	11.37	49.16	14.02	96.25
Radnor, PA[2]	35.83	83.99	23.05	11.26	72.45	13.50	53.42
Randolph, NJ[2]	33.76	85.56	23.37	11.27	82.52	18.60	98.44
Rexburg, ID	n/a	n/a	n/a	n/a	n/a	n/a	n/a
Rio Rancho, NM	22.28	50.82	20.78	10.69	50.94	11.54	126.36
Rye, NY[2]	40.29	102.01	25.05	12.50	82.38	18.07	99.14
Sammamish, WA[2]	33.41	71.14	25.89	15.01	67.78	21.28	116.93
San Ramon, CA[2]	41.84	75.56	23.31	13.08	71.42	16.33	n/a
Saratoga, CA	37.50	83.75	24.67	13.30	76.91	14.05	100.79
Shrewsbury, MA[3]	34.21	60.54	20.03	12.83	58.63	14.93	102.79
South Brunswick, NJ[2]	40.29	102.01	25.05	12.50	82.38	18.07	99.14
South Jordan, UT	25.96	57.80	19.73	11.71	45.07	11.90	117.22
South Kingstown, RI[3]	27.18	67.30	23.44	13.06	63.80	13.31	110.91
South Portland, ME[3]	24.68	62.86	21.42	11.71	53.35	11.73	94.87
Sparks, NV	27.15	59.36	19.06	9.74	56.89	10.44	n/a
State College, PA	21.80	65.67	18.59	11.41	57.98	14.29	n/a
Sugar Land, TX	26.60	79.13	21.23	11.38	72.37	16.50	64.84
Sun Prairie, WI	26.41	62.80	20.99	11.48	60.40	17.16	108.93
Syracuse, UT	24.32	47.30	19.13	10.04	37.10	10.30	121.23
Tredyffrin, PA[2]	32.95	77.12	23.30	11.87	71.35	14.53	72.25
Upper Dublin, PA[2]	32.95	77.12	23.30	11.87	71.35	14.53	72.25
Urbandale, IA	25.69	61.27	20.70	12.09	53.57	17.44	n/a
Vestal, NY	26.72	60.05	20.87	11.41	51.53	17.08	n/a
Vestavia Hills, AL	22.64	69.31	21.18	10.42	60.37	11.55	n/a
Webster, NY	28.00	74.38	20.96	11.86	61.79	13.95	n/a
Wellesley, MA[4]	33.06	73.25	22.73	14.24	71.68	18.96	117.53
West Fargo, ND	25.29	62.05	20.00	12.54	50.64	14.88	n/a
West Lafayette, IN	29.95	51.34	17.11	10.88	44.52	15.00	n/a
Weston, FL[2]	22.76	66.88	22.64	11.58	59.24	15.47	85.80
Wilmette, IL[2]	38.07	69.07	21.43	11.77	64.78	13.83	104.71
Yorba Linda, CA[2]	28.42	69.46	21.56	12.55	70.39	13.36	108.07
Zionsville, IN	27.93	64.87	19.38	10.77	53.29	13.03	124.42

Notes: (1) Figures cover the Metropolitan Statistical Area (MSA) except where noted. See Appendix B for areas included; (2) Metropolitan Division; (3) New England City and Town Area; (4) New England City and Town Area Division; n/a not available

Source: Bureau of Labor Statistics, May 2017 Metro Area Occupational Employment and Wage Estimates

Average Hourly Wages: Occupations J – N

Metro Area	Janitors/ Cleaners	Landscapers	Lawyers	Maids/ House-keepers	Main-tenance Repairers	Marketing Managers	Nuclear Medicine Techs
Aberdeen, SD	n/a	n/a	n/a	n/a	n/a	n/a	n/a
Aliso Viejo, CA[2]	14.17	14.71	90.94	12.89	21.38	71.48	50.56
Allen, TX[2]	11.64	13.94	74.27	10.22	18.82	68.55	38.32
Ames, IA	13.65	14.79	52.99	10.99	19.39	50.56	n/a
Amherst, MA[3]	15.05	15.59	63.30	12.80	20.49	53.46	39.21
Apex, NC	11.28	14.52	70.13	10.46	20.16	73.07	33.44
Beavercreek, OH	13.24	13.53	52.78	10.52	19.36	57.48	35.17
Bellevue, NE	12.57	14.98	53.76	10.95	19.63	52.30	32.99
Bend, OR	15.38	14.79	57.41	12.13	17.54	47.19	n/a
Benicia, CA	14.87	15.09	70.74	13.56	22.05	78.45	59.39
Bentonville, AR	11.36	12.49	66.63	9.95	17.11	77.33	n/a
Bethlehem, NY	13.53	15.24	52.28	11.50	20.31	76.36	41.21
Blacksburg, VA	13.26	12.89	48.68	9.44	17.24	n/a	n/a
Bowie, MD[2]	14.08	15.39	85.57	13.60	22.45	80.64	40.46
Bozeman, MT	n/a	n/a	n/a	n/a	n/a	n/a	n/a
Brentwood, TN	12.25	12.56	57.01	10.71	19.14	58.04	35.65
Burlington, VT[3]	14.36	16.71	54.73	11.66	19.40	59.05	n/a
Cabot, AR	10.91	11.86	44.25	9.87	15.73	54.56	34.81
Carmel, IN	12.09	13.41	53.89	11.14	19.51	54.84	34.33
Cedar Falls, IA	12.71	12.89	60.44	10.93	19.63	43.06	n/a
Cedar Park, TX	11.56	13.91	62.43	10.39	18.24	71.33	36.16
Central, LA	9.97	13.42	49.10	9.58	17.53	50.28	29.73
Chapel Hill, NC	11.71	13.73	67.34	10.53	19.97	68.75	n/a
Cheshire, CT[3]	15.20	17.83	70.35	12.67	22.95	57.04	n/a
Chino Hills, CA	15.45	13.87	71.14	12.96	20.03	59.58	49.42
Cibolo, TX	11.75	13.02	53.94	10.27	16.70	79.46	32.81
Cicero, NY	14.81	13.81	45.36	12.23	19.07	70.96	38.63
Collierville, TN	12.49	12.82	61.20	10.29	17.91	53.27	28.76
Coppell, TX[2]	11.64	13.94	74.27	10.22	18.82	68.55	38.32
Cornelius, NC	11.68	13.23	71.22	9.98	19.62	69.20	32.69
Cranberry, PA	13.12	13.77	66.30	11.08	18.78	69.78	28.71
Crown Point, IN[2]	13.35	12.15	n/a	11.12	18.65	42.35	39.80
Dublin, OH	13.30	13.83	55.56	10.64	19.19	69.96	33.95
East Fishkill, NY[2]	15.06	15.82	70.70	11.88	19.61	n/a	n/a
Eden Prairie, MN	14.97	17.05	62.88	13.41	22.03	69.20	40.23
Edmond, OK	11.50	12.92	50.69	9.74	16.23	49.15	34.70
Edwardsville, IL	12.55	14.52	61.51	11.27	20.31	66.18	35.78
Evesham, NJ[2]	14.44	13.47	57.98	12.21	21.88	66.59	42.78
Flower Mound, TX[2]	11.64	13.94	74.27	10.22	18.82	68.55	38.32
Folsom, CA	15.04	16.06	62.92	14.02	20.50	69.77	59.63
Friendswood, TX	11.34	13.44	84.07	9.96	18.70	87.13	38.25
Gaines, MI	11.92	14.08	47.65	11.60	18.46	57.83	33.13
Glastonbury, CT[3]	16.60	16.93	66.33	13.56	22.37	69.83	39.07
Grand Blanc, MI	12.55	13.20	54.75	12.37	15.92	53.59	n/a
Hampden, PA	12.23	13.97	64.25	9.90	19.00	60.45	n/a
Hilliard, OH	13.30	13.83	55.56	10.64	19.19	69.96	33.95
Hillsborough, NJ[2]	15.05	14.41	69.73	12.64	21.89	91.54	46.41
Holly Springs, NC	11.28	14.52	70.13	10.46	20.16	73.07	33.44
Independence, KY	12.64	13.91	57.80	10.99	20.16	61.03	33.28
Juneau, AK	n/a	n/a	n/a	n/a	n/a	n/a	n/a
Kaysville, UT	12.91	13.52	37.29	11.27	18.64	57.76	n/a
Keller, TX[2]	12.27	12.43	61.37	10.55	20.21	64.84	41.26
Lafayette, CA[2]	17.54	17.95	77.79	15.57	23.89	81.08	54.91
Lafayette, CO	14.30	16.07	n/a	12.58	21.59	89.28	n/a
Lake Oswego, OR	14.36	16.84	60.18	12.81	20.42	60.81	41.94
Laramie, WY	n/a	n/a	n/a	n/a	n/a	n/a	n/a
Leander, TX	11.56	13.91	62.43	10.39	18.24	71.33	36.16
Leawood, KS	13.14	14.73	54.01	10.69	19.06	66.26	35.39
Lee's Summit, MO	13.14	14.73	54.01	10.69	19.06	66.26	35.39
Leesburg, VA[2]	14.08	15.39	85.57	13.60	22.45	80.64	40.46
Lehi, UT	9.93	13.52	58.96	10.58	18.59	51.89	n/a
Lexington, MA[4]	17.90	17.46	81.07	16.71	23.82	72.56	37.56
Los Altos, CA	15.34	17.35	95.24	15.62	25.39	93.76	56.31
Loveland, CO	14.12	15.73	64.55	11.12	19.20	78.40	n/a
Lower Macungie, PA	14.62	13.08	58.23	11.01	19.23	69.33	35.50
Madison, AL	11.25	12.03	57.65	8.99	20.05	76.04	25.10
Madison, MS	10.33	12.27	52.78	9.51	16.16	45.41	33.26

Table continued on next page.

Metro Area	Janitors/ Cleaners	Landscapers	Lawyers	Maids/ House-keepers	Main-tenance Repairers	Marketing Managers	Nuclear Medicine Techs
Maple Valley, WA[2]	15.98	17.89	68.30	13.84	22.79	75.75	44.70
Marion, IA	13.49	14.59	56.98	10.51	21.72	55.29	n/a
Marlboro, NJ[2]	16.77	16.81	86.28	17.63	22.69	93.94	43.34
Mason, OH	12.64	13.91	57.80	10.99	20.16	61.03	33.28
Menomonee Falls, WI	12.58	14.49	n/a	11.23	19.95	60.43	37.02
Meridian, ID	11.53	13.50	52.61	10.13	16.34	55.18	n/a
Meridian, MI	11.92	14.10	48.22	12.18	18.31	57.53	34.36
Merrimack, NH[4]	14.31	14.62	53.01	10.80	20.60	69.94	n/a
Milton, GA	12.06	14.24	71.06	9.85	18.38	69.00	36.83
Moon, PA	13.12	13.77	66.30	11.08	18.78	69.78	28.71
Moorpark, CA	15.09	14.95	83.86	13.24	21.63	73.37	53.07
Morgantown, WV	13.13	12.27	49.59	10.68	17.16	n/a	n/a
Mount Pleasant, SC	10.53	12.90	39.04	10.36	18.91	48.00	35.95
Newark, DE[2]	13.41	14.03	n/a	11.44	21.22	81.53	39.56
Newtown, CT[3]	14.60	18.36	73.48	11.22	22.04	65.73	n/a
North Attleborough, MA[3]	14.54	15.92	61.71	13.06	n/a	70.12	42.22
North Port, FL	11.93	12.57	57.99	11.51	17.34	56.04	35.30
North Ridgeville, OH	12.84	13.70	52.80	10.87	19.79	66.17	34.32
Northville, MI[2]	12.63	15.08	54.14	11.79	19.24	71.04	32.78
O'Fallon, MO	12.55	14.52	61.51	11.27	20.31	66.18	35.78
Orchard Park, NY	14.28	14.78	54.26	11.94	18.64	66.80	34.68
Oro Valley, AZ	12.07	13.61	52.74	10.80	17.05	54.17	n/a
Oviedo, FL	11.30	12.54	71.69	10.99	16.80	55.42	33.18
Parker, CO	13.61	15.17	70.29	11.95	20.22	78.23	39.06
Parkland, FL[2]	11.76	13.27	n/a	11.03	17.49	60.51	34.13
Peachtree City, GA	12.06	14.24	71.06	9.85	18.38	69.00	36.83
Pittsfield, MI	16.20	12.95	64.86	11.64	18.19	56.74	n/a
Plainfield, IL[2]	14.61	15.59	71.28	13.84	21.85	59.67	39.33
Pleasant Grove, UT	9.93	13.52	58.96	10.58	18.59	51.89	n/a
Poway, CA	15.05	15.55	73.79	13.44	19.93	71.00	51.97
Princeton, NJ	15.08	17.63	63.90	12.26	22.35	n/a	45.63
Queen Creek, AZ	12.43	13.23	70.28	11.44	18.18	56.60	39.83
Radnor, PA[2]	14.81	15.73	75.57	12.93	20.42	77.55	41.09
Randolph, NJ[2]	15.05	14.41	69.73	12.64	21.89	91.54	46.41
Rexburg, ID	n/a	n/a	n/a	n/a	n/a	n/a	n/a
Rio Rancho, NM	11.51	12.60	49.01	9.90	17.22	42.49	37.83
Rye, NY[2]	16.77	16.81	86.28	17.63	22.69	93.94	43.34
Sammamish, WA[2]	15.98	17.89	68.30	13.84	22.79	75.75	44.70
San Ramon, CA[2]	17.54	17.95	77.79	15.57	23.89	81.08	54.91
Saratoga, CA	15.34	17.35	95.24	15.62	25.39	93.76	56.31
Shrewsbury, MA[3]	15.35	15.29	52.87	13.84	20.69	63.04	n/a
South Brunswick, NJ[2]	16.77	16.81	86.28	17.63	22.69	93.94	43.34
South Jordan, UT	11.13	13.68	54.14	11.76	19.74	56.20	35.11
South Kingstown, RI[3]	14.54	15.92	61.71	13.06	n/a	70.12	42.22
South Portland, ME[3]	14.02	15.87	57.83	11.56	19.10	48.21	n/a
Sparks, NV	11.52	14.55	77.15	10.16	18.58	61.59	n/a
State College, PA	13.99	14.90	48.77	11.52	18.49	73.44	n/a
Sugar Land, TX	11.34	13.44	84.07	9.96	18.70	87.13	38.25
Sun Prairie, WI	13.39	15.00	60.31	11.11	19.87	58.82	n/a
Syracuse, UT	12.91	13.52	37.29	11.27	18.64	57.76	n/a
Tredyffrin, PA[2]	15.18	15.35	65.40	12.16	20.49	78.42	38.33
Upper Dublin, PA[2]	15.18	15.35	65.40	12.16	20.49	78.42	38.33
Urbandale, IA	13.36	14.11	62.19	11.15	19.32	57.49	n/a
Vestal, NY	12.78	13.49	40.63	11.15	17.99	82.71	n/a
Vestavia Hills, AL	11.12	11.83	61.64	9.44	19.80	57.13	31.17
Webster, NY	13.21	15.10	45.29	11.87	19.83	66.11	38.57
Wellesley, MA[4]	17.90	17.46	81.07	16.71	23.82	72.56	37.56
West Fargo, ND	13.14	15.96	54.35	11.44	19.38	50.85	n/a
West Lafayette, IN	11.89	13.13	39.46	10.21	19.43	51.05	n/a
Weston, FL[2]	11.76	13.27	n/a	11.03	17.49	60.51	34.13
Wilmette, IL[2]	14.61	15.59	71.28	13.84	21.85	59.67	39.33
Yorba Linda, CA[2]	14.17	14.71	90.94	12.89	21.38	71.48	50.56
Zionsville, IN	12.09	13.41	53.89	11.14	19.51	54.84	34.33

Notes: (1) Figures cover the Metropolitan Statistical Area (MSA) except where noted. See Appendix B for areas included; (2) Metropolitan Division; (3) New England City and Town Area; (4) New England City and Town Area Division; n/a not available
Source: Bureau of Labor Statistics, May 2017 Metro Area Occupational Employment and Wage Estimates

Average Hourly Wages: Occupations N – R

Metro Area	Nurses, Licensed Practical	Nurses, Registered	Nursing Assistants	Packers/ Packagers	Physical Therapists	Postal Mail Carriers	R.E. Brokers
Aberdeen, SD	n/a	n/a	n/a	n/a	n/a	n/a	n/a
Aliso Viejo, CA[2]	25.53	42.01	15.18	13.12	49.25	25.17	n/a
Allen, TX[2]	23.08	35.81	12.85	11.53	46.48	24.53	38.66
Ames, IA	20.72	27.60	14.06	9.27	51.73	24.19	n/a
Amherst, MA[3]	24.92	37.17	14.89	15.32	42.36	23.62	n/a
Apex, NC	21.55	30.78	12.00	12.08	41.09	24.09	28.09
Beavercreek, OH	21.10	32.28	13.29	10.13	46.40	23.79	n/a
Bellevue, NE	20.57	30.52	13.32	11.61	36.77	24.25	28.39
Bend, OR	24.28	43.56	15.34	13.13	36.39	24.05	25.71
Benicia, CA	27.53	57.61	16.26	12.50	49.48	25.08	n/a
Bentonville, AR	20.61	27.81	11.49	11.26	37.20	24.20	n/a
Bethlehem, NY	20.13	32.20	13.47	16.35	37.27	23.84	n/a
Blacksburg, VA	18.33	26.92	12.25	10.27	41.71	24.58	n/a
Bowie, MD[2]	23.78	39.18	14.92	12.28	44.22	23.72	34.13
Bozeman, MT	n/a	n/a	n/a	n/a	n/a	n/a	n/a
Brentwood, TN	20.05	29.96	12.56	11.65	40.41	24.47	36.87
Burlington, VT[3]	25.12	33.99	14.34	13.07	37.08	24.59	n/a
Cabot, AR	19.59	30.25	12.53	10.18	38.71	24.18	32.82
Carmel, IN	21.05	32.06	13.07	11.83	40.92	23.80	n/a
Cedar Falls, IA	19.46	26.51	13.44	15.91	39.25	24.43	n/a
Cedar Park, TX	22.13	33.07	13.17	11.83	47.04	23.97	n/a
Central, LA	18.18	28.63	10.93	10.33	43.06	23.57	21.67
Chapel Hill, NC	22.35	32.39	12.72	10.85	39.58	23.67	26.54
Cheshire, CT[3]	27.99	39.71	16.82	13.40	41.77	24.34	n/a
Chino Hills, CA	23.26	46.88	15.87	13.70	45.20	24.66	n/a
Cibolo, TX	21.76	32.70	12.42	10.68	44.06	23.97	27.39
Cicero, NY	19.50	31.13	13.92	13.74	37.93	23.70	n/a
Collierville, TN	20.35	31.52	12.84	11.74	41.83	24.10	29.72
Coppell, TX[2]	23.08	35.81	12.85	11.53	46.48	24.53	38.66
Cornelius, NC	20.91	30.00	11.59	11.30	40.06	23.78	37.46
Cranberry, PA	21.30	31.43	14.33	11.66	38.11	23.70	37.49
Crown Point, IN[2]	21.32	32.36	12.20	9.95	44.25	23.74	30.41
Dublin, OH	20.20	32.25	12.69	11.53	38.85	23.75	64.98
East Fishkill, NY[2]	22.18	38.01	16.48	13.92	40.18	24.03	n/a
Eden Prairie, MN	22.77	39.19	16.47	13.45	39.54	24.13	33.93
Edmond, OK	19.76	30.65	12.42	11.16	39.74	23.81	n/a
Edwardsville, IL	21.53	31.69	12.87	12.46	38.96	23.90	n/a
Evesham, NJ[2]	25.11	37.17	13.31	12.28	46.76	24.02	28.22
Flower Mound, TX[2]	23.08	35.81	12.85	11.53	46.48	24.53	38.66
Folsom, CA	26.81	55.85	17.62	13.89	47.82	24.50	54.75
Friendswood, TX	23.53	38.01	13.34	11.54	44.66	23.97	37.97
Gaines, MI	20.14	30.78	13.80	11.54	40.23	23.88	37.29
Glastonbury, CT[3]	27.27	38.21	15.76	16.78	44.73	24.22	70.94
Grand Blanc, MI	23.62	36.05	13.22	19.22	41.42	24.05	n/a
Hampden, PA	23.69	33.95	15.14	13.87	42.72	24.26	41.02
Hilliard, OH	20.20	32.25	12.69	11.53	38.85	23.75	64.98
Hillsborough, NJ[2]	27.31	40.53	14.42	11.18	48.39	24.46	50.29
Holly Springs, NC	21.55	30.78	12.00	12.08	41.09	24.09	28.09
Independence, KY	21.64	32.14	13.53	12.12	41.64	24.38	51.21
Juneau, AK	n/a	n/a	n/a	n/a	n/a	n/a	n/a
Kaysville, UT	23.12	29.68	11.67	11.61	47.16	23.72	n/a
Keller, TX[2]	24.11	36.10	12.92	13.16	45.02	24.25	n/a
Lafayette, CA[2]	28.17	56.09	16.90	13.34	44.57	24.73	39.99
Lafayette, CO	25.05	36.12	15.33	12.61	36.70	23.91	35.39
Lake Oswego, OR	24.34	43.78	15.55	13.84	41.47	23.67	35.51
Laramie, WY	n/a	n/a	n/a	n/a	n/a	n/a	n/a
Leander, TX	22.13	33.07	13.17	11.83	47.04	23.97	n/a
Leawood, KS	21.39	31.48	13.05	13.01	36.40	23.73	30.23
Lee's Summit, MO	21.39	31.48	13.05	13.01	36.40	23.73	30.23
Leesburg, VA[2]	23.78	39.18	14.92	12.28	44.22	23.72	34.13
Lehi, UT	19.60	29.55	12.23	11.40	42.50	23.64	28.14
Lexington, MA[4]	30.49	46.70	16.28	13.52	43.69	25.03	51.23
Los Altos, CA	29.50	62.09	18.47	13.20	48.13	25.32	n/a
Loveland, CO	23.57	33.83	14.94	12.06	36.74	23.48	30.84
Lower Macungie, PA	23.15	32.65	14.85	13.42	41.51	24.07	n/a
Madison, AL	17.87	27.08	11.63	12.07	43.18	24.20	n/a
Madison, MS	18.40	29.97	11.34	10.11	39.29	23.95	n/a

Table continued on next page.

Metro Area	Nurses, Licensed Practical	Nurses, Registered	Nursing Assistants	Packers/ Packagers	Physical Therapists	Postal Mail Carriers	R.E. Brokers
Maple Valley, WA[2]	27.55	39.36	15.23	14.09	43.21	24.22	32.17
Marion, IA	20.41	27.38	13.36	13.16	38.01	24.30	n/a
Marlboro, NJ[2]	25.93	43.67	17.06	12.09	44.62	24.27	49.22
Mason, OH	21.64	32.14	13.53	12.12	41.64	24.38	51.21
Menomonee Falls, WI	22.37	33.60	13.68	12.91	38.07	24.07	n/a
Meridian, ID	21.03	31.94	13.18	13.23	38.93	23.88	22.11
Meridian, MI	23.16	35.75	14.87	10.21	42.94	23.69	n/a
Merrimack, NH[4]	24.01	33.62	15.19	11.11	38.04	24.09	n/a
Milton, GA	20.61	33.92	12.80	11.68	42.20	24.15	33.52
Moon, PA	21.30	31.43	14.33	11.66	38.11	23.70	37.49
Moorpark, CA	25.65	40.34	14.67	11.98	41.51	24.53	n/a
Morgantown, WV	18.29	31.12	13.07	n/a	44.89	24.22	n/a
Mount Pleasant, SC	20.08	35.64	13.79	10.54	36.99	23.57	29.74
Newark, DE[2]	26.24	35.73	14.73	11.71	44.53	23.79	n/a
Newtown, CT[3]	26.33	42.99	15.50	13.75	44.43	24.33	n/a
North Attleborough, MA[3]	26.42	36.74	14.63	12.33	40.28	23.80	45.28
North Port, FL	20.56	31.33	13.59	9.93	43.96	23.99	30.82
North Ridgeville, OH	21.94	32.85	12.98	11.18	42.14	24.22	n/a
Northville, MI[2]	25.19	34.04	14.02	13.54	43.94	24.20	34.47
O'Fallon, MO	21.53	31.69	12.87	12.46	38.96	23.90	n/a
Orchard Park, NY	20.45	35.22	14.23	11.80	35.15	23.79	n/a
Oro Valley, AZ	23.96	34.80	13.71	12.21	41.41	24.46	n/a
Oviedo, FL	20.79	30.42	12.15	12.15	41.70	23.98	47.24
Parker, CO	25.54	35.58	16.64	12.46	38.33	23.98	n/a
Parkland, FL[2]	22.13	33.18	12.30	11.10	46.94	24.67	49.48
Peachtree City, GA	20.61	33.92	12.80	11.68	42.20	24.15	33.52
Pittsfield, MI	24.46	35.88	15.28	11.91	n/a	23.42	n/a
Plainfield, IL[2]	26.18	36.84	14.01	11.91	44.33	24.44	39.54
Pleasant Grove, UT	19.60	29.55	12.23	11.40	42.50	23.64	28.14
Poway, CA	26.09	45.55	15.99	12.84	44.77	24.71	48.96
Princeton, NJ	26.56	36.63	13.33	13.82	44.92	24.33	n/a
Queen Creek, AZ	26.23	36.61	14.92	12.44	42.46	24.33	33.34
Radnor, PA[2]	26.12	39.55	14.95	11.71	42.83	24.69	45.32
Randolph, NJ[2]	27.31	40.53	14.42	11.18	48.39	24.46	50.29
Rexburg, ID	n/a	n/a	n/a	n/a	n/a	n/a	n/a
Rio Rancho, NM	23.28	35.32	13.47	10.95	42.17	23.95	n/a
Rye, NY[2]	25.93	43.67	17.06	12.09	44.62	24.27	49.22
Sammamish, WA[2]	27.55	39.36	15.23	14.09	43.21	24.22	32.17
San Ramon, CA[2]	28.17	56.09	16.90	13.34	44.57	24.73	39.99
Saratoga, CA	29.50	62.09	18.47	13.20	48.13	25.32	n/a
Shrewsbury, MA[3]	27.13	40.49	15.03	13.31	39.24	23.82	n/a
South Brunswick, NJ[2]	25.93	43.67	17.06	12.09	44.62	24.27	49.22
South Jordan, UT	26.48	31.17	13.05	11.77	40.96	24.18	29.37
South Kingstown, RI[3]	26.42	36.74	14.63	12.33	40.28	23.80	45.28
South Portland, ME[3]	22.30	33.28	14.29	12.23	36.48	24.32	42.09
Sparks, NV	25.15	37.67	15.88	11.95	40.69	24.16	30.95
State College, PA	18.22	28.07	14.26	17.46	39.29	23.18	n/a
Sugar Land, TX	23.53	38.01	13.34	11.54	44.66	23.97	37.97
Sun Prairie, WI	22.25	37.94	15.32	16.44	38.57	23.80	n/a
Syracuse, UT	23.12	29.68	11.67	11.61	47.16	23.72	n/a
Tredyffrin, PA[2]	26.10	34.89	14.70	14.20	41.15	24.32	37.70
Upper Dublin, PA[2]	26.10	34.89	14.70	14.20	41.15	24.32	37.70
Urbandale, IA	20.93	28.97	14.51	12.85	40.07	23.98	n/a
Vestal, NY	20.50	29.96	13.37	14.77	40.26	23.86	n/a
Vestavia Hills, AL	19.16	28.91	11.63	12.76	41.04	24.35	n/a
Webster, NY	19.92	30.90	13.63	12.72	36.57	23.74	n/a
Wellesley, MA[4]	30.49	46.70	16.28	13.52	43.69	25.03	51.23
West Fargo, ND	21.08	30.40	15.15	12.39	36.95	23.53	n/a
West Lafayette, IN	21.68	30.04	12.73	10.03	37.57	24.25	n/a
Weston, FL[2]	22.13	33.18	12.30	11.10	46.94	24.67	49.48
Wilmette, IL[2]	26.18	36.84	14.01	11.91	44.33	24.44	39.54
Yorba Linda, CA[2]	25.53	42.01	15.18	13.12	49.25	25.17	n/a
Zionsville, IN	21.05	32.06	13.07	11.83	40.92	23.80	n/a

Notes: (1) Figures cover the Metropolitan Statistical Area (MSA) except where noted. See Appendix B for areas included; (2) Metropolitan Division; (3) New England City and Town Area; (4) New England City and Town Area Division; n/a not available

Source: Bureau of Labor Statistics, May 2017 Metro Area Occupational Employment and Wage Estimates

Average Hourly Wages: Occupations R – T

Metro Area	Retail Salespersons	Sales Reps., Except Tech./Scien.	Sales Reps., Tech./Scien.	Secretaries, Exc. Leg./ Med./Exec.	Security Guards	Surgeons	Teacher Assistants
Aberdeen, SD	n/a	n/a	n/a	n/a	n/a	n/a	n/a
Aliso Viejo, CA[2]	14.85	33.06	40.87	20.26	14.36	67.69	18.13
Allen, TX[2]	12.92	35.50	46.25	18.51	14.49	95.39	12.35
Ames, IA	12.51	29.25	45.90	18.65	n/a	n/a	10.95
Amherst, MA[3]	14.12	33.52	39.47	19.96	14.54	110.66	16.42
Apex, NC	12.43	34.15	49.11	17.60	13.21	n/a	11.37
Beavercreek, OH	12.11	31.08	37.39	17.14	12.89	117.20	13.00
Bellevue, NE	13.53	30.87	36.06	16.81	15.44	n/a	12.44
Bend, OR	14.91	31.71	n/a	17.04	13.31	n/a	16.50
Benicia, CA	13.37	31.85	37.81	18.97	14.40	n/a	15.01
Bentonville, AR	12.35	36.48	33.52	15.66	12.53	n/a	10.49
Bethlehem, NY	13.22	31.91	47.26	19.39	16.56	129.94	14.37
Blacksburg, VA	12.30	26.74	46.29	15.96	16.80	n/a	10.80
Bowie, MD[2]	13.45	38.69	44.61	21.77	19.97	121.03	16.30
Bozeman, MT	n/a	n/a	n/a	n/a	n/a	n/a	n/a
Brentwood, TN	13.79	27.81	45.45	16.98	12.35	117.14	11.72
Burlington, VT[3]	13.93	33.21	47.98	17.44	16.92	132.28	15.47
Cabot, AR	11.86	27.21	33.20	15.69	13.08	137.83	10.57
Carmel, IN	12.19	35.14	56.29	16.64	12.64	125.38	12.09
Cedar Falls, IA	11.23	31.47	49.52	16.40	13.33	n/a	11.97
Cedar Park, TX	13.50	31.25	58.15	17.10	15.40	n/a	12.25
Central, LA	11.53	29.04	41.40	15.29	13.95	126.86	9.83
Chapel Hill, NC	12.95	33.37	51.56	19.27	16.10	n/a	11.94
Cheshire, CT[3]	14.38	37.16	41.56	20.93	15.83	122.11	14.88
Chino Hills, CA	14.83	32.25	37.38	18.48	13.59	n/a	15.92
Cibolo, TX	13.66	31.71	39.98	16.55	13.67	101.09	12.13
Cicero, NY	13.45	35.85	37.24	17.70	22.95	138.35	13.93
Collierville, TN	12.74	33.63	45.71	17.12	13.70	133.23	12.73
Coppell, TX[2]	12.92	35.50	46.25	18.51	14.49	95.39	12.35
Cornelius, NC	12.41	36.93	44.69	17.59	13.64	127.11	11.53
Cranberry, PA	12.76	35.29	41.62	16.98	11.70	135.87	13.11
Crown Point, IN[2]	11.64	30.57	39.03	13.89	13.95	137.88	9.88
Dublin, OH	12.95	31.18	37.44	18.06	15.30	123.63	13.91
East Fishkill, NY[2]	13.32	33.03	48.99	18.99	18.43	n/a	13.58
Eden Prairie, MN	13.51	38.16	56.01	20.30	16.42	n/a	15.68
Edmond, OK	14.29	27.58	35.23	15.58	14.53	113.44	9.82
Edwardsville, IL	13.59	33.72	40.98	17.38	n/a	127.24	13.48
Evesham, NJ[2]	14.10	37.92	50.36	19.30	15.04	n/a	12.45
Flower Mound, TX[2]	12.92	35.50	46.25	18.51	14.49	95.39	12.35
Folsom, CA	13.84	33.86	39.59	18.56	13.98	128.49	15.32
Friendswood, TX	12.56	35.48	50.17	18.10	14.68	111.21	11.30
Gaines, MI	12.79	35.08	40.09	17.13	12.70	n/a	12.97
Glastonbury, CT[3]	14.85	33.96	49.71	22.19	17.26	133.31	14.89
Grand Blanc, MI	11.93	33.75	32.64	16.05	15.01	n/a	13.17
Hampden, PA	12.49	32.93	40.60	18.01	15.37	n/a	11.52
Hilliard, OH	12.95	31.18	37.44	18.06	15.30	123.63	13.91
Hillsborough, NJ[2]	13.45	37.60	45.88	20.16	14.92	135.41	14.51
Holly Springs, NC	12.43	34.15	49.11	17.60	13.21	n/a	11.37
Independence, KY	13.06	35.56	40.41	17.68	12.79	109.37	12.62
Juneau, AK	n/a	n/a	n/a	n/a	n/a	n/a	n/a
Kaysville, UT	12.68	33.52	42.12	15.70	15.74	132.35	12.56
Keller, TX[2]	12.81	34.21	43.05	16.54	14.04	134.41	10.15
Lafayette, CA[2]	15.01	35.36	47.04	22.27	16.43	125.87	17.70
Lafayette, CO	15.27	40.46	43.59	18.63	15.69	n/a	15.92
Lake Oswego, OR	13.77	33.99	43.91	19.42	14.07	n/a	15.88
Laramie, WY	n/a	n/a	n/a	n/a	n/a	n/a	n/a
Leander, TX	13.50	31.25	58.15	17.10	15.40	n/a	12.25
Leawood, KS	12.97	31.28	42.74	17.18	16.81	105.45	12.50
Lee's Summit, MO	12.97	31.28	42.74	17.18	16.81	105.45	12.50
Leesburg, VA[2]	13.45	38.69	44.61	21.77	19.97	121.03	16.30
Lehi, UT	12.22	28.33	33.75	15.26	14.50	n/a	12.08
Lexington, MA[4]	14.21	37.58	46.95	23.14	16.62	104.24	16.27
Los Altos, CA	14.88	37.29	47.64	22.30	17.17	129.45	17.95
Loveland, CO	13.27	35.39	51.48	17.19	12.14	119.77	12.87
Lower Macungie, PA	12.67	34.95	43.54	17.31	12.69	82.63	12.62
Madison, AL	12.51	26.54	41.98	17.98	12.11	n/a	n/a
Madison, MS	12.77	29.10	25.22	16.11	13.26	125.04	9.10

Table continued on next page.

Metro Area	Retail Salespersons	Sales Reps., Except Tech./Scien.	Sales Reps., Tech./Scien.	Secretaries, Exc. Leg./ Med./Exec.	Security Guards	Surgeons	Teacher Assistants
Maple Valley, WA[2]	17.29	35.61	43.93	21.37	17.25	120.52	17.44
Marion, IA	13.81	32.64	35.22	16.72	13.67	n/a	13.40
Marlboro, NJ[2]	13.21	35.80	51.24	20.14	16.26	119.74	14.74
Mason, OH	13.06	35.56	40.41	17.68	12.79	109.37	12.62
Menomonee Falls, WI	12.28	37.38	44.24	18.40	13.15	132.61	14.65
Meridian, ID	13.28	30.26	39.27	15.91	14.71	133.29	12.00
Meridian, MI	11.70	27.06	32.51	19.30	12.67	n/a	12.89
Merrimack, NH[4]	14.02	38.91	51.13	17.75	17.37	n/a	16.48
Milton, GA	12.00	31.04	39.95	17.61	13.97	130.27	10.56
Moon, PA	12.76	35.29	41.62	16.98	11.70	135.87	13.11
Moorpark, CA	13.53	32.49	44.41	19.50	14.11	99.32	15.64
Morgantown, WV	11.95	24.43	38.57	15.65	16.25	n/a	11.88
Mount Pleasant, SC	12.15	29.45	32.94	17.21	14.89	n/a	10.20
Newark, DE[2]	11.96	32.58	49.47	19.11	13.45	138.34	14.19
Newtown, CT[3]	15.94	37.24	53.31	20.12	15.99	92.96	14.67
North Attleborough, MA[3]	14.68	34.46	44.01	19.85	14.64	117.82	14.65
North Port, FL	12.59	28.14	36.81	16.78	12.31	n/a	11.84
North Ridgeville, OH	15.17	32.33	39.96	17.67	14.97	130.61	13.32
Northville, MI[2]	13.21	35.18	40.50	17.85	13.33	n/a	12.49
O'Fallon, MO	13.59	33.72	40.98	17.38	n/a	127.24	13.48
Orchard Park, NY	13.13	31.41	43.36	17.18	12.61	82.41	12.36
Oro Valley, AZ	12.09	26.48	31.52	16.32	12.52	n/a	12.15
Oviedo, FL	11.96	29.24	40.95	16.58	11.73	100.89	11.13
Parker, CO	14.39	36.97	50.26	19.07	15.67	123.85	14.49
Parkland, FL[2]	12.53	27.35	43.55	16.91	12.63	n/a	11.46
Peachtree City, GA	12.00	31.04	39.95	17.61	13.97	130.27	10.56
Pittsfield, MI	12.71	36.21	37.60	19.59	12.81	n/a	13.54
Plainfield, IL[2]	13.66	35.10	37.26	18.71	15.46	115.09	13.82
Pleasant Grove, UT	12.22	28.33	33.75	15.26	14.50	n/a	12.08
Poway, CA	14.99	31.82	37.76	20.18	15.21	125.71	16.35
Princeton, NJ	11.90	39.36	41.09	22.87	17.40	n/a	14.85
Queen Creek, AZ	12.62	31.33	39.40	17.56	13.57	n/a	11.99
Radnor, PA[2]	13.34	36.21	41.91	18.93	13.30	63.22	12.25
Randolph, NJ[2]	13.45	37.60	45.88	20.16	14.92	135.41	14.51
Rexburg, ID	n/a	n/a	n/a	n/a	n/a	n/a	n/a
Rio Rancho, NM	13.36	26.13	32.30	16.99	12.86	132.84	10.90
Rye, NY[2]	13.21	35.80	51.24	20.14	16.26	119.74	14.74
Sammamish, WA[2]	17.29	35.61	43.93	21.37	17.25	120.52	17.44
San Ramon, CA[2]	15.01	35.36	47.04	22.27	16.43	125.87	17.70
Saratoga, CA	14.88	37.29	47.64	22.30	17.17	129.45	17.95
Shrewsbury, MA[3]	13.88	38.38	43.04	20.84	15.51	131.00	16.15
South Brunswick, NJ[2]	13.21	35.80	51.24	20.14	16.26	119.74	14.74
South Jordan, UT	12.75	31.20	49.75	16.47	14.98	n/a	11.64
South Kingstown, RI[3]	14.68	34.46	44.01	19.85	14.64	117.82	14.65
South Portland, ME[3]	13.17	29.97	36.87	18.70	13.93	n/a	16.33
Sparks, NV	12.90	31.12	39.27	18.34	11.64	n/a	13.43
State College, PA	12.07	30.68	n/a	16.85	13.56	n/a	12.85
Sugar Land, TX	12.56	35.48	50.17	18.10	14.68	111.21	11.30
Sun Prairie, WI	12.18	32.50	34.99	18.69	14.21	136.45	14.05
Syracuse, UT	12.68	33.52	42.12	15.70	15.74	132.35	12.56
Tredyffrin, PA[2]	14.11	38.62	53.25	18.31	13.23	115.69	14.12
Upper Dublin, PA[2]	14.11	38.62	53.25	18.31	13.23	115.69	14.12
Urbandale, IA	13.63	33.02	40.89	18.34	14.14	87.79	12.30
Vestal, NY	12.97	25.11	40.89	17.64	16.16	n/a	11.50
Vestavia Hills, AL	13.61	32.02	48.35	17.55	11.68	n/a	10.55
Webster, NY	13.48	32.00	43.98	17.69	15.18	135.07	12.83
Wellesley, MA[4]	14.21	37.58	46.95	23.14	16.62	104.24	16.27
West Fargo, ND	14.63	31.04	30.65	18.15	15.78	n/a	14.84
West Lafayette, IN	10.82	29.73	34.45	16.22	15.34	134.64	10.74
Weston, FL[2]	12.53	27.35	43.55	16.91	12.63	n/a	11.46
Wilmette, IL[2]	13.66	35.10	37.26	18.71	15.46	115.09	13.82
Yorba Linda, CA[2]	14.85	33.06	40.87	20.26	14.36	67.69	18.13
Zionsville, IN	12.19	35.14	56.29	16.64	12.64	125.38	12.09

Notes: (1) Figures cover the Metropolitan Statistical Area (MSA) except where noted. See Appendix B for areas included; (2) Metropolitan Division; (3) New England City and Town Area; (4) New England City and Town Area Division; n/a not available
Source: Bureau of Labor Statistics, May 2017 Metro Area Occupational Employment and Wage Estimates

Average Hourly Wages: Occupations T – Z

Metro Area	Teachers, Elementary School	Teachers, Secondary School	Tele-marketers	Truck Driv., Heavy/ Trac. Trail.	Truck Drivers, Light	Waiters/ Waitresses
Aberdeen, SD	n/a	n/a	n/a	n/a	n/a	n/a
Aliso Viejo, CA[2]	41.36	41.41	15.01	22.45	17.54	14.48
Allen, TX[2]	28.98	30.02	14.70	22.55	18.42	13.47
Ames, IA	24.76	29.17	n/a	20.52	16.78	9.67
Amherst, MA[3]	37.25	38.46	16.53	22.93	19.23	12.57
Apex, NC	23.37	22.64	12.79	22.04	16.18	11.50
Beavercreek, OH	28.89	30.45	11.90	19.48	16.19	11.19
Bellevue, NE	27.11	26.81	13.13	20.50	16.69	12.89
Bend, OR	37.44	32.10	n/a	23.42	19.84	14.00
Benicia, CA	35.17	29.47	11.69	22.28	14.67	14.84
Bentonville, AR	25.89	26.88	13.34	21.26	15.11	9.43
Bethlehem, NY	30.24	34.41	12.94	20.55	17.68	13.08
Blacksburg, VA	21.97	22.05	17.28	18.48	13.11	12.09
Bowie, MD[2]	37.55	37.59	14.20	21.54	18.11	13.19
Bozeman, MT	n/a	n/a	n/a	n/a	n/a	n/a
Brentwood, TN	23.48	24.07	14.61	21.85	17.08	9.47
Burlington, VT[3]	29.72	31.59	11.86	22.16	18.77	14.91
Cabot, AR	24.56	25.47	10.61	20.64	15.57	10.49
Carmel, IN	25.50	26.49	15.34	22.61	16.42	10.44
Cedar Falls, IA	26.77	n/a	12.26	20.79	15.76	9.86
Cedar Park, TX	26.92	26.61	17.74	19.00	17.85	12.09
Central, LA	24.14	25.18	13.80	21.15	15.42	8.76
Chapel Hill, NC	22.24	23.49	11.00	21.03	16.80	11.38
Cheshire, CT[3]	36.90	38.98	20.68	23.26	18.21	11.63
Chino Hills, CA	40.08	36.72	12.38	22.96	19.11	14.17
Cibolo, TX	27.51	27.64	13.79	22.12	14.49	11.75
Cicero, NY	30.86	35.77	12.08	21.80	16.76	12.55
Collierville, TN	26.02	25.88	11.92	20.31	18.19	9.48
Coppell, TX[2]	28.98	30.02	14.70	22.55	18.42	13.47
Cornelius, NC	22.69	23.52	15.83	20.51	15.89	9.95
Cranberry, PA	30.36	32.72	11.84	22.40	16.44	10.83
Crown Point, IN[2]	23.88	25.10	11.02	23.73	15.77	10.41
Dublin, OH	29.63	30.34	13.39	22.21	16.82	10.98
East Fishkill, NY[2]	40.98	39.04	n/a	22.75	15.25	14.34
Eden Prairie, MN	32.12	33.06	16.51	24.10	19.87	12.77
Edmond, OK	20.26	20.66	12.01	20.26	18.65	10.57
Edwardsville, IL	26.81	29.01	13.03	23.68	18.09	10.26
Evesham, NJ[2]	32.41	35.51	13.33	22.40	16.58	11.95
Flower Mound, TX[2]	28.98	30.02	14.70	22.55	18.42	13.47
Folsom, CA	34.04	35.84	11.88	21.53	19.24	14.00
Friendswood, TX	30.16	29.87	13.59	20.84	17.06	11.73
Gaines, MI	28.51	28.53	11.85	20.84	16.76	11.28
Glastonbury, CT[3]	36.55	35.61	16.45	23.13	18.35	11.85
Grand Blanc, MI	27.46	32.45	12.44	18.48	17.64	10.49
Hampden, PA	29.34	24.23	9.99	22.02	15.67	10.34
Hilliard, OH	29.63	30.34	13.39	22.21	16.82	10.98
Hillsborough, NJ[2]	33.05	36.38	13.84	23.59	17.83	14.31
Holly Springs, NC	23.37	22.64	12.79	22.04	16.18	11.50
Independence, KY	30.46	28.67	12.96	21.44	17.03	10.07
Juneau, AK	n/a	n/a	n/a	n/a	n/a	n/a
Kaysville, UT	24.75	26.90	11.72	20.70	14.38	12.20
Keller, TX[2]	27.99	28.91	12.09	23.05	17.09	10.51
Lafayette, CA[2]	37.42	37.54	16.34	23.15	19.13	16.05
Lafayette, CO	29.04	29.94	16.41	20.12	16.63	12.82
Lake Oswego, OR	32.66	35.05	14.66	22.83	18.14	13.39
Laramie, WY	n/a	n/a	n/a	n/a	n/a	n/a
Leander, TX	26.92	26.61	17.74	19.00	17.85	12.09
Leawood, KS	27.07	25.78	12.86	23.07	17.44	10.87
Lee's Summit, MO	27.07	25.78	12.86	23.07	17.44	10.87
Leesburg, VA[2]	37.55	37.59	14.20	21.54	18.11	13.19
Lehi, UT	30.62	30.59	17.43	19.71	16.14	10.88
Lexington, MA[4]	37.71	37.48	n/a	26.13	19.96	15.39
Los Altos, CA	36.78	38.20	15.06	22.68	20.42	15.36
Loveland, CO	25.14	25.42	14.96	18.91	18.31	13.94
Lower Macungie, PA	33.32	31.97	16.01	23.22	17.67	11.59
Madison, AL	23.75	25.15	10.98	20.22	15.02	8.95
Madison, MS	20.48	21.96	n/a	20.92	16.27	10.73

Table continued on next page.

Metro Area	Teachers, Elementary School	Teachers, Secondary School	Tele-marketers	Truck Driv., Heavy/ Trac. Trail.	Truck Drivers, Light	Waiters/ Waitresses
Maple Valley, WA[2]	30.93	31.86	17.50	23.87	19.46	18.07
Marion, IA	27.18	25.62	12.11	20.11	16.29	10.49
Marlboro, NJ[2]	38.25	41.32	13.67	24.54	18.59	15.27
Mason, OH	30.46	28.67	12.96	21.44	17.03	10.07
Menomonee Falls, WI	28.74	30.69	15.42	22.13	16.94	9.94
Meridian, ID	23.36	23.51	14.28	20.35	15.83	10.16
Meridian, MI	27.59	29.80	11.19	19.10	15.78	10.97
Merrimack, NH[4]	29.02	29.13	16.77	22.32	17.03	10.50
Milton, GA	26.80	27.63	12.57	20.85	18.36	9.25
Moon, PA	30.36	32.72	11.84	22.40	16.44	10.83
Moorpark, CA	36.30	34.40	20.75	20.98	17.60	13.73
Morgantown, WV	n/a	n/a	n/a	19.99	13.68	11.48
Mount Pleasant, SC	22.53	23.74	11.87	21.87	15.64	10.36
Newark, DE[2]	29.63	32.09	14.40	23.33	18.02	11.50
Newtown, CT[3]	39.13	41.36	n/a	21.74	17.79	11.88
North Attleborough, MA[3]	32.70	32.62	15.86	22.35	16.36	12.54
North Port, FL	22.18	27.06	15.89	17.95	15.49	15.36
North Ridgeville, OH	28.13	31.03	11.26	20.91	16.99	11.36
Northville, MI[2]	31.11	31.06	12.62	20.38	19.13	11.53
O'Fallon, MO	26.81	29.01	13.03	23.68	18.09	10.26
Orchard Park, NY	32.05	34.60	14.73	20.83	15.87	13.34
Oro Valley, AZ	20.21	19.40	12.62	21.95	16.75	13.26
Oviedo, FL	22.50	23.37	12.05	20.87	15.88	14.34
Parker, CO	26.89	28.20	14.03	23.53	19.14	11.37
Parkland, FL[2]	24.84	27.99	11.27	20.65	16.74	12.90
Peachtree City, GA	26.80	27.63	12.57	20.85	18.36	9.25
Pittsfield, MI	29.82	27.66	14.04	21.96	18.80	11.02
Plainfield, IL[2]	31.99	35.68	13.37	23.91	18.95	11.97
Pleasant Grove, UT	30.62	30.59	17.43	19.71	16.14	10.88
Poway, CA	35.55	35.86	14.72	20.44	17.80	16.37
Princeton, NJ	34.20	36.05	13.32	22.09	16.11	11.28
Queen Creek, AZ	21.89	24.28	14.92	21.84	18.30	12.54
Radnor, PA[2]	33.10	31.52	11.16	22.67	18.92	11.98
Randolph, NJ[2]	33.05	36.38	13.84	23.59	17.83	14.31
Rexburg, ID	n/a	n/a	n/a	n/a	n/a	n/a
Rio Rancho, NM	29.40	23.44	11.39	20.39	16.91	10.51
Rye, NY[2]	38.25	41.32	13.67	24.54	18.59	15.27
Sammamish, WA[2]	30.93	31.86	17.50	23.87	19.46	18.07
San Ramon, CA[2]	37.42	37.54	16.34	23.15	19.13	16.05
Saratoga, CA	36.78	38.20	15.06	22.68	20.42	15.36
Shrewsbury, MA[3]	34.89	34.72	22.81	24.54	18.02	13.93
South Brunswick, NJ[2]	38.25	41.32	13.67	24.54	18.59	15.27
South Jordan, UT	26.16	26.63	13.88	21.28	16.78	11.71
South Kingstown, RI[3]	32.70	32.62	15.86	22.35	16.36	12.54
South Portland, ME[3]	28.10	28.12	14.69	20.44	15.76	12.74
Sparks, NV	27.55	27.93	13.73	23.36	18.57	9.74
State College, PA	31.48	30.42	n/a	22.69	19.22	11.64
Sugar Land, TX	30.16	29.87	13.59	20.84	17.06	11.73
Sun Prairie, WI	27.78	26.68	14.27	23.09	18.42	14.07
Syracuse, UT	24.75	26.90	11.72	20.70	14.38	12.20
Tredyffrin, PA[2]	36.63	35.24	15.44	23.25	17.31	11.15
Upper Dublin, PA[2]	36.63	35.24	15.44	23.25	17.31	11.15
Urbandale, IA	27.69	29.49	12.34	22.77	16.73	11.93
Vestal, NY	28.88	31.83	n/a	19.15	15.76	11.99
Vestavia Hills, AL	24.55	24.79	n/a	20.07	14.05	10.16
Webster, NY	30.56	32.87	14.74	21.87	16.18	14.01
Wellesley, MA[4]	37.71	37.48	n/a	26.13	19.96	15.39
West Fargo, ND	24.82	23.89	14.17	22.93	17.54	9.81
West Lafayette, IN	23.18	25.82	n/a	24.68	15.71	9.81
Weston, FL[2]	24.84	27.99	11.27	20.65	16.74	12.90
Wilmette, IL[2]	31.99	35.68	13.37	23.91	18.95	11.97
Yorba Linda, CA[2]	41.36	41.41	15.01	22.45	17.54	14.48
Zionsville, IN	25.50	26.49	15.34	22.61	16.42	10.44

Notes: (1) Figures cover the Metropolitan Statistical Area (MSA) except where noted. See Appendix B for areas included; (2) Metropolitan Division; (3) New England City and Town Area; (4) New England City and Town Area Division; Hourly wages for elementary and secondary school teachers were calculated by the editors from annual wage data assuming a 40 hour work week; n/a not available
Source: Bureau of Labor Statistics, May 2017 Metro Area Occupational Employment and Wage Estimates

Means of Transportation to Work: City

City	Car/Truck/Van: Drove Alone	Car/Truck/Van: Car-pooled	Public Transportation: Bus	Public Transportation: Subway	Public Transportation: Railroad	Bicycle	Walked	Other Means	Worked at Home
Aberdeen, SD	82.6	8.3	0.3	0.0	0.0	0.8	2.9	2.1	3.0
Aliso Viejo, CA	81.8	7.7	0.7	0.0	0.1	0.1	1.4	0.5	7.6
Allen, TX	81.6	7.0	0.1	0.4	0.9	0.0	0.9	1.1	7.9
Ames, IA	68.4	5.9	8.3	0.0	0.0	3.1	10.2	0.4	3.7
Amherst, MA	48.7	6.3	8.1	0.2	0.1	2.8	23.1	0.8	9.9
Apex, NC	81.4	7.8	0.4	0.0	0.0	0.2	0.6	0.9	8.7
Beavercreek, OH	88.7	5.2	0.1	0.0	0.0	0.1	1.3	0.6	4.0
Bellevue, NE	85.1	10.6	0.2	0.0	0.0	0.0	0.7	1.2	2.1
Bend, OR	75.1	7.5	0.6	0.0	0.0	3.1	3.3	1.0	9.4
Benicia, CA	75.2	10.3	1.0	2.5	0.2	0.4	1.4	2.9	6.2
Bentonville, AR	83.7	9.5	0.0	0.0	0.0	0.2	2.4	0.6	3.6
Bethlehem, NY	84.3	6.0	1.2	0.0	0.2	0.1	1.0	0.9	6.3
Blacksburg, VA	62.7	5.9	11.0	0.6	0.0	2.8	11.3	1.5	4.2
Bowie, MD	74.2	9.0	1.5	7.9	1.2	0.0	1.1	0.7	4.4
Bozeman, MT	70.2	7.7	0.9	0.0	0.0	5.6	9.3	0.7	5.6
Brentwood, TN	83.9	5.6	0.2	0.0	0.1	0.1	0.5	1.1	8.5
Burlington, VT	52.9	8.3	5.2	0.0	0.0	5.6	21.7	0.8	5.3
Cabot, AR	86.2	9.0	0.1	0.0	0.0	0.1	1.7	0.6	2.4
Carmel, IN	83.0	7.7	0.2	0.0	0.0	0.2	0.8	0.5	7.7
Cedar Falls, IA	80.3	5.4	0.2	0.0	0.0	0.9	9.9	0.5	2.9
Cedar Park, TX	81.9	7.6	0.4	0.0	0.3	0.4	0.8	0.7	8.0
Central, LA	87.1	8.6	0.3	0.0	0.0	0.0	0.5	0.4	3.1
Chapel Hill, NC	54.9	6.9	11.8	0.0	0.0	1.9	13.7	2.0	8.8
Cheshire, CT	83.1	7.8	0.6	0.0	0.3	0.0	1.5	0.8	5.8
Chino Hills, CA	80.0	11.8	0.6	0.1	0.8	0.3	0.5	0.7	5.3
Cibolo, TX	85.8	7.6	0.1	0.0	0.0	0.1	0.8	1.7	4.0
Cicero, NY	89.1	5.5	0.5	0.0	0.0	0.2	1.2	1.1	2.5
Collierville, TN	88.3	5.3	0.1	0.0	0.0	0.0	0.4	0.6	5.3
Coppell, TX	81.2	6.0	0.1	0.4	0.4	0.1	0.5	1.4	9.8
Cornelius, NC	76.7	6.7	0.9	0.0	0.0	0.4	2.0	1.5	11.8
Cranberry, PA	83.3	8.4	1.0	0.0	0.0	0.0	0.6	0.6	6.0
Crown Point, IN	87.6	4.1	0.1	0.2	1.2	0.0	1.7	2.0	3.1
Dublin, OH	85.8	4.5	0.4	0.0	0.0	0.2	0.5	1.4	7.2
East Fishkill, NY	85.2	4.8	0.3	0.0	3.3	0.1	0.4	0.5	5.3
Eden Prairie, MN	80.9	6.4	2.8	0.0	0.0	0.3	1.4	0.9	7.2
Edmond, OK	84.7	6.3	0.3	0.0	0.0	0.2	2.0	1.0	5.4
Edwardsville, IL	85.6	3.9	1.9	0.0	0.0	0.6	1.5	0.8	5.6
Evesham, NJ	84.8	5.8	0.6	1.2	1.1	0.1	0.6	0.7	5.1
Flower Mound, TX	82.1	5.2	0.1	0.1	0.3	0.0	0.8	1.1	10.4
Folsom, CA	80.0	8.2	0.3	0.7	0.8	0.7	0.7	1.4	7.0
Friendswood, TX	86.3	5.9	0.8	0.0	0.0	0.2	0.9	0.7	5.3
Gaines, MI	86.7	6.3	1.4	0.0	0.0	0.2	1.8	0.8	2.8
Glastonbury, CT	85.0	4.8	0.8	0.0	0.1	0.2	1.5	0.5	7.2
Grand Blanc, MI	89.8	5.9	0.1	0.0	0.0	0.0	0.4	0.4	3.5
Hampden, PA	87.5	6.8	0.4	0.0	0.0	0.3	0.4	0.4	4.0
Hilliard, OH	84.2	8.3	0.4	0.0	0.0	0.1	1.0	0.8	5.2
Hillsborough, NJ	84.3	5.2	0.4	0.0	2.7	0.1	0.6	0.5	6.1
Holly Springs, NC	80.4	7.1	0.5	0.0	0.0	0.0	0.5	1.6	9.9
Independence, KY	84.8	10.5	0.5	0.0	0.0	0.1	0.4	1.2	2.6
Juneau, AK	69.6	14.0	3.4	0.0	0.0	1.2	6.9	1.9	3.1
Kaysville, UT	76.3	8.9	2.7	0.4	1.3	0.0	1.0	1.7	7.6
Keller, TX	83.2	5.7	0.0	0.1	0.1	0.2	0.6	0.9	9.4
Lafayette, CA	65.1	3.0	0.0	17.2	1.1	0.4	2.3	0.8	9.9
Lafayette, CO	77.2	6.4	2.7	0.0	0.0	1.3	1.1	1.6	9.7
Lake Oswego, OR	72.3	7.9	3.9	0.1	0.0	0.8	1.5	0.5	13.1
Laramie, WY	65.3	10.6	2.9	0.0	0.0	5.1	10.8	0.7	4.6
Leander, TX	78.9	10.2	0.7	0.0	0.3	0.3	0.3	0.9	8.4
Leawood, KS	84.2	4.2	0.2	0.0	0.0	0.1	0.5	0.7	10.2
Lee's Summit, MO	87.0	5.5	0.3	0.1	0.0	0.0	0.4	0.9	5.9
Leesburg, VA	77.2	10.5	3.3	0.3	0.1	0.3	2.1	0.9	5.2
Lehi, UT	76.2	10.6	0.6	0.2	1.3	0.4	1.0	1.7	7.9
Lexington, MA	72.1	6.7	2.5	5.7	0.5	1.2	1.9	0.8	8.6
Los Altos, CA	77.5	5.5	1.2	0.0	1.3	3.1	2.2	0.5	8.6
Loveland, CO	80.6	8.6	0.4	0.0	0.0	0.9	1.4	1.8	6.2
Lower Macungie, PA	87.1	3.9	1.0	0.1	0.0	0.2	0.6	0.3	6.9
Madison, AL	91.8	4.5	0.1	0.0	0.0	0.1	0.2	1.1	2.2
Madison, MS	90.3	4.6	0.0	0.0	0.0	0.1	0.2	1.2	3.6

Table continued on next page.

City	Car/Truck/Van		Public Transportation			Bicycle	Walked	Other Means	Worked at Home
	Drove Alone	Car-pooled	Bus	Subway	Railroad				
Maple Valley, WA	77.4	9.6	2.5	0.5	0.8	0.2	0.9	1.2	7.0
Marion, IA	85.9	8.1	0.2	0.0	0.0	0.2	1.3	0.6	3.7
Marlboro, NJ	72.0	6.3	11.3	0.4	3.5	0.0	0.6	1.0	4.8
Mason, OH	87.4	4.8	0.6	0.0	0.0	0.0	0.7	0.3	6.2
Menomonee Falls, WI	87.7	6.6	0.3	0.0	0.1	0.1	0.9	0.3	3.9
Meridian, ID	82.9	7.7	0.2	0.0	0.0	0.5	0.8	0.4	7.5
Meridian, MI	80.1	8.8	2.8	0.0	0.0	1.0	1.8	0.3	5.3
Merrimack, NH	85.6	4.9	0.3	0.0	0.0	0.1	0.8	0.9	7.4
Milton, GA	77.8	5.5	0.0	0.3	0.2	0.5	0.8	0.6	14.2
Moon, PA	79.5	10.0	3.3	0.0	0.0	0.0	2.5	1.1	3.6
Moorpark, CA	81.0	9.4	0.4	0.0	1.0	0.1	1.4	1.1	5.6
Morgantown, WV	63.6	7.2	3.0	0.8	0.0	0.9	16.4	0.8	7.3
Mount Pleasant, SC	82.3	5.2	0.4	0.0	0.0	0.6	1.5	0.6	9.5
Newark, DE	66.1	6.5	3.9	0.1	0.4	2.8	15.8	0.4	4.0
Newtown, CT	82.8	6.5	0.0	0.0	1.2	0.0	1.1	0.6	7.8
North Attleborough, MA	82.9	7.1	0.6	1.0	2.6	0.0	1.5	0.9	3.4
North Port, FL	88.6	5.5	1.1	0.0	0.0	0.5	0.0	1.0	3.2
North Ridgeville, OH	87.1	6.8	0.8	0.1	0.0	0.2	0.5	0.9	3.6
Northville, MI	88.1	4.5	0.4	0.0	0.0	0.1	0.4	0.6	5.9
O'Fallon, MO	85.9	6.7	0.1	0.0	0.0	0.2	0.6	1.0	5.5
Orchard Park, NY	89.1	5.1	0.6	0.0	0.0	0.1	1.2	0.7	3.2
Oro Valley, AZ	78.8	7.0	1.1	0.1	0.0	0.6	1.1	2.8	8.5
Oviedo, FL	82.6	8.2	0.3	0.0	0.0	0.4	0.9	0.9	6.7
Parker, CO	81.4	6.4	1.3	0.6	0.5	0.2	0.7	1.3	7.7
Parkland, FL	82.2	5.8	0.1	0.0	0.2	0.0	0.7	1.4	9.6
Peachtree City, GA	76.7	8.3	0.6	0.1	0.0	0.1	0.3	3.3	10.6
Pittsfield, MI	80.4	8.6	3.4	0.0	0.0	0.6	0.9	1.1	5.0
Plainfield, IL	85.0	5.5	0.3	0.1	3.3	0.0	0.9	0.5	4.4
Pleasant Grove, UT	77.5	10.8	1.6	0.0	0.3	0.6	1.1	1.7	6.5
Poway, CA	80.4	7.9	1.4	0.0	0.0	1.0	1.7	0.7	7.0
Princeton, NJ	49.6	4.3	4.9	0.7	5.9	5.8	15.8	0.3	12.8
Queen Creek, AZ	79.0	9.3	0.3	0.0	0.0	0.1	0.8	1.2	9.3
Radnor, PA	59.4	5.1	0.9	2.1	8.5	0.7	14.1	0.6	8.7
Randolph, NJ	78.7	7.3	0.8	0.1	3.8	0.1	1.9	0.3	6.9
Rexburg, ID	64.1	8.5	0.3	0.0	0.0	5.2	11.3	2.0	8.7
Rio Rancho, NM	84.4	8.1	0.5	0.0	0.7	0.1	0.9	1.4	3.9
Rye, NY	56.7	8.5	5.1	0.9	12.2	0.3	7.6	5.5	3.2
Sammamish, WA	69.0	11.8	6.9	0.0	0.0	0.5	0.9	0.6	10.4
San Ramon, CA	75.1	7.8	1.3	4.7	0.8	0.4	1.0	0.8	8.3
Saratoga, CA	80.5	6.9	0.3	0.1	0.7	0.3	0.8	0.3	10.0
Shrewsbury, MA	81.8	8.4	0.2	0.1	1.6	0.2	1.6	1.0	5.0
South Brunswick, NJ	77.2	7.2	6.4	0.3	2.8	0.1	0.8	1.1	4.2
South Jordan, UT	75.6	9.5	0.5	1.2	1.6	0.7	1.8	1.0	8.1
South Kingstown, RI	77.9	6.5	1.0	0.1	0.6	0.2	7.1	1.0	5.6
South Portland, ME	78.3	10.0	1.5	0.0	0.1	1.2	2.6	1.5	4.9
Sparks, NV	81.0	11.3	1.6	0.0	0.0	0.4	1.7	1.1	3.0
State College, PA	36.5	5.7	10.3	0.1	0.0	7.5	35.7	0.8	3.4
Sugar Land, TX	80.3	9.6	2.3	0.0	0.0	0.0	0.6	0.8	6.3
Sun Prairie, WI	83.4	8.9	0.3	0.0	0.0	0.5	1.9	0.7	4.3
Syracuse, UT	80.0	11.0	0.3	0.0	1.2	0.2	1.8	0.9	4.6
Tredyffrin, PA	74.5	4.9	0.4	0.9	7.4	0.4	2.5	0.7	8.3
Upper Dublin, PA	78.8	5.7	0.7	0.3	4.9	0.5	1.3	0.6	7.1
Urbandale, IA	86.2	5.2	0.8	0.0	0.0	0.1	0.5	0.6	6.6
Vestal, NY	79.5	5.6	2.8	0.2	0.1	0.2	7.3	0.5	3.8
Vestavia Hills, AL	86.3	6.6	0.1	0.0	0.0	0.2	0.9	0.5	5.5
Webster, NY	86.7	7.4	0.3	0.0	0.0	0.0	1.1	0.7	3.8
Wellesley, MA	59.9	5.9	1.0	1.7	8.1	0.6	11.7	1.1	9.9
West Fargo, ND	84.9	10.0	0.2	0.0	0.0	0.2	1.1	0.9	2.8
West Lafayette, IN	50.0	7.2	6.4	0.1	0.0	4.9	25.8	0.7	4.8
Weston, FL	79.9	8.1	0.3	0.1	0.0	0.1	0.4	0.9	10.3
Wilmette, IL	58.6	5.5	1.5	3.0	16.5	0.3	2.3	0.4	11.7
Yorba Linda, CA	82.0	7.2	0.5	0.0	0.4	0.4	0.6	1.0	7.8
Zionsville, IN	85.6	4.6	0.0	0.1	0.0	0.2	0.8	1.0	7.7
U.S.	76.4	9.3	2.6	1.9	0.6	0.6	2.8	1.3	4.6

Note: Figures are percentages and cover workers 16 years of age and older
Source: U.S. Census Bureau, 2012-2016 American Community Survey 5-Year Estimates

Means of Transportation to Work: Metro Area

Metro Area	Car/Truck/Van		Public Transportation			Bicycle	Walked	Other Means	Worked at Home
	Drove Alone	Car-pooled	Bus	Subway	Railroad				
Aberdeen, SD	81.5	8.7	0.2	0.0	0.0	0.7	3.2	1.5	4.2
Aliso Viejo, CA	74.6	9.8	4.8	0.4	0.3	0.9	2.6	1.4	5.3
Allen, TX	80.7	9.9	1.0	0.2	0.3	0.2	1.2	1.5	5.0
Ames, IA	72.3	7.1	5.7	0.0	0.0	2.3	7.5	0.5	4.7
Amherst, MA	79.4	7.5	2.2	0.1	0.0	0.6	4.8	0.9	4.5
Apex, NC	80.2	9.1	0.9	0.0	0.0	0.3	1.2	1.0	7.2
Beavercreek, OH	83.4	8.0	1.6	0.0	0.0	0.2	2.6	0.7	3.3
Bellevue, NE	83.9	8.6	0.9	0.0	0.0	0.2	1.8	0.9	3.5
Bend, OR	74.9	9.0	0.4	0.0	0.0	2.2	2.7	1.2	9.5
Benicia, CA	76.9	13.5	1.4	0.6	0.2	0.5	1.5	1.5	3.8
Bentonville, AR	81.7	10.9	0.4	0.0	0.0	0.3	1.8	0.7	4.1
Bethlehem, NY	79.8	7.9	3.3	0.1	0.1	0.3	3.7	0.9	4.0
Blacksburg, VA	78.1	9.2	2.7	0.1	0.0	0.9	4.2	1.4	3.3
Bowie, MD	65.9	9.7	5.2	8.0	0.8	0.8	3.3	1.1	5.2
Bozeman, MT	72.9	9.3	0.7	0.0	0.0	3.2	6.0	0.9	7.1
Brentwood, TN	82.0	9.3	1.0	0.0	0.1	0.2	1.4	1.0	5.0
Burlington, VT	74.7	8.7	2.0	0.0	0.0	1.6	6.6	0.8	5.6
Cabot, AR	84.4	9.7	0.6	0.0	0.0	0.1	1.2	1.0	3.0
Carmel, IN	83.8	8.5	0.9	0.0	0.0	0.3	1.5	0.9	4.0
Cedar Falls, IA	82.2	7.9	0.4	0.0	0.0	0.4	5.0	1.0	3.2
Cedar Park, TX	76.5	9.9	2.2	0.0	0.1	0.8	1.7	1.3	7.4
Central, LA	84.8	8.9	1.0	0.0	0.0	0.3	1.5	0.8	2.7
Chapel Hill, NC	74.2	10.1	4.4	0.0	0.0	0.9	3.4	1.1	5.9
Cheshire, CT	78.6	8.3	3.2	0.1	1.0	0.6	3.5	0.7	4.0
Chino Hills, CA	77.7	12.9	1.0	0.0	0.4	0.4	1.6	1.1	4.9
Cibolo, TX	79.6	10.9	2.2	0.0	0.0	0.2	1.7	1.1	4.4
Cicero, NY	80.0	8.2	2.4	0.0	0.0	0.4	4.6	0.8	3.6
Collierville, TN	83.9	9.5	1.1	0.0	0.0	0.1	1.2	1.3	2.9
Coppell, TX	80.7	9.9	1.0	0.2	0.3	0.2	1.2	1.5	5.0
Cornelius, NC	80.7	9.6	1.4	0.1	0.1	0.1	1.4	1.1	5.4
Cranberry, PA	77.5	8.4	4.9	0.2	0.0	0.4	3.4	1.1	4.1
Crown Point, IN	70.7	8.0	4.6	3.9	3.2	0.7	3.1	1.2	4.6
Dublin, OH	82.5	7.9	1.7	0.0	0.0	0.4	2.2	0.9	4.4
East Fishkill, NY	50.1	6.6	7.7	19.1	3.8	0.6	6.0	1.8	4.2
Eden Prairie, MN	77.9	8.2	4.2	0.2	0.1	1.0	2.2	0.9	5.2
Edmond, OK	83.3	9.9	0.4	0.0	0.0	0.3	1.6	1.0	3.5
Edwardsville, IL	82.8	7.4	2.2	0.3	0.1	0.3	1.7	0.9	4.4
Evesham, NJ	73.1	7.7	5.4	1.7	2.3	0.6	3.7	1.0	4.3
Flower Mound, TX	80.7	9.9	1.0	0.2	0.3	0.2	1.2	1.5	5.0
Folsom, CA	76.2	10.3	1.8	0.2	0.3	1.8	2.1	1.4	5.9
Friendswood, TX	80.2	10.7	2.2	0.0	0.0	0.3	1.4	1.5	3.7
Gaines, MI	82.1	8.8	1.5	0.0	0.0	0.5	2.2	0.9	3.9
Glastonbury, CT	81.4	7.9	2.8	0.0	0.1	0.2	2.5	0.9	4.1
Grand Blanc, MI	84.6	9.1	1.2	0.0	0.0	0.2	1.2	0.6	3.0
Hampden, PA	80.8	9.1	1.4	0.0	0.0	0.4	3.4	0.8	3.9
Hilliard, OH	82.5	7.9	1.7	0.0	0.0	0.4	2.2	0.9	4.4
Hillsborough, NJ	50.1	6.6	7.7	19.1	3.8	0.6	6.0	1.8	4.2
Holly Springs, NC	80.2	9.1	0.9	0.0	0.0	0.3	1.2	1.0	7.2
Independence, KY	82.8	8.0	1.9	0.0	0.0	0.2	2.1	0.7	4.2
Juneau, AK	69.6	14.0	3.4	0.0	0.0	1.2	6.9	1.9	3.1
Kaysville, UT	79.5	10.7	1.4	0.1	0.6	0.5	1.5	1.1	4.7
Keller, TX	80.7	9.9	1.0	0.2	0.3	0.2	1.2	1.5	5.0
Lafayette, CA	59.3	9.8	7.6	6.9	1.2	2.0	4.5	2.6	6.1
Lafayette, CO	65.2	7.6	4.9	0.0	0.0	4.4	5.3	1.3	11.3
Lake Oswego, OR	70.4	9.8	4.8	0.7	0.3	2.4	3.4	1.7	6.6
Laramie, WY	66.6	10.4	2.5	0.0	0.0	4.4	9.8	0.7	5.5
Leander, TX	76.5	9.9	2.2	0.0	0.1	0.8	1.7	1.3	7.4
Leawood, KS	83.4	8.5	1.0	0.0	0.0	0.2	1.3	0.9	4.6
Lee's Summit, MO	83.4	8.5	1.0	0.0	0.0	0.2	1.3	0.9	4.6
Leesburg, VA	65.9	9.7	5.2	8.0	0.8	0.8	3.3	1.1	5.2
Lehi, UT	73.1	12.1	0.9	0.2	0.7	1.1	4.1	1.4	6.3
Lexington, MA	67.7	7.2	4.2	6.3	2.0	1.0	5.3	1.6	4.8
Los Altos, CA	75.7	10.5	2.3	0.2	1.4	1.8	2.0	1.5	4.7
Loveland, CO	75.1	8.5	1.3	0.0	0.0	3.9	2.7	1.1	7.4
Lower Macungie, PA	81.7	8.5	1.8	0.0	0.0	0.3	2.6	1.1	4.0
Madison, AL	87.5	7.2	0.2	0.0	0.0	0.1	0.8	1.2	3.0
Madison, MS	86.0	9.4	0.3	0.0	0.0	0.1	1.0	1.0	2.1

Table continued on next page.

Metro Area	Car/Truck/Van: Drove Alone	Car/Truck/Van: Car-pooled	Public Transportation: Bus	Public Transportation: Subway	Public Transportation: Railroad	Bicycle	Walked	Other Means	Worked at Home
Maple Valley, WA	69.1	10.0	8.4	0.2	0.4	1.1	3.8	1.3	5.7
Marion, IA	83.2	8.9	0.8	0.0	0.0	0.3	2.3	0.8	3.7
Marlboro, NJ	50.1	6.6	7.7	19.1	3.8	0.6	6.0	1.8	4.2
Mason, OH	82.8	8.0	1.9	0.0	0.0	0.2	2.1	0.7	4.2
Menomonee Falls, WI	80.5	8.2	3.6	0.0	0.1	0.6	2.8	0.8	3.6
Meridian, ID	79.3	9.2	0.4	0.0	0.0	1.3	1.8	1.2	6.8
Meridian, MI	79.6	8.8	2.4	0.0	0.0	1.2	3.6	0.6	3.7
Merrimack, NH	81.6	8.5	0.7	0.0	0.1	0.1	2.3	0.7	5.9
Milton, GA	77.9	9.9	2.1	0.8	0.1	0.2	1.4	1.3	6.3
Moon, PA	77.5	8.4	4.9	0.2	0.0	0.4	3.4	1.1	4.1
Moorpark, CA	77.5	12.3	1.0	0.0	0.3	0.6	1.8	1.0	5.4
Morgantown, WV	76.6	10.0	1.7	0.2	0.0	0.5	5.4	0.7	4.9
Mount Pleasant, SC	81.1	8.5	1.2	0.0	0.0	0.9	2.7	1.0	4.6
Newark, DE	73.1	7.7	5.4	1.7	2.3	0.6	3.7	1.0	4.3
Newtown, CT	72.1	8.1	2.8	0.3	7.1	0.3	2.7	0.9	5.7
North Attleborough, MA	80.7	8.5	1.7	0.1	0.9	0.3	3.4	0.9	3.5
North Port, FL	81.0	8.3	0.9	0.0	0.0	0.8	1.2	1.2	6.6
North Ridgeville, OH	82.1	7.2	2.9	0.2	0.1	0.3	2.3	1.0	3.9
Northville, MI	84.2	8.5	1.5	0.0	0.0	0.3	1.3	0.9	3.4
O'Fallon, MO	82.8	7.4	2.2	0.3	0.1	0.3	1.7	0.9	4.4
Orchard Park, NY	82.5	7.8	3.0	0.2	0.0	0.4	2.6	0.8	2.7
Oro Valley, AZ	76.5	9.9	2.7	0.0	0.0	1.8	2.3	2.0	4.7
Oviedo, FL	80.5	9.5	1.8	0.0	0.1	0.5	1.0	1.4	5.3
Parker, CO	75.9	8.6	3.3	0.6	0.3	0.8	2.2	1.2	7.1
Parkland, FL	78.0	9.3	3.4	0.2	0.2	0.6	1.8	1.4	5.1
Peachtree City, GA	77.9	9.9	2.1	0.8	0.1	0.2	1.4	1.3	6.3
Pittsfield, MI	72.3	7.9	5.1	0.0	0.0	1.8	6.3	0.7	5.9
Plainfield, IL	70.7	8.0	4.6	3.9	3.2	0.7	3.1	1.2	4.6
Pleasant Grove, UT	73.1	12.1	0.9	0.2	0.7	1.1	4.1	1.4	6.3
Poway, CA	75.9	9.1	2.5	0.0	0.2	0.7	2.9	1.6	7.0
Princeton, NJ	71.8	10.3	3.1	0.3	4.4	0.8	3.1	1.3	4.9
Queen Creek, AZ	76.8	10.9	1.9	0.0	0.0	0.8	1.5	1.8	6.1
Radnor, PA	73.1	7.7	5.4	1.7	2.3	0.6	3.7	1.0	4.3
Randolph, NJ	50.1	6.6	7.7	19.1	3.8	0.6	6.0	1.8	4.2
Rexburg, ID	70.1	11.0	0.5	0.0	0.0	2.9	6.7	1.7	7.0
Rio Rancho, NM	80.4	9.2	1.4	0.0	0.3	1.0	1.8	1.4	4.5
Rye, NY	50.1	6.6	7.7	19.1	3.8	0.6	6.0	1.8	4.2
Sammamish, WA	69.1	10.0	8.4	0.2	0.4	1.1	3.8	1.3	5.7
San Ramon, CA	59.3	9.8	7.6	6.9	1.2	2.0	4.5	2.6	6.1
Saratoga, CA	75.7	10.5	2.3	0.2	1.4	1.8	2.0	1.5	4.7
Shrewsbury, MA	81.3	8.6	0.8	0.2	0.6	0.1	2.8	1.1	4.5
South Brunswick, NJ	50.1	6.6	7.7	19.1	3.8	0.6	6.0	1.8	4.2
South Jordan, UT	75.0	12.0	2.4	0.4	0.6	0.8	2.2	1.6	5.1
South Kingstown, RI	80.7	8.5	1.7	0.1	0.9	0.3	3.4	0.9	3.5
South Portland, ME	78.0	9.1	0.9	0.0	0.0	0.7	4.0	1.2	6.1
Sparks, NV	77.7	11.1	2.0	0.0	0.0	0.5	2.9	1.5	4.2
State College, PA	68.2	9.4	4.3	0.1	0.0	2.0	9.8	1.2	4.9
Sugar Land, TX	80.2	10.7	2.2	0.0	0.0	0.3	1.4	1.5	3.7
Sun Prairie, WI	74.2	8.3	4.4	0.0	0.0	2.4	5.2	0.9	4.7
Syracuse, UT	79.5	10.7	1.4	0.1	0.6	0.5	1.5	1.1	4.7
Tredyffrin, PA	73.1	7.7	5.4	1.7	2.3	0.6	3.7	1.0	4.3
Upper Dublin, PA	73.1	7.7	5.4	1.7	2.3	0.6	3.7	1.0	4.3
Urbandale, IA	83.9	8.3	1.0	0.0	0.0	0.2	1.8	0.7	4.0
Vestal, NY	80.7	8.4	2.6	0.2	0.0	0.4	3.8	0.8	3.2
Vestavia Hills, AL	85.2	9.2	0.6	0.0	0.0	0.1	1.0	0.9	3.0
Webster, NY	81.3	7.9	2.3	0.1	0.0	0.5	3.5	0.8	3.7
Wellesley, MA	67.7	7.2	4.2	6.3	2.0	1.0	5.3	1.6	4.8
West Fargo, ND	82.1	8.6	0.8	0.0	0.0	0.5	3.4	0.8	3.7
West Lafayette, IN	75.3	10.3	2.9	0.0	0.0	1.3	6.0	1.1	3.1
Weston, FL	78.0	9.3	3.4	0.2	0.2	0.6	1.8	1.4	5.1
Wilmette, IL	70.7	8.0	4.6	3.9	3.2	0.7	3.1	1.2	4.6
Yorba Linda, CA	74.6	9.8	4.8	0.4	0.3	0.9	2.6	1.4	5.3
Zionsville, IN	83.8	8.5	0.9	0.0	0.0	0.3	1.5	0.9	4.0
U.S.	76.4	9.3	2.6	1.9	0.6	0.6	2.8	1.3	4.6

Note: Figures are percentages and cover workers 16 years of age and older; (1) Figures cover the Metropolitan Statistical Area—see Appendix B for areas included

Source: U.S. Census Bureau, 2012-2016 American Community Survey 5-Year Estimates

Travel Time to Work: City

City	Less Than 10 Minutes	10 to 19 Minutes	20 to 29 Minutes	30 to 44 Minutes	45 to 59 Minutes	60 to 89 Minutes	90 Minutes or More
Aberdeen, SD	43.2	47.9	4.0	2.5	1.1	1.0	0.3
Aliso Viejo, CA	11.2	23.9	26.9	23.4	6.4	6.3	1.8
Allen, TX	10.9	23.3	23.8	22.8	11.1	7.2	0.9
Ames, IA	25.6	50.0	10.1	6.6	5.8	1.3	0.6
Amherst, MA	25.0	43.7	13.6	9.8	4.1	2.2	1.6
Apex, NC	10.2	25.5	31.6	24.8	4.6	1.9	1.3
Beavercreek, OH	10.1	48.4	26.7	8.5	2.6	3.0	0.8
Bellevue, NE	12.2	36.3	29.5	17.2	2.6	1.4	1.0
Bend, OR	24.2	54.7	11.0	6.1	1.6	0.9	1.5
Benicia, CA	13.2	22.2	18.2	16.6	9.7	13.9	6.1
Bentonville, AR	18.9	46.9	23.3	8.2	1.8	0.3	0.5
Bethlehem, NY	10.9	36.4	32.1	14.6	2.9	1.9	1.2
Blacksburg, VA	33.6	46.4	9.8	6.6	2.0	1.3	0.4
Bowie, MD	5.8	14.6	15.4	27.0	14.9	17.8	4.5
Bozeman, MT	29.8	52.5	10.1	3.7	0.9	1.6	1.3
Brentwood, TN	6.1	29.3	29.7	26.7	4.9	1.9	1.4
Burlington, VT	18.4	43.1	19.7	12.5	3.8	2.0	0.5
Cabot, AR	14.1	20.5	21.4	29.0	9.9	4.2	0.9
Carmel, IN	11.9	32.0	17.1	26.9	8.5	2.8	0.8
Cedar Falls, IA	32.1	47.8	15.1	2.5	0.7	1.2	0.6
Cedar Park, TX	10.5	22.3	23.3	24.2	12.3	6.6	0.8
Central, LA	4.1	18.2	30.0	29.8	10.8	4.5	2.6
Chapel Hill, NC	15.7	38.7	24.8	13.5	4.3	2.2	0.7
Cheshire, CT	12.6	22.8	23.1	28.2	8.4	3.1	1.8
Chino Hills, CA	6.0	14.1	16.1	27.8	14.1	15.2	6.7
Cibolo, TX	6.0	25.1	21.9	28.0	12.7	4.4	1.9
Cicero, NY	12.7	39.3	35.5	7.7	2.8	0.7	1.2
Collierville, TN	11.3	23.7	25.2	28.7	8.5	1.4	1.2
Coppell, TX	8.4	27.8	25.2	26.9	8.2	2.2	1.3
Cornelius, NC	12.8	23.5	17.8	26.0	11.7	6.1	2.1
Cranberry, PA	9.8	27.3	12.9	29.2	14.4	3.9	2.5
Crown Point, IN	15.5	24.7	16.5	22.4	9.2	6.8	4.9
Dublin, OH	15.2	22.3	26.0	27.8	5.1	2.0	1.7
East Fishkill, NY	7.4	17.0	19.2	23.5	13.0	11.4	8.4
Eden Prairie, MN	11.0	35.4	25.9	19.4	5.1	2.4	0.8
Edmond, OK	13.5	31.2	28.3	20.5	3.9	1.1	1.5
Edwardsville, IL	17.8	30.5	14.5	22.3	11.3	2.8	0.8
Evesham, NJ	9.2	28.5	21.7	18.8	9.9	8.0	3.9
Flower Mound, TX	10.1	20.6	20.0	29.4	13.1	5.2	1.5
Folsom, CA	14.0	32.3	18.6	22.4	6.5	3.7	2.5
Friendswood, TX	9.9	20.4	18.5	23.6	13.9	10.5	3.2
Gaines, MI	16.3	36.5	28.3	11.3	4.8	1.4	1.4
Glastonbury, CT	10.5	31.3	26.9	21.5	5.1	3.1	1.6
Grand Blanc, MI	12.3	33.1	20.9	12.5	8.6	10.9	1.6
Hampden, PA	10.4	43.5	27.3	13.1	2.2	1.6	1.9
Hilliard, OH	10.9	27.7	31.6	23.2	4.4	1.9	0.4
Hillsborough, NJ	7.8	20.2	18.7	27.5	12.3	8.9	4.5
Holly Springs, NC	6.7	18.0	27.1	33.9	9.5	3.4	1.4
Independence, KY	6.5	25.3	27.8	25.7	7.4	4.8	2.4
Juneau, AK	23.9	48.8	17.6	6.9	1.0	0.5	1.3
Kaysville, UT	14.3	30.8	20.8	22.9	5.2	5.6	0.5
Keller, TX	8.1	19.5	19.9	29.8	14.4	6.5	1.8
Lafayette, CA	10.6	26.5	15.1	20.5	14.0	10.2	3.1
Lafayette, CO	10.3	25.9	33.0	20.1	5.8	3.2	1.8
Lake Oswego, OR	12.1	27.3	26.1	24.2	6.6	2.2	1.5
Laramie, WY	50.7	38.3	4.5	1.7	2.2	1.8	0.8
Leander, TX	7.5	20.5	20.5	27.5	14.8	7.4	1.8
Leawood, KS	11.5	34.3	28.1	21.4	3.3	0.5	0.9
Lee's Summit, MO	11.8	25.4	21.9	28.8	9.4	2.0	0.7
Leesburg, VA	13.0	23.3	15.8	22.8	10.7	9.5	4.9
Lehi, UT	16.6	27.6	22.2	22.0	7.1	3.1	1.3
Lexington, MA	9.4	19.6	19.4	24.1	15.5	10.0	2.1
Los Altos, CA	7.6	29.1	35.3	19.5	3.6	3.3	1.6
Loveland, CO	14.7	29.6	23.3	19.2	5.6	5.7	1.8
Lower Macungie, PA	15.5	33.2	21.0	13.8	5.8	7.6	3.0
Madison, AL	10.6	39.4	31.6	15.6	1.5	0.7	0.6
Madison, MS	9.4	32.1	32.8	18.1	4.3	1.9	1.5
Maple Valley, WA	7.4	11.3	12.5	31.9	17.2	14.2	5.4

Table continued on next page.

City	Less Than 10 Minutes	10 to 19 Minutes	20 to 29 Minutes	30 to 44 Minutes	45 to 59 Minutes	60 to 89 Minutes	90 Minutes or More
Marion, IA	16.2	39.5	28.5	10.7	2.6	1.5	1.1
Marlboro, NJ	6.5	16.2	13.9	16.7	11.8	17.7	17.2
Mason, OH	10.8	25.0	28.7	24.0	7.5	2.6	1.4
Menomonee Falls, WI	14.7	29.5	31.0	18.5	3.2	2.0	1.3
Meridian, ID	8.2	32.2	33.4	21.7	2.1	1.0	1.4
Meridian, MI	15.4	42.1	27.1	7.6	2.7	3.5	1.6
Merrimack, NH	9.7	30.2	27.8	13.2	7.3	8.6	3.1
Milton, GA	9.3	31.3	20.5	13.1	12.8	12.4	0.6
Moon, PA	13.8	35.4	16.0	18.9	8.7	5.3	1.8
Moorpark, CA	10.9	26.9	24.0	22.3	7.6	5.6	2.6
Morgantown, WV	21.2	52.0	13.7	6.7	2.7	3.2	0.5
Mount Pleasant, SC	11.3	32.6	28.6	21.6	3.5	1.3	1.3
Newark, DE	13.4	37.2	20.5	17.6	4.9	5.2	1.2
Newtown, CT	7.6	20.9	17.9	26.8	11.9	10.3	4.7
North Attleborough, MA	11.5	26.4	20.6	19.6	9.1	9.7	3.2
North Port, FL	5.1	19.7	24.2	36.3	8.3	3.2	3.1
North Ridgeville, OH	7.5	22.7	26.5	28.0	9.3	4.6	1.4
Northville, MI	6.8	22.1	20.7	34.4	11.4	3.6	0.9
O'Fallon, MO	9.1	24.4	23.3	28.0	11.1	2.8	1.4
Orchard Park, NY	14.2	30.1	25.8	23.0	3.7	1.9	1.4
Oro Valley, AZ	11.8	23.0	22.9	25.6	11.1	3.2	2.4
Oviedo, FL	7.6	19.3	20.7	31.5	13.5	4.7	2.7
Parker, CO	10.3	26.3	20.7	25.4	10.9	4.8	1.8
Parkland, FL	5.5	23.4	20.0	33.2	11.8	4.7	1.4
Peachtree City, GA	13.7	27.0	12.1	24.9	11.2	8.6	2.5
Pittsfield, MI	7.8	37.9	23.5	19.0	6.5	4.4	0.9
Plainfield, IL	6.5	17.8	18.1	19.7	14.4	16.9	6.6
Pleasant Grove, UT	17.2	34.4	23.5	13.9	6.1	3.2	1.6
Poway, CA	10.6	27.6	20.4	29.7	6.4	3.0	2.3
Princeton, NJ	20.7	37.9	11.1	12.4	4.7	5.5	7.7
Queen Creek, AZ	8.8	15.0	21.5	29.3	15.5	7.4	2.6
Radnor, PA	19.9	26.6	17.9	17.9	10.6	4.9	2.2
Randolph, NJ	8.0	20.5	20.1	23.0	12.4	8.5	7.5
Rexburg, ID	49.7	30.7	5.0	12.0	0.7	1.0	0.9
Rio Rancho, NM	9.4	24.5	17.0	25.9	14.6	6.2	2.4
Rye, NY	14.1	34.4	17.6	14.3	5.5	9.0	5.0
Sammamish, WA	5.5	14.5	22.1	35.8	13.9	6.7	1.7
San Ramon, CA	8.0	25.8	13.6	17.6	12.3	17.0	5.8
Saratoga, CA	4.6	17.8	28.0	33.6	8.9	5.1	2.0
Shrewsbury, MA	9.8	29.1	23.3	17.3	8.0	8.4	4.0
South Brunswick, NJ	6.1	20.7	19.8	20.2	10.9	11.2	11.0
South Jordan, UT	9.5	25.2	26.6	28.5	6.1	3.1	1.1
South Kingstown, RI	19.5	28.1	15.5	20.7	8.7	5.1	2.4
South Portland, ME	17.5	47.6	20.0	7.7	2.2	3.4	1.6
Sparks, NV	9.0	40.2	27.8	16.8	2.6	1.8	1.8
State College, PA	22.2	48.9	17.0	7.1	2.1	1.1	1.4
Sugar Land, TX	7.7	20.9	18.2	29.6	14.9	6.4	2.4
Sun Prairie, WI	18.3	35.3	21.7	18.2	3.5	1.9	1.0
Syracuse, UT	10.2	30.4	17.1	23.9	10.8	4.8	2.7
Tredyffrin, PA	14.5	29.7	18.6	15.9	9.4	9.7	2.2
Upper Dublin, PA	12.1	24.6	18.3	24.1	11.3	7.0	2.8
Urbandale, IA	14.5	42.3	31.3	9.2	1.4	0.6	0.7
Vestal, NY	16.9	49.2	22.4	5.8	1.1	2.1	2.3
Vestavia Hills, AL	9.6	42.4	29.4	14.6	1.8	1.2	1.1
Webster, NY	14.6	30.0	33.0	17.6	2.8	1.4	0.6
Wellesley, MA	15.5	21.1	14.3	25.0	14.4	7.6	2.0
West Fargo, ND	19.1	53.5	16.6	7.2	0.8	2.0	0.8
West Lafayette, IN	23.3	54.9	13.9	4.3	0.8	1.6	1.1
Weston, FL	10.5	22.2	18.6	22.7	14.4	9.3	2.4
Wilmette, IL	9.5	18.3	13.3	24.7	17.7	14.7	1.9
Yorba Linda, CA	7.0	20.0	17.5	31.6	11.7	8.5	3.8
Zionsville, IN	10.4	24.2	24.9	30.8	5.8	2.3	1.7
U.S.	12.9	29.2	20.9	20.4	8.0	6.0	2.7

Note: Figures are percentages and include workers 16 years old and over
Source: U.S. Census Bureau, 2012-2016 American Community Survey 5-Year Estimates

Travel Time to Work: Metro Area

Metro Area	Less Than 10 Minutes	10 to 19 Minutes	20 to 29 Minutes	30 to 44 Minutes	45 to 59 Minutes	60 to 89 Minutes	90 Minutes or More
Aberdeen, SD	37.3	43.3	10.1	6.5	1.3	1.0	0.5
Aliso Viejo, CA	7.6	25.4	20.2	25.0	9.6	8.8	3.3
Allen, TX	9.4	25.8	21.1	25.0	10.3	6.3	2.0
Ames, IA	23.8	43.7	14.9	9.9	5.4	1.7	0.7
Amherst, MA	14.5	32.6	24.1	17.9	6.1	3.3	1.6
Apex, NC	9.9	28.5	25.1	23.2	7.7	3.8	1.7
Beavercreek, OH	15.1	35.5	25.7	15.8	3.8	2.7	1.4
Bellevue, NE	14.4	36.8	27.0	15.9	3.3	1.6	1.0
Bend, OR	21.7	43.8	15.9	12.7	2.9	1.4	1.6
Benicia, CA	12.0	29.2	15.2	17.1	9.7	11.3	5.6
Bentonville, AR	15.8	36.5	22.6	16.3	5.4	2.2	1.2
Bethlehem, NY	12.9	32.3	24.6	20.4	5.8	2.6	1.4
Blacksburg, VA	20.2	36.3	18.5	14.6	5.3	3.5	1.5
Bowie, MD	6.1	19.2	18.0	25.8	13.7	12.8	4.4
Bozeman, MT	24.1	44.9	18.0	7.5	1.7	1.8	1.8
Brentwood, TN	9.4	27.1	22.4	23.5	9.9	5.9	1.7
Burlington, VT	14.7	33.4	22.7	18.8	6.3	2.9	1.1
Cabot, AR	13.0	32.0	24.7	19.8	6.4	2.9	1.3
Carmel, IN	11.8	27.8	24.8	23.4	7.1	3.5	1.6
Cedar Falls, IA	26.5	42.9	18.2	8.2	1.7	1.3	1.2
Cedar Park, TX	10.2	28.3	22.3	22.7	9.2	5.5	1.9
Central, LA	10.3	27.2	23.0	21.9	9.5	5.8	2.3
Chapel Hill, NC	10.6	34.4	24.3	19.4	5.9	3.6	1.7
Cheshire, CT	11.8	32.4	22.8	19.7	6.2	4.4	2.5
Chino Hills, CA	10.1	26.6	18.6	19.4	8.6	10.3	6.4
Cibolo, TX	10.0	28.8	24.7	22.6	7.7	4.1	2.1
Cicero, NY	15.8	36.1	25.5	14.6	4.1	2.3	1.5
Collierville, TN	10.5	28.6	25.9	24.0	7.1	2.7	1.2
Coppell, TX	9.4	25.8	21.1	25.0	10.3	6.3	2.0
Cornelius, NC	10.1	28.2	22.8	23.6	8.9	4.5	1.9
Cranberry, PA	12.1	27.3	21.4	22.1	9.3	5.9	2.0
Crown Point, IN	8.7	22.1	18.6	24.8	12.1	10.4	3.3
Dublin, OH	11.4	30.6	26.7	21.0	6.0	3.0	1.4
East Fishkill, NY	7.4	19.3	16.4	23.7	12.4	14.4	6.5
Eden Prairie, MN	10.7	27.7	25.0	23.1	7.9	4.2	1.3
Edmond, OK	13.3	32.5	25.8	19.6	5.0	2.2	1.5
Edwardsville, IL	10.7	27.7	24.1	23.5	8.2	4.2	1.6
Evesham, NJ	9.8	24.7	20.5	23.5	10.7	7.9	3.0
Flower Mound, TX	9.4	25.8	21.1	25.0	10.3	6.3	2.0
Folsom, CA	11.2	29.2	22.8	22.2	7.4	4.1	3.2
Friendswood, TX	8.3	24.1	19.6	25.8	11.3	8.5	2.4
Gaines, MI	15.3	35.0	24.6	16.2	4.7	2.6	1.6
Glastonbury, CT	12.4	30.9	24.3	21.2	6.1	3.4	1.7
Grand Blanc, MI	13.4	32.0	23.2	13.6	7.9	7.3	2.6
Hampden, PA	14.2	34.3	24.3	16.7	5.8	3.0	1.8
Hilliard, OH	11.4	30.6	26.7	21.0	6.0	3.0	1.4
Hillsborough, NJ	7.4	19.3	16.4	23.7	12.4	14.4	6.5
Holly Springs, NC	9.9	28.5	25.1	23.2	7.7	3.8	1.7
Independence, KY	11.1	28.5	25.4	23.0	7.2	3.3	1.5
Juneau, AK	23.9	48.8	17.6	6.9	1.0	0.5	1.3
Kaysville, UT	16.0	33.7	22.3	16.3	6.2	3.9	1.6
Keller, TX	9.4	25.8	21.1	25.0	10.3	6.3	2.0
Lafayette, CA	7.1	23.5	18.4	23.9	11.8	11.4	3.9
Lafayette, CO	15.5	35.4	21.3	16.4	6.0	3.9	1.5
Lake Oswego, OR	10.9	28.2	23.0	22.4	8.4	5.2	2.0
Laramie, WY	46.1	39.3	6.3	2.9	2.7	1.8	0.9
Leander, TX	10.2	28.3	22.3	22.7	9.2	5.5	1.9
Leawood, KS	12.8	31.1	25.2	21.2	6.3	2.4	1.1
Lee's Summit, MO	12.8	31.1	25.2	21.2	6.3	2.4	1.1
Leesburg, VA	6.1	19.2	18.0	25.8	13.7	12.8	4.4
Lehi, UT	19.1	35.9	19.7	14.6	5.3	3.6	1.6
Lexington, MA	9.6	23.1	18.3	24.1	11.6	10.1	3.2
Los Altos, CA	7.5	27.0	24.9	23.6	8.3	6.3	2.4
Loveland, CO	15.5	36.9	21.3	14.5	5.4	4.8	1.6
Lower Macungie, PA	12.7	28.3	21.8	18.3	7.4	7.5	4.1
Madison, AL	10.6	33.8	28.1	20.1	4.9	1.4	1.1
Madison, MS	10.5	29.4	26.1	23.2	6.3	3.0	1.5
Maple Valley, WA	8.2	23.9	21.5	25.1	10.5	7.9	2.9

Table continued on next page.

Metro Area	Less Than 10 Minutes	10 to 19 Minutes	20 to 29 Minutes	30 to 44 Minutes	45 to 59 Minutes	60 to 89 Minutes	90 Minutes or More
Marion, IA	18.4	39.8	21.2	13.6	3.6	2.2	1.2
Marlboro, NJ	7.4	19.3	16.4	23.7	12.4	14.4	6.5
Mason, OH	11.1	28.5	25.4	23.0	7.2	3.3	1.5
Menomonee Falls, WI	12.2	31.5	25.8	20.7	5.6	2.7	1.5
Meridian, ID	13.2	34.0	26.5	19.1	4.2	2.0	1.1
Meridian, MI	15.4	38.8	23.5	13.9	3.6	3.0	1.8
Merrimack, NH	12.3	29.3	19.9	19.6	8.3	7.1	3.4
Milton, GA	7.6	23.0	20.1	24.5	12.0	9.4	3.3
Moon, PA	12.1	27.3	21.4	22.1	9.3	5.9	2.0
Moorpark, CA	12.1	29.7	23.1	19.7	6.7	5.7	3.1
Morgantown, WV	13.0	37.1	22.3	15.4	5.9	4.2	2.1
Mount Pleasant, SC	10.0	28.1	24.8	23.7	8.3	3.6	1.5
Newark, DE	9.8	24.7	20.5	23.5	10.7	7.9	3.0
Newtown, CT	11.5	30.9	18.1	17.0	7.3	9.3	5.9
North Attleborough, MA	12.6	31.1	22.2	18.7	7.1	5.5	2.9
North Port, FL	9.4	30.6	27.5	22.1	5.9	2.9	1.7
North Ridgeville, OH	11.2	28.1	25.0	23.6	7.4	3.4	1.4
Northville, MI	9.6	27.0	22.8	24.2	9.4	5.2	1.8
O'Fallon, MO	10.7	27.7	24.1	23.5	8.2	4.2	1.6
Orchard Park, NY	14.3	33.9	26.4	18.4	4.1	1.8	1.2
Oro Valley, AZ	11.1	29.4	24.7	23.0	7.0	3.1	1.7
Oviedo, FL	7.3	25.2	23.6	27.0	9.9	4.9	2.1
Parker, CO	8.7	25.5	23.4	25.7	9.5	5.4	1.9
Parkland, FL	7.0	24.2	22.7	27.2	9.6	6.9	2.3
Peachtree City, GA	7.6	23.0	20.1	24.5	12.0	9.4	3.3
Pittsfield, MI	11.5	33.6	24.3	18.7	6.8	3.9	1.1
Plainfield, IL	8.7	22.1	18.6	24.8	12.1	10.4	3.3
Pleasant Grove, UT	19.1	35.9	19.7	14.6	5.3	3.6	1.6
Poway, CA	9.0	30.6	25.1	22.2	6.8	4.3	2.1
Princeton, NJ	11.5	32.9	21.4	15.4	6.3	6.9	5.7
Queen Creek, AZ	10.0	27.3	23.6	24.0	8.7	4.9	1.6
Radnor, PA	9.8	24.7	20.5	23.5	10.7	7.9	3.0
Randolph, NJ	7.4	19.3	16.4	23.7	12.4	14.4	6.5
Rexburg, ID	36.3	35.7	9.6	12.0	2.0	1.9	2.6
Rio Rancho, NM	11.5	32.9	25.3	19.7	5.8	3.2	1.7
Rye, NY	7.4	19.3	16.4	23.7	12.4	14.4	6.5
Sammamish, WA	8.2	23.9	21.5	25.1	10.5	7.9	2.9
San Ramon, CA	7.1	23.5	18.4	23.9	11.8	11.4	3.9
Saratoga, CA	7.5	27.0	24.9	23.6	8.3	6.3	2.4
Shrewsbury, MA	12.1	27.1	19.5	20.1	9.8	8.2	3.2
South Brunswick, NJ	7.4	19.3	16.4	23.7	12.4	14.4	6.5
South Jordan, UT	10.8	32.8	27.7	19.8	5.2	2.5	1.2
South Kingstown, RI	12.6	31.1	22.2	18.7	7.1	5.5	2.9
South Portland, ME	13.7	30.7	22.1	19.5	7.7	4.1	2.2
Sparks, NV	12.3	40.0	25.4	14.4	3.7	2.5	1.7
State College, PA	17.2	39.8	21.3	13.8	4.0	2.0	1.8
Sugar Land, TX	8.3	24.1	19.6	25.8	11.3	8.5	2.4
Sun Prairie, WI	16.3	33.1	24.2	17.9	4.8	2.5	1.2
Syracuse, UT	16.0	33.7	22.3	16.3	6.2	3.9	1.6
Tredyffrin, PA	9.8	24.7	20.5	23.5	10.7	7.9	3.0
Upper Dublin, PA	9.8	24.7	20.5	23.5	10.7	7.9	3.0
Urbandale, IA	15.5	36.7	27.0	15.1	3.0	1.5	1.2
Vestal, NY	17.3	40.0	22.9	12.1	3.2	2.7	1.8
Vestavia Hills, AL	9.6	27.3	23.9	23.8	9.0	4.8	1.6
Webster, NY	15.6	34.4	25.9	16.1	4.3	2.4	1.3
Wellesley, MA	9.6	23.1	18.3	24.1	11.6	10.1	3.2
West Fargo, ND	20.2	49.6	18.2	7.6	1.9	1.6	0.9
West Lafayette, IN	18.0	44.7	19.4	11.2	3.4	2.3	1.2
Weston, FL	7.0	24.2	22.7	27.2	9.6	6.9	2.3
Wilmette, IL	8.7	22.1	18.6	24.8	12.1	10.4	3.3
Yorba Linda, CA	7.6	25.4	20.2	25.0	9.6	8.8	3.3
Zionsville, IN	11.8	27.8	24.8	23.4	7.1	3.5	1.6
U.S.	12.9	29.2	20.9	20.4	8.0	6.0	2.7

Note: Figures are percentages and include workers 16 years old and over; Figures cover the Metropolitan Statistical Area—see Appendix B for areas included

Source: U.S. Census Bureau, 2012-2016 American Community Survey 5-Year Estimates

2016 Presidential Election Results

City	Area Covered	Clinton	Trump	Johnson	Stein	Other
Aberdeen, SD	Brown County	33.8	59.7	5.7	0.0	0.8
Aliso Viejo, CA	Orange County	50.9	42.3	3.9	1.5	1.4
Allen, TX	Collin County	38.6	55.2	3.8	0.7	1.8
Ames, IA	Story County	50.7	38.4	5.9	1.0	3.9
Amherst, MA	Hampshire County	65.8	25.9	3.7	3.1	1.6
Apex, NC	Wake County	57.4	37.2	3.7	0.3	1.4
Beavercreek, OH	Greene County	34.9	58.5	4.0	0.8	1.8
Bellevue, NE	Sarpy County	34.8	56.0	5.8	1.0	2.3
Bend, OR	Deschutes County	43.1	46.4	5.2	2.0	3.3
Benicia, CA	Solano County	60.9	30.9	3.7	1.6	2.9
Bentonville, AR	Benton County	28.9	62.9	4.0	1.0	3.2
Bethlehem, NY	Albany County	59.4	34.2	3.4	1.8	1.2
Blacksburg, VA	Montgomery County	46.5	45.2	4.7	0.9	2.6
Bowie, MD	Prince George's County	88.1	8.4	1.2	1.2	1.1
Bozeman, MT	Gallatin County	45.1	44.2	7.5	2.0	1.3
Brentwood, TN	Williamson County	29.2	64.2	4.3	0.5	1.9
Burlington, VT	Chittenden County	65.7	22.3	3.0	2.2	6.9
Cabot, AR	Lonoke County	20.9	73.6	2.8	0.6	2.0
Carmel, IN	Hamilton County	36.7	56.0	5.8	0.2	1.2
Cedar Falls, IA	Black Hawk County	50.0	42.7	3.7	0.9	2.7
Cedar Park, TX	Williamson County	41.3	50.9	5.0	1.0	1.8
Central, LA	East Baton Rouge Parish	52.3	43.1	2.5	0.8	1.2
Chapel Hill, NC	Orange County	72.8	22.5	2.9	0.6	1.2
Cheshire, CT	New Haven County	54.2	42.0	2.4	1.3	0.1
Chino Hills, CA	San Bernardino County	52.1	41.5	3.2	1.6	1.6
Cibolo, TX	Guadalupe County	31.6	63.0	3.5	0.7	1.1
Cicero, NY	Onondaga County	53.9	40.1	4.1	1.5	0.4
Collierville, TN	Shelby County	61.9	34.5	2.1	0.6	0.9
Coppell, TX	Dallas County	60.2	34.3	3.1	0.8	1.5
Cornelius, NC	Mecklenburg County	62.3	32.9	3.3	0.3	1.3
Cranberry, PA	Butler County	29.2	65.7	3.1	0.6	1.4
Crown Point, IN	Lake County	57.7	37.3	3.8	0.4	0.8
Dublin, OH	Franklin County	59.8	33.9	3.4	1.0	1.9
East Fishkill, NY	Dutchess County	47.5	47.2	2.7	1.5	1.0
Eden Prairie, MN	Hennepin County	63.1	28.2	3.6	1.5	3.6
Edmond, OK	Oklahoma County	41.2	51.7	7.1	0.0	0.0
Edwardsville, IL	Madison County	38.9	54.1	4.2	1.4	1.4
Evesham, NJ	Burlington County	55.0	40.3	2.2	1.1	1.4
Flower Mound, TX	Denton County	37.1	57.1	3.9	0.9	1.0
Folsom, CA	Sacramento County	58.0	33.8	4.3	1.8	2.2
Friendswood, TX	Galveston County	35.5	60.0	3.3	0.7	0.5
Gaines, MI	Kent County	44.6	47.7	4.6	1.3	1.9
Glastonbury, CT	Hartford County	59.1	36.4	2.9	1.4	0.2
Grand Blanc, MI	Genesee County	52.0	42.6	3.1	1.1	1.2
Hampden, PA	Cumberland County	38.1	55.9	3.2	0.8	2.0
Hilliard, OH	Franklin County	59.8	33.9	3.4	1.0	1.9
Hillsborough, NJ	Somerset County	54.5	41.7	2.4	1.0	0.4
Holly Springs, NC	Wake County	57.4	37.2	3.7	0.3	1.4
Independence, KY	Kenton County	33.6	59.7	4.3	1.0	1.4
Juneau, AK	House Districts 33 & 34	52.7	34.5	5.8	2.8	4.2
Kaysville, UT	Davis County	20.5	44.4	3.8	0.6	30.7
Keller, TX	Tarrant County	43.1	51.7	3.6	0.8	0.7
Lafayette, CA	Contra Costa County	67.5	24.5	3.4	1.8	2.8
Lafayette, CO	Boulder County	70.3	22.0	4.3	2.0	1.4
Lake Oswego, OR	Clackamas County	47.7	41.3	5.2	1.9	4.0
Laramie, WY	Albany County	40.4	44.6	8.2	2.0	4.9
Leander, TX	Williamson County	41.3	50.9	5.0	1.0	1.8
Leawood, KS	Johnson County	44.1	46.7	5.2	1.7	2.3
Lee's Summit, MO	Jackson County	55.5	38.1	3.6	1.2	1.7
Leesburg, VA	Loudoun County	55.1	38.2	3.1	0.7	2.9
Lehi, UT	Utah County	14.0	50.2	3.2	0.5	32.2
Lexington, MA	Middlesex County	65.3	27.6	4.1	1.3	1.7
Los Altos, CA	Santa Clara County	72.7	20.6	3.6	1.8	1.3
Loveland, CO	Larimer County	47.5	42.6	5.9	1.6	2.4
Lower Macungie, PA	Lehigh County	50.0	45.3	2.5	0.9	1.4
Madison, AL	Madison County	38.4	54.8	4.1	0.8	1.9
Madison, MS	Madison County	40.6	56.4	1.7	0.3	1.1
Maple Valley, WA	King County	69.8	21.0	4.0	1.7	3.4
Marion, IA	Linn County	50.3	41.3	4.7	0.9	2.7

Table continued on next page.

City	Area Covered	Clinton	Trump	Johnson	Stein	Other
Marlboro, NJ	Monmouth County	43.2	52.5	2.0	1.0	1.3
Mason, OH	Warren County	28.5	65.6	3.7	0.6	1.6
Menomonee Falls, WI	Waukesha County	33.3	60.0	3.7	0.7	2.2
Meridian, ID	Ada County	38.7	47.9	5.1	1.6	6.7
Meridian, MI	Ingham County	59.9	33.2	4.0	1.4	1.5
Merrimack, NH	Hillsborough County	46.5	46.7	4.3	0.8	1.7
Milton, GA	Fulton County	67.7	26.8	3.6	0.1	1.8
Moon, PA	Allegheny County	55.9	39.5	2.5	0.8	1.4
Moorpark, CA	Ventura County	54.6	37.2	3.8	1.8	2.6
Morgantown, WV	Monongalia County	40.0	50.1	5.0	2.2	2.7
Mount Pleasant, SC	Charleston County	50.6	42.8	4.1	1.0	1.5
Newark, DE	New Castle County	62.0	32.5	3.5	1.5	0.6
Newtown, CT	Fairfield County	57.9	38.0	2.8	1.2	0.2
North Attleborough, MA	Bristol County	51.4	41.8	4.0	1.5	1.3
North Port, FL	Sarasota County	42.3	53.8	2.0	0.7	1.2
North Ridgeville, OH	Lorain County	47.6	47.5	3.2	0.9	0.7
Northville, MI	Wayne County	66.4	29.3	2.4	1.0	1.0
O'Fallon, MO	St. Charles County	33.8	59.9	3.9	0.8	1.6
Orchard Park, NY	Erie County	50.9	44.5	3.0	1.5	0.2
Oro Valley, AZ	Pima County	53.3	39.7	3.7	1.5	1.8
Oviedo, FL	Seminole County	46.6	48.1	3.0	0.9	1.5
Parker, CO	Douglas County	36.6	54.7	5.4	0.8	2.4
Parkland, FL	Broward County	66.1	31.2	1.3	0.6	0.8
Peachtree City, GA	Fayette County	37.9	57.0	3.4	0.2	1.6
Pittsfield, MI	Washtenaw County	67.6	26.6	3.1	1.3	1.4
Plainfield, IL	Will County	49.9	43.6	3.9	1.3	1.3
Pleasant Grove, UT	Utah County	14.0	50.2	3.2	0.5	32.2
Poway, CA	San Diego County	56.3	36.6	4.0	1.7	1.4
Princeton, NJ	Mercer County	66.3	29.2	2.1	1.1	1.4
Queen Creek, AZ	Maricopa County	44.8	47.7	4.3	1.2	2.0
Radnor, PA	Delaware County	59.3	37.0	2.0	0.9	0.9
Randolph, NJ	Morris County	45.5	49.7	2.3	1.0	1.5
Rexburg, ID	Madison County	7.7	57.0	3.9	0.4	31.0
Rio Rancho, NM	Sandoval County	44.9	42.0	10.8	1.0	1.3
Rye, NY	Westchester County	64.9	31.2	1.9	1.0	1.0
Sammamish, WA	King County	69.8	21.0	4.0	1.7	3.4
San Ramon, CA	Contra Costa County	67.5	24.5	3.4	1.8	2.8
Saratoga, CA	Santa Clara County	72.7	20.6	3.6	1.8	1.3
Shrewsbury, MA	Worcester County	51.0	40.4	5.4	1.5	1.7
South Brunswick, NJ	Middlesex County	58.8	37.4	1.7	1.1	1.1
South Jordan, UT	Salt Lake County	41.5	32.6	3.8	1.2	20.9
South Kingstown, RI	Washington County	50.8	41.0	3.8	1.6	2.7
South Portland, ME	Cumberland County	59.9	33.6	4.3	1.9	0.3
Sparks, NV	Washoe County	46.4	45.1	4.4	0.0	4.0
State College, PA	Centre County	48.0	45.6	3.4	1.0	1.9
Sugar Land, TX	Fort Bend County	51.4	44.8	2.6	0.7	0.5
Sun Prairie, WI	Dane County	70.4	23.0	3.4	1.4	1.8
Syracuse, UT	Davis County	20.5	44.4	3.8	0.6	30.7
Tredyffrin, PA	Chester County	51.9	42.5	2.9	0.8	1.8
Upper Dublin, PA	Montgomery County	58.4	37.1	2.5	0.8	1.2
Urbandale, IA	Polk County	51.7	40.4	4.3	0.8	2.8
Vestal, NY	Broome County	45.6	47.6	3.8	1.8	1.3
Vestavia Hills, AL	Jefferson County	51.6	44.3	2.2	0.5	1.4
Webster, NY	Monroe County	54.2	39.3	3.8	1.5	1.2
Wellesley, MA	Norfolk County	60.3	32.6	4.2	1.1	1.8
West Fargo, ND	Cass County	38.8	49.3	7.5	1.5	2.9
West Lafayette, IN	Tippecanoe County	43.1	48.6	6.3	0.5	1.5
Weston, FL	Broward County	66.1	31.2	1.3	0.6	0.8
Wilmette, IL	Cook County	73.9	20.8	2.7	1.5	1.1
Yorba Linda, CA	Orange County	50.9	42.3	3.9	1.5	1.4
Zionsville, IN	Boone County	31.3	60.4	6.8	0.2	1.2
U.S.	U.S.	48.0	45.9	3.3	1.1	1.7

Note: Results are percentages and may not add to 100% due to rounding
Source: Dave Leip's Atlas of U.S. Presidential Elections

House Price Index (HPI)

Metro Area[1]	National Ranking[3]	Quarterly Change (%)	One-Year Change (%)	Five-Year Change (%)
Aberdeen, SD	n/a	n/a	n/a	n/a
Aliso Viejo, CA[2]	118	1.26	6.37	45.90
Allen, TX[2]	20	1.01	10.57	57.15
Ames, IA	n/r	n/a	7.41	26.00
Amherst, MA	202	-0.43	3.56	9.58
Apex, NC	95	0.62	7.09	29.98
Beavercreek, OH	136	0.69	5.68	15.17
Bellevue, NE	110	0.37	6.59	22.66
Bend, OR	49	0.93	9.28	84.38
Benicia, CA	31	2.33	10.09	87.20
Bentonville, AR	105	0.51	6.77	28.33
Bethlehem, NY	192	0.96	3.96	9.14
Blacksburg, VA	179	1.46	4.26	10.88
Bowie, MD[2]	178	0.59	4.26	24.94
Bozeman, MT	n/a	n/a	n/a	n/a
Brentwood, TN	25	1.67	10.32	48.69
Burlington, VT	200	1.29	3.69	12.41
Cabot, AR	182	0.46	4.21	10.91
Carmel, IN	117	0.65	6.40	22.61
Cedar Falls, IA	247	-0.97	-0.30	8.25
Cedar Park, TX	85	0.63	7.61	55.90
Central, LA	154	0.07	5.26	18.27
Chapel Hill, NC	54	0.98	9.08	28.49
Cheshire, CT	232	1.10	1.90	3.96
Chino Hills, CA	56	1.84	9.05	67.18
Cibolo, TX	81	1.04	7.81	34.40
Cicero, NY	226	-2.00	2.51	9.09
Collierville, TN	165	-1.27	4.84	19.45
Coppell, TX[2]	20	1.01	10.57	57.15
Cornelius, NC	80	0.07	7.93	35.37
Cranberry, PA	186	0.79	4.10	19.67
Crown Point, IN[2]	173	0.34	4.41	15.32
Dublin, OH	72	-0.08	8.20	30.85
East Fishkill, NY[2]	208	-0.39	3.44	10.16
Eden Prairie, MN	94	0.10	7.14	32.42
Edmond, OK	206	-1.23	3.46	19.45
Edwardsville, IL	146	0.66	5.38	17.44
Evesham, NJ[2]	231	0.47	2.08	9.04
Flower Mound, TX[2]	20	1.01	10.57	57.15
Folsom, CA	24	1.84	10.34	67.38
Friendswood, TX	149	1.74	5.34	40.98
Gaines, MI	33	-0.39	10.01	43.75
Glastonbury, CT	244	-0.78	0.78	2.23
Grand Blanc, MI	91	-0.63	7.31	40.14
Hampden, PA	224	1.40	2.62	9.23
Hilliard, OH	72	-0.08	8.20	30.85
Hillsborough, NJ[2]	213	0.97	3.29	14.23
Holly Springs, NC	95	0.62	7.09	29.98
Independence, KY	120	0.30	6.32	19.53
Juneau, AK	n/a	n/a	n/a	n/a
Kaysville, UT	18	1.67	10.80	39.80
Keller, TX[2]	15	1.36	11.00	48.21
Lafayette, CA[2]	34	2.16	9.81	74.66
Lafayette, CO	48	1.86	9.30	60.66
Lake Oswego, OR	78	0.16	8.04	61.46
Laramie, WY	n/a	n/a	n/a	n/a
Leander, TX	85	0.63	7.61	55.90
Leawood, KS	103	0.21	6.79	27.28
Lee's Summit, MO	103	0.21	6.79	27.28
Leesburg, VA[2]	178	0.59	4.26	24.94
Lehi, UT	41	0.30	9.55	45.03
Lexington, MA[2]	93	0.75	7.15	31.86
Los Altos, CA	83	1.44	7.77	65.37
Loveland, CO	44	0.28	9.43	58.82
Lower Macungie, PA	168	0.38	4.57	11.64
Madison, AL	229	1.40	2.35	7.47
Madison, MS	250	-0.13	-1.24	7.97
Maple Valley, WA[2]	2	1.73	14.34	69.01

Table continued on next page.

Metro Area[1]	National Ranking[3]	Quarterly Change (%)	One-Year Change (%)	Five-Year Change (%)
Marion, IA	215	-0.27	3.18	9.54
Marlboro, NJ[2]	148	1.22	5.35	20.60
Mason, OH	120	0.30	6.32	19.53
Menomonee Falls, WI	157	0.11	5.20	17.25
Meridian, ID	7	1.26	12.29	62.51
Meridian, MI	127	-0.08	6.09	27.73
Merrimack, NH	96	1.00	7.05	22.90
Milton, GA	69	0.94	8.31	48.08
Moon, PA	186	0.79	4.10	19.67
Moorpark, CA	114	1.43	6.44	47.48
Morgantown, WV	n/r	n/a	-0.30	13.09
Mount Pleasant, SC	53	1.29	9.10	47.71
Newark, DE[2]	233	0.85	1.89	10.18
Newtown, CT	240	0.23	1.19	6.28
North Attleborough, MA	119	0.64	6.36	22.49
North Port, FL	77	1.91	8.05	68.92
North Ridgeville, OH	177	-0.82	4.38	18.06
Northville, MI[2]	86	0.52	7.51	44.53
O'Fallon, MO	146	0.66	5.38	17.44
Orchard Park, NY	111	0.42	6.57	23.19
Oro Valley, AZ	70	0.38	8.30	30.79
Oviedo, FL	28	1.99	10.23	61.52
Parker, CO	23	1.45	10.35	67.81
Parkland, FL[2]	73	0.58	8.17	62.29
Peachtree City, GA	69	0.94	8.31	48.08
Pittsfield, MI	68	-0.86	8.31	42.37
Plainfield, IL[2]	169	0.37	4.56	22.32
Pleasant Grove, UT	41	0.30	9.55	45.03
Poway, CA	74	1.34	8.14	51.58
Princeton, NJ	234	1.68	1.83	8.55
Queen Creek, AZ	55	1.14	9.05	59.50
Radnor, PA[2]	99	0.25	6.92	20.17
Randolph, NJ[2]	213	0.97	3.29	14.23
Rexburg, ID	n/a	n/a	n/a	n/a
Rio Rancho, NM	184	-0.26	4.18	14.18
Rye, NY[2]	148	1.22	5.35	20.60
Sammamish, WA[2]	2	1.73	14.34	69.01
San Ramon, CA[2]	34	2.16	9.81	74.66
Saratoga, CA	83	1.44	7.77	65.37
Shrewsbury, MA	121	0.74	6.27	20.53
South Brunswick, NJ[2]	148	1.22	5.35	20.60
South Jordan, UT	22	1.27	10.46	45.01
South Kingstown, RI	119	0.64	6.36	22.49
South Portland, ME	109	0.32	6.61	22.23
Sparks, NV	11	2.69	11.81	93.61
State College, PA	n/r	n/a	2.07	17.01
Sugar Land, TX	149	1.74	5.34	40.98
Sun Prairie, WI	131	-0.22	5.95	20.83
Syracuse, UT	18	1.67	10.80	39.80
Tredyffrin, PA[2]	181	0.74	4.24	14.38
Upper Dublin, PA[2]	181	0.74	4.24	14.38
Urbandale, IA	150	0.04	5.34	21.64
Vestal, NY	n/r	n/a	2.16	1.50
Vestavia Hills, AL	153	0.30	5.28	18.93
Webster, NY	183	-0.11	4.20	12.33
Wellesley, MA[2]	108	0.48	6.71	30.49
West Fargo, ND	225	-0.33	2.56	33.44
West Lafayette, IN	158	1.29	5.18	19.20
Weston, FL[2]	73	0.58	8.17	62.29
Wilmette, IL[2]	169	0.37	4.56	22.32
Yorba Linda, CA[2]	118	1.26	6.37	45.90
Zionsville, IN	117	0.65	6.40	22.61
U.S.[4]	–	1.61	6.68	34.71

Note: The HPI is a weighted repeat sales index. It measures average price changes in repeat sales or refinancings on the same properties. This information is obtained by reviewing repeat mortgage transactions on single-family properties whose mortgages have been purchased or securitized by Fannie Mae or Freddie Mac in January 1975; (1) figures cover the Metropolitan Statistical Area (MSA) unless noted otherwise—see Appendix B for areas included; (2) Metropolitan Division—see Appendix B for areas included; (3) Rankings are based on annual percentage change, for all MSAs containing at least 15,000 transactions over the last 10 years and ranges from 1 to 253; (4) figures based on a weighted division average; all figures are for the period ended December 31, 2017; n/a not available; n/r not ranked
Source: Federal Housing Finance Agency, House Price Index, February 28, 2018

Home Value Distribution: City

Area	Under $50,000	$50,000 -$99,999	$100,000 -$149,999	$150,000 -$199,999	$200,000 -$299,999	$300,000 -$499,999	$500,000 -$999,999	$1,000,000 or more
Aberdeen, SD	9.5	19.3	26.8	20.9	13.1	8.8	1.3	0.3
Aliso Viejo, CA	1.5	0.0	0.4	1.1	5.6	35.9	49.8	5.6
Allen, TX	1.1	3.5	12.1	21.3	30.2	24.2	7.0	0.8
Ames, IA	6.8	3.4	23.1	27.3	24.3	12.7	2.3	0.1
Amherst, MA	1.9	0.5	1.0	5.9	26.6	48.5	15.7	0.0
Apex, NC	1.6	0.7	5.4	13.7	37.4	36.6	4.2	0.3
Beavercreek, OH	1.4	4.9	23.1	32.6	26.7	9.9	1.0	0.3
Bellevue, NE	3.7	11.5	46.1	27.5	8.7	2.0	0.5	0.1
Bend, OR	6.3	2.3	7.1	10.4	25.2	31.6	14.8	2.4
Benicia, CA	2.6	1.7	2.0	4.1	8.1	36.4	44.1	1.0
Bentonville, AR	2.7	11.3	22.7	18.2	21.1	17.7	5.8	0.6
Bethlehem, NY	3.0	0.9	3.6	15.7	38.4	32.3	5.4	0.6
Blacksburg, VA	5.8	1.3	3.7	10.8	36.7	31.5	9.6	0.7
Bowie, MD	2.3	1.0	2.0	8.5	35.0	45.1	5.5	0.6
Bozeman, MT	4.3	2.6	4.7	10.8	35.4	31.0	10.4	0.9
Brentwood, TN	1.2	0.6	1.0	2.0	4.4	32.9	49.7	8.2
Burlington, VT	3.1	1.4	3.1	15.4	37.5	29.0	9.5	0.9
Cabot, AR	2.8	11.4	39.2	26.2	16.3	3.7	0.3	0.1
Carmel, IN	1.2	1.8	4.6	10.6	30.4	34.2	15.1	2.1
Cedar Falls, IA	6.5	6.7	21.7	27.8	22.9	11.7	2.5	0.1
Cedar Park, TX	2.2	1.6	10.3	21.8	37.9	23.5	2.5	0.2
Central, LA	8.6	3.8	18.8	23.2	28.2	14.4	2.2	0.8
Chapel Hill, NC	1.1	2.0	6.2	6.4	16.2	36.0	27.9	4.1
Cheshire, CT	1.6	1.5	3.9	4.7	28.8	48.9	9.9	0.7
Chino Hills, CA	2.3	1.0	1.1	1.7	5.7	31.9	52.2	4.1
Cibolo, TX	2.6	3.8	9.3	30.3	45.3	8.1	0.6	0.0
Cicero, NY	3.4	14.9	32.0	21.1	22.3	5.2	0.7	0.3
Collierville, TN	1.8	2.2	3.4	9.7	40.9	35.5	6.0	0.5
Coppell, TX	3.9	0.7	3.6	10.2	27.4	39.2	13.6	1.6
Cornelius, NC	2.2	2.0	14.9	14.2	26.6	18.9	12.6	8.6
Cranberry, PA	3.9	3.1	9.1	13.6	26.5	33.3	9.4	1.0
Crown Point, IN	3.5	3.9	19.1	36.0	25.1	8.4	3.4	0.5
Dublin, OH	1.4	2.3	4.0	4.6	21.1	50.8	15.2	0.6
East Fishkill, NY	2.1	0.8	1.4	4.2	25.8	49.2	16.2	0.5
Eden Prairie, MN	1.9	1.6	6.8	10.6	24.9	34.9	17.0	2.3
Edmond, OK	2.7	4.1	18.9	22.5	23.3	19.2	8.2	1.1
Edwardsville, IL	2.1	9.4	23.7	16.4	27.8	15.1	4.5	1.1
Evesham, NJ	1.8	0.5	5.0	11.9	40.3	35.9	4.5	0.1
Flower Mound, TX	1.6	1.0	4.7	12.8	32.4	35.9	10.6	1.0
Folsom, CA	3.2	1.5	0.7	1.8	10.9	51.6	29.4	0.9
Friendswood, TX	2.6	4.6	20.2	13.1	21.2	28.8	8.3	1.2
Gaines, MI	16.4	6.3	20.9	27.9	19.5	7.2	1.5	0.4
Glastonbury, CT	2.1	1.0	3.7	7.9	22.9	41.2	19.8	1.3
Grand Blanc, MI	9.2	17.6	27.5	19.0	19.6	5.3	0.7	1.0
Hampden, PA	5.2	2.4	8.1	16.3	35.1	26.7	5.1	1.0
Hilliard, OH	1.2	4.7	20.2	18.7	36.0	18.3	0.9	0.0
Hillsborough, NJ	1.4	0.4	1.6	3.1	25.6	37.3	30.0	0.7
Holly Springs, NC	1.5	2.1	6.0	17.0	36.6	31.0	5.4	0.4
Independence, KY	3.6	6.6	31.7	34.3	19.4	4.2	0.1	0.2
Juneau, AK	4.7	2.6	3.0	5.8	25.2	47.4	10.8	0.6
Kaysville, UT	3.1	0.4	4.1	12.9	35.4	34.9	7.1	2.1
Keller, TX	2.0	2.6	8.3	7.4	26.8	37.3	14.4	1.1
Lafayette, CA	0.5	0.2	0.1	0.2	0.8	2.4	33.7	62.1
Lafayette, CO	5.4	1.3	5.2	7.4	28.4	34.6	15.9	1.7
Lake Oswego, OR	0.5	1.2	3.3	3.2	8.1	32.8	40.1	10.9
Laramie, WY	11.9	3.1	10.6	22.0	31.6	19.2	1.3	0.3
Leander, TX	2.7	2.5	26.1	25.3	21.8	15.2	6.0	0.3
Leawood, KS	1.6	0.5	2.9	3.2	16.0	43.8	26.0	6.0
Lee's Summit, MO	2.3	5.2	18.6	25.7	28.7	16.5	2.7	0.3
Leesburg, VA	2.4	1.1	1.7	4.5	17.6	46.0	26.4	0.3
Lehi, UT	1.9	1.0	3.0	14.9	42.3	31.5	4.9	0.5
Lexington, MA	0.9	0.7	0.3	1.2	1.6	11.0	57.8	26.5
Los Altos, CA	0.7	0.2	0.4	0.2	1.0	1.5	5.5	90.5
Loveland, CO	4.0	1.0	3.7	21.9	42.5	21.3	4.8	0.8
Lower Macungie, PA	6.2	4.3	7.2	12.7	34.9	31.2	3.2	0.3
Madison, AL	1.5	4.8	12.2	22.9	28.5	25.7	3.8	0.5
Madison, MS	1.3	2.4	7.7	20.9	34.9	24.3	6.9	1.6
Maple Valley, WA	1.6	0.3	1.7	7.8	34.6	46.5	6.8	0.6

Table continued on next page.

Area	Under $50,000	$50,000 -$99,999	$100,000 -$149,999	$150,000 -$199,999	$200,000 -$299,999	$300,000 -$499,999	$500,000 -$999,999	$1,000,000 or more
Marion, IA	9.3	8.6	29.4	25.3	18.2	7.7	1.3	0.1
Marlboro, NJ	2.6	1.7	0.6	1.2	7.7	34.7	47.7	3.8
Mason, OH	2.5	5.8	16.8	18.5	22.3	25.9	7.1	1.1
Menomonee Falls, WI	2.1	1.9	5.1	28.1	35.7	23.2	3.7	0.3
Meridian, ID	2.9	3.4	14.1	30.1	32.8	14.8	1.5	0.3
Meridian, MI	3.2	10.7	19.1	23.4	24.7	14.4	3.8	0.8
Merrimack, NH	2.2	1.3	9.1	13.7	44.0	27.6	1.9	0.2
Milton, GA	1.4	1.7	3.1	8.0	12.3	27.3	39.1	7.1
Moon, PA	2.8	9.4	17.2	23.7	26.0	17.4	3.3	0.2
Moorpark, CA	1.4	1.6	1.1	1.0	3.5	29.5	56.6	5.2
Morgantown, WV	8.0	9.1	15.6	26.8	21.6	12.7	5.5	0.6
Mount Pleasant, SC	1.2	1.1	3.7	5.7	16.4	39.8	26.6	5.4
Newark, DE	1.4	1.5	8.2	9.0	44.2	32.6	2.6	0.6
Newtown, CT	1.9	0.4	1.7	2.9	15.7	46.5	28.1	3.0
North Attleborough, MA	2.8	2.4	4.3	6.1	28.6	42.1	12.9	0.8
North Port, FL	5.6	18.8	27.1	23.9	15.9	7.6	1.1	0.1
North Ridgeville, OH	5.0	10.0	28.7	26.4	26.9	2.6	0.1	0.3
Northville, MI	2.3	7.6	6.7	6.1	14.9	35.0	25.5	2.0
O'Fallon, MO	3.9	2.7	17.3	27.2	37.8	9.7	1.1	0.3
Orchard Park, NY	1.1	4.4	18.3	18.5	28.4	24.5	4.3	0.5
Oro Valley, AZ	2.8	1.6	3.4	10.7	37.7	30.4	11.6	1.7
Oviedo, FL	1.1	2.4	12.0	18.9	35.1	26.6	3.7	0.2
Parker, CO	1.1	0.6	3.3	5.1	29.7	51.3	8.8	0.1
Parkland, FL	0.8	2.1	0.4	1.4	7.2	40.1	43.2	4.7
Peachtree City, GA	1.8	2.3	5.4	12.4	33.2	34.9	9.5	0.5
Pittsfield, MI	7.0	2.1	8.6	17.1	28.4	27.6	8.2	0.9
Plainfield, IL	1.4	0.8	2.8	11.6	40.3	39.5	3.3	0.3
Pleasant Grove, UT	2.9	2.0	11.6	20.8	33.3	23.0	5.9	0.5
Poway, CA	2.5	2.3	1.2	1.4	2.9	29.2	46.9	13.5
Princeton, NJ	0.9	1.1	0.5	0.5	2.9	10.4	50.8	32.8
Queen Creek, AZ	2.2	0.9	5.7	14.7	32.2	35.9	8.1	0.4
Radnor, PA	1.0	0.2	3.0	3.1	6.5	22.7	45.7	17.8
Randolph, NJ	1.1	0.6	0.3	0.9	5.3	41.0	48.6	2.1
Rexburg, ID	8.2	2.7	18.8	31.5	29.5	8.0	0.9	0.4
Rio Rancho, NM	2.9	6.5	23.7	29.0	26.9	9.4	1.4	0.1
Rye, NY	1.4	2.8	1.8	2.4	6.5	31.2	44.7	9.2
Sammamish, WA	0.7	0.1	0.4	1.3	5.1	21.4	62.3	8.7
San Ramon, CA	0.8	0.5	0.5	0.7	2.3	7.8	64.6	22.8
Saratoga, CA	1.6	0.4	0.1	0.7	1.1	1.5	8.3	86.3
Shrewsbury, MA	2.7	0.6	2.5	3.9	19.9	44.7	24.6	1.0
South Brunswick, NJ	2.5	1.7	1.8	3.0	13.0	48.6	28.4	1.0
South Jordan, UT	1.6	0.0	0.7	5.7	25.9	53.0	12.9	0.2
South Kingstown, RI	2.1	1.0	3.2	5.7	27.3	45.5	13.8	1.5
South Portland, ME	3.2	1.2	5.2	26.3	39.6	21.2	2.8	0.5
Sparks, NV	5.4	7.4	14.0	20.2	30.8	19.6	2.2	0.5
State College, PA	2.4	2.1	5.0	11.4	37.3	32.8	8.6	0.4
Sugar Land, TX	1.3	1.2	10.6	14.6	26.9	30.5	13.0	1.9
Sun Prairie, WI	1.6	0.9	12.5	32.4	38.3	13.4	0.6	0.2
Syracuse, UT	2.9	0.5	5.3	16.4	44.8	28.3	1.3	0.5
Tredyffrin, PA	2.0	0.6	1.1	7.4	12.0	29.6	39.2	8.2
Upper Dublin, PA	2.0	0.5	1.5	2.6	18.4	49.5	24.9	0.6
Urbandale, IA	2.3	5.0	12.5	28.4	33.0	14.2	4.0	0.6
Vestal, NY	4.8	19.1	27.2	21.4	16.3	8.1	2.4	0.6
Vestavia Hills, AL	2.1	2.0	3.8	7.4	23.7	38.1	21.1	1.7
Webster, NY	2.8	4.4	25.5	31.9	26.1	7.1	1.5	0.7
Wellesley, MA	0.4	0.3	0.6	0.4	1.3	4.6	44.4	48.0
West Fargo, ND	5.0	6.6	18.8	23.0	27.8	15.8	2.9	0.1
West Lafayette, IN	1.7	2.3	23.7	25.5	26.0	18.2	2.7	0.0
Weston, FL	2.0	0.6	3.4	7.2	13.6	39.5	29.3	4.5
Wilmette, IL	1.4	0.4	1.2	2.3	5.9	25.6	40.5	22.7
Yorba Linda, CA	1.4	1.2	0.4	0.3	1.8	11.4	63.2	20.3
Zionsville, IN	2.2	1.6	4.4	10.2	21.2	38.0	19.3	3.1
U.S.	8.8	14.8	15.3	14.9	18.4	16.4	9.0	2.5

Note: Figures are percentages and cover owner-occupied housing units.
Source: U.S. Census Bureau, 2012-2016 American Community Survey 5-Year Estimates

Home Value Distribution: Metro Area

MSA[1]	Under $50,000	$50,000 -$99,999	$100,000 -$149,999	$150,000 -$199,999	$200,000 -$299,999	$300,000 -$499,999	$500,000 -$999,999	$1,000,000 or more
Aberdeen, SD	13.2	17.8	20.1	19.0	16.0	11.5	2.0	0.4
Aliso Viejo, CA	2.9	1.8	1.8	2.7	9.8	32.0	37.2	11.8
Allen, TX	6.4	17.3	20.6	17.5	18.4	13.4	4.9	1.5
Ames, IA	6.7	8.4	25.0	23.3	21.6	11.4	2.8	0.8
Amherst, MA	3.4	3.7	13.9	23.7	31.8	19.1	3.9	0.5
Apex, NC	4.5	6.5	16.2	18.2	24.8	21.9	6.9	1.1
Beavercreek, OH	9.2	29.4	23.2	17.2	13.5	5.9	1.3	0.3
Bellevue, NE	5.3	14.9	28.7	19.5	18.7	9.8	2.5	0.6
Bend, OR	5.0	4.9	8.6	12.4	25.0	26.5	15.6	2.0
Benicia, CA	4.4	3.0	6.4	10.2	24.8	36.8	13.3	1.3
Bentonville, AR	8.1	17.7	23.4	18.5	16.8	11.0	3.7	0.8
Bethlehem, NY	5.2	8.1	14.3	22.3	29.1	17.1	3.4	0.5
Blacksburg, VA	9.6	15.7	18.1	19.8	19.3	12.5	4.2	0.7
Bowie, MD	2.2	1.4	3.2	6.9	19.4	33.8	27.5	5.6
Bozeman, MT	6.8	2.6	5.1	10.9	29.1	28.5	13.1	3.9
Brentwood, TN	4.3	10.1	21.3	19.3	20.8	15.7	7.0	1.5
Burlington, VT	4.6	2.5	6.3	14.9	36.8	26.1	7.7	1.1
Cabot, AR	10.0	20.5	23.2	18.6	16.0	8.5	2.4	0.8
Carmel, IN	7.3	19.7	25.6	17.9	15.6	9.9	3.3	0.7
Cedar Falls, IA	8.7	22.6	25.0	20.1	15.4	6.4	1.4	0.4
Cedar Park, TX	4.5	6.2	14.1	18.3	24.9	20.4	9.3	2.2
Central, LA	10.9	14.1	17.6	21.1	20.5	11.6	3.3	0.8
Chapel Hill, NC	5.5	8.9	16.7	18.1	21.9	19.1	8.4	1.4
Cheshire, CT	3.0	4.8	11.2	17.5	28.8	25.8	7.7	1.2
Chino Hills, CA	7.0	5.7	8.7	12.0	24.4	30.2	10.6	1.5
Cibolo, TX	9.3	23.2	19.7	17.1	16.1	10.0	3.6	0.9
Cicero, NY	7.6	26.1	26.9	17.4	13.8	5.9	1.8	0.5
Collierville, TN	11.0	25.0	19.6	15.8	16.3	8.7	2.9	0.7
Coppell, TX	6.4	17.3	20.6	17.5	18.4	13.4	4.9	1.5
Cornelius, NC	6.1	14.6	20.8	17.6	19.3	14.2	5.9	1.5
Cranberry, PA	11.1	23.5	20.5	17.3	15.2	9.3	2.7	0.5
Crown Point, IN	4.3	9.3	14.7	17.5	24.1	19.7	8.4	2.1
Dublin, OH	5.9	16.9	21.7	19.7	19.7	12.0	3.6	0.5
East Fishkill, NY	2.8	1.8	2.9	5.0	16.2	37.0	26.9	7.3
Eden Prairie, MN	3.8	4.9	13.3	20.9	29.2	20.1	6.6	1.2
Edmond, OK	9.1	21.0	23.8	19.0	15.7	8.0	2.7	0.6
Edwardsville, IL	8.2	17.8	19.7	19.1	19.7	10.9	3.8	0.9
Evesham, NJ	4.7	7.9	10.8	15.6	27.1	23.9	8.5	1.4
Flower Mound, TX	6.4	17.3	20.6	17.5	18.4	13.4	4.9	1.5
Folsom, CA	4.5	3.1	6.0	10.5	23.8	34.2	16.1	1.9
Friendswood, TX	7.0	18.8	21.1	17.1	16.9	12.1	5.3	1.7
Gaines, MI	9.1	17.4	25.3	19.9	16.7	8.6	2.4	0.6
Glastonbury, CT	2.6	3.1	10.3	18.2	32.9	25.3	6.6	1.0
Grand Blanc, MI	26.8	27.5	21.6	12.3	7.8	3.0	0.9	0.3
Hampden, PA	6.2	10.8	19.7	24.6	23.8	11.4	2.8	0.5
Hilliard, OH	5.9	16.9	21.7	19.7	19.7	12.0	3.6	0.5
Hillsborough, NJ	2.8	1.8	2.9	5.0	16.2	37.0	26.9	7.3
Holly Springs, NC	4.5	6.5	16.2	18.2	24.8	21.9	6.9	1.1
Independence, KY	6.2	17.9	23.2	19.1	18.7	10.9	3.3	0.7
Juneau, AK	4.7	2.6	3.0	5.8	25.2	47.4	10.8	0.6
Kaysville, UT	4.6	4.2	16.5	22.3	29.1	18.7	3.7	0.8
Keller, TX	6.4	17.3	20.6	17.5	18.4	13.4	4.9	1.5
Lafayette, CA	2.2	1.4	1.7	2.3	6.5	19.6	44.2	22.3
Lafayette, CO	3.9	0.9	2.5	7.2	18.6	32.8	27.9	6.3
Lake Oswego, OR	4.8	1.8	5.2	12.0	30.0	31.9	12.6	1.6
Laramie, WY	11.0	3.5	10.7	17.8	30.4	20.5	4.0	2.2
Leander, TX	4.5	6.2	14.1	18.3	24.9	20.4	9.3	2.2
Leawood, KS	7.7	16.3	20.4	19.7	20.1	11.6	3.5	0.8
Lee's Summit, MO	7.7	16.3	20.4	19.7	20.1	11.6	3.5	0.8
Leesburg, VA	2.2	1.4	3.2	6.9	19.4	33.8	27.5	5.6
Lehi, UT	3.3	1.5	9.8	20.0	34.6	23.1	6.7	1.0
Lexington, MA	2.4	1.3	2.5	5.2	19.7	39.5	24.0	5.2
Los Altos, CA	2.3	1.9	1.2	1.2	3.2	14.4	46.3	29.5
Loveland, CO	5.4	1.6	3.9	12.2	32.3	32.3	10.9	1.4
Lower Macungie, PA	4.9	8.7	15.5	20.9	27.8	18.3	3.4	0.5
Madison, AL	7.9	16.7	18.8	18.4	21.4	12.9	3.1	0.8
Madison, MS	14.1	22.0	18.7	17.0	15.9	8.6	2.7	0.9
Maple Valley, WA	3.8	1.8	4.3	9.1	23.4	32.3	21.1	4.2

Table continued on next page.

MSA[1]	Under $50,000	$50,000 -$99,999	$100,000 -$149,999	$150,000 -$199,999	$200,000 -$299,999	$300,000 -$499,999	$500,000 -$999,999	$1,000,000 or more
Marion, IA	6.9	16.1	28.6	20.0	18.5	7.4	2.0	0.6
Marlboro, NJ	2.8	1.8	2.9	5.0	16.2	37.0	26.9	7.3
Mason, OH	6.2	17.9	23.2	19.1	18.7	10.9	3.3	0.7
Menomonee Falls, WI	4.5	10.3	16.9	20.3	26.6	15.8	4.7	0.9
Meridian, ID	5.4	10.4	21.1	21.4	22.4	14.6	4.1	0.5
Meridian, MI	10.8	23.6	22.8	20.1	15.2	5.9	1.3	0.3
Merrimack, NH	2.8	2.9	7.2	16.5	39.4	25.6	4.8	0.8
Milton, GA	6.2	15.7	18.4	17.5	18.9	15.6	6.4	1.3
Moon, PA	11.1	23.5	20.5	17.3	15.2	9.3	2.7	0.5
Moorpark, CA	3.0	2.3	1.7	2.0	9.0	35.5	39.7	6.9
Morgantown, WV	17.3	15.5	16.6	17.4	18.4	10.0	4.3	0.5
Mount Pleasant, SC	8.1	10.0	15.3	18.0	20.5	16.0	8.9	3.3
Newark, DE	4.7	7.9	10.8	15.6	27.1	23.9	8.5	1.4
Newtown, CT	2.2	2.0	3.5	6.7	16.3	29.4	25.6	14.2
North Attleborough, MA	3.2	2.7	8.3	17.8	32.8	26.3	7.5	1.5
North Port, FL	9.9	13.9	13.8	15.1	19.9	17.3	7.6	2.5
North Ridgeville, OH	8.6	22.5	23.1	17.8	16.7	8.5	2.3	0.6
Northville, MI	16.6	20.7	16.5	15.5	16.5	10.5	3.0	0.7
O'Fallon, MO	8.2	17.8	19.7	19.1	19.7	10.9	3.8	0.9
Orchard Park, NY	9.5	24.0	25.7	17.1	14.8	6.8	1.7	0.4
Oro Valley, AZ	10.1	15.5	19.6	18.2	18.1	12.4	5.1	1.0
Oviedo, FL	8.6	16.2	17.8	18.8	20.5	12.7	4.1	1.3
Parker, CO	3.4	2.7	6.5	12.3	28.6	31.1	13.1	2.3
Parkland, FL	6.9	12.4	12.9	14.2	21.3	20.0	8.8	3.4
Peachtree City, GA	6.2	15.7	18.4	17.5	18.9	15.6	6.4	1.3
Pittsfield, MI	7.6	9.2	11.6	16.7	25.0	21.1	7.6	1.2
Plainfield, IL	4.3	9.3	14.7	17.5	24.1	19.7	8.4	2.1
Pleasant Grove, UT	3.3	1.5	9.8	20.0	34.6	23.1	6.7	1.0
Poway, CA	3.8	2.2	2.0	2.9	10.7	36.5	33.8	8.1
Princeton, NJ	2.9	7.6	7.2	11.6	26.3	24.7	16.2	3.5
Queen Creek, AZ	7.8	11.0	15.0	17.2	22.3	17.9	7.0	1.8
Radnor, PA	4.7	7.9	10.8	15.6	27.1	23.9	8.5	1.4
Randolph, NJ	2.8	1.8	2.9	5.0	16.2	37.0	26.9	7.3
Rexburg, ID	8.4	9.9	20.9	22.9	23.2	10.9	2.8	1.0
Rio Rancho, NM	7.1	8.8	19.7	22.6	23.9	13.3	4.0	0.6
Rye, NY	2.8	1.8	2.9	5.0	16.2	37.0	26.9	7.3
Sammamish, WA	3.8	1.8	4.3	9.1	23.4	32.3	21.1	4.2
San Ramon, CA	2.2	1.4	1.7	2.3	6.5	19.6	44.2	22.3
Saratoga, CA	2.3	1.9	1.2	1.2	3.2	14.4	46.3	29.5
Shrewsbury, MA	2.6	2.8	9.1	18.8	32.9	25.6	7.4	0.9
South Brunswick, NJ	2.8	1.8	2.9	5.0	16.2	37.0	26.9	7.3
South Jordan, UT	4.3	2.1	11.1	18.7	30.7	23.9	8.1	1.1
South Kingstown, RI	3.2	2.7	8.3	17.8	32.8	26.3	7.5	1.5
South Portland, ME	4.7	3.9	9.1	18.1	32.6	22.5	7.6	1.5
Sparks, NV	6.5	7.6	11.1	14.8	25.9	22.8	8.8	2.5
State College, PA	7.2	7.7	12.5	20.7	27.4	17.0	6.3	1.2
Sugar Land, TX	7.0	18.8	21.1	17.1	16.9	12.1	5.3	1.7
Sun Prairie, WI	3.0	4.5	11.8	21.3	32.2	20.4	5.8	0.9
Syracuse, UT	4.6	4.2	16.5	22.3	29.1	18.7	3.7	0.8
Tredyffrin, PA	4.7	7.9	10.8	15.6	27.1	23.9	8.5	1.4
Upper Dublin, PA	4.7	7.9	10.8	15.6	27.1	23.9	8.5	1.4
Urbandale, IA	5.3	14.4	22.6	22.3	21.6	10.3	3.0	0.4
Vestal, NY	10.1	32.4	26.0	15.8	10.5	3.6	1.2	0.3
Vestavia Hills, AL	12.3	20.2	17.9	16.5	17.0	11.3	3.9	0.9
Webster, NY	6.9	22.0	29.1	19.3	14.3	6.4	1.7	0.4
Wellesley, MA	2.4	1.3	2.5	5.2	19.7	39.5	24.0	5.2
West Fargo, ND	5.0	8.7	22.1	23.4	25.6	12.5	2.5	0.3
West Lafayette, IN	7.2	24.5	26.4	17.0	15.0	7.9	1.8	0.3
Weston, FL	6.9	12.4	12.9	14.2	21.3	20.0	8.8	3.4
Wilmette, IL	4.3	9.3	14.7	17.5	24.1	19.7	8.4	2.1
Yorba Linda, CA	2.9	1.8	1.8	2.7	9.8	32.0	37.2	11.8
Zionsville, IN	7.3	19.7	25.6	17.9	15.6	9.9	3.3	0.7
U.S.	8.8	14.8	15.3	14.9	18.4	16.4	9.0	2.5

Note: (1) Figures cover the Metropolitan Statistical Area (MSA)—see Appendix B for areas included; Figures are percentages and cover owner-occupied housing units.
Source: U.S. Census Bureau, 2012-2016 American Community Survey 5-Year Estimates

Homeownership Rate

Metro Area	2009	2010	2011	2012	2013	2014	2015	2016	2017
Aberdeen, SD	n/a	n/a	n/a	n/a	n/a	n/a	n/a	n/a	n/a
Aliso Viejo, CA	50.4	49.7	50.1	49.9	48.7	49.0	49.1	47.1	49.1
Allen, TX	61.6	63.8	62.6	61.8	59.9	57.7	57.8	59.7	61.8
Ames, IA	n/a	n/a	n/a	n/a	n/a	n/a	n/a	n/a	n/a
Amherst, MA	n/a	n/a	n/a	n/a	n/a	n/a	n/a	n/a	n/a
Apex, NC	65.7	65.9	66.7	67.7	65.5	65.5	67.4	65.9	68.2
Beavercreek, OH	67.9	67.4	68.4	67.1	64.4	65.0	60.8	66.0	63.5
Bellevue, NE	73.1	73.2	71.6	72.4	70.6	68.7	69.6	69.2	65.5
Bend, OR	n/a	n/a	n/a	n/a	n/a	n/a	n/a	n/a	n/a
Benicia, CA	n/a	n/a	n/a	n/a	n/a	n/a	n/a	n/a	n/a
Bentonville, AR	n/a	n/a	n/a	n/a	n/a	n/a	n/a	n/a	n/a
Bethlehem, NY	71.1	72.8	72.4	70.6	67.9	67.5	65.9	61.3	64.1
Blacksburg, VA	n/a	n/a	n/a	n/a	n/a	n/a	n/a	n/a	n/a
Bowie, MD	67.2	67.3	67.6	66.9	66.0	65.0	64.6	63.1	63.3
Bozeman, MT	n/a	n/a	n/a	n/a	n/a	n/a	n/a	n/a	n/a
Brentwood, TN	71.8	70.4	69.6	64.9	63.9	67.1	67.4	65.0	69.4
Burlington, VT	n/a	n/a	n/a	n/a	n/a	n/a	n/a	n/a	n/a
Cabot, AR	n/a	n/a	n/a	n/a	n/a	n/a	65.8	64.9	61.0
Carmel, IN	71.0	68.8	68.3	67.1	67.5	66.9	64.6	63.9	63.9
Cedar Falls, IA	n/a	n/a	n/a	n/a	n/a	n/a	n/a	n/a	n/a
Cedar Park, TX	64.0	65.8	58.4	60.1	59.6	61.1	57.5	56.5	55.6
Central, LA	70.4	70.3	72.0	71.4	66.6	64.8	64.2	64.8	66.9
Chapel Hill, NC	n/a	n/a	n/a	n/a	n/a	n/a	n/a	n/a	n/a
Cheshire, CT	64.1	65.6	66.3	62.2	62.0	62.4	64.6	59.4	58.7
Chino Hills, CA	65.9	63.9	59.2	58.2	56.3	56.8	61.1	62.9	59.9
Cibolo, TX	69.8	70.1	66.5	67.5	70.1	70.2	66.0	61.6	62.5
Cicero, NY	61.3	61.1	61.5	57.0	58.9	60.4	62.8	61.0	63.1
Collierville, TN	61.5	61.9	60.1	60.5	56.2	57.2	59.6	61.8	62.4
Coppell, TX	61.6	63.8	62.6	61.8	59.9	57.7	57.8	59.7	61.8
Cornelius, NC	66.1	66.1	63.6	58.3	58.9	58.1	62.3	66.2	64.6
Cranberry, PA	71.7	70.4	70.3	67.9	68.3	69.1	71.0	72.2	72.7
Crown Point, IN	69.2	68.2	67.7	67.1	68.2	66.3	64.3	64.5	64.1
Dublin, OH	61.5	62.2	59.7	60.7	60.5	60.0	59.0	57.5	57.9
East Fishkill, NY	51.7	51.6	50.9	51.5	50.6	50.7	49.9	50.4	49.9
Eden Prairie, MN	70.9	71.2	69.1	70.8	71.7	69.7	67.9	69.1	70.1
Edmond, OK	69.0	70.0	69.6	67.3	67.6	65.7	61.4	63.1	64.7
Edwardsville, IL	72.5	72.2	71.1	72.0	72.7	71.1	68.7	66.4	65.6
Evesham, NJ	69.7	70.7	69.7	69.5	69.1	67.0	67.0	64.7	65.6
Flower Mound, TX	61.6	63.8	62.6	61.8	59.9	57.7	57.8	59.7	61.8
Folsom, CA	64.3	61.1	57.2	58.6	60.4	60.1	60.8	60.5	60.1
Friendswood, TX	63.6	61.4	61.3	62.1	60.5	60.4	60.3	59.0	58.9
Gaines, MI	75.6	76.4	76.4	76.9	73.7	71.6	75.8	76.2	71.7
Glastonbury, CT	72.1	71.3	71.4	70.8	69.8	68.5	66.1	63.7	66.5
Grand Blanc, MI	n/a	n/a	n/a	n/a	n/a	n/a	n/a	n/a	n/a
Hampden, PA	n/a	n/a	n/a	n/a	n/a	n/a	n/a	n/a	n/a
Hilliard, OH	61.5	62.2	59.7	60.7	60.5	60.0	59.0	57.5	57.9
Hillsborough, NJ	51.7	51.6	50.9	51.5	50.6	50.7	49.9	50.4	49.9
Holly Springs, NC	65.7	65.9	66.7	67.7	65.5	65.5	67.4	65.9	68.2
Independence, KY	62.4	62.8	65.2	63.4	63.3	65.5	65.9	64.9	65.7
Juneau, AK	n/a	n/a	n/a	n/a	n/a	n/a	n/a	n/a	n/a
Kaysville, UT	n/a	n/a	n/a	n/a	n/a	n/a	n/a	n/a	n/a
Keller, TX	61.6	63.8	62.6	61.8	59.9	57.7	57.8	59.7	61.8
Lafayette, CA	57.3	58.0	56.1	53.2	55.2	54.6	56.3	55.8	55.7
Lafayette, CO	n/a	n/a	n/a	n/a	n/a	n/a	n/a	n/a	n/a
Lake Oswego, OR	64.0	63.7	63.7	63.9	60.9	59.8	58.9	61.8	61.1
Laramie, WY	n/a	n/a	n/a	n/a	n/a	n/a	n/a	n/a	n/a
Leander, TX	64.0	65.8	58.4	60.1	59.6	61.1	57.5	56.5	55.6
Leawood, KS	69.5	68.8	68.5	65.1	65.6	66.1	65.0	62.4	62.4
Lee's Summit, MO	69.5	68.8	68.5	65.1	65.6	66.1	65.0	62.4	62.4
Leesburg, VA	67.2	67.3	67.6	66.9	66.0	65.0	64.6	63.1	63.3
Lehi, UT	n/a	n/a	n/a	n/a	n/a	n/a	n/a	n/a	n/a
Lexington, MA	65.5	66.0	65.5	66.0	66.3	62.8	59.3	58.9	58.8
Los Altos, CA	57.2	58.9	60.4	58.6	56.4	56.4	50.7	49.9	50.4
Loveland, CO	n/a	n/a	n/a	n/a	n/a	n/a	n/a	n/a	n/a
Lower Macungie, PA	72.4	71.5	75.7	75.5	71.5	68.2	69.2	68.9	73.1
Madison, AL	n/a	n/a	n/a	n/a	n/a	n/a	n/a	n/a	n/a
Madison, MS	n/a	n/a	n/a	n/a	n/a	n/a	n/a	n/a	n/a
Maple Valley, WA	61.2	60.9	60.7	60.4	61.0	61.3	59.5	57.7	59.5
Marion, IA	n/a	n/a	n/a	n/a	n/a	n/a	n/a	n/a	n/a

Table continued on next page.

Metro Area	2009	2010	2011	2012	2013	2014	2015	2016	2017
Marlboro, NJ	51.7	51.6	50.9	51.5	50.6	50.7	49.9	50.4	49.9
Mason, OH	62.4	62.8	65.2	63.4	63.3	65.5	65.9	64.9	65.7
Menomonee Falls, WI	61.6	62.4	62.3	61.9	60.0	55.9	57.0	60.4	63.9
Meridian, ID	n/a	n/a	n/a	n/a	n/a	n/a	n/a	n/a	n/a
Meridian, MI	n/a	n/a	n/a	n/a	n/a	n/a	n/a	n/a	n/a
Merrimack, NH	n/a	n/a	n/a	n/a	n/a	n/a	n/a	n/a	n/a
Milton, GA	67.7	67.2	65.8	62.1	61.6	61.6	61.7	61.5	62.4
Moon, PA	71.7	70.4	70.3	67.9	68.3	69.1	71.0	72.2	72.7
Moorpark, CA	n/a	n/a	n/a	n/a	n/a	n/a	n/a	n/a	n/a
Morgantown, WV	n/a	n/a	n/a	n/a	n/a	n/a	n/a	n/a	n/a
Mount Pleasant, SC	n/a	n/a	n/a	n/a	n/a	n/a	65.8	62.1	67.7
Newark, DE	69.7	70.7	69.7	69.5	69.1	67.0	67.0	64.7	65.6
Newtown, CT	70.3	71.3	71.6	70.6	70.7	67.7	66.6	65.9	67.3
North Attleborough, MA	61.7	61.0	61.3	61.7	60.1	61.6	60.0	57.5	58.6
North Port, FL	n/a	n/a	n/a	n/a	n/a	n/a	71.3	73.4	65.0
North Ridgeville, OH	70.9	70.7	69.8	64.2	65.8	69.2	68.4	64.8	66.6
Northville, MI	73.9	73.6	73.5	73.4	71.7	71.2	74.0	71.6	70.2
O'Fallon, MO	72.5	72.2	71.1	72.0	72.7	71.1	68.7	66.4	65.6
Orchard Park, NY	60.3	64.5	67.6	63.5	65.5	64.1	63.9	62.6	62.4
Oro Valley, AZ	65.5	64.3	67.2	64.9	66.1	66.7	61.4	56.0	60.1
Oviedo, FL	72.4	70.8	68.6	68.0	65.5	62.3	58.4	58.5	59.5
Parker, CO	65.3	65.7	63.0	61.8	61.0	61.9	61.6	61.6	59.3
Parkland, FL	67.1	63.8	64.2	61.8	60.1	58.8	58.6	58.4	57.9
Peachtree City, GA	67.7	67.2	65.8	62.1	61.6	61.6	61.7	61.5	62.4
Pittsfield, MI	n/a	n/a	n/a	n/a	n/a	n/a	n/a	n/a	n/a
Plainfield, IL	69.2	68.2	67.7	67.1	68.2	66.3	64.3	64.5	64.1
Pleasant Grove, UT	n/a	n/a	n/a	n/a	n/a	n/a	n/a	n/a	n/a
Poway, CA	56.4	54.4	55.2	55.4	55.0	57.4	51.8	53.3	56.0
Princeton, NJ	n/a	n/a	n/a	n/a	n/a	n/a	n/a	n/a	n/a
Queen Creek, AZ	69.8	66.5	63.3	63.1	62.2	61.9	61.0	62.6	64.0
Radnor, PA	69.7	70.7	69.7	69.5	69.1	67.0	67.0	64.7	65.6
Randolph, NJ	51.7	51.6	50.9	51.5	50.6	50.7	49.9	50.4	49.9
Rexburg, ID	n/a	n/a	n/a	n/a	n/a	n/a	n/a	n/a	n/a
Rio Rancho, NM	65.7	65.5	67.1	62.8	65.9	64.4	64.3	66.9	67.0
Rye, NY	51.7	51.6	50.9	51.5	50.6	50.7	49.9	50.4	49.9
Sammamish, WA	61.2	60.9	60.7	60.4	61.0	61.3	59.5	57.7	59.5
San Ramon, CA	57.3	58.0	56.1	53.2	55.2	54.6	56.3	55.8	55.7
Saratoga, CA	57.2	58.9	60.4	58.6	56.4	56.4	50.7	49.9	50.4
Shrewsbury, MA	64.4	64.1	65.8	61.9	63.3	62.5	64.2	65.5	64.9
South Brunswick, NJ	51.7	51.6	50.9	51.5	50.6	50.7	49.9	50.4	49.9
South Jordan, UT	68.8	65.5	66.4	66.9	66.8	68.2	69.1	69.2	68.1
South Kingstown, RI	61.7	61.0	61.3	61.7	60.1	61.6	60.0	57.5	58.6
South Portland, ME	n/a	n/a	n/a	n/a	n/a	n/a	n/a	n/a	n/a
Sparks, NV	n/a	n/a	n/a	n/a	n/a	n/a	n/a	n/a	n/a
State College, PA	n/a	n/a	n/a	n/a	n/a	n/a	n/a	n/a	n/a
Sugar Land, TX	63.6	61.4	61.3	62.1	60.5	60.4	60.3	59.0	58.9
Sun Prairie, WI	n/a	n/a	n/a	n/a	n/a	n/a	n/a	n/a	n/a
Syracuse, UT	n/a	n/a	n/a	n/a	n/a	n/a	n/a	n/a	n/a
Tredyffrin, PA	69.7	70.7	69.7	69.5	69.1	67.0	67.0	64.7	65.6
Upper Dublin, PA	69.7	70.7	69.7	69.5	69.1	67.0	67.0	64.7	65.6
Urbandale, IA	n/a	n/a	n/a	n/a	n/a	n/a	n/a	n/a	n/a
Vestal, NY	n/a	n/a	n/a	n/a	n/a	n/a	n/a	n/a	n/a
Vestavia Hills, AL	75.1	76.2	76.1	73.2	72.1	71.9	71.3	68.7	70.6
Webster, NY	74.7	71.4	68.3	68.2	69.3	68.0	64.9	58.0	63.1
Wellesley, MA	65.5	66.0	65.5	66.0	66.3	62.8	59.3	58.9	58.8
West Fargo, ND	n/a	n/a	n/a	n/a	n/a	n/a	n/a	n/a	n/a
West Lafayette, IN	n/a	n/a	n/a	n/a	n/a	n/a	n/a	n/a	n/a
Weston, FL	67.1	63.8	64.2	61.8	60.1	58.8	58.6	58.4	57.9
Wilmette, IL	69.2	68.2	67.7	67.1	68.2	66.3	64.3	64.5	64.1
Yorba Linda, CA	50.4	49.7	50.1	49.9	48.7	49.0	49.1	47.1	49.1
Zionsville, IN	71.0	68.8	68.3	67.1	67.5	66.9	64.6	63.9	63.9
U.S.	67.4	66.9	66.1	65.4	65.1	64.5	63.7	63.4	63.9

Note: Figures are percentages and cover the Metropolitan Statistical Area—see Appendix B for areas included
Source: U.S. Census Bureau, Housing Vacancies and Homeownership Annual Statistics: 2009-2017

Year Housing Structure Built: City

City	2010 or Later	2000 -2009	1990 -1999	1980 -1989	1970 -1979	1960 -1969	1950 -1959	1940 -1949	Before 1940	Median Year
Aberdeen, SD	5.0	9.0	7.2	8.3	17.4	14.4	9.7	6.8	22.1	1968
Aliso Viejo, CA	2.3	12.9	55.4	23.5	4.3	0.7	0.2	0.2	0.4	1994
Allen, TX	9.7	40.1	26.3	13.7	7.3	1.4	0.9	0.3	0.3	2000
Ames, IA	3.8	18.8	19.1	10.2	15.4	12.4	6.9	3.6	10.0	1982
Amherst, MA	1.0	4.4	11.9	14.8	20.0	13.3	8.3	2.5	23.8	1971
Apex, NC	10.2	37.5	38.7	6.6	3.0	1.0	0.8	0.8	1.4	1999
Beavercreek, OH	2.5	22.0	15.0	9.9	19.4	12.6	13.6	2.5	2.6	1980
Bellevue, NE	1.6	7.4	12.2	17.4	25.2	18.5	9.9	3.7	4.1	1975
Bend, OR	3.4	33.1	24.1	12.0	15.4	3.3	2.3	1.2	5.0	1994
Benicia, CA	0.3	7.2	13.2	32.7	27.2	4.5	2.5	6.2	6.3	1981
Bentonville, AR	8.6	34.9	27.0	11.3	9.2	3.8	1.9	1.3	2.1	1998
Bethlehem, NY	2.1	11.1	15.5	14.0	11.7	10.8	12.5	6.8	15.5	1974
Blacksburg, VA	2.8	14.2	18.7	19.9	21.7	8.3	7.6	3.4	3.4	1983
Bowie, MD	0.8	10.5	25.3	17.6	8.3	33.0	2.7	1.0	0.8	1982
Bozeman, MT	6.2	30.1	15.7	9.0	14.5	7.0	5.6	2.0	10.0	1991
Brentwood, TN	5.2	27.8	20.3	19.9	17.3	7.7	0.4	0.6	0.8	1992
Burlington, VT	1.3	3.5	8.0	9.5	10.5	9.6	11.9	4.6	41.2	1954
Cabot, AR	6.3	34.5	30.9	12.5	10.2	3.7	1.1	0.2	0.6	1997
Carmel, IN	6.3	27.1	26.0	14.2	14.5	7.1	3.3	0.8	0.7	1994
Cedar Falls, IA	4.5	11.6	10.6	6.9	15.4	15.3	17.3	4.6	13.7	1969
Cedar Park, TX	12.4	43.7	27.9	11.3	3.5	0.7	0.2	0.1	0.3	2001
Central, LA	7.7	12.3	14.1	24.5	31.3	4.4	3.3	1.3	1.0	1984
Chapel Hill, NC	2.5	18.3	18.7	19.0	14.2	13.1	8.3	2.7	3.3	1985
Cheshire, CT	0.6	7.5	10.1	16.9	14.2	18.6	18.4	6.4	7.4	1970
Chino Hills, CA	0.8	12.6	32.8	36.7	11.1	2.2	1.6	1.4	0.7	1989
Cibolo, TX	15.5	60.2	9.3	7.4	4.5	0.6	1.2	0.4	1.1	2004
Cicero, NY	1.1	16.0	15.7	15.0	11.9	12.5	14.9	5.1	7.7	1978
Collierville, TN	3.5	29.4	38.2	16.6	6.6	2.3	1.2	0.4	1.7	1996
Coppell, TX	3.8	12.9	40.4	34.1	5.7	1.2	0.9	0.5	0.4	1992
Cornelius, NC	5.4	39.6	30.3	14.8	5.6	1.7	0.5	0.5	1.6	1998
Cranberry, PA	6.8	21.6	28.4	18.6	13.9	4.6	4.4	0.5	1.1	1992
Crown Point, IN	4.2	26.1	14.0	9.4	15.3	10.8	7.4	3.4	9.5	1984
Dublin, OH	4.2	24.1	29.6	29.0	8.2	1.7	1.8	0.2	1.0	1993
East Fishkill, NY	1.7	15.2	13.2	16.9	21.3	13.7	9.0	2.8	6.2	1979
Eden Prairie, MN	1.2	16.2	24.4	35.0	15.7	3.9	2.0	0.5	1.0	1988
Edmond, OK	6.8	20.4	19.6	20.8	19.0	7.1	3.3	1.2	1.8	1988
Edwardsville, IL	3.2	12.1	18.0	11.2	10.5	7.4	15.2	7.0	15.3	1975
Evesham, NJ	1.3	11.2	20.0	30.9	18.8	11.1	5.1	0.6	1.1	1984
Flower Mound, TX	3.7	21.9	50.4	16.8	4.8	1.2	0.7	0.4	0.2	1995
Folsom, CA	2.6	30.6	31.1	19.1	8.5	2.5	3.0	1.3	1.3	1995
Friendswood, TX	5.1	22.6	18.9	14.8	27.1	10.4	0.9	0.1	0.1	1988
Gaines, MI	3.6	24.2	24.1	16.2	11.6	7.0	7.2	2.8	3.2	1991
Glastonbury, CT	1.0	6.8	15.9	17.2	19.5	11.7	12.0	4.4	11.5	1975
Grand Blanc, MI	0.5	25.5	18.6	11.6	16.5	13.4	8.7	2.8	2.5	1985
Hampden, PA	3.9	19.4	19.1	13.1	19.3	12.6	9.8	1.3	1.5	1984
Hilliard, OH	6.4	15.3	39.0	14.0	5.7	4.3	13.1	0.8	1.5	1993
Hillsborough, NJ	3.3	6.8	17.1	30.6	21.4	8.6	6.8	1.6	3.8	1983
Holly Springs, NC	10.3	52.5	28.6	4.5	1.6	0.7	0.8	0.7	0.3	2002
Independence, KY	5.8	37.4	19.9	6.7	16.4	7.8	2.9	1.0	2.0	1997
Juneau, AK	1.6	7.5	12.4	28.3	26.7	10.8	4.1	2.4	6.3	1980
Kaysville, UT	4.6	25.0	22.4	15.9	15.0	8.2	3.2	2.3	3.4	1991
Keller, TX	6.4	33.0	31.0	19.0	7.8	1.8	0.6	0.3	0.1	1997
Lafayette, CA	0.2	5.2	4.5	6.5	16.7	21.7	30.5	10.0	4.6	1962
Lafayette, CO	7.1	11.7	29.6	23.3	18.2	2.6	2.3	1.4	3.7	1989
Lake Oswego, OR	2.1	8.9	17.3	22.6	23.7	9.7	7.4	3.7	4.6	1980
Laramie, WY	3.9	19.5	12.3	9.1	14.7	9.9	10.0	3.9	16.7	1976
Leander, TX	14.5	51.2	17.0	11.0	3.8	0.8	0.0	0.4	1.3	2003
Leawood, KS	2.5	18.0	22.9	20.5	10.2	8.6	13.9	2.1	1.4	1987
Lee's Summit, MO	2.5	24.4	27.4	18.1	14.9	6.9	3.5	0.6	1.7	1992
Leesburg, VA	2.7	25.6	29.6	20.4	10.2	5.0	3.2	0.6	2.7	1993
Lehi, UT	11.7	51.8	17.1	4.2	5.1	1.8	1.9	2.6	3.9	2003
Lexington, MA	2.5	10.3	6.0	7.1	7.5	13.5	22.5	7.7	22.9	1959
Los Altos, CA	2.3	6.4	5.7	5.3	12.2	18.9	38.1	7.3	3.9	1960
Loveland, CO	3.1	25.6	17.9	12.0	20.1	8.1	4.8	1.5	6.6	1987
Lower Macungie, PA	1.5	36.5	12.8	14.6	13.3	10.4	3.3	2.3	5.4	1991
Madison, AL	5.4	29.6	32.1	20.8	6.2	3.5	1.2	0.3	0.8	1995
Madison, MS	4.3	28.7	34.7	18.4	8.2	3.7	0.9	0.6	0.5	1995
Maple Valley, WA	5.5	34.9	29.3	16.4	8.3	2.9	0.2	0.6	1.8	1997

Table continued on next page.

City	2010 or Later	2000 -2009	1990 -1999	1980 -1989	1970 -1979	1960 -1969	1950 -1959	1940 -1949	Before 1940	Median Year
Marion, IA	5.4	24.3	22.0	7.1	12.3	11.9	8.8	1.4	6.8	1991
Marlboro, NJ	1.8	13.3	25.5	27.3	13.9	12.2	2.6	0.8	2.6	1987
Mason, OH	1.5	27.2	35.9	10.3	11.8	1.8	8.5	0.5	2.6	1994
Menomonee Falls, WI	2.6	12.2	21.5	8.7	8.5	21.1	19.1	2.7	3.6	1974
Meridian, ID	9.5	43.8	29.7	6.6	7.0	0.8	0.6	0.5	1.3	2001
Meridian, MI	2.4	8.5	16.6	20.8	19.8	13.7	10.8	2.3	5.2	1979
Merrimack, NH	0.7	7.3	12.7	33.5	25.8	11.0	4.9	1.1	2.9	1981
Milton, GA	4.9	38.6	42.5	6.7	2.8	1.9	1.6	0.4	0.6	1998
Moon, PA	4.1	9.6	14.4	10.8	20.4	19.3	12.7	4.8	3.9	1975
Moorpark, CA	1.5	16.5	14.4	48.0	9.8	3.0	5.1	0.8	0.9	1986
Morgantown, WV	3.1	9.9	10.6	7.3	9.8	12.8	13.3	7.6	25.5	1963
Mount Pleasant, SC	5.9	32.2	24.8	15.3	11.6	5.8	2.9	0.7	0.7	1995
Newark, DE	2.2	9.8	17.9	12.4	15.7	17.8	13.9	3.1	7.2	1975
Newtown, CT	0.7	13.7	15.6	12.0	14.9	15.4	11.2	3.7	12.8	1975
North Attleborough, MA	0.5	9.2	8.6	17.9	13.7	10.4	11.8	4.5	23.4	1970
North Port, FL	1.8	58.2	16.4	8.7	9.8	4.0	0.9	0.0	0.3	2002
North Ridgeville, OH	6.5	30.1	10.9	5.7	20.6	10.8	8.4	2.4	4.6	1986
Northville, MI	3.9	26.0	19.3	15.8	21.2	6.2	3.6	1.1	2.8	1990
O'Fallon, MO	5.5	38.6	33.8	10.6	4.1	3.3	1.8	0.7	1.5	1998
Orchard Park, NY	1.3	11.9	12.3	10.5	19.5	12.7	16.5	5.6	9.7	1973
Oro Valley, AZ	2.9	24.3	44.8	17.4	6.6	2.3	1.1	0.4	0.1	1995
Oviedo, FL	4.2	23.0	41.2	23.1	5.2	1.3	0.6	0.8	0.7	1994
Parker, CO	4.7	39.7	37.8	14.6	2.0	0.4	0.2	0.2	0.3	1999
Parkland, FL	5.9	41.4	32.4	16.5	1.6	1.8	0.3	0.1	0.0	1999
Peachtree City, GA	1.7	17.1	33.3	32.2	13.4	1.2	0.5	0.2	0.4	1991
Pittsfield, MI	1.9	20.0	33.8	15.3	16.2	6.6	2.9	0.7	2.5	1992
Plainfield, IL	3.3	64.2	21.6	3.4	3.1	0.7	1.9	0.4	1.5	2003
Pleasant Grove, UT	6.0	33.0	23.2	7.1	16.7	2.1	4.4	2.8	4.7	1995
Poway, CA	1.1	8.3	13.7	19.9	34.4	14.0	6.3	1.1	1.1	1978
Princeton, NJ	1.5	8.5	9.1	9.6	7.9	11.9	18.6	5.9	27.0	1959
Queen Creek, AZ	13.0	74.4	5.4	3.8	2.3	0.4	0.1	0.4	0.2	2005
Radnor, PA	1.1	4.1	6.0	10.1	13.7	14.3	22.9	5.9	22.0	1960
Randolph, NJ	0.2	5.9	17.9	16.9	24.4	15.9	11.5	3.5	3.8	1976
Rexburg, ID	9.7	34.6	14.8	12.7	15.9	6.1	2.9	1.4	1.8	1996
Rio Rancho, NM	3.8	37.8	21.2	21.9	11.9	2.3	0.7	0.1	0.2	1996
Rye, NY	0.5	4.7	4.7	5.2	4.8	15.6	20.3	8.3	35.9	1953
Sammamish, WA	4.4	21.9	29.3	28.7	10.5	2.5	1.2	0.5	1.0	1992
San Ramon, CA	4.2	30.2	18.4	21.1	17.3	7.8	0.7	0.2	0.2	1991
Saratoga, CA	0.7	6.3	4.4	7.0	23.0	25.6	24.4	4.8	3.7	1967
Shrewsbury, MA	2.0	9.3	18.8	10.7	16.0	8.9	14.9	5.4	14.0	1974
South Brunswick, NJ	1.4	11.2	25.8	26.7	14.7	9.4	6.9	1.5	2.2	1986
South Jordan, UT	16.8	41.4	25.6	6.6	6.3	1.7	0.5	0.4	0.8	2002
South Kingstown, RI	2.1	12.0	13.7	14.1	15.2	6.6	11.2	5.8	19.3	1975
South Portland, ME	0.4	11.8	7.9	12.3	12.0	7.7	8.9	11.3	27.7	1963
Sparks, NV	2.2	28.4	17.9	15.9	17.6	9.0	6.0	1.5	1.6	1989
State College, PA	0.7	3.8	9.9	17.0	17.1	20.2	13.9	7.1	10.2	1969
Sugar Land, TX	6.4	19.8	22.2	32.3	15.6	1.7	0.7	0.4	0.9	1990
Sun Prairie, WI	3.3	32.0	19.0	9.2	12.7	10.6	5.6	2.1	5.5	1992
Syracuse, UT	8.5	56.2	17.3	3.5	7.6	3.2	1.6	0.6	1.4	2003
Tredyffrin, PA	0.3	2.0	8.0	23.9	14.9	18.3	18.1	4.1	10.3	1970
Upper Dublin, PA	1.4	4.9	12.9	14.0	19.5	20.0	14.9	4.0	8.3	1971
Urbandale, IA	4.2	25.9	18.3	15.3	13.9	11.1	6.9	1.7	2.8	1989
Vestal, NY	1.6	5.3	8.1	9.5	16.3	18.7	20.8	7.5	12.1	1965
Vestavia Hills, AL	1.3	14.6	14.7	15.6	19.3	19.1	12.6	2.2	0.6	1978
Webster, NY	2.7	16.2	15.9	13.8	14.8	12.4	14.6	2.5	7.2	1979
Wellesley, MA	3.5	7.9	3.9	3.8	7.3	7.2	16.0	12.5	37.9	1950
West Fargo, ND	12.3	35.9	14.2	7.8	15.0	6.1	5.8	0.9	1.9	1999
West Lafayette, IN	3.8	13.5	16.9	13.8	15.1	16.2	9.7	3.2	7.8	1979
Weston, FL	0.0	23.2	51.4	16.8	6.2	0.7	1.1	0.3	0.3	1995
Wilmette, IL	0.7	6.8	4.4	2.9	5.3	15.0	25.1	8.2	31.5	1954
Yorba Linda, CA	2.4	12.9	12.8	31.5	22.6	13.3	2.7	0.7	1.2	1983
Zionsville, IN	11.5	32.7	19.1	8.5	12.3	5.5	3.7	0.5	6.1	1997
U.S.	2.3	14.7	14.0	13.7	15.6	10.9	10.6	5.2	13.0	1977

Note: Figures are percentages except for Median Year
Source: U.S. Census Bureau, 2012-2016 American Community Survey 5-Year Estimates

Year Housing Structure Built: Metro Area

Metro Area	2010 or Later	2000 -2009	1990 -1999	1980 -1989	1970 -1979	1960 -1969	1950 -1959	1940 -1949	Before 1940	Median Year
Aberdeen, SD	4.5	10.9	10.5	7.2	16.7	12.6	8.7	6.1	22.8	1970
Aliso Viejo, CA	1.3	6.6	7.6	12.6	16.3	15.9	19.0	8.7	12.1	1966
Allen, TX	4.5	22.2	16.8	19.1	14.9	9.0	7.7	2.9	2.9	1987
Ames, IA	3.1	17.2	17.8	9.1	16.6	11.7	7.0	3.8	13.6	1978
Amherst, MA	1.0	5.7	6.6	9.7	13.1	11.2	15.4	6.6	30.8	1958
Apex, NC	5.6	28.6	24.7	16.2	10.1	6.2	4.1	1.7	2.8	1994
Beavercreek, OH	1.0	8.2	8.8	8.0	16.7	16.7	17.2	6.8	16.5	1966
Bellevue, NE	3.4	15.3	12.7	10.1	15.1	12.0	9.3	3.8	18.1	1974
Bend, OR	2.6	29.7	24.9	13.7	18.0	3.7	2.4	1.3	3.7	1993
Benicia, CA	1.8	14.0	13.6	21.9	20.6	9.1	8.3	4.4	6.4	1981
Bentonville, AR	4.1	26.3	24.8	15.7	13.3	6.5	3.5	2.0	3.8	1992
Bethlehem, NY	2.0	8.8	9.9	11.1	12.2	9.3	10.7	6.1	30.0	1963
Blacksburg, VA	2.2	14.9	16.2	15.4	18.4	10.4	8.0	6.4	8.2	1979
Bowie, MD	3.0	15.3	14.5	16.3	14.8	12.5	9.8	5.2	8.6	1979
Bozeman, MT	4.7	29.0	19.5	11.4	15.6	5.6	4.3	1.8	8.0	1992
Brentwood, TN	4.1	21.2	18.9	15.4	14.4	10.1	7.7	3.3	4.9	1986
Burlington, VT	2.6	12.7	13.3	16.2	14.7	9.3	7.1	3.1	21.0	1976
Cabot, AR	4.6	19.5	17.9	15.7	17.6	10.6	7.0	3.3	3.7	1985
Carmel, IN	3.1	16.8	16.8	10.8	13.0	11.3	10.6	4.7	13.0	1978
Cedar Falls, IA	2.4	7.8	6.9	6.1	15.9	13.8	16.5	6.7	23.9	1962
Cedar Park, TX	7.0	28.6	19.4	18.2	13.1	5.4	3.7	2.0	2.5	1993
Central, LA	4.4	21.9	14.9	15.5	18.1	11.2	7.3	3.1	3.6	1984
Chapel Hill, NC	4.3	20.7	19.1	16.8	13.0	9.8	6.9	3.5	5.8	1987
Cheshire, CT	0.9	5.6	7.3	12.3	13.1	12.5	15.0	7.2	26.1	1961
Chino Hills, CA	1.8	21.6	14.5	22.2	16.4	9.1	8.7	2.9	2.9	1985
Cibolo, TX	5.5	22.7	14.9	16.2	14.5	9.0	8.0	4.4	4.8	1986
Cicero, NY	1.3	6.3	8.6	11.8	12.7	11.7	14.8	6.6	26.3	1962
Collierville, TN	2.1	16.9	17.0	13.7	16.5	11.2	11.7	5.5	5.5	1980
Coppell, TX	4.5	22.2	16.8	19.1	14.9	9.0	7.7	2.9	2.9	1987
Cornelius, NC	3.8	25.7	20.4	14.5	12.2	8.8	6.8	3.3	4.5	1990
Cranberry, PA	1.3	6.7	7.6	7.4	12.1	11.4	17.0	9.2	27.4	1958
Crown Point, IN	1.0	11.8	11.0	9.0	14.1	12.0	13.3	6.0	21.8	1967
Dublin, OH	2.6	14.9	16.8	12.0	14.8	11.6	10.5	4.3	12.5	1977
East Fishkill, NY	1.3	7.2	6.1	7.9	10.0	13.8	16.2	9.1	28.3	1958
Eden Prairie, MN	2.1	15.0	14.7	14.7	15.1	10.0	9.9	3.9	14.6	1978
Edmond, OK	4.7	15.9	11.5	15.3	17.8	12.6	10.1	5.4	6.8	1979
Edwardsville, IL	1.7	12.2	12.3	11.5	13.2	12.8	13.5	6.1	16.7	1971
Evesham, NJ	1.4	8.3	9.4	10.2	12.3	12.1	15.9	8.5	21.8	1963
Flower Mound, TX	4.5	22.2	16.8	19.1	14.9	9.0	7.7	2.9	2.9	1987
Folsom, CA	1.5	18.3	14.7	16.6	19.0	11.2	10.5	3.8	4.4	1981
Friendswood, TX	5.6	23.9	14.8	15.7	18.8	9.1	6.7	2.8	2.7	1986
Gaines, MI	1.7	13.3	16.4	12.6	14.2	9.8	11.0	5.3	15.5	1976
Glastonbury, CT	0.9	7.0	7.7	13.4	13.7	14.3	16.2	7.4	19.3	1965
Grand Blanc, MI	0.4	10.0	11.7	7.5	16.5	16.3	18.4	7.6	11.5	1968
Hampden, PA	2.3	10.5	12.1	11.8	14.4	10.7	12.8	5.4	20.2	1971
Hilliard, OH	2.6	14.9	16.8	12.0	14.8	11.6	10.5	4.3	12.5	1977
Hillsborough, NJ	1.3	7.2	6.1	7.9	10.0	13.8	16.2	9.1	28.3	1958
Holly Springs, NC	5.6	28.6	24.7	16.2	10.1	6.2	4.1	1.7	2.8	1994
Independence, KY	1.8	12.6	14.7	10.8	13.4	11.0	12.3	5.3	18.1	1972
Juneau, AK	1.6	7.5	12.4	28.3	26.7	10.8	4.1	2.4	6.3	1980
Kaysville, UT	4.5	21.9	17.1	12.8	15.6	8.5	8.8	4.3	6.4	1985
Keller, TX	4.5	22.2	16.8	19.1	14.9	9.0	7.7	2.9	2.9	1987
Lafayette, CA	1.3	8.1	8.3	11.2	15.1	13.3	14.1	8.2	20.3	1965
Lafayette, CO	2.7	13.4	19.9	16.5	21.3	12.1	5.2	1.7	7.1	1982
Lake Oswego, OR	2.5	15.7	18.9	11.4	17.8	8.9	7.3	4.7	12.6	1979
Laramie, WY	3.7	19.3	13.0	9.1	17.0	9.8	9.3	3.9	15.0	1977
Leander, TX	7.0	28.6	19.4	18.2	13.1	5.4	3.7	2.0	2.5	1993
Leawood, KS	1.9	14.6	14.5	12.5	15.9	12.2	12.0	4.8	11.6	1976
Lee's Summit, MO	1.9	14.6	14.5	12.5	15.9	12.2	12.0	4.8	11.6	1976
Leesburg, VA	3.0	15.3	14.5	16.3	14.8	12.5	9.8	5.2	8.6	1979
Lehi, UT	5.5	29.0	20.6	9.6	15.7	5.4	5.2	3.5	5.4	1992
Lexington, MA	1.7	7.8	7.4	10.6	11.1	10.4	10.9	5.7	34.4	1959
Los Altos, CA	2.2	9.5	10.7	12.8	22.3	18.5	14.9	4.1	5.1	1973
Loveland, CO	3.9	21.1	20.7	14.4	20.2	7.6	4.1	2.0	6.1	1987
Lower Macungie, PA	1.4	11.5	10.6	10.8	12.8	9.6	11.8	5.4	26.1	1967
Madison, AL	5.6	21.4	19.5	15.2	12.5	13.7	7.2	2.0	2.8	1988
Madison, MS	2.9	17.6	17.6	15.1	18.1	12.0	9.3	3.9	3.5	1982
Maple Valley, WA	3.4	16.1	16.1	15.1	15.1	11.2	7.8	4.5	10.7	1980

Table continued on next page.

Metro Area	2010 or Later	2000 -2009	1990 -1999	1980 -1989	1970 -1979	1960 -1969	1950 -1959	1940 -1949	Before 1940	Median Year
Marion, IA	3.2	14.9	15.7	7.1	14.3	12.2	10.4	4.0	18.3	1974
Marlboro, NJ	1.3	7.2	6.1	7.9	10.0	13.8	16.2	9.1	28.3	1958
Mason, OH	1.8	12.6	14.7	10.8	13.4	11.0	12.3	5.3	18.1	1972
Menomonee Falls, WI	1.1	8.3	10.7	7.8	13.2	11.4	17.3	7.5	22.6	1962
Meridian, ID	4.1	26.7	22.1	10.7	17.6	5.1	5.0	3.5	5.2	1991
Meridian, MI	1.3	11.0	12.7	11.3	16.9	13.1	11.5	5.9	16.4	1972
Merrimack, NH	1.4	10.1	10.3	21.2	15.5	9.5	7.5	3.6	20.9	1976
Milton, GA	2.3	26.2	22.4	18.0	13.0	8.0	4.9	2.1	3.2	1990
Moon, PA	1.3	6.7	7.6	7.4	12.1	11.4	17.0	9.2	27.4	1958
Moorpark, CA	1.1	10.9	10.7	17.7	23.3	20.1	10.0	2.9	3.3	1976
Morgantown, WV	3.8	17.6	15.9	13.0	14.7	7.5	6.9	5.1	15.5	1980
Mount Pleasant, SC	4.9	24.6	16.5	17.7	15.0	9.1	5.5	2.7	4.0	1988
Newark, DE	1.4	8.3	9.4	10.2	12.3	12.1	15.9	8.5	21.8	1963
Newtown, CT	1.8	7.0	6.7	11.5	13.0	14.7	16.2	7.8	21.3	1963
North Attleborough, MA	0.9	6.6	8.1	10.9	12.3	10.4	11.8	6.7	32.4	1959
North Port, FL	2.5	20.7	14.7	20.3	21.6	10.0	7.0	1.4	1.7	1984
North Ridgeville, OH	1.0	7.4	8.6	6.6	12.5	13.3	18.6	8.0	24.1	1960
Northville, MI	0.9	8.7	11.3	8.8	14.6	12.6	19.6	10.3	13.3	1965
O'Fallon, MO	1.7	12.2	12.3	11.5	13.2	12.8	13.5	6.1	16.7	1971
Orchard Park, NY	1.2	5.2	6.8	6.3	10.3	11.1	17.9	8.8	32.4	1955
Oro Valley, AZ	2.1	18.9	18.1	17.6	20.1	8.9	9.1	2.8	2.5	1984
Oviedo, FL	3.2	25.9	21.6	21.1	13.6	6.2	5.5	1.4	1.5	1990
Parker, CO	3.0	17.7	15.6	14.6	19.2	10.0	9.8	3.0	7.0	1981
Parkland, FL	1.4	13.9	15.1	19.7	21.7	12.7	10.2	3.0	2.2	1980
Peachtree City, GA	2.3	26.2	22.4	18.0	13.0	8.0	4.9	2.1	3.2	1990
Pittsfield, MI	1.6	13.9	16.8	11.2	16.4	12.2	11.0	4.6	12.3	1976
Plainfield, IL	1.0	11.8	11.0	9.0	14.1	12.0	13.3	6.0	21.8	1967
Pleasant Grove, UT	5.5	29.0	20.6	9.6	15.7	5.4	5.2	3.5	5.4	1992
Poway, CA	1.6	12.1	12.4	19.6	23.1	12.2	10.9	3.6	4.4	1978
Princeton, NJ	1.2	9.0	9.0	11.5	10.7	12.9	15.8	7.1	22.7	1963
Queen Creek, AZ	2.6	27.2	20.8	17.9	16.6	7.2	5.4	1.4	1.0	1990
Radnor, PA	1.4	8.3	9.4	10.2	12.3	12.1	15.9	8.5	21.8	1963
Randolph, NJ	1.3	7.2	6.1	7.9	10.0	13.8	16.2	9.1	28.3	1958
Rexburg, ID	5.9	26.7	15.1	11.1	20.5	7.2	4.3	2.9	6.3	1988
Rio Rancho, NM	1.9	18.8	18.3	16.7	18.0	9.9	9.5	3.7	3.1	1983
Rye, NY	1.3	7.2	6.1	7.9	10.0	13.8	16.2	9.1	28.3	1958
Sammamish, WA	3.4	16.1	16.1	15.1	15.1	11.2	7.8	4.5	10.7	1980
San Ramon, CA	1.3	8.1	8.3	11.2	15.1	13.3	14.1	8.2	20.3	1965
Saratoga, CA	2.2	9.5	10.7	12.8	22.3	18.5	14.9	4.1	5.1	1973
Shrewsbury, MA	1.3	9.1	9.3	12.6	11.8	8.5	10.5	5.8	31.1	1963
South Brunswick, NJ	1.3	7.2	6.1	7.9	10.0	13.8	16.2	9.1	28.3	1958
South Jordan, UT	3.9	16.5	16.3	13.2	19.4	9.0	9.3	3.9	8.4	1980
South Kingstown, RI	0.9	6.6	8.1	10.9	12.3	10.4	11.8	6.7	32.4	1959
South Portland, ME	1.7	13.6	12.2	15.7	13.5	6.9	7.0	5.3	24.2	1975
Sparks, NV	1.9	23.2	20.3	16.1	18.9	9.2	5.5	2.2	2.7	1987
State College, PA	2.3	12.8	14.4	14.5	14.9	12.0	9.5	4.7	15.0	1976
Sugar Land, TX	5.6	23.9	14.8	15.7	18.8	9.1	6.7	2.8	2.7	1986
Sun Prairie, WI	2.6	17.6	16.1	11.3	16.3	9.6	8.5	3.7	14.4	1978
Syracuse, UT	4.5	21.9	17.1	12.8	15.6	8.5	8.8	4.3	6.4	1985
Tredyffrin, PA	1.4	8.3	9.4	10.2	12.3	12.1	15.9	8.5	21.8	1963
Upper Dublin, PA	1.4	8.3	9.4	10.2	12.3	12.1	15.9	8.5	21.8	1963
Urbandale, IA	5.1	18.6	13.9	8.8	13.9	9.0	10.0	4.7	16.0	1977
Vestal, NY	1.1	4.3	6.6	10.3	11.0	13.0	14.1	9.1	30.5	1957
Vestavia Hills, AL	2.8	16.7	16.9	13.1	16.0	11.4	10.8	5.1	7.1	1980
Webster, NY	1.3	7.2	9.3	11.0	13.3	12.6	11.5	5.7	28.1	1964
Wellesley, MA	1.7	7.8	7.4	10.6	11.1	10.4	10.9	5.7	34.4	1959
West Fargo, ND	6.6	19.5	16.4	11.4	16.7	7.8	8.4	2.8	10.4	1983
West Lafayette, IN	3.3	14.9	15.7	9.9	14.0	12.0	9.5	4.7	16.0	1976
Weston, FL	1.4	13.9	15.1	19.7	21.7	12.7	10.2	3.0	2.2	1980
Wilmette, IL	1.0	11.8	11.0	9.0	14.1	12.0	13.3	6.0	21.8	1967
Yorba Linda, CA	1.3	6.6	7.6	12.6	16.3	15.9	19.0	8.7	12.1	1966
Zionsville, IN	3.1	16.8	16.8	10.8	13.0	11.3	10.6	4.7	13.0	1978
U.S.	2.3	14.7	14.0	13.7	15.6	10.9	10.6	5.2	13.0	1977

Note: Figures are percentages except for Median Year; Figures cover the Metropolitan Statistical Area—see Appendix B for areas included
Source: U.S. Census Bureau, 2012-2016 American Community Survey 5-Year Estimates

Gross Monthly Rent: City

City	Under $500	$500 -$999	$1,000 -$1,499	$1,500 -$1,999	$2,000 -$2,499	$2,500 -$2,999	$3,000 and up	Median ($)
Aberdeen, SD	29.3	60.3	7.2	2.5	0.7	0.0	0.0	616
Aliso Viejo, CA	1.7	3.9	10.1	39.5	25.1	13.7	5.9	1,933
Allen, TX	1.4	18.1	49.1	19.1	8.4	2.5	1.5	1,299
Ames, IA	8.3	63.7	19.7	6.8	1.3	0.1	0.0	835
Amherst, MA	7.4	27.4	37.6	15.3	10.6	1.3	0.4	1,201
Apex, NC	0.1	32.2	47.8	16.8	2.7	0.5	0.0	1,162
Beavercreek, OH	3.9	30.7	44.5	17.8	3.1	0.0	0.0	1,135
Bellevue, NE	7.5	56.5	28.2	5.8	1.3	0.3	0.3	880
Bend, OR	5.1	42.9	34.9	12.1	3.1	0.5	1.4	1,024
Benicia, CA	3.9	11.8	39.9	25.3	12.5	5.1	1.5	1,429
Bentonville, AR	6.3	67.8	20.6	4.4	0.2	0.4	0.5	831
Bethlehem, NY	1.9	40.3	42.0	9.6	3.8	1.0	1.4	1,098
Blacksburg, VA	5.1	48.9	34.2	8.6	3.1	0.0	0.0	964
Bowie, MD	0.8	4.4	23.7	34.9	28.7	4.8	2.8	1,803
Bozeman, MT	8.7	51.5	30.6	7.2	1.7	0.0	0.3	901
Brentwood, TN	2.7	5.1	19.4	27.1	13.1	10.0	22.7	1,922
Burlington, VT	11.8	32.0	36.5	14.4	4.0	1.0	0.4	1,071
Cabot, AR	12.0	57.1	24.4	5.1	0.0	0.0	1.3	738
Carmel, IN	0.9	34.4	43.5	12.5	6.8	1.6	0.4	1,132
Cedar Falls, IA	11.0	57.8	18.6	10.0	2.7	0.0	0.0	793
Cedar Park, TX	0.6	30.6	40.8	20.3	5.9	0.9	0.7	1,195
Central, LA	12.8	67.3	14.5	5.4	0.0	0.0	0.0	772
Chapel Hill, NC	3.4	40.4	35.4	12.7	5.0	2.2	0.9	1,061
Cheshire, CT	12.7	25.8	33.5	22.2	4.4	0.0	1.3	1,148
Chino Hills, CA	0.8	3.4	20.7	30.2	30.5	10.8	3.7	1,916
Cibolo, TX	4.3	11.2	33.5	41.8	9.2	0.0	0.0	1,512
Cicero, NY	20.2	44.7	27.2	7.5	0.1	0.3	0.0	835
Collierville, TN	0.9	21.9	56.6	12.1	7.2	0.8	0.5	1,153
Coppell, TX	0.2	25.5	44.3	18.5	4.5	3.9	3.2	1,225
Cornelius, NC	1.3	32.7	43.5	18.0	3.6	0.3	0.6	1,149
Cranberry, PA	2.8	21.4	53.0	8.9	7.3	3.2	3.4	1,201
Crown Point, IN	4.1	55.8	28.5	8.7	1.9	0.0	1.0	945
Dublin, OH	0.5	23.8	46.5	16.4	7.9	3.9	1.0	1,266
East Fishkill, NY	3.7	32.2	36.4	8.5	10.9	4.8	3.4	1,191
Eden Prairie, MN	4.9	19.8	47.3	17.0	6.3	2.0	2.9	1,237
Edmond, OK	6.0	49.1	30.3	10.8	1.9	0.8	1.1	962
Edwardsville, IL	4.0	54.8	35.0	4.4	1.8	0.0	0.0	929
Evesham, NJ	4.1	12.0	43.1	23.8	15.0	1.4	0.6	1,355
Flower Mound, TX	0.7	12.5	28.4	37.7	11.9	6.3	2.4	1,611
Folsom, CA	1.8	12.7	39.0	29.1	12.2	3.3	2.0	1,465
Friendswood, TX	0.0	39.6	38.7	15.2	4.2	1.9	0.4	1,097
Gaines, MI	2.6	65.1	24.2	7.8	0.4	0.0	0.0	828
Glastonbury, CT	12.9	21.6	43.7	11.4	5.7	1.7	3.0	1,194
Grand Blanc, MI	4.3	70.8	20.5	2.5	1.9	0.0	0.0	786
Hampden, PA	1.2	46.1	29.7	11.4	3.8	2.3	5.5	1,031
Hilliard, OH	8.6	41.0	39.6	9.2	1.2	0.0	0.4	1,004
Hillsborough, NJ	0.5	1.2	52.2	26.9	13.8	1.6	3.9	1,445
Holly Springs, NC	13.5	20.4	36.1	20.0	6.9	3.1	0.0	1,231
Independence, KY	11.0	45.1	38.0	5.4	0.0	0.4	0.0	952
Juneau, AK	10.2	24.6	40.8	15.3	5.9	2.6	0.5	1,184
Kaysville, UT	18.9	52.8	12.4	14.3	1.6	0.0	0.0	760
Keller, TX	0.0	23.1	56.2	9.9	3.0	4.5	3.3	1,207
Lafayette, CA	5.7	6.7	19.8	28.1	18.2	9.4	12.0	1,816
Lafayette, CO	6.3	22.7	39.2	23.7	5.4	0.8	1.8	1,260
Lake Oswego, OR	2.7	11.6	46.7	25.1	4.9	3.0	6.0	1,371
Laramie, WY	16.8	56.6	21.4	4.9	0.2	0.0	0.0	728
Leander, TX	0.8	19.9	31.6	40.7	6.4	0.5	0.0	1,461
Leawood, KS	2.5	28.2	27.4	8.8	21.4	3.8	7.8	1,235
Lee's Summit, MO	5.3	45.2	36.5	8.6	3.1	1.0	0.3	996
Leesburg, VA	4.7	14.1	36.8	33.8	8.5	1.6	0.5	1,446
Lehi, UT	2.4	21.9	37.8	32.5	5.1	0.3	0.0	1,306
Lexington, MA	18.8	5.8	14.2	18.7	15.3	12.8	14.4	1,799
Los Altos, CA	0.0	1.1	9.6	22.4	13.9	13.1	39.8	2,611
Loveland, CO	6.5	42.1	33.2	12.6	3.5	1.5	0.6	1,018
Lower Macungie, PA	0.0	18.6	53.4	26.5	1.6	0.0	0.0	1,247
Madison, AL	6.3	60.6	21.9	7.8	0.8	2.3	0.3	864
Madison, MS	4.0	9.6	36.7	22.2	12.5	2.9	12.1	1,492
Maple Valley, WA	5.3	12.6	22.7	25.6	27.5	5.6	0.7	1,684

Table continued on next page.

City	Under $500	$500 -$999	$1,000 -$1,499	$1,500 -$1,999	$2,000 -$2,499	$2,500 -$2,999	$3,000 and up	Median ($)
Marion, IA	24.4	54.7	17.3	2.8	0.4	0.0	0.3	658
Marlboro, NJ	1.0	8.0	11.9	21.5	51.9	2.5	3.2	2,074
Mason, OH	4.4	41.1	40.7	10.2	1.5	0.3	1.8	1,056
Menomonee Falls, WI	4.0	52.2	34.2	5.2	3.4	0.7	0.3	946
Meridian, ID	5.3	42.6	42.1	8.1	1.5	0.5	0.0	1,020
Meridian, MI	11.1	63.1	17.4	4.7	2.3	1.2	0.3	828
Merrimack, NH	3.6	8.5	56.7	27.1	4.1	0.0	0.0	1,375
Milton, GA	0.5	22.6	50.3	15.8	6.5	0.7	3.7	1,234
Moon, PA	1.4	61.2	30.9	3.7	2.7	0.0	0.0	919
Moorpark, CA	2.6	10.2	15.3	36.9	19.6	8.4	7.0	1,797
Morgantown, WV	18.0	52.7	23.7	4.4	1.2	0.0	0.0	742
Mount Pleasant, SC	1.3	10.5	46.1	23.0	9.3	4.2	5.5	1,403
Newark, DE	6.1	28.7	35.8	17.6	4.9	4.9	2.0	1,177
Newtown, CT	5.8	21.4	32.2	19.7	12.1	5.3	3.5	1,366
North Attleborough, MA	11.9	42.3	35.2	6.5	2.8	0.8	0.6	975
North Port, FL	3.7	48.6	39.4	8.0	0.0	0.3	0.0	985
North Ridgeville, OH	4.0	40.7	40.2	9.8	1.0	0.0	4.4	1,071
Northville, MI	0.0	28.6	51.2	13.1	2.2	1.2	3.7	1,174
O'Fallon, MO	3.4	44.7	38.8	9.3	1.1	0.7	2.1	1,020
Orchard Park, NY	4.5	64.4	24.1	6.0	0.5	0.0	0.6	915
Oro Valley, AZ	1.1	43.8	34.5	14.0	3.5	1.6	1.5	1,068
Oviedo, FL	1.1	15.6	43.0	35.0	3.3	0.9	1.0	1,392
Parker, CO	0.4	13.3	50.4	22.3	10.8	2.4	0.3	1,350
Parkland, FL	1.9	0.0	3.2	27.1	12.9	15.0	39.9	2,663
Peachtree City, GA	7.0	20.6	43.5	18.0	6.9	2.4	1.6	1,270
Pittsfield, MI	4.2	49.3	33.2	8.2	2.5	2.0	0.6	982
Plainfield, IL	2.2	16.9	23.6	21.9	27.1	3.7	4.6	1,665
Pleasant Grove, UT	3.7	39.2	46.4	7.3	2.9	0.2	0.3	1,051
Poway, CA	6.8	13.8	29.6	22.1	15.1	6.4	6.1	1,497
Princeton, NJ	6.1	19.6	28.2	14.7	9.3	8.9	13.2	1,396
Queen Creek, AZ	2.3	20.4	41.4	21.2	13.2	0.9	0.6	1,258
Radnor, PA	1.3	7.6	48.7	26.6	8.4	3.7	3.7	1,432
Randolph, NJ	4.2	3.3	66.8	18.7	3.7	1.3	2.1	1,341
Rexburg, ID	16.4	68.7	8.9	3.2	2.3	0.0	0.5	655
Rio Rancho, NM	1.0	38.1	42.5	14.1	3.0	0.0	1.2	1,114
Rye, NY	8.4	10.5	29.0	32.3	11.1	5.9	2.9	1,532
Sammamish, WA	0.7	7.9	15.9	26.5	21.1	14.5	13.4	1,982
San Ramon, CA	1.3	3.4	14.8	31.3	21.0	11.8	16.4	1,987
Saratoga, CA	13.4	6.5	9.3	12.5	10.2	7.2	41.0	2,410
Shrewsbury, MA	5.0	22.6	50.7	14.1	4.4	1.9	1.4	1,225
South Brunswick, NJ	5.0	6.6	40.7	35.7	7.1	2.3	2.7	1,475
South Jordan, UT	2.5	7.5	50.7	23.8	13.0	2.5	0.0	1,399
South Kingstown, RI	19.3	27.5	27.8	16.5	4.5	2.0	2.5	1,038
South Portland, ME	13.3	25.8	48.7	10.2	2.0	0.0	0.0	1,086
Sparks, NV	3.6	49.2	34.0	9.2	2.9	0.1	1.0	971
State College, PA	4.3	50.1	25.3	11.2	6.1	2.5	0.6	968
Sugar Land, TX	0.0	3.7	39.5	29.2	13.2	7.5	6.9	1,617
Sun Prairie, WI	3.2	50.5	38.4	6.8	1.0	0.0	0.0	976
Syracuse, UT	4.2	22.7	24.3	33.5	15.4	0.0	0.0	1,478
Tredyffrin, PA	0.4	12.3	49.6	19.1	8.7	5.8	4.1	1,392
Upper Dublin, PA	2.3	7.7	42.2	21.0	11.1	11.7	4.0	1,463
Urbandale, IA	3.2	66.4	16.0	9.8	1.8	1.5	1.4	850
Vestal, NY	9.2	53.5	22.4	7.0	0.6	2.5	4.8	906
Vestavia Hills, AL	0.4	49.2	26.6	11.6	5.4	4.5	2.3	1,005
Webster, NY	9.9	44.7	30.9	12.0	0.3	1.8	0.4	970
Wellesley, MA	19.8	7.9	14.5	11.1	17.2	14.3	15.2	1,852
West Fargo, ND	9.3	63.8	21.8	3.4	0.6	0.7	0.4	770
West Lafayette, IN	4.6	59.0	19.4	12.0	3.1	0.1	1.8	852
Weston, FL	0.0	3.9	17.8	32.8	22.2	12.3	11.1	1,933
Wilmette, IL	4.4	20.5	20.0	12.0	16.8	13.3	12.9	1,713
Yorba Linda, CA	1.7	11.7	21.3	27.6	14.8	12.6	10.2	1,777
Zionsville, IN	9.0	26.1	47.0	15.4	0.5	1.0	1.0	1,182
U.S.	11.3	43.3	27.7	10.7	4.0	1.6	1.5	949

Note: Figures are percentages except for Median; Gross rent is the contract rent plus the estimated average monthly cost of utilities (electricity, gas, and water and sewer) and fuels (oil, coal, kerosene, wood, etc.) if these are paid by the renter (or paid for the renter by someone else).

Source: U.S. Census Bureau, 2012-2016 American Community Survey 5-Year Estimates

Gross Monthly Rent: Metro Area

MSA[1]	Under $500	$500 -$999	$1,000 -$1,499	$1,500 -$1,999	$2,000 -$2,499	$2,500 -2,999	$3,000 and up	Median ($)
Aberdeen, SD	29.2	60.3	7.7	2.2	0.6	0.0	0.0	622
Aliso Viejo, CA	4.8	20.6	36.0	21.6	9.6	4.1	3.2	1,334
Allen, TX	4.6	49.0	32.4	10.0	2.5	0.8	0.7	969
Ames, IA	9.7	63.8	18.7	6.1	1.3	0.1	0.3	814
Amherst, MA	20.3	44.9	26.6	5.4	1.7	0.4	0.7	871
Apex, NC	5.9	49.1	34.2	7.8	1.8	0.5	0.6	963
Beavercreek, OH	16.8	61.5	17.5	2.9	0.8	0.2	0.3	756
Bellevue, NE	10.9	58.8	23.9	4.5	1.3	0.4	0.4	833
Bend, OR	5.4	46.8	34.7	9.3	2.4	0.5	0.8	981
Benicia, CA	4.4	20.3	36.3	25.2	10.3	2.7	0.7	1,337
Bentonville, AR	13.1	65.8	16.9	2.7	1.0	0.4	0.1	752
Bethlehem, NY	9.6	49.9	30.7	6.9	1.8	0.6	0.5	923
Blacksburg, VA	14.8	56.3	21.5	5.4	1.6	0.2	0.3	797
Bowie, MD	5.0	11.2	31.5	28.0	14.1	5.7	4.5	1,541
Bozeman, MT	9.7	50.8	30.2	7.1	1.6	0.3	0.3	895
Brentwood, TN	10.3	51.2	28.6	6.8	1.9	0.6	0.5	899
Burlington, VT	10.8	31.5	37.2	15.2	3.5	1.0	0.7	1,089
Cabot, AR	12.4	64.6	19.6	2.5	0.5	0.2	0.2	780
Carmel, IN	8.7	62.8	23.0	4.0	0.9	0.3	0.3	828
Cedar Falls, IA	16.9	64.8	12.5	3.8	1.6	0.0	0.4	701
Cedar Park, TX	3.7	36.9	38.9	15.0	3.5	1.0	0.9	1,098
Central, LA	10.5	57.0	23.7	6.5	1.7	0.4	0.2	841
Chapel Hill, NC	8.5	52.9	28.4	6.8	1.9	0.8	0.7	910
Cheshire, CT	11.0	31.5	39.6	13.2	3.2	0.8	0.7	1,075
Chino Hills, CA	5.2	30.0	37.1	18.4	6.4	2.2	0.7	1,176
Cibolo, TX	9.1	51.0	29.6	7.5	1.7	0.5	0.5	909
Cicero, NY	14.5	63.7	17.8	2.6	0.8	0.2	0.3	780
Collierville, TN	10.0	56.2	27.0	5.1	1.1	0.2	0.5	863
Coppell, TX	4.6	49.0	32.4	10.0	2.5	0.8	0.7	969
Cornelius, NC	8.0	54.4	28.9	6.2	1.4	0.4	0.5	893
Cranberry, PA	19.5	56.6	17.3	4.0	1.5	0.5	0.5	749
Crown Point, IN	8.3	41.4	31.8	12.1	3.9	1.4	1.1	1,005
Dublin, OH	9.9	58.4	25.2	4.6	1.3	0.3	0.3	855
East Fishkill, NY	9.7	18.7	35.2	19.8	8.3	3.8	4.5	1,297
Eden Prairie, MN	10.3	43.7	30.9	11.1	2.5	0.8	0.6	963
Edmond, OK	10.6	62.4	20.6	4.7	1.1	0.3	0.3	800
Edwardsville, IL	11.8	57.9	23.4	4.5	1.3	0.5	0.5	832
Evesham, NJ	9.0	37.4	35.4	11.9	3.9	1.3	1.1	1,040
Flower Mound, TX	4.6	49.0	32.4	10.0	2.5	0.8	0.7	969
Folsom, CA	5.3	36.2	35.2	16.5	4.7	1.2	0.8	1,106
Friendswood, TX	5.2	49.7	30.4	10.1	2.7	1.0	1.0	955
Gaines, MI	10.4	64.7	19.1	4.2	0.8	0.2	0.5	786
Glastonbury, CT	11.7	35.5	39.1	10.4	2.0	0.6	0.6	1,028
Grand Blanc, MI	16.6	66.1	14.7	1.8	0.7	0.0	0.1	720
Hampden, PA	10.7	55.6	26.5	4.9	1.0	0.5	0.7	873
Hilliard, OH	9.9	58.4	25.2	4.6	1.3	0.3	0.3	855
Hillsborough, NJ	9.7	18.7	35.2	19.8	8.3	3.8	4.5	1,297
Holly Springs, NC	5.9	49.1	34.2	7.8	1.8	0.5	0.6	963
Independence, KY	15.7	58.5	20.2	3.6	1.0	0.4	0.5	767
Juneau, AK	10.2	24.6	40.8	15.3	5.9	2.6	0.5	1,184
Kaysville, UT	10.6	55.4	25.7	6.6	1.0	0.3	0.4	856
Keller, TX	4.6	49.0	32.4	10.0	2.5	0.8	0.7	969
Lafayette, CA	6.9	13.4	26.5	23.7	14.1	7.7	7.7	1,567
Lafayette, CO	4.5	26.2	37.2	20.2	7.5	2.3	2.2	1,236
Lake Oswego, OR	5.8	40.2	35.7	13.0	3.3	1.1	0.9	1,047
Laramie, WY	17.4	56.4	21.3	4.7	0.2	0.0	0.0	729
Leander, TX	3.7	36.9	38.9	15.0	3.5	1.0	0.9	1,098
Leawood, KS	10.5	55.4	26.9	5.1	1.3	0.4	0.5	863
Lee's Summit, MO	10.5	55.4	26.9	5.1	1.3	0.4	0.5	863
Leesburg, VA	5.0	11.2	31.5	28.0	14.1	5.7	4.5	1,541
Lehi, UT	8.3	49.5	28.3	10.3	2.6	0.6	0.3	916
Lexington, MA	13.7	18.4	32.2	20.7	8.7	3.5	2.9	1,274
Los Altos, CA	4.3	8.4	21.3	26.6	19.1	10.9	9.5	1,801
Loveland, CO	5.2	38.3	35.9	15.5	3.6	1.0	0.4	1,077
Lower Macungie, PA	10.4	44.3	34.3	8.2	1.8	0.4	0.7	961
Madison, AL	15.3	61.2	18.9	3.1	0.7	0.5	0.3	759
Madison, MS	13.8	59.6	22.2	3.0	0.8	0.3	0.4	810
Maple Valley, WA	6.1	27.3	35.9	19.6	6.9	2.5	1.8	1,212

Table continued on next page.

MSA[1]	Under $500	$500 -$999	$1,000 -$1,499	$1,500 -$1,999	$2,000 -$2,499	$2,500 -2,999	$3,000 and up	Median ($)
Marion, IA	22.0	62.5	12.6	1.7	0.6	0.1	0.4	696
Marlboro, NJ	9.7	18.7	35.2	19.8	8.3	3.8	4.5	1,297
Mason, OH	15.7	58.5	20.2	3.6	1.0	0.4	0.5	767
Menomonee Falls, WI	9.2	60.9	23.5	4.5	1.3	0.2	0.3	841
Meridian, ID	11.0	58.0	25.4	3.7	1.1	0.2	0.5	842
Meridian, MI	11.4	62.9	20.2	3.4	1.3	0.4	0.4	803
Merrimack, NH	7.5	31.8	43.5	14.6	2.0	0.5	0.2	1,099
Milton, GA	5.3	44.4	38.2	9.0	2.1	0.6	0.5	1,003
Moon, PA	19.5	56.6	17.3	4.0	1.5	0.5	0.5	749
Moorpark, CA	4.7	12.5	28.9	27.6	16.3	5.5	4.5	1,572
Morgantown, WV	16.4	56.5	19.8	6.3	0.7	0.1	0.1	743
Mount Pleasant, SC	6.9	42.3	34.7	11.1	2.9	1.0	1.1	1,009
Newark, DE	9.0	37.4	35.4	11.9	3.9	1.3	1.1	1,040
Newtown, CT	8.9	17.0	31.7	22.1	10.5	4.8	5.0	1,385
North Attleborough, MA	16.7	44.7	28.6	7.3	1.7	0.5	0.5	901
North Port, FL	5.2	41.9	35.8	10.3	3.3	1.4	2.1	1,032
North Ridgeville, OH	15.7	61.3	18.7	2.8	0.8	0.3	0.4	758
Northville, MI	11.4	53.5	26.9	5.6	1.6	0.5	0.5	866
O'Fallon, MO	11.8	57.9	23.4	4.5	1.3	0.5	0.5	832
Orchard Park, NY	17.3	64.9	14.1	2.4	0.6	0.3	0.3	738
Oro Valley, AZ	10.6	55.5	26.1	5.3	1.2	0.5	0.8	831
Oviedo, FL	3.3	40.0	42.4	11.4	1.9	0.5	0.5	1,063
Parker, CO	5.9	34.3	36.1	16.7	4.8	1.1	1.1	1,119
Parkland, FL	5.9	27.8	38.8	17.8	5.8	2.0	1.7	1,182
Peachtree City, GA	5.3	44.4	38.2	9.0	2.1	0.6	0.5	1,003
Pittsfield, MI	6.2	46.4	31.6	10.0	3.5	1.3	1.2	980
Plainfield, IL	8.3	41.4	31.8	12.1	3.9	1.4	1.1	1,005
Pleasant Grove, UT	8.3	49.5	28.3	10.3	2.6	0.6	0.3	916
Poway, CA	4.1	17.7	35.2	22.8	12.5	4.7	3.1	1,395
Princeton, NJ	10.5	26.0	37.9	14.9	6.4	2.4	1.9	1,144
Queen Creek, AZ	5.2	46.0	35.1	9.6	2.5	0.9	0.8	989
Radnor, PA	9.0	37.4	35.4	11.9	3.9	1.3	1.1	1,040
Randolph, NJ	9.7	18.7	35.2	19.8	8.3	3.8	4.5	1,297
Rexburg, ID	17.1	67.9	9.3	3.3	1.9	0.0	0.4	656
Rio Rancho, NM	10.5	56.4	26.4	5.0	0.9	0.3	0.5	830
Rye, NY	9.7	18.7	35.2	19.8	8.3	3.8	4.5	1,297
Sammamish, WA	6.1	27.3	35.9	19.6	6.9	2.5	1.8	1,212
San Ramon, CA	6.9	13.4	26.5	23.7	14.1	7.7	7.7	1,567
Saratoga, CA	4.3	8.4	21.3	26.6	19.1	10.9	9.5	1,801
Shrewsbury, MA	14.7	41.8	33.5	7.4	1.8	0.6	0.4	943
South Brunswick, NJ	9.7	18.7	35.2	19.8	8.3	3.8	4.5	1,297
South Jordan, UT	6.8	47.1	33.6	9.7	1.8	0.5	0.5	967
South Kingstown, RI	16.7	44.7	28.6	7.3	1.7	0.5	0.5	901
South Portland, ME	13.0	42.8	32.9	8.2	2.2	0.5	0.4	948
Sparks, NV	7.5	50.7	29.2	9.7	2.0	0.4	0.5	917
State College, PA	6.1	51.0	26.8	9.3	5.1	1.2	0.5	930
Sugar Land, TX	5.2	49.7	30.4	10.1	2.7	1.0	1.0	955
Sun Prairie, WI	6.3	54.2	29.0	7.4	2.1	0.5	0.5	919
Syracuse, UT	10.6	55.4	25.7	6.6	1.0	0.3	0.4	856
Tredyffrin, PA	9.0	37.4	35.4	11.9	3.9	1.3	1.1	1,040
Upper Dublin, PA	9.0	37.4	35.4	11.9	3.9	1.3	1.1	1,040
Urbandale, IA	9.8	60.7	23.5	4.1	1.0	0.4	0.4	831
Vestal, NY	16.4	67.2	12.5	2.4	0.5	0.3	0.7	709
Vestavia Hills, AL	15.6	56.1	22.4	3.9	1.0	0.5	0.5	806
Webster, NY	12.1	60.7	21.4	3.4	1.1	0.6	0.7	821
Wellesley, MA	13.7	18.4	32.2	20.7	8.7	3.5	2.9	1,274
West Fargo, ND	12.5	68.6	13.4	3.8	1.3	0.3	0.1	733
West Lafayette, IN	8.3	64.7	20.0	5.5	1.0	0.0	0.6	794
Weston, FL	5.9	27.8	38.8	17.8	5.8	2.0	1.7	1,182
Wilmette, IL	8.3	41.4	31.8	12.1	3.9	1.4	1.1	1,005
Yorba Linda, CA	4.8	20.6	36.0	21.6	9.6	4.1	3.2	1,334
Zionsville, IN	8.7	62.8	23.0	4.0	0.9	0.3	0.3	828
U.S.	11.3	43.3	27.7	10.7	4.0	1.6	1.5	949

Note: (1) Figures cover the Metropolitan Statistical Area (MSA)—see Appendix B for areas included; Figures are percentages except for Median; Gross rent is the contract rent plus the estimated average monthly cost of utilities (electricity, gas, and water and sewer) and fuels (oil, coal, kerosene, wood, etc.) if these are paid by the renter (or paid for the renter by someone else).
Source: U.S. Census Bureau, 2012-2016 American Community Survey 5-Year Estimates

Highest Level of Education: City

City	Less than H.S.	H.S. Diploma	Some College, No Deg.	Associate Degree	Bachelors Degree	Masters Degree	Profess. School Degree	Doctorate Degree
Aberdeen, SD	8.5	32.0	21.0	10.2	20.8	5.2	1.0	1.3
Aliso Viejo, CA	3.2	10.3	20.4	8.5	38.6	13.7	3.4	1.9
Allen, TX	4.8	13.7	21.2	7.2	34.7	14.3	2.4	1.8
Ames, IA	2.6	12.2	14.4	7.3	32.6	18.9	2.2	9.8
Amherst, MA	5.5	12.2	11.8	5.0	23.6	22.4	4.3	15.3
Apex, NC	4.9	10.2	15.3	8.9	39.1	16.5	2.6	2.4
Beavercreek, OH	2.7	18.7	19.5	8.9	25.0	18.3	2.9	3.8
Bellevue, NE	7.5	27.3	27.8	8.9	19.3	7.9	0.9	0.5
Bend, OR	5.3	17.3	26.2	9.6	26.9	10.2	3.1	1.4
Benicia, CA	4.5	16.5	26.6	9.9	26.5	11.1	3.2	1.7
Bentonville, AR	6.8	22.7	18.7	4.5	30.2	14.1	2.0	1.1
Bethlehem, NY	3.0	16.2	12.0	10.1	25.1	22.4	7.8	3.5
Blacksburg, VA	5.1	9.5	9.7	4.3	31.1	21.4	4.4	14.4
Bowie, MD	3.7	18.1	22.4	5.8	28.1	17.2	2.1	2.5
Bozeman, MT	1.3	13.3	23.7	6.1	34.5	14.5	2.6	3.9
Brentwood, TN	2.1	9.6	12.5	4.9	42.3	19.3	5.6	3.7
Burlington, VT	10.2	17.8	16.2	4.8	29.7	14.2	4.0	3.0
Cabot, AR	8.9	27.9	30.0	10.3	15.6	6.0	1.0	0.3
Carmel, IN	2.1	9.5	13.9	4.5	41.0	18.2	6.3	4.5
Cedar Falls, IA	4.4	22.8	18.7	10.7	26.0	10.9	2.5	4.0
Cedar Park, TX	4.4	17.1	25.6	8.4	30.7	11.2	1.5	1.0
Central, LA	7.1	37.5	24.0	7.5	17.5	4.6	1.4	0.5
Chapel Hill, NC	4.1	7.6	9.4	4.3	30.6	22.7	8.2	13.0
Cheshire, CT	4.9	20.6	14.3	6.3	27.0	18.7	5.0	3.1
Chino Hills, CA	6.6	17.4	22.4	8.7	30.4	10.3	2.2	1.9
Cibolo, TX	4.4	19.0	24.3	13.7	23.4	13.3	1.3	0.6
Cicero, NY	5.1	28.9	21.8	13.5	18.3	10.3	1.1	0.8
Collierville, TN	3.6	14.8	20.4	6.3	35.5	14.9	2.8	1.8
Coppell, TX	3.3	10.4	15.8	5.7	38.5	19.8	4.3	2.1
Cornelius, NC	2.9	14.3	18.2	10.4	35.6	13.3	3.4	1.9
Cranberry, PA	3.2	18.1	14.0	7.7	36.3	16.0	2.7	2.0
Crown Point, IN	8.1	33.2	18.7	8.4	21.9	7.3	1.8	0.6
Dublin, OH	1.5	7.3	10.9	5.0	44.6	20.9	5.8	4.1
East Fishkill, NY	7.2	26.0	18.1	8.2	23.0	14.0	2.5	0.9
Eden Prairie, MN	3.2	10.2	16.2	8.2	39.0	16.7	3.3	3.1
Edmond, OK	3.9	15.6	21.5	5.9	31.6	14.4	4.3	2.7
Edwardsville, IL	2.8	19.9	20.4	7.3	30.3	13.7	3.3	2.3
Evesham, NJ	4.4	22.7	18.9	8.1	30.6	11.1	2.8	1.4
Flower Mound, TX	3.4	11.6	18.3	6.9	40.7	15.3	2.4	1.3
Folsom, CA	7.5	16.3	19.4	8.5	29.2	14.1	3.1	1.9
Friendswood, TX	4.9	16.0	21.9	9.2	31.5	12.0	2.7	1.7
Gaines, MI	11.3	29.6	22.1	9.9	17.9	7.3	0.7	1.1
Glastonbury, CT	4.0	15.7	13.6	6.5	28.4	21.7	7.4	2.7
Grand Blanc, MI	3.5	21.9	21.9	14.2	21.9	12.2	3.1	1.1
Hampden, PA	6.0	21.4	15.1	7.4	30.4	14.1	3.5	2.1
Hilliard, OH	3.7	18.3	17.9	8.0	31.6	13.4	4.6	2.4
Hillsborough, NJ	2.5	20.8	14.0	6.8	34.5	16.5	2.5	2.4
Holly Springs, NC	4.3	12.8	17.2	9.0	38.6	14.7	1.2	2.1
Independence, KY	10.5	29.6	22.3	8.7	19.8	6.6	1.7	0.7
Juneau, AK	4.4	21.2	27.6	7.4	25.3	10.2	2.6	1.4
Kaysville, UT	2.3	14.5	25.5	9.9	32.7	12.5	2.2	0.6
Keller, TX	3.5	13.1	20.0	6.4	37.9	14.3	3.3	1.5
Lafayette, CA	2.2	6.4	13.5	5.4	38.1	20.7	8.6	5.2
Lafayette, CO	5.2	15.9	15.8	7.9	32.9	15.7	2.3	4.2
Lake Oswego, OR	1.5	9.0	17.8	4.7	39.3	16.7	8.2	2.8
Laramie, WY	4.3	15.1	22.5	8.6	28.4	11.8	2.6	6.7
Leander, TX	7.4	19.8	25.9	11.2	24.4	8.6	1.4	1.3
Leawood, KS	0.7	6.0	14.7	4.5	41.2	18.7	11.9	2.3
Lee's Summit, MO	3.6	20.3	23.9	8.7	27.9	11.4	2.4	1.7
Leesburg, VA	9.8	16.0	15.8	7.3	32.1	15.3	1.7	2.1
Lehi, UT	3.1	16.1	27.3	12.7	29.4	9.1	1.3	1.1
Lexington, MA	2.7	7.2	6.7	3.9	27.3	31.5	7.8	13.1
Los Altos, CA	1.4	4.3	8.3	5.0	33.3	30.1	9.0	8.5
Loveland, CO	5.1	24.7	25.4	9.9	23.2	8.5	1.4	1.7
Lower Macungie, PA	6.0	22.1	14.3	8.4	26.9	16.1	3.1	3.1
Madison, AL	3.8	12.2	18.3	8.4	34.9	17.3	2.6	2.6
Madison, MS	1.9	9.2	19.0	7.4	37.3	16.1	6.1	3.1

Table continued on next page.

City	Less than H.S.	H.S. Diploma	Some College, No Deg.	Associate Degree	Bachelors Degree	Masters Degree	Profess. School Degree	Doctorate Degree
Maple Valley, WA	2.4	18.8	27.9	10.2	27.9	11.1	0.8	0.9
Marion, IA	3.9	26.9	22.0	13.1	24.1	8.5	0.9	0.7
Marlboro, NJ	4.2	16.9	12.3	6.1	33.5	18.4	5.7	3.0
Mason, OH	2.5	18.6	13.3	6.2	33.4	18.9	4.4	2.7
Menomonee Falls, WI	4.5	25.8	19.1	9.6	26.8	10.9	2.0	1.3
Meridian, ID	4.7	24.5	28.0	9.4	24.2	7.0	1.5	0.7
Meridian, MI	3.9	9.6	14.6	6.9	29.9	19.4	6.2	9.6
Merrimack, NH	3.9	24.8	17.5	9.4	29.7	12.1	1.0	1.6
Milton, GA	2.7	10.6	13.7	5.9	43.7	18.1	3.8	1.6
Moon, PA	5.2	20.9	15.2	8.9	31.3	13.6	2.6	2.2
Moorpark, CA	11.6	14.6	23.5	10.6	25.9	9.7	2.6	1.6
Morgantown, WV	7.1	20.9	17.6	5.7	24.9	13.5	4.6	5.8
Mount Pleasant, SC	2.2	13.2	18.1	7.2	38.4	13.6	4.3	3.0
Newark, DE	3.6	17.4	16.4	5.7	31.0	17.5	1.9	6.6
Newtown, CT	4.2	18.7	15.2	6.6	31.0	18.0	4.7	1.6
North Attleborough, MA	5.8	25.3	19.9	8.4	24.6	12.7	2.5	0.9
North Port, FL	9.2	37.9	23.4	10.8	13.1	4.0	0.6	1.1
North Ridgeville, OH	7.7	28.9	21.5	9.4	21.1	8.9	1.6	1.0
Northville, MI	2.6	12.6	15.0	7.5	32.0	21.3	6.2	2.8
O'Fallon, MO	5.0	24.3	24.2	8.0	25.0	11.6	1.0	0.9
Orchard Park, NY	3.5	21.3	15.4	13.8	24.6	15.3	4.6	1.5
Oro Valley, AZ	2.5	15.2	22.0	9.7	27.8	15.2	4.2	3.5
Oviedo, FL	5.5	17.8	20.0	14.5	26.8	11.3	2.0	2.1
Parker, CO	2.0	14.0	21.4	9.0	35.9	14.4	1.6	1.6
Parkland, FL	3.1	15.0	14.8	8.8	34.0	14.0	7.1	3.1
Peachtree City, GA	3.7	13.2	17.9	7.8	37.3	15.2	3.3	1.6
Pittsfield, MI	7.6	13.2	17.2	7.0	27.4	17.5	4.2	6.0
Plainfield, IL	3.1	17.5	18.8	9.7	31.9	15.8	1.4	1.9
Pleasant Grove, UT	5.3	17.6	27.8	12.5	26.7	8.5	0.6	1.0
Poway, CA	7.0	16.4	21.9	8.8	29.2	11.4	2.8	2.4
Princeton, NJ	4.3	7.6	6.9	2.5	24.4	29.9	7.9	16.5
Queen Creek, AZ	3.6	17.5	28.2	11.0	24.6	11.0	2.9	1.2
Radnor, PA	2.5	11.7	9.2	3.9	33.2	22.9	11.0	5.7
Randolph, NJ	3.5	14.4	13.4	5.8	34.7	20.5	5.0	2.8
Rexburg, ID	1.9	10.6	28.6	18.6	27.5	8.2	1.5	3.1
Rio Rancho, NM	7.1	24.0	28.1	10.8	18.2	9.1	1.3	1.4
Rye, NY	22.5	23.4	14.5	4.4	19.7	11.7	3.1	0.8
Sammamish, WA	1.8	6.2	11.7	7.4	43.5	22.6	3.0	3.7
San Ramon, CA	2.5	8.8	14.4	7.4	39.2	20.4	3.8	3.5
Saratoga, CA	2.4	5.5	10.4	4.7	36.3	28.3	6.0	6.3
Shrewsbury, MA	5.1	17.8	12.5	8.5	29.4	18.0	4.4	4.4
South Brunswick, NJ	4.9	15.2	12.3	6.6	35.7	19.5	3.5	2.2
South Jordan, UT	3.3	16.7	28.3	11.7	25.7	10.7	2.1	1.4
South Kingstown, RI	5.6	20.8	16.7	5.4	27.0	15.1	4.2	5.2
South Portland, ME	4.5	23.3	19.9	9.7	28.2	10.9	2.7	0.9
Sparks, NV	14.0	27.1	26.9	9.4	15.3	5.6	1.0	0.6
State College, PA	3.0	12.1	10.2	4.9	28.8	24.9	2.1	14.1
Sugar Land, TX	7.1	12.4	17.9	6.0	33.4	16.2	3.4	3.5
Sun Prairie, WI	4.0	19.8	22.7	12.4	27.3	10.4	2.2	1.1
Syracuse, UT	2.7	20.6	27.4	12.6	25.3	9.4	1.2	0.8
Tredyffrin, PA	1.8	9.2	9.3	3.4	39.8	24.2	7.3	4.9
Upper Dublin, PA	3.2	15.9	11.5	6.1	32.7	19.7	7.3	3.6
Urbandale, IA	3.4	17.8	19.3	10.1	35.3	9.7	3.4	1.1
Vestal, NY	4.2	22.5	16.7	12.4	21.2	16.0	3.6	3.3
Vestavia Hills, AL	2.8	9.4	15.9	4.1	36.5	17.2	9.7	4.4
Webster, NY	4.7	20.9	16.9	13.8	24.3	15.4	1.6	2.4
Wellesley, MA	1.8	5.6	5.7	3.0	33.7	29.8	11.2	9.2
West Fargo, ND	4.3	19.2	22.9	17.1	25.6	8.1	1.2	1.6
West Lafayette, IN	5.5	10.5	12.4	2.5	27.9	22.6	3.1	15.5
Weston, FL	3.3	12.0	16.3	9.7	34.4	16.2	6.3	1.8
Wilmette, IL	1.5	5.5	9.0	3.0	33.9	27.0	13.8	6.4
Yorba Linda, CA	4.2	12.7	22.8	8.3	32.8	13.0	3.9	2.2
Zionsville, IN	2.1	11.6	11.0	5.3	35.0	20.6	8.6	5.9
U.S.	13.0	27.5	21.0	8.2	18.8	8.2	2.0	1.3

Note: Figures cover persons age 25 and over
Source: U.S. Census Bureau, 2012-2016 American Community Survey 5-Year Estimates

Highest Level of Education: Metro Area

Metro Area	Less than H.S.	H.S. Diploma	Some College, No Deg.	Associate Degree	Bachelors Degree	Masters Degree	Profess. School Degree	Doctorate Degree
Aberdeen, SD	8.1	32.8	20.8	10.9	19.8	5.2	1.1	1.4
Aliso Viejo, CA	20.7	19.9	19.7	7.1	21.2	7.6	2.4	1.3
Allen, TX	15.4	22.5	22.2	6.7	21.9	8.5	1.7	1.0
Ames, IA	3.7	18.5	18.4	9.2	28.0	13.7	2.1	6.5
Amherst, MA	12.5	28.9	18.3	9.6	17.2	9.7	2.0	1.8
Apex, NC	9.2	19.0	18.7	8.8	28.6	11.5	2.1	2.1
Beavercreek, OH	9.8	28.7	24.1	9.5	16.3	8.8	1.5	1.2
Bellevue, NE	8.9	24.4	23.6	8.5	22.9	8.3	2.1	1.2
Bend, OR	7.0	23.6	26.9	9.1	20.9	8.9	2.3	1.2
Benicia, CA	12.5	23.5	28.9	9.9	17.6	5.1	1.6	0.8
Bentonville, AR	14.7	30.0	20.6	5.2	18.5	7.6	2.0	1.3
Bethlehem, NY	7.8	27.3	17.3	12.1	19.7	11.7	2.2	1.9
Blacksburg, VA	11.9	28.2	18.9	8.4	17.2	9.4	1.8	4.1
Bowie, MD	9.6	18.7	16.8	5.6	25.3	16.8	4.2	3.1
Bozeman, MT	3.2	19.5	22.9	6.4	31.6	11.0	2.6	2.9
Brentwood, TN	11.4	28.1	20.7	6.9	21.4	8.1	2.0	1.4
Burlington, VT	7.1	24.7	16.7	8.7	25.8	11.6	3.2	2.1
Cabot, AR	10.2	30.0	24.0	6.9	18.6	7.2	1.9	1.4
Carmel, IN	10.8	28.7	20.4	7.9	20.9	8.0	2.1	1.2
Cedar Falls, IA	8.1	33.1	20.3	11.5	18.2	6.0	1.3	1.3
Cedar Park, TX	11.1	19.2	21.3	6.4	27.4	10.6	2.3	1.8
Central, LA	12.8	32.6	21.6	5.8	18.0	6.2	1.7	1.4
Chapel Hill, NC	11.7	18.8	16.9	6.7	23.7	13.1	3.9	5.2
Cheshire, CT	10.5	30.3	17.6	7.3	18.5	10.8	2.9	2.1
Chino Hills, CA	20.3	26.0	25.3	8.0	13.0	5.2	1.3	0.8
Cibolo, TX	15.7	26.2	23.3	7.8	17.4	7.0	1.6	1.0
Cicero, NY	10.2	29.1	18.3	11.9	17.2	9.8	2.0	1.5
Collierville, TN	13.5	28.7	24.0	6.9	17.0	7.0	1.8	1.1
Coppell, TX	15.4	22.5	22.2	6.7	21.9	8.5	1.7	1.0
Cornelius, NC	12.2	24.5	21.7	8.7	22.3	8.0	1.6	0.9
Cranberry, PA	7.1	34.3	16.3	9.8	19.9	9.0	2.1	1.5
Crown Point, IN	12.4	24.4	20.0	7.1	22.0	10.3	2.5	1.3
Dublin, OH	9.3	28.5	20.1	7.4	22.3	8.8	2.1	1.5
East Fishkill, NY	14.3	25.3	15.5	6.7	22.3	11.3	3.0	1.5
Eden Prairie, MN	6.8	22.1	20.9	10.2	26.4	9.6	2.4	1.5
Edmond, OK	11.9	27.2	24.5	7.2	19.1	7.0	1.8	1.2
Edwardsville, IL	9.0	26.6	23.0	8.7	19.8	9.4	2.0	1.3
Evesham, NJ	10.3	30.0	17.3	6.9	21.3	9.9	2.5	1.8
Flower Mound, TX	15.4	22.5	22.2	6.7	21.9	8.5	1.7	1.0
Folsom, CA	11.5	21.5	25.3	9.8	20.5	7.4	2.5	1.4
Friendswood, TX	17.7	23.3	21.3	6.5	20.1	7.8	1.9	1.4
Gaines, MI	9.9	27.7	22.4	9.2	20.4	7.8	1.6	1.1
Glastonbury, CT	9.6	27.2	17.4	8.2	21.3	12.0	2.8	1.5
Grand Blanc, MI	10.4	32.3	27.0	10.5	12.4	5.8	1.1	0.6
Hampden, PA	10.0	35.0	16.6	8.3	18.7	8.1	2.2	1.2
Hilliard, OH	9.3	28.5	20.1	7.4	22.3	8.8	2.1	1.5
Hillsborough, NJ	14.3	25.3	15.5	6.7	22.3	11.3	3.0	1.5
Holly Springs, NC	9.2	19.0	18.7	8.8	28.6	11.5	2.1	2.1
Independence, KY	9.9	30.3	19.8	8.2	20.0	8.6	1.9	1.3
Juneau, AK	4.4	21.2	27.6	7.4	25.3	10.2	2.6	1.4
Kaysville, UT	6.8	25.3	28.2	10.2	20.4	7.1	1.2	0.8
Keller, TX	15.4	22.5	22.2	6.7	21.9	8.5	1.7	1.0
Lafayette, CA	11.7	16.2	18.7	6.9	27.8	12.4	3.7	2.7
Lafayette, CO	5.5	12.9	16.2	6.0	31.7	18.5	3.8	5.3
Lake Oswego, OR	8.8	20.9	24.8	8.8	23.1	9.6	2.4	1.6
Laramie, WY	4.2	16.8	22.2	8.9	27.4	11.6	2.5	6.3
Leander, TX	11.1	19.2	21.3	6.4	27.4	10.6	2.3	1.8
Leawood, KS	8.6	26.3	22.6	7.6	22.3	9.4	2.2	1.1
Lee's Summit, MO	8.6	26.3	22.6	7.6	22.3	9.4	2.2	1.1
Leesburg, VA	9.6	18.7	16.8	5.6	25.3	16.8	4.2	3.1
Lehi, UT	6.4	17.0	27.8	11.1	26.0	8.3	1.6	1.8
Lexington, MA	8.9	23.3	15.2	7.2	25.1	14.1	3.3	3.0
Los Altos, CA	13.2	15.0	16.5	7.0	26.3	15.9	2.6	3.4
Loveland, CO	4.3	19.4	22.1	8.9	27.8	12.2	2.1	3.2
Lower Macungie, PA	10.7	35.0	17.7	8.9	17.5	7.6	1.5	1.2
Madison, AL	10.8	23.2	21.0	8.0	23.4	10.7	1.5	1.5
Madison, MS	13.2	25.7	23.3	8.5	17.7	7.8	2.4	1.4

Table continued on next page.

Metro Area	Less than H.S.	H.S. Diploma	Some College, No Deg.	Associate Degree	Bachelors Degree	Masters Degree	Profess. School Degree	Doctorate Degree
Maple Valley, WA	8.0	20.3	22.3	9.2	25.4	10.4	2.5	1.8
Marion, IA	5.8	29.1	22.8	12.4	20.6	6.9	1.5	0.9
Marlboro, NJ	14.3	25.3	15.5	6.7	22.3	11.3	3.0	1.5
Mason, OH	9.9	30.3	19.8	8.2	20.0	8.6	1.9	1.3
Menomonee Falls, WI	9.6	26.8	21.2	8.6	22.1	8.4	2.1	1.1
Meridian, ID	9.0	25.7	26.1	8.8	20.7	6.9	1.7	1.2
Meridian, MI	7.1	24.7	25.0	9.8	19.5	9.0	2.3	2.6
Merrimack, NH	8.4	27.1	18.6	9.6	23.3	10.3	1.5	1.2
Milton, GA	11.5	24.3	20.5	7.2	23.1	9.6	2.3	1.4
Moon, PA	7.1	34.3	16.3	9.8	19.9	9.0	2.1	1.5
Moorpark, CA	16.6	18.8	23.6	8.9	20.1	8.2	2.3	1.5
Morgantown, WV	10.7	35.5	16.4	5.3	16.7	9.5	2.9	3.1
Mount Pleasant, SC	10.4	25.3	21.8	9.2	21.6	8.3	2.2	1.3
Newark, DE	10.3	30.0	17.3	6.9	21.3	9.9	2.5	1.8
Newtown, CT	10.1	22.4	15.2	6.0	25.9	15.0	3.9	1.6
North Attleborough, MA	14.2	28.5	18.2	8.7	18.5	8.6	1.8	1.5
North Port, FL	9.3	30.3	21.1	8.5	18.6	8.4	2.3	1.4
North Ridgeville, OH	10.4	29.7	22.0	8.1	18.1	8.2	2.3	1.2
Northville, MI	10.9	27.2	23.7	8.7	17.8	8.9	1.9	1.0
O'Fallon, MO	9.0	26.6	23.0	8.7	19.8	9.4	2.0	1.3
Orchard Park, NY	9.2	29.5	18.9	11.9	17.0	10.2	2.0	1.3
Oro Valley, AZ	12.3	22.6	25.8	8.6	17.8	8.9	2.1	2.0
Oviedo, FL	11.4	27.5	20.9	10.8	19.7	7.0	1.8	0.9
Parker, CO	9.6	20.3	21.2	7.6	26.3	11.0	2.5	1.5
Parkland, FL	15.2	27.2	18.2	9.2	19.2	7.1	2.7	1.2
Peachtree City, GA	11.5	24.3	20.5	7.2	23.1	9.6	2.3	1.4
Pittsfield, MI	5.3	15.6	18.8	7.1	25.3	17.8	4.4	5.8
Plainfield, IL	12.4	24.4	20.0	7.1	22.0	10.3	2.5	1.3
Pleasant Grove, UT	6.4	17.0	27.8	11.1	26.0	8.3	1.6	1.8
Poway, CA	13.6	18.8	22.4	8.7	22.5	9.2	2.7	2.1
Princeton, NJ	12.3	25.2	16.3	5.8	21.0	13.1	2.6	3.7
Queen Creek, AZ	13.2	23.5	24.9	8.5	19.0	7.8	1.8	1.1
Radnor, PA	10.3	30.0	17.3	6.9	21.3	9.9	2.5	1.8
Randolph, NJ	14.3	25.3	15.5	6.7	22.3	11.3	3.0	1.5
Rexburg, ID	6.8	21.5	25.6	14.7	21.0	7.0	1.3	2.1
Rio Rancho, NM	12.2	24.7	24.1	8.2	17.2	9.5	1.9	2.1
Rye, NY	14.3	25.3	15.5	6.7	22.3	11.3	3.0	1.5
Sammamish, WA	8.0	20.3	22.3	9.2	25.4	10.4	2.5	1.8
San Ramon, CA	11.7	16.2	18.7	6.9	27.8	12.4	3.7	2.7
Saratoga, CA	13.2	15.0	16.5	7.0	26.3	15.9	2.6	3.4
Shrewsbury, MA	10.2	29.5	17.9	8.9	20.4	9.8	1.7	1.5
South Brunswick, NJ	14.3	25.3	15.5	6.7	22.3	11.3	3.0	1.5
South Jordan, UT	10.1	23.1	25.6	8.9	20.7	7.9	2.1	1.6
South Kingstown, RI	14.2	28.5	18.2	8.7	18.5	8.6	1.8	1.5
South Portland, ME	6.3	27.3	18.9	9.5	24.5	9.5	2.5	1.5
Sparks, NV	12.9	23.9	26.3	7.9	18.2	7.1	2.0	1.6
State College, PA	6.7	31.1	12.1	7.6	22.3	12.7	1.7	5.7
Sugar Land, TX	17.7	23.3	21.3	6.5	20.1	7.8	1.9	1.4
Sun Prairie, WI	5.2	21.8	18.8	10.2	26.6	11.3	2.9	3.0
Syracuse, UT	6.8	25.3	28.2	10.2	20.4	7.1	1.2	0.8
Tredyffrin, PA	10.3	30.0	17.3	6.9	21.3	9.9	2.5	1.8
Upper Dublin, PA	10.3	30.0	17.3	6.9	21.3	9.9	2.5	1.8
Urbandale, IA	7.4	25.4	20.9	10.3	25.2	7.4	2.2	1.1
Vestal, NY	9.8	32.6	18.2	12.2	15.4	8.9	1.5	1.3
Vestavia Hills, AL	12.5	28.1	22.6	8.0	18.0	7.2	2.4	1.3
Webster, NY	9.8	27.3	17.9	12.0	18.5	11.0	2.0	1.6
Wellesley, MA	8.9	23.3	15.2	7.2	25.1	14.1	3.3	3.0
West Fargo, ND	5.5	22.3	21.7	14.3	25.7	7.1	1.6	1.8
West Lafayette, IN	9.6	29.1	21.0	7.9	18.5	9.0	1.5	3.3
Weston, FL	15.2	27.2	18.2	9.2	19.2	7.1	2.7	1.2
Wilmette, IL	12.4	24.4	20.0	7.1	22.0	10.3	2.5	1.3
Yorba Linda, CA	20.7	19.9	19.7	7.1	21.2	7.6	2.4	1.3
Zionsville, IN	10.8	28.7	20.4	7.9	20.9	8.0	2.1	1.2
U.S.	13.0	27.5	21.0	8.2	18.8	8.2	2.0	1.3

Note: Figures cover persons age 25 and over; Figures cover the Metropolitan Statistical Area—see Appendix B for areas included
Source: U.S. Census Bureau, 2012-2016 American Community Survey 5-Year Estimates

School Enrollment by Grade and Control: City

City	Preschool (%)		Kindergarten (%)		Grades 1 - 4 (%)		Grades 5 - 8 (%)		Grades 9 - 12 (%)	
	Public	Private	Public	Private	Public	Private	Public	Private	Public	Private
Aberdeen, SD	69.3	30.7	76.1	23.9	80.8	19.2	78.7	21.3	81.5	18.5
Aliso Viejo, CA	27.4	72.6	84.4	15.6	84.4	15.6	88.0	12.0	89.9	10.1
Allen, TX	33.8	66.2	86.6	13.4	92.9	7.1	93.3	6.7	95.7	4.3
Ames, IA	60.5	39.5	88.1	11.9	85.2	14.8	97.6	2.4	93.6	6.4
Amherst, MA	62.9	37.1	86.4	13.6	84.3	15.7	84.1	15.9	93.1	6.9
Apex, NC	29.3	70.7	90.6	9.4	86.4	13.6	87.2	12.8	93.7	6.3
Beavercreek, OH	32.7	67.3	74.0	26.0	87.6	12.4	85.9	14.1	84.4	15.6
Bellevue, NE	56.4	43.6	88.5	11.5	91.5	8.5	91.4	8.6	91.4	8.6
Bend, OR	22.2	77.8	85.5	14.5	89.7	10.3	90.6	9.4	94.4	5.6
Benicia, CA	62.3	37.7	90.0	10.0	93.3	6.7	91.7	8.3	94.5	5.5
Bentonville, AR	34.2	65.8	86.3	13.7	92.6	7.4	95.1	4.9	97.8	2.2
Bethlehem, NY	37.2	62.8	94.4	5.6	92.1	7.9	94.1	5.9	87.1	12.9
Blacksburg, VA	11.7	88.3	81.4	18.6	84.8	15.2	90.5	9.5	89.8	10.2
Bowie, MD	40.7	59.3	85.3	14.7	72.2	27.8	74.0	26.0	71.5	28.5
Bozeman, MT	26.9	73.1	87.2	12.8	92.8	7.2	89.8	10.2	88.5	11.5
Brentwood, TN	31.3	68.8	81.5	18.5	90.4	9.6	81.4	18.6	79.8	20.2
Burlington, VT	47.2	52.8	89.8	10.2	93.0	7.0	94.3	5.7	91.9	8.1
Cabot, AR	47.2	52.8	96.7	3.3	96.1	3.9	95.3	4.7	94.2	5.8
Carmel, IN	21.7	78.3	80.4	19.6	83.3	16.7	89.9	10.1	84.6	15.4
Cedar Falls, IA	63.9	36.1	93.5	6.5	91.7	8.3	92.8	7.2	96.4	3.6
Cedar Park, TX	31.5	68.5	87.0	13.0	95.1	4.9	90.2	9.8	93.9	6.1
Central, LA	61.3	38.7	78.2	21.8	85.0	15.0	74.7	25.3	76.7	23.3
Chapel Hill, NC	28.7	71.3	85.6	14.4	93.4	6.6	93.5	6.5	89.2	10.8
Cheshire, CT	21.0	79.0	89.9	10.1	92.8	7.2	92.8	7.2	91.3	8.7
Chino Hills, CA	36.5	63.5	86.8	13.2	87.9	12.1	91.2	8.8	92.7	7.3
Cibolo, TX	60.7	39.3	76.2	23.8	89.8	10.2	96.4	3.6	96.8	3.2
Cicero, NY	57.9	42.1	92.1	7.9	90.4	9.6	96.1	3.9	93.6	6.4
Collierville, TN	22.3	77.7	63.3	36.7	82.7	17.3	81.8	18.2	80.3	19.7
Coppell, TX	31.0	69.0	84.5	15.5	90.5	9.5	87.3	12.7	91.6	8.4
Cornelius, NC	17.8	82.2	77.0	23.0	87.1	12.9	85.1	14.9	90.8	9.2
Cranberry, PA	32.7	67.3	80.8	19.2	82.1	17.9	85.7	14.3	85.4	14.6
Crown Point, IN	44.7	55.3	73.6	26.4	81.5	18.5	81.0	19.0	88.0	12.0
Dublin, OH	27.6	72.4	73.1	26.9	89.6	10.4	87.4	12.6	92.0	8.0
East Fishkill, NY	5.1	94.9	87.0	13.0	84.5	15.5	89.6	10.4	91.7	8.3
Eden Prairie, MN	49.6	50.4	81.0	19.0	81.7	18.3	82.2	17.8	91.4	8.6
Edmond, OK	53.7	46.3	79.3	20.7	82.8	17.2	84.3	15.7	90.9	9.1
Edwardsville, IL	53.0	47.0	67.4	32.6	76.8	23.2	85.0	15.0	95.1	4.9
Evesham, NJ	30.1	69.9	90.7	9.3	96.0	4.0	90.8	9.2	93.0	7.0
Flower Mound, TX	29.3	70.7	77.7	22.3	91.7	8.3	93.6	6.4	92.2	7.8
Folsom, CA	48.2	51.8	70.6	29.4	89.2	10.8	92.1	7.9	95.7	4.3
Friendswood, TX	31.6	68.4	89.5	10.5	92.2	7.8	92.9	7.1	95.9	4.1
Gaines, MI	66.5	33.5	95.2	4.8	85.1	14.9	86.9	13.1	77.0	23.0
Glastonbury, CT	42.4	57.6	97.3	2.7	97.3	2.7	86.4	13.6	89.0	11.0
Grand Blanc, MI	83.0	17.0	84.8	15.2	90.2	9.8	90.9	9.1	96.2	3.8
Hampden, PA	43.7	56.3	90.7	9.3	96.1	3.9	94.8	5.2	91.8	8.2
Hilliard, OH	31.3	68.8	94.1	5.9	92.3	7.7	87.9	12.1	87.5	12.5
Hillsborough, NJ	38.2	61.8	80.2	19.8	93.9	6.1	90.8	9.2	90.9	9.1
Holly Springs, NC	15.1	84.9	84.2	15.8	92.2	7.8	87.4	12.6	94.9	5.1
Independence, KY	37.2	62.8	86.9	13.1	82.2	17.8	86.6	13.4	91.8	8.2
Juneau, AK	79.4	20.6	93.9	6.1	96.7	3.3	92.1	7.9	94.0	6.0
Kaysville, UT	38.9	61.1	92.7	7.3	98.0	2.0	96.8	3.2	99.5	0.5
Keller, TX	27.6	72.4	85.0	15.0	83.7	16.3	85.2	14.8	82.1	17.9
Lafayette, CA	36.2	63.8	85.1	14.9	93.4	6.6	87.3	12.7	92.4	7.6
Lafayette, CO	50.3	49.7	84.0	16.0	92.9	7.1	95.3	4.7	89.0	11.0
Lake Oswego, OR	27.5	72.5	84.9	15.1	86.1	13.9	89.0	11.0	90.5	9.5
Laramie, WY	62.5	37.5	100.0	0.0	89.8	10.2	93.4	6.6	92.4	7.6
Leander, TX	52.2	47.8	82.8	17.2	98.0	2.0	94.8	5.2	97.2	2.8
Leawood, KS	25.4	74.6	71.8	28.2	64.8	35.2	66.5	33.5	69.5	30.5
Lee's Summit, MO	39.4	60.6	87.9	12.1	90.7	9.3	91.7	8.3	91.7	8.3
Leesburg, VA	31.5	68.5	93.0	7.0	93.9	6.1	94.6	5.4	96.0	4.0
Lehi, UT	42.4	57.6	96.3	3.7	96.3	3.7	97.1	2.9	96.9	3.1
Lexington, MA	23.1	76.9	88.3	11.7	94.5	5.5	90.9	9.1	90.9	9.1
Los Altos, CA	18.0	82.0	83.8	16.2	80.7	19.3	78.0	22.0	73.8	26.2
Loveland, CO	56.0	44.0	90.1	9.9	91.8	8.2	90.3	9.7	93.8	6.2
Lower Macungie, PA	16.5	83.5	62.9	37.1	91.2	8.8	89.2	10.8	93.6	6.4
Madison, AL	56.2	43.8	89.4	10.6	92.3	7.7	88.1	11.9	92.6	7.4
Madison, MS	17.9	82.1	73.9	26.1	74.9	25.1	73.0	27.0	79.6	20.4
Maple Valley, WA	31.4	68.6	79.9	20.1	91.9	8.1	94.2	5.8	97.1	2.9

Table continued on next page.

City	Preschool (%)		Kindergarten (%)		Grades 1 - 4 (%)		Grades 5 - 8 (%)		Grades 9 - 12 (%)	
	Public	Private	Public	Private	Public	Private	Public	Private	Public	Private
Marion, IA	53.8	46.2	82.1	17.9	89.6	10.4	93.8	6.2	95.1	4.9
Marlboro, NJ	19.6	80.4	87.5	12.5	98.4	1.6	98.2	1.8	91.3	8.7
Mason, OH	54.7	45.3	70.3	29.7	83.7	16.3	92.6	7.4	83.5	16.5
Menomonee Falls, WI	41.3	58.7	88.1	11.9	77.9	22.1	81.3	18.7	86.9	13.1
Meridian, ID	34.2	65.8	86.9	13.1	91.9	8.1	94.8	5.2	94.4	5.6
Meridian, MI	49.9	50.1	71.0	29.0	90.3	9.7	93.6	6.4	92.8	7.2
Merrimack, NH	38.1	61.9	79.5	20.5	95.0	5.0	90.1	9.9	85.3	14.7
Milton, GA	16.0	84.0	81.6	18.4	85.2	14.8	82.5	17.5	89.8	10.2
Moon, PA	42.0	58.0	84.1	15.9	87.2	12.8	90.3	9.7	92.5	7.5
Moorpark, CA	62.4	37.6	92.8	7.2	91.7	8.3	87.0	13.0	89.8	10.2
Morgantown, WV	54.2	45.8	93.3	6.7	78.4	21.6	86.4	13.6	94.0	6.0
Mount Pleasant, SC	32.5	67.5	73.3	26.7	89.1	10.9	82.4	17.6	90.7	9.3
Newark, DE	33.1	66.9	87.9	12.1	74.0	26.0	65.9	34.1	84.7	15.3
Newtown, CT	48.6	51.4	85.1	14.9	93.9	6.1	90.3	9.7	89.7	10.3
North Attleborough, MA	36.7	63.3	87.4	12.6	79.4	20.6	87.1	12.9	86.1	13.9
North Port, FL	42.7	57.3	90.0	10.0	91.8	8.2	93.4	6.6	90.3	9.7
North Ridgeville, OH	36.3	63.7	70.4	29.6	83.0	17.0	82.5	17.5	84.5	15.5
Northville, MI	35.7	64.3	79.8	20.2	89.8	10.2	88.8	11.2	85.7	14.3
O'Fallon, MO	32.8	67.2	87.5	12.5	79.7	20.3	84.9	15.1	83.2	16.8
Orchard Park, NY	61.3	38.7	72.9	27.1	83.7	16.3	82.0	18.0	85.9	14.1
Oro Valley, AZ	34.7	65.3	65.4	34.6	86.9	13.1	92.2	7.8	88.1	11.9
Oviedo, FL	43.8	56.2	74.3	25.7	83.2	16.8	83.9	16.1	95.5	4.5
Parker, CO	43.5	56.5	92.4	7.6	89.9	10.1	90.9	9.1	93.5	6.5
Parkland, FL	15.4	84.6	89.1	10.9	84.4	15.6	88.9	11.1	75.8	24.2
Peachtree City, GA	42.9	57.1	89.5	10.5	85.2	14.8	86.8	13.2	91.5	8.5
Pittsfield, MI	45.9	54.1	85.4	14.6	90.6	9.4	89.3	10.7	90.0	10.0
Plainfield, IL	42.9	57.1	100.0	0.0	94.4	5.6	93.5	6.5	95.3	4.7
Pleasant Grove, UT	57.0	43.0	89.1	10.9	93.9	6.1	92.7	7.3	97.7	2.3
Poway, CA	56.6	43.4	90.7	9.3	92.3	7.7	91.9	8.1	93.1	6.9
Princeton, NJ	13.6	86.4	66.4	33.6	85.5	14.5	88.3	11.7	83.0	17.0
Queen Creek, AZ	48.5	51.5	89.0	11.0	92.1	7.9	88.3	11.7	95.0	5.0
Radnor, PA	10.4	89.6	77.4	22.6	74.0	26.0	78.1	21.9	78.2	21.8
Randolph, NJ	34.3	65.7	66.7	33.3	89.2	10.8	95.7	4.3	90.3	9.7
Rexburg, ID	71.2	28.8	95.2	4.8	96.0	4.0	97.7	2.3	100.0	0.0
Rio Rancho, NM	65.0	35.0	86.6	13.4	87.3	12.7	89.8	10.2	92.1	7.9
Rye, NY	46.2	53.8	85.8	14.2	93.9	6.1	85.5	14.5	88.8	11.2
Sammamish, WA	24.0	76.0	74.8	25.2	89.5	10.5	91.8	8.2	89.2	10.8
San Ramon, CA	22.9	77.1	89.6	10.4	94.2	5.8	96.2	3.8	95.2	4.8
Saratoga, CA	22.0	78.0	80.9	19.1	79.2	20.8	83.8	16.2	77.3	22.7
Shrewsbury, MA	54.2	45.8	92.3	7.7	88.8	11.2	91.6	8.4	85.4	14.6
South Brunswick, NJ	31.1	68.9	77.1	22.9	95.6	4.4	94.5	5.5	93.3	6.7
South Jordan, UT	51.9	48.1	97.5	2.5	95.5	4.5	96.8	3.2	96.3	3.7
South Kingstown, RI	55.3	44.7	100.0	0.0	93.1	6.9	97.3	2.7	86.0	14.0
South Portland, ME	29.9	70.1	100.0	0.0	89.4	10.6	84.1	15.9	92.8	7.2
Sparks, NV	59.6	40.4	89.4	10.6	93.8	6.2	93.0	7.0	96.9	3.1
State College, PA	29.3	70.7	96.7	3.3	89.1	10.9	72.1	27.9	91.2	8.8
Sugar Land, TX	28.4	71.6	80.5	19.5	83.8	16.2	89.2	10.8	91.6	8.4
Sun Prairie, WI	52.1	47.9	84.8	15.2	93.0	7.0	93.2	6.8	96.1	3.9
Syracuse, UT	58.1	41.9	98.5	1.5	95.6	4.4	96.3	3.7	94.9	5.1
Tredyffrin, PA	18.5	81.5	86.6	13.4	92.1	7.9	90.5	9.5	85.9	14.1
Upper Dublin, PA	10.7	89.3	89.5	10.5	84.0	16.0	85.3	14.7	80.4	19.6
Urbandale, IA	59.9	40.1	80.3	19.7	84.6	15.4	81.6	18.4	82.1	17.9
Vestal, NY	61.9	38.1	91.8	8.2	96.2	3.8	98.7	1.3	88.5	11.5
Vestavia Hills, AL	26.6	73.4	74.0	26.0	89.9	10.1	86.8	13.2	90.6	9.4
Webster, NY	51.8	48.2	82.5	17.5	91.4	8.6	88.7	11.3	87.5	12.5
Wellesley, MA	17.1	82.9	76.0	24.0	80.3	19.7	79.4	20.6	76.3	23.7
West Fargo, ND	66.8	33.2	100.0	0.0	94.1	5.9	87.6	12.4	93.7	6.3
West Lafayette, IN	38.5	61.5	85.7	14.3	91.9	8.1	86.5	13.5	92.6	7.4
Weston, FL	31.3	68.7	76.5	23.5	84.1	15.9	86.3	13.7	84.1	15.9
Wilmette, IL	32.8	67.2	76.7	23.3	81.6	18.4	82.2	17.8	89.5	10.5
Yorba Linda, CA	40.9	59.1	78.7	21.3	81.0	19.0	88.6	11.4	88.2	11.8
Zionsville, IN	27.7	72.3	76.6	23.4	96.7	3.3	92.7	7.3	91.6	8.4
U.S.	58.4	41.6	87.7	12.3	89.8	10.2	89.7	10.3	90.4	9.6

Note: Figures shown cover persons 3 years old and over
Source: U.S. Census Bureau, 2012-2016 American Community Survey 5-Year Estimates

School Enrollment by Grade and Control: Metro Area

Metro Area	Preschool (%)		Kindergarten (%)		Grades 1 - 4 (%)		Grades 5 - 8 (%)		Grades 9 - 12 (%)	
	Public	Private	Public	Private	Public	Private	Public	Private	Public	Private
Aberdeen, SD	71.0	29.0	81.2	18.8	85.6	14.4	81.8	18.2	83.1	16.9
Aliso Viejo, CA	58.6	41.4	88.8	11.2	90.7	9.3	90.8	9.2	91.6	8.4
Allen, TX	57.4	42.6	89.3	10.7	92.6	7.4	92.0	8.0	92.3	7.7
Ames, IA	70.4	29.6	92.0	8.0	87.3	12.7	96.2	3.8	96.4	3.6
Amherst, MA	63.4	36.6	90.6	9.4	91.8	8.2	92.0	8.0	93.2	6.8
Apex, NC	40.5	59.5	87.6	12.4	89.6	10.4	89.5	10.5	89.8	10.2
Beavercreek, OH	60.7	39.3	83.5	16.5	86.9	13.1	86.9	13.1	87.5	12.5
Bellevue, NE	57.5	42.5	85.8	14.2	87.9	12.1	88.2	11.8	88.3	11.7
Bend, OR	30.0	70.0	92.5	7.5	90.1	9.9	89.6	10.4	95.0	5.0
Benicia, CA	53.6	46.4	91.5	8.5	91.3	8.7	91.8	8.2	92.9	7.1
Bentonville, AR	60.7	39.3	90.8	9.2	91.6	8.4	90.8	9.2	93.7	6.3
Bethlehem, NY	47.9	52.1	88.0	12.0	91.0	9.0	91.3	8.7	91.1	8.9
Blacksburg, VA	48.1	51.9	89.6	10.4	91.0	9.0	88.7	11.3	90.5	9.5
Bowie, MD	43.0	57.0	85.5	14.5	88.7	11.3	88.1	11.9	88.6	11.4
Bozeman, MT	30.3	69.7	81.7	18.3	86.3	13.7	87.9	12.1	83.2	16.8
Brentwood, TN	48.9	51.1	87.9	12.1	88.9	11.1	85.9	14.1	85.1	14.9
Burlington, VT	49.8	50.2	93.5	6.5	94.3	5.7	92.6	7.4	93.9	6.1
Cabot, AR	59.7	40.3	84.7	15.3	88.0	12.0	86.9	13.1	87.0	13.0
Carmel, IN	48.9	51.1	85.2	14.8	89.4	10.6	89.0	11.0	89.3	10.7
Cedar Falls, IA	72.0	28.0	88.1	11.9	90.6	9.4	90.1	9.9	90.0	10.0
Cedar Park, TX	50.0	50.0	88.8	11.2	91.4	8.6	91.6	8.4	93.5	6.5
Central, LA	59.4	40.6	76.9	23.1	82.7	17.3	82.3	17.7	82.5	17.5
Chapel Hill, NC	42.6	57.4	89.1	10.9	89.7	10.3	89.9	10.1	89.2	10.8
Cheshire, CT	60.5	39.5	85.5	14.5	91.6	8.4	91.8	8.2	90.0	10.0
Chino Hills, CA	66.2	33.8	92.1	7.9	94.0	6.0	94.5	5.5	94.7	5.3
Cibolo, TX	67.1	32.9	90.9	9.1	93.1	6.9	92.4	7.6	93.6	6.4
Cicero, NY	64.3	35.7	91.4	8.6	92.5	7.5	92.3	7.7	93.6	6.4
Collierville, TN	62.4	37.6	85.1	14.9	86.2	13.8	85.5	14.5	85.3	14.7
Coppell, TX	57.4	42.6	89.3	10.7	92.6	7.4	92.0	8.0	92.3	7.7
Cornelius, NC	49.5	50.5	90.0	10.0	90.4	9.6	90.0	10.0	90.4	9.6
Cranberry, PA	48.3	51.7	84.3	15.7	87.5	12.5	88.2	11.8	89.7	10.3
Crown Point, IN	58.7	41.3	85.0	15.0	88.7	11.3	89.1	10.9	90.5	9.5
Dublin, OH	50.6	49.4	87.5	12.5	89.9	10.1	88.5	11.5	89.2	10.8
East Fishkill, NY	51.9	48.1	81.6	18.4	86.1	13.9	86.3	13.7	85.9	14.1
Eden Prairie, MN	57.8	42.2	87.3	12.7	88.5	11.5	89.1	10.9	90.8	9.2
Edmond, OK	72.0	28.0	89.9	10.1	91.3	8.7	90.7	9.3	91.7	8.3
Edwardsville, IL	52.8	47.2	83.0	17.0	84.0	16.0	84.4	15.6	85.6	14.4
Evesham, NJ	43.6	56.4	81.7	18.3	85.0	15.0	83.6	16.4	83.6	16.4
Flower Mound, TX	57.4	42.6	89.3	10.7	92.6	7.4	92.0	8.0	92.3	7.7
Folsom, CA	57.7	42.3	88.6	11.4	91.7	8.3	92.3	7.7	92.8	7.2
Friendswood, TX	58.9	41.1	90.0	10.0	92.8	7.2	93.4	6.6	93.4	6.6
Gaines, MI	64.5	35.5	83.6	16.4	84.8	15.2	86.4	13.6	86.2	13.8
Glastonbury, CT	57.3	42.7	91.2	8.8	93.7	6.3	93.3	6.7	91.1	8.9
Grand Blanc, MI	83.9	16.1	93.5	6.5	92.0	8.0	92.1	7.9	92.8	7.2
Hampden, PA	49.4	50.6	80.3	19.7	85.7	14.3	88.0	12.0	88.6	11.4
Hilliard, OH	50.6	49.4	87.5	12.5	89.9	10.1	88.5	11.5	89.2	10.8
Hillsborough, NJ	51.9	48.1	81.6	18.4	86.1	13.9	86.3	13.7	85.9	14.1
Holly Springs, NC	40.5	59.5	87.6	12.4	89.6	10.4	89.5	10.5	89.8	10.2
Independence, KY	54.2	45.8	80.9	19.1	82.7	17.3	83.1	16.9	82.8	17.2
Juneau, AK	79.4	20.6	93.9	6.1	96.7	3.3	92.1	7.9	94.0	6.0
Kaysville, UT	55.7	44.3	93.2	6.8	96.6	3.4	96.6	3.4	96.9	3.1
Keller, TX	57.4	42.6	89.3	10.7	92.6	7.4	92.0	8.0	92.3	7.7
Lafayette, CA	41.7	58.3	84.5	15.5	86.4	13.6	85.9	14.1	87.9	12.1
Lafayette, CO	47.6	52.4	90.3	9.7	90.3	9.7	92.6	7.4	94.4	5.6
Lake Oswego, OR	40.3	59.7	84.9	15.1	88.9	11.1	89.9	10.1	91.2	8.8
Laramie, WY	65.9	34.1	100.0	0.0	90.4	9.6	92.7	7.3	90.6	9.4
Leander, TX	50.0	50.0	88.8	11.2	91.4	8.6	91.6	8.4	93.5	6.5
Leawood, KS	53.4	46.6	87.9	12.1	89.0	11.0	88.8	11.2	90.3	9.7
Lee's Summit, MO	53.4	46.6	87.9	12.1	89.0	11.0	88.8	11.2	90.3	9.7
Leesburg, VA	43.0	57.0	85.5	14.5	88.7	11.3	88.1	11.9	88.6	11.4
Lehi, UT	46.7	53.3	91.9	8.1	94.6	5.4	95.0	5.0	95.0	5.0
Lexington, MA	44.7	55.3	86.6	13.4	90.6	9.4	89.7	10.3	87.0	13.0
Los Altos, CA	35.4	64.6	81.9	18.1	86.7	13.3	87.3	12.7	88.0	12.0
Loveland, CO	47.8	52.2	89.9	10.1	91.7	8.3	91.8	8.2	95.2	4.8
Lower Macungie, PA	45.3	54.7	80.4	19.6	90.6	9.4	89.9	10.1	90.4	9.6
Madison, AL	47.5	52.5	85.3	14.7	85.3	14.7	86.6	13.4	88.5	11.5
Madison, MS	60.5	39.5	76.8	23.2	85.4	14.6	85.0	15.0	84.9	15.1
Maple Valley, WA	40.4	59.6	83.9	16.1	88.6	11.4	88.5	11.5	90.7	9.3

Table continued on next page.

Metro Area	Preschool (%)		Kindergarten (%)		Grades 1 - 4 (%)		Grades 5 - 8 (%)		Grades 9 - 12 (%)	
	Public	Private	Public	Private	Public	Private	Public	Private	Public	Private
Marion, IA	65.1	34.9	86.9	13.1	88.4	11.6	91.4	8.6	92.4	7.6
Marlboro, NJ	51.9	48.1	81.6	18.4	86.1	13.9	86.3	13.7	85.9	14.1
Mason, OH	54.2	45.8	80.9	19.1	82.7	17.3	83.1	16.9	82.8	17.2
Menomonee Falls, WI	53.5	46.5	77.3	22.7	80.4	19.6	79.7	20.3	85.4	14.6
Meridian, ID	40.4	59.6	90.3	9.7	92.1	7.9	93.6	6.4	91.8	8.2
Meridian, MI	65.6	34.4	87.0	13.0	89.3	10.7	89.6	10.4	92.8	7.2
Merrimack, NH	38.3	61.7	78.5	21.5	89.0	11.0	90.2	9.8	89.2	10.8
Milton, GA	56.5	43.5	86.6	13.4	90.5	9.5	89.4	10.6	89.9	10.1
Moon, PA	48.3	51.7	84.3	15.7	87.5	12.5	88.2	11.8	89.7	10.3
Moorpark, CA	53.7	46.3	90.4	9.6	91.4	8.6	90.5	9.5	91.6	8.4
Morgantown, WV	70.3	29.7	92.1	7.9	89.7	10.3	90.2	9.8	91.1	8.9
Mount Pleasant, SC	49.7	50.3	86.5	13.5	90.1	9.9	88.8	11.2	88.6	11.4
Newark, DE	43.6	56.4	81.7	18.3	85.0	15.0	83.6	16.4	83.6	16.4
Newtown, CT	39.1	60.9	85.0	15.0	87.7	12.3	86.3	13.7	85.7	14.3
North Attleborough, MA	53.0	47.0	87.5	12.5	89.7	10.3	88.8	11.2	86.8	13.2
North Port, FL	59.8	40.2	87.3	12.7	91.3	8.7	90.2	9.8	89.6	10.4
North Ridgeville, OH	51.4	48.6	80.5	19.5	81.2	18.8	81.5	18.5	84.0	16.0
Northville, MI	65.4	34.6	88.2	11.8	90.1	9.9	90.6	9.4	91.1	8.9
O'Fallon, MO	52.8	47.2	83.0	17.0	84.0	16.0	84.4	15.6	85.6	14.4
Orchard Park, NY	66.4	33.6	87.6	12.4	89.5	10.5	89.1	10.9	88.8	11.2
Oro Valley, AZ	61.1	38.9	88.9	11.1	92.6	7.4	92.1	7.9	92.3	7.7
Oviedo, FL	54.9	45.1	83.8	16.2	88.6	11.4	87.9	12.1	90.8	9.2
Parker, CO	58.1	41.9	90.4	9.6	92.9	7.1	92.0	8.0	92.5	7.5
Parkland, FL	49.8	50.2	83.6	16.4	86.5	13.5	87.4	12.6	87.4	12.6
Peachtree City, GA	56.5	43.5	86.6	13.4	90.5	9.5	89.4	10.6	89.9	10.1
Pittsfield, MI	49.0	51.0	87.3	12.7	88.3	11.7	86.2	13.8	91.0	9.0
Plainfield, IL	58.7	41.3	85.0	15.0	88.7	11.3	89.1	10.9	90.5	9.5
Pleasant Grove, UT	46.7	53.3	91.9	8.1	94.6	5.4	95.0	5.0	95.0	5.0
Poway, CA	56.6	43.4	89.9	10.1	92.5	7.5	92.0	8.0	92.6	7.4
Princeton, NJ	46.4	53.6	88.9	11.1	90.4	9.6	91.2	8.8	88.0	12.0
Queen Creek, AZ	58.7	41.3	91.8	8.2	92.9	7.1	93.7	6.3	93.7	6.3
Radnor, PA	43.6	56.4	81.7	18.3	85.0	15.0	83.6	16.4	83.6	16.4
Randolph, NJ	51.9	48.1	81.6	18.4	86.1	13.9	86.3	13.7	85.9	14.1
Rexburg, ID	66.2	33.8	96.9	3.1	97.9	2.1	98.7	1.3	98.3	1.7
Rio Rancho, NM	62.8	37.2	87.7	12.3	90.5	9.5	88.8	11.2	90.0	10.0
Rye, NY	51.9	48.1	81.6	18.4	86.1	13.9	86.3	13.7	85.9	14.1
Sammamish, WA	40.4	59.6	83.9	16.1	88.6	11.4	88.5	11.5	90.7	9.3
San Ramon, CA	41.7	58.3	84.5	15.5	86.4	13.6	85.9	14.1	87.9	12.1
Saratoga, CA	35.4	64.6	81.9	18.1	86.7	13.3	87.3	12.7	88.0	12.0
Shrewsbury, MA	58.2	41.8	92.4	7.6	92.6	7.4	91.9	8.1	91.2	8.8
South Brunswick, NJ	51.9	48.1	81.6	18.4	86.1	13.9	86.3	13.7	85.9	14.1
South Jordan, UT	54.4	45.6	91.1	8.9	93.1	6.9	92.8	7.2	93.8	6.2
South Kingstown, RI	53.0	47.0	87.5	12.5	89.7	10.3	88.8	11.2	86.8	13.2
South Portland, ME	39.2	60.8	88.9	11.1	92.4	7.6	92.6	7.4	90.4	9.6
Sparks, NV	54.4	45.6	90.1	9.9	92.5	7.5	91.6	8.4	94.6	5.4
State College, PA	37.8	62.2	85.1	14.9	87.0	13.0	83.7	16.3	91.8	8.2
Sugar Land, TX	58.9	41.1	90.0	10.0	92.8	7.2	93.4	6.6	93.4	6.6
Sun Prairie, WI	61.1	38.9	89.5	10.5	89.9	10.1	90.3	9.7	94.8	5.2
Syracuse, UT	55.7	44.3	93.2	6.8	96.6	3.4	96.6	3.4	96.9	3.1
Tredyffrin, PA	43.6	56.4	81.7	18.3	85.0	15.0	83.6	16.4	83.6	16.4
Upper Dublin, PA	43.6	56.4	81.7	18.3	85.0	15.0	83.6	16.4	83.6	16.4
Urbandale, IA	65.9	34.1	90.0	10.0	90.8	9.2	90.4	9.6	91.0	9.0
Vestal, NY	74.1	25.9	90.9	9.1	91.9	8.1	94.0	6.0	93.8	6.2
Vestavia Hills, AL	44.4	55.6	84.2	15.8	90.8	9.2	90.8	9.2	90.2	9.8
Webster, NY	60.3	39.7	89.9	10.1	90.6	9.4	90.0	10.0	90.1	9.9
Wellesley, MA	44.7	55.3	86.6	13.4	90.6	9.4	89.7	10.3	87.0	13.0
West Fargo, ND	63.9	36.1	90.7	9.3	88.5	11.5	88.4	11.6	91.8	8.2
West Lafayette, IN	42.1	57.9	89.2	10.8	89.1	10.9	86.7	13.3	89.0	11.0
Weston, FL	49.8	50.2	83.6	16.4	86.5	13.5	87.4	12.6	87.4	12.6
Wilmette, IL	58.7	41.3	85.0	15.0	88.7	11.3	89.1	10.9	90.5	9.5
Yorba Linda, CA	58.6	41.4	88.8	11.2	90.7	9.3	90.8	9.2	91.6	8.4
Zionsville, IN	48.9	51.1	85.2	14.8	89.4	10.6	89.0	11.0	89.3	10.7
U.S.	58.4	41.6	87.7	12.3	89.8	10.2	89.7	10.3	90.4	9.6

Note: Figures shown cover persons 3 years old and over; Figures cover the Metropolitan Statistical Area—see Appendix B for areas included;

Source: U.S. Census Bureau, 2012-2016 American Community Survey 5-Year Estimates

Educational Attainment by Race: City

City	High School Graduate or Higher (%)					Bachelor's Degree or Higher (%)				
	Total	White	Black	Asian	Hisp.[1]	Total	White	Black	Asian	Hisp.[1]
Aberdeen, SD	91.5	92.4	76.2	60.1	69.7	28.3	28.9	26.7	29.6	23.7
Aliso Viejo, CA	96.8	97.6	100.0	98.6	87.2	57.5	56.5	54.1	71.5	35.5
Allen, TX	95.2	95.5	98.9	91.7	77.9	53.1	51.4	52.1	68.7	30.8
Ames, IA	97.4	98.3	81.9	94.9	94.0	63.4	61.6	45.1	86.7	49.3
Amherst, MA	94.5	96.9	74.9	89.5	73.9	65.5	70.1	24.6	64.7	42.6
Apex, NC	95.1	95.5	89.6	94.6	67.0	60.7	61.1	40.5	80.5	28.1
Beavercreek, OH	97.3	97.4	98.2	93.0	96.7	50.0	48.2	62.3	76.7	55.4
Bellevue, NE	92.5	93.1	93.9	81.8	72.6	28.5	27.7	36.3	36.0	14.5
Bend, OR	94.7	95.4	92.3	82.1	74.8	41.6	42.5	48.2	27.8	22.0
Benicia, CA	95.5	97.0	87.0	95.4	87.4	42.4	42.5	28.8	55.2	27.3
Bentonville, AR	93.2	93.2	91.5	96.8	79.9	47.4	42.5	43.5	87.9	30.1
Bethlehem, NY	97.0	97.7	82.0	93.3	85.1	58.7	58.7	35.0	79.5	43.2
Blacksburg, VA	94.9	95.0	84.9	97.5	88.3	71.3	70.5	54.1	89.9	63.5
Bowie, MD	96.3	96.4	97.2	90.3	86.9	49.9	46.4	52.8	58.9	32.1
Bozeman, MT	98.7	98.9	99.3	100.0	100.0	55.6	56.2	58.4	67.1	24.3
Brentwood, TN	97.9	98.2	96.8	94.5	88.2	70.9	71.2	45.5	80.9	51.9
Burlington, VT	89.8	93.1	75.5	52.4	88.8	50.9	54.1	21.7	28.9	42.5
Cabot, AR	91.1	91.3	76.3	86.3	92.2	22.9	23.3	0.0	33.7	14.2
Carmel, IN	97.9	98.2	99.7	96.5	81.9	70.0	69.0	58.9	82.8	44.0
Cedar Falls, IA	95.6	96.2	89.6	90.1	93.8	43.4	43.0	46.7	61.2	44.7
Cedar Park, TX	95.6	95.7	92.6	96.2	89.5	44.5	42.8	23.9	70.9	29.0
Central, LA	92.9	92.8	96.8	94.3	73.2	23.9	23.3	23.5	54.9	24.3
Chapel Hill, NC	95.9	97.7	86.7	93.7	85.2	74.6	79.8	37.9	79.1	48.8
Cheshire, CT	95.1	96.6	77.1	94.8	81.0	53.8	55.4	4.2	77.9	28.1
Chino Hills, CA	93.4	94.8	95.9	94.2	85.7	44.8	39.4	44.8	63.4	21.4
Cibolo, TX	95.6	95.7	96.4	88.5	91.8	38.6	38.7	46.8	31.3	38.6
Cicero, NY	94.9	95.0	97.7	83.1	93.7	30.6	30.5	20.8	59.5	28.1
Collierville, TN	96.4	97.9	86.2	95.8	97.5	54.9	54.1	51.4	70.0	40.3
Coppell, TX	96.7	97.2	99.3	95.4	84.8	64.7	63.1	56.5	75.1	43.8
Cornelius, NC	97.1	97.8	89.2	94.0	92.1	54.2	55.6	37.9	54.5	40.1
Cranberry, PA	96.8	97.2	95.9	89.8	86.1	57.0	56.8	65.6	62.3	52.9
Crown Point, IN	91.9	92.1	88.8	95.1	86.9	31.6	31.2	17.2	70.1	32.7
Dublin, OH	98.5	98.6	99.6	98.2	95.4	75.3	74.1	58.9	84.6	76.3
East Fishkill, NY	92.8	93.9	92.6	91.7	72.7	40.4	39.7	54.7	70.9	22.1
Eden Prairie, MN	96.8	98.1	86.3	91.5	76.5	62.2	61.8	39.3	77.5	36.8
Edmond, OK	96.1	96.7	96.3	94.0	75.8	53.0	53.9	40.0	73.2	33.0
Edwardsville, IL	97.2	97.5	95.4	100.0	80.9	49.6	50.3	41.1	65.2	5.7
Evesham, NJ	95.6	96.0	93.8	95.2	86.9	45.9	46.0	31.7	64.4	33.5
Flower Mound, TX	96.6	97.0	96.7	95.9	87.7	59.8	58.6	53.7	78.8	47.3
Folsom, CA	92.5	95.7	72.2	94.3	78.0	48.3	47.5	12.4	77.8	29.4
Friendswood, TX	95.1	96.0	97.0	86.6	89.2	48.0	47.8	54.5	56.6	43.8
Gaines, MI	88.7	90.2	83.8	61.7	64.9	27.1	28.0	22.2	17.8	10.6
Glastonbury, CT	96.0	96.9	95.4	91.7	81.4	60.2	60.7	53.3	63.4	37.1
Grand Blanc, MI	96.5	96.5	96.1	98.7	83.5	38.4	37.8	29.3	66.2	28.3
Hampden, PA	94.0	94.9	94.3	88.2	91.1	50.1	48.5	36.8	66.6	32.0
Hilliard, OH	96.3	96.3	93.3	98.1	66.6	52.1	51.5	30.1	74.8	29.4
Hillsborough, NJ	97.5	97.7	96.9	97.3	93.5	55.9	50.9	55.3	81.8	30.2
Holly Springs, NC	95.7	98.4	84.8	95.6	77.0	56.7	60.6	35.3	66.9	44.5
Independence, KY	89.5	89.7	72.7	100.0	100.0	28.9	29.1	13.7	30.2	16.5
Juneau, AK	95.6	97.1	95.2	89.7	95.5	39.4	44.6	43.3	22.6	26.8
Kaysville, UT	97.7	98.0	83.3	100.0	76.4	47.9	48.8	19.7	27.6	14.5
Keller, TX	96.5	97.2	98.9	97.6	80.7	57.0	56.3	72.5	78.4	38.4
Lafayette, CA	97.8	98.5	94.9	92.6	93.5	72.6	72.8	44.3	77.5	35.0
Lafayette, CO	94.8	95.9	100.0	90.4	74.5	55.1	56.8	57.5	49.3	22.1
Lake Oswego, OR	98.5	98.7	100.0	99.9	90.6	67.0	67.6	46.7	69.0	55.1
Laramie, WY	95.7	96.1	100.0	100.0	77.3	49.5	49.2	80.7	85.9	20.6
Leander, TX	92.6	93.7	89.5	81.6	81.0	35.7	36.2	34.5	63.9	17.8
Leawood, KS	99.3	99.4	97.2	98.9	100.0	74.1	74.1	59.1	87.4	85.8
Lee's Summit, MO	96.4	96.9	95.8	92.7	75.0	43.5	44.6	39.2	42.4	29.7
Leesburg, VA	90.2	92.1	90.4	81.9	64.1	51.2	54.1	33.9	52.1	19.4
Lehi, UT	96.9	96.9	100.0	96.5	85.7	40.8	40.5	27.3	67.7	23.2
Lexington, MA	97.3	97.6	86.4	97.2	100.0	79.6	78.6	58.4	84.1	96.6
Los Altos, CA	98.6	98.6	94.9	98.5	94.4	80.9	79.5	71.8	85.1	64.3
Loveland, CO	94.9	95.7	75.5	96.0	80.9	34.8	34.8	31.4	61.0	18.5
Lower Macungie, PA	94.0	93.9	96.1	92.0	97.6	49.2	48.0	51.4	72.9	32.6
Madison, AL	96.2	97.0	97.7	91.2	81.3	57.4	61.0	37.0	67.6	52.4
Madison, MS	98.1	98.4	96.2	94.9	96.7	62.5	63.5	51.4	70.1	68.7
Maple Valley, WA	97.6	97.5	94.4	100.0	96.2	40.7	40.2	43.6	45.2	44.5

Table continued on next page.

City	High School Graduate or Higher (%)					Bachelor's Degree or Higher (%)				
	Total	White	Black	Asian	Hisp.[1]	Total	White	Black	Asian	Hisp.[1]
Marion, IA	96.1	96.3	90.7	96.2	94.0	34.2	34.0	10.3	52.4	34.0
Marlboro, NJ	95.8	96.6	100.0	92.2	88.6	60.6	57.1	45.6	76.9	40.1
Mason, OH	97.5	97.7	95.4	98.2	88.9	59.3	57.3	65.4	81.1	68.9
Menomonee Falls, WI	95.5	95.7	87.2	96.3	93.7	41.1	39.3	41.8	77.7	34.0
Meridian, ID	95.3	95.7	100.0	90.2	73.8	33.4	32.9	73.1	57.8	14.2
Meridian, MI	96.1	96.7	96.6	95.0	76.5	65.1	63.2	64.9	82.5	59.5
Merrimack, NH	96.1	96.1	70.6	95.6	100.0	44.4	43.0	35.3	73.5	75.0
Milton, GA	97.3	96.9	99.2	100.0	82.5	67.2	68.6	49.4	82.5	53.1
Moon, PA	94.8	96.0	87.8	82.0	76.6	49.8	49.6	35.9	73.6	35.6
Moorpark, CA	88.4	88.9	100.0	96.8	61.6	39.7	39.3	43.6	67.3	14.5
Morgantown, WV	92.9	92.9	89.1	100.0	50.1	48.7	49.4	21.4	74.5	23.4
Mount Pleasant, SC	97.8	98.8	86.0	85.2	93.8	59.3	61.9	16.1	55.0	64.1
Newark, DE	96.4	96.2	96.6	99.1	89.0	57.0	55.8	40.2	85.8	56.1
Newtown, CT	95.8	96.7	84.9	74.7	90.8	55.3	56.2	31.2	54.8	40.5
North Attleborough, MA	94.2	94.5	100.0	94.5	77.0	40.6	38.9	53.7	79.6	27.2
North Port, FL	90.8	91.3	88.6	58.8	82.4	18.7	19.5	10.3	26.9	12.3
North Ridgeville, OH	92.3	93.4	89.1	72.2	84.6	32.6	32.2	30.4	45.7	26.6
Northville, MI	97.4	97.8	92.3	97.0	100.0	62.3	59.5	53.0	81.4	55.4
O'Fallon, MO	95.0	95.0	94.4	96.5	85.4	38.6	36.8	43.6	79.5	40.8
Orchard Park, NY	96.5	96.6	91.3	90.8	99.3	45.9	45.7	33.5	76.9	62.7
Oro Valley, AZ	97.5	98.0	92.2	93.2	94.9	50.7	51.2	29.6	55.8	35.9
Oviedo, FL	94.5	95.8	84.8	89.3	91.0	42.2	43.0	36.9	56.5	28.5
Parker, CO	98.0	98.3	82.7	98.0	92.5	53.6	53.8	41.6	68.7	41.0
Parkland, FL	96.9	97.8	94.0	88.6	93.8	58.3	58.7	51.8	63.4	49.6
Peachtree City, GA	96.3	97.1	91.4	97.0	81.3	57.5	58.1	38.6	75.3	33.4
Pittsfield, MI	92.4	93.7	85.8	94.1	73.7	55.1	57.3	31.3	77.2	28.3
Plainfield, IL	96.9	97.4	98.2	95.0	88.2	50.9	51.0	47.6	70.9	31.2
Pleasant Grove, UT	94.7	95.0	100.0	96.1	74.0	36.8	37.1	0.0	37.4	30.5
Poway, CA	93.0	94.6	82.8	90.8	78.1	45.8	46.3	25.5	54.2	24.3
Princeton, NJ	95.7	96.1	87.6	97.3	85.2	78.7	81.0	41.9	86.7	32.9
Queen Creek, AZ	96.4	97.4	84.5	94.6	91.0	39.8	40.2	22.8	55.3	31.0
Radnor, PA	97.5	97.5	94.6	98.6	98.2	72.7	73.6	40.2	83.6	69.7
Randolph, NJ	96.5	97.3	93.1	95.3	91.7	63.0	63.1	37.1	78.3	35.5
Rexburg, ID	98.1	98.0	100.0	100.0	98.4	40.4	40.9	64.7	34.3	22.0
Rio Rancho, NM	92.9	94.2	97.4	91.4	88.0	30.0	31.2	31.9	49.3	22.0
Rye, NY	77.5	84.5	83.4	93.6	55.3	35.3	43.7	29.1	70.0	11.1
Sammamish, WA	98.2	98.6	89.7	97.2	95.9	72.9	69.4	63.7	83.4	65.7
San Ramon, CA	97.5	97.5	99.2	97.7	96.0	66.8	58.7	62.5	79.2	39.1
Saratoga, CA	97.6	97.6	87.0	98.1	87.4	77.0	70.9	32.5	86.0	37.2
Shrewsbury, MA	94.9	95.9	98.3	89.9	88.0	56.2	53.5	59.7	70.4	27.4
South Brunswick, NJ	95.1	96.5	93.1	94.3	94.6	60.9	47.8	60.3	79.7	30.4
South Jordan, UT	96.7	97.6	83.2	93.3	86.1	40.1	39.7	37.1	56.1	40.0
South Kingstown, RI	94.4	95.3	74.8	100.0	83.8	51.6	52.8	36.1	85.1	45.1
South Portland, ME	95.5	95.9	98.4	86.0	86.5	42.6	43.3	44.2	20.2	55.6
Sparks, NV	86.0	87.2	88.4	91.8	58.4	22.6	22.8	24.0	38.0	9.6
State College, PA	97.0	97.3	100.0	98.7	89.4	69.8	68.8	46.9	88.2	51.8
Sugar Land, TX	92.9	95.5	96.8	89.6	86.9	56.5	53.0	59.9	62.7	37.2
Sun Prairie, WI	96.0	96.6	94.5	93.3	80.7	41.1	41.7	20.5	62.1	28.3
Syracuse, UT	97.3	97.2	100.0	93.8	91.0	36.7	37.9	33.0	0.0	16.1
Tredyffrin, PA	98.2	98.9	96.1	94.5	87.0	76.2	75.5	51.9	88.5	61.0
Upper Dublin, PA	96.8	97.6	93.8	91.1	87.8	63.3	65.2	32.1	66.1	35.3
Urbandale, IA	96.6	97.7	83.1	93.9	66.2	49.5	49.9	34.1	62.2	25.7
Vestal, NY	95.8	96.2	89.6	93.5	97.3	44.1	42.0	37.4	72.9	52.8
Vestavia Hills, AL	97.2	97.8	91.8	100.0	71.6	67.9	69.0	36.4	82.6	31.9
Webster, NY	95.3	95.8	96.9	83.3	97.0	43.7	43.3	40.8	59.8	24.4
Wellesley, MA	98.2	98.5	87.3	96.8	98.1	83.8	84.2	41.0	83.9	86.0
West Fargo, ND	95.7	96.8	65.6	68.3	96.2	36.6	37.1	24.6	32.1	46.9
West Lafayette, IN	94.5	95.5	93.3	93.1	90.4	69.1	64.1	59.6	85.4	64.6
Weston, FL	96.7	96.7	96.2	95.0	96.6	58.7	58.6	59.9	70.0	57.1
Wilmette, IL	98.5	98.7	95.0	98.5	97.3	81.1	81.9	65.5	77.6	75.2
Yorba Linda, CA	95.8	96.0	100.0	95.6	85.1	52.0	48.0	28.7	72.2	32.8
Zionsville, IN	97.9	98.4	100.0	90.2	100.0	70.1	69.7	42.0	81.7	78.7
U.S.	87.0	88.9	84.3	86.3	65.7	30.3	31.6	20.0	52.1	14.7

Note: Figures shown cover persons 25 years old and over; (1) People of Hispanic origin can be of any race
Source: U.S. Census Bureau, 2012-2016 American Community Survey 5-Year Estimates

Educational Attainment by Race: Metro Area

Metro Area	High School Graduate or Higher (%)					Bachelor's Degree or Higher (%)				
	Total	White	Black	Asian	Hisp.[1]	Total	White	Black	Asian	Hisp.[1]
Aberdeen, SD	91.9	92.6	83.2	62.7	73.0	27.4	27.7	36.7	33.6	23.1
Aliso Viejo, CA	79.3	81.8	89.2	87.6	59.2	32.6	34.5	25.0	51.0	11.8
Allen, TX	84.6	85.2	89.6	88.0	56.8	33.1	34.1	24.8	58.8	12.0
Ames, IA	96.3	96.9	78.1	95.3	78.2	50.3	48.3	43.2	81.9	32.4
Amherst, MA	87.5	89.4	82.8	81.5	65.9	30.7	32.2	19.2	44.5	11.4
Apex, NC	90.8	92.9	87.5	91.3	59.1	44.3	47.8	29.0	68.3	19.5
Beavercreek, OH	90.2	90.9	86.4	87.6	80.5	27.8	28.6	18.9	56.7	27.0
Bellevue, NE	91.1	92.6	86.8	76.6	54.9	34.6	35.7	22.5	49.5	13.1
Bend, OR	93.0	93.7	92.5	86.4	72.7	33.3	33.9	32.2	24.5	18.8
Benicia, CA	87.5	89.6	89.4	89.9	68.2	25.1	25.4	16.8	39.7	12.0
Bentonville, AR	85.3	87.3	90.5	90.6	47.9	29.4	29.6	32.0	68.4	9.2
Bethlehem, NY	92.2	93.3	86.1	87.4	80.7	35.5	36.2	18.0	61.7	26.3
Blacksburg, VA	88.1	88.0	84.8	95.3	74.8	32.5	31.1	27.2	85.3	38.7
Bowie, MD	90.4	93.2	90.5	90.7	66.0	49.4	57.0	32.7	63.4	24.4
Bozeman, MT	96.8	97.0	94.3	95.3	85.5	48.0	48.4	38.7	65.7	28.0
Brentwood, TN	88.6	89.9	86.0	83.6	60.9	33.0	34.3	24.5	49.3	15.0
Burlington, VT	92.9	93.8	85.0	70.3	87.3	42.8	43.1	39.6	42.6	43.7
Cabot, AR	89.8	90.9	87.0	89.8	66.3	29.0	31.0	20.1	59.2	12.7
Carmel, IN	89.2	90.7	85.5	84.7	60.9	32.2	34.2	18.7	57.5	14.3
Cedar Falls, IA	91.9	93.4	77.1	82.9	65.5	27.0	27.6	14.1	50.8	18.5
Cedar Park, TX	88.9	90.1	89.6	91.8	70.4	42.0	43.6	25.5	67.7	20.2
Central, LA	87.2	90.2	82.1	84.6	73.5	27.2	31.4	18.0	54.1	18.6
Chapel Hill, NC	88.3	90.8	86.0	91.6	48.6	45.9	52.4	29.2	72.9	15.0
Cheshire, CT	89.5	91.2	86.3	90.6	73.0	34.3	36.2	20.8	65.8	14.9
Chino Hills, CA	79.7	82.2	89.3	89.2	63.8	20.3	20.5	21.4	46.9	9.1
Cibolo, TX	84.3	85.0	90.4	86.4	74.6	27.0	27.7	26.1	51.4	15.8
Cicero, NY	89.8	91.4	77.5	71.0	78.2	30.6	31.5	14.6	47.0	26.8
Collierville, TN	86.5	91.1	82.7	87.7	53.2	26.9	34.1	17.7	54.4	11.8
Coppell, TX	84.6	85.2	89.6	88.0	56.8	33.1	34.1	24.8	58.8	12.0
Cornelius, NC	87.8	89.6	86.4	84.7	60.6	32.9	35.3	23.8	54.8	15.4
Cranberry, PA	92.9	93.3	88.9	88.4	86.2	32.5	32.9	18.6	71.7	35.8
Crown Point, IN	87.6	90.4	86.5	90.8	64.3	36.1	39.4	21.3	63.4	13.6
Dublin, OH	90.7	91.8	86.0	88.4	72.0	34.8	36.2	20.6	63.9	22.6
East Fishkill, NY	85.7	90.0	84.1	82.9	68.9	38.1	43.2	23.8	53.1	17.7
Eden Prairie, MN	93.2	95.7	82.0	79.7	66.4	40.0	41.9	20.8	43.5	19.1
Edmond, OK	88.1	89.2	89.7	82.5	57.1	29.1	30.5	20.2	44.2	11.0
Edwardsville, IL	91.0	92.5	84.6	88.0	77.3	32.6	34.9	18.0	62.8	26.0
Evesham, NJ	89.7	92.3	85.7	83.4	68.1	35.5	39.5	19.2	55.0	16.3
Flower Mound, TX	84.6	85.2	89.6	88.0	56.8	33.1	34.1	24.8	58.8	12.0
Folsom, CA	88.5	91.4	88.5	82.3	71.6	31.8	33.4	20.4	40.6	16.1
Friendswood, TX	82.3	82.5	89.4	86.7	60.6	31.3	31.9	25.9	56.2	13.1
Gaines, MI	90.1	92.1	82.3	73.9	59.5	30.8	32.3	15.7	36.1	12.9
Glastonbury, CT	90.4	92.5	85.5	89.5	70.9	37.7	39.9	20.5	66.5	16.3
Grand Blanc, MI	89.6	90.6	85.8	93.2	80.9	19.9	21.1	12.7	62.0	14.4
Hampden, PA	90.0	91.3	85.6	81.5	71.1	30.1	31.2	16.4	50.5	16.3
Hilliard, OH	90.7	91.8	86.0	88.4	72.0	34.8	36.2	20.6	63.9	22.6
Hillsborough, NJ	85.7	90.0	84.1	82.9	68.9	38.1	43.2	23.8	53.1	17.7
Holly Springs, NC	90.8	92.9	87.5	91.3	59.1	44.3	47.8	29.0	68.3	19.5
Independence, KY	90.1	91.0	84.9	87.4	72.2	31.7	33.0	17.2	63.4	24.7
Juneau, AK	95.6	97.1	95.2	89.7	95.5	39.4	44.6	43.3	22.6	26.8
Kaysville, UT	93.2	94.3	92.6	88.9	71.4	29.5	30.5	19.9	33.0	10.9
Keller, TX	84.6	85.2	89.6	88.0	56.8	33.1	34.1	24.8	58.8	12.0
Lafayette, CA	88.3	92.1	89.7	86.2	69.0	46.6	52.0	24.7	52.4	19.1
Lafayette, CO	94.5	95.4	92.2	91.0	68.9	59.3	60.6	38.4	66.6	21.9
Lake Oswego, OR	91.2	92.9	87.9	85.0	65.0	36.8	37.6	24.6	47.0	17.4
Laramie, WY	95.8	96.2	100.0	100.0	77.9	47.9	47.5	79.5	81.8	23.3
Leander, TX	88.9	90.1	89.6	91.8	70.4	42.0	43.6	25.5	67.7	20.2
Leawood, KS	91.4	93.1	87.6	83.8	66.1	35.0	37.5	19.0	53.2	16.1
Lee's Summit, MO	91.4	93.1	87.6	83.8	66.1	35.0	37.5	19.0	53.2	16.1
Leesburg, VA	90.4	93.2	90.5	90.7	66.0	49.4	57.0	32.7	63.4	24.4
Lehi, UT	93.6	94.2	90.6	92.0	70.5	37.7	37.9	37.1	57.1	18.1
Lexington, MA	91.1	93.8	83.4	85.0	69.8	45.4	47.8	24.6	59.4	20.3
Los Altos, CA	86.8	89.0	91.2	89.7	66.0	48.3	46.3	34.7	62.8	15.2
Loveland, CO	95.7	96.3	90.7	95.4	81.2	45.3	45.8	33.6	63.5	24.8
Lower Macungie, PA	89.3	90.5	87.2	87.6	73.2	27.7	28.1	19.7	57.5	12.6
Madison, AL	89.2	90.4	85.8	90.7	65.9	37.1	39.2	27.8	56.4	23.3
Madison, MS	86.8	91.9	81.5	89.2	61.4	29.3	37.2	19.9	56.2	18.2
Maple Valley, WA	92.0	94.2	88.2	87.2	71.5	40.1	41.0	22.2	52.0	20.3

Table continued on next page.

Metro Area	High School Graduate or Higher (%)					Bachelor's Degree or Higher (%)				
	Total	White	Black	Asian	Hisp.[1]	Total	White	Black	Asian	Hisp.[1]
Marion, IA	94.2	94.8	81.1	96.4	81.9	29.9	29.8	15.3	65.3	22.8
Marlboro, NJ	85.7	90.0	84.1	82.9	68.9	38.1	43.2	23.8	53.1	17.7
Mason, OH	90.1	91.0	84.9	87.4	72.2	31.7	33.0	17.2	63.4	24.7
Menomonee Falls, WI	90.4	93.5	80.9	83.6	66.0	33.8	37.6	13.6	51.3	12.9
Meridian, ID	91.0	92.1	86.1	85.6	64.4	30.5	30.9	25.7	46.8	10.5
Meridian, MI	92.9	93.9	88.9	88.2	81.7	33.3	33.1	26.2	65.6	21.1
Merrimack, NH	91.6	92.0	85.9	87.3	71.9	36.3	35.8	23.8	61.6	17.7
Milton, GA	88.5	89.7	89.2	86.7	62.8	36.5	40.2	28.3	55.5	17.8
Moon, PA	92.9	93.3	88.9	88.4	86.2	32.5	32.9	18.6	71.7	35.8
Moorpark, CA	83.4	83.6	92.5	93.3	61.0	32.2	31.2	35.2	58.8	12.4
Morgantown, WV	89.3	89.4	84.4	98.0	66.5	32.2	31.4	20.6	76.4	29.2
Mount Pleasant, SC	89.6	92.7	82.6	86.8	69.4	33.4	40.1	15.4	42.9	22.8
Newark, DE	89.7	92.3	85.7	83.4	68.1	35.5	39.5	19.2	55.0	16.3
Newtown, CT	89.9	92.6	86.3	90.6	70.2	46.4	51.4	20.8	68.6	18.7
North Attleborough, MA	85.8	87.6	80.9	82.7	67.2	30.4	31.7	20.9	48.0	12.4
North Port, FL	90.7	91.6	82.6	85.7	70.8	30.7	31.7	13.3	44.3	16.6
North Ridgeville, OH	89.6	91.5	82.8	88.5	73.3	29.7	32.6	14.6	63.4	15.0
Northville, MI	89.1	90.7	84.9	89.3	70.2	29.5	31.5	17.3	64.7	18.6
O'Fallon, MO	91.0	92.5	84.6	88.0	77.3	32.6	34.9	18.0	62.8	26.0
Orchard Park, NY	90.8	92.8	82.8	78.6	74.2	30.5	32.2	15.5	55.3	20.1
Oro Valley, AZ	87.7	90.1	88.0	86.6	73.7	30.8	33.2	21.9	50.3	14.4
Oviedo, FL	88.6	90.2	84.0	87.6	81.6	29.5	30.8	20.1	49.4	19.9
Parker, CO	90.4	91.8	89.4	85.0	67.8	41.3	43.4	24.5	50.2	14.3
Parkland, FL	84.8	86.3	79.8	86.5	78.8	30.1	32.8	18.2	48.7	25.2
Peachtree City, GA	88.5	89.7	89.2	86.7	62.8	36.5	40.2	28.3	55.5	17.8
Pittsfield, MI	94.7	95.6	88.7	95.8	83.3	53.2	55.1	25.1	81.0	36.9
Plainfield, IL	87.6	90.4	86.5	90.8	64.3	36.1	39.4	21.3	63.4	13.6
Pleasant Grove, UT	93.6	94.2	90.6	92.0	70.5	37.7	37.9	37.1	57.1	18.1
Poway, CA	86.4	87.5	90.6	88.6	66.7	36.5	37.5	23.4	48.6	16.0
Princeton, NJ	87.7	89.2	84.5	93.6	61.6	40.4	42.8	18.2	77.4	13.3
Queen Creek, AZ	86.8	88.5	88.6	87.8	64.9	29.8	30.8	23.6	55.3	11.6
Radnor, PA	89.7	92.3	85.7	83.4	68.1	35.5	39.5	19.2	55.0	16.3
Randolph, NJ	85.7	90.0	84.1	82.9	68.9	38.1	43.2	23.8	53.1	17.7
Rexburg, ID	93.2	94.2	100.0	100.0	61.1	31.4	31.9	47.3	35.7	17.0
Rio Rancho, NM	87.8	89.9	91.3	84.8	78.8	30.8	34.1	29.8	44.6	17.6
Rye, NY	85.7	90.0	84.1	82.9	68.9	38.1	43.2	23.8	53.1	17.7
Sammamish, WA	92.0	94.2	88.2	87.2	71.5	40.1	41.0	22.2	52.0	20.3
San Ramon, CA	88.3	92.1	89.7	86.2	69.0	46.6	52.0	24.7	52.4	19.1
Saratoga, CA	86.8	89.0	91.2	89.7	66.0	48.3	46.3	34.7	62.8	15.2
Shrewsbury, MA	89.8	91.1	84.9	83.9	68.4	33.4	33.7	25.7	55.7	14.3
South Brunswick, NJ	85.7	90.0	84.1	82.9	68.9	38.1	43.2	23.8	53.1	17.7
South Jordan, UT	89.9	93.1	84.8	83.8	64.8	32.2	33.8	25.0	49.5	12.7
South Kingstown, RI	85.8	87.6	80.9	82.7	67.2	30.4	31.7	20.9	48.0	12.4
South Portland, ME	93.7	94.2	84.6	76.6	85.9	37.9	38.3	22.8	37.9	33.8
Sparks, NV	87.1	88.6	88.6	87.0	58.3	28.9	30.2	19.9	38.7	10.1
State College, PA	93.3	93.6	88.3	93.3	81.9	42.4	41.4	33.0	72.5	38.4
Sugar Land, TX	82.3	82.5	89.4	86.7	60.6	31.3	31.9	25.9	56.2	13.1
Sun Prairie, WI	94.8	95.9	88.0	87.7	70.9	43.9	44.4	20.9	65.8	24.5
Syracuse, UT	93.2	94.3	92.6	88.9	71.4	29.5	30.5	19.9	33.0	10.9
Tredyffrin, PA	89.7	92.3	85.7	83.4	68.1	35.5	39.5	19.2	55.0	16.3
Upper Dublin, PA	89.7	92.3	85.7	83.4	68.1	35.5	39.5	19.2	55.0	16.3
Urbandale, IA	92.6	93.9	85.0	80.1	61.1	35.9	36.9	19.6	43.3	13.7
Vestal, NY	90.2	91.1	79.7	84.1	76.3	27.2	27.1	15.9	54.5	21.4
Vestavia Hills, AL	87.5	88.8	86.0	88.5	56.4	28.8	32.3	19.7	55.9	13.6
Webster, NY	90.2	92.3	78.8	81.0	70.4	33.0	35.0	13.8	53.0	16.0
Wellesley, MA	91.1	93.8	83.4	85.0	69.8	45.4	47.8	24.6	59.4	20.3
West Fargo, ND	94.5	95.5	82.4	74.8	80.2	36.2	36.9	22.1	42.5	16.2
West Lafayette, IN	90.4	90.9	91.3	92.5	60.0	32.3	30.7	20.2	81.0	13.2
Weston, FL	84.8	86.3	79.8	86.5	78.8	30.1	32.8	18.2	48.7	25.2
Wilmette, IL	87.6	90.4	86.5	90.8	64.3	36.1	39.4	21.3	63.4	13.6
Yorba Linda, CA	79.3	81.8	89.2	87.6	59.2	32.6	34.5	25.0	51.0	11.8
Zionsville, IN	89.2	90.7	85.5	84.7	60.9	32.2	34.2	18.7	57.5	14.3
U.S.	87.0	88.9	84.3	86.3	65.7	30.3	31.6	20.0	52.1	14.7

Note: Figures shown cover persons 25 years old and over; Figures cover the Metropolitan Statistical Area—see Appendix B for areas included; (1) People of Hispanic origin can be of any race

Source: U.S. Census Bureau, 2012-2016 American Community Survey 5-Year Estimates

Cost of Living Index

Urban Area	Composite	Groceries	Housing	Utilities	Transp.	Health	Misc.
Aberdeen, SD	n/a	n/a	n/a	n/a	n/a	n/a	n/a
Aliso Viejo, CA[1]	152.5	113.9	257.0	103.4	132.4	104.7	108.4
Allen, TX[2]	107.2	99.6	120.8	97.9	103.9	85.0	105.6
Ames, IA[3]	92.5	90.7	95.4	79.7	106.9	99.7	89.8
Amherst, MA	n/a	n/a	n/a	n/a	n/a	n/a	n/a
Apex, NC[4]	96.2	105.7	83.4	97.5	99.7	100.5	101.1
Beavercreek, OH[5]	90.8	96.0	68.1	83.5	104.0	87.0	106.4
Bellevue, NE[6]	92.0	94.2	88.8	85.9	92.1	100.6	94.2
Bend, OR	n/a	n/a	n/a	n/a	n/a	n/a	n/a
Benicia, CA	n/a	n/a	n/a	n/a	n/a	n/a	n/a
Bentonville, AR[7]	89.2	93.3	75.8	94.6	85.1	88.4	98.1
Bethlehem, NY[8]	107.3	107.7	115.8	98.4	104.8	99.1	104.6
Blacksburg, VA[9]	90.4	88.2	66.2	117.7	88.2	111.1	100.9
Bowie, MD[10]	140.2	115.2	219.2	100.1	105.8	93.6	112.6
Bozeman, MT[11]	100.2	101.8	107.8	77.0	95.3	103.1	100.8
Brentwood, TN[12]	96.6	96.9	91.1	89.9	100.3	81.7	103.7
Burlington, VT[13]	120.5	111.9	146.9	119.1	111.7	104.5	107.2
Cabot, AR[14]	78.1	86.0	64.7	81.6	89.3	85.6	80.9
Carmel, IN[15]	92.4	93.0	80.8	97.7	94.2	93.8	99.5
Cedar Falls, IA[16]	94.6	94.9	88.6	84.0	99.5	91.1	101.6
Cedar Park, TX[17]	97.3	87.7	101.8	87.7	93.3	99.4	100.8
Central, LA[18]	94.8	101.8	84.4	79.5	96.8	116.2	101.4
Chapel Hill, NC[19]	93.9	92.5	99.1	91.4	94.1	97.5	90.3
Cheshire, CT[20]	117.7	104.3	130.1	102.4	106.5	114.4	120.6
Chino Hills, CA	n/a	n/a	n/a	n/a	n/a	n/a	n/a
Cibolo, TX[21]	88.6	92.1	75.9	115.7	83.5	92.5	90.5
Cicero, NY	n/a	n/a	n/a	n/a	n/a	n/a	n/a
Collierville, TN[22]	83.2	91.0	65.8	103.2	89.1	84.8	86.7
Coppell, TX[23]	107.2	99.6	120.8	97.9	103.9	85.0	105.6
Cornelius, NC[24]	96.0	96.3	86.7	99.5	96.3	105.1	101.2
Cranberry, PA[25]	99.4	110.4	91.5	110.0	106.7	93.8	97.4
Crown Point, IN	n/a	n/a	n/a	n/a	n/a	n/a	n/a
Dublin, OH[26]	89.6	98.9	76.8	77.7	96.9	92.1	97.4
East Fishkill, NY	n/a	n/a	n/a	n/a	n/a	n/a	n/a
Eden Prairie, MN[27]	104.7	106.6	104.8	91.1	107.9	104.5	107.0
Edmond, OK[28]	89.5	87.9	86.4	84.5	95.4	91.7	92.2
Edwardsville, IL[29]	90.4	104.8	71.7	113.9	95.8	95.6	91.2
Evesham, NJ[30]	117.0	116.2	129.5	124.5	114.9	105.7	107.2
Flower Mound, TX[31]	107.2	99.6	120.8	97.9	103.9	85.0	105.6
Folsom, CA[32]	116.9	116.7	136.8	89.3	122.6	103.7	109.1
Friendswood, TX[33]	86.6	83.2	89.3	72.0	93.4	101.4	86.2
Gaines, MI[34]	94.3	97.1	87.8	86.8	106.1	95.2	97.3
Glastonbury, CT[35]	116.6	100.6	131.7	96.4	112.8	113.6	117.7
Grand Blanc, MI	n/a	n/a	n/a	n/a	n/a	n/a	n/a
Hampden, PA[36]	99.3	98.8	92.6	119.1	105.9	88.3	98.9
Hilliard, OH[37]	89.6	98.9	76.8	77.7	96.9	92.1	97.4
Hillsborough, NJ[38]	122.9	106.7	152.8	115.4	112.7	101.9	112.5
Holly Springs, NC[39]	96.2	105.7	83.4	97.5	99.7	100.5	101.1
Independence, KY[40]	87.6	89.1	72.4	93.8	101.9	101.4	91.3
Juneau, AK[41]	133.2	143.5	150.5	119.9	128.3	155.6	117.3
Kaysville, UT[42]	100.1	103.9	105.5	76.0	101.8	113.4	99.0
Keller, TX[43]	99.1	101.2	90.0	108.7	102.9	103.8	101.4
Lafayette, CA[44]	149.2	125.5	217.5	113.6	130.3	123.1	121.8
Lafayette, CO	n/a	n/a	n/a	n/a	n/a	n/a	n/a
Lake Oswego, OR[45]	129.1	115.2	178.9	78.0	106.4	107.1	117.6
Laramie, WY[46]	95.3	109.3	81.9	109.3	94.6	98.6	96.6
Leander, TX[47]	97.3	87.7	101.8	87.7	93.3	99.4	100.8
Leawood, KS[48]	91.4	101.0	81.9	76.6	95.0	98.9	97.5
Lee's Summit, MO[49]	91.4	101.0	81.9	76.6	95.0	98.9	97.5
Leesburg, VA[50]	144.0	114.4	233.7	89.4	105.5	97.8	114.6
Lehi, UT[51]	98.0	100.0	100.4	72.6	101.9	110.9	99.8
Lexington, MA[52]	140.5	110.8	188.0	120.1	114.4	120.1	128.7
Los Altos, CA	n/a	n/a	n/a	n/a	n/a	n/a	n/a
Loveland, CO	n/a	n/a	n/a	n/a	n/a	n/a	n/a
Lower Macungie, PA[53]	105.7	100.1	115.9	97.7	109.5	101.4	101.6
Madison, AL[54]	95.1	96.1	74.4	109.7	95.4	96.6	107.1
Madison, MS[55]	88.5	88.5	75.5	104.4	86.7	89.0	95.0
Maple Valley, WA[56]	148.8	126.7	194.2	123.1	133.1	124.2	135.3
Marion, IA[57]	94.8	95.8	87.2	101.4	104.4	104.2	95.0

Table continued on next page.

Urban Area	Composite	Groceries	Housing	Utilities	Transp.	Health	Misc.
Marlboro, NJ[58]	116.7	104.2	134.1	114.5	111.1	106.7	110.9
Mason, OH[59]	92.3	91.3	76.2	95.4	100.7	98.4	101.9
Menomonee Falls, WI[60]	97.1	97.9	93.9	107.2	95.5	113.4	94.7
Meridian, ID[61]	92.3	89.5	87.9	85.7	107.5	103.4	93.4
Meridian, MI	n/a	n/a	n/a	n/a	n/a	n/a	n/a
Merrimack, NH[62]	114.7	113.6	110.1	131.2	105.1	115.0	116.7
Milton, GA[63]	98.8	105.2	94.4	85.3	101.0	107.5	102.0
Moon, PA[64]	99.4	110.4	91.5	110.0	106.7	93.8	97.4
Moorpark, CA	n/a	n/a	n/a	n/a	n/a	n/a	n/a
Morgantown, WV[65]	95.7	103.1	87.3	88.3	97.7	91.4	101.8
Mount Pleasant, SC[66]	103.9	100.9	96.9	118.1	94.8	103.8	108.9
Newark, DE[67]	107.7	109.4	110.0	104.8	95.2	100.4	110.3
Newtown, CT[68]	142.0	109.2	206.9	111.5	115.2	113.6	121.5
North Attleborough, MA[69]	123.4	115.0	140.7	126.7	101.5	110.0	119.1
North Port, FL[70]	108.6	119.5	102.3	105.7	91.6	116.9	113.7
North Ridgeville, OH[71]	101.1	111.2	88.3	104.7	102.5	101.2	106.0
Northville, MI[72]	96.8	90.7	94.1	102.1	107.9	94.2	97.2
O'Fallon, MO[73]	90.4	104.8	71.7	113.9	95.8	95.6	91.2
Orchard Park, NY[74]	100.1	97.2	102.5	108.7	102.5	85.5	98.0
Oro Valley, AZ[75]	94.0	102.7	80.0	90.2	96.6	101.2	101.3
Oviedo, FL[76]	95.3	102.1	88.9	111.2	94.0	88.2	94.6
Parker, CO[77]	111.8	97.9	133.5	93.5	105.5	105.3	107.4
Parkland, FL[78]	119.3	104.2	160.2	98.2	112.7	95.9	102.9
Peachtree City, GA[79]	98.8	105.2	94.4	85.3	101.0	107.5	102.0
Pittsfield, MI	n/a	n/a	n/a	n/a	n/a	n/a	n/a
Plainfield, IL[80]	100.2	101.8	105.3	83.9	111.4	108.6	96.1
Pleasant Grove, UT[81]	98.0	100.0	100.4	72.6	101.9	110.9	99.8
Poway, CA[82]	145.9	114.3	237.8	117.0	122.8	106.6	103.4
Princeton, NJ	n/a	n/a	n/a	n/a	n/a	n/a	n/a
Queen Creek, AZ[83]	94.8	97.3	95.2	96.1	91.7	97.7	93.7
Radnor, PA[84]	117.0	116.2	129.5	124.5	114.9	105.7	107.2
Randolph, NJ[85]	122.9	106.7	152.8	115.4	112.7	101.9	112.5
Rexburg, ID	n/a	n/a	n/a	n/a	n/a	n/a	n/a
Rio Rancho, NM[86]	94.7	92.9	93.5	83.9	101.4	101.0	96.9
Rye, NY	n/a	n/a	n/a	n/a	n/a	n/a	n/a
Sammamish, WA[87]	148.8	126.7	194.2	123.1	133.1	124.2	135.3
San Ramon, CA[88]	149.2	125.5	217.5	113.6	130.3	123.1	121.8
Saratoga, CA	n/a	n/a	n/a	n/a	n/a	n/a	n/a
Shrewsbury, MA[89]	116.1	99.6	120.3	127.4	98.0	118.1	120.4
South Brunswick, NJ[90]	116.7	104.2	134.1	114.5	111.1	106.7	110.9
South Jordan, UT[91]	96.9	106.8	94.1	75.2	103.5	98.6	99.5
South Kingstown, RI[92]	123.4	115.0	140.7	126.7	101.5	110.0	119.1
South Portland, ME[93]	113.4	100.3	124.9	116.6	108.1	107.7	110.3
Sparks, NV[94]	106.6	100.1	106.8	84.6	113.0	110.2	113.1
State College, PA	n/a	n/a	n/a	n/a	n/a	n/a	n/a
Sugar Land, TX[95]	98.1	86.8	104.8	110.6	97.4	91.2	94.5
Sun Prairie, WI[96]	107.4	102.9	109.4	105.2	107.3	122.4	106.1
Syracuse, UT[97]	100.1	103.9	105.5	76.0	101.8	113.4	99.0
Tredyffrin, PA[98]	117.0	116.2	129.5	124.5	114.9	105.7	107.2
Upper Dublin, PA[99]	117.0	116.2	129.5	124.5	114.9	105.7	107.2
Urbandale, IA[100]	89.4	90.4	82.4	99.2	98.6	97.0	88.5
Vestal, NY	n/a	n/a	n/a	n/a	n/a	n/a	n/a
Vestavia Hills, AL[101]	91.2	95.6	86.4	100.8	91.0	83.8	91.7
Webster, NY[102]	98.0	100.9	88.0	92.0	110.0	93.5	104.1
Wellesley, MA[103]	140.5	110.8	188.0	120.1	114.4	120.1	128.7
West Fargo, ND[104]	99.8	108.2	98.0	86.6	98.9	114.8	100.1
West Lafayette, IN[105]	88.7	96.8	65.9	107.3	97.3	93.7	95.9
Weston, FL[106]	119.3	104.2	160.2	98.2	112.7	95.9	102.9
Wilmette, IL[107]	123.4	108.2	155.6	90.2	126.6	101.3	114.8
Yorba Linda, CA[108]	152.5	113.9	257.0	103.4	132.4	104.7	108.4
Zionsville, IN[109]	92.4	93.0	80.8	97.7	94.2	93.8	99.5
U.S.	100.0	100.0	100.0	100.0	100.0	100.0	100.0

Note: The Cost of Living Index measures regional differences in the cost of consumer goods and services, excluding taxes and non-consumer expenditures, for professional and managerial households in the top income quintile. It is based on more than 50,000 prices covering almost 60 different items for which prices are collected three times a year by chambers of commerce, economic development organizations or university applied economic centers in each participating urban area. The numbers shown should be read as a percentage above or below the national average of 100. For example, a value of 115.4 in the groceries column indicates that grocery prices are 15.4% higher than the national average. Small differences in the index numbers should not be interpreted as significant. In cases where data is not available for the city, data for the metro area or for a neighboring city has been provided and noted as follows: (1) Orange County CA; (2) Plano TX; (3) Ames IA; (4) Raleigh NC; (5) Dayton OH; (6) Omaha NE; (7) Fayetteville AR; (8) Albany NY; (9) Blacksburg VA; (10) Bethesda-Gaithersburg-Frederick MD; (11) Bozeman MT; (12) Nashville-Murfreesboro TN; (13) Burlington-Chittenden County VT;
Table continued on next page.

(14) Conway AR; (15) Indianapolis IN; (16) Waterloo-Cedar Falls IA; (17) Austin TX; (18) Baton Rouge LA; (19) Chapel Hill NC; (20) New Haven CT; (21) Seguin TX; (22) Memphis TN; (23) Plano TX; (24) Charlotte NC; (25) Pittsburgh PA; (26) Columbus OH; (27) Minneapolis MN; (28) Edmond OK; (29) St. Louis MO-IL; (30) Philadelphia PA; (31) Plano TX; (32) Sacramento CA; (33) Brazoria County TX; (34) Grand Rapids MI; (35) Hartford CT; (36) Harrisburg PA; (37) Columbus OH; (38) Newark-Elizabeth NJ; (39) Raleigh NC; (40) Covington KY; (41) Juneau AK; (42) Ogden UT; (43) Fort Worth TX; (44) Oakland CA; (45) Portland OR; (46) Laramie WY; (47) Austin TX; (48) Kansas City MO-KS; (49) Kansas City MO-KS; (50) Arlington VA; (51) Provo-Orem UT; (52) Framingham-Natick MA; (53) Allentown PA; (54) Huntsville AL; (55) Jackson MS; (56) Seattle WA; (57) Cedar Rapids IA; (58) Middlesex-Monmouth NJ; (59) Cincinnati OH; (60) Milwaukee-Waukesha WI; (61) Boise ID; (62) Manchester NH; (63) Atlanta GA; (64) Pittsburgh PA; (65) Morgantown WV; (66) Charleston-N Charleston SC; (67) Wilmington DE; (68) Stamford CT; (69) Providence RI; (70) Sarasota FL; (71) Cleveland OH; (72) Detroit MI; (73) St. Louis MO-IL; (74) Buffalo NY; (75) Tucson AZ; (76) Orlando FL; (77) Denver CO; (78) Fort Lauderdale FL; (79) Atlanta GA; (80) Joliet-Will County IL; (81) Provo-Orem UT; (82) San Diego CA; (83) Phoenix AZ; (84) Philadelphia PA; (85) Newark-Elizabeth NJ; (86) Albuquerque NM; (87) Seattle WA; (88) Oakland CA; (89) Fitchburg-Leominster MA; (90) Middlesex-Monmouth NJ; (91) Salt Lake City UT; (92) Providence RI; (93) Portland ME; (94) Reno-Sparks NV; (95) Houston TX; (96) Madison WI; (97) Ogden UT; (98) Philadelphia PA; (99) Philadelphia PA; (100) Des Moines IA; (101) Birmingham AL; (102) Rochester NY; (103) Framingham-Natick MA; (104) Fargo-Moorhead ND-MN; (105) Lafayette IN; (106) Fort Lauderdale FL; (107) Chicago IL; (108) Orange County CA; (109) Indianapolis IN

Source: The Council for Community and Economic Research (formerly ACCRA), Cost of Living Index, 2017

Grocery Prices

Urban Area	T-Bone Steak ($/pound)	Frying Chicken ($/pound)	Whole Milk ($/half gal.)	Eggs ($/dozen)	Orange Juice ($/64 oz.)	Coffee ($/11.5 oz.)
Aberdeen, SD	n/a	n/a	n/a	n/a	n/a	n/a
Aliso Viejo, CA[1]	12.43	1.04	2.23	2.11	3.65	6.36
Allen, TX[2]	11.99	1.19	1.82	1.82	3.99	4.43
Ames, IA[3]	10.98	1.53	1.91	1.05	2.98	4.38
Amherst, MA	n/a	n/a	n/a	n/a	n/a	n/a
Apex, NC[4]	12.34	1.69	2.00	2.92	3.57	4.42
Beavercreek, OH[5]	13.13	1.77	1.57	1.10	3.67	4.27
Bellevue, NE[6]	11.04	1.48	1.73	1.29	3.16	3.84
Bend, OR	n/a	n/a	n/a	n/a	n/a	n/a
Benicia, CA	n/a	n/a	n/a	n/a	n/a	n/a
Bentonville, AR[7]	10.12	1.41	1.91	1.10	3.43	4.39
Bethlehem, NY[8]	11.52	1.40	2.32	1.66	3.30	3.97
Blacksburg, VA[9]	10.99	1.06	1.88	1.12	3.23	4.01
Bowie, MD[10]	13.62	1.89	2.32	1.72	4.49	3.59
Bozeman, MT[11]	11.13	1.54	1.94	1.42	3.51	5.38
Brentwood, TN[12]	12.68	1.46	1.82	1.31	3.51	4.66
Burlington, VT[13]	11.60	1.37	2.67	2.43	3.36	4.14
Cabot, AR[14]	10.72	1.18	2.00	1.45	2.88	3.88
Carmel, IN[15]	12.44	1.29	1.22	1.19	3.39	4.30
Cedar Falls, IA[16]	11.64	1.53	1.94	1.22	3.14	3.89
Cedar Park, TX[17]	9.91	1.15	1.81	1.34	3.14	3.97
Central, LA[18]	10.94	1.28	2.54	1.26	3.86	4.40
Chapel Hill, NC[19]	9.70	1.22	2.42	1.49	3.16	3.33
Cheshire, CT[20]	11.92	1.55	2.07	1.50	2.98	3.95
Chino Hills, CA	n/a	n/a	n/a	n/a	n/a	n/a
Cibolo, TX[21]	10.48	1.18	2.07	1.49	3.96	4.12
Cicero, NY	n/a	n/a	n/a	n/a	n/a	n/a
Collierville, TN[22]	10.52	1.12	1.86	1.14	3.53	4.19
Coppell, TX[23]	11.99	1.19	1.82	1.82	3.99	4.43
Cornelius, NC[24]	10.92	1.17	1.87	1.53	3.44	3.82
Cranberry, PA[25]	13.40	1.57	1.90	1.05	3.91	4.74
Crown Point, IN	n/a	n/a	n/a	n/a	n/a	n/a
Dublin, OH[26]	12.96	1.30	1.43	1.39	3.01	7.48
East Fishkill, NY	n/a	n/a	n/a	n/a	n/a	n/a
Eden Prairie, MN[27]	13.89	2.05	2.30	1.89	3.66	4.70
Edmond, OK[28]	12.13	1.17	1.83	0.98	3.14	3.54
Edwardsville, IL[29]	15.14	1.93	2.49	1.55	3.18	4.83
Evesham, NJ[30]	11.82	1.46	2.11	1.74	3.92	4.10
Flower Mound, TX[31]	11.99	1.19	1.82	1.82	3.99	4.43
Folsom, CA[32]	11.84	1.40	2.85	1.84	3.65	6.40
Friendswood, TX[33]	9.80	0.99	1.47	1.26	3.06	4.41
Gaines, MI[34]	12.04	1.26	1.59	1.09	3.67	3.84
Glastonbury, CT[35]	12.16	1.67	2.01	1.76	3.16	3.99
Grand Blanc, MI	n/a	n/a	n/a	n/a	n/a	n/a
Hampden, PA[36]	12.35	1.42	2.10	1.55	3.09	3.55
Hilliard, OH[37]	12.96	1.30	1.43	1.39	3.01	7.48
Hillsborough, NJ[38]	11.80	1.69	2.27	1.72	3.04	3.82
Holly Springs, NC[39]	12.34	1.69	2.00	2.92	3.57	4.42
Independence, KY[40]	n/a	n/a	n/a	n/a	n/a	n/a
Juneau, AK[41]	13.59	2.23	2.81	2.53	5.04	5.89
Kaysville, UT[42]	10.69	1.86	1.87	2.61	3.76	4.32
Keller, TX[43]	12.84	1.09	1.67	1.47	3.93	4.76
Lafayette, CA[44]	12.72	1.51	2.74	2.66	4.38	6.65
Lafayette, CO	n/a	n/a	n/a	n/a	n/a	n/a
Lake Oswego, OR[45]	12.94	1.58	2.06	1.78	3.92	5.88
Laramie, WY[46]	12.92	1.28	2.56	1.57	3.85	4.95
Leander, TX[47]	9.91	1.15	1.81	1.34	3.14	3.97
Leawood, KS[48]	11.94	1.62	2.27	1.05	3.17	4.18
Lee's Summit, MO[49]	11.94	1.62	2.27	1.05	3.17	4.18
Leesburg, VA[50]	10.29	1.98	2.53	1.62	3.35	4.55
Lehi, UT[51]	10.90	1.47	1.57	1.89	3.84	4.40
Lexington, MA[52]	12.27	1.71	2.49	1.84	3.53	4.19
Los Altos, CA	n/a	n/a	n/a	n/a	n/a	n/a
Loveland, CO	n/a	n/a	n/a	n/a	n/a	n/a
Lower Macungie, PA[53]	11.88	1.41	1.86	1.24	3.21	3.68
Madison, AL[54]	10.82	1.19	1.71	1.13	3.29	3.94
Madison, MS[55]	9.01	1.05	1.78	2.36	3.34	3.70

Table continued on next page.

Urban Area	T-Bone Steak ($/pound)	Frying Chicken ($/pound)	Whole Milk ($/half gal.)	Eggs ($/dozen)	Orange Juice ($/64 oz.)	Coffee ($/11.5 oz.)
Maple Valley, WA[56]	15.36	1.88	2.03	1.68	4.11	5.76
Marion, IA[57]	11.33	1.47	1.97	1.07	3.00	4.40
Marlboro, NJ[58]	11.10	1.47	2.24	1.66	3.35	3.57
Mason, OH[59]	12.29	1.07	1.31	1.19	3.30	4.16
Menomonee Falls, WI[60]	12.83	1.95	1.85	1.00	3.68	4.46
Meridian, ID[61]	10.22	1.27	1.34	1.23	3.09	4.60
Meridian, MI	n/a	n/a	n/a	n/a	n/a	n/a
Merrimack, NH[62]	12.82	1.82	3.56	1.66	3.52	4.62
Milton, GA[63]	12.05	1.27	1.98	1.58	3.56	4.66
Moon, PA[64]	13.40	1.57	1.90	1.05	3.91	4.74
Moorpark, CA	n/a	n/a	n/a	n/a	n/a	n/a
Morgantown, WV[65]	11.00	1.33	1.55	1.75	3.55	4.73
Mount Pleasant, SC[66]	11.15	1.40	1.98	1.46	3.71	3.78
Newark, DE[67]	12.05	1.72	2.13	1.70	3.59	4.77
Newtown, CT[68]	12.74	1.44	1.96	2.20	3.50	3.99
North Attleborough, MA[69]	12.39	1.62	2.39	1.99	4.36	4.32
North Port, FL[70]	11.20	1.72	2.93	2.20	4.26	4.28
North Ridgeville, OH[71]	15.83	2.05	1.88	1.18	3.81	4.95
Northville, MI[72]	12.84	1.15	1.73	1.20	3.11	3.89
O'Fallon, MO[73]	15.14	1.93	2.49	1.55	3.18	4.83
Orchard Park, NY[74]	12.85	1.23	1.95	1.17	3.48	4.14
Oro Valley, AZ[75]	12.56	1.61	1.55	1.34	3.07	5.19
Oviedo, FL[76]	9.24	1.23	2.43	1.85	3.14	3.80
Parker, CO[77]	12.90	1.35	1.72	1.83	3.52	4.59
Parkland, FL[78]	10.52	1.30	2.49	1.38	3.67	3.62
Peachtree City, GA[79]	12.05	1.27	1.98	1.58	3.56	4.66
Pittsfield, MI	n/a	n/a	n/a	n/a	n/a	n/a
Plainfield, IL[80]	11.30	1.77	2.41	1.40	3.56	6.51
Pleasant Grove, UT[81]	10.90	1.47	1.57	1.89	3.84	4.40
Poway, CA[82]	11.76	1.14	2.16	2.11	3.72	6.36
Princeton, NJ	n/a	n/a	n/a	n/a	n/a	n/a
Queen Creek, AZ[83]	12.16	1.52	1.49	1.55	3.85	4.98
Radnor, PA[84]	11.82	1.46	2.11	1.74	3.92	4.10
Randolph, NJ[85]	11.80	1.69	2.27	1.72	3.04	3.82
Rexburg, ID	n/a	n/a	n/a	n/a	n/a	n/a
Rio Rancho, NM[86]	10.82	1.11	1.52	1.40	3.44	4.27
Rye, NY	n/a	n/a	n/a	n/a	n/a	n/a
Sammamish, WA[87]	15.36	1.88	2.03	1.68	4.11	5.76
San Ramon, CA[88]	12.72	1.51	2.74	2.66	4.38	6.65
Saratoga, CA	n/a	n/a	n/a	n/a	n/a	n/a
Shrewsbury, MA[89]	12.11	1.48	1.97	1.06	3.48	5.01
South Brunswick, NJ[90]	11.10	1.47	2.24	1.66	3.35	3.57
South Jordan, UT[91]	10.77	1.50	1.74	2.60	3.85	4.39
South Kingstown, RI[92]	12.39	1.62	2.39	1.99	4.36	4.32
South Portland, ME[93]	12.05	1.64	1.79	1.26	3.32	4.19
Sparks, NV[94]	12.86	1.55	2.16	1.43	3.47	5.35
State College, PA	n/a	n/a	n/a	n/a	n/a	n/a
Sugar Land, TX[95]	10.13	1.04	1.55	1.50	3.07	4.05
Sun Prairie, WI[96]	12.91	1.77	1.97	1.21	3.58	4.65
Syracuse, UT[97]	10.69	1.86	1.87	2.61	3.76	4.32
Tredyffrin, PA[98]	11.82	1.46	2.11	1.74	3.92	4.10
Upper Dublin, PA[99]	11.82	1.46	2.11	1.74	3.92	4.10
Urbandale, IA[100]	10.31	1.60	1.79	1.14	3.09	4.21
Vestal, NY	n/a	n/a	n/a	n/a	n/a	n/a
Vestavia Hills, AL[101]	10.45	1.26	2.26	1.65	3.53	4.42
Webster, NY[102]	11.62	1.30	1.74	1.23	3.46	4.23
Wellesley, MA[103]	12.27	1.71	2.49	1.84	3.53	4.19
West Fargo, ND[104]	12.56	1.84	2.96	1.24	4.12	4.32
West Lafayette, IN[105]	12.20	1.41	1.59	1.20	3.58	4.64
Weston, FL[106]	10.52	1.30	2.49	1.38	3.67	3.62
Wilmette, IL[107]	12.21	1.28	1.95	1.65	4.55	4.53
Yorba Linda, CA[108]	12.43	1.04	2.23	2.11	3.65	6.36
Zionsville, IN[109]	12.44	1.29	1.22	1.19	3.39	4.30
Average*	11.29	1.40	2.02	1.47	3.55	4.37
Minimum*	7.71	0.93	1.04	0.70	2.86	3.24
Maximum*	15.83	2.39	4.03	3.92	6.29	8.16

Note: ***T-Bone Steak*** *(price per pound);* ***Frying Chicken*** *(price per pound, whole fryer);* ***Whole Milk*** *(half gallon carton);* ***Eggs*** *(price per dozen, Grade A, large);* ***Orange Juice*** *(64 oz. Tropicana or Florida Natural);* ***Coffee*** *(11.5 oz. can, vacuum-packed, Maxwell House, Hills*

Table continued on next page.

Bros, or Folgers); (*) Values for the local area are compared with the average, minimum, and maximum values for all 294 areas in the Cost of Living Index report; n/a not available; In cases where data is not available for the city, data for the metro area or for a neighboring city has been provided and noted as follows: (1) Orange County CA; (2) Plano TX; (3) Ames IA; (4) Raleigh NC; (5) Dayton OH; (6) Omaha NE; (7) Fayetteville AR; (8) Albany NY; (9) Blacksburg VA; (10) Bethesda-Gaithersburg-Frederick MD; (11) Bozeman MT; (12) Nashville-Murfreesboro TN; (13) Burlington-Chittenden County VT; (14) Conway AR; (15) Indianapolis IN; (16) Waterloo-Cedar Falls IA; (17) Austin TX; (18) Baton Rouge LA; (19) Chapel Hill NC; (20) New Haven CT; (21) Seguin TX; (22) Memphis TN; (23) Plano TX; (24) Charlotte NC; (25) Pittsburgh PA; (26) Columbus OH; (27) Minneapolis MN; (28) Edmond OK; (29) St. Louis MO-IL; (30) Philadelphia PA; (31) Plano TX; (32) Sacramento CA; (33) Brazoria County TX; (34) Grand Rapids MI; (35) Hartford CT; (36) Harrisburg PA; (37) Columbus OH; (38) Newark-Elizabeth NJ; (39) Raleigh NC; (40) Covington KY; (41) Juneau AK; (42) Ogden UT; (43) Fort Worth TX; (44) Oakland CA; (45) Portland OR; (46) Laramie WY; (47) Austin TX; (48) Kansas City MO-KS; (49) Kansas City MO-KS; (50) Arlington VA; (51) Provo-Orem UT; (52) Framingham-Natick MA; (53) Allentown PA; (54) Huntsville AL; (55) Jackson MS; (56) Seattle WA; (57) Cedar Rapids IA; (58) Middlesex-Monmouth NJ; (59) Cincinnati OH; (60) Milwaukee-Waukesha WI; (61) Boise ID; (62) Manchester NH; (63) Atlanta GA; (64) Pittsburgh PA; (65) Morgantown WV; (66) Charleston-N Charleston SC; (67) Wilmington DE; (68) Stamford CT; (69) Providence RI; (70) Sarasota FL; (71) Cleveland OH; (72) Detroit MI; (73) St. Louis MO-IL; (74) Buffalo NY; (75) Tucson AZ; (76) Orlando FL; (77) Denver CO; (78) Fort Lauderdale FL; (79) Atlanta GA; (80) Joliet-Will County IL; (81) Provo-Orem UT; (82) San Diego CA; (83) Phoenix AZ; (84) Philadelphia PA; (85) Newark-Elizabeth NJ; (86) Albuquerque NM; (87) Seattle WA; (88) Oakland CA; (89) Fitchburg-Leominster MA; (90) Middlesex-Monmouth NJ; (91) Salt Lake City UT; (92) Providence RI; (93) Portland ME; (94) Reno-Sparks NV; (95) Houston TX; (96) Madison WI; (97) Ogden UT; (98) Philadelphia PA; (99) Philadelphia PA; (100) Des Moines IA; (101) Birmingham AL; (102) Rochester NY; (103) Framingham-Natick MA; (104) Fargo-Moorhead ND-MN; (105) Lafayette IN; (106) Fort Lauderdale FL; (107) Chicago IL; (108) Orange County CA; (109) Indianapolis IN

Source: The Council for Community and Economic Research (formerly ACCRA), Cost of Living Index, 2017

Housing and Utility Costs

Urban Area	New Home Price ($)	Apartment Rent ($/month)	All Electric ($/month)	Part Electric ($/month)	Other Energy ($/month)	Telephone ($/month)
Aberdeen, SD	n/a	n/a	n/a	n/a	n/a	n/a
Aliso Viejo, CA[1]	924,177	2,233	-	123.56	67.24	25.97
Allen, TX[2]	387,838	1,300	-	110.21	55.03	27.72
Ames, IA[3]	324,094	999	-	77.51	57.88	22.40
Amherst, MA	n/a	n/a	n/a	n/a	n/a	n/a
Apex, NC[4]	261,414	1,013	-	81.95	61.55	31.92
Beavercreek, OH[5]	222,925	747	-	76.40	66.28	23.32
Bellevue, NE[6]	281,754	1,047	-	88.31	73.05	21.01
Bend, OR	n/a	n/a	n/a	n/a	n/a	n/a
Benicia, CA	n/a	n/a	n/a	n/a	n/a	n/a
Bentonville, AR[7]	262,934	738	-	79.29	56.63	31.66
Bethlehem, NY[8]	389,074	1,207	-	82.48	66.79	31.34
Blacksburg, VA[9]	202,531	859	-	84.93	58.72	44.61
Bowie, MD[10]	746,332	2,163	-	108.03	68.22	26.86
Bozeman, MT[11]	367,460	1,086	-	77.55	61.50	20.00
Brentwood, TN[12]	295,539	1,009	-	91.73	64.72	24.50
Burlington, VT[13]	500,962	1,489	-	100.24	128.91	28.00
Cabot, AR[14]	214,000	692	-	59.86	54.30	27.95
Carmel, IN[15]	247,691	1,014	-	102.60	72.06	25.68
Cedar Falls, IA[16]	342,156	674	-	93.18	66.87	20.10
Cedar Park, TX[17]	301,734	1,305	-	103.67	53.64	22.94
Central, LA[18]	275,985	906	127.49	-	-	23.88
Chapel Hill, NC[19]	345,150	975	-	82.94	61.22	27.99
Cheshire, CT[20]	401,985	1,663	-	131.81	66.14	23.90
Chino Hills, CA	n/a	n/a	n/a	n/a	n/a	n/a
Cibolo, TX[21]	249,814	816	156.37	-	-	40.74
Cicero, NY	n/a	n/a	n/a	n/a	n/a	n/a
Collierville, TN[22]	215,913	686	-	113.27	43.60	32.78
Coppell, TX[23]	387,838	1,300	-	110.21	55.03	27.72
Cornelius, NC[24]	267,863	1,061	154.11	-	-	31.00
Cranberry, PA[25]	281,247	1,110	-	96.22	90.24	30.99
Crown Point, IN	n/a	n/a	n/a	n/a	n/a	n/a
Dublin, OH[26]	238,079	952	-	52.90	65.42	24.67
East Fishkill, NY	n/a	n/a	n/a	n/a	n/a	n/a
Eden Prairie, MN[27]	352,818	1,128	-	95.84	62.02	24.99
Edmond, OK[28]	301,277	837	-	91.58	62.81	21.55
Edwardsville, IL[29]	223,050	877	-	96.99	71.90	37.05
Evesham, NJ[30]	424,983	1,411	-	107.26	69.96	42.00
Flower Mound, TX[31]	387,838	1,300	-	110.21	55.03	27.72
Folsom, CA[32]	410,200	1,820	-	124.54	43.93	21.67
Friendswood, TX[33]	279,516	1,054	-	93.44	38.40	18.33
Gaines, MI[34]	274,936	1,031	-	97.29	71.79	20.00
Glastonbury, CT[35]	445,407	1,420	-	106.10	68.07	24.99
Grand Blanc, MI	n/a	n/a	n/a	n/a	n/a	n/a
Hampden, PA[36]	322,594	888	210.14	-	-	31.90
Hilliard, OH[37]	238,079	952	-	52.90	65.42	24.67
Hillsborough, NJ[38]	507,404	1,663	-	126.69	64.16	33.50
Holly Springs, NC[39]	261,414	1,013	-	81.95	61.55	31.92
Independence, KY[40]	n/a	n/a	n/a	n/a	n/a	n/a
Juneau, AK[41]	509,408	1,498	-	84.91	177.94	21.66
Kaysville, UT[42]	393,127	890	-	69.29	68.50	19.62
Keller, TX[43]	267,887	1,164	-	128.21	57.85	30.25
Lafayette, CA[44]	751,609	2,176	-	150.90	79.34	24.33
Lafayette, CO	n/a	n/a	n/a	n/a	n/a	n/a
Lake Oswego, OR[45]	507,368	2,482	-	76.08	69.16	19.33
Laramie, WY[46]	276,055	858	-	65.31	66.99	41.62
Leander, TX[47]	301,734	1,305	-	103.67	53.64	22.94
Leawood, KS[48]	260,080	957	-	88.23	65.63	16.67
Lee's Summit, MO[49]	260,080	957	-	88.23	65.63	16.67
Leesburg, VA[50]	799,297	2,344	-	77.90	63.27	27.32
Lehi, UT[51]	353,645	992	-	67.76	62.38	19.00
Lexington, MA[52]	650,928	1,854	-	79.83	137.46	31.08
Los Altos, CA	n/a	n/a	n/a	n/a	n/a	n/a
Loveland, CO	n/a	n/a	n/a	n/a	n/a	n/a
Lower Macungie, PA[53]	354,972	1,436	-	101.48	75.53	25.24
Madison, AL[54]	243,562	823	155.88	-	-	37.04
Madison, MS[55]	265,054	748	-	76.16	46.19	40.59

Table continued on next page.

Urban Area	New Home Price ($)	Apartment Rent ($/month)	All Electric ($/month)	Part Electric ($/month)	Other Energy ($/month)	Telephone ($/month)
Maple Valley, WA[56]	649,370	2,366	190.91	-	-	38.34
Marion, IA[57]	323,005	766	-	125.87	63.55	25.00
Marlboro, NJ[58]	456,663	1,380	-	124.44	63.78	33.50
Mason, OH[59]	242,171	887	-	84.08	78.14	26.78
Menomonee Falls, WI[60]	324,408	977	-	98.69	61.89	34.53
Meridian, ID[61]	297,092	893	-	68.75	75.75	24.32
Meridian, MI	n/a	n/a	n/a	n/a	n/a	n/a
Merrimack, NH[62]	342,782	1,358	-	121.03	105.09	36.25
Milton, GA[63]	290,041	1,169	-	86.30	40.60	27.67
Moon, PA[64]	281,247	1,110	-	96.22	90.24	30.99
Moorpark, CA	n/a	n/a	n/a	n/a	n/a	n/a
Morgantown, WV[65]	311,942	785	-	74.32	58.69	28.31
Mount Pleasant, SC[66]	275,736	1,354	260.94	-	-	20.88
Newark, DE[67]	364,276	1,162	-	108.61	83.40	26.64
Newtown, CT[68]	681,279	2,371	-	95.13	105.06	29.17
North Attleborough, MA[69]	435,485	1,746	-	110.50	101.89	36.19
North Port, FL[70]	341,439	1,076	153.91	-	-	34.98
North Ridgeville, OH[71]	281,845	1,041	-	87.85	69.95	33.53
Northville, MI[72]	295,582	1,094	-	84.61	66.23	33.31
O'Fallon, MO[73]	223,050	877	-	96.99	71.90	37.05
Orchard Park, NY[74]	369,768	866	-	81.57	69.97	37.33
Oro Valley, AZ[75]	258,912	885	-	105.66	56.63	23.48
Oviedo, FL[76]	276,775	1,065	181.04	-	-	32.85
Parker, CO[77]	442,949	1,414	-	77.99	51.58	32.29
Parkland, FL[78]	521,080	1,772	159.36	-	-	29.11
Peachtree City, GA[79]	290,041	1,169	-	86.30	40.60	27.67
Pittsfield, MI	n/a	n/a	n/a	n/a	n/a	n/a
Plainfield, IL[80]	298,568	1,474	-	79.40	51.44	25.99
Pleasant Grove, UT[81]	353,645	992	-	67.76	62.38	19.00
Poway, CA[82]	821,579	2,294	-	170.98	61.71	25.97
Princeton, NJ	n/a	n/a	n/a	n/a	n/a	n/a
Queen Creek, AZ[83]	317,372	1,032	197.60	-	-	19.99
Radnor, PA[84]	424,983	1,411	-	107.26	69.96	42.00
Randolph, NJ[85]	507,404	1,663	-	126.69	64.16	33.50
Rexburg, ID	n/a	n/a	n/a	n/a	n/a	n/a
Rio Rancho, NM[86]	314,655	968	-	95.47	54.10	22.15
Rye, NY	n/a	n/a	n/a	n/a	n/a	n/a
Sammamish, WA[87]	649,370	2,366	190.91	-	-	38.34
San Ramon, CA[88]	751,609	2,176	-	150.90	79.34	24.33
Saratoga, CA	n/a	n/a	n/a	n/a	n/a	n/a
Shrewsbury, MA[89]	390,660	1,377	-	85.28	159.71	29.97
South Brunswick, NJ[90]	456,663	1,380	-	124.44	63.78	33.50
South Jordan, UT[91]	317,989	1,010	-	74.59	63.74	19.00
South Kingstown, RI[92]	435,485	1,746	-	110.50	101.89	36.19
South Portland, ME[93]	389,935	1,535	-	96.60	135.40	25.89
Sparks, NV[94]	347,722	1,164	-	68.86	44.40	30.01
State College, PA	n/a	n/a	n/a	n/a	n/a	n/a
Sugar Land, TX[95]	307,633	1,337	-	147.08	37.96	31.67
Sun Prairie, WI[96]	388,298	1,048	-	105.90	70.78	29.99
Syracuse, UT[97]	393,127	890	-	69.29	68.50	19.62
Tredyffrin, PA[98]	424,983	1,411	-	107.26	69.96	42.00
Upper Dublin, PA[99]	424,983	1,411	-	107.26	69.96	42.00
Urbandale, IA[100]	309,691	672	-	97.96	59.19	30.20
Vestal, NY	n/a	n/a	n/a	n/a	n/a	n/a
Vestavia Hills, AL[101]	267,638	1,051	-	109.87	80.89	24.33
Webster, NY[102]	278,085	1,047	-	76.56	69.20	27.99
Wellesley, MA[103]	650,928	1,854	-	79.83	137.46	31.08
West Fargo, ND[104]	342,347	952	-	75.25	67.27	25.30
West Lafayette, IN[105]	220,878	704	-	90.93	67.76	34.99
Weston, FL[106]	521,080	1,772	159.36	-	-	29.11
Wilmette, IL[107]	487,764	1,831	-	79.20	51.49	29.99
Yorba Linda, CA[108]	924,177	2,233	-	123.56	67.24	25.97
Zionsville, IN[109]	247,691	1,014	-	102.60	72.06	25.68
Average*	335,956	1,047	175.01	97.34	67.93	28.71
Minimum*	187,788	491	109.48	49.33	35.44	12.39
Maximum*	1,739,087	4,559	432.62	227.09	353.33	44.61

*Note: **New Home Price** (2,400 sf living area, 8,000 sf lot, in urban area with full utilities); **Apartment Rent** (950 sf 2 bedroom/1.5 or 2 bath, unfurnished, excluding all utilities except water); **All Electric** (average monthly cost for an all-electric home); **Part Electric** (average*

Table continued on next page.

monthly cost for a part-electric home); ***Other Energy*** *(average monthly cost for natural gas, fuel oil, coal, wood, and any other forms of energy except electricity);* ***Telephone*** *(price includes basic monthly rate for a private residential line plus additional local usage charges incurred by a family of four); (*) Values for the local area are compared with the average, minimum, and maximum values for all 294 areas in the Cost of Living Index report; n/a not available; In cases where data is not available for the city, data for the metro area or for a neighboring city has been provided and noted as follows: (1) Orange County CA; (2) Plano TX; (3) Ames IA; (4) Raleigh NC; (5) Dayton OH; (6) Omaha NE; (7) Fayetteville AR; (8) Albany NY; (9) Blacksburg VA; (10) Bethesda-Gaithersburg-Frederick MD; (11) Bozeman MT; (12) Nashville-Murfreesboro TN; (13) Burlington-Chittenden County VT; (14) Conway AR; (15) Indianapolis IN; (16) Waterloo-Cedar Falls IA; (17) Austin TX; (18) Baton Rouge LA; (19) Chapel Hill NC; (20) New Haven CT; (21) Seguin TX; (22) Memphis TN; (23) Plano TX; (24) Charlotte NC; (25) Pittsburgh PA; (26) Columbus OH; (27) Minneapolis MN; (28) Edmond OK; (29) St. Louis MO-IL; (30) Philadelphia PA; (31) Plano TX; (32) Sacramento CA; (33) Brazoria County TX; (34) Grand Rapids MI; (35) Hartford CT; (36) Harrisburg PA; (37) Columbus OH; (38) Newark-Elizabeth NJ; (39) Raleigh NC; (40) Covington KY; (41) Juneau AK; (42) Ogden UT; (43) Fort Worth TX; (44) Oakland CA; (45) Portland OR; (46) Laramie WY; (47) Austin TX; (48) Kansas City MO-KS; (49) Kansas City MO-KS; (50) Arlington VA; (51) Provo-Orem UT; (52) Framingham-Natick MA; (53) Allentown PA; (54) Huntsville AL; (55) Jackson MS; (56) Seattle WA; (57) Cedar Rapids IA; (58) Middlesex-Monmouth NJ; (59) Cincinnati OH; (60) Milwaukee-Waukesha WI; (61) Boise ID; (62) Manchester NH; (63) Atlanta GA; (64) Pittsburgh PA; (65) Morgantown WV; (66) Charleston-N Charleston SC; (67) Wilmington DE; (68) Stamford CT; (69) Providence RI; (70) Sarasota FL; (71) Cleveland OH; (72) Detroit MI; (73) St. Louis MO-IL; (74) Buffalo NY; (75) Tucson AZ; (76) Orlando FL; (77) Denver CO; (78) Fort Lauderdale FL; (79) Atlanta GA; (80) Joliet-Will County IL; (81) Provo-Orem UT; (82) San Diego CA; (83) Phoenix AZ; (84) Philadelphia PA; (85) Newark-Elizabeth NJ; (86) Albuquerque NM; (87) Seattle WA; (88) Oakland CA; (89) Fitchburg-Leominster MA; (90) Middlesex-Monmouth NJ; (91) Salt Lake City UT; (92) Providence RI; (93) Portland ME; (94) Reno-Sparks NV; (95) Houston TX; (96) Madison WI; (97) Ogden UT; (98) Philadelphia PA; (99) Philadelphia PA; (100) Des Moines IA; (101) Birmingham AL; (102) Rochester NY; (103) Framingham-Natick MA; (104) Fargo-Moorhead ND-MN; (105) Lafayette IN; (106) Fort Lauderdale FL; (107) Chicago IL; (108) Orange County CA; (109) Indianapolis IN*

Source: The Council for Community and Economic Research (formerly ACCRA), Cost of Living Index, 2017

Health Care, Transportation, and Other Costs

Urban Area	Doctor ($/visit)	Dentist ($/visit)	Optometrist ($/visit)	Gasoline ($/gallon)	Beauty Salon ($/visit)	Men's Shirt ($)
Aberdeen, SD	n/a	n/a	n/a	n/a	n/a	n/a
Aliso Viejo, CA[1]	96.00	106.60	101.17	3.03	60.87	39.89
Allen, TX[2]	80.02	73.81	108.39	2.18	48.10	29.06
Ames, IA[3]	107.67	92.06	89.00	2.32	32.70	19.00
Amherst, MA	n/a	n/a	n/a	n/a	n/a	n/a
Apex, NC[4]	99.19	98.93	103.10	2.26	51.86	23.44
Beavercreek, OH[5]	82.67	82.00	96.33	2.24	34.33	33.18
Bellevue, NE[6]	137.37	74.14	97.13	1.82	32.86	27.45
Bend, OR	n/a	n/a	n/a	n/a	n/a	n/a
Benicia, CA	n/a	n/a	n/a	n/a	n/a	n/a
Bentonville, AR[7]	91.83	78.83	85.33	1.99	24.78	18.40
Bethlehem, NY[8]	102.72	93.90	99.72	2.35	30.79	28.31
Blacksburg, VA[9]	120.31	111.97	102.22	2.02	33.44	37.57
Bowie, MD[10]	94.00	86.00	72.75	2.35	55.00	40.00
Bozeman, MT[11]	133.00	84.00	84.93	2.30	37.52	21.49
Brentwood, TN[12]	83.40	71.60	77.07	2.11	46.12	32.33
Burlington, VT[13]	113.28	94.00	130.00	2.32	49.11	29.00
Cabot, AR[14]	103.33	66.00	87.67	2.04	30.00	23.42
Carmel, IN[15]	92.24	91.22	72.00	2.16	36.97	39.13
Cedar Falls, IA[16]	101.67	81.66	120.17	2.29	27.50	18.93
Cedar Park, TX[17]	98.76	99.00	109.83	2.11	46.34	29.05
Central, LA[18]	136.79	102.88	156.41	2.01	45.13	42.04
Chapel Hill, NC[19]	80.00	105.00	104.06	2.24	33.50	11.33
Cheshire, CT[20]	130.03	114.44	119.32	2.38	55.01	35.75
Chino Hills, CA	n/a	n/a	n/a	n/a	n/a	n/a
Cibolo, TX[21]	94.61	85.54	98.68	1.99	26.70	26.28
Cicero, NY	n/a	n/a	n/a	n/a	n/a	n/a
Collierville, TN[22]	70.43	87.60	64.31	2.08	29.50	25.17
Coppell, TX[23]	80.02	73.81	108.39	2.18	48.10	29.06
Cornelius, NC[24]	102.91	113.63	113.53	2.14	33.80	36.82
Cranberry, PA[25]	98.75	86.30	86.58	2.61	32.20	26.61
Crown Point, IN	n/a	n/a	n/a	n/a	n/a	n/a
Dublin, OH[26]	99.16	86.52	59.51	2.29	33.40	29.68
East Fishkill, NY	n/a	n/a	n/a	n/a	n/a	n/a
Eden Prairie, MN[27]	132.41	84.22	82.63	2.23	34.28	34.59
Edmond, OK[28]	92.73	82.67	113.11	1.93	31.85	24.00
Edwardsville, IL[29]	81.57	97.45	78.31	2.23	34.20	20.75
Evesham, NJ[30]	130.24	96.14	100.71	2.48	56.27	31.77
Flower Mound, TX[31]	80.02	73.81	108.39	2.18	48.10	29.06
Folsom, CA[32]	100.28	96.52	122.96	2.82	51.92	32.88
Friendswood, TX[33]	110.52	96.61	102.00	2.02	33.50	37.83
Gaines, MI[34]	97.56	88.11	91.22	2.49	37.45	22.99
Glastonbury, CT[35]	125.00	123.03	120.00	2.39	51.67	32.49
Grand Blanc, MI	n/a	n/a	n/a	n/a	n/a	n/a
Hampden, PA[36]	89.29	82.49	51.78	2.45	23.12	21.84
Hilliard, OH[37]	99.16	86.52	59.51	2.29	33.40	29.68
Hillsborough, NJ[38]	96.29	99.80	100.58	2.39	37.53	38.16
Holly Springs, NC[39]	99.19	98.93	103.10	2.26	51.86	23.44
Independence, KY[40]	n/a	n/a	n/a	n/a	n/a	n/a
Juneau, AK[41]	193.50	151.00	229.28	3.08	35.78	45.33
Kaysville, UT[42]	103.34	124.99	109.34	2.32	30.34	26.97
Keller, TX[43]	120.46	93.52	96.19	2.19	57.67	42.84
Lafayette, CA[44]	138.93	122.57	120.71	2.93	69.62	39.77
Lafayette, CO	n/a	n/a	n/a	n/a	n/a	n/a
Lake Oswego, OR[45]	107.61	102.69	131.19	2.88	48.67	33.62
Laramie, WY[46]	104.92	86.92	140.76	2.16	30.00	50.83
Leander, TX[47]	98.76	99.00	109.83	2.11	46.34	29.05
Leawood, KS[48]	99.13	97.70	98.24	2.13	29.57	30.66
Lee's Summit, MO[49]	99.13	97.70	98.24	2.13	29.57	30.66
Leesburg, VA[50]	97.42	95.33	77.00	2.44	56.89	37.78
Lehi, UT[51]	105.68	119.67	92.59	2.23	33.57	31.19
Lexington, MA[52]	151.91	110.63	136.98	2.42	50.37	59.13
Los Altos, CA	n/a	n/a	n/a	n/a	n/a	n/a
Loveland, CO	n/a	n/a	n/a	n/a	n/a	n/a
Lower Macungie, PA[53]	92.57	105.22	122.49	2.53	38.21	29.58
Madison, AL[54]	93.11	94.44	113.35	2.16	41.22	29.69
Madison, MS[55]	90.50	86.63	83.00	2.01	23.38	14.57

Table continued on next page.

Urban Area	Doctor ($/visit)	Dentist ($/visit)	Optometrist ($/visit)	Gasoline ($/gallon)	Beauty Salon ($/visit)	Men's Shirt ($)
Maple Valley, WA[56]	124.00	132.64	145.72	2.88	43.43	45.00
Marion, IA[57]	128.23	82.63	120.35	2.16	37.28	21.54
Marlboro, NJ[58]	93.87	115.62	108.67	2.36	36.33	38.93
Mason, OH[59]	100.96	95.10	95.13	2.30	38.07	39.56
Menomonee Falls, WI[60]	163.66	98.09	53.85	2.27	34.01	35.41
Meridian, ID[61]	127.33	86.44	111.38	2.35	27.62	20.02
Meridian, MI	n/a	n/a	n/a	n/a	n/a	n/a
Merrimack, NH[62]	145.00	106.67	102.92	2.21	39.33	31.66
Milton, GA[63]	105.10	114.97	102.23	2.32	46.88	32.61
Moon, PA[64]	98.75	86.30	86.58	2.61	32.20	26.61
Moorpark, CA	n/a	n/a	n/a	n/a	n/a	n/a
Morgantown, WV[65]	91.50	82.50	94.75	2.41	35.37	45.75
Mount Pleasant, SC[66]	114.72	96.39	105.51	2.10	44.38	35.38
Newark, DE[67]	87.50	107.42	114.17	2.17	38.67	37.67
Newtown, CT[68]	124.71	112.48	115.59	2.55	64.81	39.16
North Attleborough, MA[69]	146.33	91.00	125.67	2.21	55.55	33.33
North Port, FL[70]	154.87	94.94	114.72	2.29	34.84	49.29
North Ridgeville, OH[71]	110.20	90.67	80.26	2.24	36.88	33.63
Northville, MI[72]	97.01	91.17	74.88	2.40	47.07	26.23
O'Fallon, MO[73]	81.57	97.45	78.31	2.23	34.20	20.75
Orchard Park, NY[74]	86.67	78.97	60.23	2.36	37.27	17.38
Oro Valley, AZ[75]	110.67	92.14	104.38	2.10	47.43	42.77
Oviedo, FL[76]	79.27	79.99	79.06	2.12	41.60	19.86
Parker, CO[77]	131.22	91.02	100.38	2.25	37.83	29.14
Parkland, FL[78]	83.20	97.89	94.17	2.36	61.89	26.39
Peachtree City, GA[79]	105.10	114.97	102.23	2.32	46.88	32.61
Pittsfield, MI	n/a	n/a	n/a	n/a	n/a	n/a
Plainfield, IL[80]	145.88	91.90	102.46	2.38	36.33	30.13
Pleasant Grove, UT[81]	105.68	119.67	92.59	2.23	33.57	31.19
Poway, CA[82]	105.00	104.33	107.20	2.91	57.00	29.46
Princeton, NJ	n/a	n/a	n/a	n/a	n/a	n/a
Queen Creek, AZ[83]	99.17	99.17	72.44	2.12	35.00	25.43
Radnor, PA[84]	130.24	96.14	100.71	2.48	56.27	31.77
Randolph, NJ[85]	96.29	99.80	100.58	2.39	37.53	38.16
Rexburg, ID	n/a	n/a	n/a	n/a	n/a	n/a
Rio Rancho, NM[86]	103.83	100.33	101.52	2.21	45.00	30.00
Rye, NY	n/a	n/a	n/a	n/a	n/a	n/a
Sammamish, WA[87]	124.00	132.64	145.72	2.88	43.43	45.00
San Ramon, CA[88]	138.93	122.57	120.71	2.93	69.62	39.77
Saratoga, CA	n/a	n/a	n/a	n/a	n/a	n/a
Shrewsbury, MA[89]	140.02	123.73	123.27	2.21	73.51	35.79
South Brunswick, NJ[90]	93.87	115.62	108.67	2.36	36.33	38.93
South Jordan, UT[91]	107.86	86.24	89.33	2.23	31.67	27.18
South Kingstown, RI[92]	146.33	91.00	125.67	2.21	55.55	33.33
South Portland, ME[93]	134.00	98.00	127.00	2.26	52.89	30.82
Sparks, NV[94]	138.14	99.33	108.47	2.73	46.47	34.11
State College, PA	n/a	n/a	n/a	n/a	n/a	n/a
Sugar Land, TX[95]	80.33	92.07	106.05	2.09	49.70	25.00
Sun Prairie, WI[96]	182.00	101.89	60.83	2.21	41.66	33.66
Syracuse, UT[97]	103.34	124.99	109.34	2.32	30.34	26.97
Tredyffrin, PA[98]	130.24	96.14	100.71	2.48	56.27	31.77
Upper Dublin, PA[99]	130.24	96.14	100.71	2.48	56.27	31.77
Urbandale, IA[100]	118.76	78.86	99.16	2.20	31.92	16.38
Vestal, NY	n/a	n/a	n/a	n/a	n/a	n/a
Vestavia Hills, AL[101]	86.11	71.22	116.33	2.01	34.18	41.00
Webster, NY[102]	91.47	94.93	111.54	2.42	38.00	29.43
Wellesley, MA[103]	151.91	110.63	136.98	2.42	50.37	59.13
West Fargo, ND[104]	157.22	95.33	93.17	2.11	34.13	28.47
West Lafayette, IN[105]	90.00	90.00	100.00	2.27	30.01	36.66
Weston, FL[106]	83.20	97.89	94.17	2.36	61.89	26.39
Wilmette, IL[107]	100.00	102.33	95.00	2.93	69.87	42.99
Yorba Linda, CA[108]	96.00	106.60	101.17	3.03	60.87	39.89
Zionsville, IN[109]	92.24	91.22	72.00	2.16	36.97	39.13
Average*	108.00	92.54	101.93	2.25	37.58	30.92
Minimum*	30.39	60.00	49.75	1.82	16.11	11.20
Maximum*	193.50	161.94	229.28	3.16	77.35	59.13

*Note: **Doctor** (general practitioners routine exam of an established patient); **Dentist** (adult teeth cleaning and periodic oral examination); **Optometrist** (full vision eye exam for established adult patient); **Gasoline** (one gallon regular unleaded, national brand, including all taxes,*

Table continued on next page.

cash price at self-service pump if available); ***Beauty Salon*** *(woman's shampoo, trim, and blow-dry);* ***Men's Shirt*** *(cotton/polyester dress shirt, pinpoint weave, long sleeves); (*) Values for the local area are compared with the average, minimum, and maximum values for all 294 areas in the Cost of Living Index report; n/a not available; In cases where data is not available for the city, data for the metro area or for a neighboring city has been provided and noted as follows: (1) Orange County CA; (2) Plano TX; (3) Ames IA; (4) Raleigh NC; (5) Dayton OH; (6) Omaha NE; (7) Fayetteville AR; (8) Albany NY; (9) Blacksburg VA; (10) Bethesda-Gaithersburg-Frederick MD; (11) Bozeman MT; (12) Nashville-Murfreesboro TN; (13) Burlington-Chittenden County VT; (14) Conway AR; (15) Indianapolis IN; (16) Waterloo-Cedar Falls IA; (17) Austin TX; (18) Baton Rouge LA; (19) Chapel Hill NC; (20) New Haven CT; (21) Seguin TX; (22) Memphis TN; (23) Plano TX; (24) Charlotte NC; (25) Pittsburgh PA; (26) Columbus OH; (27) Minneapolis MN; (28) Edmond OK; (29) St. Louis MO-IL; (30) Philadelphia PA; (31) Plano TX; (32) Sacramento CA; (33) Brazoria County TX; (34) Grand Rapids MI; (35) Hartford CT; (36) Harrisburg PA; (37) Columbus OH; (38) Newark-Elizabeth NJ; (39) Raleigh NC; (40) Covington KY; (41) Juneau AK; (42) Ogden UT; (43) Fort Worth TX; (44) Oakland CA; (45) Portland OR; (46) Laramie WY; (47) Austin TX; (48) Kansas City MO-KS; (49) Kansas City MO-KS; (50) Arlington VA; (51) Provo-Orem UT; (52) Framingham-Natick MA; (53) Allentown PA; (54) Huntsville AL; (55) Jackson MS; (56) Seattle WA; (57) Cedar Rapids IA; (58) Middlesex-Monmouth NJ; (59) Cincinnati OH; (60) Milwaukee-Waukesha WI; (61) Boise ID; (62) Manchester NH; (63) Atlanta GA; (64) Pittsburgh PA; (65) Morgantown WV; (66) Charleston-N Charleston SC; (67) Wilmington DE; (68) Stamford CT; (69) Providence RI; (70) Sarasota FL; (71) Cleveland OH; (72) Detroit MI; (73) St. Louis MO-IL; (74) Buffalo NY; (75) Tucson AZ; (76) Orlando FL; (77) Denver CO; (78) Fort Lauderdale FL; (79) Atlanta GA; (80) Joliet-Will County IL; (81) Provo-Orem UT; (82) San Diego CA; (83) Phoenix AZ; (84) Philadelphia PA; (85) Newark-Elizabeth NJ; (86) Albuquerque NM; (87) Seattle WA; (88) Oakland CA; (89) Fitchburg-Leominster MA; (90) Middlesex-Monmouth NJ; (91) Salt Lake City UT; (92) Providence RI; (93) Portland ME; (94) Reno-Sparks NV; (95) Houston TX; (96) Madison WI; (97) Ogden UT; (98) Philadelphia PA; (99) Philadelphia PA; (100) Des Moines IA; (101) Birmingham AL; (102) Rochester NY; (103) Framingham-Natick MA; (104) Fargo-Moorhead ND-MN; (105) Lafayette IN; (106) Fort Lauderdale FL; (107) Chicago IL; (108) Orange County CA; (109) Indianapolis IN*

Source: The Council for Community and Economic Research (formerly ACCRA), Cost of Living Index, 2017

Number of Medical Professionals

City	Area Covered	MDs[1]	DOs[1,2]	Dentists	Podiatrists	Chiropractors	Optometrists
Aberdeen, SD	Brown County	213.0	18.2	51.4	10.3	51.4	25.7
Aliso Viejo, CA	Orange County	316.6	21.5	108.1	6.1	46.2	25.3
Allen, TX	Collin County	268.4	18.7	66.5	4.0	32.2	16.3
Ames, IA	Story County	158.8	27.0	46.5	6.2	36.2	16.5
Amherst, MA	Hampshire County	376.1	27.4	69.3	5.6	40.8	16.7
Apex, NC	Wake County	273.3	9.8	68.2	3.2	24.4	15.1
Beavercreek, OH	Greene County	312.7	70.1	82.4	5.5	22.4	25.4
Bellevue, NE	Sarpy County	142.1	14.3	69.0	2.8	26.9	16.3
Bend, OR	Deschutes County	297.2	29.8	82.5	6.1	55.3	21.6
Benicia, CA	Solano County	202.2	27.1	92.0	7.0	15.4	16.4
Bentonville, AR	Benton County	132.3	14.3	43.3	1.9	32.1	13.5
Bethlehem, NY	Albany County	566.4	38.9	89.3	8.4	19.1	16.2
Blacksburg, VA	Montgomery County	160.0	95.4	43.7	1.0	21.3	8.1
Bowie, MD	Prince George's County	164.3	5.1	60.4	5.9	9.5	8.6
Bozeman, MT	Gallatin County	224.3	14.0	70.1	4.8	51.9	18.3
Brentwood, TN	Williamson County	576.0	24.1	76.3	3.7	46.1	22.4
Burlington, VT	Chittenden County	824.2	19.9	91.6	3.7	47.1	20.4
Cabot, AR	Lonoke County	35.1	4.2	25.1	1.4	13.9	13.9
Carmel, IN	Hamilton County	564.8	24.6	74.3	4.1	36.0	22.1
Cedar Falls, IA	Black Hawk County	218.1	32.2	71.5	14.3	42.9	18.1
Cedar Park, TX	Williamson County	172.2	17.7	54.2	4.2	26.9	17.4
Central, LA	E. Baton Rouge Parish	380.1	5.8	71.2	4.2	11.4	13.4
Chapel Hill, NC	Orange County	1,443.9	18.4	210.2	3.5	14.0	11.9
Cheshire, CT	New Haven County	555.9	11.6	76.7	9.2	25.7	16.4
Chino Hills, CA	San Bernardino County	185.1	20.2	68.3	3.5	14.2	12.3
Cibolo, TX	Guadalupe County	89.7	12.6	31.7	1.3	10.3	9.7
Cicero, NY	Onondaga County	477.3	17.7	74.8	10.1	27.2	15.2
Collierville, TN	Shelby County	392.9	7.9	70.6	3.5	12.0	29.7
Coppell, TX	Dallas County	324.9	20.7	80.2	3.9	34.2	13.0
Cornelius, NC	Mecklenburg County	313.2	10.8	67.9	3.1	31.0	13.2
Cranberry, PA	Butler County	140.4	37.1	69.8	6.4	58.5	25.2
Crown Point, IN	Lake County	160.6	23.6	59.0	9.0	16.6	16.2
Dublin, OH	Franklin County	415.2	64.7	84.7	6.8	24.1	26.3
East Fishkill, NY	Dutchess County	250.9	17.9	71.6	10.9	27.8	13.6
Eden Prairie, MN	Hennepin County	496.2	17.9	93.9	4.0	68.8	18.5
Edmond, OK	Oklahoma County	397.5	46.1	99.5	5.0	25.9	18.0
Edwardsville, IL	Madison County	114.7	7.1	81.3	4.1	44.4	16.2
Evesham, NJ	Burlington County	256.9	73.5	70.5	8.0	24.8	16.1
Flower Mound, TX	Denton County	174.7	18.7	53.3	3.6	36.5	16.8
Folsom, CA	Sacramento County	302.9	13.9	75.9	4.5	22.4	17.6
Friendswood, TX	Galveston County	472.8	17.7	42.8	3.6	28.5	17.3
Gaines, MI	Kent County	318.6	66.6	69.7	4.8	32.7	23.3
Glastonbury, CT	Hartford County	423.9	22.6	104.0	6.7	22.6	19.9
Grand Blanc, MI	Genesee County	224.7	72.2	71.7	7.3	24.7	18.4
Hampden, PA	Cumberland County	242.4	44.3	71.4	7.3	23.4	21.8
Hilliard, OH	Franklin County	415.2	64.7	84.7	6.8	24.1	26.3
Hillsborough, NJ	Somerset County	442.1	29.7	95.1	7.2	29.6	16.1
Holly Springs, NC	Wake County	273.3	9.8	68.2	3.2	24.4	15.1
Independence, KY	Kenton County	270.6	11.6	51.0	6.1	20.0	12.8
Juneau, AK	Juneau (B) Borough	230.0	18.4	104.9	9.3	52.5	33.9
Kaysville, UT	Davis County	144.0	16.4	64.2	4.7	26.1	10.8
Keller, TX	Tarrant County	176.3	38.3	57.4	4.2	24.6	14.4
Lafayette, CA	Contra Costa County	293.8	12.9	84.3	4.3	30.5	17.6
Lafayette, CO	Boulder County	353.8	29.9	97.5	5.9	72.9	25.8
Lake Oswego, OR	Clackamas County	248.9	25.3	77.9	3.7	37.4	14.3
Laramie, WY	Albany County	163.0	21.0	52.6	2.6	21.1	26.3
Leander, TX	Williamson County	172.2	17.7	54.2	4.2	26.9	17.4
Leawood, KS	Johnson County	488.7	48.5	81.2	3.6	64.0	25.7
Lee's Summit, MO	Jackson County	295.4	57.2	81.8	6.5	42.1	19.8
Leesburg, VA	Loudoun County	192.2	8.0	60.3	3.4	22.3	16.8
Lehi, UT	Utah County	118.8	18.0	61.1	4.1	23.9	10.3
Lexington, MA	Middlesex County	557.9	10.0	94.8	7.3	22.0	18.5
Los Altos, CA	Santa Clara County	395.2	8.6	111.9	6.3	39.9	25.4
Loveland, CO	Larimer County	241.0	28.8	81.2	4.7	52.6	19.8
Lower Macungie, PA	Lehigh County	339.0	84.9	84.5	14.3	29.2	18.7
Madison, AL	Madison County	276.1	11.9	55.3	3.9	23.3	18.2
Madison, MS	Madison County	628.2	15.6	70.3	5.8	12.5	15.4
Maple Valley, WA	King County	473.0	15.1	105.3	6.4	45.8	21.3
Marion, IA	Linn County	180.0	21.8	71.7	7.7	56.8	17.1

Table continued on next page.

City	Area Covered	MDs[1]	DOs[1,2]	Dentists	Podiatrists	Chiropractors	Optometrists
Marlboro, NJ	Monmouth County	391.8	39.4	101.9	15.2	54.2	19.6
Mason, OH	Warren County	250.7	33.5	36.2	4.0	23.0	12.4
Menomonee Falls, WI	Waukesha County	469.4	27.5	90.4	5.8	45.5	22.1
Meridian, ID	Ada County	289.1	28.2	79.0	3.4	52.4	18.2
Meridian, MI	Ingham County	308.4	156.8	72.9	4.9	24.7	19.1
Merrimack, NH	Hillsborough County	230.5	21.7	76.8	4.9	26.0	18.6
Milton, GA	Fulton County	500.1	10.8	71.3	4.9	50.9	15.5
Moon, PA	Allegheny County	621.0	37.6	94.4	10.5	42.5	19.1
Moorpark, CA	Ventura County	224.4	11.9	88.4	5.1	35.0	16.7
Morgantown, WV	Monongalia County	948.6	51.0	115.5	6.7	17.2	15.3
Mount Pleasant, SC	Charleston County	780.1	27.7	102.9	5.0	45.9	20.9
Newark, DE	New Castle County	308.9	40.9	59.7	6.5	25.6	13.8
Newtown, CT	Fairfield County	387.8	15.2	91.8	9.5	34.2	12.7
North Attleborough, MA	Bristol County	154.3	8.4	63.6	4.7	27.2	16.8
North Port, FL	Sarasota County	289.3	27.2	72.2	10.2	50.6	14.5
North Ridgeville, OH	Lorain County	139.9	25.9	46.6	7.8	16.3	17.0
Northville, MI	Wayne County	303.6	42.1	66.9	9.3	18.3	10.1
O'Fallon, MO	St. Charles County	96.9	17.9	54.5	5.1	59.1	15.9
Orchard Park, NY	Erie County	381.4	23.6	80.4	8.3	39.0	15.3
Oro Valley, AZ	Pima County	353.0	23.8	60.3	5.4	19.0	14.8
Oviedo, FL	Seminole County	188.8	20.9	58.7	6.8	30.7	18.2
Parker, CO	Douglas County	201.6	36.1	66.8	4.9	36.0	20.7
Parkland, FL	Broward County	245.2	38.1	73.8	10.7	34.5	21.9
Peachtree City, GA	Fayette County	298.3	12.7	95.3	10.8	53.0	18.0
Pittsfield, MI	Washtenaw County	1,196.7	37.0	168.1	5.8	24.7	17.0
Plainfield, IL	Will County	129.9	20.1	53.6	6.2	32.0	12.3
Pleasant Grove, UT	Utah County	118.8	18.0	61.1	4.1	23.9	10.3
Poway, CA	San Diego County	310.8	16.5	85.2	3.9	32.8	17.0
Princeton, NJ	Mercer County	389.4	25.7	78.1	8.3	26.2	19.0
Queen Creek, AZ	Maricopa County	241.4	33.2	65.9	6.0	33.5	14.7
Radnor, PA	Delaware County	373.1	61.6	81.0	12.9	25.4	18.1
Randolph, NJ	Morris County	400.0	39.1	110.9	12.0	42.7	17.2
Rexburg, ID	Madison County	92.4	39.6	59.3	5.2	33.5	30.9
Rio Rancho, NM	Sandoval County	141.0	10.1	43.5	1.4	10.0	10.7
Rye, NY	Westchester County	646.7	18.9	108.2	14.0	26.4	16.6
Sammamish, WA	King County	473.0	15.1	105.3	6.4	45.8	21.3
San Ramon, CA	Contra Costa County	293.8	12.9	84.3	4.3	30.5	17.6
Saratoga, CA	Santa Clara County	395.2	8.6	111.9	6.3	39.9	25.4
Shrewsbury, MA	Worcester County	364.6	19.3	70.8	5.8	20.6	17.7
South Brunswick, NJ	Middlesex County	363.7	19.3	85.4	9.8	24.2	17.6
South Jordan, UT	Salt Lake County	359.5	14.4	75.2	5.9	26.6	13.3
South Kingstown, RI	Washington County	225.9	29.3	55.6	6.4	22.2	21.4
South Portland, ME	Cumberland County	549.8	107.1	89.0	10.0	40.9	20.6
Sparks, NV	Washoe County	290.5	20.3	69.6	4.2	25.6	20.6
State College, PA	Centre County	208.0	38.0	56.8	4.3	31.5	17.9
Sugar Land, TX	Fort Bend County	252.7	17.2	51.8	3.1	12.9	14.7
Sun Prairie, WI	Dane County	581.7	19.9	67.9	5.1	41.3	22.3
Syracuse, UT	Davis County	144.0	16.4	64.2	4.7	26.1	10.8
Tredyffrin, PA	Chester County	241.8	44.6	66.2	9.3	27.3	19.2
Upper Dublin, PA	Montgomery County	583.1	83.3	104.9	13.2	39.7	23.0
Urbandale, IA	Polk County	202.2	110.0	68.0	9.1	50.8	22.5
Vestal, NY	Broome County	262.4	34.1	68.3	17.5	21.6	16.9
Vestavia Hills, AL	Jefferson County	597.0	15.5	85.0	4.4	15.5	32.1
Webster, NY	Monroe County	479.2	16.6	80.3	6.3	27.4	17.8
Wellesley, MA	Norfolk County	593.4	11.1	118.7	6.7	26.0	20.1
West Fargo, ND	Cass County	393.7	17.0	78.5	2.9	61.8	29.2
West Lafayette, IN	Tippecanoe County	213.4	9.7	46.1	3.7	14.8	17.0
Weston, FL	Broward County	245.2	38.1	73.8	10.7	34.5	21.9
Wilmette, IL	Cook County	422.2	22.2	87.7	12.0	26.7	19.2
Yorba Linda, CA	Orange County	316.6	21.5	108.1	6.1	46.2	25.3
Zionsville, IN	Boone County	796.4	42.8	45.1	3.1	18.7	21.8
U.S.	U.S.	276.5	22.3	67.3	6.0	26.7	15.9

Note: All figures are rates per 100,000 population; Data as of 2016 unless noted; (1) Data as of 2015 and includes all active,, non-federal physicians; (2) Doctor of Osteopathic Medicine

Source: U.S. Department of Health and Human Services, Health Resources and Services Administration, Bureau of Health Professions, Area Resource File (ARF) 2016-2017

Health Insurance Coverage: City

City	With Health Insurance	With Private Health Insurance	With Public Health Insurance	Without Health Insurance	Population Under Age 18 Without Health Insurance
Aberdeen, SD	90.3	74.5	28.3	9.7	5.9
Aliso Viejo, CA	94.3	86.4	12.6	5.7	2.6
Allen, TX	90.2	81.5	14.8	9.8	6.6
Ames, IA	95.4	88.0	16.1	4.6	1.1
Amherst, MA	96.4	85.7	17.7	3.6	3.7
Apex, NC	94.2	88.7	11.1	5.8	2.8
Beavercreek, OH	96.6	88.0	23.4	3.4	3.2
Bellevue, NE	90.0	74.3	29.5	10.0	5.7
Bend, OR	86.3	66.7	33.1	13.7	9.9
Benicia, CA	94.7	82.2	27.5	5.3	3.7
Bentonville, AR	91.7	79.4	17.9	8.3	2.8
Bethlehem, NY	97.3	90.2	22.8	2.7	1.8
Blacksburg, VA	94.5	89.9	9.8	5.5	2.5
Bowie, MD	94.2	85.9	21.1	5.8	2.6
Bozeman, MT	91.2	83.1	15.4	8.8	5.3
Brentwood, TN	96.6	91.2	13.9	3.4	1.7
Burlington, VT	95.4	73.3	30.6	4.6	1.8
Cabot, AR	92.5	75.2	29.8	7.5	2.5
Carmel, IN	96.2	89.3	15.8	3.8	2.6
Cedar Falls, IA	95.4	87.1	20.8	4.6	5.1
Cedar Park, TX	90.1	83.0	13.7	9.9	6.3
Central, LA	92.1	75.6	28.1	7.9	0.9
Chapel Hill, NC	94.1	88.4	15.1	5.9	6.1
Cheshire, CT	96.5	87.0	21.5	3.5	2.0
Chino Hills, CA	91.7	77.9	18.9	8.3	3.9
Cibolo, TX	91.8	84.6	19.0	8.2	4.6
Cicero, NY	96.4	80.8	28.2	3.6	1.6
Collierville, TN	95.4	87.8	16.7	4.6	3.3
Coppell, TX	91.8	86.2	10.3	8.2	6.7
Cornelius, NC	93.9	86.4	16.6	6.1	2.9
Cranberry, PA	96.4	90.0	16.2	3.6	2.9
Crown Point, IN	92.7	81.2	26.2	7.3	3.9
Dublin, OH	97.9	93.5	11.4	2.1	1.2
East Fishkill, NY	94.8	82.5	23.2	5.2	4.6
Eden Prairie, MN	97.2	87.5	18.7	2.8	0.6
Edmond, OK	92.1	81.5	22.3	7.9	3.9
Edwardsville, IL	96.5	86.6	19.7	3.5	1.5
Evesham, NJ	96.2	86.9	23.4	3.8	2.8
Flower Mound, TX	95.1	90.4	10.7	4.9	3.5
Folsom, CA	96.1	87.8	18.9	3.9	1.4
Friendswood, TX	90.8	83.3	18.4	9.2	5.8
Gaines, MI	92.5	74.2	30.3	7.5	1.7
Glastonbury, CT	96.1	85.3	23.0	3.9	1.8
Grand Blanc, MI	95.9	81.1	29.1	4.1	0.2
Hampden, PA	97.3	87.6	25.9	2.7	1.1
Hilliard, OH	94.6	84.7	18.3	5.4	2.2
Hillsborough, NJ	95.4	88.9	14.6	4.6	3.2
Holly Springs, NC	95.5	89.1	12.9	4.5	2.4
Independence, KY	96.3	83.1	22.8	3.7	1.7
Juneau, AK	87.7	77.4	22.7	12.3	8.7
Kaysville, UT	94.1	87.4	13.5	5.9	4.6
Keller, TX	94.2	88.0	14.9	5.8	3.0
Lafayette, CA	97.7	89.0	23.4	2.3	0.6
Lafayette, CO	91.3	75.9	23.3	8.7	1.9
Lake Oswego, OR	95.5	85.8	22.8	4.5	2.9
Laramie, WY	91.2	81.2	17.3	8.8	3.8
Leander, TX	89.5	78.8	19.0	10.5	6.9
Leawood, KS	98.7	92.4	18.7	1.3	0.4
Lee's Summit, MO	95.0	86.5	19.6	5.0	3.1
Leesburg, VA	89.3	82.9	12.5	10.7	7.1
Lehi, UT	93.4	86.1	13.0	6.6	4.1
Lexington, MA	98.9	90.2	22.2	1.1	0.5
Los Altos, CA	98.5	90.9	20.0	1.5	0.3
Loveland, CO	90.3	69.3	33.3	9.7	5.8
Lower Macungie, PA	94.9	85.0	25.2	5.1	2.5
Madison, AL	93.9	87.8	17.5	6.1	3.0
Madison, MS	97.2	92.0	17.9	2.8	1.2

Table continued on next page.

City	With Health Insurance	With Private Health Insurance	With Public Health Insurance	Without Health Insurance	Population Under Age 18 Without Health Insurance
Maple Valley, WA	95.4	85.8	17.4	4.6	4.0
Marion, IA	94.8	78.9	29.6	5.2	1.4
Marlboro, NJ	96.6	88.8	17.7	3.4	2.4
Mason, OH	96.7	89.4	17.1	3.3	2.0
Menomonee Falls, WI	96.9	85.5	26.1	3.1	2.0
Meridian, ID	90.3	79.1	21.2	9.7	7.1
Meridian, MI	93.2	84.7	23.1	6.8	4.1
Merrimack, NH	94.5	87.2	20.3	5.5	2.1
Milton, GA	93.1	88.0	11.3	6.9	4.9
Moon, PA	96.4	88.0	20.9	3.6	0.3
Moorpark, CA	91.9	80.7	18.5	8.1	4.9
Morgantown, WV	91.5	80.4	20.1	8.5	3.6
Mount Pleasant, SC	92.7	84.3	19.1	7.3	5.6
Newark, DE	95.4	86.7	19.1	4.6	3.0
Newtown, CT	97.1	85.9	21.5	2.9	1.0
North Attleborough, MA	97.8	83.2	26.6	2.2	0.4
North Port, FL	86.9	63.5	41.3	13.1	7.7
North Ridgeville, OH	95.5	83.1	27.6	4.5	1.6
Northville, MI	97.0	90.7	22.5	3.0	1.6
O'Fallon, MO	94.5	87.4	15.9	5.5	4.2
Orchard Park, NY	98.2	89.4	25.4	1.8	0.5
Oro Valley, AZ	95.2	79.5	36.5	4.8	3.4
Oviedo, FL	90.9	78.7	19.7	9.1	3.9
Parker, CO	95.9	88.8	13.8	4.1	2.3
Parkland, FL	95.1	86.8	15.9	4.9	1.3
Peachtree City, GA	92.3	83.8	21.4	7.7	6.4
Pittsfield, MI	94.3	83.2	20.7	5.7	2.2
Plainfield, IL	96.7	89.0	12.1	3.3	1.4
Pleasant Grove, UT	90.0	79.9	16.2	10.0	7.6
Poway, CA	95.2	79.9	25.8	4.8	2.2
Princeton, NJ	96.8	90.8	17.4	3.2	0.2
Queen Creek, AZ	95.1	86.0	15.4	4.9	3.4
Radnor, PA	97.0	89.5	16.6	3.0	0.2
Randolph, NJ	95.6	90.1	15.3	4.4	2.4
Rexburg, ID	92.1	75.6	23.4	7.9	5.2
Rio Rancho, NM	92.2	70.9	33.2	7.8	3.3
Rye, NY	81.7	60.3	30.3	18.3	2.8
Sammamish, WA	97.8	94.1	9.3	2.2	1.5
San Ramon, CA	96.9	90.3	12.9	3.1	1.4
Saratoga, CA	97.9	89.2	23.0	2.1	1.4
Shrewsbury, MA	97.7	88.0	22.7	2.3	2.4
South Brunswick, NJ	94.6	85.6	16.6	5.4	3.7
South Jordan, UT	93.4	86.5	13.9	6.6	5.5
South Kingstown, RI	94.9	83.8	25.7	5.1	3.3
South Portland, ME	92.5	75.0	29.2	7.5	6.2
Sparks, NV	86.6	67.4	29.8	13.4	8.7
State College, PA	95.0	90.0	10.0	5.0	1.7
Sugar Land, TX	89.9	79.7	17.8	10.1	8.4
Sun Prairie, WI	93.5	79.6	26.5	6.5	1.7
Syracuse, UT	95.3	87.4	14.4	4.7	2.5
Tredyffrin, PA	97.6	91.0	21.0	2.4	0.9
Upper Dublin, PA	96.7	88.4	22.5	3.3	0.9
Urbandale, IA	95.2	84.6	21.9	4.8	3.6
Vestal, NY	97.2	85.6	26.5	2.8	2.1
Vestavia Hills, AL	96.2	90.0	19.4	3.8	0.3
Webster, NY	96.6	83.5	28.2	3.4	2.4
Wellesley, MA	98.9	92.9	17.3	1.1	0.6
West Fargo, ND	94.2	86.7	18.0	5.8	4.7
West Lafayette, IN	94.1	89.7	10.4	5.9	3.3
Weston, FL	90.2	80.2	14.9	9.8	8.8
Wilmette, IL	96.7	89.5	20.0	3.3	2.9
Yorba Linda, CA	95.1	82.9	21.5	4.9	3.4
Zionsville, IN	97.2	91.7	13.0	2.8	0.7
U.S.	88.3	66.7	33.0	11.7	5.9

Note: Figures are percentages that cover the civilian noninstitutionalized population
Source: U.S. Census Bureau, 2012-2016 American Community Survey 5-Year Estimates

Health Insurance Coverage: Metro Area

Metro Area	With Health Insurance	With Private Health Insurance	With Public Health Insurance	Without Health Insurance	Population Under Age 18 Without Health Insurance
Aberdeen, SD	92.0	77.5	27.4	8.0	4.3
Aliso Viejo, CA	85.0	58.1	33.5	15.0	5.9
Allen, TX	81.5	63.6	25.2	18.5	10.8
Ames, IA	95.7	86.4	19.5	4.3	1.4
Amherst, MA	96.6	66.9	42.8	3.4	1.5
Apex, NC	88.8	74.4	23.4	11.2	5.2
Beavercreek, OH	91.6	68.4	36.6	8.4	4.0
Bellevue, NE	91.0	75.5	26.0	9.0	4.1
Bend, OR	86.9	64.9	36.9	13.1	8.3
Benicia, CA	90.8	69.7	34.2	9.2	4.2
Bentonville, AR	87.1	66.6	29.6	12.9	6.0
Bethlehem, NY	94.8	77.3	31.8	5.2	2.1
Blacksburg, VA	91.5	77.4	26.2	8.5	4.3
Bowie, MD	90.4	77.4	23.2	9.6	4.7
Bozeman, MT	89.8	78.4	20.2	10.2	6.0
Brentwood, TN	88.8	70.3	28.3	11.2	5.0
Burlington, VT	95.7	75.2	32.3	4.3	1.9
Cabot, AR	89.1	66.4	34.9	10.9	4.8
Carmel, IN	89.0	69.9	29.4	11.0	5.9
Cedar Falls, IA	94.1	77.6	31.3	5.9	4.2
Cedar Park, TX	85.1	71.7	21.8	14.9	8.7
Central, LA	87.9	66.4	30.8	12.1	3.4
Chapel Hill, NC	87.8	71.0	28.0	12.2	6.4
Cheshire, CT	92.9	68.7	35.5	7.1	3.1
Chino Hills, CA	85.6	55.6	37.7	14.4	6.9
Cibolo, TX	83.7	63.6	30.7	16.3	8.3
Cicero, NY	94.0	71.8	36.6	6.0	3.1
Collierville, TN	86.8	63.0	33.9	13.2	6.0
Coppell, TX	81.5	63.6	25.2	18.5	10.8
Cornelius, NC	87.1	68.5	28.5	12.9	5.7
Cranberry, PA	94.1	76.7	33.5	5.9	2.4
Crown Point, IN	89.2	68.1	30.2	10.8	3.4
Dublin, OH	91.0	71.2	29.7	9.0	4.3
East Fishkill, NY	89.8	65.8	33.7	10.2	3.6
Eden Prairie, MN	94.0	78.1	27.2	6.0	3.7
Edmond, OK	85.7	66.9	29.8	14.3	7.0
Edwardsville, IL	91.3	73.4	29.1	8.7	4.0
Evesham, NJ	92.0	72.6	31.5	8.0	3.5
Flower Mound, TX	81.5	63.6	25.2	18.5	10.8
Folsom, CA	90.4	67.7	34.6	9.6	4.3
Friendswood, TX	80.1	60.5	26.1	19.9	11.0
Gaines, MI	92.4	74.2	30.3	7.6	3.1
Glastonbury, CT	94.5	74.0	32.2	5.5	2.4
Grand Blanc, MI	92.5	63.4	45.3	7.5	2.7
Hampden, PA	92.5	76.5	30.7	7.5	5.3
Hilliard, OH	91.0	71.2	29.7	9.0	4.3
Hillsborough, NJ	89.8	65.8	33.7	10.2	3.6
Holly Springs, NC	88.8	74.4	23.4	11.2	5.2
Independence, KY	92.2	72.4	30.4	7.8	3.8
Juneau, AK	87.7	77.4	22.7	12.3	8.7
Kaysville, UT	90.5	79.0	21.0	9.5	5.8
Keller, TX	81.5	63.6	25.2	18.5	10.8
Lafayette, CA	92.2	73.7	28.6	7.8	3.3
Lafayette, CO	92.6	78.5	23.1	7.4	4.0
Lake Oswego, OR	90.5	71.4	30.7	9.5	3.6
Laramie, WY	91.3	80.5	19.3	8.7	3.8
Leander, TX	85.1	71.7	21.8	14.9	8.7
Leawood, KS	89.4	74.2	26.3	10.6	5.5
Lee's Summit, MO	89.4	74.2	26.3	10.6	5.5
Leesburg, VA	90.4	77.4	23.2	9.6	4.7
Lehi, UT	89.7	79.5	17.2	10.3	7.2
Lexington, MA	96.5	76.5	31.6	3.5	1.4
Los Altos, CA	92.2	74.3	26.0	7.8	2.9
Loveland, CO	91.5	75.6	26.9	8.5	5.4
Lower Macungie, PA	91.9	73.4	32.5	8.1	3.6
Madison, AL	89.2	74.5	28.5	10.8	3.0
Madison, MS	87.1	62.8	34.8	12.9	5.6

Table continued on next page.

Metro Area	With Health Insurance	With Private Health Insurance	With Public Health Insurance	Without Health Insurance	Population Under Age 18 Without Health Insurance
Maple Valley, WA	91.2	74.6	27.0	8.8	3.8
Marion, IA	95.1	78.4	30.1	4.9	2.4
Marlboro, NJ	89.8	65.8	33.7	10.2	3.6
Mason, OH	92.2	72.4	30.4	7.8	3.8
Menomonee Falls, WI	92.5	70.3	33.3	7.5	2.9
Meridian, ID	87.1	69.6	28.8	12.9	6.3
Meridian, MI	92.8	75.2	31.9	7.2	3.1
Merrimack, NH	91.8	76.8	26.1	8.2	2.4
Milton, GA	84.6	67.2	25.8	15.4	7.9
Moon, PA	94.1	76.7	33.5	5.9	2.4
Moorpark, CA	87.7	67.3	30.4	12.3	5.4
Morgantown, WV	90.8	73.0	28.5	9.2	3.2
Mount Pleasant, SC	87.0	69.0	30.3	13.0	5.7
Newark, DE	92.0	72.6	31.5	8.0	3.5
Newtown, CT	89.9	71.5	28.5	10.1	5.7
North Attleborough, MA	93.6	70.2	36.3	6.4	2.8
North Port, FL	86.1	64.6	42.9	13.9	8.9
North Ridgeville, OH	92.2	69.5	35.6	7.8	3.8
Northville, MI	91.4	69.9	35.3	8.6	3.2
O'Fallon, MO	91.3	73.4	29.1	8.7	4.0
Orchard Park, NY	95.1	72.0	37.7	4.9	2.1
Oro Valley, AZ	87.7	61.3	39.4	12.3	9.4
Oviedo, FL	83.3	61.9	30.7	16.7	9.4
Parker, CO	89.2	70.9	27.2	10.8	5.9
Parkland, FL	80.2	54.9	32.8	19.8	9.9
Peachtree City, GA	84.6	67.2	25.8	15.4	7.9
Pittsfield, MI	94.3	82.5	24.0	5.7	2.4
Plainfield, IL	89.2	68.1	30.2	10.8	3.4
Pleasant Grove, UT	89.7	79.5	17.2	10.3	7.2
Poway, CA	87.8	67.0	30.2	12.2	6.2
Princeton, NJ	90.3	73.1	28.1	9.7	3.8
Queen Creek, AZ	86.5	63.6	33.2	13.5	9.3
Radnor, PA	92.0	72.6	31.5	8.0	3.5
Randolph, NJ	89.8	65.8	33.7	10.2	3.6
Rexburg, ID	90.2	73.4	26.1	9.8	5.8
Rio Rancho, NM	87.7	59.0	40.1	12.3	5.2
Rye, NY	89.8	65.8	33.7	10.2	3.6
Sammamish, WA	91.2	74.6	27.0	8.8	3.8
San Ramon, CA	92.2	73.7	28.6	7.8	3.3
Saratoga, CA	92.2	74.3	26.0	7.8	2.9
Shrewsbury, MA	96.6	73.8	35.1	3.4	1.4
South Brunswick, NJ	89.8	65.8	33.7	10.2	3.6
South Jordan, UT	86.8	74.5	20.2	13.2	9.8
South Kingstown, RI	93.6	70.2	36.3	6.4	2.8
South Portland, ME	92.0	73.9	31.8	8.0	5.1
Sparks, NV	85.9	66.7	30.0	14.1	10.5
State College, PA	93.4	83.5	21.8	6.6	6.1
Sugar Land, TX	80.1	60.5	26.1	19.9	11.0
Sun Prairie, WI	94.5	82.3	24.1	5.5	2.8
Syracuse, UT	90.5	79.0	21.0	9.5	5.8
Tredyffrin, PA	92.0	72.6	31.5	8.0	3.5
Upper Dublin, PA	92.0	72.6	31.5	8.0	3.5
Urbandale, IA	94.2	76.4	29.4	5.8	2.7
Vestal, NY	94.1	69.6	39.8	5.9	3.3
Vestavia Hills, AL	89.5	69.4	32.4	10.5	3.8
Webster, NY	94.1	73.0	35.6	5.9	3.9
Wellesley, MA	96.5	76.5	31.6	3.5	1.4
West Fargo, ND	93.0	81.1	23.4	7.0	4.4
West Lafayette, IN	89.0	74.9	23.9	11.0	5.6
Weston, FL	80.2	54.9	32.8	19.8	9.9
Wilmette, IL	89.2	68.1	30.2	10.8	3.4
Yorba Linda, CA	85.0	58.1	33.5	15.0	5.9
Zionsville, IN	89.0	69.9	29.4	11.0	5.9
U.S.	88.3	66.7	33.0	11.7	5.9

Note: Figures are percentages that cover the civilian noninstitutionalized population; Figures cover the Metropolitan Statistical Area (MSA)—see Appendix B for areas included

Source: U.S. Census Bureau, 2012-2016 American Community Survey 5-Year Estimates

Crime Rate: City

City	All Crimes	Violent Crimes				Property Crimes		
		Murder	Rape	Robbery	Aggrav. Assault	Burglary	Larceny -Theft	Motor Vehicle Theft
Aberdeen, SD	2,649.3	0.0	101.8	17.5	350.9	410.6	1,638.7	129.8
Aliso Viejo, CA	869.5	0.0	7.9	9.9	39.5	120.5	638.3	53.4
Allen, TX	1,210.7	0.0	24.7	10.9	43.6	151.5	927.5	52.5
Ames, IA	1,784.9	1.5	58.8	22.6	78.4	247.2	1,307.0	69.3
Amherst, MA	816.2	2.5	49.9	10.0	154.8	164.7	406.9	27.5
Apex, NC	1,354.5	2.1	*4.2	27.5	50.7	175.4	1,058.7	35.9
Beavercreek, OH	2,359.6	0.0	30.1	28.0	10.8	137.7	2,084.3	68.8
Bellevue, NE	1,897.2	0.0	65.7	24.9	40.9	202.5	1,335.8	227.4
Bend, OR	2,359.8	0.0	19.0	22.4	66.1	199.5	1,949.7	103.1
Benicia, CA	1,968.3	0.0	14.1	28.2	24.6	496.5	1,052.8	352.1
Bentonville, AR	1,612.2	0.0	30.1	6.5	146.4	178.7	1,158.0	92.6
Bethlehem, NY	1,394.1	0.0	31.3	5.7	25.6	150.8	1,163.7	17.1
Blacksburg, VA	1,015.1	0.0	42.7	6.7	47.2	139.2	747.8	31.4
Bowie, MD	1,383.2	1.7	6.8	42.6	42.6	204.7	980.7	104.0
Bozeman, MT	3,136.0	2.2	98.3	15.6	214.6	277.2	2,371.5	156.5
Brentwood, TN	987.4	2.3	4.7	11.7	39.8	124.0	760.4	44.5
Burlington, VT[1]	3,674.1	2.4	35.6	42.7	154.2	540.8	2,898.5	0.0
Cabot, AR	2,264.0	3.9	65.6	34.7	135.0	381.8	1,504.2	138.9
Carmel, IN	913.7	0.0	14.3	7.7	5.5	64.0	779.1	43.0
Cedar Falls, IA	1,858.3	0.0	48.0	21.6	88.8	283.3	1,342.1	74.4
Cedar Park, TX	1,564.1	0.0	59.4	24.6	84.0	220.1	1,125.3	50.7
Central, LA	n/a	n/a	n/a	n/a	n/a	n/a	n/a	n/a
Chapel Hill, NC	2,459.8	3.3	*25.0	55.0	105.0	466.6	1,694.9	110.0
Cheshire, CT	847.6	0.0	6.8	0.0	6.8	99.1	628.9	106.0
Chino Hills, CA	1,357.1	1.3	10.1	15.2	48.1	419.0	753.3	110.1
Cibolo, TX	1,161.1	0.0	10.7	14.2	60.5	110.4	901.1	64.1
Cicero, NY	1,014.2	0.0	0.0	6.8	23.7	128.9	841.2	13.6
Collierville, TN	1,655.5	0.0	12.1	20.2	129.2	179.7	1,257.8	56.5
Coppell, TX	1,303.6	0.0	19.2	9.6	36.0	177.7	998.7	62.4
Cornelius, NC[1]	1,503.3	3.6	*7.1	21.3	92.4	213.2	1,137.2	28.4
Cranberry, PA	1,312.2	0.0	6.5	12.9	29.1	74.3	1,173.2	16.2
Crown Point, IN	1,275.5	0.0	0.0	24.1	6.9	106.6	1,100.2	37.8
Dublin, OH	1,175.3	0.0	19.6	10.9	17.4	211.5	885.3	30.5
East Fishkill, NY	624.2	0.0	10.2	0.0	34.1	37.5	508.3	34.1
Eden Prairie, MN	1,194.6	3.1	23.4	12.5	17.2	117.1	979.1	42.2
Edmond, OK	1,664.3	1.1	25.0	22.9	95.8	280.8	1,168.0	70.8
Edwardsville, IL	1,277.2	0.0	23.9	27.9	79.6	131.3	986.8	27.9
Evesham, NJ	1,520.4	0.0	6.6	28.5	35.1	173.3	1,226.4	50.5
Flower Mound, TX	873.3	0.0	9.6	5.5	30.3	88.2	698.3	41.3
Folsom, CA	1,890.1	0.0	11.7	44.0	42.7	341.8	1,302.3	147.6
Friendswood, TX	835.0	0.0	27.9	15.2	25.4	91.4	634.5	40.6
Gaines, MI	n/a	n/a	n/a	n/a	n/a	n/a	n/a	n/a
Glastonbury, CT[1]	1,039.3	0.0	0.0	23.0	23.0	97.6	861.3	34.5
Grand Blanc, MI[1]	1,841.0	0.0	65.7	24.6	90.3	341.9	1,258.3	60.2
Hampden, PA	828.7	0.0	6.7	20.2	10.1	101.1	680.5	10.1
Hilliard, OH	1,082.3	0.0	31.6	25.8	37.3	192.4	726.3	68.9
Hillsborough, NJ	694.4	0.0	25.0	5.0	7.5	124.9	514.5	17.5
Holly Springs, NC	925.1	0.0	*3.0	6.1	18.3	136.9	745.5	15.2
Independence, KY	635.4	0.0	36.7	14.7	18.4	102.8	411.4	51.4
Juneau, AK	5,694.1	0.0	109.2	94.0	652.2	940.4	3,676.7	221.5
Kaysville, UT	937.0	0.0	22.5	12.9	22.5	173.9	679.4	25.8
Keller, TX	627.0	0.0	17.0	6.4	40.4	102.0	446.4	14.9
Lafayette, CA	1,550.2	0.0	19.0	19.0	11.4	247.6	1,097.0	156.2
Lafayette, CO	2,550.9	0.0	123.1	35.2	147.8	186.5	1,917.6	140.7
Lake Oswego, OR	1,227.5	0.0	23.2	12.9	43.7	159.5	952.1	36.0
Laramie, WY	1,382.2	0.0	37.0	6.2	74.0	175.9	1,036.7	52.5
Leander, TX	1,232.5	0.0	46.7	9.8	56.6	140.2	927.4	51.7
Leawood, KS	1,212.3	0.0	2.8	17.1	65.5	176.4	887.9	62.6
Lee's Summit, MO	1,805.4	2.1	21.9	36.5	48.0	213.9	1,396.4	86.6
Leesburg, VA	1,752.3	5.7	54.7	22.6	122.6	34.0	1,452.4	60.4
Lehi, UT	1,391.3	0.0	59.2	13.2	54.3	213.8	985.1	65.8
Lexington, MA	460.7	0.0	8.9	3.0	56.5	65.4	321.0	5.9
Los Altos, CA	1,148.4	0.0	9.7	9.7	22.6	429.0	622.6	54.8
Loveland, CO	2,821.8	1.3	53.3	26.0	158.6	250.9	2,234.3	97.5
Lower Macungie, PA	n/a	n/a	n/a	n/a	n/a	n/a	n/a	n/a
Madison, AL	2,556.1	2.1	23.0	50.3	362.5	240.9	1,730.6	146.7

Table continued on next page.

City	All Crimes	Violent Crimes				Property Crimes		
		Murder	Rape	Robbery	Aggrav. Assault	Burglary	Larceny -Theft	Motor Vehicle Theft
Madison, MS	811.7	0.0	*0.0	15.3	38.3	53.6	670.0	34.5
Maple Valley, WA	1,452.3	0.0	*19.0	38.0	22.8	330.7	821.2	220.5
Marion, IA	1,783.6	0.0	37.0	21.1	129.5	375.2	1,130.9	89.8
Marlboro, NJ	620.6	0.0	2.5	4.9	17.2	61.3	495.5	39.3
Mason, OH	1,017.4	0.0	9.1	6.1	3.0	51.5	923.5	24.2
Menomonee Falls, WI	1,248.0	0.0	0.0	22.1	22.1	69.0	1,054.7	80.1
Meridian, ID	1,659.7	0.0	25.5	5.3	80.8	239.1	1,238.9	70.1
Meridian, MI	2,370.0	0.0	44.5	23.4	133.5	224.8	1,901.6	42.2
Merrimack, NH	743.9	0.0	0.0	0.0	0.0	85.7	646.5	11.7
Milton, GA	902.7	2.6	*7.8	2.6	13.0	127.1	736.7	13.0
Moon, PA	1,052.4	0.0	15.5	7.7	50.3	174.1	789.3	15.5
Moorpark, CA	914.3	0.0	32.9	11.0	57.7	162.0	584.8	65.9
Morgantown, WV	2,452.7	6.4	38.6	61.1	180.0	414.7	1,661.9	90.0
Mount Pleasant, SC	1,851.0	0.0	7.1	23.7	119.8	200.5	1,423.9	75.9
Newark, DE	2,562.9	0.0	20.4	116.6	195.4	247.8	1,906.9	75.8
Newtown, CT	306.0	0.0	0.0	3.6	7.1	71.2	206.4	17.8
North Attleborough, MA	1,613.1	0.0	17.2	17.2	86.2	186.1	1,258.1	48.3
North Port, FL	1,498.8	1.6	33.1	17.4	88.3	261.9	1,053.9	42.6
North Ridgeville, OH	619.4	3.0	12.1	9.1	12.1	111.8	465.3	6.0
Northville, MI	1,228.8	0.0	20.8	0.0	20.8	86.5	1,035.0	65.8
O'Fallon, MO	1,256.8	1.2	12.8	10.5	58.1	86.0	1,046.5	41.8
Orchard Park, NY	1,221.4	3.4	23.6	3.4	37.0	137.9	999.3	16.8
Oro Valley, AZ	1,546.9	0.0	9.1	15.9	40.8	158.8	1,258.8	63.5
Oviedo, FL	1,107.6	10.1	35.3	17.7	133.7	184.2	709.0	17.7
Parker, CO	1,265.6	0.0	21.8	4.0	65.5	170.6	914.5	89.3
Parkland, FL	595.5	0.0	12.7	9.5	34.8	85.5	411.8	41.2
Peachtree City, GA	1,593.8	0.0	*8.5	19.8	25.4	124.3	1,288.6	127.2
Pittsfield, MI	1,806.0	0.0	62.0	25.8	116.3	160.2	1,348.7	93.0
Plainfield, IL	852.2	0.0	16.3	7.0	62.7	81.3	650.2	34.8
Pleasant Grove, UT	677.2	2.6	2.6	0.0	25.7	105.2	520.7	20.5
Poway, CA	1,027.5	0.0	15.8	27.7	85.0	183.8	650.1	65.2
Princeton, NJ	836.1	0.0	6.7	0.0	43.8	114.6	654.1	16.9
Queen Creek, AZ	n/a	n/a	n/a	n/a	n/a	n/a	n/a	n/a
Radnor, PA	989.7	0.0	3.2	0.0	66.4	94.9	793.7	31.6
Randolph, NJ	510.1	0.0	0.0	7.7	11.6	81.2	386.4	23.2
Rexburg, ID	704.3	0.0	10.7	0.0	21.3	106.7	544.3	21.3
Rio Rancho, NM	2,582.4	1.0	*44.0	34.6	145.6	371.9	1,660.5	324.8
Rye, NY	391.1	0.0	0.0	0.0	6.2	49.7	310.4	24.8
Sammamish, WA	865.4	0.0	*16.9	3.7	15.0	157.3	612.5	59.9
San Ramon, CA	1,120.9	0.0	11.7	15.6	23.4	182.1	801.0	87.1
Saratoga, CA	1,008.0	0.0	12.8	19.3	57.8	510.4	385.2	22.5
Shrewsbury, MA	488.1	0.0	0.0	2.7	8.1	127.5	311.9	38.0
South Brunswick, NJ	872.2	0.0	6.5	17.4	15.3	172.3	597.4	63.2
South Jordan, UT	2,276.9	0.0	27.1	10.0	38.4	280.5	1,775.7	145.2
South Kingstown, RI	848.7	0.0	6.5	3.2	32.4	204.1	550.7	51.8
South Portland, ME	2,492.8	0.0	23.4	42.8	105.2	292.1	1,967.0	62.3
Sparks, NV	2,966.0	3.1	26.7	91.5	325.9	460.6	1,708.7	349.5
State College, PA	911.9	0.0	13.8	17.2	36.1	60.2	769.1	15.5
Sugar Land, TX	1,706.1	0.0	17.8	47.7	20.0	277.5	1,289.8	53.3
Sun Prairie, WI	1,885.1	0.0	*15.2	18.2	72.9	109.3	1,602.8	66.8
Syracuse, UT	1,135.3	0.0	17.9	3.6	21.4	153.5	917.5	21.4
Tredyffrin, PA	817.5	3.4	6.8	20.3	43.9	84.5	625.0	33.8
Upper Dublin, PA	884.8	0.0	11.4	19.0	11.4	68.4	725.3	49.4
Urbandale, IA	1,704.0	2.2	20.0	17.8	108.9	388.8	1,066.4	100.0
Vestal, NY	1,773.3	0.0	14.2	21.2	21.2	120.3	1,571.5	24.8
Vestavia Hills, AL	1,234.2	0.0	0.0	23.4	49.7	210.6	854.0	96.5
Webster, NY	1,056.5	0.0	4.5	18.0	33.7	116.9	856.4	27.0
Wellesley, MA	592.1	0.0	3.4	10.3	31.0	113.6	430.3	3.4
West Fargo, ND	1,568.3	2.8	65.0	17.0	101.7	390.0	861.8	130.0
West Lafayette, IN	1,099.7	0.0	*21.6	21.6	79.9	153.4	777.8	45.4
Weston, FL	534.7	0.0	7.1	18.3	25.4	60.7	368.2	55.0
Wilmette, IL	1,161.1	0.0	10.9	10.9	18.2	185.6	895.4	40.0
Yorba Linda, CA	1,115.0	0.0	16.0	8.7	34.9	218.3	748.2	88.8
Zionsville, IN	517.2	7.4	*7.4	0.0	100.5	18.6	353.5	29.8
U.S.	2,847.8	5.3	40.4	102.8	248.5	468.9	1,745.0	236.9

Note: Figures are crimes per 100,000 population in 2016 except where noted; n/a not available; (1) 2015 data; (*) Figures shown were reported using the legacy Uniform Crime Reporting (UCR) definition of rape. The U.S. figure for rape is 29.6 using the legacy definition.
Source: FBI Uniform Crime Reports, 2015, 2016

Crime Rate: Metro Area

Metro Area[1]	All Crimes	Violent Crimes				Property Crimes		
		Murder	Rape[4]	Robbery	Aggrav. Assault	Burglary	Larceny -Theft	Motor Vehicle Theft
Aberdeen, SD	n/a	n/a	n/a	n/a	n/a	n/a	n/a	n/a
Aliso Viejo, CA[2]	2,306.5	1.8	25.5	67.2	134.4	346.8	1,462.8	268.0
Allen, TX[2]	2,776.8	5.2	40.2	141.3	170.0	488.1	1,640.0	292.0
Ames, IA	1,849.8	1.0	55.6	17.5	88.5	269.5	1,330.2	87.4
Amherst, MA	2,828.2	2.9	51.2	123.9	359.8	530.6	1,583.5	176.2
Apex, NC	n/a	n/a	n/a	n/a	n/a	n/a	n/a	n/a
Beavercreek, OH	3,240.6	7.9	56.4	107.5	139.6	672.4	2,045.8	211.0
Bellevue, NE	3,102.6	3.9	42.1	78.2	227.0	361.2	1,948.4	441.8
Bend, OR	2,322.4	1.1	26.1	16.7	107.7	243.2	1,793.2	134.4
Benicia, CA	3,139.8	5.5	46.6	147.8	262.1	776.2	1,407.1	494.5
Bentonville, AR	n/a	n/a	n/a	n/a	n/a	n/a	n/a	n/a
Bethlehem, NY	2,299.2	2.0	38.9	68.7	180.0	281.5	1,646.0	82.0
Blacksburg, VA	1,879.8	2.8	63.4	14.9	116.9	259.1	1,363.8	59.0
Bowie, MD[2]	2,278.3	5.3	31.2	120.4	174.4	183.0	1,624.9	139.2
Bozeman, MT	n/a	n/a	n/a	n/a	n/a	n/a	n/a	n/a
Brentwood, TN	3,099.9	6.2	45.0	130.7	439.7	446.6	1,865.1	166.6
Burlington, VT[3]	n/a	n/a	n/a	n/a	n/a	n/a	n/a	n/a
Cabot, AR	n/a	10.0	59.3	136.8	553.9	n/a	3,116.5	379.6
Carmel, IN	3,920.2	9.2	46.8	218.9	438.5	665.1	2,202.8	339.0
Cedar Falls, IA	2,423.8	1.8	53.8	42.1	344.7	525.5	1,338.9	117.0
Cedar Park, TX	2,872.1	3.4	57.4	68.7	187.4	421.9	1,968.3	165.1
Central, LA	3,902.9	9.5	33.5	140.1	321.9	721.1	2,507.8	169.0
Chapel Hill, NC	n/a	n/a	n/a	n/a	n/a	n/a	n/a	n/a
Cheshire, CT	2,854.4	3.7	23.0	110.0	186.1	406.3	1,821.5	303.9
Chino Hills, CA	3,064.6	5.1	26.7	115.0	250.6	581.1	1,570.1	516.0
Cibolo, TX	4,608.3	7.7	65.8	104.9	348.0	663.3	3,055.2	363.3
Cicero, NY	2,234.6	5.3	51.3	65.6	154.2	347.9	1,516.3	94.0
Collierville, TN	4,950.3	18.5	54.6	269.4	739.6	934.3	2,623.2	310.6
Coppell, TX[2]	2,776.8	5.2	40.2	141.3	170.0	488.1	1,640.0	292.0
Cornelius, NC[3]	n/a	n/a	n/a	n/a	n/a	n/a	n/a	n/a
Cranberry, PA	2,035.5	5.1	22.9	82.9	178.1	309.5	1,349.8	87.2
Crown Point, IN[2]	2,830.1	10.6	22.3	93.9	145.6	419.7	1,917.4	220.7
Dublin, OH	3,196.0	5.2	59.7	125.1	94.9	594.4	2,100.6	216.1
East Fishkill, NY[2]	1,209.5	1.0	30.9	30.9	92.2	145.8	882.7	26.0
Eden Prairie, MN	2,603.3	2.2	43.1	94.9	147.5	354.4	1,771.6	189.7
Edmond, OK	3,600.1	6.7	54.8	104.4	324.9	686.7	2,093.3	329.3
Edwardsville, IL	n/a	11.1	38.1	122.5	n/a	442.5	1,801.5	246.3
Evesham, NJ[2]	2,221.1	6.7	22.6	89.2	153.9	411.9	1,422.1	114.6
Flower Mound, TX[2]	2,776.8	5.2	40.2	141.3	170.0	488.1	1,640.0	292.0
Folsom, CA	2,802.0	4.2	26.1	120.1	260.7	458.9	1,565.7	366.4
Friendswood, TX	3,502.0	7.2	39.9	215.5	315.6	548.2	2,035.1	340.5
Gaines, MI	1,953.1	2.1	78.8	50.6	205.7	280.3	1,245.2	90.4
Glastonbury, CT[3]	2,428.2	4.4	22.5	94.7	131.2	325.4	1,637.0	213.0
Grand Blanc, MI[3]	3,067.1	12.9	64.6	107.5	396.3	707.2	1,632.9	145.6
Hampden, PA	1,734.5	3.4	38.0	54.7	159.1	272.4	1,144.8	62.1
Hilliard, OH[2]	3,196.0	5.2	59.7	125.1	94.9	594.4	2,100.6	216.1
Hillsborough, NJ[2]	1,683.1	6.0	16.9	134.2	126.5	248.6	943.7	207.1
Holly Springs, NC	n/a	n/a	n/a	n/a	n/a	n/a	n/a	n/a
Independence, KY	2,873.9	4.7	41.1	102.3	109.2	525.9	1,954.4	136.2
Juneau, AK	n/a	n/a	n/a	n/a	n/a	n/a	n/a	n/a
Kaysville, UT	2,374.8	1.4	41.5	27.2	85.5	377.4	1,686.1	155.7
Keller, TX[2]	2,952.5	4.9	50.8	90.6	219.3	467.5	1,910.3	209.1
Lafayette, CA[2]	3,684.7	6.1	33.6	237.3	226.1	445.2	1,998.9	737.5
Lafayette, CO	2,550.7	0.3	68.5	25.3	142.2	348.0	1,812.7	153.7
Lake Oswego, OR	3,070.3	1.7	49.2	68.4	156.8	370.7	2,033.5	390.0
Laramie, WY	n/a	n/a	n/a	n/a	n/a	n/a	n/a	n/a
Leander, TX	2,872.1	3.4	57.4	68.7	187.4	421.9	1,968.3	165.1
Leawood, KS	n/a	n/a	n/a	n/a	n/a	n/a	n/a	n/a
Lee's Summit, MO	n/a	n/a	n/a	n/a	n/a	n/a	n/a	n/a
Leesburg, VA[2]	2,278.3	5.3	31.2	120.4	174.4	183.0	1,624.9	139.2
Lehi, UT	1,838.9	0.8	27.4	10.7	38.7	207.1	1,462.7	91.6
Lexington, MA[2]	1,465.4	1.1	19.1	44.8	170.3	181.5	945.0	103.6
Los Altos, CA	2,456.7	2.9	33.0	82.6	161.6	384.7	1,286.3	505.5
Loveland, CO	2,419.2	2.6	30.3	20.9	155.4	267.0	1,829.7	113.4
Lower Macungie, PA	n/a	2.6	19.4	58.3	n/a	264.7	n/a	89.1
Madison, AL	3,751.0	4.9	53.2	112.5	386.4	608.7	2,305.3	280.0

Table continued on next page.

Metro Area[1]	All Crimes	Violent Crimes				Property Crimes		
		Murder	Rape[4]	Robbery	Aggrav. Assault	Burglary	Larceny -Theft	Motor Vehicle Theft
Madison, MS	n/a	n/a	n/a	n/a	n/a	n/a	n/a	n/a
Maple Valley, WA[2]	4,169.6	2.4	36.9	105.6	168.5	697.7	2,632.0	526.5
Marion, IA	n/a	1.9	37.4	43.0	138.1	n/a	1,716.8	175.2
Marlboro, NJ[2]	1,805.2	3.1	22.2	136.2	255.9	160.0	1,152.5	75.3
Mason, OH	2,873.9	4.7	41.1	102.3	109.2	525.9	1,954.4	136.2
Menomonee Falls, WI	3,373.6	9.9	40.5	232.1	373.5	512.0	1,746.6	459.0
Meridian, ID	2,014.6	2.5	50.3	14.8	176.4	316.1	1,317.4	136.9
Meridian, MI	2,301.5	3.4	91.2	74.7	289.2	378.1	1,315.6	149.3
Merrimack, NH	1,794.1	1.2	39.7	61.0	166.6	209.4	1,245.6	70.5
Milton, GA	3,401.4	6.8	24.0	144.1	228.2	576.2	2,100.8	321.3
Moon, PA	2,035.5	5.1	22.9	82.9	178.1	309.5	1,349.8	87.2
Moorpark, CA	2,189.4	3.6	31.7	85.3	137.3	342.4	1,395.0	194.2
Morgantown, WV	1,879.0	2.2	46.8	24.5	190.0	361.3	1,168.0	86.4
Mount Pleasant, SC	3,264.1	9.4	33.1	87.9	287.8	481.3	2,107.4	257.2
Newark, DE[2]	3,298.2	7.3	26.4	163.4	315.9	503.5	2,085.9	195.7
Newtown, CT	1,663.9	1.5	18.7	85.6	124.0	228.3	1,034.8	170.9
North Attleborough, MA	n/a	2.4	38.8	65.7	208.2	367.3	n/a	n/a
North Port, FL	2,364.7	4.1	30.7	54.6	252.0	359.8	1,560.2	103.3
North Ridgeville, OH	2,829.3	9.2	43.8	195.1	197.4	565.2	1,535.3	283.3
Northville, MI[2]	4,166.7	19.4	63.2	220.9	730.7	735.0	1,725.4	672.1
O'Fallon, MO	n/a	11.1	38.1	122.5	n/a	442.5	1,801.5	246.3
Orchard Park, NY	2,828.4	4.9	33.1	138.9	234.2	461.7	1,822.8	132.9
Oro Valley, AZ	4,763.1	4.8	57.2	141.0	293.4	599.7	3,401.9	265.0
Oviedo, FL	3,467.8	8.1	50.1	99.3	346.8	683.1	2,065.3	215.2
Parker, CO	3,343.0	4.3	67.0	86.2	231.5	435.8	2,055.3	462.9
Parkland, FL[2]	3,441.1	4.2	29.0	140.7	217.3	456.6	2,302.1	291.3
Peachtree City, GA	3,401.4	6.8	24.0	144.1	228.2	576.2	2,100.8	321.3
Pittsfield, MI	1,965.2	0.6	52.6	51.5	212.8	254.8	1,271.9	121.2
Plainfield, IL[2]	2,678.9	11.9	35.4	199.0	266.6	345.2	1,609.3	211.6
Pleasant Grove, UT	1,838.9	0.8	27.4	10.7	38.7	207.1	1,462.7	91.6
Poway, CA	2,180.4	3.0	32.8	83.7	210.8	313.2	1,204.5	332.4
Princeton, NJ	2,181.1	6.8	28.9	158.6	208.3	429.5	1,203.1	146.1
Queen Creek, AZ	3,297.0	5.5	46.1	112.7	262.6	552.3	2,028.6	289.2
Radnor, PA[2]	3,618.8	14.6	62.8	324.5	424.8	389.4	2,117.7	285.0
Randolph, NJ[2]	1,683.1	6.0	16.9	134.2	126.5	248.6	943.7	207.1
Rexburg, ID	n/a	n/a	n/a	n/a	n/a	n/a	n/a	n/a
Rio Rancho, NM	6,189.7	8.3	57.3	238.7	596.7	951.1	3,319.6	1,018.0
Rye, NY[2]	1,805.2	3.1	22.2	136.2	255.9	160.0	1,152.5	75.3
Sammamish, WA[2]	4,169.6	2.4	36.9	105.6	168.5	697.7	2,632.0	526.5
San Ramon, CA[2]	3,684.7	6.1	33.6	237.3	226.1	445.2	1,998.9	737.5
Saratoga, CA	2,456.7	2.9	33.0	82.6	161.6	384.7	1,286.3	505.5
Shrewsbury, MA	n/a	1.4	34.3	70.4	n/a	339.9	1,148.7	111.7
South Brunswick, NJ[2]	1,805.2	3.1	22.2	136.2	255.9	160.0	1,152.5	75.3
South Jordan, UT	5,009.9	3.9	69.5	103.9	233.2	612.4	3,396.6	590.4
South Kingstown, RI	n/a	2.4	38.8	65.7	208.2	367.3	n/a	n/a
South Portland, ME	1,825.3	1.5	27.4	24.0	81.4	285.5	1,349.9	55.5
Sparks, NV	3,107.8	3.1	42.2	107.3	361.9	419.4	1,777.7	396.2
State College, PA	1,159.2	1.2	40.3	11.8	40.9	147.5	899.6	18.0
Sugar Land, TX	3,502.0	7.2	39.9	215.5	315.6	548.2	2,035.1	340.5
Sun Prairie, WI	2,118.5	2.0	30.7	48.0	122.0	268.1	1,556.5	91.1
Syracuse, UT	2,374.8	1.4	41.5	27.2	85.5	377.4	1,686.1	155.7
Tredyffrin, PA[2]	1,533.9	1.7	11.8	33.4	72.5	161.9	1,194.9	57.6
Upper Dublin, PA[2]	1,533.9	1.7	11.8	33.4	72.5	161.9	1,194.9	57.6
Urbandale, IA	n/a	4.0	42.2	61.0	264.6	546.5	n/a	227.9
Vestal, NY	2,416.9	2.5	62.9	60.0	164.0	438.9	1,602.8	85.9
Vestavia Hills, AL	n/a	n/a	n/a	n/a	n/a	n/a	n/a	n/a
Webster, NY	2,276.5	4.7	42.7	85.1	148.3	329.9	1,562.2	103.6
Wellesley, MA[2]	n/a	3.0	32.9	115.4	n/a	234.7	1,255.0	122.5
West Fargo, ND	2,742.3	2.1	57.5	38.7	172.0	414.6	1,846.2	211.1
West Lafayette, IN	2,464.4	1.4	32.3	61.9	152.0	452.7	1,631.6	132.6
Weston, FL[2]	3,441.1	4.2	29.0	140.7	217.3	456.6	2,302.1	291.3
Wilmette, IL[2]	2,678.9	11.9	35.4	199.0	266.6	345.2	1,609.3	211.6
Yorba Linda, CA[2]	2,306.5	1.8	25.5	67.2	134.4	346.8	1,462.8	268.0
Zionsville, IN	3,920.2	9.2	46.8	218.9	438.5	665.1	2,202.8	339.0
U.S.	2,847.8	5.3	40.4	102.8	248.5	468.9	1,745.0	236.9

Note: Figures are crimes per 100,000 population in 2016 except where noted; n/a not available; (1) Figures cover the Metropolitan Statistical Area except where noted; (2) Metropolitan Division (MD); (3) 2015 data; (4) The metro area figures for rape are an aggregate total of the data submitted using both the revised and legacy Uniform Crime Reporting (UCR) definitions. The U.S. figure for rape is 29.6 using the legacy definition.
Source: FBI Uniform Crime Reports, 2015, 2016

Temperature & Precipitation: Yearly Averages and Extremes

City	Extreme Low (°F)	Average Low (°F)	Average Temp. (°F)	Average High (°F)	Extreme High (°F)	Average Precip. (in.)	Average Snow (in.)
Aberdeen, SD	-44	30	42	54	109	15.8	44
Aliso Viejo, CA	25	53	64	75	112	11.9	Trace
Allen, TX	-2	56	67	77	112	33.9	3
Ames, IA	-24	40	50	60	108	31.8	33
Amherst, MA	-9	43	n/a	58	97	48.9	36.2
Apex, NC	-9	48	60	71	105	42.0	8
Beavercreek, OH	-25	42	52	62	102	37.4	29
Bellevue, NE	-23	40	51	62	110	30.1	29
Bend, OR	-12	42	53	63	108	47.3	7
Benicia, CA	17	45	n/a	71	110	23.5	n/a
Bentonville, AR	-10	49	61	73	111	41.8	6
Bethlehem, NY	-28	37	48	58	100	35.8	63
Blacksburg, VA	-11	46	57	67	105	40.8	23
Bowie, MD	-5	49	58	67	104	39.5	18
Bozeman, MT	-32	36	47	59	105	14.6	59
Brentwood, TN	-17	49	60	70	107	47.4	11
Burlington, VT	-30	35	45	54	100	34.0	79
Cabot, AR	-5	51	62	73	112	50.7	5
Carmel, IN	-23	42	53	62	104	40.2	25
Cedar Falls, IA	-34	36	47	57	105	34.4	33
Cedar Park, TX	-2	58	69	79	109	31.1	1
Central, LA	8	57	68	78	103	58.5	Trace
Chapel Hill, NC	-9	48	60	71	105	42.0	8
Cheshire, CT	-7	44	52	60	103	41.4	25
Chino Hills, CA	24	53	66	78	114	n/a	n/a
Cibolo, TX	0	58	69	80	108	29.6	1
Cicero, NY	-26	38	48	57	98	38.5	107
Collierville, TN	0	52	65	77	107	54.8	1
Coppell, TX	-2	56	67	77	112	33.9	3
Cornelius, NC	-5	50	61	71	104	42.8	6
Cranberry, PA	-18	41	51	60	103	37.1	43
Crown Point, IN	-27	40	49	59	104	35.4	39
Dublin, OH	-19	42	52	62	104	37.9	28
East Fishkill, NY	-23	38	n/a	61	102	41.0	35.6
Eden Prairie, MN	-34	35	45	54	105	27.1	52
Edmond, OK	-8	49	60	71	110	32.8	10
Edwardsville, IL	-18	46	56	66	115	36.8	20
Evesham, NJ	-7	45	55	64	104	41.4	22
Flower Mound, TX	-2	56	67	77	112	33.9	3
Folsom, CA	18	48	61	73	115	17.3	Trace
Friendswood, TX	7	58	69	79	107	46.9	Trace
Gaines, MI	-22	38	48	57	102	34.7	73
Glastonbury, CT	-26	40	50	60	102	44.2	46
Grand Blanc, MI	-25	38	47	57	101	30.5	47
Hampden, PA	-9	44	53	62	107	39.0	35
Hilliard, OH	-19	42	52	62	104	37.9	28
Hillsborough, NJ	-2	47	55	62	104	47.0	23
Holly Springs, NC	-9	48	60	71	105	42.0	8
Independence, KY	-25	44	54	64	103	40.9	23
Juneau, AK	-22	34	41	47	90	55.2	102
Kaysville, UT	-22	40	52	64	107	15.6	63
Keller, TX	-2	56	67	77	112	33.9	3
Lafayette, CA	27	52	59	66	106	17.6	Trace
Lafayette, CO	-25	37	51	64	103	15.5	63
Lake Oswego, OR	-3	45	54	62	107	37.5	7
Laramie, WY	-29	33	46	58	100	14.6	53
Leander, TX	-2	58	69	79	109	31.1	1
Leawood, KS	-23	44	54	64	109	38.1	21
Lee's Summit, MO	-23	44	54	64	109	38.1	21
Leesburg, VA	-5	49	58	67	104	39.5	18
Lehi, UT	-22	40	52	64	107	15.6	63
Lexington, MA	-12	44	52	59	102	42.9	41
Los Altos, CA	21	50	59	68	105	13.5	Trace
Loveland, CO	-25	37	51	64	103	15.5	63
Lower Macungie, PA	-12	42	52	61	105	44.2	32
Madison, AL	-11	50	61	71	104	56.8	4
Madison, MS	2	53	65	76	106	55.4	1
Maple Valley, WA	0	44	52	59	99	38.4	13

Table continued on next page.

City	Extreme Low (°F)	Average Low (°F)	Average Temp. (°F)	Average High (°F)	Extreme High (°F)	Average Precip. (in.)	Average Snow (in.)
Marion, IA	-34	36	47	57	105	34.4	33
Marlboro, NJ	-2	47	55	62	104	47.0	23
Mason, OH	-25	44	54	64	103	40.9	23
Menomonee Falls, WI	-26	38	47	55	103	32.0	49
Meridian, ID	-25	39	51	63	111	11.8	22
Meridian, MI	-24	37	48	57	100	30.6	51
Merrimack, NH	-33	34	46	57	102	36.9	63
Milton, GA	-8	52	62	72	105	49.8	2
Moon, PA	-18	41	51	60	103	37.1	43
Moorpark, CA	27	51	60	68	105	12.0	0
Morgantown, WV	-18	41	51	60	103	37.1	43
Mount Pleasant, SC	6	55	66	76	104	52.1	1
Newark, DE	-7	45	55	64	104	41.4	22
Newtown, CT	-16	39	n/a	60	100	48.8	38.6
North Attleborough, MA	-13	42	51	60	104	45.3	35
North Port, FL	26	65	75	84	103	53.9	0
North Ridgeville, OH	-19	41	50	59	104	37.1	55
Northville, MI	-21	39	49	58	104	32.4	41
O'Fallon, MO	-18	46	56	66	115	36.8	20
Orchard Park, NY	-20	40	48	56	99	38.1	90
Oro Valley, AZ	16	55	69	82	117	11.6	2
Oviedo, FL	19	62	72	82	100	47.7	Trace
Parker, CO	-25	37	51	64	103	15.5	63
Parkland, FL	30	69	76	83	98	57.1	0
Peachtree City, GA	-8	52	62	72	105	49.8	2
Pittsfield, MI	-21	39	49	58	104	32.4	41
Plainfield, IL	-27	40	49	59	104	35.4	39
Pleasant Grove, UT	-22	40	52	64	107	15.6	63
Poway, CA	29	57	64	71	111	9.5	Trace
Princeton, NJ	-7	45	55	64	104	41.4	22
Queen Creek, AZ	17	59	72	86	122	7.3	Trace
Radnor, PA	-7	45	55	64	104	41.4	22
Randolph, NJ	-2	47	55	62	104	47.0	23
Rexburg, ID	-33	34	47	60	104	11.5	43
Rio Rancho, NM	-17	43	57	70	105	8.5	11
Rye, NY	-2	47	55	62	104	47.0	23
Sammamish, WA	0	44	52	59	99	38.4	13
San Ramon, CA	27	52	59	66	106	17.6	Trace
Saratoga, CA	21	50	59	68	105	13.5	Trace
Shrewsbury, MA	-13	38	47	56	99	47.6	62
South Brunswick, NJ	-2	47	55	62	104	47.0	23
South Jordan, UT	-22	40	52	64	107	15.6	63
South Kingstown, RI	-13	42	51	60	104	45.3	35
South Portland, ME	-26	36	46	55	103	43.6	71
Sparks, NV	-16	33	50	67	105	7.2	24
State College, PA	-9	44	53	62	107	39.0	35
Sugar Land, TX	7	58	69	79	107	46.9	Trace
Sun Prairie, WI	-37	35	46	57	104	31.1	42
Syracuse, UT	-22	40	52	64	107	15.6	63
Tredyffrin, PA	-7	45	55	64	104	41.4	22
Upper Dublin, PA	-7	45	55	64	104	41.4	22
Urbandale, IA	-24	40	50	60	108	31.8	33
Vestal, NY	-26	38	46	55	98	37.1	81
Vestavia Hills, AL	-6	51	63	74	106	53.5	2
Webster, NY	-19	39	48	57	100	31.8	92
Wellesley, MA	-12	44	52	59	102	42.9	41
West Fargo, ND	-36	31	41	52	106	19.6	40
West Lafayette, IN	-23	42	53	62	104	40.2	25
Weston, FL	30	69	76	83	98	57.1	0
Wilmette, IL	-27	40	49	59	104	35.4	39
Yorba Linda, CA	25	53	64	75	112	11.9	Trace
Zionsville, IN	-23	42	53	62	104	40.2	25

Source: National Climatic Data Center, International Station Meteorological Climate Summary, 9/96

Weather Conditions

City	Temperature			Daytime Sky			Precipitation		
	10°F & below	32°F & below	90°F & above	Clear	Partly cloudy	Cloudy	0.01 inch or more precip.	1.0 inch or more snow/ice	Thunder-storms
Aberdeen, SD	n/a	187	22	84	144	137	96	41	35
Aliso Viejo, CA	0	2	18	95	192	78	41	0	4
Allen, TX	1	34	102	108	160	97	78	2	49
Ames, IA	n/a	137	26	99	129	137	106	25	46
Amherst, MA	n/a	101	2	n/a	n/a	n/a	n/a	n/a	16
Apex, NC	n/a	n/a	39	98	143	124	110	3	42
Beavercreek, OH	18	117	17	80	121	164	133	28	40
Bellevue, NE	n/a	139	35	100	142	123	97	20	46
Bend, OR	n/a	n/a	15	75	115	175	136	4	3
Benicia, CA	n/a	23	25	n/a	n/a	n/a	n/a	n/a	2
Bentonville, AR	3	76	76	117	121	127	98	5	59
Bethlehem, NY	n/a	147	11	58	149	158	133	36	24
Blacksburg, VA	4	89	31	90	152	123	119	11	35
Bowie, MD	2	71	34	84	144	137	112	9	30
Bozeman, MT	n/a	149	29	75	163	127	97	41	27
Brentwood, TN	5	76	51	98	135	132	119	8	54
Burlington, VT	n/a	156	7	49	146	170	154	55	22
Cabot, AR	1	57	73	110	142	113	104	4	57
Carmel, IN	19	119	19	83	128	154	127	24	43
Cedar Falls, IA	n/a	156	16	89	132	144	109	28	42
Cedar Park, TX	< 1	20	111	105	148	112	83	1	41
Central, LA	< 1	21	86	99	150	116	113	< 1	73
Chapel Hill, NC	n/a	n/a	39	98	143	124	110	3	42
Cheshire, CT	n/a	n/a	7	80	146	139	118	17	22
Chino Hills, CA	0	4	82	124	178	63	n/a	n/a	5
Cibolo, TX	n/a	n/a	112	97	153	115	81	1	36
Cicero, NY	n/a	136	9	56	135	174	170	67	27
Collierville, TN	1	53	86	101	152	112	104	2	59
Coppell, TX	1	34	102	108	160	97	78	2	49
Cornelius, NC	1	65	44	98	142	125	113	3	41
Cranberry, PA	n/a	121	8	62	137	166	154	42	35
Crown Point, IN	n/a	132	17	83	136	146	125	31	38
Dublin, OH	n/a	118	19	72	137	156	136	29	40
East Fishkill, NY	n/a	146	7	n/a	n/a	n/a	n/a	n/a	25
Eden Prairie, MN	n/a	156	16	93	125	147	113	41	37
Edmond, OK	5	79	70	124	131	110	80	8	50
Edwardsville, IL	13	100	43	97	138	130	109	14	46
Evesham, NJ	5	94	23	81	146	138	117	14	27
Flower Mound, TX	1	34	102	108	160	97	78	2	49
Folsom, CA	0	21	73	175	111	79	58	< 1	2
Friendswood, TX	n/a	n/a	96	83	168	114	101	1	62
Gaines, MI	n/a	146	11	67	119	179	142	57	34
Glastonbury, CT	n/a	134	18	69	151	145	126	26	20
Grand Blanc, MI	n/a	143	8	74	122	169	133	47	33
Hampden, PA	n/a	106	22	83	134	148	124	20	31
Hilliard, OH	n/a	118	19	72	137	156	136	29	40
Hillsborough, NJ	n/a	n/a	18	85	166	114	120	11	20
Holly Springs, NC	n/a	n/a	39	98	143	124	110	3	42
Independence, KY	14	107	23	80	126	159	127	25	39
Juneau, AK	n/a	139	n/a	40	78	247	219	50	1
Kaysville, UT	n/a	128	56	94	152	119	92	38	38
Keller, TX	1	34	102	108	160	97	78	2	49
Lafayette, CA	0	< 1	3	99	168	98	59	0	6
Lafayette, CO	24	155	33	99	177	89	90	38	39
Lake Oswego, OR	n/a	37	11	67	116	182	152	4	7
Laramie, WY	n/a	173	9	94	172	99	99	44	51
Leander, TX	< 1	20	111	105	148	112	83	1	41
Leawood, KS	22	110	39	112	134	119	103	17	51
Lee's Summit, MO	22	110	39	112	134	119	103	17	51
Leesburg, VA	2	71	34	84	144	137	112	9	30
Lehi, UT	n/a	128	56	94	152	119	92	38	38
Lexington, MA	n/a	97	12	88	127	150	253	48	18
Los Altos, CA	0	5	5	106	180	79	57	< 1	6
Loveland, CO	24	155	33	99	177	89	90	38	39
Lower Macungie, PA	n/a	123	15	77	148	140	123	20	31
Madison, AL	2	66	49	70	118	177	116	2	54

Table continued on next page.

City	Temperature			Daytime Sky			Precipitation		
	10°F & below	32°F & below	90°F & above	Clear	Partly cloudy	Cloudy	0.01 inch or more precip.	1.0 inch or more snow/ice	Thunder-storms
Madison, MS	1	50	84	103	144	118	106	2	68
Maple Valley, WA	n/a	38	3	57	121	187	157	8	8
Marion, IA	n/a	156	16	89	132	144	109	28	42
Marlboro, NJ	n/a	n/a	18	85	166	114	120	11	20
Mason, OH	14	107	23	80	126	159	127	25	39
Menomonee Falls, WI	n/a	141	10	90	118	157	126	38	35
Meridian, ID	n/a	124	45	106	133	126	91	22	14
Meridian, MI	n/a	149	11	71	131	163	142	47	32
Merrimack, NH	n/a	171	12	87	131	147	125	32	19
Milton, GA	1	49	38	98	147	120	116	3	48
Moon, PA	n/a	121	8	62	137	166	154	42	35
Moorpark, CA	0	1	2	114	155	96	34	< 1	1
Morgantown, WV	n/a	121	8	62	137	166	154	42	35
Mount Pleasant, SC	< 1	33	53	89	162	114	114	1	59
Newark, DE	5	94	23	81	146	138	117	14	27
Newtown, CT	n/a	132	9	n/a	n/a	n/a	n/a	n/a	21
North Attleborough, MA	n/a	117	9	85	134	146	123	21	21
North Port, FL	n/a	n/a	115	93	220	52	110	0	92
North Ridgeville, OH	n/a	123	12	63	127	175	157	48	34
Northville, MI	n/a	136	12	74	134	157	135	38	32
O'Fallon, MO	13	100	43	97	138	130	109	14	46
Orchard Park, NY	n/a	131	4	47	144	174	169	65	30
Oro Valley, AZ	0	18	140	177	119	69	54	2	42
Oviedo, FL	n/a	n/a	90	76	208	81	115	0	80
Parker, CO	24	155	33	99	177	89	90	38	39
Parkland, FL	n/a	n/a	55	48	263	54	128	0	74
Peachtree City, GA	1	49	38	98	147	120	116	3	48
Pittsfield, MI	n/a	136	12	74	134	157	135	38	32
Plainfield, IL	n/a	132	17	83	136	146	125	31	38
Pleasant Grove, UT	n/a	128	56	94	152	119	92	38	38
Poway, CA	0	< 1	4	115	126	124	40	0	5
Princeton, NJ	5	94	23	81	146	138	117	14	27
Queen Creek, AZ	0	10	167	186	125	54	37	< 1	23
Radnor, PA	5	94	23	81	146	138	117	14	27
Randolph, NJ	n/a	n/a	18	85	166	114	120	11	20
Rexburg, ID	n/a	165	33	91	149	125	95	42	25
Rio Rancho, NM	4	114	65	140	161	64	60	9	38
Rye, NY	n/a	n/a	18	85	166	114	120	11	20
Sammamish, WA	n/a	38	3	57	121	187	157	8	8
San Ramon, CA	0	< 1	3	99	168	98	59	0	6
Saratoga, CA	0	5	5	106	180	79	57	< 1	6
Shrewsbury, MA	n/a	141	4	81	144	140	131	32	23
South Brunswick, NJ	n/a	n/a	18	85	166	114	120	11	20
South Jordan, UT	n/a	128	56	94	152	119	92	38	38
South Kingstown, RI	n/a	117	9	85	134	146	123	21	21
South Portland, ME	n/a	155	5	83	128	154	130	31	16
Sparks, NV	14	178	50	143	139	83	50	17	14
State College, PA	n/a	106	22	83	134	148	124	20	31
Sugar Land, TX	n/a	n/a	96	83	168	114	101	1	62
Sun Prairie, WI	n/a	161	14	88	119	158	118	38	40
Syracuse, UT	n/a	128	56	94	152	119	92	38	38
Tredyffrin, PA	5	94	23	81	146	138	117	14	27
Upper Dublin, PA	5	94	23	81	146	138	117	14	27
Urbandale, IA	n/a	137	26	99	129	137	106	25	46
Vestal, NY	n/a	145	3	53	137	175	159	67	29
Vestavia Hills, AL	1	57	59	91	161	113	119	1	57
Webster, NY	n/a	135	11	58	137	170	157	65	27
Wellesley, MA	n/a	97	12	88	127	150	253	48	18
West Fargo, ND	n/a	180	15	81	145	139	100	38	31
West Lafayette, IN	19	119	19	83	128	154	127	24	43
Weston, FL	n/a	n/a	55	48	263	54	128	0	74
Wilmette, IL	n/a	132	17	83	136	146	125	31	38
Yorba Linda, CA	0	2	18	95	192	78	41	0	4
Zionsville, IN	19	119	19	83	128	154	127	24	43

Note: Figures are average number of days per year
Source: National Climatic Data Center, International Station Meteorological Climate Summary, 9/96

Air Quality Index

MSA[1] (Days[2])	Percent of Days when Air Quality was...					AQI Statistics	
	Good	Moderate	Unhealthy for Sensitive Groups	Unhealthy	Very Unhealthy	Maximum	Median
Aberdeen, SD (122)	95.9	4.1	0.0	0.0	0.0	97	23
Aliso Viejo, CA (365)	10.4	56.2	20.8	10.4	2.2	224	79
Allen, TX (365)	52.6	40.8	6.6	0.0	0.0	147	50
Ames, IA (n/a)	n/a	n/a	n/a	n/a	n/a	n/a	n/a
Amherst, MA (365)	81.9	16.7	1.4	0.0	0.0	122	40
Apex, NC (365)	66.3	33.7	0.0	0.0	0.0	100	45
Beavercreek, OH (365)	70.4	28.8	0.8	0.0	0.0	108	43
Bellevue, NE (365)	54.2	45.2	0.5	0.0	0.0	114	48
Bend, OR (273)	79.9	9.9	0.7	5.5	4.0	365	18
Benicia, CA (365)	66.8	30.4	1.4	1.4	0.0	175	44
Bentonville, AR (365)	70.1	29.9	0.0	0.0	0.0	81	44
Bethlehem, NY (365)	83.8	16.2	0.0	0.0	0.0	90	39
Blacksburg, VA (365)	59.2	20.8	12.6	7.4	0.0	200	44
Bowie, MD (365)	40.0	57.8	2.2	0.0	0.0	133	53
Bozeman, MT (365)	78.9	20.3	0.5	0.3	0.0	152	23
Brentwood, TN (365)	63.8	35.9	0.3	0.0	0.0	133	45
Burlington, VT (365)	93.7	6.3	0.0	0.0	0.0	74	35
Cabot, AR (365)	69.0	30.7	0.3	0.0	0.0	115	44
Carmel, IN (365)	54.0	43.6	2.5	0.0	0.0	122	48
Cedar Falls, IA (363)	63.6	36.4	0.0	0.0	0.0	93	46
Cedar Park, TX (365)	71.8	27.1	1.1	0.0	0.0	130	43
Central, LA (365)	62.5	35.3	2.2	0.0	0.0	140	46
Chapel Hill, NC (365)	72.3	27.4	0.3	0.0	0.0	110	44
Cheshire, CT (365)	78.6	18.1	2.2	1.1	0.0	179	40
Chino Hills, CA (365)	6.8	45.2	26.0	14.5	7.4	366	99
Cibolo, TX (362)	72.4	26.0	1.1	0.6	0.0	188	43
Cicero, NY (365)	92.6	7.4	0.0	0.0	0.0	93	36
Collierville, TN (365)	66.8	32.1	0.8	0.3	0.0	161	44
Coppell, TX (365)	52.6	40.8	6.6	0.0	0.0	147	50
Cornelius, NC (365)	58.6	40.0	1.4	0.0	0.0	115	48
Cranberry, PA (365)	25.2	66.0	8.5	0.3	0.0	164	59
Crown Point, IN (365)	43.0	50.1	6.3	0.5	0.0	177	53
Dublin, OH (365)	77.3	21.9	0.8	0.0	0.0	112	42
East Fishkill, NY (365)	42.2	52.6	4.7	0.5	0.0	159	52
Eden Prairie, MN (365)	47.7	52.1	0.3	0.0	0.0	115	51
Edmond, OK (365)	62.2	35.9	1.9	0.0	0.0	119	47
Edwardsville, IL (365)	45.8	51.0	3.0	0.3	0.0	159	52
Evesham, NJ (365)	34.5	59.5	5.5	0.5	0.0	166	55
Flower Mound, TX (365)	52.6	40.8	6.6	0.0	0.0	147	50
Folsom, CA (365)	35.6	47.7	15.9	0.8	0.0	164	61
Friendswood, TX (365)	50.4	42.7	6.0	0.8	0.0	177	50
Gaines, MI (365)	77.8	22.2	0.0	0.0	0.0	100	40
Glastonbury, CT (365)	74.0	23.6	2.2	0.3	0.0	151	42
Grand Blanc, MI (365)	83.8	16.2	0.0	0.0	0.0	93	38
Hampden, PA (365)	72.9	26.8	0.3	0.0	0.0	110	43
Hilliard, OH (365)	77.3	21.9	0.8	0.0	0.0	112	42
Hillsborough, NJ (365)	42.2	52.6	4.7	0.5	0.0	159	52
Holly Springs, NC (365)	66.3	33.7	0.0	0.0	0.0	100	45
Independence, KY (365)	47.1	50.1	2.7	0.0	0.0	129	51
Juneau, AK (347)	87.0	12.7	0.3	0.0	0.0	103	15
Kaysville, UT (365)	48.8	41.1	9.6	0.5	0.0	162	51
Keller, TX (365)	52.6	40.8	6.6	0.0	0.0	147	50
Lafayette, CA (365)	46.6	49.0	2.2	1.9	0.3	205	52
Lafayette, CO (357)	67.2	29.7	3.1	0.0	0.0	149	45
Lake Oswego, OR (365)	76.4	19.2	2.7	1.4	0.3	212	38
Laramie, WY (365)	61.6	37.5	0.5	0.3	0.0	153	48
Leander, TX (365)	71.8	27.1	1.1	0.0	0.0	130	43
Leawood, KS (365)	55.3	42.7	1.9	0.0	0.0	129	48
Lee's Summit, MO (365)	55.3	42.7	1.9	0.0	0.0	129	48
Leesburg, VA (365)	40.0	57.8	2.2	0.0	0.0	133	53
Lehi, UT (365)	50.1	46.0	3.0	0.8	0.0	161	50
Lexington, MA (365)	48.8	49.9	1.4	0.0	0.0	147	51
Los Altos, CA (365)	61.4	35.3	2.5	0.8	0.0	182	45
Loveland, CO (365)	53.7	43.0	3.0	0.3	0.0	153	49
Lower Macungie, PA (365)	49.0	50.7	0.3	0.0	0.0	119	51
Madison, AL (336)	89.9	10.1	0.0	0.0	0.0	100	39
Madison, MS (365)	70.1	29.9	0.0	0.0	0.0	90	43

Table continued on next page.

MSA[1] (Days[2])	Percent of Days when Air Quality was...					AQI Statistics	
	Good	Moderate	Unhealthy for Sensitive Groups	Unhealthy	Very Unhealthy	Maximum	Median
Maple Valley, WA (365)	60.8	32.6	3.6	2.7	0.3	202	47
Marion, IA (365)	76.7	23.3	0.0	0.0	0.0	100	40
Marlboro, NJ (365)	42.2	52.6	4.7	0.5	0.0	159	52
Mason, OH (365)	47.1	50.1	2.7	0.0	0.0	129	51
Menomonee Falls, WI (365)	72.1	25.8	2.2	0.0	0.0	136	42
Meridian, ID (365)	49.9	42.5	6.3	0.8	0.5	243	51
Meridian, MI (365)	84.4	15.6	0.0	0.0	0.0	97	38
Merrimack, NH (365)	93.7	6.0	0.3	0.0	0.0	101	37
Milton, GA (365)	47.9	49.0	3.0	0.0	0.0	150	51
Moon, PA (365)	25.2	66.0	8.5	0.3	0.0	164	59
Moorpark, CA (365)	44.9	46.0	5.5	2.2	1.4	537	53
Morgantown, WV (362)	92.8	7.2	0.0	0.0	0.0	90	35
Mount Pleasant, SC (360)	83.6	16.1	0.3	0.0	0.0	101	40
Newark, DE (365)	34.5	59.5	5.5	0.5	0.0	166	55
Newtown, CT (365)	73.2	22.5	3.3	1.1	0.0	179	42
North Attleborough, MA (365)	73.2	24.9	1.4	0.5	0.0	151	43
North Port, FL (365)	78.1	21.1	0.8	0.0	0.0	133	41
North Ridgeville, OH (365)	56.4	40.3	3.3	0.0	0.0	147	46
Northville, MI (365)	41.6	54.0	4.1	0.3	0.0	186	54
O'Fallon, MO (365)	45.8	51.0	3.0	0.3	0.0	159	52
Orchard Park, NY (365)	78.9	20.8	0.3	0.0	0.0	119	39
Oro Valley, AZ (365)	39.7	58.4	1.9	0.0	0.0	122	53
Oviedo, FL (365)	73.4	25.8	0.8	0.0	0.0	147	43
Parker, CO (365)	19.7	69.3	10.7	0.3	0.0	155	62
Parkland, FL (357)	59.4	38.4	2.2	0.0	0.0	143	47
Peachtree City, GA (365)	47.9	49.0	3.0	0.0	0.0	150	51
Pittsfield, MI (365)	77.8	21.4	0.8	0.0	0.0	119	40
Plainfield, IL (365)	43.0	50.1	6.3	0.5	0.0	177	53
Pleasant Grove, UT (365)	50.1	46.0	3.0	0.8	0.0	161	50
Poway, CA (365)	22.7	60.3	15.3	1.6	0.0	174	65
Princeton, NJ (365)	76.4	22.5	1.1	0.0	0.0	133	40
Queen Creek, AZ (365)	8.8	65.2	22.5	3.0	0.5	365	84
Radnor, PA (365)	34.5	59.5	5.5	0.5	0.0	166	55
Randolph, NJ (365)	42.2	52.6	4.7	0.5	0.0	159	52
Rexburg, ID (n/a)	n/a	n/a	n/a	n/a	n/a	n/a	n/a
Rio Rancho, NM (365)	45.2	53.7	1.1	0.0	0.0	119	52
Rye, NY (365)	42.2	52.6	4.7	0.5	0.0	159	52
Sammamish, WA (365)	60.8	32.6	3.6	2.7	0.3	202	47
San Ramon, CA (365)	46.6	49.0	2.2	1.9	0.3	205	52
Saratoga, CA (365)	61.4	35.3	2.5	0.8	0.0	182	45
Shrewsbury, MA (365)	88.5	10.7	0.8	0.0	0.0	143	38
South Brunswick, NJ (365)	42.2	52.6	4.7	0.5	0.0	159	52
South Jordan, UT (365)	44.7	43.0	12.1	0.3	0.0	155	53
South Kingstown, RI (365)	73.2	24.9	1.4	0.5	0.0	151	43
South Portland, ME (365)	87.1	12.3	0.3	0.3	0.0	159	38
Sparks, NV (365)	55.3	43.6	1.1	0.0	0.0	126	49
State College, PA (365)	69.3	30.7	0.0	0.0	0.0	100	45
Sugar Land, TX (365)	50.4	42.7	6.0	0.8	0.0	177	50
Sun Prairie, WI (365)	80.5	19.5	0.0	0.0	0.0	93	39
Syracuse, UT (365)	48.8	41.1	9.6	0.5	0.0	162	51
Tredyffrin, PA (365)	34.5	59.5	5.5	0.5	0.0	166	55
Upper Dublin, PA (365)	34.5	59.5	5.5	0.5	0.0	166	55
Urbandale, IA (365)	80.0	19.7	0.3	0.0	0.0	135	40
Vestal, NY (n/a)	n/a	n/a	n/a	n/a	n/a	n/a	n/a
Vestavia Hills, AL (365)	38.1	59.2	2.7	0.0	0.0	129	55
Webster, NY (365)	85.2	14.0	0.8	0.0	0.0	112	39
Wellesley, MA (365)	48.8	49.9	1.4	0.0	0.0	147	51
West Fargo, ND (362)	84.5	15.5	0.0	0.0	0.0	77	37.5
West Lafayette, IN (365)	77.0	23.0	0.0	0.0	0.0	81	42
Weston, FL (357)	59.4	38.4	2.2	0.0	0.0	143	47
Wilmette, IL (365)	43.0	50.1	6.3	0.5	0.0	177	53
Yorba Linda, CA (365)	10.4	56.2	20.8	10.4	2.2	224	79
Zionsville, IN (365)	54.0	43.6	2.5	0.0	0.0	122	48

Note: The Air Quality Index (AQI) is an index for reporting daily air quality. EPA calculates the AQI for five major air pollutants regulated by the Clean Air Act: ground-level ozone, particle pollution (also known as particulate matter), carbon monoxide, sulfur dioxide, and nitrogen dioxide. The AQI runs from 0 to 500. The higher the AQI value, the greater the level of air pollution and the greater the health concern. There are six AQI categories: "Good" The AQI is between 0 and 50. Air quality is considered satisfactory; "Moderate" The AQI is between 51 and 100. Air quality is acceptable; "Unhealthy for Sensitive Groups" When AQI values are between 101 and 150, members of sensitive groups may experience health effects; "Unhealthy" When AQI values are between 151 and 200 everyone may begin to experience health effects; "Very Unhealthy" AQI values between 201 and 300 trigger a health alert; "Hazardous" AQI values over 300 trigger health warnings of emergency conditions; Data covers the entire county unless noted otherwise; (1) Data covers the Metropolitan Statistical Area—see Appendix B for areas included; (2) Number of days with AQI data in 2017

Source: U.S. Environmental Protection Agency, Air Quality Index Report, 2017

Air Quality Index Pollutants

MSA[1] (Days[2])	Percent of Days when AQI Pollutant was...					
	Carbon Monoxide	Nitrogen Dioxide	Ozone	Sulfur Dioxide	Particulate Matter 2.5	Particulate Matter 10
Aberdeen, SD (122)	0.0	0.0	0.0	0.0	91.0	9.0
Aliso Viejo, CA (365)	0.0	6.8	48.2	0.0	44.4	0.5
Allen, TX (365)	0.0	2.7	57.0	0.0	40.3	0.0
Ames, IA (n/a)	n/a	n/a	n/a	n/a	n/a	n/a
Amherst, MA (365)	0.0	0.5	74.2	0.0	25.2	0.0
Apex, NC (365)	0.0	0.5	42.7	0.0	56.7	0.0
Beavercreek, OH (365)	0.0	0.0	56.7	0.0	43.3	0.0
Bellevue, NE (365)	0.0	0.0	29.9	6.0	51.8	12.3
Bend, OR (273)	0.0	0.0	0.0	0.0	100.0	0.0
Benicia, CA (365)	0.0	0.3	53.2	0.0	46.6	0.0
Bentonville, AR (365)	0.0	0.0	46.6	0.0	53.4	0.0
Bethlehem, NY (365)	0.0	0.0	67.7	0.0	32.3	0.0
Blacksburg, VA (365)	0.0	0.0	54.8	45.2	0.0	0.0
Bowie, MD (365)	0.0	5.8	44.1	0.0	50.1	0.0
Bozeman, MT (365)	0.5	3.8	0.0	0.0	95.6	0.0
Brentwood, TN (365)	0.0	3.8	36.4	0.5	59.2	0.0
Burlington, VT (365)	0.0	1.4	77.3	0.0	21.1	0.3
Cabot, AR (365)	0.0	0.5	39.2	0.0	60.3	0.0
Carmel, IN (365)	0.0	0.3	36.2	2.5	61.1	0.0
Cedar Falls, IA (363)	0.0	0.0	18.7	0.0	81.3	0.0
Cedar Park, TX (365)	0.0	3.8	49.9	0.0	46.3	0.0
Central, LA (365)	0.0	0.5	36.4	2.7	60.3	0.0
Chapel Hill, NC (365)	0.0	0.0	47.4	0.5	52.1	0.0
Cheshire, CT (365)	0.0	9.0	60.5	0.0	30.4	0.0
Chino Hills, CA (365)	0.0	3.0	61.1	0.3	26.8	8.8
Cibolo, TX (362)	0.0	1.7	55.0	0.6	42.8	0.0
Cicero, NY (365)	0.0	0.0	86.0	0.0	14.0	0.0
Collierville, TN (365)	0.0	1.4	52.3	0.0	46.3	0.0
Coppell, TX (365)	0.0	2.7	57.0	0.0	40.3	0.0
Cornelius, NC (365)	0.0	0.0	55.3	0.0	44.7	0.0
Cranberry, PA (365)	0.0	0.0	22.7	7.4	69.6	0.3
Crown Point, IN (365)	0.0	4.7	40.5	3.0	47.1	4.7
Dublin, OH (365)	0.0	7.4	53.7	0.0	38.1	0.8
East Fishkill, NY (365)	0.0	13.2	31.8	0.0	55.1	0.0
Eden Prairie, MN (365)	0.0	0.5	27.1	0.0	38.4	34.0
Edmond, OK (365)	0.0	4.1	58.1	0.0	37.8	0.0
Edwardsville, IL (365)	0.0	3.3	44.1	1.4	46.6	4.7
Evesham, NJ (365)	0.0	0.3	31.2	0.5	67.7	0.3
Flower Mound, TX (365)	0.0	2.7	57.0	0.0	40.3	0.0
Folsom, CA (365)	0.0	0.0	64.1	0.0	34.5	1.4
Friendswood, TX (365)	0.0	4.4	47.4	0.0	47.9	0.3
Gaines, MI (365)	0.0	0.0	63.0	0.3	36.7	0.0
Glastonbury, CT (365)	0.0	11.8	48.5	0.0	39.5	0.3
Grand Blanc, MI (365)	0.0	0.0	56.2	0.0	43.8	0.0
Hampden, PA (365)	0.0	0.0	46.6	0.0	53.4	0.0
Hilliard, OH (365)	0.0	7.4	53.7	0.0	38.1	0.8
Hillsborough, NJ (365)	0.0	13.2	31.8	0.0	55.1	0.0
Holly Springs, NC (365)	0.0	0.5	42.7	0.0	56.7	0.0
Independence, KY (365)	0.0	3.3	35.6	1.4	59.7	0.0
Juneau, AK (347)	0.0	0.0	0.0	0.0	99.7	0.3
Kaysville, UT (365)	0.0	8.5	69.0	0.0	21.6	0.8
Keller, TX (365)	0.0	2.7	57.0	0.0	40.3	0.0
Lafayette, CA (365)	0.0	3.8	27.7	0.0	68.5	0.0
Lafayette, CO (357)	0.0	0.0	91.6	0.0	8.4	0.0
Lake Oswego, OR (365)	0.0	4.1	48.8	0.0	47.1	0.0
Laramie, WY (365)	0.0	0.5	88.5	0.0	2.2	8.8
Leander, TX (365)	0.0	3.8	49.9	0.0	46.3	0.0
Leawood, KS (365)	0.0	1.6	44.9	0.5	46.8	6.0
Lee's Summit, MO (365)	0.0	1.6	44.9	0.5	46.8	6.0
Leesburg, VA (365)	0.0	5.8	44.1	0.0	50.1	0.0
Lehi, UT (365)	0.0	6.8	70.1	0.0	21.6	1.4
Lexington, MA (365)	0.0	0.3	27.1	0.0	72.6	0.0
Los Altos, CA (365)	0.0	1.4	60.3	0.0	37.8	0.5
Loveland, CO (365)	0.0	0.0	87.7	0.0	12.3	0.0
Lower Macungie, PA (365)	0.0	0.3	33.2	0.0	66.6	0.0
Madison, AL (336)	0.0	0.0	67.9	0.0	16.1	16.1
Madison, MS (365)	0.0	0.0	31.2	0.0	68.8	0.0

Table continued on next page.

MSA[1] (Days[2])	Percent of Days when AQI Pollutant was...					
	Carbon Monoxide	Nitrogen Dioxide	Ozone	Sulfur Dioxide	Particulate Matter 2.5	Particulate Matter 10
Maple Valley, WA (365)	0.0	5.8	49.0	0.0	45.2	0.0
Marion, IA (365)	0.0	0.0	43.6	5.2	51.0	0.3
Marlboro, NJ (365)	0.0	13.2	31.8	0.0	55.1	0.0
Mason, OH (365)	0.0	3.3	35.6	1.4	59.7	0.0
Menomonee Falls, WI (365)	0.0	1.9	58.4	0.0	39.7	0.0
Meridian, ID (365)	0.3	2.2	52.9	0.0	43.8	0.8
Meridian, MI (365)	0.0	0.8	67.7	0.0	31.5	0.0
Merrimack, NH (365)	0.0	0.0	96.4	0.3	3.3	0.0
Milton, GA (365)	0.0	3.6	43.0	0.0	53.4	0.0
Moon, PA (365)	0.0	0.0	22.7	7.4	69.6	0.3
Moorpark, CA (365)	0.0	0.0	66.0	0.0	31.8	2.2
Morgantown, WV (362)	0.0	0.0	61.0	22.1	16.9	0.0
Mount Pleasant, SC (360)	0.0	1.1	54.2	0.0	43.9	0.8
Newark, DE (365)	0.0	0.3	31.2	0.5	67.7	0.3
Newtown, CT (365)	0.0	2.7	46.3	0.0	51.0	0.0
North Attleborough, MA (365)	0.0	3.3	55.9	0.0	40.8	0.0
North Port, FL (365)	0.0	0.0	58.1	0.3	41.6	0.0
North Ridgeville, OH (365)	0.3	1.9	46.8	2.5	47.4	1.1
Northville, MI (365)	0.0	2.2	28.8	14.8	47.4	6.8
O'Fallon, MO (365)	0.0	3.3	44.1	1.4	46.6	4.7
Orchard Park, NY (365)	0.0	3.8	53.2	0.0	43.0	0.0
Oro Valley, AZ (365)	0.0	0.0	54.2	0.0	11.0	34.8
Oviedo, FL (365)	0.0	3.0	58.9	0.0	37.8	0.3
Parker, CO (365)	0.0	17.8	63.8	0.0	13.7	4.7
Parkland, FL (357)	0.0	1.4	20.7	0.0	73.4	4.5
Peachtree City, GA (365)	0.0	3.6	43.0	0.0	53.4	0.0
Pittsfield, MI (365)	0.0	0.0	63.3	0.0	36.7	0.0
Plainfield, IL (365)	0.0	4.7	40.5	3.0	47.1	4.7
Pleasant Grove, UT (365)	0.0	6.8	70.1	0.0	21.6	1.4
Poway, CA (365)	0.0	0.3	65.2	0.0	34.5	0.0
Princeton, NJ (365)	0.0	0.0	58.1	0.0	41.9	0.0
Queen Creek, AZ (365)	0.0	2.2	37.5	0.0	16.4	43.8
Radnor, PA (365)	0.0	0.3	31.2	0.5	67.7	0.3
Randolph, NJ (365)	0.0	13.2	31.8	0.0	55.1	0.0
Rexburg, ID (n/a)	n/a	n/a	n/a	n/a	n/a	n/a
Rio Rancho, NM (365)	0.0	0.5	68.8	0.0	8.8	21.9
Rye, NY (365)	0.0	13.2	31.8	0.0	55.1	0.0
Sammamish, WA (365)	0.0	5.8	49.0	0.0	45.2	0.0
San Ramon, CA (365)	0.0	3.8	27.7	0.0	68.5	0.0
Saratoga, CA (365)	0.0	1.4	60.3	0.0	37.8	0.5
Shrewsbury, MA (365)	0.0	4.9	77.8	0.0	17.3	0.0
South Brunswick, NJ (365)	0.0	13.2	31.8	0.0	55.1	0.0
South Jordan, UT (365)	0.0	3.0	69.3	0.0	26.8	0.8
South Kingstown, RI (365)	0.0	3.3	55.9	0.0	40.8	0.0
South Portland, ME (365)	0.0	4.1	69.9	0.0	25.2	0.8
Sparks, NV (365)	0.0	1.9	74.5	0.0	20.8	2.7
State College, PA (365)	0.0	0.0	54.8	0.0	45.2	0.0
Sugar Land, TX (365)	0.0	4.4	47.4	0.0	47.9	0.3
Sun Prairie, WI (365)	0.0	0.0	53.2	1.9	44.9	0.0
Syracuse, UT (365)	0.0	8.5	69.0	0.0	21.6	0.8
Tredyffrin, PA (365)	0.0	0.3	31.2	0.5	67.7	0.3
Upper Dublin, PA (365)	0.0	0.3	31.2	0.5	67.7	0.3
Urbandale, IA (365)	0.0	0.5	56.4	0.0	43.0	0.0
Vestal, NY (n/a)	n/a	n/a	n/a	n/a	n/a	n/a
Vestavia Hills, AL (365)	0.0	0.5	21.9	20.0	57.3	0.3
Webster, NY (365)	0.0	0.3	66.3	0.3	33.2	0.0
Wellesley, MA (365)	0.0	0.3	27.1	0.0	72.6	0.0
West Fargo, ND (362)	0.0	0.3	45.6	0.0	49.7	4.4
West Lafayette, IN (365)	0.0	0.0	39.2	0.0	60.8	0.0
Weston, FL (357)	0.0	1.4	20.7	0.0	73.4	4.5
Wilmette, IL (365)	0.0	4.7	40.5	3.0	47.1	4.7
Yorba Linda, CA (365)	0.0	6.8	48.2	0.0	44.4	0.5
Zionsville, IN (365)	0.0	0.3	36.2	2.5	61.1	0.0

Note: The Air Quality Index (AQI) is an index for reporting daily air quality. EPA calculates the AQI for five major air pollutants regulated by the Clean Air Act: ground-level ozone, particle pollution (also known as particulate matter), carbon monoxide, sulfur dioxide, and nitrogen dioxide. The AQI runs from 0 to 500. The higher the AQI value, the greater the level of air pollution and the greater the health concern; (1) Data covers the Metropolitan Statistical Area—see Appendix B for areas included; (2) Number of days with AQI data in 2017
Source: U.S. Environmental Protection Agency, Air Quality Index Report, 2017

Air Quality Trends: Ozone

MSA[1]	1990	1995	2000	2005	2010	2012	2013	2014	2015	2016
Aberdeen, SD	n/a	n/a	n/a	n/a	n/a	n/a	n/a	n/a	n/a	n/a
Aliso Viejo, CA	0.129	0.110	0.089	0.082	0.074	0.077	0.073	0.082	0.081	0.081
Allen, TX	0.095	0.105	0.096	0.097	0.080	0.080	0.081	0.076	0.077	0.070
Ames, IA	n/a	n/a	n/a	n/a	n/a	n/a	n/a	n/a	n/a	n/a
Amherst, MA	0.092	0.091	0.075	0.086	0.073	0.073	0.066	0.065	0.067	0.070
Apex, NC	0.093	0.081	0.087	0.082	0.071	0.071	0.061	0.063	0.065	0.069
Beavercreek, OH	0.074	0.087	0.074	0.080	0.071	0.077	0.067	0.065	0.067	0.069
Bellevue, NE	0.053	0.066	0.061	0.070	0.061	0.072	0.060	0.060	0.058	0.062
Bend, OR	n/a	n/a	n/a	n/a	n/a	n/a	n/a	n/a	n/a	n/a
Benicia, CA	0.066	0.071	0.051	0.048	0.060	0.056	0.055	0.064	0.064	0.061
Bentonville, AR	n/a	n/a	n/a	n/a	n/a	n/a	n/a	n/a	n/a	n/a
Bethlehem, NY	0.086	0.079	0.070	0.082	0.072	0.071	0.063	0.061	0.062	0.068
Blacksburg, VA	n/a	n/a	n/a	n/a	n/a	n/a	n/a	n/a	n/a	n/a
Bowie, MD	0.088	0.093	0.082	0.081	0.077	0.075	0.065	0.065	0.067	0.068
Bozeman, MT	n/a	n/a	n/a	n/a	n/a	n/a	n/a	n/a	n/a	n/a
Brentwood, TN	0.089	0.092	0.084	0.078	0.073	0.079	0.065	0.067	0.065	0.068
Burlington, VT	0.072	0.074	0.071	0.069	0.063	0.065	0.062	0.059	0.066	0.063
Cabot, AR	0.080	0.086	0.090	0.083	0.072	0.078	0.067	0.066	0.063	0.064
Carmel, IN	0.086	0.095	0.082	0.080	0.069	0.074	0.062	0.063	0.064	0.068
Cedar Falls, IA	n/a	n/a	n/a	n/a	n/a	n/a	n/a	n/a	n/a	n/a
Cedar Park, TX	0.088	0.089	0.088	0.082	0.074	0.074	0.069	0.062	0.073	0.064
Central, LA	0.105	0.091	0.090	0.090	0.075	0.074	0.064	0.071	0.069	0.066
Chapel Hill, NC	n/a	n/a	n/a	n/a	n/a	n/a	n/a	n/a	n/a	n/a
Cheshire, CT	n/a	n/a	n/a	n/a	n/a	n/a	n/a	n/a	n/a	n/a
Chino Hills, CA	0.146	0.129	0.104	0.102	0.093	0.095	0.091	0.091	0.094	0.096
Cibolo, TX	0.090	0.095	0.078	0.084	0.072	0.081	0.076	0.069	0.079	0.071
Cicero, NY	0.089	0.090	0.074	0.077	0.073	0.074	0.065	0.063	0.063	0.067
Collierville, TN	0.088	0.095	0.092	0.086	0.076	0.080	0.066	0.067	0.065	0.069
Coppell, TX	0.095	0.105	0.096	0.097	0.080	0.080	0.081	0.076	0.077	0.070
Cornelius, NC	0.098	0.094	0.094	0.088	0.080	0.079	0.064	0.066	0.066	0.066
Cranberry, PA	0.080	0.095	0.082	0.082	0.075	0.079	0.067	0.065	0.069	0.068
Crown Point, IN	0.074	0.094	0.073	0.084	0.070	0.082	0.066	0.068	0.066	0.074
Dublin, OH	0.090	0.091	0.085	0.084	0.073	0.077	0.065	0.067	0.066	0.069
East Fishkill, NY	0.101	0.106	0.090	0.091	0.081	0.079	0.071	0.069	0.075	0.073
Eden Prairie, MN	0.068	0.084	0.065	0.074	0.066	0.073	0.066	0.063	0.061	0.061
Edmond, OK	0.078	0.086	0.082	0.077	0.071	0.080	0.071	0.068	0.067	0.066
Edwardsville, IL	0.085	0.092	0.082	0.087	0.075	0.085	0.069	0.068	0.067	0.072
Evesham, NJ	0.102	0.109	0.099	0.091	0.083	0.084	0.069	0.071	0.074	0.075
Flower Mound, TX	0.095	0.105	0.096	0.097	0.080	0.080	0.081	0.076	0.077	0.070
Folsom, CA	0.088	0.093	0.087	0.087	0.074	0.079	0.070	0.073	0.074	0.077
Friendswood, TX	0.119	0.114	0.102	0.087	0.079	0.080	0.075	0.064	0.083	0.066
Gaines, MI	0.102	0.089	0.073	0.085	0.071	0.083	0.069	0.069	0.066	0.075
Glastonbury, CT	0.103	0.097	0.082	0.094	0.079	0.080	0.080	0.078	0.075	0.076
Grand Blanc, MI	0.076	0.081	0.073	0.080	0.068	0.084	0.066	0.068	0.067	0.073
Hampden, PA	0.091	0.086	0.080	0.084	0.075	0.072	0.066	0.063	0.066	0.067
Hilliard, OH	0.090	0.091	0.085	0.084	0.073	0.077	0.065	0.067	0.066	0.069
Hillsborough, NJ	0.101	0.106	0.090	0.091	0.081	0.079	0.071	0.069	0.075	0.073
Holly Springs, NC	0.093	0.081	0.087	0.082	0.071	0.071	0.061	0.063	0.065	0.069
Independence, KY	0.092	0.090	0.082	0.086	0.076	0.082	0.065	0.069	0.069	0.072
Juneau, AK	n/a	n/a	n/a	n/a	n/a	n/a	n/a	n/a	n/a	n/a
Kaysville, UT	n/a	n/a	n/a	n/a	n/a	n/a	n/a	n/a	n/a	n/a
Keller, TX	0.095	0.105	0.096	0.097	0.080	0.080	0.081	0.076	0.077	0.070
Lafayette, CA	0.058	0.074	0.057	0.055	0.061	0.057	0.056	0.065	0.062	0.059
Lafayette, CO	n/a	n/a	n/a	n/a	n/a	n/a	n/a	n/a	n/a	n/a
Lake Oswego, OR	0.081	0.065	0.059	0.059	0.056	0.059	0.053	0.057	0.064	0.057
Laramie, WY	n/a	n/a	n/a	n/a	n/a	n/a	n/a	n/a	n/a	n/a
Leander, TX	0.088	0.089	0.088	0.082	0.074	0.074	0.069	0.062	0.073	0.064
Leawood, KS	0.075	0.098	0.088	0.084	0.072	0.085	0.067	0.066	0.063	0.066
Lee's Summit, MO	0.075	0.098	0.088	0.084	0.072	0.085	0.067	0.066	0.063	0.066
Leesburg, VA	0.088	0.093	0.082	0.081	0.077	0.075	0.065	0.065	0.067	0.068
Lehi, UT	0.070	0.068	0.083	0.078	0.070	0.077	0.077	0.068	0.073	0.072
Lexington, MA	n/a	n/a	n/a	n/a	n/a	n/a	n/a	n/a	n/a	n/a
Los Altos, CA	0.079	0.085	0.070	0.065	0.073	0.064	0.064	0.069	0.067	0.063
Loveland, CO	0.066	0.072	0.074	0.076	0.072	0.077	0.074	0.071	0.069	0.070
Lower Macungie, PA	0.093	0.091	0.091	0.086	0.080	0.075	0.068	0.068	0.070	0.071
Madison, AL	0.079	0.080	0.088	0.075	0.071	0.076	0.064	0.064	0.063	0.066
Madison, MS	0.079	0.075	0.080	0.072	0.067	0.066	0.059	0.060	0.060	0.060
Maple Valley, WA	0.082	0.062	0.056	0.053	0.053	0.059	0.048	0.052	0.059	0.054
Marion, IA	n/a	n/a	n/a	n/a	n/a	n/a	n/a	n/a	n/a	n/a

Table continued on next page.

MSA[1]	1990	1995	2000	2005	2010	2012	2013	2014	2015	2016
Marlboro, NJ	0.101	0.106	0.090	0.091	0.081	0.079	0.071	0.069	0.075	0.073
Mason, OH	0.092	0.090	0.082	0.086	0.076	0.082	0.065	0.069	0.069	0.072
Menomonee Falls, WI	0.095	0.106	0.082	0.092	0.079	0.092	0.069	0.072	0.069	0.074
Meridian, ID	n/a	n/a	n/a	n/a	n/a	n/a	n/a	n/a	n/a	n/a
Meridian, MI	0.080	0.082	0.076	0.080	0.065	0.080	0.065	0.066	0.064	0.073
Merrimack, NH	n/a	n/a	n/a	n/a	n/a	n/a	n/a	n/a	n/a	n/a
Milton, GA	0.104	0.103	0.101	0.087	0.076	0.079	0.066	0.072	0.070	0.073
Moon, PA	0.080	0.095	0.082	0.082	0.075	0.079	0.067	0.065	0.069	0.068
Moorpark, CA	0.100	0.100	0.083	0.077	0.073	0.068	0.066	0.074	0.067	0.069
Morgantown, WV	n/a	n/a	n/a	n/a	n/a	n/a	n/a	n/a	n/a	n/a
Mount Pleasant, SC	0.068	0.071	0.078	0.073	0.067	0.063	0.059	0.060	0.054	0.058
Newark, DE	0.102	0.109	0.099	0.091	0.083	0.084	0.069	0.071	0.074	0.075
Newtown, CT	0.106	0.103	0.088	0.094	0.081	0.087	0.083	0.075	0.083	0.081
North Attleborough, MA	0.106	0.107	0.087	0.090	0.072	0.072	0.073	0.067	0.070	0.075
North Port, FL	0.075	0.076	0.084	0.076	0.069	0.063	0.066	0.062	0.062	0.060
North Ridgeville, OH	0.085	0.092	0.076	0.083	0.077	0.087	0.068	0.069	0.071	0.072
Northville, MI	0.083	0.088	0.076	0.083	0.074	0.081	0.068	0.069	0.068	0.073
O'Fallon, MO	0.085	0.092	0.082	0.087	0.075	0.085	0.069	0.068	0.067	0.072
Orchard Park, NY	0.089	0.088	0.083	0.090	0.072	0.081	0.068	0.062	0.069	0.072
Oro Valley, AZ	0.073	0.078	0.074	0.075	0.068	0.069	0.069	0.065	0.065	0.065
Oviedo, FL	0.081	0.075	0.080	0.083	0.069	0.071	0.063	0.062	0.060	0.063
Parker, CO	0.077	0.070	0.069	0.072	0.070	0.079	0.079	0.070	0.073	0.071
Parkland, FL	0.068	0.072	0.075	0.065	0.064	0.062	0.061	0.062	0.061	0.061
Peachtree City, GA	0.104	0.103	0.101	0.087	0.076	0.079	0.066	0.072	0.070	0.073
Pittsfield, MI	n/a	n/a	n/a	n/a	n/a	n/a	n/a	n/a	n/a	n/a
Plainfield, IL	0.074	0.094	0.073	0.084	0.070	0.082	0.066	0.068	0.066	0.074
Pleasant Grove, UT	0.070	0.068	0.083	0.078	0.070	0.077	0.077	0.068	0.073	0.072
Poway, CA	0.105	0.087	0.075	0.070	0.069	0.066	0.066	0.068	0.064	0.065
Princeton, NJ	0.105	0.107	0.099	0.089	0.086	0.080	0.070	0.071	0.073	0.074
Queen Creek, AZ	0.080	0.087	0.082	0.077	0.076	0.080	0.076	0.075	0.072	0.071
Radnor, PA	0.102	0.109	0.099	0.091	0.083	0.084	0.069	0.071	0.074	0.075
Randolph, NJ	0.101	0.106	0.090	0.091	0.081	0.079	0.071	0.069	0.075	0.073
Rexburg, ID	n/a	n/a	n/a	n/a	n/a	n/a	n/a	n/a	n/a	n/a
Rio Rancho, NM	0.072	0.070	0.072	0.073	0.066	0.070	0.067	0.062	0.066	0.065
Rye, NY	0.101	0.106	0.090	0.091	0.081	0.079	0.071	0.069	0.075	0.073
Sammamish, WA	0.082	0.062	0.056	0.053	0.053	0.059	0.048	0.052	0.059	0.054
San Ramon, CA	0.058	0.074	0.057	0.055	0.061	0.057	0.056	0.065	0.062	0.059
Saratoga, CA	0.079	0.085	0.070	0.065	0.073	0.064	0.064	0.069	0.067	0.063
Shrewsbury, MA	0.097	0.096	0.076	0.085	0.070	0.070	0.067	0.065	0.063	0.066
South Brunswick, NJ	0.101	0.106	0.090	0.091	0.081	0.079	0.071	0.069	0.075	0.073
South Jordan, UT	n/a	n/a	n/a	n/a	n/a	n/a	n/a	n/a	n/a	n/a
South Kingstown, RI	0.106	0.107	0.087	0.090	0.072	0.072	0.073	0.067	0.070	0.075
South Portland, ME	0.099	0.100	0.070	0.072	0.072	0.072	0.074	0.066	0.066	0.067
Sparks, NV	0.074	0.070	0.067	0.069	0.068	0.072	0.067	0.069	0.071	0.070
State College, PA	n/a	n/a	n/a	n/a	n/a	n/a	n/a	n/a	n/a	n/a
Sugar Land, TX	0.119	0.114	0.102	0.087	0.079	0.080	0.075	0.064	0.083	0.066
Sun Prairie, WI	0.077	0.084	0.072	0.079	0.062	0.074	0.067	0.068	0.064	0.068
Syracuse, UT	n/a	n/a	n/a	n/a	n/a	n/a	n/a	n/a	n/a	n/a
Tredyffrin, PA	0.102	0.109	0.099	0.091	0.083	0.084	0.069	0.071	0.074	0.075
Upper Dublin, PA	0.102	0.109	0.099	0.091	0.083	0.084	0.069	0.071	0.074	0.075
Urbandale, IA	n/a	n/a	n/a	n/a	n/a	n/a	n/a	n/a	n/a	n/a
Vestal, NY	n/a	n/a	n/a	n/a	n/a	n/a	n/a	n/a	n/a	n/a
Vestavia Hills, AL	0.094	0.098	0.091	0.084	0.075	0.078	0.065	0.064	0.068	0.070
Webster, NY	0.087	0.096	0.070	0.065	0.071	0.072	0.066	0.064	0.061	0.067
Wellesley, MA	n/a	n/a	n/a	n/a	n/a	n/a	n/a	n/a	n/a	n/a
West Fargo, ND	n/a	n/a	n/a	n/a	n/a	n/a	n/a	n/a	n/a	n/a
West Lafayette, IN	n/a	n/a	n/a	n/a	n/a	n/a	n/a	n/a	n/a	n/a
Weston, FL	0.068	0.072	0.075	0.065	0.064	0.062	0.061	0.062	0.061	0.061
Wilmette, IL	0.074	0.094	0.073	0.084	0.070	0.082	0.066	0.068	0.066	0.074
Yorba Linda, CA	0.129	0.110	0.089	0.082	0.074	0.077	0.073	0.082	0.081	0.081
Zionsville, IN	0.086	0.095	0.082	0.080	0.069	0.074	0.062	0.063	0.064	0.068
U.S.	0.087	0.089	0.081	0.079	0.073	0.075	0.069	0.067	0.068	0.069

Note: (1) Data covers the Metropolitan Statistical Area—see Appendix B for areas included; n/a not available. The values shown are the composite ozone concentration averages among trend sites based on the highest fourth daily maximum 8-hour concentration in parts per million. These trends are based on sites having an adequate record of monitoring data during the trend period. Data from exceptional events are included.

Source: U.S. Environmental Protection Agency, Air Quality Monitoring Information, "Air Quality Trends by City, 1990-2016"

Maximum Air Pollutant Concentrations: Particulate Matter, Ozone, CO and Lead

Metro Aea	PM 10 (ug/m^3)	PM 2.5 Wtd AM (ug/m^3)	PM 2.5 24-Hr (ug/m^3)	Ozone (ppm)	Carbon Monoxide (ppm)	Lead (ug/m^3)
Aberdeen, SD	65	5.4	14	n/a	n/a	n/a
Aliso Viejo, CA	127	12	29	0.1	4	0.03
Allen, TX	52	8.5	19	0.076	1	0.06
Ames, IA	n/a	n/a	n/a	0.06	n/a	n/a
Amherst, MA	33	6.2	17	0.076	2	n/a
Apex, NC	26	7.6	16	0.069	2	n/a
Beavercreek, OH	39	8.9	21	0.072	1	0
Bellevue, NE	134	8	18	0.063	2	0.07
Bend, OR	n/a	n/a	n/a	n/a	n/a	n/a
Benicia, CA	23	7.4	19	0.067	2	n/a
Bentonville, AR	n/a	8.1	18	0.058	n/a	n/a
Bethlehem, NY	n/a	6.3	18	0.068	1	n/a
Blacksburg, VA	n/a	n/a	n/a	0.064	n/a	n/a
Bowie, MD	41	8.5	20	0.076	2	0.01
Bozeman, MT	n/a	n/a	n/a	n/a	4	n/a
Brentwood, TN	34	8.9	18	0.068	2	n/a
Burlington, VT	33	5.4	13	0.063	1	n/a
Cabot, AR	44	9.8	21	0.065	1	n/a
Carmel, IN	85	10.4	22	0.073	3	0.01
Cedar Falls, IA	40	7.5	20	0.063	n/a	n/a
Cedar Park, TX	72	n/a	n/a	0.064	n/a	n/a
Central, LA	69	9.9	26	0.071	1	n/a
Chapel Hill, NC	29	8.9	20	0.063	n/a	n/a
Cheshire, CT	35	6.8	20	0.08	1	n/a
Chino Hills, CA	449	14.8	36	0.116	2	0.06
Cibolo, TX	47	7.9	16	0.071	n/a	n/a
Cicero, NY	n/a	5	12	0.067	n/a	n/a
Collierville, TN	40	8.4	17	0.071	1	n/a
Coppell, TX	52	8.5	19	0.076	1	0.06
Cornelius, NC	44	9	21	0.074	1	n/a
Cranberry, PA	84	12.8	40	0.073	3	0.02
Crown Point, IN	131	9.4	20	0.08	1	0.05
Dublin, OH	52	8.7	18	0.072	2	0.01
East Fishkill, NY	33	9.2	20	0.078	3	0.03
Eden Prairie, MN	127	7.8	22	0.061	2	0.11
Edmond, OK	68	7.8	17	0.068	1	n/a
Edwardsville, IL	82	10	21	0.076	2	0.14
Evesham, NJ	113	11	24	0.08	2	0.04
Flower Mound, TX	52	8.5	19	0.076	1	0.06
Folsom, CA	53	8.8	28	0.093	2	n/a
Friendswood, TX	81	10.1	23	0.079	2	0
Gaines, MI	56	8.8	23	0.075	1	0
Glastonbury, CT	46	7.2	19	0.08	2	n/a
Grand Blanc, MI	n/a	7.2	19	0.073	n/a	n/a
Hampden, PA	41	8.9	25	0.07	n/a	n/a
Hilliard, OH	52	8.7	18	0.072	2	0.01
Hillsborough, NJ	33	9.2	20	0.078	3	0.03
Holly Springs, NC	26	7.6	16	0.069	2	n/a
Independence, KY	85	10.9	25	0.076	1	n/a
Juneau, AK	32	n/a	n/a	n/a	n/a	n/a
Kaysville, UT	62	9	39	0.076	3	n/a
Keller, TX	52	8.5	19	0.076	1	0.06
Lafayette, CA	29	8.7	19	0.082	2	0.03
Lafayette, CO	44	6.9	26	0.053	n/a	n/a
Lake Oswego, OR	32	5.9	18	0.064	1	n/a
Laramie, WY	114	3.9	11	0.064	n/a	n/a
Leander, TX	72	n/a	n/a	0.064	n/a	n/a
Leawood, KS	84	8.9	20	0.069	1	n/a
Lee's Summit, MO	84	8.9	20	0.069	1	n/a
Leesburg, VA	41	8.5	20	0.076	2	0.01
Lehi, UT	66	8.8	37	0.072	1	n/a
Lexington, MA	30	7	16	0.07	1	n/a
Los Altos, CA	43	9.1	19	0.072	2	0.08
Loveland, CO	50	n/a	n/a	0.076	n/a	n/a
Lower Macungie, PA	31	10.5	25	0.075	n/a	0.11
Madison, AL	68	n/a	n/a	0.066	n/a	n/a
Madison, MS	49	8.4	17	0.063	1	n/a

Table continued on next page.

Metro Aea	PM 10 (ug/m³)	PM 2.5 Wtd AM (ug/m³)	PM 2.5 24-Hr (ug/m³)	Ozone (ppm)	Carbon Monoxide (ppm)	Lead (ug/m³)
Maple Valley, WA	n/a	6.9	31	0.061	1	n/a
Marion, IA	48	7.8	19	0.064	1	n/a
Marlboro, NJ	33	9.2	20	0.078	3	0.03
Mason, OH	85	10.9	25	0.076	1	n/a
Menomonee Falls, WI	48	8.3	20	0.079	1	n/a
Meridian, ID	72	8.4	21	0.072	3	n/a
Meridian, MI	n/a	7.3	18	0.073	n/a	n/a
Merrimack, NH	n/a	4.2	10	0.069	0	n/a
Milton, GA	43	10.8	24	0.078	2	n/a
Moon, PA	84	12.8	40	0.073	3	0.02
Moorpark, CA	71	9.6	19	0.077	n/a	n/a
Morgantown, WV	n/a	7.4	16	0.059	n/a	n/a
Mount Pleasant, SC	66	7.7	17	0.058	n/a	n/a
Newark, DE	113	11	24	0.08	2	0.04
Newtown, CT	30	9.4	23	0.087	2	n/a
North Attleborough, MA	39	9.3	20	0.076	2	n/a
North Port, FL	32	6.4	15	0.062	n/a	n/a
North Ridgeville, OH	86	10.7	22	0.077	4	0.03
Northville, MI	181	11.3	26	0.075	2	0.07
O'Fallon, MO	82	10	21	0.076	2	0.14
Orchard Park, NY	n/a	6.8	15	0.074	1	n/a
Oro Valley, AZ	165	6.4	19	0.069	1	n/a
Oviedo, FL	33	7	15	0.064	1	n/a
Parker, CO	109	9.5	25	0.083	2	n/a
Parkland, FL	197	7.6	16	0.062	2	n/a
Peachtree City, GA	43	10.8	24	0.078	2	n/a
Pittsfield, MI	n/a	7.9	18	0.074	n/a	n/a
Plainfield, IL	131	9.4	20	0.08	1	0.05
Pleasant Grove, UT	66	8.8	37	0.072	1	n/a
Poway, CA	66	8.7	18	0.084	2	0.01
Princeton, NJ	n/a	8.6	17	0.074	n/a	n/a
Queen Creek, AZ	357	12	34	0.075	2	0.05
Radnor, PA	113	11	24	0.08	2	0.04
Randolph, NJ	33	9.2	20	0.078	3	0.03
Rexburg, ID	n/a	n/a	n/a	n/a	n/a	n/a
Rio Rancho, NM	205	7.6	19	0.067	2	0
Rye, NY	33	9.2	20	0.078	3	0.03
Sammamish, WA	n/a	6.9	31	0.061	1	n/a
San Ramon, CA	29	8.7	19	0.082	2	0.03
Saratoga, CA	43	9.1	19	0.072	2	0.08
Shrewsbury, MA	40	5.8	15	0.074	1	n/a
South Brunswick, NJ	33	9.2	20	0.078	3	0.03
South Jordan, UT	78	9.4	43	0.076	n/a	0.05
South Kingstown, RI	39	9.3	20	0.076	2	n/a
South Portland, ME	62	6.5	15	0.068	1	n/a
Sparks, NV	78	7	21	0.073	2	n/a
State College, PA	n/a	n/a	n/a	0.065	n/a	n/a
Sugar Land, TX	81	10.1	23	0.079	2	0
Sun Prairie, WI	34	8.1	19	0.07	n/a	n/a
Syracuse, UT	62	9	39	0.076	3	n/a
Tredyffrin, PA	113	11	24	0.08	2	0.04
Upper Dublin, PA	113	11	24	0.08	2	0.04
Urbandale, IA	37	7.1	18	0.061	1	n/a
Vestal, NY	n/a	n/a	n/a	n/a	n/a	n/a
Vestavia Hills, AL	66	10.8	22	0.073	2	n/a
Webster, NY	n/a	6.3	15	0.067	1	n/a
Wellesley, MA	30	7	16	0.07	1	n/a
West Fargo, ND	63	n/a	n/a	0.054	0	n/a
West Lafayette, IN	n/a	7.6	18	0.066	n/a	n/a
Weston, FL	197	7.6	16	0.062	2	n/a
Wilmette, IL	131	9.4	20	0.08	1	0.05
Yorba Linda, CA	127	12	29	0.1	4	0.03
Zionsville, IN	85	10.4	22	0.073	3	0.01
NAAQS[1]	150	15	35	0.075	9	0.15

Note: Data from exceptional events are included; Data covers the Metropolitan Statistical Area—see Appendix B for areas included; (1) National Ambient Air Quality Standards; ppm = parts per million; ug/m³ = micrograms per cubic meter; n/a not available Concentrations: Particulate Matter 10 (coarse particulate)—highest second maximum 24-hour concentration; Particulate Matter 2.5 Wtd AM (fine particulate)—highest weighted annual mean concentration; Particulate Matter 2.5 24-Hour (fine particulate)—highest 98th percentile 24-hour concentration; Ozone—highest fourth daily maximum 8-hour concentration; Carbon Monoxide—highest second maximum non-overlapping 8-hour concentration; Lead—maximum running 3-month average

Source: U.S. Environmental Protection Agency, Air Quality Monitoring Information, "Air Quality Statistics by City, 2016"

Maximum Air Pollutant Concentrations: Nitrogen Dioxide and Sulfur Dioxide

Metro Area	Nitrogen Dioxide AM (ppb)	Nitrogen Dioxide 1-Hr (ppb)	Sulfur Dioxide AM (ppb)	Sulfur Dioxide 1-Hr (ppb)	Sulfur Dioxide 24-Hr (ppb)
Aberdeen, SD	n/a	n/a	n/a	n/a	n/a
Aliso Viejo, CA	24	77	n/a	12	n/a
Allen, TX	12	45	n/a	8	n/a
Ames, IA	n/a	n/a	n/a	n/a	n/a
Amherst, MA	11	38	n/a	3	n/a
Apex, NC	9	39	n/a	3	n/a
Beavercreek, OH	n/a	n/a	n/a	16	n/a
Bellevue, NE	n/a	n/a	n/a	65	n/a
Bend, OR	n/a	n/a	n/a	n/a	n/a
Benicia, CA	7	36	n/a	5	n/a
Bentonville, AR	n/a	n/a	n/a	n/a	n/a
Bethlehem, NY	n/a	n/a	n/a	4	n/a
Blacksburg, VA	n/a	n/a	n/a	n/a	n/a
Bowie, MD	18	59	n/a	8	n/a
Bozeman, MT	2	n/a	n/a	n/a	n/a
Brentwood, TN	16	54	n/a	2	n/a
Burlington, VT	6	n/a	n/a	2	n/a
Cabot, AR	8	41	n/a	7	n/a
Carmel, IN	13	n/a	n/a	23	n/a
Cedar Falls, IA	n/a	n/a	n/a	n/a	n/a
Cedar Park, TX	14	47	n/a	4	n/a
Central, LA	11	45	n/a	22	n/a
Chapel Hill, NC	n/a	n/a	n/a	4	n/a
Cheshire, CT	14	53	n/a	4	n/a
Chino Hills, CA	31	74	n/a	46	n/a
Cibolo, TX	8	42	n/a	7	n/a
Cicero, NY	n/a	n/a	n/a	3	n/a
Collierville, TN	10	38	n/a	n/a	n/a
Coppell, TX	12	45	n/a	8	n/a
Cornelius, NC	11	40	n/a	4	n/a
Cranberry, PA	11	40	n/a	64	n/a
Crown Point, IN	17	61	n/a	31	n/a
Dublin, OH	12	42	n/a	4	n/a
East Fishkill, NY	20	60	n/a	7	n/a
Eden Prairie, MN	13	43	n/a	13	n/a
Edmond, OK	17	47	n/a	3	n/a
Edwardsville, IL	12	45	n/a	27	n/a
Evesham, NJ	16	58	n/a	19	n/a
Flower Mound, TX	12	45	n/a	8	n/a
Folsom, CA	13	43	n/a	9	n/a
Friendswood, TX	14	54	n/a	23	n/a
Gaines, MI	n/a	n/a	n/a	20	n/a
Glastonbury, CT	16	54	n/a	2	n/a
Grand Blanc, MI	n/a	n/a	n/a	n/a	n/a
Hampden, PA	n/a	n/a	n/a	n/a	n/a
Hilliard, OH	12	42	n/a	4	n/a
Hillsborough, NJ	20	60	n/a	7	n/a
Holly Springs, NC	9	39	n/a	3	n/a
Independence, KY	21	56	n/a	43	n/a
Juneau, AK	n/a	n/a	n/a	n/a	n/a
Kaysville, UT	15	n/a	n/a	n/a	n/a
Keller, TX	12	45	n/a	8	n/a
Lafayette, CA	17	51	n/a	13	n/a
Lafayette, CO	n/a	n/a	n/a	n/a	n/a
Lake Oswego, OR	13	35	n/a	3	n/a
Laramie, WY	n/a	n/a	n/a	n/a	n/a
Leander, TX	14	47	n/a	4	n/a
Leawood, KS	13	46	n/a	10	n/a
Lee's Summit, MO	13	46	n/a	10	n/a
Leesburg, VA	18	59	n/a	8	n/a
Lehi, UT	15	60	n/a	n/a	n/a
Lexington, MA	15	49	n/a	13	n/a
Los Altos, CA	16	46	n/a	2	n/a
Loveland, CO	n/a	n/a	n/a	n/a	n/a
Lower Macungie, PA	11	48	n/a	19	n/a
Madison, AL	n/a	n/a	n/a	n/a	n/a
Madison, MS	n/a	n/a	n/a	13	n/a

Table continued on next page.

Metro Area	Nitrogen Dioxide AM (ppb)	Nitrogen Dioxide 1-Hr (ppb)	Sulfur Dioxide AM (ppb)	Sulfur Dioxide 1-Hr (ppb)	Sulfur Dioxide 24-Hr (ppb)
Maple Valley, WA	21	49	n/a	n/a	n/a
Marion, IA	n/a	n/a	n/a	54	n/a
Marlboro, NJ	20	60	n/a	7	n/a
Mason, OH	21	56	n/a	43	n/a
Menomonee Falls, WI	14	49	n/a	6	n/a
Meridian, ID	10	41	n/a	4	n/a
Meridian, MI	7	n/a	n/a	10	n/a
Merrimack, NH	n/a	n/a	n/a	2	n/a
Milton, GA	20	61	n/a	32	n/a
Moon, PA	11	40	n/a	64	n/a
Moorpark, CA	8	35	n/a	n/a	n/a
Morgantown, WV	n/a	n/a	n/a	9	n/a
Mount Pleasant, SC	n/a	n/a	n/a	10	n/a
Newark, DE	16	58	n/a	19	n/a
Newtown, CT	n/a	n/a	n/a	3	n/a
North Attleborough, MA	20	56	n/a	7	n/a
North Port, FL	2	15	n/a	8	n/a
North Ridgeville, OH	11	50	n/a	370	n/a
Northville, MI	16	50	n/a	59	n/a
O'Fallon, MO	12	45	n/a	27	n/a
Orchard Park, NY	11	48	n/a	18	n/a
Oro Valley, AZ	8	34	n/a	1	n/a
Oviedo, FL	4	29	n/a	2	n/a
Parker, CO	29	77	n/a	20	n/a
Parkland, FL	8	43	n/a	5	n/a
Peachtree City, GA	20	61	n/a	32	n/a
Pittsfield, MI	n/a	n/a	n/a	n/a	n/a
Plainfield, IL	17	61	n/a	31	n/a
Pleasant Grove, UT	15	60	n/a	n/a	n/a
Poway, CA	17	53	n/a	n/a	n/a
Princeton, NJ	n/a	n/a	n/a	n/a	n/a
Queen Creek, AZ	31	63	n/a	7	n/a
Radnor, PA	16	58	n/a	19	n/a
Randolph, NJ	20	60	n/a	7	n/a
Rexburg, ID	n/a	n/a	n/a	n/a	n/a
Rio Rancho, NM	10	44	n/a	6	n/a
Rye, NY	20	60	n/a	7	n/a
Sammamish, WA	21	49	n/a	n/a	n/a
San Ramon, CA	17	51	n/a	13	n/a
Saratoga, CA	16	46	n/a	2	n/a
Shrewsbury, MA	12	49	n/a	5	n/a
South Brunswick, NJ	20	60	n/a	7	n/a
South Jordan, UT	7	48	n/a	n/a	n/a
South Kingstown, RI	20	56	n/a	7	n/a
South Portland, ME	6	40	n/a	9	n/a
Sparks, NV	13	46	n/a	5	n/a
State College, PA	5	31	n/a	7	n/a
Sugar Land, TX	14	54	n/a	23	n/a
Sun Prairie, WI	n/a	n/a	n/a	1	n/a
Syracuse, UT	15	n/a	n/a	n/a	n/a
Tredyffrin, PA	16	58	n/a	19	n/a
Upper Dublin, PA	16	58	n/a	19	n/a
Urbandale, IA	8	33	n/a	1	n/a
Vestal, NY	n/a	n/a	n/a	n/a	n/a
Vestavia Hills, AL	14	53	n/a	11	n/a
Webster, NY	10	41	n/a	27	n/a
Wellesley, MA	15	49	n/a	13	n/a
West Fargo, ND	4	27	n/a	2	n/a
West Lafayette, IN	n/a	n/a	n/a	n/a	n/a
Weston, FL	8	43	n/a	5	n/a
Wilmette, IL	17	61	n/a	31	n/a
Yorba Linda, CA	24	77	n/a	12	n/a
Zionsville, IN	13	n/a	n/a	23	n/a
NAAQS[1]	53	100	30	75	140

Note: Data from exceptional events are included; Data covers the Metropolitan Statistical Area—see Appendix B for areas included; (1) National Ambient Air Quality Standards; ppb = parts per billion; n/a not available Concentrations: Nitrogen Dioxide AM—highest arithmetic mean concentration; Nitrogen Dioxide 1-Hr—highest 98th percentile 1-hour daily maximum concentration; Sulfur Dioxide AM—highest annual mean concentration; Sulfur Dioxide 1-Hr—highest 99th percentile 1-hour daily maximum concentration; Sulfur Dioxide 24-Hr—highest second maximum 24-hour concentration

Source: U.S. Environmental Protection Agency, Air Quality Monitoring Information, "Air Quality Statistics by City, 2016"

Appendix B: Metropolitan Area Definitions

Metropolitan and Micropolitan Statistical Areas (MSA), Metropolitan Divisions (MD), New England City and Town Areas (NECTA), and New England City and Town Area Divisions (NECTAD)

Note: *In February 2013, the Office of Management and Budget (OMB) announced significant changes to metropolitan area definitions. Both current and historical definitions are shown below. If the change only affected the name of the metro area, the counties included were not repeated.*

Aberdeen, SD MSA
Brown and Edmunds Counties

Akron, OH MSA
Portage and Summit Counties

Albuquerque, NM MSA
Bernalillo, Sandoval, Torrance, and Valencia Counties

Aliso Viejo, CA
See Los Angeles, CA (Anaheim-Santa Ana-Irvine, CA MD)

Allen, TX
See Dallas, TX (Dallas-Plano-Irving, TX MD)

Allentown-Bethlehem-Easton, PA-NJ MSA
Carbon, Lehigh, and Northampton Counties, PA; Warren County, NJ

Ames, IA MSA
Story County

Amherst, MA
See Springfield, MA

Ann Arbor, MI MSA
Washtenaw County

Apex, NC
See Raleigh, NC MSA

Atlanta-Sandy Springs-Roswell, GA MSA
Barrow, Bartow, Butts, Carroll, Cherokee, Clayton, Cobb, Coweta, Dawson, DeKalb, Douglas, Fayette, Forsyth, Fulton, Gwinnett, Haralson, Heard, Henry, Jasper, Lamar, Meriwether, Morgan, Newton, Paulding, Pickens, Pike, Rockdale, Spalding, and Walton Counties
Previous name: Atlanta-Sandy Springs-Marietta, GA MSA
Barrow, Bartow, Butts, Carroll, Cherokee, Clayton, Cobb, Coweta, Dawson, DeKalb, Douglas, Fayette, Forsyth, Fulton, Gwinnett, Haralson, Heard, Henry, Jasper, Lamar, Meriwether, Newton, Paulding, Pickens, Pike, Rockdale, Spalding, and Walton Counties

Austin-Round Rock, TX MSA
Previous name: Austin-Round Rock-San Marcos, TX MSA
Bastrop, Caldwell, Hays, Travis, and Williamson Counties

Baton Rouge, LA MSA
Ascension, East Baton Rouge, East Feliciana, Iberville, Livingston, Pointe Coupee, St. Helena, West Baton Rouge, and West Feliciana Parishes
Previously Baton Rouge, LA MSA
Ascension, East Baton Rouge, Livingston, and West Baton Rouge Parishes

Beavercreek, OH
See Dayton, OH MSA

Bellevue, NE
See Omaha-Council Bluffs, NE-IA MSA

Bend, OR
See Bend-Redmond, OR MSA

Bend-Redmond, OR MSA
Deschutes County

Benicia, CA
See Vallejo-Fairfield, CA MSA

Bentonville, AR
See Fayetteville-Springdale-Rogers, AR-MO MSA

Bethlehem, NY
See Albany-Schenectady-Troy, NY MSA

Binghamton, NY MSA
Broome and Tioga Counties

Birmingham-Hoover, AL MSA
Bibb, Blount, Chilton, Jefferson, St. Clair, Shelby, and Walker Counties

Blacksburg, VA
See Blacksburg-Christiansburg-Radford, VA MSA

Blacksburg-Christiansburg-Radford, VA MSA
Floyd, Giles, Montgomery, and Pulaski Counties; Radford city

Boise City, ID MSA
Previous name: Boise City-Nampa, ID MSA
Ada, Boise, Canyon, Gem, and Owyhee Counties

Boston, MA
Boston-Cambridge-Newton, MA-NH MSA
Previous name: Boston-Cambridge-Quincy, MA-NH MSA
Essex, Middlesex, Norfolk, Plymouth, and Suffolk Counties, MA; Rockingham and Strafford Counties, NH

Boston, MA MD
Previous name: Boston-Quincy, MA MD
Norfolk, Plymouth, and Suffolk Counties

Cambridge-Newton-Framingham, MA MD
Essex and Middlesex Counties

Boston-Cambridge-Nashua, MA-NH NECTA
Includes 157 cities and towns in Massachusetts and 34 cities and towns in New Hampshire
Previous name: Boston-Cambridge-Quincy, MA-NH NECTA
Includes 155 cities and towns in Massachusetts and 38 cities and towns in New Hampshire

Boston-Cambridge-Newton, MA NECTA Division
Includes 92 cities and towns in Massachusetts
Previous name: Boston-Cambridge-Quincy, MA NECTA Division
Includes 97 cities and towns in Massachusetts

Boulder, CO MSA
Boulder County

Bowie, MD
See Washington, DC (Washington-Arlington-Alexandria, DC-VA-MD-WV MD)

Bozeman, MT MSA
Gallatin County

Brentwood, TN
See Nashville-Davidson-Murfreesboro-Franklin, TN MSA

Bridgeport, CT
Bridgeport-Stamford-Norwalk, CT MSA
Fairfield County

Bridgeport-Stamford-Norwalk, CT NECTA
Includes 24 cities and towns in Connecticut

Buffalo-Cheektowaga-Niagara Falls, NY MSA
Previous name: Buffalo-Niagara Falls, NY MSA
Erie and Niagara Counties

Burlington, VT
Burlington-South Burlington, VT MSA
Chittenden, Franklin, and Grand Isle Counties

Burlington-South Burlington, VT NECTA
Includes 33 cities and towns in Vermont

Cabot, AR
See Little Rock-North Little Rock-Conway, AR MSA

Carmel, IN
See Indianapolis-Carmel-Anderson, IN MSA

Cedar Falls, IA
See Waterloo-Cedar Falls, IA MSA

Cedar Park, TX
See Austin-Round Rock, TX MSA

Cedar Rapids, IA MSA
Benton, Jones, and Linn Counties

Central, LA
See Baton Rouge, LA MSA

Chapel Hill, NC
See Durham-Chapel Hill, NC MSA

Charleston-North Charleston, SC MSA
Previous name: Charleston-North Charleston- Summerville, SC MSA
Berkeley, Charleston, and Dorchester Counties

Charlotte-Concord-Gastonia, NC-SC MSA
Cabarrus, Gaston, Iredell, Lincoln, Mecklenburg, Rowan, and Union Counties, NC; Chester, Lancaster, and York Counties, SC
Previous name: Charlotte-Gastonia-Rock Hill, NC-SC MSA
Anson, Cabarrus, Gaston, Mecklenburg, and Union Counties, NC; York County, SC

Cheshire, CT
See New Haven-Milford, CT MSA

Chicago, IL

Chicago-Naperville-Elgin, IL-IN-WI MSA
Previous name: Chicago-Joliet-Naperville, IL-IN-WI MSA
Cook, DeKalb, DuPage, Grundy, Kane, Kendall, Lake, McHenry, and Will Counties, IL; Jasper, Lake, Newton, and Porter Counties, IN; Kenosha County, WI

Chicago-Naperville-Arlington Heights, IL MD
Cook, DuPage, Grundy, Kendall, McHenry, and Will Counties
Previous name: Chicago-Joliet-Naperville, IL MD
Cook, DeKalb, DuPage, Grundy, Kane, Kendall, McHenry, and Will Counties

Elgin, IL MD
DeKalb and Kane Counties
Previously part of the Chicago-Joliet-Naperville, IL MD

Gary, IN MD
Jasper, Lake, Newton, and Porter Counties

Lake County-Kenosha County, IL-WI MD
Lake County, IL; Kenosha County, WI

Chino Hills, CA
See Riverside-San Bernardino-Ontario, CA MSA

Cibolo, TX
See San Antonio-New Braunfels, TX MSA

Cicero, NY
See Syracuse, NY MSA

Cincinnati, OH-KY-IN MSA
Previous name: Cincinnati-Middletown, OH-KY-IN MSA
Dearborn, Ohio, and Union Counties, OH; Boone, Bracken, Campbell, Gallatin, Grant, Kenton, and Pendleton County, KY; Brown, Butler, Clermont, Hamilton, and Warren Counties, IN

Cleveland-Elyria, OH MSA
Previous name: Cleveland-Elyria-Mentor, OH MSA
Cuyahoga, Geauga, Lake, Lorain, and Medina Counties

Collierville, TN
See Memphis, TN-MS-AR MSA

Columbus, OH MSA
Delaware, Fairfield, Franklin, Licking, Madison, Morrow, Pickaway, and Union Counties

Coppell, TX
See Dallas, TX (Dallas-Plano-Irving, TX MD)

Cornelius, NC
See Charlotte-Concord-Gastonia, NC-SC MSA

Cranberry, PA
See Pittsburgh, PA MSA

Crown Point, IN
See Chicago, IL (Gary, IN MD)

Dallas, TX

Dallas-Fort Worth-Arlington, TX MSA
Collin, Dallas, Denton, Ellis, Hunt, Johnson, Kaufman, Parker, Rockwall, Tarrant, and Wise Counties

Dallas-Plano-Irving, TX MD
Collin, Dallas, Denton, Ellis, Hunt, Kaufman, and Rockwall Counties

Dayton, OH MSA
Greene, Miami, and Montgomery Counties
Previous name: Dayton, OH MSA
Greene, Miami, Montgomery, and Preble Counties

Denver-Aurora-Lakewood, CO MSA
Previous name: Denver-Aurora-Broomfield, CO MSA
Adams, Arapahoe, Broomfield, Clear Creek, Denver, Douglas, Elbert, Gilpin, Jefferson, and Park Counties

Des Moines-West Des Moines, IA MSA
Dallas, Guthrie, Madison, Polk, and Warren Counties

Detroit, MI

Detroit-Warren-Dearborn, MI MSA
Previous name: Detroit-Warren-Livonia, MI MSA
Lapeer, Livingston, Macomb, Oakland, St. Clair, and Wayne Counties

Detroit-Dearborn-Livonia, MI MD
Previous name: Detroit-Livonia-Dearborn, MI MD
Wayne County

Warren-Troy-Farmington Hills, MI MD
Lapeer, Livingston, Macomb, Oakland, and St. Clair Counties

Dublin, OH
See Columbus, OH MSA

Durham-Chapel Hill, NC MSA
Chatham, Durham, Orange, and and Person Counties

East Fishkill, NY
See New York, NY (Dutchess County-Putnam County, NY MD)

Eden Prairie, MN
See Minneapolis-St. Paul-Bloomington, MN-WI, MSA

Edmond, OK
See Oklahoma City, OK MSA

Edwardsville, IL
See Saint Louis, MO-IL MSA

Evesham, NJ
See Philadelphia, PA (Camden, NJ MD)

Fargo, ND-MN MSA
Cass County, ND; Clay County, MN

Fayetteville-Springdale-Rogers, AR-MO MSA
Benton, Madison, and Washington Counties, AR; McDonald County, MO

Flint, MI MSA
Genesee County

Flower Mound, TX
See Dallas, TX (Dallas-Plano-Irving, TX MD)

Folsom, CA
See Sacramento-Roseville-Arden-Arcade, CA MSA

Fort Collins, CO MSA
Larimer County

Fort Worth, TX

Dallas-Fort Worth-Arlington, TX MSA
Collin, Dallas, Denton, Ellis, Hunt, Johnson, Kaufman, Parker, Rockwall, Tarrant, and Wise Counties

Fort Worth-Arlington, TX MD
Hood, Johnson, Parker, Somervell, Tarrant, and Wise Counties

Friendswood, TX
See Houston-The Woodlands-Sugar Land, TX MSA

Gaines, MI
See Grand Rapids-Wyoming, MI MSA

Glastonbury, CT
See Hartford-West Hartford-East Hartford, CT MSA

Grand Blanc, MI
See Flint, MI MSA

Grand Rapids-Wyoming, MI MSA
Barry, Kent, Montcalm, and Ottawa Counties

Hampden, PA
See Harrisburg-Carlisle, PA MSA

Harrisburg-Carlisle, PA MSA
Cumberland, Dauphin, and Perry Counties

Hartford, CT

Hartford-West Hartford-East Hartford, CT MSA
Hartford, Middlesex, and Tolland Counties

Hartford-West Hartford-East Hartford, CT NECTA
Includes 54 cities and towns in Connecticut
Previous name: Hartford-West Hartford-East Hartford, CT NECTA
Includes 52 cities and towns in Connecticut

Hilliard, OH
See Columbus, OH MSA

Hillsborough, NJ
See New York, NY (Newark, NJ-PA MD)

Holly Springs, NC
See Raleigh, NC MSA

Houston-The Woodlands-Sugar Land-Baytown, TX MSA
Austin, Brazoria, Chambers, Fort Bend, Galveston, Harris, Liberty, Montgomery, and Waller Counties
Previous name: Houston-Sugar Land-Baytown, TX MSA
Austin, Brazoria, Chambers, Fort Bend, Galveston, Harris, Liberty, Montgomery, San Jacinto, and Waller Counties

Huntsville, AL MSA
Limestone and Madison Counties

Independence, KY
See Cincinnati, OH-KY-IN MSA

Indianapolis-Carmel-Anderson, IN MSA
Boone, Brown, Hamilton, Hancock, Hendricks, Johnson, Marion, Morgan, Putnam, and Shelby Counties

Jackson, MS MSA
Copiah, Hinds, Madison, Rankin, Simpson, and Yazoo Counties

Juneau, AK MSA
Juneau City and Borough

Kansas City, MO-KS MSA
Franklin, Johnson, Leavenworth, Linn, Miami, and Wyandotte Counties, KS; Bates, Caldwell, Cass, Clay, Clinton, Jackson, Lafayette, Platte, and Ray Counties, MO

Kaysville, UT
See Ogden-Clearfield, UT MSA

Keller, TX
See Fort Worth, TX (Fort Worth-Arlington, TX MD)

Kennewick-Richland, WA MSA
Previous name: Kennewick-Pasco-Richland, WA MSA
Benton and Franklin Counties

Lafayette, CA
See San Francisco, CA (Oakland-Hayward-Berkeley, CA MD)

Lafayette, CO
See Boulder, CO MSA

Lafayette-West Lafayette, IN MSA
Benton, Carroll, and Tippecanoe Counties

Lake Oswego, OR
See Portland-Vancouver-Hillsboro, OR-WA MSA

Lancaster, PA
Lancaster County

Lansing-East Lansing, MI MSA
Clinton, Eaton, and Ingham Counties

Laramie, WY MSA
Albany County

Leander, TX
See Austin-Round Rock, TX MSA

Leawood, KS
See Kansas City, MO-KS MSA

Lee's Summit, MO
See Kansas City, MO-KS MSA

Leesburg, VA
See Washington, DC (Washington-Arlington-Alexandria, DC-VA-MD-WV MD)

Lehi, UT
See Provo-Orem, UT MSA

Lexington, MA
See Boston, MA (Cambridge-Newton-Framingham, MA MD)

Little Rock-North Little Rock-Conway, AR MSA
Faulkner, Grant, Lonoke, Perry, Pulaski, and Saline Counties

Los Altos, CA
See San Jose-Sunnyvale-Santa Clara, CA MSA

Los Angeles, CA

Los Angeles-Long Beach-Anaheim, CA MSA
Previous name: Los Angeles-Long Beach-Santa Ana, CA MSA
Los Angeles and Orange Counties

Los Angeles-Long Beach-Glendale, CA MD
Los Angeles County

Anaheim-Santa Ana-Irvine, CA MD
Previous name: Santa Ana-Anaheim-Irvine, CA MD
Orange County

Loveland, CO
See Fort Collins, CO MSA

Lower Macungie, PA
See Allentown-Bethlehem-Easton, PA-NJ MSA

Madison, AL
See Huntsville, AL MSA

Madison, MS
See Jackson, MS MSA

Madison, WI MSA
Columbia, Dane, and Iowa Counties

Manchester, NH

Manchester-Nashua, NH MSA
Hillsborough County

Manchester, NH NECTA
Includes 11 cities and towns in New Hampshire
Previous name: Manchester, NH NECTA
Includes 9 cities and towns in New Hampshire

Maple Valley, WA
See Seattle, WA (Seattle-Bellevue-Everett, WA MD)

Marion, IA
See Cedar Rapids, IA MSA

Marlboro, NJ
See New York, NY (New York-Jersey City-White Plains, NY-NJ MD)

Mason, OH
See Cincinnati, OH-KY-IN MSA

Memphis, TN-MS-AR MSA
Crittenden County, AR; Benton, DeSoto, Marshall, Tate, and Tunica Counties, MS; Fayette, Shelby, and Tipton Counties, TN
Previous name: Memphis, TN-MS-AR MSA
Crittenden County, AR; DeSoto, Marshall, Tate, and Tunica Counties, MS; Fayette, Shelby, and Tipton Counties, TN

Menomonee Falls, WI
See Milwaukee-Waukesha-West Allis, WI MSA

Meridian, ID
See Boise City, ID MSA

Meridian, MI
See Lansing-East Lansing, MI MSA

Merrimack, NH
See Manchester-Nashua, NH MSA

Miami, FL

Miami-Fort Lauderdale-West Palm Beach, FL MSA
Previous name: Miami-Fort Lauderdale-Pompano Beach, FL MSA
Broward, Miami-Dade, and Palm Beach Counties

Fort Lauderdale-Pompano Beach-Deerfield Beach, FL MD
Broward County

Miami-Miami Beach-Kendall, FL MD
Miami-Dade County

Milwaukee-Waukesha-West Allis, WI MSA
Milwaukee, Ozaukee, Washington, and Waukesha Counties

Milton, GA
See Atlanta-Sandy Springs-Roswell, GA MSA

Minneapolis-St. Paul-Bloomington, MN-WI MSA
Anoka, Carver, Chisago, Dakota, Hennepin, Isanti, Le Sueur, Mille Lacs, Ramsey, Scott, Sherburne, Sibley, Washington, and Wright Counties, MN; Pierce and St. Croix Counties, WI

Moon, PA
See Pittsburgh, PA MSA

Moorpark, CA
See Oxnard-Thousand Oaks-Ventura, CA MSA

Morgantown, WV MSA
Monongalia and Preston Counties

Mount Pleasant, SC
See Charleston-North Charleston, SC MSA

Nashville-Davidson-Murfreesboro-Franklin, TN MSA
Cannon, Cheatham, Davidson, Dickson, Hickman, Macon, Robertson, Rutherford, Smith, Sumner, Trousdale, Williamson, and Wilson Counties

New Haven, CT

New Haven-Milford, CT MSA
New Haven County

New Haven, CT NECTA
Includes 23 cities and towns in Connecticut
Previous name: New Haven, CT NECTA
Includes 22 cities and towns in Connecticut

New York, NY

New York-Newark-Jersey City, NY-NJ-PA MSA
Bergen, Essex, Hudson, Hunterdon, Middlesex, Monmouth, Morris, Ocean, Passaic, Somerset, Sussex, and Union Counties, NJ; Bronx, Dutchess, Kings, Nassau, New York, Orange, Putnam, Queens, Richmond, Rockland, Suffolk, and Westchester Counties, NY; Pike County, PA
Previous name: New York-Northern New Jersey-Long Island, NY-NJ-PA MSA
Bergen, Essex, Hudson, Hunterdon, Middlesex, Monmouth, Morris, Ocean, Passaic, Somerset, Sussex, and Union Counties, NJ; Bronx, Kings, Nassau, New York, Putnam, Queens, Richmond, Rockland, Suffolk, and Westchester Counties, NY; Pike County, PA

Dutchess County-Putnam County, NY MD
Dutchess and Putnam Counties
Dutchess County was previously part of the Poughkeepsie-Newburgh-Middletown, NY MSA. Putnam County was previously part of the New York-Wayne-White Plains, NY-NJ MD

Nassau-Suffolk, NY MD
Nassau and Suffolk Counties

New York-Jersey City-White Plains, NY-NJ MD
Bergen, Hudson, Middlesex, Monmouth, Ocean, and Passaic Counties, NJ; Bronx, Kings, New York, Orange, Queens, Richmond, Rockland, and Westchester Counties, NY
Previous name: New York-Wayne-White Plains, NY-NJ MD
Bergen, Hudson, and Passaic Counties, NJ; Bronx, Kings, New York, Putnam, Queens, Richmond, Rockland, and Westchester Counties, NY

Newark, NJ-PA MD
Essex, Hunterdon, Morris, Somerset, Sussex, and Union Counties, NJ; Pike County, PA
Previous name: Newark-Union, NJ-PA MD
Essex, Hunterdon, Morris, Sussex, and Union Counties, NJ; Pike County, PA

Newark, DE
See Philadelphia, PA (Wilmington, DE-MD-NJ MD)

Newtown, CT
See Bridgeport, CT

North Attleborough, MA
See Providence, RI (Providence-Warwick, RI-MA NECTA)

North Port, FL
See North Port-Sarasota-Bradenton, FL MSA

North Port-Sarasota-Bradenton, FL MSA
Manatee and Sarasota Counties

North Ridgeville, OH
See Cleveland-Elyria, OH MSA

Northville, MI
See Detroit, MI (Detroit-Dearborn-Livonia, MI MD)

O'Fallon, MO
See St. Louis, MO-IL MSA

Ogden-Clearfield, UT MSA
Box Elder, Davis, Morgan, and Weber Counties
Previous name: Ogden-Clearfield, UT MSA
Davis, Morgan, and Weber Counties

Oklahoma City, OK MSA
Canadian, Cleveland, Grady, Lincoln, Logan, McClain, and Oklahoma Counties

Omaha-Council Bluffs, NE-IA MSA
Harrison, Mills, and Pottawattamie Counties, IA; Cass, Douglas, Sarpy, Saunders, and Washington Counties, NE

Orchard Park, NY
See Buffalo-Cheektowaga-Niagara Falls, NY MSA

Orlando-Kissimmee-Sanford, FL MSA
Lake, Orange, Osceola, and Seminole Counties

Oro Valley, AZ
See Tucson, AZ MSA

Oviedo, FL
See Orlando-Kissimmee-Sanford, FL MSA

Oxnard-Thousand Oaks-Ventura, CA MSA
Ventura County

Parker, CO
See Denver-Aurora-Lakewood, CO MSA

Parkland, FL
See Miami, FL (Fort Lauderdale-Pompano Beach-Deerfield Beach, FL MD)

Peachtree City, GA
See Atlanta-Sandy Springs-Roswell, GA MSA

Philadelphia, PA

Philadelphia-Camden-Wilmington, PA-NJ-DE-MD MSA
New Castle County, DE; Cecil County, MD; Burlington, Camden, Gloucester, and Salem Counties, NJ; Bucks, Chester, Delaware, Montgomery, and Philadelphia Counties, PA

Camden, NJ MD
Burlington, Camden, and Gloucester Counties

Montgomery County-Bucks County-Chester County, PA MD
Bucks, Chester, and Montgomery Counties
Previously part of the Philadelphia, PA MD

Philadelphia, PA MD
Delaware and Philadelphia Counties
Previous name: Philadelphia, PA MD
Bucks, Chester, Delaware, Montgomery, and Philadelphia Counties

Wilmington, DE-MD-NJ MD
New Castle County, DE; Cecil County, MD; Salem County, NJ

Pittsburgh, PA MSA
Allegheny, Armstrong, Beaver, Butler, Fayette, Washington, and Westmoreland Counties

Pittsfield, MI
See Ann Arbor, MI MSA

Plainfield, IL
See Chicago, IL (Chicago-Naperville-Arlington Heights, IL MD)

Pleasant Grove, UT
See Provo-Orem, UT MSA

Portland, ME

Portland-South Portland, ME MSA
Cumberland, Sagadahoc, and York Counties

Portland-South Portland, ME NECTA
Includes 39 towns and cities in Maine

Portland-Vancouver-Hillsboro, OR-WA MSA
Clackamas, Columbia, Multnomah, Washington, and Yamhill Counties, OR; Clark and Skamania Counties, WA

Poway, CA
See San Diego-Carlsbad, CA MSA

Princeton, NJ
See Trenton, NJ MSA

Providence, RI

Providence-Warwick, RI-MA MSA
Previous name: Providence-New Bedford-Fall River, RI-MA MSA
Bristol County, MA; Bristol, Kent, Newport, Providence, and Washington Counties, RI

Providence-Warwick, RI-MA NECTA
Includes 12 cities and towns in Massachusetts and 36 cities and towns in Rhode Island
Previous name: Providence-Fall River-Warwick, RI-MA NECTA
Includes 12 cities and towns in Massachusetts and 37 cities and towns in Rhode Island

Provo-Orem, UT MSA
Juab and Utah Counties

Queen Creek, AZ
See Phoenix-Mesa-Scottsdale, AZ MSA

Radnor, PA
See Philadelphia, PA (Philadelphia, PA MD)

Raleigh, NC MSA
Previous name: Raleigh-Cary, NC MSA
Franklin, Johnston, and Wake Counties

Randolph, NJ
See New York, NY (Newark, NJ-PA MD)

Reno, NV MSA
Storey and Washoe Counties

Rexburg, ID MSA
Fremont and Madison Counties

Rio Rancho, NM
See Albuquerque, NM MSA

Rochester, NY MSA
Livingston, Monroe, Ontario, Orleans, Wayne, and Yates Counties
Previous name: Rochester, NY MSA
Livingston, Monroe, Ontario, Orleans, and Wayne Counties

Rye, NY
See New York, NY (New York-Jersey City-White Plains, NY-NJ MD)

Sacramento-Roseville-Arden- Arcade, CA MSA
El Dorado, Placer, Sacramento, and Yolo Counties
Previous name: Sacramento-Arden-Arcade - Roseville, CA MSA
El Dorado, Placer, Sacramento, and Yolo Counties

Saint Louis, MO-IL MSA
Bond, Calhoun, Clinton, Jersey, Macoupin, Madison, Monroe, Saint Clair Counties, IL; Franklin, Jefferson, Lincoln, Saint Charles, Saint Louis, and Warren Counties, MO; Saint Louis city, MO
Previous name: Saint Louis, MO-IL MSA
Bond, Calhoun, Clinton, Jersey, Macoupin, Madison, Monroe, Saint Clair Counties, IL; Franklin, Jefferson, Lincoln, Saint Charles, Saint Louis, Warren, and Washington Counties, MO; Saint Louis city, MO

Salt Lake City, UT MSA
Salt Lake and Tooele Counties

Sammamish, WA
See Seattle, WA (Seattle-Bellevue-Everett, WA MD)

San Antonio-New Braunfels, TX MSA
Atascosa, Bandera, Bexar, Comal, Guadalupe, Kendall, Medina, and Wilson Counties

San Francisco, CA

San Francisco-Oakland-Hayward, CA MSA
Previous name: San Francisco-Oakland-Fremont, CA MSA
Alameda, Contra Costa, Marin, San Francisco, and San Mateo Counties

Oakland-Hayward-Berkeley, CA MD
Previous name: Oakland-Fremont-Hayward, CA MD
Alameda and Contra Costa Counties

San Francisco-Redwood City-South San Francisco, CA MD
San Francisco and San Mateo Counties
Previous name: San Francisco-San Mateo-Redwood City, CA MD
Marin, San Francisco, and San Mateo Counties

San Jose-Sunnyvale-Santa Clara, CA MSA
San Benito and Santa Clara Counties

San Ramon, CA
See San Francisco, CA (Oakland-Hayward-Berkeley, CA MD)

Saratoga, CA
See San Jose-Sunnyvale-Santa Clara, CA MSA

Seattle, WA

Seattle-Tacoma-Bellevue, WA MSA
King, Pierce, and Snohomish Counties

Seattle-Bellevue-Everett, WA MD
King and Snohomish Counties

Shrewsbury, MA
See Worcester, MA-CT MSA

South Brunswick, NJ
See New York, NY (New York-Jersey City-White Plains, NY-NJ MD)

South Jordan, UT
See Salt Lake City, UT MSA

South Kingstown, RI
See Providence-Warwick, RI-MA MSA

South Portland, ME
See Portland, ME

Sparks, NV
See Reno, NV MSA

Springfield, MA

Springfield, MA MSA
Hampden and Hampshire Counties

Springfield, MA-CT NECTA
Includes 47 cities and towns in Massachusetts and 5 towns in Connecticut

State College, PA MSA
Centre County

Sugar Land, TX
See Houston-The Woodlands-Sugar Land, TX MSA

Sun Prairie, WI
See Madison, WI MSA

Syracuse, NY MSA
Madison, Onondaga, and Oswego Counties

Syracuse, UT
See Ogden-Clearfield, UT MSA

Tredyffrin, PA
See Philadelphia, PA (Montgomery County-Bucks County-Chester County, PA MD)

Trenton, NJ MSA
Previous name: Trenton-Ewing, NJ MSA
Mercer County

Tucson, AZ MSA
Pima County

Upper Dublin, PA
See Philadelphia, PA (Montgomery County-Bucks County-Chester County, PA MD)

Urbandale, IA
See Des Moines-West Des Moines, IA MSA

Vallejo-Fairfield, CA MSA
Solano County

Vestal, NY
See Binghamton, NY MSA

Vestavia Hills, AL
See Birmingham-Hoover, AL MSA

Washington, DC

Washington-Arlington-Alexandria, DC-VA-MD-WV MSA
District of Columbia; Calvert, Charles, Frederick, Montgomery, and Prince George's Counties, MD; Alexandria, Fairfax, Falls Church, Fredericksburg, Manassas Park, and Manassas cities, VA; Arlington, Clarke, Culpepper, Fairfax, Fauquier, Loudoun, Prince William, Rappahannock, Spotsylvania, Stafford, and Warren Counties, VA; Jefferson County, WV
Previous name: Washington-Arlington-Alexandria, DC-VA-MD-WV MSA
District of Columbia; Calvert, Charles, Frederick, Montgomery, and Prince George's Counties, MD; Alexandria, Fairfax, Falls Church, Fredericksburg, Manassas Park, and Manassas cities, VA; Arlington, Clarke, Fairfax, Fauquier, Loudoun, Prince William, Spotsylvania, Stafford, and Warren Counties, VA; Jefferson County, WV

Washington-Arlington-Alexandria, DC-VA-MD-WV MD
District of Columbia; Calvert, Charles, and Prince George's Counties, MD; Alexandria, Fairfax, Falls Church, Fredericksburg, Manassas Park, and Manassas cities, VA; Arlington, Clarke, Culpepper, Fairfax, Fauquier, Loudoun, Prince William, Rappahannock, Spotsylvania, Stafford, and Warren Counties, VA; Jefferson County, WV
Previous name: Washington-Arlington-Alexandria, DC-VA-MD-WV MD
District of Columbia; Calvert, Charles, and Prince George's Counties, MD; Alexandria, Fairfax, Falls Church, Fredericksburg, Manassas Park, and Manassas cities, VA; Arlington, Clarke, Fairfax, Fauquier, Loudoun, Prince William, Spotsylvania, Stafford, and Warren Counties, VA; Jefferson County, WV

Waterloo-Cedar Falls, IA MSA
Black Hawk, Bremer, and Grundy Counties

Webster, NY
See Rochester, NY MSA

Wellesley, MA
See Boston, MA (Boston, MA MD)

West Fargo, ND
See Fargo, ND-MN MSA

West Lafayette, IN
See Lafayette-West Lafayette, IN MSA

Weston, FL
See Miami, FL (Fort Lauderdale-Pompano Beach-Deerfield Beach, FL MD)

Wilmette, IL
See Chicago, IL (Chicago-Naperville-Arlington Heights, IL MD)

Worcester, MA

Worcester, MA-CT MSA
Windham County, CT; Worcester County, MA
Previous name: Worcester, MA MSA
Worcester County

Worcester, MA-CT NECTA
Includes 40 cities and towns in Massachusetts and 8 cities and towns in Connecticut
Previous name: Worcester, MA-CT NECTA
Includes 37 cities and towns in Massachusetts and 3 cities and towns in Connecticut

Yorba Linda, CA
See Los Angeles, CA (Anaheim-Santa Ana-Irvine, CA MD)

Zionsville, IN
See Indianapolis-Carmel-Anderson, IN MSA

Appendix C: Government Type & Primary County

This appendix includes the government structure of each place included in this book. It also includes the county or county equivalent in which each place is located. If a place spans more that one county, the county in which the majority of the population resides is shown.

Aberdeen, SD
Government Type: City
County: Brown

Aliso Viejo, CA
Government Type: City
County: Orange

Allen, TX
Government Type: City
County: Collin

Ames, IA
Government Type: City
County: Story

Amherst, MA
Government Type: Town
County: Hampshire

Apex, NC
Government Type: Town
County: Wake

Beavercreek, OH
Government Type: City
County: Greene

Bellevue, NE
Government Type: City
County: Sarpy

Bend, OR
Government Type: City
County: Deschutes

Benicia, CA
Government Type: City
County: Solano

Bentonville, AR
Government Type: City
County: Benton

Bethlehem, NY
Government Type: Town
County: Albany

Blacksburg, VA
Government Type: Town
County: Montgomery

Bowie, MD
Government Type: City
County: Prince George's

Bozeman, MT
Government Type: City
County: Gallatin

Brentwood, TN
Government Type: City
County: Williamson

Burlington, VT
Government Type: City
County: Chittenden

Cabot, AR
Government Type: City
County: Lonoke

Carmel, IN
Government Type: City
County: Hamilton

Cedar Falls, IA
Government Type: City
County: Black Hawk

Cedar Park, TX
Government Type: City
County: Williamson

Central, LA
Government Type: City
Parish: East Baton Rouge

Chapel Hill, NC
Government Type: Town
County: Orange

Cheshire, CT
Government Type: Town
County: New Haven

Chino Hills, CA
Government Type: City
County: San Bernardino

Cibolo, TX
Government Type: City
County: Guadalupe

Cicero, NY
Government Type: Town
County: Onondaga

Collierville, TN
Government Type: Town
County: Shelby

Coppell, TX
Government Type: City
County: Dallas

Cornelius, NC
Government Type: Town
County: Mecklenburg

Cranberry, PA
Government Type: Township
County: Butler

Crown Point, IN
Government Type: City
County: Lake

Dublin, OH
Government Type: City
County: Franklin

East Fishkill, NY
Government Type: Town
County: Dutchess

Eden Prairie, MN
Government Type: City
County: Hennepin

Edmond, OK
Government Type: City
County: Oklahoma

Edwardsville, IL
Government Type: City
County: Madison

Evesham, NJ
Government Type: Township
County: Burlington

Flower Mound, TX
Government Type: Town
County: Denton

Folsom, CA
Government Type: City
County: Sacramento

Friendswood, TX
Government Type: City
County: Galveston

Gaines, MI
Government Type: Township
County: Kent

Glastonbury, CT
Government Type: Town
County: Hartford

Grand Blanc, MI
Government Type: Township
County: Genesee

Hampden, PA
Government Type: Township
County: Cumberland

Hilliard, OH
Government Type: City
County: Franklin

Hillsborough, NJ
Government Type: Township
County: Somerset

Holly Springs, NC
Government Type: Town
County: Wake

Independence, KY
Government Type: City
County: Kenton

Juneau, AK
Government Type: City and Borough
Borough: Juneau

Kaysville, UT
Government Type: City
County: Davis

Keller, TX
Government Type: City
County: Tarrant

Lafayette, CA
Government Type: City
County: Contra Costa

Lafayette, CO
Government Type: City
County: Boulder

Lake Oswego, OR
Government Type: City
County: Clackamas

Laramie, WY
Government Type: City
County: Albany

Leander, TX
Government Type: City
County: Williamson

Leawood, KS
Government Type: City
County: Johnson

Lee's Summit, MO
Government Type: City
County: Jackson

Leesburg, VA
Government Type: Town
County: Loudoun

Lehi, UT
Government Type: City
County: Utah

Lexington, MA
Government Type: Town
County: Middlesex

Los Altos, CA
Government Type: City
County: Santa Clara

Loveland, CO
Government Type: City
County: Larimer

Lower Macungie, PA
Government Type: Township
County: Lehigh

Madison, AL
Government Type: City
County: Madison

Madison, MS
Government Type: City
County: Madison

Maple Valley, WA
Government Type: City
County: King

Marion, IA
Government Type: City
County: Linn

Marlboro, NJ
Government Type: Township
County: Monmouth

Mason, OH
Government Type: City
County: Warren

Menomonee Falls, WI
Government Type: Village
County: Waukesha

Meridian, ID
Government Type: City
County: Ada

Meridian, MI
Government Type: Township
County: Ingham

Merrimack, NH
Government Type: Town
County: Hillsborough

Milton, GA
Government Type: City
County: Fulton

Moon, PA
Government Type: Township
County: Allegheny

Moorpark, CA
Government Type: City
County: Ventura

Morgantown, WV
Government Type: City
County: Monongalia

Mount Pleasant, SC
Government Type: Town
County: Charleston

Newark, DE
Government Type: City
County: New Castle

Newtown, CT
Government Type: Town
County: Fairfield

North Attleborough, MA
Government Type: Town
County: Bristol

North Port, FL
Government Type: City
County: Sarasota

North Ridgeville, OH
Government Type: City
County: Lorain

Northville, MI
Government Type: Township
County: Wayne

O'Fallon, MO
Government Type: City
County: Saint Charles

Orchard Park, NY
Government Type: Town
County: Erie

Oro Valley, AZ
Government Type: Town
County: Pima

Oviedo, FL
Government Type: City
County: Seminole

Parker, CO
Government Type: Town
County: Douglas

Parkland, FL
Government Type: City
County: Broward

Peachtree City, GA
Government Type: City
County: Fayette

Pittsfield, MI
Government Type: Township
County: Washtenaw

Plainfield, IL
Government Type: Village
County: Will

Pleasant Grove, UT
Government Type: City
County: Utah

Poway, CA
Government Type: City
County: San Diego

Princeton, NJ
Government Type: Municipality
County: Mercer

Queen Creek, AZ
Government Type: Town
County: Maricopa

Radnor, PA
Government Type: Township
County: Delaware

Randolph, NJ
Government Type: Township
County: Morris

Rexburg, ID
Government Type: City
County: Madison

Rio Rancho, NM
Government Type: City
County: Sandoval

Rye, NY
Government Type: Town
County: Westchester

Sammamish, WA
Government Type: City
County: King

San Ramon, CA
Government Type: City
County: Contra Costa

Saratoga, CA
Government Type: City
County: Santa Clara

Shrewsbury, MA
Government Type: Town
County: Worcester

South Brunswick, NJ
Government Type: Township
County: Middlesex

South Jordan, UT
Government Type: City
County: Salt Lake

South Kingstown, RI
Government Type: Town
County: Washington

South Portland, ME
Government Type: City
County: Cumberland

Sparks, NV
Government Type: City
County: Washoe

State College, PA
Government Type: Borough
County: Centre

Sugar Land, TX
Government Type: City
County: Fort Bend

Sun Prairie, WI
Government Type: City
County: Dane

Syracuse, UT
Government Type: City
County: Davis

Tredyffrin, PA
Government Type: Township
County: Chester

Upper Dublin, PA
Government Type: Township
County: Montgomery

Urbandale, IA
Government Type: City
County: Polk

Vestal, NY
Government Type: Town
County: Broome

Vestavia Hills, AL
Government Type: City
County: Jefferson

Webster, NY
Government Type: Town
County: Monroe

Wellesley, MA
Government Type: Town
County: Norfolk

West Fargo, ND
Government Type: City
County: Cass

West Lafayette, IN
Government Type: City
County: Tippecanoe

Weston, FL
Government Type: City
County: Broward

Wilmette, IL
Government Type: Village
County: Cook

Yorba Linda, CA
Government Type: City
County: Orange

Zionsville, IN
Government Type: Town
County: Boone

Appendix D: Chambers of Commerce

Aberdeen, SD
Aberdeen Area Chamber of Commerce
516 South Main Street
PO Box 1179
Aberdeen, SD 57402
Phone: 605-225-2860
Fax: 605-225-2437
http://www.aberdeen-chamber.com

Aliso Viejo, CA
Alisa Viejo Chamber of Commerce
12 Journey
Suite 100
Alisa Viejo, CA 92656-5335
Phone: 949-243-7042
http://alisoviejochamber.com

Allen, TX
Allen Chamber of Commerce
210 West McDermott Drive
Allen, TX 75013
Phone: 972-727-5585
Fax: 972-727-9000
http://www.allenfairviewchamber.com

Ames, IA
Ames Chamber of Commerce
304 Main Street
Ames, IA 50010
Phone: 515-232-2310
Fax: 515-233-3203
https://www.ameschamber.com

Amherst, MA
Amherst Chamber of Commerce
35 South Pleasant Street
Amherst, MA 01002
Phone: 413-253-0700
https://www.amherstarea.com

Apex, NC
Apex Chamber of Commerce
220 North Salem Street
Apex, NC 27502
Phone: 919-362-6456
Fax: 919-362-9050
http://www.apexchamber.com/

Beavercreek, OH
Beavercreek Chamber of Commerce
3210 Beaver-Vu Drive
Beavercreek, OH 45434
Phone: 937-426-2202
Fax: 937-426-2204
http://www.beavercreekchamber.org

Bellevue, NE
Greater Bellevue Area Chamber of Commerce
1102 Gavin Road South
Bellevue, NE 68005
Phone: 402-898-3000
Fax: 402-291-8729
https://www.bellevuenebraska.com

Bend, OR
Bend Chamber of Commerce
777 Northwest Wall Street
Suite 200
Bend, OR 97701
Phone: 541-382-3221
Fax: 541-385-9929
https://bendchamber.org

Benicia, CA
Benicia Chamber of Commerce
601 First Street
Suite 100
Benicia, CA 94510
Phone: 707-745-2120
http://www.beniciachamber.com

Bentonville, AR
Bentonville-Bella Vista Chamber of Commerce
412 South Main
Bentonville, AR 72712
Phone: 479-273-2841
Fax: 497-273-2180
http://www.bentonvillebellavistachamber.com

Bethlehem, NY
Bethlehem Chamber of Commerce
318 Delaware Avenue
Suite 11
Delmar, NY 12054
Phone: 518-439-0512
Fax: 518-475-0910
http://www.bethlehemchamber.com

Blacksburg, VA
Montgomery County Chamber of Commerce
103 Professional Park Drive
Blacksburg, VA 24060
Phone: 540-552-2636
Fax: 540-552-2639
http://www.montgomerycountychamber.org

Bowie, MD
Greater Bowie Chamber of Commerce
2614 Kenhill Drive
Suite 117
Bowie, MD 20715
Phone: 301-262-0920
Fax: 304-262-0921
http://www.bowiechamber.org

Bozeman, MT
Bozeman Chamber of Commerce
2000 Commerce Way
Bozeman, MT 59715
Phone: 406-586-5421
Fax: 406-586-8286
http://bozemanchamber.com

Brentwood, TN
Wlliamson, Inc.
5005 Meridian Boulevard
Franklin, TN 37067
Phone: 615-771-1912
http://www.williamsonchamber.com

Burlington, VT
Lake Champlain Regional Chamber of Commerce
60 Main Street
Suite 100
Burlington, VT 05401
Phone: 802-863-3489
Fax: 802-863-1538
http://www.vermont.org

Cabot, AR
Cabot Chamber of Commerce
110 S. 1st Street.
Cabot, AR 72023
Phone: 501-843-2136
Fax: 501-843-1861
http://www.cabotcc.org

Carmel, IN
OneZone - Carmel and Fishers Chambers of Commerce
10305 Allisonville Road
Suite B
Fishers, IN 46038
Phone: 317-436-4653
http://www.onezonecommerce.com

Cedar Falls, IA
Greater Cedar Valley Alliance & Chamber
360 Westfield Ave
Suite 200
Waterloo, IA 50701
Phone: 319-266-3593
Fax: 319-233-4580
https://www.cedarvalleyalliance.com

Cedar Park, TX
Cedar Park Chamber of Commerce
1460 E. Whitestone Blvd.
Suite 180
Cedar Park, TX 78630
Phone: 512-260-7800
Fax: 512-260-9269
http://www.cedarparkchamber.org

Central, LA
Central Louisiana Regional Chamber of Commerce
1118 Third Street
Alexandria, LA 71301
Phone: 318-442-6671
http://www.cenlachamber.org

Chapel Hill, NC
Chapel Hill-Carrboro Chamber of Commerce
104 S. Estes Drive
P.O. Box 2897
Chapel Hill, NC 27515
Phone: 919-967-7075
Fax: 919-968-6874
https://www.carolinachamber.org

Cheshire, CT
Cheshire Chamber of Commerce
195 South Main Street
Cheshire, CT 06410
Phone: 203-272-2345
Fax: 203-271-3044
http://www.cheshirechamber.org

Chino Hills, CA
Chino Valley Chamber of Commerce
13150 Seventh Street
Chino Hills, CA 91710
Phone: 909-627-6177
Fax: 909-627-4180
https://www.chinohills.org

Cibolo, TX
The Chamber (Schertz-Cibolo-Selma Area)
1730 Schertz Parkway
Schertz, TX 78154
Phone: 210-619-1950
Fax: 210-619-1959
https://www.thechamber.info

Cicero, NY
Greater Cicero Chamber of Commerce
5701 East Circle Dr.
Suite 302
Cicero, NY 13039
Phone: 315-699-1358
https://www.cicerochamber.com

Collierville, TN
Collierville Chamber of Commerce
485 Halle Park Drive
Collierville, TN 38017
Phone: 901-853-1949
Fax: 901-853-2399
http://www.colliervillechamber.com

Coppell, TX
Coppell Chamber of Commerce
708 Main St
Coppell, TX 75019
Phone: 972-393-2829
Fax: 972-393-0659
http://coppellchamber.org

Cornelius, NC
Lake Norman Chamber of Commerce
19900 W. Catawba Ave
Cornelius, NC 28031
Phone: 704-892-1922
Fax: 704-892-5313
https://www.lakenormanchamber.org

Cranberry, PA
Pittsburgh North Regional Chamber - Cranberry Twp Satellite Office
2525 Rochester Road
Suite 200
Cranberry Twp, PA 16066
Phone: 724-934-9700
http://www.pghnorthchamber.com

Crown Point, IN
Crossroads Regional Chamber of Commerce
440 West 84th Drive
Merrillville, IN 46410
Phone: 219-769-8180
Fax: 219-736-6223
https://www.crossroadschamber.org

Dublin, OH
Dublin Chamber of Commerce
129 South High Street
Dublin, OH 43017
Phone: 614-889-2001
Fax: 614-889-2888
http://www.dublinchamber.org

East Fishkill, NY
Dutchess County Regional Chamber of Commerce
One Civic Center Plaza
Suite 400
Poughkeepsie, NY 12601
Phone: 845-454-1700
Fax: 845-454-1702
https://www.dcrcoc.org

Eden Prairie, MN
Eden Prairie Chamber of Commerce
11455 Viking Drive
Suite 270
Eden Prairie, MN 55344
Phone: 952-944-2830
Fax: 952-944-0229
http://epchamber.org

Edmond, OK
Edmond Area Chamber of Commerce
825 East 2nd Street
Suite 100
Edmond, OK 73003
Phone: 405-341-2808
Fax: 405-340-5512
http://www.edmondchamber.com

Edwardsville, IL
Edwardsville-Glen Carbon Chamber of Commerce
1 North Research Drive
Edwardsville, IL 62025
Phone: 618-656-7600
Fax: 618-656-7611
https://www.edglenchamber.com

Evesham, NJ
Burlington County Regional Chamber of Commerce
520 Fellowship Road
Suite E502
Mount Laurel, NJ 08054
Phone: 856-439-2520
Fax: 856-439-2523
http://www.bcrcc.com

Flower Mound, TX
Flower Mound Chamber of Commerce
700 Parker Square
Suite 100
Flower Mound, TX 75028
Phone: 972-539-0500
Fax: 972-539-4307
http://www.flowermoundchamber.com

Folsom, CA
Folsom Chamber of Commerce
200 Wool Street
Folsom, CA 95630
Phone: 916-985-2698
http://www.folsomchamber.com

Friendswood, TX
Friendswood Chamber of Commerce
1100 South Friendswood Drive
Friendswood, TX 77546
Phone: 281-482-3329
Fax: 281-482-3911
http://www.friendswoodchamber.com

Gaines, MI
Cutlerville-Gaines Area Chamber of Commerce
8561 Kalamazoo Ave SE
Caledonia, MI 49316
Phone: 616-890-1378
http://www.cutlerville-gaineschamber.org

Glastonbury, CT
CT River Valley Chamber of Commerce
2400 Main Street
Suite 2
Glastonbury, CT 06033
Phone: 860-659-3587
Fax: 860-659-0102
http://www.crvchamber.org

Grand Blanc, MI
Grand Blanc Chamber of Commerce
512 E. Grand Blanc Rd.
Grand Blanc, MI 48439
Phone: 810-695-4222
http://grandblancchamber.com

Hampden, PA
West Shore Chamber of Commerce
4211 Trindle Road
Camp Hill, PA 17011
Phone: 717-761-0702
Fax: 717-761-4315
https://www.wschamber.org

Hilliard, OH
Hilliard Area Chamber of Commerce
4081 Main Street
Hilliard, OH 43026
Phone: 614-876-7666
Fax: 614-876-3113
http://www.hilliardchamber.org

Hillsborough, NJ
Somerset County Business Partnership
360 Grove Street
Bridgewater, NJ 08807
Phone: 908-218-4300
Fax: 908-722-7823
http://www.scbp.org

Holly Springs, NC
Holly Springs Chamber of Commerce
344 Raleigh Street
Suite 100
Holly Springs, NC 27540
Phone: 919-567-1796
Fax: 919-567-1380
http://www.hollyspringschamber.org

Independence, KY
Northern Kentucky Chamber of Commerce
300 Buttermilk Pike
Suite 330
Fort Mitchell, KY 17416
Phone: 859-578-8800
Fax: 859-578-8802
http://www.nkychamber.com

Juneau, AK
Juneau Chamber of Commerce
9301 Glacier Hwy
Suite 110
Juneau, AK 99801
Phone: 907-463-3488
Fax: 907-463-3483
http://www.juneauchamber.com

Kaysville, UT
Davis Chamber of Commerce
450 S. Simmons Way
Suite 220
Kaysville, UT 84037
Phone: 801-593-2200
Fax: 801-593-2212
https://davischamberofcommerce.com

Keller, TX
Greater Keller Chamber of Commerce
420 Johnson Road
Keller, TX 76248
Phone: 817-431-2169
Fax: 817-431-3789
http://www.kellerchamber.com

Lafayette, CA
Lafayette Chamber of Commerce
251 Lafayette Circle
Suite 150
Lafayette, CA 94549
Phone: 925-284-7404
http://www.lafayettechamber.org

Lafayette, CO
Lafayette Chamber
1290 S. Public Road
Lafayette, CO 80026
Phone: 303-666-9555
Fax: 303-666-4392
http://www.lafayettecolorado.com

Lake Oswego, OR
Lake Oswego Chamber of Commerce
459 3rd Street
Lake Oswego, OR 97034
Phone: 503-636-3634
Fax: 503-636-7427
http://www.lake-oswego.com

Laramie, WY
Laramie Chamber Business Alliance
800 S. 3rd Street
Laramie, WY 82070
Phone: 307-745-7339
Fax: 307-745-4624
https://laramie.org

Leander, TX
Leander Chamber of Commerce
100 North Brushy
Leander, TX 78641
Phone: 512-259-1907
http://www.leandercc.org

Leawood, KS
Leawood Chamber of Commerce
13451 Briar
Suite 201
Leawood, KS 66209
Phone: 913-498-1514
Fax: 913-491-0134
http://www.leawoodchamber.org

Lee's Summit, MO
Lee's Summit Chamber of Commerce
220 SE Main Street
Lee's Summit, MO 64063-2332
Phone: 816-524-2424
Fax: 816-524-5246
http://www.lschamber.com

Leesburg, VA
Loudoun County Chamber of Commerce
19301 Winmeade Drive
Suite 210
Lansdowne, VA 20176
Phone: 703-777-2176
Fax: 703-777-1392
http://www.loudounchamber.org

Lehi, UT
Lehi Area Chamber of Commerce
235 East State Street
Lehi, UT 84043
Phone: 801-901-6664
http://lehiareachamber.com

Lexington, MA
Lexington Chamber of Commerce
1875 Massachusetts Avenue
Lexington, MA 02420
Phone: 781-862-2480
Fax: 781-862-1450
http://www.lexingtonchamber.org

Los Altos, CA
Los Altos Chamber of Commerce
321 University Avenue
Los Altos, CA 94022
Phone: 650-948-1455
Fax: 650-948-6238
http://losaltoschamber.org

Loveland, CO
Loveland Chamber of Commerce
5400 Stone Creek Circle
Loveland, CO 80538
Phone: 970-667-6311
http://www.loveland.org

Lower Macungie, PA
Greater Lehigh Valley Chamber of Commerce
840 Hamilton Street
Siote 205
Allentown, PA 18101
Phone: 610-739-1513
http://www.lehighvalleychamber.org

Madison, AL
Madison Chamber of Commerce
130 Park Square Lane
Madison, AL 35758
Phone: 256-325-8317
Fax: 256-461-0840
http://www.madisonalchamber.com

Madison, MS
Madison The City Chamber of Commerce
2023 Main Street
Madison, MS 39110
Phone: 601-856-7060
http://www.madisonthecitychamber.com

Maple Valley, WA
Maple Valley Black Diamond Chamber
23745 225 Way SE
Suite 205
Maple Valley, WA 98038
Phone: 425-432-0222
http://www.maplevalleychamber.org

Marion, IA
Cedar Rapids Metro Economic Alliance
501 First St. SE
Cedar Rapids, IA 52401
Phone: 319-398-5317
Fax: 319-398-5228
http://www.cedarrapids.org

Marlboro, NJ
Greater Monmouth Chamber of Commerce
10 East Main Street
Suite 1A
Freehold, NJ 07728
Phone: 732-462-3030
Fax: 732-462-2123
http://www.greatermonmouthchamber.com

Mason, OH
Mason Deerfield Chamber
316 W. Main Street
Mason, OH 45040
Phone: 513-336-0125
Fax: 513-398-6371
http://business.madechamber.org

Menomonee Falls, WI
Menomonee Falls Chamber of Commerce
N88 W16621 Appleton Avenue
Menomonee Falls, WI 53051
Phone: 262-251-2430
Fax: 262-251-0969
http://www.fallschamber.com

Meridian, ID
Meridan Chamber of Commerce
215 East Franklin Road
Meridian, ID 83642
Phone: 208-888-2817
Fax: 208-888-2682
http://www.meridianchamber.org

Meridian, MI
Lansing Regional Chamber of Commerce
500 E. Michigan Ave
Suite 200
Lansing, MI 48912
Phone: 517-487-6340
https://www.lansingchamber.org

Merrimack, NH
Merrimack Chamber of Commerce
246 Daniel Webster Highway
Merrimack, NH 03054
Phone: 603-424-3669
Fax: 603-429-4325
http://www.merrimackchamber.org

Milton, GA
Greater North Fulton Chamber of Commerce
11605 Haynes Bridge Road
Suite 100
Alpharetta, GA 30009
Phone: 866-840-5770
Fax: 770-594-1059
https://www.gnfcc.com

Moon, PA
Pittsburgh Airport Area Chamber of Commerce
850 Beaver Grade Rd
Suite 101
Moon, PA 15108
Phone: 412-264-6270
https://www.paacc.com

Moorpark, CA
Moorpark Chamber of Commerce
18 High Street
Moorpark, CA 93021
Phone: 805-529-0322
http://www.moorparkchamber.com

Morgantown, WV
Morgantown Area Chamber of Commerce
1029 University Avenue
Suite 101
Morgantown, WV 26505
Phone: 304-292-3311
Fax: 304-296-6619
http://www.morgantownchamber.org

Mount Pleasant, SC
Charleston Metro Chamber of Commerce
4500 Leeds Avenue
Suite 100
North Charleston, SC 29405
Phone: 843-577-2510
http://www.charlestonchamber.net

Newark, DE
New Castle County Chamber of Commerce
12 Penns Way
New Castle, DE 19720
Phone: 302-737-4343
Fax: 302-322-3593
http://www.ncccc.com

Newtown, CT
Chamber of Commerce of Newtown, Inc
45 Main Street
Newtown, CT 06470
Phone: 203-426-2695
http://www.newtown-ct.com

North Attleborough, MA
United Regional Chamber of Commerce
310 South Street
Plainville, MA 02762
Phone: 508-316-0861
Fax: 508-316-1992
http://www.unitedregionalchamber.org

North Port, FL
North Port Area Chamber of Commerce
15141 Tamiami Trail
North Port, FL 34287
Phone: 941-564-3040
Fax: 941-423-5042
http://www.northportareachamber.com

North Ridgeville, OH
North Ridgeville Chamber of Commerce
34845 Lorain Road
North Ridgeville, OH 44039
Phone: 440-327-3737
Fax: 440-327-1474
https://nrchamber.com

Northville, MI
Northville Chamber of Commerce
195 S. Main Street
Northville, MI 48167
Phone: 248-349-7640
Fax: 248-349-8730
http://www.northville.org

O'Fallon, MO
O'Fallon Chamber of Commerce & Industries
2145 Bryan Valley Commercial Dr
O'Fallon, MO 63366
Phone: 636-240-1818
Fax: 888-349-1897
http://www.ofallonchamber.org

Orchard Park, NY
The Orchard Park Chamber of Commerce
4211 North Buffalo Street
Orchard Park, NY 14127
Phone: 716-662-3366
Fax: 716-662-5946
http://orchardparkchamber.org

Oro Valley, AZ
Greater Oro Valley Chamber of Commerce
7435 N. Oracle Road
Suite 107
Tucson, AZ 85704
Phone: 520-597—2191
http://www.orovalleychamber.com

Oviedo, FL
Oviedo Winter Springs Regional Chamber of Commerce
376 North Central Ave
Oviedo, FL 32765
Phone: 407-365-6500
Fax: 407- 650-2712
http://www.oviedowintersprings.org

Parker, CO
Parker Area Chamber of Commerce
19590 E Mainstreet
Suite 100
Parker, CO 80138
Phone: 303-841-4268
Fax: 303-841-8061
http://www.parkerchamber.com

Parkland, FL
Parkland Chamber of Commerce
10561 Trails End
Parkland, FL
Phone: 954-937-0232
http://www.parklandchamber.org

Peachtree City, GA
Fayette Chamber of Commerce
600 West Lanier Avenue
Suite 205
Fayetteville, GA 30214
Phone: 770-461-9983
Fax: 770-461-9622
http://fayettechamber.org

Pittsfield, MI
Saline Area Chamber of Commerce
141 E. Michigan Ave
Suite B
Saline, MI 48176
Phone: 734-429-4494
https://www.salinechamber.org

Plainfield, IL
Plainfield Area Chamber of Commerce
24109 W. Lockport Street
Plainfield, IL 60544
Phone: 815-436-4431
Fax: 815-436-0520
http://www.plainfieldchamber.com

Pleasant Grove, UT
Pleasant Grove Chamber of Commerce
70 S 100 E
Pleasant Grove, UT 84062
Phone: 801-922-4555
Fax: 801-785-8923
https://www.pglindonchamber.org

Poway, CA
Poway Chamber of Commerce
13117 Quate Court
Suite E
Poway, CA 92064
Phone: 858-748-0016
Fax: 858-748-1710
http://poway.com

Princeton, NJ
Princeton Regional Chamber of Commerce
182 Nassau St.
Suite 301
Princeton, NJ 08542
Phone: 609-924-1776
Fax: 609-924-5776
http://www.princetonchamber.org

Queen Creek, AZ
Queen Creek Chamber of Commerce
22246 South Ellsworth Rd
Queen Creek, AZ 85142
Phone: 480-888-1709
Fax: 480-289-4801
http://www.queencreekchamber.com

Radnor, PA
The Main Line Chamber of Commerce
175 Strafford Avenue
Suite 130
Wayne, PA 19087
Phone: 610-687-6232
Fax: 610-687-8085
http://www.mlcc.org

Randolph, NJ
Randolph Area Chamber of Commerce
PO Box 391
Mount Freedom, NJ 07970
Phone: 973-361-3462
Fax: 973-895-3297
http://randolphchamber.org

Rexburg, ID
Rexburg Area Chamber of Commerce
167 W Main Street
Suite 2
Rexburg, ID 83440
Phone: 208-356-5700
Fax: 208-356-5799
http://rexburgchamber.org

Rio Rancho, NM
Rio Rancho Regional Chamber of Commerce
4001 Southern Blvd SE
Suite B
Rio Rancho, NM 87124
Phone: 505-892-1533
Fax: 505-892-6157
http://rrrcc.org

Rye, NY
Rye Chamber of Commerce
PO Box 72
Rye, NY 10580
Phone: 914-967-5188
http://www.ryechamberofcommerce.com

Sammamish, WA
Sammamish Chamber of Commerce
704 228th Avenue Northeast
Suite 123
Sammamish, WA 98074
Phone: 425-681-4910
Fax: 425-484-6266
http://sammamishchamber.org

San Ramon, CA
San Ramon Chamber of Commerce
2410 Camino Ramon
Suite 125
San Ramon, CA 94583
Phone: 925-242-0600
Fax: 925-242-0603
http://sanramon.org

Saratoga, CA
Saratoga Chamber of Commerce
14460 Big Basin Way
Saratoga, CA 95070
Phone: 408-867-0753
http://www.saratogachamber.org

Shrewsbury, MA
Corridor Nine Area Chamber of Commerce
30 Lyman Street
Westborough, MA 01581
Phone: 508-836-4444
Fax: 508-836-2652
http://www.corridornine.org

South Brunswick, NJ
Middlesex County Regional Chamber of Commerce
109 Church Street
New Brunswick, NJ 08901
Phone: 732-745-8090
https://www.mcrcc.org

South Jordan, UT
South Jordan Chamber of Commerce
11565 S District Main Drive
Suite 600
South Jordan, UT 84095
Phone: 801-253-5200
Fax: 801-253-5201
http://www.southjordanchamber.com

South Kingstown, RI
Southern Rhode Island Chamber of Commerce
230 Old Tower Hill Road
Wakefield, RI 02879
Phone: 401-783-2801
Fax: 401-789-3120
http://www.srichamber.com

South Portland, ME
Portland Regional Chamber of Commerce
443 Congress Street
Portland, ME 04101
Phone: 207-772-2811
Fax: 207-772-1179
http://www.portlandregion.com

Sparks, NV
Reno-Sparks Chamber of Commerce
449 South Virginia Street
Reno, NV 89501
Phone: 775-636-9550
Fax: 775-337-3038
http://www.thechambernv.org

State College, PA
Chamber of Business & Industry of Centre County
131 S. Fraser Street
State College, PA 16801
Phone: 814-234-1829
http://www.cbicc.org

Sugar Land, TX
Fort Bend Chamber of Commerce
445 Commerce Green Blvd
Sugar Land, TX 77478
Phone: 281-491-0800
Fax: 281-491-0112
http://www.fortbendchamber.com

Sun Prairie, WI
Sun Prairie Chamber Of Commerce
109 East Main Street
Sun Prairie, WI 53590
Phone: 608-837-4547
Fax: 608-837-8765
http://www.sunprairiechamber.com

Syracuse, UT
Syracuse Chamber of Commerce
PO Box 160595
Clearfield, UT 84016
Phone: 801-645-0247
http://syracuseutahchamber.com

Tredyffrin, PA
The Main Line Chamber of Commerce
175 Strafford Avenue
Suite 130
Wayne, PA 19087
Phone: 610-687-6232
Fax: 610-687-8085
http://www.mlcc.org

Upper Dublin, PA
Eastern Montgomery County Chamber of Commerce
436 Old York Rd
Jenkintown, PA 19046
Phone: 215-887-5122
http://www.emccc.org

Urbandale, IA
Urbandale Chamber of Commerce
2900 Justin Drive
Suite L
Urbandale, IA 50322
Phone: 515-331-6855
Fax: 515-331-2987
http://uniquelyurbandale.com

Vestal, NY
Greater Binghamton Chamber of Commerce
5 South College Drive
Binghamton, NY 13905
Phone: 607-772-8860
Fax: 607-722-4513
http://greaterbinghamtonchamber.com

Vestavia Hills, AL
Vestavia Hills Chamber of Commerce
1975 Merryvale Road
Vestavia Hills, AL 35216
Phone: 205-823-5011
Fax: 205-823-8974
http://vestaviahills.org

Webster, NY
Webster Chamber of Commerce
1110 Crosspointe Lane
Suite C
Webster, NY 14580
Phone: 585-265-3960
Fax: 585-265-3702
http://www.websterchamber.com

Wellesley, MA
Wellesley Chamber of Commerce
One Hollis Street
Suite 232
Wellesley, MA 02482-4671
Phone: 781-235-2446
Fax: 781-235-7326
http://wellesleychamber.org

West Fargo, ND
West Fargo Chamber of Commerce
202 First Avenue North
Moorhead, ND 56560
Phone: 218-223-1100
Fax: 218-233-1200
http://www.fmwfchamber.com

West Lafayette, IN
Greater Lafayette Commerce
337 Columbia Street
Lafayette, IN 47901
Phone: 765-742-4044
Fax: 765-742-6276
http://www.greaterlafayettecommerce.com

Weston, FL
Weston Area Chamber of Commerce
9001-B Pembroke Road
Pembroke Pines, FL 33025
Phone: 954-432-9808
https://westonflchamber.com

Wilmette, IL
The Wilmette/Kenilworth Chamber of Commerce
351 Linden Avenue
Wilmette, IL 60091
Phone: 847-251-3800
Fax: 847-251-6321
http://www.wilmettechamber.org

Yorba Linda, CA
Yorba Linda Chamber of Commerce
17670 Yorba Linda Boulevard
Yorba Linda, CA 92886
Phone: 714-993-9537
http://www.yorbalindachamber.org

Zionsville, IN
Zionsville Chamber of Commerce
1100 West Oak Street
Suite 214
Zionsville, IN 46077
Phone: 317-873-3836
https://www.zionsvillechamber.org

Appendix E: State Departments of Labor

Alabama
Alabama Department of Labor
P.O. Box 303500
Montgomery, AL 36130-3500
Phone: (334) 242-3072
https://www.labor.alabama.gov

Alaska
Dept of Labor and Workforce Devel.
P.O. Box 11149
Juneau, AK 99822-2249
Phone: (907) 465-2700
http://www.labor.state.ak.us

Arizona
Industrial Commission or Arizona
800 West Washington Street
Phoenix, AZ 85007
Phone: (602) 542-4411
https://www.azica.gov

Arkansas
Department of Labor
10421 West Markham
Little Rock, AR 72205
Phone: (501) 682-4500
http://www.labor.ar.gov

California
Labor and Workforce Development
445 Golden Gate Ave., 10th Floor
San Francisco, CA 94102
Phone: (916) 263-1811
http://www.labor.ca.gov

Colorado
Dept of Labor and Employment
633 17th St., 2nd Floor
Denver, CO 80202-3660
Phone: (888) 390-7936
https://www.colorado.gov/CDLE

Connecticut
Department of Labor
200 Folly Brook Blvd.
Wethersfield, CT 06109-1114
Phone: (860) 263-6000
http://www.ctdol.state.ct.us

Delaware
Department of Labor
4425 N. Market St., 4th Floor
Wilmington, DE 19802
Phone: (302) 451-3423
http://dol.delaware.gov

District of Columbia
Department of Employment Services
614 New York Ave., NE, Suite 300
Washington, DC 20002
Phone: (202) 671-1900
http://does.dc.gov

Florida
Florida Department of Economic Opportunity
The Caldwell Building
107 East Madison St. Suite 100
Tallahassee, FL 32399-4120
Phone: (800) 342-3450
http://www.floridajobs.org

Georgia
Department of Labor
Sussex Place, Room 600
148 Andrew Young Intl Blvd., NE
Atlanta, GA 30303
Phone: (404) 656-3011
http://dol.georgia.gov

Hawaii
Dept of Labor & Industrial Relations
830 Punchbowl Street
Honolulu, HI 96813
Phone: (808) 586-8842
http://labor.hawaii.gov

Idaho
Department of Labor
317 W. Main St.
Boise, ID 83735-0001
Phone: (208) 332-3579
http://www.labor.idaho.gov

Illinois
Department of Labor
160 N. LaSalle Street, 13th Floor
Suite C-1300
Chicago, IL 60601
Phone: (312) 793-2800
https://www.illinois.gov/idol

Indiana
Indiana Department of Labor
402 West Washington Street, Room W195
Indianapolis, IN 46204
Phone: (317) 232-2655
http://www.in.gov/dol

Iowa
Iowa Workforce Development
1000 East Grand Avenue
Des Moines, IA 50319-0209
Phone: (515) 242-5870
http://www.iowadivisionoflabor.gov

Kansas
Department of Labor
401 S.W. Topeka Blvd.
Topeka, KS 66603-3182
Phone: (785) 296-5000
http://www.dol.ks.gov

Kentucky
Department of Labor
1047 U.S. Hwy 127 South, Suite 4
Frankfort, KY 40601-4381
Phone: (502) 564-3070
http://www.labor.ky.gov

Louisiana
Louisiana Workforce Commission
1001 N. 23rd Street
Baton Rouge, LA 70804-9094
Phone: (225) 342-3111
http://www.laworks.net

Maine
Department of Labor
45 Commerce Street
Augusta, ME 04330
Phone: (207) 623-7900
http://www.state.me.us/labor

Maryland
Department of Labor, Licensing & Regulation
500 N. Calvert Street
Suite 401
Baltimore, MD 21202
Phone: (410) 767-2357
http://www.dllr.state.md.us

Massachusetts
Dept of Labor & Workforce Development
One Ashburton Place
Room 2112
Boston, MA 02108
Phone: (617) 626-7100
http://www.mass.gov/lwd

Michigan
Department of Licensing and Regulatory Affairs
611 W. Ottawa
P.O. Box 30004
Lansing, MI 48909
Phone: (517) 373-1820
http://www.michigan.gov/lara

Minnesota
Dept of Labor and Industry
443 Lafayette Road North
Saint Paul, MN 55155
Phone: (651) 284-5070
http://www.doli.state.mn.us

Mississippi
Dept of Employment Security
P.O. Box 1699
Jackson, MS 39215-1699
Phone: (601) 321-6000
http://www.mdes.ms.gov

Missouri
Labor and Industrial Relations
P.O. Box 599
3315 W. Truman Boulevard
Jefferson City, MO 65102-0599
Phone: (573) 751-7500
https://labor.mo.gov

Montana
Dept of Labor and Industry
P.O. Box 1728
Helena, MT 59624-1728
Phone: (406) 444-9091
http://www.dli.mt.gov

Nebraska
Department of Labor
550 S 16th Street
Lincoln, NE 68508
Phone: (402) 471-9000
https://dol.nebraska.gov

Nevada
Dept of Business and Industry
3300 W. Sahara Ave
Suite 425
Las Vegas, NV 89102
Phone: (702) 486-2750
http://business.nv.gov

New Hampshire
Department of Labor
State Office Park South
95 Pleasant Street
Concord, NH 03301
Phone: (603) 271-3176
https://www.nh.gov/labor

New Jersey
Department of Labor & Workforce Development
John Fitch Plaza, 13th Floor
Suite D
Trenton, NJ 08625-0110
Phone: (609) 777-3200
http://lwd.dol.state.nj.us/labor

New Mexico
Department of Workforce Solutions
401 Broadway, NE
Albuquerque, NM 87103-1928
Phone: (505) 841-8450
https://www.dws.state.nm.us

New York
Department of Labor
State Office Bldg. # 12
W.A. Harriman Campus
Albany, NY 12240
Phone: (518) 457-9000
https://www.labor.ny.gov

North Carolina
Department of Labor
4 West Edenton Street
Raleigh, NC 27601-1092
Phone: (919) 733-7166
https://www.labor.nc.gov

North Dakota
North Dakota Department of Labor and Human Rights
State Capitol Building
600 East Boulevard, Dept 406
Bismark, ND 58505-0340
Phone: (701) 328-2660
http://www.nd.gov/labor

Ohio
Department of Commerce
77 South High Street, 22nd Floor
Columbus, OH 43215
Phone: (614) 644-2239
http://www.com.state.oh.us

Oklahoma
Department of Labor
4001 N. Lincoln Blvd.
Oklahoma City, OK 73105-5212
Phone: (405) 528-1500
https://www.ok.gov/odol

Oregon
Bureau of Labor and Industries
800 NE Oregon St., #32
Portland, OR 97232
Phone: (971) 673-0761
http://www.oregon.gov/boli

Pennsylvania
Dept of Labor and Industry
1700 Labor and Industry Bldg
7th and Forster Streets
Harrisburg, PA 17120
Phone: (717) 787-5279
http://www.dli.pa.gov

Rhode Island
Department of Labor and Training
1511 Pontiac Avenue
Cranston, RI 02920
Phone: (401) 462-8000
http://www.dlt.state.ri.us

South Carolina
Dept of Labor, Licensing & Regulations
P.O. Box 11329
Columbia, SC 29211-1329
Phone: (803) 896-4300
http://www.llr.state.sc.us

South Dakota
Department of Labor & Regulation
700 Governors Drive
Pierre, SD 57501-2291
Phone: (605) 773-3682
http://dlr.sd.gov

Tennessee
Dept of Labor & Workforce Development
Andrew Johnson Tower
710 James Robertson Pkwy
Nashville, TN 37243-0655
Phone: (615) 741-6642
http://www.tn.gov/workforce

Texas
Texas Workforce Commission
101 East 15th St.
Austin, TX 78778
Phone: (512) 475-2670
http://www.twc.state.tx.us

Utah
Utah Labor Commission
160 East 300 South, 3rd Floor
Salt Lake City, UT 84114-6600
Phone: (801) 530-6800
https://laborcommission.utah.gov

Vermont
Department of Labor
5 Green Mountain Drive
P.O. Box 488
Montpelier, VT 05601-0488
Phone: (802) 828-4000
http://labor.vermont.gov

Virginia
Dept of Labor and Industry
Powers-Taylor Building
13 S. 13th Street
Richmond, VA 23219
Phone: (804) 371-2327
http://www.doli.virginia.gov

Washington
Dept of Labor and Industries
P.O. Box 44001
Olympia, WA 98504-4001
Phone: (360) 902-4200
http://www.lni.wa.gov

West Virginia
Division of Labor
749 B Bulding 6
Capitol Complex
Charleston, WV 25305
Phone: (304) 558-7890
https://labor.wv.gov

Wisconsin
Dept of Workforce Development
201 E. Washington Ave., #A400
P.O. Box 7946
Madison, WI 53707-7946
Phone: (608) 266-6861
http://dwd.wisconsin.gov

Wyoming
Department of Workforce Services
1510 East Pershing Blvd.
Cheyenne, WY 82002
Phone: (307) 777-7261
http://www.wyomingworkforce.org

Source: *U.S. Department of Labor; Original research*

Grey House Publishing

2018 Title List

Visit www.GreyHouse.com for Product Information, Table of Contents, and Sample Pages

General Reference
America's College Museums
American Environmental Leaders: From Colonial Times to the Present
Encyclopedia of African-American Writing
Encyclopedia of Constitutional Amendments
Encyclopedia of Human Rights and the United States
Encyclopedia of Invasions & Conquests
Encyclopedia of Prisoners of War & Internment
Encyclopedia of Religion & Law in America
Encyclopedia of Rural America
Encyclopedia of the Continental Congress
Encyclopedia of the United States Cabinet, 1789-2010
Encyclopedia of War Journalism
Encyclopedia of Warrior Peoples & Fighting Groups
The Environmental Debate: A Documentary History
The Evolution Wars: A Guide to the Debates
From Suffrage to the Senate: America's Political Women
Gun Debate: An Encyclopedia of Gun Rights & Gun Control in the U.S.
Opinions throughout History: National Security vs. Civil and Privacy Rights
Opinions throughout History: Immigration
Opinions throughout History: Drug Abuse & Drug Epidemics
Political Corruption in America
Privacy Rights in the Digital Era
The Religious Right: A Reference Handbook
Speakers of the House of Representatives, 1789-2009
This is Who We Were: 1880-1900
This is Who We Were: A Companion to the 1940 Census
This is Who We Were: In the 1900s
This is Who We Were: In the 1910s
This is Who We Were: In the 1920s
This is Who We Were: In the 1940s
This is Who We Were: In the 1950s
This is Who We Were: In the 1960s
This is Who We Were: In the 1970s
This is Who We Were: In the 1980s
This is Who We Were: In the 1990s
This is Who We Were: In the 2000s
U.S. Land & Natural Resource Policy
The Value of a Dollar 1600-1865: Colonial Era to the Civil War
The Value of a Dollar: 1860-2014
Working Americans 1770-1869 Vol. IX: Revolutionary War to the Civil War
Working Americans 1880-1999 Vol. I: The Working Class
Working Americans 1880-1999 Vol. II: The Middle Class
Working Americans 1880-1999 Vol. III: The Upper Class
Working Americans 1880-1999 Vol. IV: Their Children
Working Americans 1880-2015 Vol. V: Americans At War
Working Americans 1880-2005 Vol. VI: Women at Work
Working Americans 1880-2006 Vol. VII: Social Movements
Working Americans 1880-2007 Vol. VIII: Immigrants
Working Americans 1880-2009 Vol. X: Sports & Recreation
Working Americans 1880-2010 Vol. XI: Inventors & Entrepreneurs
Working Americans 1880-2011 Vol. XII: Our History through Music
Working Americans 1880-2012 Vol. XIII: Education & Educators
Working Americans 1880-2016 Vol. XIV: Industry Through the Ages
Working Americans 1880-2017 Vol. XV: Politics & Politicians
World Cultural Leaders of the 20th & 21st Centuries

Education Information
Charter School Movement
Comparative Guide to American Elementary & Secondary Schools
Complete Learning Disabilities Directory
Educators Resource Handbook
Special Education: Policy and Curriculum Development

Health Information
Comparative Guide to American Hospitals
Complete Directory for Pediatric Disorders
Complete Directory for People with Chronic Illness
Complete Directory for People with Disabilities
Complete Mental Health Directory
Diabetes in America: Analysis of an Epidemic
Guide to Health Care Group Purchasing Organizations
Guide to U.S. HMO's & PPO's
Medical Device Market Place
Older Americans Information Directory

Business Information
Complete Television, Radio & Cable Industry Directory
Directory of Business Information Resources
Directory of Mail Order Catalogs
Directory of Venture Capital & Private Equity Firms
Environmental Resource Handbook
Financial Literacy Starter Kit
Food & Beverage Market Place
Grey House Homeland Security Directory
Grey House Performing Arts Directory
Grey House Safety & Security Directory
Hudson's Washington News Media Contacts Directory
New York State Directory
Sports Market Place Directory

Statistics & Demographics
American Tally
America's Top-Rated Cities
America's Top-Rated Smaller Cities
Ancestry & Ethnicity in America
The Asian Databook
Comparative Guide to American Suburbs
The Hispanic Databook
Profiles of America
"Profiles of" Series - State Handbooks
Weather America

Financial Ratings Series
Financial Literacy Basics
TheStreet Ratings' Guide to Bond & Money Market Mutual Funds
TheStreet Ratings' Guide to Common Stocks
TheStreet Ratings' Guide to Exchange-Traded Funds
TheStreet Ratings' Guide to Stock Mutual Funds
TheStreet Ratings' Ultimate Guided Tour of Stock Investing
Weiss Ratings' Consumer Guides
Weiss Ratings' Financial Literary Basic Guides
Weiss Ratings' Guide to Banks
Weiss Ratings' Guide to Credit Unions
Weiss Ratings' Guide to Health Insurers
Weiss Ratings' Guide to Life & Annuity Insurers
Weiss Ratings' Guide to Property & Casualty Insurers

Bowker's Books In Print® Titles
American Book Publishing Record® Annual
American Book Publishing Record® Monthly
Books In Print®
Books In Print® Supplement
Books Out Loud™
Bowker's Complete Video Directory™
Children's Books In Print®
El-Hi Textbooks & Serials In Print®
Forthcoming Books®
Law Books & Serials In Print™
Medical & Health Care Books In Print™
Publishers, Distributors & Wholesalers of the US™
Subject Guide to Books In Print®
Subject Guide to Children's Books In Print®

Canadian General Reference
Associations Canada
Canadian Almanac & Directory
Canadian Environmental Resource Guide
Canadian Parliamentary Guide
Canadian Venture Capital & Private Equity Firms
Canadian Who's Who
Financial Post Directory of Directors
Financial Services Canada
Governments Canada
Health Guide Canada
The History of Canada
Libraries Canada
Major Canadian Cities

2018 Title List

Visit **www.SalemPress.com** for Product Information, Table of Contents, and Sample Pages

Science, Careers & Mathematics

Ancient Creatures
Applied Science
Applied Science: Engineering & Mathematics
Applied Science: Science & Medicine
Applied Science: Technology
Biomes and Ecosystems
Careers in the Arts: Fine, Performing & Visual
Careers in Building Construction
Careers in Business
Careers in Chemistry
Careers in Communications & Media
Careers in Environment & Conservation
Careers in Financial Services
Careers in Green Energy
Careers in Healthcare
Careers in Hospitality & Tourism
Careers in Human Services
Careers in Law, Criminal Justice & Emergency Services
Careers in Manufacturing
Careers in Outdoor Jobs
Careers in Overseas Jobs
Careers in Physics
Careers in Sales, Insurance & Real Estate
Careers in Science & Engineering
Careers in Sports & Fitness
Careers in Social Media
Careers in Sports Medicine & Training
Careers in Technology Services & Repair
Computer Technology Innovators
Contemporary Biographies in Business
Contemporary Biographies in Chemistry
Contemporary Biographies in Communications & Media
Contemporary Biographies in Environment & Conservation
Contemporary Biographies in Healthcare
Contemporary Biographies in Hospitality & Tourism
Contemporary Biographies in Law & Criminal Justice
Contemporary Biographies in Physics
Earth Science
Earth Science: Earth Materials & Resources
Earth Science: Earth's Surface and History
Earth Science: Physics & Chemistry of the Earth
Earth Science: Weather, Water & Atmosphere
Encyclopedia of Energy
Encyclopedia of Environmental Issues
Encyclopedia of Environmental Issues: Atmosphere and Air Pollution
Encyclopedia of Environmental Issues: Ecology and Ecosystems
Encyclopedia of Environmental Issues: Energy and Energy Use
Encyclopedia of Environmental Issues: Policy and Activism
Encyclopedia of Environmental Issues: Preservation/Wilderness Issues
Encyclopedia of Environmental Issues: Water and Water Pollution
Encyclopedia of Global Resources
Encyclopedia of Global Warming
Encyclopedia of Mathematics & Society
Encyclopedia of Mathematics & Society: Engineering, Tech, Medicine
Encyclopedia of Mathematics & Society: Great Mathematicians
Encyclopedia of Mathematics & Society: Math & Social Sciences
Encyclopedia of Mathematics & Society: Math Development/Concepts
Encyclopedia of Mathematics & Society: Math in Culture & Society
Encyclopedia of Mathematics & Society: Space, Science, Environment
Encyclopedia of the Ancient World
Forensic Science
Geography Basics
Internet Innovators
Inventions and Inventors
Magill's Encyclopedia of Science: Animal Life
Magill's Encyclopedia of Science: Plant life
Notable Natural Disasters
Principles of Artificial Intelligence & Robotics
Principles of Astronomy
Principles of Biology
Principles of Biotechnology
Principles of Chemistry
Principles of Climatology
Principles of Physical Science
Principles of Physics
Principles of Programming & Coding
Principles of Research Methods
Principles of Sustainability
Science and Scientists
Solar System
Solar System: Great Astronomers
Solar System: Study of the Universe
Solar System: The Inner Planets
Solar System: The Moon and Other Small Bodies
Solar System: The Outer Planets
Solar System: The Sun and Other Stars
World Geography

Literature

American Ethnic Writers
Classics of Science Fiction & Fantasy Literature
Critical Approaches: Feminist
Critical Approaches: Multicultural
Critical Approaches: Moral
Critical Approaches: Psychological
Critical Insights: Authors
Critical Insights: Film
Critical Insights: Literary Collection Bundles
Critical Insights: Themes
Critical Insights: Works
Critical Survey of American Literature
Critical Survey of Drama
Critical Survey of Graphic Novels: Heroes & Super Heroes
Critical Survey of Graphic Novels: History, Theme & Technique
Critical Survey of Graphic Novels: Independents/Underground Classics
Critical Survey of Graphic Novels: Manga
Critical Survey of Long Fiction
Critical Survey of Mystery & Detective Fiction
Critical Survey of Mythology and Folklore: Heroes and Heroines
Critical Survey of Mythology and Folklore: Love, Sexuality & Desire
Critical Survey of Mythology and Folklore: World Mythology
Critical Survey of Novels into Film
Critical Survey of Poetry
Critical Survey of Poetry: American Poets
Critical Survey of Poetry: British, Irish & Commonwealth Poets
Critical Survey of Poetry: Cumulative Index
Critical Survey of Poetry: European Poets
Critical Survey of Poetry: Topical Essays
Critical Survey of Poetry: World Poets
Critical Survey of Science Fiction & Fantasy
Critical Survey of Shakespeare's Plays
Critical Survey of Shakespeare's Sonnets
Critical Survey of Short Fiction
Critical Survey of Short Fiction: American Writers
Critical Survey of Short Fiction: British, Irish, Commonwealth Writers
Critical Survey of Short Fiction: Cumulative Index
Critical Survey of Short Fiction: European Writers
Critical Survey of Short Fiction: Topical Essays
Critical Survey of Short Fiction: World Writers
Critical Survey of World Literature
Critical Survey of Young Adult Literature
Cyclopedia of Literary Characters
Cyclopedia of Literary Places
Holocaust Literature
Introduction to Literary Context: American Poetry of the 20th Century
Introduction to Literary Context: American Post-Modernist Novels
Introduction to Literary Context: American Short Fiction
Introduction to Literary Context: English Literature
Introduction to Literary Context: Plays
Introduction to Literary Context: World Literature
Magill's Literary Annual 2018
Masterplots
Masterplots II: African American Literature
Masterplots II: American Fiction Series
Masterplots II: British & Commonwealth Fiction Series
Masterplots II: Christian Literature
Masterplots II: Drama Series
Masterplots II: Juvenile & Young Adult Literature, Supplement
Masterplots II: Nonfiction Series
Masterplots II: Poetry Series
Masterplots II: Short Story Series
Masterplots II: Women's Literature Series
Notable African American Writers
Notable American Novelists
Notable Playwrights
Notable Poets
Recommended Reading: 600 Classics Reviewed
Short Story Writers

SALEM PRESS

SALEM PRESS

2018 Title List

Visit www.SalemPress.com for Product Information, Table of Contents, and Sample Pages

History and Social Science

The 2000s in America
50 States
African American History
Agriculture in History
American First Ladies
American Heroes
American Indian Culture
American Indian History
American Indian Tribes
American Presidents
American Villains
America's Historic Sites
Ancient Greece
The Bill of Rights
The Civil Rights Movement
The Cold War
Countries, Peoples & Cultures
Countries, Peoples & Cultures: Central & South America
Countries, Peoples & Cultures: Central, South & Southeast Asia
Countries, Peoples & Cultures: East & South Africa
Countries, Peoples & Cultures: East Asia & the Pacific
Countries, Peoples & Cultures: Eastern Europe
Countries, Peoples & Cultures: Middle East & North Africa
Countries, Peoples & Cultures: North America & the Caribbean
Countries, Peoples & Cultures: West & Central Africa
Countries, Peoples & Cultures: Western Europe
Defining Documents: American Revolution
Defining Documents: American West
Defining Documents: Ancient World
Defining Documents: Asia
Defining Documents: Civil Rights
Defining Documents: Civil War
Defining Documents: Court Cases
Defining Documents: Dissent & Protest
Defining Documents: Emergence of Modern America
Defining Documents: Exploration & Colonial America
Defining Documents: Immigration & Immigrant Communities
Defining Documents: LGBTQ
Defining Documents: Manifest Destiny
Defining Documents: Middle Ages
Defining Documents: Middle East
Defining Documents: Nationalism & Populism
Defining Documents: Native Americans
Defining Documents: Political Campaigns, Candidates & Discourse
Defining Documents: Postwar 1940s
Defining Documents: Reconstruction
Defining Documents: Renaissance & Early Modern Era
Defining Documents: Secrets, Leaks & Scandals
Defining Documents: 1920s
Defining Documents: 1930s
Defining Documents: 1950s
Defining Documents: 1960s
Defining Documents: 1970s
Defining Documents: The 17th Century
Defining Documents: The 18th Century
Defining Documents: The 19th Century
Defining Documents: The 20th Century: 1900-1950
Defining Documents: Vietnam War
Defining Documents: Women
Defining Documents: World War I
Defining Documents: World War II
Education Today
The Eighties in America
Encyclopedia of American Immigration
Encyclopedia of Flight
Encyclopedia of the Ancient World
Fashion Innovators
The Fifties in America
The Forties in America
Great Athletes
Great Athletes: Baseball
Great Athletes: Basketball
Great Athletes: Boxing & Soccer
Great Athletes: Cumulative Index
Great Athletes: Football
Great Athletes: Golf & Tennis
Great Athletes: Olympics
Great Athletes: Racing & Individual Sports
Great Contemporary Athletes
Great Events from History: 17th Century
Great Events from History: 18th Century
Great Events from History: 19th Century
Great Events from History: 20th Century (1901-1940)
Great Events from History: 20th Century (1941-1970)
Great Events from History: 20th Century (1971-2000)
Great Events from History: 21st Century (2000-2016)
Great Events from History: African American History
Great Events from History: Cumulative Indexes
Great Events from History: LGBTG
Great Events from History: Middle Ages
Great Events from History: Secrets, Leaks & Scandals
Great Events from History: Renaissance & Early Modern Era
Great Lives from History: 17th Century
Great Lives from History: 18th Century
Great Lives from History: 19th Century
Great Lives from History: 20th Century
Great Lives from History: 21st Century (2000-2017)
Great Lives from History: American Women
Great Lives from History: Ancient World
Great Lives from History: Asian & Pacific Islander Americans
Great Lives from History: Cumulative Indexes
Great Lives from History: Incredibly Wealthy
Great Lives from History: Inventors & Inventions
Great Lives from History: Jewish Americans
Great Lives from History: Latinos
Great Lives from History: Notorious Lives
Great Lives from History: Renaissance & Early Modern Era
Great Lives from History: Scientists & Science
Historical Encyclopedia of American Business
Issues in U.S. Immigration
Magill's Guide to Military History
Milestone Documents in African American History
Milestone Documents in American History
Milestone Documents in World History
Milestone Documents of American Leaders
Milestone Documents of World Religions
Music Innovators
Musicians & Composers 20th Century
The Nineties in America
The Seventies in America
The Sixties in America
Sociology Today
Survey of American Industry and Careers
The Thirties in America
The Twenties in America
United States at War
U.S. Court Cases
U.S. Government Leaders
U.S. Laws, Acts, and Treaties
U.S. Legal System
U.S. Supreme Court
Weapons and Warfare
World Conflicts: Asia and the Middle East

Health

Addictions & Substance Abuse
Adolescent Health & Wellness
Cancer
Complementary & Alternative Medicine
Community & Family Health
Genetics & Inherited Conditions
Health Issues
Infectious Diseases & Conditions
Magill's Medical Guide
Nutrition
Nursing
Psychology & Behavioral Health
Psychology Basics

WILSON WILSON

2018 Title List

Visit **www.HWWilsonInPrint.com** for Product Information, Table of Contents and Sample Pages

Current Biography
Current Biography Cumulative Index 1946-2013
Current Biography Monthly Magazine
Current Biography Yearbook: 2003
Current Biography Yearbook: 2004
Current Biography Yearbook: 2005
Current Biography Yearbook: 2006
Current Biography Yearbook: 2007
Current Biography Yearbook: 2008
Current Biography Yearbook: 2009
Current Biography Yearbook: 2010
Current Biography Yearbook: 2011
Current Biography Yearbook: 2012
Current Biography Yearbook: 2013
Current Biography Yearbook: 2014
Current Biography Yearbook: 2015
Current Biography Yearbook: 2016
Current Biography Yearbook: 2017

Core Collections
Children's Core Collection
Fiction Core Collection
Graphic Novels Core Collection
Middle & Junior High School Core
Public Library Core Collection: Nonfiction
Senior High Core Collection
Young Adult Fiction Core Collection

The Reference Shelf
Aging in America
Alternative Facts: Post Truth & the Information War
The American Dream
American Military Presence Overseas
The Arab Spring
Artificial Intelligence
The Brain
The Business of Food
Campaign Trends & Election Law
Conspiracy Theories
The Digital Age
Dinosaurs
Embracing New Paradigms in Education
Faith & Science
Families: Traditional and New Structures
The Future of U.S. Economic Relations: Mexico, Cuba, and Venezuela
Global Climate Change
Graphic Novels and Comic Books
Guns in America
Immigration
Immigration in the U.S.
Internet Abuses & Privacy Rights
Internet Safety
LGBTQ in the 21st Century
Marijuana Reform
The News and its Future
The Paranormal
Politics of the Ocean
Prescription Drug Abuse
Racial Tension in a "Postracial" Age
Reality Television
Representative American Speeches: 2008-2009
Representative American Speeches: 2009-2010
Representative American Speeches: 2010-2011
Representative American Speeches: 2011-2012
Representative American Speeches: 2012-2013
Representative American Speeches: 2013-2014
Representative American Speeches: 2014-2015
Representative American Speeches: 2015-2016
Representative American Speeches: 2016-2017
Representative American Speeches: 2017-2018
Rethinking Work
Revisiting Gender
Robotics
Russia
Social Networking
Social Services for the Poor
South China Seas Conflict
Space Exploration & Development
Sports in America
The Supreme Court
The Transformation of American Cities
U.S. Infrastructure
U.S. National Debate Topic: Educational Reform
U.S. National Debate Topic: Surveillance
U.S. National Debate Topic: The Ocean
U.S. National Debate Topic: Transportation Infrastructure
Whistleblowers

Readers' Guide
Abridged Readers' Guide to Periodical Literature
Readers' Guide to Periodical Literature

Indexes
Index to Legal Periodicals & Books
Short Story Index
Book Review Digest

Sears List
Sears List of Subject Headings
Sears: Lista de Encabezamientos de Materia

Facts About Series
Facts About American Immigration
Facts About China
Facts About the 20th Century
Facts About the Presidents
Facts About the World's Languages

Nobel Prize Winners
Nobel Prize Winners: 1901-1986
Nobel Prize Winners: 1987-1991
Nobel Prize Winners: 1992-1996
Nobel Prize Winners: 1997-2001

World Authors
World Authors: 1995-2000
World Authors: 2000-2005

Famous First Facts
Famous First Facts
Famous First Facts About American Politics
Famous First Facts About Sports
Famous First Facts About the Environment
Famous First Facts: International Edition

American Book of Days
The American Book of Days
The International Book of Days

Monographs
American Reformers
The Barnhart Dictionary of Etymology
Celebrate the World
Guide to the Ancient World
Indexing from A to Z
Nobel Prize Winners
The Poetry Break
Radical Change: Books for Youth in a Digital Age
Speeches of American Presidents

Wilson Chronology
Wilson Chronology of Asia and the Pacific
Wilson Chronology of Human Rights
Wilson Chronology of Ideas
Wilson Chronology of the Arts
Wilson Chronology of the World's Religions
Wilson Chronology of Women's Achievements